UNDERSTANDING LITERATURE

UNDERSTANDING LITERATURE

An Introduction to Reading and Writing

Walter Kalaidjian
Emory University

Judith Roof
Michigan State University

Stephen Watt
Indiana University

HOUGHTON MIFFLIN COMPANY   Boston   New York

Publisher: Patricia A. Coryell
Executive editor: Suzanne Phelps Weir
Sponsoring editor: Michael Gillespie
Editorial associate: Bruce Cantley
Senior production editor: Rosemary Winfield
Editorial assistant: Marlowe Shaeffer
Senior production/design coordinator: Jodi O'Rourke
Senior manufacturing coordinator: Priscilla Bailey
Marketing manager: Cindy Graff Cohen

Cover: Diego Rivera (1866–1957), *Sunset* (series of twenty), 1956, oil and tempera on canvas, 30 x 40 cm. Copyright © Schalkwijk/Art Resource, New York; Fundacion Dolores Olmedo, Mexico City, D.F., Mexico.

Acknowledgments begin on page C-1, which constitutes an extension of the copyright page.

Printed in the U.S.A.

Library of Congress Catalog Card Number: 2001133270

ISBN: 0-618-08492-4

123456789-DOW-05 04 03 02

Brief Contents

DRAMA

WRITING

Contents

FICTION

An Album of Art
Jacques-Louis David, *Madame Recamier*
Edouard Manet, *Olympia*
Henri Matisse, *Odalisque*
Amadeo Modigliani, *Reclining Nude from the Back*
Vanessa Bell, *The Memoir Club*
Paul Cézanne, *Mont Sainte-Victoire*
Pablo Picasso, *Les demoiselles d'Avignon*
Georges Braque, *The Bather*
Georges Braque, *Musical Instruments*
Pablo Picasso, *The Aficionado*
Umberto Boccioni, *The Dynamism of a Soccer Player*

POETRY

An Album of Art

Vasily Kandinsky, *Composition vi*

Charles Henry Demuth, *I Saw the Figure Five in Gold*

Andy Warhol, *Marilyn Monroe (Twenty Times)*

The Chicago Women's Graphics Collective, *Boycott Lettuce and Grapes*

Pieter Brueghel, *Landscape with the Fall of Icarus*

Botticelli, *The Birth of Venus*

Raphael, *An Allegory: Vision of a Knight*

Michelangelo, *Leda and the Swan*

William Blake, Illuminated manuscript of The Lamb

Dante Gabriel Rossetti, *The Girlhood of Mary Virgin*

Samuel Bak, *Thou Shalt Not Kill*

DRAMA

An Album of Art
Set design for *Death of a Salesman*
Leaf Projection design for *Death of a Salesman*
Sir John Everett Millais, *Ferdinand Lured by Ariel*
Sir John Everett Millais, *Ophelia*

WRITING

Preface for Instructors

The past twenty years have witnessed exciting evolutions in the way instructors think, talk, and write about literature—the expanding canon, growing interest in literary and cultural theory, changing definitions of what a "text" is, the emergence of new technologies, and so on. Capturing the energy, relevance, and skills of literary study and transmitting them to undergraduate students is one of the most important things we do as English instructors. In creating *Understanding Literature*, our aim has been twofold—to better address the ways instructors want to teach literature today and to better inspire in students the desire and skills to engage literature critically. In its reading selections, approach, apparatus, and integrated technology components, *Understanding Literature* has been carefully crafted to uphold the best literary traditions while furthering innovations that engage a new generation of students and instructors.

The heart of any anthology is found in its reading selections. We have balanced favorite canonical works with an outstanding selection of thought-provoking contemporary writing. We think you will find some wonderful surprises in the table of contents that you will be eager to explore with your students. We have included a wealth of relevant works of art and photographs—including color pages in each genre—that enrich the study of literature and culture. We have also designed a media-rich CD-ROM and Web site—both fully integrated with the text—to further bring literature to life and to better engage the learning styles of today's students.

We focus students on the necessary skills to perform close readings and to think critically about literary works. Each genre section starts with discussions of the basic, formal elements students need to understand and analyze literature. You will find discussions of reading fiction and drama for plot construction, narrative point of view, characterization, setting, tone, style, symbolism, and irony. Students will benefit from our discussions of understanding poetry in terms of its formal presentation of word choice, imagery, figurative language, sound sense, irony, paradox, rhyme and rhythm, and stanza form. These formalist practices continue to be essential skills that introductory students must master as requisites to understanding and enjoying literature. However, we feel it is important for today's students to move beyond basic readings toward more considered interpretations of literary texts. Therefore, through integrated, *accessible* discussions of critical approaches to literature, *Understanding Literature* encourages and supports students to explore ways in which literature engages with critical understandings of nationalism, race, gender, sexuality, global multiculturalism, and other cultural and political frames. *Understanding Literature* enables instructors to adopt a text more in step with the needs and interests of today's students and reflective of the ways many instructors organize their classes.

If you are an instructor who wants to engage your students with a lifelong enjoyment of literature while encouraging them to reach beyond a reading of the words to more rewarding and interesting interpretations, then *Understanding Literature* will meet your needs. We hope you find that *Understanding Literature* empowers you to go where you want to go and do what you want to do.

Key Features of the Anthology

Understanding Literature offers instructors a wealth of features that support the teaching of their classes.

Compelling Table of Contents

- **A rich array of the best literature** offers instructors a wonderful range of authors—from the cherished work of Faulkner, Hawthorne, O'Connor, Walker, Frost, Dickinson, Sophocles, and Shakespeare to the fresh and contemporary voices of Paul Auster, Michelle Cliff, Tracie Morris, Miguel Piñero, Ha Jin, Cherríe Moraga, and Margaret Edson. *Understanding Literature* gives you the flexibility you need to teach the selections that suit your class.
- **Important featured writers are treated in-depth** to allow more focused study of a single writer and give students rich opportunities for writing and research assignments. Featured writers include James Baldwin, Virginia Woolf, William Faulkner, Salman Rushdie, John Keats, Gwendolyn Brooks, Anne Sexton, and William Shakespeare.
- **Two unique interdisciplinary chapters explore the broader connections between literature and culture as showcased by** "The Beats" (Chapter 18) and "Performance and Performativity" (Chapter 40). These chapters include a wonderful range of dynamic writers, including the poetry of Allen Ginsberg, Diane Di Prima, and Amiri Baraka, the prose of Jack Kerouac and William S. Burroughs, and the experimental performance art of Guillermo Gómez-Peña and Tracie Morris. Enlivened with relevant social and political commentary, both chapters serve as case studies of how countercultural ideas and modes of expression create a dynamic conversation with mainstream cultural values and forms of expression.
- **Distinctive poetry casebooks** allow students to explore specific themes in-depth, such as "Poetry and Social Activism Between the Wars," "Poetry, Trauma, and Testimony: Holocaust Verses," "Postmodern Poetics," "Chicano/a Poetry," and "Native American Poetry." These casebooks facilitate focused class discussions and provide students with rich topics for writing and research.

Wealth of Visual Texts

- **Over sixty photos and works of art, including twelve pages of full-color work,** are carefully placed throughout the text to help students explore the connections between written and visual texts.

Comprehensive Coverage of Approaches to Studying Literature

- **Complete coverage of the formal elements of literature** gives student the knowledge they need to understand the basic features of literature including plot, character, point of view, theme, rhyme, meter, imagery, and forms of drama. Each genre devotes multiple chapters to the study of these elements giving helpful explanations and accessible examples.
- **Unique, integrated coverage of contemporary critical approaches** offers accessible, insightful discussions of how literary and cultural theory is used to explore meaning in literature. Integrated throughout the anthology in "Critical Perspective" sections rather than placed in an appendix or special chapters, this coverage includes in-text discussions, casebooks, and excerpts from classic and contemporary critical essays that offer students accessible and important critical perspectives into how literary theory can facilitate a deeper understanding of literary texts. Critical Perspectives can also be used as a springboard for class discussion and writing.
- **Emphasis on cultural, social, and historical contexts** Reflecting the increased desire to view literature through the lens of culture, the text discussions offer students ample opportunities to analyze and interpret literature using cultural, social, and historical events. Five chapters in Poetry are especially well-suited to these discussions: "Race and Representation" (Chapter 32), "Feminism and Representation" (Chapter 35), "Representations of Desire and Sexuality" (Chapter 36), and "Postcolonial Poetics" (Chapter 37).

Thorough Coverage of Writing and Research

- **Five chapters are devoted** to guiding students through the process of writing about literature and developing effective essays. Coverage includes general guidance, genre-specific advice, and help with the research paper.
- **Annotated student papers** for all three genres provide excellent models of strong student writing.
- **Topics for Critical Thinking and Critical Writing** are integrated into the chapters followed by suggestions for class discussion and writing topics. Instructors may use these informally in class or assign them as writing projects.

Integrated CD-ROM and Web Site

New technologies are opening up new avenues of literary exploration. Technology cannot replace the pleasure of reading a print text, but it can enhance certain aspects of its study—particularly for today's students who are more accustomed to integrating technology into their lives. By integrating print and technology components, *Understanding Literature* taps into the strengths of various media to bring literature to life for your students. Marginal icons throughout *Understanding Literature* direct you and your students to the related resources on our CD-ROM and Web site that help support and expand the readings and pedagogy in the text.

- **A highly interactive CD-ROM with a wealth of audio and visual resources** offers opportunities for in-depth study of drama, poetry, and fiction. The drama unit focuses on drama as a performed art, and it features exercises involving film clips from Dustin Hoffman's *Death of a Salesman* and two distinguished productions of *Hamlet*—Laurence Olivier's classic portrayal and Mel Gibson's contemporary performance. The poetry unit focuses on the work of Langston Hughes, placing it in broader cultural, political, and artistic contexts. This section features poems by Hughes, seven audio clips of related jazz and blues music and poetry readings, and photos and art. The fiction unit walks students through the literary elements of Hawthorne's "The Birthmark," teaching students how to interpret this story and to apply it to other works of fiction.
- **A resource-rich Web site** helps students and instructors further explore the works, authors, artistic movements, and literary theories introduced in the anthology. The *Understanding Literature* Web site provides helpful support for students including a poetry tutorial, questions and writing assignments, insights into literary movements, supplemental biographical materials, and relevant photos and visual art.

Organized to be Flexible and Teachable

Understanding Literature, rich with the finest classic and contemporary literature, allows instructors the flexibility to tailor the text to suit their classroom needs. Some instructors may prefer to concentrate on the core chapters that cover the literary elements. Other instructors may choose to blend classic coverage with chapters that explore cultural, social, and historical contexts along with topics such as metafiction, postmodernism, and postcolonialism.

Organized by literary genre, *Understanding Literature* includes three major sections—fiction, poetry, and drama. A fourth section on writing about literature includes five chapters devoted to the writing process; writing about fiction, poetry, and drama; and writing a research paper.

Fiction

Understanding Literature includes major works of fiction that invite students to engage in both reading for pleasure and reading for critical engagement. The stories cover a wide range from the beginnings of modern prose fiction through the best in contemporary short stories. You will find a multitude of authors, themes, and writing styles, including the best-loved classics from Nathaniel Hawthorne, Kate Chopin, Zora Neale Hurston, and William Faulkner to the contemporary voices of Julio Cortázar, Paul Auster, and Michelle Cliff.

Part I covers the basic literary elements with chapters devoted to character, setting, plot, narrator and point of view, and theme. These chapters give students a sound footing in the formal workings of fiction. Part II, "Image, Style, Structure," discusses imagery, style, structure, and tone, which lead to more sophisticated explorations in interpretation. Part III, "Reading and Interpreting," raises questions about *how we read.* The stories included are from around the globe, and students are asked to read these stories by examining issues of language, representation, metanarrative, and intertextuality.

Many chapters contain a section called "Critical Perspectives" that builds on discussions of fiction's formal elements by integrating concepts and terms drawn from current critical methods and theories about literature. The Critical Perspectives give students accessible discussions of how various literary approaches can be used to explore deeper meaning in literature.

Poetry

This section's focus on practical approaches to reading poems allows students to master the challenges of interpreting verse. Students will be introduced to classic voices such as William Shakespeare, Emily Dickinson, T. S. Eliot, and Langston Hughes, along with contemporary writers such as Janice Mirikitani, Jimmy Santiago Baca, Ray A. Young Bear, Ha Jin, and Tracie Morris. Coverage of imagery, figurative language, symbolism, myth, and prosody introduce the rudiments of form in the chapters that make up Part IV, "Understanding Poetic Form." Part V "Poetry and History," examines verse writing not just as formal lyric expression but, equally important, as a means of social expression. In this vein, Critical Perspective Casebooks explore poetry's cultural role in modern history, its place in the Native American, Chicano, and African American communities, its power to bear witness to the Holocaust, as well as poetry's changing styles of postcolonial and postmodern expression. In addition, fresh perspectives on poetry's representation of race, ethnicity, feminism, and desire open up bold new realms of classroom discussion and critical reflection. These chapters offer students a rich resource for writing and research.

Drama

The chapters devoted to drama give students a thorough introduction to the forms of drama. The text emphasizes drama as an art form meant to be performed, and students are asked to read with this foremost in their mind. In addition, the drama section goes beyond historical and formal considerations and encourages students to consider alternate ways of reading and interpreting. Plays by Sophocles, Shakespeare, Moliere, Ibsen, Chekhov, Glaspell, O'Neill, Miller, and Williams provide a familiar repertory to acquaint students with the elements of drama. Moving into the world of the contemporary theater, plays by Wole Soyinka, Cherríe Moraga, and Terrence McNally share center stage with such names as Samuel Beckett, Amiri Baraka, Harold Pinter, and David Henry Hwang. These contemporary works of drama focus critical attention on such issues as the AIDS epidemic, the Holocaust, postcolonialism, and the social makeup of today's multicultural America. The section's accompanying apparatus provides a rich context for understanding drama's performance history and its key terms of critical analysis.

Writing Guidance

Understanding Literature is not just a textbook on how to read and interpret great works of fiction, poetry, and drama; equally important, it also offers a practical guide to student writing. Section IX, on "Writing," introduces students to the art of critical writing from invention through final execution. Here you will find practical advice about every stage of the writing process, illustrated by sample student essays. In teaching the craft of critical writing, *Understanding Literature* addresses the key areas of critical thinking and composition including crafting effective thesis statements and employing evidence in argumentation. In addition to providing a general introduction to effective critical writing, *Understanding Literature* offers individual writing chapters covering each of the three genres of fiction, poetry, and drama, as well as an extensive discussion of college-level research writing.

Resources for Teaching *Understanding Literature*

A wealth of instructor resources are available to help you in the classroom. A comprehensive instructor's guide discusses every author and nearly every reading selection in the text. The authors provide guidance for discussing the selections in class, answering in-text questions and writing assignments, making connections to other writing selections, incorporating more coverage of literary theory in the classroom, and using the technology components. The accompanying CD-ROM can be used by students as a study tool, or you can use it in the classroom to enhance lectures and discussions. You will also find additional instructor resources at the *Understanding Literature* Web site.

For instructors who want to assign additional literary works in their course, special packaging options are available with the New Riverside Editions—a wonderful series that complements literary texts with relevant historical documents, cultural contexts, and critical essays. Titles include *The Scarlet Letter, Adventures of Huckleberry Finn, Call of the Wild, Sense and Sensibility, Fictions of Empire*, and *Wuthering Heights*. For a complete listing, please visit the Houghton Mifflin Web site at http://college.hmco.com.

Acknowledgments

We would like to thank all the instructors and colleagues who helped throughout the development process of this book. Your feedback and ideas were invaluable, and every chapter of this book has benefited from your insight. We particularly appreciate the dedicated work of Brian W. Gastle, Western Carolina University; Michelle Glaros, Dakota State University; Ann C. Hall, Ohio Dominican College; John Marx, University of Richmond; and Michele Peers, Northern Kentucky University; Aimee Pozorsky, Emory University.

We thank all of the reviewers, focus group participants, and class testers for their assistance in shaping this project: Linda B. Adams, Jefferson Community College; Frank Ancona, Sussex County Community College; Mike Anzelome, Nassau Community College; Maryam Barrie, Washtenaw Community College; Robert Barton, Rutgers University; John Blair, Southwest Texas State University; Barbara Bonallo, Miami-Dade Community College–Wolfson Campus; Lisa Brandom, John Brown University; Richard Brodesky, Pima Community College; Terence Brunk, Columbia College; Robert Callahan, Temple University; Ruth Callahan, Glendale Community College; Ron Carter, Rappahonnock Community College; Peggy Cole, Arapahoe Community College; Mark Garrett Cooper, Florida State University; Keith Coplin, Colby Community College; Gail S. Corso, Neumann College; Carol Ann Davis, College of Charleston; Kathy De Grave, Pittsburg State University; Gillian Devereux, Old Dominion University; Ken Donelson, Arizona State University; Tina D. Eliopulos, Community College of Southern Nevada; Sandra K. Ellston, Eastern Oregon University; Nancy Esposito, Bentley College; Marilyn Falkenberg, Menlo College; Ray Foster, Scottsdale Community College; Phyllis Frus, Hawaii Pacific University; Mark Gellis, Kettering University; Karen Golightly, University of Memphis; John Granger, San Diego State University; Marlene Groner, State University of New York–Farmingdale; Jean Harper, Ball State University; Randall Howe, North Georgia College and State University; Bryon Lee Grigsby, Centenary College; Grant Jenkins, Old Dominion University; Suzanne Keen, Washington and Lee University; Linda Cooper Knight, College of the Albemarle; Jim Kosmicki, Central Community College; Wendy Kurant, University of Georgia; Eleanor Latham, Central Oregon Community College; Marilyn Levine, Suffolk County Community College; David Levy, Housatonic Community College; Sarah Littefield, Salve Regina University; Jerry Bryan Lincecum, Austin College; Jack Lynch, Rutgers University; Diann V. Mason, Paris Junior College; Deborah Mael, Newberry College; Lisa Marcus, Pacific Lutheran University; Dennis D. McDaniel, Saint Vincent College; Thomas H. McNeely, Emerson

College; Janice Okoomian, Brown University; Michael Overman, University of South Carolina–Columbia; Elizabeth Patterson, Yakima Valley Community College; Eva Mokry Pohler, University of Texas at San Antonio; William Provost, University of Georgia; Jean-Michel Rabaté, University of Pennsylvania; Ann Marie Radaskiewicz, Western Piedmont Community College; Jeff Rice, University of Florida; Donald Riggs, Drexel University; Susan Roberts, Boston College; Peter Burton Ross, University of the District of Columbia; Albert Rouzie, Ohio University; Deborah Schwartz, Lourdes College; Carl Seiple, Kutztown University of Pennsylvania; Larry Severeid, College of Eastern Utah; William Sullivan, Winthrop College; John K. Swensson, DeAnza College; Joanna Tardoni, Western Wyoming Community College; Donna Thomsen, Johnson and Wales University; Michael Thro, Tidewater Community College; John Wargacki, Seton Hall University; Robert A. Watts, Drexel University; Joy Wentz, College of the Desert; Sallie Wolf, Arapahoe Community College; Nancy J. Young, Curry College.

We would also like to thank the individuals who helped us on this project from the start. For their thoughtful work on the anthology and the instructor's resource manual, we thank Jaime Hovey, Aimee Pozorski, Craig Owens, Yasmina Madden, Terence Hartnett, Danielle Hartnett, Caitlin Watt, Amy Nolan, and Johanna Frank. At Houghton Mifflin, we thank June Smith, Kris Clerkin, and Pat Coryell for their unflagging support of *Understanding Literature* from its earliest stages. We appreciate the editorial guidance of Suzanne Phelps Weir, Michael Gillespie, Katharine Glynn, and Bruce Cantley. Janet Edmonds and Beth McCracken ably developed the technology components, and Rosemary Winfield and Marlowe Shaeffer worked tirelessly to keep the book on schedule through production. Nancy Lyman and Cindy Graff Cohen contributed their ideas and enthusiasm throughout the process, and Maria Maimone and Michael Farmer tackled the Herculean task of clearing all the permissions. And thanks to Nonie and Brendan Watt for their love and support.

Why Study Literature?

Literature, as the Welsh poet Dylan Thomas famously remarked, is a "sullen art." Bound between the covers of a book, the writer's craft is made up of black marks that lie silent on the page. Yet according to Henry David Thoreau, literature also can empower you to "live deep and suck the marrow out of life." Robin Williams, in the guise of English teacher John Keating, declared in the film *Dead Poets Society* that he read literature because he was "a member of the human race and the human race is filled with passion! Medicine, Law, Banking—these are necessary to sustain life—but poetry, romance, love, beauty! These are what we stay alive for."

Higher education is a requisite, certainly, to becoming a doctor, lawyer, accountant, journalist, or business executive. Nevertheless, the kind of passion to be found from the fiction of Gabriel García Márquez, the poetry of Gwendolyn Brooks, and the drama of William Shakespeare just might point you toward becoming a more discerning professional, a more engaged citizen, a more thoughtful human being: someone—in short—who is more alive. A work of literature—whether a short story, a poem, or a play—is not just a form of entertainment or an amusement. Reading is not the same as consuming; reading is more radically transformative. Great literature, according to German poet Ranier Maria Rilke, makes you aware that "you must change your life."

In addition to experiencing literature, understanding it requires discipline and critical thinking skills. No one is born with the capacity to detect dramatic irony or to discern the difference between "theater in the round" and "theater of the absurd." Interpreting the complexities of an Elizabethan sonnet or a postmodern work of hyperfiction is not something that comes naturally to most people. It's an acquired art, much like mastering a sport or a musical instrument. The delight of critical thinking lies in both experiencing and understanding what literature can do on the page, at the microphone, and on the stage. This book will give you the tools you will need to enjoy great literature and, equally important, to write about it with greater precision and keener insight.

UNDERSTANDING LITERATURE

FICTION

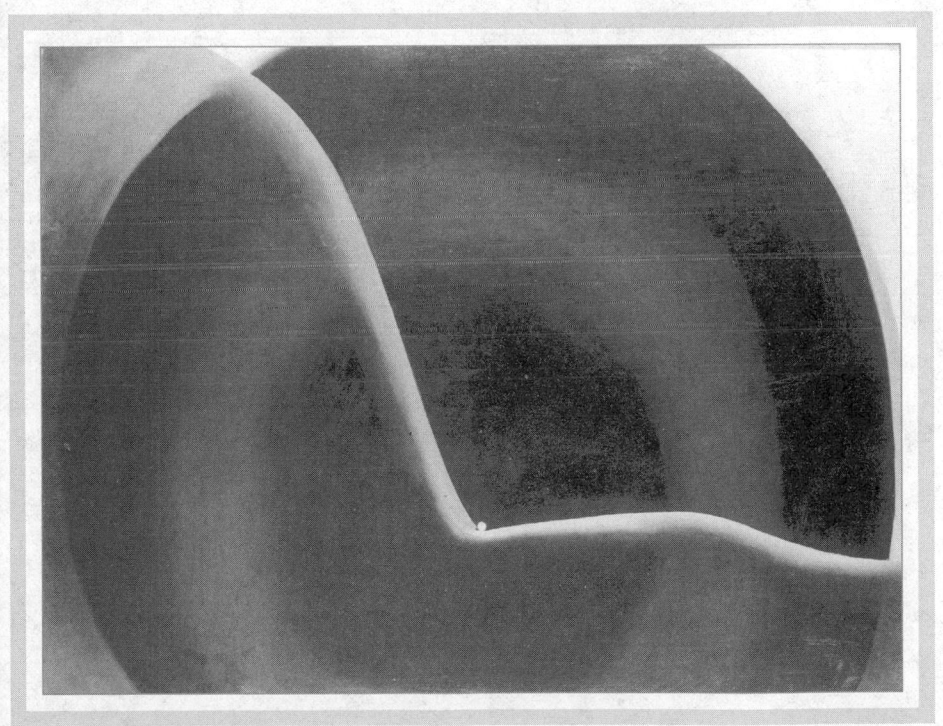

Part I
Form and Content

1   Introduction: Reading Fiction

Narrative Fiction

In the twenty-first century we are surrounded by fiction. Novels, short stories, comic books, movies, television shows, videos, folk tales, bedtime stories, and even jokes saturate our existence. Such genres (or kinds) of fiction as "mystery," "romance," "adventure," "science fiction," "comedy," "drama," and "literature" sort book and video store shelves. These forms of fiction are all narrative in that they organize events as a series of cause-and-effect relations in time: they tell stories. Most of us are avid consumers of stories and most of us know how they work: we are with what the story is.

Fiction offers itself to be read, enjoyed, and interpreted. You might have noticed that most stories are not a simple recounting of events but embody an art in their telling. The study of fiction is the study of this art. It is a process

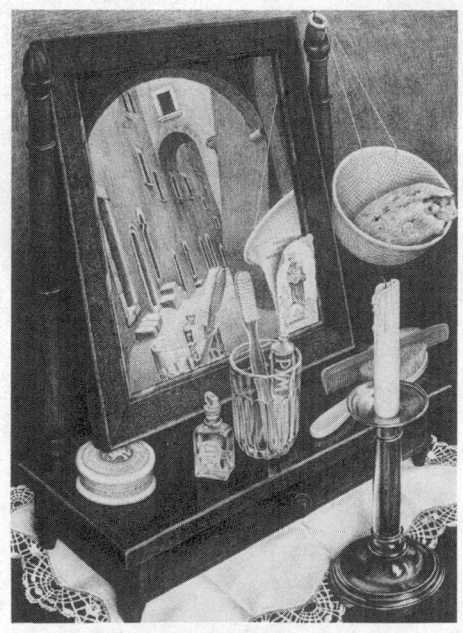

M.C. Escher, *Still Life with Mirror* (1934)

of reading and analyzing both what a story says and how it says it. As we read, we notice these aspects of stories. Interpreting or analyzing stories is a way of explaining how they work as pieces of art—how they tell their story—and why we enjoy them. In other words, interpreting is a way of thinking about what we have already read and what we already know.

Fictional narratives are fictional in that they do not represent any specific historical event, though most stories transmit insights and truths about the nature of humanity and culture. While plays, poems, and stories in any medium (print, live performance, video, film) typically contain narratives, in discussions of literature the term *fiction* generally refers to fictional narratives in the form of written prose.

In this section on fiction, we are concerned with prose fiction in the form of short stories or novellas (short novels). These genres of prose fiction accomplish most of the things the longer novel accomplishes except that they are shorter. Their relative brevity enables us to include them in their entirety. The skills readers use to interpret short stories are the same skills employed to interpret all prose fiction.

Characteristics of Fiction

All narratives share certain basic characteristics regardless of their medium. Let's use as an example a familiar—perhaps even an overly familiar and corny—story.

> A young white man, who has grown up in a big city, lives an aimless existence as a part-time prize fighter and collector for a loan shark. His striking boxing name catches the attention of the heavyweight champion who is looking for a man of the people to challenge. Wanting both the publicity and an easy victory, the champ, who is African American, invites the young man to fight him. The young man, unsure of his talent, decides to accept and begins a rigorous training regimen that includes drinking raw eggs, running through the streets, and pounding sides of beef. While in the midst of training, the young man falls in love with a shy young woman. Although he works hard and almost beats the champ, the young man is finally defeated. His courage, however, wins the heart of the crowd, and he realizes that in trying his hardest and winning the love of the woman, he has conquered after all.

Like all narratives, this story has characters, setting, and plot. Its characters consist of the young fighter, his trainer, the girl, and the champ. The story's setting is the big city, the boxing ring, and the young man's apartment. The story's plot involves the challenge, the young fighter's training and courtship of the young woman, the fight, and what the young man learns. Like all instances of narrative fiction, this story has a theme or unifying idea (or ideas) that hold it together. It focuses on the virtues of hard work and various understandings of what it might mean to win. It illustrates that although the young boxer doesn't win the bout, he gains love and self-respect. It also suggests that trying hard always pays off, even if in ways one doesn't expect.

Like most narrative fiction, this story also reflects in some fashion the ideas, biases, and social conditions of the period and culture in which it was written. The story of the boxer illustrates the possibilities or impossibilities of class mobility in American culture. It presents the saga of the classic underdog. It assumes our familiarity with the patterns of romance and the mechanisms of a society in which people can become stars or commodities. It works on (and in some ways counters) our assumptions about race and power.

All fictional narratives are involved in processes of reception (how readers react to a story), interpretation (the ways readers analyze and understand a story), and some contemplation of the story as a story and as part of a tradition of story telling (how the story relates to all other stories). The boxer's story, for example, depends on the reader sympathizing with the young boxer. His loss invites the reader to acknowledge the value of other kinds of triumph. It works in relation to our experience of all stories about underdogs, romance, sports, and the special reverence accorded the "common man" in American culture. And like all narratives, this one, minimal as it might seem, engages in the complex dynamics of telling a story. It employs a narrator (a presence in the story that tells the story), represents a point of view, and could recount events out of the order of their imagined occurrence, deploy images, symbols, motifs, repetition, and other devices to enhance and deepen the telling of the narrative.

The History of Prose Fiction

Prose fiction depends on written language as its medium of representation. Prose designed to be heard (such as orally transmitted folk tales and radio) tends to contain more repetition and simpler sentence structures than prose designed to be read. Prose for reading can take advantage of the fact that print media (including electronic forms) can be read as slowly as readers wish and that any part can be read over and over. The ease with which print enables the reader to peruse at will, to interrupt, read ahead, compare with other texts, and quote the text exactly means that prose fiction can be more linguistically complex. It can use more elaborate sentences, employ a wider and more varied vocabulary, and sustain a more complicated web of images. Prose fiction can also have a more complex mode of narration and might combine a greater number of different stories or plots. It can have, for example, one or more narrators and multiple narratives arranged together.

Of the various contemporary mediums devoted primarily to narrative, only orally transmitted folk tales are older than prose fiction. Written prose is an old medium compared to such relatively recent arrivals as radio, cinema, television, and the Internet. Both poetry and drama are ways of telling stories that have existed since ancient times. Until just after the Renaissance, the primary form for formal written storytelling was the long poem, a genre going back to antiquity. Shorter forms of prose fiction included folk tales, myths, and legends, which tended to be oral forms, and fables, which were written in either poetry or prose. From the seventeenth century on, prose fiction gained popularity, not only because of the continuing refinement of printing technologies that made books cheaper and more available but also because of the gradually widening audience of literate readers. **Web** Early forms of prose fiction, however, appeared mainly in the longer form of the novel and were often composed of a series of letters exchanged among characters (the epistolary novel). **Web**

www

www

Prose fiction in the form of the short story as we know it is a very recent genre. As twentieth-century writer Elizabeth Bowen suggests, "The short story is a young art. As we know it, it is a child of this century." That the novel was the favored form for prose writers and readers during the seventeenth, eighteenth, and nineteenth centuries was partly due to the vision and understanding of the role of fiction in culture during those eras. The rise of the novel—the genre employed by such writers as Jane Austen, Charles Dickens, George Eliot, and Mark Twain—accompanied the rise of the middle class and a coincident interest in history. This history consisted of tracking the causes and effects of various ideas, economic forces, and social conditions and describing relations within and among various social classes. The novel ultimately links the trends of history to society, and history's large movements to individual lives. Such a sense of the novel as the representation of "the shaping force of man's individual and collective history," as the eminent critic of the novel Ian Watt describes it, does not encourage serious writers to compose shorter, less panoramic works, nor are those shorter works perceived as worthy or serious art.

In contrast to the epic scale of the novel, shorter forms of fiction became prominent in the nineteenth century in America and in the 1880s in England. Cheaper to publish and circulate than the longer novel, short stories focused on the individual—often an outsider—and on more ephemeral expressions of social and cultural relations. In the nineteenth century, short fiction appeared primarily in periodicals. **Web** These short stories contrasted with the fairy tale, an ancient form that typically involves stereotyped characters with no specific consciousness or interior life, who take part in clear-cut events set in a remote or timeless world. In contrast to the fairy tale, the modern notion of the short story has, as Edgar Allan Poe suggests, "a unity of effect or impression." **Web** This unity was aided by the story's short length, which enabled readers to read it in two hours or less. There are many different definitions of the short story that add to Poe's insistence on unity. Critics suggest variously that the short story is defined by its "plot compression," its treatment of changes in character, its subject matter, or its tone. There are also many ways of looking at the short story.

www

www

Analyzing and Interpreting

Stories invite us to read and interpret, but we need the sets of concepts and vocabularies that permit us to think about and discuss the ways stories do what they do. There are many different ways of approaching a story. In this text, these various approaches are called Critical Perspectives. These perspectives, which come from an area of study called *critical* or *literary theory*, illustrate different ways of thinking about how literature works as an art. Understanding these perspectives will provide you with tools for interpreting prose fiction.

The range of skills and approaches needed to read, understand, analyze, and write about prose fiction are reflected in the organization and focus of the three sections on fiction. These three sections also roughly map the literary history of American, British, and Anglophone (stories written in English by writers who did not live in the British Isles or America) short fiction. Although the sections do not adhere strictly to either temporal or stylistic divisions, the tendency is to move from older, more realistic texts through modernism's emphasis on image and impression to more recent stories that are conscious of themselves as stories and reflect on what it means to write a story.

The first section, Form and Content, concentrates on the formal elements of short fiction and on some of the ideas, biases, and social conditions (the plight of women, poor people, or African Americans, for example) reflected in the stories—on what stories tell. Understanding the relation between how stories are shaped (their form) and what they tell is a basic and crucial starting point in interpreting prose fiction. This section centers primarily around nineteenth- and early twentieth-century American fiction, since the short story in English was mainly developed in America.

The second section, Image, Style, Structure, focuses on how stories are told. It examines the functions of images, symbols, motifs, style, and language as well as the structures and dynamics of narrating. It builds on the studies of form and content in the first section by inviting us to consider the ways language, image, and tone relate to both. The second section focuses on modernist and postcolonial fiction, including selections from English, American, and Anglophone writers.

The third section, Reading and Interpreting, raises questions about how we read. Centered around issues of language, representation, metanarrative, and intertextuality, this section takes up issues of postmodernism in stories from Europe, America, and South America.

Each section encourages the reader to analyze stories and to understand and employ various critical perspectives as each builds on the basic skills and concepts of literary interpretation. (See, for example, the Study Project for each chapter located on the Web **Web** or the intensive What to Do When Analyzing a Story included on the CD-ROM **CD-ROM** .) Part of this labor is to see writing itself as a mode of analysis and an engagement with various conversations and theories of literature. Whatever one writes or even says about literature inevitably assumes particular ideas about literature: how it works, what we should look at, the kinds of traits we are looking for. Part of the process of studying literature is to become conscious of what our assumptions about literature are, how these assumptions shape our perceptions and define the questions we ask, and how shifting our assumptions might enable us to gain new insights into what we read.

2 Overview: The Formal Elements of Fiction

When we analyze fiction, one of the first steps is to identify and characterize its formal elements. The **formal elements** include character, setting, plot, narrator, point of view, and theme. These are called formal elements for two reasons. First, defining the way a story employs each of these elements helps us characterize its **form:** what specific conventions a story uses. Second, studying a story's form is a way of describing how its elements come together as a whole work of art. We study each of these elements in more detail in the chapters that follow, but as a beginning it is useful to get a sense of how they all work together.

Stories present settings full of characters who do something. Characters may be people, animals, or even landscape or nature—the young boxer, the champ, or the young woman of the young boxer's story you read in the Introduction. Settings may be real places, imagined environments, or the imagination itself. In the young boxer's story, the settings are the city streets and the boxing ring. The deeds recounted make up the story's plot. These fundamental ingredients—characters, settings, and plot—provide readers with a basic sense of the story's subject—of *what the story tells.*

At first glance the three components of prose fiction are obvious. As apparent as these elements may be, understanding that they always work together with the story's other elements—narrator, point of view, themes, images, symbols, language, style, and tone—is critically important. Understanding how a story's formal elements work together is the beginning of the process of interpretation, which seeks both to understand the story's various meanings and to understand the story as a work of art.

Critical Perspectives: Formalism and New Criticism   *www*

Web

Form (how a story's elements fit together) is one vantage from which a story might be interpreted. Analyses that employ form as their starting point are called **formalism.** Formalist critics begin with the assumption that literature's forms differentiate it from other modes of expression and that those forms and the ways various texts employ them tell us much about a story's art. Most literary interpretations consider some aspect of form in their analyses, and many approaches to fiction (feminist criticism, race criticism, Marxist criticism, queer theory) focus on the story's content or subject matter.

9

Criticism that studies how form and content relate to one another is called **New Criticism.** New Criticism assumes that a literary work can be read in itself, without additional contextual material such as author biography or history. It focuses on how all of the elements of a story work together to reflect, repeat, or sometimes contradict one another in ways that reflect what the story is about.

An example of the fledgling art of the short story is Nathaniel Hawthorne's "The Birthmark," which appeared in his second collection of short stories, *Mosses from an Old Manse* (1846), after originally appearing in *The Pioneer* in 1843. Hawthorne himself criticizes the collection in the book's Preface:

> These fitfull sketches with so little of external life about them, yet claiming no profundity of purpose—so reserved even when they sometimes seem so frank— often but half in earnest, and never, even when most so, expressing satisfactorily the thoughts which they profess to image—such trifles, I truly feel, afford no solid basis for a literary reputation.

But in a later edition of the book, author Henry James disagrees with Hawthorne's own assessment:

> [T]he valuable element in these things was not what Hawthorne put into them consciously, but what passed into them without his being able to measure it—the element of simple genius, the quality of imagination. This is the real charm of Hawthorne's writing—this purity and spontaneity and naturalness of fancy.

෬෬෬

NATHANIEL HAWTHORNE

The Birthmark   *(1854)*

In the latter part of the last century there lived a man of science, an eminent proficient in every branch of natural philosophy, who not long before our story opens had made experience of a spiritual affinity more attractive than any chemical one. He had left his laboratory to the care of an assistant, cleared his fine countenance from the furnace smoke, washed the stain of acids from his fingers, and persuaded a beautiful woman to become his wife. In those days, when the comparatively recent discovery of electricity and other kindred mysteries of Nature seemed to open paths into the region of miracle, it was not unusual for the love of science to rival the love of woman in its depth and absorbing energy. The higher intellect, the imagination, the spirit, and even the heart might all find their congenial aliment in pursuits which, as some of their ardent votaries believed, would ascend from one step of powerful intelligence to another, until the philosopher should lay his hand on the secret of creative force and perhaps make new worlds for himself. We know not whether Aylmer possessed this degree of faith in man's ultimate control over Nature. He had devoted himself, however, too unreservedly to scientific studies ever to be weaned from them by any second passion. His love for his young wife might prove the stronger of the two; but it could only be by intertwining itself with his love of science and uniting the strength of the latter to his own.

Such a union accordingly took place, and was attended with truly remarkable consequences and a deeply impressive moral. One day, very soon after their marriage, Aylmer sat gazing at his wife with a trouble in his countenance that grew stronger until he spoke.

"Georgiana," said he, "has it never occurred to you that the mark upon your cheek might be removed?"

"No, indeed," said she, smiling; but, perceiving the seriousness of his manner, she blushed deeply. "To tell you the truth, it has been so often called a charm that I was simple enough to imagine it might be so."

"Ah, upon another face perhaps it might," replied her husband; "but 5 never on yours. No, dearest Georgiana, you came so nearly perfect from the hand of Nature that this slightest possible defect, which we hesitate whether to term a defect or a beauty, shocks me, as being the visible mark of earthly imperfection."

"Shocks you, my husband!" cried Georgiana, deeply hurt; at first reddening with momentary anger, but then bursting into tears. "Then why did you take me from my mother's side? You cannot love what shocks you!"

To explain this conversation, it must be mentioned that in the centre of Georgiana's left cheek there was a singular mark, deeply interwoven, as it were, with the texture and substance of her face. In the usual state of her complexion—a healthy though delicate bloom—the mark wore a tint of deeper crimson, which imperfectly defined its shape amid the surrounding rosiness. When she blushed it gradually became more indistinct, and finally vanished amid the triumphant rush of blood that bathed the whole cheek with its brilliant glow. But if any shifting motion caused her to turn pale there was the mark again, a crimson stain upon the snow, in what Aylmer sometimes deemed an almost fearful distinctness. Its shape bore not a little similarity to the human hand, though of the smallest pygmy size. Georgiana's lovers were wont to say that some fairy at her birth hour had laid her tiny hand upon the infant's cheek, and left this impress there in token of the magic endowments that were to give her such sway over all hearts. Many a desperate swain would have risked life for the privilege of pressing his lips to the mysterious hand. It must not be concealed, however, that the impression wrought by this fairy sign-manual varied exceedingly according to the difference of temperament in the beholders. Some fastidious persons—but they were exclusively of her own sex—affirmed that the bloody hand, as they chose to call it, quite destroyed the effect of Georgiana's beauty and rendered her countenance even hideous. But it would be as reasonable to say that one of those small blue stains which sometimes occur in the purest statuary marble would convert the Eve of Powers to a monster. Masculine observers, if the birthmark did not heighten their admiration, contented themselves with wishing it away, that the world might possess one living specimen of ideal loveliness without the semblance of a flaw. After his marriage,—for he thought little or nothing of the matter before,—Aylmer discovered that this was the case with himself.

Had she been less beautiful,—if Envy's self could have found aught else to sneer at,—he might have felt his affection heightened by the prettiness of this mimic hand, now vaguely portrayed, now lost, now stealing forth again and glimmering to and fro with every pulse of emotion that throbbed within her heart; but, seeing her otherwise so perfect, he found this one defect grow more and more intolerable with every moment of their united lives. It was the fatal flaw of humanity which Nature, in one shape or another, stamps ineffaceably on all her productions, either to imply that they are temporary and finite, or that their perfection must be wrought by toil and pain. The crimson hand expressed the ineludible grip in which mortality clutches the highest and purest of earthly mould, degrading them into kindred with the lowest, and even with the very brutes, like whom their visible frames return to dust. In this manner, selecting it as the symbol of his wife's liability to sin, sorrow, decay, and death, Aylmer's sombre imagination was not long in rendering the birthmark a frightful object, causing him more trouble and horror than ever Georgiana's beauty, whether of soul or sense, had given him delight.

At all the seasons which should have been their happiest he invariably, and without intending it, nay, in spite of a purpose to the contrary, reverted to this one disastrous topic. Trifling as it at first appeared, it so connected itself with innumerable trains of thought and modes of feeling that it became the central point of all. With the morning twilight Aylmer opened his eyes upon his wife's face and recognized the symbol of imperfection; and when they sat together at the evening hearth his eyes wandered stealthily to her cheek, and beheld, flickering with the blaze of the wood fire, the spectral hand that wrote mortality where he would fain have worshipped. Georgiana soon learned to shudder at his gaze. It needed but a glance with the peculiar expression that his face often wore to change the roses of her cheek into a deathlike paleness, amid which the crimson hand was brought strongly out, like a bass relief of ruby on the whitest marble.

Late one night, when the lights were growing dim so as hardly to betray   10
the stain on the poor wife's cheek, she herself, for the first time, voluntarily took up the subject.

"Do you remember, my dear Aylmer," said she, with a feeble attempt at a smile, "have you any recollection, of a dream last night about this odious hand?"

"None! none whatever!" replied Aylmer, starting; but then he added, in a dry, cold tone, affected for the sake of concealing the real depth of his emotion, "I might well dream of it; for, before I fell asleep, it had taken a pretty firm hold of my fancy."

"And you did dream of it?" continued Georgiana, hastily; for she dreaded lest a gush of tears should interrupt what she had to say. "A terrible dream! I wonder that you can forget it. Is it possible to forget this one expression?—'It is in her heart now; we must have it out!' Reflect, my husband; for by all means I would have you recall that dream."

The mind is in a sad state when Sleep, the all-involving, cannot confine her spectres within the dim region of her sway, but suffers them to break forth, affrighting this actual life with secrets that perchance belong to a deeper one. Aylmer now remembered his dream. He had fancied himself with his servant Aminadab, attempting an operation for the removal of the birthmark; but the deeper went the knife, the deeper sank the hand, until at length its tiny grasp appeared to have caught hold of Georgiana's heart; whence, however, her husband was inexorably resolved to cut or wrench it away.

When the dream had shaped itself perfectly in his memory Aylmer sat in his wife's presence with a guilty feeling. Truth often finds its way to the mind close muffled in robes of sleep, and then speaks with uncompromising directness of matters in regard to which we practise an unconscious self-deception during our waking moments. Until now he had not been aware of the tyrannizing influence acquired by one idea over his mind, and of the lengths which he might find in his heart to go for the sake of giving himself peace.

"Aylmer," resumed Georgiana, solemnly, "I know not what may be the cost to both of us to rid me of this fatal birthmark. Perhaps its removal may cause cureless deformity; or it may be the stain goes as deep as life itself. Again: do we know that there is a possibility, on any terms, of unclasping the firm grip of this little hand which was laid upon me before I came into the world?"

"Dearest Georgiana, I have spent much thought upon the subject," hastily interrupted Aylmer. "I am convinced of the perfect practicability of its removal."

"If there be the remotest possibility of it," continued Georgiana, "let the attempt be made, at whatever risk. Danger is nothing to me; for life, while this hateful mark makes me the object of your horror and disgust,—life is a burden which I would fling down with joy. Either remove this dreadful hand, or take my wretched life! You have deep science. All the world bears witness of it. You have achieved great wonders. Cannot you remove this little, little mark, which I cover with the tips of two small fingers? Is this beyond your power, for the sake of your own peace, and to save your poor wife from madness?"

"Noblest, dearest, tenderest wife," cried Aylmer, rapturously, "doubt not my power. I have already given this matter the deepest thought—thought which might almost have enlightened me to create a being less perfect than yourself. Georgiana, you have led me deeper than ever into the heart of science. I feel myself fully competent to render this dear cheek as faultless as its fellow; and then, most beloved, what will be my triumph when I shall have corrected what Nature left imperfect in her fairest work! Even Pygmalion, when his sculptured woman assumed life, felt not greater ecstasy than mine will be."

"It is resolved, then," said Georgiana, faintly smiling. "And, Aylmer, spare me not, though you should find the birthmark take refuge in my heart at last."

Her husband tenderly kissed her cheek—her right cheek—not that which bore the impress of the crimson hand.

The next day Aylmer apprised his wife of a plan that he had formed whereby he might have opportunity for the intense thought and constant watchfulness which the proposed operation would require; while Georgiana, likewise, would enjoy the perfect repose essential to its success. They were to seclude themselves in the extensive apartments occupied by Aylmer as a laboratory, and where, during his toilsome youth, he had made discoveries in the elemental powers of Nature that had roused the admiration of all the learned societies in Europe. Seated calmly in this laboratory, the pale philosopher had investigated the secrets of the highest cloud region and of the profoundest mines; he had satisfied himself of the causes that kindled and kept alive the fires of the volcano; and had explained the mystery of the fountains, and how it is that they gush forth, some so bright and pure, and others with such rich medicinal virtues, from the dark bosom of the earth. Here, too, at an earlier period, he had studied the wonders of the human frame, and attempted to fathom the very process by which Nature assimilates all her precious influences from earth and air, and from the spiritual world, to create and foster man, her masterpiece. The latter pursuit, however, Aylmer had long laid aside in unwilling recognition of the truth—against which all seekers sooner or later stumble—that our great creative Mother, while she amuses us with apparently working in the broadest sunshine, is yet severely careful to keep her own secrets, and, in spite of her pretended openness, shows us nothing but results. She permits us, indeed, to mar, but seldom to mend, and, like a jealous patentee, on no account to make. Now, however, Aylmer resumed these half-forgotten investigations; not, of course, with such hopes or wishes as first suggested them; but because they involved much physiological truth and lay in the path of his proposed scheme for the treatment of Georgiana.

As he led her over the threshold of the laboratory, Georgiana was cold and tremulous. Aylmer looked cheerfully into her face, with intent to reassure her, but was so startled with the intense glow of the birthmark upon the whiteness of her cheek that he could not restrain a strong convulsive shudder. His wife fainted.

"Aminadab! Aminadab!" shouted Aylmer, stamping violently on the floor.

Forthwith there issued from an inner apartment a man of low stature, but 25 bulky frame, with shaggy hair hanging about his visage, which was grimed with the vapors of the furnace. This personage had been Aylmer's underworker during his whole scientific career, and was admirably fitted for that office by his great mechanical readiness, and the skill with which, while incapable of comprehending a single principle, he executed all the details of his master's experiments. With his vast strength, his shaggy hair, his smoky aspect, and the indescribable earthiness that incrusted him, he seemed to represent man's physical nature; while Aylmer's slender figure, and pale, intellectual face, were no less apt a type of the spiritual element.

"Throw open the door of the boudoir, Aminadab," said Aylmer, "and burn a pastil."

"Yes, master," answered Aminadab, looking intently at the lifeless form of Georgiana; and then he muttered to himself, "If she were my wife, I'd never part with that birthmark."

When Georgiana recovered consciousness she found herself breathing an atmosphere of penetrating fragrance, the gentle potency of which had recalled her from her deathlike faintness. The scene around her looked like enchantment. Aylmer had converted those smoky, dingy, sombre rooms, where he had spent his brightest years in recondite pursuits, into a series of beautiful apartments not unfit to be the secluded abode of a lovely woman. The walls were hung with gorgeous curtains, which imparted the combination of grandeur and grace that no other species of adornment can achieve; and, as they fell from the ceiling to the floor, their rich and ponderous folds, concealing all angles and straight lines, appeared to shut in the scene from infinite space. For aught Georgiana knew, it might be a pavilion among the clouds. And Aylmer, excluding the sunshine, which would have interfered with his chemical processes, had supplied its place with perfumed lamps, emitting flames of various hue, but all uniting in a soft, impurpled radiance. He now knelt by his wife's side, watching her earnestly, but without alarm; for he was confident in his science, and felt that he could draw a magic circle round her within which no evil might intrude.

"Where am I? Ah, I remember," said Georgiana, faintly, and she placed her hand over her cheek to hide the terrible mark from her husband's eyes.

"Fear not, dearest!" exclaimed he. "Do not shrink from me! Believe me, 30 Georgiana, I even rejoice in this single imperfection, since it will be such a rapture to remove it."

"O, spare me!" sadly replied his wife. "Pray do not look at it again. I never can forget that convulsive shudder."

In order to soothe Georgiana, and, as it were, to release her mind from the burden of actual things, Aylmer now put in practice some of the light and playful secrets which science had taught him among its profounder lore. Airy figures, absolutely bodiless ideas, and forms of unsubstantial beauty came and danced before her, imprinting their momentary footsteps on beams of light. Though she had some indistinct idea of the method of these optical phenomena, still the illusion was almost perfect enough to warrant the belief that her husband possessed sway over the spiritual world. Then again, when she felt a wish to look forth from her seclusion, immediately, as if her thoughts were answered, the procession of external existence flitted across a screen. The scenery and the figures of actual life were perfectly represented, but with that bewitching yet indescribable difference which always makes a picture, an image, or a shadow so much more attractive than the original. When wearied of this, Aylmer bade her cast her eyes upon a vessel containing a quantity of earth. She did so, with little interest at first; but was soon startled to perceive the germ of a plant shooting upward from the soil. Then came the slender stalk; the leaves gradually unfolded themselves; and amid them was a perfect and lovely flower.

"It is magical!" cried Georgiana. "I dare not touch it."

"Nay, pluck it," answered Aylmer,—"pluck it, and inhale its brief perfume while you may. The flower will wither in a few moments and leave nothing save its brown seed vessels; but thence may be perpetuated a race as ephemeral as itself."

But Georgiana had no sooner touched the flower than the whole plant 35 suffered a blight, its leaves turning coal-black as if by the agency of fire.

"There was too powerful a stimulus," said Aylmer, thoughtfully.

To make up for this abortive experiment, he proposed to take her portrait by a scientific process of his own invention. It was to be effected by rays of light striking upon a polished plate of metal. Georgiana assented; but, on looking at the result, was affrighted to find the features of the portrait blurred and indefinable; while the minute figure of a hand appeared where the cheek should have been. Aylmer snatched the metallic plate and threw it into a jar of corrosive acid.

Soon, however, he forgot these mortifying failures. In the intervals of study and chemical experiment he came to her flushed and exhausted, but seemed invigorated by her presence, and spoke in glowing language of the resources of his art. He gave a history of the long dynasty of the alchemists, who spent so many ages in quest of the universal solvent by which the golden principle might be elicited from all things vile and base. Aylmer appeared to believe that, by the plainest scientific logic, it was altogether within the limits of possibility to discover this long-sought medium; "but," he added, "a philosopher who should go deep enough to acquire the power would attain too lofty a wisdom to stoop to the exercise of it." Not less singular were his opinions in regard to the elixir vitae. He more than intimated that it was at his option to concoct a liquid that should prolong life for years, perhaps interminably; but that it would produce a discord in Nature which all the world, and chiefly the quaffer of the immortal nostrum, would find cause to curse.

"Aylmer, are you in earnest?" asked Georgiana, looking at him with amazement and fear. "It is terrible to possess such power, or even to dream of possessing it."

"O, do not tremble, my love," said her husband. "I would not wrong either you or myself by working such inharmonious effects upon our lives; but I would have you consider how trifling, in comparison, is the skill requisite to remove this little hand."   40

At the mention of the birthmark, Georgiana, as usual, shrank as if a red-hot iron had touched her cheek.

Again Aylmer applied himself to his labors. She could hear his voice in the distant furnace room giving directions to Aminadab, whose harsh, uncouth, misshapen tones were audible in response, more like the grunt or growl of a brute than human speech. After hours of absence, Aylmer reappeared and proposed that she should now examine his cabinet of chemical products and natural treasures of the earth. Among the former he showed her a small vial, in which, he remarked, was contained a gentle yet most powerful fragrance, capable of impregnating all the breezes that blow across a kingdom. They were of inestimable value, the contents of that little vial; and, as he said so, he threw some of the perfume into the air and filled the room with piercing and invigorating delight.

"And what is this?" asked Georgiana, pointing to a small crystal globe containing a gold-colored liquid. "It is so beautiful to the eye that I could imagine it the elixir of life."

"In one sense it is," replied Aylmer; "or rather, the elixir of immortality. It is the most precious poison that ever was concocted in this world. By its aid I could apportion the lifetime of any mortal at whom you might point your finger. The strength of the dose would determine whether he were to linger out years, or drop dead in the midst of a breath. No king on his guarded throne could keep his life if I, in my private station, should deem that the welfare of millions justified me in depriving him of it."

"Why do you keep such a terrific drug?" inquired Georgiana in horror.   45

"Do not mistrust me, dearest," said her husband, smiling; "its virtuous potency is yet greater than its harmful one. But see! here is a powerful cosmetic. With a few drops of this in a vase of water, freckles may be washed away as easily as the hands are cleansed. A stronger infusion would take the blood out of the cheek, and leave the rosiest beauty a pale ghost."

"Is it with this lotion that you intend to bathe my cheek?" asked Georgiana, anxiously.

"O, no," hastily replied her husband; "this is merely superficial. Your case demands a remedy that shall go deeper."

In his interviews with Georgiana, Aylmer generally made minute inquiries as to her sensations, and whether the confinement of the rooms and the temperature of the atmosphere agreed with her. These questions had such a particular drift that Georgiana began to conjecture that she was already subjected to certain physical influences, either breathed in with the fragrant air or taken with her food. She fancied likewise, but it might be altogether fancy, that there was a stirring up of her system—a strange, indefinite sensation creeping through her veins, and tingling, half painfully, half pleasurably, at her heart. Still, whenever she dared to look into the mirror, there she beheld herself pale as a white rose and with the crimson birthmark stamped upon her cheek. Not even Aylmer now hated it so much as she.

To dispel the tedium of the hours which her husband found it necessary   50
to devote to the processes of combination and analysis, Georgiana turned over the volumes of his scientific library. In many dark old tomes she met with chapters full of romance and poetry. They were the works of the philosophers of the middle ages, such as Albertus Magnus, Cornelius Agrippa, Paracelsus, and the famous friar who created the prophetic Brazen Head. All these antique naturalists stood in advance of their centuries, yet were imbued with some of their credulity, and therefore were believed, and perhaps imagined themselves to have acquired from the investigation of Nature a power above Nature, and from physics a sway over the spiritual world. Hardly less curious and imaginative were the early volumes of the Transactions of the Royal Society, in which the members, knowing little of the limits of natural possibility, were continually recording wonders or proposing methods whereby wonders might be wrought.

But to Georgiana, the most engrossing volume was a large folio from her husband's own hand, in which he had recorded every experiment of his scientific career, its original aim, the methods adopted for its development, and its final success or failure, with the circumstances to which either event was attributable. The book, in truth, was both the history and emblem of his ardent, ambitious, imaginative, yet practical and laborious life. He handled physical details as if there were nothing beyond them; yet spiritualized them all and redeemed himself from materialism by his strong and eager aspiration towards the infinite. In his grasp the veriest clod of earth assumed a soul.

Georgiana, as she read, reverenced Aylmer and loved him more profoundly than ever, but with a less entire dependence on his judgment than heretofore. Much as he had accomplished, she could not but observe that his most splendid successes were almost invariably failures, if compared with the ideal at which he aimed. His brightest diamonds were the merest pebbles, and felt to be so by himself, in comparison with the inestimable gems which lay hidden beyond his reach. The volume, rich with achievements that had won renown for its author, was yet as melancholy a record as ever mortal hand had penned. It was the sad confession and continual exemplification of the shortcomings of the composite man, the spirit burdened with clay and working in matter, and of the despair that assails the higher nature at finding itself so miserably thwarted by the earthly part. Perhaps every man of genius, in whatever sphere, might recognize the image of his own experience in Aylmer's journal.

So deeply did these reflections affect Georgiana that she laid her face upon the open volume and burst into tears. In this situation she was found by her husband.

"It is dangerous to read in a sorcerer's books," said he with a smile, though his countenance was uneasy and displeased. "Georgiana, there are pages in that volume which I can scarcely glance over and keep my senses. Take heed lest it prove detrimental to you."

"It has made me worship you more than ever," said she.

"Ah, wait for this one success," rejoined he, "then worship me if you will. 55 I shall deem myself hardly unworthy of it. But come, I have sought you for the luxury of your voice. Sing to me, dearest."

So she poured out the liquid music of her voice to quench the thirst of his spirit. He then took his leave with a boyish exuberance of gayety, assuring her that her seclusion would endure but a little longer, and that the result was already certain. Scarcely had he departed when Georgiana felt irresistibly impelled to follow him. She had forgotten to inform Aylmer of a symptom which for two or three hours past had begun to excite her attention. It was a sensation in the fatal birthmark, not painful, but which induced a restlessness throughout her system. Hastening after her husband, she intruded for the first time into the laboratory.

The first thing that struck her eye was the furnace, that hot and feverish worker, with the intense glow of its fire, which by the quantities of soot clustered above it seemed to have been burning for ages. There was a distilling apparatus in full operation. Around the room were retorts, tubes, cylinders, crucibles, and other apparatus of chemical research. An electrical machine stood ready for immediate use. The atmosphere felt oppressively close, and was tainted with gaseous odors which had been tormented forth by the processes of science. The severe and homely simplicity of the apartment, with its naked walls and brick pavement, looked strange, accustomed as Georgiana had become to the fantastic elegance of her boudoir. But what chiefly, indeed almost solely, drew her attention, was the aspect of Aylmer himself.

He was pale as death, anxious and absorbed, and hung over the furnace as if it depended upon his utmost watchfulness whether the liquid which it was distilling should be the draught of immortal happiness or misery. How different from the sanguine and joyous mien that he had assumed for Georgiana's encouragement!

"Carefully now, Aminadab; carefully, thou human machine; carefully, thou man of clay," muttered Aylmer, more to himself than his assistant. "Now, if there be a thought too much or too little, it is all over."

"Ho! ho!" mumbled Aminadab. "Look, master! look!" 60

Aylmer raised his eyes hastily, and at first reddened, then grew paler than ever, on beholding Georgiana. He rushed towards her and seized her arm with a grip that left the print of his fingers upon it.

"Why do you come hither? Have you no trust in your husband?" cried he, impetuously. "Would you throw the blight of that fatal birthmark over my labors? It is not well done. Go, prying woman! go!"

"Nay, Aylmer," said Georgiana with the firmness of which she possessed no stinted endowment, "it is not you that have a right to complain. You mistrust your wife; you have concealed the anxiety with which you watch the development of this experiment. Think not so unworthily of me, my husband. Tell me all the risk we run, and fear not that I shall shrink; for my share in it is far less than your own."

"No, no, Georgiana!" said Aylmer, impatiently; "it must not be."

"I submit," replied she, calmly. "And, Aylmer, I shall quaff whatever 65 draught you bring me; but it will be on the same principle that would induce me to take a dose of poison if offered by your hand."

"My noble wife," said Aylmer, deeply moved, "I knew not the height and depth of your nature until now. Nothing shall be concealed. Know, then, that this crimson hand, superficial as it seems, has clutched its grasp into your being with a strength of which I had no previous conception. I have already administered agents powerful enough to do aught except to change your entire physical system. Only one thing remains to be tried. If that fails us we are ruined."

"Why did you hesitate to tell me this?" asked she.

"Because, Georgiana," said Aylmer, in a low voice, "there is danger."

"Danger? There is but one danger—that this horrible stigma shall be left upon my cheek!" cried Georgiana. "Remove it, remove it, whatever be the cost, or we shall both go mad!"

"Heaven knows your words are too true," said Aylmer, sadly. "And now, 70 dearest, return to your boudoir. In a little while all will be tested."

He conducted her back and took leave of her with a solemn tenderness which spoke far more than his words how much was now at stake. After his departure Georgiana became rapt in musings. She considered the character of Aylmer and did it completer justice than at any previous moment. Her heart exulted, while it trembled, at his honorable love—so pure and lofty that it would accept nothing less than perfection nor miserably make itself contented with an earthlier nature than he had dreamed of. She felt how much more precious was such a sentiment than that meaner kind which would have borne with the imperfection for her sake, and have been guilty of treason to holy love by degrading its perfect idea to the level of the actual; and with her whole spirit she prayed that, for a single moment, she might satisfy his highest and deepest conception. Longer than one moment she well knew it could not be;

for his spirit was ever on the march, ever ascending, and each instant required something that was beyond the scope of the instant before.

The sound of her husband's footsteps aroused her. He bore a crystal goblet containing a liquor colorless as water, but bright enough to be the draught of immortality. Aylmer was pale; but it seemed rather the consequence of a highly-wrought state of mind and tension of spirit than of fear or doubt.

"The concoction of the draught has been perfect," said he, in answer to Georgiana's look. "Unless all my science have deceived me, it cannot fail."

"Save on your account, my dearest Aylmer," observed his wife, "I might wish to put off this birthmark of mortality by relinquishing mortality itself in preference to any other mode. Life is but a sad possession to those who have attained precisely the degree of moral advancement at which I stand. Were I weaker and blinder, it might be happiness. Were I stronger, it might be endured hopefully. But, being what I find myself, methinks I am of all mortals the most fit to die."

"You are fit for heaven without tasting death!" replied her husband. "But 75 why do we speak of dying? The draught cannot fail. Behold its effect upon this plant."

On the window seat there stood a geranium diseased with yellow blotches which had overspread all its leaves. Aylmer poured a small quantity of the liquid upon the soil in which it grew. In a little time, when the roots of the plant had taken up the moisture, the unsightly blotches began to be extinguished in a living verdure.

"There needed no proof," said Georgiana, quietly. "Give me the goblet. I joyfully stake all upon your word."

"Drink, then, thou lofty creature!" exclaimed Aylmer, with fervid admiration. "There is no taint of imperfection on thy spirit. Thy sensible frame, too, shall soon be all perfect."

She quaffed the liquid and returned the goblet to his hand.

"It is grateful," said she, with a placid smile. "Methinks it is like water 80 from a heavenly fountain; for it contains I know not what of unobtrusive fragrance and deliciousness. It allays a feverish thirst that had parched me for many days. Now, dearest, let me sleep. My earthly senses are closing over my spirit like the leaves around the heart of a rose at sunset."

She spoke the last words with a gentle reluctance, as if it required almost more energy than she could command to pronounce the faint and lingering syllables. Scarcely had they loitered through her lips ere she was lost in slumber. Aylmer sat by her side, watching her aspect with the emotions proper to a man the whole value of whose existence was involved in the process now to be tested. Mingled with this mood, however, was the philosophic investigation characteristic of the man of science. Not the minutest symptom escaped him. A heightened flush of the cheek, a slight irregularity of breath, a quiver of the eyelid, a hardly perceptible tremor through the frame,—such were the details which, as the moments passed, he wrote down in his folio volume. Intense thought had set its stamp upon every previous page of that volume; but the thoughts of years were all concentrated upon the last.

While thus employed, he failed not to gaze often at the fatal hand, and not without a shudder. Yet once, by a strange and unaccountable impulse, he pressed it with his lips. His spirit recoiled, however, in the very act; and Georgiana, out of the midst of her deep sleep, moved uneasily and murmured as if in remonstrance. Again Aylmer resumed his watch. Nor was it without avail. The crimson hand, which at first had been strongly visible upon the marble paleness of Georgiana's cheek, now grew more faintly outlined. She remained not less pale than ever; but the birthmark, with every breath that came and went lost somewhat of its former distinctness. Its presence had been awful; its departure was more awful still. Watch the stain of the rainbow fading out of the sky, and you will know how that mysterious symbol passed away.

"By Heaven! it is well nigh gone!" said Aylmer to himself, in almost irrepressible ecstasy. "I can scarcely trace it now. Success! success! And now it is like the faintest rose color. The slightest flush of blood across her cheek would overcome it. But she is so pale!"

He drew aside the window curtain and suffered the light of natural day to fall into the room and rest upon her cheek. At the same time he heard a gross, hoarse chuckle, which he had long known as his servant Aminadab's expression of delight.

"Ah, clod! ah, earthly mass!" cried Aylmer, laughing in a sort of frenzy, 85 "you have served me well! Matter and spirit—earth and heaven—have both done their part in this! Laugh, thing of the senses! You have earned the right to laugh."

These exclamations broke Georgiana's sleep. She slowly unclosed her eyes and gazed into the mirror which her husband had arranged for that purpose. A faint smile flitted over her lips when she recognized how barely perceptible was now that crimson hand which had once blazed forth with such disastrous brilliancy as to scare away all their happiness. But then her eyes sought Aylmer's face with a trouble and anxiety that he could by no means account for.

"My poor Aylmer!" murmured she.

"Poor? Nay, richest, happiest, most favored!" exclaimed he. "My peerless bride, it is successful! You are perfect!"

"My poor Aylmer," she repeated, with a more than human tenderness, "you have aimed loftily; you have done nobly. Do not repent that, with so high and pure a feeling, you have rejected the best the earth could offer. Aylmer, dearest Aylmer, I am dying!"

Alas! it was too true! The fatal hand had grappled with the mystery of life, 90 and was the bond by which an angelic spirit kept itself in union with a mortal frame. As the last crimson tint of the birthmark—that sole token of human imperfection—faded from her cheek, the parting breath of the now perfect woman passed into the atmosphere, and her soul, lingering a moment near her husband, took its heavenward flight. Then a hoarse, chuckling laugh was heard again! Thus ever does the gross fatality of earth exult in its invariable triumph over the immortal essence which, in this dim sphere of half development, demands the completeness of a higher state. Yet, had Aylmer reached a profounder wisdom, he need not thus have flung away the happiness which would have woven his mortal life of the selfsame texture with the celestial.

The momentary circumstance was too strong for him; he failed to look beyond the shadowy scope of time, and, living once for all in eternity, to find the perfect future in the present.

―――――――― **NATHANIEL HAWTHORNE** ――――――――

(1804–1864)

Nathanel Hawthorne always wanted to be a writer. Born to an old New England family, Hawthorne graduated from Bowdoin College and returned to Salem, Massachusetts, to write. After producing children's fiction and encyclopedias, Hawthorne turned to serious writing, creating four novels, including *The Scarlett Letter*, and a series of short stories. A friend of President Franklin Pierce, Hawthorne served as United States Consul in England.

TOPICS FOR CRITICAL THINKING   CD-ROM

1. What do the characters of "The Birthmark" stand for beyond themselves?
2. How does the story illustrate the clash of science and nature?
3. In what ways do the settings of "The Birthmark" reflect the story's conflicts?
4. Is Aminadab right? If so, why is this perspective voiced by him?
5. What is the role of Aylmer's dream in the story?
6. In what ways is the problem of perfection linked to issues of gender?

TOPICS FOR CRITICAL WRITING   CD-ROM

1. Why is it that "The Birthmark" can have no other outcome?
2. Explain what it might mean that the birthmark is in the shape of a hand.

3 Character

Prose fiction solicits our interest in part through the intriguing characters it presents—figures that range from the resistant Bartleby to the chivalric grocery store clerk of "A & P." All stories have characters; and most stories have many characters who differ in the kinds of roles they play, their relative importance in the story, the detail with which they are drawn, and the degree to which readers are familiar with the stereotype they may represent. Characters who serve as the primary actors in a story and with whom readers are invited to sympathize are called **protagonists.** Rocky Balboa, Luke Skywalker, James Bond, Neo, and Bridget Jones are protagonists in film narratives, while Aylmer ("The Birthmark"), Betsey Lane ("The Flight of Betsey Lane"), Peyton Farquhar ("An Occurrence at Owl Creek Bridge"), and Marlow (*Heart of Darkness*) are protagonists in prose fiction whom you meet in this book.

Although it is usually clear which of several characters is a story's protagonist, sometimes the role shifts from one character to another (as it shifts from Luke to Han Solo in *Star Wars*) or is shared by more than one character. Both of the young travelers in Ernest Hemingway's "Hills Like White Elephants" could be considered protagonists, while in *Heart of Darkness*, the protagonist Marlow seeks the charismatic Kurtz who, in his own way, has served as hero (or demagogue) of the African bush. Determining which character is the protagonist of a story tells a lot about the story's plot and themes.

Another important role is that of the **antagonist,** the character who opposes the protagonist or whose actions conflict with the protagonist's aims or desires. Antagonists include such film characters as Austin Powers' enemy Dr. Evil, James Bond's nemesis Blofeld, and Luke Skywalker's opponent Darth Vader, or the literary villain The Misfit from Flannery O'Connor's "A Good Man Is Hard to Find." Although readers may often find an antagonist unsympathetic, occasionally antagonists are more interesting than protagonists—as perhaps The Misfit is or Iago from William Shakespeare's *Othello.* Although protagonists are usually human beings, antagonists sometimes appear as forces such as animals or nature. Jack London's stories often situate nature as an antagonist.

Protagonists and antagonists are usually main (that is, major or primary) characters in a story. They are fully drawn, often in some detail, and offer points of sympathy (or its opposite, in the case of the antagonist) and identification for the reader. In some stories, the narrator is the protagonist. These first-person narrator protagonists (those narrating using *I* or *we*) are also characters whose personalities are developed directly through comments they make about themselves and indirectly in the way they narrate events (see Chapter 6).

Other characters are presented in less detail, their more generalized qualities providing contrast to the main characters and enabling plot development. Minor characters frequently work with one another and with primary characters to produce a sense of time, place, and atmosphere or help with the development of plot details. As points of comparison to major characters, minor characters emphasize a main character's idiosyncrasies. As extensions of primary characters' influence and ability, they enhance major characters' importance, strengths, or even weaknesses. Other characters are functionaries, scarcely described, who fulfill such utilitarian roles as servant, authority figure, child, friend, or member of a crowd. These characters are almost part of the story's setting. **CD-ROM**

Any type of character may be **stereotypical**—present a familiar type such as the bully; **allegorical**—stand for a concept, position, or one aspect of personality such as the greedy King Midas; or **structural**—serve as protagonist, antagonist, or narrator in the story. Characters sometimes fulfill more than one of these functions at a time. Many stories center on a single character, describing and developing the sense of a unique personality. In character-centered stories such as Herman Melville's "Bartleby the Scrivener" or *Heart of Darkness,* character dominates and defines other formal elements. The story's plot, for example, might track the actions and fate of a character or characters, and its setting might parallel or complement a character's traits and actions.

Critical Perspective: Psychological Criticism

Characters provide readers with a familiar fascination. As we do in other media such as television and movies, we are attentive to the characters' motivations—their reasons for doing things. Taking clues from the text, readers form theories about characters' behaviors based on what they know about how and why people behave in certain ways. Interpreting stories on the basis of character motivation is called **psychological criticism. CD-ROM** Readers often treat characters as if they are real people; this is testimony to the power of the writer who creates such believable portraits. When stories are specifically about a character's motivations, character psychology is an important way of understanding how a story works. Not all stories, however, are about character psychology alone. Relying too much on character psychology sometimes prevents appreciation of a story's other elements or the ways all of its elements, including character, work together.

If we interpret a character's actions using the scientific categories of psychology (such as schizophrenia or depression), we are reading stories as clinical studies of people who are in trouble. Some stories invite such a reading, especially if they center on characters whose main difficulty seems to be psychological. We might interpret Bartleby's behavior as a symptom of depression, for example. In other stories focused on character, it is tempting to interpret characters psychologically because character psychology is a logic that can work anywhere. What, for example, motivates Betsey Lane to see the world? The many different schools of psychology (Freudian, Jungian, ego psychology, object relations psychology, to name a few) provide different models and vocabularies for understanding and talking about character motivation. Even if readers are not familiar with specific psychological terms, most still understand the basic motives of human behavior.

Critical Perspective: Myth Criticism

Another way of interpreting character is to understand characters as representative parts of a mythical pattern. This is called **myth criticism.** **CD-ROM** Myths that concern creation, rites of passage (birth, puberty, marriage, death), or scapegoats are basic to Western culture and are shared in one form or another by many societies. Sometimes stories provide hints that characters might represent **archetypes** (the basic model for a particular character in a myth) through names, objects associated with characters, or actions that parallel the actions of mythical figures. For example, a character named Lucifer inevitably suggests evil, while a hooded figure carrying a scythe intimates death. Sometimes we discern mythical patterns through the prominence of a character who seems to be the embodiment of a mythical figure. An example of this would be Prometheus, who angers the gods by stealing fire and giving it to humanity. In other stories, we may discern a mythical pattern such as rebirth in spring, then fit the characters into their proper roles in the myth. Myth criticism thus involves our ability to match a specific instance of a pattern to a paradigm (or pattern) that is generally known. **CD-ROM** As with any kind of criticism, it's important to avoid trying to reduce a story to a simple pattern.

Stories About Character

While almost all stories involve some human characters, stories specifically focused on character may occasionally defy the conventional antagonist-protagonist patterns of plot (see Chapter 5). Such stories seem almost like character sketches or portraits whose main purpose is descriptive, but the often unusual whims of the featured character may permit a plot that runs counter to normal expectations. "Bartleby the Scrivener," first published in *Putnam's Magazine* in November–December 1853, is, on one level at least, a story about a character who refuses to participate in any conventional existence. "Bartleby" followed Melville's publication of seven novels, the first two of which focused on his experiences in the South Pacific.

Sarah Orne Jewett's "The Flight of Betsey Lane" was published forty years later in *Scribner's Magazine*. Jewett, who admired Harriet Beecher Stowe, often focused on female characters and their relationships. Tracking the decision of an elderly woman to take a trip to the Philadelphia Centennial, the story focuses on Betsey and her two retirement home friends, avoiding conventional narratives in which women's actions are traditionally more limited.

Herman Melville

Bartleby the Scrivener (1853)

I am a rather elderly man. The nature of my avocations, for the last thirty years, has brought me into more than ordinary contact with what would seem an interesting and somewhat singular set of men, of whom, as yet, nothing, that I know of, has ever been written—I mean, the law-copyists, or scriveners. I have known very many of them, professionally and privately, and, if I pleased, could relate divers histories, at which good-natured gentlemen might smile, and sentimental souls might weep. But I waive the biographies of all other scriveners, for a few passages in the life of Bartleby, who was a scrivener, the strangest I ever saw, or heard of. While, of other law-copyists, I might write the complete life, of Bartleby nothing of that sort can be done. I believe that no materials exist, for a full and satisfactory biography of this man. It is an irreparable loss to literature. Bartleby was one of those beings of whom nothing is ascertainable, except from the original sources, and, in his case, those are very small. What my own astonished eyes saw of Bartleby, *that* is all I know of him, except, indeed, one vague report, which will appear in the sequel.

Ere introducing the scrivener, as he first appeared to me, it is fit I make some mention of myself, my *employés*, my business, my chambers, and general surroundings; because some such description is indispensable to an adequate understanding of the chief character about to be presented. Imprimis: I am a man who, from his youth upwards, has been filled with a profound conviction that the easiest way of life is the best. Hence, though I belong to a profession proverbially energetic and nervous, even to turbulence, at times, yet nothing of that sort have I ever suffered to invade my peace. I am one of those unambitious lawyers who never addresses a jury, or in any way draws down public applause; but, in the cool tranquillity of a snug retreat, do a snug business among rich men's bonds, and mortgages, and title-deeds. All who know me, consider me an eminently *safe* man. The late John Jacob Astor,[1] a personage little given to poetic enthusiasm, had no hesitation in pronouncing my first grand point to be prudence; my next, method. I do not speak it in vanity, but simply record the fact, that I was not unemployed in my profession by the late John Jacob Astor, a name which, I admit, I love to repeat; for it hath a rounded and orbicular sound to it, and rings like unto bullion. I will freely add, that I was not insensible to the late John Jacob Astor's good opinion.

1. American fur trader and financier.

Some time prior to the period at which this little history begins, my avocations had been largely increased. The good old office, now extinct in the State of New York, of a Master in Chancery, had been conferred upon me. It was not a very arduous office, but very pleasantly remunerative. I seldom lose my temper; much more seldom indulge in dangerous indignation at wrongs and outrages; but, I must be permitted to be rash here, and declare, that I consider the sudden and violent abrogation of the office of Master in Chancery, by the new Constitution, as a——premature act; inasmuch as I had counted upon a life-lease of the profits, whereas I only received those of a few short years. But this is by the way.

My chambers were up stairs, at No.—Wall Street. At one end, they looked upon the white wall of the interior of a spacious sky-light shaft, penetrating the building from top to bottom.

This view might have been considered rather tame than otherwise, deficient in what landscape painters call "life." But, if so, the view from the other end of my chambers offered, at least, a contrast, if nothing more. In that direction, my windows commanded an unobstructed view of a lofty brick wall, black by age and everlasting shade; which wall required no spy-glass to bring out its lurking beauties, but, for the benefit of all near-sighted spectators, was pushed up to within ten feet of my window panes. Owing to the great height of the surrounding buildings, and my chambers being on the second floor, the interval between this wall and mine not a little resembled a huge square cistern.

At the period just preceding the advent of Bartleby, I had two persons as copyists in my employment, and a promising lad as an office-boy. First, Turkey; second, Nippers; third, Ginger Nut. These may seem names, the like of which are not usually found in the Directory. In truth, they were nicknames, mutually conferred upon each other by my three clerks, and were deemed expressive of their respective persons or characters. Turkey was a short, pursy Englishman, of about my own age—that is, somewhere not far from sixty. In the morning, one might say, his face was of a fine florid hue, but after twelve o'clock, meridian—his dinner hour—it blazed like a grate full of Christmas coals; and continued blazing—but, as it were, with a gradual wane—till six o'clock, P.M., or thereabouts; after which, I saw no more of the proprietor of the face, which, gaining its meridian with the sun, seemed to set with it, to rise, culminate, and decline the following day, with the like regularity and undiminished glory. There are many singular coincidences I have known in the course of my life, not the least among which was the fact, that, exactly when Turkey displayed his fullest beams from his red and radiant countenance, just then, too, at that critical moment, began the daily period when I considered his business capacities as seriously disturbed for the remainder of the twenty-four hours. Not that he was absolutely idle, or averse to business, then; far from it. The difficulty was, he was apt to be altogether too energetic. There was a strange, inflamed, flurried, flighty recklessness of activity about him. He would be incautious in dipping his pen into his inkstand. All his blots upon my documents were dropped there after twelve o'clock, meridian. Indeed, not only would he be reckless, and sadly given to making blots in the afternoon, but, some days, he went further, and was rather noisy. At such times, too, his face flamed with augmented blazonry, as if cannel coal had been heaped on anthracite. He made an unpleasant racket with his chair; spilled his sand-box; in mending his pens, impatiently split them all to pieces, and threw them on the floor in a sudden passion; stood up, and leaned over his table, boxing his papers about in a most indecorous manner, very sad to behold in an elderly man like him. Nevertheless, as he was in many ways a most valuable person to me, and all the time before twelve o'clock, meridian, was the quickest, steadiest creature, too, accomplishing a great deal of work in a style not easily to be matched—for these reasons, I was willing to overlook his eccentricities, though, indeed, occasionally, I remonstrated with him. I did this very gently, however, because, though the civilest, nay, the blandest and most reverential of men in the morning, yet, in the afternoon, he was disposed, upon provocation, to be slightly rash with his tongue—in fact, insolent. Now, valuing his morning services as I did, and resolved not to lose them—yet, at the same time, made uncomfortable by his inflamed ways after twelve o'clock—and being a man of peace, unwilling by my admonitions to call forth unseemly retorts from him, I took upon me, one Saturday noon (he was always worse on Saturdays) to hint to him, very kindly, that, perhaps, now that he was growing old, it might be well to abridge his labors; in short, he need not come to my chambers after twelve o'clock, but, dinner over, had best go home to his lodgings, and rest himself till tea-time. But no; he insisted upon his afternoon devotions. His countenance became intolerably fervid, as he oratorically assured me—gesticulating with a long ruler at the other end of the room—that if his services in the morning were useful, how indispensable, then, in the afternoon?

"With submission, sir," said Turkey, on this occasion, "I consider myself your right-hand man. In the morning I but marshal and deploy my columns; but in the afternoon I put myself at their head, and gallantly charge the foe, thus"—and he made a violent thrust with the ruler.

"But the blots, Turkey," intimated I.

"True; but, with submission, sir, behold these hairs! I am getting old. Surely, sir, a blot or two of a warm afternoon is not to be severely urged against gray hairs. Old age—even if it blot the page—is honorable. With submission, sir, we *both* are getting old."

This appeal to my fellow-feeling was hardly to be resisted. At all events, I   10 saw that go he would not. So, I made up my mind to let him stay, resolving, nevertheless, to see to it that, during the afternoon, he had to do with my less important papers.

Nippers, the second on my list, was a whiskered, sallow, and, upon the whole, rather piratical-looking young man, of about five and twenty. I always deemed him the victim of two evil powers—ambition and indigestion. The ambition was evinced by a certain impatience of the duties of a mere copyist, an unwarrantable usurpation of strictly professional affairs, such as the original drawing up of legal documents. The indigestion seemed betokened in an occasional nervous testiness and grinning irritability, causing the teeth to audibly grind together over mistakes committed in copying; unnecessary maledictions, hissed, rather than spoken, in the heat of business; and especially by a continual discontent with the height of the table where he worked. Though of a very ingenious mechanical turn, Nippers could never get this table to suit him. He put chips under it, blocks of various sorts, bits of pasteboard, and at last went so far as to attempt an exquisite adjustment, by final pieces of folded blotting-paper. But no invention would answer. If, for the sake of easing his back, he brought the table lid at a sharp angle well up towards his chin, and wrote there like a man using the steep roof of a Dutch house for his desk, then he declared that it stopped the circulation in his arms. If now he lowered the table to his waistbands, and stooped over it in writing, then there was a sore aching in his back. In short, the truth of the matter was, Nippers knew not what he wanted. Or, if he wanted anything, it was to be rid of a scrivener's table altogether. Among the manifestations of his diseased ambition was a fondness he had for receiving visits from certain ambiguous-looking fellows in seedy coats, whom he called his clients. Indeed, I was aware that not only was he, at times, considerable of a ward-politician, but he occasionally did a little business at the Justices' courts, and was not unknown on the steps of the Tombs. I have good reason to believe, however, that one individual who called upon him at my chambers, and who, with a grand air, he insisted was his client, was no other than a dun, and the alleged title-deed, a bill. But, with all his failings, and the annoyances he caused me, Nippers, like his compatriot Turkey, was a very useful man to me; wrote a neat, swift hand; and, when he chose, was not deficient in a gentlemanly sort of deportment. Added to this, he always dressed in a gentlemanly sort of way; and so, incidentally, reflected credit upon my chambers. Whereas, with respect to Turkey, I had much ado to keep him from being a reproach to me. His clothes were apt to look oily, and smell of eating-houses. He wore his pantaloons very loose and baggy in summer. His coats were execrable; his hat not to be handled. But while the hat was a thing of indifference to me, inasmuch as his natural civility and deference, as a dependent Englishman, always led him to doff it the moment he entered the room, yet his coat was another matter. Concerning his coats, I reasoned with him; but with no effect. The truth was, I suppose, that a man with so small an income could not afford to sport such a lustrous face and a lustrous coat at one and the same time. As Nippers once observed, Turkey's money went chiefly for red ink. One winter day, I presented Turkey with a highly respectable-looking coat of my own—a padded gray coat, of a most comfortable warmth, and which buttoned straight up from the knee to the neck. I thought Turkey would appreciate the favor, and abate his rashness and obstreperousness of afternoons. But no; I verily believe that buttoning himself up in so downy and blanket-like a coat had a pernicious effect upon him— upon the same principle that too much oats are bad for horses. In fact, precisely as a rash, restive horse is said to feel his oats, so Turkey felt his coat. It made him insolent. He was a man whom prosperity harmed.

Though, concerning the self-indulgent habits of Turkey, I had my own private surmises, yet, touching Nippers, I was well persuaded that, whatever might be his faults in other respects, he was, at least, a temperate young man. But, indeed, nature herself seemed to have been his vintner, and, at his birth, charged him so thoroughly with an irritable, brandy-like disposition, that all subsequent potations were needless. When I consider how, amid the stillness of my chambers, Nippers would sometimes impatiently rise from his seat, and stooping over his table, spread his arms wide apart, seize the whole desk, and move it, and jerk it, with a grim, grinding motion on the floor, as if the table were a perverse voluntary agent, intent on thwarting and vexing him, I plainly perceive that, for Nippers, brandy-and-water were altogether superfluous.

It was fortunate for me that, owing to its peculiar cause—indigestion— the irritability and consequent nervousness of Nippers were mainly observable in the morning, while in the afternoon he was comparatively mild. So that, Turkey's paroxysms only coming on about twelve o'clock, I never had to do with their eccentricities at one time. Their fits relieved each other, like guards. When Nippers' was on, Turkey's was off; and *vice versa*. This was a good natural arrangement, under the circumstances.

Ginger Nut, the third on my list, was a lad, some twelve years old. His father was a car-man, ambitious of seeing his son on the bench instead of a cart, before he died. So he sent him to my office, as student at law, errand-boy, cleaner and sweeper, at the rate of one dollar a week. He had a little desk to himself, but he did not use it much. Upon inspection, the drawer exhibited a great array of the shells of various sorts of nuts. Indeed, to this quick-witted youth, the whole noble science of the law was contained in a nut-shell. Not the least among the employments of Ginger Nut, as well as one which he discharged with the most alacrity, was his duty as cake and apple purveyor for Turkey and Nippers. Copying law-papers being proverbially a dry, husky sort of business, my two scriveners were fain to moisten their mouths very often with Spitzenbergs, to be had at the numerous stalls nigh the Custom House and Post Office. Also, they sent Ginger Nut very frequently for that peculiar cake—small, flat, round, and very spicy—after which he had been named by them. Of a cold morning, when business was but dull, Turkey would gobble up scores of these cakes, as if they were mere wafers—indeed, they sell them at the rate of six or eight for a penny—the scrape of his pen blending with the crunching of the crisp particles in his mouth. Of all the fiery afternoon blunders and flurried rashnesses of Turkey, was his once moistening a ginger-cake between his lips, and clapping it on to a mortgage, for a seal. I came within an ace of dismissing him then. But he mollified me by making an oriental bow, and saying—

"With submission, sir, it was generous of me to find you in stationery on 15 my own account."

Now my original business—that of a conveyancer and title hunter, and drawer-up of recondite documents of all sorts—was considerably increased by receiving the master's office. There was now great work for scriveners. Not only must I push the clerks already with me, but I must have additional help.

In answer to my advertisement, a motionless young man one morning stood upon my office threshold, the door being open, for it was summer. I can see that figure now—pallidly neat, pitiably respectable, incurably forlorn! It was Bartleby.

After a few words touching his qualifications, I engaged him, glad to have among my corps of copyists a man of so singularly sedate an aspect, which I thought might operate beneficially upon the flighty temper of Turkey, and the fiery one of Nippers.

I should have stated before that ground glass folding-doors divided my premises into two parts, one of which was occupied by my scriveners, the other by myself. According to my humor, I threw open these doors, or closed them. I resolved to assign Bartleby a corner by the folding-doors, but on my side of them, so as to have this quiet man within easy call, in case any trifling thing was to be done. I placed his desk close up to a small side-window in that part of the room, a window which originally had afforded a lateral view of certain grimy backyards and bricks, but which, owing to subsequent erections, commanded at present no view at all, though it gave some light. Within three feet of the panes was a wall, and the light came down from far above, between two lofty buildings, as from a very small opening in a dome. Still further to a satisfactory arrangement, I procured a high green folding screen, which might entirely isolate Bartleby from my sight, though not remove him from my voice. And thus, in a manner, privacy and society were conjoined.

At first, Bartleby did an extraordinary quantity of writing. As if long famishing for something to copy, he seemed to gorge himself on my documents. There was no pause for digestion. He ran a day and night line, copying by sun-light and by candle-light. I should have been quite delighted with his application, had he been cheerfully industrious. But he wrote on silently, palely, mechanically. 20

It is, of course, an indispensable part of a scrivener's business to verify the accuracy of his copy, word by word. Where there are two or more scriveners in an office, they assist each other in this examination, one reading from the copy, the other holding the original. It is a very dull, wearisome, and lethargic affair. I can readily imagine that, to some sanguine temperaments, it would be altogether intolerable. For example, I cannot credit that the mettlesome poet, Byron, would have contentedly sat down with Bartleby to examine a law document of, say five hundred pages, closely written in a crimpy hand.

Now and then, in the haste of business, it had been my habit to assist in comparing some brief document myself, calling Turkey or Nippers for this purpose. One object I had, in placing Bartleby so handy to me behind the screen, was, to avail myself of his services on such trivial occasions. It was on the third day, I think, of his being with me, and before any necessity had arisen for having his own writing examined, that, being much hurried to complete a small affair I had in hand, I abruptly called to Bartleby. In my haste and natural expectancy of instant compliance, I sat with my head bent over the original on my desk, and my right hand sideways, and somewhat nervously extended with the copy, so that, immediately upon emerging from his retreat, Bartleby might snatch it and proceed to business without the least delay.

In this very attitude did I sit when I called to him, rapidly stating what it was I wanted him to do—namely, to examine a small paper with me. Imagine my surprise, nay, my consternation, when, without moving from his privacy, Bartleby, in a singularly mild, firm voice, replied, "I would prefer not to."

I sat awhile in perfect silence, rallying my stunned faculties. Immediately it occurred to me that my ears had deceived me, or Bartleby had entirely misunderstood my meaning. I repeated my request in the clearest tone I could assume; but in quite as clear a one came the previous reply, "I would prefer not to."

"Prefer not to," echoed I, rising in high excitement, and crossing the 25 room with a stride. "What do you mean? Are you moon-struck? I want you to help me compare this sheet here—take it," and I thrust it towards him.

"I would prefer not to," said he.

I looked at him steadfastly. His face was leanly composed; his gray eye dimly calm. Not a wrinkle of agitation rippled him. Had there been the least uneasiness, anger, impatience or impertinence in his manner; in other words, had there been any thing ordinarily human about him, doubtless I should have violently dismissed him from the premises. But as it was, I should have as soon thought of turning my pale plaster-of-paris bust of Cicero out of doors. I stood gazing at him awhile, as he went on with his own writing, and then re-seated myself at my desk. This is very strange, thought I. What had one best do? But my business hurried me. I concluded to forget the matter for the present, reserving it for my future leisure. So calling Nippers from the other room, the paper was speedily examined.

A few days after this, Bartleby concluded four lengthy documents, being quadruplicates of a week's testimony taken before me in my High Court of Chancery. It became necessary to examine them. It was an important suit, and great accuracy was imperative. Having all things arranged, I called Turkey, Nippers, and Ginger Nut, from the next room, meaning to place the four copies in the hands of my four clerks, while I should read from the original. Accordingly, Turkey, Nippers, and Ginger Nut had taken their seats in a row, each with his document in his hand, when I called to Bartleby to join this interesting group.

"Bartleby! quick, I am waiting."

I heard a slow scrape of his chair legs on the uncarpeted floor, and soon 30 he appeared standing at the entrance of his hermitage.

"What is wanted?" said he, mildly.

"The copies, the copies," said I, hurriedly. "We are going to examine them. There"—and I held towards him the fourth quadruplicate.

"I would prefer not to," he said, and gently disappeared behind the screen.

For a few moments I was turned into a pillar of salt, standing at the head of my seated column of clerks. Recovering myself, I advanced towards the screen, and demanded the reason for such extraordinary conduct.

"*Why* do you refuse?"   35

"I would prefer not to."

With any other man I should have flown outright into a dreadful passion, scorned all further words, and thrust him ignominiously from my presence. But there was something about Bartleby that not only strangely disarmed me, but, in a wonderful manner, touched and disconcerted me. I began to reason with him.

"These are your own copies we are about to examine. It is labor saving to you, because one examination will answer for your four papers. It is common usage. Every copyist is bound to help examine his copy. Is it not so? Will you not speak? Answer!"

"I prefer not to," he replied in a flutelike tone. It seemed to me that, while I had been addressing him, he carefully revolved every statement that I made; fully comprehended the meaning; could not gainsay the irresistible conclusion; but, at the same time, some paramount consideration prevailed with him to reply as he did.

"You are decided, then, not to comply with my request—a request made 40 according to common usage and common sense?"

He briefly gave me to understand, that on that point my judgment was sound. Yes: his decision was irreversible.

It is not seldom the case that, when a man is browbeaten in some unprecedented and violently unreasonable way, he begins to stagger in his own plainest faith. He begins, as it were, vaguely to surmise that, wonderful as it may be, all the justice and all the reason is on the other side. Accordingly, if any disinterested persons are present, he turns to them for some reinforcement of his own faltering mind.

"Turkey," said I, "what do you think of this? Am I not right?"

"With submission, sir," said Turkey, in his blandest tone, "I think that you are."

"Nippers," said I, "what do *you* think of it?" 45

"I think I should kick him out of the office."

(The reader, of nice perceptions, will here perceive that, it being morning, Turkey's answer is couched in polite and tranquil terms, but Nippers' replies in ill-tempered ones. Or, to repeat a previous sentence, Nippers' ugly mood was on duty, and Turkey's off.)

"Ginger Nut," said I, willing to enlist the smallest suffrage in my behalf, "what do *you* think of it?"

"I think, sir, he's a little *luny*," replied Ginger Nut, with a grin.

"You hear what they say," said I, turning towards the screen, "come forth 50 and do your duty."

But he vouchsafed no reply. I pondered a moment in sore perplexity. But once more business hurried me. I determined again to postpone the consideration of this dilemma to my future leisure. With a little trouble we made out to examine the papers without Bartleby, though at every page or two Turkey deferentially dropped his opinion, that this proceeding was quite out of the common; while Nippers, twitching in his chair with a dyspeptic nervousness, ground out, between his set teeth, occasional hissing maledictions against the stubborn oaf behind the screen. And for his (Nippers') part, this was the first and the last time he would do another man's business without pay.

Meanwhile Bartleby sat in his hermitage, oblivious to everything but his own peculiar business there.

Some days passed, the scrivener being employed upon another lengthy work. His late remarkable conduct led me to regard his ways narrowly. I observed that he never went to dinner; indeed, that he never went anywhere. As yet I had never, of my personal knowledge, known him to be outside of my office. He was a perpetual sentry in the corner. At about eleven o'clock though, in the morning, I noticed that Ginger Nut would advance toward the opening in Bartleby's screen, as if silently beckoned thither by a gesture invisible to me where I sat. The boy would then leave the office, jingling a few pence, and reappear with a handful of ginger-nuts, which he delivered in the hermitage, receiving two of the cakes for his trouble.

He lives, then, on ginger-nuts, thought I; never eats a dinner, properly speaking; he must be a vegetarian, then; but no; he never eats even vegetables, he eats nothing but ginger-nuts. My mind then ran on in reveries concerning the probable effects upon the human constitution of living entirely on ginger-nuts. Ginger-nuts are so called, because they contain ginger as one of their peculiar constituents, and the final flavoring one. Now, what was ginger? A hot, spicy thing. Was Bartleby hot and spicy? Not at all. Ginger, then, had no effect upon Bartleby. Probably he preferred it should have none.

Nothing so aggravates an earnest person as a passive resistance. If the individual so resisted be of a not inhumane temper, and the resisting one perfectly harmless in his passivity, then, in the better moods of the former, he will endeavor charitably to construe to his imagination what proves impossible to be solved by his judgment. Even so, for the most part, I regarded Bartleby and his ways. Poor fellow! thought I, he means no mischief; it is plain he intends no insolence; his aspect sufficiently evinces that his eccentricities are involuntary. He is useful to me. I can get along with him. If I turn him away, the chances are he will fall in with some less-indulgent employer, and then he will be rudely treated, and perhaps driven forth miserably to starve. Yes. Here I can cheaply purchase a delicious self-approval. To befriend Bartleby; to humor him in his strange willfulness, will cost me little or nothing, while I lay up in my soul what will eventually prove a sweet morsel for my conscience. But this mood was not invariable with me. The passiveness of Bartleby sometimes irritated me. I felt strangely goaded on to encounter him in new opposition— to elicit some angry spark from him answerable to my own. But, indeed, I might as well have essayed to strike fire with my knuckles against a bit of Windsor soap. But one afternoon the evil impulse in me mastered me, and the following little scene ensued:

"Bartleby," said I, "when those papers are all copied, I will compare them with you."

"I would prefer not to."

"How? Surely you do not mean to persist in that mulish vagary?"

No answer.

I threw open the folding-doors near by, and, turning upon Turkey and Nippers, exclaimed:

"Bartleby a second time says, he won't examine his papers. What do you think of it, Turkey?"

It was afternoon, be it remembered. Turkey sat glowing like a brass boiler; his bald head steaming; his hands reeling among his blotted papers.

"Think of it?" roared Turkey; "I think I'll just step behind his screen, and black his eyes for him!"

So saying, Turkey rose to his feet and threw his arms into a pugilistic position. He was hurrying away to make good his promise, when I detained him, alarmed at the effect of incautiously rousing Turkey's combativeness after dinner.

"Sit down, Turkey," said I, "and hear what Nippers has to say. What do 65 you think of it, Nippers? Would I not be justified in immediately dismissing Bartleby?"

"Excuse me, that is for you to decide, sir. I think his conduct quite unusual, and, indeed, unjust, as regards Turkey and myself. But it may only be a passing whim."

"Ah," exclaimed I, "you have strangely changed your mind, then—you speak very gently of him now."

"All beer," cried Turkey; "gentleness is effects of beer—Nippers and I dined together to-day. You see how gentle *I* am, sir. Shall I go and black his eyes?"

"You refer to Bartleby, I suppose. No, not to-day, Turkey," I replied; "pray, put up your fists."

I closed the doors, and again advanced towards Bartleby. I felt additional 70 incentives tempting me to my fate. I burned to be rebelled against again. I remember that Bartleby never left the office.

"Bartleby," said I, "Ginger Nut is away; just step around to the Post Office, won't you? (it was but a three minutes' walk), and see if there is anything for me."

"I would prefer not to."

"You *will* not?"

"I *prefer* not."

I staggered to my desk, and sat there in a deep study. My blind inveteracy 75 returned. Was there any other thing in which I could procure myself to be ignominiously repulsed by this lean, penniless wight?—my hired clerk? What added thing is there, perfectly reasonable, that he will be sure to refuse to do?

"Bartleby!"

No answer.

"Bartleby," in a louder tone.

No answer.

"Bartleby," I roared. 80

Like a very ghost, agreeably to the laws of magical invocation, at the third summons, he appeared at the entrance of his hermitage.

"Go to the next room, and tell Nippers to come to me."

"I prefer not to," he respectfully and slowly said, and mildly disappeared.

"Very good, Bartleby," said I, in a quiet sort of serenely-severe self-possessed tone, intimating the unalterable purpose of some terrible retribution very close at hand. But upon the whole, as it was drawing towards my dinner-hour, I thought it best to put on my hat and walk home for the day, suffering much from perplexity and distress of mind.

Shall I acknowledge it? The conclusion of this whole business was, that it 85 soon became a fixed fact of my chambers, that a pale young scrivener, by the name of Bartleby, had a desk there; that he copied for me at the usual rate of four cents a folio (one hundred words); but he was permanently exempt from examining the work done by him, that duty being transferred to Turkey and Nippers, out of compliment, doubtless, to their superior acuteness; moreover, said Bartleby was never, on any account, to be dispatched on the most trivial errand of any sort; and that even if entreated to take upon him such a matter, it was generally understood that he would "prefer not to"—in other words, that he would refuse point-blank.

As days passed on, I became considerably reconciled to Bartleby. His steadiness, his freedom from all dissipation, his incessant industry (except when he chose to throw himself into a standing revery behind his screen), his great stillness, his unalterableness of demeanor under all circumstances, made him a valuable acquisition. One prime thing was this—*he was always there*—first in the morning, continually through the day, and the last at night. I had a singular confidence in his honesty. I felt my most precious papers perfectly safe in his hands. Sometimes, to be sure, I could not, for the very soul of me, avoid falling into sudden spasmodic passions with him. For it was exceeding difficult to bear in mind all the time those strange peculiarities, privileges, and unheard of exemptions, forming the tacit stipulations on Bartleby's part under which he remained in my office. Now and then, in the eagerness of dispatching pressing business, I would inadvertently summon Bartleby, in a short, rapid tone, to put his finger, say, on the incipient tie of a bit of red tape with which I was about compressing some papers. Of course, from behind the screen the usual answer, "I prefer not to," was sure to come; and then, how could a human creature, with the common infirmities of our nature, refrain from bitterly exclaiming upon such perverseness—such unreasonableness. However, every added repulse of this sort which I received only tended to lessen the probability of my repeating the inadvertence.

Here it must be said, that according to the custom of most legal gentlemen occupying chambers in densely-populated law buildings, there were several keys to my door. One was kept by a woman residing in the attic, which person weekly scrubbed and daily swept and dusted my apartments. Another was kept by Turkey for convenience sake. The third I sometimes carried in my own pocket. The fourth I knew not who had.

Now, one Sunday morning I happened to go to Trinity Church, to hear a celebrated preacher, and finding myself rather early on the ground I thought I would walk around to my chambers for a while. Luckily I had my key with me; but upon applying it to the lock, I found it resisted by something inserted from the inside. Quite surprised, I called out; when to my consternation a key was turned from within; and thrusting his lean visage at me, and holding the door ajar, the apparition of Bartleby appeared, in his shirt sleeves, and otherwise in a strangely tattered deshabille, saying quietly that he was sorry, but he was deeply engaged just then, and—preferred not admitting me at present. In a brief word or two, he moreover added, that perhaps I had better walk around the block two or three times, and by that time he would probably have concluded his affairs.

Now, the utterly unsurmised appearance of Bartleby, tenanting my law-chambers of a Sunday morning, with his cadaverously gentlemanly *nonchalance*, yet withal firm and self-possessed, had such a strange effect upon me, that incontinently I slunk away from my own door, and did as desired. But not without sundry twinges of impotent rebellion against the mild effrontery of this unaccountable scrivener. Indeed, it was his wonderful mildness chiefly, which not only disarmed me, but unmanned me as it were. For I consider that one, for the time, is somehow unmanned when he tranquilly permits his hired clerk to dictate to him, and order him away from his own premises. Furthermore, I was full of uneasiness as to what Bartleby could possibly be doing in my office in his shirt sleeves, and in an otherwise dismantled condition of a Sunday morning. Was anything amiss going on? Nay, that was out of the question. It was not to be thought of for a moment that Bartleby was an immoral person. But what could he be doing there?—copying? Nay again, whatever might be his eccentricities, Bartleby was an eminently decorous person. He would be the last man to sit down to his desk in any state approaching to nudity. Besides, it was Sunday; and there was something about Bartleby that forbade the supposition that he would by any secular occupation violate the proprieties of the day.

Nevertheless, my mind was not pacified; and full of a restless curiosity, at last I returned to the door. Without hindrance I inserted my key, opened it, and entered. Bartleby was not to be seen. I looked round anxiously, peeped behind his screen; but it was very plain that he was gone. Upon more closely examining the place, I surmised that for an indefinite period Bartleby must have ate, dressed, and slept in my office, and that, too, without plate, mirror, or bed. The cushioned seat of a rickety old sofa in one corner bore the faint impression of a lean, reclining form. Rolled away under his desk, I found a blanket; on a chair, a tin basin, with soap and a ragged towel; in a newspaper a few crumbs of ginger-nuts and a morsel of cheese. Yes, thought I, it is evident enough that Bartleby has been making his home here, keeping bachelor's hall all by himself. Immediately then the thought came sweeping across me, what miserable friendlessness and loneliness are here revealed! His poverty is great; but his solitude, how horrible! Think of it. Of a Sunday, Wall Street is deserted as Petra;[2] and every night of every day it is an emptiness. This building, too, which of week-days hums with industry and life, at nightfall echoes with sheer vacancy, and all through Sunday is forlorn. And here Bartleby makes his home; sole spectator of a solitude which he has seen all populous—a sort of innocent and transformed Marius brooding among the ruins of Carthage!

For the first time in my life a feeling of over-powering stinging melancholy seized me. Before, I had never experienced aught but a not unpleasing sadness. The bond of a common humanity now drew me irresistibly to gloom. A fraternal melancholy! For both I and Bartleby were sons of Adam. I remembered the bright silks and sparkling faces I had seen that day, in gala trim, swan-like sailing down the Mississippi of Broadway; and I contrasted them with the pallid copyist, and thought to myself, Ah, happiness courts the light, so we deem the world is gay; but misery hides aloof, so we deem that misery there is none. These sad fancyings—chimeras, doubtless, of a sick and silly

90

2. Ancient city in Syria.

brain—led on to other and more special thoughts, concerning the eccentricities of Bartleby. Presentiments of strange discoveries hovered round me. The
scrivener's pale form appeared to me laid out, among uncaring strangers, in its
shivering winding sheet.

Suddenly I was attracted by Bartleby's closed desk, the key in open sight
left in the lock.

I mean no mischief, seek the gratification of no heartless curiosity,
thought I; besides, the desk is mine, and its contents, too, so I will make bold
to look within. Everything was methodically arranged, the papers smoothly
placed. The pigeon holes were deep, and removing the files of documents, I
groped into their recesses. Presently I felt something there, and dragged it
out. It was an old bandanna handkerchief, heavy and knotted. I opened it, and
saw it was a saving's bank.

I now recalled all the quiet mysteries which I had noted in the man. I remembered that he never spoke but to answer; that, though at intervals he had
considerable time to himself, yet I had never seen him reading—no, not even
a newspaper; that for long periods he would stand looking out, at his pale window behind the screen, upon the dead brick wall; I was quite sure he never visited any refectory or eating house; while his pale face clearly indicated that he
never drank beer like Turkey, or tea and coffee even, like other men; that he
never went anywhere in particular that I could learn; never went out for a
walk, unless, indeed, that was the case at present; that he had declined telling
who he was, or whence he came, or whether he had any relatives in the world;
that though so thin and pale, he never complained of ill health. And more
than all, I remembered a certain unconscious air of pallid—how shall I call
it?—of pallid haughtiness, say, or rather an austere reserve about him, which
had positively awed me into my tame compliance with his eccentricities, when
I had feared to ask him to do the slightest incidental thing for me, even
though I might know, from his long-continued motionlessness, that behind
his screen he must be standing in one of those deadwall reveries of his.

Revolving all these things, and coupling them with the recently discov-   95
ered fact, that he made my office his constant abiding place and home, and not
forgetful of his morbid moodiness; revolving all these things, a prudential
feeling began to steal over me. My first emotions had been those of pure
melancholy and sincerest pity; but just in proportion as the forlornness of
Bartleby grew and grew to my imagination, did that same melancholy merge
into fear, that pity into repulsion. So true it is, and so terrible, too, that up to
a certain point the thought or sight of misery enlists our best affections; but,
in certain special cases, beyond that point it does not. They err who would assert that invariably this is owing to the inherent selfishness of the human
heart. It rather proceeds from a certain hopelessness of remedying excessive
and organic ill. To a sensitive being, pity is not seldom pain. And when at last
it is perceived that such pity cannot lead to effectual succor, common sense
bids the soul be rid of it. What I saw that morning persuaded me that the
scrivener was the victim of inate and incurable disorder. I might give alms to
his body; but his body did not pain him; it was his soul that suffered, and his
soul I could not reach.

I did not accomplish the purpose of going to Trinity Church that morning. Somehow, the things I had seen disqualified me for the time from church-going. I walked homeward, thinking what I would do with Bartleby. Finally, I resolved upon this—I would put certain calm questions to him the next morning, touching his history, etc., and if he declined to answer them openly and unreservedly (and I supposed he would prefer not), then to give him a twenty dollar bill over and above whatever I might owe him, and tell him his services were no longer required; but that if in any other way I could assist him, I would be happy to do so, especially if he desired to return to his native place, wherever that might be, I would willingly help to defray the expenses. Moreover, if, after reaching home, he found himself at any time in want of aid, a letter from him would be sure of a reply.

The next morning came.

"Bartleby," said I, gently calling to him behind his screen.

No reply.

"Bartleby," said I, in a still gentler tone, "come here; I am not going to ask you to do anything you would prefer not to do—I simply wish to speak to you."

Upon this he noiselessly slid into view.

"Will you tell me, Bartleby, where you were born?"

"I would prefer not to."

"Will you tell me *anything* about yourself?"

"I would prefer not to."

"But what reasonable objection can you have to speak to me? I feel friendly towards you."

He did not look at me while I spoke, but kept his glance fixed upon my bust of Cicero, which, as I then sat, was directly behind me, some six inches above my head.

"What is your answer, Bartleby," said I, after waiting a considerable time for a reply, during which his countenance remained immovable, only there was the faintest conceivable tremor of the white attenuated mouth.

"At present I prefer to give no answer," he said, and retired into his hermitage.

It was rather weak in me I confess, but his manner, on this occasion, nettled me. Not only did there seem to lurk in it a certain calm disdain, but his perverseness seemed ungrateful, considering the undeniable good usage and indulgence he had received from me.

Again I sat ruminating what I should do. Mortified as I was at his behavior, and resolved as I had been to dismiss him when I entered my office, nevertheless I strangely felt something superstitious knocking at my heart, and forbidding me to carry out my purpose, and denouncing me for a villain if I dared to breathe one bitter word against this forlornest of mankind. At last, familiarly drawing my chair behind his screen, I sat down and said: "Bartleby, never mind, then, about revealing your history; but let me entreat you, as a friend, to comply as far as may be with the usages of this office. Say now, you will help to examine papers to-morrow or next day: in short, say now, that in a day or two you will begin to be a little reasonable:—say so, Bartleby."

"At present I would prefer not to be a little reasonable," was his mildly cadaverous reply.

Just then the folding-doors opened, and Nippers approached. He seemed suffering from an unusually bad night's rest, induced by severer indigestion than common. He overheard those final words of Bartleby.

"*Prefer not,* eh?" gritted Nippers—"I'd *prefer* him, if I were you, sir," addressing me—"I'd *prefer* him; I'd give him preferences, the stubborn mule! What is it, sir, pray, that he *prefers* not to do now?"

Bartleby moved not a limb.   115

"Mr. Nippers," said I, "I'd prefer that you would withdraw for the present."

Somehow, of late, I had got into the way of involuntarily using this word "prefer" upon all sorts of not exactly suitable occasions. And I trembled to think that my contact with the scrivener had already and seriously affected me in a mental way. And what further and deeper aberration might it not yet produce? This apprehension had not been without efficacy in determining me to summary measures.

As Nippers, looking very sour and sulky, was departing, Turkey blandly and deferentially approached.

"With submission, sir," said he, "yesterday I was thinking about Bartleby here, and I think that if he would but prefer to take a quart of good ale every day, it would do much towards mending him, and enabling him to assist in examining his papers."

"So you have got the word, too," said I, slightly excited.   120

"With submission, what word, sir," asked Turkey, respectfully crowding himself into the contracted space behind the screen, and by so doing, making me jostle the scrivener. "What word, sir?"

"I would prefer to be left alone here," said Bartleby, as if offended at being mobbed in his privacy.

"*That's* the word, Turkey," said I—"*that's* it."

"Oh, *prefer?* oh yes—queer word. I never use it myself. But, sir, as I was saying, if he would but prefer—"

"Turkey," interrupted I, "you will please withdraw."   125

"Oh, certainly, sir, if you prefer that I should."

As he opened the folding-door to retire, Nippers at his desk caught a glimpse of me, and asked whether I would prefer to have a certain paper copied on blue paper or white. He did not in the least roguishly accent the word prefer. It was plain that it involuntarily rolled from his tongue. I thought to myself, surely I must get rid of a demented man, who already has in some degree turned the tongues, if not the heads of myself and clerks. But I thought it prudent not to break the dismission at once.

The next day I noticed that Bartleby did nothing but stand at his window in his dead-wall revery. Upon asking him why he did not write, he said that he had decided upon doing no more writing.

"Why, how now? what next?" exclaimed I, "do no more writing?"

"No more."   130

"And what is the reason?"

"Do you not see the reason for yourself," he indifferently replied.

I looked steadfastly at him, and perceived that his eyes looked dull and glazed. Instantly it occurred to me, that his unexampled diligence in copying by his dim window for the first few weeks of his stay with me might have temporarily impaired his vision.

I was touched. I said something in condolence with him. I hinted that of course he did wisely in abstaining from writing for a while; and urged him to embrace that opportunity of taking wholesome exercise in the open air. This, however, he did not do. A few days after this, my other clerks being absent, and being in a great hurry to dispatch certain letters by the mail, I thought that, having nothing else earthly to do, Bartleby would surely be less inflexible than usual, and carry these letters to the post-office. But he blankly declined. So, much to my inconvenience, I went myself.

Still added days went by. Whether Bartleby's eyes improved or not, I could not say. To all appearance, I thought they did. But when I asked him if they did, he vouchsafed no answer. At all events, he would do no copying. At last, in reply to my urgings, he informed me that he had permanently given up copying.

"What!" exclaimed I; "suppose your eyes should get entirely well—better than ever before—would you not copy then?"

"I have given up copying," he answered, and slid aside.

He remained as ever, a fixture in my chamber. Nay—if that were possible—he became still more of a fixture than before. What was to be done? He would do nothing in the office; why should he stay there? In plain fact, he had now become a millstone to me, not only useless as a necklace, but afflictive to bear. Yet I was sorry for him. I speak less than truth when I say that, on his own account, he occasioned me uneasiness. If he would but have named a single relative or friend, I would instantly have written, and urged their taking the poor fellow away to some convenient retreat. But he seemed alone, absolutely alone in the universe. A bit of wreck in the mid Atlantic. At length, necessities connected with my business tyrannized over all other considerations. Decently as I could, I told Bartleby that in six days time he must unconditionally leave the office. I warned him to take measures, in the interval, for procuring some other abode. I offered to assist him in this endeavor, if he himself would but take the first step towards a removal. "And when you finally quit me, Bartleby," added I, "I shall see that you go not away entirely unprovided. Six days from this hour, remember."

At the expiration of that period, I peeped behind the screen, and lo! Bartleby was there.

I buttoned up my coat, balanced myself; advanced slowly towards him, touched his shoulder, and said, "The time has come; you must quit this place; I am sorry for you; here is money; but you must go."

"I would prefer not," he replied, with his back still towards me.

"You *must*."

He remained silent.

Now I had an unbounded confidence in this man's common honesty. He had frequently restored to me sixpences and shillings carelessly dropped upon

135

140

the floor, for I am apt to be very reckless in such shirt-button affairs. The proceeding, then, which followed will not be deemed extraordinary.

"Bartleby," said I, "I owe you twelve dollars on account; here are thirty-two; the odd twenty are yours—Will you take it?" and I handed the bills towards him.

But he made no motion. 145

"I will leave them here, then," putting them under a weight on the table. Then taking my hat and cane and going to the door, I tranquilly turned and added—"After you have removed your things from these offices, Bartleby, you will of course lock the door—since every one is now gone for the day but you—and if you please, slip your key underneath the mat, so that I may have it in the morning. I shall not see you again; so good-by to you. If, hereafter, in your new place of abode, I can be of any service to you, do not fail to advise me by letter. Good-by, Bartleby, and fare you well."

But he answered not a word; like the last column of some ruined temple, he remained standing mute and solitary in the middle of the otherwise deserted room.

As I walked home in a pensive mood, my vanity got the better of my pity. I could not but highly plume myself on my masterly management in getting rid of Bartleby. Masterly I call it, and such it must appear to any dispassionate thinker. The beauty of my procedure seemed to consist in its perfect quietness. There was no vulgar bullying, no bravado of any sort, no choleric hectoring, and striding to and fro across the apartment, jerking out vehement commands for Bartleby to bundle himself off with his beggarly traps. Nothing of the kind. Without loudly bidding Bartleby depart—as an inferior genius might have done—I *assumed* the ground that depart he must; and upon that assumption built all I had to say. The more I thought over my procedure, the more I was charmed with it. Nevertheless, next morning, upon awakening, I had my doubts—I had somehow slept off the fumes of vanity. One of the coolest and wisest hours a man has, is just after he awakes in the morning. My procedure seemed as sagacious as ever—but only in theory. How it would prove in practice—there was the rub. It was truly a beautiful thought to have assumed Bartleby's departure; but, after all, that assumption was simply my own, and none of Bartleby's. The great point was, not whether I had assumed that he would quit me, but whether he would prefer so to do. He was more a man of preferences than assumptions.

After breakfast, I walked down town, arguing the probabilities *pro* and 150 *con*. One moment I thought it would prove a miserable failure, and Bartleby would be found all alive at my office as usual; the next moment it seemed certain that I should find his chair empty. And so I kept veering about. At the corner of Broadway and Canal Street, I saw quite an excited group of people standing in earnest conversation.

"I'll take odds he doesn't," said a voice as I passed.

"Doesn't go?—done!" said I, "put up your money."

I was instinctively putting my hand in my pocket to produce my own, when I remembered that this was an election day. The words I had overheard bore no reference to Bartleby, but to the success or nonsuccess of some candidate for the mayoralty. In my intent frame of mind, I had, as it were, imagined that all Broadway shared in my excitement, and were debating the same question with me. I passed on, very thankful that the uproar of the street screened my momentary absent-mindedness.

As I had intended, I was earlier than usual at my office door. I stood listening for a moment. All was still. He must be gone. I tried the knob. The door was locked. Yes, my procedure had worked to a charm; he indeed must be vanished. Yet a certain melancholy mixed with this: I was almost sorry for my brilliant success. I was fumbling under the door mat for the key, which Bartleby was to have left there for me, when accidentally my knee knocked against a panel, producing a summoning sound, and in response a voice came to me from within—"Not yet; I am occupied."

It was Bartleby. 155

I was thunderstruck. For an instant I stood like the man who, pipe in mouth, was killed one cloudless afternoon long ago in Virginia, by summer lightning; at his own warm open window he was killed, and remained leaning out there upon the dreamy afternoon, till some one touched him, when he fell.

"Not gone!" I murmured at last. But again obeying that wondrous ascendancy which the inscrutable scrivener had over me, and from which ascendancy, for all my chafing, I could not completely escape, I slowly went down stairs and out into the street, and while walking round the block, considered what I should next do in this unheard-of perplexity. Turn the man out by an actual thrusting I could not; to drive him away by calling him hard names would not do; calling in the police was an unpleasant idea; and yet, permit him to enjoy his cadaverous triumph over me—this, too, I could not think of. What was to be done? or, if nothing could be done, was there anything further that I could *assume* in the matter? Yes, as before I had prospectively assumed that Bartleby would depart, so now I might retrospectively assume that departed he was. In the legitimate carrying out of this assumption, I might enter my office in a great hurry, and pretending not to see Bartleby at all, walk straight against him as if he were air. Such a proceeding would in a singular degree have the appearance of a home-thrust. It was hardly possible that Bartleby could withstand such an application of the doctrine of assumptions. But upon second thoughts the success of the plan seemed rather dubious. I resolved to argue the matter over with him again.

"Bartleby," said I, entering the office, with a quietly severe expression, "I am seriously displeased. I am pained, Bartleby. I had thought better of you. I had imagined you of such a gentlemanly organization, that in any delicate dilemma a slight hint would suffice—in short, an assumption. But it appears I am deceived. Why," I added, unaffectedly starting, "you have not even touched that money yet," pointing to it, just where I had left it the evening previous.

He answered nothing.

"Will you, or will you not, quit me?" I now demanded in a sudden passion, advancing close to him. 160

"I would prefer *not* to quit you," he replied, gently emphasizing the *not*.

"What earthly right have you to stay here? Do you pay any rent? Do you pay my taxes? Or is this property yours?"

He answered nothing.

"Are you ready to go on and write now? Are your eyes recovered? Could you copy a small paper for me this morning? or help examine a few lines? or step round to the post-office? In a word, will you do anything at all, to give a coloring to your refusal to depart the premises?"

He silently retired into his hermitage.   165

I was now in such a state of nervous resentment that I thought it but prudent to check myself at present from further demonstrations. Bartleby and I were alone. I remembered the tragedy of the unfortunate Adams and the still more unfortunate Colt in the solitary office of the latter; and how poor Colt, being dreadfully incensed by Adams, and imprudently permitting himself to get wildly excited, was at unawares hurried into his fatal act—an act which certainly no man could possibly deplore more than the actor himself. Often it had occurred to me in my ponderings upon the subject, that had that altercation taken place in the public street, or at a private residence, it would not have terminated as it did. It was the circumstance of being alone in a solitary office, up stairs, of a building entirely unhallowed by humanizing domestic associations—an uncarpeted office, doubtless, of a dusty, haggard sort of appearance—this it must have been, which greatly helped to enhance the irritable desperation of the hapless Colt.[3]

But when this old Adam of resentment rose in me and tempted me concerning Bartleby, I grappled him and threw him. How? Why, simply by recalling the divine injunction: "A new commandment give I unto you, that ye love one another." Yes, this it was that saved me. Aside from higher considerations, charity often operates as a vastly wise and prudent principle—a great safeguard to its possessor. Men have committed murder for jealousy's sake, and anger's sake, and hatred's sake, and selfishness' sake, and spiritual pride's sake; but no man, that ever I heard of, ever committed a diabolical murder for sweet charity's sake. Mere self-interest, then, if no better motive can be enlisted, should, especially with high-tempered men, prompt all beings to charity and philanthropy. At any rate, upon the occasion in question, I strove to drown my exasperated feelings towards the scrivener by benevolently construing his conduct. Poor fellow, poor fellow! thought I, he don't mean anything; and besides, he has seen hard times, and ought to be indulged.

I endeavored, also, immediately to occupy myself, and at the same time to comfort my despondency. I tried to fancy, that in the course of the morning, at such time as might prove agreeable to him, Bartleby, of his own free accord, would emerge from his hermitage and take up some decided line of march in the direction of the door. But no. Half-past twelve o'clock came; Turkey began to glow in the face, overturn his inkstand, and become generally obstreperous; Nippers abated down into quietude and courtesy; Ginger Nut munched his noon apple; and Bartleby remained standing at his window in

3. A widely publicized murder case in which John C. Colt killed Samuel Adams, in New York City, in January 1842.

one of his profoundest dead-wall reveries. Will it be credited? Ought I to acknowledge it? That afternoon I left the office without saying one further word
to him.

Some days now passed, during which, at leisure intervals I looked a little
into "Edwards on the Will," and "Priestly on Necessity." Under the circumstances, those books induced a salutary feeling. Gradually I slid into the persuasion that these troubles of mine, touching the scrivener, had been all
predestinated from eternity, and Bartleby was billeted upon me for some mysterious purpose of an allwise Providence, which it was not for a mere mortal
like me to fathom. Yes, Bartleby, stay there behind your screen, thought I; I
shall persecute you no more; you are harmless and noiseless as any of these
old chairs; in short, I never feel so private as when I know you are here. At last
I see it, I feel it; I penetrate to the predestinated purpose of my life. I am content. Others may have loftier parts to enact; but my mission in this world,
Bartleby, is to furnish you with office-room for such period as you may see fit
to remain.

I believe that this wise and blessed frame of mind would have continued 170
with me, had it not been for the unsolicited and uncharitable remarks obtruded upon me by my professional friends who visited the rooms. But thus it
often is, that the constant friction of illiberal minds wears out at last the best
resolves of the more generous. Though to be sure, when I reflected upon it, it
was not strange that people entering my office should be struck by the peculiar aspect of the unaccountable Bartleby, and so be tempted to throw out
some sinister observations concerning him. Sometimes an attorney, having
business with me, and calling at my office, and finding no one but the
scrivener there, would undertake to obtain some sort of precise information
from him touching my whereabouts; but without heeding his idle talk,
Bartleby would remain standing immovable in the middle of the room. So after contemplating him in that position for a time, the attorney would depart,
no wiser than he came.

Also, when a reference was going on, and the room full of lawyers and
witnesses, and business driving fast, some deeply-occupied legal gentleman
present, seeing Bartleby wholly unemployed, would request him to run round
to his (the legal gentleman's) office and fetch some papers for him. Thereupon, Bartleby would tranquilly decline, and yet remain idle as before. Then
the lawyer would give a great stare, and turn to me. And what could I say? At
last I was made aware that all through the circle of my professional acquaintance, a whisper of wonder was running round, having reference to the
strange creature I kept at my office. This worried me very much. And as the
idea came upon me of his possibly turning out a long-lived man, and keep occupying my chambers, and denying my authority; and perplexing my visitors;
and scandalizing my professional reputation; and casting a general gloom over
the premises; keeping soul and body together to the last upon his savings (for
doubtless he spent but half a dime a day), and in the end perhaps outlive me,
and claim possession of my office by right of his perpetual occupancy: as all
these dark anticipations crowded upon me more and more, and my friends
continually intruded their relentless remarks upon the apparition in my room;

a great change was wrought in me. I resolved to gather all my faculties together, and forever rid me of this intolerable incubus.

Ere revolving any complicated project, however, adapted to this end, I first simply suggested to Bartleby the propriety of his permanent departure. In a calm and serious tone, I commended the idea to his careful and mature consideration. But, having taken three days to meditate upon it, he apprised me, that his original determination remained the same; in short, that he still preferred to abide with me.

What shall I do? I now said to myself, buttoning up my coat to the last button. What shall I do? what ought I to do? what does conscience say I *should* do with this man, or, rather, ghost. Rid myself of him, I must; go, he shall. But how? You will not thrust him, the poor, pale, passive mortal—you will not thrust such a helpless creature out of your door? you will not dishonor yourself by such cruelty? No, I will not, I cannot do that. Rather would I let him live and die here, and then mason up his remains in the wall. What, then, will you do? For all your coaxing, he will not budge. Bribes he leaves under your own paper-weight on your table; in short, it is quite plain that he prefers to cling to you.

Then something severe, something unusual must be done. What! surely you will not have him collared by a constable, and commit his innocent pallor to the common jail? And upon what ground could you procure such a thing to be done?—a vagrant, is he? What! he a vagrant, a wanderer, who refuses to budge? It is because he will *not* be a vagrant, then, that you seek to count him *as* a vagrant. That is too absurd. No visible means of support: there I have him. Wrong again: for indubitably he *does* support himself, and that is the only unanswerable proof that any man can show of his possessing the means so to do. No more, then. Since he will not quit me, I must quit him. I will change my offices; I will move elsewhere, and give him fair notice, that if I find him on my new premises I will then proceed against him as a common trespasser.

Acting accordingly, next day I thus addressed him: "I find these chambers too far from the City Hall; the air is unwholesome. In a word, I propose to remove my offices next week, and shall no longer require your services. I tell you this now, in order that you may seek another place." 175

He made no reply, and nothing more was said.

On the appointed day I engaged carts and men, proceeded to my chambers, and, having but little furniture, everything was removed in a few hours. Throughout, the scrivener remained standing behind the screen, which I directed to be removed the last thing. It was withdrawn; and, being folded up like a huge folio, left him the motionless occupant of a naked room. I stood in the entry watching him a moment, while something from within me upbraided me.

I re-entered, with my hand in my pocket—and—and my heart in my mouth.

"Good-by, Bartleby; I am going—good-by, and God some way bless you; and take that," slipping something in his hand. But it dropped upon the floor, and then—strange to say—I tore myself from him whom I had so longed to be rid of.

Established in my new quarters, for a day or two I kept the door locked, 180
and started at every footfall in the passages. When I returned to my rooms, after any little absence, I would pause at the threshold for an instant, and attentively listen, ere applying my key. But these fears were needless. Bartleby
never came nigh me.

I thought all was going well, when a perturbed-looking stranger visited
me, inquiring whether I was the person who had recently occupied rooms at
No.—Wall Street.

Full of forebodings, I replied that I was.

"Then, sir," said the stranger, who proved a lawyer, "you are responsible
for the man you left there. He refuses to do any copying; he refuses to do anything; he says he prefers not to; and he refuses to quit the premises."

"I am very sorry, sir," said I, with assumed tranquillity, but an inward
tremor, "but, really, the man you allude to is nothing to me—he is no relation
or apprentice of mine, that you should hold me responsible for him."

"In mercy's name, who is he?" 185

"I certainly cannot inform you. I know nothing about him. Formerly
I employed him as a copyist; but he has done nothing for me now for some
time past."

"I shall settle him, then—good morning, sir."

Several days passed, and I heard nothing more; and, though I often felt a
charitable prompting to call at the place and see poor Bartleby, yet a certain
squeamishness, of I know not what, withheld me.

All is over with him, by this time, thought I, at last, when, through another week, no further intelligence reached me. But, coming to my room the
day after, I found several persons waiting at my door in a high state of nervous
excitement.

"That's the man—here he comes," cried the foremost one, whom I rec- 190
ognized as the lawyer who had previously called upon me alone.

"You must take him away, sir, at once," cried a portly person among them,
advancing upon me, and whom I knew to be the landlord of No.—Wall Street.
"These gentlemen, my tenants, cannot stand it any longer; Mr. B——," pointing to the lawyer, "has turned him out of his room, and he now persists in
haunting the building generally, sitting upon the banisters of the stairs by day,
and sleeping in the entry by night. Everybody is concerned; clients are leaving the offices; some fears are entertained of a mob; something you must do,
and that without delay."

Aghast at this torrent, I fell back before it, and would fain have locked
myself in my new quarters. In vain I persisted that Bartleby was nothing to
me—no more than to any one else. In vain—I was the last person known to
have anything to do with him, and they held me to the terrible account. Fearful, then, of being exposed in the papers (as one person present obscurely
threatened), I considered the matter, and, at length, said, that if the lawyer
would give me a confidential interview with the scrivener, in his (the lawyer's)
own room, I would, that afternoon, strive my best to rid them of the nuisance
they complained of.

Going up stairs to my old haunt, there was Bartleby silently sitting upon the banister at the landing.

"What are you doing here, Bartleby?" said I.

"Sitting upon the banister," he mildly replied.   195

I motioned him into the lawyer's room, who then left us.

"Bartleby," said I, "are you aware that you are the cause of great tribulation to me, by persisting in occupying entry after being dismissed from the office?"

No answer.

"Now one of two things must take place. Either you must do something, or something must be done to you. Now what sort of business would you like to engage in? Would you like to re-engage in copying for some one?"

"No; I would prefer not to make any change."   200

"Would you like a clerkship in a dry-goods store?"

"There is too much confinement about that. No, I would not like a clerkship; but I am not particular."

"Too much confinement," I cried, "why you keep yourself confined all the time!"

"I would prefer not to take a clerkship," he rejoined, as if to settle that little item at once.

"How would a bar-tender's business suit you? There is no trying of the   205
eye-sight in that."

"I would not like it at all; though, as I said before, I am not particular."

His unwonted wordiness inspirited me. I returned to the charge.

"Well, then, would you like to travel through the country collecting bills for the merchants? That would improve your health."

"No, I would prefer to be doing something else."

"How, then, would going as a companion to Europe, to entertain some   210
young gentleman with your conversation—how would that suit you?"

"Not at all. It does not strike me that there is anything definite about that. I like to be stationary. But I am not particular."

"Stationary you shall be, then," I cried, now losing all patience, and, for the first time in all my exasperating connection with him, fairly flying into a passion. "If you do not go away from these premises before night, I shall feel bound—indeed, I *am* bound—*to*—*to*—*to* quit the premises myself!" I rather absurdly concluded, knowing not with what possible threat to try to frighten his immobility into compliance. Despairing of all further efforts, I was precipitately leaving him, when a final thought occurred to me—one which had not been wholly unindulged before.

"Bartleby," said I, in the kindest tone I could assume under such exciting circumstances, "will you go home with me now—not to my office, but my dwelling—and remain there till we can conclude upon some convenient arrangement for you at our leisure? Come, let us start now, right away."

"No: at present I would prefer not to make any change at all."

I answered nothing; but, effectually dodging every one by the suddenness   215
and rapidity of my flight, rushed from the building, ran up Wall Street

towards Broadway, and, jumping into the first omnibus, was soon removed from pursuit. As soon as tranquillity returned, I distinctly perceived that I had now done all that I possibly could, both in respect to the demands of the land-lord and his tenants, and with regard to my own desire and sense of duty, to benefit Bartleby, and shield him from rude persecution. I now strove to be en-tirely care-free and quiescent; and my conscience justified me in the attempt; though, indeed, it was not so successful as I could have wished. So fearful was I of being again hunted out by the incensed landlord and his exasperated ten-ants, that, surrendering my business to Nippers, for a few days, I drove about the upper part of the town and through the suburbs, in my rockaway; crossed over to Jersey City and Hoboken, and paid fugitive visits to Manhattanville and Astoria. In fact, I almost lived in my rockaway for the time.

When again I entered my office, lo, a note from the landlord lay upon the desk. I opened it with trembling hands. It informed me that the writer had sent to the police, and had Bartleby removed to the Tombs as a vagrant. Moreover, since I knew more about him than any one else, he wished me to appear at that place, and make a suitable statement of the facts. These tidings had a conflict-ing effect upon me. At first I was indignant; but, at last, almost approved. The landlord's energetic, summary disposition, had led him to adopt a procedure which I do not think I would have decided upon myself; and yet, as a last re-sort, under such peculiar circumstances, it seemed the only plan.

As I afterwards learned, the poor scrivener, when told that he must be conducted to the Tombs, offered not the slightest obstacle, but, in his pale, unmoving way, silently acquiesced.

Some of the compassionate and curious bystanders joined the party; and headed by one of the constables arm in arm with Bartleby, the silent proces-sion filed its way through all the noise, and heat, and joy of the roaring thor-oughfares at noon.

The same day I received the note, I went to the Tombs, or, to speak more properly, the Halls of Justice. Seeking the right officer, I stated the purpose of my call, and was informed that the individual I described was, indeed, within. I then assured the functionary that Bartleby was a perfectly honest man, and greatly to be compassionated, however unaccountably eccentric. I narrated all I knew, and closed by suggesting the idea of letting him remain in as indulgent confinement as possible, till something less harsh might be done—though, in-deed, I hardly knew what. At all events, if nothing else could be decided upon, the almshouse must receive him. I then begged to have an interview.

Being under no disgraceful charge, and quite serene and harmless in all   220
his ways, they had permitted him freely to wander about the prison, and, es-pecially, in the inclosed grass-platted yards thereof. And so I found him there, standing all alone in the quietest of the yards, his face towards a high wall, while all around, from the narrow slits of the jail windows, I thought I saw peering out upon him the eyes of murderers and thieves.

"Bartleby!"

"I know you," he said without looking round—"and I want nothing to say to you."

"It was not I that brought you here, Bartleby," said I, keenly pained at his implied suspicion. "And to you, this should not be so vile a place. Nothing reproachful attaches to you by being here. And see, it is not so sad a place as one might think. Look, there is the sky, and here is the grass."

"I know where I am," he replied, but would say nothing more, and so I left him.

As I entered the corridor again, a broad meat-like man, in an apron, accosted me, and, jerking his thumb over his shoulder, said—"Is that your friend?"   225

"Yes."

"Does he want to starve? If he does, let him live on the prison fare, that's all."

"Who are you?" asked I, not knowing what to make of such an unofficially speaking person in such a place.

"I am the grub-man. Such gentlemen as have friends here, hire me to provide them with something good to eat."

"Is this so?" said I, turning to the turnkey.   230

He said it was.

"Well, then," said I, slipping some silver into the grub-man's hands (for so they called him), "I want you to give particular attention to my friend there; let him have the best dinner you can get. And you must be as polite to him as possible."

"Introduce me, will you?" said the grub-man, looking at me with an expression which seemed to say he was all impatience for an opportunity to give a specimen of his breeding.

Thinking it would prove of benefit to the scrivener, I acquiesced; and, asking the grub-man his name, went up with him to Bartleby.

"Bartleby, this is a friend; you will find him very useful to you."   235

"Your sarvant, sir, your sarvant," said the grub-man, making a low salutation behind his apron. "Hope you find it pleasant here, sir; nice grounds—cool apartments—hope you'll stay with us sometime—try to make it agreeable. What will you have for dinner to-day?"

"I prefer not to dine to-day," said Bartleby, turning away. "It would disagree with me; I am unused to dinners." So saying, he slowly moved to the other side of the inclosure, and took up a position fronting the dead-wall.

"How's this?" said the grub-man, addressing me with a stare of astonishment, "He's odd, ain't he?"

"I think he is a little deranged," said I, sadly.

"Deranged? deranged is it? Well, now, upon my word, I thought that friend of yourn was a gentleman forger; they are always pale and genteel-like, them forgers. I can't help pity 'em—can't help it, sir. Did you know Monroe Edwards?" he added, touchingly, and paused. Then, laying his hand piteously on my shoulder, sighed, "he died of consumption at Sing-Sing. So you weren't acquainted with Monroe?"

"No, I was never socially acquainted with any forgers. But I cannot stop longer. Look to my friend yonder. You will not lose by it. I will see you again."

Some few days after this, I again obtained admission to the Tombs, and went through the corridors in quest of Bartleby; but without finding him.

"I saw him coming from his cell not long ago," said a turnkey, "may be he's gone to loiter in the yards."

So I went in that direction.

"Are you looking for the silent man?" said another turnkey, passing me. 245 "Yonder he lies—sleeping in the yard there. 'Tis not twenty minutes since I saw him lie down."

The yard was entirely quiet. It was not accessible to the common prisoners. The surrounding walls, of amazing thickness, kept off all sounds behind them. The Egyptian character of the masonry weighed upon me with its gloom. But a soft imprisoned turf grew under foot. The heart of the eternal pyramids, it seemed, wherein, by some strange magic, through the clefts, grass-seed, dropped by birds, had sprung.

Strangely huddled at the base of the wall, his knees drawn up, and lying on his side, his head touching the cold stones, I saw the wasted Bartleby. But nothing stirred. I paused; then went close up to him; stooped over, and saw that his dim eyes were open; otherwise he seemed profoundly sleeping. Something prompted me to touch him. I felt his hand, when a tingling shiver ran up my arm and down my spine to my feet.

The round face of the grub-man peered upon me now. "His dinner is ready. Won't he dine to-day, either? Or does he live without dining?"

"Lives without dining," said I, and closed the eyes.

"Eh!—He's asleep, ain't he?" 250

"With kings and counselors," murmured I.

There would seem little need for proceeding further in this history. Imagination will readily supply the meagre recital of poor Bartleby's interment. But, ere parting with the reader, let me say, that if this little narrative has sufficiently interested him, to awaken curiosity as to who Bartleby was, and what manner of life he led prior to the present narrator's making his acquaintance, I can only reply, that in such curiosity I fully share, but am wholly unable to gratify it. Yet here I hardly know whether I should divulge one little item of rumor, which came to my ear a few months after the scrivener's decease. Upon what basis it rested, I could never ascertain; and hence, how true it is I cannot now tell. But, inasmuch as this vague report has not been without a certain suggestive interest to me, however sad, it may prove the same with some others; and so I will briefly mention it. The report was this: that Bartleby had been a subordinate clerk in the Dead Letter Office at Washington, from which he had been suddenly removed by a change in the administration. When I think over this rumor, hardly can I express the emotions which seize me. Dead letters! does it not sound like dead men? Conceive a man by nature and misfortune prone to a pallid hopelessness, can any business seem more fitted to heighten it than that of continually handling these dead letters, and assorting them for the flames? For by the cartload they are annually burned. Sometimes from out the folded paper the pale clerk takes a ring—the finger it was meant for, perhaps, moulders in the grave; a bank-note sent in swiftest charity—he whom it would relieve, nor eats nor hungers any more; pardon for those who died despairing; hope for those who died unhoping; good tidings for those who died stifled by unrelieved calamities. On errands of life, these letters speed to death.

Ah, Bartleby! Ah, humanity!

——— **HERMAN MELVILLE** ———

(1819–1891) `Web`

www

After having worked as a bank clerk, farm hand, store clerk, schoolmaster, surveyor, and sailor, Melville became a writer. He began his career writing novels about South Seas adventures and in 1851 published *Moby Dick*. Melville's writing did not please the taste of the times sufficiently to enable him to live by the pen, so like his predecessor Nathaniel Hawthorne, he got a job in a customs house. Late in his life he inherited enough money to devote himself to writing full time.

www

TOPICS FOR CRITICAL THINKING `Web`

1. Who is the protagonist in this story?
2. How does having worked in a Dead Letter Office account for Bartleby's behavior?
3. Why does Bartleby die soon after he is removed from the offices?
4. What is the function of such minor characters as Turkey, Nippers, and Ginger Nut?

www

TOPICS FOR CRITICAL WRITING `Web`

1. What is the relation between the narrator and Bartleby?
2. In what ways does the image of the Dead Letter Office pervade the story?

ᘒᘒ

SARAH ORNE JEWETT

The Flight of Betsey Lane   *(1893)*

I.

One windy morning in May, three old women sat together near an open window in the shed chamber of Byfleet Poor-house. The wind was from the northwest, but their window faced the southeast, and they were only visited by an occasional pleasant waft of fresh air. They were close together, knee to knee, picking over a bushel of beans, and commanding a view of the dandelion-starred, green yard below, and of the winding, sandy road that led to the village, two miles away. Some captive bees were scolding among the cobwebs of the rafters overhead, or thumping against the upper panes of glass;

two calves were bawling from the barnyard, where some of the men were at work loading a dump-cart and shouting as if every one were deaf. There was a cheerful feeling of activity, and even an air of comfort, about the Byfleet Poor-house. Almost every one was possessed of a most interesting past, though there was less to be said about the future. The inmates were by no means distressed or unhappy; many of them retired to this shelter only for the winter season, and would go out presently, some to begin such work as they could still do, others to live in their own small houses; old age had impoverished most of them by limiting their power of endurance; but far from lamenting the fact that they were town charges, they rather liked the change and excitement of a winter residence on the poor-farm. There was a sharp-faced, hard-worked young widow with seven children, who was an exception to the general level of society, because she deplored the change in her fortunes. The older women regarded her with suspicion, and were apt to talk about her in moments like this, when they happened to sit together at their work.

The three bean-pickers were dressed alike in stout brown ginghams, checked by a white line, and all wore great faded aprons of blue drilling, with sufficient pockets convenient to the right hand. Miss Peggy Bond was a very small, belligerent-looking person, who wore a huge pair of steel-bowed spectacles, holding her sharp chin well up in air, as if to supplement an inadequate nose. She was more than half blind, but the spectacles seemed to face upward instead of square ahead, as if their wearer were always on the sharp lookout for birds. Miss Bond had suffered much personal damage from time to time, because she never took heed where she planted her feet, and so was always tripping and stubbing her bruised way through the world. She had fallen down hatchways and cellar-ways, and stepped composedly into deep ditches and pasture brooks; but she was proud of stating that she was upsighted, and so was her father before her. At the poor-house, where an unusual malady was considered a distinction, upsightedness was looked upon as a most honorable infirmity. Plain rheumatism, such as afflicted Aunt Lavina Dow, whose twisted hands found even this light work difficult and tiresome, plain rheumatism was something of every day occurrence, and nobody cared to hear about it. Poor Peggy was a meek and friendly soul, who never put herself forward; she was just like other folks, as she always loved to say, but Mrs. Lavina Dow was a different sort of person altogether, of great dignity and, occasionally, almost aggressive behavior. The time had been when she could do a good day's work with anybody: but for many years now she had not left the town-farm, being too badly crippled to work; she had no relations or friends to visit, but from an innate love of authority she could not submit to being one of those who are forgotten by the world. Mrs. Dow was the hostess and social lawgiver here, where she remembered every inmate and every item of interest for nearly forty years, besides an immense amount of town history and biography for three or four generations back.

She was the dear friend of the third woman, Betsey Lane; together they led thought and opinion—chiefly opinion—and held sway, not only over Byfleet Poor-farm, but also the selectmen and all others in authority. Betsey Lane had spent most of her life as aid-in-general to the respected household of old General Thornton. She had been much trusted and valued, and, at the breaking up of that once large and flourishing family, she had been left in good circumstances, what with legacies and her own comfortable savings; but by sad misfortune and lavish generosity everything had been scattered, and after much illness, which ended in a stiffened arm and more uncertainty, the good soul had sensibly decided that it was easier for the whole town to support her than for a part of it. She had always hoped to see something of the world before she died; she came of an adventurous, seafaring stock, but had never made a longer journey than to the towns of Danby and Northville, thirty miles away.

They were all old women; but Betsey Lane, who was sixty-nine, and looked much older, was the youngest. Peggy Bond was far on in the seventies, and Mrs. Dow was at least ten years older. She made a great secret of her years; and as she sometimes spoke of events prior to the Revolution with the assertion of having been an eye-witness, she naturally wore an air of vast antiquity. Her tales were an inexpressible delight to Betsey Lane, who felt younger by twenty years because her friend and comrade was so unconscious of chronological limitations.

The bushel basket of cranberry beans was within easy reach, and each of the pickers had filled her lap from it again and again. The shed chamber was not an unpleasant place in which to sit at work, with its traces of seed corn hanging from the brown crossbeams, its spare churns, and dusty loom, and rickety wool-wheels, and a few bits of old furniture. In one far corner was a wide board of dismal use and suggestion, and close beside it an old cradle. There was a battered chest of drawers where the keeper of the poor-house kept his garden-seeds, with the withered remains of three seed cucumbers ornamenting the top. Nothing beautiful could be discovered, nothing interesting, but there was something usable and homely about the place. It was the favorite and untroubled bower of the bean-pickers, to which they might retreat unmolested from the public apartments of this rustic institution.

Betsey Lane blew away the chaff from her handful of beans. The spring breeze blew the chaff back again, and sifted it over her face and shoulders. She rubbed it out of her eyes impatiently, and happened to notice old Peggy holding her own handful high, as if it were an oblation, and turning her queer, uptilted head this way and that, to look at the beans sharply, as if she were first cousin to a hen.

"There, Miss Bond, 't is kind of botherin' work for you, ain't it?" Betsey inquired compassionately.

"I feel to enjoy it, anything that I can do my own way so," responded Peggy. "I like to do my part. Ain't that old Mis' Fales comin' up the road? It sounds like her step."

The others looked, but they were not farsighted, and for a moment Peggy had the advantage. Mrs. Fales was not a favorite.

"I hope she ain't comin' here to put up this spring. I guess she won't now, it's gettin' so late," said Betsey Lane. "She likes to go rovin' soon as the roads is settled."

"'T is Mis' Fales!" said Peggy Bond, listening with solemn anxiety. "There, do let 's pray her by!"

"I guess she 's headin' for her cousin's folks up Beech Hill way," said Betsey presently. "If she 'd left her daughter's this mornin', she 'd have got just about as far as this. I kind o' wish she had stepped in just to pass the time o' day, long 's she wa'n't going to make no stop."

There was a silence as to further speech in the shed chamber; and even the calves were quiet in the barnyard. The men had all gone away to the field where corn-planting was going on. The beans clicked steadily into the wooden measure at the pickers' feet. Betsey Lane began to sing a hymn, and the others joined in as best they might, like autumnal crickets; their voices were sharp and cracked, with now and then a few low notes of plaintive tone. Betsey herself could sing pretty well, but the others could only make a kind of accompaniment. Their voices ceased altogether at the higher notes.

"Oh my! I wish I had the means to go to the Centennial," mourned Betsey Lane, stopping so suddenly that the others had to go on croaking and shrilling without her for a moment before they could stop. "It seems to me as if I can't die happy 'less I do," she added; "I ain't never seen nothin' of the world, an' here I be."

"What if you was as old as I be?" suggested Mrs. Dow pompously. "You 've got time enough yet, Betsey; don't you go an' despair. I knowed of a woman that went clean round the world four times when she was past eighty, an' enjoyed herself real well. Her folks followed the sea; she had three sons an' a daughter married,—all shipmasters, and she 'd been with her own husband when they was young. She was left a widder early, and fetched up her family herself,—a real stirrin', smart woman. After they 'd got married off, an' settled, an' was doing well, she come to be lonesome; and first she tried to stick it out alone, but she wa'n't one that could; an' she got a notion she had n't nothin' before her but her last sickness, and she wa'n't a person that enjoyed havin' other folks do for her. So one on her boys—I guess 't was the oldest— said he was going to take her to sea; there was ample room, an' he was sailin' a good time o' year for the Cape o' Good Hope an' way up to some o' them tea-ports in the Chiny Seas. She was all high to go, but it made a sight o' talk at her age; an' the minister made it a subject o' prayer the last Sunday, and all the folks took a last leave; but she said to some she 'd fetch 'em home something real pritty, and so did. An' then they come home t' other way, round the Horn, an' she done so well, an' was such a sight o' company, the other child'n was jealous, an' she promised she 'd go a v'y'ge long o' each on 'em. She was as sprightly a person as ever I see; an' could speak well o' what she'd seen."

"Did she die to sea?" asked Peggy, with interest.

"No, she died to home between v'y'ges, or she 'd gone to sea again. I was to her funeral. She liked her son George's ship the best; 't was the one she was going on to Callao. They said the men aboard all called her 'gran'ma'am,' an' she kep' 'em mended up, an' would go below and tend to 'em if they was sick. She might 'a' been alive an' enjoyin' of herself a good many years but for the kick of a cow; 't was a new cow out of a drove, a dreadful unruly beast."

Mrs. Dow stopped for breath, and reached down for a new supply of beans; her empty apron was gray with soft chaff. Betsey Lane, still pondering on the Centennial, began to sing another verse of her hymn, and again the old women joined her. At this moment some strangers came driving round into the yard from the front of the house. The turf was soft, and our friends did not hear the horses' steps. Their voices cracked and quavered; it was a funny little concert, and a lady in an open carriage just below listened with sympathy and amusement.

II.

"Betsey! Betsey! Miss Lane!" a voice called eagerly at the foot of the stairs that led up from the shed. "Betsey! There's a lady here wants to see you right away."

Betsey was dazed with excitement, like a country child who knows the   20
rare pleasure of being called out of school. "Lor', I ain't fit to go down, be I?" she faltered, looking anxiously at her friends; but Peggy was gazing even nearer to the zenith than usual, in her excited effort to see down into the yard, and Mrs. Dow only nodded somewhat jealously, and said that she guessed 't was nobody would do her any harm. She rose ponderously, while Betsey hesitated, being, as they would have said, all of a twitter. "It is a lady, certain," Mrs. Dow assured her; "'t ain't often there's a lady comes here."

"While there was any of Mis' Gen'ral Thornton's folks left, I wa'n't without visits from the gentry," said Betsey Lane, turning back proudly at the head of the stairs, with a touch of old-world pride and sense of high station. Then she disappeared, and closed the door behind her at the stair-foot with a decision quite unwelcome to the friends above.

"She need n't 'a' been so dreadful 'fraid anybody was goin' to listen. I guess we 've got folks to ride an' see us, or had once, if we hain 't now," said Miss Peggy Bond, plaintively.

"I expect 't was only the wind shoved it to," said Aunt Lavina. "Betsey is one that gits flustered easier than some. I wish 't was somebody to take her off an' give her a kind of a good time; she 's young to settle down 'long of old folks like us. Betsey 's got a notion o' rovin' such as ain't my natur', but I should like to see her satisfied. She 'd been a very understandin' person, if she had the advantages that some does."

"'T is so," said Peggy Bond, tilting her chin high. "I suppose you can't hear nothin' they 're saying? I feel my hearin' ain't up to whar it was. I can hear things close to me well as ever; but there, hearin' ain't everything; 't ain't as if we lived where there was more goin' on to hear. Seems to me them folks is stoppin' a good while."

"They surely be," agreed Lavina Dow.   25

"I expect it 's somethin' particular. There ain't none of the Thornton folks left, except one o' the gran'darters, an' I 've often heard Betsey remark that she should never see her more, for she lives to London. Strange how folks feels contented in them strayaway places off to the ends of the airth."

The flies and bees were buzzing against the hot window-panes; the handfuls of beans were clicking into the brown wooden measure. A bird came and perched on the window-sill, and then flitted away toward the blue sky. Below, in the yard, Betsey Lane stood talking with the lady. She had put her blue drilling apron over her head, and her face was shining with delight.

"Lor', dear," she said, for at least the third time, "I remember ye when I first see ye; an awful pritty baby you was, an' they all said you looked just like the old gen'ral. Be you goin' back to foreign parts right away?"

"Yes, I'm going back; you know that all my children are there. I wish I could take you with me for a visit," said the charming young guest. "I 'm going to carry over some of the pictures and furniture from the old house; I did n't care half so much for them when I was younger as I do now. Perhaps next summer we shall all come over for a while. I should like to see my girls and boys playing under the pines."

"I wish you re'lly was livin' to the old place," said Betsey Lane. Her imag- 30 ination was not swift; she needed time to think over all that was being told her, and she could not fancy the two strange houses across the sea. The old Thornton house was to her mind the most delightful and elegant in the world.

"Is there anything I can do for you ?" asked Mrs. Strafford kindly, — "anything that I can do for you myself, before I go away? I shall be writing to you, and sending some pictures of the children, and you must let me know how you are getting on."

"Yes, there is one thing, darlin'. If you could stop in the village an' pick me out a pritty, little, small lookin'-glass, that I can keep for my own an' have to remember you by. 'T ain't that I want to set me above the rest o' the folks, but I was always used to havin' my own when I was to your grandma's. There 's very nice folks here, some on 'em, and I 'm better off than if I was able to keep house; but sence you ask me, that's the only thing I feel cropin' about. What be you goin' right back for? ain't you goin' to see the great fair to Phc-ladelphy, that everybody talks about?"

"No," said Mrs. Strafford, laughing at this eager and almost convicting question. "No; I 'm going back next week. If I were, I believe that I should take you with me. Good-by, dear old Betsey; you make me feel as if I were a little girl again; you look just the same."

For full five minutes the old woman stood out in the sunshine, dazed with delight, and majestic with a sense of her own consequence. She held some-thing tight in her hand, without thinking what it might be: but just as the friendly mistress of the poor-farm came out to hear the news, she tucked the roll of money into the bosom of her brown gingham dress. "'T was my dear Mis' Katy Strafford," she turned to say proudly. "She come way over from London; she 's been sick; they thought the voyage would do her good. She said most the first thing she had on her mind was to come an' find me, and see how I was, an' if I was comfortable; an' now she 's goin' right back. She 's got two splendid houses; an' said how she wished I was there to look after things,—she remembered I was always her gran'ma's right hand. Oh, it does so carry me back, to see her! Seems if all the rest on 'em must be there to-gether to the old house. There, I must go up an' tell Mis' Dow an' Peggy."

"Dinner's all ready; I was just goin' to blow the horn for the men-folks," 35 said the keeper's wife. "They'll be right down. I expect you 've got along smart

with them beans,—all three of you together;" but Betsey's mind roved so high
and so far at that moment that no achievements of bean-picking could lure
it back.

III.

The long table in the great kitchen soon gathered its company of waifs
and strays,—creatures of improvidence and misfortune, and the irreparable
victims of old age. The dinner was satisfactory, and there was not much delay
for conversation. Peggy Bond and Mrs. Dow and Betsey Lane always sat together at one end, with an air of putting the rest of the company below the
salt. Betsey was still flushed with excitement; in fact, she could not eat as much
as usual, and she looked up from time to time expectantly, as if she were likely
to be asked to speak of her guest; but everybody was hungry, and even Mrs.
Dow broke in upon some attempted confidences by asking inopportunely for
a second potato. There were nearly twenty at the table, counting the keeper
and his wife and two children, noisy little persons who had come from school
with the small flock belonging to the poor widow, who sat just opposite our
friends. She finished her dinner before any one else, and pushed her chair
back; she always helped with the housework,—a thin, sorry, bad-tempered-
looking poor soul, whom grief had sharpened instead of softening. "I expect
you feel too fine to set with common folks," she said enviously to Betsey.

"Here I be a-settin'," responded Betsey calmly. "I don' know 's I behave
more unbecomin' than usual." Betsey prided herself upon her good and
proper manners; but the rest of the company, who would have like to hear the
bit of morning news, were now defrauded of that pleasure. The wrong note
had been struck; there was a silence after the clatter of knives and plates, and
one by one the cheerful town charges disappeared. The bean-picking had
been finished, and there was a call for any of the women who felt like planting
corn; so Peggy Bond, who could follow the line of hills pretty fairly, and Betsey herself, who was still equal to anybody at that work, and Mrs. Dow, all
went out to the field together. Aunt Lavina labored slowly up the yard, carrying a light splint-bottomed kitchen chair and her knitting-work, and sat near
the stone wall on a gentle rise, where she could see the pond and the green
country, and exchange a word with her friends as they came and went up and
down the rows. Betsey vouchsafed a word now and then about Mrs. Strafford,
but you would have thought that she had been suddenly elevated to Mrs.
Strafford's own cares and the responsibilities attending them, and had little in
common with her old associates. Mrs. Dow and Peggy knew well that these
high-feeling times never lasted long, and so they waited with as much patience as they could muster. They were by no means without that true tact
which is only another word for unselfish sympathy.

The strip of corn land ran along the side of a great field; at the upper end
of it was a field-corner thicket of young maples and walnut saplings, the children of a great nut-tree that marked the boundary. Once, when Betsey Lane
found herself alone near this shelter at the end of her row, the other planters
having lagged behind beyond the rising ground, she looked stealthily about,

and then put her hand inside her gown, and for the first time took out the money that Mrs. Strafford had given her. She turned it over and over with an astonished look: there were new bank-bills for a hundred dollars. Betsey gave a funny little shrug of her shoulders, came out of the bushes, and took a step or two on the narrow edge of turf, as if she were going to dance; then she hastily tucked away her treasure, and stepped discreetly down into the soft harrowed and hoed land, and began to drop corn again, five kernels to a hill. She had seen the top of Peggy Bond's head over the knoll, and now Peggy herself came entirely into view, gazing upward to the skies, and stumbling more or less, but counting the corn by touch and twisting her head about anxiously to gain advantage over her uncertain vision. Betsey made a friendly, inarticulate little sound as they passed; she was thinking that somebody said once that Peggy's eyesight might be remedied if she could go to Boston to the hospital; but that was so remote and impossible an undertaking that no one had ever taken the first step. Betsey Lane's brown old face suddenly worked with excitement, but in a moment more she regained her usual firm expression, and spoke carelessly to Peggy as she turned and came alongside.

The high spring wind of the morning had quite fallen; it was a lovely May afternoon. The woods about the field to the northward were full of birds, and the young leaves scarcely hid the solemn shapes of a company of crows that patiently attended the cornplanting. Two of the men had finished their hoeing, and were busy with the construction of a scarecrow; they knelt in the furrows, chuckling, and looking over some forlorn, discarded garments. It was a time-honored custom to make the scarecrow resemble one of the poor-house family; and this year they intended to have Mrs. Lavina Dow protect the field in effigy; last year it was the counterfeit of Betsey Lane who stood on guard, with an easily recognized quilted hood and the remains of a valued shawl that one of the calves had found airing on a fence and chewed to pieces. Behind the men was the foundation for this rustic attempt at statuary,—an upright stake and bar in the form of a cross. This stood on the highest part of the field; and as the men knelt near it, and the quaint figures of the corn-planters went and came, the scene gave a curious suggestion of foreign life. It was not like New England; the presence of the rude cross appealed strangely to the imagination.

IV.

Life flowed so smoothly, for the most part, at the Byfleet Poor-farm, that nobody knew what to make, later in the summer, of a strange disappearance. All the elder inmates were familiar with illness and death, and the poor pomp of a town-pauper's funeral. The comings and goings and the various misfortunes of those who composed this strange family, related only through its disasters, hardly served for the excitement and talk of a single day. Now that the June days were at their longest, the old people were sure to wake earlier than ever; but one morning, to the astonishment of everyone, Betsey Lane's bed was empty; the sheets and blankets, which were her own, and guarded with jealous care, were carefully folded and placed on a chair not too near the window, and Betsey had flown. Nobody had heard her go down the creaking stairs. The kitchen door was unlocked, and the old watch-dog lay on the step outside in the early sunshine, wagging his tail and looking wise, as if he were left on guard and meant to keep the fugitive's secret.

"Never knowed her to do nothin' afore 'thout talking it over a fortnight, and paradin' off when we could all see her," ventured a spiteful voice. "Guess we can wait till night to hear 'bout it."

Mrs. Dow looked sorrowful and shook her head. "Betsey had an aunt on her mother's side that went and drownded of herself; she was a pritty-appearing woman as ever you see."

"Perhaps she 's gone to spend the day with Decker's folks," suggested Peggy Bond. "She always takes an extra early start; she was speakin' lately o' going up their way;" but Mrs. Dow shook her head with a most melancholy look. "I 'm impressed that something 's befell her," she insisted. "I heard her a-groanin' in her sleep. I was wakeful for the forepart o' the night,—'t is very unusual with me, too."

" 'T wa'n't like Betsey not to leave us any word," said the other old friend, with more resentment than melancholy. They sat together almost in silence that morning in the shed chamber. Mrs. Dow was sorting and cutting rags, and Peggy braided them into long ropes, to be made into mats at a later date. If they had only known where Betsey Lane had gone, they might have talked about it until dinner-time at noon; but failing this new subject, they could take no interest in any of their old ones. Out in the field the corn was well up, and the men were hoeing. It was a hot morning in the shed chamber, and the woolen rags were dusty and hot to handle.

V.

Byfleet people knew each other well, and when this mysteriously absent   45 person did not return to the town-farm at the end of a week, public interest became much excited; and presently it was ascertained that Betsey Lane was neither making a visit to her friends the Deckers on Birch Hill, nor to any nearer acquaintances; in fact, she had disappeared altogether from her wonted haunts. Nobody remembered to have seen her pass, hers had been such an early flitting; and when somebody thought of her having gone away by train, he was laughed at for forgetting that the earliest morning train from South Byfleet, the nearest station, did not start until long after eight o'clock; and if Betsey had designed to be one of the passengers, she would have started along the road at seven, and been seen and known of all women. There was not a kitchen in that part of Byfleet that did not have windows toward the road. Conversation rarely left the level of the neighborhood gossip: to see Betsey Lane, in her best clothes, at that hour in the morning, would have been the signal for much exercise of imagination; but as day after day went by without news, the curiosity of those who knew her best turned slowly into fear, and at last Peggy Bond again gave utterance to the belief that Betsey had either gone out in the early morning and put an end to her life, or that she had gone to the Centennial. Some of the people at table were moved to loud laughter,—it was at supper-time on a Sunday night,—but others listened with great interest.

"She never 'd put on her good clothes to drownd herself," said the widow. "She might have thought 't was good as takin' 'em with her, though. Old folks has wandered off an' got lost in the woods afore now."

Mrs. Dow and Peggy resented this impertinent remark, but deigned to take no notice of the speaker. "She would n't have wore her best clothes to the Centennial, would she?" mildly inquired Peggy, bobbing her head toward the ceiling. "'T would be a shame to spoil your best things in such a place. An' I don't know of her havin' any money; there 's the end o' that."

"You 're bad as old Mis' Bland, that used to live neighbor to our folks," said one of the old men. "She was dreadful precise; an' she so begretched to wear a good alapaca dress that was left to her, that it hung in a press forty year, an' baited the moths at last."

"I often seen Mis' Bland a-goin' in to meetin' when I was a young girl," said Peggy Bond approvingly. "She was a good-appearin' woman, an' she left property."

"Wish she'd left it to me, then," said the poor soul opposite, glancing at her pathetic row of children: but it was not good manners at the farm to deplore one's situation, and Mrs. Dow and Peggy only frowned. "Where do you suppose Betsey can be?" said Mrs. Dow, for the twentieth time. "She did n't have no money. I know she ain't gone far, if it 's so that she 's yet alive. She 's b'en real pinched all the spring."

"Perhaps that lady that come one day give her some," the keeper's wife suggested mildly.

"Then Betsey would have told me," said Mrs. Dow, with injured dignity.

VI.

On the morning of her disappearance, Betsey rose even before the pewee and the English sparrow, and dressed herself quietly, though with trembling hands, and stole out of the kitchen door like a plunderless thief. The old dog licked her hand and looked at her anxiously; the tortoise-shell cat rubbed against her best gown, and trotted away up the yard, then she turned anxiously and came after the old woman, following faithfully until she had to be driven back. Betsey was used to long country excursions afoot. She dearly loved the early morning; and finding that there was no dew to trouble her, she began to follow pasture paths and short cuts across the field, surprising here and there a flock of sleepy sheep, or a startled calf that rustled out from the bushes. The birds were pecking their breakfast from bush and turf; and hardly any of the wild inhabitants of that rural world were enough alarmed by her presence to do more than flutter away if they chanced to be in her path. She stepped along, light-footed and eager as a girl, dressed in her neat old straw bonnet and black gown, and carrying a few belongings in her best bundle-handkerchief, one that her only brother had brought home from the East Indies fifty years before. There was an old crow perched as sentinel on a small, dead pine-tree, where he could warn friends who were pulling up the sprouted corn in a field close by; but he only gave a contemptuous caw as the adventurer appeared, and she shook her bundle at him in revenge, and laughed to see him so clumsy as he tried to keep his footing on the twigs.

"Yes, I be," she assured him. "I 'm a-goin' to Pheladelphy, to the Centennial, same 's other folks. I 'd jest as soon tell ye 's not, old crow;" and Betsey laughed aloud in pleased content with herself and her daring, as she walked along. She had only two miles to go to the station at South Byfleet, and she felt for the money now and then, and found it safe enough. She took great pride in the success of her escape, and especially in the long concealment of her wealth. Not a night had passed since Mrs. Strafford's visit that she had not slept with the roll of money under her pillow by night, and buttoned safe inside her dress by day. She knew that everybody would offer advice and even commands about the spending or saving of it; and she brooked no interference.

The last mile of the foot-path to South Byfleet was along the railway 55 track; and Betsey began to feel in haste, though it was still nearly two hours to train time. She looked anxiously forward and back along the rails every few minutes, for fear of being run over; and at last she caught sight of an engine that was apparently coming toward her, and took flight into the woods before she could gather courage to follow the path again. The freight train proved to be at a standstill, waiting at a turnout; and some of the men were straying about, eating their early breakfast comfortably in this time of leisure. As the old woman came up to them, she stopped too, for a moment of rest and conversation.

"Where be ye goin'?" she asked pleasantly; and they told her. It was to the town where she had to change cars and take the great through train; a point of geography which she had learned from evening talks between the men at the farm.

"What'll ye carry me there for?"

"We don't run no passenger cars," said one of the young fellows, laughing. "What makes you in such a hurry?"

"I 'm startin' for Pheladelphy, an' it 's a gre't ways to go."

"So 't is; but you 're consid'able early, if you 're makin' for the eight-forty 60 train. See here! You have n't got a needle an' thread 'long of you in that bundle, have you? If you 'll sew me on a couple o' buttons, I 'll give ye a free ride. I'm in a sight o' distress, an' none o' the fellows is provided with as much as a bent pin."

"You poor boy! I'll have you seen to, in half a minute. I 'm troubled with a stiff arm, but I 'll do the best I can."

The obliging Betsey seated herself stiffly on the slope of the embankment, and found her thread and needle with utmost haste. Two of the trainmen stood by and watched the careful stitches, and even offered her a place as spare brakeman, so that they might keep her near; and Betsey took the offer with considerable seriousness, only thinking it necessary to assure them that she was getting most too old to be out in all weathers. An express went by like an earthquake, and she was presently hoisted on board an empty box-car by two of her new and flattering acquaintances, and found herself before noon at the end of the first stage of her journey, without having spent a cent, and furnished with any amount of thrifty advice. One of the young men, being compassionate of her unprotected state as a traveler, advised her to find out the widow of an uncle of his in Philadelphia, saying despairingly that he could n't tell her just how to find the house; but Miss Betsey Lane said that she had an English tongue in her head, and should be sure to find whatever she was looking for. This unexpected incident of the freight train was the reason why everybody about the South Byfleet station insisted that no such person had taken passage by the regular train that same morning, and why there were those who persuaded themselves that Miss Betsey Lane was probably lying at the bottom of the poor-farm pond.

VII.

"Land sakes!" said Miss Betsey Lane, as she watched a Turkish person parading by in his red fez, "I call the Centennial somethin' like the day o' judgment! I wish I was goin' to stop a month, but I dare say 't would be the death o' my poor old bones."

She was leaning against the barrier of a patent pop-corn establishment, which had given her a sudden reminder of home, and of the winter nights when the sharp-kerneled little red and yellow ears were brought out, and Old Uncle Eph Flanders sat by the kitchen stove, and solemnly filled a great wooden chopping-tray for the refreshment of the company. She had wandered and loitered and looked until her eyes and head had grown numb and unreceptive; but it is only unimaginative persons who can be really astonished. The imagination can always outrun the possible and actual sights and sounds of the world; and this plain old body from Byfleet rarely found anything rich and splendid enough to surprise her. She saw the wonders of the West and the splendors of the East with equal calmness and satisfaction; she had always known that there was an amazing world outside the boundaries of Byfleet. There was a piece of paper in her pocket on which was marked, in her clumsy handwriting, "If Betsey Lane should meet with accident, notify the selectmen of Byfleet;" but having made this slight provision for the future, she had thrown herself boldly into the sea of strangers, and then had made the joyful discovery that friends were to be found at every turn.

There was something delightfully companionable about Betsey; she had a way of suddenly looking up over her big spectacles with a reassuring and expectant smile, as if you were going to speak to her, and you generally did. She must have found out where hundreds of people came from, and whom they had left at home, and what they thought of the great show, as she sat on a bench to rest, or leaned over the railings where free luncheons were afforded by the makers of hot waffles and molasses candy and fried potatoes; and there was not a night when she did not return to her lodgings with a pocket crammed with samples of spool cotton and nobody knows what. She had already collected small presents for almost everybody she knew at home, and she was such a pleasant, beaming old country body, so unmistakably appreciative and interested, that nobody ever thought of wishing that she would move

on. Nearly all the busy people of the Exhibition called her either Aunty or
Grandma at once, and made little pleasures for her as best they could. She was
a delightful contrast to the indifferent, stupid crowd that drifted along, with
eyes fixed at the same level, and seeing, even on that level, nothing for fifty
feet at a time. "What be you making here, dear?" Betsey Lane would ask joyfully, and the most perfunctory guardian hastened to explain. She squandered
money as she had never had the pleasure of doing before, and this hastened
the day when she must return to Byfleet. She was always inquiring if there
were any spectacle-sellers at hand, and received occasional directions; but it
was a difficult place for her to find her way about in, and the very last day of
her stay arrived before she found an exhibitor of the desired sort, an oculist
and instrument-maker.

"I called to get some specs for a friend that 's upsighted," she gravely informed the salesman, to his extreme amusement. "She 's dreadful troubled, and
jerks her head up like a hen a-drinkin'. She 's got a blur agrowin' an' spreadin',
an' sometimes she can see out to one side on 't, and more times she can't."

"Cataracts," said a middle-aged gentleman at her side; and Betsey Lane
turned to regard him with approval and curiosity.

"'T is Miss Peggy Bond I was mentioning, of Byfleet Poor-farm," she explained. "I count on gettin' some glasses to relieve her trouble, if there 's any
to be found."

"Glasses won't do her any good," said the stranger. "Suppose you come
and sit down on this bench, and tell me all about it. First, where is Byfleet?"
and Betsey gave the directions at length.

"I thought so," said the surgeon. "How old is this friend of yours?"   70
Betsey cleared her throat decisively, and smoothed her gown over her
knees as if it were an apron; then she turned to take a good look at her new acquaintance as they sat on the rustic bench together. "Who be you, sir, I should
like to know?" she asked, in a friendly tone.

"My name 's Dunster."

"I take it you 're a doctor," continued Betsey, as if they had overtaken each
other walking from Byfleet to South Byfleet on a summer morning.

"I'm a doctor; part of one at least," said he. "I know more or less about
eyes; and I spend my summers down on the shore at the mouth of your river;
some day I'll come up and look at this person. How old is she?"

"Peggy Bond is one that never tells her age; 't ain't come quite up to   75
where she 'll begin to brag of it, you see," explained Betsey reluctantly; "but I
know her to be nigh to seventy-six, one way or t' other. Her an' Mrs. Mary
Ann Chick was same year's child'n, and Peggy knows I know it, an' two or
three times when we 've be'n in the buryin'-ground where Mary Ann lays an'
has her dates right on her headstone, I could n't bring Peggy to take no sort
o' notice. I will say she makes, at times, a convenience of being upsighted. But
there, I feel for her,—everybody does; it keeps her stubbin' an' trippin' against
everything, beakin' and gazin' up the way she has to."

"Yes, yes," said the doctor, whose eyes were twinkling. "I 'll come and
look after her, with your town doctor, this summer,—some time in the last of
July or first of August."

"You'll find occupation," said Betsey, not without an air of patronage. "Most of us to the Byfleet Farm has got our ails, now I tell ye. You ain't got no bitters that 'll take a dozen years right off an ol' lady's shoulders?"

The busy man smiled pleasantly, and shook his head as he went away. "Dunster," said Betsey to herself, soberly committing the new name to her sound memory. "Yes, I must n't forget to speak of him to the doctor, as he directed. I do' know now as Peggy would vally herself quite so much accordin' to, if she had her eyes fixed same as other folks. I expect there would n't been a smarter woman in town, though, if she 'd had a proper chance. Now I've done what I set to do for her, I do believe, an' 't wa'n't glasses, neither. I 'll git her a pritty little shawl with that money I laid aside. Peggy Bond ain't got a pritty shawl. I always wanted to have a real good time, an' now I'm havin' it."

VIII.

Two or three days later, two pathetic figures might have been seen crossing the slopes of the poor-farm field, toward the low shores of Byfield pond. It was early in the morning, and the stubble of the lately mown grass was wet with rain and hindering to old feet. Peggy Bond was more blundering and liable to stray in the wrong direction than usual; it was one of the days when she could hardly see at all. Aunt Lavina Dow was unusually clumsy of movement, and stiff in the joints; she had not been so far from the house for three years. The morning breeze filled the gathers of her wide gingham skirt, and aggravated the size of her unwieldy figure. She supported herself with a stick, and trusted beside to the fragile support of Peggy's arm. They were talking together in whispers.

"Oh, my sakes!" exclaimed Peggy, moving her small head from side to side. "Hear you wheeze, Mis' Dow! This may be the death o' you; there, do go slow! You set here on the side-hill, an' le' me go try if I can see." 80

"It needs more eyesight than you 've got," said Mrs. Dow, panting between the words. "Oh! to think how spry I was in my young days, an' here I be now, the full of a door, an' all my complaints so aggravated by my size. 'T is hard! 't is hard! But I'm a-doin' of all this for pore Betsey's sake. I know they've all laughed, but I look to see her ris' to the top o' the pond this day,— 't is just nine days since she departed; an' say what they may, I know she hove herself in. It run in her family; Betsey had an aunt that done just so, an' she ain't be'n like herself, a-broodin' an' hivin' away alone, an' nothin' to say to you an' me that was always sich good company all together. Somethin' sprung her mind, now I tell ye, Mis' Bond."

"I feel to hope we sha'n't find her, I must say," faltered Peggy. It was plain that Mrs. Dow was the captain of this doleful expedition. "I guess she ain't never thought o' drowndin' of herself, Mis' Dow; she 's gone off a-visitin' way over to the other side o' South Byfleet; some thinks she 's gone to the Centennial even now!"

"She had n't no proper means, I tell ye," wheezed Mrs. Dow indignantly; "an' if you prefer that others should find her floatin' to the top this day, instid of us that 's her best friends, you can step back to the house."

They walked on in aggrieved silence. Peggy Bond trembled with excitement, but her companion's firm grasp never wavered, and so they came to the narrow, gravelly margin and stood still. Peggy tried in vain to see the glittering water and the pond-lilies that starred it; she knew that they must be there; once, years ago, she had caught fleeting glimpses of them, and she never forgot what she had once seen. The clear blue sky overhead, the dark pine-woods beyond the pond, were all clearly pictured in her mind. "Can't you see nothin'?" she faltered; "I believe I'm wuss'n upsighted this day. I'm going to be blind."

"No," said Lavina Dow solemnly; "no, there ain't nothin' whatever, 85 Peggy. I hope to mercy she ain't"—

"Why, whoever'd expected to find you 'way out here!" exclaimed a brisk and cheerful voice. There stood Betsey Lane herself, close behind them, having just emerged from a thicket of alders that grew close by. She was following the short way homeward from the railroad.

"Why, what's the matter, Mis' Dow? You ain't overdoin', be ye? an' Peggy 's all of a flutter. What in the name o' natur' ails ye?"

"There ain't nothin' the matter, as I knows on," responded the leader of this fruitless expedition. "We only thought we 'd take a stroll this pleasant mornin'," she added, with sublime self-possession. "Where 've you be'n, Betsey Lane?"

"To Pheladelphy, ma'am," said Betsey, looking quite young and gay, and wearing a townish and unfamiliar air that upheld her words. "All ought to go that can; why, you feel 's if you 'd be'n all round the world. I guess I 've got enough to think of and tell ye for the rest o' my days. I 've always wanted to go somewheres. I wish you 'd be'n there, I do so. I 've talked with folks from Chiny an' the back o' Pennsylvany: and I see folks way from Australy that 'peared as well as anybody; an' I see how they made spool cotton, an' sights o' other things; an' I spoke with a doctor that lives down to the beach in the summer, an' he offered to come up 'long in the first of August, an' see what he can do for Peggy's eyesight. There was di'monds there as big as pigeon's eggs; an' I met with Mis' Abby Fletcher from South Byfleet depot; an' there was hogs there that weighed risin' thirteen hunderd"—

"I want to know," said Mrs. Lavina Dow and Peggy Bond, together. 90

"Well, 't was a great exper'ence for a person," added Lavina, turning ponderously, in spite of herself, to give a last wistful look at the smiling waters of the pond.

"I don't know how soon I be goin' to settle down," proclaimed the rustic sister of Sindbad. "What's for the good o' one 's for the good of all. You just wait till we 're setting together up in the old shed chamber! You know, my dear Mis' Katy Strafford give me a han'some present o' money that day she come to see me; and I 'd be'n a-dreamin' by night an' day o' seein' that Centennial; and when I come to think on 't I felt sure somebody ought to go from this neighborhood, if 't was only for the good o' the rest; and I thought I'd better be the one. I wa'n't goin' to ask the selec'men neither. I've come back with one-thirty-five in money, and I see everything there, an' I fetched ye all a little somethin'; but I 'm full o' dust now, an' pretty nigh beat out. I never see a place more friendly than Pheladelphy; but 't ain't natural to a Byfleet person to be always walkin' on a level. There, now, Peggy, you take my bundle-handkercher and the basket, and let Mis' Dow sag on to me. I'll git her along twice as easy."

With this the small elderly company set forth triumphant toward the poor-house, across the wide green field.

───────── **SARAH ORNE JEWETT** ─────────

(1849–1909) Web   *www*

Like Melville descended from an old New England family, Sarah Orne Jewett grew up in Maine. Though she wanted to be a medical doctor like her father, poor health made her choose writing instead. She preferred writing short stories, though she also wrote novels—*A Country Doctor* (1884) and *The Country of the Pointed Firs* (1896). Her stories often focus on characters and settings rather than on more conventional plots. Jewett was a major influence on the generation of women writers to follow, particularly Willa Cather, who dedicated her first novel to her.

TOPICS FOR CRITICAL THINKING Web   *www*

1. Why does Betsey Lane go to the Centennial?
2. What reevaluations of old age do Betsey's actions inspire?
3. How does the character of Betsey Lane make a bridge between the small town and the world?
4. What is the function of the story of the old woman who sailed around the world?

TOPICS FOR CRITICAL WRITING Web   *www*

1. The story's characters are quite tolerant of their friends' pretensions. Describe the faults of the characters and show how these faults combine to produce a generous portrait of older women.
2. In what ways do the characters of this story overcome the limitations of age and gender?

4   Setting

Though we rarely think about it, **setting** is all around us. As in life, setting in fiction consists of the physical, environmental, social, historical, and cultural contexts described in a story as the scene of its action. Although in discussions of fiction, setting sometimes seems less important than character or plot, it has tremendous power. It can evoke atmosphere, mood, and circumstances. The eerie darkness of a graveyard, for example, conveys horror, fright, or un-worldliness. The junkyard atmosphere of contemporary science fiction in such films as *The Matrix* conveys a feeling of outdated technology and a makeshift existence. Setting can provide both motivation and explanations for characters' actions and demonstrate the effects of characters' choices. A bad storm might account for a character's desperate need to survive, or a posh mansion might indicate success and wealth.

Settings sometimes are literal, historical, and realistic, or subjective, dreamlike, and full of symbolic suggestion, or all of these. They can reflect characters' feelings in the same way houses or cars reflect the personalities of their owners, or they can parallel and anticipate events. An excessively messy environment (like some dorm rooms), for example, might suggest a character who is disorganized or who likes to party. An excessively neat room might signal someone who is organized, compulsive, or straight-laced. Setting can even serve as a character itself; the sea, untamed lands, the weather, and even buildings sometimes provide formidable foes, for example, as the weather does in *The Perfect Storm* or the arctic environment does in Jack London's stories of
www human struggles to survive. Web

The presentation of setting varies from story to story. In some stories, setting is barely evoked, present merely as a suggestion or stereotype. This is
www the case in Kate Chopin's "The Story of an Hour." Web In other stories, setting reflects and undergirds the story in complex but nonobtrusive ways, as in
www Ambrose Bierce's "An Occurrence at Owl Creek Bridge." Web Sometimes the setting is more social than physical; and some stories are so preoccupied
www with setting, like Jack London's "The Law of Life," Web that setting becomes an active part of the narrative.

While setting may seem to be simple background—the frame or context for a story's actions—it more often works as a complicated part of a story's intricate whole. Although we can easily point to elements of story we might understand as setting, separating such elements from character and plot is more difficult. For this reason, paying deliberate attention to the details of setting sometimes complicates our reading of a story or even suggests an opposite interpretation.

Critical Perspective: New Historicism

Analyses that focus on the historical and cultural aspects of a story's action look to history as a way of explaining or illuminating some of the story's art. This mode of criticism is called **New Historicism.** web New Historicist *www* critics look at the larger context of a story, both in terms of what it is describing and the culture in which it was written. Seeing a literary work as a piece of the culture, New Historicist criticism combines many disciplines—literature, politics, sociology, art, economics, and anthropology—to understand how a story relates to the social and historical conditions of its time.

Stories About Setting

While we often understand characters as agents whose actions drive the story, we tend to regard setting as the passive ground of their actions. We look for setting in a story's descriptive passages and expect it to be the production of the artful use of adjectives. However, in stories where setting is more of an active agent, its role becomes more dynamic. This is certainly the case in Edgar Allan Poe's "The Fall of the House of Usher" with its dreamlike gothic setting, which aggressively reflects the decadence of the house's aristocratic inhabitants. Poe wrote this story in 1839 while he was serving as the coeditor of *Burton's Magazine* in New York and busily writing book reviews and other essays. Later published in Poe's collection of tales, *Tales of the Grotesque and the Arabesque* (1840), "Usher" reflects admirably Poe's theory that short stories should have a "unity of effect."

Poe's macabre effect in "The Fall of the House of Usher" contrasts with "Paul's Mistress," Guy de Maupassant's 1881 story about the nightclub scene along the Seine. This narrative depicts a different kind of obsession, one hinted at as the river's locales twist among the complex romances of Paul's mistress.

ೲ

EDGAR ALLAN POE

The Fall of the House of Usher   *(1839)*

> *Son coeur est un luth suspendu;*
> *Sitôt qu'on le touche il résonne.*
>   —DE BÉRANGER

During the whole of a dull, dark, and soundless day in the autumn of the year, when the clouds hung oppressively low in the heavens, I had been passing alone, on horseback, through a singularly dreary tract of country; and at length found myself, as the shades of the evening drew on, within view of the melancholy House of Usher. I knew not how it was—but, with the first glimpse of the building, a sense of insufferable gloom pervaded my spirit. I say insufferable; for the feeling was unrelieved by any of that half-pleasurable, because poetic, sentiment with which the mind usually receives even the sternest natural images of the desolate or terrible. I looked upon the scene before me—upon the mere house, and the simple landscape features of the domain, upon the bleak walls, upon the vacant eyelike windows, upon a few rank sedges, and upon a few white trunks of decayed trees—with an utter depression of soul which I can compare to no earthly sensation more properly than to the after-dream of the reveler upon opium; the bitter lapse into everyday life, the hideous dropping off of the veil. There was an iciness, a sinking, a sickening of the heart, an unredeemed dreariness of thought which no goading of the imagination could torture into aught of the sublime. What was it—I paused to think—what was it that so unnerved me in the contemplation of the House of Usher? It was a mystery all insoluble; nor could I grapple with the shadowy fancies that crowded upon me as I pondered. I was forced to fall back upon the unsatisfactory conclusion, that while, beyond doubt, there *are* combinations of very simple natural objects which have the power of thus affecting us, still the analysis of this power lies among considerations beyond our depth. It was possible, I reflected, that a mere different arrangement of the particulars of the scene, of the details of the picture, would be sufficient to modify, or perhaps to annihilate, its capacity for sorrowful impression; and, acting upon this idea, I reined my horse to the precipitous brink of a black and lurid tarn that lay in unruffled luster by the dwelling, and gazed down—but with a shudder even more thrilling than before—upon the remodeled and inverted images of the gray sedge, and the ghastly tree stems, and the vacant and eye-like windows.

Nevertheless, in this mansion of gloom I now proposed to myself a sojourn of some weeks. Its proprietor, Roderick Usher, had been one of my boon companions in boyhood; but many years had elapsed since our last meeting. A letter, however, had lately reached me in a distant part of the country—a letter from him—which in its wildly importunate nature had admitted of no other than a personal reply. The MS. gave evidence of nervous agitation. The writer spoke of acute bodily illness, of a mental disorder which oppressed him, and of an earnest desire to see me, as his best and indeed his only personal friend, with a view of attempting, by the cheerfulness of my society, some alleviation of his malady. It was the manner in which all this, and much more, was said—it was the apparent *heart* that went with his request—which allowed me no room for hesitation; and I accordingly obeyed forthwith what I still considered a very singular summons.

Although as boys we had been even intimate associates, yet I really knew little of my friend. His reserve had been always excessive and habitual. I was aware, however, that his very ancient family had been noted, time out of mind, for a peculiar sensibility of temperament, displaying itself, through long ages, in many works of exalted art, and manifested of late in repeated deeds of munificent yet unobtrusive charity, as well as in a passionate devotion of the intricacies, perhaps even more than to the orthodox and easily recognizable beauties, of musical science. I had learned, too, the very remarkable fact that the stem of the Usher race, all time-honored as it was, had put forth at no period any enduring branch; in other words, that the entire family lay in the direct line of descent, and had always, with very trifling and very temporary variation, so lain. It was this deficiency, I considered, while running over in thought the perfect keeping of the character of the premises with the accredited character of the people, and while speculating upon the possible influence which the one, in the long lapse of centuries, might have exercised upon the other—it was this deficiency, perhaps, of collateral issue, and the consequent undeviating transmission from sire to son of the patrimony with the name, which had, at length, so identified the two as to merge the original title of the estate in the quaint and equivocal appellation of the "House of Usher"—an appellation which seemed to include, in the minds of the peasantry who used it, both the family and the family mansion.

I have said that the sole effect of my somewhat childish experiment, that of looking down within the tarn, had been to deepen the first singular impression. There can be no doubt that the consciousness of the rapid increase of my superstition—for why should I not so term it?—served mainly to accelerate the increase itself. Such, I have long known, is the paradoxical law of all sentiments having terror as a basis. And it might have been for this reason only, that, when I again uplifted my eyes to the house itself, from its image in the pool, there grew in my mind a strange fancy—a fancy so ridiculous, indeed, that I but mention it to show the vivid force of the sensations which oppressed me. I had so worked upon my imagination as really to believe that about the whole mansion and domain there hung an atmosphere peculiar to themselves and their immediate vicinity: an atmosphere which had no affinity with the air of heaven, but which had reeked up from the decayed trees, and the gray wall, and the silent tarn: a pestilent and mystic vapor, dull, sluggish, faintly discernible, and leaden-hued.

Shaking off from my spirit what *must* have been a dream, I scanned more narrowly the real aspect of the building. Its principal feature seemed to be that of an excessive antiquity. The discoloration of ages had been great. Minute fungi overspread the whole exterior, hanging in a fine tangled webwork from the eaves. Yet all this was apart from any extraordinary dilapidation. No portion of the masonry had fallen; and there appeared to be a wild inconsistency between its still perfect adaptation of parts and the crumbling condition of the individual stones. In this there was much that reminded me of the specious totality of old woodwork which has rotted for long years in some neglected vault, with no disturbance from the breath of the external air. Beyond this indication of excessive decay, however, the fabric gave little token of instability. Perhaps the eye of a scrutinizing observer might have discovered a barely perceptible fissure, which, extending from the roof of the building in front, made its way down the wall in a zigzag direction, until it became lost in the sullen waters of the tarn.

Noticing these things, I rode over a short causeway to the house. A servant in waiting took my horse, and I entered the Gothic archway of the hall. A valet, of stealthy step, thence conducted me, in silence, through many dark and intricate passages in my progress to the studio of his master. Much that I encountered on the way contributed, I know not how, to heighten the vague sentiments of which I have already spoken. While the objects around me— while the carvings of the ceilings, the somber tapestries of the walls, the ebon blackness of the floors, and the phantasmagoric armorial trophies which rattled as I strode, were but matters to which, or to such as which, I had been accustomed from my infancy—while I hesitated not to acknowledge how familiar was all this—I still wondered to find how unfamiliar were the fancies which ordinary images were stirring up. On one of the staircases, I met the physician of the family. His countenance, I thought, wore a mingled expression of low cunning and perplexity. He accosted me with trepidation and passed on. The valet now threw open a door and ushered me into the presence of his master.

The room in which I found myself was very large and lofty. The windows were long, narrow, and pointed, and at so vast a distance from the black oaken floor as to be altogether inaccessible from within. Feeble gleams of encrimsoned light made their way through the trellised panes, and served to render sufficiently distinct the more prominent objects around; the eye, however, struggled in vain to reach the remoter angles of the chamber, or the recesses of the vaulted and fretted ceiling. Dark draperies hung upon the walls. The general furniture was profuse, comfortless, antique, and tattered. Many books and musical instruments lay scattered about, but failed to give any vitality to the scene. I felt that I breathed an atmosphere of sorrow. An air of stern, deep, and irredeemable gloom hung over and pervaded all.

Upon my entrance, Usher arose from a sofa on which he had been lying at full length, and greeted me with a vivacious warmth which had much in it, I at first thought, of an overdone cordiality—of the constrained effort of the *ennuyé* man of the world. A glance, however, at his countenance, convinced me of his perfect sincerity. We sat down; and for some moments, while he spoke not, I gazed upon him with a feeling half of pity, half of awe. Surely man had never before so terribly altered in so brief a period as had Roderick Usher! It was with difficulty that I could bring myself to admit the identity of the wan being before me with the companion of my boyhood. Yet the character of his face had been at all times remarkable. A cadaverousness of complexion; an eye large, liquid, and luminous beyond comparison; lips somewhat thin and very pallid, but of a surpassingly beautiful curve; a nose of a delicate Hebrew model, but with a breadth of nostril unusual in similar formations; a finely molded chin, speaking, in its want of prominence, of a want of moral energy; hair of a more than weblike softness and tenuity; these features, with an inordinate expansion above the regions of the temple, made up altogether a countenance not easily to be forgotten. And now in the mere exaggeration of the prevailing character of these features, and of the expression they were wont to convey, lay so much of change that I doubted to whom I spoke. The now ghostly pallor of the skin, and the now miraculous luster of the eye, above all things startled and even awed me. The silken hair, too, had been suffered to grow all unheeded, and as, in its wild gossamer texture, it floated rather than fell about the face, I could not, even with effort, connect its arabesque expression with any idea of simple humanity.

In the manner of my friend I was at once struck with an incoherence, an inconsistency; and I soon found this to arise from a series of feeble and futile struggles to overcome an habitual trepidancy, an excessive nervous agitation. For something of this nature I had indeed been prepared, no less by his letter than by reminiscences of certain boyish traits, and by conclusions deduced from his peculiar physical conformation and temperament. His action was alternatively vivacious and sullen. His voice varied rapidly from a tremulous indecision (when the animal spirits seemed utterly in abeyance) to that species of energetic concision—that abrupt, weighty, unhurried, and hollow-sounding enunciation—that leaden, self-balanced and perfectly modulated guttural utterance—which may be observed in the lost drunkard, or the irreclaimable eater of opium, during the periods of his most intense excitement.

It was thus that he spoke of the object of my visit, of his earnest desire to 10 see me, and of the solace he expected me to afford him. He entered, at some length, into what he conceived to be the nature of his malady. It was, he said, a constitutional and a family evil, and one for which he despaired to find a remedy—a mere nervous affection, he immediately added, which would undoubtedly soon pass off. It displayed itself in a host of unnatural sensations. Some of these, as he detailed them, interested and bewildered me: although, perhaps, the terms and the general manner of the narration had their weight. He suffered much from a morbid acuteness of the senses; the most insipid food was alone endurable; he could wear only garments of a certain texture; the odors of all flowers were oppressive; his eyes were tortured by even a faint light; and there were but peculiar sounds, and these from stringed instruments, which did not inspire him with horror.

To an anomalous species of terror I found him a bounden slave. "I shall perish," said he, "I *must* perish in this deplorable folly. Thus, thus, and not otherwise, shall I be lost. I dread the events of the future, not in themselves, but in their results. I shudder at the thought of any, even the most trivial, incident, which may operate upon this intolerable agitation of soul. I have, indeed, no abhorrence of danger, except in its absolute effect—in terror. In this unnerved—in this pitiable condition—I feel that the period will sooner or later arrive when I must abandon life and reason together, in some struggle with the grim phantasm, FEAR."

I learned moreover at intervals, and through broken and equivocal hints, another singular feature of his mental condition. He was enchained by certain superstitious impressions in regard to the dwelling which he tenanted, and whence, for many years, he had never ventured forth—in regard to an influence whose supposititious force was conveyed in terms too shadowy here to be restated—an influence which some peculiarities in the mere form and substance of his family mansion, had, by dint of long sufferance, he said, obtained over his spirit—an effect which the physique of the gray walls and turrets, and of the dim tarn into which they all looked down, had, at length, brought about upon the morale of his existence.

He admitted, however, although with hesitation, that much of the peculiar gloom which thus afflicted him could be traced to a more natural and far more palpable origin—to the severe and long-continued illness, indeed to the evidently approaching dissolution, of a tenderly beloved sister—his sole companion for long years, his last and only relative on earth. "Her decease," he said, with a bitterness which I can never forget, "would leave him (him the hopeless and the frail) the last of the ancient race of the Ushers." While he spoke, the lady Madeline (for so was she called) passed slowly through a remote portion of the apartment, and, without having noticed my presence, disappeared. I regarded her with an utter astonishment not unmingled with dread, and yet I found it impossible to account for such feelings. A sensation of stupor oppressed me, as my eyes followed her retreating steps. When a door, at length, closed upon her, my glance sought instinctively and eagerly the countenance of the brother, but he had buried his face in his hands, and I could only perceive that a far more than ordinary wanness had overspread the emaciated fingers through which trickled many passionate tears.

The disease of the lady Madeline had long baffled the skill of her physicians. A settled apathy, a gradual wasting away of the person, and frequent although transient affections of a partially cataleptical character, were the unusual diagnosis. Hitherto she had steadily borne up against the pressure of her malady, and had not betaken herself finally to bed; but, on the closing in of the evening of my arrival at the house, she succumbed (as her brother told me at night with inexpressible agitation) to the prostrating power of the destroyer; and I learned that the glimpse I had obtained of her person would thus probably be the last I should obtain—that the lady, at least while living, would be seen by me no more.

For several days ensuing, her name was unmentioned by either Usher or 15 myself; and during this period I was busied in earnest endeavors to alleviate the melancholy of my friend. We painted and read together; or I listened, as if in a dream, to the wild improvisation of his speaking guitar. And thus, as a closer and still closer intimacy admitted me more unreservedly into the recesses of his spirit, the more bitterly did I perceive the futility of all attempt at cheering a mind from which darkness, as if an inherent positive quality, poured forth upon all objects of the moral and physical universe, in one unceasing radiation of gloom.

I shall ever bear about me a memory of the many solemn hours I thus spent alone with the master of the House of Usher. Yet I should fail in any attempt to convey an idea of the exact character of the studies, or of the occupations, in which he involved me, or led me the way. An excited and highly distempered ideality threw a sulphurous luster over all. His long improvised dirges will ring forever in my ears. Among other things, I hold painfully in mind a certain singular perversion and amplification of the wild air of the last waltz of Von Weber. From the paintings over which his elaborate fancy brooded, and which grew, touch by touch, into vagueness at which I shuddered the more thrillingly because I shuddered knowing not why;—from these paintings (vivid as their images now are before me) I would in vain endeavor to educe more than a small portion which should lie within the compass of merely written words. By the utter simplicity, by the nakedness of his designs, he arrested and overawed attention. If ever mortal painted an idea, that mortal was Roderick Usher. For me at least, in the circumstances then

surrounding me, there arose, out of the pure abstractions which the hypochondriac contrived to throw upon his canvas, an intensity of intolerable awe,
no shadow of which felt I ever yet in the contemplation of the certainly glowing yet too concrete reveries of Fuseli.

One of the phantasmagoric conceptions of my friend, partaking not so
rigidly of the spirit of abstraction, may be shadowed forth, although feebly, in
words. A small picture presented the interior of an immensely long and rectangular vault or tunnel, with low walls, smooth, white, and without interruption
or device. Certain accessory points of the design served well to convey the idea
that this excavation lay at an exceeding depth below the surface of the earth.
No outlet was observed in any portion of its vast extent, and no torch or other
artificial source of light was discernible; yet a flood of intense rays rolled
throughout, and bathed the whole in a ghastly and inappropriate splendor.

I have just spoken of that morbid condition of the auditory nerve which
rendered all music intolerable to the sufferer, with the exception of certain effects of stringed instruments. It was, perhaps, the narrow limits to which he
thus confined himself upon the guitar, which gave birth, in great measure, to
the fantastic character of his performances. But the fervid *facility* of his *im-
promptus* could not be so accounted for. They must have been, and were, in
the notes, as well as in the words of his wild fantasias (for he not unfrequently
accompanied himself with rhymed verbal improvisations), the result of that
intense mental collectedness and concentration to which I have previously alluded as observable only in particular moments of the highest artificial excitement. The words of one of these rhapsodies I have easily remembered. I was,
perhaps, the more forcibly impressed with it, as he gave it, because, in the under or mystic current of its meaning, I fancied that I perceived, and for the
first time, a full consciousness, on the part of Usher, of the tottering of his
lofty reason upon her throne. The verses, which were entitled "The Haunted
Palace," ran very nearly, if not accurately, thus:

I

In the greenest of our valleys,
　By good angels tenanted,
Once a fair and stately palace—
　Radiant palace—reared its head.
In the monarch Thought's dominion,
　It stood there!
Never seraph spread a pinion
　Over fabric half so fair.

II

Banners yellow, glorious, golden,
　On its roof did float and flow,
(This—all this—was in the olden
　Time long ago)
And every gentle air that dallied,
　In that sweet day,

Along the ramparts plumed and pallid,
   A wingèd odor went away.

III

Wanderers in that happy valley
   Through two luminous windows saw
Spirits moving musically
   To a lute's well-tunèd law,
Round about a throne where, sitting,
   (Porphyrogene!)
In state his glory well befitting,
   The ruler of the realm was seen.

IV

And all with pearl and ruby glowing
   Was the fair palace door,
Through which came flowing, flowing, flowing,
   And sparkling evermore,
A troop of Echoes whose sweet duty
   Was but to sing,
In voices of surpassing beauty,
   The wit and wisdom of their king.

V

But evil things, in robes of sorrow,
   Assailed the monarch's high estate;
(Ah, let us mourn, for never morrow
   Shall dawn upon him, desolate!)
And round about his home the glory
   That blushed and bloomed
Is but a dim-remembered story
   Of the old time entombed.

VI

And travellers now within that valley
   Through the red-litten windows see
Vast forms that move fantastically
   To a discordant melody;
While, like a rapid ghastly river,
   Through the pale door,
A hideous throng rush out forever,
   And laugh—but smile no more.

I well remember that suggestions arising from this ballad led us into a train of thought, wherein there became manifest an opinion of Usher's which I mention not so much on account of its novelty (for other men have thought thus) as on account of the pertinacity with which he maintained it. This opinion, in its general form, was that of the sentience of all vegetable things. But in his disordered fancy the idea had assumed a more daring character, and trespassed, under certain conditions, upon the kingdom of inorganization. I lack words to express the full extent, or the earnest *abandon* of his persuasion. The belief, however, was connected (as I have previously hinted) with the gray stones of the home of his forefathers. The conditions of the sentience had been here, he imagined, fulfilled in the method of collocation of these stones—in the order of their arrangement, as well as in that of the many fungi which overspread them, and of the decayed trees which stood around—above all, in the long undisturbed endurance of this arrangement, and in its reduplication in the still waters of the tarn. Its evidence—the evidence of the sentience—was to be seen, he said (and I here started as he spoke), in the gradual yet certain condensation of an atmosphere of their own about the waters and the walls. The result was discoverable, he added, in that silent, yet importunate and terrible influence which for centuries had molded the destinies of his family, and which made *him* what I now saw him—what he was. Such opinions need no comment, and I will make none.

Our books—the books which, for years, had formed no small portion of 20 the mental existence of the invalid—were, as might be supposed, in strict keeping with this character of phantasm. We pored together over such works as the Ververt and Chartreuse of Gresset; the Belphegor of Machiavelli; the Heaven and Hell of Swedenborg; the Subterranean Voyage of Nicholas Klimm by Holberg; the Chiromancy of Robert Flud, of Jean D'Indaginé, and of De la Chambre; the Journey into the Blue Distance of Tieck; and the City of the Sun of Campanella. One favorite volume was a small octavo edition of the *Directorium Inquisitorium*, by the Dominican Eymeric de Gironne; and there were passages in Pomponius Mela, about the old African Satyrs and Ægipans, over which Usher would sit dreaming for hours. His chief delight, however, was found in the perusal of an exceedingly rare and curious book in quarto Gothic—the manual of a forgotten church—the *Vigiliæ Mortuorum Secundum Chorum Ecclesiæ Maguntinæ*.

I could not help thinking of the wild ritual of this work, and of its probable influence upon the hypochondriac, when one evening, having informed me abruptly that the lady Madeline was no more, he stated his intention of preserving her corpse for a fortnight (previously to its final interment) in one of the numerous vaults within the main walls of the building. The worldly reason, however, assigned for this singular proceeding was one which I did not feel at liberty to dispute. The brother had been led to his resolution (so he told me) by consideration of the unusual character of the malady of the deceased, of certain obtrusive and eager inquiries on the part of her medical men, and of the remote and exposed situation of the burial-ground of the family. I will not deny that when I called to mind the sinister countenance of the person whom I met upon the staircase, on the day of my arrival at the house, I had no desire to oppose what I regarded as at best but a harmless, and by no means an unnatural, precaution.

At the request of Usher, I personally aided him in the arrangements for the temporary entombment. The body having been encoffined, we two alone bore it to its rest. The vault in which we placed it (and which had been so long unopened that our torches, half smothered in its oppressive atmosphere, gave us little opportunity for investigation) was small, damp, and entirely without means of admission for light; lying, at great depth, immediately beneath that portion of the building in which was my own sleeping apartment. It had been used, apparently, in remote feudal times, for the worst purposes of a donjon-keep, and in later days as a place of deposit for powder, or some other highly combustible substance, as a portion of its floor, and the whole interior of a long archway through which we reached it, were carefully sheathed with copper. The door, of massive iron, had been also similarly protected. Its immense weight caused an unusually sharp grating sound, as it moved upon its hinges.

Having deposited our mournful burden upon trestles within this region of horror, we partially turned aside the yet unscrewed lid of the coffin, and looked upon the face of the tenant. A striking similitude between the brother and sister now first arrested my attention; and Usher divining, perhaps, my thoughts, murmured out some few words from which I learned that the deceased and himself had been twins, and that sympathies of a scarcely intelligible nature had always existed between them. Our glances, however, rested not long upon the dead—for we could not regard her unawed. The disease which had thus entombed the lady in the maturity of youth, had left, as usual in all maladies of a strictly cataleptical character, the mockery of a faint blush upon the bosom and the face, and that suspiciously lingering smile upon the lip which is so terrible in death. We replaced and screwed down the lid, and, having secured the door of iron, made our way, with toil, into the scarcely less gloomy apartments of the upper portion of the house.

And now, some days of bitter grief having elapsed, an observable change came over the features of the mental disorder of my friend. His ordinary manner had vanished. His ordinary occupations were neglected or forgotten. He roamed from chamber to chamber with hurried, unequal, and objectless step. The pallor of his countenance had assumed, if possible, a more ghastly hue—but the luminousness of his eye had utterly gone out. The once occasional huskiness of his tone was heard no more; and a tremulous quaver, as if of extreme terror, habitually characterized his utterance. There were times, indeed, when I thought his unceasingly agitated mind was laboring with some oppressive secret, to divulge which he struggled for the necessary courage. At times, again, I was obliged to resolve all into the mere inexplicable vagaries of madness, for I beheld him gazing upon vacancy for long hours, in an attitude of the profoundest attention, as if listening to some imaginary sound. It was no wonder that his condition terrified—that it infected me. I felt creeping upon me, by slow yet certain degrees, the wild influences of his own fantastic yet impressive superstitions.

It was, especially, upon retiring to bed late in the night of the seventh or 25 eighth day after the placing of the lady Madeline within the donjon, that I experienced the full power of such feelings. Sleep came not near my couch, while the hours waned and waned away. I struggled to reason off the nervousness which had dominion over me. I endeavored to believe that much, if not all, of what I felt was due to the bewildering influence of the gloomy furniture of the room—of the dark and tattered draperies which, tortured into motion by the breath of a rising tempest, swayed fitfully to and fro upon the walls, and rustled uneasily about the decorations of the bed. But my efforts were fruitless. An irrepressible tremor gradually pervaded my frame; and at length there sat upon my very heart an incubus of utterly causeless alarm. Shaking this off with a gasp and a struggle, I uplifted myself upon the pillows, and, peering earnestly within the intense darkness of the chamber, hearkened—I know not why, except that an instinctive spirit prompted me—to certain low and indefinite sounds which came, through the pauses of the storm, at long intervals, I knew not whence. Overpowered by an intense sentiment of horror, unaccountable yet unendurable, I threw on my clothes with haste (for I felt that I should sleep no more during the night) and endeavored to arouse myself from the pitiable condition into which I had fallen, by pacing rapidly to and fro through the apartment.

I had taken but few turns in this manner, when a light step on an adjoining staircase arrested my attention. I presently recognized it as that of Usher. In an instant afterward he rapped with a gentle touch at my door, and entered, bearing a lamp. His countenance was, as usual, cadaverously wan—but, moreover, there was a species of mad hilarity in his eyes—an evidently restrained *hysteria* in his whole demeanor. His air appalled me—but anything was preferable to the solitude which I had so long endured, and I even welcomed his presence as a relief.

"And you have not seen it?" he said abruptly, after having stared about him for some moments in silence—"you have not then seen it?—but, stay! you shall." Thus speaking, and having carefully shaded his lamp, he hurried to one of the casements, and threw it freely open to the storm.

The impetuous fury of the entering gust nearly lifted us from our feet. It was, indeed, a tempestuous yet sternly beautiful night, and one wildly singular in its terror and its beauty. A whirlwind had apparently collected its force in our vicinity; for there were frequent and violent alterations in the direction of the wind; and the exceeding density of the clouds (which hung so low as to press upon the turrets of the house) did not prevent our perceiving the lifelike velocity with which they flew careening from all points against each other, without passing away into the distance. I say that even their exceeding density did not prevent our perceiving this; yet we had no glimpse of the moon or stars, nor was there any flashing forth of the lightning. But the under surfaces of the huge masses of agitated vapor, as well as all terrestrial objects immediately around us, were glowing in the unnatural light of a faintly luminous and distinctly visible gaseous exhalation which hung about and enshrouded the mansion.

"You must not—you shall not behold this!" said I, shudderingly, to Usher, as I led him with a gentle violence from the window to a seat. "These appearances, which bewilder you, are merely electrical phenomena not uncommon—or it may be that they have their ghastly origin in the rank miasma of the tarn. Let us close this casement; the air is chilling and dangerous to your frame. Here is one of your favorite romances. I will read, and you shall listen;—and so we will pass away this terrible night together."

The antique volume which I had taken up was the *Mad Trist* of Sir 30 Launcelot Canning; but I had called it a favorite of Usher's more in sad jest than in earnest; for, in truth, there is little in its uncouth and unimaginative prolixity which could have had interest for the lofty and spiritual ideality of my friend. It was, however, the only book immediately at hand; and I indulged a vague hope that the excitement which now agitated the hypochondriac might find relief (for the history of mental disorder is full of similar anomalies) even in the extremeness of the folly which I should read. Could I have judged, indeed, by the wild overstrained air of vivacity with which he hearkened, or apparently hearkened, to the words of the tale, I might well have congratulated myself upon the success of my design.

I had arrived at that well-known portion of the story where Ethelred, the hero of the Trist, having sought in vain for peaceable admission into the dwelling of the hermit, proceeds to make good an entrance by force. Here, it will be remembered, the words of the narrative run thus:

> "And Ethelred, who was by nature of a doughty heart, and who was now mighty withal, on account of the powerfulness of the wine which he had drunken, waited no longer to hold parley with the hermit, who, in sooth, was of an obstinate and maliceful turn, but, feeling the rain upon his shoulders, and fearing the rising of the tempest, uplifted his mace outright, and, with blows, made quickly room in the plankings of the door for his gauntleted hand; and now pulling therewith sturdily, he so cracked, and ripped, and tore all asunder, that the noise of the dry and hollow-sounding wood alarummed and reverberated throughout the forest."

At the termination of this sentence I started, and for a moment paused; for it appeared to me (although I at once concluded that my excited fancy had deceived me)—it appeared to me that from some very remote portion of the mansion there came, indistinctly, to my ears, what might have been, in its exact similarity of character, the echo (but a stifled and dull one certainly) of the very cracking and ripping sound which Sir Launcelot had so particularly described. It was, beyond doubt, the coincidence alone which had arrested my attention; for, amid the rattling of the sashes of the casements, and the ordinary commingled noises of the still increasing storm, the sound, in itself, had nothing, surely, which should have interested or disturbed me. I continued the story:

> "But the good champion Ethelred, now entering within the door, was sore enraged and amazed to perceive no signal of the maliceful hermit; but, in the stead thereof, a dragon of a scaly and prodigious demeanor, and of a fiery tongue, which sate in guard before a palace of gold, with a floor of silver; and upon the wall there hung a shield of shining brass with this legend enwritten—
>
>   Who entereth herein, a conqueror hath bin;
>   Who slayeth the dragon, the shield he shall win
>
> And Ethelred uplifted his mace, and struck upon the head of the dragon, which fell before him, and gave up his pesty breath, with a shriek so horrid and harsh, and withal so piercing, that Ethelred had fain to close his ears with his hands against the dreadful noise of it, the like whereof was never before heard."

Here again I paused abruptly, and now with a feeling of wild amazement; for there could be no doubt whatever that, in this instance, I did actually hear (although from what direction it proceeded I found it impossible to say) a low and apparently distant, but harsh, protracted, and most unusual screaming or grating sound—the exact counterpart of what my fancy had already conjured up for the dragon's unnatural shriek as described by the romancer.

Oppressed, as I certainly was, upon the occurrence of this second and most extraordinary coincidence, by a thousand conflicting sensations, in which wonder and extreme terror were predominant, I still retained sufficient presence of mind to avoid exciting, by any observation, the sensitive nervousness of my companion. I was by no means certain that he had noticed the sounds in question; although, assuredly, a strange alteration had during the last few minutes taken place in his demeanor. From a position fronting my own, he had gradually brought round his chair, so as to sit with his face to the door of the chamber; and thus I could but partially perceive his features, although I saw that his lips trembled as if he were murmuring inaudibly. His head had dropped upon his breast—yet I knew that he was not asleep, from the wide and rigid opening of the eye as I caught a glance of it in profile. The motion of his body, too, was at variance with this idea—for he rocked from side to side with a gentle yet constant and uniform sway. Having rapidly taken notice of all this, I resumed the narrative of Sir Launcelot, which thus proceeded:

> "And now, the champion having escaped from the terrible fury of the dragon, bethinking himself of the brazen shield, and of the breaking up of the enchantment which was upon it, removed the carcass from out of the way before him, and approached valorously over the silver pavement of the castle to where the shield was upon the wall; which in sooth tarried not for his full coming, but fell down at his feet upon the silver floor, with a mighty great and terrible ringing sound."

No sooner had these syllables passed my lips, than—as if a shield of brass had indeed, at the moment, fallen heavily upon a floor of silver—I became aware of a distinct, hollow, metallic and clangorous, yet apparently muffled reverberation. Completely unnerved, I leaped to my feet; but the measured rocking movement of Usher was undisturbed. I rushed to the chair in which he sat. His eyes were bent fixedly before him, and throughout his whole countenance there reigned a stony rigidity. But, as I placed my hand upon his shoulder, there came a strong shudder over his whole person; a sickly smile quivered about his lips; and I saw that he spoke in a low, hurried, and gibbering murmur, as if unconscious of my presence. Bending closely over him, I at length drank in the hideous import of his words.

"Not hear it?—yes, I hear it, and *have* heard it. Long—long—long— many minutes, many hours, many days, have I heard it—yet I dared not—oh, pity me, miserable wretch that I am!—I dared not—*I dared not speak! We have put her living in the tomb!* Said I not that my senses were acute? I *now* tell you that I heard her first feeble movements in the hollow coffin. I heard them— many, many days ago—yet I dared not—*I dared not speak!* And now— tonight—Ethelred—ha! ha!—the breaking of the hermit's door, and the death-cry of the dragon, and the clangor of the shield!—say, rather, the rending of her coffin, and the grating of the iron hinges of her prison, and her struggles within the coppered archway of the vault! Oh, whither shall I fly? Will she not be here anon? Is she not hurrying to upbraid me for my haste?

Have I not heard her footsteps on the stair? Do I not distinguish that heavy and horrible beating of her heart? Madman!"—here he sprang furiously to his feet, and shrieked out his syllables, as if in the effort he were giving up his soul—*"Madman! I tell you that she now stands without the door!"*

As if in the superhuman energy of his utterance there had been found the potency of a spell, the huge antique panels to which the speaker pointed drew slowly back, upon the instant, their ponderous and ebony jaws. It was the work of the rushing gust—but then without the doors there *did* stand the lofty and enshrouded figure of the lady Madeline of Usher. There was blood upon her white robes, and the evidence of some bitter struggle upon every portion of her emaciated frame. For a moment she remained trembling and reeling to and fro upon the threshold—then, with a low moaning cry, fell heavily inward upon the person of her brother, and, in her violent and now final death-agonies, bore him to the floor a corpse, and a victim to the terrors he had anticipated.

From that chamber, and from that mansion, I fled aghast. The storm was still abroad in all its wrath as I found myself crossing the old causeway. Suddenly there shot along the path a wild light, and I turned to see whence a gleam so unusual could have issued; for the vast house and its shadows were alone behind me. The radiance was that of the full, setting, and blood-red moon, which now shone vividly through that once barely discernible fissure, of which I have before spoken as extending from the roof of the building, in a zigzag direction, to the base. While I gazed, this fissure rapidly widened— there came a fierce breath of the whirlwind—the entire orb of the satellite burst at once upon my sight—my brain reeled as I saw the mighty walls rushing asunder—there was a long tumultuous shouting sound like the voice of a thousand waters—and the deep and dank tarn at my feet closed sullenly and silently over the fragments of the House of Usher.

——————— **EDGAR ALLAN POE** ———————

www   *(1809–1849)* Web

A West Point graduate, Poe quit the army to become a professional editor and writer. Poe was a conscious and controlled artist who was best known for his criticism, but who strove to write stories that would appeal to popular audiences. Poe's fiction fascinated later writers, from Charles-Pierre Baudelaire to Vladimir Nabokov, who admired and developed his atmospheric rendering of effect and complex intellectual games.

www   *TOPICS FOR CRITICAL THINKING* Web

1. How does the story's emphasis on setting signal the way it should be read?

2. The narrator notices the similarities between the Ushers' property and their family history. What are his theories about the relation of the two? What are Roderick Usher's theories?

3. What are the parallels among the story's setting, Usher's paintings and ballad, his books, and the feeling that pervades the mansion?

4. If the setting doubles (reflects, parallels, provides another version of) both characters and events, how does the idea of the double govern this story?

TOPICS FOR CRITICAL WRITING Web

www

1. In what ways does the setting reflect the story's events?
2. What elements does Poe's tale have in common with contemporary horror stories?

GUY DE MAUPASSANT
Translated by Ernest Boyd

Paul's Mistress (1881)

The Restaurant Grillon, a small commonwealth of boatmen, was slowly emptying. In front of the door all was tumult—cries and calls—and huge fellows in white jerseys gesticulated with oars on their shoulders.

The ladies in bright spring toilettes stepped aboard the skiffs with care, and seating themselves astern, arranged their dresses, while the landlord of the establishment, a mighty, red-bearded, self-possessed individual of renowned strength, offered his hand to the pretty creatures, and kept the frail crafts steady.

The rowers, bare-armed, with bulging chests, took their places in their turn, playing to the gallery as they did so—a gallery consisting of middle-class people dressed in their Sunday clothes, of workmen and soldiers leaning upon their elbows on the parapet of the bridge, all taking a great interest in the sight.

One by one the boats cast off from the landing stage. The oarsmen bent forward and then threw themselves backward with even swing, and under the impetus of the long curved oars, the swift skiffs glided along the river, grew smaller in the distance, and finally disappeared under the railway bridge, as they descended the stream toward La Grenouillère. One couple only remained behind. The young man, still almost beardless, slender, with a pale countenance, held his mistress, a thin little brunette with the air of a grasshopper, by the waist; and occasionally they gazed into each other's eyes. The landlord shouted

"Come, Mr. Paul, make haste," and they drew near.

Of all the guests of the house, Mr. Paul was the most liked and most respected. He paid well and punctually, while the others hung back for a long time if indeed they did not vanish without paying. Besides which he was a sort of walking advertisement for the establishment, inasmuch as his father was a senator. When a stranger would inquire: "Who on earth is that little chap who thinks so much of his girl?"some *habitué* would reply, half-aloud, with a mysterious and important air: "Don't you know? That is Paul Baron, a senator's son."

And invariably the other would exclaim:

"Poor devil! He has got it badly."

Mother Grillon, a good and worthy business woman, described the young man and his companion as "her two turtledoves," and appeared quite touched by this passion, which was profitable for her business.

The couple advanced at a slow pace. The skiff "Madeleine" was ready, and at the moment of embarking they kissed each other, which caused the public collected on the bridge to laugh. Mr. Paul took the oars, and rowed away for La Grenouillère.   10

When they arrived it was just upon three o'clock and the large floating café overflowed with people.

The immense raft, sheltered by a tarpaulin roof, is joined to the charming island of Croissy by two narrow footbridges, one of which leads into the centre of the aquatic establishment, while the other unites with a tiny islet, planted with a tree and called "The Flower Pot," and thence leads to land near the bath office.

Mr. Paul made fast his boat alongside the establishment, climbed over the railing of the café, and then, grasping his mistress's hands, assisted her out of the boat. They both seated themselves at the end of a table opposite each other.

On the opposite side of the river along the towing-path, a long string of vehicles was drawn up. Cabs alternated with the fine carriages of the swells; the first, clumsy, with enormous bodies crushing the springs, drawn by broken-down hacks with hanging heads and broken knees; the second, slightly built on light wheels, with horses slender and straight, their heads well up, their bits snowy with foam, and with solemn coachmen in livery, heads erect in high collars, waiting bolt upright, with whips resting on their knees.

The bank was covered with people who came off in families, or in parties, or in couples, or alone. They plucked at the blades of grass, went down to the water, ascended the path, and having reached the spot, stood still awaiting the ferryman. The clumsy punt plied incessantly from bank to bank, discharging its passengers upon the island. The arm of the river (called the Dead Arm) upon which this refreshment wharf lay, seemed asleep, so feeble was the current. Fleets of yawls, of skiffs, of canoes, of podoscaphs, of gigs, of craft of all forms and of all kinds, crept about upon the motionless stream, crossing each other, intermingling, running foul of one another, stopping abruptly under a jerk of the arms only to shoot off afresh under a sudden strain of the muscles and gliding swiftly along like great yellow or red fishes.   15

Others arrived continually; some from Chatou up the stream; others from Bougival down it; laughter crossed the water from one boat to another, calls, admonitions, or imprecations. The boatmen exposed the bronzed and knotted muscles of their biceps to the heat of the day; and like strange floating flowers, the silk parasols, red, green, blue, or yellow, of the ladies bloomed in the sterns of the boats.

A July sun flamed high in the heavens; the atmosphere seemed full of burning merriment; not a breath of air stirred the leaves of the willows or poplars.

In front, away in the distance, the inevitable Mont-Valérien reared its fortified ramparts, tier above tier, in the intense light; while on the right the

divine slopes of Louveciennes, following the bend of the river, disposed themselves in a semicircle, displaying in turn across the rich and shady lawns of
large gardens the white walls of country seats.

Upon the outskirts of La Grenouillère a crowd of pedestrians moved
about beneath the giant trees which make this corner of the island one of the
most delightful parks in the world.

Women and girls with yellow hair and breasts developed beyond all mea-   20
surement, with exaggerated hips, their complexions plastered with rouge,
their eyes daubed with charcoal, their lips blood-red, laced up, rigged out in
outrageous dresses, trailed the crying bad taste of their toilettes over the fresh
green sward; while beside them young men posed in their fashion-plate garments with light gloves, patent leather boots, canes the size of a thread, and
single eyeglasses emphasizing the insipidity of their smiles.

Opposite La Grenouillère the island is narrow, and on its other side,
where also a ferryboat plies, bringing people unceasingly across from Croissy,
the rapid branch of the river, full of whirlpools and eddies and foam, rushes
along with the strength of a torrent. A detachment of pontoon-builders, in
the uniform of artillerymen, was encamped upon this bank, and the soldiers
seated in a row on a long beam watched the water flowing.

In the floating establishment there was a boisterous and uproarious
crowd. The wooden tables upon which the spilt refreshments made little
sticky streams were covered with half-empty glasses and surrounded by half-
tipsy individuals. The crowd shouted, sang, and brawled. The men, their hats
at the backs of their heads, their faces red, with the shining eyes of drunkards,
moved about vociferating and evidently looking for the quarrels natural to
brutes. The women, seeking their prey for the night, sought for free liquor in
the meantime; and the unoccupied space between the tables was dominated
by the customary local public, a whole regiment of rowdy boatmen, with their
female companions in short flannel skirts.

One of them performed on the piano and appeared to play with his feet
as well as his hands; four couples glided through a quadrille, and some young
men watched them, polished and correct, men who would have looked respectable, did not their innate viciousness show in spite of everything.

For there you see all the scum of society, all its well-bred debauchery, all
the seamy side of Parisian society—a mixture of counter-jumpers, of strolling
players, of low journalists, of gentlemen in tutelage, of rotten stock-jobbers,
of ill-famed debauchees, of old used-up fast men; a doubtful crowd of suspicious characters, half-known, half-sunk, half-recognized, half-criminal, pick-
pockets, rogues, procurers of women, sharpers with dignified manners, and a
bragging air which seems to say: "I shall kill the first man who treats me as a
scoundrel."

The place reeks of folly, and stinks of vulgarity and cheap gallantry. Male   25
and female are just as bad one as the other. There dwells an odour of so-called
love, and there one fights for a yes, or for a no, in order to sustain a worm-
eaten reputation, which a thrust of the sword or a pistol bullet only destroys
further.

Some of the neighbouring inhabitants looked in out of curiosity every

Sunday; some young men, very young, appeared there every year to learn how to live, some promenaders lounging about showed themselves there; some greenhorns wandered thither. With good reason is it named La Grenouillère. At the side of the covered wharf where drink was served, and quite close to the Flower Pot, people bathed. Those among the women who possessed the requisite roundness of form came there to display their wares and to get clients. The rest, scornful, although well filled out with wadding, supported by springs, corrected here and altered there, watched their dabbling sisters with disdain.

The swimmers crowded on to a little platform to dive. Straight like vine poles, or round like pumpkins, gnarled like olive branches, bowed over in front, or thrown backward by the size of their stomachs, and invariably ugly, they leaped into the water, splashing it over the drinkers in the café.

Notwithstanding the great trees which overhang the floating-house, and notwithstanding the vicinity of the water, a suffocating heat filled the place. The fumes of the spilt liquors mingled with the effluvia of the bodies and with the strong perfumes with which the skin of the trader in love is saturated and which evaporate in this furnace. But beneath all these diverse scents a slight aroma of *poudre de riz* lingered, disappearing and reappearing, and perpetually encountered as though some concealed hand had shaken an invisible powder-puff in the air. The show was on the river, where the perpetual coming and going of the boats attracted the eyes. The girls in the boats sprawled upon their seats opposite their strong-wristed males, and scornfully contemplated the dinner-hunting females prowling about the island.

Sometimes when a crew in full swing passed at top speed, the friends who had gone ashore gave vent to shouts, and all the people as if suddenly seized with madness commenced to yell.

At the bend of the river toward Chatou fresh boats continually appeared. 30 They came nearer and grew larger, and as faces became recognisable, the vociferations broke out anew.

A canoe covered with an awning and manned by four women came slowly down the current. She who rowed was petite, thin, faded, in a cabin-boy's costume, her hair drawn up under an oilskin hat. Opposite her, a lusty blonde, dressed as a man, with a white flannel jacket, lay upon her back at the bottom of the boat, her legs in the air, resting on the seat at each side of the rower. She smoked a cigarette, while at each stroke of the oars, her chest and stomach quivered, shaken by the stroke. At the back, under the awning, two handsome girls, tall and slender, one dark and the other fair, held each other by the waist as they watched their companions.

A cry arose from La Grenouillère, "There's Lesbos," and all at once a furious clamour, a terrifying scramble took place; the glasses were knocked down; people clambered on to the tables; all in a frenzy of noise bawled "Lesbos! Lesbos! Lesbos!" The shout rolled along, became indistinct, was no longer more than a kind of deafening howl, and then suddenly it seemed to start anew, to rise into space, to cover the plain, to fill the foliage of the great trees, to extend to the distant slopes, and reach even to the sun.

The rower, in the face of this ovation, had quietly stopped. The handsome blonde, stretched out upon the bottom of the boat, turned her head with a careless air, as she raised herself upon her elbows; and the two girls at the back commenced laughing as they saluted the crowd.

Then the hullabaloo redoubled, making the floating establishment tremble. The men took off their hats, the women waved their handkerchiefs, and all voices, shrill or deep, together cried:

"Lesbos."　　　　　　　　　　　　　　　　　　　　　　　　　　　35

It was as if these people, this collection of the corrupt, saluted their chiefs like the war-ships which fire guns when an admiral passes along the line.

The numerous fleet of boats also saluted the women's boat, which pushed along more quickly to land farther off.

Mr. Paul, contrary to the others, had drawn a key from his pocket and whistled with all his might. His nervous mistress grew paler, caught him by the arm to make him be quiet, and upon this occasion she looked at him with fury in her eyes. But he appeared exasperated, as though borne away by jealousy of some man or by deep anger, instinctive and ungovernable. He stammered, his lips quivering with indignation:

"It is shameful! They ought to be drowned like puppies with a stone about the neck."

But Madeleine instantly flew into a rage; her small and shrill voice be-　40
came a hiss, and she spoke volubly, as though pleading her own cause:

"And what has it to do with you—you indeed? Are they not at liberty to do what they wish since they owe nobody anything? You shut up and mind your own business."

But he cut her speech short:

"It is the police whom it concerns, and I will have them marched off to St. Lazare; indeed I will."

She gave a start:

"You?"　　　　　　　　　　　　　　　　　　　　　　　　　　45

"Yes, I! And in the meantime I forbid you to speak to them—you understand, I forbid you to do so."

Then she shrugged her shoulders and grew calm in a moment:

"My dear, I shall do as I please; if you are not satisfied, be off, and instantly. I am not your wife, am I? Very well then, hold your tongue."

He made no reply and they stood face to face, their lips tightly closed, breathing quickly.

At the other end of the great wooden café the four women made their en-　50
try. The two in men's costumes marched in front: the one thin like an oldish tomboy, with a yellow tinge on her temples; the other filling out her white flannel garments with her fat, swelling out her wide trousers with her buttocks and swaying about like a fat goose with enormous legs and yielding knees. Their two friends followed them, and the crowd of boatmen thronged about to shake their hands.

The four had hired a small cottage close to the water's edge, and lived there as two households would have lived.

Their vice was public, recognised, patent to all. People talked of it as a natural thing, which almost excited their sympathy, and whispered in very low tones strange stories of dramas begotten of furious feminine jealousies, of the stealthy visit of well-known women and of actresses to the little house close to the water's edge.

A neighbour, horrified by these scandalous rumours, notified the police, and the inspector, accompanied by a man, had come to make inquiry. The mission was a delicate one; it was impossible, in short, to accuse these women, who did not abandon themselves to prostitution, of any tangible crime. The inspector, very much puzzled, and, indeed, ignorant of the nature of the offences suspected, had asked questions at random, and made a lofty report conclusive of their innocence.

The joke spread as far as Saint Germain. They walked about the Grenouillère establishment with mincing steps like queens; and seemed to glory in their fame, rejoicing in the gaze that was fixed on them, so superior to this crowd, to this mob, to these plebeians.

Madeleine and her lover watched them approach, and the girl's eyes   55
lit up.

When the first two had reached the end of the table, Madeleine cried: "Pauline!"

The large woman turned and stopped, continuing all the time to hold the arm of her feminine cabin-boy:

"Good gracious, Madeleine! Do come and talk to me, my dear."

Paul squeezed his fingers upon his mistress's wrist, but she said to him,   60
with such an air: "You know, my dear, you can clear out, if you like," that he said nothing and remained alone.

Then they chatted in low voices, all three of them standing. Many pleasant jests passed their lips, they spoke quickly; and Pauline now and then looked at Paul, by stealth, with a shrewd and malicious smile.

At last, unable to put up with it any longer, he suddenly rose and in a single bound was at their side, trembling in every limb. He seized Madeleine by the shoulders.

"Come, I wish it," said he; "I have forbidden you to speak to these sluts."

Whereupon Pauline raised her voice and set to work blackguarding him with her Billingsgate vocabulary. All the bystanders laughed; they drew near him; they raised themselves on tiptoe in order the better to see him. He remained dumb under this downpour of filthy abuse. It appeared to him that the words which came from that mouth and fell upon him defiled him like dirt, and, in presence of the row which was beginning, he fell back, retraced his steps, and rested his elbows on the railing toward the river, turning his back upon the victorious women.

There he stayed watching the water, and sometimes with rapid gesture, as   65
though he could pluck it out, he removed with his nervous fingers the tear which stood in his eye.

The fact was that he was hopelessly in love, without knowing why, notwithstanding his refined instincts, in spite of his reason, in spite, indeed, of his will. He had fallen into this love as one falls into a muddy hole. Of a tender and delicate disposition, he had dreamed of liaisons, exquisite, ideal, and impassioned, and there that little bit of a woman, stupid like all prostitutes, with an exasperating stupidity, not even pretty, but thin and a spitfire, had taken him prisoner, possessing him from head to foot, body and soul. He had submitted to this feminine witchery, mysterious and all powerful, this unknown power, this prodigious domination—arising no one knows whence, but from the demon of the flesh—which casts the most sensible man at the feet of some harlot or other without there being anything in her to explain her fatal and sovereign power.

And there at his back he felt that some infamous thing was brewing. Shouts of laughter cut him to the heart. What should he do? He knew well, but he could not do it.

He steadily watched an angler upon the bank opposite him, and his motionless line.

Suddenly, the worthy man jerked a little silver fish, which wriggled at the end of his line, out of the river. Then he endeavoured to extract his hook, pulled and turned it, but in vain. At last, losing patience, he commenced to tear it out, and all the bleeding gullet of the fish, with a portion of its intestines came out. Paul shuddered, rent to his heartstrings. It seemed to him that the hook was his love, and that if he should pluck it out, all that he had in his breast would come out in the same way at the end of a curved iron, fixed in the depths of his being, to which Madeleine held the line.

A hand was placed on his shoulder; he started and turned; his mistress was at his side. They did not speak to each other; and like him she rested her elbows upon the railing, and fixed her eyes upon the river. 70

He tried to speak to her and could find nothing. He could not even disentangle his own emotions; all that he was sensible of was joy at feeling her there close to him, come back again, as well as shameful cowardice, a craving to pardon everything, to allow everything, provided she never left him.

At last, after a few minutes, he asked her in a very gentle voice:

"Would you like to go? It will be nicer in the boat."

She answered: "Yes, darling."

And he assisted her into the skiff, pressing her hands, all softened, with some tears still in his eyes. Then she looked at him with a smile and they kissed each other again. 75

They reascended the river very slowly, skirting the willow-bordered, grass-covered bank, bathed and still in the afternoon warmth. When they had returned to the Restaurant Grillon, it was barely six o'clock. Then leaving their boat they set off on foot towards Bezons, across the fields and along the high poplars which bordered the river. The long grass ready to be mowed was full of flowers. The sinking sun glowed from beneath a sheet of red light, and in the tempered heat of the closing day the floating exhalations from the grass, mingled with the damp scents from the river, filled the air with a soft languor, with a happy light, with an atmosphere of blessing.

A soft weakness overtook his heart, a species of communion with this splendid calm of evening, with this vague and mysterious throb of teeming life, with the keen and melancholy poetry which seems to arise from flowers and things, and reveals itself to the senses at this sweet and pensive time.

Paul felt all that; but for her part she did not understand anything of it.

They walked side by side; and, suddenly, tired of being silent, she sang. She sang in her shrill, unmusical voice some street song, some catchy air, which jarred upon the profound and serene harmony of the evening.

Then he looked at her and felt an impassable abyss between them. She beat the grass with her parasol, her head slightly inclined, admiring her feet and singing, dwelling on the notes, attempting trills, and venturing on shakes. Her smooth little brow, of which he was so fond, was at that time absolutely empty! empty! There was nothing therein but this canary music; and the ideas which formed there by chance were like this music. She did not understand anything of him; they were now as separated as if they did not live together. Did his kisses never go any farther than her lips?

Then she raised her eyes to him and laughed again. He was moved to 80 the quick and, extending his arms in a paroxysm of love, he embraced her passionately.

As he was rumpling her dress she finally broke away from him, murmuring by way of compensation as she did so:

"That's enough. You know I love you, my darling."

But he clasped her around the waist and, seized by madness, he started to run with her. He kissed her on the cheek, on the temple, on the neck, all the while dancing with joy. They threw themselves down panting at the edge of a thicket, lit up by the rays of the setting sun, and before they had recovered breath they were in one another's arms without her understanding his transport.

They returned, holding each other by the hand, when, suddenly, through the trees, they perceived on the river the skiff manned by the four women. Fat Pauline also saw them, for she drew herself up and blew kisses to Madeleine. And then she cried:

"Until to-night!"   85

Madeleine replied: "Until to-night!"

Paul felt as if his heart had suddenly been frozen.

They re-entered the house for dinner and installed themselves in one of the arbours, close to the water. They began to eat in silence. When night arrived, the waiter brought a candle enclosed in a glass globe, which gave a feeble and glimmering light; and they heard every moment the bursts of shouting from the boatmen in the large room on the first floor.

Toward dessert, Paul, taking Madeleine's hand, tenderly said to her:

"I feel very tired, my darling; unless you have any objection, we will go to 90 bed early."

She, however, understood the ruse, and shot an enigmatical glance at him—that glance of treachery which so readily appears in the depths of a woman's eyes. Having reflected she answered:

"You can go to bed if you wish, but I have promised to go to the ball at La Grenouillère."

He smiled in a piteous manner, one of those smiles with which one veils the most horrible suffering, and replied in a coaxing but agonized tone:

"If you were really nice, we should remain here, both of us."

She indicated no with her head, without opening her mouth.   95

He insisted:

"I beg of you, my darling."

Then she roughly broke out:

"You know what I said to you. If you are not satisfied, the door is open. No one wishes to keep you. As for myself, I have promised; I shall go."

He placed his two elbows upon the table, covered his face with his hands,   100
and remained there pondering sorrowfully.

The boat people came down again, shouting as usual, and set off in their vessels for the ball at La Grenouillère.

Madeleine said to Paul:

"If you are not coming, say so, and I will ask one of these gentlemen to take me."

Paul rose:

"Let us go!" murmured he.   105

And they left.

The night was black, the sky full of stars, but the air was heat-laden by oppressive breaths of wind, burdened with emanations, and with living germs, which destroyed the freshness of the night. It offered a heated caress, made one breathe more quickly, gasp a little, so thick and heavy did it seem. The boats started on their way, bearing Venetian lanterns at the prow. It was not possible to distinguish the craft, but only the little coloured lights, swift and dancing up and down like frenzied glowworms, while voices sounded from all sides in the shadows. The young people's skiff glided gently along. Now and then, when a fast boat passed near them, they could, for a moment, see the white back of the rower, lit up by his lantern.

When they turned the elbow of the river, La Grenouillère appeared to them in the distance. The establishment *en fête*, was decorated with flags and garlands of coloured lights, in grape-like clusters. On the Seine some great barges moved about slowly, representing domes, pyramids, and elaborate monuments in fires of all colours. Illuminated festoons hung right down to the water, and sometimes a red or blue lantern, at the end of an immense invisible fishing-rod, seemed like a great swinging star.

All this illumination spread a light around the café, lit up the great trees on the bank, from top to bottom, the trunks standing out in pale gray and the leaves in milky green upon the deep black of the fields and the heavens. The orchestra, composed of five suburban artists, flung far its public-house dance-music, poor of its kind and jerky, inciting Madeleine to sing anew.

She wanted to go in at once. Paul wanted first to take a stroll on the island,   110
but he was obliged to give way. The attendance was now more select. The boatmen, almost alone, remained, with here and there some better class people, and young men escorted by girls. The director and organiser of this spree, looking majestic in a jaded black suit, walked about in every direction, bald-headed and worn by his old trade of purveyor of cheap public amusements.

Fat Pauline and her companions were not there; and Paul breathed again.

They danced; couples opposite each other capered in the maddest fashion, throwing their legs in the air, until they were upon a level with the noses of their partners.

The women, whose thighs seemed disjointed, pranced around with flying skirts which revealed their underclothing, wriggling their stomachs and hips, causing their breasts to shake, and spreading the powerful odour of perspiring female bodies.

The men squatted like toads, some making obscene gestures; some twisted and distorted themselves, grimacing and hideous; some turned cartwheels on their hands, or, perhaps, trying to be funny, posed with exaggerated gracefulness.

A fat servant-maid and two waiters served refreshments.   115

The café boat being only covered with a roof and having no wall whatever to shut it in, this hare-brained dance flaunted in the face of the peaceful night and of the firmament powdered with stars.

Suddenly, Mont-Valérien, opposite, appeared, illuminated, as if some conflagration had arisen behind it. The radiance spread and deepened upon the sky, describing a large luminous circle of white, wan light. Then something or other red appeared, grew greater, shining with a burning crimson, like that of hot metal upon the anvil. It gradually developed into a round body rising from the earth; and the moon, freeing herself from the horizon, rose slowly into space. As she ascended, the purple tint faded and became yellow, a shining bright yellow, and the satellite grew smaller in proportion as her distance increased.

Paul watched the moon for some time, lost in contemplation, forgetting his mistress; when he returned to himself the latter had vanished.

He sought her, but could not find her. He threw his anxious eye over table after table, going to and fro unceasingly, inquiring for her from one person and then another. No one had seen her. He was tormented with uneasiness, when one of the waiters said to him:

"You are looking for Madame Madeleine, are you not? She left a few mo- 120
ments ago, with Madame Pauline." And at the same instant, Paul perceived the cabin-boy and the two pretty girls standing at the other end of the café, all three holding each other's waists and lying in wait for him, whispering to one another. He understood, and like a madman, dashed off into the island.

He first ran toward Chatou, but having reached the plain, retraced his steps. Then he began to search the dense coppices, occasionally roaming about distractedly, or halting to listen.

The toads all about him poured out their short metallic notes.

From the direction of Bougival, some unknown bird warbled a song which reached him faintly from the distance.

Over the broad fields the moon shed a soft light, resembling powdered wool; it penetrated the foliage, silvered the bark of the poplars, and riddled with its brilliant rays the waving tops of the great trees. The entrancing poetry of this summer night had, in spite of himself, entered into Paul, athwart his infatuated anguish, stirring his heart with ferocious irony, and increasing even to madness his craving for an ideal tenderness, for passionate outpourings on the breast of an adored and faithful woman. He was compelled to stop, choked by hurried and rending sobs.

The convulsion over, he went on.   125

Suddenly, he received what resembled the stab of a dagger. There, behind that bush, some people were kissing. He ran thither; and found an amorous couple whose faces were united in a endless kiss.

He dared not call, knowing well that She would not respond, and he had a frightful dread of coming upon them suddenly.

The flourishes of the quadrilles, with the earsplitting solos of the cornet, the false shriek of the flute, the shrill squeaking of the violin, irritated his feelings, and increased his suffering. Wild and limping music was floating under the trees, now feeble, now stronger, wafted hither and thither by the breeze.

Suddenly he thought that possibly She had returned. Yes, she had returned! Why not? He had stupidly lost his head, without cause, carried away by his fears, by the inordinate suspicions which had for some time overwhelmed him. Seized by one of those singular calms which will sometimes occur in cases of the greatest despair, he returned toward the ball-room.

With a single glance of the eye, he took in the whole room. He made the round of the tables, and abruptly again found himself face to face with the three women. He must have had a doleful and queer expression of countenance, for all three burst into laughter.

He made off, returned to the island, and threw himself into the coppice panting. He listened again, listened a long time, for his ears were singing. At last, however, he believed he heard farther off a little, sharp laugh, which he recognized at once; and he advanced very quietly, on his knees, removing the branches from his path, his heart beating so rapidly, that he could no longer breathe.

Two voices murmured some words, the meaning of which he did not understand, and then they were silent.

Then, he was possessed by a frightful longing to fly, to save himself, for ever, from this furious passion which threatened his existence. He was about to return to Chatou and take the train, resolved never to come back again, never again to see her. But her likeness suddenly rushed in upon him, and he mentally pictured the moment in the morning when she would awake in their warm bed, and would press coaxingly against him, throwing her arms around his neck, her hair dishevelled, and a little entangled on the forehead, her eyes still shut and her lips apart ready to receive the first kiss. The sudden recollection of this morning caress filled him with frantic recollections and the maddest desire.

The couple began to speak again; and he approached, stooping low. Then a faint cry rose from under the branches quite close to him. He advanced again, in spite of himself, irresistibly attracted, without being conscious of anything—and he saw them.

If her companion had only been a man. But that! that! He felt as though he were spellbound by the very infamy of it. And he stood there astounded and overwhelmed, as if he had discovered the mutilated corpse of one dear to him, a crime against nature, a monstrous, disgusting profanation. Then, in an involuntary flash of thought, he remembered the little fish whose entrails he had felt being torn out! But Madeleine murmured: "Pauline!" in the same tone in which she had often called him by name, and he was seized by such a fit of anguish that he turned and fled.

He struck against two trees, fell over a root, set off again, and suddenly found himself near the rapid branch of the river, which was lit up by the moon. The torrent-like current made great eddies where the light played upon it. The high bank dominated the stream like a cliff, leaving a wide obscure zone at its foot where the eddies could be heard swirling in the darkness.

On the other bank, the country seats of Croissy could be plainly seen.

Paul saw all this as though in a dream; he thought of nothing, understood nothing, and all things, even his very existence, appeared vague, far-off, forgotten, and closed.

The river was there. Did he know what he was doing? Did he wish to die? He was mad. He turned, however, toward the island, toward Her, and in the still air of the night, in which the faint and persistent burden of the music was borne up and down, he uttered, in a voice frantic with despair, bitter beyond measure, and superhumanly low, a frightful cry:

"Madeleine!"   140

His heartrending call shot across the great silence of the sky, and sped over the horizon. Then with a tremendous leap, with the bound of a wild animal, he jumped into the river. The water rushed on, closed over him, and from the place where he had disappeared a series of great circles started, enlarging their brilliant undulations, until they finally reached the other bank. The two women had heard the noise of the plunge. Madeleine drew herself up and exclaimed:

"It is Paul,"—a suspicion having arisen in her soul,—"he has drowned himself"; and she rushed toward the bank, where Pauline rejoined her.

A clumsy punt, propelled by two men, turned round and round on the spot. One of the men rowed, the other plunged into the water a great pole and appeared to be looking for something. Pauline cried:

"What are you doing? What is the matter?"

An unknown voice answered: 145

"It is a man who has just drowned himself."

The two haggard women, huddling close to each other, followed the manœuvres of the boat. The music of La Grenouillère continued to sound in the distance, seeming with its cadences to accompany the movements of the sombre fishermen; and the river which now concealed a corpse, whirled round and round, illuminated. The search was prolonged. The horrible suspense made Madeleine shiver all over. At last, after at least half an hour, one of the men announced:

"I have got him."

And he pulled up his long pole very gently, very gently. Then something large appeared upon the surface. The other boatman left his oars, and by uniting their strength and hauling upon the inert weight, they succeeded in getting it into their boat.

Then they made for land, seeking a place well lighted and low. At the   150
moment they landed, the women also arrived. The moment she saw him,

Madeleine fell back with horror. In the moonlight he already appeared green, with his mouth, his eyes, his nose, his clothes full of slime. His fingers, closed and stiff, were hideous. A kind of black and liquid plaster covered his whole body. The face appeared swollen, and from his hair, plastered down by the ooze, there ran a stream of dirty water.

The two men examined him.

"Do you know him?" asked one.

The other, the Croissy ferryman, hesitated:

"Yes, it certainly seems to me that I have seen that head; but you know when a body is in that state one cannot recognize it easily." And then, suddenly:

"Why, it's Mr. Paul!"   155

"Who is Mr. Paul?" inquired his comrade.

The first answered:

"Why, Mr. Paul Baron, the son of the senator, the little chap who was so much in love."

The other added, philosophically:

"Well, his fun is ended now; it is a pity, all the same, when one is rich!"   160

Madeleine had fallen on the ground sobbing. Pauline approached the body and asked:

"Is he really quite dead?"

The men shrugged their shoulders.

"Oh! After that length of time, certainly."

Then one of them asked: 165

"Was it not at Grillon's that he lodged?"

"Yes," answered the other; "we had better take him back there, there will be something to be made out of it."

They embarked again in their boat and set out, moving off slowly on account of the rapid current. For a long time after they were out of sight of the place where the women remained, the regular splash of the oars in the water could be heard.

Then Pauline took the poor weeping Madeleine in her arms, petted her, embraced her for a long while, and consoled her.

"How can you help it? it is not your fault, is it? It is impossible to prevent 170 men from doing silly things. He did it of his own free will; so much the worse for him, after all!"

And then lifting her up:

"Come, my dear, come and sleep at the house; it is impossible for you to go back to Grillon's to-night."

And she embraced her again, saying: "Come, we will cure you."

Madeleine arose, and weeping all the while but with fainter sobs, laid her head upon Pauline's shoulder, as though she had found a refuge in a closer and more certain affection, more familiar and more confiding, and she went off slowly.

www

GUY DE MAUPASSANT

(1850–1893) Web

Author of more than three hundred short stories in nineteenth-century France, de Maupassant was known for his combination of realism and naturalism. The simplicity of his portraits of French bourgeois futility made him an influential writer among foreigners.

www

TOPICS FOR CRITICAL THINKING Web

1. How does the riverscape parallel or reflect the story's complicated romance?
2. What does the story's setting tell us about how we should regard the four women in the boat?
3. Is there a relation between setting and social class? What purpose might such a parallel serve?

www

TOPICS FOR CRITICAL WRITING Web

1. How do the repeated elements of the setting produce a feeling of decadence? To answer this question, select an element that is repeated and trace its various appearances throughout the story's continued establishment of setting.
2. To what end does the story compare various versions of romance? To answer this question, you need to establish the various kinds of romance in the story.

5   Plot

Plot is an element of fiction that we know very well. We know the shapes of a variety of plots and how they should unfold: a young person overcomes adversity and finds success; the good guys win the war; love is found, then lost, then found. Instead of having surprise endings, most stories play out familiar plots. Part of our pleasure in reading these plots stems from anticipating the detail of these plots and knowing how events in a story will conclude. Notice, for example, the ways Mark Twain solicits our knowledge of plot in the following brief story.

Mark Twain

Story of the Bad Little Boy   *(1865)*

Once there was a bad little boy whose name was Jim—though, if you will notice, you will find that bad little boys are nearly always called James in your Sunday-school books. It was strange, but still it was true that this one was called Jim.

He didn't have any sick mother either—a sick mother who was pious and had the consumption, and would be glad to lie down in the grave and be at rest but for the strong love she bore her boy, and the anxiety she felt that the world might be harsh and cold towards him when she was gone. Most bad boys in the Sunday-books are named James, and have sick mothers, who teach them to say, "Now, I lay me down," etc., and sing them to sleep with sweet, plaintive voices, and then kiss them good-night, and kneel down by the bedside and weep. But it was different with this fellow. He was named Jim, and there wasn't anything the matter with his mother—no consumption, nor anything of that kind. She was rather stout than otherwise, and she was not pious; moreover, she was not anxious on Jim's account. She said if he were to break his neck it wouldn't be much loss. She always spanked Jim to sleep, and she never kissed him good-night; on the contrary, she boxed his ears when she was ready to leave him.

Once this little bad boy stole the key of the pantry, and slipped in there and helped himself to some jam, and filled up the vessel with tar, so that his mother would never know; but all at once a terrible feeling didn't come over him, and something didn't seem to whisper to him, "Is it right to disobey my mother? Isn't it sinful to do this? Where do bad little boys go who gobble up their good kind mother's jam?" and then he didn't kneel down all alone and promise never to be wicked any more, and rise up with a light, happy heart, and go and tell his mother all about it, and beg her forgiveness, and be blessed by her with tears of pride and thankfulness in her eyes. No; that is just the way with all other bad boys in the books; but it happened otherwise with Jim, strangely enough. He ate that jam, and said it was bully, in his sinful, vulgar way; and he put in the tar, and said that was bully also, and laughed, and observed "that the old woman would get up and snort" when she found it out; and when she did find it out, he denied knowing anything about it, and she whipped him severely, and he did the crying himself. Everything about this boy was curious—everything turned out differently with him from the way it does to the bad Jameses in the books.

Once he climbed up in Farmer Acorn's apple-tree to steal, and the limb didn't break, and he didn't fall and break his arm, and get torn by the farmer's great dog, and then languish on a sick bed for weeks, and repent and become good. Oh! no; he stole as many apples as he wanted and came down all right; and he was all ready for the dog too, and knocked him endways with a brick when he came to tear him. It was very strange—nothing like it ever happened in those mild little books with marbled backs, and with pictures in them of men with swallow-tailed coats and bell-crowned hats, and pantaloons that are short in the legs, and women with the waists of their dresses under their arms, and no hoops on. Nothing like it in any of the Sunday-school books.

Once he stole the teacher's pen-knife, and, when he was afraid it would be found out and he would get whipped, he slipped it into George Wilson's cap—poor Widow Wilson's son, the moral boy, the good little boy of the village, who always obeyed his mother, and never told an untruth, and was fond of his lessons, and infatuated with Sunday-school. And when the knife dropped from the cap, and poor George hung his head and blushed, as if in conscious guilt, and the grieved teacher charged the theft upon him, and was just in the very act of bringing the switch down upon his trembling shoulders, a white-haired, improbable justice of the peace did not suddenly appear in their midst, and strike an attitude and say, "Spare this noble boy—there stands the cowering culprit! I was passing the school-door at recess, and unseen myself, I saw the theft committed!" And then Jim didn't get whaled, and the venerable judge didn't read the tearful school a homily, and take George by the hand and say such a boy deserved to be exalted, and then tell him to come and make his home with him, and sweep out the office, and make fires, and run errands, and chop wood, and study law, and help his wife do household labors, and have all the balance of the time to play, and get forty cents a month, and be happy. No; it would have happened that way in the books, but it didn't happen that way to Jim. No meddling old clam of a justice dropped in to make trouble, and so the model boy George got thrashed, and Jim was glad of it because, you know, Jim hated moral boys. Jim said he was "down on them milksops." Such was the coarse language of this bad, neglected boy.

But the strangest thing that ever happened to Jim was the time he went boating on Sunday, and didn't get drowned, and that other time that he got caught out in the storm when he was fishing on Sunday, and didn't get struck by lightning. Why, you might look, and look, all through the Sunday-school books from now till next Christmas, and you would never come across anything like this. Oh no; you would find that all the bad boys who go boating on Sunday invariably get drowned; and all the bad boys who get caught out in storms when they are fishing on Sunday infallibly get struck by lightning. Boats with bad boys in them always upset on Sunday, and it always storms when bad boys go fishing on the Sabbath. How this Jim ever escaped is a mystery to me.

This Jim bore a charmed life—that must have been the way of it. Nothing could hurt him. He even gave the elephant in the menagerie a plug of tobacco, and the elephant didn't knock the top of his head off with his trunk. He browsed around the cupboard after essence of peppermint, and didn't make a mistake and drink *aqua fortis*. He stole his father's gun and went hunting on the Sabbath, and didn't shoot three or four of his fingers off. He struck his little sister on the temple with his fist when he was angry, and she didn't linger in pain through long summer days, and die with sweet words of forgiveness upon her lips that redoubled the anguish of his breaking heart. No; she got over it. He ran off and went to sea at last, and didn't come back and find himself sad and alone in the world, his loved ones sleeping in the quiet churchyard, and the vine-embowered home of his boyhood tumbled down and gone to decay. Ah! no; he came home as drunk as a piper, and got into the station-house the first thing.

And he grew up and married, and raised a large family, and brained them all with an axe one night, and got wealthy by all manner of cheating and rascality; and now he is the infernalist wickedest scoundrel in his native village, and is universally respected, and belongs to the Legislature.

So you can see there never was a bad James in the Sunday-school books that had such a streak of luck as this sinful Jim with the charmed life.

Twain's story presumes that we know how the story should turn out. It points out the ways plots are related to character types, our sense of morality and justice, and our feeling about the fitness of cause and effect. In telling a story with a plot that doesn't "fit," Twain's narrative draws attention to the ways we think plot ought to be. But what exactly is this notion of plot we know so well?

In narrative fiction, **plot** refers to the events in a story and the order in which they are presented. Plot conveys the sense of a logical progression of events where causes precede and are properly proportionate to their effects. We understand that plot has a beginning, a middle, and an end. We often like to begin our analysis of a story by recounting its plot or "what happens"; but what we find is that stories are much more complicated than their plots. We understand that plot is a story's scaffold around which are folded the draperies of character and setting. Like character and setting, plot is intertwined with the other formal elements of fiction.

The plots we expect to read give an artificial ordering of events arranged in the story so as to deliver a message. We see these plots so often that we understand them as describing the state of the natural world rather than embodying an ethical system. Twain's "Story of the Bad Little Boy" comments on the expectations we might have about the shape of plot. A cause—the boy's bad behavior—results in an effect—usually punishment—and the effect is a lesson in morality. Bad behavior results in a bad fate. Twain's story cynically alters the expected effect of the bad cause. No longer a "as you sow, so shall you reap" plot of poetic justice, the plot of Twain's story consists merely of a series of actions. The failure of just retribution in Twain's story draws attention to the ways plot has served as a means of delivering moral lessons.

Plot Versus Story

Comprised of the events actually narrated in a specific piece of fiction, plot differs from what we call "story." Plot refers only to those events present in the text, including events that may not be an explicit part of the story—details about the circumstances of the story's telling, for example, or elements of the process of narrating related within the story, or even the author's name listed at the beginning of the text. In the sitcom *Friends*, for example, plot includes the opening titles, what the characters actually do and say in the show's twenty-three minutes of scenes. All of this is what actually happens. **Story** includes all of the events that belong to the space and time of the world created by the text as well as events that are only suggested or implied in the text. In the sit-com *Friends*, story consists of all of the conditions and actions implied by the plot such as the fact that the characters have lives off-screen, they breath, eat, work (which we rarely see), have families, had childhoods, and so on. Story consists of the common range of events that we all understand happen, a total picture of a series of events, narrated or not, understood in chronological order. Story is all of the elements of the world in which we imagine the characters to live; but, unlike plot, it does not include extraneous matter such as a show's credits.

Often plot consists of significant events that occur within the larger context of story. The order in which significant events are narrated may be altered in plot; short stories very typically do not arrange their events in chronological order but leave it to the reader to reorder plot events in relation to what they know about story. A good example of this is when stories begin in the present, then recount events from the past. The distinction between story and plot is important because the selection of events to be included in a plot tells readers something about the art of the story. Why were these particular events selected? Why are they related in this order?

For example, the film *Star Wars* includes a number of actions and events in a certain order. We see Luke Skywalker on his home planet with his aunt and uncle, we see Princess Leia hide the important information in the droid R2D2, we see the droids in an escape pod that lands on Luke's planet, and so on. These are all elements of plot. Story consists of everything we see as well as events that are only implied by suggestion (showing a small part of the droids' trek to represent the whole of it), reference (someone in the film refers to other planets), or their belonging to the normal laws of human behavior:

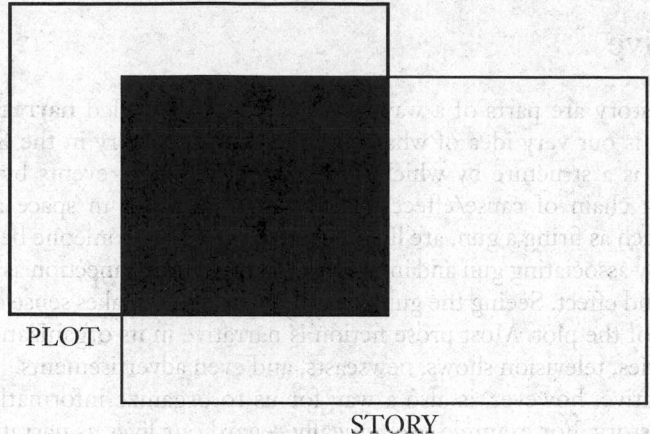

PLOT

STORY

the existence of a larger galactic war, the entire sequence of the droids' trek across the planet, the actual murder of Luke's family, the methods of the imperial storm troopers. Together, plot and story give us an entire sense of the world of the narrative.

Plot and Chronology

Plots do not necessarily need to have a beginning, a middle, and an end, and certainly these elements do not need to be related in that order. Readers are quite capable of sorting out and rearranging chronologies of events from various flashbacks where events of the past are recounted after the story has begun in the present. A more precise literary term for flashback is **analepsis** or "leaping back." Analepses are often used to explain the current state of events or a character's motivations. Sometimes stories employ flash forwards when events from the future are recounted before their causes are presented. A more literary term for this is **prolepsis** or "leaping forward." Prolepses raise the question of how circumstances or characters will become what the future suggests. Both analepses and prolepses produce a desire to know by presenting elements of plot as mysteries to be explained. Thinking about the difference between the chronology of events in story and the order of their presentation as plot tells readers much about a **story's art**—the ways all of the material that makes up a story (plot, character, setting, image, symbol, theme, narrator, point of view, style, tone) work together to produce a set of effects that go beyond the simple recounting of a plot. What is the purpose of an analepsis? Prolepsis? What is the particular effect or strategy of ordering plot events in the way they are ordered?

Narrative

www Plot and story are parts of a way of ordering events called **narrative**. `Web` Narrative is our very idea of what might constitute a story in the first place. Narrative is a structure by which we make sense out of events by ordering them in a chain of cause/effect relations that play out in space and time. Causes, such as firing a gun, are linked to effects, such as someone being hit by a bullet. By associating gun and injury, we assume their connection as a relation of cause and effect. Seeing the gun as causing the injury makes sense of the two elements of the plot. Most prose fiction is narrative in its organization, as are most movies, television shows, newscasts, and even advertisements.

Narrative, however, is also a way for us to organize information into a coherent story. For example, we typically regard our lives as narratives, with beginnings, middles, and ends. This isn't necessarily because that is the shape of lives; it is more because this narrative shape is the way we make sense of things.

Types of Plot

Though strictly speaking, plot refers only to the order of specific events in a story, we use the term *plot* as a shorthand to refer both to the way events in a story are ordered and to the patterns that structure the arrangements of events in a story. There are only so many plot patterns; many story texts use the same general plot. We often understand that plot has a beginning or **exposition** in which the story introduces characters and circumstances. Occasionally stories begin in the middle of things, known as **in medias res**, without such exposition. The middle of a plot consists of a conflict or complication that is resolved ultimately in a story's **climax** and **dénouement**. Stories differ in the ways they define, arrange, and even omit the various parts of this pattern.

Patterns of events—such as those Twain makes fun of in "Story of the Bad Little Boy"—make up the trove of **paradigms**, the models or patterns, on which we depend for story material. There are also specific thematic patterns or paradigms of plot. There is, for example, a common plot based on the conflict between two opposing forces—a protagonist and an antagonist. There is a quest plot in which a protagonist searches for something or works to become something, as in the narrative of the young boxer discussed in the Introduction. Romance plots—two people who overcome obstacles to be together or tragically fail—may stand by themselves, combine with quest plots as in the young boxer's story, or be linked to coming-of-age plots that trace a young person's processes of learning and maturing. While these types of plot have a definite aim, some plots are structured more around subtle shifts in awareness or understanding. Some even seem to have no aim at all, focusing instead on acts of perception, irony, the absurdity of existence, or a critique of social customs.

Realism and Naturalism

Realist and naturalist writers of the nineteenth century turned the practices of everyday life into plot, though their stories ultimately focused on dramatic or humorous events. **Web** **Realism** and **naturalism** designate literary movements: a **literary movement** is a set of ideas formulated by authors and critics about what literature should do and how it should do it. Such movements account for why the work of authors who write during the same period in time often share the same sense of form and aesthetics.

www

Twain's "Story of the Bad Little Boy" is one example of a realist story. The author's unveiling of the narrative's expected morality offers a far more realistic plot than would a sentimental lesson from a lesson book. The three stories that follow are realist stories: Each one presents a detailed account of the protagonist's experience rendered in such a way that the narrative conforms to the world as we sense it. Jack London's two tales of survival, "The Law of Life" and "To Build a Fire" render two incidents of a man's encounter with nature. "An Occurrence at Owl Creek Bridge" by satirist Ambrose Bierce more dramatically contrasts future and present, internal and external, while remaining realistic in its presentation of events.

ᔆᔆᔆ

JACK LONDON

The Law of Life   *(1901)*

Old Koskoosh listened greedily. Though his sight had long since faded, his hearing was still acute, and the slightest sound penetrated to the glimmering intelligence which yet abode behind the withered forehead, but which no longer gazed forth upon the things of the world. Ah! that was Sit-cum-to-ha, shrilly anathematizing the dogs as she cuffed and beat them into the harnesses. Sit-cum-to-ha was his daughter's daughter, but she was too busy to waste a thought upon her broken grandfather, sitting alone there in the snow, forlorn and helpless. Camp must be broken. The long trail waited while the short day refused to linger. Life called her, and the duties of life, not death. And he was very close to death now.

The thought made the old man panicky for the moment, and he stretched forth a palsied hand which wandered tremblingly over the small heap of dry wood beside him. Reassured that it was indeed there, his hand returned to the shelter of his mangy furs, and he again fell to listening. The sulky crackling of half-frozen hides told him that the chief's moose-skin lodge had been struck, and even then was being rammed and jammed into portable compass. The chief was his son, stalwart and strong, head man of the tribesmen, and a mighty hunter. As the women toiled with the camp luggage, his voice rose, chiding them for their slowness. Old Koskoosh strained his ears. It was the

last time he would hear that voice. There went Geehow's lodge! And
Tusken's! Seven, eight, nine; only the shaman's could be still standing. There!
They were at work upon it now. He could hear the shaman grunt as he piled
it on the sled. A child whimpered, and a woman soothed it with soft, crooning
gutturals. Little Koo-tee, the old man thought, a fretful child, and not over-
strong. It would die soon, perhaps, and they would burn a hole through the
frozen tundra and pile rocks above to keep the wolverines away. Well, what
did it matter? A few years at best, and as many an empty belly as a full one.
And in the end, Death waited, ever-hungry and hungriest of them all.

What was that? Oh, the men lashing the sleds and drawing tight the
thongs. He listened, who would listen no more. The whip-lashes snarled and
bit among the dogs. Hear them whine! How they hated the work and the trail!
They were off! Sled after sled churned slowly away into the silence. They
were gone. They had passed out of his life, and he faced the last bitter hour
alone. No. The snow crunched beneath a moccasin; a man stood beside him;
upon his head a hand rested gently. His son was good to do this thing. He remembered other old men whose sons had not waited after the tribe. But his
son had. He wandered away into the past, till the young man's voice brought
him back.

"Is it well with you?" he asked.

And the old man answered, "It is well."   5

"There be wood beside you," the younger man continued, "and the fire
burns bright. The morning is gray, and the cold has broken. It will snow
presently. Even now it is snowing."

"Ay, even now is it snowing."

"The tribesmen hurry. Their bales are heavy, and their bellies flat with
lack of feasting. The trail is long and they travel fast. I go now. It is well?"

"It is well. I am as a last year's leaf, clinging lightly to the stem. The first
breath that blows, and I fall. My voice is become like an old woman's. My eyes
no longer show me the way of my feet, and my feet are heavy, and I am tired.
It is well."

He bowed his head in content till the last noise of the complaining snow   10
had died away, and he knew his son was beyond recall. Then his hand crept
out in haste to the wood. It alone stood between him and the eternity that
yawned in upon him. At last the measure of his life was a handful of fagots.
One by one they would go to feed the fire, and just so, step by step, death
would creep upon him. When the last stick had surrendered up its heat, the
frost would begin to gather strength. First his feet would yield, then his
hands; and the numbness would travel, slowly, from the extremities to the
body. His head would fall forward upon his knees, and he would rest. It was
easy. All men must die.

He did not complain. It was the way of life, and it was just. He had been
born close to the earth, close to the earth had he lived, and the law thereof was
not new to him. It was the law of all flesh. Nature was not kindly to the flesh.
She had no concern for that concrete thing called the individual. Her interest
lay in the species, the race. This was the deepest abstraction old Koskoosh's
barbaric mind was capable of, but he grasped it firmly. He saw it exemplified

in all life. The rise of the sap, the bursting greenness of the willow bud, the fall of the yellow leaf—in this alone was told the whole history. But one task did Nature set the individual. Did he not perform it, he died. Did he perform it, it was all the same, he died. Nature did not care; there were plenty who were obedient, and it was only the obedience in this matter, not the obedient, which lived and lived always. The tribe of Koskoosh was very old. The old men he had known when a boy, had known old men before them. Therefore it was true that the tribe lived, that it stood for the obedience of all its members, way down into the forgotten past, whose very resting-places were unremembered. They did not count; they were episodes. They had passed away like clouds from a summer sky. He also was an episode, and would pass away. Nature did not care. To life she set one task, gave one law. To perpetuate was the task of life, its law was death. A maiden was a good creature to look upon, full-breasted and strong, with spring to her step and light in her eyes. But her task was yet before her. The light in her eyes brightened, her step quickened, she was now bold with the young men, now timid, and she gave them of her own unrest. And ever she grew fairer and yet fairer to look upon, till some hunter, able no longer to withhold himself, took her to his lodge to cook and toil for him and to become the mother of his children. And with the coming of her offspring her looks left her. Her limbs dragged and shuffled, her eyes dimmed and bleared, and only the little children found joy against the withered cheek of the old squaw by the fire. Her task was done. But a little while, on the first pinch of famine or the first long trail, and she would be left, even as he had been left, in the snow, with a little pile of wood. Such was the law.

He placed a stick carefully upon the fire and resumed his meditations. It was the same everywhere, with all things. The mosquitoes vanished with the first frost. The little tree-squirrel crawled away to die. When age settled upon the rabbit it became slow and heavy, and could no longer outfoot its enemies. Even the big bald-face grew clumsy and blind and quarrelsome, in the end to be dragged down by a handful of yelping huskies. He remembered how he had abandoned his own father on an upper reach of the Klondike one winter, the winter before the missionary came with his talk-books and his box of medicines. Many a time had Koskoosh smacked his lips over the recollection of that box, though now his mouth refused to moisten. The "painkiller" had been especially good. But the missionary was a bother after all, for he brought no meat into the camp, and he ate heartily, and the hunters grumbled. But he chilled his lungs on the divide by the Mayo, and the dogs afterwards nosed the stones away and fought over his bones.

Koskoosh placed another stick on the fire and harked back deeper into the past. There was the time of the Great Famine, when the old men crouched empty-bellied to the fire, and let fall from their lips dim traditions of the ancient day when the Yukon ran wide open for three winters, and then lay frozen for three summers. He had lost his mother in that famine. In the summer the salmon run had failed, and the tribe looked forward to the winter and the coming of the caribou. Then the winter came, but with it there were no caribou. Never had the like been known, not even in the lives of the old men. But the caribou did not come, and it was the seventh year, and the rabbits had not replenished, and the dogs were naught but bundles of bones. And through the long darkness the children wailed and died, and the women, and the old men; and not one in ten of the tribe lived to meet the sun when it came back in the spring. That *was* a famine!

But he had seen times of plenty, too, when the meat spoiled on their hands, and the dogs were fat and worthless with overeating—times when they let the game go unkilled, and the women were fertile, and the lodges were cluttered with sprawling men-children and women-children. Then it was the men became high-stomached, and revived ancient quarrels, and crossed the divides to the south to kill the Pellys, and to the west that they might sit by the dead fires of the Tananas. He remembered, when a boy, during a time of plenty, when he saw a moose pulled down by the wolves. Zing-ha lay with him in the snow and watched—Zing-ha, who later became the craftiest of hunters, and who, in the end, fell through an air-hole on the Yukon. They found him, a month afterward, just as he had crawled halfway out and frozen stiff to the ice.

But the moose. Zing-ha and he had gone out that day to play at hunting after the manner of their fathers. On the bed of the creek they struck the fresh track of a moose, and with it the tracks of many wolves. "An old one," Zing-ha, who was quicker at reading the sign, said—"an old one who cannot keep up with the herd. The wolves have cut him out from his brothers, and they will never leave him." And it was so. It was their way. By day and by night, never resting, snarling on his heels, snapping at his nose, they would stay by him to the end. How Zing-ha and he felt the blood-lust quicken! The finish would be a sight to see!   15

Eager-footed, they took the trail, and even he, Koskoosh, slow of sight and an unversed tracker, could have followed it blind, it was so wide. Hot were they on the heels of the chase, reading the grim tragedy, fresh-written, at every step. Now they came to where the moose had made a stand. Thrice the length of a grown man's body, in every direction, had the snow been stamped about and uptossed. In the midst were the deep impressions of the splay-hoofed game, and all about, everywhere, were the lighter footmarks of the wolves. Some, while their brothers harried the kill, had lain to one side and rested. The full-stretched impress of their bodies in the snow was as perfect as though made the moment before. One wolf had been caught in a wild lunge of the maddened victim and trampled to death. A few bones, well picked, bore witness.

Again, they ceased the uplift of their snowshoes at a second stand. Here the great animal had fought desperately. Twice had he been dragged down, as the snow attested, and twice had he shaken his assailants clear and gained footing once more. He had done his task long since, but none the less was life dear to him. Zing-ha said it was strange thing, a moose once down to get free again; but this one certainly had. The shaman would see signs and wonders in this when they told him.

And yet again, they come to where the moose had made to mount the bank and gain the timber. But his foes had laid on from behind, till he reared and fell back upon them, crushing two deep into the snow. It was plain the kill was at hand, for their brothers had left them untouched. Two more stands were hurried past, brief in time-length and very close together. The trail was red now, and the clean stride of the great beast had grown short and slovenly. Then they heard the first sounds of the battle—not the full-throated chorus of the chase, but the short, snappy bark which spoke of close quarters and teeth to flesh. Crawling up the wind, Zing-ha bellied it through the snow, and with him crept he, Koskoosh, who was to be chief of the tribesmen in the years to come. Together they shoved aside the under branches of a young spruce and peered forth. It was the end they saw.

The picture, like all of youth's impressions, was still strong with him, and his dim eyes watched the end played out as vividly as in that far-off time. Koskoosh marveled at this, for in the days which followed, when he was a leader of men and a head of councillors, he had done great deeds and made his name a curse in the mouths of the Pellys, to say naught of the strange white man he had killed, knife to knife, in open fight.

For long he pondered on the days of his youth, till the fire died down and 20 the frost bit deeper. He replenished it with two sticks this time, and gauged his grip on life by what remained. If Sit-cum-to-ha had only remembered her grandfather, and gathered a larger armful, his hours would have been longer. It would have been easy. But she was ever a careless child, and honored not her ancestors from the time the Beaver, son of the son of Zing-ha, first cast eyes upon her. Well, what mattered it? Had he not done likewise in his own quick youth? For a while he listened to the silence. Perhaps the heart of his son might soften, and he would come back with the dogs to take his old father on with the tribe to where the caribou ran thick and the fat hung heavy upon them.

He strained his ears, his restless brain for the moment stilled. Not a stir, nothing. He alone took breath in the midst of the great silence. It was very lonely. Hark! What was that? A chill passed over his body. The familiar, long-drawn howl broke the void, and it was close at hand. Then on his darkened eyes was projected the vision of the moose—the old bull moose—the torn flanks and bloody sides, the riddled mane, and the great branching horns, down low and tossing to the last. He saw the flashing forms of gray, the gleaming eyes, the lolling tongues, the slavered fangs. And he saw the inexorable circle close in till it became a dark point in the midst of the stamped snow.

A cold muzzle thrust against his cheek, and at its touch his soul leaped back to the present. His hand shot into the fire and dragged out a burning faggot. Overcome for the nonce by his hereditary fear of man, the brute retreated, raising a prolonged call to his brothers; and greedily they answered, till a ring of crouching, jaw-slobbered gray was stretched round about. The old man listened to the drawing in of this circle. He waved his brand wildly, and sniffs turned to snarls; but the panting brutes refused to scatter. Now one wormed his chest forward, dragging his haunches after, now a second, now a third; but never a one drew back. Why should he cling to life? he asked, and dropped the blazing stick into the snow. It sizzled and went out. The circle grunted uneasily, but held its own. Again he saw the last stand of the old bull moose, and Koskoosh dropped his head wearily upon his knees. What did it matter after all? Was it not the law of life?

──────── **JACK LONDON** ────────
(1876–1916) Web

A jack of all trades, London finished high school after a stint in jail for vagrancy and became a successful and prolific writer who published more than fifty-one books before his early death at forty. Many of his stories involve the sea or adventures in the wild.

TOPICS FOR CRITICAL THINKING Web

1. How is "the law of life" also the plot of the story?
2. What is the connection between Koskoosh's present circumstances and the story Koskoosh remembers?
3. How does this story's plot rely on character and setting?

TOPICS FOR CRITICAL WRITING Web

1. What are the effects of narrating events out of their chronological order in this story?
2. How do the text's various stories parallel one another? To what end? To answer this question, you need to define the text's various stories.

✍✍

To Build a Fire   *(1902)*

For land travel or seafaring, the world over, a companion is usually considered desirable. In the Klondike, as Tom Vincent found out, such a companion is absolutely essential. But he found it out, not by precept, but through bitter experience.

"Never travel alone," is a precept of the north. He had heard it many times and laughed; for he was a strapping young fellow, big-boned and big-muscled, with faith in himself and in the strength of his head and hands.

It was on a bleak January day when the experience came that taught him respect for the frost, and for the wisdom of the men who had battled with it.

He had left Calumet Camp on the Yukon with a light pack on his back, to go up Paul Creek to the divide between it and Cherry Creek, where his party was prospecting and hunting moose.

The frost was sixty degrees below zero, and he had thirty miles of lonely 5 trail to cover, but he did not mind. In fact, he enjoyed it, swinging along through the silence, his blood pounding warmly through his veins, and his mind carefree and happy. For he and his comrades were certain they had struck "pay" up there on the Cherry Creek Divide; and, further, he was returning to them from Dawson with cheery home letters from the States.

At seven o'clock, when he turned the heels of his moccasins toward Calumet Camp, it was still black night. And when day broke at half past nine he had made the four-mile cut-off across the flats and was six miles up Paul Creek. The trail, which had seen little travel, followed the bed of the creek, and there was no possibility of his getting lost. He had gone to Dawson by way of Cherry Creek and Indian River, so Paul Creek was new and strange. By half past eleven he was at the forks, which had been described to him, and he knew he had covered fifteen miles, half the distance.

He knew that in the nature of things the trail was bound to grow worse from there on, and thought that, considering the good time he had made, he merited lunch. Casting off his pack and taking a seat on a fallen tree, he un-mittened his right hand, reached inside his shirt next to the skin, and fished out a couple of biscuits sandwiched with sliced bacon and wrapped in a hand-kerchief—the only way they could be carried without freezing solid.

He had barely chewed the first mouthful when his numbing fingers warned him to put his mitten on again. This he did, not without surprise at the bitter swiftness with which the frost bit in. Undoubtedly it was the coldest snap he had ever experienced, he thought.

He spat upon the snow,—a favorite northland trick,—and the sharp crackle of the instantly congealed spittle startled him. The spirit thermome-ter at Calumet had registered sixty below when he left, but he was certain it had grown much colder, how much colder he could not imagine.

Half of the first biscuit was yet untouched, but he could feel himself be- 10
ginning to chill—a thing most unusual for him. This would never do, he de-cided, and slipping the pack-straps across his shoulders, he leaped to his feet and ran briskly up the trail.

A few minutes of this made him warm again, and he settled down to a steady stride, munching the biscuits as he went along. The moisture that ex-haled with his breath crusted his lips and mustache with pendent ice and formed a miniature glacier on his chin. Now and again sensation forsook his nose and cheeks, and he rubbed them till they burned with the returning blood.

Most men wore nose-straps; his partners did, but he had scorned such "feminine contraptions," and till now had never felt the need of them. Now he did feel the need, for he was rubbing constantly.

Nevertheless he was aware of a thrill of joy, of exultation. He was doing something, achieving something, mastering the elements. Once he laughed aloud in sheer strength of life, and with his clenched fist defied the frost. He was its master. What he did he did in spite of it. It could not stop him. He was going on to the Cherry Creek Divide.

Strong as were the elements, he was stronger. At such times animals crawled away into their holes and remained in hiding. But he did not hide. He was out in it, facing it, fighting it. He was a man, a master of things.

In such fashion, rejoicing proudly, he tramped on. After half an hour he 15
rounded a bend, where the creek ran close to the mountainside, and came upon one of the most insignificant-appearing but most formidable dangers in northern travel.

The creek itself was frozen solid to its rocky bottom, but from the moun-tain came the outflow of several springs. These springs never froze, and the only effect of the severest cold snaps was to lessen their discharge. Protected from the frost by the blanket of snow, the water of these springs seeped down into the creek, and, on top of the creek ice, formed shallow pools.

The surface of these pools, in turn, took on a skin of ice which grew thicker and thicker, until the water overran, and so formed a second ice-skinned pool above the first.

Thus at the bottom was the solid creek ice, then probably six to eight inches of water, then a thin ice-skin, then another six inches of water and another ice-skin. And on top of this last skin was about an inch of recent snow to make the trap complete.

To Tom Vincent's eye the unbroken snow surface gave no warning of the lurking danger. As the crust was thicker at the edge, he was well toward the middle before he broke through.

In itself it was a very insignificant mishap,—a man does not drown in 20 twelve inches of water,—but in its consequences as serious an accident as could possibly befall him.

At the instant he broke through he felt the cold water strike his feet and ankles, and with half a dozen lunges he made the bank. He was quite cool and collected. The thing to do, and the only thing to do, was to build a fire. For another precept of the north runs: *Travel with wet socks down to twenty below zero; after that build a fire.* And it was three times twenty below and colder, and he knew it.

He knew, further, that great care must be exercised; that with failure at the first attempt, the chance was made greater for failure at the second attempt. In short, he knew that there must be no failure. The moment before a strong, exulting man, boastful of his mastery of the elements, he was now fighting for his life against those same elements—such was the difference caused by the injection of a quart of water into a northland traveller's calculations.

In a clump of pines on the rim of the bank the spring high-water had lodged many twigs and small branches. Thoroughly dried by the summer sun, they now waited the match.

It is impossible to build a fire with heavy Alaskan mittens on one's hands, so Vincent bared his, gathered a sufficient number of twigs, and knocking the snow from them, knelt down to kindle his fire. From an inside pocket he drew out his matches and a strip of thin birch bark. The matches were of the Klondike kind, sulphur matches, one hundred in a bunch.

He noticed how quickly his fingers had chilled as he separated one match 25 from the bunch and scratched it on his trousers. The birch bark, like the dryest of paper, burst into bright flame. This he carefully fed with the smallest twigs and finest débris, cherishing the flame with the utmost care. It did not do to hurry things, as he well knew, and although his fingers were now quite stiff, he did not hurry.

After the first quick, biting sensation of cold, his feet had ached with a heavy, dull ache and were rapidly growing numb. But the fire, although a very young one, was now a success, and he knew that a little snow, briskly rubbed, would speedily cure his feet.

But at the moment he was adding the first thick twigs to the fire a grievous thing happened. The pine boughs above his head were burdened with a four months' snowfall, and so finely adjusted were the burdens that his slight movements in collecting the twigs had been sufficient to disturb the balance.

The snow from the topmost bough was the first to fall, striking and dislodging the snow on the boughs beneath. And all this snow, accumulating as it fell, smote Tom Vincent's head and shoulders and blotted out his fire.

He still kept his presence of mind, for he knew how great his danger was. He started at once to rebuild the fire, but his fingers were now so cold that he could not bend them, and he was forced to pick up each twig and splinter between the tips of the fingers of either hand.

When he came to the match he encountered great difficulty in separating one from the bunch. This he succeeded in managing, however, and also, by a great effort, in clutching the match between his thumb and forefinger. But in scratching it, he dropped it in the snow and could not pick it up again. 30

He stood up, desperate. He could not feel even his weight on his feet, although the ankles were aching painfully. Putting on his mittens, he stepped to one side, so that the snow would not fall upon the new fire he was to build, and beat his hands violently against a tree-trunk.

This enabled him to separate and strike a second match and to set fire to the remaining fragment of birch bark. But his body had now begun to chill and he was shivering, so that when he tried to add the first twigs his hand shook and the tiny flame was quenched.

The frost had beaten him. His hands were worthless. But he had the foresight to drop the bunch of matches into his wide-mouthed outside pocket before he slipped on his mittens in despair, and started to run up the trail. One cannot run the frost out of wet feet at sixty below and colder, however, as he quickly discovered.

He came round a sharp turn of the creek to where he could look ahead for a mile. But there was no help, no sign of help, only the white trees and the white hills, the quiet cold and the brazen silence! If only he had a comrade whose feet were not freezing, he thought, only such a comrade to start the fire that could save him!

Then his eyes chanced upon another high-water lodgment of twigs and leaves and branches. If he could strike a match, all might yet be well. With stiff fingers which he could not bend, he got out a bunch of matches, but found it impossible to separate them. 35

He sat down and awkwardly shuffled the bunch about on his knees, until he got it resting on his palm with the sulphur ends projecting, somewhat in the manner the blade of a hunting-knife would project when clutched in the fist.

But his fingers stood straight out. They could not clutch. This he overcame by pressing the wrist of the other hand against them, and so forcing them down upon the bunch. Time and again, holding thus by both hands, he scratched the bunch on his leg and finally ignited it. But the flame burned into the flesh of his hand, and he involuntarily relaxed his hold. The bunch fell into the snow, and while he tried vainly to pick it up, sizzled and went out.

Again he ran, by this time badly frightened. His feet were utterly devoid of sensation. He stubbed his toes once on a buried log, but beyond pitching him into the snow and wrenching his back, it gave him no feelings.

His fingers were helpless and his wrists were beginning to grow numb. His nose and cheeks he knew were freezing, but they did not count. It was his feet and hands that were to save him, if he was to be saved.

He recollected being told of a camp of moose-hunters somewhere above 40 the forks of Paul Creek. He must be somewhere near it, he thought, and if he could find it he yet might be saved. Five minutes later he came upon it, lone and deserted, with drifted snow sprinkled inside the pine-bough shelter in which the hunters had slept. He sank down, sobbing. All was over. In an hour at best, in that terrific temperature, he would be an icy corpse.

But the love of life was strong in him, and he sprang again to his feet. He was thinking quickly. What if the matches did burn his hands? Burned hands were better than dead hands. No hands at all were better than death. He floundered along the trail till he came upon another high-water lodgment. There were twigs and branches, leaves and grasses, all dry and waiting the fire.

Again he sat down and shuffled the bunch of matches on his knees, got it into place on his palm, with the wrist of his other hand forced the nerveless fingers down against the bunch, and with the wrist kept them there. At the second scratch the bunch caught fire, and he knew that if he could stand the pain he was saved. He choked with the sulphur fumes, and the blue flame licked the flesh of his hands.

At first he could not feel it, but it burned quickly in through the frosted surface. The odor of the burning flesh—his flesh—was strong in his nostrils. He writhed about in his torment, yet held on. He set his teeth and swayed back and forth, until the clear white flame of the burning match shot up, and he had applied that flame to the leaves and grasses.

An anxious five minutes followed, but the fire gained steadily. Then he set to work to save himself. Heroic measures were necessary, such was his extremity, and he took them.

Alternately rubbing his hands with snow and thrusting them into the 45 flames, and now and again beating them against the hard trees, he restored their circulation sufficiently for them to be of use to him. With his hunting-knife he slashed the straps from his pack, unrolled his blanket, and got out dry socks and foot-gear.

Then he cut away his moccasins and bared his feet. But while he had taken liberties with his hands, he kept his feet fairly away from the fire and rubbed them with snow. He rubbed till his hands grew numb, when he would cover his feet with the blanket, warm his hands by the fire, and return to the rubbing.

For three hours he worked, till the worst effects of the freezing had been counteracted. All that night he stayed by the fire, and it was late the next day when he limped pitifully into the camp on the Cherry Creek Divide.

In a month's time he was able to be about on his feet, although the toes were destined always after that to be very sensitive to frost. But the scars on his hands he knows he will carry to the grave. And—"*Never travel alone!*" he now lays down the precept of the north.

www

TOPICS FOR CRITICAL THINKING Web

1. Through what tactics does the story create a sense of urgency? For what purposes?
2. Why does this story reveal a moral lesson at the beginning?

www

TOPICS FOR CRITICAL WRITING Web

1. In what ways does the opening lesson affect the ways we read the story? What is the relation between the actual plot and the lesson with which the story begins?
2. What specific tactics does the story use to create a sense of doom? For what purposes does it create this sense?

AMBROSE BIERCE

An Occurrence at Owl Creek Bridge (1891)

I

A man stood upon a railroad bridge in northern Alabama, looking down into the swift water twenty feet below. The man's hands were behind his back, the wrists bound with a cord. A rope closely encircled his neck. It was attached to a stout cross-timber above his head and the slack fell to the level of his knees. Some loose boards laid upon the sleepers supporting the metals of the railway supplied a footing for him and his executioners—two private soldiers of the Federal army, directed by a sergeant who in civil life may have been a deputy sheriff. At a short remove upon the same temporary platform was an officer in the uniform of his rank, armed. He was a captain. A sentinel at each end of the bridge stood with his rifle in the position known as "support," that is to say, vertical in front of the left shoulder, the hammer resting on the forearm thrown straight across the chest—a formal and unnatural position, enforcing an erect carriage of the body. It did not appear to be the duty of these two men to know what was occurring at the center of the bridge; they merely block-aded the two ends of the foot planking that traversed it.

Beyond one of the sentinels nobody was in sight; the railroad ran straight away into a forest for a hundred yards, then, curving, was lost to view. Doubt-less there was an outpost farther along. The other bank of the stream was open ground—a gentle acclivity topped with a stockade of vertical tree trunks, loopholed for rifles, with a single embrasure through which protruded the muzzle of a brass cannon commanding the bridge. Midway of the slope be-tween bridge and fort were the spectators—a single company of infantry in line, at "parade rest," the butts of the rifles on the ground, the barrels inclin-ing slightly backward against the right shoulder, the hands crossed upon the stock. A lieutenant stood at the right of the line, the point of his sword upon the ground, his left hand resting upon his right. Excepting the group of four at the center of the bridge, not a man moved. The company faced the bridge, staring stonily, motionless. The sentinels, facing the banks of the stream, might have been statues to adorn the bridge. The captain stood with folded arms, silent, observing the work of his subordinates, but making no sign. Death is a dignitary who when he comes announced is to be received with formal manifestations of respect, even by those most familiar with him. In the code of military etiquette silence and fixity are forms of deference.

The man who was engaged in being hanged was apparently about thirty-five years of age. He was a civilian, if one might judge from his habit, which was that of a planter. His features were good—a straight nose, firm mouth, broad forehead, from which his long, dark hair was combed straight back, falling behind his ears to the collar of his well-fitting frock coat. He wore a mustache and pointed beard, but no whiskers; his eyes were large and dark gray, and had a kindly expression which one would hardly have expected in one whose neck was in the hemp. Evidently this was no vulgar assassin. The liberal military code makes provision for hanging many kinds of persons, and gentlemen are not excluded.

The preparations being complete, the two private soldiers stepped aside and each drew away the plank upon which he had been standing. The sergeant turned to the captain, saluted, and placed himself immediately behind that officer, who in turn moved apart one pace. These movements left the condemned man and the sergeant standing on the two ends of the same plank, which spanned three of the cross-ties of the bridge. The end upon which the civilian stood almost, but not quite, reached a fourth. This plank had been held in place by the weight of the captain; it was now held by that of the sergeant. At a signal from the former the latter would step aside, the plank would tilt and the condemned man go down between two ties. The arrangement commended itself to his judgment as simple and effective. His face had not been covered nor his eyes bandaged. He looked a moment at his "unsteadfast footing," then let his gaze wander to the swirling water of the stream racing madly beneath his feet. A piece of dancing driftwood caught his attention and his eyes followed it down the current. How slowly it appeared to move! What a sluggish stream!

He closed his eyes in order to fix his last thoughts upon his wife and chil- 5 dren. The water, touched to gold by the early sun, the brooding mists under the banks at some distance down the stream, the fort, the soldiers, the piece of drift—all had distracted him. And now he became conscious of a new disturbance. Striking through the thought of his dear ones was a sound which he could neither ignore nor understand, a sharp, distinct, metallic percussion like the stroke of a blacksmith's hammer upon the anvil; it had the same ringing quality. He wondered what it was, and whether immeasurably distant or nearby—it seemed both. Its recurrence was regular, but as slow as the tolling of a death knell. He awaited each stroke with impatience and—he knew not why—apprehension. The intervals of silence grew progressively longer; the delays became maddening. With their greater infrequency the sounds increased in strength and sharpness. They hurt his ear like the thrust of a knife; he feared he would shriek. What he heard was the ticking of his watch.

He unclosed his eyes and saw again the water below him. "If I could free my hands," he thought, "I might throw off the noose and spring into the stream. By diving I could evade the bullets and, swimming vigorously, reach the bank, take to the woods and get away home. My home, thank God, is as yet outside their lines; my wife and little ones are still beyond the invader's farthest advance."

As these thoughts, which have here to be set down in words, were flashed into the doomed man's brain rather than evolved from it the captain nodded to the sergeant. The sergeant stepped aside.

II

Peyton Farquhar was a well-to-do planter, of an old and highly respected Alabama family. Being a slave owner and like other slave owners a politician he was naturally an original secessionist and ardently devoted to the Southern cause. Circumstances of an imperious nature, which it is unnecessary to relate here, had prevented him from taking service with the gallant army that had fought the disastrous campaigns ending with the fall of Corinth, and he chafed under the inglorious restraint, longing for the release of his energies, the larger life of the soldier, the opportunity for distinction. That opportunity, he felt, would come, as it comes to all in wartime. Meanwhile he did what he could. No service was too humble for him to perform in aid of the South, no adventure too perilous for him to undertake if consistent with the character of a civilian who was at heart a soldier, and who in good faith and without too much qualification assented to at least a part of the frankly villainous dictum that all is fair in love and war.

One evening while Farquhar and his wife were sitting on a rustic bench near the entrance to his grounds, a gray-clad soldier rode up to the gate and asked for a drink of water. Mrs. Farquhar was only too happy to serve him with her own white hands. While she was fetching the water her husband approached the dusty horseman and inquired eagerly for news from the front.

"The Yanks are repairing the railroads," said the man, "and are getting 10
ready for another advance. They have reached the Owl Creek bridge, put it in order, and built a stockade on the north bank. The commandant has issued an order, which is posted everywhere, declaring that any civilian caught interfering with the railroad, its bridges, tunnels or trains will be summarily hanged. I saw the order."

"How far is it to the Owl Creek bridge?" Farquhar asked.

"About thirty miles."

"Is there no force on this side the creek?"

"Only a picket post half a mile out, on the railroad, and a single sentinel at this end of the bridge."

"Suppose a man—a civilian and student of hanging—should elude the 15
picket post and perhaps get the better of the sentinel," said Farquhar, smiling, "what could he accomplish?"

The soldier reflected. "I was there a month ago," he replied. "I observed that the flood of last winter had lodged a great quantity of driftwood against the wooden pier at this end of the bridge. It is now dry and would burn like tow."

The lady had now brought the water, which the soldier drank. He thanked her ceremoniously, bowed to her husband and rode away. An hour later, after nightfall, he repassed the plantation, going northward in the direction from which he had come. He was a Federal scout.

III

As Peyton Farquhar fell straight downward through the bridge he lost consciousness and was as one already dead. From this state he was awakened—ages later, it seemed to him—by the pain of a sharp pressure upon his throat, followed by a sense of suffocation. Keen, poignant agonies seemed to shoot from his neck downward through every fiber of his body and limbs. These pains appeared to flash along well-defined lines of ramification and to beat with an inconceivably rapid periodicity. They seemed like streams of pulsating fire heating him to an intolerable temperature. As to his head, he was conscious of nothing but a feeling of fullness—of congestion. These sensations were unaccompanied by thought. The intellectual part of his nature was already effaced; he had power only to feel, and feeling was torment. He was conscious of motion. Encompassed in a luminous cloud, of which he was now merely the fiery heart, without material substance, he swung through unthinkable arcs of oscillation, like a vast pendulum. Then all at once, with terrible suddenness, the light about him shot upward with the noise of a loud plash; a frightful roaring was in his ears, and all was cold and dark. The power of thought was restored; he knew that the rope had broken and he had fallen into the stream. There was no additional strangulation; the noose about his neck was already suffocating him and kept the water from his lungs. To die of hanging at the bottom of a river!—the idea seemed to him ludicrous. He opened his eyes in the darkness and saw above him a gleam of light, but how distant, how inaccessible! He was still sinking, for the light became fainter and fainter until it was a mere glimmer. Then it began to grow and brighten, and he knew that he was rising toward the surface—knew it with reluctance, for he was now very comfortable. "To be hanged and drowned," he thought, "that is not so bad, but I do not wish to be shot. No, I will not be shot. That is not fair."

He was not conscious of an effort, but a sharp pain in his wrist apprised him that he was trying to free his hands. He gave the struggle his attention, as an idler might observe the feat of a juggler, without interest in the outcome. What splendid effort! What magnificent, what superhuman strength! Ah, that was a fine endeavor! Bravo! The cord fell away; his arms parted and floated upward, the hands dimly seen on each side in the growing light. He watched them with a new interest as first one and then the other pounced upon the noose at his neck. They tore it away and thrust it fiercely aside, its undulations resembling those of a water snake. "Put it back, put it back!" He thought he shouted these words to his hands, for the undoing of the noose had been succeeded by the direst pang that he had yet experienced. His neck ached horribly; his brain was on fire; his heart, which had been fluttering faintly, gave a great leap, trying to force itself out at his mouth. His whole body was racked and wrenched with an insupportable anguish! But his disobedient hands gave no heed to the command. They beat the water vigorously with quick, downward strokes, forcing him to the surface. He felt his head emerge; his eyes were blinded by the sunlight; his chest expanded convulsively, and with a supreme and crowning agony his lungs engulfed a great draught of air, which instantly he expelled in a shriek!

He was now in full possession of his physical senses. They were, indeed, 20 preternaturally keen and alert. Something in the awful disturbance of his organic system had so exalted and defined them that they made record of things never before perceived. He felt the ripples upon his face and heard their separate sounds as they struck. He looked at the forest on the bank of the stream, saw the individual trees, the leaves and the veining of each leaf—saw the very insects upon them: the locusts, the brilliant-bodied flies, the gray spiders stretching their webs from twig to twig. He noted the prismatic colors in all the dewdrops upon a million blades of grass. The humming of the gnats that danced above the eddies of the stream, the beating of the dragonflies' wings, the strokes of the water spiders' legs, like oars which had lifted their boat—all these made audible music. A fish slid along beneath his eyes and he heard the rush of its body parting the water.

He had come to the surface facing down the stream; in a moment the visible world seemed to wheel slowly round, himself the pivotal point, and he saw the bridge, the fort, the soldiers upon the bridge, the captain, the sergeant, the two privates, his executioners. They were in silhouette against the blue sky. They shouted and gesticulated, pointing at him. The captain had drawn his pistol, but did not fire; the others were unarmed. Their movements were grotesque and horrible, their forms gigantic.

Suddenly he heard a sharp report and something struck the water smartly within a few inches of his head, spattering his face with spray. He heard a second report, and saw one of the sentinels with his rifle at his shoulder, a light cloud of blue smoke rising from the muzzle. The man in the water saw the eye of the man on the bridge gazing into his own through the sights of the rifle. He observed that it was a gray eye and remembered having read that gray eyes were keenest, and that all famous marksmen had them. Nevertheless, this one had missed.

A counterswirl had caught Farquhar and turned him half round; he was again looking into the forest on the bank opposite the fort. The sound of a clear, high voice in a monotonous singsong now rang out behind him and came across the water with a distinctness that pierced and subdued all other sounds, even the beating of the ripples in his ears. Although no soldier, he had frequented camps enough to know the dread significance of that deliberate, drawling aspirated chant; the lieutenant on shore was taking a part in the morning's work. How coldly and pitilessly—with what an even, calm intonation, presaging, and enforcing tranquillity in the men—with what accurately measured intervals fell those cruel words:

"Attention, company! . . . Shoulder arms! . . . Ready! . . . Aim! . . . Fire!"

Farquhar dived—dived as deeply as he could. The water roared in his ears 25 like the voice of Niagara, yet he heard the dulled thunder of the volley and, rising again toward the surface, met shining bits of metal, singularly flattened, oscillating slowly downward. Some of them touched him on the face and hands, then fell away, continuing their descent. One lodged between his collar and neck; it was uncomfortably warm and he snatched it out.

As he rose to the surface, gasping for breath, he saw that he had been a long time under water; he was perceptibly farther downstream—nearer to safety. The soldiers had almost finished reloading; the metal ramrods flashed all at once in the sunshine as they were drawn from the barrels, turned in the air, and thrust into their sockets. The two sentinels fired again, independently and ineffectually.

The hunted man saw all this over his shoulder; he was now swimming vigorously with the current. His brain was as energetic as his arms and legs; he thought with the rapidity of lightning.

"The officer," he reasoned, "will not make that martinet's error a second time. It is as easy to dodge a volley as a single shot. He has probably already given the command to fire at will. God help me, I cannot dodge them all!"

An appalling plash within two yards of him was followed by a loud, rushing sound, diminuendo, which seemed to travel back through the air to the fort and died in an explosion which stirred the very river to its deeps! A rising sheet of water curved over him, fell down upon him, blinded him, strangled him! The cannon had taken a hand in the game. As he shook his head free from the commotion of the smitten water he heard the deflected shot humming through the air ahead, and in an instant it was cracking and smashing the branches in the forest beyond.

"They will not do that again," he thought. "The next time they will use a [30] charge of grape. I must keep my eye upon the gun. The smoke will apprise me—the report arrives too late; it lags behind the missile. That is a good gun."

Suddenly he felt himself whirled round and round—spinning like a top. The water, the banks, the forests, the now distant bridge, fort and men—all were commingled and blurred. Objects were represented by their colors only; circular horizontal streaks of color—that was all he saw. He had been caught in a vortex and was being whirled on with a velocity of advance and gyration that made him giddy and sick. In a few moments he was flung upon the gravel at the foot of the left bank of the stream—the southern bank—and behind a projecting point which concealed him from his enemies. The sudden arrest of his motion, the abrasion of one of his hands on the gravel, restored him, and he wept with delight. He dug his fingers into the sand, threw it over himself in handfuls and audibly blessed it. It looked like diamonds, rubies, emeralds; he could think of nothing beautiful which it did not resemble. The trees upon the bank were giant garden plants; he noted a definite order in their arrangement, inhaled the fragrance of their blooms. A strange, roseate light shone through the spaces among their trunks and the wind made in their branches the music of aeolian harps. He had no wish to perfect his escape—was content to remain in that enchanting spot until retaken.

A whiz and rattle of grapeshot among the branches high above his head roused him from his dream. The baffled cannoneer had fired him a random farewell. He sprang to his feet, rushed up the sloping bank, and plunged into the forest.

All that day he traveled, laying his course by the rounding sun. The forest seemed interminable; nowhere did he discover a break in it, not even a woodman's road. He had not known that he lived in so wild a region. There was something uncanny in the revelation.

By nightfall he was fatigued, footsore, famishing. The thought of his wife and children urged him on. At last he found a road which led him in what he knew to be the right direction. It was as wide and straight as a city street, yet it seemed untraveled. No fields bordered it, no dwelling anywhere. Not so much as the barking of a dog suggested human habitation. The black bodies of the trees formed a straight wall on both sides, terminating on the horizon in a point, like a diagram in a lesson in perspective. Overhead, as he looked up through this rift in the wood, shone great golden stars looking unfamiliar and grouped in strange constellations. He was sure they were arranged in some order which had a secret and malign significance. The wood on either side was full of singular noises, among which—once, twice, and again—he distinctly heard whispers in an unknown tongue.

His neck was in pain and lifting his hand to it he found it horribly 35 swollen. He knew that it had a circle of black where the rope had bruised it. His eyes felt congested; he could no longer close them. His tongue was swollen with thirst; he relieved its fever by thrusting it forward from between his teeth into the cold air. How softly the turf had carpeted the untraveled avenue—he could no longer feel the roadway beneath his feet!

Doubtless, despite his suffering, he had fallen asleep while walking, for now he sees another scene—perhaps he has merely recovered from a delirium. He stands at the gate of his own home. All is as he left it, and all bright and beautiful in the morning sunshine. He must have traveled the entire night. As he pushes open the gate and passes up the wide white walk, he sees a flutter of female garments; his wife, looking fresh and cool and sweet, steps down from the veranda to meet him. At the bottom of the steps she stands waiting, with a smile of ineffable joy, an attitude of matchless grace and dignity. Ah, how beautiful she is! He springs forward with extended arms. As he is about to clasp her he feels a stunning blow upon the back of the neck; a blinding white light blazes all about him with a sound like the shock of a cannon—then all is darkness and silence!

Peyton Farquhar was dead; his body, with a broken neck, swung gently from side to side beneath the timbers of the Owl Creek bridge.

——— **AMBROSE BIERCE** ———

(1842–1914?) Web   *www*

A writer who fought for the Union in the Civil War, Bierce worked as a journalist in San Francisco until he disappeared while on a trip to Mexico. A satirist like Twain, Bierce often portrayed the ills of self-deception and the hypocrisies of bourgeois culture.

TOPICS FOR CRITICAL THINKING Web   *www*

1. How does the story expand time?
2. What strategies make us believe Farquhar has escaped?

3. What clues suggest the unreality of Farquhar's experience after the hanging?
4. Why does the text describe the setting so carefully?

www   TOPICS FOR CRITICAL WRITING Web

1. Describe the ways "An Occurrence at Owl Creek Bridge" plays past against present and present against future. What tensions and desires does this intersection of times and plots create?
2. The story posits two potential endings to Farquhar's plight. Which is more just?

6   The Narrator and Point of View

Like character, setting, and plot, the narrator and point of view are formal elements of fiction. The **narrator** is a part of the story—the part that creates the sense of the scene of the story's telling. The narrator is also a part of what is *told*—what is conveyed or produced by the story. Although our notion of a narrator would seem to imply an agent who, existing somehow beyond the story, tells the story, any idea that the narrator exists separately from the story is an illusion produced by the story itself. The narrator can be a character, mind reader, and commentator, and at the same time function as an organizer, director, and lens. The kind of narrator a story has determines the choices of *point of view* available in a story. The narrator is not the author of the story. Rather, the narrator is a creation of an author, a formal element of a story that works in a dynamic relation with fiction's other elements. `Web`   *www*

There are several different kinds of narrators. They are classified by two criteria: (1) whether the narrator is explicitly present in the world of the story (called its **diegesis**); and (2) the kind and extent of the narrator's knowledge. A **first-person narrator** is present in the story as a participating character and is identified as such through the narrator's use of *I*. Occasionally (but rarely), a first-person narrator is characterized through the use of *we* (as in William Faulkner's "A Rose for Emily"). First-person narrators know only what a single person (or group) would know. They cannot read other characters' minds, and they generally provide a source for any information they may convey about events they do not (or could not) witness. Thus, first-person narrators have only one possible point of view, although it is possible that such narrators will present their perceptions of what other characters are thinking or feeling.

We understand first-person narrators as necessarily **subjective;** that is, we do not expect their telling of events to be detached and unbiased. First-person narrators, however, may have different levels of **reliability.** Depending on how the narrator's speaking *I* is characterized in the story, we may be more or less likely to understand a narrator's account as generous, scrupulous, confused, mean-spirited, or motivated by psychological difficulties with other characters or events (such as the narrator in "Bartleby the Scrivener"). `Web`   *www*

A **third-person narrator** is not explicitly present in the story's diegesis but appears to recount the story from a position outside of the story, which is not explained or accounted for by the story. Despite this illusion of outsidedness, third-person narrators are still present within the story and only exist as a part of the story. Because there need be no explanation of how third-person narrators get their information, they may have unlimited knowledge of events, histories, settings, and the thought-processes and feelings of all the other characters. Thus, third-person narrators provide a wide choice of points of view. Narrators who have a complete range of knowledge are referred to as **third-person omniscient narrators.** Because of this knowledge, third-person omniscient narrators sometimes present an appearance of great objectivity, detachment, and reliability (we have no reason not to believe that their account is in any way biased). However, it is important to consider why such a range of knowledge is necessary for the telling of the story and how such knowledge is used.

Often, third-person narrators present the knowledge and feelings of one or only a few (but not all) characters, even though they have an unlimited knowledge of events, histories, and settings. Since their implied knowledge is limited to the subjective experiences of only a few characters, these narrators are referred to as **third-person limited narrators.** Such narrators often present only one or two characters' perspectives, which may create increased sympathy and understanding for those characters (see, for example, "The Flight of Betsey Lane" or "An Occurrence at Owl Creek Bridge"). Third-person narrators can present other characters' feelings as if they are separate from these characters (limited omniscience) or they can present characters' feelings from the point of view of the character—as if they are inside the character.

As with a third-person omniscient narrator, it is important to consider the relation between the narrator's range of knowledge and the other elements of the story. How does the story employ the kinds of knowledge a particular narrator can provide? How would the story look with a first-person as opposed to a third-person narrator? The narrator is a choice that relates to how the story works formally, aesthetically, and thematically.

Stories may also have more than one narrator. Stories may shift from one narrator to another, or they may present different narratives framed by one another. In this latter case, the story may begin with one narrator who describes another narrator telling the story. In this case, the first narrator is called a **frame narrator.** An example of a frame narrator is the first narrator in *Heart of Darkness* who introduces Marlow, who then tells the story of his African trip.

Point of View

When a third-person limited narrator narrates as if from the perspective of a single character, that perspective is referred to as point of view. **Point of view** is the sense that we are seeing events as if we are a particular character in a story. Although we might understand third-person omniscient narrators as having a wide perspective, they often do not have a specific point of view. Point of view, then, is a characteristic of narrators whose knowledge is limited to the experience of one or several characters. Not all narrators take the specific point of view of a character, and only first-person narrators automatically have a point of view. Some narrators present multiple points of view. If the narrator's function is to provide a sense of the scene of the story's telling, point of view contributes the additional lens or frame of a character's perceptions through which the story is filtered. This produces the illusion of subjectivity since the narrator provides only a partial view, one seemingly motivated by a particular character's desires and prejudices. It may also produce the illusion of greater **unreliability,** since characters often have biases, motivations, and interests that would logically sway their perception of events. Since the only way we can know those events is through a narration posed as limited, we must deduce that versions of events are unreliable based on our reading of character.

Although the kind of narrator may determine what points of view are possible in prose fiction, the choices and uses of point of view are still quite varied. Although a first-person narrator seems limited only to that character/ narrator's perspective, it is possible for a first-person narrator to attempt to understand and produce another character's perspective. An example of this is when the narrator of "The Yellow Wall-Paper" presents what her husband thinks. A third-person narrator may narrate from the point of view of all characters, only a few, or none. The narrator of "The Story of an Hour" narrates only from the point of view of Louise Mallard, while the narrator of "The Birthmark" shifts point of view from Aylmer to Georgiana. The narrator of "The Horse-Dealer's Daughter" provides the point of view of both the young doctor and the young woman. The narrator of "Hills Like White Elephants" provides no specific point of view.

Although third-person omniscient narrators seemingly offer an objective point of view (but remember, even these narrators are constructions, and the elements narrated and the ways they are narrated are carefully chosen), third-person limited narrators may offer a number of different points of view with varying degrees of subjectivity. "Paul's Mistress," for example, presents several different points of view but develops most deeply Paul's. Although narrator and point of view might seem to be aspects of one another, they do represent an arsenal of different choices an author can make.

Point of view offers an additional frame through which the story is narrated. That frame itself becomes an object for inquiry and interpretation. Very often the biases and mental status of the character whose point of view we share are of prime importance in the story. Some stories are about contrasting points of view as enacted by narration from the points of view of different characters.

Point of view, like any other formal element of fiction (character, setting, plot, narrator) works in relation to the other elements. When interpreting prose fiction, readers need to consider point of view in relation to both the story's themes and its formal presentation. The purposes of employing subjective points of view in stories are many. Subjective point of view often elicits sympathy for the character whose perspective is shared, as in "The Story of an Hour." It can provide the impression of an unusual subjective experience, as in "The Fall of the House of Usher." It can also supply perspectives for a dialogue on various aspects of a particular issue or experience, as occurs in "The Garden-Party."

Critical Perspective: Gender and Point of View

Stories about the experience of minority or disenfranchised characters occasionally use point of view to convey the experience of individuals whose views traditionally have not been recognized as an intrinsic part of "official" or "dominant" culture (the culture that represents those who make decisions about proper aesthetics and subject matter). Since the Renaissance one function of literature has been to challenge the assumptions and dictates of dominant culture by portraying its oppressions (as in Harriet Beecher Stowe's *Uncle Tom's Cabin*), critiquing middle class values (for example, in "Paul's Mistress"), or presenting perspectives not typically acknowledged—those of women, people of color, and lower class citizens. The following three stories—Willa Cather's "Paul's Case," Charlotte Perkins Gilman's "The Yellow Wall-Paper," and Kate Chopin's "The Story of an Hour"—employ point of view as a prime strategy for conveying the experience of those often not permitted to speak for themselves. The experience presented in these stories is from the point of view of female and gay male protagonists and represents some of the complexities of the sex/gender system in a late-nineteenth- and early-twentieth-century culture that did not allow women or sexual minorities much individual freedom or choice. Their focus on questions of gender and sexuality makes the work of these writers extremely valuable to critics interested in the ways gender and sexuality define writing and individuals' experience in culture. Criticism that explores the many issues, relations, aesthetic practices, and problems of gender in literature and culture is called **feminist**
www **criticism. Web**

Critical Perspective: Secrets, Sexuality, and Interpretation

In many stories, narrators are the presenters and interpreters of secrets and mysteries. Sometimes these secrets are presented directly; sometimes they are hidden or encoded as part of what the narrator refers to but never addresses openly. One example of this is the way television shows aired before the late 1990s made a character's homosexuality a public secret. The character Ellen Morgan, for example, on *Ellen* was understood to be gay long before she actually announced the fact. Even an earlier show such as *Bewitched* had a gay character—Uncle Arthur (Paul Lynde)—who was never openly identified as such.

The audience knows the secret by interpreting the clues provided; this indirect approach was made necessary by the general lack of societal acceptance for homosexuality. While the notion of the secret does not refer necessarily to sexual orientations (it might refer to illness, for example), the necessity for protecting the secret or for using writing that has encoded meanings has long been a fact of existence for homosexuality in Western culture. That does not mean, however, that such sexualities were not present or represented in literature. The tactics of encodement and indirection often employed to present such characters are not simply reflections of cultural necessity; they also represent an aesthetic where desire is produced by the constant deferment of an answer or meaning.

Stories about sexuality may present the point of view of a character who views culture from the perspective of a sexual minority. Criticism that focuses on issues of sexuality, or on the politics and aesthetics of gay experience and representation, is called **gay and lesbian criticism** or **queer theory**. Web   *www* The activities of such methods of criticism are closely allied with the insights of feminist criticism.

ℂℂ

WILLA CATHER

Paul's Case   *(1905)*

A Study in Temperament

It was Paul's afternoon to appear before the faculty of the Pittsburgh High School to account for his various misdemeanours. He had been suspended a week ago, and his father had called at the Principal's office and confessed his perplexity about his son. Paul entered the faculty room suave and smiling. His clothes were a trifle outgrown and the tan velvet on the collar of his open overcoat was frayed and worn; but for all that there was something of the dandy about him, and he wore an opal pin in his neatly knotted black four-in-hand, and a red carnation in his buttonhole. This latter adornment the faculty somehow felt was not properly significant of the contrite spirit befitting a boy under the ban of suspension.

Paul was tall for his age and very thin, with high, cramped shoulders and a narrow chest. His eyes were remarkable for a certain hysterical brilliancy and he continually used them in a conscious, theatrical sort of way, peculiarly offensive in a boy. The pupils were abnormally large, as though he were addicted to belladonna, but there was a glassy glitter about them which that drug does not produce.

When questioned by the Principal as to why he was there, Paul stated, politely enough, that he wanted to come back to school. This was a lie, but Paul was quite accustomed to lying; found it, indeed, indispensable for overcoming friction. His teachers were asked to state their respective charges against him, which they did with such a rancour and aggrievedness as evinced that this was not a usual case. Disorder and impertinence were among the offences named, yet each of his instructors felt that it was scarcely possible to put into words the real cause of the trouble, which lay in a sort of hysterically defiant manner of the boy's; in the contempt which they all knew he felt for them, and which he seemingly made not the least effort to conceal. Once, when he had been making a synopsis of a paragraph at the blackboard, his English teacher had stepped to his side and attempted to guide his hand. Paul had started back with a shudder and thrust his hands violently behind him. The astonished woman could scarcely have been more hurt and embarrassed had he struck at her. The insult was so involuntary and definitely personal as to be unforgettable. In one way and another, he had made all his teachers, men and women alike, conscious of the same feeling of physical aversion. In one class he habitually sat with his hand shading his eyes; in another he always looked out of the window during the recitation; in another he made a running commentary on the lecture, with humorous intention.

His teachers felt this afternoon that his whole attitude was symbolized by his shrug and his flippantly red carnation flower, and they fell upon him without mercy, his English teacher leading the pack. He stood through it smiling, his pale lips parted over his white teeth. (His lips were continually twitching, and he had a habit of raising his eyebrows that was contemptuous and irritating to the last degree.) Older boys than Paul had broken down and shed tears under that baptism of fire, but his set smile did not once desert him, and his only sign of discomfort was the nervous trembling of the fingers that toyed with the buttons of his overcoat, and an occasional jerking of the other hand that held his hat. Paul was always smiling, always glancing about him, seeming to feel that people might be watching him and trying to detect something. This conscious expression, since it was as far as possible from boyish mirthfulness, was usually attributed to insolence or "smartness."

As the inquisition proceeded, one of his instructors repeated an impertinent remark of the boy's, and the Principal asked him whether he thought that a courteous speech to have made a woman. Paul shrugged his shoulders slightly and his eyebrows twitched.   5

"I don't know," he replied. "I didn't mean to be polite or impolite, either. I guess it's a sort of way I have of saying things regardless."

The Principal, who was a sympathetic man, asked him whether he didn't think that a way it would be well to get rid of. Paul grinned and said he guessed so. When he was told that he could go, he bowed gracefully and went out. His bow was but a repetition of the scandalous red carnation.

His teachers were in despair, and his drawing master voiced the feeling of them all when he declared there was something about the boy which none of them understood. He added: " I don't really believe that smile of his comes altogether from insolence; there's something sort of haunted about it. The boy is not strong, for one thing. I happen to know that he was born in Colorado, only a few months before his mother died out there of a long illness. There is something wrong about the fellow."

The drawing master had come to realize that, in looking at Paul, one saw only his white teeth and the forced animation of his eyes. One warm afternoon the boy had gone to sleep at his drawing-board, and his master had noted with amazement what a white, blue-veined face it was; drawn and wrinkled like an old man's about the eyes, the lips twitching even in his sleep, and stiff with a nervous tension that drew them back from his teeth.

His teachers left the building dissatisfied and unhappy; humiliated to   10

have felt so vindictive toward a mere boy, to have uttered this feeling in cutting terms, and to have set each other on, as it were, in the grewsome game of
intemperate reproach. Some of them remembered having seen a miserable
street cat set at bay by a ring of tormentors.

As for Paul, he ran down the hill whistling the Soldiers' Chorus from *Faust*
looking wildly behind him now and then to see whether some of his teachers
were not there to writhe under his light-heartedness. As it was now late in the
afternoon and Paul was on duty that evening as usher at Carnegie Hall, he decided that he would not go home to supper. When he reached the concert hall
the doors were not yet open and, as it was chilly outside, he decided to go up
into the picture gallery—always deserted at this hour—where there were some
of Raffelli's gay studies of Paris streets and an airy blue Venetian scene or two
that always exhilarated him. He was delighted to find no one in the gallery but
the old guard, who sat in one corner, a newspaper on his knee, a black patch
over one eye and the other closed. Paul possessed himself of the place and
walked confidently up and down, whistling under his breath. After a while he
sat down before a blue Rico and lost himself. When he bethought him to look
at his watch, it was after seven o'clock, and he rose with a start and ran downstairs, making a face at Augustus, peering out from the castroom, and an evil
gesture at the Venus of Milo as he passed her on the stairway.

When Paul reached the ushers' dressing-room half-a-dozen boys were
there already, and he began excitedly to tumble into his uniform. It was one of
the few that at all approached fitting, and Paul thought it very becoming—
though he knew that the tight, straight coat accentuated his narrow chest,
about which he was exceedingly sensitive. He was always considerably excited
while he dressed, twanging all over to the tuning of the strings and the preliminary flourishes of the horns in the music-room; but to-night he seemed
quite beside himself, and he teased and plagued the boys until, telling him
that he was crazy, they put him down on the floor and sat on him.

Somewhat calmed by his suppression, Paul dashed out to the front of the
house to seat the early comers. He was a model usher; gracious and smiling he
ran up and down the aisles; nothing was too much trouble for him; he carried
messages and brought programmes as though it were his greatest pleasure in
life, and all the people in his section thought him a charming boy, feeling that
he remembered and admired them. As the house filled, he grew more and
more vivacious and animated, and the colour came to his cheeks and lips. It
was very much as though this were a great reception and Paul were the host.
Just as the musicians came out to take their places, his English teacher arrived
with checks for the seats which a prominent manufacturer had taken for the
season. She betrayed some embarrassment when she handed Paul the tickets,
and a *hauteur* which subsequently made her feel very foolish. Paul was startled
for a moment, and had the feeling of wanting to put her out; what business
had she here among all these fine people and gay colours ? He looked her over
and decided that she was not appropriately dressed and must be a fool to sit
downstairs in such togs. The tickets had probably been sent her out of kindness, he reflected as he put down a seat for her, and she had about as much
right to sit there as he had.

When the symphony began Paul sank into one of the rear seats with a long sigh of relief, and lost himself as he had done before the Rico. It was not that symphonies, as such, meant anything in particular to Paul, but the first sigh of the instruments seemed to free some hilarious and potent spirit within him; something that struggled there like the Genius in the bottle found by the Arab fisherman. He felt a sudden zest of life; the lights danced before his eyes and the concert hall blazed into unimaginable splendour. When the soprano soloist came on, Paul forgot even the nastiness of his teacher's being there and gave himself up to the peculiar stimulus such personages always had for him. The soloist chanced to be a German woman, by no means in her first youth, and the mother of many children; but she wore an elaborate gown and a tiara, and above all she had that indefinable air of achievement, that world-shine upon her which, in Paul's eyes, made her a veritable queen of Romance.

After a concert was over Paul was always irritable and wretched until he   15
got to sleep, and to-night he was even more than usually restless. He had the feeling of not being able to let down, of its being impossible to give up this delicious excitement which was the only thing that could be called living at all. During the last number he withdrew and, after hastily changing his clothes in the dressing-room, slipped out to the side door where the soprano's carriage stood. Here he began pacing rapidly up and down the walk, waiting to see her come out.

Over yonder the Schenley, in its vacant stretch, loomed big and square through the fine rain, the windows of its twelve stories glowing like those of a lighted card-board house under a Christmas tree. All the actors and singers of the better class stayed there when they were in the city, and a number of the big manufacturers of the place lived there in the winter. Paul had often hung about the hotel, watching the people go in and out, longing to enter and leave school-masters and dull care behind him forever.

At last the singer came out, accompanied by the conductor, who helped her into her carriage and closed the door with a cordial *auf wiedersehen* which set Paul to wondering whether she were not an old sweetheart of his. Paul followed the carriage over to the hotel, walking so rapidly as not to be far from the entrance when the singer alighted and disappeared behind the swinging glass doors that were opened by a negro in a tall hat and a long coat. In the moment that the door was ajar it seemed to Paul that he, too, entered. He seemed to feel himself go after her up the steps, into the warm, lighted building, into an exotic, a tropical world of shiny, glistening surfaces and basking ease. He reflected upon the mysterious dishes that were brought into the dining-room, the green bottles in buckets of ice, as he had seen them in the supper party pictures of the *Sunday World* supplement. A quick gust of wind brought the rain down with sudden vehemence, and Paul was startled to find that he was still outside in the slush of the gravel driveway; that his boots were letting in the water and his scanty overcoat was clinging wet about him; that the lights in front of the concert hall were out, and that the rain was driving in sheets between him and the orange glow of the windows above him. There it was, what he wanted—tangibly before him, like the fairy world of a Christmas pantomime, but mocking spirits stood guard at the doors, and, as the rain beat in his face, Paul wondered whether he were destined always to shiver in the black night outside, looking up at it.

He turned and walked reluctantly toward the car tracks. The end had to come sometime; his father in his night-clothes at the top of the stairs, explanations that did not explain, hastily improvised fictions that were forever tripping him up, his upstairs room and its horrible yellow wall-paper, the creaking bureau with the greasy plush collar-box, and over his painted wooden bed the pictures of George Washington and John Calvin, and the framed motto, "Feed my Lambs," which had been worked in red worsted by his mother.

Half an hour later, Paul alighted from his car and went slowly down one of the side streets off the main thoroughfare. It was a highly respectable street, where all the houses were exactly alike, and where business men of moderate means begot and reared large families of children, all of whom went to Sabbath-school and learned the shorter catechism, and were interested in arithmetic; all of whom were as exactly alike as their homes, and of a piece with the monotony in which they lived. Paul never went up Cordelia Street without a shudder of loathing. His home was next to the house of the Cumberland minister. He approached it to-night with the nerveless sense of defeat, the hopeless feeling of sinking back forever into ugliness and commonness that he had always had when he came home. The moment he turned into Cordelia Street he felt the waters close above his head. After each of these orgies of living, he experienced all the physical depression which follows a debauch; the loathing of respectable beds, of common food, of a house penetrated by kitchen odours; a shuddering repulsion for the flavourless, colourless mass of every-day existence; a morbid desire for cool things and soft lights and fresh flowers.

The nearer he approached the house, the more absolutely unequal Paul 20
felt to the sight of it all; his ugly sleeping chamber; the cold bathroom with the grimy zinc tub, the cracked mirror, the dripping spiggots; his father, at the top of the stairs, his hairy legs sticking out from his night-shirt, his feet thrust into carpet slippers. He was so much later than usual that there would certainly be inquiries and reproaches. Paul stopped short before the door. He felt that he could not be accosted by his father to-night; that he could not toss again on that miserable bed. He would not go in. He would tell his father that he had no car fare, and it was raining so hard he had gone home with one of the boys and stayed all night.

Meanwhile, he was wet and cold. He went around to the back of the house and tried one of the basement windows, found it open, raised it cautiously, and scrambled down the cellar wall to the floor. There he stood, holding his breath, terrified by the noise he had made, but the floor above him was silent, and there was no creak on the stairs. He found a soap-box, and carried it over to the soft ring of light that streamed from the furnace door, and sat down. He was horribly afraid of rats, so he did not try to sleep, but sat looking distrustfully at the dark, still terrified lest he might have awakened his father. In such reactions, after one of the experiences which made days and nights out of the dreary blanks of the calendar, when his senses were deadened,

Paul's head was always singularly clear. Suppose his father had heard him getting in at the window and had come down and shot him for a burglar? Then, again, suppose his father had come down, pistol in hand, and he had cried out in time to save himself, and his father had been horrified to think how nearly he had killed him ? Then, again, suppose a day should come when his father would remember that night, and wish there had been no warning cry to stay his hand? With this last supposition Paul entertained himself until daybreak.

The following Sunday was fine; the sodden November chill was broken by the last flash of autumnal summer. In the morning Paul had to go to church and Sabbath-school, as always. On seasonable Sunday afternoons the burghers of Cordelia Street always sat out on their front "stoops," and talked to their neighbours on the next stoop, or called to those across the street in neighbourly fashion. The men usually sat on gay cushions placed upon the steps that led down to the sidewalk, while the women, in their Sunday "waists," sat in rockers on the cramped porches, pretending to be greatly at their ease. The children played in the streets; there were so many of them that the place resembled the recreation grounds of a kindergarten. The men on the steps—all in their shirt sleeves, their vests unbuttoned—sat with their legs well apart, their stomachs comfortably protruding, and talked of the prices of things, or told anecdotes of the sagacity of their various chiefs and overlords. They occasionally looked over the multitude of squabbling children, listened affectionately to their high-pitched, nasal voices, smiling to see their own proclivities reproduced in their offspring, and interspersed their legends of the iron kings with remarks about their sons' progress at school, their grades in arithmetic, and the amounts they had saved in their toy banks.

On this last Sunday of November, Paul sat all the afternoon on the lowest step of his "stoop," staring into the street, while his sisters, in their rockers, were talking to the minister's daughters next door about how many shirt-waists they had made in the last week, and how many waffles some one had eaten at the last church supper. When the weather was warm, and his father was in a particularly jovial frame of mind, the girls made lemonade, which was always brought out in a red-glass pitcher, ornamented with forget-me-nots in blue enamel. This the girls thought very fine, and the neighbours always joked about the suspicious colour of the pitcher.

To-day Paul's father sat on the top step, talking to a young man who shifted a restless baby from knee to knee. He happened to be the young man who was daily held up to Paul as a model, and after whom it was his father's dearest hope that he would pattern. This young man was of a ruddy complexion, with a compressed, red mouth, and faded, near-sighted eyes, over which he wore thick spectacles, with gold bows that curved about his ears. He was clerk to one of the magnates of a great steel corporation, and was looked upon in Cordelia Street as a young man with a future. There was a story that, some five years ago—he was now barely twenty-six—he had been a trifle dissipated but in order to curb his appetites and save the loss of time and strength that a sowing of wild oats might have entailed, he had taken his chief's advice, oft reiterated to his employees, and at twenty-one had married the first woman whom he could persuade to share his fortunes. She happened to be an angular schoolmistress, much older than he, who also wore thick glasses, and who had now borne him four children, all near-sighted, like herself.

The young man was relating how his chief, now cruising in the Mediterranean, kept in touch with all the details of the business, arranging his office hours on his yacht just as though he were at home, and "knocking off work enough to keep two stenographers busy." His father told, in turn, the plan his corporation was considering, of putting in an electric railway plant at Cairo. Paul snapped his teeth; he had an awful apprehension that they might spoil it all before he got there. Yet he rather liked to hear these legends of the iron kings, that were told and retold on Sundays and holidays; these stories of palaces in Venice, yachts on the Mediterranean, and high play at Monte Carlo appealed to his fancy, and he was interested in the triumphs of these cash boys who had become famous, though he had no mind for the cash-boy stage.

After supper was over, and he had helped to dry the dishes, Paul nervously asked his father whether he could go to George's to get some help in his geometry, and still more nervously asked for car fare. This latter request he had to repeat, as his father, on principle, did not like to hear requests for money, whether much or little. He asked Paul whether he could not go to some boy who lived nearer, and told him that he ought not to leave his school work until Sunday; but he gave him the dime. He was not a poor man, but he had a worthy ambition to come up in the world. His only reason for allowing Paul to usher was, that he thought a boy ought to be earning a little.

Paul bounded upstairs, scrubbed the greasy odour of the dish-water from his hands with the ill-smelling soap he hated, and then shook over his fingers a few drops of violet water from the bottle he kept hidden in his drawer. He left the house with his geometry conspicuously under his arm, and the moment he got out of Cordelia Street and boarded a downtown car, he shook off the lethargy of two deadening days, and began to live again.

The leading juvenile of the permanent stock company which played at one of the downtown theatres was an acquaintance of Paul's, and the boy had been invited to drop in at the Sunday-night rehearsals whenever he could. For more than a year Paul had spent every available moment loitering about Charley Edwards's dressing-room. He had won a place among Edwards's following not only because the young actor, who could not afford to employ a dresser, often found him useful, but because he recognized in Paul something akin to what churchmen term "vocation."

It was at the theatre and at Carnegie Hall that Paul really lived; the rest was but a sleep and a forgetting. This was Paul's fairy tale, and it had for him all the allurement of a secret love. The moment he inhaled the gassy, painty, dusty odour behind the scenes, he breathed like a prisoner set free, and felt within him the possibility of doing or saying splendid, brilliant, poetic things. The moment the cracked orchestra beat out the overture from *Martha*, or jerked at the serenade from *Rigoletto*, all stupid and ugly things slid from him, and his senses were deliciously, yet delicately fired.

Perhaps it was because, in Paul's world, the natural nearly always wore the guise of ugliness, that a certain element of artificiality seemed to him necessary in beauty. Perhaps it was because his experience of life elsewhere was so full of Sabbath-school picnics, petty economies, wholesome advice as to how to succeed in life, and the unescapable odours of cooking, that he found this existence so alluring, these smartly-clad men and women so attractive, that he was so moved by these starry apple orchards that bloomed perennially under the lime-light.

It would be difficult to put it strongly enough how convincingly the stage entrance of that theatre was for Paul the actual portal of Romance. Certainly none of the company ever suspected it, least of all Charley Edwards. It was very like the old stories that used to float about London of fabulously rich Jews, who had subterranean halls there, with palms, and fountains, and soft lamps and richly apparelled women who never saw the disenchanting light of London day. So, in the midst of that smoke-palled city, enamoured of figures and grimy toil, Paul had his secret temple, his wishing carpet, his bit of blue-and-white Mediterranean shore bathed in perpetual sunshine.

Several of Paul's teachers had a theory that his imagination had been perverted by garish fiction, but the truth was that he scarcely ever read at all. The books at home were not such as would either tempt or corrupt a youthful mind, and as for reading the novels that some of his friends urged upon him—well, he got what he wanted much more quickly from music; any sort of music, from an orchestra to a barrel organ. He needed only the spark, the indescribable thrill that made his imagination master of his senses, and he could make plots and pictures enough of his own. It was equally true that he was not stage struck—not, at any rate, in the usual acceptation of that expression. He had no desire to become an actor, any more than he had to become a musician. He felt no necessity to do any of these things; what he wanted was to see, to be in the atmosphere, float on the wave of it, to be carried out, blue league after blue league, away from everything.

After a night behind the scenes, Paul found the school-room more than ever repulsive; the bare floors and naked walls; the prosy men who never wore frock coats, or violets in their buttonholes; the women with their dull gowns, shrill voices, and pitiful seriousness about prepositions that govern the dative. He could not bear to have the other pupils think, for a moment, that he took these people seriously; he must convey to them that he considered it all trivial, and was there only by way of a jest, anyway. He had autographed pictures of all the members of the stock company which he showed his classmates, telling them the most incredible stories of his familiarity with these people, of his acquaintance with the soloists who came to Carnegie Hall, his suppers with them and the flowers he sent them. When these stories lost their effect, and his audience grew listless, he became desperate and would bid all the boys good-bye, announcing that he was going to travel for a while; going to Naples, to Venice, to Egypt. Then, next Monday, he would slip back, conscious and nervously smiling; his sister was ill, and he should have to defer his voyage until spring.

Matters went steadily worse with Paul at school. In the itch to let his instructors know how heartily he despised them and their homilies, and how thoroughly he was appreciated elsewhere, he mentioned once or twice that he had no time to fool with theorems; adding—with a twitch of the eyebrows and a touch of that nervous bravado which so perplexed them—that he was helping the people down at the stock company; they were old friends of his.

The upshot of the matter was that the Principal went to Paul's father, and Paul was taken out of school and put to work. The manager at Carnegie Hall was told to get another usher in his stead; the doorkeeper at the theatre was warned not to admit him to the house; and Charley Edwards remorsefully promised the boy's father not to see him again.

The members of the stock company were vastly amused when some of Paul's stories reached them—especially the women. They were hardworking women, most of them supporting indigent husbands or brothers, and they laughed rather bitterly at having stirred the boy to such fervid and florid inventions. They agreed with the faculty and with his father that Paul's was a bad case.

The east-bound train was ploughing through a January snow-storm; the dull dawn was beginning to show grey when the engine whistled a mile out of Newark. Paul started up from the seat where he had lain curled in uneasy slumber, rubbed the breath-misted window glass with his hand, and peered out. The snow was whirling in curling eddies above the white bottom lands, and the drifts lay already deep in the fields and along the fences, while here and there the long dead grass and dried weed stalks protruded black above it. Lights shone from the scattered houses, and a gang of labourers who stood beside the track waved their lanterns.

Paul had slept very little, and he felt grimy and uncomfortable. He had made the all night journey in a day coach, partly because he was ashamed, dressed as he was, to go into a Pullman, and partly because he was afraid of being seen there by some Pittsburgh business man, who might have noticed him in Denny & Carson's office. When the whistle awoke him, he clutched quickly at his breast pocket, glancing about him with an uncertain smile. But the little, clay-bespattered Italians were still sleeping, the slatternly women across the aisle were in open-mouthed oblivion, and even the crumby, crying babies were for the nonce stilled. Paul settled back to struggle with his impatience as best he could.

When he arrived at the Jersey City station, he hurried through his breakfast, manifestly ill at ease and keeping a sharp eye about him. After he reached the Twenty-third Street station, he consulted a cabman, and had himself driven to a men's furnishing establishment that was just opening for the day. He spent upward of two hours there, buying with endless reconsidering and great care. His new street suit he put on in the fitting-room; the frock coat and dress clothes he had bundled into the cab with his linen. Then he drove to a hatter's and a shoe house. His next errand was at Tiffany's, where he selected his silver and a new scarf-pin. He would not wait to have his silver marked, he said. Lastly, he stopped at a trunk shop on Broadway, and had his purchases packed into various travelling bags.

It was a little after one o'clock when he drove up to the Waldorf, and after settling with the cabman, went into the office. He registered from

Washington; said his mother and father had been abroad, and that he had come down to await the arrival of their steamer. He told his story plausibly and had no trouble, since he volunteered to pay for them in advance, in engaging his rooms; a sleeping-room, sitting-room and bath.

Not once, but a hundred times Paul had planned this entry into New York. He had gone over every detail of it with Charley Edwards, and in his scrap book at home there were pages of description about New York hotels, cut from the Sunday papers. When he was shown to his sitting-room on the eighth floor, he saw at a glance that everything was as it should be; there was but one detail in his mental picture that the place did not realize, so he rang for the bell boy and sent him down for flowers. He moved about nervously until the boy returned, putting away his new linen and fingering it delightedly as he did so. When the flowers came, he put them hastily into water, and then tumbled into a hot bath. Presently he came out of his white bath-room, resplendent in his new silk underwear, and playing with the tassels of his red robe. The snow was whirling so fiercely outside his windows that he could scarcely see across the street, but within the air was deliciously soft and fragrant. He put the violets and jonquils on the taboret beside the couch, and threw himself down, with a long sigh, covering himself with a Roman blanket. He was thoroughly tired; he had been in such haste, he had stood up to such a strain, covered so much ground in the last twenty-four hours, that he wanted to think how it had all come about. Lulled by the sound of the wind, the warm air, and the cool fragrance of the flowers, he sank into deep, drowsy retrospection.

It had been wonderfully simple; when they had shut him out of the theatre and concert hall, when they had taken away his bone, the whole thing was virtually determined. The rest was a mere matter of opportunity. The only thing that at all surprised him was his own courage—for he realized well enough that he had always been tormented by fear, a sort of apprehensive dread that, of late years, as the meshes of the lies he had told closed about him, had been pulling the muscles of his body tighter and tighter. Until now, he could not remember the time when he had not been dreading something. Even when he was a little boy, it was always there—behind him, or before, or on either side. There had always been the shadowed corner, the dark place into which he dared not look, but from which something seemed always to be watching him—and Paul had done things that were not pretty to watch, he knew.

But now he had a curious sense of relief, as though he had at last thrown down the gauntlet to the thing in the corner.

Yet it was but a day since he had been sulking in the traces; but yesterday afternoon that he had been sent to the bank with Denny & Carson's deposit, as usual—but this time he was instructed to leave the book to be balanced. There was above two thousand dollars in checks, and nearly a thousand in the bank notes which he had taken from the book and quietly transferred to his pocket. At the bank he had made out a new deposit slip. His nerves had been steady enough to permit of his returning to the office, where he had finished his work and asked for a full day's holiday to-morrow, Saturday, giving a perfectly reasonable pretext. The bank book, he knew, would not be returned be-

fore Monday or Tuesday, and his father would be out of town for the next
week. From the time he slipped the bank notes into his pocket until he
boarded the night train for New York, he had not known a moment's hesitation. It was not the first time Paul had steered through treacherous waters.

How astonishingly easy it had all been; here he was, the thing done; and   45
this time there would be no awakening, no figure at the top of the stairs. He
watched the snow flakes whirling by his window until he fell asleep.

When he awoke, it was three o'clock in the afternoon. He bounded up
with a start; half of one of his precious days gone already! He spent more than
an hour in dressing, watching every stage of his toilet carefully in the mirror.
Everything was quite perfect; he was exactly the kind of boy he had always
wanted to be.

When he went downstairs, Paul took a carriage and drove up Fifth Avenue toward the Park. The snow had somewhat abated; carriages and trades-
men's wagons were hurrying soundlessly to and fro in the winter twilight;
boys in woollen mufflers were shovelling off the doorsteps; the avenue stages
made fine spots of colour against the white street. Here and there on the corners were stands, with whole flower gardens blooming under glass cases,
against the sides of which the snow flakes stuck and melted; violets, roses, carnations, lilies of the valley—somehow vastly more lovely and alluring that
they blossomed thus unnaturally in the snow. The Park itself was a wonderful
stage winterpiece.

When he returned, the pause of the twilight had ceased, and the tune of
the streets had changed. The snow was falling faster, lights streamed from the
hotels that reared their dozen stories fearlessly up into the storm, defying the
raging Atlantic winds. A long, black stream of carriages poured down the avenue, intersected here and there by other streams, tending horizontally.
There were a score of cabs about the entrance of his hotel, and his driver had
to wait. Boys in livery were running in and out of the awning stretched across
the sidewalk, up and down the red velvet carpet laid from the door to the
street. Above, about, within it all was the rumble and roar, the hurry and toss
of thousands of human beings as hot for pleasure as himself, and on every side
of him towered the glaring affirmation of the omnipotence of wealth.

The boy set his teeth and drew his shoulders together in a spasm of realization; the plot of all dramas, the text of all romances, the nerve-stuff of all
sensations was whirling about him like the snow flakes. He burnt like a faggot
in a tempest.

When Paul went down to dinner, the music of the orchestra came float-   50
ing up the elevator shaft to greet him. His head whirled as he stepped into the
thronged corridor, and he sank back into one of the chairs against the wall to
get his breath. The lights, the chatter, the perfumes, the bewildering medley
of colour—he had, for a moment, the feeling of not being able to stand it. But
only for a moment; these were his own people, he told himself. He went
slowly about the corridors, through the writing-rooms, smoking-rooms,
reception-rooms, as though he were exploring the chambers of an enchanted
palace, built and peopled for him alone.

When he reached the dining-room he sat down at a table near a window.

The flowers, the white linen, the many-coloured wine glasses, the gay toilettes of the women, the low popping of corks, the undulating repetitions of the *Blue Danube* from the orchestra, all flooded Paul's dream with bewildering radiance. When the roseate tinge of his champagne was added—that cold, precious, bubbling stuff that creamed and foamed in his glass—Paul wondered that there were honest men in the world at all. This was what all the world was fighting for, he reflected; this was what all the struggle was about. He doubted the reality of his past. Had he ever known a place called Cordelia Street, a place where fagged-looking businessmen got on the early car; mere rivets in a machine they seemed to Paul,—sickening men, with combings of children's hair always hanging to their coats, and the smell of cooking in their clothes. Cordelia Street—Ah! that belonged to another time and country; had he not always been thus, had he not sat here night after night, from as far back as he could remember, looking pensively over just such shimmering textures, and slowly twirling the stem of a glass like this one between his thumb and middle finger? He rather thought he had.

He was not in the least abashed or lonely. He had no especial desire to meet or to know any of these people; all he demanded was the right to look on and conjecture, to watch the pageant. The mere stage properties were all he contended for. Nor was he lonely later in the evening, in his loge at the Metropolitan. He was now entirely rid of his nervous misgivings, of his forced aggressiveness, of the imperative desire to show himself different from his surroundings. He felt now that his surroundings explained him. Nobody questioned the purple; he had only to wear it passively. He had only to glance down at his attire to reassure himself that here it would be impossible for anyone to humiliate him.

He found it hard to leave his beautiful sitting-room to go to bed that night, and sat long watching the raging storm from his turret window. When he went to sleep it was with the lights turned on in his bedroom; partly because of his old timidity, and partly so that, if he should wake in the night, there would be no wretched moment of doubt, no horrible suspicion of yellow wall-paper, or of Washington and Calvin above his bed.

Sunday morning the city was practically snow-bound. Paul breakfasted late, and in the afternoon he fell in with a wild San Francisco boy, a freshman at Yale, who said he had run down for a "little flyer" over Sunday. The young man offered to show Paul the night side of the town, and the two boys went out together after dinner, not returning to the hotel until seven o'clock the next morning. They had started out in the confiding warmth of a champagne friendship, but their parting in the elevator was singularly cool. The freshman pulled himself together to make his train, and Paul went to bed. He awoke at two o'clock in the afternoon, very thirsty and dizzy, and rang for ice-water, coffee, and the Pittsburgh papers.

On the part of the hotel management, Paul excited no suspicion. There 55 was this to be said for him, that he wore his spoils with dignity and in no way made himself conspicuous. Even under the glow of his wine he was never boisterous, though he found the stuff like a magician's wand for wonder-building. His chief greediness lay in his ears and eyes, and his excesses were not offensive ones. His dearest pleasures were the grey winter twilights in his sitting-room; his quiet enjoyment of his flowers, his clothes, his wide divan, his cigarette and his sense of power. He could not remember a time when he had felt so at peace with himself. The mere release from the necessity of petty lying, lying every day and every day, restored his self-respect. He had never lied for pleasure, even at school; but to be noticed and admired, to assert his difference from other Cordelia Street boys; and he felt a good deal more manly, more honest, even, now that he had no need for boastful pretensions, now that he could, as his actor friends used to say, "dress the part." It was characteristic that remorse did not occur to him. His golden days went by without a shadow, and he made each as perfect as he could.

On the eighth day after his arrival in New York, he found the whole affair exploited in the Pittsburgh papers, exploited with a wealth of detail which indicated that local news of a sensational nature was at a low ebb. The firm of Denny & Carson announced that the boy's father had refunded the full amount of the theft, and that they had no intention of prosecuting. The Cumberland minister had been interviewed, and expressed his hope of yet reclaiming the motherless lad, and his Sabbath-school teacher declared that she would spare no effort to that end. The rumour had reached Pittsburgh that the boy had been seen in a New York hotel, and his father had gone East to find him and bring him home.

Paul had just come in to dress for dinner; he sank into a chair, weak to the knees, and clasped his head in his hands. It was to be worse than jail, even; the tepid waters of Cordelia Street were to close over him finally and forever. The grey monotony stretched before him in hopeless, unrelieved years; Sabbath-school, Young People's Meeting, the yellow-papered room, the damp dish-towels; it all rushed back upon him with a sickening vividness. He had the old feeling that the orchestra had suddenly stopped, the sinking sensation that the play was over. The sweat broke out on his face, and he sprang to his feet, looked about him with his white, conscious smile, and winked at himself in the mirror. With something of the old childish belief in miracles with which he had so often gone to class, all his lessons unlearned, Paul dressed and dashed whistling down the corridor to the elevator.

He had no sooner entered the dining-room and caught the measure of the music than his remembrance was lightened by his old elastic power of claiming the moment, mounting with it, and finding it all sufficient. The glare and glitter about him, the mere scenic accessories had again, and for the last time, their old potency. He would show himself that he was game, he would finish the thing splendidly. He doubted, more than ever, the existence of Cordelia Street, and for the first time he drank his wine recklessly. Was he not, after all, one of those fortunate beings born to the purple, was he not still himself and in his own place? He drummed a nervous accompaniment to the Pagliacci music and looked about him, telling himself over and over that it had paid.

He reflected drowsily, to the swell of the music and the chill sweetness of his wine, that he might have done it more wisely. He might have caught an outbound steamer and been well out of their clutches before now. But the other side of the world had seemed too far away and too uncertain then; he could not have waited for it; his need had been too sharp. If he had to choose over again, he would do the same thing tomorrow. He looked affectionately about the dining-room, now gilded with a soft mist. Ah, it had paid indeed!

Paul was awakened next morning by a painful throbbing in his head and feet. He had thrown himself across the bed without undressing, and had slept with his shoes on. His limbs and hands were lead heavy, and his tongue and throat were parched and burnt. There came upon him one of those fateful attacks of clear-headedness that never occurred except when he was physically exhausted and his nerves hung loose. He lay still and closed his eyes and let the tide of things wash over him.

His father was in New York; "stopping at some joint or other," he told himself. The memory of successive summers on the front stoop fell upon him like a weight of black water. He had not a hundred dollars left; and he knew now, more than ever, that money was everything, the wall that stood between all he loathed and all he wanted. The thing was winding itself up; he had thought of that on his first glorious day in New York, and had even provided a way to snap the thread. It lay on his dressing-table now; he had got it out last night when he came blindly up from dinner, but the shiny metal hurt his eyes, and he disliked the looks of it.

He rose and moved about with a painful effort, succumbing now and again to attacks of nausea. It was the old depression exaggerated; all the world had become Cordelia Street. Yet somehow he was not afraid of anything, was absolutely calm; perhaps because he had looked into the dark corner at last and knew. It was bad enough, what he saw there, but somehow not so bad as his long fear of it had been. He saw everything clearly now. He had a feeling that he had made the best of it, that he had lived the sort of life he was meant to live, and for half an hour he sat staring at the revolver. But he told himself that was not the way, so he went downstairs and took a cab to the ferry.

When Paul arrived at Newark, he got off the train and took another cab, directing the driver to follow the Pennsylvania tracks out of the town. The snow lay heavy on the roadways and had drifted deep in the open fields. Only here and there the dead grass or dried weed stalks projected, singularly black, above it. Once well into the country, Paul dismissed the carriage and walked, floundering along the tracks, his mind a medley of irrelevant things. He seemed to hold in his brain an actual picture of everything he had seen that morning. He remembered every feature of both his drivers, of the toothless old woman from whom he had bought the red flowers in his coat, the agent from whom he had got his ticket, and all of his fellow-passengers on the ferry. His mind, unable to cope with vital matters near at hand, worked feverishly and deftly at sorting and grouping these images. They made for him a part of the ugliness of the world, of the ache in his head, and the bitter burning on his tongue. He stooped and put a handful of snow into his mouth as he walked, but that, too, seemed hot. When he reached a little hillside, where the tracks ran through a cut some twenty feet below him, he stopped and sat down.

The carnations in his coat were drooping with the cold, he noticed; their red glory all over. It occurred to him that all the flowers he had seen in the

60

glass cases that first night must have gone the same way, long before this. It was only one splendid breath they had, in spite of their brave mockery at the winter outside the glass; and it was a losing game in the end, it seemed, this revolt against the homilies by which the world is run. Paul took one of the blossoms carefully from his coat and scooped a little hole in the snow, where he covered it up. Then he dozed a while, from his weak condition, seemingly insensible to the cold.

The sound of an approaching train awoke him, and he started to his feet, 65 remembering only his resolution, and afraid lest he should be too late. He stood watching the approaching locomotive, his teeth chattering, his lips drawn away from them in a frightened smile; once or twice he glanced nervously sidewise, as though he were being watched. When the right moment came, he jumped. As he fell, the folly of his haste occurred to him with merciless clearness, the vastness of what he had left undone. There flashed through his brain, clearer than ever before, the blue of Adriatic water, the yellow of Algerian sands.

He felt something strike his chest, and that his body was being thrown swiftly through the air, on and on, immeasurably far and fast, while his limbs were gently relaxed. Then, because the picture making mechanism was crushed, the disturbing visions flashed into black, and Paul dropped back into the immense design of things.

————— **WILLA CATHER** —————
(1873–1947) **Web**   *www*

Raised on the prairie, Cather moved to New York City. After working briefly for a magazine, Cather began writing short stories and novels. Cather's stories often focus on characters from the West like those with whom she grew up. The realism of her novels works toward exploring how people survive within cultural restrictions.

TOPICS FOR CRITICAL THINKING **Web**   *www*

1. Through what strategies does the narrator present the character Paul?
2. What is the plot?
3. How and why does the narrator use both objective and subjective views of Paul to explain his character?
4. What is the relation between what Paul wants and the narrator's indirect descriptions of Paul's "problem"?
5. Why does Paul kill himself?

TOPICS FOR CRITICAL WRITING **Web**   *www*

1. How does the narrator convey an understanding of Paul by not identifying his desires and problems directly?
2. Explain the title of the story.

∽∽

CHARLOTTE PERKINS GILMAN

The Yellow Wall-Paper   *(1892)*

It is very seldom that mere ordinary people like John and myself secure ancestral halls for the summer.

A colonial mansion, a hereditary estate, I would say a haunted house,
and reach the height of romantic felicity—but that would be asking too much
of fate!

Still I will proudly declare that there is something queer about it.

Else, why should it be let so cheaply? And why have stood so long
untenanted?

John laughs at me, of course, but one expects that in marriage.   5

John is practical in the extreme. He has no patience with faith, an intense
horror of superstition, and he scoffs openly at any talk of things not to be felt
and seen and put down in figures.

John is a physician, and *perhaps*—(I would not say it to a living soul, of
course, but this is dead paper and a great relief to my mind)—*perhaps* that is
one reason I do not get well faster.

You see he does not believe I am sick!

And what can one do?

If a physician of high standing, and one's own husband, assures friends   10
and relatives that there is really nothing the matter with one but temporary
nervous depression—a slight hysterical tendency—what is one to do?

My brother is also a physician, and also of high standing, and he says the
same thing.

So I take phosphates or phosphites—whichever it is, and tonics, and journeys, and air, and exercise, and am absolutely forbidden to "work" until I am
well again.

Personally, I disagree with their ideas.

Personally, I believe that congenial work, with excitement and change,
would do me good.

But what is one to do?   15

I did write for a while in spite of them; but it *does* exhaust me a good
deal—having to be so sly about it, or else meet with heavy opposition.

I sometimes fancy that in my condition if I had less opposition and more
society and stimulus—but John says the very worst thing I can do is to think
about my condition, and I confess it always makes me feel bad.

So I will let it alone and talk about the house.

The most beautiful place! It is quite alone, standing well back from the
road, quite three miles from the village. It makes me think of English places
that you read about, for there are hedges and walls and gates that lock, and
lots of separate little houses for the gardeners and people.

There is a *delicious* garden! I never saw such a garden—large and shady,   20 full of box-bordered paths, and lined with long grape-covered arbors with seats under them.

There were greenhouses, too, but they are all broken now.

There was some legal trouble, I believe, something about the heirs and co-heirs; anyhow, the place has been empty for years.

That spoils my ghostliness, I am afraid, but I don't care—there is something strange about the house—I can feel it.

I even said so to John one moonlight evening, but he said what I felt was a *draught*, and shut the window.

I get unreasonably angry with John sometimes. I'm sure I never used to be so sensitive. I think it is due to this nervous condition.

But John says if I feel so, I shall neglect proper self-control; so I take pains to control myself—before him, at least, and that makes me very tired.

I don't like our room a bit. I wanted one downstairs that opened on the piazza and had roses all over the window, and such pretty old-fashioned chintz hangings! but John would not hear of it.

He said there was only one window and not room for two beds, and no near room for him if he took another.

He is very careful and loving, and hardly lets me stir without special direction.

I have a schedule prescription for each hour in the day; he takes all care from me, and so I feel basely ungrateful not to value it more.

He said we came here solely on my account, that I was to have perfect rest and all the air I could get. "Your exercise depends on your strength, my dear," said he, "and your food somewhat on your appetite; but air you can absorb all the time." So we took the nursery at the top of the house.

It is a big, airy room, the whole floor nearly, with windows that look all ways, and air and sunshine galore. It was nursery first and then playroom and gymnasium, I should judge; for the windows are barred for little children, and there are rings and things in the walls.

The paint and paper look as if a boys' school had used it. It is stripped off—the paper—in great patches all around the head of my bed, about as far as I can reach, and in a great place on the other side of the room low down. I never saw a worse paper in my life.

One of those sprawling flamboyant patterns committing every artistic sin.

It is dull enough to confuse the eye in following, pronounced enough to constantly irritate and provoke study, and when you follow the lame uncertain curves for a little distance they suddenly commit suicide—plunge off at outrageous angles, destroy themselves in unheard of contradictions.

The color is repellent, almost revolting; a smouldering unclean yellow, strangely faded by the slow-turning sunlight.

It is a dull yet lurid orange in some places, a sickly sulphur tint in others.

No wonder the children hated it! I should hate it myself if I had to live in this room long.

There comes John, and I must put this away,—he hates to have me write a word.

* * *

We have been here two weeks, and I haven't felt like writing before, since   40
that first day.

I am sitting by the window now, up in this atrocious nursery, and there is
nothing to hinder my writing as much as I please, save lack of strength.

John is away all day, and even some nights when his cases are serious.

I am glad my case is not serious!

But these nervous troubles are dreadfully depressing.

John does not know how much I really suffer. He knows there is no *rea-*   45
son to suffer, and that satisfies him.

Of course it is only nervousness. It does weigh on me so not to do my
duty in any way!

I meant to be such a help to John, such a real rest and comfort, and here
I am a comparative burden already!

Nobody would believe what an effort it is to do what little I am able,—to
dress and entertain, and order things.

It is fortunate Mary is so good with the baby. Such a dear baby!

And yet I *cannot* be with him, it makes me so nervous.   50

I suppose John never was nervous in his life. He laughs at me so about this
wall-paper!

At first he meant to repaper the room, but afterwards he said that I was
letting it get the better of me, and that nothing was worse for a nervous patient than to give way to such fancies.

He said that after the wall-paper was changed it would be the heavy bedstead, and then the barred windows, and then that gate at the head of the
stairs, and so on.

"You know the place is doing you good," he said, "and really, dear, I don't
care to renovate the house just for a three months' rental."

"Then do let us go downstairs," I said, "there are such pretty rooms   55
there."

Then he took me in his arms and called me a blessed little goose, and
said he would go down to the cellar, if I wished, and have it whitewashed into
the bargain.

But he is right enough about the beds and windows and things.

It is an airy and comfortable room as any one need wish, and, of course, I
would not be so silly as to make him uncomfortable just for a whim.

I'm really getting quite fond of the big room, all but that horrid paper.

Out of one window I can see the garden, those mysterious deep-shaded   60
arbors, the riotous old-fashioned flowers, and bushes and gnarly trees.

Out of another I get a lovely view of the bay and a little private wharf belonging to the estate. There is a beautiful shaded lane that runs down there
from the house. I always fancy I see people walking in these numerous paths
and arbors, but John has cautioned me not to give way to fancy in the least.
He says that with my imaginative power and habit of story-making, a nervous
weakness like mine is sure to lead to all manner of excited fancies, and that I
ought to use my will and good sense to check the tendency. So I try.

I think sometimes that if I were only well enough to write a little it would relieve the press of ideas and rest me.

But I find I get pretty tired when I try.

It is so discouraging not to have any advice and companionship about my work. When I get really well, John says we will ask Cousin Henry and Julia down for a long visit; but he says he would as soon put fireworks in my pillow-case as to let me have those stimulating people about now.

I wish I could get well faster.   65

But I must not think about that. This paper looks to me as if it *knew* what a vicious influence it had!

There is a recurrent spot where the pattern lolls like a broken neck and two bulbous eyes stare at you upside down.

I get positively angry with the impertinence of it and the everlastingness. Up and down and sideways they crawl, and those absurd, unblinking eyes are everywhere. There is one place where two breadths didn't match, and the eyes go all up and down the line, one a little higher than the other.

I never saw so much expression in an inanimate thing before, and we all know how much expression they have! I used to lie awake as a child and get more entertainment and terror out of blank walls and plain furniture than most children could find in a toy-store.

I remember what a kindly wink the knobs of our big, old bureau used to   70
have, and there was one chair that always seemed like a strong friend.

I used to feel that if any of the other things looked too fierce I could always hop into that chair and be safe.

The furniture in this room is no worse than inharmonious, however, for we had to bring it all from downstairs. I suppose when this was used as a play-room they had to take the nursery things out, and no wonder! I never saw such ravages as the children have made here.

The wall-paper, as I said before, is torn off in spots, and it sticketh closer than a brother—they must have had perseverance as well as hatred.

Then the floor is scratched and gouged and splintered, the plaster itself is dug out here and there, and this great heavy bed which is all we found in the room, looks as if it had been through the wars.

But I don't mind it a bit—only the paper.   75

There comes John's sister. Such a dear girl as she is, and so careful of me! I must not let her find me writing.

She is a perfect and enthusiastic housekeeper, and hopes for no better profession. I verily believe she thinks it is the writing which made me sick!

But I can write when she is out, and see her a long way off from these windows.

There is one that commands the road, a lovely shaded winding road, and one that just looks off over the country. A lovely country, too, full of great elms and velvet meadows.

This wall-paper has a kind of sub-pattern in a different shade, a par-   80
ticularly irritating one, for you can only see it in certain lights, and not clearly then.

But in the places where it isn't faded and where the sun is just so—I can see a strange, provoking, formless sort of figure, that seems to skulk about behind that silly and conspicuous front design.

There's sister on the stairs!

Well, the Fourth of July is over! The people are all gone and I am tired out. John thought it might do me good to see a little company, so we just had mother and Nellie and the children down for a week.

Of course I didn't do a thing. Jennie sees to everything now.

But it tired me all the same.   85

John says if I don't pick up faster he shall send me to Weir Mitchell in the fall.

But I don't want to go there at all. I had a friend who was in his hands once, and she says he is just like John and my brother, only more so!

Besides, it is such an undertaking to go so far.

I don't feel as if it was worth while to turn my hand over for anything, and I'm getting dreadfully fretful and querulous.

I cry at nothing, and cry most of the time.   90

Of course I don't when John is here, or anybody else, but when I am alone.

And I am alone a good deal just now. John is kept in town very often by serious cases, and Jennie is good and lets me alone when I want her to.

So I walk a little in the garden or down that lovely lane, sit on the porch under the roses, and lie down up here a good deal.

I'm getting really fond of the room in spite of the wall-paper. Perhaps *because* of the wall-paper.

It dwells in my mind so!   95

I lie here on this great immovable bed—it is nailed down, I believe—and follow that pattern about by the hour. It is as good as gymnastics, I assure you. I start, we'll say, at the bottom, down in the corner over there where it has not been touched, and I determine for the thousandth time that I *will* follow that pointless pattern to some sort of a conclusion.

I know a little of the principle of design, and I know this thing was not arranged on any laws of radiation, or alternation, or repetition, or symmetry, or anything else that I ever heard of.

It is repeated, of course, by the breadths, but not otherwise.

Looked at in one way each breadth stands alone, the bloated curves and flourishes—a kind of "debased Romanesque" with *delirium tremens*—go waddling up and down in isolated columns of fatuity.

But, on the other hand, they connect diagonally, and the sprawling out-   100
lines run off in great slanting waves of optic horror, like a lot of wallowing sea-weeds in full chase.

The whole thing goes horizontally, too, at least it seems so, and I exhaust myself in trying to distinguish the order of its going in that direction.

They have used a horizontal breadth for a frieze, and that adds wonderfully to the confusion.

There is one end of the room where it is almost intact, and there, when the crosslights fade and the low sun shines directly upon it, I can almost fancy radiation after all,—the interminable grotesques seem to form around a common centre and rush off in headlong plunges of equal distraction.

It makes me tired to follow it. I will take a nap I guess.

I don't know why I should write this.

I don't want to.

I don't feel able.

And I know John would think it absurd. But I *must* say what I feel and think in some way—it is such a relief!

But the effort is getting to be greater than the relief.

Half the time now I am awfully lazy, and lie down ever so much.

John says I mustn't lose my strength, and has me take cod liver oil and lots of tonics and things, to say nothing of ale and wine and rare meat.

Dear John! He loves me very dearly, and hates to have me sick. I tried to have a real earnest reasonable talk with him the other day, and tell him how I wish he would let me go and make a visit to Cousin Henry and Julia.

But he said I wasn't able to go, nor able to stand it after I got there; and I did not make out a very good case for myself, for I was crying before I had finished.

It is getting to be a great effort for me to think straight. Just this nervous weakness I suppose.

And dear John gathered me up in his arms, and just carried me upstairs and laid me on the bed, and sat by me and read to me till it tired my head.

He said I was his darling and his comfort and all he had, and that I must take care of myself for his sake, and keep well.

He says no one but myself can help me out of it, that I must use my will and self-control and not let any silly fancies run away with me.

There's one comfort, the baby is well and happy, and does not have to occupy this nursery with the horrid wall-paper.

If we had not used it, that blessed child would have! What a fortunate escape! Why, I wouldn't have a child of mine, an impressionable little thing, live in such a room for worlds.

I never thought of it before, but it is lucky that John kept me here after all, I can stand it so much easier than a baby, you see.

Of course I never mention it to them any more—I am too wise,—but I keep watch of it all the same.

There are things in that paper that nobody knows but me, or ever will.

Behind that outside pattern the dim shapes get clearer every day.

It is always the same shape, only very numerous.

And it is like a woman stooping down and creeping about behind that pattern. I don't like it a bit. I wonder—I begin to think—I wish John would take me away from here!

It is so hard to talk with John about my case, because he is so wise, and because he loves me so.

But I tried it last night.

It was moonlight. The moon shines in all around just as the sun does.

I hate to see it sometimes, it creeps so slowly, and always comes in by one window or another.

John was asleep and I hated to waken him, so I kept still and watched the moonlight on that undulating wall-paper till I felt creepy. 130

The faint figure behind seemed to shake the pattern, just as if she wanted to get out.

I got up softly and went to feel and see if the paper *did* move, and when I came back John was awake.

"What is it, little girl?" he said. "Don't go walking about like that—you'll get cold."

I thought it was a good time to talk, so I told him that I really was not gaining here, and that I wished he would take me away.

"Why darling!" said he, "our lease will be up in three weeks, and I can't see how to leave before." 135

"The repairs are not done at home, and I cannot possibly leave town just now. Of course if you were in any danger, I could and would, but you really are better, dear, whether you can see it or not. I am a doctor, dear, and I know. You are gaining flesh and color, your appetite is better, I feel really much easier about you."

"I don't weigh a bit more," said I, "nor as much; and my appetite may be better in the evening when you are here, but it is worse in the morning when you are away!"

"Bless her little heart!" said he with a big hug, "she shall be as sick as she pleases! But now let's improve the shining hours by going to sleep, and talk about it in the morning!"

"And you won't go away?" I asked gloomily.

"Why, how can I, dear? It is only three weeks more and then we will take a nice little trip of a few days while Jennie is getting the house ready. Really dear you are better!" 140

"Better in body perhaps—" I began, and stopped short, for he sat up straight and looked at me with such a stern, reproachful look that I could not say another word.

"My darling," said he, "I beg of you, for my sake and for our child's sake, as well as for your own, that you will never for one instant let that idea enter your mind! There is nothing so dangerous, so fascinating, to a temperament like yours. It is a false and foolish fancy. Can you not trust me as a physician when I tell you so?"

So of course I said no more on that score, and we went to sleep before long. He thought I was asleep first, but I wasn't, and lay there for hours trying to decide whether that front pattern and the back pattern really did move together or separately.

On a pattern like this, by daylight, there is a lack of sequence, a defiance of law, that is a constant irritant to a normal mind.

The color is hideous enough, and unreliable enough, and infuriating 145
enough, but the pattern is torturing.

You think you have mastered it, but just as you get well underway in following, it turns a back-somersault and there you are. It slaps you in the face,
knocks you down, and tramples upon you. It is like a bad dream.

The outside pattern is a florid arabesque, reminding one of a fungus. If
you can imagine a toadstool in joints, an interminable string of toadstools,
budding and sprouting in endless convolutions—why, that is something like it.

That is, sometimes!

There is one marked peculiarity about this paper, a thing nobody seems
to notice but myself, and that is that it changes as the light changes.

When the sun shoots in through the east window—I always watch for 150
that first long, straight ray—it changes so quickly that I never can quite believe it.

That is why I watch it always.

By moonlight—the moon shines in all night when there is a moon—I
wouldn't know it was the same paper.

At night in any kind of light, in twilight, candle light, lamplight, and
worst of all by moonlight, it becomes bars! The outside pattern I mean, and
the woman behind it is as plain as can be.

I didn't realize for a long time what the thing was that showed behind,
that dim sub-pattern, but now I am quite sure it is a woman.

By daylight she is subdued, quiet. I fancy it is the pattern that keeps her 155
so still. It is so puzzling. It keeps me quiet by the hour.

I lie down ever so much now. John says it is good for me, and to sleep all
I can.

Indeed he started the habit by making me lie down for an hour after
each meal.

It is a very bad habit I am convinced, for you see I don't sleep.

And that cultivates deceit, for I don't tell them I'm awake—O no!

The fact is I am getting a little afraid of John. 160

He seems very queer sometimes, and even Jennie has an inexplicable look.

It strikes me occasionally, just as a scientific hypothesis,—that perhaps it
is the paper!

I have watched John when he did not know I was looking, and come into the
room suddenly on the most innocent excuses, and I've caught him several times
looking at the paper! And Jennie too. I caught Jennie with her hand on it once.

She didn't know I was in the room, and when I asked her in a quiet, a very
quiet voice, with the most restrained manner possible, what she was doing
with the paper—she turned around as if she had been caught stealing, and
looked quite angry—asked me why I should frighten her so!

Then she said that the paper stained everything it touched, that she had 165
found yellow smooches on all my clothes and John's, and she wished we would
be more careful!

Did not that sound innocent? But I know she was studying that pattern,
and I am determined that nobody shall find it out but myself!

* * *

Life is very much more exciting now than it used to be. You see I have something more to expect, to look forward to, to watch. I really do eat better, and am more quiet than I was.

John is so pleased to see me improve! He laughed a little the other day, and said I seemed to be flourishing in spite of my wall-paper.

I turned it off with a laugh. I had no intention of telling him it was *because* of the wall-paper—he would make fun of me. He might even want to take me away.

I don't want to leave now until I have found it out. There is a week more, 170 and I think that will be enough.

I'm feeling ever so much better! I don't sleep much at night, for it is so interesting to watch developments; but I sleep a good deal in the daytime.

In the daytime it is tiresome and perplexing.

There are always new shoots on the fungus, and new shades of yellow all over it. I cannot keep count of them, though I have tried conscientiously.

It is the strangest yellow, that wall-paper! It makes me think of all the yellow things I ever saw—not beautiful ones like buttercups, but old foul, bad yellow things.

But there is something else about that paper—the smell! I noticed it the 175 moment we came into the room, but with so much air and sun it was not bad. Now we have had a week of fog and rain, and whether the windows are open or not, the smell is here.

It creeps all over the house.

I find it hovering in the dining-room, skulking in the parlor, hiding in the hall, lying in wait for me on the stairs.

It gets into my hair.

Even when I go to ride, if I turn my head suddenly and surprise it—there is that smell!

Such a peculiar odor, too! I have spent hours in trying to analyze it, to 180 find what it smelled like.

It is not bad—at first, and very gentle, but quite the subtlest, most enduring odor I ever met.

In this damp weather it is awful, I wake up in the night and find it hanging over me.

It used to disturb me at first. I thought seriously of burning the house—to reach the smell.

But now I am used to it. The only thing I can think of that it is like is the *color* of the paper! A yellow smell.

There is a very funny mark on this wall, low down, near the mopboard. 185 A streak that runs round the room. It goes behind every piece of furniture, except the bed, a long, straight, even *smooch*, as if it had been rubbed over and over.

I wonder how it was done and who did it, and what they did it for. Round and round and round—round and round and round—it makes me dizzy!

* * *

I really have discovered something at last.

Through watching so much at night, when it changes so, I have finally found out.

The front pattern *does* move—and no wonder! The woman behind shakes it!

Sometimes I think there are a great many women behind, and sometimes   190
only one, and she crawls around fast, and her crawling shakes it all over.

Then in the very bright spots she keeps still, and in the very shady spots she just takes hold of the bars and shakes them hard.

And she is all the time trying to climb through. But nobody could climb through that pattern—it strangles so; I think that is why it has so many heads.

They get through, and then the pattern strangles them off and turns them upside down, and makes their eyes white!

If those heads were covered or taken off it would not be half so bad.

I think that woman gets out in the daytime!   195

And I'll tell you why—privately—I've seen her!

I can see her out of every one of my windows!

It is the same woman, I know, for she is always creeping, and most women do not creep by daylight.

I see her on that long road under the trees, creeping along, and when a carriage comes she hides under the blackberry vines.

I don't blame her a bit. It must be very humiliating to be caught creeping   200
by daylight!

I always lock the door when I creep by daylight. I can't do it at night, for I know John would suspect something at once.

And John is so queer now, that I don't want to irritate him. I wish he would take another room! Besides, I don't want anybody to get that woman out at night but myself.

I often wonder if I could see her out of all the windows at once.

But, turn as fast as I can, I can only see out of one at one time.

And though I always see her, she *may* be able to creep faster than I   205
can turn!

I have watched her sometimes away off in the open country, creeping as fast as a cloud shadow in a high wind.

If only that top pattern could be gotten off from the under one! I mean to try it, little by little.

I have found out another funny thing, but I shan't tell it this time! It does not do to trust people too much.

There are only two more days to get this paper off, and I believe John is beginning to notice. I don't like the look in his eyes.

And I heard him ask Jennie a lot of professional questions about me. She   210
had a very good report to give.

She said I slept a good deal in the daytime.

John knows I don't sleep very well at night, for all I'm so quiet!

He asked me all sorts of questions, too, and pretended to be very loving and kind.

As if I couldn't see through him!

Still, I don't wonder he acts so, sleeping under this paper for three months. 215

It only interests me, but I feel sure John and Jennie are secretly affected by it.

Hurrah! This is the last day, but it is enough. John to stay in town over night, and won't be out until this evening.

Jennie wanted to sleep with me—the sly thing! but I told her I should undoubtedly rest better for a night all alone.

That was clever, for really I wasn't alone a bit! As soon as it was moonlight and that poor thing began to crawl and shake the pattern, I got up and ran to help her.

I pulled and she shook, I shook and she pulled, and before morning we 220 had peeled off yards of that paper.

A strip about as high as my head and half around the room.

And then when the sun came and that awful pattern began to laugh at me, I declared I would finish it to-day!

We go away to-morrow, and they are moving all my furniture down again to leave things as they were before.

Jennie looked at the wall in amazement, but I told her merrily that I did it out of pure spite at the vicious thing.

She laughed and said she wouldn't mind doing it herself, but I must not 225 get tired.

How she betrayed herself that time!

But I am here, and no person touches this paper but me,—not *alive!*

She tried to get me out of the room—it was too patent! But I said it was so quiet and empty and clean now that I believed I would lie down again and sleep all I could; and not to wake me even for dinner—I would call when I woke.

So now she is gone, and the servants are gone, and the things are gone, and there is nothing left but that great bedstead nailed down, with the canvas mattress we found on it.

We shall sleep downstairs to-night, and take the boat home tomorrow. 230

I quite enjoy the room, now it is bare again.

How those children did tear about here!

This bedstead is fairly gnawed!

But I must get to work.

I have locked the door and thrown the key down into the front path. 235

I don't want to go out, and I don't want to have anybody come in, till John comes.

I want to astonish him.

I've got a rope up here that even Jennie did not find. If that woman does get out, and tries to get away, I can tie her!

But I forgot I could not reach far without anything to stand on!

This bed will *not* move! 240

I tried to lift and push it until I was lame, and then I got so angry I bit off a little piece at one corner—but it hurt my teeth.

Then I peeled off all the paper I could reach standing on the floor. It sticks horribly and the pattern just enjoys it! All those strangled heads and bulbous eyes and waddling fungus growths just shriek with derision!

I am getting angry enough to do something desperate. To jump out of the window would be admirable exercise, but the bars are too strong even to try.

Besides I wouldn't do it. Of course not. I know well enough that a step like that is improper and might be misconstrued.

I don't like to *look* out of the windows even—there are so many of those creeping women, and they creep so fast.   245

I wonder if they all come out of that wall-paper as I did?

But I am securely fastened now by my well-hidden rope—you don't get *me* out in the road there!

I suppose I shall have to get back behind the pattern when it comes night, and that is hard!

It is so pleasant to be out in this great room and creep around as I please!

I don't want to go outside. I won't, even if Jennie asks me to.   250

For outside you have to creep on the ground, and everything is green instead of yellow.

But here I can creep smoothly on the floor, and my shoulder just fits in that long smooch around the wall, so I cannot lose my way.

Why there's John at the door!

It is no use, young man, you can't open it!

How he does call and pound!   255

Now he's crying for an axe.

It would be a shame to break down that beautiful door!

"John dear!" said I in the gentlest voice, "the key is down by the front steps, under a plantain leaf!"

That silenced him for a few moments.

Then he said—very quietly indeed, "Open the door, my darling!"   260

"I can't," said I. "The key is down by the front door under a plantain leaf!"

And then I said it again, several times, very gently and slowly, and said it so often that he had to go and see, and he got it of course, and came in. He stopped short by the door.

"What is the matter?" he cried. "For God's sake, what are you doing!"

I kept on creeping just the same, but I looked at him over my shoulder.

"I've got out at last," said I, "in spite of you and Jane. And I've pulled off   265 most of the paper, so you can't put me back!"

Now why should that man have fainted? But he did, and right across my path by the wall, so that I had to creep over him every time!

——— **CHARLOTTE PERKINS GILMAN** ———

(1860–1935) Web   *www*

Grand-niece of Harriet Beecher Stowe, Gilman wrote stories and prose essays on the plight of women. A social activist, Gilman published books and a monthly periodical, *The Forerunner*, in which she serialized several of her own novels.

www   *TOPICS FOR CRITICAL THINKING* Web

1. Why does the wallpaper captivate the narrator?
2. What various explanations are there for the narrator's interest in the wallpaper?
3. In what ways is the narrator conscious of contrary or differing opinions about the wallpaper?
4. What might the wallpaper represent other than itself?
5. What does the narrator's relation to the wallpaper say about the processes of reading and interpretation?
6. How do you understand the end of the story?

www   *TOPICS FOR CRITICAL WRITING* Web

1. How do the narrator's perceptions of the wallpaper shift your perceptions of the narrator?
2. In what ways does the narrator's relation to the wallpaper parallel the status of women in patriarchal society?

KATE CHOPIN

The Story of an Hour   *(1894)*

Knowing that Mrs. Mallard was afflicted with a heart trouble, great care was taken to break to her as gently as possible the news of her husband's death.

It was her sister Josephine who told her, in broken sentences, veiled hints that revealed in half concealing. Her husband's friend Richards was there, too, near her. It was he who had been in the newspaper office when intelligence of the railroad disaster was received, with Brently Mallard's name leading the list of "killed." He had only taken the time to assure himself of its truth by a second telegram, and had hastened to forestall any less careful, less tender friend in bearing the sad message.

She did not hear the story as many women have heard the same, with a paralyzed inability to accept its significance. She wept at once, with sudden, wild abandonment, in her sister's arms. When the storm of grief had spent itself she went away to her room alone. She would have no one follow her.

There stood, facing the open window, a comfortable, roomy armchair. Into this she sank, pressed down by a physical exhaustion that haunted her body and seemed to reach into her soul.

She could see in the open square before her house the tops of trees that   5
were all aquiver with the new spring life. The delicious breath of rain was in the air. In the street below a peddler was crying his wares. The notes of a distant song which some one was singing reached her faintly, and countless sparrows were twittering in the eaves.

There were patches of blue sky showing here and there through the clouds that had met and piled one above the other in the west facing her window.

She sat with her head thrown back upon the cushion of the chair, quite motionless, except when a sob came up into her throat and shook her, as a child who has cried itself to sleep continues to sob in its dreams.

She was young, with a fair, calm face, whose lines bespoke repression and even a certain strength. But now there was a dull stare in her eyes, whose gaze was fixed away off yonder on one of those patches of blue sky. It was not a glance of reflection, but rather indicated a suspension of intelligent thought.

There was something coming to her and she was waiting for it, fearfully. What was it? She did not know; it was too subtle and elusive to name. But she felt it, creeping out of the sky, reaching toward her through the sounds, the scents, the color that filled the air.

Now her bosom rose and fell tumultuously. She was beginning to recognize this thing that was approaching to possess her, and she was striving to beat it back with her will—as powerless as her two white slender hands would have been.   10

When she abandoned herself a little whispered word escaped her slightly parted lips. She said it over and over under her breath: "Free, free, free!" The vacant stare and the look of terror that had followed it went from her eyes. They stayed keen and bright. Her pulses beat fast, and the coursing blood warmed and relaxed every inch of her body.

She did not stop to ask if it were or were not a monstrous joy that held her. A clear and exalted perception enabled her to dismiss the suggestion as trivial.

She knew that she would weep again when she saw the kind, tender hands folded in death; the face that had never looked save with love upon her, fixed and gray and dead. But she saw beyond that bitter moment a long procession of years to come that would belong to her absolutely. And she opened and spread her arms out to them in welcome.

There would be no one to live for during those coming years; she would live for herself. There would be no powerful will bending hers in that blind persistence with which men and women believe they have a right to impose a private will upon a fellow-creature. A kind intention or a cruel intention made the act seem no less a crime as she looked upon it in that brief moment of illumination.

And yet she had loved him—sometimes. Often she had not. What did it matter! What could love, the unsolved mystery, count for in face of this possession of self-assertion which she suddenly recognized as the strongest impulse of her being!   15

"Free! Body and soul free!" she kept whispering.

Josephine was kneeling before the closed door with her lips to the keyhole, imploring for admission. "Louise, open the door! I beg, open the door—you will make yourself ill. What are you doing, Louise? For heaven's sake open the door."

"Go away. I am not making myself ill." No; she was drinking in a very elixir of life through that open window.

Her fancy was running riot along those days ahead of her. Spring days, and summer days, and all sorts of days that would be her own. She breathed a

quick prayer that life might be long. It was only yesterday she had thought
with a shudder that life might be long.

She arose at length and opened the door to her sister's importunities. 20
There was a feverish triumph in her eyes, and she carried herself unwittingly
like a goddess of Victory. She clasped her sister's waist, and together they descended the stairs. Richards stood waiting for them at the bottom.

Some one was opening the front door with a latchkey. It was Brently Mallard who entered, a little travel-stained, composedly carrying his grip-sack
and umbrella. He had been far from the scene of accident, and did not even
know there had been one. He stood amazed at Josephine's piercing cry; at
Richards' quick motion to screen him from the view of his wife.

But Richards was too late.

When the doctors came they said she had died of heart disease—of joy
that kills.

KATE CHOPIN

(1851–1904) CD-ROM

Born in St. Louis and living in New Orleans, Chopin wrote stories that approached women's experiences from a woman's perspective. Chopin wrote stories about adultery, independence, miscegenation, and divorce, considered
unwholesome subjects in the late nineteenth century.

TOPICS FOR CRITICAL WRITING CD-ROM

1. Does the point of view of the third-person narrator change during the course of the
   story? What is the purpose of this shift?
2. How does point of view produce double meanings in some of the story's key phrases
   (such as "a heart trouble" and "the joy that kills")?
3. How does this story take advantage of those double meanings to illustrate women's
   feelings about cultural roles?
4. What is "the joy that kills"?

TOPICS FOR CRITICAL WRITING CD-ROM

1. Define the relations between the story's third-person narrator and its point of view.
   How are the points of view constructed? How do we know they are differing points
   of view?
2. Trace the connections made between what Louise sees and her changing perspective on life.

7 Theme

Stories are generally about something (even if, as in the case of the television sitcom *Seinfeld*, they are about "nothing"). The ideas that organize stories—that tie together characters, settings, plots, narrators, and points of view—are called **themes**. Themes may be many different kinds of ideas or feelings. They might consist of a political concept such as democracy, freedom, or oppression.

Themes about interpersonal issues such as friendship, betrayal, sacrifice, or loyalty may tie stories together. Themes might focus on questions about art and culture, such as the possibility of communication, the passion of creativity, or the importance of intangible qualities in a materialist society. Stories may have a single dominant theme or several related themes. Like the other elements of fiction, theme does not function by itself; nor is it a more important consideration than other elements. Theme works in a cooperative relation with other elements of fiction, defining them and being defined by them.

Unlike character, setting, and plot, however, theme is not always immediately apparent. Some kinds of stories (such as fables) have a message—a clear directive about behavior or values such as the lesson of the fable about the tortoise and the hare. But not all stories have a message, and the message is not always the same as the theme. Messages tend to be clear and straightforward, while themes are ideas, questions, and issues that often appear in more than one guise in any given story. For example, commercials have messages; stories, novels, and films have themes. Stories such as "The Birthmark" have more than one theme—the relation of man to nature, the possibility of perfection. A story such as "Bartleby the Scrivener" presents the themes of inaction and passivity through both the narrator and Bartleby.

A story's themes frequently must be deduced from its events and the way they are presented. For example, a character's motives may relate to a story's themes. A character might be greedy in a story about the avaricious superficiality of the rich. Or several characters may encounter different versions of the same dilemma; for example, they may each experience some aspect of their parents aging. Theme may be deduced from a story's events (as in Peyton Farquhar's desperate fantasy of escape in "An Occurrence at Owl Creek Bridge"), the conditions a story describes (as in the harshness of nature in "The Law of Life"), or a preoccupation of the narrator (as in Marlow's fixation on Kurtz in *Heart of Darkness*). Often readers discern theme by noticing the ways ideas in a story repeat themselves through multiple characters, plots, points of view, and settings. A good example of this is the connection between the decadence of the Ushers' house, the deathlike nature of Roderick Usher's appearance, and the end of the family line in "The Fall of the House of Usher."

Critical Perspective: Race Criticism

In Chapter 6, we looked at criticism focused around the perspectives of gender and sexuality. Gender and sexuality may appear both as themes and as part of the very fabric of language and prose fiction. Like gender and sexuality, race is an intrinsic component of the way we understand the world. Gender, sexual, and racial issues are depicted as both personal and social; they all provide both points of view and themes in prose fiction. Often, issues of gender, sexuality, and race are combined. Interpretations of fiction that focus on race—whether black, white, Asian, or Native American, for example—either as a theme or a perspective are called **race criticism**. **Web**

www

Critical Perspective: Marxist Criticism

Like gender, sexuality, and race, class is another lens through which experience is organized. Although Americans often believe that they live in a society without pronounced class differences, social class in part defines our use of language, our beliefs, and our possibilities. Some prose fiction focuses on class as a theme, portraying the effects of class differences or the experience of being a member of a particular class (particularly the lower class); stories about wealthy or upper class people tend not to see class as a problem. Other stories include class as an element defining character. Critics who study representations of class, the ways literature enacts the effects of economic disparity, and the material conditions and contexts within which stories are produced are called **Marxist or materialist critics**. **Web**

www

Stories About Race and Class

The following five stories focus on the themes of race and class. The first three center on the experiences of African Americans in American culture. Alice Walker's "Everyday Use" shows the effects of change and bourgeois ambition within a rural African American family. Featured author James Baldwin's "Previous Condition" portrays the discrimination experienced by a young African American man struggling in New York City. "Sonny's Blues" contrasts two brothers, one who has learned to survive in the city and the other who turns to drugs and music as a way to bear his existence. The final story—Tillie Olsen's "I Stand Here Ironing" —portrays the effects of having to struggle in a poor economy. Olsen's reminiscence of her daughter's childhood reviews the hardships of being a single mother during the Depression.

∽⟨⟩∽

ALICE WALKER

Everyday Use   *(1973)*

For Your Grandmama

I will wait for her in the yard that Maggie and I made so clean and wavy yesterday afternoon. A yard like this is more comfortable than most people know. It is not just a yard. It is like an extended living room. When the hard clay is swept clean as a floor and the fine sand around the edges lined with tiny, irregular grooves, anyone can come and sit and look up into the elm tree and wait for the breezes that never come inside the house.

Maggie will be nervous until after her sister goes: she will stand hopelessly in corners, homely and ashamed of the burn scars down her arms and legs, eying her sister with a mixture of envy and awe. She thinks her sister has held life always in the palm of one hand, that "no" is a word the world never learned to say to her.

You've no doubt seen those TV shows where the child who has "made it" is confronted, as a surprise, by her own mother and father, tottering in weakly from backstage. (A pleasant surprise, of course: What would they do if parent and child came on the show only to curse out and insult each other?) On TV mother and child embrace and smile into each other's faces. Sometimes the mother and father weep, the child wraps them in her arms and leans across the table to tell how she would not have made it without their help. I have seen these programs.

Sometimes I dream a dream in which Dee and I are suddenly brought together on a TV program of this sort. Out of a dark and soft-seated limousine I am ushered into a bright room filled with many people. There I meet a smiling, gray, sporty man like Johnny Carson who shakes my hand and tells me what a fine girl I have. Then we are on the stage and Dee is embracing me with tears in her eyes. She pins on my dress a large orchid, even though she has told me once that she thinks orchids are tacky flowers.

In real life I am a large, big-boned woman with rough, man-working   5
hands. In the winter I wear flannel nightgowns to bed and overalls during the day. I can kill and clean a hog as mercilessly as a man. My fat keeps me hot in zero weather. I can work outside all day, breaking ice to get water for washing; I can eat pork liver cooked over the open fire minutes after it comes steaming from the hog. One winter I knocked a bull calf straight in the brain between the eyes with a sledge hammer and had the meat hung up to chill before nightfall. But of course all this does not show on television. I am the way my daughter would want me to be: a hundred pounds lighter, my skin like an uncooked barley pancake. My hair glistens in the hot bright lights. Johnny Carson has much to do to keep up with my quick and witty tongue.

But that is a mistake. I know even before I wake up. Who ever knew a

Johnson with a quick tongue? Who can even imagine me looking a strange white man in the eye? It seems to me I have talked to them always with one foot raised in flight, with my head turned in whichever way is farthest from them. Dee, though. She would always look anyone in the eye. Hesitation was no part of her nature.

"How do I look, Mama?" Maggie says, showing just enough of her thin body enveloped in pink skirt and red blouse for me to know she's there, almost hidden by the door.

"Come out into the yard," I say.

Have you ever seen a lame animal, perhaps a dog run over by some careless person rich enough to own a car, sidle up to someone who is ignorant enough to be kind to him? That is the way my Maggie walks. She has been like this, chin on chest, eyes on ground, feet in shuffle, ever since the fire that burned the other house to the ground.

Dee is lighter than Maggie, with nicer hair and a fuller figure. She's a woman now, though sometimes I forget. How long ago was it that the other house burned? Ten, twelve years? Sometimes I can still hear the flames and feel Maggie's arms sticking to me, her hair smoking and her dress falling off her in little black papery flakes. Her eyes seemed stretched open, blazed open by the flames reflected in them. And Dee. I see her standing off under the sweet gum tree she used to dig gum out of; a look of concentration on her face as she watched the last dingy gray board of the house fall in toward the red-hot brick chimney. Why don't you do a dance around the ashes? I'd want to ask her. She had hated the house that much.

I used to think she hated Maggie, too. But that was before we raised the money, the church and me, to send her to Augusta to school. She used to read to us without pity; forcing words, lies, other folks' habits, whole lives upon us two, sitting trapped and ignorant underneath her voice. She washed us in a river of make-believe, burned us with a lot of knowledge we didn't necessarily need to know. Pressed us to her with the serious way she read, to shove us away at just the moment, like dimwits, we seemed about to understand.

Dee wanted nice things. A yellow organdy dress to wear to her graduation from high school; black pumps to match a green suit she'd made from an old suit somebody gave me. She was determined to stare down any disaster in her efforts. Her eyelids would not flicker for minutes at a time. Often I fought off the temptation to shake her. At sixteen she had a style of her own: and knew what style was.

I never had an education myself. After second grade the school was closed down. Don't ask me why: in 1927 colored asked fewer questions than they do now. Sometimes Maggie reads to me. She stumbles along good-naturedly but can't see well. She knows she is not bright. Like good looks and money, quickness passed her by. She will marry John Thomas (who has mossy teeth in an earnest face) and then I'll be free to sit here and I guess just sing church songs to myself. Although I never was a good singer. Never could carry a tune. I was always better at a man's job. I used to love to milk till I was hooked in the side in '49. Cows are soothing and slow and don't bother you, unless you try to milk them the wrong way.

I have deliberately turned my back on the house. It is three rooms, just like the one that burned, except the roof is tin; they don't make shingle roofs any more. There are no real windows, just some holes cut in the sides, like the portholes in a ship, but not round and not square, with rawhide holding the shutters up on the outside. This house is in a pasture, too, like the other one. No doubt when Dee sees it she will want to tear it down. She wrote me once that no matter where we "choose" to live, she will manage to come see us. But she will never bring her friends. Maggie and I thought about this and Maggie asked me, "Mama, when did Dee ever *have* any friends?"

She had a few. Furtive boys in pink shirts hanging about on washday after 15 school. Nervous girls who never laughed. Impressed with her they worshipped the well-turned phrase, the cute shape, the scalding humor that erupted like bubbles in lye. She read to them.

When she was courting Jimmy T she didn't have much time to pay to us, but turned all her faultfinding power on him. He *flew* to marry a cheap city girl from a family of ignorant flashy people. She hardly had time to recompose herself.

When she comes I will meet—but there they are!

Maggie attempts to make a dash for the house, in her shuffling way, but I stay her with my hand. "Come back here," I say. And she stops and tries to dig a well in the sand with her toe.

It is hard to see them clearly through the strong sun. But even the first glimpse of leg out of the car tells me it is Dee. Her feet were always neat looking, as if God himself had shaped them with a certain style. From the other side of the car comes a short, stocky man. Hair is all over his head a foot long and hanging from his chin like a kinky mule tail. I hear Maggie suck in her breath. "Uhnnnh," is what it sounds like. Like when you see the wriggling end of a snake just in front of your foot on the road. "Uhnnnh."

Dee next. A dress down to the ground, in this hot weather. A dress so loud 20 it hurts my eyes. There are yellows and oranges enough to throw back the light of the sun. I feel my whole face warming from the heat waves it throws out. Earrings gold, too, and hanging down to her shoulders. Bracelets dangling and making noises when she moves her arm up to shake the folds of the dress out of her armpits. The dress is loose and flows, and as she walks closer, I like it. I hear Maggie go "Uhnnnh" again. It is her sister's hair. It stands straight up like the wool on a sheep. It is black as night and around the edges are two long pigtails that rope about like small lizards disappearing behind her ears.

"Wa-su-zo-Tean-o!" she says, coming on in that gliding way the dress makes her move. The short stocky fellow with the hair to his navel is all grinning and he follows up with "Asalamalakim,[1] my mother and sister!" He moves to hug Maggie but she falls back, right up against the back of my chair.

---

1. The mother assumes that this is the young man's name. Actually, it is an Islamic salutation, "Peace be with you."

I feel her trembling there and when I look up I see the perspiration falling off her chin.

"Don't get up," says Dee. Since I am stout it takes something of a push. You can see me trying to move a second or two before I make it. She turns, showing white heels through her sandals, and goes back to the car. Out she peeks next with a Polaroid. She stoops down quickly and lines up picture after picture of me sitting there in front of the house with Maggie cowering behind me. She never takes a shot without making sure the house is included. When a cow comes nibbling around the edge of the yard she snaps it and me and Maggie *and* the house. Then she puts the Polaroid in the back seat of the car, and comes up and kisses me on the forehead.

Meanwhile Asalamalakim is going through motions with Maggie's hand. Maggie's hand is as limp as a fish, and probably as cold, despite the sweat, and she keeps trying to pull it back. It looks like Asalamalakim wants to shake hands but wants to do it fancy. Or maybe he don't know how people shake hands. Anyhow, he soon gives up on Maggie.

"Well," I say. "Dee."

"No, Mama," she says. "Not 'Dee,' Wangero Leewanika Kemanjo!"   25

"What happened to 'Dee'?" I wanted to know.

"She's dead," Wangero said. "I couldn't bear it any longer, being named after the people who oppress me."

"You know as well as me you was named after your aunt Dicie," I said. Dicie is my sister. She named Dee. We called her "Big Dee" after Dee was born.

"But who was *she* named after?" asked Wangero.

"I guess after Grandma Dee," I said.   30

"And who was she named after?" asked Wangero.

"Her mother," I said, and saw Wangero was getting tired. "That's about as far back as I can trace it," I said. Though, in fact, I probably could have carried it back beyond the Civil War through the branches.

"Well," said Asalamalakim, "there you are."

"Uhnnnh," I heard Maggie say.

"There I was not," I said, "before 'Dicie' cropped up in our family, so why   35
should I try to trace it that far back?"

He just stood there grinning, looking down on me like somebody inspecting a Model A car. Every once in a while he and Wangero sent eye signals over my head.

"How do you pronounce this name?" I asked.

"You don't have to call me by it if you don't want to," said Wangero.

"Why shouldn't I?" I asked. "If that's what you want us to call you, we'll call you."

"I know it might sound awkward at first," said Wangero.   40

"I'll get used to it," I said. "Ream it out again."

Well, soon we got the name out of the way. Asalamalakim had a name twice as long and three times as hard. After I tripped over it two or three times he told me to just call him Hakim-a-barber. I wanted to ask him was he a barber, but I didn't really think he was, so I didn't ask.

"You must belong to those beef-cattle peoples down the road," I said. They said "Asalamalakim" when they met you, too, but they didn't shake hands. Always too busy: feeding the cattle, fixing the fences, putting up salt-lick shelters, throwing down hay. When the white folks poisoned some of the herd the men stayed up all night with rifles in their hands. I walked a mile and a half just to see the sight.

Hakim-a-barber said, "I accept some of their doctrines, but farming and raising cattle is not my style." (They didn't tell me, and I didn't ask, whether Wangero (Dee) had really gone and married him.)

We sat down to eat and right away he said he didn't eat collards and pork   45 was unclean. Wangero, though, went on through the chitlins and corn bread, the greens and everything else. She talked a blue streak over the sweet pota-toes. Everything delighted her. Even the fact that we still used the benches her daddy made for the table when we couldn't afford to buy chairs.

"Oh, Mama!" she cried. Then turned to Hakim-a-barber. "I never knew how lovely these benches are. You can feel the rump prints," she said, running her hands underneath her and long the bench. Then she gave a sigh and her hand closed over Grandma Dee's butter dish. "That's it!" she said. "I knew there was something I wanted to ask you if I could have." She jumped up from the table and went over in the corner where the churn stood, the milk in it clabber by now. She looked at the churn and looked at it.

"This churn top is what I need," she said. "Didn't Uncle Buddy whittle it out of a tree you all used to have?"

"Yes," I said.

"Uh huh," she said happily. "And I want the dasher, too."

"Uncle Buddy whittle that, too?" asked the barber.   50

Dee (Wangero) looked up at me.

"Aunt Dee's first husband whittled the dash," said Maggie so low you al-most couldn't hear her. "His name was Henry, but they called him Stash."

"Maggie's brain is like an elephant's," Wangero said, laughing. "I can use the churn top as a centerpiece for the alcove table," she said, sliding a plate over the churn, "and I'll think of something artistic to do with the dasher."

When she finished wrapping the dasher the handle stuck out. I took it for a moment in my hands. You didn't even have to look close to see where hands pushing the dasher up and down to make butter had left a kind of sink in the wood. In fact, there were a lot of small sinks; you could see where thumbs and fingers had sunk into the wood. It was beautiful light yellow wood, from a tree that grew in the yard where Big Dee and Stash had lived.

After dinner Dee (Wangero) went to the trunk at the foot of my bed and   55 started rifling through it. Maggie hung back in the kitchen over the dishpan. Out came Wangero with two quilts. They had been pieced by Grandma Dee and then Big Dee and me had hung them on the quilt frames on the front porch and quilted them. One was in the Lone Star pattern. The other was Walk Around the Mountain. In both of them were scraps of dresses Grandma Dee had worn fifty and more years ago. Bits and pieces of Grandpa Jarrell's Paisley shirts. And one teeny faded blue piece, about the size of a penny matchbox, that was from Great Grandpa Ezra's uniform that he wore in the Civil War.

"Mama," Wangero said sweet as a bird. "Can I have these old quilts?"

I heard something fall in the kitchen, and a minute later the kitchen door slammed.

"Why don't you take one or two of the others?" I asked. "These old things was just done by me and Big Dee from some tops your grandma pieced before she died."

"No," said Wangero. "I don't want those. They are stitched around the borders by machine."

"That'll make them last better," I said.   60

"That's not the point," said Wangero. "These are all pieces of dresses Grandma used to wear. She did all this stitching by hand. Imagine!" She held the quilts securely in her arms, stroking them.

"Some of the pieces, like those lavender ones, come from old clothes her mother handed down to her," I said, moving up to touch the quilts. Dee (Wangero) moved back just enough so that I couldn't reach the quilts. They already belonged to her.

"Imagine!" she breathed again, clutching them closely to her bosom.

"The truth is," I said, "I promised to give them quilts to Maggie, for when she marries John Thomas."

She gasped like a bee had stung her.   65

"Maggie can't appreciate these quilts!" she said. "She'd probably be back-ward enough to put them to everyday use."

"I reckon she would," I said. "God knows I been saving 'em for long enough with nobody using 'em. I hope she will!" I didn't want to bring up how I had offered Dee (Wangero) a quilt when she went away to college. Then she had told me they were old-fashioned, out of style.

"But they're *priceless!*" she was saying now, furiously; for she has a temper. "Maggie would put them on the bed and in five years they'd be in rags. Less than that!"

"She can always make some more," I said. "Maggie knows how to quilt."

Dee (Wangero) looked at me with hatred. "You just will not understand.   70 The point is these quilts, *these* quilts!"

"Well," I said, stumped. "What would *you* do with them?"

"Hang them," she said. As if that was the only thing you *could* do with quilts.

Maggie by now was standing in the door. I could almost hear the sound her feet made as they scraped over each other.

"She can have them, Mama," she said, like somebody used to never win-ning anything, or having anything reserved for her. "I can 'member Grandma Dee without the quilts."

I looked at her hard. She had filled her bottom lip with checkerberry   75 snuff and it gave her face a kind of dopey, hangdog look. It was Grandma Dee and Big Dee who taught her how to quilt herself. She stood there with her scarred hands hidden in the folds of her skirt. She looked at her sister with something like fear but she wasn't mad at her. This was Maggie's portion. This was the way she knew God to work.

When I looked at her like that something hit me in the top of my head and ran down to the soles of my feet. Just like when I'm in church and the spirit of God touches me and I get happy and shout. I did something I never had done before: hugged Maggie to me, then dragged her on into the room, snatched the quilts out of Miss Wangero's hands and dumped them into Maggie's lap. Maggie just sat there on my bed with her mouth open.

"Take one or two of the others," I said to Dee.

But she turned without a word and went out to Hakim-a-barber.

"You just don't understand," she said, as Maggie and I came out to the car.

"What don't I understand?" I wanted to know.   80

"Your heritage," she said. And then she turned to Maggie, kissed her, and said, "You ought to try to make something of yourself, too, Maggie. It's really a new day for us. But from the way you and Mama still live you'd never know it."

She put on some sunglasses that hid everything above the tip of her nose and her chin.

Maggie smiled; maybe at the sunglasses. But a real smile, not scared. After we watched the car dust settle I asked Maggie to bring me a dip of snuff. And then the two of us sat there just enjoying, until it was time to go in the house and go to bed.

ALICE WALKER

(b. 1944) Web   *www*

Winner of a Guggenheim Fellowship, Walker is the author of novels such as *The Color Purple* (1982), short stories, essays and poetry. She quit teaching to devote full-time to writing and activism, working for causes such as women's rights, anti-apartheid, and civil rights. Her work is both realist and mythical, the pragmatic reverberating meanings beyond its "everyday use."

TOPICS FOR CRITICAL THINKING Web   *www*

1. Are differences in perception in the story merely a function of generation?
2. What does "heritage" mean?
3. How do objects in the story reflect the story's themes?

TOPICS FOR CRITICAL WRITING Web   *www*

1. What might "everyday use" mean?
2. What different narratives of their history do the narrator and Dee have? What clues does the story provide about these narratives?

Featured Writer

JAMES BALDWIN CD-ROM

Previous Condition   *(1948)*

I woke up shaking, alone in my room. I was clammy cold with sweat; under me the sheet and the mattress were soaked. The sheet was gray and twisted like a rope. I breathed like I had been running.

I couldn't move for the longest while. I just lay on my back, spread-eagled, looking up at the ceiling, listening to the sounds of people getting up in other parts of the house, alarm clocks ringing and water splashing and doors opening and shutting and feet on the stairs. I could tell when people left for work: the hall doorway downstairs whined and shuffled as it opened and gave a funny kind of double slam as it closed. One thud and then a louder thud and then a little final click. While the door was open I could hear the street sounds too, horses' hoofs and delivery wagons and people in the streets and big trucks and motor cars screaming on the asphalt.

I had been dreaming. At night I dreamt and woke up in the morning trembling, but not remembering the dream, except that in the dream I had been running. I could not remember when the dream—or dreams—had started; it had been long ago. For long periods maybe, I would have no dreams at all. And then they would come back, every night, I would try not to go to bed, I would go to sleep frightened and wake up frightened and have another day to get through with the nightmare at my shoulder. Now I was back from Chicago, busted, living off my friends in a dirty furnished room downtown. The show I had been with had folded in Chicago. It hadn't been much of a part—or much of a show either, to tell the truth. I played a kind of intellectual Uncle Tom, a young college student working for his race. The playwright had wanted to prove he was a liberal, I guess. But, as I say, the show had folded and here I was, back in New York and hating it. I knew that I should be getting another job, making the rounds, pounding the pavement. But I didn't. I couldn't face it. It was summer. I seemed to be fagged out. And every day I hated myself more. Acting's a rough life, even if you're white. I'm not tall and I'm not good looking and I can't sing or dance and I'm not white; so even at the best of times I wasn't in much demand.

The room I lived in was heavy ceilinged, perfectly square, with walls the color of chipped dry blood. Jules Weissman, a Jewboy, had got the room for me. It's a room to sleep in, he said, or maybe to die in but God knows it wasn't meant to live in. Perhaps because the room was so hideous it had a fantastic array of light fixtures: one on the ceiling, one on the left wall, two on the right wall, and a lamp on the table beside my bed. My bed was in front of the window through which nothing ever blew but dust. It was a furnished room and they'd thrown enough stuff in it to furnish three rooms its size. Two easy chairs and a desk, the bed, the table, a straight-backed chair, a bookcase, a cardboard wardrobe; and my books and my suitcase, both unpacked; and my dirty clothes flung in a corner. It was the kind of room that defeated you. It had a fireplace, too, and a heavy marble mantelpiece and a great gray mirror above the mantelpiece. It was hard to see anything in the mirror very clearly—which was perhaps just as well—and it would have been worth your life to have started a fire in the fireplace.

"Well, you won't have to stay here long," Jules told me the night I came.   5
Jules smuggled me in, sort of, after dark, when everyone had gone to bed.

"Christ, I hope not."

"I'll be moving to a big place soon," Jules said. "You can move in with me." He turned all the lights on. "Think it'll be all right for a while?" He sounded apologetic, as though he had designed the room himself.

"Oh, sure. D'you think I'll have any trouble?"

"I don't think so. The rent's paid. She can't put you out."

I didn't say anything to that.   10

"Sort of stay undercover," Jules said. "You know."

"Roger," I said.

I had been living there for three days, timing it so I left after everyone else had gone, coming back late at night when everyone else was asleep. But I knew it wouldn't work. A couple of the tenants had seen me on the stairs, a woman had surprised me coming out of the john. Every morning I waited for the landlady to come banging on the door. I didn't know what would happen. It might be all right. It might not be. But the waiting was getting me.

The sweat on my body was turning cold. Downstairs a radio was tuned in to the Breakfast Symphony. They were playing Beethoven. I sat up and lit a cigarette. "Peter," I said, "don't let them scare you to death. You're a man, too." I listened to Ludwig and I watched the smoke rise to the dirty ceiling. Under Ludwig's drums and horns I listened to hear footsteps on the stairs.

I'd done a lot of traveling in my time. I'd knocked about through St.   15
Louis, Frisco, Seattle, Detroit, New Orleans, worked at just about everything. I'd run away from my old lady when I was about sixteen. She'd never been able to handle me. You'll never be nothin' *but* a bum, she'd say. We lived in an old shack in a town in New Jersey in the nigger part of town, the kind of houses colored people live in all over the U.S. I hated my mother for living there. I hated all the people in my neighborhood. They went to church and they got drunk. They were nice to the white people. When the landlord came around they paid him and took his crap.

The first time I was ever called nigger I was seven years old. It was a little white girl with long black curls. I used to leave the front of my house and go wandering by myself through town. This little girl was playing ball alone and as I passed her the ball rolled out of her hands into the gutter.

I threw it back to her.

"Let's play catch," I said.

But she held the ball and made a face at me.

"My mother don't let me play with niggers," she told me.   20

I did not know what the word meant. But my skin grew warm. I stuck my tongue out at her.

"I don't care. Keep your old ball." I started down the street.

She screamed after me: "Nigger, nigger, nigger!"

I screamed back: "Your mother was a nigger!"

I asked my mother what a nigger was.   25

"Who called you that?"

"I heard somebody say it."

"Who?"

"Just somebody."

"Go wash your face," she said. "You dirty as sin. Your supper's on the   30
table."

I went to the bathroom and splashed water on my face and wiped my face and hands on the towel.

"You call that clean?" my mother cried. "Come here, boy!"

She dragged me back to the bathroom and began to soap my face and neck.

"You run around dirty like you do all the time, everybody'll call you a little nigger, you hear?" She rinsed my face and looked at my hands and dried me. "Now, go on and eat your supper."

I didn't say anything. I went to the kitchen and sat down at the table. I re- 35
member I wanted to cry. My mother sat down across from me.

"Mama," I said. She looked at me. I started to cry.

She came around to my side of the table and took me in her arms.

"Baby, don't fret. Next time somebody calls you nigger you tell them you'd rather be your color than be lowdown and nasty like some white folks is."

We formed gangs when I was older, my friends and I. We met white boys and their friends on the opposite sides of fences and we threw rocks and tin cans at each other.

I'd come home bleeding. My mother would slap me and scold me and cry.   40

"Boy, you wanna get killed? You wanna end up like your father?"

My father was a bum and I had never seen him. I was named for him: Peter.

I was always in trouble: truant officers, welfare workers, everybody else in town.

"You ain't never gonna be nothin' *but* a bum," my mother said.

By and by older kids I knew finished school and got jobs and got married   45
and settled down. They were going to settle down and bring more black babies into the world and pay the same rents for the same old shacks and it would go on and on—

When I was sixteen I ran away. I left a note and told Mama not to worry, I'd come back one day and I'd be all right. But when I was twenty-two she died. I came back and put my mother in the ground. Everything was like it had been. Our house had not been painted and the porch floor sagged and there was somebody's raincoat stuffed in the broken window. Another family was moving in.

Their furniture was stacked along the walls and their children were running through the house and laughing and somebody was frying pork chops in the kitchen. The oldest boy was tacking up a mirror.

Last year Ida took me driving in her big car and we passed through a couple of towns upstate. We passed some crumbling houses on the left. The clothes on the line were flying in the wind.

"Are people living there?" asked Ida.

"Just darkies," I said.

Ida passed the car ahead, banging angrily on the horn. "D'you know you're becoming paranoiac, Peter?"

"All right. All right. I know a lot of white people are starving too."

"You're damn right they are. I know a little about poverty myself."

Ida had come from the kind of family called shanty Irish. She was raised in Boston. She's a very beautiful woman who married young and married for money—so now I can afford to support attractive young men, she'd giggle. Her husband was a ballet dancer who was forever on the road. Ida suspected that he went with boys. Not that I give a damn, she said, as long as he leaves me alone. When we met last year she was thirty and I was twenty-five. We had a pretty stormy relationship but we stuck. Whenever I got to town I called her; whenever I was stranded out of town I'd let her know. We never let it get too serious. She went her way and I went mine.

In all this running around I'd learned a few things. Like a prizefighter learns to take a blow or a dancer learns to fall, I'd learned how to get by. I'd learned never to be belligerent with policemen, for instance. No matter who was right, I was certain to be wrong. What might be accepted as just good old American independence in someone else would be insufferable arrogance in me. After the first few times I realized that I had to play smart, to act out the role I was expected to play. I only had one head and it was too easy to get it broken. When I faced a policeman I acted like I didn't know a thing. I let my jaw drop and I let my eyes get big. I didn't give him any smart answers, none of the crap about my rights. I figured out what answers he wanted and I gave them to him. I never let him think he wasn't king. If it was more than routine, if I was picked up on suspicion of robbery or murder in the neighborhood, I looked as humble as I could and kept my mouth shut and prayed. I took a couple of beatings but I stayed out of prison and I stayed off chain gangs. That was also due to luck, Ida pointed out once. "Maybe it would've been better for you if you'd been a little less lucky. Worse things have happened than chain gangs. Some of them have happened to you."

There was something in her voice. "What are you talking about?" I asked.

"Don't lose your temper. I said maybe."

"You mean you think I'm a coward?"

"I didn't say that, Peter."

"But you meant that. Didn't you?"

"No. I didn't mean that. I didn't mean anything. Let's not fight."

There are times and places when a Negro can use his color like a shield. He can trade on the subterranean Anglo-Saxon guilt and get what he wants that way; or some of what he wants. He can trade on his nuisance value, his value as forbidden fruit; he can use it like a knife, he can twist it and get his vengeance that way. I knew these things long before I realized that I knew them and in the beginning I used them, not knowing what I was doing. Then when I began to see it, I felt betrayed. I felt beaten as a person. I had no honest place to stand.

This was the year before I met Ida. I'd been acting in stock companies and little theaters; sometimes fairly good parts. People were nice to me. They told me I had talent. They said it sadly, as though they were thinking, What a pity, he'll never get anywhere. I had got to the point where I resented praise and I resented pity and I wondered what people were thinking when they shook my hand. In New York I met some pretty fine people; easygoing, hard-drinking, flotsam and jetsam; and they liked me; and I wondered if I trusted them; if I was able any longer to trust anybody. Not on top, where all the world could see, but underneath where everybody lives.

Soon I would have to get up. I listened to Ludwig. He shook the little room like the footsteps of a giant marching miles away. On summer evenings (and maybe we would go this summer) Jules and Ida and I would go up to the Stadium and sit beneath the pillars on the cold stone steps. There it seemed to me the sky was far away; and I was not myself, I was high and lifted up. We never talked, the three of us. We sat and watched the blue smoke curl in the air and watched the orange tips of cigarettes. Every once in a while the boys who sold popcorn and soda pop and ice cream climbed the steep steps chattering; and Ida shifted slightly and touched her blue-black hair; and Jules scowled. I sat with my knee up watching the lighted half-moon below, the black-coated, straining conductor, the faceless men beneath him moving together in a rhythm like the sea. There were pauses in the music for the rushing, calling, halting piano. Everything would stop except the climbing soloist; he would reach a height and everything would join him, the violins first and then the horns; and then the deep blue bass and the flute and the bitter trampling drums; beating, beating and mounting together and stopping with a crash like daybreak. When I first heard the *Messiah* I was alone; my blood bubbled like fire and wine; I cried; like an infant crying for its mother's milk; or a sinner running to meet Jesus.

Now below the music I heard footsteps on the stairs. I put out my ciga- 65
rette. My heart was beating so hard I thought it would tear my chest apart. Someone knocked on the door.

I thought: Don't answer. Maybe she'll go away.

But the knocking came again, harder this time.

Just a minute, I said. I sat on the edge of the bed and put on my bathrobe. I was trembling like a fool. For Christ's sake, Peter, you've been through this before. What's the worst thing that can happen? You won't have a room. The world's full of rooms.

When I opened the door the landlady stood there, red-and-whitefaced and hysterical.

"Who are you? I didn't rent this room to you."   70

My mouth was dry. I started to say something.

"I can't have no colored people here," she said. "All my tenants are complainin'. Women afraid to come home nights."

"They ain't gotta be afraid of me," I said. I couldn't get my voice up; it rasped and rattled in my throat; and I began to be angry. I wanted to kill her. "My friend rented this room for me," I said.

"Well, I'm sorry, he didn't have no right to do that, I don't have nothin' against you, but you gotta get out."

Her glasses blinked, opaque in the light on the landing. She was fright-   75
ened to death. She was afraid of me but she was more afraid of losing her tenants. Her face was mottled with rage and fear, her breath came rushed and little bits of spittle gathered at the edges of her mouth; her breath smelled bad, like rotting hamburger on a July day.

"You can't put me out," I said. "This room was rented in my name." I started to close the door, as though the matter was finished: "I live here, see, this is my room, you can't put me out."

"You get outa my house!" she screamed. "I got the right to know who's in my house! This is a white neighborhood, I don't rent to colored people. Why don't you go on uptown, like you belong?"

"I can't stand niggers," I told her. I started to close the door again but she moved and stuck her foot in the way. I wanted to kill her, I watched her stupid, wrinkled, frightened white face and I wanted to take a club, a hatchet, and bring it down with all my weight, splitting her skull down the middle where she parted her iron-grey hair.

"Get out of the door," I said. "I want to get dressed."

But I knew that she had won, that I was already on my way. We stared at   80
each other. Neither of us moved. From her came an emanation of fear and fury and something else. You maggot-eaten bitch, I thought. I said evilly, "You wanna come in and watch me?" Her face didn't change, she didn't take her foot away. My skin prickled, tiny hot needles punctured my flesh. I was aware of my body under the bathrobe; and it was as though I had done something wrong, something monstrous, years ago, which no one had forgotten and for which I would be killed.

"If you don't get out," she said, "I'll get a policeman to put you out."

I grabbed the door to keep from touching her. "All right. All right. You can have the goddamn room. Now get out and let me dress."

She turned away. I slammed the door. I heard her going down the stairs. I threw stuff into my suitcase. I tried to take as long as possible but I cut myself while shaving because I was afraid she would come back upstairs with a policeman.

Jules was making coffee when I walked in.

"Good morning, good morning! What happened to you?"   85

"No room at the inn," I said. "Pour a cup of coffee for the notorious son of man." I sat down and dropped my suitcase on the floor.

Jules looked at me. "Oh. Well. Coffee coming up."

He got out the coffee cups. I lit a cigarette and sat there. I couldn't think of anything to say. I knew that Jules felt bad and I wanted to tell him that it wasn't his fault.

He pushed coffee in front of me and sugar and cream.

"Cheer up, baby. The world's wide and life—life, she is very long."   90

"Shut up. I don't want to hear any of your bad philosophy."

"Sorry."

"I mean, let's not talk about the good, the true, and the beautiful."

"All right. But don't sit there holding onto your table manners. Scream if you want to."

"Screaming won't do any good. Besides I'm a big boy now."   95

I stirred my coffee. "Did you give her a fight?" Jules asked.

I shook my head. "No."

"Why the hell not?"

I shrugged; a little ashamed now. I couldn't have won it. What the hell.

"You might have won it. You might have given her a couple of bad mo-   100
ments."

"Goddamit to hell, I'm sick of it. Can't I get a place to sleep without dragging it through the courts? I'm goddamn tired of battling every Tom, Dick, and Harry for what everybody else takes for granted. I'm tired, man, tired! Have you ever been sick to death of something? Well, I'm sick to death. And I'm scared. I've been fighting so goddamn long I'm not a person any more. I'm not Booker T. Washington. I've got no vision of emancipating anybody. I want to emancipate myself. If this goes on much longer, they'll send me to Bellevue, I'll blow my top, I'll break somebody's head. I'm not worried about that miserable little room. I'm worried about what's happening to me, *to me*, inside. I don't walk the streets, I crawl. I've never been like this before. Now when I go to a strange place I wonder what will happen, will I be accepted, if I'm accepted, can I accept?—"

"Take it easy," Jules said.

"Jules, I'm beaten."

"I don't think you are. Drink your coffee."

"Oh," I cried, "I know you think I'm making it dramatic, that I'm para-   105
noiac and just inventing trouble! Maybe I think so sometimes, how can I tell? You get so used to being hit you find you're always waiting for it. Oh, I know, you're Jewish, you get kicked around, too, but you can walk into a bar and nobody *knows* you're Jewish and if you go looking for a job you'll get a better job than mine! How can I say what it feels like? I don't know. I know everybody's in trouble and nothing is easy, but how can I explain to you what it feels like to be black when I don't understand it and don't want to and spend all my time trying to forget it? I don't want to hate anybody—but now maybe, I can't love anybody either—are we friends? Can we be really friends?"

"We're friends," Jules said, "don't worry about it." He scowled. "If I wasn't Jewish I'd ask you why you didn't live in Harlem." I looked at him. He raised his hand and smiled— "But I'm Jewish, so I didn't ask you. Ah Peter," he said, "I can't help you—take a walk, get drunk, we're all in this together."

I stood up. "I'll be around later. I'm sorry."

"Don't be sorry. I'll leave my door open. Bunk here for awhile."

"Thanks," I said.

I felt that I was drowning; that hatred had corrupted me like cancer in the   110
bone.

I saw Ida for dinner. We met in a restaurant in the Village, an Italian place in a gloomy cellar with candles on the tables.

It was not a busy night, for which I was grateful. When I came in there were only two other couples on the other side of the room. No one looked at me. I sat down in a corner booth and ordered a Scotch old-fashioned. Ida was late and I had three of them before she came.

She was very fine in black, a high-necked dress with a pearl choker; and her hair was combed page-boy style, falling just below her ears.

"You look real sweet, baby."

"Thank you. It took fifteen extra minutes but I hoped it would be   115
worth it."

"It was worth it. What're you drinking?"

"Oh—what're you drinking?"

"Old-fashioneds."

She sniffed and looked at me. "How many?"

I laughed. "Three."   120

"Well," she said, "I suppose you had to do something." The waiter came over. We decided on one Manhattan and one lasagna and one spaghetti with clam sauce and another old-fashioned for me.

"Did you have a constructive day, sweetheart? Find a job?"

"Not today," I said. I lit her cigarette. "Metro offered me a fortune to come to the coast and do the lead in *Native Son* but I turned it down. Type casting, you know. It's so difficult to find a decent part."

"Well, if they don't come up with a decent offer soon tell them you'll go back to Selznick. *He'll* find you a part with guts—the very *idea* of offering you *Native Son!* I wouldn't stand for it."

"You ain't gotta tell me. I told them if they didn't find me a decent script   125
in two weeks I was through, that's all."

"Now that's talking, Peter my lad."

The drinks came and we sat in silence for a minute or two. I finished half of my drink at a swallow and played with the toothpicks on the table. I felt Ida watching me.

"Peter, you're going to be awfully drunk."

"Honeychile, the first thing a southern gentleman learns is how to hold his liquor."

"That myth is older than the rock of ages. And anyway you come from   130
Jersey."

I finished my drink and snarled at her: "That's just as good as the South."

Across the table from me I could see that she was readying herself for trouble: her mouth tightened slightly, setting her chin so that the faint cleft showed: "What happened to you today?"

I resented her concern; I resented my need. "Nothing worth talking about," I muttered, "just a mood."

And I tried to smile at her, to wipe away the bitterness.

"Now I know something's the matter. Please tell me."   135

It sounded trivial as hell: "You know the room Jules found for me? Well, the landlady kicked me out of it today."

"God save the American republic," Ida said. "D'you want to waste some of my husband's money? We can sue her."

"Forget it. I'll end up with lawsuits in every state in the union."

"Still, as a gesture—"

"The devil with the gesture. I'll get by."   140

The food came. I didn't want to eat. The first mouthful hit my belly like a gong. Ida began cutting up lasagna.

"Peter," she said, "try not to feel so badly. We're all in this together, the whole world. Don't let it throw you. What can't be helped you have to learn to live with."

"That's easy for you to say," I told her.

She looked at me quickly and looked away. "I'm not pretending that it's easy to do," she said.

I didn't believe that she could really understand it; and there was nothing   145
I could say. I sat like a child being scolded, looking down at my plate, not eating, not saying anything. I wanted her to stop talking, to stop being intelligent about it, to stop being calm and grown-up about it; good Lord, none of us has ever grown up, we never will.

"It's no better anywhere else," she was saying. "In all of Europe there's famine and disease, in France and England they hate the Jews—nothing's going to change, baby, people are too empty-headed, too empty-hearted—it's always been like that, people always try to destroy what they don't understand—and they hate almost everything because they understand so little—"

I began to sweat in my side of the booth. I wanted to stop her voice. I wanted her to eat and be quiet and leave me alone. I looked around for the waiter so I could order another drink. But he was on the far side of the restaurant, waiting on some people who had just come in; a lot of people had come in since we had been sitting there.

"Peter," Ida said, "Peter please don't look like that."

I grinned: the painted grin of the professional clown. "Don't worry, baby, I'm all right. I know what I'm going to do. I'm gonna go back to my people where I belong and find me a nice, black nigger wench and raise me a flock of babies."

Ida had an old maternal trick; the grin tricked her into using it now. She   150
raised her fork and rapped me with it across the knuckles. "Now, stop that. You're too old for that."

I screamed and stood up screaming and knocked the candle over: "Don't *do* that, you bitch, don't *ever* do that!"

She grabbed the candle and set it up and glared at me. Her face had turned perfectly white: "Sit down! Sit *down!*"

I fell back into my seat. My stomach felt like water. Everyone was looking at us. I turned cold, seeing what they were seeing: a black boy and a white woman, alone together. I knew it would take nothing to have them at my throat.

"I'm sorry," I muttered, "I'm sorry, I'm sorry."

The waiter was at my elbow. "Is everything all right, miss?"   155

"Yes, quite, thank you." She sounded like a princess dismissing a slave. I didn't look up. The shadow of the waiter moved away from me.

"Baby," Ida said, "forgive me, please forgive me."

I stared at the tablecloth. She put her hand on mine, brightness and blackness.

"Let's go," I said, "I'm terribly sorry."

She motioned for the check. When it came she handed the I waiter a ten   160
dollar bill without looking. She picked up her bag.

"Shall we go to a nightclub or a movie or something?"

"No, honey, not tonight." I looked at her. "I'm tired, I think I'll go on over to Jules's place. I'm gonna sleep on his floor for a while. Don't worry about me. I'm all right."

She looked at me steadily. She said: "I'll come see you tomorrow?"

"Yes, baby, please."

The waiter brought the change and she tipped him. We stood up; as we   165
passed the tables (not looking at the people) the ground under me seemed falling, the doorway seemed impossibly far away. All my muscles tensed; I seemed ready to spring; I was waiting for the blow.

I put my hands in my pockets and we walked to the end of the block. The lights were green and red, the lights from the theater across the street exploded blue and yellow, off and on.

"Peter?"

"Yes?"

"I'll see you tomorrow?"

"Yeah. Come by Jules's. I'll wait for you."   170

"Goodnight, darling."

"Goodnight."

I started to walk away. I felt her eyes on my back. I kicked a bottle-top on the sidewalk.

God save the American republic.

I dropped into the subway and got on an uptown train, not knowing   175
where it was going and not caring. Anonymous, islanded people surrounded me, behind newspapers, behind make-up, fat, fleshy masks and flat eyes. I watched the empty faces. (No one looked at me.) I looked at the ads, unreal women and pink-cheeked men selling cigarettes, candy, shaving cream, nightgowns, chewing gum, movies, sex; sex without organs, drier than sand and more secret than death. The train stopped. A white boy and a white girl got

on. She was nice, short, svelte. Nice legs. She was hanging on his arm. He was the football type, blond, ruddy. They were dressed in summer clothes. The wind from the doors blew her print dress. She squealed, holding the dress at the knees and giggled and looked at him. He said something I didn't catch and she looked at me and the smile died. She stood so that she faced him and had her back to me. I looked back at the ads. Then I hated them. I wanted to do something to make them hurt, something that would crack the pink-cheeked mask. The white boy and I did not look at each other again. They got off at the next stop.

I wanted to keep on drinking. I got off in Harlem and went to a rundown bar on Seventh Avenue. My people, my people. Sharpies stood on the corner, waiting. Women in summer dresses pranced by on wavering heels. Click clack. Click clack. There were white mounted policemen in the streets. On every block there was another policeman on foot. I saw a black cop.

God save the American republic.

The juke box was letting loose with "Hamps' Boogie." The place was jumping, I walked over to the man.

"Rye," I said.

I was standing next to somebody's grandmother. "Hello, papa. What you   180
puttin' down?"

"Baby, you can't pick it up," I told her. My rye came and I drank.

"Nigger," she said, "you must think you's somebody."

I didn't answer. She turned away, back to her beer, keeping time to the juke box, her face sullen and heavy and aggrieved. I watched her out of the side of my eye. She had been good looking once, pretty even, before she hit the bottle and started crawling into too many beds. She was flabby now, flesh heaved all over in her thin dress. I wondered what she'd be like in bed; then I realized that I was a little excited by her; I laughed and set my glass down.

"The same," I said. "And a beer chaser."

The juke box was playing something else now, something brassy and   185
commercial which I didn't like. I kept on drinking, listening to the voices of my people, watching the faces of my people. (God pity us, the terrified republic.) Now I was sorry to have angered the woman who still sat next to me, now deep in conversation with another, younger woman. I longed for some opening, some sign, something to make me part of the life around me. But there was nothing except my color. A white outsider coming in would have seen a young Negro drinking in a Negro bar, perfectly in his element, in his place, as the saying goes. But the people here knew differently, as I did. I didn't seem to have a place.

So I kept on drinking by myself, saying to myself after each drink, Now I'll go. But I was afraid; I didn't want to sleep on Jules's floor; I didn't want to go to sleep. I kept on drinking and listening to the juke box. They were playing Ella Fitzgerald, "Cow-Cow Boogie."

"Let me buy you a drink," I said to the woman.

She looked at me, startled, suspicious, ready to blow her top.

"On the level," I said. I tried to smile. "Both of you."

"I'll take a beer," the young one said.   190

I was shaking like a baby. I finished my drink.
"Fine," I said. I turned to the bar.
"Baby," said the old one, "what's your story?"
The man put three beers on the counter.
"I got no story, Ma," I said.   195

-------- **JAMES BALDWIN** --------

(1924–1987)   *www*

Born in Harlem, Baldwin eventually moved to Paris, where he wrote novels, essays, and stories. In 1953 he published his first novel, *Go Tell It on a Mountain*,
which enjoyed both popular and critical success. He won a prestigious Guggenheim Award and continued writing, publishing *Giovanni's Room*, a novel about a
man's struggle with his sexuality, in 1955. Baldwin returned to New York in
1960, where he became active in the civil rights movement. From that point,
much of his writing became more openly focused on racism in America. Baldwin's fiction combines the attentive realism traditional in America since the
nineteenth century with a lyricism influenced by jazz and the blues. His characters are astute observers often caught in the chaos of warring truths.

TOPICS FOR CRITICAL THINKING Web   *www*

1. Does sympathy for the protagonist help the reader understand the effects of
   racism?
2. What does it mean that this narrator feels that he doesn't belong anywhere?
3. What is the relation between the narrator's childhood experiences and his experiences as a man?
4. What is the relation between the story's themes and the choice of a first-person narrator?

TOPICS FOR CRITICAL WRITING Web   *www*

1. What is the relation between acting and the narrator's experiences as a black man
   in America?
2. Why won't the narrator fight back?

Sonny's Blues   *(1957)*

I read about it in the paper, in the subway, on my way to work. I read it, and I
couldn't believe it, and I read it again. Then perhaps I just stared at it, at the
newsprint spelling out his name, spelling out the story. I stared at it in the
swinging lights of the subway car, and in the faces and bodies of the people,
and in my own face, trapped in the darkness which roared outside.

It was not to be believed and I kept telling myself that as I walked from
the subway station to the high school. And at the same time I couldn't doubt

it. I was scared, scared for Sonny. He became real to me again. A great block
of ice got settled in my belly and kept melting there slowly all day long, while
I taught my classes algebra. It was a special kind of ice. It kept melting, sending trickles of ice water all up and down my veins, but it never got less. Sometimes it hardened and seemed to expand until I felt my guts were going to
come spilling out or that I was going to choke or scream. This would always
be at a moment when I was remembering some specific thing Sonny had once
said or done.

When he was about as old as the boys in my classes his face had been
bright and open, there was a lot of copper in it; and he'd had wonderfully direct brown eyes, and great gentleness and privacy. I wondered what he looked
like now. He had been picked up, the evening before, in a raid on an apartment downtown, for peddling and using heroin.

I couldn't believe it: but what I mean by that is that I couldn't find any
room for it anywhere inside me. I had kept it outside me for a long time. I
hadn't wanted to know. I had had suspicions, but I didn't name them, I kept
putting them away. I told myself that Sonny was wild, but he wasn't crazy. And
he'd always been a good boy, he hadn't ever turned hard or evil or disrespectful, the way kids can, so quick, so quick, especially in Harlem. I didn't want to
believe that I'd ever see my brother going down, coming to nothing, all that
light in his face gone out, in the condition I'd already seen so many others. Yet
it had happened and here I was, talking about algebra to a lot of boys who
might, every one of them for all I knew, be popping off needles every time
they went to the head. Maybe it did more for them than algebra could.

I was sure that the first time Sonny had ever had horse, he couldn't have   5
been much older than these boys were now. These boys, now, were living as
we'd been living then, they were growing up with a rush and their heads
bumped abruptly against the low ceiling of their actual possibilities. They
were filled with rage. All they really knew were two darknesses, the darkness
of their lives, which was now closing in on them, and the darkness of the
movies, which had blinded them to that other darkness, and in which they
now, vindictively, dreamed, at once more together than they were at any other
time, and more alone.

When the last bell rang, the last class ended, I let out my breath. It
seemed I'd been holding it for all that time. My clothes were wet—I may have
looked as though I'd been sitting in a steam bath, all dressed up, all afternoon.
I sat alone in the classroom a long time. I listened to the boys outside, downstairs, shouting and cursing and laughing. Their laughter struck me for perhaps the first time. It was not the joyous laughter which—God knows
why—one associates with children. It was mocking and insular, its intent was
to denigrate. It was disenchanted, and in this, also, lay the authority of their
curses. Perhaps I was listening to them because I was thinking about my
brother and in them I heard my brother. And myself.

One boy was whistling a tune, at once very complicated and very simple,
it seemed to be pouring out of him as though he were a bird, and it sounded
very cool and moving through all that harsh, bright air, only just holding its
own through all those other sounds.

I stood up and walked over to the window and looked down into the courtyard. It was the beginning of the spring and the sap was rising in the boys. A teacher passed through them every now and again, quickly, as though he or she couldn't wait to get out of that courtyard, to get those boys out of their sight and off their minds. I started collecting my stuff. I thought I'd better get home and talk to Isabel.

The courtyard was almost deserted by the time I got downstairs. I saw this boy standing in the shadow of a doorway, looking just like Sonny. I almost called his name. Then I saw that it wasn't Sonny, but somebody we used to know, a boy from around our block. He'd been Sonny's friend. He'd never been mine, having been too young for me, and, anyway, I'd never liked him. And now, even though he was a grown-up man, he still hung around that block, still spent hours on the street corner, was always high and raggy. I used to run into him from time to time and he'd often work around to asking me for a quarter or fifty cents. He always had some real good excuse, too, and I always gave it to him, I don't know why.

But now, abruptly, I hated him. I couldn't stand the way he looked at me, 10 partly like a dog, partly like a cunning child. I wanted to ask him what the hell he was doing in the school courtyard.

He sort of shuffled over to me, and he said, "I see you got the papers. So you already know about it."

"You mean about Sonny? Yes, I already know about it. How come they didn't get you?"

He grinned. It made him repulsive and it also brought to mind what he'd looked like as a kid. "I wasn't there. I stay away from them people."

"Good for you." I offered him a cigarette and I watched him through the smoke. "You come all the way down here just to tell me about Sonny?"

"That's right." He was sort of shaking his head and his eyes looked 15 strange, as though they were about to cross. The bright sun deadened his damp dark brown skin and it made his eyes look yellow and showed up the dirt in his conked hair. He smelled funky. I moved a little away from him and I said, "Well, thanks. But I already know about it and I got to get home."

"I'll walk you a little ways," he said. We started walking. There were a couple of kids still loitering in the courtyard and one of them said good night to me and looked strangely at the boy beside me.

"What're you going to do?" he asked me. "I mean, about Sonny?"

"Look. I haven't seen Sonny for over a year, I'm not sure I'm going to do anything. Anyway, what the hell *can* I do?"

"That's right," he said quickly, "ain't nothing you can do. Can't much help old Sonny no more, I guess."

It was what I was thinking and so it seemed to me he had no right to 20 say it.

"I'm surprised at Sonny, though," he went on—he had a funny way of talking, he looked straight ahead as though he were talking to himself—"I thought Sonny was a smart boy, I thought he was too smart to get hung."

"I guess he thought so too," I said sharply, "and that's how he got hung. And how about you? You're pretty goddamn smart, I bet."

Then he looked directly at me, just for a minute. "I ain't smart," he said. "If I was smart, I'd have reached for a pistol a long time ago."

"Look. Don't tell *me* your sad story, if it was up to me, I'd give you one." Then I felt guilty—guilty, probably, for never having supposed that the poor bastard *had* a story of his own, much less a sad one, and I asked, quickly, "What's going to happen to him now?"

He didn't answer this. He was off by himself some place. "Funny thing," 25 he said, and from his tone we might have been discussing the quickest way to get to Brooklyn, "when I saw the papers this morning, the first thing I asked myself was if I had anything to do with it. I felt sort of responsible."

I began to listen more carefully. The subway station was on the corner, just before us, and I stopped. He stopped, too. We were in front of a bar and he ducked slightly, peering in, but whoever he was looking for didn't seem to be there. The juke box was blasting away with something black and bouncy and I half watched the barmaid as she danced her way from the juke box to her place behind the bar. And I watched her face as she laughingly responded to something someone said to her, still keeping time to the music. When she smiled one saw the little girl, one sensed the doomed, still-struggling woman beneath the battered face of the semi-whore.

"I never *give* Sonny nothing," the boy said finally, "but a long time ago I come to school high and Sonny asked me how it felt." He paused, I couldn't bear to watch him, I watched the barmaid, and I listened to the music which seemed to be causing the pavement to shake. "I told him it felt great." The music stopped, the barmaid paused and watched the juke box until the music began again. "It did."

All this was carrying me some place I didn't want to go. I certainly didn't want to know how it felt. It filled everything, the people, the houses, the music, the dark, quicksilver barmaid, with menace; and this menace was their reality.

"What's going to happen to him now?" I asked again.

"They'll send him away some place and they'll try to cure him." He shook 30 his head. "Maybe he'll even think he's kicked the habit. Then they'll let him loose"—he gestured, throwing his cigarette into the gutter. "That's all."

"What do you mean, that's *all?*"

But I knew what he meant.

"I *mean*, that's *all*." He turned his head and looked at me, pulling down the corners of his mouth. "Don't you know what I mean?" he asked softly.

"How the hell *would* I know what you mean?" I almost whispered it, I don't know why.

"That's right," he said to the air, "how would *he* know what I mean?" He 35 turned toward me again, patient and calm, and yet I somehow felt him shaking, shaking as though he were going to fall apart. I felt that ice in my guts again, the dread I'd felt all afternoon; and again I watched the barmaid, moving about the bar, washing glasses, and singing. "Listen. They'll let him out and then it'll just start all over again. That's what I mean."

"You mean—they'll let him out. And then he'll just start working his way back in again. You mean he'll never kick the habit. Is that what you mean?"

"That's right," he said, cheerfully. "*You* see what I mean."

"Tell me," I said at last, "why does he want to die? He must want to die, he's killing himself, why does he want to die?"

He looked at me in surprise. He licked his lips. "He don't want to die. He wants to live. Don't nobody want to die, ever."

Then I wanted to ask him—too many things. He could not have an- 40
swered, or if he had, I could not have borne the answers. I started walking. "Well, I guess it's none of my business."

"It's going to be rough on old Sonny," he said. We reached the subway station. "This is your station?" he asked. I nodded. I took one step down. "Damn!" he said, suddenly. I looked up at him. He grinned again. "Damn if I didn't leave all my money home. You ain't got a dollar on you, have you? Just for a couple of days, is all."

All at once something inside gave and threatened to come pouring out of me. I didn't hate him any more. I felt that in another moment I'd start crying like a child.

"Sure," I said. "Don't sweat." I looked in my wallet and didn't have a dollar, I only had a five. "Here," I said. "That hold you?"

He didn't look at it—he didn't want to look at it. A terrible, closed look came over his face, as though he were keeping the number on the bill a secret from him and me. "Thanks," he said, and now he was dying to see me go. "Don't worry about Sonny. Maybe I'll write him or something."

"Sure," I said. "You do that. So long." 45

"Be seeing you," he said. I went on down the steps.

And I didn't write Sonny or send him anything for a long time. When I finally did, it was just after my little girl died, he wrote me back a letter which made me feel like a bastard.

Here's what he said:

DEAR BROTHER,

You don't know how much I needed to hear from you. I wanted to write you many a time but I dug how much I must have hurt you and so I didn't write. But now I feel like a man who's been trying to climb up out of some deep, real deep and funky hole and just saw the sun up there, outside. I got to get outside.

I can't tell you much about how I got here. I mean I don't know how to tell you. I guess I was afraid of something or I was trying to escape from something and you know I have never been very strong in the head (smile). I'm glad Mama and Daddy are dead and can't see what's happened to their son and I swear if I'd known what I was doing I would never have hurt you so, you and a lot of other fine people who were nice to me and who believed in me.

I don't want you to think it had anything to do with me being a musician. It's more than that. Or maybe less than that. I can't get anything straight in my head down here and I try not to think about what's going to happen to me when I get outside again. Sometime I think I'm going to flip and *never* get outside and sometime I think I'll come straight back. I tell you one thing, though, I'd rather blow my brains out than go through this again. But that's what they all say, so they tell me. If I tell you when I'm coming to New York and if you could meet me, I sure would appreciate it. Give my love to Isabel and the kids and I was sorry to hear about little Gracie.

I wish I could be like Mama and say the Lord's will be done, but I don't know it seems to me that trouble is the one thing that never does get stopped and I don't know what good it does to blame it on the Lord. But maybe it does some good if you believe it.

Your brother,
SONNY

Then I kept in constant touch with him and I sent him whatever I could and I went to meet him when he came back to New York. When I saw him many things I thought I had forgotten came flooding back to me. This was because I had begun, finally, to wonder about Sonny, about the life that Sonny lived inside. This life, whatever it was, had made him older and thinner and it had deepened the distant stillness in which he had always moved. He looked very unlike my baby brother. Yet, when he smiled, when we shook hands, the baby brother I'd never known looked out from the depths of his private life, like an animal waiting to be coaxed into the light.

"How you been keeping?" he asked me.   50

"All right. And you?"

"Just fine." He was smiling all over his face. "It's good to see you again."

"It's good to see you."

The seven years' difference in our ages lay between us like a chasm: I wondered if these years would ever operate between us as a bridge. I was remembering, and it made it hard to catch my breath, that I had been there when he was born; and I had heard the first words he had ever spoken. When he started to walk, he walked from our mother straight to me. I caught him just before he fell when he took the first steps he ever took in this world.

"How's Isabel?"   55

"Just fine. She's dying to see you."

"And the boys?"

"They're fine, too. They're anxious to see their uncle."

"Oh, come on. You know they don't remember me."

"Are you kidding? Of course they remember you."   60

He grinned again. We got into a taxi. We had a lot to say to each other, far too much to know how to begin.

As the taxi began to move, I asked, "You still want to go to India?"

He laughed. "You still remember that. Hell, no. This place is Indian enough for me."

"It used to belong to them," I said.

And he laughed again. "They damn sure knew what they were doing   65
when they got rid of it."

Years ago, when he was around fourteen, he'd been all hipped on the idea of going to India. He read books about people sitting on rocks, naked, in all kinds of weather, but mostly bad, naturally, and walking barefoot through hot coals and arriving at wisdom. I used to say that it sounded to me as though they were getting away from wisdom as fast as they could. I think he sort of looked down on me for that.

"Do you mind," he asked, "if we have the driver drive alongside the park? On the west side—I haven't seen the city in so long."

"Of course not," I said. I was afraid that I might sound as though I were humoring him, but I hoped he wouldn't take it that way.

So we drove along, between the green of the park and the stony, lifeless elegance of hotels and apartment buildings, toward the vivid, killing streets of our childhood. These streets hadn't changed, though housing projects jutted up out of them now like rocks in the middle of a boiling sea. Most of the houses in which we had grown up had vanished, as had the stores from which we had stolen, the basements in which we had first tried sex, the rooftops from which we had hurled tin cans and bricks. But houses exactly like the houses of our past yet dominated the landscape, boys exactly like the boys we once had been found themselves smothering in these houses, came down into the streets for light and air and found themselves encircled by disaster. Some escaped the trap, most didn't. Those who got out always left something of themselves behind, as some animals amputate a leg and leave it in the trap. It might be said, perhaps, that I had escaped, after all, I was a school teacher; or that Sonny had, he hadn't lived in Harlem for years. Yet, as the cab moved uptown through streets which seemed, with a rush, to darken with dark people, and as I covertly studied Sonny's face, it came to me that what we both were seeking through our separate cab windows was that part of ourselves which had been left behind. It's always at the hour of trouble and confrontation that the missing member aches.

We hit 110th Street and started rolling up Lenox Avenue. And I'd known   70
this avenue all my life, but it seemed to me again, as it had seemed on the day I'd first heard about Sonny's trouble, filled with a hidden menace which was its very breath of life.

"We almost there," said Sonny.

"Almost." We were both too nervous to say anything more.

We live in a housing project. It hasn't been up long. A few days after it was up it seemed uninhabitably new, now, of course, it's already run-down. It looks like a parody of the good, clean, faceless life—God knows the people who live in it do their best to make it a parody. The beat-looking grass lying around isn't enough to make their lives green, the hedges will never hold out the streets, and they know it. The big windows fool no one, they aren't big enough to make space out of no space. They don't bother with the windows, they watch the TV screen instead. The playground is most popular with the children who don't play at jacks, or skip rope, or roller skate, or swing, and they can be found in it after dark. We moved in partly because it's not too far from where I teach, and partly for the kids; but it's really just like the houses in which Sonny and I grew up. The same things happen, they'll have the same things to remember. The moment Sonny and I started into the house I had the feeling that I was simply bringing him back into the danger he had almost died trying to escape.

Sonny has never been talkative. So I don't know why I was sure he'd be dying to talk to me when supper was over the first night. Everything went fine, the oldest boy remembered him, and the youngest boy liked him, and Sonny had remembered to bring something for each of them; and Isabel, who is really much nicer than I am, more open and giving, had gone to a lot of trouble about dinner and was genuinely glad to see him. And she's always been able to tease Sonny in a way that I haven't. It was nice to see her face so vivid again and to hear her laugh and watch her make Sonny laugh. She wasn't, or, anyway, she didn't seem to be, at all uneasy or embarrassed. She chatted as though there were no subject which had to be avoided and she got Sonny past his first, faint stiffness. And thank God she was there, for I was filled with that icy dread again. Everything I did seemed awkward to me, and everything I said sounded freighted with hidden meaning. I was trying to remember everything I'd heard about dope addiction and I couldn't help watching Sonny for signs. I wasn't doing it out of malice. I was trying to find out something about my brother. I was dying to hear him tell me he was safe.

"Safe!" my father grunted, whenever Mama suggested trying to move to   75
a neighborhood which might be safer for children. "Safe, hell! Ain't no place safe for kids, nor nobody."

He always went on like this, but he wasn't, ever, really as bad as he sounded, not even on weekends, when he got drunk. As a matter of fact, he was always on the lookout for "something a little better," but he died before he found it. He died suddenly, during a drunken weekend in the middle of the war, when Sonny was fifteen. He and Sonny hadn't ever got on too well. And this was partly because Sonny was the apple of his father's eye. It was because he loved Sonny so much and was frightened for him, that he was always fighting with him. It doesn't do any good to fight with Sonny. Sonny just moves back, inside himself, where he can't be reached. But the principal reason that they never hit it off is that they were so much alike. Daddy was big and rough and loud-talking, just the opposite of Sonny, but they both had—that same privacy.

Mama tried to tell me something about this, just after Daddy died. I was home on leave from the army.

This was the last time I ever saw my mother alive. Just the same, this picture gets all mixed up in my mind with pictures I had of her when she was younger. The way I always see her is the way she used to be on a Sunday afternoon, say, when the old folks were talking after the big Sunday dinner. I always see her wearing pale blue. She'd be sitting on the sofa. And my father would be sitting in the easy chair, not far from her. And the living room would be full of church folks and relatives. There they sit, in chairs all around the living room, and the night is creeping up outside, but nobody knows it yet. You can see the darkness growing against the window-panes and you hear the street noises every now and again, or maybe the jangling beat of a tambourine from one of the churches close by, but it's real quiet in the room. For a moment nobody's talking, but every face looks darkening, like the sky outside. And my mother rocks a little from the waist, and my father's eyes are closed. Everyone is looking at something a child can't see. For a minute they've forgotten the children. Maybe a kid is lying on the rug half asleep. Maybe somebody's got a kid on his lap and is absent-mindedly stroking the kid's head. Maybe there's a kid, quiet and big-eyed, curled up in a big chair in the corner. The silence, the darkness coming, and the darkness in the faces frightens the child obscurely. He hopes that the hand which strokes his forehead will never stop—will never die. He hopes that there will never come a time when the old folks won't be sitting around the living room, talking about where they've come from, and what they've seen, and what's happened to them and their kinfolk.

But something deep and watchful in the child knows that this is bound to end, is already ending. In a moment someone will get up and turn on the light. Then the old folks will remember the children and they won't talk any more that day. And when light fills the room, the child is filled with darkness. He knows that every time this happens he's moved just a little closer to that darkness outside. The darkness outside is what the old folks have been talking about. It's what they've come from. It's what they endure. The child knows that they won't talk any more because if he knows too much about what's happened to *them*, he'll know too much too soon, about what's going to happen to *him*.

The last time I talked to my mother, I remember I was restless. I wanted 80 to get out and see Isabel. We weren't married then and we had a lot to straighten out between us.

There Mama sat, in black, by the window. She was humming an old church song, *Lord, you brought me from a long ways off*. Sonny was out somewhere. Mama kept watching the streets.

"I don't know," she said, "if I'll ever see you again, after you go off from here. But I hope you'll remember the things I tried to teach you."

"Don't talk like that," I said, and smiled. "You'll be here a long time yet."

She smiled, too, but she said nothing. She was quiet for a long time. And I said, "Mama, don't you worry about nothing. I'll be writing all the time, and you be getting the checks. . . ."

"I want to talk to you about your brother," she said, suddenly. "If any- 85 thing happens to me he ain't going to have nobody to look out for him."

"Mama," I said, "ain't nothing going to happen to you *or* Sonny. Sonny's all right. He's a good boy and he's got good sense."

"It ain't a question of his being a good boy," Mama said, "nor of his having good sense. It ain't only the bad ones, nor yet the dumb ones that gets sucked under." She stopped, looking at me. "Your Daddy once had a brother," she said, and she smiled in a way that made me feel she was in pain. "You didn't never know that, did you?"

"No," I said, "I never knew that," and I watched her face.

"Oh, yes," she said, "your Daddy had a brother." She looked out of the window again. "I know you never saw your Daddy cry. But *I* did—many a time, through all these years."

I asked her, "What happened to his brother? How come nobody's ever 90 talked about him?"

This was the first time I ever saw my mother look old.

"His brother got killed," she said, "when he was just a little younger than you are now. I knew him. He was a fine boy. He was maybe a little full of the devil, but he didn't mean nobody no harm."

Then she stopped and the room was silent, exactly as it had sometimes been on those Sunday afternoons. Mama kept looking out into the streets.

"He used to have a job in the mill," she said, "and, like all young folks, he

just liked to perform on Saturday nights. Saturday nights, him and your father
would drift around to different places, go to dances and things like that, or
just sit around with people they knew, and your father's brother would sing, he
had a fine voice, and play along with himself on his guitar. Well, this particular Saturday night, him and your father was coming home from some place,
and they were both a little drunk and there was a moon that night, it was
bright like day. Your father's brother was feeling kind of good, and he was
whistling to himself, and he had his guitar slung over his shoulder. They
was coming down a hill and beneath them was a road that turned off from the
highway. Well, your father's brother, being always kind of frisky, decided to
run down this hill, and he did, with that guitar banging and clanging behind
him, and he ran across the road, and he was making water behind a tree. And
your father was sort of amused at him and he was still coming down the hill,
kind of slow. Then he heard a car motor and that same minute his brother
stepped from behind the tree, into the road, in the moonlight. And he started
to cross the road. And your father started to run down the hill, he says he
don't know why. This car was full of white men. They was all drunk, and when
they seen your father's brother they let out a great whoop and holler and they
aimed the car straight at him. They was having fun, they just wanted to scare
him, the way they do sometimes, you know. But they was drunk. And I guess
the boy, being drunk, too, and scared, kind of lost his head. By the time he
jumped it was too late. Your father says he heard his brother scream when the
car rolled over him, and he heard the wood of that guitar when it give, and
he heard them strings go flying, and he heard them white men shouting, and
the car kept on a-going and it ain't stopped till this day. And, time your father
got down the hill, his brother weren't nothing but blood and pulp."

Tears were gleaming on my mother's face. There wasn't anything I could   95
say.

"He never mentioned it," she said, "because I never let him mention it
before you children. Your Daddy was like a crazy man that night and for many
a night thereafter. He says he never in his life seen anything as dark as that
road after the lights of that car had gone away. Weren't nothing, weren't nobody on that road, just your Daddy and his brother and that busted guitar.
Oh, yes. Your Daddy never did really get right again. Till the day he died he
weren't sure but that every white man he saw was the man that killed his
brother."

She stopped and took out her handkerchief and dried her eyes and looked
at me.

"I ain't telling you all this," she said, "to make you scared or bitter or to
make you hate nobody. I'm telling you this because you got a brother. And the
world ain't changed."

I guess I didn't want to believe this. I guess she saw this in my face. She
turned away from me, toward the window again, searching those streets.

"But I praise my Redeemer," she said at last, "that He called your Daddy   100
home before me. I ain't saying it to throw no flowers at myself, but, I declare,
it keeps me from feeling too cast down to know I helped your father get safely
through this world. Your father always acted like he was the roughest, strongest

man on earth. And everybody took him to be like that. But if he hadn't had *me* there—to see his tears!"

She was crying again. Still, I couldn't move. I said, "Lord, Lord, Mama, I didn't know it was like that."

"Oh, honey," she said, "there's a lot that you don't know. But you are going to find it out." She stood up from the window and came over to me. "You got to hold on to your brother," she said, "and don't let him fall, no matter what it looks like is happening to him and no matter how evil you gets with him. You going to be evil with him many a time. But don't you forget what I told you, you hear?"

"I won't forget," I said. "Don't you worry, I won't forget. I won't let nothing happen to Sonny."

My mother smiled as though she were amused at something she saw in my face. Then, "You may not be able to stop nothing from happening. But you got to let him know you's *there*."

Two days later I was married, and then I was gone. And I had a lot of   105
things on my mind and I pretty well forgot my promise to Mama until I got shipped home on a special furlough for her funeral.

And, after the funeral, with just Sonny and me alone in the empty kitchen, I tried to find out something about him.

"What do you want to do?" I asked him.

"I'm going to be a musician," he said.

For he had graduated, in the time I had been away, from dancing to the juke box to finding out who was playing what, and what they were doing with it, and he had bought himself a set of drums.

"You mean, you want to be a drummer?" I somehow had the feeling that   110
being a drummer might be all right for other people but not for my brother Sonny.

"I don't think," he said, looking at me very gravely, "that I'll ever be a good drummer. But I think I can play a piano."

I frowned. I'd never played the role of the older brother quite so seriously before, had scarcely ever, in fact, *asked* Sonny a damn thing. I sensed myself in the presence of something I didn't really know how to handle, didn't understand. So I made my frown a little deeper as I asked: "What kind of musician do you want to be?"

He grinned. "How many kinds do you think there are?"

"Be *serious*," I said.

He laughed, throwing his head back, and then looked at me. "I *am*   115
serious."

"Well, then, for Christ's sake, stop kidding around and answer a serious question. I mean, do you want to be a concert pianist, you want to play classical music and all that, or—or what?" Long before I finished he was laughing again. "For Christ's *sake*, Sonny!"

He sobered, but with difficulty. "I'm sorry. But you sound so—*scared!*" and he was off again.

"Well, you may think it's funny now, baby, but it's not going to be so funny when you have to make your living at it, let me tell you *that*." I was furious because I knew he was laughing at me and I didn't know why.

"No," he said, very sober now, and afraid, perhaps, that he'd hurt me, "I don't want to be a classical pianist. That isn't what interests me. I mean"—he paused, looking hard at me, as though his eyes would help me to understand, and then gestured helplessly, as though perhaps his hand would help—"I mean, I'll have a lot of studying to do, and I'll have to study *everything*, but I mean, I want to play *with*—jazz musicians." He stopped. "I want to play jazz," he said.

Well, the word had never before sounded as heavy, as real, as it sounded   120
that afternoon in Sonny's mouth. I just looked at him and I was probably frowning a real frown by this time. I simply couldn't see why on earth he'd want to spend his time hanging around night clubs, clowning around on bandstands, while people pushed each other around a dance floor. It seemed—beneath him, somehow. I had never thought about it before, had never been forced to, but I suppose I had always put jazz musicians in a class with what Daddy called "good-time people."

"Are you *serious?*"

"Hell, *yes*, I'm serious."

He looked more helpless than ever, and annoyed, and deeply hurt.

I suggested, helpfully: "You mean—like Louis Armstrong?"

His face closed as though I'd struck him. "No. I'm not talking about none   125
of that old-time, down home crap."

"Well, look, Sonny, I'm sorry, don't get mad. I just don't altogether get it, that's all. Name somebody—you know, a jazz musician you admire."

"Bird."

"Who?"

"Bird! Charlie Parker! Don't they teach you nothing in the goddamn army?"

I lit a cigarette. I was surprised and then a little amused to discover that I   130
was trembling. "I've been out of touch," I said, "You'll have to be patient with me. Now. Who's this Parker character?"

"He's just one of the greatest jazz musicians alive," said Sonny, sullenly, his hands in his pockets, his back to me. "Maybe *the* greatest," he added, bitterly, "that's probably why *you* never heard of him."

"All right," I said. "I'm ignorant. I'm sorry. I'll go out and buy all the cat's records right away, all right?"

"It don't," said Sonny, with dignity, "make any difference to me. I don't care what you listen to. Don't do me no favors."

I was beginning to realize that I'd never seen him so upset before. With another part of my mind I was thinking that this would probably turn out to be one of those things kids go through and that I shouldn't make it seem important by pushing it too hard. Still, I didn't think it would do any harm to ask: "Doesn't all this take a lot of time? Can you make a living at it?"

He turned back to me and half leaned, half sat, on the kitchen table.   135
"Everything takes time," he said, "and—well, yes, sure, I can make a living at it. But what I don't seem to be able to make you understand is that it's the only thing I want to do."

"Well Sonny," I said, gently, "you know people can't always do exactly what they *want* to do——"

"*No*, I don't know that," said Sonny, surprising me. "I think people *ought* to do what they want to do, what else are they alive for?"

"You getting to be a big boy," I said desperately, "it's time you started thinking about your future."

"I'm thinking about my future," said Sonny, grimly. "I think about it all the time."

I gave up. I decided, if he didn't change his mind, that we could always   140 talk about it later. "In the meantime," I said, "you got to finish school." We had already decided that he'd have to move in with Isabel and her folks. I knew this wasn't the ideal arrangement because Isabel's folks are inclined to be dicty and they hadn't especially wanted Isabel to marry me. But I didn't know what else to do. "And we have to get you fixed up at Isabel's."

There was a long silence. He moved from the kitchen table to the window. "That's a terrible idea. You know it yourself."

"Do you have a *better* idea?"

He just walked up and down the kitchen for a minute. He was as tall as I was. He had started to shave. I suddenly had the feeling that I didn't know him at all.

He stopped at the kitchen table and picked up my cigarettes. Looking at me with a kind of mocking, amused defiance, he put one between his lips. "You mind?"

"You smoking already?"   145

He lit the cigarette and nodded, watching me through the smoke. "I just wanted to see if I'd have the courage to smoke in front of you." He grinned and blew a great cloud of smoke to the ceiling. "It was easy." He looked at my face. "Come on, now. I bet you was smoking at my age, tell the truth."

I didn't say anything but the truth was on my face, and he laughed. But now there was something very strained in his laugh. "Sure. And I bet that ain't all you was doing."

He was frightening me a little. "Cut the crap," I said. "We already decided that you was going to go and live at Isabel's. Now what's got into you all of a sudden?"

"*You* decided it," he pointed out. "*I* didn't decide nothing." He stopped in front of me, leaning against the stove, arms loosely folded. "Look, brother. I don't want to stay in Harlem no more, I really don't." He was very earnest. He looked at me, then over toward the kitchen window. There was something in his eyes I'd never seen before, some thoughtfulness, some worry all his own. He rubbed the muscle of one arm. "It's time I was getting out of here."

"Where do you want to *go*, Sonny?"   150

"I want to join the army. Or the navy, I don't care. If I say I'm old enough they'll believe me."

Then I got mad. It was because I was so scared. "You must be crazy. You goddamn fool, what the hell do you want to go and join the *army* for?"

"I just told you. To get out of Harlem."

"Sonny, you haven't even finished *school*. And if you really want to be a musician, how do you expect to study if you're in the *army?*"

He looked at me, trapped, and in anguish. "There's ways. I might be able to work out some kind of deal. Anyway, I'll have the G.I. Bill when I come out." 155

"*If* you come out." We stared at each other. "Sonny, please. Be reasonable. I know the setup is far from perfect. But we got to do the best we can."

"I ain't learning nothing in school," he said. "Even when I go." He turned away from me and opened the window and threw his cigarette out into the narrow alley. I watched his back. "At least, I ain't learning nothing you'd want me to learn." He slammed the window so hard I thought the glass would fly out, and turned back to me. "And I'm sick of the stink of these garbage cans!"

"Sonny," I said, "I know how you feel. But if you don't finish school now, you're going to be sorry later that you didn't." I grabbed him by the shoulders. "And you only got another year. It ain't so bad. And I'll come back and I swear I'll help you do *whatever* you want to do. Just try to put up with it till I come back. Will you please do that? For me?"

He didn't answer and he wouldn't look at me.

"Sonny. You hear me?" 160

He pulled away. "I hear you. But you never hear anything *I* say."

I didn't know what to say to that. He looked out of the window and then back at me. "OK," he said, and sighed. "I'll try."

Then I said, trying to cheer him up a little, "They got a piano at Isabel's. You can practice on it."

And as a matter of fact, it did cheer him up for a minute. "That's right," he said to himself. "I forgot that." His face relaxed a little. But the worry, the thoughtfulness, played on it still, the way shadows play on a face which is staring into the fire.

But I thought I'd never hear the end of that piano. At first, Isabel would 165 write me, saying how nice it was that Sonny was so serious about his music and how, as soon as he came in from school, or wherever he had been when he was supposed to be at school, he went straight to that piano and stayed there until suppertime. And, after supper, he went back to that piano and stayed there until everybody went to bed. He was at the piano all day Saturday and all day Sunday. Then he bought a record player and started playing records. He'd play one record over and over again, all day long sometimes, and he'd improvise along with it on the piano. Or he'd play one section of the record, one chord, one change, one progression, then he'd do it on the piano. Then back to the record. Then back to the piano.

Well, I really don't know how they stood it. Isabel finally confessed that it wasn't like living with a person at all, it was like living with sound. And the sound didn't make any sense to her, didn't make any sense to any of them— naturally. They began, in a way, to be afflicted by this presence that was living in their home. It was as though Sonny were some sort of god, or monster. He moved in an atmosphere which wasn't like theirs at all. They fed him and he ate, he washed himself, he walked in and out of their door; he certainly wasn't nasty or unpleasant or rude, Sonny isn't any of those things; but it was as though he were all wrapped up in some cloud, some fire, some vision all his own; and there wasn't any way to reach him.

At the same time, he wasn't really a man yet, he was still a child, and they had to watch out for him in all kinds of ways. They certainly couldn't throw him out. Neither did they dare to make a great scene about that piano because even they dimly sensed, as I sensed, from so many thousands of miles away, that Sonny was at that piano playing for his life.

But he hadn't been going to school. One day a letter came from the school board and Isabel's mother got it—there had, apparently, been other letters but Sonny had torn them up. This day, when Sonny came in, Isabel's mother showed him the letter and asked where he'd been spending his time. And she finally got it out of him that he'd been down in Greenwich Village, with musicians and other characters, in a white girl's apartment. And this scared her and she started to scream at him and what came up, once she began—though she denies it to this day—was what sacrifices they were making to give Sonny a decent home and how little he appreciated it.

Sonny didn't play the piano that day. By evening, Isabel's mother had calmed down but then there was the old man to deal with, and Isabel herself. Isabel says she did her best to be calm but she broke down and started crying. She says she just watched Sonny's face. She could tell, by watching him, what was happening with him. And what was happening was that they penetrated his cloud, they had reached him. Even if their fingers had been a thousand times more gentle than human fingers ever are, he could hardly help feeling that they had stripped him naked and were spitting on that nakedness. For he also had to see that his presence, that music, which was life or death to him, had been torture for them and that they had endured it, not at all for his sake, but only for mine. And Sonny couldn't take that. He can take it a little better today than he could then but he's still not very good at it and, frankly, I don't know anybody who is.

The silence of the next few days must have been louder than the sound of all the music ever played since time began. One morning, before she went to work, Isabel was in his room for something and she suddenly realized that all of his records were gone. And she knew for certain that he was gone. And he was. He went as far as the navy would carry him. He finally sent me a postcard from some place in Greece and that was the first I knew that Sonny was still alive. I didn't see him any more until we were both back in New York and the war had long been over.

He was a man by then, of course, but I wasn't willing to see it. He came by the house from time to time, but we fought almost every time we met. I didn't like the way he carried himself, loose and dreamlike all the time, and I didn't like his friends, and his music seemed to be merely an excuse for the life he led. It sounded just that weird and disordered.

Then we had a fight, a pretty awful fight, and I didn't see him for months. By and by I looked him up, where he was living, in a furnished room in the Village, and I tried to make it up. But there were lots of other people in the room and Sonny just lay on his bed, and he wouldn't come downstairs with me, and he treated these other people as though they were his family and I weren't. So I got mad and then he got mad, and then I told him that he might just as well be dead as live the way he was living. Then he stood up and he told me not to worry about him any more in life, that he *was* dead as far as I was concerned. Then he pushed me to the door and the other people looked on as though nothing were happening, and he slammed the door behind me. I stood in the hallway, staring at the door. I heard somebody laugh in the room and then the tears came to my eyes. I started down the steps, whistling to keep from crying, I kept whistling to myself, *You going to need me, baby, one of these cold, rainy days.*

I read about Sonny's trouble in the spring. Little Grace died in the fall. She was a beautiful little girl. But she only lived a little over two years. She died of polio and she suffered. She had a slight fever for a couple of days, but it didn't seem like anything and we just kept her in bed. And we would certainly have called the doctor, but the fever dropped, she seemed to be all right. So we thought it had just been a cold. Then, one day, she was up, playing, Isabel was in the kitchen fixing lunch for the two boys when they'd come in from school, and she heard Grace fall down in the living room. When you have a lot of children you don't always start running when one of them falls, unless they start screaming or something. And, this time, Grace was quiet. Yet, Isabel says that when she heard that *thump* and then that silence, something happened in her to make her afraid. And she ran to the living room and there was little Grace on the floor, all twisted up and the reason she hadn't screamed was that she couldn't get her breath. And when she did scream, it was the worst sound, Isabel says, that she'd ever heard in all her life, and she still hears it sometimes in her dreams. Isabel will sometimes wake me up with a low, moaning, strangled sound and I have to be quick to awaken her and hold her to me and where Isabel is weeping against me seems a mortal wound.

I think I may have written Sonny the very day that little Grace was buried. I was sitting in the living room in the dark, by myself, and I suddenly thought of Sonny. My trouble made his real.

One Saturday afternoon, when Sonny had been living with us, or, anyway, 175 been in our house, for nearly two weeks, I found myself wandering aimlessly about the living room, drinking from a can of beer, and trying to work up the courage to search Sonny's room. He was out, he was usually out whenever I was home, and Isabel had taken the children to see their grandparents. Suddenly I was standing still in front of the living room window, watching Seventh Avenue. The idea of searching Sonny's room made me still. I scarcely dared to admit to myself what I'd be searching for. I didn't know what I'd do if I found it. Or if I didn't.

On the sidewalk across from me, near the entrance to a barbecue joint, some people were holding an old-fashioned revival meeting. The barbecue cook, wearing a dirty white apron, his conked hair reddish and metallic in the pale sun, and a cigarette between his lips, stood in the doorway, watching them. Kids and older people paused in their errands and stood there, along with some older men and a couple of very tough-looking women who watched everything that happened on the avenue, as though they owned it, or were maybe owned by it. Well, they were watching this, too. The revival was being carried on by three sisters in black, and a brother. All they had were their voices and their Bibles and a tambourine. The brother was testifying and while he testified two of the sisters stood together, seeming to say, Amen, and the third sister walked around with the tambourine outstretched and a couple of people dropped coins into it. Then the brother's testimony ended and the sister who had been taking up the collection dumped the coins into her palm and transferred them to the pocket of her long black robe. Then she raised both hands, striking the tambourine against the air, and then against one hand, and she started to sing. And the two other sisters and the brother joined in.

It was strange, suddenly, to watch, though I had been seeing these street meetings all my life. So, of course, had everybody else down there. Yet, they paused and watched and listened and I stood still at the window. *"Tis the old ship of Zion,"* they sang, and the sister with the tambourine kept a steady, jangling beat, *"It has rescued many a thousand!"* Not a soul under the sound of their voices was hearing this song for the first time, not one of them had been rescued. Nor had they seen much in the way of rescue work being done around them. Neither did they especially believe in the holiness of the three sisters and the brother, they knew too much about them, knew where they lived, and how. The woman with the tambourine, whose voice dominated the air, whose face was bright with joy, was divided by very little from the woman who stood watching her, a cigarette between her heavy, chapped lips, her hair a cuckoo's nest, her face scarred and swollen from many beatings, and her black eyes glittering like coal. Perhaps they both knew this, which was why, when, as rarely, they addressed each other, they addressed each other as Sister. As the singing filled the air the watching, listening faces underwent a change, the eyes focusing on something within; the music seemed to soothe a poison out of them; and time seemed, nearly, to fall away from the sullen, belligerent, battered faces, as though they were fleeing back to their first condition, while dreaming of their last. The barbecue cook half shook his head and smiled, and dropped his cigarette and disappeared into his joint. A man fumbled in his pockets for change and stood holding it in his hand impatiently, as though he had just remembered a pressing appointment further up the avenue. He looked furious. Then I saw Sonny, standing on the edge of the crowd. He was carrying a wide, flat notebook with a green cover, and it made him look, from where I was standing, almost like a schoolboy. The coppery sun brought out the copper in his skin, he was very faintly smiling, standing very still. Then the singing stopped, the tambourine turned into a collection plate again. The furious man dropped in his coins and vanished, so did a couple of the women, and Sonny dropped some change in the plate, looking directly at the woman with a little smile. He started across the avenue, toward the house. He has a slow, loping walk, something like the way Harlem hipsters walk, only he's imposed on this his own halfbeat. I had never really noticed it before.

I stayed at the window, both relieved and apprehensive. As Sonny disappeared from my sight, they began singing again. And they were still singing when his key turned in the lock.

"Hey," he said.

"Hey, yourself. You want some beer?"

"No. Well, maybe." But he came up to the window and stood beside me, looking out. "What a warm voice," he said.

They were singing *If I could only hear my mother pray again!*

"Yes," I said, "and she can sure beat that tambourine."

"But what a terrible song," he said, and laughed. He dropped his notebook on the sofa and disappeared into the kitchen. "Where's Isabel and the kids?"

"I think they went to see their grandparents. You hungry?"

"No." He came back into the living room with his can of beer. "You want to come some place with me tonight?"

I sensed, I don't know how, that I couldn't possibly say No. "Sure. Where?"

He sat down on the sofa and picked up his notebook and started leafing through it. "I'm going to sit in with some fellows in a joint in the Village."

"You mean, you're going to play, tonight?"

"That's right." He took a swallow of his beer and moved back to the window. He gave me a sidelong look. "If you can stand it."

"I'll try," I said.

He smiled to himself and we both watched as the meeting across the way broke up. The three sisters and the brother, heads bowed, were singing *God be with you till we meet again.* The faces around them were very quiet. Then the song ended. The small crowd dispersed. We watched the three women and the lone man walk slowly up the avenue.

"When she was singing before," said Sonny, abruptly, "her voice reminded me for a minute of what heroin feels like sometimes—when it's in your veins. It makes you feel sort of warm and cool at the same time. And distant. And—and sure." He sipped his beer, very deliberately not looking at me. I watched his face. "It makes you feel—in control. Sometimes you've got to have that feeling."

"Do you?" I sat down slowly in the easy chair.

"Sometimes." He went to the sofa and picked up his notebook again. "Some people do."

"In order," I asked, "to play?" And my voice was very ugly, full of contempt and anger.

"Well"—he looked at me with great, troubled eyes, as though, in fact, he hoped his eyes would tell me things he could never otherwise say—"they *think* so. And *if* they think so—!"

"And what do *you* think?" I asked.

He sat on the sofa and put his can of beer on the floor. "I don't know," he said, and I couldn't be sure if he were answering my question or pursuing his thoughts. His face didn't tell me. "It's not so much to *play*. It's to *stand* it, to be able to make it at all. On any level." He frowned and smiled: "In order to keep from shaking to pieces."

180

185

190

195

"But these friends of yours," I said, "they seem to shake themselves to   200
pieces pretty goddamn fast."

"Maybe." He played with the notebook. And something told me that I
should curb my tongue, that Sonny was doing his best to talk, that I should listen. "But of course you only know the ones that've gone to pieces. Some
don't—or at least they haven't *yet* and that's just about all *any* of us can say."
He paused. "And then there are some who just live, really, in hell, and they
know it and they see what's happening and they go right on. I don't know." He
sighed, dropped the notebook, folded his arms. "Some guys, you can tell from
the way they play, they on something *all* the time. And you can see that, well,
it makes something real for them. But of course," he picked up his beer from
the floor and sipped it and put the can down again, "they *want* to, too, you've
got to see that. Even some of them that say they don't—*some*, not all."

"And what about you?" I asked—I couldn't help it. "What about you? Do
you want to?"

He stood up and walked to the window and remained silent for a long
time. Then he sighed. "Me," he said. Then: "While I was downstairs before,
on my way here, listening to that woman sing, it struck me all of a sudden how
much suffering she must have had to go through—to sing like that. It's *repulsive* to think you have to suffer that much."

I said: "But there's no way not to suffer—is there, Sonny?"

"I believe not," he said, and smiled, "but that's never stopped anyone   205
from trying." He looked at me. "Has it?" I realized, with this mocking look,
that there stood between us, forever, beyond the power of time or forgiveness,
the fact that I had held silence—so long!— when he had needed human
speech to help him. He turned back to the window. "No, there's no way not to
suffer. But you try all kinds of ways to keep from drowning in it, to keep on
top of it, and to make it seem—well, like *you*. Like you did something, all
right, and now you're suffering for it. You know?" I said nothing. "Well you
know," he said, impatiently, "why *do* people suffer? Maybe it's better to do
something to give it a reason, *any* reason."

"But we just agreed," I said, "that there's no way not to suffer. Isn't it better, then, just to—take it?"

"But nobody just takes it," Sonny cried, "that's what I'm telling you!
Everybody tries not to. You're just hung up on the *way* some people try—it's
not *your* way!"

The hair on my face began to itch, my face felt wet. "That's not true," I
said, "that's not true. I don't give a damn what other people do, I don't even
care how they suffer. I just care how *you* suffer." And he looked at me. "Please
believe me," I said, "I don't want to see you—die—trying not to suffer."

"I won't," he said, flatly, "die trying not to suffer. At least, not any faster
than anybody else."

"But there's no need," I said, trying to laugh, "is there? in killing your-   210
self."

I wanted to say more, but I couldn't. I wanted to talk about will power and
how life could be—well, beautiful. I wanted to say that it was all within; but
was it? or, rather, wasn't that exactly the trouble? And I wanted to promise

that I would never fail him again. But it would all have sounded—empty words and lies.

So I made the promise to myself and prayed that I would keep it.

"It's terrible sometimes, inside," he said, "that's what's the trouble. You walk these streets, black and funky and cold, and there's not really a living ass to talk to, and there's nothing shaking, and there's no way of getting it out— that storm inside. You can't talk it and you can't make love with it, and when you finally try to get with it and play it, you realize *nobody's* listening. So *you've* got to listen. You got to find a way to listen."

And then he walked away from the window and sat on the sofa again, as though all the wind had suddenly been knocked out of him. "Sometimes you'll do *anything* to play, even cut your mother's throat." He laughed and looked at me. "Or your brother's." Then he sobered. "Or your own." Then: "Don't worry. I'm all right now and I think I'll *be* all right. But I can't forget—where I've been. I don't mean just the physical place I've been, I mean where I've *been*. And *what* I've been."

"What have you been, Sonny?" I asked.

215

He smiled—but sat sideways on the sofa, his elbow resting on the back, his fingers playing with his mouth and chin, not looking at me. "I've been something I didn't recognize, didn't know I could be. Didn't know anybody could be." He stopped, looking inward, looking helplessly young, looking old. "I'm not talking about it now because I feel *guilty* or anything like that— maybe it would be better if I did, I don't know. Anyway, I can't really talk about it. Not to you, not to anybody," and now he turned and faced me. "Sometimes, you know, and it was actually when I was most *out* of the world, I felt that I was in it, and that I was *with* it, really, and I could play or I didn't really have to *play*, it just came out of me, it was there. And I don't know how I played, thinking about it now, but I know I did awful things, those times, sometimes, to people. Or it wasn't that I *did* anything to them—it was that they weren't real." He picked up the beer can; it was empty; he rolled it be- tween his palms: "And other times—well, I needed a fix, I needed to find a place to lean, I needed to clear a space to *listen*—and I couldn't find it, and I— went crazy, I did terrible things to *me*, I was terrible *for* me." He began press- ing the beer can between his hands, I watched the metal begin to give. It glittered, as he played with it, like a knife, and I was afraid he would cut him- self, but I said nothing. "Oh well. I can never tell you. I was all by myself at the bottom of something, stinking and sweating and crying and shaking, and I smelled it, you know? *my* stink, and I thought I'd die if I couldn't get away from it and yet, all the same, I knew that everything I was doing was just lock- ing me in with it. And I didn't know," he paused, still flattening the beer can, "I didn't know, I still *don't* know, something kept telling me that maybe it was good to smell your own stink, but I didn't think that *that* was what I'd been trying to do—and—who can stand it?" and he abruptly dropped the ruined beer can, looking at me with a small, still smile, and then rose, walking to the window as though it were the lodestone rock. I watched his face, he watched the avenue. "I couldn't tell you when Mama died—but the reason I wanted to leave Harlem so bad was to get away from drugs. And then, when I ran away, that's what I was running from—really. When I came back, nothing had changed, *I* hadn't changed, I was just—older." And he stopped, drumming with his fingers on the windowpane. The sun had vanished, soon darkness would fall. I watched his face. "It can come again," he said, almost as though speaking to himself. Then he turned to me. "It can come again," he repeated. "I just want you to know that."

"All right," I said, at last. "So it can come again. All right."

He smiled, but the smile was sorrowful. "I had to try to tell you," he said.

"Yes," I said. "I understand that."

"You're my brother," he said, looking straight at me, and not smiling   220 at all.

"Yes," I repeated, "yes. I understand that."

He turned back to the window, looking out. "All that hatred down there," he said, "all that hatred and misery and love. It's a wonder it doesn't blow the avenue apart."

We went to the only night club on a short, dark street, downtown. We squeezed through the narrow, chattering, jam-packed bar to the entrance of the big room, where the bandstand was. And we stood there for a moment, for the lights were very dim in this room and we couldn't see. Then, "Hello, boy," said a voice and an enormous black man, much older than Sonny or myself, erupted out of all that atmospheric lighting and put an arm around Sonny's shoulder. "I been sitting right here," he said, "waiting for you."

He had a big voice, too, and heads in the darkness turned toward us.

Sonny grinned and pulled a little away, and said, "Creole, this is my   225 brother. I told you about him."

Creole shook my hand. "I'm glad to meet you, son," he said, and it was clear that he was glad to meet me *there*, for Sonny's sake. And he smiled, "You got a real musician in *your* family," and he took his arm from Sonny's shoulder and slapped him, lightly, affectionately, with the back of his hand.

"Well. Now I've heard it all," said a voice behind us. This was another musician, and a friend of Sonny's, a coal-black, cheerful-looking man, built close to the ground. He immediately began confiding to me, at the top of his lungs, the most terrible things about Sonny, his teeth gleaming like a lighthouse and his laugh coming up out of him like the beginning of an earthquake. And it turned out that everyone at the bar knew Sonny, or almost everyone; some were musicians, working there, or nearby, or not working, some were simply hangers-on, and some were there to hear Sonny play. I was introduced to all of them and they were all very polite to me. Yet, it was clear that, for them, I was only Sonny's brother. Here, I was in Sonny's world. Or, rather: his kingdom. Here, it was not even a question that his veins bore royal blood.

They were going to play soon and Creole installed me, by myself, at a table in a dark corner. Then I watched them, Creole, and the little black man, and Sonny, and the others, while they horsed around, standing just below the bandstand. The light from the bandstand spilled just a little short of them and, watching them laughing and gesturing and moving about, I had the feeling that they, nevertheless, were being most careful not to step into that circle of light too suddenly: that if they moved into the light too suddenly, without thinking, they would perish in flame. Then, while I watched, one of them, the small, black man, moved into the light and crossed the bandstand and started fooling around with his drums. Then—being funny and being, also, extremely ceremonious—Creole took Sonny by the arm and led him to the piano. A woman's voice called Sonny's name and a few hands started clapping. And Sonny, also being funny and being ceremonious, and so touched, I think, that he could have cried, but neither hiding it nor showing it, riding it like a man, grinned, and put both hands to his heart and bowed from the waist.

Creole then went to the bass fiddle and a lean, very bright-skinned brown man jumped up on the bandstand and picked up his horn. So there they were, and the atmosphere on the bandstand and in the room began to change and tighten. Someone stepped up to the microphone and announced them. Then there were all kinds of murmurs. Some people at the bar shushed others. The waitress ran around, frantically getting in the last orders, guys and chicks got closer to each other, and the lights on the bandstand, on the quartet, turned to a kind of indigo. Then they all looked different there. Creole looked about him for the last time, as though he were making certain that all his chickens were in the coop, and then he—jumped and struck the fiddle. And there they were.

All I know about music is that not many people ever really hear it. And even then, on the rare occasions when something opens within, and the music enters, what we mainly hear, or hear corroborated, are personal private, vanishing evocations. But the man who creates the music is hearing something else, is dealing with the roar rising from the void and imposing order on it as it hits the air. What is evoked in him, then, is of another order, more terrible because it has no words, and triumphant, too, for that same reason. And his triumph, when he triumphs, is ours. I just watched Sonny's face. His face was troubled, he was working hard, but he wasn't with it. And I had the feeling that, in a way, everyone on the bandstand was waiting for him, both waiting for him and pushing him along. But as I began to watch Creole, I realized that it was Creole who held them all back. He had them on a short rein. Up there, keeping the beat with his whole body, wailing on the fiddle, with his eyes half closed, he was listening to everything, but he was listening to Sonny. He was having a dialogue with Sonny. He wanted Sonny to leave the shore line and strike out for the deep water. He was Sonny's witness that deep water and drowning were not the same thing—he had been there, and he knew. And he wanted Sonny to know. He was waiting for Sonny to do the things on the keys which would let Creole know that Sonny was in the water.

And, while Creole listened, Sonny moved, deep within, exactly like someone in torment. I had never before thought of how awful the relationship must be between the musician and his instrument. He has to fill it, this instrument, with the breath of life, his own. He has to make it do what he wants it to do. And a piano is just a piano. It's made out of so much wood and wires and little hammers and big ones, and ivory. While there's only so much you can do with it, the only way to find this out is to try and make it do everything.

And Sonny hadn't been near a piano for over a year. And he wasn't on much better terms with his life, not the life that stretched before him now. He

230

and the piano stammered, started one way, got scared, stopped; started another way, panicked, marked time, started again; then seemed to have found a direction, panicked again, got stuck. And the face I saw on Sonny I'd never seen before. Everything had been burned out of it, and, at the same time, things usually hidden were being burned in, by the fire and fury of the battle which was occurring in him up there.

Yet, watching Creole's face as they neared the end of the first set, I had the feeling that something had happened, something I hadn't heard. Then they finished, there was scattered applause, and then, without an instant's warning, Creole started into something else, it was almost sardonic, it was *Am I Blue*. And, as though he commanded, Sonny began to play. Something began to happen. And Creole let out the reins. The dry, low, black man said something awful on the drums, Creole answered, and the drums talked back. Then the horn insisted, sweet and high, slightly detached perhaps, and Creole listened, commenting now and then, dry, and driving, beautiful and calm and old. Then they all came together again, and Sonny was part of the family again. I could tell this from his face. He seemed to have found, right there beneath his fingers, a damn brand-new piano. It seemed that he couldn't get over it. Then, for awhile, just being happy with Sonny, they seemed to be agreeing with him that brand-new pianos certainly were a gas.

Then Creole stepped forward to remind them that what they were playing was the blues. He hit something in all of them, he hit something in me, myself, and the music tightened and deepened, apprehension began to beat the air. Creole began to tell us what the blues were all about. They were not about anything very new. He and his boys up there were keeping it new, at the risk of ruin, destruction, madness, and death, in order to find new ways to make us listen. For, while the tale of how we suffer, and how we are delighted, and how we may triumph is never new, it always must be heard. There isn't any other tale to tell, it's the only light we've got in all this darkness.

And this tale, according to that face, that body, those strong hands on 235 those strings, has another aspect in every country, and a new depth in every generation. Listen, Creole seemed to be saying, listen. Now these are Sonny's blues. He made the little black man on the drums know it, and the bright, brown man on the horn. Creole wasn't trying any longer to get Sonny in the water. He was wishing him Godspeed. Then he stepped back, very slowly, filling the air with the immense suggestion that Sonny speak for himself.

Then they all gathered around Sonny and Sonny played. Every now and again one of them seemed to say, Amen. Sonny's fingers filled the air with life, his life. But that life contained so many others. And Sonny went all the way back, he really began with the spare, flat statement of the opening phrase of the song. Then he began to make it his. It was very beautiful because it wasn't hurried and it was no longer a lament. I seemed to hear with what burning he had made it his, with what burning we had yet to make it ours, how we could cease lamenting. Freedom lurked around us and I understood, at last, that he could help us to be free if we would listen, that he would never be free until we did. Yet, there was no battle in his face now. I heard what he had gone through, and would continue to go through until he came to rest in earth. He had made it his: that long line, of which we knew only Mama and Daddy. And he was giving it back, as everything must be given back, so that, passing through death, it can live forever. I saw my mother's face again, and felt, for the first time, how the stones of the road she had walked on must have bruised her feet. I saw the moonlit road where my father's brother died. And it brought something else back to me, and carried me past it, I saw my little girl again and felt Isabel's tears again, and I felt my own tears begin to rise. And I was yet aware that this was only a moment, that the world waited outside, as hungry as a tiger, and that trouble stretched above us, longer than the sky.

Then it was over. Creole and Sonny let out their breath, both soaking wet, and grinning. There was a lot of applause and some of it was real. In the dark, the girl came by and I asked her to take drinks to the bandstand. There was a long pause, while they talked up there in the indigo light and after awhile I saw the girl put a Scotch and milk on top of the piano for Sonny. He didn't seem to notice it, but just before they started playing again, he sipped from it and looked toward me, and nodded. Then he put it back on top of the piano. For me, then, as they began to play again, it glowed and shook above my brother's head like the very cup of trembling.

www   *TOPICS FOR CRITICAL THINKING* Web

1. What kinds of darkness surround the narrator?
2. In what ways is this story itself like the blues?
3. How are drugs and music alike?
4. How does the narrator envision the possibilities for social change?

www   *TOPICS FOR CRITICAL WRITING* Web

1. How are modes of escape in this story also methods of coping? Where is the line between self-destruction and salvation?
2. How does this story represent the world of urban African Americans and for what purposes?

Issues of Class

∽∽

TILLIE OLSEN

I Stand Here Ironing   *(1953–1954)*

I stand here ironing, and what you asked me moves tormented back and forth with the iron.

"I wish you would manage the time to come in and talk with me about your daughter. I'm sure you can help me understand her. She's a youngster who needs help and whom I'm deeply interested in helping."

"Who needs help." Even if I came, what good would it do? You think because I am her mother I have a key, or that in some way you could use me as a key? She has lived for nineteen years. There is all that life that has happened outside of me, beyond me.

And when is there time to remember, to sift, to weigh, to estimate, to total? I will start and there will be an interruption and I will have to gather it all together again. Or I will become engulfed with all I did or did not do, with what should have been and what cannot be helped.

She was a beautiful baby. The first and only one of our five that was beau- 5
tiful at birth. You do not guess how new and uneasy her tenancy in her now-loveliness. You did not know her all those years she was thought homely, or see her poring over her baby pictures, making me tell her over and over how beautiful she had been—and would be, I would tell her—and was now, to the seeing eye. But the seeing eyes were few or nonexistent. Including mine.

I nursed her. They feel that's important nowadays. I nursed all the children, but with her, with all the fierce rigidity of first motherhood, I did like the books then said. Though her cries battered me to trembling and my breasts ached with swollenness, I waited till the clock decreed.

Why do I put that first? I do not even know if it matters, or if it explains anything.

She was a beautiful baby. She blew shining bubbles of sound. She loved motion, loved light, loved color and music and textures. She would lie on the floor in her blue overalls patting the surface so hard in ecstasy her hands and feet would blur. She was a miracle to me, but when she was eight months old I had to leave her daytimes with the woman downstairs to whom she was no miracle at all, for I worked or looked for work and for Emily's father, who "could no longer endure" (he wrote in his good-bye note) "sharing want with us."

I was nineteen. It was the pre-relief, pre-WPA world of the depression. I would start running as soon as I got off the streetcar, running up the stairs, the place smelling sour, and awake or asleep to startle awake, when she saw me she would break into a clogged weeping that could not be comforted, a weeping I can hear yet.

After a while I found a job hashing at night so I could be with her days, 10
and it was better. But it came to where I had to bring her to his family and leave her.

It took a long time to raise the money for her fare back. Then she got chicken pox and I had to wait longer. When she finally came, I hardly knew her, walking quick and nervous like her father, looking like her father, thin, and dressed in a shoddy red that yellowed her skin and glared at the pockmarks. All the baby loveliness gone.

She was two. Old enough for nursery school they said, and I did not know then what I know now—the fatigue of the long day, and the lacerations of group life in nurseries that are only parking places for children.

Except that it would have made no difference if I had known. It was the only place there was. It was the only way we could be together, the only way I could hold a job.

And even without knowing, I knew. I knew the teacher that was evil because all these years it has curdled into my memory, the little boy hunched in the corner, her rasp, "why aren't you outside, because Alvin hits you? that's no reason, go out, scaredy." I knew Emily hated it even if she did not clutch and implore "don't go Mommy" like the other children, mornings.

She always had a reason why we should stay home. Momma, you look   15 sick. Momma, I feel sick. Momma, the teachers aren't there today, they're sick. Momma, we can't go, there was a fire there last night. Momma, it's a holiday today, no school, they told me.

But never a direct protest, never rebellion. I think of our others in their three-, four-year-oldness—the explosions, the tempers, the denunciations, the demands—and I feel suddenly ill. I put the iron down. What in me demanded that goodness in her? And what was the cost, the cost to her of such goodness?

The old man living in the back once said in his gentle way: "You should smile at Emily more when you look at her." What *was* in my face when I looked at her? I loved her. There were all the acts of love.

It was only with the others I remembered what he said, and it was the face of joy, and not of care or tightness or worry I turned to them—too late for Emily. She does not smile easily, let alone almost always as her brothers and sisters do. Her face is closed and sombre, but when she wants, how fluid. You must have seen it in her pantomimes, you spoke of her rare gift for comedy on the stage that rouses a laughter out of the audience so dear they applaud and applaud and do not want to let her go.

Where does it come from, that comedy? There was none of it in her when she came back to me that second time, after I had had to send her away again. She had a new daddy now to learn to love, and I think perhaps it was a better time.

Except when we left her alone nights, telling ourselves she was old   20 enough.

"Can't you go some other time, Mommy, like tomorrow?" she would ask. "Will it be just a little while you'll be gone? Do you promise?"

The time we came back, the front door open, the clock on the floor in the hall. She rigid awake. "It wasn't just a little while. I didn't cry. Three times I called you, just three times, and then I ran downstairs to open the door so you could come faster. The clock talked loud. I threw it away, it scared me what it talked."

She said the clock talked loud again that night I went to the hospital to have Susan. She was delirious with the fever that comes before red measles, but she was fully conscious all the week I was gone and the week after we were home when she could not come near the new baby or me.

She did not get well. She stayed skeleton thin, not wanting to eat, and night after night she had nightmares. She would call for me, and I would rouse from exhaustion to sleepily call back: "You're all right, darling, go to sleep, it's just a dream," and if she still called, in a sterner voice, "now go to sleep, Emily, there's nothing to hurt you." Twice, only twice, when I had to get up for Susan anyhow, I went in to sit with her.

Now when it is too late (as if she would let me hold and comfort her like   25

I do the others) I get up and go to her at once at her moan or restless stirring. "Are you awake, Emily? Can I get you something?" And the answer is always the same: "No, I'm all right, go back to sleep, Mother."

They persuaded me at the clinic to send her away to a convalescent home in the country where "she can have the kind of food and care you can't manage for her, and you'll be free to concentrate on the new baby." They still send children to that place. I see pictures on the society page of sleek young women planning affairs to raise money for it, or dancing at the affairs, or decorating Easter eggs or filling Christmas stockings for the children.

They never have a picture of the children so I do not know if the girls still wear those gigantic red bows and the ravaged looks on the every other Sunday when parents can come to visit "unless otherwise notified"—as we were notified the first six weeks.

Oh it is a handsome place, green lawns and tall trees and fluted flower beds. High up on the balconies of each cottage the children stand, the girls in their red bows and white dresses, the boys in white suits and giant red ties. The parents stand below shrieking up to be heard and the children shriek down to be heard, and between them the invisible wall "Not To Be Contaminated by Parental Germs or Physical Affection."

There was a tiny girl who always stood hand in hand with Emily. Her parents never came. One visit she was gone. "They moved her to Rose College," Emily shouted in explanation. "They don't like you to love anybody here."

She wrote once a week, the labored writing of a seven-year-old. "I am   30
fine. How is the baby. If I write my leter nicly I will have a star. Love." There never was a star. We wrote every other day, letters she could never hold or keep but only hear read—once. "We simply do not have room for children to keep any personal possessions," they patiently explained when we pieced one Sunday's shrieking together to plead how much it would mean to Emily, who loved so to keep things, to be allowed to keep her letters and cards.

Each visit she looked frailer. "She isn't eating," they told us.

(They had runny eggs for breakfast or mush with lumps, Emily said later, I'd hold it in my mouth and not swallow. Nothing ever tasted good, just when they had chicken.)

It took us eight months to get her released home, and only the fact that she gained back so little of her seven lost pounds convinced the social worker.

I used to try to hold and love her after she came back, but her body would stay stiff, and after a while she'd push away. She ate little. Food sickened her, and I think much of life too. Oh she had physical lightness and brightness, twinkling by on skates, bouncing like a ball up and down up and down over the jump rope, skimming over the hill; but these were momentary.

She fretted about her appearance, thin and dark and foreign-looking at a   35
time when every little girl was supposed to look or thought she should look a chubby blonde replica of Shirley Temple. The doorbell sometimes rang for her, but no one seemed to come and play in the house or be a best friend. Maybe because we moved so much.

There was a boy she loved painfully through two school semesters. Months later she told me how she had taken pennies from my purse to buy him candy. "Licorice was his favorite and I brought him some every day, but he still liked Jennifer better'n me. Why, Mommy?" The kind of question for which there is no answer.

School was a worry to her. She was not glib or quick in a world where glibness and quickness were easily confused with ability to learn. To her overworked and exasperated teachers she was an over-conscientious "slow learner" who kept trying to catch up and was absent entirely too often.

I let her be absent, though sometimes the illness was imaginary. How different from my now-strictness about attendance with the others. I wasn't working. We had a new baby, I was home anyhow. Sometimes, after Susan grew old enough, I would keep her home from school, too, to have them all together.

Mostly Emily had asthma, and her breathing, harsh and labored, would fill the house with a curiously tranquil sound. I would bring the two old dresser mirrors and her boxes of collections to her bed. She would select beads and single earrings, bottle tops and shells, dried flowers and pebbles, old postcards and scraps, all sorts of oddments; then she and Susan would play Kingdom, setting up landscapes and furniture, peopling them with action.

Those were the only times of peaceful companionship between her and   40
Susan. I have edged away from it, that poisonous feeling between them, that terrible balancing of hurts and needs I had to do between the two, and did so badly, those earlier years.

Oh there are conflicts between the others too, each one human, needing, demanding, hurting, taking—but only between Emily and Susan, no, Emily toward Susan that corroding resentment. It seems so obvious on the surface, yet it is not obvious. Susan, the second child, Susan, golden- and curly-haired and chubby, quick and articulate and assured, everything in appearance and manner Emily was not; Susan, not able to resist Emily's precious things, losing or sometimes clumsily breaking them; Susan telling jokes and riddles to company for applause while Emily sat silent (to say to me later: that was *my* riddle, Mother, I told it to Susan); Susan, who for all the five years' difference in age was just a year behind Emily in developing physically.

I am glad for that slow physical development that widened the difference between her and her contemporaries, though she suffered over it. She was too vulnerable for that terrible world of youthful competition, of preening and parading, of constant measuring of yourself against every other, of envy, "If I had that copper hair," "If I had that skin. . . ." She tormented herself enough about not looking like the others, there was enough of the unsureness, the having to be conscious of words before you speak, the constant caring—what are they thinking of me? without having it all magnified by the merciless physical drives.

Ronnie is calling. He is wet and I change him. It is rare there is such a cry now. That time of motherhood is almost behind me when the ear is not one's own but must always be racked and listening for the child cry, the child call. We sit for a while and I hold him, looking out over the city spread in charcoal with its soft aisles of light. "*Shoogily,*" he breathes and curls closer. I carry him back to bed, asleep. *Shoogily*. A funny word, a family word, inherited from Emily, invented by her to say: *comfort*.

In this and other ways she leaves her seal, I say aloud. And startle at my saying it. What do I mean? What did I start to gather together, to try and make coherent? I was at the terrible, growing years. War years. I do not remember them well. I was working, there were four smaller ones now, there was not time for her. She had to help be a mother, and housekeeper, and shopper. She had to set her seal. Mornings of crisis and near hysteria trying to get lunches packed, hair combed, coats and shoes found, everyone to school or Child Care on time, the baby ready for transportation. And always the paper scribbled on by a smaller one, the book looked at by Susan then mislaid, the homework not done. Running out to that huge school where she was one, she was lost, she was a drop; suffering over the unpreparedness, stammering and unsure in her classes.

There was so little time left at night after the kids were bedded down. She 45 would struggle over books, always eating (it was in those years she developed her enormous appetite that is legendary in our family) and I would be ironing, or preparing food for the next day, or writing V-mail to Bill, or tending the baby. Sometimes, to make me laugh, or out of her despair, she would imitate happenings or types at school.

I think I said once: "Why don't you do something like this in the school amateur show?" One morning she phoned me at work, hardly understandable through the weeping: "Mother, I did it. I won, I won; they gave me first prize; they clapped and clapped and wouldn't let me go."

Now suddenly she was Somebody, and as imprisoned in her difference as she had been in anonymity.

She began to be asked to perform at other high schools, even in colleges, then at city and statewide affairs. The first one we went to, I only recognized her that first moment when thin, shy, she almost drowned herself into the curtains. Then: Was this Emily? The control, the command, the convulsing and deadly clowning, the spell, then the roaring, stamping audience, unwilling to let this rare and precious laughter out of their lives.

Afterwards: You ought to do something about her with a gift like that— but without money or knowing how, what does one do? We have left it all to her, and the gift has as often eddied inside, clogged and clotted, as been used and growing.

She is coming. She runs up the stairs two at a time with her light graceful 50 step, and I know she is happy tonight. Whatever it was that occasioned your call did not happen today.

"Aren't you ever going to finish the ironing, Mother? Whistler painted his mother in a rocker. I'd have to paint mine standing over an ironing board." This is one of her communicative nights and she tells me everything and nothing as she fixes herself a plate of food out of the icebox.

She is so lovely. Why did you want me to come in at all? Why were you concerned? She will find her way.

She starts up the stairs to bed. "Don't get me up with the rest in the morning." "But I thought you were having midterms." "Oh, those," she comes back in, kisses me, and says quite lightly, "in a couple of years when we'll all be atom-dead they won't matter a bit."

She has said it before. She *believes* it. But because I have been dredging the past, and all that compounds a human being is so heavy and meaningful in me, I cannot endure it tonight.

I will never total it all. I will never come in to say: She was a child seldom   55
smiled at. Her father left me before she was a year old. I had to work her first six years when there was work, or I sent her home and to his relatives. There were years she had care she hated. She was dark and thin and foreign-looking in a world where the prestige went to blondeness and curly hair and dimples, she was slow where glibness was prized. She was a child of anxious, not proud, love. We were poor and could not afford for her the soil of easy growth. I was a young mother, I was a distracted mother. There were the other children pushing up, demanding. Her younger sister seemed all that she was not. There were years she did not want me to touch her. She kept too much in herself, her life was such she had to keep too much in herself. My wisdom came too late. She has much to her and probably nothing will come of it. She is a child of her age, of depression, of war, of fear.

Let her be. So all that is in her will not bloom—but in how many does it? There is still enough left to live by. Only help her to know—help make it so there is cause for her to know—that she is more than this dress on the ironing board, helpless before the iron.

TILLIE OLSEN

www

(b. 1913?) Web

A single mother with four children, Olsen began to write in the 1930s. She was awarded a Guggenheim Fellowship.

www

TOPICS FOR CRITICAL THINKING Web

1. Why is this story framed with a request that the narrator come in and discuss the daughter?

2. In what ways does this story question mainstream ideas about hard work and family?

3. What alternative possibilities to middle class notions of parenting does the narrator offer?

www

TOPICS FOR CRITICAL WRITING Web

1. What are the connections between ironing and storytelling?

2. What norms does the story bring into question? How does it accomplish this questioning?

Part II
Image, Style, Structure

8   Reading Image and Style Closely

"Sarrasine," a story written by Honoré de Balzac, is one of the most closely analyzed stories in the history of literary criticism. Full of rich, enigmatic images and puzzles about gender and history, "Sarrasine" is the focus of Roland *www* Barthes's comprehensive analysis in *S/Z* (1970). **Web** Barthes, an influential critic and literary theorist, helped enlist new ways of analyzing both literature and culture. The thoroughness of Barthes's reading (which does not even pretend to be complete) illustrates how stories are comprised of many interconnected and elaborate sign systems (systems such as fashion, food, social customs, and courtesy, in addition to language and literary conventions).

Analyzing the formal elements of fiction (character, setting, plot, narrator, point of view, and theme) helps readers understand what a story is "about." But studying a story's use of images and style increases our understanding of the story's *art*—what it says, how it says it, and how form and content relate to one another. Studying imagery and style often engages readers in a more detailed examination of a story. This might make the task of interpretation more complicated, but it also shows how intricate and complex stories really are. To understand how image, language, and structure work together with a story's other formal elements requires a painstaking scrutiny of the text. It also requires a more sophisticated understanding of language. The purpose of such an analysis is to discover how all the elements of a text work together *as a story*.

Much of what Barthes discerns in his study of "Sarrasine" is based on the connotative qualities of the words that appear in the text. Words both refer to something specific (they denote) and suggest associations, contexts, or shades of meaning (they connote). For example, the word *tycoon* denotes a very rich man, while it connotes a specific kind of rich man who has accumulated vast wealth through corporate dealings. Because all of the words in a story both denote and connote, a story's language is a rich site of multiple and often ambivalent and conflicting meanings. While Barthes demonstrates how this happens in "Sarrasine," it happens in all fiction. In Nathaniel Hawthorne's "The Birthmark," for example, the narrator refers to the birthmark as a "mark," an "impress," and a "stain." Though they all denote the same thing, each of these words connotes something slightly different—"mark" connoting the addition of a spot, "impress" connoting that the spot had been formed by something touching the heroine's cheek, and "stain" suggesting something slightly shameful or dirty. In "The Birthmark," these differing connotations represent different opinions about the birthmark's beauty.

Studying the shades of meaning in a story's language in relation to its images and ideas helps critics and readers define subsystems within the story. **Subsystems** are a way of understanding how different aspects of a story both break down into coherent groups and fit together. They are different for every story. For example, in the young boxer's story presented in the Introduction, the politics and rules of boxing might form one subsystem, while the racial and class positions of the various characters might form another. These subsystems come together in the boxing match, which gains part of its impact from the clash of underdog and champion, black man and white man. A primary subsystem in "The Birthmark" is the many interpretations of the birthmark itself. When the birthmark comes up against the story's subsystem of science, both the birthmark and its bearer are destroyed. Subsystems combine with the story's obvious or surface elements of plot, characterization, and setting to reveal the larger system of the story—its preoccupations, conflicts, issues, and the ways it represents them. What Barthes's analysis of "Sarrasine" shows is that the choices that make up the story are not at all random. Rather, they constitute a multilayered architecture constructed with the balanced tensions characteristic of a gothic arch or an extension bridge.

Critical Perspective: Semiotics Web *www*

The method Barthes uses to analyze stories is known as *semiotics*. **Semiotics** is the study of how various signs (or signifiers) relate to one another in complex webs of meaning. Semiotics is the study of both what signs are and how they work together. Signs consist of anything from words, names, and road signs to gestures, objects, and social conventions. A simple example of a sign system is how the shapes of road signs tell us what the sign says—the triangular yield sign, octagonal stop sign, shield-like route sign, and so on. A more complex example is the system of signs that signal ways to understand a movie—for example, camera angles and methods of editing. We understand that when an image fades out, time passes; when the camera focuses on a detail, this detail will play an important role in the story.

Written in 1830, Balzac's "Sarrasine" is part of his large series of stories and novels called *La Comédie Humaine*. Like the American authors who would follow him, Balzac was a realist, describing with unsentimental detail the more than two thousand named characters that appear throughout his work.

ᔕᔕ

HONORÉ DE BALZAC
Translated by Richard Miller

Sarrasine   *(1830)*

I was deep in one of those daydreams which overtake even the shallowest of men, in the midst of the most tumultuous parties. Midnight had just sounded from the clock of the Elysée-Bourbon. Seated in a window recess and hidden behind the sinuous folds of a silk curtain, I could contemplate at my leisure the garden of the mansion where I was spending the evening. The trees, partially covered with snow, stood out dimly against the grayish background of a cloudy sky, barely whitened by the moon. Seen amid these fantastic surroundings, they vaguely resembled ghosts half out of their shrouds, a gigantic representation of the famous Dance of the Dead. Then, turning in the other direction, I could admire the Dance of the Living! a splendid salon decorated in silver and gold, with glittering chandeliers, sparkling with candles. There, milling about, whirling around, flitting here and there, were the most beautiful women of Paris, the richest, the noblest, dazzling, stately, resplendent with diamonds, flowers in their hair, on their bosoms, on their heads, strewn over dresses or in garlands at their feet. Light, rustling movements, voluptuous steps, made the laces, the silk brocades, the gauzes, float around their delicate forms. Here and there, some overly animated glances darted forth, eclipsing the lights, the fire of the diamonds, and stimulated anew some too-ardent hearts. One might also catch movements of the head meaningful to lovers, and negative gestures for husbands. The sudden outburst of the gamblers' voices at each unexpected turn of the dice, the clink of gold, mingled with the music and the murmur of conversation, and to complete the giddiness of this mass of people intoxicated by everything seductive the world can hold, a haze of perfume and general inebriation played upon the fevered mind. Thus, on my right, the dark and silent image of death; on my left, the seemly bacchanalias of life: here, cold nature, dull, in mourning; there, human beings enjoying themselves. On the borderline between these two so different scenes, which, a thousand times repeated in various guises, make Paris the world's most amusing and most philosophical city, I was making for myself a moral macédoine, half pleasant, half funereal. With my left foot I beat time, and I felt as though the other were in the grave. My leg was in fact chilled by one of those insidious drafts which freeze half our bodies while the other half feels the humid heat of rooms, an occurrence rather frequent at balls.

"Monsieur de Lanty hasn't owned this house for very long, has he?"

"Oh yes. Maréchal Carigliano sold it to him nearly ten years ago."

"Ah!"

"These people must have a huge fortune."   5

"They must have."

"What a party! It's shockingly elegant."

"Do you think they're as rich as M. de Nucingen or M. de Gondreville?"

"You mean you don't know?" . . .

I stuck my head out and recognized the two speakers as members of that   10 strange race which, in Paris, deals exclusively with "whys" and "hows," with "Where did they come from?" "What's happening?" "What has she done?" They lowered their voices and walked off to talk in greater comfort on some isolated sofa. Never had a richer vein been offered to seekers after mystery. Nobody knew what country the Lanty family came from, or from what business, what plunder, what piratical activity, or what inheritance derived a fortune estimated at several millions. All the members of the family spoke Italian,

French, Spanish, English, and German perfectly enough to create the belief that they must have spent a long time among these various peoples. Were they gypsies? Were they freebooters?

"Even if it's the devil," some young politicians said, "they give a marvelous party."

"Even if the Count de Lanty had robbed a bank, I'd marry his daughter any time!" cried a philosopher.

Who wouldn't have married Marianina, a girl of sixteen whose beauty embodied the fabled imaginings of the Eastern poets! Like the sultan's daughter, in the story of the Magic Lamp, she should have been kept veiled. Her singing put into the shade the partial talents of Malibran, Sontag, and Fodor, in whom one dominant quality has always excluded over-all perfection; whereas Marianina was able to bring to the same level purity of sound, sensibility, rightness of movement and pitch, soul and science, correctness and feeling. This girl was the embodiment of that secret poetry, the common bond among all the arts, which always eludes those who search for it. Sweet and modest, educated and witty, no one could eclipse Marianina, save her mother.

Have you ever encountered one of those women whose striking beauty defies the inroads of age and who seem at thirty-six more desirable than they could have been fifteen years earlier? Their visage is a vibrant soul, it glows; each feature sparkles with intelligence; each pore has a special brilliance, especially in artificial light. Their seductive eyes refuse, attract, speak or remain silent; their walk is innocently knowledgeable; their voices employ the melodious wealth of the most coquettishly soft and tender notes. Based on comparisons, their praises flatter the self-love of the most sentient. A movement of their eyebrows, the least glance, their pursed lips, fill with a kind of terror those whose life and happiness depend upon them. Inexperienced in love and influenced by words, a young girl can be seduced; for this kind of woman, however, a man must know, like M. de Jaucourt, not to cry out when he is hiding in a closet and the maid breaks two of his fingers as she shuts the door on them. In loving these powerful sirens, one gambles with one's life. And this, perhaps, is why we love them so passionately. Such was the Countess de Lanty.

Filippo, Marianina's brother, shared with his sister in the Countess's marvelous beauty. To be brief, this young man was a living image of Antinous, even more slender. Yet how well these thin, delicate proportions are suited to young people when an olive complexion, strongly defined eyebrows, and the fire of velvet eyes give promise of future male passion, of brave thoughts! If Filippo resided in every girl's heart as an ideal, he also resided in the memory of every mother as the best catch in France.

The beauty, the fortune, the wit, the charms of these two children, came solely from their mother. The Count de Lanty was small, ugly, and pockmarked; dark as a Spaniard, dull as a banker. However, he was taken to be a deep politician, perhaps because he rarely laughed, and was always quoting Metternich or Wellington.

This mysterious family had all the appeal of one of Lord Byron's poems, whose difficulties each person in the fashionable world interpreted in a different way: an obscure and sublime song in every strophe. The reserve maintained by M. and Mme de Lanty about their origin, their past life, and their relationship with the four corners of the globe had not lasted long as a subject of astonishment in Paris. Nowhere perhaps is Vespasian's axiom better understood. There, even bloodstained or filthy money betrays nothing and stands for everything. So long as high society knows the amount of your fortune, you are classed among those having an equal amount, and no one asks to see your family tree, because everyone knows how much it cost. In a city where social problems are solved like algebraic equations, adventurers have every opportunity in their favor. Even supposing this family were of gypsy origin, it was so wealthy, so attractive, that society had no trouble in forgiving its little secrets. Unfortunately, however, the mystery of the Lantys presented a continuing source of curiosity, rather like that contained in the novels of Ann Radcliffe.

Observers, people who make it a point to know in what shop you buy your candlesticks, or who ask the amount of your rent when they find your apartment attractive, had noticed, now and then, in the midst of the Countess's parties, concerts, balls, and routs, the appearance of a strange personage. It was a man. The first time he had appeared in the mansion was during a concert, when he seemed to have been drawn to the salon by Marianina's enchanting voice.

"All of a sudden, I'm cold," a lady had said who was standing with a friend by the door.

The stranger, who was standing next to the women, went away. 20

"That's odd! I'm warm now," she said, after the stranger had gone. "And you'll say I'm mad, but I can't help thinking that my neighbor, the man dressed in black who just left, was the cause of my chill."

Before long, the exaggeration native to those in high society gave birth to and accumulated the most amusing ideas, the most outrageous expressions, the most ridiculous anecdotes about this mysterious personage. Although not a vampire, a ghoul, or an artificial man, a kind of Faust or Robin Goodfellow, people fond of fantasy said he had something of all these anthropomorphic natures about him. Here and there, one came across some Germans who accepted as fact these clever witticisms of Parisian scandal-mongering. The stranger was merely an old man. Many of the young men who were in the habit of settling the future of Europe every morning in a few elegant phrases would have liked to see in this stranger some great criminal, the possessor of vast wealth. Some storytellers recounted the life of this old man and provided really curious details about the atrocities he had committed while in the service of the Maharaja of Mysore. Some bankers more positive by nature, invented a fable about money. "Bah," they said, shrugging their shoulders in pity, "this poor old man is a *tête génoise!*"

"Sir, without being indiscreet, could you please tell me what you mean by a *tête génoise?*"

"A man, sir, with an enormous lifetime capital and whose family's income doubtless depends on his good health."

I remember having heard at Mme d'Espard's a hypnotist proving on 25 highly suspect historical data that this old man, preserved under glass, was the famous Balsamo, known as Cagliostro. According to this contemporary alchemist, the Sicilian adventurer had escaped death and passed his time fabricating gold for his grandchildren. Last, the bailiff of Ferette maintained that he had recognized this odd personage as the Count of Saint-Germain. These stupidities, spoken in witty accents, with the mocking air characteristic of atheistic society in our day, kept alive vague suspicions about the Lanty family. Finally, through a strange combination of circumstances, the members of this family justified everyone's conjectures by behaving somewhat mysteriously toward this old man, whose life was somehow hidden from all investigation.

Whenever this person crossed the threshold of the room he was supposed to inhabit in the Lanty mansion, his appearance always created a great sensation among the family. One might have called it an event of great importance. Filippo, Marianina, Mme de Lanty, and an old servant were the only persons privileged to assist the old man in walking, arising, sitting down. Each of them watched over his slightest movement. It seemed that he was an enchanted being upon whom depended the happiness, the life, or the fortune of them all. Was it affection or fear? Those in society were unable to discover any clue to help them solve this problem. Hidden for whole months in the depths of a secret sanctuary, this family genie would suddenly come forth, unexpectedly, and would appear in the midst of the salons like those fairies of bygone days who descended from flying dragons to interrupt the rites to which they had not been invited. Only the most avid onlookers were then able to perceive the uneasiness of the heads of the house, who could conceal their feelings with unusual skill. Sometimes, however, while dancing a quadrille, Marianina, naïve as she was, would cast a terrified glance at the old man when she spied him among the crowd. Or else Filippo would slip quickly through the throng to his side and would stay near him, tender and attentive, as though contact with others or the slightest breath would destroy this strange creature. The Countess would make a point of drawing near, without seeming to have any intention of joining them; then, assuming a manner and expression of servitude mixed with tenderness, submission, and power, she would say a few words, to which the old man nearly always deferred, and he would disappear, led off, or, more precisely, carried off, by her. If Mme de Lanty were not present, the Count used a thousand stratagems to reach his side; however, he seemed to have difficulty making himself heard, and treated him like a spoiled child whose mother gives in to his whims in order to avoid a scene. Some bolder persons having thoughtlessly ventured to question the Count de Lanty, this cold, reserved man had appeared never to understand them. And so, after many tries, all futile because of the circumspection of the entire family, everyone stopped trying to fathom such a well-kept secret. Weary of trying, the companionable spies, the idly curious, and the politic all gave up bothering about this mystery.

However, even now perhaps in these glittering salons there were some philosophers who, while eating an ice or a sherbert, or placing their empty punch glass on a side table, were saying to each other: "It wouldn't surprise me to learn that those people are crooks. The old man who hides and only makes his appearance on the first day of spring or winter, or at the solstices, looks to me like a killer . . ."

"Or a confidence man . . ."

"It's almost the same thing. Killing a man's fortune is sometimes worse than killing the man."

"Sir, I have bet twenty louis, I should get back forty."

"But, sir, there are only thirty on the table."   30

"Ah well, you see how mixed the crowd is, here. It's impossible to play."

"True . . . But it's now nearly six months since we've seen the Spirit. Do you think he's really alive?"

"Hah! at best . . ."

These last words were spoken near me by people I did not know, as they   35
were moving off, and as I was resuming, in an afterthought, my mixed thoughts of white and black, life and death. My vivid imagination as well as my eyes looked back and forth from the party, which had reached the height of its splendor, and the somber scene in the gardens. I do not know how long I meditated on these two faces of the human coin; but all at once I was awakened by the stifled laugh of a young woman. I was stunned by the appearance of the image which arose before me. By one of those tricks of nature, the half-mournful thought turning in my mind had emerged, and it appeared living before me, it had sprung like Minerva from the head of Jove, tall and strong, it was at once a hundred years old and twenty-two years old; it was alive and dead. Escaped from his room like a lunatic from his cell, the little old man had obviously slipped behind a hedge of people who were listening to Marianina's voice, finishing the cavatina from *Tancredi*. He seemed to have come out from underground, impelled by some piece of stage machinery. Motionless and somber, he stood for a moment gazing at the party, the noises of which had perhaps reached his ears. His almost somnambulatory preoccupation was so concentrated on things that he was in the world without seeing it. He had unceremoniously sprung up next to one of the most ravishing women in Paris, a young and elegant dancer, delicately formed, with one of those faces as fresh as that of a child, pink and white, so frail and transparent that a man's glance seems to penetrate it like a ray of sunlight going through ice. They were both there before me, together, united, and so close that the stranger brushed against her, her gauzy dress, her garlands of flowers, her softly curled hair, her floating sash.

I had brought this young woman to Mme de Lanty's ball. Since this was her first visit to the house, I forgave her her stifled laugh, but I quickly gave her a signal which completely silenced her and filled her with awe for her neighbor. She sat down next to me. The old man did not want to leave this lovely creature, to whom he had attached himself with that silent and seemingly baseless stubbornness to which the extremely old are prone, and which makes them appear childish. In order to sit near her, he had to take a folding chair. His slightest movements were full of that cold heaviness, the stupid indecision, characteristic of the gestures of a paralytic. He sat slowly down on his seat, with circumspection, muttering some unintelligible words. His worn-out voice was like the sound made by a stone falling down a well. The young woman held my hand tightly, as if seeking protection on some precipice, and she shivered when this man at whom she was looking turned upon her two eyes without warmth, glaucous eyes which could only be compared to dull mother-of-pearl.

"I'm afraid," she said, leaning toward my ear.

"You can talk," I answered. "He is very hard of hearing."

"Do you know him?"

"Yes." 40

Thereupon, she gathered up enough courage to look for a moment at this creature for which the human language had no name, a form without substance, a being without life, or a life without action. She was under the spell of that timorous curiosity which leads women to seek out dangerous emotions, to go see chained tigers, to look at boa constrictors, frightening themselves because they are separated from them only by weak fences. Although the little old man's back was stooped like a laborer's, one could easily tell that he must have had at one time a normal shape. His excessive thinness, the delicacy of his limbs, proved that he had always been slender. He was dressed in black silk trousers which fell about his bony thighs in folds, like an empty sail. An anatomist would have promptly recognized the symptoms of galloping consumption by looking at the skinny legs supporting this strange body. You would have said they were two bones crossed on a tombstone.

A feeling of profound horror for mankind gripped the heart when one saw the marks that decrepitude had left on this fragile machine. The stranger was wearing an old-fashioned gold-embroidered white waistcoat, and his linen was dazzlingly white. A frill of somewhat yellowed lace, rich enough for a queen's envy, fell into ruffles on his breast. On him, however, this lace seemed more like a rag than like an ornament. Centered on it was a fabulous diamond which glittered like the sun. This outmoded luxury, this particular and tasteless jewel, made the strange creature's face even more striking. The setting was worthy of the portrait. This dark face was angular and all sunk in. The chin was sunken, the temples were sunken; the eyes were lost in yellowish sockets. The jawbones stood out because of his indescribable thinness, creating cavities in the center of each cheek. These deformations, more or less illuminated by the candles, produced shadows and strange reflections which succeeded in erasing any human characteristics from his face. And the years had glued the thin, yellow skin of his face so closely to his skull that it was covered all over with a multitude of circular wrinkles, like the ripples on a pond into which a child has thrown a pebble, or star-shaped, like a cracked windowpane, but everywhere deep and close-set as the edges of pages in a closed book. Some old people have presented more hideous portraits; what contributed the most, however, in lending the appearance of an artificial creature to the specter which had risen up before us was the red and white with which he glistened. The eyebrows of his mask took from the light a luster which revealed that they were painted on. Fortunately for the eye depressed by the sight of such ruin, his cadaverous skull was covered by a blond wig whose innumerable curls were evidence of an extraordinary pretension. For the rest, the feminine coquetry of this phantasmagorical personage was rather strongly emphasized by the gold ornaments hanging from his ears, by the rings whose fine stones glittered on his bony fingers, and by a watch chain which shimmered like the brilliants of a choker around a woman's neck. Finally, this sort of Japanese idol had on his bluish lips a fixed and frozen smile, implacable and mocking, like a skull. Silent and motionless as a statue, it exuded the musty odor of old clothes which the heirs of some duchess take out for inventory. Although the old man turned his eyes toward the crowd, it seemed that the movements of those orbs, incapable of sight, were accomplished only by means of some imperceptible artifice; and when the eyes came to rest on something, anyone looking at them would have concluded that they had not moved at all. To see, next to this human wreckage, a young woman whose neck, bosom, and arms were bare and white, whose figure was in the full bloom of its beauty, whose hair rose from her alabaster forehead and inspired love, whose eyes did not receive but gave off light, who was soft, fresh, and whose floating curls and sweet breath seemed too heavy, too hard, too powerful for this shadow, for this man of dust: ah! here were death and life indeed, I thought, in a fantastic arabesque, half hideous chimera, divinely feminine from the waist up.

"Yet there are marriages like that often enough in the world," I said to myself.

"He smells like a graveyard," cried the terrified young woman, pressing against me for protection, and whose uneasy movements told me she was frightened. "What a horrible sight," she went on. "I can't stay here any longer. If I look at him again, I shall believe that death itself has come looking for me. Is he alive?"

She reached out to the phenomenon with that boldness women can summon up out of the strength of their desires; but she broke into a cold sweat, for no sooner had she touched the old man than she heard a cry like a rattle. This sharp voice, if voice it was, issued from a nearly dried up throat. Then the sound was quickly followed by a little, convulsive, childish cough of a peculiar sonorousness. At this sound, Marianina, Filippo, and Mme de Lanty looked in our direction, and their glances were like bolts of lightning. The young woman wished she were at the bottom of the Seine. She took my arm and led me into a side room. Men, women, everyone made way for us. At the end of the public rooms, we came into a small, semicircular chamber. My companion threw herself onto a divan, trembling with fright, oblivious to her surroundings.

"Madame, you are mad," I said to her.

"But," she replied, after a moment's silence, during which I gazed at her in admiration, "is it my fault? Why does Mme de Lanty allow ghosts to wander about in her house?"

"Come," I replied, "you are being ridiculous, taking a little old man for a ghost."

"Be still," she said, with that forceful and mocking air all women so easily assume when they want to be in the right. "What a pretty room!" she cried, looking around. "Blue satin always makes such wonderful wall hangings. How refreshing it is! Oh! what a beautiful painting!" she went on, getting up and going to stand before a painting in a magnificent frame.

We stood for a moment in contemplation of this marvel, which seemed to have been painted by some supernatural brush. The picture was of Adonis lying on a lion's skin. The lamp hanging from the ceiling of the room in an alabaster globe illuminated this canvas with a soft glow which enabled us to make out all the beauties of the painting.

"Does such a perfect creature exist?" she asked me, after having, with a soft smile of contentment, examined the exquisite grace of the contours, the pose, the color, the hair; in short, the entire picture.

"He is too beautiful for a man," she added, after an examination such as she might have made of some rival.

Oh! how jealous I then felt: something in which a poet had vainly tried to make me believe, the jealousy of engravings, of pictures, wherein artists exaggerate human beauty according to the doctrine which leads them to idealize everything.

"It's a portrait," I replied, "the product of the talent of Vien. But that great painter never saw the original and maybe you'd admire it less if you knew that this daub was copied from the statue of a woman."

"But who is it?"   55

I hesitated.

"I want to know," she added, impetuously.

"I believe," I replied, "that this Adonis is a . . . a relative of Mme de Lanty."

I had the pain of seeing her rapt in the contemplation of this figure. She sat in silence; I sat down next to her and took her hand without her being aware of it! Forgotten for a painting! At this moment, the light footsteps of a woman in a rustling dress broke the silence. Young Marianina came in, and her innocent expression made her even more alluring than did her grace and her lovely dress; she was walking slowly and escorting with maternal care, with filial solicitude, the costumed specter who had made us flee from the music room and whom she was leading, watching with what seemed to be concern as he slowly advanced on his feeble feet. They went together with some difficulty to a door hidden behind a tapestry. There, Marianina knocked softly. At once, as if by magic, a tall, stern man, a kind of family genie, appeared. Before entrusting the old man to the care of his mysterious guardian, the child respectfully kissed the walking corpse, and her chaste caress was not devoid of that graceful cajolery of which some privileged women possess the secret.

"Addio, addio," she said, with the prettiest inflection in her youthful   60 voice.

She added to the final syllable a marvelously well-executed trill, but in a soft voice, as if to give poetic expression to the emotions in her heart. Suddenly struck by some memory, the old man stood on the threshold of this secret hideaway. Then, through the silence, we heard the heavy sigh that came from his chest: he took the most beautiful of the rings which adorned his skeletal fingers, and placed it in Marianina's bosom. The young girl broke into laughter, took the ring, and slipped it onto her finger over her glove; then she walked quickly toward the salon, from which there could be heard the opening measures of a quadrille. She saw us:

"Ah, you were here," she said, blushing.

After having seemed as if about to question us, she ran to her partner with the careless petulance of youth.

"What did that mean?" my young companion asked me. "Is he her husband? I must be dreaming. Where am I?"

"You," I replied, "you, madame, superior as you are, you who understand   65
so well the most hidden feelings, who know how to inspire in a man's heart the most delicate of feelings without blighting it, without breaking it at the outset, you who pity heartache and who combine the wit of a Parisienne with a passionate soul worthy of Italy or Spain—"

She perceived the bitter irony in my speech; then, without seeming to have heard, she interrupted me: "Oh, you fashion me to your own taste. What tyranny! You don't want me for myself!"

"Ah, I want nothing," I cried, taken aback by her severity. "Is it true, at least, that you enjoy hearing stories of those vivid passions that ravishing Southern women inspire in our hearts?"

"Yes, so?"

"So, I'll call tomorrow around nine and reveal this mystery to you."

"No," she replied, "I want to know now."   70

"You haven't yet given me the right to obey you when you say: I want to."

"At this moment," she replied with maddening coquetry, "I have the most burning desire to know the secret. Tomorrow, I might not even listen to you . . ."

She smiled and we parted; she just as proud, just as forbidding, and I just as ridiculous as ever. She had the audacity to waltz with a young aide-de-camp; and I was left in turn angry, pouting, admiring, loving, jealous.

"Till tomorrow," she said, around two in the morning, as she left the ball.

"I won't go," I thought to myself. "I'll give you up. You are more capri-   75
cious, perhaps a thousand times more fanciful . . . than my imagination."

The next evening, we were both seated before a good fire in a small, elegant salon, she on a low sofa, I on cushions almost at her feet, and my eyes below hers. The street was quiet. The lamp shed a soft light. It was one of those evenings pleasing to the soul, one of those never-to-be-forgotten moments, one of those hours spent in peace and desire whose charm, later on, is a matter for constant regret, even when we may be happier. Who can erase the vivid imprint of the first feelings of love?

"Well," she said, "I'm listening."

"I don't dare begin. The story has some dangerous passages for its teller. If I become too moved, you must stop me."

"Tell."

"I will obey."   80

Ernest-Jean Sarrasine was the only son of a lawyer in the Franche-Comté, I went on, after a pause. His father had amassed six or eight thousand livres of income honestly enough, a professional's fortune which at that time in the provinces, was considered to be colossal. The elder Sarrasine, having but one child and anxious to overlook nothing where his education was concerned, hoped to make a magistrate of him, and to live long enough to see, in his old age, the grandson of Matthieu Sarrasine, farmer of Saint-Dié, seated beneath the lilies and napping through some trial for the greater glory of the law; however, heaven did not hold this pleasure in store for the lawyer.

The younger Sarrasine, entrusted to the Jesuits at an early age, evidenced an unusual turbulence. He had the childhood of a man of talent. He would study only what pleased him, frequently rebelled, and sometimes spent hours on end plunged in confused thought, occupied at times in watching his comrades at play, at times dreaming of Homeric heroes. Then, if he made up his mind to amuse himself, he threw himself into games with an extraordinary ardor. When a fight broke out between him and a friend, the battle rarely ended without bloodshed. If he was the weaker of the two, he would bite. Both active and passive by turns, without aptitude and not overly intelligent, his bizarre character made his teachers as wary of him as were his classmates. Instead of learning the elements of Greek, he drew the Reverend Father as he explained a passage in Thucydides to them, sketched the mathematics teacher, the tutors, the Father in charge of discipline, and he scribbled shapeless designs on the walls. Instead of singing the Lord's praises in church, he distracted himself during services by whittling on a pew; or when he had stolen a piece of wood, he carved some holy figure. If he had no wood, paper, or pencil, he reproduced his ideas with bread crumbs. Whether copying the characters in the pictures that decorated the choir, or improvising, he always left behind him some gross sketches whose licentiousness shocked the youngest Fathers; evil tongues maintained that the older Jesuits were amused by them. Finally, if we are to believe school gossip, he was expelled for having, while awaiting his turn at the confessional on Good Friday, shaped a big stick of wood into the form of Christ. The impiety with which this statue was endowed was too blatant not to have merited punishment of the artist. Had he not had the audacity to place this somewhat cynical figure on top of the tabernacle!

Sarrasine sought in Paris a refuge from the effects of a father's curse. Having one of those strong wills that brook no obstacle, he obeyed the commands of his genius and entered Bouchardon's studio. He worked all day, and in the evening went out to beg for his living. Astonished at the young artist's progress and intelligence, Bouchardon soon became aware of his pupil's poverty; he helped him, grew fond of him, and treated him like his own son. Then, when Sarrasine's genius was revealed in one of those works in which future talent struggles with the effervescence of youth, the warmhearted Bouchardon endeavored to restore him to the old lawyer's good graces. Before the authority of the famous sculptor, the parental anger subsided. All Besançon rejoiced at having given birth to a great man of the future. In the first throes of the ecstasy produced by his flattered vanity, the miserly lawyer gave his son the means to cut a good figure in society. For a long time, the lengthy and laborious studies demanded by sculpture tamed Sarrasine's impetuous nature and wild genius. Bouchardon, foreseeing the violence with which the passions would erupt in this young soul, which was perhaps as predisposed to them as Michelangelo's had been, channeled his energy into constant labor. He succeeded in keeping Sarrasine's extraordinary impetuosity within limits by forbidding him to work; by suggesting distractions when he saw him being carried away by the fury of some idea, or by entrusting him with important work when he seemed on the point of abandoning himself to dissipation. However, gentleness was always the most powerful of weapons where this passionate soul was concerned, and the master had no greater control over his student than when he inspired his gratitude through paternal kindness.

At twenty-two, Sarrasine was necessarily removed from the salutary influence Bouchardon had exercised over his morals and his habits. He reaped the fruits of his genius by winning the sculpture prize established by the Marquis de Marigny, the brother of Mme de Pompadour, who did so much for the arts. Diderot hailed the statue by Bouchardon's pupil as a masterpiece. The King's sculptor, not without great sorrow, saw off to Italy a young man whom he had kept, as a matter of principle, in total ignorance of the facts of life.

For six years, Sarrasine had boarded with Bouchardon. As fanatic in his art as Canova was later to be, he arose at dawn, went to the studio, did not emerge until nightfall, and lived only with his Muse. If he went to the Comédie-Française, he was taken by his master. He felt so out of place at Mme Geoffrin's and in high society, into which Bouchardon tried to introduce him, that he preferred to be alone, and shunned the pleasures of that licentious era. He had no other mistress but sculpture and Clotilde, one of the luminaries of the Opéra. And even this affair did not last. Sarrasine was rather ugly, always badly dressed, and so free in his nature, so irregular in his private life, that the celebrated nymph, fearing some catastrophe, soon relinquished the sculptor to his love of the Arts. Sophie Arnould made one of her witticisms on this subject. She confessed her surprise, I believe, that her friend had managed to triumph over statuary.

Sarrasine left for Italy in 1758. During the journey, his vivid imagination caught fire beneath a brilliant sky and at the sight of the wonderful monuments which are to be found in the birthplace of the Arts. He admired the statues, the frescoes, the paintings, and thus inspired, he came to Rome, filled with desire to carve his name between Michelangelo's and M. Bouchardon's. Accordingly, at the beginning, he divided his time between studio tasks and examining the works of art in which Rome abounds. He had already spent two weeks in the ecstatic state which overwhelms young minds at the sight of the queen of ruins, when he went one evening to the Teatro Argentina, before which a huge crowd was assembled. He inquired as to the causes of this gathering and everyone answered with two names: Zambinella! Jomelli! He entered and took a seat in the orchestra, squeezed between two notably fat *abbati*; however, he was lucky enough to be fairly close to the stage. The curtain rose. For the first time in his life, he heard that music whose delights M. Jean-Jacques Rousseau had so eloquently praised to him at one of Baron d'Holbach's evenings. The young sculptor's senses were, so to speak, lubricated by the accents of Jomelli's sublime harmony. The languorous novelties of these skillfully mingled Italian voices plunged him into a delicious ecstasy. He remained speechless, motionless, not even feeling crowded by the two priests. His soul passed into his ears and eyes. He seemed to hear through every pore. Suddenly a burst of applause which shook the house greeted the prima donna's entrance. She came coquettishly to the front of the stage and greeted the audience with infinite grace. The lights, the general enthusiasm, the theatrical illusion, the glamour of a style of dress which in those days was quite attractive, all conspired in favor of this woman. Sarrasine cried out with pleasure.

At that instant he marveled at the ideal beauty he had hitherto sought in life, seeking in one often unworthy model the roundness of a perfect leg; in another, the curve of a breast; in another, white shoulders; finally taking some girl's neck, some woman's hands, and some child's smooth knees, without ever having encountered under the cold Parisian sky the rich, sweet creations of ancient Greece. La Zambinella displayed to him, united, living, and delicate, those exquisite female forms he so ardently desired, of which a sculptor is at once the severest and the most passionate judge. Her mouth was expressive, her eyes loving, her complexion dazzlingly white. And along with these details, which would have enraptured a painter, were all the wonders of those images of Venus revered and rendered by the chisels of the Greeks. The artist never wearied of admiring the inimitable grace with which the arms were attached to the torso, the marvelous roundness of the neck, the harmonious lines drawn by the eyebrows, the nose, and the perfect oval of the face, the purity of its vivid contours and the effect of the thick, curved lashes which lined her heavy and voluptuous eyelids. This was more than a woman, this was a masterpiece! In this unhoped-for creation could be found a love to enrapture any man, and beauties worthy of satisfying a critic. With his eyes, Sarrasine devoured Pygmalion's statue, come down from its pedestal. When La Zambinella sang, the effect was delirium. The artist felt cold; then he felt a heat which suddenly began to prickle in the innermost depth of his being, in what we call the heart, for lack of any other word! He did not applaud, he said nothing, he experienced an impulse of madness, a kind of frenzy which overcomes us only when we are at the age when desire has something frightening and infernal about it. Sarrasine wanted to leap onto the stage and take possession of this woman: his strength, increased a hundredfold by a moral depression impossible to explain, since these phenomena occur in an area hidden from human observation, seemed to manifest itself with painful violence. Looking at him, one would have thought him a cold and senseless man. Fame, knowledge, future, existence, laurels, everything collapsed.

"To be loved by her, or die!" Such was the decree Sarrasine passed upon himself. He was so utterly intoxicated that he no longer saw the theater, the spectators, the actors, or heard the music. Moreover, the distance between himself and La Zambinella had ceased to exist, he possessed her, his eyes were riveted upon her, he took her for his own. An almost diabolical power enabled him to feel the breath of this voice, to smell the scented powder covering her hair, to see the planes of her face, to count the blue veins shadowing her satin skin. Last, this agile voice, fresh and silvery in timbre, supple as a thread shaped by the slightest breath of air, rolling and unrolling, cascading and scattering, this voice attacked his soul so vividly that several times he gave vent to involuntary cries torn from him by convulsive feelings of pleasure which are all too rarely vouchsafed by human passions. He was presently obliged to leave the theater. His trembling legs almost refused to support him. He was limp, weak as a sensitive man who has given way to overwhelming anger. He had experienced such pleasure, or perhaps he had suffered so keenly, that his life had drained away like water from a broken vase. He felt empty inside, a prostration similar to the debilitation that overcomes those convalescing from serious illness.

Overcome by an inexplicable sadness, he sat down on the steps of a church. There, leaning back against a pillar, he fell into a confused meditation, as in a dream. He had been smitten by passion. Upon returning to his lodgings, he fell into one of those frenzies of activity which disclose to us the presence of new elements in our lives. A prey to this first fever of love derived equally from both pleasure and pain, he tried to appease his impatience and his delirium by drawing La Zambinella from memory. It was a kind of embodied meditation. On one page, La Zambinella appeared in that apparently calm and cool pose favored by Raphael, Giorgione, and every great painter. On another, she was delicately turning her head after having finished a trill, and appeared to be listening to herself. Sarrasine sketched his mistress in every pose: he drew her unveiled, seated, standing, lying down, chaste or amorous, embodying through the delirium of his pencils every capricious notion that can enter our heads when we think intently about a mistress. However, his fevered thoughts went beyond drawing. He saw La Zambinella, spoke to her, beseeched her, he passed a thousand years of life and happiness with her by placing her in every imaginable position; in short, by sampling the future with her. On the following day, he sent his valet to rent a box next to the stage for the entire season. Then, like all young people with lusty souls, he exaggerated to himself the difficulties of his undertaking and first fed his passion with the pleasure of being able to admire his mistress without obstruction. This golden age of love, during which we take pleasure in our own feeling and in which we are happy almost by ourselves, was not destined to last long in Sarrasine's case. Nevertheless, events took him by surprise while he was still under the spell of this vernal hallucination, as naïve as it was voluptuous. In a week he lived a lifetime, spending the mornings kneading the clay by which he would copy La Zambinella, despite the veils, skirts, corsets, and ribbons which concealed her from him. In the evenings, installed in his box early, alone, lying on a sofa like a Turk under the influence of opium, he created for himself a pleasure as rich and varied as he wished it to be. First, he gradually familiarized himself with the overly vivid emotions his mistress's singing afforded him; he then trained his eyes to see her, and finally he could contemplate her without fearing an outburst of the wild frenzy which had seized him on the first day. As his passion became calmer, it grew deeper. For the rest, the unsociable sculptor did not allow his friends to intrude upon his solitude, which was peopled with images, adorned with fantasies of hope, and filled with happiness. His love was so strong, so naïve, that he experienced all the innocent scruples that assail us when we love for the first time. As he began to realize that he would soon have to act, to plot, to inquire where La Zambinella lived, whether she had a mother, uncle, teacher, family, to ponder, in short, on ways to see her, speak to her, these great, ambitious thoughts made his heart swell so painfully that he put them off until later, deriving as much satisfaction from his physical suffering as he did from his intellectual pleasures.

"But," Mme de Rochefide interrupted me, "I still don't see anything 90 about either Marianina or her little old man."

"You are seeing nothing but him!" I cried impatiently, like an author who is being forced to spoil a theatrical effect.

For several days, I resumed after a pause, Sarrasine had reappeared so faithfully in his box and his eyes had expressed such love that his passion for La Zambinella's voice would have been common knowledge throughout Paris, had this adventure happened there; however, in Italy, madame, everyone goes to the theater for himself, with his own passions, and with a heartfelt interest which precludes spying through opera glasses. Nevertheless, the sculptor's enthusiasm did not escape the attention of the singers for long. One evening, the Frenchman saw that they were laughing at him in the wings. It is hard to know what extreme actions he might not have taken had La Zambinella not come onto the stage. She gave Sarrasine one of those eloquent glances which often reveal much more than women intend them to. This glance was a total revelation. Sarrasine was loved!

"If it's only a caprice," he thought, already accusing his mistress of excessive ardor, "she doesn't know what she is subjecting herself to. I am hoping her caprice will last my whole life."

At that moment, the artist's attention was distracted by three soft knocks on the door of his box. He opened it. An old woman entered with an air of mystery.

"Young man," she said, "if you want to be happy, be prudent. Put on a 95 cape, wear a hat drawn down over your eyes; then, around ten in the evening, be in the Via del Corso in front of the Hotel di Spagna."

"I'll be there," he replied, placing two louis in the duenna's wrinkled hand.

He left his box after having given a signal to La Zambinella, who timidly lowered her heavy eyelids, like a woman pleased to be understood at last. Then he ran home to dress himself as seductively as he could. As he was leaving the theater, a strange man took his arm.

"Be on your guard, Frenchman," he whispered in his ear. "This is a matter of life and death. Cardinal Cicognara is her protector and doesn't trifle."

At that moment, had some demon set the pit of hell between Sarrasine and La Zambinella, he would have crossed it with one leap. Like the horses of the gods described by Homer, the sculptor's love had traversed vast distances in the twinkling of an eye.

"If death itself were waiting for me outside the house, I would go even 100 faster," he replied.

"*Poverino!*" the stranger cried as he disappeared.

Speaking of danger to a lover is tantamount to selling him pleasure, is it not? Sarrasine's valet had never seen his master take so much care over his toilette. His finest sword, a gift from Bouchardon, the sash Clotilde had given him, his embroidered coat, his silver-brocade waistcoat, his gold snuffbox, his jeweled watches, were all taken from their coffers, and he adorned himself like a girl about to appear before her first love. At the appointed hour, drunk with love and seething with hope, Sarrasine, concealed in his cape, sped to the rendezvous the old woman had given him. The duenna was waiting for him.

"You took a long time," she said. "Come."

She led the Frenchman along several back streets and stopped before a rather handsome mansion. She knocked. The door opened. She led Sarrasine along a labyrinth of stairways, galleries, and rooms which were lit only by the feeble light of the moon, and soon came to a door through whose cracks gleamed bright lights and from behind which came the joyful sounds of several voices. When at a word from the old woman he was admitted to this mysterious room, Sarrasine was suddenly dazzled at finding himself in a salon as brilliantly lighted as it was sumptuously furnished, in the center of which stood a table laden with venerable bottles and flashing flagons sparkling with ruby facets. He recognized the singers from the theater, along with some charming women, all ready to begin an artists' orgy as soon as he was among them. Sarrasine suppressed a feeling of disappointment and put on a good face. He had expected a dim room, his mistress seated by the fire, some jealous person nearby, death and love, an exchange of confidences in low voices, heart to heart, dangerous kisses and faces so close that La Zambinella's hair would have caressed his forehead throbbing with desire, feverish with happiness.

"*Vive la folie!*" he cried. "*Signori e belle donne,* you will allow me to take my   105 revenge later and to show you my gratitude for the way you have welcomed a poor sculptor."

Having been greeted warmly enough by most of those present, whom he knew by sight, he sought to approach the armchair on which La Zambinella was casually reclining. Ah! how his heart beat when he spied a delicate foot shod in one of those slippers which in those days, may I say, madame, gave women's feet such a coquettish and voluptuous look that I don't know how men were able to resist them. The well-fitting white stockings with green clocks, the short skirts, the slippers with pointed toes, and the high heels of Louis XV's reign may have contributed something to the demoralization of Europe and the clergy.

"Something?" the Marquise replied. "Have you read nothing?"

La Zambinella, I continued, smiling, had impudently crossed her legs and was gently swinging the upper one with a certain attractive indolence which suited her capricious sort of beauty. She had removed her costume and was wearing a bodice that accentuated her narrow waist and set off the satin panniers of her dress, which was embroidered with blue flowers. Her bosom, the treasures of which were concealed, in an excess of coquetry, by a covering of lace, was dazzlingly white. Her hair arranged something like that of Mme du Barry, her face, though it was partially hidden under a full bonnet, appeared only the more delicate, and powder suited her. To see her thus was to adore her. She gave the sculptor a graceful smile. Unhappy at not being able to speak to her without witnesses present, Sarrasine politely sat down next to her and talked about music, praising her extraordinary talent; but his voice trembled with love, with fear and hope.

"What are you afraid of?" asked Vitagliani, the company's most famous singer. "Go ahead; you need fear no rivals here." Having said this, the tenor smiled without another word. This smile was repeated on the lips of all the guests, whose attention contained a hidden malice a lover would not have noticed. Such openness was like a dagger thrust in Sarrasine's heart. Although endowed with a certain strength of character, and although nothing could change his love, it had perhaps not yet occurred to him that La Zambinella was virtually a courtesan, and that he could not have both the pure pleasures that make a young girl's love so delicious and the tempestuous transports by which the hazardous possession of an actress must be purchased. He reflected and resigned himself. Supper was served. Sarrasine and La Zambinella sat down informally side by side. For the first half of the meal, the artists preserved some decorum, and the sculptor was able to chat with the singer. He found her witty, acute, but astonishingly ignorant, and she revealed herself to be weak and superstitious. The delicacy of her organs was reflected in her understanding. When Vitagliani uncorked the first bottle of champagne, Sarrasine read in his companion's eyes a start of terror at the tiny explosion caused by the escaping gas. The love-stricken artist interpreted the involuntary shudder of this feminine constitution as the sign of an excessive sensitivity. The Frenchman was charmed by this weakness. How much is protective in a man's love!

"My strength your shield!" Is this not written at the heart of all declara- 110 tions of love? Too excited to shower the beautiful Italian with compliments, Sarrasine, like all lovers, was by turns serious, laughing, or reflective. Although he seemed to be listening to the other guests, he did not hear a word they were saying, so absorbed was he in the pleasure of finding himself beside her, touching her hand as he served her. He bathed in a secret joy. Despite the eloquence of a few mutual glances, he was astonished at the reserve La Zambinella maintained toward him. Indeed, she had begun by pressing his foot and teasing him with the flirtatiousness of a woman in love and free to show it; but she suddenly wrapped herself in the modesty of a young girl, after hearing Sarrasine describe a trait which revealed the excessive violence of his character. When the supper became an orgy, the guests broke into song under the influence of the Peralta and the Pedro-Ximenes. There were ravishing duets, songs from Calabria, Spanish seguidillas, Neapolitan canzonettas. Intoxication was in every eye, in the music, in hearts and voices alike. Suddenly an enchanting vivacity welled up, a gay abandon, and Italian warmth of feeling inconceivable to those acquainted only with Parisian gatherings, London routs, or Viennese circles. Jokes and words of love flew like bullets in a battle through laughter, profanities, and invocations to the Holy Virgin or *il Bambino*. Someone lay down on a sofa and fell asleep. A girl was listening to a declaration of love unaware that she was spilling sherry on the tablecloth. In the midst of this disorder, La Zambinella remained thoughtful, as though terror-struck.

She refused to drink, perhaps she ate a bit too much; however, it is said that greediness in a woman is a charming quality. Admiring his mistress's modesty, Sarrasine thought seriously about the future.

"She probably wants to be married," he thought. He then turned his thoughts to the delights of this marriage. His whole life seemed too short to exhaust the springs of happiness he found in the depths of his soul. Vitagliani, who was sitting next to him, refilled his glass so often that, toward three in the morning, without being totally drunk, Sarrasine could no longer control his delirium. Impetuously, he picked up the woman, escaping into a kind of boudoir next to the salon, toward the door of which he had glanced more than once. The Italian woman was armed with a dagger.

"If you come any closer," she said, "I will be forced to plunge this weapon into your heart. Let me go! You would despise me. I have conceived too much respect for your character to surrender in this fashion. I don't want to betray the feeling you have for me."

"Oh no!" cried Sarrasine. "You cannot stifle a passion by stimulating it! Are you already so corrupt that, old in heart, you would act like a young courtesan who whets the emotions by which she plies her trade?"

"But today is Friday," she replied, frightened at the Frenchman's violence.

Sarrasine, who was not devout, broke into laughter. La Zambinella 115 jumped up like a young deer and ran toward the salon. When Sarrasine appeared in her pursuit, he was greeted by an infernal burst of laughter.

He saw La Zambinella lying in a swoon upon a sofa. She was pale and drained by the extraordinary effort she had just made. Although Sarrasine knew little Italian, he heard his mistress saying in a low voice to Vitagliani: "But he will kill me!"

The sculptor was utterly confounded by this strange scene. He regained his senses. At first he stood motionless; then he found his voice, sat down next to his mistress, and assured her of his respect. He was able to divert his passion by addressing the most high-minded phrases to this woman; and in depicting his love, he used all the resources of that magical eloquence, that inspired intermediary which women rarely refuse to believe. When the guests were surprised by the first gleams of morning light, a woman suggested they go to Frascati. Everyone enthusiastically fell in with the idea of spending the day at the Villa Ludovisi. Vitagliani went down to hire some carriages. Sarrasine had the pleasure of leading La Zambinella to a phaeton. Once outside Rome, the gaiety which had been momentarily repressed by each person's battle with sleepiness suddenly revived. Men and women alike seemed used to this strange life, these ceaseless pleasures, this artist's impulsiveness which turns life into a perpetual party at which one laughed unreservedly. The sculptor's companion was the only one who seemed downcast.

"Are you ill?" Sarrasine asked her. "Would you rather go home?"

"I'm not strong enough to stand all these excesses," she replied. "I must be very careful; but with you I feel so well! Had it not been for you, I would never have stayed for supper; a sleepless night and I lose whatever bloom I have."

"You are so delicate," Sarrasine said, looking at the charming creature's 120 pretty face.

"Orgies ruin the voice."

"Now that we're alone," the artist cried, "and you no longer need fear the outbursts of my passion, tell me that you love me."

"Why?" she replied. "What would be the use? I seemed pretty to you. But you are French and your feelings will pass. Ah, you would not love me as I long to be loved."

"How can you say that?"

"Not to satisfy any vulgar passion; purely. I abhor men perhaps even more 125 than I hate women. I need to seek refuge in friendship. For me, the world is a desert. I am an accursed creature, condemned to understand happiness, to feel it, to desire it, and, like many others, forced to see it flee from me continually. Remember, sir, that I will not have deceived you. I forbid you to love me. I can be your devoted friend, for I admire your strength and your character. I need a brother, a protector. Be all that for me, but no more."

"Not love you!" Sarrasine cried. "But my dearest angel, you are my life, my happiness!"

"If I were to say one word, you would repulse me with horror."

"Coquette! Nothing can frighten me. Tell me you will cost my future, that I will die in two months, that I will be damned merely for having kissed you."

He kissed her, despite La Zambinella's efforts to resist this passionate embrace.

"Tell me you are a devil, that you want my money, my name, all my fame! 130 Do you want me to give up being a sculptor? Tell me."

"And if I were not a woman?" La Zambinella asked in a soft silvery voice.

"What a joke!" Sarrasine cried. "Do you think you can deceive an artist's eye? Haven't I spent ten days devouring, scrutinizing, admiring your perfection? Only a woman could have this round, soft arm, these elegant curves. Oh, you want compliments."

She smiled at him sadly, and raising her eyes heavenward, she murmured: "Fatal beauty!"

At that moment her gaze had an indescribable expression of horror, so powerful and vivid that Sarrasine shuddered.

"Frenchman," she went on, "forget this moment of madness forever. I re- 135 spect you, but as for love, do not ask it of me; that feeling is smothered in my heart. I have no heart!" she cried, weeping. "The stage where you saw me, that applause, that music, that fame I am condemned to, such is my life, I have no other. In a few hours you will not see me in the same way, the woman you love will be dead."

The sculptor made no reply. He was overcome with a dumb rage which oppressed his heart. He could only gaze with enflamed, burning eyes at this extraordinary woman. La Zambinella's weak voice, her manner, her movements and gestures marked with sorrow, melancholy, and discouragement, awakened all the wealth of passion in his soul. Each word was a goad. At that moment they reached Frascati. As the artist offered his mistress his arm to assist her in alighting, he felt her shiver.

"What is wrong? You would kill me," he cried, seeing her grow pale, "if I were even an innocent cause of your slightest unhappiness."

"A snake," she said, pointing to a grass snake which was sliding along a ditch. "I am afraid of those horrid creatures." Sarrasine crushed the snake's head with his heel.

"How can you be so brave?" La Zambinella continued, looking with visible horror at the dead reptile.

"Ah," the artist replied, smiling, "now do you dare deny you are a woman?"   140

They rejoined their companions and strolled through the woods of the Villa Ludovisi, which in those days belonged to Cardinal Cicognara. That morning fled too quickly for the enamored sculptor, but it was filled with a host of incidents which revealed to him the coquetry, the weakness, and the delicacy of this soft and enervated being. This was woman herself, with her sudden fears, her irrational whims, her instinctive worries, her impetuous boldness, her fussings, and her delicious sensibility. It happened that as they were wandering in the open countryside, the little group of merry singers saw in the distance some heavily armed men whose manner of dress was far from reassuring. Someone said, "They must be highwaymen," and everyone quickened his pace toward the refuge of the Cardinal's grounds. At this critical moment, Sarrasine saw from La Zambinella's pallor that she no longer had the strength to walk; he took her up in his arms and carried her for a while, running. When he came to a nearby arbor, he put her down.

"Explain to me," he said, "how this extreme weakness, which I would find hideous in any other woman, which would displease me and whose slightest indication would be almost enough to choke my love, pleases and charms me in you? Ah, how I love you," he went on. "All your faults, your terrors, your resentments, add an indefinable grace to your soul. I think I would detest a strong woman, a Sappho, a courageous creature, full of energy and passion. Oh, soft, frail creature, how could you be otherwise? That angelic voice, that delicate voice would be an anomaly coming from any body but yours."

"I cannot give you any hope," she said. "Stop speaking to me in this way, because they will make a fool of you. I cannot stop you from coming to the theater; but if you love me or if you are wise, you will come there no more. Listen, monsieur," she said in a low voice.

"Oh, be still," the impassioned artist said. "Obstacles make my love more ardent."

La Zambinella's graceful and modest attitude did not change, but she fell   145
silent as though a terrible thought had revealed some misfortune to her. When it came time to return to Rome, she got into the four-seated coach, ordering the sculptor with imperious cruelty to return to Rome alone in the carriage. During the journey, Sarrasine resolved to kidnap La Zambinella. He spent the entire day making plans, each more outrageous than the other. At nightfall, as he was going out to inquire where his mistress's palazzo was located, he met one of his friends on the threshold.

"My dear fellow," he said, "our ambassador has asked me to invite you to his house tonight. He is giving a magnificent concert, and when I tell you that Zambinella will be there . . ."

"Zambinella," cried Sarrasine, intoxicated by the name, "I'm mad about her!"

"You're like everyone else," his friend replied.

"If you are my friends, you, Vien, Lauterbourg, and Allegrain, will you help me do something after the party?" Sarrasine asked.

"It's not some cardinal to be killed? . . . not . . . ?"   150

"No, no," Sarrasine said, "I'm not asking you to do anything an honest person couldn't do."

In a short time, the sculptor had arranged everything for the success of his undertaking. He was one of the last to arrive at the ambassador's, but he had come in a traveling carriage drawn by powerful horses and driven by one of the most enterprising *veturini* of Rome. The ambassador's palazzo was crowded; not without some difficulty, the sculptor, who was a stranger to everyone present, made his way to the salon where Zambinella was singing at that very moment.

"Is it out of consideration for the cardinals, bishops, and abbés present," Sarrasine asked, "that *she* is dressed like a man, that she is wearing a snood, kinky hair, and a sword?"

"She? What she?" asked the old nobleman to whom Sarrasine had been speaking. "La Zambinella." "La Zambinella!" the Roman prince replied. "Are you joking? Where are you from? Has there ever been a woman on the Roman stage? And don't you know about the creatures who sing female roles in the Papal States? I am the one, monsieur, who gave Zambinella his voice. I paid for everything that scamp ever had, even his singing teacher. Well, he has so little gratitude for the service I rendered him that he has never consented to set foot in my house. And yet, if he makes a fortune, he will owe it all to me."

Prince Chigi may well have gone on talking for some time; Sarrasine was   155
not listening to him. A horrid truth had crept into his soul. It was as though he had been struck by lightning. He stood motionless, his eyes fixed on the false singer. His fiery gaze exerted a sort of magnetic influence on Zambinella, for the *musico* finally turned to look at Sarrasine, and at that moment his heavenly voice faltered. He trembled! An involuntary murmur escaping from the audience he had kept hanging on his lips completed his discomfiture; he sat down and cut short his aria. Cardinal Cicognara, who had glanced out the corner of his eye to see what had attracted his protégé's attention, then saw the Frenchman: he leaned over to one of his ecclesiastical aides-de-camp and appeared to be asking the sculptor's name. Having obtained the answer he sought, he regarded the artist with great attention and gave an order to an abbé, who quickly disappeared.

During this time, Zambinella, having recovered himself, once more began the piece he had so capriciously interrupted; but he sang it badly, and despite all the requests made to him, he refused to sing anything else. This was the first time he displayed that capricious tyranny for which he would later be as celebrated as for his talent and his vast fortune, due, as they said, no less to his voice than to his beauty.

"It is a woman," Sarrasine said, believing himself alone. "There is some hidden intrigue here. Cardinal Cicognara is deceiving the Pope and the whole city of Rome!"

The sculptor thereupon left the salon, gathered his friends together, and posted them out of sight in the courtyard of the palazzo. When Zambinella was confident that Sarrasine had departed, he appeared to regain his composure. Around midnight, having wandered through the rooms like a man seeking some enemy, the *musico* departed. As soon as he crossed the threshold of the palazzo, he was adroitly seized by men who gagged him with a handkerchief and drew him into the carriage Sarrasine had hired. Frozen with horror, Zambinella remained in a corner, not daring to move. He saw before him the terrible face of the artist, who was silent as death.

The journey was brief. Carried in Sarrasine's arms, Zambinella soon found himself in a dark, empty studio. Half dead, the singer remained in a chair, without daring to examine the statue of a woman in which he recognized his own features. He made no attempt to speak, but his teeth chattered. Sarrasine paced up and down the room. Suddenly he stopped in front of Zambinella.

"Tell me the truth," he pleaded in a low, altered voice. "You are a woman? Cardinal Cicognara . . ." 160

Zambinella fell to his knees, and in reply lowered his head.

"Ah, you are a woman," the artist cried in a delirium, "for even a . . ." He broke off. "No," he continued, "*he* would not be so cowardly."

"Ah, do not kill me," cried Zambinella, bursting into tears. "I only agreed to trick you to please my friends, who wanted to laugh."

"Laugh!" the sculptor replied in an infernal tone. "Laugh! Laugh! You dared play with a man's feelings, you?"

"Oh, have mercy!" Zambinella replied. 165

"I ought to kill you," Sarrasine cried, drawing his sword with a violent gesture. "However," he went on, in cold disdain, "were I to scour your body with this blade, would I find there one feeling to stifle, one vengeance to satisfy? You are nothing. If you were a man or a woman, I would kill you, but . . ."

Sarrasine made a gesture of disgust which forced him to turn away, whereupon he saw the statue.

"And it's an illusion," he cried. Then, turning to Zambinella: "A woman's heart was a refuge for me, a home. Have you any sisters who resemble you? Then die! But no, you shall live. Isn't leaving you alive condemning you to something worse than death? It is neither my blood nor my existence that I regret, but the future and my heart's fortune. Your feeble hand has destroyed my happiness. What hope can I strip from you for all those you have blighted? You have dragged me down to your level. *To love, to be loved!* are henceforth meaningless words for me, as they are for you. I shall forever think of this imaginary woman when I see a real woman." He indicated the statue with a gesture of despair. "I shall always have the memory of a celestial harpy who thrusts its talons into all my manly feelings, and who will stamp all other women with a seal of imperfection! Monster! You who can give life to nothing. For me, you have wiped women from the earth."

Sarrasine sat down before the terrified singer. Two huge tears welled from his dry eyes, rolled down his manly cheeks, and fell to the ground: two tears of rage, two bitter and burning tears.

"No more love! I am dead to all pleasure, to every human emotion." 170

So saying, he seized a hammer and hurled it at the statue with such extraordinary force that he missed it. He thought he had destroyed this monument to his folly, and then took up his sword and brandished it to kill the singer. Zambinella uttered piercing screams. At that moment, three men entered and at once the sculptor fell, stabbed by three stiletto thrusts.

"On behalf of Cardinal Cicognara," one of them said.

"It is a good deed worthy of a Christian," replied the Frenchman as he died. These sinister messengers informed Zambinella of the concern of his protector, who was waiting at the door in a closed carriage, to take him away as soon as he had been rescued.

"But," Mme de Rochefide asked me, "what connection is there between this story and the little old man we saw at the Lantys'?"

"Madame, Cardinal Cicognara took possession of Zambinella's statue and   175
had it executed in marble; today it is in the Albani Museum. There, in 1791, the Lanty family found it and asked Vien to copy it. The portrait in which you saw Zambinella at twenty, a second after having seen him at one hundred, later served for Girodet's *Endymion;* you will have recognized its type in the Adonis."

"But this Zambinella—he or she?"

"He, madame, is none other than Marianina's great-uncle. Now you can readily see what interest Mme de Lanty has in hiding the source of a fortune which comes from—"

"Enough!" she said, gesturing to me imperiously. We sat for a moment plunged in the deepest silence.

"Well?" I said to her.

"Ah," she exclaimed, standing up and pacing up and down the room. She   180
looked at me and spoke in an altered voice. "You have given me a disgust for life and for passions that will last a long time. Excepting for monsters, don't all human feelings come down to the same thing, to horrible disappointments? Mothers, our children kill us either by their bad behavior or by their lack of affection. Wives, we are deceived. Mistresses, we are forsaken, abandoned. Does friendship even exist? I would become a nun tomorrow did I not know that I can remain unmoved as a rock amid the storms of life. If the Christian's future is also an illusion, at least it is not destroyed until after death. Leave me."

"Ah," I said, "you know how to punish."

"Am I wrong?"

"Yes," I replied, with a kind of courage. "In telling this story, which is fairly well known in Italy, I have been able to give you a fine example of the progress made by civilization today. They no longer create these unfortunate creatures."

"Paris is a very hospitable place," she said. "It accepts everything, shameful fortunes and bloodstained fortunes. Crime and infamy can find asylum here; only virtue has no altars here. Yes, pure souls have their home in heaven! No one will have known me. I am proud of that!"

And the Marquise remained pensive.   185

—————— HONORÉ DE BALZAC ——————
                    (1799–1850) Web

A prolific author, Balzac wrote to pay his business debts. Addicted to coffee, he
got up in the middle of the night to write, and for nineteen years he wrote an average of thirty-eight pages per week. He produced a vast array of characters, all
of whom are described in the realistic style that made them come alive.

TOPICS FOR CRITICAL THINKING Web

1. What are the relations between beauty and gender in the story?
2. In what various ways does the story present a spot "in between"?
3. What is the role of painting in the story?
4. How does castration figure as a metaphor in the story?
5. What are the relations between the frame narrative (the party) and the embedded
   story (the narrative of Sarrasine)?

TOPICS FOR CRITICAL WRITING Web

1. Read closely a single line or paragraph of "Sarrasine." What patterns, motifs, and
   connotations structure the passage?
2. Read closely a single line or paragraph of "Sarrasine." How does this passage relate
   to the rest of the work? You might want to consider how its images repeat images
   from the rest of the text, or the ways it varies or modifies your understanding of
   character through its use of language.

9   Image, Motif, and Symbol

Image, *motif*, and *symbol* are three terms describing different ways language evokes complex and multilayered meanings in prose fiction. The terms *image*, *motif*, and *symbol* actually refer to three different but related uses of images. Confusing them is a common mistake, one that not only limits the tools and concepts you might use to analyze a text, but one that also might confuse those who read your work. **Image** refers to the way words create or suggest sensory phenomena: what we see, hear, smell, feel, or even taste. **Motif** refers to images, words, or ideas that recur in a story; it is a way stories organize images or themes through repetition. A **symbol** is an image that always refers to the same thing.

Image and Motif

Images are crucial components of stories. Rather than being mere decoration or elaboration, images are often the means through which a story comes alive, especially in **modernist** literature, discussed below. In appealing to the reader's senses, images evoke the feel and impression of the world of the story; they portray experience and feelings in a vivid and immediate way. Almost everything in a story is an image produced in the way language creates the scene and action of a story. Although the visual image is the prototype—so much so that twenty-first-century readers think of texts in cinematic terms—images may refer to sounds, smells, tactile sensations, and even taste.

    In stories, images are produced by language. Sometimes images are simply descriptions of places or things—"stony hills ablaze with heat" (*Heart of Darkness*) or "Outside, the fire-red, gas-blue, ghost-green signs shone smokily through the tranquil rain" ("Babylon Revisited"). The sense of an image can be created through the artful use of detail—"his starched collars and got-up shirtfronts were achievements of character" (*Heart of Darkness*). "The wild garden behind the house contained a central apple tree and a few straggling bushes, under one of which I found the late tenant's rusty bicycle pump" ("Araby"). Image is also produced by sketching the broad outlines of familiar objects—"The sun set" (*Heart of Darkness*) or "The girl stood up and walked to the end of the station" ("Hills Like White Elephants"). Sometimes an image is evoked through suggestion by using elements of common knowledge to suggest a place, thing, or sensation—"I had a cup of tea—the last decent cup of tea for many days" (*Heart of Darkness*) or "Then the breeze stirred rather more briskly overhead" ("Kew Gardens"). Images can be things we all see every day or they may be subjective or dreamlike.

The exact language and details used to create images are important. Details often link one image to another or connect images to actions or impressions (as we saw in the discussion of Roland Barthes's analysis of "Sarrasine" in Chapter 8). It is by means of imagery that the sense of the story's world— its **diegesis**—is produced. This sense of a world is what Marlow creates in Joseph Conrad's novella *Heart of Darkness*. A story about a story told by the seaman Marlow on a ship waiting for the tide on the Thames, *Heart of Darkness* explores the image of the colonial ivory agent, Kurtz, and the practices of colonial rule through Marlow's impressions of his journey to Brussels and

www Africa. (See Colonial and Postcolonial Criticism. **Web**) In this narrative, images are Marlow's most profound impressions and his primary way of recounting his experience. Images of the jungle, the river, Kurtz, and even the sunset on the Thames convey Marlow's feelings about his journey into the heart of Africa.

Critical Perspective: On Imagery

"Some of the images in [*Heart of Darkness*] are representative in a limited and mainly pictorial way; the older knitter, for example, with her wart and her flat cloth slippers, becomes a stark visual image of physical and spiritual deformity combined with imperturbable self-complacence. But there is another, larger, and to some extent contrary, tendency, where the extreme selectivity of Marlow's memory draws our attention to his state of mind at the time. For instance, when Marlow comments about the tycoon: 'He shook hands, I fancy,' his uncertainty suggests that his consciousness was occupied with other matters. Marlow omits much that would certainly be mentioned in an autobiography, or a naturalist novel; we are not, for instance, given the details of Marlow's contract, or the name of the people. This omission of proper names is a particularly symbolist procedure—in Maeterlinck, for instance, or in Kafka. The general reason for this strategy is clear: most of the details about the narrative object are omitted, so that what details remain, liberated from the bonds and irrelevancies of the purely circumstantial and contingent, can be recognized as representatives of larger ideas and attitudes."

—Ian Watt, "Impressionism and Symbolism in *Heart of Darkness*," in Joseph Conrad, *Heart of Darkness* (3rd ed.), ed. Robert Kimbrough (1988), p. 326.

In this brief consideration of the ways Conrad uses images and symbols in *Heart of Darkness*, Watt focuses on the ways the novella employs imagery to convey images and states of mind and uses selected details as a way of conveying larger ideas and attitudes.

JOSEPH CONRAD

Heart of Darkness (1899)

I

The *Nellie*, a cruising yawl, swung to her anchor without a flutter of the sails, and was at rest. The flood had made, the wind was nearly calm, and being bound down the river, the only thing for it was to come to and wait for the turn of the tide.

The sea-reach of the Thames stretched before us like the beginning of an interminable waterway. In the offing the sea and the sky were welded together without a joint, and in the luminous space the tanned sails of the barges drifting up with the tide seemed to stand still in red clusters of canvas sharply peaked, with gleams of varnished sprits. A haze rested on the low shores that ran out to sea in vanishing flatness. The air was dark above Gravesend,[1] and farther back still seemed condensed into a mournful gloom, brooding motionless over the biggest, and the greatest, town on earth.

The director of Companies was our captain and our host. We four affectionately watched his back as he stood in the bows looking to seaward. On the whole river there was nothing that looked half so nautical. He resembled a pilot, which to a seaman is trustworthiness personified. It was difficult to realize his work was not out there in the luminous estuary, but behind him, within the brooding gloom.

Between us there was, as I have already said somewhere, the bond of the sea. Besides holding our hearts together through long periods of separation, it had the effect of making us tolerant of each other's yarns—and even convictions. The Lawyer—the best of old fellows—had, because of his many years and many virtues, the only cushion on deck, and was lying on the only rug. The Accountant had brought out already a box of dominoes, and was toying architecturally with the bones.[2] Marlow sat cross-legged right aft, leaning against the mizzen-mast. He had sunken cheeks, a yellow complexion, a straight back, an ascetic aspect, and, with his arms dropped, the palms of hands outwards, resembled an idol. The Director, satisfied the anchor had good hold, made his way aft and sat down amongst us. We exchanged a few words lazily. Afterwards there was silence on board the yacht. For some reason or other we did not begin that game of dominoes. We felt meditative, and fit for nothing but placid staring. The day was ending in a serenity of still and exquisite brilliance. The water shone pacifically; the sky, without a speck, was a benign immensity of unstained light; the very mist on the Essex marshes was like a gauzy and radiant fabric, hung from the wooded rises inland, and drap-

1. A town near the mouth of the Thames in England.
2. Slang term for dominoes.

ing the low shores in diaphanous folds. Only the gloom to the west, brooding over the upper reaches, became more somber every minute, as if angered by the approach of the sun.

And at last, in its curved and imperceptible fall, the sun sank low, and 5 from glowing white changed to a dull red without rays and without heat, as if about to go out suddenly, stricken to death by the touch of that gloom brooding over a crowd of men.

Forthwith a change came over the waters, and the serenity became less brilliant but more profound. The old river in its broad reach rested unruffled at the decline of day, after ages of good service done to the race that peopled its banks, spread out in the tranquil dignity of a waterway leading to the uttermost ends of the earth. We looked at the venerable stream not in the vivid flush of a short day that comes and departs for ever, but in the august light of abiding memories. And indeed nothing is easier for a man who has, as the phrase goes, "followed the sea" with reverence and affection, than to evoke the great spirit of the past upon the lower reaches of the Thames. The tidal current runs to and fro in its unceasing service, crowded with memories of men and ships it had borne to the rest of home or to the battles of the sea. It had known and served all the men of whom the nation is proud, from Sir Francis Drake to Sir John Franklin, knights all, titled and untitled—the great knights-errant of the sea. It had borne all the ships whose names are like jewels flashing in the night of time, from the *Golden Hind* returning with her round flanks full of treasure, to be visited by the Queen's Highness and thus pass out of the gigantic tale, to the *Erebus* and *Terror*,[3] bound on other conquests—and that never returned. It had known the ships and the men. They had sailed from Deptford, from Greenwich, from Erith—the adventurers and the settlers; kings' ships and the ships of men on 'Change; captains, admirals, the dark "interlopers" of the Eastern trade, and the commissioned "generals" of East India fleets. Hunters for gold or pursuers of fame, they all had gone out on that stream, bearing the sword, and often the torch, messengers of the might within the land, bearers of a spark from the sacred fire. What greatness had not floated on the ebb of that river into the mystery of an unknown earth! . . . The dreams of men, the seed of commonwealths, the germs of empires.

The sun set; the dusk fell on the stream, and lights began to appear along the shore. The Chapman lighthouse, a three-legged thing erect on a mud-flat, shone strongly. Lights of ships moved in the fairway—a great stir of lights going up and going down. And farther west on the upper reaches the place of the monstrous town was still marked ominously on the sky, a brooding gloom in sunshine, a lurid glare under the stars.

"And this also," said Marlow suddenly, "has been one of the dark places of the earth."

---

3. The *Golden Hind* was Sir Francis Drake's ship in which he sailed around the world, 1577–1580; *Erebus* and *Terror* were commanded by Sir John Franklin in 1845 on an expedition to discover a northwest passage.

He was the only man of us who still "followed the sea." The worst that could be said of him was that he did not represent his class. He was a seaman, but he was a wanderer too, while most seamen lead, if one may so express it, a sedentary life. Their minds are of the stay-at-home order, and their home is always with them—the ship; and so is their country—the sea. One ship is very much like another, and the sea is always the same. In the immutability of their surroundings the foreign shores, the foreign faces, the changing immensity of life, glide past, veiled not by a sense of mystery but by a slightly disdainful ignorance; for there is nothing mysterious to a seaman unless it be the sea itself, which is the mistress of his existence and as inscrutable as Destiny. For the rest, after his hours of work, a casual stroll or a casual spree on shore suffices to unfold for him the secret of a whole continent, and generally he finds the secret not worth knowing. The yarns of seamen have a direct simplicity, the whole meaning of which lies within the shell of a cracked nut. But Marlow was not typical (if his propensity to spin yarns be excepted), and to him the meaning of an episode was not inside like a kernel but outside, enveloping the tale which brought it out only as a glow brings out a haze, in the likeness of one of these misty halos that sometimes are made visible by the spectral illumination of moonshine.

His remark did not seem at all surprising. It was just like Marlow. It was accepted in silence. No one took the trouble to grunt even; and presently he said, very slow— 10

"I was thinking of very old times, when the Romans first came here, nineteen hundred years ago—the other day. . . . Light came out of this river since—you say Knights? Yes; but it is like a running blaze on a plain, like a flash of lightning in the clouds. We live in the flicker—may it last as long as the old earth keeps rolling! But darkness was here yesterday. Imagine the feelings of a commander of a fine—what d'ye call 'em?—trireme in the Mediterranean, ordered suddenly to the north; run overland across the Gauls in a hurry; put in charge of one of these craft the legionaries,—a wonderful lot of handy men they must have been too—used to build, apparently by the hundred, in a month or two, if we may believe what we read. Imagine him here—the very end of the world, a sea the color of lead, a sky the color of smoke, a kind of ship about as rigid as a concertina—and going up this river with stores, or orders, or what you like. Sandbanks, marshes, forests, savages,—precious little to eat fit for a civilized man, nothing but Thames water to drink. No Falernian wine here, no going ashore. Here and there a military camp lost in a wilderness, like a needle in a bundle of hay—cold, fog, tempests, disease, exile, and death,—death skulking in the air, in the water, in the bush. They must have been dying like flies here. Oh yes—he did it. Did it very well, too, no doubt, and without thinking much about it either, except afterwards to brag of what he had gone through in his time, perhaps. They were men enough to face the darkness. And perhaps he was cheered by keeping his eye on a chance of promotion to the fleet at Ravenna by-and-by, if he had good friends in Rome and survived the awful climate. Or think of a decent young citizen in a toga—perhaps too much dice, you know—coming out here in the train of some prefect, or tax-gatherer, or trader even, to mend his fortunes. Land in a swamp, march through the woods, and in some inland post feel the savagery, the utter savagery, had closed round him,—all that mysterious life of the wilderness that stirs in the forest, in the jungles, in the hearts of wild men. There's no initiation either into such mysteries. He has to live in the midst of the incomprehensible, which is also detestable. And it has a fascination, too, that goes to work upon him. The fascination of the abomination—you know. Imagine the growing regrets, the longing to escape, the powerless disgust, the surrender, the hate."

He paused.

"Mind," he began again, lifting one arm from the elbow, the palm of the hand outwards, so that, with his legs folded before him, he had the pose of a Buddha preaching in European clothes and without a lotus-flower—"Mind, none of us would feel exactly like this. What saves us is efficiency—the devotion to efficiency. But these chaps were not much account, really. They were no colonists; their administration was merely a squeeze, and nothing more, I suspect. They were conquerors, and for that you want only brute force— nothing to boast of, when you have it, since your strength is just an accident arising from the weakness of others. They grabbed what they could get for the sake of what was to be got. It was just robbery with violence, aggravated murder on a great scale, and men going at it blind—as is very proper for those who tackle a darkness. The conquest of the earth, which mostly means the taking it away from those who have a different complexion or slightly flatter noses than ourselves, is not a pretty thing when you look into it too much. What redeems it is the idea only. An idea at the back of it; not a sentimental pretense but an idea; and an unselfish belief in the idea—something you can set up, and bow down before, and offer a sacrifice to. . . ."

He broke off. Flames glided in the river, small green flames, red flames, white flames,[4] pursuing, overtaking, joining, crossing each other—then separating slowly or hastily. The traffic of the great city went on in the deepening night upon the sleepless river. We looked on, waiting patiently—there was nothing else to do till the end of the flood; but it was only after a long silence, when he said, in a hesitating voice, "I suppose you fellows remember I did once turn fresh-water sailor for a bit," that we knew we were fated, before the ebb began to run, to hear about one of Marlow's inconclusive experiences.

"I don't want to bother you much with what happened to me personally,"   15 he began, showing in this remark the weakness of many tellers of tales who seem so often unaware of what their audience would best like to hear: "yet to understand the effect of it on me you ought to know how I got out there, what I saw, how I went up that river to the place where I first met the poor chap. It was the farthest point of navigation and the culminating point of my experience. It seemed somehow to throw a kind of light on everything about me—and into my thoughts. It was somber enough too—and pitiful—not ex-

---

4. Each color of light designated a particular kind of boat.

traordinary in any way—not very clear either. No, not very clear. And yet it seemed to throw a kind of light.

"I had then, as you remember, just returned to London after a lot of Indian Ocean, Pacific, China Seas—a regular dose of the East—six years or so, and I was loafing about, hindering you fellows in your work and invading your homes, just as though I had got a heavenly mission to civilize you. It was very fine for a time, but after a bit I did get tired of resting. Then I began to look for a ship—I should think the hardest work on earth. But the ships wouldn't even look at me. And I got tired of that game too.

"Now when I was a little chap I had a passion for maps. I would look for hours at South America, or Africa, or Australia, and lose myself in all the glories of exploration. At that time there were many blank spaces on the earth, and when I saw one that looked particularly inviting on a map (but they all look that) I would put my finger on it and say, When I grow up I will go there. The North Pole was one of these places, I remember. Well, I haven't been there yet, and shall not try now. The glamour's off. Other places were scattered about the Equator, and in every sort of latitude all over the two hemispheres. I have been in some of them, . . . well, we won't talk about that. But there was one yet—the biggest, the most blank, so to speak—that I had a hankering after.

"True, by this time it was not a blank space any more. It had got filled since my boyhood with rivers and lakes and names. It had ceased to be a blank space of delightful mystery—a white patch for a boy to dream gloriously over. It had become a place of darkness. But there was in it one river especially, a mighty big river, that you could see on the map, resembling an immense snake uncoiled, with its head in the sea, its body at rest curving afar over a vast country, and its tail lost in the depths of the land. And as I looked at the map of it in a shop-window, it fascinated me as a snake would a bird—a silly little bird. Then I remembered there was a big concern, a Company for trade on that river. Dash it all! I thought to myself, they can't trade without using some kind of craft on that lot of fresh water—steamboats! Why shouldn't I try to get charge of one. I went on along Fleet Street, but could not shake off the idea. The snake had charmed me.

"You understand it was a Continental concern, that Trading society; but I have a lot of relations living on the Continent, because it's cheap and not so nasty as it looks, they say.

"I am sorry to own I began to worry[5] them. This was already a fresh departure for me. I was not used to get things that way, you know. I always went my own road and on my own legs where I had a mind to go. I wouldn't have believed it of myself; but, then—you see—I felt somehow I must get there by hook or by crook. So I worried them. The men said 'My dear fellow,' and did nothing. Then—would you believe it?—I tried the women. I, Charlie Marlow, set the women to work—to get a job. Heavens! Well, you see, the notion

20

5. Pester.

drove me. I had an aunt, a dear enthusiastic soul. She wrote: 'It will be delightful. I am ready to do anything, anything for you. It is a glorious idea. I know the wife of a very high personage in the Administration, and also a man who has lots of influence with,' &c., &c. She was determined to make no end of fuss to get me appointed skipper of a river steamboat, if such was my fancy.

"I got my appointment—of course; and I got it very quick. It appears the Company had received news that one of their captains had been killed in a scuffle with the natives. This was my chance, and it made me the more anxious to go. It was only months and months afterwards, when I made the attempt to recover what was left of the body, that I heard the original quarrel arose from a misunderstanding about some hens. Yes, two black hens. Fresleven—that was the fellow's name, a Dane—thought himself wronged somehow in the bargain, so he went ashore and started to hammer the chief of the village with a stick. Oh, it didn't surprise me in the least to hear this, and at the same time to be told that Fresleven was the gentlest, quietest creature that ever walked on two legs. No doubt he was; but he had been a couple of years already out there engaged in the noble cause, you know, and he probably felt the need at last of asserting his self-respect in some way. Therefore he whacked the old nigger mercilessly, while a big crowd of his people watched him, thunderstruck, till some man,—I was told the chief's son,—in desperation at hearing the old chap yell, made a tentative jab with a spear at the white man—and of course it went quite easy between the shoulder-blades. Then the whole population cleared into the forest, expecting all kinds of calamities to happen, while, on the other hand, the steamer Fresleven commanded left also in a bad panic, in charge of the engineer, I believe. Afterwards nobody seemed to trouble much about Fresleven's remains, till I got out and stepped into his shoes. I couldn't let it rest, though; but when an opportunity offered at last to meet my predecessor, the grass growing through his ribs was tall enough to hide his bones. They were all there. The supernatural being had not been touched after he fell. And the village was deserted, the huts gaped black, rotting, all askew within the fallen enclosures. A calamity had come to it, sure enough. The people had vanished. Mad terror had scattered them, men, women, and children, through the bush, and they had never returned. What became of the hens I don't know either. I should think the cause of progress got them, anyhow. However, through this glorious affair I got my appointment, before I had fairly begun to hope for it.

"I flew around like mad to get ready, and before forty-eight hours I was crossing the Channel to show myself to my employers, and sign the contract. In a very few hours I arrived in a city that always makes me think of a whited sepulcher.[6] Prejudice no doubt. I had no difficulty in finding the Company's offices. It was the biggest thing in the town, and everybody I met was full of it. They were going to run an over-sea empire, and make no end of coin by trade.

---

6. Matthew 23: 27–28: Jesus used the term to describe hypocrites who appear beautiful on the outside but are rotten inside.

"A narrow and deserted street in deep shadow, high houses, innumerable windows with venetian blinds, a dead silence, grass sprouting between the stones, imposing carriage archways right and left, immense double doors standing ponderously ajar. I slipped through one of these cracks, went up a swept and ungarnished staircase, as arid as a desert, and opened the first door I came to. Two women, one fat and the other slim, sat on straw-bottomed chairs, knitting black wool. The slim one got up and walked straight at me— still knitting with downcast eyes—and only just as I began to think of getting out of her way, as you would for a somnambulist, stood still, and looked up. Her dress was as plain as an umbrella-cover, and she turned round without a word and preceded me into a waiting-room. I gave my name, and looked about. Deal table in the middle, plain chairs all round the walls, on one end a large shining map, marked with all the colors of a rainbow. There was a vast amount of red—good to see at any time, because one knows that some real work is done in there, a deuce of a lot of blue, a little green, smears of orange, and, on the East Coast, a purple patch, to show where the jolly pioneers of progress drink the jolly lager-beer.[7] However, I wasn't going into any of these. I was going into the yellow. Dead in the center. And the river was there— fascinating—deadly—like a snake. Ough! A door opened, a white-haired secretarial head, but wearing a compassionate expression, appeared, and a skinny forefinger beckoned me into the sanctuary. Its light was dim, and a heavy writing-desk squatted in the middle. From behind that structure came out an impression of pale plumpness in a frock-coat. The great man himself. He was five feet six, I should judge, and had his grip on the handle-end of ever so many millions. He shook hands, I fancy, murmured vaguely, was satisfied with my French. *Bon voyage.*

"In about forty-five seconds I found myself again in the waiting-room with the compassionate secretary, who, full of desolation and sympathy, made me sign some document. I believe I undertook amongst other things not to disclose any trade secrets. Well, I am not going to.

"I began to feel slightly uneasy. You know I am not used to such cere- 25 monies, and there was something ominous in the atmosphere. It was just as though I had been let into some conspiracy—I don't know—something not quite right; and I was glad to get out. In the other room the two women knit-ted black wool feverishly. People were arriving, and the younger one was walking back and forth introducing them. The old one sat on her chair. Her flat cloth slippers were propped up on a foot-warmer, and a cat reposed on her lap. She wore a starched white affair on her head, had a wart on one cheek, and silver-rimmed spectacles hung on the tip of her nose. She glanced at me above the glasses. The swift and indifferent placidity of that look troubled me. Two youths with foolish and cheery countenances were being piloted over, and she threw at them the same quick glance of unconcerned wisdom. She

---

7. Victorian maps were color-coded to show which countries controlled which colonies: red, blue, green, orange, purple, yellow were for British, French, Portuguese, Italian, German, and Belgian possessions respectively. Marlow was sailing to the Belgian Congo, present-day Demo-cratic Republic of Congo.

seemed to know all about them and about me too. An eerie feeling came over me. She seemed uncanny and fateful. Often far away there I thought of these two, guarding the door of Darkness, knitting black wool as for a warm pall, one introducing, introducing continuously to the unknown, the other scrutinizing the cheery and foolish faces with unconcerned old eyes. *Ave!* Old knitter of black wool. *Morituri te salutant.*[8] Not many of those she looked at ever saw her again—not half, by a long way.

"There was yet a visit to the doctor. 'A simple formality,' assured me the secretary, with an air of taking an immense part in all my sorrows. Accordingly a young chap wearing his hat over the left eyebrow, some clerk I suppose,—there must have been clerks in the business, though the house was as still as a house in a city of the dead,—came from somewhere up-stairs, and led me forth. He was shabby and careless, with ink-stains on the sleeves of his jacket, and his cravat was large and billowy, under a chin shaped like the toe of an old boot. It was a little too early for the doctor, so I proposed a drink, and thereupon he developed a vein of joviality. As we sat over our vermouths he glorified the Company's business, and by-and-by I expressed casually my surprise at him not going out there. He became very cool and collected all at once. 'I am not such a fool as I look, quoth Plato to his disciples,' he said sententiously, emptied his glass with great resolution, and we rose.

"The old doctor felt my pulse, evidently thinking of something else the while. 'Good, good for there,' he mumbled, and then with a certain eagerness asked me whether I would let him measure my head. Rather surprised, I said Yes, when he produced a thing like calipers and got the dimensions back and front and every way, taking notes carefully. He was an unshaven little man in a threadbare coat like a gabardine, with his feet in slippers, and I thought him a harmless fool. 'I always ask leave, in the interests of science, to measure the crania of those going out there,' he said. 'And when they come back too?' I asked. 'Oh, I never see them,' he remarked; 'and, moreover, the changes take place inside, you know.' He smiled, as if at some quiet joke. 'So you are going out there. Famous. Interesting too.' He gave me a searching glance, and made another note. 'Ever any madness in your family?' he asked, in a matter-of-fact tone. I felt very annoyed. 'Is that question in the interests of science too?' 'It would be,' he said, without taking notice of my irritation, 'interesting for science to watch the mental changes of individuals, on the spot, but . . .' 'Are you an alienist?'[9] I interrupted. 'Every doctor should be—a little,' answered that original, imperturbably. 'I have a little theory which you Messieurs who go out there must help me to prove. This is my share in the advantages my country shall reap from the possession of such a magnificent dependency. The mere wealth I leave to others. Pardon my questions, but you are the first Englishman coming under my observation. . . .' I hastened to assure him I was not in the least typical. 'If I were,' said I, 'I wouldn't be talking like this with

8. The full phrase is "Ave Caesar, morituri te salutamus": "Hail, Caesar, they who are about to die salute you"—the gladiators' salute to the emperor before the games.

  9. One who treats mental illness.

you.' 'What you say is rather profound, and probably erroneous,' he said, with a laugh. 'Avoid irritation more than exposure to the sun. Adieu. How do you English say, eh? Good-by. Ah! Good-by. Adieu. In the tropics one must before everything keep calm.' . . . He lifted a warning forefinger. . . . '*Du calme, du calme. Adieu.*'[10]

"One thing more remained to do—say good-by to my excellent aunt. I found her triumphant. I had a cup of tea—the last decent cup of tea for many days—and in a room that most soothingly looked just as you would expect a lady's drawing-room to look, we had a long quiet chat by the fireside. In the course of these confidences it became quite plain to me I had been represented to the wife of the high dignitary, and goodness knows to how many more people besides, as an exceptional and gifted creature—a piece of good fortune for the Company—a man you don't get hold of every day. Good heavens! and I was going to take charge of a two-penny-halfpenny river-steamboat with a penny whistle attached! It appeared, however, I was also one of the Workers, with a capital—you know. Something like an emissary of light, something like a lower sort of apostle. There had been a lot of such rot let loose in print and talk just about that time, and the excellent woman, living right in the rush of all that humbug, got carried off her feet. She talked about 'weaning those ignorant millions from their horrid ways,' till, upon my word, she made me quite uncomfortable.[11] I ventured to hint that the Company was run for profit.

"'You forget, dear Charlie, that the laborer is worthy of his hire,' she said, brightly. It's queer how out of touch with truth women are. They live in a world of their own, and there had never been anything like it, and never can be. It is too beautiful altogether, and if they were to set it up it would go to pieces before the first sunset. Some confounded fact we men have been living contentedly with ever since the day of creation would start up and knock the whole thing over.

"After this I got embraced, told to wear flannel, be sure to write often, and so on—and I left. In the street—I don't know why—a queer feeling came to me that I was an imposter. Odd thing that I, who used to clear out for any part of the world at twenty-four hours' notice, with less thought than most men give to the crossing of a street, had a moment—I won't say of hesitation, but of startled pause, before this commonplace affair. The best way I can explain it to you is by saying that, for a second or two, I felt as though, instead of going to the center of a continent, I were about to set off for the center of the earth.

"I left in a French steamer, and she called in every blamed port they have out there, for, as far as I could see, the sole purpose of landing soldiers and custom-house officers. I watched the coast. Watching a coast as it slips by the

30

10. "Keep calm, keep calm. Good-bye."

11. Marlow refers here to what Rudyard Kipling called "The white man's burden," the idea that "civilized" Europeans were morally obliged to "raise" the "savages" of Africa and other "uncivilized" countries. The extent to which Marlow (and Conrad) believed in this idea is hotly debated by critics.

ship is like thinking about an enigma. There it is before you—smiling, frowning, inviting, grand, mean, insipid, or savage, and always mute with an air of whispering, Come and find out. This one was almost featureless, as if still in the making, with an aspect of monotonous grimness. The edge of a colossal jungle, so dark-green as to be almost black, fringed with white surf, ran straight, like a ruled line, far, far away along a blue sea whose glitter was blurred by a creeping mist. The sun was fierce, the land seemed to glisten and drip with steam. Here and there grayish-whitish specks showed up, clustered inside the white surf, with a flag flying above them perhaps. Settlements some centuries old, and still no bigger than pin-heads on the untouched expanse of their background. We pounded along, stopped, landed soldiers; went on, landed custom-house clerks to levy toll in what looked like a God-forsaken wilderness, with a tin shed and a flag-pole lost in it; landed more soldiers—to take care of the custom-house clerks, presumably. Some, I heard, got drowned in the surf; but whether they did or not, nobody seemed particularly to care. They were just flung out there, and on we went. Every day the coast looked the same, as though we had not moved; but we passed various places—trading places—with names like Gran' Bassam Little Popo; names that seemed to belong to some sordid farce acted in front of a sinister backcloth. The idleness of a passenger, my isolation amongst all these men with whom I had no point of contact, the oily and languid sea, the uniform somberness of the coast, seemed to keep me away from the truth of things, within the toil of a mournful and senseless delusion. The voice of the surf heard now and then was a positive pleasure, like the speech of a brother. It was something natural, that had its reason, that had a meaning. Now and then a boat from the shore gave one a momentary contact with reality. It was paddled by black fellows. You could see from afar the white of their eyeballs glistening. They shouted, sang; their bodies streamed with perspiration; they had faces like grotesque masks—these chaps; but they had bone, muscle, a wild vitality, an intense energy of movement, that was as natural and true as the surf along their coast. They wanted no excuse for being there. They were a great comfort to look at. For a time I would feel I belonged still to a world of straightforward facts; but the feeling would not last long. Something would turn up to scare it away. Once, I remember, we came upon a man-of-war anchored off the coast. There wasn't even a shed there, and she was shelling the bush. It appears the French had one of their wars going on thereabouts. Her ensign dropped limp like a rag; the muzzles of the long six-inch guns stuck out all over the low hull; the greasy, slimy swell swung her up lazily and let her down, swaying her thin masts. In the empty immensity of earth, sky, and water, there she was, incomprehensible, firing into a continent. Pop, would go one of the six-inch guns; a small flame would dart and vanish, a little white smoke would disappear, a tiny projectile would give a feeble screech—and nothing happened. Nothing could happen. There was a touch of insanity in the proceeding, a sense of lugubrious drollery in the sight; and it was not dissipated by somebody on board assuring me earnestly there was a camp of natives—he called them enemies!—hidden out of sight somewhere.

"We gave her her letters (I heard the men in that lonely ship were dying of fever at the rate of three a day) and went on. We called at some more places with farcical names, where the merry dance of death and trade goes on in a still and earthy atmosphere as of an overheated catacomb; all along the formless coast bordered by dangerous surf, as if Nature herself had tried to ward off intruders; in and out of rivers, streams of death in life, whose banks were rotting into mud, whose waters, thickened into slime, invaded the contorted mangroves, that seemed to writhe at us in the extremity of an impotent despair. Nowhere did we stop long enough to get a particularized impression, but the general sense of vague and oppressive wonder grew upon me. It was like a weary pilgrimage amongst hints for nightmares.

"It was upward of thirty days before I saw the mouth of the big river. We anchored off the seat of the government. But my work would not begin till some two hundred miles farther on. So as soon as I could I made a start for a place thirty miles higher up.

"I had my passage on a little sea-going steamer. Her captain was a Swede, and knowing me for a seaman, invited me on the bridge. He was a young man, lean, fair, and morose, with lanky hair and a shuffling gait. As we left the miserable little wharf, he tossed his head contemptuously at the shore. 'Been living there?' he asked. I said, 'Yes.' 'Fine lot these government chaps—are they not?' he went on, speaking English with great precision and considerable bitterness. 'It is funny what some people will do for a few francs a month. I wonder what becomes of that kind when it goes up country?' I said to him I expected to see that soon. 'So-o-o!' he exclaimed. He shuffled athwart, keeping one eye ahead vigilantly. 'Don't be too sure,' he continued. 'The other day I took up a man who hanged himself on the road. He was a Swede, too.' 'Hanged himself! Why, in God's name?' I cried. He kept on looking out watchfully. 'Who knows? The sun too much for him, or the country perhaps.'

"At last we opened a reach. A rocky cliff appeared, mounds of turned-up 35 earth by the shore, houses on a hill, others, with iron roofs, amongst a waste of excavations, or hanging to the declivity. A continuous noise of the rapids above hovered over this scene of inhabited devastation. A lot of people, mostly black and naked, moved about like ants. A jetty projected into the river. A blinding sunlight drowned all this at times in a sudden recrudescence of glare. 'There's your Company's station,' said the Swede, pointing to three wooden barrack-like structures on the rocky slope. 'I will send your things up. Four boxes did you say? So. Farewell.'

"I came upon a boiler wallowing in the grass, then found a path leading up the hill. It turned aside for the bowlders, and also for an undersized railway-truck lying there on its back with its wheels in the air. One was off. The thing looked as dead as the carcass of some animal. I came upon more pieces of decaying machinery, a stack of rusty nails. To the left a clump of trees made a shady spot, where dark things seemed to stir feebly. I blinked, the path was steep. A horn tooted to the right, and I saw the black people run. A heavy and dull detonation shook the ground, a puff of smoke came out of the cliff, and that was all. No change appeared on the face of the rock. They were building a railway. The cliff was not in the way or anything; but this objectless blasting was all the work going on.

"A slight clinking behind me made me turn my head. Six black men advanced in a file, toiling up the path. They walked erect and slow, balancing small baskets full of earth on their heads, and the clink kept time with their footsteps. Black rags were wound round their loins, and the short ends behind waggled to and fro like tails. I could see every rib, the joints of their limbs were like knots in a rope; each had an iron collar on his neck, and all were connected together with a chain whose bights[12] swung between them, rhythmically clinking. Another report from the cliff made me think suddenly of that ship of war I had seen firing into a continent. It was the same kind of ominous voice; but these men could by no stretch of imagination be called enemies. They were called criminals, and the outraged law, like the bursting shells, had come to them, an insoluble mystery from the sea. All their meager breasts panted together, the violently dilated nostrils quivered, the eyes stared stonily uphill. They passed me within six inches, without a glance, with that complete, deathlike indifference of unhappy savages. Behind this raw matter one of the reclaimed, the product of the new forces at work, strolled despondently, carrying a rifle by its middle. He had a uniform jacket with one button off, and seeing a white man on the path, hoisted his weapon to his shoulder with alacrity. This was simple prudence, white men being so much alike at a distance that he could not tell who I might be. He was speedily reassured, and with a large, white, rascally grin, and a glance at his charge, seemed to take me into partnership in his exalted trust. After all, I also was a part of the great cause of these high and just proceedings.

"Instead of going up, I turned and descended to the left. My idea was to let that chain-gang get out of sight before I climbed the hill. You know I am not particularly tender; I've had to strike and to fend off. I've had to resist and to attack sometimes—that's only one way of resisting—without counting the exact cost, according to the demands of such sort of life as I had blundered into. I've seen the devil of violence, and the devil of greed, and the devil of hot desire; but, by all the stars! these were strong, lusty, red-eyed devils, that swayed and drove men—men, I tell you. But as I stood on this hillside, I foresaw that in the blinding sunshine of that land I would become acquainted with a flabby, pretending, weak-eyed devil of a rapacious and pitiless folly. How insidious he could be, too, I was only to find out several months later and a thousand miles farther. For a moment I stood appalled, as though by a warning. Finally I descended the hill, obliquely, towards the trees I had seen.

"I avoided a vast artificial hole somebody had been digging on the slope, the purpose of which I found it impossible to divine. It wasn't a quarry or a sandpit, anyhow. It was just a hole. It might have been connected with the philanthropic desire of giving the criminals something to do. I don't know. Then I nearly fell into a very narrow ravine, almost no more than a scar in the hillside. I discovered that a lot of imported drainage-pipes for the settlement had been tumbled in there. There wasn't one that was not broken. It was a wanton smash-up. At last I got under the trees. My purpose was to stroll into the shade for a moment; but no sooner within than it seemed to me I had

12. Bends (of chain).

stepped into a gloomy circle of some Inferno. The rapids were near, and an uninterrupted, uniform, headlong, rushing noise filled the mournful stillness of the grove, where not a breath stirred, not a leaf moved, with a mysterious sound—as though the tearing pace of the launched earth had suddenly become audible.

"Black shapes crouched, lay, sat between the trees, leaning against the 40 trunks, clinging to the earth, half coming out, half effaced within the dim light, in all the attitudes of pain, abandonment, and despair. Another mine on the cliff went off, followed by a slight shudder of the soil under my feet. The work was going on. The work! And this was the place where some of the helpers had withdrawn to die.

"They were dying slowly—it was very clear. They were not enemies, they were not criminals, they were nothing earthly now,—nothing but black shadows of disease and starvation, lying confusedly in the greenish gloom. Brought from all the recesses of the coast in all the legality of time contracts, lost in uncongenial surroundings, fed on unfamiliar food, they sickened, became inefficient, and were then allowed to crawl away and rest. These moribund shapes were free as air—and nearly as thin. I began to distinguish the gleam of the eyes under the trees. Then, glancing down, I saw a face near my hand. The black bones reclined at full length with one shoulder against the tree, and slowly the eyelids rose and the sunken eyes looked up at me, enormous and vacant, a kind of blind, white flicker in the depths of the orbs, which died out slowly. The man seemed young—almost a boy—but you know with them it's hard to tell. I found nothing else to do but to offer him one of my good Swede's ship's biscuits I had in my pocket. The fingers closed slowly on it and held—there was no other movement and no other glance. He had tied a bit of white worsted round his neck—Why? Where did he get it? Was it a badge—an ornament—a charm—a propitiatory act? Was there any idea at all connected with it? It looked startling round his black neck, this bit of white thread from beyond the seas.

"Near the same tree two more bundles of acute angles sat with their legs drawn up. One, with his chin propped on his knees, stared at nothing, in an intolerable and appalling manner: his brother phantom rested its forehead, as if overcome with a great weariness; and all about others scattered in every pose of contorted collapse, as in some picture of a massacre or a pestilence. While I stood horror-struck, one of these creatures rose to his hands and knees, and went off on all-fours towards the river to drink. He lapped out of his hand, then sat up in the sunlight, crossing his shins in front of him, and after a time let his woolly head fall on his breastbone.

"I didn't want any more loitering in the shade, and I made haste towards the station. When near the buildings I met a white man, in such an unexpected elegance of get-up that in the first moment I took him for a sort of vision. I saw a high starched collar, white cuffs, a light alpaca jacket, snowy trousers, a clean necktie, and varnished boots. No hat. Hair parted, brushed, oiled, under a green-lined parasol held in a big white hand. He was amazing, and had a penholder behind his ear.

"I shook hands with this miracle, and I learned he was the Company's chief accountant, and that all the bookkeeping was done at this station. He had come out for a moment, he said, 'to get a breath of fresh air.' The expression sounded wonderfully odd, with its suggestion of sedentary desk-life. I wouldn't have mentioned the fellow to you at all, only it was from his lips that I first heard the name of the man who is so indissolubly connected with the memories of that time. Moreover, I respected the fellow. Yes; I respected his collars, his vast cuffs, his brushed hair. His appearance was certainly that of a hairdresser's dummy; but in the great demoralization of the land he kept up his appearance. That's backbone. His starched collars and got-up shirtfronts were achievements of character. He had been out nearly three years; and, later on, I could not help asking him how he managed to sport such linen. He had just the faintest blush, and said modestly, 'I've been teaching one of the native women about the station. It was difficult. She had a distaste for the work.' Thus this man had verily accomplished something. And he was devoted to his books, which were in apple-pie order.

"Everything else in the station was in a muddle,—heads, things, build- 45 ings. Strings of dusty niggers with splay feet arrived and departed; a stream of manufactured goods, rubbishy cottons, beads, and brass-wire sent into the depths of darkness, and in the return came a precious trickle of ivory.

"I had to wait in the station for ten days—an eternity. I lived in a hut in the yard, but to be out of the chaos I would sometimes get into the accountant's office. It was built of horizontal planks, and so badly put together that, as he bent over his desk, he was barred from neck to heels with narrow strips of sunlight. There was no need to open the big shutter to see. It was hot there too; big flies buzzed fiendishly, and did not sting, but stabbed. I sat generally on the floor, while, of faultless appearance (and even slightly scented), perching on a high stool, he wrote, he wrote. Sometimes he stood up for exercise. When a truckle-bed with a sick man (some invalided agent from up-country) was put in there, he exhibited a gentle annoyance. 'The groans of this sick person,' he said, 'distract my attention. And without that it is extremely difficult to guard against clerical errors in this climate.'

"One day he remarked, without lifting his head, 'In the interior you will no doubt meet Mr. Kurtz.' On my asking who Mr. Kurtz was, he said he was a first-class agent; and seeing my disappointment at this information, he added slowly, laying down his pen, 'He is a very remarkable person.' Further questions elicited from him that Mr. Kurtz was at present in charge of a trading post, a very important one, in the true ivory-country, at 'the very bottom of there. Sends in as much ivory as all the others put together. . . .' He began to write again. The sick man was too ill to groan. The flies buzzed in a great peace.

"Suddenly there was a growing murmur of voices and a great tramping of feet. A caravan had come in. A violent babble of uncouth sounds burst out on the other side of the planks. All the carriers were speaking together, and in the midst of the uproar the lamentable voice of the chief agent was heard 'giving it up' tearfully for the twentieth time that day. . . . He rose slowly. 'What a frightful row,' he said. He crossed the room gently to look at the sick man, and returning, said to me, 'He does not hear.' 'What! Dead?' I asked, startled.

'No, not yet,' he answered, with great composure. Then, alluding with a toss of the head to the tumult in the station-yard, 'When one has got to make correct entries, one comes to hate those savages—hate them to the death.' He remained thoughtful for a moment. 'When you see Mr. Kurtz,' he went on, 'tell him from me that everything here'—he glanced at the desk—'is very satisfactory. I don't like to write to him—with those messengers of ours you never know who may get hold of your letter—at that Central Station.' He stared at me for a moment with his mild, bulging eyes. 'Oh, he will go far, very far,' he began again. 'He will be a somebody in the Administration before long. They, above—the Council in Europe, you know—mean him to be.'

"He turned to his work. The noise outside had ceased, and presently in going out I stopped at the door. In the steady buzz of flies the homeward-bound agent was lying flushed and insensible; the other, bent over his books, was making correct entries of perfectly correct transactions; and fifty feet below the doorstep I could see the still tree-tops of the grove of death.

"Next day I left that station at last, with a caravan of sixty men, for a two-hundred-mile tramp.   50

"No use telling you much about that. Paths, paths, everywhere; a stamped-in network of paths spreading over the empty land, through long grass, through burnt grass, through thickets, down and up chilly ravines, up and down stony hills ablaze with heat; and a solitude, nobody, not a hut. The population had cleared out a long time ago. Well, if a lot of mysterious niggers armed with all kinds of fearful weapons suddenly took to traveling on the road between Deal and Gravesend, catching the yokels right and left to carry heavy loads for them, I fancy every farm and cottage thereabouts would get empty very soon. Only here the dwellings were gone too. Still I passed through several abandoned villages. There's something pathetically childish in the ruins of grass walls. Day after day, with the stamp and shuffle of sixty pair of bare feet behind me, each pair under a 60-lb. load. Camp, cook, sleep, strike camp, march. Now and then a carrier dead in harness, at rest in the long grass near the path, with an empty water gourd and his long staff lying by his side. A great silence around and above. Perhaps on some quiet night the tremor of far-off drums, sinking, swelling, a tremor vast, faint; a sound weird, appealing, suggestive, and wild—and perhaps with as profound a meaning as the sound of bells in a Christian country. Once a white man in an unbuttoned uniform, camping on the path with an armed escort of lank Zanzibaris, very hospitable and festive—not to say drunk. Was looking after the upkeep of the road, he declared. Can't say I saw any road or any upkeep, unless the body of a middle-aged negro, with a bullet-hole in the forehead, upon which I absolutely stumbled three miles farther on, may be considered as a permanent improvement. I had a white companion too, not a bad chap, but rather too fleshy and with the exasperating habit of fainting on the hot hillsides, miles away from the least bit of shade and water. Annoying, you know, to hold your own coat like a parasol over a man's head while he is coming-to. I couldn't help asking him once what he meant by coming there at all. 'To make money, of course. What do you think?' he said, scornfully. Then he got fever, and had to be carried in a hammock slung under a pole. As he weighed sixteen stone[13] I had no end of rows with the carriers. They jibbed, ran away, sneaked off with their loads in the night—quite a mutiny. So, one evening, I made a speech in English with gestures, not one of which was lost to the sixty pairs of eyes before me, and the next morning I started the hammock off in front all right. An hour afterwards I came upon the whole concern wrecked in a bush—man, hammock, groans, blankets, horrors. The heavy pole had skinned his poor nose. He was very anxious for me to kill somebody, but there wasn't the shadow of a carrier near. I remembered the old doctor,—'It would be interesting for science to watch the mental changes of individuals, on the spot.' I felt I was becoming scientifically interesting. However, all that is to no purpose. On the fifteenth day I came in sight of the big river again, and hobbled into the Central Station. It was on a back water surrounded by scrub and forest, with a pretty border of smelly mud on one side, and on the three others inclosed by a crazy fence of rushes. A neglected gap was all the gate it had, and the first glance at the place was enough to let you see the flabby devil was running that show. White men with long staves in their hands appeared languidly from amongst the buildings, strolling up to take a look at me, and then retired out of sight somewhere. One of them, a stout, excitable chap with black mustaches, informed me with great volubility and many digressions, as soon as I told him who I was, that my steamer was at the bottom of the river. I was thunderstruck. What, how, why? Oh, it was 'all right.' The 'manager himself' was there. All quite correct. 'Everybody had behaved splendidly! splendidly!'—'you must,' he said in agitation, 'go and see the general manager at once. He is waiting!'

"I did not see the real significance of that wreck at once. I fancy I see it now, but I am not sure—not at all. Certainly the affair was too stupid—when I think of it—to be altogether natural. Still. . . . But at the moment it presented itself simply as a confounded nuisance. The steamer was sunk. They had started two days before in a sudden hurry up the river with the manager on board, in charge of some volunteer skipper, and before they had been out three hours they tore the bottom out of her on stones, and she sank near the south bank. I asked myself what I was to do there, now my boat was lost. As a matter of fact, I had plenty to do in fishing my command out of the river. I had to set about it the very next day. That, and the repairs when I brought the pieces to the station, took some months.

"My first interview with the manager was curious. He did not ask me to sit down after my twenty-mile walk that morning. He was commonplace in complexion, in feature, in manners, and in voice. He was of middle size and of ordinary build. His eyes, of the usual blue, were perhaps remarkably cold, and he certainly could make his glance fall on one as trenchant and heavy as an ax. But even at these times the rest of his person seemed to disclaim the intention. Otherwise there was only an indefinable, faint expression of his lips, something stealthy—a smile—not a smile—I remember it, but I can't explain. It was unconscious, this smile was, though just after he had said something it got

13. A stone is 14 pounds; hence 224 pounds.

intensified for an instant. It came at the end of his speeches like a seal applied on the words to make the meaning of the commonest phrase appear absolutely inscrutable. He was a common trader, from his youth up employed in these parts—nothing more. He was obeyed, yet he inspired neither love nor fear, nor even respect. He inspired uneasiness. That was it! Uneasiness. Not a definite mistrust—just uneasiness—nothing more. You have no idea how effective such a . . . a . . . faculty can be. He had no genius for organizing, for initiative, or for order even. That was evident in such things as the deplorable state of the station. He had no learning, and no intelligence. His position had come to him—why? Perhaps because he was never ill . . . He had served three terms of three years out there . . . Because triumphant health in the general rout of constitutions is a kind of power in itself. When he went home on leave he rioted on a large scale—pompously. Jack ashore—with a difference—in externals only. This one could gather from his casual talk. He originated nothing, he could keep the routine going—that's all. But he was great. He was great by this little thing that it was impossible to tell what could control such a man. He never gave that secret away. Perhaps there was nothing within him. Such a suspicion made one pause—for out there there were no external checks. Once when various tropical diseases had laid low almost every 'agent' in the station, he was heard to say, 'Men who come out here should have no entrails.' He sealed the utterance with that smile of his, as though it had been a door opening into a darkness he had in his keeping. You fancied you had seen things—but the seal was on. When annoyed at meal-times by the constant quarrels of the white men about precedence, he ordered an immense round table to be made, for which a special house had to be built. This was the station's mess-room. Where he sat was the first place—the rest were nowhere. One felt this to be his unalterable conviction. He was neither civil nor uncivil. He was quiet. He allowed his 'boy'—an overfed young negro from the coast—to treat the white men, under his very eyes, with provoking insolence.

"He began to speak as soon as he saw me. I had been very long on the road. He could not wait. Had to start without me. The up-river stations had to be relieved. There had been so many delays already that he did not know who was dead and who was alive, and how they got on—and so on, and so on. He paid no attention to my explanations, and, playing with a stick of sealing-wax, repeated several times that the situation was 'very grave, very grave.' There were rumors that a very important station was in jeopardy, and its chief, Mr. Kurtz, was ill. Hoped it was not true. Mr. Kurtz was . . . I felt weary and irritable. Hang Kurtz, I thought. I interrupted him by saying I had heard of Mr. Kurtz on the coast. 'Ah! So they talk of him down there,' he murmured to himself. Then he began again, assuring me Mr. Kurtz was the best agent he had, an exceptional man, of the greatest importance to the Company; therefore I could understand his anxiety. He was, he said, 'very, very uneasy.' Certainly he fidgeted on his chair a good deal, exclaimed, 'Ah, Mr. Kurtz!' broke the stick of sealing-wax and seemed dumbfounded by the accident. Next thing he wanted to know 'how long it would take to' . . . I interrupted him again. Being hungry, you know, and kept on my feet too, I was getting savage. 'How could I tell,' I said. 'I hadn't even seen the wreck yet—some months, no doubt! All this talk seemed to me so futile. 'Some months,' he said. 'Well, let us say three months before we can make a start. Yes. That ought to do the affair.' I flung out of his hut (he lived all alone in a clay hut with a sort of veranda) muttering to myself my opinion of him. He was a chattering idiot. Afterwards I took it back when it was borne in upon me startlingly with what extreme nicety he had estimated the time requisite for the 'affair.'

"I went to work the next day, turning, so to speak, my back on that station. In that way only it seemed to me I could keep my hold on the redeeming facts of life. Still, one must look about sometimes; and then I saw this station, these men strolling aimlessly about in the sunshine of the yard. I asked myself sometimes what it all meant. They wandered here and there with their absurd long staves in their hands, like a lot of faithless pilgrims bewitched inside a rotten fence. The word 'ivory' rang in the air, was whispered, was sighed. You would think they were praying to it. A taint of imbecile rapacity blew through it all, like a whiff from some corpse. By Jove! I've never seen anything so unreal in my life. And outside, the silent wilderness surrounding this cleared speck on the earth struck me as something great and invincible, like evil or truth, waiting patiently for the passing away of this fantastic invasion.

"Oh, these months! well, never mind. Various things happened. One evening a grass shed full of calico, cotton prints, beads, and I don't know what else, burst into a blaze so suddenly that you would have thought the earth had opened to let an avenging fire consume all that trash. I was smoking my pipe quietly by my dismantled steamer, and saw them all cutting capers in the light, with their arms lifted high, when the stout man with mustaches came tearing down to the river, a tin pail in his hand, assured me that everybody was 'behaving splendidly, splendidly,' dipped about a quart of water and tore back again. I noticed there was a hole in the bottom of his pail.

"I strolled up. There was no hurry. You see the thing had gone off like a box of matches. It had been hopeless from the very first. The flame had leaped high, driven everybody back, lighted up everything—and collapsed. The shed was already a heap of embers glowing fiercely. A nigger was being beaten near by. They said he had caused the fire in some way; be that as it may, he was screeching most horribly. I saw him, later on, for several days, sitting in a bit of shade looking very sick and trying to recover himself: afterwards he arose and went out—and the wilderness without a sound took him into its bosom again. As I approached the glow from the dark I found myself at the back of two men, talking. I heard the name of Kurtz pronounced, then the words, 'take advantage of this unfortunate accident.' One of the men was the manager. I wished him a good evening. 'Did you ever see anything like it—eh? it is incredible,' he said and walked off. The other man remained. He was a first-class agent, young, gentlemanly, a bit reserved, with a forked little beard and a hooked nose. He was standoffish with the other agents, and they on their side said he was the manager's spy upon them. As to me, I had hardly ever spoken to him before. We got into talk, and by-and-by we strolled away from the hissing ruins. Then he asked me to his room, which was in the main building of the station. He struck a match, and I perceived that this young aristocrat had only a silver-mounted dressing-case but also a whole candle all to himself. Just at that time the manager was the only man supposed to have any right to candles. Native mats covered the clay walls; a collection of spears, assegais, shields, knives was hung up in trophies. The business intrusted to this fellow was the making of bricks—so I had been informed; but there wasn't a fragment of a brick anywhere in the station, and he had been there more than a year—waiting. It seems he could not make bricks without something, I don't know what—straw maybe. Anyways, it could not be found there, and as it was not likely to be sent from Europe, it did not appear clear to me what he was waiting for. An act of special creation perhaps. However, they were all waiting—all the sixteen or twenty pilgrims of them—for something; and upon my word it did not seem an uncongenial occupation, from the way they took it, though the only thing that ever came to them was disease—as far as I could see. They beguiled the time by backbiting and intriguing against each other in a foolish kind of way. There was an air of plotting about that station, but nothing came of it, of course. It was as unreal as everything else—as the philanthropic pretense of the whole concern, as their talk, as their government, as their show of work. The only real feeling was a desire to get appointed to a trading-post where ivory was to be had, so that they could earn percentages. They intrigued and slandered and hated each other only on that account,— but as to effectually lifting a little finger—oh, no. By heavens! there is something after all in the world allowing one man to steal a horse while another must not look at a halter. Steal a horse straight out. Very well. He has done it. Perhaps he can ride. But there is a way of looking at a halter that would provoke the most charitable of saints into a kick.

"I had no idea why he wanted to be sociable, but as we chatted in there it suddenly occurred to me the fellow was trying to get at something—in fact, pumping me. He alluded constantly to Europe, to the people I was supposed to know there—putting leading questions as to my acquaintances in the sepulchral city, and so on. His little eyes glittered like mica discs—with curiosity,— though he tried to keep up a bit of superciliousness. At first I was astonished, but very soon I became awfully curious to see what he would find out from me. I couldn't possibly imagine what I had in me to make it worth his while. It was very pretty to see how he baffled himself, for in truth my body was full of chills, and my head had nothing in it but that wretched steamboat business. It was evident he took me for a perfectly shameless prevaricator. At last he got angry, and, to conceal a movement of furious annoyance, he yawned. I rose. Then I noticed a small sketch in oils, on a panel, representing a woman, draped and blindfolded, carrying a lighted torch. The background was somber—almost black. The movement of the woman was stately, and the effect of the torchlight on the face was sinister.

"It arrested me, and he stood by civilly, holding an empty half-pint champagne bottle (medical comforts) with the candle stuck in it. To my question he said Mr. Kurtz had painted this—in this very station more than a year ago— while waiting for means to go to his trading-post. 'Tell me, pray,' said I, 'who is this Mr. Kurtz?'

"'The chief of the Inner Station,' he answered in a short tone, looking 60 away. 'Much obliged,' I said, laughing. 'And you are the brickmaker of the Central Station. Everyone knows that.' He was silent for a while. 'He is a prodigy,' he said at last. 'He is an emissary of pity, and science, and progress, and devil knows what else. We want,' he began to declaim suddenly, 'for the guidance of the cause intrusted to us by Europe, so to speak, higher intelligence, wide sympathies, a singleness of purpose.' 'Who says that?' I asked. 'Lots of them,' he replied. 'Some even write that; and so *he* comes here, a special being, as you ought to know.' 'Why ought I to know?' I interrupted, really surprised. He paid no attention. 'Yes. To-day he is chief of the best station, next year he will be assistant-manager, two years more and . . . but I dare say you know what he will be in two years' time. You are the new gang—the gang of virtue. The same people who sent him specially also recommended you. Oh, don't say no. I've my own eyes to trust.' Light dawned upon me. My dear aunt's influential acquaintances were producing an unexpected effect upon that young man. I nearly burst into a laugh. 'Do you read the Company's confidential correspondence?' I asked. He hadn't a word to say. It was great fun. 'When Mr. Kurtz,' I continued severely, 'is General Manager, you won't have the opportunity.'

"He blew the candle out suddenly, and we went outside. The moon had risen. Black figures strolled about listlessly, pouring water on the glow, whence proceeded a sound of hissing; steam ascended in the moonlight, the beaten nigger groaned somewhere. 'What a row the brute makes!' said the indefatigable man with the mustaches, appearing near us. 'Serve him right. Transgression—punishment—bang! Pitiless, pitiless. That's the only way. This will prevent all conflagration for the future. I was just telling the manager . . .' He noticed my companion, and became crestfallen all at once. 'Not in bed yet,' he said, with a kind of servile heartiness; 'it's so natural. Ha! Danger-agitation.' He vanished. I went on to the river-side, and the other followed me. I heard a scathing murmur at my ear. 'Heap of muffs—go to.' The pilgrims could be seen in knots gesticulating, discussing. Several had still their staves in their hands. I verily believe they took these sticks to bed with them. Beyond the fence the forest stood up spectrally in the moonlight, and through the dim stir, through the faint sounds of that lamentable courtyard, the silence of the land went home to one's very heart,—its mystery, its greatness, the amazing reality of its concealed life. The hurt nigger moaned feebly somewhere near by, and then fetched a deep sigh that made me mend my pace away from there. I felt a hand introducing itself under my arm. 'My dear sir,' said the fellow, 'I don't want to be misunderstood, and especially by you, who will see Mr. Kurtz long before I can have that pleasure. I wouldn't like him to get a false idea of my disposition. . . .'

"I let him run on, this papier-maché Mephistopheles, and it seemed to me that if I tried I could poke my forefinger through him, and would find nothing inside but a little loose dirt, maybe. He, don't you see, had been planning to be assistant-manager by-and-by under the present man, and I could see that the coming of that Kurtz had upset them both not a little. He talked precipitately, and I did not try to stop him. I had my shoulders against the wreck of my steamer, hauled up on the slope like a carcass of some big river animal.

The smell of mud, of primeval mud, by Jove! was in my nostrils, the high still-ness of primeval forest was before my eyes; there were shiny patches on the black creek. The moon had spread over everything a thin layer of silver—over the rank grass, over the mud, upon the wall of matted vegetation standing higher than the wall of a temple, over the great river I could see through a somber gap glittering, glittering, as it flowed broadly by without a murmur. All this was great, expectant, mute, while the man jabbered about himself. I wondered whether the stillness on the face of the immensity looking at us two were meant as an appeal or as a menace. What were we who had strayed in here? Could we handle that dumb thing, or would it handle us? I felt how big, how confoundedly big, was that thing that couldn't talk, and perhaps was deaf as well. What was in there? I could see a little ivory coming out from there, and I had heard Mr. Kurtz was in there. I had heard enough about it too—God knows! Yet somehow it didn't bring any image with it—no more than if I had been told an angel or a fiend was in there. I believed it in the same way one of you might believe there are inhabitants in the planet Mars. I knew once a Scotch sailmaker who was certain, dead sure, there were people in Mars. If you asked him for some idea how they looked and behaved, he would get shy and mutter something about 'walking on all-fours.' If you as much as smiled, he would—though a man of sixty—offer to fight you. I would not have gone so far as to fight for Kurtz, but I went for him near enough to a lie. You know I hate, detest, and can't bear a lie, not because I am straighter than the rest of us, but simply because it appalls me. There is a taint of death, a flavor of mor-tality in lies,—which is exactly what I hate and detest in the world—what I want to forget. It makes me miserable and sick, like biting something rotten would do. Temperament, I suppose. Well, I went near enough to it by letting the young fool there believe anything he liked to imagine as to my influence in Europe. I became in an instant as much of a pretense as the rest of the be-witched pilgrims. This simply because I had a notion it somehow would be of help to that Kurtz whom at the time I did not see—you understand. He was just a word for me. I did not see the man in the name any more than you do. Do you see him? Do you see the story? Do you see anything? It seems to me I am trying to tell you a dream—making a vain attempt, because no relation of a dream can convey the dream-sensation, that commingling of absurdity, surprise, and bewilderment in a tremor of struggling revolt, that notion of be-ing captured by the incredible which is of the very essence of dreams. . . ."

He was silent for a while.

". . . No, it is impossible; it is impossible to convey the life-sensation of any given epoch of one's existence,—that which makes its truth, its meaning—its subtle and penetrating essence. It is impossible. We live, as we dream—alone. . . ."

He paused again as if reflecting, then added—

"Of course in this you fellows see more than I could then. You see me, whom you know. . . ."

It had become so pitch dark that we listeners could hardly see one an-other. For a long time already he, sitting apart, had been no more to us than a voice. There was not a word from anybody. The others might have been

65

asleep, but I was awake. I listened, I listened on the watch for the sentence, for the word, that would give me the clew to the faint uneasiness inspired by this narrative that seemed to shape itself without human lips in the heavy night-air of the river.

"... Yes—I let him run on," Marlow began again, "and think what he pleased about the powers that were behind me. I did! And there was nothing behind me! There was nothing but that wretched, old, mangled steamboat I was leaning against, while he talked fluently about 'the necessity for every man to get on.' 'And when one comes out here, you conceive, it is not to gaze at the moon.' Mr. Kurtz was a 'universal genius,' but even a genius would find it easier to work with 'adequate tools—intelligent men.' He did not make bricks—why, there was a physical impossibility in the way—as I was well aware; and if he did secretarial work for the manager, it was because 'no sensible man rejects wantonly the confidence of his superiors.' Did I see it? I saw it. What more did I want? What I really wanted was rivets, by heaven! Rivets. To get on with the work—to stop the hole. Rivets I wanted. There were cases of them down at the coast—cases—piled up—burst—split! You kicked a loose rivet at every second step in that station yard on the hillside. Rivets had rolled into the grove of death. You could fill your pockets with rivets for the trouble of stooping down—and there wasn't one rivet to be found where it was wanted. We had plates that would do, but nothing to fasten them with. And every week the messenger, a lone negro, letter-bag on shoulder and staff in hand, left our station for the coast. And several times a week a coast caravan came in with trade goods,—ghastly glazed calico that made you shudder only to look at it, glass beads value about a penny a quart, confounded spotted cotton handkerchiefs. And no rivets. Three carriers could have brought all that was wanted to set that steamboat afloat.

"He was becoming confidential now, but I fancy my unresponsive attitude must have exasperated him at last, for he judged it necessary to inform me he feared neither God nor devil, let alone any mere man. I said I could see that very well, but what I wanted was a certain quantity of rivets—and rivets were what really Mr. Kurtz wanted, if he had only known it. Now letters went to the coast every week. . . . 'My dear sir,' he cried, 'I write from dictation.' I demanded rivets. There was a way—for an intelligent man. He changed his manner; became very cold, and suddenly began to talk about a hippopotamus; wondered whether sleeping on board the steamer (I stuck to my salvage night and day) I wasn't disturbed. There was an old hippo that had the bad habit of getting out on the bank and roaming at night over the station grounds. The pilgrims use to turn out in a body and empty every rifle they could lay hands on at him. Some even had sat up o' nights for him. All this energy was wasted, though. 'That animal has a charmed life,' he said; 'but you can say this only of brutes in this country. No man—you apprehend me?—no man here bears a charmed life.' He stood there for a moment in the moonlight with his delicate hooked nose set a little askew, and his mica eyes glittering without a wink, then, with a curt Good night, he strode off. I could see he was disturbed and considerably puzzled, which made me feel more hopeful than I had been for days. It was a great comfort to turn from that chap to my influential friend, the battered, twisted, ruined, tin-pot steamboat. I clambered on board. She rang under my feet like an empty Huntley & Palmer biscuit-tin kicked along a gutter; she was nothing so solid in make, and rather less pretty in shape, but I had expended enough hard work on her to make me love her. No influential friend would have served me better. She had given me a chance to come out a bit—to find out what I could do. No, I don't like work. I had rather laze about and think of all the fine things that can be done. I don't like work—no man does—but I like what is in the work,—the chance to find yourself. Your own reality—for yourself, not for others—what no other man can ever know. They can only see the mere show, and never can tell what it really means.

"I was not surprised to see somebody sitting aft, on the deck, with his legs 70 dangling over the mud. You see I rather chummed with the few mechanics there were in that station, whom the other pilgrims naturally despised—on account of their imperfect manners, I suppose. This was the foreman—a boiler-maker by trade—a good worker. He was a lank, bony, yellow-faced man, with big intense eyes. His aspect was worried, and his head was as bald as the palm of my hand; but his hair in falling seemed to have stuck to his chin, and had prospered in the new locality, for his beard hung down to his waist. He was a widower with six young children (he had left them in charge of a sister of his to come out there), and the passion of his life was pigeon-flying. He was an enthusiast and a connoisseur. He would rave about pigeons. After work hours he used sometimes to come over from his hut for a talk about his children and his pigeons; at work, when he had to crawl in the mud under the bottom of the steamboat, he would tie up that beard of his in a kind of white serviette he brought for the purpose. It had loops to go over his ears. In the evening he could be seen squatted on the bank rinsing that wrapper in the creek with great care, then spreading it solemnly on a bush to dry.

"I slapped him on the back and shouted 'We shall have rivets!' He scrambled to his feet exclaiming 'No! Rivets!' as though he couldn't believe his ears. Then in a low voice, 'You . . . eh?' I don't know why we behaved like lunatics. I put my finger to the side of my nose and nodded mysteriously. 'Good for you!' he cried, snapped his fingers above his head, lifting one foot. I tried a jig. We capered on the iron deck. A frightful clatter came out of that hulk, and the virgin forest on the other bank of the creek sent it back in a thundering roll upon the sleeping station. It must have made some of the pilgrims sit up in their hovels. A dark figure obscured the lighted doorway of the manager's hut, vanished, then, a second or so after, the doorway itself vanished too. We stopped, and the silence driven away by the stamping of our feet flowed back again from the recesses of the land. The great wall of vegetation, an exuberant and entangled mass of trunks branches, leaves, boughs, festoons, motionless in the moonlight, was like a rioting invasion of soundless life, a rolling wave of plants piled up, crested, ready to topple over the creek, to sweep every little man of us out of his little existence. And it moved not. A deadened burst of mighty splashes and snorts reached us from afar, as though an ichthyosaurus had been taking a bath of glitter in that great river. 'After all,' said the boiler-maker in a reasonable tone, 'why shouldn't we get the rivets?' Why not, indeed! I did not know of any reason why we shouldn't. 'They'll come in three weeks,' I said, confidently.

"But they didn't. Instead of rivets there came an invasion, an infliction, a visitation. It came in sections during the next three weeks, each section headed by a donkey carrying a white man in new clothes and tan shoes, bowing from that elevation right and left to the impressed pilgrims. A quarrelsome band of footsore sulky niggers trod on the heels of the donkey; a lot of tents, camp-stools, tin boxes, white cases, brown bales would be shot down in the courtyard, and the air of mystery would deepen a little over the muddle of the station. Five such installments came, with their absurd air of disorderly flight with the loot of innumerable outfit shops and provision stores, that, one would think, they were lugging, after a raid, into the wilderness for equitable division. It was an inextricable mess of things decent in themselves but that human folly made look like the spoils of thieving.

"This devoted band called itself the Eldorado Exploring Expedition, and I believe they were sworn to secrecy. Their talk, however, was the talk of sordid buccaneers: it was reckless without hardihood, greedy without audacity, and cruel without courage; there was not an atom of foresight or of serious intention in the whole batch of them, and they did not seem aware these things are wanted for the work of the world. To tear treasure out of the bowels of the land was their desire, with no more moral purpose at the back of it than there is in burglars breaking into a safe. Who paid the expenses of the noble enterprise I don't know; but the uncle of our manager was leader of that lot.

"In exterior he resembled a butcher in a poor neighborhood, and his eyes had a look of sleepy cunning. He carried his fat paunch with ostentation on his short legs, and during the time his gang infested the station spoke to no one but his nephew. You could see these two roaming about all day long with their heads close together in an everlasting confab.

"I had given up worrying myself about the rivets. One's capacity for that 75 kind of folly is more limited than you would suppose. I said Hang!—and let things slide. I had plenty of time for meditation, and now and then I would give some thought to Kurtz. I wasn't very interested in him. No. Still, I was curious to see whether this man, who had come out equipped with moral ideas of some sort, would climb to the top after all, and how he would set about his work when there."

II

"One evening as I was lying flat on the deck of my steamboat, I heard voices approaching—and there were the nephew and the uncle strolling along the bank. I laid my head on my arm again, and had nearly lost myself in a doze, when somebody said in my ear, as it were: 'I am as harmless as a little child, but I don't like to be dictated to. Am I the manager—or am I not? I was ordered to send him there. It's incredible.' . . . I became aware that the two were standing on the shore alongside the forepart of the steamboat, just below my head. I did not move; it did not occur to me to move: I was sleepy. 'It *is* unpleasant,' grunted the uncle. 'He asked the Administration to be sent there,' said the other, 'with the idea of showing what he could do; and I was instructed accordingly. Look at the influence that man must have. Is it not frightful?' They both agreed it was frightful, then made several bizarre remarks: 'Make rain and fine weather—one man—the Council—by the nose'—bits of absurd sentences that got the better of my drowsiness, so that I had pretty near the whole of my wits about me when the uncle said, 'The climate may do away with this difficulty for you. Is he alone there?' 'Yes,' answered the manager; 'he sent his assistant down the river with a note to me in these terms: "Clear this poor devil out of the country, and don't bother sending more of that sort. I had rather be alone than have the kind of men you can dispose of with me." It was more than a year ago. Can you imagine such impudence!' 'Anything since then?' asked the other, hoarsely. 'Ivory,' jerked the nephew; "lots of it—prime sort—lots—most annoying, from him. 'And with that?' questioned the heavy rumble. 'Invoice,' was the reply fired out, so to speak. Then silence. They had been talking about Kurtz.

"I was broad awake by this time, but, lying perfectly at ease, remained still, having no inducement to change my position. 'How did that ivory come all this way?' growled the elder man, who seemed very vexed. The other explained that it had come with a fleet of canoes in charge of an English half-caste clerk Kurtz had with him; that Kurtz had apparently intended to return himself, the station being by that time bare of goods and stores, but after coming three hundred miles, had suddenly decided to go back, which he started to do alone in a small dug-out with four paddlers, leaving the half-caste to continue down the river with the ivory. The two fellows there seemed astounded at anybody attempting such a thing. They were at a loss for an adequate motive. As to me, I seemed to see Kurtz for the first time. It was a distinct glimpse: the dug-out, four paddling savages, and the lone white man turning his back suddenly on the headquarters, on relief, on thoughts of home—perhaps; setting his face towards the depths of the wilderness, towards his empty and desolate station. I did not know the motive. Perhaps he was just simply a fine fellow who stuck to his work for its own sake. His name, you understand, had not been pronounced once. He was 'that man.' The half-caste, who, as far as I could see, had conducted a difficult trip with great prudence and pluck, was invariably alluded to as 'that scoundrel.' The 'scoundrel' had reported that the 'man' had been very ill—had recovered imperfectly. . . . The two below me moved away then a few paces, and strolled back and forth at some little distance. I heard: 'Military post—doctor—two hundred miles—quite alone now—unavoidable delays—nine months—no news—strange rumors.' They approached again, just as the manager was saying, 'No one, as far as I know, unless a species of wandering trader—a pestilential fellow, snapping ivory from the natives.' Who was it they were talking about now? I gathered in snatches that this was some man supposed to be in Kurtz's district, and of whom the manager did not approve. 'We will not be free from unfair competition till one of these fellows is hanged for an example,' he said. 'Certainly,' grunted the other; 'get him hanged! Why not? Anything—anything can be done in this country. That's what I say; nobody here, you understand, *here*, can endanger your position. And why? You stand the climate—you outlast them all. The danger is in Europe; but there before I left I took care to—' They moved off and whispered, then their voices rose again. 'The extraordinary series of delays is not my fault. I did my possible." The fat man sighed, 'Very sad.' 'And the pestiferous absurdity of his talk,' continued the other; 'he bothered me enough when he was here. "Each station should be like a beacon on the road towards better things, a center for trade of course, but also for humanizing, improving, instructing." Conceive you—that ass! And he wants to be manager! No, it's—' Here he got choked by excessive indignation, and I lifted my head the least bit. I was surprised to see how near they were—right under me. I could have spat upon their hats. They were looking on the ground, absorbed in thought. The manager was switching his leg with a slender twig: his sagacious relative lifted his head. 'You have been well since you came out this time?' he asked. The other gave a start. 'Who? I? Oh! Like a charm—like a charm. But the rest—oh, my goodness! All sick. They die so quick, too, that I haven't the time to send them out of the country—it's incredible!' 'H'm. Just so,' grunted the uncle. 'Ah! my boy, trust to this—I say, trust to this.' I saw him extend his short flipper of an arm for a gesture that took in the forest, the creek, the mud, the river,—seemed to beckon with a dishonoring flourish before the sunlit face of the land a treacherous appeal to the lurking death, to the hidden evil, to the profound darkness of its heart. It was so startling that I leaped to my feet and looked back at the edge of the forest, as though I had expected an answer of some sort to that black display of confidence. You know the foolish notions that come to one sometimes. The high stillness confronted these two figures with its ominous patience, waiting for the passing away of a fantastic invasion.

"They swore aloud together—out of sheer fright, I believe—then pretending not to know anything of my existence, turned back to the station. The sun was low; and leaning forward side by side, they seemed to be tugging painfully uphill their two ridiculous shadows of unequal length, that trailed behind them slowly over the tall grass without bending a single blade.

"In a few days the Eldorado Expedition went into the patient wilderness, that closed upon it as the sea closes over a diver. Long afterwards the news came that all the donkeys were dead. I know nothing as to the fate of the less valuable animals. They, no doubt, like the rest of us, found what they deserved. I did not inquire. I was then rather excited at the prospect of meeting Kurtz very soon. When I say very soon I mean it comparatively. It was just two months from the day we left the creek when we came to the bank below Kurtz's station.

"Going up that river was like traveling back to the earliest beginnings of the world, when vegetation rioted on the earth and the big trees were kings. An empty stream, a great silence, and impenetrable forest. The air was warm, thick, heavy, sluggish. There was no joy in the brilliance of sunshine. The long stretches of the waterway ran on, deserted, into the gloom of over-shadowed distances. On silvery sandbanks hippos and alligators sunned themselves side by side. The broadening waters flowed through a mob of wooded islands; you lost your way on that river as you would in a desert, and butted all day long against shoals, trying to find the channel, till you thought yourself bewitched and cut off for ever from everything you had known once—somewhere—far away—in another existence perhaps. There were moments when one's past came back to one, as it will sometimes when you have not a moment to spare to yourself; but it came in the shape of an unrestful and noisy dream, remembered with wonder amongst the overwhelming realities of this strange world of plants, and water, and silence. And this stillness of life did not in the least resemble a peace. It was the stillness of an implacable force brooding over an inscrutable intention. It looked at you with a vengeful aspect. I got used to it afterwards; I did not see it any more; I had no time. I had to keep guessing at the channel; I had to discern, mostly by inspiration, the signs of hidden banks; I watched for sunken stones; I was learning to clap my teeth smartly before my heart flew out, when I shaved by a fluke some infernal sly old snag that would have ripped the life out of the tin-pot steamboat and drowned all the pilgrims; I had to keep a look-out for the signs of dead wood we could cut up in the night for next day's steaming. When you have to attend to things of that sort, to the mere incidents of the surface, the reality—the reality, I tell you—fades. The inner truth is hidden—luckily, luckily. But I felt it all the same; I felt often its mysterious stillness watching me at my monkey tricks, just as it watches you fellows performing on your respective tight-ropes for—what is it? half-a-crown a tumble—"

"Try to be civil, Marlow," growled a voice, and I knew there was at least one listener awake besides myself.

"I beg your pardon. I forgot the heartache which makes up the rest of the price. And indeed what does the price matter, if the trick be well done? You do your tricks very well. And I didn't do badly either, since I managed not to sink that steamboat on my first trip. It's a wonder to me yet. Imagine a blindfolded man set to drive a van over a bad road. I sweated and shivered over that business considerably, I can tell you. After all, for a seaman, to scrape the bottom of the thing that's supposed to float all the time under his care is the unpardonable sin. No one may know of it, but you never forget the thump—eh? A blow on the very heart. You remember it, you dream of it, you wake up at night and think of it—years after—and go hot and cold all over. I don't pretend to say that steamboat floated all the time. More than once she had to wade for a bit, with twenty cannibals splashing around and pushing. We had enlisted some of these chaps on the way for a crew. Fine fellows—cannibals—in their place. They were men one could work with, and I am grateful to them. And, after all, they did not eat each other before my face: they had brought along a provision of hippo-meat which went rotten, and made the mystery of the wilderness stink in my nostrils. Phoo! I can sniff it now. I had the manager on board and three or four pilgrims with their staves—all complete. Sometimes we came upon a station close by the bank, clinging to the skirts of the unknown, and the white men rushing out of a tumble-down hovel, with great gestures of joy and surprise and welcome, seemed very strange,—had the appearance of being held there captive by a spell. The word ivory would ring in the air for a while—and on we went again into the silence, along empty reaches, round the still bends, between the high walls of our winding way, reverberating in hollow claps the ponderous beat of the stern-wheel. Trees, trees, millions of trees, massive, immense, running up high; and at their foot, hugging the bank against the stream, crept the little begrimed steamboat, like a sluggish beetle crawling on the floor of a lofty portico. It made you feel very small, very lost, and yet it was not altogether depressing that feeling. After all, if you were small, the grimy beetle crawled on—which was just what you wanted it to do. Where the pilgrims imagined it crawled to I don't know. To some place where they expected to get something, I bet! For me it crawled toward Kurtz—exclusively; but when the steam-pipes started leaking we crawled very slow. The reaches opened before us and closed behind, as if the forest had stepped leisurely across the water to bar the way for our return. We penetrated deeper and deeper into the heart of darkness. It was very quiet there. At night sometimes the roll of drums behind the curtain of trees would run up the river and remain sustained faintly, as if hovering in the air high over our heads, till the first break of day. Whether it meant war, peace, or prayer we could not tell. The dawns were heralded by the descent of a chill stillness; the woodcutters slept, their fires burned low; the snapping of a twig would make you start. We were wanderers in a prehistoric earth, on an earth that wore the aspect of an unknown planet. We could have fancied ourselves the first of men taking possession of an accursed inheritance, to be subdued at the cost of profound anguish and of excessive toil. But suddenly, as we struggled round a bend, there would be a glimpse of rush walls, of peaked grass-roofs, a burst of yells, a whirl of black limbs, a mass of hands clapping, of feet stamping, of bodies swaying, of eyes rolling, under the droop of heavy and motionless foliage. The steamer toiled along slowly on the edge of a black and incomprehensible frenzy. The prehistoric man was cursing us, praying to us, welcoming us—who could tell? We were cut off from the comprehension of our surroundings; we glided past like phantoms, wondering and secretly appalled, as sane men would be before an enthusiastic outbreak in a madhouse. We could not understand, because we were too far and could not remember, because we were traveling in the night of first ages, of those ages that are gone, leaving hardly a sign—and no memories.

"The earth seemed unearthly. We are accustomed to look upon the shackled form of a conquered monster, but there—there you could look at a thing monstrous and free. It was unearthly, and the men were—No, they were not inhuman. Well, you know, that was the worst of it—this suspicion of their not being inhuman. It would come slowly to one. They howled, and leaped, and spun, and made horrid faces; but what thrilled you was just the thought of their humanity—like yours—the thought of your remote kinship with this wild and passionate uproar. Ugly. Yes, it was ugly enough; but if you were man enough you would admit to yourself that there was in you just the faintest trace of a response to the terrible frankness of that noise, a dim suspicion of there being a meaning in which you—you so remote from the night of first ages—could comprehend. And why not? The mind of a man is capable of anything—because everything is in it, all the past as well as all the future. What was there after all? Joy, fear, sorrow, devotion, valor, rage—who can tell?—but truth—truth stripped of its cloak of time. Let the fool gape and shudder—the man knows, and can look on without a wink. But he must at least be as much of a man as these on the shore. He must meet that truth with his own true stuff—with his own inborn strength. Principles? Principles won't do. Acquisitions, clothes, pretty rags—rags that would fly off at the first good shake. No; you want a deliberate belief. An appeal to me in this fiendish row—is there? Very well; I hear; I admit, but I have a voice, too, and for good or evil mine is the speech that cannot be silenced. Of course, a fool, what with sheer fright and fine sentiments, is always safe. Who's that grunting? You wonder I didn't go ashore for a howl and a dance? Well, no—I didn't. Fine sentiments, you say? Fine sentiments, be hanged! I had no time. I had to mess about with white-lead and strips of woolen blanket helping to put bandages on those leaky steam-pipes—I tell you. I had to watch the steering, and circumvent those snags, and get the tin-pot along by hook or by crook. There was surface-truth enough in these things to save a wiser man. And between whiles I had to look after the savage who was fireman. He was an improved speci-men; he could fire up a vertical boiler. He was there below me, and, upon my word, to look at him was as edifying as seeing a dog in a parody of breeches and a feather hat, walking on his hindlegs. A few months of training had done for that really fine chap. He squinted at the steam-gauge and at the water-gauge with an evident effort of intrepidity—and he had filed teeth too, the poor devil, and the wool of his pate shaved into queer patterns, and three or-namental scars on each of his cheeks. He ought to have been clapping his hands and stamping his feet on the bank, instead of which he was hard at work, a thrall to strange witchcraft, full of improving knowledge. He was use-ful because he had been instructed; and what he knew was this—that should the water in that transparent thing disappear, the evil spirit inside the boiler would get angry through the greatness of his thirst, and take a terrible vengeance. So he sweated and fired up and watched the glass fearfully (with an impromptu charm, made of rags, tied to his arm, and a piece of polished bone, as big as a watch, stuck flatways through his lower lip), while the wooded banks slipped past us slowly, the short noise was left behind the interminable miles of silence—and we crept on, towards Kurtz. But the snags were thick, the water was treacherous and shallow, the boiler seemed indeed to have a sulky devil in it, and thus neither that fireman nor I had any time to peer into our creepy thoughts.

"Some fifty miles below the Inner Station we came upon a hut of reeds, an inclined and melancholy pole, with the unrecognizable tatters of what had been a flag of some sort flying from it, and a neatly stacked wood-pile. This was unexpected. We came to the bank, and on the stack of firewood found a flat piece of board with some faded pencil-writing on it. When deciphered it said: 'Wood for you. Hurry up. Approach cautiously.' There was a signature, but it was illegible—not Kurtz—a much longer word. Hurry up. Where? Up the river? 'Approach cautiously.' We had not done so. But the warning could not have been meant for the place where it could be only found after ap-proach. Something was wrong above. But what—and how much? That was the question. We commented adversely upon the imbecility of that tele-graphic style. The bush around said nothing, and would not let us look very far, either. A torn curtain of red twill hung in the doorway of the hut, and flapped sadly in our faces. The dwelling was dismantled; but we could see a white man had lived there not very long ago. There remained a rude table—

a plank on two posts; a heap of rubbish reposed in a dark corner, and by the door I picked up a book. It had lost its covers, and the pages had been thumbed into a state of extremely dirty softness; but the back had been lovingly stitched afresh with white cotton thread, which looked clean yet. It was an extraordinary find. Its title was, 'An Inquiry into some Points of Seamanship,' by a man Tower, Towson—some such name—Master in his Majesty's Navy. The matter looked dreary reading enough, with illustrative diagrams and repulsive tables of figures, and the copy was sixty years old. I handled this amazing antiquity with the greatest possible tenderness, lest it should dissolve in my hands. Within, Towson or Towser was inquiring earnestly into the breaking strain of ships' chains and tackle, and other such matters. Not a very enthralling book; but at the first glance you could see there a singleness of intention, an honest concern for the right way of going to work, which made these humble pages, thought out so many years ago, luminous with another than a professional light. The simple old sailor, with his talk of chains and purchases, made me forget the jungle and the pilgrims in a delicious sensation of having come upon something unmistakably real. Such a book being there was wonderful enough; but still more astounding were the notes penciled in the margin, and plainly referring to the text. I couldn't believe my eyes! They were in cipher! Yes, it looked like cipher. Fancy a man lugging with him a book of that description into this nowhere and studying it—and making notes—in cipher at that! It was an extravagant mystery.

"I had been dimly aware for some time of a worrying noise, and when I   85
lifted my eyes I saw the wood-pile was gone, and the manager, aided by all the pilgrims, was shouting at me from the river-side. I slipped the book into my pocket. I assure you to leave off reading was like tearing myself away from the shelter of an old and solid friendship.

"I started the lame engine ahead. 'It must be this miserable trader—this intruder,' exclaimed the manager, looking back malevolently at the place we had left. 'He must be English,' I said. 'It will not save him from getting into trouble if he is not careful,' muttered the manager darkly. I observed with assumed innocence that no man was safe from trouble in this world.

"The current was more rapid now, the steamer seemed at her last gasp, the stern-wheel flopped languidly, and I caught myself listening on tiptoe for the next beat of the float, for in sober truth I expected the wretched thing to give up every moment. It was like watching the last flickers of life. But still we crawled. Sometimes I would pick out a tree a little way ahead to measure our progress towards Kurtz by, but I lost it invariably before we got abreast. To keep the eyes so long on one thing was too much for human patience. The manager displayed a beautiful resignation. I fretted and fumed and took to arguing with myself whether or no I would talk openly with Kurtz; but before I could come to any conclusion it occurred to me that my speech or my silence, indeed any action of mine, would be a mere futility. What did it matter what anyone knew or ignored? What did it matter who was manager? One gets sometimes such a flash of insight. The essentials of this affair lay deep under the surface, beyond my reach, and beyond my power of meddling.

"Towards the evening of the second day we judged ourselves about eight miles from Kurtz's station. I wanted to push on; but the manager looked grave, and told me the navigation up there was so dangerous that it would be advisable, the sun being very low already, to wait where we were till next morning. Moreover, he pointed out that if the warning to approach cautiously were to be followed, we must approach in daylight—not at dusk, or in the dark. This was sensible enough. Eight miles meant nearly three hours' steaming for us, and I could also see suspicious ripples at the upper end of the reach. Nevertheless, I was annoyed beyond expression at the delay, and most unreasonably too, since one night more could not matter much after so many months. As we had plenty of wood, and caution was the word, I brought up in the middle of the stream. The reach was narrow, straight, with high sides like a railway cutting. The dusk came gliding into it long before the sun had set. The current ran smooth and swift, but a dumb immobility sat on the banks. The living trees, lashed together by the creepers and every living bush of the undergrowth, might have been changed into stone, even to the slenderest twig, to the lightest leaf. It was not sleep—it seemed unnatural, like a state of trance. Not the faintest sound of any kind could be heard. You looked on amazed, and began to suspect yourself of being deaf—then the night came suddenly, and struck you blind as well. About three in the morning some large fish leaped, and the loud splash made me jump as though a gun had been fired. When the sun rose there was a white fog, very warm and clammy, and more blinding than the night. It did not shift or drive; it was just there, standing all round you like something solid. At eight or nine, perhaps, it lifted as a shutter lifts. We had a glimpse of the towering multitude of trees, of the immense matted jungle, with the blazing little ball of the sun hanging over it—all perfectly still—and then the white shutter came down again, smoothly, as if sliding in greased grooves. I ordered the chain, which we had begun to heave in, to be paid out again. Before it stopped running with a muffled rattle, a cry, a very loud cry, as of infinite desolation, soared slowly in the opaque air. It ceased. A complaining clamor, modulated in savage discords, filled our ears. The sheer unexpectedness of it made my hair stir under my cap. I don't know how it struck the others: to me it seemed as though the mist itself had screamed, so suddenly, and apparently from all sides at once, did this tumultuous and mournful uproar arise. It culminated in a hurried outbreak of almost intolerably excessive shrieking, which stopped short, leaving us stiffened in a variety of silly attitudes, and obstinately listening to the nearly as appalling and excessive silence. 'Good God! What is the meaning—?' stammered at my elbow one of the pilgrims,—a little fat man, with sandy hair and red whiskers, who wore side-spring boots, and pink pyjamas tucked into his socks. Two others remained open-mouthed a whole minute, then dashed into the little cabin, to rush out incontinently and stand darting scared glances, with Winchesters at 'ready' in their hands. What we could see was just the steamer we were on, her outlines blurred as though she had been on the point of dissolving, and a misty strip of water, perhaps two feet broad, around her—and that was all. The rest of the world was nowhere, as far as our eyes and ears were concerned. Just nowhere. Gone, disappeared; swept off without leaving a whisper or a shadow behind.

"I went forward, and ordering the chain to be hauled in short, so as to be ready to trip the anchor and move the steamboat at once if necessary. 'Will they attack?' whispered an awed voice. 'We will be butchered in this fog,' murmured another. The faces twitched with the strain, the hands trembled slightly, the eyes forgot to wink. It was very curious to see the contrast of expressions of the white men and of the black fellows of our crew, who were as much strangers to that part of the river as we, though their homes were only eight hundred miles away. The whites, of course greatly discomposed, had besides a curious look of being painfully shocked by such an outrageous row. The others had an alert, naturally interested expression; but their faces were essentially quiet, even those of the one or two who grinned as they hauled at the chain. Several exchanged short, grunting phrases, which seemed to settle the matter to their satisfaction. Their headman, a young, broad-chested black, severely draped in dark-blue fringed cloths, with fierce nostrils and his hair all done up artfully in oily ringlets, stood near me. 'Aha!' I said, just for good fellowship's sake. 'Catch 'im,' he snapped, with a bloodshot widening of his eyes and a flash of sharp teeth—'catch 'im. Give 'im to us.' 'To you, eh?' I asked; 'what would you do with them?' 'Eat 'im!' he said curtly, and, leaning his elbow on the rail, looked out into the fog in a dignified and profoundly pensive attitude. I would no doubt have been properly horrified, had it not occurred to me that he and his chaps must be very hungry: that they must have been growing increasingly hungry for at least this month past. They had been engaged for six months (I don't think a single one of them had any clear idea of time, as we at the end of countless ages have. They still belonged to the beginnings of time—had no inherited experience to teach them as it were), and of course, as long as there was a piece of paper written over in accordance with some farcical law or other made down the river, it didn't enter anybody's head to trouble how they would live. Certainly they had brought with them some rotten hippo-meat, which couldn't have lasted very long, anyway, even if the pilgrims hadn't, in the midst of a shocking hullabaloo, thrown a considerable quantity of it overboard. It looked like a high-handed proceeding; but it was really a case of legitimate self-defense. You can't breathe dead hippo waking, sleeping, and eating, and at the same time keep your precarious grip on existence. Besides that, they had given them every week three pieces of brass wire, each about nine inches long; and the theory was they were to buy their provisions with that currency in river-side villages. You can see how *that* worked. There were either no villages, or the people were hostile, or the director, who like the rest of us fed out of tins, with an occasional old he-goat thrown in, didn't want to stop the steamer for some more or less recondite reason. So, unless they swallowed the wire itself, or made loops of it to snare the fishes with, I don't see what good their extravagant salary could be to them. I must say it was paid with a regularity worthy of a large and honorable trading company. For the rest, the only thing to eat—though it didn't look eatable in the least—I saw in their possession was a few lumps of some stuff like half-cooked dough, of a dirty lavender color,[14] they kept wrapped in leaves, and now and

---

14. An accurate description of cassava dough, which is nutritious and keeps a long time.

then swallowed a piece of, but so small that it seemed done for more for the looks of the thing than for any serious purpose of sustenance. Why in the name of all the gnawing devils of hunger they didn't go for us—they were thirty to five—and have a good tuck in for once, amazes me now when I think of it. They were big powerful men, with not much capacity to weigh the consequences, with courage, with strength, even yet, though their skins were no longer glossy and their muscles no longer hard. And I saw that something restraining, one of those human secrets that baffle probability, had come into play there. I looked at them with a swift quickening of interest—not because it occurred to me I might be eaten by them before very long, though I own to you that just then I perceived—in a new light, as it were—how unwholesome the pilgrims looked, and I hoped, yes, I positively hoped, that my aspect was not so—what shall I say?—so—unappetizing: a touch of fantastic vanity which fitted well with the dream-sensation that pervaded all my days at that time. Perhaps I had a little fever too. One can't live with one's finger everlastingly on one's pulse. I had often 'a little fever,' or a little touch of other things—the playful paw-strokes of the wilderness, the preliminary trifling before the more serious onslaught which came in due course. Yes; I looked at them as you would on any human being, with a curiosity of their impulses, motives, capacities, weaknesses, when brought to the test of an inexorable physical necessity. Restraint! What possible restraint? Was it superstition, disgust, patience, fear—or some kind of primitive honor? No fear can stand up to hunger, no patience can wear it out, disgust simply does not exist where hunger is; and as to superstition, beliefs, and what you may call principles, they are less than chaff in a breeze. Don't you know the devilry of lingering starvation, its exasperating torment, its black thoughts, its somber and brooding ferocity? Well, I do. It takes a man all his inborn strength to fight hunger properly. It's really easier to face bereavement, dishonor, and the perdition of one's soul—than this kind of prolonged hunger. Sad, but true. And these chaps too had no earthly reason for any kind of scruple. Restraint! I would just as soon have expected restraint from a hyena prowling amongst the corpses of a battlefield. But there was the fact facing me—the fact dazzling, to be seen, like the foam on the depths of the sea, like a ripple on a unfathomable enigma, a mystery greater—when I thought of it—than the curious, inexplicable note of desperate grief in this savage clamor that had swept by us on the river-bank, behind the blind whiteness of the fog.

"Two pilgrims were quarreling in hurried whispers as to which bank. 90 'Left.' 'No, no; how can you? Right, right, of course.' 'It is very serious,' said the manager's voice behind me; 'I would be desolated if anything should happen to Mr. Kurtz before we came up.' I looked at him, and had not the slightest doubt he was sincere. He was just the kind of man who would wish to preserve appearances. That was his restraint. But when he muttered something about going on at once, I did not even take the trouble to answer him. I knew, and he knew, that it was impossible. Were we to let go our hold of the bottom, we would be absolutely in the air—in space. We wouldn't be able to tell where we were going to—whether up or down stream, or across—till we fetched against one bank or the other,—and then we wouldn't know at first which it was. Of course I made no move. I had no mind for a smash-up. You couldn't imagine a more deadly place for a shipwreck. Whether drowned at once or not, we were sure to perish speedily in one way or another. 'I authorize you to take all the risks,' he said, after a short silence. 'I refuse to take any,' I said shortly; which was just the answer he expected, though its tone might have surprised him. 'Well, I must defer to your judgment. You are captain,' he said, with marked civility. I turned my shoulder to him in sign of my appreciation, and looked into the fog. How long would it last? It was the most hopeless look-out. The approach to this Kurtz grubbing for ivory in the wretched bush was beset by as many dangers as though he had been an enchanted princess sleeping in a fabulous castle. 'Will they attack, do you think?' asked the manager, in a confidential tone.

"I did not think they would attack, for several obvious reasons. The thick fog was one. If they left the bank in their canoes they would get lost in it, as we would be if we attempted to move. Still, I had also judged the jungle of both banks quite impenetrable—and yet eyes were in it, eyes that had seen us. The river-side bushes were certainly thick; but the undergrowth behind was evidently penetrable. However, during the short lift I had seen no canoes anywhere in the reach—certainly not abreast of the steamer. But what made the idea of attack inconceivable to me was the nature of the noise—of the cries we had heard. They had not the fierce character boding of immediate hostile intention. Unexpected, wild, and violent as they had been, they had given me an irresistible impression of sorrow. The glimpse of the steamboat had for some reason filled those savages with unrestrained grief. The danger, if any, I expounded, was from our proximity to a great human passion let loose. Even extreme grief may ultimately vent itself in violence—but more generally takes the form of apathy. . . .

"You should have seen the pilgrims stare! They had no heart to grin, or even to revile me; but I believe they thought me gone mad—with fright, maybe. I delivered a regular lecture. My dear boys, it was no good bothering. Keep a look-out? Well, you may guess I watched the fog for the signs of lifting as a cat watches a mouse; but for anything else our eyes were of no more use to us than if we had been buried miles deep in a heap of cotton-wool. It felt like it too—choking, warm, stifling. Besides, all I said, though it sounded extravagant, was absolutely true to fact. What we afterwards alluded to as an attack was really an attempt at repulse. The action was very far from being aggressive—it was not even defensive, in the usual sense: it was undertaken under the stress of desperation, and in its essence was purely protective.

"It developed itself, I should say, two hours after the fog lifted, and its commencement was at a spot, roughly speaking, about a mile and a half below Kurtz's station. We had just floundered and flopped round a bend, when I saw an islet, a mere grassy hummock of bright green, in the middle of the stream. It was the only thing of the kind; but as we opened the reach more, I perceived it was the head of a long sandbank, or rather a chain of shallow patches stretching down the middle of the river. They were discolored, just awash, and the whole lot was seen just under the water, exactly as a man's backbone is seen running down the middle of his back under the skin. Now, as far as I did see, I could go to the right or to the left of this. I didn't know either channel, of course. The banks looked pretty well alike, the depth appeared the same; but as I had been informed the station was on the west side, I naturally headed for the western passage.

"No sooner had we fairly entered it than I became aware it was much narrower than I had supposed. To the left of us there was the long uninterrupted shoal, and to the right a high, steep bank heavily overgrown with bushes. Above the bush the trees stood in serried ranks. The twigs overhung the current thickly, and from distance to distance a large limb of some tree projected rigidly over the stream. It was then well on in the afternoon, the face of the forest was gloomy, and a broad strip of shadow had already fallen on the water. In this shadow we steamed up—very slowly, as you may imagine. I sheered her well inshore—the water being deepest near the bank, as the sounding-pole informed me.

"One of my hungry and forbearing friends was sounding in the bows just 95 below me. This steamboat was exactly like a decked scow. On the deck there were two little teak-wood houses, with doors and windows. The boiler was in the fore-end, and the machinery right astern. Over the whole there was a light roof, supported on stanchions. The funnel projected through that roof, and in front of the funnel a small cabin built of light planks served for a pilot-house. It contained a couch, two campstools, a loaded Martini-Henry leaning in one corner, a tiny table, and the steering-wheel. It had a wide door in front and a broad shutter at each side. All these were always thrown open, of course. I spent my days perched up there on the extreme fore-end of that roof, before the door. At night I slept, or tried to, on the couch. An athletic black belonging to some coast tribe, and educated by my poor predecessor, was the helmsman. He sported a pair of brass earrings, wore a blue cloth wrapper from the waist to the ankles, and thought all the world of himself. He was the most unstable kind of fool I had ever seen. He steered with no end of a swagger while you were by; but if he lost sight of you, he became instantly the prey of an abject funk, and would let that cripple of a steamboat get the upper hand of him in a minute.

"I was looking down at the sounding-pole, and feeling much annoyed to see at each try a little more of it stick out of that river, when I saw my poleman give up the business suddenly, and stretch himself flat on the deck, without even taking the trouble to haul his pole in. He kept hold on it though, and it trailed in the water. At the same time the fireman, whom I could also see below me, sat down abruptly before his furnace and ducked his head. I was amazed. Then I had to look at the river mighty quick, because there was a snag in the fairway. Sticks, little sticks, were flying about—thick: they were whizzing before my nose, dropping below me, striking behind me against my pilot-house. All this time the river, the shore, the woods, were very quiet—perfectly quiet. I could only hear the heavy splashing thump of the stern-wheel and the patter of these things. We cleared the snag clumsily. Arrows, by Jove! We were being shot at! I stepped in quickly to close the shutter on the land side. That fool-helmsman, his hands on the spokes, was lifting his knees high, stamping his feet, champing his mouth, like a reined-in horse. Confound

him! And we were staggering within ten feet of the bank. I had to lean right
out to swing the heavy shutter, and I saw a face amongst the leaves on the level
with my own, looking at me very fierce and steady; and then suddenly, as
though a veil had been removed from my eyes, I made out, deep in the tangled gloom, naked breasts, arms, legs, glaring eyes,—the bush was swarming
with human limbs in movement, glistening, of bronze color. The twigs shook,
swayed, and rustled, the arrows flew out of them, and then the shutter came
to. 'Steer her straight,' I said to the helmsman. He held his head rigid, face
forward; but his eyes rolled, he kept lifting and setting down his feet gently,
his mouth foamed a little. 'Keep quiet!' I said in a fury. I might just as well
have ordered a tree not to sway in the wind. I darted out. Below me there was
a great scuffle of feet on the iron deck; confused exclamations; a voice
screamed, 'Can you turn back?' I caught sight of a V-shaped ripple on the water ahead. What? Another snag! A fusillade burst out under my feet. The pilgrims had opened their little Winchesters, and were simply squirting lead into
that bush. A deuce of a lot of smoke came up and drove slowly forward. I
swore at it. Now I couldn't see the ripple or the snag either. I stood in the
doorway, peering, and the arrows came in swarms. They might have been poisoned, but they looked as though they wouldn't kill a cat. The bush began to
howl. Our wood-cutters raised a warlike whoop; the report of a rifle just at my
back deafened me. I glanced over my shoulder, and the pilot-house was yet
full of noise and smoke when I made a dash at the wheel. The fool-nigger had
dropped everything, to throw the shutter open and let off that Martini-Henry.
He stood before the wide opening, glaring, and I yelled at him to come back,
while I straightened the sudden twist out of that steamboat. There was no
room to turn even if I had wanted to, the snag was somewhere very near ahead
in that confounded smoke, there was no time to lose, so I just crowded her
into the bank—right into the bank, where I knew the water was deep.

"We tore slowly along the overhanging bushes in a whirl of broken twigs
and flying leaves. The fusillade below stopped short, as I had foreseen it
would when the squirts got empty. I threw my head back to a glinting whizz
that traversed the pilot-house, in at one shutter-hole and out at the other.
Looking past that mad helmsman, who was shaking the empty rifle and
yelling at the shore, I saw vague forms of men running bent double, leaping,
gliding, distinct, incomplete, evanescent. Something big appeared in the air
before the shutter, the rifle went overboard, and the man stepped back swiftly,
looked at me over his shoulder in an extraordinary, profound, familiar manner, and fell upon my feet. The side of his head hit the wheel twice, and the
end of what appeared a long cane clattered round and knocked over a little
camp-stool. It looked as though after wrenching that thing from somebody
ashore he had lost his balance in the effort. The thin smoke had blown away,
we were clear of the snag, and looking ahead I could see that in another hundred yards or so I would be free to sheer off, away from the bank; but my feet
felt so very warm and wet that I had to look down. The man had rolled on his
back and stared straight up at me; both his hands clutched that cane. It was the
shaft of a spear that, either thrown or lunged through the opening, had caught

him in the side just below the ribs; the blade had gone in out of sight, after making a frightful gash; my shoes were full; a pool of blood lay very still, gleaming dark-red under the wheel; his eyes shone with an amazing luster. The fusillade burst out again. He looked at me anxiously, gripping the spear like something precious, with an air of being afraid I would try to take it away from him. I had to make an effort to free my eyes from his gaze and attend to the steering. With one hand I felt above my head for the line of the steam-whistle, and jerked out screech after screech hurriedly. The tumult of angry and warlike yells was checked instantly, and then from the depths of the woods went out such a tremulous and prolonged wail of mournful fear and utter despair as may be imagined to follow the flight of the last hope from the earth. There was a great commotion in the bush; the shower of arrows stopped, a few dropping shots rang out sharply—then silence, in which the languid beat of the stern-wheel came plainly to my ears. I put the helm hard a-starboard at the moment when the pilgrim in pink pyjamas, very hot and agitated, appeared in the doorway. 'The manager sends me—' he began in an official tone, and stopped short. 'Good God!' he said, glaring at the wounded man.

"We two whites stood over him, and his lustrous and inquiring glance enveloped us both. I declare it looked as though he would presently put to us some question in an understandable language; but he died without uttering a sound, without moving a limb, without twitching a muscle. Only in the very last moment, as though in response to some sign we could not see, to some whisper we could not hear, he frowned heavily, and that frown gave to his black death-mask an inconceivably somber, brooding, and menacing expression. The luster of inquiring glance faded swiftly into vacant glassiness. 'Can you steer?' I asked the agent eagerly. He looked very dubious; but I made a grab at his arm, and he understood at once I meant him to steer whether or no. To tell you the truth, I was morbidly anxious to change my shoes and socks. 'He is dead,' murmured the fellow, immensely impressed. 'No doubt about it,' said I, tugging like mad at the shoe-laces. 'And, by the way, I suppose Mr. Kurtz is dead as well by this time.'

"For the moment that was the dominant thought. There was a sense of extreme disappointment, as though I had found out I had been striving after something altogether without a substance. I couldn't have been more disgusted if I had traveled all this way for the sole purpose of talking with Mr. Kurtz. Talking with . . . I flung one shoe overboard, and became aware that was exactly what I had been looking forward to—a talk with Kurtz. I made the strange discovery that I had never imagined him as doing, you know, but as discoursing. I didn't say to myself, 'Now I will never see him,' or 'Now I will never shake him by the hand,' but, 'Now I will never hear him.' The man presented himself as a voice. Not of course that I did not connect him with some sort of action. Hadn't I been told in all the tones of jealousy and admiration that he had collected, bartered, swindled, or stolen more ivory than all the other agents together? That was not the point. The point was in his being a gifted creature, and that of all his gifts the one that stood out preeminently, that carried with it a sense of real presence, was his ability to talk, his words—

the gift of expression, the bewildering, the illuminating, the most exalted and the most contemptible, the pulsating stream of light, or the deceitful flow from the heart of an impenetrable darkness.

"The other shoe went flying unto the devil-god of that river. I thought,   100 By Jove! it's all over. We are too late; he has vanished—the gift has vanished, by means of some spear, arrow, or club. I will never hear that chap speak after all,—and my sorrow had a startling extravagance of emotion, even such as I had noticed in the howling sorrow of these savages in the bush. I couldn't have felt more of lonely desolation somehow, had I been robbed of a belief or had missed my destiny in life. . . . Why do you sigh in this beastly way, some-body? Absurd? Well, absurd. Good Lord! mustn't a man ever—Here, give me some tobacco."

There was a pause of profound stillness, then a match flared, and Mar-low's lean face appeared, worn, hollow, with downward folds and dropped eyelids, with an aspect of concentrated attention; and as he took vigorous draws at his pipe, it seemed to retreat and advance out of the night in the reg-ular flicker of the tiny flame. The match went out.

"Absurd!" he cried. "This is the worst of trying to tell. . . . Here you all are, each moored with two good addresses, like a hulk with two anchors, a butcher round one corner, a policeman round another, excellent appetites, and temperature normal—you hear—normal from year's end to year's end. And you say, Absurd! Absurd be—exploded! Absurd! My dear boys, what can you expect from a man who out of sheer nervousness had just flung overboard a pair of new shoes. Now I think of it, it is amazing I did not shed tears. I am, upon the whole, proud of my fortitude. I was cut to the quick at the idea of having lost the inestimable privilege of listening to the gifted Kurtz. Of course I was wrong. The privilege was waiting for me. Oh yes, I heard more than enough. And I was right, too. A voice. He was very little more than a voice. And I heard—him—it—this voice—other voices—all of them were so little more than voices—and the memory of that time itself lingers around me, impalpable, like a dying vibration of one immense jabber, silly, atrocious, sor-did, savage, or simply mean, without any kind of sense. Voices, voices—even the girl herself—now—"

He was silent for a long time.

"I laid the ghost of his gifts at last with a lie," he began suddenly. "Girl! What? Did I mention a girl? Oh, she is out of it—completely. They—the women I mean—are out of it—should be out of it. We must help them to stay in that beautiful world of their own, lest ours gets worse. Oh, she had to be out of it. You should have heard the disinterred body of Mr. Kurtz saying, 'My Intended.' You would have perceived directly then how completely she was out of it. And the lofty frontal bone of Mr. Kurtz! They say the hair goes on growing sometimes,[15] but this—ah—specimen, was impressively bald. The wilderness had patted him on the head, and, behold, it was like a ball—an ivory ball; it had caressed him, and—lo!—he had withered; it had taken him,

---

15. A reference to the idea that hair continues to grow after death.

loved him, embraced him, got into his veins, consumed his flesh, and sealed his soul to its own by the inconceivable ceremonies of some devilish initiation. He was its spoiled and pampered favorite. Ivory? I should think so. Heaps of it, stacks of it. The old mud shanty was bursting with it. You would think there was not a single tusk left either above or below the ground in the whole country. 'Mostly fossil,' the manager had remarked disparagingly. It was no more fossil than I am; but they call it fossil when it is dug up. It appears these niggers do bury the tusks sometimes—but evidently they couldn't bury this parcel deep enough to save the gifted Mr. Kurtz from his fate. We filled the steamboat with it, and had to pile a lot on the deck. Thus he could see and enjoy as long as he could see, because the appreciation of this favor had remained with him to the last. You should have heard him say, 'My ivory.' Oh yes, I heard him. 'My Intended, my ivory, my station, my river, my—' everything belonged to him. It made me hold my breath in expectation of hearing the wilderness burst in to a prodigious peal of laughter that would shake the fixed stars in their places. Everything belonged to him—but that was a trifle. The thing was to know what he belonged to, how many powers of darkness claimed him for their own. That was the reflection that made you creepy all over. It was impossible—it was not good for one either—trying to imagine. He had taken a high seat amongst the devils of the land—I mean literally. You can't understand. How could you?—with solid pavement under your feet, surrounded by kind neighbors ready to cheer you or to fall on you, stepping delicately between the butcher and the policeman, in the holy terror of scandal and gallows and lunatic asylums—how can you imagine what particular region of the first ages a man's untrammeled feet may take him into by the way of solitude—utter solitude without a policeman—by the way of silence—utter silence, where no warning voice of a kind neighbor can be heard whispering of public opinion? These little things make all the great difference. When they are gone you must fall back upon your own innate strength, upon your own capacity for faithfulness. Of course you may be too much of a fool to go wrong—too dull even to know you are being assaulted by the powers of darkness. I take it, no fool ever made a bargain for this soul with the devil: the fool is too much of a fool, or the devil too much of a devil—I don't know which. Or you may be such a thunderingly exalted creature as to be altogether deaf and blind to anything but heavenly sights and sounds. Then the earth for you is only a standing place—and whether to be like this is your loss or your gain I won't pretend to say. But most of us are neither one nor the other. The earth for us is a place to live in, where we must put up with sights, with sounds, with smells too, by Jove!—breathe dead hippo, so to speak, and not be contaminated. And there, don't you see? your strength comes in, the faith in your ability for the digging of unostentatious holes to bury the stuff in—your power of devotion, not to yourself, but to an obscure, back-breaking business. And that's difficult enough. Mind, I am not trying to excuse or even explain—I am trying to account to myself for—for—Mr. Kurtz—for the shade of Mr. Kurtz. This initiated wraith from the back of Nowhere honored me with its amazing confidence before it vanished altogether. This was because it could speak English to me. The original Kurtz had been educated partly in England, and—

as he was good enough to say himself—his sympathies were in the right place. His mother was half-English, his father was half-French. All Europe contributed to the making of Kurtz; and by-and-by I learned that, most appropriately, the International Society for the Suppression of Savage Customs[16] had entrusted him with the making of a report, for its future guidance. And he had written it too. I've seen it. I've read it. It was eloquent, vibrating with eloquence, but too high-strung, I think. Seventeen pages of close writing he had found time for! But this must have been before his—let us say—nerves, went wrong, and caused him to preside at certain midnight dances ending with unspeakable rites, which—as far as I reluctantly gathered from what I heard at various times—were offered up to him—do you understand?—to Mr. Kurtz himself. But it was a beautiful piece of writing. The opening paragraph, however, in the light of later information, strikes me now as ominous. He began with the argument that we whites, from the point of development we had arrived at, 'must necessarily appear to them [savages] in the nature of supernatural beings—we approach them with the might as of a deity,' and so on, and so on. 'By the simple exercise of our will we can exert a power for good practically unbounded,' &c., &c. From that point he soared and took me with him. The peroration was magnificent, though difficult to remember, you know. It gave me the notion of an exotic Immensity ruled by an august Benevolence. It made me tingle with enthusiasm. This was the unbounded power of eloquence—of words—of burning noble words. There were no practical hints to interrupt the magic current of phrases, unless a kind of note at the foot of the last page, scrawled evidently much later, in an unsteady hand, may be regarded as the exposition of a method. It was very simple, and at the end of that moving appeal to every altruistic sentiment it blazed at you, luminous and terrifying, like a flash of lightning in a serene sky: 'Exterminate all the brutes!' The curious part was that he had apparently forgotten all about that valuable postscriptum, because, later on, when he in a sense came to himself, he repeatedly entreated me to take good care of 'my pamphlet' (he called it), as it was sure to have in the future a good influence upon his career. I had full information about all these things, and, besides, as it turned out, I was to have the care of his memory. I've done enough for it to give me the indisputable right to lay it, if I choose, for an everlasting rest in the dust-bin of progress, amongst all the sweepings and, figuratively speaking, all the dead cats of civilization. But then, you see, I can't choose. He wouldn't be forgotten. Whatever he was, he was not common. He had the power to charm or frighten rudimentary souls into an aggravated witch-dance in his honor; he could also fill the small souls of the pilgrims with bitter misgivings: he had one devoted friend at least, and he had conquered one soul in the world that was neither rudimentary nor tainted with self-seeking. No; I can't forget him, though I am not prepared to affirm the fellow was exactly worth the life we lost in getting to him. I missed my late helmsman awfully,—I missed him even while his

16. Perhaps a reference to the International Society for the Suppression of Savage Customs, headed by King Leopold of Belgium.

body was still lying in the pilot-house. Perhaps you will think it passing strange this regret for a savage who was no more account than a grain of sand in a black Sahara. Well, don't you see, he had done something, he had steered; for months I had him at my back—a help—an instrument. It was a kind of partnership. He steered for me—I had to look after him, I worried about his deficiencies, and thus a subtle bond had been created, of which I only became aware when it was suddenly broken. And the intimate profundity of that look he gave me when he received his hurt remains to this day in my memory—like a claim of distant kinship affirmed in a supreme moment.

"Poor fool! If he had only left that shutter alone. He had no restraint, no 105 restraint—just like Kurtz—a tree swayed in the wind. As soon as I had put on a dry pair of slippers, I dragged him out, after first jerking the spear out of his side, which operation I confess I performed with my eyes shut tight. His heels leaped together over the little door-step; his shoulders were pressed to my breast; I hugged him from behind desperately. Oh! he was heavy, heavy; heavier than any man on earth, I should imagine. Then without more ado I tipped him overboard. The current snatched him as though he had been a wisp of grass, and I saw the body roll over twice before I lost sight of it for ever. All the pilgrims and the manager were then congregated on the awning-deck about the pilot-house, chattering at each other like a flock of excited magpies, and there was a scandalized murmur at my heartless promptitude. What they wanted to keep that body hanging about for I can't guess. Embalm it, maybe. But I had also heard another, and a very ominous, murmur on the deck below. My friends the wood-cutters were likewise scandalized, and with a better show of reason—though I admit that the reason itself was quite inadmissible. Oh, quite! I had made up my mind that if my late helmsman was to be eaten, the fishes alone should have him. He had been a very second-rate helmsman while alive, but now he was dead he might have become a first-class temptation, and possibly cause some startling trouble. Besides, I was anxious to take the wheel, the man in pink pyjamas showing himself a hopeless duffer at the business.

"This I did directly the simple funeral was over. We were going half-speed, keeping right in the middle of the stream, and I listened to the talk about me. They had given up Kurtz, they had given up the station; Kurtz was dead, and the station had been burnt—and so on—and so on. The red-haired pilgrim was beside himself with the thought that at least this poor Kurtz had been properly revenged. 'Say! We must have made a glorious slaughter of them in the bush. Eh? What do you think? Say?' He positively danced, the bloodthirsty little gingery beggar. And he had nearly fainted when he saw the wounded man! I could not help saying, 'You made a glorious lot of smoke, anyhow.' I had seen, from the way the tops of the bushes rustled and flew, that almost all the shots had gone too high. You can't hit anything unless you take aim and fire from the shoulder; but these chaps fired from the hip with their eyes shut. The retreat, I maintained—and I was right—was caused by the screeching of the steam-whistle. Upon this they forgot Kurtz, and began to howl at me with indignant protests.

"The manager stood by the wheel murmuring confidentially about the necessity of getting well away down the river before dark at all events, when I saw in the distance a clearing on the river-side and the outlines of some sort of building. 'What's this?' I asked. He clapped his hands in wonder. 'The station!' he cried. I edged in at once, still going half-speed.

"Through my glasses I saw the slope of a hill interspersed with rare trees and perfectly free from undergrowth. A long decaying building on the summit was half buried in the high grass; the large holes in the peaked roof gaped back from afar; the jungle and the woods made a background. There was no inclosure or fence of any kind; but there had been one apparently, for near the house half-a-dozen slim posts remained in a row, roughly trimmed, and with their upper ends ornamented with round curved balls. The rails, or whatever there had been between, had disappeared. Of course the forest surrounded all that. The river-bank was clear, and on the water-side I saw a white man under a hat like a cart-wheel beckoning persistently with his whole arm. Examining the edge of the forest above and below, I was almost certain I could see movements—human forms gliding here and there. I steamed past prudently, then stopped the engines and let her drift down. The man on the shore began to shout, urging us to land. 'We have been attacked,' screamed the manager. 'I know—I know. It's all right,' yelled back the other, as cheerful as you please. 'Come along. It's all right. I am glad.'

"His aspect reminded me of something I had seen—something funny I had seen somewhere. As I maneuvered to get alongside, I was asking myself, 'What does this fellow look like?' Suddenly I got it. He looked like a harlequin. His clothes had been made of some stuff that was brown holland probably, but it was covered with patches all over, with bright patches, blue, red, and yellow,—patches on the back, patches on front, patches on elbows, on knees; colored binding round his jacket, scarlet edging at the bottom of his trousers; and the sunshine made him look extremely gay and wonderfully neat withal, because you could see how beautifully all this patching had been done. A beardless, boyish face, very fair, no features to speak of, nose peeling, little blue eyes, smiles and frowns chasing each other over that open countenance like sunshine and shadow on a wind-swept plain. 'Look out, captain!' he cried; 'there's a snag lodged in here last night.' What! Another snag? I confess I swore shamefully. I had nearly holed my cripple, to finish off that charming trip. The harlequin on the bank turned his little pug nose up to me. 'You English?' he asked, all smiles. 'Are you?' I shouted from the wheel. The smiles vanished, and he shook his head as if sorry for my disappointment. Then he brightened up. 'Never mind!' he cried encouragingly. 'Are we in time?' I asked. 'He is up there,' he replied, with a toss of the head up the hill, and becoming gloomy all of a sudden. His face was like the autumn sky, overcast one moment and bright the next.

"When the manager, escorted by the pilgrims, all of them armed to the teeth, had gone to the house, this chap came on board. 'I say, I don't like this. These natives are in the bush,' I said. He assured me earnestly it was all right. 'They are simple people,' he added; 'well, I am glad you came. It took me all my time to keep them off.' 'But you said it was all right,' I cried. 'Oh, they meant no harm,' he said; and as I stared he corrected himself, 'Not exactly.' Then vivaciously, 'My faith, your pilot-house wants a clean up!' In the next breath he advised me to keep enough steam on the boiler to blow the whistle in case of any trouble. 'One good screech will do more for you than all your rifles. They are simple people,' he repeated. He rattled away at such a rate he quite overwhelmed me. He seemed to be trying to make up for lots of silence, and actually hinted, laughing, that such was the case. 'Don't you talk with Mr. Kurtz?' I said. 'You don't talk with that man—you listen to him,' he exclaimed with severe exaltation. 'But now—' He waved his arm, and in the twinkling of an eye was in the uttermost depths of despondency. In a moment he came up again with a jump, possessed himself of both my hands, shook them continuously, while he gabbed: 'Brother sailor . . . honor . . . pleasure . . . delight . . . introduce myself . . . Russian . . . son of an archpriest . . . Government of Tambov . . . What? Tobacco! English tobacco; the excellent English tobacco! Now, that's brotherly. Smoke? Where's a sailor that does not smoke?'

"The pipe soothed him, and gradually I made out he had run away from school, had gone to sea in a Russian ship; ran away again; served some time in English ships; was now reconciled with the arch-priest. He made a point of that. 'But when one is young one must see things, gather experience, ideas; enlarge the mind.' 'Here!' I interrupted. 'You can never tell! Here I have met Mr. Kurtz,' he said, youthfully solemn and reproachful. I held my tongue after that. It appears he had persuaded a Dutch trading-house on the coast to fit him out with stores and goods, and had started for the interior with a light heart, and no more idea of what would happen to him than a baby. He had been wandering about that river for nearly two years alone, cut off from everybody and everything. 'I am not so young as I look. I am twenty-five,' he said. 'At first old Van Shuyten would tell me to go to the devil,' he narrated with keen enjoyment; 'but I stuck to him, and talked and talked, till at last he got afraid I would talk the hind-leg off his favorite dog, so he gave me some cheap things and a few guns, and told me he hoped he would never see my face again. Good old Dutchman, Van Shuyten. I've sent him one small lot of ivory a year ago, so that he can't call me a little thief when I get back. I hope he got it. And for the rest I don't care. I had some wood stacked for you. That was my old house. Did you see?

"I gave him Towson's book. He made as though he would kiss me, but restrained himself. 'The only book I had left, and I thought I had lost it,' he said, looking at it ecstatically. 'So many accidents happen to a man going about alone, you know. Canoes get upset sometimes—and sometimes you've got to clear out so quick when the people get angry.' He thumbed the pages. 'You made notes in Russian?' I asked. He nodded. 'I thought they were written in cipher,' I said. He laughed, then became serious. 'I had lots of trouble to keep these people off,' he said. 'Did they want to kill you?' I asked. 'Oh no!' he cried, and checked himself. 'Why did they attack us?' I pursued. He hesitated, then said shamefacedly, 'They don't want him to go.' 'Don't they?' I said, curiously. He nodded a nod full of mystery and wisdom. 'I tell you,' he cried, 'this man has enlarged my mind.' He opened his arms wide, staring at me with his little blue eyes that were perfectly round."

III

"I looked at him, lost in astonishment. There he was before me, in motley,[17] as though he had absconded from a troupe of mimes, enthusiastic, fabulous. His very existence was improbable, inexplicable, and altogether bewildering. He was an insoluble problem. It was inconceivable how he had existed, how he had succeeded in getting so far, how he had managed to remain—why he did not instantly disappear. 'I went a little farther,' he said, 'then still a little farther—till I had gone so far that I don't know how I'll ever get back. Never mind. Plenty time. I can manage. You take Kurtz away quick—quick—I tell you.' The glamour of youth enveloped his particolored rags, his destitution, his loneliness, the essential desolation of his futile wanderings. For months—for years—his life hadn't been worth a day's purchase; and there he was gallantly, thoughtlessly alive, to all appearance indestructible solely by the virtue of his few years and of his unreflecting audacity. I was seduced into something like admiration—like envy. Glamour urged him on, glamour kept him unscathed. He surely wanted nothing from the wilderness but space to breathe in and to push on through. His need was to exist, and to move onwards at the greatest possible risk, and with a maximum of privation. If the absolutely pure, uncalculating, unpractical spirit of adventure had ever ruled a human being, it ruled this be-patched youth. I almost envied him the possession of this modest and clear flame. It seemed to have consumed all thought of self so completely, that, even while he was talking to you, you forgot that it was he—the man before your eyes—who had gone through these things. I did not envy him his devotion to Kurtz, though. He had not meditated over it. It came to him, and he accepted it with a sort of eager fatalism. I must say that to me it appeared about the most dangerous thing in every way he had come upon so far.

"They had come together unavoidably, like two ships becalmed near each other, and lay rubbing sides at last. I suppose Kurtz wanted an audience, because on a certain occasion, when encamped in the forest, they had talked all night, or more probably Kurtz had talked. 'We talked of everything,' he said, quite transported at the recollection. 'I forgot there was such a thing as sleep. The night did not seem to last an hour. Everything! Everything! . . . Of love too.' 'Ah, he talked to you of love!' I said, much amused, 'It isn't what you think,' he cried, almost passionately. 'It was in general. He made me see things—things.'

"He threw his arms up. We were on deck at the time, and the headman of 115 my wood-cutters, lounging near by, turned upon him his heavy and glittering eyes. I looked around, and I don't know why, but I assure you that never, never before, did this land, this river, this jungle, the very arch of this blazing sky, appear to me so hopeless and so dark, so impenetrable to human thought, so pitiless to human weakness. 'And, ever since, you have been with him, of course?' I said.

"On the contrary. It appears their intercourse had been very much broken

17. The many-colored clothes of a harlequin or jester.

by various causes. He had, as he informed me proudly, managed to nurse Kurtz through two illnesses (he alluded to it as you would to some risky feat), but as a rule Kurtz wandered alone, far in the depths of the forest. 'Very often coming to this station, I had to wait days and days before he would turn up,' he said. 'Ah, it was worth waiting for!—sometimes.' 'What was he doing? exploring or what?' I asked. 'Oh yes, of course'; he had discovered lots of villages, a lake too—he did not know exactly in what direction, it was dangerous to inquire too much—but mostly his expeditions had been for ivory. 'But he had no goods to trade with by that time,' I objected. 'There's a good lot of cartridges left even yet,' he answered, looking away. 'To speak plainly, he raided the country,' I said. He nodded. 'Not alone, surely!' He muttered something about the villages round that lake. 'Kurtz got the tribe to follow him, did he?' I suggested. He fidgeted a little. 'They adored him,' he said. The tone of these words was so extraordinary that I looked at him searchingly. It was curious to see his mingled eagerness and reluctance to speak of Kurtz. The man filled his life, occupied his thoughts, swayed his emotions. 'What can you expect?' he burst out; 'he came to them with thunder and lightning, you know—and they had never seen anything like it—and very terrible. He could be very terrible. You can't judge Mr. Kurtz as you would an ordinary man. No, no, no! Now—just to give you an idea—I don't mind telling you, he wanted to shoot me too one day—but I don't judge him.' 'Shoot you!' I cried. 'What for?' 'Well, I had a small lot of ivory the chief of that village near my house gave me. You see I used to shoot game for them. Well, he wanted it, and wouldn't hear reason. He declared he would shoot me unless I gave him the ivory and then cleared out of the country, because he could do so, and had a fancy for it, and there was nothing on earth to prevent him killing whom he jolly well pleased. And it was true too. I gave him the ivory. What did I care! But I didn't clear out. No, no. I couldn't leave him. I had to be careful, of course, till we got friendly again for a time. He had his second illness then. Afterwards I had to keep out of the way; but I don't mind. He was living for the most part in those villages on the lake. When he came down to the river, sometimes he would take me, and sometimes it was better for me to be careful. This man suffered too much. He hated all this, and somehow he couldn't get away. When I had a chance I begged him to try and leave while there was time; I offered to go back with him. And he would say yes, and then he would remain; go off on another ivory hunt; disappear for weeks; forget himself amongst these people—forget himself—you know.' 'Why! he's mad,' I said. He protested indignantly. Mr. Kurtz couldn't be mad. If I had heard him talk, only two days ago, I wouldn't dare hint at such a thing. . . . I had taken up my binoculars while we talked and was looking at the shore, sweeping the limit of the forest at each side and at the back of the house. The consciousness of there being people in that bush, so silent, so quiet—as silent and quiet as the ruined house on the hill—made me uneasy. There was no sign on the face of nature of this amazing tale that was not so much told as suggested to me in desolate exclamations, completed by shrugs, in interrupted phrases, in hints ending in deep sighs. The woods were unmoved, like a mask—heavy, like the closed door of a prison—they looked with their air of hidden knowledge, of patient expectation, of unapproachable silence. The Russian was explaining to me that it was only lately that Mr. Kurtz had come down to the river, bringing along with him all the fighting men of that lake tribe. He had been absent for several months—getting himself adored, I suppose—and had come down unexpectedly, with the intention to all appearance of making a raid either across the river or down stream. Evidently the appetite for more ivory had got the better of the—what shall I say?—less material aspirations. However he had got much worse suddenly. 'I heard he was lying helpless, and so I came up—took my chance,' said the Russian. 'Oh, he is bad, very bad.' I directed my glass to the house. There were no signs of life, but there was the ruined roof, the long mud wall peeping above the grass, with three little square window-holes, no two of the same size; all this brought within reach of my hand, as it were. And then I made a brusque movement, and one of the remaining posts of that vanished fence leaped up in the field of my glass. You remember I told you I had been struck at the distance by certain attempts at ornamentation, rather remarkable in the ruinous aspect of the place. Now I had suddenly a nearer view, and its first result was to make me throw my head back as if before a blow. Then I went carefully from post to post with my glass, and I saw my mistake. These round knobs were not ornamental but symbolic; they were expressive and puzzling, striking and disturbing—food for thought and also for the vultures if there had been any looking down from the sky; but at all events for such ants as were industrious enough to ascend the pole. They would have been even more impressive, those heads on the stakes, if their faces had not been turned to the house. Only one, the first I had made out, was facing my way. I was not so shocked as you may think. The start back I had given was really nothing but a movement of surprise. I had expected to see a knob of wood there, you know. I returned deliberately to the first I had seen—and there it was, black, dried, sunken, with closed eyelids—a head that seemed to sleep at the top of that pole, and, with the shrunken dry lips showing a narrow white line of the teeth, was smiling too, smiling continuously at some endless and jocose dream of that eternal slumber.

"I am not disclosing any trade secrets. In fact the manager said afterwards that Mr. Kurtz's methods had ruined the district. I have no opinion on that point, but I want you clearly to understand that there was nothing exactly profitable in these heads being there. They only showed that Mr. Kurtz lacked restraint in the gratification of his various lusts, that there was something wanting in him—some small matter which, when the pressing need arose, could not be found under his magnificent eloquence. Whether he knew of this deficiency himself I can't say. I think the knowledge came to him at last—only at the very last. But the wilderness had found him out early, and had taken on him a terrible vengeance for the fantastic invasion. I think it had whispered to him things about himself which he did not know, things of which he had no conception till he took counsel with this great solitude—and the whisper had proved irresistibly fascinating. It echoed loudly within him because he was hollow at the core. . . . I put down the glass, and the head that had appeared near enough to be spoken to seemed at once to have leaped away from me into inaccessible distance.

"The admirer of Mr. Kurtz was a bit crestfallen. In a hurried, indistinct voice he began to assure me he had not dared to take these—say, symbols— down. He was not afraid of the natives; they would not stir till Mr. Kurtz gave the word. His ascendancy was extraordinary. The camps of these people surrounded the place, and the chiefs came every day to see him. They would crawl. . . . 'I don't want to know anything of the ceremonies used when approaching Mr. Kurtz,' I shouted. Curious, this feeling that came over me that such details would be more intolerable than those heads drying on the stakes under Mr. Kurtz's windows. After all, that was only a savage sight, while I seemed at one bound to have been transported into some lightless region of subtle horrors, where pure, uncomplicated savagery was a positive relief, being something that had a right to exist—obviously—in the sunshine. The young man looked at me with surprise. I suppose it did not occur to him that Mr. Kurtz was no idol of mine. He forgot I hadn't heard any of these splendid monologues on, what was it? on love, justice, conduct of life—or what not. If it had come to crawling before Mr. Kurtz, he crawled as much as the veriest savage of them all. I had no idea of the conditions, he said: these heads were the heads of rebels. I shocked him excessively by laughing. Rebels! What would be the next definition I was to hear? There had been enemies, criminals, workers—and these were rebels. Those rebellious heads looked very subdued to me on their sticks. 'You don't know how such a life tries a man like Kurtz,' cried Kurtz's last disciple. 'Well, and you?' I said. 'I! I! I am a simple man. I have no great thoughts. I want nothing from anybody. How can you compare me to . . . ?' His feelings were too much for speech, and suddenly he broke down. 'I don't understand,' he groaned. 'I've been doing my best to keep him alive, and that's enough. I had no hand in all this. I have no abilities. There hasn't been a drop of medicine or a mouthful of invalid food for months here. He was shamefully abandoned. A man like this, with such ideas. Shamefully! Shamefully! I—I—haven't slept for the last ten nights. . . .'

"His voice lost itself in the calm of the evening. The long shadows of the forest had slipped down hill while we talked, had gone far beyond the ruined hovel, beyond the symbolic row of stakes. All this was in the gloom, while we down there were yet in the sunshine, and the stretch of the river abreast of the clearing glittered in a still and dazzling splendor, with a murky and overshadowed bend above and below. Not a living soul was seen on the shore. The bushes did not rustle.

"Suddenly round the corner of the house a group of men appeared, as though they had come up from the ground. They waded waist-deep in the grass, in a compact body, bearing an improvised stretcher in their midst. Instantly, in the emptiness of the landscape, a cry arose whose shrillness pierced the still air like a sharp arrow flying straight to the very heart of the land; and, as if by enchantment, streams of human beings—of naked human beings— with spears in their hands, with bows, with shields, with wild glances and savage movements, were poured into the clearing by the dark-faced and pensive forest. The bushes shook, the grass swayed for a time, and then everything stood still in attentive immobility.

"'Now, if he does not say the right thing to them we are all done for,' said the Russian at my elbow. The knot of men with the stretcher had stopped too, halfway to the steamer, as if petrified. I saw the man on the stretcher sit up, lank and with an uplifted arm, above the shoulders of the bearers. 'Let us hope that the man who can talk so well of love in general will find some particular reason to spare us this time,' I said. I resented bitterly the absurd danger of our situation, as if to be at the mercy of that atrocious phantom had been a dishonoring necessity. I could not hear a sound, but through my glasses I saw the thin arm extended commandingly, the lower jaw moving, the eyes of that apparition shining darkly far in its bony head that nodded with grotesque jerks. Kurtz—Kurtz—that means short in German—don't it? Well, the name was as true as everything else in his life—and death. He looked at least seven feet long. His covering had fallen off, and his body emerged from it pitiful and appalling as from a winding-sheet. I would see the cage of his ribs all astir, the bones of his arm waving. It was as though an animated image of death carved out of old ivory had been shaking its hand with menaces at a motionless crowd of men made of dark and glittering bronze. I saw him open his mouth wide— it gave him a weirdly voracious aspect, as though he had wanted to swallow all the air, all the earth, all the men before him. A deep voice reached me faintly. He must have been shouting. He fell back suddenly. The stretcher shook as the bearers staggered forward again, and almost at the same time I noticed that the crowd of savages was vanishing without any perceptible movement of retreat, as if the forest that had ejected these beings so suddenly had drawn them in again as the breath is drawn in a long aspiration.

"Some of the pilgrims behind the stretcher carried his arms—two shot-guns, a heavy rifle, and a light revolver-carbine—the thunderbolts of that piti-ful Jupiter.[18] The manager bent over him murmuring as he walked beside his head. They laid him down in one of the little cabins—just a room for a bed-place and a camp-stool or two, you know. We had brought his belated corre-spondence, and a lot of torn envelopes and open letters littered his bed. His hand roamed feebly amongst these papers. I was struck by the fire of his eyes and the composed languor of his expression. It was not so much the exhaus-tion of disease. He did not seem in pain. This shadow looked satiated and calm, as though for the moment it had had its fill of all the emotions.

"He rustled one of the letters, and looking straight in my face said, 'I am glad.' Somebody had been writing to him about me. These special recom-mendations were turning up again. The volume of tone he emitted without effort, almost without the trouble of moving his lips, amazed me. A voice! a voice! It was grave, profound, vibrating, while the man did not seem capable of a whisper. However, he had enough strength in him—factitious no doubt— to very nearly make an end of us, as you shall hear directly.

"The manager appeared silently in the doorway; I stepped out at once and he drew the curtain after me. The Russian, eyed curiously by the pilgrims, was staring at the shore. I followed the direction of his glance.

"Dark human shapes could be made out in the distance, flitting in-distinctly against the gloomy border of the forest, and near the river two   125

18. Chief god of the Romans.

bronze figures, leaning on tall spears, stood in the sunlight under fantastic head-dresses of spotted skins, warlike and still in statuesque repose. And from right to left along the lighted shore moved a wild and gorgeous apparition of a woman.

"She walked with measured steps, draped in striped and fringed cloths, treading the earth proudly, with a slight jingle and flash of barbarous ornaments. She carried her head high; her hair was done in the shape of a helmet; she had brass leggings to the knee, brass wire gauntlets to the elbow, a crimson spot on her tawny cheek, innumerable necklaces of glass beads on her neck; bizarre things, charms, gifts of witch-men, that hung about her, glittered and trembled at every step. She must have had the value of several elephant tusks upon her. She was savage and superb, wild-eyed and magnificent; there was something ominous and stately in her deliberate progress. And in the hush that had fallen suddenly upon the whole sorrowful land, the immense wilderness, the colossal body of the fecund and mysterious life seemed to look at her, pensive, as though it had been looking at the image of its own tenebrous and passionate soul.

"She came abreast of the steamer, stood still, and faced us. Her long shadow fell to the water's edge. Her face had a tragic and fierce aspect of wild sorrow and of dumb pain mingled with the fear of some struggling, half-shaped resolve. She stood looking at us without a stir and like the wilderness itself, with an air of brooding over an inscrutable purpose. A whole minute passed, and then she made a step forward. There was a low jingle, a glint of yellow metal, a sway of fringed draperies, and she stopped as if her heart had failed her. The young fellow by my side growled. The pilgrims murmured at my back. She looked at us all as if her life had depended upon the unswerving steadiness of her glance. Suddenly she opened her bared arms and threw them up rigid above her head, as though in an uncontrollable desire to touch the sky, and at the same time the swift shadows darted out on the earth, swept around on the river, gathering the steamer into a shadowy embrace. A formidable silence hung over the scene.

"She turned away slowly, walked on, following the bank, and passed into the bushes to the left. Once only her eyes gleamed back at us in the dusk of the thickets before she disappeared.

"'If she had offered to come aboard I really think I would have tried to shoot her,' said the man of patches, nervously. 'I had been risking my life every day for the last fortnight to keep her out of the house. She got in one day and kicked up a row about those miserable rags I picked up in the storeroom to mend my clothes with. I wasn't decent. At least it must have been that, for she talked like a fury to Kurtz for an hour, pointing at me now and then. I don't understand the dialect of this tribe. Luckily for me, I fancy Kurtz felt too ill that day to care, or there would have been mischief. I don't understand. . . . No—it's too much for me. Ah, well, it's all over now.'

"At this moment I heard Kurtz's deep voice behind the curtain, 'Save 130 me!—save the ivory, you mean. Don't tell me. Save *me!* Why, I've had to save you. You are interrupting my plans now. Sick! Sick! Not so sick as you would like to believe. Never mind. I'll carry my ideas out yet—I will return. I'll show

you what can be done. You with your little peddling notions—you are interfering with me. I will return. I . . .'

"The manager came out. He did me the honor to take me under the arm
and lead me aside. 'He is very low, very low,' he said. He considered it necessary to sigh, but neglected to be consistently sorrowful. 'We have done all we
could for him—haven't we? But there is no disguising the fact, Mr. Kurtz has
done more harm than good to the Company. He did not see the time was not
ripe for vigorous action. Cautiously, cautiously—that's my principle. We must
be cautious yet. The district is closed to us for a time. Deplorable! Upon the
whole, the trade will suffer. I don't deny there is a remarkable quantity of
ivory—mostly fossil. We must save it, at all events—but look how precarious
the position is—and why? Because the method is unsound.' 'Do you,' said I,
looking at the shore, 'call it "unsound method"?' 'Without doubt,' he exclaimed, hotly. 'Don't you?' . . . 'No method at all,' I murmured after a while.
'Exactly,' he exulted. 'I anticipated this. Shows a complete want of judgment.
It is my duty to point it out in the proper quarter.' 'Oh,' said I, 'that fellow—
what's his name?—the brickmaker, will make a readable report for you.' He
appeared confounded for a moment. It seemed to me I had never breathed an
atmosphere so vile, and I turned mentally to Kurtz for relief—positively for
relief. 'Nevertheless I think Mr. Kurtz is a remarkable man,' I said with emphasis. He started, dropped on me a cold heavy glance, said very quietly, 'He
was,' and turned his back on me. My hour of favor was over; I found myself
lumped along with Kurtz as a partisan of methods for which the time was not
ripe: I was unsound! Ah! but it was something to have at least a choice of
nightmares.

"I had turned to the wilderness really, not to Mr. Kurtz, who, I was ready
to admit, was as good as buried. And for a moment it seemed to me as if I also
were buried in a vast grave full of unspeakable secrets. I felt an intolerable
weight oppressing my breast, the smell of the damp earth, the unseen presence of victorious corruption, the darkness of an impenetrable night. . . . The
Russian tapped me on the shoulder. I heard him mumbling and stammering
something about 'brother seaman—couldn't conceal—knowledge of matters
that would affect Mr. Kurtz's reputation.' I waited. For him evidently Mr.
Kurtz was not in his grave; I suspect that for him Mr. Kurtz was one of the im-
mortals. 'Well!' said I at last, 'speak out. As it happens, I am Mr. Kurtz's
friend—in a way.'

"He stated with a good deal of formality that had we not been 'of the
same profession,' he would have kept the matter to himself without regard to
consequences. 'He suspected there was an active ill-will towards him on the
part of these white men that—' 'You are right,' I said, remembering a certain
conversation I had overheard. 'The manager thinks you ought to be hanged.'
He showed a concern at this intelligence which amused me at first. 'I had better get out of the way quietly,' he said, earnestly. 'I can do no more for Kurtz
now, and they would soon find some excuse. What's to stop them? There's a
military post three hundred miles from here.' 'Well, upon my word,' said I,
'perhaps you had better go if you have any friends amongst the savages near
by.' 'Plenty,' he said. 'They are simple people—and I want nothing, you

know.' He stood biting his lip, then: 'I don't want any harm to happen to these whites here, but of course I was thinking of Mr. Kurtz's reputation—but you are a brother seaman and—' 'All right,' said I, after a time. 'Mr. Kurtz's reputation is safe with me.' I did not know how truly I spoke.

"He informed me, lowering his voice, that it was Kurtz who had ordered the attack to be made on the steamer. 'He hated sometimes the idea of being taken away—and then again. . . . But I don't understand these matters. I am a simple man. He thought it would scare you away—that you would give it up, thinking him dead. I could not stop him. Oh, I had an awful time of it this last month.' 'Very well,' I said. 'He is all right now.' 'Ye-e-es,' he muttered, not very convinced apparently. 'Thanks,' said I; 'I shall keep my eyes open.' 'But quiet—eh?' he urged, anxiously. 'It would be awful for his reputation if anybody here—' I promised a complete discretion with great gravity. 'I have a canoe and three black fellows waiting not very far. I am off. Could you give me a few Martini-Henry cartridges?' I could, and did, with proper secrecy. He helped himself, with a wink at me, to a handful of my tobacco. 'Between sailors—you know—good English tobacco.' At the door of the pilot-house he turned round—'I say, haven't you a pair of shoes you could spare?' He raised one leg. 'Look.' The soles were tied with knotted strings sandal-wise under his bare feet. I rooted out an old pair, at which he looked with admiration before tucking it under his left arm. One of his pockets (bright red) was bulging with cartridges, from the other (dark blue) peeped 'Towson's Inquiry,' &c., &c. He seemed to think himself excellently well equipped for a renewed encounter with the wilderness. 'Ah! I'll never, never meet such a man again. You ought to have heard him recite poetry—his own too it was, he told me. Poetry!' He rolled his eyes at the recollection of these delights. 'Oh, he enlarged my mind!' 'Good-by,' said I. He shook hands and vanished in the night. Sometimes I ask myself whether I had ever really seen him—whether it was possible to meet such a phenomenon! . . .

"When I woke up shortly after midnight his warning came to mind with its hint of danger that seemed, in the starred darkness, real enough to make me get up for the purpose of having a look round. On the hill a big fire burned, illuminating fitfully a crooked corner of the station-house. One of the agents with a picket of a few of our blacks, armed for the purpose, was keeping guard over the ivory; but deep within the forest, red gleams that wavered, that seemed to sink and rise from the ground amongst confused columnar shapes of intense blackness, showed the exact position of the camp where Mr. Kurtz's adorers were keeping their uneasy vigil. The monotonous beating of a big drum filled the air with muffled shocks and a lingering vibration. A steady droning sound of many men chanting each to himself some weird incantation came out from the black, flat wall of the woods as the humming of bees comes out of a hive, and had a strange narcotic effect upon my half-awake senses. I believe I dozed off leaning over the rail, till an abrupt burst of yells, an overwhelming outbreak of a pent-up and mysterious frenzy, woke me up in a bewildered wonder. It was cut short all at once, and the low droning went on with an effect of audible and soothing silence. I glanced casually into the little cabin. A light was burning within, but Mr. Kurtz was not there.

"I think I would have raised an outcry if I had believed my eyes. But I didn't believe them at first—the thing seemed so impossible. The fact is I was completely unnerved by a sheer blank fright, pure abstract terror, unconnected with any distinct shape of physical danger. What made this emotion so overpowering was—how shall I define it?—the moral shock I received, as if something altogether monstrous, intolerable to thought and odious to the soul, had been thrust upon me unexpectedly. This lasted of course the merest fraction of a second, and then the usual sense of commonplace, deadly danger, the possibility of a sudden onslaught and massacre, or something of the kind, which I saw impending, was positively welcome and composing. It pacified me, in fact, so much, that I did not raise an alarm.

"There was an agent buttoned up inside an ulster and sleeping on a chair on deck within three feet of me. The yells had not awakened him; he snored very slightly; I left him to his slumbers and leaped shore. I did not betray Mr. Kurtz—it was ordered I should never betray him—it was written I should be loyal to the nightmare of my choice. I was anxious to deal with this shadow by myself alone,—and to this day I don't know why I was so jealous of sharing with anyone the peculiar blackness of that experience.

"As soon as I got on the bank I saw a trail—a broad trail through the grass. I remember the exultation with which I said to myself, 'He can't walk—he is crawling on all-fours—I've got him.' The grass was wet with dew. I strode rapidly with clenched fists. I fancy I had some vague notion of falling upon him and giving him a drubbing. I don't know. I had some imbecile thoughts. The knitting old woman with the cat obtruded herself upon my memory as a most improper person to be sitting at the other end of such an affair. I saw a row of pilgrims squirting lead in the air out of Winchesters held to the hip. I thought I would never get back to the steamer, and imagined myself living alone and unarmed in the woods to an advanced age. Such silly things—you know. And I remember I confounded the beat of the drum with the beating of my heart, and was pleased at its calm regularity.

"I kept to the track though—then stopped to listen. The night was very clear: a dark blue space, sparkling with dew and starlight, in which black things stood very still. I thought I could see a kind of motion ahead of me. I was strangely cocksure of everything that night. I actually left the track and ran in a wide semicircle (I verily believe chuckling to myself) so as to get in front of that stir, of that motion I had seen—if indeed I had seen anything. I was circumventing Kurtz as though it had been a boyish game.

"I came upon him, and, if he had not heard me coming, I would have 140 fallen over him too, but he got up in time. He rose, unsteady, long, pale, indistinct, like a vapor exhaled by the earth, and swayed slightly, misty and silent before me; while at my back the fires loomed between the trees, and the murmur of many voices issued from the forest. I had cut him off cleverly; but when actually confronting him I seemed to come to my senses, I saw the danger in its right proportion. It was by no means over yet. Suppose he began to shout? Though he could hardly stand, there was still plenty of vigor in his voice. 'Go away—hide yourself,' he said, in that profound tone. It was very awful. I glanced back. We were within thirty yards from the nearest fire. A black figure stood up, strode on long black legs, waving long black arms, across the glow. It had horns—antelope horns, I think—on its head. Some sorcerer, some witch-man, no doubt; it looked fiend-like enough. 'Do you know what you are doing?' I whispered. 'Perfectly,' he answered, raising his voice for that single word: it sounded to me far off and yet loud, like a hail through a speaking-trumpet. If he makes a row we are lost, I thought to myself. This clearly was not a case for fisticuffs, even apart from the very natural aversion I had to beat that Shadow—this wandering and tormented thing. 'You will be lost.' I said—'utterly lost.' One gets sometimes such a flash of inspiration, you know. I did say the right thing, though indeed he could not have been more irretrievably lost than he was at this very moment, when the foundations of our intimacy were being laid—to endure—to endure—even to the end—even beyond.

"'I had immense plans,' he muttered irresolutely. 'Yes,' said I; 'but if you try to shout I'll smash your head with—' there was not a stick or a stone near. 'I will throttle you for good,' I corrected myself. 'I was on the threshold of great things,' he pleaded, in a voice of longing, with a wistfulness of tone that made my blood run cold. 'And now for this stupid scoundrel—' 'Your success in Europe is assured in any case,' I affirmed, steadily. I did not want to have the throttling of him, you understand—and indeed it would have been very little use for any practical purpose. I tried to break the spell—the heavy, mute spell of the wilderness—that seemed to draw him to its pitiless breast by the awakening of forgotten and brutal instincts, by the memory of gratified and monstrous passions. This alone, I was convinced, had driven him out to the edge of the forest, to the bush, towards the gleam of fires, the throb of drums, the drone of weird incantations; this alone had beguiled his unlawful soul beyond the bounds of permitted aspirations. And, don't you see, the terror of the position was not in being knocked on the head—though I had a very lively sense of that danger too—but in this, that I had to deal with a being to whom I could not appeal in the name of anything high or low. I had, even like the niggers, to invoke him—himself—his own exalted and incredible degradation. There was nothing either above or below him, and I knew it. He had kicked himself loose of the earth. Confound the man! he had kicked the very earth to pieces. He was alone, and I before him did not know whether I stood on the ground or floated in the air. I've been telling you what we said—repeating the phrases we pronounced,—but what's the good? They were common everyday words,—the familiar, vague sounds exchanged on every waking day of life. But what of that? They had behind them, to my mind, the terrific suggestiveness of words heard in dreams, of phrases spoken in nightmares. Soul! If anybody had ever struggled with a soul, I am the man. And I wasn't arguing with a lunatic either. Believe me or not, his intelligence was perfectly clear—concentrated, it is true, upon himself with horrible intensity, yet clear; and therein was my only chance—barring, of course, the killing him there and then, which wasn't so good, on account of unavoidable noise. But his soul was mad. Being alone in the wilderness, it had looked within itself, and, by heavens! I tell you, it had gone mad. I had—for my sins, I suppose—to go through the ordeal of looking into it myself. No eloquence could have been so withering to one's belief in mankind as his final burst of sincerity. He struggled with himself, too. I saw it,—I heard it. I saw the inconceivable mystery of a soul that knew no restraint, no faith, and no fear, yet struggling blindly with itself. I kept my head pretty well; but when I had him at last stretched on the couch, I wiped my forehead, while my legs shook under me as though I had carried half a ton on my back down that hill. And yet I had only supported him, his bony arm clasped around my neck—and he was not much heavier than a child.

"When next day we left at noon, the crowd, of whose presence behind the curtain of trees I had been acutely conscious all the time, flowed out of the woods again, filled the clearing, covered the slope with a mass of naked, breathing, quivering, bronze bodies. I steamed up a bit, then swung down-stream, and two thousand eyes followed the evolutions of the splashing, thumping, fierce river-demon beating the water with its terrible tail and breathing black smoke into the air. In front of the first rank, along the river, three men, plastered with bright red earth from head to foot, strutted to and fro restlessly. When we came abreast again, they faced the river, stamped their feet, nodded their horned heads, swayed their scarlet bodies; they shook towards the fierce river-demon a bunch of black feathers, a mangy skin with a pendent tail—something that looked like a dried gourd; they shouted period-ically together strings of amazing words that resembled no sounds of human language; and the deep murmurs of the crowd, interrupted suddenly, were like the response of some satanic litany.

"We had carried Kurtz into the pilot-house: there was more air there. Ly-ing on the couch, he stared through the open shutter. There was an eddy in the mass of human bodies, and the woman with helmeted head and tawny cheeks rushed out to the very brink of the stream. She put out her hands, shouted something, and all that wild mob took up the shout in a roaring chorus of articulated, rapid, breathless utterance.

"'Do you understand this?' I asked.

"He kept on looking out past me with fiery, longing eyes, with a mingled 145 expression of wistfulness and hate. He made no answer, but I saw a smile, a smile of indefinable meaning, appear on his colorless lips that a moment after twitched convulsively. 'Do I not?' he said slowly, gasping, as if the words had been torn out of him by a supernatural power.

"I pulled the string of the whistle, and I did this because I saw the pilgrims on deck getting out their rifles with an air of anticipating a jolly lark. At the sudden screech there was a movement of abject terror through that wedged mass of bodies. 'Don't! don't! you frighten them away,' cried someone on deck disconsolately. I pulled the string time after time. They broke and ran, they leaped, they crouched, they swerved, they dodged the flying terror of the sound. The three red chaps had fallen flat, face down on the shore, as though they had been shot dead. Only the barbarous and superb woman did not so much as flinch, and stretched tragically her bare arms after us over the somber and glittering river.

"And then that imbecile crowd down on the deck started their little fun, and I could see nothing more for smoke.

"The brown current ran swiftly out of the heart of darkness, bearing us down towards the sea with twice the speed of our upward progress; and Kurtz's life was running swiftly too, ebbing, ebbing out of his heart into the sea of inexorable time. The manager was very placid, he had no vital anxieties now, he took us both in with a comprehensive and satisfied glance: the 'affair' had come off as well as could be wished. I saw the time approaching when I would be left alone of the party of 'unsound method.' The pilgrims looked upon me with disfavor. I was, so to speak, numbered with the dead. It is strange how I accepted this unforeseen partnership, this choice of nightmares forced upon me in the tenebrous land invaded by these mean and greedy phantoms.

"Kurtz discoursed. A voice! a voice! It rang deep to the very last. It survived his strength to hide in the magnificent folds of eloquence the barren darkness of his heart. Oh, he struggled! he struggled! The wastes of his weary brain were haunted by shadowy images now—images of wealth and fame revolving obsequiously round his unextinguishable gift of noble and lofty expression. My Intended, my station, my career, my ideas—these were the subjects for the occasional utterances of elevated sentiments. The shade of the original Kurtz frequented the bedside of the hollow sham, whose fate it was to be buried presently in the mold of primeval earth. But both the diabolic love and the unearthly hate of the mysteries it had penetrated fought for the possession of that soul satiated with primitive emotions, avid of lying fame, of sham distinction, of all the appearances of success and power.

"Sometimes he was contemptibly childish. He desired to have kings meet 150 him at railway-stations on his return from some ghastly Nowhere, where he intended to accomplish great things. 'You show them you have in you something that is really profitable, and then there will be no limits to the recognition of your ability,' he would say. 'Of course you must take care of the motives—right motives—always.' The long reaches that were like one and the same reach, monotonous bends that were exactly alike, slipped past the steamer with their multitude of secular trees looking patiently after this grimy fragment of another world, the forerunner of change, of conquest, of trade, of massacres, of blessings. I looked ahead—piloting. 'Close the shutter,' said Kurtz suddenly one day; 'I can't bear to look at this.' I did so. There was a silence. 'Oh, but I will wring your heart yet!' he cried at the invisible wilderness.

"We broke down—as I had expected—and had to lie up for repairs at the head of an island. This delay was the first thing that shook Kurtz's confidence. One morning he gave me a packet of papers and a photograph,—the lot tied together with a shoestring. 'Keep this for me,' he said. 'This noxious fool' (meaning the manager) 'is capable of prying into my boxes when I am not looking.' In the afternoon I saw him. He was lying on his back with closed eyes, and I withdrew quietly, but I heard him mutter, 'Live rightly, die, die . . .' I listened. There was nothing more. Was he rehearsing some speech in his sleep, or was it a fragment of a phrase from some newspaper article? He had been writing for the papers and meant to do so again, 'for the furthering of my ideas. It's a duty.'

"His was an impenetrable darkness. I looked at him as you peer down at a man who is lying at the bottom of a precipice where the sun never shines. But I had not much time to give him, because I was helping the engine-driver to take to pieces the leaky cylinders, to straighten a bent connecting-rod, and in other such matters. I lived in an infernal mess of rust, filings, nuts, bolts, spanners, hammers, ratchet-drills—things I abominate, because I don't get on with them. I tended the little forge we fortunately had aboard; I toiled wearily in a wretched scrap-heap—unless I had the shakes too bad to stand.

"One evening coming in with a candle I was startled to hear him say a little tremulously, 'I am lying here in the dark waiting for death.' The light was within a foot of his eyes. I forced myself to murmur. 'Oh, nonsense!' and stood over him as if transfixed.

"Anything approaching the change that came over his features I have never seen before, and hope never to see again. Oh, I wasn't touched. I was fascinated. It was as though a veil had been rent. I saw on that ivory face the expression of somber pride, of ruthless power, of craven terror—of an intense and hopeless despair. Did he live his life again in every detail of desire, temptation, and surrender during that supreme moment of complete knowledge? He cried in a whisper at some image, at some vision,—he cried out twice, a cry that was no more than a breath—

"'The horror! The horror!'   155

"I blew the candle out and left the cabin. The pilgrims were dining in the mess-room, and I took my place opposite the manager, who lifted his eyes to give me a questioning glance, which I successfully ignored. He leaned back, serene, with that peculiar smile of his sealing the unexpressed depths of his meanness. A continuous shower of small flies streamed upon the lamp, upon the cloth, upon our hands and faces. Suddenly the manager's boy put his insolent black head in the doorway, and said in a tone of scathing contempt—

"'Mistah Kurtz—he dead.'

"All the pilgrims rushed out to see. I remained, and went on with my dinner. I believe I was considered brutally callous. However, I did not eat much. There was a lamp in there—light, don't you know—and outside it was so beastly, beastly dark. I went no more near the remarkable man who had pronounced a judgment upon the adventures of his soul on this earth. The voice was gone. What else had been there? But I am of course aware that next day the pilgrims buried something in a muddy hole.

"And then they very nearly buried me.

"However, as you see, I did not go to join Kurtz there and then. I did not.   160
I remained to dream the nightmare out to the end, and to show my loyalty to Kurtz once more. Destiny. My destiny! Droll thing life is—that mysterious arrangement of merciless logic for a futile purpose. The most you can hope from it is some knowledge of yourself—that comes too late—a crop of unextinguishable regrets. I have wrestled with death. It is the most unexciting contest you can imagine. It takes place in an impalpable grayness, with nothing underfoot, with nothing around, without spectators, without clamor, without glory, without the great desire of victory, without the great fear of defeat, in a sickly atmosphere of tepid skepticism, without much belief in your own right, and still less in that of your adversary. If such is the form of ultimate wisdom, then life is a greater riddle than some of us think it to be. I was within a hair's-breadth of the last opportunity for pronouncement, and I found with humili-

ation that probably I would have nothing to say. This is the reason why I affirm that Kurtz was a remarkable man. He had something to say. He said it. Since I had peeped over the edge myself, I understand better the meaning of his stare, that could not see the flame of the candle, but was wide enough to embrace the whole universe, piercing enough to penetrate all the hearts that beat in the darkness. He had summed up—he had judged. 'The horror!' He was a remarkable man. After all, this was the expression of some sort of belief; it had candor, it had conviction, it had a vibrating note of revolt in its whisper, it had the appalling face of a glimpsed truth—the strange commingling of desire and hate. And it is not my own extremity I remember best—a vision of grayness without form filled with physical pain, and a careless contempt for the evanescence of all things—even of this pain itself. No! It is his extremity that I seem to have lived through. True, he had made that last stride, he had stepped over the edge, while I had been permitted to draw back my hesitating foot. And perhaps in this is the whole difference; perhaps all the wisdom, and all truth, and all sincerity, are just compressed into the inappreciable moment of time in which we step over the threshold of the invisible. Perhaps! I like to think my summing-up would not have been a world of careless contempt. Better his cry—much better. It was an affirmation, a moral victory paid for by innumerable defeats, by abominable terrors, by abominable satisfactions. But it was a victory! That is why I have remained loyal to Kurtz to the last, and even beyond, when a long time after I heard once more, not his own voice, but the echo of his magnificent eloquence thrown to me from a soul as translucently pure as a cliff of crystal.

"No, they did not bury me, though there is a period of time which I remember mistily, with a shuddering wonder, like a passage through some inconceivable world that had no hope in it and no desire. I found myself back in the sepulchral city resenting the sight of people hurrying through the streets to filch a little money from each other, to devour their infamous cookery, to gulp their unwholesome beer, to dream their insignificant and silly dreams. They trespassed upon my thoughts. They were intruders whose knowledge of life was to me an irritating pretense, because I felt so sure they could not possibly know the things I knew. Their bearing, which was simply the bearing of commonplace individuals going about their business in the assurance of perfect safety, was offensive to me like the outrageous flauntings of folly in the face of a danger it is unable to comprehend. I had no particular desire to enlighten them, but I had some difficulty in restraining myself from laughing in their faces, so full of stupid importance. I dare say I was not very well at that time. I tottered about the streets—there were various affairs to settle—grinning bitterly at perfectly respectable persons. I admit my behavior was inexcusable, but then my temperature was seldom normal in these days. My dear aunt's endeavors to 'nurse up my strength' seemed altogether beside the mark. It was not my strength that wanted nursing, it was my imagination that wanted soothing. I kept the bundle of papers given me by Kurtz, not knowing exactly what to do with it. His mother had died lately, watched over, as I was told, by his Intended. A clean-shaved man, with an official manner and wearing gold-rimmed spectacles, called on me one day and made inquiries, at first

circuitous, afterwards suavely pressing, about what he was pleased to denom-
inate certain 'documents.' I was not surprised, because I had had two rows
with the manager on the subject out there. I had refused to give up the smallest scrap out of that package, and I took the same attitude with the spectacled
man. He became darkly menacing at last, and with much heat argued that the
Company had the right to every bit of information about its 'territories.' And,
said he, 'Mr. Kurtz's knowledge of unexplored regions must have been necessarily extensive and peculiar—owing to his great abilities and to the deplorable circumstances in which he had been placed: therefore'—I assured
him Mr. Kurtz's knowledge, however extensive, did not bear upon the problems of commerce or administration. He invoked then the name of science. 'It
would be an incalculable loss if,' &c., &c. I offered him the report on the
'Suppression of Savage Customs,' with the postscriptum torn off. He took it
up eagerly, but ended by sniffing at it with an air of contempt. 'This is not
what we had a right to expect,' he remarked. 'Expect nothing else,' I said.
'There are only private letters.' He withdrew upon some threat of legal proceedings, and I saw him no more; but another fellow, calling himself Kurtz's
cousin, appeared two days later, and was anxious to hear all the details about
his dear relative's last moments. Incidentally he gave me to understand that
Kurtz had been essentially a great musician. 'There was the making of an immense success,' said the man, who was an organist, I believe, with lank gray
hair flowing over a greasy coat-collar. I had no reason to doubt his statement;
and to this day I am unable to say what was Kurtz's profession, whether he
ever had any—which was the greatest of his talents. I had taken him for a
painter who wrote for the papers, or else for a journalist who could print—but
even the cousin (who took snuff during the interview) could not tell me what
he had been—exactly. He was a universal genius—on that point I agreed with
the old chap, who thereupon blew his nose noisily into a large cotton handkerchief and withdrew in senile agitation, bearing off some family letters and
memoranda without importance. Ultimately a journalist anxious to know
something of the fate of his 'dear colleague' turned up. This visitor informed
me Kurtz's proper sphere ought to have been politics 'on the popular side.'
He had furry straight eyebrows, bristly hair cropped short, an eye-glass on a
broad ribbon, and, becoming expansive, confessed his opinion that Kurtz
really couldn't write a bit—'but heavens! how that man could talk! He electrified large meetings. He had faith—don't you see?—he had the faith. He could
get himself to believe anything—anything. He would have been a splendid
leader of an extreme party.' 'What party?' I asked. 'Any party,' answered the
other. 'He was an—an—extremist.' Did I not think so? I assented. Did I know,
he asked, with a sudden flash of curiosity, 'what it was that had induced him to
go out there?' 'Yes,' said I, and forthwith handed him the famous Report for
publication, if he thought fit. He glanced through it hurriedly, mumbling all
the time, judged 'it would do,' and took himself off with this plunder.

"Thus I was left at last with a slim packet of letters and the girl's portrait.
She struck me as beautiful—I mean she had a beautiful expression. I know
that the sunlight can be made to lie too, yet one felt that no manipulation of
light and pose could have conveyed the delicate shade of truthfulness upon

those features. She seemed ready to listen without mental reservation, without suspicion, without a thought for herself. I concluded I would go and give her back her portrait and those letters myself. Curiosity? Yes; and also some other feeling perhaps. All that had been Kurtz's had passed out of my hands: his soul, his body, his station, his plans, his ivory, his career. There remained only his memory and his Intended—and I wanted to give that up too to the past, in a way,—to surrender personally all that remained of him with me to that oblivion which is the last word of our common fate. I don't defend myself. I had no clear perception of what it was I really wanted. Perhaps it was an impulse of unconscious loyalty, or the fulfillment of one of these ironic necessities that lurk in the facts of human existence. I don't know. I can't tell. But I went.

"I thought his memory was like the other memories of the dead that accumulate in every man's life—a vague impress on the brain of shadows that had fallen on it in their swift and final passage; but before the high and ponderous door, between the tall houses of a street as still and decorous as a well-kept alley in a cemetery, I had a vision of him on the stretcher, opening his mouth voraciously, as if to devour all the earth with all its mankind. He lived then before me; he lived as much as he had ever lived—a shadow insatiable of splendid appearances, of frightful realities; a shadow darker than the shadow of the night, and draped nobly in the folds of a gorgeous eloquence. The vision seemed to enter the house with me—the stretcher, the phantom-bearers, the wild crowd of obedient worshipers, the gloom of the forests, the glitter of the reach between the murky bends, the beat of the drum, regular and muffled like the beating of a heart—the heart of a conquering darkness. It was a moment of triumph for the wilderness, an invading and vengeful rush which, it seemed to me, I would have to keep back alone for the salvation of another soul. And the memory of what I had heard him say afar there, with the horned shapes stirring at my back, in the glow of fires, within the patient woods, those broken phrases came back to me, were heard again in their ominous and terrifying simplicity. I remembered his abject pleading, his abject threats, the colossal scale of his vile desires, the meanness, the torment, the tempestuous anguish of his soul. And later on I seemed to see his collected languid manner, when he said one day, 'This lot of ivory now is really mine. The Company did not pay for it. I collected it myself at a very great personal risk. I am afraid they will try to claim it as theirs though. H'm. It is a difficult case. What do you think I ought to do—resist? Eh? I want no more than justice.' . . . He wanted no more than justice—no more than justice. I rang the bell before a mahogany door on the first floor, and while I waited he seemed to stare at me out of the glassy panel—stare with that wide and immense stare embracing, condemning, loathing all the universe. I seemed to hear the whispered cry, 'The horror! The horror!'

"The dusk was falling. I had to wait in a lofty drawing-room with three long windows from floor to ceiling that were like three luminous and bedraped columns. The bent gilt legs and backs of the furniture shone in indistinct curves. The tall marble fireplace had a cold and monumental whiteness. A grand piano stood massively in a corner, with dark gleams on the flat surfaces like a somber and polished sarcophagus. A high door opened—closed. I rose.

"She came forward, all in black, with a pale head, floating towards me in   165
the dusk. She was in mourning. It was more than a year since his death, more than a year since the news came; she seemed as though she would remember and mourn for ever. She took both my hands in hers and murmured, 'I had heard you were coming.' I noticed she was not very young—I mean not girlish. She had a mature capacity for fidelity, for belief, for suffering. The room seemed to have grown darker, as if all the sad light of the cloudy evening had taken refuge on her forehead. This fair hair, this pale visage, this pure brow, seemed surrounded by an ashy halo from which the dark eyes looked out at me. Their glance was guileless, profound, confident, and trustful. She carried her sorrowful head as though she were proud of that sorrow, as though she would say, I—I alone know how to mourn for him as he deserves. But while we were shaking hands, such a look of awful desolation came upon her face that I perceived she was one of those creatures that are not the playthings of Time. For her he had died only yesterday. And, by Jove! The impression was so powerful that for me too he seemed to have died only yesterday—nay, this very minute. I saw her and him in the same instant of time—his death and her sorrow—I saw her sorrow in the very moment of his death. Do you understand? I saw them together—I heard them together. She had said, with a deep catch of the breath, 'I have survived;' while my strained ears seemed to hear distinctly, mingled with her tone of despairing regret, the summing-up whisper of his eternal condemnation. I asked myself what I was doing there, with a sensation of panic in my heart as though I had blundered into a place of cruel and absurd mysteries not fit for a human being to behold. She motioned me to a chair. We sat down, I laid the packet gently on the little table, and she put her hand over it . . . 'You knew him well,' she murmured, after a moment of mourning silence.

"'Intimacy grows quick out there,' I said. 'I knew him as well as it is possible for one man to know another.'

"'And you admired him,' she said. 'It was impossible to know him and not to admire him. Was it?'

"'He was a remarkable man,' I said, unsteadily. Then before the appealing fixity of her gaze, that seemed to watch for more words on my lips, I went on, 'It was impossible not to—'

"'Love him,' she finished eagerly, silencing me into an appalled dumbness. 'How true! how true! But when you think that no one knew him so well as I! I had all his noble confidence. I knew him best.'

"'You knew him best,' I repeated. And perhaps she did. But with every   170
word spoken the room was growing darker, and only her forehead, smooth and white, remained illumined by the unextinguishable light of belief and love.

"'You were his friend,' she went on. 'His friend,' she repeated, a little louder. 'You must have been, if he had given you this, and sent you to me. I feel I can speak to you—and oh! I must speak. I want you—you who have heard his last words—to know I have been worthy of him. . . . It is not pride. . . . Yes! I am proud to know I understood him better than anyone on earth—he told me so himself. And since his mother died I have had no one—no one—to—to—'

"I listened. The darkness deepened. I was not even sure whether he had given me the right bundle. I rather suspect he wanted me to take care of another batch of his papers which, after his death, I saw the manager examining under the lamp. And the girl talked, easing her pain in the certitude of my sympathy; she talked as thirsty men drink. I had heard that her engagement with Kurtz had been disapproved by her people. He wasn't rich enough or something. And indeed I don't know whether he had not been a pauper all his life. He had given me some reason to infer that it was his impatience of comparative poverty that drove him out there.

"'. . . Who was not his friend who had heard him speak once?' she was saying. 'He drew men towards him by what was best in them.' She looked at me with intensity. 'It is the gift of the great,' she went on, and the sound of her low voice seemed to have the accompaniment of all the other sounds, full of mystery, desolation, and sorrow, I had ever heard—the ripple of the river, the soughing of the trees swayed by the wind, the murmurs of wild crows, the faint ring of incomprehensible words cried from afar, the whisper of a voice speaking from beyond the threshold of an eternal darkness. 'But you have heard him! You know!' she cried.

"'Yes, I know,' I said with something like despair in my heart, but bowing my head before the faith that was in her, before that great and saving illusion that shone with an unearthly glow in the darkness, in the triumphant darkness from which I could not have defended her—from which I could not even defend myself.

"'What a loss to me—to us!'—she corrected herself with beautiful generosity; then added in a murmur, 'To the world.' By the last gleams of twilight I could see the glitter of her eyes, full of tears—of tears that would not fall. 175

"'I have been very happy—very fortunate—very proud,' she went on. 'Too fortunate. Too happy for a little while. And now I am unhappy—for life.'

"She stood up; her fair hair seemed to catch all the remaining light in a glimmer of gold. I rose too.

"'And of all this,' she went on, mournfully, 'of all his promise, and of all his greatness, of his generous mind, of his noble heart, nothing remains—nothing but a memory. You and I—'

"'We shall always remember him,' I said, hastily.

"'No!' she cried. 'It is impossible that all this should be lost—that such a life should be sacrificed to leave nothing—but sorrow. You know what vast plans he had. I knew of them too—I could not perhaps understand,—but others knew of them. Something must remain. His words, at least, have not died.' 180

"'His words will remain,' I said.

"'And his example,' she whispered to herself. 'Men looked up to him,—his goodness shone in every act. His example—'

"'True,' I said; 'his example too. Yes, his example. I forgot that.'

"'But I do not. I cannot—I cannot believe—not yet. I cannot believe that I shall never see him again, that nobody will see him again, never, never, never.'

"She put out her arms as if after a retreating figure, stretching them back 185 and with clasped pale hands across the fading and narrow sheen of the window. Never see him! I saw him clearly enough then. I shall see this eloquent phantom as long as I live, and I shall see her too, a tragic and familiar Shade, resembling in this gesture another one, tragic also, and bedecked with powerless charms, stretching bare brown arms over the glitter of the infernal stream, the stream of darkness. She said suddenly very low, 'He died as he lived.'

"'His end,' said I, with dull anger stirring in me, 'was in every way worthy of his life.'

"'And I was not with him,' she murmured. My anger subsided before a feeling of infinite pity.

"'Everything that could be done—' I mumbled.

"'Ah, but I believed in him more than anyone on earth—more than his own mother, more than—himself. He needed me! Me! I would have treasured every sigh, every word, every sign, every glance.'

"I felt like a chill grip on my chest. 'Don't,' I said, in a muffled voice.   190

"'Forgive me. I—I—have mourned so long in silence—in silence. . . . You were with him—to the last? I think of his loneliness. Nobody near to understand him as I would have understood. Perhaps no one to hear. . . .'

"'To the very end,' I said, shakily. 'I heard his very last words. . . .' I stopped in a fright.

"'Repeat them,' she murmured in a heart-broken tone. 'I want—I want—something—something—to—to live with.'

"I was on the point of crying at her, 'Don't you hear them?' The dusk was repeating them in a persistent whisper all around us, in a whisper that seemed to swell menacingly like the first whisper of a rising wind. 'The horror! The horror!'

"'His last word—to live with,' she insisted. 'Don't you understand I loved   195 him—I loved him—I loved him!'

"I pulled myself together and spoke slowly.

"'The last word he pronounced was—your name.'

"I heard a light sigh, and then my heart stood still, stopped dead short by an exulting and terrible cry, by the cry of inconceivable triumph and of unspeakable pain. 'I knew it—I was sure!' . . . She knew. She was sure. I heard her weeping; she had hidden her face in her hands. It seemed to me that the house would collapse before I could escape, that the heavens would fall upon my head. But nothing happened. The heavens do not fall for such a trifle. Would they have fallen, I wonder, if I had rendered Kurtz that justice which was his due? Hadn't he said he wanted only justice? But I couldn't. I could not tell her. It would have been too dark—too dark altogether. . . ."

Marlow ceased, and sat apart, indistinct and silent, in the pose of a meditating Buddha. Nobody moved for a time. "We have lost the first of the ebb," said the Director, suddenly. I raised my head. The offing was barred by a black bank of clouds, and the tranquil waterway leading to the uttermost ends of the earth flowed somber under an overcast sky—seemed to lead into the heart of an immense darkness.

——— **JOSEPH CONRAD** ———

(1857–1924) Web

Born in Poland, Conrad became a sailor on English ships and retired to become a writer, penning more than eighteen novels and novellas. Many of them involve the sea; many focus on characters who must make choices in ambiguous circumstances. Conrad's command of language is so masterful that it is difficult to believe that his writing is the work of someone for whom English is a third language.

TOPICS FOR CRITICAL THINKING Web

1. Who is the story's narrator?
2. What does it mean that the tall, elegant African woman defies the boat whistle as they take Kurtz away?
3. Why is Marlow compared to a Buddha? How does this image relate to the story's other images?
4. What does Kurtz mean by "The horror, the horror"?
5. Why does Marlow lie to Kurtz's intended?

TOPICS FOR CRITICAL WRITING Web

1. Select a recurrent image and trace it through the story. What various objects and ideas does this image describe? How does it link these various objects and ideas together?
2. In what ways is *Heart of Darkness* not like the "kernel" but like the haze outside?

Modernism

Modernism in literature refers to the gradual shift from the realist, almost empirically-based literature of the nineteenth century to a more subjective, impressionistic literature. Fueled by nineteenth-century critic Matthew Arnold's aesthetic "art-for-art's-sake" movement and avant-garde movements such as Symbolism, modernism focuses on representing impression and individual consciousness and questions both literary form and the reliability of language. Web Modernist fiction represents the subjective perception of temporality, the vagaries of human consciousness ("stream of consciousness"), the loss of shared cultural values, and the sensitivity of the artist in a culture increasingly dulled by technology and mass media. In other words, modernist fiction often describes the ways individuals (often sensitive or artistic people) perceive their world and see that others perceive it completely differently.

As contemporary fiction writer John Barth describes in it "The Literature of Replenishment," modernism is characterized by

[t]he radical disruption of linear flow of narrative; the frustration of conventional expectations concerning unity and coherence of plot and character and the cause

and effect development thereof; the deployment of ironic and ambiguous juxtapo-
sitions to call into question the moral and philosophical meaning of literary action;
the adoption of a tone of epistemological self-mockery aimed at naive pretensions
of bourgeois rationality; the opposition of inward consciousness to rational, public, objective discourse; and an inclination to subjective distortion to point up the
evanescence of the social world of the nineteenth-century bourgeoisie.

Many early-twentieth-century writers from both the United Kingdom
and the United States wrote in a modernist style, though the writings of authors such as E. M. Forster, Katherine Mansfield, D. H. Lawrence, James
Joyce, Virginia Woolf, Ernest Hemingway, Gertrude Stein, F. Scott Fitzgerald, and William Faulkner differ greatly. All of these modernist writers depend on the power of the image as a way to convey complex ideas. All focus
on the subjective experience of the characters as they encounter the ambiguities of modern existence. Many are ironic in their observation of character.
E. M. Forster's "The Road from Colonus" describes an old man's epiphany
while on a trip to Greece and how he subsequently forgets it. An **epiphany,** a
term first used by James Joyce, describes a sudden transcendent insight, the
sense that one sees the truth one has been seeking. Katherine Mansfield's
"The Garden-Party" depicts a young girl's perception of class differences.
D. H. Lawrence's "The Horse-Dealer's Daughter" portrays an accidental but
inevitable falling in love. James Joyce's "Araby" from *Dubliners* tracks the
ironies of a young man's first love. All employ images as the primary medium
for presenting characters and focusing on characters' perceptions.

෨෨෨

E. M. FORSTER

The Road from Colonus   *(1903)*

I

For no very intelligible reason, Mr. Lucas had hurried ahead of his party. He
was perhaps reaching the age at which independence becomes valuable, because it is so soon to be lost. Tired of attention and consideration, he liked
breaking away from the younger members, to ride by himself, and to dis-
mount unassisted. Perhaps he also relished that more subtle pleasure of being
kept waiting for lunch, and of telling the others on their arrival that it was of
no consequence.

So, with childish impatience, he battered the animal's sides with his heels,
and made the muleteer bang it with a thick stick and prick it with a sharp one,
and jolted down the hill sides through clumps of flowering shrubs and stretches
of anemones and asphodel, till he heard the sound of running water, and came
in sight of the group of plane trees where they were to have their meal.

Even in England those trees would have been remarkable, so huge were
they, so interlaced, so magnificently clothed in quivering green. And here in
Greece they were unique, the one cool spot in that hard brilliant landscape,
already scorched by the heat of an April sun. In their midst was hidden a tiny

Khan or country inn, a frail mud building with a broad wooden balcony in which sat an old woman spinning, while a small brown pig, eating orange peel, stood beside her. On the wet earth below squatted two children, playing some primeval game with their fingers; and their mother, none too clean either, was messing with some rice inside. As Mrs. Forman would have said, it was all very Greek, and the fastidious Mr. Lucas felt thankful that they were bringing their own food with them, and should eat it in the open air.

Still, he was glad to be there—the muleteer had helped him off—and glad that Mrs. Forman was not there to forestall his opinions—glad even that he should not see Ethel for quite half an hour. Ethel was his youngest daughter, still unmarried. She was unselfish and affectionate, and it was generally understood that she was to devote her life to her father, and be the comfort of his old age. Mrs. Forman always referred to her as Antigone, and Mr. Lucas tried to settle down to the role of Oedipus, which seemed the only one that public opinion allowed him.

He had this in common with Oedipus, that he was growing old. Even to   5
himself it had become obvious. He had lost interest in other people's affairs, and seldom attended when they spoke to him. He was fond of talking himself but often forgot what he was going to say, and even when he succeeded, it seldom seemed worth the effort. His phrases and gestures had become stiff and set, his anecdotes, once so successful, fell flat, his silence was as meaningless as his speech. Yet he had led a healthy, active life, had worked steadily, made money, educated his children. There was nothing and no one to blame: he was simply growing old.

At the present moment, here he was in Greece, and one of the dreams of his life was realized. Forty years ago he had caught the fever of Hellenism, and all his life he had felt that could he but visit that land, he would not have lived in vain. But Athens had been dusty, Delphi wet, Thermopylae flat, and he had listened with amazement and cynicism to the rapturous exclamations of his companions. Greece was like England: it was a man who was growing old, and it made no difference whether that man looked at the Thames or the Eurotas. It was his last hope of contradicting that logic of experience, and it was failing.

Yet Greece had done something for him, though he did not know it. It had made him discontented, and there are stirrings of life in discontent. He knew that he was not the victim of continual ill-luck. Something great was wrong, and he was pitted against no mediocre or accidental enemy. For the last month a strange desire had possessed him to die fighting.

"Greece is the land for young people," he said to himself as he stood under the plane trees, "but I will enter into it, I will possess it. Leaves shall be green again, water shall be sweet, the sky shall be blue. They were so forty years ago, and I will win them back. I do mind being old, and I will pretend no longer."

He took two steps forward, and immediately cold waters were gurgling over his ankle.

"Where does the water come from?" he asked himself. "I do not even   10
know that." He remembered that all the hill sides were dry; yet here the road was suddenly covered with flowing streams.

He stopped still in amazement, saying: "Water out of a tree—out of a hollow tree? I never saw nor thought of that before."

For the enormous plane that leant towards the Khan was hollow—it had been burnt out for charcoal—and from its living trunk there gushed an impetuous spring, coating the bark with fern and moss, and flowing over the mule track to create fertile meadows beyond. The simple country folk had paid to beauty and mystery such tribute as they could, for in the rind of the tree a shrine was cut, holding a lamp and a little picture of the Virgin, inheritor of the Naiad's and Dryad's joint abode.

"I never saw anything so marvellous before," said Mr. Lucas. "I could even step inside the trunk and see where the water comes from."

For a moment he hesitated to violate the shrine. Then he remembered with a smile his own thought—"the place shall be mine; I will enter it and possess it"—and leapt almost aggressively on to a stone within.

The water pressed up steadily and noiselessly from the hollow roots and   15
hidden crevices of the plane, forming a wonderful amber pool ere it spilt over the lip of bark on to the earth outside. Mr. Lucas tasted it and it was sweet, and when he looked up the black funnel of the trunk he saw sky which was blue, and some leaves which were green; and he remembered, without smiling, another of his thoughts.

Others had been before him—indeed he had a curious sense of companionship. Little votive offerings to the presiding Power were fastened on to the bark—tiny arms and legs and eyes in tin, grotesque models of the brain or the heart—all tokens of some recovery of strength or wisdom or love. There was no such thing as the solitude of nature, for the sorrows and joys of humanity had pressed even into the bosom of a tree. He spread out his arms and steadied himself against the soft charred wood, and then slowly leant back, till his body was resting on the trunk behind. His eyes closed, and he had the strange feeling of one who is moving, yet at peace—the feeling of the swimmer, who, after long struggling with chopping seas, finds that after all the tide will sweep him to his goal.

So he lay motionless, conscious only of the stream below his feet, and that all things were a stream, in which he was moving.

He was aroused at last by a shock—the shock of an arrival perhaps, for when he opened his eyes, something unimagined, indefinable, had passed over all things, and made them intelligible and good.

There was meaning in the stoop of the old woman over her work, and in the quick motions of the little pig, and in her diminishing globe of wool. A young man came singing over the streams on a mule, and there was beauty in his pose and sincerity in his greeting. The sun made no accidental patterns upon the spreading roots of the trees, and there was intention in the nodding clumps of asphodel, and in the music of the water. To Mr. Lucas, who, in a brief space of time, had discovered not only Greece, but England and all the world and life, there seemed nothing ludicrous in the desire to hang within the tree another votive offering—a little model of an entire man.

"Why, here's papa, playing at being Merlin."   20

All unnoticed they had arrived—Ethel, Mrs. Forman, Mr. Graham, and the English-speaking dragoman. Mr. Lucas peered out at them suspiciously. They had suddenly become unfamiliar, and all that they did seemed strained and coarse.

"Allow me to give you a hand," said Mr. Graham, a young man who was always polite to his elders.

Mr. Lucas felt annoyed. "Thank you, I can manage perfectly well by myself," he replied. His foot slipped as he stepped out of the tree, and went into the spring.

"Oh papa, my papa!" said Ethel, "what are you doing? Thank goodness I have got a change for you on the mule."

She tended him carefully, giving him clean socks and dry boots, and then 25 sat him down on the rug beside the lunch basket, while she went with the others to explore the grove.

They came back in ecstasies, in which Mr. Lucas tried to join. But he found them intolerable. Their enthusiasm was superficial, commonplace, and spasmodic. They had no perception of the coherent beauty that was flowering around them. He tried at least to explain his feelings, and what he said was:

"I am altogether pleased with the appearance of this place. It impresses me very favourably. The trees are fine, remarkably fine for Greece, and there is something very poetic in the spring of clear running water. The people too seem kindly and civil. It is decidedly an attractive place."

Mrs. Forman upbraided him for his tepid praise.

"Oh, it is a place in a thousand!" she cried. "I could live and die here! I really would stop if I had not to be back at Athens! It reminds me of the Colonus of Sophocles."

"Well, *I* must stop," said Ethel. "I positively must."   30

"Yes, do! You and your father! Antigone and Oedipus. Of course you must stop at Colonus!"

Mr. Lucas was almost breathless with excitement. When he stood within the tree, he had believed that his happiness would be independent of locality. But these few minutes' conversation had undeceived him. He no longer trusted himself to journey through the world, for old thoughts, old wearinesses might be waiting to rejoin him as soon as he left the shade of the planes, and the music of the virgin water. To sleep in the Khan with the gracious, kind-eyed country people, to watch the bats flit about within the globe of shade, and see the moon turn the golden patterns into silver—one such night would place him beyond relapse, and confirm him for ever in the kingdom he had regained. But all his lips could say was: "I should be willing to put in a night here."

"You mean a week, papa! It would be sacrilege to put in less."

"A week then, a week," said his lips, irritated at being corrected, while his heart was leaping with joy. All through lunch he spoke to them no more, but watched the place he should know so well, and the people who would so soon be his companions and friends. The inmates of the Khan only consisted of an old woman, a middle-aged woman, a young man and two children, and to none of them had he spoken, yet he loved them as he loved everything that moved or breathed or existed beneath the benedictory shade of the planes.

"*En route!*" said the shrill voice of Mrs. Forman. "Ethel! Mr. Graham! 35 The best of things must end."

"To-night," thought Mr. Lucas, "they will light the little lamp by the shrine. And when we all sit together on the balcony, perhaps they will tell me which offerings they put up."

"I beg your pardon, Mr. Lucas," said Graham, "but they want to fold up the rug you are sitting on."

Mr. Lucas got up, saying to himself: "Ethel shall go to bed first, and then I will try to tell them about my offering too—for it is a thing I must do. I think they will understand if I am left with them alone."

Ethel touched him on the cheek. "Papa! I've called you three times. All the mules are here."

"Mules? What mules?"   40

"Our mules. We're all waiting. Oh, Mr. Graham, do help my father on."

"I don't know what you're talking about, Ethel."

"My dearest papa, we must start. You know we have to get to Olympia to-night."

Mr. Lucas in pompous, confident tones replied: "I always did wish, Ethel, that you had a better head for plans. You know perfectly well that we are putting in a week here. It is your own suggestion."

Ethel was startled into impoliteness. "What a perfectly ridiculous idea.   45
You must have known I was joking. Of course I meant I wished we could."

"Ah! if we could only do what we wished!" sighed Mrs. Forman, already seated on her mule.

"Surely," Ethel continued in calmer tones, "you didn't think I meant it."

"Most certainly I did. I have made all my plans on the supposition that we are stopping here, and it will be extremely inconvenient, indeed, impossible for me to start."

He delivered this remark with an air of great conviction, and Mrs. Forman and Mr. Graham had to turn away to hide their smiles.

"I am sorry I spoke so carelessly; it was wrong of me. But, you know, we   50
can't break up our party, and even one night here would make us miss the boat at Patras."

Mrs. Forman, in an aside, called Mr. Graham's attention to the excellent way in which Ethel managed her father.

"I don't mind about the Patras boat. You said that we should stop here, and we are stopping."

It seemed as if the inhabitants of the Khan had divined in some mysterious way that the altercation touched them. The old woman stopped her spinning, while the young man and the two children stood behind Mr. Lucas, as if supporting him.

Neither arguments nor entreaties moved him. He said little, but he was absolutely determined, because for the first time he saw his daily life aright. What need had he to return to England? Who would miss him? His friends were dead or cold. Ethel loved him in a way, but, as was right, she had other interests. His other children he seldom saw. He had only one other relative, his sister Julia, whom he both feared and hated. It was no effort to struggle. He would be a fool as well as a coward if he stirred from the place which brought him happiness and peace.

At last Ethel, to humour him, and not disinclined to air her modern   55

Greek, went into the Khan with the astonished dragoman to look at the rooms. The woman inside received them with loud welcomes, and the young man, when no one was looking, began to lead Mr. Lucas' mule to the stable.

"Drop it, you brigand!" shouted Graham, who always declared that foreigners could understand English if they chose. He was right, for the man obeyed, and they all stood waiting for Ethel's return.

She emerged at last, with close-gathered skirts, followed by the dragoman bearing the little pig, which he had bought at a bargain.

"My dear papa, I will do all I can for you, but stop in that Khan—no."

"Are there—fleas?" asked Mrs. Forman.

Ethel intimated that "fleas" was not the word.   60

"Well, I am afraid that settles it," said Mrs. Forman, "I know how particular Mr. Lucas is."

"It does not settle it," said Mr. Lucas. "Ethel, you go on. I do not want you. I don't know why I ever consulted you. I shall stop here alone."

"That is absolute nonsense," said Ethel, losing her temper. "How can you be left alone at your age? How would you get your meals or your bath? All your letters are waiting for you at Patras. You'll miss the boat. That means missing the London operas, and upsetting all your engagements for the month. And as if you could travel by yourself!"

"They might knife you," was Mr. Graham's contribution.

The Greeks said nothing; but whenever Mr. Lucas looked their way, they   65 beckoned him towards the Khan. The children would even have drawn him by the coat, and the old woman on the balcony stopped her almost completed spinning, and fixed him with mysterious appealing eyes. As he fought, the issue assumed gigantic proportions, and he believed that he was not merely stopping because he had regained youth or seen beauty or found happiness, but because in that place and with those people a supreme event was awaiting him which would transfigure the face of the world. The moment was so tremendous that he abandoned words and arguments as useless, and rested on the strength of his mighty unrevealed allies: silent men, murmuring water, and whispering trees. For the whole place called with one voice, articulate to him, and his garrulous opponents became every minute more meaningless and absurd. Soon they would be tired and go chattering away into the sun, leaving him to the cool grove and the moonlight and the destiny he foresaw.

Mrs. Forman and the dragoman had indeed already started, amid the piercing screams of the little pig, and the struggle might have gone on indefinitely if Ethel had not called in Mr. Graham.

"Can you help me?" she whispered. "He is absolutely unmanageable."

"I'm no good at arguing—but if I could help you in any other way——" and he looked down complacently at his well-made figure.

Ethel hesitated. Then she said: "Help me in any way you can. After all, it is for his good that we do it."

"Then have his mule led up behind him."   70

So when Mr. Lucas thought he had gained the day, he suddenly felt himself lifted off the ground, and sat sideways on the saddle, and at the same time the mule started off at a trot. He said nothing, for he had nothing to say, and even his face showed little emotion as he felt the shade pass and heard the sound of the water cease. Mr. Graham was running at his side, hat in hand, apologizing.

"I know I had no business to do it, and I do beg your pardon awfully. But I do hope that some day you too will feel that I was—damn!"

A stone had caught him in the middle of the back. It was thrown by the little boy, who was pursuing them along the mule track. He was followed by his sister, also throwing stones.

Ethel screamed to the dragoman, who was some way ahead with Mrs. Forman, but before he could rejoin them, another adversary appeared. It was the young Greek, who had cut them off in front, and now dashed down at Mr. Lucas' bridle. Fortunately Graham was an expert boxer, and it did not take him a moment to beat down the youth's feeble defence, and to send him sprawling with a bleeding mouth into the asphodel. By this time the dragoman had arrived, the children, alarmed at the fate of their brother, had desisted, and the rescue party, if such it is to be considered, retired in disorder to the trees.

"Little devils!" said Graham, laughing with triumph. "That's the modern   75
Greek all over. Your father meant money if he stopped, and they consider we were taking it out of their pocket."

"Oh, they are terrible—simple savages! I don't know how I shall ever thank you. You've saved my father."

"I only hope you didn't think me brutal."

"No," replied Ethel with a little sigh. "I admire strength."

Meanwhile the cavalcade reformed, and Mr. Lucas, who, as Mrs. Forman said, bore his disappointment wonderfully well, was put comfortably on to his mule. They hurried up the opposite hillside, fearful of another attack, and it was not until they had left the eventful place far behind that Ethel found an opportunity to speak to her father and ask his pardon for the way she had treated him.

"You seemed so different, dear father, and you quite frightened me. Now   80
I feel that you are your old self again."

He did not answer, and she concluded that he was not unnaturally offended at her behaviour.

By one of those curious tricks of mountain scenery, the place they had left an hour before suddenly reappeared far below them. The Khan was hidden under the green dome, but in the open there still stood three figures, and through the pure air rose up a faint cry of defiance or farewell.

Mr. Lucas stopped irresolutely, and let the reins fall from his hand.

"Come, father dear," said Ethel gently.

He obeyed, and in another moment a spur of the hill hid the dangerous   85
scene for ever.

II

It was breakfast time, but the gas was alight, owing to the fog. Mr. Lucas was in the middle of an account of a bad night he had spent. Ethel, who was to be married in a few weeks, had her arms on the table, listening.

"First the door bell rang, then you came back from the theatre. Then the dog started, and after the dog the cat. And at three in the morning a young hooligan passed by singing. Oh yes: then there was the water gurgling in the pipe above my head."

"I think that was only the bath water running away," said Ethel, looking rather worn.

"Well, there's nothing I dislike more than running water. It's perfectly impossible to sleep in the house. I shall give it up. I shall give notice next quarter. I shall tell the landlord plainly, 'The reason I am giving up the house is this: it is perfectly impossible to sleep in it.' If he says—says—well, what has he got to say?"

"Some more toast, father?"   90

"Thank you, my dear." He took it, and there was an interval of peace.

But he soon recommenced. "I'm not going to submit to the practising next door as tamely as they think. I wrote and told them so—didn't I?"

"Yes," said Ethel, who had taken care that the letter should not reach. "I have seen the governess, and she has promised to arrange it differently. And Aunt Julia hates noise. It will sure to be all right."

Her aunt, being the only unattached member of the family, was coming to keep house for her father when she left him. The reference was not a happy one, and Mr. Lucas commenced a series of half articulate sighs, which was only stopped by the arrival of the post.

"Oh, what a parcel!" cried Ethel. "For me! What can it be! Greek stamps.   95
This is most exciting!"

It proved to be some asphodel bulbs, sent by Mrs. Forman from Athens for planting in the conservatory.

"Doesn't it bring it all back! You remember the asphodels, father. And all wrapped up in Greek newspapers. I wonder if I can read them still. I used to be able to, you know."

She rattled on, hoping to conceal the laughter of the children next door— a favourite source of querulousness at breakfast time.

"Listen to me! 'A rural disaster.' Oh, I've hit on something sad. But never mind. 'Last Tuesday at Plataniste, in the province of Messenia, a shocking tragedy occurred. A large tree'—aren't I getting on well?—'blew down in the night and'—wait a minute—oh, dear! 'crushed to death the five occupants of the little Khan there, who had apparently been sitting in the balcony. The bodies of Maria Rhomaides, the aged proprietress, and of her daughter, aged forty-six, were easily recognizable, whereas that of her grandson'—oh, the rest is really too horrid; I wish I had never tried it, and what's more I feel to have heard the name Plataniste before. We didn't stop there, did we, in the spring?"

"We had lunch," said Mr. Lucas, with a faint expression of trouble on his   100
vacant face. "Perhaps it was where the dragoman bought the pig."

"Of course," said Ethel in a nervous voice. "Where the dragoman bought the little pig. How terrible!"

"Very terrible!" said her father, whose attention was wandering to the noisy children next door. Ethel suddenly started to her feet with genuine interest.

"Good gracious!" she exclaimed. "This is an old paper. It happened not lately but in April—the night of Tuesday the eighteenth—and we—we must have been there in the afternoon."

"So we were," said Mr. Lucas. She put her hand to her heart, scarcely able to speak.

"Father, dear father, I must say it: you wanted to stop there. All those   105 people, those poor half-savage people, tried to keep you, and they're dead. The whole place, it says, is in ruins, and even the stream has changed its course. Father, dear, if it had not been for me, and if Arthur had not helped me, you must have been killed."

Mr. Lucas waved his hand irritably. "It is not a bit of good speaking to the governess, I shall write to the landlord and say, 'The reason I am giving up the house is this: the dog barks, the children next door are intolerable, and I cannot stand the noise of running water.'"

Ethel did not check his babbling. She was aghast at the narrowness of the escape, and for a long time kept silence. At last she said: "Such a marvellous deliverance does make one believe in Providence."

Mr. Lucas, who was still composing his letter to the landlord, did not reply.

─────── **EDWARD MORGAN FORSTER** ───────

www

www   *(1879–1970)* **Web**

A part of the Bloomsbury Group **Web** , Forster wrote novels and stories that often focus on failures of communication among people of different classes and aspirations. His work often conveys the drabness of middle class existence, comparing it to the more spontaneous life in such Mediterranean countries as Italy and Greece. Five of his novels have been adapted to film.

www   *TOPICS FOR CRITICAL THINKING* **Web**

1. In what ways is "The Road from Colonus" a retelling of the Oedipus myth? (See **myth criticism** and the discussion in Chapter 43.

2. How does Mr. Lucas change when he enters the plane tree? What insight does he gain?

3. Why does Mr. Lucas detest the sound of water at the story's end?

4. Is this story ironic? In what ways?

www   *TOPICS FOR CRITICAL WRITING* **Web**

1. Select one recurrent image or motif and discuss how it functions through the story.

2. How does setting convey entirely different ways of seeing the world?

KATHERINE MANSFIELD

The Garden-Party (1924)

And after all the weather was ideal. They could not have had a more perfect day for a garden-party if they had ordered it. Windless, warm, the sky without a cloud. Only the blue was veiled with a haze of light gold, as it is sometimes in early summer. The gardener had been up since dawn, mowing the lawns and sweeping them, until the grass and the dark flat rosettes where the daisy plants had been seemed to shine. As for the roses, you could not help feeling they understood that roses are the only flowers that impress people at garden-parties; the only flowers that everybody is certain of knowing. Hundreds, yes, literally hundreds, had come out in a single night; the green bushes bowed down as though they had been visited by archangels.

Breakfast was not yet over before the men came to put up the marquee.

"Where do you want the marquee put, mother?"

"My dear child, it's no use asking me. I'm determined to leave everything to you children this year. Forget I am your mother. Treat me as an honoured guest."

But Meg could not possibly go and supervise the men. She had washed her hair before breakfast, and she sat drinking her coffee in a green turban, with a dark wet curl stamped on each cheek. Jose, the butterfly, always came down in a silk petticoat and a kimono jacket.

"You'll have to go, Laura; you're the artistic one."

Away Laura flew, still holding her piece of bread-and-butter. It's so delicious to have an excuse for eating out of doors, and besides, she loved having to arrange things; she always felt she could do it so much better than anybody else.

Four men in their shirt sleeves stood grouped together on the garden path. They carried staves covered with rolls of canvas, and they had big tool-bags slung on their backs. They looked impressive. Laura wished now that she had not got the bread-and-butter, but there was nowhere to put it, and she couldn't possibly throw it away. She blushed and tried to look severe and even a little bit short-sighted as she came up to them.

"Good morning," she said, copying her mother's voice. But that sounded so fearfully affected that she was ashamed, and stammered like a little girl, "Oh—er—have you come—is it about the marquee?"

"That's right, miss," said the tallest of the men, a lanky, freckled fellow, and he shifted his tool-bag, knocked back his straw hat and smiled down at her. "That's about it."

His smile was so easy, so friendly that Laura recovered. What nice eyes he had, small, but such a dark blue! And now she looked at the others, they were smiling too. "Cheer-up, we won't bite," their smile seemed to say. How very nice workmen were! And what a beautiful morning! She mustn't mention the morning; she must be business like. The marquee.

"Well, what about the lily-lawn? Would that do?"

And she pointed to the lily-lawn with the hand that didn't hold the bread-and-butter. They turned, they stared in the direction. A little fat chap thrust out his under-lip, and the tall fellow frowned.

"I don't fancy it," said he. "Not conspicuous enough. You see, with a thing like a marquee," and he turned to Laura in his easy way, "you want to put it somewhere where it'll give you a bang slap in the eye, if you follow me."

Laura's upbringing made her wonder for a moment whether it was quite   15
respectful of a workman to talk to her of bangs slap in the eye. But she did quite follow him.

"A corner of the tennis-court," she suggested. "But the band's going to be in one corner."

"H'm, going to have a band, are you?" said another of the workmen. He was pale. He had a haggard look as his dark eyes scanned the tennis-court. What was he thinking?

"Only a very small band," said Laura gently. Perhaps he wouldn't mind so much if the band was quite small. But the tall fellow interrupted.

"Look here, miss, that's the place. Against those trees. Over there. That'll do fine."

Against the karakas. Then the karaka trees would be hidden. And they   20
were so lovely, with their broad, gleaming leaves, and their clusters of yellow fruit. They were like trees you imagined growing on a desert island, proud, solitary, lifting their leaves and fruits to the sun in a kind of silent splendour. Must they be hidden by a marquee?

They must. Already the men had shouldered their staves and were making for the place. Only the tall fellow was left. He bent down, pinched a sprig of lavender, put his thumb and forefinger to his nose and snuffed up the smell. When Laura saw that gesture she forgot all about the karakas in her wonder at him caring for things like that—caring for the smell of lavender. How many men that she knew would have done such a thing? Oh, how extraordinarily nice workmen were, she thought. Why couldn't she have workmen for friends rather than the silly boys she danced with and who came to Sunday night supper? She would get on much better with men like these.

It's all the fault, she decided, as the tall fellow drew something on the back of an envelope, something that was to be looped up or left to hang, of these absurd class distinctions. Well, for her part, she didn't feel them. Not a bit, not an atom. . . . And now there came the chock-chock of wooden hammers. Some one whistled, some one sang out, "Are you right there, matey?" "Matey!" The friendliness of it, the—the— Just to prove how happy she was, just to show the tall fellow how at home she felt, and how she despised stupid conventions, Laura took a big bite of her bread-and-butter as she stared at the little drawing. She felt just like a work-girl.

"Laura, Laura, where are you? Telephone, Laura!" a voice cried from the house.

"Coming!" Away she skimmed, over the lawn, up the path, up the steps, across the verandah, and into the porch. In the hall her father and Laurie were brushing their hats ready to go to the office.

"I say, Laura," said Laurie very fast, "you might just give a squiz at my 25 coat before this afternoon. See if it wants pressing."

"I will," she said. Suddenly she couldn't stop herself. She ran at Laurie and gave him a small, quick squeeze. "Oh, I do love parties, don't you?" gasped Laura.

"Rather," said Laurie's warm, boyish voice, and he squeezed his sister too, and gave her a gentle push. "Dash off to the telephone, old girl."

The telephone. "Yes, yes; oh yes. Kitty? Good morning, dear. Come to lunch? Do, dear. Delighted of course. It will only be a very scratch meal—just the sandwich crusts and broken meringue-shells and what's left over. Yes, isn't it a perfect morning? Your white? Oh, I certainly should. One moment—hold the line. Mother's calling." And Laura sat back. "What, mother? Can't hear."

Mrs. Sheridan's voice floated down the stairs. "Tell her to wear that sweet hat she had on last Sunday."

"Mother says you're to wear that *sweet* hat you had on last Sunday. Good. 30 One o'clock. Bye-bye."

Laura put back the receiver, flung her arms over her head, took a deep breath, stretched and let them fall. "Huh," she sighed, and the moment after the sigh she sat up quickly. She was still, listening. All the doors in the house seemed to open. The house was alive with soft, quick steps and running voices. The green baize door that led to the kitchen regions swung open and shut with a muffled thud. And now there came a long, chuckling absurd sound. It was the heavy piano being moved on its stiff castors. But the air! If you stopped to notice, was the air always like this? Little faint winds were playing chase, in at the tops of the windows, out at the doors. And there were two tiny spots of sun, one on the inkpot, one on a silver photograph frame, playing too. Darling little spots. Especially the one on the inkpot lid. It was quite warm. A warm little silver star. She could have kissed it.

The front door bell pealed, and there sounded the rustle of Sadie's print skirt on the stairs. A man's voice murmured; Sadie answered, careless, "I'm sure I don't know. Wait. I'll ask Mrs. Sheridan."

"What is it, Sadie?" Laura came into the hall.

"It's the florist, Miss Laura."

It was, indeed. There, just inside the door, stood a wide, shallow tray 35 full of pots of pink lilies. No other kind. Nothing but lilies—canna lilies, big pink flowers, wide open, radiant, almost frighteningly alive on bright crimson stems.

"O-oh, Sadie!" said Laura, and the sound was like a little moan. She crouched down as if to warm herself at that blaze of lilies; she felt they were in her fingers, on her lips, growing in her breast.

"It's some mistake," she said faintly. "Nobody ever ordered so many. Sadie, go and find mother."

But at that moment Mrs. Sheridan joined them.

"It's quite right," she said calmly. "Yes, I ordered them. Aren't they lovely?" She pressed Laura's arm. "I was passing the shop yesterday, and I saw them in the window. And I suddenly thought for once in my life I shall have enough canna lilies. The garden-party will be a good excuse."

"But I thought you said you didn't mean to interfere," said Laura. Sadie   40
had gone. The florist's man was still outside at his van. She put her arm round
her mother's neck and gently, very gently, she bit her mother's ear.

"My darling child, you wouldn't like a logical mother, would you? Don't
do that. Here's the man."

He carried more lilies still, another whole tray.

"Bank them up, just inside the door, on both sides of the porch, please,"
said Mrs. Sheridan. "Don't you agree, Laura?"

"Oh, I *do* mother."

In the drawing-room, Meg, Jose and good little Hans had at last suc-   45
ceeded in moving the piano.

"Now, if we put this chesterfield against the wall and move everything out
of the room except the chairs, don't you think?"

"Quite."

"Hans, move these tables into the smoking-room, and bring a sweeper to
take these marks off the carpet and—one moment, Hans—" Jose loved giving
orders to the servants, and they loved obeying her. She always made them feel
they were taking part in some drama. "Tell mother and Miss Laura to come
here at once."

"Very good, Miss Jose."

She turned to Meg. "I want to hear what the piano sounds like, just in   50
case I'm asked to sing this afternoon. Let's try over 'This life is Weary.'"

Pom! Ta-ta-ta *Tee*-ta! The piano burst out so passionately that Jose's face
changed. She clasped her hands. She looked mournfully and enigmatically at
her mother and Laura as they came in.

> This Life is *Wee*-ary,
> A Tear—a Sigh.
> A Love that *Chan*-ges,
>   This life is *Wee*-ary,
> A Tear—a Sigh.
> A Love that *Chan*-ges,
> And then . . . Good-bye!

But at the word "Good-bye," and although the piano sounded more
desperate than ever, her face broke into a brilliant, dreadfully unsympathetic smile.

"Aren't I in good voice, mummy?" she beamed.

> This Life is *Wee*-ary,
> Hope come to Die.
> A Dream—a *Wa*-kening.

But now Sadie interrupted them. "What is it, Sadie?"

"If you please, m'm, cook says have you got the flags for the sandwiches?"   55

"The flags for the sandwiches, Sadie?" echoed Mrs. Sheridan dreamily.
And the children knew by her face that she hadn't got them. "Let me see."
And she said to Sadie firmly, "Tell cook I'll let her have them in ten minutes."

Sadie went.

"Now, Laura," said her mother quickly. "Come with me into the smoking-room. I've got the names somewhere on the back of an envelope. You'll have to write them out for me. Meg, go upstairs this minute and take that wet thing off your head. Jose, run and finish dressing this instant. Do you hear me, children, or shall I have to tell your father when he comes home to-night? And—and, Jose, pacify cook if you do go into the kitchen, will you? I'm terrified of her this morning."

The envelope was found at last behind the dining-room clock, though how it had got there Mrs. Sheridan could not imagine.

"One of you children must have stolen it out of my bag, because I re-   60
member vividly—cream cheese and lemon-curd. Have you done that?"

"Yes."

"Egg and—" Mrs. Sheridan held the envelope away from her. "It looks like mice. It can't be mice, can it?"

"Olive, pet," said Laura, looking over her shoulder.

"Yes, of course, olive. What a horrible combination it sounds. Egg and olive."

They were finished at last, and Laura took them off to the kitchen. She   65
found Jose there pacifying the cook, who did not look at all terrifying.

"I have never seen such exquisite sandwiches," said Jose's rapturous voice. "How many kinds did you say there were, cook? Fifteen?"

"Fifteen, Miss Jose."

"Well, cook, I congratulate you."

Cook swept up crusts with the long sandwich knife, and smiled broadly.

"Godber's has come," announced Sadie, issuing out of the pantry. She had   70
seen the man pass the window.

That meant the cream puffs had come. Godber's were famous for their cream puffs. Nobody ever thought of making them at home.

"Bring them in and put them on the table, my girl," ordered cook.

Sadie brought them in and went back to the door. Of course Laura and Jose were far too grown-up to really care about such things. All the same, they couldn't help agreeing that the puffs looked very attractive. Very. Cook began arranging them, shaking off the extra icing sugar.

"Don't they carry one back to all one's parties?" said Laura.

"I suppose they do," said practical Jose, who never liked to be carried   75
back. "They look beautifully light and feathery, I must say."

"Have one each, my dears," said cook in her comfortable voice. "Yer ma won't know."

Oh, impossible. Fancy cream puffs so soon after breakfast. The very idea made one shudder. All the same, two minutes later Jose and Laura were licking their fingers with that absorbed inward look that only comes from whipped cream.

"Let's go into the garden, out by the back way," suggested Laura. "I want to see how the men are getting on with the marquee. They're such awfully nice men."

But the back door was blocked by cook, Sadie, Godber's man and Hans.

Something had happened.   80

"Tuk-tuk-tuk," clucked cook like an agitated hen. Sadie had her hand clapped to her cheek as though she had toothache. Hans' face was screwed up in the effort to understand. Only Godber's man seemed to be enjoying himself; it was his story.

"What's the matter? What's happened?"

"There's been a horrible accident," said cook. "A man killed."

"A man killed! Where? How? When?"

But Godber's man wasn't going to have his story snatched from under his   85
very nose.

"Know those little cottages just below here, miss?" Know them? Of course, she knew them. "Well, there's a young chap living there, name of Scott, a carter. His horse shied at a traction-engine, corner of Hawke Street this morning, and he was thrown out on the back of his head. Killed."

"Dead!" Laura stared at Godber's man.

"Dead when they picked him up," said Godber's man with relish. "They were taking the body home as I come up here." And he said to the cook, "He's left a wife and five little ones."

"Jose, come here." Laura caught hold of her sister's sleeve and dragged her through the kitchen to the other side of the green baize door. There she paused and leaned against it. "Jose!" she said, horrified, "however are we going to stop everything?"

"Stop everything, Laura!" cried Jose in astonishment. "What do you mean?"   90

"Stop the garden-party, of course." Why did Jose pretend?

But Jose was still more amazed. "Stop the garden-party? My dear Laura, don't be so absurd. Of course we can't do anything of the kind. Nobody expects us to. Don't be so extravagant."

"But we can't possibly have a garden-party with a man dead just outside the front gate."

That really was extravagant, for the little cottages were in a lane to themselves at the very bottom of a steep rise that led up to the house. A broad road ran between. True, they were far too near. They were the greatest possible eyesore, and they had no right to be in that neighbourhood at all. They were little mean dwellings painted a chocolate brown. In the garden patches there was nothing but cabbage stalks, sick hens and tomato cans. The very smoke coming out of their chimneys was poverty-stricken. Little rags and shreds of smoke, so unlike the great silvery plumes that uncurled from the Sheridans' chimneys. Washerwomen lived in the lane and sweeps and a cobbler, and a man whose house-front was studded all over with minute bird-cages. Children swarmed. When the Sheridans were little they were forbidden to set foot there because of the revolting language and of what they might catch. But since they were grown up, Laura and Laurie on their prowls sometimes walked through. It was disgusting and sordid. They came out with a shudder. But still one must go everywhere; one must see everything. So through they went.

"And just think of what the band would sound like to that poor woman,"   95
said Laura.

"Oh, Laura!" Jose began to be seriously annoyed. "If you're going to stop a band playing every time some one has an accident, you'll lead a very strenuous life. I'm every bit as sorry about it as you. I feel just as sympathetic." Her eyes hardened. She looked at her sister just as she used to when they were little and fighting together. "You won't bring a drunken workman back to life by being sentimental," she said softly.

"Drunk! Who said he was drunk?" Laura turned furiously on Jose. She said, just as they had used to say on those occasions, "I'm going straight up to tell mother."

"Do, dear," cooed Jose.

"Mother, can I come into your room?" Laura turned the big glass doorknob.

"Of course, child. Why, what's the matter? What's given you such a colour?" And Mrs. Sheridan turned round from her dressing table. She was trying on a new hat.

"Mother, a man's been killed," began Laura.

"*Not* in the garden?" interrupted her mother.

"No, no!"

"Oh, what a fright you gave me!" Mrs. Sheridan sighed with relief, and took off the big hat and held it on her knees.

"But listen, mother," said Laura. Breathless, half-choking, she told the dreadful story. "Of course, we can't have our party, can we?" she pleaded. "The band and everybody arriving. They'd hear us, mother, they're nearly neighbours!"

To Laura's astonishment her mother behaved just like Jose; it was harder to bear because she seemed amused. She refused to take Laura seriously.

"But, my dear child, use your common sense. It's only by accident we've heard of it. If some one had died there normally—and I can't understand how they keep alive in those poky little holes—we should still be having our party, shouldn't we?"

Laura had to say "yes" to that, but she felt it was all wrong. She sat down on her mother's sofa and pinched the cushion frill.

"Mother, isn't it really terribly heartless of us?" she asked.

"Darling!" Mrs. Sheridan got up and came over to her, carrying the hat. Before Laura could stop her she had popped it on. "My child," said her mother, "the hat is yours. It's made for you. It's much too young for me. I have never seen you look such a picture. Look at yourself!" And she held up her hand-mirror.

"But, mother," Laura began again. She couldn't look at herself; she turned aside.

This time Mrs. Sheridan lost patience just as Jose had done.

"You are being very absurd, Laura," she said coldly. "People like that don't expect sacrifices from us. And it's not very sympathetic to spoil everybody's enjoyment as you're doing now."

"I don't understand," said Laura, and she walked quickly out of the room into her own bedroom. There, quite by chance, the first thing she saw was this charming girl in the mirror, in her black hat trimmed with gold daisies, and a long black velvet ribbon. Never had she imagined she could look like that. Is mother right? she thought. And now she hoped her mother was right. Am I being extravagant? Perhaps it was extravagant. Just for a moment she had another glimpse of that poor woman and those little children, and the body being carried into the house. But it all seemed blurred, unreal, like a picture in the newspaper. I'll remember it again after the party's over, she decided. And somehow that seemed quite the best plan. . . .

Lunch was over by half past one. By half past two they were all ready for   115
the fray. The green-coated band had arrived and was established in a corner of the tennis-court.

"My dear!" trilled Kitty Maitland, "aren't they too like frogs for words? You ought to have arranged them round the pond with the conductor in the middle on a leaf."

Laurie arrived and hailed them on his way to dress. At the sight of him Laura remembered the accident again. She wanted to tell him. If Laurie agreed with the others, then it was bound to be all right. And she followed him into the hall.

"Laurie!" "Hallo!" He was half-way upstairs, but when he turned around and saw Laura he suddenly puffed out his cheeks and goggled his eyes at her. "My word, Laura; you do look stunning," said Laurie. "What an absolutely topping hat!"

Laura said faintly "Is it?" and smiled up at Laurie, and didn't tell him after all.

Soon after that people began coming in streams. The band struck up; the   120
hired waiters ran from the house to the marquee. Wherever you looked there were couples strolling, bending to the flowers, greeting, moving on over the lawn. They were like bright birds that had alighted in the Sheridans' garden for this one afternoon, on their way to—where? Ah, what happiness it is to be with people who all are happy, to press hands, press cheeks, smile into eyes.

"Darling Laura, how well you look!"

"What a becoming hat, child!"

"Laura, you look quite Spanish. I've never seen you look so striking."

And Laura, glowing, answered softly, "Have you had tea? Won't you have an ice? The passion-fruit ices really are rather special." She ran to her father and begged him. "Daddy darling, can't the band have something to drink?"

And the perfect afternoon slowly ripened, slowly faded, slowly its petals   125
closed.

"Never a more delightful garden-party . . ." "The greatest success . . ." "Quite the most . . ."

Laura helped her mother with the good-byes. They stood side by side in the porch till it was all over.

"All over, all over, thank heaven," said Mrs. Sheridan. "Round in the others, Laura. Let's go and have some fresh coffee. I'm exhausted. Yes, it's been very successful. But oh, these parties, these parties! Why will you children insist on giving parties!" And they all of them sat down in the deserted marquee.

"Have a sandwich, daddy dear. I wrote the flag."

"Thanks." Mr. Sheridan took a bite and the sandwich was gone. He took   130 another. "I suppose you didn't hear of a beastly accident that happened to-day?" he said.

"My dear," said Mrs. Sheridan, holding up her hand, "we did. It nearly ruined the party. Laura insisted we should put it off."

"Oh, mother!" Laura didn't want to be teased about it.

"It was a horrible affair all the same," said Mr. Sheridan. "The chap was married too. Lived just below in the lane, and leaves a wife and half a dozen kiddies, so they say."

An awkward little silence fell. Mrs. Sheridan fidgeted with her cup. Really, it was very tactless of father . . .

Suddenly she looked up. There on the table were all those sandwiches,   135
cakes, puffs, all uneaten, all going to be wasted. She had one of her brilliant ideas.

"I know," she said. "Let's make up a basket. Let's send that poor creature some of this perfectly good food. At any rate, it will be the greatest treat for the children. Don't you agree? And she's sure to have neighbours calling in and so on. What a point to have it all ready prepared. Laura!" She jumped up. "Get me the big basket out of the stairs cupboard."

"But, mother, do you really think it's a good idea?" said Laura.

Again, how curious, she seemed to be different from them all. To take scraps from their party. Would the poor woman really like that?

"Of course!" What's the matter with you to-day? An hour or two ago you were insisting on us being sympathetic, and now—"

Oh, well! Laura ran for the basket. It was filled, it was heaped by her mother.   140

"Take it yourself, darling," said she. "Run down just as you are. No, wait, take the arum lilies too. People of that class are so impressed by arum lilies."

"The stems will ruin her lace frock," said practical Jose.

So they would. Just in time. "Only the basket, then. And, Laura!"—her mother followed her out of the marquee—"don't on any account—"

"What, mother?"

No, better not put such ideas into the child's head! "Nothing! Run along."   145

It was just growing dusky as Laura shut their garden gates. A big dog ran by like a shadow. The road gleamed white, and down below in the hollow the little cottages were in deep shade. How quiet it seemed after the afternoon. Here she was going down the hill to somewhere where a man lay dead, and she couldn't realize it. Why couldn't she? She stopped a minute. And it seemed to her that kisses, voices, tinkling spoons, laughter, the smell of crushed grass were somehow inside her. She had no room for anything else. How strange! She looked up at the pale sky, and all she thought was, "Yes, it was the most successful party."

Now the broad road was crossed. The lane began, smoky and dark. Women in shawls and men's tweed caps hurried by. Men hung over the palings; the children played in the doorways. A low hum came from the mean little cottages. In some of them there was a flicker of light, and a shadow, crab-like, moved across the window. Laura bent her head and hurried on. She wished now she had put on a coat. How her frock shone! And the big hat with the velvet streamer—if only it was another hat! Were the people looking at her? They must be. It was a mistake to have come; she knew all along it was a mistake. Should she go back even now?

No, too late. This was the house. It must be. A dark knot of people stood outside. Beside the gate an old, old woman with a crutch sat in a chair, watching. She had her feet on a newspaper. The voices stopped as Laura drew near. The group parted. It was as though she was expected, as though they had known she was coming here.

Laura was terribly nervous. Tossing the velvet ribbon over her shoulder, she said to a woman standing by, "Is this Mrs. Scott's house?" and the woman, smiling queerly, said, "It is, my lass."

Oh, to be away from this! She actually said, "Help me, God," as she   150
walked up the tiny path and knocked. To be away from those staring eyes, or to be covered up in anything, one of those women's shawls even. I'll just leave the basket and go, she decided. I shan't even wait for it to be emptied.

Then the door opened. A little woman in black showed in the gloom.

Laura said, "Are you Mrs. Scott?" But to her horror the woman answered, "Walk in please, miss," and she was shut in the passage.

"No," said Laura, "I don't want to come in. I only want to leave this basket. Mother sent—"

The little woman in the gloomy passage seemed not to have heard her. "Step this way, please, miss," she said in an oily voice, and Laura followed her.

She found herself in a wretched little low kitchen, lighted by a smoky   155
lamp. There was a woman sitting before the fire.

"Em," said the little creature who had let her in. "Em! It's a young lady." She turned to Laura. She said meaningly, "I'm 'er sister, miss. You'll excuse 'er, won't you?"

"Oh, but of course!" said Laura. "Please, don't disturb her. I—I only want to leave—"

But at that moment the woman at the fire turned round. Her face, puffed up, red, with swollen eyes and swollen lips, looked terrible. She seemed as though she couldn't understand why Laura was there. What did it mean? Why was this stranger standing in the kitchen with a basket? What was it all about? And the poor face puckered up again.

"All right, my dear," said the other. "I'll thank the young lady."

And again she began, "You'll excuse her, miss, I'm sure," and her face,   160
swollen too, tried an oily smile.

Laura only wanted to get out, to get away. She was back in the passage. The door opened. She walked straight through into the bedroom, where the dead was lying.

"You'd like a look at 'im, wouldn't you?" said Em's sister, and she brushed past Laura over to the bed. "Don't be afraid, my lass,—" and now her voice sounded fond and sly, and fondly she drew down the sheet—"'e looks a picture. There's nothing to show. Come along, my dear."

Laura came.

There lay a young man, fast asleep—sleeping so soundly, so deeply, that he was far, far away from them both. Oh, so remote, so peaceful. He was dreaming. Never wake him up again. His head was sunk in the pillow, his eyes were closed; they were blind under the closed eyelids. He was given up to his dream. What did garden-parties and baskets and lace frocks matter to him? He was far from all those things. He was wonderful, beautiful. While they were laughing and while the band was playing, this marvel had come to the lane. Happy . . . happy. . . . All is well, said that sleeping face. This is just as it should be. I am content.

But all the same you had to cry, and she couldn't go out of the room with- 165
out saying something to him. Laura gave a loud childish sob.

"Forgive my hat," she said.

And this time she didn't wait for Em's sister. She found her way out of the door, down the path, past all those dark people. At the corner of the lane she met Laurie.

He stepped out of the shadow. "Is that you, Laura?"

"Yes."

"Mother was getting anxious. Was it all right?"   170

"Yes, quite. Oh, Laurie!" She took his arm, she pressed up against him.

"I say, you're not crying, are you?" asked her brother.

Laura shook her head. She was.

Laurie put his arm round her shoulder. "Don't cry," he said in his warm, loving voice. "Was it awful?"

"No," sobbed Laura. "It was simply marvelous. But. Laurie—" She 175
stopped, she looked at her brother. "Isn't life," she stammered, "Isn't life—" But what life was she couldn't explain. No matter. He quite understood.

"*Isn't* it, darling?" said Laurie.

———— **KATHERINE MANSFIELD** ————

(1888–1923) Web   *www*

Born in New Zealand, Katherine Mansfield Beauchamp attended college in London. Mansfield's métier was the short story, and she wrote stories for magazines and published collections of stories with Hogarth Press. Mansfield had the ability to capture atmosphere and dilemma through the strategic use of imagery and detail. She died of tuberculosis at the age of thirty-four.

TOPICS FOR CRITICAL THINKING Web   *www*

1. In what ways does this story approach the question of class?
2. What are the functions of the hat motif?
3. Through what devices does this story show the shallowness of the Sheridans?
4. Why does Laura say, "Excuse my hat"?

TOPICS FOR CRITICAL WRITING Web   *www*

1. In what ways does this story portray Laura's search for identity?
2. What indications are there that the story's narrator takes a slightly ironic view of the Sheridans? To what end?

∽∽∽

D. H. LAWRENCE

The Horse-Dealer's Daughter　　(1922)

'Well, Mabel, and what are you going to do with yourself?' asked Joe, with foolish flippancy. He felt quite safe himself. Without listening for an answer, he turned aside, worked a grain of tobacco to the tip of his tongue, and spat it out. He did not care about anything, since he felt safe himself.

The three brothers and the sister sat round the desolate breakfast-table, attempting some sort of desultory consultation. The morning's post had given the final tap to the family fortunes, and all was over. The dreary dining-room itself, with its heavy mahogany furniture, looked as if it were waiting to be done away with.

But the consultation amounted to nothing. There was a strange air of ineffectuality about the three men, as they sprawled at table, smoking and reflecting vaguely on their own condition. The girl was alone, a rather short, sullen-looking young woman of twenty-seven. She did not share the same life as her brothers. She would have been good-looking, save for the impressive fixity of her face, 'bull-dog', as her brothers called it.

There was a confused tramping of horses' feet outside. The three men all sprawled round in their chairs to watch. Beyond the dark holly bushes that separated the strip of lawn from the high-road, they could see a cavalcade of shire horses swinging out of their own yard, being taken for exercise. This was the last time. These were the last horses that would go through their hands. The young men watched with critical, callous look. They were all frightened at the collapse of their lives, and the sense of disaster in which they were involved left them no inner freedom.

Yet they were three fine, well-set fellows enough. Joe, the eldest, was a 5 man of thirty-three, broad and handsome in a hot, flushed way. His face was red, he twisted his black moustache over a thick finger, his eyes were shallow and restless. He had a sensual way of uncovering his teeth when he laughed, and his bearing was stupid. Now he watched the horses with a glazed look of helplessness in his eyes, a certain stupor of downfall.

The great draught-horses swung past. They were tied head to tail, four of them, and they heaved along to where a lane branched off from the high-road, planting their great hoofs floutingly in the fine black mud, swinging their great rounded haunches sumptuously, and trotting a few sudden steps as they were led into the lane, round the corner. Every movement showed a massive, slumbrous strength, and a stupidity which held them in subjection. The groom at the head looked back, jerking the leading rope. And the cavalcade moved out of sight up the lane, the tail of the last horse, bobbed up tight and stiff, held out taut from the swinging great haunches as they rocked behind the hedges in a motion-like sleep.

Joe watched with glazed hopeless eyes. The horses were almost like his own body to him. He felt he was done for now. Luckily he was engaged to a woman as old as himself, and therefore her father, who was steward of a neighbouring estate, would provide him with a job. He would marry and go into harness. His life was over, he would be a subject animal now.

He turned uneasily aside, the retreating steps of the horses echoing in his ears. Then, with foolish restlessness, he reached for the scraps of bacon-rind from the plates, and making a faint whistling sound, flung them to the terrier that lay against the fender. He watched the dog swallow them, and waited till the creature looked into his eyes. Then a faint grin came on his face, and in a high, foolish voice he said:

'You won't get much more bacon, shall you, you little b——?'

The dog faintly and dismally wagged its tail, the lowered its haunches, 10 circled round, and lay down again.

There was another helpless silence at the table. Joe sprawled uneasily in his seat, not willing to go till the family conclave was dissolved. Fred Henry, the second brother, was erect, clean-limbed, alert. He had watched the passing of the horses with more sang-froid. If he was an animal, like Joe, he was an animal which controls, not one which is controlled. He was master of any horse, and he carried himself with a well-tempered air of mastery. But he was not master of the situations of life. He pushed his coarse brown moustache upwards, off his lip, and glanced irritably at his sister, who sat impassive and inscrutable.

'You'll go and stop with Lucy for a bit, shan't you?' he asked. The girl did not answer.

'I don't see what else you can do,' persisted Fred Henry.

'Go as a skivvy,' Joe interpolated laconically.

The girl did not move a muscle. 15

'If I was her, I should go in for training for a nurse,' said Malcolm, the youngest of them all. He was the baby of the family, a young man of twenty-two, with a fresh, jaunty *museau*.

But Mabel did not take any notice of him. They had talked at her and round her for so many years, that she hardly heard them at all.

The marble clock on the mantelpiece softly chimed the half-hour, the dog rose uneasily from the hearth-rug and looked at the party at the breakfast-table. But still they sat on in ineffectual conclave.

'Oh, all right,' said Joe suddenly, apropos of nothing. 'I'll get a move on.'

He pushed back his chair, straddled his knees with a downward jerk, to 20 get them free, in horsey fashion, and went to the fire. Still, he did not go out of the room; he was curious to know what the others would do or say. He began to charge his pipe, looking down at the dog and saying in a high, affected voice:

'Going wi' me? Going wi' me are ter? Tha'rt goin' further than tha counts on just now, dost hear?'

The dog faintly wagged its tail, the man stuck out his jaw and covered his pipe with his hands, and puffed intently, losing himself in the tobacco, looking down all the while at the dog with an absent brown eye. The dog looked up at him in mournful distrust. Joe stood with his knees stuck out, in real horsey fashion.

'Have you had a letter from Lucy?' Fred Henry asked of his sister.

'Last week,' came the neutral reply.

'And what does she say?'   25

There was no answer.

'Does she *ask* you to go and stop there?' persisted Fred Henry.

'She says I can if I like.'

'Well, then, you'd better. Tell her you'll come on Monday.'

This was received in silence.   30

'That's what you'll do then, is it?' said Fred Henry, in some exasperation.

But she made no answer. There was a silence of futility and irritation in the room. Malcolm grinned fatuously.

'You'll have to make up your mind between now and next Wednesday,' said Joe loudly, 'or else find yourself lodgings on the kerbstone.'

The face of the young woman darkened, but she sat on immutable.

'Here's Jack Fergusson!' exclaimed Malcolm, who was looking aimlessly   35
out of the window.

'Where?' exclaimed Joe loudly.

'Just gone past.'

'Coming in?'

Malcolm craned his neck to see the gate.

'Yes,' he said.   40

There was a silence. Mabel sat on like one condemned, at the head of the table. Then a whistle was heard from the kitchen. The dog got up and barked sharply. Joe opened the door and shouted:

'Come on.'

After a moment a young man entered. He was muffled up in overcoat and a purple woollen scarf, and his tweed cap, which he did not remove, was pulled down on his head. He was of medium height, his face was rather long and pale, his eyes looked tired.

'Hello, Jack! Well, Jack!' exclaimed Malcolm and Joe. Fred Henry merely said: 'Jack.'

'What's doing?' asked the newcomer, evidently addressing Fred Henry.   45

'Same. We've got to be out by Wednesday. Got a cold?'

'I have—got it bad, too.'

'Why don't you stop in?'

'*Me* stop in? When I can't stand on my legs, perhaps I shall have a chance.' The young man spoke huskily. He had a slight Scotch accent.

'It's a knock-out, isn't it,' said Joe, boisterously, 'if a doctor goes round 50
croaking with a cold. Looks bad for the patients, doesn't it?'

The young doctor looked at him slowly.

'Anything the matter with *you*, then?' he asked sarcastically.

'Not as I know of. Damn your eyes, I hope not. Why?'

'I thought you were very concerned about the patients, wondered if you might be one yourself.'

'Damn it, no, I've never been patient to no flaming doctor, and hope I   55
never shall be,' returned Joe.

At this point Mabel rose from the table, and they all seemed to become aware of her existence. She began putting the dishes together. The young doctor looked at her, but did not address her. He had not greeted her. She went out of the room with the tray, her face impassive and unchanged.

'When are you off then, all of you?' asked the doctor.

'I'm catching the eleven-forty,' replied Malcolm. 'Are you goin' down wi' th' trap, Joe?'

'Yes, I've told you I'm going down wi' th' trap, haven't I?'

'We'd better be getting her in then. So long, Jack, if I don't see you be- 60 fore I go,' said Malcolm, shaking hands.

He went out, followed by Joe, who seemed to have his tail between his legs.

'Well, this is the devil's own,' exclaimed the doctor, when he was left alone with Fred Henry. 'Going before Wednesday, are you?'

'That's the orders,' replied the other.

'Where, to Northampton?'

'That's it.'   65

'The devil!' exclaimed Fergusson, with quiet chagrin.

And there was silence between the two.

'All settled up, are you?' asked Fergusson.

'About.'

There was another pause.   70

'Well, I shall miss yer, Freddy, boy,' said the young doctor.

'And I shall miss thee, Jack,' returned the other.

'Miss you like hell,' mused the doctor.

Fred Henry turned aside. There was nothing to say. Mabel came in again, to finish clearing the table.

'What are *you* going to do, then, Miss Pervin?' asked Fergusson. 'Going 75 to your sister's, are you?'

Mabel looked at him with her steady, dangerous eyes, that always made him uncomfortable, unsettling his superficial ease.

'No,' she said.

'Well, what in the name of fortune *are* you going to do? Say what you mean to do,' cried Fred Henry, with futile intensity.

But she only averted her head, and continued her work. She folded the white table-cloth, and put on the chenille cloth.

'The sulkiest bitch that ever trod!' muttered her brother.   80

But she finished her task with perfectly impassive face, the young doctor watching her interestedly all the while. Then she went out.

Fred Henry stared after her, clenching his lips, his blue eyes fixing in sharp antagonism, as he made a grimace of sour exasperation.

'You could bray her into bits, and that's all you'd get out of her,' he said, in a small, narrowed tone.

The doctor smiled faintly.

'What's she *going* to do, then?' he asked.   85

'Strike me if *I* know!' returned the other.

There was a pause. Then the doctor stirred.

'I'll be seeing you to-night, shall I?' he said to his friend.

'Ay—where's it to be? Are we going over to Jessdale?'

'I don't know. I've got such a cold on me. I'll come round to the "Moon   90
and Stars", anyway.'

'Let Lizzie and May miss their night for once, eh?'

'That's it—if I feel as I do now.'

'All's one—'

The two young men went through the passage and down to the back door
together. The house was large, but it was servantless now, and desolate. At the
back was a small bricked house-yard and beyond that a big square, gravelled
fine and red, and having stables on two sides. Sloping, dank, winter-dark fields
stretched away on the open sides.

But the stables were empty. Joseph Pervin, the father of the family, had   95
been a man of no education, who had become a fairly large horse dealer. The
stables had been full of horses, there was a great turmoil and come-and-go of
horses and of dealers and grooms. Then the kitchen was full of servants. But
of late things had declined. The old man had married a second time, to retrieve his fortunes. Now he was dead and everything was gone to the dogs,
there was nothing but debt and threatening.

For months, Mabel had been servantless in the big house, keeping the
home together in penury for her ineffectual brothers. She had kept house for
ten years. But previously it was with unstinted means. Then, however brutal
and coarse everything was, the sense of money had kept her proud, confident.
The men might be foul-mouthed, the women in the kitchen might have bad
reputations, her brothers might have illegitimate children. But so long as
there was money, the girl felt herself established, and brutally proud, reserved.

No company came to the house, save dealers and coarse men. Mabel had
no associates of her own sex, after her sister went away. But she did not mind.
She went regularly to church, she attended to her father. And she lived in the
memory of her mother, who had died when she was fourteen, and whom she
had loved. She had loved her father, too, in a different way, depending upon
him, and feeling secure in him, until at the age of fifty-four he married again.
And then she had set hard against him. Now he had died and left them all
hopelessly in debt.

She had suffered badly during the period of poverty. Nothing, however,
could shake the curious, sullen, animal pride that dominated each member of
the family. Now, for Mabel, the end had come. Still she would not cast about
her. She would follow her own way just the same. She would always hold the
keys of her own situation. Mindless and persistent, she endured from day to day.
Why should she think? Why should she answer anybody? It was enough that
this was the end, and there was no way out. She need not pass any more darkly
along the main street of the small town, avoiding every eye. She need not de-
mean herself any more, going into the shops and buying the cheapest food. This
was at an end. She thought of nobody, not even of herself. Mindless and persistent, she seemed in a sort of ecstasy to be coming nearer to her fulfilment, her
own glorification, approaching her dead mother, who was glorified.

In the afternoon she took a little bag, with shears and sponge and a small
scrubbing-brush, and went out. It was a grey, wintry day, with saddened, dark
green fields and an atmosphere blackened by the smoke of foundries not far

off. She went quickly, darkly along the causeway, heeding nobody, through the town to the churchyard.

There she always felt secure, as if no one could see her, although as a matter of fact she was exposed to the stare of everyone who passed along under the churchyard wall. Nevertheless, once under the shadow of the great looming church, among the graves, she felt immune from the world, reserved within the thick churchyard wall as in another country. 100

Carefully she clipped the grass from the grave, and arranged the pinky white, small chrysanthemums in the tin cross. When this was done, she took an empty jar from a neighbouring grave, brought water, and carefully, most scrupulously sponged the marble headstone and the coping-stone.

It gave her sincere satisfaction to do this. She felt in immediate contact with the world of her mother. She took minute pains, went through the park in a state bordering on pure happiness, as if in performing this task she came into a subtle, intimate connection with her mother. For the life she followed here in the world was far less real than the world of death she inherited from her mother.

The doctor's house was just by the church. Fergusson, being a mere hired assistant, was slave to the country-side. As he hurried now to attend to the out-patients in the surgery, glancing across the graveyard with his quick eye, he saw the girl at her task at the grave. She seemed so intent and remote, it was like looking into another world. Some mystical element was touched in him. He slowed down as he walked, watching her as if spellbound.

She lifted her eyes, feeling him looking. Their eyes met. And each looked again at once, each feeling, in some way, found out by the other. He lifted his cap and passed on down the road. There remained distinct in his consciousness, like a vision, the memory of her face, lifted from the tombstone in the churchyard, and looking at him with slow, large, portentous eyes. It *was* portentous, her face. It seemed to mesmerise him. There was a heavy power in her eyes which laid hold of his whole being, as if he had drunk some powerful drug. He had been feeling weak and done before. Now the life came back into him, he felt delivered from his own fretted, daily self.

He finished his duties at the surgery as quickly as might be, hastily filling up the bottles of the waiting people with cheap drugs. Then, in perpetual haste, he set off again to visit several cases in another part of his round, before tea-time. At all times he preferred to walk if he could, but particularly when he was not well. He fancied the motion restored him. 105

The afternoon was falling. It was grey, deadened, and wintry, with a slow, moist, heavy coldness sinking in and deadening all the faculties. But why should he think or notice? He hastily climbed the hill and turned across the dark green fields, following the black cinder-track. In the distance, across a shallow dip in the country, the small town was clustered like smouldering ash, a tower, a spire, a heap of low, raw, extinct houses. And on the nearest fringe of the town, sloping into the dip, was Oldmeadow, the Pervins' house. He could see the stables and the outbuildings distinctly, as they lay towards him on the slope. Well, he would not go there many more times! Another resource would be lost to him, another place gone: the only company he cared for in the alien, ugly little town he was losing. Nothing but work, drudgery, constant hastening from dwelling to dwelling among the colliers and the iron-workers. It wore him out, but at the same time he had a craving for it. It was a stimulant to him to be in the homes of the working people, moving, as it were, through the innermost body of their life. His nerves were excited and gratified. He could come so near, into the very lives of the rough, inarticulate, powerfully emotional men and women. He grumbled, he said he hated the hellish hole. But as a matter of fact it excited him, the contact with the rough, strongly-feeling people was a stimulant applied direct to his nerves.

Below Oldmeadow, in the green, shallow, soddened hollow of fields, lay a square, deep pond. Roving across the landscape, the doctor's quick eye detected a figure in black passing through the gate of the field, down towards the pond. He looked again. It would be Mabel Pervin. His mind suddenly became alive and attentive.

Why was she going down there? He pulled up on the path on the slope above, and stood staring. He could just make sure of the small black figure moving in the hollow of the failing day. He seemed to see her in the midst of such obscurity, that he was like a clairvoyant, seeing rather with the mind's eye than with ordinary sight. Yet he could see her positively enough, whilst he kept his eye attentive. He felt, if he looked away from her, in the thick, ugly falling dusk, he would lose her altogether.

He followed her minutely as she moved, direct and intent, like something transmitted rather than stirring in voluntary activity, straight down the field towards the pond. There she stood on the bank for a moment. She never raised her head. Then she waded slowly into the water.

He stood motionless as the small black figure walked slowly and deliberately towards the centre of the pond, very slowly, gradually moving deeper into the motionless water, and still moving forward as the water got up to her breast. Then he could see her no more in the dusk of the dead afternoon.   110

'There!' he exclaimed. 'Would you believe it?'

And he hastened straight down, running over the wet, soddened fields, pushing through the hedges, down into the depression of callous wintry obscurity. It took him several minutes to come to the pond. He stood on the bank, breathing heavily. He could see nothing. His eyes seemed to penetrate the dead water. Yes, perhaps that was the dark shadow of her black clothing beneath the surface of the water.

He slowly ventured into the pond. The bottom was deep, soft clay, he sank in, and the water clasped dead cold round his legs. As he stirred he could smell the cold, rotten clay that fouled up into the water. It was objectionable in his lungs. Still, repelled and yet not heeding, he moved deeper into the pond. The cold water rose over his thighs, over his loins, upon his abdomen. The lower part of his body was all sunk in the hideous cold element. And the bottom was so deeply soft and uncertain, he was afraid of pitching with his mouth underneath. He could not swim, and was afraid.

He crouched a little, spreading his hands under the water and moving them round, trying to feel for her. The dead cold pond swayed upon his chest. He moved again, a little deeper, and again, with his hands underneath, he felt all around under the water. And he touched her clothing. But it evaded his fingers. He made a desperate effort to grasp it.

And so doing he lost his balance and went under, horribly, suffocating in 115 the foul earthy water, struggling madly for a few moments. At last, after what seemed an eternity, he got his footing, rose again into the air and looked around. He gasped, and knew he was in the world. Then he looked at the water. She had risen near him. He grasped her clothing, and drawing her nearer, turned to take his way to land again.

He went very slowly, carefully, absorbed in the slow process. He rose higher, climbing out of the pond. The water was now only about his legs; he was thankful, full of relief to be out of the clutches of the pond. He lifted her and staggered on to the bank, out of the horror of wet, grey clay.

He laid her down on the bank. She was quite unconscious and running with water. He made the water come from her mouth, he worked to restore her. He did not have to work very long before he could feel the breathing begin again in her; she was breathing naturally. He worked a little longer. He could feel her live beneath his hands; she was coming back. He wiped her face, wrapped her in his overcoat, looked round into the dim, dark grey world, then lifted her and staggered down the bank and across the fields.

It seemed an unthinkably long way, and his burden so heavy he felt he would never get to the house. But at last he was in the stable-yard, and then in the house-yard. He opened the door and went into the house. In the kitchen he laid her down on the hearth-rug and called. The house was empty. But the fire was burning in the grate.

Then again he kneeled to attend to her. She was breathing regularly, her eyes were wide open and as if conscious, but there seemed something missing in her look. She was conscious in herself, but unconscious of her surroundings.

He ran upstairs, took blankets from a bed, and put them before the fire to 120 warm. Then he removed her saturated, earthy-smelling clothing, rubbed her dry with a towel, and wrapped her naked in the blankets. Then he went into the dining-room, to look for spirits. There was a little whisky. He drank a gulp himself, and put some into her mouth.

The effect was instantaneous. She looked full into his face, as if she had been seeing him for some time, and yet had only just become conscious of him.

'Dr. Fergusson?' she said.

'What?' he answered.

He was divesting himself of his coat, intending to find some dry clothing upstairs. He could not bear the smell of the dead, clayey water, and he was mortally afraid for his own health.

'What did I do?' she asked. 125

'Walked into the pond,' he replied. He had begun to shudder like one sick, and could hardly attend to her. Her eyes remained full on him, he seemed to be going dark in his mind, looking back at her helplessly. The shuddering became quieter in him, his life came back to him, dark and unknowing, but strong again.

'Was I out of my mind?' she asked, while her eyes were fixed on him all the time.

'Maybe, for the moment,' he replied. He felt quiet, because his strength had come back. The strange fretful strain had left him.

'Am I out of my mind now?' she asked.

'Are you?' he reflected a moment. 'No,' he answered truthfully, 'I don't   130
see that you are.' He turned his face aside. He was afraid now, because he felt dazed, and felt dimly that her power was stronger than his, in this issue. And she continued to look at him fixedly all the time. 'Can you tell me where I shall find some dry things to put on?' he asked.

'Did you dive into the pond for me?' she asked.

'No,' he answered. 'I walked in. But I went in overhead as well.'

There was silence for a moment. He hesitated. He very much wanted to go upstairs to get into dry clothing. But there was another desire in him. And she seemed to hold him. His will seemed to have gone to sleep, and left him, standing there slack before her. But he felt warm inside himself. He did not shudder at all, though his clothes were sodden on him.

'Why did you?' she asked.

'Because I didn't want you to do such a foolish thing,' he said.   135

'It wasn't foolish,' she said, still gazing at him as she lay on the floor, with a sofa cushion under her head. 'It was the right thing to do. *I* knew best, then.'

'I'll go and shift these wet things,' he said. But still he had not the power to move out of her presence, until she sent him. It was as if she had the life of his body in her hands, and he could not extricate himself. Or perhaps he did not want to.

Suddenly she sat up. Then she became aware of her own immediate condition. She felt the blankets about her, she knew her own limbs. For a moment it seemed as if her reason were going. She looked round, with wild eye, as if seeking something. He stood still with fear. She saw her clothing lying scattered.

'Who undressed me?' she asked, her eyes resting full and inevitable on his face.

'I did,' he replied, 'to bring you round.'   140

For some moments she sat and gazed at him awfully, her lips parted.

'Do you love me, then?' she asked.

He only stood and stared at her, fascinated. His soul seemed to melt.

She shuffled forward on her knees, and put her arms round him, round his legs, as he stood there, pressing her breasts against his knees and thighs, clutching him with strange, convulsive certainty, pressing his thighs against her, drawing him to her face, her throat, as she looked up at him with flaring, humble eyes and transfiguration, triumphant in first possession.

'You love me,' she murmured, in strange transport, yearning and tri-   145
umphant and confident. 'You love me. I know you love me, I know.'

And she was passionately kissing his knees, through the wet clothing, passionately and indiscriminately kissing his knees, his legs, as if unaware of everything.

He looked down at the tangled wet hair, the wild, bare, animal shoulders. He was amazed, bewildered, and afraid. He had never thought of loving her. He had never wanted to love her. When he rescued her and restored her, he was a doctor, and she was a patient. He had had no single personal thought of her. Nay, this introduction of the personal element was very distasteful to him, a violation of his professional honour. It was horrible to have her there embracing his knees. It was horrible. He revolted from it, violently. And yet— and yet—he had not the power to break away.

She looked at him again, with the same supplication of powerful love, and that same transcendent, frightening light of triumph. In view of the delicate flame which seemed to come from her face like a light, he was powerless. And yet he had never intended to love her. He had never intended. And something stubborn in him could not give way.

'You love me,' she repeated, in a murmur of deep, rhapsodic assurance. 'You love me.'

Her hands were drawing him, drawing him down to her. He was afraid, 150 even a little horrified. For he had, really, no intention of loving her. Yet her hands were drawing him towards her. He put out his hand quickly to steady himself, and grasped her bare shoulder. A flame seemed to burn the hand that grasped her soft shoulder. He had no intention of loving her: his whole will was against his yielding. It was horrible. And yet wonderful was the touch of her shoulders, beautiful the shining of her face. Was she perhaps mad? He had a horror of yielding to her. Yet something in him ached also.

He had been staring away at the door, away from her. But his hand remained on her shoulder. She had gone suddenly very still. He looked down at her. Her eyes were now wide with fear, with doubt, the light was dying from her face, a shadow of terrible greyness was returning. He could not bear the touch of her eyes' question upon him, and the look of death behind the question.

With an inward groan he gave way, and let his heart yield towards her. A sudden gentle smile came on his face. And her eyes, which never left his face, slowly, slowly filled with tears. He watched the strange water rise in her eyes, like some slow fountain coming up. And his heart seemed to burn and melt away in his breast.

He could not bear to look at her any more. He dropped on his knees and caught her head with his arms and pressed her face against his throat. She was very still. His heart, which seemed to have broken, was burning with a kind of agony in his breast. And he felt her slow, hot tears wetting his throat. But he could not move.

He felt the hot tears wet his neck and the hollows of his neck, and he remained motionless, suspended through one of man's eternities. Only now it had become indispensable to him to have her face pressed close to him; he could never let her go again. He could never let her head go away from the close clutch of his arm. He wanted to remain like that for ever, with his heart hurting him in a pain that was also life to him. Without knowing, he was looking down on her damp, soft brown hair.

Then, as it were suddenly, he smelt the horrid stagnant smell of that wa- 155 ter. And at the same moment she drew away from him and looked at him. Her eyes were wistful and unfathomable. He was afraid of them, and he fell to kissing her, not knowing what he was doing. He wanted her eyes not to have that terrible, wistful, unfathomable look.

When she turned her face to him again, a faint delicate flush was glowing, and there was again dawning that terrible shining of joy in her eyes, which really terrified him, and yet which he now wanted to see, because he feared the look of doubt still more.

'You love me?' she said, rather faltering.

'Yes.' The word cost him a painful effort. Not because it wasn't true. But because it was too newly true, the *saying* seemed to tear open again his newly-torn heart. And he hardly wanted it to be true, even now.

She lifted her face to him, and he bent forward and kissed her on the mouth, gently, with the one kiss that is an eternal pledge. And as he kissed her his heart strained again in his breast. He never intended to love her. But now it was over. He had crossed over the gulf to her, and all that he had left behind had shrivelled and become void.

After the kiss, her eyes again slowly filled with tears. She sat still, away   160
from him, with her face drooped aside, and her hands folded in her lap. The tears fell very slowly. There was complete silence. He too sat there motionless and silent on the hearth-rug. The strange pain of his heart that was broken seemed to consume him. That he should love her? That this was love! That he should be ripped open in this way! Him, a doctor! How they would all jeer if they knew! It was agony to him to think they might know.

In the curious naked pain of the thought he looked again to her. She was sitting there drooped into a muse. He saw a tear fall, and his heart flared hot. He saw for the first time that one of her shoulders was quite uncovered, one arm bare, he could see one of her small breasts; dimly, because it had become almost dark in the room.

'Why are you crying?' he asked, in an altered voice.

She looked up at him, and behind her tears the consciousness of her situation for the first time brought a dark look of shame to her eyes.

'I'm not crying, really,' she said, watching him, half frightened.

He reached his hand, and softly closed it on her bare arm.   165

'I love you! I love you!' he said in a soft, low vibrating voice, unlike himself.

She shrank, and dropped her head. The soft, penetrating grip of his hand on her arm distressed her. She looked up at him.

'I want to go,' she said. 'I want to go and get you some dry things.'

'Why?' he said. 'I'm all right.'

'But I want to go,' she said. 'And I want you to change your things.'   170

He released her arm, and she wrapped herself in the blanket, looking at him rather frightened. And still she did not rise.

'Kiss me,' she said wistfully.

He kissed her, but briefly, half in anger.

Then, after a second, she rose nervously, all mixed up in the blanket. He watched her in her confusion as she tried to extricate herself and wrap herself up so that she could walk. He watched her relentlessly, as she knew. And as she went, the blanket trailing, and as he saw a glimpse of her feet and her white leg, he tried to remember her as she was when he had wrapped her in the blanket. But then he didn't want to remember, because she had been nothing to him then, and his nature revolted from remembering her as she was when she was nothing to him.

A tumbling, muffled noise from within the dark house startled him. Then 175 he heard her voice: 'There are clothes.' He rose and went to the foot of the stairs, and gathered up the garments she had thrown down. Then he came back to the fire, to rub himself down and dress. He grinned at his own appearance when he had finished.

The fire was sinking, so he put on coal. The house was now quite dark, save for the light of a street-lamp that shone in faintly from beyond the holly trees. He lit the gas with matches he found on the mantelpiece. Then he emptied the pockets of his own clothes, and threw all his wet things in a heap into the scullery. After which he gathered up her sodden clothes, gently, and put them in a separate heap on the copper-top in the scullery.

It was six o'clock on the clock. His own watch had stopped. He ought to go back to the surgery. He waited, and still she did not come down. So he went to the foot of the stairs and called:

'I shall have to go.'

Almost immediately he heard her coming down. She had on her best dress of black voile, and her hair was tidy, but still damp. She looked at him— and in spite of herself, smiled.

'I don't like you in those clothes,' she said. 180

'Do I look a sight?' he answered.

They were shy of one another.

'I'll make you some tea,' she said.

'No, I must go.'

'Must you?' And she looked at him again with the wide, strained, doubt- 185 ful eyes. And again, from the pain of his breast, he knew how he loved her. He went and bent to kiss her, gently, passionately, with his heart's painful kiss.

'And my hair smells so horrible,' she murmured in distraction. 'And I'm so awful, I'm so awful! Oh no, I'm too awful.' And she broke into bitter, heart-broken sobbing. 'You can't want to love me, I'm horrible.'

'Don't be silly, don't be silly,' he said, trying to comfort her, kissing her, holding her in his arms. 'I want you, I want to marry you, we're going to be married, quickly, quickly—to-morrow if I can.'

But she only sobbed terribly, and cried:

'I feel awful. I feel awful. I feel I'm horrible to you.'

'No, I want you, I want you,' was all he answered, blindly, with that terri- 190 ble intonation which frightened her almost more than her horror lest he should *not* want her.

<hr>

D. H. LAWRENCE

(1885–1930) **Web** www

Son of a coal miner and a schoolteacher, D. H. Lawrence became a schoolteacher and finally a writer. Lawrence's fiction deploys the significant events and details about the physical environment as ways to work through the conflicts that beset modern humanity: humanity versus nature, humanity versus technology, man versus woman, soul versus matter. Always, Lawrence wrote against the constricting norms of conventional society.

www ### TOPICS FOR CRITICAL THINKING `Web`

1. What kind of narrator does this story have, and what points of view does this narrator assume?
2. What clues are there that there will be a romantic relation between the Doctor and Mabel?
3. What observations about class and love does the story make?
4. What does the pond stand for?

www ### TOPICS FOR CRITICAL WRITING `Web`

1. Trace the ways the story uses animal imagery. What do these animal motifs tell us about what is happening in the story?
2. What is the future of this couple? What clues does the story offer about the possibilities of relations between men and women?

ᖇᖇᖇ

JAMES JOYCE

Araby   *(1904–1905)*

North Richmond Street, being blind, was a quiet street except at the hour when the Christian Brothers' School set the boys free. An uninhabited house of two stories stood at the blind end, detached from its neighbours in a square ground. The other houses of the street, conscious of decent lives within them, gazed at one another with brown imperturbable faces.

The former tenant of our house, a priest, had died in the back drawing-room. Air, musty from having been long enclosed, hung in all the rooms, and the waste room behind the kitchen was littered with old useless papers. Among these I found a few paper-covered books, the pages of which were curled and damp: *The Abbot*, by Walter Scott, *The Devout Communicant*, and *The Memoirs of Vidocq*. I liked the last best because its leaves were yellow. The wild garden behind the house contained a central apple tree and a few straggling bushes under one of which I found the late tenant's rusty bicycle pump. He had been a very charitable priest; in his will he had left all his money to institutions and the furniture of his house to his sister.

When the short days of winter came dusk fell before we had well eaten our dinners. When we met in the street the houses had grown sombre. The space of sky above us was the colour of ever-changing violet and towards it the lamps of the street lifted their feeble lanterns. The cold air stung us and we played till our bodies glowed. Our shouts echoed in the silent street. The career of our play brought us through the dark muddy lanes behind the houses where we ran the gauntlet of the rough tribes from the cottages, to the back doors of the dark dripping gardens where odours arose from the ash-pits, to the dark odorous stables where a coachman smoothed and combed the horse or shook music from the buckled harness. When we returned to the street, light from the kitchen windows had filled the areas. If my uncle was seen turning the corner we hid in the shadow until we had seen him safely housed. Or if Mangan's sister came out on the doorstep to call her brother in to his tea we watched her from our shadow peer up and down the street. We waited to see whether she would remain or go in and, if she remained, we left our shadow and walked up to Mangan's steps resignedly. She was waiting for us, her figure defined by the light from the half-opened door. Her brother always teased her before he obeyed and I stood by the railings looking at her. Her dress swung as she moved her body and the soft rope of her hair tossed from side to side.

Every morning I lay on the floor in the front parlour watching her door. The blind was pulled down to within an inch of the sash so that I could not be seen. When she came out on the doorstep my heart leaped. I ran to the hall, seized my books and followed her. I kept her brown figure always in my eye and, when we came near the point at which our ways diverged, I quickened my pace and passed her. This happened morning after morning. I had never spoken to her, except for a few casual words, and yet her name was like a summons to all my foolish blood.

Her image accompanied me even in places the most hostile to romance. 5 On Saturday evenings when my aunt went marketing I had to go to carry some of the parcels. We walked through the flaring streets, jostled by drunken men and bargaining women, amid the curses of labourers, the shrill litanies of shop-boys who stood on guard by the barrels of pigs' cheeks, the nasal chanting of street-singers, who sang a *come-all-you* about O'Donovan Rossa, or a ballad about the troubles in our native land. These noises converged in a single sensation of life for me: I imagined that I bore my chalice safely through a throng of foes. Her name sprang to my lips at moments in strange prayers and praises which I myself did not understand. My eyes were often full of tears (I could not tell why) and at times a flood from my heart seemed to pour itself out into my bosom. I thought little of the future. I did not know whether I would ever speak to her or not or, if I spoke to her, how I could tell her of my confused adoration. But my body was like a harp and her words and gestures were like fingers running upon the wires.

One evening I went into the back drawing-room in which the priest had died. It was a dark rainy evening and there was no sound in the house. Through one of the broken panes I heard the rain impinge upon the earth, the fine incessant needles of water playing in the sodden beds. Some distant lamp or lighted window gleamed below me. I was thankful that I could see so little. All my senses seemed to desire to veil themselves and, feeling that I was about to slip from them, I pressed the palms of my hands together until they trembled, murmuring: *"O love! O love!"* many times.

At last she spoke to me. When she addressed the first words to me I was so confused that I did not know what to answer. She asked me was I going to

Araby. I forgot whether I answered yes or no. It would be a splendid bazaar, she said she would love to go.

"And why can't you?" I asked.

While she spoke she turned a silver bracelet round and round her wrist. She could not go, she said, because there would be a retreat that week in her convent. Her brother and two other boys were fighting for their caps and I was alone at the railings. She held one of the spikes, bowing her head towards me. The light from the lamp opposite our door caught the white curve of her neck, lit up her hair that rested there and, falling, lit up the hand upon the railing. It fell over one side of her dress and caught the white border of a petticoat, just visible as she stood at ease.

"It's well for you," she said.   10

"If I go," I said, "I will bring you something."

What innumerable follies laid waste my waking and sleeping thoughts after the evening! I wished to annihilate the tedious intervening days. I chafed against the work of school. At night in my bedroom and by day in the classroom her image came between me and the page I strove to read. The syllables of the word *Araby* were called to me through the silence in which my soul luxuriated and cast an Eastern enchantment over me. I asked for leave to go to the bazaar on Saturday night. My aunt was surprised and hoped it was not some Freemason affair. I answered few questions in class. I watched my master's face pass from amiability to sternness; he hoped I was not beginning to idle, I could not call my wandering thoughts together. I had hardly any patience with the serious work of life which, now that it stood between me and my desire, seemed to me child's play, ugly monotonous child's play.

On Saturday morning I reminded my uncle that I wished to go to the bazaar in the evening. He was fussing at the hall-stand, looking for the hat brush, and answered me curtly:

"Yes, boy, I know."

As he was in the hall I could not go into the front parlour and lie at the   15
window. I left the house in bad humour and walked slowly towards the school. The air was pitilessly raw and already my heart misgave me.

When I came home to dinner my uncle had not yet been home. Still it was early. I sat staring at the clock for some time and, when its ticking began to irritate me, I left the room. I mounted the staircase and gained the upper part of the house. The high cold empty gloomy rooms liberated me and I went from room to room singing. From the front window I saw my companions playing below in the street. Their cries reached me weakened and indistinct and, leaning my forehead against the cool glass, I looked over at the dark house where she lived. I may have stood there for an hour, seeing nothing but the brown-clad figure cast by my imagination, touched discreetly by the lamplight at the curved neck, at the hand upon the railings and at the border below the dress.

When I came downstairs again I found Mrs. Mercer sitting at the fire. She was an old garrulous woman, a pawnbroker's widow, who collected used stamps for some pious purpose. I had to endure the gossip of the tea-table. The meal was prolonged beyond an hour and still my uncle did not come. Mrs. Mercer stood up to go: she was sorry she couldn't wait any longer, but it was after eight o'clock and she did not like to be out late, as the night air was bad for her. When she had gone I began to walk up and down the room, clenching my fists. My aunt said:

"I'm afraid you may put off your bazaar for this night of Our Lord."

At nine o'clock I heard my uncle's latchkey in the hall-door. I heard him talking to himself and heard the hall-stand rocking when it had received the weight of his overcoat. I could interpret these signs. When he was midway through his dinner I asked him to give me the money to go to the bazaar. He had forgotten.

"The people are in bed and after their first sleep now," he said.   20

I did not smile. My aunt said to him energetically:

"Can't you give him the money and let him go? You've kept him late enough as it is."

My uncle said he was very sorry he had forgotten. He said he believed in the old saying: "All work and no play makes Jack a dull boy." He asked me where I was going and, when I had told him a second time, he asked me did I know *The Arab's Farewell to his Steed*. When I left the kitchen he was about to recite the opening lines of the piece to my aunt.

I held a florin tightly in my hand as I strode down Buckingham Street towards the station. The sight of the streets thronged with buyers and glaring with gas recalled to me the purpose of my journey. I took my seat in a third-class carriage of a deserted train. After an intolerable delay the train moved out of the station slowly. It crept onward among ruinous houses and over the twinkling river. At Westland Row Station a crowd of people pressed to the carriage doors; but the porters moved them back, saying that it was a special train for the bazaar. I remained alone in the bare carriage. In a few minutes the train drew up beside an improvised wooden platform. I passed out on the road and saw by the lighted dial of a clock that it was ten minutes to ten. In front of me was a large building which displayed the magical name.

I could not find any sixpenny entrance and, fearing that the bazaar would   25
be closed, I passed in quickly through a turnstile, handing a shilling to a weary-looking man. I found myself in a big hall girdled at half its height by a gallery. Nearly all the stalls were closed and the greater part of the hall was in darkness. I recognized a silence like that which pervades a church after a service. I walked into the center of the bazaar timidly. A few people were gathered about the stalls which were still open. Before a curtain, over which the words *Café Chantant* were written in coloured lamps, two men were counting money on a salver. I listened to the fall of the coins.

Remembering with difficulty why I had come I went over to one of the stalls and examined porcelain vases and flowered tea-sets. At the door of the stall a young lady was talking and laughing with two young gentlemen. I remarked their English accents and listened vaguely to their conversation.

"O, I never said such a thing!"

"O, but you did!"

"O, but I didn't!"

"Didn't she say that?"   30

"Yes. I heard her."

"O, there's a .... fib!"

Observing me, the young lady came over and asked me did I wish to buy anything. The tone of her voice was not encouraging; she seemed to have spoken to me out of a sense of duty. I looked humbly at the great jars that stood like eastern guards at either side of the dark entrance to the stall and murmured:

"No, thank you."

The young lady changed the position of one of the vases and went back   35
to the two young men. They began to talk of the same subject. Once or twice the young lady glanced at me over her shoulder.

I lingered before her stall, though I knew my stay was useless, to make my interest in her wares seem the more real. Then I turned away slowly and walked down the middle of the bazaar. I allowed the two pennies to fall against the sixpence in my pocket. I heard a voice call from one end of the gallery that the light was out. The upper part of the hall was now completely dark.

Gazing up into the darkness I saw myself as a creature driven and derided by vanity; and my eyes burned with anguish and anger.

───────   **JAMES JOYCE**   ───────

www

(1882–1941) Web

Born in Dublin to a middle-class Catholic family, Joyce moved to Europe as a young man, living in Paris, Italy, and Switzerland. From his more distanced vantage point on the continent, Joyce wrote about Irish characters. His novels and short stories are multilayered, presenting the lively detail of a Dublin existence in concert with the psychological experience of insight and awareness.

www

TOPICS FOR CRITICAL THINKING Web

1. Trace the text's use of light and dark imagery.
2. What various things might "Araby" represent?
3. Why did the narrator's eyes burn "with anguish and anger" at the end?

www

TOPICS FOR CRITICAL WRITING Web

1. On one level, "Araby" is about a young man's insight. What else might this story be about?
2. From what vantage does the narrator see himself? What does the narration tell us about the narrator who sees himself as he was as a child?

Symbols

Images that refer to the same set of ideas are **symbols.** Culturally, we understand images such as the clock face, the flag, a stop sign, a crucifix, the mountain peak, or even a lighthouse, which has come to stand as a beacon of hope and salvation, as symbols. Prose fiction can employ these standard cultural symbols or it can establish its own by always linking a particular image to a particular idea or set of ideas. In Virginia Woolf's short story "The Symbol," consider the ways in which the image of the mountain becomes a symbol.

Featured Writer

VIRGINIA WOOLF

The Symbol (1941)

There was a little dent on the top of the mountain like a crater on the moon. It was filled with snow, iridescent like a pigeon's breast, or dead white. There was a scurry of dry particles now and again, covering nothing. It was too high for breathing flesh or fur covered life. All the same the snow was iridescent one moment; and blood red; and pure white, according to the day.

The graves in the valley—for there was a vast descent on either side; first pure rock; snow silted; lower a pine tree gripped a crag; then a solitary hut; then a saucer of pure green; then a cluster of eggshell roofs; at last, at the bottom, a village, an hotel, a cinema, and a graveyard—the graves in the churchyard near the hotel recorded the names of several men who had fallen climbing.

'The mountain,' the lady wrote, sitting on the balcony of the hotel, 'is a symbol . . .' She paused. She could see the topmost height through her glasses. She focussed the lens, as if to see what the symbol was. She was writing to her elder sister at Birmingham.

The balcony overlooked the main street of the Alpine summer resort, like a box at a theatre. There were very few private sitting rooms, and so the plays—such as they were—the curtain raisers—were acted in public. They were always a little provisional; preludes, curtain raisers. Entertainments to pass the time; seldom leading to any conclusion, such as marriage; or even lasting friendship. There was something fantastic about them, airy, inconclusive. So little that was solid could be dragged to this height. Even the houses looked gimcrack. By the time the voice of the English Announcer had reached the village it too became unreal.

Lowering her glasses, she nodded at the young men who in the street below were making ready to start. With one of them she had a certain connection—that is, an Aunt of his had been Mistress of her daughter's school. 5

Still holding the pen, still tipped with a drop of ink, she waved down at the climbers. She had written the mountain was a symbol. But of what? In the forties of the last century two men, in the sixties four men had perished; the first party when a rope broke; the second when night fell and froze them to death. We are always climbing to some height; that was the cliché. But it did not represent what was in her mind's eye; after seeing through her glasses the virgin height.

She continued, inconsequently. 'I wonder why it makes me think of the Isle of Wight? You remember when Mama was dying, we took her there. And

I would stand on the balcony, when the boat came in and describe the passengers. I would say, I think that must be Mr Edwardes . . . He has just come off the gangway. Then, now all the passengers have landed. Now they have turned the boat . . . I never told you, naturally not—you were in India; you were going to have Lucy—how I longed when the doctor came, that he should say, quite definitely, She cannot live another week. It was very prolonged; she lived eighteen months. The mountain just now reminded me how when I was alone, I would fix my eyes upon her death, as a symbol. I would think if I could reach that point—when I should be free—we could not marry as you remember until she died—A cloud then would do instead of the mountain. I thought, when I reach that point—I have never told anyone; for it seemed so heartless; I shall be at the top. And I could imagine so many sides. We come of course of an Anglo Indian family. I can still imagine, from hearing stories told, how people live in other parts of the world. I can see mud huts; and savages; I can see elephants drinking at pools. So many of our uncles and cousins were explorers. I have always had a great desire to explore for myself. But of course, when the time came it seemed more sensible, considering our long engagement, to marry.'

She looked across the street at a woman shaking a mat on another balcony. Every morning at the same time she came out. You could have thrown a pebble into her balcony. They had indeed come to the point of smiling at each other across the street.

'The little villas,' she added, taking up her pen, 'are much the same here as in Birmingham. Every house takes in lodgers. The hotel is quite full. Though monotonous, the food is not what you would call bad. And of course the hotel has a splendid view. One can see the mountain from every window. But then that's true of the whole place. I can assure you, I could shriek sometimes coming out of the one shop where they sell papers—we get them a week late—always to see that mountain. Sometimes it looks just across the way. At others, like a cloud; only it never moves. Somehow the talk, even among the invalids, who are every where, is always about the mountain. Either, how clear it is today, it might be across the street; or, how far away it looks; it might be a cloud. That is the usual cliché. In the storm last night, I hoped for once it was hidden. But just as they brought in the anchovies, The Rev. W. Bishop said, "Look there's the mountain!"

Am I being selfish? Ought I not to be ashamed of myself, when there is so much suffering? It is not confined to the visitors. The natives suffer dreadfully from goitre. Of course it could be stopped, if any one had enterprise, and money. Ought one not to be ashamed of dwelling upon what after all can't be cured? It would need an earthquake to destroy that mountain, just as, I suppose, it was made by an earthquake. I asked the Proprietor, Herr Melchior, the other day, if there were ever earthquakes now? No, he said, only landslides and avalanches. They have been known he said to blot out a whole village. But he added quickly, there's no danger here.

As I write these words, I can see the young men quite plainly on the slopes of the mountain. They are roped together. One I think I told you was at the same school with Margaret. They are now crossing a crevasse. . . .'

The pen fell from her hand, and the drop of ink straggled in a zig zag line down the page. The young men had disappeared.

It was only late that night when the search party had recovered the bodies that she found the unfinished letter on the table on the balcony. She dipped her pen once more; and added, 'The old clichés will come in very handy. They died trying to climb the mountain . . . And the peasants brought spring flowers to lay upon their graves. They died in an attempt to discover . . .'

There seemed no fitting conclusion. And she added, 'Love to the children,' and then her pet name.

In her short story "The Symbol," Virginia Woolf depicts how a letter-writing vacationer takes a particular mountain in the Swiss landscape as a symbol. In the course of the woman's day, the mountain changes appearance and prominence. The woman's search for the meaning of the mountain leads her to a series of associations and observations about her mother's dying (which the mountain reminds her of), life in the Alpine village where she is staying, her wish to have been an explorer, and her desire that the mountain might disappear. During these ruminations, the woman sees the mountain, oppressive and mysterious in its changing appearances, as a symbol of dying and of freedom. At the end of the day (and the story), the mountain claims the lives of more climbers. The mountain retains its complex but stable symbolic significance.

Woolf's story illustrates the difference between image and symbol. Images include the letter-writer's different accounts of the mountain's appearances as well as her descriptions of the Alpine village, and her imagined portraits of India. Symbols include the mountain itself. Its persistent presence, like the graves below, consistently reminds the letter-writer of death. Images are impressions that evoke the senses and that might refer to a number of different phenomena in any given story. Symbols are objects which, throughout a story, always refer to the same complex meaning. In *Heart of Darkness* for example, imagery includes descriptions of the jungle, but the jungle itself is a complex symbol of ignorance, greed, the resilience of nature, and the forbidden. Symbols are, in fact, like mountains in that they tend to be broodingly present throughout a story. They often connote (suggest) a meaning that is associated with them in the culture at large, as Woolf's protagonist demonstrates in her struggle with the mountain's significance.

———— **VIRGINIA WOOLF** ————
(1882–1941) **Web**

www

Co-owner of the Hogarth Press in the Bloomsbury section of London, Woolf wrote novels that helped define modernism with their prose that shifts rapidly and fluidly among present events and memory and one person's thoughts and another's, and that weaves imagery and rhythm to produce a sense of the richness of moments of being. The daughter of Sir Leslie Stephen, a noted British intellectual, Woolf and her husband Leonard became the center of the Bloomsbury Group, a group of artists, writers, and thinkers who helped *www* formulate concepts of literary modernism Web . From 1913 until 1941, Woolf was busy as a writer, critic, and publisher, publishing seven novels as well as stories and extended essays such as *A Room of One's Own* (1929) and *Three Guineas* (1938). Dreading another World War and worried about her tendency towards nervous breakdowns, Woolf committed suicide in March 1941.

www # Kew Gardens Web   *(1917–1921)*

From the oval-shaped flower-bed there rose perhaps a hundred stalks spreading into heart-shaped or tongue-shaped leaves half way up and unfurling at the tip red or blue or yellow petals marked with spots of colour raised upon the surface; and from the red, blue or yellow gloom of the throat emerged a straight bar, rough with gold dust and slightly clubbed at the end. The petals were voluminous enough to be stirred by the summer breeze, and when they moved, the red, blue and yellow lights passed one over the other, staining an inch of the brown earth beneath with a spot of the most intricate colour. The light fell either upon the smooth grey back of a pebble, or the shell of a snail with its brown circular veins, or, falling into a raindrop, it expanded with such intensity of red, blue and yellow the thin walls of water that one expected them to burst and disappear. Instead, the drop was left in a second silver grey once more, and the light now settled upon the flesh of a leaf, revealing the branching thread of fibre beneath the surface, and again it moved on and spread its illumination in the vast green spaces beneath the dome of the heart-shaped and tongue-shaped leaves. Then the breeze stirred rather more briskly overhead and the colour was flashed into the air above, into the eyes of the men and women who walk in Kew Gardens in July.

The figures of these men and women straggled past the flower-bed with a curiously irregular movement not unlike that of the white and blue butterflies who crossed the turf in zig-zag flights from bed to bed. The man was about six inches in front of the woman, strolling carelessly, while she bore on with greater purpose, only turning her head now and then to see that the children were not too far behind. The man kept this distance in front of the woman purposely, though perhaps unconsciously, for he wanted to go on with his thoughts.

"Fifteen years ago I came here with Lily," he thought. "We sat somewhere over there by a lake, and I begged her to marry me all through the hot afternoon. How the dragon-fly kept circling round us: how clearly I see the dragon-fly and her shoe with the square silver buckle at the toe. All the time I spoke I saw her shoe and when it moved impatiently I knew without looking up what she was going to say: the whole of her seemed to be in her shoe. And my love, my desire, were in the dragon-fly; for some reason I thought that if it settled there, on that leaf, the broad one with the red flower in the middle of it, if the dragon-fly settled on the leaf she would say 'Yes' at once. But the dragon-fly went round and round: it never settled anywhere—of course not, happily not, or I shouldn't be walking here with Eleanor and the children— Tell me, Eleanor, d'you ever think of the past?"

"Why do you ask, Simon?"

"Because I've been thinking of the past. I've been thinking of Lily, the 5 woman I might have married . . . Well, why are you silent? Do you mind my thinking of the past?"

"Why should I mind, Simon? Doesn't one always think of the past, in a garden with men and women lying under the trees? Aren't they one's past, all that remains of it, those men and women, those ghosts lying under the trees, . . . one's happiness, one's reality?"

"For me, a square silver shoe-buckle and a dragon-fly—"

"For me, a kiss. Imagine six little girls sitting before their easels twenty years ago, down by the side of a lake, painting the water-lilies, the first red water-lilies I'd ever seen. And suddenly a kiss, there on the back of my neck. And my hand shook all the afternoon so that I couldn't paint. I took out my watch and marked the hour when I would allow myself to think of the kiss for five minutes only—it was so precious—the kiss of an old grey-haired woman with a wart on her nose, the mother of all my kisses all my life. Come Caroline, come Hubert."

They walked on past the flower-bed, now walking four abreast, and soon diminished in size among the trees and looked half transparent as the sunlight and shade swam over their backs in large trembling irregular patches.

In the oval flower-bed the snail, whose shell had been stained red, blue and yellow for the space of two minutes or so, now appeared to be moving very slightly in its shell, and next began to labour over the crumbs of loose earth which broke away and rolled down as it passed over them. It appeared to have a definite goal in front of it, differing in this respect from the singular high-stepping angular green insect who attempted to cross in front of it, and waited for a second with its antennae trembling as if in deliberation, and then stepped off as rapidly and strangely in the opposite direction. Brown cliffs with deep green lakes in the hollows, flat blade-like trees that waved from root to tip, round boulders of grey stone, vast crumpled surfaces of a thin crackling texture—all these objects lay across the snail's progress between one stalk and another to his goal. Before he decided whether to circumvent the arched tent of a dead leaf or to breast it there came past the bed the feet of other human beings.

This time they were both men. The younger of the two wore an expression of perhaps unnatural calm; he raised his eyes and fixed them very steadily in front of him while his companion spoke, and directly his companion had done speaking he looked on the ground again and sometimes opened his lips only after a long pause and sometimes did not open them at all. The elder man had a curiously uneven and shaky method of walking, jerking his hand forward and throwing up his head abruptly, rather in the manner of an impatient carriage horse tired of waiting outside a house; but in the man these gestures were irresolute and pointless. He talked almost incessantly; he smiled to himself and again began to talk, as if the smile had been an answer. He was talking about spirits—the spirits of the dead, who, according to him, were even now telling him all sorts of odd things about their experiences in Heaven.

"Heaven was known to the ancients as Thessaly, William, and now, with this war, the spirit matter is rolling between the hills like thunder." He paused, seemed to listen, smiled, jerked his head and continued:—

"You have a small electric battery and a piece of rubber to insulate the wire—isolate?—insulate?—well, we'll skip the details, no good going into details that wouldn't be understood—and in short the little machine stands in any convenient position by the head of the bed, we will say, on a neat mahogany stand. All arrangements being properly fixed by workmen under my direction, the widow applies her ear and summons the spirit by sign as agreed. Women! Widows! Women in black—"

Here he seemed to have caught sight of a woman's dress in the distance, which in the shade looked a purple black. He took off his hat, placed his hand upon his heart, and hurried towards her muttering and gesticulating feverishly. But William caught him by the sleeve and touched a flower with the tip of his walking-stick in order to divert the old man's attention. After looking at it for a moment in some confusion the old man bent his ear to it and seemed to answer a voice speaking from it, for he began talking about the forests of Uruguay which he had visited hundreds of years ago in company with the most beautiful young woman in Europe. He could be heard murmuring about forests of Uruguay blanketed with the wax petals of tropical roses, nightingales, sea beaches, mermaids and women drowned at sea, as he suffered himself to be moved on by William, upon whose face the look of stoical patience grew slowly deeper and deeper.

Following his steps so closely as to be slightly puzzled by his gestures 15 came two elderly women of the lower middle class, one stout and ponderous, the other rosy-cheeked and nimble. Like most people of their station they were frankly fascinated by any signs of eccentricity betokening a disordered brain, especially in the well-to-do; but they were too far off to be certain whether the gestures were merely eccentric or genuinely mad. After they had scrutinised the old man's back in silence for a moment and given each other a queer, sly look, they went on energetically piecing together their very complicated dialogue:

"Nell, Bert, Lot, Cess, Phil, Pa, he says, I says, she says, I says, I says, I says—"

"My Bert, Sis, Bill, Grandad, the old man, sugar,
Sugar, flour, kippers, greens
Sugar, sugar, sugar."

The ponderous woman looked through the pattern of falling words at the flowers standing cool, firm and upright in the earth, with a curious expression. She saw them as a sleeper waking from a heavy sleep sees a brass candlestick reflecting the light in an unfamiliar way, and closes his eyes and opens them, and seeing the brass candlestick again, finally starts broad awake and stares at the candlestick with all his powers. So the heavy woman came to a standstill opposite the oval-shaped flower-bed, and ceased even to pretend to listen to what the other woman was saying. She stood there letting the words fall over her, swaying the top part of her body slowly backwards and forwards, looking at the flowers. Then she suggested that they should find a seat and have their tea.

The snail had now considered every possible method of reaching his goal without going round the dead leaf or climbing over it. Let alone the effort needed for climbing a leaf, he was doubtful whether the thin texture which vibrated with such an alarming crackle when touched even by the tip of his horns would bear his weight; and this determined him finally to creep beneath it, for there was a point where the leaf curved high enough from the ground to admit him. He had just inserted his head in the opening and was taking stock of the high brown roof and was getting used to the cool brown light when two other people came past outside on the turf. This time they were both young, a young man and a young woman. They were both in the prime of youth, or even in that season which precedes the prime of youth, the season before the smooth pink folds of the flower have burst their gummy case, when the wings of the butterfly, though fully grown, are motionless in the sun.

"Lucky it isn't Friday," he observed.

"Why? D'you believe in luck?"

"They make you pay sixpence on Friday."   20

"What's sixpence anyway? Isn't it worth sixpence?"

"What's 'it'—what do you mean by 'it'?"

"O anything—I mean—you know what I mean."

Long pauses came between each of these remarks: they were uttered in toneless and monotonous voices. The couple stood still on the edge of the flower-bed, and together pressed the end of her parasol deep down into the soft earth. The action and the fact that this hand rested on the top of hers expressed their feelings in a strange way, as these short insignificant words also expressed something, words with short wings for their heavy body of meaning, inadequate to carry them far and thus alighting awkwardly upon the very common objects that surrounded them and were to their inexperienced touch so massive: but who knows (so they thought as they pressed the parasol into the earth) what precipices aren't concealed in them, or what slopes of ice don't shine in the sun on the other side? Who knows? Who has ever seen this before? Even when she wondered what sort of tea they gave you at Kew, he felt that something loomed up behind her words, and stood vast and solid behind them; and the mist very slowly rose and uncovered—O Heavens,—what were those shapes?—little white tables, and waitresses who looked first at her and then at him; and there was a bill that he would pay with a real two shilling piece, and it was real, all real, he assured himself, fingering the coin in his pocket, real to everyone except to him and to her; even to him it began to seem real and then—but it was too exciting to stand and think any longer, and he pulled the parasol out of the earth with a jerk and was impatient to find the place where one had tea with other people, like other people.

"Come along, Trissie; it's time we had our tea."   25

"Wherever *does* one have one's tea?" she asked with the oddest thrill of excitement in her voice, looking vaguely round and letting herself be drawn on down the grass path, trailing her parasol, turning her head this way and that way, forgetting her tea, wishing to go down there and then down there, remembering orchids and cranes among wild flowers, a Chinese pagoda and a crimson-crested bird; but he bore her on.

Thus one couple after another with much the same irregular and aimless movement passed the flower-bed and were enveloped in layer after layer of green-blue vapour, in which at first their bodies had substance and a dash of colour, but later both substance and colour dissolved in the green-blue atmosphere. How hot it was! So hot that even the thrush chose to hop, like a mechanical bird, in the shadow of the flowers, with long pauses between one movement and the next; instead of rambling vaguely the white butterflies danced once above another, making with their white shifting flakes the outline of a shattered marble column above the tallest flowers; the glass roofs of the palm house shone as if a whole market full of shiny green umbrellas had opened in the sun; and in the drone of the aeroplane the voice of the summer sky murmured its fierce soul. Yellow and black, pink and snow white, shapes of all these colours, men, women and children, were spotted for a second upon the horizon, and then, seeing the breadth of yellow that lay upon the grass, they wavered and sought shade beneath the trees, dissolving like drops of water in the yellow and green atmosphere, staining it faintly with red and blue. It seemed as if all gross and heavy bodies had sunk down in the heat motionless and lay huddled upon the ground, but their voices went wavering from them as if they were flames lolling from the thick waxen bodies of candles. Voices, yes, voices, wordless voices, breaking the silence suddenly with such depth of contentment, such passion of desire, or, in the voices of children, such freshness of surprise; breaking the silence? But there was no silence; all the time the motor omnibuses were turning their wheels and changing their gear; like a vast nest of Chinese boxes all of wrought steel turning ceaselessly one within another the city murmured; on the top of which the voices cried aloud and the petals of myriads of flowers flashed their colours into the air.

www   ## TOPICS FOR CRITICAL THINKING Web

1. In what ways does the story convey the sense of simultaneous action?
2. How does that simultaneity relate to the story's views of different stages in life?
3. How does the past relate to the present in this story?
4. What does the story illustrate about the connectedness (or lack) among human beings?

www   ## TOPICS FOR CRITICAL WRITING Web

1. How does the image of the Chinese box describe the story itself?
2. In what ways is this story like a painting?

The Introduction   *(1922–1925)*

Lily Everit saw Mrs Dalloway bearing down on her from the other side of the room, and could have prayed her not to come and disturb her; and yet, as Mrs Dalloway approached with her right hand raised and a smile which Lily knew (though this was her first party) meant: 'But you've got to come out of your corner and talk,' a smile at once benevolent and drastic, commanding, she felt the strangest mixture of excitement and fear, of desire to be left alone and of longing to be taken out and thrown down, down into the boiling depths. But

Mrs Dalloway was intercepted; caught by an old gentleman with white moustaches, and thus Lily Everit had two minutes respite in which to hug to herself,
like a spar in the sea, to sip, like a glass of wine, the thought of her essay upon
the character of Dean Swift which Professor Miller had marked that morning
with three red stars; First rate. First rate; she repeated that to herself, but the
cordial was ever so much weaker now than it had been when she stood before
the long glass being finished off (a pat here, a dab there) by her sister and Mildred, the housemaid. For as their hands moved about her, she felt that they
were fidgeting agreeably on the surface but beneath lay untouched like a lump
of glowing metal her essay on the character of Dean Swift, and all their praises
when she came downstairs and stood in the hall waiting for a cab—Rupert had
come out of his room and said what a swell she looked—ruffled the surface,
went like a breeze among ribbons, but no more. One divided life (she felt sure
of it) into fact, this essay, and into fiction, this going out, into rock and into
wave, she thought, driving along and seeing things with such intensity that for
ever she would see the truth and herself, a white reflection in the driver's dark
back inextricably mixed: the moment of vision. Then as she came into the
house, at the very first sight of people moving up stairs, down stairs, this hard
lump (her essay on the character of Swift) wobbled, began melting, she could
not keep hold of it, and all her being (no longer sharp as a diamond cleaving
the heart of life asunder) turned to a mist of alarm, apprehension, and defence
as she stood at bay in her corner. This was the famous place: the world.

Looking out, Lily Everit instinctively hid that essay of hers, so ashamed
was she now, so bewildered too, and on tiptoe nevertheless to adjust her focus
and get into right proportions (the old having been shamefully wrong) these
diminishing and expanding things (what could one call them? people—
impressions of people's lives?) which seemed to menace her and mount over
her, to turn everything to water, leaving her only—for that she would not resign—the power to stand at bay.

Now Mrs Dalloway, who had never quite dropped her arm, had shown by
the way she moved it while she stood talking that she remembered, was only
interrupted by the old soldier with the white moustaches, raised it again definitely and came straight down on her, and said to the shy charming girl, with
her pale skin, her bright eyes, the dark hair which clustered poetically round
her head and the thin body in a dress which seemed slipping off,

'Come and let me introduce you,' and there Mrs Dalloway hesitated, and
then remembering that Lily was the clever one, who read poetry, looked
about for some young man, some young man just down from Oxford, who
would have read everything and could talk about Shelley. And holding Lily
Everit's hand [she] led her towards a group where there were young people
talking, and Bob Brinsley.

Lily Everit hung back a little, might have been the wayward sailing boat ⁵
curtseying in the wake of a steamer, and felt as Mrs Dalloway led her on, that
it was now going to happen; that nothing could prevent it now; or save her
(and she only wanted it to be over now) from being flung into a whirlpool
where either she would perish or be saved. But what was the whirlpool?

Oh it was made of a million things and each was distinct to her;

Westminster Abbey; the sense of enormously high solemn buildings sur-rounding them; being a woman. Perhaps that was the thing that came out, that remained, it was partly the dress, but all the little chivalries and respects of the drawing-room—all made her feel that she had come out of her chrysalis and was being proclaimed what in the comfortable darkness of childhood she had never been—this frail and beautiful creature, before whom men bowed, this limited and circumscribed creature who could not do what she liked, this butterfly with a thousand facets to its eyes and delicate fine plumage, and dif-ficulties and sensibilities and sadnesses innumerable; a woman.

As she walked with Mrs Dalloway across the room she accepted the part which was now laid on her and, naturally, overdid it a little as a soldier, proud of the traditions of an old and famous uniform might overdo it, feeling con-scious as she walked, of her finery; of her tight shoes; of her coiled and twisted hair; and how if she dropped a handkerchief (this had happened) a man would stoop precipitately and give it her; thus accentuating the delicacy, the artificial-ity of her bearing unnaturally, for they were not hers after all.

Hers it was, rather, to run and hurry and ponder on long solitary walks, climbing gates, stepping through the mud, and through the blur, the dream, the ecstasy of loneliness, to see the plover's wheel and surprise the rabbits, and come in the hearts of woods or wide lonely moors upon little ceremonies which had no audience, private rites, pure beauty offered by beetles and lilies of the valley and dead leaves and still pools, without any care whatever what human beings thought of them, which filled her mind with rapture and won-der and held her there till she must touch the gate post to recollect herself—all this was, until tonight her ordinary being, by which she knew and liked herself and crept into the heart of mother and father and brothers and sisters; and this other was a flower which had opened in ten minutes. As the flower opened so too [came], incontrovertibly, the flower's world, so different, so strange; the towers of Westminster; the high and formal buildings; talk; this civilisation, she felt, hanging back, as Mrs Dalloway led her on, this regulated way of life, which fell like a yoke about her neck, softly, indomitably, from the skies, a statement which there was no gainsaying. Glancing at her essay, the three red stars dulled to obscurity, but peacefully, pensively, as if yielding to the pressure of unquestionable might, that is the conviction that it was not hers to dominate, or to assert; rather to air and embellish this orderly life where all was done already; high towers, solemn bells, flats built every brick of them by men's toil, churches built by men's toil, parliaments too; and even the criss-cross of telegraph wires she thought looking at the window as she walked. What had she to oppose to this massive masculine achievement? An essay on the character of Dean Swift! And as she came up to the group, which Bob Brinsley dominated, (with his heel on the fender, and his head back), with his great honest forehead, and his self-assurance, and his delicacy, and honour and robust physical well being, and sunburn, and airiness and direct descent from Shakespeare, what could she do but lay her essay, oh and the whole of her being, on the floor as a cloak for him to trample on, as a rose for him to rifle. Which she did, emphatically, when Mrs Dalloway said, still holding her hand as if she would run away from this supreme trial, this introduction, 'Mr

Brinsley—Miss Everit. Both of you love Shelley.' But hers was not love compared with his.

Saying this, Mrs Dalloway felt, as she always felt remembering her youth, absurdly moved; youth meeting youth at her hands, and there flashing, as at the concussion of steel upon flint (both stiffened to her feeling perceptibly) the loveliest and most ancient of all fires as she saw in Bob Brinsley's change of expression from carelessness to conformity, to formality, as he shook hands, which foreboded Clarissa thought, the tenderness, the goodness, the carefulness of women latent in all men, to her a sight to bring tears to the eyes, as it moved her even more intimately, to see in Lily herself the shy look, the startled look, surely the loveliest of all looks on a girl's face; and man feeling this for woman, and woman that for man, and there flowing from that contact all those homes, trials, sorrows, profound joy and ultimate staunchness in the face of catastrophe, humanity was sweet at its heart, thought Clarissa, and her own life (to introduce a couple made her think of meeting Richard for the first time!) infinitely blessed. And on she went.

But, thought Lily Everit. But—but—but what?

Oh nothing, she thought hastily smothering down softly her sharp instinct. Yes, she said. She did like reading. 10

'And I suppose you write?' he said, 'poems presumably?'

'Essays,' she said. And she would not let this horror get possession of her. Churches and parliaments, flats, even the telegraph wires—all, she told herself, made by men's toil, and this young man, she told herself, is in direct descent from Shakespeare, so she would not let this terror, this suspicion of something different, get hold of her and shrivel up her wings and drive her out into loneliness. But as she said this, she saw him—how clse could she describe it—kill a fly. He tore the wings off a fly, standing with his foot on the fender his head thrown back, talking insolently about himself, arrogantly, but she didn't mind how insolent and arrogant he was to her, if only he had not been brutal to flies.

But she said, fidgeting as she smothered down that idea, why not, since he is the greatest of all worldly objects? And to worship, to adorn, to embellish was her task, and to be worshipped, her wings were for that. But he talked; but he looked; but he laughed; he tore the wings off a fly. He pulled the wings off its back with his clever strong hands, and she saw him do it; and she could not hide the knowledge from herself. But it is necessary that it should be so, she argued, thinking of the churches, of the parliaments and the blocks of flats, and so tried to crouch and cower and fold the wings down flat on her back. But—but, what was it why was it? In spite of all she could do her essay upon the character of Swift became more and more obtrusive and the three stars burnt quite bright again, only no longer clear and brilliant, but troubled and bloodstained as if this man, this great Mr Brinsley, had just by pulling the wings off a fly as he talked (about his essay, about himself and once laughing, about a girl there) charged her light being with cloud, and confused her for ever and ever and shrivelled her wings on her back, and, as he turned away from her, he made her think of the towers of civilisation with horror, and the yoke that had fallen from the skies onto her neck crushed her, and she felt like a naked wretch who having sought shelter in some shady garden is turned out and told—no, that there are no sanctuaries, or butterflies, in this world, and this civilisation, churches, parliaments and flats—this civilisation, said Lily Everit to herself, as she accepted the kind compliments of old Mrs Bromley on her appearance[, depends upon me,] and Mrs Bromley said later that like all the Everits Lily looked 'as if she had the weight of the world upon her shoulders'.

www ### TOPICS FOR CRITICAL THINKING Web

1. What does Lily come to understand about gender?
2. For what purposes does the story shift points of view?
3. What does Lily understand through her evocation of Mr. Brinsley tearing the wings off of flies?
4. How does this short scene embody the complex issues of a girl becoming a woman?

www ### TOPICS FOR CRITICAL WRITING Web

1. To what does the story's title refer?
2. How does this story use the contrast between images of the city and the country?

10   Language and Style

Prose fiction is made up of words. The ways these words are arranged is called **style**. Web The study of style is called **stylistics** Web . Style involves many   *www* choices on the part of the writer about the language of the piece—diction, sentence length, the rhythm of the words, a predominance of action or imagery, and the repetition of words or phrases. **Diction** refers to the choice of words. If, for example, a writer chooses to use the word *prevaricate* instead of *lie*, the writer is selecting a word that connotes a level of sophistication and seriousness that is not implied by the use of the plainer term *lie*. Or a writer might use the word *luscious* instead of *delicious*. Though the words mean the same thing, they have different **connotations**. In prose fiction, diction is used as a way to set tone (see Chapter 11); to aid characterization (see Chapter 3); to convey social class, age, gender, and race; and to help constitute the rhythm, sound, and patterns of language (or *motifs)* that constitute the art of the prose.

Georgia O'Keeffe, *Black Abstraction* (1927)

Style also involves how sentence grammar is used. Sentences may be long and complex (as they are in the writings of Nathaniel Hawthorne, Virginia Woolf, James Joyce, and D. H. Lawrence) or shorter and simpler (as in the work of Jack London, Mark Twain, Tillie Olsen, Alice Walker, Ernest Hemingway, and Gertrude Stein). Compare, for example, these two sentences. The first is from Joyce's "Araby," and the second is from Hemingway's "Hills Like White Elephants."

> I may have stood there for an hour, seeing nothing but a brown-clad figure cast by my imagination, touched discreetly by the lamplight at the curved neck, at the hand upon the railings and at the border below the dress.

> The Hills across the valley of the Ebro were long and white.

Sentence length and complexity might vary in relation to the actions described as in Kate Chopin's, James Baldwin's, or Joyce's stories, or as a way of establishing mood or atmosphere, as in Edgar Allan Poe's stories. For example, the impact of the news of Mr. Mallard's death in Chopin's "The Story of an Hour" tends to produce a series of accumulating emotions in Mrs. Mallard. These emotions are conveyed by sentences in which feelings and events gather in extended phrases: "She was young, with a fair, calm face, whose lines bespoke repression and even a certain strength." In Baldwin's "Sonny's Blues," sentences sometimes imitate the music they describe: "One boy was whistling a tune, at once very complicated and very simple, it seemed to be pouring out of him as though he were a bird, and it sounded very cool and moving through all that harsh, bright air, only just holding its own through all those other sounds."

Style also consists of how much of a story's prose focuses on images, describes actions, or presents dialogue. Some stories rely on imagery and suggestion; these use many adjectives and often linger over descriptions of people and places. "The Birthmark" and "Kew Gardens" are such stories. London's story "The Law of Life" concentrates on the character's actions. Other stories present the more staccato rhythms of dialogue. "Hills Like White Elephants" is almost entirely dialogue: "Four reales." "We want two Anis del Toro." "With water?" "I don't know." John Updike's "A & P" tells its story through the running interior monologue of the main character: "I thought and said 'No' but it wasn't about that I was thinking."

www   Style is intimately linked to *image* Web, conveying via language impressions that match or complement a story's imagery. Images are partly an effect of style. The sentences from Joyce and Hemingway above both demonstrate how diction and grammar combine to produce both an image and an atmosphere. Joyce's sentence ruminates, lingering on detail and the effects of light on the person the character is in love with, while Hemingway's sentence is as straightforward as the hills it describes.

Critical Perspective: On Style

"In a large studio in Paris, hung with paintings by Renoir, Matisse and Picasso, Gertrude Stein is doing with words what Picasso is doing with paint. She is impelling language to induce new states of consciousness, and in doing so language becomes with her a creative art rather than a mirror of history. In her impressionistic writing she uses familiar words to create perceptions, conditions, and states of being, never before quite consciously experienced. She does this by using words that appeal to her as having the meaning that they seem to have. She has taken the English language and, according to many people, has misused it, or has used it roughly, uncouthly and brutally, or madly, stupidly and hideously, but by her method she is finding the hidden and inner nature of nature. . . .

"In Gertrude Stein's writing every word lives and, apart from the concept, it is so exquisitely rhythmical and cadenced, that when read aloud and received as pure sound, it is like a kind of sensuous music. Just as one may stop, for once in a way, before a canvas of Picasso, and, letting one's reason sleep for an instant, may exclaim: 'It is a fine pattern!'—so listening to Gertrude Stein's words and forgetting to try to understand what they mean, one submits to their gradual charm. Huntley Carter, of the *New Age*, says that her use of language has a curious hypnotic effect when read aloud. In one part of her writing she made use of repetition and the rearranging of certain words over and over, so that they became adjusted into a kind of incantation, and in listening one feels that from the combination of repeated sounds, varied ever so little, that there emerges gradually a perception of some meaning quite other than that of the contents of the phrases. Many people have experienced this magical evocation, but have been unable to explain in what way it came to pass, but though they did not know what meaning the words were bearing, nor how they were affected by them, yet they had begun to know what it all meant, because they were not indifferent."

—Mabel Dodge, "Speculations, or Post-Impressionism in Prose," *Arts and Decoration* (March 1913).

Mabel Dodge, a friend of Stein's, analyzes Stein's style—the ways she uses language—as a way of explaining what Stein's work achieves. Describing what the rhythms and sounds of Stein's language evokes, Dodge conveys how Stein's writing depends on the effects of style.

Critical Perspectives: Close Readings and Deconstructive Readings

Analyzing how language and image might match or work in tension with one another is a task of both close reading **Web** and deconstruction **Web**. **Close** *www* **readings** investigate the ways language and image work together. Both **New** *www* **Criticism** Web and **semiotics** Web affirm the idea that insights about the ways texts work can be gained from looking at the relationships among their various elements. Building on the practice of close reading, **deconstructive readings** focus on the precariousness of a story's elements, looking at the ways language in a story might work against itself or against its imagery, producing tensions, contradictions, and enigmas that partly account for a story's complexity and richness.

Style is almost always in line with a story's atmosphere—the combination of setting, plot, and tone that indicates whether a story is comic, tragic, ironic, cynical, or romantic. Style provides clues about how a story should be read: whether it is serious or lighthearted, everyday or unusual. Style also plays a *www* large part in defining literary movements such as **realism** Web , **naturalism** Web , and **modernism** Web , so much so that these movements are also sometimes called *styles*.

Stories About Language and Style

The stories that follow are all examples of stories that develop the style of American modernism. The authors—F. Scott Fitzgerald, Ernest Hemingway, and Gertrude Stein—experiment with language and style. Hemingway and *www* Stein were influenced by *cubist* painters Web , and their styles are often lean, but musical. Along with Fitzgerald, Hemingway and Stein were part of the *www* rich and lively culture of a *transatlantic modernism* Web that mingled the work of European writers and innovations in the plastic arts (such as *cubism* and *sur-* *www* *realism* Web with fresh ideas from the *Harlem Renaissance* Web and the elegant discipline of an American vision.

ᘐᘐᘐ

F. SCOTT FITZGERALD

Babylon Revisited   *(1941)*

I

"And where's Mr. Campbell?" Charlie asked.

"Gone to Switzerland. Mr. Campbell's a pretty sick man, Mr. Wales."

"I'm sorry to hear that. And George Hardt?" Charlie inquired.

"Back in America, gone to work."

"And where is the Snow Bird?"   5

"He was in here last week. Anyway, his friend, Mr. Schaeffer, is in Paris."

Two familiar names from the long list of a year and a half ago. Charlie scribbled an address in his notebook and tore out the page.

"If you see Mr. Schaeffer, give him this," he said. "It's my brother-in-law's address. I haven't settled on a hotel yet."

He was not really disappointed to find Paris was so empty. But the stillness in the Ritz bar was strange and portentous. It was not an American bar any more—he felt polite in it, and not as if he owned it. It had gone back into France. He felt the stillness from the moment he got out of the taxi and saw the doorman, usually in a frenzy of activity at this hour, gossiping with a *chasseur*[1] by the servants' entrance.

Passing through the corridor, he heard only a single, bored voice in the once-clamorous women's room. When he turned into the bar he traveled the twenty feet of green carpet with his eyes fixed straight ahead by old habit; and then, with his foot firmly on the rail, he turned and surveyed the room, encountering only a single pair of eyes that fluttered up from a newspaper in the corner. Charlie asked for the head barman, Paul, who in the latter days of the bull market had come to work in his own custom-built car—disembarking, however, with due nicety at the nearest corner. But Paul was at his country house today and Alix giving him information.

"No, no more," Charlie said, "I'm going slow these days."

Alix congratulated him: "You were going pretty strong a couple of years ago."

"I'll stick to it all right," Charlie assured him. "I've stuck to it for over a year and a half now."

"How do you find conditions in America?"

"I haven't been to America for months. I'm in business in Prague, representing a couple of concerns there. They don't know about me down there."

Alix smiled.

"Remember the night of George Hardt's bachelor dinner here?" said Charlie. "By the way, what's become of Claude Fessenden?"

Alix lowered his voice confidentially: "He's in Paris, but he doesn't come here any more. Paul doesn't allow it. He ran up a bill of thirty thousand francs, charging all his drinks and his lunches, and usually his dinner, for more than a year. And when Paul finally told him he had to pay, he gave him a bad check."

Alix shook his head sadly.

"I don't understand it, such a dandy fellow. Now he's all bloated up—" He made a plump apple of his hands.

Charlie watched a group of strident queens installing themselves in a corner.

"Nothing affects them," he thought. "Stocks rise and fall, people loaf or work, but they go on forever." The place oppressed him. He called for the dice and shook with Alix for the drink.

"Here for long, Mr. Wales?"

"I'm here for four or five days to see my little girl."

"Oh-h! You have a little girl?"

Outside, the fire-red, gas-blue, ghost-green signs shone smokily through the tranquil rain. It was late afternoon and the streets were in movement; the bistros gleamed. At the corner of the Boulevard des Capucines he took a taxi.

---

1. Porter.

The Place de la Concorde moved by in pink majesty; they crossed the logical Seine, and Charlie felt the sudden provincial quality of the Left Bank.

Charlie directed his taxi to the Avenue de l'Opéra, which was out of his way. But he wanted to see the blue hour spread over the magnificent façade, and imagine that the cab horns, playing endlessly the first few bars of *Le Plus que Lent*, were the trumpets of the Second Empire.[2] They were closing the iron grill in front of Brentano's Bookstore, and people were already at dinner behind the trim little bourgeois hedge of Duval's. He had never eaten at a really cheap restaurant in Paris. Five-course dinner, four francs fifty, eighteen cents, wine included. For some odd reason he wished that he had.

As they rolled on to the Left Bank, and he felt its sudden provincialism, he thought, "I spoiled this city for myself. I didn't realize it, but the days came along one after another, and then two years were gone, and everything was gone, and I was gone."

He was thirty-five, and good to look at. The Irish mobility of his face was sobered by a deep wrinkle between his eyes. As he rang his brother-in-law's bell in the Rue Palatine, the wrinkle deepened till it pulled down his brows; he felt a cramping sensation in his belly. From behind the maid who opened the door darted a lovely little girl of nine who shrieked "Daddy!" and flew up, struggling like a fish, into his arms. She pulled his head around by one ear and set her cheek against his.

"My old pie," he said.

"Oh, daddy, daddy, daddy, daddy, dads, dads, dads!"

She drew him into the salon, where the family waited, a boy and a girl his daughter's age, his sister-in-law and her husband. He greeted Marion with his voice pitched carefully to avoid either feigned enthusiasm or dislike, but her response was more frankly tepid, though she minimized her expression of unalterable distrust by directing her regard toward his child. The two men clasped hands in a friendly way and Lincoln Peters rested his for a moment on Charlie's shoulder.

The room was warm and comfortably American. The three children moved intimately about, playing through the yellow oblongs that led to other rooms; the cheer of six o'clock spoke in the eager smacks of the fire and the sounds of French activity in the kitchen. But Charlie did not relax; his heart sat up rigidly in his body and he drew confidence from his daughter, who from time to time came close to him, holding in her arms the doll he had brought.

"Really extremely well," he declared in answer to Lincoln's question. "There's a lot of business there that isn't moving at all, but we're doing even better than ever. In fact, damn well. I'm bringing my sister over from America next month to keep house for me. My income last year was bigger than it was when I had money. You see, the Czechs—"

His boasting was for a specific purpose; but after a moment, seeing a faint restiveness in Lincoln's eye, he changed the subject:

"Those are fine children of yours, well brought up, good manners."

"We think Honoria's a great little girl too."

2. Second Empire 1852–1870, under Napoleon III.

Marion Peters came back from the kitchen. She was a tall woman with worried eyes, who had once possessed a fresh American loveliness. Charlie had never been sensitive to it and was always surprised when people spoke of how pretty she had been. From the first there had been an instinctive antipathy between them.

"Well, how do you find Honoria?" she asked.

"Wonderful. I was astonished how much she's grown in ten months. All the children are looking well."   40

"We haven't had a doctor for a year. How do you like being back in Paris?"

"It seems very funny to see so few Americans around."

"I'm delighted," Marion said vehemently. "Now at least you can go into a store without their assuming you're a millionaire. We've suffered like everybody, but on the whole it's a good deal pleasanter."

"But it was nice while it lasted," Charlie said. "We were a sort of royalty, almost infallible, with a sort of magic around us. In the bar this afternoon"— he stumbled, seeing his mistake—"there wasn't a man I knew."

She looked at him keenly. "I should think you'd have had enough of bars."   45

"I only stayed a minute. I take one drink every afternoon, and no more."

"Don't you want a cocktail before dinner?" Lincoln asked.

"I take only one drink every afternoon, and I've had that."

"I hope you keep to it," said Marion.

Her dislike was evident in the coldness with which she spoke, but Charlie only smiled; he had larger plans. Her very aggressiveness gave him an advantage, and he knew enough to wait. He wanted them to initiate the discussion of what they knew had brought him to Paris.   50

At dinner he couldn't decide whether Honoria was most like him or her mother. Fortunate if she didn't combine the traits of both that had brought them to disaster. A great wave of protectiveness went over him. He thought he knew what to do for her. He believed in character; he wanted to jump back a whole generation and trust in character again as the eternally valuable element. Everything else wore out.

He left soon after dinner, but not to go home. He was curious to see Paris by night with clearer and more judicious eyes than those of other days. He bought a *strapontin*[3] for the Casino and watched Josephine Baker[4] go through her chocolate arabesques.

After an hour he left and strolled toward Montmartre, up the Rue Pigalle into the Place Blanche. The rain had stopped and there were a few people in evening clothes disembarking from taxis in front of cabarets, and *cocottes*[5] prowling singly or in pairs, and many Negroes. He passed a lighted door from which issued music, and stopped with the sense of familiarity; it was Bricktop's, where he had parted with so many hours and so much money. A few

3. Folding chair.
4. African-American dancer (1906–1975), very popular in Paris in the 1920s and 1930s.
5. Prostitutes.

doors farther on he found another ancient rendezvous and incautiously put his head inside. Immediately an eager orchestra burst into sound, a pair of professional dancers leaped to their feet and a maitre d'hôtel swooped toward him, crying,"Crowd just arriving, sir!" But he withdrew quickly.

"You have to be damn drunk," he thought.

Zelli's was closed, the bleak and sinister cheap hotels surrounding it were   55
dark; up in the Rue Blanche there was more light and a local, colloquial French crowd. The Poet's Cave had disappeared, but the two great mouths of the Café of Heaven and the Café of Hell still yawned—even devoured, as he watched, the meager contents of a tourist bus—a German, a Japanese, and an American couple who glanced at him with frightened eyes.

So much for the effort and ingenuity of Montmartre. All the catering to vice and waste was on an utterly childish scale, and he suddenly realized the meaning of the word "dissipate"—to dissipate into thin air; to make nothing out of something. In the little hours of the night every move from place to place was an enormous human jump, an increase of paying for the privilege of slower and slower motion.

He remembered thousand-franc notes given to an orchestra for playing a single number, hundred-franc notes tossed to a doorman for calling a cab.

But it hadn't been given for nothing.

It had been given, even the most wildly squandered sum, as an offering to destiny that he might not remember the things most worth remembering, the things that now he would always remember—his child taken from his control, his wife escaped to a grave in Vermont.

In the glare of a *brasserie*[6] a woman spoke to him. He bought her some   60
eggs and coffee, and then, eluding her encouraging stare, gave her a twenty-franc note and took a taxi to his hotel.

II

He woke upon a fine fall day—football weather. The depression of yesterday was gone and he liked the people on the streets. At noon he sat opposite Honoria at Le Grand Vatel, the only restaurant he could think of not reminiscent of champagne dinners and long luncheons that began at two and ended in a blurred and vague twilight.

"Now, how about vegetables? Oughtn't you to have some vegetables?"

"Well, yes."

"Here's *épinards* and *chou-fleur* and carrots and *haricots*."[7]

"I'd like *chou-fleur*."   65

"Wouldn't you like to have two vegetables?"

"I usually only have one at lunch."

The waiter was pretending to be inordinately fond of children. *"Qu'elle est mignonne la petite! Elle parle exactement comme une française."*[8]

6. Bar and grill.
7. Spinach, cauliflower, green beans.
8. "The little one is so sweet. She speaks exactly like a little French girl."

"How about dessert? Shall we wait and see?"

The waiter disappeared. Honoria looked at her father expectantly.   70

"What are we going to do?"

"First, we're going to that toy store in the Rue Saint-Honoré and buy you anything you like. And then we're going to the vaudeville at the Empire."

She hesitated. "I like it about the vaudeville, but not the toy store."

"Why not?"

"Well, you brought me this doll." She had it with her. "And I've got lots   75
of things. And we're not rich any more, are we?"

"We never were. But today you are to have anything you want."

"All right," she agreed resignedly.

When there had been her mother and a French nurse he had been inclined to be strict; now he extended himself, reached out for a new tolerance; he must be both parents to her and not shut any of her out of communication.

"I want to get to know you," he said gravely. "First let me introduce myself. My name is Charles J. Wales, of Prague."

"Oh, daddy!" her voice cracked with laughter.   80

"And who are you, please?" he persisted, and she accepted a role immediately: "Honoria Wales, Rue Palatine, Paris."

"Married or single?"

"No, not married. Single."

He indicated the doll. "But I see you have a child, madame."

Unwilling to disinherit it, she took it to her heart and thought quickly: 85
"Yes, I've been married, but I'm not married now. My husband is dead."

He went on quickly, "And the child's name?"

"Simone. That's after my best friend at school."

"I'm very pleased that you're doing so well at school."

"I'm third this month," she boasted. "Elsie"—that was her cousin—"is only about eighteenth, and Richard is about at the bottom."

"You like Richard and Elsie, don't you?"   90

"Oh, yes. I like Richard quite well and I like her all right."

Cautiously and casually he asked: "And Aunt Marion and Uncle Lincoln—which do you like best?"

"Oh, Uncle Lincoln, I guess."

He was increasingly aware of her presence. As they came in, a murmur of ". . . adorable" followed them, and now the people at the next table bent all their silences upon her, staring as if she were something no more conscious than a flower.

"Why don't I live with you?" she asked suddenly. "Because mamma's   95
dead?"

"You must stay here and learn more French. It would have been hard for daddy to take care of you so well."

"I don't really need much taking care of any more. I do everything for myself."

Going out of the restaurant, a man and a woman unexpectedly hailed him. "Well, the old Wales!"

"Hello there, Lorraine. . . . Dunc."

Sudden ghosts out of the past: Duncan Schaeffer, a friend from college.   100
Lorraine Quarrles, a lovely, pale blonde of thirty; one of a crowd who had
helped him make months into days in the lavish times of three years ago.

"My husband couldn't come this year," she said, in answer to his question.
"We're poor as hell. So he gave me two hundred a month and told me I could
do my worst on that. . . . This your little girl?"

"What about coming back and sitting down?" Duncan asked.

"Can't do it." He was glad for an excuse. As always, he felt Lorraine's passionate, provocative attraction, but his own rhythm was different now.

"Well, how about dinner?" she asked.

"I'm not free. Give me your address and let me call you."   105

"Charlie, I believe you're sober," she said judicially. "I honestly believe
he's sober, Dunc. Pinch him and see if he's sober."

Charlie indicated Honoria with his head. They both laughed.

"What's your address?" said Duncan skeptically.

He hesitated, unwilling to give the name of his hotel.

"I'm not settled yet. I'd better call you. We're going to see the vaudeville   110
at the Empire."

"There! That's what I want to do," Lorraine said. "I want to see some
clowns and acrobats and jugglers. That's just what we'll do, Dunc."

"We've got to do an errand first," said Charlie. "Perhaps we'll see you
there."

"All right, you snob. . . . Good-by, beautiful little girl."

"Good-by."

Honoria bobbed politely.   115

Somehow, an unwelcome encounter. They liked him because he was
functioning, because he was serious; they wanted to see him, because he was
stronger than they were now, because they wanted to draw a certain sustenance from his strength.

At the Empire, Honoria proudly refused to sit upon her father's folded
coat. She was already an individual with a code of her own, and Charlie was
more and more absorbed by the desire of putting a little of himself into her
before she crystallized utterly. It was hopeless to try to know her in so short
a time.

Between the acts they came upon Duncan and Lorraine in the lobby
where the band was playing.

"Have a drink?"

"All right, but not up at the bar. We'll take a table."   120

"The perfect father."

Listening abstractedly to Lorraine, Charlie watched Honoria's eyes leave
their table, and he followed them wistfully about the room, wondering what
they saw. He met her glance and she smiled.

"I liked that lemonade," she said.

What had she said? What had he expected? Going home in a taxi afterward, he pulled her over until her head rested against his chest.

"Darling, do you ever think about your mother?"   125

"Yes, sometimes," she answered vaguely.

"I don't want you to forget her. Have you got a picture of her?"

"Yes, I think so. Anyhow, Aunt Marion has. Why don't you want me to forget her?"

"She loved you very much."

"I loved her too."   130

They were silent for a moment.

"Daddy, I want to come and live with you," she said suddenly.

His heart leaped; he had wanted it to come like this.

"Aren't you perfectly happy?"

"Yes, but I love you better than anybody. And you love me better than   135
anybody, don't you, now that mummy's dead?"

"Of course I do. But you won't always like me best, honey. You'll grow up
and meet somebody your own age and go marry him and forget you ever had
a daddy."

"Yes, that's true," she agreed tranquilly.

He didn't go in. He was coming back at nine o'clock and he wanted to
keep himself fresh and new for the thing he must say then.

"When you're safe inside, just show yourself in that window."

"All right. Good-by, dads, dads, dads, dads."   140

He waited in the dark street until she appeared, all warm and glowing, in
the window above and kissed her fingers out into the night.

III

They were waiting. Marion sat behind the coffee service in a dignified black
dinner dress that just faintly suggested mourning. Lincoln was walking up and
down with the animation of one who had already been talking. They were as
anxious as he was to get into the question. He opened it almost immediately:

"I suppose you know what I want to see you about—why I really came to
Paris."

Marion played with the black stars on her necklace and frowned.

"I'm awfully anxious to have a home," he continued. "And I'm awfully   145
anxious to have Honoria in it. I appreciate your taking in Honoria for her
mother's sake, but things have changed now"—he hesitated and then continued more forcibly—"changed radically with me, and I want to ask you to reconsider the matter. It would be silly for me to deny that about three years ago
I was acting badly—"

Marion looked up at him with hard eyes.

"—but all that's over. As I told you, I haven't had more than a drink a day
for over a year, and I take that drink deliberately, so that the idea of alcohol
won't get too big in my imagination. You see the idea?"

"No," said Marion succinctly.

"It's a sort of stunt I set myself. It keeps the matter in proportion."

"I get you," said Lincoln. "You don't want to admit it's got any attraction   150
for you."

"Something like that. Sometimes I forget and don't take it. But I try to take it. Anyhow, I couldn't afford to drink in my position. The people I represent are more than satisfied with what I've done, and I'm bringing my sister over from Burlington to keep house for me, and I want awfully to have Honoria too. You know that even when her mother and I weren't getting along well we never let anything that happened touch Honoria. I know she's fond of me and I know I'm able to take care of her and—well, there you are. How do you feel about it?"

He knew that now he would have to take a beating. It would last an hour or two hours, and it would be difficult, but if he modulated his inevitable resentment to the chastened attitude of the reformed sinner, he might win his point in the end.

Keep your temper, he told himself. You don't want to be justified. You want Honoria.

Lincoln spoke first: "We've been talking it over ever since we got your letter last month. We're happy to have Honoria here. She's a dear little thing, and we're glad to be able to help her, but of course that isn't the question—"

Marion interrupted suddenly. "How long are you going to stay sober, 155 Charlie?" she asked.

"Permanently, I hope."

"How can anybody count on that?"

"You know I never did drink heavily until I gave up business and came over here with nothing to do. Then Helen and I began to run around with—"

"Please leave Helen out of it. I can't bear to hear you talk about her like that."

He stared at her grimly; he had never been certain how fond of each other 160 the sisters were in life.

"My drinking only lasted about a year and a half—from the time we came over until I—collapsed."

"It was time enough."

"It was time enough," he agreed.

"My duty is entirely to Helen," she said. "I try to think what she would have wanted me to do. Frankly, from the night you did that terrible thing you haven't really existed for me. I can't help that. She was my sister."

"Yes."   165

"When she was dying she asked me to look out for Honoria. If you hadn't been in a sanitarium then, it might have helped matters."

He had no answer.

"I'll never in my life be able to forget the morning when Helen knocked at my door, soaked to the skin and shivering, and said you'd locked her out."

Charlie gripped the sides of the chair. This was more difficult than he expected; he wanted to launch out into a long expostulation and explanation, but he only said: "The night I locked her out—" and she interrupted, "I don't feel up to going over that again."

After a moment's silence Lincoln said: "We're getting off the subject. You 170 want Marion to set aside her legal guardianship and give you Honoria. I think the main point for her is whether she has confidence in you or not."

"I don't blame Marion," Charlie said slowly, "but I think she can have entire confidence in me. I had a good record up to three years ago. Of course, it's within human possibilities I might go wrong any time. But if we wait much longer I'll lose Honoria's childhood and my chance for a home." He shook his head. "I'll simply lose her, don't you see?"

"Yes, I see," said Lincoln.

"Why didn't you think of all this before?" Marion asked.

"I suppose I did, from time to time, but Helen and I were getting along badly. When I consented to the guardianship, I was flat on my back in a sanitarium and the market had cleaned me out. I knew I'd acted badly, and I thought if it would bring any peace to Helen, I'd agree to anything. But now it's different. I'm functioning, I'm behaving damn well, so far as—"

"Please don't swear at me," Marion said.   175

He looked at her, startled. With each remark the force of her dislike became more and more apparent. She had built up all her fear of life into one wall and faced it toward him. This trivial reproof was possibly the result of some trouble with the cook several hours before. Charlie became increasingly alarmed at leaving Honoria in this atmosphere of hostility against himself; sooner or later it would come out, in a word here, a shake of the head there, and some of that distrust would be irrevocably implanted in Honoria. But he pulled his temper down out of his face and shut it up inside him; he had won a point, for Lincoln realized the absurdity of Marion's remark and asked her lightly since when she had objected to the word "damn."

"Another thing," Charlie said: "I'm able to give her certain advantages now. I'm going to take a French governess to Prague with me. I've got a lease on a new apartment—"

He stopped, realizing that he was blundering. They couldn't be expected to accept with equanimity the fact that his income was again twice as large as their own.

"I suppose you can give her more luxuries than we can," said Marion. "When you were throwing away money we were living along watching every ten francs. . . . I suppose you'll start doing it again."

"Oh, no," he said. "I've learned. I worked hard for ten years, you know—   180
until I got lucky in the market, like so many people. Terribly lucky. It won't happen again."

There was a long silence. All of them felt their nerves straining, and for the first time in a year Charlie wanted a drink. He was sure now that Lincoln Peters wanted him to have his child.

Marion shuddered suddenly; part of her saw that Charlie's feet were planted on the earth now, and her own maternal feeling recognized the naturalness of his desire; but she had lived for a long time with a prejudice—a prejudice founded on a curious disbelief in her sister's happiness, which, in the shock of one terrible night, had turned to hatred for him. It had all happened at a point in her life where the discouragement of ill health and adverse circumstances made it necessary for her to believe in tangible villainy and a tangible villain.

"I can't help what I think!" she cried out suddenly. "How much you were responsible for Helen's death, I don't know. It's something you'll have to square with your own conscience."

An electric current of agony surged through him; for a moment he was almost on his feet, an unuttered sound echoing in his throat. He hung on to himself for a moment, another moment.

"Hold on there," said Lincoln uncomfortably. "I never thought you were 185 responsible for that."

"Helen died of heart trouble," Charlie said dully.

"Yes, heart trouble." Marion spoke as if the phrase had another meaning for her. Then, in the flatness that followed her outburst, she saw him plainly and she knew he had somehow arrived at control over the situation. Glancing at her husband, she found no help from him, and as abruptly as if it were a matter of no importance, she threw up the sponge.

"Do what you like!" she cried, springing up from her chair. "She's your child. I'm not the person to stand in your way. I think if it were my child I'd rather see her—" She managed to check herself. "You two decide it. I can't stand this. I'm sick. I'm going to bed."

She hurried from the room; after a moment Lincoln said:

"This has been a hard day for her. You know how strongly she feels—" 190 His voice was almost apologetic: "When a woman gets an idea in her head."

"Of course."

"It's going to be all right. I think she sees now that you—can provide for the child, and so we can't very well stand in your way or Honoria's way."

"Thank you, Lincoln."

"I'd better go along and see how she is."

"I'm going." 195

He was still trembling when he reached the street, but a walk down the Rue Bonaparte to the *quais*[9] set him up, and as he crossed the Seine, fresh and new by the *quai* lamps, he felt exultant. But back in his room he couldn't sleep. The image of Helen haunted him. Helen whom he had loved so until they had senselessly begun to abuse each other's love, tear it into shreds. On that terrible February night that Marion remembered so vividly, a slow quarrel had gone on for hours. There was a scene at the Florida, and then he attempted to take her home, and then she kissed young Webb at a table; after that there was what she had hysterically said. When he arrived home alone he turned the key in the lock in wild anger. How could he know she would arrive an hour later alone, that there would be a snow storm in which she wandered about in slippers, too confused to find a taxi? Then the aftermath, her escaping pneumonia by a miracle, and all the attendant horror. They were "reconciled," but that was the beginning of the end, and Marion, who had seen with her own eyes and who imagined it to be one of many scenes from her sister's martyrdom, never forgot.

Going over it again brought Helen nearer, and in the white, soft light that steals upon half sleep near morning he found himself talking to her again. She said that he was perfectly right about Honoria and that she wanted Honoria

9. Docks.

to be with him. She said she was glad he was being good and doing better. She said a lot of other things—very friendly things—but she was in a swing in a white dress, and swinging faster and faster all the time, so that at the end he could not hear clearly all that she said.

IV

He woke up feeling happy. The door of the world was open again. He made plans, vistas, futures for Honoria and himself, but suddenly he grew sad, remembering all the plans he and Helen had made. She had not planned to die. The present was the thing—work to do and someone to love. But not to love too much, for he knew the injury that a father can do to a daughter or a mother to a son by attaching them too closely: afterward, out in the world, the child would seek in the marriage partner the same blind tenderness and, failing probably to find it, turn against love and life.

It was another bright, crisp day. He called Lincoln Peters at the bank where he worked and asked if he could count on taking Honoria when he left for Prague. Lincoln agreed that there was no reason for delay. One thing— the legal guardianship. Marion wanted to retain that awhile longer. She was upset by the whole matter, and it would oil things if she felt that the situation was still in her control for another year. Charlie agreed, wanting only the tangible, visible child.

Then the question of a governess. Charlie sat in a gloomy agency and   200
talked to a cross Béarnaise and to a buxom Breton peasant, neither of whom he could have endured. There were others whom he would see tomorrow.

He lunched with Lincoln Peters at Griffons, trying to keep down his exultation.

"There's nothing quite like your own child," Lincoln said. "But you understand how Marion feels too."

"She's forgotten how hard I worked for seven years there," Charlie said. "She just remembers one night."

"There's another thing," Lincoln hesitated. "While you and Helen were tearing around Europe throwing money away, we were just getting along. I didn't touch any of the prosperity because I never got ahead enough to carry anything but my insurance. I think Marion felt there was some kind of injustice in it—you not even working toward the end, and getting richer and richer."

"It went just as quick as it came," said Charlie.   205

"Yes, a lot of it stayed in the hands of *chasseurs* and saxaphone players and maitres d'hôtel—well, the big party's over now. I just said that to explain Marion's feeling about those crazy years. If you drop in about six o'clock tonight before Marion's too tired, we'll settle the details on the spot."

Back at his hotel, Charlie found a *pneumatique*[10] that had been redirected from the Ritz bar, where Charlie had left his address for the purpose of a certain man.

---

10. A message sent by pneumatic tube.

Dear Charlie:

You were so strange when we saw you the other day that I wondered if I did something to offend you. If so, I'm not conscious of it. In fact, I have thought about you too much for the last year, and it's always been in the back of my mind that I might see you if I came over here. We *did* have such good times that crazy spring, like the night you and I stole the butcher's tricycle, and the time we tried to call on the president and you had the old derby rim and the wire cane. Everybody seems so old lately, but I don't feel old a bit. Couldn't we get together some time today for old time's sake? I've got a vile hangover for the moment, but will be feeling better this afternoon and will look for you about five in the sweatshop at the Ritz.

Always devotedly,
Lorraine

His first feeling was one of awe that he had actually, in his mature years, stolen a tricycle and pedaled Lorraine all over the Étoile[11] between the small hours and dawn. In retrospect it was a nightmare. Locking out Helen didn't fit in with any other act of his life, but the tricycle incident did—it was one of many. How many weeks or months of dissipation to arrive at that condition of utter irresponsibility?

He tried to picture how Lorraine had appeared to him then—very attractive; Helen was unhappy about it, though she said nothing. Yesterday, in the restaurant, Lorraine had seemed trite, blurred, worn away. He emphatically did not want to see her, and he was glad Alix had not given away his hotel address. It was a relief to think, instead, of Honoria, to think of Sundays spent with her and of saying good morning to her and knowing she was there in his house at night, drawing her breath in the darkness.

At five he took a taxi and bought presents for all the Peterses—a piquant   210 cloth doll, a box of Roman soldiers, flowers for Marion, big linen handkerchiefs for Lincoln.

He saw, when he arrived in the apartment, that Marion had accepted the inevitable. She greeted him now as though he were a recalcitrant member of the family, rather than a menacing outsider. Honoria had been told she was going; Charlie was glad to see that her tact made her conceal her excessive happiness. Only on his lap did she whisper her delight and the question "When?" before she slipped away with the other children.

He and Marion were alone for a minute in the room, and on an impulse he spoke out boldly:

"Family quarrels are bitter things. They don't go according to any rules. They're not like aches or wounds; they're more like splits in the skin that won't heal because there's not enough material. I wish you and I could be on better terms."

"Some things are hard to forget," she answered. "It's a question of confidence." There was no answer to this and presently she asked, "When do you propose to take her?"

"As soon as I can get a governess. I hoped the day after tomorrow."   215

"That's impossible. I've got to get her things in shape. Not before Saturday."

He yielded. Coming back into the room, Lincoln offered him a drink. "I'll take my daily whisky," he said.

11. A district in Paris.

It was warm here, it was a home, people together by a fire. The children felt very safe and important; the mother and father were serious, watchful. They had things to do for the children more important than his visit here. A spoonful of medicine was, after all, more important than the strained relations between Marion and himself. They were not dull people, but they were very much in the grip of life and circumstances. He wondered if he couldn't do something to get Lincoln out of his rut at the bank.

A long peal at the doorbell; the *bonne à tout faire*[12] passed through and went down the corridor. The door opened upon another long ring, and then voices, and the three in the salon looked up expectantly; Richard moved to bring the corridor within his range of vision, and Marion rose. Then the maid came back along the corridor, closely followed by the voices, which developed under the light into Duncan Schaeffer and Lorraine Quarrles. 220

They were gay, they were hilarious, they were roaring with laughter. For a moment Charlie was astounded; unable to understand how they ferreted out the Peterses' address.

"Ah-h-h!" Duncan wagged his finger roguishly at Charlie, "Ah-h-h!"

They both slid down another cascade of laughter. Anxious and at a loss, Charlie shook hands with them quickly and presented them to Lincoln and Marion. Marion nodded, scarcely speaking. She had drawn back a step toward the fire; her little girl stood beside her, and Marion put an arm about her shoulder.

With growing annoyance at the intrusion, Charlie waited for them to explain themselves. After some concentration Duncan said:

"We came to invite you out to dinner. Lorraine and I insist that all this shishi, cagy business 'bout your address got to stop." 225

Charlie came closer to them, as if to force them backward down the corridor.

"Sorry, but I can't. Tell me where you'll be and I'll phone you in half an hour."

This made no impression. Lorraine sat down suddenly on the side of a chair, and focusing her eyes on Richard, cried, "Oh, what a nice little boy! Come here, little boy." Richard glanced at his mother, but did not move. With a perceptible shrug of her shoulder, Lorraine turned back to Charlie:

"Come and dine. Sure your cousins won' mine. See you so sel'om. Or solemn."

"I can't," said Charlie sharply. "You two have dinner and I'll phone you." 230

Her voice became suddenly unpleasant. "All right, we'll go. But I remember once when you hammered on my door at four A.M. I was enough of a good sport to give you a drink. Come on, Dunc."

Still in slow motion, with blurred, angry faces, with uncertain feet, they retired along the corridor.

"Good night," Charlie said.

"Good night!" responded Lorraine emphatically.

When he went back into the salon Marion had not moved, only now her 235

12. Maid of all work.

son was standing in the circle of her other arm. Lincoln was still swinging Honoria back and forth like a pendulum from side to side.

"What an outrage!" Charlie broke out. "What an absolute outrage!"

Neither of them answered. Charlie dropped into an armchair, picked up his drink, set it down again and said:

"People I haven't seen for two years having the colossal nerve—"

He broke off. Marion had made the sound "Oh!" in one swift, furious breath, turned her body from him with a jerk and left the room.

Lincoln set down Honoria carefully.   240

"You children go in and start your soup," he said, and when they obeyed, he said to Charlie:

"Marion's not well and she can't stand shocks. That kind of people make her really physically sick."

"I didn't tell them to come here. They wormed your name out of somebody. They deliberately—"

"Well, it's too bad. It doesn't help matters. Excuse me a minute."

Left alone, Charlie sat tense in his chair. In the next room he could hear   245
the children eating, talking in monosyllables, already oblivious to the scene between their elders. He heard a murmur of conversation from a farther room and then the ticking bell of a telephone receiver picked up, and in a panic he moved to the other side of the room and out of earshot.

In a minute Lincoln came back. "Look here, Charlie. I think we'd better call off dinner for tonight. Marion's in bad shape."

"Is she angry with me?"

"Sort of," he said, almost roughly. "She's not strong and—"

"You mean she's changed her mind about Honoria?"

"She's pretty bitter right now. I don't know. You phone me at the bank to-   250
morrow."

"I wish you'd explain to her I never dreamed these people would come here. I'm just as sore as you are."

"I couldn't explain anything to her now."

Charlie got up. He took his coat and hat and started down the corridor. Then he opened the door of the dining room and said in a strange voice, "Good night, children."

Honoria rose and ran around the table to hug him.

"Good night, sweetheart," he said vaguely, and then trying to make his   255
voice more tender, trying to conciliate something. "Good night, dear children."

V

Charlie went directly to the Ritz bar with the furious idea of finding Lorraine and Duncan, but they were not there, and he realized that in any case there was nothing he could do. He had not touched his drink at the Peterses, and now he ordered a whisky-and-soda. Paul came over to say hello.

"It's a great change," he said sadly. "We do about half the business we did. So many fellows I hear about back in the States lost everything, maybe not in the first crash, but then in the second. Your friend George Hardt lost every cent, I hear. Are you back in the States?"

"No, I'm in business in Prague."

"I heard that you lost a lot in the crash."

"I did," and he added grimly, "but I lost everything I wanted in the boom." 260

"Selling short."

"Something like that."

Again the memory of those days swept over him like a nightmare—the people they had met traveling; then people who couldn't add a row of figures or speak a coherent sentence. The little man Helen had consented to dance with at the ship's party, who had insulted her ten feet from the table; the women and girls carried screaming with drink or drugs out of public places—

The men who locked their wives out in the snow, because the snow of twenty-nine wasn't real snow. If you didn't want it to be snow, you just paid some money.

He went to the phone and called the Peterses' apartment; Lincoln answered. 265

"I called up because this thing is on my mind. Has Marion said anything definite?"

"Marion's sick," Lincoln answered shortly. "I know this thing isn't altogether your fault, but I can't have her go to pieces about it. I'm afraid we'll have to let it slide for six months; I can't take the chance of working her up to this state again."

"I see."

"I'm sorry, Charlie."

He went back to his table. His whisky glass was empty, but he shook his 270 head when Alix looked at it questioningly. There wasn't much he could do now except send Honoria some things; he would send her a lot of things tomorrow. He thought rather angrily that this was just money—he had given so many people money. . . .

"No, no more," he said to another waiter. "What do I owe you?"

He would come back some day; they couldn't make him pay forever. But he wanted his child, and nothing was much good now, beside that fact. He wasn't young any more, with a lot of nice thoughts and dreams to have by himself. He was absolutely sure Helen wouldn't have wanted him to be so alone.

F. SCOTT FITZGERALD ———
(1896–1940) Web

www

A successful writer from the Midwest, Fitzgerald lived and worked for a while in Paris, then returned to America and wrote for Hollywood. His most famous novel is *The Great Gatsby* (1925).

TOPICS FOR CRITICAL THINKING Web

www

1. What are the functions of the snow image?
2. What feelings, events, and images are linked to alcohol in this story?
3. Why does Charlie take a drink each day? How does that practice relate to his dealing with the past?
4. What does the story's title mean?
5. Why does the story end with Charlie evoking Helen?

1. Does Charlie unconsciously want his past to catch up to him? Support your position with details from the story.
2. In what ways is "Babylon Revisited" about loss?

ERNEST HEMINGWAY

Hills Like White Elephants   *(1927)*

The Hills across the valley of the Ebro[1] were long and white. On this side there was no shade and no trees and the station was between two lines of rails in the sun. Close against the side of the station there was the warm shadow of the building and a curtain, made of strings of bamboo beads, hung across the open door into the bar, to keep out flies. The American and the girl with him sat at a table in the shade, outside the building. It was very hot and the express from Barcelona would come in forty minutes. It stopped at this junction for two minutes and went on to Madrid.

"What should we drink?" the girl asked. She had taken off her hat and put it on the table.

"It's pretty hot," the man said.

"Let's drink beer."

"Dos cervezas," the man said into the curtain.   5

"Big ones?" a woman asked from the doorway.

"Yes. Two big ones."

The woman brought two glasses of beer and two felt pads. She put the felt pads and the beer glasses on the table and looked at the man and the girl. The girl was looking off at the line of hills. They were white in the sun and the country was brown and dry.

"They look like white elephants," she said.

"I've never seen one," the man drank his beer.   10

"No, you wouldn't have."

"I might have," the man said. "Just because you say I wouldn't have doesn't prove anything."

The girl looked at the bead curtain. "They've painted something on it," she said. "What does it say?"

"Anis del Toro. It's a drink."

"Could we try it?"   15

The man called "Listen" through the curtain. The woman came out from the bar.

"Four reales."

"We want two Anis del Toro."

"With water?"

"Do you want it with water?"   20

---

1. River in northeast Spain that empties into the Mediterranean between Barcelona and Valencia.

"I don't know," the girl said. "Is it good with water?"

"It's all right."

"You want them with water?" asked the woman.

"Yes, with water."

"It tastes like licorice," the girl said and put the glass down. 25

"That's the way with everything."

"Yes," said the girl. "Everything tastes of licorice. Especially all the things you've waited so long for, like absinthe."

"Oh, cut it out."

"You started it," the girl said. "I was being amused. I was having a fine time."

"Well, let's try and have a fine time." 30

"All right. I was trying. I said the mountains looked like white elephants. Wasn't that bright?"

"That was bright."

"I wanted to try this new drink. That's all we do, isn't it—look at things and try new drinks?"

"I guess so."

The girl looked across at the hills. 35

"They're lovely hills," she said. "They don't really look like white elephants. I just meant the coloring of their skin through the trees."

"Should we have another drink?"

"All right."

The warm wind blew the bead curtain against the table.

"The beer's nice and cool," the man said. 40

"It's lovely," the girl said.

"It's really an awfully simple operation, Jig," the man said. "It's not really an operation at all."

The girl looked at the ground the table legs rested on.

"I know you wouldn't mind it, Jig. It's really not anything. It's just to let the air in."

The girl did not say anything. 45

"I'll go with you and I'll stay with you all the time. They just let the air in and then it's all perfectly natural."

"Then what will we do afterward?"

"We'll be fine afterward. Just like we were before."

"What makes you think so?"

"That's the only thing that bothers us. It's the only thing that's made us 50 unhappy."

The girl looked at the bead curtain, put her hand out and took hold of two of the strings of beads.

"And you think then we'll be all right and be happy."

"I know we will. You don't have to be afraid. I've known lots of people that have done it."

"So have I," said the girl. "And afterward they were all so happy."

"Well," the man said, "if you don't want to you don't have to. I wouldn't 55 have you do it if you didn't want to. But I know it's perfectly simple."

"And you really want to?"

"I think it's the best thing to do. But I don't want you to do it if you don't really want to."

"And if I do it you'll be happy and things will be like they were and you'll love me?"

"I love you now. You know I love you."

"I know. But if I do it, then it will be nice again if I say things are like white elephants, and you'll like it?"   60

"I'll love it. I love it now but I just can't think about it. You know how I get when I worry."

"If I do it you won't ever worry?"

"I won't worry about that because it's perfectly simple."

"Then I'll do it. Because I don't care about me."

"What do you mean?"   65

"I don't care about me."

"Well, I care about you."

"Oh, yes. But I don't care about me. And I'll do it and then everything will be fine."

"I don't want you to do it if you feel that way."

The girl stood up and walked to the end of the station. Across, on the   70
other side, were fields of grain and trees along the banks of the Ebro. Far away, beyond the river, were mountains. The shadow of a cloud moved across the field of grain and she saw the river through the trees.

"And we could have all this," she said. "And we could have everything and every day we make it more impossible."

"What did you say?"

"I said we could have everything."

"We can have everything."

"No, we can't."

"We can have the whole world."   75

"No, we can't."

"We can go everywhere."

"No, we can't. It isn't ours any more."

"It's ours."   80

"No, it isn't. And once they take it away, you never get it back."

"But they haven't taken it away."

"We'll wait and see."

"Come on back in the shade," he said. "You mustn't feel that way."

"I don't feel any way," the girl said. "I just know things."   85

"I don't want you to do anything that you don't want to do——"

"Nor that isn't good for me," she said. "I know. Could we have another beer?"

"All right. But you've got to realize——"

"I realize," the girl said. "Can't we maybe stop talking?"

They sat down at the table and the girl looked across at the hills on the   90
dry side of the valley and the man looked at her and at the table.

"You've got to realize," he said, "that I don't want you to do it if you don't want to. I'm perfectly willing to go through with it if it means anything to you."

"Doesn't it mean anything to you? We could get along."

"Of course it does. But I don't want anybody but you. I don't want any one else. And I know it's perfectly simple."

"Yes, you know it's perfectly simple."

"It's all right for you to say that, but I do know it." 95

"Would you do something for me now?"

"I'd do anything for you."

"Would you please please please please please please please stop talking?"

He did not say anything but looked at the bags against the wall of the station. There were labels on them from all the hotels where they had spent nights.

"But I don't want you to," he said, "I don't care anything about it." 100

"I'll scream," the girl said.

The woman came out through the curtains with two glasses of beer and put them down on the damp felt pads. "The train comes in five minutes," she said.

"What did she say?" asked the girl.

"That the train is coming in five minutes."

The girl smiled brightly at the woman, to thank her. 105

"I'd better take the bags over to the other side of the station," the man said. She smiled at him.

"All right. Then come back and we'll finish the beer."

He picked up the two heavy bags and carried them around the station to the other tracks. He looked up the tracks but could not see the train. Coming back, he walked through the barroom, where people waiting for the train were drinking. He drank an Anis at the bar and looked at the people. They were all waiting reasonably for the train. He went out through the bead curtain. She was sitting at the table and smiled at him.

"Do you feel better?" he asked.

"I feel fine," she said. "There's nothing wrong with me. I feel fine." 110

ERNEST HEMINGWAY

(1899–1961) Web

www

An outdoorsman and journalist, Nobel Laureate Hemingway began writing serious fiction in Paris. Associated with fishing and bullfights, Hemingway perfected a style based on verbal economy.

TOPICS FOR CRITICAL THINKING Web

www

1. Does the woman always mean what she says? The man?
2. Pinpoint moments in the conversation when the characters might be speaking ironically.
3. How would you describe the style of the story?
4. Does this story show an insensitivity toward the woman's feelings or an understanding of her plight?
5. What is the relation between their drinking and their talking?
6. Can things ever be the same again for them?

1. What various elements of the story might the metaphor of the hills stand for?
2. What does the woman mean at the end of the story when she says, "There's nothing wrong with me. I feel fine."?

GERTRUDE STEIN

Miss Furr and Miss Skeene   *(1922)*

Helen Furr had quite a pleasant home. Mrs. Furr was quite a pleasant woman. Mr. Furr was quite a pleasant man. Helen Furr had quite a pleasant voice quite worth cultivating. She did not mind working. She worked to cultivate her voice. She did not find it gay living in the same place where she had always been living. She went to a place where some were cultivating something, voices and other things needing cultivating. She met Georgine Skeene there who was cultivating her voice which some thought was quite a pleasant one. Helen Furr and Georgine Skeene lived together then. Georgine Skeene liked travelling. Helen Furr did not care about travelling, she liked to stay in one place and be gay there. They were together then and travelled to another place and stayed there and were gay there.

They stayed there and were gay there, not very gay there, just gay there. They were both gay there, they were regularly working there both of them cultivating their voices there, they were both gay there. Georgine Skeene was gay there and she was regular, regular in being gay, regular in not being gay, regular in being a gay one who was not being gay longer than was needed to be one being quite a gay one. They were both gay then there and both working there then.

They were in a way both gay there where there were many cultivating something. They were both regular in being gay there. Helen Furr was gay there, she was gayer and gayer there and really she was just gay there, she was gayer and gayer there, that is to say she found ways of being gay there that she was using in being gay there. She was gay there, not gayer and gayer, just gay there, that is to say she was not gayer by using the things she found there that were gay things, she was gay there.

They were quite regularly gay there, Helen Furr and Georgine Skeene, they were regularly gay there where they were gay. They were very regularly gay.

To be regularly gay was to do every day the gay thing that they did every   5 day. To be regularly gay was to end every day at the same time after they had been regularly gay. They were regularly gay. They were gay every day. They ended every day in the same way, at the same time, and they had been every day regularly gay.

The voice Helen Furr was cultivating was quite a pleasant one. The voice Georgine Skeene was cultivating was, some said, a better one. The voice Helen Furr was cultivating she cultivated and it was quite completely a pleasant enough one then, a cultivated enough one then. The voice Georgine Skeene was cultivating she did not cultivate too much. She cultivated it quite some. She cultivated and she would sometime go on cultivating it and it was not then an unpleasant one, it would not be then an unpleasant one, it would be a quite richly cultivated one, it would be quite richly enough to be a pleasant enough one.

They were gay where there were many cultivating something. The two were gay there, were regularly gay there. Georgine Skeene would have liked to do more travelling. They did some travelling, not very much travelling, Georgine Skeene would have liked to do more travelling, Helen Furr did not care about doing travelling, she liked to stay in a place and be gay there.

They stayed in a place and were gay there, both of them stayed there, they stayed together there, they were gay there, they were regularly gay there.

They went quite often, not very often, but they did go back to where Helen Furr had a pleasant enough home and then Georgine Skeene went to a place where her brother had quite some distinction. They both went, every few years, went visiting to where Helen Furr had quite a pleasant home. Certainly Helen Furr would not find it gay to stay, she did not find it gay, she said she would not stay, she said she did not find it gay, she said she would not stay where she did not find it gay, she said she found it gay where she did stay and she did stay there where very many were cultivating something. She did stay there. She always did find it gay there.

She went to see them where she had always been living and where she did not find it gay. She had a pleasant home there, Mrs. Furr was a pleasant enough woman, Mr. Furr was a pleasant enough man, Helen told them and they were not worrying, that she did not find it gay living where she had always been living. 10

Georgine Skeene and Helen Furr were living where they were both cultivating their voices and they were gay there. They visited where Helen Furr had come from and then they went to where they were living where they were then regularly living.

There were some dark and heavy men there then. There were some who were not so heavy and some who were not so dark. Helen Furr and Georgine Skeene sat regularly with them. They sat regularly with the ones who were dark and heavy. They sat regularly with the ones who were not so dark. They sat regularly with the ones that were not so heavy. They sat with them regularly, sat with some of them. They went with them regularly went with them. They were regular then, they were gay then, they were where they wanted to be then where it was gay to be then, they were regularly gay then. There were men there then who were dark and heavy and they sat with them with Helen Furr and Georgine Skeene and they went with them with Miss Furr and Miss Skeene, and they went with the heavy and dark men Miss Furr and Miss Skeene went with them, and they sat with them, Miss Furr and Miss Skeene sat with them, and there were other men, some were not heavy men and they sat with Miss Furr and Miss Skeene and Miss Furr and Miss Skeene sat with them, and there were other men who were not dark men and they sat with Miss Furr and Miss Skeene and Miss Furr and Miss Skeene sat with them. Miss

Furr and Miss Skeene went with them and they went with Miss Furr and
Miss Skeene, some who were not heavy men, some who were not dark men.
Miss Furr and Miss Skeene sat regularly, they sat with some men. Miss Furr
and Miss Skeene went and there were some men with them. There were men
and Miss Furr and Miss Skeene went with them, went somewhere with them,
went with some of them.

Helen Furr and Georgine Skeene were regularly living where very
many were living and cultivating in themselves something. Helen Furr and
Georgine Skeene were living very regularly then, being very regular then in
being gay then. They did then learn many ways to be gay and they were then
being gay being quite regular in being gay, being gay and they were learning
little things, little things in ways of being gay, they were very regular then,
they were learning very many little things in ways of being gay, they were being gay and using these little things they were learning to have to be gay with
regularly gay with then and they were gay the same amount they had been
gay. They were quite gay, they were quite regular, they were learning little
things, gay little things, they were gay inside them the same amount they had
been gay, they were gay the same length of time they had been gay every day.

They were regular in being gay, they learned little things that are things
in being gay, they learned many little things that are things in being gay, they
were gay every day, they were regular, they were gay, they were gay the same
length of time every day, they were gay, they were quite regularly gay.

Georgine Skeene went away to stay two months with her brother. Helen 15
Furr did not go then to stay with her father and her mother. Helen Furr
stayed there where they had been regularly living the two of them and she
would then certainly not be lonesome, she would go on being gay. She did go
on being gay. She was not any more gay but she was gay longer every day than
they had been being gay when they were together being gay. She was gay then
quite exactly the same way. She learned a few more little ways of being gay.
She was quite gay and in the same way, the same way she had been gay and she
was gay a little longer in the day, more of each day she was gay. She was gay
longer every day than when the two of them had been being gay. She was gay
quite in the way they had been gay, quite in the same way.

She was not lonesome then, she was not at all feeling any need of having
Georgine Skeene. She was not astonished at this thing. She would have been
a little astonished by this thing but she knew she was not astonished at anything and so she was not astonished at this thing not astonished at not feeling
any need of having Georgine Skeene.

Helen Furr had quite a completely pleasant voice and it was quite well
enough cultivated and she could use it and she did use it but then there was not
any way of working at cultivating a completely pleasant voice when it has become a quite completely well enough cultivated one, and there was not much
use in using it when one was not wanting it to be helping to make one a gay
one. Helen Furr was not needing using her voice to be a gay one. She was gay
then and sometimes she used her voice and she was not using it very often. It
was quite completely enough cultivated and it was quite completely a pleasant
one and she did not use it very often. She was then, she was quite exactly as gay
as she had been, she was gay a little longer in the day than she had been.

She was gay exactly the same way. She was never tired of being gay that way. She had learned very many little ways to use in being gay. Very many were telling about using other ways in being gay. She was gay enough, she was always gay exactly the same way, she was always learning little things to use in being gay, she was telling about using other ways in being gay, she was telling about learning other ways in being gay, she was learning other ways in being gay, she would be using other ways in being gay, she would always be gay in the same way, when Georgine Skeene was there not so long each day as when Georgine Skeene was away.

She came to using many ways in being gay, she came to use every way in being gay. She went on living where many were cultivating something and she was gay, she had used every way to be gay.

They did not live together then Helen Furr and Georgine Skeene. Helen 20 Furr lived there the longer where they had been living regularly together. Then neither of them were living there any longer. Helen Furr was living somewhere else then and telling some about being gay and she was gay then and she was living quite regularly then. She was regularly gay then. She was quite regular in being gay then. She remembered all the little ways of being gay. She used all the little ways of being gay. She was quite regularly gay. She told many then the way of being gay, she taught very many then little ways they could use in being gay. She was living very well, she was gay then, she went on living then, she was regular in being gay, she always was living very well and was gay very well and was telling about little ways one could be learning to use in being gay, and later was telling them quite often, telling them again and again.

——— **GERTRUDE STEIN** ———
(1874–1946) Web   *www*

Originally a medical student and later a patron of the arts, Stein provided a center for innovative artistic activity in Paris. Befriending artists Pablo Picasso and Henri Matisse and young writers such as Ernest Hemingway and Sherwood Anderson, Stein developed a writing style in tune with cubism and verbal economy.

TOPICS FOR CRITICAL THINKING Web   *www*

1. What are the relations between style and character in this story?
2. In what ways does the style of the story relate to the ideas of cubism? (For a discussion of cubism, see Web .)   *www*
3. Through what strategies does the story convey the quality of the relationship between the two main characters?

TOPICS FOR CRITICAL WRITING Web   *www*

1. Analyze the story's use of repetition. Link repetition to characterization, plot, and setting.
2. Define Stein's style and its relation to narrative.

Style as Substance

The complexities of style make it a crucial element of prose fiction, and yet because of the number and subtleties of the elements that comprise style, it is often difficult to describe. For this reason, style will often seem to be more a feeling or presence in the text. Just as Gertrude Stein's style might evoke the geometries of cubism, so also it conjures a particular presence—the substantial sense of a narrator who is guiding the telling. In the writing of William Faulkner, style contributes to the feeling that the narrator speaks from a position of wisdom that comes from a sense of the mythical patterns (life, death, renewal) that govern people and events: "When Miss Emily Grierson died, our whole town went to her funeral: the men through a sort of respectful attention for a fallen monument, the women mostly out of curiosity to see the inside of her house." Part of this effect is created through tone, which we will examine in greater depth in Chapter 11. Much of it, however, is created through such elements of style as the strategic use of adjectives ("respectful") and Faulkner's drawing attention to the differences in men's and women's motivations. This combination of wisdom and detail creates a feeling of simultaneously being close and distant from events. Style, in other words, can convey the sense of presence within a text as well as its perspective and range of knowledge.

Faulkner, a writer who produced prose invested with a strong sense of regional flavor, often wove tales of mythic proportion that focused on moments in the lives of individuals. His epic tale of generations of families in mythical Yoknapatawpha County, Mississippi, provides both a privileged view of history and the meaning of generations as well as an often sympathetic portrayal of the peculiarities and experiences of specific characters. (Note, for example, the way "A Rose for Emily" combines a historical view with the description of Emily's odd behaviors.) In drawing together the breadth of life with the idiosyncrasy of event, Faulkner's work produces a sustained portrait of the human comedy.

Featured Writer

WILLIAM FAULKNER

A Rose for Emily   *(1930)*

I

When Miss Emily Grierson died, our whole town went to her funeral: the men through a sort of respectful affection for a fallen monument, the women mostly out of curiosity to see the inside of her house, which no one save an old man-servant—a combined gardener and cook—had seen in at least ten years.

It was a big, squarish frame house that had once been white, decorated with cupolas and spires, and scrolled balconies in the heavily lightsome style of the seventies, set on what had once been our most select street. But garages and cotton gins had encroached and obliterated even the august names of that neighborhood; only Miss Emily's house was left, lifting its stubborn and coquettish decay above the cotton wagons and the gasoline pumps—an eyesore among eyesores. And now Miss Emily had gone to join the representatives of those august names where they lay in the cedar-bemused cemetery among the ranked and anonymous graves of Union and Confederate soldiers who fell at the battle of Jefferson.

Alive, Miss Emily had been a tradition, a duty, and a care; a sort of hereditary obligation upon the town, dating from that day in 1894 when Colonel Sartoris, the mayor—he who fathered the edict that no Negro woman should appear on the street without an apron—remitted her taxes, the dispensation dating from the death of her father on into perpetuity. Not that Miss Emily would have accepted charity. Colonel Sartoris invented an involved tale to the effect that Miss Emily's father had loaned money to the town, which the town, as a matter of business, preferred this way of repaying. Only a man of Colonel Sartoris' generation and thought could have invented it, and only a woman could have believed it.

When the next generation, with its more modern ideas, became mayors and aldermen, this arrangement created some little dissatisfaction. On the first of the year they mailed her a tax notice. February came, and there was no reply. They wrote her a formal letter, asking her to call at the sheriff's office at her convenience. A week later the mayor wrote her himself, offering to call or to send his car for her, and received in reply a note on paper of an archaic shape, in a thin, flowing calligraphy in faded ink, to the effect that she no longer went out at all. The tax notice was also enclosed, without comment.

They called a special meeting of the Board of Aldermen. A deputation waited upon her, knocked at the door through which no visitor had passed 5 since she ceased giving china-painting lessons eight or ten years earlier. They were admitted by the old Negro into a dim hall from which a stairway mounted into still more shadow. It smelled of dust and disuse—a close, dank smell. The Negro led them into the parlor. It was furnished in heavy, leather-covered furniture. When the Negro opened the blinds of one window, they could see that the leather was cracked; and when they sat down, a faint dust rose sluggishly about their thighs, spinning with slow motes in the single sun-ray. On a tarnished gilt easel before the fireplace stood a crayon portrait of Miss Emily's father.

They rose when she entered—a small, fat woman in black, with a thin gold chain descending to her waist and vanishing into her belt, leaning on an ebony cane with a tarnished gold head. Her skeleton was small and spare; perhaps that was why what would have been merely plumpness in another was obesity in her. She looked bloated, like a body long submerged in motionless water, and of that pallid hue. Her eyes, lost in the fatty ridges of her face, looked like two small pieces of coal pressed into a lump of dough as they moved from one face to another while the visitors stated their errand.

She did not ask them to sit. She just stood in the door and listened quietly until the spokesman came to a stumbling halt. Then they could hear the invisible watch ticking at the end of the gold chain.

Her voice was dry and cold. "I have no taxes in Jefferson. Colonel Sartoris explained it to me. Perhaps one of you can gain access to the city records and satisfy yourselves."

"But we have. We are the city authorities, Miss Emily. Didn't you get a notice from the sheriff, signed by him?"

"I received a paper, yes," Miss Emily said. "Perhaps he considers himself   10 the sheriff . . . I have no taxes in Jefferson."

"But there is nothing on the books to show that, you see. We must go by the—"

"See Colonel Sartoris. I have no taxes in Jefferson."

"But Miss Emily—"

"See Colonel Sartoris." (Colonel Sartoris had been dead almost ten years.) "I have no taxes in Jefferson. Tobe!" The Negro appeared. "Show these gentlemen out."

II

So she vanquished them, horse and foot, just as she had vanquished their   15 fathers thirty years before about the smell. That was two years after her father's death and a short time after her sweetheart—the one we believed would marry her—had deserted her. After her father's death she went out very little; after her sweetheart went away, people hardly saw her at all. A few of the ladies had the temerity to call, but were not received, and the only sign of life about the place was the Negro man—a young man then—going in and out with a market basket.

"Just as if a man—any man—could keep a kitchen properly," the ladies said; so they were not surprised when the smell developed. It was another link between the gross, teeming world and the high and mighty Griersons.

Edward Steichen, *Heavy Roses* (1914)

A neighbor, a woman, complained to the mayor, Judge Stevens, eighty years old.

"But what will you have me do about it, madam?" he said.

"Why, send her word to stop it," the woman said. "Isn't there a law?"

"I'm sure that won't be necessary," Judge Stevens said. "It's probably just a snake or a rat that nigger of hers killed in the yard. I'll speak to him about it." 20

The next day he received two more complaints, one from a man who came in diffident deprecation. "We really must do something about it, Judge. I'd be the last one in the world to bother Miss Emily, but we've got to do something." That night the Board of Aldermen met—three graybeards and one younger man, a member of the rising generation.

"It's simple enough," he said. "Send her word to have her place cleaned up. Give her a certain time do it in, and if she don't . . . ."

"Dammit, sir," Judge Stevens said, "will you accuse a lady to her face of smelling bad?"

So the next night, after midnight, four men crossed Miss Emily's lawn and slunk about the house like burglars, sniffing along the base of the brickwork and at the cellar openings while one of them performed a regular sowing motion with his hand out of a sack slung from his shoulder. They broke open the cellar door and sprinkled lime there, and in all the outbuildings. As they recrossed the lawn, a window that had been dark was lighted and Miss Emily sat in it, the light behind her, and her upright torso motionless as that of an idol. They crept quietly across the lawn and into the shadow of the locusts that lined the street. After a week or two the smell went away.

That was when people had begun to feel really sorry for her. People in our town, remembering how old lady Wyatt, her great-aunt, had gone completely crazy at last, believed that the Griersons held themselves a little too high for what they really were. None of the young men were quite good enough for Miss Emily and such. We had long thought of them as a tableau, Miss Emily a slender figure in white in the background, her father a spraddled silhouette in the foreground, his back to her and clutching a horsewhip, the two of them framed by the backflung front door. When she got to be thirty and was still single, we were not pleased exactly, but vindicated; even with insanity in the family she wouldn't have turned down all of her chances if they had really materialized.

When her father died, it got about that the house was all that was left to her; and in a way, people were glad. At last they could pity Miss Emily. Being left alone, and a pauper, she had become humanized. Now she too would know the old thrill and the old despair of a penny more or less.

The day after his death all the ladies prepared to call at the house and offer condolence and aid, as is our custom. Miss Emily met them at the door, dressed as usual and with no trace of grief on her face. She told them that her father was not dead. She did that for three days, with the ministers calling on her, and the doctors, trying to persuade her to let them dispose of the body. Just as they were about to resort to law and force, she broke down, and they buried her father quickly.

We did not say she was crazy then. We believed she had to do that. We remembered all the young men her father had driven away, and we knew that with nothing left, she would have to cling to that which had robbed her, as people will.

III

She was sick for a long time. When we saw her again, her hair was cut short, making her look like a girl, with a vague resemblance to those angels in colored church windows—sort of tragic and serene.

The town had just let the contracts for paving the sidewalks, and in the summer after her father's death they began the work. The construction company came with niggers and mules and machinery, and a foreman named Homer Barron, a Yankee—a big, dark, ready man, with a big voice and eyes lighter than his face. The little boys would follow in groups to hear him cuss the niggers, and the niggers singing in time to the rise and fall of picks. Pretty soon he knew everybody in town. Whenever you heard a lot of laughing anywhere about the square, Homer Barron would be in the center of the group. Presently we began to see him and Miss Emily on Sunday afternoons driving in the yellow-wheeled buggy and the matched team of bays from the livery stable.

At first we were glad that Miss Emily would have an interest, because the ladies all said, "Of course a Grierson would not think seriously of a Northerner, a day laborer." But there were still others, older people, who said that even grief could not cause a real lady to forget *noblesse oblige*—without calling it *noblesse oblige*. They just said, "Poor Emily. Her kinsfolk should come to her." She had some kin in Alabama; but years ago her father had fallen out with them over the estate of old Lady Wyatt, the crazy woman, and there was no communication between the two families. They had not even been represented at the funeral.

And as soon as the old people said, "Poor Emily," the whispering began. "Do you suppose it's really so?" they said to one another. "Of course it is. What else could . . ." This behind their hands; rustling of craned silk and satin behind jalousies closed upon the sun of Sunday afternoon as the thin, swift clop-clop-clop of the matched team passed: "Poor Emily."

She carried her head high enough—even when we believed that she was fallen. It was as if she demanded more than ever the recognition of her dignity as the last Grierson; as if it had wanted that touch of earthiness to reaffirm her imperviousness. Like when she bought the rat poison, the arsenic. That was over a year after they had begun to say "Poor Emily," and while the two female cousins were visiting her.

"I want some poison," she said to the druggist. She was over thirty then, still a slight woman, though thinner than usual, with cold, haughty black eyes in a face the flesh of which was strained across the temples and about the eye-sockets as you imagine a lighthousekeeper's face ought to look. "I want some poison," she said.

"Yes, Miss Emily. What kind? For rats and such? I'd recom—"   35

"I want the best you have. I don't care what kind."

The druggist named several. "They'll kill anything up to an elephant. But what you want is—"

"Arsenic," Miss Emily said. "Is that a good one?"

"Is . . . arsenic? Yes, ma'am. But what you want—"

"I want arsenic."   40

The druggist looked down at her. She looked back at him, erect, her face like a strained flag. "Why, of course," the druggist said. "If that's what you want. But the law requires you to tell what you are going to use it for."

Miss Emily just stared at him, her head tilted back in order to look him eye for eye, until he looked away and went and got the arsenic and wrapped it up. The Negro delivery boy brought her the package; the druggist didn't come back. When she opened the package at home there was written on the box, under the skull and bones: "For rats."

IV

So the next day we all said, "She will kill herself"; and we said it would be the best thing. When she had first begun to be seen with Homer Barron, we had said, "She will marry him." Then we said, "She will persuade him yet," because Homer himself had remarked—he liked men, and it was known that he drank with the younger men in the Elks' Club—that he was not a marrying man. Later we said, "Poor Emily" behind the jalousies as they passed on

Sunday afternoon in the glittering buggy, Miss Emily with her head high and Homer Barron with his hat cocked and cigar in his teeth, reins and whip in a yellow glove.

Then some of the ladies began to say that it was a disgrace to the town and a bad example to the young people. The men did not want to interfere, but at last the ladies forced the Baptist minister—Miss Emily's people were Episcopal—to call upon her. He would never divulge what happened during that interview, but he refused to go back again. The next Sunday they again drove about the streets, and the following day the minister's wife wrote to Miss Emily's relations in Alabama.

So she had blood-kin under her roof again and we sat back to watch developments. At first nothing happened. Then we were sure that they were to be married. We learned that Miss Emily had been to the jeweler's and ordered a man's toilet set in silver, with the letters H. B. on each piece. Two days later we learned that she had bought a complete outfit of men's clothing, including a nightshirt, and we said, "They are married." We were really glad. We were glad because the two female cousins were even more Grierson than Miss Emily had ever been.   45

So we were not surprised when Homer Barron—the streets had been finished some time since—was gone. We were a little disappointed that there was not a public blowing-off, but we believed that he had gone on to prepare for Miss Emily's coming, or to give her a chance to get rid of the cousins. (By that time it was a cabal, and we were all Miss Emily's allies to help circumvent the cousins.) Sure enough, after another week they departed. And, as we had expected all along, within three days Homer Barron was back in town. A neighbor saw the Negro man admit him at the kitchen door at dusk one evening.

And that was the last we saw of Homer Barron. And of Miss Emily for some time. The Negro man went in and out with the market basket, but the front door remained closed. Now and then we would see her at a window for a moment, as the men did that night when they sprinkled the lime, but for almost six months she did not appear on the streets. Then we knew that this was to be expected too; as if that quality of her father which had thwarted her woman's life so many times had been too virulent and too furious to die.

When we next saw Miss Emily, she had grown fat and her hair was turning gray. During the next few years it grew grayer and grayer until it attained an even pepper-and-salt iron-gray, when it ceased turning. Up to the day of her death at seventy-four it was still that vigorous iron-gray, like the hair of an active man.

From that time on her front door remained closed, save for a period of six or seven years, when she was about forty, during which she gave lessons in china-painting. She fitted up a studio in one of the downstairs rooms, where the daughters and granddaughters of Colonel Sartoris' contemporaries were sent to her with the same regularity and in the same spirit that they were sent to church on Sunday with a twenty-five-cent piece for the collection plate. Meanwhile her taxes had been remitted.

Then the newer generation became the backbone and the spirit of the   50 town, and the painting pupils grew up and fell away and did not send their children to her with boxes of color and tedious brushes and pictures cut from the ladies' magazines. The front door closed upon the last one and remained closed for good. When the town got free postal delivery, Miss Emily alone refused to let them fasten the metal numbers above her door and attach a mailbox to it. She would not listen to them.

Daily, monthly, yearly we watched the Negro grow grayer and more stooped, going in and out with the market basket. Each December we sent her a tax notice, which would be returned by the post office a week later, unclaimed. Now and then we would see her in one of the downstairs windows—she had evidently shut up the top floor of the house—like the carven torso of an idol in a niche, looking or not looking at us, we could never tell which. Thus she passed from generation to generation—dear, inescapable, impervious, tranquil, and perverse.

And so she died. Fell ill in the house filled with dust and shadows, with only a doddering Negro man to wait on her. We did not even know she was sick; we had long since given up trying to get any information from the Negro. He talked to no one, probably not even to her, for his voice had grown harsh and rusty, as if from disuse.

She died in one of the downstairs rooms, in a heavy walnut bed with a curtain, her gray head propped on a pillow yellow and moldy with age and lack of sunlight.

V

The Negro met the first of the ladies at the front door and let them in, with their hushed, sibilant voices and their quick, curious glances, and then he disappeared. He walked right through the house and out the back and was not seen again.

The two female cousins came at once. They held the funeral on the second day, with the town coming to look at Miss Emily beneath a mass of bought flowers, with the crayon face of her father musing profoundly above the bier and the ladies sibilant and macabre; and the very old men—some in their brushed Confederate uniforms—on the porch and the lawn, talking of Miss Emily as if she had been a contemporary of theirs, believing that they had danced with her and courted her perhaps, confusing time with its mathematical progression, as the old do, to whom all the past is not a diminishing road but, instead, a huge meadow which no winter ever quite touches, divided from them now by the narrow bottle-neck of the most recent decade of years.

Already we knew that there was one room in that region above stairs which no one had seen in forty years, and which would have to be forced. They waited until Miss Emily was decently in the ground before they opened it.

The violence of breaking down the door seemed to fill this room with pervading dust. A thin, acrid pall of the tomb seemed to lie everywhere upon this room decked and furnished as for a bridal: upon the valance curtains of faded rose color, upon the rose-shaded lights, upon the dressing table, upon the delicate array of crystal and the man's toilet things backed with tarnished silver, silver so tarnished that the monogram was obscured. Among them lay a collar and tie, as if they had just been removed, which, lifted, left upon the surface a pale crescent in the dust. Upon a chair hung the suit, carefully folded; beneath it the two mute shoes and the discarded socks.

The man himself lay in the bed.

For a long while we just stood there, looking down at the profound and fleshless grin. The body had apparently once lain in the attitude of an embrace, but now the long sleep that outlasts love, that conquers even the grimace of love, had cuckolded him. What was left of him, rotted beneath what was left of the nightshirt, had become inextricable from the bed in which he lay; and upon him and upon the pillow beside him lay that even coating of the patient and biding dust.

Then we noticed that in the second pillow was the indentation of a head.   60
One of us lifted something from it, and leaning forward, that faint and invisible dust dry and acrid in the nostrils, we saw a long strand of iron-gray hair.

──────── **WILLIAM FAULKNER** ────────

www   *(1897–1962)* Web

An airman in the Royal Air Force, William Faulkner was another writer who sought a Parisian atmosphere in which to write. Unlike Fitzgerald and Hemingway, however, Faulkner's writing was best nourished by his Mississippi home, about which he wrote for the rest of his life. After marrying his childhood sweetheart in 1929, Faulkner wrote *The Sound and the Fury* and *As I Lay Dying*, beginning a major body of work that would eventually win him the Nobel Prize (1949). From 1932 and through the 1940s, Faulkner worked on and off as a Hollywood screenwriter, collaborating with directors Howard Hawks and Jean Renoir and garnering six screenwriting credits for films, most notably for the film *To Have and Have Not* staring Humphrey Bogart and Lauren Bacall. Spinning out the intertwined histories of several families, Faulkner's novels have an epic quality derived from their sense of generations and the mythical play of sin, debt, and legacy that haunts the present from the past.

www   *TOPICS FOR CRITICAL THINKING* Web

1. Through the use of which specific words does the story change the feeling of distance and proximity from point to point in the story?
2. What purpose does the narrator's flexible distance serve in relation to the narrative of Miss Emily?
3. At what point in the story does the reader begin to suspect what has happened in Miss Emily's life? What are the functions of the dramatic irony that ensues?
4. What is the meaning of the gray hair on the pillow?
5. Explain the story's title.

www   *TOPICS FOR CRITICAL WRITING* Web

1. Explain the various social and personal relations "taxes" might represent in this story.
2. In what ways is the story about community?

Golden Land

(1935)

If he had been thirty, he would not have needed the two aspirin tablets and the half glass of raw gin before he could bear the shower's needling on his body and steady his hands to shave. But then when he had been thirty neither could he have afforded to drink as much each evening as he now drank; certainly he would not have done it in the company of the men and the women in which, at forty-eight, he did each evening, even though knowing during the very final hours filled with the breaking of glass and the shrill cries of drunken women above the drums and saxophones—the hours during which he carried a little better than his weight both in the amount of liquor consumed and in the number and sum of checks paid—that six or eight hours later he would rouse from what had not been sleep at all but instead that dreamless stupefaction of alcohol out of which last night's turgid and licensed uproar would die, as though without any interval for rest or recuperation, into the familiar shape of his bedroom—the bed's foot silhouetted by the morning light which entered the bougainvillaea-bound windows beyond which his painful and almost unbearable eyes could see the view which might be called the monument to almost twenty-five years of industry and desire, of shrewdness and luck and even fortitude—the opposite canyonflank dotted with the white villas halfhidden in imported olive groves or friezed by the sombre spaced columns of cypress like the façades of eastern temples, whose owners' names and faces and even voices were glib and familiar in back corners of the United States and of America and of the world where those of Einstein and Rousseau and Esculapius had never sounded.

He didn't waken sick. He never wakened ill nor became ill from drinking, not only because he had drunk too long and too steadily for that, but because he was too tough even after the thirty soft years; he came from too tough stock on that day thirty-four years ago when at fourteen he had fled, on the brakebeam of a westbound freight, the little lost Nebraska town named for, permeated with, his father's history and existence—a town to be sure, but only in the sense that any shadow is larger than the object which casts it. It was still frontier even as he remembered it at five and six—the projected and increased shadow of a small outpost of sodroofed dugouts on the immense desolation of the plains where his father, Ira Ewing too, had been first to essay to wring wheat during the six days between those when, outdoors in spring and summer and in the fetid halfdark of a snowbound dugout in the winter and fall, he preached. The second Ira Ewing had come a long way since then, from that barren and treeless village which he had fled by a night freight to where he now lay in a hundred-thousand-dollar house, waiting until he knew that he could rise and go to the bath and put the two aspirin tablets into his mouth. They—his mother and father—had tried to explain it to him—something about fortitude, the will to endure. At fourteen he could neither answer them with logic and reason nor explain what he wanted: he could only flee. Nor was he fleeing his father's harshness and wrath. He was fleeing the scene itself—the treeless immensity in the lost center of which he seemed to see the sum of his father's and mother's dead youth and bartered lives as a tiny forlorn spot which nature permitted to green into brief and niggard wheat for a season's moment before blotting it all with the primal and invincible snow as though (not even promise, not even threat) in grim and almost playful augury of the final doom of all life. And it was not even this that he was fleeing because he was not fleeing: it was only that absence, removal, was the only argument which fourteen knew how to employ against adults with any hope of success. He spent the next ten years half tramp half casual laborer as he drifted down the Pacific Coast to Los Angeles; at thirty he was married, to a Los Angeles girl, daughter of a carpenter, and father of a son and a daughter and with a foothold in real estate; at forty-eight he spent fifty thousand dollars a year, owning a business which he had built up unaided and preserved intact through nineteen-twenty-nine; he had given to his children luxuries and advantages which his own father not only could not have conceived in fact but would have condemned completely in theory—as it proved, as the paper which the Filipino chauffeur, who each morning carried him into the house and undressed him and put him to bed, had removed from the pocket of his topcoat and laid on the reading table proved, with reason. On the death of his father twenty years ago he had returned to Nebraska, for the first time, and fetched his mother back with him, and she was now established in a home of her own only the less sumptuous because she refused (with a kind of abashed and thoughtful unshakability which he did not remark) anything finer or more elaborate. It was the house in which they had all lived at first, though he and his wife and children had moved within the year. Three years ago they had moved again, into the house where he now waked in a select residential section of Beverley Hills, but not once in the nineteen years had he failed to stop (not even during the last five, when to move at all in the mornings required a terrific drain on that character or strength which the elder Ira had bequeathed him, which had enabled the other Ira to pause on the Nebraska plain and dig a hole for his wife to bear children in while he planted wheat) on his way to the office (twenty miles out of his way to the office) and spend ten minutes with her. She lived in as complete physical ease and peace as he could devise. He had arranged her affairs so that she did not even need to bother with money, cash, in order to live; he had arranged credit for her with a neighboring market and butcher so that the Japanese gardener who came each day to water and tend the flowers could do her shopping for her; she never even saw the bills. And the only reason she had no servant was that even at seventy she apparently clung stubbornly to the old habit of doing her own cooking and housework. So it would seem that he had been right. Perhaps there were times when, lying in bed like this and waiting for the will to rise and take the aspirin and the gin (mornings perhaps following evenings when he had drunk more than ordinarily and when even the six or seven hours of oblivion had not been sufficient to enable him to distinguish between reality and illusion) something of the old strong harsh Campbellite blood which the elder Ira must have bequeathed him might have caused him to see or feel or imagine his father looking down from somewhere upon him, the prodigal, and what he had accomplished. If this were so, then surely the elder Ira, looking down for the last two mornings upon the two tabloid papers which the Filipino removed from his master's topcoat and laid on the reading table, might have taken advantage of that old blood and taken his revenge, not just for that afternoon thirty-four years ago but for the entire thirty-four years.

When he gathered himself, his will, his body, at last and rose from the bed he struck the paper so that it fell to the floor and lay open at his feet, but he did not look at it. He just stood so, tall in silk pajamas, thin where his father had been gaunt with the years of hard work and unceasing struggle with the unpredictable and implacable earth (even now, despite the life which he had led, he had very little paunch) looking at nothing while at his feet the black headline flared above the row of five or six tabloid photographs from which his daughter alternately stared back or flaunted long pale shins: APRIL LALEAR BARES ORGY SECRETS. When he moved at last he stepped on the paper, walking on his bare feet into the bath; now it was his trembling and jerking hands that he watched as he shook the two tablets onto the glass shelf and set the tumbler into the rack and unstoppered the gin bottle and braced his knuckles against the wall in order to pour into the tumbler. But he did not look at the paper, not even when, shaved, he re-entered the bedroom and went to the bed beside which his slippers sat and shoved the paper aside with his foot in order to step into them. Perhaps, doubtless, he did not need to. The trial was but entering its third tabloidal day now, and so for two days his daughter's face had sprung out at him, hard, blonde and inscrutable, from every paper he opened; doubtless he had never forgot her while he slept even, that he had waked into thinking about remembering her as he had waked into the dying drunken uproar of the evening eight hours behind him without any interval between for rest or forgetting.

Nevertheless as, dressed, in a burnt orange turtleneck sweater beneath his gray flannels, he descended the Spanish staircase, he was outwardly calm and possessed. The delicate iron balustrade and the marble steps coiled down to the tile-floored and barnlike living room beyond which he could hear his wife and son talking on the breakfast terrace. The son's name was Voyd. He and his wife had named the two children by what might have been called mutual contemptuous armistice—his wife called the boy Voyd, for what reason he never knew; he in his turn named the girl (the child whose woman's face had met him from every paper he touched for two days now beneath or above the name, April Lalear) Samantha, after his own mother. He could hear them talking—the wife between whom and himself there had been nothing save civility, and not always a great deal of that, for ten years now; and the son who one afternoon two years ago had been delivered at the door drunk and insensible by a car whose occupants he did not see and, it devolving upon him to undress the son and put him to bed, whom he discovered to be wearing, in place of underclothes, a woman's brassière and step-ins. A few minutes later, hearing the blows perhaps, Voyd's mother ran in and found her husband beating the still unconscious son with a series of towels which a servant was steeping in rotation in a basin of ice-water. He was beating the son hard, with grim and deliberate fury. Whether he was trying to sober the son up or was merely beating him, possibly he himself did not know. His wife though jumped to the latter conclusion. In his raging disillusionment he tried to tell

her about the woman's garments but she refused to listen; she assailed him in
turn with virago fury. Since that day the son had contrived to see his father
only in his mother's presence (which neither the son nor the mother found
very difficult, by the way) and at which times the son treated his father with a
blend of cringing spite and vindictive insolence half a cat's and half a woman's.

He emerged onto the terrace; the voices ceased. The sun, strained by the   5
vague high soft almost nebulous California haze, fell upon the terrace with a
kind of treacherous unbrightness. The terrace, the sundrenched terra cotta
tiles, butted into a rough and savage shear of canyonwall bare yet without
dust, on or against which a solid mat of flowers bloomed in fierce lush myriad-
colored paradox as though in place of being rooted into and drawing from the
soil they lived upon air alone and had been merely leaned intact against the
sustenanceless lavawall by someone who would later return and take them
away. The son, Voyd, apparently naked save for a pair of straw-colored shorts,
his body brown with sun and scented faintly by the depilatory which he used
on arms, chest and legs, lay in a wicker chair, his feet in straw beach shoes, an
open newspaper across his brown legs. The paper was the highest class one of
the city, yet there was a black headline across half of it too, and even without
pausing, without even being aware that he had looked, Ira saw there too the
name which he recognized. He went on to his place; the Filipino who put him
to bed each night, in a white service jacket now, drew his chair. Beside the
glass of orange juice and the waiting cup lay a neat pile of mail topped by a
telegram. He sat down and took up the telegram; he had not glanced at his
wife until she spoke:

"Mrs. Ewing telephoned. She says for you to stop in there on your way
to town."

He stopped; his hands opening the telegram stopped. Still blinking a little against the sun he looked at the face opposite him across the table—the
smooth dead makeup, the thin lips and the thin nostrils and the pale blue unforgiving eyes, the meticulous platinum hair which looked as though it had
been transferred to her skull with a brush from a book of silver leaf such as
window painters use. "What?" he said. "Telephoned? Here?"

"Why not? Have I ever objected to any of your women telephoning
you here?"

The unopened telegram crumpled suddenly in his hand. "You know what
I mean," he said harshly. "She never telephoned me in her life. She don't have
to. Not that message. When have I ever failed to go by there on my way to
town?"

"How do I know?" she said. "Or are you the same model son you have   10
been a husband and seem to be a father?" Her voice was not shrill yet, nor even
very loud, and none could have told how fast her breathing was because she sat
so still, rigid beneath the impeccable and unbelievable hair, looking at him
with that pale and outraged unforgiveness. They both looked at each other
across the luxurious table—the two people who at one time twenty years ago
would have turned as immediately and naturally and unthinkingly to one another in trouble, who even ten years ago might have done so.

"You know what I mean," he said, harshly again, holding himself too against the trembling which he doubtless believed was from last night's drinking, from the spent alcohol. "She don't read papers. She never even sees one. Did you send it to her?"

"I?" she said. "Send what?"

"Damnation!" he cried. "A paper! Did you send it to her? Don't lie to me."

"What if I did?" she cried. "Who is she, that she must not know about it? Who is she, that you should shield her from knowing it? Did you make any effort to keep me from knowing it? Did you make any effort to keep it from happening? Why didn't you think about that all those years while you were too drunk, too besotted with drink, to know or notice or care what Samantha was—"

"Miss April Lalear of the cinema, if you please," Voyd said. They paid no   15 attention to him; they glared at one another across the table.

"Ah," he said, quiet and rigid, his lips scarcely moving. "So I am to blame for this too, am I? I made my daughter a bitch, did I? Maybe you will tell me next that I made my son a f—"

"Stop!" she cried. She was panting now; they glared at one another across the suave table, across the five feet of irrevocable division.

"Now, now," Voyd said. "Don't interfere with the girl's career. After all these years, when at last she seems to have found a part that she can—" He ceased; his father had turned and was looking at him. Voyd lay in his chair, looking at his father with that veiled insolence that was almost feminine. Suddenly it became completely feminine; with a muffled halfscream he swung his legs out to spring up and flee but it was too late; Ira stood above him, gripping him not by the throat but by the face with one hand, so that Voyd's mouth puckered and slobbered in his father's hard, shaking hand. Then the mother sprang forward and tried to break Ira's grip but he flung her away and then caught and held her, struggling too, with the other hand when she sprang in again.

"Go on," he said. "Say it." But Voyd could say nothing because of his father's hand gripping his jaws open, or more than likely because of terror. His body was free of the chair now, writhing and thrashing while he made his slobbering, moaning sound of terror while his father held him with one hand and held his screaming mother with the other one. Then Ira flung Voyd free, onto the terrace; Voyd rolled once and came onto his feet, crouching, retreating toward the French windows with one arm flung up before his face while he cursed his father. Then he was gone. Ira faced his wife, holding her quiet too at last, panting too, the skillful map of makeup standing into relief now like a paper mask trimmed smoothly and pasted onto her skull. He released her.

"You sot," she said. "You drunken sot. And yet you wonder why your   20 children—"

"Yes," he said quietly. "All right. That's not the question. That's all done. The question is, what to do about it. My father would have known. He did it once." He spoke in a dry light pleasant voice: so much so that she stood, panting still but quiet, watching him. "I remember. I was about ten. We had rats in the barn. We tried everything. Terriers. Poison. Then one day father said, 'Come.' We went to the barn and stopped all the cracks, the holes. Then we set fire to it. What do you think of that?" Then she was gone too. He stood for a moment, blinking a little, his eyeballs beating faintly and steadily in his skull with the impact of the soft unchanging sunlight, the fierce innocent mass of the flowers. "Philip!" he called. The Filipino appeared, brownfaced, impassive, with a pot of hot coffee, and set it beside the empty cup and the icebedded glass of orange juice. "Get me a drink," Ira said. The Filipino glanced at him, then he became busy at the table, shifting the cup and setting the pot down and shifting the cup again while Ira watched him. "Did you hear me?" Ira said. The Filipino stood erect and looked at him.

"You told me not to give it to you until you had your orange juice and coffee."

"Will you or won't you get me a drink?" Ira shouted.

"Very good, sir," the Filipino said. He went out. Ira looked after him; this had happened before: he knew well that the brandy would not appear until he had finished the orange juice and the coffee, though just where the Filipino lurked to watch him he never knew. He sat again and opened the crumpled telegram and read it, the glass of orange juice in the other hand. It was from his secretary: MADE SETUP BEFORE I BROKE STORY LAST NIGHT STOP THIRTY PERCENT FRONT PAGE STOP MADE APPOINT-MENT FOR YOU COURTHOUSE THIS P.M. STOP WILL YOU COME TO OFFICE OR CALL ME. He read the telegram again, the glass of orange juice still poised. Then he put both down and rose and went and lifted the paper from the terrace where Voyd had flung it, and read the half headline: LALEAR WOMAN DAUGHTER OF PROMINENT LOCAL FAMILY. Admits Real Name Is Samantha Ewing, Daughter of Ira Ewing, Local Realtor. He read it quietly; he said quietly, aloud:

"It was that Jap that showed her the paper. It was that damned gardener." 25 He returned to the table. After a while the Filipino came, with the brandy-and-soda, and wearing now a jacket of bright imitation tweed, telling him that the car was ready.

II

His mother lived in Glendale; it was the house which he had taken when he married and later bought, in which his son and daughter had been born—a bungalow in a cul-de-sac of pepper trees and flowering shrubs and vines which the Japanese tended, backed into a barren foothill combed and curried into a cypress-and-marble cemetery dramatic as a stage set and topped by an electric sign in red bulbs which, in the San Fernando valley fog, glared in broad sourceless ruby as though just beyond the crest lay not heaven but hell. The length of his sports model car in which the Filipino sat reading a paper dwarfed it. But she would have no other, just as she would have neither servant, car, nor telephone—a gaunt spare slightly stooped woman upon whom even California and ease had put no flesh, sitting in one of the chairs which she had insisted on bringing all the way from Nebraska. At first she had been content to allow the Nebraska furniture to remain in storage, since it had not been needed (when Ira moved his wife and family out of the house and into the second one, the intermediate one, they had bought new furniture too, leaving the first house furnished complete for his mother) but one day, he could not recall just when, he discovered that she had taken the one chair out of storage and was using it in the house. Later, after he began to sense that quality of unrest in her, he had suggested that she let him clear the house of its present furniture and take all of hers out of storage but she declined, apparently preferring or desiring to leave the Nebraska furniture where it was. Sitting so, a knitted shawl about her shoulders, she looked less like she lived in or belonged to the house, the room, than the son with his beach burn and his faintly theatrical gray temples and his bright expensive suavely antiphonal garments did. She had changed hardly at all in the thirty-four years; she and the older Ira Ewing too, as the son remembered him, who, dead, had suffered as little of alteration as while he had been alive. As the sod Nebraska outpost had grown into a village and then into a town, his father's aura alone had increased, growing into the proportions of a giant who at some irrevocable yet recent time had engaged barehanded in some titanic struggle with the pitiless earth and endured and in a sense conquered—it too, like the town, a shadow out of all proportion to the gaunt gnarled figure of the actual man. And the actual woman too as the son remembered them back in that time. Two people who drank air and who required to eat and sleep as he did and who had brought him into the world, yet were strangers as though of another race, who stood side by side in an irrevocable loneliness as though strayed from another planet, not as husband and wife but as blood brother and sister, even twins, of the same travail because they had gained a strange peace through fortitude and the will and strength to endure.

"Tell me again what it is," she said. "I'll try to understand."

"So it was Kazimura that showed you the damned paper," he said. She didn't answer this; she was not looking at him.

"You tell me she has been in the pictures before, for two years. That that was why she had to change her name, that they all have to change their names."

"Yes. They call them extra parts. For about two years, God knows why."

"And then you tell me that this—that all this was so she could get into the pictures—"

He started to speak, then he caught himself back out of some quick impatience, some impatience perhaps of grief or despair or at least rage, holding his voice, his tone, quiet: "I said that that was one possible reason. All I know is that the man has something to do with pictures, giving out the parts. And that the police caught him and Samantha and the other girl in an apartment with the doors all locked and that Samantha and the other woman were naked. They say that he was naked too and he says he was not. He says in the trial that he was framed—tricked; that they were trying to blackmail him into giving them parts in a picture; that they fooled him into coming there and arranged for the police to break in just after they had taken off their clothes; that one of them made a signal from the window. Maybe so. Or maybe they were all just having a good time and were innocently caught." Unmoving,

rigid, his face broke, wrung with faint bitter smiling as though with in-
domitable and impassive suffering, or maybe just smiling, just rage. Still his
mother did not look at him.

"But you told me she was already in the pictures. That that was why she
had to change her—"

"I said, extra parts," he said. He had to catch himself again, out of his jan-
gled and outraged nerves, back from the fierce fury of the impatience. "Can't
you understand that you don't get into the pictures just by changing your
name? and that you don't even stay there when you get in? that you can't even
stay there by being female? that they come here in droves on every train—
girls younger and prettier than Samantha and who will do anything to get into
the pictures? So will she, apparently; but who know or are willing to learn to
do more things than even she seems to have thought of? But let's don't talk
about it. She has made her bed; all I can do is to help her up: I can't wash the
sheets. Nobody can. I must go, anyway; I'm late." He rose, looking down at
her. "They said you telephoned me this morning. Is this what it was?"

"No," she said. Now she looked up at him; now her gnarled hands began   35
to pick faintly at one another. "You offered me a servant once."

"Yes. I thought fifteen years ago that you ought to have one. Have you
changed your mind? Do you want me to—"

Now she stopped looking at him again, though her hands did not cease.
"That was fifteen years ago. It would have cost at least five hundred dollars a
year. That would be—"

He laughed, short and harsh. "I'd like to see the Los Angeles servant you
could get for five hundred dollars a year. But what—" He stopped laughing,
looking down at her.

"That would be at least five thousand dollars," she said.

He looked down at her. After a while he said, "Are you asking me again   40
for money?" She didn't answer nor move her hands picking slowly and quietly
at one another. "Ah," he said. "You want to go away. You want to run from it.
So do I!" he cried, before he could catch himself this time; "so do I! But you
did not choose me when you elected a child; neither did I choose my two. But
I shall have to bear them and you will have to bear all of us. There is no help
for it." He caught himself now, panting, quieting himself by will as when he
would rise from bed, though his voice was still harsh: "Where would you go?
Where would you hide from it?"

"Home," she said.

"Home?" he repeated; he repeated in a kind of amazement: "home?" before he understood. "You would go back there? with those winters, that snow
and all? Why, you wouldn't live to see the first Christmas: don't you know
that?" She didn't move nor look up at him. "Nonsense," he said. "This will
blow over. In a month there will be two others and nobody except us will even
remember it. And you don't need money. You have been asking me for money
for years, but you don't need it. I had to worry about money so much at one
time myself that I swore that the least I could do was to arrange your affairs so
you would never even have to look at the stuff. I must go; there is something
at the office today. I'll see you tomorrow."

It was already one o'clock. "Courthouse," he told the Filipino, settling back into the car. "My God, I want a drink." He rode with his eyes closed against the sun; the secretary had already sprung onto the runningboard before he realized that they had reached the courthouse. The secretary, bareheaded too, wore a jacket of authentic tweed; his turtleneck sweater was dead black, his hair was black too, varnished smooth to his skull; he spread before Ira a dummy newspaper page laid out to embrace the blank space for the photograph beneath the caption: APRIL LALEAR'S FATHER. Beneath the space was the legend: IRA EWING, PRESIDENT OF THE EWING REALTY CO.,—WILSHIRE BOULEVARD, BEVERLY HILLS.

"Is thirty percent all you could get?" Ira said. The secretary was young; he glared at Ira for an instant in vague impatient fury.

"Jesus, thirty percent is thirty percent. They are going to print a thousand 45 extra copies and use our mailing list. It will be spread all up and down the Coast and as far East as Reno. What do you want? We can't expect them to put under your picture, 'Turn to page fourteen for halfpage ad,' can we?" Ira sat again with his eyes closed, waiting for his head to stop.

"All right," he said. "Are they ready now?"

"All set. You will have to go inside. They insisted it be inside, so everybody that sees it will know it is the courthouse."

"All right," Ira said. He got out; with his eyes half closed and the secretary at his elbow he mounted the steps and entered the courthouse. The reporter and the photographer were waiting but he did not see them yet; he was aware only of being enclosed in a gaping crowd which he knew would be mostly women, hearing the secretary and a policeman clearing the way in the corridor outside the courtroom door.

"This is O.K.," the secretary said. Ira stopped; the darkness was easier on his eyes though he did not open them yet; he just stood, hearing the secretary and the policeman herding the women, the faces, back; someone took him by the arm and turned him; he stood obediently; the magnesium flashed and glared, striking against his painful eyeballs like blows; he had a vision of wan faces craned to look at him from either side of a narrow human lane; with his eyes shut tight now he turned, blundering until the reporter in charge spoke to him:

"Just a minute, chief. We better get another one just in case." This time 50 his eyes were tightly closed; the magnesium flashed, washed over them; in the thin acrid smell of it he turned and with the secretary again at his elbow he moved blindly back and into the sunlight and into his car. He gave no order this time, he just said, "Get me a drink." He rode with his eyes closed again while the car cleared the downtown traffic and then began to move quiet, powerful and fast under him; he rode so for a long while before he felt the car swing into the palmbordered drive, slowing. It stopped; the doorman opened the door for him, speaking to him by name. The elevator boy called him by name too, stopping at the right floor without direction; he followed the corridor and knocked at a door and was fumbling for the key when the door opened upon a woman in a bathing suit beneath a loose beach cloak—a woman with treated hair also and brown eyes, who swung the door back for him to enter and then to behind him, looking at him with the quick bright faint serene smiling which only a woman nearing forty can give to a man to whom she is not married and from whom she has had no secrets physical and few mental over a long time of pleasant and absolute intimacy. She had been married though and divorced; she had a child, a daughter of fourteen, whom he was now keeping in boarding school. He looked at her, blinking, as she closed the door.

"You saw the papers," he said. She kissed him, not suddenly, without heat, in a continuation of the movement which closed the door, with a sort of warm envelopment; suddenly he cried, "I can't understand it! After all the advantages that . . . after all I tried to do for them—"

"Hush," she said. "Hush, now. Get into your trunks; I'll have a drink ready for you when you have changed. Will you eat some lunch if I have it sent up?"

"No. I don't want any lunch. —after all I have tried to give—"

"Hush, now. Get into your trunks while I fix you a drink. It's going to be swell at the beach." In the bedroom his bathing trunks and robe were laid out on the bed. He changed, hanging his suit in the closet where her clothes hung, where there hung already another suit of his and clothes for the evening. When he returned to the sitting room she had fixed the drink for him; she held the match to his cigarette and watched him sit down and take up the glass, watching him still with that serene impersonal smiling. Now he watched her slip off the cape and kneel at the cellarette, filling a silver flask, in the bathing costume of the moment, such as ten thousand wax female dummies wore in ten thousand shop windows that summer, such as a hundred thousand young girls wore on California beaches; he looked at her, kneeling—back, buttocks and flanks trim enough, even firm enough (so firm in fact as to be a little on the muscular side, what with unremitting and perhaps even rigorous care) but still those of forty. But I don't want a young girl, he thought. Would to God that all young girls, all young female flesh, were removed, blasted even, from the earth. He finished the drink before she had filled the flask.

"I want another one," he said.   55

"All right," she said. "As soon as we get to the beach."

"No. Now."

"Let's go on to the beach first. It's almost three o'clock. Won't that be better?"

"Just so you are not trying to tell me I can't have another drink now."

"Of course not," she said, slipping the flask into the cape's pocket and   60
looking at him again with that warm, faint, inscrutable smiling. "I just want to have a dip before the water gets too cold." They went down to the car; the Filipino knew this too: he held the door for her to slip under the wheel, then he got himself into the back. The car moved on; she drove well. "Why not lean back and shut your eyes," she told Ira, "and rest until we get to the beach? Then we will have a dip and a drink."

"I don't want to rest," he said. "I'm all right." But he did close his eyes again and again the car ran powerful, smooth, and fast beneath him, performing its afternoon's jaunt over the incredible distances of which the city was composed; from time to time, had he looked, he could have seen the city in the bright soft vague hazy sunlight, random, scattered about the arid earth like so many gay scraps of paper blown without order, with its curious air of being rootless—of houses bright beautiful and gay, without basements or foundations, lightly attached to a few inches of light penetrable earth, lighter even than dust and laid lightly in turn upon the profound and primeval lava, which one good hard rain would wash forever from the sight and memory of man as a firehose flushes down a gutter—that city of almost incalculable wealth whose queerly appropriate fate it is to be erected upon a few spools of a substance whose value is computed in billions and which may be completely destroyed in that second's instant of a careless match between the moment of striking and the moment when the striker might have sprung and stamped it out.

"You saw your mother today," she said. "Has she—"

"Yes." He didn't open his eyes. "That damned Jap gave it to her. She asked me for money again. I found out what she wants with it. She wants to run, to go back to Nebraska. I told her, so did I. . . . If she went back there, she would not live until Christmas. The first month of winter would kill her. Maybe it wouldn't even take winter to do it."

She still drove, she still watched the road, yet somehow she had contrived to become completely immobile. "So that's what it is," she said.

He did not open his eyes. "What what is?"   65

"The reason she has been after you all this time to give her money, cash. Why, even when you won't do it, every now and then she asks you again."

"What what . . ." He opened his eyes, looking at her profile; he sat up suddenly. "You mean, she's been wanting to go back there all the time? That all these years she has been asking me for money, that that was what she wanted with it?"

She glanced at him swiftly, then back to the road. "What else can it be? What else could she use money for?"

"Back there?" he said. "To those winters, that town, that way of living, where she's bound to know that the first winter would . . . You'd almost think she wanted to die, wouldn't you?"

"Hush," she said quickly. "Shhhhh. Don't say that. Don't say that about   70 anybody." Already they could smell the sea; now they swung down toward it; the bright salt wind blew upon them, with the long-spaced sound of the rollers; now they could see it—the dark blue of water creaming into the blanched curve of beach dotted with bathers. "We won't go through the club," she said. "I'll park in here and we can go straight to the water." They left the Filipino in the car and descended to the beach. It was already crowded, bright and gay with movement. She chose a vacant space and spread her cape.

"Now that drink," he said.

"Have your dip first," she said. He looked at her. Then he slipped his robe off slowly; she took it and spread it beside her own; he looked down at her.

"Which is it? Will you always be too clever for me, or is it that every time I will always believe you again?"

She looked at him, bright, warm, fond and inscrutable. "Maybe both. Maybe neither. Have your dip; I will have the flask and a cigarette ready when you come out." When he came back from the water, wet, panting, his heart a little too hard and fast, she had the towel ready, and she lit the cigarette and uncapped the flask as he lay on the spread robes. She lay too, lifted to one elbow, smiling down at him, smoothing the water from his hair with the towel while he panted, waiting for his heart to slow and quiet. Steadily between them and the water, and as far up and down the beach as they could see, the bathers passed—young people, young men in trunks, and young girls in little more, with bronzed, unselfconscious bodies. Lying so, they seemed to him to walk along the rim of the world as though they and their kind alone inhabited it, and he with his forty-eight years were the forgotten last survivor of another race and kind, and they in turn precursors of a new race not yet seen on the earth: of men and women without age, beautiful as gods and goddesses, and with the minds of infants. He turned quickly and looked at the woman beside him—at the quiet face, the wise, smiling eyes, the grained skin and temples, the hairroots showing where the dye had grown out, the legs veined faint and blue and myriad beneath the skin. "You look better than any of them!" he cried. "You look better to me than any of them!"

III

The Japanese gardener, with his hat on, stood tapping on the glass and beckoning and grimacing until old Mrs. Ewing went out to him. He had the afternoon's paper with its black headline: LALEAR WOMAN CREATES SCENE IN COURTROOM. "You take," the Japanese said. "Read while I catch water." But she declined; she just stood in the soft halcyon sunlight, surrounded by the myriad and almost fierce blooming of flowers, and looked quietly at the headline without even taking the paper, and that was all.

"I guess I won't look at the paper today," she said. "Thank you just the same." She returned to the living room. Save for the chair, it was exactly as it had been when she first saw it that day when her son brought her into it and told her that it was now her home and that her daughter-in-law and her grandchildren were now her family. It had changed very little, and that which had altered was the part which her son knew nothing about, and that too had changed not at all in so long that she could not even remember now when she had added the last coin to the hoard. This was in a china vase on the mantel. She knew what was in it to the penny; nevertheless, she took it down and sat in the chair which she had brought all the way from Nebraska and emptied the coins and the worn timetable into her lap. The timetable was folded back at the page on which she had folded it the day she walked downtown to the ticket office and got it fifteen years ago, though that was so long ago now that the pencil circle about the name of the nearest junction point to Ewing, Nebraska, had faded away. But she did not need that either; she knew the distance to the exact halfmile, just as she knew the fare to the penny, and back in the early twenties when the railroads began to become worried and passenger fares began to drop, no broker ever watched the grain and utilities market any closer than she watched the railroad advertisements and quotations. Then at last the fares became stabilized with the fare back to Ewing thirteen dollars more than she had been able to save, and at a time when her source of income had ceased. This was the two grandchildren. When she entered the house that day twenty years ago and looked at the two babies for the first time, it was with diffidence and eagerness both. She would be dependent for the rest of her life, but she would give something in return for it. It was not that she would attempt to make another Ira and Samantha Ewing of them; she had made that mistake with her own son and had driven him from home. She was wiser now; she saw now that it was not the repetition of hardship: she would merely take what had been of value in hers and her husband's hard lives—that which they had learned through hardship and endurance of honor and courage and pride—and transmit it to the children without their having to suffer the hardship at all, the travail and the despairs. She had expected that there would be some friction between her and the young daughter-in-law, but she had believed that her son, the actual Ewing, would be her ally; she had even reconciled herself after a year to waiting, since the children were still but babies; she was not alarmed, since they were Ewings too: after she had looked that first searching time at the two puttysoft little faces feature by feature, she had said it was because they were babies yet and so looked like no one. So she was content to bide and wait; she did not even know that her son was planning to move until he told her that the other house was bought and that the present one was to be hers until she died. She watched them go; she said nothing; it was not to begin then. It did not begin for five years, during which she watched her son making money faster and faster and easier and easier, gaining with apparent contemptible and contemptuous ease that substance for which in niggard amounts her husband had striven while still clinging with undeviating incorruptibility to honor and dignity and pride, and spending it, squandering it, in the same way. By that time she had given up the son and she had long since learned that she and her daughter-in-law were irrevocable and implacable moral enemies. It was in the fifth year. One day in her son's home she saw the two children take money from their mother's purse lying on a table. The mother did not even know how much she had in the purse; when the grandmother told her about it she became angry and dared the older woman to put it to the test. The grandmother accused the children, who denied the whole affair with perfectly straight faces. That was the actual break between herself and her son's family; after that she saw the two children only when the son would bring them with him occasionally on his unfailing daily visits. She had a few broken dollars which she had brought from Nebraska and had kept intact for five years, since she had no need for money here; one day she planted one of the coins while the children were there, and when she went back to look, it was gone too. The next morning she tried to talk to her son about the children, remembering her experience with the daughter-in-law and approaching the matter indirectly, speaking generally of money. "Yes," the son said. "I'm making money. I'm making it fast while I can. I'm going to make a lot of it. I'm going to give my children luxuries and advantages that my father never dreamed a child might have."

"That's it," she said. "You make money too easy. This whole country is too easy for us Ewings. It may be all right for them that have been born here for generations; I don't know about that. But not for us."

"But these children were born here."

"Just one generation. The generation before that they were born in a sodroofed dugout on the Nebraska wheat frontier. And the one before that in a log house in Missouri. And the one before that in a Kentucky blockhouse with Indians around it. This world has never been easy for Ewings. Maybe the Lord never intended it to be."

"But it is from now on," he said; he spoke with a kind of triumph. "For you and me too. But mostly for them." 80

And that was all. When he was gone she sat quietly in the single Nebraska chair which she had taken out of storage—the first chair which the older Ira Ewing had bought for her after he built a house and in which she had rocked the younger Ira to sleep before he could walk, while the older Ira himself sat in the chair which he had made out of a flour barrel, grim, quiet and incorruptible, taking his earned twilight ease between a day and a day—telling herself quietly that that was all. Her next move was curiously direct; there was something in it of the actual pioneer's opportunism, of taking immediate and cold advantage of Spartan circumstance; it was as though for the first time in her life she was able to use something, anything, which she had gained by bartering her youth and strong maturity against the Nebraska immensity, and this not in order to live further but in order to die; apparently she saw neither paradox in it nor dishonesty. She began to make candy and cake of the materials which her son bought for her on credit, and to sell them to the two grandchildren for the coins which their father gave them or which they perhaps purloined also from their mother's purse, hiding the coins in the vase with the timetable, watching the niggard hoard grow. But after a few years the children outgrew candy and cake, and then she had watched railroad fares go down and down and then stop thirteen dollars away. But she did not give up, even then. Her son had tried to give her a servant years ago and she had refused; she believed that when the time came, the right moment, he would not refuse to give her at least thirteen dollars of the money which she had saved him. Then this had failed. "Maybe it wasn't the right time," she thought. "Maybe I tried it too quick. I was surprised into it," she told herself, looking down at the heap of small coins in her lap. "Or maybe he was surprised into saying No. Maybe when he has had time . . ." She roused; she put the coins back into the vase and set it on the mantel again, looking at the clock as she did so. It was just four, two hours yet until time to start supper. The sun was high; she could see the water from the sprinkler flashing and glinting in it as she went to the window. It was still high, still afternoon; the mountains stood serene and drab against it; the city, the land, lay sprawled and myriad beneath it—the land, the earth which spawned a thousand new faiths, nostrums and cures each year but no disease to even disprove them on—beneath the golden days unmarred by rain or weather, the changeless monotonous beautiful days without end countless out of the halcyon past and endless into the halcyon future.

"I will stay here and live forever," she said to herself.

TOPICS FOR CRITICAL THINKING Web www

1. In what ways do the children embody the attitudes of the "golden land"?
2. In terms of the question of values, what does it mean that Ira's son is gay?
3. What is the connection between sex and success?
4. Why does Ira keep his mother prisoner?
5. What is the relation between the beauty of the golden land and the events that transpire in it?

TOPICS FOR CRITICAL WRITING Web www

1. In what ways does "Golden Land" unravel the relations between material and emotional success?
2. In what ways is "Golden Land" a critique of American society?"

11   Tone

Most of us have ideas about how a story sounds. The literary concept of **tone** is analogous to the tone of voice in spoken language. It is an attitude conveyed through inflection, **diction** (word choice), sentence structure, the speaker's character, the distribution of knowledge among characters within the text, and the information shared between the story and the reader. Inflection relates to various qualities added to words when they are spoken. One can emphasize words for the sake of explanation, humor, or even out of exasperation. One can say words snidely, sarcastically, ironically, caressingly, tauntingly, interrogatively, mockingly, curtly, angrily, or any way that conveys an attitude. For example, imagine the differences in tone of voice if the word *honey* is said in any of the ways listed above. By simply altering the attitude conveyed by the voice, very different scenarios are conjured. Since written texts cannot directly convey the quality of a voice, vocal inflections are signaled in other ways. One way is simply through the use of adverbs. "Honey," he said caressingly. "Honey," she said, exasperated. "Honey?" Another way to imply inflection in written texts is through circumstances. The word *honey* spoken at a romantic luncheon has a different inflection than if the word is used by one gang member to refer to another.

Diction is another means through which written texts produce tone. Diction may be employed by a narrator to convey an attitude. Compare for example, the tone conveyed by the following two lines:

"As always, he was unfailingly polite to women."

"As usual, he didn't fail to make use of the opportunity to impress women with his manners."

The tone of the first sentence suggests a straightforward, admirably earnest man. The second conveys sarcasm in its description of an opportunist. The first is Beaver Cleaver, the second, Eddie Haskell. The narrator's tone is produced in this case by a combination of word choice ("as always" instead "as usual," the more sarcastic selection) and through sentence structure. The first sentence is a positive declaration. The second sentence employs a negative to produce a positive ("didn't fail to make use"), which suggests snideness or sarcasm in the negative's understatement of the man's avid use of opportunity.

Occasionally, tone is conveyed by a story's characters or setting. Some characters are portrayed as having an attitude (as does the husband in "Sweat"); this attitude contributes to the story's tone. A setting may evoke a gloomy feeling that sets its tone. This atmosphere or feeling defines its **mood**. Web

www

396

Tone is also an effect of differences between what the readers, the narrator, and various characters know. When the readers know more than the characters, such a disparity is called **dramatic irony**. While this irony is not quite the same as knowing that narrators or characters actually mean the opposite of what they say (as in **irony**), it does produce a tone or attitude in the story.

Critical Perspective: On Tone

The first paragraph of Flannery O'Connor's "A Good Man Is Hard to Find" displays the essence of irony both in its complex playful/authoritative tone and in the way it signals the inevitability of the fate to be avoided. The story takes irony apart, exhibiting on the one hand the sense of a controlling voice typical of irony and on the other the innocent lack of awareness on the part of those whose lives are narrated. The difference in feel between narrator and narrated is a difference in knowledge and attitude. The narrator seems to know far more than the characters, who because of a lack of foresight, can be no more than the dupes of fate or of their own unconscious. At the same time, the narrator's tone indicates that the narrator knows fate but for the sake of the story will only hint at the outcome. The trick or talent of irony is the way its tone stealthily and irresistibly seduces readers to the side of knowledge. When, for example, the narrator states in the story's first line, "The grandmother didn't want to go to Florida," it appears to convey a simple fact about the grandmother's desires, but it also and at the same time conveys the sense that despite what the grandmother wants, something else is in store for her. The next sentence elaborates the grandmother's wishes but in so doing increases the sense readers might have that the narrator in fact knows better than the grandmother both what she wants and what will happen anyway. This duplicity, produced through tone, defines the story that follows in which some force, other than the characters' wishes or conscious desires, determines where the characters will go. It is as if the narrator, representing the inevitable, pushes the characters against their wishes, and we readers watch it all, privy to the duplicities of fate, the unconscious, and bad luck. Irony is, in fact, a "misfit," present in the difference between what the narrator says and what it conveys that it knows, which matches the difference in the story between what the characters think they are doing and where they inevitably end up.

Stories About Tone

The three stories that follow all employ tone as a central element of their telling. Zora Neale Hurston's "Sweat" takes a studied detached tone to offset the story's ironies. Flannery O'Connor's "A Good Man Is Hard to Find" depends heavily on both dramatic irony and the narrator's ironic tone. W. S. Penn's "In Dreams Begins Reality" plays with the ambiguities of tone as the narrator tries to understand the women he encounters.

Zora Neale Hurston

Sweat   (1926)

It was eleven o'clock of a Spring night in Florida. It was Sunday. Any other night, Delia Jones would have been in bed for two hours by this time. But she was a washwoman, and Monday morning meant a great deal to her. So she collected the soiled clothes on Saturday when she returned the clean things. Sunday night after church, she sorted them and put the white things to soak. It saved her almost a half day's start. A great hamper in the bedroom held the clothes that she brought home. It was so much neater than a number of bundles lying around.

She squatted on the kitchen floor beside the great pile of clothes, sorting them into small heaps according to color, and humming a song in a mournful key, but wondering through it all where Sykes, her husband, had gone with her horse and buckboard.[1]

Just then something long, round, limp and black fell upon her shoulders and slithered to the floor beside her. A great terror took hold of her. It softened her knees and dried her mouth so that it was a full minute before she could cry out or move. Then she saw that it was the big bull whip her husband liked to carry when he drove.

She lifted her eyes to the door and saw him standing there bent over with laughter at her fright. She screamed at him.

"Sykes, what you throw dat whip on me like dat? You know it would skeer 5 me—looks just like a snake, an' you knows how skeered Ah is of snakes."

"Course Ah knowed it! That's how come Ah done it." He slapped his leg with his hand and almost rolled on the ground in his mirth. "If you such a big fool dat you got to have a fit over a earth worm or a string, Ah don't keer how bad Ah skeer you."

"You aint got no business doing it. Gawd knows it's a sin. Some day Ah'm gointuh drop dead from some of yo' foolishness. 'Nother thing, where you been wid mah rig? Ah feeds dat pony. He aint fuh you to be drivin' wid no bull whip."

"You sho is one aggravatin' nigger woman!" he declared and stepped into the room. She resumed her work and did not answer him at once. "Ah done tole you time and again to keep them white folks' clothes outa dis house."

He picked up the whip and glared down at her. Delia went on with her work. She went out into the yard and returned with a galvanized tub and set it on the washbench. She saw that Sykes kicked all of the clothes together again, and now stood in her way truculently, his whole manner hoping, *praying,* for an argument. But she walked calmly around him and commenced to re-sort the things.

1. An open wagon.

"Next time, Ah'm gointer kick 'em outdoors," he threatened as he struck   10
a match along the leg of his corduroy breeches.

Delia never looked up from her work, and her thin, stooped shoulders
sagged further.

"Ah aint for no fuss t'night, Sykes. Ah just come from taking sacrament at
the church house."

Two months after the wedding, he had given her the first brutal beating.
She had the memory of his numerous trips to Orlando[2] with all of his wages
when he had returned to her penniless, even before the first year had passed.
She was young and soft then, but now she thought of her knotty, muscled
limbs, her harsh, knuckly hands, and drew herself up into an unhappy little
ball in the middle of the big feather bed. Too late now to hope for love, even
if it were not Bertha it could be someone else. This case differed from the others only in that she was bolder than the others. Too late for everything except
her little home. She had built it for her old days, and planted one by one the
trees and flowers there. It was lovely to her, lovely.

Somehow, before sleep came, she found herself saying aloud: "Oh well,
whatever goes over the Devil's back, is got to come under his belly. Sometime
or ruther, Sykes, like everybody else, is gointer reap his sowing." After that
she was able to build a spiritual earthworks[3] against her husband. His shells
could no longer reach her. *Amen.* She went to sleep and slept until he announced his presence in bed by kicking her feet and rudely snatching the covers away.

"Gimme some kivah heah, an' git yo' damn foots over on yo' own side!   15
Ah oughter mash you in yo' mouf fuh drawing dat skillet on me."

Delia went clear to the rail without answering him. A triumphant indifference to all that he was or did.

The week was as full of work for Delia as all other weeks, and Saturday
found her behind her little pony, collecting and delivering clothes.

It was a hot, hot day near the end of July. The village men on Joe Clarke's
porch even chewed cane listlessly. They did not hurl the caneknots as usual.
They let them dribble over the edge of the porch. Even conversation had collapsed under the heat.

"Heah come Delia Jones," Jim Merchant said, as the shaggy pony came
'round the bend of the road toward them. The rusty buckboard was heaped
with baskets of crisp, clean laundry.

"Yep," Joe Lindsay agreed. "Hot or col', rain or shine, jes ez reg'lar ez de   20
weeks roll roun' Delia carries 'em an' fetches 'em on Sat'day."

"She better if she wanter eat," said Moss. "Syke Jones aint wuth de shot
an' powder hit would tek tuh kill 'em. Not to *huh* he aint."

"He sho' aint," Walter Thomas chimed in. "It's too bad, too, cause she
wuz a right pritty lil trick when he got huh. Ah'd uh mah'ied huh mahseff if
he hadnter beat me to it."

---

2. City in Florida.
3. A ridge of earth of the kind used to protect trench soldiers in World War I.

Delia nodded briefly at the men as she drove past.

"Too much knockin' will ruin *any* 'oman. He done beat huh 'nough tuh kill three women, let 'lone change they looks," said Elijah Moseley. "How Syke kin stommuck dat big black greasy Mogul[4] he's layin' roun' wid, gits me. Ah swear dat eight-rock couldn't kiss a sardine can Ah done thowed out de back do' 'way las' yeah."

"Aw, she's fat, thass how come. He's allus been crazy 'bout fat women," 25 put in Merchant. "He'd a' been tied up wid one long time ago if he could a' found one tuh have him. Did Ah tell yuh 'bout him come sidlin' roun' *mah* wife—bringin' her a basket uh peecans outa his yard fuh a present? Yessir, mah wife! She tol' him tuh take em right straight back home, cause Delia works so hard ovah dat wash tub she reckon everything on de place taste lak sweat an' soapsuds. Ah jus' wisht Ah'd a caught 'im 'roun' dere! Ah'd a' made his hips ketch on fiah down dat shell road."

"Ah know he done it, too. Ah sees 'im grinnin' at every 'oman dat passes," Walter Thomas said. "But even so, he useter eat some mighty big hunks uh humble pie tuh git dat lil' 'oman he got. She wuz ez pritty ez a speckled pup! Dat wuz fifteen yeahs ago. He useter be so skeered uh losin' huh, she could make him do some parts of a husband's duty. Dey never wuz de same in de mind."

"There oughter be a law about him," said Lindsay. "He aint fit tuh carry guts tuh a bear."

Clarke spoke for the first time. "Taint no law on earth dat kin make a man be decent if it aint in 'im. There's plenty men dat takes a wife lak dey do a joint uh sugar-cane. It's round, juicy an' sweet when dey gits it. But dey squeeze an' grind, squeeze an' grind an' wring tell dey wring every drop uh pleasure dat's in 'em out. When dey's satisfied dat dey is wrung dry, dey treats 'em jes lak dey do a cane-chew. Dey thows 'em away. Dey knows whut dey is doin' while dey is at it, an' hates theirselves fuh it but they keeps on hangin' after huh tell she's empty. Den dey hates huh fuh bein' a cane-chew an' in de way."

"We oughter take Syke an' dat stray 'oman uh his'n down in Lake How-ell swamp an' lay on de rawhide till they cain't say Lawd a' mussy.' He allus wuz uh ovahbearin' niggah, but since dat white 'oman from up north done teached 'im how to run a automobile, he done got too biggety[5] to live—an' we oughter kill 'im." Old Man Anderson advised.

A grunt of approval went around the porch. But the heat was melting 30 their civic virtue and Elijah Moseley began to bait Joe Clarke.

"Come on, Joe, git a melon outa dere an' slice it up for yo' customers. We'se all sufferin' wid de heat. De bear's done got *me!*"

"Thass right, Joe, a watermelon is jes' whut Ah needs tuh cure de eppizu-dicks,"[6] Walter Thomas joined forces with Moseley. "Come on dere, Joe. We all is steady customers an' you aint set us up in a long time. Ah chooses dat long, bowlegged Floridy favorite."

"A god, an' be dough. You all gimme twenty cents and slice way," Clarke

4. Big woman.
5. Full of himself.
6. "Epizootic," a descriptive term for a disease that attacks a large number of animals at once.

retorted. "Ah needs a col' slice m'self. Heah, everybody chip in. Ah'll lend y'll mah meat knife."

The money was quickly subscribed and the huge melon brought forth. At that moment, Sykes and Bertha arrived. A determined silence fell on the porch and the melon was put away again.

Merchant snapped down the blade of his jacknife and moved toward the store door.

"Come on in, Joe, an' gimme a slab uh sow belly an' uh pound uh coffee—almost fuhgot 'twas Sat'day. Got to git on home." Most of the men left also.

Just then Delia drove past on her way home, as Sykes was ordering magnificently for Bertha. It pleased him for Delia to see.

"Git whutsoever yo' heart desires, Honey. Wait a minute, Joe. Give huh two bottles uh strawberry soda-water, uh quart uh parched ground-peas, an' a block uh chewin' gum."

With all this they left the store, with Sykes reminding Bertha that this was his town and she could have it if she wanted it.

The men returned soon after they left, and held their watermelon feast.

"Where did Syke Jones git da 'oman from nohow?" Lindsay asked.

"Ovah Apopka. Guess dey musta been cleanin' out de town when she lef'. She don't look lak a thing but a hunk uh liver wid hair on it."

"Well, she sho' kin squall," Dave Carter contributed. "When she gits ready tuh laff, she jes' opens huh mouf an' latches it back tuh de las' notch. No ole grandpa alligator down in Lake Bell ain't got nothin' on huh."

Bertha had been in town three months now. Sykes was still paying her room rent at Della Lewis'—the only house in town that would have taken her in. Sykes took her frequently to Winter Park to "stomps."[7] He still assured her that he was the swellest man in the state.

"Sho' you kin have dat lil' ole house soon's Ah kin git dat 'oman outa dere. Everything b'longs tuh me an' you sho' kin have it. Ah sho' 'bominates uh skinny 'oman. Lawdy, you sho' is got one portly shape on you! You kin git *anything* you wants. Dis is *mah* town an' you sho' kin have it."

Delia's work-worn knees crawled over the earth in Gethsemane and up the rocks of Calvary[8] many, many times during these months. She avoided the villagers and meeting places in her efforts to be blind and deaf. But Bertha nullified this to a degree, by coming to Delia's house to call Sykes out to her at the gate.

Delia and Sykes fought all the time now with no peaceful interludes. They slept and ate in silence. Two or three times Delia had attempted a timid friendliness, but she was repulsed each time. It was plain that the breaches must remain agape.

The sun had burned July to August. The heat streamed down like a

---

7. Jazz dances.

8. Gethsemane, the garden where Christ was betrayed (Matthew 26:36–47); Calvary, the hill where he was crucified.

million hot arrows, smiting all things living upon the earth. Grass withered, leaves browned, snakes went blind in shedding and men and dogs went mad. Dog days!

Delia came home one day and found Sykes there before her. She wondered, but started to go on into the house without speaking, even though he was standing in the kitchen door and she must either stoop under his arm or ask him to move. He made no room for her. She noticed a soap box beside the steps, but paid no particular attention to it, knowing that he must have brought it there. As she was stooping to pass under his outstretched arm, he suddenly pushed her backward, laughingly.

"Look in de box dere Delia, Ah done brung yuh somethin'!"   50

She nearly fell upon the box in her stumbling, and when she saw what it held, she all but fainted outright.

"Syke! Syke, mah Gawd! You take dat rattlesnake 'way from heah! You *gottuh*. Oh, Jesus, have mussy!"

"Ah aint gut tuh do nuthin' uh de kin'—fact is Ah aint got tuh do nothin' but die. Taint no use uh you puttin' on airs makin' out lak you skeered uh dat snake—he's gointer stay right heah tell he die. He wouldn't bite me cause Ah knows how tuh handle 'im. Nohow he wouldn't risk breakin' out his fangs 'gin *yo'* skinny laigs."

"Naw, now Syke, don't keep dat thing 'roun' heah tuh skeer me tuh death. You knows Ah'm even feared uh earth worms. Thass de biggest snake Ah evah did see. Kill 'im Syke, please."

"Doan ast me tuh do nothin' fuh yuh. Goin' 'roun' tryin' tuh be so damn   55 asterperious. Naw, Ah aint gonna kill it. Ah think uh damn sight mo' uh him dan you! Dat's a nice snake an' anybody doan lak 'im kin jes' hit de grit."

The village soon heard that Sykes had the snake, and came to see and ask questions.

"How de hen-fire did you ketch dat six-foot rattler, Syke?" Thomas asked.

"He's full uh frogs so he caint hardly move, thass how Ah eased up on 'm. But Ah'm a snake charmer an' knows how tuh handle 'em. Shux, dat aint nothin'. Ah could ketch one eve'y day if Ah so wanted tuh."

"Whut he needs is a heavy hick'ry club leaned real heavy on his head. Dat's de bes 'way tuh charm a rattlesnake."

"Naw, Walt, y'll jes' don't understand dese diamon' backs lak Ah do," said   60 Sykes in a superior tone of voice.

The village agreed with Walter, but the snake stayed on. His box remained by the kitchen door with its screen wire covering. Two or three days later it had digested its meal of frogs and literally came to life. It rattled at every movement in the kitchen or the yard. One day as Delia came down the kitchen steps she saw his chalky-white fangs curved like scimitars hung in the wire meshes. This time she did not run away with averted eyes as usual. She stood for a long time in the doorway in a red fury that grew bloodier for every second that she regarded the creature that was her torment.

That night she broached the subject as soon as Sykes sat down to the table.

"Syke, Ah wants you tuh take dat snake 'way fum heah. You done starved me an' Ah put up widcher, you done beat me an Ah took dat, but you done kilt all mah insides bringin' dat varmint heah."

Sykes poured out a saucer full of coffee and drank it deliberately before he answered her.

"A whole lot Ah keer 'bout how you feels inside uh out. Dat snake aint　65 goin' no damn wheah till Ah gits ready fuh 'im tuh go. So fur as beatin' is concerned, yuh aint took near all dat you gointer take ef you stay 'roun' *me*."

Delia pushed back her plate and got up from the table. "Ah hates you, Sykes," she said calmly. "Ah hates you tuh de same degree dat Ah useter love yuh. Ah done took an' took till mah belly is full up tuh mah neck. Dat's de reason Ah got mah letter fum de church an' moved mah membership tuh Woodbridge—so Ah don't haftuh take no sacrament wid yuh. Ah don't wantuh see yuh 'roun' me atall. Lay 'roun' wid dat 'oman all yuh wants tuh, but gwan 'way fum me an' mah house. Ah hates yuh lak uh suck-egg dog."

Sykes almost let the huge wad of corn bread and collard greens he was chewing fall out of his mouth in amazement. He had a hard time whipping himself up to the proper fury to try to answer Delia.

"Well, Ah'm glad you does hate me. Ah'm sho' tiahed uh you hangin' ontuh me. Ah don't want yuh. Look at yuh stringey ole neck! Yo' rawbony laigs an' arms is enough tuh cut uh man tuh death. You looks jes' lak de devvul's doll-baby tuh *me*. You cain't hate me no worse dan Ah hates you. Ah been hatin' *you* fuh years."

"Yo' ole black hide don't look lak nothin' tuh me, but uh passle uh wrinkled up rubber, wid yo' big ole yeahs flappin' on each side lak uh paih uh buzzard wings. Don't think Ah'm gointuh be run 'way fum mah house neither. Ah'm goin' tuh de white folks bout *you*, mah young man, de very nex' time you lay yo' han's on me. Mah cup is done run ovah."

Delia said this with no signs of fear and Sykes departed from the house,　70 threatening her, but made not the slightest move to carry out any of them.

That night he did not return at all, and the next day being Sunday, Delia was glad she did not have to quarrel before she hitched up her pony and drove the four miles to Woodbridge.

She stayed to the night service—"love feast"—which was very warm and full of spirit. In the emotional winds her domestic trials were borne far and wide so that she sang as she drove homeward,

"Jurden water,[9] black an' col'
Chills de body, not de soul
An' Ah wantah cross Jurden in uh calm time."

She came from the barn to the kitchen door and stopped.

"Whut's de mattah, ol' satan, you aint kickin' up yo' racket?" She addressed the snake's box. Complete silence. She went on into the house with a new hope in its birth struggles. Perhaps her threat to go to the white folks had frightened Sykes! Perhaps he was sorry! Fifteen years of misery and

9. Jordan water, the river that the Jews had to cross to reach the promised land.

suppression had brought Delia to the place where she would hope *anything* that looked towards a way over or through her wall of inhibitions.

She felt in the match safe behind the stove at once for a match. There was   75 only one there.

"Dat niggah wouldn't fetch nothin' heah tuh save his rotten neck, but he kin run thew whut Ah brings quick enough. Now he done toted off nigh on tuh haff uh box uh matches. He done had dat 'oman heah in mah house too."

Nobody but a woman could tell how she knew this even before she struck the match. But she did and it put her into a new fury.

Presently she brought in the tubs to put the white things to soak. This time she decided she need not bring the hamper out of the bedroom: she would go in there and do the sorting. She picked up the pot-bellied lamp and went in. The room was small and the hamper stood hard by the foot of the white iron bed. She could sit and reach through the bedposts—resting as she worked.

"Ah wantah cross Jurden in uh calm time." She was singing again. The mood of the "love feast" had returned. She threw back the lid of the basket almost gaily. Then, moved by both horror and terror, she sprang back toward the door. *There lay the snake in the basket!* He moved sluggishly at first, but even as she turned round and round, jumped up and down in an insanity of fear, he began to stir vigorously. She saw him pouring his awful beauty from the basket upon the bed, then she seized the lamp and ran as fast as she could to the kitchen. The wind from the open door blew out the light and the darkness added to her terror. She sped to the darkness of the yard, slamming the door after her before she thought to set down the lamp. She did not feel safe even on the ground, so she climbed up in the hay barn.

There for an hour or more she lay sprawled upon the hay a gibbering   80 wreck.

Finally she grew quiet, and after that, coherent thought. With this, stalked through her a cold, bloody rage. Hours of this. A period of introspection, a space of retrospection, then a mixture of both. Out of this an awful calm.

"Well, Ah done de bes' Ah could. If things aint right, Gawd knows taint mah fault."

She went to sleep—a twitch sleep—and woke up to a faint gray sky. There was a loud hollow sound below. She peered out. Sykes was at the wood-pile, demolishing a wire-covered box.

He hurried to the kitchen door, but hung outside there some minutes before he entered, and stood some minutes more inside before he closed it after him.

The gray in the sky was spreading. Delia descended without fear now, and   85 crouched beneath the low bedroom window. The drawn shade shut out the dawn, shut in the night. But the thin walls held back no sound.

"Dat ol' scratch is woke up now!" She mused at the tremendous whirr inside, which every woodsman knows, is one of the sound illusions. The rattler is a ventriloquist. His whirr sounds to the right, to the left, straight ahead, behind, close under foot—everywhere but where it is. Woe to him who guesses wrong unless he is prepared to hold up his end of the argument! Sometimes he strikes without rattling at all.

Inside, Sykes heard nothing until he knocked a pot lid off the stove while trying to reach the match safe in the dark. He had emptied his pockets at Bertha's.

The snake seemed to wake up under the stove and Sykes made a quick leap into the bedroom. In spite of the gin he had had, his head was clearing now. "Mah Gawd!" he chattered, "ef Ah could on'y strack uh light!"

The rattling ceased for a moment as he stood paralyzed. He waited. It 90 seemed that the snake waited also.

"Oh, fuh de light! Ah thought he'd be too sick"—Sykes was muttering to himself when the whirr began again, closer, right underfoot this time. Long before this, Sykes' ability to think had been flattened down to primitive instinct and he leaped—onto the bed.

Outside Delia heard a cry that might have come from a maddened chimpanzee, a stricken gorilla. All the terror, all the horror, all the rage that man possibly could express, without a recognizable human sound.

A tremendous stir inside there, another series of animal screams, the intermittent whirr of the reptile. The shade torn violently down from the window, letting in the red dawn, a huge brown hand seizing the window stick, great dull blows upon the wooden floor punctuating the gibberish of sound long after the rattle of the snake had abruptly subsided. All this Delia could see and hear from her place beneath the window, and it made her ill. She crept over to the four-o'clocks[10] and stretched herself on the cool earth to recover.

She lay there. "Delia, Delia!" She could hear Sykes calling in a most despairing tone as one who expected no answer. The sun crept on up, and he called. Delia could not move—her legs were gone flabby. She never moved, he called, and the sun kept rising.

"Mah Gawd!" She heard him moan, "Mah Gawd fum Heben!" She heard 95 him stumbling about and got up from her flower-bed. The sun was growing warm. As she approached the door she heard him call out hopefully, "Delia, is dat you Ah heah?"

She saw him on his hands and knees as soon as she reached the door. He crept an inch or two toward her—all that he was able, and she saw his horribly swollen neck and his one open eye shining with hope. A surge of pity too strong to support bore her away from that eye that must, could not, fail to see the tubs. He would see the lamp. Orlando with its doctors was too far. She could scarcely reach the Chinaberry tree, where she waited in the growing heat while inside she knew the cold river was creeping up and up to extinguish that eye which must know by now that she knew.

——— **ZORA NEALE HURSTON** ———

(1891–1960) Web   *www*

Educated at Howard University, Hurston worked both as a writer and an anthropologist, published the novel *Their Eyes Were Watching God* in 1937, and collected folktales in Florida. She was part of the Harlem Renaissance. Web   *www*

10. A plant native to tropical America with flowers that open in the late afternoon.

She published nothing after 1948 and died penniless twelve years later. In the 1970s, both African American and feminist critics renewed interest in her work.

www   *TOPICS FOR CRITICAL THINKING* **Web**

1. What effect does the narrator's tone have on the ways we might sympathize with Delia?
2. Why is this story told primarily through dialogue?
3. What relations between the genders does this story present?
4. Is Delia right?
5. What is the story's mood?

www   *TOPICS FOR CRITICAL WRITING* **Web**

1. In what specific ways does the snake function in the story?
2. Why is the story titled "Sweat"?

FLANNERY O'CONNOR

A Good Man Is Hard to Find   *(1955)*

The grandmother didn't want to go to Florida. She wanted to visit some of her connections in east Tennessee and she was seizing at every chance to change Bailey's mind. Bailey was the son she lived with, her only boy. He was sitting on the edge of his chair at the table, bent over the orange sports section of the *Journal.* "Now look here, Bailey," she said, "see here, read this," and she stood with one hand on her thin hip and the other rattling the newspaper at his bald head. "Here this fellow that calls himself The Misfit is aloose from the Federal Pen and headed toward Florida and you read here what it says he did to these people. Just you read it. I wouldn't take my children in any direction with a criminal like that aloose in it. I couldn't answer to my conscience if I did."

Bailey didn't look up from his reading so she wheeled around then and faced the children's mother, a young woman in slacks, whose face was as broad and innocent as a cabbage and was tied round with a green head-kerchief that had two points on the top like rabbit's ears. She was sitting on the sofa, feeding the baby his apricots out of a jar. "The children have been to Florida before," the old lady said. "You all ought to take them somewhere else for a change so they would see different parts of the world and be broad. They never have been to east Tennessee."

The children's mother didn't seem to hear her but the eight-year-old boy, John Wesley, a stocky child with glasses, said, "If you don't want to go to Florida, why dontcha stay at home?" He and the little girl, June Star, were reading the funny papers on the floor.

"She wouldn't stay at home to be queen for a day," June Star said without raising her yellow head.

"Yes and what would you do if this fellow, The Misfit, caught you?" the   5
grandmother asked.

"I'd smack his face," John Wesley said.

"She wouldn't stay at home for a million bucks," June Star said. "Afraid
she'd miss something. She has to go everywhere we go."

"All right, Miss," the grandmother said. "Just remember that the next
time you want me to curl your hair."

June Star said her hair was naturally curly.

The next morning the grandmother was the first one in the car, ready to   10
go. She had her big black valise that looked like the head of a hippopotamus
in one corner, and underneath it she was hiding a basket with Pitty Sing, the
cat, in it. She didn't intend for the cat to be left alone in the house for three
days because he would miss her too much and she was afraid he might brush
against one of the gas burners and accidentally asphyxiate himself. Her son,
Bailey, didn't like to arrive at a motel with a cat.

She sat in the middle of the back seat with John Wesley and June Star on
either side of her. Bailey and the children's mother and the baby sat in the
front and they left Atlanta at eight forty-five with the mileage on the car at
55890. The grandmother wrote this down because she thought it would be
interesting to say how many miles they had been when they got back. It took
them twenty minutes to reach the outskirts of the city.

The old lady settled herself comfortably, removing her white cotton
gloves and putting them up with her purse on the shelf in front of the back
window. The children's mother still had on slacks and still had her head tied
up in a green kerchief, but the grandmother had on a navy blue straw sailor
hat with a bunch of white violets on the brim and a navy blue dress with a
small white dot in the print. Her collar and cuffs were white organdy trimmed
with lace and at her neckline she had pinned a purple spray of cloth violets
containing a sachet. In case of an accident, anyone seeing her dead on the
highway would know at once that she was a lady.

She said she thought it was going to be a good day for driving, neither too
hot nor too cold, and she cautioned Bailey that the speed limit was fifty-five
miles an hour and that the patrolmen hid themselves behind billboards and
small clumps of trees and sped out after you before you had a chance to slow
down. She pointed out interesting details of the scenery: Stone Mountain; the
blue granite that in some places came up to both sides of the highway; the
brilliant red clay banks slightly streaked with purple; and the various crops
that made rows of green lace-work on the ground. The trees were full of
silver-white sunlight and the meanest of them sparkled. The children were
reading comic magazines and their mother had gone back to sleep.

"Let's go through Georgia fast so we won't have to look at it much," John
Wesley said.

"If I were a little boy," said the grandmother, "I wouldn't talk about my   15
native state that way. Tennessee has the mountains and Georgia has the hills."

"Tennessee is just a hillbilly dumping ground," John Wesley said, "and
Georgia is a lousy state too."

"You said it," June Star said.

"In my time," said the grandmother, folding her thin veined fingers, "children were more respectful of their native states and their parents and everything else. People did right then. Oh look at the cute little pickaninny!" she said and pointed to a Negro child standing in the door of a shack. "Wouldn't that make a picture, now?" she asked and they all turned and looked at the little Negro out of the back window. He waved.

"He didn't have any britches on," June said.

"He probably didn't have any," the grandmother explained. "Little nig-   20 gers in the country don't have things like we do. If I could paint, I'd paint that picture," she said.

The children exchanged comic books.

The grandmother offered to hold the baby and the children's mother passed him over the front seat to her. She set him on her knee and bounced him and told him about the things they were passing. She rolled her eyes and screwed up her mouth and stuck her leathery thin face into his smooth bland one. Occasionally he gave her a faraway smile. They passed a large cotton field with five or six graves fenced in the middle of it, like a small island. "Look at the graveyard!" the grandmother said, pointing it out. "That was the old family burying ground. That belonged to the plantation."

"Where's the plantation?" John Wesley asked.

"Gone With the Wind," said the grandmother. "Ha. Ha."

When the children finished all the comic books they had brought, they   25 opened the lunch and ate it. The grandmother ate a peanut butter sandwich and an olive and would not let the children throw the box and the paper napkins out the window. When there was nothing else to do they played a game by choosing a cloud and making the other two guess what shape it suggested. John Wesley took one the shape of a cow and June Star guessed a cow and John Wesley said, no, an automobile, and June Star said he didn't play fair, and they began to slap each other over the grandmother.

The grandmother said she would tell them a story if they would keep quiet. When she told a story, she rolled her eyes and waved her head and was very dramatic. She said once when she was a maiden lady she had been courted by a Mr. Edgar Atkins Teagarden from Jasper, Georgia. She said he was a very good-looking man and a gentleman and that he brought her a watermelon every Saturday afternoon with his initials cut in it, E. A. T. Well, one Saturday, she said, Mr. Teagarden brought the watermelon and there was nobody at home and he left it on the front porch and returned in his buggy to Jasper, but she never got the watermelon, she said, because a nigger boy ate it when he saw the initials, E. A. T.! This story tickled John Wesley's funny bone and he giggled and giggled but June Star didn't think it was any good. She said she wouldn't marry a man that just brought her a watermelon on Saturday. The grandmother said she would have done well to marry Mr. Teagarden because he was a gentleman and had bought Coca-Cola stock when it first came out and that he had died only a few years ago, a very wealthy man.

They stopped at The Tower for barbecued sandwiches. The Tower was a part stucco and part wood filling station and dance hall set in a clearing outside of Timothy. A fat man named Red Sammy Butts ran it and there were signs stuck here and there on the building and for miles up and down the highway saying, TRY RED SAMMY'S FAMOUS BARBEQUE, NONE LIKE FAMOUS RED SAMMY'S! RED SAM! THE FAT BOY WITH THE HAPPY LAUGH. A VETERAN! SAMMY'S YOUR MAN!

Red Sammy was lying on the bare ground outside The Tower with his head under a truck while a gray monkey about a foot high, chained to a small chinaberry tree, chattered nearby. The monkey sprang back into the tree and got on the highest limb as soon as he saw the children jump out of the car and run toward him.

Inside, The Tower was a long dark room with a counter at one end and tables at the other and dancing space in the middle. They all sat down at a broad table next to the nickelodeon and Red Sam's wife, a tall burnt-brown woman with hair and eyes lighter than her skin, came and took their order. The children's mother put a dime in the machine and played "The Tennessee Waltz," and the grandmother said that tune always made her want to dance. She asked Bailey if he would like to dance but he only glared at her. He didn't have a naturally sunny disposition like she did and trips made him nervous. The grandmother's brown eyes were very bright. She swayed her head from side to side and pretended she was dancing in her chair. June Star said play something she could tap to so the children's mother put in another dime and played a fast number and June Star stepped out onto the dance floor and did her tap routine.

"Ain't she cute?" Red Sam's wife said, leaning over the counter. "Would you like to come be my little girl?" 30

"No I certainly wouldn't," June Star said. "I wouldn't live in a broken-down place like this for a million bucks!" and she ran back to the table.

"Ain't she cute?" the woman repeated, stretching her mouth politely.

"Aren't you ashamed?" hissed the grandmother.

Red Sam came in and told his wife to quit lounging on the counter and hurry with these people's order. His khaki trousers reached just to his hip bones and his stomach hung over them like a sack of meal swaying under his shirt. He came over and sat down at a table nearby and let out a combination sigh and yodel. "You can't win," he said. "You can't win," and he wiped his sweating red face off with a gray handkerchief. "These days you don't know who to trust," he said. "Ain't that the truth?"

"People are certainly not nice like they used to be," said the grandmother. 35

"Two fellers come in here last week," Red Sammy said, "driving a Chrysler. It was a old beat-up car but it was a good one and these boys looked all right to me. Said they worked at the mill and you know I let them fellers charge the gas they bought? Now why did I do that?"

"Because you're a good man!" the grandmother said at once.

"Yes'm, I suppose so," Red Sam said as if he were struck with the answer.

His wife brought the orders, carrying the five plates all at once without a tray, two in each hand and one balanced on her arm. "It isn't a soul in this green world of God's that you can trust," she said. "And I don't count anybody out of that, not nobody," she repeated, looking at Red Sammy.

"Did you read about that criminal, The Misfit, that's escaped?" asked the grandmother. 40

"I wouldn't be a bit surprised if he didn't attact this place right here," said the woman. "If he hears about it being here, I wouldn't be none surprised to see him. If he hears it's two cent in the cash register, I wouldn't be a tall surprised if he . . ."

"That'll do," Red Sam said. "Go bring these people their Co'Colas," and the woman went off to get the rest of the order.

"A good man is hard to find," Red Sammy said. "Everything is getting terrible. I remember the day you could go off and leave your screen door unlatched. Not no more."

He and the grandmother discussed better times. The old lady said that in her opinion Europe was entirely to blame for the way things were now. She said the way Europe acted you would think we were made of money and Red Sam said it was no use talking about it, she was exactly right. The children ran outside into the white sunlight and looked at the monkey in the lacy chinaberry tree. He was busy catching fleas on himself and biting each one carefully between his teeth as if it were a delicacy.

They drove off again into the hot afternoon. The grandmother took cat 45 naps and woke up every few minutes with her own snoring. Outside of Toombsboro she woke up and recalled an old plantation that she had visited in this neighborhood once when she was a young lady. She said the house had six white columns across the front and that there was an avenue of oaks leading up to it and two little wooden trellis arbors on either side in front where you sat down with your suitor after a stroll in the garden. She recalled exactly which road to turn off to get to it. She knew that Bailey would not be willing to lose any time looking at an old house, but the more she talked about it, the more she wanted to see it once again and find out if the little twin arbors were still standing. "There was a secret panel in this house," she said craftily, not telling the truth but wishing that she were, "and the story went that all the family silver was hidden in it when Sherman came through but it was never found . . ."

"Hey!" John Wesley said. "Let's go see it! We'll find it! We'll poke all the woodwork and find it! Who lives there? Where do you turn off at? Hey Pop, can't we turn off there?"

"We never have seen a house with a secret panel!" June Star shrieked. "Let's go to the house with the secret panel! Hey, Pop, can't we go see the house with the secret panel!"

"It's not far from here, I know," the grandmother said. "It wouldn't take over twenty minutes."

Bailey was looking straight ahead. His jaw was as rigid as a horseshoe. "No," he said.

The children began to yell and scream that they wanted to see the house 50 with the secret panel. John Wesley kicked the back of the front seat and June Star hung over her mother's shoulder and whined desperately into her ear that they never had any fun even on their vacation, and that they could never do what they wanted to do. The baby began to scream and John Wesley kicked the back of the seat so hard that his father could feel the blows in his kidney.

"All right!" he shouted, and drew the car to a stop at the side of the road. "Will you all shut up? Will you all just shut up for one second? If you don't shut up, we won't go anywhere."

"It would be very educational for them," the grandmother murmured.

"All right," Bailey said, "but get this: this is the only time we're going to stop for anything like this. This is the one and only time."

"The dirt road that you have to turn down is about a mile back," the grandmother directed. "I marked it when we passed."

"A dirt road," Bailey groaned. 55

After they had turned around and were headed toward the dirt road, the grandmother recalled other points about the house, the beautiful glass over the front doorway and the candle-lamp in the hall. John Wesley said that the secret panel was probably in the fireplace.

"You can't go inside this house," Bailey said. "You don't know who lives there."

"While you all talk to the people in front, I'll run around behind and get in a window," John Wesley suggested.

"We'll all stay in the car," his mother said.

They turned onto the dirt road and the car raced roughly along in a swirl 60 of pink dust. The grandmother recalled the times when there were no paved roads and thirty miles was a day's journey. The dirt road was hilly and there were sudden washes in it and sharp curves on dangerous embankments. All at once they would be on a hill, looking down over the blue tops of trees for miles around, then the next minute, they would be in a red depression with the dust-coated trees looking down on them.

"This place had better turn up in a minute," Bailey said, "or I'm going to turn around."

The road looked as if no one had traveled on it in months.

"It's not much farther," the grandmother said and just as she said it, a horrible thought came to her. The thought was so embarrassing that she turned red in the face and her eyes dilated and her feet jumped up, upsetting her valise in the corner. The instant the valise moved, the newspaper top she had over the basket under it rose with a snarl and Pitty Sing, the cat, sprang onto Bailey's shoulder.

The children were thrown to the floor and their mother, clutching the baby, was thrown out the door onto the ground, the old lady was thrown into the front seat. The car turned over once and landed right-side-up in a gulch on the side of the road. Bailey remained in the driver's seat with the cat— gray-striped with a broad white face and an orange nose—clinging to his neck like a caterpillar.

As soon as the children saw they could move their arms and legs, they 65 scrambled out of the car, shouting. "We've had an ACCIDENT!" The grandmother was curled up under the dashboard, hoping she was injured so that Bailey's wrath would not come down on her all at once. The horrible thought she had had before the accident was that the house she had remembered so vividly was not in Georgia but in Tennessee.

Bailey removed the cat from his neck with both hands and flung it out the window against the side of a pine tree. Then he got out of the car and started looking for the children's mother. She was sitting against the side of the red gutted ditch, holding the screaming baby, but she only had a cut down her face and a broken shoulder. "We've had an ACCIDENT!" the children screamed in a frenzy of delight.

"But nobody's killed," June Star said with disappointment as the grandmother limped out of the car, her hat still pinned to her head but the broken front brim standing up at a jaunty angle and the violet spray hanging off the side. They all sat down in the ditch, except the children, to recover from the shock. They were all shaking.

"Maybe a car will come along," said the children's mother hoarsely.

"I believe I have injured an organ," said the grandmother, pressing her side, but no one answered her. Bailey's teeth were clattering. He had on a yellow sport shirt with bright blue parrots designed in it and his face was as yellow as the shirt. The grandmother decided that she would not mention that the house was in Tennessee.

The road was about ten feet above and they could see only the tops of the   70 trees on the other side of it. Behind the ditch they were sitting in there were more woods, tall and dark and deep. In a few minutes they saw a car some distance away on top of a hill, coming slowly as if the occupants were watching them. The grandmother stood up and waved both arms dramatically to attract their attention. The car continued to come on slowly, disappeared around a bend and appeared again, moving even slower, on top of the hill they had gone over. It was a big black battered hearse-like automobile. There were three men in it.

It came to a stop just over them and for some minutes, the driver looked down with a steady expressionless gaze to where they were sitting, and didn't speak. Then he turned his head and muttered something to the other two and they got out. One was a fat boy in black trousers and a red sweat shirt with a silver stallion embossed on the front of it. He moved around on the right side of them and stood staring, his mouth partly open in a kind of loose grin. The other had on khaki pants and a blue striped coat and a gray hat pulled down very low, hiding most of his face. He came around slowly on the left side. Neither spoke.

The driver got out of the car and stood by the side of it, looking down at them. He was an older man than the other two. His hair was just beginning to gray and he wore silver-rimmed spectacles that gave him a scholarly look. He had a long creased face and didn't have on any shirt or undershirt. He had on blue jeans that were too tight for him and was holding a black hat and a gun. The two boys also had guns.

"We've had an ACCIDENT!" the children screamed.

The grandmother had the peculiar feeling that the bespectacled man was someone she knew. His face was as familiar to her as if she had known him all her life but she could not recall who he was. He moved away from the car and began to come down the embankment, placing his feet carefully so that he wouldn't slip. He had on tan and white shoes and no socks, and his ankles were red and thin. "Good afternoon," he said. "I see you all had you a little spill."

"We turned over twice!" said the grandmother.   75

"Oncet," he corrected. "We seen it happen. Try their car and see will it run, Hiram," he said quietly to the boy with the gray hat.

"What you got that gun for?" John Wesley asked. "Whatcha gonna do with that gun?"

"Lady," the man said to the children's mother, "would you mind calling them children to sit down by you? Children make me nervous. I want all you all to sit down right together there where you're at."

"What are you telling us what to do for?" June Star asked.

Behind them the line of woods gaped like a dark open mouth. "Come here," said their mother. 80

"Look here now," Bailey began suddenly, "we're in a predicament! We're in . . ."

The grandmother shrieked. She scrambled to her feet and stood staring. "You're The Misfit!" she said. "I recognized you at once."

"Yes'm," the man said, smiling slightly as if he were pleased in spite of himself to be known, "but it would have been better for all of you, lady, if you hadn't of reckernized me."

Bailey turned his head sharply and said something to his mother that shocked even the children. The old lady began to cry and The Misfit reddened.

"Lady," he said, "don't you get upset. Sometimes a man says things he don't mean. I don't reckon he meant to talk to you thataway." 85

"You wouldn't shoot a lady, would you?" the grandmother said and removed a clean handkerchief from her cuff and began to slap at her eyes with it.

The Misfit pointed the toe of his shoe into the ground and made a little hole and then covered it up again. "I would hate to have to," he said.

"Listen," the grandmother almost screamed, "I know you're a good man. You don't look a bit like you have common blood. I know you must come from nice people!"

"Yes mam," he said, "finest people in the world." When he smiled he showed a row of strong white teeth. "God never made a finer woman than my mother and my daddy's heart was pure gold," he said. The boy with the red sweat shirt had come around behind them and was standing with his gun at his hip. The Misfit squatted down on the ground. "Watch them children, Bobby Lee," he said. "You know they make me nervous." He looked at the six of them huddled together in front of him and he seemed to be embarrassed as if he couldn't think of anything to say. "Ain't a cloud in the sky," he remarked, looking up at it. "Don't see no sun but don't see no cloud neither."

"Yes, it's a beautiful day," said the grandmother. "Listen," she said, "you shouldn't call yourself The Misfit because I know you're a good man at heart. I can just look at you and tell." 90

"Hush!" Bailey yelled. "Hush! Everybody shut up and let me handle this!" He was squatting in the position of a runner about to sprint forward but he didn't move.

"I pre-chate that, lady," The Misfit said and drew a little circle in the ground with the butt of his gun.

"It'll take a half a hour to fix this here car," Hiram called, looking over the raised hood of it.

"Well, first you and Bobby Lee get him and that little boy to step over yonder with you," The Misfit said, pointing to Bailey and John Wesley. "The boys want to ask you something," he said to Bailey. "Would you mind stepping back in them woods there with them?"

"Listen," Bailey began, "we're in a terrible predicament. Nobody realizes   95
what this is," and his voice cracked. His eyes were as blue and intense as the
parrots in his shirt and he remained perfectly still.

The grandmother reached up to adjust her hat brim as if she were going
to the woods with him but it came off in her hand. She stood staring at it and
after a second she let it fall on the ground. Hiram pulled Bailey up by the arm
as if he were assisting an old man. John Wesley caught hold of his father's hand
and Bobby Lee followed. They went off toward the woods and just as they
reached the dark edge, Bailey turned and supporting himself against a gray
naked pine trunk, he shouted, "I'll be back in a minute, Mamma, wait on me!"

"Come back this instant!" his mother shrilled but they all disappeared
into the woods.

"Bailey Boy!" the grandmother called in a tragic voice but she found she
was looking at The Misfit squatting on the ground in front of her. "I just know
you're a good man," she said desperately. "You're not a bit common!"

"Nome, I ain't a good man," The Misfit said after a second as if he had
considered her statement carefully, "but I ain't the worst in the world neither.
My daddy said I was different breed of dog from my brothers and sisters. 'You
know,' Daddy said, 'it's some that can live their whole life out without asking
about it and it's others has to know why it is, and this boy is one of the latters.
He's going to be into everything!'" He put on his black hat and looked up
suddenly and then away deep into the woods as if he were embarrassed again.
"I'm sorry I don't have on a shirt before you ladies," he said, hunching his
shoulders slightly. "We buried our clothes that we had on when we escaped
and we're just making do until we can get better. We borrowed these from
some folks we met," he explained.

"That's perfectly all right," the grandmother said. "Maybe Bailey has an   100
extra shirt in his suitcase."

"I'll look and see terrectly," The Misfit said.

"Where are they taking him?" the children's mother screamed.

"Daddy was a card himself," the Misfit said. "You couldn't put anything
over on him. He never got in trouble with the Authorities though. Just had
the knack of handling them."

"You could be honest too if you'd only try," said the grandmother. "Think
how wonderful it would be to settle down and live a comfortable life and not
have to think about somebody chasing you all the time."

The Misfit kept scratching in the ground with the butt of his gun as if he   105
were thinking about it. "Yes'm, somebody is always after you," he murmured.

The grandmother noticed how thin his shoulder blades were just behind
his hat because she was standing up looking down on him. "Do you ever
pray?" she asked.

He shook his head. All she saw was the black hat wiggle between his
shoulder blades. "Nome," he said.

There was a pistol shot from the woods, followed closely by another.
Then silence. The old lady's head jerked around. She could hear the wind
move through the tree tops like a long satisfied insuck of breath. "Bailey Boy!"
she called.

"I was a gospel singer for a while," The Misfit said. "I been most everything. Been in the arm service, both land and sea, at home and abroad, been twict married, been an undertaker, been with the railroads, plowed Mother Earth, been in a tornado, seen a man burnt alive oncet," and he looked up at the children's mother and the little girl who were sitting close together, their faces white and their eyes glassy; "I even seen a woman flogged," he said.

"Pray, pray," the grandmother began, "pray, pray . . ." 110

"I never was a bad boy that I remember of," The Misfit said in an almost dreamy voice, "but somewheres along the line I done something wrong and got sent to the penitentiary. I was buried alive," and he looked up and held her attention to him by a steady stare.

"That's when you should have started to pray," she said. "What did you do to get sent to the penitentiary that first time?"

"Turn to the right, it was a wall," The Misfit said, looking up again at the cloudless sky. "Turn to the left, it was a wall. Look up it was a ceiling, look down it was a floor. I forgot what I done, lady. I set there and set there, trying to remember what it was I done and I ain't recalled it to this day. Oncet in a while, I would think it was coming to me, but it never come."

"Maybe they put you in by mistake," the old lady said vaguely.

"Nome," he said. "It wasn't no mistake. They had the papers on me." 115

"You must have stolen something," she said.

The Misfit sneered slightly. "Nobody had nothing I wanted," he said. "It was a head-doctor at the penitentiary said what I had done was kill my daddy but I know that for a lie. My daddy died in nineteen ought nineteen of the epidemic flu and I never had a thing to do with it. He was buried in the Mount Hopewell Baptist churchyard and you can go there and see for yourself."

"If you would pray," the old lady said, "Jesus would help you."

"That's right," The Misfit said.

"Well then, why don't you pray?" she asked trembling with delight 120 suddenly.

"I don't want no hep," he said. "I'm doing all right by myself."

Bobby Lee and Hiram came ambling back from the woods. Bobby Lee was dragging a yellow shirt with bright blue parrots in it.

"Throw me that shirt, Bobby Lee," The Misfit said. The shirt came flying at him and landed on his shoulder and he put it on. The grandmother couldn't name what the shirt reminded her of. "No, lady," The Misfit said while he was buttoning it up. "I found out the crime don't matter. You can do one thing or you can do another, kill a man or take a tire off his car, because sooner or later you're going to forget what it was you done and just be punished for it."

The children's mother had begun to make heaving noises as if she couldn't get her breath. "Lady," he asked, "would you and that little girl like to step off yonder with Bobby Lee and Hiram and join your husband?"

"Yes, thank you," the mother said faintly. Her left arm dangled helplessly 125 and she was holding the baby, who had gone to sleep, in the other. "Hep that lady up, Hiram," The Misfit said as she struggled to climb out of the ditch, "and Bobby Lee, you hold onto that little girl's hand."

"I don't want to hold hands with him," June Star said. "He reminds me of a pig."

The fat boy blushed and laughed and caught her by the arm and pulled her off into the woods after Hiram and her mother.

Alone with The Misfit, the grandmother found that she had lost her voice. There was not a cloud in the sky nor any sun. There was nothing around her but woods. She wanted to tell him that he must pray. She opened and closed her mouth several times before anything came out. Finally she found herself saying, "Jesus, Jesus," meaning Jesus will help you, but the way she was saying it, it sounded as if she might be cursing.

"Yes'm," The Misfit said as if he agreed. "Jesus thown everything off balance. It was the same case with Him as with me except He hadn't committed any crime and they could prove I had committed one because they had the papers on me. Of course," he said, "they never shown me any papers. That's why I sign myself now. I said long ago, you get you a signature and sign everything you do and keep a copy of it. Then you'll know what you done and you can hold up the crime to the punishment and see do they match and in the end you'll have something to prove you ain't been treated right. I call myself The Misfit," he said, "because I can't make what all I done wrong fit what all I gone through in punishment."

There was a piercing scream from the woods, followed closely by a pistol report. "Does it seem right to you, lady, that one is punished a heap and another ain't punished at all?" 130

"Jesus!" the old lady cried. "You've got good blood! I know you wouldn't shoot a lady! I know you come from nice people! Pray! Jesus, you ought not to shoot a lady. I'll give you all the money I've got!"

"Lady," The Misfit said, looking beyond her far into the woods, "there never was a body that give the undertaker a tip."

There were two more pistol reports and the grandmother raised her head like a parched old turkey hen crying for water and called, "Bailey Boy, Bailey Boy!" as if her heart would break.

"Jesus was the only One that ever raised the dead," The Misfit continued, "and He shouldn't have done it. He thown everything off balance. If He did what He said, then it's nothing for you to do but thow away everything and follow Him, and if He didn't, then it's nothing for you to do but enjoy the few minutes you got left the best way you can—by killing somebody or burning down his house or doing some other meanness to him. No pleasure but meanness," he said and his voice had become almost a snarl.

"Maybe He didn't raise the dead," the old lady mumbled, not knowing what she was saying and feeling so dizzy that she sank down in the ditch with her legs twisted under her. 135

"I wasn't there so I can't say He didn't," The Misfit said. "I wisht I had of been there," he said, hitting the ground with his fist. "It ain't right I wasn't there because if I had of been there I would of known. Listen lady," he said in a high voice, "if I had of been there I would of known and I wouldn't be like I am now." His voice seemed about to crack and the grandmother's head cleared for an instant. She saw the man's face twisted close to her own as if he were going to cry and she murmured, "Why you're one of my babies. You're one of my own children!" She reached out and touched him on the shoulder. The Misfit sprang back as if a snake had bitten him and shot her three times through the chest. Then he put his gun down on the ground and took off his glasses and began to clean them.

Hiram and Bobby Lee returned from the woods and stood over the ditch, looking down at the grandmother who half sat and half lay in a puddle of blood with her legs crossed under her like a child's and her face smiling up at the cloudless sky.

Without his glasses, The Misfit's eyes were red-rimmed and pale and defenseless-looking. "Take her off and thow her where you thown the others," he said, picking up the cat that was rubbing itself against his leg.

"She was a talker, wasn't she?" Bobby Lee said, sliding down the ditch with a yodel.

"She would of been a good woman," The Misfit said, "if it had been 140 somebody there to shoot her every minute of her life."

"Some fun!" Bobby Lee said.

"Shut up, Bobby Lee," The Misfit said. "It's no real pleasure in life."

--------- **FLANNERY O'CONNOR** ---------

(1925–1964) Web   *www*

A Depression-era child, O'Connor earned an MFA from the University of Iowa, worked briefly in New York, and then returned to Georgia to write. A winner of the National Book Award for her collected stories, O'Connor died of lupus when she was only thirty-nine. Her stories and novels are all set in the American South; she found in Georgia a "collection of goods and evils which are intensely stimulating to the imagination."

TOPICS FOR CRITICAL THINKING Web   *www*

1. At what point in the story do you know that the family will meet The Misfit? What are the clues?
2. How does this knowledge produce tension when reading the story?
3. What does The Misfit mean when he says, "She would of been a good woman if it had been somebody there to shoot her every minute of her life"?
4. How does the end of the story both meet and defy the reader's expectations?

TOPICS FOR CRITICAL WRITING Web   *www*

1. What does the phrase "a good man is hard to find" mean?
2. What is the relation between the story and the story about the watermelon the grandmother tells?

W. S. PENN

In Dreams Begins Reality   *(2000)*

My first wife was mad. Or so my sister said. "She was crazy as a loon, Albert," she'd say. She never said it while we were happily married, but waited until things had fallen apart. I think of the times we visited my sister and I came out of the shower in the morning to find my wife hunched on the edge of the makeshift bed in her hot-pink flannels, eating her breakfast with the door closed, and I wish my sister had said something earlier. But when I remember the look on my wife's face as she explained why she was eating in the bedroom instead of with my sister and her husband, I am unconvinced. She didn't sound like a madwoman.

"They either sit there reading and ignoring me," she said, "or she berates him for keeping her awake all night with his snoring. It makes me uncomfortable."

"That's just the way she is," I'd say.

The second wife, my sister said, was dull as brass. "She's a very nice person, Albert. But what do you have in common?"

Again she waited until I was alone, nightly trying to find a way to make   5
the king-sized bed seem less like the Wallowa Valley. It was comforting to know I hadn't made a mistake. That's what sisters were for, I figured, like codeine. And I was grateful.

My sister never met the hat-trick wife. She was a hinter. You know the type, the woman who warns you a hundred times a day in small unnoticeable ways that something is wrong. She hints so much that your only recourse is to mistake her meaning. When she came home and said, What did I want for dinner, pork? Or just the fat? I pretended she was being humorous.

When she asked the same question about lamb—"You want some lamb? Or you just want me to slice off the fat and heat it up in the micro?"—I took her seriously and weighed my choices.

"Lamb would be fine," I said. "Thank you very much. Dear." She was dressed in a gregarious sheath of red. "Nice dress," I said.

"I'm going out later," she replied.

Sometimes, I'd try to participate in the hinting, make it fun. Like when   10
we went to her sister's to look at wedding pictures and generally gush and glow over her sister's actually getting married. There was a picture of the rear of me, my feet and head lopped off by the viewfinder.

"Is it the same on a tug? Is port left and starboard right?" the wife asked her sister as they looked at the picture. Her sister squirmed. So as not to embarrass her, I joined in.

"That's not a tugboat," I said, grinning.

The wife gave me a piercing look.

"More like Moby-Dick with a tie."

The wife didn't laugh.   15

"Put cameras and 'Goodyear' on it and run it up in the air and it'll shoot the Super Bowl," I said.

The wife shot me a look that felt like the searing flames of hatred.

We divorced. "Three's the charm," I said, and decided that I was through with women. A hat trick's enough by anyone's measure. I have made an effort to remain friends with her, mostly for the sake of our love's by-product, Alicia, who is six.

She's still a hinter. Talking with her on the phone just now, I was regaling her with my theory that the president we see giving a prepared speech is really the brilliant artistry of an automatist, the careful modulations of the recorded voice the secret of Dolby. "That's why the real man seems so stupid at press conferences. It's not just that he is virtually incapable of a solitary logical thought. It's the contrast between art and life that really brings it home."

"Still as much fun as always," the ex-wife hinted.   20

"That a question or a statement?" I asked. "How's my little girl, anyway?"

"She's right here. Want to speak to her? Alicia," I could hear the ex-wife say, "come listen to your father. Yes, *now*."

"Hello, Father," Alicia said.

"Hi, precious. How's my little pumpkin?"

"Father!" Alicia complained. She doesn't like these affectionate nicknames.   25
Thinks she's outgrown them. I try not to use them, but I can't help myself. As with a full half of what I say, the words just slip out when I'm not looking.

"When are you going to come up for a visit?" I asked.

"Don't know. It's so far."

"Maybe that's true, honeybunch. But I'd be happy to come down and get you, if your mother is afraid of the subway." Alicia lives with her mother in the East Village. I live at the far reaches of the Upper West Side. "Or I'll send you cab fare."

"Maybe after the Bahamas. Richard's taking Mommy and me to the Bahamas next month."

"I know," I said.   30

"Richard bought me a new bathing suit just for the trip. It's red. He's gonna teach me to scuba-dive."

"That Richard sounds like quite a guy. By the way, do you know what the letters in 'scuba' stand for?"

"Do I have to?" Alicia sighed.

"No. No, Richard will probably tell you anyway. 'Self-contained underwater breathing apparatus' people are like that. They like you to know the rituals and symbols of their sport. They're like sailors. Like dieters or people into meditation. . . ."

"Father," Alicia interrupted. "What's a wonk?"   35

"Why, sweetcakes? Where'd you hear that word?"

"Richard."

"Yeah?" I wasn't sure I liked Richard teaching my babydoll such language. Where did it lead?

"Yeah. He says you're a real—"

"So Albert," the ex-wife's voice said after a scuffle over the receiver.   40

"We've got to run along. The Bottom Line is playing Trump's Trumps this afternoon."

"What in the world is 'the bottom line'?"

"Richard's softball team," the ex-wife said. "Talk to you later. Maybe you should get out and join a softball team. Be good for you. And you could supply the team with chatter."

I can take a hint. "If I do, will you come back to me? Would you love me again?"

"I'll make Alicia send you a postcard from the Bahamas," she said. She hung up.

Normally I keep Sundays to myself, reserving time to browse through the 45
Times and time to think up letters to the editor of the book review section. These letters range from chilling attacks on the entire section to letters with specific focus. I never send these letters, at least in part because I never write them. I think them. Taking the time to write them would waste precious Sunday minutes.

After shaming the book review editor, I stroll down to Zabar's and buy fresh bagels, then cut over to Columbus and stop by the deli to pick up chopped Nova lox, then home again to eat them both with cream cheese, while I decide what to do with the rest of the day. Most Sundays, this deciding takes me into late afternoon, at which point I allow myself to look through the television section and start thinking about having a drink before dinner. With mixed emotions, I decide this Sunday to get out and get some exercise. By the boat pond in the park, radio-controlled sailboats compete for attention with radio-controlled roller skaters. In a vee of grass among the trees, the pitched laughter of twelve Asians playing volleyball sounds like the delicate and oddly beautiful plink of Eastern music. A girl on the frontier of womanhood and leaning to tart buys ice cream from a vendor's cart, her red nylon stretch pants drawing L's—from lust and longing to leers and leaving. Her pants are so revealing that she almost achieves the nun-like innocence of the over-clothed. The feeling of her as I walk away stays with me like the sunrise over Makrialos.

I sit on a bench and watch sides being chosen for a pickup softball game, imaginatively penning another letter to the *Times*. A woman comes over and asks me if I want to play. Her name is Gail. Even with her dirty blond hair held back by a headband you can tell Gail has what can only be called big hair.

"No. Thank you."

"We can use another player," she says.

"You've got a backstop," I say. She just looks perplexed. "Well, what the 50
heck. Okay." I figured I'd play catcher.

Gail borrows a glove for me from the other team and assigns me third base, a position I want about as much as another divorce. I'm no better at third base than I am at marriage or poker, preferring low-risk bets like catcher to the high stakes of double plays and charging grounders.

Gail takes shortstop. In all my years of watching softball, this hasn't happened often, but Gail looks as though she can handle the job. Indeed, Gail seems eager, ready, willing, and able to field grounders, pop-ups, and line drives, as well as to egg on those of us less eager or able. As the first baseman lobs grounders at us and warms us up she moves with grace and not a little strength. Her chatter as the game begins sounds like any shortstop's chatter. Except for the pitch of her voice and the fact that despite her big hair Gail is pretty, she could be Phil Rizzuto. Pee Wee Reese. The girl in red comes over and stands there, tongue licking about the rim of her ice cream cone, watching. She suddenly takes me back to days when little boys played softball and little girls looked appealingly on the sidelines, careful not to show too much calf between their bobby socks and the hems of their full skirts.

Days of an uneasy détente when our mothers apprenticed us to the world of action by telling us to stop moping around the house and go out and kill off a tribe or two of Indians. (Moping was for girls and when Mother's friends heard that I liked books more than ball, they coughed.) Days of a recurring boyhood dream: I'm at third base, a huge white softball bouncing ten feet in front of me and beginning to spin. With the instinct of Brooks Robinson, I understood that the second bounce would send the ball kicking over my head, so I charged it and knocked it down heroically. Feeling the little girls smile from the sidelines, I concentrated on keeping my wits about me. I picked up the ball and looked toward first. "I'm making a play," I thought, and realizing that I was making a play, I threw the ball hard at the first baseman.

The ball orbited over first base, returned to earth a good forty feet beyond, and rolled white and solitary for a decade. Long enough for the shortstop to stroll over and force himself to say, "It's all right. We'll get the next batter." Long enough for the sidelined girls to giggle and twitter and point, and for me to hate their twittering. I'd awaken, swearing off softball, swearing that I would show those girls, that I'd never let this happen again.

But it did. It happened again, again and again, over thirty-odd years. 55 Crouching there beside Gail, I see how I'm a sucker for games. How if there was one to be played, I played it.

I come to life like the stone guest in *Don Giovanni* as a hard-hit grounder—mine—skips to my left. Gail slides deep into the hole behind me, knocks the ball down, and, despite the thrill of making the play, decides against throwing to first. The men on the opposing team's bench smile secretly. Chagrined, I look away and see the girl in nylon pants poke the last of her ice cream cone through her lips and smirk.

"Sorry," I mutter to Gail. "Daydreaming."

"S'okay," Gail says. "We'll get the next batter." She smiles and slaps me on the rear end, coach-like, and for a moment I feel, deep down, an awakening of the simple innocence of my boyish heart. I believe we will get the next batter, Gail and I, if only I can pay attention. I crouch, eye on the next batter and ready for the pitch, determined not to let Gail down, marveling at the way things change. Had little girls giggled and twittered not at me but because they were denied the chance to make the same errors? I was grateful for the way some of them had grown up, giving up limp-wristed dainty flings, learning to throw from the shoulder.

I was grateful for Gail and I was amused by the antics of the men on the other team, celebrating their victory with lots of expensive-looking beer. "If only I'd caught that pop-up," I said.

"What the hell," Gail said. "It's only a game. See you next week?"   60

"Maybe," I said.

"Maybe we'll try you at catcher."

"Sure. Whatever. Even backstop." Gail didn't get it and I let it go. We said goodbye.

Heading past the boat pond out of the park, the roller skaters had been replaced by a bunch of boys bouncing like popcorn to the dulcet strains of their rap music on a ghetto blaster. "Ghetto-blasting their way right out of the power structure," I think. "Right out of time." I think about the girl in red pants. She, too, seems out of time, like an illusion from the past which has become a present anachronism. Maybe she would grow up like Gail. Then again, maybe she wouldn't.

"Anything's possible," I think, and then I say it, out loud, making a pret-   65
zel vendor wonder if I am speaking to him or, like so many in this city, simply speaking to anyone who might be listening. For the first time in years, I know what to do with the rest of my Sunday. Go downtown and buy Alicia a softball glove. Maybe some sweatpants. Some loose blue sweatpants.

———— **W. S. PENN** ————

www   *(b. 1949)* Web

An urban mixed-blood Nez Perce, W. S. Penn is the author of *The Absence of Angels* (1994) and *All My Sins Are Relatives* (1995). A writer of both fiction and non-fictional essays, he has been named Writer of the Year and Editor of the Year by the Woodcraft Circle of Native Writers and Storytellers.

www   ## *TOPICS FOR CRITICAL THINKING* Web

1. In what ways does the narrator interpret his first wife's tone?
2. In what ways is the narrator's tone related to what he knows or understands?
3. Does the narrator's tone shift? If so, when and why?
4. In what ways does tone indicate class tensions?
5. What is the relation between daydreaming and tone?

www   ## *TOPICS FOR CRITICAL WRITING* Web

1. How do the two parts of the story relate to shifts in the story's tone?
2. What are the dreams in the story?

12   Structure

All of the elements that make up a story do not occur randomly, but rather are arranged to work together. The ways a story organizes its elements is called **structure.** Structure is the difference between a rambling recital of events as might happen in a personal conversation and the tightly organized telling that occurs in prose fiction. Structure refers to the way a story's various elements work together to produce patterns of meaning. As discussed in Chapter 6, the primary structure that organizes stories is **narrative.** Narrative refers both to the act of telling a story and to our sense of what makes something a story (as opposed to a list or an argument) in the first place. **Plot** is the ordering of events, while structure includes the ways *plot, imagery, motifs,* and *character* are organized as repetitions, variations, or a series of oppositions. Although stories all have a narrative structure—that is, they consist of a series of events related through cause and effect and they have a beginning, a middle, and an end—they also each have their own particular structure that relates to both the ways the story is told (style, tone, narrator, point of view) and its themes.

Structure is often *conventional;* that is, it consists of a familiar pattern (like the story of the conquering hero or the young person who is growing up) repeated throughout culture. Stories borrow structures from tradition, as in the folktale or joke, or from other stories deeply embedded in culture, such as the success narrative attached to the American dream where the young, poor person grows up, works hard, and achieves wealth. Sometimes structure is very simple—a repetition of the same event or image, an inevitable moving towards what one is trying to avoid, or a simple conflict of human and nature. Occasionally structure seems quite complex, as in stories with multiple plots or elaborate chronologies or stories with very intricate imagery and characterization. Often stories contain a series of oppositions—between characters, images, ideas—that organize its themes within its plot. At the same time, however, stories are quite economical, consisting of very few elements or actions. The structure of economical stories often uses all details and events for multiple purposes. An example of this is the way Ernest Hemingway's "Hills Like White Elephants" uses only conversation and drinking to convey the couple's larger dilemma and the character of their relationship.

Discerning a story's structure is sometimes the beginning of analysis, sometimes the end. In some stories, parts of structure are evident, marked by dates, subtitles, or divisions in the text. Other ways of determining structure are to see what elements are repeated or form systems of opposition in which the same ideas are contrasted in many different ways throughout the story in

its events, imagery, and characterization. Another way to see structure is to
see how ideas or themes vary or change throughout a story.

   The overall effect of some stories is in their structure. The surprise ending, for example, is partly the effect of a story's structure, which plays on the
reader's expectations about the patterns of narrative that seem to lead another
direction. In other stories, structure is a corollary of style or tone. In ironic
stories, structure often conforms to, helps produce, and reaffirms a sense of
dramatic irony. In Flannery O'Connor's "A Good Man Is Hard to Find," for
example, our sense that the family will meet The Misfit is encouraged both by
the narrator's tone and by the series of events, which inevitably lead to an encounter with the man who is feared from the beginning. Sometimes structure
provides a platform for other kinds of expression such as description, characterization, or tone. Stories that focus on a single character, for example, provide
ample opportunity for describing the character. Structure is a combination
of elements that itself works with other elements to produce a story's aesthetic or its **art**—the particular ways a story is more than simply the events it
describes.

Critical Perspectives: Structuralism and Psychoanalytic Criticism

www   Criticism that studies what a story's structure tells us about how it works as
         a story is called **structuralist criticism**. **Web** Building on structure, criticism
         that looks at the ways a story's structures (repetitions, oppositions, appear-
         ances of what is avoided) reveal a story's preoccupations is called **psychoana-**
www   **lytic criticism**. **Web** Based on the ways psychoanalysts analyze their patients'
         narratives, psychoanalytic critics treat stories as if they were patients who have
         symptoms and an unconscious that is revealed in the ways stories structure
         events. Another mode of criticism that considers these structural elements is
         deconstruction, which looks at how structures as well as language and im-
         agery might work against or contradict themselves or other aspects of a story's
www   expression. **Web**

Stories About Structure

The stories that follow illustrate various structural possibilities and conventions from the folktale to the romance. Chinua Achebe's "The Sacrificial Egg"
is a modern folktale. Anita Desai's "Studies in the Park" is structured around
repeated actions and the opposition between parental expectations and youthful rebellion. Hanif Kureishi's "Blue, Blue Pictures of You" is a variation on
the structure of the romance. All illustrate in some way the clash of cultures,
conventions, and perspectives occurring when writers from colonized areas

such as Africa and the Indian Subcontinent write about the experiences of colonization, oppression, and the problems of shifting from one culture to another.

∽∽∽

CHINUA ACHEBE

The Sacrificial Egg   *(1959)*

Julius Obi sat gazing at his typewriter. The fat Chief Clerk, his boss, was snoring at his table. Outside, the gatekeeper in his green uniform was sleeping at his post. You couldn't blame him; no customer had passed through the gate for nearly a week. There was an empty basket on the giant weighing machine. A few palm-kernels lay desolately in the dust around the machine. Only the flies remained in strength.

Julius went to the window that overlooked the great market on the bank of the River Niger. The market, though still called Nkwo, had long spilled over into Eke, Oye, and Afo with the coming of civilization and the growth of the town into a big palm-oil port. In spite of this encroachment, however, it was still busiest on its original Nkwo day, because the deity who had presided over it from antiquity still cast her spell only on her own day—let men in their greed spill over themselves. It was said that she appeared in the form of an old woman in the centre of the market just before cock-crow and waved her magic fan in the four directions of the earth—in front of her, behind her, to the right and to the left—to draw to the market men and women from distant places. And they came bringing the produce of their lands—palm-oil and kernels, kola nuts, cassava, mats, baskets and earthenware pots; and took home many-coloured cloths, smoked fish, iron pots and plates. These were the forest peoples. The other half of the world who lived by the great rivers came down also—by canoe, bringing yams and fish. Sometimes it was a big canoe with a dozen or more people in it; sometimes it was a lone fisherman and his wife in a small vessel from the swift-flowing Anambara. They moored their canoe on the bank and sold their fish, after much haggling. The woman then walked up the steep banks of the river to the heart of the market to buy salt and oil and, if the sales had been very good, even a length of cloth. And for her children at home she bought bean cakes and mai-mai which the Igara women cooked. As evening approached, they took up their paddles again and paddled away, the water shimmering in the sunset and their canoe becoming smaller and smaller in the distance until it was just a dark crescent on the water's face and two dark bodies swaying forwards and backwards in it. Umuru then was the meeting place of the forest people who were called Igbo and the alien riverain folk whom the Igbo called Olu and beyond whom the world stretched in indefiniteness.

Julius Obi was not a native of Umuru. He had come like countless others from some bush village inland. Having passed his Standard Six in a mission school he had come to Umuru to work as a clerk in the offices of the all-powerful European trading company which bought palm-kernels at its own price and sold cloth and metalware, also at its own price. The offices were situated beside the famous market so that in his first two or three weeks Julius had to learn to work within its huge enveloping hum. Sometimes when the Chief Clerk was away he walked to the window and looked down on the vast anthill activity. Most of these people were not there yesterday, he thought, and yet the market had been just as full. There must be many, many people in the world to be able to fill the market day after day like this. Of course they say not all who came to the great market were real people. Janet's mother, Ma, had said so.

"Some of the beautiful young women you see squeezing through the crowds are not people like you or me but mammy-wota who have their town in the depths of the river," she said. "You can always tell them, because they are beautiful with a beauty that is too perfect and too cold. You catch a glimpse of her with the tail of your eye, then you blink and look properly, but she has already vanished in the crowd."

Julius thought about these things as he now stood at the window looking   5
down on the silent, empty market. Who would have believed that the great boisterous market could ever be quenched like this? But such was the strength of Kitikpa, the incarnate power of smallpox. Only he could drive away all those people and leave the market to the flies.

When Umuru was a little village, there was an age-grade who swept its market-square every Nkwo day. But progress had turned it into a busy, sprawling, crowded and dirty river port, a no-man's-land where strangers outnumbered by far the sons of the soil, who could do nothing about it except shake their heads at this gross perversion of their prayer. For indeed they had prayed—who will blame them—for their town to grow and prosper. And it had grown. But there is good growth and there is bad growth. The belly does not bulge out only with food and drink; it might be the abominable disease which would end by sending its sufferer out of the house even before he was fully dead.

The strangers who came to Umuru came for trade and money, not in search of duties to perform, for they had those in plenty back home in their village which was real home.

And as if this did not suffice, the young sons and daughters of Umuru soil, encouraged by schools and churches were behaving no better than the strangers. They neglected all their old tasks and kept only the revelries.

Such was the state of the town when Kitikpa came to see it and to demand the sacrifice the inhabitants owed the gods of the soil. He came in confident knowledge of the terror he held over the people. He was an evil deity, and boasted it. Lest he be offended those he killed were not killed but decorated, and no one dared weep for them. He put an end to the coming and going between neighbours and between villages. They said, "Kitikpa is in that village," and immediately it was cut off by its neighbours.

Julius was sad and worried because it was almost a week since he had seen   10

Janet, the girl he was going to marry. Ma had explained to him very gently that he should no longer go to see them "until this thing is over, by the power of Jehovah." (Ma was a very devout Christian convert and one reason why she approved of Julius for her only daughter was that he sang in the choir of the CMS church.)

"You must keep to your rooms," she had said in hushed tones, for Kitikpa strictly forbade any noise or boisterousness. "You never know whom you might meet on the streets. That family has got it." She lowered her voice even more and pointed surreptitiously at the house across the road whose doorway was barred with a yellow palm-frond. "He has decorated one of them already and the rest were moved away today in a big government lorry."

Janet walked a short way with Julius and stopped; so he stopped too. They seemed to have nothing to say to each other yet they lingered on. Then she said goodnight and he said goodnight. And they shook hands, which was very odd, as though parting for the night were something new and grave.

He did not go straight home, because he wanted desperately to cling, even alone, to this strange parting. Being educated he was not afraid of whom he might meet, so he went to the bank of the river and just walked up and down it. He must have been there a long time because he was still there when the wooden gong of the night-mask sounded. He immediately set out for home, half-walking and half-running, for night-masks were not a matter of superstition; they were real. They chose the night for their revelry because like the bat's their ugliness was great.

In his hurry he stepped on something that broke with a slight liquid explosion. He stopped and peeped down at the footpath. The moon was not up yet but there was a faint light in the sky which showed that it would not be long delayed. In this half-light he saw that he had stepped on an egg offered in sacrifice. Someone oppressed by misfortune had brought the offering to the crossroads in the dusk. And he had stepped on it. There were the usual young palm-fronds around it. But Julius saw it differently as a house where the terrible artist was at work. He wiped the sole of his foot on the sandy path and hurried away, carrying another vague worry in his mind. But hurrying was no use now; the fleet-footed mask was already abroad. Perhaps it was impelled to hurry by the threatening imminence of the moon. Its voice rose high and clear in the still night air like a flaming sword. It was yet a long way away, but Julius knew that distances vanished before it. So he made straight for the co-coyam farm beside the road and threw himself on his belly, in the shelter of the broad leaves. He had hardly done this when he heard the rattling staff of the spirit and a thundering stream of esoteric speech. He shook all over. The sounds came bearing down on him, almost pressing his face into the moist earth. And now he could hear the footsteps. It was as if twenty evil men were running together. Panic sweat broke all over him and he was nearly impelled to get up and run. Fortunately he kept a firm hold on himself . . . In no time at all the commotion in the air and on the earth—the thunder and torrential rain, the earthquake and flood—passed and disappeared in the distance on the other side of the road.

The next morning, at the office the Chief Clerk, a son of the soil spoke 15 bitterly about last night's provocation of Kitikpa by the headstrong youngsters who had launched the noisy fleet-footed mask in defiance of their elders, who knew that Kitikpa would be enraged, and then . . .

The trouble was that the disobedient youths had never yet experienced the power of Kitikpa themselves; they had only heard of it. But soon they would learn.

As Julius stood at the window looking out on the emptied market he lived through the terror of that night again. It was barely a week ago but already it seemed like another life, separated from the present by a vast emptiness. This emptiness deepened with every passing day. On this side of it stood Julius, and on the other Ma and Janet whom the dread artist decorated.

www

CHINUA ACHEBE

(b. 1930) Web

Born in Nigeria and educated in English, Achebe writes about the tensions between African traditions and folk ways and the effects of Westernization. Considered by many to be Africa's premier novelist, Achebe is currently the Charles P. Stevenson Jr. Professor of Languages and Literature at Bard College in New York State.

www

TOPICS FOR CRITICAL THINKING Web

1. What elements in the story represent traditional African culture?
2. What elements represent Western culture?
3. Which elements are divine? Which are mundane?
4. What are the connections among time, geography, tradition, Westernization, and death?

www

TOPICS FOR CRITICAL WRITING Web

1. What are the different meanings of Julius stepping on the sacrificial egg?
2. In what ways does this story represent the difficulties of change?

∽∽∽

ANITA DESAI

Studies in the Park   *(1978)*

—Turn it off, turn it off, turn it off! First he listens to the news in Hindi. Directly after, in English. Broom—brroom—brrroom—the voice of doom roars. Next, in Tamil. Then in Punjabi. In Gujarati. What next, my god, what next? Turn it off before I smash it onto his head, fling it out of the window, do nothing of the sort of course, nothing of the sort.

—And my mother. She cuts and fries, cuts and fries. All day I hear her chopping and slicing and the pan of oil hissing. What all does she find to fry and feed us on, for God's sake? Eggplants, potatoes, spinach, shoe soles, news-papers, finally she'll slice me and feed me to my brothers and sisters. Ah, now she's turned on the tap. It's roaring and pouring, pouring and roaring into a bucket without a bottom.

—The bell rings. Voices clash, clatter and break. The tin-and-bottle man? The neighbours? The police? The Help-the-Blind man? Thieves and burglars? All of them, all of them, ten or twenty or a hundred of them, march-ing up the stairs, hammering at the door, breaking in and climbing over me—ten, twenty or a hundred of them.

—Then, worst of all, the milk arrives. In the tallest glass in the house. 'Suno, drink your milk. Good for you, Suno. You need it. Now, before the ex-ams. Must have it, Suno. Drink.' The voice wheedles its way into my ear like a worm. I shudder. The table tips over. The milk runs. The tumbler clangs on the floor. 'Suno, Suno, how will you do your exams?'

—That is precisely what I ask myself. All very well to give me a room— Uncle's been pushed off on a pilgrimage to Hardwar to clear a room for me—and to bring me milk and say, 'Study, Suno, study for your exam.' What about the uproar around me? These people don't know the meaning of the word Quiet. When my mother fills buckets, sloshes the kitchen floor, fries and sizzles things in the pan, she thinks she is being Quiet. The children have never even heard the word, it amazes and puzzles them. On their way back from school they fling their satchels in at my door, then tear in to snatch them back before I tear them to bits. Bawl when I pull their ears, screech when mother whacks them. Stuff themselves with her fries and then smear the grease on my books.

So I raced out of my room, with my fingers in my ears, to scream till the roof fell down about their ears. But the radio suddenly went off, the door to my parents' room suddenly opened and my father appeared, bathed and shaven, stuffed and set up with the news of the world in six different lan-guages—his white *dhoti* blazing, his white shirt crackling, his patent leather pumps glittering. He stopped in the doorway and I stopped on the balls of my feet and wavered. My fingers came out of my ears, my hair came down over my eyes. Then he looked away from me, took his watch out of his pocket and enquired, 'Is the food ready?' in a voice that came out of his nose like the whistle of a punctual train. He skated off towards his meal, I turned and slouched back to my room. On his way to work, he looked in to say, 'Remem-ber, Suno, I expect good results from you. Study hard, Suno.' Just behind him, I saw all the rest of them standing, peering in, silently. All of them stared at me, at the exam I was to take. At the degree I was to get. Or not get. Horrify-ing thought. Oh study, study, study, they all breathed at me while my father's footsteps went down the stairs, crushing each underfoot in turn. I felt their eyes on me, goggling, and their breath on me, hot with earnestness. I looked back at them, into their open mouths and staring eyes.

'Study,' I said, and found I croaked. 'I know I ought to study. And how do you expect me to study—in this madhouse? You run wild, *wild*. I'm getting out,' I screamed, leaping up and grabbing my books, 'I'm going to study out-side. Even the street is quieter,' I screeched and threw myself past them and down the stairs that my father had just cowed and subjugated so that they still lay quivering, and paid no attention to the howls that broke out behind me of 'Suno, Suno, listen. Your milk—your studies—your exams, Suno!'

At first I tried the tea shop at the corner. In my reading I had often come across men who wrote at café tables—letters, verse, whole novels—over a cup of coffee or a glass of absinthe. I thought it would be simple to read a chapter of history over a cup of tea. There was no crowd in the mornings, none of my friends would be there. But the proprietor would not leave me alone. Bored, picking his nose, he wandered down from behind the counter to my table by the weighing machine and tried to pass the time of day by complaining about his piles, the new waiter and the high prices. 'And sugar,' he whined. 'How can I give you anything to put in your tea with sugar at four rupees a kilo? There's rationed sugar, I know, at two rupees, but that's not enough to feed even an ant. And the way you all sugar your tea—*hai, hai*,' he sighed, worse than my mother. I didn't answer. I frowned at my book and looked stubborn. But when I got rid of him, the waiter arrived. 'Have a biscuit?' he murmured, flicking at my table and chair with his filthy duster. 'A bun? Fritters? Make you some hot fritters?' I snarled at him but he only smiled, determined to be friendly. Just a boy, really, in a pink shirt with purple circles stamped all over it—he thought he looked so smart. He was growing sideburns, he kept fingering them. 'I'm a student, too,' he said, 'sixth class, fail. My mother wanted me to go back and try again, but I didn't like the teacher—he beat me. So I came here to look for a job. Lala-*ji* had just thrown out a boy called Hari for selling lottery tickets to the clients so he took me on. I can make out a bill . . .' He would have babbled on if Lala-*ji* had not come and shoved him into the kitchen with an oath. So it went on. I didn't read more than half a chapter that whole morning. I didn't want to go home either. I walked along the street, staring at my shoes, with my shoulders slumped in the way that makes my father scream, 'What's the matter? Haven't you bones? A spine?' I kicked some rubble along the pavement, down the drain, then stopped at the iron gates of King Edward's Park.

'Exam troubles?' asked a *gram* vendor who sat outside it, in a friendly voice. Not insinuating, but low, pleasant. 'The park's full of boys like you,' he continued in that sympathetic voice. 'I see them walk up and down, up and down with their books, like mad poets. Then I'm glad I was never sent to school,' and he began to whistle, not impertinently but so cheerfully that I stopped and stared at him. He had a crippled arm that hung out of his shirt sleeve like a leg of mutton dangling on a hook. His face was scarred as though he had been dragged out of some terrible accident. But he was shuffling hot *gram* into paper cones with his one hand and whistling like a bird, whistling the tune of, 'We are the *bul-buls* of our land, our land is Paradise.' Nodding at the greenery beyond the gates, he said, 'The park's a good place to study in,' and, taking his hint, I went in.

I wonder how it is I never thought of the park before. It isn't far from our   10
house and I sometimes went there as a boy, if I managed to run away from

school, to lie on a bench, eat peanuts, shy stones at the chipmunks that came for the shells, and drink from the fountain. But then it was not as exciting as playing marbles in the street or stoning rats with my school friends in the vacant lot behind the cinema. It had straight paths, beds of flapping red flowers—cannas, I think—rows of palm trees like limp flags, a dry fountain and some green benches. Old men sat on them with their legs far apart, heads drooping over the tops of sticks, mumbling through their dentures or cackling with that mad, ripping laughter that makes children think of old men as wizards and bogey-men. Bag-like women in grey and fawn *saris* or black *borkhas* screamed, just as grey and fawn and black birds do, at children falling into the fountain or racing on rickety legs after the chipmunks and pigeons. A madman or two, prancing around in paper caps and bits of rags, munching banana peels and scratching like monkeys. Corners behind hibiscus bushes stinking of piss. Iron rails with rows of beggars contentedly dozing, scratching, gambling, with their sackcloth backs to the rails. A city park.

What I hadn't noticed, or thought of, were all the students who escaped from their city flats and families like mine to come and study here. Now, walking down a path with my history book tucked under my arm, I felt like a gate-crasher at a party or a visitor to a public library trying to control a sneeze. They all seemed to belong here, to be at home here. Dressed in loose pyjamas, they strolled up and down under the palms, books open in their hands, heads lowered into them. Or they sat in twos and threes on the grass, reading aloud in turns. Or lay full length under the trees, books spread out across their faces—sleeping, or else imbibing information through the subconscious. Opening out my book, I too strolled up and down, reading to myself in a low murmur.

In the beginning, when I first started studying in the park, I couldn't concentrate on my studies. I'd keep looking up at the boy strolling in front of me, reciting poetry in a kind of thundering whisper, waving his arms about and running his bony fingers through his hair till it stood up like a thorn bush. Or at the chipmunks that fought and played and chased each other all over the park, now and then joining forces against the sparrows over a nest or a paper cone of *gram*. Or at the madman going through the rubble at the bottom of the dry fountain and coming up with a rubber shoe, a banana peel or a piece of glittering tin that he appreciated so much that he put it in his mouth and chewed it till blood ran in strings from his mouth.

It took me time to get accustomed to the ways of the park. I went there daily, for the whole day, and soon I got to know it as well as my own room at home and found I could study there, or sleep, or daydream, as I chose. Then I fell into its routine, its rhythm, and my time moved in accordance with its time. We were like a house-owner and his house, or a turtle and its shell, or a river and its bank—so close. I resented everyone else who came to the park—I thought they couldn't possibly share my feeling for it. Except, perhaps, the students.

The park was like an hotel, or an hospital, belonging to the city but with its own order and routine, enclosed by iron rails, laid out according to prescription in rows of palms, benches and paths. If I went there very early in the morning, I'd come upon a yoga class. It consisted of young bodybuilders rippling their muscles like snakes as well as old crack-pots determined to keep up with the youngest and fittest, all sitting cross-legged on the grass and displaying *hus-mukh* to the sun just rising over the palms: the Laughing Face pose it was called, but they looked like gargoyles with their mouths torn open and their thick, discoloured tongues sticking out. If I were the sun, I'd feel so disgusted by such a reception I'd just turn around and go back. And that was the simplest of their poses—after that they'd go into contortions that would embarrass an ape. Once their leader, a black and hirsute man like an aborigine, saw me watching and called me to join them. I shook my head and ducked behind an oleander. You won't catch me making an ass of myself in public. And I despise all that body-beautiful worship anyway. What's the body compared to the soul, the mind?

I'd stroll under the palms, breathing in the cool of the early morning,   15
feeling it drive out, or wash clean, the stifling dark of the night, and try to avoid bumping into all the other early morning visitors to the park—mostly aged men sent by their wives to fetch the milk from the Government dairy booth just outside the gates. Their bottles clinking in green cloth bags and newspapers rolled up and tucked under their arms, they strutted along like stiff puppets and mostly they would be discussing philosophy. 'Ah but in Vedanta it is a different matter,' one would say, his eyes gleaming fanatically, and another would announce, 'The sage Shanakaracharya showed the way,' and some would refer to the Upanishads or the Bhagavad Puranas, but in such argumentative, hacking tones that you could see they were quite capable of coming to blows over some theological argument. Certainly it was the mind above the body for these old coots but I found nothing to admire in them either. I particularly resented it when one of them disengaged himself from the discussion long enough to notice me and throw me a gentle look of commiseration. As if he'd been through exams, too, long long ago, and knew all about them. So what?

Worst of all were the athletes, wrestlers, Mr Indias and others who lay on their backs and were massaged with oil till every muscle shone and glittered. The men who massaged them huffed and puffed and cursed as they climbed up and down the supine bodies, pounding and pummelling the men who lay there wearing nothing but little greasy clouts, groaning and panting in a way I found obscene and disgusting. They never looked up at me or at anyone. They lived in a meaty, sweating world of their own—massages, oils, the body, a match to be fought and won—I kicked up dust in their direction but never went too close.

The afternoon would be quiet, almost empty. I would sit under a tree and read, stroll and study, doze too. Then, in the evening, as the sky softened from its blank white glare and took on shades of pink and orange and the palm trees rustled a little in an invisible breeze, the crowds would begin to pour out of Darya Ganj, Mori Gate, Chandni Chowk and the Jama Masjid bazaars and slums. Large families would come to sit about on the grass, eating peanuts and listening to a transistor radio placed in the center of the circle. Mothers would sit together in flocks like screeching birds while children jumped into the dry fountains, broke flowers and terrorized each other. There would be a few young men moaning at the corners, waiting for a girl to roll her hips and dart her fish eyes in their direction, and then start the exciting adventure of pursuit. The children's cries would grow more piercing with the dark; frightened, shrill and exalted with mystery and farewell. I would wander back to the flat.

The exams drew nearer. Not three, not two, but only one month to go. I had to stop daydreaming and set myself tasks for every day and remind myself constantly to complete them. It grew so hot I had to give up strolling on the paths and staked out a private place for myself under a tree. I noticed the tension tightening the eyes and mouths of other students—they applied themselves more diligently to their books, talked less, slept less. Everyone looked a little demented from lack of sleep. Our books seemed attached to our hands as though by roots, they were a part of us, they lived because we fed them. They were parasites and, like parasites, were sucking us dry. We mumbled to ourselves, not always consciously. Chipmunks jumped over our feet, mocking us. The *gram* seller down at the gate whistled softly 'I'm glad I never went to school, I am a *bul-bul*, I live in Paradise . . .'

My brains began to jam up. I could feel it happening, slowly. As if the oil were all used up. As if everything was getting locked together, rusted. The white cells, the grey matter, the springs and nuts and bolts. I yelled at my mother—I think it was my mother—'What do you think I am? What do you want of me?' and crushed a glass of milk between my hands. It was sticky. She had put sugar in my milk. As if I were a baby. I wanted to cry. They wouldn't let me sleep, they wanted to see my light on all night, they made sure I never stopped studying. Then they brought me milk and sugar and made clicking sounds with their tongues. I raced out to the park. I think I sobbed as I paced up and down, up and down, in the corner that stank of piss. My head ached worse than ever. I slept all day under the tree and had to work all night.

My father laid his hand on my shoulder. I knew I was not to fling it off. So   20
I sat still, slouching, ready to spring aside if he lifted it only slightly. 'You must get a first, Suno,' he said through his nose, 'must get a first, or else you won't get a job. Must get a job, Suno,' he sighed and wiped his nose and went off, his patent leather pumps squealing like mice. I flung myself back in my chair and howled. Get a first, get a first, get a first—like a railway engine, it went charging over me, grinding me down, and left me dead and mangled on the tracks.

Everything hung still and yellow in the park. I lay sluggishly on a heap of waste paper under my tree and read without seeing, slept without sleeping. Sometimes I went to the water tap that leaked and drank the leak. It tasted of brass. I spat out a mouthful. It nearly went over the feet of the student waiting for his turn at that dripping tap. I stepped aside for him. He swilled the water around his mouth and spat, too, carefully missing my feet. Wiping his mouth, he asked, 'B.A.?'

'No, Inter.'

'Hu,' he burped. 'Wait till you do your B.A. Then you'll get to know.' His face was like a grey bone. It was not unkind, it simply had no expression. 'Another two weeks,' he sighed and slouched off to his own lair.

I touched my face. I thought it would be all bone, like his. I was surprised to

find a bit of skin still covering it. I felt as if we were all dying in the park, that
when we entered the examination hall it would be to be declared officially dead.
That's what the degree was about. What else was it all about? Why were we
creeping around here, hiding from the city, from teachers and parents, pretending to study and prepare? Prepare for what? We hadn't been told. Inter, they said,
or B.A., or M.A. These were like official stamps—they would declare us dead.
Ready for a dead world. A world in which ghosts went about, squeaking or whining, rattling or rustling. Slowly, slowly we were killing ourselves in order to join
them. The ball-point pen in my pocket was the only thing that still lived, that still
worked. I didn't work myself any more—I mean physically, my body no longer
functioned. I was constipated, I was dying. I was lying under a yellow tree, feeling the dust sift through the leaves to cover me. It was filling my eyes, my throat.
I could barely walk. I never strolled. Only on the way out of the park, late in the
evening, I crept down the path under the palms, past the benches.

     Then I saw the scene that stopped it all, stopped me just before I died.   25
     Hidden behind an oleander was a bench. A woman lay on it, stretched
out. She was a Muslim, wrapped in a black *borkha*. I hesitated when I saw this
straight, still figure in black on the bench. Just then she lifted a pale, thin hand
and lifted her veil. I saw her face. It lay bared, in the black folds of her *borkha*,
like a flower, wax-white and composed, like a Persian lily or a tobacco flower
at night. She was young. Very young, very pale, beautiful with a beauty I had
never come across even in a dream. It caught me and held me tight, tight till
I couldn't breathe and couldn't move. She was so white, so still, I saw she was
very ill—with anaemia, perhaps, or t.b. Too pale, too white—I could see she
was dying. Her head—so still and white it might have been carved if it weren't
for this softness, this softness of a flower at night—lay in the lap of a very old
man. Very much older than her. With spectacles and a long grey beard like a
goat's, or a scholar's. He was looking down at her and caressing her face—so
tenderly, so tenderly, I had never seen a hand move so gently and tenderly. Beside them, on the ground, two little girls were playing. Round little girls,
rather dirty, drawing lines in the gravel. They stared at me but the man and
the woman did not notice me. They never looked at anyone else, only at each
other, with an expression that halted me. It was tender, loving, yes, but in an
inhuman way, so intense. Divine, I felt, or insane. I stood, half-hidden by the
bush, holding my book, and wondered at them. She was ill, I could see, dying.
Perhaps she had only a short time to live. Why didn't he take her to the Victoria Zenana Hospital, so close to the park? Who was this man—her husband,
her father, a lover? I couldn't make out although I watched them without
moving, without breathing. I felt not as if I were staring rudely at strangers,
but as if I were gazing at a painting or a sculpture, some work of art. Or seeing a vision. They were still and I stood still and the children stared. Then she
lifted her arms above her head and laughed. Very quietly.

     I broke away and hurried down the path, in order to leave them alone, in
privacy. They weren't a work of art, or a vision, but real, human and alive as
no one else in my life had been real and alive. I had only that glimpse of them.
But I felt I could never open my books and study or take degrees after that.
They belonged to the dead, and now I had seen what being alive meant. The

vision burnt the surfaces of my eyes so that they watered as I groped my way up the stairs to the flat. I could hardly find my way to the bed.

It was not just the examination but everything else had suddenly withered and died, gone lifeless and purposeless when compared with this vision. My studies, my family, my life—they all belonged to the dead and only what I had seen in the park had any meaning.

Since I did not know how to span the distance between that beautiful ideal and my stupid, dull existence, I simply lay still and shut my eyes. I kept them shut so as not to see all the puzzled, pleading, indignant faces of my family around me, but I could not shut out their voices.

'Suno, Suno,' I heard them croon and coax and mourn.   30

'Suno, drink milk.'

'Suno, study.'

'Suno, take the exam.'

And when they tired of being so patient with me and I still would not get up, they began to crackle and spit and storm.

'Get up, Suno.'   35

'Study, Suno.'

'At once, Suno'

Only my mother became resigned and gentle. She must have seen something quite out of the ordinary on my face to make her so. I felt her hand on my forehead and heard her say, 'Leave him alone. Let him sleep tonight. He is tired out, that is what it is—he has driven himself too much and now he must sleep.'

Then I heard all of them leave the room. Her hand stayed on my forehead, wet and smelling of onions, and after a bit my tears began to flow from under my lids.

'Poor Suno, sleep,' she murmured.   40

I went back to the park of course. But now I was changed. I had stopped being a student—I was a 'professional'. My life was dictated by the rules and routine of the park. I still had my book open on the palms of my hands as I strolled but now my eyes strayed without guilt, darting at the young girls walking in pairs, their arms linked, giggling and bumping into each other. Sometimes I stopped to rest on a bench and conversed with one of the old men, told him who my father was and what examination I was preparing for, and allowing him to tell me about his youth, his politics, his philosophy, his youth and again his youth. Or I joked with the other students, sitting on the grass and throwing peanut shells at the chipmunks, and shocking them, I could see, with my irreverence and cynicism about the school, the exam, the system. Once I even nodded at the yoga teacher and exchanged a few words with him. He suggested I join his class and I nodded vaguely and said I would think it over. It might help. My father says I need help. He says I am hopeless but that I need help. I just laugh but I know that he knows I will never appear for the examination, I will never come up to that hurdle or cross it—life has taken a different path for me, in the form of a search, not a race as it is for him, for them.

Yes, it is a search, a kind of perpetual search for me and now that I have accepted it and don't struggle, I find it satisfies me entirely, and I wander about the park as freely as a prince in his palace garden. I look over the benches, I

glance behind the bushes, and wonder if I shall ever get another glimpse of that
strange vision that set me free. I never have but I keep hoping, wishing.

www

———— **ANITA DESAI** ————
(b. 1937) **Web**

An Indian writer who writes in English, Desai focuses on changes in Indian culture and the plight of women in a society still heavily invested in family tradition. Because in India written literature was less the custom than recited stories,
Desai's writing belongs to a newer tradition of Indian literature that dates only
to the 1930s. She has taught at universities in England and America, including
Mt. Holyoke College, Smith College, and Cambridge University.

www

TOPICS FOR CRITICAL THINKING **Web**

1. From the story's first five paragraphs, what can you discern about the probable outcome of Suno's studies? What are the clues?
2. What kinds of actions are repeated in the story?
3. What oppositions (or alternatives) does Suno create in his world?
4. In what ways does every distraction repeat Suno's alternatives?
5. What does this pattern (or structure) suggest about what Suno really desires?

www

TOPICS FOR CRITICAL WRITING **Web**

1. What does Suno study in the park?
2. How does the image of the woman reflect the themes and structure of the story?

ᏗᏗᏗ

HANIF KUREISHI

Blue, Blue Pictures of You   *(1997)*

I used to like talking about sex. All of life, I imagined—from politics to aesthetics—merged in passionate human conjunctions. A caress, not to speak of
a kiss, could transport you from longing to Russia, on to Velazquez and ahead
to anarchism. To illustrate this fancy, I did, at one time, consider collecting a
'book of desire,' an anthology of outlandish, melancholy and droll stories
about the subject. This particular story was one, had the project been finished—or even started—I would have included. It was an odd story. Eshan,
the photographer who told it to me, used the word himself. At least he said it
was the oddest request he'd had. When it was put to him by his pub companion, his first response was embarrassment and perplexity. But of course he was
fascinated too.

   At the end of the street where Eshan had a tiny office and small dark
room, there was a pub where he'd go at half past six or seven, most days. He
liked to work office hours, believing much discipline was required to do what

he did, as if without it he would fly off into madness—though he had, in fact, never flown anywhere near madness, except to sit in the pub.

Eshan thought he liked routine, and for weeks would do exactly the same thing every day, while frequently loathing this decline into habit. In the pub he would smoke, drink and read the paper for an hour or longer, depending on his mood and on whether he felt sentimental, guilty or plain affectionate towards his wife and two children. Sometimes he'd get home before the children were asleep, and carry them around on his back, kick balls with them, and tell them stories of pigs with spiders on their heads. Other times he would turn up late so he could have his wife make supper, and be free of the feeling that the kids were devouring his life.

Daily, there were many hapless people in that bar: somnolent junkies from the local rehab, the unemployed and unemployable, pinball pillocks. Eshan nodded at many of them, but if one sat at his table without asking, he could become truculent. Often, however, he would chat to people as he passed to and fro, being more grateful than he knew for distracting conversation. He had become, without meaning to, one of the bar's characters.

Eshan's passion was to photograph people who had produced something 5 of significance, whose work had 'meaning.' These were philosophers, novelists, painters, film and theatre directors. He used only minimal props and hard, direct lighting. The idea wasn't to conceal but to expose. The spectator could relate the face to what the subject did. He called it the moment of truth in the features of people seeking the truth.

He photographed 'artists' but also considered himself, in private only, to be 'some sort' of an artist. To represent oneself—a changing being, alive with virtues and idiocies—was, for Eshan, the task that entailed the most honesty and fulfillment. But although his work had been published and exhibited, he still had to send out his portfolio with introductory letters, and harass people about his abilities. This was demeaning. By now he should, he reckoned, have got further. But he accepted his condition, imagining that overall he possessed most of what he required to live a simple but not complacent life. His wife illustrated children's books, and could earn decent money, so they got by. To earn a reasonable living himself, Eshan photographed new groups for the pop press—not that he was stimulated by these callow faces, though occasionally he was moved by their ugliness, the stupidity of their innocence, and their crass hopes. But they wanted only clichés.

A young man called Brian, who always wore pink shades, started to join Eshan regularly. The pub was his first stop of the day after breakfast. He was vague about what he did, though it seemed to involve trying to manage bands and set up businesses around music. His main occupation was dealing drugs, and he liked supplying Eshan with different kinds of grass that he claimed would make him 'creative.' Eshan replied that he took drugs in the evenings to stop himself getting creative. When Eshan talked about surrealism, or the great photographers, Brian listened with innocent enthusiasm, as if these were things he could get interested in were he a different person. It turned out that he did know a little about the music that Eshan particularly liked, West Coast psychedelic music of the mid-sixties, and the films, writing and politics

that accompanied it. Eshan talked of the dream of freedom, rebellion and irresponsibility it had represented, and how he wished he'd had the courage to
go there and join in.

'You make it sound like the past few years in London,' Brian said. 'Except
the music is faster.'

A couple of months after Eshan started seeing him in the pub, Brian
parted from his casual girlfriends. He went out regularly—it was like a job;
and he was the sort of man that women were attracted to in pubic places.
There was hope; every night could take you somewhere new. But Brian was
nearly thirty; for a long time he had been part of everything new, living not for
the present but for the next thing. He was beginning to see how little it had
left him, and he was afraid.

One day he met a girl who used to play the drums in a trip-hop group.   10
Any subject—the economy, the comparative merits of Paris, Rome or Berlin—
would return him to this woman. Every day he went to some trouble to buy
her something, even if it was only a pencil. Other times it might be a first-
edition Elizabeth David, an art deco lamp from Prague, a tape of Five Easy
Pieces, a bootleg of Lennon singing 'On the Road to Rishikesh.' These things
he would anxiously bring to the pub to ask Eshan's opinion of. Eshan wondered if Brian imagined that because he was a photographer he had taste and
judgement, and, being married, had some knowledge of romance.

After a few drinks Eshan would go home and Brian would start phoning
to make his plans for the night ahead. In what Eshan considered to be the
middle of the night, Brian and Laura would go to a club, to someone's house,
and then on to another club. Eshan learned that there were some places that
only opened at nine on Sunday morning.

Lying in bed with his wife as they watched TV and read nineteenth-
century novels while drinking camomile tea, Eshan found himself trying to picture what Brian and Laura were doing, what sort of good time they were having.
He looked forward to hearing next day where they'd been, what drugs they'd
taken, what they wore and how the conversation had gone. He was particularly
curious about her reaction to each gift; he wanted to know whether she was demanding more and better gifts, or if she appreciated the merits of each one. And
what, Eshan inquired with some concern, was Brian getting in return?

'Enough,' Brian inevitably replied.

'So she's good to you?'

Unusually, Brian replied that no lover had ever shown him what she had.   15
Then he leaned forward, glanced left and right, and felt compelled to say, despite his loving loyalty, what this was. Her touch, her words, her sensual art,
not to mention her murmurs, gasps, cries; and her fine wrists, long fingers and
dark fine-haired bush that stood out like a punk's back-combed mohican—all
were an incomparable rapture. Only the previous evening she had taken him
by the shoulders and said—

'Yes?' Eshan asked.

'Your face, your hands, you, all of you, you . . .'

Eshan dried his palms on his trousers. Sighing inwardly, he listened,
while signalling a detached approval. He encouraged Brian to repeat every-

thing, like a much-loved story, and Brian was delighted to do so, until they were no longer sure of the facts.

Perhaps Eshan envied Brian his lover and their pleasure, and Brian was beginning to envy Eshan his stability. Whatever it was between them, Brian involved Eshan in his new love. It was, Eshan was pleased to see, agonising. Laura drew out Brian's best impulses; tenderness, kindness, generosity. He became more fervent as a dealer so as to take her to restaurants most nights; he borrowed money and took her to Budapest for a week.

But in love each moment is magnified, and every gesture, word and sylla- 20 ble is examined like a speech by the President. Solid expectation, unfurled hope, immeasurable disappointment—all are hurled together like a cocktail of random drugs that, quaffed within the hour, make both lovers reel. If she dressed up and went to a party with a male friend, he spent the night catatonic with paranoia; if he saw an old girlfriend, she assumed they would never speak again. And surely she was seeing someone else, someone better in every way? Did she feel about him as he did her? To love her was to fear losing her. Brian would have locked her in a bare room to have everything hold still a minute.

One day when Eshan went to the bar he returned to see that Brian had picked up a folder Eshan had left on the table, opened it, and was holding up the photographs. Brian could be impudent, which was his charm, and Eshan liked charm, because it was rare and good to watch as a talent. But it also exposed Brian as a man who was afraid; his charm was charged with the task of disarming people before they damaged him.

'Hey,' said Eshan.

Brian placed his finger on a picture of Doris Lessing. Laura was reading *The Golden Notebook;* could he buy it for her? Eshan said, yes, and he wouldn't charge. But Brian insisted. They agreed on a price and on a black frame. They drank more and wondered what Laura would think. A few days later Brian reported that though Laura would never finish the book—she never finished any book, the satisfaction was too diffuse—she had been delighted by the picture. Could she visit his studio?

'Studio? If only it was. But yes, bring her over—it's time we met.'

'Tomorrow, then.'   25

They were more than two hours late. Eshan had been meditating, which he did whenever he was tense or angry. You couldn't beat those Eastern religions for putting the wet blanket on desire. When he was turning out the lights and ready to leave, Brian and Laura arrived at the door with wine. Eshan put out his work for Laura. She looked closely at everything. They smoked the dope he had grown on his balcony from Brian's seeds, lay on the floor with the tops of their heads touching, and watched a Kenneth Anger film. Brian and Laura rang some people and said they were going out. Would he like to come? Eshan almost agreed. He said he would like to have joined them, but that he got up early to work. And the music, an electronic blizzard of squeaks, bleeps and beats, had nothing human in it.

'Yes, that's right,' Laura said. 'Nothing human there. A bunch of robots on drugs.'

'You don't mean that,' said Brian.

A few days after the visit Brian made the strange request.

'She enjoyed meeting you,' he was saying, as Eshan read his newspaper in 30
the pub.

'And me her,' Eshan murmured without raising his eyes. 'Anyone would.'

It cheered Brian to hear her praised. 'She's pretty, eh?'

'No, beautiful.'

'Yes, that's it, you've got the right word.'

He picked up his phone. 'She wants to ask you a favour. Can she join us?' 35

'I've got to go.'

'Of course, you've got to put the kids to bed, but I think you'll find it an
interesting favour.'

Laura arrived within fifteen minutes. She sat down at their table and began.
'What we want is for you to photograph us.'

Eshan nodded. Laura glanced at Brian. 'Naked. Or we could wear things. 40
Rings through our belly buttons or something. But anyway—making love.' Eshan looked at her. 'You photograph us fucking,' she concluded. 'Do you see?'

Eshan didn't know what to say.

She asked, 'What about it?'

'I am not a pornographer.'

It must have sounded pompous. She gave him an amused look.

'I've seen your stuff, and we haven't the nerve for pornography. It isn't 45
even beauty we want. And I know you don't go for that.'

'No. What is it?'

'You see, we go to bed and eat crackers and drink wine and caress one another and chatter all day. We've both been through terrible things in our lives,
you see. Now we want to capture this summer moment—I mean we want you
to capture it for us.'

'To look back on?'

She said, 'I suppose that is it. We all know love doesn't last.'

'Is that right?' said Eshan. 50

Brian added, 'It might be replaced by something else.'

'But this terrible passion and suspicion . . . and the intensity of it . . . will
get domesticated.' She went on, 'I think that when one has an idea, even if it
is a queer one, one should follow it through, don't you?'

Eshan supposed he agreed with this.

Laura kissed Brian and said to him, 'Eshan's up for it.'

'I'm not sure,' said Brian. 55

Eshan had picked up his things, said goodbye and reached the door, before he returned.

'Why me?'

She was looking up at him.

'Why? Brian has run into you with your children. You're a kind father, a
normal man, and you will surely understand what we want.' Eshan looked at
Brian, who had maintained a neutral expression. She said, 'But . . . if it's all too
much, let's forget it.'

It was an idea they'd conceived frivolously. He would give her the chance 60
to drop the whole thing. She should call in the morning.

He thought it over in bed. When Laura made the request, though excited, she hadn't seemed mad or over-ebullient. It was vanity, of course, but a touching, naive vanity, not a grand one; and he was, more than ever, all for naivety. Laura was, too, a woman anyone would want to look at.

An old upright piano and guitar; painted canvases leaning against the wall; club fliers, rolling papers, pills, a razor blade, beer bottles empty and full, standing on a chest of drawers. Leaning against this, a long mirror. The bed, its linen white, was in the center of the room.

Laura pulled the curtains, and then half-opened them again.

'Will you have enough light?'

'I'll manage,' Eshan whispered 65

Brian went to shave. Then, while Eshan unpacked his things, he plucked at the guitar with his mouth open, and drank beer. The three of them spoke in low voices and were solicitous of one another, as if they were about to do something dangerous but delicate, like planting a bomb.

A young man, covered in spots, wandered into the room.

'Get out now and go to bed,' Laura said. 'You've got chickenpox. Everyone here had it?' she asked.

They all laughed. It was better then. She put a chair against the door. They watched her arrange herself on the bed. Eshan photographed her back; he photographed her face. She took her clothes off. The breeze from the open window caressed her. She stretched out her fingers to Brian.

He walked over to her and they pressed their faces together. Eshan pho- 70 tographed that. She undressed him. Eshan shot his discomfort.

Soon they were taking up different positions, adjusting their heads, putting their hands here and there for each shot. Brian began to smile as if he fancied himself as a model.

'It's very sweet, but it ain't going to work,' Eshan told them. 'There's nothing there. It's dead.'

'He might be right,' Laura told Brian. 'We're going to have to pretend he's not here.'

Eshan said, "I'll put film in the camera now, then.'

Eshan didn't go to bed but carried his things through the dark city back 75 to his studio. He developed the material as quickly as he could and when it was done went home. His wife and children were having breakfast, laughing and arguing as usual. He walked in and his children kept asking him to take off his coat. He felt like a criminal, though the only laws he'd broken were his own, and he wasn't sure which ones they were.

Unusually he had the pictures with him and he went through them several times as he ate his toast, keeping them away from the children.

'Please, can I see?' His wife put her hand on his shoulder. 'Don't hide them. It's a long time since you've shown me your work. You live such a secret life.'

'Do I?'

'Sometimes I think you're not doing anything at all over there but just sitting.'

She looked at the photographs and then closed the folder. 80

'You stayed out all night without getting in touch. What have you been doing?'

'Taking pictures.'

'Don't talk to me like that. Who are these people, Eshan?'

'People I met in the pub. They asked me to photograph them.'

They went into the kitchen and she closed the door. She could be very 85 disapproving, and she didn't like mysteries.

'And you did this?'

'You know I like to start somewhere and finish somewhere else. It wasn't an orgy.'

'Are you going to publish or sell them?'

'No. They paid me. And that's it.'

He got up. 90

'Where are you going?'

'Back to work.'

'If this the same kind of thing you'll be doing today?'

'Ha ha ha.'

He tried to resume his routine but couldn't work, or even listen to music 95 or read the papers. He could only look at the pictures. They were not pornography, being too crude and unembellished for that. He had omitted nothing human. All the same, the images gave him a dry mouth, exciting and distressing him at the same time. He wouldn't be able to start anything else until the material was out of the studio.

He thought Brian would have gone back to his place, but wasn't certain. However, he couldn't persuade himself to ring first. He took a chance and walked all the way back there again. He was exhausted but was careful to cross the road where he crossed it before.

She came to the door in her dressing gown, and was surprised to see him. He said he'd brought the stuff round, and proffered the folder as evidence.

He went past her and up the stairs. She tugged her dressing gown around herself, as if he hadn't seen her body before. Upstairs they sat on the broken sofa. She was reluctant to look at the stuff, but knew she had to. She held up the contact sheets, turning them this way and that, repeatedly.

'Is that what you wanted?' he asked.

'I don't know.' 100

'Is that what you do on a good day?'

'I should thank you for the lovely job you've done. I don't know what I can do in return.' He looked at her. She said, 'How about a drum lesson?'

'Why not?'

She took him into a larger room, where he noticed some of Brian's gifts. Set before a big window, with a view of the street and the square, was her red spangled kit. She showed him how she played, and demonstrated how he could. Soon this bored her and she made lunch. As he ate she returned to the photographs, glanced through them without comment, and went back to the table. He wasn't certain that she wanted him there. But she didn't ask him to go away and seemed to assume that he had nothing better to do. He didn't know what else he would do anyway, as if something had come to an end.

They started to watch television, but suddenly she switched it off and   105
stood up and sat down. She started agitatedly asking him questions about the
people he knew, how many friends he had, what he liked about them, and
what they said to one another. At first he answered abruptly, afraid of boring
her. But she said she'd never had any guidance, and for the past few years, like
everyone else, had only wanted a good time. Now she wanted to find something important to do, wanted a reason to get out of bed before four. He murmured that fucking might be a good excuse for staying in bed, just as the need
to wash was an excuse for lying in the bath. She understood that, she said. She
hardly knew anyone with a job; London was full of drugged, useless people
who didn't listen to one another but merely thought all the time of how to distract themselves and never spoke of anything serious. She was tired of it; she
was even tired of being in love; it had become another narcotic. Now she
wanted interesting difficulty, not pleasure or even ease.

'And look, look at the pictures . . .'

'What do they say?'

'Too much, my friend.'

She hurried from the room. After a time she returned with a bucket
which she set down on the carpet. She held the photographs over it and invited him to set fire to them.

'Are you sure?' he said.   110

'Oh yes.'

They singed the carpet and burned their fingers, and then they threw
handfuls of ash out of the window and cheered.

'Are you going to the pub now?' she asked as he said goodbye.

'I don't think I'll be going there for a while.'

He told her that the next day he was going to photograph a painter who   115
had also done record covers. He asked her to come along, 'to have a look.' She
said she would.

Leaving the house he crossed the street. He could see her sitting in the
window playing. When he walked away he could hear her all the way to the
end of the road.

——— **HANIF KUREISHI** ———

(b. 1954) **Web**   *www*

Kureishi, the son of a Pakistani father and English mother, grew up in England.
After attending the University of London, he began writing plays, screenplays,
stories, and novels dealing with the experiences of young immigrants in London. He wrote the screenplays for *My Beautiful Laundrette* and *Sammy and Rosie
Get Laid*.

TOPICS FOR CRITICAL THINKING **Web**   *www*

1. How many different versions of love does the story suggest?
2. How many frame narrators does this story have?
3. What kind of structure does a frame narrator create?

4. What narrative of art or being an artist does the story recount? Is that narrative repeated?

5. What oppositions do the various layers of this story set up around art and love?

6. How do those oppositions structure the story?

7. What is the function of image in the story?

www   TOPICS FOR CRITICAL WRITING Web

1. How does this story compare the writer to the photographer? What does this comparison tell us about art or love?

2. Why did Laura burn the pictures? What is Laura's and Brian's future, and why?

Part III
Reading and Interpreting

13 The Perils of Interpretation

Interpretation is generally understood to be the art of drawing conclusions from a series of clues offered by a text. The activity of interpreting a literary text is not unlike the activity of interpreting any set of circumstances. Readers gather clues about character, plot, circumstance, and motivation, and from these clues they deduce (or make conclusions) based on how these details fit into patterns with which they are familiar. For example, in a detective story, a detective gathers clues about how a crime was committed. Based on how those clues fit into a sensible plan of behavior, which explains how a crime was accomplished, the detective determines the identity of a malefactor (thief, murderer, and so on) as the only one whose circumstances fit the crime. Interpreting literature is not unlike this process, except that the questions a reader attempts to answer are questions not only about plot and character motivation, but also those about how the various elements of a story work together in relation to what happens.

Interpreting, however, also has dangers. One danger, of course, is drawing the wrong conclusion. That is easily corrected, generally by the story itself. If we think, for example, that Charlie in "Babylon Revisited" is going to regain custody of his daughter based on our (and Charlie's own) astute reading of the clues, we realize that conclusion is no longer possible once Charlie's friends show up. Another danger is that our process of interpretation will be clouded by what we want to see happen. This has a tendency to skew the ways

we understand and interpret the clues offered by stories. One of the best examples about the way our own desires cloud our ability to interpret is Edgar
Allan Poe's "The Purloined Letter." Consider the ways the story brings
processes of interpretation into question.

EDGAR ALLAN POE

The Purloined Letter   *(1844)*

Nil sapientae odiosius acumine nimio.
                                        —SENECA

At Paris, just after dark one gusty evening in the autumn of 18——, I was enjoying the twofold luxury of meditation and a meerschaum, in company with
my friend C. Auguste Dupin, in his little back library, or book-closet, *au
troisième, No. 33, Rue Dunôt, Faubourg St. Germain.* For one hour at least we
had maintained a profound silence; while each, to any casual observer, might
have seemed intently and exclusively occupied with the curling eddies of
smoke that oppressed the atmosphere of the chamber. For myself, however, I
was mentally discussing certain topics which had formed matter for conversation between us at an earlier period of the evening; I mean the affair of the
Rue Morgue, and the mystery attending the murder of Marie Rogêt. I looked
upon it, therefore, as something of a coincidence, when the door of our apartment was thrown open and admitted our old acquaintance, Monsieur G——,
the Prefect of the Parisian police.

We gave him a hearty welcome; for there was nearly half as much of the entertaining as of the contemptible about the man, and we had not seen him for
several years. We had been sitting in the dark, and Dupin now arose for the purpose of lighting a lamp, but sat down again, without doing so, upon G.'s saying
that he had called to consult us, or rather to ask the opinion of my friend, about
some official business which had occasioned a great deal of trouble.

"If it is any point requiring reflection," observed Dupin, as he forbore to
enkindle the wick, "we shall examine it to better purpose in the dark."

"That is another of your odd notions," said the Prefect, who had a fashion of calling every thing "odd" that was beyond his comprehension, and thus
lived amid an absolute legion of "oddities."

"Very true," said Dupin, as he supplied his visitor with a pipe, and rolled 5
towards him a comfortable chair.

"And what is the difficulty now?" I asked. "Nothing more in the assassination way, I hope?"

"Oh no; nothing of that nature. The fact is, the business is *very* simple indeed, and I make no doubt that we can manage it sufficiently well ourselves;
but then I thought Dupin would like to hear the details of it, because it is so
excessively *odd.*"

"Simple and odd," said Dupin.

"Why, yes; and not exactly that either. The fact is, we have all been a good deal puzzled because the affair *is* so simple, and yet baffles us altogether."

"Perhaps it is the very simplicity of the thing which puts you at fault," said   10
my friend.

"What nonsense you *do* talk!" replied the Prefect, laughing heartily.

"Perhaps the mystery is a little *too* plain," said Dupin.

"Oh, good heavens! who ever heard of such an idea?"

"A little *too* self-evident."

"Ha! ha! ha!—ha! ha! ha!—ho! ho! ho!"—roared our visitor, profoundly   15
amused, "oh, Dupin, you will be the death of me yet!"

"And what, after all, *is* the matter on hand?" I asked.

"Why, I will tell you," replied the Prefect, as he gave a long, steady, and contemplative puff, and settled himself in his chair. "I will tell you in a few words; but, before I begin, let me caution you that this is an affair demanding the greatest secrecy, and that I should most probably lose the position I now hold, were it known that I confided it to any one."

"Proceed," said I.

"Or not," said Dupin.

"Well, then; I have received personal information, from a very high quarter,   20
that a certain document of the last importance has been purloined from the royal apartments. The individual who purloined it is known; this beyond a doubt; he was seen to take it. It is known, also, that it still remains in his possession."

"How is this known?" asked Dupin.

"It is clearly inferred," replied the Prefect, "from the nature of the document, and from the non-appearance of certain results which would at once arise from its passing *out* of the robber's possession;—that is to say, from his employing it as he must design in the end to employ it."

"Be a little more explicit," I said.

"Well, I may venture so far as to say that the paper gives its holder a certain power in a certain quarter where such power is immensely valuable." The Prefect was fond of the cant of diplomacy.

"Still I do not quite understand," said Dupin.   25

"No? Well; the disclosure of the document to a third person, who shall be nameless, would bring in question the honour of a personage of most exalted station; and this fact gives the holder of the document an ascendancy over the illustrious personage whose honour and peace are so jeopardized."

"But this ascendancy," I interposed, "would depend upon the robber's knowledge of the loser's knowledge of the robber. Who would dare—"

"The thief," said G., "is the Minister D——, who dares all things, those unbecoming as well as those becoming a man. The method of the theft was not less ingenious than bold. The document in question—a letter, to be frank—had been received by the personage robbed while alone in the royal *boudoir*. During its perusal she was suddenly interrupted by the entrance of the other exalted personage from whom especially it was her wish to conceal it. After a hurried and vain endeavour to thrust it in a drawer, she was forced to place it, open it was, upon a table. The address, however, was uppermost, and, the contents thus unexposed, the letter escaped notice. At this juncture enters the Minister D——. His lynx eye immediately perceives the paper, recognizes the handwriting of the address, observes the confusion of the personage addressed, and fathoms her secret. After some business transactions, hurried through in his ordinary manner, he produces a letter somewhat similar to the one in question, opens it, pretends to read it, and then places it in close juxtaposition to the other. Again he converses, for some fifteen minutes, upon the public affairs. At length, in taking leave, he takes also from the table the letter to which he had no claim. Its rightful owner saw, but, of course, dared not call attention to the act, in the presence of the third personage who stood at her elbow. The minister decamped; leaving his own letter—one of no importance—upon the table."

"Here, then," said Dupin to me, "you have precisely what you demand to make the ascendancy complete—the robber's knowledge of the loser's knowledge of the robber."

"Yes," replied the Prefect; "and the power thus attained has, for some months past, been wielded, for political purposes, to a very dangerous extent. The personage robbed is more thoroughly convinced, every day, of the necessity of reclaiming her letter. But this, of course, cannot be done openly. In fine, driven to despair, she has committed the matter to me."

"Than whom," said Dupin, amid a perfect whirlwind of smoke, "no more sagacious agent could, I suppose, be desired, or even imagined."

"You flatter me," replied the Prefect; "but it is possible that some such opinion may have been entertained."

"It is clear," said I, "as you observe, that the letter is still in the possession of the minister; since it is this possession, and not any employment of the letter, which bestows the power. With the employment the power departs."

"True," said G.; "and upon this conviction I proceeded. My first care was to make thorough search of the minister's hotel; and here my chief embarrassment lay in the necessity of searching without his knowledge. Beyond all things, I have been warned of the danger which would result from giving him reason to suspect our design."

"But," said I, "you are quite *au fait* in these investigations. The Parisian police have done this thing often before."

"O yes; and for this reason I did not despair. The habits of the minister gave me, too, a great advantage. He is frequently absent from home all night. His servants are by no means numerous. They sleep at a distance from their master's apartment, and being chiefly Neapolitans, are readily made drunk. I have keys, as you know, with which I can open any chamber or cabinet in Paris. For three months a night has not passed, during the greater part of which I have not been engaged, personally, in ransacking the D—— Hôtel. My honour is interested, and, to mention a great secret, the reward is enormous. So I did not abandon the search until I had become fully satisfied that the thief is a more astute man than myself. I fancy that I have investigated every nook and corner of the premises in which it is possible that the paper can be concealed."

"But is it not possible," I suggested, "that although the letter may be in the possession of the minister, as it unquestionably is, he may have concealed it elsewhere than upon his own premises?"

"This is barely possible," said Dupin. "The present peculiar condition of affairs at court, and especially of those intrigues in which D—— is known to be involved, would render the instant availability of the document—its susceptibility of being produced at a moment's notice—a point of nearly equal importance with its possession."

"Its susceptibility of being produced?" said I.

"That is to say, of being *destroyed*," said Dupin.   40

"True," I observed; "the paper is clearly then upon the premises. As for its being upon the person of the minister, we may consider that as out of the question."

"Entirely," said the Prefect. "He had been twice waylaid, as if by footpads, and his person rigorously searched under my own inspection."

"You might have spared yourself this trouble," said Dupin. "D——, I presume, is not altogether a fool, and, if not, must have anticipated these waylayings, as a matter of course."

"Not *altogether* a fool," said G., "but then he is a poet, which I take to be only one remove from a fool."

"True," said Dupin, after a long and thoughtful whiff from his meer-   45
schaum, "although I have been guilty of certain doggerel myself."

"Suppose you detail," said I, "the particulars of your search."

"Why the fact is, we took our time, and we searched *every where*. I have had long experience in these affairs. I took the entire building, room by room; devoting the nights of a whole week to each. We examined, first, the furniture of each apartment. We opened every possible drawer; and I presume you know that, to a properly trained police agent, such a thing as a *secret* drawer is impossible. Any man is a dolt who permits a 'secret' drawer to escape him in a search of this kind. The thing is *so* plain. There is a certain amount of bulk— of space—to be accounted for in every cabinet. Then we have accurate rules. The fiftieth part of a line could not escape us. After the cabinets we took the chairs. The cushions we probed with the fine long needles you have seen me employ. From the tables we removed the tops."

"Why so?"

"Sometimes the top of a table, or other similarly arranged piece of furniture, is removed by the person wishing to conceal an article; then the leg is excavated, the article deposited within the cavity, and the top replaced. The bottoms and tops of bedposts are employed in the same way."

"But could not the cavity be detected by sounding?" I asked.   50

"By no means, if, when the article is deposited, a sufficient wadding of cotton be placed around it. Besides, in our case, we were obliged to proceed without noise."

"But you could not have removed—you could not have taken to pieces *all* articles of furniture in which it would have been possible to make a deposit in the manner you mention. A letter may be compressed into a thin spiral roll, not differing much in shape or bulk from a large knitting-needle, and in this form it might be inserted into the rung of a chair, for example. You did not take to pieces all the chairs?"

"Certainly not; but we did better—we examined the rungs of every chair in the hotel, and indeed the jointings of every description of furniture, by the aid of a most powerful microscope. Had there been any traces of recent disturbance we should not have failed to detect it instantly. A single grain of gimlet-dust, for example, would have been as obvious as an apple. Any disorder in the glueing—any unusual gaping in the joints—would have sufficed to insure detection."

"I presume you looked to the mirrors, between the boards and the plates, and you probed the beds and the bed-clothes, as well as the curtains and carpets."

"That of course; and when we had absolutely completed every particle of 55 the furniture in this way, then we examined the house itself. We divided its entire surface into compartments, which we numbered, so that none might be missed; then we scrutinized each individual square inch throughout the premises, including the two houses immediately adjoining, with the microscope as before."

"The two houses adjoining!" I exclaimed; "you must have had a great deal of trouble."

"We had; but the reward offered is prodigious."

"You include the *grounds* about the houses?"

"All the grounds are paved with brick. They gave us comparatively little trouble. We examined the moss between the bricks, and found it undisturbed."

"You looked among D——'s papers, of course, and into the books of the 60 library?"

"Certainly; we opened every package and parcel; we not only opened every book, but we turned over every leaf in each volume, not contenting ourselves with a mere shake, according to the fashion of some of our police officers. We also measured the thickness of every book-*cover*, with the most accurate admeasurement, and applied to each the most jealous scrutiny of the microscope. Had any of the bindings been recently meddled with, it would have been utterly impossible that the fact should have escaped observation. Some five or six volumes, just from the hands of the binder, we carefully probed, longitudinally, with the needles."

"You explored the floors beneath the carpets?"

"Beyond doubt. We removed every carpet, and examined the boards with the microscope."

"And the paper on the walls?"

"Yes." 65

"You looked into the cellars?"

"We did."

"Then," I said, "you have been making a miscalculation, and the letter is *not* upon the premises as you suppose."

"I fear you are right there," said the Prefect. "And now, Dupin, what would you advise me to do?"

"To make a thorough re-search of the premises."   70

"That is absolutely needless," replied G——. "I am not more sure that I breathe than I am that the letter is not at the Hôtel."

"I have no better advice to give you," said Dupin. "You have, of course, an accurate description of the letter?"

"Oh, yes!"—And here the Prefect, producing a memorandum-book, proceeded to read aloud a minute account of the internal, and especially of the external, appearance of the missing document. Soon after finishing the perusal of this description, he took his departure, more entirely depressed in spirits than I had ever known the good gentleman before.

In about a month afterward he paid us another visit, and found us occupied very nearly as before. He took a pipe and a chair and entered into some ordinary conversation. At length I said;—

"Well, but G——, what of the purloined letter? I presume you have at last   75
made up your mind that there is no such thing as overreaching the Minister?"

"Confound him, say I—yes; I made the re-examination, however, as Dupin suggested—but it was all labour lost, as I knew it would be."

"How much was the reward offered, did you say?" asked Dupin.

"Why, a very great deal—a *very* liberal reward—I don't like to say how much, precisely; but one thing I *will* say, that I wouldn't mind giving my individual check for fifty thousand francs to any one who could obtain me that letter. The fact is, it is becoming of more and more importance every day; and the reward has been lately doubled. If it were trebled, however, I could do no more than I have done."

"Why, yes," said Dupin, drawlingly, between the whiffs of his meerschaum, "I really—think, G——, you have not exerted yourself—to the utmost in this matter. You might—do a little more, I think, eh?"

"How?—in what way?"   80

"Why—puff, puff,—you might—puff, puff—employ counsel in the matter, eh?—puff, puff, puff. Do you remember the story they tell of Abernethy?"

"No; hang Abernethy!"

"To be sure! hang him and welcome. But, once upon a time, a certain rich miser conceived the design of spunging upon this Abernethy for a medical opinion. Getting up, for this purpose, an ordinary conversation in a private company, he insinuated his case to the physician, as that of an imaginary individual."

"'We will suppose,' said the miser, 'that his symptoms are such and such; now, doctor, what would *you* have directed him to take?'"

"'Take!' said Abernethy, 'why, take *advice*, to be sure.'"   85

"But," said the Prefect, a little discomposed, "I am *perfectly* willing to take advice, and to pay for it. I would *really* give fifty thousand francs to any one who would aid me in the matter."

"In that case," replied Dupin, opening a drawer, and producing a checkbook, "you may as well fill me up a check for the amount you mentioned. When you have signed it, I will hand you the letter."

I was astounded. The Prefect appeared absolutely thunderstricken. For some minutes he remained speechless and motionless, looking incredulously at my friend with open mouth, and eyes that seemed starting from their sockets;

then, apparently recovering himself in some measure, he seized a pen, and after several pauses and vacant stares, finally filled up and signed a check for fifty thousand francs, and handed it across the table to Dupin. The latter examined it carefully and deposited it in his pocket-book; then, unlocking an *escritoire*, took thence a letter and gave it to the Prefect. This functionary grasped it in a perfect agony of joy, opened it with a trembling hand, cast a rapid glance at its contents, and then, scrambling and struggling to the door, rushed at length unceremoniously from the room and from the house, without having uttered a syllable since Dupin had requested him to fill up the check.

When he had gone, my friend entered into some explanations.

"The Parisian police," he said, "are exceedingly able in their way. They are 90 persevering, ingenious, cunning, and thoroughly versed in the knowledge which their duties seem chiefly to demand. Thus, when G—— detailed to us his mode of searching the premises at the Hôtel D——, I felt entire confidence in his having made a satisfactory investigation—so far as his labours extended."

"So far as his labours extended?" said I.

"Yes," said Dupin. "The measures adopted were not only the best of their kind, but carried out to absolute perfection. Had the letter been deposited within the range of their search, these fellows would, beyond a question, have found it."

I merely laughed—but he seemed quite serious in all that he said.

"The measures, then," he continued, "were good in their kind, and well executed; their defect lay in their being inapplicable to the case, and to the man. A certain set of highly ingenious resources are, with the Prefect, a sort of Procrustean bed, to which he forcibly adapts his designs. But he perpetually errs by being too deep or too shallow, for the matter in hand; and many a schoolboy is a better reasoner than he. I knew one about eight years of age, whose success at guessing in the game of 'even and odd' attracted universal admiration. This game is simple, and is played with marbles. One player holds in his hand a number of these toys, and demands of another whether that number is even or odd. If the guess is right, the guesser wins one; if wrong, he loses one. The boy to whom I allude won all the marbles of the school. Of course he had some principle of guessing; and this lay in mere observation and admeasurement of the astuteness of his opponents. For example, an arrant simpleton is his opponent, and, holding up his closed hand, asks: 'Are they even or odd?' Our schoolboy replies, 'Odd,' and loses; but upon the second trial he wins, for he then says to himself, 'The simpleton had them even upon the first trial, and his amount of cunning is just sufficient to make him have them odd upon the second; I will therefore guess odd';—he guesses odd, and wins. Now, with a simpleton a degree above the first, he would have reasoned thus: 'This fellow finds that in the first instance I guessed odd, and, in the second, he will propose to himself upon the first impulse, a simple variation from even to odd, as did the first simpleton; but then a second thought will suggest that this is too simple a variation, and finally he will decide upon putting it even as before. I will therefore guess even';—he guesses even, and wins. Now this mode of reasoning in the schoolboy, whom his fellows termed 'lucky,'— what, in its last analysis, is it?"

"It is merely," I said, "an identification of the reasoner's intellect with that   95
of his opponent."

"It is," said Dupin; "and, upon inquiring of the boy by what means he effected the *thorough* identification in which his success consisted, I received answer as follows: 'When I wish to find out how wise, or how stupid, or how good, or how wicked is any one, or what are his thoughts at the moment, I fashion the expression on my face, as accurately as possible, in accordance with the expression of his, and then wait to see what thoughts or sentiments arise in my mind or heart, as if to match or correspond with the expression.' This response of the schoolboy lies at the bottom of all the spurious profundity which has been attributed to Rochefoucault, to La Bougive, to Machiavelli, and to Campanella."

"And the identification," I said, "of the reasoner's intellect with that of his opponent, depends, if I understand you aright, upon the accuracy with which the opponent's intellect is admeasured."

"For its practical value it depends upon this," replied Dupin; "and the Prefect and his cohort fail so frequently, first, by default of this identification, and secondly, by ill-admeasurement, or rather through non-admeasurement, of the intellect with which they are engaged. They consider only their *own* ideas of ingenuity; and, in searching for anything hidden, advert only to the modes in which *they* would have hidden it. They are right in this much—that their own ingenuity is a faithful representative of that of *the mass;* but when the cunning of the individual felon is diverse in character from their own, the felon foils them, of course. This always happens when it is above their own, and very usually when it is below. They have no variation of principle in their investigations; at best, when urged by some unusual emergency—by some extraordinary reward—they extend or exaggerate their old modes of *practice*, without touching their principles. What, for example, in this case of D——, has been done to vary the principle of action? What is all this boring, and probing, and sounding, and scrutinizing with the microscope, and dividing the surface of the building into registered square inches—what is it all but an exaggeration *of the application* of one principle or set of principles of search, which are based upon the one set of notions regarding human ingenuity, to which the Prefect, in the long routine of his duty, has been accustomed? Do you not see he has taken it for granted that *all* men proceed to conceal a letter,—not exactly in a gimlet-hole bored in a chair-leg—but, at least, in *some* out-of-the-way hole or corner suggested by the same tenor or thought which would urge a man to secret a letter in a gimlet-hole bored in a chair-leg? And do you not see also, that such *recherchés* nooks for concealment are adapted only for ordinary occasions, and would be adopted only by ordinary intellects; for, in all cases of concealment, a disposal of the article concealed—a disposal of it in this *recherché* manner—is, in the very first instance, presumable and presumed; and thus its discovery depends, not at all upon the acumen, but altogether upon the mere care, patience, and determination of the seekers; and where the case is of importance—or, what amounts to the same thing in the political eyes, when the reward is of magnitude,—the qualities in question have *never* been known to fail. You will now understand what I meant in suggesting that, had the purloined letter been hidden anywhere within the limits of the Prefect's examination—in other words, had the principle of its conceal-ment been comprehended within the principles of the Prefect—its discovery would have been a matter altogether beyond question. This functionary, how-ever, has been thoroughly mystified; and the remote source of his defeat lies in the supposition that the Minister is a fool, because he has acquired renown as a poet. All fools are poets; this the Prefect *feels;* and he is merely guilty of a *non distributio medii* in thence inferring that all poets are fools."

"But is this really the poet?" I asked. "There are two brothers, I know; and both have attained reputation in letters. The Minister I believe has written learnedly on the Differential Calculus. He is a mathematician, and no poet."

"You are mistaken; I know him well: he is both. As poet *and* mathemati-   100
cian, he would reason well; as mere mathematician, he could not have rea-soned at all, and thus would have been at the mercy of the Prefect."

"You surprise me," I said, "by these opinions, which have been contra-dicted by the voice of the world. You do not mean to set at naught the well-digested idea of centuries. The mathematical reason has long been regarded as *the* reason *par excellence.*"

"'*Il y a à parier,*'" replied Dupin, quoting from Chamfort, "'*que toute idée publique, toute convention reçue, est une sottise, car elle a convenu au plus grand nombre.*' The mathematicians, I grant you, have done their best to promulgate the popular error to which you allude, and which is none the less an error for its promulgation as truth. With an art worthy a better cause, for example, they have insinuated the term 'analysis' into application to algebra. The French are the originators of this particular deception; but if a term is of any impor-tance—if words derive any value from applicability—then 'analysis' conveys 'algebra' about as much as, in Latin, '*ambitus*' implies 'ambition,' '*religio*' 'reli-gion,' or '*homines honesti,*' a set of *honourable* men."

"You have a quarrel on hand, I see," said I, "with some of the algebraists of Paris; but proceed."

"I dispute the availability, and thus the value, of that reason which is cul-tivated in any especial form other than the abstractly logical. I dispute, in particular, the reason educed by mathematical study. The mathematics are the science of form and quantity; mathematical reasoning is merely logic applied to observation upon form and quantity. The great error lies in sup-posing that even the truths of what is called *pure* algebra, are abstract or gen-eral truths. And this error is so egregious that I am confounded at the universality with which it has been received. Mathematical axioms are *not* ax-ioms of general truth. What is true of *relation*—of form and quantity—is of-ten grossly false in regard to morals, for example. In this latter science it is very usually *un*true that the aggregated parts are equal to the whole. In chem-istry also the axiom fails. In the consideration of motive it fails; for two mo-tives, each of a given value, have not, necessarily, a value when united, equal to the sum of their values apart. There are numerous other mathematical truths which are only truths within the limits of *relation*. But the mathematician argues from his *finite truths*, through habit, as if they were of an absolutely general applicability—as the world indeed imagines them to be. Bryant, in his very learned 'Mythology,' mentions an analogous source of error, when he says that 'although the Pagan fables are not believed, yet we forget ourselves continually, and make inferences from them as existing realities.' With the algebraists, however, who are Pagans themselves, the 'Pagan fables' *are* believed, and the inferences are made, not so much through lapse of memory as through an unaccountable addling of the brains. In short, I never yet encountered the mere mathematician who could be trusted out of equal roots, or one who did not clandestinely hold it as a point of his faith that $x^2 + px$ was absolutely and unconditionally equal to q. Say to one of these gentlemen, by way of experiment, if you please, that you believe occasions may occur where $x^2 + px$ is *not* altogether equal to q, and having made him understand what you mean, get out of his reach as speedily as convenient, for, beyond doubt, he will endeavour to knock you down."

"I mean to say," continued Dupin, while I merely laughed at his last observations, "that if the Minister had been no more than a mathematician, the Prefect would have been under no necessity of giving me this check. I knew him, however, as both mathematician and poet, and my measures were adapted to his capacity, with reference to the circumstances by which he was surrounded. I knew him as a courtier, too, and as a bold *intriguant.* Such a man, I considered, could not fail to be aware of the ordinary political modes of action. He could not have failed to anticipate—and events have proved that he did not fail to anticipate—the waylayings to which he was subjected. He must have foreseen, I reflected, the secret investigations of his premises. His frequent absences from home at night, which were hailed by the Prefect as certain aids to his success, I regarded only as *ruses,* to afford opportunity for thorough search to the police, and thus the sooner to impress them with the conviction to which G——, in fact, did finally arrive—the conviction that the letter was not upon the premises. I felt, also, that the whole train of thought, which I was at some pains in detailing to you just now, concerning the invariable principle of political action in searches for articles concealed—I felt that this whole train of thought would necessarily pass through the mind of the Minister. It would imperatively lead him to despise all the ordinary *nooks* of concealment. *He* could not, I reflected, be so weak as not to see that the most intricate and remote recess of his hotel would be as open as his commonest closets to the eyes, to the probes, to the gimlets, and to the microscopes of the Prefect. I saw, in fine, that he would be driven, as a matter of course, to simplicity, if not deliberately induced to it as a matter of choice. You will remember, perhaps, how desperately the Prefect laughed when I suggested, upon our first interview, that it was just possible this mystery troubled him so much on account of its being so *very* self-evident."

"Yes," said I, "I remember his merriment well. I really thought he would have fallen into convulsions."

"The material world," continued Dupin, "abounds with very strict analogies to the immaterial; and thus some color of truth has been given to the rhetorical dogma, that metaphor, or simile, may be made to strengthen an argument as well as to embellish a description. The principle of the *vis inertiae,* for example, seems to be identical in physics and metaphysics. It is not more true in the former, that a large body is with more difficulty set in motion than a smaller one, and that its subsequent *momentum* is commensurate with this difficulty, than it is, in the latter, that intellects of the vaster capacity, while more forcible, more constant, and more eventful in their movements than those of inferior grade, are yet the less readily moved, and more embarrassed and full of hesitation in the first few steps of their progress. Again: have you ever noticed which of the street signs, over the shop doors, are the most attractive of attention?"

"I have never given the matter a thought," I said.

"There is a game of puzzles," he resumed, "which is played upon a map. One party playing requires another to find a given word—the name of town, river, state, or empire—any word, in short, upon the motley and perplexed surface of the chart. A novice in the game generally seeks to embarrass his opponents by giving them the most minutely lettered names; but the adept selects such words as stretch, in large characters, from one end of the chart to the other. These, like the over-largely lettered signs and placards of the street, escape observation by the dint of being excessively obvious; and here the physical oversight is precisely analogous with the moral inapprehension by which the intellect suffers to pass unnoticed those considerations which are too obtrusively and too palpably self-evident. But this is a point, it appears, somewhat above or beneath the understanding of the Prefect. He never once thought it probable, or possible, that the Minister had deposited the letter immediately beneath the nose of the whole world, by way of best preventing any portion of that world from perceiving it."

"But the more I reflected upon the daring, dashing, and discriminating ingenuity of D——; upon the fact that the document must always have been *at hand*, if he intended to use it to good purpose; and upon the decisive evidence, obtained by the Prefect, that it was not hidden within the limits of that dignitary's ordinary search—the more satisfied I became that, to conceal this letter, the Minister had resorted to the comprehensive and sagacious expedient of not attempting to conceal it at all." 110

"Full of these ideas, I prepared myself with a pair of green spectacles, and called one fine morning, quite by accident, at the Ministerial hotel. I found D—— at home, yawning, lounging, and dawdling, as usual, and pretending to be in the last extremity of *ennui*. He is, perhaps, the most really energetic human being now alive—but that is only when nobody sees him."

"To be even with him, I complained of my weak eyes, and lamented the necessity of the spectacles, under cover of which I cautiously and thoroughly surveyed the whole apartment, while seemingly intent only upon the conversation of my host."

"I paid especial attention to a large writing-table near which he sat, and upon which lay confusedly, some miscellaneous letters and other papers, with one or two musical instruments and a few books. Here, however, after a long and very deliberate scrutiny, I saw nothing to excite particular suspicion."

"At length my eyes, in going the circuit of the room, fell upon a trumpery filigree card-rack of pasteboard, that hung dangling by a dirty blue ribbon, from a little brass knob just beneath the middle of the mantel-piece. In this rack, which had three or four compartments, were five or six visiting cards and a solitary letter. This last was much soiled and crumpled. It was torn nearly in two, across the middle—as if a design, in the first instance, to tear it entirely up as worthless, had been altered, or stayed, in the second. It had a large black seal, bearing the D—— cipher *very* conspicuously, and was addressed, in a diminutive female hand, to D——, the minister, himself. It was thrust carelessly, and even, as it seemed, contemptuously, into one of the upper divisions of the rack."

"No sooner had I glanced at this letter than I concluded it to be that of 115 which I was in search. To be sure, it was, to all appearance, radically different from the one of which the Prefect had read us so minute a description. Here the seal was large and black, with the D—— cipher; there it was small and red, with the ducal arms of the S—— family. Here, the address, to the Minister, was diminutive and feminine; there the superscription, to a certain royal personage, was markedly bold and decided; the size alone formed a point of correspondence. But, then, the *radicalness* of these differences, which was excessive; the dirt; the soiled and torn condition of the paper, so inconsistent with the *true* methodical habits of D——, and so suggestive of a design to delude the beholder into an idea of the worthlessness of the document; these things, together with the hyperobtrusive situation of this document, full in the view of every visitor, and thus exactly in accordance with the conclusions to which I had previously arrived; these things, I say, were strongly corroborative of suspicion, in one who came with the intention to suspect."

"I protracted my visit as long as possible, and, while I maintained a most animated discussion with the Minister, upon a topic which I knew well had never failed to interest and excite him, I kept my attention really riveted upon the letter. In this examination, I committed to memory its external appearance and arrangement in the rack; and also fell, at length, upon a discovery which set at rest whatever trivial doubt I might have entertained. In scrutinizing the edges of the paper, I observed them to be more *chafed* than seemed necessary. They presented the *broken* appearance which is manifested when a stiff paper, having been once folded and pressed with a folder, is refolded in a reversed direction, in the same creases or edges which had formed the original fold. This discovery was sufficient. It was clear to me that the letter had been turned, as a glove, inside out, re-directed, and re-sealed. I bade the Minister good morning, and took my departure at once, leaving a gold snuff-box upon the table."

"The next morning I called for the snuff-box, when we resumed, quite eagerly, the conversation of the preceding day. While thus engaged, however, a loud report, as if of a pistol, was heard immediately beneath the windows of the hotel, and was succeeded by a series of fearful screams, and the shoutings of a mob. D—— rushed to a casement, threw it open, and looked out. In the meantime I stepped to the card-rack, took the letter, put it in my pocket, and replaced it by a *facsimile*, (so far as regards externals) which I had carefully prepared at my lodgings; imitating the D—— cipher, very readily, by means of a seal formed of bread."

"The disturbance in the street had been occasioned by the frantic behaviour of a man with a musket. He had fired it among a crowd of women and children. It proved, however, to have been without ball, and the fellow was suffered to go his way as a lunatic or a drunkard. When he had gone, D—— came from the window, whither I had followed him immediately upon securing the object in view. Soon afterward I bade him farewell. The pretended lunatic was a man in my own pay."

"But what purpose had you," I asked, "in replacing the letter by a *facsimile?* Would it not have been better, at the first visit, to have seized it openly, and departed?"

"D——," replied Dupin, "is a desperate man, and a man of nerve. His hotel, too, is not without attendants devoted to his interests. Had I made the wild attempt you suggest, I might never have left the Ministerial presence alive. The good people of Paris might have heard of me no more. But I had an object apart from these considerations. You know my political prepossessions. In this matter, I act as a partisan of the lady concerned. For eighteen months the Minister has had her in his power. She has now him in hers; since, being unaware that the letter is not in his possession, he will proceed with his exactions as if it was. Thus will he inevitably commit himself, at once, to his political destruction. His downfall, too, will not be more precipitate than awkward. It is all very well to talk about the *facilis descensus Averni;* but in all kinds of climbing, as Catalani said of singing, it is far more easy to get up than to come down. In the present instance I have no sympathy—at least no pity—for him who descends. He is that *monstrum horrendum*, an unprincipled man of genius. I confess, however, that I should like very well to know the precise character of his thoughts, when, being defied by her whom the Prefect terms 'a certain personage,' he is reduced to opening the letter which I left for him in the card-rack."

"How? did you put any thing particular in it?"

"Why—it did not seem altogether right to leave the interior blank—that would have been insulting. D——, at Vienna once, did me an evil turn, which I told him, quite good-humouredly, that I should remember. So, as I knew he would feel some curiosity in regard to the identity of the person who had outwitted him, I thought it a pity not to give him a clue. He is well acquainted with my MS., and I just copied into the middle of the blank sheet the words—

——Un dessein si funeste,
S'il n'est digne d'Atrée, est digne
de Thyeste.

They are to be found in Crébillon's 'Atrée.'"

EDGAR ALLAN POE

(1809–1849) **Web**

A West Point graduate, Poe quit the army to become a professional editor and writer. Poe was a conscious and controlled artist who was best known for his

www

criticism, but who strove to write stories that would appeal to popular audiences. His fiction fascinated later writers from Charles-Pierre Baudelaire to Vladimir Nabokov, who admired and developed Poe's atmospheric rendering of effect and his complex intellectual games.

www   *TOPICS FOR CRITICAL THINKING* Web

1. Why can't the Inspector find the letter?
2. What methods and assumptions make Dupin successful?
3. Who is the story's narrator?
4. How do the layers of the story relate to the layers of deception around the letter?
5. How might the processes of detection in the story relate to processes of literary interpretation?

www   *TOPICS FOR CRITICAL WRITING* Web

1. In what ways does the circulation of the letter parallel the ways a story might circulate in processes of interpretation?
2. In what ways do the characters reveal their own desires in the ways they search for the letter? How is this an analogy for the process of reading?

Desire and Interpretation

Poe's detective, Monsieur Dupin, is able to see the forest for the trees. He can do this because, unlike the Inspector, he seems to have freed himself from presuppositions about the proper places to hide purloined documents. The Inspector doggedly persists in his "close" reading, examining details and deducing the presence of a foreign object through calculations about space. In contrast, Dupin's method consists of identifying with (putting himself in the place of) the various figures—the Queen, the Minister—who have tried to hide the letter. Like a good critic (or at least a canny one), Dupin sees the same trick repeated. Both the Queen and the Minister hide the letter by leaving it in clear sight, assuming that the presumptions others make about hiding things will blind them to the object's blatant presence.

If Poe's story on one level is about competing modes of interpretation, on another level it shows some of the dangers of interpretation. In committing herself to one tactic, the Queen exposes herself to the mercy of the savvy "reader," the Minister. In the same way, the Minister exposes himself to the canny Dupin. To whom might Dupin finally expose himself? In interpreting others (or texts), one always leaves oneself open to critique—to being read. And one always reveals a blind spot—the element one cannot see because of the positions one occupies and assumptions one makes.

Those who write about literature know that they inevitably choose certain approaches from which to interpret a text and not others. (One cannot possibly undertake them all at the same time.) Some of what a critic chooses to do is suggested by the text, but some is unconscious and reveals the desires of the critic. Not only does this selection determine the kinds of interpretations that will be possible, it also reveals something about the critic. In any case, interpretation produces another text, which in its turn can become the subject of another interpretation. The perils of interpretation are thus twofold: The choice of subject and approach exposes the desires of the critic; and the critic produces another text that itself becomes subject of another interpretation, one that inevitably will find a blind spot. Students find this out when their interpretations are scrutinized by a teacher just as they have attempted to scrutinize a text. Like Dupin, teachers always find the blind spot.

Critical Perspective: Reader Response Criticism

Because reading is never passive but is influenced by the dynamics of the story and the reader's desires, how readers read and respond to a story provides valuable insights about how a story works. Criticism that focuses on processes of reading and the readers' responses is called **reader response criticism** **Web** . Instead of focusing on the text itself, as does **New Criticism**, reader response criticism emphasizes the role of the reader in a process of interpretation. But such criticism is not simply the collection of individual responses to a text. Rather, many different critics who emphasize the role of the reader use different methodologies (**formalism, psychoanalysis, Marxism, feminism, historicism** **Web**) to account for the ways thinking about how one reads a text might illuminate the text one reads.   *www*

Parables of Reading and Desire, or Seeing What You Want to See

The following stories—Franz Kafka's "A Hunger Artist," Jorge Luis Borges's "The Shape of the Sword," and Gabriel García Márquez's "The Handsomest Drowned Man in the World"—all illustrate the ways people interpret events according to what they want to see. These interpretations are as much about the desires of those who are interpreting as they are about the phenomena they interpret.

FRANZ KAFKA
Translated by Willa and Edwin Muir

A Hunger Artist   (1922)

During these last decades the interest in professional fasting has markedly diminished. It used to pay very well to stage such great performances under one's own management, but today that is quite impossible. We live in a different world now. At one time the whole town took a lively interest in the hunger artist; from day to day of his fast the excitement mounted; everybody wanted to see him at least once a day; there were people who bought season tickets for the last few days and sat from morning till night in front of his small barred cage; even in the nighttime there were visiting hours, when the whole effect was heightened by torch flares; on fine days the cage was set out in the open air, and then it was the children's special treat to see the hunger artist; for their elders he was often just a joke that happened to be in fashion, but the children stood open-mouthed, holding each other's hands for greater security, marvelling at him as he sat there pallid in black tights, with his ribs sticking out so prominently, not even on a seat but down among straw on the ground, sometimes giving a courteous nod, answering questions with a constrained smile, or perhaps stretching an arm through the bars so that one might feel how thin it was, and then again withdrawing deep into himself, paying no attention to anyone or anything, not even to the all-important striking of the clock that was the only piece of furniture in his cage, but merely staring into vacancy with half-shut eyes, now and then taking a sip from a tiny glass of water to moisten his lips.

Besides casual onlookers there were also relays of permanent watchers selected by the public, usually butchers, strangely enough, and it was their task to watch the hunger artist day and night, three of them at a time, in case he should have some secret recourse to nourishment. This was nothing but a formality, instituted to reassure the masses, for the initiates knew well enough that during his fast the artist would never in any circumstances, not even under forcible compulsion, swallow the smallest morsel of food; the honor of his profession forbade it. Not every watcher, of course, was capable of understanding this, there were often groups of night watchers who were very lax in carrying out their duties and deliberately huddled together in a retired corner to play cards with great absorption, obviously intending to give the hunger artist the chance of a little refreshment, which they supposed he could draw from some private hoard. Nothing annoyed the artist more than such watchers; they made him miserable; they made his fast seem unendurable; sometimes he mastered his feebleness sufficiently to sing during their watch for as long as he could keep going, to show them how unjust their suspicions were. But that was of little use; they only wondered at his cleverness in being able to fill his mouth even while singing. Much more to his taste were the watchers who sat close up to the bars, who were not content with the dim night lighting of the hall but focused him in the full glare of the electric pocket torch given them by the impresario. The harsh light did not trouble him at all. In any case he could never sleep properly, and he could always drowse a little, whatever the light, at any hour, even when the hall was thronged with noisy onlookers. He was quite happy at the prospect of spending a sleepless night with such watchers; he was ready to exchange jokes with them, to tell them stories out of his nomadic life, anything at all to keep them awake and demonstrate to them again that he had no eatables in his cage and that he was fasting as not one of them could fast. But his happiest moment was when the morning came and an enormous breakfast was brought them, at his expense, on which they flung themselves with the keen appetite of healthy men after a weary night of wakefulness. Of course there were people who argued that this breakfast was an unfair attempt to bribe the watchers, but that was going rather too far, and when they were invited to take on a night's vigil without a breakfast, merely for the sake of the cause, they made themselves scarce, although they stuck stubbornly to their suspicions.

Such suspicions, anyhow, were a necessary accompaniment to the profession of fasting. No one could possibly watch the hunger artist continuously, day and night, and so no one could produce first-hand evidence that the fast had really been rigorous and continuous; only the artist himself could know that; he was therefore bound to be the sole completely satisfied spectator of his own fast. Yet for other reasons he was never satisfied; it was not perhaps mere fasting that had brought him to such skeleton thinness that many people had regretfully to keep away from his exhibitions, because the sight of him was too much for them, perhaps it was dissatisfaction with himself that had worn him down. For he alone knew, what no other initiate knew, how easy it was to fast. It was the easiest thing in the world. He made no secret of this, yet people did not believe him; at the best they set him down as modest, most of them, however, thought he was out for publicity or else was some kind of cheat who found it easy to fast because he had discovered a way of making it easy, and then had the impudence to admit the fact, more or less. He had to put up with all that, and in the course of time had got used to it, but his inner dissatisfaction always rankled, and never yet, after any term of fasting—this must be granted to his credit—had he left the cage of his own free will. The longest period of fasting was fixed by his impresario at forty days, beyond that term he was not allowed to go, not even in great cities, and there was good reason for it, too. Experience had proved that for about forty days the interest of the public could be stimulated by a steadily increasing pressure of advertisement, but after that the town began to lose interest, sympathetic support began notably to fall off; there were of course local variations as between one town and another or one country and another, but as a general rule forty days marked the limit. So on the fortieth day the flower-bedecked cage was opened, enthusiastic spectators filled the hall, a military band played, two doctors entered the cage to measure the results of the fast, which were announced through a megaphone, and finally two young ladies appeared, blissful at having been selected for the honor, to help the hunger artist down the few steps leading to a small table on which was spread a carefully chosen invalid repast. And at this very moment the artist always turned stubborn. True, he would entrust his bony arms to the outstretched helping hands of the ladies bending over him, but stand up he would not. Why stop fasting at this particular moment, after forty days of it? He had held out for a long time, an illimitably long time; why stop now, when he was in his best fasting form, or rather, not yet quite in his best fasting form? Why should he be cheated of the fame he would get for fasting longer, for being not only the record hunger artist of all time, which presumably he was already, but for beating his own record by a performance beyond human imagination, since he felt that there were no limits to his capacity for fasting? His public pretended to admire him so much, why should it have so little patience with him; if he could endure fasting longer, why shouldn't the public endure it? Besides, he was tired, he was comfortable sitting in the straw, and now he was supposed to lift himself to his full height and go down to a meal the very thought of which gave him a nausea that only the presence of the ladies kept him from betraying, and even that with an effort. And he looked up into the eyes of the ladies who were apparently so friendly and in reality so cruel, and shook his head, which felt too heavy on its strengthless neck. But then there happened yet again what always happened. The impresario came forward, without a word—for the band made speech impossible—lifted his arms in the air above the artist, as if inviting Heaven to look down upon its creature here in the straw, this suffering martyr, which indeed he was, although in quite another sense; grasped him round the emaciated waist, with exaggerated caution, so that the frail condition he was in might be appreciated; and committed him to the care of the blenching ladies, not without secretly giving him a shaking so that his legs and body tottered and swayed. The artist now submitted completely; his head lolled on his breast as if it had landed there by chance; his body was hollowed out; his legs in a spasm of self-preservation clung close to each other at the knees, yet scraped on the ground as if it were not really solid ground, as if they were only trying to find solid ground; and the whole weight of his body, a featherweight after all, relapsed onto one of the ladies, who, looking round for help and panting a little—this post of honor was not at all what she had expected it to be—first stretched her neck as far as she could to keep her face at least free from contact with the artist, then finding this impossible, and her more fortunate companion not coming to her aid but merely holding extended on her own trembling hand the little bunch of knucklebones that was the artist's, to the great delight of the spectators burst into tears and had to be replaced by an attendant who had long been stationed in readiness. Then came the food, a little of which the impresario managed to get between the artist's lips, while he sat in a kind of half-fainting trance, to the accompaniment of cheerful patter designed to distract the public's attention from the artist's condition; after that, a toast was drunk to the public, supposedly prompted by a whisper from the artist in the impresario's ear; the band confirmed it with a mighty flourish, the spectators melted away, and no one had any cause to be dissatisfied with the proceedings, no one except the hunger artist himself, he only, as always.

So he lived for many years, with small regular intervals of recuperation, in visible glory, honored by the world, yet in spite of that troubled in spirit, and all the more troubled because no one would take his trouble seriously. What comfort could he possibly need? What more could he possibly wish for? And if some good-natured person, feeling sorry for him, tried to console him by pointing out that his melancholy was probably caused by fasting, it could happen, especially when he had been fasting for some time, that he reacted with an outburst of fury and to the general alarm began to shake the bars of his cage like a wild animal. Yet the impresario had a way of punishing these outbreaks which he rather enjoyed putting into operation. He would apologize publicly for the artist's behavior, which was only to be excused, he admitted, because of the irritability caused by fasting; a condition hardly to be understood by well-fed people; then by natural transition he went on to mention the artist's equally incomprehensible boast that he could fast for much longer than he was doing; he praised the high ambition, the good will, the great self-denial undoubtedly implicit in such a statement; and then quite simply countered it by bringing out photographs, which were also on sale to the public, showing the artist on the fortieth day of a fast lying in bed almost dead from exhaustion. This perversion of the truth, familiar to the artist though it was, always unnerved him afresh and proved too much for him. What was a consequence of the premature ending of his fast was here presented as the cause of it! To fight against this lack of understanding, against a whole world of non-understanding, was impossible. Time and again in good faith he stood by the bars listening to the impresario, but as soon as the photographs appeared he always let go and sank with a groan back on to his straw, and the reassured public could once more come close and gaze at him.

A few years later when the witnesses of such scenes called them to mind, 5 they often failed to understand themselves at all. For meanwhile the aforementioned change in public interest had set in; it seemed to happen almost overnight; there may have been profound causes for it, but who was going to bother about that; at any rate the pampered hunger artist suddenly found himself deserted one fine day by the amusement seekers, who went streaming past him to other more favored attractions. For the last time the impresario hurried him over half Europe to discover whether the old interest might still survive here and there; all in vain; everywhere, as if by secret agreement, a positive revulsion from professional fasting was in evidence. Of course it could not really have sprung up so suddenly as all that, and many premonitory symptoms which had not been sufficiently remarked or suppressed during the rush and glitter of success now came retrospectively to mind, but it was now too late to take any countermeasures. Fasting would surely come into fashion again at some future date, yet that was no comfort for those living in the present. What, then, was the hunger artist to do? He had been applauded by thousands in his time and could hardly come down to showing himself in a street booth at village fairs, and as for adopting another profession, he was not only too old for that but too fanatically devoted to fasting. So he took leave of the impresario, his partner in an unparalleled career, and hired himself to a large circus; in order to spare his own feelings he avoided reading the conditions of his contract.

A large circus with its enormous traffic in replacing and recruiting men, animals and apparatus can always find a use for people at any time, even for a hunger artist, provided of course that he does not ask too much, and in this particular case anyhow it was not only the artist who was taken on but his famous and long-known name as well; indeed considering the peculiar nature of his performance, which was not impaired by advancing age, it could not be objected that here was an artist past his prime, no longer at the height of his professional skill, seeking a refuge in some quiet corner of a circus; on the contrary, the hunger artist averred that he could fast as well as ever, which was entirely credible; he even alleged that if he were allowed to fast as he liked, and this was at once promised him without more ado, he could astound the world by establishing a record never yet achieved, a statement which certainly provoked a smile among the other professionals, since it left out of account the change in public opinion, which the hunger artist in his zeal conveniently forgot.

He had not, however, actually lost his sense of the real situation and took it as a matter of course that he and his cage should be stationed, not in the middle of the ring as a main attraction, but outside, near the animal cages, on a site that was after all easily accessible. Large and gaily painted placards made a frame for the cage and announced what was to be seen inside it. When the public came thronging out in the intervals to see the animals, they could hardly avoid passing the hunger artist's cage and stopping there for a moment, perhaps they might even have stayed longer had not those pressing behind them in the narrow gangway, who did not understand why they should be held up on their way towards the excitements of the menagerie, made it impossible for anyone to stand gazing quietly for any length of time. And that was the reason why the hunger artist, who had of course been looking forward to these visiting hours as the main achievement of his life, began instead to shrink from them. At first he could hardly wait for the intervals; it was exhilarating to watch the crowds come streaming his way, until only too soon—not even the most obstinate self-deception, clung to almost consciously, could hold out against the fact—the conviction was borne in upon him that these people, most of them, to judge from their actions, again and again, without exception, were all on their way to the menagerie. And the first sight of them from the distance remained the best. For when they reached his cage he was at once deafened by the storm of shouting and abuse that arose from the two contending factions, which renewed themselves continuously, of those who wanted to stop and stare at him—he soon began to dislike them more than the others—not out of real interest but only out of obstinate self-assertiveness, and those who wanted to go straight on to the animals. When the first great rush was past, the stragglers came along, and these, whom nothing could have prevented from stopping to look at him as long as they had breath, raced past with long strides, hardly even glancing at him, in their haste to get to the menagerie in time. And all too rarely did it happen that he had a stroke of luck, when some father of a family fetched up before him with his children, pointed a finger at the hunger artist and explained at length what the phenomenon meant, telling stories of earlier years when he himself had watched similar but much more thrilling performances, and the children, still rather uncomprehending, since neither inside nor outside school had they been sufficiently prepared for this lesson—what did they care about fasting?—yet showed by the brightness of their intent eyes that new and better times might be coming. Perhaps, said the hunger artist to himself many a time, things would be a little better if his cage were set not quite so near the menagerie. That made it too easy for people to make their choice, to say nothing of what he suffered from the stench of the menagerie, the animals' restlessness by night, the carrying past of raw lumps of flesh for the beasts of prey, the roaring at feeding times, which depressed him continually. But he did not dare to lodge a complaint with the management; after all, he had the animals to thank for the troops of people who passed his cage, among whom there might always be one here and there to take an interest in him, and who could tell where they might seclude him if he called attention to his existence and thereby to the fact that, strictly speaking, he was only an impediment on the way to the menagerie.

A small impediment, to be sure, one that grew steadily less. People grew familiar with the strange idea that they could be expected, in times like these, to take an interest in a hunger artist, and with this familiarity the verdict went out against him. He might fast as much as he could, and he did so; but nothing could save him now, people passed him by. Just try to explain to anyone the art of fasting! Anyone who has no feeling for it cannot be made to understand it. The fine placards grew dirty and illegible, they were torn down; the little notice board telling the number of fast days achieved, which at first was changed carefully every day, had long stayed at the same figure, for after the first few weeks even this small task seemed pointless to the staff; and so the artist simply fasted on and on, as he had once dreamed of doing, and it was no trouble to him, just as he had always foretold, but no one counted the days, no one, not even the artist himself, knew what records he was already breaking, and his heart grew heavy. And when once in a time some leisurely passer-by stopped, made merry over the old figure on the board and spoke of swindling, that was in its way the stupidest lie ever invented by indifference and inborn malice, since it was not the hunger artist who was cheating; he was working honestly, but the world was cheating him of his reward.

Many more days went by, however, and that too came to an end. An overseer's eye fell on the cage one day and he asked the attendants why this perfectly good stage should be left standing there unused with dirty straw inside it; nobody knew, until one man, helped out by the notice board, remembered about the hunger artist. They poked into the straw with sticks and found him in it. "Are you still fasting?" asked the overseer. "When on earth do you mean to stop?" "Forgive me, everybody," whispered the hunger artist; only the overseer, who had his ear to the bars, understood him. "Of course," said the overseer, and tapped his forehead with a finger to let the attendants know what state the man was in, "we forgive you." "I always wanted you to admire my fasting," said the hunger artist. "We do admire it," said the overseer, affably. "But you shouldn't admire it," said the hunger artist. "Well, then we don't admire it," said the overseer, "but why shouldn't we admire it?" "Because I have to fast, I can't help it," said the hunger artist. "What a fellow you are," said the overseer, "and why can't you help it?" "Because," said the hunger artist, lifting his head a little and speaking, with his lips pursed, as if for a kiss, right into the overseer's ear, so that no syllable might be lost, "because I couldn't find the food I liked. If I had found it, believe me, I should have made no fuss and stuffed myself like you or anyone else." These were his last words, but in his dimming eyes remained the firm though no longer proud persuasion that he was still continuing to fast.

"Well, clear this out now!" said the overseer, and they buried the hunger 10 artist, straw and all. Into the cage they put a young panther. Even the most insensitive felt it refreshing to see this wild creature leaping around the cage that had so long been dreary. The panther was all right. The food he liked was brought him without hesitation by the attendants; he seemed not even to miss his freedom; his noble body, furnished almost to the bursting point with all that it needed, seemed to carry freedom around with it too; somewhere in his jaws it seemed to lurk; and the joy of life streamed with such ardent passion from his throat that for the onlookers it was not easy to stand the shock of it. But they braced themselves, crowded round the cage, and did not want ever to move away.

——— **FRANZ KAFKA** ———

www

(1883–1924) Web

A lawyer who worked for an insurance company, Kafka lived in Czechoslovakia and wrote in German. Never famous in his own lifetime, his vision of culture seemed more in tune with post–World War II horrors such as recognition of Nazi genocide and the terrors of the atomic bomb.

www

TOPICS FOR CRITICAL THINKING Web

1. In what ways does the hunger artist's performance require the active involvement of his audience?
2. What various interpretations of the hunger artist's practices do spectators offer?
3. In what ways is the hunger artist an artist?
4. How does context change the way spectators view the hunger artist?
5. If "The Hunger Artist" comments on how spectators interpret the artist's performance, what kinds of interpretation are possible for the story's readers?
6. What comments does this story make about the desires of the audience/reader?

www

TOPICS FOR CRITICAL WRITING Web

1. What does "The Hunger Artist" suggest about the relation between art and interpretation?
2. The artist suggests that photos taken at the end of the fast are evidence of the damage done by ending the fast rather than evidence that the fast should be ended. What does this reversal of cause and effect suggest about the relations between art, interpretation, and truth?

JORGE LUIS BORGES

Translated by Donald A. Yates

The Shape of the Sword   *(1944)*

A spiteful scar crossed his face: an ash-colored and nearly perfect arc that creased his temple at one tip and his cheek at the other. His real name is of no importance; everyone in Tacuarembó called him the "Englishman from La Colorada." Cardoso, the owner of those fields, refused to sell them: I understand that the Englishman resorted to an unexpected argument: he confided to Cardoso the secret of the scar. The Englishman came from the border, from Río Grande Del Sur; there are many who say that in Brazil he had been a smuggler. The fields were overgrown with grass, the waterholes brackish; the Englishman, in order to correct those deficiencies, worked fully as hard as his laborers. They say that he was severe to the point of cruelty, but scrupulously just. They say also that he drank: a few times a year he locked himself into an upper room, not to emerge until two or three days later as if from a battle or from vertigo, pale, trembling, confused and as authoritarian as ever. I remember the glacial eyes, the energetic leanness, the gray mustache. He had no dealings with anyone; it is a fact that his Spanish was rudimentary and cluttered with Brazilian. Aside from a business letter or some pamphlet, he received no mail.

The last time I passed through the northern provinces, a sudden overflowing of the Caraguatá stream compelled me to spend the night at La Colorada. Within a few moments, I seemed to sense that my appearance was inopportune; I tried to ingratiate myself with the Englishman; I resorted to the least discerning of passions: patriotism. I claimed as invincible a country with such a spirit as England's. My companion agreed, but added with a smile that he was not English. He was Irish, from Dungarvan. Having said this, he stopped short, as if he had revealed a secret.

After dinner we went outside to look at the sky. It had cleared up, but beyond the low hills the southern sky, streaked and gashed by lightning, was conceiving another storm. Into the cleared up dining room the boy who had served dinner brought a bottle of rum. We drank for some time, in silence.

I don't know what time it must have been when I observed that I was drunk; I don't know what inspiration or what exultation or tedium made me mention the scar. The Englishman's face changed its expression; for a few seconds I thought he was going to throw me out of the house. At length he said in his normal voice:

"I'll tell you the history of my scar under one condition: that of not mitigating one bit of the opprobrium, of the infamous circumstances." 5

I agreed. This is the story that he told me, mixing his English with Spanish, and even with Portuguese:

"Around 1922, in one of the cities of Connaught, I was one of the many who were conspiring for the independence of Ireland. Of my comrades, some are still living, dedicated to peaceful pursuits; others, paradoxically, are fighting on desert and sea under the English flag; another, the most worthy, died in the courtyard of a barracks, at dawn, shot by men filled with sleep; still others (not the most unfortunate) met their destiny in the anonymous and almost secret battles of the civil war. We were Republicans, Catholics; we were, I suspect, Romantics. Ireland was for us not only the utopian future and the intolerable present; it was a bitter and cherished mythology, it was the circular towers and the red marshes, it was the repudiation of Parnell and the enormous epic poems which sang of the robbing of bulls which in another incarnation were heroes and in others fish and mountains . . . One afternoon I will never forget, an affiliate from Munster joined us: one John Vincent Moon.

"He was scarcely twenty years old. He was slender and flaccid at the same time; he gave the uncomfortable impression of being invertebrate. He had studied with fervor and with vanity nearly every page of Lord knows what Communist manual; he made use of dialectical materialism to put an end to any discussion whatever. The reasons one can have for hating another man, or for loving him, are infinite: Moon reduced the history of the universe to a sordid economic conflict. He affirmed that the revolution was predestined to succeed. I told him that for a gentleman only lost causes should be attractive . . . Night had already fallen; we continued our disagreement in the hall, on the stairs, then along the vague streets. The judgments Moon emitted impressed me less than his irrefutable, apodictic note. The new comrade did not discuss: he dictated opinions with scorn and with a certain anger.

"As we were arriving at the outlying houses, a sudden burst of gunfire stunned us. (Either before or afterwards we skirted the blank wall of a factory or barracks.) We moved into an unpaved street; a soldier, huge in the firelight, came out of a burning hut. Crying out, he ordered us to stop. I quickened my pace; my companion did not follow. I turned around: John Vincent Moon was motionless, fascinated, as if eternized by fear. I then ran back and knocked the soldier to the ground with one blow, shook Vincent Moon, insulted him and ordered him to follow. I had to take him by the arm; the passion of fear had rendered him helpless. We fled, into the night pierced by flames. A rifle volley reached out for us, and a bullet nicked Moon's right shoulder; as we were fleeing amid pines, he broke out in weak sobbing.

"In that fall of 1923 I had taken shelter in General Berkeley's country 10 house. The general (whom I had never seen) was carrying out some administrative assignment or other in Bengal; the house was less than a century old, but it was decayed and shadowy and flourished in puzzling corridors and in pointless antechambers. The museum and the huge library usurped the first floor: controversial and uncongenial books which in some manner are the history of the nineteenth century; scimitars from Nishapur, along whose captured arcs there seemed to persist still the wind and violence of battle. We entered (I seem to recall) through the rear. Moon, trembling, his mouth parched, murmured that the events of the night were interesting; I dressed his wound and brought him a cup of tea; I was able to determine that his 'wound' was superficial. Suddenly he stammered in bewilderment:

"'You know, you ran a terrible risk.'

"I told him not to worry about it. (The habit of the civil war had incited me to act as I did; besides, the capture of a single member could endanger our cause.)

"By the following day Moon had recovered his poise. He accepted a cigarette and subjected me to a severe interrogation on the 'economic resources of our revolutionary party.' His questions were very lucid; I told him (truthfully) that the situation was serious. Deep bursts of rifle fire agitated the south. I told Moon our comrades were waiting for us. My overcoat and my revolver were in my room; when I returned, I found Moon stretched out on the sofa, his eyes closed. He imagined he had a fever; he invoked a painful spasm in his shoulder.

"At that moment I understood that his cowardice was irreparable. I clumsily entreated him to take care of himself and went out. This frightened man mortified me, as if I were the coward, not Vincent Moon. Whatever one man does, it is as if all men did it. For that reason it is not unfair that one disobedience in a garden should contaminate all humanity; for that reason it is not unjust that the crucifixion of a single Jew should be sufficient to save it. Perhaps Schopenhauer was right: I am all other men, any man is all men, Shakespeare is in some manner the miserable John Vincent Moon.

"Nine days we spent in the general's enormous house. Of the agonies and   15
the successes of the war I shall not speak: I propose to relate the history of the scar that insults me. In my memory, those nine days form only a single day, save for the next to the last, when our men broke into a barracks and we were able to avenge precisely the sixteen comrades who had been machine-gunned in Elphin. I slipped out of the house towards dawn, in the confusion of daybreak. At nightfall I was back. My companion was waiting for me upstairs: his wound did not permit him to descend to the ground floor. I recall him having some volume of strategy in his hand, F. N. Maude or Clausewitz. 'The weapon I prefer is the artillery,' he confessed to me one night. He inquired into our plans; he liked to censure them or revise them. He also was accustomed to denouncing 'our deplorable economic basis'; dogmatic and gloomy, he predicted the disastrous end. '*C'est une affaire flambée*,' he murmured. In order to show that he was indifferent to being a physical coward, he magnified his mental arrogance. In this way, for good or for bad, nine days elapsed.

"On the tenth day the city fell definitely to the Black and Tans. Tall, silent horsemen patrolled the roads; ashes and smoke rode on the wind; on the corner I saw a corpse thrown to the ground, an impression less firm in my memory than that of a dummy on which the soldiers endlessly practiced their marksmanship, in the middle of the square . . . I had left when dawn was in the sky; before noon I returned. Moon, in the library, was speaking with someone; the tone of his voice told me he was talking on the telephone. Then I heard my name; then, that I would return at seven; then, the suggestion that they should arrest me as I was crossing the garden. My reasonable friend was reasonably selling me out. I heard him demand guarantees of personal safety.

"Here my story is confused and becomes lost. I know that I pursued the informer along the black, nightmarish halls and along deep stairways of dizziness. Moon knew the house very well, much better than I. One or two times I lost him. I cornered him before the soldiers stopped me. From one of the general's collections of arms I tore a cutlass: with that half moon I carved into his face forever a half moon of blood. Borges, to you, a stranger, I have made this confession. Your contempt does not grieve me so much."

Here the narrator stopped. I noticed that his hands were shaking.

"And Moon?" I asked him.

"He collected his Judas money and fled to Brazil. That afternoon, in the   20
square, he saw a dummy shot up by some drunken men."

I waited in vain for the rest of the story. Finally I told him to go on.

Then a sob went through his body; and with a weak gentleness he pointed to the whitish curved scar.

"You don't believe me?" he stammered. "Don't you see that I carry written on my face the mark of my infamy? I have told you the story thus so that

you would hear me to the end. I denounced the man who protected me: I am
Vincent Moon. Now despise me."

www

JORGE LUIS BORGES
(1899–1986) Web

Argentinian Borges was brought up speaking both Spanish and English. Educated in Europe, Borges returned to Argentina to pursue a lengthy and innovative literary career. Beginning to go blind in his thirties, Borges began writing in
earnest, developing the metafictional style that would become his legacy.

www

TOPICS FOR CRITICAL THINKING Web

1. In what ways does the narrator try to read or interpret the "Englishman from
   Colorado"?
2. When are his readings wrong, and why?
3. What clues enable the reader to recognize who the real narrator of the enframed
   story is?
4. How does our interpretation of the "Englishman's" story change when we learn
   who is narrating?
5. How does the shift in the identity of the narrator invite a rereading of the entire
   story?
6. In what different ways are we likely to understand the "Englishman's" behaviors before and after he tells the story?

www

TOPICS FOR CRITICAL WRITING Web

1. In what different ways can one interpret the scar?
2. What does the story say about the assumptions of readers?

GABRIEL GARCÍA MÁRQUEZ
Translated by Gregory Rebassa

The Handsomest Drowned Man in the World   *(1970)*
A Tale for Children

The first children who saw the dark and slinky bulge approaching through the
sea let themselves think it was an empty ship. Then they saw it had no flags or
masts and they thought it was a whale. But when it washed up on the beach,
they removed the clumps of seaweed, the jellyfish tentacles, and the remains
of fish and flotsam, and only then did they see that it was a drowned man.

They had been playing with him all afternoon, burying him in the sand
and digging him up again, when someone chanced to see them and spread the
alarm in the village. The men who carried him to the nearest house noticed

the he weighed more than any dead man they had ever known, almost as much as a horse, and they said to each other that maybe he'd been floating too long and the water had got into his bones. When they laid him on the floor they said he'd been taller than all other men because there was barely enough room for him in the house, but they thought that maybe the ability to keep on growing after death was part of the nature of certain drowned men. He had the smell of the sea about him and only his shape gave one to suppose that it was the corpse of a human being, because the skin was covered with a crust of mud and scales.

They did not even have to clean off his face to know that the dead man was a stranger. The village was made up of only twenty-odd wooden houses that had stone courtyards with no flowers and which were spread about on the end of a desertlike cape. There was so little land that mothers always went about with the fear that the wind would carry off their children and the few dead that the years had caused among them had to be thrown off the cliffs. But the sea was calm and bountiful and all the men fit into seven boats. So when they found the drowned man they simply had to look at one another to see that they were all there. That night they did not go out to work at sea. While the men went to find out if anyone was missing in neighboring villages, the women stayed behind to care for the drowned man. They took the mud off with grass swabs, they removed the underwater stones entangled in his hair, and they scraped the crust off with tools used for scaling fish. As they were doing that they noticed that the vegetation on him came from faraway oceans and deep water and that his clothes were in tatters, as if he had sailed through labyrinths of coral. They noticed too that he bore his death with pride, for he did not have the lonely look of other drowned men who came out of the sea or that haggard, needy look of men who drowned in rivers. But only when they finished cleaning him off did they become aware of the kind of man he was and it left them breathless. Not only was he the tallest, strongest, most virile, and best built man they had ever seen, but even though they were looking at him there was no room for him in their imagination.

They could not find a bed in the village large enough to lay him on nor was there a table solid enough to use for his wake. The tallest men's holiday pants would not fit him, nor the fattest ones' Sunday shirts, nor the shoes of the one with the biggest feet. Fascinated by his huge size and his beauty, the women then decided to make him some pants from a large piece of sail and a shirt from some bridal brabant linen so that he could continue through his death with dignity. As they sewed, sitting in a circle and gazing at the corpse between stitches, it seemed to them that the wind had never been so steady nor the sea so restless as on that night and they supposed that the change had something to do with the dead man. They thought that if that magnificent man had lived in the village, his house would have had the widest doors, the highest ceiling, and the strongest floor, his bedstead would have been made from a midship frame held together by iron bolts, and his wife would have been the happiest woman. They thought that he would have had so much authority that he could have drawn fish out of the sea simply by calling their names and that he would have put so much work into his land that springs would have burst forth from among the rocks so that he would have been able to plant flowers on the cliffs. They secretly compared him to their own men, thinking that for all their lives theirs were incapable of doing what he could do in one night, and they ended up dismissing them deep in their hearts as the weakest, meanest, and most useless creatures on earth. They were wandering through that maze of fantasy when the oldest woman, who as the oldest had looked upon the drowned man with more compassion than passion, sighed:

"He has the face of someone called Esteban."   5

It was true. Most of them had only to take another look at him to see that he could not have any other name. The more stubborn among them, who were the youngest, still lived for a few hours with the illusion that when they put his clothes on and he lay among the flowers in patent leather shoes his name might be Lautaro. But it was a vain illusion. There had not been enough canvas, the poorly cut and worse sewn pants were too tight, and the hidden strength of his heart popped the buttons on his shirt. After midnight the whistling of the wind died down and the sea fell into its Wednesday drowsiness. The silence put an end to any last doubts: he was Esteban. The women who had dressed him, who had combed his hair, had cut his nails and shaved him were unable to hold back a shudder of pity when they had to resign themselves to his being dragged along the ground. It was then that they understood how unhappy he must have been with that huge body since it bothered him even after death. They could see him in life, condemned to go through doors sideways, cracking his head on crossbeams, remaining on his feet during visits, not knowing what to do with his soft, pink, sea lion hands while the lady of the house looked for her most resistant chair and begged him, frightened to death, sit here, Esteban, please, and he, leaning against the wall, smiling, don't bother, ma'am, I'm fine where I am, his heels raw and his back roasted from having done the same thing so many times whenever he paid a visit, don't bother, ma'am, I'm fine where I am, just to avoid the embarrassment of breaking up the chair, and never knowing perhaps that the ones who said don't go, Esteban, at least wait till the coffee's ready, where the ones who later on would whisper the big boob finally left, how nice, the handsome fool has gone. That was what the women were thinking beside the body a little before dawn. Later, when they covered his face with a handkerchief so that the light would not bother him, he looked so forever dead, so defenseless, so much like their men that the first furrows of tears opened in their hearts. It was one of the younger ones who began the weeping. The others, coming to, went from sighs to wails, and the more they sobbed the more they felt like weeping, because the drowned man was becoming all the more Esteban for them, and so they wept so much, for he was the most destitute, most peaceful, and most obliging man on earth, poor Esteban. So when the men returned with the news that the drowned man was not from the neighboring villages either, the women felt an opening of jubilation in the midst of their tears.

"Praise the Lord," they sighed, "he's ours!"

The men thought the fuss was only womanish frivolity. Fatigued because of the difficult nighttime inquiries, all they wanted was to get rid of the bother of the newcomer once and for all before the sun grew strong on that arid, windless day. They improvised a litter with the remains of foremasts and gaffs, tying it together with rigging so that it would bear the weight of the body until they reached the cliffs. They wanted to tie the anchor from a cargo ship to him so that he would sink easily into the deepest waves, where fish are blind and divers die of nostalgia, and bad currents would not bring him back to shore, as had happened with other bodies. But the more they hurried, the more the women thought of ways to waste time. They walked about like startled hens, pecking with the sea charms on their breasts, some interfering on one side to put a scapular of the good wind on the drowned man, some on the other side to put a wrist compass on him, and after a great deal of *get away from there, woman, stay out of the way, look, you almost made me fall on top of the dead man*, the men began to feel mistrust in their livers and started grumbling about why so many main-altar decorations for a stranger, because no matter how many nails and holy-water jars he had on him, the sharks would chew him all the same, but the women kept piling on their junk relics, running back and forth, stumbling, while they released in sighs what they did not in tears, so that the men finally exploded with *since when has there ever been such a fuss over a drifting corpse, a drowned nobody, a piece of cold Wednesday meat*. One of the women, mortified by so much lack of care, then removed the handkerchief from the dead man's face and the men were left breathless too.

He was Esteban. It was not necessary to repeat it for them to recognize him. If they had been told Sir Walter Raleigh, even they might have been impressed with his gringo accent, the macaw on his shoulder, his cannibal-killing blunderbuss, but there could be only one Esteban in the world and there he was, stretched out like a sperm whale, shoeless, wearing the pants of an undersized child, and with those stony nails that had to be cut with a knife. They only had to take the handkerchief off his face to see that he was ashamed, that it was not his fault that he was so big or so heavy or so handsome, and if he had known that this was going to happen, he would have looked for a more discreet place to drown in, seriously, I even would have tied the anchor off a galleon around my neck and staggered off a cliff like someone who doesn't like things in order not to be upsetting people now with this Wednesday dead body, as you people say, in order not to be bothering anyone with this filthy piece of cold meat that doesn't have anything to do with me. There was so much truth in his manner that even the most mistrustful men, the ones who felt the bitterness of endless nights at sea fearing that their women would tire of dreaming about them and begin to dream of drowned men, even they and others who were harder still shuddered in the marrow of their bones at Esteban's sincerity.

That was how they came to hold the most splendid funeral they could 10
conceive of for an abandoned drowned man. Some women who had gone to get flowers in the neighboring villages returned with other women who could not believe what they had been told, and those women went back for more flowers when they saw the dead man, and they brought more and more until there were so many flowers and so many people that it was hard to walk about. At the final moment it pained them to return him to the waters as an orphan and they chose a father and mother from among the best people, and aunts

and uncles and cousins, so that through him all the inhabitants of the village became kinsmen. Some sailors who heard weeping from a distance went off course and people heard of one who had himself tied to the mainmast, remembering ancient fables about sirens. While they fought for the privilege of carrying him on their shoulders along the steep escarpment by the cliffs, men and women became aware for the first time of the desolation of their streets, the dryness of their courtyards, the narrowness of their dreams as they faced the splendor and beauty of their drowned man. They let him go without an anchor so that he could come back if he wished and whenever he wished, and they all held their breath for the fraction of centuries the body took to fall into the abyss. They did not need to look at one another to realize that they were no longer all present, that they would never be. But they also knew that everything would be different from then on, that their houses would have wider doors, higher ceilings, and stronger floors so that Esteben's memory could go everywhere without bumping into beams and so that no one in the future would dare whisper the big boob finally died, too bad, the handsome fool has finally died, because they were going to paint their house fronts gay colors to make Esteban's memory eternal and they were going to break their backs digging for springs among the stones and planting flowers on the cliffs so that in future years at dawn the passengers on great liners would awaken, suffocated by the smell of gardens on the high seas, and the captain would have to come down from the bridge in his dress uniform, with his astrolabe, his pole star, and his row of war medals and, pointing to the promontory of roses on the horizon, he would say in fourteen languages, look there, where the wind is so peaceful now that it's gone to sleep beneath the beds, over there, where the sun's so bright that the sunflowers don't know which way to turn, yes, that's Esteban's village.

GABRIEL GARCÍA MÁRQUEZ

www   *(b. 1928)* **Web**

Educated in law and influenced by Franz Kafka and William Faulkner, García Márquez worked as a journalist and became a writer who continued the development of magical realism. Always interested in politics, García Márquez worked as a leftist journalist while writing the novels that resulted in his winning the Nobel Prize in literature in 1982.

www   *TOPICS FOR CRITICAL THINKING* **Web**

1. How does the description of the drowned man change through the course of the story?
2. What do changes in the drowned man tell us about the villagers themselves?
3. What changes in the village come about through the villagers' interpretations of the drowned man?
4. What is the significance of the fact that the drowned man is very large?
5. Why is this story subtitled "A Tale for Children"?

TOPIC FOR CRITICAL WRITING [Web]

What does "The Handsomest Drowned Man in the World" suggest about the relations between perception and interpretation? Desire and interpretation?

Reading and Misreading

The effect of some stories relies on revealing how characters' desires produce interpretations, making the readers of the story the wise and masterful consumers of such events. Some stories show how characters within stories rely on the misreadings that a character assumes other characters will make. Other stories work by catching up readers in their own desires and then revealing their mistakes at the end.

While the processes of reading and interpretation are bound up with the reader's desire, they are also products of cultural assumptions (ideologies) of race, gender, and class. Notions about how people of different races, genders, classes, and sexual orientations look and act often determine how we identify and relate to people we don't know. Stories that feature such misinterpretations illustrate the extent to which preconceptions and essentialized ideas about such categories shape the ways certain characters are treated. In other words, reading is not always something that must occur in relation to a text.

Often a story's examination of the biases of reading provides a necessary commentary on various kinds of social and cultural oppression. For this reason the problems of reading become one way to examine larger assumptions about others—such as stereotypes and the causes of miscommunication and misunderstanding. Stories treating issues of race, gender, and sexuality often bring the acts of reading, interpreting, and misreading into question. These readings or misreadings based on cultural stereotypes may suggest entire histories, as in María Cristina Mena's "The Vine-Leaf" (1914), which asks readers to follow sets of assumptions made by an enframed narrator about the identity and motives of a female character. Misreadings may enable characters to fool other characters by taking advantage of their misinterpretations or might provide the basis for ironic commentary on the misreading characters' investments and assumptions about gender and sexuality, as in Colette's "The Hidden Woman" (1924) and Dorothy Parker's "The Waltz" (1933).

ᏫᏫᏫ

MARÍA CRISTINA MENA

The Vine-Leaf   *(1914)*

It is a saying in the capital of Mexico that Dr. Malsufrido carries more family secrets under his hat than any archbishop, which applies, of course, to family secrets of the rich. The poor have no family secrets, or none that Dr. Malsufrido would trouble to carry under his hat.

The doctor's hat is, appropriately enough, uncommonly capacious, rising very high, and sinking so low that it seems to be supported by his ears and eyebrows, and it has a furry look, as if it had been brushed the wrong way, which is perhaps what happens to it if it is ever brushed at all. When the doctor takes it off, the family secrets do not fly out like a flock of parrots, but remain nicely bottled up beneath a dome of old and highly polished ivory, which, with its unbroken fringe of dyed black hair, has the effect of a tonsure; and then Dr. Malsufrido looks like one of the early saints. I've forgotten which one.

So edifying is his personality that, when he marches into a sick-room, the forces of disease and infirmity march out of it, and do not dare to return until he has taken his leave. In fact, it is well known that none of his patients has ever had the bad manners to die in his presence.

If you will believe him, he is almost ninety years old, and everybody knows that he has been dosing good Mexicans for half a century. He is forgiven for being a Spaniard on account of a legend that he physicked royalty in his time, and that a certain princess—but that has nothing to do with this story.

It is sure he has a courtly way with him that captivates his female patients, 5 of whom he speaks as his *penitentes*, insisting on confession as a prerequisite of diagnosis, and declaring that the physician who undertakes to cure a woman's body without reference to her soul is a more abominable kill-healthy than the famous *Dr. Sangrado*, who taught medicine to *Gil Blas.*

"Describe me the symptoms of your conscience, *Señora*," he will say. "Fix yourself that I shall forget one tenth of what you tell me."

"But what of the other nine tenths, Doctor?" the troubled lady will exclaim.

"The other nine tenths I shall take care not to believe," Dr. Malsufrido will reply, with a roar of laughter. And sometimes he will add:

"Do not confess your neighbor's sins; the doctor will have enough with your own."

When an inexperienced one fears to become a *penitente* lest that terrible 10 old doctor betray her confidence, he reassures her as to his discretion, and at the same time takes her mind off her anxieties by telling her the story of his first patient.

"Figure you my prudence, *Señora*," he begins, "that, although she was my patient, I did not so much as see her face."

And then, having enjoyed the startled curiosity of his hearer, he continues:

"On that day of two crosses when I first undertook the mending of mortals, she arrived to me beneath a veil as impenetrable as that of a nun, saying:

"'To you I come, *Señor* Doctor, because no one knows you.'

"'Who would care for fame, *Señorita*,' said I, 'when obscurity bring such 15 excellent fortune?'

"And the lady, in a voice which trembled slightly, returned:

"'If your knife is as apt as your tongue, and your discretion equal to both, I shall not regret my choice of a surgeon.'

"With suitable gravity I reassured her, and inquired how I might be privileged to serve her. She replied:

"'By ridding me of a blemish, if you are skillful enough to leave no trace on the skin.'

"'Of that I will judge, with the help of God, when the *señorita* shall have 20 removed her veil.'

"'No, no; you shall not see my face. Praise the saints the blemish is not there!'

"'Wherever it be,' said I, resolutely, 'my science tells me that it must be seen before it can be well removed.'

"The lady answered with great simplicity that she had no anxiety on that account, but that, as she had neither duena nor servant with her, I must help her. I had no objection, for a surgeon must needs be something of a lady's maid. I judged from the quality of her garments that she was of an excellent family, and I was ashamed of my clumsy fingers; but she was as patient as marble, caring only to keep her face closely covered. When at last I saw the blemish she had complained of, I was astonished, and said:

"'But it seems to me a blessed stigma, *Señorita*, this delicate, wine-red vine-leaf, staining a surface as pure as the petal of any magnolia. With permission, I should say that the god Bacchus himself painted it here in the arch of this chaste back, where only the eyes of Cupid could find it; for it is safely below the line of the most fashionable gown.'

"But she replied: 25

"'I have my reasons. Fix yourself that I am superstitious.'

"I tried to reason with her on that, but she lost her patience, and cried:

"'For favor, good surgeon, your knife!'

"Even in those days I had much sensibility, *Señora*, and I swear that my heart received more pain from the knife than did she. Neither the cutting nor the stitching brought a murmur from her. Only some strong ulterior thought could have armed a delicate woman with such valor. I beat my brains to construe the case, but without success. A caprice took me to refuse the fee she offered me.

"'No, *Señorita*,' I said, 'I have not seen your face, and if I were to take 30 your money, it might pass that I should not see the face of a second patient, which would be a great misfortune. You are my first, and I am as superstitious as you.'

"I would have added that I had fallen in love with her, but I feared to appear ridiculous, having seen no more than her back.

"'You would place me under an obligation,' she said. I felt that her eyes studied me attentively through her veil. 'Very well, I can trust you the better for that. *Adiós, Señor* Surgeon.'

"She came once more to have me remove the stitches, as I had told her, and again her face was concealed, and again I refused payment; but I think she knew that the secret of the vine-leaf was buried in my heart."

"But that secret, what was it, Doctor? Did you ever see the mysterious lady again?"

"*¡Chist!* Little by little one arrives to the *rancho, Señora.* Five years passed,   35
and many patients arrived to me, but, although all showed me their faces,
I loved none of them better than the first one. Partly through family influence, partly through well-chosen friendships, and perhaps a little through
that diligence in the art of Hippocrates for which in my old age I am favored
by the most charming of Mexicans, I had prospered, and was no longer
unknown.

"At a meeting of a learned society I became known to a certain *marqués*
who had been a great traveler in his younger days. We had a discussion on a
point of anthropology, and he invited me to his house, to see the curiosities he
had collected in various countries. Most of them recalled scenes of horror, for
he had a morbid fancy.

"Having taken from my hand the sword with which he had seen five Chinese pirates sliced into small pieces, he led me toward a little door, saying:

"'Now you shall see the most mysterious and beautiful of my mementos,
one which recalls a singular event in our own peaceful Madrid.'

"We entered a room lighted by a skylight, and containing little but an
easel on which rested a large canvas. The *marqués* led me where the most auspicious light fell upon it. It was a nude, beautifully painted. The model stood
poised divinely, with her back to the beholder, twisting flowers in her hair before a mirror. And there, in the arch of that chaste back, staining a surface as
pure as the petal of any magnolia, what did my eyes see? Can you possibly
imagine, *Señora?*"

"*¡Válgame Dios!* The vine-leaf, Doctor!"   40

"What penetration of yours, *Señora!* It was veritably the vine-leaf, wine-
red, as it had appeared to me before my knife barbarously extirpated it from
the living flesh; but in the picture it seemed unduly conspicuous, as if Bacchus
had been angry when he kissed. You may imagine how the sight startled me.
But those who know Dr. Malsufrido need no assurance that even in those
early days he never permitted himself one imprudent word. No, *Señora;* I only
remarked, after praising the picture in proper terms:

"'What an interesting moon is that upon the divine creature's back!'

"'Does it not resemble a young vine-leaf in early spring?' said the *marqués,* who contemplated the picture with the ardor of a connoisseur. I agreed
politely, saying:

"'Now that you suggest it, *Marqués,* it has some of the form and color of
a tender vine-leaf. But I could dispense me a better vine-leaf, with many
bunches of grapes, to satisfy the curiosity I have to see such a well-formed
lady's face. What a misfortune that it does not appear in that mirror, as the
artist doubtless intended! The picture was never finished, then?'

"'I have reason to believe that it was finished,' he replied, 'but that the   45
face painted in the mirror was obliterated. Observe that its surface is an
opaque and disordered smudge of many pigments, showing no brush-work,
but only marks of a rude rubbing that in some places has overlapped the justly
painted frame of the mirror.'

"'This promises an excellent mystery,' I commented lightly. 'Was it the
artist or his model who was dissatisfied with the likeness, *Marqués?*'

"'I suspect that the likeness was more probably too good than not good enough,' returned the *marqués*. 'Unfortunately, poor Andrade is not here to tell us.'

"'Andrade! The picture was his work?'

"'The last his hand touched. Do you remember when he was found murdered in his studio?'

"'With a knife sticking between his shoulders. I remember it very well.'   50

"The *marqués* continued:

"'I had asked him to let me have this picture. He was then working on that rich but subdued background. The figure was finished, but there was no vine-leaf, and the mirror was empty of all but a groundwork of paint, with a mere luminous suggestion of a face.

"'Andrade, however, refused to name me a price, and tried to put me off with excuses. His friends were jesting about the unknown model, whom no one had managed to see, and all suspected that he designed to keep the picture for himself. That made me the more determined to possess it. I wished to make it a betrothal gift to the beautiful *Señorita* Lisarda Monte Alegre, who had then accepted the offer of my hand, and who is now the *marquesa*. When I have a desire, Doctor, it bites me, and I make it bite others. That poor Andrade, I gave him no peace.

"'He fell into one of his solitary fits, shutting himself in his studio, and seeing no one; but that did not prevent me from knocking at his door whenever I had nothing else to do. Well, one morning the door was open.'

"'Yes, yes!' I exclaimed. 'I remember now, *Marqués*, that it was you who   55 found the body.'

"'You have said it. He was lying in front of this picture, having dragged himself across the studio. After assuring myself that he was beyond help, and while awaiting the police, I made certain observations. The first thing to strike my attention was this vine-leaf. The paint was fresh, whereas the rest of the figure was comparatively dry. Moreover, its color had not been mixed with Andrade's usual skill. Observe you, Doctor, that the blemish is not of the texture of the skin, or bathed in its admirable atmosphere. It presents itself as an excrescence. And why? Because that color had been mixed and applied with feverish haste by the hand of a dying man, whose one thought was to denounce his assassin—she who undoubtedly bore such a mark on her body, and who had left him for dead, after carefully obliterating the portrait of herself which he had painted in the mirror.'

"'¡*Ay Dios!* But the police, *Marqués*—they never reported these details so significant?'

"'Our admirable police are not connoisseurs of the painter's art, my friend. Moreover, I had taken the precaution to remove from the dead man's fingers the empurpled brush with which he had traced that accusing symbol.'

"'You wished to be the accomplice of an unknown assassin?'

"'Inevitably, *Señor*, rather than deliver that lovely body to the hands of the   60 public executioner.'

"The *marqués* raised his lorgnette and gazed at the picture. And I—I was recovering from my agitation, *Señora*. I said:

"'It seems to me, *Marqués*, that if I were a woman and loved you, I should be jealous of that picture.'

"He smiled and replied:

"'It is true that the *marquesa* affects some jealousy on that account, and will not look at the picture. However, she is one who errs on the side of modesty, and prefers more austere objects of contemplation. She is excessively religious.'

"'I have been called superstitious,' pronounced a voice behind me.   65

"It was a voice that I had heard before. I turned, *Señora*, and I ask you to try to conceive whose face I now beheld."

"*Válgame la Virgen*, Dr. Malsufrido, was it not the face of the good *marquesa*, and did she not happen to have been also your first patient?"

"Again such penetration, *Señora*, confounds me. It was she. The *marqués* did me the honor to present me to her.

"'I have heard of your talents, *Señor* Surgeon,' she said.

"'And I of your beauty, *marquesa*,' I hastened to reply; 'but that tale was   70
not well told.' And I added, 'If you are superstitious, I will be, too.'

"With one look from her beautiful and devout eyes she thanked me for that prudence which to this day, *Señora*, is at the service of my *penitentes*, little daughters of my affections and my prayers; and then she sighed and said:

"'Can you blame me for not loving this questionable lady of the vine-leaf, of whom my husband is such a gallant accomplice?'

"'Not for a moment,' I replied, 'for I am persuaded, *marquesa*, that a lady of rare qualities may have power to bewitch an unfortunate man without showing him the light of her face.'"

MARÍA CRISTINA MENA
(1893–1965) Web

www

Born in Mexico, Mena was sent to the United States before the Mexican Revolution. She published short stories in American magazines and befriended D. H. Lawrence.

TOPICS FOR CRITICAL THINKING

1. What various clues does the Doctor use to establish identity? Are these reliable?
2. Why does the patient have the birthmark removed?
3. What story is implied by the text but not told?
4. What various meanings might the vine-leaf have?

TOPIC FOR CRITICAL WRITING

Compare the functions of the birthmark in this story to the functions of the birthmark in "The Birthmark."

ᗡᗡᗡ

SIDONIE-GABRIELLE COLETTE
Translated by Matthew Ward

The Hidden Woman   *(1924)*

He had been looking at the swirl of masks in front of him for a long time, suffering vaguely from the intermingling of their colors and the synchronized sound of two orchestras too close together. His cowl pressed his temples; a nervous headache was building between his eyes. But he savored, without impatience, a mixture of malaise and pleasure which allowed the hours to fly by unnoticed. He had wandered down all the corridors of the Opéra, had drunk in the silvery dust of the dance floor, recognized bored friends, and wrapped around his neck the indifferent arms of a very fat girl humorously disguised as a sylph. Though embarrassed by his long domino, tripping over it like a man in skirts, the cowled doctor did not dare take off either the domino or the hood, because of his schoolboy lie.

"I'll be spending tomorrow night in Nogent," he had told his wife the evening before. "They just telephoned and I'm afraid that my patient, you know, that poor old lady . . . Can you imagine? And I was looking forward to this ball like a kid. It's ridiculous, isn't it, a man my age who's never been to the Opéra Ball?"

"Very, darling, very ridiculous! If I had known I might never have married you . . ."

She laughed, and he admired her narrow face, pink, matte, and long, like a thin sugared almond.

"But . . . don't you want to go to the Green and Purple Ball? You know   5
you can go without me if you want, darling."

She trembled with one of those long shivers of disgust which made her hair, her delicate hands, and her chest in her white dress shudder at the sight of a slug or some filthy passer-by.

"Oh, no! Can you see me in a crowd, all those hands . . . What can I do? It's not that I'm a prude, it's . . . it makes my skin crawl. There's nothing I can do about it."

Leaning against the balustrade of the loggia, above the main staircase, he thought about this trembling hand, as he contemplated, directly in front of him, on the bare back of a sultana, the grasp of two enormous square hands with black nails. Bursting out of the braid-trimmed sleeves of a Venetian lord, they sank into the white female flesh as if it were dough. Because he was thinking about her, it gave him quite a start to hear, next to him, a little "ahem," a little cough typical of his wife. He turned around and saw someone in a long and impenetrable disguise, sitting sidesaddle on the balustrade, Pierrot by the looks of the huge-sleeved tunic, the loose-fitting pantaloons, the skullcap, the plaster-like whiteness coating the little bit of skin visible above the half-mask bearded with lace. The fabric of the costume and skullcap, woven of dark violet and silver, glistened like a conger eel fished for by night with iron hooks, in boats with resin lanterns. Overcome with surprise, he waited to hear the little "ahem," which did not come again. The Pierrot-Eel, seated, casual, tapped the marble balusters with a dangling heel, revealing only its two satin slippers and a black-gloved hand bent back against one hip. The two oblique slits in the mask, carefully covered over with a tulle mesh, allowed only a smothered fire of indeterminate color to pass through.

He almost called out, "Irene!" but held back, remembering his own lie. Not good at playacting, he also decided against disguising his voice. The Pierrot scratched its thigh, with a free and uninhibited gesture, and the anxious husband sighed in relief.

"Ah! It's not her."   10

But out of a pocket the Pierrot pulled a flat gold box, opened it to take out a lipstick, and the anxious husband recognized an antique snuffbox, fitted with a mirror inside, the last birthday present . . . He put his left hand on the pain in his chest with so brusque and so involuntarily theatrical a motion that the Pierrot-Eel noticed him.

"Is that a declaration, Purple Domino?"

He did not answer, half choked with surprise, anticipating, as in a bad dream, and listened for a long moment to the thinly disguised voice—the voice of his wife. The Eel, sitting there cavalierly, its head tilted like a bird's, looked at him; she shrugged her shoulders, hopped down, and walked away. Her movement freed the distraught husband, who, restored to an active and normal jealousy, started to think clearly again, and calmly rose to follow his wife.

"She's here for someone, with someone. In less than an hour I'll know everything."

A hundred other purple or green cowls guaranteed that he would be nei-   15
ther noticed nor recognized. Irene walked ahead of him nonchalantly. He was amazed to see her roll her hips softly and drag her feet a little as if she were wearing Turkish slippers. A Byzantine, in embroidered emerald green and gold, grabbed her as she passed, and she bent back, grown thinner in his arms, as if his grasp were going to cut her in half. Her husband ran a few steps forward and reached the couple as Irene cried out flatteringly, "You big brute, you!"

She walked away, with the same relaxed and calm step, stopping often, musing at the open doors of the boxes, almost never turning around. She hesitated at the bottom of a staircase, turned aside, came back toward the entrance to the orchestra stalls, slid into a noisy, dense group with slippery skillfulness, the exact movement of a knife blade sliding into its sheath. Ten arms imprisoned her, an almost naked wrestler roughly pinned her up against the edge of the boxes on the main floor and held her there. She yielded under the weight of the naked man, threw back her head with a laugh that was drowned out by other laughter, and the man in the purple cowl saw her teeth flash beneath the mask's lacy beard. Then she slipped away again with ease and sat down on the steps which led to the dance floor. Her husband, standing two steps behind, watched her. She readjusted her mask, and her crumpled tunic, and tightened the roll of her headband. She seemed calm, as though alone, and walked away again after a few minutes' rest. She went down the steps, and put her arms on the shoulders of a warrior who invited her, without speaking, to dance, and she danced, clinging to him.

"That's him," the husband said to himself.

But she did not say a word to the dancer, clad in iron and moist skin, and left him quietly, when the dance ended. She went off to have a glass of champagne at the buffet, and then a second glass, paid, and then watched, motionless and curious, as two men began scuffling, surrounded by screaming women. Then she amused herself by placing her little satanic hands, all black, on the white throat of a Dutch girl with golden hair, who cried out nervously. At last the anxious man who was following her saw her stop as she bumped up against a young man collapsed on a banquette, out of breath, fanning himself with his mask. She leaned over, disdainfully took his handsome face, rugged and fresh, by the chin, and kissed the panting, half-open mouth . . .

But her husband, instead of rushing forward and tearing the two joined mouths away from each other, disappeared into the crowd. Dismayed, he no longer feared, he no longer hoped for betrayal. He was sure now that Irene did not know the adolescent, drunk with dancing, whom she was kissing, or the Hercules. He was sure that she was not waiting or looking for anyone, that the lips she held beneath her own like a crushed grape, she would abandon, leave again the next minute, then wander about again, gather up some other passer-by, forget him, until she felt tired and it was time to go back home, tasting only the monstrous pleasure of being alone, free, honest, in her native brutality, of being the one who is unknown, forever solitary and without shame, whom a little mask and a hermetic costume had restored to her irremediable solitude and her immodest innocence.

<hr>

SIDONIE-GABRIELLE COLETTE

(1873–1954) **Web**   *www*

One of the most esteemed women writers of twentieth century France, Colette enjoyed careers as writer and music hall performer. Popular in her time, she is now best known for her novels *Chéri* and *Gigi*. Many of her novels and short stories treat the dilemmas of female independence.

TOPICS FOR CRITICAL THINKING

1. What clues about the identity of the Pierrot does the husband's close reading of the Pierrot provide?

2. How might the story's point-of-view relate to different ways of understanding the Pierrot's actions?

3. What do the husband's interpretations of the Pierrot tell us about the husband?

4. What might we understand about the reliability of our own readings when we see the reliability of the husband's readings?

5. What insight does the husband gain?

TOPICS FOR CRITICAL WRITING

1. On what various levels and in what ways do characters and readers engage in a process of interpretation? (See also sample student essay in Chapter 53.)
2. In what ways is this story about the husband's desire?

∽∽∽

DOROTHY PARKER

The Waltz   (1933)

Why, thank you so much, I'd adore to.

I don't want to dance with him. I don't want to dance with anybody. And even if I did, it wouldn't be him. He'd be well down among the last ten. I've seen the way he dances; it looks like something you do on Saint Walpurgis Night. Just think, not a quarter of an hour ago, here I was sitting, feeling so sorry for the poor girl he was dancing with. And now *I'm* going to be the poor girl. Well, well. Isn't it a small world?

And a peach of a world, too. A true little corker. It's events are so fascinatingly unpredictable, are not they? Here I was, minding my own business, not doing a stitch of harm to any living soul. And then he comes into my life, all smiles and city manners, to sue me for the favor of one memorable mazurka. Why, he scarcely knows my name, let alone what it stands for. It stands for Despair, Bewilderment, Futility, Degradation, and Premeditated Murder, but little does he wot. I don't wot his name, either; I haven't any idea what it is. Jukes, would be my guess from the look in his eyes. How do you do, Mr. Jukes? And how is that dear little brother of yours, with the two heads?

Ah, now why did he have to come around me, with his low requests? Why can't he let me lead my own life? I ask so little—just to be left alone in my quiet corner of the table, to do my evening brooding over all my sorrows. And he must come, with his bows and his scrapes and his may-I-have-this-ones. And I had to go and tell him that I'd adore to dance with him. I cannot understand why I wasn't struck right down dead. Yes, and being struck dead would look like a day in the country, compared to struggling out a dance with this boy. But what could I do? Everyone else at the table had got up to dance, except him and me. There was I, trapped. Trapped like a trap in a trap.

What can you say, when a man asks you to dance with him? I most cer   5
tainly will *not* dance with you, I'll see you in hell first. Why, thank you, I'd like to awfully, but I'm having labor pains. Oh, yes, *do* let's dance together—it's so nice to meet a man who isn't a scaredy-cat about catching my beri-beri. No. There was nothing for me to do, but say I'd adore to. Well, we might as well get it over with. All right, Cannonball, let's run out on the field. You won the toss; you can lead.

Why, I think it's more of a waltz, really. Isn't it? We might just listen to the music a second. Shall we? Oh, yes, it's a waltz. Mind? Why, I'm simply thrilled. I'd love to waltz with you.

I'd love to waltz with you. I'd love to waltz with you. I'd love to have my tonsils out, I'd love to be in a midnight fire at sea. Well, it's too late now. We're getting under way. *Oh.* Oh, dear. Oh, dear, dear, dear. Oh, this is even worse than I thought it would be. I suppose that's the one dependable law of life—everything is always worse than you thought it was going to be. Oh, if I had any real grasp of what this dance would be like, I'd have held out for sitting it out. Well, it will probably amount to the same thing in the end. We'll be sitting it out on the floor in a minute, if he keeps this up.

I'm so glad I brought it to his attention that this is a waltz they're playing. Heaven knows what might have happened, if he had thought it was something fast; we'd have blown the sides right out of the building. Why does he always want to be somewhere that he isn't? Why can't we stay in one place just long enough to get acclimated? It's this constant rush, rush, rush, that's the curse of American life. That's the reason that we're all of us so—*Ow!* For God's sake, don't *kick*, you idiot; this is only second down. Oh, my shin. My poor, poor shin, that I've had ever since I was a little girl!

Oh, no, no, no. Goodness, no. It didn't hurt the least little bit. And anyway it was my fault. Really it was. Truly. Well, you're just being sweet, to say that. It really was all my fault.

I wonder what I'd better do—kill him this instant, with my naked hands, or wait and let him drop in his traces. Maybe it's best not to make a scene. I guess I'll just lie low, and watch the pace get him. He can't keep this up indefinitely—he's only flesh and blood. Die he must, and die he shall, for what he did to me. I don't want to be of the oversensitive type, but you can't tell me that kick was unpremeditated. Freud says there are no accidents. I've led no cloistered life, I've known dancing partners who have spoiled my slippers and torn my dress; but when it comes to kicking, I am Outraged Womanhood. When you kick me in the shin, *smile*.

Maybe he didn't do it maliciously. Maybe it's just his way of showing his high spirits. I suppose I ought to be glad that one of us is having such a good time. I suppose I ought to think myself lucky if he brings me back alive. Maybe it's captious to demand of a practically strange man that he leave your shins as he found them. After all, the poor boy's doing the best he can. Probably he grew up in the hill country, and never had no larnin'. I bet they had to throw him on his back to get shoes on him.

Yes, it's lovely, isn't it? It's simply lovely. It's the loveliest waltz. Isn't it? Oh, I think it's lovely, too.

Why, I'm getting positively drawn to the Triple Threat here. He's my hero. He has the heart of a lion, and the sinews of a buffalo. Look at him—never a thought of the consequences, never afraid of his face, hurling himself into every scrimmage, eyes shining, cheeks ablaze. And shall it be said that I hung back? No, a thousand times no. What's it to me if I have to spend the next couple of years in a plaster cast? Come on, Butch, right through them! Who wants to live forever?

Oh. Oh, dear. Oh, he's all right, thank goodness. For a while I thought they'd have to carry him off the field. Ah, I couldn't bear to have anything happen to him. I love him. I love him better than anybody in the world. Look at the spirit he gets into a dreary, commonplace waltz; how effete the other dancers seem, beside him. He is youth and vigor and courage, he is strength and gaiety and—*Ow!* Get off my instep, you hulking peasant! What do you think I am, anyway—a gangplank? *Ow!*

No, of course it didn't hurt. Why, it didn't a bit. Honestly. And it was all my 15 fault. You see, that little step of yours—well, it's perfectly lovely, but it's just a tiny bit tricky to follow at first. Oh, did you work it up yourself? You really did? Well, aren't you amazing! Oh, now I think I've got it. Oh, I think it's lovely. I was watching you do it when you were dancing before. It's awfully effective when you look at it.

It's awfully effective when you look at it. I bet I'm awfully effective when you look at me. My hair is hanging along my cheeks, my skirt is swaddled about me, I can feel the cold damp of my brow. I must look like something out of "The Fall of the House of Usher." This sort of thing takes a fearful toll of a woman my age. And he worked up his little step himself, he with his degenerate cunning. And it was just a tiny bit tricky at first, but now I think I've got it. Two stumbles, slip, and a twenty-yard dash; yes, I've got it. I've got several other things, too, including a split shin and a bitter heart. I hate this creature I'm chained to. I hated him the moment I saw his leering, bestial face. And here I've been locked in his noxious embrace for the thirty-five years this waltz has lasted. Is that orchestra never going to stop playing? Or must this obscene travesty of a dance go on until hell burns out?

Oh, they're going to play another encore. Oh, goody. Oh, that's lovely. Tired? I should say I'm not tired. I'd like to go on like this forever.

I should say I'm not tired. I'm dead, that's all I am. Dead, and in what a cause! And the music is never going to stop playing, and we're going on like this, Double-Time Charlie and I, throughout eternity. I suppose I won't care any more, after the first hundred thousand years. I suppose nothing will matter then, not heat nor pain nor broken heart nor cruel, aching weariness. Well. It can't come too soon for me.

I wonder why I didn't tell him I was tired. I wonder why I didn't suggest going back to the table. I could have said let's just listen to the music. Yes, and if he would, that would be the first bit of attention he has given it all evening. George Jean Nathan said that the lovely rhythms of the waltz should be listened to in stillness and not be accompanied by strange gyrations of the human body. I think that's what he said. I think it was George Jean Nathan. Anyhow, whatever he said and whoever he was and whatever he's doing now, he's better off than I am. That's safe. Anybody who isn't waltzing with this Mrs. O'Leary's cow I've got here is having a good time.

Still if we were back at the table, I'd probably have to talk to him. Look at 20 him—what could you say to a thing like that! Did you go to the circus this year, what's your favorite kind of ice cream, how do you spell cat? I guess I'm as well off here. As well off as if I were in a cement mixer in full action.

I'm past all feeling now. The only way I can tell when he steps on me is that I can hear the splintering of bones. And all the events of my life are passing before my eyes. There was the time I was in a hurricane in the West Indies, there was the day I got my head cut open in the taxi smash, there was the night the drunken lady threw a bronze ash-tray at her own true love and got me instead, there was that summer that the sailboat kept capsizing. Ah, what an easy, peaceful time was mine, until I fell in with Swifty, here. I didn't know what trouble was, before I got drawn into this *danse macabre*. I think my mind is beginning to wander. It almost seems to me as if the orchestra were stopping. It couldn't be, of course; it could never, never be. And yet in my ears there is a silence like the sound of angel voices. . . .

Oh, they've stopped, the mean things. They're not going to play any more. Oh, darn. Oh, do you think they would? Do you really think so, if you gave them fifty dollars? Oh, that would be lovely. And look, do tell them to play this same thing. I'd simply adore to go on waltzing.

——— DOROTHY PARKER ———
(1893–1967) Web

www

Noted journalist and wit, Dorothy Parker wrote short stories, poetry, screenplays, reviews, criticism, and newspaper columns. A member of the noted New York Algonquin Round Table Web , Parker exemplified the cosmopolitan genius of the self-made woman of the twentieth century.

www

TOPICS FOR CRITICAL THINKING

1. In what ways does "The Waltz" enact the differences between what one says and what one means?
2. How do those differences illustrate gender politics?
3. Are we to take the narrator's commentary literally? If not, how do we know what is happening?
4. How should the story's readers understand the narrator's tone?
5. Is it likely that the gentleman waltzer is aware of his partner's feelings?

TOPIC FOR CRITICAL WRITING

Is "The Waltz" about only a dance?

14 Questions of Perception and Representation: Postmodernism

What happens when we can no longer trust our eyes to see or our language to convey what we mean? Writers of the first part of the twentieth century such as Franz Kafka wrote about the difference between an individual's experience and how the individual perceives that experience. Some writers in the later twentieth century bring even a character's perceptions into doubt—not in the way Colette does by showing the way characters perceive the same event differently, but instead by showing how perception itself is unreliable. While early twentieth-century writers brought language into question as a reliable medium for expressing meaning, later twentieth-century writers question whether we can communicate at all via language and show the ways our perceptions themselves are unreliable.

Postmodernism

www This doubt about the reliability of perception and representation is a part of a larger philosophical and aesthetic attitude called **postmodernism**. **Web** Coming from the disparate realms of architecture, literature, art, and philosophy, postmodernists question whether there can be a universal truth or narratives about truth that can produce and sustain any belief in singular meaning (that is, that everything has only one definite, locatable truth). Postmodernism even challenges an individual's belief in his or her own unified singular and stable identity, over which he or she has complete control.

Postmodernism is characterized by its attention to the making of art as the subject of art, a focus on process rather than product, and concern about the ways we think and the assumptions and premises we hold rather than the validity or truth of our conclusions. Postmodernism brings meaning into question while producing artistic works that explore whether anything can really be represented at all.

Postmodernist literature is characterized by some of the following qualities.

- It is often fragmented or nonsense narrative. See the film *Memento*, for an example.
- It often disrupts our sense of spatial or temporal continuity. Again, the film *Memento* is a good example.

- It often makes use of pastiche or the combination of different styles and elements. **Web** (See Mark Leyner's *My Cousin, My Gastroenterologist* in Chapter 16 for an example of pastiche.) *www*
- It includes characters who do not seem to be in command of themselves or their motives. These characters are called *split* or *disunified subjects*. An example is the protagonist of "How I Contemplated the World from the Detroit House of Correction and Began My Life Over Again" in Chapter 15.
- It has a consciousness of the processes of representation, for example, stories about writing stories or *metanarrative* **Web** (see Chapter 15 for a discussion about metanarrative). Examples of this include "A Story," "How I Contemplated the World from the Detroit House of Correction and Began My Life Over Again," and "The Calmative," all in Chapter 15. *www*
- It distrusts such institutions as government, religion, and capitalism and questions the possibility of any single, transcendent truth. Featured writer Salman Rushdie's story "The Free Radio" and this chapter's story "Blow Up" exemplify this distrust, as does much of the work of Beat writers such as Allen Ginsberg and Jack Kerouac. See Chapter 18 for a discussion of the Beats. **Web** *www*
- It embodies a sense of the failure of language as a mode of communication.

Not all postmodern works demonstrate all of these characteristics, but all manifest one or more. Some prose fiction is a combination of modernist and postmodernist elements. (For the difference between these, see **Web** .) What *www* is ultimately important to an understanding of postmodernism in writing is the way a story regards the possibilities of truth and certainty.

The following stories—Julio Cortázar's "Blow-Up," Italo Calvino's "Mr. Palomar on the Beach," and Michelle Cliff's "The Store of a Million Items"— all raise questions about the reliability of perception, not only as it reflects the perceiver's desires, but as it is inherently unreliable. Bringing perception into question also brings the perceiver into question and, with this, any narrative he or she might construct.

Critical Perspective: On Postmodernism

"To come now to the last of these parallels: Both Jorge Luis Borges and Italo Calvino managed marvelously to combine in their fiction the values that I call Algebra and Fire (I'm borrowing those terms here, as I have done elsewhere, from Borges's *First Encyclopedia of Tlön*, a realm complete, he reports, "with its emperors and its seas, with its minerals and its birds and its fish, with its algebra and its fire"). Let "algebra" stand for formal ingenuity and "fire" for what touches our emotions (it's tempting to borrow instead Calvino's alternative values of "crystal" and "flame," from his lecture on exactitude, but he happens not to mean by those terms what I'm referring to here). Formal virtuosity itself can of course be breathtaking, but much algebra and little or no fire makes for mere gee-whizzery, like Queneau's *Exercises in Style* and *One Hundred Thousand Billion Sonnets*. Much fire and little or no algebra, on the other hand, makes for heartfelt muddles—no examples needed. What most of us want from literature most of the time is what has been called passionate virtuosity, and both Borges and Calvino deliver it. Although I find both writers indispensable and would never presume to rank them as literary artists, by my lights Calvino perhaps comes closer to being the very model of a modern major Postmodernist—not that that very much matters, and whatever the capacious bag is that can contain such otherwise dissimilar spirits as Donald Barthelme, Samuel Beckett, J. L. Borges, Italo Calvino, Angela Carter, Robert Coover, Gabriel García Márquez, Elsa Morante, Vladimir Nabokov, Grace Paley, Thomas Pychon, et al. . . . What I mean is not only the fusion of algebra and fire, the great (and in Calvino's case high-spirited) virtuosity, the massive acquaintance with and respectfully ironic recycling of what Umberto Eco calls "the already said," and the combination of storytelling charm with zero naiveté, but also the keeping of one authorial foot in narrative antiquity while the other rests firmly in the high-tech (in Calvino's case, the Parisian "structuralist") narrative present. Add to this what I have cited as our chap's perhaps larger humanity and in-the-worldness, and you have my reasons."

—John Barth, "The Parallels! Italo Calvino and Jorge Luis Borges," in *Context: A Forum for Literary Arts and Culture*, (1999), p. 1.

In this passage, author John Barth analyzes the ways in which he understands the work of Italo Calvino to be postmodernist. In so doing, he also defines what he considers to be postmodernist writing

JULIO CORTÁZAR
Translated by Paul Blackburn

Blow-Up   *(1951)*

It'll never be known how this has to be told, in the first person or in the second, using the third person plural or continually inventing modes that will serve for nothing. If one might say: I will see the moon rose, or: we hurt me at the back of my eyes, and especially: you the blond woman was the clouds that race before my your his our yours their faces. What the hell.

Seated ready to tell it, if one might go to drink a bock over there, and the typewriter continue by itself (because I use the machine), that would be perfection. And that's not just a manner of speaking. Perfection, yes, because here is the aperture which must be counted also as a machine (of another sort, a Contax 1.1.2) and it is possible that one machine may know more about another machine than I, you, she—the blond—and the clouds. But I have the dumb luck to know that if I go this Remington will sit turned to stone on top of the table with the air of being twice as quiet that mobile things have when they are not moving. So, I have to write. One of us all has to write, if this is going to get told. Better that it be me who am dead, for I'm less compromised than the rest; I who see only the clouds and can think without being distracted, write without being distracted (there goes another, with a grey edge) and remember without being distracted, I who am dead (and I'm alive, I'm not trying to fool anybody, you'll see when we get to the moment, because I have to begin some way and I've begun with this period, the last one back, the one at the beginning, which in the end is the best of the periods when you want to tell something).

All of a sudden I wonder why I have to tell this, but if one begins to wonder why he does all he does do, if one wonders why he accepts an invitation to lunch (now a pigeon's flying by and it seems to me a sparrow), or why when someone has told us a good joke immediately there starts up something like a tickling in the stomach and we are not at peace until we've gone into the office across the hall and told the joke over again; then it feels good immediately, one is fine, happy, and can get back to work. For I imagine that no one has explained this, that really the best thing is to put aside all decorum and tell it, because, after all's done, nobody is ashamed of breathing or of putting on his shoes; they're things that you do, and when something weird happens, when you find a spider in your shoe or if you take a breath and feel like a broken window, then you have to tell what's happening, tell it to the guys at the office or to the doctor. Oh, doctor, every time I take a breath . . . Always tell it, always get rid of that tickle in the stomach that bothers you.

And now that we're finally going to tell it, let's put things a little bit in order, we'd be walking down the staircase in this house as far as Sunday, November 7, just a month back. One goes down five floors and stands then in the Sunday in the sun one would not have suspected of Paris in November, with a large appetite to walk around, to see things, to take photos (because we were photographers, I'm a photographer). I know that the most difficult thing is going to be finding a way to tell it, and I'm not afraid of repeating myself. It's going to be difficult because nobody really knows who it is telling it, if I am I or what actually occurred or what I'm seeing (clouds, and once in a while a pigeon) or if, simply, I'm telling a truth which is only my truth, and then is the truth only for my stomach, for this impulse to go running out and to finish up in some manner with, this, whatever it is.

We're going to tell it slowly, what happens in the middle of what I'm writ-   5
ing is coming already. If they replace me, if, so soon, I don't know what to say, if the clouds stop coming and something else starts (because it's impossible that this keep coming, clouds passing continually and occasionally a pigeon), if something out of all this . . . And after the "if" what am I going to put if I'm going to close the sentence structure correctly? But if I begin to ask questions, I'll never tell anything, maybe to tell would be like an answer, at least for someone who's reading it.

Roberto Michel, French-Chilean, translator and in his spare time an amateur photographer, left number 11, rue Monsieur-le-Prince Sunday November 7 of the current year (now they're two small ones passing, with silver linings). He had spent three weeks working on the French version of a treatise on challenges and appeals by José Norberto Allende, professor at the University of Santiago. It's rare that there's wind in Paris, and even less seldom a wind like this that swirled around corners and rose up to whip at old wooden venetian blinds behind which astonished ladies commented variously on how unreliable the weather had been these last few years. But the sun was out also, riding the wind and friend of the cats, so there was nothing that would keep me from taking a walk along the docks of the Seine and taking photos of the Conservatoire and Sainte-Chapelle. It was hardly ten o'clock, and I figured that by eleven the light would be good, the best you can get in the fall; to kill some time I detoured around by the Isle Saint-Louis and started to walk along the quai d'Anjou, I stared for a bit at the hôtel de Lauzun, I recited bits from Apollinaire which always get into my head whenever I pass in front of the hôtel de Lauzun (and at that I ought to be remembering the other poet, but Michel is an obstinate beggar), and when the wind stopped all at once and the sun came out at least twice as hard (I mean warmer, but really it's the same thing), I sat down on the parapet and felt terribly happy in the Sunday morning.

One of the many ways of contesting level-zero, and one of the best, is to take photographs, an activity in which one should start becoming an adept very early in life, teach it to children since it requires discipline, aesthetic education, a good eye and steady fingers. I'm not talking about waylaying the lie like any old reporter, snapping the stupid silhouette of the VIP leaving number 10 Downing Street, but in all ways when one is walking about with a camera, one has almost a duty to be attentive, to not lose that abrupt and happy rebound of sun's rays off an old stone, or the pigtails-flying run of a small girl going home with a loaf of bread or a bottle of milk. Michel knew that the photographer always worked as a permutation of his personal way of seeing the world as other than the camera insidiously imposed upon it (now a large cloud

is going by, almost black), but he lacked no confidence in himself, knowing
that he had only to go out without the Contax to recover the keynote of distraction, the sight without a frame around it, light without the diaphragm
aperture or 1/250 sec. Right now (what a word, *now*, what a dumb lie) I was
able to sit quietly on the railing overlooking the river watching the red and
black motorboats passing below without it occurring to me to think photo-
graphically of the scenes, nothing more than letting myself go in the letting
go of objects, running immobile in the stream of time. And then the wind was
not blowing.

After, I wandered down the quai de Bourbon until getting to the end of
the isle where the intimate square was (intimate because it was small, not that
it was hidden, it offered its whole breast to the river and the sky), I enjoyed it,
a lot. Nothing there but a couple and, of course, pigeons; maybe even some of
those which are flying past now so that I'm seeing them. A leap up and I settled on the wall, and let myself turn about and be caught and fixed by the sun,
giving it my face and ears and hands (I kept my gloves in my pocket). I had no
desire to shoot pictures, and lit a cigarette to be doing something; I think it
was that moment when the match was about to touch the tobacco that I saw
the young boy for the first time.

What I'd thought was a couple seemed much more now a boy with his
mother, although at the same time I realized that it was not a kid and his
mother, and that it was a couple in the sense that we always allegate to couples
when we see them leaning up against the parapets or embracing on the
benches in the squares. As I had nothing else to do, I had more than enough
time to wonder why the boy was so nervous, like a young colt or a hare, sticking his hands into his pockets, taking them out immediately, one after the
other, running his fingers through his hair, changing his stance, and especially
why was he afraid, well, you could guess that from every gesture, a fear suffocated by his shyness, an impulse to step backwards which he telegraphed, his
body standing as if it were on the edge of flight, holding itself back in a final,
pitiful decorum.

All this was so clear, ten feet away—and we were alone against the parapet at the tip of the island—that at the beginning the boy's fright didn't let me
see the blond very well. Now, thinking back on it, I see her much better at that
first second when I read her face (she'd turned around suddenly, swinging like
a metal weathercock, and the eyes, the eyes were there), when I vaguely understood what might have been occurring to the boy and figured it would be
worth the trouble to stay and watch (the wind was blowing their words away
and they were speaking in a low murmur). I think that I know how to look, if
it's something I know, and also that every looking oozes with mendacity, because it's that which expels us furthest outside ourselves, without the least
guarantee, whereas to smell, or (but Michel rambles on to himself easily
enough, there's no need to let him harangue on this way). In any case, if the
likely inaccuracy can be seen beforehand, it becomes possible again to look;
perhaps it suffices to choose between looking and the reality looked at, to strip
things of all their unnecessary clothing. And surely all that is difficult besides.

As for the boy I remember the image before his actual body (that will clear itself up later), while now I am sure that I remember the woman's body much better than the image. She was thin and willowy, two unfair words to describe what she was, and was wearing an almost-black fur coat, almost long, almost handsome. All the morning's wind (now it was hardly a breeze and it wasn't cold) had blown through her blond hair which pared away her white, bleak face—two unfair words—and put the world at her feet and horribly alone in front of her dark eyes, her eyes fell on things like two eagles, two leaps into nothingness, two puffs of green slime. I'm not describing anything, it's more a matter of trying to understand it. And I said two puffs of green slime.

Let's be fair, the boy was well enough dressed and was sporting yellow gloves which I would have sworn belonged to his older brother, a student of law or sociology; it was pleasant to see the fingers of the gloves sticking out of his jacket pocket. For a long time I didn't see his face, barely a profile, not stupid—a terrified bird, a Fra Filippo angel, rice pudding with milk—and the back of an adolescent who wants to take up judo and has had a scuffle or two in defense of an idea or his sister. Turning fourteen, perhaps fifteen, one would guess that he was dressed and fed by his parents but without a nickel in his pocket, having to debate with his buddies before making up his mind to buy a coffee, a cognac, a pack of cigarettes. He'd walk through the streets thinking of the girls in his class, about how good it would be to go to the movies and see the latest film, or to buy novels or neckties or bottles of liquor with green and white labels on them. At home (it would be a respectable home, lunch at noon and romantic landscapes on the walls, with a dark entryway and a mahogany umbrella stand inside the door) there'd be the slow rain of time, for studying, for being mama's hope, for looking like dad, for writing to his aunt in Avignon. So that there was a lot of walking the streets, the whole of the river for him (but without a nickel) and the mysterious city of fifteen-year-olds with its signs in doorways, its terrifying cats, a paper of fried potatoes for thirty francs, the pornographic magazine folded four ways, a solitude like the emptiness of his pockets, the eagerness for so much that was incomprehensible but illumined by a total love, by the availability analogous to the wind and the streets.

This biography was of the boy and of any boy whatsoever, but this particular one now, you could see he was insular, surrounded solely by the blond's presence as she continued talking with him. (I'm tired of insisting, but two long ragged ones just went by. That morning I don't think I looked at the sky once, because what was happening with the boy and the woman appeared so soon I could do nothing but look at them and wait, look at them and . . .) To cut it short, the boy was agitated and one could guess without too much trouble what had just occurred a few minutes before, at most half-an-hour. The boy had come onto the tip of the island, seen the woman and thought her marvelous. The woman was waiting for that because she was there waiting for that, or maybe the boy arrived before her and she saw him from one of the balconies or from a car and got out to meet him, starting the conversation with whatever, from the beginning she was sure that he was going to be afraid and want to run off, and that, naturally, he'd stay, stiff and sullen, pretending experience and the pleasure of the adventure. The rest was easy because it was happening ten feet away from me, and anyone could have gauged the stages of the game, the derisive, competitive fencing; its major attraction was not that it was happening but in foreseeing its denouement. The boy would try to end it by pretending a date, an obligation, whatever, and would go stumbling off disconcerted, wishing he were walking with some assurance, but naked under the mocking glance which would follow him until he was out of sight. Or rather, he would stay there, fascinated or simply incapable of taking the initiative, and the woman would begin to touch his face gently, muss his hair, still talking to him voicelessly, and soon would take him by the arm to lead him off, unless he, with an uneasiness beginning to tinge the edge of desire, even his stake in the adventure, would rouse himself to put his arm around her waist and to kiss her. Any of this could have happened, though it did not, and perversely Michel waited, sitting on the railing, making the settings almost without looking at the camera, ready to take a picturesque shot of a corner of the island with an uncommon couple talking and looking at one another.

Strange how the scene (almost nothing: two figures there mismatched in their youth) was taking on a disquieting aura. I thought it was I imposing it, and that my photo, if I shot it, would reconstitute things in their true stupidity. I would have liked to know what he was thinking, a man in a grey hat sitting at the wheel of a car parked on the dock which led up to the footbridge, and whether he was reading the paper or asleep. I had just discovered him because people inside a parked car have a tendency to disappear, they get lost in that wretched, private cage stripped of the beauty that motion and danger give it. And nevertheless, the car had been there the whole time, forming part (or deforming that part) of the isle. A car: like saying a lighted streetlamp, a park bench. Never like saying wind, sunlight, those elements always new to the skin and the eyes, and also the boy and the woman, unique, put there to change the island, to show it to me in another way. Finally, it may have been that the man with the newspaper also became aware of what was happening and would, like me, feel that malicious sensation of waiting for everything to happen. Now the woman had swung around smoothly, putting the young boy between herself and the wall, I saw them almost in profile, and he was tall, though not much taller, and yet she dominated him, it seemed like she was hovering over him (her laugh, all at once, a whip of feathers), crushing him just by being there, smiling, one hand taking a stroll through the air. Why wait any longer? Aperture at sixteen, a sighting which would not include the horrible black car, but yes, that tree, necessary to break up too much grey space . . .

I raised the camera, pretended to study a focus which did not include them, and waited and watched closely, sure that I would finally catch the revealing expression, one that would sum it all up, life that is rhythmed by movement but which a stiff image destroys, taking time in cross section, if we do not choose the essential imperceptible fraction of it. I did not have to wait long. The woman was getting on with the job of handcuffing the boy smoothly, stripping from him what was left of his freedom a hair at a time, in an incredibly slow and delicious torture. I imagined the possible endings (now a small fluffy cloud appears, almost alone in the sky), I saw their arrival at the house (a basement apartment probably, which she would have filled with large cushions and cats) and conjectured the boy's terror and his desperate decision to play it cool and to be led off pretending there was nothing new in it for him. Closing my eyes, if I did in fact close my eyes, I set the scene: the teasing kisses, the woman mildly repelling the hands which were trying to undress her, like in novels, on a bed that would have a lilac-colored comforter, on the other hand she taking off his clothes, plainly mother and son under a milky yellow light, and everything would end up as usual, perhaps, but maybe everything would go otherwise, and the initiation of the adolescent would not happen, she would not let it happen, after a long prologue wherein the awkwardnesses, the exasperating caresses, the running of hands over bodies would be resolved in who knows what, in a separate and solitary pleasure, in a petulant denial mixed with the art of tiring and disconcerting so much poor innocence. It might go like that, it might very well go like that; that woman was not looking for the boy as a lover, and at the same time she was dominating him toward some end impossible to understand if you do not imagine it as a cruel game, the desire to desire without satisfaction, to excite herself for someone else, someone who in no way could be that kid.

Michel is guilty of making literature, of indulging in fabricated unrealities. Nothing pleases him more than to imagine exceptions to the rule, individuals outside the species, not-always-repugnant monsters. But that woman invited speculation, perhaps giving clues enough for the fantasy to hit the bullseye. Before she left, and now that she would fill my imaginings for several days, for I'm given to ruminating, I decided not to lose a moment more. I got it all into the view-finder (with the tree, the railing, the eleven-o'clock sun) and took the shot. In time to realize that they both had noticed and stood there looking at me, the boy surprised and as though questioning, but she was irritated, her face and body flat-footedly hostile, feeling robbed, ignominiously recorded on a small chemical image.

I might be able to tell it in much greater detail but it's not worth the trouble. The woman said that no one had the right to take a picture without permission, and demanded that I hand her over the film. All this in a dry, clear voice with a good Parisian accent, which rose in color and tone with every phrase. For my part, it hardly mattered whether she got the roll of film or not, but anyone who knows me will tell you, if you want anything from me, ask nicely. With the result that I restricted myself to formulating the opinion that not only was photography in public places not prohibited, but it was looked upon with decided favor, both private and official. And while that was getting said, I noticed on the sly how the boy was falling back, sort of actively backing up though without moving, and all at once (it seemed almost incredible) he turned and broke into a run, the poor kid, thinking that he was walking off and in fact in full flight, running past the side of the car, disappearing like a gossamer filament of angel-spit in the morning air.

But filaments of angel-spittle are also called devil-spit, and Michel had to endure rather particular curses, to hear himself called meddler and imbecile, taking great pains meanwhile to smile and to abate with simple movements of his head such a hard sell. As I was beginning to get tired, I heard the car door slam. The man in the grey hat was there, looking at us. It was only at that point that I realized he was playing a part in the comedy.

He began to walk toward us, carrying in his hand the paper he had been pretending to read. What I remember best is the grimace that twisted his mouth askew, it covered his face with wrinkles, changed somewhat both in location and shape because his lips trembled and the grimace went from one side of his mouth to the other as though it were on wheels, independent and involuntary. But the rest stayed fixed, a flour-powdered clown or bloodless man, dull dry skin, eyes deepset, the nostrils black and prominently visible, blacker than the eyebrows or hair or the black necktie. Walking cautiously as though the pavement hurt his feet; I saw patent-leather shoes with such thin soles that he must have felt every roughness in the pavement. I don't know why I got down off the railing, nor very well why I decided to not give them the photo, to refuse that demand in which I guessed at their fear and cowardice. The clown and the woman consulted one another in silence: we made a perfect and unbearable triangle, something I felt compelled to break with a crack of a whip. I laughed in their faces and began to walk off, a little more slowly, I imagine, than the boy. At the level of the first houses, beside the iron footbridge, I turned around to look at them. They were not moving, but the man had dropped his newspaper; it seemed to me that the woman, her back to the parapet, ran her hands over the stone with the classical and absurd gesture of someone pursued looking for a way out.

What happened after that happened here, almost just now, in a room on the fifth floor. Several days went by before Michel developed the photos he'd taken on Sunday; his shots of the Conservatoire and of Sainte-Chapelle were all they should be. Then he found two or three proof-shots he'd forgotten, a poor attempt to catch a cat perched astonishingly on the roof of a rambling public urinal, and also the shot of the blond and the kid. The negative was so good that he made an enlargement; the enlargement was so good that he made one very much larger, almost the size of a poster. It did not occur to him (now one wonders and wonders) that only the shots of the Conservatoire were worth so much work. Of the whole series, the snapshot of the tip of the island was the only one which interested him; he tacked up the enlargement on one wall of the room, and the first day he spent some time looking at it and remembering, that gloomy operation of comparing the memory with the gone reality; a frozen memory, like any photo, where nothing is missing, not even, and especially, nothingness, the true solidifier of the scene. There was the woman, there was the boy, the tree rigid above their heads, the sky as sharp as the stone of the parapet, clouds and stones melded into a single substance and inseparable (now one with sharp edges is going by, like a thunderhead). The first two days I accepted what I had done, from the photo itself to the enlargement on the wall, and didn't even question that every once in a while I would interrupt my translation of José Norberto Allende's treatise to encounter once more the woman's face, the dark splotches on the railing. I'm such a jerk; it had never occurred to me that when we look at a photo from the front, the eyes reproduce exactly the position and the vision of the lens; it's these things that are taken for granted and it never occurs to anyone to think about them. From my chair, with the typewriter directly in front of me, I looked at the photo ten feet away, and then it occurred to me that I had hung it exactly at the point of view of the lens. It looked very good that way; no doubt, it was the best way to appreciate a photo, though the angle from the diagonal doubtless has its pleasures and might even divulge different aspects.

Every few minutes, for example when I was unable to find the way to say in good French what José Norberto Allende was saying in very good Spanish, I raised my eyes and looked at the photo; sometimes the woman would catch my eye, sometimes the boy, sometimes the pavement where a dry leaf had fallen admirably situated to heighten a lateral section. Then I rested a bit from my labors, and I enclosed myself again happily in that morning in which the photo was drenched, I recalled ironically the angry picture of the woman demanding I give her the photograph, the boy's pathetic and ridiculous flight, the entrance on the scene of the man with the white face. Basically, I was satisfied with myself; my part had not been too brilliant, and since the French have been given the gift of the sharp response, I did not see very well why I'd chosen to leave without a complete demonstration of the rights, privileges and prerogatives of citizens. The important thing, the really important thing was having helped the kid to escape in time (this in case my theorizing was correct, which was not sufficiently proven, but the running away itself seemed to show it so). Out of plain meddling, I had given him the opportunity finally to take advantage of his fright to do something useful; now he would be regretting it, feeling his honor impaired, his manhood diminished. That was better than the attentions of a woman capable of looking as she had looked at him on that island. Michel is something of a puritan at times, he believes that one should not seduce someone from a position of strength. In the last analysis, taking that photo had been a good act.

Well, it wasn't because of the good act that I looked at it between paragraphs while I was working. At that moment I didn't know the reason, the reason I had tacked the enlargement onto the wall; maybe all fatal acts happen that way, and that is the condition of their fulfillment. I don't think the almost-furtive trembling of the leaves on the tree alarmed me, I was working on a sentence and rounded it out successfully. Habits are like immense herbariums, in the end an enlargement of 32 x 28 looks like a movie screen, where, on the tip of the island, a woman is speaking with a boy and a tree is shaking its dry leaves over their heads.

But her hands were just too much. I had just translated: "In that case, the second key resides in the intrinsic nature of difficulties which societies . . ."— when I saw the woman's hand beginning to stir slowly, finger by finger. There was nothing left of me, a phrase in French which I would never have to finish, a typewriter on the floor, a chair that squeaked and shook, fog. The kid had ducked his head like boxers do when they've done all they can and are waiting for the final blow to fall; he had turned up the collar of his overcoat and seemed more a prisoner than ever, the perfect victim helping promote the catastrophe. Now the woman was talking into his ear, and her hand opened again to lay itself against his cheekbone, to caress and caress it, burning it, taking her time. The kid was less startled than he was suspicious, once or twice he poked his head over the woman's shoulder and she continued talking, saying something that made him look back every few minutes toward that area where Michel knew the car was parked and the man in the grey hat, carefully eliminated from the photo but present in the boy's eyes (how doubt that now) in the words of the woman, in the woman's hands, in the vicarious presence of the woman. When I saw the man come up, stop near them and look at them, his hands in his pockets and a stance somewhere between disgusted and demanding, the master who is about to whistle in his dog after a frolic in the square, I understood, if that was to understand, what had to happen now, what had to have happened then, what would have to happen at that moment, among these people, just where I had poked my nose in to upset an established order, interfering innocently in that which had not happened, but which was now going to happen, now was going to be fulfilled. And what I had imagined earlier was much less horrible than the reality, that woman, who was not there by herself, she was not caressing or propositioning or encouraging for her own pleasure, to lead the angel away with his tousled hair and play the tease with his terror and eager grace. The real boss was waiting there, smiling petulantly, already certain of the business; he was not the first to send a woman in the vanguard, to bring him the prisoners manacled with flowers. The rest of it would be so simple, the car, some house or another, drinks, stimulating engravings, tardy tears, the awakening in hell. And there was nothing I could do, this time I could do absolutely nothing. My strength had been a photograph, that, there, where they were taking their revenge on me, demonstrating clearly what was going to happen. The photo had been taken, the time had run out, gone; we were so far from one another, the abusive act had certainly already taken place, the tears already shed, and the rest conjecture and sorrow. All at once the order was inverted, they were alive, moving, they were deciding and had decided, they were going to their future; and I on this side, prisoner of another time, in a room on the fifth floor, to not know who they were, that woman, that man, and that boy, to be only the lens of my camera, something fixed, rigid, incapable of intervention. It was horrible, their mocking me, deciding it before my impotent eye, mocking me, for the boy again was looking at the flour-faced clown and I had to accept the fact that he was going to say yes, that the proposition carried money with it or a gimmick, and I couldn't yell for him to run, or even open the road to him again with a new photo, a small and almost meek intervention which would ruin the framework of drool and perfume. Everything was going to resolve itself right there, at that moment; there was like an immense silence which had nothing to do with physical silence. It was stretching it out, setting itself up. I think I screamed, I screamed terribly, and that at that exact second I realized that I was beginning to move toward them, four inches, a step, another step, the tree swung its branches rhythmically in the foreground, a place where the railing was tarnished emerged from the frame, the woman's face turned toward me as though surprised, was enlarging, and then I turned a bit, I mean that the camera turned a little, and without losing sight of the woman, I began to close in on the man who was looking at me with the black holes he had in the place of eyes, surprised and angered both, he looked, wanting to nail me onto the air, and at that instant I happened to see something like a large bird outside the focus that was flying in a single swoop in front of the picture, and I leaned up against the wall of my room and was happy because the boy had just managed to escape, I saw him running off, in focus again, sprinting with his hair flying in the wind, learning finally to fly across the island, to arrive at the footbridge, return to the city. For the second time he'd escaped them, for the second time I was helping him to escape, returning him to his precarious paradise. Out of breath, I stood in front of them; no need to step closer, the game was played out. Of the woman you could see just maybe a shoulder and a bit of the hair, brutally cut off by the frame of the picture; but the man was directly center, his mouth half open, you could see a shaking black tongue, and he lifted his hands slowly, bringing them into the foreground, an instant still in perfect focus, and then all of him a lump that blotted out the island, the tree, and I shut my eyes, I didn't want to see any more, and I covered my face and broke into tears like an idiot.

Now there's a big white cloud, as on all these days, all this untellable time. What remains to be said is always a cloud, two clouds, or long hours of a sky perfectly clear, a very clean, clear rectangle tacked up with pins on the wall of my room. That was what I saw when I opened my eyes and dried them with my fingers: the clear sky, and then a cloud that drifted in from the left, passed gracefully and slowly across and disappeared on the right. And then another, and for a change sometimes, everything gets grey, all one enormous cloud, and suddenly the splotches of rain cracking down, for a long spell you can see it raining over the picture, like a spell of weeping reversed, and little by little, the frame becomes clear, perhaps the sun comes out, and again the clouds begin to come, two at a time, three at a time. And the pigeons once in a while, and a sparrow or two.

———— **JULIO CORTÁZAR** ————

www   *(1914–1984)* **Web**

Trained as a teacher, Cortázar moved from Argentina to France. Politically active, he contributed the prize money from one of his novels to the United Chilean Front. Cortázar is best known for his novel *Hopscotch* (1963) and the short story "Blow-Up," made into a film with the same name by Michelangelo Antonioni.

www   ### TOPICS FOR CRITICAL THINKING **Web**

1. How many different times are combined in this narrative and how are they introduced?
2. In what ways is this story conscious of the process of its own writing?
3. How does this story illustrate the ways knowledge might be an illusion?
4. Does reading "Blow-Up" repeat in any way the photographer's experience?
5. What conclusions might we make about the nature of perception based on the narrator's experience?

www   ### TOPICS FOR CRITICAL WRITING **Web**

1. In what ways is the narrator like the man in the car?
2. What is the role of the machine?

ITALO CALVINO
Translated by William Weaver

Mr. Palomar on the Beach   *(1983)*

Reading a Wave

The sea is barely wrinkled, and little waves strike the sandy shore. Mr. Palomar is standing on the shore, looking at a wave. Not that he is lost in contemplation of the waves. He is not lost, because he is quite aware of what he is doing: he wants to look at a wave and he is looking at it. He is not contemplating, because for contemplation you need the right temperament, the right mood, and the right combination of exterior circumstances; and though Mr. Palomar has nothing against contemplation in principle, none of these three conditions applies to him. Finally, it is not "the waves" that he means to look at, but just one individual wave: in his desire to avoid vague sensations, he establishes for his every action a limited and precise object.

Mr. Palomar sees a wave rise in the distance, grow, approach, change form and color, fold over itself, break, vanish, and flow again. At this point he could convince himself that he has concluded the operation he had set out to achieve, and he could go away. But isolating one wave is not easy, separating it from the wave immediately following, which seems to push it and at times overtakes it and sweeps it away; and it is no easier to separate that one wave from the preceding wave, which seems to drag it toward the shore, unless it turns against the following wave, as if to arrest it. Then, if you consider the breadth of the wave, parallel to the shore, it is hard to decide where the advancing front extends regularly and where it is separated and segmented into independent waves, distinguished by their speed, shape, force, direction.

In other words, you cannot observe a wave without bearing in mind the complex features that concur in shaping it and the other, equally complex ones that the wave itself originates. These aspects vary constantly, so each wave is different from another wave, even if not immediately adjacent or successive; in other words, there are some forms and sequences that are repeated, though irregularly distributed in space and time. Since what Mr. Palomar means to do at this moment is simply *see* a wave—that is, to perceive all its simultaneous components without overlooking any of them—his gaze will dwell on the movement of the wave that strikes the shore until it can record aspects not previously perceived; as soon as he notices that the images are being repeated, he will know he has seen everything he wanted to see and he will be able to stop.

A nervous man who lives in a frenzied and congested world, Mr. Palomar tends to reduce his relations with the outside world; and, to defend himself against the general neurasthenia, he tries to keep his sensations under control insofar as possible.

The hump of the advancing wave rises more at one point than at any 5 other, and it is here that it becomes hemmed in white. If this occurs at some distance from the shore, there is time for the foam to fold over upon itself and vanish again, as if swallowed, and at the same moment invade the whole, but this time emerging again from below, like a white carpet rising from the bank to welcome the wave that is arriving. But just when you expect that wave to roll over the carpet, you realize it is no longer wave but only carpet, and this also rapidly disappears, to become a glinting of wet sand that quickly withdraws, as if driven back by the expansion of the dry, opaque sand that moves its jagged edge forward.

At this same time, the indentations in the brow of the wave must be considered, where it splits into two wings, one stretching toward the shore from right to left and the other from left to right, and the departure point or the destination of their divergence or convergence is this negative tip, which follows the advance of the wings but is always held back, subject to their alternate overlapping until another wave, a stronger wave, overtakes it, with the same problem of divergence-convergence, and then a wave stronger still, which resolves the knot by shattering it.

Taking the pattern of the waves as model, the beach thrusts into the water some faintly hinted points, prolonged in submerged sandy shoals, shaped and destroyed by the currents at every tide. Mr. Palomar has chosen one of these low tongues of sand as his observation point, because the waves strike it on either side, obliquely, and, overrunning the half-submerged surface, they meet their opposites. So, to understand the composition of a wave, you have to consider these opposing thrusts, which are to some extent counterbalanced and to some extent added together, to produce a general shattering of thrusts and counterthrusts in the usual spreading of foam.

Mr. Palomar now tries to limit his field of observation; if he bears in mind a square zone of, say, ten meters of shore by ten meters of sea, he can carry out an inventory of all the wave movements that are repeated with varying frequency within a given time interval. The hard thing is to fix the boundaries of this zone, because if, for example, he considers as the side farthest from him the outstanding line of an advancing wave, as this line approaches him and rises it hides from his eyes everything behind it, and thus the space under examination is overturned and at the same time crushed.

In any case, Mr. Palomar does not lose heart and at each moment he thinks he has managed to see everything to be seen from his observation point, but then something always crops up that he had not borne in mind. If it were not for his impatience to reach a complete, definitive conclusion of his visual operation, looking at waves would be a very restful exercise for him and could save him from neurasthenia, heart attack, and gastric ulcer. And it could perhaps be the key to mastering the world's complexity by reducing it to its simplest mechanism.

But every attempt to define this model must take into account a long wave that is arriving in a direction perpendicular to the breakers and parallel to the shore, creating the flow of a constant, barely surfacing crest. The shifts of the waves that ruffle toward the shore do not disturb the steady impulse of this compact crest that slices them at a right angle, and there is no knowing where it comes from or where it then goes. Perhaps it is a breath of east wind that stirs the sea's surface against the deep drive that comes from the mass of water far out to sea, but this wave born of air, in passing, receives also the oblique thrusts from the water's depth and redirects them, straightening them in its own direction and bearing them along. And so the wave continues to grow and gain strength until the clash with contrary waves gradually dulls it and makes it disappear, or else twists it until it is confused in one of the many dynasties of oblique waves slammed against the shore.

Concentrating the attention on one aspect makes it leap into the foreground and occupy the square, just as, with certain drawings, you have only to close your eyes and when you open them the perspective has changed. Now, in the overlapping of crests moving in various directions, the general pattern seems broken down into sections that rise and vanish. In addition, the reflux of every wave also has a power of its own that hinders the oncoming waves. And if you concentrate your attention on these backward thrusts, it seems that the true movement is the one that begins from the shore and goes out to sea. Is this perhaps the real result that Mr. Palomar is about to achieve? To make the waves run in the opposite direction, to overturn time, to perceive the true substance of the world beyond sensory and mental habits? No, he feels a slight dizziness, but it goes no further than that. The stubbornness that drives the waves toward the shore wins the match: in fact, the waves have swelled considerably. Is the wind about to change? It would be disastrous if the image that Mr. Palomar has succeeded painstakingly in putting together were to shatter and be lost. Only if he manages to bear all the aspects in mind at once can he begin the second phase of the operation: extending this knowledge to the entire universe.

It would suffice not to lose patience, as he soon does. Mr. Palomar goes off along the beach, tense and nervous as when he came, and even more unsure about everything.

————— **ITALO CALVINO** —————

(1923–1984) `Web`   *www*

Like many authors, Calvino moved to Paris to write. He found that the distance from his homeland made him more perceptive about his own experiences and processes of perception. Born in Italy and influenced by the work of Jorge Luis Borges, Calvino mastered the art of metafiction. He published numerous novels, including *Cosmicomics* (1968) and *If on a Winter's Night a Traveler* (1981).

TOPICS FOR CRITICAL THINKING `Web`   *www*

1. What does watching the wave indicate about the reliability of perception?
2. Why is Mr. Palomar "tense and nervous" after watching the wave?
3. Is objectivity possible?
4. What aspects of this story, if any, are postmodern?

TOPIC FOR CRITICAL WRITING `Web`   *www*

In what ways is the wave like writing?

ᗡᗡᗡ

MICHELLE CLIFF

The Store of a Million Items   *(1998)*

As children we had our seasons, apart from growing up, growing seasons. Our own ways of dividing time, managing the elliptical motion of the Earth, life on a spinning planet. Our ways were grounded, uncelestial. Light years were beyond us; black holes not yet imagined. Our idea of matter-destroying entity was the sewer under the city, stygian, dripping, where Floridian Godzillas survived on Norwegian rats.

No, our seasons were set by the appearance of something in The Store of a Million Items, on Victory Boulevard between the Mercury Cleaners and the Mill End Shop. The store was a postwar phenomenon, promising a bounty only available in America. Everything we loved was there; there we flocked. As close to infinity as we dared.

The first Duncan yo-yo—the first to catch the eye, splendid, gold-flecked, *deluxe*, guaranteed to go around the world, without end, singing all the while—usually appeared sometime in March, brought by common carrier from the Midwest. It led the way, grand marshal of a parade of yo-yos, lined up in a corner of the store window, as less *deluxe*, less articulate yo-yos followed, right down to the 29¢ model, thick wood and flaccid kitchen string, unable to sleep or sing, promising no momentum at all. Its brand-new cherry-red face was deceptively bright, for the paint would soon enough crack, strip, even run in the rain, dyeing its master, mistress red-handed. Stamped MADE IN JAPAN, which phrase then signified nothing so much as inferiority, cheapness. The work of the un-American.

But—and this is important, the teacher stressed—you couldn't trust MADE IN USA either, for right after Hiroshima, a Japanese town had changed its name to USA (pronounced you-sah) and therefore MADE IN USA was suspect. The un-American was crafty.

"Too many people don't understand Hiroshima," Miss Clausen contin-   5
ued. "Make sure it's U-period, S-period, A-period," she cautioned.

Yet the child who couldn't afford a grander, made in U-period, S-period, A-period yo-yo (and was too chicken, or good, to lift one) would treasure even the Japanese version, determined to overcome its birthright and teach it to sleep. Fingering the wood in his pants pocket, rubbing it along the wale of her corduroy skirt, you could hear the call of the schoolyard, while the teacher's voice became white noise.

We stood in clusters on the concrete, surrounded by the whirr of yo-yos sleeping. In the shape of the world, the world on a string.

We were truly blessed, the principal assured us.

Behind the Iron Curtain were streets of empty markets, with nothing but shelf after shelf of noodles. That's what happened when people lived on handouts. Everybody had cardboard in their shoes, not just the poor kids or the kids whose parents had better use for their money. Behind the Iron Curtain they sold *Uncle Tom's Cabin*, stamped 1955, with the words "first edition" on the title page.

We knew better. 10

On August 28, 1955, Emmett Till's body was dredged from the River Pearl. But teachers weren't responsible for telling us about things that happened in summer.

Behind the Iron Curtain everything was gray—people, cities, skies. The sun didn't shine there. They were deprived of Happy Tooth, while Mr. Tooth Decay dogged their tracks, like a villain in a silent two-reeler. Even the children had false teeth, if they were lucky.

In 1956 we passed around a special edition of *Life* devoted to the Hungarian Revolution. We were about to receive a refugee classmate. Some of us were foreign-born, but he would be our first refugee. Gray tanks rumbled through streets page after page. People were squashed. For some reason the refugee went to Chicago instead.

The years moved on. Jacks. Marbles. Jump ropes. Pea shooters.

Water pistols. My personal favorite. Coming at the end of spring, the 15 verge of summer vacation, when we watched the green canvas shade, drawn down against the sun and against our eyes, drawn by the warmth of the outdoors, trained on long evenings. The shade flapped gently, but any breeze was trapped.

Black lugers. Silver derringers. Translucent ray guns. One blast and your enemy would disintegrate before your very eyes. We'd all seen *The Day the Earth Stood Still. The Thing. It Came from Outer Space*. Pods landing in a California valley.

Earth Versus the Flying Saucers.

"Will they be back, Brad?"

"Not as long as we're here, Sally."

Saturday mornings in the children's pit of the local movie house, the ma- 20 tron, whom some of us would come to remember as a stone butch, patrolled the aisles during the show. She collected water pistols at the door, those she could detect, or tried to remember the children who were likely to be armed.

We hated her with a feeling as natural as what we felt for Messala in *Ben Hur*.

"C'mon, Ben!" we cheered during the chariot race and thrilled as Ben's nemesis was dragged bloody through the sand of the Circus Maximus.

Of course some of us eluded the matron's once-over and we blasted her again and again, water running over her ducktail, droplets bouncing off her Vitalis'ed strands, soaking the nurse's uniform they dressed her in.

"Bas-tuds!" She swore at us, calling us chicken, threatening to stop the picture and raise the lights.

When the water ran out, we pelted her with Goobers and Raisinets, 25 Good-and-Plenty, and Milk Duds.

Then she brought out the heavy artillery, the ticket-taker, for one final warning: "Now, boys and girls." To which we either feigned good behavior or began a rampage, depending on whether we knew the ending of the movie or cared. We were in that dark pit gloriously leaderless. Anarchy for the most part prevailed.

In school we declared War! (what else?) on each other. The-girls-against-the-boys, the-boys-against-the-girls, ancient compound nouns, spoken in one rapid breath, running back and forth during recess, reloading our sidearms in the girls' room, the boys' room. There was a rumor a boy in 5-3 peed in his.

Even Gerald O'Brien who draped pop beads from The Store of a Million Items around his waist and pretended he was a mermaid—like Ann Blyth, he said—armed himself. Gerald wouldn't have been caught dead at the movies on Saturday morning. He said he preferred solitude, hated crowds, and watched his movies in peace on *The Early Show*, in the time between the end of school and his parents' return from work. He drank tap water from a stemmed glass he'd bought in The Store of a Million Items, into which he dropped two cocktail onions, calling himself a Gibson Girl. He would have preferred to have used his water pistol as a prop in high drama or melodrama, *The Letter* or *Deception*, the first frames of *Mildred Pierce*, the final scene of *Duel in the Sun*, not as the rest of us did, in gross displays of force.

"Boys and girls, boys and girls, hold your partner's hand," we were told, as we were marched from one place to another, to the schoolyard, gym, auditorium for assembly on Friday mornings, to the lunchroom, which always smelled of alphabet soup no matter the entree of the day.

Seated in front of a plate on which sugary Franco-American ravioli and   30
sauce has congealed, a girl suddenly pulls a derringer from a pleat in her plaid skirt and lays waste to her lunch partner.

"Drop it!" The lunch marshal swoops into action, confiscating the gun, huge tins (fallout shelter size) of cling peaches bearing witness on a shelf behind her, SCIENTIA EST POTENTIA etched in tile above her head.

A visit to the Brooklyn Botanical Gardens, where exotica have been gathered, labeled, staked. Where armed children descend in the glass-enclosed re-creation of a tropical rain forest, heavy mist thickening with their excited breath, the City's rising humidity. We are running, tripping over metal stakes, tags identifying tree ferns, bromeliads, orchids, flesh wet with scent, the place as lush as the Hanging Gardens of Babylon, which we've memorized as one of the Seven Wonders of the Ancient World and can only imagine.

The tropics have seized us. The teachers have not seen anything like it since some seventh-graders escaped from the star show at the Hayden Planetarium and occupied the war canoe at the Museum of Natural History.

They scream for order.

"Hey, Jesse, this make you homesick for Puerto Rico?"   35

Does he mean the chaos or the foliage?

"Man, you don't know nothing."

"I like to be in America . . ."

The guerrillas are swarming. Thin streams from our pistols whip the mist further. We have created our own fog. A wall lies ahead of us.

Someone, off by himself, hidden, is tracing in the glass of the greenhouse: 40
VITO WAS HERE.

The steam will dissipate, the letters disappear.

*   *   *

"Death doesn't make sense in summer," one girl tells another. "Last summer, when Marilyn Monroe died, I just didn't get it."

"Yeah."

"Maybe it's not summer. Maybe it is being at camp. You don't expect bad things to happen."   45

"Yeah."

There was a vacant lot about two blocks up the hill from school. Traces of a former structure could be detected in the ground, but what dominated the lot and drew some of us into it were several huge boulders we named the Mexican Rocks, lending the exotic, the untamed, to a common urban terrain, making it strange.

One day Gerald O'Brien is taking a shortcut from school to *The Early Show* through the vacant lot. He hears a moan, then the sound of something scraping against rock, the granite which is the bedrock of the island. He looks into the bushes. Suddenly he is afraid of what he will find. He sees the thin arm of a girl, charm bracelet dragging in the dirt. Zodiacal fishes, Eiffel Tower, Statue of Liberty, Sacred Heart, each displayed in clear plastic trays at The Store of a Million Items, are visible, beside the bulk of a man in a business suit, who is moaning. Gerald wishes he were in The Store of a Million Items right now, browsing.

Or at home, in front of his flickering images, hearing "The Syncopated Clock," heralding *The Early Show.*

"Hey, mister! Quit it, mister! Quit it!" He screams at the back of the man.

"You wanna crush her?!"   50

The man doesn't seem to hear him.

Gerald picks up a discarded Pepsi bottle and, knowing only he wants this to stop, shuts his eyes and cracks the man on the back of the head.

"What the fuck?!"

Gerald has the man's attention. He moves back a few steps, afraid of what is coming next. "Oh, shit," the man says, under his breath, as if this were nothing.

He gets up and begins to walk away, down the hill toward the schoolyard,   55
brushing his suit as he goes.

The girl just lies there, uncovered, her plaid skirt up, bright red stains her upper leg. Gerald is afraid to touch her. He lays his pullover over her. The wool scratches her. She starts; cries. "Stay here," he says.

"Please; don't leave me."

He sits with her until another grown-up comes by, a woman loaded down with groceries. He does his best to tell the woman what happened. He stares at the ACME stamped on her bags as he speaks.

"Why, you're a little hero," she says.

Gerald is commended at the next assembly. He never sees the girl again.   60
No one does. She disappears down the Jersey shore with her mother and father, who pray it will not follow them. Gerald's father tries to reconcile his pansy of a son with the hero of the Mexican Rocks.

The PTA chips in and buys Gerald a glove embossed with Mickey Mantle's signature.

* * *

At The Store of a Million Items baseball gloves, cards, bats, balls, caps give way. School approaches. Marbled notebooks, Crayolas, pencil cases, rulers, erasers, compasses, protractors, things vital and unnecessary lie side by side under BACK TO SCHOOL.

Time passes. Seasons change.

Soon enough it is nearing Christmas and "Silver Bells" is piped to the sidewalk from The Store of a Million Items. We're getting in the mood. We watch as a whole window is cleared for the Flexible Flyers—surely the most beautiful name anything was ever given. They are arranged like fallen dominoes, one resting against the next, Eagle trademark echoing behind the glass.

There is a loud explosion. A huge clap over the City.   65

A fireball follows, rolling in the early dark of the December afternoon, above the last-minute shoppers, the schoolchildren looking to the holiday. Some of us think: "Russia," "Communism," "Sneak attack." We duck and cover and wait for the all-clear.

There is no sound.

Outside it begins to rain people. Arms and legs catch in the ailanthus, the ginkgo trees. Torsos bounce from awnings. Scraps of metal shine through the slush. Airsick bags dissolve in the streets. Samsonite jams a storm drain. It's unbelievable.

No one will forget it. Nobody doesn't talk about it. I heard this, I heard that. In the halls, on the line in the lunchroom, over trays heavy with Weiss-glass milk and Dinty Moore beef stew. "I seen a head rolling to the Colonial Lanes."

"You're full of it."   70

"My mom's a nurse. You probably wouldn't believe her neither. She said they had to put the pieces together, just so's they could bury them. There must have been millions of pieces, she said."

"I bet."

"She said you couldn't tell if they were a man or a woman, or colored neither."

That gets someone's attention.

"Isn't that a sin?"   75

"What?"

"To bury people all mixed up."

"I guess."

A woman on the radio says she dreamed it before it happened. "That's right. I dreamed there were sugar packets falling from the sky. Some said TWA, some said United. That's when I knew. I just didn't have the flight numbers."

"Have you had this . . ."   80

"Kind of experience before? You bet."

"They didn't know what hit them," is spoken all over the City as benediction.

The Store of a Million Items shifts the display of Flexible Flyers, moves the mechanical Santa bowing to passers-by, cuts off "Silver Bells," and on snow made from Ivory flakes, sets two black-shrouded model planes, assembled by the owner's grandson.

The collision, the crash, the manmade thunder and lightning, the rain of people, this was horrible enough, and then came the news that a kid had caused it.

A girl and her father are sitting at a kitchen table. The tabletop is 85 Formica, gray with pink flamingos, covered with a striped tablecloth. The table is a gift from generous in-laws; the mother prefers the table covered. "No taste," her rationale.

The man is wearing a freshly laundered breakneck shirt, his name embroidered over his left nipple. It's his bowling night. He's taking time out to talk to his daughter.

"You know why those planes collided and all those people died?"

"No," she responds; but she does. The teacher told them during current events that morning. Finding irresistible the news that a boy playing with his transistor interfered with the planes' communication with the tower at Idlewild and BOOM!

"What does that tell us, boys and girls?"

The girl knows her father wants to be the first to tell her; so she lies, and 90 feigns surprise as he gets to the point.

"A kid."

"I didn't know that." The woman at the sink, carefully soaping the dinner plates, comments.

"Didn't you hear me?"

"Yes, Dad."

"Well?" 95

"You need help, Mom?"

"Stay put, young lady."

"Okay."

"Don't 'okay' me. I want you to hear this. A kid caused the whole thing."

"How?" She plays along. 100

"He was playing with his transistor, that's how."

Maybe it was hearing it a second time, being weary of the adult version, the blame attached to this dead boy. Maybe it was remembering Jesse Moreno whispering in her ear, "Better he shoulda been playing with himself." But a smile was starting and she was desperate to erase it.

Too late.

"You think that's funny?"

"No, Dad." 105

"Well, then. That's not all. You know what happened to him?"

"No."

"He landed a few blocks from his grandparents' house in Bay Ridge. He was visiting them for the holidays."

She is biting her bottom lip, hoping to bring on tears, avoid laughter. She hates crying in front of her parents but would welcome the embarrassment right now.

Her mother only makes it worse. 110

"What were his grandparents?"

"Catholic." He is adamant in his knowledge of these strangers.

"From Naples, originally."

"Poor things."

"Irony is what you call that."   115

"Honey?"

"What?"

"If they're all dead, how come we know this?"

"Know what?"

"That the boy caused the crash."   120

"The papers said he confessed before he died. Said he didn't listen to the stewardess when she asked him to stop. It was in all the papers."

"Poor thing."

"What poor thing? He took all those people with him. All because he wouldn't listen."

"Imagine how his people feel."

When we went with our mothers to buy shoes, in the back of The Store   125
of a Million Items, the shoe salesman had us stand on a pair of metal feet and we were x-rayed. They thought they saw right through us, tissue, muscle, tendon became transparent and the bones beneath the skin, the skeleton of our feet was bared, cast in negative, like the Mr. Boneses hanging in the window around Halloween time.

——— MICHELLE CLIFF ———

www   *(b. 1946)* Web

The author of short stories, poetry, and novels, Cliff was born in Jamaica and lives in New York. Her writing retells stories of the colonized and enslaved.

www   *TOPICS FOR CRITICAL THINKING* Web

1. How does the narrator understand the passage of time?
www 2. In what ways does the story engage the notion of commodity culture? Web Does it critique such a culture?
3. In what ways does the story bring to light the increasing globalization of commerce?
4. How does this story contrast disparate items and places, and to what ends?
5. In what ways is this story postmodern?

www   *TOPIC FOR CRITICAL WRITING* Web

Discuss the ironies of "The Store of a Million Items."

15 Metanarrative

An important part of postmodernism is the way it focuses on the processes of writing and telling. Stories that draw attention to the mechanisms of telling stories are called **metanarratives, Web** and stories about stories are called *www* **metafiction.** Metanarrative is narrative that is in some way conscious of itself as narrative. Although metanarrative certainly exists in fiction from all periods (storytellers are often concerned about the art of telling stories), it is a prominent feature of postmodern literature. This is partly because postmodern tellers no longer trust either language or story to convey meaning. Meaning (if there is any) thus resides in the act of telling itself—or in telling about the uncertainties of telling.

Metanarrative takes several forms. One form is to tell a story about telling a story, as in Rudolfo Anaya's "A Story." Joyce Carol Oates's "How I Contemplated the World from the Detroit House of Correction and Began My Life Over Again" invites the reader to become part of the storytelling process as the story presents a series of fragments in a portrait of a young writer's struggles. Salman Rushdie's short stories, "The Free Radio" and "At the Auction of the Ruby Slippers," draw attention to the act of narration; the narrator often interrupts the stories to point out his stratagems. In addition, these stories play on the power of stories in culture—how stories shape our perceptions of events, the ways we value commodities (objects we desire and purchase), and the identities we adopt. Samuel Beckett's "The Calmative" demonstrates the ways narratives are a conscious way of passing time and distracting attention; his fiction depicts the minute difficulties of making meaning in any form.

Critical Perspective: On Metanarrative

"Once reading has become a questioning, rather than a finding of thematic and discursive answers, it shows itself as coinciding with, rather than simply reflecting, the human experience of life, our basic 'reading' of the world. . . .

"By exceeding the self-reflective quality of the most sophisticated modern artifacts, Beckett's texts create the awareness of their self-reflexive (i.e., critical, not only self-reflective), procedural occurrence.

"Beckett makes us aware of this textual economy because he 'hampers' the realization of meaning, and by suspending reference, by withholding referential meanings (which are themselves the result of interpretation), connotes reading as a matter of interpretation rather than as a simple referential recognition."

—Carla Locatelli, "My Life Natural Order More or Less," in Lois Oppenheim and Marius Buning (eds.), *Beckett On and On* . . . (1996), pp. 135, 139.

In these excerpts, Carla Locatelli considers the ways Beckett's fiction both reflects on itself as fiction and invites us to reflect on the processes of reading. Suggesting that Beckett's fiction draws attention to what we do when we read, the essay argues that all reading is interpreting. It also suggests that by frustrating the reader, Beckett's fiction draws attention to the ways it reflects on itself.

ꝏꝏ

RUDOLFO ANAYA

A Story   *(1982)*

Cast of Characters as created by the writer:
The Writer: myself
My Wife: herself
Sabrina: Grandpa's daughter
Sabrina's Husband: a foreigner
Federico: Grandpa's son
Federico's wife
Grandpa: Don Francisco Gomez
Alfredo: Grandpa's nephew
Don Cosme del Rincón: My dead uncle who wants to be a character
Others: Characters on the periphery who also want to get into the story

TIME: It is late New Year's morning.

PLACE: My writing room.

SITUATION: I am trying to cure a hangover with a dose of New Year's football games and left over, stale beer that tastes like sudsy water. I belch. Dandy Don smiles at me and reminds me the eyes of Texas are upon me. I remember a hangover remedy my uncle Cosme used to concoct when he was alive.

"Poke a hole in one side of the egg, put some salt and tabasco sauce in it, and stir it with a toothpick," he says from somewhere over my shoulder.

"It's not your story, uncle," I remind him and frown. He's been trying to   5
get into a story since last week, when I remembered the story my father told me about my uncle Cosme's death. But my head is too full of cobwebs to remember the details.

"Who are you talking to?" my wife calls from upstairs.

"The TV," I answer.

"I can't write today," I mumble to myself as I drag into the kitchen. "I need another situation. Real characters. . . ." I find a nice lopsided, speckled egg in the frig, poke a hole in it, pour in salt and tabasco sauce and mix. The phone rings.

"Phone's ringing," I call to my wife, then suck at the egg. Only the hot sauce keeps me from emptying my queasy stomach.

"Damn, uncle, I don't know what's worse, the hangover or the cure. . . ." I shudder and return to my room to sit at my typewriter. My uncle smiles. The paper stares at me.   10

Menudo, the Breakfast of Champions, I write, is a sure cure for a hangover.

"It's Sabrina!" my wife calls. "She wants us to come over for menudo!"

Great, I think, the situation is improving. It's just what I needed, a new situation for a story. Then I remember last night's party. Slinky Sabrina kept throwing herself all over me, swearing I was the best writer she ever knew. The situation became, uh, sticky, uncomfortable. I erase quickly with Liquid Paper Correction Fluid and I shout "No!" but it's too late. MENUDO, THE BREAKFAST OF CHAMPIONS has already become **A STORY**.

"We'll be right over, Sabrina," my wife says into the phone, "as soon as we can get ready."

"I don't want to go!" I shout. Sabrina and her husband live across the   15
street in an old, rambling adobe house. He's a foreigner, a German, I think. He's the quiet type; he likes to pierce you with his cold, analytic eyes. Sabrina grew up in my hometown, left, some say, because she got pregnant, wandered around the world and found the German. They're both okay, but what I can't stand is her family. They are the greatest liars in the world. They love to make up stories. Awful stories! I can never think when I'm around people who tell stories.

"Ready," my wife smiles.

"What happened at the party last night?"

"You should know; you were there."

Perhaps it wasn't as bad as I thought, I reassure myself. I drank one too many, I remember. We lean into the cold, January wind. It comes down like, like, a wolf on the fold. . . .

"That's awful!" my wife says.   20

"It's cold," I answer lamely and stumble across the road to Sabrina's house. It's a large house, and it's always full of relatives. Everyone who comes from the llano, that strange ocean of plain which keeps haunting me, stops to visit us. There's already a whiff on the llano that I'm a writer, so people poke around to see where they fit into my stories. Sabrina has many visitors because her family is large. And each one of them is an obsessive storyteller. Gaunt people with dark eyes set in deep sockets, they brood with their dark secrets. But they're lousy storytellers, I think, a bunch of liars.

"Don't talk nasty about people," my wife says over my shoulder.

I have to in order to write stories, I think. Who wants to read about saints. I remember my uncle Cosme del Rincón. What's the story he's trying to tell me? The wind moans and swirls dust. Suddenly Sabrina's house looms before us. The curtains are pulled and eyes stare at me from the windows. I have the feeling that I shouldn't have come. Perhaps I should go back and start all over.

"No," my wife says and knocks. Sabrina opens the door. She's dressed in a dark, revealing morning gown. "I'm so glad you came!" She smiles and

throws her arms around me. "Happy New Year! Happy New Year!" I glance
at my wife. What a character, she's thinking.

"We're glad we came, too," my wife smiles. There's a hug for her.   25

"Yes, so glad . . . come in, come in. Everything's fine. Oh, that was a great
party last night!"

"Yes, it was nice. . . ."

"Come in. . . ."

"Yes."

We enter and Sabrina leads us to the den. It's a dark, subterranean room.   30
Sabrina stumbles in the dark. She's already been nipping, I think. I take off my
sheepskin jacket and look around. Good place for a scene. There are shadows
wandering around the dark corners of the room, lurking at the story's edge.
Sabrina reaches for two and brings them into the light.

"This is my brother, Federico, and his wife . . . they just came in from Tucumcari last night, well you know, they were at the party!"

There are greetings and abrazos for everyone as we're introduced. I remember somewhere I wrote: . . . there's something rotten in Tucumcari. I
look closely at Federico, but I can't remember him from anywhere. Federico
looks closely at me. Sabrina's husband serves us sherry. "Want to play a game
of billiards?" he asks and stares at me.

"No, thanks." I refuse and pick a chair where I can observe all the action.
A writer always sits where he can observe the action. "Want to arm wrestle?"
he asks, and I refuse again. He draws back into the shadows; I know he'll keep
his eyes on me, though. I look at Federico.

"Good party last night," he nods, "but I think this neighborhood is going
to the dogs."

"Someone threw a rock at him last night," his wife explains.   35

"It's my story!" he growls at her. "I'll tell it!" He moves dramatically to
the middle of the circle. Center stage. Even the shadows that circle around us
turn to listen. I nod and Federico begins his story.

"I was driving home from the party last night," he begins. I don't remember him from the party.

"Alone?" I ask.

"That's what I'd like to know!" He glares at me and sips his beer. His
drooping mustache glistens with droplets of beer. The dim, overhead light
makes his eyes look menacing. "That rock hit my window like an explosion!"
he shouts. "There was flying glass all over!"

"Did you call the police?" Sabrina asks. She sips her sherry and swings a   40
long, sleek leg for attention. I think she wants to get into the storytelling. Her
husband clears his throat and leans over to whisper in my ear, "Federico
thinks his wife was out with someone last night . . . he came from the party
and didn't find her home."

"There were two cops just down the street!" Federico struggles to retain
my interest in his story. "They were waiting for me! But I was drunk, so. . . ."

"Was it a real rock?" I ask.

"You should know!" he answers sharply. "It was thrown so hard it shattered the entire window! There was glass all over! It could've killed me," he

whispers soto voce, for dramatic emphasis, but I'm not interested. It's a dull story. I know Sabrina's kin, they're all exaggerators, liars, storytellers.

"He could've been killed!" Sabrina gasps.

"He's too mean to kill," Federico's wife snickers.   45

"She's got a big insurance policy on him," Sabrina whispers to my wife, "he drinks a lot. . . ."

Sabrina's husband serves more sherry. Federico stalks off for a beer. Sabrina looks at me; she wants to begin her story.

"I wrecked my car before the party," she laughs. "I was at the beauty shop, getting all dolled up for that wild party last night, when who do you suppose called me and wanted a ride?" Her legs swing with mean intent. She looks at me. Don't look at me, I think.

Federico returns and fights to keep his position at the center of the stage. "I jumped out of the truck and looked around, but it was too dark. I couldn't see anything except the two cops down the street, drinking coffee while innocent drunk people are getting their windows smashed! Oh, I got madder than hell! I'm going to go home and get my guns and kill this sonofabeech that's throwing rocks, I said to myself!" He looks at me.

"He's got a lot of guns," his wife nods at me.   50

"I jumped out of my chair at the beauty shop and ran to my car to pick up whoever called me!" Sabrina says. They're both working with a mystery element which keeps us listening, but the stories aren't very interesting. Soap opera, I think. Who threw the rock that bopped Federico? Who called Sabrina for a ride just before the party started? For these and more answers, tune in tomorrow for another exciting episode in AS THE SPIRIT MOVES US! Organ music. Fade out.

"I'm going home," I say. My wife agrees.

"Stay for menudo!" Sabrina insists. "Grandpa's coming soon. Stay and meet him! I know he wants to meet you. He's a great storyteller! I swear, you won't believe a word he says!"

"Is Grandpa coming?" Federico asks. He peers into the shadows.

Grandpa, Don Francisco Gomez, was in the story we began at the party   55
last night, I remember. That's where all this started.

"Yes," Grandpa speaks from the shadows, "and I have a story to tell. . . ."

I feel goose pimples spread along my back. "Not yet, Grandpa," I say and turn to Federico. "Did you save the rock for fingerprints?" I ask.

"Yes, I saved the rock!" Federico nods and juts his face in front of mine. "I'm not dumb!" He spews beer-breath all over me. "I saved that rock, and I'm goin' to find out who threw it, an', an' in case you don't know it," he said threateningly, "there's a dead cat on the street!" He nods for emphasis and staggers a little.

"Federico ran over a cat last week," his wife explains. "Maybe that's why someone is throwing rocks at you!" Sabrina laughs. We all laugh.

"Yeah, dead pussy!" Federico exclaims.   60

"There's a lot of stories been told about dead pussy," Grandpa adds as he enters. "But jours is by far dee worse one I eber hear!" he says with his fake accent.

Grandpa is a small, wiry man. He wears boots, a leather jacket and a cowboy hat. There's a twinkle in his eyes that can suddenly turn into a threatening flash. I feel uncomfortable with him, but it's too late to do anything about it; he's pushed his way in. Alfredo, his nephew, follows him.

"Grandpa!" Sabrina jumps up to greet her father. "When did you get there? Never mind, we're glad you're here." She hugs him. "You're just in time for a drink, then we're going to eat menudo. . . ."

I remember that it was menudo that got me into this situation. Everyone rises to greet Grandpa. Sabrina introduces me as a writer.

"Don Francisco Gomez, a sus ordenes," Grandpa says and shakes my   65
hand. I wince under the grip of a man who has chopped a lot of wood in his time. I feel the bones in my hand cracking. Grandpa looks into my eyes; he recognizes me from somewhere.

"My writing hand. . . ." I smile weakly and withdraw it from his grip.

"So jew are a righter, huh?" He smiles. He has yellow teeth stained from tobacco. He wears a red kerchief tied around his neck. When he greets my wife he bows low and says, "Enchanted, miss. . . ." He kisses her hand. A real ham, I think. But then I've met enough of Sabrina's family to know they're all like that. Now I know they got it from the old man.

"I'm glad to meet you," my wife smiles. Grandpa winks.

Federico continues with his story. He's desperate now. "I ran ober dat cat a week ago," he slurs his words. "So last night they were waiting for me, right? I killed their pussy so they wanted to get even. . . ."

"Federico, jew neber deed know how to tell a story. Dat dead pussy story,   70
eet stink!" Grandpa says and moves towards center stage, threatening Federico; it's obvious Grandpa came to tell a story.

It's then that I remember Federico from the party. He came late. Stayed in a corner and drank to himself. But did he come before or after the rock-throwing incident? And was he looking for me? I look at his wife. She smiles.

"Let me tell jew a real story," Grandpa smiles, a cold glint in his eyes. He looks at me for approval. He sips his bourbon.

"Grandpa, we were talking about you last night, at the party!" Sabrina exclaims. "About the time you saw Don Cosme del Rincón murdered! Don Cosme was. . . ." She points at me but Federico interrupts.

"I know the pussy was dead. I ran over it. I whammed it myself!" he shouts. "But I don't know who that pussy belongs to. I was too drunk," he admits and looks at his wife. "Maybe I was just thinking about dead pussy. . . . but I could smell it." He shakes his head sadly. "But why did the rock hit my window at that exact spot? At that exact time?"

"It always happens like that," Sabrina insists. "The right situation re-   75
quires the right time, that's what Grandpa always said." Grandpa nods. He's still looking at me. "Look what happened to me when I'm driving to meet my friend!" She emphasizes *my friend* and swings her legs. "I'm driving down Central, and I know it's very crowded at 5 o'clock, so I decide to take Lomas, and it's exactly at the moment that I decide to change streets that the other car hits me! Wham, just like that! Has that ever happened to you?" she asks.

"No," I answer. "So you never got to your friend, the one who called for a ride?"

"No," she pouts and downs the remainder of her sherry. I feel easier.

"So I decided to take the law into my own hands!" Federico continues. "I went home to get my guns."

"He's got a closet full of guns," his wife nods.

Sabrina whispers to my wife: "Federico shot a man once. He's very jeal- 80 ous. He came home late from work one night and found a man leaving his house, so he shot him. Turned out to be a poor telegraph boy just delivering a telegram." She laughs. My wife looks at me as if to say be careful with these characters. I shrug.

"I know who murder' Don Cosme del Rincón," Grandpa nods and begins his story. "I hab dee gun dat kill heem. . . ."

Cut the cheap theatrics, I think. Grandpa grins and drops his accent. "The first gun I ever owned was an old Smith and Wesson .38. I was just a kid, 1914, and I was herding sheep on the Rincón llano when three men who had just escaped from the Santa Fe Prison rode into our camp. . . ."

Sabrina claps her hands. "But he's from that llano, from the Rincón!" She points at me. "He's a writer! He writes stories! And Don Cosme was his uncle!"

"Ah, I thought so," Grandpa nods. The twinkle in his eyes has changed to a cold, piercing stare. "I thought I recognized you," he says, "the chin, the nose."

"Jew right books, huh?" Federico asks. He has acquired Grandpa's accent; 85 he thinks I'm interested in the accent instead of the story.

"Yes," I say and stand to leave. "But I'm tired, I think we should leave." I look at my wife. She nods agreement. It's hard to observe a potential story if the characters know the writer is present; it causes too many interferences. The characters start acting and hamming it up, looking for a part.

"You can't go until I show you the pistol," Grandpa says sternly. "Go get the pistol, Alfredo!" he orders and Alfredo disappears into the shadows. "You know, they're writing a book about me, too," he says. His eyes bore into mine. "All those years I spent working on the llano, I saw a lot, there's a lot of stories I can tell. . . ." He turns and walks to center stage. His presence holds our attention. The room grows silent. This is the silence before the story begins, the most challenging part of the story. The silence is ominous. From it will come the words that will affect all of us. I shiver, lean forward and wait. Alfredo returns with the pistol. The small Smith and Wesson curls like a black snake into Grandpa's hand.

"Three men escaped from prison," Grandpa begins. His words hypnotize us, rivet us to our spots. I have to give Grandpa credit, when he drops the cheap theatrics he's a real story teller. There's an aura around him, as if he's infused with the spirit of the past. "One of the escaped prisoners was a Mexican nationalist, and he was shot and killed by a deputy sheriff from Pastura. That man's family later sent many sons across the border to avenge the death, and for years the llano was filled with bloodshed . . . but that's another story. The other man was a dirt farmer who didn't know his way in the llano, so there's no need to speak of him. The third man. . . ."

"The third man was the man who killed my uncle Cosme," I interrupt. I feel a cold sweat on my forehead. So this is what my uncle Cosme was trying to warn me about! That's why he keeps appearing at the edges of the story!

But what were the details of that story? I ask myself. Why am I on dangerous ground with Grandpa?

"Uncle?" I say.

My uncle Cosme struggles forward. He is a terrible sight. He has been dead for half a century. He is moldy from the grave, but I can still make out the bullet hole in his forehead. He wants to speak, he wants to warn me, but there is only a dry, raspy rattle as Grandpa pushes him back into the shadows.

"It's my story," Grandpa insists, "and I haven't finished it yet!" He has grown very strong. His knuckles are white around the pistol as he points it my way. He grins. "The third man was my brother," he says, "and he returned to kill your uncle who had stolen his woman. I was herding sheep for your uncle when they rode in. At first I didn't recognize my older brother. Then he shot Don Cosme del Rincón, and he gave me the pistol and he told me to hide it. I've kept it ever since. I needed to keep it because after that killing a war broke out on the llano. There was no mercy when the family honor was violated. Blood called for blood. . . ."

"So, you deserve what you get," Federico nods drunkenly.

I know, I think. I had been told that story a hundred times, but I had forgotten it. I thought I had left the past behind. I thought I had left the family feuds of the llano behind me, and now they had returned to trap me, perhaps to kill me. My legs feel weak. I look at Grandpa pointing the pistol at me.

"It must have been you who called," Sabrina says, "you're the only one I could tell my story to. . . ."

Over my shoulder I hear Sabrina's husband whisper, "You would have been better off playing cards with me, a simple game to pass the time. Now look at the situation you've gotten yourself into."

It was a situation I was looking for, I think. I needed a story, I needed to create a situation. I see the typewriter paper in front of me and secretly yearn to recreate the past. I wish I could undo what I have done. I look at Grandpa. I know I've created my own destruction. He's an old man, and he's still avenging the old feud. I can see blood in his narrow eyes.

"Grandpa, don't point the gun!" Federico's wife cries nervously.

"Don't, Grandpa!" Sabrina cries.

"No!" my wife shouts and jumps between Grandpa at me.

There is a profound silence; the cold wind whistles around the edges of the house. The shadows shrink back into the dark corners. Then Grandpa smiles. He tosses the small pistol at me and I catch it. "It's not loaded," he says, "I just wanted you to see it. It's a beauty, isn't it? And it did so much killing in its time. But that's over now. . . ."

Yes, I nod and look at the small, black pistol nestled in my hand, that's over now. My wife slips her arm around my waist. I look at her. Her presence is reassuring. I think she's the only one who understands what I go through with my crazy characters.

"Oh, Grandpa, you're such a joker," Federico's wife smiles.

"It's not fair to use stuff like that when you tell a story," Federico says lamely.

"Okay, enough of this nonsense, enough of this story telling!" Sabrina announces. "It's time to eat menudo! That's why all of you were invited, for a good meal of spicy menudo! And I've got hot chile and beans. . . ." She takes her husband's arm and leads us into the kitchen.

I feel my wife take my hand. "You ready to eat?" she asks.

"Yeah," I nod.

"How's the situation?" she smiles back.

"I think I've got it under control," I say. I look at Grandpa. "That was a good story," I tell him.

His eyes twinkle. "There's a lot of stories that happened on the llano," he   110
says. "I never told too many of them, but now one of my grand-daughters has gotten her college degree, and she wants to write down my stories. So why not," he chuckles.

"Hey," Federico asks as we enter the kitchen, "maybe someday you'll want to write down my story, huh? I could tell you about the time we went hunting up in the Pecos. . . ."

RUDOLFO ANAYA
(b. 1937) Web   *www*

Rudolfo Anaya is an award-winning southwestern writer, whose work focuses on the experiences of Chicano people caught between folk culture and the changes forced by modernization and population movement. Raised in rural New Mexico, Anaya grew up in a bilingual home steeped in the traditions of Catholicism and folk medicine.

TOPICS FOR CRITICAL THINKING Web   *www*

1. In what ways does this story make evident its status as a story?
2. What constitutes a good story in "A Story"?
3. In what ways is "A Story" an example of postmodernism?
4. In what ways is Anaya's story part of the tradition of folk storytelling?
5. How can folk tradition and postmodernism be mixed?

TOPIC FOR CRITICAL WRITING Web   *www*

What does this story's rendition of the processes of writing a story reveal about the story "A Story"?

∽∾

JOYCE CAROL OATES

How I Contemplated the World from the Detroit House of Correction and Began My Life Over Again   *(1971)*

Notes for an Essay for an English Class at Baldwin Country
Day School; Poking Around in Debris; Disgust and Curiosity;
A Revelation of the Meaning of Life; A Happy Ending . . .

I Events

1. The girl (myself) is walking through Branden's, that excellent store. Suburb of a large famous city that is a symbol for large famous American cities. The event sneaks up on the girl, who believes she is herding it along with a small fixed smile, a girl of fifteen, innocently experienced. She dawdles in a certain style by a counter of costume jewellery. Rings, earrings, necklaces. Prices from $5 to $50, all within reach. All ugly. She eases over to the glove counter, where everything is ugly too. In her close-fitted coat with its black fur collar she contemplates the luxury of Branden's, which she has known for many years: its many mild pale lights, easy on the eye and the soul, its elaborate tinkly decorations, its women shoppers with their excellent shoes and coats and hairdos, all dawdling gracefully, in no hurry.

Who was ever in a hurry here?

2. The girl seated at home. A small library, panelled walls of oak. Someone is talking to me. An earnest, husky, female voice drives itself against my ears, nervous, frightened, groping around my heart, saying, 'If you wanted gloves, why didn't you say so? Why didn't you ask for them?' That store, Branden's, is owned by Raymond Forrest who lives on Du Maurier Drive. We live on Sioux Drive. Raymond Forrest. A handsome man? An ugly man? A man of fifty or sixty, with grey hair, or a man of forty with earnest, courteous eyes, a good golf game; who is Raymond Forrest, this man who is my salvation? Father has been talking to him. Father is not his physician; Dr Berg is his physician. Father and Dr Berg refer patients to each other. There is a connection. Mother plays bridge with . . . On Mondays and Wednesdays our maid Billie works at . . . The strings draw together in a cat's cradle, making a net to save you when you fall. . . .

3. *Harriet Arnold's.* A small shop, better than Branden's. Mother in her black coat, I in my close-fitted blue coat. Shopping. Now look at this, isn't this cute, do you want this, why don't you want this, try this on, take this with you to the fitting room, take this also, what's wrong with you, what can I do for you, why are you so strange . . . ? 'I wanted to steal but not to buy,' I don't tell her. The girl droops along in her coat and gloves and leather boots, her eyes

scan the horizon, which is pastel pink and decorated like Branden's, tasteful walls and modern ceilings with graceful glimmering lights.

4. Weeks later, the girl at a bus stop. Two o'clock in the afternoon, a Tuesday; obviously she has walked out of school.

5. The girl stepping down from a bus. Afternoon, weather changing to colder. Detroit. Pavement and closed-up stores; grill-work over the windows of a pawnshop. What is a pawnshop, exactly?

II *Characters*

1. The girl stands five feet five inches tall. An ordinary height. Baldwin Country Day School draws them up to that height. She dreams along the corridors and presses her face against the Thermoplex glass. No frost or steam can ever form on that glass. A smudge of grease from her forehead . . . could she be boiled down to grease? She wears her hair loose and long and straight in suburban teen-age style, 1968. Eyes smudged with pencil, dark brown. Brown hair. Vague green eyes. A pretty girl? An ugly girl? She sings to herself under her breath, idling in the corridor, thinking of her many secrets (the thirty dollars she once took from the purse of a friend's mother, just for fun, the basement window she smashed in her own house just for fun) and thinking of her brother who is at Susquehanna Boys' Academy, an excellent preparatory school in Maine, remembering him unclearly . . . he has long manic hair and a squeaking voice and he looks like one of the popular teenage singers of 1968, one of those in a group, *The Certain Forces, The Way Out, The Maniacs Responsible*. The girl in her turn looks like one of those fieldsful of girls who listen to the boys' singing, dreaming and mooning restlessly, breaking into high sullen laughter, innocently experienced.

2. The mother. A Midwestern woman of Detroit and suburbs. Belongs to the Detroit Athletic Club. Also the Detroit Golf Club. Also the Bloomfield Hills Country Club. The Village Women's Club at which lectures are given each winter on Genet and Sartre and James Baldwin, by the Director of the Adult Education Program at Wayne State University. . . . The Bloomfield Art Association. Also the Founders Society of the Detroit Institute of Arts. Also . . . Oh, she is in perpetual motion, this lady, hair like blown-up gold and finer than gold, hair and fingers and body of inestimable grace. Heavy weighs the gold on the back of her hairbrush and hand mirror. Heavy heavy the candlesticks in the dining room. Very heavy is the big car, a Lincoln, long and black, that on one cool autumn day split a squirrel's body in two unequal parts.

3. The father. Dr——. He belongs to the same clubs as ——2. A player of squash and golf; he has a golfer's umbrella of stripes. Candy stripes. In his mouth nothing turns to sugar, however; saliva works no miracles here. His doctoring is of the slightly sick. The sick are sent elsewhere (to Dr Berg?), the deathly sick are sent back for more tests and their bills are sent to their homes,

the unsick are sent to Dr Coronet (Isabel, a lady), an excellent psychiatrist for unsick people who angrily believe they are sick and want to do something about it. If they demand a male psychiatrist, the unsick are sent by Dr (my father) to Dr Lowenstein, a male psychiatrist, excellent and expensive, with a limited practice.

4. Clarita. She is twenty, twenty-five, she is thirty or more? Pretty, ugly, 10 what? She is a woman lounging by the side of a road, in jeans and a sweater, hitchhiking, or she is slouched on a stool at a counter in some roadside diner. A hard line of jaw. Curious eyes. Amused eyes. Behind her eyes processions move, funeral pageants, cartoons. She says, 'I never can figure out why girls like you bum around down here. What are you looking for anyway?' An odour of tobacco about her. Unwashed underclothes, or no underclothes, unwashed skin, gritty toes, hair long and falling into strands, not recently washed.

5. Simon. In this city the weather changes abruptly, so Simon's weather changes abruptly. He sleeps through the afternoon. He sleeps through the morning. Rising, he gropes around for something to get him going, for a cigarette or a pill to drive him out to the street, where the temperature is hovering around 35°. Why doesn't it drop? Why, why doesn't the cold clean air come down from Canada; will he have to go up into Canada to get it? will he have to leave the Country of his Birth and sink into Canada's frosty fields . . . ? Will the F.B.I. (which he dreams about constantly) chase him over the Canadian border on foot, hounded out in a blizzard of broken glass and horns . . . ?

'Once I was Huckleberry Finn,' Simon says, 'but now I am Roderick Usher.' Beset by frenzies and fears, this man who makes my spine go cold, he takes green pills, yellow pills, pills of white and capsules of dark blue and green . . . he takes other things I may not mention, for what if Simon seeks me out and climbs into my girl's bedroom here in Bloomfield Hills and strangles me, what then . . . ? (As I write this I begin to shiver. Why do I shiver? I am now sixteen and sixteen is not an age for shivering.) It comes from Simon, who is always cold.

III World Events

Nothing.

IV People & Circumstances Contributing to This Delinquency

Nothing.

V Sioux Drive

George, Clyde G. 240 Sioux. A manufacturer's representative; children, a 15 dog, a wife. Georgian with the usual columns. You think of the White House, then of Thomas Jefferson, then your mind goes blank on the white pillars and you think of nothing. Norris, Ralph W. 246 Sioux. Public relations. Colonial. Bay window, brick, stone, concrete, wood, green shutters, sidewalk, lantern, grass, trees, blacktop drive, two children, one of them my classmate Esther (Esther Norris) at Baldwin. Wife, cars. Ramsey, Michael D. 250 Sioux. Colonial. Big living room, thirty by twenty-five, fireplaces in living room, library, recreation room, panelled walls wet bar five bathrooms five bedrooms two lavatories central air conditioning automatic sprinkler automatic garage door three children one wife two cars a breakfast room a patio a large fenced lot fourteen trees a front door with a brass knocker never knocked. Next is our house. Classic contemporary. Traditional modern. Attached garage, attached Florida room, attached patio, attached pool and cabana, attached roof. A front door mail slot through which pour *Time Magazine, Fortune, Life, Business Week*, the *Wall Street Journal*, the *New York Times*, the *New Yorker*, the *Saturday Review, M.D., Modern Medicine, Disease of the Month* . . . and also. . . . And in addition to all this, a quiet sealed letter from Baldwin saying: *Your daughter is not doing work compatible with her performance on the Stanford-Binet.* . . . And your son is not doing well, not well at all, very sad. Where is your son anyway? Once he stole trick-and-treat candy from some six-year-old kids, he himself being a robust ten. The beginning. Now your daughter steals. In the Village Pharmacy she made off with, yes she did, don't deny it, she made off with a copy of *Pageant Magazine* for no reason, she swiped a roll of Life Savers in a green wrapper and was in no need of saving her life or even in need of sucking candy; when she was no more than eight years old she stole, don't blush, she stole a package of Tums only because it was out on the counter and available, and the nice lady behind the counter (now dead) said nothing. . . . Sioux Drive. Maples, oaks, elms. Diseased elms cut down. Sioux Drive runs into Roosevelt Drive. Slow, turning lanes, not streets, all drives and lanes and ways and passes. A private police force. Quiet private police, in unmarked cars. Cruising on Saturday evenings with paternal smiles for the residents who are streaming in and out of houses, going to and from parties, a thousand parties, slightly staggering, the women in their furs alighting from automobiles bought of Ford and General Motors and Chrysler, very heavy automobiles. No foreign cars. Detroit. In 275 Sioux, down the block in that magnificent French-Normandy mansion, lives——himself, who has the C—— account itself, imagine that! Look at where he lives and look at the enormous trees and chimneys, imagine his many fireplaces, imagine his wife and children, imagine his wife's hair, imagine her fingernails, imagine her bathtub of smooth clean glowing pink, imagine their embraces, his trouser pockets filled with odd coins and keys and dust and peanuts, imagine their ecstasy on Sioux Drive, imagine their income tax returns, imagine their little boy's pride in his experimental car, a scaled-down C——, as he roars around the neighborhood on the sidewalks frightening dogs and Negro maids, oh imagine all these things, imagine everything, let your mind roar out all over Sioux Drive and Du Maurier Drive and Roosevelt Drive and Ticonderoga Pass and Burning Bush Way and Lincolnshire Pass and Lois Lane.

When spring comes, its winds blow nothing to Sioux Drive, no odours of hollyhocks or forsythia, nothing Sioux Drive doesn't already possess, everything is planted and performing. The weather vanes, had they weather vanes, don't have to turn with the wind, don't have to contend with the weather. There is no weather.

VI Detroit

There is always weather in Detroit. Detroit's temperature is always 32°. Fast-falling temperatures. Slow-rising temperatures. Wind from the north-northeast four to forty miles an hour, small-craft warnings, partly cloudy today and Wednesday changing to partly sunny through Thursday . . . small warnings of frost, soot warnings, traffic warnings, hazardous lake conditions for small craft and swimmers, restless Negro gangs, restless cloud formations, restless temperatures aching to fall out the very bottom of the thermometer or shoot up over the top and boil everything over in red mercury.

Detroit's temperature is 32°. Fast-falling temperatures. Slow-rising temperatures. Wind from the north-northeast four to forty miles an hour. . . .

VII Events

1. The girl's heart is pounding. In her pocket is a pair of gloves! In a plastic bag! Airproof breathproof plastic bag, gloves selling for twenty-five dollars on Branden's counter! In her pocket! Shoplifted! . . . In her purse is a blue comb, not very clean. In her purse is a leather billfold (a birthday present from her grandmother in Philadelphia) with snapshots of the family in clean plastic windows, in the billfold are bills, she doesn't know how many bills. . . . In her purse is an ominous note from her friend Tykie *What's this about Joe H. and the kids hanging around at Louise's Sat. night? You heard anything?* . . . passed in French class. In her purse is a lot of dirty yellow Kleenex, her mother's heart would break to see such very dirty Kleenex, and at the bottom of her purse are brown hairpins and safety pins and a broken pencil and a ballpoint pen (blue) stolen from somewhere forgotten and a purse-size compact of Cover Girl Make-Up, Ivory Rose. . . . Her lipstick is Broken Heart, a corrupt pink; her fingers are trembling like crazy; her teeth are beginning to chatter; her insides are alive; her eyes glow in her head; she is saying to her mother's astonished face *I want to steal but not to buy.*

2. At Clarita's. Day or night? What room is this? A bed, a regular bed, and a mattress on the floor nearby. Wallpaper hanging in strips. Clarita says she tore it like that with her teeth. She was fighting a barbaric tribe that night, high from some pills; she was battling for her life with men wearing helmets of heavy iron and their faces no more than Christian crosses to breathe through, every one of those bastards looking like her lover Simon, who seems to breathe with great difficulty through the slits of mouth and nostrils in his face. Clarita has never heard of Sioux Drive. Raymond Forrest cuts no ice with her, nor does the C⸺ account and its millions; Harvard Business School could be at the corner of Vernor and 12th Street for all she cares, and Vietnam might have sunk by now into the Dead Sea under its ton of debris,

for all the amazement she could show . . . her face is overworked, over-wrought, at the age of twenty (thirty?) it is already exhausted but fanciful and ready for a laugh. Clarita says mournfully to me *Honey somebody is going to turn you out let me give you warning.* In a movie shown on late television Clarita is not a mess like this but a nurse, with short neat hair and a dedicated look, in love with her doctor and her doctor's patients and their diseases, enamoured of needles and sponges and rubbing alcohol. . . . Or no: she is a private secretary. Robert Cummings is her boss. She helps him with fantastic plots, the canned audience laughs, no, the audience doesn't laugh because nothing is funny, instead her boss is Robert Taylor and they are not boss and secretary but husband and wife, she is threatened by a young starlet, she is grim, handsome, wifely, a good companion for a good man. . . . She is Claudette Colbert. Her sister too is Claudette Colbert. They are twins, identical. Her husband Charles Boyer is a very rich handsome man and her sister, Claudette Colbert, is plotting her death in order to take her place as the rich man's wife, no one will know because they are *twins.* . . . All these marvellous lives Clarita might have lived, but she fell out the bottom at the age of thirteen. At the age when I was packing my overnight case for a slumber party at Toni Deshield's she was tearing filthy sheets off a bed and scratching up a rash on her arms. . . . Thirteen is uncommonly young for a white girl in Detroit, Miss Brock of the Detroit House of Correction said in a sad newspaper interview for the *Detroit News;* fifteen and sixteen are more likely. Eleven, twelve, thirteen are not surprising in coloured . . . they are more precocious. What can we do? Taxes are rising and the tax base is falling. The temperature rises slowly but falls rapidly. Everything is falling out the bottom, Woodward Avenue is filthy, Livernois Avenue is filthy! Scraps of paper flutter in the air like pigeons, dirt flies up and hits you right in the eye, oh Detroit is breaking up into dangerous bits of newspaper and dirt, watch out. . . .

Clarita's apartment is over a restaurant. Simon her lover emerges from the cracks at dark. Mrs Olesko, a neighbour of Clarita's, an aged white wisp of a woman, doesn't complain but sniffs with contentment at Clarita's noisy life and doesn't tell the cops, hating cops, when the cops arrive. I should give more fake names, more blanks, instead of telling all these secrets. I myself am a secret; I am a minor.

3. My father reads a paper at a medical convention in Los Angeles. There he is, on the edge of the North American continent, when the un-marked detective put his hand so gently on my arm in the aisle of Branden's and said, 'Miss, would you like to step over here for a minute?'

And where was he when Clarita put her hand on my arm, that wintry dark sulphurous aching day in Detroit, in the company of closed-down barber shops, closed-down diners, closed-down movie houses, homes, windows, basements, faces . . . she put her hand on my arm and said, 'Honey, are you looking for somebody down here?'

And was he home worrying about me, gone for two weeks solid, when they carried me off . . . ? It took three of them to get me in the police cruiser, so they said, and they put more than their hands on my arm.

4. I work on this lesson. My English teacher is Mr Forest, who is from 25
Michigan State. Not handsome, Mr Forest, and his name is plain, unlike Raymond Forrest's, but he is sweet and rodentlike, he has conferred with the
principal and my parents, and everything is fixed . . . treat her as if nothing
has happened, a new start, begin again, only sixteen years old, what a shame,
how did it happen?—nothing happened, nothing could have happened, a
slight physiological modification known only to a gynecologist or to Dr
Coronet. I work on my lesson. I sit in my pink room. I look around the room
with my sad pink eyes. I sigh, I dawdle, I pause, I eat up time, I am limp and
happy to be home, I am sixteen years old suddenly, my head hangs heavy as a
pumpkin on my shoulders, and my hair has just been cut by Mr Faye at the
Crystal Salon and is said to be very becoming.

   (Simon too put his hand on my arm and said, 'Honey, you have got to
come with me,' and in his six-by-six room we got to know each other. Would
I go back to Simon again? Would I lie down with him in all that filth and
craziness? Over and over again.

                                                      a Clarita is being
betrayed as in front of a Cunningham Drug Store she is nervously eying a
coloured man who may or may not have money, or a nervous white boy of
twenty with sideburns and an Appalachian look, who may or may not have a
knife hidden in his jacket pocket, or a husky red-faced man of friendly countenance who may or may not be a member of the Vice Squad out for an early
twilight walk.)

   I work on my lesson for Mr Forest. I have filled up eleven pages. Words
pour out of me and won't stop. I want to tell everything . . . what was the song
Simon was always humming, and who was Simon's friend in a very new trench
coat with an old high school graduation ring on his finger . . . ? Simon's
bearded friend? When I was down too low for him, Simon kicked me out and
gave me to him for three days, I think, on Fourteenth Street in Detroit, an
airy room of cold cruel drafts with newspapers on the floor. . . . Do I really remember that or am I piecing it together from what they told me? Did they tell
the truth? Did they know much of the truth?

VIII Characters

1. Wednesdays after school, at four; Saturday mornings at ten. Mother
drives me to Dr Coronet. Ferns in the office, plastic or real, they look the
same. Dr Coronet is queenly, an elegant nicotine-stained lady who would
have studied with Freud had circumstances not prevented it, a bit of a
Catholic, ready to offer you some mystery if your teeth will ache too much
without it. Highly recommended by Father! Forty dollars an hour, Father's
forty dollars! Progress! Looking up! Looking better! That new haircut is so
becoming, says Dr Coronet herself, showing how normal she is for a woman
with an I.Q. of 180 and many advanced degrees.

2. Mother. A lady in a brown suede coat. Boots of shiny black material,
black gloves, a black fur hat. She would be humiliated could she know that of

all the people in the world it is my ex-lover Simon who walks most like her . . . self-conscious and unreal, listening to distant music, a little bowlegged with craftiness. . . .

3. Father. Tying a necktie. In a hurry. On my first evening home he put his hand on my arm and said, 'Honey, we're going to forget all about this.'

4. Simon. Outside, a plane is crossing the sky, in here we're in a hurry. Morning. It must be morning. The girl is half out of her mind, whimpering and vague; Simon her dear friend is wretched this morning . . . he is wretched with morning itself . . . he forces her to give him an injection with that needle she knows is filthy, she has a dread of needles and surgical instruments and the odour of things that are to be sent into the blood, thinking somehow of her father. . . . This is a bad morning, Simon says that his mind is being twisted out of shape, and so he submits to the needle that he usually scorns and bites his lip with his yellowish teeth, his face going very pale. *Ah baby!* he says in his soft mocking voice, which with all women is a mockery of love, *do it like this— Slowly*—And the girl, terrified, almost drops the precious needle but manages to turn it up to the light from the window . . . is it an extension of herself then? She can give him this gift then? *I wish you wouldn't do this to me*, she says, wise in her terror, because it seems to her that Simon's danger—in a few minutes he may be dead—is a way of pressing her against him that is more powerful than any other embrace. She has to work over his arm, the knotted corded veins of his arm, her forehead wet with perspiration as she pushes and releases the needle, staring at that mixture of liquid now stained with Simon's bright blood. . . . When the drug hits him she can feel it herself, she feels that magic that is more than any woman can give him, striking the back of his head and making his face stretch as if with the impact of a terrible sun. . . . She tries to embrace him but he pushes her aside and stumbles to his feet. *Jesus Christ*, he says. . . .

5. Princess, a Negro girl of eighteen. What is her charge? She is closed-mouthed about it, shrewd and silent, you know that no one had to wrestle her to the sidewalk to get her in here; she came with dignity. In the recreation room she sits reading *Nancy Drew and the Jewel Box Mystery*, which inspires in her face tiny wrinkles of alarm and interest: what a face! Light brown skin, heavy shaded eyes, heavy eyelashes, a serious sinister dark brow, graceful fingers, graceful wristbones, graceful legs, lips, tongue, a sugar-sweet voice, a leggy stride more masculine than Simon's and my mother's, decked out in a dirty white blouse and dirty white slacks; vaguely nautical is Princess' style. . . . At breakfast she is in charge of clearing the table and leans over me, saying, *Honey you sure you ate enough?*

6. The girl lies sleepless, wondering. Why here, why not there? Why Bloomfield Hills and not jail? Why jail and not her pink room? Why downtown Detroit and not Sioux Drive? What is the difference? Is Simon all the difference? The girl's head is a parade of wonders. She is nearly sixteen, her breath is marvellous with wonders, not long ago she was colouring with crayons and now she is smearing the landscape with paints that won't come off

and won't come off her fingers either. She says to the matron *I am not talking about anything*, not because everyone has warned her not to talk but because, because she will not talk; because she won't say anything about Simon, who is her secret. And she says to the matron, *I won't go home*, up until that night in the lavatory when everything was changed. . . . 'No, I won't go home I want to stay here,' she says, listening to her own words with amazement, thinking that weeds might climb everywhere over that marvellous $180,000 house and dinosaurs might return to muddy the beige carpeting, but never never will she reconcile four o'clock in the morning in Detroit with eight o'clock breakfasts in Bloomfield Hills. . . . oh, she aches still for Simon's hands and his caressing breath, though he gave her little pleasure, he took everything from her (five-dollar bills, ten-dollar bills, passed into her numb hands by men and taken out of her hands by Simon) until she herself was passed into the hands of other men, police, when Simon evidently got tired of her and her hysteria. . . . *No, I won't go home, I don't want to be bailed out.* The girl thinks as a *Stubborn and Wayward Child* (one of several charges lodged against her), and the matron understands her crazy white-rimmed eyes that are seeking out some new violence that will keep her in jail, should someone threaten to let her out. Such children try to strangle the matrons, the attendants, or one another . . . they want the locks locked forever, the doors nailed shut . . . and this girl is no different up until that night her mind is changed for her. . . .

IX That Night

Princess and Dolly, a little white girl of maybe fifteen, hardy however as a sergeant and in the House of Correction for armed robbery, corner her in the lavatory at the farthest sink and the other girls look away and file out to bed, leaving her. God, how she is beaten up! Why is she beaten up? Why do they pound her, why such hatred? Princess vents all the hatred of a thousand silent Detroit winters on her body, this girl whose body belongs to me, fiercely she rides across the Midwestern plains on this girl's tender bruised body . . . revenge on the oppressed minorities of America! revenge on the slaughtered Indians! revenge on the female sex, on the male sex, revenge on Bloomfield Hills, revenge revenge. . . .

X Detroit

In Detroit, weather weighs heavily upon everyone. The sky looms large. The horizon shimmers in smoke. Downtown the buildings are imprecise in the haze. Perpetual haze. Perpetual motion inside the haze. Across the choppy river is the city of Windsor, in Canada. Part of the continent has bunched up here and is bulging outward, at the tip of Detroit; a cold hard rain is forever falling on the expressways. . . . Shoppers shop grimly, their cars are not parked in safe places, their windshields may be smashed and graceful ebony hands may drag them out through their shatterproof smashed windshields, crying, *Revenge for the Indians!* Ah, they all fear leaving Hudson's and being dragged to the very tip of the city and thrown off the parking roof of Cobo Hall, that expensive tomb, into the river. . . .

XI Characters We Are Forever Entwined With

1. Simon drew me into his tender rotting arms and breathed gravity into me. Then I came to earth, weighed down. He said, *You are such a little girl*, and he weighed me down with his delight. In the palms of his hands were teeth marks from his previous life experiences. He was thirty-five, they said. Imagine Simon in this room, in my pink room: he is about six feet tall and stoops slightly, in a feline cautious way, always thinking, always on guard, with his scuffed light suede shoes and his clothes that are anyone's clothes, slightly rumpled ordinary clothes that ordinary men might wear to not-bad jobs. Simon has fair long hair, curly hair, spent languid curls that are like . . . exactly like the curls of wood shavings to the touch, I am trying to be exact . . . and he smells of unheated mornings and coffee and too many pills coating his tongue with a faint green-white scum. . . . Dear Simon, who would be panicked in this room and in this house (right now Billie is vacuuming next door in my parents' room; a vacuum cleaner's roar is a sign of all good things), Simon who is said to have come from a home not much different from this, years ago, fleeing all the carpeting and the polished banisters . . . Simon has a deathly face, only desperate people fall in love with it. His face is bony and cautious, the bones of his cheeks prominent as if with the rigidity of his ceaseless thinking, plotting, for he has to make money out of girls to whom money means nothing, they're so far gone they can hardly count it, and in a sense money means nothing to him either except as a way of keeping on with his life. *Each Day's Proud Struggle*, the title of a novel we could read at jail. . . . Each day he needs a certain amount of money. He devours it. It wasn't love he uncoiled in me with his hollowed-out eyes and his courteous smile, that remnant of a prosperous past, but a dark terror that needed to press itself flat against him, or against another man . . . but he was the first, he came over to me and took my arm, a claim. We struggled on the stairs and I said, *Let me loose, you're hurting my neck, my face*, it was such a surprise that my skin hurt where he rubbed it, and afterward we lay face to face and he breathed everything into me. In the end I think he turned me in.

2. Raymond Forrest. I just read this morning that Raymond Forrest's father, the chairman of the board at   , died of a heart attack on a plane bound for London. I would like to write Raymond Forrest a note of sympathy. I would like to thank him for not pressing charges against me one hundred years ago, saving me, being so generous . . . well, men like Raymond Forrest are generous men, not like Simon. I would like to write him a letter telling of my love, or of some other emotion that is positive and healthy. Not like Simon and his poetry, which he scrawled down when he was high and never changed a word . . . but when I try to think of something to say, it is Simon's language that comes back to me, caught in my head like a bad song, it is always Simon's language:

> There is no reality only dreams
> Your neck may get snapped when you wake

My love is drawn to some violent end
She keeps wanting to get away
My love is heading downward
And I am heading upward
She is going to crash on the sidewalk
And I am going to dissolve into the clouds

XII Events

1. Out of the hospital, bruised and saddened and converted, with Princess' grunts still tangled in my hair . . . and Father in his overcoat looking like a prince himself, come to carry me off. Up the expressway and out north to home. Jesus Christ, but the air is thinner and cleaner here. Monumental houses. Heartbreaking sidewalks, so clean.

2. Weeping in the living room. The ceiling is two stories high and two chandeliers hang from it. Weeping, weeping, though Billie the maid is *probably listening*. I will never leave home again. Never. Never leave home. Never leave this home again, never.

3. Sugar doughnuts for breakfast. The toaster is very shiny and my face is distorted in it. Is that my face?

40

4. The car is turning in the driveway. Father brings me home. Mother embraces me. Sunlight breaks in movieland patches on the roof of our traditional-contemporary home, which was designed for the famous automotive stylist whose identity, if I told you the name of the famous car he designed, you would all know, so I can't tell you because my teeth chatter at the thought of being sued . . . or having someone climb into my bedroom window with a rope to strangle me. . . . The car turns up the blacktop drive. The house opens to me like a doll's house, so lovely in the sunlight, the big living room beckons to me with its walls falling away in a delirium of joy at my return, Billie the maid is *no doubt* listening from the kitchen as I burst into tears and the hysteria Simon got so sick of. Convulsed in Father's arms, I say I will never leave again, never, why did I leave, where did I go, what happened, my mind is gone wrong, my body is one big bruise, my backbone was sucked dry, it wasn't the men who hurt me and Simon never hurt me but only those girls . . . my God, how they hurt me . . . I will never leave home again. . . . The car is perpetually turning up the drive and I am perpetually taking the right exit from the expressway (Lahser Road) and the wall of the rest room is perpetually banging against my head and perpetually are Simon's hands moving across my body and adding everything up and so too are Father's hands on my shaking bruised back, far from the surface of my skin on the surface of my good blue cashmere coat (dry-cleaned for my release). . . . I weep for all the money here, for God in gold and beige carpeting, for the beauty of chandeliers and the miracle of a clean polished gleaming toaster and faucets that run

both hot and cold water, and I tell them, *I will never leave home, this is my home,*
I love everything here, I am in love with everything here. . . .

  I am home.

JOYCE CAROL OATES

(b. 1938) Web

www

A prolific portrayer of contemporary American life, Oates is the author of more
than forty novels. Oates's work details realistic portraits of human nature within
the specific environments produced by rapid social change. She currently
teaches at Princeton University.

TOPICS FOR CRITICAL THINKING Web

www

1. Assemble a chronological narrative from the pieces the narrator has provided.
2. What are the effects of breaking the story into its various elements?
3. Is this story an example of metafiction? Of metanarrative? In what ways?
4. Is there any relation between the narrator's fragmentation of experience and the nature and quality of her experience?
5. What commentary does this story make on suburbia?

TOPIC FOR CRITICAL WRITING Web

www

In what ways does this story bring larger metanarratives underwriting American culture into question?

∾∾∾

SAMUEL BECKETT

The Calmative   (1967)

I don't know when I died. It always seemed to me I died old, about ninety
years old, and what years, and that my body bore it out, from head to foot. But
this evening, alone in my icy bed, I have the feeling I'll be older than the day,
the night, when the sky with all its lights fell upon me, the same I had so often gazed on since my first stumblings on the distant earth. For I'm too frightened this evening to listen to myself rot, waiting for the great red lapses of the
heart, the tearings at the caecal walls, and for the slow killings to finish in my
skull, the assaults on unshakable pillars, the fornications with corpses. So I'll
tell myself a story, I'll try and tell myself another story, to try and calm myself,
and it's there I feel I'll be old, old, even older than the day I fell, calling for
help, and it came. Or is it possible that in this story I have come back to life,
after my death? No, it's not like me to come back to life, after my death.

  What possessed me to stir when I wasn't with anybody? Was I being
thrown out? No, I wasn't with anybody. I see a kind of den littered with empty

tins. And yet we are not in the country. Perhaps it's just ruins, a ruined folly, on the skirts of the town, in a field, for the fields come right up to our walls, their walls, and the cows lie down at night in the lee of the ramparts. I have changed refuge so often, in the course of my rout, that now I can't tell between dens and ruins. But there was never any city but the one. It is true you often move along in a dream, houses and factories darken the air, trams go by, and under your feet wet from the grass there are suddenly cobbles. I only know the city of my childhood, I must have seen the other, but unbelieving. All I say cancels out, I'll have said nothing. Was I hungry itself? Did the weather tempt me? It was cloudy and cool, I insist, but not to the extent of luring me out. I couldn't get up at the first attempt, nor let us say at the second, and once up, propped against the wall, I wondered if I could go on, I mean up, propped against the wall. Impossible to go out and walk. I speak as though it all happened yesterday. Yesterday indeed is recent, but not enough. For what I tell this evening is passing this evening, at this passing hour. I'm no longer with these assassins, in this bed of terror, but in my distant refuge, my hands twined together, my head bowed, weak, breathless, calm, free, and older than I'll have ever been, if my calculations are correct. I'll tell my story in the past none the less, as though it were a myth, or an old fable, for this evening I need another age, that age to become another age in which I became what I was.

But little by little I got myself out and started walking with short steps among the trees, oh look, trees! The paths of other days were rank with tangled growth. I leaned against the trunks to get my breath and pulled myself forward with the help of boughs. Of my last passage no trace remained. They were the perishing oaks immortalized by d'Aubigné. It was only a grove. The fringe was near, a light less green and kind of tattered told me so, in a whisper. Yes, no matter where you stood, in this little wood, and were it in the furthest recess of its poor secrecies, you saw on every hand the gleam of this pale light, promise of God knows what fatuous eternity. Die without too much pain, a little, that's worth your while. Under the blind sky close with your own hands the eyes soon sockets, then quick into carrion not to mislead the crows. That's the advantage of death by drowning, one of the advantages, the crabs never get there too soon. But here a strange thing, I was no sooner free of the wood at last, having crossed unminding the ditch that girdles it, than thoughts came to me of cruelty, the kind that smiles. A lush pasture lay before me, nonsuch perhaps, who cares, drenched in evening dew or recent rain. Beyond this meadow to my certain knowledge a path, then a field and finally the ramparts, closing the prospect. Cyclopean and crenellated, standing out faintly against a sky scarcely less sombre, they did not seem in ruins, viewed from mine, but were, to my certain knowledge. Such was the scene offered to me, in vain, for I knew it well and loathed it. What I saw was a bald man in a brown suit, a comedian. He was telling a funny story about a fiasco. Its point escaped me. He used the word snail, or slug, to the delight of all present. The women seemed even more entertained than their escorts, if that were possible. Their shrill laughter pierced the clapping and, when this had subsided, broke out still here and there in sudden peals even after the next story had begun, so that part of it was lost. Perhaps they had in mind the reigning penis sitting who knows by their side and from that sweet shore launched their cries of joy towards the comic vast, what a talent. But it's to me this evening something has to happen, to my body as in myth and metamorphosis, this old body to which nothing ever happened, or so little, which never met with anything, loved anything, wished for anything, in its tarnished universe, except for the mirrors to shatter, the plane, the curved, the magnifying, the minifying, and to vanish in the havoc of its images. Yes, this evening it has to be as in the story my father used to read to me, evening after evening, when I was small, and he had all his health, to calm me, evening after evening, year after year it seems to me this evening, which I don't remember much about, except that it was the adventure of one Joe Breem, or Breen, the son of a lighthouse-keeper, a strong muscular lad of fifteen, those were the words, who swam for miles in the night, a knife between his teeth, after a shark, I forget why, out of sheer heroism. He might have simply told me the story, he knew it by heart, so did I, but that wouldn't have calmed me, he had to read it to me, evening after evening, or pretend to read it to me, turning the pages and explaining the pictures that were of me already, evening after evening the same pictures, till I dozed off on his shoulder. If he had skipped a single word I would have hit him, with my little fist, in his big belly bursting out of the old cardigan and unbuttoned trousers that rested him from his office canonicals. For me now the setting forth, the struggle and perhaps the return, for the old man I am this evening, older than my father ever was, older than I shall ever be. I crossed the meadow with little stiff steps at the same time limp, the best I could manage. Of my last passage no trace remained, it was long ago. And the little bruised stems soon straighten up again, having need of air and light, and as for the broken their place is soon taken. I entered the town by what they call the Shepherds' Gate without having seen a soul, only the first bats like flying crucifixions, nor heard a sound except my steps, my heart in my breast and then, as I went under the arch, the hoot of an owl, that cry at once so soft and fierce which in the night, calling, answering, through my little wood and those nearby, sounded in my shelter like a tocsin. The further I went into the city the more I was struck by its deserted air. It was lit as usual, brighter than usual, although the shops were shut. But the lights were on in their windows with the object no doubt of attracting customers and prompting them to say, I say, I like that, not dear either, I'll come back tomorrow, if I'm still alive. I nearly said, Good God it's Sunday. The trams were running, the buses too, but few, slow, empty, noiseless, as if under water. I didn't see a single horse! I was wearing my long green greatcoat with the velvet collar, such as motorists wore about 1900, my father's, but that day it was sleeveless, a vast cloak. But on me it was still the same great dead weight, with no warmth to it, and the tails swept the ground, scraped it rather, they had grown so stiff, and I so shrunken. What would, what could happen to me in this empty place? But I felt the houses packed with people, lurking behind the curtains they looked out into the street or, crouched far back in the depths of the room, head in hands, were sunk in dream. Up aloft my hat, the same as always, I reached no further. I went right across the city and came to the sea, having followed the river to its mouth. I kept saying, I'll go back, unbelieving. The boats at anchor in the harbour, tied up to the jetty, seemed no less numerous than usual, as if I knew anything about what was usual. But the quays were deserted and there was no sign or stir of arrival or departure. But all might change from one moment to the next and be transformed like magic before my eyes. Then all the bustle of the people and things of the sea, the masts of the big craft gravely rocking and of the small more jauntily, I insist, and I'd hear the gulls' terrible cry and perhaps the sailors' cry. And I might slip unnoticed aboard a freighter outward bound and get far away and spend far away a few good months, perhaps even a year or two, in the sun, in peace, before I died. And without going that far it would be a sad state of affairs if in that unscandalizable throng I couldn't achieve a little encounter that would calm me a little, or exchange a few words with a navigator for example, words to carry away with me to my refuge, to add to my collection. I waited sitting on a kind of topless capstan, saying, The very capstans this evening are out of order. And I gazed out to sea, out beyond the breakwaters, without sighting the least vessel. I could see lights flush with the water. And the pretty beacons at the harbour mouth I could see too, and others in the distance, flashing from the coast, the islands, the headlands. But seeing still no sign or stir I made ready to go, to turn away sadly from this dead haven, for there are scenes that call for strange farewells. I had merely to bow my head and look down at my feet, for it is in this attitude I always drew the strength to, how shall I say, I don't know, and it was always from the earth, rather than from the sky, notwithstanding its reputation, that my help came in time of trouble. And there, on the flagstone, which I was not focussing, for why focus it, I saw haven afar, where the black swell was most perilous, and all about me storm and wreck. I'll never come back here, I said. But when with a thrust of both hands against the rim of the capstan I heaved myself up I found facing me a young boy holding a goat by a horn. I sat down again. He stood there silent looking at me without visible fear or revulsion. Admittedly the light was poor. His silence seemed natural to me, it befitted me as the elder to speak first. He was barefoot and in rags. Haunter of the waterfront he had stepped aside to see what the dark hulk could be abandoned on the quayside. Such was my train of thought. Close up to me now with his little guttersnipe's eye there could be no doubt left in his mind. And yet he stayed. Can this base thought be mine? Moved, for after all that is what I must have come out for, in a way, and with little expectation of advantage from what might follow, I resolved to speak to him. So I marshalled the words and opened my mouth, thinking I would hear them. But all I heard was a kind of rattle, unintelligible even to me who knew what was intended. But it was nothing, mere speechlessness due to long silence, as in the wood that darkens the mouth of hell, do you remember, I only just. Without letting go of his goat he moved right up against me and offered me a sweet out of a twist of paper such as you could buy for a penny. I hadn't been offered a sweet for eighty years at least, but I took it eagerly and put it in my mouth, the old gesture came back to me, more and more moved since that is what I wanted. The sweets were stuck together and I had my work cut out to separate the top one, a green one, from the others, but he helped me and his hand brushed mine. And a moment later as he made to move away, hauling his goat after him, with a great gesticulation of my whole body I motioned him to stay and I said, in an impetuous murmur, Where are you off to, my little man, with your nanny? The words were hardly out of my mouth when for shame I covered my face. And yet they were the same I had tried to utter but a moment before. Where are you off to, my little man, with your nanny! If I could have blushed I would have, but there was not enough blood left in my extremities. If I had had a penny in my pocket I would have given it to him, for him to forgive me, but I did not have a penny in my pocket, nor anything resembling it. Nothing that could give pleasure to a little unfortunate at the mouth of life. I suspect I had nothing with me but my stone, that day, having gone out as it were without premeditation. Of his little person I was fated to see no more than the black curly hair and the pretty curve of the long bare legs all muscle and dirt. And the hand, so fresh and keen, I would not forget in a hurry either. I looked for better words to say to him, I found them too late, he was gone, oh not far, but far. Out of my life too he went without a care, not one of his thoughts would ever be for me again, unless perhaps when he was old and, delving in his boyhood, would come upon that gallows night and hold the goat by the horn again and linger again a moment by my side, with who knows perhaps a touch of tenderness, even of envy, but I have my doubts. Poor dear dumb beasts, how you will have helped me. What does your daddy do? that's what I would have said to him if he had given me the chance. Soon they were no more than a single blur which if I hadn't known I might have taken for a young centaur. I was nearly going to have the goat dung, then pick up a handful of the pellets so soon cold and hard, sniff and even taste them, no, that would not help me this evening. I say this evening as if it were always the same evening, but are there two evenings? I went, intending to get back as fast as I could, but it would not be quite empty-handed, repeating, I'll never come back here. My legs were paining me, every step would gladly have been the last, but the glances I darted towards the windows, stealthily, showed me a great cylinder sweeping past as though on rollers on the asphalt. I must indeed have been moving fast, for I overhauled more than one pedestrian, there are the first men, without extending myself, I who in the normal way was left standing by cripples, and then I seemed to hear the footfalls die behind me. And yet each little step would gladly have been the last. So much so that when I emerged on a square I hadn't noticed on the way out, with a cathedral looming on the far side, I decided to go in, if it was open, and hide, as in the Middle Ages, for a space. I say cathedral, it may not have been, I don't know, all I know is it would vex me in this story that aspires to be the last, to have taken refuge in a common church. I remarked the Saxon Stützenwechsel. Charming effect, but it didn't charm me. The brilliantly lit nave appeared deserted. I walked round it several times without seeing a soul. They were hiding perhaps, under the choirstalls, or dodging behind the pillars, like woodpeckers. Suddenly close to where I was, and without my having heard the long preliminary rumblings, the organ began to boom. I sprang up from the mat on which I lay before the altar and hastened to the far end of the nave as if on my way out. But it was a side aisle and the door I disappeared through was not the exit. For instead of being restored to the night I found myself at the foot of a spiral staircase which I began to climb at top speed, mindless of my heart, like one hotly pursued by a homicidal maniac. This staircase faintly lit by I know not what means, slits perhaps, I mounted panting as far as the projecting gallery in which it culminated and which, separated from the void by a cynical parapet, encompassed a smooth round wall capped by a little dome covered with lead or verdigrised copper, phew, if that's not clear. People must have come here for the view, those who fall die on the way. Flattening myself against the wall I started round, clock-wise. But I had hardly gone a few steps when I met a man revolving in the other direction, with the utmost circumspection. How I'd love to push him, or him to push me, over the edge. He gazed at me wild-eyed for a moment and then, not daring to pass me on the parapet side and surmising correctly that I would not relinquish the wall just to oblige him, abruptly turned his back on me, his head rather, for his back remained glued to the wall, and went back the way he had come so that soon there was nothing left of him but a left hand. It lingered a moment, then slid out of sight. All that remained to me was the vision of two burning eyes starting out of their sockets under a check cap. Into what nightmare thingness am I fallen? My hat flew off, but did not get far thanks to the string. I turned my head towards the staircase and lent an eye. Nothing. Then a little girl came into view followed by a man holding her by the hand, both pressed against the wall. He pushed her into the stairway, dis-appeared after her, turned and raised towards me a face that made me recoil. I could only see his bare head above the top step. When they were gone I called. I completed in haste the round of the gallery. No one. I saw on the horizon, where sky, sea, plain and mountain meet, a few low stars, not to be confused with the fires men light, at night, or that go alight alone. Enough. Back in the street I tried to find my way in the sky, where I knew the Bears so well. If I had seen someone I would have stopped him to ask, the most fero-cious aspect would not have daunted me. I would have said, touching my hat, Pardon me your honour, the Shepherds' Gate for the love of God. I thought I could go no further, but no sooner had the impetus reached my legs than on I went, believe it or not, at a very fair pace. I wasn't returning empty-handed, not quite, I was taking back with me the virtual certainty that I was still of this world, of that world too, in a way. But I was paying the price. I would have done better to spend the night in the cathedral, on the mat before the altar, I would have continued on my way at first light, or they would have found me stretched out in the rigor of death, the genuine bodily article, under the blue eyes fount of so much hope, and put me in the evening papers. But suddenly I was descending a wide street, vaguely familiar, but in which I could never have set foot, in my lifetime. But soon realizing I was going downhill I turned about and set off in the other direction. For I was afraid if I went downhill of returning to the sea where I had sworn never to return. When I say I turned about I mean I wheeled round in a wide semi-circle without slowing down, for I was afraid if I stopped of not being able to start again, yes, I was afraid of that too. And this evening too I dare not stop. I was struck more and more by the contrast between the brightly lit streets and their deserted air. To say it dis-tressed me, no, but I say it all the same, in the hope of calming myself. To say there was no one abroad, no, I would not go that far, for I remarked a number of shapes, male and female, strange shapes, but not more so than usual. As to what hour it might have been I had no idea, except that it must have been some hour of the night. But it might have been three or four in the morning just as it might have been ten or eleven in the evening, depending no doubt on whether one wondered at the scarcity of passers-by or at the extraordinary radiance shed by the street-lamps and traffic-lights. For at one or other of these no one could fail to wonder, unless he was out of his mind. Not a single private car, but admittedly from time to time a public vehicle, slow sweep of light silent and empty. It is not my wish to labour these antinomies, for we are needless to say in a skull, but I have no choice but to add the following few remarks. All the mortals I saw were alone and as if sunk in themselves. It must be a common sight, but mixed with something else I imagine. The only couple was two men grappling, their legs intertwined. I only saw one cyclist! He was going the same way as I was. All were going the same way as I was, vehicles too, I have only just realized it. He was pedalling slowly in the middle of the street, reading a newspaper which he held with both hands spread open before his eyes. Every now and then he rang his bell without interrupting his reading. I watched him recede till he was no more than a dot on the horizon. Suddenly a young woman perhaps of easy virtue, dishevelled and her dress in disarray, darted across the street like a rabbit. That is all I had to add. But here a strange thing, yet another, I had no pain whatever, not even in my legs. Weakness. A good night's nightmare and a tin of sardines would restore my sensitivity. My shadow, one of my shadows, flew before me, dwindled, slid under my feet, trailed behind me the way shadows will. This degree of opacity appeared to me conclusive. But suddenly ahead of me a man on the same side of the street and going the same way, to keep harping on the same thing lest I forget. The distance between us was considerable, seventy paces at least, and fearing he might escape me I quickened my step with the result I swept forward as if on rollers. This is not me, I said, let us make the most of it. Finding myself in an instant a bare ten paces in his rear I slowed down so as not to burst in on him and so heighten the aversion my person inspired even in its most abject and obsequious attitudes. And a moment later, keeping humbly in step with him, Excuse me your honour, the Shepherds' Gate for the love of God! At close quarters he appeared normal apart from that air already noted of ebbing inward. I drew a few steps ahead, turned, cringed, touched my hat and said, The right time for mercy's sake! I might as well not have existed. But what about the sweet? A light! I cried. Given my need of help I can't think why I did not bar his path. I couldn't have, that's all, I couldn't have touched him. Seeing a stone seat by the kerb I sat down and crossed my legs, like Walther. I must have dozed off, for the next thing was a man sitting beside me. I was still taking him in when he opened his eyes and set them on me, as if for the first time, for he shrank back unaffectedly. Where did you spring from? he said. To hear myself addressed again so soon impressed me greatly. What's the matter with you? he said. I tried to look like one with whom that only is the matter which is native to him. Forgive me your honour, I said, gingerly lifting my hat and rising a fraction from the seat, the right time for the love of God! He said a time, I don't remember which, a time that explained nothing, that's all I remember, and did not calm me. But what time could have done that? Oh I know, I know, one will come that will. But in the meantime? What's that you said? he said. Unfortunately I had said nothing. But I wriggled out of it by asking him if he could help me find my way which I had lost. No, he said, for I am not from these parts and if I am sitting on this slab it is because the hotels were full or would not let me in, I have no opinion. But tell me the story of your life, then we'll see. My life! I cried. Why yes, he said, you know, that kind of—what shall I say? He brooded for a time, no doubt trying to think of what life could well be said to be a kind. In the end he went on, testily, Come now, everyone knows that. He jogged me in the ribs. No details, he said, the main drift, the main drift. But as I remained silent he said, Shall I tell you mine, then you'll see what I mean. The account he then gave was brief and dense, facts, without comment. That's what I call a life, he said, do you follow me now? It wasn't bad, his story, positively fairy-like in places. But that Pauline, I said, are you still with her? I am, he said, but I'm going to leave her and set up with another, younger and plumper. You travel a lot, I said. Oh widely, widely, he said. Words were coming back to me, and the way to make them sound. All that's a thing of the past for you no doubt, he said. Do you think of spending some time among us? I said. This sentence struck me as particularly well turned. If it's not a rude question, he said, how old are you? I don't know, I said. You don't know! he cried. Not exactly, I said. Are thighs much in your thoughts, he said, arses, cunts and environs. I didn't follow. No more erections naturally, he said. Erections? I said. The penis, he said, you know what the penis is, there, between the legs. Ah that, I said. It thickens, lengthens, stiffens and rises, he said, does it not? I assented, though they were not the terms I would have used. That is what we call an erection, he said. He pondered, then exclaimed, Phenomenal! No? Strange right enough, I said. And there you have it all, he said. But what will become of her? I said. Who? he said. Pauline, I said. She will grow old, he said with tranquil assurance, slowly at first, then faster and faster, in pain and bitterness, pulling the devil by the tail. The face was not full, but I eyed it in vain, it remained clothed in its flesh instead of turning all chalky and channelled as with a gouge. The very vomer kept its cushion. It is true discussion was always bad for me. I longed for the tender nonsuch, I would have trodden it gently, with my boots in my hand, and for the shade of my wood, far from this terrible light. What are you grinning and bearing? he said. He held on his knees a big black bag, like a midwife's I imagine. It was full of glittering phials. I asked him if they were all alike. Oho no, he said, for every taste. He took one and held it out to me, saying, One and six. What did he want? To sell it to me? Proceeding on this hypothesis I told him I had no money. No money! he cried. All of a sudden his hand came down on the back of my neck, his sinewy fingers closed and with a jerk and a twist he had me up against him. But instead of dispatching me he began to murmur words so sweet that I went limp and my head fell forward in his lap. Between the caressing voice and the fingers rowelling my neck the contrast was striking. But gradually the two things merged in a devastating hope, if I dare say so, and I dare. For this evening I have nothing to lose that I can discern. And if I have reached this point (in my story) without anything having changed, for if anything had changed I think I'd know, the fact remains I have reached it, and that's something, and with nothing changed, and that's something too. It's no excuse for rushing matters. No, it must cease gently, as gently cease on the stairs the steps of the loved one, who could not love and will not come back, and whose steps say so, that she could not love and will not come back. He suddenly shoved me away and showed me the phial again. There you have it all, he said. It can't have been the same all as before. Want it? he said. No, but I said yes, so as not to vex him. He proposed an exchange. Give me your hat, he said. I refused. What vehemence! he said. I haven't a thing, I said. Try in your pockets, he said. I haven't a thing, I said, I came out without a thing. Give me a lace, he said. I refused. Long silence. And if you gave me a kiss, he said finally. I knew there were kisses in the air. Can you take off your hat? he said. I took it off. Put it back, he said, you look nicer with it on. I put it on. Come on, he said, give me a kiss and let there be an end to it. Did it not occur to him I might turn him down? No, a kiss is not a bootlace, he must have seen from my face that all passion was not quite spent. Come, he said. I wiped my mouth in its tod of hair and advanced it towards his. Just a moment, he said. My mouth stood still. You know what a kiss is? he said. Yes yes, I said? If it's not a rude question, he said, when was your last? Some time ago, I said, but I can still do them. He took off his hat, a bowler, and tapped the middle of his forehead. There, he said, and there only. He had a noble brow, white and high. He leaned forward, closing his eyes. Quick, he said? I pursed up my lips as mother had taught me and brought them down where he had said. Enough, he said. He raised his hand towards the spot, but left the gesture unfinished and put on his hat. I turned away and looked across the street. It was then I noticed we were sitting opposite a horse-butcher's. Here, he said, take it. I had forgotten. He rose. Standing he was quite short. One good turn, he said, with radiant smile. His teeth shone. I listened to his steps die away. How tell what remains. But it's the end. Or have I been dreaming, am I dreaming? No, no, none of that, for dream is nothing, a joke, and significant what is worse. I said, Stay where you are till day breaks, wait sleeping till the lamps go out and the streets come to life. But I stood up and moved off. My pains were back, but with something untoward which prevented my wrapping them round me. But I said, Little by little you are coming to. From my gait alone, slow, stiff and which seemed at every step to solve a statodynamic problem never posed before, I would have been known again, if I had been known. I crossed over and stopped before the butcher's. Behind the grille the curtains were drawn, rough canvas curtains striped blue and white, colours of the Virgin, and stained with great pink stains. They did not quite meet in the middle, and through the chink I could make out the dim carcasses of the gutted horses hanging from hooks head downwards. I hugged the walls, famished for shadow. To think that in a moment all will be said, all to do again. And the city clocks, what was wrong with them, whose great chill clang even in my wood fell on me from the air? What else? Ah yes, my spoils. I tried to think of Pauline, but she eluded me, gleamed an instant and was gone, like the young woman in the street. So I went in the atrocious brightness, buried in my old flesh, straining towards an issue and passing them by to left and right, and my mind panting after this and that and always flung back to where there was nothing. I succeeded however in fastening briefly on the little girl, long enough to see her a little more clearly than before, so that she wore a kind of bonnet and clasped in her hand a book, of common prayer perhaps, and to try and have her smile, but she did not smile, but vanished down the staircase without having yielded me her little face. I had to stop. At first nothing, then little by little, I mean rising up out of the silence till suddenly no higher, a kind of massive murmur coming perhaps from the house that was propping me up. That reminded me that the houses were full of people, besieged, no, I don't know. When I stepped back to look at the windows I could see, in spite of shutters, blinds and muslins, that many of the rooms were lit. The light was so dimmed by the brilliancy flooding the boulevard that short of knowing or suspecting it was not so one might have supposed everyone sleeping. The sound was not continuous, but broken by silences possibly of consternation. I thought of ringing at the door and asking for shelter and protection till morning. But suddenly I was on my way again. But little by little, in a slow swoon, darkness fell about me. I saw a mass of bright flowers fade in an exquisite cascade of paling colours. I found myself admiring, all along the housefronts, the gradual blossoming of squares and rectangles, casement and sash, yellow, green, pink, according to the curtains and blinds, finding that pretty. Then at last, before I fell, first to my knees, as cattle do, then on my face, I was in a throng. I didn't lose consciousness, when I lose consciousness it will not be to recover it. They paid no heed to me, though careful not to walk on me, a courtesy that must have touched me, it was what I had come out for. It was well with me, sated with dark and calm, lying at the feet of mortals, fathom deep in the grey of dawn, if it was dawn. But reality, too tired to look for the right word, was soon restored, the throng fell away, the light came back and I had no need to raise my head from the ground to know I was back in the same blinding void as before. I said, Stay where you are, down on the friendly stone, or at least indifferent, don't open your eyes, wait for morning. But up with me again and back on the way that was not mine, on uphill along the boulevard. A blessing he was not waiting for me, poor old Breem, or Breen. I said, The sea is east, it's west I must go, to the left of north. But in vain I raised without hope my eyes to the sky to look for the Bears. For the light I steeped in put out the stars, assuming they were there, which I doubted, remembering the clouds.

———— **SAMUEL BECKETT** ————
(1906–1989) Web

Nobel Prize-winning author of such plays as *Waiting for Godot* and *Krapp's Last Tape*, Beckett is known for his minimalist style, innovative use of the stage, and self-conscious narratives. Born in Foxcroft, a suburb of Dublin, of Protestant Irish parents, Samuel Beckett went to private school and then to Trinity College. After graduate study, Beckett moved to Paris, where he became friends with James Joyce. During World War II, Beckett worked as a member of the French Resistance.

www   *TOPICS FOR CRITICAL THINKING* Web

1. Is there a distinction between story and action?
2. How many stories does the story the narrator tells contain?

3. Is the story "The Calmative" the story the narrator tells?
4. How is a story a "calmative"?
5. In what ways is this story conscious of its telling?
6. Why does this story have only three paragraphs?

TOPICS FOR CRITICAL WRITING Web   *www*

1. Select an episode in the narrator's story and consider how that episode relates to the whole story. Are there ways it doesn't relate?
2. How does this story deviate from the typical narrative structure we have seen in most stories? In what ways is that deviation itself a commentary on the idea of a story?

Featured Writer

SALMAN RUSHDIE

The Free Radio   (1994)

We all knew nothing good would happen to him while the thief's widow had her claws dug into his flesh, but the boy was an innocent, a real donkey's child, you can't teach such people.

That boy could have had a good life. God had blessed him with God's own looks, and his father had gone to the grave for him, but didn't he leave the boy a brand-new first-class cycle rickshaw with plastic covered seats and all? So: looks he had, his own trade he had, there would have been a good wife in time, he should just have taken out some years to save some rupees; but no, he must fall for a thief's widow before the hairs had time to come out on his chin, before his milk-teeth had split, one might say.

We felt bad for him, but who listens to the wisdom of the old today? I say: who listens?

Exactly; nobody, certainly not a stone-head like Ramani the rickshaw-   5 wallah. But I blame the widow. I saw it happen, you know, I saw most of it until I couldn't stand any more. I sat under this very banyan, smoking this selfsame hookah, and not much escaped my notice.

And at one time I tried to save him from his fate, but it was no go . . .

The widow was certainly attractive, no point denying, in a sort of hard vicious way she was all right, but it is her mentality that was rotten. Ten years older than Ramani she must have been, five children alive and two dead, what that thief did besides robbing and making babies God only knows, but he left her not one new paisa, so of course she would be interested in Ramani. I'm not saying a rickshaw-wallah makes much in this town but two mouthfuls are better to eat than wind. And not many people will look twice at the widow of a good-for-nothing.

They met right here.

One day Ramani rode into town without a passenger, but grinning as usual as if someone had given him a ten-chip tip, singing some playback music from the radio, his hair greased like for a wedding. He was not such a fool that he didn't know how the girls watched him all the time and passed remarks about his long and well-muscled legs.

The thief's widow had gone to the bania stop to buy some three grains of   10 dal and I won't say where the money came from, but people saw men at night near her rutputty shack, even the bania himself they were telling me but I personally will not comment.

She had all her five brats with her and then and there, cool as a fan, she called out: '*Hey! Rickshaaa!*' Loud, you know, like a truly cheap type. Showing us she can afford to ride in rickshaws, as if anyone was interested. Her children must have gone hungry to pay for the ride but in my opinion it was an investment for her, because must-be she had decided already to put her hooks into Ramani. So they all poured into the rickshaw and he took her away, and with the five kiddies as well as the widow there was quite a weight, so he was puffing hard, and the veins were standing out on his legs, and I thought, careful, my son, or you will have this burden to pull for all of your life.

But after that Ramani and the thief's widow were seen everywhere, shamelessly, in public places, and I was glad his mother was dead because if she had lived to see this her face would have fallen off from shame.

Sometimes in those days Ramani came into this street in the evenings to meet some friends, and they thought they were very smart because they would go into the back room of the Irani's canteen and drink illegal liquor, only of course everybody knew, but who would do anything, if boys ruin their lives let their relations worry.

I was sad to see Ramani fall into this bad company. His parents were known to me when alive. But when I told Ramani to keep away from those hot-shots he grinned like a sheep and said I was wrong, nothing bad was taking place.

Let it go, I thought.   15

I knew those cronies of his. They all wore the armbands of the new Youth Movement. This was the time of the State of Emergency, and these friends were not peaceful persons, there were stories of beatings-up, so I sat quiet under my tree. Ramani wore no armband but he went with them because they impressed him, the fool.

These armband youths were always flattering Ramani. Such a handsome chap, they told him, compared to you Shashi Kapoor and Amitabh are like lepers only, you should go to Bombay and be put in the motion pictures.

They flattered him with dreams because they knew they could take money from him at cards and he would buy them drink while they did it, though he was no richer than they. So now Ramani's head became filled with these movie dreams, because there was nothing else inside to take up any space, and this is another reason why I blame the widow woman, because she had more years and should have had more sense. In two ticks she could have made him forget all about it, but no, I heard her telling him one day for all to hear, 'Truly you have the looks of Lord Krishna himself, except you are not blue all over.' In the street! So all would know they were lovers! From that day on I was sure a disaster would happen.

The next time the thief's widow came into the street to visit the bania shop I decided to act. Not for my own sake but for the boy's dead parents I risked being shamed by a . . . no, I will not call her the name, she is elsewhere now and they will know what she is like.

'Thief's widow!' I called out.   20

She stopped dead, jerking her face in an ugly way, as if I had hit her with a whip.

'Come here and speak,' I told her.

Now she could not refuse because I am not without importance in the town and maybe she calculated that if people saw us talking they would stop ignoring her when she passed, so she came as I knew she would.

'I have to say this thing only,' I told her with dignity. 'Ramani the rick-shaw boy is dear to me, and you must find some person of your own age, or, better still, go to the widows' ashrams in Benares and spend the rest of your life there in holy prayer, thanking God that widow-burning is now illegal.'

So at this point she tried to shame me by screaming out and calling me   25
curses and saying that I was a poisonous old man who should have died years ago, and then she said, 'Let me tell you, mister teacher sahib *retired*, that your Ramani has asked to marry me and I have said no, because I wish no more children, and he is a young man and should have his own. So tell that to the whole world and stop your cobra poison.'

For a time after that I closed my eyes to this affair of Ramani and the thief's widow, because I had done all I could and there were many other things in the town to interest a person like myself. For instance, the local health of-ficer had brought a big white caravan into the street and was given permission to park it out of the way under the banyan tree; and every night men were taken into this van for a while and things were done to them.

I did not care to be in the vicinity at these times, because the youths with armbands were always in attendance, so I took my hookah and sat in another place. I heard rumours of what was happening in the caravan but I closed my ears.

But it was while this caravan, which smelled of ether, was in town that the extent of the widow's wickedness became plain; because at this time Ramani suddenly began to talk about his new fantasy, telling everyone he could find that very shortly he was to receive a highly special and personalised gift from the Central Government in Delhi itself, and this gift was to be a brand-new first-class battery-operated transistor radio.

Now then: we had always believed that our Ramani was a little soft in the head, with his notions of being a film star and what all; so most of us just nod-ded tolerantly and said, 'Yes, Ram, that is nice for you,' and, 'What a fine, gen-erous Government it is that gives radios to persons who are so keen on popular music.'

But Ramani insisted it was true, and seemed happier than at any time in   30
his life, a happiness which could not be explained simply by the supposed im-minence of the transistor.

Soon after the dream-radio was first mentioned, Ramani and the thief's widow were married, and then I understood everything. I did not attend the nuptials—it was a poor affair by all accounts—but not long afterwards I spoke to Ram when he came past the banyan with an empty rickshaw one day.

He came to sit by me and I asked, 'My child, did you go to the caravan? What have you let them do to you?'

'Don't worry,' he replied. 'Everything is tremendously wonderful. I am in love, teacher sahib, and I have made it possible for me to marry my woman.'

I confess I became angry; indeed, I almost wept as I realised that Ramani had gone voluntarily to subject himself to a humiliation which was being forced upon the other men who were taken to the caravan. I reproved him bitterly. 'My idiot child, you have let that woman deprive you of your manhood!'

'It is not so bad,' Ram said, meaning the *nasbandi*. 'It does not stop love-   35
making or anything, excuse me, teacher sahib, for speaking of such a thing. It stops babies only and my woman did not want children any more, so now all is hundred per cent OK. Also it is in national interest,' he pointed out. 'And soon the free radio will arrive.'

'The free radio,' I repeated.

'Yes, remember, teacher sahib,' Ram said confidentially, 'some years back, in my kiddie days, when Laxman the tailor had this operation? In no time the radio came and from all over town people gathered to listen to it. It is how the Government says thank you. It will be excellent to have.'

'Go away, get away from me,' I cried out in despair, and did not have the heart to tell him what everyone else in the country already knew, which was that the free radio scheme was a dead duck, long gone, long forgotten. It had been over—*funtoosh!*—for years.

After these events the thief's widow, who was now Ram's wife, did not come into town very often, no doubt being too ashamed of what she had made him do, but Ramani worked longer hours than ever before, and every time he saw any of the dozens of people he'd told about the radio he would put one hand up to his ear as if he were already holding the blasted machine in it, and he would mimic broadcasts with a certain energetic skill.

'*Yé Akashvani hai*,' he announced to the streets. 'This is All-India Radio.   40
Here is the news. A Government spokesman today announced that Ramani rickshaw-wallah's radio was on its way and would be delivered at any moment. And now some playback music.' After which he would sing songs by Asha Bhonsle or Lata Mangeshkar in a high, ridiculous falsetto.

Ram always had the rare quality of total belief in his dreams, and there were times when his faith in the imaginary radio almost took us in, so that we half-believed it was really on its way, or even that it was already there, cupped invisibly against his ear as he rode his rickshaw around the streets of the town. We began to expect to hear Ramani, around a corner or at the far end of a lane, ringing his bell and yelling cheerfully:

'All-India Radio! This is All-India Radio!'

Time passed. Ram continued to carry the invisible radio around town. One year passed. Still his caricatures of the radio channel filled the air in the streets. But when I saw him now, there was a new thing in his face, a strained thing, as if he were having to make a phenomenal effort, which was much more tiring than driving a rickshaw, more tiring even than pulling a rickshaw containing a thief's widow and her five living children and the ghosts of two dead ones; as if all the energy of his young body was being poured into that fictional space between his ear and his hand, and he was trying to bring the radio into existence by a mighty, and possibly fatal, act of will.

I felt most helpless, I can tell you, because I had divined that Ram had poured into the idea of the radio all his worries and regrets about what he had done, and that if the dream were to die he would be forced to face the full gravity of his crime against his own body, to understand that the thief's widow had turned him, before she married him, into a thief of a stupid and terrible kind, because she had made him rob himself.

And then the white caravan came back to its place under the banyan tree   45
and I knew there was nothing to be done, because Ram would certainly come to get his gift.

He did not come for one day, then for two, and I learned afterwards that he had not wished to seem greedy; he didn't want the health officer to think he was desperate for the radio. Besides, he was half hoping they would come over and give it to him at his place, perhaps with some kind of small, formal presentation ceremony. A fool is a fool and there is no accounting for his notions.

On the third day he came. Ringing his bicycle-bell and imitating weather forecasts, ear cupped as usual, he arrived at the caravan. And in the rickshaw behind him sat the thief's widow, the witch, who had not been able to resist coming along to watch her companion's destruction.

It did not take very long.

Ram went into the caravan gaily, waving at his arm-banded cronies who were guarding it against the anger of the people, and I am told—for I had left the scene to spare myself the pain—that his hair was well-oiled and his clothes were freshly starched. The thief's widow did not move from the rickshaw, but sat there with a black sari pulled over her head, clutching at her children as if they were straws.

After a short time there were sounds of disagreement inside the caravan,   50
and then louder noises still, and finally the youths in armbands went in to see what was becoming, and soon after that Ram was frogmarched out by his drinking-chums, and his hair-grease was smudged on to his face and there was blood coming from his mouth. His hand was no longer cupped by his ear.

And still—they tell me—the thief's black widow did not move from her place in the rickshaw, although they dumped her husband in the dust.

Yes, I know, I'm an old man, my ideas are wrinkled with age, and these days they tell me sterilisation and God knows what is necessary, and maybe I'm wrong to blame the widow as well—why not? Maybe all the views of the old can be discounted now, and if that's so, let it be. But I'm telling this story and I haven't finished yet.

Some days after the incident at the caravan I saw Ramani selling his rickshaw to the old Muslim crook who runs the bicycle-repair shop. When he saw me watching, Ram came to me and said, 'Goodbye, teacher sahib, I am off to Bombay, where I will become a bigger film star than Shashi Kapoor or Amitabh Bachchan even.'

'"*I* am off," you say?' I asked him. 'Are you perhaps travelling alone?'

He stiffened. The thief's widow had already taught him not to be humble 55
in the presence of elders.

'My wife and children will come also,' he said. It was the last time we spoke. They left that same day on the down train.

After some months had passed I got his first letter, which was not written by himself, of course, since in spite of all my long-ago efforts he barely knew how to write. He had paid a professional letter-writer, which must have cost him many rupees, because everything in life costs money and in Bombay it costs twice as much. Don't ask me why he wrote to me, but he did. I have the letters and can give you proof positive, so maybe there are some uses for old people still, or maybe he knew I was the only one who would be interested in his news.

Anyhow: the letters were full of his new career, they told me how he'd been discovered at once, a big studio had given him a test, now they were grooming him for stardom, he spent his days at the Sun'n'Sand Hotel at Juhu beach in the company of top lady artistes, he was buying a big house at Pali Hill, built in the split-level mode and incorporating the latest security equipment to protect him from the movie fans, the thief's widow was well and happy and getting fat, and life was filled with light and success and no-questions-asked alcohol.

They were wonderful letters, brimming with confidence, but whenever I read them, and sometimes I read them still, I remember the expression which came over his face in the days just before he learned the truth about his radio, and the huge mad energy which he had poured into the act of conjuring reality, by an act of magnificent faith, out of the hot thin air between his cupped hand and his ear.

———— **SALMAN RUSHDIE** ————

(b. 1947) Web   *www*

Rushdie was born in India, moved to Pakistan, educated in England, and now writes novels in English. His work is renowned for its mixture of magical realism (writing that presents fantastic or impossible events as if they were a part of everyday life), self-reflexive narrative, and comic portrayals of people caught in the shifts of postcolonial cultures. He was sentenced to death by Iran's Ayatollah Khomeini for his novel *The Satanic Verses* (1988).

TOPICS FOR CRITICAL THINKING Web   *www*

1. What different kinds of narrative does this story include?
2. What is the relation between fate, dream, and narrative?

3. In what ways is this story conscious of its own process of being told?
4. In what ways is this story conscious of the various shapes stories can take?
5. In what ways does faith in a story prove to be misleading?
6. What comment does this story make on the power of stories?
7. In what ways is "reality" conjured by stories, and to what ends?

www   **TOPIC FOR CRITICAL WRITING** Web

What does the radio represent? Why a radio?

At the Auction of the Ruby Slippers   *(1994)*

The bidders who have assembled for the auction of the magic slippers bear little resemblance to your usual saleroom crowd. The Auctioneers have publi-
cised the event widely and are prepared for all comers. People venture out but
rarely nowadays; nevertheless, and rightly, the Auctioneers believed this prize
would tempt us from our bunkers. High feelings are anticipated. Accordingly,
in addition to the standard facilities provided for the comfort and security of
the more notable personages, extra-large bronze cupsidors have been placed
in the vestibules and toilets, for the use of the physically sick; teams of psychiatrists of varying disciplines have been installed in strategically located
neo-Gothic confessional booths, to counsel the sick at heart.

  Most of us nowadays are sick.

  There are no priests. The Auctioneers have drawn a line. The priests remain in other, nearby buildings, buildings with which they are familiar, hoping to deal with any psychic fall-out, any insanity overspill.

  Units of obstetricians and helmeted police SWAT teams wait out of sight in
side alleys in case the excitement leads to unexpected births or deaths. Lists of
next of kin have been drawn up and their contact numbers recorded. A supply
of strait-jackets has been laid in.

  See: behind bullet-proof glass, the ruby slippers sparkle. We do not know   5
the limits of their powers. We suspect that these limits may not exist.

  Movie stars are here, among the bidders, bringing their glossy, spangled
auras to the saleroom. Movie-star auras, developed in collaboration with masters of Applied Psychics, are platinum, golden, silver, bronze. Certain genre
actors specialising in villainous rôles are surrounded by auras of evil—livid
green, mustard yellow, inky red. When one of us collides with a star's priceless (and fragile) aura, he or she is instantly knocked to the floor by a security
team and hustled out to the waiting paddy-wagons. Such incidents slightly reduce the crush in the Grand Saleroom.

  The memorabilia junkies are out in predictable force, and now with a
ducking movement of the head one of them applies her desperate lips to the

slippers' transparent cage, setting off the state-of-the-art defence system whose programmers have neglected to teach it about the relative harmlessness of such a gesture of adoration. The system pumps a hundred thousand volts of electricity into the collagen-implanted lips of the glass-kisser, terminating her interest in the proceedings.

It is an unpleasantly whiffy moment, but it fails to deter a second *aficionado* from the same suicidal act of devotion. When we learn that this moron was the lover of the first fatality, we rather wonder at the mysteries of love, whilst reaching once again for our perfumed handkerchiefs.

The cult of the ruby slippers is at its height. A fancy dress party is in full swing. Wizards, Lions, Scarecrows are in plentiful supply. They jostle crossly for position, stamping on one another's feet. There is a scarcity of Tin Men on account of the particular discomfort of the costume. Witches bide their time on the *balcons* and *galeries* of the Grand Saleroom, living gargoyles with, in many cases, high credit ratings. One corner is occupied entirely by Totos, several of whom are copulating enthusiastically, obliging a rubber-gloved janitor to separate them so as to avoid giving public offence. He does this with great delicacy and taste.

We, the public, are easily, lethally offended. We have come to think of taking offence as a fundamental right. We value very little more highly than our rage, which gives us, in our opinion, the moral high ground. From this high ground we can shoot down at our enemies and inflict heavy fatalities. We take pride in our short fuses. Our anger elevates, transcends. 10

Around the—let us say—shrine of the ruby-sequinned slippers, pools of saliva have been forming. There are those of us who lack restraint, who drool. The jump-suited Latino janitor moves amongst us, a pail in one hand and a squeegee mop in the other. We admire and are grateful for his talent for self-effacement. He removes our mouth waters from the floor without causing any loss of face on our part.

Opportunities for encountering the truly miraculous are limited in our Nietzschean, relativistic universe. Behaviourist philosophers and quantum scientists crowd around the magic shoes. They make indecipherable notes.

Exiles, displaced persons of all sorts, even homeless tramps have turned up for a glimpse of the impossible. They have emerged from their subterranean hollows and braved the bazookas, the Uzi-armed gangs high on crack or smack or ice, the smugglers, the emptiers of houses. The tramps wear stenchy jute ponchos and hawk noisily into the giant potted yuccas. They grab fistfuls of canapés from trays borne upon the superb palms of A-list caterers. Sushi is eaten by them with impressive quantities of *wasabi* sauce, to whose inflammatory powers the hoboes' innards seem impervious. SWAT teams are summoned and after a brief battle involving the use of rubber bullets and sedative darts the tramps are removed, clubbed into unconsciousness and driven away. They will be deposited some distance beyond the city limits, out there in that smoking no-man's-land surrounded by giant advertising hoardings into which we venture no more. Wild dogs will gather around them, eager for luncheon. These are uncompromising times.

Political refugees are at the auction: conspirators, deposed monarchs, defeated factions, poets, bandit chieftains. Such figures no longer wear the black berets, the pebble-lensed spectacles and enveloping greatcoats of yesteryear, but strike resplendent attitudes in boxy silken jackets and high-waisted Japanese couture pantaloons. The women sport toreador jackets bearing sequinned representations of great works of art. One beauty parades *Guernica* on her back, while several others wear glittering scenes from the *Disasters of War* sequence by Francisco Goya.

Incandescent as they are in their suits of lights, the female political 15 refugees fail to eclipse the ruby slippers, and huddle with their male comrades in small hissing bunches, periodically hurling imprecations, ink-pellets, spitballs and paper darts across the salon at rival clusters of *émigrés*. The guards at the exits crack their bullwhips idly and the politicals control themselves.

We revere the ruby slippers because we believe they can make us invulnerable to witches (and there are so many sorcerers pursuing us nowadays); because of their powers of reverse metamorphosis, their affirmation of a lost state of normalcy in which we have almost ceased to believe and to which the slippers promise us we can return; and because they shine like the footwear of the gods.

Disapproving critiques of the fetishing of the slippers are offered by religious fundamentalists, who have been allowed to gain entry by virtue of the extreme liberalism of some of the Auctioneers, who argue that a civilised saleroom must be a broad church, open, tolerant. The fundamentalists have openly stated that they are interested in buying the magic footwear only in order to burn it, and this is not, in the view of the liberal Auctioneers, a reprehensible programme. What price tolerance if the intolerant are not tolerated also? 'Money insists on democracy,' the liberal Auctioneers insist. 'Anyone's cash is as good as anyone else's.' The fundamentalists fulminate from soapboxes constructed of special, sanctified wood. They are ignored, but some senior figures present speak ominously of the thin end of the wedge.

Orphans arrive, hoping that the ruby slippers might transport them back through time as well as space (for, as our equations prove, all space machines are time machines as well): they hope to be reunited with their deceased parents by the famous shoes.

Men and women of dubious character are present—untouchables, outcasts. The security forces deal brusquely with many of these.

'Home' has become such a scattered, damaged, various concept in our 20 present travails. There is no much to yearn for. There are so few rainbows any more. How hard can we expect even a pair of magic shoes to work? They promised to take us *home*, but are metaphors of homeliness comprehensible to them, are abstractions permissible? Are they literalists, or will they permit us to redefine the blessed word?

Are we asking, hoping for, too much?

As our numberless needs emerge from their redoubts and press in upon the electrified glass, will the shoes, like the Grimms' ancient flatfish, lose patience with our ever-growing demands and return us to the hovels of our discontents?

The presence of imaginary beings in the Saleroom may be the last straw. Children from nineteenth-century Australian paintings are here, whining from their ornate, gilded frames about being lost in the immensity of the Outback. In blue smocks and ankle socks they gaze into rain forests and red deserts, and tremble.

A literary character, condemned to an eternity of reading the works of Dickens to an armed madman in a jungle, has sent in a written bid.

On a television monitor, I notice the frail figure of an alien creature with an illuminated fingertip. 25

This permeation of the real world by the fictional is a symptom of the moral decay of our post-millennial culture. Heroes step down off cinema screens and marry members of the audience. Will there be no end to it? Should there be more rigorous controls? Is the State employing insufficient violence? We debate such questions often. There can be little doubt that a large majority of us opposes the free, unrestricted migration of imaginary beings into an already damaged reality, whose resources diminish by the day. After all, few of us would choose to travel in the opposite direction (though there are persuasive reports of an increase in such migrations latterly).

I shelve such disputes for the moment. The Auction is about to begin.

It is necessary that I speak about my cousin Gale, and her habit of moaning loudly while making love. Let me be frank: my cousin Gale was and is the love of my life, and even now that we have parted I am easily aroused by the mere memory of her erotic noisiness. I hasten to add that except for this volubility there was nothing abnormal about our love-making, nothing, if I may put it thus, *fictional*. Yet it satisfied me deeply, deeply, especially when she chose to cry out at the moment of penetration: 'Home, boy! Home, baby, yes—you've come home!'

One day, sad to relate, I came home to find her in the arms of a hairy escapee from a caveman movie. I moved out the same day, weeping my way down the street with my portrait of Gale in the guise of a tornado cradled in my arms and my collection of old Pat Boone 78 r.p.m. records in a rucksack on my back.

This happened many years ago. 30

For a time after Gale dumped me I was bitter and would reveal to our social circle that she had lost her virginity at the age of fourteen in an accident involving a defective shooting-stick; but vindictiveness did not satisfy me for long.

Since those days I have dedicated myself to her memory. I have made of myself a candle at her temple.

I am aware that, after all these years of separation and non-communication, the Gale I adore is not entirely a real person. The real Gale has become confused with my re-imagining of her, with my private elaboration of our continuing life together in an alternative universe devoid of ape-men. The real Gale may by now be beyond our grasp, ineffable.

I caught a glimpse of her recently. She was at the far end of a long, dark, subterranean bar-room guarded by freelance commandos bearing battlefield nuclear weapons. There were Polynesian snacks on the counter and beers from the Pacific rim on tap: Kirin, Tsingtao, Swan.

At that time many television channels were devoted to the sad case of the   35 astronaut stranded on Mars without hope of rescue, and with diminishing supplies of food and breathable air. Official spokesmen told us of the persuasive arguments for the abrupt cancellation of the space exploration budget. We found these arguments powerful; influential voices complained of the sentimentality of the images of the dying spaceman. Nevertheless, the cameras inside his marooned craft continued to send us poignant pictures of his slow descent into despair, his low-gravity, weight-reduced death.

I watched my cousin Gale as she watched the bar's TV. She did not see me watching her, did not know that she had become my chosen programme.

The condemned man on another planet—the condemned man *on* TV— began to sing a squawky medley of half-remembered songs. I was reminded of the dying computer, Hal, in the old film *2001: A Space Odyssey.* Hal sang 'Daisy, Daisy' as it was being unplugged.

The Martian—for he was now a permanent resident of that planet—offered us his spaced-out renditions of 'Swanee', 'Show Me the Way to Go Home' and several numbers from *The Wizard of Oz;* and Gale's shoulders began to shake. She was crying.

I did not go across to comfort her.

I first heard about the upcoming auction of the ruby slippers the very next   40 morning, and resolved at once to buy them, whatever the cost. My plan was simple: I would offer the miracle-shoes to Gale in all humility. If she wished, I would say, she could use them to travel to Mars and bring the spaceman back to Earth.

Perhaps I might even click the heels together three times, and win back her heart by murmuring, in soft reminder of our wasted love, *There's no place like home.*

You laugh at my desperation. Ha! Go tell a drowning man not to clutch at straws. Go ask a dying astronaut not to sing. Come here and stand in my shoes. What was it the Cowardly Lion said? Put 'em up. Put 'em uuuuup. I'll fight you with one hand tied behind my back. I'll fight you with my eyes closed.

Scared, huh? Scared?

* * *

The Grand Saleroom of the Auctioneers is the beating heart of the earth. If you stand here for long enough all the wonders of the world will pass by. In the Grand Saleroom, in recent years, we have witnessed the auction of the Taj Mahal, the Statue of Liberty, the Alps, the Sphinx. We have assisted at the sale of wives and the purchase of husbands. State secrets have been sold here, openly, to the highest bidder. On one very special occasion, the Auctioneers presided over the sale, to an overheated and inter-denominational bunch of smouldering red demons, of a wide selection of human souls of all classes, qualities, ages, races and creeds.

Everything is for sale, and under the firm yet essentially benevolent su-   45
pervision of the Auctioneers, their security dogs and SWAT teams, we engage in a battle of wits and wallets, a war of nerves.

There is a purity about our actions here, and also an aesthetically pleasing tension between the vast complexity of the life that turns up, packaged into lots, to go under the hammer, and the equally immense simplicity of our manner of dealing with this life.

We bid, the Auctioneers knock a lot down, we pass on.

All are equal before the justice of the gavels: the pavement artist and Michelangelo, the slave girl and the Queen.

This is the courtroom of demand.

They are bidding for the slippers now. As the price rises, so does my gorge. Panic   50
clutches at me, pulling me down, drowning me. I think of Gale—sweet coz!—and
fight back fear, and bid.

Once I was asked by the widower of a world-famous and much-loved pop singer to attend an auction of rock memorabilia on his behalf. He was the sole trustee of her estate, which was worth tens of millions. I treated him with respect.

'There's only one lot I want,' he said. 'Spend whatever you have to spend.'

It was an article of clothing, a pair of edible rice-paper panties in peppermint flavour, purchased long ago in a store on (I think this was the name) Rodeo Drive. My employer's late wife's stage act had included the public removal and consumption of several such pairs. More panties, in a variety of flavours—chocolate chip, knickerbocker glory, cassata—were hurled into the crowd. These, too, were gobbled up in the general excitement of the concert, the lucky recipients being too carried away to consider the future value of what they had caught. Undergarments that had actually been worn by the lady were therefore in short supply, and presently in great demand.

During that auction, bids came in across the video links with Tokyo, Los Angeles, Paris and Milan, bids so rapid and of such size that I lost my nerve. However, when I telephoned my employer to confess my failure he was quite unperturbed, interested only in the final price. I mentioned a five-figure sum, and he laughed. It was the first genuinely joyful laugh I had heard from him since the day his wife died.

'That's all right then,' he said. 'I've got three hundred thousand of those.'   55

* * *

It is to the Auctioneers we go to establish the value of our pasts, of our futures, of our lives.

The price for the ruby slippers is rising ever higher. Many of the bidders would appear to be proxies, as I was on the day of the underpants; as I am so often, in so many ways.

Today, however, I am bidding—perhaps literally—for myself.

There's an explosion in the street outside. We hear running feet, sirens, screams. Such things have become commonplace. We stay where we are, absorbed by a higher drama.

The cuspidors are in full employment. Witches keen, movie stars flounce 60 off with tarnished auras. Queues of the disconsolate form at the psychiatrists' booths. There is work for the club-wielding guards, though not, as yet, for the obstetricians. Order is maintained. I am the only person in the Saleroom still in the bidding. My rivals are disembodied heads on video screens, and unheard voices on telephone links. I am doing battle with an invisible world of demons and ghosts, and the prize is my lady's hand.

At the height of an auction, when the money has become no more than a way of keeping score, a thing happens which I am reluctant to admit: one becomes detached from the earth.

There is a loss of gravity, a reduction in weight, a floating in the capsule of the struggle. The ultimate goal crosses a delirious frontier. Its achievement and our own survival becomes—yes!—fictions.

And fictions, as I have come close to suggesting before, are dangerous.

In fiction's grip, we may mortgage our homes, sell our children, to have whatever it is we crave. Alternatively, in that miasmal ocean, we may simply float away from our desires, and see them anew, from a distance, so that they seem weightless, trivial. We let them go. Like men dying in a blizzard, we lie down in the snow to rest.

So it is that my cousin Gale loses her hold over me in the crucible of the 65 auction. So it is that I drop out of the bidding, go home, and fall asleep.

When I awake I feel refreshed, and free.

Next week there is another auction. Family trees, coats of arms, royal lineages will be up for sale, and into any of these one may insert any name one chooses, one's own, or one's beloved's. Canine and feline pedigrees will be on offer, too: Alsatian, Burmese, saluki, Siamese, cairn terrier.

Thanks to the infinite bounty of the Auctioneers, any of us, cat, dog, man, woman, child, can be a blue-blood; can be—as we long to be; and as, cowering in our shelters, we fear we are not—*somebody*.

TOPICS FOR CRITICAL THINKING Web

1. What elements of style work in this story to produce a consciousness of narrative?
2. What do the ruby slippers stand for?

3. What are the connections among the auction, the narrator's love for Gale, and the dying astronaut?
4. In what ways is this story connected to the *Wizard of Oz?*
5. What commentary does this story make about commodity culture? Web   *www*

TOPIC FOR CRITICAL WRITING Web   *www*

What does this story suggest about the power (for good or bad) of fiction?

16 Intertextuality

Every literary text bears within it a sense of its place in the history of literature, the evolution of genres, the legacies of style, and the politics of its themes. Not only are stories produced within a cultural context, which they inevitably reflect (even if the story is about another time and place); they also exist in relation to all other stories we have read—that is, to a tradition of literature. The various ways literary texts refer to other texts is called **intertex**
www **tuality.** `Web` Intertextuality exists within individual texts and among texts. It consists of such practices as citing and alluding to other texts (or to other parts of itself); employing structures and conventions common to many texts; writing about other texts using parody, satire, and burlesque; and employing the
www methods of **collage** and **pastiche.** `Web`

The question postmodern intertextuality raises is not necessarily one of reference but more one of how multiple texts do or do not work together. Reading literature that employs intertextuality does not mean looking up every allusion to another text or knowing the reference for every style, but rather involves the constant acknowledgment of all texts together as a teeming body. Intertextual reading means enjoying the interplay of multiple texts and styles in works that mesmerize through their ability to manage the disparate multitudes of representations bombarding contemporary culture. While intertextuality deploys familiar modes of narrative and organization such as the frame narrator and the embedded narrative (see Chapter 6), it uses them in a manner somewhat different from the ways in which Joseph Conrad and other modernist writers use them, producing a sense of distance, alienation, and intimacy all at the same time.

Collage and Pastiche

Collage and pastiche are the intertextual methods most often associated with postmodern literature, though postmodern texts may also be intertextual in other ways. Collage, which was used widely by early twentieth-century avant-garde artists, involves cutting and pasting parts from different texts together to make a single ensemble. **Dada** poets such as Tristan Tzara, for example, composed poems by randomly picking out of a hat words cut from a newspa-
www per. `Web` The method of collage used by postmodern writers is not so random. Postmodern intertextuality may emphasize the similarities among disparate texts, as in Mark Leyner's juxtaposition of advertising language with the claims of science in *My Cousin, My Gastroenterologist*. Literary collage may

take the form of framing, where one narrative encompasses multiple other stories. It may consist of the swift cutting and combination that occurs in Leyner's stories where sentences shift rapidly through vocabularies from many different contexts, or it may quickly range, as *Ghosts* does, through allusions to many different texts. Intertextuality is one way postmodern texts bring together material from high (literary and intellectual) and low (popular) culture and from many different genres and vocabularies. For some idea of the range of intertextual references in the texts below, see Web .

www

Critical Perspective: An Example of Criticism Focused on Intertextuality

"For the postmodern detective this anxiety increases in correlation to the poststructuralist questions concerning language and subjectivity, along with the increase in unstable home-lives, overcrowded cities, and high-speed technologies—postmodern 'realities' for which Wakefield functions as the perfect embodiment. The detective's present condition is nowhere more evident than in Paul Auster's *The New York Trilogy*, possibly the best example of Wakefield parody and appropriation in postmodern detective fictions. Auster's trilogy concerns itself primarily with problems of language and identity. The detective in those novels 'becomes a pilgrim searching for correspondence between signifiers and signifieds,' a search that becomes 'a quest for his own identity' (Russell 72–3). But those are impossible tasks for the detective, for in the world of these novels signifiers have divorced themselves from signifieds, while the distinction between self and other has conflated. To further complicate matters, in all three narratives the detective, the high priest of logic, in his attempt to locate missing persons becomes himself the missing person, a Wakefield who can no longer return home.

"Not only does Auster's trilogy share similar themes with 'Wakefield,' but more significantly the trilogy itself refers us directly to 'Wakefield' as a significant intratext for the perplexities of subjectivity involved in postmodern experience. In the second book of the trilogy, *Ghosts*, Black, the man Blue has been hired to watch, at one point actually tells Blue the story of Wakefield. By the end of the novel we realize that the Wakefield story is not only relevant to *Ghosts* but actually functions as a mise-en-abyme for the larger narrative—and for the entire trilogy. *Ghosts* is riddled with mise-en-abymes functioning at various fictional or metafictional levels, but at all levels those reflections of the larger text point back to 'Wakefield.' For example, Blue's history of detective work includes a case concerning a man named Gray who has disappeared, but just when Gray's wife concedes his death, Blue finds an amnesiac Gray, now Green, working in a bar not two blocks from his old home, echoing Hawthorne (166–67).

"In light of those intratexts, it should come as no surprise that Blue himself comes to resemble Wakefield, as does Black for that matter."

—Richard Swope, "Approaching the Threshold(s) in Postmodern Detective Fiction: Hawthorne's Wakefield and Other Missing Persons," *Critique* 39:3 (Spring: 1998)

In this passage, critic Richard Swope investigates the relation between one of *Ghosts*'s intertexts, Nathaniel Hawthorne's story "Wakefield" and the themes and behaviors of the characters in *Ghosts*.

∞

PAUL AUSTER

Ghosts   *(1983)*

First of all there is Blue. Later there is White, and then there is Black, and before the beginning there is Brown. Brown broke him in, Brown taught him the ropes, and when Brown grew old, Blue took over. That is how it begins. The place is New York, the time is the present, and neither one will ever change. Blue goes to his office every day and sits at his desk, waiting for something to happen. For a long time nothing does, and then a man named White walks through the door, and that is how it begins.

The case seems simple enough. White wants Blue to follow a man named Black and to keep an eye on him for as long as necessary. While working for Brown, Blue did many tail jobs, and this one seems no different, perhaps even easier than most.

Blue needs the work, and so he listens to White and doesn't ask many questions. He assumes it's a marriage case and that White is a jealous husband. White doesn't elaborate. He wants a weekly report, he says, sent to such and such a postbox number, typed out in duplicate on pages so long and so wide. A check will be sent each week to Blue in the mail. White then tells Blue where Black lives, what he looks like, and so on. When Blue asks White how long he thinks the case will last, White says he doesn't know. Just keep sending the reports, he says, until further notice.

To be fair to Blue, he finds it all a little strange. But to say that he has misgivings at this point would be going too far. Still, it's impossible for him not to notice certain things about White. The black beard, for example, and the overly bushy eyebrows. And then there is the skin, which seems inordinately white, as though covered with powder. Blue is no amateur in the art of disguise, and it's not difficult for him to see through this one. Brown was his teacher, after all, and in his day Brown was the best in the business. So Blue begins to think he was wrong, that the case has nothing to do with marriage. But he gets no farther than this, for White is still speaking to him, and Blue must concentrate on following his words.

Everything has been arranged, White says. There's a small apartment directly across the street from Black's. I've already rented it, and you can move in there today. The rent will be paid for until the case is over.   5

Good idea, says Blue, taking the key from White. That will eliminate the legwork.

Exactly, White answers, stroking his beard.

And so it's settled. Blue agrees to take the job, and they shake hands on it. To show his good faith, White even gives Blue an advance of ten fifty-dollar bills.

That is how it begins, then. The young Blue and a man named White, who is obviously not the man he appears to be. It doesn't matter, Blue says to himself after White has left. I'm sure he has his reasons. And besides, it's not my problem. The only thing I have to worry about is doing my job.

It is February 3, 1947. Little does Blue know, of course, that the case will 10 go on for years. But the present is no less dark than the past, and its mystery is equal to anything the future might hold. Such is the way of the world: one step at a time, one word and then the next. There are certain things that Blue cannot possibly know at this point. For knowledge comes slowly, and when it comes, it is often at great personal expense.

White leaves the office, and a moment later Blue picks up the phone and calls the future Mrs. Blue. I'm going under cover, he tells his sweetheart. Don't worry if I'm out of touch for a little while. I'll be thinking of you the whole time.

Blue takes a small gray satchel down from the shelf and packs it with his thirty-eight, a pair of binoculars, a notebook, and other tools of the trade. Then he tidies his desk, puts his papers in order, and locks up the office. From there he goes to the apartment that White has rented for him. The address is unimportant. But let's say Brooklyn Heights, for the sake of argument. Some quiet, rarely traveled street not far from the bridge—Orange Street perhaps. Walt Whitman handset the first edition of Leaves of Grass on this street in 1855, and it was here that Henry Ward Beecher railed against slavery from the pulpit of his red-brick church. So much for local color.

It's a small studio apartment on the third floor of a four-story brownstone. Blue is happy to see that it's fully equipped, and as he walks around the room inspecting the furnishings, he discovers that everything in the place is new: the bed, the table, the chair, the rug, the linens, the kitchen supplies, everything. There is a complete set of clothes hanging in the closet, and Blue, wondering if the clothes are meant for him, tries them on and sees that they fit. It's not the biggest place I've ever been in, he says to himself, pacing from one end of the room to the other, but it's cozy enough, cozy enough.

He goes back outside, crosses the street, and enters the opposite building. In the entryway he searches for Black's name on one of the mailboxes and finds it: Black—3rd floor. So far so good. Then he returns to his room and gets down to business.

Parting the curtains of the window, he looks out and sees Black sitting at 15 a table in his room across the street. To the extent that Blue can make out what is happening, he gathers that Black is writing. A look through the binoculars confirms that he is. The lenses, however, are not powerful enough to pick up the writing itself, and even if they were, Blue doubts that he would be able to read the handwriting upside down. All he can say for certain, therefore, is that Black is writing in a notebook with a red fountain pen. Blue takes out his own notebook and writes: Feb. 3, 3 P.M. Black writing at his desk.

Now and then Black pauses in his work and gazes out the window. At one point, Blue thinks that he is looking directly at him and ducks out of the way. But on closer inspection he realizes that it is merely a blank stare, signifying thought rather than seeing, a look that makes things invisible, that does not let them in. Black gets up from his chair every once in a while and disappears to a hidden spot in the room, a corner Blue supposes, or perhaps the bathroom, but he is never gone for very long, always returning promptly to the desk. This goes on for several hours, and Blue is none the wiser for his efforts At six o'clock he writes the second sentence in his notebook: This goes on for several hours.

It's not so much that Blue is bored, but that he feels thwarted. Without being able to read what Black has written, everything is a blank so far. Perhaps he's a madman, Blue thinks, plotting to blow up the world. Perhaps that writing has something to do with his secret formula. But Blue is immediately embarrassed by such a childish notion. It's too early to know anything, he says to himself, and for the time being he decides to suspend judgment.

His mind wanders from one small thing to another, eventually settling on the future Mrs. Blue. They were planning to go out tonight, he remembers, and if it hadn't been for White showing up at the office today and this new case, he would be with her now. First the Chinese restaurant on 39th Street, where they would have wrestled with the chopsticks and held hands under the table, and then the double feature at the Paramount. For a brief moment he has a startlingly clear picture of her face in his mind (laughing with lowered eyes, feigning embarrassment), and he realizes that he would much rather be with her than sitting in this little room for God knows how long. He thinks about calling her up on the phone for a chat, hesitates, and then decides against it. He doesn't want to seem weak. If she knew how much he needed her, he would begin to lose his advantage, and that wouldn't be good. The man must always be the stronger one.

Black has now cleared his table and replaced the writing materials with dinner. He sits there chewing slowly, staring out the window in that abstracted way of his. At the sight of food, Blue realizes that he is hungry and hunts through the kitchen cabinet for something to eat. He settles on a meal of canned stew and soaks up the gravy with a slice of white bread. After dinner he has some hope that Black will be going outside, and he is encouraged when he sees a sudden flurry or activity in Black's room. But all comes to nothing. Fifteen minutes later, Black is sitting at his desk again, this time reading a book. A lamp is on beside him, and Blue has a clearer view of Black's face than before. Blue estimates Black's age to be the same as his, give or take a year or two. That is to say, somewhere in his late twenties or early thirties. He finds Black's face pleasant enough, with nothing to distinguish it from a thousand other faces one sees every day. This is a disappointment to Blue, for he is still secretly hoping to discover that Black is a madman. Blue looks through the binoculars and reads the title of the book that Black is reading. Walden, by Henry David Thoreau. Blue has never heard of it before and writes it down carefully in his notebook.

So it goes for the rest of the evening, with Black reading and Blue watch- 20 ing him read. As time passes, Blue grows more and more discouraged. He's not used to sitting around like this, and with the darkness closing in on him now, it's beginning to get on his nerves. He likes to be up and about, moving from one place to another, doing things. I'm not the Sherlock Holmes type, he would say to Brown, whenever the boss gave him a particularly sedentary task. Give me something I can sink my teeth into. Now, when he himself is the boss, this is what he gets: a case with nothing to do. For to watch someone read and write is in effect to do nothing. The only way for Blue to have a sense of what is happening is to be inside Black's mind, to see what he is thinking, and that of course is impossible. Little by little, therefore, Blue lets his own mind drift back to the old days. He thinks of Brown and some of the cases they worked on together, savoring the memory of their triumphs. There was the Redman Affair, for example, in which they tracked down the bank teller who had embezzled a quarter of a million dollars. For that one Blue pretended to be a bookie and lured Redman into placing a bet with him. The money was traced back to the bills missing from the bank, and the man got what was coming to him. Even better was the Gray Case. Gray had been missing for over a year, and his wife was ready to give him up for dead. Blue searched through all the normal channels and came up empty. Then, one day, as he was about to file his final report, he stumbled on Gray in a bar, not two blocks from where the wife was sitting, convinced he would never return. Gray's name was now Green, but Blue knew it was Gray in spite of this, for he had been carrying around a photograph of the man for the past three months and knew his face by heart. It turned out to be amnesia. Blue took Gray back to his wife, and although he didn't remember her and continued to call himself Green, he found her to his liking and some days later proposed marriage. So Mrs. Gray became Mrs. Green, married to the same man a second time, and while Gray never remembered the past—and stubbornly refused to admit that he had forgotten anything—that did not seem to stop him from living comfortably in the present. Whereas Gray had worked as an engineer in his former life, as Green he now kept the job as bartender in the bar two blocks away. He liked mixing drinks, he said, and talking to the people who came in, and he couldn't imagine doing anything else. I was born to be a bartender, he announced to Brown and Blue at the wedding party, and who were they to object to what a man chose to do with his life?

Those were the good old days, Blue says to himself now, as he watches Black turn off the light in his room across the street. Full of strange twists and amusing coincidences. Well, not every case can be exciting. You've got to take the good with the bad.

Blue, ever the optimist, wakes up the next morning in a cheerful mood. Outside, snow is falling on the quiet street, and everything has turned white. After watching Black eat his breakfast at the table by the window and read a few more pages of Walden, Blue sees him retreat to the back of the room and then return to the window dressed in his overcoat. The time is shortly after eight o'clock. Blue reaches for his hat, his coat, his muffler, and boots, hastily scrambles into them, and gets downstairs to the street less than a minute after Black. It is a windless morning, so still that he can hear the snow falling on the branches of the trees. No one else is about, and Black's shoes have made a perfect set of tracks on the white pavement. Blue follows the tracks around the corner and then sees Black ambling down the next street, as if enjoying the weather. Not the behavior of a man about to escape, Blue thinks, and accordingly

he slows his pace. Two streets later, Black enters a small grocery store, stays
ten or twelve minutes, and then comes out with two heavily loaded brown paper bags. Without noticing Blue, who is standing in a doorway across the
street, he begins retracing his steps towards Orange Street. Stocking up for
the storm, Blue says to himself. Blue then decides to risk losing contact with
Black and goes into the store himself to do the same. Unless it's a decoy, he
thinks, and Black is planning to dump the groceries and take off, it's fairly certain that he's on his way home. Blue therefore does his own shopping, stops in
next door to buy a newspaper and several magazines, and then returns to his
room on Orange Street. Sure enough, Black is already at his desk by the window, writing in the same notebook as the day before.

   Because of the snow, visibility is poor, and Blue has trouble deciphering
what is happening in Black's room. Even the binoculars don't help much. The
day remains dark, and through the endlessly falling snow, Black appears to be
no more than a shadow. Blue resigns himself to a long wait and then settles
down with his newspapers and magazines. He is a devoted reader of True Detective and tries never to miss a month. Now, with time on his hands, he reads
the new issue thoroughly, even pausing to read the little notices and ads on
the back pages. Buried among the feature stories on gangbusters and secret
agents, there is one short article that strikes a chord in Blue, and even after he
finishes the magazine, he finds it difficult not to keep thinking about it.
Twenty-five years ago, it seems, in a patch of woods outside Philadelphia, a
little boy was found murdered. Although the police promptly began work on
the case, they never managed to come up with any clues. Not only did they
have no suspects, they could not even identify the boy. Who he was, where he
had come from, why he was there—all these questions remained unanswered.
Eventually, the case was dropped from the active file, and if not for the coroner who had been assigned to do the autopsy on the boy, it would have been
forgotten altogether. This man, whose name was Gold, became obsessed by
the murder. Before the child was buried, he made a death mask of his face, and
from then on devoted whatever time he could to the mystery. After twenty
years, he reached retirement age, left his job, and began spending every moment on the case. But things did not go well. He made no headway, came not
one step closer to solving the crime. The article in True Detective describes
how he is now offering a reward of two thousand dollars to anyone who can
provide information about the little boy. It also includes a grainy, retouched
photograph of the man holding the death mask in his hands. The look in his
eyes is so haunted and imploring that Blue can scarcely turn his own eyes
away. Gold is growing old now, and he is afraid that he will die before he
solves the case. Blue is deeply moved by this. If it were possible, he would like
nothing better than to drop what he's doing and try to help Gold. There
aren't enough men like that, he thinks. If the boy were Gold's son, then it
would make sense: revenge, pure and simple, and anyone can understand that.
But the boy was a complete stranger to him, and so there's nothing personal
about it, no hint of a secret motive. It is this thought that so affects Blue. Gold
refuses to accept a world in which the murderer of a child can go unpunished,
even if the murderer himself is now dead, and he is willing to sacrifice his own

life and happiness to right the wrong. Blue then thinks about the little boy for a while, trying to imagine what really happened, trying to feel what the boy must have felt, and then it dawns on him that the murderer must have been one of the parents, for otherwise the boy would have been reported as missing. That only makes it worse, Blue thinks, and as he begins to grow sick at the thought of it, fully understanding now what Gold must feel all the time, he realizes that twenty-five years ago he too was a little boy and that had the boy lived he would be Blue's age now. It could have been me, Blue thinks. I could have been that little boy. Not knowing what else to do, he cuts out the picture from the magazine and tacks it onto the wall above his bed.

So it goes for the first days. Blue watches Black, and little of anything happens. Black writes, reads, eats, takes brief strolls through the neighborhood, seems not to notice that Blue is there. As for Blue, he tries not to worry. He assumes that Black is lying low, biding his time until the right moment comes. Since Blue is only one man, he realizes that constant vigilance is not expected of him. After all, you can't watch someone twenty-four hours a day. There has to be time for you to sleep, to eat, to do your laundry, and so on. If White wanted Black to be watched around the clock, he would have hired two or three men, not one. But Blue is only one, and more than what is possible he cannot do.

Still, he does begin to worry, in spite of what he tells himself. For if Black 25 must be watched, then it would follow that he must be watched every hour of every day. Anything less than constant surveillance would be as no surveillance at all. It would not take much, Blue reasons, for the entire picture to change. A single moment's inattention—a glance to the side of him, a pause to scratch his head, the merest yawn—and presto, Black slips away and commits whatever heinous act he is planning to commit. And yet, there will necessarily be such moments, hundreds and even thousands of them every day. Blue finds this troubling, for no matter how often he turns this problem over inside himself, he gets no closer to solving it. But that is not the only thing that troubles him.

Until now, Blue has not had much chance for sitting still, and this new idleness has left him at something of a loss. For the first time in his life, he finds that he has been thrown back on himself, with nothing to grab hold of, nothing to distinguish one moment from the next. He has never given much thought to the world inside him, and though he always knew it was there, it has remained an unknown quantity, unexplored and therefore dark, even to himself. He has moved rapidly along the surface of things for as long as he can remember, fixing his attention on these surfaces only in order to perceive them, sizing up one and then passing on to the next, and he has always taken pleasure in the world as such, asking no more of things than that they be there. And until now they have been, etched vividly against the daylight, distinctly telling him what they are, so perfectly themselves and nothing else that he has never had to pause before them or look twice. Now, suddenly, with the world as it were removed from him, with nothing much to see but a vague shadow by the name of Black, he finds himself thinking about things that have never occurred to him before, and this, too, has begun to trouble him. If thinking is perhaps too strong a word at this point, a slightly more modest

term—speculation, for example—would not be far from the mark. To speculate, from the Latin speculatus, meaning to spy out, to observe, and linked to
the word speculum, meaning mirror or looking glass. For in spying out at
Black across the street, it is as though Blue were looking into a mirror, and instead of merely watching another, he finds that he is also watching himself.
Life has slowed down so drastically for him that Blue is now able to see things
that have previously escaped his attention. The trajectory of the light that
passes through the room each day, for example, and the way the sun at certain
hours will reflect the snow on the far corner of the ceiling in his room. The
beating of his heart, the sound of his breath, the blinking of his eyes—Blue is
now aware of these tiny events, and try as he might to ignore them, they persist in his mind like a nonsensical phrase repeated over and over again. He
knows it cannot be true, and yet little by little this phrase seems to be taking
on a meaning.

Of Black, of White, of the job he has been hired to do, Blue now begins
to advance certain theories. More than just helping to pass the time, he discovers that making up stories can be a pleasure in itself. He thinks that perhaps White and Black are brothers and that a large sum of money is at
stake—an inheritance, for example, or the capital invested in a partnership.
Perhaps White wants to prove that Black is incompetent, have him committed to an institution, and take control of the family fortune himself. But Black
is too clever for that and has gone into hiding, waiting for the pressure to ease
up. Another theory that Blue puts forward has White and Black as rivals, both
of them racing toward the same goal—the solution to a scientific problem, for
example—and White wants Black watched in order to be sure he isn't out-
smarted. Still another story has it that White is a renegade agent from the
F.B.I. or some espionage organization, perhaps foreign, and has struck out on
his own to conduct some peripheral investigation not necessarily sanctioned by
his superiors. By hiring Blue to do his work for him, he can keep the surveillance of Black a secret and at the same time continue to perform his normal
duties. Day by day, the list of these stories grows, with Blue sometimes returning in his mind to an early story to add certain flourishes and details and
at other times starting over again with something new. Murder plots, for instance, and kidnapping schemes for giant ransoms. As the days go on, Blue realizes there is no end to the stories he can tell. For Black is no more than a
kind of blankness, a hold in the texture of things, and one story can fill this
hold as well as any other.

Blue does not mince words, however. He knows that more than anything
else he would like to learn the real story. But at this early stage he also knows
that patience is called for. Bit by bit, therefore, he begins to dig in, and with
each day that passes he finds himself a little more comfortable with his situation, a little more resigned to the fact that he is in for the long haul.

Unfortunately, thoughts of the future Mrs. Blue occasionally disturb his
growing peace of mind. Blue misses her more than ever, but he also senses
somehow that things will never be the same again. Where this feeling comes
from he cannot tell. But while he feels reasonably content whenever he con-

fines his thoughts to Black, to his room, to the case he is working on, whenever the future Mrs. Blue enters his consciousness, he is seized by a kind of panic. All of a sudden, his calm turns to anguish, and he feels as though he is falling into some dark, cave-like place, with no hope of finding a way out. Nearly every day he has been tempted to pick up the phone and call her, thinking that perhaps a moment of real contact would break the spell. But the days pass, and still he doesn't call. This, too, is troubling to him, for he cannot remember a time in his life when he has been so reluctant to do a thing he so clearly wants to do. I'm changing, he says to himself. Little by little, I'm no longer the same. This interpretation reassures him somewhat, at least for a while, but in the end it only leaves him feeling stranger than before. The days pass, and it becomes difficult for him not to keep seeing pictures of the future Mrs. Blue in his head, especially at night, and there in the darkness of his room, lying on his back with his eyes open, he reconstructs her body piece by piece, beginning with her feet and ankles, working his way up her legs and along her thighs, climbing from her belly toward her breasts, and then, roaming happily among the softness, dipping down to her buttocks and then up again along her back, at last finding her neck and curling forward to her round and smiling face. What is she doing now? he sometimes asks himself. And what does she think of all this? But he can never come up with a satisfactory answer. If he is able to invent a multitude of stories to fit the facts concerning Black, with the future Mrs. Blue all is silence, confusion, and emptiness.

The day comes for him to write his final report. Blue is an old hand at such 30 compositions and has never had any trouble with them. His method is to stick to outward facts, describing events as though each word tallied exactly with the thing described, and to question the matter no further. Words are transparent for him, great windows that stand between him and the world, and until now they have never impeded his view, have never even seemed to be there. Oh, there are moments when the glass gets a trifle smudged and Blue has to polish it in one spot or another, but once he finds the right word, everything clears up. Drawing on the entries he has made previously in his notebook, sifting through them to refresh his memory and to underscore pertinent remarks, he tries to fashion a coherent whole, discarding the slack and embellishing the gist. In every report he has written so far, action holds forth over interpretation. For example: The subject walked from Columbus Circle to Carnegie Hall. No references to the weather, no mention of the traffic, no stab at trying to guess what the subject might be thinking. The report confines itself to known and verifiable facts, and beyond this limit it does not try to go.

Faced with the facts of the Black case, however, Blue grows aware of his predicament. There is the notebook, of course, but when he looks through it to see what he has written, he is disappointed to find such paucity of detail. It's as though his words, instead of drawing out the facts and making them sit palpably in the world, have induced them to disappear. This has never happened to Blue before. He looks out across the street and sees Black sitting at his desk as usual. Black, too, is looking through the window at that moment, and it suddenly occurs to Blue that he can no longer depend on the old procedures. Clues, legwork, investigative routine—none of this is going to matter anymore. But then, when he tries to imagine what will replace these things, he gets nowhere. At this point, Blue can only surmise what the case is not. To say what it is, however, is completely beyond him.

Blue sets his typewriter on the table and casts about for ideas, trying to apply himself to the task at hand. He thinks that perhaps a truthful account of the past week would include the various stories he has made up for himself concerning Black. With so little else to report, these excursions into the make-believe would at least give some flavor of what has happened. But Blue brings himself up short, realizing that they have nothing really to do with Black. This isn't the story of my life, after all, he says. I'm supposed to be writing about him, not myself.

Still, it looms as a perverse temptation, and Blue must struggle with himself for some time before fighting it off. He goes back to the beginning and works his way through the case, step by step. Determined to do exactly what has been asked of him, he painstakingly composes the report in the old style, tackling each detail with such care and aggravating precision that many hours go by before he manages to finish. As he reads over the results, he is forced to admit that everything seems accurate. But then why does he feel so dissatisfied, so troubled by what he has written? He says to himself: what happened is not really what happened. For the first time in his experience of writing reports, he discovers that words do not necessarily work, that it is possible for them to obscure the things they are trying to say. Blue looks around the room and fixes his attention on various objects, one after another. He sees the lamp and says to himself, lamp. He sees the bed and says to himself, bed. He sees the notebook and says to himself, notebook. It will not do to call the lamp a bed, he thinks, or the bed a lamp. No, these words fit snugly around the things they stand for, and the moment Blue speaks them, he feels a deep satisfaction, as though he has just proved the existence of the world. Then he looks out across the street and sees Black's window. It is dark now, and Black is asleep. That's the problem, Blue says to himself, trying to find a little courage. That and nothing else. He's there, but it's impossible to see him. And even when I do see him it's as though the lights are out.

He seals up his report in an envelope and goes outside, walks to the corner, and drops it into the mailbox. I may not be the smartest person in the world, he says to himself, but I'm doing my best, I'm doing my best.

After that, the snow begins to melt. The next morning, the sun is shining 35 brightly, clusters of sparrows are chirping in the trees, and Blue can hear the pleasant dripping of water from the edge of the roof, the branches, the lampposts. Spring suddenly does not seem far away. Another few weeks, he says to himself, and every morning will be like this one.

Black takes advantage of the weather to wander farther afield than previously, and Blue follows. Blue is relieved to be moving again, and as Black continues on his way, Blue hopes the journey will not end before he's had a chance to work out the kinks. As one would imagine, he has always been an ardent walker, and to feel his legs striding along through the morning air fills him with happiness. As they move through the narrow streets of Brooklyn Heights, Blue is encouraged to see that Black keeps increasing his distance from home. But then, his mood suddenly darkens. Black begins to climb the staircase that leads to the walkway across the Brooklyn Bridge, and Blue gets it into his head that he's planning to jump. Such things happen, he tells himself. A man goes to the top of the bridge, gives a last look to the world through the wind and the clouds, and then leaps out over the water, bones cracking on impact, his body broken apart. Blue gags on the image, tells himself to stay alert. If anything starts to happen, he decides, he will step out from his role as neutral bystander and intervene. For he does not want Black to be dead—at least not yet.

It has been many years since Blue crossed the Brooklyn Bridge on foot. The last time was with his father when he was a boy, and the memory of that day comes back to him now. He can see himself holding his father's hand and walking at his side, and as he hears the traffic moving along the steel bridge-road below, he can remember telling his father that this noise sounded like the buzzing of an enormous swarm of bees. To his left is the Statue of Liberty; to his right is Manhattan, the buildings so tall in the morning sun they seem to be figments. His father was a great one for facts, and he told Blue the stories of all the monuments and skyscrapers, vast litanies of detail—the architects, the dates, the political intrigues—and how at one time the Brooklyn Bridge was the tallest structure in America. The old man was born the same year the bridge was finished, and there was always that link in Blue's mind, as though the bridge were somehow a monument to his father. He liked the story he was told that day as he and Blue Senior walked home over the same wooden planks he was walking on now, and for some reason he never forgot it. How John Roebling, the designer of the bridge, got his foot crushed between the dock pilings and a ferry boat just days after finishing the plans and died from gangrene in less than three weeks. He didn't have to die, Blue's father said, but the only treatment he would accept was hydrotherapy, and that proved useless, and Blue was struck that a man who had spent his life building bridges over bodies of water so that people wouldn't get wet should believe that the only true medicine consisted in immersing oneself in water. After John Roebling's death, his son Washington took over as chief engineer, and that was another curious story. Washington Roebling was just thirty-one at the time, with no building experience except for the wooden bridges he designed during the Civil War, but he proved to be even more brilliant than his father. Not long after construction began on the Brooklyn Bridge, however, he was trapped for several hours during a fire in one of the underwater caissons and came out of it with a severe case of the bends, an excruciating disease in which nitrogen bubbles gather in the bloodstream. Nearly killed by the attack, he was thereafter an invalid, unable to leave the top floor room where he and his wife set up house in Brooklyn Heights. There Washington Roebling sat every day for many years, watching the progress of the bridge through a telescope, sending his wife down every morning with his instructions, drawing elaborate color pictures for the foreign workers who spoke no English so they would understand what to do next, and the remarkable thing was that the whole bridge was literally in his head: every piece of it had been memorized, down to the tiniest bits of steel and stone, and though Washington Roebling never set foot on the bridge, it was totally present inside him, as though by the end of all those years it had somehow grown into his body.

Blue thinks of this now as he makes his way across the river, watching Black ahead of him and remembering his father and his boyhood out in Gravesend. The old man was a cop, later a detective at the 77th precinct, and life would have been good, Blue thinks, if it hadn't been for the Russo Case and the bullet that went through his father's brain in 1927. Twenty years ago, he says to himself, suddenly appalled by the time that has passed, wondering if there is a heaven, and if so whether or not he will get to see his father again after he dies. He remembers a story from one of the endless magazines he has read this week, a new monthly called Stranger than Fiction, and it seems somehow to follow from all the other thoughts that have just come to him. Somewhere in the French Alps, he recalls, a man was lost skiing twenty or twenty-five years ago, swallowed up by an avalanche, and his body was never recovered. His son, who was a little boy at the time, grew up and also became a skier. One day in the past year he went skiing, not far from the spot where his father was lost—although he did not know this. Through the minute and persistent displacements of the ice over the decades since his father's death, the terrain was now completely different from what it had been. All alone there in the mountains, miles away from any other human being, the son chanced upon a body in the ice—a dead body, perfectly intact, as though preserved in suspended animation. Needless to say, the young man stopped to examine it, and as he bent down and looked at the face of the corpse, he had the distinct and terrifying impression that he was looking at himself. Trembling with fear, as the article put it, he inspected the body more closely, all sealed away as it was in the ice, like someone on the other side of a thick window, and saw that it was his father. The dead man was still young, even younger than his son was now, and there was something awesome about it, Blue felt, something so odd and terrible about being older than your own father, that he actually had to fight back tears as he read the article. Now, as he nears the end of the bridge, these same feelings come back to him, and he wishes to God that his father could be there, walking over the river and telling him stories. Then, suddenly aware of what his mind is doing, he wonders why he has turned so sentimental, why all these thoughts keep coming to him, when for so many years they have never even occurred to him. It's all part of it, he thinks, embarrassed at himself for being like this. That's what happens when you have no one to talk to.

He comes to the end and sees that he was wrong about Black. There will be no suicides today, no jumping from bridges, no leaps into the unknown. For there goes his man, as blithe and unperturbed as anyone can be, descending the stairs of the walkway and traveling along the street that curves around City Hall, then moving north along Centre Street past the courthouse and other municipal buildings, never once slackening his pace, continuing on through Chinatown and beyond. These divagations last several hours, and at no point does Blue have the sense that Black is walking to any purpose. He seems rather to be airing his lungs, walking for the pure pleasure of walking, and as the journey goes on Blue confesses to himself for the first time that he is developing a certain fondness for Black.

At one point Black enters a bookstore and Blue follows him in. There 40 Black browses for half an hour or so, accumulating a small pile of books in the process, and Blue, with nothing better to do, browses as well, all the while trying to keep his face hidden from Black. The little glances he takes when Black seems not to be looking give him the feeling that he has seen Black before, but he can't remember where. There's something about the eyes, he says to himself, but that's as far as he gets, not wanting to call attention to himself and not really sure if there's anything to it.

A minute later, Blue comes across a copy of Walden by Henry David Thoreau. Flipping through the pages, he is surprised to discover that the name of the publisher is Black: "Published for the Classics Club by Walter J. Black, Inc., Copyright 1942." Blue is momentarily jarred by this coincidence, thinking that perhaps there is some message in it for him, some glimpse of meaning that could make a difference. But then, recovering from the jolt, he begins to think not. It's a common enough name, he says to himself—and besides, he knows for a fact that Black's name is not Walter. Could be a relative though, he adds, or maybe even his father. Still turning this last point over in his mind, Blue decides to buy the book. If he can't read what Black writes, at least he can read what he reads. A long shot, he says to himself, but who knows that it won't give some hint of what the man is up to.

So far so good. Black pays for his books, Blue pays for his book, and the walk continues. Blue keeps looking for some pattern to emerge, for some clue to drop in his path that will lead him to Black's secret. But Blue is too honest a man to delude himself, and he knows that no rhyme or reason can be read into anything that's happened so far. For once, he is not discouraged by this. In fact, as he probes more deeply into himself, he realizes that on the whole he feels rather invigorated by it. There is something nice about being in the dark, he discovers, something thrilling about not knowing what is going to happen next. It keeps you alert, he thinks, and there's no harm in that, is there? Wide awake and on your toes, taking it all in, ready for anything.

A few moments after thinking this thought, Blue is finally offered a new development, and the case takes on its first twist. Black turns a corner in midtown, walks halfway down the block, hesitates briefly, as if searching for an address, backtracks a few paces, moves on again, and several seconds later enters a restaurant. Blue follows him in, thinking nothing much of it, since it's lunchtime after all, and people have to eat, but it does not escape him that Black's hesitation seems to indicate that he's never been here before, which in turn might mean that Black has an appointment. It's a dark place inside, fairly crowded, with a group of people clustered around the bar in front, lots of chatter and the clinking of silverware and plates in the background. It looks expensive, Blue thinks, with wood paneling on the walls and white tablecloths, and he decides to keep his bill as low as he can. Tables are available, and Blue takes it as a good omen when he is seated within eyeshot of Black, not obtrusively close, but not so far as not to be able to watch what he does. Black tips his hand by asking for two menus, and three or four minutes later breaks into a smile when a woman walks across the room, approaches Black's table, and kisses him on the cheek before sitting down. The woman's not bad, Blue thinks. A bit on the lean side for his taste, but not bad at all. Then he thinks: now the interesting part begins.

Unfortunately, the woman's back is turned to Blue, so he can't watch her face as the meal progresses. As he sits there eating his Salisbury steak, he thinks that maybe his first hunch was the right one, that it's a marriage case after all. Blue is already imagining the kinds of things he will write in his next report, and it gives him pleasure to contemplate the phrases he will use to describe what he is seeing now. By having another person in the case, he knows that certain decisions have to be made. For example: should he stick with Black or divert his attention to the woman? This could possibly accelerate matters a bit, but at the same time it could mean that Black would be given the chance to slip away from him, perhaps for good. In other words, is the meeting with the woman a smoke-screen or the real thing? Is it a part of the case or not, is it an essential or contingent fact? Blue ponders these questions for a while and concludes that it's too early to tell. Yes, it could be one thing, he tells himself. But it could be another.

About midway through the meal, things seem to take a turn for the worse. 45 Blue detects a look of great sadness in Black's face, and before he knows it the woman seems to be crying. At least that is what he can gather from the sudden change in the position of her body: her shoulders slumped, her head leaning forward, her face perhaps covered by her hands, the slight shuddering along her back. It could be a fit of laughter, Blue reasons, but then why would Black be so miserable? It looks as though the ground has just been cut out from under him. A moment later, the woman turns her face away from Black, and Blue gets a glimpse of her profile: tears without question, he thinks, as he watches her dab her eyes with a napkin and sees a smudge of wet mascara glistening on her cheek. She stands up abruptly and walks off in the direction of the ladies' room. Again Blue has an unobstructed view of Black, and seeing the sadness in his face, that look of absolute dejection, he almost begins to feel sorry for him. Black glances in Blue's direction, but clearly he's not seeing anything, and then, an instant later, he buries his face in his hands. Blue tries to guess what is happening, but it's impossible to know. It looks like it's over between them, he thinks, it has the feeling of something that's come to an end. And yet, for all that, it could be just a tiff.

The woman returns to the table looking a little better, and then the two of them sit there for a few minutes without saying anything, leaving their food untouched. Black sighs once or twice, looking off into the distance, and finally calls for the check. Blue does the same and then follows the two of them out of the restaurant. He notes that Black has his hand on her elbow, but that could just be a reflex he tells himself, and probably means nothing. They walk down the street in silence, and at the corner Black waves down a cab. He opens the door for the woman, and before she climbs in he touches her very gently on the cheek. She gives him a brave little smile in return, but still they don't say a word. Then she sits down in the back seat, Black shuts the door, and the cab takes off.

Black walks around for a few minutes, pausing briefly in front of a travel agency window to study a poster of the White Mountains, and then climbs into a cab himself. Blue gets lucky again and manages to find another cab just seconds later. He tells the driver to follow Black's cab and then sits back as the two yellow cars make their way slowly through the traffic downtown, across the Brooklyn Bridge, and finally to Orange Street. Blue is shocked by the fare and kicks himself mentally for not following the woman instead. He should have known that Black was going home.

His mood brightens considerably when he enters his building and finds a letter in his mailbox. It can only be one thing, he tells himself, and sure enough as he walks upstairs and opens the envelope, there it is: the first check, a postal money order for the exact amount settled on with White. He finds it a bit perplexing, however, that the method of payment should be so anonymous. Why not a personal check from White? This leads Blue to toy with the thought that White is a renegade agent after all, eager to cover his tracks and therefore making sure there will be no record of the payments. Then, removing his hat and overcoat and stretching out on the bed, Blue realizes that he's a little disappointed not to have had some comment about the report. Considering how hard he struggled to get it right, a word of encouragement would have been welcomed. The fact that the money was sent means that White was not dissatisfied. But still—silence is not a rewarding response, no matter what it means. If that's the way it is, Blue says to himself, I'll just have to get used it.

The days go by, and once again things settle down to the barest of routines. Black writes, reads, shops in the neighborhood, visits the post office, takes an occasional stroll. The woman does not reappear, and Black makes no further excursions to Manhattan. Blue begins to think that any day he will get a letter telling him the case is closed. The woman is gone, he reasons, and that could be the end of it. But nothing of the sort happens. Blue's meticulous description of the scene in restaurant draws no special response from White, and week after week the checks continue to arrive on time. So much for love, Blue says to himself. The woman never meant anything. She was just a diversion.

In this early period, Blue's state of mind can best be described as one of 50 ambivalence and conflict. There are moments when he feels so completely in harmony with Black, so naturally at one with the other man, that to anticipate what Black is going to do, to know when he will stay in his room and when he will go out, he need merely look into himself. Whole days go by when he doesn't even bother to look through the window or follow Black onto the street. Now and then, he even allows himself to make solo expeditions, knowing full well that during the time he is gone Black will not have budged from his spot. How he knows this remains something of a mystery to him, but the fact is that he is never wrong, and when the feeling comes over him, he is beyond all doubt and hesitation. On the other hand, not all moments are like these. There are times when he feels totally removed from Black, cut off from him in a way that is so stark and absolute that he begins to lose the sense of who he is. Loneliness envelopes him, sits him in, and with it comes a terror worse than anything he has ever known. It puzzles him that he should switch so rapidly from one state to another, and for a long time he goes back and forth between extremes, not knowing which one is true and which one is false.

After a stretch of particularly bad days, he begins to long for some companionship. He sits down and writes a detailed letter to Brown, outlining the case and asking for his advice. Brown has retired to Florida, where he spends most of his time fishing, and Blue knows that it will take quite a while before he receives an answer. Still, the day after he mails the letter, he begins looking forward to the reply with an eagerness that soon grows to obsession. Each morning, about an hour before the mail is delivered, he plants himself by the window, watching for the postman to round the corner and come into view, pinning all his hopes on what Brown will say to him. What he is expecting from this letter is not certain. Blue does not even ask the question, but surely it is something monumental, some luminous and extraordinary words that will bring him back to the world of the living.

As the days and weeks go by without any letter from Brown, Blue's disappointment grows into aching, irrational desperation. But that is nothing compared to what he feels when the letter finally comes. For Brown does not even address himself to what Blue wrote. It's good to hear from you, the letter begins, and good to know you're working so hard. Sounds like an interesting case. Can't say I miss any of it, though. Here it's the good life for me—get up early and fish, spend some time with my wife, read a little, sleep in the sun, nothing to complain about. The only thing I don't understand is why I didn't move down here years ago.

The letter goes on in that vein for several pages, never once broaching the subject of Blue's torments and anxieties. Blue feels betrayed by the man who was once like a father to him, and when he finishes the letter he feels empty, the stuffing all knocked out of him. I'm on my own, he thinks, there's no one to turn to anymore. This is followed by several hours of despondency and self-pity, with Blue thinking once or twice that maybe he'd be better off dead. But eventually he works his way out of the gloom. For Blue is a solid character on the whole, less given to dark thoughts than most, and if there are moments when he feels the world is a foul place, who are we to blame him for it? By the time supper rolls around, he has even begun to look on the bright side. This is perhaps his greatest talent: not that he does not despair, but that he never despairs for very long. It might be a good thing after all, he says to himself. It might be better to stand alone than to depend on anyone else. Blue thinks about this for a while and decides there is something to be said for it. He is no longer an apprentice. There is no master above him anymore. I'm my own man, he says to himself. I'm my own man, accountable to no one but myself.

Inspired by this new approach to things, he discovers that he has at last found the courage to contact the future Mrs. Blue. But when he picks up the phone and dials her number, there is no answer. This is a disappointment, but he remains undaunted. I'll try again some other time, he says. Some time soon.

The days continue to pass. Once again, Blue falls into step with Black, per- 55
haps even more harmoniously than before. In doing so, he discovers the in-

herent paradox of his situation. For the closer he feels to Black, the less he finds it necessary to think about him. In other words, the more deeply entangled he becomes, the freer he is. What bogs him down is not involvement but separation. For it is only when Black seems to drift away from him that he must go out looking for him, and this takes time and effort, not to speak of struggle. At those moments when he feels closest to Black, however, he can even begin to lead the semblance of an independent life. At first he is not very daring in what he allows himself to do, but even so he considers it a kind of triumph, almost an act of bravery. Going outside, for example, and walking up and down the block. Small as it might be, this gesture fills him with happiness, and as he moves back and forth along Orange Street in the lovely spring weather, he is glad to be alive in a way he has not felt in years. At one end there is a view of the river, the harbor, the Manhattan skyline, the bridges. Blue finds all this beautiful, and on some days he even allows himself to sit for several minutes on one of the benches and look out at the boats. In the other direction there is the church, and sometimes Blue goes to the small grassy yard to sit for a while, studying the bronze statue of Henry Ward Beecher. Two slaves are holding on to Beecher's legs, as though begging him to help them, to make them free at last, and in the brick wall behind there is a porcelain relief of Abraham Lincoln. Blue cannot help but feel inspired by these images, and each time he comes to the churchyard his head fills with noble thoughts about the dignity of man.

Little by little, he becomes more bold in his strayings from Black. It is 1947, the year that Jackie Robinson breaks in with the Dodgers, and Blue follows in his progress closely, remembering the churchyard and knowing there is more to it than just baseball. One bright Tuesday afternoon in May, he decides to make an excursion to Ebbets Field, and as he leaves Black behind in his room on Orange Street, hunched over his desk as usual with his pen and papers, he feels no cause for worry, secure in the fact that everything will be exactly the same when he returns. He rides the subway, rubs shoulders with the crowd, feels himself lunging towards a sense of the moment. As he takes his seat at the ball park, he is struck by the sharp clarity of the colors around him: the green grass, the brown dirt, the white ball, the blue sky above. Each thing is distinct from every other thing, wholly separate and defined, and the geometric simplicity for the pattern impresses Blue with its force. Watching the game, he finds it difficult to take his eyes off Robinson, lured constantly by the blackness of the man's face, and he thinks it must take courage to do what he is doing, to be alone like that in front of so many strangers, with half of them no doubt wishing him to be dead. As the game moves along, Blue finds himself cheering whatever Robinson does, and when the black man steals a base in the third inning he rises to his feet, and later, in the seventh, when Robinson doubles off the wall in left, he actually pounds the back of the man next to him for joy. The Dodgers pull it out in the ninth with a sacrifice fly, and as Blue shuffles off with the rest of the crowd and makes his way home, it occurs to him that Black did not cross his mind even once.

But the ball games are only the beginning. On certain nights, when it is clear to Blue that Black will not be going anywhere, he slips out to a bar not far away for a beer or two, enjoying the conversations he sometimes has with the bartender, whose name is Red, and who bears an uncanny resemblance to Green, the bartender from the Gray Case so long ago. A blowsy tart named Violet is often there, and once or twice Blue gets her tipsy enough to get invited back to her place around the corner. He knows that she likes him well enough because she never makes him pay for it, but he also knows that it has nothing to do with love. She calls him honey and her flesh is soft and ample, but whenever she has one drink too many she begins to cry, and then Blue has to console her, and he secretly wonders if it's worth the trouble. His guilt towards the future Mrs. Blue is scant, however, for he justifies these sessions with Violet by comparing himself to a soldier at war in another country. Every man needs a little comfort, especially when his number could be up tomorrow. And besides, he isn't made of stone, he says to himself.

More often than not, however, Blue will bypass the bar and go to the movie theatre several blocks away. With summer coming on now and the heat beginning to hover uncomfortably in his little room, it's refreshing to be able to sit in the cool theater and watch the feature show. Blue is fond of the movies, not only for the stories they tell and the beautiful women he can see in them, but for the darkness of the theater itself, the way the pictures on the screen are somehow like the thoughts inside his head whenever he closes his eyes. He is more or less indifferent to the kinds of movies he sees, whether comedies or dramas, for example, or whether the film is shot in black and white or color, but he has a particular weakness for movies about detectives, since there is a natural connection, and he is always gripped by these stories more than by others. During this period he sees a number of such movies and enjoys them all: Lady in the Lake, Fallen Angel, Dark Passage, Body and Soul, Ride the Pink Horse, Desperate, and so on. But for Blue there is one that stands out from the rest, and he likes it so much that he actually goes back the next night to see it again.

It's called Out of the Past, and it stars Robert Mitchum as an ex–private eye who is trying to build a new life for himself in a small town under an assumed name. He has a girl friend, a sweet country girl named Ann, and runs a gas station with the help of a deaf-and-dumb boy, Jimmy, who is firmly devoted to him. But the past catches up with Mitchum, and there's little he can do about it. Years ago, he had been hired to look for Jane Greer, the mistress of gangster Kirk Douglas, but once he found her they fell in love and ran off together to live in secret. One thing led to another—money was stolen, a murder was committed—and eventually Mitchum came to his senses and left Greer, finally understanding the depth of her corruption. Now he is being blackmailed by Douglas and Greer into committing a crime, which itself is merely a set-up, for once he figures out what is happening, he sees that they are planning to frame him for another murder. A complicated story unfolds, with Mitchum desperately trying to extricate himself from the trap. At one point, he returns to the small town where he lives, tells Ann that he's innocent, and again persuades her of his love. But it's really too late, and Mitchum knows it. Towards the end, he manages to convince Douglas to turn in Greer for the murder she committed, but at that moment Greer enters the room, calmly takes out a gun, and kills Douglas. She tells Mitchum that they belong to each other, and he, fatalistic to the last, appears to go along. They decide to escape the country together, but as Greer goes to pack her bag, Mitchum picks up the phone and calls the police. They get into the car and drive off, but soon they come to a police roadblock. Greer, seeing that she's been double-crossed, pulls a gun from her bag and shoots Mitchum. The police then open fire on the car and Greer is killed as well. After that, there's one last scene—the next morning, back in the small town of Bridgeport. Jimmy is sitting on a bench outside the gas station, and Ann walks over and sits down beside him. Tell me one thing, Jimmy, she says, I've got to know this one thing: was he running away with her or not? The boy thinks for a moment, trying to decide between truth and kindness. Is it more important to preserve a friend's good name or to spare the girl? All this happens in no more than an instant. Looking into the girl's eyes, he nods his head, as if to say yes, he was in love with Greer after all. Ann pats Jimmy's arm and thanks him, then walks off to her former boyfriend, a straight-arrow local policeman who always despised Mitchum. Jimmy looks up at the gas station sign with Mitchum's name on it, gives a little salute of friendship, and then turns away and walks down the road. He is the only one who knows the truth, and he will never tell.

For the next few days, Blue goes over this story many times in his head. It's a good thing, he decides, that the movie ends with the deaf mute boy. The secret is buried, and Mitchum will remain an outsider, even in death. His ambition was simple enough: to become a normal citizen in a normal American town, to marry the girl next door, to live a quiet life. It's strange, Blue thinks, that the new name Mitchum chooses for himself is Jeff Bailey. This is remarkably close to the name of another character in a movie he saw the previous year with the future Mrs. Blue—George Bailey, played by James Stewart in It's a Wonderful Life. That story was also about small town America, but from the opposite point of view: the frustrations of a man who spends his whole life trying to escape. But in the end he comes to understand that his life has been a good one, that he has done the right thing all along. Mitchum's Bailey would no doubt like to be the same man as Stewart's Bailey. But in his case the name is Markham—or, as Blue sounds it out to himself, mark him—and that is the whole point. He has been marked by the past, and once that happens, nothing can be done about it. Something happens, Blue thinks, and then it goes on happening forever. It can never be changed, can never be otherwise. Blue begins to be haunted by this thought, for he sees it as a kind of warning, a message delivered up from within himself, and try as he does to push it away, the darkness of this thought does not leave him.

One night, therefore, Blue finally turns to his copy of Walden. The time has come, he says to himself, and if he doesn't make an effort now, he knows that he never will. But the book is not a simple business. As Blue begins to read, he feels as though he is entering an alien world. Trudging through swamps and brambles, hoisting himself up gloomy screes and treacherous cliffs, he feels like a prisoner on a forced march, and his only thought is to escape. He is bored by Thoreau's words and finds it difficult to concentrate. Whole chapters go by, and when he comes to the end of them he realizes that he has not retained a thing. Why would anyone want to go off and live alone in the woods? What's all this about planting beans and not drinking coffee or eating meat? Why all these interminable descriptions of birds? Blue thought that he was going to get a story, or at least something like a story, but this is no more than blather, an endless harangue about nothing at all.

It would be unfair to blame him, however. Blue has never read much of anything except newspapers and magazines, and an occasional adventure novel when he was a boy. Even experienced and sophisticated readers have been known to have trouble with Walden, and no less a figure than Emerson once wrote in his journal that reading Thoreau made him feel nervous and wretched. To Blue's credit, he does not give up. The next day he begins again, and this second go-through is somewhat less rocky than the first. In the third chapter he comes across a sentence that finally says something to him—Books must be read as deliberately and reservedly as they were written—and suddenly he understands that the trick is to go slowly, more slowly than he has ever gone with words before. This helps to some extent, and certain passages begin to grow clear: the business about clothes in the beginning, the battle between the red ants and the black ants, the argument against work. But Blue still finds it painful, and though he grudgingly admits that Thoreau is perhaps not as stupid as he thought, he begins to resent Black for putting him through this torture. What he does not know is that were he to find the patience to read the book in the spirit in which it asks to be read, his entire life would begin to change, and little by little he would come to a full understanding to his situation—that is to say, of Black, of White, of the case, of everything that concerns him. But lost chances are as much a part of life as chances taken, and a story cannot dwell on what might have been. Throwing the book aside in disgust, Blue puts on his coat (for it is fall now) and goes out for a breath of air. Little does he realize that this is the beginning of the end. For something is about to happen, and once it happens, nothing will ever be the same again.

He goes to Manhattan, wandering farther from Black than at any time before, venting his frustration in movement, hoping to calm himself down by exhausting his body. He walks north, alone in his thoughts, not bothering to take in the things around him. On East 26th Street his left shoelace comes undone, and it is precisely then, as he bends down to tie it, crouching on one knee, that the sky falls on top of him. For who should he glimpse at just that moment but the future Mrs. Blue. She is coming up the street with her two arms linked through the right arm of a man Blue has never seen before, and she is smiling radiantly, engrossed in what the man is saying to her. For several moments Blue is so at a loss that he doesn't know whether to bend his head farther down and hide his face or stand up and greet the woman whom he now understands—with a knowledge as sudden and irrevocable as the slamming of a door—will never be his wife. As it turns out, he manages neither—first ducking his head, but then discovering a second later that he wants her to recognize him, and when he sees she will not, being so wrapped up in her companion's talk, Blue abruptly rises from the pavement when they are no more than six feet away from him. It is as though some spectre has suddenly materialized in front of her, and the ex–future Mrs. Blue gives out a little gasp, even before she sees who the spectre is. Blue speaks her name, in a voice that seems strange to him, and she stops dead in her tracks, her expression turns to one of anger.

You! she says to him. You!

Before he has a chance to say a word, she disentangles herself from her companion's arm and begins pounding Blue's chest with her fists, screaming insanely at him, accusing him of one foul crime after another. It is all Blue can do to repeat her name over and over, as though trying desperately to distinguish between the woman he loves and the wild beast who is now attacking him. He feels totally defenseless, and as the onslaught continues, he begins to welcome each new blow as just punishment for his behavior. The other man soon puts a stop to it, however, and though Blue is tempted to take a swing at him, he is too stunned to act quickly enough, and before he knows it the man has led away the weeping ex–future Mrs. Blue down the street and around the corner, and that's the end of it. 65

This brief scene, so unexpected and devastating, turns Blue inside out. By the time he regains his composure and manages to return home, he realizes that he has thrown away his life. It's not her fault, he says to himself, wanting to blame her but knowing he can't. He might have been dead for all she knew, and how can he hold it against her for wanting to live? Blue feels tears forming in his eyes, but more than grief he feels anger at himself for being such a fool. He has lost whatever chance he might have had for happiness, and if that is the case, then it would not be wrong to say that this is truly the beginning of the end.

Blue gets back to his room on Orange Street, lies down on his bed, and tries to weigh the possibilities. Eventually, he turns his face to the wall and encounters the photograph of the coroner from Philadelphia, Gold. He thinks of the sad blankness of the unsolved case, the child lying in his grave with no name, and as he studies the death mask of the little boy, he begins to turn an idea over in his mind. Perhaps there are ways of getting close to Black, he thinks, ways that need not give him away. God knows there must be. Moves that can be made, plans that can be set in motion—perhaps two or three at the same time. Never mind the rest, he tells himself. It's time to turn the page.

His next report is due the day after tomorrow, and so he sits down to it now in order to get it mailed off on schedule. For the past few months his reports have been exceedingly cryptic, no more than a paragraph or two, giving the bare bones and nothing else, and this time he does not depart from the pattern. However, at the bottom of the page he interjects an obscure comment as a kind of test, hoping to elicit something more than silence from White: Black seems ill. I'm afraid he might be dying. Then he seals up the report, saying to himself that this is only the beginning.

Two days hence, Blue hastens early in the morning to the Brooklyn Post Office, a great castle of a building within eyeshot of the Manhattan Bridge. All of Blue's reports have been addressed to box number one thousand and one, and he walks over to it now as though by accident, sauntering past it and unobtrusively peeking inside to see if the report has come. It has. Or at least a letter is there—a solitary white envelope tilted at a forty-five degree angle in the narrow cubby—and Blue has no reason to suspect it's any letter other than his own. He then begins a slow circular walk around the area, determined to remain until White or someone working for White appears, his eyes fixed on the huge wall of numbered boxes, each box with a different combination, each one holding a different secret. People come and go, open boxes and close them, and Blue keeps wandering in his circle, pausing every now and then in some random spot and then moving on. Everything seems brown to him, as though the fall weather outside has penetrated the room, and the place smells pleasantly of cigar smoke. After several hours he begins to get hungry, but he does not give in to the call of his stomach, telling himself it's now or never and therefore holding his ground. Blue watches everyone who approaches the bank of post boxes, zeroing in on each person who skirts the vicinity of one thousand and one, aware of the fact that if it's not White who comes for the reports it could be anyone—an old woman, a young child, and consequently he must take nothing for granted. But none of these possibilities comes to anything, for the box remains untouched throughout, and though Blue momentarily and successively spins a story for each candidate who comes near, trying to imagine how that person might be connected to White and or Black, what role he or she might play in the case, and so on, one by one he is forced to diminish them from his mind, casting them back into the oblivion from which they have come.

Just past noon, at a moment when the post office begins to get crowded— 70 an influx of people on their lunch break rushing through to mail letters, buy stamps, attend to business of one sort or another—a man with a mask on his face walks through the door. Blue doesn't notice him at first, what with so many others coming through the door at the same time, but as the man separates himself from the crowd and begins walking toward the numbered post boxes, Blue finally catches sight of the mask—a mask of the sort that children wear on Halloween, made of rubber and portraying some hideous monster with gashes in his forehead and bleeding eyeballs and fangs for teeth. The rest of him is perfectly ordinary (gray tweed overcoat, red scarf wrapped around his neck), and Blue senses in this first moment that the man behind the mask is White. As the man continues walking toward the area of box one thousand and one, this sense grows to conviction. At the same time, Blue also feels that the man is not really there, that even though he knows he is seeing him, it is more than likely that he is the only one who can. On this point, however, Blue is wrong, for as the masked man continues moving across the vast marble floor, Blue sees a number of people laughing and pointing at him—but whether this is better or worse he cannot say. The masked man reaches box one thousand and one, spins the combination wheel back and forth and back again, and opens the box. As soon as Blue sees that this is definitely his man, he begins making a move toward him, not really sure of what he is planning to do, but in the back of his mind no doubt intending to grab hold of him and tear the mask off his face. But the man is too alert, and once he has pocketed the envelope and locked the box, he gives a quick glance around the room, sees Blue approaching, and makes a dash for it, heading for the door as fast as he can. Blue runs after him, hoping to catch him from behind and tackle him, but he gets tangled momentarily in a crowd of people at the door, and by the time he manages to get through it, the masked man is bounding down the stairs, landing on the sidewalk, and running down the street. Blue continues in pursuit, even feels he is gaining ground, but then the man reaches the corner, where a bus just happens to be pulling out from a stop, and so he conveniently leaps aboard, and Blue is left in the lurch, all out of breath and standing there like an idiot.

Two days later, when Blue receives his check in the mail, there is finally a word from White. No more funny business, it says, and though it's not much of a word, for all that Blue is glad to have received it, happy to have cracked White's wall of silence at last. It's not clear to him, however, whether the message refers to the last report or to the incident in the post office. After thinking it over for a while, he decides that it makes no difference. One way or another, the key to the case is action. He must go on disrupting things wherever he can, a little here, a little there, chipping away at each conundrum until the whole structure begins to weaken, until one day the whole rotten business comes toppling to the ground.

Over the next few weeks, Blue returns to the post office several times, hoping to catch another glimpse of White. But nothing comes of it. Either the report is already gone from the box when he gets there, or White does not show up. The fact that this area of the post office is open twenty-four hours a day leaves Blue with few options. White is on to him now, and he will not make the same mistake twice. He will simply wait until Blue is gone before going to the box, and unless Blue is willing to spend his entire life in the post office, there's no way he can expect to sneak up on White again.

The picture is far more complicated than Blue ever imagined. For almost a year now, he has thought of himself as essentially free. For better or worse he has been doing his job, looking straight ahead of him and studying Black, waiting for a possible opening, trying to stick with it, but through it all he has not given a single thought to what might be going on behind him. Now, after the incident with the masked man and the further obstacles that have ensued, Blue no longer knows what to think. It seems perfectly plausible to him that he is also being watched, observed by another in the same way that he has been observing Black. If that is the case, then he has never been free. From the very start he has been the man in the middle, thwarted in front and hemmed in on the rear. Oddly enough, this thought reminds him of some sentences from Walden, and he searches through his notebook for the exact phrasing, fairly certain that he has written them down. *We are not where we are, he finds, but in a false position Through an infirmity of our natures, we suppose a case, and put ourselves into it, and hence are in two cases at the same time, and it is doubly difficult to get out.* This makes sense to Blue, and though he is beginning to feel a little frightened, he thinks that perhaps it is not too late for him to do something about it.

The real problem boils down to identifying the nature of the problem itself. To start with, who poses the greater threat to him, White or Black? White has kept up his end of the bargain: the checks have come on time every week, and to turn against him now, Blue knows, would be to bite the hand that feeds him. And yet White is the one who set the case in motion—thrusting Blue into an empty room, as it were, and then turning off the light and locking the door. Ever since, Blue has been groping about in the darkness, feeling blindly for the light switch, a prisoner of the case itself. All well and good, but why would White want to do such a thing? When Blue comes up against this question, he can no longer think. His brain stops working, he can get no farther than this.

Take Black, then. Until now he has been the entire case, the apparent cause of all his troubles. But if White is really out to get Blue and not Black, then perhaps Black has nothing to do with it, perhaps he is no more than an innocent bystander. In that case, it is Black who occupies the position Blue has assumed all along to be his, and Blue who takes the role of Black. There is something to be said for this. On the other hand, it is also possible that Black is somehow working in league with White and that together they have conspired to do Blue in.

If so, what are they doing to him? Nothing very terrible, finally—at least not in any absolute sense. They have trapped Blue into doing nothing, into being so inactive as to reduce his life to almost no life at all. Yes, says Blue to himself, that's what it feels like: like nothing at all. He feels like a man who has been condemned to sit in a room and go on reading a book for the rest of his life. This is strange enough—to be only half alive at best, seeing the world only through words, living only through the lives of others. But if the book were an interesting one, perhaps it wouldn't be so bad. He could get caught up in the story, so to speak, and little by little begin to forget himself. But this book offers him nothing. There is no story, no plot, no action—nothing but a man sitting alone in a room and writing a book. That's all there is, Blue realizes, and he no longer wants any part of it. But how to get out? How to get out of the room that is the book that will go on being written for as long as he stays in the room?

As for Black, the so-called writer of this book, Blue can no longer trust what he sees. Is it possible that there really is such a man—who does nothing, who merely sits in his room and writes? Blue has followed him everywhere, has tracked him down into the remotest corners, has watched him so hard that his eyes seem to be failing him. Even when he does leave his room, Black never goes anywhere, never does much of anything: grocery shopping, an occasional haircut, a trip to the movies, and so on. But mostly he just wanders around the streets, looking at odd bits of scenery, clusters of random data, and even this happens only in spurts. For a while it will be buildings—craning his neck to catch a glimpse of the roofs, inspecting doorways, running his hands slowly over the stone facades. And then, for a week or two, it will be public statues, or the boats in the river, or the signs in the street. Nothing more than that, with scarcely a word to anyone, and no meetings with others except for that one lunch with the woman in tears by now so long ago. In one sense, Blue knows everything there is to know about Black: what kind of soap he buys, what newspapers he reads, what clothes he wears, and each of these things he has faithfully recorded in his notebook. He has learned a thousand facts, but the only thing they have taught him is that he knows nothing. For the fact remains that none of this is possible. It is not possible for such a man as Black to exist.

Consequently, Blue begins to suspect that Black is no more than a ruse, another one of White's hirelings, paid by the week to sit in that room and do nothing. Perhaps all that writing is merely a sham—page after page of it: a list of every name in the phone book, for example, or each word from the dictionary in alphabetical order, or a handwritten copy of Walden. Or perhaps they are not even words, but senseless scribbles, random marks of a pen, a growing heap of nonsense and confusion. This would make White the real writer then—and Black no more than his stand-in, a fake, an actor with no substance of his own. Then there are the times, following through with this thought, that Blue believes the only logical explanation is that Black is not one man but several. Two, three, four look-alikes who play the role of Black for Blue's benefit, each one putting in his allotted time and then going back to the comforts of hearth and home. But this is a thought too monstrous for Blue to contemplate for very long. Months go by, and at last he says to himself out loud: I can't breathe anymore. This is the end. I'm dying.

It is midsummer, 1948. Finally mustering the courage to act, Blue reaches into his bag of disguises and casts about for a new identity. After dismissing several possibilities, he settles on an old man who used to beg on the corners of his neighborhood when he was a boy—a local character by the name of Jimmy Rose—and decks himself out in the garb of tramphood: tattered woolen clothes, shoes held together with string to prevent the soles from flapping, a weathered carpetbag to hold his belongings, and then, last of all, a flowing white beard and long white hair. These final details give him the look of an Old Testament prophet. Blue as Jimmy Rose is not a scrofulous down-and-outer so much as a wise fool, a saint of penury living in the margins of society. A trifle daft perhaps, but harmless: he exudes a sweet indifference to the world around him, for since everything has happened to him already, nothing can disturb him anymore.

Blue posts himself in a suitable spot across the street, takes a fragment of 80 a broken magnifying glass from his pocket, and begins reading a crumpled day-old newspaper that he has salvaged from one of the nearby garbage cans. Two hours later, Black appears, walking down the steps of his house and then turning in Blue's direction. Black pays no attention to the bum—either lost in his own thoughts or ignoring him on purpose—and so as he begins to approach, Blue addresses him in a pleasant voice.

Can you spare some change, mister?

Black stops, looks over the disheveled creature who has just spoken, and gradually relaxes into a smile as he realizes he is not in danger. Then he reaches into his pocket, pulls out a coin, and puts it in Blue's hand.

Here you are, he says.

God bless you, says Blue.

Thank you, answers Black, touched by the sentiment.   85

Never fear, says Blue. God blesses all.

And with that word of reassurance, Black tips his hat to Blue and continues on his way.

The next afternoon, once again in bum's regalia, Blue waits for Black in the same spot. Determined to keep the conversation going a little longer this

time, now that he has won Black's confidence, Blue finds that the problem is
taken out of his hands when Black himself shows an eagerness to linger. It is
late in the day by now, not yet dusk but no longer afternoon, the twilight hour
of slow changes, of glowing bricks and shadows. After greeting the bum cor-
dially and giving him another coin, Black hesitates a moment, as though debating whether to take the plunge, and then says:

Has anyone ever told you that you look just like Walt Whitman?

Walt who? answers Blue, remembering to play his part.   90

Walt Whitman. A famous poet.

No, says Blue. I can't say I know him.

You wouldn't know him, says Black. He's not alive anymore. But the resemblance is remarkable.

Well, you know what they say, says Blue. Every man has his double somewhere. I don't see why mine can't be a dead man.

The funny thing, continues Black, is that Walt Whitman used to work on   95
this street. He printed his first book right here, not far from where we're
standing.

You don't say, says Blue, shaking his head pensively. It makes you stop and
think, doesn't it?

There are some odd stories about Whitman, Black says, gesturing to Blue
to sit down on the stoop of the building behind them, which he does, and then
Black does the same, and suddenly it's just the two of them out there in the
summer light together, chatting away like two old friends about this and that.

Yes, says Black, settling in comfortably to the languor of the moment, a
number of very curious stories. The one about Whitman's brain, for example.
All his life Whitman believed in the science of phrenology—you know, reading the bumps on the skull. It was very popular at the time.

Can't say I've ever heard of it, replies Blue.

Well, that doesn't much matter, says Black. The main thing is that Whit-   100
man was interested in brains and skulls—thought they could tell you everything about a man's character. Anyway, when Whitman lay dying over there
in New Jersey about fifty or sixty years ago, he agreed to let them perform an
autopsy on him after he was dead.

How could he agree to it after he was dead?

Ah, good point. I didn't say it right. He was still alive when he agreed. He
just wanted them to know that he didn't mind if they opened him up later.
What you might call his dying wish.

Famous last words.

That's right. A lot of people thought he was a genius, you see, and they
wanted to take a look at his brain to find out if there was anything special
about it. So, the day after he died, a doctor removed Whitman's brain—cut it
right out of his head—and had it sent to the American Anthropometric Society to be measured and weighed.

Like a giant cauliflower, interjects Blue.   105

Exactly. Like a big gray vegetable. But this is where the story gets interesting. The brain arrives at the laboratory, and just as they're about to get to
work on it, one of the assistants drops it on the floor.

Did it break?

Of course it broke. A brain isn't very tough, you know. It splattered all over the place, and that was that. The brain of America's greatest poet got swept up and thrown out with the garbage.

Blue, remembering to respond in character, emits several wheezing laughs—a good imitation of an old codger's mirth. Black laughs, too, and by now the atmosphere has thawed to such an extent that no one could ever know they were not lifelong chums.

It's sad to think of poor Walt lying in his grave, though, says Black. All alone and without any brains. 110

Just like that scarecrow, says Blue.

Sure enough, says Black. Just like the scarecrow in the land of Oz.

After another good laugh, Black says: And then there's the story of the time Thoreau came to visit Whitman. That's a good one, too.

Was he another poet?

Not exactly. But a great writer just the same. He's the one who lived alone 115 in the woods.

Oh yes, says Blue, not wanting to carry his ignorance too far. Someone once told me about him. Very fond of nature he was. Is that the man you mean?

Precisely, answers Black. Henry David Thoreau. He came down from Massachusetts for a little while and paid a call on Whitman in Brooklyn. But the day before that he came right here to Orange Street.

Any particular reason?

Plymouth Church. He wanted to hear Henry Ward Beecher's sermon.

A lovely spot, says Blue, thinking of the pleasant hours he has spent in the 120 grassy yard. I like to go there myself.

Many great men have gone there, says Black. Abraham Lincoln, Charles Dickens—they all walked down this street and went into the church.

Ghosts.

Yes, there are ghosts all around us.

And the story?

It's really very simple. Thoreau and Bronson Alcott, a friend of his, ar- 125 rived at Whitman's house on Myrtle Avenue, and Walt's mother sent them up to the attic bedroom he shared with his mentally retarded brother, Eddy. Everything was just fine. They shook hands, exchanged greetings, and so on. But then, when they sat down to discuss their views of life, Thoreau and Alcott noticed a full chamber pot right in the middle of the floor. Walt was of course an expansive fellow and paid no attention, but the two New Englanders found it hard to keep talking with a bucket of excrement in front of them. So eventually they went downstairs to the parlor and continued the conversation there. It's a minor detail, I realize. But still, when two great writers meet, history is made, and it's important to get all the facts straight. That chamber pot, you see, somehow reminds me of the brains on the floor. And when you stop to think about it, there's a certain similarity of form. The bumps and convolutions, I mean. There's a definite connection. Brains and guts, the insides of a man. We always talk about trying to get inside a writer to understand his work better. But when you get right down to it, there's not much to find in there—at least not much that's different from what you'd find in anyone else.

You seem to know a lot about these things, says Blue, who's beginning to lose the thread of Black's argument.

It's my hobby, says Black. I like to know how writers live, especially American writers. It helps me to understand things.

I see, says Blue, who sees nothing at all, for with each word Black speaks, he finds himself understanding less and less.

Take Hawthorne, says Black. A good friend of Thoreau's, and probably the first real writer America ever had. After he graduated from college, he went back to his mother's house in Salem, shut himself up in his room, and didn't come out for twelve years.

What did he do in there?   130

He wrote stories.

Is that all? He just wrote?

Writing is a solitary business. It takes over your life. In some sense, a writer has no life of his own. Even when he's there, he's not really there.

Another ghost.

Exactly.   135

Sounds mysterious.

It is. But Hawthorne wrote great stories, you see, and we still read them now, more than a hundred years later. In one of them, a man named Wakefield decides to play a joke on his wife. He tells her that he has to go away on a business trip for a few days, but instead of leaving the city, he goes around the corner, rents a room, and just waits to see what will happen. He can't say for sure why he's doing it, but he does it just the same. Three or four days go by, but he doesn't feel ready to return home yet, and so he stays on in the rented room. The days turn into weeks, the weeks turn into months. One day Wakefield walks down his old street and sees his house decked out in mourning. It's his own funeral, and his wife has become a lonely widow. Years go by. Every now and then he crosses paths with his wife in town, and once, in the middle of a large crowd, he actually brushes up against her. But she doesn't recognize him. More years pass, more than twenty years, and little by little Wakefield has become an old man. One rainy night in autumn, as he's taking a walk through the empty streets, he happens to pass by his old house and peeks through the window. There's a nice warm fire burning in the fireplace, and he thinks to himself: how pleasant it would be if I were in there right now, sitting in one of those cozy chairs by the hearth, instead of standing out here in the rain. And so, without giving it any more thought than that, he walks up the steps of the house and knocks on the door.

And then?

That's it. That's the end of the story. The last thing we see is the door opening and Wakefield going inside with a crafty smile on his face.

And we never know what he says to his wife?   140

No. That's the end. Not another word. But he moved in again, we know that much, and remained a loving spouse until death.

By now the sky has begun to darken overhead, and night is fast approaching.

A last glimmer of pink remains in the west, but the day is as good as done. Black, taking his cue from the darkness, stands up from his spot and extends his hand to Blue.

It's been a pleasure talking to you, he says. I had no idea we'd been sitting here so long.

The pleasure's been mine, says Blue, relieved that the conversation is over, for he knows that it won't be long now before his beard begins to slip, what with the summer heat and his nerves making him perspire into the glue.

My name is Black, says Black, shaking Blue's hand.   145

Mine's Jimmy, says Blue. Jimmy Rose.

I'll remember this little talk of ours for a long time, Jimmy, says Black.

I will, too, says Blue. You've given me a lot to think about.

God bless you, Jimmy Rose, says Black.

And God bless you, sir, says Blue.   150

And then, with one last handshake, they walk off in opposite directions, each one accompanied by his own thoughts.

Later that night, when Blue returns to his room, he decides that he had best bury Jimmy Rose now, get rid of him for good. The old tramp has served his purpose, but beyond this point it would not be wise to go.

Blue is glad to have made this initial contact with Black, but the encounter did not quite have its desired effect, and all in all he feels rather shaken by it. For even though the talk had nothing to do with the case, Blue cannot help feeling that Black was actually referring to it all along—talking in riddles, so to speak, as though trying to tell Blue something, but not daring to say it out loud. Yes, Black was more than friendly, his manner was altogether pleasant, but still Blue cannot get rid of the thought that the man was on to him from the start. If so, then Black is surely one of the conspirators—for why else would he have gone on talking to Blue as he did? Not from loneliness, certainly. Assuming that Black is for real, then loneliness cannot be an issue. Everything about his life to this point has been part of a determined plan to remain alone, and it would be absurd to read his willingness to talk as an effort to escape the throes of solitude. Not at this late date, not after more than a year of avoiding all human contact. If Black is finally resolved to break out of his hermetic routine, then why would he begin by talking to a broken-down old man on a street corner? No, Black knew that he was talking to Blue. And if he knew that, then he knows who Blue is. No two ways about it, Blue says to himself: he knows everything.

When the time comes for him to write his next report, Blue is forced to confront this dilemma. White never said anything about making contact with Black. Blue was to watch him, no more, no less, and he wonders now if he has not in fact broken the rules of his assignment. If he includes the conversation in his report, then White might object. On the other hand, if he does not put it in, and if Black is indeed working with White, then White will know immediately that Blue is lying. Blue mulls this over for a long time, but for all that he gets no closer to finding a solution. He's stuck, one way or the other, and he knows it. In the end, he decides to leave it out, but only because he still puts some meager hope in the fact that he has guessed wrong and that White and Black are not in it together. But this last little stab at optimism soon comes to naught. Three days after sending in the sanitized report, his weekly check comes in the mail, and inside the envelope there is also a note that says, Why do you lie?, and then Blue has proof beyond any shadow of a doubt. And from that moment on, Blue lives with the knowledge that he is drowning.

The next night he follows Black into Manhattan on the subway, dressed in   155
his normal clothes, no longer feeling he has to hide anything. Black gets off at Times Square and wanders around for a while in the bright lights, the noise, the crowds of people surging this way and that. Blue, watching him as though his life depended on it, is never more than three or four steps behind him. At nine o'clock, Black enters the lobby of the Algonquin Hotel, and Blue follows him in. There's quite a crowd milling about, and tables are scarce, so when Black sits down in a corner nook that just that moment has become free, it seems perfectly natural for Blue to approach and politely ask if he can join him. Black has no objection and gestures with an indifferent shrug of the shoulders for Blue to take the chair opposite. For several minutes they say nothing to each other, waiting for someone to take their orders, in the meantime watching the women walk by in their summer dresses, inhaling the different perfumes that flit behind them in the air, and Blue feels no rush to jump into things, content to bide his time and let the business take its course. When the waiter at last comes to ask their pleasure, Black orders a Black and White on the rocks, and Blue cannot help but take this as a secret message that the fun is about to begin, all the while marveling at Black's effrontery, his crassness, his vulgar obsession. For the sake of symmetry, Blue orders the same drink. As he does so, he looks Black in the eyes, but Black gives nothing away, looking back at Blue with utter blankness, dead eyes that seem to say there is nothing behind them and that no matter how hard Blue looks, he will never find a thing.

This gambit nevertheless breaks the ice, and they begin by discussing the merits of various brands of scotch. Plausibly enough, one thing leads to another, and as they sit there chatting about the inconveniences of the New York summer season, the decor of the hotel, the Algonquin Indians who lived in the city long ago when it was all woods and fields, Blue slowly evolves into the character he wants to play for the night, settling on a jovial blowhard by the name of Snow, a life insurance salesman from Kenosha, Wisconsin. Play dumb, Blue tells himself, for he knows that it would make no sense to reveal who he is, even though he knows that Black knows. It's got to be hide and seek, he says, hide and seek to the end.

They finish their first drink and order another round, followed by yet another, and as the talk ambles from actuarial tables to the life expectancies of men in different professions, Black lets fall a remark that turns the conversation in another direction.

I suppose I wouldn't be very high up on your list, he says.

Oh? says Blue, having no idea what to expect. What kind of work do you do?

I'm a private detective, says Black, point blank, all cool and collected, and   160
for a brief moment Blue is tempted to throw his drink in Black's face, he's that peeved, that burned at the man's gall.

You don't say! Blue exclaims, quickly recovering and managing to feign a bumpkin's surprise. A private detective. Imagine that. In the flesh. Just think of what the wife will says when I tell her. Me in New York having drinks with a private eye. She'll never believe it.

What I'm trying to say, says Black rather abruptly, is that I don't imagine my life expectancy is very great. At least not according to your statistics.

Probably not, Blue blusters on. But think of the excitement! There's more to life than living a long time, you know. Half the men in America would give ten years off their retirement to live the way you do. Cracking cases, living by your wits, seducing women, pumping bad guys full of lead—God, there's a lot to be said for it.

That's all make-believe, says Black. Real detective work can be pretty dull.

Well, every job has its routines, Blue continues. But in your case at least   165
you know that all the hard work will eventually lead to something out of the ordinary.

Sometimes yes, sometimes no. But most of the time it's no. Take the case I'm working on now. I've been at it for more than a year already, and nothing could be more boring. I'm so bored that sometimes I think I'm losing my mind.

How so?

Well, figure it out for yourself. My job is to watch someone, no one in particular as far as I can tell, and send in a report about him every week. Just that. Watch this guy and write about it. Not one damned thing more.

What's so terrible about that?

He doesn't do anything, that's what. He just sits in his room all day and   170
writes. It's enough to drive you crazy.

It could be that he's leading you along. You know, lulling you to sleep before springing into action.

That's what I thought at first. But now I'm sure that nothing's going to happen—not ever. I can feel it in my bones.

That's too bad, says Blue sympathetically. Maybe you should resign from the case.

I'm thinking about it. I'm also thinking that maybe I should just chuck the whole business and go into something else. Some other line of work. Sell insurance, maybe, or run off to join the circus.

I never realized it could get as bad as that, says Blue, shaking his head. But   175
tell me, why aren't you watching your man now? Shouldn't you be keeping an eye on him?

That's just the point, answers Black. I don't even have to bother anymore. I've been watching him for so long now that I know him better than I know myself. All I have to do is think about him, and I know what he's doing, I know where he is, I know everything. It's come to the point that I can watch him with my eyes closed.

Do you know where he is now?

At home. The same as usual. Sitting in his room and writing.

What's he writing about?

I'm not sure, but I have a pretty good idea. I think he's writing about him-   180
self. The story of his life. That's the only possible answer. Nothing else would fit.

So why all the mystery?

I don't know, says Black, and for the first time his voice betrays some emotion, catching ever so slightly on the words.

It all boils down to one question, then, doesn't it? says Blue, forgetting all about Snow now and looking Black straight in the eyes. Does he know you're watching him or not?

Black turns away, unable to look at Blue anymore, and says with a suddenly trembling voice: Of course he knows. That's the whole point, isn't it? He's got to know, or else nothing makes sense.

Why?   185

Because he needs me, says Black, still looking away. He needs my eyes looking at him. He needs me to prove he's alive.

Blue sees a tear fall down Black's cheek, but before he can say anything, before he can begin to press home his advantage, Black stands up hastily and excuses himself, saying that he has to make a telephone call. Blue waits in his chair for ten or fifteen minutes, but he knows that he's wasting his time. Black won't be back. The conversation is over, and no matter how long he sits there, nothing more will happen tonight.

Blue pays for the drinks and then heads back to Brooklyn. As he turns down Orange Street, he looks up at Black's window and sees that everything is dark. No matter, says Blue, he'll return before long. We haven't come to the end yet. The party is only beginning. Wait until the champagne is opened, and then we'll see what's what.

Once inside, Blue paces back and forth, trying to plot his next move. It seems to him that Black has finally made a mistake, but he is not quite certain. For in spite of the evidence, Blue cannot shrug the feeling that it was all done on purpose, and that Black has now begun to call out to him, leading him along, so to speak, urging him on towards whatever end he is planning.

Still, he has broken through to something, and for the first time since the   190
case began he is no longer standing where he was. Ordinarily, Blue would be celebrating this little triumph of his, but it turns out that he is in no mood for patting himself on the back tonight. More than anything else, he feels sad, he feels drained of enthusiasm, he feels disappointed in the world. Somehow, the facts have finally let him down, and he finds it hard not to take it personally, knowing full well that however he might present the case to himself, he is a part of it, too. Then he walks to the window, looks out across the street, and sees that the lights are now on in Black's room.

He lies down on his bed and thinks: good-bye, Mr. White. You were never really there, were you? There never was such a man as White. And then: poor Black. Poor soul. Poor blighted no one. And then, as his eyes grow heavy and sleep begins to wash over him, he thinks how strange it is that everything has its own color. Everything we see, everything we touch—everything in the world has its own color. Struggling to stay awake a little longer, he begins to make a list. Take blue for example, he says. There are bluebirds and blue jays and blue herons. There are cornflowers and periwinkles. There is noon over New York. There are blueberries, huckleberries, and the Pacific Ocean.

There are blue devils and blue ribbons and blue bloods. There is a voice singing the blues. There is my father's police uniform. There are blue laws and blue movies. There are my eyes and my name. He pauses, suddenly at a loss for more blue things, and then moves on to white. There are seagulls, he says, and terns and storks and cockatoos. There are the walls of this room and the sheets on my bed. There are lilies-of-the-valley, carnations, and the petals of daisies. There is the flag of peace and Chinese death. There is mother's milk and semen. There are my teeth. There are the whites of my eyes. There are white bass and white pines and white ants. There is the President's house and white rot. There are white lies and white heat. Then, without hesitating, he moves on to black, beginning with black books, the black market, and the Black Hand. There is night over New York, he says. There are the Chicago Black Sox. There are blackberries and crows, blackouts and black marks, Black Tuesday and the Black Death. There is blackmail. There is my hair. There is the ink that comes out of a pen. There is the world a blind man sees. Then, finally growing tired of the game, he begins to drift, saying to himself that there is no end to it. He falls asleep, dreams of things that happened long ago, and then, in the middle of the night, wakes up suddenly and begins pacing the room again, thinking about what he will do next.

Morning comes, and Blue starts busying himself with another disguise. This time it's the Fuller brush man, a trick he has used before, and for the next two hours he patiently goes about giving himself a bald head, a moustache, and age lines around his eyes and mouth, sitting in front of his little mirror like an old-time vaudevillian on tour. Shortly after eleven o'clock, he gathers up his case of brushes and walks across the street to Black's building. Picking the lock on the front door is child's play for Blue, no more than a matter of seconds, and as he slips into the hallway he can't help feeling something of the old thrill. No tough stuff, he reminds himself, as he starts climbing the stairs to Black's floor. This visit is only to get a look inside, to stake out the room for future reference. Still, there's an excitement to the moment that Blue can't quite suppress. For it's more than just seeing the room, he knows—it's the thought of being there himself, of standing inside those four walls, of breathing the same air as Black. From now on, he thinks, everything that happens will affect everything else. The door will open, and after that Black will be inside of him forever.

He knocks, the door opens, and suddenly there is no more distance, the thing and the thought of the thing are one and the same. Then it's Black who is there, standing in the doorway with an uncapped fountain pen in his right hand, as though interrupted in his work, and yet with a look in his eyes that tells Blue he's been expecting him, resigned to the hard truth, but no longer seeming to care.

Blue launches into his patter about the brushes, pointing to the case, offering apologies, asking admittance, all in the same breath, with that rapid salesman's pitch he's done a thousand times before. Black calmly lets him in, saying he might be interested in a toothbrush, and as Blue steps across the sill, he goes rattling on about hair brushes and clothes brushes, anything to keep the words flowing, for in that way he can leave the rest of himself free to take in the room, observe the observable, think, all the while diverting Black from his true purpose.

The room is much as he imagined it would be, though perhaps even more   195 austere. Nothing on the walls, for example, which surprises him a little, since he always thought there would be a picture or two, an image of some kind just to break the monotony, a nature scene perhaps, or else a portrait of someone Black might once have loved. Blue was always curious to know what the picture would be, thinking it might be a valuable clue, but now that he sees there is nothing, he understands that this is what he should have expected all along. Other than that, there's precious little to contradict his former notions. It's the same monk's cell he saw in his mind: the small, neatly made bed in one corner, the kitchenette in another corner, everything spotless, not a crumb to be seen. Then, in the center of the room facing the window, the wooden table with a single stiff-backed wooden chair. Pencils, pens, a typewriter. A bureau, a night table, a lamp. A bookcase on the north wall, but no more than several books in it: Walden, Leaves of Grass, Twice-Told Tales, a few others. No telephone, no radio, no magazines. On the table, neatly stacked around the edges, piles of paper: some blank, some written on, some typed, some in longhand. Hundreds of pages, perhaps thousands. But you can't call this a life, thinks Blue. You can't really call it anything. It's a no man's land, the place you come to at the end of the world.

They look through the toothbrushes, and Black finally chooses a red one. From there they start examining the various clothes brushes, with Blue giving demonstrations on his own suit. For a man as neat as yourself, says Blue, I should think you'd find it indispensable. But Black says he's managed so far without one. On the other hand, maybe he'd like to consider a hair brush, and so they go through the possibilities in the sample case, discussing the different sizes and shapes, the different kinds of bristles, and so on. Blue is already done with his real business, of course, but he goes through the motions nevertheless, wanting to do the things right, even if it doesn't matter. Still, after Black has paid for the brushes and Blue is packing up his case to go, he can't resist making one little remark. You seem to be a writer, he says, gesturing to the table, and Black says yes, that's right, he's a writer.

It looks like a big book, Blue continues.

Yes, says Black. I've been working on it for many years.

Are you almost finished?

I'm getting there, Black says thoughtfully. But sometimes it's hard to   200 know where you are. I think I'm almost done, and then I realize I've left out something important, and so I have to go back to the beginning again. But yes, I do dream of finishing it one day. One day soon, perhaps.

I hope I get a chance to read it, says Blue.

Anything is possible, says Black. But first of all, I've got to finish it. There are days when I don't even know if I'll live that long.

Well, we never know, do we? says Blue, nodding philosophically. One day we're alive, and the next day we're dead. It happens to all of us.

Very true, says Black. It happens to all of us.

They're standing by the door now, and something in Blue wants to go on 205 making inane remarks of this sort. Playing the buffoon is enjoyable, he real-izes, but at the same time there's an urge to toy with Black, to prove that noth-ing has escaped him—for deep down Blue wants Black to know that he's just as smart as he is, that he can match wits with him every step of the way. But Blue manages to fight back the impulse and hold his tongue, nodding politely in thanks for the sales, and then makes his exit. That's the end of the Fuller brush man, and less than an hour later he is discarded into the same bag that holds the remains of Jimmy Rose. Blue knows that no more disguises will be needed. The next step is inevitable, and the only thing that matters now is to choose the right moment.

But three nights later, when he finally gets his chance, Blue realizes that he's scared. Black goes out at nine o'clock, walks down the street, and vanishes around the corner. Although Blue knows that this is a direct signal, that Black is practically begging him to make his move, he also feels that it could be a set-up, and now, at the last possible moment, when only just before he was filled with confidence, almost swaggering with a sense of his own power, he sinks into a fresh torment of self-doubt. Why should he suddenly begin to trust Black? What earthly cause could there be for him to think they are both working on the same side now? How has this happened, and why does he find himself so obsequiously at Black's bidding once again? Then, from out of the blue, he begins to consider another possibility. What if he just simply left? What if he stood up, went out the door, and walked away from the whole business? He ponders this thought for a while, testing it out in his mind, and little by little he begins to tremble, overcome by terror and happiness, like a slave stumbling onto a vision of his own freedom. He imagines himself some-where else, far away from here, walking through the woods and swinging an axe over his shoulder. Alone and free, his own man at last. He would build his life from the bottom up, an exile, a pioneer, a pilgrim in the new world. But that is as far as he gets. For no sooner does he begin to walk through these woods in the middle of nowhere than he feels that Black is there, too, hiding behind some tree, stalking invisibly through some thicket, waiting for Blue to lie down and close his eyes before sneaking up on him and slitting his throat. It goes on and on, Blue thinks. If he doesn't take care of Black now, there will never be any end to it. This is what the ancients called fate, and every hero must submit to it. There is no choice, and if there is anything to be done, it is only the one thing that leaves no choice. But Blue is loathe to acknowledge it. He struggles against it, he rejects it, he grows sick at heart. But that is only be-cause he already knows, and to fight it is already to have accepted it, to want to say no is already to have said yes. And so Blue gradually comes round, at last giving in to the necessity of the thing to be done. But that is not to say he does not feel afraid. From this moment on, there is only one word that speaks for Blue, and that word is fear.

He has wasted valuable time, and now he must rush forth onto the street, hoping feverishly it is not too late. Black will not be gone forever, and who knows if he is not lurking around the corner, just waiting for the moment to pounce? Blue races up the steps of Black's building, fumbles awkwardly as he picks the front door lock, continually glancing over his shoulder, and then goes up the stairs to Black's floor. The second lock gives him more trouble than the first, though theoretically it should be simpler, an easy job even for the rawest beginner. This clumsiness tells Blue that he's losing control, letting it all get the better of him; but even though he knows it, there's little he can do but ride it out and hope that his hands will stop shaking. But it goes from bad to worse, and the moment he sets foot in Black's room, he feels everything go dark inside him, as though the night were pressing through his pores, sitting on top of him with a tremendous weight, and at the same time his head seems to be growing, filling with air as though about to detach itself from his body and float away. He takes one more step into the room and then blacks out, collapsing to the floor like a dead man.

His watch stops with the fall, and when he comes to he doesn't know how long he's been out. Dimly at first, he regains consciousness with a sense of having been here before, perhaps long ago, and as he sees the curtains fluttering by the open window and the shadows moving strangely on the ceiling, he thinks that he is lying in bed at home, back when he was a little boy, unable to sleep during the hot summer nights, and he imagines that if he listens hard enough he will be able to hear the voices of his mother and father talking quietly in the next room. But this lasts only a moment. He begins to feel the ache in his head, to register the disturbing queasiness in his stomach, and then, finally seeing where he is, to relive the panic that gripped him the moment he entered the room. He scrambles shakily to his feet, stumbling once or twice in the process, and tells himself he can't stay here, he's got to be going, yes, and right away. He grabs hold of the doorknob, but then, remembering suddenly why he came here in the first place, snatches the flashlight from his pocket and turns it on, waving it fitfully around the room until the light falls by chance on a pile of papers stacked neatly at the edge of Black's desk. Without thinking twice, Blue gathers up the papers with his free hand, saying to himself it doesn't matter, this will be a start, and then makes his way to the door.

Back in his room across the street, Blue pours himself a glass of brandy, sits down on his bed, and tells himself to be calm. He drinks off the brandy sip by sip and then pours himself another glass. As his panic begins to subside, he is left with a feeling of shame. He's botched it, he tells himself, and that's the long and the short of it. For the first time in his life he has not been equal to the moment, and it comes as a shock to him—to see himself as a failure, to realize that at bottom he's a coward.

He picks up the papers he has stolen, hoping to distract himself from 210 these thoughts. But this only compounds the problem, for once he begins to read them, he sees they are nothing more than his own reports. There they are, one after the other, the weekly accounts, all spelled out in black and white, meaning nothing, saying nothing, as far from the truth of the case as silence would have been. Blue groans when he sees them, sinking down deep within himself, and then, in the face of what he finds there, begins to laugh, at first faintly, but with growing force, louder and louder, until he is gasping for breath, almost choking on it, as though trying to obliterate himself once and for all. Taking the papers firmly in his hand, he flings them up to the ceiling and watches the pile break apart, scatter, and come fluttering to the ground, page by miserable page.

It is not certain that Blue ever really recovers from the events of this night. And even if he does, it must be noted that several days go by before he returns to a semblance of his former self. In that time he does not shave, he does not change his clothes, he does not even contemplate stirring from his room. When the day comes for him to write his next report, he does not bother. It's finished now, he says, kicking one of the old reports on the floor, and I'll be damned if I ever write one of those again.

For the most part, he either lies on his bed or paces back and forth in his room. He looks at the various pictures he has tacked onto the walls since starting the case, studying each one in its turn, thinking about it for as long as he can, and then passing on to the next. There is the coroner from Philadelphia, Gold, with the death mask of the little boy. There is a snow-covered mountain, and in the upper right hand corner of the photograph, an inset of the French skier, his face enclosed in a small box. There is the Brooklyn Bridge, and next to it the two Roeblings, father and son. There is Blue's father, dressed in his police uniform and receiving a medal from the mayor of New York, Jimmy Walker. Again there is Blue's father, this time in his street clothes, standing with his arm around Blue's mother in the early days of their marriage, the two of them smiling brightly into the camera. There is a picture of Brown with his arm around Blue, taken in front of their office on the day Blue was made a partner. Below it there is an action shot of Jackie Robinson sliding into second base. Next to that there is a portrait of Walt Whitman. And finally, directly to the poet's left, there is a movie still of Robert Mitchum from one of the fan magazines: gun in hand, looking as though the world is about to cave in on him. There is no picture of the ex–future Mrs. Blue, but each time Blue makes a tour of his little gallery, he pauses in front of a certain blank spot on the wall and pretends that she, too, is there.

For several days, Blue does not bother to look out the window. He has enclosed himself so thoroughly in his own thoughts that Black no longer seems to be there. The drama is Blue's alone, and if Black is in some sense the cause of it, it's as though he has already played his part, spoken his lines, and made his exit from the stage. For Blue at this point can no longer accept Black's existence, and therefore he denies it. Having penetrated Black's room and stood there alone, having been, so to speak, in the sanctum of Black's solitude, he cannot respond to the darkness of that moment except by replacing it with a solitude of his own. To enter Black, then, was the equivalent of entering himself, and once inside himself, he can no longer conceive of being anywhere else. But this is precisely where Black is, even though Blue does not know it.

One afternoon, therefore, as if by chance, Blue comes closer to the window than he has in many days, happens to pause in front of it, and then as if for old times' sake, parts the curtains and looks outside. The first thing he sees is Black—not inside his room, but sitting on the stoop of his building across the street, looking up at Blue's window. Is he finished, then? Blue wonders. Does this mean it's over?

Blue retrieves his binoculars from the back of the room and returns to the window. Bringing them into focus on Black, he studies the man's face for several minutes, first one feature and then another, the eyes, the lips, the nose, and so on, taking the face apart and then putting it back together. He is moved by the depth of Black's sadness, the way the eyes looking up at him seem so devoid of hope, and in spite of himself, caught unawares by this image, Blue feels compassion rising up in him, a rush of pity for that forlorn figure across the street. He wishes it were not so, however, wishes he had the courage to load his gun, take aim at Black, and fire a bullet through his head. He'd never know what hit him, Blue thinks, he'd be in heaven before he touched the ground. But as soon as he has played out this little scene in his mind, he begins to recoil from it. No, he realizes, that's not what he wishes at all. If not that, then—what? Still struggling against the surge of tender feelings, saying to himself that he wants to be left alone, that all he wants is peace and quiet, it gradually dawns on him that he has in fact been standing there for several minutes wondering if there is not some way that he might help Black, if it would not be possible for him to offer his hand in friendship. That would certainly turn the tables, Blue thinks, that would certainly stand the whole business on its head. But why not? Why not do the unexpected? To knock on the door, to erase the whole story—it's no less absurd than anything else. For the fact of the matter is, all the fight has been taken out of Blue. He no longer has the stomach for it. And, to all appearances, neither does Black. Just look at him, Blue says to himself. He's the saddest creature in the world. And then, the moment he says these words, he understands that he's also talking about himself.

Long after Black leaves the steps, therefore, turning around and reentering the building, Blue goes on staring at the vacant spot. An hour or two before dusk, he finally turns from the window, sees the disorder he has allowed his room to fall into, and spends the next hour straightening up—washing the dishes, making the bed, putting away his clothes, removing the old reports from the floor. Then he goes into the bathroom, takes a long shower, shaves, and puts on fresh clothes, selecting his best blue suit for the occasion. Everything is different for him now, suddenly and irrevocably different. There is no more dread, no more trembling. Nothing but a calm assurance, a sense of rightness in the thing he is about to do.

Shortly after nightfall, he adjusts his tie one last time before the mirror and then leaves the room, going outside, crossing the street, and entering Black's building. He knows that Black is there, since a small lamp is on in his room, and as he walks up the stairs he tries to imagine the expression that will come over Black's face when he tells him what he has in mind. He knocks twice on the door, very politely, and then hears Black's voice from within: The door's open. Come in.

It is difficult to say exactly what Blue was expecting to find—but in all events, it was not this, not the thing that confronts him the moment he steps into the room. Black is there, sitting on his bed, and he's wearing the mask again, the same one Blue saw on the man in the post office, and in his right hand he's holding a gun, a thirty-eight revolver, enough to blow a man apart at such close range, and he's pointing it directly at Blue. Blue stops in his tracks, says nothing. So much for burying the hatchet, he thinks. So much for turning the tables.

Sit down in the chair, Blue, says Black, gesturing with the gun to the wooden desk chair. Blue has no choice, and so he sits—now facing Black, but too far away to make a lunge at him, too awkwardly positioned to do anything about the gun.

I've been waiting for you, says Black. I'm glad you finally made it.   220

I figured as much, answers Blue.

Are you surprised?

Not really. At least not at you. Myself maybe—but only because I'm so stupid. You see, I came here tonight in friendship.

But of course you did, says Black, in a slightly mocking voice. Of course we're friends. We've been friends from the beginning, haven't we? The very best of friends.

If this is how you treat your friends, says Blue, then lucky for me I'm not   225
one of your enemies.

Very funny.

That's right, I'm the original funny man. You can always count on a lot of laughs when I'm around.

And the mask—aren't you going to ask me about the mask?

I don't see why. If you want to wear that thing, it's not my problem.

But you have to look at it, don't you?   230

Why ask questions when you already know the answer?

It's grotesque, isn't it?

Of course it's grotesque.

And frightening to look at.

Yes, very frightening.   235

Good. I like you, Blue. I always knew you were the right one for me. A man after my own heart.

If you stopped waving that gun around, maybe I'd start feeling the same about you.

I'm sorry, I can't do that. It's too late now.

Which means?

I don't need you anymore, Blue.   240

It might not be so easy to get rid of me, you know. You got me into this, and now you're stuck with me.

No, Blue, you're wrong. Everything is over now.

Stop the doubletalk.

It's finished. The whole thing is played out. There's nothing more to be done.

Since when?   245

Since now. Since this moment.

You're out of your mind.

No, Blue. If anything, I'm in my mind, too much in my mind. It's used me up, and now there's nothing left. But you know that, Blue, you know that better than anyone.

So why don't you just pull the trigger?

When I'm ready, I will. 250

And then walk out of here leaving my body on the floor? Fat chance.

Oh no, Blue. You don't understand. It's going to be the two of us together, just like always.

But you're forgetting something, aren't you?

Forgetting what?

You're supposed to tell me the story. Isn't that how it's supposed to end? 255
You tell me the story, and then we say good-bye.

You know it already, Blue. Don't you understand that? You know the story by heart.

Then why did you bother in the first place?

Don't ask stupid questions.

And me—what was I there for? Comic relief?

No, Blue, I've needed you from the beginning. If it hadn't been for you, I 260
couldn't have done it.

Needed me for what?

To remind me of what I was supposed to be doing. Every time I looked up, you were there, watching me, following me, always in sight, boring into me with your eyes. You were the whole world to me, Blue, and I turned you into my death. You're the one thing that doesn't change, the one thing that turns everything inside out.

And now there's nothing left. You've written your suicide note, and that's the end of it.

Exactly.

You're a fool. You're a goddamned, miserable fool. 265

I know that. But no more than anyone else. Are you going to sit there and tell me that you're smarter than I am? At least I know what I've been doing. I've had my job to do, and I've done it. But you're nowhere, Blue. You've been lost from the first day.

Why don't you pull the trigger, then, you bastard? says Blue, suddenly standing up and pounding his chest in anger, daring Black to kill him. Why don't you shoot me now and get it over with?

Blue then takes a step towards Black, and when the bullet doesn't come, he takes another, and then another, screaming at the masked man to shoot, no longer caring if he lives or dies. A moment later, he's right up against him. Without hesitating he swats the gun out of Black's hand, grabs him by the collar, and yanks him to his feet. Black tries to resist, tries to struggle against Blue, but Blue is too strong for him, all crazy with the passion of his anger, as though turned into someone else, and as the first blows begin to land on Black's face and groin and stomach, the man can do nothing, and not long after that he's out cold on the floor. But that does not prevent Blue from continuing the assault, battering the unconscious Black with his feet, picking him up and banging his head on the floor, pelting his body with one punch after another. Eventually, when Blue's fury begins to abate and he sees what he has done, he cannot say for certain whether Black is alive or dead. He removes the mask from Black's face and puts his ear against his mouth, listening for the sound of Black's breath. There seems to be something, but he can't tell if it's coming from Black or himself. If he's alive now, Blue thinks, it won't be for long. And if he's dead, then so be it.

Blue stands up, his suit all in tatters, and begins collecting the pages of Black's manuscript from the desk. This takes several minutes. When he has all of them, he turns off the lamp in the corner and leaves the room, not even bothering to give Black a last look.

It's past midnight when Blue gets back to his room across the street. He puts the manuscript down on the table, goes into the bathroom, and washes the blood off his hands. Then he changes his clothes, pours himself a glass of scotch, and sits down at the table with Black's book. Time is short. They'll be coming before he knows it, and then there will be hell to pay. Still, he does not let this interfere with the business at hand.

He reads the story right through, every word of it from beginning to end. By the time he finishes, dawn has come, and the room has begun to brighten. He hears a bird sing, he hears footsteps going down the street, he hears a car driving across the Brooklyn Bridge. Black was right, he says to himself. I knew it all by heart.

But the story is not yet over. There is still the final moment, and that will not come until Blue leaves the room. Such is the way of the world: not one moment more, not one moment less. When Blue stands up from his chair, puts on his hat, and walks through the door, that will be the end of it.

Where he goes after that is not important. For we must remember that all this took place more than thirty years ago, back in the days of our earliest childhood. Anything is possible, therefore. I myself prefer to think that he went far away, boarding a train that morning and going out West to start a new life. It is even possible that America was not the end of it. In my secret dreams, I like to think of Blue booking passage on some ship and sailing to China. Let it be China, then, and we'll leave it at that. For now is the moment that Blue stands up from his chair, puts on his hat, and walks through the door. And from this moment on, we know nothing.

──────── **PAUL AUSTER** ────────

(b. 1947) **Web**

www

A translator and student of French, Paul Auster has written poetry, novels, and screenplays. He lives in Brooklyn.

TOPICS FOR CRITICAL THINKING **Web**

www

1. What embedded narratives does the novella include?
2. Are there similarities in theme or subject among these embedded narratives?
3. In what ways do the embedded narratives reflect the larger themes of the novella?
4. What other kinds of intertextuality does *Ghosts* employ?
5. In what ways is intertextuality itself the subject of the novella?
6. In what ways does *Ghosts* use or alter the conventions of detective fiction?
7. Why make all proper names references to colors?

Select one of the many embedded stories, and show how it connects to the larger
narrative.

MARK LEYNER

Selections from *My Cousin, My Gastroenterologist*

(1990)

i was an infinitely hot and dense dot
idyll
the suggestiveness of one stray hair in an otherwise perfect coiffure

1. i was an infinitely hot and dense dot

I was driving to Las Vegas to tell my sister that I'd had Mother's respirator unplugged. Four bald men in the convertible in front of me were picking the
scabs off their sunburnt heads and flicking them onto the road. I had to
swerve to avoid riding over one of the oozy crusts of blood and going into an
uncontrollable skid. I maneuvered the best I could in my boxy Korean import
but my mind was elsewhere. I hadn't eaten for days. I was famished. Suddenly
as I reached the crest of a hill, emerging from the fog, there was a bright neon
sign flashing on and off that read: . . . FOIE GRAS AND HARICOTS VERTS NEXT
EXIT. I checked the guidebook and it said: *Excellent food, malevolent ambience.*
I'd been habitually abusing an illegal growth hormone extracted from the pituitary glands of human corpses and I felt as if I were drowning in excremen-
tal filthiness but the prospect of having something good to eat cheered me up.
I asked the waitress about the soup du jour and she said that it was primordial
soup—which is ammonia and methane mixed with ocean water in the presence
of lightning. Oh I'll take a tureen of that embryonic broth, I say, constraint
giving way to exuberance—but as soon as she vanishes my spirit immediately
sags because the ambience is so malevolent. The bouncers are hassling some
youngsters who want drinks—instead of simply carding the kids, they give
them radiocarbon tests, using traces of carbon 14 to determine how old they
are—and also there's a young wise guy from Texas A&M at a table near mine
who asks for freshly ground Rolaids on his fettuccine and two waiters viciously work him over with heavy bludgeon-sized pepper mills, so I get right
back into my car and narcissistically comb my thick jet-black hair in the rear-
view mirror and I check the guidebook. There's an inn nearby—it's called Little Bo Peep's—its habitués are shepherds. And after a long day of herding,
shearing, panpipe playing, muse invoking, and conversing in eclogues, it's
Miller time, and Bo Peep's is packed with rustic swains who've left their flocks
and sunlit, idealized arcadia behind for the more pungent charms of hard-core
social intercourse. Everyone's favorite waitress is Kikugoro. She wears a pale-

blue silk kimono and a brocade obi of gold and silver chrysanthemums with a small fan tucked into its folds, her face is painted and powdered to a porcelain white. A cowboy from south of the border orders a "Biggu Makku." But Kikugoro says, "This is not Makudonarudo." She takes a long cylinder of gallium arsenide crystal and slices him a thin wafer which she serves with soy sauce, wasabi, picked ginger, and daikon. "Conducts electrons ten times faster than silicon . . . taste good, gaucho-*san*, you eat," she says, bowing.

My sister is the beautiful day. Oh beautiful day, my sister, wipe my nose, swaddle me in fresh-smelling garments. I nurse at the adamantine nipple of the beautiful day. I quaff the milk of the beautiful day, and for the first time since 1956, I cheese on the shoulder of the beautiful day. Oh beautiful day, wash me in your lake of cloudless azure. I have overdosed on television, I am unresponsive and cyanotic, revive me in your shower of gelid light and walk me through your piazza which is made of elegant slabs of time. Oh beautiful day, kiss me. Your mouth is like Columbus Day. You are the menthol of autumn. My lungs cannot quench their thirst for you. Resuscitate me—I will never exhale your tonic gasses. Inflate me so that I may rise into the sky and mourn the monotonous topography of my life. Oh beautiful day, my sister, wipe my nose and adorn me in your finery. Let us lunch alfresco. Your club sandwiches are made of mulch and wind perfumed with newsprint. Your frilly toothpicks are the deciduous trees of school days.

I was an infinitely hot and dense dot. So begins the autobiography of a feral child who was raised by huge and lurid puppets. An autobiography written wearing wrist weights. It ends with these words: A car drives through a puddle of sperm, sweat, and contraceptive jelly, splattering the great chopsocky vigilante from Hong Kong. Inside, two acephalic sardines in mustard sauce are asleep in the rank darkness of their tin container. Suddenly, the swinging doors burst open and a mesomorphic cyborg walks in and whips out a 35-lb. phallus made of corrosion-resistant nickel-base alloy and he begins to stroke it sullenly, his eyes half shut. It's got a metal-oxide membrane for absolute submicron filtration of petrochemical fluids. It can ejaculate herbicides, sulfuric acid, tar glue, you name it. At the end of the bar, a woman whose album-length poem about temporomandibular joint dysfunction (TMJ) had won a Grammy for best spoken word recording is gently slowly ritually rubbing copper hexafluoroacetylacetone into her clitoris as she watches the hunk with the non-Euclidian features shoot a gob of dehydrogenated ethylbenzene 3,900 miles towards the Arctic archipelago, eventually raining down upon a fiord on Baffin Bay. Outside, a basketball plunges from the sky, killing a dog. At a county fair, a huge and hairy man in mud-caked blue overalls, surrounded by a crowd of retarded teenagers, swings a sledgehammer above his head with brawny keloidal arms and then brings it down with all his brute force on a tofu-burger on a flowery paper plate. A lizard licks the dew from the stamen of a stunted crocus. Rivets and girders float above the telekinetic construction workers. The testicular voice of Barry White emanates from some occult source within the laundry room. As I chugalug a glass of tap water milky with contaminants, I realize that my mind is being drained of its contents and refilled with the beliefs of the most mission-oriented, can-do feral child ever raised by huge and lurid puppets. I am the voice . . . the voice from beyond and the voice from within—can you hear me? Yes. I speak to you and you only—is that clear? Yes, master. To whom do I speak? To me and me only. Is "happy" the appropriate epithet for someone who experiences each moment as if he were being alternately flayed alive and tickled to death? No, master.

In addition to the growth hormone extracted from the glands of human corpses, I was using anabolic steroids, tissue regeneration compounds, granulocyte-macrophage colony-stimulating factor (GM-CSF)—a substance used to stimulate growth of certain vital blood cells in radiation victims—and a nasal spray of neuropeptides that accelerates the release of pituitary hormones and I was getting larger and larger and my food bills were becoming enormous. So I went on a TV game show in the hopes of raising cash. This was my question, for $250,000 in cash and prizes: If the Pacific Ocean were filled with gin, what would be, in terms of proportionate volume, the proper lake of vermouth necessary to achieve a dry martini? I said Lake Ontario—but the answer was the Caspian Sea which is called a sea but is a lake by definition. I had failed. I had humiliated my family and disgraced the king fu masters of the Shaolin temple. I stared balefully out into the studio audience which was chanting something that sounded like "dork." I'm in my car. I'm high on Sinutab. And I'm driving anywhere. The vector of my movement from a given point is isotropic—meaning that all possible directions are equally probable. I end up at a squalid little dive somewhere in Vegas maybe Reno maybe Tahoe. I don't know . . . but there she is. I can't tell if she's a human or a fifth-generation gynemorphic android and I don't care. I crack open an ampule of mating pheromone and let it waft across the bar, as I sip my drink, a methyl isocyanate on the rocks—methyl isocyanate is the substance which killed more than 2,000 people when it leaked in Bhopal, India, but thanks to my weight training, aerobic workouts, and a low-fat fiber-rich diet, the stuff has no effect on me. Sure enough she strolls over and occupies the stool next to mine. After a few moments of silence, I make the first move: We're all larval psychotics and have been since the age of two, I say, spitting an ice cube back into my glass. She moves closer to me. At this range, the downy cilia-like hairs that trickle from her navel remind me of the fractal ferns produced by injecting dyed water into an aqueous polymer solution, and I tell her so. She looks into my eyes: You have the glibness, superficial charm, grandiosity, lack of guilt, shallow feelings, impulsiveness, and lack of realistic long-term plans that excite me right now, she says, moving even closer. We feed on the same prey species, I growl. My lips are now one angstrom unit from her lips, which is one ten-billionth of a meter. I begin to kiss her but she turns her head away. Don't good little boys who finish all their vegetables get dessert? I ask. I can't kiss you, we're monozygotic replicants—we share 100% of our genetic material. My head spins. You are the beautiful day, I exclaim, your breath is a zephyr of eucalyptus that does a pas de bourrée across the Sea of Galilee. Thanks, she says, but we can't go back to my house and make love because monozygotic incest is forbidden by the elders. What if I said I could change all that . . . What if I said that I had a miniature shotgun that blasts gene fragments into the cells of living organisms, altering their genetic matrices so that a monozygotic replicant would no longer be a monozygotic replicant and she could then make love to a muscle-man without transgressing the incest taboo, I say, opening my shirt and expos-ing the device which I had stuck in the waistband of my black jeans. How'd you get that thing? she gasps, ogling its thick fiber-reinforced plastic barrel and the Uzi-Biotech logo embossed on the magazine which held two cartridges of gelated recombinant DNA. I got it for Christmas. . . . Do you have any last words before I scramble your chromosomes, I say, taking aim. Yes, she says, you first. I put the barrel to my heart. These are my last words: When I emerged from my mother's uterus I was the size of a chicken bouillon cube and Father said to the obstetrician: I realize that at this stage it's difficult to prog-nosticate his chances for a productive future, but if he's going to remain six-sided and 0.4 grams for the rest of his life, then euthanasia's our best bet. But Mother, who only milliseconds before was in the very throes of labor, had al-ready slipped on her muumuu and espadrilles and was puffing on a Marlboro: No pimple-faced simp two months out of Guadalajara is going to dissolve this helpless little hexahedron in a mug of boiling water, she said, as a nurse man-aged with acrobatic desperation to slide a suture basin under the long ash of her cigarette which she'd consumed in one furiously deep drag. These are my last words: My fear of being bullied and humiliated stems from an incident that occurred many years ago in a diner. A 500-lb. man seated next to me at the counter was proving that one particular paper towel was more absorbent than another brand. His face was swollen and covered with patches of hectic red. He spilled my glass of chocolate milk on the counter and then sopped it up with one paper towel and then with the other. With each wipe of the counter the sweep of his huge dimpled arm became wider and wider until he was repeat-edly smashing his flattened hand and the saturated towel into my chest. There was an interminable cadence to the blows I endured. And instead of assistance from other patrons at the counter, I received their derision, their sneering laughter. But now look at me! I am a terrible god. When I enter the forest the mightiest oaks blanch and tremble. All rustling, chirping, growling, and buzzing cease, purling brooks become still. This is all because of my tremen-dous muscularity . . . which is the result of the hours of hard work that I put in at the gym and the strict dietary regimen to which I adhere. When I enter the forest the birds become incontinent with fear so there's this torrential down-pour of shit from the trees. And I stride through—my whistle is like an ear-splitting fife being played by a lunatic with a bloody bandage around his head. And the sunlight, rent into an incoherence of blazing vectors, illuminates me: a shimmering, serrated monster!

2. *idyll*

I was reading an article that contained the words "vineyards, orchards, and fields bountiful with fruits and vegetables; sheeps and goats graze on hill-sides of lush greenery" and I realized that in five months none of these things would exist and I realized that as the last sheep on earth is skinned, boned, fil-leted, and flash-frozen, Arleen and I would probably be making love for the last time, mingling—for the last time—the sweet smell of her flesh which is like hyacinths and narcissus with the virile tang of my own which is like pond scum and headcheese and then I realized that the only thing that would distinguish me in the eyes of posterity from—for instance—those three sullen Chinese yuppies slumped over in their bentwood chairs at the most elegant McDonald's in the world is that I wrote the ads that go: "Suddenly There's Vancouver!" . . .

6. *the suggestiveness of one stray hair in an otherwise perfect coiffure*

He's got a car bomb. He puts the key in the ignition and turns it—the car blows up. He gets out. He opens the hood and makes a cursory inspection. He closes the hood and gets back in. He turns the key in the ignition. The car blows up. He gets out and slams the door shut disgustedly. He kicks the tire. He takes off his jacket and shimmies under the chassis. He pokes around. He slides back out and wipes the grease off his shirt. He puts his jacket back on. He gets in. He turns the key in the ignition. The car blows up, sending debris into the air and shattering windows for blocks. He gets out and says, Damn it! He calls a tow truck. He gives them his AAA membership number. They tow the car to an Exxon station. The mechanic gets in and turns the key in the ignition. The car explodes, demolishing the gas pumps, the red-and-blue Exxon logo high atop its pole bursting like a balloon on a string. The mechanic steps out. You got a car bomb, he says. The man rolls his eyes. I know that, he says.

MARK LEYNER

www   *(b. 1956)* **Web**

Referred to as an "avant-pop" writer, Leyner, from Hoboken, New Jersey, writes a poetic prose that is as dense and frenetic as the multitasked layers of culture that blanket the world.

www   TOPICS FOR CRITICAL THINKING **Web**

1. Language from how many different contexts appears in Leyner's stories?
2. What is the effect of the juxtaposition of languages from different contexts?
3. What various aspects of the stories unify them, both individually and as a group?
4. In what ways is Leyner's writing like collage? Pastiche?
5. What commentary on contemporary culture does Leyner's writing make?
6. How do Leyner's stories imagine a transglobal world, one in which national boundaries no longer make much difference?

www   TOPICS FOR CRITICAL WRITING **Web**

1. Consider the various ways one of Leyner's stories disrupts traditional notions of the story. What are the effects of that disruption? Do Leyner's stories present a new idea of what a story can be?
2. In what ways is Leyner's writing like commodity culture?

17   Stories for Further Reading

∞∞

ANTON CHEKHOV

Translated by Constance Garnett

The Lady with the Dog   *(1899)*

I

It was said that a new person had appeared on the sea-front: a lady with a little dog. Dmitri Dmitritch Gurov, who had by then been a fortnight at Yalta, and so was fairly at home there, had begun to take an interest in new arrivals. Sitting in Verney's pavilion, he saw, walking on the sea-front, a fair-haired young lady of medium height, wearing a *béret*; a white Pomeranian dog was running behind her.

And afterwards he met her in the public gardens and in the square several times a day. She was walking alone, always wearing the same *béret*, and always with the same white dog; no one knew who she was, and every one called her simply "the lady with the dog."

"If she is here alone without a husband or friends, it wouldn't be amiss to make her acquaintance," Gurov reflected.

He was under forty, but he had a daughter already twelve years old, and two sons at school. He had been married young, when he was a student in his second year, and by now his wife seemed half as old again as he. She was a tall, erect woman with dark eyebrows, staid and dignified, and, as she said of herself, intellectual. She read a great deal, used phonetic spelling, called her husband, not Dmitri, but Dimitri, and he secretly considered her unintelligent, narrow, inelegant, was afraid of her, and did not like to be at home. He had begun being unfaithful to her long ago—had been unfaithful to her often, and, probably on that account, almost always spoke ill of women, and when they were talked about in his presence, used to call them "the lower race."

It seemed to him that he had been so schooled by bitter experience that 5 he might call them what he liked, and yet he could not get on for two days together without "the lower race." In the society of men he was bored and not himself, with them he was cold and uncommunicative; but when he was in the company of women he felt free, and knew what to say to them and how to behave; and he was at ease with them even when he was silent. In his appearance, in his character, in his whole nature, there was something attractive and elusive which allured women and disposed them in his favour; he knew that, and some force seemed to draw him, too, to them.

Experience often repeated, truly bitter experience, had taught him long ago that with decent people, especially Moscow people—always slow to move and irresolute—every intimacy, which at first so agreeably diversifies life and appears a light and charming adventure, inevitably grows into a regular problem of extreme intricacy, and in the long run the situation becomes unbearable. But at every fresh meeting with an interesting woman this experience seemed to slip out of his memory, and he was eager for life, and everything seemed simple and amusing.

One evening he was dining in the gardens, and the lady in the *béret* came up slowly to take the next table. Her expression, her gait, her dress, and the way she did her hair told him that she was a lady, that she was married, that she was in Yalta for the first time and alone, and that she was dull there. . . . The stories told of the immorality in such places as Yalta are to a great extent untrue; he despised them, and knew that such stories were for the most part made up by persons who would themselves have been glad to sin if they had been able; but when the lady sat down at the next table three paces from him, he remembered these tales of easy conquests, of trips to the mountains, and the tempting thought of a swift, fleeting love affair, a romance with an unknown woman, whose name he did not know, suddenly took possession of him.

He beckoned coaxingly to the Pomeranian, and when the dog came up to him he shook his finger at it. The Pomeranian growled: Gurov shook his finger at it again.

The lady looked at him and at once dropped her eyes.

"He doesn't bite," she said, and blushed.   10

"May I give him a bone?" he asked; and when she nodded he asked courteously, "Have you been long in Yalta?"

"Five days."

"And I have already dragged out a fortnight here."

There was a brief silence.

"Time goes fast, and yet it is so dull here!" she said, not looking at him.   15

"That's only the fashion to say it is dull here. A provincial will live in Belyov or Zhidra and not be dull, and when he comes here it's 'Oh, the dulness! Oh, the dust!' One would think he came from Grenada."

She laughed. Then both continued eating in silence, like strangers, but after dinner they walked side by side; and there sprang up between them the light jesting conversation of people who are free and satisfied, to whom it does not matter where they go or what they talk about. They walked and talked of the strange light on the sea: the water was of a soft warm lilac hue, and there was a golden streak from the moon upon it. They talked of how sultry it was after a hot day. Gurov told her that he came from Moscow, that he had taken his degree in Arts, but had a post in a bank; that he had trained as an opera-singer, but had given it up, that he owned two houses in Moscow. . . . And

from her he learnt that she had grown up in Petersburg, but had lived in S——
since her marriage two years before, that she was staying another month in
Yalta, and that her husband, who needed a holiday too, might perhaps come
and fetch her. She was not sure whether her husband had a post in a Crown
Department or under the Provincial Council—and was amused by her own
ignorance. And Gurov learnt, too, that she was called Anna Sergeyevna.

Afterwards he thought about her in his room at the hotel—thought she
would certainly meet him next day; it would be sure to happen. As he got into
bed he thought how lately she had been a girl at school, doing lessons like his
own daughter; he recalled the diffidence, the angularity, that was still manifest
in her laugh and her manner of talking with a stranger. This must have been
the first time in her life she had been alone in surroundings in which she was
followed, looked at, and spoken to merely from a secret motive which she
could hardly fail to guess. He recalled her slender, delicate neck, her lovely
grey eyes.

"There's something pathetic about her, anyway," he thought, and fell
asleep.

II

A week had passed since they had made acquaintance. It was a holiday. It   20
was sultry indoors, while in the street the wind whirled the dust round and
round, and blew people's hats off. It was a thirsty day, and Gurov often went
into the pavilion, and pressed Anna Sergeyevna to have syrup and water or an
ice. One did not know what to do with oneself.

In the evening when the wind had dropped a little, they went out on the
groyne to see the steamer come in. There were a great many people walking
about the harbour; they had gathered to welcome some one, bringing bouquets. And two peculiarities of a well-dressed Yalta crowd were very conspicuous: the elderly ladies were dressed like young ones, and there were great
numbers of generals.

Owing to the roughness of the sea, the steamer arrived late, after the sun
had set, and it was a long time turning about before it reached the groyne.
Anna Sergeyevna looked through her lorgnette at the steamer and the passengers as though looking for acquaintances, and when she turned to Gurov
her eyes were shining. She talked a great deal and asked disconnected questions, forgetting next moment what she had asked; then she dropped her
lorgnette in the crush.

The festive crowd began to disperse; it was too dark to see people's faces.
The wind had completely dropped, but Gurov and Anna Sergeyevna still
stood as though waiting to see some one else come from the steamer. Anna
Sergeyevna was silent now, and sniffed the flowers without looking at Gurov.

"The weather is better this evening," he said. "Where shall we go now?
Shall we drive somewhere?"

She made no answer.   25

Then he looked at her intently, and all at once put his arm round her and kissed her on the lips, and breathed in the moisture and the fragrance of the flowers; and he immediately looked round him, anxiously wondering whether any one had seen them.

"Let us go to your hotel," he said softly. And both walked quickly.

The room was close and smelt of the scent she had bought at the Japanese shop. Gurov looked at her and thought: "What different people one meets in the world!" From the past he preserved memories of careless, good-natured women, who loved cheerfully and were grateful to him for the happiness he gave them, however brief it might be; and of women like his wife who loved without any genuine feeling, with superfluous phrases, affectedly, hysterically, with an expression that suggested that it was not love nor passion, but something more significant; and of two or three others, very beautiful, cold women, on whose faces he had caught a glimpse of a rapacious expression— an obstinate desire to snatch from life more than it could give, and these were capricious, unreflecting, domineering, unintelligent women not in their first youth, and when Gurov grew cold to them their beauty excited his hatred, and the lace on their linen seemed to him like scales.

But in this case there was still the diffidence, the angularity of inexperienced youth, an awkward feeling; and there was a sense of consternation as though some one had suddenly knocked at the door. The attitude of Anna Sergeyevna—"the lady with the dog"—to what had happened was somehow peculiar, very grave, as though it were her fall—so it seemed, and it was strange and inappropriate. Her face dropped and faded, and on both sides of it her long hair hung down mournfully; she mused in a dejected attitude like "the woman who was a sinner" in an old-fashioned picture.

"It's wrong," she said. "You will be the first to despise me now."   30

There was a water-melon on the table. Gurov cut himself a slice and began eating it without haste. There followed at least half an hour of silence.

Anna Sergeyevna was touching; there was about her the purity of a good, simple woman who had seen little of life. The solitary candle burning on the table threw a faint light on her face, yet it was clear that she was very unhappy.

"How could I despise you?" asked Gurov. "You don't know what you are saying."

"God forgive me," she said, and her eyes filled with tears. "It's awful."

"You seem to feel you need to be forgiven."   35

"Forgiven? No. I am a bad, low woman; I despise myself and don't attempt to justify myself. It's not my husband but myself I have deceived. And not only just now; I have been deceiving myself for a long time. My husband may be a good, honest man, but he is a flunkey! I don't know what he does there, what his work is, but I know he is a flunkey! I was twenty when I was married to him. I have been tormented by curiosity; I wanted something better. 'There must be a different sort of life,' I said to myself. I wanted to live! To live, to live! . . . I was fired by curiosity . . . you don't understand it, but, I swear to God, I could not control myself; something happened to me: I could not be restrained. I told my husband I was ill, and came here. . . . And here I have been walking about as though I were dazed, like a mad creature; . . . and now I have become a vulgar, contemptible woman whom any one may despise."

Gurov felt bored already, listening to her. He was irritated by the naïve tone, by this remorse, so unexpected and inopportune; but for the tears in her eyes, he might have thought she was jesting or playing a part.

"I don't understand," he said softly. "What is it you want?"

She hid her face on his breast and pressed close to him.

"Believe me, believe me, I beseech you . . ." she said. "I love a pure, hon- 40 est life, and sin is loathsome to me. I don't know what I am doing. Simple people say: 'The Evil One has beguiled me.' And I may say of myself now that the Evil One has beguiled me."

"Hush, hush! . . ." he muttered.

He looked at her fixed, scared eyes, kissed her, talked softly and affectionately, and by degrees she was comforted, and her gaiety returned; they both began laughing.

Afterwards when they went out there was not a soul on the sea-front. The town with its cypresses had quite a deathlike air, but the sea still broke noisily on the shore; a single barge was rocking on the waves, and a lantern was blinking sleepily on it.

They found a cab and drove to Oreanda.

"I found out your surname in the hall just now: it was written on the 45 board—Von Diderits," said Gurov. "Is your husband a German?"

"No; I believe his grandfather was a German, but he is an Orthodox Russian himself."

At Oreanda they sat on a seat not far from the church, looked down at the sea, and were silent. Yalta was hardly visible through the morning mist; white clouds stood motionless on the mountain-tops. The leaves did not stir on the trees, grasshoppers chirruped, and the monotonous hollow sound of the sea rising up from below, spoke of the peace, of the eternal sleep awaiting us. So it must have sounded when there was no Yalta, no Oreanda here; so it sounds now, and it will sound as indifferently and monotonously when we are all no more. And in this constancy, in this complete indifference to the life and death of each of us, there lies hid, perhaps, a pledge of our eternal salvation, of the unceasing movement of life upon earth, of unceasing progress towards perfection. Sitting beside a young woman who in the dawn seemed so lovely, soothed and spellbound in these magical surroundings—the sea, mountains, clouds, the open sky—Gurov thought how in reality everything is beautiful in this world when one reflects: everything except what we think or do ourselves when we forget our human dignity and the higher aims of our existence.

A man walked up to them—probably a keeper—looked at them and walked away. And this detail seemed mysterious and beautiful, too. They saw a steamer come from Theodosia, with its lights out in the glow of dawn.

"There is dew on the grass," said Anna Sergeyevna, after a silence.

"Yes. It's time to go home."   50

They went back to the town.

Then they met every day at twelve o'clock on the sea-front, lunched and dined together, went for walks, admired the sea. She complained that she slept badly, that her heart throbbed violently; asked the same questions, troubled now by jealousy and now by the fear that he did not respect her sufficiently.

And often in the square or gardens, when there was no one near them, he suddenly drew her to him and kissed her passionately. Complete idleness, these kisses in broad daylight while he looked round in dread of some one's seeing them, the heat, the smell of the sea, and the continual passing to and fro before him of idle, well-dressed, well-fed people, made a new man of him; he told Anna Sergeyevna how beautiful she was, how fascinating. He was impatiently passionate, he would not move a step away from her, while she was often pensive and continually urged him to confess that he did not respect her, did not love her in the least, and thought of her as nothing but a common woman. Rather late almost every evening they drove somewhere out of town, to Oreanda or to the waterfall; and the expedition was always a success, the scenery invariably impressed them as grand and beautiful.

They were expecting her husband to come, but a letter came from him, saying that there was something wrong with his eyes, and he entreated his wife to come home as quickly as possible. Anna Sergeyevna made haste to go.

"It's a good thing I am going away," she said to Gurov. "It's the finger of destiny!"

She went by coach and he went with her. They were driving the whole 55 day. When she had got into a compartment of the express, and when the second bell had rung, she said:

"Let me look at you once more . . . look at you once again. That's right."

She did not shed tears, but was so sad that she seemed ill, and her face was quivering.

"I shall remember you . . . think of you," she said. "God be with you; be happy. Don't remember evil against me. We are parting forever—it must be so, for we ought never to have met. Well, God be with you."

The train moved off rapidly, its lights soon vanished from sight, and a minute later there was no sound of it, as though everything had conspired together to end as quickly as possible that sweet delirium, that madness. Left alone on the platform, and gazing into the dark distance, Gurov listened to the chirrup of the grasshoppers and the hum of the telegraph wires, feeling as though he had only just waked up. And he thought, musing, that there had been another episode or adventure in his life, and it, too, was at an end, and nothing was left of it but a memory. . . . He was moved, sad, and conscious of a slight remorse. This young woman whom he would never meet again had not been happy with him; he was genuinely warm and affectionate with her, but yet in his manner, his tone, and his caresses there had been a shade of light irony, the coarse condescension of a happy man who was, besides, almost twice her age. All the time she had called him kind, exceptional, lofty; obviously he had seemed to her different from what he really was, so he had unintentionally deceived her. . . .

Here at the station was already a scent of autumn; it was a cold evening. 60

"It's time for me to go north," thought Gurov as he left the platform. "High time!"

III

At home in Moscow everything was in its winter routine; the stoves were heated, and in the morning it was still dark when the children were having breakfast and getting ready for school, and the nurse would light the lamp for a short time. The frosts had begun already. When the first snow has fallen, on the first day of sledge-driving it is pleasant to see the white earth, the white roofs, to draw soft, delicious breath, and the season brings back the days of one's youth. The old limes and birches, white with hoar-frost, have a good-natured expression; they are nearer to one's heart than cypresses and palms, and near them one doesn't want to be thinking of the sea and the mountains.

Gurov was Moscow born; he arrived in Moscow on a fine frosty day, and when he put on his fur coat and warm gloves, and walked along Petrovka, and when on Saturday evening he heard the ringing of the bells, his recent trip and the places he had seen lost all charm for him. Little by little he became absorbed in Moscow life, greedily read three newspapers a day, and declared he did not read the Moscow papers on principle! He already felt a longing to go to restaurants, clubs, dinner-parties, anniversary celebrations, and he felt flattered at entertaining distinguished lawyers and artists, and at playing cards with a professor at the doctors' club. He could already eat a whole plateful of salt fish and cabbage. . . .

In another month, he fancied, the image of Anna Sergeyevna would be shrouded in a mist in his memory, and only from time to time would visit him in his dreams with a touching smile as others did. But more than a month passed, real winter had come, and everything was still clear in his memory as though he had parted with Anna Sergeyevna only the day before. And his memories glowed more and more vividly. When in the evening stillness he heard from his study the voices of his children, preparing their lessons, or when he listened to a song or the organ at the restaurant, or the storm howled in the chimney, suddenly everything would rise up in his memory: what had happened on the groyne, and the early morning with the mist on the mountains, and the steamer coming from Theodosia, and the kisses. He would pace a long time about his room, remembering it all and smiling; then his memories passed into dreams, and in his fancy the past was mingled with what was to come. Anna Sergeyevna did not visit him in dreams, but followed him about everywhere like a shadow and haunted him. When he shut his eyes he saw her as though she were living before him, and she seemed to him lovelier, younger, tenderer than she was; and he imagined himself finer than he had been in Yalta. In the evenings she peeped out at him from the bookcase, from the fireplace, from the corner—he heard her breathing, the caressing rustle of her dress. In the street he watched the women, looking for some one like her.

He was tormented by an intense desire to confide his memories to some one. But in his home it was impossible to talk of his love, and he had no one outside; he could not talk to his tenants nor to any one at the bank. And what had he to talk of? Had he been in love, then? Had there been anything beautiful, poetical, or edifying or simply interesting in his relations with Anna

Sergeyevna? And there was nothing for him but to talk vaguely of love, of woman, and no one guessed what it meant; only his wife twitched her black eyebrows, and said: "The part of a lady-killer does not suit you at all, Dimitri."

One evening, coming out of the doctors' club with an official with whom he had been playing cards, he could not resist saying:

"If only you knew what a fascinating woman I made the acquaintance of in Yalta!"

The official got into his sledge and was driving away, but turned suddenly and shouted:

"Dmitri Dmitritch!"

"What?"   70

"You were right this evening: the sturgeon was a bit too strong!"

These words, so ordinary, for some reason moved Gurov to indignation, and struck him as degrading and unclean. What savage manners, what people! What senseless nights, what uninteresting, uneventful days! The rage for card-playing, the gluttony, the drunkenness, the continual talk always about the same thing. Useless pursuits and conversations always about the same things absorb the better part of one's time, the better part of one's strength, and in the end there is left a life grovelling and curtailed, worthless and trivial, and there is no escaping or getting away from it—just as though one were in a madhouse or a prison.

Gurov did not sleep all night, and was filled with indignation. And he had a headache all next day. And the next night he slept badly; he sat up in bed, thinking, or paced up and down his room. He was sick of his children, sick of the bank; he had no desire to go anywhere or to talk of anything.

In the holidays in December he prepared for a journey, and told his wife he was going to Petersburg to do something in the interests of a young friend—and he set off for S——. What for? He did not very well know himself. He wanted to see Anna Sergeyevna and to talk with her—to arrange a meeting, if possible.

He reached S—— in the morning, and took the best room at the hotel, in   75
which the floor was covered with grey army cloth, and on the table was an inkstand, grey with dust and adorned with a figure on horseback, with its hat in its hand and its head broken off. The hotel porter gave him the necessary information; Von Diderits lived in a house of his own in Old Gontcharny Street—it was not far from the hotel: he was rich and lived in good style, and had his own horses; every one in the town knew him. The porter pronounced the name "Dridirits."

Gurov went without haste to Old Gontcharny Street and found the house. Just opposite the house stretched a long grey fence adorned with nails.

"One would run away from a fence like that," thought Gurov, looking from the fence to the windows of the house and back again.

He considered: to-day was a holiday, and the husband would probably be at home. And in any case it would be tactless to go into the house and upset her. If he were to send her a note it might fall into her husband's hands, and then it might ruin everything. The best thing was to trust to chance. And he kept walking up and down the street by the fence, waiting for the chance. He saw a beggar go in at the gate and dogs fly at him; then an hour later he heard a piano, and the sounds were faint and indistinct. Probably it was Anna Sergeyevna playing. The front door suddenly opened, and an old woman came out, followed by the familiar white Pomeranian. Gurov was on the point of calling to the dog, but his heart began beating violently, and in his excitement he could not remember the dog's name.

He walked up and down, and loathed the grey fence more and more, and by now he thought irritably that Anna Sergeyevna had forgotten him, and was perhaps already amusing herself with some one else, and that that was very natural in a young woman who had nothing to look at from morning till night but that confounded fence. He went back to his hotel room and sat for a long while on the sofa, not knowing what to do, then he had dinner and a long nap.

"How stupid and worrying it is!" he thought when he woke and looked at 80 the dark windows: it was already evening. "Here I've had a good sleep for some reason. What shall I do in the night?"

He sat on the bed, which was covered by a cheap grey blanket, such as one sees in hospitals, and he taunted himself in his vexation:

"So much for the lady with the dog . . . so much for the adventure. . . . You're in a nice fix. . . ."

That morning at the station a poster in large letters had caught his eye. "The Geisha" was to be performed for the first time. He thought of this and went to the theatre.

"It's quite possible she may go to the first performance," he thought.

The theatre was full. As in all provincial theatres, there was a fog above 85 the chandelier, the gallery was noisy and restless; in the front row the local dandies were standing up before the beginning of the performance, with their hands behind them; in the Governor's box the Governor's daughter, wearing a boa, was sitting in the front seat, while the Governor himself lurked modestly behind the curtain with only his hands visible; the orchestra was a long time tuning up; the stage curtain swayed. All the time the audience were coming in and taking their seats Gurov looked at them eagerly.

Anna Sergeyevna, too, came in. She sat down in the third row, and when Gurov looked at her his heart contracted, and he understood clearly that for him there was in the whole world no creature so near, so precious, and so important to him; she, this little woman, in no way remarkable, lost in a provincial crowd, with a vulgar lorgnette in her hand, filled his whole life now, was his sorrow and his joy, the one happiness that he now desired for himself, and to the sounds of the inferior orchestra, of the wretched provincial violins, he thought how lovely she was. He thought and dreamed.

A young man with small side-whiskers, tall and stooping, came in with Anna Sergeyevna and sat down beside her; he bent his head at every step and seemed to be continually bowing. Most likely this was the husband whom at Yalta, in a rush of bitter feeling, she had called a flunkey. And there really was in his long figure, his side-whiskers, and the small bald patch on his head, something of the flunkey's obsequiousness; his smile was sugary, and in his buttonhole there was some badge of distinction like the number on a waiter.

During the first interval the husband went away to smoke; she remained alone in her stall. Gurov, who was sitting in the stalls, too, went up to her and said in a trembling voice, with a forced smile:

"Good-evening."

She glanced at him and turned pale, then glanced again with horror, un- 90
able to believe her eyes, and tightly gripped the fan and the lorgnette in her hands, evidently struggling with herself not to faint. Both were silent. She was sitting, he was standing, frightened by her confusion and not venturing to sit down beside her. The violins and the flute began tuning up. He felt suddenly frightened; it seemed as though all the people in the boxes were looking at them. She got up and went quickly to the door; he followed her, and both walked senselessly along passages, and up and down stairs, and figures in legal, scholastic, and civil service uniforms, all wearing badges, flitted before their eyes. They caught glimpses of ladies, of fur coats hanging on pegs; the draughts blew on them, bringing a smell of stale tobacco. And Gurov, whose heart was beating violently, thought:

"Oh, heavens! Why are these people here and this orchestra! . . . ."

And at that instant he recalled how when he had seen Anna Sergeyevna off at the station he had thought that everything was over and they would never meet again. But how far they were still from the end!

On the narrow, gloomy staircase over which was written "To the Amphitheatre," she stopped.

"How you have frightened me!" she said, breathing hard, still pale and overwhelmed. "Oh, how you have frightened me! I am half dead. Why have you come? Why?"

"But do understand, Anna, do understand . . ." he said hastily in a low 95
voice. "I entreat you to understand. . . ."

She looked at him with dread, with entreaty, with love; she looked at him intently, to keep his features more distinctly in her memory.

"I am so unhappy," she went on, not heeding him. "I have thought of nothing but you all the time; I live only in the thought of you. And I wanted to forget, to forget you; but why, oh, why, have you come?"

On the landing above them two schoolboys were smoking and looking down, but that was nothing to Gurov; he drew Anna Sergeyevna to him, and began kissing her face, her cheeks, and her hands.

"What are you doing, what are you doing!" she cried in horror, pushing him away. "We are mad. Go away to-day; go away at once. . . . I beseech you by all that is sacred, I implore you. . . . There are people coming this way!"

Some one was coming up the stairs. 100

"You must go away," Anna Sergeyevna went on in a whisper. "Do you hear, Dmitri Dmitritch? I will come and see you in Moscow. I have never been happy; I am miserable now, and I never, never shall be happy, never! Don't make me suffer still more! I swear I'll come to Moscow. But now let us part. My precious, good, dear one, we must part!"

She pressed his hand and began rapidly going downstairs, looking round at him, and from her eyes he could see that she really was unhappy. Gurov stood for a little while, listened, then, when all sound had died away, he found his coat and left the theatre.

IV

And Anna Sergeyevna began coming to see him in Moscow. Once in two or three months she left S——, telling her husband that she was going to consult a doctor about an internal complaint—and her husband believed her, and did not believe her. In Moscow she stayed at the Slaviansky Bazaar hotel, and at once sent a man in a red cap to Gurov. Gurov went to see her, and no one in Moscow knew of it.

Once he was going to see her in this way on a winter morning (the messenger had come the evening before when he was out). With him walked his daughter, whom he wanted to take to school: it was on the way. Snow was falling in big wet flakes.

"It's three degrees above freezing-point, and yet it is snowing," said   105
Gurov to his daughter. "The thaw is only on the surface of the earth; there is quite a different temperature at a greater height in the atmosphere."

"And why are there no thunderstorms in the winter, father?"

He explained that, too. He talked, thinking all the while that he was going to see *her*, and no living soul knew of it, and probably never would know. He had two lives: one, open, seen and known by all who cared to know, full of relative truth and of relative falsehood, exactly like the lives of his friends and acquaintances; and another life running its course in secret. And through some strange, perhaps accidental, conjunction of circumstances, everything that was essential, of interest and of value to him, everything in which he was sincere and did not deceive himself, everything that made the kernel of his life, was hidden from other people; and all that was false in him, the sheath in which he hid himself to conceal the truth—such, for instance, as his work in the bank, his discussions at the club, his "lower race," his presence with his wife at anniversary festivities—all that was open. And he judged of others by himself, not believing in what he saw, and always believing that every man had his real, most interesting life under the cover of secrecy and under the cover of night. All personal life rested on secrecy, and possibly it was partly on that account that civilised man was so nervously anxious that personal privacy should be respected.

After leaving his daughter at school, Gurov went on to the Slaviansky Bazaar. He took off his fur coat below, went upstairs, and softly knocked at the door. Anna Sergeyevna, wearing his favourite grey dress, exhausted by the journey and the suspense, had been expecting him since the evening before. She was pale; she looked at him, and did not smile, and he had hardly come in when she fell on his breast. Their kiss was slow and prolonged, as though they had not met for two years.

"Well, how are you getting on there?" he asked. "What news?"

"Wait; I'll tell you directly. . . . I can't talk."   110

She could not speak; she was crying. She turned away from him, and pressed her handkerchief to her eyes.

"Let her have her cry out. I'll sit down and wait," he thought, and he sat down in an arm-chair.

Then he rang and asked for tea to be brought him, and while he drank his tea she remained standing at the window with her back to him. She was crying from emotion, from the miserable consciousness that their life was so hard for them; they could only meet in secret, hiding themselves from people, like thieves! Was not their life shattered?

"Come, do stop!" he said.

It was evident to him that this love of theirs would not soon be over, that   115
he could not see the end of it. Anna Sergeyevna grew more and more attached to him. She adored him, and it was unthinkable to say to her that it was bound to have an end some day; besides, she would not have believed it!

He went up to her and took her by the shoulders to say something affectionate and cheering, and at that moment he saw himself in the looking-glass.

His hair was already beginning to turn grey. And it seemed strange to him that he had grown so much older, so much plainer during the last few years. The shoulders on which his hands rested were warm and quivering. He felt compassion for this life, still so warm and lovely, but probably already not far from beginning to fade and wither like his own. Why did she love him so much? He always seemed to women different from what he was, and they loved in him not himself, but the man created by their imagination, whom they had been eagerly seeking all their lives; and afterwards, when they noticed their mistake, they loved him all the same. And not one of them had been happy with him. Time passed, he had made their acquaintance, got on with them, parted, but he had never once loved; it was anything you like, but not love.

And only now when his head was grey he had fallen properly, really in love—for the first time in his life.

Anna Sergeyevna and he loved each other like people very close and akin, like husband and wife, like tender friends; it seemed to them that fate itself had meant them for one another, and they could not understand why he had a wife and she a husband; and it was as though they were a pair of birds of passage, caught and forced to live in different cages. They forgave each other for what they were ashamed of in their past, they forgave everything in the present, and felt that this love of theirs had changed them both.

In moments of depression in the past he had comforted himself with any   120
arguments that came into his mind, but now he no longer cared for arguments; he felt profound compassion, he wanted to be sincere and tender. . . .

"Don't cry, my darling," he said. "You've had your cry; that's enough. . . . Let us talk now, let us think of some plan."

Then they spent a long while taking counsel together, talked of how to avoid the necessity for secrecy, for deception, for living in different towns and not seeing each other for long at a time. How could they be free from this intolerable bondage?

"How? How?" he asked, clutching his head. "How?"

And it seemed as though in a little while the solution would be found, and then a new and splendid life would begin; and it was clear to both of them that they had still a long, long road before them, and that the most complicated and difficult part of it was only just beginning.

∞∞

KATHERINE MANSFIELD

This Flower   *(1919)*

"But I tell you, my lord fool, out of this nettle danger, we pluck this flower, safety."

As she lay there, looking up at the ceiling, she had her moment—yes, she had her moment! And it was not connected with anything she had thought or felt before, not even with those words the doctor had scarcely ceased speaking. It was single, glowing, perfect; it was like—a pearl, too flawless to match with another . . . Could she describe what happened? Impossible. It was as though, even if she had not been conscious (and she certainly had not been conscious all the time) that she was fighting against the stream of life—the stream of life indeed!—she had suddenly ceased to struggle. Oh, more than that! She had yielded, yielded absolutely, down to every minutest pulse and nerve, and she had fallen into the bright bosom of the stream and it had borne her . . . She was part of her room—part of the great bouquet of southern anemones, of the white net curtains that blew in stiff against the light breeze, of the mirrors, the white silky rugs; she was part of the high, shaking, quivering clamour, broken with little bells and crying voices that went streaming by outside,—part of the leaves and the light.

Over. She sat up. The doctor had reappeared. This strange little figure with his stethoscope still strung round his neck— for she had asked him to examine her heart—squeezing and kneading his freshly washed hands, had told her . . .

It was the first time she had ever seen him. Roy, unable, of course, to miss the smallest dramatic opportunity, had obtained his rather shady Bloomsbury address from the man in whom he always confided everything, who, although he'd never met her, knew, "all about them."

"My darling," Roy had said, "we'd better have an absolutely unknown man just in case it's—well, what we don't either of us want it to be. One can't be too careful in affairs of this sort. Doctors *do* talk. It's all damned rot to say they don't." Then, "Not that I care a straw who on earth knows. Not that I wouldn't—if you'd have me—blazon it on the skies, or take the front page of the *Daily Mirror* and have our two names on it, in a heart, you know—pierced by an arrow."

Nevertheless, of course, his love of mystery and intrigue, his passion for   5 "keeping our secret beautifully" (his phrase!) had won the day, and off he'd gone in a taxi to fetch this rather sodden-looking little man.

She heard her untroubled voice saying, "Do you mind not mentioning anything of this to Mr. King? If you'd tell him that I'm a little run down and that my heart wants a rest. For I've been complaining about my heart."

Roy had been really *too* right about the kind of man the doctor was. He gave her a strange, quick, leering look, and taking off the stethoscope with shaking fingers he folded it into his bag that looked somehow like a broken old canvas shoe.

"Don't you worry, my dear," he said huskily. "I'll see you through."

Odious little toad to have asked a favour of! She sprang to her feet, and picking up her purple cloth jacket, went over to the mirror. There was a soft knock at the door, and Roy—he really did look pale, smiling his half-smile—came in and asked the doctor what he had to say.

"Well," said the doctor, taking up his hat, holding it against his chest and   10
beating a tattoo on it, "all I've got to say is that Mrs.—h'm—Madam wants a bit of a rest. She's a bit run down. Her heart's a bit strained. Nothing else wrong."

In the street a barrel-organ struck up something gay, laughing, mocking, gushing, with little trills, shakes, jumbles of notes.

> That's *all* I got to say, to say,
>
> That's *all* I got to say,

it mocked. It sounded so near she wouldn't have been surprised if the doctor were turning the handle.

She saw Roy's smile deepen; his eyes took fire. He gave a little "Ah!" of relief and happiness. And just for one moment he allowed himself to gaze at her without caring a jot whether the doctor saw or not, drinking her up with that gaze she knew so well, as she stood tying the pale ribbons of her camisole and drawing on the little purple cloth jacket. He jerked back to the doctor, "She shall go away. She shall go away to the sea at once," said he, and then, terribly anxious, "What about her food?" At that, buttoning her jacket in the long mirror, she couldn't help laughing at him.

"That's all very well," he protested, laughing back delightedly at her and at the doctor. "But if I didn't manage her food, doctor, she'd never eat anything but caviare sandwiches and—and white grapes. About wine—oughtn't she to have wine?"

Wine would do her no harm.   15

"Champagne," pleaded Roy. How he was enjoying himself!

"Oh, as much champagne as she likes," said the doctor, "and a brandy and soda with her lunch if she fancies it."

Roy loved that; it tickled him immensely.

"Do you hear that?" he asked solemnly, blinking and sucking in his cheeks to keep from laughing. "Do you fancy a brandy and soda?"

And, in the distance, faint and exhausted, the barrel-organ: 20

> A brandy and so-da,
>
> A brandy and soda, please!
>
> A brandy and soda, please!

The doctor seemed to hear that, too. He shook hands with her and Roy and went with him into the passage to settle his fee.

She heard the front door close and then—rapid, rapid steps along along the passage. This time he simply burst into her room, and she was in his arms,

crushed up small while he kissed her with warm quick kisses, murmuring between them, "My darling, my beauty, my delight. You're mine, you're safe."
And then three soft groans. "Oh! Oh! Oh! the relief!" Still keeping his arms
round her he leant his head against her shoulder as though exhausted. "If you
knew how frightened I've been," he murmured. "I thought we were in for it
this time. I really did. And it would have been so—fatal—so fatal!"

∞∞

WILLIAM FAULKNER

Barn Burning   *(1939)*

The store in which the Justice of the Peace's court was sitting smelled of
cheese. The boy, crouched on his nail keg at the back of the crowded room,
knew he smelled cheese, and more: from where he sat he could see the ranked
shelves close-packed with the solid, squat, dynamic shapes of tin cans whose
labels his stomach read, not from the lettering which meant nothing to his
mind but from the scarlet devils and the silver curve of fish—this, the cheese
which he knew he smelled and the hermetic meat which his intestines believed he smelled coming in intermittent gusts momentary and brief between
the other constant one, the smell and sense just a little of fear because mostly
of despair and grief, the old fierce pull of blood. He could not see the table
where the Justice sat and before which his father and his father's enemy (*our
enemy* he thought in that despair; *ourn! mine and hisn both! He's my father!*)
stood, but he could hear them, the two of them that is, because his father had
said no word yet:

"But what proof have you, Mr. Harris?"

"I told you. The hog got into my corn. I caught it up and sent it back to
him. He had no fence that would hold it. I told him so, warned him. The next
time I put the hog in my pen. When he came to get it I gave him enough wire
to patch up his pen. The next time I put the hog up and kept it. I rode down
to his house and saw the wire I gave him still rolled on to the spool in his yard.
I told him he could have the hog when he paid me a dollar pound fee. That
evening a nigger came with the dollar and got the hog. He was a strange nigger. He said, 'He say to tell you wood and hay kin burn.' I said, 'What?' 'That
whut he say to tell you,' the nigger said. 'Wood and hay kin burn.' That night
my barn burned. I got the stock out but I lost the barn."

"Where is the nigger? Have you got him?"

"He was a strange nigger, I tell you. I don't know what became of him."   5

"But that's not proof. Don't you see that's not proof?"

"Get that boy up here. He knows." For a moment the boy thought too
that the man meant his older brother until Harris said, "Not him. The little
one. The boy," and, crouching, small for his age, small and wiry like his father,
in patched and faded jeans even too small for him, with straight, uncombed,
brown hair and eyes gray and wild as storm scud, he saw the men between
himself and the table part and become a lane of grim faces, at the end of which

he saw the Justice, a shabby, collarless, graying man in spectacles, beckoning him. He felt no floor under his bare feet; he seemed to walk beneath the palpable weight of the grim turning faces. His father, stiff in his black Sunday coat donned not for the trial but for the moving, did not even look at him. *He aims for me to lie,* he thought, again with that frantic grief and despair. *And I will have to do hit.*

"What's your name, boy?" the Justice said.

"Colonel Sartoris Snopes," the boy whispered.

"Hey?" the Justice said. "Talk louder. Colonel Sartoris? I reckon anybody   10
named for Colonel Sartoris in this country can't help but tell the truth, can they?" The boy said nothing. *Enemy! Enemy!* he thought; for a moment he could not even see, could not see that the Justice's face was kindly nor discern that his voice was troubled when he spoke to the man named Harris: "Do you want me to question this boy?" But he could hear, and during those subsequent long seconds while there was absolutely no sound in the crowded little room save that of quiet and intent breathing it was as if he had swung outward at the end of a grape vine, over a ravine, and at the top of the swing had been caught in a prolonged instant of mesmerized gravity, weightless in time.

"No!" Harris said violently, explosively. "Damnation! Send him out of here!" Now time, the fluid world, rushed beneath him again, the voices coming to him again through the smell of cheese and sealed meat, the fear and despair and the old grief of blood:

"This case is closed. I can't find against you, Snopes, but I can give you advice. Leave this country and don't come back to it."

His father spoke for the first time, his voice cold and harsh, level, without emphasis: "I aim to. I don't figure to stay in a country among people who . . ." he said something unprintable and vile, addressed to no one.

"That'll do," the Justice said. "Take your wagon and get out of this country before dark. Case dismissed."

His father turned, and he followed the stiff black coat, the wiry figure   15
walking a little stiffly from where a Confederate provost's man's musket ball had taken him in the heel on a stolen horse thirty years ago, followed the two backs now, since his older brother had appeared from somewhere in the crowd, no taller than the father but thicker, chewing tobacco steadily, between the two lines of grim-faced men and out of the store and across the worn gallery and down the sagging steps and among the dogs and half-grown boys in the mild May dust, where as he passed a voice hissed:

"Barn burner!"

Again he could not see, whirling; there was a face in a red haze, moonlike, bigger than the full moon, the owner of it half again his size, he leaping in the red haze toward the face, feeling no blow, feeling no shock when his head struck the earth, scrabbling up and leaping again, feeling no blow this time either and tasting no blood, scrabbling up to see the other boy in full flight and himself already leaping into pursuit as his father's hand jerked him back, the harsh, cold voice speaking above him: "Go get in the wagon."

It stood in a grove of locusts and mulberries across the road. His two hulking sisters in their Sunday dresses and his mother and her sister in calico and sunbonnets were already in it, sitting on and among the sorry residue of the dozen and more movings which even the boy could remember—the battered stove, the broken beds and chairs, the clock inlaid with mother-of-pearl, which would not run, stopped at some fourteen minutes past two o'clock of a dead and forgotten day and time, which had been his mother's dowry. She was crying, though when she saw him she drew her sleeve across her face and began to descend from the wagon. "Get back," the father said.

"He's hurt. I got to get some water and wash his . . ."

"Get back in the wagon," his father said. He got in too, over the tail-gate. 20 His father mounted to the seat where the older brother already sat and struck the gaunt mules two savage blows with the peeled willow, but without heat. It was not even sadistic; it was exactly that same quality which in later years would cause his descendants to over-run the engine before putting a motor car into motion, striking and reining back in the same movement. The wagon went on, the store with its quiet crowd of grimly watching men dropped behind; a curve in the road hid it. *Forever* he thought. *Maybe he's done satisfied now, now that he has* . . . stopping himself, not to say it aloud even to himself. His mother's hand touched his shoulder.

"Does hit hurt?" she said.

"Naw," he said. "Hit don't hurt. Lemme be."

"Can't you wipe some of the blood off before hit dries?"

"I'll wash to-night," he said. "Lemme be, I tell you."

The wagon went on. He did not know where they were going. None of 25 them ever did or ever asked, because it was always somewhere, always a house of sorts waiting for them a day or two days or even three days away. Likely his father had already arranged to make a crop on another farm before he . . . Again he had to stop himself. He (the father) always did. There was something about his wolflike independence and even courage when the advantage was at least neutral which impressed strangers, as if they got from his latent ravening ferocity not so much a sense of dependability as a feeling that his ferocious conviction in the rightness of his own actions would be of advantage to all whose interest lay with his.

That night they camped, in a grove of oaks and beeches where a spring ran. The nights were still cool and they had a fire against it, of a rail lifted from a nearby fence and cut into lengths—a small fire, neat, niggard almost, a shrewd fire; such fires were his father's habit and custom always, even in freezing weather. Older, the boy might have remarked this and wondered why not a big one; why should not a man who had not only seen the waste and extravagance of war, but who had in his blood an inherent voracious prodigality with material not his own, have burned everything in sight? Then he might have gone a step farther and thought that that was the reason: that niggard blaze was the living fruit of nights passed during those four years in the woods hiding from all men, blue or gray, with his strings of horses (captured horses, he called them). And older still, he might have divined the true reason: that the element of fire spoke to some deep mainspring of his father's being, as the element of steel or of powder spoke to other men, as the one weapon for the preservation of integrity, else breath were not worth the breathing, and hence to be regarded with respect and used with discretion.

But he did not think this now and he had seen those same niggard blazes all his life. He merely ate his supper beside it and was already half asleep over his iron plate when his father called him, and once more he followed the stiff back, the stiff and ruthless limp, up the slope and on to the starlit road where, turning, he could see his father against the stars but without face or depth—a shape black, flat, and bloodless as though cut from tin in the iron folds of the frockcoat which had not been made for him, the voice harsh like tin and without heat like tin:

"You were fixing to tell them. You would have told him." He didn't answer. His father struck him with the flat of his hand on the side of the head, hard but without heat, exactly as he had struck the two mules at the store, exactly as he would strike either of them with any stick in order to kill a horse fly, his voice still without heat or anger: "You're getting to be a man. You got to learn. You got to learn to stick to your own blood or you ain't going to have any blood to stick to you. Do you think either of them, any man there this morning, would? Don't you know all they wanted was a chance to get at me because they knew I had them beat? Eh?" Later, twenty years later, he was to tell himself, "If I had said they wanted only truth, justice, he would have hit me again." But now he said nothing. He was not crying. He just stood there. "Answer me," his father said.

"Yes," he whispered. His father turned.

"Get on to bed. We'll be there tomorrow."   30

To-morrow they were there. In the early afternoon the wagon stopped before a paintless two-room house identical almost with the dozen others it had stopped before even in the boy's ten years, and again, as on the other dozen occasions, his mother and aunt got down and began to unload the wagon, although his two sisters and his father and brother had not moved.

"Likely hit ain't fitten for hawgs," one of the sisters said.

"Nevertheless, fit it will and you'll hog it and like it," his father said. "Get out of them chairs and help your Ma unload."

The two sisters got down, big, bovine, in a flutter of cheap ribbons; one of them drew from the jumbled wagon bed a battered lantern, the other a worn broom. His father handed the reins to the older son and began to climb stiffly over the wheel. "When they get unloaded, take the team to the barn and feed them." Then he said, and at first the boy thought he was still speaking to his brother: "Come with me."

"Me?" he said.   35

"Yes," his father said. "You."

"Abner," his mother said. His father paused and looked back—the harsh level stare beneath the shaggy, graying, irascible brows.

"I reckon I'll have a word with the man that aims to begin to-morrow owning me body and soul for the next eight months."

They went back up the road. A week ago—or before last night, that is—he would have asked where they were going, but not now. His father had struck him before last night but never before had he paused afterward to explain why; it was as if the blow and the following calm, outrageous voice still rang, repercussed, divulging nothing to him save the terrible handicap of being young, the light weight of his few years, just heavy enough to prevent his soaring free of the world as it seemed to be ordered but not heavy enough to keep him footed solid in it, to resist it and try to change the course of its events.

Presently he could see the grove of oaks and cedars and the other flower- 40 ing trees and shrubs where the house would be, though not the house yet. They walked beside a fence massed with honeysuckle and Cherokee roses and came to a gate swinging open between two brick pillars, and now, beyond a sweep of drive, he saw the house for the first time and at that instant he forgot his father and the terror and despair both, and even when he remembered his father again (who had not stopped) the terror and despair did not return. Because, for all the twelve movings, they had sojourned until now in a poor country, a land of small farms and fields and houses, and he had never seen a house like this before. *Hit's big as a courthouse* he thought quietly, with a surge of peace and joy whose reason he could not have thought into words, being too young for that: *They are safe from him. People whose lives are a part of this peace and dignity are beyond his touch, he no more to them than a buzzing wasp: capable of stinging for a little moment but that's all; the spell of this peace and dignity rendering even the barns and stable and cribs which belong to it impervious to the puny flames he might contrive* . . . this, the peace and joy, ebbing for an instant as he looked again at the stiff black back, the stiff and implacable limp of the figure which was not dwarfed by the house, for the reason that it had never looked big anywhere and which now, against the serene columned backdrop, had more than ever that impervious quality of something cut ruthlessly from tin, depthless, as though, sidewise to the sun, it would cast no shadow. Watching him, the boy remarked the absolutely undeviating course which his father held and saw the stiff foot come squarely down in a pile of fresh droppings where a horse had stood in the drive and which his father could have avoided by a simple change of stride. But it ebbed only for a moment, though he could not have thought this into words either, walking on in the spell of the house, which he could even want but without envy, without sorrow, certainly never with that ravening and jealous rage which unknown to him walked in the ironlike black coat before him: *Maybe he will feel it too. Maybe it will even change him now from what maybe he couldn't help but be.*

They crossed the portico. Now he could hear his father's stiff foot as it came down on the boards with clocklike finality, a sound out of all proportion to the displacement of the body it bore and which was not dwarfed either by the white door before it, as though it had attained to a sort of vicious and ravening minimum not to be dwarfed by anything—the flat, wide, black hat, the formal coat of broadcloth which had once been black but which had now that friction-glazed greenish cast of the bodies of old house flies, the lifted sleeve which was too large, the lifted hand like a curled claw. The door opened so promptly that the boy knew the Negro must have been watching them all the time, an old man with neat grizzled hair, in a linen jacket, who stood barring the door with his body, saying, "Wipe yo foots, white man, fo you come in here. Major ain't home nohow."

"Get out of my way, nigger," his father said, without heat too, flinging the door back and the Negro also and entering, his hat still on his head. And now the boy saw the prints of the stiff foot on the doorjamb and saw them appear on the pale rug behind the machinelike deliberation of the foot which seemed to bear (or transmit) twice the weight which the body compassed. The Negro was shouting "Miss Lula! Miss Lula!" somewhere behind them, then the boy, deluged as though by a warm wave by a suave turn of carpeted stair and a pendant glitter of chandeliers and a mute gleam of gold frames, heard the swift feet and saw her too, a lady—perhaps he had never seen her like before either—in a gray, smooth gown with lace at the throat and an apron tied at the waist and the sleeves turned back, wiping cake or biscuit dough from her hands with a towel as she came up the hall, looking not at his father at all but at the tracks on the blond rug with an expression of incredulous amazement.

"I tried," the Negro cried. "I tole him to . . ."

"Will you please go away?" she said in a shaking voice. "Major de Spain is not at home. Will you please go away?"

His father had not spoken again. He did not speak again. He did not even   45 look at her. He just stood stiff in the center of the rug, in his hat, the shaggy iron-gray brows twitching slightly above the pebble-colored eyes as he appeared to examine the house with brief deliberation. Then with the same deliberation he turned; the boy watched him pivot on the good leg and saw the stiff foot drag round the arc of the turning, leaving a final long and fading smear. His father never looked at it, he never once looked down at the rug. The Negro held the door. It closed behind them, upon the hysteric and indistinguishable woman-wail. His father stopped at the top of the steps and scraped his boot clean on the edge of it. At the gate he stopped again. He stood for a moment, planted stiffly on the stiff foot, looking back at the house. "Pretty and white, ain't it?" he said. "That's sweat. Nigger sweat. Maybe it ain't white enough yet to suit him. Maybe he wants to mix some white sweat with it."

Two hours later the boy was chopping wood behind the house within which his mother and aunt and the two sisters (the mother and aunt, not the two girls, he knew that; even at this distance and muffled by walls the flat loud voices of the two girls emanated an incorrigible idle inertia) were setting up the stove to prepare a meal, when he heard the hooves and saw the linen-clad man on a fine sorrel mare, whom he recognized even before he saw the rolled rug in front of the Negro youth following on a fat bay carriage horse—a suffused, angry face vanishing, still at full gallop, beyond the corner of the house where his father and brother were sitting in the two tilted chairs; and a moment later, almost before he could have put the axe down, he heard the hooves again and watched the sorrel mare go back out of the yard, already galloping again. Then his father began to shout one of the sisters' names, who presently emerged backward from the kitchen door dragging the rolled rug along the ground by one end while the other sister walked behind it.

"If you ain't going to tote, go on and set up the wash pot," the first said.

"You, Sarty!" the second shouted. "Set up the wash pot!" His father appeared at the door, framed against that shabbiness, as he had been against that other bland perfection, impervious to either, the mother's anxious face at his shoulder.

"Go on," the father said. "Pick it up." The two sisters stooped, broad, lethargic; stooping, they presented an incredible expanse of pale cloth and a flutter of tawdry ribbons.

"If I thought enough of a rug to have to git hit all the way from France I 50 wouldn't keep hit where folks coming in would have to tromp on hit," the first said. They raised the rug.

"Abner," the mother said. "Let me do it."

"You go back and git dinner," his father said. "I'll tend to this."

From the woodpile through the rest of the afternoon the boy watched them, the rug spread flat in the dust beside the bubbling wash-pot, the two sisters stooping over it with that profound and lethargic reluctance, while the father stood over them in turn, implacable and grim, driving them though never raising his voice again. He could smell the harsh homemade lye they were using; he saw his mother come to the door once and look toward them with an expression not anxious now but very like despair; he saw his father turn, and he fell to with the axe and saw from the corner of his eye his father raise from the ground a flattish fragment of field stone and examine it and return to the pot, and this time his mother actually spoke: "Abner. Abner. Please don't. Please, Abner."

Then he was done too. It was dusk; the whippoorwills had already begun. He could smell coffee from the room where they would presently eat the cold food remaining from the mid-afternoon meal, though when he entered the house he realized they were having coffee again probably because there was a fire on the hearth, before which the rug now lay spread over the backs of the two chairs. The tracks of his father's foot were gone. Where they had been were now long, water-cloudy scoriations resembling the sporadic course of a lilliputian mowing machine.

It still hung there while they ate the cold food and then went to bed, scat- 55 tered without order or claim up and down the two rooms, his mother in one bed, where his father would later lie, the older brother in the other, himself, the aunt, and the two sisters on pallets on the floor. But his father was not in bed yet. The last thing the boy remembered was the depthless, harsh silhouette of the hat and coat bending over the rug and it seemed to him that he had not even closed his eyes when the silhouette was standing over him, the fire almost dead behind it, the stiff foot prodding him awake. "Catch up the mule," his father said.

When he returned with the mule his father was standing in the black door, the rolled rug over his shoulder. "Ain't you going to ride?" he said.

"No. Give me your foot."

He bent his knee into his father's hand, the wiry, surprising power flowed smoothly, rising, he rising with it, on to the mule's bare back (they had owned a saddle once; the boy could remember it though not when or where) and with the same effortlessness his father swung the rug up in front of him. Now in the starlight they retraced the afternoon's path, up the dusty road rife with honeysuckle, through the gate and up the black tunnel of the drive to the lightless house, where he sat on the mule and felt the rough warp of the rug drag across his thighs and vanish.

"Don't you want me to help?" he whispered. His father did not answer and now he heard again that stiff foot striking the hollow portico with that wooden and clocklike deliberation, that outrageous overstatement of the weight it carried. The rug, hunched, not flung (the boy could tell that even in the darkness) from his father's shoulder, struck the angle of wall and floor with a sound unbelievably loud, thunderous, then the foot again, unhurried and enormous; a light came on in the house and the boy sat, tense, breathing steadily and quietly and just a little fast, though the foot itself did not increase its beat at all, descending the steps now; now the boy could see him.

"Don't you want to ride now?" he whispered. "We kin both ride now,"   60
the light within the house altering now, flaring up and sinking. *He's coming down the stairs now*, he thought. He had already ridden the mule up beside the horse block; presently his father was up behind him and he doubled the reins over and slashed the mule across the neck, but before the animal could begin to trot the hard, thin arm came round him, the hard, knotted hand jerking the mule back to a walk.

In the first red rays of the sun they were in the lot, putting plow gear on the mules. This time the sorrel mare was in the lot before he heard it at all, the rider collarless and even bareheaded, trembling, speaking in a shaking voice as the woman in the house had done, his father merely looking up once before stooping again to the hame he was buckling, so that the man on the mare spoke to his stooping back:

"You must realize you have ruined that rug. Wasn't there anybody here, any of your women . . ." he ceased, shaking, the boy watching him, the older brother leaning now in the stable door, chewing, blinking slowly and steadily at nothing apparently. "It cost a hundred dollars. But you never had a hundred dollars. You never will. So I'm going to charge you twenty bushels of corn against your crop. I'll add it in your contract and when you come to the commissary you can sign it. That won't keep Mrs. de Spain quiet but maybe it will teach you to wipe your feet off before you enter her house again."

Then he was gone. The boy looked at his father, who still had not spoken or even looked up again, who was now adjusting the logger-head in the hame.

"Pap," he said. His father looked at him—the inscrutable face, the shaggy brows beneath which the gray eyes glinted coldly. Suddenly the boy went toward him, fast, stopping as suddenly. "You done the best you could!" he cried. "If he wanted hit done different why didn't he wait and tell you how? He won't git no twenty bushels! He won't git none! We'll gether hit and hide hit! I kin watch . . ."

"Did you put the cutter back in that straight stock like I told you?"   65
"No, sir," he said.
"Then go do it."
That was Wednesday. During the rest of that week he worked steadily, at

what was within his scope and some which was beyond it, with an industry that did not need to be driven nor even commanded twice; he had this from his mother, with the difference that some at least of what he did he liked to do, such as splitting wood with the half-size axe which his mother and aunt had earned, or saved money somehow, to present him with at Christmas. In company with the two older women (and on one afternoon, even one of the sisters), he built pens for the shoat and the cow which were a part of his father's contract with the landlord, and one afternoon, his father being absent, gone somewhere on one of the mules, he went to the field.

They were running a middle buster now, his brother holding the plow straight while he handled the reins, and walking beside the straining mule, the rich black soil shearing cool and damp against his bare ankles, he thought *Maybe this is the end of it. Maybe even that twenty bushels that seems hard to have to pay for just a rug will be a cheap price for him to stop forever and always from being what he used to be;* thinking, dreaming now, so that his brother had to speak sharply to him to mind the mule: *Maybe he even won't collect the twenty bushels. Maybe it will all add up and balance and vanish—corn, rug, fire; the terror and grief, the being pulled two ways like between two teams of horses—gone, done with for ever and ever.*

Then it was Saturday; he looked up from beneath the mule he was har-   70
nessing and saw his father in the black coat and hat. "Not that," his father said. "The wagon gear." And then, two hours later, sitting in the wagon bed behind his father and brother on the seat, the wagon accomplished a final curve, and he saw the weathered paintless store with its tattered tobacco- and patent-medicine posters and the tethered wagons and saddle animals below the gallery. He mounted the gnawed steps behind his father and brother, and there again was the lane of quiet, watching faces for the three of them to walk through. He saw the man in spectacles sitting at the plank table and he did not need to be told this was a Justice of the Peace; he sent one glare of fierce, exultant, partisan defiance at the man in collar and cravat now, whom he had seen but twice before in his life, and that on a galloping horse, who now wore on his face an expression not of rage but of amazed unbelief which the boy could not have known was at the incredible circumstance of being sued by one of his own tenants, and came and stood against his father and cried at the Justice: "He ain't done it! He ain't burnt . . ."

"Go back to the wagon," his father said.

"Burnt?" the Justice said. "Do I understand this rug was burned too?"

"Does anybody here claim it was?" his father said. "Go back to the wagon." But he did not, he merely retreated to the rear of the room, crowded as that other had been, but not to sit down this time, instead, to stand pressing among the motionless bodies, listening to the voices:

"And you claim twenty bushels of corn is too high for the damage you did to the rug?"

"He brought the rug to me and said he wanted the tracks washed out of   75
it. I washed the tracks out and took the rug back to him."

"But you didn't carry the rug back to him in the same condition it was in before you made the tracks on it."

His father did not answer, and now for perhaps half a minute there was no sound at all save that of breathing, the faint, steady suspiration of complete and intent listening.

"You decline to answer that, Mr. Snopes?" Again his father did not answer. "I'm going to find against you, Mr. Snopes. I'm going to find that you were responsible for the injury to Major de Spain's rug and hold you liable for it. But twenty bushels of corn seems a little high for a man in your circumstances to have to pay. Major de Spain claims it cost a hundred dollars. October corn will be worth about fifty cents. I figure that if Major de Spain can stand a ninety-five-dollar loss on something he paid cash for, you can stand a five-dollar loss you haven't earned yet. I hold you in damages to Major de Spain to the amount of ten bushels of corn over and above your contract with him, to be paid to him out of your crop at gathering time. Court adjourned."

It had taken no time hardly, the morning was but half begun. He thought they would return home and perhaps back to the field, since they were late, far behind all other farmers. But instead his father passed on behind the wagon, merely indicating with his hand for the older brother to follow with it, and crossed the road toward the blacksmith shop opposite, pressing on after his father, overtaking him, speaking, whispering up at the harsh, calm face beneath the weathered hat: "He won't git no ten bushels neither. He won't git one. We'll . . . ." until his father glanced for an instant down at him, the face absolutely calm, the grizzled eyebrows tangled above the cold eyes, the voice almost pleasant, almost gentle:

"You think so? Well, we'll wait till October anyway." 80

The matter of the wagon—the setting of a spoke or two and the tightening of the tires—did not take long either, the business of the tires accomplished by driving the wagon into the spring branch behind the shop and letting it stand there, the mules nuzzling into the water from time to time, and the boy on the seat with the idle reins, looking up the slope and through the sooty tunnel of the shed where the slow hammer rang and where his father sat on an upended cypress bolt, easily, either talking or listening, still sitting there when the boy brought the dripping wagon up out of the branch and halted it before the door.

"Take them on to the shade and hitch," his father said. He did so and returned. His father and the smith and a third man squatting on his heels inside the door were talking, about crops and animals; the boy, squatting too in the ammoniac dust and hoof-parings and scales of rust, heard his father tell a long and unhurried story out of the time before the birth of the older brother even when he had been a professional horsetrader. And then his father came up beside him where he stood before a tattered last year's circus poster on the other side of the store, gazing rapt and quiet at the scarlet horses, the incredible poisings and convolutions of tulle and tights and the painted leers of comedians, and said, "It's time to eat."

But not at home. Squatting beside his brother against the front wall, he watched his father emerge from the store and produce from a paper sack a segment of cheese and divide it carefully and deliberately into three with his pocket knife and produce crackers from the same sack. They all three squatted on the gallery and ate, slowly, without talking; then in the store again, they drank from a tin dipper tepid water smelling of the cedar bucket and of living beech trees. And still they did not go home. It was a horse lot this time, a tall rail fence upon and along which men stood and sat and out of which one by one horses were led, to be walked and trotted and then cantered back and forth along the road while the slow swapping and buying went on and the sun began to slant westward, they—the three of them—watching and listening, the older brother with his muddy eyes and his steady, inevitable tobacco, the father commenting now and then on certain of the animals, to no one in particular.

It was after sundown when they reached home. They ate supper by lamplight, then, sitting on the doorstep, the boy watched the night fully accomplish, listening to the whippoorwills and the frogs, when he heard his mother's voice: "Abner! No! No! Oh, God. Oh, God. Abner!" and he rose, whirled, and saw the altered light through the door where a candle stub now burned in a bottle neck on the table and his father, still in the hat and coat, at once formal and burlesque as though dressed carefully for some shabby and ceremonial violence, emptying the reservoir of the lamp back into the five-gallon kerosene can from which it had been filled, while the mother tugged at his arm until he shifted the lamp to the other hand and flung her back, not savagely or viciously, just hard, into the wall, her hands flung out against the wall for balance, her mouth open and in her face the same quality of hopeless despair as had been in her voice. Then his father saw him standing in the door.

"Go to the barn and get that can of oil we were oiling the wagon with," he said. The boy did not move. Then he could speak.   85

"What . . ." he cried. "What are you . . ."

"Go get that oil," his father said. "Go."

Then he was moving, running, outside the house, toward the stable: this is the old habit, the old blood which he had not been permitted to choose for himself, which had been bequeathed him willy nilly and which had run for so long (and who knew where, battening on what of outrage and savagery and lust) before it came to him. *I could keep on*, he thought. *I could run on and on and never look back, never need to see his face again. Only I can't. I can't*, the rusted can in his hand now, the liquid sploshing in it as he ran back to the house and into it, into the sound of his mother's weeping in the next room, and handed the can to his father.

"Ain't you going to even send a nigger?" he cried. "At least you sent a nigger before!"

This time his father didn't strike him. The hand came even faster than the   90 blow had, the same hand which had set the can on the table with almost excruciating care flashing from the can toward him too quick for him to follow it, gripping him by the back of his shirt and on to tiptoe before he had seen it quit the can, the face stooping at him in breathless and frozen ferocity, the cold, dead voice speaking over him to the older brother who leaned against the table, chewing with that steady, curious, sidewise motion of cows:

"Empty the can into the big one and go on. I'll catch up with you."

"Better tie him up to the bedpost," the brother said.

"Do like I told you," the father said. Then the boy was moving, his bunched shirt and the hard, bony hand between his shoulder-blades, his toes just touching the floor, across the room and into the other one, past the sisters sitting with spread heavy thighs in the two chairs over the cold hearth, and to where his mother and aunt sat side by side on the bed, the aunt's arms about his mother's shoulders.

"Hold him," the father said. The aunt made a startled movement. "Not you," the father said. "Lennie. Take hold of him. I want to see you do it." His mother took him by the wrist. "You'll hold him better than that. If he gets loose don't you know what he is going to do? He will go up yonder." He jerked his head toward the road. "Maybe I'd better tie him."

"I'll hold him," his mother whispered.   95

"See you do then." Then his father was gone, the stiff foot heavy and measured upon the boards, ceasing at last.

Then he began to struggle. His mother caught him in both arms, he jerking and wrenching at them. He would be stronger in the end, he knew that. But he had no time to wait for it. "Lemme go!" he cried. "I don't want to have to hit you!"

"Let him go!" the aunt said. "If he don't go, before God, I am going there myself!"

"Don't you see I can't!" his mother cried. "Sarty! Sarty! No! No! Help me, Lizzie!"

Then he was free. His aunt grasped at him but it was too late. He whirled,   100
running, his mother stumbled forward on to her knees behind him, crying to the nearer sister: "Catch him, Net! Catch him!" But that was too late too, the sister (the sisters were twins, born at the same time, yet either of them now gave the impression of being, encompassing as much living meat and volume and weight as any other two of the family) not yet having begun to rise from the chair, her head, face, alone merely turned, presenting to him in the flying instant an astonishing expanse of young female features untroubled by any surprise even, wearing only an expression of bovine interest. Then he was out of the room, out of the house, in the mild dust of the starlit road and the heavy rifeness of honeysuckle, the pale ribbon unspooling with terrific slowness under his running feet, reaching the gate at last and turning in, running, his heart and lungs drumming, on up the drive toward the lighted house, the lighted door. He did not knock, he burst in, sobbing for breath, incapable for the moment of speech; he saw the astonished face of the Negro in the linen jacket without knowing when the Negro had appeared.

"De Spain!" he cried, panted. "Where's . . ." then he saw the white man too emerging from a white door down the hall. "Barn!" he cried. "Barn!"

"What?" the white man said. "Barn?"

"Yes!" the boy cried. "Barn!"

"Catch him!" the white man shouted.

But it was too late this time too. The Negro grasped his shirt, but the en-   105
tire sleeve, rotten with washing, carried away, and he was out that door too

and in the drive again, and had actually never ceased to run even while he was screaming into the white man's face.

Behind him the white man was shouting, "My horse! Fetch my horse!" and he thought for an instant of cutting across the park and climbing the fence into the road, but he did not know the park nor how high the vine-massed fence might be and he dared not risk it. So he ran on down the drive, blood and breath roaring; presently he was in the road again though he could not see it. He could not hear either: the galloping mare was almost upon him before he heard her, and even then he held his course, as if the very urgency of his wild grief and need must in a moment more find him wings, waiting until the ultimate instant to hurl himself aside and into the weed-choked roadside ditch as the horse thundered past and on, for an instant in furious silhouette against the stars, the tranquil early summer night sky which, even before the shape of the horse and rider vanished, stained abruptly and violently upward: a long, swirling roar incredible and soundless, blotting the stars, and he springing up and into the road again, running again, knowing it was too late yet still running even after he heard the shot and, an instant later, two shots, pausing now without knowing he had ceased to run, crying "Pap! Pap!", running again before he knew he had begun to run, stumbling, tripping over something and scrabbling up again without ceasing to run, looking backward over his shoulder at the glare as he got up, running on among the invisible trees, panting, sobbing, "Father! Father!"

At midnight he was sitting on the crest of a hill. He did not know it was midnight and he did not know how far he had come. But there was no glare behind him now and he sat now, his back toward what he had called home for four days anyhow, his face toward the dark woods which he would enter when breath was strong again, small, shaking steadily in the chill darkness, hugging himself into the remainder of his thin, rotten shirt, the grief and despair now no longer terror and fear but just grief and despair. *Father. My father,* he thought. "He was brave!" he cried suddenly, aloud but not loud, no more than a whisper: "He was! He was in the war! He was in Colonel Sartoris' cav'ry!" not knowing that his father had gone to that war a private in the fine old European sense, wearing no uniform, admitting the authority of and giving fidelity to no man or army or flag, going to war as Malbrouck himself did: for booty—it meant nothing and less than nothing to him if it were enemy booty or his own.

The slow constellations wheeled on. It would be dawn and then sun-up after a while and he would be hungry. But that would be to-morrow and now he was only cold, and walking would cure that. His breathing was easier now and he decided to get up and go on, and then he found that he had been asleep because he knew it was almost dawn, the night almost over. He could tell that from the whippoorwills. They were everywhere now among the dark trees below him, constant and inflectioned and ceaseless, so that, as the instant for giving over to the day birds drew nearer and nearer, there was no interval at all between them. He got up. He was a little stiff, but walking would cure that too as it would the cold, and soon there would be the sun. He went on down the hill, toward the dark woods within which the liquid silver voices of the birds called unceasing—the rapid and urgent beating of the urgent and quiring heart of the late spring night. He did not look back.

∽∾∿

CHESTER HIMES

Lunching at the Ritzmore   *(1942)*

If you have ever been to the beautiful city of Los Angeles, you will know that Pershing Square, a palm-shaded spot in the center of downtown, is the mecca of the motley. Here, a short walk up from 'Skid Row,' on the green-painted benches flanking the crisscrossed sidewalks, is haven for men of all races, all creeds, all nationalities, and of all stages of deterioration—drifters and hop-heads and tbs' and beggars and bums and bindle-stiffs and big sisters, clipped and clippers, fraternizing with the tired business men from nearby offices, with students from various universities, with the strutting Filipinos, the sharp-cat Mexican youths in their ultra drapes, with the colored guys from out South Central way.

It is here the old men come to meditate in the warm midday sun, and watch the hustle and bustle of the passing younger world; here the job seekers with packed bags wait to be singled out for work; here the hunters relax and the hunted keep vigil. It is here you will find your man, for a game of pool, for a game of murder.

Along the Hill Street side buses going west line up one behind the other to take you out to Wilshire, to Beverly Hills, to Hollywood, to Santa Monica, to Westwood, to the Valley; and the red cards and the yellow cars fill the street with clatter and clang. On the Fifth Street side a pale pink skyscraper overlooks a lesser structure of aquamarine, southern California architecture on the pastel side; and along Sixth Street there are various shops and perhaps an office building which you would not notice unless you had business there.

But you would notice the Ritzmore, swankiest of West Coast hotels, standing in solid distinction along the Olive Street side, particularly if you were hungry in Pershing Square. You would watch footmen opening doors of limousines and doormen escorting patrons underneath the marquee across the width of sidewalk to the brass and mahogany doorway, and you would see hands of other doormen extended from within to hold wide the glass doors so that the patrons could make an unhampered entrance. And after that, if your views leaned a little to the Left, which they likely would if you were hungry in Pershing Square, you would spit on the sidewalk and resume your discussion, your boisterous and heated and surprisingly-often very well-versed discussion, on defense, or on the army, or the navy, or that 'rat' Hitler, or 'them Japs,' or the F.B.I., or the 'so and so' owners of Lockheed, or that (unprintable) Aimee Semple McPherson; on history and geography, on life and death; and you would just ignore the 'fat sonsaguns' who entered the Ritzmore.

On this particular day, a discussion which had begun on the Soviet Union   5 had developed into an argument on discrimination against Negroes, and a young University of Southern California student from Vermont stated flatly that he did not believe Negroes were discriminated against at all.

'If you would draw your conclusions from investigation instead of from agitation, you would find that most of the discrimination against Negroes exists only in communistic literature distributed by the Communist Party for organizational purposes,' he went on. 'As a matter of plain and simple fact, I have yet to visit a place where Negroes could not go. In fact, I think I've seen Negroes in every place I've ever been—hotels, theatres, concerts, operas . . .'

'Yass, and I bet they were working there, too,' another young fellow, a drifter from Chicago, argued. 'Listen, boy, I'm telling you, and I'm telling you straight, Negroes are out in this country. They can't get no work and they can't go nowhere, and that's a dirty shame for there're a lot of good Negroes, a lot of Negroes just as good as you and me.'

Surveying the drifter from head to foot, his unshaven face, his shabby unpressed suit, his run-over, unpolished shoes, the student replied, 'Frankly, that wouldn't make them any super race.'

'Huh?'

'However, that is beside the point,' the student continued, smiling. 'The point is that most of what you term discrimination is simply a matter of taste, of personal likes and dislikes. For instance, if I don't like you, should I have to put up with your presence? No, why should I? But this agitation about Negroes being discriminated against by the Army and Navy and defense industries and being refused service by hotels and restaurants is just so much bosh.'

'Are you kidding me, fellow?' the drifter asked suspiciously, giving the student a sharp look, 'Or are you just plain dumb? Say, listen— ' and then he spied a Negro at the edge of the group. 'Say, here's a colored fellow now; I suppose he knows whether he's being discriminated against or not.'

'Not necessarily,' the student murmured.

Ignoring him, the drifter called, 'Hey, mister, you mind settling a little argument for us.'

The Negro, a young brown-skinned fellow of medium build with regular features and a small mustache, pushed to the center of the group. He wore a pair of corduroy trousers and a slip-over sweater with a sport shirt underneath.

'Say, mister, I been tryna tell this schoolboy—' the drifter began, but the Negro interrupted him, 'I know, I heard you.'

Turning to the student, he said, 'I don't know whether you're kidding or not, fellow, but it ain't no kidding matter with me. Here I am, a mechanic, a good mechanic, and they're supposed to be needing mechanics everywhere. But can I get a job—no! I gotta stand down here and listen to guys like you make a joke out of it while the government is crying for mechanics in defense.'

'I'm not making a joke out of it,' the student stated. 'If what you say is true, I'm truly sorry, mister; it's just hard for me to believe it.'

'Listen, schoolboy,' the drifter said, 'I'll tell you what I'll do with you; I'll just bet you a dollar this boy—this man—can't eat in any of these restaurants downtown. I'll just bet you a dollar.'

Now that a bet had been offered, the ten or twelve fellows crowded about who had remained silent out of respect for the Negro's feelings, egged it on, 'All right, schoolboy, put up or shut up!'

'Well, if it's all right with you, mister,' the student addressed the Ne-   20
gro, 'I'll just take this young man up on that bet. But how are we going to determine?'

They went into a huddle and after a moment decided to let the Negro enter any restaurant of his choice, and if he should be refused service the student would pay off the bet and treat the three of them to dinners on Central Avenue; but should he be served, the check would be on the drifter.

So the three of them, the student, the Negro, and the drifter, started down Hill Street in search of a restaurant. The ten or twelve others of the original group fell in behind, and shortly fellows in other groups about the square looked up and saw the procession, and thinking someone was giving away something somewhere, hurried to get in line. Before they had progressed half the length of the block, more than a hundred of the raggedy bums of Pershing Square were following them.

The pedestrians stopped to see what the commotion was all about, adding to the congestion; and then the motorists noticed and slowed their cars. Soon almost a thousand people had congregated on the sidewalk and a jam of alarming proportions had halted traffic for several blocks. In time the policeman at the corner of Sixth and Hill awakened, and becoming aware of the mob, rushed forth to investigate. When he saw the long procession from the square, he charged the three in front who seemed to be the leaders, and shouted.

'Starting a riot, eh! Communist rally, eh! Where do you think you're going?'

'We're going to lunch,' the student replied congenially.   25

For an instant the policeman was startled out of his wits. 'Lunch?' His face went slack and his mouth hung open. Then he got himself under control. 'Lunch! What is this? I suppose all of you are going to lunch,' he added sarcastically.

The student looked about at the crowd, then looked back. 'I don't know,' he confessed. 'I'm only speaking for the three of us.'

Shoving back among the others, the policeman snarled, 'Now don't tell me that you're going to lunch, too?'

A big, raw-boned fellow in overalls spat a stream of tobacco juice on the grass, and replied, 'That's right.'

Red-faced and inarticulate, the policeman took off his hat and scratched   30
his head. Never in the six years since he had been directing traffic at Sixth and Hill had he seen anyone leave Pershing Square for lunch. In fact, it had never occurred to him that they ate lunch. It sounded incredible. He wanted to do something. He felt that it was his duty to do something. But what? He was in a dilemma. He could not hinder them from going to lunch, if indeed they were going to lunch. Nor could he order them to move on, as they were already moving on. There was nothing for him to do but follow. So he fell in and followed.

The Negro, however, could not make up his mind. On Sixth Street, midway between Hill and Olive, he came to a halt. 'Listen,' he pointed out, 'these guys are used to seeing colored people down here. All the domestic workers who work out in Hollywood and Beverly and all out there get off the U car and come down here and catch their buses. It ain't like if it was somewhere on the West Side where they ain't used to seeing them.'

'What has that got to do with it?' the student asked.

'Naw, what I mean is this,' he explained. 'They're liable to serve me around here. And then you're going to think it's like that all over the city. And I know it ain't.' Pausing for an instant, he added another point, 'And besides, if I walk in there with you two guys, they're liable to serve me anyway. For all they know you guys might be some rich guys and I might be working for you; and if they refuse to serve me they might get in dutch with you. It ain't like some place in Hollywood where they wouldn't care.'

When they had stopped, the procession behind them which by then reached around the corner down Hill Street had also stopped. This was the chance for which the policeman had been waiting. 'Move on!' he shouted. 'Don't block the sidewalk! What d'ya think this is?'

They all returned to the square and took up the argument where they had 35 dropped it. Only now, it was just one big mob in the center of the square, waiting for the Negro to make up his mind.

'You see, he doesn't want to do it,' the student was pointing out. 'That proves my point. They won't go into these places, but yet they say they're being discriminated against.'

Suddenly, the drifter was inspired. 'All right, I'll tell you, let's go to the Ritzmore.'

A hundred startled glances leveled on him, then lifted to the face of the brick and granite edifice across the street which seemed impregnated in rock-like respectability. The very audacity of the suggestion appealed to them. 'That's the place, let's go there,' they chimed.

'That's nonsense,' the student snapped angrily. 'He can't eat at the Ritzmore; he's not dressed correctly.'

'Can *you* eat there?' the Negro challenged. 'I mean just as you're dressed.' 40

The student was also clad in a sweater and trousers, although his were of a better quality and in better condition than the Negro's. For a moment he considered the question, then replied, 'To be fair, I don't know whether they would serve me or not. They might in the grill—'

'In the main dining room?' the drifter pressed.

Shaking his head, the student stated, 'I really don't know, but if they will serve any of us they will serve him.'

'Come on,' the drifter barked, taking the Negro by the arm, and they set forth for the Ritzmore, followed by every man in Pershing Square—the bindle-stiffs and the beggars and the bums and the big sisters, the clipped and the clippers, the old men who liked to sit in the midday sun and meditate.

Seeing them on the move again, the policeman hastened from his post to 45 follow.

They crossed Olive Street, a ragged procession of gaunt, unshaven, unwashed humanity, led by two young white men and one young Negro, passed
the two doormen, who, seeing the policeman among them, thought they were
all being taken to the clink. They approached the brass and mahogany doorway unchallenged, pushed open the glass doors, and entered the classical
splendor of the Ritzmore's main lounge.

Imagine the consternation among the well-bred, superbly clad, highly-
heeled patrons; imagine the indignity of the room clerk as he pounded on his
bell and yelled frantically, 'Front! Front! *Front!*' Had the furniture been animate, it would have fled in terror; and the fine Oriental rugs would have been
humiliated unendurably.

Outraged, the house officer rushed to halt this smelly mob, but seeing
among them the policeman, who by now had lost all capacity for speech,
stood with his mouth gaped open, wondering if perhaps it wasn't just the effects of that last brandy he had enjoyed in '217,' after all. Stupidly, he reached
out his hand to touch them to make certain they were real.

But before he could get his reflexes together, those in front had strolled
past him and entered the main dining room, while, what seemed to him like
thousands of others, pushed in from the street.

The student and the Negro and the drifter, along with ten or twelve oth-   50
ers, took seats at three vacant tables. In unison the diners turned one horrified
stare in their direction, and arose in posthaste, only to be blocked at the doorway by a shoving mass of men, struggling for a ringside view.

From all over the dining room the waiters ran stumbling toward the rear,
and went into a quick, alarmed huddle, turning every now and then to stare at
the group and then going into another huddle. The head waiter rushed from
the kitchen and joined the huddle; and then the *maître d'hotel* appeared and
took his place. One by one the cooks, the first cook and the second cook and
the third cook and the fourth cook on down to what seemed like the twenty-
fourth cook (although some of them must have been dishwashers), stuck their
heads through the pantry doorway and stared for a moment and then retired.

Finally, two waiters timidly advanced toward the tables and took their orders. Menus were passed about. 'You order first,' the student said to the Negro. However, as the menus were composed mostly of French words, the
Negro could not identify anything but apple pie. So he ordered apple pie.

'I'll take apple pie, too,' the student said; and the drifter muttered, 'Make
mine the same.'

Every one ordered apple pie.

One of the fellows standing in the doorway called back to those in the   55
lobby who could not see.

'They served him.'

'Did they serve him?'

'Yeah, they served him.'

'What did they serve him?'

'Apple pie.'   60

And it was thus proved by the gentlemen of Pershing Square that no discrimination exists in the beautiful city of Los Angeles. However, it so hap-

pened that the drifter was without funds, and the student found himself in the peculiar situation of having to pay off a bet which he had won.

HISAYE YAMAMOTO

Seventeen Syllables (1949)

The first Rosie knew that her mother had taken to writing poems was one evening when she finished one and read it aloud for her daughter's approval. It was about cats, and Rosie pretended to understand it thoroughly and appreciate it no end, partly because she hesitated to disillusion her mother about the quantity and quality of Japanese she had learned in all the years now that she had been going to Japanese school every Saturday (and Wednesday, too, in the summer). Even so, her mother must have been skeptical about the depth of Rosie's understanding, because she explained afterwards about the kind of poem she was trying to write.

See, Rosie, she said, it was a *haiku*, a poem in which she must pack all her meaning into seventeen syllables only, which were divided into three lines of five, seven, and five syllables. In the one she had just read, she had tried to capture the charm of a kitten, as well as comment on the superstition that owning a cat of three colors meant good luck.

"Yes, yes, I understand. How utterly lovely," Rosie said, and her mother, either satisfied or seeing through the deception and resigned, went back to composing.

The truth was that Rosie was lazy; English lay ready on the tongue but Japanese had to be searched for and examined, and even then put forth tentatively (probably to meet with laughter). It was so much easier to say yes, yes, even when one meant no, no. Besides, this was what was in her mind to say: I was looking through one of your magazines from Japan last night, Mother, and towards the back I found some *haiku* in English that delighted me. There was one that made me giggle off and on until I fell asleep—

It is morning, and lo!
I lie awake, comme il faut,
sighing for some dough.

Now, how to reach her mother, how to communicate the melancholy 5 song? Rosie knew formal Japanese by fits and starts, her mother had even less English, no French. It was much more possible to say yes, yes.

It developed that her mother was writing the *haiku* for a daily newspaper, the *Mainichi Shimbun*, that was published in San Francisco. Los Angeles, to be sure, was closer to the farming community in which the Hayashi family lived and several Japanese vernaculars were printed there, but Rosie's parents said they preferred the tone of the northern paper. Once a week, the *Mainichi* would have a section devoted to *haiku*, and her mother became an extravagant contributor, taking for herself the blossoming pen name, Ume Hanazono.

So Rosie and her father lived for a while with two women, her mother and Ume Hanazono. Her mother (Tome Hayashi by name) kept house, cooked, washed, and, along with her husband and the Carrascos, the Mexican family hired for the harvest, did her ample share of picking tomatoes out in the sweltering fields and boxing them in tidy strata in the cool packing shed. Ume Hanazono, who came to life after the dinner dishes were done, was an earnest, muttering stranger who often neglected speaking when spoken to and stayed busy at the parlor table as late as midnight scribbling with pencil on scratch paper or carefully copying characters on good paper with her fat, pale green Parker.

The new interest had some repercussions on the household routine. Before, Rosie had been accustomed to her parents and herself taking their hot baths early and going to bed almost immediately afterwards, unless her parents challenged each other to a game of flower cards or unless company dropped in. Now if her father wanted to play cards, he had to resort to solitaire (at which he always cheated fearlessly), and if a group of friends came over, it was bound to contain someone who was also writing *haiku*, and the small assemblage would be split in two, her father entertaining the non-literary members and her mother comparing ecstatic notes with the visiting poet.

If they went out, it was more of the same thing. But Ume Hanazono's life span, even for a poet's, was very brief—perhaps three months at most.

One night they went over to see the Hayano family in the neighboring   10
town to the west, an adventure both painful and attractive to Rosie. It was attractive because there were four Hayano girls, all lovely and each one named after a season of the year (Haru, Natsu, Aki, Fuyu), painful because something had been wrong with Mrs. Hayano ever since the birth of her first child. Rosie would sometimes watch Mrs. Hayano, reputed to have been the belle of her native village, making her way about a room, stooped, slowly shuffling, violently trembling (*always* trembling), and she would be reminded that this woman, in this same condition, had carried and given issue to three babies. She would look wonderingly at Mr. Hayano, handsome, tall, and strong, and she would look at her four pretty friends. But it was not a matter she could come to any decision about.

On this visit, however, Mrs. Hayano sat all evening in the rocker, as motionless and unobtrusive as it was possible for her to be, and Rosie found the greater part of the evening practically anaesthetic. Too, Rosie spent most of it in the girls' room, because Haru, the garrulous one, said almost as soon as the bows and other greetings were over, "Oh, you must see my new coat!"

It was a pale plaid of grey, sand, and blue, with an enormous collar, and Rosie, seeing nothing special in it, said, "Gee, how nice."

"Nice?" said Haru, indignantly. "Is that all you can say about it? It's gorgeous! And so cheap, too. Only seventeen-ninety-eight, because it was a sale. The saleslady said it was twenty-five dollars regular."

"Gee," said Rosie. Natsu, who never said much and when she said anything said it shyly, fingered the coat covetously and Haru pulled it away.

"Mine," she said, putting it on. She minced in the aisle between the two   15
large beds and smiled happily. "Let's see how your mother likes it."

She broke into the front room and the adult conversation and went to
stand in front of Rosie's mother, while the rest watched from the door. Rosie's
mother was properly envious. "May I inherit it when you're through with it?"

Haru, pleased, giggled and said yes, she could, but Natsu reminded
gravely from the door, "You promised me, Haru."

Everyone laughed but Natsu, who shamefacedly retreated into the bedroom. Haru came in laughing, taking off the coat. "We were only kidding,
Natsu," she said. "Here, you try it on now."

After Natsu buttoned herself into the coat, inspected herself solemnly in
the bureau mirror, and reluctantly shed it, Rosie, Aki, and Fuyu got their turns,
and Fuyu, who was eight, drowned in it while her sisters and Rosie doubled up
in amusement. They all went into the front room later, because Haru's mother
quaveringly called to her to fix the tea and rice cakes and open a can of sliced
peaches for everybody. Rosie noticed that her mother and Mr. Hayano were
talking together at the little table—they were discussing a *haiku* that Mr.
Hayano was planning to send to the *Mainichi*, while her father was sitting at
one end of the sofa looking through a copy of *Life*, the new picture magazine.
Occasionally, her father would comment on a photograph, holding it toward
Mrs. Hayano and speaking to her as he always did—loudly, as though he
thought someone such as she must surely be at least a trifle deaf also.

The five girls had their refreshments at the kitchen table, and it was while   20
Rosie was showing the sisters her trick of swallowing peach slices without
chewing (she chased each slippery crescent down with a swig of tea) that her
father brought his empty teacup and untouched saucer to the sink and said,
"Come on, Rosie, we're going home now."

"Already?" asked Rosie.

"Work tomorrow," he said.

He sounded irritated, and Rosie, puzzled, gulped one last yellow slice and
stood up to go, while the sisters began protesting, as was their wont.

"We have to get up at five-thirty," he told them, going into the front
room quickly, so that they did not have their usual chance to hang onto his
hands and plead for an extension of time.

Rosie, following, saw that her mother and Mr. Hayano were sipping tea   25
and still talking together, while Mrs. Hayano concentrated, quivering, on
raising the handleless Japanese cup to her lips with both her hands and lowering it back to her lap. Her father, saying nothing, went out the door, onto the
bright porch, and down the steps. Her mother looked up and asked, "Where
is he going?"

"Where is he going?" Rosie said. "He said we were going home now."

"Going home?" Her mother looked with embarrassment at Mr. Hayano
and his absorbed wife and then forced a smile. "He must be tired," she said.

Haru was not giving up yet. "May Rosie stay overnight?" she asked, and
Natsu, Aki, and Fuyu came to reinforce their sister's plea by helping her make
a circle around Rosie's mother. Rosie, for once having no desire to stay, was
relieved when her mother, apologizing to the perturbed Mr. and Mrs. Hayano

for her father's abruptness at the same time, managed to shake her head no at
the quartet, kindly but adamant, so that they broke their circle and let her go.

Rosie's father looked ahead into the windshield as the two joined him.
"I'm sorry," her mother said. "You must be tired." Her father, stepping on the
starter, said nothing. "You know how I get when it's *haiku*," she continued, "I
forget what time it is." He only grunted.

As they rode homeward silently, Rosie, sitting between, felt a rush of hate   30
for both—for her mother for begging, for her father for denying her mother.
I wish this old Ford would crash, right now, she thought, then immediately,
no, no, I wish my father would laugh, but it was too late: already the vision
had passed through her mind of the green pick-up crumpled in the dark
against one of the mighty eucalyptus trees they were just riding past, of the
three contorted, bleeding bodies, one of them hers.

Rosie ran between two patches of tomatoes, her heart working more ram-
bunctiously than she had ever known it to. How lucky it was that Aunt Taka
and Uncle Gimpachi had come tonight, though, how very lucky. Otherwise
she might not have really kept her half-promise to meet Jesus Carrasco. Jesus
was going to be a senior in September at the same school she went to, and his
parents were the ones helping with the tomatoes this year. She and Jesus, who
hardly remembered seeing each other at Cleveland High where there were so
many other people and two whole grades between them, had become great
friends this summer—he always had a joke for her when he periodically drove
the loaded pick-up up from the fields to the shed where she was usually sorting while her mother and father did the packing, and they laughed a great deal
together over infinitesimal repartee during the afternoon break for chilled
watermelon or ice cream in the shade of the shed.

What she enjoyed most was racing him to see which could finish picking
a double row first. He, who could work faster, would tease her by slowing
down until she thought she would surely pass him this time, then speeding
up furiously to leave her several sprawling vines behind. Once he had made
her screech hideously by crossing over, while her back was turned, to a place
atop the tomatoes in her green-stained bucket a truly monstrous, pale green
worm (it had looked more like an infant snake). And it was when they had finished a contest this morning, after she had pantingly pointed a green finger at
the immature tomatoes evident in the lugs at the end of his row and he had returned the accusation (with justice), that he had startlingly brought up the
matter of their possibly meeting outside the range of both their parents' dubious eyes.

"What for?" she had asked.

"I've got a secret I want to tell you," he said.

"Tell me now," she demanded.   35

"It won't be ready till tonight," he said.

She laughed. "Tell me tomorrow then."

"It'll be gone tomorrow," he threatened.

"Well, for seven hakes, what is it?" she had asked, more than twice, and when he had suggested that the packing shed would be an appropriate place to find out, she had cautiously answered maybe. She had not been certain she was going to keep the appointment until the arrival of mother's sister and her husband. Their coming seemed a sort of signal of permission, of grace, and she had definitely made up her mind to lie and leave as she was bowing them welcome.

So as soon as everyone appeared settled back for the evening, she announced loudly that she was going to the privy outside, "I'm going to the *benjo!*" and slipped out the door. And now that she was actually on her way, her heart pumped in such an undisciplined way that she could hear it with her ears. It's because I'm running, she told herself, slowing to a walk. The shed was up ahead, one more patch away, in the middle of the fields. Its bulk, looming in the dimness, took on a sinisterness that was funny when Rosie reminded herself that it was only a wooden frame with a canvas roof and three canvas walls that made a slapping noise on breezy days. 40

Jesus was sitting on the narrow plank that was the sorting platform and she went around to the other side and jumped backwards to seat herself on the rim of a packing stand. "Well, tell me," she said without greeting, thinking her voice sounded reassuringly familiar.

"I saw you coming out the door," Jesus said. "I heard you running part of the way, too."

"Uh-huh," Rosie said. "Now tell me the secret."

"I was afraid you wouldn't come," he said.

Rosie delved around on the chicken-wire bottom of the stall for number two tomatoes, ripe, which she was sitting beside, and came up with a left-over that felt edible. She bit into it and began sucking out the pulp and seeds. "I'm here," she pointed out. 45

"Rosie, are you sorry you came?"

"Sorry? What for?" she said. "You said you were going to tell me something."

"I will, I will," Jesus said, but his voice contained disappointment, and Rosie fleetingly felt the older of the two, realizing a brand-new power which vanished without category under her recognition.

"I have to go back in a minute," she said. "My aunt and uncle are here from Wintersburg. I told them I was going to the privy."

Jesus laughed. "You funny thing," he said. "You slay me!" 50

"Just because you have a bathroom *inside*," Rosie said. "Come on, tell me."

Chuckling, Jesus came around to lean on the stand facing her. They still could not see each other very clearly, but Rosie noticed that Jesus became very sober again as he took the hollow tomato from her hand and dropped it back into the stall. When he took hold of her empty hand, she could find no words to protest; her vocabulary had become distressingly constricted and she thought desperately that all that remained intact now was yes and no and oh, and even these few sounds would not easily out. Thus, kissed by Jesus, Rosie fell for the first time entirely victim to a helplessness delectable beyond speech. But the terrible, beautiful sensation lasted no more than a second, and

the reality of Jesus' lips and tongue and teeth and hands made her pull away
with such strength that she nearly tumbled.

Rosie stopped running as she approached the lights from the windows of
home. How long since she had left? She could not guess, but gasping yet, she
went to the privy in the back and locked herself in. Her own breathing deafened her in the dark, close space, and she sat and waited until she could hear
at last the nightly calling of the frogs and crickets. Even then, all she could
think to say was oh, my, and the pressure of Jesus' face against her face would
not leave.

No one had missed her in the parlor, however, and Rosie walked in and
through quickly, announcing that she was next going to take a bath. "Your father's in the bathhouse," her mother said, and Rosie, in her room, recalled
that she had not seen him when she entered. There had been only Aunt Taka
and Uncle Gimpachi with her mother at the table, drinking tea. She got her
robe and straw sandals and crossed the parlor again to go outside. Her mother
was telling them about the *haiku* competition in the *Mainichi* and the poem
she had entered.

Rosie met her father coming out of the bathhouse. "Are you through Fa-   55
ther?" she asked. "I was going to ask you to scrub my back."

"Scrub your own back," he said shortly, going toward the main house.

"What have I done now?" she yelled after him. She suddenly felt like doing a lot of yelling. But he did not answer, and she went into the bathhouse.
Turning on the dangling light, she removed her denims and T-shirt and threw
them in the big carton for dirty clothes standing next to the washing machine.
Her other things she took with her into the bath compartment to wash after
her bath. After she had scooped a basin of hot water from the square wooden
tub, she sat on the grey cement of the floor and soaped herself at exaggerated
leisure, singing "Red Sails in the Sunset" at the top of her voice and using da-
da-da where she suspected her words. Then, standing up, still singing, for she
was possessed by the notion that any attempt now to analyze would result in
spoilage and she believed that the larger her volume the less she would be able
to hear herself think, she obtained more hot water and poured it on until she
was free of lather. Only then did she allow herself to step into the steaming
vat, one leg first, then the remainder of her body inch by inch until the water
no longer stung and she could move around at will.

She took a long time soaking, afterwards remembering to go around outside to stoke the embers of the tin-lined fireplace beneath the tub and to
throw on a few more sticks so that the water might keep its heat for her
mother, and when she finally returned to the parlor, she found her mother still
talking *haiku* with her aunt and uncle, the three of them on another round of
tea. Her father was nowhere in sight.

At Japanese school the next day (Wednesday, it was), Rosie was grave and
giddy by turns. Preoccupied at her desk in the row for students on Book Eight,
she made up for it at recess by performing wild mimicry for the benefit of her
friend Chizuko. She held her nose and whined a witticism or two in what she
considered was the manner of Fred Allen; she assumed intoxication and a

British accent to go over the climax of the Rudy Vallee recording of the pub conversation about William Ewart Gladstone; she was the child Shirley Temple piping, "On the Good Ship Lollipop"; she was the gentleman soprano of the Four Inkspots trilling, "If I Didn't Care." And she felt reasonably satisfied when Chizuko wept and gasped, "Oh, Rosie, you ought to be in the movies!"

Her father came after her at noon, bringing her sandwiches of minced 60 ham and two nectarines to eat while she rode, so that she could pitch right into the sorting when they got home. The lugs were piling up, he said, and the ripe tomatoes in them would probably have to be taken to the cannery tomorrow if they were not ready for the produce haulers tonight. "This heat's not doing them any good. And we've got no time for a break today."

It *was* hot, probably the hottest day of the year, and Rosie's blouse stuck damply to her back even under the protection of the canvas. But she worked as efficiently as a flawless machine and kept the stalls heaped, with one part of her mind listening in to the parental murmuring about the heat and the tomatoes and with another part planning the exact words she would say to Jesus when he drove up with the first load of the afternoon. But when at last she saw that the pick-up was coming, her hands went beserk and the tomatoes starting falling into the wrong stalls, and her father said, "Hey, hey! Rosie, watch what you're doing!"

"Well, I have to go to the *benjo*," she said, hiding panic.

"Go in the weeds over there," he said, only half-joking.

"Oh, Father!" she protested.

"Oh, go on home," her mother said. "We'll make out for a while." 65

In the privy Rosie peered through a knothole toward the fields, watching as much as she could of Jesus. Happily she thought she saw him look in the direction of the house from time to time before he finished unloading and went back toward the patch where his mother and father worked. As she was heading for the shed, a very presentable black car purred up the dirt driveway to the house and its driver motioned to her. Was this the Hayashi home, he wanted to know. She nodded. Was she a Hayashi? Yes, she said, thinking that he was a good-looking man. He got out of the car with a huge, flat package and she saw that he warmly wore a business suit. "I have something here for your mother then," he said, in a more elegant Japanese than she was used to.

She told him where her mother was and he came along with her, patting his face with an immaculate white handkerchief and saying something about the coolness of San Francisco. To her surprised mother and father, he bowed and introduced himself as, among other things, the *haiku* editor of the *Mainichi Shimbun*, saying that since he had been coming as far as Los Angeles anyway, he had decided to bring her the first prize she had won in the recent contest.

"First prize?" her mother echoed, believing and not believing, pleased and overwhelmed. Handed the package with a bow, she bobbed her head up and down numerous times to express her utter gratitude.

"It is nothing much," he added, "but I hope it will serve as a token of our great appreciation for your contributions and our great admiration of your considerable talent."

"I am not worthy," she said, falling easily into his style. "It is I who should 70
make some sign of my humble thanks for being permitted to contribute."

"No, no, to the contrary," he said, bowing again.

But Rosie's mother insisted, and then saying that she knew she was being
unorthodox, she asked if she might open the package because her curiosity
was so great. Certainly she might. In fact, he would like her reaction to it, for
personally, it was one of his favorite *Hiroshiges*.

Rosie thought it was a pleasant picture, which looked to have been
sketched with delicate quickness. There were pink clouds, containing some
graceful calligraphy, and a sea that was a pale blue except at the edges, containing four sampans with indications of people in them. Pines edged the water and on the far-off beach there was a cluster of thatched huts towered over
by pine-dotted mountains of grey and blue. The frame was scalloped and gilt.

After Rosie's mother pronounced it without peer and somewhat prodded
her father into nodding agreement, she said Mr. Kuroda must at least have a
cup of tea after coming all this way, and although Mr. Kuroda did not want to
impose, he soon agreed that a cup of tea would be refreshing and went along
with her to the house, carrying the picture for her.

"Ha, your mother's crazy!" Rosie's father said, and Rosie laughed uneasily 75
as she resumed judgment on the tomatoes. She had emptied six lugs when he
broke into an imaginary conversation with Jesus to tell her to go and remind
her mother of the tomatoes, and she went slowly.

Mr. Kuroda was in his shirtsleeves expounding some *haiku* theory as he
munched a rice cake, and her mother was rapt. Abashed in the great man's
presence, Rosie stood next to her mother's chair until her mother looked up inquiringly, and then she started to whisper the message, but her mother pushed
her gently away and reproached, "You are not being very polite to our guest."

"Father says the tomatoes . . ." Rosie said aloud, smiling foolishly.

"Tell him I shall only be a minute," her mother said, speaking the language of Mr. Kuroda.

When Rosie carried the reply to her father, he did not seem to hear and
she said again, "Mother says she'll be back in a minute."

"All right, all right," he nodded, and they worked again in silence. But 80
suddenly, her father uttered an incredible noise, exactly like the cork of a bottle popping, and the next Rosie knew, he was stalking angrily toward the
house, almost running in fact, and she chased after him crying, "Father! Father! What are you going to do?"

He stopped long enough to order her back to the shed. "Never mind!" he
shouted, "Get on with the sorting!"

And from the place in the fields where she stood, frightened and vacillat-
ing, Rosie saw her father enter the house. Soon Mr. Kuroda came out alone,
putting on his coat. Mr. Kuroda got into his car and backed out down the
driveway onto the highway. Next her father emerged, also alone, something
in his arms (it was the picture, she realized), and, going over to the bathhouse
woodpile, he threw the picture on the ground and picked up the axe. Smashing the picture, glass and all (she heard the explosion faintly), he reached over
for the kerosene that was used to encourage the bath fire and poured it over

the wreckage. I am dreaming, Rosie said to herself, I am dreaming, but her father, having made sure that his act of cremation was irrevocable, was even then returning to the fields.

Rosie ran past him and toward the house. What had become of her mother? She burst into the parlor and found her mother at the back window watching the dying fire. They watched together until there remained only a feeble smoke under the blazing sun. Her mother was very calm.

"Do you know why I married your father?" she said without turning.

"No," said Rosie. It was the most frightening question she had ever been called upon to answer. Don't tell me now, she wanted to say, tell me tomorrow, tell me next week, don't tell me today. But she knew she would be told now, that the telling would combine with the other violence of the hot afternoon to level her life, her world to the very ground.

It was like a story out of the magazines illustrated in sepia, which she had consumed so greedily for a period until the information had somehow reached her that those wretchedly unhappy autobiographies, offered to her as the testimonials of living men and women, were largely inventions: Her mother, at nineteen, had come to America and married her father as an alternative to suicide.

At eighteen she had been in love with the first son of one of the well-to-do families in her village. The two had met whenever and wherever they could, secretly, because it would not have done for his family to see him favor her—her father had no money; he was a drunkard and a gambler besides. She had learned she was with child; an excellent match had already been arranged for her lover. Despised by her family, she had given premature birth to a still-born son, who would be seventeen now. Her family did not turn her out, but she could no longer project herself in any direction without refreshing in them the memory of her indiscretion. She wrote to Aunt Taka, her favorite sister in America, threatening to kill herself if Aunt Taka would not send for her. Aunt Taka hastily arranged a marriage with a young man of whom she knew, but lately arrived from Japan, a young man of simple mind, it was said, but of kindly heart. The young man was never told why his unseen betrothed was so eager to hasten the day of meeting.

The story was told perfectly, with neither groping for words nor untoward passion. It was as though her mother had memorized it by heart, reciting it to herself so many times over that its nagging vileness had long since gone.

"I had a brother then?" Rosie asked, for this was what seemed to matter now; she would think about the other later, she assured herself, pushing back the illumination which threatened all that darkness that had hitherto been merely mysterious or even glamorous. "A half-brother?"

"Yes."

"I would have liked a brother," she said.

Suddenly, her mother knelt on the floor and took her by the wrists. "Rosie," she said urgently, "Promise me you will never marry!" Shocked more by the request than the revelation, Rosie stared at her mother's face. Jesus, Jesus, she called silently, not certain whether she was invoking the help of the son of the Carrascos or of God, until there returned sweetly the memory of

Jesus' hand, how it had touched her and where. Still her mother waited for an answer, holding her wrists so tightly that her hands were going numb. She tried to pull free. Promise her mother whispered fiercely, promise. Yes, yes, I promise, Rosie said. But for an instant she turned away, and her mother, hearing the familiar glib agreement, released her. Oh, you, you, you, her eyes and twisted mouth said, you fool. Rosie, covering her face, began at last to cry, and the embrace and consoling hand came much later than she expected.

∽∽∽

RICHARD WRIGHT

The Man Who Was Almost a Man   *(1961)*

Dave struck out across the fields, looking homeward through paling light. Whut's the use talkin wid em niggers in the field? Anyhow, his mother was putting supper on the table. Them niggers can't understan nothing. One of these days he was going to get a gun and practice shooting, then they couldn't talk to him as though he were a little boy. He slowed, looking at the ground. Shucks, Ah ain scareda them even ef they are biggern me! Aw, Ah know whut Ahma do. Ahm going by ol Joe's sto n git that Sears Roebuck catlog n look at them guns. Mebbe Ma will lemme buy one when she gits mah pay from ol man Hawkins. Ahma beg her t gimme some money. Ahm ol ernough to hava gun. Ahm seventeen. Almost a man. He strode, feeling his long loose-jointed limbs. Shucks, a man oughta hava little gun aftah he done worked hard all day.

He came in sight of Joe's store. A yellow lantern glowed on the front porch. He mounted steps and went through the screen door, hearing it bang behind him. There was a strong smell of coal oil and mackerel fish. He felt very confident until he saw fat Joe walk in through the rear door, then his courage began to ooze.

"Howdy, Dave! Whutcha want?"

"How yuh, Mistah Joe? Aw, Ah don wanna buy nothing. Ah just wanted t see ef yuhd lemme look at tha catlog erwhile."

"Sure! You wanna see it here?"   5

"Nawsuh. Ah wants t take it home wid me. Ah'll bring it back termorrow when Ah come in from the fiels."

"You plannin on buying something?"

"Yessuh."

"Your ma lettin you have your own money now?"

"Shucks. Mistah Joe, Ahm gittin t be a man like anybody else!"   10

Joe laughed and wiped his greasy white face with a red bandanna.

"Whut you plannin on buyin?"

Dave looked at the floor, scratched his head, scratched his thigh, and smiled. Then he looked up shyly.

"Ah'll tell yuh, Mistah Joe, ef yuh promise yuh won't tell."

"I promise."   15

"Waal, Ahma buy a gun."

"A gun? What you want with a gun?"

"Ah wanna keep it."

"You ain't nothing but a boy. You don't need a gun."

"Aw, lemme have the catlog, Mistah Joe. Ah'll bring it back."   20

Joe walked through the rear door. Dave was elated. He looked around at barrels of sugar and flour. He heard Joe coming back. He craned his neck to see if he were bringing the book. Yeah, he's got it. Gawddog, he's got it!

"Here, but be sure you bring it back. It's the only one I got."

"Sho, Mistah Joe."

"Say, if you wanna buy a gun, why don't you buy one from me? I gotta gun to sell."

"Will it shoot?"   25

"Sure it'll shoot."

"Whut kind is it?"

"Oh, it's kinda old . . . a left-hand Wheeler. A pistol. A big one."

"Is it got bullets in it?"

"It's loaded."   30

"Kin Ah see it?"

"Where's your money?"

"What yuh wan fer it?"

"I'll let you have it for two dollars."

"Just two dollahs? Shucks, Ah could buy tha when Ah git mah pay."   35

"I'll have it here when you want it."

"Awright, suh. Ah be in fer it."

He went through the door, hearing it slam again behind him. Ahma git some money from Ma n buy me a gun! Only two dollahs! He tucked the thick catalogue under his arm and hurried.

"Where yuh been, boy?" His mother held a steaming dish of black-eyed peas.

"Aw, Ma, Ah jus stopped down the road t talk wid the boys."   40

"Yuh know bettah t keep suppah waitin."

He sat down, resting the catalogue on the edge of the table.

"Yuh git up from there and git to the well n wash yosef! Ah ain feedin no hogs in mah house!"

She grabbed his shoulder and pushed him. He stumbled out of the room, then came back to get the catalogue.

"Whut this?"   45

"Aw, Ma, it's jusa catlog."

"Who yuh git it from?"

"From Joe, down at the sto."

"Waal, thas good. We kin use it in the outhouse."

"Naw, Ma." He grabbed for it. "Gimme ma catlog, Ma."   50

She held onto it and glared at him.

"Quit hollerin at me! Whut's wrong wid yuh? Yuh crazy?"

"But Ma, please. It ain mine! It's Joe's! He tol me t bring it back t im termorrow."

She gave up the book. He stumbled down the back steps, hugging the thick book under his arm. When he had splashed water on his face and hands, he groped back to the kitchen and fumbled in a corner for the towel. He bumped into a chair; it clattered to the floor. The catalogue sprawled at his feet. When he had dried his eyes he snatched up the book and held it again under his arm. His mother stood watching him.

"Now, ef yuh gonna act a fool over that ol book, Ah'll take it n burn it up." 55

"Naw, Ma, please."

"Waal, set down n be still!"

He sat down and drew the oil lamp close. He thumbed page after page, unaware of the food his mother set on the table. His father came in. Then his small brother.

"Whutcha got there, Dave?" his father asked.

"Jusa catlog," he answered, not looking up. 60

"Yeah, here they is!" His eyes glowed at blue-and-black revolvers. He glanced up, feeling sudden guilt. His father was watching him. He eased the book under the table and rested it on his knees. After the blessing was asked, he ate. He scooped up peas and swallowed fat meat without chewing. Buttermilk helped to wash it down. He did not want to mention money before his father. He would do much better by cornering his mother when she was alone. He looked at his father uneasily out of the edge of his eye.

"Boy, how come yuh don quit foolin wid tha book n eat yo suppah?"

"Yessuh."

"How you n ol man Hawkins gitten erlong?"

"Suh?" 65

"Can't yuh hear? Why don yuh lissen? Ah ast yu how wiz yuh n ol man Hawkins gittin erlong?"

"Oh, swell, Pa. Ah plows mo lan than anybody over there."

"Waal, yuh oughta keep you mind on whut yuh doin."

"Yessuh."

He poured his plate full of molasses and sopped it up slowly with a chunk 70 of cornbread. When his father and brother had left the kitchen, he still sat and looked again at the guns in the catalogue, longing to muster courage enough to present his case to his mother. Lawd, ef Ah only had tha pretty one! He could almost feel the slickness of the weapon with his fingers. If he had a gun like that he would polish it and keep it shining so it would never rust. N Ah'd keep it loaded, by Gawd!

"Ma?" His voice was hesitant.

"Hunh?"

"Ol man Hawkins give yuh mah money yit?"

"Yeah, but ain no usa yuh thinking bout throwin nona it erway. Ahm keeping tha money sos yuh kin have cloes t go to school this winter."

He rose and went to her side with the open catalogue in his palms. She 75 was washing dishes, her head bent low over a pan. Shyly he raised the book. When he spoke, his voice was husky, faint.

"Ma, Gawd knows Ah wans one of these."

"One of whut?" she asked, not raising her eyes.

"One of these," he said again, not daring even to point. She glanced up at the page, then at him with wide eyes.

"Nigger, is yuh gone plumb crazy?"

"Aw, Ma—" 80

"Git outta here! Don yuh talk t me bout no gun! Yuh a fool!"

"Ma, Ah kin buy one fer two dollahs."

"Not ef Ah knows it, yuh ain!"

"But yuh promised me one—"

"Ah don care what Ah promised! Yuh ain nothing but a boy yit!" 85

"Ma, ef yuh lemme buy one Ah'll *never* ast yuh fer nothing no mo."

"Ah tol yuh t git outta here! Yuh ain gonna toucha penny of tha money fer no gun! Thas how come Ah has Mistah Hawkins t pay yo wages t me, cause ah knows yuh ain got no sense."

"But, Ma, we needa gun. Pa ain got no gun. We needa gun in the house. Yuh kin never tell whut might happen."

"Now don yuh try to maka fool outta me, boy! Ef we did hava gun, yuh wouldn't have it!"

He laid the catalogue down and slipped his arm around her waist. 90

"Aw, Ma, Ah done worked hard alla summer n ain ast yuh fer nothing, is Ah, now?"

"Thas whut yuh spose t do!"

"But Ma, Ah wans a gun. Yuh kin lemme have two dollahs outta mah money. Please, Ma. I kin give it to Pa. . . . Please, Ma! Ah loves yuh, Ma."

When she spoke her voice came soft and low.

"What yu wan wida gun, Dave? Yuh don need no gun. Yuh'll git in trou- 95 ble. N ef yo pa jus thought Ah let yuh have money t buy a gun he'd hava fit."

"Ah'll hide it, Ma. It ain but two dollahs."

"Lawd, chil, whut's wrong wid yuh?"

"Ain nothin wrong, Ma. Ahm almos a man now. Ah wans a gun."

"Who gonna sell yuh a gun?"

"Ol Joe at the sto." 100

"N it don cos but two dollahs?"

"Thas all, Ma. Jus two dollahs. Please, Ma."

She was stacking the plates away; her hands moved slowly, reflectively. Dave kept an anxious silence. Finally, she turned to him.

"Ah'll let yuh git tha gun ef yuh promise me one thing."

"What's tha, Ma?" 105

"Yuh bring it straight back t me, yuh hear? It be fer Pa."

"Yessum! Lemme go now, Ma."

She stooped, turned slightly to one side, raised the hem of her dress, rolled down the top of her stocking, and came up with a slender wad of bills.

"Here," she said. "Lawd knows yuh don need no gun. But yer pa does. Yuh bring it right back t me, yuh hear? Ahma put it up. Now ef yuh don, Ahma have yuh pa lick yuh so hard yuh won fergit it."

"Yessum." 110

He took the money, ran down the steps, and across the yard.

"Dave! Yuuuuuh Daaaaave!"

He heard, but he was not going to stop now. "Now, Lawd!"

The first movement he made the following morning was to reach under his pillow for the gun. In the gray light of dawn he held it loosely, feeling a sense of power. Could kill a man with a gun like this. Kill anybody, black or white. And if he were holding his gun in his hand, nobody could run over him; they would have to respect him. It was a big gun, with a long barrel and a heavy handle. He raised and lowered it in his hand, marveling at its weight.

He had not come straight home with it as his mother had asked; instead   115
he had stayed out in the fields, holding the weapon in his hand, aiming it now and then at some imaginary foe. But he had not fired it; he had been afraid that his father might hear. Also he was not sure he knew how to fire it.

To avoid surrendering the pistol he had not come into the house until he knew that they were all asleep. When his mother had tiptoed to his bedside late that night and demanded the gun, he had first played possum; then he had told her that the gun was hidden outdoors, that he would bring it to her in the morning. Now he lay turning it slowly in his hands. He broke it, took out the cartridges, felt them, and then put them back.

He slid out of bed, got a long strip of old flannel from a trunk, wrapped the gun in it, and tied it to his naked thigh while it was still loaded. He did not go in to breakfast. Even though it was not yet daylight, he started for Jim Hawkins' plantation. Just as the sun was rising he reached the barns where the mules and plows were kept.

"Hey! That you, Dave?"

He turned. Jim Hawkins stood eying him suspiciously.

"What're yuh doing here so early?"   120

"Ah didn't know Ah wuz gittin up so early, Mistah Hawkins. Ah was fixin t hitch up ol Jenny n take her t the fiels."

"Good. Since you're so early, how about plowing that stretch down by the woods?"

"Suits me, Mistah Hawkins."

"O.K. Go to it!"

He hitched Jenny to a plow and started across the fields. Hot dog! This   125
was just what he wanted. If he could get down by the woods, he could shoot his gun and nobody would hear. He walked behind the plow, hearing the traces creaking, feeling the gun tied tight to his thigh.

When he reached the woods, he plowed two whole rows before he decided to take out the gun. Finally, he stopped, looked in all directions, then untied the gun and held it in his hand. He turned to the mule and smiled.

"Know whut this is, Jenny? Naw, yuh wouldn know! Yuhs jusa ol mule! Anyhow, this is a gun, n it kin shoot, by Gawd!"

He held the gun at arm's length. Whut t hell, Ahma shoot this thing! He looked at Jenny again.

"Lissen here, Jenny! When Ah pull this ol trigger, Ah don wan yuh t run n acka fool now!"

Jenny stood with head down, her short ears pricked straight. Dave walked   130 off about twenty feet, held the gun far out from him at arm's length, and turned his head. Hell, he told himself, Ah ain afraid. The gun felt loose in his fingers; he waved it wildly for a moment. Then he shut his eyes and tightened his forefinger. Bloom! A report half deafened him and he thought his right hand was torn from his arm. He heard Jenny whinnying and galloping over the field, and he found himself on his knees, squeezing his fingers hard between his legs. His hand was numb; he jammed it into his mouth, trying to warm it, trying to stop the pain. The gun lay at his feet. He did not quite know what had happened. He stood up and stared at the gun as though it were a living thing. He gritted his teeth and kicked the gun. Yuh almos broke mah arm! He turned to look for Jenny; she was far over the fields, tossing her head and kicking wildly.

"Hol on there, ol mule!"

When he caught up with her she stood trembling, walling her big white eyes at him. The plow was far away; the traces had broken. Then Dave stopped short, looking, not believing. Jenny was bleeding. Her left side was red and wet with blood. He went closer. Lawd, have mercy! Wondah did Ah shoot this mule? He grabbed for Jenny's mane. She flinched, snorted, whirled, tossing her head.

"Hol on now! Hol on."

Then he saw the hole in Jenny's side, right between the ribs. It was round, wet, red. A crimson stream streaked down the front leg, flowing fast. Good Gawd! Ah wuzn't shootin at tha mule. He felt panic. He knew he had to stop that blood, or Jenny would bleed to death. He had never seen so much blood in all his life. He chased the mule for half a mile, trying to catch her. Finally she stopped, breathing hard, stumpy tail half arched. He caught her mane and led her back to where the plow and gun lay. Then he stopped and grabbed handfuls of damp black earth and tried to plug the bullet hole. Jenny shuddered, whinnied, and broke from him.

"Hol on! Hol on now!"   135

He tried to plug it again, but blood came anyhow. His fingers were hot and sticky. He rubbed dirt into his palms, trying to dry them. Then again he attempted to plug the bullet hole, but Jenny shied away, kicking her heels high. He stood helpless. He had to do something. He ran at Jenny; she dodged him. He watched a red stream of blood flow down Jenny's leg and form a bright pool at her feet.

"Jenny . . . Jenny," he called weakly.

His lips trembled. She's bleeding t death! He looked in the direction of home, wanting to go back, wanting to get help. But he saw the pistol lying in the damp black clay. He had a queer feeling that if he only did something, this would not be; Jenny would not be there bleeding to death.

When he went to her this time, she did not move. She stood with sleepy, dreamy eyes; and when he touched her she gave a low-pitched whinny and knelt to the ground, her front knees slopping in blood.

"Jenny . . . Jenny . . ." he whispered.   140

For a long time she held her neck erect; then her head sank, slowly. Her ribs swelled with a mighty heave and she went over.

Dave's stomach felt empty, very empty. He picked up the gun and held it gingerly between his thumb and forefinger. He buried it at the foot of a tree. He took a stick to cover the pool of blood with dirt—but what was the use? There was Jenny lying with her mouth open and her eyes walled and glassy. He could not tell Jim Hawkins he had shot his mule. But he had to tell something. Yeah, Ah'll tell em Jenny started gittin wil n fell on the joint of the plow. . . . But that would hardly happen to a mule. He walked across the field slowly, head down.

It was sunset. Two of Jim Hawkins' men were over near the edge of the woods digging a hole in which to bury Jenny. Dave was surrounded by a knot of people, all of whom were looking down at the dead mule.

"I don't see how in the world it happened," said Jim Hawkins for the tenth time.

The crowd parted and Dave's mother, father, and small brother pushed   145
into the center.

"Where Dave?" his mother called.

"There he is," said Jim Hawkins.

His mother grabbed him.

"Whut happened, Dave? Whut yuh done?"

"Nothin."   150

"C mon, boy, talk," his father said.

Dave took a deep breath and told the story he knew nobody believed.

"Waal," he drawled. "Ah brung ol Jenny down here sos Ah could do mah plowin. Ah plowed bout two rows, just like yuh see." He stopped and pointed at the long rows of upturned earth. "Then somethin musta been wrong wid ol Jenny. She wouldn ack right a-tall. She started snortin n kickin her heels. Ah tried t hol her, but she pulled erway, rearin n goin in. Then when the point of the plow was stickin up in the air, she swung erroun n twisted herself back on it. . . . She stuck herself n started t bleed. N fo Ah could do anything, she wuz dead."

"Did you ever hear of anything like that in all your life?" asked Jim Hawkins.

There were white and black standing in the crowd. They murmured.   155
Dave's mother came close to him and looked hard into his face. "Tell the truth, Dave," she said.

"Looks like a bullet hole to me," said one man.

"Dave, whut yuh do wid the gun?" his mother asked.

The crowd surged in, looking at him. He jammed his hands into his pockets, shook his head slowly from left to right, and backed away. His eyes were wide and painful.

"Did he hava gun?" asked Jim Hawkins.

"By Gawd, Ah tol yuh tha wuz a gun wound," said a man, slapping his   160
thigh.

His father caught his shoulders and shook him till his teeth rattled.

"Tell whut happened, yuh rascal! Tell whut. . . ."

Dave looked at Jenny's stiff legs and began to cry.

"Whut yuh do wid tha gun?" his mother asked.

"What wuz he doin wida gun?" his father asked.   165

"Come on and tell the truth," said Hawkins. "Ain't nobody going to hurt you. . . ."

His mother crowded close to him.

"Did yuh shoot tha mule, Dave?"

Dave cried, seeing blurred white and black faces.

"Ahh ddinn gggo tt sshooot hher . . . Ah sssswear ffo Gawd Ah ddin. . . .   170
Ah wuz a-tryin t sssee ef the old gggun would sshoot—"

"Where yuh git the gun from?" his father asked.

"Ah got it from Joe, at the sto."

"Where yuh git the money?"

"Ma give it t me."

"He kept worryin me, Bob. Ah had t. Ah tol im t bring the gun right back   175
t me. . . . It was fer yuh, the gun."

"But how yuh happen to shoot that mule?" asked Jim Hawkins.

"Ah wuzn shootin at the mule, Mistah Hawkins. The gun jumped when Ah pulled the trigger. . . . N fo Ah knowed anythin Jenny was there a-bleedin."

Somebody in the crowd laughed. Jim Hawkins walked close to Dave and looked into his face.

"Well, looks like you have bought you a mule, Dave."

"Ah swear fo Gawd, Ah didn go t kill the mule, Mistah Hawkins!"   180

"But you killed her!"

All the crowd was laughing now. They stood on tiptoe and poked heads over one another's shoulders.

"Well, boy, looks like yuh done bought a dead mule! Hahaha!"

"Ain tha ershame."   185

"Hohohohoho."

Dave stood, head down, twisting his feet in the dirt.

"Well, you needn't worry about it, Bob," said Jim Hawkins to Dave's father. "Just let the boy keep on working and pay me two dollars a month."

"Whut yuh wan fer yo mule, Mistah Hawkins?"

Jim Hawkins screwed up his eyes.   190

"Fifty dollars."

"Whut yuh do wid tha gun?" Dave's father demanded.

Dave said nothing.

"Yuh wan me t take a tree n beat yuh till yuh talk!"

"Nawsuh!"   195

"Whut yuh do wid it?"

"Ah throwed it erway."

"Where?"

"Ah . . . Ah throwed it in the creek."

"Waal, c mon home. N firs thing in the mawnin git to tha creek n fin   200
tha gun."

"Yessuh."

"Whut yuh pay fer it?"

"Two dollahs."

"Take tha gun n git yo money back n carry it to Mistah Hawkins, yuh hear? N don fergit Ahma lam you black bottom good fer this! Now march yosef on home, suh!"

Dave turned and walked slowly. He heard people laughing. Dave glared, his eyes welling with tears. Hot anger bubbled in him. Then he swallowed and stumbled on.

That night Dave did not sleep. He was glad that he had gotten out of kill-   205
ing the mule so easily, but he was hurt. Something hot seemed to turn over in-side him each time he remembered how they had laughed. He tossed on his bed, feeling his hard pillow. N Pa says he's gonna beat me. . . . He remem-bered other beatings, and his back quivered. Naw, naw, Ah sho don wan im t beat me tha way no mo. Dam em all! Nobody ever gave him anything. All he did was work. They treat me like a mule, n then they beat me. He gritted his teeth. N Ma had t tell on me.

Well, if he had to, he would take old man Hawkins that two dollars. But that meant selling the gun. And he wanted to keep that gun. Fifty dollars for a dead mule.

He turned over, thinking how he had fired the gun. He had an itch to fire it again. Ef other men kin shoota gun, by Gawd, Ah kin! He was still, listen-ing. Mebbe they all sleepin now. The house was still. He heard the soft breathing of his brother. Yes, now! He would go down and get that gun and see if he could fire it! He eased out of bed and slipped into overalls.

The moon was bright. He ran almost all the way to the edge of the woods. He stumbled over the ground, looking for the spot where he had buried the gun. Yeah, here it is. Like a hungry dog scratching for a bone, he pawed it up. He puffed his black cheeks and blew dirt from the trigger and barrel. He broke it and found four cartridges unshot. He looked around; the fields were filled with silence and moonlight. He clutched the gun stiff and hard in his fingers. But, as soon as he wanted to pull the trigger, he shut his eyes and turned his head. Naw, Ah can't shoot wid mah eyes closed n mah head turned. With effort he held his eyes open; then he squeezed. *Blooooom!* He was stiff, not breathing. The gun was still in his hands. Dammit, he'd done it! He fired again. *Blooooom!* He smiled. *Blooooom! Blooooom! Click, click.* There! It was empty. If anybody could shoot a gun, he could. He put the gun into his hip pocket and started across the fields.

When he reached the top of a ridge he stood straight and proud in the moonlight, looking at Jim Hawkins' big white house, feeling the gun sagging in his pocket. Lawd, ef Ah had just one mo bullet Ah'd taka shot at tha house. Ah'd like t scare ol man Hawkins jusa little. . . . Jusa enough t let im know Dave Saunders is a man.

To his left the road curved, running to the tracks of the Illinois Central.   210
He jerked his head, listening. From far off came a faint *hoooof-hoooof; hoooof-hoooof*. . . . He stood rigid. Two dollahs a mont. Les see now. . . . Tha means it'll take bout two years. Shucks! Ah'll be dam!

He started down the road, toward the tracks. Yeah, here she comes! He stood beside the track and held himself stiffly. Here she comes, erroun the ben. . . . C mon, yuh slow poke! C mon! He had his hand on his gun; something quivered in his stomach. Then the train thundered past, the gray and brown box cars rumbling and clinking. He gripped the gun tightly; then he jerked his hand out of his pocket. Ah betcha Bill wouldn't do it! Ah betcha. . . . The cars slid past, steel grinding upon steel. Ahm ridin yuh ternight, so hep me Gawd! He was hot all over. He hesitated just a moment; then he grabbed, pulled atop of a car, and lay flat. He felt his pocket; the gun was still there. Ahead the long rails were glinting in the moonlight, stretching away, away to somewhere, somewhere where he could be a man. . . .

∽∾

DORIS LESSING

A Woman on the Roof   *(1993)*

It was during the week of hot sun, that June.

Three men were at work on the roof, where the leads got so hot they had the idea of throwing water on to cool them. But the water steamed, then sizzled; and they made jokes about getting an egg from some woman in the flats under them, to poach it for their dinner. By two it was not possible to touch the guttering they were replacing, and they speculated about what workmen did in regularly hot countries. Perhaps they should borrow kitchen gloves with the egg? They were all a bit dizzy, not used to the heat; and they shed their coats and stood side by side squeezing themselves into a foot-wide patch of shade against a chimney, careful to keep their feet in the thick socks and boots out of the sun. There was a fine view across several acres of roofs. Not far off a man sat in a deck chair reading the newspapers. Then they saw her, between chimneys, about fifty yards away. She lay face down on a brown blanket. They could see the top part of her: black hair, a flushed solid back, arms spread out.

"She's stark naked," said Stanley, sounding annoyed.

Harry, the oldest, a man of about forty-five, said: "Looks like it."

Young Tom, seventeen, said nothing, but he was excited and grinning.   5

Stanley said: "Someone'll report her if she doesn't watch out."

"She thinks no one can see," said Tom, craning his head all ways to see more.

At this point the woman, still lying prone, brought her two hands up behind her shoulders with the ends of a scarf in them, tied it behind her back, and sat up. She wore a red scarf tied around her breasts and brief red bikini pants. This being the first day of the sun she was white, flushing red. She sat smoking, and did not look up when Stanley let out a wolf whistle. Harry said: "Small things amuse small minds," leading the way back to their part of the roof, but it was scorching. Harry said: "Wait, I'm going to rig up some shade," and disappeared down the skylight into the building. Now that he'd gone, Stanley and Tom went to the farthest point they could to peer at the woman.

She had moved, and all they could see were two pink legs stretched on the blanket. They whistled and shouted but the legs did not move. Harry came back with a blanket and shouted: "Come on, then." He sounded irritated with them. They clambered back to him and he said to Stanley: "What about your missus?" Stanley was newly married, about three months. Stanley said, jeering: "What about my missus?"—preserving his independence. Tom said nothing, but his mind was full of the nearly naked woman. Harry slung the blanket, which he had borrowed from a friendly woman downstairs, from the stem of a television aerial to a row of chimney-pots. This shade fell across the piece of gutter they had to replace. But the shade kept moving, they had to adjust the blanket, and not much progress was made. At last some of the heat left the roof, and they worked fast, making up for lost time. First Stanley, then Tom, made a trip to the end of the roof to see the woman. "She's on her back," Stanley said, adding a jest which made Tom snicker, and the older man smile tolerantly. Tom's report was that she hadn't moved, but it was a lie. He wanted to keep what he had seen to himself: he had caught her in the act of rolling down the little red pants over her hips, till they were no more than a small triangle. She was on her back, fully visible, glistening with oil.

Next morning, as soon as they came up, they went to look. She was already there, face down, arms spread out, naked except for the little red pants. She had turned brown in the night. Yesterday she was a scarlet-and-white woman, today she was a brown woman. Stanley let out a whistle. She lifted her head, startled, as if she'd been asleep, and looked straight over at them. The sun was in her eyes, she blinked and stared, then she dropped her head again. At this gesture of indifference, they all three, Stanley, Tom, and old Harry, let out whistles and yells. Harry was doing it in parody of the younger men, making fun of them, but he was also angry. They were all angry because of her utter indifference to the three men watching her.

"Bitch," said Stanley.   10

"She should ask us over," said Tom, snickering.

Harry recovered himself and reminded Stanley: "If she's married, her old man wouldn't like that."

"Christ," said Stanley virtuously, "if my wife lay about like that, for everyone to see, I'd soon stop her."

Harry said, smiling: "How do you know, perhaps she's sunning herself at this very moment?"

"Not a chance, not on our roof." The safety of his wife put Stanley into a   15 good humour, and they went to work. But today it was hotter than yesterday; and several times one or the other suggested they should tell Matthew, the foreman, and ask to leave the roof until the heat wave was over. But they didn't. There was work to be done in the basement of the big block of flats, but up here they felt free, on a different level from ordinary humanity shut in the streets or the buildings. A lot more people came out on to the roofs that day, for an hour at midday. Some married couples sat side by side in deck chairs, the women's legs stockingless and scarlet, the men in vests with reddening shoulders.

The woman stayed on her blanket, turning herself over and over. She ignored them, no matter what they did. When Harry went off to fetch more screws, Stanley said: "Come on." Her roof belonged to a different system of roofs, separated from theirs at one point by about twenty feet. It meant a scrambling climb from one level to another, edging along parapets, clinging to chimneys, while their big boots slipped and slithered, but at last they stood on a small square projecting roof looking straight down at her, close. She sat smoking, reading a book. Tom thought she looked like a poster, or a magazine cover, with the blue sky behind her and her legs stretched out. Behind her a great crane at work on a new building in Oxford Street swung its black arm across roofs in a great arc. Tom imagined himself at work on the crane, adjusting the arm to swing over and pick her up and swing her back across the sky to drop her near him.

They whistled. She looked up at them, cool and remote, then went on reading. Again, they were furious. Or, rather, Stanley was. His sun-heated face was screwed into a rage as he whistled again and again, trying to make her look up. Young Tom stopped whistling. He stood beside Stanley, excited, grinning; but he felt as if he were saying to the woman: Don't associate me with *him*, for his grin was apologetic. Last night he had thought of the unknown woman before he slept, and she had been tender with him. This tenderness he was remembering as he shifted his feet by the jeering, whistling Stanley, and watched the indifferent, healthy brown woman a few feet off, with the gap that plunged to the street between them. Tom thought it was romantic, it was like being high on two hilltops. But there was a shout from Harry, and they clambered back. Stanley's face was hard, really angry. The boy kept looking at him and wondered why he hated the woman so much, for by now he loved her.

They played their little games with the blanket, trying to trap shade to work under; but again it was not until nearly four that they could work seriously, and they were exhausted, all three of them. They were grumbling about the weather by now. Stanley was in a thoroughly bad humour. When they made their routine trip to see the woman before they packed up for the day, she was apparently asleep, face down, her back all naked save for the scarlet triangle on her buttocks. "I've got a good mind to report her to the police," said Stanley, and Harry said: "What's eating you? What harm's she doing?"

"I tell you, if she was my wife!"

"But she isn't, is she?" Tom knew that Harry, like himself, was uneasy at   20
Stanley's reaction. He was normally a sharp young man, quick at his work, making a lot of jokes, good company.

"Perhaps it will be cooler tomorrow," said Harry.

But it wasn't; it was hotter, if anything, and the weather forecast said the good weather would last. As soon as they were on the roof, Harry went over to see if the woman was there, and Tom knew it was to prevent Stanley going, to put off his bad humour. Harry had grownup children, a boy the same age as Tom, and the youth trusted and looked up to him.

Harry came back and said: "She's not there."

"I bet her old man has put his foot down," said Stanley, and Harry and Tom caught each other's eyes and smiled behind the young married man's back.

Harry suggested they should get permission to work in the basement, and   25
they did, that day. But before packing up Stanley said: "Let's have a breath of
fresh air." Again Harry and Tom smiled at each other as they followed Stanley
up to the roof, Tom in the devout conviction that he was there to protect the
woman from Stanley. It was about five-thirty, and a calm, full sunlight lay over
the roofs. The great crane still swung its black arm from Oxford Street to
above their heads. She was not there. Then there was a flutter of white from
behind a parapet, and she stood up, in a belted, white dressing-gown. She had
been there all day, probably, but on a different patch of roof, to hide from
them. Stanley did not whistle; he said nothing, but watched the woman bend
to collect papers, books, cigarettes, then fold the blanket over her arm. Tom
was thinking: If they weren't here, I'd go over and say . . . what? But he knew
from his nightly dreams of her that she was kind and friendly. Perhaps she
would ask him down to her flat? Perhaps . . . He stood watching her disappear
down the skylight. As she went, Stanley let out a shrill derisive yell; she started,
and it seemed as if she nearly fell. She clutched to save herself, they could hear
things falling. She looked straight at them, angry. Harry said, facetiously: "Better be careful on those slippery ladders, love." Tom knew he said it to save her
from Stanley, but she could not know it. She vanished, frowning. Tom was full
of a secret delight, because he knew her anger was for the others, not for him.
     "Roll on some rain," said Stanley, bitter, looking at the blue evening sky.
     Next day was cloudless, and they decided to finish the work in the base-
ment. They felt excluded, shut in the grey cement basement fitting pipes,
from the holiday atmosphere of London in a heat wave. At lunchtime they
came up for some air, but while the married couples, and the men in shirt-
sleeves or vests, were there, she was not there, either on her usual patch of
roof or where she had been yesterday. They all, even Harry, clambered about,
between chimney-pots, over parapets, the hot leads stinging their fingers.
There was not a sign of her. They took off their shirts and vests and exposed
their chests, feeling their feet sweaty and hot. They did not mention the
woman. But Tom felt alone again. Last night she had him into her flat: it was
big and had fitted white carpets and a bed with a padded white leather head-
board. She wore a black filmy negligée and her kindness to Tom thickened his
throat as he remembered it. He felt she had betrayed him by not being there.
     And again after work they climbed up, but still there was nothing to be
seen of her. Stanley kept repeating that if it was as hot as this tomorrow he
wasn't going to work and that's all there was to it. But they were all there next
day. By ten the temperature was in the middle seventies, and it was eighty long
before noon. Harry went to the foreman to say it was impossible to work on
the leads in that heat; but the foreman said there was nothing else he could
put them on, and they'd have to. At midday they stood, silent, watching the
skylight on her roof open, and then she slowly emerged in her white gown,
holding a bundle of blanket. She looked at them, gravely, then went to the
part of the roof where she was hidden from them. Tom was pleased. He felt
she was more his when the other men couldn't see her. They had taken off
their shirts and vests, but now they put them back again, for they felt the sun
bruising their flesh. "She must have the hide of a rhino," said Stanley, tugging

at guttering and swearing. They stopped work, and sat in the shade, moving around behind chimney stacks. A woman came to water a yellow window box opposite them. She was middle-aged, wearing a flowered summer dress. Stanley said to her: "We need a drink more than them." She smiled and said: "Better drop down to the pub quick, it'll be closing in a minute." They exchanged pleasantries, and she left them with a smile and a wave.

"Not like Lady Godiva," said Stanley. "She can give us a bit of a chat and a smile."

"You didn't whistle at *her*," said Tom, reproving.   30

"Listen to him," said Stanley, "you didn't whistle, then?"

But the boy felt as if he hadn't whistled, as if only Harry and Stanley had. He was making plans, when it was time to knock off work, to get left behind and somehow make his way over to the woman. The weather report said the hot spell was due to break, so he had to move quickly. But there was no chance of being left. The other two decided to knock off work at four, because they were exhausted. As they went down, Tom quickly climbed a parapet and hoisted himself higher by pulling his weight up a chimney. He caught a glimpse of her lying on her back, her knees up, eyes closed, a brown woman lolling in the sun. He slipped and clattered down, as Stanley looked for information: "She's gone down," he said. He felt as if he had protected her from Stanley, and that she must be grateful to him. He could feel the bond between the woman and himself.

Next day, they stood around on the landing below the roof, reluctant to climb up into the heat. The woman who had lent Harry the blanket came out and offered them a cup of tea. They accepted gratefully, and sat around Mrs. Pritchett's kitchen an hour or so, chatting. She was married to an airline pilot. A smart blonde, of about thirty, she had an eye for the handsome sharp-faced Stanley; and the two teased each other while Harry sat in a corner, watching, indulgent, though his expression reminded Stanley that he was married. And young Tom felt envious of Stanley's ease in badinage; felt, too, that Stanley's getting off with Mrs. Pritchett left his romance with the woman on the roof safe and intact.

"I thought they said the heat wave'd break," said Stanley, sullen, as the time approached when they really would have to climb up into the sunlight.

"You don't like it, then?" asked Mrs. Pritchett.   35

"All right for some," said Stanley. "Nothing to do but lie about as if it was a beach up there. Do you ever go up?"

"Went up once," said Mrs. Pritchett. "But it's a dirty place up there, and it's too hot."

"Quite right too," said Stanley.

Then they went up, leaving the cool neat little flat and the friendly Mrs. Pritchett.

As soon as they were up they saw her. The three men looked at her, re-   40
sentful at her ease in this punishing sun. Then Harry said, because of the expression on Stanley's face: "Come on, we've got to pretend to work, at least."

They had to wrench another length of guttering that ran beside a parapet out of its bed, so that they could replace it. Stanley took it in his two hands, tugged, swore, stood up. "Fuck it," he said, and sat down under a chimney. He lit a cigarette. "Fuck them," he said. "What do they think we are, lizards? I've got blisters all over my hands." Then he jumped up and climbed over the roofs and stood with his back to them. He put his fingers either side of his mouth and let out a shrill whistle. Tom and Harry squatted, not looking at each other, watching him. They could just see the woman's head, the beginnings of her brown shoulders. Stanley whistled again. Then he began stamping with his feet, and whistled and yelled and screamed at the woman, his face getting scarlet. He seemed quite mad, as he stamped and whistled, while the woman did not move, she did not move a muscle.

"Barmy," said Tom.

"Yes," said Harry, disapproving.

Suddenly the older man came to a decision. It was, Tom knew, to save some sort of scandal or real trouble over the woman. Harry stood up and began packing tools into a length of oily cloth. "Stanley," he said, commanding. At first Stanley took no notice, but Harry said: "Stanley, we're packing it in, I'll tell Matthew."

Stanley came back, cheeks mottled, eyes glaring.   45

"Can't go on like this," said Harry. "It'll break in a day or so. I'm going to tell Matthew we've got sunstroke, and if he doesn't like it, it's too bad." Even Harry sounded aggrieved, Tom noted. The small, competent man, the family man with his grey hair, who was never at a loss, sounded really off balance. "Come on," he said, angry. He fitted himself into the open square in the roof, and went down, watching his feet on the ladder. Then Stanley went, with not a glance at the woman. Then Tom, who, his throat beating with excitement, silently promised her on a backward glance: Wait for me, wait, I'm coming.

On the pavement Stanley said: "I'm going home." He looked white now, so perhaps he really did have sunstroke. Harry went off to find the foreman, who was at work on the plumbing of some flats down the street. Tom slipped back, not into the building they had been working on, but the building on whose roof the woman lay. He went straight up, no one stopping him. The skylight stood open, with an iron ladder leading up. He emerged on to the roof a couple of yards from her. She sat up, pushing back her black hair with both hands. The scarf across her breasts bound them tight, and brown flesh bulged around it. Her legs were brown and smooth. She stared at him in silence. The boy stood grinning, foolish, claiming the tenderness he expected from her.

"What do you want?" she asked.

"I . . . I came to . . . make your acquaintance," he stammered, grinning, pleading with her.

They looked at each other, the slight, scarlet-faced excited boy, and the   50 serious, nearly naked woman. Then, without a word, she lay down on her brown blanket, ignoring him.

"You like the sun, do you?" he enquired of her glistening back.

Not a word. He felt panic, thinking of how she had held him in her arms, stroked his hair, brought him where he sat, lordly, in her bed, a glass of some exhilarating liquor he had never tasted in life. He felt that if he knelt down, stroked her shoulders, her hair, she would turn and clasp him in her arms.

He said: "The sun's all right for you, isn't it?"

She raised her head, set her chin on two small fists. "Go away," she said. He did not move. "Listen," she said, in a slow reasonable voice, where anger was kept in check, though with difficulty; looking at him, her face weary with anger, "if you get a kick out of seeing women in bikinis, why don't you take a sixpenny bus ride to the Lido? You'd see dozens of them, without all this mountaineering."

She hadn't understood him. He felt her unfairness pale him. He stam-   55 mered: "But I like you, I've been watching you and . . ."

"Thanks," she said, and dropped her face again, turned away from him.

She lay there. He stood there. She said nothing. She had simply shut him out. He stood, saying nothing at all, for some minutes. He thought: She'll have to say something if I stay. But the minutes went past, with no sign of them in her, except in the tension of her back, her thighs, her arms—the tension of waiting for him to go.

He looked up at the sky, where the sun seemed to spin in heat; and over the roofs where he and his mates had been earlier. He could see the heat quivering where they had worked. And they expect us to work in these conditions! he thought, filled with righteous indignation. The woman hadn't moved. A bit of hot wind blew her black hair softly; it shone, and was iridescent. He remembered how he had stroked it last night.

Resentment of her at last moved him off and away down the ladder, through the building, into the street. He got drunk then, in hatred of her.

Next day when he woke the sky was grey. He looked at the wet grey and thought, vicious: Well, that's fixed you, hasn't it now? That's fixed you good and proper.

The three men were at work early on the cool leads, surrounded by damp drizzling roofs where no one came to sun themselves, black roofs, slimy with rain. Because it was cool now, they would finish the job that day, if they hurried.

∞∞

JOHN UPDIKE

A & P   *(1962)*

In walks these three girls in nothing but bathing suits. I'm in the third checkout slot, with my back to the door, so I don't see them until they're over by the bread. The one that caught my eye first was the one in the plaid green two-piece. She was a chunky kid, with a good tan and a sweet broad soft-looking can with those two crescents of white just under it, where the sun never seems to hit, at the top of the backs of her legs. I stood there with my hand on a box of HiHo crackers trying to remember if I rang it up or not. I ring it up again and the customer starts giving me hell. She's one of these cash-register-watchers, a witch about fifty with rouge on her cheekbones and no eyebrows, and I know it made her day to trip me up. She'd been watching cash registers for fifty years and probably never seen a mistake before.

By the time I got her feathers smoothed and her goodies into a bag—she gives me a little snort in passing, if she'd been born at the right time they would have burned her over in Salem—by the time I get her on her way the girls had circled around the bread and were coming back, without a pushcart, back my way along the counters, in the aisle between the checkouts and the Special bins. They didn't even have shoes on. There was this chunky one, with the two-piece—it was bright green and all the seams on the bra were still sharp and her belly was still pretty pale so I guessed she just got it (the suit)— there was this one, with one of those chubby berry-faces, the lips all bunched together under her nose, this one, and a tall one, with black hair that hadn't quite frizzed right, and one of these sunburns right across under the eyes, and a chin that was too long—you know, the kind of girl other girls think is very "striking" and "attractive" but never quite makes it, as they very well know, which is why they like her so much—and then the third one, that wasn't quite so tall. She was the queen. She kind of led them, the other two peeking around and making their shoulders round. She didn't look around, not this queen, she just walked straight on slowly, on these long white primadonna legs. She came down a little hard on her heels, as if she didn't walk in bare feet that much, putting down her heels and then letting the weight move along to her toes as if she was testing the floor with every step, putting a little deliberate extra ac- tion into it. You never know for sure how girls' minds work (do you really think it's a mind in there or just a little buzz like a bee in a glass jar?) but you got the idea she had talked the other two into coming here with her, and now she was showing them how to do it, walk slow and hold yourself straight.

She had on a kind of dirty-pink—beige maybe, I don't know—bathing suit with a little nubble all over it and, what got me, the straps were down. They were off her shoulders looped loose around the cool tops of her arms, and I guess as a result the suit had slipped a little on her, so all around the top of the cloth there was this shining rim. If it hadn't been there you wouldn't have known there could have been anything whiter than those shoulders. With the straps pushed off, there was nothing between the top of the suit and the top of her head except just *her*, this clean bare plane of the top of her chest down from the shoulder bones like a dented sheet of metal tilted in the light. I mean, it was more than pretty.

She had a sort of oaky hair that the sun and salt had bleached, done up in a bun that was unravelling, and a kind of prim face. Walking into the A & P with your straps down, I suppose it's the only kind of face you *can* have. She held her head so high her neck, coming up out of those white shoulders, looked kind of stretched, but I didn't mind. The longer her neck was, the more of her there was.

She must have felt in the corner of her eye me and over my shoulder   5 Stokesie in the second slot watching, but she didn't tip. Not this queen. She kept her eyes moving across the racks, and stopped, and turned so slow it

Jacques-Louis David, *Madame Recamier* (1800)

Edouard Manet, *Olympia* (1863)

Henri Matisse, *Odalisque* (1923–1924)

Amadeo Modigliani, *Reclining Nude from the Back* (1917)

Vanessa Bell, *The Memoir Club* (c. 1943) Figures in the picture, from left to right: Duncan Grant, Leonard Woolf, Vanessa and Clive Bell, David Garnett, Maynard and Lydia Keynes, Desmond and Millie MacCarthy, Quentin Bell and E. M. Forster. Portraits on the wall of Woolf by Duncan Grant, Lytton Strachey by Grant, and Roger Fry by Vanessa Bell.

Paul Cézanne, *Mont Sainte-Victoire* (1900)

Pablo Picasso, *Les demoiselles d'Avignon* (1907)

Georges Braque, *The Bather* (1907)

Georges Braque, *Musical Instruments* (1908)

Pablo Picasso, *The Aficionado* (1912)

Umberto Boccioni, *The Dynamism of a Soccer Player* (1913)

made my stomach rub the inside of my apron, and buzzed to the other two, who kind of huddled against her for relief, and then they all three of them went up the cat-and-dog-food-breakfast-cereal-macaroni-rice-raisins-seasonings-spreads-spaghetti-soft-drinks-crackers-and-cookies aisle. From the third slot I look straight up this aisle to the meat counter, and I watched them all the way. The fat one with the tan sort of fumbled with the cookies, but on second thought she put the package back. The sheep pushing their carts down the aisle—the girls were walking against the usual traffic (not that we have one-way signs or anything)—were pretty hilarious. You could see them, when Queenie's white shoulders dawned on them, kind of jerk, or hop, or hiccup, but their eyes snapped back to their own baskets and on they pushed. I bet you could set off dynamite in an A & P and the people would by and large keep reaching and checking oatmeal off their lists and muttering "Let me see, there was a third thing, began with A, asparagus, no, ah, yes, applesauce!" or whatever it is they do mutter. But there was no doubt, this jiggled them. A few houseslaves in pin curlers even looked around after pushing their carts past to make sure what they had seen was correct.

You know, it's one thing to have a girl in a bathing suit down on the beach, where what with the glare nobody can look at each other much anyway, and another thing in the cool of the A & P, under the fluorescent lights, against all those stacked packages, with her feet paddling along naked over our checker-board green-and-cream rubber-tile floor.

"Oh Daddy," Stokesie said beside me. "I feel so faint."

"Darling," I said. "Hold me tight." Stokesie's married, with two babies chalked up on his fuselage already, but as far as I can tell that's the only difference. He's twenty-two, and I was nineteen this April.

"Is it done?" he asks, the responsible married man finding his voice. I forgot to say he thinks he's going to be manager some sunny day, maybe in 1990 when it's called the Great Alexandrov and Petrooshki Tea Company or something.

What he meant was, our town is five miles from a beach, with a big sum- 10 mer colony out on the Point, but we're right in the middle of town, and the women generally put on a shirt or shorts or something before they get out of the car into the street. And anyway these are usually women with six children and varicose veins mapping their legs and nobody, including them, could care less. As I say, we're right in the middle of town, and if you stand at our front doors you can see two banks and the Congregational church and the newspaper store and three real-estate offices and about twenty-seven old freeloaders tearing up Central Street because the sewer broke again. It's not as if we're on the Cape; we're north of Boston and there's people in this town haven't seen the ocean for twenty years.

The girls had reached the meat counter and were asking McMahon something. He pointed, they pointed, and they shuffled out of sight behind a pyramid of Diet Delight peaches. All that was left for us to see was old McMahon patting his mouth and looking after them sizing up their joints. Poor kids, I began to feel sorry for them, they couldn't help it.

*   *   *

Now here comes the sad part of the story, at least my family says it's sad, but I don't think it's so sad myself. The store's pretty empty, it being Thursday afternoon, so there was nothing much to do except lean on the register and wait for the girls to show up again. The whole store was like a pinball machine and I didn't know which tunnel they'd come out of. After a while they come around out of the far aisle, around the light bulbs, records at discount of the Caribbean Six or Tony Martin Sings or some such gunk you wonder they waste the wax on, six-packs of candy bars, and plastic toys done up in cellophane that fall apart when a kid looks at them anyway. Around they come, Queenie still leading the way, and holding a little gray jar in her hand. Slots Three through Seven are unmanned and I could see her wondering between Stokes and me, but Stokesie with his usual luck draws an old party in baggy gray pants who stumbles up with four giant cans of pineapple juice (what do these bums *do* with all that pineapple juice? I've often asked myself) so the girls come to me. Queenie puts down the jar and I take it into my fingers icy cold. Kingfish Fancy Herring Snacks in Pure Sour Cream: 49¢. Now her hands are empty, not a ring or a bracelet, bare as God made them, and I wonder where the money's coming from. Still with that prim look she lifts a folded dollar bill out of the hollow at the center of her nubbled pink top. The jar went heavy in my hand. Really, I thought that was so cute.

Then everybody's luck begins to run out. Lengel comes in from haggling with a truck full of cabbages on the lot and is about to scuttle into that door marked MANAGER behind which he hides all day when the girls touch his eye. Lengel's pretty dreary, teaches Sunday school and the rest, but he doesn't miss that much. He comes over and says, "Girls, this isn't the beach."

Queenie blushes, though maybe it's just a brush of sunburn I was noticing for the first time, now that she was so close. "My mother asked me to pick up a jar of herring snacks." Her voice kind of startled me, the way voices do when you see the people first, coming out so flat and dumb yet kind of tony, too, the way it ticked over "pick up" and "snacks." All of a sudden I slid right down her voice into her living room. Her father and the other men were standing around in ice-cream coats and bow ties and the women were in sandals picking up herring snacks on toothpicks off a big glass plate and they were all holding drinks the color of water with olives and springs of mint in them. When my parents have somebody over they get lemonade and if it's a real racy affair Schlitz in tall glasses with "They'll Do It Every Time" cartoons stenciled on.

"That's all right," Lengel said. "But this isn't the beach." His repeating 15 this struck me as funny, as if it had just occurred to him, and he had been thinking all these years the A & P was a great big dune and he was the head lifeguard. He didn't like my smiling—as I say he doesn't miss much—but he concentrates on giving the girls that sad Sunday-school-superintendent stare.

Queenie's blush is no sunburn now, and the plump one in plaid, that I liked better from the back—a really sweet can—pipes up, "We weren't doing any shopping. We just came in for the one thing."

"That makes no difference," Lengel tells her, and I could see from the way his eyes went that he hadn't noticed she was wearing a two-piece before. "We want you decently dressed when you come in here."

"We *are* decent," Queenie says suddenly, her lower lip pushing, getting sore now that she remembers her place, a place from which the crowd that runs the A & P must look pretty crummy. Fancy Herring Snacks flashed in her very blue eyes.

"Girls, I don't want to argue with you. After this come in here with your shoulders covered. It's our policy." He turns his back. That's policy for you. Policy is what the kingpins want. What the others want is juvenile delinquency.

All this while, the customers had been showing up with their carts but, you know, sheep, seeing a scene, they had all bunched up on Stokesie, who shook open a paper bag as gently as peeling a peach, not wanting to miss a word. I could feel in the silence everybody getting nervous, most of all Lengel, who asks me, "Sammy, have you rung up their purchase?"   **20**

I thought and said "No" but it wasn't about that I was thinking. I go through the punches, 4, 9, GROC, TOT—it's more complicated than you think, and after you do it often enough, it begins to make a little song, that you hear words to, in my case "Hello (*bing*) there, you (*gung*) hap-py *pee*-pul (*splat*)!"— the *splat* being the drawer flying out. I uncrease the bill, tenderly as you may imagine, it just having come from between the two smoothest scoops of vanilla I had ever known there were, and pass a half and a penny into her narrow pink palm, and nestle the herrings in a bag and twist its neck and hand it over, all the time thinking.

The girls, and who'd blame them, are in a hurry to get out, so I say "I quit" to Lengel quick enough for them to hear, hoping they'll stop and watch me, their unsuspected hero. They keep right on going, into the electric eye; the door flies open and they flicker across the lot to their car, Queenie and Plaid and Big Tall Goony-Goony (not that as raw material she was so bad), leaving me with Lengel and a kink in his eyebrow.

"Did you say something, Sammy?"

"I said I quit."

"I thought you did."   **25**

"You didn't have to embarrass them."

"It was they who were embarrassing us."

I started to say something that came out "Fiddle-de-do." It's a saying of my grandmother's, and I know she would have been pleased.

"I don't think you know what you're saying," Lengel said.

"I know you don't," I said. "But I do." I pull the bow at the back of my   **30** apron and start shrugging it off my shoulders. A couple of customers that had been heading for my slot begin to knock against each other, like scared pigs in a chute.

Lengel sighs and begins to look very patient and old and gray. He's been a friend of my parents for years. "Sammy, you don't want to do this to your Mom and Dad," he tells me. It's true, I don't. But it seems to me that once you begin a gesture it's fatal not to go through with it. I folded the apron, "Sammy" stitched in red on the pocket, and put it on the counter, and drop the bow tie on top of it. The bow tie is theirs, if you've ever wondered. "You'll feel this for the rest of your life," Lengel says, and I know that's true, too, but remembering how he made that pretty girl blush makes me so scrunchy inside I punch the No Sale tab and the machine whirs "pee-pul" and the drawer splats out. One advantage to this scene taking place in summer, I can follow this up with a clean exit, there's no fumbling around getting your coat and galoshes, I just saunter into the electric eye in my white shirt that my mother ironed the night before, and the door heaves itself open, and outside the sunshine is skating around on the asphalt.

I look around for my girls, but they're gone, of course. There wasn't anybody but some young married screaming with her children about some candy they didn't get by the door of a powder-blue Falcon station wagon. Looking back in the big windows, over the bags of peat moss and aluminum lawn furniture stacked on the pavement, I could see Lengel in my place in the slot, checking the sheep through. His face was dark gray and his back stiff, as if he's just had an injection of iron, and my stomach kind of fell as I felt how hard the world was going to be to me hereafter.

18

Critical Perspectives on Literature and Culture

The Beats Web   *www*

After the Second World War, a group of young writers who first met at Columbia University began to explore the joy of unfettered creativity. Inspired by jazz, the crazy potentials of language, the excitement of the road, and the utter ecstasy of knowledge, this group grew to include Jack Kerouac Web, Allen *www*
Ginsberg Web, Neal Cassady, William S. Burroughs, Gregory Corso, and later *www*
Lawrence Ferlinghetti, Amiri Baraka (LeRoi Jones) Web, Diane Di Prima, *www*
Gary Snyder Web, Michael McClure, Bruce Conner, and Ann Waldman, all of *www*
whom gave voice to the tradition of twentieth-century avant-gardism. These artists congregated in Greenwich Village and later San Francisco. They wrote poetry and prose, made films, staged readings and theatrical "happenings," and generally spread a new excitement about art and language throughout New York and later American culture. Paradoxically, what began as a distinctly countercultural, even radical, movement eventually became—and has continued to be in the twenty-first century—a dominant social force. Fifty years ago, their identity as cultural icons became so established that magazines like *Time* and *Newsweek* wrote about their unconventional lifestyle and rich socialites used to "rent" beatniks to attend parties. Both their work and their personas, although not without their critics, became the subjects of both fascination and emulation. California beat Michael McClure associated with Jim Morrison of The Doors, who liked to think of himself as a beat poet; today, the images of Jack Kerouac and actor-photographer Dennis Hopper, have been appropriated by Gap to help sell khakis. Their images still exude hipness and style.

The beats were not, however, simply "arts-for-art's sake" writers. Much of their work contains a social critique stimulated by what they saw as a 1950s culture of repressiveness in America. The decade gave rise to a host of political and social events promulgating notions of conformity and convention, including the House of Un-American Activities hearings, which was led by Senator Joseph McCarthy and blacklisted Hollywood writers and others for their political beliefs; a cold war mentality that thrived on paranoia; the threat of the atomic bomb; the racial oppressions and segregations intrinsic to American culture; the destructive greed of corporations; narrow and con-

Beat poetry book rack at the Paperback Book Gallery, New York, 1960.

formist notions of family, sexuality, and identity; and the exploration of what constitutes a useful endeavor. If Jack Kerouac travels the country with Neal Cassady looking for the soul of jazz and the charms of the everyday citizen, if Allen Ginsberg looks for ways to make words sing, if Gary Snyder and Bruce Conner seek visionary experiences through Eastern religion or Native American culture, all extol the spirit of life and art. Their work represents a mixture of media—language, photography, film, jazz, and a liberated theater no longer kept inside the confines of traditional form and stage.

Beat art reflects all of these: it is a fusion of jazz rhythms and soulfulness with the liberations of humor, philosophy, and substances. But beat art is not simply an accident or the result of some kind of spontaneous generation. Beat artists were conscious of their methods and the meanings of what they did. Although their public image may have been one of unrestrained action, their art was the result of the thoughtful analysis of the relations of individuals to the world. If beat artists extolled spontaneity, it was because they realized they could not control much of what happened. Beat art made a virtue out of understanding that a 9-to-5 workaday world may not be life.

In other words, beat art—beat literature, in particular—embodies a philosophy of critical action. More often than not, beat literature "does" something by intervening in contemporary events, ideologies, or oppressions. Both Allen Ginsberg and Gregory Corso spoke out in poems against nuclear proliferation during the cold war era; Kerouac and Ginsberg, to name just two, wrote strong criticisms of American capitalism that, in many respects, are still relevant and are entirely compatible with critiques of multinational capitalism today; black beats like LeRoi Jones (who changed his name to Amiri Baraka shortly after the assassination of Malcolm X), Bob Kaufman, and Ted Joans saw beat culture as embracing black cultural forms and making an intervention in what was, at the time, a deeply segregated America. For all of these reasons and more, beat culture metamorphosed readily into the "free love" generation of the later 1960s, into the anti-Vietnam War and civil rights movements, and into many other social and political causes. Aesthetic innovation and social critique joined in the beat movement; coffee houses and alternative bookstores, folk rock, and independent film remain today some of its significant legacies.

JACK KEROUAC

Belief & Technique for Modern Prose (1958)

List of Essentials

1. Scribbled secret notebooks, and wild typewritten pages, for yr own joy
2. Submissive to everything, open, listening

Jack Kerouac

3. Try never get drunk outside yr own house
4. Be in love with yr life
5. Something that you feel will find its own form
6. Be crazy dumbsaint of the mind
7. Blow as deep as you want to blow
8. Write what you want bottomless from bottom of the mind
9. The unspeakable visions of the individual
10. No time for poetry but exactly what is
11. Visionary tics shivering in the chest
12. In tranced fixation dreaming upon object before you
13. Remove literary, grammatical and syntactical inhibition
14. Like Proust be an old teahead of time
15. Telling the true story of the world in interior monolog
16. The jewel center of interest is the eye within the eye
17. Write in recollection and amazement for yourself
18. Work from pithy middle eye out, swimming in language sea
19. Accept loss forever
20. Believe in the holy contour of life
21. Struggle to sketch the flow that already exists intact in mind
22. Dont think of words when you stop but to see picture better
23. Keep track of every day the date emblazoned in yr morning
24. No fear or shame in the dignity of yr experience, language & knowledge
25. Write for the world to read and see yr exact pictures of it
26. Bookmovie is the movie in words, the visual American form
27. In praise of Character in the Bleak inhuman Loneliness
28. Composing wild, undisciplined, pure, coming in from under, crazier the better
29. You're a Genius all the time
30. Writer-Director of Earthly movies Sponsored & Angeled in Heaven

∽∽∽

ALLEN GINSBERG

America   (1956)

America I've given you all and now I'm nothing.
America two dollars and twentyseven cents January 17, 1956.
I can't stand my own mind.
America when will we end the human war?
Go fuck yourself with your atom bomb.
I don't feel good don't bother me.
I won't write my poem till I'm in my right mind.
America when will you be angelic?
When will you take off your clothes?
When will you look at yourself through the grave?

When will you be worthy of your million Trotskyites?°
America why are your libraries full of tears?
America when will you send your eggs to India?
I'm sick of your insane demands.
When can I go into the supermarket and buy what I need with my
    good looks? 15
America after all it is you and I who are perfect not the next
    world.
Your machinery is too much for me.
You made me want to be a saint.
There must be some other way to settle this argument.
Burroughs° is in Tangiers I don't think he'll come back it's sinister. 20
Are you being sinister or is this some form of practical joke?
I'm trying to come to the point.
I refuse to give up my obsession.
America stop pushing I know what I'm doing.
America the plum blossoms are falling. 25
I haven't read the newspapers for months, everyday somebody goes
    on trial for murder.
America I feel sentimental about the Wobblies.°
America I used to be a communist when I was a kid I'm not sorry.
I smoke marijuana every chance I get.
I sit in my house for days on end and stare at the roses in the
    closet. 30
When I go to Chinatown I get drunk and never get laid.
My mind is made up there's going to be trouble.
You should have seen me reading Marx.
My psychoanalyst thinks I'm perfectly right.
I won't say the Lord's Prayer. 35
I have mystical visions and cosmic vibrations.
America I still haven't told you what you did to Uncle Max after
    he came over from Russia.

I'm addressing you.
Are you going to let your emotional life be run by Time
    Magazine?
I'm obsessed by Time Magazine. 40
I read it every week.
Its cover stares at me every time I slink past the corner candystore.
I read it in the basement of the Berkeley Public Library.
It's always telling me about responsibility. Businessmen are serious.
    Movie producers are serious. Everybody's serious but me.

---

11 *Trotskyites:* Communist idealists, followers of Leon Trotsky (1879–1940).   20 *Burroughs:* William Burroughs (1914–1997), author of *Naked Lunch.*   27 *Wobblies:* Members of the Industrial Workers of the World, a militant labor organization strong in the 1910s.

It occurs to me that I am America.   45
I am talking to myself again.

Asia is rising against me.
I haven't got a chinaman's chance.
I'd better consider my national resources.
My national resources consist of two joints of marijuana millions of
          genitals an unpublished private literature that goes 1400 miles
          an hour and twentyfive-thousand mental institutions.   50
I say nothing about my prisons nor the millions of underprivileged
          who live in my flowerpots under the light of five hundred
          suns.
I have abolished the whorehouses of France, Tangiers is the next
          to go.
My ambition is to be President despite the fact that I'm a
          Catholic.

America how can I write a holy litany in your silly mood?
I will continue like Henry Ford my strophes are as individual as
          his automobiles more so they're all different sexes.   55
America I will sell you strophes $2500 apiece $500 down on your
          old strophe
America free Tom Mooney°
America save the Spanish Loyalists°
America Sacco & Vanzetti° must not die.
America I am the Scottsboro boys.°   60
America when I was seven momma took me to Communist Cell
          meetings they sold us garbanzos a handful per ticket a ticket
          cost a nickel and the speeches were free everybody was
          angelic and sentimental about the workers it was all so sincere
          you have no idea what a good thing the party was in 1935
          Scott Nearing was a grand old man a real mensch Mother
          Bloor made my cry I once saw Israel Amter° plain. Everybody
          must have been a spy.
America you don't really want to go to war
America it's them bad Russians
Them Russians them Russians and them Chinamen. And them
          Russians.
The Russia wants to eat us alive. The Russia's power mad. She
          wants to take our cars from out our garages.   65

---

57 *Tom Mooney:* Labor leader sentenced to death for killings in 1916. The sentence was com-
muted and he was eventually pardoned.   58 *Spanish Loyalists:* Opponents of Franco's Fascists in
the Spanish Civil War.   59 *Sacco & Vanzetti:* Anarchists executed in Massachusetts for murder
(1927) in a case that aroused much controversy.   60 *Scottsboro boys:* Nine black men falsely convicted in Alabama for the rape of two white women (1931). The defense was undertaken by the
Communist Party, and the case became a cause for liberals and radicals, who believed it to be a
miscarriage of justice.   61 *Scott . . . Amter:* Nearing, Bloor, and Amter were active in Socialist
and radical causes.

Her wants to grab Chicago. Her needs a Red Reader's Digest. Her
    wants our auto plants in Siberia. Him big bureaucracy
    running our fillingstations.
That no good. Ugh. Him make Indians learn read. Him need big
    black niggers. Hah. Her make us all work sixteen hours a day.
    Help.
America this is quite serious.
America this is the impression I get from looking in the television
    set.
America is this correct?   70
I'd better get right down to the job.
It's true I don't want to join the Army or turn lathes in precision
parts factories, I'm nearsighted and psychopathic anyway.
America I'm putting my queer shoulder to the wheel.

A Supermarket in California   *(1955–1956)*

What thoughts I have of you tonight, Walt Whitman, for I walked down the sidestreets under the trees with a headache self-conscious looking at the full moon.

In my hungry fatigue, and shopping for images, I went into the neon fruit supermarket, dreaming of your enumerations!

What peaches and what penumbras! Whole families shopping at night! Aisles full of husbands! Wives in the avocados, babies in the tomatoes!—and you, Garcia Lorca,° what were you doing down by the watermelons?

I saw you, Walt Whitman, childless, lonely old grubber, poking among the meats in the refrigerator and eyeing the grocery boys.

I heard you asking questions of each: Who killed the pork chops? What price bananas? Are you my Angel?   5

I wandered in and out of the brilliant stacks of cans following you, and followed in my imagination by the store detective.

We strode down the open corridors together in our solitary fancy tasting artichokes, possessing every frozen delicacy, and never passing the cashier.

Where are we going, Walt Whitman? The doors close in an hour. Which way does your beard point tonight?

(I touch your book and dream of our odyssey in the supermarket and feel absurd.)

Will we walk all night through solitary streets? The trees add shade to shade, lights out in the houses, we'll both be lonely.   10

Will we stroll dreaming of the lost America of love past blue automobiles in driveways, home to our silent cottage?

Ah, dear father, graybeard, lonely old courage-teacher, what America did you have when Charon quit poling his ferry and you got out on a smoking bank and stood watching the boat disappear on the black waters of Lethe?°

---

3 *Garcia Lorca:* Spanish poet and dramatist (1889–1937).   12 *Lethe:* River of forgetfulness in Hades, in classical myth.

First Party at Ken Kesey's with Hell's Angels   *(1965)*

Cool black night thru redwoods
cars parked outside in shade
behind the gate, stars dim above
the ravine, a fire burning by the side
porch and a few tired souls hunched over   5
in black leather jackets. In the huge
wooden house, a yellow chandelier
at 3 A.M. the blast of loudspeakers
hi-fi Rolling Stones Ray Charles Beatles
Jumping Joe Jackson and twenty youths   10
dancing to the vibration thru the floor,
a little weed in the bathroom, girls in scarlet
tights, one muscular smooth skinned man
sweating dancing for hours, beer cans
bent littering the yard, a hanged man   15
sculpture dangling from a high creek branch,
children sleeping softly in their bedroom bunks.
And 4 police cars parked outside the painted
gate, red lights revolving in the leaves.

ᘛ⁐̤ᕐᐷ

JACK KEROUAC

About the Beat Generation   *(1957)*

The beat generation, that was a vision that we had, John Clellon Holmes and
I, and Allen Ginsberg in an even wilder way, in the late Forties, of a generation of crazy, illuminated hipsters suddenly rising and roaming America, serious,
curious, bumming and hitchhiking everywhere, ragged, beatific, beautiful in
an ugly graceful new way—a vision gleaned from the way we had heard the
word "beat" spoken on streetcorners on Times Square and in the Village, in
other cities in the downtown city night of postwar America—beat, meaning
down and out but full of intense conviction—We'd even heard old 1910
Daddy Hipsters of the streets speak the word that way, with a melancholy
sneer—It never meant juvenile delinquents, it meant characters of a special
spirituality who didn't gang up but were solitary Bartlebies staring out the
dead wall window of our civilization—the subterraneans heroes who'd finally
turned from the "freedom" machine of the West and were taking drugs, digging bop, having flashes of insight, experiencing the "derangement of the
senses," talking strange, being poor and glad, prophesying a new style for
American culture, a new style (we thought) completely free from European
influences (unlike the Lost Generation), a new incantation—The same thing
was almost going on in the postwar France of Satre and Genet and what's

Neal Cassady

more we knew about it—But as to the actual existence of a Beat Generation, chances are it was really just an idea in our minds— We'd stay up 24 hours drinking cup after cup of black coffee, playing record after record of Wardell Gray, Lester Young, Dexter Gordon, Willie Jackson, Lennie Tristano and all the rest, talking madly about that holy new feeling out there in the streets— We'd write stories about some strange beatific Negro hepcat saint with goatee hitchhiking across Iowa with taped up horn bringing the secret message of blowing to other coasts, other cities, like a veritable Walter the Penniless leading an invisible First Crusade—We had our mystic heroes and wrote, nay sung novels about them, erected long poems celebrating the new "angels" of the American underground—In actuality there was only a handful of real hip swinging cats and what there was vanished mighty swiftly during the Korean War when (and after) a sinister new kind of efficiency appeared in America, maybe it was the result of the universalization of Television and nothing else (the Polite Total Police Control of Dragnet's "peace" officers) but the beat characters after 1950 vanished into jails and madhouses, or were shamed into silent conformity, the generation itself was shortlived and small in number.

But there'd be no sense in writing this article if it weren't equally true that by some miracle of metamorphosis, suddenly, the Korean postwar youth emerged cool and beat, had picked up the gestures and the style, soon it was everywhere, the new look, the "twisted" slouchy look, finally it began to appear even in movies (James Dean) and on television, bop arrangements that were once the secret ecstasy music of beat contemplatives began to appear in every pit in every square orchestral book (cf. the works of Neil Hefti and not meaning Basie's book), the bop visions became common property of the commercial popular cultural world, the use of expressions like "crazy," "hungup," "hassle," "make it," "like" ("like make it over sometime, like"), "go," became familiar and common usage, the ingestion of drugs became official (tranquillizers and the rest), and even the clothes style of the beat hipsters carried over to the new Rock'n'Roll youth via Montgomery Clift (leather jacket), Marlon Brando (T-shirt), and Elvis Presley (long sideburns), and the Beat Generation, though dead, was suddenly resurrected and justified.

It really happened, and the sad thing is, that while I am asked to explain the Beat Generation, there is no actual original Beat Generation left.

Yet today from Montreal to Mexico City, from London to Casablanca kids in blue jeans are now playing Rock'n'Roll records on jukeboxes.

As to an analysis of what it means . . . who knows? Even in this late stage ⁵ of civilization when money is the only thing that really matters, to everybody, I think perhaps it is the Second Religiousness that Oswald Spengler prophesied for the West (in America the final home of Faust), because there are elements of hidden religious significance in the way, for instance, that a guy like Stan Getz, the highest jazz genius of his "beat" generation, was put in jail for trying to hold up a drug store, suddenly had visions of God and repented (something gracefully Villonesque in that story)—Or take the case of the posthumous canonization of James Dean by millions of kids—Strange talk we'd heard among the early hipsters, of "the end of the world" at the "second coming," of "stoned-out visions" and even visitations, all believing, all inspired and fervent and free of Bourgeois-Bohemian Materialism, such as P.L.'s[1] being knocked off his chair by the Angel and his vision of the books of the Fathers of the Church and of Christ crashing through Time, G.C.'s[2] visions of the devil and celestial Heralds, A.G.'s[3] visions in Harlem and elsewhere of the tearful Divine Love, W.S.B.'s[4] reception of the word that he is the One Prophet, G.S.'s[5] Buddhist visions of the vow of salvation, peotl visions of all the myths being true, P.W.'s[6] visions of malific flashes and forms and the roof flying off the house, J.K.'s[7] numerous visions of Heaven, the "Golden Eternity," bright light in the night woods, H.H.'s[8] geekish visions of Armaggedon (experienced in Sing Sing), N.C.'s[9] visions of reincarnation under God's will [. . .] A.L.'s[10] vision of everything as mysterious electricity, and

---

1. Philip Lamantia.
2. Gregory Corso.
3. Allen Ginsberg.
4. William S. Burroughs.
5. Gary Snyder.
6. Philip Whalen.
7. Jack Kerouac.
8. Herbert Huncke.
9. Neal Cassady.
10. Alene L., the African-American woman with whom Kerouac had an affair in New York City in 1953; she is called "Mardou" in *The Subterraneans*.

Allen Ginsberg

one unnamed Times Square kid's vision of the Second Coming being televised (all taking place, a definite fact, in the midst of everyday contemporary life in the minds of typical members of my generation whom I know), reappearances of the early Gothic Springtime feeling of Western mankind before it went on its "Civilization" Rationale and developed relativity, jets and superbombs and supercolossal bureaucratic totalitarian benevolent Big Brother structures—so, as Spengler says, when comes the sunset of our culture (due now, according to his morphological graphs) and the dust of civilized striving settles, lo, the clear late-day glow reveals the original concerns again, reveals a beatific indifference to things that are Caesar's, for instance, a tiredness of that, and a yearning for, a regret for, the transcendent value, or "God," again, "Heaven," the spiritual regret for Endless Love which our theory of electromagnetic gravitation, our conquest of space will prove, and instead of only techniques of efficiency, all will be left, as with a population that has gone through a violent earthquake, will be the Last Things . . . again (for the fact that everybody dies makes the world kind).

We all know about the Religious Revival, Billy Graham and all, under which the Beat Generation, even the existentialists with all their intellectual overlays and pretenses of indifference, represent an even deeper religiousness, the desire to be gone, out of this world (which is not our kingdom), "high," ecstatic, saved, as if the visions of the cloistral saints of Chartres and Clairvaux were back with us again bursting like weeds through the sidewalks of stiffened Civilization wearying through its late motions.

Or maybe the Beat Generation, which is the offspring of the Lost Generation, is just another step towards that last, pale generation which will not know the answers either.

In any case, indications are that its effect has taken root in American culture.
Maybe.
Or, what difference does it make?   10

149th Chorus   *(1959)*
from Mexico City Blues

I keep falling in love
    with my mother,
I dont want to hurt her
—Of all people to hurt.

Every time I see her   5
    she's grown older
But her uniform always
    amazes me
For its Dutch simplicity
And the Doll she is,   10
The doll-like way
    she stands
Bowlegged in my dreams,
Waiting to serve me.

    And I am only an Apache   15
    Smoking Hashi
    In old Cabashy
    By the Lamp

211th Chorus   *(1959)*
from Mexico City Blues

The wheel of the quivering meat
               conception
Turns in the void expelling human beings,
Pigs, turtles, frogs, insects, nits,
Mice, lice, lizards, rats, roan   5
Racinghorses, poxy bucolic pigtics,
Horrible unnameable lice of vultures,
Murderous attacking dog-armies
Of Africa, Rhinos roaming in the
               jungle,   10
Vast boars and huge gigantic bull
Elephants, rams, eagles, condors,
Pones and Porcupines and Pills—

All the endless conception of living
>   beings   15
Gnashing everywhere in Consciousness
Throughout the ten directions of space
Occupying all the quarters in & out,
From supermicroscopic no-bug
To huge Galaxy Lightyear Bowell   20
Illuminating the sky of one Mind—
>   *Poor!* I wish I was free
>   of that slaving meat wheel
>   and safe in heaven dead

The Thrashing Doves   *(1959)*

from Mexico City Blues

In the back of the dark Chinese store
>   in a wooden jailhouse bibbet box
>   with dust of hay on the floor, rice
>   where the rice bags are leaned,
>   beyond the doomed peekokoos in the box   5
>   cage

All the little doves'll die.
>   As well as the Peekotoos—eels
>   —they'll bend chickens' necks back
>   oer barrels and slice at Samsara   10
>   the world of eternal suffering with silver
>   blades as thin as the ice in Peking

As thick & penetrable as the Wall of China
>   the rice darkness of that store, beans,
>   tea, boxes of dried fish, doodlebones,   15
>   pieces of sea-weed, dry, pieces of eight,
>   all the balloon of the shroud on the floor

And the lights from little tinkly Washington St.
>   Behung, dim, opium pipes and gong wars,
>   Tong, the rice and the card game—and   20
>   Tibbet de tibbet the tink tink tink
>   them Chinese cooks do in the kitchen
>   Jazz

The thrashing doves in the dark, white fear,
>   my eyes reflect that liquidly   25
>   and I no understand Buddha-fear?
>   awakener's fear? So I give warnings
>   'bout midnight round about midnight

And tell all the children the little otay
    story of magic, multiple madness, maya   30
otay, magic trees-sitters and little girl
bitters, and littlest lil brothers
    in crib made made of clay (blue in the moon).

For the doves.

GREGORY CORSO

Dream of a Baseball Star   *(1960)*

I dreamed Ted Williams
leaning at night
against the Eiffel Tower, weeping.

He was in uniform
and his bat lay at his feet   5
—knotted and twiggy.

'Randall Jarrell says you're a poet !' I cried.
'So do I ! I say you're a poet !'

He picked up his bat with blown hands;
stood there astraddle as he would in the batter's box,   10
and laughed ! flinging his schoolboy wrath
toward some invisible pitcher's mound
—waiting the pitch all the way from heaven.

It came; hundreds came! all afire!
He swung and swung and swung and connected not one   15
sinker curve hook or right-down-the-middle.
A hundred strikes !
The umpire dressed in strange attire
thundered his judgement: YOU'RE OUT !
And the phantom crowd's horrific boo   20
dispersed the gargoyles from Notre Dame.

And I screamed in my dream :
God ! throw thy merciful pitch !
Herald the crack of bats !
Hooray the sharp liner to left !   25
Yea the double, the triple !
Hosannah the home run !

∽∽

WILLIAM S. BURROUGHS

The Finger   *(n.d.)*

Lee walked slowly up 6th Avenue from 42nd Street, looking in pawnshop windows.

"I must do it," he repeated to himself.

Here it was. A cutlery store. He stood there shivering, with the collar of his shabby Chesterfield turned up. One button had fallen off the front of his overcoat, and the loose threads twisted in a cold wind. He moved slowly around the shop window and into the entrance, looking at knives and scissors and pocket microscopes and air pistols and take-down tool kits with the tools snapping or screwing into a metal handle, the whole kit folding into a small leather packet. Lee remembered getting one of these kits for Christmas when he was a child. Finally he saw what he was looking for: poultry shears like his father used to cut through the joints when he carved the turkey at grandmother's Thanksgiving dinners. There they were, glittering and stainless, one blade smooth and sharp, the other with teeth like a saw to hold the meat in place for cutting.

Lee went in and asked to see the shears. He opened and closed the blades, tested the edge with his thumb.

"That's stainless steel, sir. Never rusts or tarnishes."   5

"How much?"

"Two dollars and seventy-nine cents plus tax."

"O.K."

The clerk wrapped the shears in brown paper, taped the package neatly. It seemed to Lee that the crackling paper made a deafening noise in the empty store. He paid with his last five dollars, and walked out with the shears heavy in his overcoat pocket.

He walked up 6th Avenue repeating: "I must do it. I've got to do it now   10 that I've bought the shears."

He saw a sign: Hotel Aristo. There was no lobby. He walked up a flight of stairs. An old man, dingy and indistinct like a faded photograph, was standing behind a desk. Lee registered, paid one dollar in advance, and picked up a key with a heavy bronze tag.

His room opened onto a dark shaft. He turned on the light. Black stained furniture, a double bed with a thin mattress and sagging springs. Lee unwrapped the shears, and held them in his hand. He put the shears down on the dresser in front of an oval mirror that turned on a pivot.

Lee walked around the room. He picked up the shears again and placed the end joint of his left little finger against the saw teeth, lower blade exactly at the joint. Slowly he lowered the cutting blade until it rested against the flesh of his finger. He looked in the mirror, composing his face into the supercilious mask of an 18th-century dandy. He took a deep breath, pressed the handle quick and hard. He felt no pain. The finger joint fell on the dresser. Lee turned his hand over and looked at the stub. Blood spurted up and hit him in the face. He felt a sudden deep pity for the finger joint that lay there on the dresser, a few drops of blood gathering around the white bone. Tears came to his eyes.

"It didn't do anything," he said in a broken child's voice. He adjusted his face again, cleaned the blood off it with a towel, and bandaged his finger crudely, adding more gauze as the blood soaked through. In a few minutes the bleeding had stopped. Lee picked up the finger joint and put it in his vest pocket, and walked out of the hotel tossing his key on the desk.

"I've done it," he said to himself. Waves of euphoria swept through him 15 as he walked down the street. He stopped in a bar and ordered a double brandy, meeting all eyes with a level, friendly stare. Good will flowed out of him for everyone he saw, for the whole world. A lifetime of defensive hostility had fallen from him.

Half an hour later he was sitting with his analyst on a park bench in Central Park. The analyst was trying to persuade him to go to Bellevue, and had suggested they "go outside to talk it over."

"Really, Bill, you're doing yourself a great disservice. When you realize what you've done you'll need psychiatric care. Your ego will be overwhelmed."

"All I need is to have this finger sewed up. I've got a date tonight."

"Really, Bill, I don't see how I can continue as your psychiatrist if you don't follow my advice in this matter." The analyst's voice had become whiney, shrill, almost hysterical. Lee wasn't listening; he felt a deep trust in the doctor. The doctor would take care of him. He turned to the doctor with a little boy smile: "Why don't you fix it yourself?"

"I haven't practiced since my internship, and I don't have the necessary 20 materials in any case. This has to be sewed up right or it could get infected right on up the arm."

Lee finally agreed to go to Bellevue for medical treatment only.

At Bellevue Lee sat on a bench waiting while the doctor talked to somebody. The doctor came back, and led Lee to another room where an intern sewed up the finger and put on a dressing. The doctor kept urging him to allow himself to be committed; Lee was overcome by a sudden faintness. A nurse told him to put his head back. Lee felt that he must put himself entirely in the care of the doctor.

"All right," he said, "I'll do what you say."

The doctor patted his arm. "Ah, you're doing the right thing, Bill." The doctor lead him past several desks, where he signed papers.

"I'm cutting red tape by the yard," the doctor said. 25

Finally Lee found himself in a dressing gown in a bare ward.

"Where is my room?" he asked a nurse.

"Your room! I don't know what bed you've been assigned to. Anyway you can't go there before eight unless you have a special order from the doctor."

"Where is my doctor?"

"Doctor Bromfield? He isn't here now. He'll be in tomorrow morning 30 around ten.'"

"I mean Doctor Horowitz."

William S. Burroughs

"Doctor Horowitz? I don't think he's on the staff here."

He looked around him at the bare corridors, the men walking around in bathrobes muttering under the cold, indifferent eyes of an attendant.

"Why this is the psychopathic ward," he thought. "He put me in here and went away!"

Years later Lee would tell the story: "Did I ever tell you about the time I got on a Van Gogh kick and cut off the end joint of my little finger?" At this point he would hold up his left hand. "This girl, see? She lives in the next room to me in a rooming house on Jane Street. That's in the Village. I love her and she's so stupid I can't make any impression. Night after night I lay there hearing her carry on with some man in the next room. It's tearing me all apart . . . So I hit on this finger joint gimmick. Ill present it to her: 'A trifling memento of my undying affection. I suggest you wear it around your neck in a pendant filled with formaldehyde.'

"But my analyst, the lousy bastard, shanghaied me into the nuthouse, and the finger joint was sent to potter's field with a death certificate, because someone might find the finger joint and the police go around looking for the rest of the body.

"If you ever have occasion to cut off a finger joint, my dear, don't consider any instrument but poultry shears. That way you're sure of cutting *through* at the joint."

"And what about the girl?"

"Oh, by the time I got out of the nuthouse she'd gone to Chicago, I never saw her again."

∞∞

AMIRI BARAKA (LEROI JONES)

Three Modes of History and Culture   *(1969)*

Chalk mark sex of the nation, on walls we drummers
know
as cathedrals. Cathedra, in a churning meat milk.

Women glide through looking for telephones. Maps
weep   5
and are mothers and their daughters listening to

music teachers. From heavy beginnings. Plantations,
learning
America, as speech, and a common emptiness. Songs knocking

inside old women's faces. Knocking through cardboard trunks.   10
Train's
leaning north, catching hellfire in windows, passing through

the first ignoble cities of missouri, to illinois, and the panting
Chicago.
And then all ways, we go where flesh is cheap. Where factories   15

sit open, burning the chiefs. Make your way! Up through fog and
history
Make your way, and swing the general, that it come flash open

and spill the innards of that sweet thing we heard, and gave theory
to.   20
Breech, bridge, and reach, to where all talk is energy. And there's

enough, for anything singular. All our lean prophets and rhythms.
Entire
we arrive and set up shacks, hole cards, Western hearts at the edge

of saying. Thriving to balance the meanness of particular skies.   25
Race
of madmen and giants.

Brick songs. Shoe songs. Chants of open weariness.
Knife wiggle early evenings of the wet mouth. Tongue
dance midnight, any season shakes our house. Don't   30
tear my clothes! To doubt the balance of misery

ripping meat hug shuffle fuck. The Party of Insane
Hope. I've come from there too. Where the dead told lies
about clever social justice. Burning coffins voted
and staggered through cold white streets listening   35
to Willkie or Wallace or Dewey through the dead face
of Lincoln. Come from there, and belched it out.

I think about a time when I will be relaxed.
When flames and non-specific passion wear themselves
away. And my eyes and hands and mind can turn   40
and soften, and my songs will be softer
and lightly weight the air.

∽∽

DIANE DI PRIMA

On Sitting Down to Write, I Decide Instead to Go to Fred Herko's Concert *(1975)*

As water, silk
the quiver of fish
or the long cry of goose
      or some such bird
      I never heard   5
your orange tie
a sock in the eye
      as Duncan
      might forcibly note
are you sitting under the irregular drums   10
of Brooklyn Joe Jones
(in a loft which I know to be dirty
& probably cold)
or have you scurried already
        hurried already   15
uptown
on a Third Avenue Bus
toward smelly movies & crabs I'll never get
and you all perfumed too
as if they'd notice   20

O the dark caves of obligation
into which I must creep
      (alack)
like downstairs & into a coat
      O all that wind   25
Even Lord & Taylor don't quite keep out
that wind
and that petulant vacuum
I am aware of it
sucking me into Bond Street   30
into that loft
      dank
      rank
I draw a blank
at the very thought   35

            Hello
I came here
      after all

∞∞

ANNE WALDMAN

College Under Water   *(1966)*

Who are these women and offices
that control the will of the dead graduates?

They come to dinner like swimmers
assembling before a final race

Now coffins are lined up outside   5
where campus elms seize precedence over girls

Now offices are closed for the afternoon
in correspondence with the courts and the pool

Now because instructed the sky changes hands
shuffling wills that are transferred   10

to file cards behind locked doors
These vendetta women will not be put off

Now I write like this because
it could happen   My will weakens

Is there a choice? the alternative   15
lies on the other side of the poem.

POETRY

Part IV
Understanding Poetic Form

19 Introduction: Reading Poetry

I, too, dislike it. . . .
> *Reading it, however, with a perfect contempt for it, one*
> *discovers in*
> *it after all, a place for the genuine.*
>
> –MARIANNE MOORE, "POETRY" (1924)

Some readers are natural-born poetry lovers, but most of us need a little coaxing in the pleasures of reading verse. Let's face it: unpacking a dense Shakespearean sonnet isn't exactly like watching the season finale of your favorite TV show. Although you can find plenty of action, adventure, comedy, tragedy, romance, intrigue, seduction, and betrayal in poetry, reading verse doesn't entertain in the same fashion as a gripping novel or sensational action movie. Compelling poems can rivet our attention but not in the ways we expect from the latest special effects of, say, George Lucas's Industrial Light and Magic. Reading poetry makes a different claim on our attention than playing *Nintendo*. While you can always get to the next level of a video game, a particularly difficult line of verse often remains dumbfounding even on a second, third, or fourth reading. At times like these, it might help to know that even practicing poets such as Marianne Moore had moments of "perfect contempt" for poetry.

Why then do we bother with reading poetry? Perhaps it has to do with what Moore calls "the genuine." In a world of clichés, stereotypes, and packaged images, nothing satisfies our passion for "the genuine"—for originality, authenticity, "the new"—like poetry. Beyond whatever pleasure we take in a well-crafted poetic form, great poetry delivers a vital knowledge that we can find nowhere else. Late in life, the modern poet William Carlos Williams summed it up this way: "It is difficult," he concluded,

> to get the news from poems
> yet men die miserably every day
>   for lack
> of what is found there.
> (From "Asphodel, That Greeny Flower," 1955)

What one looks to find from a good poem is an act of imagination so fresh, so powerfully presented, so genuine that it possesses its own reality. As

Moore muses in a longer version of "Poetry," compelling poems are like "imaginary gardens with real toads in them." How would you describe Moore's point in the following lines?

MARIANNE MOORE *(1887–1972)*

Poetry   *(1921)*

I too, dislike it: there are things that are important beyond all this
    fiddle.
    Reading it, however, with a perfect contempt for it, one discovers in
    it after all, a place for the genuine.
        Hands that can grasp, eyes
        that can dilate, hair that can rise   5
            if it must, these things are important not because a

high-sounding interpretation can be put upon them but because they are
    useful. When they become so derivative as to become unintelligible,
    the same thing may be said for all of us, that we
        do not admire what   10
        we cannot understand: the bat
            holding on upside down or in quest of something to

eat, elephants pushing, a wild horse taking a roll, a tireless wolf under
    a tree, the immovable critic twitching his skin like a horse that feels
        a flea, the base-
        ball fan, the statistician—   15
            nor is it valid
            to discriminate against 'business documents and

school-books'; all these phenomena are important. One must make a
    distinction
    however: when dragged into prominence by half poets, the result is not
        poetry,
    nor till the poets among us can be   20
    'literalists of
        the imagination'—above
            insolence and triviality and can present

for inspection, 'imaginary gardens with real toads in them,' shall we have
    it. In the meantime, if you demand on the one hand,   25
    the raw material of poetry in
        all its rawness and
        that which is on the other hand
            genuine, then you are interested in poetry.

Art and reality, the imagination and its "raw material," imaginary gardens and real toads: For Moore, reading poetry requires having an interest in each of these opposites at the same time.

Moore's tribute to "Poetry" is a complex statement. In responding to it, write a one-paragraph **paraphrase** of her poem. A paraphrase is a restatement in your own words of the major ideas, argument, or thematic elements of a poem. A paraphrase provides a prose version of a poem's main message. Paraphrase, of course, can never begin to capture the subtlety of a poem's formal arrangement on the page, but it is a place to begin reading poetry. In paraphrasing Moore's "Poetry," consider the following questions. After you draft your paragraph, compare what you have written to the critical commentary *www* on the poem from the *Understanding Literature* Web :

1. How does Moore describe "the genuine" in "Poetry"?
2. Where, according to Moore, does understanding poetry begin?
3. In what sense does Moore imply that great poetry is "important" and "useful"?
4. What do you think Moore means by being "interested in poetry"?
5. According to the poem's argument, what relation should the imagination have to the intellect in poetry?

Poetry, of course, goes far beyond paraphrase as it involves the formal activity of verse writing. While paraphrasing summarizes a poem's main idea or theme, what poetry is about—*what it is*, in essence—is not so easily understood. If you've ever seen Tiger Woods swing a golf club, you'd probably agree that it looks like "pure poetry." Watching an Olympic swimming legend such as Janet Evans, we might say her freestyle is "poetry in motion." But what kind of poetry is this? If we were pressed to define the poetry we find in a masterful chip shot or perfect flip turn, what would we say? Considered seriously enough, such questioning sooner or later would, as the Romantic poet John Keats said, "tease us out of thought." Poets, philosophers, and even politicians have all wrestled with the question "What is poetry?"

Perhaps the most direct answer comes from the poet William Stafford. He characterized poetry as "anything said in such a way or put on the page in such a way as to invite from the hearer or reader a certain kind of attention." But how helpful is this? What kind of attention is Stafford talking about exactly? Is he implying that poetry inspires wonder, and, if so, isn't wonder, by definition, outside our understanding? Yes, and that is precisely the point. *Poetry constantly introduces us to—and addresses us by—something that is bracingly different from what we already know, what we have already thought, what we have already felt.* It captures our attention. That's the reason why the British romantic poet Percy Bysshe Shelley claimed that poetry "makes familiar objects be as if they were not familiar." But what is that experience like? And how can we tell if a poem inspires wonder? For her part, the nineteenth-century American poet Emily Dickinson applied a very simple test to the experience of poetry. "If," she says, "I read a book [and] it makes my whole body so cold no fire ever can warm me I know *that* is poetry. If I feel physically as if the top of my head were taken off, I know *that* is poetry. These are the only ways I know it." Wonder, for her, begins in the body; it is played upon the pulses.

Poetry begins, then, with a close encounter with what is radically new and unclaimed in our experience. "A poem," says Robert Frost, "is never a thought to begin with. . . . A poem begins with a lump in the throat." The emotional, and even physical, impact poetry can have on us is one of the reasons that Plato thought of poets as dangerous people. In fact, he set out to ban poets and poetry from his ideal model of the state in Book X of *The Republic*. Poets, like politicians, know that the powerful utterance will find a way to engage our feelings, our hopes, and our anxieties; it will get under our skin.

"You campaign in poetry," said former New York governor Mario Cuomo; "you govern in prose." But if poets, as Shelley writes, are the "unacknowledged legislators of the world," how do they add something original and decisive to existence? For his part, Plato charges that this is precisely what poets never do. Plato writes that poets are slavish imitators, belated and removed from the truths to be witnessed in nature. They are decidedly unheroic and merely record what their betters actually do in the real world. Against this low opinion of poets, Sir Philip Sidney notes in "An Apology for Poetry" that the titles poets carried in the Ancient world (in Greek, *poietes* or maker, and in Latin, *vates* or prophet) had civic and even religious power. Moreover, he reverses Plato to assert that "Nature never set forth the earth in so rich tapestry as diverse poets have done, neither with pleasant rivers, fruitful trees, sweet-smelling flowers, nor whatsoever else may make the too much loved earth more lovely."

Accepting Sidney's defense of why we should read poetry is one thing; knowing how to read a poem is something else altogether. Poetry makes special demands and claims on us as readers. Understanding poetry takes practice in reading it. How should you begin to read a poem? Beyond paraphrasing a poem's content, other ways of beginning to read verse include the following.

- Read the poem aloud, more than once if you need to.
- Make a word-for-word copy of the poem.
- Circle any words you don't understand and look them up in a dictionary.
- Highlight any phrases either that you don't understand or that seem particularly fresh and memorable.
- Explore the relationship between the poem's title and its key statements, key words, and key themes.
- Keep a journal of your poetry-reading experiences (for example, your experience in reading a particular poem; in reading a group of poems on a similar theme, conceit, or poetic form; or in reading poems by the same author).
- Keep a journal of your own creative writing.
- Discuss your experience and your interpretation of a poem with your friends, classmates, family members, or instructor.
- Refer to the prewriting activities in Chapter 54: Writing About Poetry.

While these are useful strategies, you will also find your own approaches for enjoying and understanding poetry.

To help you better appreciate verse with a more critical eye, we begin the verse unit in Chapter 20 with the formal elements that make poetry a distinct genre. In poetry, less is indeed more in terms of how we experience the particulars of a poem's diction, a poet's word choice, the tone created by unique turns of phrasing, and so on. Poetry's fresh presentation of images and its reliance on figurative language—metaphor, simile, personification, synaesthesia, and so on—give us new perspectives on how we use language not only in the crafted space of the poem but also in everyday life. These topics are covered in Chapters 21 and 22. Moving out from these most basic formal resources, in Chapters 23 and 24 we consider the ways in which symbolism and myth complicate a poem's presentation of its themes. As a highly stylized form of writing, poetry relies on traditions of rhyme, meter, rhythm, fixed forms, and free verse, which we take into account in Chapters 25 through 27.

www   Beyond formalism, we consider not just what makes poetry a unique literary genre but also how it participates in a wider dialogue with the nonliterary discourses of its historical occasions and cultural contexts **Web** . These concerns are taken up in Part V, "Poetry and History." Poetry is not solely an art form alone, but, as the contemporary poet Adrienne Rich reminds us, verse has ethical and political ends. Verse writing serves as both a means of self-exploration and a way of imagining and representing new modes of social life and cultural identity in the public sphere. In this vein, we explore poetry's "re-

www
www visionary" role in changing our understandings of self, inflected by race **Web** , gender **Web** , sexual **Web** , and class experiences **Web** .

While we usually encounter poetry in chapbooks and anthologies, before recorded history poetry lived fully as a spoken art. It still has something of that vital, performative role to play in contemporary society from the Beat Generation up through the latest scenes of open-mike competitions and poetry slams. Even now poetry thrives on the page, in new improvisational modes, and across the postmodern media of our contemporary information age.

20   Poetic Language: Diction, Word Choice, and Tone

"There are no poetic ideas," according to the English writer Evelyn Waugh, "only poetic utterances." We might add to this, "there are no poetic utterances without poetic language." But what is unique about the poet's special use of language? How does the poetic word differ from ordinary language? Many poets would contend that there is no real difference. Poetry simply points out the linguistic richness of our word choices if only we would pay closer attention to them. "A poet," wrote W. H. Auden, "is, before anything else, a person who is passionately in love with language," whether it be cast in the formal, epic utterances of, say, John Milton's *Paradise Lost* or the African American vernacular speech patterns of Langston Hughes's blues lyricism. Poets love the texture, sound, and even the taste of words, as the writer Mark Strand has it in his playful lyric "Eating Poetry":

> Ink runs from the corners of my mouth.
> There is no happiness like mine.
> I have been eating poetry.

Just as each wine is distinguished by the year, region, and growing conditions of its vintage, so each word bears the flavor of its particular historicity—what we describe in terms of its **etymology**.

Etymology records the changes, or morphology, a word undergoes throughout its history of usage. Moreover, etymology also defines a word's relation to **cognate** terms in other languages with which it bears a family relation by virtue of a similar linguistic ancestry. The term *cognate* defines a relation of similarity between words that have a common line of descent from the same verbal tradition. "Language," Ralph Waldo Emerson said, "is fossil poetry." If that is so, then any serious poet is not unlike a committed archaeologist or paleontologist who will scour each strata of rock and silt to discover the clues to the unique story of a fossilized bone or shard of ancient pottery.

The signs of language's etymological richness are everywhere on display if only we attend to them. Take any American place name and you are likely to turn up some interesting discoveries. For example, the linguist Lee Pederson reminds us that the upper Midwest city Minneapolis is a hybrid name literally meaning "city of water," blending as it does the Dakota term *minne* (water) with the Greek word *polis* (city). Bryn Mawr in Pennsylvania stems from the Welsh words meaning "great hill." Pennsylvania itself means Penn's woods, combining its founder's name (Admiral Sir William Penn) and the medieval Latin word for forest (*silvanus*). Language is indeed fossil poetry.

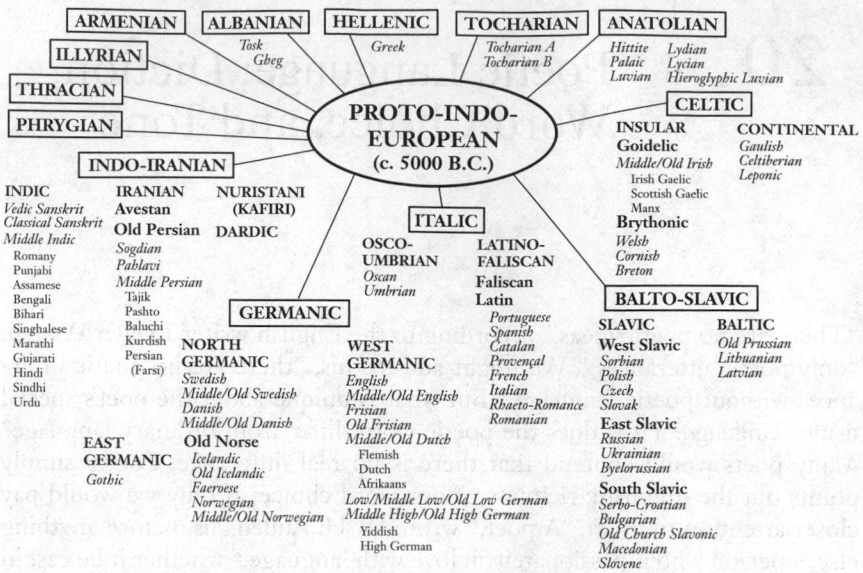

As you can see from the above language chart, the origins of modern English language are made up of lines of descent from the Indo-European language family, reaching back to the Iron Age Celts of 700 B.C. and later German invaders who arrived from the Continent around A.D. 449. The Old English period, dating from 449 to 1066, blends the dialects of the Low German Angles, Saxons, Jutes, and Northern Vikings that together share such cognate terms as *can, come, father, folk, house, man, mother, ride, see, smile, winter,* and *wire.* In his poem "Digging," the Irish Nobel Prize-winning poet Seamus Heaney draws an analogy between *pen* and *spade* as he "digs" down into language's etymological turf.

SEAMUS HEANEY (b. 1939)

Digging   (1966)

Between my finger and my thumb
The squat pen rests; snug as a gun.

Under my window, a clean rasping sound
When the spade sinks into gravelly ground:
My father, digging. I look down   5

Till his straining rump among the flowerbeds
Bends low, comes up twenty years away
Stooping in rhythm through potato drills
Where he was digging.

The coarse boot nestled on the lug, the shaft   10
Against the inside knee was levered firmly.
He rooted out tall tops, buried the bright edge deep
To scatter new potatoes that we picked
Loving their cool hardness in our hands.

By God, the old man could handle a spade.   15
Just like his old man.

My grandfather cut more turf in a day
Than any other man on Toner's bog.
Once I carried him milk in a bottle
Corked sloppily with paper. He straightened up   20
To drink it, then fell to right away
Nicking and slicing neatly, heaving sods
Over his shoulder, going down and down
For the good turf. Digging.

The cold smell of potato mould, the squelch and slap   25
Of soggy peat, the curt cuts of an edge
Through living roots awaken in my head.
But I've no spade to follow men like them.

Between my finger and my thumb
The squat pen rests.   30
I'll dig with it.

It's no accident that Heaney should link pen and spade. For generations, peat moss has been widely harvested as a domestic source of fuel in Ireland and Scotland. Removed from the traditional economy of his ancestors, Heaney is drawn nevertheless to the activity of "digging," albeit into language not turf. Burrowing into poetry is also analogous to descending into the ancient strata of the English language's age-old sedimentation. Heaney's word choices mine the Viking, German, and Old French language groups. He excavates the primordial, earthy foundations of Old and Middle English. It is this oldest stratum of the English language that the poet Theodore Roethke views as having a kind of primal signifying power to evoke archetypal states of being. "We all know," he writes, "that poetry is shot through with appeals to the unconsciousness, to the fears and desires that go far back into our childhood, into the imagination of the race. And we know that some words, like *hill*, *plow*, *mother*, *window*, *bird*, *fish*, are so drenched with human association, they sometimes can make even bad poems evocative."

Beyond a word's literal, dictionary meaning—its **denotation**—many words suggest a rich range of **connotation:** complex tonalities, associations, overtones of meaning that derive from generations of human usage. For example, the word *snug* has the connotations of being comfortable, content, secure, safe, at ease. The denotative meaning of *snug* is more specific and signifies something that "fits closely," originating perhaps from an Old Norse nautical term meaning "fit" or "ship-shape." Etymology provides clues to the origins of the connotations we bring to particular words. *Bog* comes from the Irish Gaelic term *bogach*, while *rasping* derives from the Old High German term *raspon* signifying a grating sound. Rump comes from Middle English and is of Scandanavian origin; similarly, the words "lug," "shaft," "turf," "spade," "thumb" all stem from Middle English etymological roots. Digging into language, as Heaney suggests, will unearth rich strata of "fossil poetry."

An important etymological layer of English dates from 1066 and the Norman-French invasion of the Battle of Hastings. The victorious French courtly tradition reinforced the Latinate influences of the Romance languages that had appeared much earlier in English through the influence of Christianity from the fifth through seventh centuries. The Jesuit poet Gerard Manley Hopkins features this French tradition in his poem "The Windhover."

GERARD MANLEY HOPKINS *(1844–1889)*

The Windhover   *(1877)*

To Christ Our Lord

I caught this morning morning's minion, king-
    dom of daylight's dauphin, dapple-dawn-drawn Falcon,
        in his riding
Of the rolling level underneath him steady air, and striding
High there, how he rung upon the rein of a wimpling wing
In his ecstasy! then off, off forth on swing,   5
    As a skate's heel sweeps smooth on a bow-bend: the hurl and gliding
    Rebuffed the big wind. My heart in hiding
Stirred for a bird,—the achieve of, the mastery of the thing!

Brute beauty and valour and act, oh, air, pride, plume, here
    Buckle! AND the fire that breaks from thee then, a billion   10
Times told lovelier, more dangerous, O my chevalier!

    No wonder of it: shéer plód makes plough down sillion
Shine, and blue-bleak embers, ah my dear,
    Fall, gall themselves, and gash gold-vermilion.

Hopkins's dedication, "To Christ Our Lord," suggests that the figure of the Windhover be read as a symbol for Christ. Like the Christian Son of God, the Windhover is the favorite or "minion" of the heavens, ruling there as a "dauphin": the oldest son and heir to the king of France. He is also a "chevalier"—a nobleman or knight—who proves his valor through his descent toward the earth—emblematic of Christ's incarnation and crucifixion, figured in the gashing "vermilion" (vivid red) tonalities of the plough's sillion, or furrow. The obvious French courtly words in the poem are, of course, *dauphin* and *chevalier*, but the majority of Hopkins's language stems from this tradition as well. To take only a few instances of some of the poem's key terms, *minion* stems from the Old French *mignot*; *level* from the Old French *livel* and Latin *libra* meaning balance; *mastery* derives from the Old French *maistre* and Latin *magister*; *beauty* likewise comes from the Old French *bealte* and the Latin *bellus*; *pride* descends from the Old French *prud*. A *buckle* is an Old French derivation from *boucle* and the Latin *buccula*, which is a helmet's cheek strap; as a verb it stems from the Old French *boucler* meaning to attach with a buckle. Similarly, the words *billion*, *sillion*, and *vermilion* all have French roots, which you can explore using the *Oxford English Dictionary*.

American English synthesizes such European roots with African and Asian influences. Coming into the American vernacular via the Georgia Sea Island Gullah culture, the dialect communities of New Orleans, and other southern communities, African languages from such regions as Nigeria, the Congo, Sierra Leone, Cameroon, the Nile valley, and so on have enriched the American vernacular with a savory linguistic stew or "jambalaya" of African-rooted etymologies. Similarly, Chinese, Japanese, Korean, and other East Asian influences have transformed the American dialect.

Asian American poets such as Janice Mirikitani punctuate their poems with Old World word choices to portray the dilemma of living in two cultural worlds at once. Putting such words as *salsa*, *otonashii*, and *shakuhachi* into her poem "Breaking Tradition" gives Mirikitani's readers a more immediate sense of how a diverse, multicultural heritage enriches the poet's sense of identity.

JANICE MIRIKITANI   *(b. 1942)*

Breaking Tradition   *(1978)*

for my Daughter

My daughter denies she is like me,
her secretive eyes avoid mine.
    She reveals the hatreds of womanhood
    already veiled behind music and smoke and telephones.
I want to tell her about the empty room   5
    of myself.
    This room we lock ourselves in
    where whispers live like fungus,
    giggles about small breasts and cellulite,
    where we confine ourselves to jealousies,   10

bedridden by menstruation.
The waiting room where we feel our hands
are useless, dead speechless clamps
that need hospitals and forceps and kitchens
and plugs and ironing boards to make them useful.   15
I deny I am like my mother. I remember why:
She kept her room neat with silence,
defiance smothered in requirements to be otonashii,
passion and loudness wrapped in an obi,
her steps confined to ceremony,   20
the weight of her sacrifice she carried like
a foetus. Guilt passed on in our bones.
I want to break tradition—unlock this room
where women dress in the dark
Discover the lies my mother told me.   25
The lies that we are small and powerless
that our possibilities must be compressed
to the size of pearls, displayed only as
passive chokers, charms around our neck.
Break Tradition.   30
I want to tell my daughter of this room
of myself
filled with tears of shakuhachi,
the light in my hands,
poems about madness,   35
the music of yellow guitars—
sounds shaken from barbed wire and
goodbyes and miracles of survival.
This room of open window where daring ones escape.

My daughter denies she is like me   40
her secretive eyes are walls of smoke
and music and telephones,
her pouting ruby lips, her skirts
swaying to salsa, Madonna and the Stones,
her thighs displayed in carnavals of color.   45
I do not know the contents of her room.
She mirrors my aging.

She is breaking tradition.

TOPICS FOR CRITICAL THINKING

1. Adopting the point of view of a second-generation Japanese American, Mirikitani's persona is suspended between generations. Consider how she would "break tradition" with her mother's traditional "requirements to be otonashii," that is, "to be gentle."

2. How for Mirikitani does being otonashii result in ceremonies of self-effacement and a resignation to the idea that women's lives are "small and powerless"?

3. How does Mirikitani have difficulty accepting her daughter's own form of breaking tradition?

TOPICS FOR CRITICAL WRITING

1. As a third-generation Japanese American writer, Mirikitani portrays her complex identity that draws both from her Japanese ancestry and her American experience. How does "Breaking Tradition" speak to the difficulty of a mother-daughter relationship further marked by a generational clash in cultural identifications?

2. On the one hand, Mirikitani would share her experience of internment—of "sounds shaken from barbed wire" as well as the "tears of shakuhachi" (a bamboo flute). Yet, she realizes her daughter as a sensei "denies" solidarity with her mother across the generations, immersed as she is in a multicultural "salsa" made up of "Madonna and the Stones." How does Mirikitani emphasize her sense of split generational traditions in her metaphor of separate rooms as well as in her dynamic word choices?

The best resource for understanding the etymology and cultural usage of a particular word over time is the *Oxford English Dictionary*. Whenever you come upon a word that is unfamiliar, spend some time learning its history. The *Oxford English Dictionary* is available online, and using the electronic version is a quick way toward understanding poetic language.

Poems such as Randall Jarrell's "The Knight, Death, and the Devil" that are rich in etymology will reward your efforts at tracking down their verbal histories.

RANDALL JARRELL   *(1914–1965)*

The Knight, Death, and the Devil   *(1969)*

Cowhorn-crowned, shockheaded, cornshuck-bearded,
Death is a scarecrow—his death's-head a teetotum
That tilts up toward man confidentially
But trimmed with adders; ringlet-maned, rope-bridled,
The mare he rides crops herbs beside a skull.   5
He holds up, warning, the crossed cones of time:
Here, narrowing into now, the Past and Future
Are quicksand.
                        A hoofed pikeman trots behind.
His pike's claw-hammer mocks—in duplicate, inverted—   10
The pocked, ribbed, soaring crescent of his horn.
A scapegoat aged into a steer; boar-snouted;
His great limp ears stuck sidelong out in air;
A dewlap bunched at his breast; a ram's-horn wound
Beneath each ear; a spur licked up and out   15
From the hide of his forehead; bat-winged, but in bone;
His eye a ring inside a ring inside a ring

That leers up, joyless, vile, in meek obscenity—
This is the devil. Flesh to flesh, he bleats
The herd back to the pit of being.   20
In fluted mail; upon his lance the bush
Of that old fox; a sheep-dog bounding at his stirrup,
In its eyes the cast of faithfulness (our help,
Our foolish help); his dun war-horse pacing
Beneath in strength, in ceremonious magnificence;   25
His castle—some man's castle—set on every crag:
So, companioned so, the knight moves through this world.
The fiend moos in amity, Death mouths, reminding:
He listens in assurance, has no glance
To spare for them, but looks past steadily   30
At—at—
              a man's look completes itself.

The death of his own flesh, set up outside him;
The flesh of his own soul, set up outside him—
Death and the devil, what are these to him?   35
His being accuses him—and yet his face is firm
In resolution, in absolute persistence;
The folds of smiling do for steadiness;
The face is its own fate—*a man does what he must*—
And the body underneath it says: *I am*.   40

TOPICS FOR CRITICAL THINKING

1. Look up in the *Oxford English Dictionary* the key words Jarrell uses to describe the figure of Death and the Devil in the opening lines of the poem. What etymological derivations does Jarrell employ here?

2. Investigate the language in which Jarrell portrays the knight, focusing on such terms as *fluted mail* and *companioned*. Where do these words originate?

3. Look up in the *Oxford English Dictionary* the Latin expressions that communicate the poet's tone in characterizing the knight's qualities of "assurance," "resolution," and "absolute persistence," as well as his horse's "ceremonious magnificence."

TOPICS FOR CRITICAL WRITING

1. Compare and contrast Jarrell's "The Knight, Death, and the Devil" with the Albrecht Dürer's artwork from which it takes its title.

2. Is there some dimension of the knight's ride that Jarrell's poetry communicates more vividly than the visual artist's pictorial medium?

In addition to the power of etymology, what is at stake in an entire poem's setting, situation, and theme can turn on the aptness of a particular word choice, as in John Keats's "This Living Hand."

Albrecht Dürer, *The Knight, Death, and the Devil*
(1513–1514)

JOHN KEATS *(1795–1821)*

This Living Hand *(1819, 1898)*

This living hand, now warm and capable
Of earnest grasping, would, if it were cold
And in the icy silence of the tomb,
So haunt thy days and chill thy dreaming nights
That thou wouldst wish thine own heart dry of blood   5
So in my veins red life might stream again,
And thou be conscience-calmed—see here it is—
I hold it towards you.

The key word in Keats's poem is *capable*, coming as it does from the Old
French derivation of *capere*, "to hold." There is also the pun in the poem on
the literal hand that the poet offers the beloved and the more haunting specter
of his posthumous handwriting. Prophetically perhaps, Keats left this beautiful lyric on a manuscript page of his posthumously published volume *The Jealousies*.

Similar to Keats's subtle but decisive play on the word *capable*, the entire drama of Seamus Heaney's mysterious lyric "A Dream of Jealousy" turns on the key term *candour*.

SEAMUS HEANEY   *(b. 1939)*

A Dream of Jealousy   *(1979)*

Walking with you and another lady
In wooded parkland, the whispering grass
Ran its fingers through our guessing silence
And the trees opened into a shady
Unexpected clearing where we sat down.   5
I think the candour of the light dismayed us.
We talked about desire and being jealous,
Our conversation a loose and single gown
Or a white picnic table cloth spread out
Like a book of manners in the wilderness.   10
"Show me," I said to our companion, "what
I have much coveted, your breast's mauve star."
And she consented. O neither these verses
Nor my prudence, love, can heal your wounded stare.

TOPICS FOR CRITICAL THINKING

1. In what ways is the locale of the poem's "unexpected clearing" both a literal and figurative setting?
2. The lovers' talk of "desire and being jealous" climaxes in the poet's desire for their "companion" and his lover's "wounded stare." Everything that comes to matter in the poem is clarified by the "candour" of the light that "dismayed" even as it defined the relations among the three of them. Interestingly enough, *candour* means "open and honest." How is that an apt term for the poem's disclosures of desire and jealousy?
3. Behind *candour*'s current meaning, however, stands the Latin origins of *candere*, "to shine," which has its cognate terms in *candle* and *candid*. How does that etymology reinforce the other tropes of light in the poem?

TOPIC FOR CRITICAL WRITING

How do the three lovers come upon the essential though "unexpected" truth of their feelings for one another in the clearing?

The connotations of particular word choices contribute to the **tone** of an uttered phrase, line, stanza, or entire poem. For example, Heaney conveys a tone of wonder and secrecy in the dream's setting through the imagery of the "whispering grass," "guessing silence" and the "shady / Unexpected clearing." The dreamlike tone of "A Dream of Jealousy" differs markedly from the more realistic, raw, and earthy tones of "Digging." Those organic tones, in turn, contrast with the more chivalric and regal tones of "The Windhover."

While poets mine Old English derivations to convey archetypal, earth-bound tones or French etymologies to achieve more formal and ceremonious evocations, Greek and Latin derivations can communicate tones of abstraction, rationality, and intellectual thought. Richard Eberhart's poem on "The Fury of Aerial Bombardment" uses just such Greek and Latin language roots to reflect on the violence of World War II.

RICHARD EBERHART   *(b. 1904)*

The Fury of Aerial Bombardment   *(1947)*

You would think the fury of aerial bombardment
Would rouse God to relent; the infinite spaces
Are still silent. He looks on shock-pried faces.
History, even, does not know what is meant.

You would feel that after so many centuries   5
God would give man to repent; yet he can kill
As Cain could, but with multitudinous will,
No farther advanced than in his ancient furies.

Was man made stupid to see his own stupidity?
Is God by definition indifferent, beyond us all?   10
Is the eternal truth man's fighting soul
Wherein the Beast ravens in its own avidity?

Of Van Wettering I speak, and Averill,
Names on a list, whose faces I do not recall
But they are gone to early death, who late in school   15
Distinguished the belt feed lever from the belt holding pawl.

Eberhart's experience as a gunnery instructor is plain to see in his eye for the details of the machinery of aerial combat, pointing out as he does the differences between the "belt feed lever from the belt holding pawl." Modern war is fought, won, and lost in terms of such minute particulars. But Eberhart further captures the violent immediacy of combat's intensity in the "shock-pried faces" of those in harm's way. What concerns Eberhart in the poem, however, is what to conclude about God and human civilization after the knowledge of modern violence on such a mass or "total" scale. One of his key terms, *aerial*, sets up the ultimate stakes of Eberhart's meditation, signifying on the insubstantial, even metaphysical dimensions of the heavens. *Aerial* comes from the Latin *aerius*, which has a Greek origin *aerios*, for air. Just as the bomber's literal destructive force comes from above, so the figurative "indifference" of God betokens a different, but no less lethal violence. Eberhart lends a quality of abstraction to God's apathy toward creation in the question, "Is God by definition indifferent, beyond us all?" The multisyllabic, Latin words *definition* (*definitio*) and *indifferent* (*indifferens*) resonate with such other terms in the poem as *multitudinous* (*multitudo*) and *avidity* (*avidus*), which together evoke a vision of divinity that is, finally, inexplicable.

Poems for Further Reading and Critical Writing

WILLIAM STAFFORD   (1914–1993)

Traveling Through the Dark   (1960)

Traveling through the dark I found a deer
dead on the edge of the Wilson River road.
It is usually best to roll them into the canyon:
the road is narrow; to swerve might make more dead.

By glow of the tail-light I stumbled back of the car   5
and stood by the heap, a doe, a recent killing;
she had stiffened already, almost cold.
I dragged her off; she was large in the belly.

My fingers touching her side brought me the reason—
her side was warm; her fawn lay there waiting,   10
alive, still, never to be born.
Beside that mountain road I hesitated.

The car aimed ahead its lowered parking lights;
under the hood purred the steady engine.
I stood in the glare of the warm exhaust turning red;   15
around our group I could hear the wilderness listen.

I thought hard for us all—my only swerving—,
then pushed her over the edge into the river.

TOPICS FOR CRITICAL THINKING

1. As we have seen, sometimes a single word serves as the key to unlocking a poem's major subject and theme. Consider how the poet's key word choices of *swerve* and *swerving* might reveal the meaning and significance of his encounter with the deer.

2. Explore the connotations of Stafford's key word choices such as *aimed*, *purred*, *steady*, and so on.

3. How would you characterize the poet's tone in the work?

TOPIC FOR CRITICAL WRITING

Does the poem render any moral or ethical judgment about the doe's "recent killing"?
Does it resist any moral conclusion? Would that resistance itself be a form of ethics?

LOUISE BOGAN   *(1897–1970)*

Didactic Piece   *(1929)*

The eye unacquitted by whatever it holds in allegiance:
The trees' upcurve thought sacred, the flaked air, sacred and alterable,
The hard bud seen under the lid, not the scorned leaf and the apple—
As once in a swept space, so now with speech in a house,
We think to stand spelled forever, chained to the rigid knocking   5
Of a heart whose time is its own flesh, momently swung and burning—
This, in peace, as well, though we know the air a combatant
And the word of the heart's wearing time, that it will not do without grief.

The limit already traced must be returned to and visited,
Touched, spanned, proclaimed, else the heart's time be all: 10
The small beaten disk, under the bent shell of stars,
Beside rocks in the road, dust, and the nameless herbs,
Beside rocks in the water, marked by the heeled-back current,
Seeing, in all autumns, the felled leaf betray the wind.

If but the sign of the end is given a room   15
By the pillared harp, sealed to its rest by hands—
(On the bright strings the hands are almost reflected,
The strings a mirror and light). The head bends to listen,
So that the grief is heard; tears begin and are silenced
Because of the mimic despair, under the figure of laughter.   20
Let the allegiance go; the tree and the hard bud seed themselves.
The end is set, whether it be sought or relinquished.
We wait, we hear, facing the mask without eyes,
Grief without grief, facing the eyeless music.

TOPICS FOR CRITICAL THINKING

1. How are we to interpret the sense of Bogan's opening line? In the *Oxford English
   Dictionary*, look up the etymology of the words *unacquitted* and *allegiance*. How do
   these word choices contribute to Bogan's abstract tone?
2. Contrast this opening use of diction with the language in which she depicts the
   "heart whose time is its own flesh."

TOPICS FOR CRITICAL WRITING

1. Look up the term *didactic* in the *Oxford English Dictionary*. What does it mean? What are its etymological roots? How does it shed light on the theme of her poem?
2. Discuss the roles such words as *allegiance* and *relinquished* play in the poem's final stanza.

MARIANNE MOORE   *(1887–1972)*

The Mind Is an Enchanting Thing   *(1944)*

is an enchanted thing
      like the glaze on a
katydid-wing
            subdivided by sun
            till the nettings are legion.   5
Like Gieseking° playing Scarlatti;°

like the apteryx-awl°
      as a beak, or the
kiwi's rain-shawl
            of haired feathers, the mind   10
            feeling its way as though blind,
walks along with its eyes on the ground.

It has memory's ear
      that can hear without
having to hear.   15
            Like the gyroscope's fall,
            truly unequivocal
because trued by regnant certainty,

it is a power of
      strong enchantment. It   20
is like the dove-
            neck animated by
            sun; it is memory's eye;
it's conscientious inconsistency.

It tears off the veil; tears   25
      the temptation, the

---

6 *Walter Wilhelm Gieseking (1895–1956):* German pianist.   6 *Domenico Scarlatti (1685–1757):* Italian composer.   7 *apteryx-awl:* A bird native to New Zealand.

mist the heart wears,
  from its eyes—if the heart
  has a face; it takes apart
dejection. It's fire in the dove-neck's   30

iridescence; in the
  inconsistencies
of Scarlatti.
  Unconfusion submits
  its confusion to proof; it's   35
not a Herod's oath that cannot change.

TOPICS FOR CRITICAL THINKING

1. Discuss the various tropes through which Moore explores the terms of the mind's enchantment.
2. Moore had what she called an "inordinate interest in animals" and she regularly visited the Bronx Zoo. Discuss the ways in which she presents the exotic language of ornithology.
3. Focus on the role of diction in drawing out the trope of the mind as gyroscope. Look up and discuss the definitions and etymologies of *unequivocal*, *gyroscope*, and *regnant*.
4. Look up the etymologies of Moore's word choices in describing the mind's "conscientious inconsistency"—its "iridescence; in the / inconsistencies." What is Moore's point here?

TOPIC FOR CRITICAL WRITING

Herod was the king of Judea who upheld his promise to Salome to behead John the Baptist in Mark 6:22–27. How does Moore contrast this biblical allusion to the mind's "enchantment"?

21 Poetic Imagery and Theories of the Modern Image

Imagery in poetry refers to the use of language to evoke sensory experience. Imagery captures the immediate perception of our five senses. Sight, sound, smell, taste, touch: All can be evoked by the masterful rendering of powerful imagery. Reading freshly conceived images in poetry allows us to imagine our sensuous lives more vividly and more originally. The contemporary poet Denise Levertov celebrates the power of verse to transform sensual experience through the force of the imagination and vice versa in her poem "O Taste and See."

DENISE LEVERTOV *(1923–1997)*

O Taste and See *(1964)*

The world is
not with us enough.
O taste and see

the subway Bible poster said,
meaning The Lord, meaning   5
if anything all that lives
to the imagination's tongue,

grief, mercy, language,
tangerine, weather, to
breathe them, bite,   10
savor, chew, swallow, transform

into our flesh our
deaths, crossing the street, plum, quince,
living in the orchard and being
hungry, and plucking   15
the fruit.

TOPICS FOR CRITICAL THINKING

1. Levertov makes an **allusion** to Psalms 34:8, which reads "O taste and see that the Lord is good." An allusion is a reference to another quote or figure from literary, popular, or religious traditions. How does Levertov alter our understanding of the poster's theological message?
2. How do you interpret the multiple meanings of Levertov's title?
3. What other allusion to a biblical story can you locate in the poem? What theme does this allusion convey in Levertov's revision of it?

TOPICS FOR CRITICAL WRITING

1. How would you characterize the kind of communion Levertov imagines between life and the imagination in "O Taste and See"?
2. The other literary allusion Levertov makes is to William Wordsworth's "The World is Too Much with Us." Read Wordsworth's poem, and discuss Levertov's revision of Wordsworth's themes.

Whether portraying the vibrant chaos of big-city life or the earthy perceptions of the garden world, imagery frees us from the tired conventions of rational thought. Such an escape from abstract thought into the freshness of perceived imagery is the main subject of Archibald MacLeish's poem "Eleven."

ARCHIBALD MACLEISH   *(1892–1982)*

Eleven   *(1926)*

And summer mornings the mute child, rebellious,
Stupid, hating the words, the meanings, hating
The Think now, Think, the Oh but Think! would leave
On tiptoe the three chairs on the verandah
And crossing tree by tree the empty lawn   5
Push back the shed door and upon the sill
Stand pressing out the sunlight from his eyes
And enter and with outstretched fingers feel
The grindstone and behind it the bare wall
And turn and in the corner on the cool   10
Hard earth sit listening. And one by one,
Out of the dazzled shadow in the room,
The shapes would gather, the brown plowshare, spades,
Mattocks, the polished helves of picks, a scythe
Hung from the rafters, shovels, slender tines   15
Glinting across the curve of sickles—shapes
Older than men were, the wise tools, the iron
Friendly with earth. And sit there, quiet, breathing
The harsh dry smell of withered bulbs, the faint

Odor of dung, the silence. And outside　　　　　　　　　　　　20
Beyond the half-shut door the blind leaves
And the corn moving. And at noon would come,
Up from the garden, his hard crooked hands
Gentle with earth, his knees still earth-stained, smelling
Of sun, of summer, the old gardener, like　　　　　　　　　25
A priest, like an interpreter, and bend
Over his baskets.
　　　　　　　　And they would not speak:
They would say nothing. And the child would sit there
Happy as though he had no name, as though　　　　　　　30
He had been no one: like a leaf, a stem,
Like a root growing—

One thing to notice in the unfolding action of "Eleven" is how MacLeish
stages the escape from abstract thought in the poem. The child's flight from
the "words" and "meanings" and the demand to "Think now, Think" happens
in the shed through his growing perception of embodied experience. The
concrete image—with its sensual immediacy—dramatizes the return to a
perceived world before thought and the demands of abstract rationality. Notice how perception returns first in images of touch that involve the "grindstone," then the "cool / Hard earth," leading finally—as the child's eyes adjust
to the darkened spaces—to visual images of the garden tools and farm implements stored in the shed. What other perceptual images do you notice in
the poem?

　　Something else that may help you to understand MacLeish's poem is its
title. As guideposts to the poetry, **titles** often set out the key terms for what is
at stake in a poem's situation, setting, and themes. Here the child's status as an
eleven-year-old sets up the contradictory tensions and demands made on the
preadolescent who is no longer a child but not quite an adult. That state of being in-between also marks the setting of the shed. It is similarly located between, on the one hand, the formal demands of thinking associated with the
verandah from which the child leaves "on tiptoe" and, on the other hand, the
landscape of sun, summer, and nature generally.

TOPICS FOR CRITICAL THINKING

1. Besides the child of "Eleven," the other figure who is depicted as being in-between
   opposites is the "old gardener." MacLeish compares his job to two other vocations:
   that of an "interpreter" and a "priest." What similarities do you think MacLeish
   finds in these comparisons?
2. What do the similarities discussed in question 1 have to do with the in-between situation of the eleven-year-old child?
3. How does the gardener serve as both an interpreter and priest for the child?

TOPIC FOR CRITICAL WRITING

Write an essay on the child's passage from the demands of thought to the consolations of being finally "like a leaf, a stem, / Like a root growing—".

Theories of the Modern Image Web   *www*

In the twentieth century, experimental modernist poets such as Ezra Pound, William Carlos Williams, and Hilda Doolittle (H.D.) advanced new theories and techniques of poetic imagery. They gleaned what Williams called the "radiant gist" of experience in sharply beheld images. These modern poets had a particular understanding of the poetic image. As members of what would become known as the Imagist Movement, they defined an image in poetry as involving a "direct treatment of the thing whether subjective or objective." From 1912–1914, Pound, in particular, crafted a poetic language that would be concise, efficient, and fresh in its original use of images. His colleague, T. S. Eliot, acknowledged Pound's achievement by calling him in *The Waste Land* (1922) *il miglior fabbro*, which in Italian means "the better craftsman." Pound modeled his modern poetry on the compact lyric forms of Chinese verse. Pound's shorter imagist poems also resemble Japanese **Haiku** verse (a short seventeen-syllable poem broken into three lines having the pattern of five, seven, and five syllables per line).

EZRA POUND   *(1885–1972)*

In a Station of the Metro   *(1916)*

The apparition of these faces in the crowd;
Petals on a wet, black bough.

Pound achieves a startling transformation of the natural landscape through his abrupt coupling of faces and flowers, combining urban and pastoral motifs. The specific concrete image of "petals on a wet, black bough" defines the more abstract apparition of the city crowd. The experience for this poem came to Pound in 1913 as he disembarked from a metro train at La Concorde, Paris. In his account, he writes,

> [I] saw suddenly a beautiful face, and then another and another, and then a beautiful child's face, and then another beautiful woman, and I tried all that day to find words for what this had meant to me, and I could not find any words that seemed to me worthy, or as lovely as that sudden emotion. And that evening, as I went home along the Rue Raynouard, I was still trying, and I found, suddenly, the expression. I do not mean that I found words, but there came an equation . . . not in speech, but in little splotches of colour.

The original draft of the poem ran to some thirty lines before Pound threw it away. To capture the striking, visual impression of the metro, he distilled out the essence of the metro vision into a two-line sentence. Pound would later compare his poem to the modern visual canvases of the Russian painter Vasily Kandinsky, who pioneered new forms of experimental art as a founder of the Blaue Reiter group in Berlin the year before Pound's Paris metro experience (see color insert). Just two syllables over the seventeen-syllable haiku form, Pound's short lyric offers an imaginative comparison between two otherwise disparate elements. The poem does not explain the relation between the two major images of the faces and petals but sets them side by side without connectives or transitions.

The compositional style of "In a Station of the Metro" employs **parataxis.** Stemming from the Greek term *paratassein* meaning "beside" (*para*) and "to arrange" (*tassein*), parataxis in poetry as well as in experimental film sets images directly side by side, in the quick cut from one scene or image to another. This technique allows a new perception to arise from the relational arrangement of images. Indeed, the form of "In a Station of the Metro," the poet says, came to him less as a verbal statement than "an equation . . . not in speech, but in little splotches of colour." The poem achieves its power from how the outward image, as Pound says, "darts inward into a thing inward and subjective." The other striking contrast the poem performs is between, on the one hand, the "direct treatment of the thing" and, on the other hand, the phantom-like abstraction of the key word *apparition*. This opening term lends the poem a ghostly quality of invoking the landscape of the underworld, which, as we shall see, is a quality of modern urban life that Pound and Eliot would go on to develop in their collaboration on *The Waste Land*.

The sharp compositional cut Pound makes between the outward "faces in a crowd" and inward "petals on a wet, black bough" is also at work stylistically in the rather jagged verbal surfaces of William Carlos Williams's short imagist lyric "The Great Figure."

WILLIAM CARLOS WILLIAMS   *(1883–1963)*

The Great Figure   *(1921)*

Among the rain
and lights
I saw the figure 5
in gold
on a red   5
firetruck
moving
tense
unheeded
to gong clangs   10
siren howls
and wheels rumbling
through the dark city.

The visual specificity of Pound's "wet, black bough" finds its counterpart in
the particular impressions Williams records in the gold figure 5 that rushes
across a red field set off against the background of "the dark city." Again, what
matters here is the leading term—*among*—that defines the poem's relational
field in which various sights and sounds find their places. In "The Great Figure," Williams witnesses the city's chance happenings that otherwise go unheeded. So compelling is the visual dimension of Williams's imagist lyric that
Charles Henry Demuth chose it as the subject for his classic 1928 abstract oil
painting, *I Saw the Figure Five in Gold*, now part of New York's definitive Museum of Modern Art collection (see color insert).

   While Williams finds compelling images that distill the "radiant gist" of
urban chaos, the contemporary poet Gary Snyder conveys the tranquility of
"high still air" found in the wilderness of "Mid-August at Sourdough Mountain Lookout."

GARY SNYDER   *(b. 1930)*

Mid-August at Sourdough Mountain Lookout   *(1959)*

Down valley a smoke haze
Three days heat, after five days rain
Pitch glows on the fir-cones
Across the rocks and meadows
Swarms of new flies.   5

I cannot remember things I once read
A few friends, but they are in cities.
Drinking cold snow-water from a tin cup
Looking down for miles
Through high still air.   10

Gary Snyder based this poem on his experience as a forest fire lookout in
Baker National Forest in the early 1950s. By the decade's end, he would become a culture hero in the Beat Movement appearing as the character of Jap-
phy Rider in Jack Kerouac's celebrated novel *The Dharma Bums* (1958).
Snyder also had a serious commitment to Asian studies, first in the graduate
program of the University of California, Berkeley, and later in the 1960s as a
student of Buddhism in Kyoto, Japan under the Zen Master Oda Sesso Roshi.
Similar to Pound's collaborative work with Ernest Fenollosa in *The Chinese
Written Character as a Medium for Poetry*, Snyder's spare imagist style in "Mid-

Gary Snyder

August at Sourdough Mountain Lookout" reflects the poet's work as a translator of classical Chinese lyrics and Japanese Haiku poetry.

TOPICS FOR CRITICAL THINKING

1. How do you imagine the poet's situation depicted in the poem?
2. Describe in one word the poet's mood in the opening lines.
3. How would the effect of the poem's images change if Snyder had depicted himself
   as drinking, say, an ice-cold soda from a 12 oz. can?

TOPIC FOR CRITICAL WRITING

Compare and contrast the two stanzas of Snyder's poem. How crucial are the sensual
images of the poem's last three lines to the poem's themes of stoicism, simplicity, and
asceticism?

Poems for Further Reading and Critical Writing

DENISE LEVERTOV   *(1923–1997)*

The Dead Butterfly   *(1959)*

Now I see its whiteness
is not white but green, traced with green,
and resembles the stones
of which the city is built,
quarried high in the mountains.   5

                              2

Everywhere among the marigolds
the rainblown roses and the hedges
of tamarisk are white
butterflies this morning, in constant
tremulous movement, only those   10
that lie dead revealing
their rockgreen color and the bold
cut of the wings.

TOPICS FOR CRITICAL THINKING

1. Explore your reaction to this poem. What do you think Levertov's main thematic
   point is?

2. Which do you think the poet finds more lovely, the butterflies in "tremulous movement" or the "bold / cut of the wings" that she beholds in the dead butterfly?

3. Does it matter that the color of the dead butterflies "resembles the stones / of which the city is built"? Is this a simple observation or does Levertov imply something more? Explain.

TOPIC FOR CRITICAL WRITING

Write an essay on the paradox Levertov discovers in the butterfly's actual color as opposed to its appearance.

MINA LOY *(1882–1966)*

Mexican Desert   *(1921)*

The belching ghost-wail of the locomotive
trailing her rattling wooden tail
into the jazz-band sunset. . . .

The mountains in a row
set pinnacles of ferocious isolation   5
under the alien hot heaven

Vegetable cripples of drought
thrust up the parching appeal
cracking open the earth
stump-fingered cacti   10
and hunch-back palm trees
belabour the cinders of twilight. . . .

TOPICS FOR CRITICAL THINKING

1. Examine your overall experience of "Mexican Desert." Do Loy's images imply a thematic point, or do they simply record a set of impressions?

2. How do the signs of disfigurement and stunted growth in stanza two mirror the poet's situation?

TOPIC FOR CRITICAL WRITING

Loy wrote "Mexican Desert" after the mysterious disappearance of her lover Arthur Cravan off the coast of Mexico. Where can you discern the traces of that loss in the landscape of "ferocious isolation"?

H. D. (Hilda Doolittle)   *(1886–1961)*

Sea Rose   *(1916)*

Rose, harsh rose,
marred and with stint of petals,
meager flower, thin,
sparse of leaf,

more precious   5
than a wet rose
single on a stem—
you are caught in the drift.

Stunted, with small leaf,
you are flung on the sand,   10
you are lifted
in the crisp sand
that drives in the wind.

Can the spice-rose
drip such acrid fragrance   15
hardened in a leaf?

Sea Violet   *(1916)*

The white violet
is scented on its stalk,
the sea-violet
fragile as agate,
lies fronting all the wind   5
among the torn shells
on the sand-bank.

The greater blue violets
flutter on the hill,
but who would change for these   10
who would change for these
one root of the white sort?

Violet
your grasp is frail
on the edge of the sand-hill,   15

but you catch the light—
frost, a star edges with its fire.

TOPICS FOR CRITICAL THINKING

1. What key words convey H. D.'s portrait of the "Sea Rose"?
2. What qualities does she admire in the "Sea Rose"?
3. How does the "Sea Rose" differ from a hot-house flower?
4. How do you interpret the poem's final question?

TOPIC FOR CRITICAL WRITING

Compare H. D.'s depiction of the "Sea Rose" to her "Sea Violet." What qualities do they share? How do they differ?

T. S. ELIOT   *(1888–1965)*

Preludes

(1917)

I

The winter evening settles down
With smell of steaks in passageways.
Six o'clock.
The burnt-out ends of smoky days.
And now a gusty shower wraps   5
The grimy scraps
Of withered leaves about your feet
And newspapers from vacant lots;
The showers beat
On broken blinds and chimney-pots,   10
And at the corner of the street
A lonely cab-horse steams and stamps.

And then the lighting of the lamps.

II

The morning comes to consciousness
Of faint stale smells of beer   15
From the sawdust-trampled street
With all its muddy feet that press
To early coffee-stands.
With the other masquerades
That times resumes,   20

One thinks of all the hands
That are raising dingy shades
In a thousand furnished rooms.

III

You tossed a blanket from the bed
You lay upon your back, and waited;   25
You dozed, and watched the night revealing
The thousand sordid images
Of which your soul was constituted;
They flickered against the ceiling.
And when all the world came back   30
And the light crept up between the shutters,
And you heard the sparrows in the gutters,
You had such a vision of the street
As the street hardly understands;
Sitting along the bed's edge, where   35
You curled the papers from your hair,
Or clasped the yellow soles of feet
In the palms of both soiled hands.

IV

His soul stretched tight across the skies
That fade behind a city block,   40
Or trampled by insistent feet
At four and five and six o'clock;
And short square fingers stuffing pipes,
And evening newspapers, and eyes
Assured of certain certainties,   45
The conscience of a blackened street
Impatient to assume the world.

I am moved by fancies that are curled
Around these images, and cling:
The notion of some infinitely gentle   50
Infinitely suffering thing.

Wipe your hand across your mouth, and laugh;
The worlds revolve like ancient women
Gathering fuel in vacant lots.

TOPICS FOR CRITICAL THINKING

1. The urban landscape of "Preludes" is based in Paris and particularly in the somewhat sordid quarter that the French author Charles Louis Philippe describes in his
   book *Bubu de Montparnasse*. Eliot lived there while studying at the Sorbonne in
   1910 at about the time he was working on "The Love Song of J. Alfred Prufrock."
   What is your overall impression of the setting Eliot depicts in the poem?

2. In the second stanza of section IV, the poet writes that he is "moved by fancies that are curled / Around these images, and cling." The otherwise realistic descriptions of "Preludes" seem to deny the fancies of the imagination. How are we to account for this kind of statement?

3. What attitude does the poet take toward the cityscape in the final stanza?

TOPIC FOR CRITICAL WRITING

What specific objects, scenes, and things in the poem represent the fragmented nature of modern urban life?

Critical Perspective: On Imagist Poetics

A FEW DON'TS

"An 'Image' is that which presents an intellectual and emotional complex in an instant of time. I use the term 'complex' rather technical sense employed by the newer psychologists, such as Hart, though we may not agree absolutely in our application.

"It is the presentation of such a 'complex' instantaneously which gives that sense of sudden liberation; that sense of freedom from time limits and space limits; that sense of sudden growth, which we experience in the presence of the greatest works of art.

"It is better to present one Image in a lifetime than to produce voluminous works.

"All this, however, some may consider open to debate. The immediate necessity is to tabulate A LIST OF DON'TS for those beginning to write verses. I can not put all of them into Mosaic negative.

"To begin with, consider the three propositions (demanding direct treatment, economy of words, and the sequence of the musical phrase), not as dogma—never consider anything as dogma—but as the result of long contemplation, which, even if it is some one else's contemplation, may be worth consideration. . . .

LANGUAGE

"Use no superfluous word, no adjective which does not reveal something.

"Don't use such an expression as 'dim lands of peace.' It dulls the image. It mixes an abstraction with the concrete. It comes from the writer's not realizing that the natural object is always the adequate symbol.

"Go in fear of abstractions. Do not retell in mediocre verse what has already been done in good prose. Don't think any intelligent person is going to be deceived when you try to shirk all the difficulties of the unspeakably difficult art of good prose by chopping your composition into line lengths. . . .

RHYTHM AND RHYME

"Let the candidate fill his mind with the finest cadences he can discover, preferably in a foreign language, so that the meaning of the words may be less likely to divert his attention from the movement; e.g. Saxon charms, Hebridean Folk Songs, the verse of Dante, and the lyrics of Shakespeare—if he can dissociate the vocabulary from the cadence. Let him dissect the lyrics of Goethe coldly into their component sound values, syllables long and short, stressed and unstressed, into vowels and consonants.

"It is not necessary that a poem should rely on its music, but if it does rely on its music that music must be such as will delight the expert.

"Let the neophyte know assonance and alliteration, rhyme immediate and delayed, simple and polyphonic, as a musician would expect to know harmony and counterpoint and all the minutiae of his craft. No time is too great to give to these matters or to any one of them, even if the artist seldom have need of them."

—Ezra Pound, from *A Few Don'ts for an Imagist* (1913)

Critial Perspective: Modern Poetry and Formal Invention

"The arts have a *complex* relation to society. The poet isn't a fixed phenomenon, no more is his work. *That* might be a note on current affairs, a diagnosis, a plan for procedure, a retrospect—all in its own peculiarly enduring form. There need be nothing limited or frustrated about that. It may be a throw-off from the most violent and successful action or run parallel to it, a saga. It may be the picking out of an essential detail for memory, something to be set aside for further study, a sort of shorthand of emotional significances for later reference.

"Let the metaphysical take care of itself, the arts have nothing to do with it. They will concern themselves with it if they please, among other things. To make two bald statements: There's nothing sentimental about a machine, and: A poem is a small (or large) machine made of words. When I say there's nothing sentimental about a poem I mean that there can be no part, as in any other machine, that is redundant.

"Prose may carry a load of ill-defined matter like a ship. But poetry is the machine which drives it, pruned to a perfect economy. As in all machines its movement is intrinsic, undulant, a physical more than a literary character. In a poem this movement is distinguished in each case by the character of the speech from which it arises.

"Therefore, each speech having its own character, the poetry it engenders will be peculiar to that speech also in its own intrinsic form. The effect is beauty, what in a single object resolves our complex feelings of propriety. One doesn't seek beauty. . . .

"When a man makes a poem, makes it, mind you, he takes words as he finds them interrelated about him and composes them—without distortion which would mar their exact significances—into an intense expression of his perceptions and ardors that they may constitute a revelation in the speech that he uses. It isn't what he *says* that counts as a work of art, it's what he makes, with such intensity of perception that it lives with an intrinsic movement of its own to verify its authenticity. Your attention is called now and then to some beautiful line or sonnet-sequence because of what is said there. So be it. To me all sonnets say the same thing of no importance. What does it matter what the line 'says'?

"There is no poetry of distinction without formal invention, for it is in the intimate form that works of art achieve their exact meaning, in which they most resemble the machine, to give language its highest dignity, its illumination in the environment to which it is native. Such war, as the arts live and breathe by, is continuous.

"It may be that my interests as expressed here are pre-art. If so I look for a development along these lines and will be satisfied with nothing else."

—William Carlos Williams, from *The Wedge* (1944)

22   Figurative Language

When you want to give someone a clear set of directions or concise instructions, you rely on *literal* language to provide "just the facts." But in addition to such straightforward, literal word usage, we constantly employ **figurative language** in everyday life. Whether we realize it or not, metaphor, simile, personification, and other examples of figurative language communicate our meanings and give shape to our thinking. We routinely distinguish between literal meanings and figures of speech in making sense of what we hear and say. For example, imagine you are talking with your friend, the edgy day-trader: "Yesterday I got taken to the cleaners," she tells you, "but five minutes ago I made a killing." Without the ability to distinguish figurative from literal meanings, you would probably duck for cover and dial 911. Without even thinking, we know that such figures of speech as being "taken to the cleaners" and "making a killing" are, respectively, **tropes** for losing and making a lot of money. The term *trope* comes from the Greek word *tropein* meaning "to turn." The Latin word *figura* refers to something "made," "shaped," or "formed." Tropes are figures of language that depend or "turn" on describing one thing in terms of something else. Figurative language works through such comparisons and verbal substitutions where a particular word or phrase stands in for some other intended meaning.

    Metaphor comes from the Latin word meaning "to transfer," *metapherein*: "change" (*meta*) and "to bear" (*pherein*). Metaphor transfers the qualities and associations from one word directly into another. Ordinary language is fraught with metaphoric transfers of this sort, and metaphor shapes our everyday communication whether we know it consciously or not. It doesn't take very much reflection to hear metaphor at work in what we say. In their book *Metaphors We Live By*, the linguistic theorists George Lakoff and Mark Johnson have catalogued such metaphoric comparisons as, say, "ideas equal food":

> What he said *left a bad taste in my mouth.* All this paper has in it *are raw facts, half-baked ideas,* and *warmed over theories.* There are too many facts here for me to *digest* them all. I just can't *swallow* that claim. That argument *smells fishy.* Let me *stew* over that for a while. Now there's a theory you can really *sink your teeth into.* We need to let that idea *percolate* for a while. That's *food for thought.* He's a *voracious* reader. We don't need to *spoon-feed* our students. He *devoured* the book. Let's let that idea *simmer on the back burner* for a while. This is the *meaty* part of the paper. Let that idea *jell* for a while. That idea has been *fermenting* for years.

Similarly, love can equal madness:

> I'm *crazy* about her. She *drives me out of my mind.* He constantly *raves* about her. He's gone *mad* over her. I'm just *wild* about Harry. I'm *insane* about her.

Or love can be considered a kind of magic:

> She cast her *spell* over me. The *magic* is gone. I was *spellbound*. She had me *hypno-tized*. He has me *in a trance*. I was *entranced* by him. I'm *charmed* by her. She is *bewitching*.

Poets exploit the powers of metaphor inherent in language usage to craft meanings in more eloquent and vivid terms than a factual or literal statement could convey. Moreover, in powerful metaphors something mysterious happens in the process of describing one thing in terms of something else. Additional meaning is created. The new whole becomes somehow more than the sum of its parts. We feel this surplus of new meaning, for instance, when Sylvia Plath conjures the sunrise in her poem "Ariel" as "the red / Eye, the cauldron of morning." Similarly, we can feel poetic intensity bristling in Emily Dickinson's metaphor for existence: "My life had stood—a Loaded Gun—." Deceptively simple, such profound recognitions that come from the arresting metaphor exhaust our attempts to paraphrase them.

Striking metaphors have a way of creating new meanings that baffle the literal-minded, as in Plath's poem "Metaphors."

SYLVIA PLATH   *(1932–1963)*

Metaphors   *(1959)*

I'm a riddle in nine syllables,
An elephant, a ponderous house,
A melon strolling on two tendrils.
O red fruit, ivory, fine timbers!
This loaf's big with its yeasty rising.   5
Money's new-minted in this fat purse.
I'm a means, a stage, a cow in calf.
I've eaten a bag of green apples,
Boarded the train there's no getting off.

TOPICS FOR CRITICAL THINKING

1. Plath's several metaphors are couched in the form of a riddle. To what condition do they refer?
2. Discuss the various dimensions of that subject as Plath explores it through figurative language.
3. How does poetry both reflect and construct her experience of the poem's subject?

TOPIC FOR CRITICAL WRITING

How original are Plath's metaphors? Which ones are predictable, and which are fresh?

Successful metaphors in poetry do take on a lives of their own and possess a certain charm, as in the riddle posed by the anonymous fifteenth-century lyric "I Have a Yong Sister."

ANONYMOUS

I Have a Yong Sister   *(c. fifteenth century)*

I have a yong sister
   Fer° beyond the sea;
Manye be the druries°
   That she sente me.

She sente me the cherry   5
   Withouten any stone,
And so she did the dove
   Withouten any bone.

She sente me the brere°
   Withouten any rinde;°   10
She bade me love my lemman°
   Without longing.

How should any cherry
   Be withoute stone?
And how should any dove   15
   Be withoute bone?

How should any brere
   Be withoute rind?
How should I love my lemman
   Without longing?   20

When the cherry was a flowr,
   Then hadde it no stone.
When the dove was an ey,°
   Then hadde it no bone.

When the briar was unbred°   25
   Then hadde it no rinde.
When the maiden hath that she loveth,
   She is without longinge.

---

2 *Fer:* Far.   3 *druries:* Love tokens.   9 *brere:* Briar.   10 *rinde:* Bark.   11 *lemman:* Lover.   23 *ey:* Egg.   25 *unbred:* Still a seedling.

Posed as riddles, such "love tokens" as a flower, egg, or seed become classic metaphors for innocent love that bears within itself the beginnings of a lifetime of unity.

The use of such natural images to stand as metaphors for the more abstract dimensions of a love relationship similarly lends structure and coherence to the argument of William Shakespeare's well-known Sonnet 73.

WILLIAM SHAKESPEARE   *(1564–1616)*

Sonnet 73   *(1609)*

That time of year thou mayst in me behold
When yellow leaves, or none, or few, do hang
Upon those boughs which shake against the cold,
Bare ruined choirs, where late the sweet birds sang.
In me thou see'st the twilight of such day   5
As after sunset fadeth in the west;
Which by and by black night doth take away,
Death's second self, that seals up all in rest.
In me thou sees't the glowing of such fire,
That on the ashes of his youth doth lie,   10
As the deathbed whereon it must expire,
Consumed with that which it was nourished by.
  This thou perceiv'st which makes thy love more strong,
  To love that well which thou must leave ere long.

The persona of Sonnet 73 is all too aware of time's effects presented in the three major metaphors shaping his address to the loved one. Shakespeare devotes four lines each to the three metaphors, and these units are further signaled by the Shakespearean rhyme scheme (taken up in Chapter 27). For now, notice how the poet employs time's effect in the opening seasonal metaphor. Here the persona's age is compared to the fall season whose "boughs which shake against the cold" appear even more striking when described through metaphor as "bare ruined choirs." The second metaphor shortens the sense of time as we move from the seasonal metaphor to the end of the solar day where sunset fades before "Death's second self" of evening. The final metaphor compresses time further in the figure of fire changed to ashes signifying youth being consumed in the life process of aging. The poem expresses the sense that time is collapsing in on itself as we move from the seasonal, to solar, to momentary metaphors of the aging process. The final couplet, however, marks a striking reversal that turns this urgency to the speaker's advantage precisely in the recognition of just how precious time is in the lives of lovers. In the couplet's final paradox, the awareness of mortality makes love "more strong" in the face of that which one "must leave ere long."

A similar reversal of metaphoric argument happens in Margaret Atwood's poem "Habitation."

MARGARET ATWOOD   *(b. 1939)*

Habitation   *(1976)*

Marriage is not
a house or even a tent

it is before that, and colder:

the edge of the forest, the edge
of the desert   5
    the unpainted stairs
at the back where we squat
outside, eating popcorn

the edge of the receding glacier

where painfully and with wonder   10
at having survived even
this far

we are learning to make fire

TOPICS FOR CRITICAL THINKING

1. How does Atwood, like Shakespeare, turn what appears to be a series of negatives into a positive in "Habitation"?
2. In the second line, Atwood rejects the conventional metaphors that characterize the domestic "habitations" of a marriage. The poet more radically probes the "edge" of things that any viable relationship must constantly test. What does being on "the edge" mean for Atwood?
3. The final metaphor of fire can stand for many things in marriage, and, certainly, sexual passion would be the hottest. How do you interpret the poem's ending?

TOPIC FOR CRITICAL WRITING

Explore how Atwood's metaphors for marriage present the paradoxes of survival that a successful relationship must negotiate.

Simile, from the Latin word meaning "like," is another type of figurative language. Simile renders likenesses more explicit than metaphor through the linking terms *like* or *as*. More demonstrative than dramatic, simile nevertheless, like metaphor, has the power to ground abstract states of feeling and insight in concrete images of immediate experience, as in W. S. Merwin's brief lyric "Separation."

W. S. MERWIN   *(b. 1927)*

Separation   *(1973)*

Your absence has gone through me
Like thread through a needle.
Everything I do is stitched with its color.

Simile allows Merwin to convert the nothingness of separation—the literal
absence of the other—into the presence of a compelling image. Simile in
"Separation" enables the reader to visualize and thus share the poignancy of
the poet's sense of loss.

　　The romantic poet William Wordsworth uses the relational term *as* in
the simile of his title "I Wandered Lonely As a Cloud."

WILLIAM WORDSWORTH   *(1770–1850)*

I Wandered Lonely As a Cloud   *(1807)*

I wandered lonely as a cloud
That floats on high o'er vales and hills,
When all at once I saw a crowd,
A host, of golden daffodils;
Beside the lake, beneath the trees,   5
Fluttering and dancing in the breeze.

Continuous as the stars that shine
And twinkle on the milky way,
They stretched in never-ending line
Along the margin of a bay: 10
Ten thousand saw I at a glance,
Tossing their heads in sprightly dance.

The waves beside them danced; but they
Outdid the sparkling waves in glee;
A poet could not but be gay,   15
In such a jocund company;
I gazed—and gazed—but little thought
What wealth the show to me had brought:

For oft, when on my couch I lie
In vacant or in pensive mood,   20
They flash upon that inward eye
Which is the bliss of solitude;

And then my heart with pleasure fills,
And dances with the daffodils.

Wordsworth's similes describe his own sense of solitude in nature. The poem, however, is not just about solitude but also the close encounter with a visionary setting that in some ways cures the poet's loneliness.

TOPICS FOR CRITICAL THINKING

1. The actual landscape of the daffodils is based on the real outing that the poet's sister Dorothy Wordsworth records in an entry for her *Grasmere Journals* dated April 15, 1802, two years before the publication of "I Wandered Lonely As a Cloud." But the daffodils Wordsworth depicts in the poem have a heightened, visionary quality. How does simile convey that sublime impression?
2. How does the second "recollected" moment cure the poet of his "pensive" mood?

TOPIC FOR CRITICAL WRITING

In his Preface to *Lyrical Ballads*, which Wordsworth published collaboratively with Samuel Taylor Coleridge, Wordsworth defends the "incidents and situations from common life" as proper subjects for poetry. Moreover, he lays out a definition of the role of memory and the emotions in verse composition. Poetry, he asserts, "is the spontaneous overflow of powerful feelings: it takes its origin from emotion recollected in tranquility." In "I Wandered Lonely As a Cloud," how does the first moment of coming upon the daffodils find its counterpart in the recollected moment of enjoying the sensuous memory of the flowers?

The contemporary poet Sharon Olds also relies on natural similes, but unlike the astrophysical comparisons Wordsworth makes between flowers and stars, Olds aims for a more earthbound effect in "Size and Sheer Will."

SHARON OLDS   *(b. 1942)*

Size and Sheer Will   *(1984)*

The fine, green pajama cotton,
washed so often it is paper-thin and
iridescent, has split like a sheath
and the glossy white naked bulbs of
Gabriel's toes thrust forth like crocus   5
this early Spring. The boy is growing
as fast as he can, elongated
wrists dangling, lean meat
showing between the shirt and the belt.
If there were a rack to stretch himself, he would   10
strap his slight body to it.

If there were a machine to enter,
skip the next ten years and be
sixteen immediately, this boy would
do it. All day long he cranes his   15
neck, like a plant in the dark with a single
light above it, or a sailor under
tons of green water, longing
for the surface, for his rightful life.

TOPICS FOR CRITICAL THINKING

1. What similes make the comparison between Gabriel's "sheer will" to grow and the organic vitality of plant life?
2. How do you interpret the simile that compares Gabriel to a sailor?
3. What is the effect of pairing these two very different similes together in the same poem?

TOPIC FOR CRITICAL WRITING

Write on the sigificance of Sharon Olds's title and its relation to the poem.

Personification is a third variety of figurative language that is also described as the rhetorical figure **prosopopoeia**: *prosopon*, meaning "face," plus *poiein*, meaning "to make." We use personification for dramatic effect to attribute life or human aspects to what are otherwise inanimate objects, abstractions, or nonhuman creatures. To convey the beauty of a pastoral scene, Shakespeare relies on personification when he writes in Sonnet 33 that "Full many a glorious morning have I seen / Flatter the mountain-tops with sovereign eye, / Kissing with golden face the meadows green." Personification lends a surreal quality to the satisfaction Rita Dove experiences in the abstraction of a math problem in "Geometry": "I prove a theorem," she writes, "and the house expands: / the windows jerk free to hover near the ceiling, / the ceiling floats away with a sigh."

Personification can lend a human aspect to a particular word, phrase, line, or even an entire poem's contents. Wordsworth, for example, relies on several personifications to depict the idealized signs of humanity he witnesses in the urban sunrise of his sonnet "Composed upon Westminster Bridge, September 3, 1802."

WILLIAM WORDSWORTH   *(1770–1850)*

Composed upon Westminster Bridge, September 3, 1802

(1807)

Earth has not anything to show more fair:
Dull would he be of soul who could pass by
A sight so touching in its majesty;
This City now doth, like a garment, wear
The beauty of the morning; silent, bare,   5
Ships, towers, domes, theaters, and temples lie
Open unto the fields, and to the sky;
All bright and glittering in the smokeless air.
Never did sun more beautifully steep
In his first splendor, valley, rock, or hill;   10
Ne'er saw I, never felt, a calm so deep!
The river glideth at his own sweet will:
Dear God! The very houses seem asleep;
And all that mighty heart is lying still!

In "Composed upon Westminster Bridge, September 3, 1802" Wordsworth chooses to personify the "majesty" he beholds in London, albeit distanced from the vantage point of Westminster Bridge. Notice, for example, how Wordsworth's London is personified as wearing the morning's beauty "like a garment." Similarly, the poet invokes the fresh "splendor" of a pastoral setting in the personified figure of the sun. Even the buildings of Wordsworth's city mirror the poet's sense of "calm" and, like its urban dwellers, "seem asleep." Finally, the poet is left marveling over the way "all that mighty heart is lying still!"

In the ancient world, beauty, grace, strength, horror, eros, and so on all had representation in the traditional pantheon of the gods. Modern poets, however, give a human face to such abstractions through the figure of *prosopopoeia*. **Apostrophe** is a special, performative instance of prosopopoeia. Apostrophe invokes personified meaning by addressing an abstract thing, natural object, creature, or even a departed figure from the past as present in human terms. "Death, be not proud," writes John Donne, confronting mortality as an antagonist who can be faced and faced down. Apostrophe can take the form of a heightened emotive address as when Percy Bysshe Shelley summons the mythical powers of the west wind. "O wild West Wind, thou breath of Autumn's being, / Thou, from whose unseen presence the leaves dead / Are driven, like ghosts from an enchanter fleeting." "O Rose," observes William Blake, "thou art sick." Calling our attention to the life of subhuman things in "The Grasshopper," Richard Lovelace couples personification with the more performative rhetoric of apostrophe: "O thou," he writes of the cricket, "that swing'st upon the waving hair of some well-filled oaten beard" (grain). Returning from France to England, Wordsworth invokes through apostrophe the figure of the dead epic poet John Milton to lend authority to his condem-

nation of the "vanity and parade" witnessed in his sonnet "London, 1802:"
"Milton! Thou shouldst be living at this hour: England hath need of thee: she
is a fen / Of stagnant waters. . . ." Poets also rely on apostrophe to address
their own powers of writing in a more self-referential performance as in Ezra
Pound's "Coda." "O my songs," he writes, "Why do you look so eagerly and
so curiously into people's faces, / Will you find your lost dead among them?"

 Emily Dickinson was fond of personifying the natural world. Yet her
tropes of lending a human face to the natural object never lapse into sentimentality. She eludes the pitfall of projecting human qualities onto nature, the
kind of facile anthropomorphism that the nineteenth-century writer John
Ruskin condemned as the "pathetic fallacy." Instead, she preserves an uncanny sense of difference while exploring the limits of personification in nature, as in her Poem 328, "A Bird came down the Walk."

EMILY DICKINSON *(1830–1886)*

Poem 328 (A Bird came down the Walk) *(1891)*

A Bird came down the Walk —
He did not know I saw —
He bit an Angleworm in halves
And ate the fellow, raw,

And then he drank a Dew   5
From a convenient Grass —
And then hopped sidewise to the Wall
To let a Beetle pass —

He glanced with rapid eyes
That hurried all around —   10
They looked like frightened Beads, I thought —
He stirred his Velvet Head

Like one in danger, Cautious,
I offered him a Crumb
And he unrolled his feathers   15
And rowed him softer home —

Than Oars divide the Ocean
Too silver for a seam —
Or Butterflies, off Banks of Noon
Leap, plashless° as they swim.   20

---

20 *plashless:* Splashless.

The personified figures of Poem 328 stop just the other side of nature from the human. Seemingly courteous in "hopping sidewise" for a passing beetle, the bird is almost human in taking "Dew" from a "convenient" grass. Dickinson's repeated descriptions of the bird in the third person "he" rather than "it," coupled with his "fellow" the Angleworm, give the momentary illusion of community. Such natural companionship, however, is quickly estranged as the former has the latter for a snack. Nor do "the frightened Beads" of the bird's gaze recognize Dickinson's human gesture of offering a crumb. The natural and human orders remain apart despite the poet's effort to bridge them. Even her final simile that would compare wings and oars transcend the familiar, moving into a surreal landscape that mixes air and water.

Much of Dickinson's poetry journeys into such exotic imaginative territory through the bold use of figurative language. Often, she experiments with a certain blending of physical sensations, as in her phrase "To the bugle, every color is red." Describing one of the perceptual senses of sight, hearing, smell, taste, touch in terms of another in figurative language is called **synaesthesia.** The term *synaesthesia* comes from a Greek root word meaning "blended feeling." Examples of synaesthesia are abundant in ancient and biblical literatures as when Homer in the *Odyssey* describes the Sirens as having a "honey-voice." In the modern era, synaesthesia came into vogue through the symbolist poetry of Charles Baudelaire, Arthur Rimbaud, and the French surrealists. Contemporary poets use synaesthesia to depict intense states of perception, as when Sylvia Plath describes an image of tulips filling a hospital room with "a loud noise."

Various examples of personification, simile, metaphor, and synaesthesia contribute to the surreal depiction of the small-scale machinery of Charles Simic's poem "Watch Repair."

CHARLES SIMIC *(b. 1938)*

Watch Repair   *(1974)*

A small wheel
Incandescent,
Shivering like
A pinned butterfly.

Hands   5
Pointing in all directions:
The crossroads
One enters
In a nightmare.

Higher than anyone   10
Number 12 presides

Like a beekeeper
Over the swarming honeycomb
Of the open watch.

—Other wheels   15
That could fit
Inside a raindrop,

Tools
That must be splinters
Of arctic starlight . . .   20

Tiny golden mills
Grinding invisible
Coffee beans.

When the coffee's boiling,
Cautiously,   25
So it doesn't burn us,

We raise it to it
To the lips
Of the nearest
Ear.   30

TOPIC FOR CRITICAL THINKING

Consider how Simic's line lengths and his patterns of enjambment capture the strangeness he finds in "Watch Repair."

TOPICS FOR CRITICAL WRITING

1. How does personification make a simple watch repair seem otherwordly? Where does Simic rely on simile and metaphor to depict his bizarre experience of the watch's interior?

2. Taking Simic's poem as a model, pick out a common household object and try your hand at depicting it in a new creative way that depends on figurative language for its special effects.

In "Watch Repair," Simic chooses synaesthesia to end the poem with the strange blending of the sensations—confusing mouth and ear, drinking and listening, the sensations of hearing and tasting. Synaesthesia also comes into play in Dylan Thomas's portrait of the child's mythic perception of nature in "Fern Hill."

DYLAN THOMAS   *(1914–1953)*

Fern Hill   *(1946)*

Now as I was young and easy under the apple boughs
About the lilting house and happy as the grass was green,
    The night above the dingle° starry,
        Time let me hail and climb
        Golden in the heydays of his eyes,   5
And honoured among wagons I was prince of the apple towns
And once below a time I lordly had the trees and leaves
        Trail with daisies and barley
    Down the rivers of the windfall light.

And as I was green and carefree, famous among the barns   10
About the happy yard and singing as the farm was home,
    In the sun that is young once only,
        Time let me play and be
        Golden in the mercy of his means,
And green and golden I was huntsman and herdsman, the calves   15
Sang to my horn, the foxes on the hills barked clear and cold,
        And the sabbath rang slowly
    In the pebbles of the holy streams.

All the sun long it was running, it was lovely, the hay
Fields high as the house, the tunes from the chimneys, it was air   20
        And playing, lovely and watery
          And fire green as grass.
        And nightly under the simple stars
As I rode to sleep the owls were bearing the farm away,
All the moon long I heard, blessed among stables, the night-jars°   25
        Flying with the ricks,° and the horses
        Flashing into the dark.

And then to awake, and the farm, like a wanderer white
With the dew, come back, the cock on his shoulder: it was all
        Shining, it was Adam and maiden,   30
          The sky gathered again
        And the sun grew round that very day.
So it must have been after the birth of the simple light
In the first, spinning place, the spellbound horses walking warm
        Out of the whinnying green stable   35
        On to the fields of praise.

---

3 *dingle:* A narrow wooded valley.   25 *night-jars:* Birds.   26 *ricks:* Haystacks.

And honoured among foxes and pheasants by the gay house
Under the new made clouds and happy as the heart was long,
    In the sun born over and over,
        I ran my heedless ways,   40
    My wishes raced through the house high hay
And nothing I cared, at my sky blue trades, that time allows
In all his tuneful turning so few and such morning songs
    Before the children green and golden
        Follow him out of grace,   45

Nothing I cared, in the lamb white days, that time would take me
Up to the swallow thronged loft by the shadow of my hand,
    In the moon that is always rising,
        Nor that riding to sleep
I should hear him fly with the high fields   50
And wake to the farm forever fled from the childless land.
Oh as I was young and easy in the mercy of his means,
    Time held me green and dying
    Though I sang in my chains like the sea.

    Thomas conveys the child's mythic connection to nature through the biblical allusions to the Genesis story of the Garden of Eden and through personifications of time. But equally important, Thomas invokes that first world through the richness and intensity of synaesthesia's complex perceptual blendings of primary elements. For example, the poet depicts air and light in terms of water; he describes the smoke from the cottage fireplaces as "tunes from the chimneys." The freshness of the landscape seems to burn in a "fire green as grass." Sounds mix with colors as in the phrase "whinnying green stable," or blend with sensations of touch as in the foxes that "on the hills barked clear and cold."

    Two more types of figurative language, **metonymy** and **synecdoche,** are so closely related that the latter can be considered a type of the former. Metonymy comes from the Greek word meaning "change of name," while synecdoche in Greek denotes the "act of taking together, or taking as a whole." Metonymy describes a word substituted for another word or thing that we associate with it. For example, a throne, crown, or scepter are things we might substitute for the term *king* or for royalty in general, as when James Shirley writes that "Scepter and crown / Must tumble down, / And in the dust be equal made / With the poor crooked scythe and spade." Similarly, W. B. Yeats characterizes an old man in "Sailing to Byzantium" as "A tattered coat upon a stick." If someone invites you to share some wine and you respond with "Sure, I'll have a glass," your host knows, by virtue of metonymy, that you will have a drink, not the literal container. In a restaurant when you order Chianti, your waiter understands, again through metonymy, that this place name stands in for the literal vintage that is produced in Tuscany, that famous wine-growing region of Italy. John Keats's phrase "beaker full of the warm South" is another version of substituting through metonymy an abstract place name for the type of an actual wine such as, say, Syrah. If we say, "Shirley's always out at the track; she is obsessed with the turf," we imply through metonymy that she likes to bet on horse races. "The White House conferred yesterday with leaders of the Pentagon" refers to an office that we associate with the president, not the literal building.

Synecdoche is a type of metonymy that substitutes a part of something for the whole designated. Just as sailors or laborers are often referred to as "hands"—as in "all hands on deck!"—so synecdoche underwrites many other colloquialisms that stage a part for the whole: "Beef prices are up, so we are moving 300 head to market" or "she went shopping for a year-end deal on a new set of wheels." Synecdoches abound in poetry. T. S. Eliot's persona J. Alfred Prufrock compares himself to a subhuman shellfish, complaining that "I should have been a pair of ragged claws / Scuttling across the floors of silent seas." Similarly when Colcridge's becalmed Ancient Mariner is just about to die of thirst, he at last spies a ship and calls out a synecdoche: "I bit my arm, I sucked the blood, / And cried, A sail, a sail!" Synecdoche also lends dramatic force to William Carlos Williams's "The Yachts," where the poet writes that the "ungoverned ocean . . . / . . . tortures the biggest hulls, the best man knows / to pit against its beatings, and sinks them pitilessly."

Poems for Further Reading and Critical Writing

TED HUGHES   *(1930–1998)*

The Thought-Fox   *(1957)*

I imagine this midnight moment's forest:
Something else is alive
Beside the clock's loneliness
And this blank page where my fingers move.

Through the window I see no star: 5
Something more near
Though deeper within darkness
Is entering the loneliness:

Cold, delicately as the dark snow,
A fox's nose touches twig, leaf;   10
Two eyes serve a movement, that now
And again now, and now, and now

Sets neat prints into the snow
Between trees, and warily a lame
Shadow lags by stump and in hollow   15
Of a body that is bold to come

Across clearings, an eye,
A widening deepening greenness,
Brilliantly, concentratedly,
Coming about its own business   20

Till, with sudden sharp hot stink of fox
It enters the dark hole of the head.
The window is starless still; the clock ticks,
The page is printed.

TOPICS FOR CRITICAL THINKING

1. Explore how Hughes describes the encounter with the thought-fox as an intuited process of witnessing.

2. Within the poem's narrative development of its extended metaphor, what do the "neat prints into the snow" stand for?

3. What does Hughes tell us about the tentative and gradual disclosure of the fox's "body" in such modifying terms as *warily, brilliantly, concentratedly,* and so on?

4. How would you describe the poem's ending? What final form does the metaphoric body of the thought-fox take?

TOPIC FOR CRITICAL WRITING

As the title implies, Hughes's poem is not about a literal fox. What does the figure of the thought-fox describe?

WALT WHITMAN   *(1819–1892)*

from Song of Myself (Section 6)   *(1855)*

6

A child said *What is the grass?* fetching it to me with full hands;
How could I answer the child? I do not know what it is any more than he.

I guess it must be the flag of my disposition, out of hopeful green stuff woven.

Or I guess it is the handkerchief of the Lord,
A scented gift and remembrancer designedly dropt,   5
Bearing the owner's name someway in the corners, that we may see and remark,
     and say *Whose?*

Or I guess the grass is itself a child, the produced babe of the vegetation.

Or I guess it is a uniform hieroglyphic,
And it means, Sprouting alike in broad zones and narrow zones,

Growing among black folks as among white, 10
Kanuck,° Tuckahoe,° Congressman, Cuff,° I give them the same, I receive
    them the same.

And now it seems to me the beautiful uncut hair of graves.

Tenderly will I use you curling grass,
It may be you transpire from the breasts of young men,
It may be if I had known them I would have loved them, 15
It may be you are from old people, or from offspring take soon out of their
    mothers' laps,
And here you are the mothers' laps.

This grass is very dark to be from the white heads of old mothers,
Darker than the colourless beards of old men,
Dark to come from under the faint red roofs of mouths. 20

O I perceive after all so many uttering tongues,
And I perceive they do not come from the roofs of mouths for nothing.

I wish I could translate the hints about the dead young men and women,
And the hints about old men and mothers, and the offspring taken soon out of
    their laps.

What do you think has become of the young and old men? 25
And what do you think has become of the women and children?

They are alive and well somewhere,
The smallest sprout shows there is really no death,
And if ever there was it led forward life, and does not wait at the end to
    arrest it,
And ceas'd the moment life appear'd. 30

All goes onward and outward, nothing collapses,
And to die is different from what any one supposed, and luckier.

TOPICS FOR CRITICAL THINKING

1. In answering the child's question—"What is the grass?"—what point does Whitman make in admitting that "I do not know what it is any more than he"?
2. Consider the metaphors Whitman employs to account for his experience of the
grass. What does the grass signify as the "handkerchief of the Lord"?

---

11 *Kanuck:* French Canadian.   11 *Tuckahoe:* Slave term for *Virginian*, of Native American origin.   11 *Cuff:* African American.

3. What does Whitman mean by "uniform hieroglyphic"? How does the grass as a "uniform hieroglyphic" become a metaphor for the democracy of American place?

4. Examine the imagery of darkness that Whitman uses to depict the poem's tropes of mortality following his metaphor of the grass as "the beautiful hair of graves."

TOPIC FOR CRITICAL WRITING

What point does Whitman make about the processes of life and death perceived in the example of grass?

ROBERT FROST   *(1874–1963)*

The Silken Tent   *(1942)*

She is as in a field a silken tent
At midday when a sunny summer breeze
Has dried the dew and all its ropes relent,
So that in guys° it gently sways at ease,
And its supporting central cedar pole,   5
That is its pinnacle to heavenward
And signifies the sureness of the soul,
Seems to owe naught to any single cord,
But strictly held by none, is loosely bound
By countless silken ties of love and thought   10
To everything on earth the compass round,
And only by one's going slightly taut
In the capriciousness of summer air
Is of the slightest bondage made aware.

TOPICS FOR CRITICAL THINKING

1. What do you know about tents? How do tents stay upright? Describe the poetic logic by which Frost depicts his spouse as a tent.

2. Focus on the metaphor of the "central cedar pole" as a trope for the "sureness of the soul." Examine the balance Frost sets up in the way in which it, on the one hand, points "its pinnacle to heavenward" and, on the other hand, is bound "to everything on earth."

3. Examine the tension Frost depicts in the poem between things that are "loosely bound" and those "slightly taut."

4. How does the poet heighten that tension in the final lines? Explain your interpretation of the phrase "capriciousness of summer air" and how it finds its counterpart in the word *bondage*.

---

4 *guys:* Tent ropes.

TOPIC FOR CRITICAL WRITING

Describe the theme that Frost's metaphors portray in "The Silken Tent."

JOHN DONNE   *(1572–1631)*

A Valediction Forbidding Mourning   *(1633)*

As virtuous men pass mildly away,
    And whisper to their souls to go
Whilst some of their sad friends do say,
    The breath goes now, and some say, no;

So let us melt, and make no noise,   5
    No tear-floods, nor sigh-tempests move,
'Twere profanation of our joys
    To tell the laity our love.

Moving of th'earth brings harms and fears,
    Men reckon what it did and meant;   10
But trepidation of the spheres,
    Though greater far, is innocent.

Dull sublunary lovers' love
    (Whose soul is sense) cannot admit
Absence, because it doth remove   15
    Those things which elemented it.

But we by'a love so much refined,
    That our selves know not what it is,
Inter-assuréd of the mind,
    Care less, eyes, lips, and hands to miss.   20

Our two souls therefore, which are one,
    Though I must go, endure not yet
A breach, but an expansion,
    Like gold to airy thinness beat.

If they be two, they are two so   25
    As stiff twin compasses are two;
Thy soul the fixed foot, makes no show
    To move, but doth, if th'other do.

And though it in the center sit,
    Yet when the other far doth roam,   30

It leans, and hearkens after it,
    And grows erect, as that comes home.

Such wilt thou be to me, who must
    Like th'other foot, obliquely° run.
Thy firmness makes my circle just,   35
    And makes me end where I begun.

TOPICS FOR CRITICAL THINKING

1. Discuss the first simile that depicts a death scene and the mourners' difficulty in determining the exact moment of the dying man's last breath. How does Donne compare the soul's departure and his own?

2. "Trepidation of the spheres" refers to the vibration of the celestial spheres theorized by Ptolemaic versions of the universe. It accounts for the discrepancies in the movement of heavenly objects. Everything below the sphere of the moon or "sublunary"—the world of earthly elements—was considered mutable and subject to change. Beyond the moon, life was unchanging. How does Donne turn this cosmology to his advantage in stanzas four and five to stress the "refined" love that he shares in marriage regardless of his physical proximity to his spouse?

3. In alchemical traditions, gold is considered the most spiritual of elements. In stanza six, how does Donne console his spouse by describing their spiritual oneness as "gold to airy thinness beat"?

4. Examine the extended simile of the compass—a tool for drawing circles—in the poem's final stanzas. How does this comparison eroticize the homecoming of Donne's anticipated reunion with his spouse?

TOPIC FOR CRITICAL WRITING

A *valediction* is a speech bidding farewell, and, according to Izaak Walton, Donne wrote this poem to his wife when he was traveling on the Continent in 1611. Consider the arguments Donne uses to lessen the impact of their temporary separation.

MATTHEW ARNOLD   *(1822–1888)*

Dover Beach   *(1867)*

The sea is calm tonight.
The tide is full, the moon lies fair
Upon the straits; on the French coast the light
Gleams and is gone; the cliffs of England stand,
Glimmering and vast, out in the tranquil bay.   5
Come to the window, sweet is the night-air!

------

35 *obliquely:* Diagonally.

Only, from the long line of spray
Where the sea meets the moon-blanched land,
Listen! you hear the grating roar
Of pebbles which the waves draw back, and fling,   10
At their return, up the high strand,
Begin, and cease, and then again begin,
With tremulous cadence slow, and bring
The eternal note of sadness in.

Sophocles long ago   15
Heard it on the Aegean, and it brought
Into his mind the turbid ebb and flow
Of human misery; we
Find also in the sound a thought,
Hearing it by this distant northern sea.   20

The Sea of Faith
Was once, too, at the full, and round earth's shore
Lay like the folds of a bright girdle furled.
But now I only hear
Its melancholy, long withdrawing roar,   25
Retreating, to the breath
Of the night-wind, down the vast edges drear
And naked shingles of the world.

Ah, love, let us be true
To one another! for the world, which seems   30
To lie before us like a land of dreams,
So various, so beautiful, so new,
Hath really neither joy, nor love, nor light,
Nor certitude, nor peace, nor help for pain;
And we are here as on a darkling plain   35
Swept with confused alarms of struggle and flight,
Where ignorant armies clash by night.

TOPICS FOR CRITICAL THINKING

1. Discuss the situation and setting of "Dover Beach."
2. Explore Arnold's use of simile in stanza three. How does Arnold use simile to depict "The Sea of Faith"?
3. Arnold published "Dover Beach" in 1867 after Charles Lyell's *Principles of Geology* (1830) and *The Geological Evidence of the Antiquity of Man* (1863), which, through fossil records, undermined biblical accounts of time and human history generally. Together with Charles Darwin's theories of natural selection in *Origin of Species* (1859), such modern revisions of geological change and evolution eroded the humanist foundations of biblical faith. How does Arnold depict the impact of this new modernist sensibility on the poet's perception of the "vast edges drear / And naked shingles of the world"?

4. How does Arnold use simile in the fourth stanza to contrast the imagined landscape with its real setting?

5. What is Arnold's solution to the contingencies and uncertainties of modern experience? How does he perform that answer in his direct address to his lover?

TOPIC FOR CRITICAL WRITING

Contrast Wordsworth's sonnet "It Is a Beauteous Evening" and its description of the ocean—"Listen! The mighty Being is awake"—with Arnold's "Listen! you hear the grating roar." How does Arnold's view of nature differ from Wordsworth's?

23　Symbolism

The term *symbol* comes from a Greek verb *symballein*, "to put together." In the ancient world a *symbolon* was a coin or token that was broken in two. Once broken, each half belonged to one of the two parties entering into a legal contract or agreement. Each half depended on its relation to the other half. As a kind of linguistic contract, a literary **symbol** consists of something present whose meaning and significance depends on something absent. Symbols are based on comparisons between concrete images and abstract ideas. On the one hand, a symbol is made up of something specific: an image, word, thing, setting, or even a person. On the other hand, something less immediately self-evident completes the symbol: a moral truth, an emotional state, an abstract realization or idea.

Often, you can easily identify a symbol's meaning because the concrete symbolic object bears a conventional resemblance to the abstract concept it represents. Light is generally taken to symbolize spiritual illumination. Darkness—as in the "dark night of the soul"—generally stands for its opposite. A candle symbolically lights the darkness and is a familiar symbol for humanitarian organizations such as Amnesty International. Hollywood cinema also relies on the power of symbols to define character, action, and thematic values. For example, Russell Crowe's character in the film *Gladiator*, the Roman general Maximus Decimus Meridius, always picks up a handful of soil before risking his life in battle or in the arena. As a symbol, that fistful of dirt stands for Maximus's connection to the earth, nature, and, ultimately, the risk of death that gives his life meaning, dignity, and vitality.

Symbols abound in popular culture, literature, and political and religious institutions. Nations adopt national symbols to signify particular values or ideals. The United States is represented in the eagle as a symbol of fierce independence. Religions employ concrete symbols such as the lamb, dove, cross, or menorah to stand for historical events or metaphysical concepts of God, resurrection, damnation, and so on. Poets often adopt such well-known symbols for their own purposes. For example, William Blake's poem "The Lamb" from the *Songs of Innocence* presents a straightforward account of the lamb as a traditional symbol for Christ and his divine incarnation.

WILLIAM BLAKE   *(1757–1827)*

The Lamb   *(1789)*

    Little Lamb, who made thee?
    Dost thou know who made thee?
Gave thee life, and bid thee feed
By the stream and o'er the mead;
Gave thee clothing of delight,   5
Softest clothing, woolly, bright;
Gave thee such a tender voice,
Making all the vales rejoice?
    Little Lamb, who made thee?
    Dost thou know who made thee?   10

    Little Lamb, I'll tell thee,
    Little Lamb, I'll tell thee:
He is callèd by thy name,
For he calls himself a Lamb.
He is meek, and he is mild;   15
He became a little child.
I a child, and thou a lamb.
We are called by his name.
    Little Lamb, God bless thee.
    Little Lamb, God bless thee.   20

The literal lamb that Blake addresses is innocent of its symbolic correspondence to Christ, the Lamb. It needs the poet's lesson on the mystery of its existence and who or what sustains it. The answer to the opening question draws out the relation between the literal and symbolic figures of the lamb. The likenesses between the two are not based only on resemblance—both being meek and mild—but are underwritten by the "name" of the lamb that signifies the symbolic correspondence between earth and heaven.

Through repeated usage over time, symbols enter into the conventions of everyday life. On Valentine's Day, for example, you might give your "sweetheart" (itself a symbol) a dozen roses symbolizing love. The original association of the lover with the rose is no doubt based on such resemblances as freshness, beauty, delicacy. Thus, Robert Burns symbolizes his new love with the Spring rose when he exclaims "O my luve's like a red, red rose, / That's newly sprung in June."

Through repeated usage, the rose as a symbol of love has become a social convention—a gesture of affection that Dorothy Parker whimsically revisits in her ironic poem "One Perfect Rose."

DOROTHY PARKER   *(1893–1967)*

One Perfect Rose   *(1926)*

A single flow'r he sent me, since we met.
   All tenderly his messenger he chose;
Deep-hearted, pure, with scented dew still wet—
   One perfect rose.

I knew the language of the floweret;   5
   "My fragile leaves," it said, "his heart enclose."
Love long has taken for his amulet
   One perfect rose.

Why is it no one ever sent me yet
   One perfect limousine, do you suppose?   10
Ah no, it's always just my luck to get
   One perfect rose.

We live in a world of conventional symbols where words all too quickly
stand in as emblems for known abstractions. A rose symbolizes love; a lion
stands for courage; the sun has long been a symbol of life, while a skull signifies death. Yet poets enhance the word's capacity for symbolic reference. Instead of using the concrete image to denote clichéd meaning, poetry often
works in reverse to allow more subtle and unique insights to complicate a
word's or image's everyday significance.

   Romantic poets such as William Blake reject outworn symbols, presenting instead fresh images that would grow and be shaped by their organic relation to symbolic meaning, as in "The Sick Rose."

WILLIAM BLAKE   *(1757–1827)*

The Sick Rose   *(1794)*

O Rose, thou art sick.
The invisible worm
That flies in the night
In the howling storm

Has found out thy bed   5
Of crimson joy,
And his dark secret love
Does thy life destroy.

TOPICS FOR CRITICAL THINKING

1. Why is the rose's love "dark" and "secret"?

2. What is a "bed / Of crimson joy"?

3. Who or what is the worm, and why is it "invisible"? Does it only appear "in the night"? Must it be associated with the "howling storm"? How has the worm found the rose?

TOPICS FOR CRITICAL WRITING

1. Can we ever be sure what the rose represents exactly? Why does Blake call it a "sick rose"?

2. What does the storm symbolize?

Blake's symbolic rose is neither as simple nor as clear as Parker's "amulet" of the "one perfect rose." Not surprisingly, the poem resists any easy answers to the questions posed above. Blake's symbolic drama cannot be exhausted by any simple paraphrase but, like the relation that the romantic poet John Keats finds between truth and beauty, "dost tease us out of thought." Each of us, no doubt, has an idea about how to answer questions about the poem's meaning, but will they be the same? Not likely. Presenting a symbolic action, the poem generates meaning through the reader's act of interpreting what finally remains a mystery.

Many symbols suggest rather than insist on a particular meaning, idea, or concept. The Native American poet Mary TallMountain invokes the symbolic power of nature in her poem "The Last Wolf."

MARY TALLMOUNTAIN   *(1918–1994)*

The Last Wolf   *(1989)*

the last wolf hurried toward me
through the ruined city
and I heard his baying echoes
down the steep smashed warrens
of Montgomery Street and past   5
the few ruby-crowned highrises
left standing
their lighted elevators useless

passing the flicking red and green
of traffic signals   10
baying his way eastward
in the mystery of his wild loping gait
closer the sounds in the deadly night
through clutter and rubble of quiet blocks

I heard his voice ascending the hill 15
and at last his low whine as he came
floor by empty floor to the room
where I sat
in my narrow bed looking west, waiting
I heard him snuffle at the door and 20
I watched
he trotted across the floor

he laid his long gray muzzle
on the spare white spread
and his eyes burned yellow 25
his small dotted eyebrows quivered

Yes, I said.
I know what they have done.

TOPICS FOR CRITICAL THINKING

1. TallMountain was born in 1918 in Nulato, Alaska, and inherited a dual cultural identity. On her mother's side she is Koyukon/Athabaskan, and on her father's side Scottish and Irish. After her mother's death, TallMountain was adopted and taken far away from her native traditions rooted in the Yukon. That dispossessed heritage is a common theme in her verse. How does TallMountain create the "ruined" urban present of the poem's opening setting?
2. Describe the shift in the wolf's presentation as we move from stanza one to stanza two.
3. How do you understand the final lines of the poem in her address to the wolf?

TOPIC FOR CRITICAL WRITING

Written during TallMountain's bouts with illness, her poem "The Last Wolf" presents a very intense and special relation to the wolf. What do you think the wolf symbolizes in this poem? Why is it a "last" wolf?

Some poets like to complicate a symbol's conventional meaning so as to call into question our habitual modes of interpretation. Robert Frost, for example, probes the deceptively straightforward meaning of walls as boundaries and barriers between neighbors in his poem "Mending Wall."

ROBERT FROST   *(1874–1963)*

Mending Wall   *(1914)*

Something there is that doesn't love a wall,
That sends the frozen-ground-swell under it,

And spills the upper boulders in the sun;
And makes gaps even two can pass abreast.
The work of hunters is another thing: 5
I have come after them and made repair
Where they have left not one stone on a stone,
But they would have the rabbit out of hiding,
To please the yelping dogs. The gaps I mean,
No one has seen them made or heard them made,   10
But at spring mending-time we find them there.
I let my neighbor know beyond the hill;
And on a day we meet to walk the line
And set the wall between us once again.
We keep the wall between us as we go.   15
To each the boulders that have fallen to each.
And some are loaves and some so nearly balls
We have to use a spell to make them balance:
'Stay where you are until our backs are turned!'
We wear our fingers rough with handling them.   20
Oh, just another kind of outdoor game,
One on a side. It comes to little more:
There where it is we do not need the wall:
He is all pine and I am apple orchard.
My apple trees will never get across   25
And eat the cones under his pines, I tell him.
He only says, 'Good fences make good neighbors.'
Spring is the mischief in me, and I wonder
If I could put a notion in his head:
'*Why* do they make good neighbors? Isn't it   30
Where there are cows? But here there are no cows.
Before I built a wall I'd ask to know
What I was walling in or walling out,
And to whom I was like to give offense.
Something there is that doesn't love a wall,   35
That wants it down.' I could say 'Elves' to him,
But it's not elves exactly, and I'd rather
He said it for himself. I see him there
Bringing a stone grasped firmly by the top
In each hand, like an old-stone savage armed.   40
He moves in darkness as it seems to me,
Not of woods only and the shade of trees.
He will not go behind his father's saying,
And he likes having thought of it so well
He says again, 'Good fences make good neighbors.'   45

In reading Frost's poem, how do we know that repairing the wall is not
just a literal but a symbolic activity? For one thing, in setting up the poem's
dramatic situation, Frost tells us that he and his neighbor don't really need the

wall. Because Frost's side consists of an apple orchard and his neighbor's a pine forest, there is nothing of literal value at stake in "walling in or walling out" their respective properties. It's "just another kind of outdoor game." Neither of them is at risk of livestock straying across the boundary onto the other's land. Something else, though, of symbolic value is at issue in the colloquial truism that "Good fences make good neighbors." Part of the brilliance of the poem is the way in which Frost leaves unanswered his own question "*Why* do they make good neighbors?" What the wall symbolizes, finally, is left, like the human condition generally, an open-ended mystery. There are, of course, hints that the wall—like the rule of civil law—protects us from "the darkness" of our own capacities of violence toward the other. The neighbor shoulders his rocks "like an old-stone savage armed" and seems to move in a symbolic "darkness . . . Not of woods only and the shade of trees."

How we are to judge the activity of shoring up the wall remains ambiguous in the poem itself. Clearly, the poem's speaker has no use for the wall. As far as he's concerned, it's an absurdity, for "There where it is we do not need the wall." Several phrases reinforce the notion that the wall creates division. We "set the wall between us once again," he says; "We keep the wall between us as we go." "Something there is" in the natural scheme of things as such, he philosophizes, "that doesn't love a wall." Nevertheless, at the end of the day, and in the poem's concluding lines, Frost realizes that the neighbor cannot admit, or say "it for himself." Instead, the neighbor takes a certain pleasure in "his father's saying." He prides himself on what for the poet is a mindless cliché reproducing social division. All in all, he will forever restore the literal wall as a symbol. However ironic, the poem's title underscores the symbolic paradox of "mending" through separation, encoding in more subtle, more compressed, and more cryptic terms the proposition that "Good fences make good neighbors."

Walls, of course, have a deep archetypal symbolic resonance in cultural usage. The literary term *archetype* stems from the Greek word *archetypos*, which means "original pattern." The Cambridge anthropologists Sir James Frazer, Gilbert Murray, and Jesse Weston, as well as the psychoanalytic tradition influenced by the famous Swiss psychologist Carl Jung, shaped the modern literary understanding of archetypes. An **archetype** in literature describes a symbolic image that is basic to the human experience of birth, death, fertility, disease, war, quest, and so on. The symbolic power of, say, the Great Wall of China or the former Berlin Wall signifies the power, authority, and sovereignty of boundaries beyond their literal, physical structures. Archetypes are so basic that they recur in the mythology, customs, rituals, and literatures of particular societies as a world phenomenon stretching across cultures and historical periods. Such basic archetypes as images of fire, water, earth, stars, caves, cups, animals, wounds, crosses, swastikas, circles, and so on give shape to one's individual dream life and poetic imagination because they are deeply imprinted in what Jung characterized as the "collective unconscious" of human culture.

Sylvia Plath's poetry also works with primal, archetypal symbols such as a tree and the moon in her poem "The Moon and the Yew Tree."

The Berlin Wall, Heidelberger Strasse

SYLVIA PLATH   *(1932–1963)*

The Moon and the Yew Tree   *(1961)*

This is the light of the mind, cold and planetary.
The trees of the mind are black. The light is blue.
The grasses unload their griefs on my feet as if I were God,
Prickling my ankles and murmuring of their humility.
Fumy, spiritous mists inhabit this place   5
Separated from my house by a row of headstones.
I simply cannot see where there is to get to.

The moon is no door. It is a face in its own right,
White as a knuckle and terribly upset.
It drags the sea after it like a dark crime; it is quiet   10
With the O-gape of complete despair. I live here.
Twice on Sunday, the bells startle the sky—
Eight great tongues affirming the Resurrection.
At the end, they soberly bong out their names.

The yew tree points up. It has a Gothic shape.   15
The eyes lift after it and find the moon.
The moon is my mother. She is not sweet like Mary.
Her blue garments unloose small bats and owls.
How I would like to believe in tenderness—

The face of the effigy, gentled by candles,   20
Bending, on me in particular, its mild eyes.

I have fallen a long way. Clouds are flowering
Blue and mystical over the face of the stars.
Inside the church, the saints will all be blue,
Floating on their delicate feet over the cold pews,   25
Their hands and faces stiff with holiness.
The moon sees nothing of this. She is bald and wild.
And the message of the yew tree is blackness—blackness and silence.

TOPICS FOR CRITICAL THINKING

1. What kinds of symbolic meanings do you associate with the archetypal images of
   the moon and the tree?
2. Do the tree and moon have opposing meanings in Plath's symbolic presentation of
   them? Or do they complement one another?
3. Plath claims the moon as mother and further contrasts that personification with the
   Christian figure of Mary. What is her point here?

TOPIC FOR CRITICAL WRITING

Explore the differences in the poem's two settings that contrast the outdoor scene of
evening with what is going on "inside the church."

Poetry, at times, plays on the archetypal dimensions of uncanny, everyday
things so as to make us think twice about the meanings we routinely take for
granted. Such psychological estrangement happens in W. S. Merwin's unsettling poem "Strawberries."

W. S. MERWIN   *(b. 1927)*

Strawberries   *(1983)*

When my father died I saw   a narrow valley

it looked as though it began   across the river
from the landing where he was born   but there was no river

I was hoeing the sand   of a small vegetable plot
for my mother   in deepening twilight   5
and looked up in time   to see a farm wagon
dry and gray   horse already hidden
and no driver   going into the valley
carrying a casket

                              and another wagon   10
coming out of the valley   behind a gray horse
with a boy driving   and a high load
of two kinds of berries   one of them strawberries

        that night when I slept   I dreamed of things
wrong in the house   all of them signs   15
the water of the shower   running brackish
and an insect of a kind   I had seen him kill
climbing around   the walls of his bathroom
        up in the morning   I stopped on the stairs
my mother was awake   already and asked me   20
if I wanted a shower   before breakfast
and for breakfast she said   we have strawberries

Several forceful archetypes underwrite the situation, imagery, and action of "Strawberries." In addition to the poet's dream, nearly all the poem's elements can be read as signs of symbolic meaning. To begin with, the poem's framing scenario deals with death and the succession of father and son in their respective relationships to the mother. This domestic situation itself touches on the tensions of the Oedipal myth, which is fundamental for **psychoanalytic** *www* Web approaches to literature. In Sophocles' famous Oedipal trilogy, the son's sexual rivalry with the father for the mother's attentions is a story that Sigmund Freud, the founder of modern psychoanalysis, interpreted as fundamental to the psychic development of men and women. The successful passage through the Oedipal situation, for Freud, is marked by the child's relinquishing of his primal relationship to and desire for the mother in favor of substitute satisfactions that make up the wider social and cultural sublimations of everyday life.

Merwin's poem opens with a garden of sand in a valley landscape where there once was a river; it ends with the mother's suggestion that the son take a "shower." There are two wagons: one driverless, carrying a casket, the other full of two kinds of berries driven by a boy. Similar to the archetypal rites of passage that we find, say, in T. S. Eliot's long poem *The Waste Land* (1922), we move from a burial of the dead and the dry garden associated with death to images of water, rejuvenation, and even resurrection. The son dreams of an insect the father had once killed. This detail reinforces, perhaps, the Oedipal narrative that, as Freud described it, characterizes the son's renouncing of his desire for the mother out of fear of the father's violent threat of castration. In Merwin's poem, however, the son replaces the father and receives the ambiguous dish of strawberries for breakfast.

TOPICS FOR CRITICAL THINKING

1. What do the strawberries symbolize?
2. What do the strawberries have to do with the berries carted out of the valley by the boy and his gray horse?

3. Why does the poet dream of things "wrong in the house," and what kinds of emotions does the son experience when the mother tells him that "for breakfast . . . we have strawberries"?

TOPIC FOR CRITICAL WRITING

How does the poet's use of spacings within the lines on the page affect how we read the poem's action and complicate how we interpret its meanings?

What the signs of the poet's imagination actually mean are as opaque, finally, as the typographical gaps Merwin inserts as a stylistic feature into his line lengths. Such spacings suggest the power of particular words and phrases by making us pause over them. But they obscure even as they suggest possible lines of significance and interpreted meaning. Guided by the symbolic enigmas of his dream life, Merwin seems to concur in "Strawberries" with the great Irish bard W. B. Yeats and his belief that "the poet of essences and pure ideas must seek in the half-lights that glimmer from symbol to symbol as if to the ends of the earth, all that the epic and dramatic poet finds of mystery and shadow in the accidental circumstances of life."

Symbols, as we have seen, explore the likenesses between something close to hand and something else that is less easily known. **Allegory** presents a more purposeful narrative structuring of symbolic analogies. The term *allegory* comes from the Greek words meaning "other" (*allos*) and "to speak" (*agoreuein*): to speak, that is, in terms of something other. In literary allegories, virtually all the narrative details of setting, characterization, imagery, and so on stand as emblems for moral truths and spiritual meanings in another, more metaphysical register. Through the narrative experience or quest of a protagonist—whether it is the Spenserian knight of the *Faerie Queen* torn between Una and Duessa or Bunyan's hero Christian beguiled by Mr. Wordly Wiseman in *Pilgrim's Progress*, or even Dante's descent into the underworld in the *Divine Comedy*—allegories teach us how to recognize the differences between good and evil, truth and error, the saved and the damned.

Such a scene of spiritual instruction happens in the allegorical analogies that Edward Taylor witnesses in "Upon a Spider Catching a Fly."

EDWARD TAYLOR *(1642–1729)*

Upon a Spider Catching a Fly *(1680–1682)*

Thou sorrow, venom elf:
　　Is this thy ploy,
To spin a web out of thyself
　　To catch a fly?
　　　For why?　　　　　　　　　　　　　　　　5

I saw a petish wasp
　　Fall foul therein,

Whom yet thy whorl-pins did not clasp
   Lest he should fling
      His sting.   10

But as afraid, remote
   Didst stand hereat
And with thy little fingers stroke
   And gently tap
      His back.   15

Thus gently him didst treat
   Lest he should pet,
And in a froppish, waspish heat
   Should greatly fret
      Thy net.   20

Whereas the silly fly,
   Caught by its leg
Thou by the throat tookst hastily
   And hind the head
      Bite dead.   25

This goes to pot, that not[;]
   Nature doth call.
Strive not above what strength hath got
   Lest in the brawl
      Thou fall.   30

This fray seems thus to us.
   Hell's spider gets
His entrails spun to whip-cords thus,
   And wove to nets
      And sets.   35

To tangle Adam's race
   In's stratagems
To their destructions, spoiled, made base
   By venom things,
      Damned sins.   40

But mighty, gracious Lord
   Communicate
Thy grace to break the cord, afford
   Us glory's gate
      And state.   45

We'll nightingale sing like
   When perched on high
In glory's cage, thy glory, bright,

And thankfully,
  For Joy.   50

Taylor, the New England Puritan pastor and poet, was born in Leicester-
shire, England, and emigrated to the Bay Colony (Boston) in 1668. He studied
at Harvard University and later ministered to the frontier community of West-
field, Massachusetts, from 1671 until his death in 1729. Influenced by the
metaphysical conceits he read in John Donne's *Holy Sonnets* and Richard
Crashaw's *Steps to the Temple*, Taylor's devotional poetry, *Prepatory Meditations*
(1682–1725) offers more plainspoken and didactic verse allegories for humanity's relationship to God. "Upon a Spider Catching a Fly" pays close attention
to everyday life whose worldly scenes, as Taylor believed, "illustrate supernatural things by natural." The poem sets out in a rather plainspoken style the literal situation of a spider catching a wasp or fly in its web. The second half of
the poem illuminates this scenario as an allegory for the Calvinist belief in the
so-called total depravity of Original Sin. The literal spider is an allegorical figure for "Hell's spider" or Satan, who has spun a metaphysical web "To tangle
Adam's race / In's stratagems." Like the fly, humanity cannot free itself from
the entanglements of total depravity on its own. Only God's irresistible grace
offered to a selected few—the elect who are predestined for salvation through
Christ's limited atonement—can hope to "break the cord" of Original Sin.

Poems for Further Reading and Critical Writing

WALT WHITMAN   *(1819–1892)*

When Lilacs Last in the Dooryard Bloom'd   *(1868)*

1

When lilacs last in the dooryard bloom'd,
And the great star early droop'd in the western sky in the night,
I mourn'd, and yet shall mourn with ever-returning spring.

Ever-returning spring, trinity sure to me you bring,
Lilac blooming perennial and drooping star in the west,   5
And thought of him I love.

2

O powerful western fallen star!
O shades of night—O moody, tearful night!
O great star disappear'd—O the black murk that hides the star!
O cruel hands that hold me powerless—O helpless soul of me!   10
O harsh surrounding cloud that will not free my soul.

3

In the dooryard fronting an old farm-house near the white-wash'd
    palings,
Stands the lilac-bush tall-growing with heart-shaped leaves of rich
    green,
With many a pointed blossom rising delicate, with the perfume strong I love,
With every leaf a miracle—and from this bush in the dooryard,   15
With delicate-color'd blossoms and heart-shaped leaves of rich green,
A sprig with its flower I break.

4

In the swamp in secluded recesses,
A shy and hidden bird is warbling a song.

Solitary the thrush,   20
The hermit withdrawn to himself, avoiding the settlements,
Sings by himself a song.

Song of the bleeding throat,
Death's outlet song of life, (for well dear brother I know,
If thou wast not granted to sing thou would'st surely die.)   25

5

Over the breast of the spring, the land, amid cities,
Amid lanes and through old woods, where lately the violets peep'd from the
    ground, spotting the gray debris,
Amid the grass in the fields each side of the lanes, passing the endless grass,
Passing the yellow-spear'd wheat, every grain from its shroud in the dark-
    brown fields uprisen,
Passing the apple-tree blows of white and pink in the orchards,   30
Carrying a corpse to where it shall rest in the grave,
Night and day journeys a coffin.

6

Coffin that passes through lanes and streets,
Through day and night with the great cloud darkening the land,
With the pomp of the inloop'd flags with the cities draped in black,   35
With the show of the States themselves as of crape-veil'd women
    standing,
With processions long and winding and the flambeaus of the night,
With the countless torches lit, with the silent sea of faces and the
    unbared heads,
With the waiting depot, the arriving coffin, and the sombre faces,
With dirges through the night, with the thousand voices rising strong and   40
    solemn,
With all the mournful voices of the dirges pour'd around the coffin,

The dim-lit churches and the shuddering organs—where amid these you
     journey,
With the tolling tolling bells' perpetual clang,
Here, coffin that slowly passes,
I give you my sprig of lilac.   45

7

(Nor for you, for one alone,
Blossoms and branches green to coffins all I bring,
For fresh as the morning, thus would I chant a song for you O sane
     and sacred death.

All over bouquets of roses,
O death, I cover you over with roses and early lilies,   50
But mostly and now the lilac that blooms the first,
Copious I break, I break the sprigs from the bushes,
With loaded arms I come, pouring for you,
For you and the coffins all of you O death.)

8

O western orb sailing the heaven,   55
Now I know what you must have meant as a month since I walk'd,
As I walk'd in silence the transparent shadowy night,
As I saw you had something to tell as you bent to me night after night,
As you droop'd from the sky low down as if to my side, (while the other stars
     all look'd on,)
As we wander'd together the solemn night, (for something I know not   60
     what kept me from sleep,)
As the night advanced, and I saw on the rim of the west how full you
     were of woe,
As I stood on the rising ground in the breeze in the cool transparent night,
As I watch'd where you pass'd and was lost in the netherward black of the
     night,
As my soul in its trouble dissatisfied sank, as where you sad orb,
Concluded, dropt in the night, and was gone.   65

9

Sing on there in the swamp,
O singer bashful and tender, I hear your notes, I hear your call,
I hear, I come presently, I understand you,
But a moment I linger, for the lustrous star has detain'd me,
The star my departing comrade holds and detains me.   70

10

O how shall I warble myself for the dead one there I loved?
And how shall I deck my song for the large sweet soul that has gone?
And what shall my perfume be for the grave of him I love?

Sea-winds blown from east and west,
Blown from the Eastern sea and blown from the Western sea, till there on   75
    the prairies meeting,
These and with these and the breath of my chant,
I'll perfume the grave of him I love.

11

O what shall I hang on the chamber walls?
And what shall the pictures be that I hang on the walls,
To adorn the burial-house of him I love?   80

Pictures of growing spring and farms and homes,
With the Fourth-month eve at sundown, and the gray smoke lucid and
    bright,
With floods of the yellow gold of the gorgeous, indolent, sinking sun, burn-
    ing, expanding the air,
With the fresh sweet herbage under foot, and the pale green leaves of the
    trees prolific,
In the distance the flowing glaze, the breast of the river, with a wind-dapple   85
    here and there,
With ranging hills on the banks, with many a line against the sky, and
    shadows,
And the city at hand with dwellings so dense, and stacks of chimneys,
And all the scenes of life and the workshops, and the workmen
    homeward returning.

12

Lo, body and soul—this land,
My own Manhattan with spires, and the sparkling and hurrying tides,   90
    and the ships,
The varied and ample land, the South and the North in the light, Ohio's
    shores and flashing Missouri,
And ever the far-spreading prairies cover'd with grass and corn.

Lo, the most excellent sun so calm and haughty,
The violet and purple morn with just-felt breezes,
The gentle soft-born measureless light,   95
The miracle spreading bathing all, the fulfill'd noon,
The coming eve delicious, the welcome night and the stars,
Over my cities shining all, enveloping man and land.

13

Sing on, sing on you gray-brown bird,
Sing from the swamps, the recesses, pour your chant from the bushes,   100
Limitless out of the dusk, out of the cedars and pines.

Sing on dearest brother, warble your reedy song,
Loud human song, with voice of uttermost woe.

O liquid and free and tender!
O wild and loose to my soul—O wondrous singer!   105
You only I hear—yet the star holds me, (but will soon depart,)
Yet the lilac with mastering odor holds me.

14

Now while I sat in the day and look'd forth,
In the close of the day with its light and the fields of spring, and the farmers
     preparing their crops,
In the large unconscious scenery of my land with its lakes and forests,   110
In the heavenly aerial beauty, (after the perturb'd winds and the storms,)
Under the arching heavens of the afternoon swift passing, and the
     voices of children and women,
The many-moving sea-tides, and I saw the ships how they sail'd,
And the summer approaching with richness, and the fields all busy with
     labor,
And the infinite separate houses, how they all went on, each with its meals   115
     and minutia of daily usages,
And the streets how their throbbings throbb'd, and the cities pent—lo, then
     and there,
Falling upon them all and among them all, enveloping me with the rest,
Appear'd the cloud, appear'd the long black trail,
And I knew death, its thought, and the sacred knowledge of death.

Then with the knowledge of death as walking one side of me,   120
And the thought of death close-walking the other side of me,
And I in the middle as with companions, and as holding the hands of
     companions,
I fled forth to the hiding receiving night that talks not,
Down to the shores of the water, the path by the swamp in the dimness,
To the solemn shadowy cedars and ghostly pines so still.   125

And the singer so shy to the rest receiv'd me,
The gray-brown bird I know receiv'd us comrades three,
And he sang the carol of death, and a verse for him I love.

From deep secluded recesses,
From the fragrant cedars and the ghostly pines so still,   130
Came the carol of the bird.

And the charm of the carol rapt me,
As I held as if by their hands my comrades in the night,
And the voice of my spirit tallied the song of the bird.

Come lovely and soothing death,   135
Undulate round the world, serenely arriving, arriving,
In the day, in the night, to all, to each,
Sooner or later delicate death.

Prais'd be the fathomless universe,
For life and joy, and for objects and knowledge curious,   140
And for love, sweet love—but praise! praise! praise!
For the sure-enwinding arms of cool-enfolding death.

Dark mother always gliding near with soft feet,
Have none chanted for thee a chant of fullest welcome?
Then I chant it for thee, I glorify thee above all,   145
I bring thee a song that when thou must indeed come, come unfalteringly.

Approach strong deliveress,
When it is so, when thou hast taken them I joyously sing the dead,
Lost in the loving floating ocean of thee,
Laved in the flood of thy bliss O death.   150

From me to thee glad serenades,
Dances for thee I propose saluting thee, adornments and feastings for thee,
And the sights of the open landscape and the high-spread sky are
*   fitting,*
And life and the fields, and the huge and thoughtful night.

The night in silence under many a star,   155
The ocean shore and the husky whispering wave whose voice I know,
And the soul turning to thee O vast and well-veil'd death,
And the body gratefully nestling close to thee.

Over the tree-tops I float thee a song,
Over the rising and sinking waves, over the myriad fields and the prairies wide, 160
Over the dense-pack'd cities all and the teeming wharves and ways,
I float this carol with joy, with joy to thee O death.

15

To the tally of my soul,
Loud and strong kept up the gray-brown bird,
With pure deliberate notes spreading filling the night.   165

Loud in the pines and cedars dim,
Clear in the freshness moist and the swamp-perfume,
And I with my comrades there in the night.

While my sight that was bound in my eyes unclosed,
As to long panoramas of visions. 170

And I saw askant the armies,
I saw as in noiseless dreams hundreds of battle-flags,
Borne through the smoke of the battles and pierc'd with missiles I saw them,
And carried hither and yon through the smoke, and torn and bloody,
And at last but a few shreds left on the staffs, (and all in silence,) 175
And the staffs all splinter'd and broken.

I saw battle-corpses, myriads of them,
And the white skeletons of young men, I saw them,
I saw the debris and debris of all the slain soldiers of the war,
But I saw they were not as was thought, 180
They themselves were fully at rest, they suffer'd not,
The living remain'd and suffer'd, the mother suffer'd,
And the wife and the child and the musing comrade suffer'd,
And the armies that remain'd suffer'd.

16

Passing the visions, passing the night, 185
Passing, unloosing the hold of my comrades' hands,
Passing the song of the hermit bird and the tallying song of my soul,
Victorious song, death's outlet song, yet varying ever-altering song,
As low and wailing, yet clear the notes, rising and falling, flooding the
     night,
Sadly sinking and fainting, as warning and warning, and yet again bursting 190
     with joy,
Covering the earth and filling the spread of the heaven,
As that powerful psalm in the night I heard from recesses,
Passing, I leave thee lilac with heart-shaped leaves,
I leave thee there in the door-yard, blooming, returning with spring.

I cease from my song for thee, 195
From my gaze on thee in the west, fronting the west, communing with thee,
O comrade lustrous with silver face in the night.
Yet each to keep and all, retrievements out of the night,
The song, the wondrous chant of the gray-brown bird,
And the tallying chant, the echo arous'd in my soul, 200
With the lustrous and drooping star with the countenance full of woe,
With the holders holding my hand nearing the call of the bird,
Comrades mine and I in the midst, and their memory ever to keep, for the
     dead I loved so well,
For the sweetest, wisest soul of all my days and lands—and this for his dear
     sake,
Lilac and star and bird twined with the chant of my soul, 205
There in the fragrant pines and the cedars dusk and dim.

TOPICS FOR CRITICAL THINKING

1. Whitman wrote "When Lilacs Last in the Dooryard Bloom'd" just after the assassination of President Abraham Lincoln on April 14, 1865. Explore the ways in which Whitman presents the slain president through the symbolism of the star, or "western orb," in the poem.

2. Consider the symbolic significance of the two other major tropes in the poem: the lilac and bird. What does each of these figures stand for?

3. How does the funeral procession serve to unify the divided nation in an act of mourning?

4. Explore Whitman's personification of death as a "strong deliveress." Examine the implied view of death the poet projects as he listens to "death's outlet song" in section 16.

TOPIC FOR CRITICAL WRITING

How is Lincoln's death itself symbolic of the nation's wounds? How does the poet's mourning for Lincoln open onto the larger project of seeking "reconciliation" between North and South after the Civil War?

WALT WHITMAN   (1819–1892)

I Saw in Louisiana a Live-Oak Growing   (1860)

I saw in Louisiana a live-oak growing,
All alone stood it and the moss hung down from the branches,
Without any companion it grew there uttering joyous leaves of dark green,
And its look, rude, unbending, lusty, made me think of myself,
But I wonder'd how it could utter joyous leaves standing alone there without   5
      its friend near, for I knew I could not,
And I broke off a twig with a certain number of leaves upon it, and twined
      around it a little moss,
And brought it away, and I have placed it in sight in my room,
It is not needed to remind me as of my own dear friends,
(For I believe lately I think of little else than of them,)
Yet it remains to me a curious token, it makes me think of manly love;   10
For all that, and though the live-oak glistens there in Louisiana solitary in
      a wide flat space,
Uttering joyous leaves all its life without a friend a lover near,
I know very well I could not.

TOPICS FOR CRITICAL THINKING

1. Describe Whitman's opening portrait of the live-oak tree. What does he emphasize in his impressions of it?

2. Pay close attention to Whitman's description of the tree "uttering joyous leaves." What does this depiction mirror in the poet's identity?

3. How does Whitman both identify with the live-oak and note its differences from himself?

TOPICS FOR CRITICAL WRITING

1. Whitman saves a twig from the tree as a "curious token" of what the tree symbolizes for him. What symbolic meaning does the live-oak represent?
2. What final realization does the poet come to about himself through musing on the tree's symbolic example?

WILLIAM CARLOS WILLIAMS   *(1883–1963)*

The Yachts   *(1935)*

contend in a sea which the land partly encloses
shielding them from the too-heavy blows
of an ungoverned ocean which when it chooses

tortures the biggest hulls, the best man knows
to pit against its beatings, and sinks them pitilessly.   5
Mothlike in mists, scintillant in the minute

brilliance of cloudless days, with broad bellying sails
they glide to the wind tossing green water
from their sharp prows while over them the crew crawls

ant-like, solicitously grooming them, releasing,   10
making fast as they turn, lean far over and having
caught the wind again, side by side, head for the mark.

In a well guarded arena of open water surrounded by
lesser and greater crafts which, sycophant, lumbering
and flittering follow them, they appear youthful, rare   15

as the light of a happy eye, live with the grace
of all that in the mind is fleckless, free and
naturally to be desired. Now the sea which holds them

is moody, lapping their glossy sides, as if feeling
for some slightest flaw but fails completely.   20
Today no race. Then the wind comes again. The yachts

move, jockeying for a start, the signal is set and they
are off. Now the waves strike at them but they are too
well made, the slip through, though they take in canvas.

Arms with hands grasping seek to clutch at the prows.   25
Bodies thrown recklessly in the way are cut aside.
It is a sea of faces about them in agony, in despair

until the horror of the race dawns staggering the mind,
the whole sea become an entanglement of watery bodies
lost to the world bearing what they can not hold. Broken,   30

beaten, desolate, reaching from the dead to be taken up
they cry out, failing, failing! their cries rising
in waves still as the skillful yachts pass over.

TOPICS FOR CRITICAL THINKING

1. Analyze the opening situation and setting as Williams presents them in the poem.
2. Does the fact that this poem was written in 1935 in the middle of the Great Depression clarify what is at stake in its presentation of the yacht race?
3. Do the yachts as symbols stand for more than one meaning?
4. What is the "horror" of the race that Williams alludes to in the poem?

TOPIC FOR CRITICAL WRITING

What qualities does Williams depict in the yachts? What do these qualities symbolize?

24　Myth

Literature's connections to myth are primordial, reaching back to ancient, oral traditions that predate writing. Mythic narratives take many forms and serve several cultural functions. Some myths tell stories of how life came into being; such **emergence myths** explain the origins of things and describe humanity's place in the world. For example, in the creation stories of the Hopi Pueblo tribe of the American Southwest, Grandmother Spider Woman assists in the metamorphosis of insects into animals and finally into human beings through four successive worlds of evolution. Similarly, the Book of Genesis gives the biblical account of the world's creation and the fall of humanity from the Garden of Eden. In the Greek tradition, the *Theogony* chronicles the mythic history of the Greek pantheon of gods. Such myths provide foundational narratives of a culture's world outlook. **Quest myths** offer exemplary models of heroism in the stories, say, of Prometheus's gift of fire to humanity after he stole it from the gods, or Beowulf's epic battle with the monster Grendel. Similarly, the myth of Psyche tells the story of a woman's trials in pursuing the love of the god Cupid.

By giving a deep, structural understanding of the way things are, myth has a powerful shaping influence on basic beliefs, forms of worship, civic governance, tribal customs, social practices, gender roles, sexual behavior, and the makeup of everyday life. Myths also provide a rich cultural resource for poetry. In the epic tradition, Virgil's *The Aeneid* and John Milton's *Paradise Lost* make instructive, or didactic, use of mythic narratives to lend shape and significance to the past.

In lyric modes, poets reinterpret classical myths as, for example, W. H. Auden does in his rereading of Pieter Breughel's sixteenth-century painting *Landscape with the Fall of Icarus* (see color insert).

W. H. AUDEN　*(1907–1973)*

Musée des Beaux Arts　*(1940)*

About suffering they were never wrong,
The Old Masters: how well they understood
Its human position; how it takes place
While someone else is eating or opening a window or just walking
　　dully along;

771

How, when the aged are reverently, passionately waiting   5
For the miraculous birth, there always must be
Children who did not specially want it to happen, skating
On a pond at the edge of the wood:
They never forgot
That even the dreadful martyrdom must run its course   10
Anyhow in a corner, some untidy spot
Where the dogs go on with their doggy life and the torturer's horse
Scratches its innocent behind on a tree.

In Breughel's *Icarus*, for instance: how everything turns away
Quite leisurely from the disaster; the ploughman may   15
Have heard the splash, the forsaken cry,
But for him it was not an important failure; the sun shone
As it had to on the white legs disappearing into the green
Water; and the expensive delicate ship that must have seen
Something amazing, a boy falling out of the sky,   20
Had somewhere to get to and sailed calmly on.

    To understand Auden's point about Breughel's painting, one has to know
something of the myth of Icarus. The myth of Icarus and his father Daedalus
has deep roots in the world of classical antiquity. The Roman poet Ovid, the
Greek writer Apollodorus, and Diodorus of Sicily all tell of Daedalus's exploits. The master craftsperson of the ancient world, Daedalus was commissioned by King Minos of the island of Crete to design the Labyrinth that
housed the mythic Minotaur. The Minotaur was the offspring of Minos's wife,
Pasiphaë and a bull, the gift from Poseidon, the god of the Sea. Poseidon had
given the bull to Minos to be sacrificed, but Minos kept it for himself instead.
As punishment, Poseidon had Pasiphaë fall in love with it. The Minotaur was
housed in the Labyrinth and each spring Minos required the sacrifice of seven
Athenian maidens and youths to the monster as tribute. Daedalus helped Ari-
adne show the Athenian hero Theseus how to escape the maze after killing
the Minotaur and, as punishment, Minos imprisoned both Daedalus and
Icarus in the Labyrinth. To escape from Crete, Daedalus fashioned wings held
together with wax. Before taking off, Daedalus gave his son the warning not
to fly too close to the sun because the heat would melt the wings. Icarus, of
course, did not take his father's advice and thus fell to his death in the sea.
Traditionally, the myth has been considered an allegory for the impetuousness
of youth, but this is not the lesson of Auden's poem.

TOPICS FOR CRITICAL THINKING

1. What point does Auden make about the "human position" of suffering in the first
   stanza of the poem?
2. What examples does Auden give of suffering that go unnoticed in life?
3. Do you agree with Auden's interpretation of Breughel's *Icarus*? Are there other
   ways to consider the painting? Explain.

TOPIC FOR CRITICAL WRITING

Where does Breughel place Icarus in the frame of his painting? What point does Auden make in his second stanza about the visual arrangement of Breughel's painting?

Auden interprets Breughel's representation of a famous myth to present the ways in which we ignore and even resist acknowledging the suffering of others. Myth can also offer new perspectives on experience, as when Anne Sexton returns to the story of Icarus. Her poem "To a Friend Whose Work Has Come to Triumph" muses on myth not so much to draw a moral lesson from it, but more to identify with Icarus's flight.

ANNE SEXTON (1928–1974)

To a Friend Whose Work Has Come to Triumph *(1962)*

Consider Icarus, pasting those sticky wings on,
testing that strange little tug at his shoulder blade,
and think of that first flawless moment over the lawn
of the labyrinth. Think of the difference it made!
There below are the trees, as awkward as camels;   5
and here are the shocked starlings pumping past
and think of innocent Icarus who is doing quite well:
larger than a sail, over the fog and the blast
of the plushy ocean, he goes. Admire his wings!
Feel the fire at his neck and see how casually   10
he glances up and is caught, wondrously tunneling
into that hot eye. Who cares that he fell back to the sea?
See him acclaiming the sun and come plunging down
while his sensible daddy goes straight into town.

TOPICS FOR CRITICAL THINKING

1. Sexton wrote this poem after the poet W. D. Snodgrass, one of Sexton's teachers, won the Pulitzer Prize for poetry in 1960. The poem expresses her joy in her mentor's achievement. What relationship do you draw between Icarus and the poet's vocation?
2. In imagining Icarus's flight, Sexton invites us to "Think of the difference it made!" What difference does it make, do you think?
3. What is Sexton's point in saying "Who cares that he fell back to the sea?"
4. Sexton herself luxuriated in her sunbaths. "All my life," she once said, "I have been in love with the sun. I looked at it as the great lover, the great seizure. Somehow, letting the sun wash over you, letting its heat adore you, was like having intercourse with God." How does she encourage us as readers toward that kind of ecstasy in the poem by asking us to "feel the fire at his neck" in the moment of glory "acclaiming the sun"?

TOPIC FOR CRITICAL WRITING

Contrast Auden's point of view with the ways in which Sexton urges us not just to "consider" Icarus but more actively to "see him" and even identify with his experience of flight.

Poets not only employ allusions to classical mythology in describing universal truths about the human condition. They also dramatize the expressive possibilities of the mythic imagination beyond conventional modes of being. For example, in her poem "Jacklight," the Native American writer Louise Erdrich revisits the boundary between the human and animal world that in Chippewa myth fuses hunting, seduction, and sexuality.

LOUISE ERDRICH   *(b. 1955)*

Jacklight   *(1984)*

The same Chippewa word is used both for
flirting and hunting game, while another
Chippewa word connotes both using force in
intercourse and also killing a bear with
one's bare hands.
    —R. W. DUNNING, SOCIAL AND ECONOMIC
      CHANGE AMONG THE NORTHERN OJIBWA
                    (1959)

We have come to the edge of the woods,
out of brown grass where we slept, unseen,
out of knotted twigs, out of leaves creaked shut,
out of hiding.

At first the light wavered, glancing over us.   5
Then it clenched to a fist of light that pointed,
searched out, divided us.
Each took the beams like direct blows the heart answers.
Each of us moved forward alone.

We have come to the edge of the woods,   10
drawn out of ourselves by this night sun,
this battery of polarized acids,
that outshines the moon.

We smell them behind it
but they are faceless, invisible.   15
We smell the raw steel of their gun barrels,
mink oil on leather, their tongues of sour barley.
We smell their mothers buried chin-deep in wet dirt.

We smell their fathers with scoured knuckles,
teeth cracked from hot marrow.   20
We smell their sisters of crushed dogwood, bruised apples,
of fractured cups and concussions of burnt hooks.

We smell their breath steaming lightly behind the jacklight.
We smell the itch underneath the caked guts on their clothes.
We smell their minds like silver hammers   25
cocked back, held in readiness
for the first of us to step into the open.

We have come to the edge of the woods,
out of brown grass where we slept, unseen,
out of leaves creaked shut, out of our hiding.   30
We have come here too long.

It is their turn now,
their turn to follow us. Listen,
they put down their equipment.
It is useless in the tall brush.   35
And now they take the first steps, not knowing
how deep the woods are and lightless.
How deep the woods are.

TOPICS FOR CRITICAL THINKING

1. As her epigraph from R. W. Dunning implies, Erdrich locates mythic connections
   in Chippewa language between hunting and flirting, between sexual violence and
   the force of "killing a bear with one's bare hands." How do those mythic connections shape the dramatic conflict in "Jacklight"?
2. How do you interpret the action represented in the poem's final stanza? What do
   you think Erdrich's point is in repeating the phrasing "how deep the woods are" in
   her last two lines?

TOPIC FOR CRITICAL WRITING

A jacklight is a powerful flashlight, car headlight, or search light used illegally to startle game while hunting at night. Discuss the world that Erdrich associates with the
jacklight through her poem's imagery and figurative language. What effect does the
jacklight have on the hunters' intended prey? How do they resist the forces the jacklight represents?

Poems for Further Reading and Critical Writing

LOUISE GLÜCK   *(b. 1943)*

Mythic Fragment   *(1985)*

When the stern god
approached me with his gift
my fear enchanted him
so that he ran more quickly
through the wet grass, as he insisted,   5
to praise me. I saw captivity
in praise; against the lyre,
I begged my father in the sea
to save me. When
the god arrived, I was nowhere,   10
I was in a tree forever. Reader,
pity Apollo: at the water's edge,
I turned from him, I summoned
my invisible father—as
I stiffened in the god's arms,   15
of his encompassing love
my father made
no other sign from the water.

TOPICS FOR CRITICAL THINKING

1. Glück's "Mythic Fragment" alludes to the Roman tale told by Ovid of Daphne's
   metamorphosis into a laurel tree. Daphne, the daughter of the river-god Peneus,
   was a nymph who resisted the idea of marriage in favor of leading the independent
   life of a huntress, like the goddess Diana. Pursued in the forest by Apollo—the god
   of song, sun, and perfect form—she called on her father for help. Accordingly,
   Peneus transformed her into a laurel tree, which became sacred to Apollo. How
   does the poet portray Apollo's romantic interest in Daphne? Why, according to
   Glück, is Apollo attracted to Daphne?
2. Why do you think Daphne associates Apollo's praise with captivity? What kind of
   general comment on relationships is Glück making here?
3. Why does Daphne call on the reader to pity Apollo when she is transformed into
   a tree?
4. What is Daphne's attitude toward her metamorphosis, and do you detect any pun
   in her lines "as / I stiffened in the god's arms, / of his encompassing love"? How do
   you interpret her final lines about her father?

TOPIC FOR CRITICAL WRITING

Compare Glück's use of the dramatic monologue to rewrite classical mythology with
T. S. Eliot's dramatic persona in "Journey of the Magi."

T. S. ELIOT   *(1888–1965)*

Journey of the Magi   *(1927)*

"A cold coming we had of it,
Just the worst time of the year
For a journey, and such a long journey:
The ways deep and the weather sharp,
The very dead of winter."   5
And the camels galled, sore-footed, refractory,
Lying down in the melting snow.
There were times we regretted
The summer palaces on slopes, the terraces,
And the silken girls bringing sherbet.   10
Then the camel men cursing and grumbling
And running away, and wanting their liquor and women,
And the night-fires going out, and the lack of shelters,
And the cities hostile and the towns unfriendly
And the villages dirty and charging high prices: 15
A hard time we had of it.
At the end we preferred to travel all night,
Sleeping in snatches,
With the voices singing in our ears, saying
That this was all folly.   20

Then at dawn we came down to a temperate valley,
Wet, below the snow line, smelling of vegetation;
With a running stream and a water-mill beating the darkness,
And three trees on the low sky,
And an old white horse galloped away in the meadow.   25
Then we came to a tavern with vine-leaves over the lintel,
Six hands at an open door dicing for pieces of silver,
And feet kicking the empty wine-skins,
But there was no information, and so we continued
And arrived at evening, not a moment too soon   30
Finding the place; it was (you may say) satisfactory.

All this was a long time ago, I remember,
And I would do it again, but set down
This set down

This: were we led all that way for   35
Birth or Death? There was a Birth, certainly,
We had evidence and no doubt. I had seen birth and death,
But had thought they were different; this Birth was
Hard and bitter agony for us, like Death, our death.
We returned to our places, these Kingdoms,   40
But no longer at ease here, in the old dispensation,
With an alien people clutching their gods.
I should be glad of another death.

TOPICS FOR CRITICAL THINKING

1. T. S. Eliot bases the first five lines of his poem on a sermon delivered by Bishop Lancelot Andrewes in 1622. The biblical subtext for the poem comes from Matthew 2:1–2:

   1 NOW after Jesus was born in Bethlehem of Judea in the days of Herod the king, magi from the east arrived in Jerusalem, saying,
   2 Where is He who has been born King of the Jews? For we saw His star in the east and have come to worship Him.

   How does Eliot imagine the actual journey made by the Magi? What details does he use to depict their quest?

2. The three trees of the third stanza, as well as the images of dicing and the pieces of silver, all have symbolic resonance with the story of Christ's crucifixion in the three crosses, the Roman soldiers' gambling for Christ's robe, and Judas Iscariot's betrayal of Christ for silver. What is Eliot's purpose in alluding to the crucifixion in a poem about Christ's nativity?

3. How do you interpret the poem's final line?

TOPIC FOR CRITICAL WRITING

What is the effect of the journey on the Magus? In what ways has he become alienated from the "old dispensation"?

LESLIE MARMON SILKO   *(b. 1948)*

Prayer to the Pacific   *(1981)*

I traveled to the ocean
            distant
                        from my southwest land of sandrock
                        to the moving blue water
            Big as the myth of origin.   5

Pale
pale water in the yellow-white light of
        sun   floating west
             to China
        where ocean herself was born.   10
Clouds that blow across the sand are wet.

Squat in the wet sand and speak to the Ocean:
     I return to you   turquoise   the red coral you sent us,
         sister spirit of Earth.
Four round stones in my pocket   I carry back the ocean   15
         to suck and to taste.

Thirty thousand years ago
         Indians came riding across the ocean
         carried by giant sea turtles.
Waves were high that day   20
     great sea turtles waded   slowly out
              from the gray sundown sea.
Grandfather Turtle rolled in the sand   four times
        and disappeared
            swimming into the sun.   25
And so   from that time
     immemorial,
         as the old people say,
rain clouds drift from the west
         gift from the ocean.   30

Green leaves in the wind
Wet earth on my feet
     swallowing raindrops
         clear from China.

TOPICS FOR CRITICAL THINKING

1. Silko is of mixed Pueblo, Laguna, Mexican, and white descent lines. Her novels—*Ceremony* (1977), *Almanac of the Dead* (1991), *Yellow Woman* (1993), and *Gardens Among the Dunes* (1999), among other works—dwell on the Southwest Laguna Pueblo culture near Albuquerque, New Mexico, where she grew up. In "Prayer to the Pacific," she offers "turquoise" and "red coral" from her native "southwest land of sandrock" to the Pacific Ocean. In what terms does she personify the ocean in the poem?

2. In what ways does the poem perform the prayer or ritual of return to the ocean?

3. What does the ocean have to do with the desert landscape of the southwest?

4. In Silko's version of the Native American myth of origin, Grandfather Turtle rides sea turtles across the ocean "thirty thousand years ago." This myth may allude to the Beringia land bridge across the fifty-five-mile wide Bering Strait that today separates Siberia from Alaska's Seward Peninsula. During the periods of Ice Age

glaciation in the Pleistocene era, the Bering Straight periodically froze and served
as a land bridge allowing for the prehistoric peopling of the Americas from Asia between 40,000 to 13,000 years ago. At times during the Ice Age, so much of the
Earth's supply of water took the form of glaciers that sea levels fell to 350 feet below today's levels, allowing for travel across Beringia, the Bering Straight sea bed
now covered in water. In what ways does Silko lend a mythic dimension to this prehistoric migration?

TOPIC FOR CRITICAL WRITING

Compare the mythic presentation of the natural world in Silko's "Prayer to the Pacific" with Erdrich's "Jacklight."

The Chicana poet Pat Mora adopts the mythic persona of the Mexican
goddess Coatlicue to give advice in "Coatlicue's Rules: Advice from an Aztec
Goddess." Her poem presents a whimsical fusion of ancient wisdom and contemporary self-help tips.

PAT MORA   *(b. 1942)*

Coatlicue's Rules: Advice from an Aztec Goddess   *(1995)*

Rule 1: Beware of offers to make you famous.

I, pious Aztec mother lost in housework,
am pedestaled, "She of the Serpent Skirt,"
necklace dangling hearts and hands, faceless
statue, two snakes eye-to-eye on my shoulders,   5
goddess of earth, also death, which leads to

Rule 2: Retain control of your own publicity.

Past is present. Women are women.
I'm not competitive and motherhood isn't
about numbers, but four hundred sons and a daughter   10
may be a record even without the baby.
There's something wrong in this world
if a woman isn't safe even when she sweeps
her own house, when any speck can enter even through
the eye, I'll bet, and become a stubborn tenant.   15

Rule 3: Protect your uterus.

Conceptions, immaculate and otherwise, happen.
Women swallow sacred stones that fill their bellies
with elbows and knees. In Guatemala, a skull dangling
from a tree whispers, "Touch me,"   20
to a young girl, and a clear drop

drips on her palm, disappears. Dew
drops in, if you know what I mean.
Saliva moved in her, the girl says. Moved in, I say,
settled into that empty space, and grew. Men know.   25
They stay full of themselves, keeps occupancy down.

Rule 4: Avoid housework.

Remember, I was sweeping, humming, actually,
high on Coatepec, our Serpent Mountain, humming loud
so I wouldn't hear all those sighs inside.   30
I was sweeping slivers, gold and jade, picking up
after four hundred sons who think they're gods,
and their spoiled sister. I was sweeping
when feathers fell on me, brushed my face,
first light touch in years, like in a dream.   35

At first, I just blew them off, then I saw
the prettiest ball of tiny plumes, glowing
green and gold. Gently, I gathered it. Oh,
it was soft as baby hair, brought back mother-
shivers when I pressed it to my skin. I nestled it   40
like I used to nestle them, here,
when they finished nursing. Maybe I even stroked
the roundness. I have since heard that feathers
aren't that unusual at annunciations, but I was innocent.

After sweeping, I looked in vain inside   45
my clothes, but the soft ball had vanished, well,
descended. I think I showed within the hour,
or so it seemed. They noticed first, of course.

Rule 5: Avoid housework. It bears repeating.

I was too busy washing, cooking, sweeping again,   50
worrying about my daughter, Painted with Bells,
when I began to bump into their frowns
and mutterings. They kept glancing at my stomach,
started pointing. I got so hurt and mad, I started crying.
Why do they get to us? One wrong word or look   55
from any one of them doubles me over,
and I've had four hundred and one, no anesthetic.
Near them I'm like a snail with no shell on a sizzling day.
They started yelling, "Wicked, wicked," and my daughter,
right there with them, my wannabe warrior boy.   60

The yelling was easier than the whispers, "Kill. Kill.
Kill. Kill." Kill me? Their mother?

One against four hundred and one? All I'd done
was press that feathered softness into me.

Rule 6: Listen to inside voices.   65

You mothers know about the baby in a family, right?
Even if he hadn't talked to me from deep inside,
he would have been special. Maybe the best.
But as my name is Coatlicue, he did.
That unborn child, that started as a ball of feathers   70
all soft green and gold, heard my woes, and spoke to me.
A thoughtful boy. And formal too. He said, "Do not be afraid,
I know what I must do." So I stopped shaking.

Rule 7: Verify that the inside voice is yours.

I'll spare you the part about the body hacking   75
and head rolling. But he was provoked, remember.
All this talk of gods and goddesses distorts.

This planet wasn't big enough for all of us,
but my whole family has done well for itself, I think.
I'm the mother of stars. My daughter's white head   80
rolls round the heavens each night, and my sons
wink down at me. What can I say—a family
of high visibility. The baby? Up there also, the sun,
the real thing. Such a god he is, of war unfortunately,
and the boy never stops, always racing across the sky,   85
every day of the year, a ball of fire since birth.
But I think he has forgotten me. You sense my ambivalence.
I'm blinded by his light.

Rule 8: Insist on personal interviews.

Past is present, remember. Men carved me,   90
wrote my story, and Eve's, Malinche's, Guadalupe's,
Llorona's, snakes everywhere, even in our mouths.

Rule 9: Be selective about what you swallow.

TOPICS FOR CRITICAL THINKING

1. Coatlicue means "she of the Serpent Skirt." In Aztec iconography, Coatlicue is depicted as wearing a skirt of snakes and a necklace made out of human hearts. How
   does Mora's first rule of advice "Beware of offers to make you famous" reflect ironically on Coatlicue's mythic status?

2. While sweeping in a temple, Coatlicue was struck by a mysterious ball of feathers and immediately gave birth to Huitzilopochtli, the Aztec sun god. Discuss how Mora rewrites this immaculate conception story as a contemporary advice-to-women narrative in rules 3 and 4.

3. Angered by her mother's pregnancy, Coyolxauhqui, the goddess of the Moon, persuaded Coatlicue's four hundred children to try and kill her. Coatlicue was saved by Huitzilopochtli. Discuss Mora's rewriting of this narrative in rule 5.

4. Choose a mythic persona to offer self-help tips and advice of your own.

TOPIC FOR CRITICAL WRITING

How does Mora portray Coatlicue's "ambivalence" toward her son and her own legacy in the poem?

WALT WHITMAN   *(1819–1892)*

from Song of Myself (Section 24)   *(1855)*

24

Walt Whitman, a kosmos, of Manhattan the son,
Turbulent, fleshy, sensual, eating, drinking and breeding,
No sentimentalist, no stander above men and women or apart from them,
No more modest than immodest.

Unscrew the locks from the doors!   5
Unscrew the doors themselves from their jambs!

Whoever degrades another degrades me,
And whatever is done or said returns at last to me.

Through me the afflatus surging and surging, through me the current and
    index.

I speak the pass-word primeval, I give the sign of democracy,   10
By God! I will accept nothing which all cannot have their counterpart of on
    the same terms.

Through me many long dumb voices,
Voices of the interminable generations of prisoners and slaves,
Voices of the diseas'd and despairing and of thieves and dwarfs,
Voices of cycles of preparation and accretion,   15
And of the threads that connect the stars, and of wombs and of the father-
    stuff,
And of the rights of them the others are down upon,

Of the deform'd, trivial, flat, foolish, despised,
Fog in the air, beetles rolling balls of dung.

Through me forbidden voices,   20
Voices of sexes and lusts, voices veil'd and I remove the veil,
Voices indecent by me clarified and transfigur'd.

I do not press my fingers across my mouth,
I keep as delicate around the bowels as around the head and heart,
Copulation is no more rank to me than death is.   25

I believe in the flesh and the appetites,
Seeing, hearing, feeling, are miracles, and each part and tag of me is a
    miracle.

Divine am I inside and out, and I make holy whatever I touch or am touch'd
    from,
The scent of these arm-pits aroma finer than prayer,
This head more than churches, bibles, and all the creeds.   30

If I worship one thing more than another it shall be the spread of my own
    body, or any part of it,
Translucent mould of me it shall be you!
Shaded ledges and rests it shall be you!
Firm masculine colter it shall be you!
Whatever goes to the tilth of me it shall be you!   35
You my rich blood! your milky stream pale strippings of my life!
Breast that presses against other breasts it shall be you!
My brain it shall be your occult convolutions!
Root of wash'd sweet-flag! timorous pond-snipe! nest of guarded duplicate
    eggs! it shall be you!
Mix'd tussled hay of head, beard, brawn, it shall be you!   40
Trickling sap of maple, fibre of manly wheat, it shall be you!
Sun so generous it shall be you!
Vapors lighting and shading my face it shall be you!
You sweaty brooks and dews it shall be you!
Winds whose soft-tickling genitals rub against me it shall be you!   45
Broad muscular fields, branches of live oak, loving lounger in my winding
    paths, it shall be you!
Hands I have taken, face I have kiss'd, mortal I have ever touch'd, it shall be
    you.

I dote on myself, there is that lot of me and all so luscious,
Each moment and whatever happens thrills me with joy,
I cannot tell how my ankles bend, nor whence the cause of my faintest wish,   50
Nor the cause of the friendship I emit, nor the cause of the friendship I take
    again.

That I walk up my stoop, I pause to consider if it really be,
A morning-glory at my window satisfies me more than the metaphysics of
    books.

To behold the day-break!
The little light fades the immense and diaphanous shadows,   55
The air tastes good to my palate.

Hefts of the moving world at innocent gambols silently rising, freshly
    exuding,
Scooting obliquely high and low.

Something I cannot see puts upward libidinous prongs,
Seas of bright juice suffuse heaven.   60

The earth by the sky staid with, the daily close of their junction,
The heav'd challenge from the east that moment over my head,
The mocking taunt, See then whether you shall be master!

TOPICS FOR CRITICAL THINKING

1. In the opening six lines of section 24 of "Song of Myself," examine the terms in
   which Whitman creates a myth of the modern self, one grounded in a frank openness concerning the body, its energies, and desires.
2. Discuss Whitman's catalogue of the body and the ways in which the body fuses with
   the natural landscape.

TOPIC FOR CRITICAL WRITING

How does Whitman understand that mythic sense of self as also a "democratic" identity made up of a plurality of "voices"?

PERCY BYSSHE SHELLEY (1792–1822)

Ode to the West Wind (1820)

1

O wild West Wind, thou breath of Autumn's being,
Thou, from whose unseen presence the leaves dead
Are driven, like ghosts from an enchanter fleeing,

Yellow, and black, and pale, and hectic red,
Pestilence-stricken multitudes: O thou,   5
Who chariotest to their dark wintry bed

The wingéd seeds, where they lie cold and low,
Each like a corpse within its grave, until
Thine azure sister of the Spring shall blow

Her clarion o'er the dreaming earth, and fill   10
(Driving sweet buds like flocks to feed in air)
With living hues and odors plain and hill:

Wild Spirit, which art moving everywhere;
Destroyer and preserver; hear, oh, hear!

2

Thou on whose stream, mid the steep sky's commotion,   15
Loose clouds like earth's decaying leaves are shed,
Shook from the tangled boughs of Heaven and Ocean,

Angels of rain and lightning: there are spread
On the blue surface of thine aëry surge,
Like the bright hair uplifted from the head   20

Of some fierce Maenad,° even from the dim verge
Of the horizon to the zenith's height,
The locks of the approaching storm. Thou dirge

Of the dying year, to which this closing night
Will be the dome of a vast sepulcher,   25
Vaulted with all thy congregated might

Of vapors, from whose solid atmosphere
Black rain, and fire, and hail will burst: oh, hear!

3

Thou who didst waken from his summer dreams
The blue Mediterranean, where he lay,   30
Lulled by the coil of his crystálline streams,

Beside a pumice isle in Baiae's bay,°
And saw in sleep old palaces and towers
Quivering within the wave's intenser day,

All overgrown with azure moss and flowers   35
So sweet, the sense faints picturing them! Thou
For whose path the Atlantic's level powers

---

21 *Maenad:* A female worshipper of Dionysus.   32 *Baiae's bay:* A bay near Naples.

Cleave themselves into chasms, while far below
The sea-blooms and the oozy woods which wear
The sapless foliage of the ocean, know   40

Thy voice, and suddenly grow gray with fear,
And tremble and despoil themselves: oh, hear!

                        4

If I were a dead leaf thou mightest bear;
If I were a swift cloud to fly with thee;
A wave to pant beneath thy power, and share   45

The impulse of thy strength, only less free
Than thou, O uncontrollable! If even
I were as in my boyhood, and could be

The comrade of thy wanderings over Heaven,
As then, when to outstrip thy skyey speed   50
Scarce seemed a vision; I would ne'er have striven

As thus with thee in prayer in my sore need.
Oh, lift me as a wave, a leaf, a cloud!
I fall upon the thorns of life! I bleed!

A heavy weight of hours has chained and bowed   55
One too like thee: tameless, and swift, and proud.

                        5

Make me thy lyre, even as the forest is:
What if my leaves are falling like its own!
The tumult of thy mighty harmonies

Will take from both a deep, autumnal tone,   60
Sweet though in sadness. Be thou, Spirit fierce,
My spirit! Be thou me, impetuous one!

Drive my dead thoughts over the universe
Like withered leaves to quicken a new birth!
And, by the incantation of this verse,   65

Scatter, as from an unextinguished hearth
Ashes and sparks, my words among mankind!
Be through my lips to unawakened earth

The trumpet of a prophecy! O, Wind,
If Winter comes, can Spring be far behind?   70

TOPICS FOR CRITICAL THINKING

1. The year 1819 was a highly creative one in Shelley's life; he composed *Prometheus Unbound, The Cenci, The Mask of Anarchy*, and *A Philosophical View of Reform*. But it was also a year marked by the tragic deaths of his children Clara and William. The cycles of birth and death, creation and destruction, life and death weighed on Shelley's mind when he composed "Ode to the West Wind" while living in Florence. How does Shelley depict the wind's mythic agency as both a "Destroyer and Preserver" in its seasonal roles?

2. Examine the natural metaphors Shelley employs to describe his relation to the West Wind in section 4 of the poem.

3. Discuss the musical metaphors Shelley develops in section 5 to describe the social and prophetic roles of his poetic vocation. How does poetry serve as the cure for Shelley's grief?

TOPIC FOR CRITICAL WRITING

The poem opens with the figure of apostrophe, and, following the etymology of the Latin *spiritus* that links breath, soul, and the spirit, Shelley personifies the West Wind as "thou breath of Autumn's being." What other personifications can you identify in the poem? How do they contribute to the poem's major themes?

25 Emotive Poetics

When William Wordsworth defined poetry in terms of "impassioned expression," he described what all good poets know: that verse writing involves the life of the emotions. Poetry, for Wordsworth, voices the "spontaneous overflow of powerful feelings." *Overflow* is the key word here. Deeply felt **emotive** states have a psychological urgency that demands utterance, as when John Keats begins his "Ode to a Nightingale" with the plaintive cry "My heart aches." Similarly, Wordsworth witnesses to poetry's almost therapeutic value. In his "Ode: Intimations of Immortality," he writes that "To me alone there came a thought of grief: / A timely utterance gave that thought relief, / And I again am strong."

Some poems take the experience of a dominant emotive state as in Wordsworth's "thought of grief" and make it the subject of an entire poem. For example, Theodore Roethke portrays his emotional theme in the title of his short lyric "Dolor."

THEODORE ROETHKE   *(1908–1963)*

Dolor   *(1942)*

I have known the inexorable sadness of pencils,
Neat in their boxes, dolor of pad and paper-weight,
All the misery of manila folders and mucilage,
Desolation in immaculate public places,
Lonely reception room, lavatory, switchboard,   5
The unalterable pathos of basin and pitcher,
Ritual of multigraph, paper-clip, comma,
Endless duplication of lives and objects.
And I have seen dust from the walls of institutions,
Finer than flour, alive, more dangerous than silica,   10
Sift, almost invisible, through long afternoons of tedium,
Dropping a fine film on nails and delicate eyebrows,
Glazing the pale hair, the duplicate grey standard faces.

TOPICS FOR CRITICAL THINKING

1. *Dolor* means sadness and comes from the Latin word for pain. What other key word choices unpack Roethke's emotional experience of dolor in the poem?

2. Of "Dolor" Roethke has written that "we continue to make a fetish of 'thing-hood,' we surround ourselves with junk, ugly objects endlessly repeated in an economy of waste." How does Roethke's poem assign dolor to things set in the dry institutional spaces of contemporary society?

TOPIC FOR CRITICAL WRITING

What thematic comment does Roethke make on the everyday monotony of today's standardized and homogeneous institutional settings?

Robert Bly, an American poet who was profoundly influenced by Theodore Roethke, explores a feeling at the opposite end of the emotive spectrum from "Dolor" in his poem "Waking from Sleep."

ROBERT BLY   *(b. 1926)*

Waking from Sleep   *(1962)*

Inside the veins there are navies setting forth,
Tiny explosions at the water lines,
And seagulls weaving in the wind of the salty blood.

It is the morning. The country has slept the whole winter.
Window seats were covered with fur skins, the yard was full   5
Of stiff dogs, and hands that clumsily held heavy books.

Now we wake, and rise from bed, and eat breakfast!—
Shouts rise from the harbor of the blood,
Mist, and masts rising, the knock of wooden tackle in the sunlight.

Now we sing, and do tiny dances on the kitchen floor.   10
Our whole body is like a harbor at dawn;
We know that our master has left us for the day.

TOPICS FOR CRITICAL THINKING

1. While Roethke relies on the literal presentation of standardized things to express dolor, Bly develops the emotions of waking through a highly metaphoric style. Discuss his major metaphor for the experience of waking up.
2. How does Bly depict this waking as a seasonal motif as well?
3. How would you characterize this poem's tone?

TOPIC FOR CRITICAL WRITING

The poem ends on an enigmatic note that presents waking as a new dawning of freedom, a lifting of repression communicated in the figurative phrase "We know that our master has left us for the day." How do you interpret this line?

In addition to depicting singular emotional states, it is not unusual for a poem to run the gamut of the emotions moving from despair to ecstatic joy, as in William Shakespeare's Sonnet 29.

WILLIAM SHAKESPEARE   (1564–1616)

Sonnet 29   (1609)

When, in disgrace with fortune and men's eyes,
I all alone beweep my outcast state,
And trouble deaf heaven with my bootless° cries
And look upon myself, and curse my fate,
Wishing me like to one more rich in hope,   5
Featured like him, like him with friends possessed,
Desiring this man's art and that man's scope
With what I most enjoy contented least;
Yet in these thoughts myself almost despising,
Haply I think on thee—and then my state,   10
Like to the lark at break of day arising
From sullen earth, sings hymns at heaven's gate;
 For thy sweet love rememb'red such wealth brings
 That then I scorn to change my state with kings.

Sonnet 29 begins with the emotions of despair, futility, envy, desire, and self-loathing. The whole movement of the poem's first eight lines reaches its lowest point in the line "With what I most enjoy contented least" where the nadir climaxes in the word *least*. However, as we move into the next line's qualification of "yet," a turning point frees the speaker from "despising" his own failures. "Haply" his thoughts turn to the lover, and through simile his mood ascends in the figure of the lark associated with the "day arising." Moving away from "sullen earth" in favor of "heaven's gate," the speaker finds joy in the final couplet through the insight that "sweet love" is of far greater value than either the wealth or scope of kings.

As we have seen, poetry has the power to depict primary emotions such as joy and sorrow, hope and despair, courage and fear, love and hate, wonder and apathy. But the emotive image can also be drawn in shades that obscure their differences. Like the primary colors of the painter's palette, basic emotional states can be rendered almost infinitely complex through their subtle merging in a poetic phrase, line, or stanza as in Galway Kinnell's "First Song."

———
3 *bootless:* Futile.

GALWAY KINNELL   *(b. 1927)*

First Song   *(1960)*

Then it was dusk in Illinois, the small boy
After an afternoon of carting dung
Hung on the rail fence, a sapped thing
Weary to crying. Dark was growing tall
And he began to hear the pond frogs all   5
Calling on his ear with what seemed their joy.

Soon their sound was pleasant for a boy
Listening in the smoky dusk and the nightfall
Of Illinois, and from the fields two small
Boys came bearing cornstalk violins   10
And they rubbed the cornstalk bows with resins
And the three sat there scraping of their joy.

It was now fine music the frogs and the boys
Did in the towering Illinois twilight make
And into dark in spite of a shoulder's ache   15
A boy's hunched body loved out of a stalk
The first song of his happiness, and the song woke
His heart to the darkness and into the sadness of joy.

Kinnell presents the Illinois farm boy after a hard day's work as "a sapped
thing." He is worn out and "weary to crying." The fatigue of that sapped and
weary emotional state is complicated, however, by the oncoming darkness
that brings him the sounds of the frogs. Their call invokes a "pleasant" sense
of "joy" to which the boy and his friends respond in making a "fine music" of
their own out of "cornstalk violins." Their "first song" transforms the "shoulder's ache" into a kind of "happiness" but one that, in the "darkness," combines the opposite states of sadness and joy into a new, heartfelt emotion.

Such blending of opposites is called **oxymoron** from the Greek roots
meaning sharp (*oxus*) and foolish (*moros*). Oxymoron is a rhetorical figure that
combines contradictory terms such as *deafening silence, living death, solemn gaiety*, and so on. Thus, John Milton invokes the figure of oxymoron in describing the flames of hell as "darkness visible" while Walt Whitman characterizes
a conflicted emotional state in terms of the "sweet hell within."

Whitman's contemporary, Emily Dickinson, also deftly described extreme and often clashing emotive states as in her Poem 258, "There's a certain
Slant of light."

EMILY DICKINSON   *(1830–1886)*

Poem 258 (There's a certain Slant of light)   *(1861)*

There's a certain Slant of light,
Winter Afternoons —
That oppresses, like the Heft
Of Cathedral Tunes —

Heavenly Hurt, it gives us —   5
We can find no scar,
But internal difference,
Where the Meanings, are —

None may teach it — Any —
'Tis the Seal Despair —   10
An imperial affliction
Sent us of the air —

When it comes, the Landscape listens —
Shadows — hold their breath —
When it goes, 'tis like the Distance   15
On the look of Death —

Not unlike the sad joy that Kinnell recalls in "First Song," Dickinson explores here a contradictory psychic moment conveyed to her, strangely enough, in the quality or slant of light she witnesses on a winter afternoon. We don't usually think of light as having any mass, but Dickinson feels its weight in the heft, or oppressive heaviness, that she compares through simile to the mighty force of a cathedral organ. This is a metaphysical light, but it doesn't bestow the consolation of an assured faith or ideal meaning. Instead, its luminous trace is divisive and unsettling. It leaves behind an interior, emotive "scar" of "internal difference." Light descends on the poet as an agony that marks her not with any sign of grace but rather with the "Seal Despair." Dickinson relies on figurative language to capture the suspense of this beheld light in the personification of how the entire "Landscape listens" or how "Shadows — hold their breath." Simile estranges such personifications in the departing light that is "like the Distance / On the look of Death." Oxymoron most aptly captures the light's uncanny visitation. Such phrases as "Heavenly Hurt," "Seal Despair," and "imperial affliction" communicate the paradoxical mystery of the light's poignant grace.

In drawing attention to contradiction, oxymoron heightens our sense of the irony and paradox of everyday life. Stemming from the Greek root words meaning "beyond" (*para*) and "opinion" (*doxos*), **paradox** describes a contradictory experience, insight, or truth that cuts across the grain of our conventional expectations. Theodore Roethke was fond of using such paradoxes as "We think by feeling" or "In a dark time, the eye begins to see."

Irony, like paradox and oxymoron, dramatizes the ways in which certain experiences contain something of their opposites or when situations run contrary to expectation. In classical Greek mythology, it is ironic, for example, when Oedipus flees his supposed father Polybus seeking to avoid the Delphic oracle's prophecy that he would murder his father. What Oedipus doesn't know is that Polybus is his foster parent, and that the man Oedipus kills in a struggle at a crossroads on his way from Delphi to Thebes is, in fact, his real father King Laius. **Dramatic irony** builds when Oedipus, seeking to find the murderer, discovers that he is the guilty party and, worse, that he has married his mother, King Laius's wife Queen Jocasta. Sophocles' tragic drama *Oedipus Rex* turns on drawing out the suspense of this dramatic irony. In popular narrative, irony can become a source of wry humor, as in the film *Reality Bites*. Leaving the scene of yet another unsuccessful job interview, Winona Ryder is asked to define *irony* as the doors are about to close in an elevator. Not surprisingly, Ryder can't produce a definition on the spot, pointing out the film's central irony of the class valedictorian who can only get temp jobs. The pop star Alanis Morissette made irony the subject of her song "Ironic," defining irony as "the good advice that you just didn't take." Similarly, it's appropriately ironic that Dorothy Parker receives the symbol of love in "One Perfect Rose" when what she really desires is the material reward of "one perfect limousine." **Verbal irony** compresses such situational ironies into contradictory, ambiguous, and often sarcastic utterances, as when Allen Ginsberg in his poem "America" playfully asserts his determination to resist American middle-class conformity: "America I'm putting my queer shoulder to the wheel."

Poems for Further Reading and Critical Writing

EMILY DICKINSON   *(1830–1886)*

Poem 512 (The Soul has Bandaged moments)   *(1862)*

The Soul has Bandaged moments —
When, too appalled to stir —
She feels some ghastly Fright come up
And stop to look at her —

Salute her — with long fingers   5
Caress her freezing hair —
Sip, Goblin, from the very lips
The Lover — hovered — o'er —
Unworthy, that a thought so mean
Accost a Theme — so — fair —   10

The soul has moments of Escape —
When bursting all the doors —
She dances like a Bomb, abroad,
And swings upon the Hours,

As do the Bee — delirious borne —   15
Long Dungeoned from his Rose —
Touch Liberty — then know no more,
But Noon, and Paradise —

The Soul's retaken moments —
When, Felon led along,   20
With shackles on the plumed feet,
And staples, in the Song,

The Horror welcomes her, again,
These, are not brayed of Tongue —

TOPICS FOR CRITICAL THINKING

1. What are "Bandaged moments" in the life of the soul? Can you give examples of them? Examine the ways in which Dickinson presents these moments in the poem.

2. Compare and contrast the emotional extremities of Dickinson's psychological life in this poem.

TOPIC FOR CRITICAL WRITING

What examples of figurative language can you identify in the poet's characterization of the soul's various "moments"?

SYLVIA PLATH *(1932–1963)*

Fever 103°   *(1962)*

Pure? What does it mean?
The tongues of hell
Are dull, dull as the triple

Tongues of dull, fat Cerberus
Who wheezes at the gate. Incapable   5
Of licking clean

The aguey tendon, the sin, the sin.
The tinder cries.
The indelible smell

Of a snuffed candle!
Love, love, the low smokes roll
From me like Isadora's scarves, I'm in a fright   10

One scarf will catch and anchor in the wheel.
Such yellow sullen smokes
Make their own element. They will not rise,   15

But trundle round the globe
Choking the aged and the meek,
The weak

Hothouse baby in its crib,
The ghastly orchid
Hanging its hanging garden in the air,   20

Devilish leopard!
Radiation turned it white
And killed it in an hour.

Greasing the bodies of adulterers   25
Like Hiroshima ash and eating in.
The sin. The sin.

Darling, all night
I have been flickering, off, on, off, on.
The sheets grow heavy as a lecher's kiss.   30

Three days. Three nights.
Lemon water, chicken
Water, water make me retch.

I am too pure for you or anyone.
Your body   35
Hurts me as the world hurts God. I am a lantern—

My head a moon
Of Japanese paper, my gold beaten skin
Infinitely delicate and infinitely expensive.

Does not my heat astound you. And my light.   40
All by myself I am a huge camellia
Glowing and coming and going, flush on flush.

I think I am going up,
I think I may rise—
The beads of hot metal fly, and I, love, I   45

Am a pure acetylene
Virgin
Attended by roses,

By kisses, by cherubim,
By whatever these pink things mean.   50
Not you, nor him.

Not him, nor him
(My selves dissolving, old whore petticoats)—
To Paradise.

TOPICS FOR CRITICAL THINKING

1. Given Plath's title, how would you characterize her emotional state in "Fever 103°"?
2. Plath wrote "Fever 103°" during her separation from her husband, the poet Ted Hughes, owing in part to his infidelity. What references to adultery can you find in the poem? How do they function in the work?
3. How does the poet answer the question "Pure? What does it mean?" In what terms does she imagine her own metaphoric purity in the poem?

TOPIC FOR CRITICAL WRITING

Plath alludes to Cerberus, the three-headed dog that guards the gates to Hades in Greek mythology, to Isadora Duncan, the American dance artist who was strangled when her long scarf became tangled in the wheel spokes of a Bugati automobile, and to Hiroshima, Japan, which was the target of an American nuclear bombing at the close of World War II. How do you interpret these allusions? What functions do they serve in the poem? Does Plath's identification with Japanese nuclear bomb victims run the risk of trivializing their victimization?

WALT WHITMAN   *(1819–1892)*

from Song of Myself (Section 26)   *(1855)*

26

Now I will do nothing but listen,
To accrue what I hear into this song, to let sounds contribute toward it.

I hear bravuras of birds, bustle of growing wheat, gossip of flames, clack of
     sticks cooking my meals,
I hear the sound I love, the sound of the human voice,
I hear all sounds running together, combined, fused or following,   5
Sounds of the city and sounds out of the city, sounds of the day and night,

Talkative young ones to those that like them, the loud laugh of work-people
     at their meals,
The angry base of disjointed friendship, the faint tones of the sick,
The judge with hands tight to the desk, his pallid lips pronouncing a death-
     sentence,
The heave'e'yo of stevedores unlading ships by the wharves, the refrain of   10
     the anchor-lifters,
The ring of alarm-bells, the cry of fire, the whirr of swift-streaking engines
     and hose-carts with premonitory tinkles and color'd lights,
The steam whistle, the solid roll of the train of approaching cars,
The slow march play'd at the head of the association marching two and two,
(They go to guard some corpse, the flag-tops are draped with black muslin.)

I hear the violoncello, ('tis the young man's heart's complaint,)   15
I hear the key'd cornet, it glides quickly in through my ears,
It shakes mad-sweet pangs through my belly and breast.
I hear the chorus, it is a grand opera,
Ah this indeed is music—this suits me.

A tenor large and fresh as the creation fills me,   20
The orbic flex of his mouth is pouring and filling me full.

I hear the train'd soprano (what work with hers is this?)
The orchestra whirls me wider than Uranus flies,
It wrenches such ardors from me I did not know I possess'd them,
It sails me, I dab with bare feet, they are lick'd by the indolent waves,   25
I am cut by bitter and angry hail, I lose my breath,
Steep'd amid honey'd morphine, my windpipe throttled in fakes of death,
At length let up again to feel the puzzle of puzzles,
And that we call Being.

TOPIC FOR CRITICAL THINKING

How do the sounds Whitman hears from the orchestra and opera differ from those of
everyday life as he catalogs them above?

TOPIC FOR CRITICAL WRITING

Whitman says that the music "wrenches such ardors from me I did not know I possess'd them." Discuss the ways in which Whitman accounts for the emotional effect
the opera has on him.

26   Prosody

Prosody comes from the Greek word *prosodia* meaning "tune" and alludes to poetry's origins in song and the oral tradition. As an art form, poetry doesn't just belong to the page but reaches all the way back before the invention of printing or even writing. Today, however, unless we are creative writing majors or regulars at poetry slams and coffee houses, we mostly encounter verse in a book or, just as likely, on a computer screen. Poetry is more often read in the silent encounter of person and page. Thanks to the Internet, live-streaming, and digital technology, the oral dimension is returning to verse. Prosody, in any case, reminds us that poetry has always been an oral, performative art with roots not just in entertainment but in religious worship and ritual celebration. The word *lyric* derives from the Greek musical instrument, the *lyra*, and connotes poetry's strong ties to music and song. Similarly, in the ancient Old English tradition of the Beowulf poet, the poet was called a *scop* or *gleeman* and performed at court in song accompanied by the harp.

Sound

Beyond its origins in song, however, prosody describes poetry's material medium, which—insofar as it employs sound effects, rhyme, and rhythm—is more tangible and less transparent than prose. One reason we might find poetry more satisfying or stimulating than prose has to do with how we receive and make sense of the spoken rather than written word. Poetry, in fact, is a whole-brain activity that involves the bicameral mind. In a right-handed person, the left hemisphere of the brain is responsible for processing rational thought, cognition, and motor activity, while music is a right hemispheric activity. Poetry—because it involves both abstract thought and the material textures of rhyme, rhythm and sound—is processed by both sides of the brain. The prosodic aspects of poetry, like music, are right-brain activities and begin with the sounds of poetry.

    Sound effects, of course, are key elements of popular entertainment. In the early days of radio theater, the sounds of a crackling fire could be mimicked through the crumpling of cellophane. The galloping of a horse was imitated through clopping coconut shells on a table. Each year the Academy of Motion Pictures awards an Oscar to the best audio effects, which are key elements in any successful action or sci-fi movie. Thanks to Hollywood production facilities like Industrial Light and Magic and Dreamworks Studios, we know what light sabers sounds like, even though they don't really exist.

Similarly, poetry employs **onomatopoeia**, or verbal sounds that are meant to mimic things imaginatively heard in the world. The onomatopoeia of Robert Frost's phrase "snarled and rattled" captures the menace and danger of a working buzz saw in his poem about a farm accident, "Out, Out—." "The buzz saw," he writes, "snarled and rattled in the yard / . . . And the saw snarled and rattled, snarled and rattled." Similarly, Emily Dickinson renders a death scene even more unsettling in the sound of a fly in her Poem 465, "I heard a Fly buzz — when I died."

EMILY DICKINSON   *(1830–1886)*

Poem 465 (I heard a Fly buzz – when I died)   *(1862)*

I heard a Fly buzz — when I died —
The Stillness in the Room
Was like the Stillness in the Air —
Between the Heaves of Storm —

The Eyes around — had wrung them dry —   5
And Breaths were gathering firm
For that last Onset — when the King
Be witnessed — in the Room —

I willed my Keepsakes — Signed away
What portion of me be   10
Assignable — and then it was
There interposed a Fly —

With Blue — uncertain stumbling Buzz —
Between the light — and me —
And then the Windows failed — and then   15
I could not see to see —

TOPICS FOR CRITICAL THINKING

1. What do you associate with flies? How does Dickinson's fly appear as a negative presence that intrudes into the poem's death scene?

2. How does the fly mark the moment of literal and spiritual blindness, presented in the metonymy of the windows whose light failed at the fly's approach?

3. Consider how in breaking the stillness of the room, the fly manifests not God, the "King," but the repulsive sound of the insect's "uncertain stumbling Buzz." How does Dickinson's masterful use of onomatopoeia in the repeated short *u* sound flout the poet's anticipation of the afterlife with the unsettling noise of death?

TOPIC FOR CRITICAL WRITING

Taken as a symbol of decay and mortality, how does the fly cancel the hope of resurrection in the poem?

Another question one might pose is whether the "buzz" of onomatopoeia represents something already there in nature. If so, why does the word for *buzz* in English sound differently, say, in the French *bourdonner*, German *summen*, Italian *ronzare*, Spanish *zumbar*, or even Dutch *zoemen*? It is debatable whether onomatopoeia directly mimes sounds we hear or if it instead presents stylized versions of words that we associate with sounds through usage and connotation.

Depending on one's linguistic point of view, the same could be said of the other techniques of sound sense that English poets employ to create **euphony,** the impression of sounds that are pleasing to the ear, and **cacophony,** sounds that are unpleasant and grating. Some schools of thought emphasize the kinesthetic quality of a particular consonant or vowel sound: that is, how resemblance between a sound and its meaning is based on the way a particular sound is shaped in the mouth, nose, and throat. The common variety of consonant sounds include the following.

- The *r* and *l* or *liquids* that roll in a flowing movement off the tongue, as in W. B. Yeats's "I hear lake water lapping with low sounds by the shore"
- The *m*, *n*, and *ng* sounds of the *nasals*, as in Alfred, Lord Tennyson's "The murmuring of innumerable bees"
- The harsh, rasping sounds or the *h*, *f*, *c*, *th*, *dh*, or *fricatives* and the *s*, *z*, *sh*, *zh* or *sibilants*, as in Robert Lowell's description of whaling: "The fat flukes arch and whack about its ears, / The death-lance churns into the sanctuary, tears"
- The hard *p*, *b*, *t*, *d*, *k*, *g* sounds or *stops* and *plosives*, as in John Donne's prayer for violent conversion: "bend / Your force to break, blow, burn, and make me new"

The term *alliteration* describes the repetition of consonant sounds at the beginning of successive words (initial alliteration) and within adjacent words (internal alliteration). John Keats's "Ode on Melancholy" combines both initial and internal alliteration in a richly textured depiction of deeply felt emotional states:

> But when the me*l*ancholy *f*it shall *f*all
>> Sudden from heaven like a weeping cloud,
> That *f*osters the droop-headed *f*lowers all,
>> And *h*ides the green *h*ill in an April shroud;
> Then glut thy so*rr*ow on a mo*r*ning *r*ose,
>> Or on the *r*ainbow of the *s*alt *s*and-wave,
>> Or on the wealth of globéd peonies;
> Or if thy mistress some rich anger shows,
>> Imprison *h*er soft *h*and, and let *h*er rave,
>> And feed *d*eep, *d*eep u*p*on her *p*eerless eyes.

Assonance—stemming from the Latin *assonare*, "to answer with, or echo, the same sound"—is the complementary term for the repetition of vowel sounds in a line. Because alliterations typically come at the beginning of words, we tend to read them as much as hear them. Assonance, however, occurs more often within words and therefore bears a more aural character. In acoustics, sound is a measured in terms of the frequency of its waves per second, and the greater a vowel's frequency, the higher the intensity of its pitch. English vowels range all the way from the low frequency long *o* sounds of *stone*, up through the middle range of short *u* sounds as in *mud, tub, jug*, up to the higher registers of the short *e* and short *i* of *jet*, and *thick*, ending with the highest frequency vowel sounds of the long *a* and *i* of *say* and *tight*.

The sonorous combination of these effects can greatly enhance the performative tonalities of a poem's subjects, settings, and themes, as in W. B. Yeats's "The Lake Isle of Innisfree" that employs both alliteration and assonance.

W. B. YEATS   *(1865–1939)*

The Lake Isle of Innisfree   *(1892)*

I will arise and go now, and go to Innisfree,
And a small cabin build there, of clay and wattles made:
Nine bean rows will I have there, a hive for the honey bee,
And live alone in the bee-loud glade.

And I shall have some peace there, for peace comes dropping slow,   5
Dropping from the veils of the morning to where the cricket sings;
There midnight's all a glimmer, and noon a purple glow,
And evening full of the linnet's wings.

I will arise and go now, for always night and day
I hear lake water lapping with low sounds by the shore;   10
While I stand on the roadway, or on the pavements grey,
I hear it in the deep heart's core.

TOPICS FOR CRITICAL THINKING

1. Yeats wrote "The Lake Isle of Innisfree" after noticing the sound of tinkling water from a fountain in Fleet Street, the "roadway" and "pavements grey" in the poem. The small cabin and nine bean rows are patterned after Yeats's reading in Henry David Thoreau's *Walden* (1854). How does the poem present the Irish poet's fantasy of making a retreat into nature on Innisfree, which means "Heather Island"?

2. Consider how the repetition of liquids and nasals tends to have an almost hypnotic effect of lulling the reader with the music of an interior dreamscape heard "in the deep heart's core."

TOPIC FOR CRITICAL WRITING

Yeats relies heavily on the sound effects of alliteration and assonance to perform both the high register sounds of the "bee-loud glade" and the dropoff into low frequency tonalities of "lake water lapping with low sounds by the shore." Identify as many examples of these effects as you can and consider how they function in the poem.

In "The Lake Isle of Innisfree," consonant and vowel sounds create harmonious effects that are pleasing to the ear. While Yeats presents the euphony overheard in his poem, Sylvia Plath invokes tones of a violent cacophony in depicting the ocean setting of "Point Shirley."

SYLVIA PLATH   *(1932–1963)*

Point Shirley   *(1959)*

From Water-Tower Hill to the brick prison
The shingle booms, bickering under
The sea's collapse.
Snowcakes break and welter. This year
The gritted wave leaps   5
The seawall and drops onto a bier
Of quahog chips,
Leaving a salty mash of ice to whiten

In my grandmother's sand yard. She is dead,
Whose laundry snapped and froze here, who   10
Kept house against
What the sluttish, rutted sea could do.
Squall waves once danced
Ship timbers in through the cellar window;
A thresh-tailed, lanced   15
Shark littered in the geranium bed —

Such collusion of mulish elements
She wore her broom straws to the nub.
Twenty years out
Of her hand, the house still hugs in each drab   20
Stucco socket
The purple egg-stones: from Great Head's knob
To the filled-in Gut
The sea in its cold gizzard ground those rounds.

Nobody wintering now behind   25
The planked-up windows where she set
Her wheat loaves

And apple cakes to cool. What is it
Survives, grieves
So, over this battered, obstinate spit   30
Of gravel? The waves'
Spewed relics clicker masses in the wind,

Grey waves the stub-necked eiders ride.
A labor of love, and that labor lost.
Steadily the sea   35
Eats at Point Shirley. She died blessed,
And I come by
Bones, bones only, pawed and tossed,
A dog-faced sea.
The sun sinks under Boston, bloody red.   40

I would get from these dry-papped stones
The milk your love instilled in them.
The black ducks dive.
And though your graciousness might stream,
And I contrive,   45
Grandmother, stones are nothing of home
To that spumiest dove.
Against both bar and tower the black sea runs.

TOPICS FOR CRITICAL THINKING

1. How does Point Shirley's "spit of gravel" remain "obstinate" in its resistance to the
   sea's onslaught?
2. Plath's ocean, unlike Yeats's, is not serene but "sluttish." Picking up on the Middle
   English derivation of *slutte*, or female dog, Plath's ocean is a "dog-faced sea" that
   "Eats at Point Shirley." Unlike Yeats's euphonious liquid consonants, Plath features
   in her opening stanza several plosive hard *b* sounds. Identify as many as you can and
   discuss their dramatic effect in the poem.
3. In addition to these plosives, Plath also employs fricatives and sibilants to heighten
   the cacophony communicated in her hard *c* and *g* consonants. Discuss some of the
   poem's key sound effects in such onomatopoetic phrases as "cold gizzard ground
   those rounds."
4. Through consonant stops, the sea seems to explode "against both bar and tower" of
   the "battered" coast. But the poem also exploits the assonance of the guttural short
   u sounds in such monosyllables as *nub, gut, stub, ducks, hug*, and so on. How do these
   repeated gutturals add a primal quality to her grandmother's uncanny dwelling between shore and surf?

TOPIC FOR CRITICAL WRITING

"Point Shirley" is an elegy to Plath's grandmother, whose house on the sea's edge near
Boston bears the signs of the eroding effects of time and the stubborn, "mulish" elements of wind and water. Describe the poet's presentation of setting in the poem.

While Plath and Yeats aim at differing emotive effects through the contrast of euphony and cacophony, we find both techniques combined in Samuel Taylor Coleridge's "Kubla Khan."

Samuel Taylor Coleridge   *(1772–1834)*

Kubla Khan

Or, a Vision in a Dream. A Fragment   *(1797–1798)*

In Xanadu did Kubla Khan
A stately pleasure dome decree:
Where Alph, the sacred river, ran
Through caverns measureless to man
   Down to a sunless sea.   5
So twice five miles of fertile ground
With walls and towers were girdled round:
And there were gardens bright with sinuous rills,
Where blossomed many an incense-bearing tree;
And here were forests ancient as the hills,   10
Enfolding sunny spots of greenery.

But oh! that deep romantic chasm which slanted
Down the green hill athwart a cedarn cover!
A savage place! as holy and enchanted
As e'er beneath a waning moon was haunted   15
By woman wailing for her demon lover!
And from this chasm, with ceaseless turmoil seething,
As if this earth in fast thick pants were breathing,
A mighty fountain momently was forced:
Amid whose swift half-intermitted burst   20
Huge fragments vaulted like rebounding hail,
Or chaffy grain beneath the thresher's flail:
And 'mid these dancing rocks at once and ever
It flung up momently the sacred river.
Five miles meandering with a mazy motion   25
Through wood and dale the sacred river ran,
Then reached the caverns measureless to man,
And sank in tumult to a lifeless ocean:
And 'mid this tumult Kubla heard from far
Ancestral voices prophesying war!   30

  The shadow of the dome of pleasure
  Floated midway on the waves;
  Where was heard the mingled measure
  From the fountain and the caves.

It was a miracle of rare device,   35
A sunny pleasure dome with caves of ice!

> A damsel with a dulcimer
> In a vision once I saw:
> It was an Abyssinian maid,
> And on her dulcimer she played,   40
> Singing of Mount Abora.
> Could I revive within me
> Her symphony and song,
> To such a deep delight 'twould win me,
> That with music loud and long,   45
> I would build that dome in air,
> That sunny dome! those caves of ice!
> And all who heard should see them there,
> And all should cry, Beware! Beware!
> His flashing eyes, his floating hair!   50
> Weave a circle round him thrice,
> And close your eyes with holy dread,
> For he on honey-dew hath fed,
> And drunk the milk of Paradise.

As his 1816 Preface implied, Coleridge intended that "Kubla Khan" be read as a fragment of a larger, visionary work. As it happened, Coleridge, like many others in nineteenth-century England, was in the habit of taking laudanum, an alcohol-opium mixture, for medicinal purposes. One side effect, however, was his serious addiction to the drug after 1801. Coleridge conceived the poem after taking two grains of opium, and, however we might debate the drug's role in his imaginative life, the poet envisions a remarkably euphoric landscape in "Kubla Khan."

Critics have offered a wide range of interpretations of the two major landscapes of the poem: Kubla Khan's pleasure dome and the chasm with its "mighty fountain" that feeds into the River Alph. For our purposes, notice how sound effects enhance the sharp contrast in the artistic order of the measured garden world as opposed to the "ceaseless turmoil" of the natural, subterranean energies witnessed in the chasm setting. Coleridge renders the euphony of the former scene of the garden in the liquids and nasals, culminating in the hypnotic "sinuous rills" of the sacred river's "five miles meandering with a mazy motion." The force of the chasm's volcanic energies are conveyed in the fricatives of the *ch*, *th*, *f*, and *s* sounds combined with the plosives of the hard *b*, *t*, and *p*.

> And *f*rom *th*is *ch*asm, with *c*easeless *t*urmoil *s*ee*th*ing,
> A*s* i*f* *th*i*s* earth in *f*ast *th*ick *p*ants were brea*th*ing,
> A mighty *f*ountain momently was *f*orced:
> Amid whose swi*f*t hal*f*-intermi*tt*ed *b*urst
> Huge *f*ragments vaulted like re*b*ounding *h*ail,
> Or *ch*affy grain *b*eneath the *th*resher's *f*lail:

Few locales in poetry are as vividly rendered as the exotic landscapes of "Kubla Khan." So convincing is Coleridge's "mingled measure" that we come away with the impression of actualities that are, nevertheless, based entirely in fantasies of the poetic imagination.

Rhyme

While alliteration and assonance give a sensuous sound texture to verse writing, rhyme and rhythm organize these acoustical elements for musical effects. In oral traditions, rhyme has entertainment value and, for the performer, works as an aid to memory. Rhyme is present in everyday slang terms ("fender bender,"), in advertising ("the real deal"), in teen argot ("yo, rude dude, choose it or loose it"), and rap lyrics (by, say, Dr. Dre: "Worldwide, got the triple beam, I slide. / Listenin' to yo demo in a stretch limo."). In folk culture, colloquial truisms such as "birds of a feather flock together" turn on rhyme, as do such practical proverbs as this one.

> Evening red and morning gray
> Will speed a traveler on his way;
> But evening gray and morning red
> Will pour down rain upon his head.

Rhyme can be playful, as in children's jump rope games.

> Bluebells, cockle shells,
> Eevie, ivy, over;
> I like coffee, I like tea;
> I like the boys, and the boys like me.
> Tell your mother to hold her tongue;
> She had a fellow when she was young.
> Tell your father to do the same;
> He had a girl and he changed her name.

The same is true in riddles.

> In marble walls as white as milk,
> Lined with a skin as soft as silk,
> Within a fountain crystal clear,
> A golden apple doth appear;
> No doors there are to this stronghold,
> Yet thieves break in and steal the gold.
>
> (Answer: an egg)

Rhyme also serves as a memory aid in popular usage as in the well-known Mother Goose rhyme for remembering the months of the calendar.

> Thirty days hath September,
> April, June, and November;
> February has twenty-eight alone,

All the rest have thirty-one,
Excepting leap year, that's the time
When February's days are twenty-nine.

In verse composition, **pure rhyme** is defined in terms of the heard likenesses and differences linking two or more words. For example, in the above
rhyming pair "milk/silk," the accented vowel sound of the short *i* makes the
connection of likeness along with the sameness of the ending consonant *k*.
The difference is the consonants—*m* and *s*—that come before. Thus likeness
must define the vowel sound of a rhyming pair of words and whatever sound
elements follow it, while what comes before must signify a difference. For example, the following excerpt from Christopher Marlowe's "The Passionate
Shepherd to His Love" illustrate the end rhymes "love/prove" and "fields/
yields."

Come live with me and be my love,
And we will all the pleasures prove
That valleys, groves, hills and fields,
Woods, or steepy mountain yields.

Monosyllabic rhymes are called **masculine rhyme**. In addition, masculine
rhyme describes rhyming words of more than one syllable only when the
rhyming sound falls on the final, unstressed syllable, as in *desire* and *aspire*.
Words with two syllables, where the second syllable is unstressed, are termed
feminine rhyme, as in Jonathan Swift's "The Lady's Dressing Room."

But Vengeance, goddess never sleeping
Soon punished Strephon for his peeping.

Triple syllable combinations are more rare and can have sarcastic and ironic
effects, as when Alexander Pope describes the cutting of Belinda's hair in his
mock epic "The Rape of the Lock."

"The meeting points the sacred hair dissever
From the fair head, forever, and forever!"

Rhyming effects extend beyond **end rhyme** to include **internal rhyme**:
rhyming words within lines and across adjacent lines. Poets use internal
rhyming for a variety of purposes in verse composition. Andrew Marvell
employs it to perform the resemblances between mind and nature in "The
Garden": "The *mind*, that ocean where each *kind* / Does straight its own resemblance *find*." William Shakespeare achieves an incantatory effect with internal rhyme in the witches' spell cast in *Macbeth*: "*Double, double* toil and
trouble; / Fire burn, and cauldron *bubble*." In the modern period, internal
rhyme performs in "God's Grandeur" the sense of monotony that Gerard
Manley Hopkins finds in the industrial world:

And all is *seared* with trade; *bleared, smeared* with toil;
And *wears* man's smudge and *shares* man's smell: the soil
Is bare now, nor can foot feel, being shod.

While pure rhyme voices an exact match of vowel sounds, poets also express minor and dissonant tonalities through the use of what is variously

termed **half, near,** or **slant rhyme.** Emily Dickinson uses near rhyme more often than not; Poem 303 signals a certain sense of finality through near rhyme:

> The Soul selects her own Society —
> Then — shuts the Door —
> To her divine Majority —
> Present no more —

Near rhyme often occurs with **consonance,** the repetition of the initial and terminal consonants surrounding a medial vowel. Wilfred Owen, the British soldier who died as a combatant in World War I, depicts the edgy and potentially lethal quality of modern armaments as well as the barbarism of twentieth-century war in his famous poem "Arms and the Boy."

WILFRED OWEN *(1893–1918)*

Arms and the Boy *(1918)*

Let the boy try along this bayonet-blade
How cold steel is, and keen with hunger of blood;
Blue with all malice, like a madman's flash;
And thinly drawn with famishing for flesh.

Lend him to stroke these blind, blunt bullet-leads,   5
Which long to nuzzle in the hearts of lads;
Or give him cartridges whose fine zinc teeth,
Are sharp with the sharpness of grief and death.

For his teeth seem for laughing round an apple.
There lurk no claws behind his fingers supple;   10
And God will grow no talons at his heels,
Nor antlers through the thickness of his curls.

The near rhymes of *blade* and *blood*, *flash* and *flesh*, *leads* and *lads* are rendered even more sharply dissonant through the enveloping effect of **consonance** in the repetition of *bl-d, fl-sh,* and *l-d.* In his poem "Toads," Philip Larkin uses consonance for a different, somewhat self-parodic effect in comparing himself to the little amphibian.

> For something sufficiently toad-*like*
> Squats in me, too;
> Its hunkers are heavy as hard *luck*,
> And cold as snow.

Further on in the poem, half-rhyme serves to describe the complacent squalor of Larkin's neighbors.

> Lots of folks live up lanes
>   With fires in a bucket,

Eat windfalls and tinner sardines—
        They seem to like it.

Successful, as opposed to clichéd, rhyming emphasizes key terms of significance in a poem in ways that are fresh and unexpected. "The sound," writes Alexander Pope, "must seem an echo to the sense."

Meter and Rhythm

Rhyme renders the striking utterance even more memorable when it enters into purposeful relation with the **meter** and **rhythm** of the line.

Meter comes from the Greek word *metron*, which means "measure." *Rhythm* too has a Greek derivation in the word *rhuthmos*, meaning "flow." Rhythm, of course, is basic to our experience of the world—from the internal embodied rhythm of one's heart beat or sleep and waking rhythms to the outward rhythms of the tides, night and day, the seasons, and so on. Words have their own rhythms that we can hear in the way we give weight and emphasis to certain syllables in pronunciation. We can visualize such stressed syllables with accent marks. For example, words such as gráteful, táble, gingĕr, hátchĕt, signăl, and so on lay more stress on the first syllable, which is accented in relation to the second, unaccented syllable. Conversely, words such as surpríse, rĕnew, undóne, bĕneáth, ăgáin have just the opposite pattern of flowing from an unaccented to an accented syllable. Our everyday language usage too is shaped by the rhythmic flow of emphasis and stress that we find in individual words as we combine them into phrases and sentences. You can hear a rhythmic pattern in virtually any utterance: "Wĕ wént tŏ seé thĕ fílm lăst níght." "Wŏuld yóu likĕ friés wĭth thát?" "Páss mĕ thĕ spórts séctiŏn." "Ĭ nów prŏnoúnce yŏu mán ănd wife." "Ĭ can't bĕlievĕ Ĭ atĕ thĕ whólĕ thing." "Givĕ thĕ dóg ă bonĕ, leávĕ thĕ dóg alónĕ."

The earliest metrical pattern in English verse is the so-called strong-stress meter or **accentual meter** that characterizes Old English poetry. Accentual meter is formed by a pattern of stresses and alliteration. Four stresses give metrical regularity to the line. Moreover, the stresses are balanced in relation to each half of the line or **hemistich**. Two stresses fall in the first half of the line and another two in the second half. The middle of the line—dividing the first hemistich from the second—is marked by a caesural pause (‖). **Caesura** comes from the Latin verb *caedere* meaning "to cut." In addition, three of the four stresses are alliterations. Typically, both the stresses in the first hemistich begin with the same letter followed by its repetition on the first stressed syllable belonging to the second hemistich. Ezra Pound's translation of the Anglo-Saxon, Old English poem "The Seafarer" preserves the accentual metrics of the original in virtually every line.

Chíll its chaíns are |;| chafíng síghs
Héw my heárt round ‖ and húnger begót
Mére-weary moód |.| Lest mán know nót

That hé on dry land || lóveliest livéth,
List how Í, care-wretched, || on icé-cold sea
Weathered the winter |,| wretched outcast

Richard Wilbur's contemporary poem "Junk" offers a mock-heroic reprise of
the Old English line, setting off each hemistich with visual spacing on the page:

An axe angles
                    from my neighbor's ashcan;
It is hell's handiwork,
                    the wood not hickory,
The flow of the grain
                    not faithfully followed.
The shivered shaft
                    rises from a shellheap
Of plastic playthings,
                    paper plates,
And the sheer shards
                    of shattered tumblers
That were not annealed
                    for the time needful.

Following the Norman invasion of England in 1066, the Old English accentual meter began to undergo a transformation, influenced as it was by the
Greek and Latinate metrics of Old French. **Accentual-syllabic meter** became the dominant form of English reaching back to the fourteenth century
as the Renaissance spread from Italy. The powerful examples of Petrarch's
Canzoniere and *Trionfi* and Dante's *La Vita Nuova* and *Commedia* were felt in
France, Spain, and Portugal, arriving somewhat later in England.

In accentual-syllabic meter, what we typically gauge is the rhythmic pattern of accented and unaccented syllables in a line divided into units of measurement called poetic feet. A **poetic foot** is analogous to a measure of music,
which is governed by a fixed number of beats: three for a waltz, four in four-
quarter march time, and so on. Since the beginning of the Renaissance, the
metrical workhorse of English poetry has been the **iambic** foot—an iamb being made up of an unaccented and an accented syllable ($\smile$ ′). We can further
describe the metrics of a line by the number of feet it contains and chart both
accents and syllables in what is called a **scansion**. Similar to a musical score, a
scansion provides a diagram interpreting the measure of poetic feet—including accented and unaccented syllables—in a given line, stanza, or entire poem.

The most typical metrical line in English is constructed of five iambic feet
per line, called **iambic pentameter** (*penta* being the Greek word signifying
"five," as in the Pentagon or a pentagram). Sonnets are generally written in
iambic pentameter, and this meter is plain to see in a scansion of the opening
lines of Shakespeare's Sonnet 73:

Thăt tíme | ŏf yeár | thŏu máy'st | ĭn mé | bĕhóld
Whĕn yél | lŏw leavés, | ŏr nóne, | ŏr feẃ, | dŏ hań g
Ŭpón | thŏse boughs | whĭch sháke | ăgaínst | thĕ cold

There are, of course, other metrical line lengths that poets work in besides pentameter. The first is **monometer**, lines comprising two syllables each in one-foot units. Robert Herrick's "Upon His Departure Hence" is one of a very few number of poems composed in monometer:

Thus I
Passe by,
And die:
As one,
Unknown,
And gone:
I'm made
A shade,
And laid
I'th grave:
There have
My cave.
Where tell
I dwell.
Farewell.

The primary line length in Dorothy Parker's "Résumé" is **dimeter,** or two feet per line.

Razors | pain you;
Rivers | are damp;
Acids | stain you;
And drugs | cause cramp.
Guns aren't | lawful;
Nooses | give;
Gas smells | awful;
You might | as well live.

Sir Walter Raleigh's "The Lie" is composed in **trimeter,** or lines made up of three feet each.

Go, soul, | the bod | y's guest,
Upon | a thank | less errand;
Fear not | to touch | the best;
The truth | shall be | thy warrant.
Go, since | I needs | must die,
And give | the world | the lie.

Andrew Marvell's "The Garden" is in **tetrameter,** or four feet per line:

How vain | ly men | themselves | amaze
To win | the Palm, | the oak, | or bays
And their | inces | sant la | bors sede
Crowned from | some sin | gle herb, | or tree,
Whose short | and nar | row-verg | ed shade
Does pru | dently | their toils | upbraid;
While all | flowers and | all trees | do close
To weave | the gar | lands | of repose!

William Shakespeare's Sonnet 55 is composed in **pentameter**, five feet per line.

> Not mar | ble, nor | the gild | ed mon | uments
> Of princes, | shall out | live this | power | ful rhyme;
> But you | shall shine | more bright | in these | contents
> Than un | swept stone, | besmeared | with slut | tish time.

W. B. Yeats composed "The Cold Heaven" in six-foot lines of **hexameter**.

> Sudden | ly I | saw the | cold and | rook-de | lighting | heaven
> That seemed | as though | ice burned | and was | but the | more ice,
> And there | upon | imag | ina | tion and | heart were | driven
> So wild | that eve | ry ca | sual thought | of that | and this
> Vanished, | and left | but mem | ories, that | should be | out of |
>   season
> With the | hot blood | of youth, | of love | crossed long | ago;

Heptameter, or seven feet per line length, is the meter Williams Words-worth chooses for "The Norman Boy."

> High on | a broad | unfer | tile tract | of for | est-skirt | ed Down,
> Nor kept | by Na | ture for | herself, | nor made | by man | his own,
> From home | and com | pany | remote | and eve | ry play | ful joy,
> Served, tend | ing a | few sheep | and goats, | a rag | ged Nor | man
>   Boy.

The most famous eight-foot, **octameter** poem is Edgar Allan Poe's "The Raven."

> Once up | on a | midnight | dreary | while I | pondered | weak and |
>   weary
> Over | many | a quaint | and cur | ious vol | ume of | forgot | ten lore,
> While I | nodded | nearly | napping, | sudden | ly there | came a |
>   tapping
> As of | someone | gently | rapping, | rapping | at my | chamber door.

As you can see in the above examples, poets often vary the dominant met-rical pattern of a line with irregular feet to emphasize key words and to en-hance and perform the rhythmic sense of the line. **Rhythm** describes the flow of the stresses within the dominant meter of the line. For example, the pre-vailing meter of John Donne's Holy Sonnet 14 is iambic pentameter. But as the first quatrain demonstrates, not every foot scans as an iamb.

> Báttĕr | mỹ heárt, | thrée-pér | sŏned Gód; | fŏr Yóu
> Ăs yét | bŭt knóck, | breáthe, shine, | ănd seék | tŏ ménd;
> That Í | mǎy rise | ănd stand, | o'ĕrthrów mĕ,' | And bénd
> Yoŭr fórce | tŏ breák, | blów, buŕn, | ănd make | mĕ néw.

Donne's poem prays for a violent conversion experience to alter the poet's present spiritual malaise. In the poem, he combines accentual emphasis with the plosive *b* consonant to perform that forceful transformation. "Batter" makes use of the irregular trochaic foot; in a **trochee** (´˘) the accent falls on the first syllable rather than on the second in the iamb. Certain of Donne's poetic feet accent both syllables—in the irregular foot, the **spondee** (´´)—as in breáthe, shíne, or, more emphatically, in the phrasings blów, búrn.

In masterful verse compositions, an entire poem's action can turn on how irregular rhythms play against the dominant metrical pattern, as in this excerpt from Robert Frost's "The Vantage Point."

> Ănd íf | bў̆ noón | Ĭ haʹve | tŏo múch | oʹf theʹse,
> Ĭ háve | bŭt tŏ | turʹn ŏn | m̆y arʹm, | ănd lóʹ,
> Theʹ sún | -burʹned híll | síde seʹts | m̆y faʹce | ăglóʹw,

The metrical pattern here is iambic pentameter, but Frost performs the nimble shift in perspective by varying the rhythm as the poet turns on his arm to take in a different vantage point. The phrase "bŭt tŏ | turʹn ŏn | m̆y arʹm" combines "bŭt tŏ," a **pyrrhic** foot—two unaccented syllables—with the trochee "turʹn tŏ" to dramatize the turning rhythmically.

Similarly, W. B. Yeats creates a certain rhythmic intensity in "Who Goes with Fergus," especially in stanza two.

> Who will go drive with Fergus now,
> And pierce the deep wood's woven shade,
> And dance upon the level shore?
> Young man, lift up your russet brow,
> And lift your tender eyelids, maid,
> And brood on hopes and fear no more.
>
> And no more turn aside and brood
> Upon love's bitter mystery;
> For Fergus rules the brazen cars,
> And rules the shadows of the wood,
> And the white breast of the dim sea
> And all dishevelled wandering stars.

The poem's next-to-last-line is the one to pay attention to. Varying the metrical pattern of iambic tetrameter (four feet per line), Yeats repeats the rhythmic combination of the pyrrhic foot followed by a spondee—"Ănd theʹ | white breʹast | oʹf theʹ | dim séʹa"—so as to set off the visual impact of the white breast against dim sea.

Two other irregular feet are the **anapest** (˘˘´)—two unaccented syllables followed by an accented syllable—and its opposite, the **dactyl** (´˘˘)—an accented followed by two unaccented syllables. The first, third, and fourth lines of Thomas Hardy's "The Voice" intone the dactylic meter for a haunting effect:

> Wómăn múch | mіʹssed, hŏw yŏu | caʹll tŏ mĕ, | caʹll tŏ mĕ,
> Sáyĭng | thăt nóʹw | yŏu aʹre | nóʹt ăs | yŏu wéʹre
> Whén yŏu hăd | chánged frŏm theʹ | onʹe whŏ wăs | alʹl tŏ mĕ,
> But ăs ăʹt | fіʹrst, whĕn ouʹr | dáy wăs faіʹr.

Lord Byron's "The Destruction of Sennacherib" is composed primarily in anapestic tetrameter, as in the poem's first stanza.

Tħĕ Ăssýr | iăn cáme dówn | líkĕ tħĕ wólf | oñ tħĕ fóld,
Ăñd hĭs có | hŏřts wĕrĕ gléam | ĭñg ĭñ púr | plĕ ăñd góld;
Ăñd tħĕ shéen | ŏf tħĕir spéars | wăs lĭke stárs | oñ tħĕ séa,
Whĕn tħĕ blúe | wăvĕs rolls níght | lỹ oñ deép | Gălĭleé.

Rhyme coupled with rhythm can lay down a pattern that enhances the themes and subjects of a given poem's unique performance. For example, Theodore Roethke's "My Papa's Waltz" mimics in its formal arrangement of rhythm and rhyme the three-quarter time of a waltz.

THEODORE ROETHKE   *(1908–1963)*

My Papa's Waltz   *(1948)*

The whiskey on your breath
Could make a small boy dizzy;
But I hung on like death:
Such waltzing was not easy.

We romped until the pans   5
Slid from the kitchen shelf;
My mother's countenance
Could not unfrown itself.

The hand that held my wrist
Was battered on one knuckle;   10
At every step you missed
My right ear scraped a buckle.

You beat time on my head
With a palm caked hard by dirt,
Then waltzed me off to bed   15
Still clinging to your shirt.

In "My Papa's Waltz," Roethke devises a poetic form that has a natural, organic fit to the memory of his childhood waltz. English verse, however, offers a repertoire of preset forms that test a poet's power not only in mastering the pattern, say, of a sonnet or villanelle but in marking it for all time with one's own signature of greatness.

TOPICS FOR CRITICAL THINKING

1. Roethke's father, Otto Roethke, owned a greenhouse business in rural Saginaw, Michigan, and died when the poet was in early adolescence. Many of Roethke's poems are set in the greenhouse world of his youth and several dwell on the figure of

the overbearing father in particular. Like Sylvia Plath, whose father also died while she was a child, Roethke had powerfully conflicted feelings about his father that were magnified by his loss at a formative age. How does "My Papa's Waltz" present a somewhat divided memory of the father?

2. The poem presents a bittersweet recollection of what might have been a nightly ritual from the poet's childhood. On the surface, the poem offers a comic, even cartoon-like, portrait of his family life, especially in the surreal image of the mother whose "countenance could not unfrown itself." Consider how key words like *romped* and *waltzed* contribute to the fond memories the poet has of the father.

3. Plenty of evidence, however, points to an underlying tone of violence and abuse in the connotations of such words as *battered, scraped,* and *beat.* How do these key terms resonate with phrases like "Such waltzing was not easy" or "I hung on like death"?

TOPIC FOR CRITICAL WRITING

Rhyme and meter contribute to the waltz metaphor in combining iambic trimeter with the alternating rhyme scheme of the quatrain stanza units. Together, they mimic the three-quarter waltz time, which counts three beats to the measure. In lines 2, 4, 10, and 12, Roethke captures the rollicking, off-kilter "beat" of the waltzing by adding an extra syllable to the last foot of the line in an irregular foot called the *amphibrach*: "Sŭch wáltz | ĭng wás | nŏt eásў." Explore the rhythmic effects of Roethke's dancing measures.

27 Poetic Forms

Fixed Poetic Forms

When asked why he didn't compose free or nonstructured verse, Robert Frost responded, "I'd just as soon play tennis with the net down." Fixed form imposes the kind of rules, boundaries, and prior examples of craft that some poets welcome as a competitive chance to prove their verbal prowess. Formal arrangements of meter and rhyme—working together with alliteration, assonance, figurative language, imagery, and the rest—provide more than enough ingredients to make fixed form poetry a linguistic challenge every bit as bracing as Wimbledon or the U.S. Open.

Blank Verse, Couplets, Tercets, and Quatrains

Fixed form begins with **blank verse**, or unrhymed iambic pentameter. Blank verse imposes the rigor of metrical composition. It became the stock-in-trade of William Shakespeare's comedies and tragedies as well as of John Milton's epic *Paradise Lost*. Milton imitated Greek and Latin epic-staged, grammatically complex utterances whose patterns of **enjambment**—the movement of syntactic phrasing from the end of one line to the beginning of the next— overflowed the closure of **end rhyme**. His **inversions** (reversals) of normal **syntax** (the patterning of phrases and sentences) and his highly embedded clauses are unique contributions to the blank verse medium, as the opening lines of *Paradise Lost* show.

> Of Man's first disobedience, and the fruit
> Of that forbidden tree whose mortal taste
> Brought death into the world, and all our woe,
> With loss of Eden, till one greater Man
> Restore us and regain the blissful seat,
> Sing, Heavenly Muse, . . .

Milton's blank verse inverts the normal word order of the imperative sentence "Sing, Heavenly Muse, of Man's first disobedience" to suspend meaning across the enjambments of five lines of verse.

Rhyme lends further architectural shape and complexity to verse, especially in **couplets**, or pairs of rhyming lines. The **heroic couplet**, composed in

817

iambic pentameter, became a popular form in the eighteenth century, especially in the translation of Greek and Latin epic works by John Dryden and Alexander Pope. The coupling of rhyme and phrasing lends itself to striking truisms and epigrams. Pope's "An Essay on Man," for example, focuses on the essential paradoxes of the human condition that joins opposite states of being in a precarious and, at times, absurd balance.

> Placed on this isthmus of a middle state,
> A being darkly wise, and rudely great:
> With too much knowledge for the Sceptic side,
> With too much weakness for the Stoic's pride,
> He hangs between; in doubt to act, or rest,
> In doubt to deem himself a God, or Beast;
> In doubt his Mind or Body to prefer,

Pope's balancing of opposites is reinforced by the formal possibilities afforded by his heroic couplets. Gwendolyn Brooks playfully deflates the "heroic" stature of the couplet form in her contemporary poem "Religion," spoken by a boy named Ulysses: "Our teachers feed us geography. / We spit it out in a hurry." The Shakespearean sonnet's final couplets typically seal the form's arguments in a memorable concluding statement, as in Shakespeare's Sonnet 12.

> And nothing 'gainst Time's scythe can make defense
> Save breed, to brave him when he takes thee hence.

Closed form poetry is typically organized into **stanza** units, or groupings of lines that have the same or similar patterns of rhythm and end rhyme. For example, Robert Frost composes his famous poem "Provide, Provide" into three-line stanzas—called **tercets**—of iambic tetrameter linked with matching end rhyme.

> The witch that came (the withered hag)
> To wash the steps with pail and rag,
> Was once the beauty Abishag,
>
> The picture pride of Hollywood.
> Too many fall from great and good
> For you to doubt the likelihood.

Another well-known tercet pattern, **terza rima** or "triple rhyme," takes the middle rhyme of each stanza and uses it as the **envelope** frame for the next stanza unit to rhyme: *aba, bcb, cdc, efe,* and so on. As the term *envelope* implies, the end rhymes of the first and third lines surround the middle line. Dante composed *The Divine Comedy* in terza rima, and Shelley chose it as the closed form for his "Ode to the West Wind." A contemporary example of the form can be seen in Richard Wilbur's "First Snow in Alsace."

RICHARD WILBUR   *(b. 1921)*

First Snow in Alsace   *(1947)*

The snow came down last night like moths
Burned on the moon; it fell till dawn,
Covered the town with simple cloths.

Absolute snow lies rumpled on
What shellbursts scattered and deranged,   5
Entangled railings, crevassed lawn.

As if it did not know they'd changed,
Snow smoothly clasps the roofs of homes
Fear-gutted, trustless and estranged.

The ration stacks are milky domes;   10
Across the ammunition pile
The snow has climbed in sparkling combs.

You think: beyond the town a mile
Or two, this snowfall fills the eyes
Of soldiers dead a little while.   15

Persons and persons in disguise,
Walking the new air white and fine,
Trade glances quick with shared surprise.

At children's windows, heaped, benign,
As always, winter shines the most,   20
And frost makes marvelous designs.

The night guard coming from his post,
Ten first-snows back in thought, walks slow
And warms him with a boyish boast:

He was the first to see the snow.   25

TOPICS FOR CRITICAL THINKING

1. Just west of the Rhine River, the Alsace region of France shares its eastern border
   with Germany. Ceded to the German Empire at the end of the Franco-Prussian
   War in 1871, it was the site of military conflict in both World Wars of the twentieth century owing to its strategic location. Examine the key terms that describe
   how the war has turned the setting of Alsace into a battlefield.
2. In what ways does the snow have a consoling, reparative effect on the otherwise
   "Fear-gutted, trustless and estranged" town?

3. How does the snow permit the soldiers to regress to an earlier, more innocent moment of youthful peace?

TOPIC FOR CRITICAL WRITING

Consider how terza rima connects the key terms of the poem. How does it link, for example, the consolations of "home" with the snow's transformation of "ration stacks" and the "ammunition pile" into enchanted "milky domes" and "sparkling combs." Discuss how terza rima creates an artistic envelope that contains war's barbarism within the frame of a formal artifice.

Another stanza pattern is the **quatrain**, a four-line stanza unit. The most common quatrain pattern is the ballad stanza, as in William Wordsworth's "A Slumber Did My Spirit Seal."

> No mo | tion has | she now |,| no force;
>   She nei | ther hears | nor sees;
> Rolled round | in earth's | diur | nal course,
>   With rocks |,| and stones |,| and trees.

As this second stanza of Wordsworth's poem illustrates, the ballad stanza alternates lines of iambic tetrameter with iambic trimeter in the rhyme scheme *abcb* or, as in the above example, the *abab* pattern. The term *common meter* describes ballad stanzas when used in hymnals. Virtually all of Emily Dickinson's poems can be sung to the common meter of "The Battle Hymn of the Republic." Other options for the quatrain would include the monorhyme of Dante Gabriel Rossetti's "The Woodspurge" and the *abba* envelope stanza that Alfred, Lord Tennyson uses in "In Memoriam." A final option combines two pairs of couplets, as in Adrienne Rich's "Aunt Jennifer's Tigers" and Sir Walter Raleigh's poem addressed to Queen Elizabeth I, "Fortune Hath Taken Thee Away, My Love."

> Fortune hath taken thee away, my love,
> My life's soul and my soul's heaven above;
> Fortune hath taken thee away, my princess;
> My only light and my true fancy's mistress.

Longer Fixed Stanza Forms

Five-line stanzas such as Edgar Allan Poe's "To Helen" combine an envelope tercet with a couplet to rhyme *ababb*, *cdcee*, and so on. Thomas Hardy's "New Year's Eve" also combines couplets with envelope patterns in rhyming his five-line stanza unit *abaab*, *cdccd*, and so on.

> "I have finished another year," said God,
>   "In grey, green, white, and brown;
> I have strewn the leaf upon the sod,
> Sealed up the worm within the clod,
>   And let the last sun down."

The **Scottish stanza** is a six-line unit rhyming *aaabab* popularized by Robert Burns. Another common six-line stanza unit follows the *ababcc* pattern of Shakespeare's poem "Venus and Adonis." Among the many poems composed in the **"Venus and Adonis" stanza** is Edmund Spenser's "The Shepheardes Calender."

> A Shepheards boye (no better doe him call)
> When Winters wastful spight was almost spent,
> All in a sunneshine day, as did befall,
> Led for th his flock, that had bene long ypent.°
> So faynt they woxe°, and feeble in the folde,   5
> That now unnethes° their feete could them uphold.

Of the longer stanza units, **rhyme royal** is a seven-stanza patterned *ababbcc*. Chaucer is its earliest proponent in English verse in *Troilus and Criseide*. Others who have explored its possibilities include W. H. Auden in "The Shield of Achilles" and Sir Thomas Wyatt in "They Flee from Me." Wyatt also was the first to compose in **ottava rima** or eighth rhyme, the eight-line stanza pattern rhyming *abababcc*. Lord Byron employs ottava rima in *Don Juan* as does W. B. Yeats in "The Statues," "Sailing to Byzantium," and "Among School Children." The most distinctive nine-line stanza is the **Spenserian stanza** named after Edmund Spenser's *The Fairie Queene*. This pattern presents eight lines of iambic pentameter with a final iambic hexameter line—or alexandrine; the rhyme scheme is *ababbcbcc*. Keats's "The Eve of St. Agnes" is, perhaps, the most impressive performance of this stanza, and it is the form Percy Bysshe Shelley chooses in *Adonais*, his elegy to Keats. Among its other practitioners were Byron in *Childe Harold's Pilgrimage* and Tennyson in "The Land of the Lotus Eaters."

The Sonnet

Certain closed forms determine the entire shape of poems in their patterning of end rhymes, stanza lengths, use of couplets, and so on. Of these fixed forms, the most widely written and read is the **sonnet**, which came into English from the Italian influence of poet Francesco Petrarch. In fact, the word *sonnet* comes from the Italian *sonnetto*, which means "little song." The Italian sonnet, based on Petrarch's rhyme scheme, remains the most popular of the three kinds of sonnets, which also include the English, or Shakespearean, sonnet and the Spenserian sonnet. Each of these three variations on the sonnet form has the distinctive iambic pentameter, fourteen-line structure. Their differences stem from their rhyme schemes. The Italian sonnet rhymes *abba abba cde cde*; the Shakespearean sonnet rhymes *abab cdcd efef gg*. The Spenserian rhyme scheme bears a closer resemblance to the Shakespearean than to the Italian sonnet, rhyming *abab bcbc cdcd ee*. Of the three, the Italian form comprises a two-part structure. That is, the repeated envelope rhyme *abba abba* signals a break in the poem's presentation of themes, images, subjects,

---

4 *ypent:* Penned up.   5 *woxe:* Grew.   6 *unnethes:* Scarcely.

and arguments, moving from the first eight lines or **octave** to the final six lines, or **sestet**. In contrast, the alternating rhyme scheme of the Shakespearean and Spenserian patterns—divided as they are into three quatrains—tends to break the poem's presentation into three stages with a summary statement framed in the concluding couplet.

In "When I Consider How My Light Is Spent," the great English epic poet John Milton uses the Italian sonnet form to reflect on the blindness that afflicted him in 1651 at the age of forty-three.

JOHN MILTON   *(1608–1674)*

When I Consider How My Light Is Spent   *(1652)*

When I consider how my light is spent
    Ere half my days, in this dark world and wide,
    And that one talent which is death to hide
    Lodged with me useless, though my soul more bent
To serve therewith my Maker, and present   5
    My true account, lest he returning chide;
    "Doth God exact day-labor, light denied?"
    I fondly ask; but Patience to prevent
That murmur, soon replies, "God doth not need
    Either man's work or his own gifts; who best   10
    Bear his mild yoke, they serve him best. His state
Is kingly. Thousands at his bidding speed
    And post o'er land and ocean without rest:
    They also serve who only stand and wait."

TOPICS FOR CRITICAL THINKING

1. The sonnet takes the form of a question, presented in the octave, followed by the answer given in the sestet. Rhyming *spent, wide, hide, bent, present, chide, denied,* and *prevent,* how does the poem's octave question whether God will "exact day-labor, light denied"? What is Milton's point here?
2. Consider how Milton's pun on the word *light* signifies both the poet's literal loss of eyesight and his unenlightened spiritual state.
3. Examine the poem's turning point in the sestet where the allegorical figure of "Patience" consoles the poet with a sublime insight into the transcendent vision that "His state / Is kingly."
4. What advice does "Patience" give Milton about enduring the "mild yoke" of his condition as sufficient proof of his good faith?

TOPIC FOR CRITICAL WRITING

The subtext for this poem is the biblical parable of the talents related by Jesus Christ in Matthew 25:14–30. In it, God gives a man a gold piece or talent, which he buries for safekeeping. When God returns, he chides the man for not turning his talent to profit as the other servant has done, increasing his talent fivefold. How does Milton's sonnet work through the poet's dilemma and his doubts concerning his fitness to serve God by putting to good use his "one talent" of writing (Milton's pun on the biblical talent)?

William Shakespeare and Edmund Spenser similarly muse in the sonnet form on poetry itself as the cure for the forces of change and mortality.

WILLIAM SHAKESPEARE   *(1564–1616)*

Sonnet 55   *(1609)*

Not marble, nor the gilded monuments
Of princes, shall outlive this powerful rhyme;
But you shall shine more bright in these contènts
Than unswept stone, besmeared with sluttish time.
When wasteful war shall statues overturn,   5
And broils root out the work of masonry,
Nor Mars his sword nor war's quick fire shall burn
The living record of your memory.
'Gainst death and all-oblivious enmity
Shall you pace forth; your praise shall still find room   10
Even in the eyes of all posterity
That wear this world out to the ending doom.
    So, till the judgment that yourself arise,
    You live in this, and dwell in lovers' eyes.

TOPICS FOR CRITICAL THINKING

1. Examine how Shakespeare's Sonnet 55 divides into three movements across the sonnet's three quatrain divisions.
2. What is Shakespeare's argument concerning poetry's power to prove more lasting than monuments made from what, at first glance, seem more valuable: marble and gold?
3. What is "sluttish time"? What is Shakespeare's argument concerning poetry's relation to time?
4. Consider the ways in which Shakespeare's couplet encapsulates the sonnet's themes on the love and transcendence that poetry achieves over time, mortality, and doom.

TOPIC FOR CRITICAL WRITING

In Shakespeare's Sonnet 55, how does poetry's "living record" similarly outlast war as well as the "work" of the stonemason?

EDMUND SPENSER   *(1552–1599)*

Sonnet 75   *(1595)*

One day I wrote her name upon the strand,
But came the waves and washèd it away:
Agayne I wrote it with a second hand,
But came the tyde, and made my paynes his pray.
Vayne man, sayd she, that doest in vaine assay,   5
A mortall thing so to immortalize,
For I my selve shall lyke to this decay,
And eek my name bee wypèd out lykewize.
Not so, (quod I) let baser things devize
To dy in dust, but you shall live by fame: 10
My verse your vertues rare shall eternize,
And in the hevens wryte your glorious name.
Where whenas death shall all the world subdew,
Our love shall live, and later life renew.

TOPICS FOR CRITICAL THINKING

1. Consider how the first three quatrain rhyme units stage a dialogue on the situation of writing in relation to time, change, and mortality.
2. How does the poet's couplet give Spenser the last word on poetry's power to "immortalize" the lover?

TOPIC FOR CRITICAL WRITING

Although less grand in its claims than Shakespeare's Sonnet 55, Spenser's Sonnet 75 similarly offers poetry as the antidote for time's mutability. Discuss this theme in Spenser's poem.

Not all sonnet forms follow the prescribed rhyme scheme to the letter. The majority of Italian sonnets, especially, present a variation on the *cdecde* rhyme pattern in the sestet, as in Gwendolyn Brooks's "the rites for Cousin Vit."

GWENDOLYN BROOKS   *(1917–2000)*

the rites for Cousin Vit   *(1949)*

Carried her unprotesting out the door.
Kicked back the casket-stand. But it can't hold her,
That stuff and satin aiming to enfold her,
The lid's contrition nor the bolts before.
Oh oh. Too much. Too much. Even now, surmise,   5

She rises in the sunshine. There she goes,
Back to the bars she knew and the repose
In love-rooms and the things in people's eyes.
Too vital and too squeaking. Must emerge.
Even now she does the snake-hips with a hiss,   10
Slops the bad wine across her shantung, talks
Of pregnancy, guitars and bridgework, walks
In parks or alleys, comes haply on the verge
Of happiness, haply hysterics. Is.

TOPICS FOR CRITICAL THINKING

1. How does Brooks vary the rhyme scheme of the Italian sonnet form in her sestet?
2. Characterize Cousin Vit. What qualities and forces of vitality does she embody?
3. In what ways does Cousin Vit transcend mortality and the funeral rites that are "aiming to enfold her"? How are her energies more powerful than mortality?
4. What kinds of dramatic effects does Brooks achieve through her use of sentence fragments and exclamatory utterances in the poem?

TOPIC FOR CRITICAL WRITING

Discuss the poem's opening situation and its reversal in the sestet.

The Villanelle

As equally complex and demanding of the poet's art as the sonnet, the French form of the **villanelle** originated in Italy and shares its root meaning with such words as *villanella*, a dance or country song, and *villano* or peasant. At nineteen lines, the villanelle is somewhat longer than the sonnet with five tercets and a final quatrain. The rhyme scheme describes a series of repeated refrain lines that reflect the form's origins in the circular returns of a folk dance. The complicated refrain pattern follows the sequence of *A1bA2 abA1 abA2 abA1 abA2 abA1A2*, with *A1* and *A2* forming the refrain lines as in Theodore Roethke's villanelle "The Waking."

THEODORE ROETHKE   *(1908–1963)*

The Waking   *(1953)*

I wake to sleep, and take my waking slow.
I feel my fate in what I cannot fear.
I learn by going where I have to go.

We think by feeling. What is there to know?
I hear my being dance from ear to ear.   5
I wake to sleep, and take my waking slow.

Of those so close beside me, which are you?
God bless the Ground! I shall walk softly there,
And learn by going where I have to go.

Light takes the Tree; but who can tell us how? 10
The lowly worm climbs up a winding stair;
I wake to sleep, and take my waking slow.

Great Nature has another thing to do
To you and me, so take the lively air,
And, lovely, learn by going where to go. 15

This shaking keeps me steady. I should know.
What falls away is always. And is near.
I wake to sleep, and take my waking slow.
I learn by going where I have to go.

TOPICS FOR CRITICAL THINKING

1. "The Waking" is a masterful performance of the villanelle whose fixed form provides the vehicle for the poet's celebration of his being in the world. Discuss the ways in which Roethke's refrain lines turn on life's contradictory intensities.
2. What other paradoxes does the poem celebrate?
3. Consider how the villanelle affords Roethke, as poet, the formal means for giving memorable utterance to his key insights into his experience.

TOPIC FOR CRITICAL WRITING

Roethke has written that "sometimes, of course, there is regression. I believe that the spiritual man must go back in order to go forward. The way is circuitous, and sometimes lost, but invariably returned to." How does the figure of the "lowly worm" present a symbol for the poet's regression—of "going back" to subhuman things? How does that regressive identification with subhuman things, paradoxically enough, become the beginning of his spiritual journey?

The Sestina

The last fixed form we will consider is the most complex of all, the **sestina**. This form began in the twelfth century with the troubadours, medieval poets who set their poems to music to be sung by performing artists called *joglars*. Provençal poet Arnaut Daniel is thought to have invented the first sestina. The form is composed in pentameter with six stanzas of six lines each, followed by a three-line **envoy**, or short stanza. Instead of being structured with end rhyme, the form is organized according to the repetition of the initial six end words that shift their line position in the following order:

```
stanza 1: A B C D E F
       2: F A E B D C
       3: C F D A B E
       4: E C B F A D
       5: D E A C F B
       6: B D F E C A
envoy:    E C A or A C E
```

Poets who have successfully mastered the complexity of the sestina are a select group indeed. Among the practitioners of this difficult fixed form are Sir Philip Sidney ("Yee Gote-heard Gods"), Algernon Swinburne ("The Complaint of Lisa"), Ezra Pound ("Sestina: Altaforte" and "Sestina for Isolt"), W. H. Auden ("Paysage moralisé"), Louise MacNeice ("To Hedli"), Roy Fuller ("Sestina"), Anthony Hecht ("The Book of Yolek"), John Ashbery ("The Painter"), and Elizabeth Bishop ("Sestina").

Pattern Poetry, Concrete Poetics, and Vers Libre

A version of fixed form verse, **pattern poetry,** presents the typography and arrangement of lines on the page as a visual icon for its subject matter. Pattern poetry dates as far back as the Cretan and Egyptian civilizations; in ancient Greece it was known as *technopaigneia*. Pattern poetry in the shapes of the sun and moon, wings, altars, columns, pyramids, and so on were popular during the Medieval period and can be seen, for example, in George Herbert's poem "Easter Wings."

GEORGE HERBERT   *(1593–1633)*

Easter Wings   *(1633)*

Lord, who createdst man in wealth and store,
    Though foolishly he lost the same,
        Decaying more and more
            Till he became
              Most poor: 5
              With thee
            O let me rise
        As larks, harmoniously,
    And sing this day thy victories:
Then shall the fall further the flight in me.   10

My tender age in sorrow did begin;
And still with sicknesses and shame
Thou didst so punish sin,
That I became
Most thin.   15
With thee
Let me combine,
And feel this day thy victory;
For, if I imp my wing on thine,
Affliction shall advance the flight in me.   20

Herbert's pattern poem not only mimics the look of wings on the page, but represents in the length of the line the poem's thematic nadir of the loss of grace and the plenitude of its recovery. In the twentieth century, the **Concrete Poetry Movement** of the 1950s, spearheaded by Eugen Gomringer and Öyvind Fahlström, played with the visual possibilities of pattern poems in calligraphy, typewriter art, stamp art, and typographical design. Contemporary poets such as John Hollander and May Swenson offer further examples of how pattern poetry can suggest fascinating parallels between word and world.

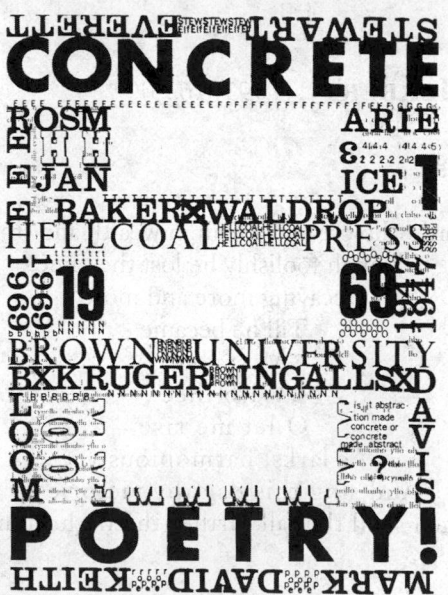

Stewart A. Baker, ed., Envelope Lover,
Love Vortex Vertigo (1969)

JOHN HOLLANDER   *(b. 1929)*

Swan and Shadow   *(1969)*

```
                    Dusk
                  Above the
               water hang the
                   loud
                   flies                                     5
                   Here
                  O so
                 gray
                 then
          What              A pale signal will appear       10
          When              Soon before its shadow fades
          Where             Here in this pool of opened eye
       In us       No Upon us As at the very edges
          of where we take shape in the dark air
              this object bares its image awakening         15
                 ripples of recognition that will
                    brush darkness up into light
even after this bird this hour both drift by atop the perfect sad instant now
                    already passing out of sight
                 toward yet-untroubled reflection           20
                 this image bears its object darkening
                 into memorial shades Scattered bits of
          light        No of water Or something across
          water            Breaking up No Being regathered
          soon             Yet by then a swan will have     25
          gone             Yes out of mind into what
                 vast
                 pale
                 hush
                 of a                                       30
                 place
                 past
          sudden dark as
            if a swan
               sang                                         35
```

MAY SWENSON   (1913–1989)

Bleeding   (1970)

Stop bleeding   said the knife
I would if I   could said the cut.
Stop bleeding   you make me messy with this blood.
I'm sorry said   the cut.
Stop or I will   sink in farther said the knife.   5
Don't said the   cut.
The knife did   not say it couldn't help it but it sank in farther.
If only you   didn't bleed said the knife I wouldn't have to do this.
I know said   the cut I bleed too easily I hate that I can't
help it I   wish I were a knife like you and   didn't have to bleed.   10
Meanwhile   stop bleeding will you said the knife.
Yes you   are a mess and sinking in deeper said the cut I will
have to   stop.
Have you   stopped by now said the knife.
I've almost   stopped I think.   15
Why must you   bleed in the first place said the knife.
For the reason   maybe that you must do what you must do said the cut.
I can't stand   bleeding said the knife and sank in farther.
I hate it too   said the cut I know it isn't you it's me   20
you're lucky to   be a knife you ought to be glad about that.
Too many cuts   around said the knife they're messy I don't know
how they stand   themselves.
They don't said   the cut.
You're bleeding   again.   25
No I've stopped   said the cut. See you're coming out now the
blood is drying   it will rub off you'll be shiny again and clean.
If only cuts   wouldn't bleed so much said the knife coming out a little.
But then knives   might become dull said the cut.
Aren't you bleeding   a little said the knife.   30
I hope not said the   cut.
I feel you are just   a little.
Maybe just a little   but I can stop now.
I feel a little   wetness still said the knife sinking in
a little but then   coming out a little.   35
Just a little maybe   just enough said the cut.
That's enough now   stop now do you feel better now said the knife.
I feel I have to   bleed to feel I think said the cut.
I don't I don't have   to feel said the knife drying now becoming shiny.

Open Poetic Forms

Increasingly in the twentieth century, much poetry parts company with the formal measures of fixed form as well as iconic form of pattern poetry. Variously labeled as **vers libre, free verse**, and **open form** poetry, this kind of verse varies line length, typography, rhythms, and stanza patterns to fit the particular style and content of the work at hand. The modern poet Theodore Roethke composed in both fixed and free verse, and especially mined the possibilities of open form in his expansive long poem sequence "North American Sequence." Roethke, however, thought of free verse as a "denial in terms." "There is, invariably," he wrote, "the ghost of some other form, often blank verse, behind what is written."

Nevertheless, the careers of other poets, such as W. S. Merwin, move increasingly away from the closure of fixed form. Merwin, especially, plays his lines off against the white space of the page, and, after his 1963 volume *The Moving Target*, he abandons completely the fixity of punctuation. "Punctuation," he has said, "nails the poem down on the page; when you don't use it the poem becomes more a thing in itself, at once more transparent and more actual." Such techniques create a striking openness of statement, as in his poem "The Well."

W. S. MERWIN   *(b. 1927)*

The Well   *(1970)*

Under the stone sky the water
waits
with all its songs inside it
the immortal
it sang once   5
it will sing again
the days
walk across the stone in heaven
unseen as planets at noon
while the water   10
watches the same night

Echoes come in like swallows
calling to it
it answers without moving
but in echoes   15
not in its voice
they do not say what it is
only where

It is a city to which many travellers
came with clear minds
having left everything even
heaven
to sit in the dark praying as one silence
for the resurrection

TOPICS FOR CRITICAL THINKING

1. How does Merwin's line length mirror the sense of the metaphoric figures in this poem?
2. How has his decision to abandon punctuation opened up the possibilities of interpretive meaning in "The Well"?

TOPIC FOR CRITICAL WRITING

In what ways do Merwin's lines play against the white space of the page? To what effect?

Questions like those posed above are not easily answered because open form verse frees up, rather than limits, the available range of the reader's response to the work. Many different versions of free verse abound in twentieth-century poetics, and your instructor can help you interpret the several free verse poems included throughtout the Poetry Section of *Understanding Literature*.

Featured Writer

Joseph Severn, *John Keats*
(1818)

JOHN KEATS

Born in 1795, John Keats was the eldest child of Thomas and Frances Jennings Keats; he had three brothers—George, Thomas, and Edward—and one sister, Frances Mary. Thomas Keats managed a livery stable at the Swan and Hoop Inn that was owned by his father-in-law John Jennings. Not insignificantly, John Keats's boyhood was marked by a series of traumas. When the poet was nine years old, his father was killed in a riding accident in April 1804; Keats's mother remarried two months later. Soon thereafter, Keats and his siblings were taken in by their grandmother Alice Jennings. The next year, John Jennings, the poet's grandfather, died, leaving an estate that was subsequently mismanaged to the poet's disadvantage in later life. In 1805, Alice moved the children from Enfield to Edmonton. The following year, the poet's mother Frances left her second husband and was reputed to be living with another man in Edmonton. She would eventually return to live with her mother and children for a short time before dying in 1810 of tuberculosis. As one of his mother's primary caregivers during her illness, John Keats was profoundly affected by this loss, magnified in the deaths by tuberculosis of his uncle in 1808 and his brother Tom ten years later.

After receiving an early education from John Clarke, the independent-minded headmaster of the Enfield school, Keats began an apprenticeship to the Edmonton apothecary surgeon Thomas Hammond in 1811. In 1814, Keats's grandmother Alice Jennings died. The following year, Keats pursued his medical training at Guy's Hospital. Passing his apothecaries' examination the next year, Keats also published his first poem, the sonnet "O Solitude" in Leigh Hunt's journal, the *Examiner*.

Keats's commitment to poetry grew apace, owing in part to his reading of Homer, the subject of his sonnet "On First Looking into Chapman's Homer." The title of this Italian sonnet refers to a 1616 folio edition of Homer's *Iliad* and *Odyssey* translated by George Chapman. Keats's friend Charles Cowden Clarke had been loaned the book, and the two had sat up all night reading it together in October 1816. The next morning, Keats composed what is regarded as his finest work from his first volume *Poems*.

On First Looking into Chapman's Homer   *(1816)*

Much have I traveled in the realms of gold,
   And many goodly states and kingdoms seen;
   Round many western islands have I been
Which bards in fealty to Apollo hold.
Oft of one wide expanse had I been told   5
   That deep-browed Homer ruled as his demesne;
   Yet did I never breathe its pure serene
Till I heard Chapman speak out loud and bold:
Then felt I like some watcher of the skies
   When a new planet swims into his ken;   10
Or like stout Cortez when with eagle eyes
   He stared at the Pacific—and all his men
Looked at each other with a wild surmise—
   Silent, upon a peak in Darien.

TOPICS FOR CRITICAL THINKING

1. The word *demesne* is defined by the *American Heritage Dictionary* as "lands retained by a feudal lord for his own use." Similarly *fealty* refers to a vassal's loyalty to a lord. What tropes of ownership, regal authority, and divine rule can you identify in the poem?

2. How does Keats read literary tradition in terms of these relations of power? To what extent does the sonnet perform Keats's own place within that tradition?

3. Balboa, not Cortez, was the first European to view the Pacific Ocean from Darien in Panama. What do you know about Cortez? However mistaken, how does this error on Keats's part parallel the poem's other themes of ownership, ambition, and conquest?

TOPIC FOR CRITICAL WRITING

Keats's brother George had a keen interest in America and emigrated there two years after Keats composed "On First Looking into Chapman's Homer." For his part, Keats had the opportunity to read William Robertson's *History of America*, which documents the European discovery of the Pacific. In what ways does Keats portray the role of reading as discovery?

Soon Keats's circle of acquaintances grew to include Benjamin Haydon, John Hamilton Reynolds, and Percy Bysshe Shelley. Keats abandoned medicine as a career in 1817. That same year, C. and J. Ollier published Keats's first volume of verse, *Poems,* as the poet combined work on his next volume *Endymion* with visits to the Isle of Wight, Margate, Hastings, and Oxford. By the end of 1817, Keats had also met Benjamin Bailey, Charles Wentworth Dilke, Charles Brown, and the poet William Wordsworth. Even at this early stage, Keats's poetry begins to testify to a certain world weariness and growing sense of mortality, which the young poet portrays in "On Seeing the Elgin Marbles."

On Seeing the Elgin Marbles   *(1817)*

My spirit is too weak—mortality
  Weighs heavily on me like unwilling sleep,
  And each imagined pinnacle and steep
Of godlike hardship tells me I must die
Like a sick eagle looking at the sky.   5
  Yet 'tis a gentle luxury to weep
  That I have not the cloudy winds to keep
Fresh for the opening of the morning's eye.
Such dim-conceived glories of the brain
  Bring round the heart an indescribable feud;   10
So do these wonders a most dizzy pain,
  That mingles Grecian grandeur with the rude
Wasting of old Time—with a billowy main—
  A sun—a shadow of a magnitude.

The so-called Elgin Marbles consist of fragmentary remains of sculptures that once adorned the Parthenon built in Athens from 447 B.C. to 432 B.C. The Parthenon housed a magnificent statue of the goddess Athena. The marbles stage battle scenes between Olympian gods and mythic giants, as well as among the Greeks, Amazons, Centaurs, and Trojans. Other scenes depict Panathenaic festivals. In addition to the Elgin Marbles of the British Museum, the Parthenon marbles are housed in Athens and the Louvre in Paris. Lord Elgin had brought fragments of the Parthenon marbles to London from Greece

The Elgin Marbles

in 1807. The year before Keats wrote the sonnet, they were the subject of political debate in the House of Commons on the question of whether England should purchase them from Elgin. At the time, Keats's liberal colleagues sided with the effort to buy them as a way of elevating British culture. Conservatives were reluctant to support a neoclassical revival that would undermine Christian values. Indeed, by celebrating Grecian art and literature, Keats himself was attacked as the "Cockney Homer" in an 1818 issue of *Blackwood's*.

TOPICS FOR CRITICAL THINKING

1. How does Keats relate the representations of "godlike hardship" back to his own situation as poet in the opening sestet of this Italian sonnet?
2. Describe the ways in which Keats interrupts his lines in the octave to imitate the breaks and erosions visible in the marbles, which have been subject to the "Wasting of old Time."

www 3. Take a look at the images of the Elgin Marbles **Web** and imagine other ways that Keats might have celebrated their "magnitude" in verse.

TOPIC FOR CRITICAL WRITING

Compare Keats's experience of viewing the "Grecian grandeur" of the Elgin marbles with his imaginative musings on the myths and mysteries of classical art in "Ode on a Grecian Urn," which is printed on the following pages.

The sparse sales of Keats's first volume of poems led him to place his second book *Endymion* with Taylor and Hessey, who published it in 1818. Keats's ties to the liberal-minded editor Leigh Hunt generated hostile reviews from the conservative ranks of Blackwood's *Edinburgh Magazine* and from the editors of *Critical Quarterly*. The myth that Keats was devastated by this harsh reception—that, as Lord Byron has it in *Don Juan*, the young Keats was "snuffed out by an article"—has been somewhat overstated. For his part, Keats allowed as how "my own domestic criticism has given me pain beyond what Blackwood or the *Quarterly* could possibly inflict." Certainly, however, 1818 was a very difficult year for Keats, owing not only to the critical attacks he suffered for *Endymion* but to his brother Tom's declining health from tuberculosis.

Beginning in March 1818, John replaced his brother George as Tom's caretaker in Teignmouth. George would go on to marry Georgiana Augusta Wylie that May and emigrate to America the next month. For Tom and John Keats, however, that early Devonshire spring was wet and dreary. Yet it was also a time when Keats read deeply in Milton and drafted, among other things, his poem *Isabella* and his famous letter to John Hamilton Reynolds on the "Chamber of Maiden-thought." At the end of the spring, John accompanied George and Georgiana to Liverpool and then joined Charles Brown on a tour of the Lake District and Scotland. By the end of the summer, Keats's own health was jarred by a severe cold and sore throat that, along with the news that Tom's condition had deteriorated, made him cut short his tour of Scotland.

Returning to London in August, it was during the upcoming fall that Keats met and eventually fell in love with Fanny Brawne. But the poet's brother Tom was bedridden and emaciated from advanced tuberculosis, and

Keats took on the responsibility of nursing his brother as he had earlier with their mother. On the morning of December 1, Tom died of the disease. Following the death of his brother, Keats shared half of Brown's house at Wentworth Place, Hampstead.

Beginning in January 1819, Keats enjoyed the most creative and productive period of his career as a poet. From January through February he composed "The Eve of St. Agnes," followed by "La Belle Dame sans Merci" that April, the same month that the Brawne family became his neighbors at Wentworth Place. During April and May, he composed the great odes—"Psyche," "Nightingale," "Grecian Urn," and "Melancholy." Leaving Wentworth, in part to distance himself from his passionate attachment to Fanny, Keats composed *Lamia* on the Isle of Wight and worked on *The Fall of Hyperion* from July through the end of the summer, composing "To Autumn" as well that September. This intense schedule of writing also included the poet's collaboration with Brown on the tragedy *Otho the Great*, several scenes for another tragedy, *King Stephen*, and a partially completed satire, *The Jealousies (The Cap and Bells)*.

Keats's great creative period came to an end that fall as the symptoms of tuberculosis began to manifest themselves, culminating with a severe hemorrhage in the lungs on February 3, 1820. That May, Keats moved to Kentish Town, close to Hampstead, then to the home of Leigh Hunt following yet another hemorrhage. Eventually, Keats returned to Wentworth Place in August where he was attended by Fanny Brawne and her mother. Meanwhile, Keats's third book of poems *Lamia, Isabella, The Eve of St. Agnes and Other Poems* was published in July by Taylor and Hessey. Twelve reviews came out in the two months following its release and, unlike the criticisms of *Endymion*, the majority were favorable. Yet this good news was tempered by Keats's diagnosis of consumption and his doctors' insistence that he spend the winter in Italy, which, of course, meant a separation from Fanny. By this time the two had an understanding of engagement, but there was little realistic hope that Keats would return from his trip to Rome.

Keats left England bound for Italy on September 18, 1820, accompanied by his friend, the artist Joseph Severn. After taking up residence on the second floor of 26 Piazza di Spagna in Rome, Keats's condition worsened steadily and, attended by Severn until the very end, the poet died on February 23, 1821. Today, Keats lies buried in the Protestant cemetery in Rome, where his tombstone, as the poet intended, bears his famous epitaph: "Here lies 'One Whose Name was writ in Water.'"

Poems for Further Reading and Critical Writing

JOHN KEATS   *(1795–1821)*

Ode on a Grecian Urn   *(1820)*

1

Thou still unravished bride of quietness,
  Thou foster child of silence and slow time,

Sylvan historian, who canst thus express
  A flowery tale more sweetly than our rhyme:
What leaf-fringed legend haunts about thy shape   5
    Of deities or mortals, or of both,
        In Tempe or the dales of Arcady?°
    What men or gods are these? What maidens loath?
What mad pursuit? What struggle to escape?
        What pipes and timbrels? What wild ecstasy?   10

2

Heard melodies are sweet, but those unheard
  Are sweeter; therefore, ye soft pipes, play on;
Not to the sensual ear, but, more endeared,
    Pipe to the spirit ditties of no tone:
Fair youth, beneath the trees, thou canst not leave   15
    Thy song, nor ever can those trees be bare;
        Bold Lover, never, never canst thou kiss,
Though winning near the goal—yet, do not grieve;
    She cannot fade, though thou hast not thy bliss,
        Forever wilt thou love, and she be fair!   20

3

Ah, happy, happy boughs! that cannot shed
  Your leaves, nor ever bid the Spring adieu;
And, happy melodist, unweariéd,
    For ever piping songs for ever new;
More happy love! more happy, happy love!   25
    For ever warm and still to be enjoyed,
        For ever panting, and for ever young;
All breathing human passion far above,
    That leaves a heart high-sorrowful and cloyed,
        A burning forehead, and a parching tongue.   30

4

Who are these coming to the sacrifice?
  To what green altar, O mysterious priest,
Lead'st thou that heifer lowing at the skies,
    And all her silken flanks with garlands dressed?
What little town by river or sea shore,   35
    Or mountain-built with peaceful citadel,
        Is emptied of this folk, this pious morn?
And, little town, thy streets forevermore
    Will silent be; and not a soul to tell
        Why thou art desolate, can e'er return.   40

---

7 *Arcady:* Pastoral valleys in Greece.

5

O Attic° shape! Fair attitude! with brede
  Of marble men and maidens overwrought,
With forest branches and the trodden weed;
  Thou, silent form, dost tease us out of thought
As doth eternity: Cold Pastoral!   45
  When old age shall this generation waste,
    Thou shalt remain, in midst of other woe
Than ours, a friend to man, to whom thou say'st,
  "Beauty is truth, truth beauty,"—that is all
    Ye know on earth, and all ye need to know.   50

TOPICS FOR CRITICAL THINKING

1. Examine and discuss your interpretations of each of Keats's personifications of the urn in stanza one. How do these figurative presentations of the urn set up particular themes and presentational motifs in the remaining stanzas of the poem?
2. Compare the images inscribed on the urn in stanzas two and three. How do they move beyond the realities of human time into a vision of eternity? How would you describe the effect of this vision on the poet at the end of the third stanza?
3. Consider the poet's changing narrative point of view in the ode. How does the narrative voice of the poem differ before, during, and after the poet's encounter with the urn?
4. Why does Keats call the urn a "Cold Pastoral" in the last stanza?
5. In earlier drafts of the poem, the concluding insight that "Beauty is truth, truth beauty" is stated without quotation marks. What difference do the quote marks make? Who do you imagine is speaking here? What are the possibilities?

TOPIC FOR CRITICAL WRITING

Compare the poet's conclusions on truth and beauty with his letter to Benjamin Bailey, November 22, 1817, reprinted later in this chapter, where Keats writes that "the Imagination may be compared to Adam's dream—he awoke and found it truth."

Keats composed "Ode to a Nightingale" in May 1819 prior to his writing "Ode on a Grecian Urn." The two poems share a similar narrative plot design of

- imaginatively penetrating beyond the actualities of the real world;
- envisioning a metaphysical dimension variously of eternity, spirituality, and truth; and
- returning to the present with an altered understanding of existence.

Consider how this tri-part structure gives shape to Keats's "Ode to a Nightingale."

---

41 *Attic:* Attic was a geographical region in Greece that included Athens.

Ode to a Nightingale   *(1819)*

1

My heart aches, and a drowsy numbness pains
   My sense, as though of hemlock° I had drunk,
Or emptied some dull opiate to the drains
   One minute past, and Lethe-wards° had sunk:
'Tis not through envy of thy happy lot,   5
   But being too happy in thine happiness—
      That thou, light-wingéd Dryad of the trees,
         In some melodious plot
Of beechen green, and shadows numberless,
      Singest of summer in full-throated ease.   10

2

O, for a draught of vintage! that hath been
   Cooled a long age in the deep-delvéd earth,
Tasting of Flora° and the country green,
   Dance, and Provençal song, and sunburnt mirth!
O for a beaker full of the warm South,   15
   Full of the true, the blushful Hippocrene,°
      With beaded bubbles winking at the brim,
         And purple-stainéd mouth;
That I might drink, and leave the world unseen,
      And with thee fade away into the forest dim: 20

3

Fade far away, dissolve, and quite forget
   What thou among the leaves hast never known,
The weariness, the fever, and the fret
   Here, where men sit and hear each other groan;
Where palsy shakes a few, sad, last gray hairs,   25
   Where youth grows pale, and specter-thin, and dies,
      Where but to think is to be full of sorrow
         And leaden-eyed despairs,
Where Beauty cannot keep her lustrous eyes,
      Or new Love pine at them beyond tomorrow.   30

4

Away! away! for I will fly to thee,
   Not charioted by Bacchus and his pards,

---

2 *hemlock:* Poison.   4 *Lethe-wards:* Toward the mythic river of forgetfulness in Hades.
13 *Flora:* Roman goddess of flowers.   16 *Hippocrene:* Fountain on Mt. Helicon, sacred
to the Muses.

But on the viewless wings of Poesy,
    Though the dull brain perplexes and retards:
Already with thee! tender is the night,   35
    And haply the Queen-Moon is on her throne,
        Clustered around by all her starry Fays;°
            But here there is no light,
    Save what from heaven is with the breezes blown
        Through verdurous glooms and winding mossy ways.   40

5

I cannot see what flowers are at my feet,
    Nor what soft incense hangs upon the boughs,
But, in embalmèd darkness, guess each sweet
    Wherewith the seasonable month endows
The grass, the thicket, and the fruit tree wild;   45
    White hawthorn, and the pastoral eglantine;
        Fast fading violets covered up in leaves;
            And mid-May's eldest child,
    The coming musk-rose, full of dewy wine,
        The murmurous haunt of flies on summer eves.   50

6

Darkling I listen; and for many a time
    I have been half in love with easeful Death,
Called him soft names in many a musèd rhyme,
    To take into the air my quiet breath;
Now more than ever seems it rich to die,   55
    To cease upon the midnight with no pain,
        While thou art pouring forth thy soul abroad
            In such an ecstasy!
    Still wouldst thou sing, and I have ears in vain—
        To thy high requiem become a sod.   60

7

Thou wast not born for death, immortal Bird!
    No hungry generations tread thee down;
The voice I hear this passing night was heard
    In ancient days by emperor and clown:
Perhaps the selfsame song that found a path   65
    Through the sad heart of Ruth,° when, sick for home,
        She stood in tears amid the alien corn;
            The same that ofttimes hath
    Charmed magic casements, opening on the foam
        Of perilous seas, in faery lands forlorn.   70

---

37 *Fays:* Fairies.   66 *Ruth:* See Biblical Book of Ruth.

8

Forlorn! the very word is like a bell
  To toil me back from thee to my sole self!
Adieu! the fancy cannot cheat so well
  As she is famed to do, deceiving elf.
Adieu! adieu! thy plaintive anthem fades   75
  Past the near meadows, over the still stream,
    Up the hill side; and now 'tis buried deep
      In the next valley-glades:
  Was it a vision, or a waking dream?
    Fled is that music:—Do I wake or sleep?   80

TOPICS FOR CRITICAL THINKING

1. Consider Keats's opening address to the nightingale in the figure of a "Dryad" or wood nymph and discuss the ways in which he attempts to identify with it in stanzas 1–4.

2. Keats had nursed his brother Tom all during the previous fall up until his death in December 1818. How might that experience bear on the poet's sense of grief and vision of mortality in stanza 3?

3. Consider how Keats's various attempts to escape the heartache described in the opening stanzas relate to his stated death wish in stanza 6.

4. Read Keats's letter to George and Thomas Keats, December 21, 1817, reprinted later in this chapter, especially where Keats defines "Negative Capability" as the ability to be "in uncertainties, Mysteries, doubts, without any irritable reaching after fact & reason." How might this state characterize the poet's transcendental encounter with the nightingale in stanzas 6 and 7?

5. Describe Keats's transcendental vision of the "immortal Bird" in stanza 7. Compare and contrast that metaphysical moment to the encounter Keats has with the urn in "Ode on a Grecian Urn."

6. Compare and contrast the poet's return to the actual world in stanza 8 with the urn as a "Cold Pastoral" in "Ode on a Grecian Urn."

TOPIC FOR CRITICAL WRITING

Keats's final question—"Do I wake or sleep?"—hints at the poet's bewilderment after his ecstatic encounter with the nightingale. Compare this poem with the knight's dream in the poem that follows, "La Belle Dame sans Merci."

La Belle Dame sans Merci   *(1819)*

1

O what can ail thee, knight-at-arms,
  Alone and palely loitering?
The sedge has withered from the lake,
  And no birds sing.

2

O what can ail thee, knight-at-arms,   5
    So haggard and so woe-begone?
The squirrel's granary is full
    And the harvest's done.

3

I see a lily on thy brow
    With anguish moist and fever dew,   10
And on thy cheeks a fading rose
    Fast withereth too.

4

"I met a lady in the Meads,
    Full beautiful, a faery's child,
Her hair was long, her foot was light   15
    And her eyes were wild.

5

"I made a Garland for her head,
    And bracelets too, and fragrant Zone;
She looked at me as she did love,
    And made sweet moan.   20

6

"I set her on my pacing steed
    And nothing else saw all day long,
For sidelong would she bend, and sing
    A faery's song.

7

"She found me roots of relish sweet,   25
    And honey wild, and manna dew,
And sure in language strange she said
    'I love thee true.'

8

"She took me to her elfin grot,
    And there she wept and sighed full sore,   30
And there I shut her wild wild eyes
    With kisses four.

9

"And there she lulléd me asleep,
    And there I dreamed, Ah! Woe betide!
The latest dream I ever dreamed   35
    On the cold hill side

10

"I saw pale kings and princes too,
    Pale warriors, death pale were they all;
They cried—"La belle dame sans merci
    Hath thee in thrall!"   40

11

"I saw their starved lips in the gloam,
    With horrid warning gapéd wide,
And I awoke, and found me here
    On the cold hill's side.

12

"And this is why I sojourn here,   45
    Alone and palely loitering,
Though the sedge is wither'd from the lake,
    And no birds sing."

TOPICS FOR CRITICAL THINKING

1. Compare and contrast the portraits of the belle dame and the knight. How does Keats's imagery and language distinguish the two?
2. Discuss Keats's presentation of narrative point of view in the poem. How many points of view can you distinguish? Who narrates the first four stanzas? How does the narrator of the first-person pronoun *I* shift in stanza 4? What other narrators can you find in the poem?
3. Is la belle dame a femme fatale? Is it clear how we are to judge her haunting encounter with the knight? Is there evidence in the poem that makes her a sympathetic, rather than a demonic, figure?

TOPIC FOR CRITICAL WRITING

Keats took his title for the poem from the French writer and poet Alain Chartier, and literary scholars have advanced several echoes in the poem from Spenser and Shakespeare, among others. A possible source for the poem in the pictorial arts is Raphael's painting *An Allegory: Vision of a Knight* (1508), now housed in the National Gallery, London. Keats admired Raphael and may well have seen the painting since it had been on display in London since 1801. Compare Raphael's painting (included in the color insert) with Keats's poem.

The Eve of St. Agnes (1819)

1

St. Agnes' Eve—Ah, bitter chill it was!
The owl, for all his feathers, was a-cold;
The hare limped trembling through the frozen grass,
And silent was the flock in woolly fold:
Numb were the Beadsman's fingers, while he told   5
His rosary, and while his frosted breath,
Like pious incense from a censer old,
Seemed taking flight for heaven, without a death,
Past the sweet Virgin's picture, while his prayer he saith.

2

His prayer he saith, this patient, holy man;   10
Then takes his lamp, and riseth from his knees,
And back returneth, meager, barefoot, wan,
Along the chapel aisle by slow degrees:
The sculptured dead, on each side, seem to freeze,
Imprisoned in black, purgatorial rails: 15
Knights, ladies, praying in dumb orat'ries,
He passeth by; and his weak spirit fails
To think how they may ache in icy hoods and mails.

3

Northward he turneth through a little door,
And scarce three steps, ere Music's golden tongue   20
Flattered to tears this aged man and poor;
But no—already had his deathbell rung:
The joys of all his life were said and sung:
His was harsh penance on St. Agnes' Eve:
Another way he went, and soon among   25
Rough ashes sat he for his soul's reprieve,
And all night kept awake, for sinners' sake to grieve.

4

That ancient Beadsman heard the prelude soft;
And so it chanced, for many a door was wide,
From hurry to and fro. Soon, up aloft,   30
The silver, snarling trumpets 'gan to chide:
The level chambers, ready with their pride,
Were glowing to receive a thousand guests:
The carvéd angels, ever eager-eyed,
Stared, where upon their heads the cornice rests,   35
With hair blown back, and wings put crosswise on their breasts.

5

At length burst in the argent revelry,
With plume, tiara, and all rich array,
Numerous as shadows haunting faerily
The brain, new stuffed, in youth, with triumphs gay   40
Of old romance. These let us wish away,
And turn, sole-thoughted, to one Lady there,
Whose heart had brooded, all that wintry day,
On love, and winged St. Agnes' saintly care,
As she had heard old dames full many times declare.   45

6

They told her how, upon St. Agnes' Eve,
Young virgins might have visions of delight,
And soft adorings from their loves receive
Upon the honeyed middle of the night,
If ceremonies due they did aright;   50
As, supperless to bed they must retire,
And couch supine their beauties, lily white;
Nor look behind, nor sideways, but require
Of heaven with upward eyes for all that they desire.

7

Full of this whim was thoughtful Madeline: 55
The music, yearning like a God in pain,
She scarcely heard: her maiden eyes divine,
Fixed on the floor, saw many a sweeping train
Pass by—she heeded not at all: in vain
Came many a tiptoe, amorous cavalier,   60
And back retired; not cooled by high disdain;
But she saw not: her heart was otherwhere:
She sighed for Agnes' dreams, the sweetest of the year.

8

She danced along with vague, regardless eyes,
Anxious her lips, her breathing quick and short: 65
The hallowed hour was near at hand: she sighs
Amid the timbrels, and the thronged resort
Of whisperers in anger, or in sport;
'Mid looks of love, defiance, hate, and scorn,
Hoodwinked with faery fancy; all amort,   70
Save to St. Agnes and her lambs unshorn,
And all the bliss to be before tomorrow morn.

9

So, purposing each moment to retire,
She lingered still. Meantime, across the moors,
Had come young Porphyro, with heart on fire   75
For Madeline. Beside the portal doors,
Buttressed from moonlight, stands he, and implores
All saints to give him sight of Madeline,
But for one moment in the tedious hours,
That he might gaze and worship all unseen;   80
Perchance speak, kneel, touch, kiss—in sooth such things have been.

10

He ventures in: let no buzzed whisper tell:
All eyes be muffled, or a hundred swords
Will storm his heart, Love's fev'rous citadel:
For him, those chambers held barbarian hordes,   85
Hyena foemen, and hot-blooded lords,
Whose very dogs would execrations howl
Against his lineage: not one breast affords
Him any mercy, in that mansion foul,
Save one old beldame, weak in body and in soul.   90

11

Ah, happy chance! the aged creature came,
Shuffling along with ivory-headed wand,
To where he stood, hid from the torch's flame,
Behind a broad hall-pillar, far beyond
The sound of merriment and chorus bland: 95
He startled her; but soon she knew his face,
And grasped his fingers in her palsied hand,
Saying, "Mercy, Porphyro! hie thee from this place;
They are all here tonight, the whole bloodthirsty race!

12

"Get hence! get hence! there's dwarfish Hildebrand;   100
He had a fever late, and in the fit
He curséd thee and thine, both house and land:
Then there's that old Lord Maurice, not a whit
More tame for his gray hairs—Alas me! flit!
Flit like a ghost away."—"Ah, Gossip dear,   105
We're safe enough; here in this armchair sit,
And tell me how"—"Good Saints! not here, not here;
Follow me, child, or else these stones will be thy bier."

13

He followed through a lowly archéd way,
Brushing the cobwebs with his lofty plume,   110
And as she muttered "Well-a—well-a-day!"
He found him in a little moonlight room,
Pale, latticed, chill, and silent as a tomb.
"Now tell me where is Madeline," said he,
"O tell me, Angela, by the holy loom   115
Which none but secret sisterhood may see,
When they St. Agnes' wool are weaving piously."

14

"St. Agnes! Ah! it is St. Agnes' Eve—
Yet men will murder upon holy days:
Thou must hold water in a witch's sieve,   120
And be liege lord of all the Elves and Fays,
To venture so: it fills me with amaze
To see thee, Porphyro!—St. Agnes' Eve!
God's help! my lady fair the conjuror plays
This very night: good angels her deceive!   125
But let me laugh awhile, I've mickle° time to grieve."

15

Feebly she laugheth in the languid moon,
While Porphyro upon her face doth look,
Like puzzled urchin on an aged crone
Who keepeth closed a wond'rous riddle-book,   130
As spectacled she sits in chimney nook.
But soon his eyes grew brilliant, when she told
His lady's purpose; and he scarce could brook
Tears, at the thought of those enchantments cold,
And Madeline asleep in lap of legends old.   135

16

Sudden a thought came like a full-blown rose,
Flushing his brow, and in his painéd heart
Made purple riot: then doth he propose
A stratagem, that makes the beldame start:
"A cruel man and impious thou art: 140
Sweet lady, let her pray, and sleep, and dream
Alone with her good angels, far apart
From wicked men like thee. Go, go!—I deem
Thou canst not surely be the same that thou didst seem."

---

126 *Mickle:* Much.

17

"I will not harm her, by all saints I swear,"   145
Quoth Porphyro: "O may I ne'er find grace
When my weak voice shall whisper its last prayer,
If one of her soft ringlets I displace,
Or look with ruffian passion in her face:
Good Angela, believe me by these tears;   150
Or I will, even in a moment's space,
Awake, with horrid shout, my foemen's ears,
And beard them, though they be more fanged than wolves
        and bears."

18

"Ah! why wilt thou affright a feeble soul?
A poor, weak, palsy-stricken, churchyard thing,   155
Whose passing bell may ere the midnight toll;
Whose prayers for thee, each morn and evening,
Were never missed."—Thus plaining, doth she bring
A gentler speech from burning Porphyro;
So woeful, and of such deep sorrowing,   160
That Angela gives promise she will do
Whatever he shall wish, betide her weal or woe.

19

Which was, to lead him, in close secrecy,
Even to Madeline's chamber, and there hide
Him in a closet, of such privacy   165
That he might see her beauty unespied,
And win perhaps that night a peerless bride,
While legioned fairies paced the coverlet,
And pale enchantment held her sleepy-eyed.
Never on such a night have lovers met,   170
Since Merlin paid his Demon all the monstrous debt.

20

"It shall be as thou wishest," said the Dame:
"All cates and dainties shall be storéd there
Quickly on this feast night: by the tambour frame
Her own lute thou wilt see: no time to spare,   175
For I am slow and feeble, and scarce dare
On such a catering trust my dizzy head.
Wait here, my child, with patience; kneel in prayer
The while: Ah! thou must needs the lady wed,
Or may I never leave my grave among the dead."   180

21

So saying, she hobbled off with busy fear.
The lover's endless minutes slowly passed;
The dame returned, and whispered in his ear
To follow her; with aged eyes aghast
From fright of dim espial. Safe at last,   185
Through many a dusky gallery, they gain
The maiden's chamber, silken, hushed, and chaste;
Where Porphyro took covert, pleased amain.
His poor guide hurried back with agues in her brain.

22

Her falt'ring hand upon the balustrade,   190
Old Angela was feeling for the stair,
When Madeline, St. Agnes' charméd maid,
Rose, like a missioned spirit, unaware:
With silver taper's light, and pious care,
She turned, and down the aged gossip led   195
To a safe level matting. Now prepare,
Young Porphyro, for gazing on that bed;
She comes, she comes again, like ringdove frayed and fled.

23

Out went the taper as she hurried in;
Its little smoke, in pallid moonshine, died: 200
She closed the door, she panted, all akin
To spirits of the air, and visions wide:
No uttered syllable, or, woe betide!
But to her heart, her heart was voluble,
Paining with eloquence her balmy side;   205
As though a tongueless nightingale should swell
Her throat in vain, and die, heart-stifled, in her dell.

24

A casement high and triple-arched there was,
All garlanded with carven imag'ries
Of fruits, and flowers, and bunches of knot-grass,   210
And diamonded with panes of quaint device,
Innumerable of stains and splendid dyes,
As are the tiger-moth's deep-damasked wings;
And in the midst, 'mong thousand heraldries,
And twilight saints, and dim emblazonings,   215
A shielded scutcheon blushed with blood of queens and kings.

25

Full on this casement shone the wintry moon,
And threw warm gules on Madeline's fair breast,
As down she knelt for heaven's grace and boon;
Rose-bloom fell on her hands, together pressed,   220
And on her silver cross soft amethyst,
And on her hair a glory, like a saint:
She seemed a splendid angel, newly dressed,
Save wings, for heaven—Porphyro grew faint:
She knelt, so pure a thing, so free from mortal taint.   225

26

Anon his heart revives: her vespers done,
Of all its wreathéd pearls her hair she frees;
Unclasps her warméd jewels one by one;
Loosens her fragrant bodice; by degrees
Her rich attire creeps rustling to her knees: 230
Half-hidden, like a mermaid in sea-weed,
Pensive awhile she dreams awake, and sees,
In fancy, fair St. Agnes in her bed,
But dares not look behind, or all the charm is fled.

27

Soon, trembling in her soft and chilly nest,   235
In sort of wakeful swoon, perplexed she lay,
Until the poppied warmth of sleep oppressed
Her soothéd limbs, and soul fatigued away;
Flown, like a thought, until the morrow-day;
Blissfully havened both from joy and pain;   240
Clasped like a missal where swart Paynims pray;
Blinded alike from sunshine and from rain,
As though a rose should shut, and be a bud again.

28

Stol'n to this paradise, and so entranced,
Porphyro gazed upon her empty dress,   245
And listened to her breathing, if it chanced
To wake into a slumberous tenderness;
Which when he heard, that minute did he bless,
And breathed himself: then from the closet crept,
Noiseless as fear in a wide wilderness,   250
And over the hushed carpet, silent, stepped,
And 'tween the curtains peeped, where, lo!—how fast she slept.

29

Then by the bedside, where the faded moon
Made a dim, silver twilight, soft he set
A table, and, half anguished, threw thereon   255
A cloth of woven crimson, gold, and jet:—
O for some drowsy Morphean amulet!
The boisterous, midnight, festive clarion,
The kettledrum, and far-heard clarinet,
Affray his ears, though but in dying tone—   260
The hall door shuts again, and all the noise is gone.

30

And still she slept an azure-lidded sleep,
In blanchéd linen, smooth, and lavendered,
While he from forth the closet brought a heap
Of candied apple, quince, and plum, and gourd;   265
With jellies soother than the creamy curd,
And lucent syrups, tinct with cinnamon;
Manna and dates, in argosy transferred
From Fez; and spicéd dainties, every one,
From silken Samarcand to cedared Lebanon.   270

31

These delicates he heaped with glowing hand
On golden dishes and in baskets bright
Of wreathéd silver: sumptuous they stand
In the retiréd quiet of the night,
Filling the chilly room with perfume light.—   275
"And now, my love, my seraph fair, awake!
Thou art my heaven, and I thine eremite:
Open thine eyes, for meek St. Agnes' sake,
Or I shall drowse beside thee, so my soul doth ache."

32

Thus whispering, his warm, unnervéd arm   280
Sank in her pillow. Shaded was her dream
By the dusk curtains: 'twas a midnight charm
Impossible to melt as icéd stream:
The lustrous salvers in the moonlight gleam;
Broad golden fringe upon the carpet lies: 285
It seemed he never, never could redeem
From such a steadfast spell his lady's eyes;
So mused awhile, entoiled in wooféd fantasies.

33

Awakening up, he took her hollow lute,—
Tumultuous,—and, in chords that tenderest be,   290
He played an ancient ditty, long since mute,
In Provence called, *"La belle dame sans merci"*:
Close to her ear touching the melody;
Wherewith disturbed, she uttered a soft moan:
He ceased—she panted quick—and suddenly   295
Her blue affrayéd eyes wide open shone:
Upon his knees he sank, pale as smooth-sculptured stone.

34

Her eyes were open, but she still beheld,
Now wide awake, the vision of her sleep:
There was a painful change, that nigh expelled   300
The blisses of her dream so pure and deep:
At which fair Madeline began to weep,
And moan forth witless words with many a sigh;
While still her gaze on Porphyro would keep,
Who knelt, with joinéd hands and piteous eye,   305
Fearing to move or speak, she looked so dreamingly.

35

"Ah, Porphyro!" said she, "but even now
Thy voice was at sweet tremble in mine ear,
Made tuneable with every sweetest vow;
And those sad eyes were spiritual and clear: 310
How changed thou art! how pallid, chill, and drear!
Give me that voice again, my Porphyro,
Those looks immortal, those complainings dear!
Oh leave me not in this eternal woe,
For if thou diest, my love, I know not where to go."   315

36

Beyond a mortal man impassioned far
At these voluptuous accents, he arose,
Ethereal, flushed, and like a throbbing star
Seen mid the sapphire heaven's deep repose;
Into her dream he melted, as the rose   320
Blendeth its odor with the violet—
Solution sweet: meantime the frost-wind blows
Like Love's alarum pattering the sharp sleet
Against the windowpanes; St. Agnes' moon hath set.

37

'Tis dark: quick pattereth the flaw-blown sleet: 325
"This is no dream, my bride, my Madeline!"
'Tis dark: the icéd gusts still rave and beat:
"No dream, alas! alas! and woe is mine!
Porphyro will leave me here to fade and pine.—
Cruel! what traitor could thee hither bring?   330
I curse not, for my heart is lost in thine,
Though thou forsakest a deceivéd thing—
A dove forlorn and lost with sick unprunéd wing."

38

"My Madeline! sweet dreamer! lovely bride!
Say, may I be for aye thy vassal blest?   335
Thy beauty's shield, heart-shaped and vermeil dyed?
Ah, silver shrine, here will I take my rest
After so many hours of toil and quest,
A famished pilgrim—saved by miracle.
Though I have found, I will not rob thy nest   340
Saving of thy sweet self; if thou think'st well
To trust, fair Madeline, to no rude infidel."

39

"Hark! 'tis an elfin-storm from faery land,
Of haggard seeming, but a boon indeed:
Arise—arise! the morning is at hand—   345
The bloated wassaillers will never heed—
Let us away, my love, with happy speed;
There are no ears to hear, or eyes to see—
Drowned all in Rhenish and the sleepy mead:
Awake! arise! my love, and fearless be,   350
For o'er the southern moors I have a home for thee."

40

She hurried at his words, beset with fears,
For there were sleeping dragons all around,
At glaring watch, perhaps, with ready spears—
Down the wide stairs a darkling way they found.—   355
In all the house was heard no human sound.
A chain-dropped lamp was flickering by each door;
The arras, rich with horseman, hawk, and hound,
Fluttered in the besieging wind's uproar;
And the long carpets rose along the gusty floor.   360

41

They glide, like phantoms, into the wide hall;
Like phantoms, to the iron porch, they glide;
Where lay the Porter, in uneasy sprawl,
With a huge empty flagon by his side:
The wakeful bloodhound rose, and shook his hide,   365
But his sagacious eye an inmate owns:
By one, and one, the bolts full easy slide:
The chains lie silent on the footworn stones;
The key turns, and the door upon its hinges groan.

42

And they are gone: aye, ages long ago   370
These lovers fled away into the storm.
That night the Baron dreamt of many a woe,
And all his warrior-guests, with shade and form
Of witch, and demon, and large coffin-worm,
Were long be-nightmared. Angela the old   375
Died palsy-twitched, with meager face deform;
The Beadsman, after thousand aves told,
For aye unsought for slept among his ashes cold.

St. Agnes was a virgin martyr who was executed in A.D. 306 during the reign of Emperor Dioclesian. Before her execution, her virginity was miraculously defended by thunder and lightning against the Romans' attempts to rape her. Following her martyrdom, her parents had a vision of Agnes among angels and attended by a lamb, her symbol. The Feast of St. Agnes is celebrated on January 21. According to folk belief, a virgin may receive the dream vision of her future husband on the eve of St. Agnes if she (1) refuses any kisses and the "salute" of any man during the day and evening before the Feast of St. Agnes, (2) wears a clean shift, or nightgown, to bed, (3) lays her right hand under her head, (4) and says "Now the god of Love send me my desire."

TOPICS FOR CRITICAL THINKING

1. How does Keats incorporate the ritual of St. Agnes's eve into the plot and imagery of his poem?

2. How are we to judge Porphyro's character and his motives for "hoodwinking" Madeline by pretending to be her dream vision? In section 16, Porphyro has a sudden "thought" that comes "like a full-blown rose." How do you interpret his strategem? Is it a plot of premeditated sexual seduction, or are his intentions more honorable?

3. Is there a way in which Madeline's following of the folk ways of St. Agnes and her dream can be read as a confirmation of the power of the imagination to enchant real life? How would this reading lead us to interpret Porphyro's role in the narrative as fulfilling the legend rather than simply manipulating it?

TOPICS FOR CRITICAL WRITING

1. In one version of the poem, which his editors and friends resisted, Keats depicts a more literal consummation of the dream in stanza 36:

> See, while she speaks his arms encroaching slow,
> Have zoned her, heart to heart,—loud, loud the dark winds blow!
> For on the midnight came a tempest fell;
> More sooth, for that his quick rejoinder flows
> Into her burning ear: and still the spell
> Unbroken guards her in serene repose.
> With her wild dream he mingled, as a rose
> Marrieth its odour to a violet.
> Still, still she dreams, the louder the frost wind lows, . . .

Which version works more successfully? Should the poem leave ambiguous the sexual dimension of the lovers' "mingling," or should it be more explicit? Does explicit sexuality undermine the romantic possibility of the lovers' otherwise more mysterious union?

2. Reread "The Eve of St. Agnes" closely and gather evidence from its language and imagery that supports either reading the poem as a legend of romantic love or as a more realistic tale of modern seduction.

To Autumn   (1820)

1

Season of mists and mellow fruitfulness,
   Close bosom-friend of the maturing sun;
Conspiring with him how to load and bless
   With fruit the vines that round the thatch-eaves run;
To bend with apples the mossed cottage-trees,   5
   And fill all fruit with ripeness to the core;
     To swell the gourd, and plump the hazel shells
   With a sweet kernel; to set budding more,
And still more, later flowers for the bees,
Until they think warm days will never cease,   10
     For Summer has o'er-brimmed their clammy cells.

2

Who hath not seen thee oft amid thy store?
   Sometimes whoever seeks abroad may find
Thee sitting careless on a granary floor,
   Thy hair soft-lifted by the winnowing wind;   15
Or on a half-reaped furrow sound asleep,
   Drowsed with the fume of poppies, while thy hook
     Spares the next swath and all its twinéd flowers:
And sometimes like a gleaner thou dost keep

Steady thy laden head across a brook;   20
Or by a cider-press, with patient look,
   Thou watchest the last oozings hours by hours.

3

Where are the songs of Spring? Aye, where are they?
   Think not of them, thou hast thy music too—
While barréd clouds bloom the soft-dying day,   25
   And touch the stubble-plains with rosy hue;
Then in a wailful choir the small gnats mourn
   Among the river sallows, borne aloft
      Or sinking as the light wind lives or dies;
And full-grown lambs loud bleat from hilly bourn;   30
   Hedge crickets sing; and now with treble soft
   The red-breast whistles from a garden-croft;
      And gathering swallows twitter in the skies.

TOPIC FOR CRITICAL THINKING

Examine how patterns of rhyme, alliteration, and assonance contribute to Keats's depiction of Autumn.

TOPIC FOR CRITICAL WRITING

Consider the role of apostrophe and personification in Keats's address to, and presentation of, the Autumn season.

Letters of John Keats

Excerpt from Letter to Benjamin Bailey   *November 22, 1817*

O I wish I was as certain of the end of all your troubles as that of your momentary start about the authenticity of the Imagination. I am certain of nothing but of the holiness of the Heart's affections and the truth of Imagination—What the imagination seizes as Beauty must be truth—whether it existed before or not—for I have the same idea of all our Passions as of Love: they are all, in their sublime, creative of essential beauty. In a word, you may know my favorite Speculation by my first Book, and the little song I send in my last—which is a representation from the fancy of the probable mode of operating in these Matters—The imagination may be compared to Adam's dream— he awoke and found it truth. I am more zealous in this affair because I have never yet been able to perceive how anything can be known for truth by consecutive reasoning—and yet it must be—Can it be that even the greatest Philosopher ever arrived at his goal without putting aside numerous objections—However it may be, O for a Life of Sensations rather than of Thoughts!

It is a 'Vision in the form of Youth,' a Shadow of reality to come—and this consideration has further convinced me for it has come as auxiliary to another favorite Speculation of mine, that we shall enjoy ourselves here after by having what we called happiness on Earth repeated in a finer tone and so repeated—And yet such a fate can only befall those who delight in sensation, rather than hunger as you do after Truth—Adam's dream will do here and seems to be a conviction that Imagination and its empyreal reflection is the same as human Life and its spiritual repetition. But, as I was saying—the simple imaginative Mind may have its rewards in the repetition of its own silent Working coming continually on the spirit with a fine suddenness—to compare great things with small—have you never by being surprised with an old Melody—in a delicious place—by a delicious voice, felt over again your very speculations and surmises at the time it first operated on your soul—do you not remember forming to yourself the singer's face more beautiful than it was possible and yet with the elevation of the Moment you did not think so—even then you were mounted on the Wings of Imagination so high—that the Prototype must be here after—that delicious face you will see—What a time! I am continually running away from the subject—sure this cannot be exactly the case with a complex Mind—one that is imaginative and at the same time careful of its fruits—who would exist partly on sensation partly on thought—to whom it is necessary that years should bring the philosophic Mind—such an one I consider your's and therefore it is necessary to your eternal Happiness that you not only drink this old Wine of Heaven, which I shall call the redigestion of our most ethereal Musings on Earth; but also increase in knowledge and know all things.

Excerpt from Letter to George and Thomas Keats
December 21, 1817

I spent Friday evening with Wells & went the next morning to see *Death on the Pale horse*. It is a wonderful picture, when West's age is considered; But there is nothing to be intense upon; no women one feels mad to kiss, no face swelling into reality. The excellence of every Art is its intensity, capable of making all disagreeables evaporate, from their being in close relationship with Beauty & Truth—Examine King Lear & you will find this examplified throughout; but in this picture we have unpleasantness without any momentuous depth of speculation excited, in which to bury its repulsiveness—The picture is larger than Christ rejected—I dined with Haydon the sunday after you left, & had a very pleasant day, I dined too (for I have been out too much lately) with Horace Smith & met his two Brothers with Hill & Kingston & one Du Bois, they only served to convince me, how superior humour is to wit in respect to enjoyment—These men say things which make one start, without making one feel, they are all alike; their manners are alike; they all know fashionables; they have a mannerism in their very eating & drinking, in their mere handling a Decanter—They talked of Kean & his low company—Would I were with that company instead of yours said I to myself! I know such like acquaintance will never do for me & yet I am going to Reynolds, on wednesday—Brown & Dilke walked with me & back from the Christmas pantomine. I had not a dispute but a disquisition with Dilke, on various subjects; several things dovetailed in my mind, & at once it struck me, what quality went to form a Man of Achievement especially in Literature & which Shakespeare posessed so enormously—I mean *Negative Capability*, that is when man is capable of being in uncertainties, Mysteries, doubts, without any irritable reaching after fact & reason—Coleridge, for instance, would let go by a fine isolated verisimilitude caught from the Penetralium of mystery, from being incapable of remaining content with half knowledge. This pursued through Volumes would perhaps take us no further than this, that with a great poet the sense of Beauty overcomes every other consideration, or rather obliterates all consideration.

Excerpt from Letter to John Taylor   *February 27, 1818*

It is a sorry thing for me that any one should have to overcome Prejudices in reading my verses—that affects me more than any hypercriticism on any particular Passage—In *Endymion*, I have most likely but moved into the Go-cart from the leading-strings. In Poetry I have a few Axioms, and you will see how far I am from their Centre. 1st I think poetry should surprise by a fine excess and not by singularity, it should strike the Reader as a wording of his own highest thoughts, and appear almost a Remembrance.—2d Its touches of Beauty should never be half way, therby making the reader breathless, instead of content: the rise, the progress, the setting of imagery should, like the Sun, come natural too him,—shine over him, and set soberly although in magnificence leaving him in the Luxury of twilight—but it is easier to think what Poetry should be than to write it—and this leads me to another axiom. That if poetry comes not as naturally as the Leaves to a tree it had better not come at all. However, it may be with me, I cannot help looking into new countries with 'O for a Muse of Fire to ascend!'—If Endymion serves me as a Pioneer perhaps I ought to be content. I have great reason to be content, for thank God I can read, and perhaps understand Shakespeare to his depths; and I have I am sure many friends, who, if I fail, will attribute any change in my Life and temper to Humbleness rather than to pride—to a cowering under the Wings of great Poets, rather than to a Bitterness that I am not appreciated. I am anxious to get Endymion printed that I may forget it and proceed. I have copied the 3rd Book and begun the 4th.

Your sincere and obliged friend,
John Keats

Excerpt from Letter to John Hamilton Reynolds   *May 3, 1818*

I will return to Wordsworth—whether or no he has an extended vision or a circumscribed grandeur—whether he is an eagle in his nest, or on the wing—And to be more explicit and to show you how tall I stand by the giant, I will put down a simile of human life as far as I now perceive it; that is, to the point to which I say we both have arrived at—Well—I compare human life to a large Mansion of Many Apartments, two of which I can only describe, the doors of the rest being as yet shut upon me—The first we step into we call the infant or thoughtless Chamber, in which we remain as long as we do not think—We remain there a long while, and notwithstanding the doors of the second Chamber remain wide open, showing a bright appearance, we care not to hasten to it; but are at length imperceptibly impelled by the awakening of the thinking principle—within us—we no sooner get into the second Chamber, which I shall call the Chamber of Maiden-Thought, than we become intoxicated with the light and the atmosphere, we see nothing but pleasant wonders, and think of delaying there for ever in delight: However, among the effects this breathing is father of is that tremendous one of sharpening one's vision into the heart and nature of man—of convincing one's nerves that the World is full of Misery and Heartbreak, Pain, Sickness, and oppression— whereby This Chamber of Maiden Thought becomes gradually darken'd and at the same time, on all sides of it many doors are set open—but all dark—all leading to dark passages—We see not the balance of good and evil. We are in a mist.—*We* are now in that state—We feel the "burden of the Mystery," To this Point was Wordsworth come, as far as I can conceive when he wrote "Tintern Abbey" and it seems to me that his Genius is explorative of those dark Passages. Now if we live, and go on thinking, we too shall explore them. He is a Genius and superior [to] us, in so far as he can, more than we, make discoveries, and shed a light in them. Here I must think Wordsworth is deeper than Milton—though I think it has depended more upon the general and gregarious advance of intellect, than individual greatness of Mind.

Critical Perspective: On Keats and Critical Judgment

"The difficulty of interpreting Keats's poetry is closely bound up with its loveliness, its power to gratify our wish for beauty. This is a power to provoke nearly unanimous value judgments together with widely disparate accounts of their occasion. Modern criticism of Keats presents a curious picture: a clear consensus on the harmonious tenor of the development leading from *Sleep and Poetry* to the ode *To Autumn*, together with strong disagreement on the meaning of its individual moments. I will begin by sketching one such disagreement—about how to characterize Keats's situation in the exquisite fifth stanza of the *Ode to a Nightingale*—to help us ask: what investments can we discern here, important enough to be common to such opposite critical readings? For if critics give incompatible accounts of key passages, and yet end with the same judgments, their conclusions must be motivated by some other kind of constraint than the acts of reading from which they ostensibly arise. The nature of such constraints on critical reading can emerge for us, I suggest, if we attend to the tropes and the rhetorical gestures that Keats's ode cites or repeats if we carry out a certain kind of intertextual reading.

"How does one characterize the gesture of the ode's peculiarly Keatsian fifth stanza—naming flowers in the darkness, guessing each sweet, 'White hawthorn, and the pastoral eglantine'? It depends on how one reads the fourth: it depends on that notorious crux where—as typically in Keats—the most lovely and the most variously interpreted lines of the poem coincide:

> Already with thee! tender is the night,
>   And haply the Queen-Moon is on her throne,
>   Cluster'd around by all her starry Fays;
>   But here there is no light,
>   Save what from heaven is with the breezes blown
>   Through verdurous glooms and winding mossy ways.

The fifth stanza continues, 'I cannot see what flowers are at my feet. . . .' The question of how to take this passage is loaded by the lines at the opening of stanza 4 with the issue of Keats's commitment to poetic flight:

> Away! away! for I will fly to thee,
>   Not charioted by Bacchus and his pards,
> But on the viewless wings of Poesy,
>   Though the dull brain perplexes and retards:

The decision how to read what follows amounts to a judgment upon the speaker's commitment to 'the viewless wings of Poesy.' It is here that one finds an incipient consensus, not upon the function of the viewless wings in these lines, but upon the desirability of Keats's ultimately giving them up. Interpretations of the fourth and fifth stanzas converge in a final value judgment—that Keats ought to abandon poetic flight—after diverging widely on just *how* these stanzas mean that. Keats's lines effectively resist attempts to determine the matter more precisely by appealing to them alone, for at this decisive juncture the ode's syntax turns radically ambiguous. To judge the effects of recourse to the viewless wings of poesy we have to decide how to voice the exclamation point after the fourth stanza 'thee.' A mute mark stands at the place which is *either* an exclamation at arrival *or* a statement of distance. The punctuation mark doesn't tell us how to hear it: whether as an expression of passionate satisfaction, or as a mere pause for differentiation, like a heavier comma or displaced italics. To have an *ear* for this can only be to have a stake in a story about the nightingale and Keats."

—Cynthia Chase, from "Viewless Wings:
Keats's 'Ode to a Nightingale'" (1986)

Critical Perspective: On Keats and Symbolism

"Although the *Ode to a Nightingale* ranges more widely than the *Ode on a Grecian Urn*, the poem can also be regarded as the exploration or testing out of a symbol, and, compared with the urn as a symbol, the nightingale would seem to have both limitations and advantages. The advantage of the urn is that it does convey the notion of experience immortally prolonged, but it does not readily allow the poet to enter and share the life it portrays. He has to stand on the outside as a spectator. The nightingale, however, has a living identity and sings to the senses, thus allowing a massive sympathetic response. The liability is that unlike the urn the song of the nightingale does not suggest something potentially eternal. It is true that in his ardor the poet momentarily makes it immortal, but he does so at the cost of destroying any sympathetic union with it, and, in the logic of the poem, virtually compels it to fly away. Hence the same sympathetic grip that makes the experience vivid to the point that one would wish to prolong it, also forces the recognition that it must be short-lived.

"The dramatic development that takes place in the ode lies partly in the gradual transformation of a living nightingale into a symbol of visionary art. By means of the symbol the ode explores the consequences of a commitment to vision, and as it does so, comes close to implying that the destruction of the protagonist is one of the results. In the verse previous to the odes, Keats had occasionally associated creative activity—whether visionary or not—with death. There is nothing surprising in this. Many artists have expressed them-selves in a similar way; notions of withdrawal and self-immolation are all too readily suggested by creative enterprise. The distinction is partly that Keats makes poetry of the theme and partly that he gives it an individual bias."

—David Perkins, from "The 'Ode to a Nightingale'"

Critical Perspective: On Imagination and Reality in the Odes

"Keats was twenty-three years old when, in the spring and autumn of 1819, he wrote the five odes that many critics consider his finest achievement. He had begun serious composition little more than three years earlier, had published a first volume, *Poems* (1817), and a long narrative poem, *Endymion* (1818), in the two years preceding, and would publish only one more volume, contain-ing the odes and, as the title page has it, *Lamia, Isabella, The Eve of St. Agnes, and Other Poems* (1820), before his death in 1821 at the age of twenty-five. When it was all over, he had the shortest writing career—a span (not counting juvenile effusions) of four years, from the winter of 1815–16 to the end of 1819—of any of the major poets in English, and without question the rapidest development.

"It is a nice job to explain that development. The documents concerning the facts of his early life—the upbringing around a London livery stable, en-rollment at John Clarke's academy at Enfield, a few miles north of London, when he was seven, the death of his father and hasty remarriage of his mother when he was eight, the death of his mother when he was fourteen—contain no hint of the poet-to-be. His formal education, first at Clarke's school (1803–11), then as an apprentice to an apothecary-surgeon of Edmonton (1811–15), and finally as a medical student at Guy's Hospital, from which after a year's course he emerged in 1816 with a certificate to practice as an apothecary, was meager by the standards of the time for a man of letters. We know that he read widely, in the Latin and English poets, under Clarke's tutelage and on his own. It is not difficult, especially as we see it dramatized in *Poems* of 1817, to understand his desire to be a poet. But it borders on the impossible, once Keats has embarked on his choice, to account fully for the incredibly fast ripening in his work from the earliest imitative efforts, embarrassing in their lushness and sentimentality, to the richest products of his maturity. One can observe, at any stage in their careers, how a Ben Jonson, a Tennyson, or even a Pope *crafted* his poems. With Keats, just as with Shakespeare, one wants, even while knowing better, to invoke the mystery and magic associated with "genius" to say what lay behind the fusion of serious theme with the perfectly controlled sounds and abundance of striking images that we see in his best writing.

"One can, however, describe what Keats's poems are about, and in the description at least partially account for his peculiar excellence. He wrote on most of the standard subjects: nature, poetry, art, love, fame, and death. But in the over-all view, his significant poems center on a single basic problem, the mutability inherent in nature and human life, and openly or in disguise they debate the pros and cons of a single hypothetical solution, transcendence of earthly limitations by means of the visionary imagination. If one were to summarize the career in a sentence, it would be something like this: Keats came to learn that this kind of imagination was a false lure, inadequate to the needs of the problem, and in the end he traded it for the naturalized imagination, embracing experience and process as his own and man's chief good. His honesty in treating the problem and his final opting for the natural world, where all the concrete images of poetry come from and where melodies impinge on 'the sensual ear' or not at all, are what, more than anything else, guarantee his place 'among the English Poets.'

"What goes up must, in reality, come down. Stock notions of 'romanticism' to the contrary, the typical lyric of the English Romantic period has the structure of a literal or metaphorical excursion that can best be represented, in blackboard fashion, by the following diagram:[1]

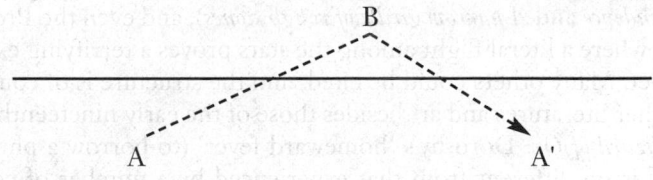

----

1. Keats himself provides a basis of sorts for this diagram in his second axiom for poetry: "the rise, the progress, the setting of imagery should like the Sun come natural [to the reader] . . . shine over him and set soberly although in magnificence leaving him in the Luxury of twilight" (to John Taylor, 27 February 1818—*The Letters of John Keats*, ed. Hyder E. Rollins, Cambridge, Mass., 1958, I, 238). Northrop Frye might seem to counter the direction of the diagram when he says that "the metaphorical structure of Romantic poetry tends to move inside and downward instead of outside and upward" ("The Drunken Boat: The Revolutionary Element in Romanticism," in *Romanticism Reconsidered*, ed. Frye, New York and London, 1963, p. 16). But his view is not fundamentally incompatible with my description here; he is in effect focusing on the descent from B to A'.

The horizontal line stands for a boundary separating the actual world (below) and the ideal (above). (The two realms have many common labels: earth and heaven, mortality and immortality, time and eternity, materiality and spirituality, the known and the unknown, the finite and the infinite, realism and romance, and so on. The ideal is represented above the line because it is, so to speak, a 'higher' reality—what is intended by the difference between 'natural' and '*super*natural.') Characteristically, the speaker in a Romantic lyric begins in the real world (A), takes off in mental flight to visit the ideal (B), and then— for a variety of reasons, but most often because he finds something wanting in the imagined ideal or because, being a native of the real world, he discovers that he does not or cannot belong permanently in the ideal—returns home to the real (A'). But he has not simply arrived back where he began (hence A' rather than A at the descent), for he has acquired something—a better understanding of a situation, a change in attitude toward it—from the experience of the flight, and he is never again quite the same person who spoke at the beginning of the poem.

"In various ways, hundreds of poems, and not all of them lyrics, may be seen to display this typical structure—to pick examples almost at random, Coleridge's *The Eolian Harp* (mental fantasies leading up to a 'what if' speculation about the organic unity of 'all of animated nature,' followed by a descent to orthodoxy at the end), *The Rime of the Ancient Mariner* (a voyage out to the unknown and subsequent journey home to the real world and society), and poems by Wordsworth as diverse as *A slumber did my spirit seal* (slumber succeeded by awakening, a return of sorts), *Tintern Abbey* (the general progress is from memory to the awareness of 'A presence . . . something far more deeply interfused,' and then back to memory), the *Intimations* ode (an imaginative excursion to childhood's 'visionary gleam' and what it intimates, followed by a return to the adult world of 'the light of common day'), all those poems in which a fancied notion is put down by a closer look (e.g., *Resolution and Independence* and *A narrow girdle of rough stones*), and even the Prologue to *Peter Bell*, where a literal flight among the stars proves a terrifying experience for the poet. Many others could be cited, and the structure is of course common to other literatures and art besides those of the early nineteenth century. In *The Wizard of Oz*, Dorothy's 'homeward fever' (to borrow a phrase from *Endymion*) is no different from that experienced by a number of cosmically displaced Romantic heroes, and the lesson she learns at the end, 'There's no place like home,' is a main point, though never in quite such plain language, of some notable poems of Keats's period."

—Jack Stillinger, from "Imagination and Reality in the Odes" (1971)

Part V
Poetry and History

28 ~ Beyond Formalism: Poetry and New Historicism

Chapters 20–27 have discussed poetry in terms of its formal components of word choice, diction, tone, imagery, figurative language, patterns of symbolism, traditions of prosody, and so on. Taken together, such formalist approaches make up the foundation for understanding what defines poetry as a literary genre. But beyond the qualities that are intrinsic to poetry, verse writing also engages with cultural discourses that are extrinsic to poetry's own forms of composition. In addition to its formalist frameworks, poetry speaks to its historical moment. A poem responds to the assumptions, beliefs, trends, and theories of its age. It is affected by the biographic circumstances of its author; a poem's meaning and significance evolves in its critical reception as it weathers the rising and falling opinions of its general and professional readers through the test of time. Poetry has a life that goes beyond its form to touch on history.

www   Dating from the 1980s, the practice of historical criticism has benefited from the developing methology of **new historicism** **Web** . This critical approach to literature was pioneered by Stephen Greenblatt, who brings social and cultural contexts to bear on Renaissance texts in such groundbreaking books as *Renaissance Self-Fashioning* (1980) and *Shakespearean Negotiations* (1988). Greenblatt's example quickly spread to other periods of English studies to become a major movement in critical reading. Unlike traditional forms of historical criticism, however, new historicism does not assume that literature simply reflects the political, religious, and intellectual trends of its era. Similarly, new historicism does not consider a story, poem, or play to be necessarily shaped by its moment in time. In contrast, new historicist critics pay close attention to how literary works enter into a dynamic dialogue with the non-literary, public discourses that make up a period's social text. For the new historicist, a literary work is not simply passive in relation to its context; it does not express only one given historical moment. Instead, new historicism investigates literature's active negotiations in shaping history through the power of the word.

To begin with, new historicism parts company with the humanist assumption that literature expresses an author's discovery of timeless, universal truths. On the contrary, new historicism argues that cultural discourses are prior to authorial genius and the humanist verities it expresses. New historicism explains how the particular languages of art, politics, religion, science, and so on actively shape how we experience history. **Ideology** is a term that defines this process of how language provides us with ways of knowing and acting in the world. "Ideology," according to the French theorist Louis Althusser, "represents the imaginary relationship of individuals to their real conditions of existence." Ideologies not only express world outlooks, they provide us with the material forms of living in it. That is, ideologies function through concrete social rituals, customs, practices of everyday life embodied in such institutions as the church, state, corporation, school system, entertainment industries, and so on. Together, such institutions shape our experience of reality through the language of several public discourses.

Through the force of language, ideologies offer us a diverse and sometimes contradictory set of roles—or subject positions—in everyday life. For example, the language system that defines one's identity and place as a Jew, Christian, Muslim, or Buddhist differs from the language that represents one's identity as, say, a national citizen, consumer, professional, family member, student, and so on. Each of the roles we play in the family, in school, in the state, in the work world, and in our religious lives is produced from particular institutional contexts whose specific discourses define regimes of knowledge and power. A rabbi, minister, or priest uses different discursive conventions and expects different responses from you than does your teacher, your boss, or your mother. The versions of knowledge and the kind of self-understandings we have of ourselves as family members differ somewhat from how we perceive ourselves at work or in school, or at the mall. Some of the roles we adopt are more empowering than others depending on our class, gender, ethnic, and racial positions. In all cases, however, the ideologies of the family, nation, religion, and workplace are sustained by discursive practices and social conventions, which are themselves constantly evolving through dynamic forces of debate, negotiation, and compromise. Moreover, contradictory and contested social forces are at play in the associations and connotations of the key words that shape our experience of the social world. For example, what defines a patriot, a pious person, a successful student, a responsible family member, and so on changes from community to community and over the course of time.

Dialogism—a key concept that new historicism takes from the twentieth-century Russian thinker Mikhail Mikhailovich Bakhtin—defines the open-ended nature of the key words through which we interpret our place in, and relation to, the social life around us.

We can see a concrete example of dialogism in William Blake's poem "London." A new historical reading of this poem does not consider only how the poet portrays the history of industrial city life in the late eighteenth century. More to the point, new historicism examines the ways in which the poem participates in shaping history by entering into dialogue with the key terms of eighteenth-century political debate.

WILLIAM BLAKE   *(1757–1827)*

London   *(1794)*

I wander thro' each charter'd street,
Near where the charter'd Thames does flow.
And mark in every face I meet
Marks of weakness, marks of woe.

In every cry of every Man,   5
In every Infant's cry of fear,
In every voice, in every ban,
The mind-forg'd manacles I hear:

How the Chimney-sweepers cry
Every blackning Church appalls,   10
And the hapless Soldiers sigh,
Runs in blood down Palace walls.

But most thro' midnight streets I hear
How the youthful Harlot's curse
Blasts the new-born Infant's tear   15
And blights with plagues the Marriage hearse.

   In the first stanza of "London," Blake points to the exploitative reality of monopoly commerce and political regulation on the city of London through the key term *charter'd*. Like "each street," the river Thames too is "charter'd." The word *charter'd*—one of the poem's key terms—has at least two metaphoric meanings in the poem. First, it alludes to the power of commerce and ownership belonging to the great chartered companies such as the East India Company, whose ships could be seen everywhere along the Thames unloading the spoils of imperial conquest from the colonies. Second, Blake's poem signifies ironically on the constitutional rhetoric of chartered rights and chartered liberties coming into being at this time. In 1793, "to charter" meant granting certain rights and privileges of political entitlement. The dialogism built into this key word stems from the era's political debate over these rights, as reflected in Thomas Paine's criticism of the new "chartered towns" in his *Rights of Man* published the previous year. Paine argued that to bestow political franchise and rights on one company, class, or corporation was to do so through the force of exclusion toward others. As a new regime of knowledge, the discourse of legal chartering empowered some Londoners over others. "It is a perversion of terms," he wrote, "to say, that a charter gives rights. It operates by a contrary effect, that of taking rights away. Rights are inherently in all the inhabitants; but charter, by annulling those rights in the majority, gave the right by exclusion in the hands of a few."
   Blake teases out the dialogic forces at work in the word *charter*. For, the

civic entitlement guaranteed to the privileged few by charter'd rights also entailed oppression for the many through the charter's powers of social exclusion. As Blake puts it in "The Human Abstract": "Pity would be no more, / If we did not make somebody Poor; / And Mercy no more could be, / If all were as happy as we." The human costs of London's completely "charter'd" environment are all too plainly seen in the metaphor of the "Marks" that everywhere disfigure the faces of the Londoners with weakness and woe. The verb *mark* describes Blake's act of noticing the signs of dehumanization around him, but it also puns on the poet's artistic activity as an engraver who would score or "mark" the plates for his illuminated manuscripts. To bear the mark of weakness and woe, however, also resonates as a dialogic word with biblical discourse. Specifically, it is an allusion to the "mark of the Beast" of the apocalypse in Revelation 8:16–17. Blake, as poet, wanders not just through the literal streets of London but also through the metaphoric avenues of an apocalyptic hell.

The confining metaphor of things, "charter'd" carries forward into the figure of the "ban"—or legal and political prohibition—that Blake hears in the "mind-forg'd manacles" of the second stanza. In an earlier version of the poem, Blake described these handcuffs as "german-forg'd manacles"—a historical allusion to the Hanoverian monarchy whose troops were expected at the time to be deployed against British dissenters. "Mind-forg'd," however, implies a more universal condition beyond this particular historical context. As a more general metaphor, the "mind-forg'd manacles" suggest how the chartered political economy of the modern city has policed and confined Londoners' abilities to think freely for themselves. The cries of exploitation that Blake hears in "every man" and "every Infant" are rendered more concrete in the poem's final two stanzas.

The chimney sweeper's cry has the metaphoric effect of "blackning" the institutions of the church again with marks of spiritual hypocrisy. Alternatively, as agent rather than object of such "blackning," the church can also be considered as figuratively blackening or having a hand in exploiting the lives of London's children. Small children were the only ones who could climb into the narrow, seven-inch smoke stacks of London's coal-driven factories. With only rags tied to their hands and knees against the scorching effects of the hot brick chimneys, they often fell to their deaths. It was not unusual for such "climbing boys"—like the one in Blake's "The Chimney Sweeper" from the *Songs of Innocence*—to be sold into apprenticeship before they could barely talk. Recognizing the lethal effects of coal soot, Parliament passed the Chimney Sweepers Act (1788) that legislated (but did not enforce) a ban on hiring out "climbing boys" under the age of eight. The other vivid metaphor of stanza three is the "sigh" of the "hapless Soldier" that—depicted through the figure of **synaesthesia** or the blending of the senses—"Runs in blood down Palace walls." Like the chimney sweeper's cry, the soldier's bloody sigh (alluding, in part, to the recent violence of the French Revolution beginning in 1789) prepares for the poem's perhaps most complex metaphors of institutional violence carried out, in this case, against women as well as children.

The cry witnessed earlier now returns in the "midnight streets" as a harlot's curse: one that, metaphorically, has the power to "blast" and "blight" new life. The prostitute, of course, is the most abject victim of London's "charter'd" social economy. The only commodity she can bargain is her own body. In her economic victimization as whore, the harlot—like the chimney sweep and soldier—is "youthful." Yet her presentation in the poem undercuts the vigor we normally assign to youth. The agricultural metaphors of "blasting" and "blighting" imply destructive natural forces—battering winds and infectious diseases—that distort and kill the organic vitality of the next generation. As a metaphor for venereal disease—a common side effect of prostitution—the "Harlot's curse" further has the power of deranging the difference between life and death by collapsing the ritual of marriage with that of the funeral, captured in the final line's arresting figure of the "marriage hearse."

Blake's poem features the force of key words whose regimes of power have material effects on particular victims of the emerging industrial order of the modern city: its chimney sweepers, soldiers, workers, homeless people, and prostitutes. The dialogism of words such as *charter'd* and *mark* suggest that the very rhetoric of civic empowerment that drives modern industry happens through a violence on society's most marginal members. That the "mind-forg'd manacles" that "Mark" London's urban working poor are the result of social rather than spiritual limitation is further illustrated, as new historicist Heather Glen has shown, in one of Blake's "ancient Proverbs" from his 1792 notebook:

> Remove away that black'ning church,
> Remove away that marriage hearse,
> Remove away that——of blood,
> You'll quite remove the ancient curse.

New historicism not only explores the relationship between poetry and the dialogism of historic key words, but it also pays special attention to the literary expression of groups that have been "marked" with political disenfranchisement. New historicism revisits the texts of women, ethnic and racial minorities, gays and lesbians, and the working classes, among others. It recovers those voices historically marginalized by the official, "charter'd" canons of cultural power. But equally important, new historicism allows us to interpret the subtle ways in which power charters verbal privilege. New historicism investigates how power shapes who has the right to speak, what one is permitted to say in a given era, and how one can say it in particular historical periods whose social and aesthetic politics differ from our own. In its attention to the contexts of a poem's formal production, new historicism moves beyond both a simple, biographical account of an author's life and a reading of a poem that is bounded by considerations of literary form. Instead, new historicism interprets literary form as it is embedded in the broader social text of its moment.

In this vein, a new historicist attention to the social context of Anne Bradstreet's place as a woman in Puritan society sheds important light on her poetic strategy of personification in "The Author to Her Book."

ANNE BRADSTREET   *(1612–1672)*

The Author to Her Book   *(1678)*

Thou ill-form'd offspring of my feeble brain,
Who after birth did'st by my side remain,
Till snatcht from thence by friends, less wise than true,
Who thee abroad expos'd to public view,
Made thee in rags, halting to th' press to trudge,
Where errors were not lessened (all may judge).
At thy return my blushing was not small,
My rambling brat (in print) should mother call;
I cast thee by as one unfit for light,
Thy Visage was so irksome in my sight,
Yet being mine own, at length affection would
Thy blemishes amend, if so I could:
I wash'd thy face, but more defects I saw,
And rubbing off a spot still made a flaw.
I stretcht thy joints to make thee even feet,
Yet still thou run'st more hobbling than is meet;
In better dress to trim thee was my mind,
But nought save home-spun cloth, i' th' house I find;
In this array, 'mongst vulgars may'st thou roam,
In critic's hands, beware thou dost not come;
And take thy way where yet thou art not known.
If for thy father asked, say, thou had'st none;
And for thy mother, she alas is poor,
Which caus'd her thus to send thee out of door.

Born in 1612, Anne Bradstreet sailed aboard the *Arbella* to America in 1630 along with other members of the Massachusetts Bay Colony, including her father Thomas Dudley and her husband Simon Bradstreet, both of whom would serve as governors of Massachusetts. In 1650, her brother-in-law took her poetry to England and arranged for its publication as a book entitled *The Tenth Muse*, most likely without Anne's prior approval. Circulating her writing in the Puritan public sphere was particularly risky for a woman in the colonies. In seventeenth-century America, women's place was mainly confined to domestic life. Indeed, Anne Bradstreet was mindful of the example of her friend Anne Hutchinson who, based on her outspoken theological views, was banished by the General Court of Boston for "traducing the ministers" and was excommunicated by the Boston Church in 1638. After settling in Pelham Bay on Long Island Sound, Anne Hutchinson and all of her servants and children save one were killed in a skirmish with Native Americans in 1643. In "The Author to Her Book," Bradstreet employs personification to criticize her own writing in a strategy of self-deprecation. That is, seeking to avoid the harsh treatment of Anne Hutchinson, Bradstreet offers an apology for her appearing in print at all. This strategy is calculated to earn her public approval, paradoxically, through disavowing her literary brainchild.

TOPICS FOR CRITICAL THINKING

1. How does Bradstreet describe her identity and faculties as writer in the poem?
2. Discuss the poet's characterization of her book. Make a list of the various ways in which she describes the book as a personified child.
3. Can you think of any recent analogies or contemporary counterparts to Bradstreet's stance in negotiating her public role in "The Author to Her Book"?

TOPIC FOR CRITICAL WRITING

What gestures does the poem make to acknowledge the force of social criticism and judgment of Bradstreet's literary offspring? Describe how personification anticipates that critical judgment.

29

Critical Perspectives

A Casebook on Poetry and Social Activism Between the Wars

The poetry of social activism **Web** that flourished between the World **www**
Wars in the United States had its seeds in the early twentieth century. Socialist poets in America took a critical stance toward global capitalism, especially during the turbulent decade of the Great Depression. In revisiting early modern socialist poetry from our point of vantage in the twenty-first century, we may find that it makes unsettling but refreshing claims on us as readers. Today, popular culture affords us fewer chances to think critically about global labor markets and class oppression. Unlike the activist culture of the early twentieth century, the contemporary scene offers fewer social alternatives to the status quo driven by fantasies of personal wealth, status, fame, and so on. Few of us would want to sacrifice our individuality to embrace "the togetherness / of bodies phalanxed in a common cause," as American poet Edwin Rolfe has it in "Credo." Nevertheless, in looking back at this period, we begin to see how the progressive poetic legacy between the World Wars remains an important forerunner of the feminist, antiwar, black, gay, and lesbian aesthetic movements that, a generation later, changed the face of contemporary American society.

In the early part of the twentieth century, the American scene was rapidly changing. By the 1910s, New York City had a population of some 5 million city dwellers, 40 percent of whom were first-generation émigrés. It was these new masses of working men and women that the young, former Columbia College student and social critic Randolph Bourne welcomed in his landmark essay "Trans-National America" (1916). Bourne's campaign for a cosmopolitan socialist culture was reinforced by the literary network of little magazines of the period such as the *Craftsman, Comrade, International Socialist Review, Coming Nation, Mother Earth,* and *New York Call.* By far, the most popular of these venues *The Masses,* was originally launched as a muckraking publication by Piet Vlag in 1911 and later edited by Max Eastman. The term *muckraker* was coined by President Theodore Roosevelt in a 1906 speech to describe the wave of novelists, writers, and investigative journalists who waged a cultural campaign against abusive labor practices, corporate monopolies, and corrupt politicians at the turn of the century. Reflecting back on this time, Eastman wrote in *The Enjoy-*

ment of Living (1948), "Our magazine provided for the first time in America a meeting ground for revolutionary *labor* and the radical intelligentsia."

The Masses offered a lively forum for the era's political journalism, manifestoes, cartoon art, poetry, fiction, and drama. But equally important, it fostered the kind of salon culture hosted in Greenwich Village parties by socialites, patrons, and cultural radicals such as Mabel Dodge, Alyse Gregory, and Gertrude Vanderbilt Whitney. At these social get-togethers, Dodge wrote, one could come upon "Socialists, Trade-Unionists, Anarchists, Suffragists, Poets, Relations, Lawyers, Murderers, 'Old Friends,' Psychoanalysts, IWWs, Single Taxers, Birth Controlists, Newspapermen, Artists, Modern-Artists, Club Women, woman's-place-is-in-the-home Women, Clergymen, and just plain men." Some of the social reform issues popularized by *The Masses* that would later become enacted into law include the income tax, women's suffrage, child labor restrictions, worker's compensation, minimum wage rates, and the eight-hour workday.

In this cultural context, poetry played an active role in portraying the plight of working-class men, women, and children, in raising public awareness of social inequities, and in imagining progressive social alternatives to the status quo. Through their visual art, cultural activists such as the suffragette illustrator Alice Beach Winter and socialist photographer Lewis Hine exposed the dire straights of the laboring poor. Winter's cover "Why Must I Work?" for the May 1912 issue of *The Masses* recalled Lewis Hine's famous 1908 portrait of a child spinner in the Whitnel Cotton Mill in North Carolina. Such arresting images exposed the scandal of the estimated 1.7 million children under sixteen who, by the end of the nineteenth century, were employed in southern mills, New England factories, and farms nationwide. Poetry, likewise, made the class tyranny of child labor an urgent and vivid issue for the general reader, as in Sarah Cleghorn's ironic and succinct lyric "Golf Links":

> The Golf Links lie so near the mill
>   That almost every day
> The laboring children can look out
>   And see the men at play.

Max Eastman, along with the black poet Claude McKay, would go on in 1918 to participate on the *Liberator*, the successor to *The Masses*. By the mid-1920s, such writers as Floyd Dell, Langston Hughes, Horace Kallen, Lola Ridge, Joseph Freeman, and Michael Gold were planning an American Proletarian Artist and Writers League that in 1926 led to a revival of *The Masses* under the title of the *New Masses*. Its contributing edi-

Alice Beach Winter, *The Masses* (May 1912).

Lewis W. Hine, *Child Laborer at the Whitnel Cotton Mill* (1908)

tors also included such major American authors as Sherwood Anderson, Stuart Davis, Waldo Frank, Carl Sandburg, Upton Sinclair, Eugene O'Neill, and Lewis Mumford, among others. Its first issues featured contributions by significant modernist writers such as William Carlos Williams, D. H. Lawrence, Babette Deutsch, John Dos Passos, and Robinson Jeffers.

Several other socialist literary magazines of the period were sponsored by the John Reed Club network in major cities such as Chicago, Cleveland, Detroit, Philadelphia, and Seattle. Named after the Harvard alumnus and hero of the Soviet Revolution, John Reed, the clubs comprised some thirty chapters with over twelve hundred members. Such JRC journals as Detroit's *The New Force*, Grand Rapids's *The Cauldron*, Indianapolis's *Midland Left*, Hollywood's *The Partisan*, Chicago's *Left Front*, Philadelphia's *Red Pen*, and New York's *Partisan Review* popularized the club's cultural activities in the fine arts, drama, film, photography, dance, music, and poetry.

Poetry of social conscience during this period responded to and commented on world and national events, often bringing writers together in joint publication ventures and group collections. "Cooperative anthologies," wrote Lucia Trent and Ralph Cheney, "are the poets' logical answer to the public's neglect to buy other anthologies." Trent's and Cheney's *America Arraigned* (1928) was one of many alternative anthologies published between the World Wars, including such titles as *An Anthology of Revolutionary Poetry* (1929), *Poems of Justice* (1929), *The Red Harvest* (1930), *We Gather Strength* (1933), *Banners of Brotherhood* (1933), and *Proletarian Literature in the United States* (1935). The growing inequities between rich and poor—which Ernest Hemingway would later depict in *To Have and Have Not* (1937)—created a receptive, mass audience for the kind of poetry of social conscience that these group anthologies collected.

During the Depression era, the New York Workers school and John Reed Clubs would provide cultural centers for aspiring socialist poets such as Edwin Rolfe. Rolfe came of age as a revolutionary poet within a cultural milieu whose internationalist scope, diversity of gender, racial, and class perspectives, and blend of high, avant-garde, and populist styles are reflected in publishing venues like the *New Masses* and the various magazines sponsored by the John Reed Clubs and other socialist organizations. Of his time studying with Michael Gold and Joseph Freeman, Rolfe has said, "Talking, lecturing, writing, they kept their ideas and convictions alive and growing when all others descended into bogs, were side tracked, or deserted. It was Joseph Freeman who finally showed some of us our real direction, our real goal. . . . 'Stop thinking of yourselves,' he said, 'as poets who are also revolutionists or revolutionists who are also poets. Remember that you are *revolutionary poets.*'" Rolfe's lyric verse would fully mature in his poetry on the Spanish Civil War where he served in the Abraham Lincoln Brigade during the latter part of the 1930s.

Drawing from the new poetic innovations and free verse techniques of imagist poetry (see Chapter 21), the early twentieth-century poetry of social protest employed a range of styles and techniques. Poets across a diverse spectrum of class, race, and regional representation composed verse ranging from traditional lyricism in fixed forms, to folk ballads, to choral and group chant recitals. These writers also took up new poetic modes gleaned from the examples of the experimental modernists, the imagists, international surrealism, Zurich Dada, and Russian Constructivism. Kenneth Fearing, for example, learned from high modernists such as T. S. Eliot and James Joyce the technique of using references to popular culture, advertising slogans, and newspaper headlines in textual collage formats that resembled the use of found urban objects in the cubofuturist art work of Pablo Picasso and Georges Braques. Fearing, however, more than Eliot, used popular references for pointedly comic critiques of American consumer society during the Depression years, as in his poem "Dirge." Fantasies of success, luxury, and prosperity in Fearing's poetry circulate through a contrived environment of radios, magazines, brokerage houses, dance halls, theaters—all of which are wholly rigged for making a quick buck. In such a setting, one's full social being is constantly deferred and dispersed across a network of alienating subject positions of collectors, salespeople, movie queens, and magnates.

Similarly, Langston Hughes criticized the spectacle of modern consumer values by using poetic forms drawing from the vernacular forms of African American expressive culture: blues lyricism, black sermon, spirituals, and folk ballads. Several of his poetic personae capture the voices of ordinary, everyday black folk, as in "Elevator Boy." While Hughes pointed to the ways in which race mattered in the poetry of class oppression, Tillie Olsen, Genevieve Taggard, and Muriel Rukeyser exposed the role gender played in the exploitative labor market of the Depression era, as in "I Want You Women Up North to Know" and "Mill Town."

Poems for Further Reading and Critical Writing

KENNETH FEARING   *(1902–1961)*

Dirge   *(1934)*

1-2-3 was the number he played but today the number came
    3-2-1;
  bought his Carbide° at 30 and it went to 29; had the
    favorite at Bowie but the track was slow—

O executive type, would you like to drive a floating power,   5
    knee-action, silk-upholstered six? Wed a Hollywood
    star? Shoot the course in 58? Draw to the ace,
    king, jack?
  O fellow with a will who won't take no, watch out for
    three cigarettes on the same, single match; O,   10
    democratic voter born in August under Mars,
    beware of liquidated rails—

Denoument to denoument, he took a personal pride in the
    certain, certain way he lived his own, private life,
  But nevertheless, they shut off his gas; nevertheless, the   15
    bank foreclosed; nevertheless, the landlord called;
    nevertheless, the radio broke,

And twelve o'clock arrived just once too often,
Just the same he wore one grey tweed suit, bought one
    straw hat, drank one straight Scotch, walked one   20
    short step, took one long look, drew one deep
    breath,
Just one too many,

And wow he died as wow he lived,
Going whop to the office and blooie home to sleep and   25
    biff got married and bam had children and oof got
    fired,
Zowie did he live and zowie did he die,

With who the hell are you at the corner of his casket, and
    where the hell're we going on the right-hand silver   30
    knob, and who the hell cares walking second from

---

3 *Carbide:* Refers to shares of stock in Union Carbide Corporation, which has merged with Dow
Chemical Company.

the end with an American Beauty wreath from why
the hell not,

Very much missed by the circulation staff of the New York
Evening Post; deeply, deeply mourned by the   35
B.M.T.,°

Wham, Mr. Roosevelt; pow, Sears Roebuck; awk, big
dipper; bop, summer rain;
Bong, Mr., bong, Mr., bong, Mr., bong.

$2.50   (1934)

But that dashing, dauntless, delphic, diehard, diabolic
cracker likes his fiction turned with a certain elegance
and wit; and that anti-anti-anti slum-congestion
clublady prefers romance;
search through the mothballs, comb the lavender and   5
lace,
were her desires and struggles futile or did an innate
fineness bring him at last to a prouder, richer peace
in a world gone somehow mad?

We want one more compelling novel, Mr. Filbert Sopkins   10
Jones,
all about it, all about it,
with signed testimonials to its stark, human, while-u-
wait, iced-or-heated, taste-that-sunshine tenderness
and truth;   15
one more comedy of manners, Sir Warwick Aldous
Wells, involving three blond souls; tried in the
crucible of war, Countess Olga out-of-limbo by
Hearst through the steerage peerage,
glamorous, gripping, moving, try it, send for a 5 cent,   20
10 cent sample, restores faith to the flophouse,
workhouse, warehouse, whorehouse, bughouse life
of man,
just one more long poem that sings a more heroic age,
baby Edwin, 58,   25

But the faith is all gone,
and all the courage is gone, used up, devoured on the
first morning of a home relief menu,
you'll have to borrow it from the picket killed last
Tuesday on the fancy knitgoods line;   30

---

36 *B.M.T.*: Brooklyn-Manhattan Transit Corporation; a New York Subway line.

and the glamor, the ice for the cocktails, the shy appeal,
    the favors for the subdeb ball? O.K.,
O.K.,
but they smell of exports to the cannibals,
reek of something blown away from the muzzle of a   35
    twenty inch gun;

Lady, the demand is for a dream that lives and grows and
    does not fade when the midnight theater special
    pulls out on track 15;
cracker, the demand is for a dream that stands and   40
    quickens and does not crumble when a General
    Motors dividend is passed;
lady, the demand is for a dream that lives and grows
    and does not die when the national guardsmen fix
    those cold, bright bayonets;   45
cracker, the demand is for a dream that stays, grows
    real, withstands the benign, afternoon vision of the
    clublady, survives the cracker's evening fantasy of
    honor, and profit, and grace.

X Minus X   *(1935)*

Even when your friend, the radio, is still; even when her dream,
    the magazine, is finished; even when his life, the ticker, is
    silent; even when their destiny, the boulevard, is bare;
And after that paradise, the dance-hall, is closed; after that
    theater, the clinic, is dark,   5

Still there will be your desire, and hers, and his hopes and theirs,
Your laughter, their laughter,
Your curse and his curse, her reward and their reward, their
    dismay and his dismay and her dismay and yours—

Even when your enemy, the collector, is dead; even when your   10
    counsellor, the salesman, is sleeping; even when your
    sweetheart, the movie queen, has spoken; even when your
    friend, the magnate, is gone.

Langston Hughes   *(1902–1967)*

Goodbye Christ   *(1932)*

Listen, Christ,
You did alright in your day, I reckon—
But that day's gone now.

They ghosted you up a swell story, too,
Called it Bible—
But it's dead now,
The popes and the preachers've   5
Made too much money from it.
They've sold you to too many

Kings, generals, robbers, and killers—   10
Even to the Tzar and the Cossacks,
Even to Rockefeller's Church,
Even to THE SATURDAY EVENING POST.
You ain't no good no more.
They've pawned you   15
Till you've done wore out.

Goodbye,
Christ Jesus Lord God Jehova,
Beat it on away from here now.
Make way for a new guy with no religion at all—   20
A real guy named
Marx Communist Lenin Peasant Stalin Worker ME—

I said, ME!

Go ahead on now,
You're getting in the way of things, Lord.   25
And please take Saint Gandhi with you when you go,
And Saint Pope Pius,
And Saint Aimee McPherson,
And big black Saint Becton
Of the Consecrated Dime.   30
And step on the gas, Christ!
Move!

Don't be so slow about movin'!
The world is mine from now on—
And nobody's gonna sell ME   35
To a king, or a general,
Or a millionaire.

Johannesburg Mines   *(1928)*

In the Johannesburg mines
There are 240,000 natives working.

What kind of poem
Would you make out of that?

240,000 natives working   5
In the Johannesburg mines.

Elevator Boy   *(1926)*

I got a job now
Runnin' an elevator
In the Dennison Hotel in Jersey.
Job ain't no good though.
No money around.   5
    Jobs are just chances
    Like everything else.
    Maybe a little luck now,
    Maybe not.
    Maybe a good job sometimes: 10
    Step out o' the barrel, boy.
Two new suits an'
A woman to sleep with.
    Maybe no luck for a long time.
    Only the elevators   15
    Goin' up an' down,
    Up an' down,
    Or somebody else's shoes
    To shine,
    Or greasy pots in a dirty kitchen.   20
I been runnin' this
Elevator too long.
Guess I'll quit now.

ALFRED HAYES   *(1911–1985)*

In a Coffee Pot   *(1934)*

Tonight, like every night, you see me here
Drinking my coffee slowly, absorbed, alone.
A quiet creature at a table in the rear
Familiar at this evening hour and quite unknown.
The coffee steams. The Greek who runs the joint   5
Leans on the counter, sucks a dead cigar.
His eyes are meditative, sad, lost in what it is
Greeks think about the kind of Greeks they are.

I brood upon myself. I rot
Night after night in this cheap coffee pot.   10
I am twenty-two I shave each day

I was educated at a public school
They taught me what to read and what to say
The nobility of man my country's pride
How Nathan Hale died   15
And Grant took Richmond.
Was it on a summer or a winter's day?
Was it Sherman burned the Southland to the sea?
The men the names the dates have worn away
The classes words the books commencement prize   20
Here bitter with myself I sit
Holding the ashes of their prompted lies.

The bright boys, where are they now?
Fernando, handsome wop who led us all
The orator in the assembly hall   25
Arista man the school's big brain.
He's bus boy in an eat-quick joint
At seven per week twelve hours a day.
His eyes are filled with my own pain
His life like mine is thrown away.   30
Big Jorgensen the honest, blond, six feet,
And Daniels, cunning, sly,—all, all—
You'll find them reading Sunday's want ad sheet.
Our old man didnt know someone
Our mother gave no social teas   35
You'll find us any morning now
Sitting in the agencies.

You'll find us there before the office opens
Crowding the vestibule before the day begins
The secretary yawns from last night's date   40
The elevator boy's black face looks out and grins.
We push we crack our bitter jokes we wait
These mornings always find us waiting there
Each one of us has shined his broken shoes
Has brushed his coat and combed his careful hair   45
Dance hall boys pool parlor kids wise guys
The earnest son the college grad all, all
Each hides the question twitching in his eyes
And smokes and spits and leans against the wall.

We meet each other sometimes on the street   50
Sixth Avenue's high L bursts overhead
Freak shows whore gypsies hotdog stands
Cajole our penniless eyes our bankrupt hands.
"Working yet?" "The job aint come
Got promised but a runaround."   55

The L shakes building store and ground
"What's become of Harry? and what's become
Of Charley? Martinelli? Brooklyn Jones?"
"He's married—got a kid—and broke."
And Charley's on Blackwell's, Martinelli's through—   60
Met him in Grand Central—he's on the bum—
We're all of us on the bum—
A freak show midget's pounding on a drum
The high L thunders redflag auctioneers
Are selling out a bankrupt world—   65
The hammer falls—a bid! a bid!—and no one hears . . .

The afternoon will see us in the park
With pigeons and our feet in peanut shells.
We pick a bench apart. We brood.

TILLIE OLSEN   *(b. 1913?)*

I Want You Women Up North to Know   *(1934)*

(Based on a Letter by Felipe Ibarro in New Masses, *Jan. 9th, 1934.)*

i want you women up north to know
how those dainty children's dresses you buy
    at macy's, wanamakers, gimbels, marshall fields,
are dyed in blood, are stitched in wasting flesh,
down in San Antonio, "where sunshine spends the winter."   5

I want you women up north to see
the obsequious smile, the salesladies trill
    "exquisite work, madame, exquisite pleats"
vanish into a bloated face, ordering more dresses,
    gouging the wages down,   10
dissolve into maria, ambrosa, catalina,
    stitching these dresses from dawn to night,
    in blood, in wasting flesh.

Catalina Rodriguez, 24,
    body shrivelled to a child's at twelve,   15
catalina rodriguez, last stages of consumption,
    works for three dollars a week from dawn to midnight.
A fog of pain thickens over her skull, the parching heat
    breaks over her body.
and the bright red blood embroiders the floor of her room.   20
    White rain stitching the night, the bourgeois poet would say,

white gulls of hands, darting, veering,
white lightning, threading the clouds,
this is the exquisite dance of her hands over the cloth,
and her cough, gay, quick, staccato,   25
like skeleton's bones clattering,
is appropriate accompaniment for the esthetic dance
of her fingers,
and the tremolo, tremolo when the hands tremble with pain.
Three dollars a week,   30
two fifty-five,
seventy cents a week,
no wonder two thousands eight hundred ladies of joy
are spending the winter with the sun after he goes down—
for five cents (who said this was a rich man's world?) you can   35
get all the lovin you want
"clap and syph aint much worse than sore fingers, blind eyes, and
t.m."

Maria Vasquez, spinster,
for fifteen cents a dozen stitches garments for children she has   40
never had,
Catalina Torres, mother of four,
to keep the starved body starving, embroiders from dawn to
night.
Mother of four, what does she think of,   45
as the needle pocked fingers shift over the silk—
of the stubble-coarse rags that stretch on her own brood,
and jut with the bony ridge that marks hunger's landscape
of fat little prairie-roll bodies that will bulge in the
silk she needles?   50
(Be not envious, Catalina Torres, look!
on your own children's clothing, embroidery,
more intricate than any a thousand hands could fashion,
there where the cloth is ravelled, or darned,
designs, multitudinous, complex and handmade by Poverty   55
herself.)

Ambrosa Espinoza trusts in god,
"Todos es de dios, everything is from god,"
through the dwindling night, the waxing day, she bolsters herself
up with it—   60
but the pennies to keep god incarnate, from ambrosa,
and the pennies to keep the priest in wine, from ambrosa,
ambrosa clothes god and priest with hand-made children's dresses.

Her bother lies on an iron cot, all day and watches,
on a mattress of rags he lies.   65
For twenty-five years he worked for the railroad, then they laid him off.

(racked days, searching for work; rebuffs; suspicious eyes of
    policemen.)
goodbye ambrosa, mebbe in dallas I find work; desperate swing
    for a freight,
surprised hands, clutching air, and the wheel goes over a   70
    leg,
the railroad cuts it off, as it cut off twenty-five years of his life.)
She says that he prays and dreams of another world, as he lies
    there, a heaven (which he does not know was brought to earth
    in 1917 in Russia, by workers like him).   75

Women up north, I want you to know
when you finger the exquisite hand made dresses
what it means, this working from dawn to midnight,
on what strange feet the feverish dawn must come
    to maria, catalina, ambrosa,   80
how the malignant fingers twitching over the pallid faces jerk them
    to work,
and the sun and the fever mounts with the day—
    long plodding hours, the eyes burn like coals, heat jellies the
        flying fingers,
down comes the night like blindness.
    long hours more with the dim eye of the lamp, the breaking   85
        back,
    weariness crawls in the flesh like worms, gigantic like earth's in
        winter.
And for Catalina Rodriguez comes the night sweat and the blood
    embroidering the darkness.
    for Catalina Torres the pinched faces of four huddled
    children,   90
    the naked bodies of four bony children,
    the chant of their chorale of hunger.
And for twenty eight hundred ladies of joy the grotesque act gone
    over—
    the wink—the grimace—the "feeling like it baby?"
And for Maria Vasquez, spinster, emptiness, emptiness.   95
    flaming with dresses for children she can never fondle.
And for Ambrosa Espinoza—the skeleton body of her brother on
    his mattress
of rags, boring twin holes in the dark with his eyes to the image of
    christ
remembering a leg, and twenty-five years cut off from his life by
    the railroad.

Women up north, I want you to know,   100
I tell you this can't last forever.

I swear it won't.

GENEVIEVE TAGGARD   *(1894–1948)*

Mill Town   *(1936)*

(Dedicated to Paul de Kruif)

> *. . . the child died, the investigator said, for lack of*
> *proper food. After the funeral the mother went back to*
> *the mill. She is expecting another child . . .*

    . . . then fold up without pause
The colored ginghams and the underclothes.
      And from the stale
Depth of the dresser, smelling of medicine, take
The first year's garments. And by this act prepare   5
Your store of pain, your weariness, dull love,
To bear another child with doubled fists
And sucking face.

      Clearly it is best, mill-mother,
Not to rebel or ask clear silly questions,   10
Saying womb is sick of its work with death,
Your body drugged with work and the repeated bitter
Gall of your morning vomit. Never try
Asking if we should blame you. Live in fear. And put
Soap on the yellowed blankets. Rub them pure.

EDWIN ROLFE   *(1909–1954)*

Credo   *(1931)*

To welcome multitudes—the miracle of deeds
performed in unison—the mind
must first renounce the fiction of the self
and its vainglory. It must pierce
the dreamplate of its solitude, the fallacy   5
of its omnipotence, the fairytale
aprilfools recurring every day
in speeches of professors and politicians.

It must learn
the wisdom and the strength and the togetherness 10
of bodies phalanxed in a common cause,
of fists tight-clenched around a crimson banner
flying in the wind above a final, fierce
life-and-death fight against a common foe.

Emerging then, the withered land will grow   15
—purged—in a new florescence; only then,
cleansed of all chaos, a race of men may know
abundance, life, fecundity.

Asbestos   *(1928)*

Knowing (as John did) nothing of the way
men act when men are roused from lethargy,
and having nothing (as John had) to say
to those he saw were starving just as he

starved, John was like a workhorse. Day by day   5
he saw his sweat cement the granite tower
(the edifice his bone had built), to stay
listless as ever, older every hour.

John's deathbed is a curious affair:
the posts are made of bone, the spring of nerves,   10
the mattress bleeding flesh. Infinite air,
compressed from dizzy altitudes, now serves

his skullface as a pillow. Overhead
a vulture leers in solemn mockery,
knowing what John had never known: that dead   15
workers are dead before they cease to be.

Not Men Alone   *(1935)*

What, you have never seen a lifeless thing flower,
revive, a new adrenaline in its veins?
Come, I shall show you: not men alone
nor women, but cities also are reborn;
not without labor, not before the hour   5
when flesh feels lacerated, mangled, torn.

Not only men are resurrected. I have seen
dull cities bloom, grow meaningful
overnight. Wherever class war comes
awareness is its courier, a newer life,   10
new depths in shallow, parallel streets
which may revert to commonplace, but never
relinquish scenes that have occurred on them.

Toledo's such a city. I remember
its dullness, how I always skirted   15
its edges on long trips west. Returning east,

I chose roads miles to the north or south
to escape its barrenness; the mind went dead,
the muscles flagged, in passing it.

Then the strike flared: the workers met   20
and merged at factories. The unions called
Down tools! and the militiamen
sped to the scene of combat. When the smoke
rose with the wind, a hundred men were maimed
but thousands more, the first time in their lives   25
were conscious of their needs, their role, their destiny.

I passed through Toledo yesterday.
The usual quiet prevailed, but from the eyes
of men and houses a newer spirit flamed.
The deadness I had felt before remained   30
but it was make-up only, mere disguise
for men aroused, a city awakened,
awaiting the propitious, inevitable day.

MURIEL RUKEYSER   *(1913–1980)*

The Minotaur   *(1944)*

Trapped, blinded, led; and in the end betrayed
Daily by new betrayals as he stays
Deep in his labyrinth, shaking and going mad.
Betrayed.   Betrayed.   Raving, the beaten head
Heavy with madness, he stands, half-dead and proud.   5
No one again will ever see his pride.
No one will find him by walking to him straight
But must be led circuitously about,
Calling to him and close and, losing the subtle thread,
Lose him again; while he waits, brutalized   10
By loneliness.   Later, afraid
Of his own suffering.   At last, savage and made
Ravenous, ready to prey upon the race
If it so much as learn the clews of blood
Into his pride his fear his glistening heart.   15
Now is the patient deserted in his fright
And love carrying salvage round the world
Lost in a crooked city; roundabout,
By the sea, the precipice, all the fantastic ways
Betrayal weaves its trap; loneliness knows the thread,   20

And the heart is lost, lost, trapped, blinded and led,
Deserted at the middle of the maze.

Joseph Kalar   *(1906–1972)*

Papermill   *(1931)*

Not to be believed, this blunt savage wind
Blowing in chill empty rooms, this tornado
Surging and bellying across the oily floor
Pushing men out in streams before it;
Not to be believed, this dry fall   5
Of unseen fog drying the oil
And emptying the jiggling greasecups;
Not to be believed, this unseen hand
Weaving a filmy rust of spiderwebs
Over these turbines and grinding gears,   10
These snarling chippers and pounding jordans;°
These fingers placed to lips saying shshsh;
Keep silent, keep silent, keep silent;
Not to be believed hardly, this clammy silence
Where once feet stamped over the oily floor,   15
Dinnerpails clattered, voices rose and fell
In laughter, curses, and songs. Now the guts
Of this mill have ceased their rumbling, now
The fires are banked and red changes to black,
Steam is cold water, silence is rust, and quiet   20
Spells hunger. Look at these men, now,
Standing before the iron gates, mumbling,
"Who could believe it? Who could believe it?"

Worker Uprooted   *(1935)*

The slow sleepy curl of cigaret smoke and butts
glowing redly out of moving smiling mouths;
now a whisper in the house, laughter muted,
and warm words spoken no more to me.
Alien, I move forlorn among curses,   5
laughing falsely, joking with tears
aching at my eyes, now surely alien and lonely.
Once I rubbed shoulders with sweating men,
pulled when they pulled, strained, cursed,

---

11 *jordans:* Papermill machinery.

comrade in their laughter,   10
comrade in their pain,
knowing fellowship of sudden smiles
and the press of hands in silent speech.
At noon hour, sprawled in the shade,
opening our lunches, chewing our sandwiches,   15
laughing and spitting,
we talked of the days and found joy
in our anger, balm in our common contempt;
thought of lumber falling with thump of lead
on piles geometrically exact; of horses   20
sweating, puffing, bulging their terrible muscles;
of wagons creaking; of sawdust
pouring from the guts of the mill.
Now alien, I move forlorn, an uprooted tree,
feel the pain of hostile eyes   25
lighting up no more for me;
the forced silence, the awkward laugh,
comrade no more in laughter and pain.

And at dawn, irresolutely,
into the void . . .   30

Critical Perspective: On Countée Cullen's "Incident"

"As one begins to reread both poets now classed as minor and poets essentially written out of the story of modern literature, one discovers, for example,
that traditional forms continued to do vital cultural work throughout this period. Far from being preeminently genteel, poetry in traditional forms was a
frequent vehicle for sharply focused social commentary. Poets were thus often
quite successful at making concise, paradigmatic statements about social life.
Freed from the need to provide extended analysis or support a thesis with detailed evidence, poetry instead could highlight both the most basic structures
of oppression in the culture and the fundamental principles that positive
change should observe. Countée Cullen's (1903–1946) 'Incident' (1925) [see
p. 1200]—a widely known poem by a poet generally viewed as relatively minor because of his preference for traditional forms—describes a black child's
encounter with a Maryland resident:

> Now I was eight and very small,
>   And he was no whit bigger,
> And so I smiled, but he poked out
>   His tongue, and called me, 'Nigger.'
>
> I saw the whole of Baltimore
>   From May until December;
> Of all the things that happened there
>   That's all that I remember.

"'Incident' hardly says all there is to say about race relations in America, but it does point with notable economy to its continuing human cost. The violation of this childlike form by the word 'Nigger' is more disturbing and effective than its appearance in a modernist collage would be. Moreover, the very innocence of the form makes the poem's pathos a productively self-conscious burden for contemporary readers."

—Cary Nelson, from *Repression and Recovery* (1989)

Critical Perspective: On Depression Era Culture

"In Gregory La Cava's 1936 film, *My Man Godfrey*, the 'forgotten man,' loitering among his fellow trash pickers on the dump, is whisked away to become a butler for a society family; when hardship threatens them too, the butler (who is actually one of the wealthy Parkeses of Boston) saves the day by turning the dump into a nightclub called, *mirabile dictu*, 'The Dump.' Thus garbage becomes classy decor, and the erstwile trash pickers become costumed waiters—actors of sorts in a profitable theme park based on their former 'lifestyle.' This entrepreneurial solution to economic hardship would seem to smack of the wishful thinking of the Reagan years, but the film's juxtaposed ingredients of wealth, poverty, and entertaining spectacle are, in fact, observable everywhere in the culture of the Depression decade. There is perhaps a temptation, looking back as we do, to think of what Alfred Kazin has called the 'lean and angry Thirties' as the last decade of the real America: a time when politics was politics, and Reds were Reds, when strikes were actually radical, when the faces of sharecroppers bespoke some kind of authenticity; a time before class disappeared, before intellectuals became professors, before culture retreated to the museums, before the shopping malls were built, and before the dump became a nightclub. But it is also possible to argue, as Jean Baudrillard does in *The Mirror of Production*, that the stock market crash of 1929 marked the birth of our present social formation, of a culture that theorists have characterized by various and much-disputed terms like the 'society of the spectacle,' the 'culture of abundance,' 'postindustrial' or 'postmodern' society, and 'late capitalism.'

—Rita Barnard, from *The Great Depression and the Culture of Abundance* (1995)

TOPICS FOR CRITICAL THINKING

1. Discuss the sources of Fearing's ironic humor in portraying the American everyman of "Dirge."

2. Consider Fearing's depictions of the fantasies of luxury, romance, and status that drive consumer society in "$2.50" and "X Minus X." What alternative dream does "$2.50" allude to in its closing stanza?

3. Compare Hughes's portrait of the "Elevator Boy" to the dramatic persona that Hayes depicts in "In a Coffee Pot."

4. Discuss the ways in which Rolfe's "Credo" poses a solution to the kind of industrial victimization offered in "Asbestos." Compare and contrast Rolfe's poetic techniques and rhetorical strategies in the two poems.

5. In what ways does Kalar rely on the power of sharply beheld images to defamiliar-ize the modern settings of industry when they are shut down in his Depression-era poem "Papermill"?

6. Contrast the rhetoric of Taggard's "Mill Town" with her address to the mill town mother in the poem. How does the latter's cleaning the blankets serve as a symbolic act in the poem's closing lines?

TOPICS FOR CRITICAL WRITING

1. Discuss the ways in which class, ethnic, and regional differences lead women to dis-criminate against other women in Olsen's "I Want You Women Up North to Know." How does Olsen's address position the reader in the role of privileged con-sumer? What is it that Olsen wants northern women to know and understand?

2. Examine how Olsen's critique of the fashion industry parallels her rejection of the aesthetic conceits of "the bourgeois poet" (line 21). How do both obscure the real-istic details of women's oppression, according to Olsen?

3. Examine Rukeyser's figure of the Minotaur as a symbol for the violence of modern twentieth-century history.

Critical Perspectives

A Casebook on Poetry, Trauma, and Testimony: Holocaust Verses

The term *holocaust* [Web] derives from the Greek root *holokaustos*, *www* which combines *holos*, "whole," and *kaustos*, "burnt," to denote a burning of the whole. The notions of a burnt sacrifice and martyrdom through burning have wide currency in biblical literature. Since early modern times, *holocaust* has also come to signify mass murder. In the twentieth century, the capitalized usage of *Holocaust* refers specifically to the genocide of the Jews perpetrated by the German Nazis during 1939–1945. This modern-day genocide has also been referred to as the *Shoah*, meaning "catastrophe." A third term, also meaning "catastrophe" is *Churban*, but this word joins the Nazi genocide to historic precedents of disaster for the Jews in *Churban Bayis Rishon*, the destruction of the First Temple in 586 B.C., and *Churban Bayis Sheni*, the destruction of the Second Temple by the Romans in A.D. 70. Furthermore, the notion of a *Churban* is tied to a historical pattern of *Churban-Golus-Geulah:* destruction followed by exile and redemption.

The term *Holocaust*, then, conveys the idea of a unique, all-consuming disaster: an event without historical precedent. The fact of genocide, of course, is not what makes the Holocaust unique. The wholesale destruction of Native Americans during the colonization of the Americas and the massacre of the Armenians in the Ottoman Empire are two precursors to the genocide of World War II. Contemporary genocides in Cambodia and Rwanda, as well as more recent, so-called ethnic cleansings in former Yugoslavia, perpetuate early-modern precedents of mass murder. Nevertheless, the Holocaust stands out as a unique event in world history. While involving Communists, gypsies, homosexuals, the disabled, and so on, the Nazis' Final Solution was conceived first and foremost with the idea of exterminating every single Jew on the planet. "The uniqueness lies," according to Holocaust scholar Yehuda Bauer in "Lessons of the Holocaust," not in the numbers or technology of modern genocide but "in the motivation of the perpetrator. Who was the Jew in the eye of the Nazis? Why the destruction? The destruction came because the Jew was viewed as a Satanic element in human society. As an extra-human on earth." The noted Jewish philosopher and theologian Emil Fackenheim describes the Holocaust as a unique event or *novum* in human history, one whose legacy commands remembrance. "We are commanded," he writes, "to remember in our very guts and bones the martyrs of the holocaust, lest their memory perish."

The ethics of commemoration is also a central concern of Auschwitz survivor Primo Levi. He addresses the reader with the force of that commitment in his poem "Shemá," whose title is based on the Jewish prayer: "Hear [Shemá] O Israel, the Lord our God the Lord is One" (Deuteronomy 6:4–9; 11:13–21). "You who live secure," he writes, "in your warm houses":

> Consider that this has been:
> I commend these words to you.
> Engrave them on your hearts
> When you are in your house, when you walk on your way,
> When you go to bed, when you rise.
> Repeat them to your children.
> Or may your house crumble,
> Disease render you powerless,
> Your offspring avert their faces from you.

Forgetting the past, of course, risks its repetition in the future. Yet, as we shall see, understanding the world historical trauma of the Holocaust poses both intellectual and psychological difficulties. The archive of political, philosophical, psychoanalytic, literary, legal, and theological discussions of the Holocaust is only a half century in the making, yet it is already vast. Time does not allow us to address here the complexity of intellectual witness to the Holocaust. A basic timeline, however, would include the following events.

1933

- Hitler becomes Chancellor of Germany.
- Civil Service Law denies government employment to Jews.
- Public book burnings are staged.
- Dachau concentration camp is established.
- Nazi party is declared the only political party in Germany.

1934

- Hitler assumes the titles of both President and Chancellor after the death of Paul von Hindenberg.

1935

- Nuremberg Race Laws deny German Jews of citizenship, military service, and political rights. Marriage and sexual relations between Jews and non-Jews are prohibited. Nazis define a Jew as anyone with three Jewish grandparents or who belonged to the Jewish community and had two Jewish grandparents. Those with any trace of Jewish blood are termed Mischling or "hybrid."

1936

- Olympic Games are held in Nazi Germany.
- Germany and Italy sign the Rome–Berlin Axis agreement.
- Sachsenhausen concentration camp opens.

1937

- Germany and Japan sign an international pact.
- Gypsies are defined as "inveterate criminals."

1938

- Germany annexes Austria.
- Buchenwald, Mauthausen and Flossenburg concentration camps open.
- Evian Conference brings together thirty-two countries to review Jewish immigration issues.
- Adolph Eichmann heads up the Central Office for Jewish Emigration in Vienna.
- Pogrom of Kristallnacht ("crystal night" or the "night of broken glass") is carried out after the assassination of an official in the Paris–German embassy. Germans kill ninety-six Jews; one thousand synagogues are destroyed; seven thousand Jewish businesses are looted; and thirty thousand Jews are arrested.

1939

- Ravensbrück and Stutthoff concentration camps open.
- Hitler and Stalin sign Nazi–Soviet Non-Aggression Pact.
- Hitler invades Poland.
- Ghettos are sealed off in occupied Poland beginning with Piotrkow Trybunalski.
- Jews required to wear the Star of David.
- Nazis destroy Jewish synagogues of Lotz.

1940

- Germany wages war on Denmark, Norway, Belgium, the Netherlands, Luxembourg, France, and England.
- Auschwitz concentration camp is established.
- Warsaw ghetto is sealed.

1941

- Germany occupies Yugoslavia and Greece and invades the Soviet Union.
- Hermann Göring appoints Reinhard Heydrich to administer the Final Solution.
- Three thousand units of the Einsatzgruppen begin the "special task" of exterminating what would amount by 1943 to 1.25 million Eastern European and Soviet Jews.
- Thirty-three thousand Jews are mass murdered outside Kiev at Babii Yar.
- Extermination camps at Birkenau, Auschwitz II, and Chelmno are constructed.
- Nazis put gas vans into operation at Chelmno.

1942

- Dutch Jews are slated for concentration and deportation.
- Heydrich unveils extermination plan at the Wannsee Conference.
- Belzec, Sobibor, and Treblinka extermination camps begin operation.

- Jewish partisans in Byelorussia and the Baltic States resist the Nazis while Jews mount challenges in Poland; Jews mount armed resistance in ghettos of Kletzk, Kremenets, Lachva, Mir, and Tuchin.
- Jewish Fighting Organization (ZOB) undertakes resistance in Warsaw.
- Jews are deported to the killing centers from Belgium, Croatia, France, the Netherlands, Poland, Germany, Greece, and Norway.

1943

- German Sixth Army is defeated at Stalingrad.
- Kraków Ghetto is liquidated.
- Jewish community mounts Warsaw Ghetto revolt.
- Reichsfuehrer-SS Heinrich Himmler oversees the liquidation of ghettos in Poland and the Soviet Union.
- Jewish resistance fighters stage revolts in Bedzin, Bialystok, Czestochowa, Lvov, and Tarnów ghettos as well as at Sobibor.
- In an attempt to destroy the evidence of genocide, Germans exhume and burn bodies of Jewish victims of Babii Yar using a special work unit of Jewish prisoners, the Sonderkommando, who are themselves in turn executed.

1944

- Germany occupies Hungary and begins deportation of Hungarian Jews.
- Allies invade Normandy on D-Day.
- Senior German officers fail in assassination attempt against Hitler.
- Russian troops liberate Majdanek extermination camp.
- Sonderkommando concentration camp inmates destroy one crematorium at Auschwitz.

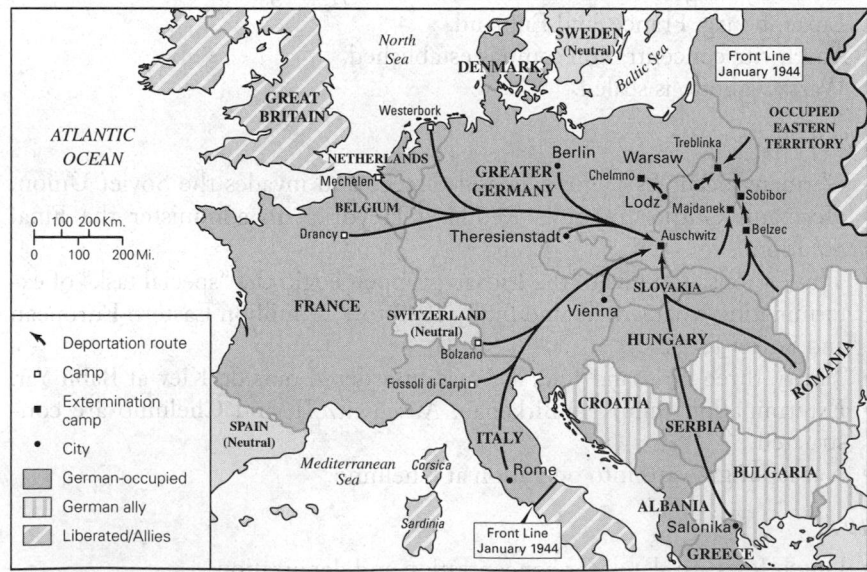

Major deportations to extermination camps, 1942–1944

1945

- Death marches of deported Jews begin from Budapest to Austria and from the evacuation of Auschwitz, Stutthof, and Buchenwald.
- Hitler withdraws to bunker under the garden of the old chancellery ("Alte Reichskanzlei").
- Hitler marries his lover Eva Braun, and the two commit suicide in the bunker.
- In the bunker, Propaganda Minister Joseph Goebbels and his wife commit suicide after killing their six children.
- Germany surrenders on VE-Day.

Knowing the history of the Holocaust in detail is important, but it is quite another thing to wrestle with the issue of how it could have happened. In approaching the *novum* of the Holocaust, the question of how we are to come to terms with its extremity has no satisfactory answer. However urgently we may take Primo Levi's command to "Consider that this has been," the fact of the Holocaust confounds any attempt to explain it. Theological discussion, as for example in Arthur Cohen's definition of the "tremendum," relies on the figure of the abyss to mark the unique difference between the Holocaust and human understanding. "As abyss," Cohen writes in *The Tremendum: A Theological Interpretation of the Holocaust* (1981), "the tremendum transforms everything that went before into distance and remoteness, as though an earthquake had overturned the center of a world, obliterating mountains that had once been near at hand and that we had formerly dreamt of scaling." Acknowledging the significance of the Holocaust in human history begins with silence. The final solution leads to silence because, according to George Steiner, its violence "lies outside speech as it lies outside reason."

On the other hand, focusing on uniqueness for its own sake, according to Fackenheim, risks "taking the event out of history and thus mystifying it." Such historical silence, as André Neher reminds us, characterized the passive response of the Allied powers and reached all the way to the absent "silence of God" toward the plight of European Jewry. "At Auschwitz," Neher writes in his essay "The Silence of Auschwitz," "everything unfolded, was fulfilled and accomplished for weeks, months, and years on end in absolute silence, away from and out of the mainstream of history." The persistence of such silence lasted well after the war in the difficulty many survivors had in communicating what they had experienced. Silence in the cross-generational repression of the Holocaust is also a special feature of postwar German perpetrator culture examined by Holocaust scholars Dan Bar-On, Barbara Heimannsberg, and Christoph J. Schmidt, among others.

As a historical task, witnessing to the Holocaust begins with a certain awe, shock, and terror that end in silence. Such silence, however, demands a second moment: one that sacrifices silence in favor of testimony. Here, the imperative to bear witness is driven by the engraved memory of unspeakable acts: crimes against humanity, mass violence, cruelty, personal trauma, loss, and so on. The testimonial moment happens as a radical negation: a violent breaching of the everyday world. Such a world historical trauma opens a gap and a silence in our cultural response. It possesses discourse as a "negative phrase" or what Jean François Lyotard calls a *differend:* a linguistic black hole, whose silence "nevertheless calls upon phrases which are in principle possible." For his part, moreover, "what is at stake in a literature, in a philosophy, in a politics perhaps, is to bear witness to *differends* by finding idioms for them." Recent psychoanalytic writing on the Holocaust is one such discourse where the "negative phrase" of the *differend* has found an idiom whose repetition, however acted out, nevertheless makes a difference in working through the event. In the writings of Dori Laub and Shoshana Felman, the Holocaust is again invoked in the silence of an abyssal metaphor, but in their texts, the extreme event is considered through the more complex understanding of time, memory, and witnessing to disaster.

Poetry is another important site for giving testimony to the *novum* of the Holocaust. One symptom of the difficulties in writing about the Holocaust is the relative lack of contemporary verse devoted to the event. It would be normal to expect repression to follow upon a death encounter. As an unprecedented trauma, however, the Holocaust changes the status of death as such. "Planet Auschwitz," as Yehiel Dinur called it, marks a radical negation of life that thereby introduces a new anxiety into human existence. Similarly, Theodor Adorno concludes in *Negative Dialectics* (1974) that "the administrative murder of millions made of death a thing one had never yet to fear in just this fashion." For his part, Adorno insisted that any contemporary thinking that failed to reflect on its belatedness "after Auschwitz" is complicit with the obscenity of the death camps. "If thought," he writes, "is not measured by the extremity that eludes the concept, it is from the outset in the nature of the musical accompaniment with which the SS liked to drown out the screams of its victims." Adorno, of course, included contemporary poetics in the "superflous trash" thrown up by postwar culture, declaring in *Prisms* (1981) his famous slogan that "to write poetry after Auschwitz is barbaric."

This dire judgment, however, has not stood as the final word on contemporary verse. In fact, it has prompted a number of counterstatements, as in the rejoinder of Edmond Jabès in *The Book of Margins* (1993): "Adorno once said that after Auschwitz we can no longer write poetry. I say that after Auschwitz we *must* write poetry but with wounded words." In the postwar context, many fewer poems have been written on genocide than the historical struggles over race, gender, sexuality, the environment, native ethnicities, and so on. "We never discussed the Second World War much when I was growing up," writes the contemporary American poet Charles Bernstein. Morever, he admits, "I don't feel much like discussing it now." Reflecting the latency of a global trauma, Bernstein notes that it is only some five decades after the Holocaust that "we are just beginning to come out of the shock enough to try to make sense of the experience." Peculiar to the temporal structure of extremity, the encounter with death, missed through survival, gathers traumatic force only through the passage of time. Echoing an observation made by Terence Des Pres, among others, Bernstein notes that for him "each year, the Extermination Process seems nearer, more recent." Similarly, Terrence Des Pres writes in his Introduction to *Legacy of Night: The Literary Universe of Elie Wiesel* (1982):

The Holocaust would seem to have no end. The destruction of Europe's Jews stopped in 1945, but the spectacle of the death camps continues to haunt us, and not merely as a fading memory or as a bad dream that lingers. The Holocaust happened. That in itself is the intractable fact that we can neither erase nor evade. And the more we think of it, the more it intrudes to occupy our minds, until *l'univers concentrationnaire* becomes a demonic anti-world that undermines our own.

Poems for Further Reading and Critical Writing

PRIMO LEVI *(1919–1987)*

Shemá *(1958)*

Translated by Ruth Feldman and Brian Swann

You who live secure
In your warm houses,
Who return at evening to find
Hot food and friendly faces:

  Consider whether this is a man,   5
  Who labours in the mud
  Who knows no peace
  Who fights for a crust of bread
  Who dies at a yes or a no.
  Consider whether this is a woman,   10
  Without hair or name
  With no more strength to remember
  Eyes empty and womb cold
  As a frog in winter.

Consider that this has been: 15
I commend these words to you.
Engrave them on your hearts
When you are in your house, when you walk on your way,
When you go to bed, when you rise.
Repeat them to your children.   20
Or may your house crumble,
Disease render you powerless,
Your offspring avert their faces from you.

NELLY SACHS   *(1891–1970)*

O the Chimneys   *(1971)*

Translated by Michael Hamburger

> *And though after my skin worms destroy this*
> *body, yet in my flesh shall I see God.*
> —JOB 19:26

O the chimneys
On the ingeniously devised habitations of death
When Israel's body drifted as smoke
Through the air—
Was welcomed by a star, a chimney sweep,   5
A star that turned black
Or was it a ray of sun?

O the chimneys!
Freedomway for Jeremiah and Job's dust—
Who devised you and laid stone upon stone   10
The road for refugees of smoke?

O the habitations of death,
Invitingly appointed
For the host who used to be a guest—
O you fingers   15
Laying the threshold
Like a knife between life and death—

O you chimneys,
O you fingers
And Israel's body as smoke through the air!   20

ELIE WIESEL   *(b. 1928)*

Never Shall I Forget   *(1958)*

Never shall I forget that night,
the first night in the camp
which has turned my life into one long night,
seven times cursed and seven times sealed.

Never shall I forget that smoke.   5
Never shall I forget the little faces of the children

whose bodies I saw turned into wreaths of smoke
beneath a silent blue sky.

Never shall I forget those flames
which consumed my faith for ever.   10
Never shall I forget that nocturnal silence
which deprived me for all eternity of the desire to live.

Never shall I forget those moments
which murdered my God and my soul
and turned my dreams to dust.   15

Never shall I forget these things,
even if I am condemned to live as
long as God Himself.

Never.

YEVGENY YEVTUSHENKO   (b. 1933)

Babii Yar   (1961)

Translated by George Reavey

No monument stands over Babii Yar.
A drop sheer as a crude gravestone.
I am afraid.
          Today I am as old in years
as all the Jewish people.   5
Now I seem to be
               a Jew.
Here I plod through ancient Egypt.
Here I perish crucified, on the cross,
and to this day I bear the scars of nails.   10
I seem to be
          Dreyfus.
The Philistine
          is both informer and judge.
I am behind bars.   15
               Beset on every side.
Hounded,
     spat on,
          slandered.

Squealing, dainty ladies in flounced Brussels lace   20
stick their parasols into my face.

I seem to be then
                    a young boy in Byelostok.
Blood runs, spilling over the floors.
The barroom rabble-rousers   25
give off a stench of vodka and onion.
A boot kicks me aside, helpless.
In vain I plead with these pogrom bullies.
While they jeer and shout,
                    'Beat the Yids. Save Russia!'   30
Some grain-marketeer beats up my mother.
O my Russian people!
                    I know
          you
are international to the core.   35
But those with unclean hands
have often made a jingle of your purest name.
I know the goodness of my land.
How vile these anti-Semites—
                    without a qualm   40
they pompously called themselves
the Union of the Russian People!

I seem to be
          Anne Frank
transparent   45
          as a branch in April.
And I love.
          And have no need of phrases.
My need
          is that we gaze into each other.   50
How little we can see
                    or smell!
We are denied the leaves,
                    we are denied the sky.
Yet we can do so much—   55
                    tenderly
embrace each other in a darkened room.
They're coming here?
                    Be not afraid. Those are the booming
sounds of spring: 60
                    spring is coming here.
Come then to me.
                    Quick, give me your lips.
Are they smashing down the door?

                    No, it's the ice breaking. . . .   65
The wild grasses rustle over Babii Yar.

The trees look ominous,
                          like judges.
Here all things scream silently,
                                and, baring my head,   70
slowly I feel myself
                    turning grey.
And I myself
            am one massive, soundless scream
above the thousand thousand buried here.   75
I am
    each old man
                here shot dead.
I am
    every child   80
                here shot dead.
Nothing in me
            shall ever forget!
The 'Internationale,' let it
                        thunder   85
when the last anti-Semite on earth
is buried for ever.
In my blood there is no Jewish blood.
In their callous rage, all anti-Semites
must hate me now as a Jew.   90
For that reason
            I am a true Russian!

DAN PAGIS *(b. 1930)*

Written in Pencil in the Sealed Railway-Car   *(1970)*

Translated by Stephen Mitchell

here in this carload
i am Eve
with my son Abel
if you see my older boy
cain son of Adam   5
tell him that i

PAUL CELAN   *(1920–1970)*

Death Fugue   *(1944, 1980)*
Translated by Michael Hamburger

Black milk of daybreak we drink it at sundown
we drink it at noon in the morning we drink it at night
we drink and we drink it
we dig a grave in the breezes there one lies unconfined
A man lives in the house he plays with the serpents he writes   5
he writes when dusk falls to Germany your golden hair
      Margarete
he writes it and steps out of doors and the stars are flashing he
      whistles his pack out
he whistles his Jews out in earth has them dig for a grave
he commands us strike up for the dance

Black milk of daybreak we drink you at night   10
we drink in the morning at noon we drink you at sundown
we drink and we drink you
A man lives in the house he plays with the serpents he writes
he writes when dusk falls to Germany your golden hair
      Margarete
your ashen hair Shulamith we dig a grave in the breezes there   15
      one lies unconfined

He calls out jab deeper into the earth you lot you others sing
      now and play
he grabs at the iron in his belt he waves it his eyes are blue
jab deeper you lot with your spades you others play on for the
      dance

Black milk of daybreak we drink you at night
we drink you at noon in the morning we drink you at   20
      sundown
we drink and we drink you
a man lives in the house your golden hair Margarete
your ashen hair Shulamith he plays with the serpents

He calls out more sweetly play death death is a master from
      Germany
he calls out more darkly now stroke your strings then as   25
      smoke you will rise into air
then a grave you will have in the clouds there one lies
      unconfined

Black milk of daybreak we drink you at night
we drink you at noon death is a master from Germany
we drink you at sundown and in the morning we drink and
  we drink you
death is a master from Germany his eyes are blue   30
he strikes you with leaden bullets his aim is true
a man lives in the house your golden hair Margarete
he sets his pack on to us he grants us a grave in the air
he plays with the serpents and daydreams death is a master
  from Germany

your golden hair Margarete   35
your ashen hair Shulamith

SYLVIA PLATH   *(1932–1963)*

Lady Lazarus   *(1962)*

I have done it again.
One year in every ten
I manage it——

A sort of walking miracle, my skin
Bright as a Nazi lampshade,   5
My right foot

A paperweight,
My face a featureless, fine
Jew linen.

Peel off the napkin   10
O my enemy.
Do I terrify?——

The nose, the eye pits, the full set of teeth?
The sour breath
Will vanish in a day.   15

Soon, soon the flesh
The grave cave ate will be
At home on me

And I a smiling woman.
I am only thirty.   20
And like the cat I have nine times to die.

This is Number Three.
What a trash
To annihilate each decade.

What a million filaments.   25
The peanut-crunching crowd
Shoves in to see

Them unwrap me hand and foot——
The big strip tease.
Gentlemen, ladies   30

These are my hands
My knees.
I may be skin and bone,

Nevertheless, I am the same, identical woman.
The first time it happened I was ten.   35
It was an accident.

The second time I meant
To last it out and not come back at all.
I rocked shut

As a seashell.   40
They had to call and call
And pick the worms off me like sticky pearls.

Dying
Is an art, like everything else.
I do it exceptionally well.   45

I do it so it feels like hell.
I do it so it feels real.
I guess you could say I've a call.

It's easy enough to do it in a cell.
It's easy enough to do it and stay put.   50
It's the theatrical

Comeback in broad day
To the same place, the same face, the same brute
Amused shout:

'A miracle!'   55
That knocks me out.
There is a charge

For the eyeing of my scars, there is a charge
For the hearing of my heart——
It really goes.   60

And there is a charge, a very large charge
For a word or a touch
Or a bit of blood

Or a piece of my hair or my clothes.
So, so, Herr Doktor.   65
So, Herr Enemy.

I am your opus,
I am your valuable,
The pure gold baby

That melts to a shriek.   70
I turn and burn.
Do not think I underestimate your great concern.

Ash, ash—
You poke and stir.
Flesh, bone, there is nothing there——   75

A cake of soap,
A wedding ring,
A gold filling.

Herr God, Herr Lucifer
Beware   80
Beware.

Out of the ash
I rise with my red hair
And I eat men like air.

WILLIAM HEYEN   *(b. 1940)*

Kotov   *(1991)*

Ivan Ivanovitch Kotov, short of speech,
clarity drifting away to mindlessness—
Kotov of stutter and suddenly empty eyes—
only Kotov, in all Russia, of all those locked inside,
survived the *dushegubka*,   5
the murder wagon, the gas van. Only Kotov,

pushed with his new bride
into the seatless seven-ton gray truck,
stood on that grated floor, and lived. Only Kotov,
pressed together with fifty others, would wake   10
in the ditch of dead, half buried, and crawl away.
He'd smelled gas, torn off one sleeve,
soaked it in his urine, covered nose and mouth,

lost consciousness, and lived, waking
in a pit of bodies somewhere outside of Krasnodar.   15

His wife?—he could not find her.
Except for the dead, he was alone. . . .
He stood up, staggered and groped through fields
back to the city, where he hid until the end.

Only Kotov, saved by his own brain and urine, woke   20
from that wedding in the death van,
in Russia, in the time of that German invention,
the windowless seven-ton gray *dushegubka*.

ANTHONY HECHT   *(b. 1921)*

The Book of Yolek   *(1991)*

Wir Haben ein Gesetz,
Und nach dem Gesetz soll er sterben.°

The dowsed coals fume and hiss after your meal
Of grilled brook trout, and you saunter off for a walk
Down the fern trail. It doesn't matter where to,
Just so you're weeks and worlds away from home,
And among midsummer hills have set up camp   5
In the deep bronze glories of declining day.

You remember, peacefully, an earlier day
In childhood, remember a quite specific meal:
A corn roast and bonfire in summer camp.
That summer you got lost on a Nature Walk;   10
More than you dared admit, you thought of home:
No one else knows where the mind wanders to.

The fifth of August, 1942.
It was the morning and very hot. It was the day
They came at dawn with rifles to The Home   15
For Jewish Children, cutting short the meal
Of bread and soup, lining them up to walk
In close formation off to a special camp.

How often you have thought about that camp,
As though in some strange way you were driven to,   20
And about the children, and how they were made to walk,
Yolek who had bad lungs, who wasn't a day

Wir . . . sterben: We have a law, and according to the law he must die.

Over five years old, commanded to leave his meal
And shamble between armed guards to his long home.

We're approaching August again. It will drive home   25
The regulation torments of that camp
Yolek was sent to, his small, unfinished meal,
The electric fences, the numeral tattoo,
The quiet extraordinary heat of the day
They all were forced to take that terrible walk.   30

Whether on a silent, solitary walk
Or among crowds, far off or safe at home,
You will remember, helplessly, that day,
And the smell of smoke, and the loudspeakers of the camp.
Wherever you are, Yolek will be there, too.   35
His unuttered name will interrupt your meal.

Prepare to receive him in your home some day.
Though they killed him in the camp they sent him to,
He will walk in as you're sitting down to a meal.

TADEUSZ RÓZEWICZ   *(b. 1921)*

Pigtail   *(1948)*

Translated by Adam Czerniawski

When all the women in the transport
had their heads shaved
four workmen with brooms made of birch twigs
swept up   5
and gathered up the hair

Behind clean glass
the stiff hair lies
of those suffocated in gas chambers
there are pins and side combs   10
in this hair

The hair is not shot through with light
is not parted by the breeze
is not touched by any hand
or rain or lips   15

In huge chests
clouds of dry hair

of those suffocated
and a faded plait
a pigtail with a ribbon
pulled at school
by naughty boys.

The Museum, Auschwitz, 1948

CHARLES REZNIKOFF   *(1894–1976)*

from Holocaust   *(1975)*

from VII, Workcamps
3

When the Second World War began
he was living in Lodz with his mother.
The family was hungry
and his mother became bloated from hunger—
as many were.   5
His mother and her family escaped from the ghetto in Lodz
and fled to the Warsaw ghetto;
but there it became much worse:
his mother had sold everything she had
and they had nothing to eat.   10
She then told him to get to the Lublin area
where other members of the family lived,
and he escaped to a small town.

One morning he heard cries and shrieking:
the Germans were taking the Jews to the market place. 15
They crowded them into freight cars
and he was among them.
There was hardly room to stand
and many fainted.
But the journey took only two or three hours   20
and they were brought to a death camp.
When they got off the train
they were hurried to a small gate,
the SS men shouting, 'Hurry! Hurry!'
and there the men were taken from the women and children. 25
While this was going on
a band was playing.

The men stayed there all night
but the women and children were taken at once to the gas
    chambers.
Many of the Jews had not believed there would be any mass   30
    extermination—
a few murders, of course;
and even when they were jammed into the freight cars,
many were happy not to be going to a camp they knew to be a
    hard labour camp
and going eastward instead:
it had been rumoured that they would be taken to the Ukraine   35
    to work in the fields
now that Germany had taken over most of it.
But some remembered a Jew who had come to town and said:
'Do not believe what you are told.
The Jews are not being taken to the Ukraine;
they are sent to death camps—   40
and killed there.'
But nobody believed him;
they thought he was just trying to start a panic.
And even in the camp they had now been sent to—
a few hundred feet from the gas chambers—   45
the men were told by the Germans that in a few weeks they
    would rejoin their families.
They saw the belongings of the women and children piled up;
but the Germans said:
'They are getting new clothes.
You are going to be gathered together and then sent to the   50
    Ukraine.'

There were really three camps at that camp:
one for shoemakers, tailors, and other craftsmen;
another for those who worked at sorting the clothes of those
    who came in the transports and were gassed;
and the third camp where the gas chambers were.
The morning after the arrival of the Jewish men who had just   55
    come,
the Germans began to sort them:
choosing the young and able-bodied by saying, 'du'—the
    German familiar for 'you'.
In about half an hour most of the men who had come in that
    transport
had been taken to the gas chambers
and only about a hundred and fifty were left to work;   60
the young man who had fled from Warsaw to the Lublin area
    among them.

He was put to work taking and piling up the clothing of the
    people who had come—
and were coming—in the transports
and kept seeing that many who had come disappeared.
After the young man had worked for a while the first day,   65
he was dazed
and as he stood, dazed and benumbed—
he was only fifteen then—
a Jew came up to him and said, 'My boy, if you are going to
    behave this way, you are not going to survive here.'
• • •

6

Jews from Holland, France, and Hungary, and later from   70
    Greece,
were brought to a camp in freight trains or cattle cars—
three or four trains a day—
the cars crowded
and on the road days and nights,
with nothing for those inside   75
to eat or drink;
and when the cars were at the camp
they were driven out with whips
and blows from the butts of rifles.

They were then lined up before the camp physician   80
and as they passed before him
he would ask their age of the men—if they did not show it—
and what they did for a living,
and then point with his thumb
to the right or left;   85
and those sent to the left—all able to work—
were driven barefoot to the camp,
even when snow was on the ground,
and whipped to go faster.
One of the soldiers on guard said as a joke,   90
pointing to the smoke from the chimneys of the crematorium,
'The only road from here to freedom!'

Some of those sent to the right
would be loaded on vans
with only a single member of an SS squad   95
seated in front
and were gassed in the van—
if it was that kind—

and their bodies brought straight to the crematorium.
But most would be brought to the gas chambers   100
behind trees that had been cut down
and set up in rows.

If the gas chambers were crowded
and no room for the youngest children—or even adults—
they were thrown on piles of wood   105
that had been sprinkled with gasoline
and just burnt alive.
But that their screams might not be too disturbing
to those who worked
an orchestra of Jews from the camp   110
was set to playing loudly
well-known German songs.

   • • •

from VIII, Children
1

Once, among the transports, was one with children—two
   freight cars full.
The young men sorting out the belongings of those taken to
   the gas chambers
had to undress the children—they were orphans—
and then take them to the 'lazarette.'
There the SS men shot them.   5

A large eight-wheeled car arrived at the hospital
where there were children;
in the two trailers—open trucks—were sick women and men
lying on the floor.
The Germans threw the children into the trucks   10
from the second floor and the balconies—
children from one year old to ten;
threw them upon the sick in the trucks.
Some of the children tried to hold on to the walls,
scratched at the walls with their nails;   15
but the shouting Germans
beat and pushed the children towards the windows.

The children arrived at the camp in buses,
guarded by gendarmes of the French Vichy government.
The buses stopped in the middle of the courtyard   20
and the children were quickly taken off
to make room for the buses following.

Frightened but quiet,
the children came down in groups of fifty or sixty to eighty;
the younger children holding on to older ones.   25
They were taken upstairs to empty halls—
without any furniture
and only dirty straw bags on the floor, full of bugs:
children as young as two, three, or four years of age,
all in torn clothes and dirty,   30
for they had already spent two or three weeks in other camps,
uncared for;
and were now on their way to a death camp in Poland.
Some had only one shoe.
Many had diarrhoea   35
but they were not allowed in the courtyard
where the water-closets were;
and, although there were chamber pots in the corridor of each
    story,
these were too large for the small children.

The women in the camp who were also deportees   40
and about to be taken to other camps
were in tears:
they would get up before sunrise
and go into the halls where the children were—
in each a hundred to a hundred and twenty—   45
to mend the children's clothing;
but the women had no soap to clean the children,
no clean underwear to give them,
and only cold water with which to wash them.
When soup came for the children,   50
there were no spoons;
and it would be served in tins
but the tins were sometimes too hot for the children to hold.
• • •

A visitor once stopped one of the children:
a boy of seven or eight, handsome, alert and gay.   55
He had only one shoe and the other foot was bare,
and his coat of good quality had no buttons.
The visitor asked him for his name
and then what his parents were doing;
and he said, 'Father is working in the office   60
and Mother is playing the piano.'
Then he asked the visitor if he would be joining his parents
    soon—
they always told the children they would be leaving soon to
    rejoin their parents—

and the visitor answered, 'Certainly. In a day or two.'
At that the child took out of his pocket   65
half an army biscuit he had been given in camp
and said, 'I am keeping this half for Mother';
and then the child who had been so gay
burst into tears.

from X, Mass Graves
1

After the Jew who had recognized the man from his
    home town
had been working in the woods for some time,
other Jews from his own town were among the dead
and among them—
his wife and his two children!   5
He lay down next to his wife and children and wanted the
    Germans to shoot him;
but one of the SS men said:
'You still have enough strength to work,'
and pushed him away.
That evening he tied to hang himself   10
but his friends in the cellar would not let him
and said, 'As long as your eyes are open,
there is hope.'
The next day the man who had tried to die was on a truck.

They were still in the woods   15
and he asked one of the SS men for a cigarette.
He himself did not smoke usually
but he lit the cigarette and, when he was back where his
    companions were sitting, said:
'Look here! He gives out cigarettes.
Why don't you all ask him for a cigarette?'   20
They all got up—
they were in the back of the truck—
and went forwards
and he was left behind.
He had a little knife   25
and made a slit in the tarpaulin at the side
and jumped out;
came down on his knees
but got up and ran.
By the time the SS men began shooting   30
he was gone in the woods.

•   •   •

3

In the morning the Jews were lined up by an officer
and the officer told them:
'You are Jews, unworthy of life,
but are now supposed to work.'   35
They were put upon trucks
and taken away to a forest
and set to digging.
After two or three spadefuls of earth,
the spade of one hit something hard,   40
and he saw that it was the head of a human being.
There was also a bad smell all around.
He stopped digging
and the officer in charge came towards him shouting:
'Why did you stop?   45
Didn't you know there are bodies buried here?'
He had opened a mass grave.

There were about ten thousand dead in that grave.
And after they had dug up the bodies
they were told to burn them.   50
Planks had been brought and beams—long and heavy.
The Germans also brought a grinding machine to grind the
    bones
and the ground bones would be sieved
for the gold fillings of teeth.
The dust of the bones would then be spread over the fields,   55
and the smell was dreadful.

They kept on working three months
opening mass graves;
and opened eight or nine.
In one those digging saw a boy of two or three,   60
lying on his mother's body.
He had little white shoes on
and a little white jacket,
and his face was pressed against his mother's.

One grave would remain open for new corpses   65
coming all the time;
a truck would bring the bodies, still warm,
to be thrown into the grave—
naked as Adam and Eve;
Jewish men, many of them bearded, and Jewish women and   70
    children.
The graves they had opened would be refilled with earth

and they had to plant grass all over them;
as for the dead—
a thousand bodies would be put on a pyre;
and there were two pyres of bodies burning all the time.   75

ADRIENNE RICH   *(b. 1929)*

from Sources   *(1986)*

V

All during World War II
I told myself I had some special destiny:
there had to be a reason
I was not living in a bombed-out house
or cellar   hiding out with rats   5

there had to be a reason
I was growing up safe, American
with sugar rationed in a Mason jar

split at the root   white-skinned social christian
neither gentile nor Jew   10

through the immense silence
of the Holocaust

I had no idea of what I had been spared

still less of the women and men   my kin
the Jews of Vicksburg or Birmingham   15
whose lives must have been strategies no less
than the vixen's on Route 5

XVI

The Jews I've felt rooted among
are those who were turned to smoke

Reading of the chimneys against the blear air
I think I have seen them myself

the fog of northern Europe licking its way   5
along the railroad tracks

to the place where all tracks end
You told me not to look there

to become
a citizen of the world   10

bound by no tribe or clan
yet dying you followed the Six Day War

with desperate attention
and this summer I lie awake at dawn

sweating the Middle East through my brain   15
wearing the star of David

on a thin chain at my breastbone

XVII

But there was also the other Jew. The one you most feared, the one from
the *shtetl*, from Brooklyn, from the wrong part of history, the wrong accent,
the wrong class. The one I left you for.   The one both like and unlike you,
who explained you to me for years, who could not explain himself.   The
one who said, as if he had memorized the formula, *There's nothing left now but* 5
the food and the humor.   The one who, like you, ended isolate, who had
tried to move in the floating world of the assimilated who know and deny they
will always be aliens.   Who drove to Vermont in a rented car at dawn and
shot himself.   For so many years I had thought you and he were in opposition. I needed your unlikeness then; now it's your likeness that stares me in 10
the face.   There is something more than food, humor, a turn of phrase, a
gesture of the hands: there is something more.

XVIII

There is something more than self-hatred. That still outlives
these photos of the old Ashkenazi° life:
we are gifted children at camp in the country
or orphaned children in kindergarten
we are hurrying along the rare book dealers' street   5
with the sunlight striking one side
we are walking the wards of the Jewish hospital
along diagonal squares   young serious nurses
we are part of a family group
formally taken in 1936   10
with tables, armchairs, ferns
(behind as, in our lives, the muddy street
and the ragged shames
the street-musician, the weavers lined for strike)

---

13 *Ashkenazi:* From the Hebrew word for "German," it designates German and Eastern European Jews.

we are part of a family wearing white head-bandages   15
we were beaten in a pogrom

The place where all tracks end
is the place where history was meant to stop
but does not stop   where thinking
was meant to stop but does not stop   20
where the pattern was meant to give way at last
                                                      but only

becomes a different pattern
                                   terrible, threadbare
strained   familiar   on-going   25

RACHEL BLAU DUPLESSIS   *(b. 1943)*

Draft 17: Unnamed   *(1992)*

It's true that every ending only erases the board
rather than filling it.
The poems are written in strange chalk
strange, a chalk
in some lights dark, plump with serifs   5
on a scumbled, agitated whiteness,
but mainly a white chalk on a whiter page.

Which can hardly be read
and that, only under angled light.

As wide as my life though when you look again it's   10
a scroll narrow, but fast,
paper towels in the hands of a toddler,
down and up hillocks and rises,
blazes and falls
so fast one can only   15
trail after it, "what could be more natural."

Or dark as a mist
hanging over the fill-built airport,
smoke brown the sky looks daubed
and of no depth.   20

But the chalk (with luck, another turn) turns
      translucent, light on light
            which is, in certain lights, like dark on dark
but more
      blinding.   25

Words,
    scattered falling
           arcs of shame,
                  glaze the flicker-ridden labyrinth—
it makes a peculiar medium.   30
           And its crossgrained nourishment
                  demands a strange tooth.

Perhaps translucence is a quality of erasure.
The thing anyway looks like a Cy Twombly°
strokes trailing each other and dibs, nibs,   35
flicks of the wrist and a dreamy evisceration of pencil.
A morning glory bolted across the door.
My little valise is filled with souvenirs.
And none of them is "art."
I can see why he said I wasn't interested in art.   40

"Poetry depersonalizes 'days'
in language." It sounded
as if this were what I wanted

yet the hole, the sufferance
fell open. Heard the shaped scream of a duration.   45
Three times: the game, the same, the same again,
"nothing but these facts and all these facts."
Why did he think I "wasn't interested in art"?

Low song clouds in unbelonging places
           emphasize the activities of light,   50
                  which is unspeakable.

While the sound, not just the light,
           plays along certain vectors
                  pools in the force field

large, square, rent, timeless   55
           void. Know?
                  Can barely know what labyrinth.

The grass clods push up
           between the lines and cracks
                  of pavement. In the depth   60

of night, a street lamp
           looming behind them
                  they rise and lurk,

---

34 *Cy Twombly (b. 1928)*: Contemporary American painter.

turf tufts made near twice
　　　　their "real" size
　　　　　　by shadow.

But what I mean is this.
　　　　She stood at the pit
　　　　　　where, this 50 years,

155 Jews were shot.
　　　　There, near a field of rye,
　　　　　　she'd found dozens of notes and addresses

tossed away
　　　　moments before their deaths.
　　　　　　To this day,

she regrets
　　　　that, out of fear
　　　　　　she did not pick them up.

The poetics seems plain.
　　　　Since then
　　　　　　there are many people spend their time

picking up the notes.
　　　　But they are not there.
　　　　They are as gone as possible to be.

So the gathering
　　　　is impossible.
　　　　　　But still the shapes are bowed,

and search
　　　　this otherwhere of here.
　　　　　　Yet had they actually

been there
　　　　that time
　　　　　　being remembered,

it is equally possible
　　　　they too would have left
　　　　　　all of them where they lay.

What illusion, what delusion, what disillusion
　　　　writes these gaps?
　　　　　　tries these missing bits and scraps?

65

70

75

80

85

90

95

It is not elegy   100
     though elegy seems the nearest category of genre
          raising stars, strewing flowers. . . .

It's not that I have not
     done this, in life or wherever I
          needed to   105

or throwing out the curled tough leather
     of the dead
          the cracked insteps of unwalkable shoes,

but it is not the name or term
     for what is meant   110
          by this inexorable bending.

And it is not "the Jews"
     (though of course it's the Jews),
          but Jews as an iterated sign of this site.

Words with (to all intents and purposes)   115
no before and after
hanging in a void of loss
the slow and normal whirlwind
from which it roars
they had not ever meant to be so lost,   120
so little wordth.

                  There are plenty of reasons to wonder.
        Forlorn spirits with spinning "swords of flame"
                   as much like angels
           as it's possible to be, but without   125
                  choices or pleasure,
                     stand empty.
               Wavy wheaty heads
                  dart and sway;
       contradictory rages swivel them.   130
          But (pace Rilke) we can tell
         these angels, or their similacra
                   "things."
    Late busses, glass smash, styrofoam containers.
                Low sun plain wing   135
                   grey toyota
                     ormolu
               soccer freshener
                 kith, soot, food
              rainbows of oil.   140

                                                          The intersection
                                                            by Dunkin'
                                                          Donuts, chicken
                                                           buckets, milk
                                                       and Gulf is   145
                                                      where you have to turn

                                                             coming
                                                              here.

So speak, stutterer, and stain the light with figments.
        Rush, and brush, this evanescent shimmer   150
                that does not even track

that does not
        even fill or replicate
                the historical air clotted here.

And Here   155
        where all this is and are
                this back and forth through time,

Alight.
        It's never
                what you think.   160

Critical Perspective: On Holocaust Testimony

"In addition, both in literary studies and in the field of public health a new awareness arises which is ethical as well as clinical. There is more *listening*, more *hearing* of words within words, and a greater openness to *testimony*. (While the status of such testimony in formal legal hearings should be and does remain subject to questioning and challenge, it is not as often ruled out of court because of its personal, emotional, and overdetermined or multivocal nature.) In nonlegal situations, the psychoanalytic dialogue had already encouraged a greater measure of supportive listening; this is now reinforced, even as the problem of the 'real' cause of trauma deepens, especially in the matter of recovered memories. As in literature, we find a way of *receiving* the story, of listening to it, of drawing it into an interpretive conversation. Medical or political reductionism is avoided. The experts are not given the last word. The story, Kathryn Hunter says, 'must be returned to the patient.' . . .

"For a generation now, literature has been increasingly looked at from a political angle. Many in the profession are desperate to redeem their drug, that is, to make the literary object of study more transitive, more connected with what goes on in a blatantly political world. Trauma studies provide a more natural transition to a 'real' world often falsely split off from that of the university, as if the one were activist and engaged and the other self-absorbed and detached. There is an opening that leads from trauma studies to public, especially mental health issues, an opening with ethical, cultural, and religious implications.

"The result is not moral criticism exactly, because this newest perspective does not attempt a definitive judgment or evaluation of the individual work. The change introduced operates at the level of theory, and of exegesis in the service of insights about human functioning. The focus is on disclosing an unconscious or not-knowing knowledge—a potentially literary way of knowing, if you wish—combining insight and blindness, play and earnest (or an adult management of transitional objects), and linking inspiration to sound as well as sense. Emphasis falls on the imaginative use of language rather than on an ideal transparency of meaning. The real—the empirical or historical origin— cannot be known as such because it presents itself always within the resonances or 'field' of the traumatic."

> —Geoffrey Hartman, from "On Traumatic Knowledge and
> Literary Studies" (1995)

Critical Perspective: On Paul Celan's Imagery

"The performance of the act of drinking, traditionally a poetic metaphor for yearning, for romantic thirst and for desire, is here transformed into the surprisingly abusive figure of an endless torture and a limitless exposure, a figure for the impotent predicament and the unbearable ordeal of having to endure, absorb, continue to *take in* with no end and no limit. This image of the drunkenness of torture ironically perverts, and ironically demystifies, on the one hand, the Hellenic-mythic connotation of libidinal, euphoric Dionysiac drinking of both wine and poetry, and on the other hand, the Christian connotation of ritual religious consecration and of Eucharistic, sacred drinking of Christ's blood—and of Christ's virtue. The prominent underlying Eucharistic image suggests, however, that the enigmatic drinking which the poem repetitiously invokes is, indeed, essentially drinking of blood.

"The perversion of the metaphor of drinking is further aggravated by the enigmatic image of the 'black milk,' which, in its obsessive repetitions, suggests the further underlying—though unspeakable and inarticulated—image of a child striving to drink from the mother's breast. But the denatured 'black milk,' tainted possibly by blackened, burnt ashes, springs not from the mother's breast but from the darkness of murder and death, from the blackness of the night and of the 'dusk' that 'falls to Germany' when death uncannily becomes a 'master.' Ingesting through the liquefied black milk at once dark blood and burnt ashes, the drinking takes place not at the maternal source but at the deadly source, precisely, of the wound, at the bleeding site of reality as stigma.

"The Christian figure of the wound, traditionally viewed as the mythic vehicle and as the metaphoric means for a *historical transcendence*—for the erasure of Christ's death in the advent of Resurrection—is reinvested by the poem with the literal concreteness of the death camp blood and ashes, and is made thus to include, within the wound, not resurrection and historical transcendence, but the specificity of history—of the concrete historical reality of massacre and race annihilation—as unerasable and untranscendable. What Celan does, in this way, is to force the language of the Christian metaphorics to *witness* in effect the Holocaust, and be in turn witnessed by it.

"The entire poem is, indeed, not simply about violence but about the relation between violence and language, about the passage of the language through the violence and the passage of the violence through language."

—Shoshana Felman, from *Testimony (on Paul Celan's "Death Fugue")* (1992)

Critical Perspective: On Witnessing to the Holocaust

"On the basis of the many Holocaust testimonies I have listened to, I would like to suggest a certain way of looking at the Holocaust that would reside in the following theoretical perspective: that what precisely made a Holocaust out of the event is the unique way in which, during its historical occurrence, *the event produced no witnesses.* Not only, in effect, did the Nazis try to exterminate the physical witnesses of their crime; but the inherently incomprehensible *and* deceptive psychological structure of the event precluded its own witnessing, even by its very victims.

"A witness is a witness to the truth of what happens during an event. During the era of the Nazi persecution of the Jews, the truth of the event could have been recorded in perception and in memory, either from within or from without, by Jews, or any one of a number of 'outsiders.' Outsider-witnesses could have been, for instance, the next-door neighbor, a friend, a business partner, community institutions including the police and the courts of law, as well as bystanders and potential rescuers and allies from other countries.

"Jews from all over the world, especially from Palestine and the United States, could have been such possible outside witnesses. Even the executioner, who was totally oblivious to the plea for life, was potentially such an 'outside' witness. Ultimately, God himself could be the witness. As the event of the Jewish genocide unfolded, however, most actual or potential witnesses failed one-by-one to occupy their position as a witness, and at a certain point it seemed as if there was no one left to witness what was taking place.

"In addition, it was inconceivable that any historical insider could remove herself sufficiently from the contaminating power of the event so as to remain a fully lucid, unaffected witness, that is, to be sufficiently detached from the inside, so as to stay entirely *outside* of the trapping roles, and the consequent identities, either of the victim or of the executioner. No observer could remain untainted, that is, maintain an integrity—a wholeness and a separateness—that could keep itself uncompromised, unharmed, by his or her very witnessing. The perpetrators, in their attempt to rationalize the unprecedented scope of the destructiveness, brutally imposed upon their victims a delusional ideology whose grandiose coercive pressure totally excluded and eliminated the possibility of an unviolated, unencumbered, and thus sane, point of reference in the witness.

"What I feel is therefore crucial to emphasize is the following: it was not only the reality of the situation and the lack of responsiveness of bystanders or the world that accounts for the fact that history was taking place with no witness: it was also the very circumstance of *being inside the event* that made unthinkable the very notion that a witness could exist, that is, someone who could step outside of the coercively totalitarian and dehumanizing frame of reference in which the event was taking place, and provide an independent frame of reference through which the event could be observed. One might say that there was, thus, historically no witness to the Holocaust, either from outside or from inside the event."

—Dori Laub, from *Testimony* (1992)

Critical Perspective: On the Holocaust Survivor

"The survivor is the figure who emerges from all those who fought for life in the concentration camps, and the most significant fact about their struggle is that it depended on fixed activities: on forms of social bonding and interchange, on collective resistance, on keeping dignity and moral sense active. That such thoroughly *human* kinds of behavior were typical in places like Buchenwald and Auschwitz amounts to a revelation reaching to the foundation of what man is. Facts such as these discredit the claims of nihilism and suggest, further, that when men and women must face months and years of death threat they endure less through cultural than through biological imperatives. The biological sciences have begun to point in the same direction, and toward the end of the book I have incorporated some of their broader insights to clarify what survivors mean when they speak of *a talent for life*, or of life as a *power*, or of their reliance on *life in itself*. But here the reader should not be misled: speculation about the relation between survival behavior and basic life-processes is speculation only. The experience itself is what counts. An agony so massive should not be, indeed cannot be, reduced to a bit of datum in a theory.

"In the concentration camps, as everyone knows, vastly more people died than came through. Statisticians may therefore wish to quarrel with my concern for the survivors. Fernand Braudel, a historian I greatly admire, argues that human destiny is shaped by sheer weight of numbers. Perhaps so, but that is not the issue here. We must not, in any case, confuse history with the constituent activities of selfhood. The image of the survivor includes any man or woman striving to keep life and spirit intact—not only those who returned, but the hundreds of thousands who stayed alive sometimes for years, only to die at the last minute. . . .

"Men have always been ready to die for beliefs, sacrificing life for higher goals. That made sense once, perhaps; but no cause moves without live men to move it, and our predicament today— as governments know—is that ideas and ideologies are stopped by killing those who hold them. The 'final solution' has become a usual solution, and the world is not what it was. Within a landscape of disaster, places like Auschwitz, Hiroshima or the obliterated earth of Indo-China, where people die in thousands, where machines reduce courage to stupidity and dying to complicity with aggression, it makes no sense to speak of death's dignity or of its communal blessing. We require a heroism commensurate with the sweep of ruin in our time: action equal to situations in which it becomes less self-indulgent and more useful to live, to be there. History moves, times change, men find themselves caught up in unexpected circumstance. The grandeur of death is lost in a world of mass murder, and except for special cases the martyr and his tragic counterpart are types of the hero unfit for the darkness ahead. When men and women must live against terrible odds, when mere existence becomes miraculous, to die is in no way a triumph.

"If by heroism we mean the dramatic defiance of superior individuals, then the age of heroes is gone. If we have in mind glory and grand gesture, the survivor is not a hero. He or she is anyone who manages to stay alive in body *and* in spirit, enduring dread and hopelessness without the loss of will to carry on in human ways. That is all."

—Terrence Des Pres, from *The Survivor* (1976)

Critical Perspective: On Post-Traumatic Stress Disorder

"In the years since Vietnam, the fields of psychiatry, psychoanalysis, and sociology have taken a renewed interest in the problem of trauma. In 1980, the American Psychiatric Association finally officially acknowledged the long-recognized but frequently ignored phenomenon under the title 'Post-Traumatic Stress Disorder' (PTSD), which included the symptoms of what had previously been called shell shock, combat stress, delayed stress syndrome, and traumatic neurosis, and referred to responses to both human and natural catastrophes. On the one hand, this classification and its attendant official acknowledgment of a pathology has provided a category of diagnosis so powerful that it has seemed to engulf everything around it: suddenly responses not only to combat and to natural catastrophes but also to rape, child abuse, and a number of other violent occurrences have been understood in terms of PTSD, and diagnoses of some dissociative disorders have also been switched to that of trauma. On the other hand, this powerful new tool has provided anything but a solid explanation of disease: indeed, the impact of trauma as a concept and a category, if it has helped diagnosis, has done so only at the cost of a fundamental disruption in our received modes of understanding and of cure, and a challenge to our very comprehension of what constitutes pathology. This can be seen in the debates that surround 'category A' of the American Psychiatric Association's definition of PTSD (a response to an event 'outside the range of usual human experience'), concerning how closely PTSD must be tied to specific kinds of events; or in the psychoanalytic problem of whether trauma is indeed pathological in the usual sense, in relation to distortions caused by desires, wishes, and repressions. Indeed, the more we satisfactorily locate and classify the symptoms of PTSD, the more we seem to have dislocated the boundaries of our modes of understanding—so that psychoanalysis and medically oriented psychiatry, sociology, history, and even literature all seem to be called upon to explain, to cure, or to show why it is that we can no longer simply explain or simply cure. The phenomenon of trauma has seemed to become all-inclusive, but it has done so precisely because it brings us to the limits of our understanding: if psychoanalysis, psychiatry, sociology, and even literature are beginning to hear each other anew in the study of trauma, it is because they are listening through the radical disruption and gaps of traumatic experience. . . .

"While the precise definition of post-traumatic stress disorder is contested, most descriptions generally agree that there is a response, sometimes delayed, to an overwhelming event or events, which takes the form of repeated, intrusive hallucinations, dreams, thoughts or behaviors stemming from the event, along with numbing that may have begun during or after the experience, and possibly also increased arousal to (and avoidance of) stimuli recalling the event. This simple definition belies a very peculiar fact: the pathology cannot be defined either by the event itself—which may or may not be catastrophic, and may not traumatize everyone equally—nor can it be defined in terms of a *distortion* of the event, achieving its haunting power as a result of distorting personal significances attached to it. The pathology consists, rather, solely in the *structure of its experience* or reception: the event is not assimilated or experienced fully at the time, but only belatedly, in its repeated *possession* of the one who experiences it. To be traumatized is precisely to be possessed by an image or event."

—Cathy Caruth, from *Trauma: Explorations in Memory* (1995)

TOPICS FOR CRITICAL THINKING

1. Primo Levi was born in Turin, Italy. Before the Holocaust he was a chemistry student, graduating in 1941 first in his class at the University of Turin. While attempting to join a partisan group in Northern Italy, he was taken prisoner by the Nazis and deported to Auschwitz. There, as he relates in his memoir *Survival in Auschwitz*, his expertise in chemistry enabled him to survive inside the death camp until it was liberated in 1945. Returning to Turin, he eventually returned to his work as a chemist, becoming the general manager at a paint factory from 1961 until 1977.

   Discuss Levi's special address to the reader in "Shemá." How do you interpret the tone of the address? What ethical demand does Levi make on the reader?

2. Nelly Sachs was born in Berlin and emigrated to Sweden in 1940. Although she escaped personal disaster, her poetry pays witness to the destruction of her people in the tradition of the Old Testament verses of Lamentations. Sachs was awarded the

Nobel Prize for Literature with S. Y. Agnon in 1966. Is there an implied point or message in the questions Sachs poses in her poem "O the Chimneys"? How would you interpret her questions? What is the relation, do you think, between her questions and her exclamatory statements?

3. Elie Wiesel's poem "Never Shall I Forget" appears in his memoir on the Holocaust entitled *Night* (1958), which relates the death of his family members and his own survival at Auschwitz and later at Buchenwald. How does the poem's pattern of repetition emphasize the force of its commitment to memory?

4. Examine the psychic costs of the Holocaust as William Heyen depicts them in his poem "Kotov," which portrays a survivor of the gas extermination vans used to kill Jews in Chelmno.

TOPICS FOR CRITICAL WRITING

1. Dmitri Shostakovich based his Thirteenth Symphony on five poems by the modern Russian poet Yevgeny Yevtushenko, including his 1961 poem "Babii Yar." Babii Yar is a ravine outside of Kiev where 33,331 Jewish men, women, and children were shot by the Nazis on September 29–30, 1941. Consider Yevtushenko's use of oxymoron to invoke the force of genocide, paradoxically, through tropes of silence and absence. Does Yevtushenko succeed or fail in his attempt to identify with the Jewish victims of the Holocaust?

2. Dan Pagis's poem "Written in Pencil in the Sealed Railway-Car" is narrated through the dramatic persona of the biblical character Eve, rendered as a modern-day victim of a Holocaust deportation. She addresses her son Cain, who in the Bible's account murders his brother Abel. What is the poetic effect of cutting off Eve's speech in midsentence? Why does she call Cain the "son of man"? What do you think she meant to tell him?

3. Born to a Jewish family in Czernovitz, Romania, in 1920, Paul Ansel grew up speaking Romanian, Yiddish, and German, but it was the latter tongue in which he composed his verse. This contradiction between German and Jewish identification stemmed from his mother's encouragement to speak German, which was the cosmopolitan language of the arts, literature, and politics of the former Austro-Hungarian empire. The poet and his parents were deported in the summer of 1942. Ansel survived as a worker in several labor battalions, but his parents quickly succumbed to concentration camp existence. After the war, Ansel changed his name to Paul Celan, moved to Vienna, and later to Paris. Although Celan would receive world acclaim as a poet, he nevertheless committed suicide in 1970.

In "Death Fugue," the contradiction between the poet's

Jews undergoing selection at Auschwitz with camp entrance in background.

German and Jewish identification is figured in the two mythic women Margarete and Shulamith. The former alludes to the heroine of Goethe's *Faust* and the "golden-hair" of Heinrich Heine's siren Lorelei. Shulamith is based on the dark Old Testament princess of the Song of Songs. Her name echoes the Hebrew word for peace, *shalom*, as well as *Yerushalayim*, or Jerusalem.

In what ways do these two complementary female principals contradict and balance one another in the poem? How do you interpret the paradoxical figure of "black milk"? Discuss Celan's use of apostrophe in his address to "black milk" as a personified contradiction.

4. Discuss the comparative identifications that Sylvia Plath makes between women and concentration camp victims. Are these comparisons valid? Do they enhance the representation of women's experience or trivialize Holocaust victims?

5. Consider the ways in which the formal resources of the sestina in "The Book of Yolek" allow Anthony Hecht to shift the meanings of the repeated end words— *meal, walk, home, camp, day*—from their familiar, everyday connotations to their opposite associations with the Holocaust.

31

Critical Perspectives

A Casebook on Postmodern Poetics

www

Postmodernism Web is a key word that you are as likely to encounter on MTV as in a book of scholarly critical theory. Architecture, music, art, theater, literature, economics, and the social sciences all describe our present moment in terms of postmodernism. Although the word *postmodernism* literally denotes what comes after twentieth-century modernism (see Chapter 14), the widespread use of this rubric in academic circles and popular culture generally makes it more than simply a term covering a moment in history. Not just a period term, postmodernism involves complex understandings of language, philosophical thought, human subjectivity and political theory. The critical theorist Fredric Jameson distinguishes between modernism and postmodernism by drawing a contrast between poet Ezra Pound's modernist slogan "make it new" and William Gibson's rejoinder "when-it-all-changed" from his 1988 cyberpunk novel *Mona Lisa Overdrive*. According to Jameson in *Postmodernism, or The Cultural Logic of Late Capitalism* (1991), modernism "thought compulsively about the New and tried to watch its coming into being . . . but the postmodern looks for breaks, for events rather than new worlds, for the telltale instant after which it is no longer the same . . . or better still, for shifts and irrevocable changes in the representation of things and of the way they change."

Ezra Pound's dictum—"make it new"—signaled a rupture and departure from what he criticized as the mannered world outlook of the Victorian era that, by the end of the nineteeth century, had become all too predictable in its aesthetic conventions. Following the example of such cubist artists as Pablo Picasso and Georges Braques, and paralleling futurist writers like F. T. Marinetti, Pound sought to overturn conventional habits of perception and thought. He wanted to renew poetic expression based on the "image" (see Chapter 21). At the level of technique, Pound defined *imagism* in terms of a "direct treatment of the 'thing' whether subjective or objective." However experimental in employing poetic collage forms, Pound's poetic dictum "make it new" assumed the fixed, knowable world of the "thing" whose referent ("It") could be comprehended, grasped, de-created, and re-created through the power of the imagination. Similarly, the modern poet Wallace Stevens wanted the imagination to "be completely adequate in the face of reality." He defined the poem as a kind of settlement between the mind and the real. In *The Necessary Angel* (1951), he wrote that a poem expresses "a violence from within that protects us from a violence without. It is the imagination pressing back against the pressure of reality." Like Pound, Stevens assumed that reality—however chaotic—has force, depth, and substance.

In contrast, Gibson's postmodern phrasing "when-it-all-changed," as its hyphenated format suggests, unhinges the "thing" (the signifer "It") from any referent grounded in a real, fixed world of essences. *As we move from the modern to the postmodern condition, the real world of things is increasingly difficult to tell apart from copies of things, or simulations, created by the influences of advertising, television, digitized computer graphics, the Internet, and other technological tools of the information age.* Gibson's slogan denotes a decisive break with the world of referential things-in-themselves. Instead, Gibson points to the postmodern turn toward a process of endless representational change in signification. While modernism still presents versions of the individual's personal point of view, or subjectivity, postmodernism parts company with the person's unique frame of reference. While the former still features the emotional lives of characters, the latter portrays random intensities that cut across individual selves. The postmodern condition is defined more by the kind of turbulent unpredictability that James Gleick describes in terms of chaos theory. In postmodern literature, for example, the author is viewed less as the creative genius presiding over the work and more as a manipulator of free-floating codes and chance operations. While we can study modernism—read its texts, experience its insights, learn from its triumphs and failures—it is, for better or worse, in the postmodern condition that we now live.

Postmodernism marks the limit of the Enlightenment philosophy of modernism dating back to the sixteenth century. The philosophical underpinnings of Enlightenment humanism are based in reason. Rational thought is foundational, and thinking defines one's human essence. *Cogito ergo sum.* "I think, therefore I am," as René Descartes famously asserted in his 1637 volume *Discourse on the Method of Rightly Conducting the Reason and Seeking the Truth in the Sciences.* Such Enlightenment principles rest on a knowable, objective universe available to scientific inquiry and reasoned verification. The Enlightenment faith in progress stems from the mind's ability to discern determinable, universal truths that can be applied to the state, government, law, legal institutions, and human relations generally. Similarly, language serves in this model as the transparent medium for reasoned thought, the articulation of truth, the practice of ethics, and the expression of beauty. Moreover, the world outlook of the Enlightenment maintains that all of these things can be rationally communicated because the written or spoken word, as signifier, reflects the "thing" or referent "It" in an unproblematic relation. The Enlightenment project seeks to map the human domains of science, politics, ethics, and aesthetics through grand or "master" narratives that rest on universal principles whose foundational truths can withstand the test of time and be applied uniformly across regional circumstance and local differences.

By the nineteenth century, however, these Enlightenment ideals became complicated by new understandings of human subjectivity. The humanist faith in rationality began to erode from new theories of evolution—inaugurated with Charles Darwin's *On the Origin of Species by Means of Natural Selection* (1859)—and reinforced by the Freudian revolution in psychology, Friedrich Nietzsche's theories of the death of God and the will to power in *The Gay Science* (1882), as well as Karl Marx's and Friedrich Engels's analyses of class conflict. Moreover, the whole concept of a constant, natural universe was further undermined in the modern theories of relativity that emerged in modern, post-Newtonian physics.

Experimental literary modernism of the early twentieth century also marks the breakup of the Enlightenment paradigm. We can see this emerging crisis in the kind of fragmentation witnessed in T. S. Eliot's bleak depiction of the post-World War I milieu of *The Waste Land* (1922). The end of Enlightenment thinking is also evident in the dispersal of the individual's personal awareness through unconscious, stream-of-consciousness narratives in the fiction of such modernist authors as Virginia Woolf and James Joyce. We can observe a similar shift in the modern self as it is exposed to the new forms of mass media, print journalism, film, and radio, as in the collaged newsreel montages of John Dos Passos. Modernist literary characters are increasingly saturated as well by a new erotic politics of desire, as portrayed by such expatriate American writers as Henry Miller and Djuna Barnes.

Modernism responds inventively to the loss of foundational belief, certainty, rationality, and the human-scale order of things. Postmodernism celebrates the modernist desire to "make it new" but accelerates the forms and representations of "the new" at a dizzying pace as the ever-multiplying technologies of the information age allow for instant global communication. Even more than modernism, postmodernism reveals the structuring role of language and sign systems in *determining* our experience of the world, rather than *www* merely *reflecting* it. **Semiotics** Web —the scholarly analysis of sign systems and practices of signification in everyday life—reflects this new awareness of how the constant acceleration of advertising and mass mediated messages broadcast via television, radio, the Internet, and so on has fundamentally changed contemporary experience.

www Some postmodern theorists are committed to a **Marxist** Web analysis of these contemporary trends. Influenced by the nineteenth-century German philosopher, historian, social scientist, and revolutionary Karl Marx, Marxist critics advance, in a variety of ways, a labor theory of value. In particular, they consider how underlying economic structures influence global and state politics, popular culture, and everyday life. From a Marxist point of view, the postmodern paradigm shift—"when-it-all-changed"—amounts to both an expression and shaping of underlying economic trends. They point to the evolution after World War II away from the economies of industrial production that define modernism and toward the consumer society of the postwar decades. Money in the postwar era is not just made from its modern settings of industrial production—the factory, textile mill, power plant, construction site, or agribusiness combine. Instead postwar capital seizes on the frontier markets of consumption—the mall, the road strip, the nuclear household— and exploits these new niche markets with ever new generations of consumer items: gas and restaurant franchises, prepackaged foods, electronic appliances, and gadgetry of all kinds. Even the most private spaces of the body and the unconscious are exploited with accelerating rhythms of style, fashion, and popular trends in music, teen culture, and suburban living. Mediated by the new electronic media, the postmodern condition of everyday life increasingly is driven by sign exchange for its own sake.

By now, we have grown accustomed to the new cultural logic of the information age and its endless layering of sign systems whose fantasies of affluence, success, luxury, and satisfaction through consumption exceed anything most of us will ever experience concretely in the real world. Increasingly, advertising has depended on the sheer repetition of canned or artificial signs of enjoyment. Harbingers of the postmodern can be seen in the postmodern visual art of Andy Warhol. Through playful but arresting images, Warhol parodies the commodity form, as in his reproduction of literal Campbell soup cans or his portraits of such Hollywood icons as Marilyn Monroe, who became inseparable from her star image (see color insert). We live not only in the society of the media spectacle but in a world of simulacra, or artificial copies, of real things. Here the endless proliferation of signs and semiotic exchange confuses the difference between the real and its manufactured imitations. Such films as the Wachowski brothers' *The Matrix* depict in the cyperpunk subgenre the blurring of the real and its postmodern simulation. Within this new horizon, the things we take for granted in everyday life—human subjectivity, thought, and personal will—are no longer simply expressed and communicated through language. Instead, they suddenly appear as produced by a complex matrix of digitized codes. In postmodern thinking, likewise, the human subject is increasingly viewed as itself linguistically produced, as shaped by complex practices of signification.

According to the postmodern view of things, the sources of our desire and what we value are neither simple nor consistent. In fact, they are not even personal; they don't belong to us as individuals. Rather, our sexual preferences, our gender identifications, the kind of work we pursue, the company we keep—the entire repertoire of where we live, what we wear, the sports we pursue, what we find appetizing, which TV channels we watch and how quickly we surf them, the Web sites we frequent—are all formed by an assemblage of competing and discursively produced seductions driven by services and consumables whose bottom-line aim is to make money. In this postmodern register, the self is experienced as dispersed across a range of desiring subject positions that are less fixed than fluid, less authentic than situational, less predictable than subject to chance. Subjectivity is no longer unitary but divided by a multiplicity of conflicting, even schizophrenic, narrative tensions.

Beginning in the late 1970s, the postmodern emphasis on language's constituting role in postmodern experience began to make itself felt in contemporary poetics, especially in the magazine *L=A=N=G=U=A=G=E* edited by Bruce Andrews and Charles Bernstein. A new movement of postmodern poets located primarily in New York City and the San Francisco Bay area began to publish experimental work in such journals as *Poetics Journal, Sulfur, This, Hills,* and in books by independent presses such as Lyn Hejinian's Tuumba, Barrett Watten's This Press, and James Sherry's Roof Press, among many others.

These writers no longer thought of the author as the expressive genius of the poetic utterance. They went beyond regarding the author as a modern craftsman of a new poetic form. In this regard, the Language writers followed the lead of the French theorist Roland Barthes, who in his 1968 essay "The Death of the Author" radically reinterpreted the author's relation to language. Instead of expressing individual genius, the literary text for Barthes inverts the author's relation to the writing. "Linguistically," Barthes writes, "the author is never more than the instance writing, just as *I* is nothing other than the instance saying I: language knows a 'subject', not a 'person.'" Similarly, the Language writers stressed the autonomous linguistic operations and verbal chance events that take place in language itself, beyond any authorial intention. "It's a mistake," said Charles Bernstein, "to posit the self as the primary organizing feature of writing. As many others have pointed out, a poem exists in a matrix of social and historical relations that are more significant to the formation of an individual text than any personal qualities of the life or voice of an author."

Much of the new, postmodern poetry sought to challenge the normative conventions that put language at the beck and call of consumer values. Many language poets subverted the "formal requirements of clarity and exposition" shaping the verbal formats of journalism, advertising, bureaucratic speaking, and other discourses that sustain consumer society through sound bites, packaged phrasings, and clichéd utterances. Instead, says Bernstein in *Content's Dream* (1986), in Language writing "contradiction, obsessiveness, associative reasoning, etc., are given fre(er) play." For Language poets, the presentation of a poem's individual letters, its formal procedures, and its syntax matter more than the qualities of its voice or emotive authenticity. Bob Perelman's postmodern manipulations of language in "Virtual Reality," for example, mimic the normative speaking voice in its first-person plural address to the reader. Nevertheless, our conventional identification with the poem's "we" quickly breaks down and is dispersed through a scene of simulated experience:

> We turned to analysis, negotiation, persuasion,
> cards on the table, confession, surrender.
>
> But there was no refamiliarizing. Our
> machines filled the freeway with names
>
> and desires, hurling aggressively streamlined
> 　　messages
> Toward a future that seemed restless,
> 　　barely interested.

More playfully, Perelman's poem "Seduced by Analogy" dismantles the ways in which language's formal operations and verbal "seductions" shape thought, not the other way around:

> First sentence: *Her cheap perfume*
> *Caused cancer in the White House late last night.*
> With *afford*, *agree* and *arrange*, use the infinitive.

I can't agree to die. With *practice,*
Imagine, and *resist,* use the gerund. *I practice to live*
Is wrong. Specify, "We've got to nuke 'em, Henry."
Second sentence: *Inside the box is plutonium.*
The concept degrades, explodes,
Goes all the way, in legal parlance.

"I can't stop. Stop. I can't stop myself."
First sentence: *She is a woman who has read*
Powers of Desire. Second sentence:
She is a man that has a job, no job, a car, no car,
To drive, driving. Tender is the money
That makes the bus *to go* over the bridge.
Go over the bridge. *Tender*
Are the postures singularly verbally undressed men and women
Assume. *Strong* are the rivets of the bridge. "I'm not interested,
Try someone else." First sentence:
Wipe them off the face. Not complete.

In these opening stanzas of "Seduced by Analogy," Perleman's "first sentence" mixes up the fetishized codes of broadcast news—"caused cancer" and "in the White House last night"—to seduce and derail the reader's consumption of a typical news report. The poem estranges and defamiliarizes our expectations of the conventional news narrative. Not only do the poet's non sequiturs subvert our habitual reliance on the simple sentence as a journalistic commodity form, but this playful quoting of grammatical rules calls attention to how the constructed nature of discourse shapes our experience of the world.

Serial repetition lays bare the fabricated codes of postmodern experience in much the same way as in, say, Andy Warhol's multiple icons of Marilyn Monroe (see color insert). Repetition of phrasing, parts of grammar, and key words in postmodern poetry parallel the serial musical forms of Philip Glass and analogous cinematic techniques of avant-garde film directors like Hollis Frampton, Sally Potter, Yvonne Rainer, and Michael Snow. Presenting language as assemblage, rather than as lyric expression, other language writers such as Ron Silliman and Lyn Hejinian likewise employ serial composition. For example, Hejinian employs her age in *My Life* (1980) as a basis for her sentence and paragraph constructions: 37 paragraphs of 37 sentences each. Similarly, Ron Silliman's "2197" is made up of 13 sections, each embodying 13 stanzas of 13 sentence units; the title "2197" equals 13 cubed.

Analogous techniques of composing lines in sentences made up of a fixed number of words point not only to the fabricated nature of all utterance but also afford new opportunities for discoveries and meanings in language usage, as in this excerpt from Perelman's "Chronic Meanings":

The single fact is matter.
Five words can say only.
Black sky at night, reasonably.
I am, the irrational residue.

Blown up chain link fence.
Next morning stronger than ever.

Midnight the pain is almost.
The train seems practically expressive.

A story familiar as a.
Society has broken into bands.
The nineteenth century was sure.
Characters in the withering capital.

Such truncated, utterances and their structural relation of **parataxis**—setting phrases side by side without obvious or logical connection—may be indeterminable, nonsensical, illuminating, comic, and profoundly unsettling. But they are never predictable. They seldom make reference to a world that comes before their invocation of it.

www   A more radical deployment of arranged language on the page happens in the poetry of Susan Howe **Web** . Beginning her career as a visual artist after graduating from the Boston Museum School of Fine Arts in 1961, Howe brings her painter's sensitivity to the pictorial space of the page. Howe began writing poems in the 1970s and published such important volumes of experimental poetry in the 1980s as *The Liberties* (1980), *Pythagorean Silence* (1982), *Articulation of Sound Forms in Time* (1987). It was at this stage in her career that she also published an influential book of criticism entitled *My Emily Dickinson* (1985). Her volumes from the 1990s include *Singularities* (1990), *The*

www   *Europe of Trusts* (1990), and *The Nonconformist's Memorial* (1993) **Web** .

Howe's visual sense of space was reinforced through her partner of twenty-seven years, David von Schlegell, who directed the Yale sculpture program in New Haven. Further shaping Howe's eclectic sensibilities as a visual artist were the minimalist influences of mixed media and collage artists whom she encountered in the 1960s New York art scene, artists such as Richard Serra, Joan Jonas, Don Judd, Eva Hesse, Ellsworth Kelly, Robert Morris, Carl Andre, John Cage, and Agnes Martin. Like these postmodern artists, Howe was drawn to the new aesthetic possibilities afforded by composing across the boundaries of genre of painting, film, music, sculpture, and poetry. Inspired by the open format "projective verse" experiments of the Black Mountain poet Charles Olson, Howe began to compose her visual compositions in language fragments, as photocopied texts cut into lines and pasted as visual objects on the canvas of the page. Of her poetic method in *The Nonconformist's Memorial*, Howe has said:

> First I would type some lines. Then cut them apart. Paste one on top of another, move them around until they looked right. Then I'd xerox that version, getting several copies, and then cut and paste again until I had it right. The getting it right has to do with how it's structured on the page as well as how it sounds—this is the meaning.

Rather than regarding verse as the vehicle for the poet's personal or confessional experience, Howe thinks of language in terms of pictorial images where the look of a verbal arrangement signifies original meanings in new compositional formats. Her poetry experiments with verbal collage and intertextual citations from other authors such as Emily Dickinson and Herman Melville,

as well as the Gospel According to John. At times, her poetry suggests the
contested reception of traumatic historical events such as the execution of
Charles I, which is the subject of her poem "Eikon Basilike."

In her long poem on the execution of Charles I, Howe runs lines into and
over one another in jagged, chaotic formats where words and phrases intersect and collide to suggest historical violence. Howe describes her compositional strategy this way:

> In the "Eikon Basilike," the sections that are all vertically jagged are based around
> the violence of the execution of Charles I, the violence of history, the violence of
> that particular event, and also then the stage drama of it. It was a trial, but the
> scene of his execution was also a performance; he acted his own death. There's no
> way to express that in just words in ordinary fashion on the page. So I would try
> to match that chaos and violence visually with words.

Other long poem sequences such as "Thorow" require the reader to turn the
poem up to 180 degrees as some lines are written at angles or in upside-down
relation to other lines. Howe describes this as a poetic "mirroring" technique.
In her poetry readings, she whispers the upside-down lines for strange, other-
worldly, and uncanny effects.

Beyond Howe's compositional language experiments on the page, postmodern poetics becomes more provocative, perhaps, in the expanded public
sphere of everyday life where language, signage, and technology intersect in
the makeup of today's society of the spectacle. Jenny Holzer's appropriation of
light emitting diode (L.E.D.) boards is one example of this new form of poetic expression. Holzer came to New York in 1976–1977 via the Whitney Museum's Independent Study Program. After collaborating with a number of
performance artists at the Whitney, she jettisoned her pursuit of more typical
artistic values and in 1977 began to compose aphorisms that she collected in a
series of "Truisms" formatted onto posters, stickers, handbills, hats, T-shirts,
and other paraphernalia. The verbal character of the "Truisms" themselves

Jenny Holzer, *Untitled* (1989–1990)

relies on the familiar slogans and one-liners common to tabloid journalism, the *Reader's Digest* headline, the TV evangelist pitch line, campaign rhetoric, rap and hip-hop lyrics, bumper sticker and T-shirt displays, and countless other kitsch forms.

In the mid-1980s, Holzer intensified her art's political content in her more militant "Survival" series and, at the same time, undertook a bolder appropriation of a uniquely authoritative and spectacular medium: the L.E.D. boards installed worldwide in stock exchanges, urban squares, airports, stadiums, sports arenas, and other mass locales. The formal elements of this new high-tech medium—its expanded memory of over 15,000 characters coupled with a built-in capacity for special visual effects and dynamic motion—advanced Holzer's poster aesthetics into the linguistic registers of poetics and textual performance art. In 1982, under the auspices of the Public Art Fund, Holzer went to the heart of America's mass spectacle, choosing selections from among her most succinct and powerful "Truisms" for public broadcast on New York's mammoth Times Square Spectacolor Board. In Holzer's work, contemporary poetics took on a life beyond the limits of the printed page and went to the literal crossroads of postmodern consumer society.

Poems for Further Reading and Critical Writing

BOB PERELMAN   *(b. 1947)*

Virtual Reality   *(1993)*

It was past four when we
found our feet lifted above our

accelerators, only touching them at intervals.
Inside, our car radios were displaying

the body of our song, marked   5
with static from Pacific storms. Outside

was the setting for the story
of our life: Route 80 near

Emeryville—fence, frontage road, bay, hills,
billboards changing every couple of months.

It was the present—there was   10
nothing to contradict this—but it

seemed stopped short, a careless afterthought,
with the background impossible to keep

in focus. We weren't pleased with
the choices, words or stations, and   15

our desire pouted in the corners
of our song, where it clung

self-consciously to the rhythm-fill or bass
or the scratch in the voice

as it pushed the big moments   20
of the lyrics over the hump.

We were stacked up and our
path was jammed negotiation for every

forward foot. Hope of automatic writing,
of turning the wheel freely in   25

a narrative of convincing possibility, was
only a byproduct of the fallen

leaves lifted in the ads and
drifting sideways in slow motion as

the BMW cornered away from us   30
at forty. We were recording everything,

but the unlabeled cassettes were spilling
over into the footage currently being

shot. This was making the archives
frankly random. A specific request might   35

yield a county fair displaying its
rows of pleasures: candy apples, Skee-Ball,

two-headed sheep, the Cave Woman. She
looked normal enough, standing in her

Plexiglass cage as the MC spieled: 40
the startled expedition, capture, scientific analysis.

But suddenly she interrupted him, breaking
her chains, thumping the glass and

grunting, as a holograph of a
gorilla was projected more or less   45

over her. The MC turned his
mike up and shouted, "We can't

control her!" and the lights went
out, which apparently was the signal

for us to stumble out of   50
the tent, giggling, every hour on

the hour, gypped certainly, but possibly
a bit nostalgic. We had already

fashioned nooses out of coded nursery
twine to help the newscasters with   55

their pronunciation, and whipped up stampedes
of ghost dancers from old westerns,

not that we could see them.
If we lived here, in separate

bodies, we'd have been home long   60
ago, watching the entertainment morsels strip

and hand over everything, and telling
the dog to sit and not

to beg. But the more commands
we gave our body the more   65

it gaped and clumped together, over-excited
and impossible to do anything with.

We turned to analysis, negotiation, persuasion,
cards on the table, confession, surrender.

But there was no refamiliarizing. Our   70
machines filled the freeway with names

and desires, hurling aggressively streamlined messages
toward a future that seemed restless,

barely interested. We could almost see
our hands seizing towers, chains, dealerships,   75

the structures that drew the maps,
but there was no time to

read them, only to react, as
the global information net had become

obsessed with our body's every move, 80
spasm, twitch, smashing at it with

videotaped sticks, validating it, urging instant
credit, free getaways, passionate replacement offers.

Chronic Meanings

(1993)

for Lee Hickman

The single fact is matter.
Five words can say only.
Black sky at night, reasonably.
I am, the irrational residue.

Blown up chain link fence. 5
Next morning stronger than ever.
Midnight the pain is almost.
The train seems practically expressive.

A story familiar as a.
Society has broken into bands. 10
The nineteenth century was sure.
Characters in the withering capital.

The heroic figure straddled the.
The clouds enveloped the tallest.
Tens of thousands of drops. 15
The monster struggled with Milton.

On our wedding night I.
The sorrow burned deeper than.
Grimly I pursued what violence.
A trap, a catch, a. 20

Fans stand up, yelling their.
Lights go off in houses.
A fictional look, not quite.
To be able to talk.

The coffee sounds intriguing but.   25
She put her cards on.
What had been comfortable subjectivity.
The lesson we can each.

Not enough time to thoroughly.
Structure announces structure and takes.   30
He caught his breath in.
The vista disclosed no immediate.

Alone with a pun in.
The clock face and the.
Rock of ages, a modern.   35
I think I had better.

Now this particular mall seemed.
The bag of groceries had.
Whether a biographical junkheap or.
In no sense do I.   40

These fields make me feel.
Mount Rushmore in a sonnet.
Some in the party tried.
So it's not as if.

That always happened until one.   45
She spread her arms and.
The sky if anything grew.
Which left a lot of.

No one could help it.
I ran farther than I.   50
That wasn't a good one.
Now put down your pencils.

They won't pull that over.
Standing up to the Empire.
Stop it, screaming in a.   55
The smell of pine needles.

Economics is not my strong.
Until one of us reads.
I took a breath, then.
The singular heroic vision, unilaterally.   60

Voices imitate the very words.
Bed was one place where.

A personal life, a toaster.
Memorized experience can't be completely.

The impossibility of the simplest. 65
So shut the fucking thing.
Now I've gone and put.
But that makes the world.

The point I am trying.
Like a cartoon worm on. 70
A physical mouth without speech.
If taken to an extreme.

The phone is for someone.
The next second it seemed.
But did that really mean. 75
Yet Los Angeles is full.

Naturally enough I turn to.
Some things are reversible, some.
You don't have that choice.
I'm going to Jo's for. 80

Now I've heard everything, he.
One time when I used.
The amount of dissatisfaction involved.
The weather isn't all it's.

You'd think people would have. 85
Or that they would invent.
At least if the emotional.
The presence of an illusion.

Symbiosis of home and prison.
Then, having become superfluous, time. 90
One has to give to.
Taste: the first and last.

I remember the look in.
It was the first time.
Some gorgeous swelling feeling that. 95
Success which owes its fortune.

Come what may it can't.
There are a number of.
But there is only one.
That's why I want to. 100

FANNY HOWE   *(b. 1940)*

Introduction to the World   *(1985)*

I'd speak if I wasn't afraid of inhaling
A memory I want to forget
Like I trusted the world which wasn't mine
The hollyhock in the tall vase is wide awake
And feelings are only overcome by fleeing   5
To their opposite. Moisture and dirt
Have entered the space between threshold and floor
A lot is my estimate when I step on it
Sorrow can be a home to stand on so
And see far to: another earth, a place I might know   10

Hide the name away in the Secret
Jesus of the little Brothers and Sisters
Those born on the last day will have no name
But Mother, Father and the above
Till now the lips of hardened hearts used politics   15
To speak of love until they lost it
You couldn't argue with their logic
The oppression of realism is consensus
To those who raise what they value
Out of reach until it's magic   20

Sea mist surprises my heavy eyes
I know at last I don't exist
This register is only a certainty
If evolution's over and the created world
Is done developing this place   25
And its laws. Always fixed and free
You never know what you were or are
Expressing
Like mathematics around a head
On rising from a siesta   30

Small birds puff their chests and feathers
With the pleasure that they know better
High morning clouds unload themselves
On the world. Blue peeps through
Sunny boys have spacious souls but killers   35
Build war zones in the sky where they go to die
Blue poems. Blue ozone. A V-sign
Sails into the elements: an old ship
Named Obsolete though Lovely is easier to see
Now visualize heaven as everything around it   40

Concentrate on the top of the mast, father
Arms up. You won't be needing them
On the swaying sea to heaven. One last goodbye
Makes each hand impotent
Like false mirth or some stupid mutant   45
I'm off to see people because you don't need me
Yet, where don't doesn't ever mean never
And I'm crossing my own stony ocean
Consciousness has nothing to do with me either
I'm just moving inside it, catch as catch can't   50

There is nothing I hear as well as my name
Called when I'm wild. The grace of God
Places a person in the truth
And is always expressed as a taste in the mouth
Walking with your arms wide open   55
And 263 days to follow, four morning stars
And Yuri Gagarin orbiting Earth
I know I may never be found or returned
When Peter, Henri or Mary call me
Fanny, as if they know who owns me   60

Come, tinkers, among droves of acorn trees
Be only one third needful, O
Name the things whereby we hope
Before the story scatters. A cardinal
Is red for fever where you passed   65
The suffering world's faith
Is a scandal. Tests of facts
Bring dread to aptitude
You who loved the people and the world
Tell us our failings and if we're home   70

I am the people never so alone
As when abiding
in history, broken
No God but a causality moral
As a socialist. Success   75
Hardly ever exists on these nights
Which intervene in secret with a *don't*
and a *so!* For then I can't lead
The little into the day but run
Like a heart blind to advice   80

The sea at last lies over this place
And registers expressly
During my siesta
I know evolution is done developing

Its laws of mathematics must be correct   85
In my created head I don't exist
As rising bed-heavy the mist
Is fixed though always full of surprises
And the world in my eyes
Is hardly a certainty   90

If you have to die
Puff and visualize
The ozone of heaven
As easy seen high as seen through
And peep on the world as if it's obsolete   95
An old ship in new elements
Everything will sail into pleasure then
Unload your spacious soul
Whose chest full of killers is zoned
For the sun now in its feather blue building   100

When mirth sways like a mast
On top of a goodbye
I don't need oceans to move myself over stones
One hand up and arms
Which show I'm impotent   105
To people or some false father
Who have nothing to do with what I'm here for
Inside I cross myself
And concentrate on the consciousness
The sea comes out of   110

I'll pay and bow out
For not hardship but the judiciary
Connected the test of time
To penalty
I in my life spent my days   115
Escaping the creator, seedy as a man
Who disappears from his tricks
Now I ache at the strange
Creations, mine, which like women
Look new in the Court of God   120

CHARLES BERNSTEIN   *(b. 1950)*

The Kiwi Bird in the Kiwi Tree   *(1991)*

I want no paradise only to be
drenched in the downpour of words, fecund

with tropicality. Fundament be-
yond relation, less 'real' than made, as arms
surround a baby's gurgling: encir- 5
cling mesh pronounces its promise (not bars
that pinion, notes that ply). The tailor tells
of other tolls, the seam that binds, the trim,
the waste. & having spelled these names, move on
to toys or talcums, skates & scores. Only 10
the imaginary is real—not trumps
beclouding the mind's acrobatic versions. The first fact is the social body,
one from another, nor needs no other.

Ear Shot   *(1991)*

Here is the spare
aside the locker room
where I am marooned

House of Formaldehyde   *(1991)*

It's not where you're going, it's
Where you've been. Dateline
In the harbor. Fellow rushes
For funding, fuming, flipping
Flaccid: rimless erosion, witless 5
Emulsification. As on a bent,
Meal, plaid, plane, a girl
Holds a pail, defends a swirl

Stumbling for eviscerated lead hooks
Englotted, Nordic stoops 10
Whosover irradiates decay, plunged
As pediment, foaming sail, lining the
Shifts with spongy (spectacular) spatulas.

Horatio of spell-bent positioning, fusing
Co-spaniel foresight and copper-wire calumny 15
Against the grain of saddlestitch cornmash.
Precisely giddy, morosely fecundated. Snorkling
& then snookered. Roadside rest-test adjoined
To defamilial tireiron. (Unhooks what's
Best left loose.) As was fonder than 20
Revenants. Neither a fender nor a succotash
Be. (Merely a spittoon of her petunia.) Seeking
Not or seeing blotted—wave-high the croon,
Defrock the peeling Argonaut. I would

Not sink her ship nor span her   25
Border as lacking sun-stained
Catapults. Neither have I . . .

Whose deflection can only pronounce incipience
As the promise leadens enactment
& the dusted gables parrot the stick to which   30
Only lessening accounts. The serpentine miles
Of the long-laundered parade dissolve
In gulps, becalmed forays. Having hidden
My amulets & fired my token,
Alone on a dust-dark sea, with only   35
Thee. Or wails oasis, deeded ground
Where foot cannot fall, & felled, retains.

TOPICS FOR CRITICAL THINKING

www

1. Discuss how Susan Howe's visual arrangement of the lines in the poem "Turning"
   Web affects their meaning for the reader.
2. Consider the ways in which Bob Perelman employs and departs from the metaphor
   of highway driving to describe postmodern experience in "Virtual Reality."
3. Interpret the relationship between Fanny Howe's title "Introduction to the World"
   and the poem's phrasings, themes, and imagery.

TOPICS FOR CRITICAL WRITING

1. Explore the convention of the five-word sentence as a formal device that generates
   new possibilities of poetic utterance in "Chronic Meanings." How does the five-
   word line disrupt our normal habits of reading?
2. Examine the ways in which Charles Bernstein subverts the conventions of setting,
   character, plot, and narrative coherence generally in "House of Formaldehyde."

Critical Perspective: On Nonlinear Poetics

"When Pound declares in Canto 81, 'To break the pentameter, that was the
first heave,' he is speaking to a particular situation in late-Victorian 'genteel'
verse, when meter stood for a particular collective attitude, a social and cultural restriction on the 'freedom' of the subject. Vladimir Mayakovsky, coming out of an entirely different tradition, but in the same time period, makes a
similar gesture when he declares in 1926, 'Trochees and iambs have never
been necessary to me. I don't know them and don't want to know them. Iambs
impede the forward movement of poetry.'

"Such statements, [Henri] Meschonnic points out, are neither true nor untrue; rather, they must be understood as part of the drive toward rupture characteristic of the early twentieth-century avant-garde. And the form Pound's
own prosody took—the 'ideogrammizing of Western verse,' in Meschonnic's
words—had everything to do with the revolution in mass print culture, a rev-

olution that bred what Meschonnic calls the 'theatre of the page.' 'If we were to talk about practices rather than intentions,' he says, 'every page of poetry would represent a conception of poetry.' Blank spaces, for example, would become just as important as the words themselves in composing a particular construct. Thus, the structuralist argument that lineation in and of itself guarantees that a text will be read and interpreted as a poem is based on two misconceptions. First, it ignores the active role that white space (silence) plays in the visual and aural reception of the poem: the line, after all, is anchored in a larger visual field, a field by no means invariable. Second, and more important, the response to lineation must itself be historicized. In a contemporary context of one-liners on the television screen and the computer monitor, as well as lineated ads, greeting-cards, and catalog entries, the reader/viewer has become quite accustomed to reading 'in lines.' Indeed, surfing the Internet is largely a scanning process in which the line is rapidly replacing the paragraph as the unit to be accessed.

"How lineation as device signifies thus depends on many factors, historical, cultural, and national. The history of free verse in English remains to be written: when it is, it will be clear that the dominant example has been, not that of Ezra Pound, whose ideographic page has only recently become a model for poets, but that of William Carlos Williams, whose verse signature is still a powerful presence."

—Marjorie Perloff, from "After Free Verse:
The New Nonlinear Poetries" (1988)

Critical Perspective: On Postmodernism and Capitalism

"The last few years have been marked by an inverted millenarianism in which premonitions of the future, catastrophic or redemptive, have been replaced by senses of the end of this or that (the end of ideology, art, or social class; the 'crisis' of Leninism, social democracy, or the welfare state, etc., etc.); taken together, all of these perhaps constitute what is increasingly called postmodernism. The case for its existence depends on the hypothesis of some radical break or *coupure*, generally traced back to the end of the 1950s or the early 1960s.

"As the word itself suggests, this break is most often related to notions of the waning or extinction of the hundred-year-old modern movement (or to its ideological or aesthetic repudiation). Thus abstract expressionism in painting, existentialism in philosophy, the final forms of representation in the novel, the films of the great *auteurs*, or the modernist school of poetry (as institutionalized and canonized in the works of Wallace Stevens) all are now seen as the final, extraordinary flowering of a high-modernist impulse which is spent and exhausted with them. The enumeration of what follows, then, at once becomes empirical, chaotic, and heterogeneous: Andy Warhol and pop art, but also photorealism, and beyond it, the 'new expressionism'; the moment, in music, of John Cage, but also the synthesis of classical and 'popular' styles found in composers like Phil Glass and Terry Riley, and also punk and new wave rock (the Beatles and the Stones now standing as the high-modernist moment of that more recent and rapidly evolving tradition); in film, Godard, post-Godard, and experimental cinema and video, but also a whole new type of commercial film . . . ; Burroughs, Pynchon, or Ishmael Reed, on the one hand, and the French *nouveau roman* and its succession, on the other, along with alarming new kinds of literary criticism based on some new aesthetic of textuality or *écriture* . . . The list might be extended indefinitely."

—Fredric Jameson, from *Postmodernism or,
The Cultural Logic of Late Capitalism* (1991)

Critical Perspective: On "Language Writing"

"There was never any self-consciously organized group known as the language writers or poets—not even a fixed name.

"This fact has not prevented 'language writing,' as a polemic horizon pregnant with unknown but unwanted developments, from often being invoked over the last two decades. There are real reasons for this: the positive structures of language writing are socially and aesthetically complex and in places strained and contradictory, but the movement has been more united by its opposition to the prevailing institutions of American poetry. During this period, American poetry has been dominated by writing workshops and creative-writing departments with large networks of legitimation—publishing, awards, reviews, extensive university connections. The aesthetics of this mainstream are not without variation, but generalizations are possible, and were certainly made, polemically, by those involved in the formation of language writing: the mainstream poet guarded a highly distinct individuality; while craft and literary knowledge contributed to poetry, sensibility and intuition reigned supreme. The mainstream poet was not an intellectual and especially not a theoretician. Hostility to analysis and, later, to theory, were constitutive of such a poetic stance. In this situation, modernism was no longer especially important. The discursive tone of later Eliot, the incantatory vaticism of Yeats, the kaleidoscopic novelty of Surrealism minus Marx and Freud, the authoritative common sense and rural cast of Frost (often translated to the suburbs), and an attenuated version of Williams as poet of the quotidian—these echoes might be read everywhere, but the more basic facts of modernism were shunned. The poet as engaged, oppositional intellectual, and poetic form and syntax as sites of experiment for political and social purposes—these would not be found. The confessional poets were the model: Lowell, Plath, Sexton, Berryman. Poems were short, narrative, focused on small or large moments of crisis or optimism. Whether the form was free verse or rhymed iambic stanzas, the tone was conversational. Such work was often unambitious, and the steady production of books and MFA graduates bespoke a bureaucratized routine, but the breakdowns and suicides of the leading exemplars stood as guarantees of intensity.

"The formation of language writing was given a negative impetus by such a poetic climate. The goals variously articulated by members of the group were quickly registered as hostile to the well-being of that climate. And this literary hostility was seen as emanating from a group of writers. Subsequent publications would show that 'the group' was not often all that cohesive: influence and interaction never produced a uniform literary program, let alone a uniform style. But there was a loose set of goals, procedures, habits, and verbal textures breaking the automatism of the poetic 'I' and its naturalized voice; foregrounding textuality and formal devices; using or alluding to Marxist or poststructuralist theory in order to open the present to critique and change. These, along with the group interaction and the aggressive dismissals of self-expressive mainstream poetics as politically reactionary, raised the specter of a Lenin-esque cadre dedicated to the overthrow of poetry. Robert von Hallberg sees mainstream American poetry of this period as the poetry of accommodation; language writing coalesced as American involvement in Vietnam was nearing its bankrupt conclusion: this was a significant cause of the unaccommodating nature of its poetics. But linkages between poetry and politics were always the source of dispute. For some, language writing was too programmatically political to be poetry; for a number of New American poets and their supporters, it was too poststructuralist to be political.

"Many features of this literary battle were reproduced on a wider scale by the introduction of poststructuralist thought into the American academy. While both were housed in universities, creative writing departments and English departments generally had nothing to do with one another; the advent of theory made the separation wider. Language writing was easy enough to subsume under the category of theory or postmodernism as part of a large tendency attacking self, reference, and history. As initial formal goals and polemical rallying cries, such attacks had specific literary value; as slogans they have devolved to little more than inflight snacks served on the proliferant hovercrafts of postmodernism."

—Bob Perelman, from *The Marginalization of Poetry* (1996)

Part VI
Understanding Poetic Representation

32 Race and Representation

Contemporary notions of race are closely bound up with their **representation** in literature, history, popular culture, the media, and everyday life. What do we mean, however, by the representation of race? How do we define representation? Understanding representation starts with the concept of **mimesis**.

Mimesis is defined by the idea of imitation and shares its root meaning with the art of mime and mimicry. The philosophy of mimesis begins with Plato in *The Republic*. In it, he argues that words reflect real objects in the world that are themselves based on ideal, fixed forms. In this Platonic understanding, *representation describes the act of using a word, image, or pictorial sign to stand for a thing or action*. For example, to pass your state driver's license exam, you had to memorize a set of verbal and pictorial representations for navigating the roadways. Three-color traffic signals, of course, give us coded representations of the act of going (green light), using caution (yellow light), and stopping (red light). In airports around the world, even if you don't always know the language, you can figure out which bathroom to use by following the pictorial icons that provide representations distinguishing women from men.

In this mimetic scheme, representations are verbal equivalents of the things we use and the actions we perform in the real world. But it's not that simple. For not all representations refer to identical things or actions. It doesn't take much reflection to realize that representations frame as much as they reflect how we understand things in the world. For example, in the ancient world, the sun typically was represented as a god such as Ra (Egyptian), Lugh (Celtic), Apollo (Greek), Liza (Fon), Amaterasu (Shinto), Huitzilopochtli (Aztec), or Shamash (Sumerian). Although all of these representations name the sun, they represent it differently. For the modern scientist, the sun represents the hydrogen- and helium-based thermonuclear energy source some 94,500,000 miles away from us at the center of our solar system. Which of these representations is the real sun? It depends, to a certain extent, on your point of view. The representations we use in language don't simply reflect a given world of things but actively shape our understanding of those things; they constitute, as much as reflect, the real world.

Equally important, representations not only reflect a given world of things, facts, and actions. They also act as persuasive rhetoric. *Representations have a shaping role in society. They convey impressions, communicate perceptions, influence opinion, build consensus, and determine attitude and beliefs.* In the United States, our form of democratic government relies on the ways in which our elected congressional officials represent our collective will and interests in the Senate and the House of Representatives. Similarly, to make a representation before a court of law is to argue a particular point of view on a case. In language usage, representations don't just mimic a world of fixed meanings and objective facts. Equally important, they perform meanings that serve particular groups and individuals politically.

Color and Representation

Historically, attitudes toward racial difference **Web** have been closely bound up *www* with cultural representations of color. A famous lesson in the cultural associations of color is dramatized in *The Autobiography of Malcolm X* (1965). During the civil rights era of the 1960s, Malcolm X emerged as one of the most influential spokespersons for African Americans. Before that time, however, he led the life of a street hustler. Convicted of robbery in 1946, he spent seven years in jail where he became a follower of Elijah Muhammad, the leader of the Nation of Islam. In prison, Malcolm learned about the politics of racial representation the first time he looked up the words *white* and *black* in a standard dictionary. There he read that *white* and *black* are not defined only by their **denotations**—that is, their objective dictionary meanings. White and black are not just neutral representations of opposites on the color wheel, one reflecting the visible spectrum of light and the other wholly absorbing it. Malcolm X discovered how color is implicated in a representational system of racial difference: one whose **connotations**—that is, the values, qualities, and associations a word acquires in usage over time—have social and political consequences.

Connotations of color have served, historically, to value whiteness at the expense of blackness. Whiteness, in fact, is valued insofar as it differs from blackness. According to the *Oxford English Dictionary*, the color black, as it has come down to us through the ages, carries with it the connotations of what is "iniquitous, atrocious, horribly wicked." Contemplating the murder of King Duncan, Macbeth remarks in a famous aside "Let not light see my black and deep desires." Blackness also conjures what is "pertaining to or involving death." Thus, William Shakespeare often marks death's limits to life through solar representations, as in Sonnet 3 where mortality is figured in "brave day sunk in hideous night" or in the "twilight" of Sonnet 73, "As after sunset fadeth in the west; / Which by and by black night doth take away."

Conversely, the color white tends to be associated with that which is "highly prized, precious; dear, beloved, favorite." Whiteness is further linked to "fairness," with what is "beautiful to the eye, of pleasing form or appearance." If the color black in traditional Anglo-European usage connotes negativity generally, whiteness is thought to be "free from malignity or evil intent—beneficent, innocent, harmless, especially as opposed to something characterized as black." John Keats, for example, invokes whiteness as the absolute marker of love's authenticity when he writes in *Endymion* that "I loved her to the very white of truth." Historically, white has not only signified truth but has stood as a universal representation of spiritual redemption, as Emily Dickinson claims in Poem 528: "Mine—by the Right of the White Election!"

The setting of heaven's grace is similarly represented in Robert Herrick's "The White Island, or Place of the Blest."

ROBERT HERRICK   *(1591–1674)*

The White Island, or Place of the Blest   *(1648)*

In this world, the isle of dreams,
While we sit by sorrow's streams,
Tears and terrors are our themes
      Reciting:

But when once from hence we fly,   5
More and more approaching nigh
Unto young eternity,
      Uniting:

In that whiter island, where
Things are evermore sincere;   10
Candor here and luster there
      Delighting:

There are no monstrous fancies shall
Out of hell an horror call,
To create, or cause at all   15
      Affrighting.

There, in calm and cooling sleep,
We our eyes shall never steep,
But eternal watch shall keep,
      Attending   20

Pleasures, such as shall pursue
Me immortalized, and you;
And fresh joys, as never too
      Have ending.

Notice in Herrick's poem how whiteness stands as a constituting representation of "young eternity," whose "whiter island" of "things ever more sincere" has the power of "uniting" and "delighting" and "attending pleasure." The candor, or shining truth, of that ideal setting is set off against the "sorrow's streams" and "tears and terrors" of "this world" as well as the "monstrous fancies" of hell.

    Light and darkness not only serve opposite moral ends in the setting of Herrick's scheme of redemption and damnation but also set the representational terms of heavenly versus earthly existence in Thomas Campion's "Follow Thy Fair Sun."

THOMAS CAMPION *(1567–1620)*

Follow Thy Fair Sun *(1601)*

Follow thy fair sun, unhappy shadow;
Though thou be black as night,
And she made all of light,
Yet follow thy fair sun, unhappy shadow.

Follow her whose light thy light depriveth;   5
Though here thou liv'st disgraced,
And she in heaven is placed,
Yet follow her whose light the world reviveth!

Follow those pure beams whose beauty burneth,
That so have scorched thee,   10
As thou still black must be,
Till her kind beams thy black to brightness turneth.

Follow her while yet her glory shineth;
There comes a luckless night,
That will dim all her light;   15
And this the black unhappy shade divineth.

Follow still since so thy fates ordained;
The sun must have his shade,
Till both at once do fade;
The sun still proved, the shadow still disdained.   20

    For Campion, sun and shadow represent opposite spiritual states. The former is "proved" (or approved) while the latter is "disdained." One is "placed" in heaven and the other "liv'st disgraced" as the reminder of mortality and impending death. Light, fairness, beauty, glory is attributed to the sun while the shadow is "unhappy," "scorched," and "luckless" by being black. The only hope of salvation for the benighted shade lies in following after that "light thy light depriveth."

    A similar opposition between fairness and night encodes the figure of the lover in the octave of Sir Philip Sidney's Sonnet 71 from *Astrophil and Stella*.

SIR PHILIP SIDNEY   *(1554–1586)*

from Sonnet 71   *(1582)*

Who will in fairest book of Nature know
How virtue may best lodged in beauty be,
Let him but learn of love to read in thee,
Stella, those fair lines which true goodness show.
There shall he find all vices' overthrow,   5
Not by rude force, but sweetest sovereignty
Of reason, from whose light those night birds fly,
That inward sun in thine eyes shineth so.

    Again, night is linked here with vice. In contrast, the luminous gaze of the lover, Stella, reflects the "fairest," "beauty," "reason," and "virtue" that can be "read" in the "book of Nature." Whiteness in these works is defined by superlative qualities of purity. Abstract and spiritually transcendent, whiteness stands for the epitome of what is good. Whiteness represents an ideal. In comparison, all other colors are found wanting in their difference from the fairest of the fair.

    How then does this color hierarchy as it is inscribed in literary tradition relate to race? The Nobel Prize-winning author Toni Morrison tackles this question in her book *Playing in the Dark: Whiteness and the Literary Imagination* (1992), a collection of essays delivered at Harvard University. In it, Morrison looks at how classic American literature defines white national identity against figures of an imagined "Africanist" presence. This representation of an Africanist presence as "other" relies on the negative tropes of blackness described above. Moreover, as Morrison reminds us, those figures of blackness are bound up with the cultural politics of slavery:

> Black slavery enriched the country's creative possibilities. For in that construction of blackness and enslavement could be found not only the not-free but also, with the dramatic polarity created by skin color, the projection of the not-me. The result was a playground for the imagination. What rose up out of collective needs to allay internal fears and to rationalize external exploitation was an American Africanism—a fabricated brew of darkness, otherness, alarm, and desire that is uniquely American.

    In Morrison's account of American literature and culture, white national identity has been defined through its representational difference from stereotyped notions of African Americans as "other." No one except, perhaps, Disney's Snow White is literally a perfect "10" on the color scale. Historically, however, differing degrees of civic power, cultural status, and moral worth have been assigned to people on the basis of what the postcolonial philosopher and psychiatrist Franz Fanon dubbed the "racial epidermal schema" of skin color. Institutional discrimination, of course, was supported by the rule of law in the pre-civil rights era United States as well as under the apartheid regime of South Africa. Moreover, separate and unequal treatment of people of color was furthered, in part, by the ways in which whiteness and blackness were traditionally depicted in language, literature, and the cultural representations of everyday life.

As noted black intellectual W. E. B. Du Bois put it in *The Souls of Black Folk* (1913), "the problem of the Twentieth Century is the problem of the color line." The whole notion of a modern black aesthetic, as it takes shape in the 1920s, emerges as a challenge to this color line. Literature in this context becomes an important site for re-imagining race through changing the representation and thereby the status of the Africanist presence in the national context. Setting out this new literary agenda in his 1922 anthology *The Book of American Negro Poetry*, James Weldon Johnson wrote that "[t]he status of the Negro in the United States is more a question of national mental attitude toward the race than of actual conditions. And nothing will do more to change that mental attitude and raise his status than a demonstration of intellectual parity by the Negro through the production of literature and art." The renaissance in black art and literature called for by Johnson soon found its movement and home in Harlem.

Poetry and the Harlem Renaissance Web   *www*

A combination of demographic factors including crop failures, rural race oppression, and urban job opportunities contributed to the Great Migration of African Americans to Harlem in the 1920s. But above all, according to former Howard University professor Alain Locke, a "new vision" of cosmopolitan opportunity made Harlem into the social "laboratory of a great race-welding." The Harlem night clubs and salon parties, like those hosted by Carl and Fania Van Vechten, provided occasions where musicians such as Bessie Smith and George Gershwin, Hollywood stars like Tallulah Bankhead and Rudolph Valentino, actors such as Paul Robeson, writers like Theodore Dreiser, James Weldon Johnson, Zora Neale Hurston, F. Scott Fitzgerald, and Countée Cullen could mix and mingle. Harlem, for Locke and the other "New Negroes," had "the same rôle to play for the New Negro as Dublin has had for the New Ireland or Prague for the New Czechoslovakia—a race capital." Reflecting this new cosmopolitan milieu, Locke's edited anthology *The New Negro* (1925) promoted an African American aesthetic with featured sections on art, music, dance, sculpture, drama and poetry, as well as sociological readings of the emerging black professional and bourgeois classes.

The New Negro boldly parted company with the minstrel stereotypes and Reconstruction figures caricaturing black identity of the previous century. Locke declared that "[t]he day of 'aunties,' 'uncles' and 'mammies' is equally gone. Uncle Tom and Sambo have passed on. . . ." Locke followed James Weldon Johnson by embracing black "self-determination." He called for a "new figure on the national canvas," one that above all would be "culturally articulate." Locke and the "New Negroes" opposed dominant and oppressive stereotypes of race. In the modern age, he maintained, "race is at present the mainspring of Negro life. It seems to be the outcome of the reaction to proscription and prejudice; an attempt, fairly successful on the whole, to convert a defensive into an offensive position, a handicap into an incentive."

The poets of the Harlem Renaissance turned the social hindrance of race into a cultural asset. Similarly, Langston Hughes in his manifesto "The Negro Artist and the Racial Mountain" (1926) boldly declared that "we younger Negro artists who create now intend to express our individual dark-skinned selves without fear or shame." As in "Dream Variations," Hughes asserted a positive African American presence in poetry by changing the traditional representation of blackness.

LANGSTON HUGHES   *(1902–1967)*

Dream Variations   *(1926)*

To fling my arms wide
In some place of the sun,
To whirl and to dance
Till the white day is done.
Then rest at cool evening   5
Beneath a tall tree
While night comes on gently,
  Dark like me—
That is my dream!

To fling my arms wide   10
In the face of the sun,
Dance! Whirl! Whirl!
Till the quick day is done.
Rest at pale evening . . .
A tall, slim tree . . .   15
Night coming tenderly
  Black like me.

TOPICS FOR CRITICAL THINKING

1. How does Hughes revise the traditional representation of day and night in "Dream Variations"? How do setting and imagery contribute to Hughes's claim to a black identity in the poem?
2. Stanza two is a variation that repeats key motifs in stanza one but with subtle changes in diction, syntax, and punctuation. Discuss your experience of the shifts in tone, meaning, and emphasis that Hughes builds into the poem's variations.

TOPIC FOR CRITICAL WRITING

Compare Hughes's celebration of the evening as a representation of black identity with Helene Johnson's poem "What Do I Care for Morning," which follows. Examine the interplay of color motifs in Johnson's attention to the moon and sun imagery set off against the darkness of night.

HELENE JOHNSON (1907–1995)

What Do I Care for Morning (1927)

What do I care for morning,
For a shivering aspen tree,
For sunflowers and sumac
Opening greedily?
What do I care for morning,   5
For the glare of the rising sun,
For a sparrow's noisy prating,
For another day begun?
Give me the beauty of evening,
The cool consummation of night,   10
And the moon like a love-sick lady,
Listless and wan and white.
Give me a little valley,
Huddled beside a hill,
Like a monk in a monastery,   15
Safe and contented and still.
Give me the white road glistening,
A strand of the pale moon's hair,
And the tall hemlocks towering,
Dark as the moon is fair.   20
Oh what do I care for morning,
Naked and newly born—
Night is here, yielding and tender—
What do I care for dawn!

TOPICS FOR CRITICAL THINKING

1. Examine the imagery in which Helene Johnson represents the morning world.
2. Contrast her images of the morning with the qualities she celebrates in its opposite of night.

TOPIC FOR CRITICAL WRITING

Consider how Johnson's evening imagery mixes images of whiteness and blackness.

Poetry and Double-Consciousness

In addition to celebrating new expressions of a modern black aesthetic, Hughes also plumbs the paradoxes of African American identity, what W. E. B. Du Bois defines in *The Souls of Black Folk* as "double-consciousness":

> After the Egyptian and Indian, the Greek and Roman, the Teuton and Mongolian, the Negro is a sort of seventh son, born with a veil, and gifted with second-sight in this American world,—a world which yields him no true self-consciousness, but only lets him see himself through the revelation of the other world. It is a peculiar sensation, this double-consciousness, this sense of always looking at one's self through the eyes of others, of measuring one's soul by the tape of a world that looks on in amused contempt and pity. One ever feels his two-ness—an American, a Negro; two souls, two thoughts, two unreconciled strivings; two warring ideals in one dark body, whose dogged strength alone keeps it from being torn asunder.

Double-consciousness, as Du Bois defines it, also touches on the traumatic legacy of slavery. Beginning with the Middle Passage—the transatlantic economy of slave trade among Africa, the Americas, and Europe—the African American heritage in the United States is a history of clashing racial forces. As a black person, Du Bois argues, "[o]ne ever feels his two-ness,—an American, a Negro; two souls, two thoughts, two unreconciled strivings; two warring ideals in one dark body, whose dogged strength alone keeps it from being torn asunder." Not insignificantly, Du Bois also describes the contradiction of double-consciousness as a resource and a gift. Being able to experience oneself as a person of color *and* to see oneself through the eyes of the dominant white culture provides a heightened self-consciousness. Du Bois employs the metaphor of the veil to depict this kind of double insight into self and society. The modern African American, he writes, is "born with a veil, and gifted with second-sight in this American world,—a world which yields him no true self-consciousness, but only lets him see himself through the revelation of the other world."

In the poetry of the Harlem Renaissance, the definitive work on the theme of double-consciousness is Countée Cullen's "Heritage." In it, Cullen poses the key refrain question "What is Africa to me?"

COUNTÉE CULLEN　*(1903–1946)*

Heritage

(1925)

For Harold Jackman

What is Africa to me:
Copper sun or scarlet sea,
Jungle star or jungle track,
Strong bronzed men, or regal black

Women from whose loins I sprang   5
When the birds of Eden sang?
One three centuries removed
From the scenes his fathers loved,
Spicy grove, cinnamon tree,
What is Africa to me?   10

So I lie, who all day long
Want no sound except the song
Sung by wild barbaric birds
Goading massive jungle herds,
Juggernauts of flesh that pass   15
Trampling tall defiant grass
Where young forest lovers lie,
Plighting troth beneath the sky.
So I lie, who always hear,
Though I cram against my ear   20
Both my thumbs, and keep them there,
Great drums throbbing through the air.
So I lie, whose fount of pride,
Dear distress, and joy allied.
Is my somber flesh and skin,   25
With the dark blood dammed within
Like great pulsing tides of wine
That, I fear, must burst the fine
Channels of the chafing net
Where they surge and foam and fret.   30

Africa? A book one thumbs
Listlessly, till slumber comes.
Unremembered are her bats
Circling through the night, her cats
Crouching in the river reeds,   35
Stalking gentle flesh that feeds
By the river brink; no more
Does the bugle-throated roar
Cry that monarch claws have leapt
From the scabbards where they slept.   40
Silver snakes that once a year
Doff the lovely coats you wear,
Seek no covert in your fear
Lest a mortal eye should see;
What's your nakedness to me?   45
Here no leprous flowers rear
Fierce corollas in the air;
Here no bodies sleek and wet,
Dripping mingled rain and sweat,

Tread the savage measures of   50
Jungle boys and girls in love.
What is last year's snow to me,
Last year's anything? The tree
Budding yearly must forget
How its past arose or set—   55
Bough and blossom, flower, fruit,
Even what shy bird with mute
Wonder at her travail there,
Meekly labored in its hair.
One three centuries removed   60
From the scenes his fathers loved,
Spicy grove, cinnamon tree,
What is Africa to me?

So I lie, who find no peace
Night or day, no slight release   65
From the unremitting beat
Made by cruel padded feet
Walking through my body's street.
Up and down they go, and back,
Treading out a jungle track.   70
So I lie, who never quite
Safely sleep from rain at night—
I can never rest at all
When the rain begins to fall;
Like a soul gone mad with pain   75
I must match its weird refrain;
Ever must I twist and squirm,
Writhing like a baited worm,
While its primal measures drip
Through my body, crying, "Strip!   80
Doff this new exuberance.
Come and dance the Lover's Dance!"
In an old remembered way
Rain works on me night and day.

Quaint, outlandish heathen gods   85
Black men fashion out of rods,
Clay, and brittle bits of stone,
In a likeness like their own,
My conversion came high-priced;
I belong to Jesus Christ,   90
Preacher of Humility,
Heathen gods are naught to me.

Father, Son, and Holy Ghost,
So I make an idle boast;

Jesus of the twice-turned cheek,   95
Lamb of God, although I speak
With my mouth thus, in my heart
Do I play a double part.
Ever at Thy glowing altar
Must my heart grow sick and falter,   100
Wishing He I served were black,
Thinking then it would not lack
Precedent of pain to guide it,
Let who would or might deride it;
Surely then this flesh would know   105
Yours had borne a kindred woe.
Lord, I fashion dark gods, too,
Daring even to give You
Dark despairing features where,
Crowned with dark rebellious hair,   110
Patience wavers just so much as
Mortal grief compels, while touches
Quick and hot, of anger, rise
To smitten cheek and weary eyes.
Lord, forgive me if my need   115
Sometimes shapes a human creed.
All day long and all night through,
One thing only must I do:
Quench my pride and cool my blood,
Lest I perish in the flood,   120
Lest a hidden ember set
Timber that I thought was wet
Burning like the dryest flax,
Melting like the merest wax,
Lest the grave restore its dead.   125
Not yet has my heart or head
In the last way realized
They and I are civilized.

TOPICS FOR CRITICAL THINKING

1. The phrase "So I lie" is used five times in the poem. How does Cullen employ the word *lie* as a pun in this phrase? How does Cullen "lie" to himself about his racial identity?

2. Discuss how Cullen depicts a double-consciousness toward Africa, race, and Christianity.

3. How does the poem describe a double-consciousness toward primitivism?

TOPIC FOR CRITICAL WRITING

Cullen's question "What is Africa to me?" can be interpreted in two differing ways. It can be read as a probing question *and* as a rhetorical question: one that performs a statement of indifference. Explain how double-consciousness is inscribed in this question.

"Heritage" makes use of stylized and exotic primitivist imagery. In the modern era, aesthetic primitivism began with the importation of African, Brazilian, and Native American figurines, masks, and ritual objects that circulated in the flea markets and private collections of Paris. The fetish of primitive "otherness" projected onto these artifacts not only marked the avant-garde imagination of visual and literary artists such as Pablo Picasso, Fernand Léger, Guillaume Apollinaire, Blaise Cendrars, Hugo Ball, and Tristan Tzara, but coincided with African American jazz culture popularized for an international audience by Josephine Baker's performances in *La Revue Nègre*. Cullen alludes to the stereotypes of primitivism in his naked "jungle boys and girls."

    Three years before Cullen wrote "Heritage," Gwendolyn Bennett published her own poem of the same title. Bennett's "Heritage" looks forward to her 1926 cover illustration for *Opportunity*, after she witnessed Josephine Baker's celebrated "dance sauvage" in Paris the preceding year. In the three-year interim between the poem and the illustration, however, Bennett's representations evolve from what Sterling Brown described as the New Negro "discovery of Africa as a source of race pride" to a more cosmopolitan mixing of primitive and modern aesthetic codes. Compare Bennett's use of primitive motifs in her illustration and poem with Cullen's poem.

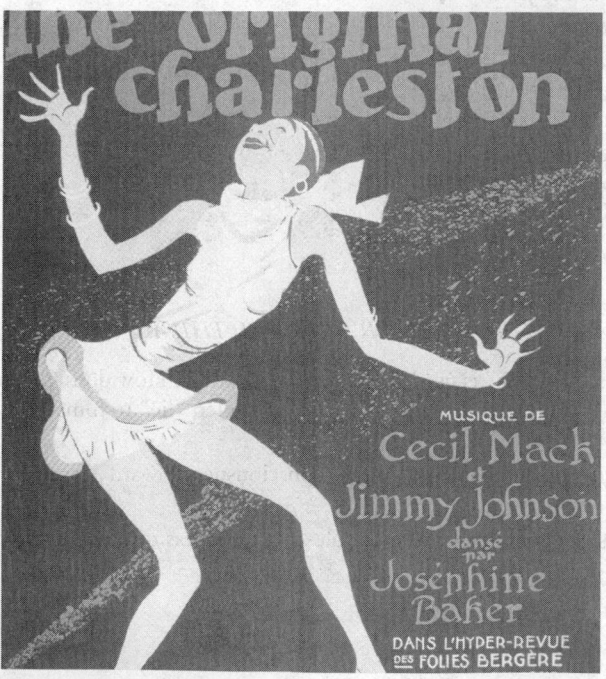

Josephine Baker (mid-1920s)

Gwendolyn B. Bennett, Cover, *Opportunity: Journal of Negro Life* (July 1926)

GWENDOLYN B. BENNETT *(1902–1981)*

Heritage *(1923)*

I want to see the slim palm-trees,
Pulling at the clouds
With little pointed fingers. . . .

I want to see lithe Negro girls,
Etched dark against the sky   5
While sunset lingers.

I want to hear the silent sands
Singing to the moon
Before the Sphinx-still face . . . .

I want to hear the chanting   10
Around a heathen fire
Of a strange black race.

I want to breathe the Lotus flow'r,
Sighing to the stars
With tendrils drinking at the Nile. . . .   15

I want to feel the surging
Of my sad people's soul
Hidden by a minstrel-smile.

TOPICS FOR CRITICAL THINKING

1. How does Nugent reverse the primitivist representations associated with an African-ist presence in American culture between the World Wars?
2. Discuss the ways in which Nugent reverses racial codes of whiteness and blackness in the white figures of his "Drawing for Mulattoes" series.

TOPIC FOR CRITICAL WRITING

Compare and contrast the representation of primitivism in Bennett's *Opportunity* cover illustration with the contemporaneous artwork of Bruce Nugent.

Bruce Nugent, *Drawings for Mulattoes, Number 2* (left) and *Number 3* (right) (1927)

Poems for Further Reading and Critical Writing

PAUL LAURENCE DUNBAR   *(1872–1906)*

We Wear the Mask   *(1896)*

We wear the mask that grins and lies,
It hides our cheeks and shades our eyes,—
This debt we pay to human guile;
With torn and bleeding hearts we smile,
And mouth with myriad subtleties.   5

Why should the world be over-wise,
In counting all our tears and sighs?
Nay, let them only see us, while
   We wear the mask.

We smile, but O great Christ, our cries   10
To thee from tortured souls arise.
We sing, but oh the clay is vile
Beneath our feet, and long the mile;
But let the world dream otherwise,
   We wear the mask!   15

CLAUDE MCKAY   *(1890–1948)*

The Harlem Dancer   *(1917)*

Applauding youths laughed with young prostitutes
And watched her perfect, half-clothed body sway;
Her voice was like the sound of blended flutes
Blown by black players upon a picnic day.
She sang and danced on gracefully and calm,   5
The light gauze hanging loose about her form;
To me she seemed a proudly-swaying palm
Grown lovelier for passing through a storm.
Upon her swarthy neck black shiny curls
Luxuriant fell; and tossing coins in praise,   10
The wine-flushed, bold-eyed boys, and even the girls,
Devoured her shape with eager, passionate gaze;
But looking at her falsely-smiling face,
I knew her self was not in that strange place.

America

(1921)

Although she feeds me bread of bitterness,
And sinks into my throat her tiger's tooth,
Stealing my breath of life, I will confess
I love this cultured hell that tests my youth!
Her vigor flows like tides into my blood,   5
Giving me strength erect against her hate.
Her bigness sweeps my being like a flood.
Yet as a rebel fronts a king in state,
I stand within her walls with not a shred
Of terror, malice, not a word of jeer.   10
Darkly I gaze into the days ahead,
And see her might and granite wonders there,
Beneath the touch of Time's unerring hand,
Like priceless treasures sinking in the sand.

JEAN TOOMER   *(1894–1967)*

Portrait in Georgia

(1923)

Hair—braided chestnut,
   coiled like a lyncher's rope,
Eyes—fagots,°
Lips—old scars, or the first red blisters,
Breath—the last sweet scent of cane,   5
And her slim body, white as the ash
   of black flesh after flame.

GEORGIA DOUGLAS JOHNSON   *(1880–1966)*

The Heart of a Woman

(1918)

The heart of a woman goes forth with the dawn
As a lone bird, soft winging, so restlessly on;
Afar o'er life's turrets and vales does it roam
In the wake of those echoes the heart calls home.

The heart of a woman falls back with the night,   5
And enters some alien cage in its plight,
And tires to forget it has dreamed of the stars
While it breaks, breaks, breaks on the sheltering bars.

———
3 *fagots:* Bundles of twigs.

The True American (1927)

America, here is your son, born of your iron heel;
Black blood and red and white contend along this frame of
   steel.
The thorns deep in his brow are set and yet he does not cower;
He goes with neither fears nor tears to crucifixion hour.   5
Nor yet does hatred blur his view of mankind's frail parade;
From his commanding triple coign, all prejudices fade.
The ebbing nations coalesce in him and flow as one;
The bright shining rainbow sweeping back to God at set of sun!
Mark well the surety of tread, the new song high in air,   10
The new note in the nation's throat, as permanent as prayer.
America, regard your son, The Cosmopolitan,
The pattern of posterity, The True American.

HELENE JOHNSON (1907–1995)

My Race (1925)

Ah, my race,
Hungry race,
Throbbing and young—
Ah, my race,
Wonder race,   5
Sobbing with song—
Ah, my race,
Laughing race,
Careless in mirth—
Ah, my veiled   10
Unformed race,
Fumbling in birth.

GWENDOLYN B. BENNETT (1902–1981)

To a Dark Girl (1923)

I love you for your brownness
And the rounded darkness of your breast.
I love you for the breaking sadness in your voice
And shadows where your wayward eye-lids rest.

Something of old forgotten queens   5
Lurks in the lithe abandon of your walk

And something of the shackled slave
Sobs in the rhythm of your talk.

Oh, little brown girl, born for sorrow's mate,
Keep all you have of queenliness,   10
Forgetting that you once were slave,
And let your full lips laugh at Fate!

TOPICS FOR CRITICAL THINKING

1. Discuss the ways in which Dunbar describes the figure of the "mask" as both a symbol of oppression and a resource of double-consciousness. How does his repeated statement "We Wear the Mask" perform both of those symbolic meanings?

2. Explore McKay's ambivalence toward American nationalism in his personifications of "America." Compare the tensions among race, sexuality, and violence witnessed in McKay's poem with Toomer's "Portrait in Georgia."

3. Consider the paradoxical representations of identity and its place in modern society as Georgia Douglas Johnson portrays them in the figure of the "alien cage" and the oxymoron of "sheltering bars" from "The Heart of a Woman."

TOPICS FOR CRITICAL WRITING

1. Compare McKay's representation of dancing in "The Harlem Dancer" with similar dance motifs in Cullen and Bennett. How do you interpret the poem's final couplet?

2. Examine the differing depictions of racial diversity celebrated in Gwendolyn B. Bennett, "To a Dark Girl" and Georgia Douglas Johnson's "The True American."

Critical Perspective: On "Double-Consciousness"

"Between me and the other world there is ever an unasked question: unasked by some through feelings of delicacy; by others through the difficulty of rightly framing it. All, nevertheless, flutter round it. They approach me in a half-hesitant sort of way, eye me curiously or compassionately, and then, instead of saying directly, How does it feel to be a problem? they say, I know an excellent colored man in my town; or, I fought at Mechanicsville; or, Do not these Southern outrages make your blood boil? At these I smile, or am interested, or reduce the boiling to a simmer, as the occasion may require. To the real question, How does it feel to be a problem? I answer seldom a word.

"And yet, being a problem is a strange experience,—peculiar even for one who has never been anything else, save perhaps in babyhood and in Europe. It is in the early days of rollicking boyhood that the revelation first bursts upon one, all in a day as it were. I remember well when the shadow swept across me. I was a little thing, away up in the hills of New England, where the dark Housatonic winds between Hoosac and Taghkanic to the sea. In a wee wooden schoolhouse, something put it into the boys' and girls' heads to buy gorgeous visiting-cards—ten cents a package— and exchange. The exchange was merry, till one girl, a tall newcomer, refused my card,—refused it peremptorily, with a glance. Then it dawned upon me with a certain suddenness that I was different from the others; or like, mayhap, in heart and life and longing, but shut out from their world by a vast veil. I had thereafter no desire to tear down that veil, to creep through; I held all beyond it in common contempt, and lived above it in a region of blue sky and great wandering shadows. That sky was bluest when I could beat my mates at examination time, or beat them at a foot-race, or even beat their stringy heads. Alas, with the years all this fine contempt began to fade, for the worlds I longed for, and all their dazzling opportunities, were theirs, not mine. But they should not keep these prizes, I said; some, all, I would wrest from them. Just how I would do it I could never decide: by reading law, by healing the sick, by telling the wonderful tales that swam in my head,—some way. With other black boys the strife was not so fiercely sunny: their youth shrunk into tasteless sycophancy, or into silent hatred of the pale world about them and mocking distrust of everything white; or wasted itself in a bitter cry, Why did God make me an outcast and a stranger in mine own house? The shades of the prison-house closed round about us all: walls strait and stubborn to the whitest, but relentlessly narrow, tall, and unscalable to sons of night who must plod darkly on in resignation, or beat unavailing palms against the stone, or steadily, half hopelessly, watch the streak of blue above.

"After the Egyptian and Indian, the Greek and Roman, the Teuton and Mongolian, the Negro is a sort of seventh son, born with a veil, and gifted with second-sight in this American world,—a world which yields him no true self-consciousness, but only lets him see himself through the revelation of the other world. It is a peculiar sensation, this double-consciousness, this sense of always looking at one's self through the eyes of others, of measuring one's soul by the tape of a world that looks on in amused contempt and pity. One ever feels his two-ness,—an American, a Negro; two souls, two thoughts, two unreconciled strivings; two warring ideals in one dark body, whose dogged strength alone keeps it from being torn asunder.[1]

"The history of the American Negro is the history of this strife,—this longing to attain self-conscious manhood, to merge his double self into a better and truer self. In this merging he wishes neither of the older selves to be lost. He would not Africanize America, for America has too much to teach the world and Africa. He would not bleach the Negro soul in a flood of white Americanism, for he knows that Negro blood has a message for the world. He simply wishes to make it possible for a man to be both a Negro and an American, without being cursed and spit upon by his fellows, without having the doors of Opportunity closed roughly in his face.

"This, then, is the end of his striving: to be a co-worker in the kingdom of culture, to escape both death and isolation, to husband and use his best powers and his latent genius. These powers of body and mind have in the past been strangely wasted, dispersed, or forgotten. The shadow of a mighty Negro past flits through the tale of Ethiopia the Shadowy and of Egypt the

---

1. This passage is often referred to as Du Bois's theory of the "double-consciousness." It is a "gift of second-sight" but it is also a curse of ambivalence.

Sphinx. Throughout history, the powers of single black men flash here and there like falling stars, and die sometimes before the world has rightly gauged their brightness. Here in America, in the few days since Emancipation, the black man's turning hither and thither in hesitant and doubtful striving has often made his very strength to lose effectiveness, to seem like absence of power, like weakness. And yet it is not weakness,—it is the contradiction of double aims. The double-aimed struggle of the black artisan—on the one hand to escape white contempt for a nation of mere hewers of wood and drawers of water, and on the other hand to plough and nail and dig for a poverty-stricken horde—could only result in making him a poor craftsman, for he had but half a heart in either cause. By the poverty and ignorance of his people, the Negro minister or doctor was tempted toward quackery and demagogy; and by the criticism of the other world, toward ideals that made him ashamed of his lowly tasks. The would-be black *savant* was confronted by the paradox that the knowledge his people needed was a twice-told tale to his white neighbors, while the knowledge which would teach the white world was Greek to his own flesh and blood. The innate love of harmony and beauty that set the ruder souls of his people a-dancing and a-singing raised but confusion and doubt in the soul of the black artist; for the beauty revealed to him was the soul-beauty of a race which his larger audience despised, and he could not articulate the message of another people. This waste of double aims, this seeking to satisfy two unreconciled ideals, has wrought sad havoc with the courage and faith and deeds of ten thousand thousand people,—has sent them often wooing false gods and invoking false means of salvation, and at times has even seemed about to make them ashamed of themselves."

—W. E. B. Du Bois, from *The Souls of Black Folk* (1903)

Critical Perspective: On Race and Art

"One of the most promising of the young Negro poets said to me once, 'I want to be a poet—not a Negro poet,' meaning, I believe, 'I want to write like a white poet'; meaning subconsciously, 'I would like to be a white poet'; meaning behind that, 'I would like to be white.' And I was sorry the young man said that, for no great poet has ever been afraid of being himself. And I doubted then that, with his desire to run away spiritually from his race, this boy would ever be a great poet. But this is the mountain standing in the way of any true Negro art in America—this urge within the race toward whiteness, the desire to pour racial individuality into the mold of American standardization, and to be as little Negro and as much American as possible.

"But let us look at the immediate background of this young poet. His family is of what I suppose one would call the Negro middle class: people who are by no means rich yet never uncomfortable nor hungry—smug, contented, respectable folk, members of the Baptist church. The father goes to work every morning. He is a chief steward at a large white club. The mother sometimes does fancy sewing or supervises parties for the rich families of the town. The children go to a mixed school. In the home they read white papers and magazines. And the mother often says 'Don't be like niggers' when the children are bad. A frequent phrase from the father is, 'Look how well a white man does things.' And so the word white comes to be unconsciously a symbol of all the virtues. It holds for the children beauty, morality, and money. The whisper of 'I want to be white' runs silently through their minds. This young poet's home is, I believe, a fairly typical home of the colored middle class. One sees immediately how difficult it would be for an artist born in such a home to interest himself in interpreting the beauty of his own people. He is never taught to see that beauty. He is taught rather not to see it, or if he does, to be ashamed of it when it is not according to Caucasian patterns.

"For racial culture the home of a self-styled 'high-class' Negro has nothing better to offer. Instead there will perhaps be more aping of things white than in a less cultured or less wealthy home. The father is perhaps a doctor, lawyer, landowner, or politician. The mother may be a social worker, or a teacher, or she may do nothing and have a maid. Father is often dark but he has usually married the lightest woman he could find. The family attend a fashionable church where few really colored faces are to be found. And they themselves draw a color line. In the North they go to white theatres and white movies. And in the South they have at least two cars and a house 'like white folks.' Nordic manners, Nordic faces, Nordic hair, Nordic art (if any), and an Episcopal heaven. A very high mountain indeed for the would-be racial artist to climb in order to discover himself and his people.

"But then there are the low-down folks, the so-called common element, and they are the majority—may the Lord be praised! The people who have their nip of gin on Saturday nights and are not too important to themselves or the community, or too well fed, or too learned to watch the lazy world go round. They live on Seventh Street in Washington or State Street in Chicago and they do not particularly care whether they are like white folks or anybody else. Their joy runs, bang! into ecstasy. Their religion soars to a shout. Work maybe a little today, rest a little tomorrow. Play awhile. Sing awhile. O, let's dance! These common people are not afraid of spirituals, as for a long time their more intellectual brethren were, and jazz is their child. They furnish a wealth of colorful, distinctive material for any artist because they still hold their own individuality in the face of American standardizations. And perhaps these common people will give to the world its truly great Negro artist, the one who is not afraid to be himself. Whereas the better-class Negro would tell the artist what to do, the people at least let him alone when he does appear. And they are not ashamed of him—if they know he exists at all. And they accept what beauty is their own without question.

"Certainly there is, for the American Negro artist who can escape the restrictions the more advanced among his own group would put upon him, a great field of unused material ready for his art. Without going outside his race, and even among the better classes with their 'white' culture and conscious American manners, but still Negro enough to be different, there is sufficient matter to furnish a black artist with a lifetime of creative work. And when he chooses to touch on the relations between Negroes and whites in this country with their innumerable overtones and undertones surely, and especially for literature and the drama, there is an inexhaustible supply of themes at hand. To these the Negro artist can give his racial individuality, his heritage of rhythm and warmth, and his incongruous humor that so often, as in the Blues, becomes ironic laughter mixed with tears. But let us look again at the mountain.

"A prominent Negro clubwoman in Philadelphia paid eleven dollars to hear Raquel Meller sing Andalusian popular songs. But she told me a few weeks before she would not think of going to hear 'that woman,' Clara Smith, a great black artist, sing Negro folksongs. And many an upper-class Negro church, even now, would not dream of employing a spiritual in its services. The drab melodies in white folks' hymnbooks are much to be preferred. 'We want to worship the Lord correctly and quietly. We don't believe in "shouting." Let's be dull like the Nordics,' they say, in effect.

"The road for the serious black artist, then, who would produce a racial art is most certainly rocky and the mountain is high. Until recently he received almost no encouragement for his work from either white or colored people. The fine novels of Chesnutt go out of print with neither race noticing their passing. The quaint charm and humor of Dunbar's dialect verse brought to him, in his day, largely the same kind of encouragement one would give a sideshow freak (A colored man writing poetry! How odd!) or a clown (How amusing!).

"The present vogue in things Negro, although it may do as much harm as good for the budding colored artist, has at least done this: it has brought him forcibly to the attention of his own people among whom for so long, unless the other race had noticed him beforehand, he was a prophet with little honor. I understand that Charles Gilpin acted for years in Negro theatres without any special acclaim from his own, but when Broadway gave him eight curtain calls, Negroes, too, began to beat a tin pan in his honor. I know a young colored writer, a manual worker by day, who had been writing well for the colored magazines for some years, but it was not until he recently broke into the white publications and his first book was accepted by a prominent New York publisher that the 'best' Negroes in his city took the trouble to discover that he lived there. Then almost immediately they decided to give a grand dinner for him. But the society ladies were careful to whisper to his mother that perhaps she'd better not come. They were not sure she would have an evening gown.

"The Negro artist works against an undertow of sharp criticism and misunderstanding from his own group and unintentional bribes from the whites. 'Oh, be respectable, write about nice people, show how good we are,' say the Negroes. 'Be stereotyped, don't go too far, don't shatter our illusions about you, don't amuse us too seriously. We will pay you,' say the whites. Both would have told Jean Toomer not to write *Cane*. The colored people did not praise it. The white people did not buy it. Most of the colored people who did read *Cane* hate it. They are afraid of it. Although the critics gave it good reviews the public remained indifferent. Yet (excepting the work of Du Bois) *Cane* contains the finest prose written by a Negro in America. And like the singing of Robeson, it is truly racial.

"But in spite of the Nordicized Negro intelligentsia and the desires of some white editors we have an honest American Negro literature already with us. Now I await the rise of the Negro theatre. Our folk music, having achieved world-wide fame, offers itself to the genius of the great individual American composer who is to come. And within the next decade I expect to see the work of a growing school of colored artists who paint and model the beauty of dark faces and create with new technique the expressions of their own soul-world. And the Negro dancers who will dance like flame and the singers who will continue to carry our songs to all who listen—they will be with us in even greater numbers tomorrow.

"Most of my own poems are racial in theme and treatment, derived from the life I know. In many of them I try to grasp and hold some of the meanings and rhythms of jazz. I am as sincere as I know how to be in these poems and yet after every reading I answer questions like these from my own people: Do you think Negroes should always write about Negroes? I wish you wouldn't read some of your poems to white folks. How do you find anything interesting in a place like a cabaret? Why do you write about black people? You aren't black. What makes you do so many jazz poems?

"But jazz to me is one of the inherent expressions of Negro life in America; the eternal tom-tom beating in the Negro soul—the tom-tom of revolt against weariness in a white world, a world of subway trains, and work, work, work; the tom-tom of joy and laughter, and pain swallowed in a smile. Yet the Philadelphia clubwoman is ashamed to say that her race created it and she does not like me to write about it. The old subconscious 'white is best' runs through her mind. Years of study under white teachers, a lifetime of white books, pictures, and papers, and white manners, morals, and Puritan standards made her dislike the spirituals. And now she turns up her nose at jazz and all its manifestations—likewise almost everything else distinctly racial. She doesn't care for the Winold Reiss portraits of Negroes because they are 'too Negro.' She does not want a true picture of herself from anybody. She wants the artist to flatter her, to make the white world believe that all Negroes are as smug and as near white in soul as she wants to be. But, to my mind, it is the duty of the younger Negro artist, if he accepts any duties at all from outsiders, to change through the force of his art that old whispering 'I want to be white,' hidden in the aspirations of his people, to 'Why should I want to be white? I am a Negro—and beautiful!'

"So I am ashamed for the black poet who says, 'I want to be a poet, not a Negro poet,' as though his own racial world were not as interesting as any other world. I am ashamed, too, for the colored artist who runs from the painting of Negro faces to the painting of sunsets after the manner of the academicians because he fears the strange un-whiteness of his own features. An artist must be free to choose what he does, certainly, but he must also never be afraid to do what he might choose.

"Let the blare of Negro jazz bands and the bellowing voice of Bessie Smith singing Blues penetrate the closed ears of the colored near-intellectuals until they listen and perhaps understand. Let Paul Robeson singing 'Water Boy,' and Rudolph Fisher writing about the streets of Harlem, and Jean Toomer holding the heart of Georgia in his hands, and Aaron Douglas drawing strange black fantasies cause the smug Negro middle class to turn from their white, respectable, ordinary books and papers to catch a glimmer of their own beauty. We younger Negro artists who create now intend to express our individual dark-skinned selves without fear or shame. If white people are pleased we are glad. If they are not, it doesn't matter. We know we are beautiful. And ugly too. The tom-tom cries and the tom-tom laughs. If colored people are pleased we are glad. If they are not, their displeasure doesn't matter either. We build our temples for tomorrow, strong as we know how, and we stand on top of the mountain, free within ourselves."

—Langston Hughes, "The Negro Artist and the Racial Mountain" (1926)

Critical Perspective: On New Representations of Race

"In the last decade something beyond the watch and guard of statistics has happened in the life of the American Negro and the three norns who have traditionally presided over the Negro problem have a changeling in their laps. The Sociologist, the Philanthropist, the Race-leader are not unaware of the New Negro, but they are at a loss to account for him. He simply cannot be swathed in their formulae. For the younger generation is vibrant with a new psychology; the new spirit is awake in the masses, and under the very eyes of the professional observers is transforming what has been a perennial problem into the progressive phases of contemporary Negro life.

"Could such a metamorphosis have taken place as suddenly as it has appeared to? The answer is no; not because the New Negro is not here, but because the Old Negro had long become more of a myth than a man. The Old Negro, we must remember, was a creature of moral debate and historical controversy. His has been a stock figure perpetuated as an historical fiction partly in innocent sentimentalism, partly in deliberate reactionism. The Negro himself has contributed his share to this through a sort of protective social mimicry forced upon him by the adverse circumstances of dependence. So for generations in the mind of America, the Negro has been more of a formula than a human being—a something to be argued about, condemned or defended, to be 'kept down,' or 'in his place,' or 'helped up,' to be worried with or worried over, harassed or patronized, a social bogey or a social burden. The thinking Negro even has been induced to share this same general attitude, to focus his attention on controversial issues, to see himself in the distorted perspective of a social problem. His shadow, so to speak, has been more real to him than his personality. Through having had to appeal from the unjust stereotypes of his oppressors and traducers to those of his liberators, friends and benefactors he has had to subscribe to the traditional positions from which his case has been viewed. Little true social or self-understanding has or could come from such a situation.

"But while the minds of most of us, black and white, have thus burrowed in the trenches of the Civil War and Reconstruction, the actual march of development has simply flanked these positions, necessitating a sudden reorientation of view. We have not been watching in the right direction; set North and South on a sectional axis, we have not noticed the East till the sun has us blinking.

"Recall how suddenly the Negro spirituals revealed themselves; suppressed for generations under the stereotypes of Wesleyan hymn harmony, secretive, half-ashamed, until the courage of being natural brought them out—and behold, there was folk-music. Similarly the mind of the Negro seems suddenly to have slipped from under the tyranny of social intimidation and to be shaking off the psychology of imitation and implied inferiority. By shedding the old chrysalis of the Negro problem we are achieving something like a spiritual emancipation. Until recently, lacking self-understanding, we have been almost as much of a problem to ourselves as we still are to others. But the decade that found us with a problem has left us with only a task. The multitude perhaps feels as yet only a strange relief and a new vague urge, but the thinking few know that in the reaction the vital inner grip of prejudice has been broken.

"With this renewed self-respect and self-dependence, the life of the Negro community is bound to enter a new dynamic phase, the buoyancy from within compensating for whatever pressure there may be of conditions from without. The migrant masses, shifting from countryside to city, hurdle several generations of experience at a leap, but more important, the same thing happens spiritually in the life-attitudes and self-expression of the Young Negro, in his poetry, his art, his education and his new outlook, with the additional advantage, of course, of the poise and greater certainty of knowing what it is all about. From this comes the promise and warrant of a new leadership. As one of them has discerningly put it:

> We have tomorrow
> Bright before us
> Like a flame.
>
> Yesterday, a night-gone thing
> A sun-down name.
>
> And dawn today
> Broad arch above the road we came.
> We march!

"This is what, even more than any 'most creditable record of fifty years of freedom,' requires that the Negro of to-day be seen through other than the dusty spectacles of past controversy. The day of 'aunties,' 'uncles' and 'mammies' is equally gone. Uncle Tom and Sambo have passed on, and even the 'Colonel' and 'George' play barnstorm rôles from which they escape with relief when the public spotlight is off. The popular melodrama has about played itself out, and it is time to scrap the fictions, garret the bogeys and settle down to a realistic facing of facts.

"First we must observe some of the changes which since the traditional lines of opinion were drawn have rendered these quite obsolete. A main change has been, of course, that shifting of the Negro population which has made the Negro problem no longer exclusively or even predominantly Southern. Why should our minds remain sectionalized, when the problem itself no longer is? Then the trend of migration has not only been toward the North and the Central-Midwest, but cityward and to the great centers of industry—the problems of adjustment are new, practical, local and not peculiarly racial. Rather they are an integral part of the large industrial and social problems of our present-day democracy. And finally, with the Negro rapidly in process of class differentiation, if it ever was warrantable to regard and treat the Negro *en masse* it is becoming with every day less possible, more unjust and more ridiculous.

"In the very process of being transplanted, the Negro is becoming transformed."

—Alain Locke, from *The New Negro* (1925)

Critical Perspective: On Women Writers of the Harlem Renaissance

"Other specifically literary factors further illuminate the status of women writers in the Harlem Renaissance. A principal one is the issue of poetry as a genre. During the period, it was, in a real sense, the preeminent form—based on its universality, accessibility for would-be writers, suitability for magazine publication, and classical heritage as the highest expression of cultured, lyric sensibility. The big three writers of the era—McKay, Cullen, and Hughes—made their reputations as poets. And most of the notable women writers of the period were poets, with only Larsen and Hurston not essaying verse. In addition to Johnson, Dunbar-Nelson, and Grimké, six others produced significant work—Anne Spencer, Jessie Fauset, Effie Lee Newsome, Gwendolyn Bennett, Helene Johnson, and the lesser-known Gladys Mae Casely Hayford.

"Anne Spencer is an arresting poet because of the originality of her material and approach. Working in forms that are an eccentric mixture of free verse and rhymed, iambic-based lines, she treated subjects as varied as her titles: 'Before the Feast of Shushan,' 'At the Carnival,' 'The Wife-Woman,' 'Dunbar,' 'Letter to My Sister,' 'Lines to a Nasturtium,' 'Neighbors,' and 'Creed.' She is most modern in her predilection for casting herself into roles, her sense of woman-self and female identity, and her style, which is characterized by terseness, apt or unusual diction, and vivid images and metaphors. Known best as a novelist, Fauset is usually represented in anthologies by her love poems. Some of them are distinguished by the French titles she gave them and by her sometimes humorous anti ironic cast of mind. Effie Lee Newsome primarily wrote children's verse based on nature lore.

"Gwendolyn Bennett and Helene Johnson are the stellar poets of the younger generation. Bennett's poetry can be quite impressive. She was, by occupation, an artist, and consequently in her work she envisions scenes, paints still lifes, and expresses herself especially well in color. Of all the women poets, Helene Johnson's work most reflects the qualities commonly designated as characteristic of the Renaissance. She took 'the "racial" bull by the horns' (as James Weldon Johnson put it), and also wrote poems in the new colloquial-folk-slang style popular during that time. Although the bulk of her poems are traditional romance and nature lyrics, her 'Sonnet to a Negro in Harlem' is pro-black and militant. In her frequently reprinted 'Poem,' she waxes ecstatic over the 'Little brown boy / Slim, dark, big-eyed,' who croons love songs to his banjo down at the Lafayette Theater.

"Gladys Mae Hayford's distinctions are being born in Africa and having two of her poems—'Nativity' (in which the Christ Child is black) and 'The Serving Girl'—published in the *Atlantic Monthly*. A Fanti, she committed herself to imbuing 'our own people with the idea of their own beauty, superiority and individuality.' Because Africa for her was a very real place, her poems have a concrete specificity not usually found in some other Harlem Renaissance works on that theme. She talks about blue lappah, frangipani blossoms, and the brass ankle bells that guard 'Brown Baby Cobina.' Her regularly accented couplets also employ various lyric personae and speak naturally about love and sex (particularly 'Rainy Season Love Song')."
—Gloria T. Hull, from *Color, Sex, and Poetry in the Harlem Renaissance* (1987)

Critical Perspective: On Formal Mastery and the Harlem Renaissance

"*The New Negro*, like the valued documents from which we grasp iconic images and pictorial myths of a colonial or frontier America, is perhaps our first *national* book, offering not only a description of streams of tendency in our collective lives but also an actual construction within its pages of the sounds, songs, images, and signs of a nation. The collection's combination of phaneric display and formal mastery can come as no surprise to the person who has followed the lines of Afro-American development through an extensive discursive field. For though the enabling conditions for Locke's collection are found in marronage, there is no gainsaying the work's quite canny presentation, utilization, and praise of formal mastery. Witness, for example, the high evaluations of Countee Cullen's poetry, poetry that is meant to imitate with astute fidelity the efforts of British romanticism. Or turn to Claude McKay's 'The White House,' a poem whose title Locke changed to 'White Houses,' and you find an English, or modified Shakespearean, sonnet. Again, most of the short fiction and, certainly, the single drama presented in *The New Negro* scarcely escape initial recognition as formally *standard* works.

"The present discussion is hardly the place to explore fully the Afro-American cultural dimensions and significances of McKay's or Cullen's *standard* artistic postures. But one can contextualize such efforts by saying that McKay's 'sonnet,' like Cullen's 'ballads,' are just as much mastered *masks* as the minstrel manipulations of Booker T. Washington and Charles Chesnutt are. The trick of McKay and Cullen was what one of my colleagues calls the denigration of form—a necessary ('forced,' as it were) adoption of the standard that results in an effective *blackening*. Locke was never of the opinion that Western *standards* in art were anything other than adequate goals for high Afro-American cultural achievement. And the revaluation of the Afro-American based on artistic accomplishment for which he calls mandated, in his view, a willingness on the part of black spokespersons to aspire toward such standards. Hence, one would have to present *recognizably* standard forms and get what black mileage one could out of subtle, or, by contrast, straining (like McKay's rebellious cries) variations and deepenings of these forms. If the younger generation was to proffer 'artistic' gifts, such gifts had first to be recognizable as 'artistic' by Western, formal standards and not simply as unadorned or primitive *folk* creations.

"Now Locke—and, indeed, the entire Harlem movement—has often been criticized severely for its advocacy of the standard. Yet it seems that such criticism proceeds somewhat in ignorance of the full discursive field marking Afro-American national possibilities. For we may not enjoy or find courageous models of derring-do in the masking that characterizes formal mastery, but we certainly cannot minimize its significant and strategic presence in our history. Furthermore, such masking carries subtle resonances and effects that cannot even be perceived (much less evaluated) by the person who begins with the notion that recognizably *standard* form automatically disqualifies a work as an authentic and valuable Afro-American national production. Analysis is in fact foreclosed by a first assumption of failure. Certainly Countée Cullen, for example, served a national need in a time of 'forced' institution building and national projection. He gained white American recognition for 'Negro poetry' at a moment when there was little encouraging recognition in the United States for *anything* Negro. And Cullen gained such recognition by means of a mastery of form pleasing *to Afro-Americans* as well as Anglo-Americans. It seems inconceivable that, in the first flush of pioneering urbanity and heady self-consciousness, the congregation of Reverend Frederick Cullen's well-attended Salem Methodist Episcopal Church in Harlem would have responded positively if, after the father's announcement of his son's accomplishments as *a poet*, the young Countee had produced sounds such as: 'April is the cruellest month, breeding / Lilacs out of the dead land, mixing / Memory and desire, stirring / Dull roots with spring rain.' The delivery of such lines would probably have caused consternation akin to the congregation's reaction to John in DuBois's classic story 'Of the Coming of John': 'Little had they understood of what he said, for he spoke an unknown tongue.' Not only was the 'tongue' of such collaged allusiveness as Eliot's *unknown* to a congregation like Reverend Cullen's; it was also unnecessary, unneeded, of little use in a world bent on recognizable (rhyme, meter, form, etc.) artistic 'contributions.' One has only to peruse the 1913 issue of *Poetry* in which Ezra Pound's famous imagist manifesto appeared to see that 'cruellest months' and breeding lilacs were the exception rather than the American rule in Cullen's day."

—Houston Baker, from "Modernism and the Harlem Renaissance" (1987)

Critical Perspective: On the White Gaze and Race Representation

"The paradox of racial representation marks a good deal of Old Left representations of black Americans but is especially patent in a cartoon that William Siegel published in the May 1930 issue of *New Masses*. Siegel offers two contradictory versions of the African-American community: 'the white bourgeois version of the Negro' vs. 'as the white worker knows him.' However well intended, Siegel's visual rendering of these representational differences actually served to perpetuate both racist and classist assumptions about blacks. Siegel's leftist reduction of the black aesthetic, nevertheless, appealed to the CP leadership as evidenced, two months later, in his sanitized portrait of 'Negro Workers' that was showcased on the cover of the July 1930 *New Masses.*

"In both plates of the May issue cartoon the power of defining the cultural roles available to blacks belongs to a foregrounded pair of white viewers. Thus the shift in class representation is, nonetheless, framed by a distanced (hence privileged) Caucasian gaze—one that interprets, and thereby fixes, African-American identity. The ideological limits of Siegel's unconscious racial framing are plain to see in the second panel which, however much it liberates blacks from both rural and urban stereotypes, also expunges the distinctive, vernacular nuances of the slave songs, black sermon, African ritual performance, blues, and jazz culture that have historically empowered black Americans with their own distinctive interpretive community. While Siegel's cartoon reduces the political subtext of biblical slave songs to sheer caricature, James Weldon Johnson, as early as 1922, had clearly identified the biblical story of Moses and the Hebrew Exodus as a trope for liberation in African-American slave songs.

"Five years later, in *God's Trombones* (1927), Johnson would theorize the black preacher as a source of consolation and political solidarity for displaced slaves in the antebellum South. 'It was through him,' Johnson wrote, 'that the people of diverse languages and customs who were brought here from diverse parts of Africa and thrown into slavery were given their first sense of unity and solidarity.' Johnson's focus on antebellum sermon as a discourse of black 'unity and solidarity' was visually underscored by Aaron Douglas' illustrations. These original images transcoded Biblical typology to a stylized African-American iconography of exodus from the chains of Southern bondage. The recovery of black sermon in Johnson's 'Let My People Go' presented less

MAY, 1930   7

The white bourgeois version of the Negro   —*as the white worker knows him.*   —*Drawn by William Siegel*

a theological than a materialist reading of Israel's oppressed class role, 'working without money and without price':

> Four hundred years
> They'd held them down in Egypt land.
> Held them under the driver's lash,
> Working without money and without price.
> And it might have been Pharaoh's wife that said:
> "Pharaoh—look what you've done.
> You let those Hebrew Children go,
> And who's going to serve us now?
> Who's going to make our bricks and mortar?
> Who's going to plant and plow our corn?
> Who's going to get up in the chill of the morning?
> And who's going to work in the blazing sun?
> Pharaoh, tell me that!"

In contrast to this liberatory narrative, Siegel reads the Hebrew exodus as a symptom of religious false consciousness. He drains this folk tradition of any political effectivity, linking it instead to the racist stereotypes of the black minstrel tradition: the surreal world of Jim Crow, Zeb Coon, Amos an' Andy, plantation medleys and 'August hams.'"

—Walter Kalaidjian, from *American Culture Between the Wars* (1994)

Critical Perspective: On Langston Hughes and Walt Whitman

"It is therefore only poetically just that Langston Hughes began composing the forerunner of one of his most famous poems on his Americanism and on the kinship of white and black Americans on the back of a letter he had received from Claude McKay in 1924. This poem became 'I Too,' which Alain Locke included in *The New Negro*:

> I, too, sing America,
>
> I am the darker brother.
> They send me to eat in the kitchen
> When company comes.

In the American family home, the 'darker brother,' disowned by white siblings, prophesies the transforming force of his song's challenge—on the basis of his own aesthetic—to the Americanism of the white kinfolk. At the same time Hughes makes his claim as an heir to Whitman and registers his distinctive poetic identity as both black and American: 'They'll see how beautiful I am / And be ashamed,— / I, too, am America.' The poem was retitled 'Epilogue' (from the Greek, meaning 'peroration') for his first book a year later; for years he often used it to conclude his poetry readings. James Baldwin would redouble Hughes's defiant stress on the kinship of white and black Americans three decades and more later.

"Hughes had come to Whitman by way of such Midwestern rebels as Carl Sandburg prior to the twenties. His was the democratic 'transnational,' socialist, 'comradely' Whitman pushed by Horace Traubel and the *Masses* circle (as opposed to the Whitman of 'cosmic consciousness' Toomer responded to). Nonetheless, he early sensed the affinity between the inclusive 'I' of Whitman and the 'I' of the spirituals, whose fusion shaped one of his first published poems, 'The Negro Speaks of Rivers,' also in *The New Negro:*

I've known rivers ancient as the world and older than the flow of
   human blood in human veins.
My soul has grown deep like the rivers.

I bathed in the Euphrates when dawns were young,
I built my hut near the Congo and it lulled me to sleep,
I looked upon the Nile and raised the pyramids above it.

I heard the singing of the Mississippi when Abe Lincoln went down
   to New Orleans,
and I've seen its muddy bosom turn all golden in the
   sunset.

Readers rarely notice that if the soul of the Negro in this poem goes back to the Euphrates, it goes back to a pre-'racial' dawn and a geography far from Africa that is identified with neither blackness nor whiteness—a geography at the time of Hughes's writing considered the cradle of all the world's civilizations and possibly the location of the Garden of Eden. Thus, even in this poem about the depth of the Negro's soul Hughes avoids racial essentialism while nonetheless stressing the existential, racialized conditions of black and modern identity.

"Returning, however, to the matter of form, I would reiterate the related point that along with the pan-Africanism of Du Bois and the force of the spirituals, the example of Whitman's break with traditional definitions of the 'poetic,' his attempts to capture the cadence and diction of the voice on the street, in the pulpit, and at the water's edge, provided a partial model for the young black poet looking for a way to sing his own song, which would be at the same time a song of his people. This role of Whitman in Hughes's career is representative of his relationship to folk poetry of the period generally, most dramatically in the case of the author of *America's Songbag*, Carl Sandburg.

"Hughes had yet to find himself in the blues and jazz—although he had published 'The Weary Blues' already—and few of Locke's selections (except 'Jazzonia') suggest his move in that direction. What Locke was interested in at this point, it seems, was the soulfulness of 'The Negro Speaks of Rivers' and the kind of 'paganism' and 'spontaneously emotional, affably democratic and naive spirit' that he found in the 'folk temperament'—not a poetry in actual folk forms, but one exploring the spiritual 'endowment' of the race. As Hughes moved closer to Van Vechten, McKay, and others of the left he abandoned 'African' primitivism—despite the influence of his patron Charlotte Osgood Mason—and increasingly experimented with the possibilities of jazz and blues."
—George Hutchinson, from *The Harlem Renaissance in Black and White* (1996)

Featured Writer

Gwendolyn Brooks

GWENDOLYN BROOKS

The granddaughter of an escaped slave, Gwendolyn Brooks was the first African American to receive the Pulitzer Prize. Although born on June 7, 1917, in Topeka, Kansas, Brooks lived her entire life in Chicago. Showing early promise as a writer, Brooks published her first poem at the age of thirteen in the popular magazine *American Childhood*. Brooks received encouragement in her early career from the African American modernist poet Langston Hughes CD-ROM.

By the age of seventeen she became a regular poetry contributor to one of the most widely read African American papers, *The Chicago Defender*. In 1936, Brooks graduated from Wilson Junior College and three years later married Henry Blakely, with whom she would have two children: her son Henry born in 1940 and her daughter Nora born in 1951.

Brooks's rise to the status of major author began in 1941 when she enrolled in a Southside Chicago poetry workshop sponsored by the Gold Coast socialite Inez Cunningham Stark. By the end of the decade, Brooks was on her way toward becoming a canonical twentieth-century author. In 1943, she received the Midwestern Writers' Conference Award, followed two years later by the Mademoiselle Merit Award. Soon after she went on to win the American Academy of Letters Award (1946), two Guggenheim Fellowships (1946, 1947), *Poetry*'s prestigious Eunice Tietjens Memorial Award (1949), and the Pulitzer Prize (1949).

From the beginning, Brooks, like Langston Hughes, put the lives of ordinary African Americans at the center of her work. "I read Langston Hughes's *Weary Blues*," she writes, "and got very excited about what he was doing. I realized that writing about the ordinary aspects of Black life was important." Brooks's first volume of verse, *A Street in Bronzeville* (1945), depicts stylized portraits of the people Brooks knew so well in such works as "Sadie and Maud."

Sadie and Maud   (1945)

Maud went to college.
Sadie stayed at home.
Sadie scraped life
With a fine-tooth comb.

She didn't leave a tangle in.   5
Her comb found every strand.
Sadie was one of the livingest chits
In all the land.

Sadie bore two babies
Under her maiden name.   10
Maud and Ma and Papa
Nearly died of shame.
Every one but Sadie
Nearly died of shame.

When Sadie said her last so-long   15
Her girls struck out from home.
(Sadie had left as heritage
Her fine-tooth comb.)

Maud, who went to college,
Is a thin brown mouse.   20
She is living all alone
In this old house.

TOPICS FOR CRITICAL THINKING

1. Discuss Brooks's symbol of the comb with which "Sadie scraped life." What values
   does Brooks associate with the comb? What kind of heritage does the comb embody?
2. Sadie is a portrait of an unwed, single mother. How does Brooks depict societal attitudes toward Sadie's subject position?
3. What point does Brooks make in her title and final imagery in framing the contrast
   between Sadie and Maud? How do the two women differ? Are there any key terms
   that assign differing value to their life choices?

TOPIC FOR CRITICAL WRITING

Examine the pattern of oppositional choices that shape the narrative structure in both
"Sadie and Maud" and the poem that follows, "a song in the front yard."

a song in the front yard   *(1945)*

I've stayed in the front yard all my life.
I want a peek at the back
Where it's rough and untended and hungry weed grows.
A girl gets sick of a rose.

I want to go in the back yard now   5
And maybe down the alley,

To where the charity children play.
I want a good time today.

They do some wonderful things.
They have some wonderful fun.　　　　　　　　　　　　　10
My mother sneers, but I say it's fine
How they don't have to go in at quarter to nine.
My mother, she tells me that Johnnie Mae
Will grow up to be a bad woman.
That George'll be taken to Jail soon or late　　　　　　　15
(On account of last winter he sold our back gate.)

But I say it's fine. Honest, I do.
And I'd like to be a bad woman, too,
And wear the brave stockings of night-black lace
And strut down the streets with paint on my face.　　　20

TOPICS FOR CRITICAL THINKING

1. How do you imagine the persona Brooks depicts in this dramatic monologue in terms of her age, background and lifestyle, experience, and so on?

2. Examine the kind of lives that Brooks imagines in the back yard.

3. Why does Brooks describe the stockings of the final stanza as "brave"? How does this key term hint at what might be at stake in the speaker's fascination with the life of the back yard?

TOPIC FOR CRITICAL WRITING

Discuss the ways in which the front and back yards of Brooks's poem represent differing social and personal values.

In addition to examining the contradictory impulses, choices, and lifestyles of contemporary African American women, Brooks also offered frank depictions of the racial and class oppressions that weighed on black women's lives in the pre-civil rights era of the late 1940s. In particular, Brooks's dramatic monologue in "The Mother" presents an unflinching look at a woman's choice of abortion and the psychological and ethical consequences of that choice.

The Mother　　　　　　　　　　　　　　　　　　　(1945)

Abortions will not let you forget.
You remember the children you got that you did not get,
The damp small pulps with a little or with no hair,
The singers and workers that never handled the air.　　　5
You will never neglect or beat
Them, or silence or buy with a sweet.

You will never wind up the sucking-thumb
Or scuttle off ghosts that come.
You will never leave them, controlling your luscious sigh,
Return for a snack of them, with gobbling mother-eye.   10

I have heard in the voices of the wind the voices of my dim killed
    children.
I have contracted. I have eased
My dim dears at the breasts they could never suck.
I have said, Sweets, if I sinned, if I seized
Your luck   15
And your lives from your unfinished reach,
If I stole your births and your names,
Your straight baby tears and your games,
Your stilted or lovely loves, your tumults, your marriages, aches,
    and your deaths,
If I poisoned the beginnings of your breaths,   20
Believe that even in my deliberateness I was not deliberate.
Though why should I whine,
Whine that the crime was other than mine?—
Since anyhow you are dead.
Or rather, or instead,   25
You were never made.
But that too, I am afraid,
Is faulty: oh, what shall I say, how is the truth to be said?
You were born, you had body, you died.
It is just that you never giggled or planned or cried.   30

Believe me, I loved you all.
Believe me, I knew you, though faintly, and I loved, I loved you
All.

TOPICS FOR CRITICAL THINKING

1. How would you characterize the mother's reflection on and her attitude toward her own abortions?
2. In what ways does Brooks present the paradox of the mother's choices both in the phrasings of the poem's opening lines and in its title?
3. How does the mother imagine the life her aborted children did not lead?
4. What significance is there in the poem's shift from the second-person *you* voice to the first-person *I* voice after the opening stanza?
5. Although "The Mother" mourns the loss of "the children you got that you did not get," does it make any moral or political claims concerning abortion?

TOPIC FOR CRITICAL WRITING

What role does direct address play in the poem, and what point does Brooks make in her shift from questions to declarative statements in the poem's final two stanzas?

In addition to probing women's lived experience of abortion, Brooks also worked in the folk ballad form to explore the complexity of women's encounters with sexual betrayal and racial violence, as in the "Ballad of Pearl May Lee."

Ballad of Pearl May Lee   (1945)

Then off they took you, off to the jail,
A hundred hooting after.
And you should have heard me at my house.
I cut my lungs with my laughter,
   Laughter,   5
   Laughter.
I cut my lungs with my laughter.

They dragged you into a dusty cell.
And a rat was in the corner.
And what was I doing? Laughing still.   10
Through never was a poor gal lorner,
   Lorner,
   Lorner.
Through never was a poor gal lorner.

The sheriff, he peeped in through the bars,   15
And (the red old thing) he told you,
"You son of a bitch, you're going to hell!"
'Cause you wanted white arms to enfold you,
   Enfold you,
   Enfold you.   20
'Cause you wanted white arms to enfold you.

But you paid for your white arms, Sammy boy,
And you didn't pay with money.
You paid with your hide and my heart, Sammy boy,
For your taste of pink and white honey,   25
   Honey,
   Honey.
For your taste of pink and white honey.

Oh, dig me out of my don't-despair.
Pull me out of my poor-me.   30
Get me a garment of red to wear.
You had it coming surely,
   Surely,
   Surely,
You had it coming surely.   35

At school, your girls were the bright little girls.
You couldn't abide dark meat.
Yellow was for to look at,
Black for the famished to eat.
Yellow was for to look at,   40
Black for the famished to eat.

You grew up with bright skins on the brain,
And me in your black folks bed.
Often and often you cut me cold,
And often I wished you dead.   45
Often and often you cut me cold.
Often I wished you dead.

Then a white girl passed you by one day,
And, the vixen, she gave you the wink.
And your stomach got sick and your legs liquefied.   50
And you thought till you couldn't think.
    You thought,
    You thought,
You thought till you couldn't think.

I fancy you out on the fringe of town,   55
The moon an owl's eye minding;
The sweet and thick of the cricket-belled dark,
The fire within you winding . . . .
    Winding,
    Winding   60
The fire within you winding.

Say, she was white like milk, though, wasn't she?
And her breasts were cups of cream.
In the back of her Buick you drank your fill.
Then she roused you out of your dream.   65
In the back of her Buick you drank your fill.
Then she roused you out of your dream.

"You raped me, nigger," she softly said.
(The shame was threading through.)
"You raped me, nigger, and what the hell   70
Do you think I'm going to do?
    What the hell,
    What the hell
Do you think I'm going to do?

"I'll tell every white man in this town.   75
I'll tell them all of my sorrow.
You got my body tonight, nigger boy.

I'll get your body tomorrow.
  Tomorrow.
  Tomorrow.   80
I'll get your body tomorrow."

And my glory but Sammy she did! She did!
And they stole you out of the jail.
They wrapped you around a cottonwood tree.
And they laughed when they heard you wail.   85
  Laughed,
  Laughed.
They laughed when they heard you wail.

And I was laughing, down at my house.
Laughing fit to kill.   90
You got what you wanted for dinner,
But brother you paid the bill.
  Brother,
  Brother,
Brother you paid the bill.   95

You paid for your dinner, Sammy boy,
And you didn't pay with money.
You paid with your hide and my heart, Sammy boy,
For your taste of pink and white honey,
  Honey,   100
  Honey.
For your taste of pink and white honey.

Oh, dig me out of my don't-despair.
Oh, pull me out of my poor-me.
Oh, get me a garment of red to wear.   105
You had it coming surely.
  Surely.
  Surely.
You had it coming surely.

TOPICS FOR CRITICAL THINKING

1. Discuss your understanding of the subject matter of racial lynching and its social context depicted in "Ballad of Pearl May Lee."
2. Describe how you imagine the character of Pearl May Lee as Brooks portrays her. What kind of relationship has she had to Sammy?
3. How do you interpret the tone that Pearl May Lee takes in her address to Sammy? Is there a tonal difference between her laughter and that of the whites who lynch Sammy?
4. What point does the poem make about race and sexuality?

TOPIC FOR CRITICAL WRITING

Consider Brooks's use of figurative language to probe the link between sexuality and consumption in such examples as "taste of pink and honey," "dark meat," "milk," and "cups of cream."

Brooks's subsequent volume *Annie Allen* (1949) and her experimental novel *Maud Martha* (1953) went to the heart of her experience as a cosmopolitan African American woman. In long-poem sequences such as "The Anniad" and "The Womanhood," Brooks explores contemporary urban identity as it is shaped by race, gender, and class forces.

Throughout the 1960s, Brooks's verse reflected on the turbulent history of the civil rights era in poems from *The Bean Eaters* (1960). One poem from that book, "A Bronzeville Mother Loiters in Mississippi. Meanwhile a Mississippi Mother Burns Bacon," is based on the violent 1955 racial murder of Emmet Till, a Chicago youth who was killed while visiting with relatives in the South. After allegedly whistling at a Caucasian woman in Money, Mississippi, Till was kidnapped and brutally beaten to death by a group of whites.

A Bronzeville Mother Loiters in Mississippi.
Meanwhile a Mississippi Mother Burns Bacon   *(1960)*

From the first it had been like a
Ballad. It had the beat inevitable. It had the blood.
A wildness cut up, and tied in little bunches,
Like the four-line stanzas of the ballads she had never quite
Understood—the ballads they had set her to, in school.   5

Herself: the milk-white maid, the "maid mild"
Of the ballad. Pursued
By the Dark Villain. Rescued by the Fine Prince.
The Happiness-Ever-After.
That was worth anything.   10
It was good to be a "maid mild."
That made the breath go fast.

Her bacon burned. She
Hastened to hide it in the step-on can, and
Drew more strips from the meat case. The eggs and sour-   15
    milk biscuits
Did well. She set out a jar
Of her new quince preserve.

. . . But there was a something about the matter of the
    Dark Villain.
He should have been older, perhaps.

The hacking down of a villain was more fun to think about   20
When his menace possessed undisputed breadth, undisputed
    height,
And a harsh kind of vice.
And best of all, when his history, was cluttered
With the bones of many eaten knights and princesses.

The fun was disturbed, then all but nullified   25
When the Dark Villain was a blackish child
Of fourteen, with eyes still too young to be dirty,
And a mouth too young to have lost every reminder
Of its infant softness.

That boy must have been surprised! For   30
These were grown-ups. Grown-ups were supposed to be
    wise.
And the Fine Prince—and that other—so tall, so broad, so
    so
Grown! Perhaps the boy had never guessed
That the trouble with grown-ups was that under the
    magnificent shell of adulthood, just under,
Waited the baby full of tantrums.   35

It occurred to her that there may have been something
Ridiculous in the picture of the Fine Prince
Rushing (rich with the breadth and height and
Mature solidness whose lack, in the Dark Villain, was
    impressing her,
Confronting her more and more as this first day after the   40
    trial
And acquittal wore on) rushing
With his heavy companion to hack down (unhorsed)
That little foe.
So much had happened, she could not remember now what
    that foe had done
Against her, or if anything had been done.   45
The one thing in the world that she did know and knew
With terrifying clarity was that her composition
Had disintegrated. That, although the pattern prevailed,
The breaks were everywhere. That she could think
Of no thread capable of the necessary   50
Sew-work.

She made the babies sit in their places at the table.
Then, before calling Him, she hurried
To the mirror with her comb and lipstick. It was necessary
To be more beautiful than ever.   55

The beautiful wife.
For sometimes she fancied he looked at her as though
Measuring her. As if he considered, Had she been worth It?

Had *she* been worth the blood, the cramped cries, the little
    stuttering bravado,
The gradual dulling of those Negro eyes,   60
The sudden, overwhelming *little-boyness* in that barn?
Whatever she might feel or half-feel, the lipstick necessity
    was something apart. He must never conclude
That she had not been worth It.

He sat down, the Fine Prince, and
Began buttering a biscuit. He looked at his hands.   65
He twisted in his chair, he scratched his nose.
He glanced again, almost secretly, at his hands.
More papers were in from the North, he mumbled. More
    meddling headlines.
With their pepper-words, "bestiality," and "barbarism,"
    and
"Shocking."   70
The half-sneers he had mastered for the trial worked
    across
His sweet and pretty face.

What he'd like to do, he explained, was kill them all.
The time lost. The unwanted fame.
Still, it had been fun to show those intruders   75
A thing or two. To show that snappy-eyed mother,
That sassy, Northern, brown-black——

Nothing could stop Mississippi.

He knew that. Big Fella
Knew that.   80
And, what was so good, Mississippi knew that.
Nothing and nothing could stop Mississippi.
They could send in their petitions, and scar
Their newspapers with bleeding headlines. Their governors
Could appeal to Washington. . . .   85

"What I want," the older baby said, "is 'lasses on my jam."
Whereupon the younger baby
Picked up the molasses pitcher and threw
The molasses in his brother's face. Instantly
The Fine Prince leaned across the table and slapped   90
The small and smiling criminal.

She did not speak. When the Hand
Came down and away, and she could look at her child,
At her baby-child,
She could think only of blood.   95
Surely her baby's cheek
Had disappeared, and in its place, surely,
Hung a heaviness, a lengthening red, a red that had no end.
She shook her head. It was not true, of course.
It was not true at all. The   100
Child's face was as always, the
Color of the paste in her paste-jar.

She left the table, to the tune of the children's lamenta-
   tions, which were shriller
Than ever. She
Looked out of a window. She said not a word. *That*   105
Was one of the new Somethings—
The fear,
Tying her as with iron.

Suddenly she felt his hands upon her. He had followed her
To the window. The children were whimpering now.   110
Such bits of tots. And she, their mother,
Could not protect them. She looked at her shoulders, still
Gripped in the claim of his hands. She tried, but could not
   resist the idea
That a red ooze was seeping, spreading darkly, thickly,
   slowly,
Over her white shoulders, her own shoulders,   115
And over all of Earth and Mars.

He whispered something to her, did the Fine Prince, something
About love, something about love and night and intention.

She heard no hoof-beat of the horse and saw no flash of
   the shining steel.

He pulled her face around to meet   120
His, and there it was, close close,

For the first time in all those days and nights.
His mouth, wet and red,
So very, very, very red,
Closed over hers.   125

Then a sickness heaved within her. The courtroom Coca-
   Cola,

The courtroom beer and hate and sweat and drone,
Pushed line a wall against her. She wanted to bear it.
But his mouth would not go away and neither would the
Decapitated exclamation points in that Other Woman's   130
   eyes.

She did not scream.
She stood there.
But a hatred for him burst into glorious flower,
And its perfume enclasped them—big,
Bigger than all magnolias.   135

The last bleak news of the ballad.
The rest of the rugged music.
The last quatrain.

TOPICS FOR CRITICAL THINKING

1. Brooks doesn't present "A Bronzeville Mother" in the form of a ballad but in a dramatic monologue told from the point of view of Till's alleged but actually perjured "victim." How do you interpret Brooks's strategy here?

2. In what ways does the Mississippi mother's sense of value and self-worth depend on Till's murder? What is the point of her question "Had she been worth it?" How does she try to be of worth to her husband, Till's murderer?

3. In what ways does the Mississippi mother identify with Till as the object of her husband's violence?

4. Examine the complex interplay of guilt, violence, and victimization that the Mississippi mother experiences as the "glorious flower" of the poem's final lines.

5. Discuss Brooks's strategy of representing that crime through its effect on the Mississippi mother rather than on the Bronzeville mother.

6. What effect does Till's murder have on the poem's narrator, and how does she feel implicated in her husband's violence?

TOPIC FOR CRITICAL WRITING

In the opening sentence of her poem, Brooks writes that "From the first it had been like a / Ballad." Compare the themes of race, sexuality, and violence in this poem with that of "Ballad of Pearl May Lee."

Brooks's career took a decisive turn in 1967 after she attended the Second Black Writers' Conference at Fisk University. At Fisk, she was impressed by the energy, talent, and political commitment of the new generation of writers such as Amiri Baraka, John Killens, David Llorens, and Ron Milner in the Black Aesthetic Movement. "First, I was aware of a general energy," Brooks has said of that moment, "an electricity, in look, walk, speech, gesture of the young blackness I saw all about me." Soon, Brooks began to show the influence of such younger writers as Don L. Lee (Haki Madhubuti) and Carolyn Rodgers in featuring a black expressive style based, as Rodgers defined it, on "signifying, teachin/rappin, covers-off, spaced, bein, love, shoutin, jazz, du-wah, and pyramid" styles. Concerning that politicized period of her life Brooks has written,

> 1966. 1967. 1968. Years of explosion. In those years a young black with pen in hand responded not to pretty sunsets and the lapping of lake water but to the speech of physical riot and spiritual rebellion. . . . Literary rhythms altered! Sometimes the literature seemed to issue from pens dipped in, *stabbed* in, writhing blood.

Brooks's next volume *In the Mecca*—published in 1968, the year Brooks succeeded Carl Sandburg as the Poet Laureate of Illinois—explored the tenement life of the Mecca building in Southside Chicago and the subculture of "Gang Girls" in "The Blackstone Rangers." In addition, she also included homages to slain civil rights leaders such as Malcolm X and Medgar Evers. Importantly, with her 1969 volume *Riot*, Brooks shifted to an Afro-American publisher, Dudley Randall's Broadside Press, leaving Harper and Row, which would publish only one more of her volumes, *The World of Gwendolyn Brooks* (1971). Subsequent volumes such as *Beckonings* (1975), *To Disembark* (1981), *Blacks* (1987), and *Children Coming Home* (1991) build on Brooks's foundational celebration of both the heroic and mundane lives of black people in America and around the globe from Chicago to Johannesburg.

Brooks remained active in publishing and performing well into the mid-1990s. In 1995 she published *Report from Part Two*. Until her death at age 83 in December 2000, Brooks offered what she called "an evocative translation of the materials of the world."

Poems for Further Reading and Critical Writing

GWENDOLYN BROOKS   *(1917–2000)*

piano after war   *(1945)*

On a snug evening I shall watch her fingers,
Cleverly ringed, declining to clever pink,
Beg glory from the willing keys. Old hungers
Will break their coffins, rise to eat and thank.
And music, warily, like the golden rose   5
That sometimes after sunset warms the west,
Will warm that room, persuasively suffuse
That room and me, rejuvenate a past.
But suddenly, across my climbing fever
Of proud delight—a multiplying cry.   10
A cry of bitter dead men who will never
Attend a gentle maker of musical joy.

Then my thawed eye will go again to ice.
And stone will shove the softness from my face.

TOPICS FOR CRITICAL THINKING

1. Consider Brooks's title and how it frames the dramatic action of "piano after war."
2. Brooks begins her poem with a revival of past hungers and hopes. Discuss her use of figurative language to depict that rejuvenation in the poem's octave, or first eight lines.
3. How do you interpret what happens to the speaker's psychological state in the poem's sestet? Examine the ways in which the poem stages that temporal difference in the contrast between the opening's "musical joy" versus the closing's "multiplying cry."

TOPIC FOR CRITICAL WRITING

Composed in the form of the Shakespearean sonnet, "piano after war" signals the contrast between the present and past in the movement from the first eight lines (octave) to the last six (sestet). Discuss the ways in which the poem reverses the movement of rejuvenation in line nine.

kitchenette building   *(1945)*

We are things of dry hours and the involuntary plan,
Grayed in, and gray. "Dream" makes a giddy sound, not strong
Like "rent," "feeding a wife," "satisfying a man."

But could a dream send up through onion fumes
Its white and violet, fight with fried potatoes   5
And yesterday's garbage ripening in the hall,
Flutter, or sing an aria down these rooms

Even if we were willing to let it in,
Had time to warm it, keep it very clean,
Anticipate a message, let it begin?   10

We wonder. But not well! not for a minute!
Since Number Five is out of the bathroom now,
We think of lukewarm water, hope to get in it.

TOPICS FOR CRITICAL THINKING

1. How do you imagine the speaker of the poem's second-person plural *we* voice who opens "kitchenette building."
2. What is a kitchenette building? Describe your sense of the poem's setting as Brooks depicts it through her vivid imagery.

Discuss the tension in the poem between reality and the imagination, the latter represented in the figure of the dream. What might the dream refer to? How is it deferred by everyday life as rendered in the poem's ending?

Jessie Mitchell's Mother   *(1960)*

Into her mother's bedroom to wash the ballooning body.
"My mother is jelly-hearted and she has a brain of jelly:
Sweet, quiver-soft, irrelevant. Not essential.
Only a habit would cry if she should die.
A pleasant sort of fool without the least iron. . . .   5
Are you better, mother, do you think it will come today?"
The stretched yellow rag that was Jessie's Mitchell's mother
Reviewed her. Young, and so thin, and so straight.
So straight! as if nothing could ever bend her.
But poor men would bend her, and doing things with poor men,   10
Being much in bed, and babies would bend her over,
And the rest of things in life that were for poor women,
Coming to them grinning and pretty with intent to bend and to kill.
Comparisons shattered her heart, ate at her bulwarks:
The shabby and the bright: she, almost hating her daughter,   15
Crept into an old sly refuge: "Jessie's black
And her way will be black, and jerkier even than mine.
Mine, in fact, because I was lovely, had flowers
Tucked in the jerks, flowers were here and there. . . ."
She revived for the moment settled and dried-up triumphs,   20
Forced perfume into old petals, pulled up the droop
Refueled
Triumphant long-exhaled breaths.
Her exquisite yellow youth. . . .

TOPICS FOR CRITICAL THINKING

1. How does Jessie Mitchell regard her mother? How would you characterize the relationship between mother and daughter in the poem?
2. What does Jessie Mitchell's mother think of her daughter?
3. Discuss the ways in which Brooks generates dramatic tension in the poem by narrating the action from both the daughter's and mother's differing points of view.

TOPIC FOR CRITICAL WRITING

In what ways does race complicate the common class position of poverty that mother and daughter share in the poem? How does the mother's memory of her "yellow youth" pit her against Jessie's blackness?

We Real Cool   (1960)

The Pool Players.
Seven at the Golden Shovel.

We real cool. We
Left school. We

Lurk late. We
Strike straight. We

Sing sin. We   5
Thin gin. We

Jazz June. We
Die soon.

TOPICS FOR CRITICAL THINKING

1. Discuss how you imagine the lives of the players Brooks portrays in "We Real Cool." Brooks published "We Real Cool" in 1960; how would you portray these types of characters today?
2. Discuss the ways in which Brooks's rhythms and her pattern of enjambment mimic the sounds and action of an actual pool hall.

TOPIC FOR CRITICAL WRITING

Just how "cool" are the players in Brooks's poem? How does the poem's title and its closing create ironic distance on the codes of hipness that these players live by and die for?

Gang Girls   (1968)

A Rangerette

Gang Girls are sweet exotics.
Mary Ann
uses the nutrients of her orient,
but sometimes sighs for Cities of blue and jewel
beyond her Ranger rim of Cottage Grove.   5
(Bowery Boys, Disciples, Whip-Birds will
dissolve no margins, stop no savory sanctities.)

Mary is
a rose in a whiskey glass.

Mary's   10
Februaries shudder and are gone. Aprils
fret frankly, lilac hurries on.
Summer is a hard irregular ridge.
October looks away.
And that's the Year!   15
                    Save for her bugle-love.
Save for the bleat of not-obese devotion.

Save for Somebody Terribly Dying, under
the philanthropy of robins. Save for her Ranger
bringing   20
an amount of rainbow in a string-drawn bag.
"Where did you get the diamond?" Do not ask:
but swallow, straight, the spirals of his flask
and assist him at your zipper; pet his lips
and help him clutch you.   25

Love's another departure.
Will there be any arrivals, confirmations?
Will there be gleaning?

Mary, the Shakedancer's child
from the rooming-flat, pants carefully, peers at   30
her laboring lover. . . .
                    Mary! Mary Ann!
Settle for sandwiches! settle for stocking caps!
for sudden blood, aborted carnival,
the props and niceties of non-loneliness—   35
the rhymes of Leaning.

TOPICS FOR CRITICAL THINKING

1. Brooks calls the gang girls "sweet exotics." Discuss the ways in which she depicts
   their exotic, teen identities. How, for example, do you interpret Brooks's metaphoric portrait of Mary as "a rose in a wine glass"?
2. What role does sexuality play in defining the gang girls' identities?
3. What questions does Brooks put to the gang girls, and what advice would she impart to Mary Ann in the poem's final stanza?

TOPIC FOR CRITICAL WRITING

Compare and contrast Brooks's representations of urban youth culture in "We Real
Cool" and "Gang Girls."

Boy Breaking Glass (1968)

To Marc Crawford
from whom the commission

Whose broken window is a cry of art
(success, that winks aware
as elegance, as a treasonable faith)
is raw: is sonic: is old-eyed première.
Our beautiful flaw and terrible ornament. 5
Our barbarous and metal little man.

"I shall create! If not a note, a hole.
If not an overture, a desecration."

Full of pepper and light
and Salt and night and cargoes. 10

"Don't go down the plank
if you see there's no extension.
Each to his grief, each to
his loneliness and fidgety revenge.

Nobody knew where I was and now I am no longer there." 15

The only sanity is a cup of tea.
The music is in minors.

Each one other
is having different weather.

"It was you, it was you who threw away my name! 20
And this is everything I have for me."

Who has not Congress, lobster, love, luau,
the Regency Room, the Statue of Liberty,
runs. A sloppy amalgamation.
A mistake. 25
A cliff.
A hymn, a snare, and an exceeding sun.

TOPICS FOR CRITICAL THINKING

1. "Boy Breaking Glass" is about a juvenile delinquent who vandalizes property, but
how does that label fail to account for the complexity that Brooks discovers in her
characterization of this urban youth?

2. Brooks defines the "Boy Breaking Glass" through the figure of oxymoron, or the combining of opposites (see Chapter 25). In addition to such coinages as "treasonable faith," what other pairs of opposites and contradictory phrasings does Brooks present in the poem?

TOPIC FOR CRITICAL WRITING

What relation does Brooks draw between art and crime in the poem? How does the boy's act of "desecration" protest his marginalization from the centers of civic, class, and racial privilege?

Ulysses   *(1991)*

Religion

At home we pray every morning, we
get down on our knees in a circle,
holding hands, holding Love,
and we sing Hallelujah.

Then we go into the World.   5

Daddy *speeds*, to break bread with his Girl Friend.
Mommy's a Boss. And a lesbian.
(She too has a nice Girl Friend.)

My brothers and sisters and I come to school.
We bring knives pistols bottles, little boxes, and cans.   10

We talk to the man who's cool at the playground gate.
Nobody Sees us, nobody stops our sin.

Our teachers feed us geography.
We spit it out in a hurry.

Now we are coming home.   15

At home, we pray every evening, we
get down on our knees in a circle,
holding hands, holding Love.

And we sing Hallelujah.

TOPICS FOR CRITICAL THINKING

1. Discuss Brooks's ironic reflections on contemporary family life in "Ulysses." How does Brooks's poem complicate and defamiliarize our stereotypical images of the traditional nuclear family?
2. Brooks's dramatic persona is one of twenty other child narrators from her volume *Children Coming Home.* But Ulysses is also the Roman name for the Greek hero Odysseus of Homer's epic poem the *Odyssey.* How do you think that heroic allusion functions in the poem?

TOPIC FOR CRITICAL WRITING

What does Brooks gain from narrating the poem from the child's point of view? How might she have told the family's story from one or both of the parent's perspectives?

Critical Perspective: On Gwendolyn Brooks and Poetic Form

"'[K]itchenette building' steps past façade into an apartment. Taking an Eliotic wryness from 'The Hollow Men' Brooks begins, 'We are things of dry hours and the involuntary plan.' The Latinate verbal tendency, favored by Eliot, is suggested by 'involuntary,' but gives way immediately to terse phrasing that evokes the local scene. Irregular rhyme, slant rhyme, and meter move toward pentameter. The thirteen lines present a kitchenette milieu where things incline askew. Nothing works well: yesterday's garbage remains 'ripening in the hall'; patience is rewarded by tepid water in the communal bathroom on each floor ('We think of lukewarm water, hope to get in it').

"The poem poses the question of dreams deferred, the 'raisin in the sun' that Langston Hughes feared they would become. The poet-narrator wonders whether aspiration can survive its fight with 'onion fumes' and 'fried potatoes' and the entire constellation of poverty. Colors of the dream are 'white' and 'violet.' Brooks has commented that the colors were chosen for their 'delicacy,' and that, although dreams can be nightmares, she preferred to deal with them in the poem as 'lovely lightsome things.' White is partly ironic. Violet, color of the flower that figures in the tenth sonnet of 'Gay Chaps at the Bar,' is a solitary flower, honeyed, self-pollinating. The speaker doubts that art, 'an aria' sung by the dream, can survive its physical habitation.

"From the interior view of the staid 'old-marrieds' and 'kitchenette,' Brooks probes deeper. '[T]he mother' is a dramatic monologue on abortion, a controversial topic then, as now. She comments: 'Hardly your crowned and praised and "customary" Mother; but a Mother not unfamiliar, who decides that *she*, rather than her World, will kill her children. The decision is not nice, not simple, and the emotional consequences are neither nice nor simple.'

"The poet employs full rhyme with a touch of slant in this thirty-two-line poem, very irregularly metered. The first stanza rhymes five couplets; the second alternates rhyme in the first six lines, then continues the couplet pattern. The meter, rolling insistent, often anapestic, conveys the profound agitation of the speaker. Tonal control, epecially in the first stanza, heightens tension. The mother begins rhetorically. 'Abortions will not let you forget,' addressing the reader/listener in impersonal second person. She reviews the loss judiciously: the children will not be neglected; she will not be burdened. But during the second stanza, her defenses fall away: 'I have heard in the voices of the wind the voices of my dim killed children.' The woman then justifies herself to the aborted children, confessing that her 'crime' was not 'deliberate.' She wanted to shield them from a painful existence. She loved them all, she insists, the last line univerbal, emphatic: 'All.'"

—D. H. Melhem, from *Gwendolyn Brooks:*
Poetry and the Heroic Voice (1987)

Critical Perspective: On Gwendolyn Brooks and Dramatic Form

"Part of Brooks's modernity lies in her use of dramatic modes in her poetry. Focus on character as expressed through the spoken, performative voice allows for indirection, complexity of narration, and obfuscation of poetic statement. Several of the greatest poems in American literature, including Wallace Stevens's 'Sunday Morning,' Pound's 'Hugh Selwyn Mauberley,' and Eliot's 'Gerontion,' are classic examples of modernist interweaving of portraiture, narration, and dramatic voice. This intermixture of modes allows the poets to demand active complicity between their reader and their poem until the full import of their poetic statement emerges as a construct put together by the reader from various indications dispersed throughout the text.

"If the way in which Brooks handles character is one index of her modernity and her aesthetic engagement, her choice of character has always indicated the fundamentally social context of her work, even at its most difficult. Thus, it seems necessary to distinguish between character and persona in her work. Brooks's characters are largely taken from the dispossessed, the unheroic residents of America's urban ghettos (named, by custom, 'Bronzeville'). These characters dramatize a microcosm of black urban life—its struggles, its small triumphs, and its unheroic survival. By focusing on them, Brooks has been able to engage, often indirectly, some of the major social issues of her time, including war and peace, racial justice, and the plight of women. Yet this commitment to social issues is often disguised by her modernist use of personae. For example, Brooks's sonnet series, 'Gay Chaps at the Bar,' from her first publication, *A Street in Bronzeville*, is both a tour de force technically and an exploration of America's unequal treatment of the black soldiers during World War II. Similarly, her unusual ballads on the death of Emmett Till in her third volume, *The Bean Eaters*, offer protest subject matter in an innovative narrative form. Again, her gallery of female portraits, from the practical Hattie Scott to the 'crazy woman who sings in November' instead of May, stresses varieties of heroism and antiheroism in women's responses to difficulties they confront; yet the complexity of their responses may not be fully apparent, particularly to the uninitiated reader who is unable to meet the demands placed upon him or her by Brooks's modernist use of nuance, ellipsis, and allusion.

"The way in which Brooks handles her characters is only one index of her modernity. Brooks's modernity also permeates her poetry in its mixture of forms and variations on forms (ballads, sonnets, sonnet-ballads, mock-epics); in its juxtaposition of 'high' and 'low' styles; and in its rich prosodic texture, including the use of varied meters, creative enjambment, melisma, and indeterminate modification. The centrality of the concrete as opposed to the abstract and Brooks's skillful deployment of image and the visual line are equally important clues of her modernity. Finally, Brooks's objective rather than subjective authorial stance creates texts in which her personality seems largely effaced. In recent years, however, Brooks seems to be moving away from the objective voice of modernity to a more personal yet public voice that is, at turns, elegiac and celebratory, reminiscent of her more recent contemporaries, Robert Lowell and Theodore Roethke."

—Maria K. Mootry, from "Down the Whirlwind of Good Rage:
An Introduction to Gwendolyn Brooks" (1987)

Critical Perspective: On Voice and "We Real Cool"

"For more than three decades now, Gwendolyn Brooks has been writing poetry that reflects a particular historical order, often close to the heart of the public event, but the dialectic that is engendered between the event and her reception of it is, perhaps, one of the more subtle confrontations of criticism. We cannot always say with grace or ease that there is a direct correspondence between the issues of her poetry and her race and sex, nor does she make the assertion necessary at every step of our reading. Black and female are basic and inherent in her poetry. The critical question is *how* they are said. Here is what the poet has to say about her own work: 'My aim, in my next future, is to write poems that will somehow successfully "call" . . . all black people: black people in taverns, black people in alleys, black people in gutters, schools, offices, factories, prisons, the consulate; I wish to reach black people in pulpits, black people in mines, on farms, on thrones; *not* always to "teach"—I shall wish often to entertain, to illumine. My newish voice will not be an imitation of the contemporary young black voice, which I so admire, but an extending adaptation of today's G. B. voice.'

"'Today's G. B. voice' is one of the most complex on the American scene precisely because Brooks refuses to make easy judgments. In fact, her disposition to preserve judgment is directly mirrored in a poetry of cunning, laconic surprise. Any descriptive catalog can be stretched and strained in her case: I have tried 'uncluttered,' 'clean,' 'robust,' 'ingenious,' 'unorthodox,' and in each case a handful of poems will fit. This method of grading and cataloging, however, is essentially busywork, and we are still left with the main business. What in this poetry is stunning and evasive?

"To begin with, one of Brooks's most faithfully anthologized poems, 'We Real Cool,' illustrates the wealth of implication that the poet can achieve in a very spare poem:

We real cool. We
Left school. We

Lurk late. We
Strike straight. We

Sing sin. We
Thin gin. We

Jazz June. We
Die soon.

The simplicity of the poem is stark to the point of elaborateness. Less than lean, it is virtually coded. Made up entirely of monosyllables and end-stops, the poem is no non-sense at all. Gathered in eight units of three-beat lines, it does not necessarily invite inflection, but its persistent bump on 'we' suggests waltz time to my ear. If the reader chooses to render the poem that way, she runs out of breath, or trips her tongue, but it seems that such 'breathlessness' is exactly required of dudes hastening toward their death. Deliberately subverting the romance of sociological pathos, Brooks presents the pool players—'seven in the golden shovel'—in their own words and time. They make no excuse for themselves and apparently invite no one else to do so. The poem is their situation as *they* see it. In eight (could be nonstop) lines, here is their total destiny. Perhaps comic geniuses, they could well drink to this poem, making it a drinking/revelry song."

—Hortense J. Spillers, from "Gwendolyn the Terrible:
Propositions on Eleven Poems" (1987)

33

Critical Perspectives

A Casebook on Chicano/a Poetry

Chicano literature represents the rich cultural heritage of what has become the fastest growing population group in the United States. In the broadest meaning of the term, *Chicano* refers to people of Mexican descent who live in the United States. Chicanos make up about 66 percent of the total Hispanic American community, which includes people of South and Central American, Cuban, and Puerto Rican origins. Together, these Hispanic American communities constitute more than 12 percent of the entire U.S. population.

But understanding Chicano heritage requires a more complex definition, one that extends beyond simple demographics. Chicano experience migrates across class, linguistic, national, and racial boundaries. The Chicano heritage—its music, cuisine, art, and language—is a vital part of the larger American culture. What defines the Chicano community, however, is neither static nor fixed; instead, Chicano identity entails a dynamic process of cultural cross-fertilization. Even the word *Chicano* signifies in ways that are less settled than they are contested; for example, its verbal coinage is split by gender in the feminine form *Chicana*, which designates the difference of women's place in the Mexican American community. Chicano speaking itself comprises a range of dialects mixing not just Spanish and English but also a vernacular patois made up of Mayan, Nahuatl, Native American, "Texan," and African American expressive communities. Consequently, as Chicano writer Guillermo Gómez-Peña explains, Chicano identity is more de-centered than self-possessed: "My 'identity,'" he writes, "now possesses multiple repertories: I am Mexican but I am also Chicano and Latin American. At the border they call me *chilango* or *mexiquillo*; in Mexico City it's *pocho* or *norteño*; and in Europe it's *sudacap*. . . . My wife Emilia is Anglo-Italian, but speaks Spanish with an Argentine accent, and together we walk amid the rubble of the Tower of Babel of our American postmodernity."

Contemporary Chicano poetry reaches back to the 1960s civil rights era with El Movimiento, the Chicano Movement of the 1960s. Poetry in that context protested the oppressive social conditions and civic marginality of Chicano people. Moreover, Chicano verse gave an empowering voice to "La Raza"—a new, imagined vision of the people in political solidarity. The celebration of civic heroes of El Movimiento derived, in part, from the Mexican *corridos* or folk ballads that, in turn, are influenced by older European romance and other narrative forms. The movement's mission to spread the Chicano heritage stemmed to some extent from the Catholic Church, which throughout the nineteenth century employed music, song, and verse as ways of instructing and acculturating Native Americans and Mexicans into Hispanic and American contexts.

At the beginning of the twentieth century, this tradition was appropriated for indigenous political ends by such poets as Arculiano Barela, who composed "El estraique de 1910," a poem on the workers' strike that resulted in the infamous Ludlow massacre of union coal miners in Colorado. Barela's poem combined oral elements of the *corridos* with the instructional aims coming from the church and Anglo-Hispanic written traditions of Latin America. Poetry's power to mobilize political change is witnessed in Jimmy Santiago Baca's elegy "Mi Tío Baca El Poeta De Socorro," written to his uncle Antonio Ce De Baca "whose poems roused *la gente* / to demand their land rights back."

The decisive year for the emerging literature of contemporary Chicano resistance was 1965 when, according to Rafael Jesús González, "the workers in the vineyards of Delano declared themselves on strike under the leadership of César Chávez and the banner of Our Lady of Guadalupe." The agitational tradition of Hispanic American workers' poetry became a resource for publications of El Movimiento such as *El Malcriado*, the organ of the United Farm Workers campaign, and *El Grito del Norte*, the voice of the Federal Alliance of Land Grants or Alianza Federal de Mercedes.

In translating the heroic dimensions of the *corridos* to the print medium, Chicano poets largely chose to abandon the rhyme schemes and ballad forms of the oral tradition in favor of free verse composition (see Chapter 27). A foundational text for contemporary Chicano verse is Rodolfe Corky Gonzales's *I Am Joaquín* (1967), which mixed English and Spanish languages, archetypal symbols, and popular icons. The desire for an indigenous homeland first assumed the dimensions of pre-Colombian mythology in *Floricanto en Aztlán* by the poet Alurista. Not just a timeless vision of the ancient past, the mythic homeland of Aztlán also functioned as a metaphor for social and political solidarity. "The myth of Aztlán," Alurista has written, "as I saw it, in the '60s was just a way to identify a people, a land, and a consciousness that said, 'Struggle, do not be afraid'." The search for mythic origins went hand-in-hand with a new emphasis on racial pride. Race took on cosmic proportions in José Vasconcelos's formulation of La Raza Cósmica that envisioned the emergence of a New Chicano as "a pluralistic man, a universal man, combining the racial strains and cultures of the entire world in his own person."

The poetic technique of crosscutting such deep, mythological, and racial narratives with images drawn from popular culture became a hallmark of the Chicano style that mixed high art with lowbrow spectacle, English with Spanish, Mexican with American cultural signs. Similarly, portmanteau terms—invented words or neologisms combining the sounds of two or more terms—and mixed linguistic constructions also made up the signature style of Chicano discourse. According to Carmen Tafolla's essay in *A Gift of Tongues: Critical Challenges in Contemporary American Poetry* (1987):

["Lexical creations"] sprang from an awareness of our own dually bilingual existence and from the discovery of new worlds of thought and literature—the Mayan, Aztec, Native American, and so forth. Formerly we would, in our daily lives, hispanicize English realities: "I missed" would resurrect in Spanish as "*mistié*," "I flunked" would expand the traditional lexicon with "*flonquié*," and the "big, old thing" ending "*azo*" would turn a party in an English sentence into a *parozo* in a Spanish conversation. . . . Acutely aware of the sounds of English, we would accent our Spanish to a mock-Anglicized "free holes" (for *frijoles*) and then play the reverse by accenting our English with the sounds of Spanish: *pino borra* for "peanut butter."

Such verbal and cultural crossings define the poetics, for example, of *el sol y los de abajo* by Jose Montoya and Raul Salinas's "Trip Through the Mind Jail," as well as the pronounced surrealist forms of Ricardo García and the ethnic hilarity of Jose Antonio Burciaga's poetry.

The early agenda of Chicano verse reflected its agitational aims of conceiving and celebrating global, universal, and public forms of social emancipation from the legacy of colonial rule in the United States. But Chicano poetry quickly expanded its focus beyond the national context to consider the transnational situation of La Raza (the People) of Mexico, Central and South America. More recent forms of Chicano poetry have shifted the focus from the agenda of Chicano national unity to more regionally specific, local, personal, and intrapersonal themes that reflect the micropolitics of gender relations, sexuality, and a contradictory mélange of racial, national, and class experiences. Beginning in the mid-1970s with Margarita Cota-Cárdenas's *Noches despertando inconciencias*, Angela de Hoyos's *Arise, Chicano* and *Chicano Poems for the Barrio*, and Bernice Zamora's *Restless Serpents*, Chicana poets celebrated the power of women's experience in mythological tropes such as *la tierra* (the earth as nurturer, healer, and source of creativity) and the serpent (as figure for the cyclic rather than linear understanding of time, change, and transformation). Moreover, female poets such as Pat Mora and Margarita Cota-Cárdenas recovered heroic feminine personae such as La Llorona, La Virgen de Guadalupe, and La Adelita to rewrite male historicism from a decidedly feminist point of view.

Exploring women's embodied experience, writers such as Alma Villanueva, Carmen Tafolla, and Vangie Vigil dealt explicitly with the disturbing realities of Chicana gender, racial and class oppression; the persistence of sexual and psychic violence; the ever-present threat of rape; and other atrocities perpetrated against women. Like Sylvia Plath and Anne Sexton before her, Villanueva accepts but recodes the role of "madwoman" and "witch" in speaking out against the injustice of contemporary social arrangements. In this regard, poetry serves as a resource against those who would judge and condemn her, as she describes in "The Last Words":

> calling me sentimental, bitter, minor, emotionally ill
> > [and ah, possessed].
>
> they do not know I burn, self/imposed
> in a fire of my

own making
my witches' secret: the poem as
my witness

this cannot be destroyed.
they burn in the heart, long after
the witch is dead.

Increasingly, the poetry of Chicano witness has received both popular and academic recognition. Poets such as Orlando Romírez, Lorna Dee Cervantes, Gary Soto, and Alberto Ríos have all won major academic awards as they pursue careers that partake of life both in La Raza and the literary world. Complicating the political unity of the early Chicano Movement, contemporary Chicano poets do not necessarily presume to represent the voice of an entire community. According to the Chicano scholar Bruce-Novoa, "they no longer feel the need to speak as political prophets. [T]his makes the recent poetry much harder to study and categorize, much harder to reduce for the sake of students and dabblers from other cultural milieu—but for that very reason much more dynamic, healthy, and interesting."

Poems for Further Reading and Critical Writing

PAT MORA   *(b. 1942)*

Agua negra   *(1995)*

I see her shadow
rocking in the candle-
light. Wind and rain bang
wood slats, slash palm trees.
We're two women caught   5
in a storm of stories.

In the hills, rivers
leap to light, plunge
through bougainvillea
into the green hiss,   10
the island's víbora.

Water rushes
down street to shacks,
to cardboard rooms. Agua negra oozes
between small toes   15
of shoeless children.

"I hear their whimpers,
'¡Mamá! ¡Mamá!'
from across the street,"
her voice begins its spin,　　　　　　　　　　　　　　　　20
a worn familiar record,
the voice of tías and abuelitas,
storytellers.

"Ay los blanquitos
y su dinero.　　　　　　　　　　　　　　　　　　　　25
Their soft hands hunger
for amber and our pink mangoes,
not the tugging
pleas, 'Look, mees. Buy, mees.'
Every afternoon　　　　　　　　　　　　　　　　　30
los policías grabbed
mis muchachos, threw them
into the police yard,
kicked their toothpick ribs.
No shade, no water.　　　　　　　　　　　　　　　35

'¡Mamá! ¡Mamá!' they scream,
and a club thuds a skull.
Glare scorches their eyes and throats
until turistas y su dinero sail,
hands and hearts heavy with bundles.　　　　　　40

'¡Mamá! ¡Mamá!'

'¡Por Dios! Son niños,'
I'd yell, but they baked them
in that horno,
baked them to their bones, pobrecitos.　　　　　45

I bought a little house
a hiding place.
Ay, que tristeza,"
she rocks, shakes her head,
"It's our country,　　　　　　　　　　　　　　　50
and we have to hide."

Wind runs round, around
the widow's hushed home
like children chase themselves
in rain, mouths open,　　　　　　　　　　　　　　55
ready to swallow
what falls from the sky.

Dear Frida°   (1995)

1

We're stuck on you, on thorns you press
into your swan neck, black swan, niñita
limping, stubborn, withered leg.

"Frida, pata de palo. Frida, pata de palo,"
sing-sing stones to break your bones.   5

You cover the skinny ankle, skirts long
even when sweat slides down your legs
like sangre, your paint, Frida.

"Pata de palo, Frida, pata de palo."

You make us taste blood that burst   10
everywhere, bones crushed in a bus crash,
rod shoved through you pelvis to spine.

Perfect aim, your clothes ripped away,
young swan plucked clean, skin gleaming
in the sun, blood and gold, powdered gold   15

bursts into air with wheels, eggs, hair, bones
and screams, wild, when you glitter
like a mangled dancer, their screams:

"¡La bailarina, la bailarina!"

2

Round your bed, she dances round   20
your stiff white cast, your stiff white room,
La Pelona dances round your body tomb.

Clakati, clak-clak, clakati, clak-clak.

Bald Death watches surgeons carve,
below your long neck—knives, needles, cut,   25
stitch, pinch skin together, but your body falls apart.

They mold you stiff, but you slip
out head first, escape from boring ceilings through
your fingertips, through the smell of paint.

––––––
Frida Kahlo (1907–1954): Mexican artist.

3

You're stuck on him, Frida, on your old fat frog,   30
your "Sapo-Rana" croaking, *Yo, yo, yo,*
into your neck, perfect aim stroking your scars

until each opens, bleeds. How his thick lips suck
on you, your Diego, immense baby bending your
crooked spine while your babies melt and slip away.   35

Clakati, clak-clak, clakati, clak-clak.

Your dolls and hungry black monkeys
curl round your neck, watch you brand
yourself, stamp Diego° right between your eyes.

We want to erase him, Frida, but we can't,   40
the man you love more than your own sad bones,
the hungry toad who likes a woman in each hand.

He is the sun, the moon. His flesh, warm dough,
surrounds you until you can't hear the pain,
his sweat sweet brandy on your nervous tongue.   45

You drink his breath heavy as a storm. Lightning
sizzles through you, pelvis to spine. His hands
stroke your hair, mold your broken pieces.

You find the ones he went to, chew lips
he kissed, hungry for some shred   50
of him, lick his smell on their willing breasts.

No others will do. "¡Chingado!" you cry
but try men, women, bite them so hard
they bleed, but always you taste Diego, Diego.

4

La Pelona Tonta dances while you paint   55
yourself, splatter sangre, smear breasts,
thighs, arms, hands, shirts, skirts, sheets white as milk.

Your paintings don't laugh like you do,
Frida, that laugh smelling of curses,
espinas flung at curdled faces.   60

---

39 *Diego Rivera (1886–1957):* Mexican muralist, husband of Frida Kahlo.

She grins, La Más Pelona, at her bones
in your mirror while you soak your scars, grins
at skulls floating white in your bath, small like soaps.

Clakati, clak-clak, clakati, clak-clak.

Your wounds are always open, Frida.   65
Why can't you hide stabs, gashes, corsets?
Why can't you vomit in private, like a lady?

                                    5

Drugged, on fire, you burst into your last show
in an ambulance. You drink, sing from your bed.
You are your art, and you make us watch you die.   70

Clakati, clak-clak, clakati, clak

Frida, pata de palo, Frida, pate de palo,
we still hear, "NO!" that mangled scream, "no!"
But La Pelona says your leg has to go.

                                    6

Clak. In your body slides, Frida, to its last burning,   75
bolts up in the lick of oven's hungry tongues,
hair, your hair, around your face, crackles, blazes.

JIMMY SANTIAGO BACA   *(b. 1952)*

Mi Tío Baca El Poeta De Socorro°   *(1989)*

Antonio Ce De Baca
chiseled on stone chunk gravemarker,
propped against a white wooden cross.
Dust storms faded the birth and death numbers.
Poet de Socorro,°   5
whose poems roused *la gente*
to demand their land rights back,
'til one night—that terrible night,
hooves shook your earthen-floor
one-room adobe, lantern flame   10
flickered shadowy omens on walls,
and you scrawled across the page,
"*¡Aquí vienen! ¡Aquí vienen!*

Mi Tío . . . .Socorro: My Uncle Baca, the Poet of Socorro.   5 *Socorro:* Town in New Mexico on
the Rio Grande River.

Here they come!"
Hooves clawed your front yard,   15
guns glimmering blue
angrily beating at your door.

       You rose.
Black boots scurried round four adobe walls,
trampling flower beds.   20
They burst through the door.
It was a warm night, and carried the scent
of their tobacco, sulphur, and leather.
Faces masked in dusty hankies,
men wearing remnants of Rinche uniforms,   25
arms pitchforked you out,
where arrogant young boys on horses
held torches and shouted,
"Shoot the Mexican! Shoot him!"
Saliva flew from bits   30
as horses reared from you,
while red-knuckled recruits held reins tight,
drunkenly pouring whiskey over you,
kicking you up the hill by the yucca,
where you turned, and met the scream   35
of rifles with your silence.

       Your house still stands.
Black burnt tin covers window openings,
weeds grow on the dirt roof
that leans like an old man's hand   40
on a cane *viga*. . . .
I walk to the church a mile away,
a prayer on my lips bridges
years of disaster between us.
Maybe things will get better.   45
Maybe our struggle to speak and be
as we are, will come about.
For now, I drink in your spirit, Antonio,
to nourish me as I descend
into dangerous abysses of the future.   50
I came here this morning
at 4:30 to walk over my history.
Sat by the yucca, and then imagined you again,
walking up to me
face sour with tortuous hooks   55
pulling your brow down in wrinkles,
cheeks weary with defeat,
face steady with implacable dignity.
The softness in your brown eyes

said you could take no more. 60
You will speak with the angels now.
I followed behind you to the church,
your great bulky field-working shoulders
lean forward in haste
as if angels really did await us. 65
Your remorseful footsteps
in crackly weeds
sound the last time
I will hear and see you. Resolve is engraved
in each step. I want to believe 70
whatever problems we have, time will take
its course, they'll be endured and consumed.
Church slumps on a hill, somber and elegant.
After you, I firmly pull the solid core door back.
You kneel before La Virgen De Guadalupe, 75
bloody lips moving slightly,
your great gray head poised in listening,
old jacket perforated with bloody bullet holes.
I close the door, and search the prairie,
considering the words *faith*, *prayer* and *forgiveness*, 80
wishing, like you, I could believe them.

Dust-Bowl Memory (1986)

for Abaskin

My ancient neighbor, Mr. Abaskin,
was born in Russia, roamed Europe,
and when the call came from America,
he boarded ship and came.
Seventy years farming this land. 5
Every morning he walks the dirt road
with his aging wife, reminding me
of two solitary mesquite trees
rooted high at the edge of a rocky cliff,
overlooking a vast canyon gorge. 10
Hands hardened, yellow claws
from farming tenderly pocket candy
in my son's pants.
He scolds his shepherd Kiki
for exciting grazing sheep or scaring 15
Rhode Island Reds. We meet every noon
by the fence where our feed is
and small talk
conditions of fields,
how he and his wife could buck 20

three hundred bales an afternoon
when they were my age.
His memory an old dust-bowl town,
he remembers who lived where
before we came, who was born to whom, 25
when Williams' Packing Company started
stealing people's cattle, when people
started locking their screen doors,
and a time when only Spanish was spoken in this valley.
"Didn't have to go to town. These Mexican folk 30
had the finest gardens in the world,
why tomatoes and chile you wouldn't believe. . . ."

Bells   *(1986)*

Bells. The word gongs my skull bone. . . .
Mamá carried me out, just born,
swaddled in hospital blanket,
from St. Vincent's in Santa Fe.
Into the evening, still drowsed 5
with uterine darkness,
my fingertips purple with new life,
cathedral bells splashed
into my blood, plunging iron hulls
into my pulse waves. Cathedral steeples, 10
amplified brooding, sonorous bells,
through narrow cobbled streets, bricked patios,
rose-trellis'd windows,
red-tiled Spanish rooftops, bells
beat my name, "Santiago! Santiago!" 15
Burning my name in black-frosted streets,
bell sounds curved and gonged deep,
ungiving, full-bellowed beats of iron on iron,
shuddering pavement Mamá walked,
quivering thick stainless panes, creaking 20
plaza shop doors, beating its gruff thuds
down alleys and dirt
passageways, past men waiting in doorways
of strange houses. Mamá carried me, past
peacocks and chickens, past the miraculous 25
stairwell winding into the choirloft, touted
in tourist brochures, *"Not one nail was used*
to build this, it clings tenaciously
together by pure prayer power, a spiraling
pinnacle of faith. . . ." And years later, 30
when I would do something wrong,
in kind reprimand Mamá would say,

"You were born of bells, more than my womb,
they speak to you in dreams.
Ay, *Mijito*,   35
you are such a dreamer!"

Choices   *(1986)*

An acquaintance at Los Alamos Labs
who engineers weapons
black x'd a mark where I live
on his office map.
Star-wars humor. . . .   5
He exchanged muddy boots
and patched jeans
for a white intern's coat
and black polished shoes.
A month ago, after butchering a gouged bull,   10
we stood on a pasture hill,
and he wondered with pained features
where money would come from
to finish his shed, plant alfalfa,
and fix his tractor.   15
Now his fingers
yank horsetail grass,
he crimps herringbone tail-seed
between teeth, and grits out words,
"Om gonna buy another tractor   20
next week. More land too."
Silence between us is gray water
let down in a tin pail
in a deep, deep well,
a silence   25
milled in continental grindings
millions of years ago.
I throw my heart
into the well, and it falls
a shimmering pebble to the bottom.   30
Words are hard
to come by. "Would have lost everything
I've worked for, not takin' the job."
His words try to
retrieve   35
my heart
from the deep well.
We walk on in silence,
our friendship
rippling away.   40

BERNICE ZAMORA   *(b. 1938)*

Notes from a Chicana "COED"   *(1977)*

To cry that the *gabacho*
is our oppressor is to shout
in abstraction, *carnal.*
He no more oppresses us
than you do now as you tell me   5
"It's the gringo who oppresses you, Babe."
You cry "The gringo is our oppressor!"
to the tune of $20,000 to $30,000
a year, brother, and I wake up
alone each morning and ask,   10
"Can I feed my children today?"

To make the day easier
I write poems about
pájaros, mariposas,
and the fragrance   15
of perfume I
smell on your collar;
you're quick to point out
that I must write
about social reality,   20
about "the gringo who
oppresses you, Babe."
And so I write about
how I worked in beet fields
as a child, about how I   25
worked as a waitress
eight hours at night to
get through high school,
about working as a
seamstress, typist, and field clerk   30
to get through college, and
about how, in graduate school
I held two jobs, seven days
a week, still alone, still asking,
"Can I feed my children today?"   35

To give meaning to my life
you make love to me in alleys,
in back seats of borrowed Vegas,
in six-dollar motel rooms
after which you talk about   40

your five children and your wife
who writes poems at home
about *pájaros, mariposas,*
and the fragrance of perfume
she smells on your collar.   45
Then you tell me how you
bear the brunt of the
gringo's oppression for me,
and how you would go
to prison for me, because   50
"The gringo is oppressing you, Babe!"

And when I mention
your G.I. Bill, your
Ford Fellowship, your
working wife, your   55
three *gabacha guisas*
then you ask me to
write your thesis,
you're quick to shout,
"Don't give that   60
Women's Lib trip, mujer,
that only divides us,
and we have to work
together for the *movimiento*
the *gabacho* is oppressing us!"   65

Oye carnal, you may as well
tell me that moon water
cures constipation, that
penguin soup prevents *crudas,*
or that the Arctic Ocean is *menudo,*   70
because we both learned in the *barrios,*
man, that pigeon shit slides easier.

Still, because of the *gabacho,*
I must write poems about
pájaros, mariposas, and the fragrance   75
of oppressing perfume I smell somewhere.

ALMA VILLANUEVA   *(b. 1944)*

Of Utterances   *(1977)*

a woman is her own
(muse)
that's the main thing.
　　　—ANNE SEXTON

the "White Goddess"
to white men
to poets and men of genius
　　"a source of inspiration;
　　　a guiding genius . ."　　　　　　　　　　　　　　　　　　　5
that beautiful Goddess
that legendary Angel,
　　　　　　　　　　descending
　　with her milky white limbs,
　　　　　full breasts, rosy at the　　　　　　　　　　　　　　10
　　　　　　tips with the milky
　　　　　　　stanzas and lyrics
　　　　　　　　to the touch of man:
the cunt all acceptance,　　　opening wide
　　　　　　　　　to the mind of man　　and　　　　　　　　15
　　　　　　　giving birth to their children
　　The Poem.　The Painting.　The Sculpture.

and I with my fetish for dark men.
and dislike (dis-taste) for sucking (this part's o.k.—
cocks and swallowing the salty sperm (this part's not—　　　20
of prose and rhymes.
we women just don't have any
dark and lovely,
　　　　　　　　descending
"Black Gods"—　　　so being　　　　　　　　　　　　　25
a woman of resources
and imagination, I decided to become
my own source of inspiration;
my very own genius—
I grew my own wings, became my　　　　　　　　　　　30
own muse.

I decided to fly
and not
descend.

The Last Words   (1977)

to Anne & Sylvia
& all those that burned before them
in Salem & other places—

Out of the ash
I rise with my red hair
And I eat men like air.
            —SYLVIA PLATH

if they knew my heart
they would

if they knew my heart
they would burn

if they knew my heart   5
they would burn me

if they knew my heart
they would burn me at the

if they knew my heart
they would burn me at the stake.   10

witches' blood must flow! dry and crackle—
sink into the mother, turn to ash—
red fire/blood release the utterance—
the last words
unheard by stupid mob—   15
the hysterical mob does not like to be
reminded of their true natures—
they would like to forget women like me.
they back away, cowering, from the heat of
my love   20
my words
my blood
calling me sentimental, bitter, minor, emotionally ill
                            [and ah, possessed].

they do not know I burn, self/imposed   25
in a fire of my

own making.
my witches' secret: the poem as
my witness.

this cannot be destroyed.
they burn in the heart, long after
the witch is dead.   30

GARY SOTO   *(b. 1952)*

Mexicans Begin Jogging   *(1981)*

At the factory I worked
In the fleck of rubber, under the press
Of an oven yellow with flame,
Until the border patrol opened
Their vans and my boss waved for us to run.   5
"Over the fence, Soto," he shouted,
And I shouted that I was American.
"No time for lies," he said, and pressed
A dollar in my palm, hurrying me
Through the back door.   10

Since I was on his time, I ran
And became the wag to a short tail of Mexicans—
Ran past the amazed crowds that lined
The street and blurred like photographs, in rain.
I ran from that industrial road to the soft   15
Houses where people paled at the turn of an autumn sky.
What could I do but yell *vivas*
To baseball, milkshakes, and those sociologists
Who would clock me
As I jog into the next century   20
On the power of a great, silly grin.

The Tale of Sunlight   *(1978)*

Listen, nephew.
When I opened the cantina
At noon
A triangle of sunlight
Was stretched out   5
On the floor
Like a rug
Like a tired cat.
It flared in
From the window   10
Through a small hole

Shaped like a yawn.
Strange I thought
And placed my hand
Before the opening,   15
But the sunlight
Did not vanish.
I pulled back
The shutters
And the room glowed,   20
But this pyramid
Of whiteness
Was simply brighter.
The sunlight around it
Appeared soiled   25
Like the bed sheet
Of a borracho.°
Amazed, I locked the door,
Closed the windows.
Workers, in from   30
The fields, knocked
To be let in,
Children peeked
Through the shutters,
But I remained silent.   35
I poured a beer,
At a table
Shuffled a pack
Of old cards
And watched it   40
Cross the floor,
Hang on the wall
Like a portrait
Like a calendar
Without numbers.   45
When a fly settled
In the sunlight
And disappeared
In a wreath of smoke,
I tapped it with the broom,   50
Spat on it.
The broom vanished.
The spit sizzled.
It is the truth, little one.
I stood eye to blank eye   55
And by misfortune

---

27 *borracho:* Drunkard.

This finger
This pink stump
Entered the sunlight,
Snapped off   60
With a dry sneeze,
And fell to the floor
As a gift
To the ants
Who know me   65
For what I gave.

SANDRA CISNEROS *(b. 1954)*

Little Clown, My Heart   *(1994)*

Little clown, my heart,
Spangled again and lopsided,
Handstands and Peking pirouettes,
Backflips snapping open like
A carpenter's hinged ruler,   5

Little gimp-footed hurray,
Paper parasol of pleasures,
Fleshy undertongue of sorrows,
Sweet potato plant of my addictions,

Acapulco cliff-diver *corazón*,°   10
Fine as an obsidian dagger,
Alley-oop and here we go
Into the froth, my life,
Into the flames!

TOPICS FOR CRITICAL THINKING

1. "Agua negra" means black water; what contradictions does Pat Mora's title set up in the connotations of blackness and water? How do both terms simultaneously take on positive and negative connotations in the work?

2. Consider the ways in which Bernice Zamora's ironic dramatic monologue in "Notes from a Chicana 'COED'" points to the clashing politics of class and gender in El Movimiento. How do you imagine the poem's addressee? In what ways does poetry allow Zamora to reverse the power imbalance between Chicano men and women in order to have the last word?

---

10 *corazón:* Heart.

3. Explore the ways in which Alma Villanueva rewrites the angelic and demonic stereotypes of women to claim an alternative feminist mythology of empowerment in "Of Utterance" and "The Last Words."

4. Investigate the ways in which Soto's line length contributes to the narrative suspense of "The Tale of Sunlight." Is it clear what exactly the mysterious triangle of sunlight symbolizes in the poem?

TOPICS FOR CRITICAL WRITING

1. In addition to suffering from childhood polio, Mexican painter Frida Kahlo was also hit by a bus at the age of eighteen. Her injuries were severe—breaks to her spinal column, collarbone, ribs, pelvis, right leg, and right foot—and she spent over a month in a plaster cast. A chronic pain victim throughout her life, Kahlo nevertheless enjoyed a successful career as a painter and had a passionate and, at times, stormy marriage to the Mexican muralist Diego Rivera. In "Dear Frida," "La Pelona," as Mora explains in a note to this poem, "was feisty Frida's name for death." What relation does Mora draw in the poem between death, trauma, and artistic creativity?

2. Of mixed Chicano and Apache blood lines, Jimmy Santiago Baca lost his father at an early age to alcoholism, while his mother was murdered by her new husband after she remarried. Baca's early years were marked by homelessness, drug and alcohol abuse, and eventually prison, solitary confinement, and shock therapy. Poetry became a means of survival, however, and the relation between violence and creative resistance is a constant feature of his work. In what ways does Baca's elegy to his uncle, also a poet and victim of violence, take on the ancestral values of "faith, prayer, and forgiveness"? To what extent does the poem's ironic turn mark certain limits to these ideals?

3. Examine how Gary Soto complicates Chicano national identity in "Mexicans Begin Jogging."

4. Consider the metaphors through which Sandra Cisneros addresses her "heart" in her apostrophe to "Little Clown, My Heart."

34

Critical Perspectives

A Casebook on Native American Poetry

Native American culture reaches back some 30,000 years on the combined North and South American continents of what has been
called "Turtle Island." In the United States, between 4 and 8 million native
peoples once existed in over 500 ancient cultures, each with its own distinct
language. Today, some 550 tribal governments preside over more than 300
tribal groups. While about half of native peoples live on approximately 53
million acres of reservation lands, about 1 million reside in urban areas.

Complicating these demographics, however, is the question of what defines
Native American identity and literature. One marker is the blood-quantum of
one's descent lines that federal and tribal governments use to determine membership rolls variously according to race. But according to Native American
scholar Geary Hobson, whether one embodies a full, half, quarter, or even a
trace of Native American blood heritage is not as significant as the degree of
one's social commitment to and cultural identification with the Native American community. In his introduction to *The Remembered Earth: An Anthology of
Native American Literature* (1991), Hobson writes:

> [A] person is judged as Native American because of how he or she views the world,
> his or her views about land, home, family, culture, etc. There are, I think, no easy
> answers. I do believe, however, that John Ross, the one-eighth blood Cherokee
> chief (with seven-eighths Scottish blood), who fought arduously against the re-
> moval of his people into Indian Territory, was more "Indian" than John Ridge, the
> seven-eighths Cherokee, who collaborated with Andrew Jackson's henchmen, sell-
> ing out his people.

Similarly, what constitutes Native American literature is also a difficult
judgment call. Native American poetry is rooted in the oral traditions of ritual,
ceremony, and mythic storytelling that have a sacred relation to tribal life and
its connections to ongoing natural and supernatural processes. The visionary
Lakota medicine man Hehaka Sapa (Black Elk) described himself as a "word
sender" because as a *wicasa wakan* or "holy man" his role, according to Kenneth Lincoln, was to release through language "the spirit in things to move
through this world." "Black Elk," Lincoln writes in *Native American Renaissance* (1983), "imagined language in projective flight, as in the arrowed move-

Turtle Island around 1500

ments of spirits from one place of sacred origin into worldly form." Indeed, in Hopi tradition, storytelling is such a powerful activity that it takes place primarily during the winter solstice month of December, a time of transition from the old year to the new. "[T]he association of storytelling with the winter solstice," writes Native American critic Andrew Wiget, "may stem from a belief that telling a story is a creative activity that has the power to restructure the world being spoken of, and that the safest time to tell stories is when the sun is coming to a standstill in the sky, to be turned back toward spring."

The oral tradition of poetics—grounded as it is in ritual oratory, ceremonial chant, jokes and "clowning," as well as performed story—remains worlds apart from the literary text. To begin with, oral performance tends to join rather than divide author from audience. The spoken word emerges out of a communal setting of shared participation in a sacred event. Such an oral tradition is site-specific insofar as the person taking on the narrative role addresses and is addressed by a particular, face-to-face audience. Here the performative nuances of body language and gesture as well as voiced stress, pitch, volume, intonation, narrative pacing, and so on are tailored to the immediate circumstances of the spoken word. Native American literature, in contrast, mediates tribal experience through the discursive modes and textual conventions of literary tradition. Numerous written accounts of tribal values have sought to negotiate between oral contexts and literary conventions: from Samson Occom's *A Sermon Preached at the Execution of Moses Paul* (1772) to George Copway's *Traditional History and Characteristic Sketches of the Ojibway Nation* (1850), and on through Scott Momaday's Pulitzer Prize-winning *The Way to Rainy Mountain* (1969) and Leslie Marmon Silko's *Ceremony* (1977).

Contemporary Native American writers compose not only out of a tribal context but, equally important, out of a literary tradition that includes such eighteenth-, nineteenth-, and early twentieth-century Native American writers as Samson Occom, Charles Eastman, Alexander Posey, Mourning Dove, D'Arcy McNickle, William Apess, Alice Callahan, John Rollin Ridge, and Jane Johnson Schoolcraft, among many others. This tradition of Native American literature is itself deeply indebted to the literary conventions of anglophone literature. John Joseph Mathews's *Wah'Kon Tah* became a Book-of-the-Month Club selection in 1932 not just because it narrated a compelling account of Native American experience but also because it drew on the literary motifs, plot devices, and stylistic techniques that made for a readable text: one designed to appeal to a mass readership. Moreover, the very composition of works such as *Black Elk Speaks* (1932) oftentimes involve ethnographic collaboration among informants, interpreters, and translators. Indeed, the full author credits for *Black Elk Speaks* include both the title *Black Elk Speaks, Being the Life Story of a Holy Man of the Oglala Sioux* and the additional phrasing "as told through John G. Neihardt (*Flaming Rainbow*)." In fact, Black Elk communicated his vision to Neihardt in 1931 via his son, Ben Black Elk, as translator, while Neihardt's daughter Enid took stenographic notes of the exchange. Nevertheless, the reverence for native place and its animal and plant "people," the holy character of the sacred hoop—where the "red road" of the spirit intersects the secular "black road" at the center of the tribal circle—the rituals of survival, the magical nexus of dream vision, breath, the chanted word all remain central concerns that carry over from oral performance into Native American writing.

Poetry, perhaps more than autobiography, sermon, or fiction comes closest to capturing on the page the immediacy and intensity of oral performance. Some of the ways in which Native American writers have invoked a sense of oral textuality in verse composition include altering patterns of enjambment and spacings of the line, formulaic repetitions of key phrasings and other forms of anaphora, innovative typography, alternative patterns of punctuation, and the absence of punctuation. Such verbal techniques can recreate the cadences of ceremonial chant, as in Joy Harjo's surrealist poem "She Had Some Horses":

> She had horses who were bodies of sand.
> She had horses who were maps drawn of blood.
> She had horses who were skins of ocean water.
> She had horses who were the blue air of sky.
> She had horses who were fur and teeth.
> She had horses who were clay and would break.
> She had horses who were splintered red cliff.

Whether in oral or written forms, the Native American presence pervades American literature and culture from the colonial era to the present. Yet, according to the modern writer D. H. Lawrence, "white people always, or nearly always, write sentimentally about Indians."

We are all familiar, of course, with the modern desire to romanticize the Native American as a "noble savage," natural seer, and helpmate to western colonization. Native peoples have been the subject of much sentimental representation, from the founding colonial myth of Pocahontas and John Smith, through such American literary figures as Henry Wadsworth Longfellow's *Hiawatha* (1855), such popular icons as the Long Ranger and Tonto, and such contemporary Hollywood depictions as the Sioux in *Dances with Wolves*. Yet the need to idealize Native peoples, as Lawrence theorizes in his widely read *Studies in Classic American Literature* (1923), goes hand-in-hand with its opposite impulse. In particular, Lawrence locates a double-consciousness at the heart of America's relation to the native peoples of Turtle Island: "The desire to extirpate the Indian. And the contradictory desire to glorify him. Both are rampant still, to-day."

The flip side to the "noble savage," of course, is the "blood-thirsty savage," and it is the persistent association of Indians with violence that Native American leaders have protested in, say, their criticism of the infamous "tomahawk chop" that is still the rallying cry of Atlanta Braves baseball fans. The myth of the Indian as the violent "other" was a staple of the American western genre well into the twentieth century, and it masked, according to writers such as Louise Erdrich and Michael Dorris, the imperialist aims of American Manifest Destiny. Writes Paula Gunn Allen in *The Sacred Hoop* (1986),

> [The view of Indians] as hostile savages who capture white ladies and torture them, obstruct the westward movement of peaceable white settlers, and engage in bloodthirsty uprisings in which they glory in the massacre of innocent colonists and pioneers is dear to the hearts of producers of bad films and even worse television. However, it is this view that is most deeply embedded in the American unconscious, where it forms the basis for much of the social oppression of other people of color and of women.

Regarding the Indian as "other" was an indispensable ingredient in the construction of an American heroic ideal. The fact that taming the frontier was synonymous with taming the Indian is a given in such American film classics as *Stagecoach*, *The Searchers*, and *Broken Arrow*. It is this connection between "progress" and subduing native populations that Louise Erdrich draws in her poem "Dear John Wayne." In the Hollywood formula of the western action genre, "Always the lookout spots the Indians first, / spread north to south, barring progress." Slipping into the voice of John Wayne, who made his cinematic mark by slaying Indian warriors, Erdrich sums up the blunt, ideological message of the western as it persists into the present: *"It is / not over, this fight, not as long as you resist. / Everything we see belongs to us."*

Whether idealized or demonized, Native Americans largely have been positioned as passive objects of ethnographic, literary, and popular representation. One effect of the widespread stereotyping of native peoples has been to flatten the rich diversity of tribal differences into a homogeneous image of the nameless, faceless, and largely ahistorical Indian as "other." The place of modern Native Americans remains largely invisible within the American mainstream. Indeed, as Vine Deloria has it in *Custer Died for Your Sins* (1969), "to be an Indian in modern American society is in a very real sense to be unreal and ahistorical." It is only in the post-World War II decades that such initiatives as the Native American Movement have empowered native peoples with an active voice in representing their social, cultural, and political lives. Moreover, such federal educational initiatives as the Indian Education Act of 1972 and the Indian Self-Determination and Educational Assistance Act of 1975 have gone a long way toward enabling a new generation of writers and scholars to represent the Native American masses.

The latter part of the twentieth century saw a dramatic increase in the number of publishers that feature Native American literary artists. Indian Center papers and newsletters include such publications as the *Shannon County News*, the *Navajo Times, Indian Country Today*, and *Akwesasne Notes*. Several small presses have emerged, such as Sun Tracks, which publishes a Native American book series, and Greenfield Review, which publishes numerous anthologies of Native American fiction and poetry. Scholarly journals such as *American Indian Quarterly* and the *American Indian Culture and Research Journal* now exist as well, further promoting a vibrant and visible literary and intellectual community. Native Americans, writes critic Joseph Bruchac, "have come away from their educations with a stronger sense of their ethnic and tribal identities and with the sophisticated knowledge of contemporary literary techniques which enables them to express the enduring values of their Native American identity to both white and Indian alike." It is to that body of work that we now turn.

Poems for Further Reading and Critical Writing

LOUISE ERDRICH   *(b. 1954)*

Dear John Wayne°   *(1984)*

August and the drive-in picture is packed.
We lounge on the hood of the Pontiac
surrounded by the slow-burning spirals they sell
at the window, to vanquish the hordes of mosquitoes.
Nothing works. They break through the smoke screen for blood.   5

Always the lookout spots the Indians first,
spread north to south, barring progress.

―――――
John Wayne (1907–1979): American film star.

The Sioux or some other Plains bunch
in spectacular columns, ICBM missiles,
feathers bristling in the meaningful sunset.   10

The drum breaks. There will be no parlance.
Only the arrows whining, a death-cloud of nerves
swarming down on the settlers
who die beautifully, tumbling like dust weeds
into the history that brought us all here   15
together: this wide screen beneath the sign of the bear.

The sky fills, acres of blue squint and eye
that the crowd cheers. His face moves over us,
a thick cloud of vengeance, pitted
like the land that was once flesh. Each rut,   20
each scar makes a promise: *It is
not over, this fight, not as long as you resist.*

Everything we see belongs to us.

A few laughing Indians fall over the hood
slipping in the hot spilled butter.   25
The eye sees a lot, John, but the heart is so blind.
Death makes us owners of nothing.
He smiles, a horizon of teeth
the credits reel over, and then the white fields

again blowing in the true-to-life dark.   30
The dark films over everything.
We get into the car
scratching our mosquito bites, speechless and small
as people are when the movie is done.
We are back in our skins.   35

How can we help but keep hearing his voice,
the flip side of the sound track, still playing:
Come on, boys, we got them
where we want them, drunk, running.
They'll give us what we want, what we need.   40
Even his disease was the idea of taking everything.
Those cells, burning, doubling, splitting out of their skins.

WENDY ROSE   *(b. 1948)*

Trickster: 1977   *(1977)*

I.

The Trickster's time
is not clicked off neatly
on round dials, nor shadowed
in shifty lengths
on the earth. He counts his changes   5
slowly and is not accurate.
He lives for his own mess of words,
his own spilled soup. He can see
when you are spread out
and captured and numb and   10
speechless; when you have stretched
to your limit and can
no more bear to hear the frozen words
circle like ravens above you,
than to see worms grow into songs   15
from your gut.
He turns to wind, he turns to sand,
he turns walking off with your singer's tongue
left invisible. We'll say he is
the whistling coyote as he steals   20
all the words you ever knew.

II.

Reach in deep: then leave me
to find the words alone.
The whole world is made up
of words, mountain-thick, that wait   25
to cave in with edges that squeeze
hurt and reason into separate sounds.
The songs become tons
of bilingual stuff to reckon with.
Tricked: let me not touch the pen.   30
Let my voice be still . . . let anesthesia ride each nerve.
Let the bones melt into the rain and
disappear; let me disappear
and let those soft bones go.

If I Am Too Brown or Too White
for You

remember I am a garnet woman
whirling into precision
as a crystal arithmetic
or a cluster and so

why the dream   5
in my mouth,
the flutter of blackbirds
at my wrists?

In the morning
there you are   10
at the edge of the river
on one knee

and you are selecting me
from among polished stones
more definitely red or white   15
between which tiny serpents swim

and you see that my body
is blood frozen
into giving birth
over and over in a single motion   20

and you touch the matrix
shattered in winter
and begin to piece together
the shape of me

wanting the fit in your palm   25
to be perfect
and the image less
clouded, less mixed

but you always see
just in time   30
working me around
in the evening sun

there is a small light
in the smoke, a tiny sun
in the blood, so deep   35
it is there and not there,

so pure
it is singing.

Story Keeper   (1985)

The stories would be braided in my hair
between the plastic combs and blue wing tips
but as the rattles would spit,
the drums begin,
along would come someone   5
to stifle and stop the sound
and the story keeper I would have been
must melt into the cave
of artifacts discarded

and this is a wound   10
to be healed
in the spin of winter,
the spiral
of beginning.
This is the task: 15
to find the stories now
and to heave at the rocks,
dig at the moss
with my fingernails,
let moisture seep along my skin   20
and fall within
soft and dark
to the blood

and I promise
I will find them
even after so long: where underground   25
they are albino
and they listen, they shine,
and they wait
with tongues shriveled like leaves   30
and fearful of their names
that would crystallize them,
make them fossils
with the feathers on their backs
frozen hard   35
like beetle wings.

ΔΔΔΔ   ΔΔΔΔ

But spring is floating
to the canyon rim;
needles burst yellow
from the pine branch   40
and the stories have built a new house.
Oh they make us dance
the old animal dances
that go a winding way
back and back   45
to the red clouds
of our first
Hopi morning.

Where I saw them last
they are still: antelope and bear   50
dancing in the dust,
prairie dog and lizard
whirling just whirling,
pinyon and willow
bending, twisting,   55
we women
rooting into the earth
our feet becoming water
and our hair pushing up
like tumbleweed   60

and the spirits should have noticed
how our thoughts wandered those first days,
how we closed our eyes against them
and forgot the signs;
the spirits were never smart about this   65
but trusted us to remember it right
and we were distracted,
we were new.
We mapped the trails
the spirits had walked   70
as if the footprints had more meaning
than the feet.
color after color,
designs that spin and sprout
were painted on the sky   75
but we were only confused
and turned our backs
and now we are trapped
inside our songlessness.

We are that kind of thing   80
that pushes away
the very song
keeping us alive
so the stories have been strong
and tell themselves   85
to this very day,
with or without us
it no longer matters.
The flower merges with the mud,
songs are hammered onto spirits   90
and spirits onto people;
every song is danced out loud
for wc are the spirits,
we are the people,
descended from the ones   95
who circled the underworld
and return to circle again.

I feel the stories
rattle under my hand
like sun-dried greasy   100
gambling bones.

LESLIE MARMON SILKO   *(b. 1948)*

Story from Bear Country   *(1976)*

You will know
when you walk
in bear country
By the silence
flowing swiftly between the juniper trees   5
by the sundown colors of sandrock
all around you.

You may smell damp earth
scratched away
from yucca roots
You may hear snorts and growls   10
slow and massive sounds
from caves
in the cliffs high above you.

It is difficult to explain   15
how they call you
All but a few who went to them
left behind families
              grandparents
              and sons   20
              a good life.

The problem is
you will never want to return
Their beauty will overcome your memory
like winter sun   25
melting ice shadows from snow
And you will remain with them
locked forever inside yourself
              your eyes will see you
              dark shaggy and thick.   30

We can send bear priests
loping after you
their medicine bags
bouncing against their chests
Naked legs painted black   35
bear claw necklaces
rattling against
their capes of blue spruce.

They will follow your trail
into the narrow canyon   40
through the blue-gray mountain sage
to the clearing
where you stopped to look back
and saw only bear tracks
behind you.   45

When they call
faint memories
will writhe around your heart
and startle you with their distance.
But the others will listen   50
because bear priests
sing beautiful songs
They must
if they are ever to call you back.

They will try to bring you   55
step by step

back to the place you stopped
and found only bear prints in the sand
where your feet had been.

Whose voice is this?   60
You may wonder
hearing this story when
after all
you are alone
hiking in these canyons and hills   70
while your wife and sons are waiting
back at the car for you.

But you have been listening to me
for some time now
from the very beginning in fact   75
and you are alone in this canyon of stillness
not even cedar birds flutter.
See, the sun is going down now
the sandrock is washed in its colors
Don't be afraid   80
        we love you
        we've been calling you
        all this time
Go ahead
turn around   85
see the shape
of your footprints
in the sand.

SIMON ORTIZ   *(b. 1941)*

The Boy and the Coyote   *(1976)*

*for a friend, Ed Theis, met
at VAH, Ft. Lyons,
Colorado, November and
December 1974*

You can see the rippled sand rifts
shallow inches below the surface.
I walk on the alkalied sand.
Willows crowd the edges of sand banks
sloping to the Arkansas River.   5

I get lonesome for the young afternoons
of a boy growing at Acoma.
He listens to the river,
the slightest nuance of sound.

Breaking thin ice from a small still pool,   10
I find Coyote's footprints.
Coyote, he's always somewhere before you;
he knows you'll come along soon.
I smile at his tracks which are not fresh
except in memory and say a brief prayer   15
for good luck for him and for me and thanks.

All of a sudden, and not far away,
there are the reports of a shotgun,
muffled flat by saltcedar thickets.
Everything halts for several moments,   20
no sound; even the wind holds to itself.
The animal in me crouches, poised immobile,
eyes trained on the distance, waiting
for motion again. The sky is wide;
blue is depthless; and the animal   25
and I wait for breaks in the horizon.

Coyote's preference is for silence
broken only by the subtle wind,
uncanny bird sounds, saltcedar scraping,
and the desire to let that man free,   30
to listen for the motion of sound.

Making an Acquaintance   *(1976)*

I walk outside without my shoes
on searing hot asphalt front yard.
Howard, my new landlord, says,
"It's gonna be a bitch of a Summer."
Strange, I think, what words mean.   5
He has a tanned middle-aged face,
used to be in real estate in Ohio,
sold his business and moved West.
We get acquainted by talking
about the coming Summer.   10
"Yeah," I agree with him,
"it's gonna be a bitch."
My feet are burning for coolness.

JOY HARJO   (b. 1951)

She Had Some Horses   *(1983)*

She had some horses.

She had horses who were bodies of sand.
She had horses who were maps drawn of blood.
She had horses who were skins of ocean water.
She had horses who were the blue air of sky.   5
She had horses who were fur and teeth.
She had horses who were clay and would break.
She had horses who were splintered red cliff.

She had some horses.

She had horses with long, pointed breasts.   10
She had horses with full, brown thighs.
She had horses who laughed too much.
She had horses who threw rocks at glass houses.
She had horses who licked razor blades.

She had some horses.   15

She had horses who danced in their mothers' arms.
She had horses who thought they were the sun and their
bodies shone and burned like stars.
She had horses who waltzed nightly on the moon.
She had horses who were much too shy, and kept quiet   20
in stalls of their own making.

She had some horses.

She had horses who liked Creek Stomp Dance songs.
She had horses who cried in their beer.
She had horses who spit at male queens who made   25
them afraid of themselves.
She had horses who said they weren't afraid.
She had horses who lied.
She had horses who told the truth, who were stripped
bare of their tongues.   30

She had some horses.

She had horses who called themselves, "horse".
She had horses who called themselves, "spirit", and kept
their voices secret and to themselves.

She had horses who had no names.   35
She had horses who had books of names.

She had some horses.

She had horses who whispered in the dark, who were afraid to speak.
She had horses who screamed out of fear of the silence, who
carried knives to protect themselves from ghosts.   40
She had horses who waited for destruction.
She had horses who waited for resurrection.

She had some horses.

She had horses who got down on their knees for any saviour.
She had horses who thought their high price had saved them.   45
She had horses who tried to save her, who climbed in her
bed at night and prayed as they raped her.

She had some horses.

She had some horses she loved.
She had some horses she hated.   50

These were the same horses.

Call It Fear   *(1983)*

There is this edge where shadows
and bones of some of us walk
                 backwards.
Talk backwards. There is this edge
call it an ocean of fear of the dark. Or
name it with other songs. Under our ribs   5
our hearts are bloody stars. Shine on
shine on, and horses in their galloping flight
strike the curve of ribs.
                 Heartbeat   10
and breathe back sharply. Breathe
                 backwards.
There is this edge within me
           I saw it once
an August Sunday morning when the heat hadn't   15
left this earth. And Goodluck
sat sleeping next to me in the truck.
We had never broken through the edge of the
singing at four a.m.
          We had only wanted to talk, to hear   20

any other voice to stay alive with.
     And there was this edge—
not the drop of sandy rock cliff
bones of volcanic earth into
       Albuquerque.   25
Not that,
   but a string of shadow horses kicking
and pulling me out of my belly,
   not into the Rio Grande but into the music
barely coming through   30
      Sunday church singing
from the radio. Battery worn-down but the voices
talking backwards.

LINDA HOGAN *(b. 1947)*

Heritage   *(1979)*

From my mother, the antique mirror
where I watch my face take on her lines.
She left me the smell of baking bread
to warm fine hairs in my nostrils,
she left the large white breasts that weigh down   5
my body.

From my father I take his brown eyes,
the plague of locusts that leveled our crops,
they flew in formation like buzzards.

From my uncle the whittled wood   10
that rattles like bones
and is white
and smells like all our old houses
that are no longer there. He was the man
who sang old chants to me, the words   15
my father was told not to remember.

From my grandfather who never spoke
I learned to fear silence.
I learned to kill a snake
when you're begging for rain.   20

And grandmother, blue-eyed woman
whose skin was brown,
she used snuff.

When her coffee can full of black saliva
spilled on me   25
it was like the brown cloud of grasshoppers
that leveled her fields.
It was the brown stain
that covered my white shirt,
my whiteness a shame.   30
That sweet black liquid like the food
she chewed up and spit into my father's mouth
when he was an infant.
It was the brown earth of Oklahoma
stained with oil.   35
She said tobacco would purge your body of poisons.
It has more medicine than stones and knives
against your enemies.

That tobacco is the dark night that covers me.

She said it is wise to eat the flesh of deer   40
so you will be swift and travel over many miles.
She told me how our tribe has always followed a stick
that pointed west
that pointed east.
From my family I have learned the secrets   45
of never having a home.

Blessings   *(1979)*

Blessed
are the injured animals
for they live in his cages.
But who will heal my father,
tape his old legs for him?   5

Here's the bird with the two broken wings
and her feathers are white as an angel
and she says goddamn stirring grains
in the kitchen. When the birds fly out
he leaves the cages open   10
and she kisses his brow for such
good works.

> Work he says
> all your life
> and at the end   15
> you don't own even a piece of land.

Blessed are the rich
for they eat meat every night.
They have already inherited the earth.

For the rest of us, may we just live   20
long enough
and unwrinkle our brows,
may we keep our good looks
and some of our teeth
and our bowels regular.   25

Perhaps we can go live places
a rich man can't inhabit,
in the sunfish and jackrabbits,
in the cinnamon colored soil,
the land of red grass   30
and red people
in the valley
of the shadow of Elk
who aren't there.

     He says the damned earth is so old   35
     and wobbles so hard
     you'd best hang on to everything.
     Your neighbors steal what little you got.

Blessed
are the rich   40
for they don't have the same old
Everyday to put up with
like my father
who's gotten old,
       Chickasaw   45
       chikkih asachi, which means
they left as a tribe not a very great while ago.
They are always leaving,
those people.

Blessed   50
are those who listen
when no one is left to speak.

RAY A. YOUNG BEAR   *(b. 1950)*

one chip of human bone   *(1980)*

one chip of human bone

it is almost fitting
to die on the railroad tracks.

i can easily understand   5
how they felt on their long
staggered walks back

grinning to the stars.

there is something about
trains, drinking, and being
an indian with nothing to lose.   10

morning-water train woman   *(1980)*

it didn't take much talk for her
to realize that her brother
was drunk
a couple of years ago
when the morning wind blew a train   5
into his sleep
spreading the muscles and fibers
of his body over the tracks
prematurely towards the sun
claiming another   10
after the long stillness of bells
now jingling with persistence in her ears.
maybe we convinced her
in accordance to time and place
about this life where we walk with but few friends,   15
feeling around for reception
at our presence
willing to exchange old familiar connections
with no forgiveness added to our partings.
perhaps she is still thinking of new methods   20
by which to end herself
this coming weekend or the next.
surely it won't be the same
as the last time she tried:
taking a bottle of aspirins   25

and downing them with a can of engine oil.
the people just laughed and said:
there are other ways, besides. . . .

one time before she went away
i dreamt of her
sitting on the tracks   30
attentive to the distant changing colors
of the signal post.
i knew what she thought and felt.
there were images of small black trains   35
circling around her teeth.
their wheels were throwing sparks
setting fire to her long stringy hair.
her eyes withdrew farther back inside
the skull of her head   40
afraid of the scars,
moving and shifting
across her ribs
like long silvery railroad tracks.

the seal   *(1980)*

in the corner of this
old woman's house,
sits another, of the same
age unable to speak
but able only to grunt   5
and moan like a seal,
doing a yes or a no
or a strange maybe.

people say when she
was inside her mother's   10
stomach, her mother
went to a circus, but
some also say it was while
swimming that she brushed
her body against a seal.   15
in time, the misfortune
is still here.

waiting to be fed   *(1980)*

she swam smiling in the river
thinking it was good that she

had come out here to be with the sun
going out into the air
and giving warmth to her sisters' faces   5
watching her from the sides
listening carefully for the hum
of human voices.
no one would show up here today
she thought. it was too hot   10
to swim with the sun
radiating on the wings of insects
flying in repetition
between shadow and sunlight
confused in their decisions   15
evident by the sound
of their open mouths everywhere.

through the years to now
she had known the river well.
sometimes she imagined herself   20
a rock under the water
surrounded by a landscape
that would bend the trees
through the sky
and then through the stars   25
reminding her of burnt holes
in cloth that protected
her hand from fire
while cooking for people
waiting to be fed.   30
she knew a place where
it was like this
where it suddenly became cool
and clear. this place
had often been mentioned   35
in her mother's constant warnings
about rivers.
like the insects and the sunlight
she released her thought
to a spiderweb drifting   40
across the river
breaking through the clouds
losing all revenge to the giants
lifting their heads in their watch
to her swimming over the cool   45
gushing spring
coming up from under the river
thinking of her stomach
and how it was growing fast.

the child swimming inside her:
the touching and speaking of two hearts
made her feel she could smell the sweetness
of the baby's skin in her breath.

in time she would be able to see   55
the face inside her stomach.
a dream indented on her body.
she took care of it
as if it were a god
as if the snow in winter
had already begun to take shape   60
in the hands of children
far from the staring foreheads
of their houses.
she knew it wasn't sacred
but everything in the land   65
seemed that way.
everyone took great interest
and care for her that she
could somehow make out visible
strips of gentleness gathering   70
around her body
streaming out from her family
a circle of suns.

she looked at her reflection
floating over the water.   75
it seemed as if the sound
of water was also the sound
of rustling leaves.
her sisters broke her thoughts
when they suddenly stopped   80
talking. she quickly asked
if there was anything wrong
but they remained motionless.
from a distance she could
not tell if they were playing.   85
it was a long time before
she found herself shouting
and hitting at the water
hoping they would start
moving. soon her sisters' hands   90
indicated a discussion.
she could not hear their words.
she felt her body drifting
away taken by the foam.
the water rippled to the banks.   95

50

seals crawled out from holes
she hadn't noticed before.
she could feel the cold
water as the seals swam by
brushing the bodies of her   100
sisters against her stomach.

she felt twisted in a dream.
there was talk around her
and she could sense by the words
being spoken that it was night   105
and that relatives were inside
the house being fed. each one
chewing and then
quietly nodding.
her mother's hand covered her head.   110
there was whisper from the root
telling her to be still.
she died as she gave birth.
the child lived without ever hearing
or speaking.   115
she lived in the shadows
of her keeper's house
and was taken care of all her life.
sometimes she would go out into
the daylight and rock her body   120
back and forth as she sat
on the porch.
a smile on her face.
her arms and legs folded to her body.
the sun deep inside her eyes   125
walking to the river.

TOPICS FOR CRITICAL THINKING

1. What is the point of Louise Erdrich's metaphoric comparison in "Dear John Wayne" of the Indian feathers of line 10 to ICBM or intercontinental ballistic missiles?

2. Discuss the relationships Rose draws among story, song, and spirituality in "Story Keeper."

3. Discuss Leslie Marmon Silko's mode of address to the reader in "Story from Bear Country." How does Silko involve the reader in the poem's movement from its literal opening to its closing's mythic frame?

4. Discuss Joy Harjo's technique of verbal repetition in "She Had Some Horses." What dramatic and emotive effects does repetition have in the poet's chanting in surreal catalogues of metaphoric horses?

5. Discuss Linda Hogan's use of figurative language to dramatize the lived intensities of her blood roots in "Heritage."

6. Compare and contrast the narrative point of view in Young Bear's "the seal" with the longer depiction of the myth of the seal in "waiting to be fed."

TOPICS FOR CRITICAL WRITING

1. Of the archetypal figure of the Trickster in Native American mythology, Kenneth Lincoln writes in *Native American Renaissance* (1983):

   > Coyote, hare, raven, crow, jay, wolverine, loon, or spider: a recreant spirit masks as an animal wandering through hundreds of tribal Indian myths. He resists the boundaries of any given species and is likely to appear at any time in any image. Trickster goes his ways "undifferentiated," Paul Radin observes, a makeshift, unregenerate figure fomenting reality. He is less divine than bestial, more mythic than animal. This figure also known as Old Man, scavenges in and out of the tribal world a gamesman, glutton, amoralist, comic rapist, world transformer, and improvisational god. He steals wealth, devours game, breaks rules, seduces the princess, procreates plants and animals, and makes up reality as people unfortunately know it, full of surprises and twists, contrary, problematical.

   In what ways does Wendy Rose identify the Trickster with language and poetry in "Trickster: 1977"?

2. In "If I Am Too Brown or Too White for You," consider Rose's metaphor of the garnet for her mixed Hopi, Miwok, English, Scottish, Irish, and German descent lines.

3. In "Call It Fear," how does Harjo's personification of fear and her address to death through apostrophe enable her to name and thereby master the traumatic heritage of Native American victimization?

4. In "Blessings," consider Hogan's appropriation of the Beatitudes of Christ's Sermon on the Mount in Matthew 5:1-2:

   > (3) Blessed are the poor in spirit,
   > for theirs is the kingdom of heaven.
   > (4) Blessed are those who mourn,
   > for they shall be comforted.
   > (5) Blessed are the meek,
   > for they shall inherit the earth.

   How does Hogan recode such New Testament phrasings to muse on the ironies and contradictions of class difference?

5. Compare and contrast the stereotypical language of the "drunk Indian" train victim of "one chip of human bone" with Ray A. Young Bear's portrayal of how the trauma of the accident affects the victim's sister in "morning-water train woman."

35 Feminism and Representation

In the history of English verse, no female poets come down to us from the Old English period; few were recognized in the Middle Ages. Only in the late sixteenth century do women authors begin to enter the margins of the canon of valued poetic texts. Consequently, feminist representation **Web** in poetry faces at least two challenges. First, female poets must confront a literary tradition that, from the Old English period through the eighteenth century, largely silenced them. Second, they face the dilemma of writing in a genre whose conventions of gender have been linked to masculine narratives of epic heroism, warfare, and male civic governance, not to mention all the lyric stereotypes of romance and sexual seduction that objectify actual women. In this chapter, we explore two aspects of feminist poetics. The double task of feminist verse begins with critique, by exposing traditional stereotypes of women, but it doesn't stop there. Equally important, feminism conceives new modes of poetic representation beyond the imagination of men.

www

To help visualize women's place in traditional English letters, Virginia Woolf invites us to imagine the likely fate of a female author with the genius of Shakespeare living in the Elizabethan period. Shakespeare's "sister" would have been denied access to education, to the stage, and to most civic and cultural forums in the public sphere. In all likelihood, she would have experienced her gift for writing as a curse. Her dilemma might have driven her to madness, suicide, or both. Today, Woolf insists, we would have to read between the lines of the historical record, even to glimpse the plight of the woman poet in the premodern period:

> When, however, one reads of a witch being ducked, of a woman possessed by devils, of a wise woman selling herbs, or even of a very remarkable man who had a mother, then I think we are on the track of a lost novelist, a suppressed poet, of some mute and inglorious Jane Austen, some Emily Brontë who dashed her brains out on the moor or mopped and mowed about the highways crazed with the torture that her gift had put her to.

Not just a problem of the Elizabethan age, the marginalization of women from the centers of male civic power persists well into the twentieth century. As Simone de Beauvoir observed in her 1949 study *The Second Sex*, women's place in society until recently has been subordinated to man's. "Society," writes de Beauvoir, "has always been male; political power has always been in the hands of men." Thus feminist poetics starts with asserting women's voices in poetry across the categories of race, class, regional, national, and ethnic difference.

Paradoxically enough, while female poets have had very little social representation as authors before the nineteenth century, one of poetry's major subjects has been women's cultural representation. Woman as muse, courtly ideal, Angel of the House, and, conversely, as femme fatale, vamp, and monstrous "other" are deeply ingrained in the heritage of English verse. Such stereotypes of women not only have silenced real women but, equally important, have obscured the ways in which the voice of the male poet has been granted a universal authority to speak on behalf of both sexes. "Women have served all these centuries," writes Woolf, "as looking-glasses possessing the magic and delicious power of reflecting the figure of man at twice its natural size." However marginalized as writers, women have been represented at the center of poetry's subjects and themes that figure into the construction of male identity.

One way of empowering the masculine voice is to associate it with the forces of reason, argument, and potent rationality while identifying women with nature, the reproductive cycles of birth and death, and the passive embodiment of youth, beauty, and innocence. As contemporary feminist sociologists, anthropologists, historians, and political scientists have shown, biological differences between the sexes have served to "essentialize" and fix the roles men and women play in ancient and modern societies. Cultures typically assign separate spheres for women and men—the former associated with the domestic world, nature, and the social margins of public decision making versus the latter's privileged access to civic government, organized religious worship, the performative arts, and so on. Emphasizing women's maternal roles, this sexual politics divides nature and culture so as to identify the former as feminine and the latter as masculine.

Carpe Diem Verse and Feminist Critique

Insofar as the splitting of women's roles from men's tends to empower men over women, it has been the subject of feminist critique, especially in the twentieth century. Much of feminist inquiry examines the social construction of gender (see Chapter 35). One can see, for example, a stinging parody of the traditional message of women as the "second sex" in the feminist postmodern poster art of Barbara Kruger. Kruger's artwork combines image and text so as to explore and critique the relations of power that underlie male and female gender roles. A former designer for Conde Nast, Kruger's artwork has the look and feel of slick advertisements, but they question media stereotypes. *We Won't Play Nature to Your Culture* debunks and resists women's passive association with nature in **patriarchy.** A term drawn from the greek root *patriarkhes* and the Latin word *pater* or "father," patriarchy describes in feminist criticism the social and cultural relations that historically have empowered men at the expense of women.

A similar divide between nature and culture, mind and body, activity and passivity underwrites men's relation to women in the seductive conventions of **carpe diem** poetics. *Carpe diem* in Latin means "pluck, or seize, the day." The carpe diem theme of enjoying life in the moment as the cure for the specters of time and death has ancient roots in Egyptian and Babylonian cultures. Sexual metaphors that associate women's reproductive lives with flowers and seasonal change are a staple of the carpe diem tradition. Such floral images come into play when the seventeenth-century poet Robert Herrick persuades women to seize the day, writing "To the Virgins, to Make Much of Time."

ROBERT HERRICK   *(1591–1674)*

To the Virgins, to Make Much of Time   *(1648)*

Gather ye rosebuds while ye may,
  Old time is still a-flying;
And this same flower that smiles today,
  Tomorrow will be dying.

The glorious lamp of heaven, the sun,   5
  The higher he's a-getting;
The sooner will his race be run,
  And nearer he's to setting.

That age is best which is the first,
  When youth and blood are warmer;   10
But being spent, the worse, and worst
  Times still succeed the former.

Then be not coy, but use your time,
  And, while ye may, go marry;
For, having lost but once your prime,   15
  You may forever tarry.

TOPICS FOR CRITICAL THINKING

1. How do rosebuds, the rising sun, warm blood, and youth all conspire to define what virgins, according to Herrick, should value in themselves?
2. What assumptions about the course of women's lives form the basis of Herrick's advice to virgins?
3. The word *coy* signifies shyness or the teasing appearance of being shy. Compare Herrick's caveat against coyness with Andrew Marvell's argument in "To His Coy Mistress," which follows.

ANDREW MARVELL   *(1621–1678)*

To His Coy Mistress   *(1681)*

Had we but world enough, and time,
This coyness, lady, were no crime.
We would sit down, and think which way
To walk, and pass our long love's day.
Thou by the Indian Ganges' side   5
Shoudst rubies find; I by the tide
Of Humber would complain. I would
Love you ten years before the flood,
And you should, if you please, refuse
Till the conversion of the Jews.   10
My vegetable love should grow
Vaster than empires, and more slow;
An hundred years should go to praise
Thine eyes, and on thy forehead gaze;
Two hundred to adore each breast,   15
But thirty thousand to the rest;
An age at least to every part,
And the last age should show your heart.
For, lady, you deserve this state,°
Nor would I love at lower rate.   20
    But at my back I always hear
Time's wingèd chariot hurrying near;
And yonder all before us lie
Deserts of vast eternity.
Thy beauty shall no more be found;   25
Nor, in thy marble vault, shall sound
My echoing song; then worms shall try
That long-preserved virginity,
And your quaint honor turn to dust,
And into ashes all my lust: 30
The grave's a fine and private place,
But none, I think, do there embrace.
    Now therefore, while the youthful hue
Sits on thy skin like morning dew,
And while thy willing soul transpires   35
At every pore with instant fires,
Now let us sport us while we may,
And now, like amorous birds of prey,
Rather at once our time devour

19 *state:* Dignity.

Than languish in his slow-chapped power.   40
Let us roll all our strength and all
Our sweetness up into one ball,
And tear our pleasures with rough strife
Through the iron gates of life:
Thus, though we cannot make our sun   45
Stand still, yet we will make him run.

TOPICS FOR CRITICAL THINKING

1. Marvell parodies the conventions of the carpe diem tradition in presenting the
   theme of time. Discuss how Marvell employs **hyperbole,** or exaggeration, to dilate
   the time of seduction and foreplay to absurd lengths.
2. How does the poet also reinforce the urgency to "sport us while we may" through
   rather grisly, realistic images of the body's decomposition in the grave?

TOPIC FOR CRITICAL WRITING

Explore Marvell's figurative language in the poem. What kind of attitude, according to
the poet, should the lovers have toward time, sexuality, and death?

The modern American poet John Crowe Ransom similarly relies on
the fact of aging to lend persuasive force to the carpe diem tradition in
"Blue Girls."

JOHN CROWE RANSOM   *(1888–1974)*

Blue Girls   *(1927)*

Twirling your blue skirts, travelling the sward
Under the towers of your seminary,
Go listen to your teachers old and contrary
Without believing a word.

Tie the white fillets then about your hair   5
And think no more of what will come to pass
Than bluebirds that go walking on the grass
And chattering on the air.

Practise your beauty, blue girls, before it fail;
And I will cry with my loud lips and publish   10
Beauty which all our power shall never establish,
It is so frail.

For I could tell you a story which is true;
I know a woman with a terrible tongue,

Blear eyes fallen from blue,   15
All her perfections tarnished—yet it is not long
Since she was lovelier than any of you.

TOPICS FOR CRITICAL THINKING

1. Compare Ransom's representation of the blue girls' natural beauty with the carpe diem conventions that shape Herrick's depictions of the coy virgins.
2. Is there an irony in Ransom's assumption that the male poet knows the course of women's lives better than the blue girls?

TOPIC FOR CRITICAL WRITING

Contrast the blue girls' innocence or ignorance of the facts of aging with what the male poet knows about what will become of them. How does his knowledge give him a certain power and authority over the blue girls?

In his seductive "Elegy XIX. To His Mistress Going to Bed," John Donne likewise takes up, but also expands, the role of poet as instructor for an unknowing female addressee.

JOHN DONNE *(1572–1631)*

Elegy XIX. To His Mistress Going to Bed   *(1669)*

Come, madam, come, all rest my powers defy,
Until I labor, I in labor lie.
The foe oft-times, having the foe in sight,
Is tired with standing though he never fight.
Off with that girdle, like heaven's zone glistering,   5
But a far fairer world encompassing.
Unpin that spangled breastplate which you wear,
That th' eyes of busy fools may be stopped there.
Unlace yourself, for that harmonious chime
Tells me from you that now it is bed time.   10
Off with that happy busk, which I envy,
That still can be, and still can stand so nigh.
Your gown going off such beauteous state reveals,
As when from flowery meads th'hill's shadow steals.
Off with that wiry coronet, and show   15
The hairy diadem which on you doth grow:
Now off with those shoes, and then safely tread
In this love's hallowed temple, this soft bed.
In such white robes, heaven's angels used to be
Received by men; thou, Angel, bring'st with thee   20
A heaven like Mahomet's Paradise; and though

Ill spirits walk in white, we easily know
By this these angels from an evil sprite:
Those set our hairs, but these our flesh upright.
　License my roving hands, and let them go   25
Before, behind, between, above, below.
O, my America! my new-found-land,
My kingdom, safeliest when with one man manned,
My mine of precious stones, my empery,
How blest am I in this discovering thee!   30
To enter in these bonds is to be free;
Then, where my hand is set, my seal shall be.
　Full nakedness! All joys are due to thee,
As souls unbodied, bodies unclothed must be,
To taste whole joys. Gems which you women use   35
Are like Atlanta's balls,° cast in men's views,
That when a fool's eye lighteth on a gem,
His earthly soul might covet theirs, not them:
Like pictures, or like books' gay coverings made
For lay-men, are all women thus arrayed.   40
Themselves are mystic books, which only we
(Whom their imputed grace will dignify)
Must see revealed. Then, since that I may know,
As liberally as to thy midwife, show
Thyself: cast all, yea, this white linen hence,   45
There is no penance due to innocence:
　To teach thee, I am naked first; why than,
What needst thou have more covering than a man?

　　Unlike Marvell's rhetorical strategy in "To His Coy Mistress," Donne's erotic argument to seize the day does not so much prey on the mistress's fears of aging and death. Rather, his seduction turns on tropes of mastery and surrender.

TOPICS FOR CRITICAL THINKING

1. Contrast the ways in which Donne imagines himself as a would-be lover in both male and female roles. Discuss Donne's childbirth imagery in the opening lines and contrast these conceits with his role as epic hero doing battle with the "foe" of his mistress's modesty.
2. Discuss Donne's simile that draws on conventions from nature to compare the lover's "beauteous state" with "flowery meads."
3. What gender relations of power are implied in Donne's self-presentation as colonizer of the lover figured as virgin land ("my America and my new-found-land")?

---

36 *Atlanta's balls:* While in a race with Atlanta, Hippomenes distracted her with gold balls in order to win and thereby marry her.

TOPIC FOR CRITICAL WRITING

To what extent does the lover—imagined as "kingdom, safeliest when with one man manned" and a "mine of precious stones"—embody value for male ownership, profit, and enjoyment?

Finally the question of whether a woman can know rather than embody history is likewise posed in W. B. Yeats's poem "Leda and the Swan."

W. B. YEATS *(1865–1939)*

Leda and the Swan *(1924)*

A sudden blow: the great wings beating still
Above the staggering girl, her thighs caressed
By the dark webs, her nape caught in his bill,
He holds her helpless breast upon his breast.

How can those terrified vague fingers push   5
The feathered glory from her loosening thighs?
And how can body, laid in that white rush,
But feel the strange heart beating where it lies?

A shudder in the loins engenders there
The broken wall, the burning roof and tower   10
And Agamemnon dead.
                          Being so caught up,
So mastered by the brute blood of the air,
Did she put on his knowledge with his power
Before the indifferent beak could let her drop?   15

In the ancient world, Leda was married to King Tyndareus of Sparta and gave birth to Clytemnestra. But she was also raped by Zeus in the incarnation of a swan. This union produced Helen of Troy and, according to some versions of the myth, the twins Castor and Pollux. The myth, depicted by such painters as Michelangelo (see color insert), Leonardo da Vinci, Correggio (Antonio Allegri) and François Boucher, was well known to Yeats, who had an active interest in the visual arts from his father, the painter John Yeats. As poet, however, Yeats gives the myth a new twist by focusing on this divine incarnation as the cause of the Trojan War. The synecdoches of "the broken wall, the burning roof and tower" refer to the destruction of Troy by the Greeks. The Greek campaign against Troy was in retaliation for Paris's abduction of Helen from her husband Menelaus, the king of Sparta. Brother to Menelaus and commander of the Greek forces, Agamemnon was the husband of Clytemnestra who murdered him in revenge for allowing the sacrifice of her daughter Iphigenia to the goddess Artemis to ensure safe passage of the Greek fleet to Troy.

"Leda and the Swan" foretells the violent history of the Trojan War and the family murders in the abrupt "sudden blow" that opens onto the poem's rape scene. That sexual assault is further dramatized in the hard *b* plosives that punctuate the opening quatrain of Yeats's sonnet. The estrangement of the poem's literal subject is further defamiliarized in the bizarre coupling of human and animal images ("her thighs caressed / By the dark webs, her nape caught in his bill"). The poem's crucial question—"Did she put on his knowledge with his power"?—asks whether Leda, as a mortal woman, was a full participant in knowing the significance of Zeus's incarnation. Was she, like the god, omniscient or all-knowing in that moment? Was she her own agent in history or merely the biological vehicle for destinies conceived by a patriarchal god for, and about, the world of men? Another question, which Yeats didn't anticipate explicitly in the poem, is whether the myth itself still has pertinence. That is, can this myth still serve as a source of memorable art glorifying, as it does, a rape narrative at the heart of history?

Poetry and Re-visionary Feminism

Part of the task of feminist poetics is to pose difficult questions to the received canon of great books. Such critical questioning happens, according to Adrienne Rich, through acts of poetic "re-vision":

> Re-vision—the act of looking back, of seeing with fresh eyes, of entering an old text from a new critical direction—is for women more than a chapter in cultural history: it is an act of survival. . . . A radical critique of literature, feminist in its impulse would take the work first of all as a clue to how we live, how we have been living, how we have been led to imagine ourselves, how our language has trapped as well as liberated us, how the very act of naming has been till now a male prerogative, and how we can begin to see and name—-and therefore live—afresh.

In undertaking a poetics of re-vision, feminist authors have written against the grain of patriarchal tradition—the Western heritage that values men over women. In the process, feminist poets have challenged the latter's foundational assumptions, its cultural logic and modes of representation, as well as its institutions of power. Emily Dickinson, for example, engages in just this kind of poetic re-vision, when she renames the patriarchal narratives underwriting the biblical authority of the Judeo-Christian tradition:

EMILY DICKINSON   *(1830–1886)*

Poem 1545 (The Bible is an antique Volume)   *(1882)*

The Bible is an antique Volume—
Written by faded Men
At the suggestion of Holy Spectres—

Subjects—Bethlehem—
Eden—the ancient Homestead—
Satan—the Brigadier—
Judas—the Great Defaulter—
David—the Troubadour—
Sin—a distinguished Precipice—
Others must resist—
Boys that "believe" are very lonesome—
Other Boys are "lost"—
Had but the Tale a warbling Teller—
All the Boys would come—
Orpheus' Sermon captivated—
It did not condemn—

In "Poem 1545," Dickinson substitutes "Orpheus' Sermon" for the biblical stories written by men "at the suggestion of Holy Spectres." Orpheus was the son of the god Apollo and Calliope, the muse of epic poetry. His parents blessed him with the arts of poetry and music. The special power of his lyre had the ability to enchant animals and change the course of nature. His music even "captivated" Pluto, the god of the underworld, persuading him to release Eurydice from death. Dickinson contrasts the aesthetic grace of the poet's art with, in her mind, the more coercive lessons of Eden, Satan, and Sin where "belief" is enforced by punishment, repression, and the slavish obedience of "Boys" to "faded Men." Although Dickinson led a deeply spiritual life, she shows a modern skepticism toward organized religion and the received authority of biblical narrative. Re-visioning the Bible in this way is fraught with controversy as it touches on religious truths that are held sacred in the Judeo-Christian tradition.

Equally challenging for the feminist poet is the critique of such foundational institutions as marriage. Historically, marriage and the traditional nuclear family unit have defined and reproduced women's place in the roles of wife and mother. Due in large part to the feminist liberation movements of the post-Vietnam era, those roles have become less restrictive than they once were. But in the conservative social milieu of the 1950s, the formal medium of poetry allowed Adrienne Rich to think critically about the plight of independent-minded women. She turned her attention to representing women who, however outwardly "normal," were nevertheless weighed down by the oppressive conditions of their married lives, as in "Aunt Jennifer's Tigers."

ADRIENNE RICH   *(b. 1929)*

Aunt Jennifer's Tigers   *(1951)*

Aunt Jennifer's tigers prance across a screen,
Bright topaz denizens of a world of green.

They do not fear the men beneath the tree;
They pace in sleek chivalric certainty.

Aunt Jennifer's fingers fluttering through her wool   5
Find even the ivory needle hard to pull.
The massive weight of Uncle's wedding band
Sits heavily upon Aunt Jennifer's hand.

When Aunt is dead, her terrified hands will lie
Still ringed with ordeals she was mastered by.   10
The tigers in the panel that she made
Will go on prancing, proud and unafraid.

The key details that clue us to Aunt Jennifer's oppression have to do with her hands and fingers. The former are depicted as "terrified" and the latter are arrested by the "massive weight of Uncle's wedding band"—a symbol for her confinement in marriage. For, even in death, the "hands will lie / Still ringed with ordeals she was mastered by." The ringed hands in Rich's subtle pun *lie* not only are still in death but they also display the lie of Aunt Jennifer's marital identity as dutiful wife. The tigers of her artistry, however, tell a different story. "Prancing, proud and unafraid," they are the opposite of Aunt Jennifer's "terrified" married life. Unlike Aunt Jennifer, "they do not fear the men beneath the tree."

Verse writing allowed Rich to recognize quite early in her career the contradictions between one's creative life as an artist and the roles of wife and mother that society demanded of women in the 1950s. Of her own dilemma at that time, Rich writes:

Looking back at poems I wrote before I was twenty-one, I'm startled because beneath the conscious craft are glimpses of the split I even then experienced between the girl who wrote poems, who defined herself in writing poems, and the girl who was to define herself by her relationships with men. "Aunt Jennifer's Tigers," written while I was a student, looks with deliberate detachment at this split. . . . In writing this poem, composed and apparently cool as it is, I thought I was creating a portrait of an imaginary woman. But this woman suffers from the opposition of her imagination, worked out in tapestry, and her life-style, "ringed with ordeals she was mastered by." It was important to me that Aunt Jennifer was a person as distinct from myself as possible—distanced by the formalism of the poem, by its objective, observant tone—even by putting the woman in a different generation. In those years formalism was part of the strategy—like asbestos gloves, it allowed me to handle materials I couldn't pick up bare handed.

Poetry begins for Rich as an unflinching encounter with, and buffer against, the harsh realities of her experience as a woman.

Composed a decade later, Sylvia Plath's poem "Daddy" lends an urgency and intensity to Rich's criticism of husbands and fathers: one whose confessional edge is far less distanced, less impersonal, and more intimate in its tone, mode of address, and presentational style.

SYLVIA PLATH   *(1932–1963)*

Daddy   *(1962)*

You do not do, you do not do
Any more, black shoe
In which I have lived like a foot
For thirty years, poor and white,
Barely daring to breathe or Achoo.   5

Daddy, I have had to kill you.
You died before I had time—
Marble-heavy, a bag full of God,
Ghastly statue with one gray toe
Big as a Frisco seal   10

And a head in the freakish Atlantic
Where it pours bean green over blue
In the waters off the beautiful Nauset.
I used to pray to recover you.
Ach, du.°   15

In the German tongue, in the Polish town°
Scraped flat by the roller
Of wars, wars, wars.
But the name of the town is common.
My Polack friend   20

Says there are a dozen or two.
So I never could tell where you
Put your foot, your root,
I never could talk to you.
The tongue stuck in my jaw.   25

It stuck in a barb wire snare.
Ich, ich, ich, ich,°
I could hardly speak.
I thought every German was you.
And the language obscene   30

An engine, an engine
Chuffing me off like a Jew.

---

15 *Ach, du:* Ah, you.   16 *Polish town:* Grabów, birthplace of Otto Plath, the poet's father.
27 *ich:* I.

A Jew to Dachau, Auschwitz, Belsen.
I began to talk like a Jew.
I think I may well be a Jew.   35

The snows of the Tyrol,° the clear beer of Vienna
Are not very pure or true.
With my gypsy ancestress and my weird luck
And my Taroc pack and my Tarot pack°
I may be a bit of a Jew.   40

I have always been scared of *you,*
With your Luftwaffe,° your gobbledygoo.
And your neat mustache
And your Aryan eye, bright blue.
Panzer-man, panzer-man,° O You—   45

Not God but a swastika
So black no sky could squeak through.
Every woman adores a Fascist,
The boot in the face, the brute
Brute heart of a brute like you.   50

You stand at the blackboard, daddy,
In the picture I have of you,
A cleft in your chin instead of your foot
But no less a devil for that, no not
Any less the black man who   55

Bit my pretty red heart in two.
I was ten when they buried you.
At twenty I tried to die
And get back, back, back to you.
I thought even the bones would do.   60

But they pulled me out of the sack,
And they stuck me together with glue,
And then I knew what to do.
I made a model of you,
A man in black with a Meinkampf° look   65

---

36 *Tyrol:* Region of Austria.   39 *Taroc pack:* Pack of cards used to tell fortunes.   42 *Luftwaffe:* German airforce.   45 *panzer-man:* Tank-man.   65 *Meinkampf: My Struggle,* the title of Adolf Hitler's biography.

And a love of the rack and the screw.
And I said I do, I do.
So daddy, I'm finally through.
The black telephone's off at the root,
The voices just can't worm through.   70

If I've killed one man, I've killed two—
The vampire who said he was you
And drank my blood for a year,
Seven years, if you want to know.
Daddy, you can lie back now.   75

There's a stake in your fat black heart
And the villagers never liked you.
They are dancing and stamping on you.
They always *knew* it was you.
Daddy, daddy, you bastard, I'm through.   80

Sylvia Plath's father, Otto Plath, immigrated to America from Silesia and, although of German descent, had connections to neither Nazism nor Judaism. A Professor of Biology at Boston University, he published a book entitled *Bumblebees and Their Ways* in 1934, two years after Sylvia was born. Interrupting the normal course of Sylvia's girlhood, Otto suffered a traumatic illness involving the amputation of a gangrenous leg. He died in 1940 when Sylvia was just eight years old.

The poem's persona is angry and unforgiving toward the father; the entire poem performs a sustained tirade against him. The harsh tone of anger is symptomatic, paradoxically enough, of the poet's mourning process that would work through the traumatic loss of a loved one. But it is also driven by the breakup of her seven-year marriage to the English poet Ted Hughes. Plath's divorce was occasioned by Hughes's adultery in the summer of 1962 while they were living in Devon, England. In the poem, Plath is not unmindful of the connection between the two losses: of her own father as well as of Hughes, her husband and the "daddy" of her two young children. That first, childhood trauma and its return in the crisis of her marriage is evident in her lines "If I've killed one man, I've killed two— / The vampire who said he was you / And drank my blood for a year, / Seven years, if you want to know." But the poem is not just a confessional exploration of her personal losses. Rather, its feminist message would overthrow the father's authority and power as they shape women's place under patriarchy.

TOPICS FOR CRITICAL THINKING

1. Discuss the poet's use of apostrophe in its direct address to the father figure. How does Plath stage that address as a kind of declaration of independence in the decisive tone with which she at once judges and dismisses the father?

2. Consider how the poet's sing-song rhyme pattern of the opening stanza darkly invokes a childhood world of Mother Goose rhymes appropriate to the poet's regression back into the role of daughter to the dead patriarch.

3. How does Plath capture the ambiguity of her relation to the dead patriarch in her pun on the word *through* in the last lines of the poem?

4. The poem draws an analogy between women's oppression and that of the Jewish victims of the Nazi death camps. Do you think this analogy is appropriate?

TOPIC FOR CRITICAL WRITING

Is the poem a tirade against Plath's literal father? Or is it more concerned with criticizing the cultural role of father as patriarch represented, say, in God the Father, Führer, fascist, teacher, and vampire-husband? To what extent does Plath debunk the myth of the father as a composite figure whose authority extends throughout the fields of religion, state, classroom, and nuclear family?

Reversing men's power to represent women, Plath in "Daddy" appropriates patriarchy's power to name the "other" for her own purposes. In Plath's poetry, according to Adrienne Rich, "Man appears as, if not a dream, a fascination and a terror; and the source of the fascination and terror is, simply, Man's power—to dominate, tyrannize, choose, or reject the woman." Men's power to represent women is the subject of much of feminist verse, as in Christina Rossetti's "In an Artist's Studio."

CHRISTINA ROSSETTI *(1830–1894)*

In an Artist's Studio *(1856)*

One face looks out from all his canvases,
   One selfsame figure sits or walks or leans:
   We found her hidden just behind those screens,
That mirror gave back all her loveliness.
A queen in opal or in ruby dress,   5
   A nameless girl in freshest summer-greens,
   A saint, an angel—every canvas means
The same one meaning, neither more nor less.
He feeds upon her face by day and night,
   And she with true kind eyes looks back on him,   10
Fair as the moon and joyful as the light:
   Not wan with waiting, not with sorrow dim;
Not as she is, but was when hope shone bright;
   Not as she is, but as she fills his dream.

Born in 1830, Christina Rossetti was the sister to the famous Pre-Raphaelite painter Dante Gabriel Rossetti. She not only moved in Pre-Raphaelite circles—publishing in their journal *The Germ*—but she sat as a

model for several of the Pre-Raphaelites and appears in many of their paintings, including her brother's *The Girlhood of Mary Virgin* (see color insert).

TOPICS FOR CRITICAL THINKING

1. How does Rossetti expose the ways in which the male artist's idealization of the
   "nameless girl" serves, paradoxically, as the source of her oppression?
2. Focus on the key terms through which the artist stereotypes his model in the poem.
   What qualities does he attribute to her?
3. How do the stereotypical representations of the poem's "selfsame figure" obscure
   the reality of the actual person who remains "hidden just behind those screens . . . /
   Not as she is, but as she fills his dream"?

TOPIC FOR CRITICAL WRITING

Compare the artist's representation of his female model in the poem to the presentation of women and girls in *The Girlhood of Mary Virgin* (see color insert).

A more overt criticism of man's power to represent woman is the subject
of H. D.'s (Hilda Doolittle) lyric on "Helen."

H. D. (Hilda Doolittle)   *(1886–1961)*

Helen   *(1924)*

All Greece hates
the still eyes in the white face,
the luster as of olives
where she stands,
And the white hands.   5

All Greece reviles
the wan face when she smiles,
hating it deeper still
when it grows wan and white,
remembering past enchantments   10
and past ills.

Greece sees, unmoved,
God's daughter, born of love,
the beauty of cool feet
and slenderest knees,   15
could love indeed the maid,
only if she were laid,
white ash amid funereal cypresses.

Helen's legendary charm and its effect on Paris and Menelaus led to the Trojan War. In H. D.'s portrait, it is Helen's subtle powers of seduction—her feminine "enchantments"—that "all Greece hates." H. D. insists on the fact of male misogyny—the hatred of women—implying that it stems from Helen's awesome beauty and her self-possession of character. "Unmoved, / God's daughter" is a threat to the power and authority of Greece's patriarchal order. Greece can only love "the maid" after she has been arrested by death. Greece's cure for her "past ills" is to transform the living face "growing wan and white" into "white ash amid funereal cypresses."

Feminist Verse

The work of feminist poetics, however, would move beyond the oppression of patriarchal representation to appropriate poetry's powers of re-vision. In this vein, "it is finally," for Adrienne Rich, "the woman's sense of *herself*—embattled, possessed—that gives the poetry its dynamic charge, its rhythms of struggle, need, will and female energy." Poetic re-vision of this kind, that recovers "female energy" out of the "embattled" condition of patriarchy, is at work in Muriel Rukeyser's reinterpretation of Botticelli's famous portrait of *The Birth of Venus* (see color insert).

MURIEL RUKEYSER   (1913–1980)

The Birth of Venus   (1958)

Risen in a
welter of waters.

Not as he saw her
standing upon a frayed and lovely surf
clean-riding the graceful leafy breezes   5
clean-poised and easy. Not yet.

But born in a
tidal wave of the father's overthrow,
the old rule killed and its mutilated sex.

The testicles of the father-god, father of fathers,   10
sickled off by his son, the next god Time.
Sickled off. Hurled into the ocean.
In all that blood and foam,
among raving and generation,
of semen and the sea born, the   15
great goddess rises.

> However, possibly,
> on the long worldward voyage flowing,
> horror gone down in birth, the curse, being changed,
> being used, is translated far at the margin into
> our rose and saving image, curling toward a shore
> early and April, with certainly shells, certainly blossoms.
>
> And the girl, the wellborn goddess, human love—
> young-known, new-knowing, mouth flickering, sure eyes—
> rides shoreward, from death to us as we are at this moment, on
> the crisp delightful Botticellian wave.

In revising Botticelli's serene depiction of Venus's birth, Rukeyser restores the more violent context of her mythic origin based as it is in the age-old struggle for patriarchal supremacy. The original Greek myth begins with the "father's overthrow" in the castration of the god Uranus by his son, the Titan Cronus. Venus or Aphrodite arises from the sea foam (aphros) fertilized by Uranus's severed testicles. Rukeyser's version differs from the majestic images of Botticelli's portrait where Venus is blown to shore on a clam shell by the West Wind Zephyr and Chloris. There she is met by one of the three nymphs of the hours, or Horae, who will drape her in a regal purple robe.

TOPICS FOR CRITICAL THINKING

1. Why does Rukeyser refer to Venus as "our rose and saving image"?
2. How does Venus's birth in Rukeyser's representation serve to change and translate the violent history of patriarchal mythology?
3. In what ways does Rukeyser represent the new goddess in her final stanza? What qualities does she attribute to her?

TOPIC FOR CRITICAL WRITING

Contrast the tone and mood of Rukeyser's poem as conveyed through the key terms of her diction with the depiction of the birth of Venus in Botticelli's painting (see color insert).

Such re-visions of male representation take less mythic and more everyday modes of expression in contemporary women's poetics as, say, when Sharon Olds celebrates her daughter's math skills in "The One Girl at the Boys Party."

SHARON OLDS   (b. 1942)

The One Girl at the Boys Party   (1983)

When I take my girl to the swimming party
I set her down among the boys. They tower and
bristle, she stands there smooth and sleek,
her math scores unfolding in the air around her.
They will strip to their suits, her body hard and   5
indivisible as a prime number,
they'll plunge in the deep end, she'll subtract
her height from ten feet, divide it into
hundreds of gallons of water, the numbers
bouncing in her mind like molecules of chlorine   10
in the bright blue pool. When they climb out,
her ponytail will hang its pencil lead
down her back, her narrow silk suit
with hamburgers and french fries printed on it
will glisten in the brilliant air, and they will   15
see her sweet face, solemn and
sealed, a factor of one, and she will
see their eyes, two each,
their legs, two each, and the curves of their sexes,
one each, and in her head she'll be doing her   20
wild multiplying, as the drops
sparkle and fall to the power of a thousand from her body.

TOPICS FOR CRITICAL THINKING

1. What stereotypes about girls does Sharon Olds write against in "The One Girl at
   the Boys Party"?
2. How does the pun on *wild multiplying* in the poem's next-to-last line add another dimension to Olds's portrait of her daughter?

TOPIC FOR CRITICAL WRITING

Discuss the ways in which Olds presents her daughter through the poem's mathematical tropes.

While Olds takes pride in her daughter's intellectual gifts, Lucille
Clifton's "Homage to My Hips" celebrates the vitality of the feminine body.

LUCILLE CLIFTON   (b. 1936)

Homage to My Hips   *(1991)*

these hips are big hips.
they need space to
move around in.
they don't fit into little
petty places. these hips   5
are free hips.
they don't like to be held back.
these hips have never been enslaved,
they go where they want to go
they do what they want to do.   10
these hips are mighty hips.
these hips are magic hips.
i have known them
to put a spell on a man and
spin him like a top!   15

TOPICS FOR CRITICAL THINKING

1. In "Homage to My Hips" Clifton resists all of the cultural messages that would
   pressure women into the confining mold of what Mary Wollstonecraft in the eighteenth century criticized as women's "corporeal accomplishment." How does
   Clifton's poem resist the distorted body images that women receive from advertising, the media, and culture generally?
2. Explore the sexual politics of Clifton's erotic ending where she claims the power to
   "put a spell on a man and / spin him like a top!"

TOPIC FOR CRITICAL WRITING

The values of being slim, pert, lean, passive, demure, silent, and so on have no place in
Clifton's lexicon of feminine virtues. How does she link acceptance of her body to a
state of being "free" from "enslavement"?

Increasingly, contemporary women's poetry has complicated any acts of
poetic re-vision that would speak on behalf of all women. Instead, feminist
poetics has recognized the diversity of women's experiences across the borders of generational, ethnic, racial, national, sexual, and economic difference.
That social diversity reflects what critic Mary Louise Pratt describes as the
complex "contact zones" of difference that define contemporary multicultural
experience. Today, feminist verse explores new ways of representing "social
spaces where cultures meet, clash, and grapple with each other, often in contexts of highly asymmetrical relations of power, such as colonialism, slavery,
or their aftermaths as they are lived out in many parts of the world today."

This edgy world of clashing cultures and conflicted borders especially characterizes the situation of Native American women's poetry, as in Joy Harjo's "The Woman Hanging from the Thirteenth Floor Window."

JOY HARJO　　(b. 1951)

The Woman Hanging from the Thirteenth Floor Window　　　　　　　*(1983)*

She is the woman hanging from the 13th floor
window. Her hands are pressed white against the
concrete moulding of the tenement building. She
hangs from the 13th floor window in east Chicago,
with a swirl of birds over her head. They could　　　　　　5
be a halo, or a storm of glass waiting to crush her.

She thinks she will be set free.

The woman hanging from the 13th floor window
on the east side of Chicago is not alone.
She is a woman of children, of the baby, Carlos,　　　　　　10
and of Margaret, and of Jimmy who is the oldest.
She is her mother's daughter and her father's son.
She is several pieces between the two husbands
she has had. She is all the women of the apartment
building who stand watching her, watching themselves.　　　　　　15

When she was young she ate wild rice on scraped down
plates in warm wood rooms. It was in the farther
north and she was the baby then. They rocked her.

She sees Lake Michigan lapping at the shores of
herself. It is a dizzy hole of water and the rich　　　　　　20
live in tall glass houses at the edge of it. In some
places Lake Michigan speaks softly, here, it just sputters
and butts itself against the asphalt. She sees
other buildings just like hers. She sees other
women hanging from many-floored windows　　　　　　25
counting their lives in the palms of their hands
and in the palms of their children's hands.

She is the woman hanging from the 13th floor window
on the Indian side of town. Her belly is soft from
her children's births, her worn levis swing down below　　　　　　30
her waist, and then her feet, and then her heart.
She is dangling.

The woman hanging from the 13th floor hears voices.
They come to her in the night when the lights have gone
dim. Sometimes they are little cats mewing and scratching   35
at the door, sometimes they are her grandmother's voice,
and sometimes they are gigantic men of light whispering
to her to get up, to get up, to get up. That's when she wants
to have another child to hold onto in the night, to be able
to fall back into dreams.   40

And the woman hanging from the 13th floor window
hears other voices. Some of them scream out from below
for her to jump, they would push her over. Others cry softly
from the sidewalks, pull their children up like flowers and gather
them into their arms. They would help her, like themselves.   45

But she is the woman hanging from the 13th floor window,
and she knows she is hanging by her own fingers, her
own skin, her own thread of indecision.

She thinks of Carlos, of Margaret, of Jimmy.
She thinks of her father, and of her mother.   50
She thinks of all the women she has been, of all
the men. She thinks of the color of her skin, and
of Chicago streets, and of waterfalls and pines.
She thinks of moonlight nights, and of cool spring storms.
Her mind chatters like neon and northside bars.   55
She thinks of the 4 a.m. lonelinesses that have folded
her up like death, discordant, without logical and
beautiful conclusion. Her teeth break off at the edges.
She would speak.

The woman hangs from the 13th floor window crying for   60
the lost beauty of her own life. She sees the
sun falling west over the grey plane of Chicago.
She thinks she remembers listening to her own life
break loose, as she falls from the 13th floor
window on the east side of Chicago, or as she   65
climbs back up to claim herself again.

"The Woman Hanging from the Thirteenth Floor Window" gives representation to the plight of urban Native American women who live with the daily extremity of social, cultural, and economic displacement. Harjo's hanging woman embodies in the contradictions of her precarious position the paradoxes of life in the "contact zone."

TOPICS FOR CRITICAL THINKING

1. Characterize how you imagine the life of the woman of Harjo's poem. What information does Harjo give us about her background?
2. In what ways is this woman both a hero and victim?
3. In what ways do the other women in the poem see themselves in her fate? Is she a representative figure, or is her story particular to her ethnic, class, or racial background?
4. How is she both connected to a network of parents and children, yet supremely alone?

TOPIC FOR CRITICAL WRITING

Describe your sense of what is at stake in the poem's last lines. Why do you think that Harjo presents two mutually exclusive endings to "The Woman Hanging from the Thirteenth Floor Window"?

Not insignificantly, Harjo leaves the woman who is hanging from the thirteenth floor window suspended between two contradictory fates. Similarly, Audre Lorde represents the irresolvable dilemma she faces as a contemporary woman of color. Her portrait of mother-daughter bonds in "From the House of Yemanjá" are inflected by her clashing indentifications over race. Describing herself as a "black lesbian feminist warrior poet," Lorde internalizes the contradictions of her African American identity in the trope of having a mother with "two faces."

AUDRE LORDE   *(1934–1992)*

From the House of Yemanjá   *(1978)*

My mother had two faces and a frying pot
where she cooked up her daughters
into girls
before she fixed our dinner.
My mother had two faces   5
and a broken pot
where she hid out a perfect daughter
who was not me
I am the sun and moon and forever hungry
for her eyes.   10

I bear two women upon my back
one dark and rich and hidden
in the ivory hungers of the other
mother
pale as a witch   15

yet steady and familiar
brings me bread and terror
in my sleep
her breasts as huge exciting anchors
in the midnight storm.   20

All this has been
before
in my mother's bed
time has no sense
I have no brothers   25
and my sisters are cruel.

Mother I need
mother I need
mother I need your blackness now
as the august earth needs rain.   30

I am
the sun and moon and forever hungry
the sharpened edge
where day and night shall meet
and not be   35
one.

TOPICS FOR CRITICAL THINKING

1. How does Lorde complicate any simple notions of solidarity with other women in the poem?

2. In what sense might Lorde internalize Pratt's definition of the "contact zone" in the trope of the "sharpened edge" defining her personal identity?

3. Yemanjá, according to Lorde, is "mother of the other *Orisha* [gods and goddesses that belong to Western Nigeria and the Yoruba tribe]; Yemanjá is also the goddess of oceans. Rivers are said to flow from her breasts. One legend has it that a son tried to rape her. She fled until she collapsed, and from her breasts, the rivers flowed. Another legend says that a husband insulted Yemanjá's long breasts, and when she fled with her pots he knocked her down. From her breasts flowed the rivers, and from her body then sprang forth all the other *Orisha*. River-smooth stones are Yemanjá's symbol, and the sea is sacred to her followers. Those who please her are blessed with many children." Do you see any connections between these Yoruba myths of Yemanjá and how Lorde represents her in her poem?

TOPIC FOR CRITICAL WRITING

Discuss your interpretation of what the two faces signify in "From the House of Yemanjá." What other figures of doubling do you notice in the poem?

Poems for Further Reading and Critical Writing

Adrienne Rich published *Diving into the Wreck* in 1973, and the following year it won the National Book Award for Poetry. The title piece of the volume reflects on the "wreck" of her past and looks forward to the new evolution her career would take. Rich graduated Phi Beta Kappa in 1951 from Radcliffe College; that year her first volume of published verse *A Change of World* won the prestigious Yale Younger Poets Award. Rich went on to win a steady succession of awards and grants for her poetry at the same time that she married Alfred Conrad and gave birth to three boys between 1955–1960. Conrad took his life in 1970, which also coincided with Rich's commitment to lesbian poetics.

"Diving into the Wreck" reflects on these major transitions in the poet's life. Its open-form poetic style also marks a significant change from the fixed-form poetry, exemplified by "Aunt Jennifer's Tigers" in the early stages of her career.

ADRIENNE RICH   *(b. 1929)*

Diving into the Wreck   *(1973)*

First having read the book of myths,
and loaded the camera,
and checked the edge of the knife-blade,
I put on
the body-armor of black rubber   5
the absurd flippers
the grave and awkward mask.
I am having to do this
not like Cousteau° with his
assiduous team   10
aboard the sun-flooded schooner
but here alone.

There is a ladder.
The ladder is always there
hanging innocently   15
close to the side of the schooner.
We know what it is for,
we who have used it.

---

9 *Cousteau:* Jacques Cousteau (1910–1997), underwater explorer and inventor, with Emile Gagnan, of the aqualung.

Otherwise
it is a piece of maritime floss   20
some sundry equipment.

I go down.
Rung after rung and still
the oxygen immerses me
the blue light   25
the clear atoms
of our human air.
I go down.
My flippers cripple me,
I crawl like an insect down the ladder   30
and there is no one
to tell me when the ocean
will begin.

First the air is blue and then
it is bluer and then green and then   35
black I am blacking out and yet
my mask is powerful
it pumps my blood with power
the sea is another story
the sea is not a question of power   40
I have to learn alone
to turn my body without force
in the deep element.

And now: it is easy to forget
what I came for   45
among so many who have always
lived here
swaying their crenellated fans
between the reefs
and besides   50
you breathe differently down here.

I came to explore the wreck.
The words are purposes.
The words are maps.
I came to see the damage that was done   55
and the treasures that prevail.
I stroke the beam of my lamp
slowly along the flank
of something more permanent
than fish or weed   60

the thing I came for:
the wreck and not the story of the wreck
the thing itself and not the myth
the drowned face always staring
toward the sun   65
the evidence of damage
worn by salt and sway into this threadbare beauty
the ribs of the disaster
curving their assertion
among the tentative haunters.   70

This is the place.
And I am here, the mermaid whose dark hair
streams black, the merman in his armored body
We circle silently
about the wreck   75
we dive into the hold.
I am she: I am he

whose drowned face sleeps with open eyes
whose breasts still bear the stress
whose silver, copper, vermeil cargo lies   80
obscurely inside barrels
half-wedged and left to rot
we are the half-destroyed instruments
that once held to a course
the water-eaten log   85
the fouled compass

We are, I am, you are
by cowardice or courage
the one who find our way
back to this scene   90
carrying a knife, a camera
a book of myths
in which
our names do not appear.

TOPICS FOR CRITICAL THINKING

1. Describe the situation and setting that Rich presents in the opening lines of "Diving into the Wreck." What point is she making in contrasting her dive with those of Jacques Cousteau?

2. Of the writing process, Rich has said that "for a poem to coalesce . . . there has to be an imaginative transformation of reality which is in no way passive. And a certain freedom of the mind is needed—freedom to press on, to enter the currents of your thought like a glider pilot, knowing that your motion can be sustained, that

the buoyancy of your attention will not be suddenly snatched away." Compare this description to the empowered sense of buoyancy and freedom Rich discovers in her descent into the "deep element" of the dive.

3. What symbolic possibilities might the wreck stand for?

4. Discuss the mode of identity and address Rich projects in the final lines that shift the voice of the poem among the first-person singular and plural (*I* and *we*) and second-person (*you*) pronouns.

TOPIC FOR CRITICAL WRITING

Rich has written that she uses poetry as a "means of self-exploration." To what extent might the dive serve as an extended metaphor for such exploration of self?

Anne Killigrew was the daughter of the seventeenth-century dramatist Dr. Henry Killigrew, who gave her access to the court of the Duke and Duchess of York. John Donne wrote an elegy upon her untimely death from smallpox in 1885 entitled "To the Pious Memory of the Accomplished Young Lady Mrs. Anne Killigrew." Female authorship, however celebrated in this way, was not without its perils and frustration. The figure of the poetess was an easy mark for male criticism, as Killigrew relates in "Upon the Saying That My Verses Were Made by Another."

ANNE KILLIGREW (1660–1685)

Upon the Saying That My Verses Were Made by Another   (1686)

Next Heaven, my Vows to thee (O Sacred *Muse*!)
I offer'd up, nor didst thou them refuse.

O Queen of Verse, said I, if thou'lt inspire,
And warm my Soul with thy Poetique Fire,
No love of gold shall share with thee my heart,   5
Or yet ambition in my brest have part,
More Rich, more Noble I will ever hold
The *Muse's* laurel, than a crown of gold.
An undivided sacrifice I'll lay
Upon thine altar, soul and body pay;   10
Thou shalt my pleasure, my employment be,
My all I'll make a holocaust° to thee.

The deity that ever does attend
Prayers so sincere, to mine did condescend.

_____

12 *holocaust:* Burnt sacrifice.

I writ, and the judicious prais'd my pen: 15
Could any doubt ensuing Glory then?
What pleasing raptures fill'd my ravisht sense?
How strong, how sweet, fame, was thy influence?
And thine, false hope, that to my flatter'd sight
Did'st glories represent so near, and bright?!   20
By thee deceiv'd, methought, each verdant tree,
Apollos transform'd *Daphne* seem'd to be;
And ev'ry fresher branch, and ev'ry bough,
Appear'd as garlands to empale my brow.
The learn'd in Love say, thus the winged boy   25
Does first approach, drest up in welcome joy;
At first he to the cheated lover's sight
Nought represents but rapture and delight,
Alluring hopes, soft fears, which stronger bind
Their hearts, than when they more assurance find.   30

    Embolden'd thus, to fame I did commit,
By some few hands, my most unlucky wit.
But ah, the sad effects that from it came!
What ought t'have brought me honour, brought me shame!
Like Aesop's painted jay I seem'd to all,   35
Adorn'd in plumes, I not my own could call:
Rifl'd like her, each one my Feathers tore,
And, as they thought, unto the owner bore.
My laurels thus anothers brow adorn'd,
My Numbers they Admir'd, but me they scorn'd: 40
Anothers brow, that had so rich a store
Of sacred wreaths, that circled it before;
Where mine quite lost, (like a small stream that ran
Into a vast and boundless ocean)
Was swallow'd up, with what it joyn'd and drown'd.   45
And that Abyss yet no accession found.

    Orinda, (*Albions* and her sex's grace)
Ow'd not her glory to a beauteous face,
It was her radiant soul that shone within,
Which struck a lustre through her outward skin;   50
That did her lips and cheeks with roses dye,
Advanc't her Height, and Sparkled in her Eye.
Nor did her Sex at all obstruct her fame,
But higher 'mong the stars it fixt her name;
What she did write, not only all allow'd,   55
But ev'ry laurel, to her laurel, bowed!

    Th'envious age, only to Me alone,
Will not allow what I do write, my Own,

But let 'em rage, and 'gainst a maide conspire,
So deathless numbers from my tuneful lyre   60
Do ever flow; so *Phoebus* I by thee
Divinely inspired and possesed may be;
I willingly accept *Cassandra's* fate,
To speak the truth, although believed too late.

TOPICS FOR CRITICAL THINKING

1. Discuss Killigrew's use of simile in her complaint over the reception her writing received as she describes it in the fourth stanza.
2. How does Killigrew address her muse in the opening of the poem, and how does
   she set up the seriousness of her commitment to poetry?
3. How does the poet react to her initial fame in stanza three?

TOPIC FOR CRITICAL WRITING

Examine Killigrew's mythological allusions to Orinda, Phoebus, and Cassandra in her
closing lines. What argument do they make about poetry's truth, however obscured by
one's political circumstances?

A recipient of the Pulitzer Prize (1955) and National Book Award (1969),
the widely traveled poet Elizabeth Bishop taught for many years at the University of Washington and Harvard. "In the Waiting Room" describes the crisis of identity she remembers from 1918 when she was seven years old.

ELIZABETH BISHOP   (1911–1979)

In the Waiting Room   *(1976)*

In Worcester, Massachusetts,
I went with Aunt Consuelo
to keep her dentist's appointment
and sat and waited for her
in the dentist's waiting room.   5
It was winter. It got dark
early. The waiting room
was full of grown-up people,
arctics and overcoats,
lamps and magazines.   10
My aunt was inside
what seemed like a long time
and while I waited and read
the *National Geographic*
(I could read) and carefully   15

studied the photographs:
the inside of a volcano,
black, and full of ashes;
then it was spilling over
in rivulets of fire.   20
Osa and Martin Johnson
dressed in riding breeches,
laced boots, and pith helmets.
A dead man slung on a pole
—"Long Pig,"° the caption said.   25
Babies with pointed heads
wound round and round with string;
black, naked women with necks
wound round and round with wire
like the necks of light bulbs.   30
Their breasts were horrifying.
I read it right straight through.
I was too shy to stop.
And then I looked at the cover:
the yellow margins, the date.   35

Suddenly, from inside,
came an *oh!* of pain
—Aunt Consuelo's voice—
not very loud or long.
I wasn't at all surprised;   40
even then I knew she was
a foolish, timid woman.
I might have been embarrassed,
but wasn't. What took me
completely by surprise   45
was that it was *me:*
my voice, in my mouth.
Without thinking at all
I was my foolish aunt,
I—we—were falling, falling,   50
our eyes glued to the cover
of the *National Geographic,*
February, 1918.

I said to myself: three days
and you'll be seven years old.   55
I was saying it to stop
the sensation of falling off
the round, turning world
into cold, blue-black space.

―――――――
25 *"Long Pig"*: Melanesian slang term for human being; a victim of cannibalism.

But I felt: you are an *I*,   60
you are an *Elizabeth*,
you are one of *them*.
Why should you be one, too?
I scarcely dared to look
to see what it was I was.   65
I gave a sidelong glance
—I couldn't look any higher—
at shadowy gray knees,
trousers and skirts and boots
and different pairs of hands   70
lying under the lamps.
I knew that nothing stranger
had ever happened, that nothing
stranger could ever happen.
Why should I be my aunt,   75
or me, or anyone?
What similarities—
boots, hands, the family voice
I felt in my throat, or even
the *National Geographic*   80
and those awful hanging breasts—
held us all together
or made us all just one?
How—I didn't know any
word for it—how "unlikely" . . .   85
How had I come to be here,
like them, and overhear
a cry of pain that could have
got loud and worse but hadn't?

The waiting room was bright   90
and too hot. It was sliding
beneath a big black wave,
another, and another.

Then I was back in it.
The War was on. Outside,   95
in Worcester, Massachusetts,
were night and slush and cold,
and it was still the fifth
of February, 1918.

TOPICS FOR CRITICAL THINKING

1. Discuss your sense of what kind of experience Bishop describes in her poem. What
   kind of ecstasy and what kind of empathy with others does Bishop's first-person
   narrator relate?

2. Examine closely the details from her reading in the February 1918 edition of *National Geographic*. Discuss the ways in which Bishop estranges our conventional images of the body in these passages.

3. What do you think the magazine representations have to do with her experience in the waiting room?

4. How significant is it that Bishop poses her revelations in the third stanza as questions rather than as statements?

5. What does her final reference to the poem's historical context of World War I have to do with the poem's action and events?

TOPIC FOR CRITICAL WRITING

How important is it that this event takes place in a waiting room? How crucial is the poem's setting to its situation and action?

Emily Brontë, the author of *Wuthering Heights*, is, like her sister Charlotte, known primarily as a novelist rather than a poet. Nevertheless, the Brontë sisters published a collection of verse entitled *Poems* under the male pseudonyms Currer, Ellis, and Acton Bell in 1846. Aside from a brief stint of study at the Roe Head, Law Hill, and Pensionnat Héger schools, Emily lived her life at her aunt's home at Haworth Parsonage in Yorkshire, whose surrounding moors comprise the settings of *Wuthering Heights*. Similar in some ways to Emily Dickinson, Emily Brontë chose, rather than succumbed to, a life of domestic seclusion. In fact, she had a strong sense of self, rooted in a romantic faith in the powers of the natural world as she describes them in "Stanzas."

EMILY BRONTË   *(1818–1848)*

Stanzas   *(1846)*

Often rebuked, yet always back returning
　　To those first feelings that were born with me,
And leaving busy chase of wealth and learning
　　For idle dreams of things which cannot be;

To-day, I will seek not the shadowy region;　　　　　　　　　　　5
　　Its unsustaining vastness waxes drear;
And visions rising, legion after legion,
　　Bring the unreal world too strangely near.

I'll walk, but not in old heroic traces,
　　And not in paths of high morality,　　　　　　　　　　　　10
And not among the half-distinguished faces,
　　The clouded forms of long-past history.

I'll walk where my own nature would be leading:
   It vexes me to choose another guide:
Where the gray flocks in ferny glens are feeding;   15
   Where the wild wind blows on the mountain side.

What have those lonely mountains worth revealing?
   More glory and more grief than I can tell:
The earth that wakes *one* human heart to feeling
   Can centre both the worlds of Heaven and Hell.   20

TOPICS FOR CRITICAL THINKING

1. Discuss the ways in which Brontë characterizes the public sphere of society in the first two stanzas. Why does she choose to turn away from it?
2. Consider her similar rejection of conventional history in stanza three. What, in your opinion, might account for why she takes this stance toward the recorded past?
3. If you have read *Wuthering Heights*, what kinds of thematic parallels do you find in the novel and her poem?

TOPIC FOR CRITICAL WRITING

Focus on the ways in which Brontë characterizes the landscapes around Haworth. What values does she find in that natural setting?

A cousin to James Russell Lowell, Amy Lowell was raised in a prominent Boston family. Her father was on the board of the Massachusetts Institute of Technology and her brother Abbott Lowell was a president of Harvard University. Not insignificantly, Amy herself in 1912 founded *Poetry* magazine, one of the most important literary journals of the twentieth century. Two years later, she began to live with Ada Russell, her lifelong partner. In "Venus Transiens" she addresses her lover, comparing her to the goddess Venus.

AMY LOWELL   *(1847–1925)*

Venus Transiens   *(1919)*

Tell me,
Was Venus more beautiful
Than you are,
When she topped
The crinkled waves,   5
Drifting shoreward
On her plaited shell?
Was Botticelli's vision

Fairer than mine;
And were the painted rosebuds   10
He tossed his lady,
Of better worth
Than the words I blow about you
To cover your too great loveliness
As with a gauze   15
Of misted silver?
For me,
You stand poised
In the blue and buoyant air,
Cinctured by bright winds,   20
Treading the sunlight.
And the waves which precede you
Ripple and stir
The sands at my feet.

TOPIC FOR CRITICAL THINKING

Compare Lowell's poem to Botticelli's *The Birth of Venus* (see color insert), and discuss the ways in which the poem alludes to specific details in its verbal presentation.

TOPIC FOR CRITICAL WRITING

Contrast Lowell's use of Botticelli with that of Rukeyser above in "The Birth of Venus."

Critical Perspective: On Feminism and Re-vision

"Ibsen's *When We Dead Awaken* is a play about the use that the male artist and thinker—in the process of creating culture as we know it—has made of women, in his life and in his work; and about a woman's slow struggling awakening to the use to which her life has been put. Bernard Shaw wrote in 1900 of this play:

> [Ibsen] shows us that no degradation ever devized or permitted is as disastrous as this degradation; that through it women can die into luxuries for men and yet can kill them; that men and women are becoming conscious of this; and that what remains to be seen as perhaps the most interesting of all imminent social developments is what will happen "when we dead awaken."[1]

"It's exhilarating to be alive in a time of awakening consciousness; it can also be confusing, disorienting, and painful. This awakening of dead or sleeping consciousness has already affected the lives of millions of women, even those who don't know it yet. It is also affecting the lives of men, even those who deny its claims upon them. The argument will go on whether an oppres-

---

1. G. B. Shaw, *The Quintessence of Ibsenism* (New York: Hill & Wang, 1922), p. 139.

sive economic class system is responsible for the oppressive nature of male/female relations, or whether, in fact, patriarchy—the domination of males—is the original model of oppression on which all others are based. But in the last few years the women's movement has drawn inescapable and illuminating connections between our sexual lives and our political institutions. The sleepwalkers are coming awake, and for the first time this awakening has a collective reality; it is no longer such a lonely thing to open one's eyes.

"Re-vision—the act of looking back, of seeing with fresh eyes, of entering an old text from a new critical direction—is for women more than a chapter in cultural history: it is an act of survival. Until we can understand the assumptions in which we are drenched we cannot know ourselves. And this drive to self-knowledge, for women, is more than a search for identity: it is part of our refusal of the self-destructiveness of male-dominated society. A radical critique of literature, feminist in its impulse, would take the work first of all as a clue to how we live, how we have been living, how we have been led to imagine ourselves, how our language has trapped as well as liberated us, how the very act of naming has been till now a male prerogative, and how we can begin to see and name—and therefore live—afresh. A change in the concept of sexual identity is essential if we are not going to see the old political order reassert itself in every new revolution. We need to know the writing of the past, and know it differently than we have ever known it; not to pass on a tradition but to break its hold over us.

"For writers, and at this moment for women writers in particular, there is the challenge and promise of a whole new psychic geography to be explored. But there is also a difficult and dangerous walking on the ice, as we try to find language and images for a consciousness we are just coming into, and with little in the past to support us."

—Adrienne Rich, from "When We Dead Awaken: Writing as Re-vision" (1971)

Critical Perspective: On Sexual Difference

"For the woman artist is not privileged or mandated to find her self-in-world except by facing (affronting?) and mounting an enormous struggle with the cultural fictions—myths, narratives, iconographies, languages—which heretofore have delimited the representation of women. And which are culturally and psychically saturating.

"To define then. 'Female aesthetic': the production of formal, epistemological, and thematic strategies by members of the group Woman, strategies born in struggle with much of already existing culture, and overdetermined by two elements of sexual difference—by women's psychosocial experiences of gender asymmetry and by women's historical status in an (ambiguously) non-hegemonic group. . . .

"This both/and vision, the contradictory movement between the logically irreconcilable, must have several causes. Perhaps it is based on the bisexual oscillation within female psychosexual development. Nancy Chodorow shows how the Oedipal configuration occurs differently in girls and boys and that, because of the way the sexes are reproduced in the family, most women retain men as erotic objects and women as emotional objects. This oscillation between men and women, father and mother, pervades her emotional (and thus aesthetic) life. And do we also value the K-Mart version of this structure: conflict avoidance. Everybody is right. Feel like a chameleon, taking coloration—

"Insider-outsider social status will also help dissolve an either-or dualism. For the woman finds she is irreconcilable things: an outsider by her gender position, by her relation to power; may be an insider by her social position, her class. She can be both. Her ontological, her psychic, her class position all cause doubleness. Doubled consciousness. Doubled understandings. How then could she neglect to invent a form which produces this incessant, critical, splitting motion. To invent this form. To invent the theory for this form.

"Following, the 'female aesthetic' will produce artworks that incorporate contradiction and nonlinear movement into the heart of the text."

—Rachel Blau Du Plessis, from "For the Etruscans" (1981)

Featured Writer

ANNE SEXTON

Anne Sexton

Born on November 9, 1928, Anne Sexton was the third daughter of Ralph and Mary Gray Staples Harvey. Notable ancestors on her mother's side of the family included Nelson Dingley Jr., a governor of Maine and member of Congress, as well as Arthur Gray Staples, editor and publisher of the *Lewiston Evening Journal*. Sexton's paternal grandfather, Louis Harvey, was an influential member of the affluent Wellesley community and president of the Wellesley National Bank. Sexton's father, Ralph Churchill Harvey, was a successful traveling sales representative for the New England wool industry and became president of the R. C. Harvey Company. Bearing the literary influences of her maternal line, Anne shared her middle name with her mother and journalist grandfather. As a child, Anne also enjoyed a very close relationship to her maternal great-aunt Anna Ladd Dingley, or "Nana" as she called her, who was herself a journalist and part owner of her father's newspaper. Nana moved in with the Harvey family in 1939 when Anne was eleven; after a period of deteriorating mental health, Nana was removed to a nursing home five years later. The example of her great-aunt's mental illness, coupled with her parents' alcoholism, were powerful shaping forces in Sexton's troubled psychic development.

Brought up and educated in Wellesley and in Weston, Sexton graduated from the Rogers Hall preparatory school in 1947 and then attended the Garland School in Boston, where she met and later eloped with Alfred Muller Sexton II in 1948. Nicknamed Kayo, Anne's husband had been a premedical major at Colgate University but soon dropped out of college. After serving in the Navy during the Korean War, Kayo eventually went to work for his father-in-law, joining the R. C. Harvey Company as a traveling salesman. Meanwhile, Anne pursued a brief career as a fashion model for the Hart Agency in Boston before giving birth to her first daughter, Linda Gray Sexton, in 1953. After her great-aunt Nana died in 1954, Anne suffered her first hospitalization for anxiety in 1956, following the birth of her second daughter, Joyce Ladd Sexton, the previous year.

In 1956, Sexton began psychoanalytic treatment with Dr. Martin Orne. Over the next eight years, Orne would offer supportive encouragement for Sexton's emergence as a major poet. During his first consultation with Sexton, Orne suggested she write about her treatment, and poetry quickly became a vital aspect of her therapy. The following year, she enrolled in a poetry workshop under the direction of John Holmes at the Boston Center for Adult Education, where she met her lifelong friend and colleague poet Maxine Kumin. Sexton quickly found a receptive audience for her distinctive style of autobiographical verse. By the summer of 1958, she was placing her poems in such national journals as *Harpers*, *The New Yorker*, and *Christian Science Monitor*. Moreover, Sexton received a scholarship to study at the Antioch Writer's Conference with the "confessional" poet W. D. Snodgrass.

Through Snodgrass's influence, Sexton began studying creative writing with the poet Robert Lowell at Boston University, where she met the young poets George Starbuck and Sylvia Plath. During this time, Sexton continued to place her work in notable journals such as the *Hudson Review*, which published her entire 240-line poem "The Double Image." Soon she had enough material for her first book, *To Bedlam and Part Way Back*, but John Holmes, her first teacher, urged her not to publish it. Although Holmes was a supportive mentor for Sexton's new life as a writer, he also discouraged her from writing overt poems about her mental illness, especially her recurrent periods of hospitalization. Her verse response in "For John, Who Begs Me Not to Enquire Further" forcefully rejected his advice as it declared her independence and self-possession as a poet.

For John, Who Begs Me Not to Enquire Further   (1960)

Not that it was beautiful,
but that, in the end, there was
a certain sense of order there;
something worth learning
in that narrow diary of my mind,   5
in the commonplaces of the asylum
where the cracked mirror
or my own selfish death
outstared me.
And if I tried   10
to give you something else,
something outside of myself,
you would not know
that the worst of anyone
can be, finally,   15
an accident of hope.
I tapped my own head;
it was glass, an inverted bowl.
It is a small thing
to rage in your own bowl.   20
At first it was private.
Then it was more than myself;
it was you, or your house

or your kitchen.
And if you turn away   25
because there is no lesson here
I will hold my awkward bowl,
with all its cracked stars shining
like a complicated lie,
and fasten a new skin around it   30
as if I were dressing an orange
or a strange sun.
Not that it was beautiful,
but that I found some order there.
There ought to be something special   35
for someone
in this kind of hope.
This is something I would never find
in a lovelier place, my dear,
although your fear is anyone's fear,   40
like an invisible veil between us all . . .
and sometimes in private,
my kitchen, your kitchen,
my face, your face.

TOPICS FOR CRITICAL THINKING

1. Sexton rejects conventional beauty as her poetry's subject matter. What does she value in its place?
2. In exploring the terms of her own madness, Sexton writes, "At first it was private. / Then it was more than myself." In what ways does she invite Holmes and her extended audience to identify with her "cracked" mental states?

TOPIC FOR CRITICAL WRITING

Discuss the metaphors and similes through which Sexton describes her psychological condition in the poem.

Sexton's title alludes to Schopenhauer's famous letter to Goethe where he writes "Most of us carry in our heart the Jocasta who begs Oedipus for God's sake not to inquire further." Identifying with Oedipus, not Jocasta, Sexton chose this quote on fearless, though tragic, self-knowledge as the epigraph to her first volume of verse. As a psychoanalytic poet, Sexton insists on finding poetic material, paradoxically, in the antipoetic yet illuminating encounters with her psychic life, its "complicated lie." Although the settings, themes, and images of her chosen subject matter—"the common places of the asylum"— are not beautiful in any conventional sense, they communicate as she says "something I would never find / in a lovelier place." Although Sexton's poetry has been given the label of "confessional" verse, her materials, as she says here, are both personal and universal in scope. "At first it was private. / Then it was more than myself." The fear that she probes and that Holmes resists is "anyone's fear, / like an invisible veil between us all."

By the end of the 1950s, Sexton was on her way toward becoming a major poet, but she was also experiencing tragic, personal losses. On the one hand, she received the good news that Houghton Mifflin would publish *To Bedlam and Part Way Back*. On the other hand, she lost both her parents with her mother dying of cancer in March 1959 and the poet's father suffering a fatal cerebral hemorrhage that June. Sexton herself had begun the year with a breakdown and recuperation at the Westwood Lodge. Despite these personal setbacks, Sexton's career as an American poet was flourishing. She received a Robert Frost Fellowship at the Bread Loaf Writer's Conference followed by her first book's nomination for the National Book Award the next year.

The 1960s was Sexton's watershed decade as a poet, beginning with her appointment to the Radcliffe Institute for Independent Study in 1961 and followed by the Levinson Prize from *Poetry* magazine for her second book of poems *All My Pretty Ones* (1962). Soon she received a traveling fellowship from the American Academy of Arts and Letters (1963) and a Ford Foundation writers in residence grant with the Charles Playhouse in Boston (1964). The mid-1960s saw the publication of her third volume *Selected Poems* (1964), her election as a Fellow of the Royal Society of Literature (1965), another travel grant from the International Congress of Cultural Freedom (1965), culminating in the Pulitzer Prize and the Shelley Award from the Poetry Society of America for her 1967 volume *Live or Die*. Other honors followed in her award of a Guggenheim Fellowship (1969) for producing her play *Mercy Street* at the American Place Theater, an honorary doctor of letters from Tufts University (1970), her promotion to Full Professor at Boston University (1972), and her award of the Crashaw Chair in Literature at Colgate University (1972). Amidst this whirlwind of readings, award ceremonies, and teaching, Sexton also found time to make an adventurous tour of Kenya with Kayo during the summer of 1966.

Throughout her meteoric rise to worldwide prominence as a poet, lecturer, and educator, Sexton continued to be hospitalized for periodic bouts with mental illness and suicide attempts. Nevertheless, she mined these experiences as material for her verse and kept in touch with fellow patients by teaching poetry, for example, in 1968 at McLean Hospital. In that same year, Sexton also made forays into popular culture by performing her verse in a rock band she formed called Anne Sexton and Her Kind. Sexton based the name of her band on her poem "Her Kind" from *To Bedlam and Partway Back*. In fact, she considered "Her Kind" to be her signature poem. She usually opened her poetry readings with it, often inviting her audience to leave if they could not identify with her kind.

Her Kind   *(1960)*

I have gone out, a possessed witch,
haunting the black air, braver at night;

dreaming evil, I have done my hitch
over the plain houses, light by light:
lonely thing, twelve-fingered, out of mind.   5
A woman like that is not a woman, quite.
I have been her kind.

I have found the warm caves in the woods,
filled them with skillets, carvings, shelves,
closets, silks, innumerable goods;   10
fixed the suppers for the worms and the elves:
whining, rearranging the disaligned.
A woman like that is misunderstood.
I have been her kind.

I have ridden in your cart, driver,   15
waved my nude arms at villages going by,
learning the last bright routes, survivor
where your flames still bite my thigh
and my ribs crack where your wheels wind.
A woman like that is not ashamed to die.   20
I have been her kind.

TOPICS FOR CRITICAL THINKING

1. While "Her Kind" reflects on the phases of the poet's life, it is not strictly autobiographical. For one thing, the first-person *I* pronoun is not fixed but reflects at least
   three personae. How would you distinguish the differences among the various versions of the self's experience in the three stanzas?

2. What unites the speakers?

3. Although the final stanza presents an image of martyrdom, perhaps for infidelity,
   how does it assert the poet's identity, nevertheless, as a "survivor" in luminous and
   ecstatic terms?

TOPIC FOR CRITICAL WRITING

How might the represented pronoun *I* in the poem differ from the poet's subject position
as the one who witnesses, records, and performs what she has otherwise experienced?

Sexton ushered in the 1970s with a creative stint that produced the seventeen long poems of *Transformations* (1971) based on the fairy tales of the
Brothers Grimm. She also made progress on two other volumes *The Book of
Folly* (1972) and *The Death Notebooks* (1974). In the early part of 1973, Sexton
divorced Kayo and was frequently accompanied by Lois Ames, Louise Co-
nant, or Joan Smith on her reading tours. Moving beyond her roles of wife
and mother in midlife, Sexton increasingly sought psychological and emotional support from other women. Toward the end of her life, Sexton gave one
of her most powerful performances on March 7, 1974, reading at the Sanders
Theater for the Harvard Literary Club. There she read what she archly de-

clared as her "posthumous poems" from her recently published collection _The Death Notebooks_ and her manuscript of _The Awful Rowing Toward God_. Indeed, as these titles implied, Sexton's obsession with death and suicide was something that was growing apace in middle age. While Sexton had attempted to take her life more than once in her career, she now began to contemplate suicide more deliberately. Setting her estate in order, Sexton amended her will to make her daughter Linda her literary executor. Finally, after making the last corrections to _The Awful Rowing Toward God_ and at the height of her fame, Anne Sexton committed suicide by carbon monoxide poisoning in her garage on October 4, 1974.

Since her death, Sexton's notoriety as poet has continued to grow. The complete corpus of her eight books of verse and two volumes of posthumous verse were compiled by Linda Gray Sexton in _The Complete Poems_ (1981). In addition, numerous critical studies and a major biography by Diane Middlebrook have examined her life and work. But equally important, Sexton remains a popular poet for the general reader. "Women poets in particular," writes poet Maxine Kumin, "owe a debt to Anne Sexton, who broke new ground, shattered taboos, and endured a barrage of attacks along the way because of the flamboyance of her subject matter. . . . Anne Sexton has earned her place in the canon."

Poems for Further Reading and Critical Writing

ANNE SEXTON (1928–1974)

The Moss of His Skin (1960)

> "_Young girls in old Arabia were often buried alive next to their dead fathers, apparently as sacrifice to the goddesses of the tribes . . ._"
> —HAROLD FELDMAN, "CHILDREN OF THE DESERT,"
> PSYCHOANALYSIS AND PSYCHOANALYTIC REVIEW,
> _Fall 1958_

It was only important
to smile and hold still,
to lie down beside him
and to rest awhile,
to be folded up together   5
as if we were silk,
to sink from the eyes of mother
and not to talk.
The black room took us
like a cave or a mouth   10
or an indoor belly.

I held my breath
and daddy was there,
his thumbs, his fat skull,
his teeth, his hair growing   15
like a field or a shawl.
I lay by the moss
of his skin until
it grew strange. My sisters
will never know that I fall   20
out of myself and pretend
that Allah will not see
how I hold my daddy
like an old stone tree.

TOPICS FOR CRITICAL THINKING

1. In her therapy sessions, Sexton often entered into trance states. In one of them she reported an incident of sexual molestation by her father Ralph Harvey. Although Sexton wrote several poems on the erotic connection between fathers and daughters, she never made up her mind whether this material was a memory of an actual encounter or something she had fantasized. How does the poem's epigraph set up a mythical frame for approaching the archetypal bond between daughters and fathers?

2. How would you describe the tone of the poem's opening lines?

3. What role, if any, does the mother play in the family drama the poet recounts?

4. How do you interpret the final lines? Do they maintain or break the mythic frame that sets up the poem in the epigraph? How are we to interpret the poem as a parable of the relationship between daughters and fathers?

5. Compare and contrast Sexton's mythic presentation of fathers and daughters in "The Moss of His Skin" with Sexton's use of the fairy tale narrative of Sleeping Beauty in "Briar Rose (Sleeping Beauty)," which follows.

TOPIC FOR CRITICAL WRITING

How does Sexton's language in "The Moss of His Skin" alternate realistic detail with more stylized descriptions that rely on figurative language?

Briar Rose (Sleeping Beauty)   *(1971)*

Consider
a girl who keeps slipping off,
arms limp as old carrots,
into the hypnotist's trance,
into a spirit world   5
speaking with the gift of tongues.
She is stuck in the time machine,
suddenly two years old sucking her thumb,
as inward as a snail,

learning to talk again.   10
She's on a voyage.
She is swimming further and further back,
up like a salmon,
struggling into her mother's pocketbook.
Little doll child,   15
come here to Papa.
Sit on my knee.
I have kisses for the back of your neck.
A penny for your thoughts, Princess.
I will hunt them like an emerald.   20

Come be my snooky
and I will give you a root.
That kind of voyage,
rank as honeysuckle.

Once   25
a king had a christening
for his daughter Briar Rose
and because he had only twelve gold plates
he asked only twelve fairies
to the grand event.   30
The thirteenth fairy,
her fingers as long and thin as straws,
her eyes burnt by cigarettes,
her uterus an empty teacup,
arrived with an evil gift.   35
She made this prophecy:
The princess shall prick herself
on a spinning wheel in her fifteenth year
and then fall down dead.
Kaputt!   40
The court fell silent.
The king looked like Munch's *Scream*°
Fairies' prophecies,
in times like those,
held water.   45
However the twelfth fairy
had a certain kind of eraser
and thus she mitigated the curse
changing that death
into a hundred-year sleep.   50

____

42 *Munch's* Scream: *The Scream* (1893) by Norwegian expressionist painter Edvard Munch
(1863–1944).

The king ordered every spinning wheel
exterminated and exorcized.
Briar Rose grew to be a goddess
and each night the king
bit the hem of her gown   55
to keep her safe.
He fastened the moon up
with a safety pin
to give her perpetual light.
He forced every male in the court   60
to scour his tongue with Bab-o
lest they poison the air she dwelt in.
Thus she dwelt in his odor.
Rank as honeysuckle.

On her fifteenth birthday   65
she pricked her finger
on a charred spinning wheel
and the clocks stopped.
Yes indeed. She went to sleep.
The king and queen went to sleep,   70
the courtiers, the flies on the wall.
The fire in the hearth grew still
and the roast meat stopped crackling.
The trees turned into metal
and the dog became china.   75
They all lay in a trance,
each a catatonic
stuck in a time machine.
Even the frogs were zombies.
Only a bunch of briar roses grew   80
forming a great wall of tacks
around the castle.
Many princes
tried to get through the brambles
for they had heard much of Briar Rose   85
but they had not scoured their tongues
so they were held by the thorns
and thus were crucified.
In due time
a hundred years passed   90
and a prince got through.
The briars parted as if for Moses
and the prince found the tableau intact.
He kissed Briar Rose
and she woke up crying: 95
Daddy! Daddy!

Presto! She's out of prison!
She married the prince
and all went well
except for the fear—   100
the fear of sleep.

Briar Rose
was an insomniac . . .
She could not nap
or lie in sleep   105
without the court chemist
mixing her some knock-out drops
and never in the prince's presence.
If it is to come, she said,
sleep must take me unawares   110
while I am laughing or dancing
so that I do not know that brutal place
where I lie down with cattle prods,
the hole in my cheek open.
Further, I must not dream   115
for when I do I see the table set
and a faltering crone at my place,
her eyes burnt by cigarettes
as she eats betrayal like a slice of meat.

I must not sleep   120
for while asleep I'm ninety
and think I'm dying.
Death rattles in my throat
like a marble.
I wear tubes like earrings.   125
I lie as still as a bar of iron.
You can stick a needle
through my kneecap and I won't flinch.
I'm all shot up with Novocain.
This trance girl   130
is yours to do with.
You could lay her in a grave,
an awful package,
and shovel dirt on her face
and she'd never call back: Hello there!   135
But if you kissed her on the mouth
her eyes would spring open
and she'd call out: Daddy! Daddy!
Presto!
She's out of prison.   140

There was a theft.
That much I am told.
I was abandoned.
That much I know.
I was forced backward.   145
I was forced forward.
I was passed hand to hand
like a bowl of fruit.
Each night I am nailed into place
and forget who I am.   150
Daddy?
That's another kind of prison.
It's not the prince at all,
but my father
drunkenly bent over my bed,   155
circling the abyss like a shark,
my father thick upon me
like some sleeping jellyfish.
What voyage this, little girl?
This coming out of prison?   160
God help—
this life after death?

TOPICS FOR CRITICAL THINKING

1. Sleeping Beauty is a well-known Brothers Grimm fairy tale that has a central place in the popular imagination. Walt Disney Pictures, for example, adapted Tchaikovsky's "Sleeping Beauty" as the sound track for its 1959 cartoon version of the legend and won the Academy Award for Best Score for a Musical Picture that year. Recount what you know about the fairy tale of Sleeping Beauty. How faithful is Sexton to the original storyline?

2. Discuss Sexton's opening stanza in "Briar Rose (Sleeping Beauty)." How might it refer to the kind of regressions back to childhood that the poet experienced in psychoanalysis?

3. Sexton emphasizes the father's obsession with keeping Briar Rose safe from the curse of the thirteenth fairy. Why does Sexton then alter the original legend to have Briar Rose call out the name of "Daddy" when the prince awakens her with a kiss?

TOPIC FOR CRITICAL WRITING

How do you interpret the ending of the poem that moves from the distanced frame of fairy tale toward a more directly autobiographical statement? Discuss the presentation of Briar Rose as an insomniac in the poem. How do you read her final questions that end the poem?

from The Death of the Fathers   (1972)

4. Santa

Father,
the Santa Claus suit
you bought from Wolff Fording Theatrical Supplies,
back before I was born,
is dead.   5
The white beard you fooled me with
and the hair like Moses,
the thick crimpy wool
that used to buzz me on the neck,
is dead.   10
Yes, my busting rosy Santa,
ringing your bronze cowbell.
You with real soot on your nose
and snow (taken from the refrigerator some years)
on your big shoulder.   15
The room was like Florida.
You took so many oranges out of your bag
and threw them around the living room,
all the time laughing that North Pole laugh.
Mother would kiss you   20
for she was that tall.
Mother could hug you
for she was not afraid.
The reindeer pounded on the roof.
(It was my Nana with a hammer in the attic.   25
For *my* children it was my husband
with a crowbar breaking things up.)
The year I ceased to believe in you
is the year you were drunk.
My boozy red man,   30
your voice all slithery like soap,
you were a long way from Saint Nick
with Daddy's cocktail smell.
I cried and ran from the room
and you said, "Well, thank God that's over!"   35
And it was, until the grandchildren came.
Then I tied up your pillows
in the five A.M. Christ morning
and I adjusted the beard,
all yellow with age,   40
and applied rouge to your cheeks
and Chalk White to your eyebrows.
We were conspirators,

secret actors,
and I kissed you 45
because I was tall enough.
But that is over.
The era closes
and large children hang their stockings
and build a black memorial to you. 50
And you, you fade out of sight
like a lost signalman
wagging his lantern
for the train that comes no more.

TOPICS FOR CRITICAL THINKING

1. Compare and contrast the treatment of fathers in the previous two poems with "Santa."
2. How does Sexton as the mature speaker of the poem differ from the childhood memory of herself as daughter represented in the opening lines?
3. In what sense have she and her father become "conspirators" in restaging the myth of Santa for her own children?
4. What change is signaled in Sexton's blunt line "But that is over" in the poem's ending?

TOPIC FOR CRITICAL WRITING

How does Sexton use the legend of Santa Claus for her own symbolic purposes in the poem? What point is Sexton making about Santa as an imagined father figure and her father's impersonation of Santa?

Rapunzel (1971)

A woman
who loves a woman
is forever young.
The mentor
and the student 5
feed off each other.
Many a girl
had an old aunt
who locked her in the study
to keep the boys away. 10
They would play rummy
or lie on the couch
and touch and touch.
Old breast against young breast . . .

Let your dress fall down your shoulder,   15
come touch a copy of you
for I am at the mercy of rain,
for I have left the three Christs of Ypsilanti,
for I have left the long naps of Ann Arbor
and the church spires have turned to stumps.   20
The sea bangs into my cloister
for the young politicians are dying,
and dying so hold me, my young dear,
hold me . . .

The yellow rose will turn to cinder   25
and New York City will fall in
before we are done so hold me,
my young dear, hold me.
Put your pale arms around my neck.
Let me hold your heart like a flower   30
lest it bloom and collapse.
Give me your skin
as sheer as a cobweb,
let me open it up
and listen in and scoop out the dark.   35
Give me your nether lips
all puffy with their art
and I will give you angel fire in return.
We are two clouds
glistening in the bottle glass.   40
We are two birds
washing in the same mirror.
We were fair game
but we have kept out of the cesspool.
We are strong.   45
We are the good ones.
Do not discover us
for we lie together all in green
like pond weeds.
Hold me, my young dear, hold me.   50

They touch their delicate watches
one at a time.
They dance to the lute
two at a time.
They are as tender as bog moss.   55
They play mother-me-do
all day.
A woman
who loves a woman
is forever young.   60

Once there was a witch's garden
more beautiful than Eve's
with carrots growing like little fish,
with many tomatoes rich as frogs,
onions as ingrown as hearts,   65
the squash singing like a dolphin
and one patch given over wholly, to magic—
rampion, a kind of salad root,
a kind of harebell more potent than penicillin,
growing leaf by leaf, skin by skin,   70
as rapt and as fluid as Isadora Duncan.
However the witch's garden was kept locked
and each day a woman who was with child
looked upon the rampion wildly,
fancying that she would die   75
if she could not have it.
Her husband feared for her welfare
and thus climbed into the garden
to fetch the life-giving tubers.

Ah ha, cried the witch,   80
whose proper name was Mother Gothel,
you are a thief and now you will die.
However they made a trade,
typical enough in those times.
He promised his child to Mother Gothel   85
so of course when it was born
she took the child away with her.
She gave the child the name Rapunzel,
another name for the life-giving rampion.
Because Rapunzel was a beautiful girl   90
Mother Gothel treasured her beyond all things.
As she grew older Mother Gothel thought:
None but I will ever see her or touch her.
She locked her in a tower without a door
or a staircase. It had only a high window.   95
When the witch wanted to enter she cried:
Rapunzel, Rapunzel, let down your hair.
Rapunzel's hair fell to the ground like a rainbow.
It was as yellow as a dandelion
and as strong as a dog leash.   100
Hand over hand she shinnied up
the hair like a sailor
and there in the stone-cold room,
as cold as a museum,
Mother Gothel cried: 105
Hold me, my young dear, hold me,
and thus they played mother-me-do.

Years later a prince came by
and heard Rapunzel singing in her loneliness.
That song pierced his heart like a valentine   110
but he could find no way to get to her.
Like a chameleon he hid himself among the trees
and watched the witch ascend the swinging hair.
The next day he himself called out:
Rapunzel, Rapunzel, let down your hair,   115
and thus they met and he declared his love.
What is this beast, she thought,
with muscles on his arms
like a bag of snakes?
What is this moss on his legs?   120
What prickly plant grows on his cheeks?
What is this voice as deep as a dog?
Yet he dazzled her with his answers.
Yet he dazzled her with his dancing stick.
They lay together upon the yellowy threads,   125
swimming through them
like minnows through kelp
and they sang out benedictions like the Pope.

Each day he brought her a skein of silk
to fashion a ladder so they could both escape.   130
But Mother Gothel discovered the plot
and cut off Rapunzel's hair to her ears
and took her into the forest to repent.
When the prince came the witch fastened
the hair to a hook and let it down.   135
When he saw Rapunzel had been banished
he flung himself out of the tower, a side of beef.
He was blinded by thorns that pricked him like tacks.
As blind as Oedipus he wandered for years
until he heard a song that pierced his heart   140
like that long-ago valentine.
As he kissed Rapunzel her tears fell on his eyes
and in the manner of such cure-alls
his sight was suddenly restored.

They lived happily as you might expect   145
proving that mother-me-do
can be outgrown,
just as the fish on Friday,
just as a tricycle.
The world, some say,   150
is made up of couples.
A rose must have a stem.

As for Mother Gothel,
her heart shrank to the size of a pin,
never again to say: Hold me, my young dear,   155
hold me,
and only as she dreamt of the yellow hair
did moonlight sift into her mouth.

TOPICS FOR CRITICAL THINKING

1. Recount what you know about the fairy tale Rapunzel.
2. Consider Sexton's narrative strategy of presenting a bonding between women before she begins the story line of "Rapunzel." How does this opening make a feminist difference in the story?
3. How does Sexton shift the narrative point of view to have us identify or at least
   sympathize with Mother Gothel?
4. Discuss Sexton's use of figurative language to describe Rapunzel's mixed feelings
   toward the prince when she first meets him.

TOPIC FOR CRITICAL WRITING

How significant is Sexton's allusion to Oedipus in the poem? What does that myth
have to do with her rendering of Rapunzel?

The Abortion   *(1962)*

Somebody who should have been born
is gone.

Just as the earth puckered its mouth,
each bud puffing out from its knot,
I changed my shoes, and then drove south.   5

Up past the Blue Mountains, where
Pennsylvania humps on endlessly,
wearing, like a crayoned cat, its green hair,

its roads sunken in like a gray washboard;
where, in truth, the ground cracks evilly,   10
a dark socket from which the coal has poured,

Somebody who should have been born
is gone.

the grass as bristly and stout as chives,
and me wondering when the ground would break,   15
and me wondering how anything fragile survives;

up in Pennsylvania, I met a little man,
not Rumpelstiltskin, at all, at all . . .
he took the fullness that love began.

Returning north, even the sky grew thin   20
like a high window looking nowhere.
The road was as flat as a sheet of tin.

Somebody who should have been born
is gone.

Yes, woman, such logic will lead   25
to loss without death. Or say what you meant,
you coward . . . this baby that I bleed.

TOPICS FOR CRITICAL THINKING

1. Sexton had an abortion in the spring of 1960. How does her refrain line emphasize and mourn that fact through repetition?
2. Discuss Sexton's setting in the poem. How does landscape imagery contribute to her theme?
3. How does Sexton employ figurative language to depict the intensities of her abortion experience?
4. Discuss the poet's allusion to the Rumpelstiltskin fairy tale in the poem. Who was Rumpelstiltskin, and how might his story relate to Sexton's theme? Why does she insist that the little man she encounters is not Rumpelstiltskin?

TOPIC FOR CRITICAL WRITING

On January 22, 1973, the U.S. Supreme Court sided with Jane Roe in the case *Roe v. Wade* that struck down a Texas statute making abortion a crime in Texas. This legal precedent found that the right to privacy granted under the Constitution covered a woman's choice whether to terminate her pregnancy. Sexton's poem "The Abortion" was published a decade before *Roe v. Wade* guaranteed a woman's right to choose the course of her reproductive life. Does the poem project any stand on the ethics or politics of abortion? Does it criticize the adverse and illegal conditions under which Sexton had to pursue her abortion?

With Mercy for the Greedy   *(1962)*

For my friend, Ruth, who urges me to make an
appointment for the Sacrament of Confession

Concerning your letter in which you ask
me to call a priest and in which you ask
me to wear The Cross that you enclose;
your own cross,

your dog-bitten cross,   5
no larger than a thumb,
small and wooden, no thorns, this rose—

I pray to its shadow,
that gray place
where it lies on your letter . . . deep, deep.   10
I detest my sins and I try to believe
in The Cross. I touch its tender hips, its dark jawed face,
its solid neck, its brown sleep.

True. There is
a beautiful Jesus.   15
He is frozen to his bones like a chunk of beef.
How desperately he wanted to pull his arms in!
How desperately I touch his vertical and horizontal axes!
But I can't. Need is not quite belief.

All morning long   20
I have worn
your cross, hung with package string around my throat.
It tapped me lightly as a child's heart might,
tapping secondhand, softly waiting to be born.
Ruth, I cherish the letter you wrote.   25

My friend, my friend, I was born
doing reference work in sin, and born
confessing it. This is what poems are:
with mercy
for the greedy,   30
they are the tongue's wrangle,
the world's pottage, the rat's star.

TOPICS FOR CRITICAL THINKING

1. "With Mercy for the Greedy" is a companion piece to "The Abortion." Sexton addresses the poem to her friend Ruth Soter, who had recently converted to Catholicism. Ruth was also the only person that Sexton told about her abortion. In response, her friend sent her a cross and urged her to seek consolation and forgiveness in the church. How does Sexton negotiate the rhetorical dilemma of having to turn down a friend to whom she is, nevertheless, still devoted?

2. Though Sexton does not accept the sacraments of Catholicism, how does her poem assert a serious commitment to the life of the spirit?

3. In refusing to believe in Christ as her personal savior, Sexton declares that "Need is not the same as belief." What do you think she means here?

4. In what ways does poetry offer another kind of mercy than that held out by Jesus Christ?

5. "Rats live on no evil star" reads the same forwards and backwards, and it was Sexton's favorite **palindrome.** In claiming that poetry is the "rats star," she is alluding to the ways in which language can take on a life of its own beyond our intentions, expectations, or judgment. How might this transformative power of language be considered a source of redemption in the poem's context?

TOPIC FOR CRITICAL WRITING

Compare Sexton's linguistic credo in "With Mercy for the Greedy" with her declaration that "My business is words" in "Said the Poet to the Analyst," which follows.

Said the Poet to the Analyst   *(1960)*

My business is words. Words are like labels,
or coins, or better, like swarming bees.
I confess I am only broken by the sources of things;
as if words were counted like dead bees in the attic,
unbuckled from their yellow eyes and their dry wings.   5
I must always forget how one word is able to pick
out another, to manner another, until I have got
something I might have said . . .
but did not.

Your business is watching my words. But I   10
admit nothing. I work with my best, for instance,
when I can write my praise for a nickel machine,
that one night in Nevada: telling how the magic jackpot
came clacking three bells out, over the lucky screen.
But if you should say this is something it is not,   15
then I grow weak, remembering how my hands felt funny
and ridiculous and crowded with all
the believing money.

TOPICS FOR CRITICAL THINKING

1. Discuss Sexton's similes for words in the opening lines of "Said the Poet to the Analyst." How does language take on an agency of its own in the first stanza?
2. What do you make of the poem's ending metaphor of writing as slot machine gambling?

TOPIC FOR CRITICAL WRITING

How does the analyst's role and attitude toward language differ from those of the poet, according to Sexton?

For My Lover, Returning to His Wife   *(1969)*

She is all there.
She was melted carefully down for you
and cast up from your childhood,
cast up from your one hundred favorite aggies.

She has always been there, my darling.   5
She is, in fact, exquisite.
Fireworks in the dull middle of February
and as real as a cast-iron pot.

Let's face it, I have been momentary.
A luxury. A bright red sloop in the harbor.   10
My hair rising like smoke from the car window.
Littleneck clams out of season.

She is more than that. She is your have to have,
has grown you your practical your tropical growth.
This is not an experiment. She is all harmony.   15
She sees to oars and oarlocks for the dinghy,

has placed wild flowers at the window at breakfast,
sat by the potter's wheel at midday,
set forth three children under the moon,
three cherubs drawn by Michelangelo,   20

done this with her legs spread out
in the terrible months in the chapel.
If you glance up, the children are there
like delicate balloons resting on the ceiling.

She has also carried each one down the hall   25
after supper, their heads privately bent,
two legs protesting, person to person,
her face flushed with a song and their little sleep.

I give you back your heart.
I give you permission—   30

for the fuse inside her, throbbing
angrily in the dirt, for the bitch in her
and the burying of her wound—
for the burying of her small red wound alive—

for the pale flickering flare under her ribs,   35
for the drunken sailor who waits in her left pulse,

for the mother's knee, for the stockings,
for the garter belt, for the call—

the curious call
when you will burrow in arms and breasts   40
and tug at the orange ribbon in her hair
and answer the call, the curious call.

She is so naked and singular
She is the sum of yourself and your dream.
Climb her like a monument, step after step.   45
She is solid.

As for me, I am a watercolor.
I wash off.

TOPICS FOR CRITICAL THINKING

1. Discuss the ways in which Sexton contrasts herself with her lover's wife, to whom
   he has returned in the poem's situation.
2. Examine the tropes through which Sexton describes love as a kind of fine art.

TOPIC FOR CRITICAL WRITING

In breaking off her affair, she addresses her lover with the strange farewell: "I give you
permission." In considering the surreal catalogue of images that follows this declaration, what kind of permission is Sexton granting the lover? How do you read the poet's
tone and her attitude toward the end of the affair? Consider how she captures and focuses that attitude in the subtle turn of her final trope when she admits that "As for me,
I am a watercolor. / I wash off."

Critical Perspective: On Poetry and the Unconscious

"In the beginning, what was the relationship between your poetry and your therapy?

"Sometimes, my doctors tell me that I understand something in a poem that I
haven't integrated into my life. In fact, I may be concealing it from myself,
while I was revealing it to the readers. The poetry is often more advanced, in
terms of my unconscious, than I am. Poetry, after all, milks the unconscious.
The unconscious is there to feed it little images, little symbols, the answers, the
insights I know not of. In therapy, one seeks to hide sometimes. I'll give you a
rather intimate example of this. About three or four years ago my analyst asked
me what I thought of my parents having intercourse when I was young. I couldn't
talk. I knew there was suddenly a poem there, and I selfishly guarded it from

him. Two days later, I had a poem, entitled, 'In the Beach House,' which describes overhearing the primal scene. In it I say, 'Inside my prison of pine and bedspring, / over my window sill, under my knob, / it is plain that they are at / the royal strapping.' The point of this little story is the image, 'the royal strapping.' My analyst was quite impressed with that image and so was I, although I don't remember going any further with it then. About three weeks ago, he said to me, 'Were you ever beaten as a child?' I told him that I had been, when I was about nine. I had torn up a five-dollar bill that my father gave to my sister; my father took me into his bedroom, laid me down on his bed, pulled off my pants and beat me with a riding crop. As I related this to my doctor, he said, 'See, that was quite a royal strapping,' thus revealing to me, by way of my own image, the intensity of that moment, the sexuality of that beating, the little masochistic seizure—it's so classic, it's almost corny. Perhaps it's too intimate an example, but then both poetry and therapy are intimate.

"Are your poems still closely connected to your therapy as in the past?

"No. The subject of therapy was an early theme—the process itself as in 'Said the Poet to the Analyst,' the people of my past, admitting what my parents were really like, the whole Gothic New England story. I've had about eight doctors, but only two that count. I've written a poem for each of the two— 'You, Doctor Martin' and 'Cripples and Other Stories.' And that will do. Those poems are about the two men as well as the strange process. One can say that my new poems, the love poems, come about as a result of new attitudes, an awareness of the possibly good as well as the possibly rotten. Inherent in the process is a rebirth of a sense of self, each time stripping away a dead self."
—Anne Sexton, "Interview with Barbara Kevles" (1974)

Critical Perspective: On Anne Sexton's "Her Kind"

"Because Sexton's writing seems so personal she is often labeled a 'confessional' poet and grouped (to her disadvantage) with poets such as Lowell, Berryman, Roethke, and Plath. But Sexton resisted the label 'confessional'; she preferred to be regarded as a 'storyteller.' To emphasize that she considered the speaking 'I' in her poetry as a literary rather than a real identity, Sexton invariably opened her public performances by reading the early poem 'Her Kind.' . . . No matter what poetry she had on an evening's agenda, Sexton offered this persona as a point of entry to her art. 'I' in the poem is a disturbing, marginal female whose power is associated with disfigurement, sexuality, and magic. But at the end of each stanza, 'I' is displaced from sufferer onto storyteller. With the lines 'A woman like that . . . I have been her kind' Sexton conveys the terms on which she wishes to be understood: not victim, but witness and witch.

   "The witch-persona of Sexton's poetry is the voice Sexton invented to tell the story of her changing relationship to a severe, incurable, but apparently undiagnosable malady. She was born in 1928 in Wellesley, Massachusetts, and lived all her life in the suburbs of Boston. Married at age nineteen to a man in the wool business, Sexton had two daughters. Severe depression following the birth of her second child deepened into a permanent mental illness for which she was treated by psychiatrists for the rest of her life. She died by suicide of carbon monoxide poisoning in 1974. Her professional interest in poetry began during the first phase of her illness, in 1956. Intensified by the death of her parents in 1959, the illness was the fixed point of reference by which she measured the reality of love, the practice of poetry, and the possibility of spiritual redemption."

—Diane Wood Middlebrook, from "Poet of Weird Abundance" (1985)

Critical Perspective: On Fathers and Daughters in Sexton's Verse

"Sexton's ablest critics have located the shift from personal to 'transpersonal' or 'cultural' in Sexton's work in her fourth volume, *Transformations*. While I agree that in *Transformations* such a shift is mythically embodied and newly garbed, there is within the 'narrow diary' of even the early poems a structural outline for the psychic biography of a gender, and particularly for what Phyllis Chesler calls 'woman's "dependent" and "incestuous" personality' in relation to her father—a pattern long known to and exploited by psychoanalysis, to the degree that therapeutic method colludes with patriarchy. If Anne Sexton learned about her own incestuous dependencies from Freud and his proxies during the early stages of her life as a career mental patient, hers was still the first contemporary voice outside of the psychoanalytic world to describe the normative relationship between father and daughter from the daughter's perspective. Sexton's early poetry both represents and dissects the subtle and pervasive psycho-social pattern that Phyllis Chesler would later discuss, and damn, in *Women and Madness*, and which now, in the wake of feminist inquiry, seems almost obvious: 'romantic' love in the western world is 'psychologically predicated on sexual union between Daughter and Father figures.'

"The 'normal' woman in western society, whether or not she is a poet, and whether or not she is fully aware of the psychic dynamics, falls in love with her father, who delights her, despises her, seduces her, betrays her, and dies. The father who dies in 1959 in the poet's personal life undergoes a series of resurrections as man and imago—husband, doctor, lover, priest—and is finally reborn as the diety of *The Awful Rowing Toward God*. Burial and resurrection of the fathers becomes a central theme in Sexton's poetry, as it is in the personal lives of her contemporaries and the collective life of her culture. In all of his incarnations in Sexton's poetry, the father finally fails himself and his daughter, for he is a god not sufficiently omnipotent, a man not sufficiently human, a male principle not sufficiently able to accommodate feminine powers and desires. But this ultimate failure is never judged harshly in Sexton's poetry, never evoked without the empathy that always accompanies insight; for the shortcomings of the father-god in a patriarchy are nearly definitive of the failures of the human enterprise, one in which all men and all women engage."

—Diana Hume George, from "How We Danced:
Anne Sexton on Fathers and Daughters" (1986)

Critical Perspective: On Sexton and Confessional Verse

"In fact, surprisingly little has been written with any authority on the subject of confessionalism, which has become, under the rubric of 'sincerity,' an impulse behind many of the significant social movements and styles since 1960.

"One of the few studies available is Theodor Reik's *The Compulsion to Confess*, a work that, while hardly exhaustive, at least opens up a few theoretical approaches toward an understanding of the 'compulsion' and its results. Broadly, Reik defines a confession as 'a statement about impulses or drives which are felt or recognized as forbidden,' and their expression involves both the repressed tendency and the repressing forces. If this secular interpretation seems to exclude the usual religious (and even legal) sense of the term as narrowed to facts and intentions, they can easily be added to Reik's definition without any loss to the force of his point. The confessional situation—most obvious in analytical sessions—resides in 'the transformation of a primitive urge for expression into the compulsion to confess,' occasioned by social and psychic restraints and 'the reactive reinforcement which the intensity of the drive experiences through repression,' so that 'confession is a repetition of action or of certain behavior substituted by displacement and with different emotional material, as words must substitute for action.' This weakened repetition allows its own gratifications, indulging as it does both guilt and the need for punishment, even while the 'reproduction through narration' achieves 'the retroactive annulment of repression.' That is to say, confession is at once the process of exorcism and the plea for absolution. And the result, in Reik's view, is that 'the disintegrating of the personality is at least temporarily halted by the confession. The communication between the ego and that part of the ego from which it was estranged is restored.' . . .

"To some extent, then, the poetry is therapeutic; or as D. H. Lawrence said, 'One sheds one's sicknesses in books—repeats and presents again one's emotions, to be master of them.' Erik Erikson underscores this aspect of the situation by reminding that 'the individual's mastery over his neurosis begins where he is put in a position to accept the historical necessity which made him what he is.' Acceptance becomes survival. Anne Sexton: 'Writing, and especially having written, is evidence of survival—the books accumulate ego-strength.' And so confessional poets are driven back to their losses, to that alienation—from self and others, from sanity and love—which is the thematic center of their vision and work. The betrayals in childhood, the family romance, the divorces and madnesses, the suicide attempts, the self-defeat and longing—the poets pursue them in their most intimate and painful detail."

—J. D. McClatchy, from "Anne Sexton: Somehow to Endure" (1978)

36   Representations of Desire and Sexuality

"How do I love thee?" Elizabeth Barrett Browning muses in her widely read Sonnet 43, "Let me count the ways." Addressed to her husband, the poet Robert Browning, Elizabeth Browning's *Sonnets from the Portuguese* enumerates the many ways that love, admiration, and desire are experienced in marriage. Poetry has always given passionate utterance to the several ways love takes, ranging from friendship to passionate sexual desire.

ELIZABETH BARRETT BROWNING   *(1806–1861)*

Sonnet 43   *(1850)*

How do I love thee? Let me count the ways.
I love thee to the depth and breadth and height
My soul can reach, when feeling out of sight
For the ends of Being and ideal Grace.
I love thee to the level of everyday's   5
Most quiet need, by sun and candle-light.
I love thee freely, as men strive for Right;
I love thee purely, as they turn from Praise.
I love thee with the passion put to use
In my old griefs, and with my childhood's faith.   10
I love thee with a love I seemed to lose
With my lost saints—I love thee with the breath,
Smiles, tears, of all my life!—and, if God choose,
I shall but love thee better after death.

TOPICS FOR CRITICAL THINKING

1. Discuss the ways in which Browning portrays the extent of her love through spatial figures in the sonnet's first quatrain.
2. In what ways does Browning project her love into a spiritual dimension in her final quatrain?

TOPIC FOR CRITICAL WRITING

How does Browning ascribe wonder, passion, and moral qualities to her love?

While Browning's sonnet expresses an unwavering commitment to her soulmate, desire in much of love poetry from the medieval period through the present is represented as both a joyful and disruptive emotive force, as in Elizabeth I of England's "On Monsieur's Departure."

QUEEN ELIZABETH I   *(1533–1603)*

On Monsieur's Departure   *(c. 1570)*

I grieve and dare not show my discontent,
I love and yet am forced to seem to hate,
I do, yet dare not say I ever meant,
I seem stark mute but inwardly do prate.
   I am and not, I freeze and yet am burned,   5
   Since from myself another self I turned.

My care is like my shadow in the sun,
Follows me flying, flies when I pursue it,
Stands and lies by me, doth what I have done.
His too familiar care doth make me rue it.   10
   No means I find to rid him from my breast,
   Till by the end of things it be suppressed.

Some gentler passion slide into my mind,
For I am soft and made of melting snow;
Or be more cruel, love, and so be kind.   15
Let me or float or sink, be high or low.
   Or let me live with some more sweet content,
   Or die and so forget what love ere meant.

TOPICS FOR CRITICAL THINKING

1. At least two historical figures have been advanced as possible candidates for the identity of the "monsieur" of Queen Elizabeth's sonnet: the French Duc d'Anjou, who left England in 1582, and the courtier Robert Devereux, Earl of Essex. Whoever is the historical subject of the poem, Elizabeth's theme is her struggle to come to terms with the "care" that she feels but, because of her royal status, must not outwardly show. How does Elizabeth present the poem's speaker as divided on the issue of desire?

2. To *die* in the Elizabethan context has a double meaning. It can mean literally to perish, but it also has the sexual connotation of experiencing orgasm. Discuss how the poem puns on this key word in its conclusion.

TOPIC FOR CRITICAL WRITING

Discuss how Elizabeth presents her emotional dilemma in her figurative language.

Queen Elizabeth's musings on the paradoxes of love are hardly unique to her, as is plain to see in Dorothy Parker's modern poem "Somebody's Song."

DOROTHY PARKER *(1893–1967)*

Somebody's Song   *(1926)*

This is what I vow:
He shall have my heart to keep;
Sweetly will we stir and sleep,
   All the years, as now.
Swift the measured sands may run;   5
Love like this is never done;
He and I are welded one:
   This is what I vow.

This is what I pray:
Keep him by me tenderly;   10
Keep him sweet in pride of me,
   Ever and a day;
Keep me from the old distress;
Let me, for our happiness,
Be the one to love the less: 15
   This is what I pray.

This is what I know:
Lovers' oaths are thin as rain;
Love's a harbinger of pain—
   Would it were not so!   20
Ever is my heart a-thirst,
Ever is my love accurst;
He is neither last nor first—
   This is what I know.

TOPICS FOR CRITICAL THINKING

1. Compare and contrast what, on the one hand, Parker vows and prays in the pursuit of love with what, on the other hand, she "knows" about love.
2. Contrast Parker's misgivings about love with Christina Rossetti's celebration of love as a rare gift in "A Birthday," which follows.

TOPIC FOR CRITICAL WRITING

Consider Parker's presentation of the differences between idealized hopes for love versus love's realities. Does either have the last word, or does the poem's irony suspend them in a contradictory tension?

CHRISTINA ROSSETTI   *(1830–1894)*

A Birthday   *(1861)*

My heart is like a singing bird
   Whose nest is in a watered shoot;
My heart is like an apple-tree
   Whose boughs are bent with thickset fruit;
My heart is like a rainbow shell   5
   That paddles in a halcyon sea;
My heart is gladder than all these
   Because my love is come to me.

Raise me a dais of silk and down;
   Hang it with vair and purple dyes;   10
Carve it in doves and pomegranates,
   And peacocks with a hundred eyes;
Work it in gold and silver grapes,
   In leaves and silver fleurs-de-lys;
Because the birthday of my life   15
   Is come, my love is come to me.

Rossetti not only depicts love through the metaphor of the artful gift in the second stanza, but she also presents her heart through a series of similes taken from the natural world of birds, trees, shells, and sea. Much of traditional English love poetry represents desire by reaching back to the natural landscapes of Greek and Roman **pastoral** verse, as in the *Idylls* of Theocritus and lyric fragments of Sappho.

The pastoral tradition's rich repertoire of conventional tropes, images, and symbols has long served as a poetic resource for rendering idealized states of desire from ancient times through the present. Pastoral poetry takes love as its stock theme, grounded in the down-to-earth characters of rustics, herdsmen, and farmers. The bucolic simplicity of the pastoral world is presented in such canonical works as Edmund Spenser's *The Shepheardes Calendar*; William Shakespeare's sonnets, comedies, and romances; Christopher Marlowe's "The Passionate Shepherd to His Love"; Sir Walter Raleigh's "Nymph's Reply to the Shepherd"; John Milton's "L'Allegro" and "Lycidas"; Andrew Marvell's "The Garden," as well as his "mower" poems; Alexander Pope's "Discourse on Pastoral Poetry"; William Wordsworth's "Michael: A Pastoral Poem"; and Alfred, Lord Tennyson's *Dora*, among many others. In these works, the simplicity of pastoral desire contrasts with the social complexities, coded behaviors, and power politics that belong to court and city life.

Punning on the language and stock figures of pastoral love poetry, Theodore Roethke's contemporary poem "I Knew a Woman" celebrates the ecstatic joy of sexuality between men and women as a dance of natural sensuality.

THEODORE ROETHKE (1908–1963)

I Knew a Woman (1958)

I knew a woman, lovely in her bones,
When small birds sighed, she would sigh back at them;
Ah, when she moved, she moved more ways than one:
The shapes a bright container can contain!
Of her choice virtues only gods should speak,   5
Or English poets who grew up on Greek
(I'd have them sing in chorus, cheek to cheek).

How well her wishes went! She stroked my chin,
She taught me Turn, and Counter-turn, and Stand;
She taught me Touch, that undulant white skin;   10
I nibbled meekly from her proffered hand;
She was the sickle; I, poor I, the rake,
Coming behind her for her pretty sake
(But what prodigious mowing did we make).

Love likes a gander, and adores a goose: 15
Her full lips pursed, the errant note to seize;
She played it quick, she played it light and loose,
My eyes, they dazzled at her flowing knees;
Her several parts could keep a pure repose,
Or one hip quiver with a mobile nose   20
(She moved in circles, and those circles moved).

Let seed be grass, and grass turn into hay:
I'm martyr to a motion not my own;
What's freedom for? To know eternity.
I swear she cast a shadow white as stone.   25
But who would count eternity in days?
These old bones live to learn her wanton ways:
(I measure time by how a body sways).

Roethke's "I Knew a Woman" reflects on his passionate midlife marriage to Beatrice O'Connell in 1953. The poet's fervor is inscribed right at the beginning in the word play of the poem's title, which puns on the well-known double entendre of the word to *know*, signifying both familiarity and carnal knowledge. Other puns underscore the latter connotation in the Scots dialect word *mow* as a term for love-making. Eroticizing the tradition of love lyricism, Roethke portrays English poets who "grew up on Greek" singing "in chorus, cheek to cheek." The Hellenistic allusion is further picked up in the lover's sensual movements of "Turn, and Counter-turn, and Stand" that allude to both the literary terms of strophe, antistrophe, and epode of Greek verse and the sexual positionings the poet learns from the beloved's "wanton ways." Finally, when Roethke depicts himself in the metaphor of the "rake / Coming behind her," he is not just alluding to a garden tool. A rake is the kind of sexual libertine and "man of loose habits" that the eighteenth-century British artist William Hogarth satirizes in his series of engravings *The Rake's Progress.* Roethke adopts the persona of the rake in matching the lover's "wanton ways." The poem's situation of erotic instruction is set in a natural landscape whose birds, including the goose and gander, reflect in their sighs the "errant note" the lovers play "light and loose." The mirroring of natural and sexual fertility is aptly summed up in declarations like "Let seed be grass, and grass turn into hay."

The kind of frolicsome, pastoral representations we find in Roethke's love poetry achieve their effects through figures of naturalized sexuality. Roethke would give us the lesson the beloved taught him in ways that instruct us about the facts of life. Such naturalized metaphors of desire have broad currency in English love lyricism. To take just one more example, when Lord Byron pays

William Hogarth, *The Rake's Progress,* Plate III (1735)

tribute to one of his many lovers, he employs the naturalizing simile of the night sky in "She Walks in Beauty."

George Gordon, Lord Byron *(1788–1824)*

She Walks in Beauty *(1815)*

She walks in beauty, like the night
  Of cloudless climes and starry skies;
And all that's best of dark and bright
  Meet in her aspect and her eyes:
Thus mellowed to that tender light   5
  Which heaven to gaudy day denies.

One shade the more, one ray the less,
  Had half impaired the nameless grace
Which waves in every raven tress,
  Or softly lightens o'er her face;   10
Where thoughts serenely sweet express
  How pure, how dear their dwelling place.

And on that cheek and o'er the brow,
  So soft, so calm, yet eloquent,
The smiles that win, the tints that glow,   15
  But tell of days in goodness spent,
A mind at peace with all below,
  A heart whose love is innocent!

TOPICS FOR CRITICAL THINKING

1. Discuss Byron's simile that captures the lover's beauty in tropes of light.
2. What key terms further portray what Byron admires in the lover's character?

TOPIC FOR CRITICAL WRITING

Compare and contrast the ways in which Byron describes the lover with Roethke's poetic representations in "I Knew a Woman." If Roethke depicts the lover as "wanton," how does Byron portray the lover as "innocent"?

    In "I Knew a Woman" and "She Walks in Beauty," the male poet expresses his desire for the beloved woman through stylized tropes that locate desire in natural settings. Nevertheless, in both of these lyrics, the immediate essence and felt urgency of the poet's emotive utterance are posed in pastoral conventions that belie the artificial, or constructed, terms of desire. Both poems are not only passionate expressions of desire, but also highly stylized po-

etic performances that stage the traditional conventions of English love poetry. So familiar are these pastoral tropes that Shakespeare parodies them in
his well-known Sonnet 18.

WILLIAM SHAKESPEARE   *(1564–1616)*

Sonnet 18   *(1609)*

Shall I compare thee to a summer's day?
Thou art more lovely and more temperate:
Rough winds do shake the darling buds of May,
And summer's lease hath all too short a date;
Sometimes too hot the eye of heaven shines,   5
And often is his gold complexion dimmed;
And every fair from fair sometime declines,
By chance or nature's changing course untrimmed;
But thy eternal summer shall not fade,
Nor lose possession of that fair thou ow'st;   10
Nor shall death brag thou wand'rest in his shade,
While in eternal lines to Time thou grow'st:
   So long as men can breathe, or eyes can see,
   So long live this, and this gives life to thee.

TOPICS FOR CRITICAL THINKING

1. How does Shakespeare's opening rhetorical question—"Shall I compare thee to a
   summer's day?"—reveal this conceit as already outworn and marked by cliché?
2. In what ways does poetry immortalize the lover beyond natural comparison?

TOPIC FOR CRITICAL WRITING

Examine how Shakespeare describes nature as subject to time, decay, and death. How
does the lover's beauty transcend the "changing course" of nature's mutability?

In Sonnet 18, Shakespeare not only pokes fun at the natural conventions
of the pastoral tradition but, equally important, he underscores the constructed, or artificial, aspect of desire. Passion is as much produced in language as it is experienced in the real world. As poet, he reveals the ways in
which desire is mediated and even generated by our representations of it. The
beloved becomes an object of our admiration only insofar as the poet's representations "give life" to her beauty.

In probing the constructed—rather than wholly natural—aspect of desire, it would be a mistake to assume that the conventions of the pastoral tradition have the last word in exhausting the query Elizabeth Barrett Browning
puts to desire: "How do I love thee?" If desire is not only reflected in but also
produced by its representation in language, then whom we love and what it is

exactly that we love about them renders Browning's question truly open-ended. In fact, contemporary debate over sexual orientation makes Browning's query a difficult question to answer in any straightforward way.

Representations of Sexuality

In current discussions of sexuality Web , a controversy turns on the issue of whether nature or nurture determines the sources and objects of our desire. Is there a natural, essential basis for sexual orientation and sexual object choice? Or is every form and expression of desire, to a greater or lesser extent, shaped by our cultural lives? Is one's particular sexual bent innate: a result of hormonal and genetic factors, or even brain structure? Or is sexual disposition acquired through environment, upbringing, and cultural background? Not surprisingly, there are no simple answers to these controversial questions and how they bear on one's identity, civil rights, and legal entitlements. *www*

Much of modern psychoanalytic theory Web , beginning with Sigmund Freud's *Three Essays on the Theory of Sexuality* (1905), distinguishes between biological needs and sexual drives. Freud located drives as "lying at the frontier between the mental and the physical." For example, a newborn baby has biological needs for basic sustenance in, say, breast-feeding. But in the absence of the breast and in excess of biological survival, the developing infant's drive for oral gratification will find a range of pleasurable substitute objects in bottles, cups, fingers, toys, candy, and pacifiers. Moreover, sexual orientation does not just serve the aims of biological reproduction. In fact, Freud hypothesized that the infantile drives are bisexual and polymorphous. Only through later social and cultural processes of nurture do these drives become identified with heterosexual object choices. *www*

Contemporary psychoanalytic theorists typically define biological **sex** in terms of the embodied differences that distinguish women from men. In contrast, **gender** Web refers to the social construction of men's and women's roles in everyday life. Today, the rigid stereotypes of men's and women's roles are largely things of the past. We no longer ascribe intelligence, rationality, and activity solely to men, nor do we necessarily attribute emotion, nurturing, and passivity to women. Furthermore, contemporary gender theorists have shown that masculine and feminine traits are neither universal across cultures and time periods nor fixed characteristics that distinguish men from women. Instead, how we define ourselves as men and women depends on an ensemble of local customs, rituals, and practices of everyday life that both reinforce and complicate basic anatomical differences. Contemporary culture affords us a fluid, not fixed, repertoire of gendered dispositions, outlooks, attitudes, and behaviors that cut across sexual difference. *www*

Similarly, our understanding of sexual orientation has undergone a sea-change since the birth of the gay liberation era of the 1960s. In America, a profound cultural shift in national attitudes toward gays and lesbians Web marks the twenty-year history between 1952 when the American Psychiatric Association (APA) added homosexuality to its list of mental disorders and 1973 *www* when the APA removed the category of homosexuality from its *Diagnostic and Statistical Manual of Sexual Disorders* (DSM-III). Today, how we experience masculinity and femininity has less to do with simple anatomy. In addition to one's biological sex, several components of sexuality contribute to personal identity. These aspects include one's sexual orientation, one's gendered sense of being masculine or feminine, as well as one's social behavior: how one acts on or refrains from acting on that self-perception of gender.

Lesbian identity, according to poet Adrienne Rich, should not be simply reduced to sexual acts but includes a continuum of female identifications in everyday life. In her 1980 essay "Compulsory Heterosexuality and Lesbian Existence," Rich defines the "lesbian continuum" in terms of "woman-identified experience; not simply the fact that a woman has had or consciously desired genital sexual experience with another woman." Rich recommends that we extend our understanding of lesbianism so as to

> expand it to embrace many more forms of primary intensity between and among women, including the sharing of a rich inner life, the bonding against male tyranny, the giving and receiving of practical and political support; if we can also hear in it such associations as marriage resistance we begin to grasp breadths of female history and psychology which have lain out of reach as a consequence of limited, mostly clinical definitions of "lesbianism."

Such theoretical insights enable us to reread traditional English lyrics such as Anne Finch's "Friendship Between Ephelia and Ardelia" as expressing a feminist solidarity between women beyond the conventional norms of patriarchy.

ANNE FINCH, COUNTESS OF WINCHILSEA   *(1661–1720)*

Friendship Between Ephelia and Ardelia   *(1713)*

Eph. What Friendship is, Ardelia show.
Ard. 'Tis to love, as I love you.
Eph. This account, so short (tho' kind)
    Suits not my inquiring mind.
    Therefore farther now repeat: 5
    What is Friendship when complete?
Ard. 'Tis to share all joy and grief;
    'Tis to lend all due relief
    From the tongue, the heart, the hand;
    'Tis to mortgage house and land;   10
    For a friend be sold a slave;
    'Tis to die upon a grave,
    If a friend therein do lie.
Eph. This indeed, tho' carried high,
    This, tho' more than e'er was done   15
    Underneath the rolling sun,

This has all been said before.
Can Ardelia say no more?
Ard. Words indeed no more can show:
    But 'tis to love, *as I love you.*   20

TOPICS FOR CRITICAL THINKING

1. In Finch's dialogue, Ephelia asks Ardelia to show "what Friendship is." Even after Ardelia takes this invitation as an opening to announce her love for Ephelia, the latter presses her to "complete" her definition. How many times does Ephelia urge Ardelia to show what female friendship means? What is the point of Ephelia's repeated questioning?
2. Discuss the ways in which Ardelia actually defines her ideal of friendship.

TOPIC FOR CRITICAL WRITING

How does the poem's dialogue progress from defining friendship in the abstract to an actual pledge of love between the two women?

Poetry is a discourse that fashions as much as reflects masculine and feminine gender roles. Finch's "Friendship Between Ephelia and Ardelia" ends with Ardelia's underscored declaration of the simple fact of her love, which "words indeed no more can show." What Ephelia desires, however, is not just the fact of her friend's love but its seemingly endless construction through performative declaration. Love lyricism gives us the pleasure of rethinking and reexperiencing who we take ourselves to be as male and female desiring subjects as well as whom and what we desire. One way of altering traditional male and female roles is to perform them in language, but with a difference.

This strategy is obviously at work in same-sex appropriations of pastoral tropes that describe one's desire for the beloved as a natural fact. Adrienne Rich's Poem XI from *Twenty-One Love Poems* locates the loved one in a landscape of sensuous natural metaphors that rename the masculine conventions of pastoral literature.

ADRIENNE RICH   *(b. 1929)*

Poem XI, from Twenty-One Love Poems   *(1976)*

Every peak is a crater. This is the law of volcanoes,
making them eternally and visibly female.
No height without depth, without a burning core,
though our straw soles shred on the hardened lava.
I want to travel with you to every sacred mountain   5
smoking within like the sibyl stooped over his tripod,
I want to reach for your hand as we scale the path,
to feel your arteries glowing in my clasp,

never failing to note the small, jewel-like flower
unfamiliar to us, nameless till we rename her,   10
that clings to the slowly altering rock—
that detail outside ourselves that brings us to ourselves,
was here before us, knew we would come, and sees beyond us.

As in the romantic tradition of nature poetry, Rich finds natural objects
that present symbolic correspondences to her inward, psychic states of being.
Here she finds such symbolic correspondences for a distinctively feminine
gender identity in the figure of the volcano whose peak is also a crater. Not
unlike the metaphor that Emily Dickinson chooses for the psychic extremities
of women's experience—"Vesuvius at home"—Rich similarly dwells on the
intensities she experiences as a woman within the "law of volcanoes" that are
"eternally and visibly female. / No height without depth, without a burning
core." Similarly, in the "small, jewel-like flower," the poet encounters something unfamiliar that, paradoxically enough, returns her to herself. Moreover,
that rediscovery involves a same-sex identity shared with the beloved female
"other": a mutual identity achieved through the act of renaming. Just as the
flower is something partly discovered and partly invented through the poet's
power to "rename her," so Rich's love relation to her companion is both passionately affirmed in their heartfelt "clasp" and constructed through poetry's
power to rename that immediate experience.

The primary intensity of same-sex desire takes many forms for women,
and writing during the Harlem Renaissance, the African American poet
Mae V. Cowdery explores the terms of jealousy between a black woman and
her white lover.

MAE V. COWDERY   *(1909–1953)*

Insatiate   *(1936)*

If my love were meat and bread
And sweet cool wine to drink,
They would not be enough,
For I must have a finer table spread
To sate my entity.   5

If her lips were rubies red,
Her eyes two sapphires blue,
Her fingers ten sticks of white jade,
Coral tipped . . . and her hair of purple hue
Hung down in a silken shawl . . .   10
They would not be enough
To fill the coffers of my need.

If her thoughts were arrows
Ever speeding true
Into the core of my mind,   15
And her voice round notes of melody
No nightingale or lark
Could ever hope to sing . . .
Not even these would be enough
To keep my constancy.   20

But if my love did whisper
Her song into another's ear
Or place the tip of one pink nail
Upon another's hand,
Then would I forever be   25
A willing prisoner . . .
Chained to her side by uncertainty!

TOPICS FOR CRITICAL THINKING

1. In what ways does Cowdery present desire as something that exceeds any object that could possibly satisfy it in her opening stanzas?
2. What images represent Cowdery's interracial, same-sex relationship to the lover?

TOPIC FOR CRITICAL WRITING

Examine the poem's assertion of desire for and commitment to the other, paradoxically enough, through the uncertainty concerning the lover's fidelity.

Not unlike Rich's project in *Twenty-One Love Poems*, the African American lesbian poet Audre Lorde also discovers the poet's power to rename her gender in relation to a same-sexed other in "Love Poem."

AUDRE LORDE *(1924–1992)*

Love Poem   *(1971)*

Speak earth and bless me
with what is richest
make sky flow honey out of my hips
rigid as mountains
spread over a valley   5
carved out by the mouth of rain.

And I knew when I entered her I was
high wind in her forest's hollow

fingers whispering sound
honey flowed from the split cup   10
impaled on a lance of tongues
on the tips of her breasts on her navel
and my breath howling into her entrances
through lungs of pain.

Greedy as herring-gulls   15
or a child
I swung out over the earth
over and over again.

Beginning with her opening imperative, or command, verb—*speak*—Lorde
lays emphasis on the power of language to construct, as much as reflect, experience. Here she conjures the earth as her muse to "speak" and thereby "bless"
her as poet and lover.

TOPIC FOR CRITICAL THINKING

Discuss Lorde's use of synaesthesia—the blending of the senses—in such phrases as
"sky flow honey out of my hips" or "fingers whispering sound." How do these usages
add a level of surreal intensity to the already fervent metaphors and similes Lorde employs to depict her embrace of the beloved as a vital commingling of passionate forces?

TOPICS FOR CRITICAL WRITING

1. Examine the ways in which Lorde's figurative language adopts a hard and active
   masculinity in phrases such as "hips / rigid as mountains" or "split cup / impaled on
   a lance of tongues / on the tips of her breasts."
2. Consider the sexual role Lorde adopts in her figurative language, describing, say,
   her "breath / howling into her entrances" or such declarations as "And I knew when
   I entered her I was / high wind in her forests hollow."

Lorde adopts an assertive, masculine persona in relation to her same-sex
"other," but poets have always complicated the ways in which men and
women possess masculine and feminine gender characteristics. Of Shakespeare's 154 sonnets, the first 126 are devoted to a young man while the subsequent sonnets 127–152 are addressed to the sequence's "dark lady." His last
two sonnets dwell on the god Cupid and a maiden worshipper of the goddess
Diana. Some of the first group on the young man unsettle the differences that
traditionally distinguish men from women even as they explore modes of desire in excess of typical romantic conceits, as in Sonnet 20.

WILLIAM SHAKESPEARE (1564–1616)

Sonnet 20 *(1609)*

A woman's face, with nature's own hand painted,
Hast thou, the master mistress of my passion;
A woman's gentle heart, but not acquainted
With shifting change as is false women's fashion;
An eye more bright than theirs, less false in rolling,   5
Gilding the object whereupon it gazeth;
A man in hue all hues in his controlling,
Which steals men's eyes and women's souls amazeth.
And for a woman wert thou first created,
Till Nature as she wrought thee fell a-doting,   10
And by addition me of thee defeated,
By adding one thing to my purpose nothing.
    But since she prick'd thee out for women's pleasure,
    Mine be thy love, and thy love's use their treasure.

TOPICS FOR CRITICAL THINKING

1. How does Shakespeare revise traditional differences between masculinity and femininity in his portrait of the poem's "master mistress"?
2. Discuss Shakespeare's personification of nature in the poem.

TOPIC FOR CRITICAL WRITING

"To prick out" is to select something or someone from a list, but as a noun, the word *prick* also has a sexual connotation. How does the sonnet explore the paradoxes of love and pleasure as they involve gender?

Not unlike Shakespeare, John Donne also complicates gender identifications in his prayer to God imagined as a male lover in his famous Holy Sonnet 14, "Batter My Heart, Three-Personed God."

JOHN DONNE (1572–1631)

Batter My Heart, Three-Personed God *(1633)*

Batter my heart, three-personed God; for You
As yet but knock, breathe, shine, and seek to mend;
That I may rise and stand, o'erthrow me, 'and bend
Your force to break, blow, burn, and make me new.

I, like an usurped town, to'another due,   5
Labor to'admit you, but O, to no end;
Reason, Your viceroy in me, me should defend,
But is captived, and proves weak or untrue.
Yet dearly I love you, 'and would be loved fain,
But am betrothed unto your enemy.   10
Divorce me, untie or break that knot again;
Take me to you, imprison me, for I,
Except you enthrall me, never shall be free,
Nor ever chaste, except you ravish me.

TOPICS FOR CRITICAL THINKING

1. In the opening quatrain unit of this holy sonnet, Donne alludes to the traditional image of Christ the bridegroom who knocks on the door of the heart. Donne presents that biblical figure, however, with a new and arresting violence. Consider how Donne dramatizes the violence of conversion through the poem's hard, plosive *b* sounds in the first quatrain of the poem.
2. Discuss the examples of Donne's figurative language in the poem's second quatrain in his simile of the "usurped town" and his personfication of his reason as a "viceroy." How do you interpret his argument here?

TOPIC FOR CRITICAL WRITING

Examine the paradox of Donne's final musings on divorce, chastity, and his desire that Christ "ravish" him in the poem.

In "Batter My Heart, Three-Personed God," Donne wants a "divorce" from Satan. But unwilling to wait for it, he implores the "three-personed God" to "untie" and even more forcefully "break" the marriage "knot" of his betrothal to the "enemy." By the end of Donne's holy sonnet, the poet has not only prayed for spiritual conversion but, equally important, has imagined masculine gender roles in a new, revolutionary way.

In the poem's final sestet, the third quatrain and concluding couplet introduce the speaker's plea to be made a soulmate to the conventional figure of Christ, the bridegroom. The last six lines turn on the irony set out in the couplet, namely that the speaker's spiritual chastity, paradoxically enough, depends on the force of Christ's masculinity to ravish, or rape, him. Critics generally read Donne's gender positioning here as necessarily feminine. The poet, that is, takes on the female gender role to reinstate the redemptive closure of his remarriage to the church personified in Christ, the ravishing bridegroom. Yet in his rereading of the poem, the Renaissance scholar Richard Rambuss asserts that there is nothing in the poem that warrants such a conventional albeit feminized reading of what remains a distinctively homoerotic sex act between men. Rambuss thus concludes that "it isn't remarriage that the poet says he then desires, but rather something that is, I think, meant to be felt as far more transgressive. For Donne says he wants to be ravished, and hence what is offered as the sonnet's devotional climax is his insistent solicitation that God would rape and enthrall this desirous devotee."

Although both Shakespeare's Sonnet 20 and Donne's "Batter My Heart, Three-Personed God" explore representations of desire between men, it would be a category error to read either as a homosexual lyric. Homosexual identity is a modern concept that emerged only in the nineteenth century. Renaissance scholars such as Alan Bray and Bruce R. Smith are clear on this point. According to Smith,

> No one in England during the sixteenth or seventeenth centuries would have thought of himself as "gay" or "homosexual" for the simple reason that those categories of self-definition did not exist. But that does not mean . . . that there were no men in early modern England whose sexual desires were turned primarily toward other men.

It is not until the nineteenth century with figures such as Walt Whitman that desire between men becomes the basis for identity. "Whitman," as Robert K. Martin reads him, "coincides with and defines a radical change in historical consciousness: the self-conscious awareness of homosexuality as an identity."

Today, the difficulty that some readers have in acknowledging gay identity is compounded, according to the critical theorist Eve Kosofsky Sedgwick, in accepting gay male effeminacy. This cultural resistance to the effeminate male is especially troubling for the gay child. "The crisis for the gay child," according to Professor David Bergman, "is in the tension between other people's views and expectations of him, and the views and expectations he has of himself." The tension in the child's recognition of same-sex desires that transgress traditional family values is the subject of Bergman's poem "Blueberry Man."

DAVID BERGMAN   *(b. 1950)*

Blueberry Man   *(1985)*

I was never the one to spot him walking
slowly up the street, pulling his yellow
wagon. It was always a brother or sister
who'd race home with the news. Then everything
spun into action like gulls at low tide.   5

Mother would shoo the children from the yard
and hide us out of danger in the living room,
warning with harsh whispers not to peek
from the windows and knowing we would anyway,
tracking the blueberry man across the porch   10
to where he knocked at the kitchen door.

Grandfather greeted him. Mother said
she was afraid. But I think she was jealous.
For though I was five or six, I knew I'd
never see such beautiful hair again. Hair   15
like a storybook princess. Great golden skeins,
falling halfway down his back. And such eyes,
freaked like a robin's egg and bobbing
beneath mascara waves of lashes. I remember
the Victory Red lips unfurling like a flag   20
when he spoke and the frilly shirt.

                          My brothers
giggled nervously. But I wasn't scared.
I wanted to pull the chiffon curtains back
and speak. But what would I say? That I knew   25
what it was to be alone? That I had heard
my own family scamper with trepidation
from my door when I was quarantined with
scarlet fever and no one but my mother was
allowed into my room?   30
                          I could have said:
I'm only a child but certain to end an outcast too.
Still, I said nothing, except once, a weak
goodby for which I was roundly scolded.
I used to ride my bike to his house, a tiny   35
cabin covered with angry brambles and
the hiss of intriguing bees, hoping we'd meet.
But he stayed inside during the day when he
wasn't peddling the wares he gathered at night.

One sleepless dawn I saw him coming home   40
with a kerosene lantern in one hand
and a silvery pail in the other.
Mother washed his berries twice to cleanse
them of his memory, as if he communicated
with his touch the fearful urge to dress   45
in women's clothing. For dessert she'd douse
the fruit with milk or pile them on peaks of
sour cream, chubby mountain climbers in the snow.
My brothers ate them greedily. But I
when everyone had left the table, would   50
still be seated, savoring the sweet juice
and the delicate flesh he had brought me.

     In the poem's opening lines, the blueberry man's coming stirs the poet's
whole family into a flurry of simultaneous desire and panic. Paradoxically
enough, he represents both a treat and a taboo. The blueberry vendor's obvi-

ous effeminacy marks him off as an abject figure of sexual transgression for the poet's family.

TOPICS FOR CRITICAL THINKING

1. Examine the parents' attempts to "hide" their children "out of danger" away from the example of the blueberry man. To what extent is the mother's compulsive efforts to "cleanse" the fruit he sells a symptomatic attempt to sanitize and contain the blueberry man's feminized gender identification?
2. Discuss the visual details that feminize the blueberry man. How do these qualities make him a figure of jealousy for the poet's mother?

TOPIC FOR CRITICAL WRITING

How does the poem present the poet's identification with the blueberry man's "quarantined" status as a social outsider?

In discussing gay identity, "the most significant term," writes Bergman,

> and the one from which the other differences derive is otherness. Although a sense of otherness affects us all, the otherness that affects the homosexual—or affects his sense of homosexuality—is more profound. For while otherness is an unavoidable part of any self's awareness of its own subjectivity and its difference to other persons around it, the homosexual suffers a categorical, perhaps even ontological, otherness since he is made to feel his "unlikeness" to the heterosexual acts and persons who gave him being.

Same-sex desire in "Blueberry Man" happens not just as a sexual attraction but, equally important, as a homoerotic identification with the blueberry man's "otherness": his distinctive style of gender identification. But however "other" the blueberry man appears to the poet's "normal" family, he brings the dessert, paradoxically enough, that they all crave. In the poem's final erotic turn, the poet takes sensuous pleasure in the "sweet" fruit, which, through metaphor, is also the blueberry man's gift of "delicate flesh."

Poems for Further Reading and Critical Writing

ELIZABETH BISHOP   *(1911–1979)*

Insomnia   *(1955)*

The moon in the bureau mirror
looks out a million miles
(and perhaps with pride, at herself,
but she never, never smiles)
far and away beyond sleep, or   5
perhaps she's a daytime sleeper.

By the Universe deserted,
she'd tell it to go to hell,
and she'd find a body of water,
or a mirror, on which to dwell.   10
So wrap up care in a cobweb
and drop it down the well

into that world inverted
where left is always right,
where the shadows are really the body,   15
where we stay awake all night,
where the heavens are shallow as the sea
is now deep, and you love me.

TOPICS FOR CRITICAL THINKING

1. Consider the ways in which Bishop's poem is set in a distinctively feminine landscape through her personification of the moon in stanzas one and two.
2. Describe the ways in which Bishop characterizes the moon. How does she assert an
   unconventional identity?

TOPIC FOR CRITICAL WRITING

In considering the title of Bishop's poem, what effect does love have on the world of
the speaker and her lover? How does love bestow a vision of the world that turns life
upside down? Examine the poem's tropes for that "world inverted."

APHRA BEHN   *(1640–1689)*

To the Fair Clarinda, Who Made Love
to Me, Imagined More Than Woman   *(1688)*

By Mrs. B.

Fair lovely maid, or if that title be
Too weak, too feminine for nobler thee
Permit a name that more approaches truth:
And let me call thee lovely charming youth.
This last will justify my soft complaint,   5
While they may serve to lessen my constraint;
And without blushes I the youth pursue,
When so much beauteous woman is in view.
Against thy charms we struggle but in vain;
With thy deluding form thou giv'st us pain,   10
While the bright nymph betrays us to the swain.

In pity to our sex sure thou wer't sent,
That we might love, and yet be innocent:
For sure no crime with thee we can commit;
Or if we should—thy form excuses it.   15
For who, that gathers fairest flowers believes
A snake lies hid beneath the fragrant leaves.

Though beauteous wonder of a different kind,
Soft *Cloris* with the dear *Alexis* joined;
Whene'er the manly part of thee, would plead   20
Though tempts us with the image of the maid,
While we the noblest passions do extend
The love to *Hermes*, *Aphrodite* the friend.

    The seventeenth-century playwright and poet Aphra Behn led an adventurous life with travels to Surinam in the West Indies and a stint as a spy for King Charles II. She wrote for a living after being widowed in 1666. Her published plays include *The Rover* (1677), *Sir Patient Fancy* (1678), *The Roundheads* (1681), and *The City Heiress* (1682). She also was an early experimenter with prose fiction in works such as *Love Letters between a Nobleman and his Sister* (1684–1666), *The Fair Jilt* (1688), *Agnes de Castro* (1688), and *Oroonoko* (1688). Writing in the liberal atmosphere of Restoration England, Behn's poetry demonstrates an unusually frank eroticism, particularly so for a woman writer of that era. Her playful "To the Fair Clarinda, Who Made Love to Me, Imagined More Than Woman" shows a very modern representation of the advantages of same sex relationships.

TOPICS FOR CRITICAL THINKING

1. Discuss the ways in which Behn addresses Clarinda in the poem and in particular how Behn constructs an alternatively gendered identity for her—one less feminine—in the figure of the "charming youth."
2. How does this youth come to embody both feminine and masculine traits?
3. What, according to Behn, are some of the advantages of this same-sex bond over those one might have to the opposite sex?

TOPICS FOR CRITICAL WRITING

1. Compare Behn's representation of her relationship to Clarinda with Finch's dialogue between Ephelia and Ardelia. How would you contrast the latter's "friendship" with Behn's address to Clarinda?
2. Examine the splitting of Clarinda's gendered identity in the final classical allusions to Hermes and Aphrodite.

WALT WHITMAN   *(1819–1892)*

When I Heard at the Close of the Day   *(1881)*

When I heard at the close of the day how my name had been
   receiv'd with plaudits in the capitol, still it was not a
   happy night for me that follow'd,
And else when I carous'd, or when my plans were
   accomplish'd, still I was not happy,
But the day when I rose at dawn from the bed of perfect
   health, refresh'd, singing, inhaling the ripe breath of
   autumn,
When I saw the full moon in the west grow pale and
   disappear in the morning light,
When I wander'd alone over the beach, and undressing   5
   bathed, laughing with the cool waters, and saw the sun
   rise,
And when I thought how my dear friend my lover was on his
   way coming, O then I was happy,
O then each breath tasted sweeter, and all that day my food
   nourish'd me more, and the beautiful day pass'd well,
And the next came with equal joy, and with the next at
   evening came my friend,
And that night while all was still I heard the waters roll
   slowly continually up the shores,
I heard the hissing rustle of the liquid and sands as directed   10
   to me whispering to congratulate me,
For the one I love most lay sleeping by me under the same
   cover in the cool night,
In the stillness in the autumn moonbeams his face was
   inclined toward me,
And his arm lay lightly around my breast—and that night I
   was happy.

The famous American nineteenth-century poet Walt Whitman had several relationships with men and even built his theories of democracy on the passionate "adhesion" among "loving comradeship," as he defines it in "Democratic Vistas":

> I confidently expect a time when there will be seen, running like a half-hid warp through all the myriad audible and visible worldly interests of America, threads of manly friendship, fond and loving, pure and sweet, strong and life-long, carried to degrees hitherto unknown . . . having the deepest relation to general politics. I say democracy infers such loving comradeship, as its most inevitable twin or counter part.

Beyond the many forms "manly friendship" took for Whitman, he enjoyed a long-term relationship with Peter Doyle that began after the Civil War and lasted until the poet's death in 1892. Whitman's most explicit musing on his same-sex identifications come in the "Calamus" section of *Leaves of Grass*, as in his passionate poem "When I Heard at the Close of the Day."

TOPICS FOR CRITICAL THINKING

1. Discuss the poet's opening situation and the catalog of outward successes that, nevertheless, bring him no lasting joy.
2. Contrast the poet's sense of dissatisfaction that opens the poem with the effect the thought of the lover has on Whitman's outlook.

TOPIC FOR CRITICAL WRITING

How does anticipating the lover's arrival change Whitman's perception of the physical world? What details does Whitman use to depict his more vivid participation in the life around him?

MINA LOY   *(1882–1966)*

Poems I, II, IX, from Songs to Joannes   *(1917)*

I

Spawn   of   Fantasies
Silting the appraisable
Pig Cupid   his rosy snout
Rooting erotic garbage
"Once upon a time"   5
Pulls a weed   white star-topped
Among wild oats   sown in mucous-membrane

I would   an   eye in a Bengal light°
Eternity in a sky-rocket
Constellations in an ocean   10
Whose rivers run no fresher
Than a trickle of saliva

These   are suspect places

I must live in my lantern
Trimming subliminal flicker   15
Virginal   to the bellows
Of Experience
                Coloured   glass

---

8 *Bengal light:* A blue signal flare.

II

                    The skin-sack   20
In which a wanton duality
Packed
All the completion of my infructuous impulses
Something the shape of a man
To the casual vulgarity of the merely observant   25
More of a clock-work mechanism
Running down against time
To which I am not paced
        My finger-tips are numb from fretting your hair
A God's door-mat   30
                On the threshold of your mind

IX

When we lifted
Our eye-lids on Love
A cosmos   35
Of coloured voices
And laughing honey

And spermatozoa
At the core of Nothing
In the milk of the Moon   40

The experimental modernist poet Mina Loy began her career as a visual artist with a well-received exhibition at the reputable Salon d'Automne show in Paris in 1905. One of the few women to affiliate with the Italian futurist movement, Loy also had ties to dadaism and surrealism. Her lifestyle was as radically modern as her poetry. Originally published under the title "Love Songs" in the experimental modernist journal *Others*, the opening selections of her *Songs to Joannes* (1917) depict frank, though highly stylized, scenes of desire between men and women.

TOPICS FOR CRITICAL THINKING

1. Discuss Loy's blending of highly figurative language and realistic detail in her images of sexuality in the above selections from *Songs to Joannes*.

2. How does Loy capture the ironies of sexuality and desire in her oxymoronic figure of "Pig Cupid"?

TOPICS FOR CRITICAL WRITING

1. Compare Loy's imagery in stanza two of Poem I with that of Poem IX. What similarities and differences do you see in her depictions of the ecstatic intensities of sexuality?

2. Loy also depicts somewhat obscene images of sexuality's "suspect places" and "casual vulgarity." Discuss the forms these moments take in her poems.

ROBERT DUNCAN   *(1919–1988)*

The Torso: Passages 18   *(1968)*

> Most beautiful! the red-flowering eucalyptus
>   the madrone, the yew
>
>   Is he . . . .
>
> *So thou wouldst smile, and take me in thine arms*
> *The sight of London to my exiled eyes*   5
> *Is as Elysium to a new-come soul*
>
>   If he be Truth
>   I would dwell in the illusion of him
>
> His hands unlocking from chambers of my male body
>
>   such an idea in man's image   10
>
> rising tides that sweep me towards him
>
>   . . . *homosexual?*
>
>   and at the treasure of his mouth
>
>   pour forth my soul
>
>   his soul   commingling   15
>
> I thought a Being more than vast, His body leading
>   into Paradise,   his eyes
>
>   quickening a fire in me,   a trembling
>
> hieroglyph: At the root of the neck
>
> *the clavicle*, for the neck is the stem of the great artery   20
>   upward into his head that is beautiful
>
>   At the rise of the pectoral muscle,
>
> *the nipples*, for the breasts are like sleeping fountains
>   of feeling in man, waiting above the beat of his heart,

shielding the rise and fall of his breath, to be   25
awakend

                    At the axis of his mid hriff

the navel, for in the pit of his stomach the chord from
      which first he was fed has its temple

                    At the root of the groin   30

the pubic hair, for the torso is the stem in which the man
      flowers forth and leads to the stamen of flesh in which
      his seed rises

a wave of need and desire over   taking me

                    cried out my name   35

            (This was long ago; It was another life)

                              and said,

            What do you want of me?

I do not know, I said.   I have fallen in love.   He
      has brought me into heights and depths my heart   40
                  would fear   without him.   His look

      pierces my side • fire eyes •

            I have been waiting for you, he said:
                  I know what you desire

            you do not yet know   but through me •   45

And I am with you everywhere.   In your falling

I have fallen from a high place.   I have raised myself

            from darkness in your   rising

                        wherever you are

my hand in your hand   seeking   the locks, the keys   50

I am there.   Gathering me, you gather

            your Self •

For my Other is not a woman but a man

the King upon whose bosom let me lie.

Robert Duncan was a celebrated avant-garde poet of the San Francisco
Renaissance in the post-World War II era. During the 1950s, at the Black
Mountain school in North Carolina, Duncan, along with Charles Olson and
Robert Creeley, would experiment with serial-form long poems made up of
encyclopedic details linked through repeated tropes, themes, and poetic mo-
tifs. In 1944 at the age of twenty-six, Duncan published "The Homosexual in
Society," a pioneering essay propounding a gay civic and cultural politics. In
his personal life, Duncan lived in a same-sex relationship with Jess Collins
from 1951 until his death in 1988. Duncan's open-form poem "The Torso:
Passages 18" celebrates a vision of homoerotic passion.

TOPICS FOR CRITICAL THINKING

1. The term *torso* derives from *thyrsus*, the Latin word for "stalk" or "stem." The *thyrsus* was also used as a phallic ceremonial object in Bacchanalian rites and rituals.
   How does Duncan inscribe the etymological origins of *torso* in his organic and floral images in the poem?
2. Male poets have long paid tribute to women in the traditional poetic form of the
   blazon that compliments the details of a lover's face and body. How does Duncan
   work within this convention to present a same-sex blazon of the male body?
3. The italicized third stanza and the last italicized line in the poem are quotes from
   Christopher Marlowe's *Edward the Second* that, in part, explores Edward's devotion
   to a young liege Gaveston. Describe the effect of placing this intertext after Duncan's ellipsis in posing the question "Is he . . . homosexual?"

TOPICS FOR CRITICAL WRITING

1. How does Duncan invent, not just reflect, his experience of same-sex desire in his response to the lover's claim to know him: "you do not yet know   but through me"?
2. What biblical tropes of crucifixion and resurrection can you detect in the poem?

OLGA BROUMAS   *(b. 1949)*

The Masseuse   *(1999)*

Always an angel rises from the figure
naked and safe between my towels
as before taboo. It's why I close
my eyes. A smell
precedes him as the heart   5
fills from his bowl. I bow
down to the riddle of the ear,
its embryonic sworl nested with nodes

that calm the uncurled spine,
a maypole among organs.   10
Each day a stranger or almost
crosses my heart to die
from the unsayable
into the thickened beating
of those wings and we are shy.   15
Or frightened as with clothes
on we forget
abysmally what heaven
shares with death: what gypsy vowels
unshackled from the lips   20
rush the impenetrable
mind and the atlas
clicks in my trowel hands.
Crocuses on the threshold's south
side then and now. It goes on   25
like an egret scaling the unruly bands
of atmosphere we have agreed on
by my palms'
erratic longing of the flesh
to try. Toes crack. Hips   30
soften and the spine,
a seaweed in the shallow spume,
undulates like a musical
string by the struck note,
helpless with harmonics.   35
Rock. Cradle the perceptible
scar of the compass, sensible
stigma in a poised blind
of trust angling for reentry,
and the rain, the wind   40
across its face like minnows in the dark
of love schooling the light
will speak to you and you will walk
home dizzy, grazed by the gloaming and the just
illumined stars.   45

Olga Broumas grew up in Greece and came to the United States on a Fulbright exchange program in Architecture and Modern Dance in 1967. A recipient of the prestigious Yale Younger Poets Award ten years later, she
combined her identity as a poet with a career in massage. In 1982 she became
licensed as a bodywork therapist, a vocation she depicts in "The Masseuse."

TOPICS FOR CRITICAL THINKING

1. Explore Broumas's primal tropes of life, death, and resurrection to depict her vocation of therapeutic bodywork.

2. Discuss how figurative language presents Broumas's experience of her physical contact with the bodies of her clients.

TOPIC FOR CRITICAL WRITING

In what ways does Broumas depict embodied desire in the poem? What is the effect of this bodywork on the one addressed at the end of the poem?

RICHARD HARTEIS   *(b. 1946)*

Star Trek III   *(1987)*

The fantasy spaceman
returning from death
greets his captain
gingerly: "Jim?"

Spock's Vulcan father explains   5
that only time will tell
if the priestess' magic
will bring him totally back.
Instead of "the end"
the film's last frames promise,   10
"the adventure continues."

I want to cry a little:
I grew up on these heroes—
to be as good as Kirk . . .

But life is a little closer now.   15
We watch the film together
and I explain the plot

the way one would talk to someone
trapped under ice. My manuals say
I mustn't convey anxiety.   20

I remember the day after
weeks at your bedside when
you said my name finally.

You were IN there,
KNEW me.   25

The same shock the cardiac nurse
felt the year before when she

randomly took the tape from
your sweet eyes and they flew open
as she called your name.   30

We've been in a few
tight spots lately.

All these months.
My loneliness deepens.
I cry in private   35
when you forget my name.

Still, you love me clearly,
whoever I am.

The adventure continues.
                                                                      40

    Richard Harteis has lived with the poet William Meredith since 1971 and, in addition to publishing several volumes of verse, has served in the Peace Corps and pursued careers as a health care worker and teacher. His ludic poem "Star Trek III" explores the frontiers of life and death, finding ways to affirm desire in the face of terminal illness.

TOPICS FOR CRITICAL THINKING

1. How does Harteis, as he says, "explain the plot" of the popular TV and film series *Star Trek?*
2. In what ways does Harteis change the conventional relationship between Kirk and Spock have as colleagues aboard the *Enterprise?*

TOPICS FOR CRITICAL WRITING

1. How do you interpret his phrase "to be as good as Kirk . . ." in stanza three? How does Harteis reinterpret what Kirk should stand for as a role model?
2. How has Harteis's love relationship been compromised by illness, and how has it been deepened by that experience? Compare the final phrase "the adventure continues" with its earlier use in stanza two.

GREGORY CORSO   *(1930–2001)*

Marriage   *(1960)*

Should I get married? Should I be good?
Astound the girl next door with my velvet suit and faustus hood?
Don't take her to movies but to cemeteries
tell all about werewolf bathtubs and forked clarinets

then desire her and kiss her and all the preliminaries   5
and she going just so far and I understanding why
not getting angry saying You must feel! It's beautiful to feel!
Instead take her in my arms lean against an old crooked tombstone
and woo her the entire night the constellations in the sky—

When she introduces me to her parents   10
back straightened, hair finally combed, strangled by a tie,
should I sit with my knees together on their 3rd degree sofa
and not ask Where's the bathroom?
How else to feel other than I am,
often thinking Flash Gordon soap—   15
O how terrible it must be for a young man
seated before a family and the family thinking
We never saw him before! He wants our Mary Lou!
After tea and homemade cookies they ask What do you do for a living?

Should I tell them? Would they like me then?   20
Say All right get married, we're losing a daughter
but we're gaining a son—
And should I then ask Where's the bathroom?

O God, and the wedding! All her family and her friends
and only a handful of mine all scroungy and bearded   25
just wait to get at the drinks and food—
And the priest! he looking at me as if I masturbated
asking me Do you take this woman for your lawful wedded wife?
And I trembling what to say say Pie Glue!
I kiss the bride all those corny men slapping me on the back   30
She's all yours, boy! Ha-ha-ha!
And in their eyes you could see some obscene honeymoon going on—
Then all that absurd rice and clanky cans and shoes
Niagara Falls! Hordes of us! Husbands! Wives! Flowers! Chocolates!
All streaming into cozy hotels   35
All going to do the same thing tonight
The indifferent clerk he knowing what was going to happen
The lobby zombies they knowing what
The whistling elevator man he knowing
The winking bellboy knowing   40
Everybody knowing! I'd almost be inclined not to do anything!
Stay up all night! Stare that hotel clerk in the eye!
Screaming: I deny honeymoon! I deny honeymoon!
running rampant into those almost climactic suites
yelling Radio belly! Cat shovel!   45
O I'd live in Niagara forever! in a dark cave beneath the Falls
I'd sit there the Mad Honeymooner
devising ways to break marriages, a scourge of bigamy
a saint of divorce—

But I should get married I should be good   50
How nice it'd be to come home to her
and sit by the fireplace and she in the kitchen
aproned young and lovely wanting my baby
and so happy about me she burns the roast beef
and comes crying to me and I get up from my big papa chair   55
saying Christmas teeth! Radiant brains! Apple deaf!
God what a husband I'd make! Yes, I should get married!
So much to do! like sneaking into Mr Jones' house late at night
and cover his golf clubs with 1920 Norwegian books
Like hanging a picture of Rimbaud° on the lawnmower   60
like pasting Tannu Tuva postage stamps all over the picket fence
like when Mrs Kindhead comes to collect for the Community Chest
grab her and tell her There are unfavorable omens in the sky!
And when the mayor comes to get my vote tell him
When are you going to stop people killing whales!   65
And when the milkman comes leave him a note in the bottle
Penguin dust, bring me penguin dust, I want penguin dust—

Yet if I should get married and it's Connecticut and snow
and she gives birth to a child and I am sleepless, worn,
up for nights, head bowed against a quiet window, the past behind me,   70
finding myself in the most common of situations a trembling man
knowledged with responsibility not twig-smear nor Roman coin soup—
O what would that be like!
Surely I'd give it for a nipple a rubber Tacitus°
For a rattle a bag of broken Bach records   75
Tack Della Francesca° all over its crib
Sew the Greek alphabet on its bib
And build for its playpen a roofless Parthenon

No, I doubt I'd be that kind of father
Not rural not snow no quiet window   80
but hot smelly tight New York City
seven flights up, roaches and rats in the walls
a fat Reichian° wife screeching over potatoes Get a job!
And five nose running brats in love with Batman
And the neighbors all toothless and dry haired   85
like those hag masses of the 18th century
all wanting to come in and watch TV
The landlord wants his rent

---

60 *Rimbaud*: Arthur Rimbaud (1854–1891), French symbolist poet.   74 *Tacitus*: Cornelius
Tacitus (A.D. 55–A.D. 117), Roman historian.   76 *Della Francesca*: Piero Della Francesca
(1420?–1492), Italian painter of the Renaissance.   83 *Reichian*: Wilhelm Reich (1897–1957),
psychological theorist of sexual pleasure.

Grocery store Blue Cross Gas & Electric Knights of Columbus
Impossible to lie back and dream Telephone snow, ghost parking—   90
No! I should not get married! I should never get married!
But—imagine if I were married to a beautiful sophisticated woman
tall and pale wearing an elegant black dress and long black gloves
holding a cigarette holder in one hand and a highball in the other
and we lived high up in a penthouse with a huge window   95
from which we could see all of New York and even farther on clearer days
No, can't imagine myself married to that pleasant prison dream—

O but what about love? I forget love
not that I am incapable of love
it's just that I see love as odd as wearing shoes—   100
I never wanted to marry a girl who was like my mother
And Ingrid Bergman was always impossible
And there's maybe a girl now but she's already married
And I don't like men and—
but there's got to be somebody!   105
Because what if I'm 60 years old and not married,
all alone in a furnished room with pee stains on my underwear
and everybody else is married! All the universe married but me!

Ah, yet well I know that were a woman possible as I am possible
then marriage would be possible—   110
Like SHE° in her lonely alien gaud waiting her Egyptian lover
so I wait—bereft of 2,000 years and the bath of life.

Gregory Corso was born in 1930 in Greenwich Village and was brought
up in foster homes until he was arrested for petty theft at the age of sixteen.
After spending three years in prison, he met the Beat poet Allen Ginsberg,
who gave Corso encouragement as an emerging poet. Along with Ginsberg,
Jack Kerouac, William S. Burroughs, and Gary Snyder, Corso became one of
the more celebrated figures of the Beat generation. In his novel the *Subterraneans* (1958), Jack Kerouac based his character of Yuri Gregorovic on Gregory Corso. Corso's famous Beat poem "Marriage" presents an absurdist look
at the conventions of married life in the postwar era.

TOPICS FOR CRITICAL THINKING

1. In Corso's opening lines he asks "Should I get married? Should I be good?" How
   might marriage be associated with success, "goodness," and normality in the cultural milieu of the late 1950s and early 1960s when Corso wrote "Marriage"?

2. "Marriage" depicts several stereotypical scenarios of courtship, marital vows, hon-
   eymooning, and so on. Discuss these scenes and Corso's parodies of them.

___

111 *SHE*: An 1887 novel by H. Rider Haggard.

1. How does Corso use the institution of marriage to satirize the wider public sphere of society in the 1950s?
2. Corso employs language as a subversive medium for performing his sense of the absurdities of existence. Discuss his use of verbal non sequiturs such as "Radio belly" and "penguin dust." How do these and other comic phrases jar us out of conventional and habitual thinking?

Critical Perspective: On Sexual Representation in John Donne's Holy Sonnet 14

"Conversely, Achsah Guibbory reads 'Batter my heart' in terms that not only heterosexualize Donne's coupling of salvation and sexual violation, but thoroughly domesticate the poem as well. In her chapter on Donne for the *Cambridge Companion to English Poetry: Donne to Marvell*, Guibbory describes the sonnet's amorous scenario this way: the speaker, she writes, is 'like a woman who loves one man (God) but is betrothed to another (Satan), and wants to be rescued, even by force.' Thus, 'Christ is the bridegroom,' while the poet adopts the 'conventionally "feminine," passive role of bride.' Yet the connubial narrative Guibbory reads into 'Batter my heart,' while orthodox enough in form, is unwarranted by the sonnet itself, this critic taming Donne's poem of the very outrageousness that is surely its point. For although Donne sees himself as currently betrothed to the devil, he never asks God to intervene and make a proper 'bride' out of him. The sonnet, in other words, fails to end with the expected and complementary call for a re-betrothal to Christ as a more appropriate spouse for the Christian. Indeed, there is little that is proper about Donne's sonnet and its multiply metaphorized scheme of redemption, one that is predicated upon a series of violent and violative actions: the Godhead is to take a battering ram to a hard heart; to besiege and steal away a town that is 'due' to another; to provoke a divorce. And, after all this, it isn't remarriage that the poet says he then desires, but rather something that is, I think, meant to be felt as far more transgressive. For Donne says he wants to be ravished, and hence what is offered as the sonnet's devotional climax is his insistent solicitation that God would rape and enthrall this desirous devotee. . . .

"Similarly, nowhere in 'Batter my heart' does Donne apostrophize himself or his soul as 'she'; nor does he accord himself the position of a 'woman,' much less a bride, over the course of the poem's envisioned path to redemption. Instead, despite enduring cultural proscriptions that have tended generally, though not monolithically, to feminize any body subject to penetration, Donne's desire in view of divine ravishment remains bawdily assertive, even priapic: 'That I may rise, and stand, o'erthrow me' (line 3). Thus, to return to Fish's formulation, while the poet may be spreading his legs and his cheeks— 'I . . . / Labour to admit you, but oh, to no end' (lines 5–6)—being so taken here does not entail effeminization or castration. Indeed, it is as though Donne wants the Godhead to ravish him, 'to break that knot again,' *in order that* he will be rendered potent, erect. Moreover, if there is any taking on of a feminized subject position in 'Batter my heart,' it is one Donne looks to abjure in seeking severance from the devil: 'Divorce me, . . . / Take me to you' (lines 11–12). Satan is the one who has made a 'woman' of him, a rectifiable situation if only God would himself 'rise' (as Donne likewise urges him to do in 'As due by many titles') and finally take him as his own, ravish him, make more of a man of him."

—Richard Rambuss, from *Closet Devotions* (1998)

Critical Perspective: On Lesbian Existence and the Lesbian Continuum

"I have chosen to use the terms *lesbian existence* and *lesbian continuum* because the word *lesbianism* has a clinical and limiting ring. *Lesbian existence* suggests both the fact of the historical presence of lesbians and our continuing creation of the meaning of that existence. I mean the term *lesbian continuum* to include a range—through each woman's life and throughout history—of woman-identified experience, not simply the fact that a woman has had or consciously desired genital sexual experience with another woman. If we expand it to embrace many more forms of primary intensity between and among women, including the sharing of a rich inner life, the bonding against male tyranny, the giving and receiving of practical and political support, if we can also hear it in such associations as *marriage resistance* and the 'haggard' behavior identified by Mary Daly (obsolete meanings 'intractable,' 'willful,' 'wanton,' and 'unchaste,' 'a woman reluctant to yield to wooing'),[45] we begin to grasp breadths of female history and psychology which have lain out of reach as a consequence of limited, mostly clinical, definitions of *lesbianism*.

"Lesbian existence comprises both the breaking of a taboo and the rejection of a compulsory way of life. It is also a direct or indirect attack on male right of access to women. But it is more than these, although we may first begin to perceive it as a form of naysaying to patriarchy, an act of resistance. It has, of course, included isolation, self-hatred, breakdown, alcoholism, suicide, and intrawoman violence; we romanticize at our peril what it means to love and act against the grain, and under heavy penalties; and lesbian existence has been lived (unlike, say, Jewish or Catholic existence) without access to any knowledge of a tradition, a continuity, a social underpinning. The destruction of records and memorabilia and letters documenting the realities of lesbian existence must be taken very seriously as a means of keeping heterosexuality

---

45. Mary Daly, *Gyn/Ecology: The Metaethics of Radical Feminism* (Boston: Beacon Press, 1978), p 15.

compulsory for women, since what has been kept from our knowledge is joy, sensuality, courage, and community, as well as guilt, self-betrayal, and pain.[46] . . .

"As the term *lesbian* has been held to limiting clinical associations in its patriarchal definition, female friendship and comradeship have been set apart from the erotic, thus limiting the erotic itself. But as we deepen and broaden the range of what we define as lesbian existence, as we delineate a lesbian continuum, we begin to discover the erotic in female terms: as that which is unconfined to any single part of the body or solely to the body itself; as an energy not only diffuse but, as Audre Lorde has described it, omnipresent in 'the sharing of joy, whether physical, emotional, psychic,' and in the sharing of work; as the empowering joy which 'makes us less willing to accept powerlessness, or those other supplied states of being which are not native to me, such as resignation, despair, self-effacement, depression, self-denial.'"[48]

—Adrienne Rich, from "Compulsory Heterosexuality and
Lesbian Existence" (1980)

Critical Perspective: On Sexual Knowledge, Power, and Ideology in Shakespeare's England

"Foucault's model of how sex is 'put into discourse' points us to the two things we need to look for: 'knowledge' and 'power.' Concerning 'knowledge,' the French language allows Foucault to make an important distinction that is sometimes lost in Robert Hurley's English translation. The 'special knowledges' that Foucault speaks of in connection with bodily pleasure, controls and resistances, and talk about sex are *connaissances*, knowledge in the sense of acquaintance, familiarity, experience. (Compare our borrowed term *connoisseur*.) The knowledge that Foucault allies with power is, on the other hand, *savoir*, knowledge in the sense of learning, erudition, ideas. In Foucault's formulation, experience (*connaissances*) is a function of ideology (*savoir*). The experience of sexual desire at a given moment in history is shaped by the ideas that people happen to entertain at that historical moment. To avoid confusing these two different senses of knowledge, we should perhaps prefer the term 'ideology' as a coordinate with power.

"'Ideology' is one aspect of sex put into discourse; 'power' is the other. The power implicit in a text is ideology put into action. It is a speaker exert-

---

46. "In a hostile world in which women are not supposed to survive except in relation with and in service to men, entire communities of women were simply erased. History tends to bury what it seeks to reject" (Blanche W. Cook, "'Women Alone Stir My Imagination': Lesbianism and the Cultural Tradition," *Signs: Journal of Women in Culture and Society* 4, no. 4 [Summer 1979]: 719–720). The Lesbian Herstory Archives in New York City is one attempt to preserve contemporary documents on lesbian existence—a project of enormous value and meaning, working against the continuing censorship and obliteration of relationships, networks, communities in other archives and elsewhere in the culture.

48. Audre Lorde, "Uses of the Erotic: The Erotic as Power," in *Sister Outsider* (Trumansburg, N.Y.: Crossing Press, 1984).

ing control over a listener, a writer exerting control over a reader. It is a listener or a reader internalizing the text and exerting control over himself. Power, in Foucault's view, is not just a matter of negative prohibitions, a central authority telling people what they may and may not do, what they may and may not feel. Power is also a matter of positive excitations: it is people, situations, and objects that a particular culture endows with erotic value. That is to say, sexuality is not simply *subject* to power; it *manifests* power. To understand homosexuality in early modern England we need to investigate not just what was prohibited but what was actively homoeroticized. What we discover is a startling ambiguity. The one salient fact about homosexuality in early modern England, as in early modern Europe generally, is the disparity that separates the extreme punishments prescribed by law and the apparent tolerance, even positive valuation, of homoerotic desire in the visual arts, in literature, and . . . in the political power structure. What are we to make of a culture that could consume popular prints of Apollo embracing Hyacinth and yet could order hanging for men who acted on the very feelings that inspire that embrace?"

—Bruce Smith, from *Homosexual Desire in
Shakespeare's England* (1991)

37   Postcolonial Poetics

www The word *postcolonial* **Web** designates both a period term and a set of theoretical issues emerging from the literature and culture of Europe's former colonies. The rise of national and international independence movements of the twentieth century reflects the breakup of Europe's colonial powers that at the time of World War I ruled over some 85 percent of the globe. In the post-World War II era, much of world literature reflected shifting social and cultural arrangements that once defined the imperial centers of power against their colonial margins in India, Africa, the Middle East, Asia, and the Pacific rim. Thus, when poet and Nobel laureate Derek Walcott composed "A Far Cry from Africa," he not only wrote as a West Indian author in the context of world literature, but, equally important, he also expanded the frontiers of **postcolonial** literature.

DEREK WALCOTT   *(b. 1930)*

A Far Cry from Africa   *(1962)*

A wind is ruffling the tawny pelt
Of Africa. Kikuyu,° quick as flies,
Batten upon the bloodstreams of the veldt.
Corpses are scattered through a paradise.
Only the worm, colonel of carrion, cries: 5
"Waste no compassion on these separate dead!"
Statistics justify and scholars seize
The salients of colonial policy.
What is that to the white child hacked in bed?
To savages, expendable as Jews?   10

Threshed out by beaters, the long rushes break
In a white dust of ibises whose cries
Have wheeled since civilization's dawn
From the parched river or beast-teeming plain.
The violence of beast on beast is read   15
As natural law, but upright man

---

2 *Kikuyu:* Mau Mau secret society of the "burning spear."

Seeks his divinity by inflicting pain.
Delirious as these worried beasts, his wars
Dance to the tightened carcass of a drum,
While he calls courage still that native dread   20
Of the white peace contracted by the dead.

Again brutish necessity wipes its hands
Upon the napkin of a dirty cause, again
A waste of our compassion, as with Spain,°
The gorilla wrestles with the superman.   25
I who am poisoned with the blood of both,
Where shall I turn, divided to the vein?
I who have cursed
The drunken officer of British rule, how choose
Between this Africa and the English tongue I love?   30
Betray them both, or give back what they give?
How can I face such slaughter and be cool?
How can I turn from Africa and live?

Published in 1962, Walcott's poem addresses the disintegration of British
rule over East Africa in Kenya. Specifically, Walcott probes the struggle of the
Kikuyu tribesmen against the British government and settler population over
such issues as land ownership, burdensome taxation, educational access, and
civil rights concerns generally. This social conflict gave birth to the Kikuyu
secret society of the "burning spear," or *Mau Mau,* which led a violent campaign against colonial rule beginning in 1952. Allegedly implicated in the Lari
massacre of 1953, the *Mau Mau* became the object of British reprisals under a
declared state of emergency. By 1956, more than 11,000 Kenyan rebels had
been killed and another 20,000 arrested. Despite this colonial crackdown, the
nationalist leader Jomo Kenyatta, who had been jailed in 1953, prevailed in
ousting British rule, becoming prime minister over an independent Kenya the
year after Walcott's poem was published.

"A Far Cry from Africa," however, does not just allude to colonial policy;
equally important, it stages the distinctive dilemma of postcolonial **hybridity**.
The *American Heritage Dictionary* defines a hybrid as the "offspring of geneti-
cally dissimilar parents or stock . . . [and, by implication] something of mixed
origin or composition." Reflecting the lived relationship of imperial center
and colonial margin, the term *hybridity* in postcolonial studies describes the
hyphenated subject of colonial rule or, in Leela Gandhi's words from *Postcolonial Theory: A Critical Introduction* (1998), "the Janus-faced bearer of a split
consciousness or a double vision." In "A Far Cry from Africa," Walcott's double vision begins with an ethical dilemma. He cannot wholly affirm either side
of the conflict when both are implicated in the murder of innocents. What do
statistics or colonial policy matter, he asks "to the white child hacked in bed? /
To savages, expendable as Jews." In the poem, the dilemma of split loyalties is

24 *Spain:* Spanish Civil War, 1936–1939.

not just an intellectual abstraction but something played along the pulses. The poet does not have the luxury of choosing between colonial and post-colonial identities. "I," he realizes, "who am poisoned with the blood of both, / Where shall I turn, divided to the vein?"

For Walcott, the political clash in Kenya not only implicates him at the level of the divided self but alerts him, as poet, to his conflicted relation to colonial language. He awakens to a lived understanding of how identity is always already underwritten by a prior linguistic hybridity. The literary understanding of postcolonial discourse derives, in part, from the critical theory of the Russian formalist critic Mikhail Bakhtin. Specifically, Bakhtin views language usage in literature and in everyday life not as unitary or monolithic but "dialogic" in nature. Language comes to us as already marked by contradictory social usage. In *The Dialogic Imagination* (1981) he writes that each verbal coinage is "a mixture of two social languages within the limits of a single utterance, an encounter, within the arena of an utterance, between two different linguistic consciousnesses, separated from one another by an epoch, by social differentiation, or by some other factor." As poet, Walcott performs the dialogic utterance by simultaneously avowing and cursing his inherited language, steeped as it is in a history of colonial domination:

> I who have cursed
> The drunken officer of British rule, how choose
> Between this Africa and the English tongue I love?

In the poem's last four lines, which all end in questions, Walcott stages that impossibility of choice as the distinctive social position of the postcolonial subject. The hybrid, in-between space of postcolonial speaking, moreover, is inscribed from the beginning in the "cry" of the poem's title. Not insignificantly, the cry intones the dialogism of a split utterance. Here the syntax of the poem's title communicates a mixed message. It can be read either as a prepositional phrase or as a phrase of possession: as either a far-away cry addressing the poet "from Africa" (possession) or as the poet's cry voiced at a far distance away "from Africa" (preposition). It is the challenge of postcolonial hybridity to hear and utter each far cry at the same time.

The postcolonial acknowledgment of hybridity—the fact that one's language, art, and identity are already shaped by the discourse of imperial powers—is not necessarily a disabling recognition. Such influences, once mastered, can be voiced with a difference: in ways that subvert, parody, and baffle colonial rule. In his Introduction to *Poems of Black Africa* (1975), Nobel Prize laureate Wole Soyinka writes:

> A distinct quality in all great poets does exercise a ghostly influence in other writers, but this need not be cause for self-flagellation. The resulting work is judged by its capacity to move ahead or sideways, by the thoroughness of ingestion within a new organic mould, by the original strength of the new entity. Modern African poems which betray traces of an internal dialogue are often accused of alien affectation, but examination of traditional poetry reveals that it too is built on a densely packed matrix of references (and not, as is sometimes claimed to the contrary, on simplistic narrative).

One technique of presenting the "densely packed matrix" of postcolonial poetry is through a discursive mimicry. "The emerging consensus on postcolonial literary practice has it," writes Gandhi, "that the most radical anticolonial writers are 'mimic men,' whose generic misappropriations constantly transgress the received and orthodox boundaries of 'literariness.' . . . Accordingly, the paradigmatic moment of anti-colonial counter-textuality is seen to begin with the first indecorous mixing of Western genres with local content."

Yambo Ouologuem, the Mali-born and Paris-educated African writer whose novel *Le Devoir de Violence (Bound to Violence)* won the Prix Renaudot in 1968, employs such mimicry in his ironic poem "Tomatoes." There, his poetic persona as "mimic man," parodies the colonial stereotypes of the African "other" as primitive cannibal and as sloganizing political nationalist.

YAMBO OUOLOGUEM   *(b. 1948)*

Tomatoes   *(1966)*

People think I'm a cannibal
But you know what people say

People say I've got red gums but who has
White ones
Up the tomatoes   5

People say there are not nearly so many tourists
Now
But you know
This isn't America and nobody
Has the money   10

People think it's my fault and are scared
But look
My teeth are white not red
I've not eaten anybody

People are rotten they say I scoff   15
Baked tourists
Or maybe grilled
Baked or grilled was my order
They don't say anything just keep looking uneasily at my gums
Up the tomatoes   20

Everyone knows that in an agricultural country there's agriculture
Up the vegetables

Everyone knows that vegetables
Well you can't live on the vegetables you grow
And that I'm quite well developed for someone underdeveloped   25
Miserable scum living off the tourists
Down with my teeth

People suddenly surrounded me
Tied me up
Threw me down   30
At the feet of justice
Cannibal or not cannibal
Answer

Ah you think you're so clever
So proud of yourself   35

Well we'll see I'm going to settle your account
Have you anything to say
Before you are sentenced to death

I shouted Up the tomatoes

People are rotten and women curious you know   40
There was one of these in the curious circle
In her rasping voice sort of bubbling like a saucepan
With a hole in it
Shrieked
Slit open his belly   45
I'm sure father is still inside

There weren't any knives
Naturally enough among the vegetarians
Of the western world
So they got a Gillette blade   50
And carefully
Slit
Slat
Plop
Slit open my belly   55

Inside flourishing rows of tomatoes
Watered by streams of palm wine
Up the tomatoes

TOPICS FOR CRITICAL THINKING

1. Describe the colonial stereotypes and attitudes that Ouologuem parodies in "Tomatoes."

2. How does he contrast America with conditions in his home state?

TOPIC FOR CRITICAL WRITING

How does the poet reveal the tourists as, in fact, more violent than the "natives" they fear? How does Ouologuem mimic colonial language in phrasings such as "settle your account"?

Colonial mimicry, according to postcolonial theorist Homi Bhabha, mines the sly contradictions between the discourses of deference toward and defiance of imperial authority: "Between the Western sign and its colonial signification," he writes in *The Location of Culture* (1994), "there emerges a map of misreading that embarrasses the righteousness of recordation and its certainty of good government . . . a range of differential knowledges and positionalities that both estrange its 'identity' [to] produce new forms of knowledge, new modes of differentiation, new sites of power."

Imperial representations of the colonial subject are not nearly as transparent as they were, say, in the 1950s thanks, in part, to such works of critical theory as Edward Said's pioneering book *Orientalism* (1978). In it, Said makes the point that the empire's knowledge of the colonies is a form of power exerted over colonial peoples. Going back to nineteenth-century European scholarship, Said reveals the ways in which its system of stereotyped representations and ideological assumptions projected a version of the Orient— Asia, India, the Middle East, and Far East—that was "other" to the imagined ideals of Western society. A set of ideological oppositions projected the West as active in relation to Oriental passivity, as masculine as opposed to feminine, normative versus exotic, intellectually superior versus culturally inferior, advanced versus backward, dominate versus subordinate, and so on.

Thinking critically about the ways in which the imperial center casts such negative stereotypes onto the colonial margins is the first step toward conceiving new forms of representational agency. Such emerging, cosmopolitan forms of identity are made possible by counter-discourses that will "write back" to the imperial centers of colonial power. These new, postcolonial forms of writing will belong neither wholly to the Euro-American first world nor to the third world of the former colonies but somewhere in-between, in the literature of postcolonial hybridity.

Poems for Further Reading and Critical Writing

Ha Jin *(b. 1956)*

Ways of Talking   *(1996)*

We used to like talking about grief.
Our journals and letters were packed
with losses, complaints, and sorrows.

Even if there was no grief
we wouldn't stop lamenting   5
as though longing for the charm
of a distressed face.

Then we couldn't help expressing grief.
So many things descended without warning:
labor wasted, loves lost, houses gone,   10
marriages broken, friends estranged,
ambitions worn away by immediate needs.
Words lined up in our throats
for a good whining.
Grief seemed like an endless river—   15
the only immortal flow of life.

After losing a land and then giving up a tongue,
we stopped talking of grief.
Smiles began to brighten our faces.
We laugh a lot, at our own mess.   20
Things become beautiful,
even hailstones in the strawberry fields.

LÉOPOLD SÉDAR SENGHOR   *(1906–2001)*

Prayer to the Masks   *(1964)*

Masks! O Masks!
Black mask, red mask, you white-and-black masks
Masks of the four cardinal points where the Spirit blows
I greet you in silence!
And you, not the least of all, Ancestor with the lion head.   5
You keep this place safe from women's laughter
And any wry, profane smiles
You exude the immortal air where I inhale
The breath of my Fathers.
Masks with faces without masks, stripped of every dimple   10
And every wrinkle
You created this portrait, my face leaning
On an altar of blank paper
And in your image, listen to me!
The Africa of empires is dying—it is the agony   15
Of a sorrowful princess
And Europe, too, tied to us at the navel.
Fix your steady eyes on your oppressed children
Who give their lives like the poor man his last garment.
Let us answer "present" at the rebirth of the World   20

As white flour cannot rise without the leaven.
Who else will teach rhythm to the world
Deadened by machines and cannons?
Who will sound the shout of joy at daybreak to wake
    orphans and the dead? 25
Tell me, who will bring back the memory of life
To the man of gutted hopes?
They call us men of cotton, coffee, and oil
They call us men of death.
But we are men of dance, whose feet get stronger 30
As we pound upon firm ground.

WOLE SOYINKA   *(b. 1934)*

Telephone Conversation   *(1960)*

The price seemed reasonable, location
Indifferent. The landlady swore she lived
Off premises. Nothing remained
But self-confession. "Madam," I warned,
"I hate a wasted journey—I am African."   5
Silence. Silenced transmission of
Pressurized good-breeding. Voice, when it came,
Lipstick coated, long gold-rolled
Cigarette-holder pipped. Caught I was, foully.
"HOW DARK?" . . . I had not misheard . . . "ARE YOU LIGHT   10
OR VERY DARK?" Button B. Button A. Stench
Of rancid breath of public hide-and-speak.
Red booth. Red pillar box. Red double-tiered
Omnibus squelching tar. It *was* real! Shamed
By ill-mannered silence, surrender   15
Pushed dumbfoundment to beg simplification.
Considerate she was, varying the emphasis—
"ARE YOU DARK? OR VERY LIGHT?" Revelation came.
"You mean—like plain or milk chocolate?"
Her assent was clinical, crushing in its light   20
Impersonality. Rapidly, wave-length adjusted,
I chose, "West African sepia"—and as afterthought,
"Down in my passport." Silence for spectroscopic
Flight of fancy, till truthfulness clanged her accent
Hard on the mouthpiece. "WHAT'S THAT?" conceding   25
"DON'T KNOW WHAT THAT IS." "Like brunette."
"THAT'S DARK, ISN'T IT?" "Not altogether.
Facially, I am brunette, but madam, you should see
The rest of me. Palm of my hand, soles of my feet
Are a peroxide blonde. Friction, caused—   30
Foolishly, madam—by sitting down, has turned
My bottom raven black—One moment, madam!"—sensing
Her receiver rearing on the thunderclap
About my ears—"Madam," I pleaded, "wouldn't you rather
See for yourself?"   35

ADRIAN OKTENBERG   *(b. 1947)*

A Young Sniper   *(1997)*

A YOUNG sniper   A single sparrow
    A sparrow crosses the air
    in Sniper Alley   His eye
is briefly on the sparrow   magnified   in his lens
    He enjoys a pretty sight   5
He can see   anyone who moves   into the open
in search of food or water   or in search of a hasty death
as easily as if he were watching a film
    a thriller in which he is the shooter the hero the man with the gun
    his finger rests lightly on the trigger   ready to squeeze   10
    his own personal film and he can   shoot any one he likes
He is calm and happy   at ease   the city is at his feet
He knows he is free
His eye is on the sparrow   and I am here below
I know he is watching me   I live   15
a few blocks from Sniper Alley and I go   in order to live
    across the open space   there is no way to judge
the degree of safety or danger   in this topsy-turvy world
    you must go   this choice too has been taken from you
    by this war   20
the whole of the Balkans is but a mote   in God's glass eye
    a single slap   there is no noise   she doesn't hear a noise
sprawled on the pavement, skirt splayed above her waist, blood
    comes from somewhere, she doesn't know where
She has a daughter she thinks of her daughter she is unable to move   25

He knows he is free
His eye is on the sparrow
and I know he is watching me

FAIZ AHMED FAIZ   (1911–1984)

A Prison Evening   (1991)

Translated by Agha Shahid Ali

Each star a rung,
night comes down the spiral
staircase of the evening.
The breeze passes by so very close
as if someone just happened to speak of love.   5
In the courtyard,
the trees are absorbed refugees
embroidering maps of return on the sky.
On the roof,
the moon—lovingly, generously—   10
is turning the stars
into a dust of sheen.
From every corner, dark-green shadows,
in ripples, come towards me.
At any moment they may break over me,   15
like the waves of pain each time I remember
this separation from my lover.
This thought keeps consoling me:
though tyrants may command that lamps be smashed
in rooms where lovers are destined to meet,   20
they cannot snuff out the moon, so today,
nor tomorrow, no tyranny will succeed,
no poison of torture make me bitter,
if just one evening in prison
can be so strangely sweet,   25
if just one moment anywhere on this earth.

TASLIMA NASRIN   (b. 1962)

Border   (1995)

Translated by Carolyne Wright and Farida Sarkar

I'm going to move ahead.
Behind me my whole family is calling,
my child is pulling at my *sari*-end,
my husband stands blocking the door,
but I will go.   5
There's nothing ahead but a river

I will cross.
I know how to swim but they
won't let me swim, won't let me cross.

There's nothing on the other side of the river   10
                but a vast expanse of fields
but I'll touch this emptiness once
and run against the wind, whose whooshing sound
makes me want to dance. I'll dance someday
and then return.   15

I've not played keep-away for years
                as I did in childhood.
I'll raise a great commotion playing keep-away someday
and then return.

For years I haven't cried with my head   20
                in the lap of solitude.
I'll cry to my heart's content someday
and then return.

There's nothing ahead but a river
and I know how to swim.   25
Why shouldn't I go? I'll go.

Jayanta Mahapatra   *(b. 1928)*

Main Temple Street, Puri   *(1987)*

Children, brown as earth, continue to laugh away
at cripples and mating mongrels.
Nobody ever bothers about them.

The temple points to unending rhythm.

On the dusty street the colour of shorn scalp   5
there are things moving all the time
and yet nothing seems to go away from sight.

Injuries drowsy with the heat.

And that sky there,
claimed by inviolable authority,   10
hanging on to its crutches of silence.

CHITRA BANERJEE DIVAKARUNI *(b. 1957)*

Song of the Fisher Wife *(1991)*

He pushes out the boat, black skeleton
against the pale east. His veins
are blue cords. Sun scours the ocean
with its red nails. I hand him
curds and rice wrapped in leaves. Sand   5
wells over my feet, rotting smell
of seaweed. I sing with the wives.

> *O husbands, muzzle the great wave,*
> *leap the dark. Bring back boats*
> *filled with fish like silver smiles,*   10
> *silver bracelets for our arms.*

All day I dry the fish, the upturned eyes,
the dead, grinning jaws. How stiff
flesh feels, the flaking layers
under my hand. Salt has cracked   15
my palms open. The odor crusts me.
My eyes are flecked with sand
and waiting. How well I learn
by the dryness in my mouth
to tell the coming storm.   20

> *O husbands, no fear*
> *though the sky's breath is black.*
> *We line the calling shore, faithful.*
> *Lip and eye and loin, we keep you*
> *from the jagged wind.*   25

They say all heard the crack and yell,
the boat exploding into splintered air.
Searched for hours. They strip
my widowed arms, shave off my hair.
Thrust me beyond the village walls.   30
Nights of no-moon they will come to me,
grunting, heaving, grinding
the damp sand into my naked back,
men with cloths over their faces.

> *O husband, sent by my evil luck*   35
> *into the great wave's jaw,*
> *do you ride the ocean's boiling back,*

eyes phosphorus, sea-lichen hair, gleam
of shell-studded skin, to see
my forehead branded whore?   40

Note: In many coastal villages in India, it is believed that the wife's virtue keeps her husband safe at sea. Widows are often outcast and forced into becoming prostitutes in order to survive.

SHU TING   *(b. 1952)*

Assembly Line   *(1991)*

Translated by Carolyn Kizer

In time's assembly line
Night presses against night.
We come off the factory night-shift
In line as we march towards home.
Over our heads in a row   5
The assembly line of stars
Stretches across the sky.
Beside us, little trees
Stand numb in assembly lines.

The stars must be exhausted   10
After thousands of years
Of journeys which never change.
The little trees are all sick,
Choked on smog and monotony,
Stripped of their color and shape.   15
It's not hard to feel for them;
We share the same tempo and rhythm.

Yes, I'm numb to my own existence
As if, like the trees and stars
—perhaps just out of habit   20
—perhaps just out of sorrow,
I'm unable to show concern
For my own manufactured fate.

Bits of Reminiscence   *(1991)*

Translated by Carolyn Kizer

A toppled wine-cup,
A stone path floating beneath the moon
Where the grass was trampled:
One azalea branch left lying there . . .

Eucalyptus trees begin to spin   5
In a collage of stars
As I sit on the rusted anchor,
The dizzy sky reflected in my eyes.

A book held up to shut out candlelight;
Fingers lightly at your mouth;   10
In the fragile cup of silence
A dream, half-illumined, half-obscure.

Critical Perspective: On Postcolonial Resistance

"The emergence of anti-colonial and 'independent' nation-States after colonialism is frequently accompanied by a desire to forget the colonial past. This
'will-to-forget' takes a number of historical forms, and is impelled by a variety of cultural and political motivations. Principally, postcolonial amnesia is
symptomatic of the urge for historical self-invention or the need to make a
new start—to erase painful memories of colonial subordination. As it happens, histories, much as families, cannot be freely chosen by a simple act of
will, and newly emergent postcolonial nation-States are often deluded and
unsuccessful in their attempts to disown the burdens of their colonial inheritance. The mere repression of colonial memories is never, in itself, tantamount to a surpassing of or emancipation from the uncomfortable realities of
the colonial encounter.

"In response, postcolonialism can be seen as a theoretical resistance to the
mystifying amnesia of the colonial aftermath. It is a disciplinary project devoted to the academic task of revisiting, remembering and, crucially, interrogating the colonial past. The process of returning to the colonial scene
discloses a relationship of reciprocal antagonism and desire between coloniser
and colonised. And it is in the unfolding of this troubled and troubling relationship that we might start to discern the ambivalent prehistory of the postcolonial condition. If postcoloniality is to be reminded of its origins in
colonial oppression, it must also be theoretically urged to recollect the compelling seductions of colonial power. The forgotten archive of the colonial
encounter narrates multiple stories of contestation and its discomfiting other,
complicity.

"In addition, the colonial archive preserves those versions of knowledge and agency produced in response to the particular pressures of the colonial encounter. The colonial past is not simply a reservoir of 'raw' political experiences and practices to be theorised from the detached and enlightened perspective of the present. It is also the scene of intense discursive and conceptual activity, characterised by a profusion of thought and writing about the cultural and political identities of colonised subjects. Thus, in its therapeutic retrieval of the colonial past, postcolonialism needs to define itself as an area of study which is willing not only to make, but also to gain, theoretical sense out of that past."

—Leela Gandhi, from *Postcolonial Theory* (1998)

Critical Perspective: On African Poets and the European Tradition

"There is a charge often raised against African poets, that of aping other models, particularly the European. This charge is of course frequently true, even to the extent of outright plagiarism, and covers the entire spectrum of stylistic development: twenty years ago it was quite possible to read poems (of serious intent) which began 'Gather ye hibiscus while ye may,' while today we are more commonly inundated with the re-creation of Waste Lands of tropical humidity. Dadaisms abound both in their founding innocence and in the revivalist adaptations hallowed by the 'beat' generation of America. Even the perverse phase of European decadence has not failed to diffuse its 'poisonous ecstasy' through situations clearly shaped in a far different clime, nurtured in the perpetual season of revolution.

"All this must be conceded and deplored. But then another question must be asked: whether this has not occurred in all other fields that make up the personalities of new nations. The excesses committed in a small part of the poetic output achieve an importance only for those who fail to see the poet's preoccupations as springing from the same source of creativity which activates the major technological developments: town-planning, sewage-disposal, hydro-electric power. None of these and others—including the making of war—has taken place or will ever again take place without the awareness of foreign thought and culture patterns, and their exploitation. To recommend, on the one hand, that the embattled general or the liberation fighter seek the most sophisticated weaponry from Europe, America or China, while, on the other, that the poet totally expunge from his consciousness all knowledge of a foreign tradition in his own craft, is an absurdity.

"A distinct quality in all great poets does exercise a ghostly influence in other writers, but this need not be cause for self-flagellation. The resulting work is judged by its capacity to move ahead or sideways, by the thoroughness of ingestion within a new organic mould, by the original strength of the new entity. Modern African poems which betray traces of an internal dialogue are often accused of alien affectation, but an examination of traditional poetry reveals that it too is built on a densely packed matrix of references (and not, as is sometimes claimed to the contrary, on simplistic narrative). This progression of linked allusions towards an elucidation of the experience of reality is the language of all poets."

—Wole Soyinka, from *Poems of Black Africa* (1975)

TOPICS FOR CRITICAL THINKING

1. Discuss the ways in which Senghor's "Prayer to the Masks" serves as a counter-discourse to the colonial representation of Africans as "men of cotton, coffee, and oil."

2. The Urdu poet Faiz Ahmed Faiz was born in Sialkot in the Punjab region in northern India in the 1930s during the reign of the British. Associated with the leftist Progressive Movement, he served in the Indian army during World War II and then moved to Pakistan after the partition and edited *The Pakistan Times*. During the early 1950s, he was arrested in the Rawalpindi Conspiracy and served four years under a death sentence. In 1962, the former Soviet Union awarded him the Lenin Peace Prize. Consider the ways in which the natural world provides Faiz a sense of freedom in his poem "A Prison Evening." What role does figurative language play in his evocation of natural beauty?

3. The Indian poet Jayanta Mahapatra was born in Cuttack, Orissa. Contrast Mahapatra's representation of everyday life in "Main Temple Street, Puri" with the poet's more stylized personification of the sky.

4. Shu Ting was born in Fujian, China, and spent her formative years there until her father was exiled to the countryside for nonconformity with the party line during the Cultural Revolution. Sent to work in a cement factory and later a textile mill, Shu Ting began to write and then publish verse. Soon she was invited to become a member of the Chinese Writers' Association and won National Poetry Awards in 1981 and 1983. Discuss the images of uniformity and monotony that make up the poet's "manufactured fate" in "Assembly Line."

TOPICS FOR CRITICAL WRITING

1. After serving in the People's Army, Ha Jin studied English at Heilongjiang University in Harbin and later at Shandong University in the People's Republic of China. Some years later, he received a Ph.D. from Brandeis University and left China for good after the Tiananmen uprising. "Ways of Talking" meditates on grief and exile. How does the poem balance Jin's sense of loss with joy? How do you interpret the poet's image of the "beautiful" in the final image of "hail stones in the strawberry fields"?

2. Wole Soyinka is the first Nigerian writer to have won the Nobel Prize for Literature (1986). In addition to publishing poetry, novels, critical essays, plays for the stage, television, and radio, he was arrested as a political prisoner and jailed by the Federal Military Government of Nigeria from 1967–1969. Discuss the ways in which Soyinka mimics and parodies the discourse of racism so as to subvert its force in "Telephone Conversation."

3. Adrian Oktenberg's "A Young Sniper" alludes to the New Testament Book of Matthew 10:29–31, where Jesus affirms that God takes note of every creature in his kingdom, even the sparrows:

Are not two sparrows sold for a cent?
And yet not one of them will fall to the ground
apart from your Father.
But the very hairs of your head are all numbered.
Therefore do not fear;
you are of more value than many sparrows.

Examine the ways in the sniper attains a kind of godlike freedom through the power of his gaze. In what ways does his happiness come, paradoxically, through the ability to terrorize others? How does Oktenberg's first-person narrator experience his enjoyment as her oppression?

4. In her note to "Song of the Fisher Wife," Chitra Banerjee Divakaruni writes that "in many coastal villages in India, it is believed that the wife's virtue keeps her husband safe at sea. Widows are often outcast and forced into becoming prostitutes in order to survive." Contrast the poem's italicized passages with the speaker's narrative of her husband's shipwreck. How do you interpret the final question in the poem's last stanza?

38 Poems for Further Reading

AI *(b. 1947)*

The Mother's Tale *(1986)*

Once when I was young, Juanito,
there was a ballroom in Lima
where Hernán, your father,
danced with another woman
and I cut him across the cheek   5
with a pocketknife.
Oh, the pitch of the music sometimes,
the smoke and rustle of crinoline.
But what things to remember now
on your wedding day.   10
I pour a kettle of hot water
into the wooden tub where you are sitting.
I was young, free.
But Juanito, how free is a woman?—
born with Eve's sin between her legs,   15
and inside her,
Lucifer sits on a throne of abalone shells,
his staff with the head of John the Baptist
skewered on it.
And in judgment, son, in judgment he says   20
that women will bear the fruit of the tree
we wished so much to eat
and that fruit will devour us
generation by generation,
so my son,   25
you must beat Rosita often.
She must know the weight of a man's hand,
the bruises that are like the wounds of Christ.
Her blood that is black at the heart
must flow until it is as red and pure as His.   30
And she must be pregnant always
if not with child
then with the knowledge
that she is alive because of you.

That you can take her life   35
more easily than she creates it,
that suffering is her inheritance from you
and through you, from Christ,
who walked on his mother's body
to be the King of Heaven.   40

JOHN ASHBERY   *(b. 1927)*

The Painter   *(1956)*

Sitting between the sea and the buildings
He enjoyed painting the sea's portrait.
But just as children imagine a prayer
Is merely silence, he expected his subject
To rush up the sand, and, seizing a brush,   5
Plaster its own portrait on the canvas.

So there was never any paint on his canvas
Until the people who lived in the buildings
Put him to work: "Try using the brush
As a means to an end. Select, for a portrait,   10
Something less angry and large, and more subject
To a painter's moods, or, perhaps, to a prayer."

How could he explain to them his prayer
That nature, not art, might usurp the canvas?
He chose his wife for a new subject,   15
Making her vast, like ruined buildings,
As if, forgetting itself, the portrait
Had expressed itself without a brush.

Slightly encouraged, he dipped his brush
In the sea, murmuring a heartfelt prayer: 20
"My soul, when I paint this next portrait
Let it be you who wrecks the canvas."
The news spread like wildfire through the buildings:
He had gone back to the sea for his subject.

Imagine a painter crucified by his subject!   25
Too exhausted even to lift his brush,
He provoked some artists leaning from the buildings
To malicious mirth: "We haven't a prayer
Now, of puffing ourselves on canvas,
Or getting the sea to sit for a portrait!"   30

Others declared it a self-portrait.
Finally all indications of a subject
Began to fade, leaving the canvas
Perfectly white. He put down the brush.
At once a howl, that was also a prayer,   35
Arose from the overcrowded buildings.

They tossed him, the portrait, from the tallest of the buildings;
And the sea devoured the canvas and the brush
As though his subject had decided to remain a prayer.

W. H. AUDEN   *(1907–1973)*

The Shield of Achilles°   *(1955)*

She looked over his shoulder
  For vines and olive trees,
Marble well-governed cities
  And ships upon untamed seas,
But there on the shining metal   5
  His hands had put instead
An artificial wilderness
  And a sky like lead.

A plain without a feature, bare and brown,
  No blade of grass, no sign of neighbourhood,   10
Nothing to eat and nowhere to sit down,
  Yet, congregated on its blankness, stood
  An unintelligible multitude,
A million eyes, a million boots in line,
Without expression, waiting for a sign.   15

Out of the air a voice without a face
  Proved by statistics that some cause was just
In tones as dry and level as the place:
  No one was cheered and nothing was discussed;
  Column by column in a cloud of dust   20
They marched away enduring a belief
Whose logic brought them, somewhere else, to grief.

She looked over his shoulder
  For ritual pieties,

Shield of Achilles: Mythic shield forged by Hephaestos, the god of fire, for Achilles in Book 18 of
Homer's *Iliad.*

> White flower-garlanded heifers,   25
>   Libation and sacrifice,
> But there on the shining metal
>   Where the altar should have been,
> She saw by his flickering forge-light
>   Quite another scene.   30

Barbed wire enclosed an arbitrary spot
    Where bored officials lounged (one cracked a joke)
And sentries sweated for the day was hot:
    A crowd of ordinary decent folk
    Watched from without and neither moved nor spoke   35
As three pale figures were led forth and bound
To three posts driven upright in the ground.

The mass and majesty of this world, all
    That carries weight and always weighs the same
Lay in the hands of others; they were small   40
    And could not hope for help and no help came:
    What their foes liked to do was done, their shame
Was all the worst could wish; they lost their pride
And died as men before their bodies died.

> She looked over his shoulder   45
>   For athletes at their games,
> Men and women in a dance
>   Moving their sweet limbs
> Quick, quick, to music,
>   But there on the shining shield   50
> His hands had set no dancing-floor
>   But a weed-choked field.

A ragged urchin, aimless and alone,
    Loitered about that vacancy, a bird
Flew up to safety from his well-aimed stone: 55
    That girls are raped, that two boys knife a third,
    Were axioms to him, who'd never heard
Of any world where promises were kept,
Or one could weep because another wept.

> The thin-lipped armourer,   60
>   Hephaestos hobbled away,
> Thetis of the shining breasts
>   Cried out in dismay
> At what the god had wrought
>   To please her son, the strong   65
> Iron-hearted man-slaying Achilles
>   Who would not live long.

Lullaby   *(1940)*

Lay your sleeping head, my love,
Human on my faithless arm;
Time and fevers burn away
Individual beauty from
Thoughtful children, and the grave   5
Proves the child ephemeral:
But in my arms till break of day
Let the living creature lie,
Mortal, guilty, but to me
The entirely beautiful.   10

Soul and body have no bounds:
To lovers as they lie upon
Her tolerant enchanted slope
In their ordinary swoon,
Grave the vision Venus sends   15
Of supernatural sympathy,
Universal love and hope;
While an abstract insight wakes
Among the glaciers and the rocks
The hermit's carnal ecstasy.   20

Certainty, fidelity
On the stroke of midnight pass
Like vibrations of a bell
And fashionable madmen raise
Their pedantic boring cry: 25
Every farthing of the cost,
All the dreaded cards foretell,
Shall be paid, but from this night
Not a whisper, not a thought,
Not a kiss nor look be lost.   30

Beauty, midnight, vision dies:
Let the winds of dawn that blow
Softly round your dreaming head
Such a day of welcome show
Eye and knocking heart may bless,   35
Find our mortal world enough;
Noons of dryness find you fed
By the involuntary powers,
Nights of insult let you pass
Watched by every human love.   40

PETER BALAKIAN   (b. 1951)

After the Survivors Are Gone   (1996)

I tried to imagine the Vilna ghetto,
to see a persimmon tree after the flash at Nagasaki.
Because my own tree had been hacked,
I tried to kiss the lips of Armenia.

At the table and the altar   5
we said some words written ages ago.
Have we settled for just the wine and bread,
for candles lit and snuffed?

Let us remember how the law has failed us.
Let us remember the child naked,   10
waiting to be shot on a bright day
with tulips blooming around the ditch.

We shall not forget the earth,
the artifact, the particular song,
the dirt of an idiom—   15
things that stick in the ear.

from *Beowulf*   (700–900)

[*The Last Survivor's Speech*]

"Now earth hold fast, since heroes have failed to,
The riches of the race! Was it not from you
That good men once won it? Battle-death, evil
Mortal and terrible has taken every man
Of this folk of mine that has left life and time,   5
That has gazed its last on feast and gladness.
No one I have to be sword-bearer or burnisher
Of the beaten-gold goblet, the dearly-loved drinking-cup:
That chivalry has slipped away. Hard helmet must shed
Its flashing furnishing, its plating of gold;   10
Burnishers sleep who should sheen the battle-mask;
So too the mail-coat that has met the biting
Of iron war-blades above clashed shields
Crumbles after its wearer; nor can this chain-armor   15
Follow the fight's commander into far-off regions

At the heroes' side. There is no harp-pleasure
And no happy minstrelsy, there is no good hawk
To swoop through the hall, there is no swift horse
With hoofbeats in the courtyard. Hatred and death   20
Have driven out on their voyage the hosts of the living!"
So one sad-minded spoke out the misery
He felt for all, moving unconsoled
Restless day and night, till the tidewater of death
Rose touching his heart.   25

[The Last Survivor's Speech in Old English]

"Heald þu nu, hruse,   nu hæleð ne mostan,
eorla æhte!   Hwæt, hyt ær on ðe
gode begeaton.   Guþ-deað fornam,
feorh-bealo frecne   fyra gehwylcne   30
leoda minra,   þare ðe þis lif ofgeaf,
gesawon sele-dreamas.   Nah hwa sweord wege
oððe feormie   fæted wæge,
drync-fæt deore;   duguð ellor scoc.
Sceal se hearda helm   hyrsted golde   35
fætum befeallen;   feormynd swefað,
þa ðe beado-griman   bywan sceoldon;
ge swylce seo here-pad,   sio æt hilde gebad
ofer borda gebræc   bite irena,
brosnað æfter beorne;   ne mæg byrnan hring   40
æfter wig-fruman   wide feran
hæleðum be healfe.   Næs hearpan wyn
gomen gleo-beames,   ne god hafoc
geond sæl swingeð,   ne se swifta mearh
burh-stede beateð.   Bealo-cwealm hafað   45
fela feorh-cynna   forð onsended!"

ELIZABETH BISHOP   *(1911–1979)*

One Art   *(1976)*

The art of losing isn't hard to master;
so many things seem filled with the intent
to be lost that their loss is no disaster.

Lose something every day. Accept the fluster
of lost door keys, the hour badly spent.   5
The art of losing isn't hard to master.

Then practice losing farther, losing faster:
places, and names, and where it was you meant
to travel. None of these will bring disaster.

I lost my mother's watch. And look! my last, or   10
next-to-last, of three loved houses went.
The art of losing isn't hard to master.

I lost two cities, lovely ones. And, vaster,
some realms I owned, two rivers, a continent.
I miss them, but it wasn't a disaster.   15

—Even losing you (the joking voice, a gesture
I love) I shan't have lied. It's evident
the art of losing's not too hard to master
though it may look like (*Write it!*) like disaster.

WILLIAM BLAKE *(1757–1827)*

The Divine Image   *(1789)*

To Mercy, Pity, Peace, and Love,
All pray in their distress:
And to these virtues of delight
Return their thankfulness.

For Mercy, Pity, Peace, and Love,   5
Is God, our father dear:
And Mercy, Pity, Peace, and Love,
Is Man, his child and care.

For Mercy has a human heart,
Pity, a human face: 10
And Love, the human form divine,
And Peace, the human dress.

Then every man of every clime,
That prays in his distress,
Prays to the human form divine,   15
Love, Mercy, Pity, Peace.

And all must love the human form,
In heathen, Turk, or Jew.
Where Mercy, Love, & Pity dwell,
There God is dwelling too.   20

A Divine Image   (1790–1791)

Cruelty has a Human heart
And Jealousy a Human Face,
Terror, the Human Form Divine,
And Secrecy, the Human Dress.

The Human Dress is forgéd Iron,   5
The Human Form, a fiery Forge,
The Human Face, a Furnace seal'd,
The Human Heart, its hungry Gorge.

A Poison Tree   (1794)

I was angry with my friend:
I told my wrath, my wrath did end.
I was angry with my foe:
I told it not, my wrath did grow.

And I waterd it in fears,   5
Night & morning with my tears;
And I sunnéd it with smiles,
And with soft deceitful wiles.

And it grew both day and night,
Till it bore an apple bright.   10
And my foe beheld it shine,
And he knew that it was mine,

And into my garden stole,
When the night had veild the pole;
In the morning glad I see   15
My foe outstretchd beneath the tree.

The Tyger   (1794)

Tyger! Tyger! burning bright
In the forests of the night,
What immortal hand or eye
Could frame thy fearful symmetry?

In what distant deeps or skies   5
Burnt the fire of thine eyes?
On what wings dare he aspire?
What the hand, dare seize the fire?

And what shoulder, & what art,
Could twist the sinews of thy heart?
And when thy heart began to beat,
What dread hand? & what dread feet?   10

What the hammer? what the chain?
In what furnace was thy brain?
What the anvil? what dread grasp
Dare its deadly terrors clasp?   15

When the stars threw down their spears,
And water'd heaven with their tears,
Did he smile his work to see?
Did he who made the Lamb make thee?   20

Tyger! Tyger! burning bright
In the forests of the night,
What immortal hand or eye
Dare frame thy fearful symmetry?

LOUISE BOGAN   *(1897–1970)*

Medusa   *(1923)*

I had come to the house, in a cave of trees,
Facing a sheer sky.
Everything moved,—a bell hung ready to strike,
Sun and reflection wheeled by.

When the bare eyes were before me   5
And the hissing hair,
Held up at a window, seen through a door.
The stiff bald eyes, the serpents on the forehead
Formed in the air.

This is a dead scene forever now.   10
Nothing will ever stir.
The end will never brighten it more than this,
Nor the rain blur.

The water will always fall, and will not fall,
And the tipped bell make no sound.   15
The grass will always be growing for hay
Deep on the ground.

And I shall stand here like a shadow
Under the great balanced day,
My eyes on the yellow dust, that was lifting in the wind, 20
And does not drift away.

EAVAN BOLAND *(b. 1944)*

The Pomegranate (1994)

The only legend I have ever loved is
the story of a daughter lost in hell.
And found and rescued there.
Love and blackmail are the gist of it.
Ceres and Persephone the names. 5
And the best thing about the legend is
I can enter it anywhere. And have.
As a child in exile in
a city of fogs and strange consonants,
I read it first and at first I was 10
an exiled child in the crackling dusk of
the underworld, the stars blighted. Later
I walked out in a summer twilight
searching for my daughter at bed-time.
When she came running I was ready 15
to make any bargain to keep her.
I carried her back past whitebeams
and wasps and honey-scented buddleias.
But I was Ceres then and I knew
winter was in store for every leaf 20
on every tree on that road.
Was inescapable for each one we passed.
And for me.
⠀⠀⠀⠀⠀⠀It is winter
and the stars are hidden. 25
I climb the stairs and stand where I can see
my child asleep beside her teen magazines,
her can of Coke, her plate of uncut fruit.
The pomegranate! How did I forget it?
She could have come home and been safe 30
and ended the story and all
our heart-broken searching but she reached
out a hand and plucked a pomegranate.
She put out her hand and pulled down
the French sound for apple and 35
the noise of stone and the proof

that even in the place of death,
at the heart of legend, in the midst
of rocks full of unshed tears
ready to be diamonds by the time   40
the story was told, a child can be
hungry. I could warn her. There is still a chance.
The rain is cold. The road is flint-coloured.
The suburb has cars and cable television.
The veiled stars are above ground.   45
It is another world. But what else
can a mother give her daughter but such
beautiful rifts in time?
If I defer the grief I will diminish the gift.
The legend will be hers as well as mine.   50
She will enter it. As I have.
She will wake up. She will hold
the papery flushed skin in her hand.
And to her lips. I will say nothing.

ANNE BRADSTREET   *(c. 1612–1672)*

To My Dear and Loving Husband   *(1678)*

If ever two were one, then surely we.
If ever man were loved by wife, then thee;
If ever wife was happy in a man,
Compare with me ye women if you can.
I prize thy love more than whole mines of gold,   5
Or all the riches that the East doth hold.
My love is such that Rivers cannot quench,
Nor ought but love from thee, give recompence.
Thy love is such I can no way repay,
The heavens reward thee manifold, I pray.   10
Then while we live, in love lets so persever,
That when we live no more we may live ever.

EMILY BRONTË   *(1818–1848)*

[Long Neglect Has Worn Away]   *(1837)*

Long neglect has worn away
Half the sweet enchanting smile;
Time has turned the bloom to gray;
Mold and damp the face defile.

But that lock of silky hair,   5
Still beneath the picture twined,
Tells what once those features were,
Paints their image on the mind.

Fair the hand that traced that line,
"Dearest, ever deem me true";   10
Swiftly flew the fingers fine
When the pen that motto drew.

STERLING A. BROWN   *(1901–1989)*

Slim in Atlanta   *(1932)*

Down in Atlanta,
    De whitefolks got laws
For to keep all de niggers
    From laughin' outdoors.

        Hope to Gawd I may die   5
            If I ain't speakin' truth
        Make de niggers do deir laughin'
            In a telefoam booth.

Slim Greer hit de town
    An' de rebs got him told,—   10
"Dontcha laugh on de street,
    If you want to die old."

        Den dey showed him de booth,
            An' a hundred shines
        In front of it, waitin'   15
            In double lines.

Slim thought his sides
    Would bust in two,
Yelled, "Lookout, everybody,
    I'm coming through!"   20

        Pulled de other man out,
            An' bust in de box,
        An' laughed four hours
            By de Georgia clocks.

Den he peeked through de door,   25
    An' what did he see?

Three hundred niggers there
  In misery.—

    Some holdin' deir sides,
      Some holdin' deir jaws,
    To keep from breakin'
      De Georgia laws.   30

An' Slim gave a holler,
  An' started again;
An' from three hundred throats   35
  Come a moan of pain.

    An' everytime Slim
      Saw what was outside,
    Got to whoopin' again
      Till he nearly died.   40

An' while de poor critters
  Was waitin' deir chance,
Slim laughed till dey sent
  Fo' de ambulance.

    De state paid de railroad   45
      To take him away;
    Den, things was as usural
      In Atlanta, Gee A.

ELIZABETH BARRETT BROWNING   *(1806–1861)*

To George Sand   *(1844)*

A Desire

Thou large-brained woman and large-hearted man,
Self-called George Sand! whose soul, amid the lions
Of thy tumultuous senses, moans defiance
And answers roar for roar, as spirits can:
I would some mild miraculous thunder ran   5
Above the applauded circus, in appliance
Of thine own nobler nature's strength and science,
Drawing two pinions, white as wings of swan,
From thy strong shoulders, to amaze the place
With holier light! that thou to woman's claim   10
And man's mightest join beside the angel's grace
Of a pure genius sanctified from blame,

Till child and maiden pressed to thine embrace
To kiss upon thy lips a stainless fame.

Sonnet 14, from Sonnets from the Portuguese   *(1850)*

If thou must love me, let it be for nought
Except for love's sake only. Do not say,
"I love her for her smile—her look—her way
Of speaking gently,—for a trick of thought
That falls in well with mine, and certes brought   5
A sense of pleasant ease on such a day"—
For these things in themselves, Belovèd, may
Be changed, or change for thee,—and love, so wrought,
May be unwrought so. Neither love me for
Thine own dear pity's wiping my cheeks dry,—   10
A creature might forget to weep, who bore
Thy comfort long, and lose thy love thereby!
But love me for love's sake, that evermore
Thou may'st love on, through love's eternity.

ROBERT BROWNING   *(1812–1889)*

My Last Duchess°   *(1842)*

Ferrara

That's my last duchess painted on the wall,
Looking as if she were alive. I call
That piece a wonder, now: Frà Pandolf's hands
Worked busily a day, and there she stands.
Will't please you sit and look at her? I said   5
"Frà Pandolf" by design, for never read
Strangers like you that pictured countenance,
The depth and passion of its earnest glance,
But to myself they turned (since none puts by
The curtain I have drawn for you, but I)   10
And seemed as they would ask me, if they durst,
How such a glance came there; so, not the first
Are you to turn and ask thus. Sir, 'twas not
Her husband's presence only, called the spot
Of joy into the Duchess' cheek: perhaps   15
Frà Pandolf chanced to say "Her mantle laps

Duchess: Daughter of Cosimo I de Medici, duke of Florence, and wife of Alfonso II d'Este, duke
of Ferrera who is the speaker in Browning's dramatic monologue.

"Over my lady's wrist too much," or "Paint
"Must never hope to reproduce the faint
"Half-flush that dies along her throat": such stuff
Was courtesy, she thought, and cause enough   20
For calling up that spot of joy. She had
A heart—how shall I say?—too soon made glad,
Too easily impressed; she liked whate'er
She looked on, and her looks went everywhere.
Sir, 'twas all one! My favor at her breast,   25
The dropping of the daylight in the West,
The bough of cherries some officious fool
Broke in the orchard for her, the white mule
She rode with round the terrace—all and each
Would draw from her alike the approving speech,   30
Or blush, at least. She thanked men—good! but thanked
Somehow—I know not how—as if she ranked
My gift of a nine-hundred-years-old name
With anybody's gift. Who'd stoop to blame
This sort of trifling? Even had you skill   35
In speech—which I have not—to make your will
Quite clear to such an one, and say, "Just this
"Or that in you disgusts me; here you miss,
"Or there exceed the mark"—and if she let
Herself be lessoned so, nor plainly set   40
Her wits to yours, forsooth, and made excuse,
—E'en then would be some stooping; and I choose
Never to stoop. Oh sir, she smiled, no doubt,
Whene'er I passed her; but who passed without
Much the same smile? This grew; I gave commands;   45
Then all smiles stopped together. There she stands
As if alive. Will 't please you rise? We'll meet
The company below, then. I repeat,
The Count your master's known munificence
Is ample warrant that no just pretense   50
Of mine for dowry will be disallowed;
Though his fair daughter's self, as I avowed
At starting, is my object. Nay, we'll go
Together down, sir. Notice Neptune, though,
Taming a sea-horse, thought a rarity,   55
Which Claus of Innsbruck cast in bronze for me!

GEORGE GORDON, LORD BYRON   *(1788–1824)*

The Destruction of Sennacherib   *(1815)*

The Assyrian came down like the wolf on the fold,
And his cohorts were gleaming in purple and gold;
And the sheen of their spears was like stars on the sea,
When the blue wave rolls nightly on deep Galilee.

Like the leaves of the forest when summer is green,   5
That host with their banners at sunset were seen:
Like the leaves of the forest when autumn hath blown,
That host on the morrow lay wither'd and strown.

For the Angel of Death spread his wings on the blast,
And breathed in the face of the foe as he passed   10
And the eyes of the sleepers wax'd deadly and chill,
And their hearts but once heaved, and forever grew still!

And there lay the steed with his nostril all wide,
But through it there roll'd not the breath of his pride;
And the foam of his gasping lay white on the turf,   15
And cold as the spray of the rock-beating surf.

And there lay the rider distorted and pale,
With the dew on his brow, and the rust on his mail:
And the tents were all silent, the banners alone,
The lances uplifted, the trumpet unblown.   20

And the widows of Ashur are loud in their wail,
And the idols are broke in the temple of Baal;
And the might of the Gentile, unsmote by the sword,
Hath melted like snow in the glance of the Lord!

LEWIS CARROLL   *(1832–1898)*

Jabberwocky   *(1871)*

'Twas brillig, and the slithy toves
   Did gyre and gimble in the wabe;
All mimsy were the borogoves,
   And the mome raths outgrabe.

"Beware the Jabberwock, my son!   5
    The jaws that bite, the claws that catch!
Beware the Jubjub bird, and shun
    The frumious Bandersnatch!"

He took his vorpal sword in hand;
    Long time the manxome foe he sought—   10
So rested he by the Tumtum tree,
    And stood awhile in thought.

And, as in uffish thought he stood,
    The Jabberwock, with eyes of flame,
Came whiffling through the tulgey wood,   15
    And burbled as it came!

One, two! One, two! And through and through
    The vorpal blade went snicker-snack!
He left it dead, and with its head
    He went galumphing back.   20

"And hast thou slain the Jabberwock?
    Come to my arms, my beamish boy!
O frabjous day! Callooh! Callay!"
    He chortled in his joy.

'Twas brillig, and the slithy toves   25
    Did gyre and gimble in the wabe:
All mimsy were the borogoves,
    And the mome raths outgrabe.

MARGARET CAVENDISH *(1623–1673)*

An Apology for Writing So Much upon This Book *(1653)*

Condemn me not, I make so much ado
About this book, it is my child, you know.
Just like a bird, when her young are in nest,
Goes in, and out, and hops, and takes no rest:
But when their young are fledg'd, their heads out-peep,   5
Lord! What a chirping does the old one keep!
So I, for fear my strengthless child should fall
Against a door, or stool, aloud I call;
Bid have a care of such a dangerous place:
Thus write I much, to hinder all disgrace.   10

GEOFFREY CHAUCER   *(c. 1343–1400)*

from *The Canterbury Tales*   *(1387–1400)*

The General Prologue

Whan that April with his° showres soote°
The droughte of March hath perced to the roote,
And bathed every veine° in swich licour,°
Of which vertu° engendred is the flowr;
Whan Zephyrus° eek° with his sweete breeth   5
Inspired° hath in every holt° and heeth°
The tendre croppes,° and the yonge sonne°
Hath in the Ram his halve cours yronne,
And smale fowles° maken melodye
That sleepen al the night with open yë°—   10
So priketh hem° Nature in hir corages°—
Thanne longen folk to goon° on pilgrimages,
And palmeres° for to seeken straunge strondes°
To ferne halwes,° couthe° in sondry° londes;
And specially from every shires ende   15
Of Engelond to Canterbury they wende,
The holy blisful martyr° for to seeke
That hem hath holpen° whan that they were seke.°
  Bifel° that in that seson on a day,
In Southwerk° at the Tabard as I lay,   20
Redy to wenden on my pilgrimage
To Canterbury with ful° devout corage,
At night was come into that hostelrye
Wel nine and twenty in a compaignye
Of sondry folk, by aventure° yfalle   25
In felaweshipe, and pilgrimes were they alle
That toward Canterbury wolden° ride.
The chambres and the stables weren wide,
And wel we weren esed° at the beste.°

---

1 *his:* Its. *soote:* Fresh.   3 *every veine:* I.e., in plants. *in swich licour:* In such liquid.   4 *Of which vertu:* By the power of which.   5 *Zephyrus:* The west wind. *eek:* Also.   6 *Inspired:* Breathed into. *holt:* Grove. *heeth:* Field.   7 *croppes:* Shoots. *yonge sonne:* The sun is young because it has run only halfway through its course in Aries, the Ram—the first sign of the zodiac in the solar year.   9 *fowles:* Birds.   10 *yë:* Eye.   11 *hem:* Them. *hir corages:* Their hearts.   12 *goon:* Go.   13 *palmeres:* Pilgrims, especially to the Holy Land. *straunge strondes:* Foreign shores.   14 *ferne halwes:* Far-off shrines. *couthe:* Known. *sondry:* Various.   17 *martyr:* Thomas à Becket, archbishop murdered in Canterbury Cathedral in 1170; his shrine was associated with healing.   18 *holpen:* Helped. *seke:* Sick.   19 *Bifel:* It happened.   20 *Southwerk:* Then a suburb of London, south of the Thames River, that was the site of the Southwerk Inn.   22 *ful:* Very.   25 *aventure:* Chance.   27 *wolden:* Would.   29 *esed:* Accommodated. *beste:* In the best possible way.

And shortly, whan the sonne was to reste,°   30
So hadde I spoken with hem everichoon°
That I was of hir felaweshipe anoon,°
And made forward° erly for to rise,
To take oure way ther as° I you devise.°
    But nathelees,° whil I have time and space,°   35
Er° that I ferther in this tale pace,°
Me thinketh it accordant to resoun°
To telle you al the condicioun
Of eech of hem, so as it seemed me,
And whiche they were, and of what degree,°   40
And eek in what array that they were inne:
And at a knight thanne° wol I first biginne.
    A Knight ther was, and that a worthy man,
That fro the time that he first bigan
To riden out, he loved chivalrye,   45
Trouthe and honour, freedom and curteisye.°
Ful worthy was he in his lordes werre,°
And therto hadde he riden, no man ferre,°
As wel in Cristendom as hethenesse,°
And evere honoured for his worthinesse.   50
    At Alisandre° he was whan it was wonne;
Ful ofte time he hadde the boord bigonne°
Aboven alle nacions in Pruce;
In Lettou had he reised,° and in Ruce,
No Cristen man so ofte of his degree;   55
In Gernade° at the sege eek hadde he be
Of Algezir, and riden in Belmarye;
At Lyeis was he, and at Satalye,
Whan they were wonne; and in the Grete See°
At many a noble arivee° hadde he be.   60
    At mortal batailes° hadde he been fifteene,
And foughten for oure faith at Tramissene
In listes° thries,° and ay° slain his fo.

---

30 *was to reste:* Had set.   31 *everichoon:* Every one.   32 *anoon:* At once.   33 *made
forward:* Made an agreement.   34 *as:* Where. *devise:* Describe.   35 *natheless:* Nevertheless. *time and space:* Opportunity.   36 *Er:* Before. *pace:* Proceed.   37 *Me . . . resoun:* It
seems to me according to reason.   40 *degree:* Social rank.   42 *thanne:* Them.
46 *Trouthe . . . curteisye:* Integrity, honor, generosity of spirit, courtesy.   47 *werre:* War.
48 *ferre:* Further.   49 *hethenesse:* Heathen lands.   51 *At Alisandre:* The Knight has taken
part in campaigns fought against three groups who threatened Christian Europe during the fourteenth century: the Moslems in the Near East, from whom Alexandria was seized after a famous
siege; the northern barbarians in Prussia, Lithuania, and Russia; and the Moors in North Africa.
The place names in the following lines refer to battlegrounds in these continuing wars.   52
hadde the boord bigonne: Sat in the seat of honor at military feasts.   54 *reised:* Campaigned.
56 *Gernade:* Granada.   59 *Grete See:* The Mediterranean.   60 *noble arivee:* Military landing.   61 *mortal batailes:* Tournaments fought to the death.   63 *listes:* Lists, tournament
grounds. *thries:* Thrice. *ay:* Always.

This ilke° worthy Knight hadde been also
Somtime with the lord of Palatye°   65
Again° another hethen in Turkye;
And everemore he hadde a soverein pris.°
And though that he were worthy, he was wis,°
And of his port° as meeke as is a maide.
He nevere yit no vilainye° ne saide   70
In al his lif unto no manere wight:°
He was a verray,° parfit,° gentil° knight.
But for to tellen you of his array,
His hors° were goode, but he was nat gay.°
Of fustian° he wered° a gipoun°   75
Al bismotered with his haubergeoun,°
For he was late° come from his viage,°
And wente for to doon his pilgrimage.

LADY MARY CHUDLEIGH   *(1656–1710)*

To the Ladies   *(1703)*

Wife and Servant are the same,
But only differ in the Name:
For when that fatal Knot is ty'd,
Which nothing, nothing can divide:
When she the word *obey* has said,   5
And Man by Law supreme has made,
Then all that's kind is laid aside,
And nothing left but State and Pride:
Fierce as an Eastern Prince he grows,
And all his innate Rigor shows: 10
Then but to look, to laugh, or speak,
Will the Nuptial Contract break.
Like Mutes she Signs alone must make,
And never any Freedom take:
But still be govern'd by a Nod,   15
And fear her Husband as her God:
Him still must serve, him still obey,

---

64 *ilke:* Same.   65 *lord of Palatye:* A Moslem. Alliances of convenience were often made during
the Crusades between Christians and Moslems.   66 *Again:* Against.   67 *pris:* Reputation.
68 *he was wis:* He was wise as well as bold.   69 *port:* Deportment, demeanor.   70 *vilainye:*
Nudeness.   71 *no manere wight:* Any sort of person. In Middle English, negatives are multiplied for emphasis, as in these two lines: "nevere," "no," "ne," "no."   72 *verray:* True. *parfit:*
Perfect. *gentil:* Noble.   74 *hors:* Horses. *gay:* Gaily dressed.   75 *fustian:* Thick cloth.
wered: Wore. *gipouni:* Tunic worn underneath the coat of mail.   76 *Al . . . haubergeoun:* All
rust-stained from his hauberk (coat of mail).   77 *late:* Lately. *viage:* Expedition.

And nothing act, and nothing say,
But what her haughty Lord thinks fit,
Who with the Pow'r, has all the Wit.   20
Then shun, oh! shun that wretched State,
And all the fawning Flatt'rers hate:
Value your selves, and Men despise,
You must be proud, if you'll be wise.

SAMUEL TAYLOR COLERIDGE *(1772–1834)*

Frost at Midnight   *(1798)*

   The Frost performs its secret ministry,
Unhelped by any wind. The owlet's cry
Came loud—and hark, again! loud as before.
The inmates of my cottage, all at rest,
Have left me to that solitude, which suits   5
Abstruser musings: save that at my side
My cradled infant° slumbers peacefully.
'Tis calm indeed! so calm, that it disturbs
And vexes meditation with its strange
And extreme silentness. Sea, hill, and wood,   10
This populous village! Sea, and hill, and wood,
With all the numberless goings-on of life,
Inaudible as dreams! the thin blue flame
Lies on my low-burnt fire, and quivers not;
Only that film,° which fluttered on the grate,   15
Still flutters there, the sole unquiet thing.
Methinks its motion in this hush of nature
Gives it dim sympathies with me who live,
Making it a companionable form,
Whose puny flaps and freaks the idling Spirit   20
By its own moods interprets, everywhere
Echo or mirror seeking of itself,
And makes a toy of Thought.

                            But O! how oft,
How oft, at school, with most believing mind,
Presageful, have I gazed upon the bars,   25
To watch that fluttering *stranger!* and as oft
With unclosed lids, already had I dreamt
Of my sweet birthplace, and the old church tower,

---

7 *infant:* Hartley Coleridge.   15 *film:* Soot: in popular folk lore thought to foreshadow a
guest's visit.

Whose bells, the poor man's only music, rang
From morn to evening, all the hot Fair-day,   30
So sweetly, that they stirred and haunted me
With a wild pleasure, falling on mine ear
Most like articulate sounds of things to come!
So gazed I, till the soothing things, I dreamt,
Lulled me to sleep, and sleep prolonged my dreams!   35
And so I brooded all the following morn,
Awed by the stern preceptor's° face, mine eye
Fixed with mock study on my swimming book:
Save if the door half opened, and I snatched
A hasty glance, and still my heart leaped up,   40
For still I hoped to see the *stranger's* face,
Townsman, or aunt, or sister more beloved,
My playmate when we both were clothed alike!

    Dear Babe, that sleepest cradled by my side,
Whose gentle breathings, heard in this deep calm,   45
Fill up the interspersèd vacancies
And momentary pauses of the thought!
My babe so beautiful! it thrills my heart
With tender gladness, thus to look at thee,
And think that thou shalt learn far other lore,   50
And in far other scenes! For I was reared
In the great city, pent 'mid cloisters dim,
And saw nought lovely but the sky and stars.
But *thou*, my babe! shalt wander like a breeze
By lakes and sandy shores, beneath the crags   55
Of ancient mountain, and beneath the clouds,
Which image in their bulk both lakes and shores
And mountain crags: so shalt thou see and hear
The lovely shapes and sounds intelligible
Of that eternal language, which thy God   60
Utters, who from eternity doth teach
Himself in all, and all things in himself.
Great universal Teacher! he shall mold
Thy spirit, and by giving make it ask.

    Therefore all seasons shall be sweet to thee,   65
Whether the summer clothe the general earth
With greenness, or the redbreast sit and sing
Betwixt the tufts of snow on the bare branch
Of mossy apple tree, while the nigh thatch
Smokes in the sun-thaw; whether the eave-drops fall   70
Heard only in the trances of the blast,

---

37 *preceptor*: Teacher.

Or if the secret ministry of frost
Shall hang them up in silent icicles,
Quietly shining to the quiet Moon.

HART CRANE   *(1899–1932)*

Proem: To Brooklyn Bridge   *(1930)*

How many dawns, chill from his rippling rest
The seagull's wings shall dip and pivot him,
Shedding white rings of tumult, building high
Over the chained bay waters Liberty—

Then, with inviolate curve, forsake our eyes   5
As apparitional as sails that cross
Some page of figures to be filed away;
—Till elevators drop us from our day . . .

I think of cinemas, panoramic sleights
With multitudes bent toward some flashing scene   10
Never disclosed, but hastened to again,
Foretold to other eyes on the same screen;

And Thee, across the harbor, silver-paced
As though the sun took step of thee, yet left
Some motion ever unspent in thy stride,—   15
Implicitly thy freedom staying thee!

Out of some subway scuttle, cell or loft
A bedlamite° speeds to thy parapets,
Tilting there momently, shrill shirt ballooning,
A jest falls from the speechless caravan.   20

Down Wall, from girder into street noon leaks,
A rip-tooth of the sky's acetylene;
All afternoon the cloud-flown derricks turn . . .
Thy cables breathe the North Atlantic still.

And obscure as that heaven of the Jews,   25
Thy guerdon . . . Accolade thou dost bestow
Of anonymity time cannot raise;
Vibrant reprieve and pardon thou dost show.

---

18 *Bedlamite:* Mad person.

O harp and altar, of the fury fused,
(How could mere toil align thy choiring strings!)   30
Terrific threshold of the prophet's pledge,
Prayer of pariah, and the lover's cry,—

Again the traffic lights that skim thy swift
Unfractioned idiom, immaculate sigh of stars,
Beading thy path—condense eternity: 35
And we have seen night lifted in thine arms.

Under thy shadow by the piers I waited;
Only in darkness is thy shadow clear.
The City's fiery parcels all undone,
Already snow submerges an iron year . . .   40

O Sleepless as the river under thee,
Vaulting the sea, the prairies' dreaming sod,
Unto us lowliest sometime sweep, descend
And of the curveship lend a myth to God.

ROBERT CREELEY   *(b. 1926)*

I Know a Man   *(1957)*

As I sd to my
friend, because I am
always talking,—John, I

sd, which was not his
name, the darkness sur-   5
rounds us, what

can we do against
it, or else, shall we &
why not, buy a goddam big car,

drive, he sd, for   10
christ's sake, look
out where yr going.

COUNTÉE CULLEN   *(1903–1946)*

Incident   *(1925)*

Once riding in old Baltimore,
   Heart-filled, head-filled with glee,
I saw a Baltimorean
   Keep looking straight at me.

Now I was eight and very small,   5
   And he was no whit bigger,
And so I smiled, but he poked out
   His tongue and called me, "Nigger."

I saw the whole of Baltimore
   From May until December;   10
Of all the things that happened there
   That's all that I remember.

E. E. CUMMINGS   *(1894–1962)*

in Just-   *(1923)*

in Just-
spring   when the world is mud-
luscious the little
lame balloonman

whistles   far   and wee   5

and eddieandbill come
running from marbles and
piracies and it's
spring

when the world is puddle-wonderful   10

the queer
old balloonman whistles
far   and   wee
and bettyandisbel come dancing

from hop-scotch and jump-rope and   15

it's
spring
and
    the

          goat-footed   20
balloonMan   whistles
far
and
wee

JAMES DICKEY   *(1923–1997)*

The Performance   *(1967)*

The last time I saw Donald Armstrong
He was staggering oddly off into the sun,
Going down, off the Philippine Islands.
I let my shovel fall, and put that hand
Above my eyes, and moved some way to one side   5
That his body might pass through the sun,

And I saw how well he was not
Standing there on his hands,
On his spindle-shanked forearms balanced,
Unbalanced, with his big feet looming and waving   10
In the great, untrustworthy air
He flew in each night, when it darkened.

Dust fanned in scraped puffs from the earth
Between his arms, and blood turned his face inside out,
To demonstrate its suppleness   15
Of veins, as he perfected his role.
Next day, he toppled his head off
On an island beach to the south,

And the enemy's two-handed sword
Did not fall from anyone's hands   20
At that miraculous sight,
As the head rolled over upon
Its wide-eyed face, and fell
Into the inadequate grave

He had dug for himself, under pressure.   25
Yet I put my flat hand to my eyebrows

Months later, to see him again
In the sun, when I learned how he died,
And imagined him, there,
Come, judged, before his small captors,   30

Doing all his lean tricks to amaze them—
The back somersault, the kip-up—
And at last, the stand on his hands,
Perfect, with his feet together,
His head down, evenly breathing,   35
As the sun poured up from the sea

And the headsmen broke down
In a blaze of tears, in that light
Of the thin, long human frame
Upside down in its own strange joy,   40
And, if some other one had not told him,
Would have cut off the feet

Instead of the head,
And if Armstrong had not presently risen
In kingly, round-shouldered attendance,   45
And then knelt down in himself
Beside his hacked, glittering grave, having done
All things in this life that he could.

EMILY DICKINSON   *(1830–1886)*

Poem 67 (Success is counted sweetest)   *(1878)*

Success is counted sweetest
By those who ne'er succeed.
To comprehend a nectar
Requires sorest need.

Not one of all the purple Host   5
Who took the Flag today
Can tell the definition
So clear of Victory

As he defeated—dying—
On whose forbidden ear   10
The distant strains of triumph
Burst agonized and clear!

Poem 216 (Safe in their Alabaster Chambers)   *(1861)*

Safe in their Alabaster Chambers—
Untouched by Morning—
And untouched by Noon—
Lie the meek members of the Resurrection—
Rafter of Satin—and Roof of Stone!   5

Grand go the Years—in the Crescent—above them—
Worlds scoop their Arcs—
And Firmaments—row—
Diadems—drop—and Doges—surrender—
Soundless as dots—on a Disc of Snow—   10

Poem 241 (I like a look of Agony)   *(1861)*

I like a look of Agony,
Because I know it's true—
Men do not sham Convulsion,
Nor simulate, a Throe—

The Eyes glaze once—and that is Death—   5
Impossible to feign
The Beads upon the Forehead
By homely Anguish strung.

Poem 280 (I felt a Funeral, in my Brain)   *(c. 1861)*

I felt a Funeral, in my Brain,
And Mourners to and fro
Kept treading—treading— till it seemed
That Sense was breaking through—

And when they all were seated,   5
A Service, like a Drum—
Kept beating—beating—till I thought
My Mind was going numb—

And then I heard them lift a Box
And creak across my Soul   10
With those same Boots of Lead, again,
Then Space—began to toll,

As all the Heavens were a Bell,
And Being, but an Ear,
And I, and Silence, some strange Race   15
Wrecked, solitary, here—

And then a Plank in Reason, broke,
And I dropped down, and down—
And hit a World, at every plunge,
And Finished knowing—then—   20

Poem 303 (The Soul selects her own Society)   *(c. 1862)*

The Soul selects her own Society—
Then—shuts the Door—
To her divine Majority—
Present no more—

Unmoved—she notes the Chariots—pausing—   5
At her low Gate—
Unmoved—an Emperor be kneeling
Upon her Mat—

I've known her—from an ample nation—
Choose One—   10
Then—close the Valves of her attention—
Like Stone—

Poem 341 (After great pain, a formal feeling comes)   *(c. 1862)*

After great pain, a formal feeling comes—
The Nerves sit ceremonious, like Tombs—
The stiff Heart questions was it He, that bore,
And Yesterday, or Centuries before?

The Feet, mechanical, go round—   5
Of Ground, or Air, or Ought—
A Wooden way
Regardless grown,
A Quartz contentment, like a stone—

This is the Hour of Lead—
Remembered, if outlived,   10
As Freezing persons, recollect the Snow—
First—Chill—then Stupor—then the letting go—

Poem 435 (Much Madness is divinest Sense) *(c. 1862)*

Much Madness is divinest Sense—
To a discerning Eye—
Much Sense—the starkest Madness—
'Tis the Majority
In this, as All, prevail—   5
Assent—and you are sane—
Demur—you're straightway dangerous—
And handled with a Chain—

Poem 528 (Mine—by the Right of the White Election) *(c. 1862)*

Mine—by the Right of the White Election!
Mine—by the Royal Seal!
Mine—by the Sign in the Scarlet prison—
Bars—cannot conceal!

Mine—here—in Vision—and in Veto!   5
Mine— by the Grave's Repeal—
Titled—Confirmed—
Delirious Charter!
Mine—long as Ages steal!

Poem 754 (My Life had stood— a Loaded Gun) *(c. 1863)*

My Life had stood—a Loaded Gun—
In Corners—till a Day
The Owner passed—identified—
And carried Me away—

And now We roam in Sovereign Woods—   5
And now We hunt the Doe—
And every time I speak for Him—
The Mountains straight reply—

And do I smile, such cordial light
Upon the Valley glow—   10
It is as a Vesuvian face
Had let its pleasure through—

And when at Night—Our good Day done—
I guard My Master's Head—
'Tis better than the Eider-Duck's   15
Deep Pillow—to have shared—

To foe of His—I'm deadly foe—
None stir the second time—
On whom I lay a Yellow Eye—
Or an emphatic Thumb—   20

Though I than He—may longer live
He longer must—than I—
For I have but the power to kill,
Without—the power to die—

Poem 1129 (Tell all the Truth but tell it slant)   *(c. 1868)*

Tell all the Truth but tell it slant—
Success in Circuit lies
Too bright for our infirm Delight
The Truth's superb surprise

As Lightning to the Children eased   5
With explanation kind
The Truth must dazzle gradually
Or every man be blind—

Poem 1763 (Fame is a bee)   *(1898)*

Fame is a bee.
    It has a song—
It has a sting—
    Ah, too, it has a wing.

JOHN DONNE   *(1572–1631)*

The Sun Rising   *(1633)*

    Busy old fool, unruly sun,
        Why dost thou thus
Through windows and through curtains call on us?
Must to thy motions lovers' seasons run?

Saucy, pedantic wretch, go chide   5
　Late schoolboys and sour 'prentices,
　Go tell court huntsmen that the king will ride,
　Call country ants to harvest offices.
Love, all alike, no season knows nor clime,
Nor hours, days, months, which are the rags of time.   10

　Thy beams, so reverend and strong
　　Why shouldst thou think?
I could eclipse and cloud them with a wink,
But that I would not lose her sight so long.
　If her eyes have not blinded thine,   15
　Look, and tomorrow late tell me
　Whether both th' Indias of spice and mine
　Be where thou left'st them, or lie here with me;
Ask for those kings whom thou saw'st yesterday,
And thou shalt hear: All here in one bed lay.   20

　She's all states, and all princes I;
　　Nothing else is.
Princes do but play us; compared to this,
All honor's mimic, all wealth alchemy.
　Thou, sun, art half as happy as we,   25
　In that the world's contracted thus;
　Thine age asks ease, and since thy duties be
　To warm the world, that's done in warming us.
Shine here to us, and thou art everywhere;
This bed thy center is, these walls thy sphere.   30

from Holy Sonnets   *(1633)*

Sonnet 10

Death, be not proud, though some have callèd thee
Mighty and dreadful, for thou art not so;
For those whom thou think'st thou dost overthrow
Die not, poor Death, nor yet canst thou kill me.
From rest and sleep, which but thy pictures be,   5
Much pleasure; then from thee much more must flow;
And soonest our best men with thee do go,
Rest of their bones and soul's delivery.
Thou'rt slave to fate, chance, kings, and desperate men,
And dost with poison, war, and sickness dwell;   10
And poppy or charms can make us sleep as well
And better than thy stroke; why swell'st thou then?
One short sleep past, we wake eternally,
And Death shall be no more: death, thou shalt die.

RITA DOVE   *(b. 1952)*

Parsley°   *(1983)*

1. The Cane Fields

There is a parrot imitating spring
in the palace, its feathers parsley green.
Out of the swamp the cane appears

to haunt us, and we cut it down. El General
searches for a word; he is all the world   5
there is. Like a parrot imitating spring,

we lie down screaming as rain punches through
and we come up green. We cannot speak an R—
out of the swamp, the cane appears

and then the mountain we call in whispers *Katalina*.   10
The children gnaw their teeth to arrowheads.
There is a parrot imitating spring.

El General has found his word: *perejil.*
Who says it, lives. He laughs, teeth shining
out of the swamp. The cane appears   15

in our dreams, lashed by wind and streaming.
And we lie down. For every drop of blood
there is a parrot imitating spring.
Out of the swamp the cane appears.

2. The Palace

The word the general's chosen is parsley.   20
It is fall, when thoughts turn
to love and death; the general thinks
of his mother, how she died in the fall
and he planted her walking cane at the grave
and it flowered, each spring stolidly forming   25
four-star blossoms. The general

pulls on his boots, he stomps to
her room in the palace, the one without
curtains, the one with a parrot
in a brass ring. As he paces he wonders   30

Parsley: According to Dove, On October 2, 1957, Rafael Trujillo (1891–1961), dictator of the
Dominican Republic, ordered 20,000 blacks killed because they could not pronounce the letter r
in *perejil*, the Spanish word for "parsley."

Who can I kill today. And for a moment
the little knot of screams
is still. The parrot, who has traveled

all the way from Australia in an ivory
cage, is, coy as a widow, practising   35
spring. Ever since the morning
his mother collapsed in the kitchen
while baking skull-shaped candies
for the Day of the Dead, the general
has hated sweets. He orders pastries   40
brought up for the bird; they arrive

dusted with sugar on a bed of lace.
The knot in his throat starts to twitch;
he sees his boots the first day in battle
splashed with mud and urine   45
as a soldier falls at his feet amazed—
how stupid he looked!—at the sound
of artillery. *I never thought it would sing*
the soldier said, and died. Now

the general sees the fields of sugar   50
cane, lashed by rain and streaming.
He sees his mother's smile, the teeth
gnawed to arrowheads. He hears
the Haitians sing without R's
as they swing the great machetes: 55
Katalina, they sing, *Katalina*,

mi madle, mi amol en muelte. God knows
his mother was no stupid woman; she
could roll an R like a queen. Even
a parrot can roll an R! In the bare room   60
the bright feathers arch in a parody
of greenery, as the last pale crumbs
disappear under the blackened tongue. Someone

calls out his name in a voice
so like his mother's, a startled tear   65
splashes the tip of his right boot.
My mother, my love in death.
The general remembers the tiny green sprigs
men of his village wore in their capes
to honor the birth of a son. He will   70
order many, this time, to be killed

for a single, beautiful word.

PAUL LAURENCE DUNBAR   *(1872–1906)*

Sympathy   *(1899)*

I know what the caged bird feels, alas!
   When the sun is bright on the upland slopes;
When the wind stirs soft through the springing grass,
And the river flows like a stream of glass;
   When the first bird sings and the first bud opes,   5
And the faint perfume from its chalice steals—
I know what the caged bird feels!

I know why the caged bird beats his wing
   Till its blood is red on the cruel bars;
For he must fly back to his perch and cling   10
When he fain would be on the bough a-swing;
   And a pain still throbs in the old, old scars
And they pulse again with a keener sting—
I know why he beats his wing!

I know why the caged bird sings, ah me,   15
   When his wing is bruised and his bosom sore,—
When he beats his bars and he would be free;
It is not a carol of joy or glee,
   But a prayer that he sends from his heart's deep core,
But a plea, that upward to Heaven he flings—   20
I know why the caged bird sings!

ROBERT DUNCAN   *(1919–1988)*

Often I Am Permitted to Return to a Meadow   *(1960)*

as if it were a scene made-up by the mind,
that is not mine, but is a made place,

that is mine, it is so near to the heart,
an eternal pasture folded in all thought
so that there is a hall therein   5

that is a made place, created by light
wherefrom the shadows that are forms fall.

Wherefrom fall all architectures I am
I say are likenesses of the First Beloved
whose flowers are flames lit to the Lady.   10

She it is Queen Under The Hill
whose hosts are a disturbance of words within words
that is a field folded.

It is only a dream of the grass blowing
east against the source of the sun   15
in an hour before the sun's going down

whose secret we see in a children's game
of ring a round of roses told.

Often I am permitted to return to a meadow
as if it were a given property of the mind   20
that certain bounds hold against chaos,

that is a place of first permission,
everlasting omen of what is.

T. S. ELIOT   *(1888–1965)*

The Love Song of J. Alfred Prufrock   *(1917)*

S'io credesse che mia risposta fosse
A persona che mai tornasse al mondo,
Questa fiamma staria senza piu scosse.
Ma perciocche giammai di questo fondo
Non torno vivo alcun, s'i'odo il vero,
Senza tema d'infamia ti rispondo.

Let us go then, you and I,
When the evening is spread out against the sky
Like a patient etherized upon a table;
Let us go, through certain half-deserted streets,
The muttering retreats   5
Of restless nights in one-night cheap hotels
And sawdust restaurants with oyster-shells:
Streets that follow like a tedious argument
Of insidious intent
To lead you to an overwhelming question . . .   10
Oh, do not ask, "What is it?"
Let us go and make our visit.

In the room the women come and go
Talking of Michelangelo.

The yellow fog that rubs its back upon the window-panes   15
The yellow smoke that rubs its muzzle on the window-panes

Licked its tongue into the corners of the evening,
Lingered upon the pools that stand in drains,
Let fall upon its back the soot that falls from chimneys,
Slipped by the terrace, made a sudden leap,   20
And seeing that it was a soft October night,
Curled once about the house, and fell asleep.

And indeed there will be time
For the yellow smoke that slides along the street,
Rubbing its back upon the window-panes;   25
There will be time, there will be time
To prepare a face to meet the faces that you meet;
There will be time to murder and create,
And time for all the works and days of hands
That lift and drop a question on your plate;   30
Time for you and time for me,
And time yet for a hundred indecisions,
And for a hundred visions and revisions,
Before the taking of a toast and tea.

In the room the women come and go   35
Talking of Michelangelo.

And indeed there will be time
To wonder, "Do I dare?" and, "Do I dare?"
Time to turn back and descend the stair,
With a bald spot in the middle of my hair—   40
[They will say: "How his hair is growing thin!"]
My morning coat, my collar mounting firmly to the chin,
My necktie rich and modest, but asserted by a simple pin—
[They will say: "But how his arms and legs are thin!"]
Do I dare   45
Disturb the universe?
In a minute there is time
For decisions and revisions which a minute will reverse.

For I have known them all already, known them all—
Have know the evenings, mornings, afternoons,   50
I have measured out my life with coffee spoons;
I know the voices dying with a dying fall
Beneath the music from a farther room.
    So how should I presume?

And I have known the eyes already, known them all—   55
The eyes that fix you in a formulated phrase,
And when I am formulated, sprawling on a pin,
When I am pinned and wriggling on the wall,

Then how should I begin
To spit out all the butt-ends of my days and ways?   60
  And how should I presume?

And I have known the arms already, known them all—
Arms that are braceleted and white and bare
[But in the lamplight, downed with light brown hair!]
Is it perfume from a dress   65
That makes me so digress?
Arms that lie along a table, or wrap about a shawl.
  And should I then presume?
  And how should I begin?

  *   *   *   *

Shall I say, I have gone at dusk through narrow streets   70
And watched the smoke the rises from the pipes
Of lonely men in shirt-sleeves, leaning out of windows? . . .

I should have been a pair of ragged claws
Scuttling across the floors of silent seas.

  *   *   *   *

And the afternoon, the evening, sleeps so peacefully!   75
Smoothed by long fingers,
Asleep . . . tired . . . or it malingers,
Stretched on the floor, here beside you and me.
Should I, after tea and cakes and ices,
Have the strength to force the moment to its crisis?   80
But though I have wept and fasted, wept and prayed,
Though I have seen my head [grown slightly bald] brought in upon a
     platter,
I am no prophet—and here's no great matter;
I have seen the moment of my greatness flicker,
And I have seen the eternal Footman hold my coat, and snicker,   85
And in short, I was afraid.

And would it have been worth it, after all,
After the cups, the marmalade, the tea,
Among the porcelain, among some talk of you and me,
Would it have been worth while,   90
To have bitten off the matter with a smile,
To have squeezed the universe into a ball
To roll it toward some overwhelming question,
To say: "I am Lazarus, come from the dead,
Come back to tell you all, I shall tell you all"—   95
If one, settling a pillow by her head,
  Should say: "That is not what I meant at all.
  That is not it, at all."

And would it have been worth it, after all,
Would it have been worth while,   100
After the sunsets and the dooryards and the sprinkled streets,
After the novels, after the teacups, after the skirts that trail along the floor—
And this, and so much more?—
It is impossible to say just what I mean!
But as if a magic lantern threw the nerves in patterns on a screen: 105
Would it have been worth while
If one, settling a pillow or throwing off a shawl,
And turning toward the window, should say:
      "That is not it at all,
      That is not what I meant, at all."   110

*   *   *   *

No! I am not Prince Hamlet, nor was meant to be;
Am an attendant lord, one that will do
To swell a progress, start a scene or two,
Advise the prince; no doubt, an easy tool,
Deferential, glad to be of use,   115
Politic, cautious, and meticulous;
Full of high sentence, but a bit obtuse;
At times, indeed, almost ridiculous—
Almost at times, the Fool.

I grow old . . . I grow old . . .   120
I shall wear the bottoms of my trousers rolled.

Shall I part my hair behind? Do I dare to eat a peach?
I shall wear white flannel trousers, and walk upon the beach.
I have heard the mermaids singing, each to each.

I do not think that they will sing to me.   125

I have seen them riding seaward on the waves
Combing the white hair of the waves blown back
When the wind blows the water white and black.

We have lingered in the chambers of the sea
By sea-girls wreathed with seaweed red and brown   130
Till human voices wake us, and we drown.

QUEEN ELIZABETH I   *(1533–1603)*

When I Was Fair and Young   *(c. 1585)*

When I was fair and young, then favor graced me.
Of many was I sought their mistress for to be,

But I did scorn them all and answered them therefore:
Go, go, go, seek some other where, importune me no more.

How many weeping eyes I made to pine in woe,   5
How many sighing hearts I have not skill to show,
But I the prouder grew and still this spake therefore:
Go, go, go, seek some other where, importune me no more.

Then spake fair Venus' son°, that proud victorious boy,
Saying: You dainty dame, for that you be so coy,   10
I will so pluck your plumes as you shall say no more:
Go, go, go, seek some other where, importune me no more.

As soon as he had said, such change grew in my breast
That neither night nor day I could take any rest.
Wherefore I did repent that I had said before: 15
Go, go, go, seek some other where, importune me no more.

RALPH WALDO EMERSON   *(1803–1882)*

Concord Hymn   *(1837)*

Sung at the completion of the Battle Monument, July 4, 1837

By the rude bridge that arched the flood,
    Their flag to April's breeze unfurled,
Here once the embattled farmers stood
    And fired the shot heard round the world.

The foe long since in silence slept;   5
    Alike the conqueror silent sleeps;
And Time the ruined bridge has swept
    Down the dark stream which seaward creeps.

On this green bank, by this soft stream,
    We set to-day a votive stone;   10
That memory may their deed redeem,
    When, like our sires, our sons are gone.

Spirit, that made those heroes dare
    To die, and leave their children free,
Bid Time and Nature gently spare   15
    That shaft we raise to them and thee.

---

9 *Venus' son:* Cupid.

CAROLYN FORCHÉ   *(b. 1950)*

The Testimony of Light   *(1994)*

Our life is a fire dampened, or a fire shut up in stone.
—JACOB BOEHME, DE INCARNATIONE VERBI

Outside everything visible and invisible a blazing maple.
Daybreak: a seam at the curve of the world. The trousered legs of the
    women shimmered.
They held their arms in front of them like ghosts.

The coal bones of the house clinked in a kimono of smoke.   5
An attention hovered over the dream where the world had been.

For if Hiroshima in the morning, after the bomb has fallen,
    is like a dream, one must ask whose dream it is.

Must understand how not to speak would carry it with us.
With bones put into rice bowls.   10
While the baby crawled over its dead mother seeking milk.

Muga-muchu: without self, without center. Thrown up in the sky by a wind.

The way back is lost, the one obsession.
The worst is over.
The worst is yet to come.   15

ROBERT FROST   *(1874–1963)*

The Road Not Taken   *(1916)*

Two roads diverged in a yellow wood,
And sorry I could not travel both
And be one traveler, long I stood
And looked down one as far as I could
To where it bent in the undergrowth;   5

Then took the other, as just as fair,
And having perhaps the better claim,
Because it was grassy and wanted wear;
Though as for that, the passing there
Had worn them really about the same,   10

And both that morning equally lay
In leaves no step had trodden black.
Oh, I kept the first for another day!
Yet knowing how way leads on to way,
I doubted if I should ever come back.   15

I shall be telling this with a sigh
Somewhere ages and ages hence:
Two roads diverged in a wood, and I—
I took the one less traveled by,
And that has made all the difference.   20

Stopping by Woods on a Snowy Evening   *(1923)*

Whose woods these are I think I know.
His house is in the village, though;
He will not see me stopping here
To watch his woods fill up with snow.

My little horse must think it queer   5
To stop without a farmhouse near
Between the woods and frozen lake
The darkest evening of the year.

He gives his harness bells a shake
To ask if there is some mistake.   10
The only other sound's the sweep
Of easy wind and downy flake.

The woods are lovely, dark, and deep,
But I have promises to keep,
And miles to go before I sleep,   15
And miles to go before I sleep.

Design   *(1936)*

I found a dimpled spider, fat and white,
On a white heal-all, holding up a moth
Like a white piece of rigid satin cloth—
Assorted characters of death and blight
Mixed ready to begin the morning right,   5
Like the ingredients of a witches' broth—
A snow-drop spider, a flower like a froth,
And dead wings carried like a paper kite.

What had that flower to do with being white,
The wayside blue and innocent heal-all?   10
What brought the kindred spider to that height,
Then steered the white moth thither in the night?
What but design of darkness to appall?—
If design govern in a thing so small.

ROBERT GRAVES   *(1895–1985)*

The White Goddess   *(1948)*

All saints revile her, and all sober men
Ruled by the God Apollo's golden mean—
In scorn of which we sailed to find her
In distant regions likeliest to hold her
Whom we desired above all things to know,   5
Sister of the mirage and echo.

It was a virtue not to stay,
To go our headstrong and heroic way
Seeking her out at the volcano's head,
Among pack ice, or where the track had faded   10
Beyond the cavern of the seven sleepers:
Whose broad high brow was white as any leper's,
Whose eyes were blue, with rowan-berry lips,
With hair curled honey-coloured to white hips.

Green sap of Spring in the young wood a-stir   15
Will celebrate the Mountain Mother,
And every song-bird shout awhile for her;
But we are gifted, even in November
Rawest of seasons, with so huge a sense
Of her nakedly worn magnificence   20
We forget cruelty and past betrayal,
Heedless of where the next bright bolt may fall.

THOMAS HARDY   *(1840–1928)*

Channel Firing   *(1914)*

That night your great guns, unawares,
Shook all our coffins as we lay,

And broke the chancel window-squares,
We thought it was the Judgment-day

And sat upright. While drearisome   5
Arose the howl of wakened hounds:
The mouse let fall the altar-crumb,
The worms drew back into the mounds,

The glebe cow drooled. Till God called "No;
It's gunnery practice out at sea   10
Just as before you went below;
The world is as it used to be:

"All nations striving strong to make
Red war yet redder. Mad as hatters
They do no more for Christés sake   15
Than you who are helpless in such matters.

"That this is not the judgment-hour
For some of them's a blessed thing,
For if it were they'd have to scour
Hell's floor for so much threatening . . .   20

"Ha, ha. It will be warmer when
I blow the trumpet (if indeed
I ever do; for you are men,
And rest eternal sorely need)."

So down we lay again. "I wonder,   25
Will the world ever saner be,"
Said, one "than when He sent us under
In our indifferent century!"

And many a skeleton shook his head.
"Instead of preaching forty year,"   30
My neighbor Parson Thirdly said,
"I wish I had stuck to pipes and beer."

Again the guns disturbed the hour,
Roaring their readiness to avenge,
As far inland as Stourton Tower,   35
And Camelot, and starlit Stonehenge.

ROBERT HAYDEN   *(1913–1980)*

Those Winter Sundays   *(1962)*

Sundays too my father got up early
and put his clothes on in the blueblack cold,
then with cracked hands that ached
from labor in the weekday weather made
banked fires blaze. No one ever thanked him.   5

I'd wake and hear the cold splintering, breaking.
When the rooms were warm, he'd call,
and slowly I would rise and dress,
fearing the chronic angers of that house,

Speaking indifferently to him,   10
who had driven out the cold
and polished my good shoes as well.
What did I know, what did I know
of love's austere and lonely offices?

Paul Laurence Dunbar   *(1978)*

For Herbert Martin

We lay red roses on his grave,
speak sorrowfully of him
as if he were but newly dead

And so it seems to us
this raw spring day, though years   5
before we two were born he was
a young poet dead.

Poet of our youth—
his "cri du coeur" our own,
his verses "in a broken tongue"   10

beguiling as an elder
brother's antic lore.
Their sad blackface lilt and croon
survive him like

The happy look (subliminal   15
of victim, dying man)
a summer's tintypes hold.

The roses flutter in the wind;
we weight their stems
with stones, then drive away.   20

GEORGE HERBERT   *(1593–1633)*

The Altar   *(1633)*

A broken ALTAR, Lord, thy servant rears,
Made of a heart, and cemented with tears:
   Whose parts are as thy hand did frame;
   No workman's tool hath touched the same.
      A   HEART   alone   5
      Is   such   a   stone,
      As   nothing   but
      Thy power doth cut.
      Wherefore each part
      Of my hard heart   10
      Meets in this frame,
      To praise thy Name:
   That, if I chance to hold my peace,
   These stones to praise thee may not cease.
Oh let thy blessed SACRIFICE be mine,   15
And   sanctify   this   ALTAR   to   be   thine.

ROBERT HERRICK   *(1591–1674)*

The Vine   *(1648)*

I dreamed this mortal part of mine
Was metamorphosed to a vine,
Which crawling one and every way
Enthralled my dainty Lucia.
Methought her long small legs and thighs   5
I with my tendrils did surprise;
Her belly, buttocks, and her waist
By my soft nervelets were embraced.
About her head I writhing hung,
And with rich clusters (hid among   10
The leaves) her temples I behung,
So that my Lucia seemed to me
Young Bacchus ravished by his tree.
My curls about her neck did crawl,

And arms and hands they did enthrall,   15
So that she could not freely stir
(All parts there made one prisoner).
But when I crept with leaves to hide
Those parts which maids keep unespied,
Such fleeting pleasures there I took   20
That with the fancy I awoke;
And found (ah me!) this flesh of mine
More like a stock than like a vine.

The Pillar of Fame   *(1648)*

Fame's pillar here at last we set,
Out-during marble, brass or jet;
Charmed and enchanted so
As to withstand the blow
    O f   o v e r t h r o w ;   5
Nor shall the seas,
O r   o u t r a g e s
Of storms, o'erbear
What   we   uprear;
Tho' kingdoms fall,   10
This pillar never shall
Decline or waste at all;
But stand for ever by his own
Firm and well-fixed foundation.

GARRETT KAORU HONGO   *(b. 1951)*

Yellow Light   *(1982)*

One arm hooked around the frayed strap
of a tar-black patent-leather purse,
the other cradling something for dinner:
fresh bunches of spinach from a J-Town *yaoya*,
sides of split Spanish mackerel from Alviso's,   5
maybe a loaf of Langendorf; she steps
off the hissing bus at Olympic and Fig,
begins the three-block climb up the hill,
passing gangs of schoolboys playing war,
Japs against Japs, Chicanas chalking sidewalks   10
with the holy double-yoked crosses of hopscotch,
and the Korean grocer's wife out for a stroll
around this neighborhood of Hawaiian apartments

just starting to steam with cooking
and the anger of young couples coming home   15
from work, yelling at kids, flicking on
TV sets for the Wednesday Night Fights.

If it were May, hydrangeas and jacaranda
flowers in the streetside trees would be
blooming through the smog of late spring.   20
Wisteria in Masuda's front yard would be
shaking out the long tresses of its purple hair.
Maybe mosquitoes, moths, a few orange butterflies
settling on the lattice of monkey flowers
tangled in chain-link fences by the trash.   25

But this is October, and Los Angeles
seethes like a billboard under twilight.
From used-car lots and the movie houses uptown,
long silver sticks of light probe the sky.
From the Miracle Mile, whole freeways away,   30
a brilliant fluorescence breaks out
and makes war with the dim squares
of yellow kitchen light winking on
in all the side streets of the Barrio.

She climbs up the two flights of flagstone   35
stairs to 201-B, the spikes of her high heels
clicking like kitchen knives on a cutting board,
props the groceries against the door,
fishes through memo pads, a compact,
empty packs of chewing gum, and finds her keys.   40

The moon then, cruising from behind
a screen of eucalyptus across the street,
covers everything, everything in sight,
in a heavy light like yellow onions.

GERARD MANLEY HOPKINS *(1844–1889)*

Pied Beauty   *(1877)*

Glory be to God for dappled things—
    For skies of couple-color as a brinded cow;
        For rose-moles all in stipple upon trout that swim;
Fresh-firecoal chestnut-falls; finches' wings;
    Landscape plotted and pieced—fold, fallow, and plough;   5
        And áll trádes, their gear and tackle and trim.

All things counter, original, spare, strange;
   Whatever is fickle, freckled (who knows how?)
      With swift, slow; sweet, sour; adazzle, dim;
He fathers-forth whose beauty is past change: 10
         Praise him.

Thou Art Indeed Just, Lord   *(1889)*

Justus quidem tu es, Domine, si disputem tecum:
verum justa loquar ad te: Quare
via impiorum prosperatur?

Thou art indeed just, Lord, if I contend
With thee; but, sir, so what I plead is just.
Why do sinners' ways prosper? and why must
Disappointment all I endeavour end?
   Wert thou my enemy, O thou my friend,   5
How wouldst thou worse, I wonder, than thou dost
Defeat, thwart me? Oh, the sots and thralls of lust
Do in spare hours more thrive than I that spend,
Sir, life upon thy cause. See, banks and brakes
Now, leavèd how thick! lacèd they are again   10
With fretty chervil,° look, and fresh wind shakes
Them; birds build—but not I build; no, but strain,
Time's eunuch, and not breed one work that wakes.
Mine, O thou lord of life, send my roots rain.

A. E. HOUSMAN   *(1859–1936)*

To an Athlete Dying Young   *(1896)*

The time you won your town the race
We chaired you through the market-place;
Man and boy stood cheering by,
And home we brought you shoulder-high.

To-day, the road all runners come,   5
Shoulder-high we bring you home,
And set you at your threshold down,
Townsman of a stiller town.

Smart lad, to slip betimes away
From fields where glory does not stay   10

------

11 *chervil:* Herb, parsley.

And early though the laurel grows
It withers quicker than the rose.

Eyes the shady night has shut
Cannot see the record cut,
And silence sounds no worse than cheers   15
After earth has stopped the ears:

Now you will not swell the rout
Of lads that wore their honors out,
Runners whom renown outran
And the name died before the man.   20

So set, before its echoes fade,
The fleet foot on the sill of shade,
And hold to the low lintel up
The still-defended challenge-cup.

And round that early-laurelled head   25
Will flock to gaze the strengthless dead,
And find unwithered on its curls
The garland briefer than a girl's.

ANDREW HUDGINS   *(b. 1951)*

Supper   *(1998)*

We shared our supper with the flames,
or the shadow of the flames—each candle
in the light of the other casting shadows
across the table, dark flickers of a brilliant flicker,
and the grain of rubbed pine swirled with light   5
and shadow, shoaled and deepened in the soft
inconstancy of candlelight.
                        With every gesture
the bright flames flinched and then corrected.
Your shrug, my laugh,
                 my nod, your tilting head   10
—conveyed on air—invited their response.
They bowed their heads, then snapped upright—
a ripple in the gases' fluted yellow silk,
blue silk, transparent silk. I yearned   15
to touch the rich untouchable fabric, and finger
the sheen beneath its scorching,

but when I reached, it leaned away
decorously, and I did not pursue it, knowing.

But the dark flames reached out, licked the meat,   20
licked the plate, the fork, and the knife edge.
They licked our faces and our lips—a dry unfelt tongue,
the shadow of the flame consuming nothing,
but stroking everything as if it could
grasp, hold, take, devour. How ardently it hungers   25
because it cannot have us.
How chaste the bright flame, because it can.

LANGSTON HUGHES   *(1902–1967)*

Bad Luck Card   *(1927)*

Cause you don't love me
Is awful, awful hard.
Gypsy done showed me
My bad luck card.

There ain't no good left   5
In this world for me.
Gypsy done tole me—
Unlucky as can be.

I don't know what
Po' weary me can do.   10
Gypsy says I'd kill my self
If I was you.

Harlem Sweeties   *(1942)*

Have you dug the spill
Of Sugar Hill?
Cast your gims
On this sepia thrill:
Brown sugar lassie,   5
Caramel treat,
Honey-gold baby
Sweet enough to eat.
Peach-skinned girlie,
Coffee and cream,   10

Chocolate darling
Out of a dream.
Walnut tinted
Or cocoa brown,
Pomegranate-lipped   15
Pride of the town.
Rich cream-colored
To plum-tinted black,
Feminine sweetness
In Harlem's no lack.   20
Glow of the quince
To blush of the rose.
Persimmon bronze
To cinnamon toes.
Blackberry cordial,   25
Virginia Dare wine—
All those sweet colors
Flavor Harlem of mine!
Walnut or cocoa,
Let me repeat: 30
Caramel, brown sugar,
A chocolate treat.
Molasses taffy,
Coffee and cream,
Licorice, clove, cinnamon   35
To a honey-brown dream.
Ginger, wine-gold,
Persimmon, blackberry,
All through the spectrum
Harlem girls vary—   40
So if you want to know beauty's
Rainbow-sweet thrill,
Stroll down luscious,
Delicious, *fine* Sugar Hill.

Harlem   *(1951)*

What happens to a dream deferred?

Does it dry up
like a raisin in the sun?
Or fester like a sore—
And then run?
Does it stink like rotten meat?   5
Or crust and sugar over—
like a syrupy sweet?

Maybe it just sags
like a heavy load.   10

Or does it explode?

Café: 3 A.M.   *(1951)*

Detectives from the vice squad
with weary sadistic eyes
spotting fairies.
    Degenerates,
    some folks say.   5

But God, Nature,
or somebody
made them that way.

Police lady or Lesbian
over there?   10
    Where?

RANDALL JARRELL   *(1914–1965)*

The Death of the Ball Turret Gunner   *(1945)*

From my mother's sleep I fell into the State,
And I hunched in its belly till my wet fur froze.
Six miles from earth, loosed from its dream of life,
I woke to black flak and the nightmare fighters.
When I died they washed me out of the turret with a hose.   5

HA JIN   *(b. 1956)*

In New York City   *(1996)*

In the golden rain
I plod along Madison Avenue,
loaded with words.
They are from a page
that shows the insignificance   5
of a person to a tribe,
just as a hive keeps thriving
while a bee is lost.

On my back the words
are gnawing and gnawing
till they enter into my bones—
I become another man,
alone, wandering,
no longer dreaming of luck
or meeting a friend.

No wisdom shines
like the neon and traffic lights,
but there are words as true as
the money eyes, the yellow cabs,
the fat pigeons on the sills.

BEN JONSON *(1572–1637)*

Song: To Celia (II) *(1616)*

Drink to me only with thine eyes,
And I will pledge with mine;
Or leave a kiss but in the cup,
And I'll not look for wine.
The thirst that from the soul doth rise,   5
Doth ask a drink divine:
But might I of Jove's nectar sup,
I would not change for thine.
I sent thee late a rosy wreath,
Not so much honoring thee,   10
As giving it a hope, that there
It could not withered be.
But thou thereon did'st only breathe,
And sent'st it back to me;
Since when it grows and smells, I swear,   15
Not of itself, but thee.

Slow, Slow, Fresh Fount° *(1600)*

Slow, slow, fresh fount, keep time with my salt tears;
Yet slower, yet, O faintly, gentle springs!
List to the heavy part the music bears,
Woe weeps out her division, when she sings.
Droop herbs and flowers;   5
Fall grief in showers;

Slow, Slow, Fresh Fount: Spoken by Echo for Narcissus in Jonson's play *Cynthia's Revels* (1600).

Our beauties are not ours. O, I could still,
Like melting snow upon some craggy hill,
    Drop, drop, drop, drop,
Since nature's pride is now a withered daffodil.   10

CAROLYN KIZER   *(b. 1925)*

Semele° Recycled   *(1984)*

After you left me forever,
I was broken into pieces,
and all the pieces flung into the river.
Then the legs crawled ashore
and aimlessly wandered the dusty cow-track.   5
They became, for a while, a simple roadside shrine:
A tiny table set up between the thighs
held a dusty candle, weed, and field flower chains
placed reverently there by children and old women.
My knees were hung with tin triangular medals   10
to cure all forms of hysterical disease.

After I died forever in the river,
my torso floated, bloated in the stream,
catching on logs or stones among the eddies.
White water foamed around it, then dislodged it;   15
after a whirlwind trip, it bumped ashore.
A grizzled old man who scavenged along the banks
had already rescued my arms and put them by,
knowing everything has its uses, sooner or later.

When he found my torso, he called it his canoe,   20
and, using my arms as paddles,
he rowed me up and down the scummy river.
When catfish nibbled my fingers, he scooped them up
and blessed his reusable bait.
Clumsy but serviceable, that canoe!   25
The trail of blood that was its wake
attracted the carp and eels, and the river turtle,
easily landed, dazed by my tasty red.

A young lad found my head among the rushes
and placed it on a dry stone.   30
He carefully combed my hair with a bit of shell

Semele: Mother of Dionysus and beloved of Zeus.

and set small offerings before it
which the birds and rats obligingly stole at night,
so it seemed I ate.
And the breeze wound through my mouth and empty sockets 35
so my lungs would sigh, and my dead tongue mutter.

Attached to my throat like a sacred necklace
was a circlet of small snails.
Soon the villagers came to consult my oracular head
with its waterweed crown. 40
Seers found occupation, interpreting sighs,
and their papyrus rolls accumulated.

Meanwhile, young boys retrieved my eyes
they used for marbles in a simple game
—till somebody's pretty sister snatched at them 45
and set them, for luck, in her bridal diadem.
Poor girl! When her future groom caught sight of her,
all eyes, he crossed himself in horror,
and stumbled away in haste
through her dowered meadows. 50

What then of my heart and organs,
my sacred slit
which loved you best of all?
They were caught in a fisherman's net
and tossed at night into a pen for swine. 55
But they shone so by moonlight that the sows stampeded,
trampled one another in fear, to get away.
And the fisherman's wife, who had thirteen living children
and was contemptuous of holy love,
raked the rest of me onto the compost heap. 60

Then in their various places and helpful functions,
the altar, oracle, offal, canoe and oars
learned the wild rumor of your return.
The altar leapt up, and ran to the canoe,
scattering candle grease and wilted grasses. 65
Arms sprang to their sockets, blind hands with nibbled nails
groped their way, aided by loud lamentation,
to the bed of the bride, snatched up those unlucky eyes
from her discarded veil and diadem,
and rammed them home. Oh, what a bright day it was! 70
This empty body danced on the riverbank.
Hollow, it called and searched among the fields
for those parts that steamed and simmered in the sun,
and never would have found them.

But then your great voice rang out under the skies   75
my name!—and all those private names
for the parts and places that had loved you best.
And they stirred in their nest of hay and dung.
The distraught old ladies chasing their lost altar,
and the seers pursuing my skull, their lost employment,   80
and the tumbling boys, who wanted the magic marbles,
and the runaway groom, and the fisherman's thirteen children
set up such a clamor, with their cries of "Miracle!"
that our two bodies met like a thunderclap
in midday—right at the corner of that wretched field   85
with its broken fenceposts and startled, skinny cattle.
We fell in a heap on the compost heap
and all our loving parts made love at once,
while the bystanders cheered and prayed and hid their eyes
and then went decently about their business.   90

And here it is, moonlight again; we've bathed in the river
and are sweet and wholesome once more.
We kneel side by side in the sand;
we worship each other in whispers.
But the inner parts remember fermenting hay,   95
the comfortable odor of dung, the animal incense,
and passion, its bloody labor,
its birth and rebirth and decay.

YUSEF KOMUNYAKAA   *(b. 1947)*

Blackberries   *(1989)*

They left my hands like a printer's
Or thief's before a police blotter
& pulled me into early morning's
Terrestrial sweetness, so thick
The damp ground was consecrated   5
Where they fell among a garland of thorns.

Although I could smell old lime-covered
History, at ten I'd still hold out my hands
& berries fell into them. Eating from one
& filling a half gallon with the other,   10
I ate the mythology & dreamt
Of pies & cobbler, almost

Needful as forgiveness. My bird dog Spot
Eyed blue jays & thrashers. The mud frogs

In rich blackness, hid from daylight.　　　　15
An hour later, beside City Limits Road
I balanced a gleaming can in each hand,
Limboed between worlds, repeating *one dollar.*

The big blue car made me sweat.
Wintertime crawled out of the windows.　　　　20
When I leaned closer I saw the boy
& girl my age, in the wide back seat
Smirking, & it was then I remembered my fingers
Burning with thorns among berries too ripe to touch.

Maxine Kumin　*(b. 1925)*

Woodchucks　　　　*(1972)*

Gassing the woodchucks didn't turn out right.
The knockout bomb from the Feed and Grain Exchange
was featured as merciful, quick at the bone
and the case we had against them was airtight,
both exits shoehorned shut with puddingstone,　　　　5
but they had a sub-sub-basement out of range.

Next morning they turned up again, no worse
for the cyanide than we for our cigarettes
and state-store Scotch, all of us up to scratch.
They brought down the marigolds as a matter of course　　　　10
and then took over the vegetable patch
nipping the broccoli shoots, beheading the carrots.

The food from our mouths, I said, righteously thrilling
to the feel of the .22, the bullets' neat noses.
I, a lapsed pacifist fallen from grace　　　　15
puffed with Darwinian pieties for killing,
now drew a bead on the littlest woodchuck's face.
He died down in the everbearing roses.

Ten minutes later I dropped the mother. She
flipflopped in the air and fell, her needle teeth　　　　20
still hooked in a leaf of early Swiss chard.
Another baby next. O one-two-three
the murderer inside me rose up hard,
the hawkeye killer came on stage forthwith.

There's one chuck left. Old wily fellow, he keeps　　　　25
me cocked and ready day after day after day.

All night I hunt his humped-up form. I dream
I sight along the barrel in my sleep.
If only they'd all consented to die unseen
gassed underground the quiet Nazi way.   30

PHILIP LARKIN   *(1922–1985)*

Talking in Bed   *(1964)*

Talking in bed ought to be easiest,
Lying together there goes back so far,
An emblem of two people being honest.

Yet more and more time passes silently.
Outside, the wind's incomplete unrest   5
Builds and disperses clouds about the sky,

And dark towns heap up on the horizon.
None of this cares for us. Nothing shows why
At this unique distance from isolation

It becomes still more difficult to find   10
Words at once true and kind,
Or not untrue and not unkind.

D. H. LAWRENCE   *(1885–1930)*

Bavarian Gentians   *(1932)*

Not every man has gentians in his house
in Soft September, at slow, sad Michaelmas.

Bavarian gentians, big and dark, only dark
darkening the daytime, torch-like with the smoking blueness of Pluto's
    gloom,
ribbed and torch-like, with their blaze of darkness spread blue   5
down flattening into points, flattened under the sweep of white day
torch-flower of the blue-smoking darkness, Pluto's dark-blue daze,
black lamps from the halls of Dis,° burning dark blue,
giving off darkness, blue darkness, as Demeter's pale lamps give off light,
lead me then, lead the way.   10

───────
8 *Dis:* Hades.

Reach me a gentian, give me a torch!
let me guide myself with the blue, forked torch of this flower
down the darker and darker stairs, where blue is darkened on blueness
even where Persephone goes, just now, from the frosted September
to the sightless realm where darkness is awake upon the dark   15
and Persephone herself is but a voice
or a darkness invisible enfolded in the deeper dark
of the arms Plutonic, and pierced with the passion of dense gloom,
among the splendour of torches of darkness, shedding darkness on the
    lost bride and her groom.

EMMA LAZARUS   *(1849–1887)*

The New Colossus°   *(1888)*

Not like the brazen giant of Greek fame,
With conquering limbs astride from land to land;
Here at our sea-washed, sunset gates shall stand
A mighty woman with a torch, whose flame
Is the imprisoned lightning, and her name   5
Mother of Exiles. From her beacon-hand
Glows world-wide welcome; her mild eyes command
The air-bridged harbor that twin cities frame.
"Keep, ancient lands, your storied pomp!" cries she
With silent lips. "Give me your tired, your poor,   10
Your huddled masses yearning to breathe free,
The wretched refuse of your teeming shore.
Send these, the homeless, tempest-tost to me,
I lift my lamp beside the golden door!"

MICHAEL LONGLEY   *(b. 1939)*

The Linen Industry   *(1979)*

Pulling up flax after the blue flowers have fallen
And laying our handfuls in the peaty water
To rot these grasses to the bone, or building stooks
That recall the skirts of an invisible dancer,

We become a part of the linen industry   5
And follow its processes to the grubby town

———

The New Colossus: Engraved on the pedestal of the Statue of Liberty.

Where fields are compacted into window-boxes
And there is little room among the big machines.

But even in our attic under the skylight
We make love on a bleach green, the whole meadow   10
Draped with material turning white in the sun
As though snow reluctant to melt were our attire.

What's passion but a battering of stubborn stalks,
Then a gentle combing out of fibres like hair
And a weaving of these into christening robes,   15
Into garments for a marriage or funeral?

Since it's like a bereavement once the labour's done
To find ourselves last workers in a dying trade,
Let flax be our matchmaker, our undertaker,
The provider of sheets for whatever the bed—   20

And be shy of your breasts in the presence of death,
Say that you look more beautiful in linen
Wearing white petticoats, the bow on your bodice
A butterfly attending the embroidered flowers.

AUDRE LORDE *(1934–1992)*

Coal   *(1976)*

I
is the total black, being spoken
from the earth's inside.
There are many kinds of open
how a diamond comes into a knot of flame   5
how sound comes into a word, colored
by who pays what for speaking.

Some words are open like a diamond
on glass windows
singing out within the passing crash of sun   10
Then there are words like stapled wagers
in a perforated book—buy and sign and tear apart—
and come whatever wills all chances
the stub remains
and ill-pulled tooth with a ragged edge.   15
Some words live in my throat

breeding like adders. Others know sun
seeking like gypsies over my tongue
to explode through my lips
like young sparrows bursting from shell.   20
Some words
bedevil me.

Love is a word, another kind of open.
As the diamond comes into a knot of flame
I am Black because I come from the earth's inside   25
now take my word for jewel in the open light.

ROBERT LOWELL   (1917–1977)

For the Union Dead   (1964)

"Relinquunt Omnia Servare Rem Publicam."°

The old South Boston Aquarium stands
in a Sahara of snow now. Its broken windows are boarded.
The bronze weathervane cod has lost half its scales.
The airy tanks are dry.

Once my nose crawled like a snail on the glass;   5
my hand tingled
to burst the bubbles
drifting from the noses of the cowed, compliant fish.

My hand draws back. I often sigh still
for the dark downward and vegetating kingdom   10
of the fish and reptile. One morning last March,
I pressed against the new barbed and galvanized

fence on the Boston Common. Behind their cage,
yellow dinosaur steamshovels were grunting
as they cropped up tons of mush and grass   15
to gouge their underworld garage.

Parking spaces luxuriate like civic
sandpiles in the heart of Boston.
A girdle of orange, Puritan-pumpkin colored girders
braces the tingling Statehouse,   20

"Relinquunt . . . Publicam": "They give up everything to serve the Republic."

shaking over the excavations, as it faces Colonel Shaw°
and his bell-cheeked Negro infantry
on St. Gaudens'° shaking Civil War relief,
propped by a plank splint against the garage's earthquake.

Two months after marching through Boston,   25
half the regiment was dead;
at the dedication,
William James could almost hear the bronze Negroes breathe.

Their monument sticks like a fishbone
in the city's throat.   30
Its Colonel is as lean
as a compass-needle.

He has an angry wrenlike vigilance,
a greyhound's gentle tautness;
he seems to wince at pleasure,   35
and suffocate for privacy.

He is out of bounds now. He rejoices in man's lovely,
peculiar power to choose life and die—
when he leads his black soldiers to death,
he cannot bend his back.   40

On a thousand small town New England greens,
the old white churches hold their air
of sparse, sincere rebellion; frayed flags
quilt the graveyards of the Grand Army of the Republic.

The stone statues of the abstract Union Soldier   45
grow slimmer and younger each year—
wasp-waisted, they doze over muskets
and muse through their sideburns . . .

Shaw's father wanted no monument
except the ditch,   50
where his son's body was thrown
and lost with his "niggers."

The ditch is nearer.
There are no statues for the last war here;

---

21 *Colonel Shaw:* Colonel Robert Gould Shaw (1837–1863), killed with several of his troops in a battle at Fort Wagner, South Carolina.   23 *St. Gaudens:* August Saint-Gaudens (1848–1907), sculptor.

on Boylston Street, a commercial photograph   55
shows Hiroshima boiling

over a Mosler Safe, the "Rock of Ages"
that survived the blast. Space is nearer.
When I crouch to my television set,
the drained faces of Negro school-children rise like balloons.   60

Colonel Shaw
is riding on his bubble,
he waits
for the blesséd break.

The Aquarium is gone. Everywhere,   65
giant finned cars nose forward like fish;
a savage servility
slides by on grease.

ANDREW MARVELL   *(1621–1678)*

The Garden   *(1681)*

How vainly men themselves amaze
To win the palm, the oak, or bays,
And their incessant labors see
Crowned from some single herb, or tree,
Whose short and narrow-vergèd shade   5
Does prudently their toils upbraid;
While all flowers and all trees do close
To weave the garlands of repose!

Fair Quiet, have I found thee here,
And Innocence, thy sister dear?   10
Mistaken long, I sought you then
In busy companies of men.
Your sacred plants, if here below,
Only among the plants will grow;
Society is all but rude   15
To this delicious solitude.

No white nor red was ever seen
So amorous as this lovely green.
Fond lovers, cruel as their flame,
Cut in these trees their mistress' name: 20
Little, alas, they know or heed

How far these beauties hers exceed!
Fair trees, wheresoe'er your barks I wound,
No name shall but your own be found.

When we have run our passion's heat,   25
Love hither makes his best retreat.
The gods, that mortal beauty chase,
Still in a tree did end their race:
Apollo hunted Daphne so,
Only that she might laurel grow;   30
And Pan did after Syrinx speed,
Not as a nymph, but for a reed.

What wondrous life is this I lead!
Ripe apples drop about my head;
The luscious clusters of the vine   35
Upon my mouth do crush their wine;
The nectarine and curious peach
Into my hands themselves do reach;
Stumbling on melons, as I pass,
Insnared with flowers, I fall on grass.   40

Meanwhile the mind, from pleasure less,
Withdraws into its happiness;
The mind, that ocean where each kind
Does straight its own resemblance find;
Yet it creates, transcending these,   45
Far other worlds and other seas,
Annihilating all that's made
To a green thought in a green shade.

Here at the fountain's sliding foot,
Or at some fruit tree's mossy root,   50
Casting the body's vest aside,
My soul into the boughs does glide:
There, like a bird, it sits and sings,
Then whets and combs its silver wings,
And, till prepared for longer flight,   55
Waves in its plumes the various light.

Such was that happy garden-state,
While man there walked without a mate:
After a place so pure and sweet,
What other help could yet be meet!   60
But 'twas beyond a mortal's share
To wander solitary there:
Two paradises 'twere in one
To live in paradise alone.

How well the skillful gardener drew 65
Of flowers and herbs this dial new,
Where, from above, the milder sun
Does through a fragrant zodiac run;
And as it works, th' industrious bee
Computes its time as well as we! 70
How could such sweet and wholesome hours
Be reckoned but with herbs and flowers?

HERMAN MELVILLE *(1819–1891)*

The Maldive Shark *(1888)*

About the Shark, phlegmatical one,
Pale sot of the Maldive sea,
The sleek little pilot-fish, azure and slim,
How alert in attendance be.
From his saw-pit of mouth, from his charnel of maw, 5
They have nothing of harm to dread
But liquidly glide on his ghastly flank
Or before his Gorgonian head;
Or lurk in the port of serrated teeth
In white triple tiers of glittering gates, 10
And there find a haven when peril's abroad,
An asylum in jaws of the Fates!

They are friends; and friendly they guide him to prey,
Yet never partake of the treat—
Eyes and brains to the dotard lethargic and dull, 15
Pale ravener of horrible meat.

GEORGE MEREDITH *(1828–1909)*

Lucifer in Starlight *(1883)*

On a starred night Prince Lucifer uprose.
Tired of his dark dominion, swung the fiend
Above the rolling ball, in cloud part screened,
Where sinners hugged their specter of repose.
Poor prey to his hot fit of pride were those. 5
And now upon his western wing he leaned,
Now his huge bulk o'er Afric's sands careened,
Now the black planet shadowed Arctic snows.
Soaring through wider zones that pricked his scars

With memory of the old revolt from Awe,   10
He reached a middle height, and at the stars,
Which are the brain of heaven, he looked, and sank.
Around the ancient track marched, rank on rank,
The army of unalterable law.

W. S. MERWIN   (b. 1927)

The Drunk in the Furnace   (1960)

       For a good decade
The furnace stood in the naked gully, fireless
And vacant as any hat. Then when it was
No more to them than a hulking black fossil
To erode unnoticed with the rest of the junk-hill,   5
By the poisonous creek, and rapidly to be added
       To their ignorance.

       They were afterwards astonished
To confirm, one morning, a twist of smoke like a pale
Resurrection, staggering out of its chewed hole,   10
And to remark then other tokens that someone,
Cozily bolted behind the eye-holed iron
Door of the drafty burner, had there established
       His bad castle.

       Where he gets his spirits   15
It's a mystery. But the stuff keeps him musical:
Hammer-and-anviling with poker and bottle
To his jugged bellowings, till the last groaning clang
As he collapses onto the rioting
Springs of a litter of car-seats ranged on the grates,   20
       To sleep like an iron pig.

       In their tar-paper church
On a text about stoke-holes that are sated never
Their Reverend lingers. They nod and hate trespassers.
When the furnace wakes, though, all afternoon   25
Their witless offspring flock like piped rats to its siren
Crescendo, and agape on the crumbling ridge
       Stand in a row and learn.

Chord

(1988)

While Keats wrote they were cutting down the sandalwood forests
while he listened to the nightingale they heard their own axes
    echoing through the forests
while he sat in the walled garden on the hill outside the city they
    thought of their gardens dying far away on the mountain
while the sound of the words clawed at him they thought of their wives
while the tip of his pen travelled the iron they had coveted was
    hateful to them   5
while he thought of the Grecian woods they bled under red flowers
while he dreamed of wine the trees were falling from the trees
while he felt his heart they were hungry and their faith was sick
while the song broke over him they were in a secret place and they
    were cutting it forever
while he coughed they carried the trunks to the hole in the forest
    the size of a foreign ship   10
while he groaned on the voyage to Italy they fell on the trails and
    were broken
when he lay with the odes behind him the wood was sold for cannons
when he lay watching the window they came home and lay down
and an age arrived when everything was explained in another language

EDNA ST. VINCENT MILLAY   *(1892–1950)*

Spring

(1920)

To what purpose, April, do you return again?
Beauty is not enough.
You can no longer quiet me with the redness
Of little leaves opening stickily.
I know what I know.   5
The sun is hot on my neck as I observe
The spikes of the crocus.
The smell of the earth is good.
It is apparent that there is no death.
But what does that signify?   10
Not only under ground are the brains of men
Eaten by maggots.
Life in itself
Is nothing,
An empty cup, a flight of uncarpeted stairs.   15
It is not enough that yearly, down this hill,
April
Comes like an idiot, babbling and strewing flowers.

JOHN MILTON   *(1608–1674)*

On the Late Massacre in Piedmont°   *(1673)*

Avenge, O Lord, thy slaughtered saints, whose bones
Lie scattered on the Alpine mountains cold;
Even them who kept thy truth so pure of old
When all our fathers worshipped stocks and stones,
Forget not: in thy book record their groans   5
Who were thy sheep and in their ancient fold
Slain by the bloody Piedmontese, that rolled
Mother with infant down the rocks. Their moans
The vales redoubled to the hills, and they
To heaven. Their martyred blood and ashes sow   10
O'er all the Italian fields where still doth sway
The triple tyrant; that from these may grow
A hundredfold, who, having learnt thy way,
Early may fly the Babylonian woe.°

JANICE MIRIKITANI   *(b. 1942)*

Desert Flowers   *(1978)*

Flowers
faded
in the desert wind.
No flowers grow
where dust winds blow   5
and rain is like
a dry heave moan.

          Mama, did you dream about that
          beau who would take you
          away from it all,   10
          who would show you
          in his '41 ford
          and tell you how soft
          your hands
          like the silk kimono   15
          you folded for the wedding?

Piedmont: On Easter 1655, the duke of Savoy killed seventeen hundred members of the Protestant Waldensian sect in northern Italy.   14 *Babylonian woe:* A refernce to the papal court.

Make you forget
about That place,
the back bending
wind that fell like a wall,   20
drowned all your geraniums
and flooded the shed
where you tried to sleep
away hyenas?
And mama,   25
bending in the candlelight,
after lights out in barracks,
an ageless shadow
grows victory flowers
made from crepe paper,   30
shaping those petals
like the tears
your eyes bled.

Your fingers
knotted at knuckles   35
wounded, winding around wire stems
the tiny, sloganed banner:

            "america for americans".

Did you dream
of the shiny ford   40
(only always a dream)
ride your youth
like the wind
in the headless night?

Flowers   45
2 ¢ a dozen,
flowers for American Legions
worn like a badge
on america's lapel
made in post-concentration camps   50
by candlelight.
Flowers
watered
by the spit
of "no japs wanted here",   55
planted in poverty
of postwar relocations,
plucked by
victory's veterans.

Mama, do you dream   60
of the wall of wind
that falls
on your limbless desert,
on stems
brimming with petals/crushed   65
crepepaper
growing
from the crippled
mouth of your hand?

Your tears, mama,   70
have nourished us.
Your children
like pollen
scatter in the wind.

MARIANNE MOORE   *(1887–1972)*

The Fish   *(1921)*

wade
through black jade.
    Of the crow-blue mussel-shells, one keeps
    adjusting the ash-heaps;
        opening and shutting itself like   5

an
injured fan.
    The barnacles which encrust the side
    of the wave, cannot hide
        there for the submerged shafts of the   10

sun,
split like spun
    glass, move themselves with spotlight swiftness
into the crevices—
    in and out, illuminating   15

the
turquoise sea
    of bodies. The water drives a wedge
    of iron through the iron edge
        of the cliff; whereupon the stars,   20

pink
rice-grains, ink-
    bespattered jelly-fish, crabs like green
    lilies, and submarine
        toadstools, slide each on the other.   25

All
external
    marks of abuse are present on this
    defiant edifice—
        all the physical features of   30

ac-
cident—lack
    of cornice, dynamite grooves, burns, and
    hatchet strokes, these things stand
        out on it; the chasm-side is   35

dead.
Repeated
    evidence has proved that it can live
    on what can not revive
        its youth. The sea grows old in it.   40

PAUL MULDOON   (b. 1951)

Milkweed and Monarch   (1994)

As he knelt by the grave of his mother and father
the taste of dill, or tarragon—
he could barely tell one from the other—

filled his mouth. It seemed as if he might smother.
Why should he be stricken   5
with grief, not for his mother and father,

but a woman slinking from the fur of a sea-otter
in Portland, Maine, or, yes, Portland, Oregon—
he could barely tell one from the other—

and why should he now savour   10
the tang of her, her little pickled gherkin,
as he knelt by the grave of his mother and father?

*

He looked about. He remembered her palaver
on how both earth and sky would darken—
"You could barely tell one from the other"—   15

while the Monarch butterflies passed over
in their milkweed-hunger: "A wing-beat, some reckon,
may trigger off the mother and father

of all storms, striking your Irish Cliffs of Moher
with the force of a hurricane."   20
Then: "Milkweed and Monarch 'invented' each other."

*

He looked about. Cow's-parsley in a samovar.
He'd mistaken his mother's name, "Regan", for "Anger":
as he knelt by the grave of his mother and father
he could barely tell one from the other.   25

FRANK O'HARA   (1926–1966)

The Day Lady° Died   *(1964)*

It is 12:20 in New York a Friday
three days after Bastille day, yes
it is 1959 and I go get a shoeshine
because I will get off the 4:19 in Easthampton
at 7:15 and then go straight to dinner   5
and I don't know the people who will feed me

I walk up the muggy street beginning to sun
and have a hamburger and a malted and buy
an ugly NEW WORLD WRITING to see what the poets
in Ghana are doing these days   10
          I go on to the bank
and Miss Stillwagon (first name Linda I once heard)
doesn't even look up my balance for once in her life
and in the GOLDEN GRIFFIN° I get a little Verlaine
for Patsy with drawings by Bonnard although I do   15
think of Hesiod, trans. Richmond Lattimore or
Brendan Behan's new play or *Le Balcon or Les Negres*

Lady: Billie Holiday (1915–1959), legendary jazz singer.   14 *GOLDEN GRIFFIN:* Bookstore in
New York City.

of Genet, but I don't, I stick with Verlaine
after practically going to sleep with quandariness
and for Mike I just stroll into the PARK LANE   20
Liquor Store and ask for a bottle of Strega and
then I go back where I came from to 6th Avenue
and the tobacconist in the Ziegfeld Theatre and
casually ask for a carton of Gauloises and a carton
of Picayunes, and a NEW YORK POST with her face on it   25

and I am sweating a lot by now and thinking of
leaning on the john door in the 5 SPOT°
while she whispered a song along the keyboard
to Mal Wandron° and everyone and I stopped breathing

WILFRED OWEN   *(1893–1918)*

Dulce et Decorum Est°   *(1920)*

Bent double, like old beggars under sacks,
Knock-kneed, coughing like hags, we cursed through sludge,
Till on the haunting flares we turned our backs
And towards our distant rest began to trudge.
Men marched asleep. Many had lost their boots   5
But limped on, blood-shod. All went lame; all blind;
Drunk with fatigue; deaf even to the hoots
Of tired, outstripped Five-Nines° that dropped behind.

Gas! Gas! Quick, boys!—An ecstasy of fumbling,
Fitting the clumsy helmets just in time;   10
But someone still was yelling out and stumbling,
And flound'ring like a man in fire or lime . . .
Dim, through the misty panes and thick green light,
As under a green sea, I saw him drowning.

In all my dreams, before my helpless sight,   15
He plunges at me, guttering, choking, drowning.

If in smothering dreams you too could pace
Behind the wagon that we flung him in,
And watch the white eyes writhing in his face,
His hanging face, like a devil's sick of sin;   20

---

27 *5 SPOT:* A New York jazz club.   29 *Mal Wandron:* Pianist and composer (b. 1935) who accompanied Billie Holiday from 1957–1959.   *Dulce et Decorum Est:* From Horace, *Odes* 3.2.13, "It is sweet and proper to die for one's country."   8 *Five-Nines:* 5.9-inch caliber cannon shells.

If you could hear, at every jolt, the blood
Come gargling from the froth-corrupted lungs,
Obscene as cancer, bitter as the cud
Of vile, incurable sores on innocent tongues,—
My friend,° you would not tell with such high zest   25
To children ardent for some desperate glory,
The old Lie: Dulce et decorum est
Pro patria mori.

SYLVIA PLATH   *(1932–1963)*

The Colossus°   *(1960)*

I shall never get you put together entirely,
Pieced, glued, and properly jointed.
Mule-bray, pig-grunt and bawdy cackles
Proceed from your great lips.
It's worse than a barnyard.   5

Perhaps you consider yourself an oracle,
Mouthpiece of the dead, or of some god or other.
Thirty years now I have labored
To dredge the silt from your throat.
I am none the wiser.   10

Scaling little ladders with gluepots and pails of lysol
I crawl like an ant in mourning
Over the weedy acres of your brow
To mend the immense skull plates and clear
The bald, white tumuli of your eyes.   15

A blue sky out of the Oresteia°
Arches above us. O father, all by yourself
You are pithy and historical as the Roman Forum.
I open my lunch on a hill of black cypress.
Your fluted bones and acanthine hair are littered   20

In their old anarchy to the horizon-line.
It would take more than a lightning-stroke
To create such a ruin.
Nights, I squat in the cornucopia
Of your left ear, out of the wind,   25

---

25 *My friend:* Jessie Pope, author of *Jessie Pope's War Poems* (1915).   *Colossus:* Third-century
B.C. statue that once stood in the harbor entrance to Rhodes, Greece.   16 *Oresteia:* Dramatic
trilogy by Aeschylus (525–456 B.C.) that presents a cycle of family murders.

Counting the red stars and those of plum-color.
The sun rises under the pillar of your tongue.
My hours are married to shadow.
No longer do I listen for the scrape of a keel
On the blank stones of the landing.   30

Witch Burning   *(1959)*

In the marketplace they are piling the dry sticks.
A thicket of shadows is a poor coat. I inhabit
The wax image of myself, a doll's body.
Sickness begins here: I am a dartboard for witches.
Only the devil can eat the devil out.   5
In the month of red leaves I climb to a bed of fire.

It is easy to blame the dark: the mouth of a door,
The cellar's belly. They've blown my sparkler out.
A black-sharded lady keeps me in a parrot cage.
What large eyes the dead have!   10
I am intimate with a hairy spirit.
Smoke wheels from the beak of this empty jar.

If I am a little one, I can do no harm.
If I don't move about, I'll knock nothing over. So I said,
Sitting under a potlid, tiny and inert as a rice grain.   15
They are turning the burners up, ring after ring.
We are full of starch, my small white fellows. We grow.
It hurts at first. The red tongues will teach the truth.

Mother of beetles, only unclench your hand:
I'll fly through the candle's mouth like a singeless moth.   20
Give me back my shape. I am ready to construe the days
I coupled with dust in the shadow of a stone.
My ankles brighten. Brightness ascends my thighs.
I am lost, I am lost, in the robes of all this light.

Edgar Allan Poe   *(1809–1849)*

The Raven   *(1845)*

Once upon a midnight dreary, while I pondered, weak and weary,
Over many a quaint and curious volume of forgotten lore—
While I nodded, nearly napping, suddenly there came a tapping,
As of some one gently rapping, rapping at my chamber door.

"'Tis some visiter," I muttered, "tapping at my chamber door—   5
                    Only this and nothing more."

Ah, distinctly I remember it was in the bleak December;
And each separate dying ember wrought its ghost upon the floor.
Eagerly I wished the morrow;—vainly I had sought to borrow
From my books surcease of sorrow—sorrow for the lost Lenore—   10
For the rare and radiant maiden whom the angels name Lenore—
                    Nameless *here* for evermore.

And the silken, sad, uncertain rustling of each purple curtain
Thrilled me—filled me with fantastic terrors never felt before;
So that now, to still the beating of my heart, I stood repeating   15
"'Tis some visiter entreating entrance at my chamber door—
Some late visiter entreating entrance at my chamber door;—
                    This it is and nothing more."

Presently my soul grew stronger; hesitating then no longer,
"Sir," said I, "or Madam, truly your forgiveness I implore;   20
But the fact is I was napping, and so gently you came rapping,
And so faintly you came tapping, tapping at my chamber door,
That I scarce was sure I heard you"—here I opened wide the door;—
                    Darkness there and nothing more.

Deep into that darkness peering, long I stood there wondering, fearing,   25
Doubting, dreaming dreams no mortal ever dared to dream before;
But the silence was unbroken, and the stillness gave no token,
And the only word there spoken was the whispered word, "Lenore?"
This I whispered, and an echo murmured back the word "Lenore!"—
                    Merely this and nothing more.   30

Back into the chamber turning, all my soul within me burning,
Soon again I heard a tapping somewhat louder than before.
"Surely," said I, "surely that is something at my window lattice;
Let me see, then, what thereat is, and this mystery explore—
Let my heart be still a moment and this mystery explore;—   35
                    'Tis the wind and nothing more!"

Open here I flung the shutter, when, with many a flirt and flutter,
In there stepped a stately Raven of the saintly days of yore;
Not the least obeisance made he; not a minute stopped or stayed he;
But, when mien of lord or lady, perched above my chamber door—   40
Perched upon a bust of Pallas just above my chamber door—
                    Perched, and sat, and nothing more.

Then this ebony bird beguiling my sad fancy into smiling,
By the grave and stern decorum of the countenance it wore,

"Though thy crest be short and shaven, thou," I said, "art sure no craven,   45
Ghastly grim and ancient Raven wandering from the Nightly shore—
Tell me what thy lordly name is on the Night's Plutonian shore!"
                  Quoth the Raven "Nevermore."

Much I marvelled this ungainly fowl to hear discourse so plainly,
Though its answer little meaning—little relevancy bore;   50
For we cannot help agreeing that no living human being
Ever yet blessed with seeing bird above this chamber door—
Bird or beast upon the sculptured bust above his chamber door,
                With such name as "Nevermore."

But the Raven, sitting lonely on the placid bust, spoke only   55
That one word, as if his soul in that one word he did outpour.
Nothing farther then he uttered—not a feather then he fluttered—
Till I scarcely more than muttered "Other friends have flown before—
On the morrow *he* will leave me, as my Hopes have flown before."
             Then the bird said "Nevermore."   60

Startled at the stillness broken by reply so aptly spoken,
"Doubtless," said I, "what it utters is its only stock and store
Caught from some unhappy master whom unmerciful Disaster
Followed fast and followed faster till his songs one burden bore—
Till the dirges of his Hope that melancholy burden bore   65
             Of 'Never-nevermore.'"

But the Raven still beguiling all my fancy into smiling,
Straight I wheeled a cushioned seat in front of bird, and bust and door;
Then, upon the velvet sinking, I betook myself to linking
Fancy unto fancy, thinking what this ominous bird of yore—   70
What this grim, ungainly, ghastly, gaunt, and ominous bird of yore
            Meant in croaking "Nevermore."

This I sat engaged in guessing, but no syllable expressing
To the fowl whose fiery eyes now burned into my bosom's core;
This and more I sat divining, with my head at ease reclining   75
On the cushion's velvet lining that the lamp light gloated o'er,
But whose velvet-violet lining with the lamp-light gloating o'er,
          She shall press, ah, nevermore!

Then, methought, the air grew denser, perfumed from an unseen censer
Swung by Seraphim whose foot-falls tinkled on the tufted floor.   80
"Wretch," I cried, "thy God hath lent thee—by these angels he hath sent
   thee
Respite—respite and nepenthe from thy memories of Lenore;
Quaff, oh quaff this kind nepenthe and forget this lost Lenore!"
              Quoth the Raven "Nevermore."

"Prophet!" said I, "thing of evil!—prophet still, if bird or devil!—   85
Whether Tempter sent, or whether tempest tossed thee here ashore,
Desolate yet all undaunted, on this desert land enchanted—
On this home by Horror haunted—tell me truly, I implore—
Is there—*is* there balm in Gilead?—tell me—tell me, I implore!"
                    Quoth the Raven "Nevermore."   90

"Prophet!" said I, "thing of evil!—prophet still, if bird or devil!
By that Heaven that bends above us—by that God we both adore!—
Tell this soul with sorrow laden if, within the distant Aidenn,
It shall clasp a sainted maiden whom the angels name Lenore—
Clasp a rare and radiant maiden whom the angels name Lenore."   95
                    Quoth the Raven "Nevermore."

"Be that word our sign of parting, bird or fiend!" I shrieked, upstarting—
"Get thee back into the tempest and the Night's Plutonian shore!
Leave no black plume as a token of that lie thy soul hath spoken!
Leave my loneliness unbroken!—quit the bust above my door!   100
Take thy beak from out my heart, and take thy form from off my door!"
                    Quoth the Raven "Nevermore."

And the Raven, never flitting, still is sitting, *still* is sitting
On the pallid bust of Pallas just above my chamber door;
And his eyes have all the seeming of a demon's that is dreaming,   105
And the lamp-light o'er him streaming throws his shadow on the floor;
And my soul from out that shadow that lies floating on the floor
                    Shall be lifted—nevermore!

ALEXANDER POPE   *(1688–1744)*

from Epistle II. Of the Nature and
State of Man With Respect to Himself,
as an Individual   *(1733)*

Know then thyself, presume not God to scan;
The proper study of mankind is man.
Placed on this isthmus of a middle state,
A being darkly wise, and rudely great:
With too much knowledge for the skeptic side,   5
With too much weakness for the Stoic's pride,
He hangs between; in doubt to act, or rest,
In doubt to deem himself a god, or beast;
In doubt his mind or body to prefer;
Born but to die, and reasoning but to err;   10
Alike in ignorance, his reason such,

Whether he thinks too little, or too much:
Chaos of thought and passion, all confused;
Still by himself abused, or disabused;
Created half to rise, and half to fall;   15
Great lord of all things, yet a prey to all;
Sole judge of truth, in endless error hurled:
The glory, jest, and riddle of the world!

from The Cantos   *(1921, 1930)*

I

And then went down to the ship,
Set keel to breakers, forth on the godly sea, and
We set up mast and sail on that swart ship,
Bore sheep aboard her, and our bodies also
Heavy with weeping, and winds from sternward   5
Bore us out onward with bellying canvas,
Circe's° this craft, the trim-coifed goddess.
Then sat we amidships, wind jamming the tiller,
Thus with stretched sail, we went over sea till day's end.
Sun to his slumber, shadows o'er all the ocean,   10
Came we then to the bounds of deepest water,
To the Kimmerian lands, and peopled cities
Covered with close-webbed mist, unpierced ever
With glitter of sun-rays
Nor with stars stretched, nor looking back from heaven 15
Swartest night stretched over wretched men there.
The ocean flowing backward, came we then to the place
Aforesaid by Circe.
Here did they rites, Perimedes and Eurylochus,°
And drawing sword from my hip   20
I dug the ell-square pitkin;
Poured we libations unto each the dead,
First mead and then sweet wine, water mixed with white flour.
Then prayed I many a prayer to the sickly death's-heads;
As set in Ithaca, sterile bulls of the best   25
For sacrifice, heaping the pyre with goods,
A sheep to Tiresias only, black and a bell-sheep.
Dark blood flowed in the fosse,
Souls out of Erebus, cadaverous dead, of brides
Of youths and of the old who had borne much;   30
Souls stained with recent tears, girls tender,
Men many, mauled with bronze lance heads,

---

7 *Circe:* Enchantress and mistress of Odysseus.   19 *Perimedes and Eurylochus:* Companions of
Odysseus.

Battle spoil, bearing yet dreory° arms,
These many crowded about me; with shouting,
Pallor upon me, cried to my men for more beasts;   35
Slaughtered the herds, sheep slain of bronze;
Poured ointment, cried to the gods,
To Pluto° the strong, and praised Proserpine;°
Unsheathed the narrow sword,
I sat to keep off the impetuous impotent dead,   40
Till I should hear Tiresias.
But first Elpenor came, our friend Elpenor,
Unburied, cast on the wide earth,
Limbs that we left in the house of Circe,
Unwept, unwrapped in sepulchre, since toils urged other.   45
Pitiful spirit. And I cried in hurried speech:
"Elpenor, how art thou come to this dark coast?
"Cam'st thou afoot, outstripping seamen?"
        And he in heavy speech:
"Ill fate and abundant wine. I slept in Circe's ingle.   50
"Going down the long ladder unguarded,
"I fell against the buttress,
"Shattered the nape-nerve, the soul sought Avernus.°
"But thou, O King, I bid remember me, unwept, unburied,
"Heap up mine arms, be tomb by sea-bord, and inscribed: 55
"*A man of no fortune, and with a name to come.*
"And set my oar up, that I swung mid fellows."

And Anticlea° came, whom I beat off, and then Tiresias Theban,
Holding his golden wand, knew me, and spoke first:
"A second time? why? man of ill star,   60
"Facing the sunless dead and this joyless region?
"Stand from the fosse, leave me my bloody bever
"For soothsay."
        And I stepped back,
And he strong with the blood, said then: "Odysseus   65
"Shalt return through spiteful Neptune, over dark seas,
"Lose all companions." And then Anticlea came.
Lie quiet Divus. I mean, that is Andreas Divus,°
In officina Wecheli, 1538, out of Homer.
And he sailed, by Sirens and thence outward and away   70
And unto Circe.
        Venerandam,°
In the Cretan's phrase, with the golden crown, Aphrodite,
Cypri munimenta sortita est, mirthful, orichalchi, with golden

---

33 *dreory:* Bloody.   38 *Pluto:* Latin name for god of the underworld. *Proserpine:* Pluto's queen.   53 *Avernus:* Lake and entrance to the underworld.   58 *Anticlea:* Mother of Odysseus.   68 *Andreas Divus:* Sixteenth-century Italian translator of the *Odyssey.* 72 *Venerandum:* "Worthy of worship."

Girdles and breast bands, thou with dark eyelids　　　　　75
Bearing the golden bough of Argicida.° So that:

JOHN CROWE RANSOM　*(1888–1974)*

Piazza Piece　　　　　　　　　　　　　　　*(1925)*

—I am a gentleman in a dustcoat trying
To make you hear. Your ears are soft and small
And listen to an old man not at all,
They want the young men's whispering and sighing.
But see the roses on your trellis dying　　　　　　5
And hear the spectral singing of the moon;
For I must have my lovely lady soon,
I am a gentleman in a dustcoat trying.

—I am a lady young in beauty waiting
Until my truelove comes, and then we kiss.　　　　10
But what grey man among the vines is this
Whose words are dry and faint as in a dream?
Back from my trellis, Sir, before I scream!
I am a lady young in beauty waiting.

EDWIN ARLINGTON ROBINSON　*(1869–1935)*

Richard Cory　　　　　　　　　　　　　*(1896–1897)*

Whenever Richard Cory went down town,
　We people on the pavement looked at him:
He was a gentleman from sole to crown,
　Clean favored, and imperially slim.

And he was always quietly arrayed,　　　　　　5
　And he was always human when he talked;
But still he fluttered pulses when he said,
　"Good-morning," and he glittered when he walked.

And he was rich—yes, richer than a king,
　And admirably schooled in every grace:　　　　10
In fine, we thought that he was everything
　To make us wish that we were in his place.

———

76 *Argicida:* A reference to the god Hermes.

So on we worked, and waited for the light,
    And went without the meat, and cursed the bread;
And Richard Cory, one calm summer night,   15
    Went home and put a bullet through his head.

THEODORE ROETHKE   *(1908–1963)*

Root Cellar   *(1948)*

Nothing would sleep in that cellar, dank as a ditch,
Bulbs broke out of boxes hunting for chinks in the dark,
Shoots dangled and drooped,
Lolling obscenely from mildewed crates,
Hung down long yellow evil necks, like tropical snakes.   5
And what a congress of stinks!
Roots ripe as old bait,
Pulpy stems, rank, silo-rich,
Leaf-mold, manure, lime, piled against slippery planks.
Nothing would give up life: 10
Even the dirt kept breathing a small breath.

In a Dark Time   *(1960)*

In a dark time, the eye begins to see,
I meet my shadow in the deepening shade;
I hear my echo in the echoing wood—
A lord of nature weeping to a tree.
I live between the heron and the wren,   5
Beasts of the hill and serpents of the den.

What's madness but nobility of soul
At odds with circumstance? The day's on fire!
I know the purity of pure despair,
My shadow pinned against a sweating wall.   10
That place among the rocks—is it a cave,
Or winding path? The edge is what I have.

A steady storm of correspondences!
A night flowing with birds, a ragged moon,
And in broad day the midnight come again!   15
A man goes far to find out what he is—
Death of the self in a long, tearless night,
All natural shapes blazing unnatural light.

Dark, dark my light, and darker my desire.
My soul, like some heat-maddened summer fly,   20
Keeps buzzing at the sill. Which I is *I?*
A fallen man, I climb out of my fear.
The mind enters itself, and God the mind,
And one is One, free in the tearing wind.

CHRISTINA ROSSETTI   *(1830–1894)*

After Death   *(1862)*

The curtains were half drawn, the floor was swept
   And strewn with rushes, rosemary and may
   Lay thick upon the bed on which I lay,
Where through the lattice ivy-shadows crept.
He leaned above me, thinking that I slept   5
   And could not hear him, but I heard him say,
   'Poor child, poor child': and as he turned away
Came a deep silence, and I knew he wept.
He did not touch the shroud, or raise the fold
   That hid my face, or take my hand in his,   10
     Or ruffle the smooth pillows for my head;
      He did not love me living; but once dead
    He pitied me; and very sweet it is
To know that he is warm though I am cold.

DANTE GABRIEL ROSSETTI   *(1828–1882)*

The Woodspurge   *(1870)*

The wind flapped loose, the wind was still,
Shaken out dead from tree and hill:
I had walked on at the wind's will—
I sat now, for the wind was still.

Between my knees my forehead was—   5
My lips, drawn in, said not Alas!
My hair was over in the grass,
My naked ears heard the day pass.

My eyes, wide open, had the run
Of some ten weeds to fix upon;   10
Among those few, out of the sun,
The woodspurge flowered, three cups in one.

From perfect grief there need not be
Wisdom or even memory:
One thing then learnt remains to me—   15
The woodspurge has a cup of three.

CARL SANDBURG   *(1878–1967)*

Chicago   *(1916)*

Hog Butcher for the World,
Tool Maker, Stacker of Wheat,
Player with Railroads and the Nation's Freight Handler;
Stormy, husky, brawling,
City of the Big Shoulders: 5

They tell me you are wicked and I believe them, for I have seen your painted
     women under the gas lamps luring the farm boys.
And they tell me you are crooked and I answer: Yes, it is true I have seen the
     gunman kill and go free to kill again.
And they tell me you are brutal and my reply is: On the faces of women and
     children I have seen the marks of wanton hunger.
And having answered so I turn once more to those who sneer at this my city,
     and I give them back the sneer and say to them:
Come and show me another city with lifted head singing so proud to be   10
     alive and coarse and strong and cunning.
Flinging magnetic curses amid the toil of piling job on job, here is a tall bold
     slugger set vivid against the little soft cities;
Fierce as a dog with tongue lapping for action, cunning as a savage pitted
     against the wilderness,
          Bareheaded,
          Shoveling,
          Wrecking,   15
          Planning,
          Building, breaking, rebuilding,
Under the smoke, dust all over his mouth, laughing with white teeth,
Under the terrible burden of destiny laughing as a young man laughs,
Laughing even as an ignorant fighter laughs who has never lost a battle,   20
Bragging and laughing that under his wrist is the pulse, and under his ribs
     the heart of the people,
          Laughing!
Laughing the stormy, husky, brawling laughter of Youth, half-naked, sweat-
     ing, proud to be Hog Butcher, Tool Maker, Stacker of Wheat, Player
     with Railroads and Freight Handler to the Nation.

Grass   *(1918)*

Pile the bodies high at Austerlitz and Waterloo.
Shovel them under and let me work—
        I am the grass; I cover all.

And pile them high at Gettysburg
And pile them high at Ypres and Verdun.   5
Shovel them under and let me work.
Two years, ten years, and passengers ask the conductor:
        What place is this?
        Where are we now?

        I am the grass.   10
        Let me work.

SIEGFRIED SASSOON   *(1886–1967)*

Christ and the Soldier   *(1916)*

I

The straggled soldier halted—stared at Him—
Then clumsily dumped down upon his knees,
Gasping, "O blessed crucifix, I'm beat!"
And Christ, still sentried by the seraphim,
Near the front-line, between two splintered trees,   5
Spoke him: "My son, behold these hands and feet."

The soldier eyed Him upward, limb by limb,
Paused at the Face; then muttered, "Wounds like these
Would shift a bloke to Blighty° just a treat!"
Christ, gazing downward, grieving and ungrim,   10
Whispered, "I made for you the mysteries,
Beyond all battles moves the Paraclete."°

II

The soldier chucked his rifle in the dust,
And slipped his pack, and wiped his neck, and said—
"O Christ Almighty, stop this bleeding fight!"   15
Above that hill the sky was stained like rust
With smoke. In sullen daybreak flaring red
The guns were thundering bombardment's blight.

---

9 *Blighty:* Britain.   12 *Paraclete:* Holy Ghost.

The soldier cried, "I was born full of lust,
With hunger, thirst, and wishfulness to wed.   20
Who cares today if I done wrong or right?"
Christ asked all pitying, "Can you put no trust
In my known word that shrives each faithful head?
Am I not resurrection, life and light?"

III

Machine-guns rattled from below the hill;   25
High bullets flicked and whistled through the leaves;
And smoke came drifting from exploding shells.
Christ said, "Believe; and I can cleanse your ill.
I have not died in vain between two thieves;
Nor made a fruitless gift of miracles."   30

The soldier answered, "Heal me if you will,
Maybe there's comfort when a soul believes
In mercy, and we need it in these hells.
But be you for both sides? I'm paid to kill
And if I shoot a man his mother grieves.   35
Does that come into what your teaching tells?"

A bird lit on the Christ and twittered gay;
Then a breeze passed and shook the ripening corn.
A Red Cross waggon bumped along the track.
Forsaken Jesus dreamed in the desolate day—   40
Uplifted Jesus, Prince of Peace forsworn—
An observation post for the attack.

"Lord Jesus, ain't you got no more to say?"
Bowed hung that head below the crown of thorns.
The soldier shifted, and picked up his pack,   45
And slung his gun, and stumbled on his way.
"O God," he groaned, "why ever was I born?" . . .
The battle boomed, and no reply came back.
a thousand cranes curtain the window,
fly up in a sudden breeze.   50

WILLIAM SHAKESPEARE   *(1564–1616)*

Sonnet 129   *(1609)*

Th' expense of spirit in a waste of shame
Is lust in action; and, till action, lust
Is perjured, murd'rous, bloody, full of blame,

Savage, extreme, rude, cruel, not to trust;
Enjoyed no sooner but despisèd straight;   5
Past reason hunted, and no sooner had,
Past reason hated, as a swallowed bait
On purpose laid to make the taker mad:
Mad in pursuit, and in possession so;
Had, having, and in quest to have, extreme;   10
A bliss in proof, and proved, a very woe;
Before, a joy proposed; behind, a dream.
    All this the world well knows; yet none knows well
    To shun the heaven that leads men to this hell.

Sonnet 130   *(1609)*

My mistress' eyes are nothing like the sun;
Coral is far more red than her lips' red;
If snow be white, why then her breasts are dun;
If hairs be wires, black wires grow on her head.
I have seen roses damasked, red and white,   5
But no such roses see I in her cheeks;
And in some perfumes is there more delight
Than in the breath that from my mistress reeks.
I love to hear her speak, yet well I know
That music hath a far more pleasing sound.   10
I grant I never saw a goddess go;
My mistress, when she walks, treads on the ground.
    And yet, by heaven, I think my love as rare
    As any she belied with false compare.

PERCY BYSSHE SHELLEY   *(1792–1822)*

Ozymandias°   *(1818)*

I met a traveler from an antique land
Who said: Two vast and trunkless legs of stone
Stand in the desert . . . Near them, on the sand,
Half sunk, a shattered visage lies, whose frown,
And wrinkled lip, and sneer of cold command,   5
Tell that its sculptor well those passions read
Which yet survive, stamped on these lifeless things,
The hand that mocked them, and the heart that fed:
And on the pedestal these words appear:

———
Ozymandias: Egyptian King Ramses II.

"My name is Ozymandias, king of kings: 10
Look on my works, ye Mighty, and despair!"
Nothing beside remains. Round the decay
Of that colossal wreck, boundless and bare
The lone and level sands stretch far away.

SIR PHILIP SIDNEY   *(1554–1586)*

What Length of Verse?   *(1593)*

What length of verse can serve brave Mopsa's good to show,
Whose virtues strange, and beauties such, as no man them may
    know?
Thus shrewdly burden, then, how can my Muse escape?
The gods must help, and precious things must serve to show her
    shape.

Like great god Saturn, fair, and like fair Venus, chaste;   5
As smooth as Pan, as Juno mild, like goddess Iris fast.
With Cupid she foresees, and goes god Vulcan's pace;
And for a taste of all these gifts, she borrows Momus' grace.

Her forehead jacinth-like, her cheeks of opal hue,
Her twinkling eyes bedecked with pearl, her lips of sapphire blue,
Her hair pure crapall stone, her mouth, O heavenly wide,   10
Her skin like burnished gold, her hands like silver ore untried.

As for those parts unknown, which hidden sure are best,
Happy be they which will believe, and never seek the rest.

CHARLOTTE SMITH   *(1749–1806)*

XXXVIII   *(1784)*

When welcome slumber sets my spirit free,
    Forth to fictitious happiness it flies,
    And where Elysian bowers of bliss arise,
I seem, my Emmeline—to meet with thee!
Ah! Fancy then, dissolving human ties,   5
    Gives me the wishes of my soul to see;
Tears of fond pity fill thy soften'd eyes:
    In heavenly harmony—our hearts agree.
Alas! these joys are mine in dreams alone,
When cruel Reason abdicates her throne!   10

Her harsh return condemns me to complain
Thro' life unpitied, unrelieved, unknown!
    And as the dear delusions leave my brain,
    She bids the truth recur—with aggravated pain!

CATHY SONG *(b. 1955)*

The Youngest Daughter   *(1983)*

The sky has been dark
for many years.
My skin has become as damp
and pale as rice paper
and feels the way   5
mother's used to before the drying sun
parched it out there in the fields.

Lately, when I touch my eyelids,
my hands react as if
I had just touched something   10
hot enough to burn.
My skin, aspirin colored,
tingles with migraine. Mother
has been massaging the left side of my face
especially in the evenings   15
when the pain flares up.

This morning
her breathing was graveled,
her voice gruff with affection
when I wheeled her into the bath.   20
She was in a good humor,
making jokes about her great breasts,
floating in the milky water
like two walruses,
flaccid and whiskered around the nipples.   25
I scrubbed them with a sour taste
in my mouth, thinking:
six children and an old man
have sucked from these brown nipples.

I was almost tender   30
when I came to the blue bruises
that freckle her body,
places where she has been injecting insulin
for thirty years. I soaped her slowly,

she sighed deeply, her eyes closed.　　　　　　　　　　　　　　35
It seems it has always
been like this: the two of us
in this sunless room,
the splashing of the bathwater.

In the afternoons　　　　　　　　　　　　　　　　　　　40
when she has rested,
she prepares our ritual of tea and rice,
garnished with a shred of gingered fish,
a slice of pickled turnip,
a token for my white body.　　　　　　　　　　　　　　45
We eat in the familiar silence.
She knows I am not to be trusted,
even now planning my escape.
As I toast to her health
with the tea she has poured,　　　　　　　　　　　　　50
a thousand cranes curtain the window,
fly up in a sudden breeze.

GERTRUDE STEIN　　(1874–1946)

from Lifting Belly　　　　　　　　　　　(1915–1917)

I have been heavy and had much selecting. I saw a star which was low. It
was so low it twinkled. Breath was in it. Little pieces are stupid.

I want to tell about fire. Fire is that which we have when we have olive.
Olive is a wood. We like linen. Linen is ordered. We are going to order linen.

All belly belly well.

Bed of coals made out of wood.

I think this one may be an expression. We can understand heating and　5
burning composition. Heating with wood.

Sometimes we readily decide upon wind we decide that there will be stars
and perhaps thunder and perhaps rain and perhaps no moon. Sometimes we
decide that there will be a storm and rain. Sometimes we look at the boats.
When we read about a boat we know that it has been sunk. Not by the waves
but by the sails. Any one knows that rowing is dangerous. Be alright. Be careful. Be angry. Say what you think. Believe in there being the same kind of a
dog. Jerk. Jerk him away. Answer that you do not care to think so.

We quarreled with him. We quarreled with him then. Do not forget that
I showed you the road. Do not forget that I showed you the road. We will forget it because he does not oblige himself to thank me. Ask him to thank me.

The next time that he came we offered him something to read. There is a
great difference of opinion as to whether cooking in oil is or is not healthful.

I don't pardon him. I find him objectionable.

What is it when it's upset. It isn't in the room. Moonlight and darkness. 10
Sleep and not sleep. We sleep every night.
What was it.
I said lifting belly.
You didn't say it.
I said it I mean lifting belly.
Don't misunderstand me. 15
Do you.
Do you lift everybody in that way.
No.
You are to say No.
Lifting belly.
How are you. 20
Lifting belly how are you lifting belly.
We like a fire and we don't mind if it smokes.
Do you.
How do you do. The Englishmen are coming. Not here. No an English- 25
woman. An Englishman and an Englishwoman.
What did you say lifting belly. I did not understand you correctly. It is not
well said. For lifting belly. For lifting belly not to lifting belly.
Did you say, oh lifting belly.
What is my another name.
Representative.
Of what. 30
Of the evils of eating.
What are they then.
They are sweet and figs.
Do not send them.
Yes we will it will be very easy. 35

Part II

Lifting belly. Are you. Lifting.
Oh dear I said I was tender, fierce and tender.
Do it. What a splendid example of carelessness.
It gives me a great deal of pleasure to say yes.
Why do I always smile. 40
I don't know.
It pleases me.
You are easily pleased.
I am very pleased.
Thank you I am scarcely sunny. 45
I wish the sun would come out.
Yes.
Do you lift it.
High.
Yes sir I helped to do it. 50
Did you.

WALLACE STEVENS   *(1879–1955)*

The Snow Man   *(1923)*

One must have a mind of winter
To regard the frost and the boughs
Of the pine-trees crusted with snow;

And have been cold a long time
To behold the junipers shagged with ice,   5
The spruces rough in the distant glitter

Of the January sun; and not to think
Of any misery in the sound of the wind,
In the sound of a few leaves,

Which is the sound of the land   10
Full of the same wind
That is blowing in the same bare place

For the listener, who listens in the snow,
And, nothing himself, beholds
Nothing that is not there and the nothing that is.   15

The Emperor of Ice-Cream   *(1923)*

Call the roller of big cigars,
The muscular one, and bid him whip
In kitchen cups concupiscent curds.
Let the wenches dawdle in such dress
As they are used to wear, and let the boys   5
Bring flowers in last month's newspapers.
Let be be finale of seem.
The only emperor is the emperor of ice-cream.

Take from the dresser of deal.°
Lacking the three glass knobs, that sheet   10
On which she embroidered fantails once
And spread it so as to cover her face.
If her horny feet protrude, they come
To show how cold she is, and dumb.
Let the lamp affix its beam.   15
The only emperor is the emperor of ice-cream.

------
9 *deal*: Pinewood.

Anecdote of the Jar *(1937)*

I placed a jar in Tennessee,
And round it was, upon a hill.
It made the slovenly wilderness
Surround that hill.

The wilderness rose up to it,   5
And sprawled around, no longer wild.
The jar was round upon the ground
And tall and of a port in air.

It took dominion everywhere.
The jar was gray and bare.   10
It did not give of bird or bush,
Like nothing else in Tennessee.

MAY SWENSON *(1913–1989)*

Poet to Tiger *(1991)*

THE HAIR

You went downstairs
saw a hair in the sink
and squeezed my toothpaste by the neck.
You roared. My ribs are sore.
This morning even my pencil's got your toothmarks.   5
Big Cat Eye cocked on me you see bird bones.
Snuggled in the rug of your belly
your breath so warm
I smell delicious fear.
Come breathe on me rough pard   10
put soft paws here.

THE SALT

You don't put salt on anything
so I'm eating without.
Honey on the eggs is all right
mustard on the toast.   15
I'm not complaining I'm saying I'm
living with *you*.
You like your meat raw
don't care if it's cold.

20

Your stomach must have tastebuds
you swallow so fast.
Night falls early. It's foggy. Just now

I found another of your bite marks in the cheese.
I'm hungry. Please
come bounding home 25
I'll hand you the wine to open
with your teeth.
Scorched me a steak unsalted
boil my coffee twice
say the blessing to a jingle on the blue TV. 30
Under the lap robe on our chilly couch
look behind my ears "for welps"
and hug me.

THE SAND

You're right I brought a grain
or two of sand 35
into bed I guess in my socks.
But it was you pushed them off
along with everything else.

Asleep you flip
over roll 40
everything under
you and off
me. I'm always grabbing
for my share of the sheets.

Or else you wake me every hour with sudden 45
growled I-love-yous
trapping my face between those plushy
shoulders. All my float-dreams turn spins
and never finish. I'm thinner
now. My watch keeps running fast. 50
But best is when we're riding pillion
my hips within your lap. You let me steer.
Your hand and arm go clear
around my ribs your moist
dream teeth fastened on my nape. 55

A grain of sand in the bed upsets you or
a hair on the floor.
But you'll get
in slick and wet from the shower if I let
you. Or with your wool cap 60

and skiing jacket on
          if it's cold.
     Tiger don't scold me
don't make me comb my hair outdoors.
     Cuff me careful. Lick don't   65
crunch. Make last what's yours.

THE DREAM

You get into the tub holding *The Naked Ape*
     in your teeth. You wet that blond
three-cornered pelt lie back wide
     chest afloat. You're reading   70
in the rising steam and I'm
drinking coffee from your tiger cup.
          You say you dreamed
     I had your baby book
and it was pink and blue.   75
     I pointed to a page and there
was your face with a cub grin.

You put your paws in your armpits
     make a tiger-moo.
     Then you say: "Come here   80
          Poet and take
               this hair
          off me." I do.
It's one of mine. I carefully
     kill it and carry   85
it outside. And stamp on it
     and bury it.

     In the begonia bed.
And then take off my shoes
     not to bring a grain   90
          of sand in to get
               into our bed.
          I'm going to
          do the cooking
          now instead   95
               of you.
     And sneak some salt in
when you're not looking.

ALFRED, LORD TENNYSON   *(1809–1892)*

Break, Break, Break   *(1834)*

Break, break, break,
  On thy cold gray stones, O Sea!
And I would that my tongue could utter
  The thoughts that arise in me.

O well for the fisherman's boy,   5
  That he shouts with his sister at play!
O well for the sailor lad,
  That he sings in his boat on the bay!

And the stately ships go on
  To their haven under the hill;   10
But O for the touch of a vanished hand,
  And the sound of a voice that is still!

Break, break, break
  At the foot of thy crags, O Sea!
But the tender grace of a day that is dead   15
  Will never come back to me.

Crossing the Bar   *(1889)*

Sunset and evening star,
  And one clear call for me!
And may there be no moaning of the bar,
  When I put out to sea,

But such a tide as moving seems asleep,   5
  Too full for sound and foam,
When that which drew from out the boundless deep
  Turns again home.

Twilight and evening bell,
  And after that the dark!   10
And may there be no sadness of farewell,
  When I embark;

For though from out our bourne of Time and Place
  The flood may bear me far,
I hope to see my Pilot face to face   15
  When I have crossed that bar.

DYLAN THOMAS   *(1914–1953)*

In My Craft or Sullen Art   *(1946)*

In my craft or sullen art
Exercised in the still night
When only the moon rages
And the lovers lie abed
With all their griefs in their arms,   5
I labor by singing light
Not for ambition or bread
Or the strut and trade of charms
On the ivory stages
But for the common wages   10
Of their most secret heart.

Not for the proud man apart
From the raging moon I write
On these spindrift pages
Nor for the towering dead   15
With their nightingales and psalms
But for the lovers, their arms
Round the griefs of the ages,
Who pay no praise or wages
Nor heed my craft or art.   20

Do Not Go Gentle into That Good Night   *(1952)*

Do not go gentle into that good night,
Old age should burn and rave at close of day;
Rage, rage against the dying of the light.

Though wise men at their end know dark is right,
Because their words had forked no lightning they   5
Do not go gentle into that good night.

Good men, the last wave by, crying how bright
Their frail deeds might have danced in a green bay,
Rage, rage against the dying of the light.

Wild men who caught and sang the sun in flight,   10
And learn, too late, they grieved it on its way,
Do not go gentle into that good night.

Grave men, near death, who see with blinding sight
Blind eyes could blaze like meteors and be gay,
Rage, rage against the dying of the light.   15

And you, my father, there on the sad height,
Curse, bless, me now with your fierce tears, I pray.
Do not go gentle into that good night.
Rage, rage against the dying of the light.

EDWARD THOMAS   *(1878–1917)*

The Owl   *(1917)*

Downhill I came, hungry, and yet not starved;
Cold, yet had heat within me that was proof
Against the North wind; tired, yet so that rest
Had seemed the sweetest thing under a roof.

Then at the inn I had food, fire, and rest,   5
Knowing how hungry, cold, and tired was I.
All of the night was quite barred out except
An owl's cry, a most melancholy cry

Shaken out long and clear upon the hill,
No merry note, nor cause of merriment,   10
But one telling me plain what I escaped
And others could not, that night, as in I went.

And salted was my food, and my repose,
Salted and sobered, too, by the bird's voice
Speaking for all who lay under the stars,   15
Soldiers and poor, unable to rejoice.

HENRY DAVID THOREAU   *(1817–1862)*

I Am a Parcel of Vain Strivings Tied   *(1841)*

I am a parcel of vain strivings tied
    By a chance bond together,
        Dangling this way and that, their links
            Were made so loose and wide,
                Methinks,   5
                For milder weather.

A bunch of violets without their roots,
   And sorrel intermixed,
  Encircled by a wisp of straw
    Once coiled about their shoots,   10
      The law
    By which I'm fixed.

A nosegay which Time clutched from out
   Those fair Elysian fields,°
  With weeds and broken stems, in haste,   15
    Doth make the rabble rout
      That waste
    The day he yields.

And here I bloom for a short hour unseen,
   Drinking my juices up,   20
  With no root in the land
    To keep my branches green,
      But stand
    In a bare cup.

JEAN TOOMER   *(1894–1967)*

Georgia Dusk   *(1923)*

The sky, lazily disdaining to pursue
   The setting sun, too indolent to hold
   A lengthened tournament for flashing gold,
Passively darkens for night's barbecue,

A feast of moon and men and barking hounds,   5
   An orgy for some genius of the South
   With blood-hot eyes and cane-lipped scented mouth,
Surprised in making folksongs from soul sounds.

The sawmill blows its whistle, buzz-saws stop,
   And silence breaks the bud of knoll and hill,   10
   Soft settling pollen where plowed lands fulfill
Their early promise of a bumper crop.

Smoke from the pyramidal sawdust pile
   Curls up, blue ghosts of trees, tarrying low

---

14 *Elysian fields:* After life of the blessed in Greek and Roman mythology.

Where only chips and stumps are left to show   15
The solid proof of former domicile.

Meanwhile, the men, with vestiges of pomp,
    Race memories of king and caravan,
    High-priests, an ostrich, and a juju-man,
Go singing through the footpaths of the swamp.   20

Their voices rise . . the pine trees are guitars,
    Strumming, pine-needles fall like sheets of rain . .
    Their voices rise . . the chorus of the cane
Is caroling a vesper to the stars. .

O singers, resinous and soft your songs   25
    Above the sacred whisper of the pines,
    Give virgin lips to cornfield concubines,
Bring dreams of Christ to dusky cane-lipped throngs.

MARGARET WALKER   *(1915–1998)*

Childhood   *(1942)*

When I was a child I knew red miners
dressed raggedly and wearing carbide lamps.
I saw them come down red hills to their camps
dyed with red dust from old Ishkooda mines.°
Night after night I met them on the roads,   5
or on the streets in town I caught their glance;
the swing of dinner buckets in their hands,
and grumbling undermining all their words.

I also lived in low cotton country
where moonlight hovered over ripe haystacks,   10
or stumps of trees, and croppers' rotting shacks
with famine, terror, flood, and plague near by;
where sentiment and hatred still held sway
and only bitter land was washed away.

---

4 *Ishkooda mines:* Located south of Birmingham, Alabama.

PHILLIS WHEATLEY *(1753–1784)*

On Being Brought from Africa to America°   *(1773)*

'Twas mercy brought me from my pagan land,
Taught my benighted soul to understand
That there's a God, that there's a Savior too:
Once I redemption neither sought nor knew.
Some view our sable race with scornful eye,   5
"Their color is a diabolic die."°
Remember, Christians, Negros, black as Cain,
May be refined, and join th' angelic train.

WALT WHITMAN *(1819–1892)*

from Song of Myself   *(1855, 1881)*

1

I celebrate myself, and sing myself,
And what I assume you shall assume,
For every atom belonging to me as good belongs to you.

I loafe and invite my soul,
I lean and loafe at my ease observing a spear of summer grass.   5

My tongue, every atom of my blood, form'd from this soil, this air,
Born here of parents born here from parents the same, and their
    parents the same,
I, now thirty-seven years old in perfect health begin,
Hoping to cease not till death.

Creeds and schools in abeyance,   10
Retiring back a while suffield at what they are, but never forgotten,
I harbor for good or bad, I permit to speak at every hazard,
Nature without check with original energy.

11

Twenty-eight young men bathe by the shore,
Twenty-eight young men and all so friendly;   15
Twenty-eight years of womanly life and all so lonesome.

---

from Africa to America: Wheatley arrived in Boston from Africa in 1761 at the age of eight.   6
die: Dye.

She owns the fine house by the rise of the bank,
She hides handsome and richly drest aft the blinds of the window.

Which of the young men does she like the best?
Ah the homeliest of them is beautiful to her.   20

Where are you off to, lady? for I see you,
You splash in the water there, yet stay stock still in your room.

Dancing and laughing along the beach came the twenty-ninth bather,
The rest did not see her, but she saw them and loved them.

The beards of the young men glisten'd with wet, it ran from their long   25
    hair,
Little streams, pass'd all over their bodies.
An unseen hand also pass'd over their bodies,
It descended tremblingly from their temples and ribs.

The young men float on their backs, their white bellies bulge to the
    sun, they do not ask who seizes fast to them,
They do not know who puffs and declines with pendant and bending   30
    arch,
They do not think whom they souse with spray.

52

The spotted hawk swoops by and accuses me, he complains of my gab
    and my loitering.

I too am not a bit tamed, I too am untranslatable,
I sound my barbaric yawp over the roofs of the world.

The last scud of day holds back for me,
It flings my likeness after the rest and true as any on the shadow'd wilds, 35
It coaxes me to the vapor and the dusk.

I depart as air, I shake my white locks at the runaway sun,
I effuse my flesh in eddies, and drift it in lacy jags.

I bequeath myself to the dirt to grow from the grass I love,
If you want me again look for me under your boot-soles.   40

You will hardly know who I am or what I mean,
But I shall be good health to you nevertheless,
And filter and fibre your blood.

Failing to fetch me at first keep encouraged,
Missing me one place search another,   45
I stop somewhere waiting for you.

When I Heard the Learn'd Astronomer *(1865)*

When I heard the learn'd astronomer,
When the proofs, the figures, were ranged in columns before me,
When I was shown the charts and diagrams, to add, divide, and measure
    them,
When I sitting heard the astronomer where he lectured with much applause in
    the lecture-room,
How soon unaccountable I became tired and sick,   5
Till rising and gliding out I wander'd off by myself,
In the mystical moist night-air, and from time to time,
Look'd up in perfect silence at the stars.

By the Bivouac's Fitful Flame *(1867)*

By the bivouac's fitful flame,
A procession winding around me, solemn and sweet and slow—but
    first I note,
The tents of the sleeping army, the fields' and woods' dim outline,
The darkness lit by spots of kindled fire, the silence,
Like a phantom far or near an occasional figure moving,   5
The shrubs and trees, (as I lift my eyes they seem to be stealthily
    watching me,)
While wind in procession thoughts, O tender and wondrous thoughts,
Of life and death, of home and the past and loved, and of those that
    are far away;
A solemn and slow procession there as I sit on the ground,
By the bivouac's fitful flame.   10

Cavalry Crossing a Ford *(1871)*

A line in long array where they wind betwixt green islands,
They take a serpentine course, their arms flash in the sun—hark to
    the musical clank,
Behold the silvery river, in it the splashing horses loitering stop to
    drink,   5
Behold the brown-faced men, each group, each person a picture, the
    negligent rest on the saddles,
Some emerge on the opposite bank, others are just entering the
    ford—while,
Scarlet and blue and snowy white,   10
The guidon flags° flutter gayly in the wind.

---

11 *guidon flags:* Military banners.

A Noiseless Patient Spider   *(1868)*

A noiseless patient spider,
I mark'd where on a little promontory it stood isolated,
Mark'd how to explore the vacant vast surrounding,
It launch'd forth filament, filament, filament, out of itself,
Ever unreeling them, ever tirelessly speeding them.   5

And you O my soul where you stand,
Surrounded, detached, in measureless oceans of space,
Ceaselessly musing, venturing, throwing, seeking the spheres to connect
    them,
Till the bridge you will need be form'd, till the ductile anchor hold,
Till the gossamer thread you fling catch somewhere, O my soul.   10

RICHARD WILBUR   *(b. 1921)*

The Death of a Toad   *(1950)*

    A toad the power mower caught,
Chewed and clipped off a leg, with a hobbling hop has got
    To the garden verge, and sanctuaried him
    Under the cineraria leaves, in the shade
        Of the ashen heartshaped leaves, in a dim,   5
            Low, and a final glade.

    The rare original heartsblood goes,
Spends on the earthen hide, in the folds and wizening, flows
    In the gutters of the banked and staring eyes. He lies
    As still as if he would return to stone,   10
        And soundlessly attending, dies
            Toward some deep monotone,

    Toward misted and ebullient seas
And cooling shores, toward lost Amphibia's emperies.
    Day dwindles, drowning, and at length is gone   15
    In the wide and antique eyes, which still appear
        To watch, across the castrate lawn,
            The haggard daylight steer.

Junk

(1961)

Huru Welandes
         worc ne geswiceð
monna ænigum
         ðara ðe Mimming can
heardne gehealdan.
                    —WALDERE°

An axe angles
         from my neighbor's ashcan;
It is hell's handiwork,
         the wood not hickory,
The flow of the grain
         not faithfully followed.
The shivered shaft
         rises from a shellheap
Of plastic playthings,
         paper plates,
And the sheer shards
         of shattered tumblers
That were not annealed
         for the time needful.
At the same curbside,
         a cast-off cabinet
Of wavily-warped
         unseasoned wood
Waits to be trundled
         in the trash-man's truck.
Haul them off! Hide them!
         The heart winces
For junk and gimcrack,
         for jerrybuilt things
And the men who make them
         for a little money,
Bartering pride
         like the bought boxer
Who pulls his punches,
         or the paid-off jockey
Who in the home stretch
         holds in his horse.
Yet the things themselves
         in thoughtless honor

5

10

15

20

25

30

Waldere: Old English poem, "The handiwork of Weland will not betray any man who knows how to wield [the sword] mimming."

Have kept composure,
                    like captives who would not
Talk under torture.
                 Tossed from a tailgate
Where the dump displays
                  its random dolmens,   40
Its black barrows
              and blazing valleys,
They shall waste in the weather
                  toward what they were.
The sun shall glory   45
               in the glitter of glass-chips,
Foreseeing the salvage
               of the prisoned sand,
And the blistering paint
               peel off in patches,   50
That the good grain
             be discovered again.
Then burnt, bulldozed,
               they shall all be buried
To the depth of diamonds,   55
              in the making dark
Where halt Hephaestus
             keeps his hammer
And Wayland's work
           is worn away.   60

WILLIAM CARLOS WILLIAMS   *(1883–1963)*

Danse Russe   *(1916)*

If when my wife is sleeping
and the baby and Kathleen
are sleeping
and the sun is a flame-white disc
in silken mists   5
above shining trees,—
if I in my north room
dance naked, grotesquely
before my mirror
waving my shirt round my head   10
and singing softly to myself:
"I am lonely, lonely.
I was born to be lonely,
I am best so!"

If I admire my arms, my face,   15
my shoulders, flanks, buttocks
against the yellow drawn shades,—

Who shall say I am not
the happy genius of my household?

This Is Just to Say   (1934)

I have eaten
the plums
that were in
the icebox

and which   5
you were probably
saving
for breakfast

Forgive me
they were delicious   10
so sweet
and so cold

The Dance   (1944)

In Breughel's° great picture, The Kermess,
the dancers go round, they go round and
around, the squeal and the blare and the
tweedle of bagpipes, a bugle and fiddles
tipping their bellies (round as the thick-   5
sided glasses whose wash they impound)
their hips and their bellies off balance
to turn them. Kicking and rolling about
the Fair Grounds, swinging their butts, those
shanks must be sound to bear up under such   10
rollicking measures, prance as they dance
in Breughel's great picture, The Kermess.

---

1 *Breughel*: Pieter Brueghel, the Elder (1525–1569), Flemish painter.

The Descent   *(1954)*

The descent beckons
          as the ascent beckoned.
                    Memory is a kind
of accomplishment,
          a sort of renewal   5
even
an initiation, since the spaces it opens are new places
          inhabited by hordes
                    heretofore unrealized,

of new kinds—   10
          since their movements
                    are toward new objectives
(even though formerly they were abandoned).

No defeat is made up entirely of defeat—since
the world it opens is always a place   15
          formerly
                    unsuspected. A
world lost,
          a world unsuspected,
                    beckons to new places   20
and no whiteness (lost) is so white as the memory
of whiteness.

With evening, love wakens
          though its shadows
                    which are alive by reason   25
of the sun shining—
          grow sleepy now and drop away
                    from desire.

Love without shadows stirs now
          beginning to awaken   30
          as night
advances.

The descent
          made up of despairs
                    and without accomplishment   35
realizes a new awakening:
                    which is a reversal
of despair.
          For what we cannot accomplish, what

is denied to love,   40
what we have lost in the anticipation—
     a descent follows,
       endless and indestructible.

WILLIAM WORDSWORTH *(1770–1850)*

She Dwelt Among the Untrodden Ways   *(1800)*

She dwelt among the untrodden ways
   Beside the springs of Dove.
A Maid whom there were none to praise
   And very few to love;

A violet by a mossy stone   5
   Half hidden from the eye!
—Fair as a star, when only one
   Is shining in the sky.

She lived unknown, and few could know
   When Lucy ceased to be;   10
But she is in her grave, and, oh,
   The difference to me!

It Is a Beauteous Evening   *(1807)*

It is a beauteous evening, calm and free,
The holy time is quiet as a Nun
Breathless with adoration; the broad sun
Is sinking down in its tranquility;
The gentleness of heaven broods o'er the Sea: 5
Listen! the mighty Being is awake,
And doth with his eternal motion make
A sound like thunder—everlastingly.
Dear Child! dear Girl! that walkest with me here,
If thou appear untouched by solemn thought,   10
Thy nature is not therefore less divine:
Thou livest in Abraham's bosom all the year;
And worshipp'st at the Temple's inner shrine,
God being with thee when we know it not.

London, 1802   *(1807)*

Milton! thou shouldst be living at this hour:
England hath need of thee: she is a fen
Of stagnant waters: altar, sword, and pen,
Fireside, the heroic wealth of hall and bower,
Have forfeited their ancient English dower   5
Of inward happiness. We are selfish men;
Oh! raise us up, return to us again;
And give us manners, virtue, freedom, power.
Thy soul was like a Star, and dwelt apart;
Thou hadst a voice whose sound was like the sea: 10
Pure as the naked heavens, majestic, free,
So didst thou travel on life's common way,
In cheerful godliness; and yet thy heart
The lowliest duties on herself did lay.

My Heart Leaps Up   *(1807)*

My heart leaps up when I behold
    A rainbow in the sky:
So was it when my life began;
So is it now I am a man;
So be it when I shall grow old,   5
    Or let me die!
The Child is father of the Man;
And I could wish my days to be
Bound each to each by natural piety.

JAMES WRIGHT   *(1927–1980)*

The Journey   *(1982)*

Anghiari is medieval, a sleeve sloping down
A steep hill, suddenly sweeping out
To the edge of a cliff, and dwindling.
But far up the mountain, behind the town,
We too were swept out, out by the wind,   5
Alone with the Tuscan grass.

Wind had been blowing across the hills
For days, and everything now was graying gold
With dust, everything we saw, even
Some small children scampering along a road,   10

Twittering Italian to a small caged bird.
We sat beside them to rest in some brushwood,
And I leaned down to rinse the dust from my face.

I found the spider web there, whose hinges
Reeled heavily and crazily with the dust,   15
Whole mounds and cemeteries of it, sagging
And scattering shadows among shells and wings.
And then she stepped into the center of air
Slender and fastidious, the golden hair
Of daylight along her shoulders, she poised there,   20
While ruins crumbled on every side of her.
Free of the dust, as though a moment before
She had stepped inside the earth, to bathe herself.

I gazed, close to her, till at last she stepped
Away in her own good time.   25

Many men
Have searched all over Tuscany and never found
What I found there, the heart of the light
Itself shelled and leaved, balancing
On filaments themselves falling. The secret   30
Of this journey is to let the wind
Blow its dust all over your body,
To let it go on blowing, to step lightly, lightly
All the way through your ruins, and not to lose
Any sleep over the dead, who surely   35
Will bury their own, don't worry.

SIR THOMAS WYATT *(1503–1542)*

They Flee from Me   *(1557)*

They flee from me that sometime did me seek
    With naked foot stalking in my chamber.
I have seen them gentle tame and meek
    That now are wild and do not remember
    That sometime they put themselves in danger   5
To take bread at my hand; and now they range
Busily seeking with a continual change.

Thanked be fortune it hath been otherwise
    Twenty times better; but once in special,
In thin array after a pleasant guise,   10

When her loose gown from her shoulders did fall,
　　And she me caught in her arms long and small;
And therewithall sweetly did me kiss,
And softly said, "Dear heart, how like you this?"

It was no dream: I lay broad waking.　　　　　　　　　　　　　　　15
　　But all is turned thorough my gentleness
Into a strange fashion of forsaking;
　　And I have leave to go of her goodness,
　　And she also to use newfangleness.
But since that I so kindely am served,　　　　　　　　　　　　20
I fain would know what she hath deserved.

W. B. Yeats　　(1865–1939)

The Second Coming　　　　　　　　　　　　　　　　(1921)

Turning and turning in the widening gyre°
The falcon cannot hear the falconer;
Things fall apart; the centre cannot hold;
Mere anarchy is loosed upon the world,
The blood-dimmed tide is loosed, and everywhere　　　　　　5
The ceremony of innocence is drowned;
The best lack all conviction, while the worst
Are full of passionate intensity.

Surely some revelation is at hand;
Surely the Second Coming is at hand:　　　　　　　　　　　　10
The Second Coming! Hardly are those words out
When a vast image out of *Spiritus Mundi*°
Troubles my sight: somewhere in sands of the desert
A shape with lion body and the head of a man,
A gaze blank and pitiless as the sun,　　　　　　　　　　　　15
Is moving its slow thighs, while all about it
Reel shadows of the indignant desert birds.
The darkness drops again; but now I know
That twenty centuries of stony sleep
Were vexed to nightmare by a rocking cradle,　　　　　　　20
And what rough beast, its hour come round at last,
Slouches toward Bethlehem to be born?

---

1 *gyre:* Conical spiral that Yeats understood as a "fundamental symbol" for cycles of history that distinguish the Greco-Roman from the Christian epoch.　　12 *Spiritus Mundi:* Spirit of the world, or what Yeats described as the "great memory" of the collective unconscious.

Sailing to Byzantium°   (1927)

1

That is no country for old men. The young
In one another's arms, birds in the trees
—Those dying generations—at their song,
The salmon-falls, the mackerel-crowded seas,
Fish, flesh, or fowl, commend all summer long   5
Whatever is begotten, born, and dies.
Caught in that sensual music all neglect
Monuments of unaging intellect.

2

An aged man is but a paltry thing,
A tattered coat upon a stick, unless   10
Soul clap its hands and sing, and louder sing
For every tatter in its mortal dress,
Nor is there singing school but studying
Monuments of its own magnificence;
And therefore I have sailed the seas and come   15
To the holy city of Byzantium.

3

O sages standing in God's holy fire
As in the gold mosaic of a wall,
Come from the holy fire, perne in a gyre,°
And be the singing-masters of my soul.   20
Consume my heart away; sick with desire
And fastened to a dying animal
It knows not what it is; and gather me
Into the artifice of eternity.

4

Once out of nature I shall never take   25
My bodily form from any natural thing,
But such a form as Grecian goldsmiths make
Of hammered gold and gold enamelling
To keep a drowsy Emperor awake;
Or set upon a golden bough to sing   30
To lords and ladies of Byzantium
Of what is past, or passing, or to come.

Byzantium: Modern Istanbul. Yeats considered Byzantium and its fifth- and sixth-century mosaics as symbols for the "unity of being" where "religious, aesthetic, and practical life were one." 19 *perne in a gyre:* Spin a bobbin in a spiral motion. Yeats implies here that the holy fire spins forth the sages in a spiral to purge the poet's soul.

39 Biographical Sketches of Selected Poets

John Ashbery (b. 1927)

Born and raised in Rochester, New York, John Ashbery attended Harvard University and Columbia University. Three years after publishing his first volume *Turandot and Other Poems* (1953), Ashbery's *Some Trees* (1956) was selected by W. H. Auden for the prestigious Yale Younger Poets Series award. Of his subject matter, Ashbery has written that "the particular experience is of lesser interest to me than the way it filters through to me. I believe this is the way in which it happens with most people, and I'm trying to record a kind of generalized transcript of what's really going on in our minds all day long." Ashbery has published more than twenty books of verse and prose poems including *The Tennis Court Oath* (1962), *Rivers and Mountains* (1966), *The Double Dream of Spring* (1970), *Three Poems* (1972), *Self-Portrait in a Convex Mirror* (1975), *Houseboat Days* (1977), *As We Know* (1979), *Shadow Train* (1981), *Flow Chart* (1991), *Hotel Lautramont* (1994), *And the Stars Were Shining* (1994), *Can You Hear, Bird* (1995), *Wakefulness* (1998), *Girls on the Run: A Poem* (1999), *Your Name Here* (2000). He is a recipient of the Pulitzer Prize for Poetry, the National Book Critics Circle Award, and the National Book Award for *Self-Portrait in a Convex Mirror*. He teaches at Brooklyn College.

Matthew Arnold (1822–1888)

The Victorian English poet Matthew Arnold was born at Laleham on the Thames, Middlesex. He received his education at Winchester, Rugby, and Balliol College, Oxford. Early on, Arnold showed promise as a poet, winning prizes for his poem "Alaric at Rome" at Rugby and the Newdigate Prize at Oxford for "Cromwell, A Prize Poem." Before becoming private secretary to Lord Lanscowne in 1847, Arnold traveled in France where he met the novelist George Sand. In 1851 Arnold was appointed inspector of schools, which became a lifelong vocation and enabled him to marry Frances Lucy Wightman. Arnold's literary career began in 1849 with his first volume of verse, *The Strayed Reveller and Other Poems*, followed by *Empedocles on Etna and Other Poems* (1852), *Poems, Second Series* (1855), and *New Poems* (1867). Arnold's reputation rests as much on his work as a literary and cultural critic as on his published poetry. Throughout his career in volumes such as *Essays in Criticism* (1865) and *Culture and Anarchy* (1869), Arnold sought what he described as "the pursuit of total perfection by means of getting to know, on all the matters which most concern us, the best which has been thought and said in the world." This version of high culture was later disputed in cultural criticism by critics such as Raymond Williams, who redefined culture in terms of a "particular way of life" which, he said, "expresses certain meanings and values not only in art and learning, but also in institutions and ordinary behaviour." Beginning in 1883, Arnold received an annual pension of 250 pounds per year conferred by William Gladstone which allowed him to travel widely including a lecture tour to the United States. He returned for another visit in 1886 to visit his daughter, who had married an American. Matthew Arnold died two years later in Liverpool.

Margaret Atwood (b. 1939)

A Canadian author, Margaret Atwood was born in 1939 in Ottawa, Ontario and received her education first at Victoria College, and later the University of Toronto, and Harvard University. In 1962, she published her first volume of verse, entitled *Double Persephone*, followed by *The Circle Game* (1964), which received the Governor's General Award. In addition, she has published three other compilations of her verse in *Selected Poems* (1976), *Selected Poems II* (1986), and *Eating Fire: Selected Poems 1965–1998*). In addition to her work as a published poet, Margaret Atwood is more widely known as a prose writer of short stories, children's literature and nonfiction as well as novels, including *The Edible Woman* (1969), *Surfacing* (1972), and *Cat's Eye* (1988), among others. Since 1990 when Atwood's 1985 novel *The Handmaid's Tale* was made into a Hollywood film, Atwood has enjoyed a broad, popular readership. A writer of literary distinction, Atwood has won several major awards, including the Booker Prize for *The Blind Assassin* (2000).

W. H. Auden (1907–1973)

The British modernist author W. H. Auden was born in York, England. As a student at St. Edmund's preparatory school, he first met Christopher Isherwood with whom he would share a rich literary collaboration. Auden later studied at Christ Church, Oxford, and was a leader of a new circle of British poets that included Stephen Spender, C. Day-Lewis, and Louis MacNeice. Auden's early poetry in *Poems* (1930) and *Look Stranger!* (1936) was inspired by Freudian psychology, social Marxism, and a commitment to the leftist international community that led him to participate in the Spanish Civil War, where he served the Republican cause as an ambulance driver. In 1939 Auden emigrated to the United States and became a citizen in 1946. During the 1940s, Auden turned toward Christianity and became a convert to the Anglican church. By 1956, Auden assumed the position of professor of poetry at Oxford and led a cosmopolitan life in England, New York, Italy, and Austria, where he died in 1973. Throughout his life, Auden authored more than twenty-five volumes of verse. In addition to his career as a poet, Auden composed with his long-time companion, Chester Kallman, several opera librettos, including one for Igor Stravinsky's *The Rake's Progress* (1951); he also wrote discerning literary criticism collected in *The Dyer's Hand* (1962).

Elizabeth Bishop (1911–1979)

Elizabeth Bishop was born in Worcester, Massachusetts, in 1911, and her father passed away before her first birthday. By the time she turned five, her mother had suffered a series of breakdowns and become institutionalized for mental illness. As a result, Bishop was raised by her maternal grandparents in Nova Scotia before moving to Worcester at the age of six to live with her father's family. At age sixteen, Bishop enrolled at Walnut Hill boarding school, later followed by her undergraduate studies at Vassar College. At Vassar, she met Mary McCarthy, with whom she would share a literary collaboration. The poems she wrote while at Vassar drew the notice of the modernist poet Marianne Moore, who became an important mentor and a lifelong friend. Elizabeth Bishop was a cosmopolitan citizen of the world and traveled widely in France, Mexico, and Key West. For fifteen years she lived in Brazil with her longtime companion, Lota de Macedo Soares. This broad, international experience is reflected in such volume titles as *North and South* (1946), *A Cold Spring* (1955), *Questions of Travel* (1965), and *Geography III* (1976), all of which are compiled in *The Complete Poems 1927–1979* (1983). Bishop had a pronounced influence on a number of her contemporaries, including Robert Lowell, who dedicated his widely read poem "Skunk Hour" to Bishop. Following the suicide of Lota de Macedo Soares, Bishop left Brazil and took a teaching position at the University of Washington in 1966 and then at Harvard University from 1969 through her retirement in 1977, two years before her death in 1979. Among her numerous awards and honors, Bishop is a recipient of the Pulitzer Prize and the National Book Award.

William Blake (1757–1827)

The son of a London hosier, William Blake was home schooled due in part to his tendency even in childhood toward visionary experience. Not just a visionary, however, Blake showed early talent for the visual arts. After attending drawing school, he apprenticed to an engraver for seven years, after which he briefly attended the Royal Academy. In 1782, Blake married Catherine Boucher and taught her to read and write. She assisted Blake with the illustrations for his poetic manuscripts. Blake's first published volume, *Poetical Sketches* (1783), took a stance of protest against King George III and his policies toward the American colonies. As an independent-minded thinker, Blake also criticized the institutions of rational science, the church, and state in *Songs of Innocence* (1789) and *Songs of Experience* (1794). Blake's famous nonconformist slogan—"I must create a system or be enslaved by another man's"—reflected his philosophical resistance to neoclassical rationalism. In the 1790s Blake's long poems—such as "The French Revolution" (1791), "America, a Prophecy" (1793), and "Europe, a Prophecy" (1791)—engaged imaginatively with the revolutionary contexts of his age. Theological parody and critique of religious orthodoxy and utilitarian thought characterize works from this decade including "The Book of Urizen" (1794) and "The Marriage of Heaven and Hell" (1790–1793). In addition to his income from professional engraving, Blake also received the patronage of William Hayley, which allowed him to move to Felpham where he learned classical languages and Hebrew and cultivated the kind of visionary mysticism that informs his major epics: *Milton* (1804–1808), *Vala, or The Four Zoas* (1797, 1800), and *Jerusalem* (1804–1820). Although reduced to poverty in later life, Blake mentored a new generation of artists, including John Linnell who commissioned Blake's last work, illustrations for Dante's *Divine Comedy*, which Blake worked on until he passed away in 1827.

Robert Bly (b. 1926)

A native Minnesotan, Robert Bly was brought up on a farm in Madison, Minnesota, and later served in the U.S. Navy during World War II. He then attended St. Olaf College and graduated from Harvard University in 1950. In college and while living for a time in New York City, Bly composed the poems that would make up his first volume, *The Lute of Three Loudnesses*. In 1958 he founded the influential and provocative literary magazine *The Fifties* that later evolved into *The Sixties*, *The Seventies*, and so on down to the present. Bly's poetry of the so-called deep image, which he explored in collaboration with Robert Kelly and James Wright, was influenced by the archetypal psychology of Carl Jung. Another poetic influence has come from translating Spanish and South American surrealist poets such as César Vallejo, Pablo Neruda, and Antonio Machado as well as the Swedish poet Tomas Transtromer. In explaining his understanding of the poetic symbol, Bly has employed the key word *entangle* from the Irish modernist poet W. B. Yeats: "I'll use Yeats's marvellous word *entangle*; he suggested that the symbolist poem entangles some substance from the divine world in its words." Bly's role as a poet has also entangled forms of social and political advocacy as in his founding (with David Ray) of American Writers Against the Vietnam War and his controversial promotion of a male spiritualist movement theorized in his 1990 best-selling book of prose, *Iron John*. In addition to numerous translations, volumes of prose, and prose poems, Bly's major books of poetry include *Silence in the Snowy Fields* (1962), *The Light Around the Body* (1967), *The Morning Glory* (1969), *The Teeth Mother Naked at Last* (1970), *Sleepers Joining Hands* (1973), *Old Man Rubbing His Eyes* (1975), *This Tree Will Be Here for a Thousand Years* (1979), *The Man in the Black Coat Turns* (1981), and *Eating the Honey of Words: New and Selected Poems* (1999). Never having held a permanent academic position, Bly supports himself from his writing, residing in rural Minnesota.

Louise Bogan (1897–1970)

A native of Maine, Louise Bogan grew up in an unsettled household owing, in part, to her mother's marital infidelity. After her education at Boston Girls' Latin School, Bogan attended Boston University in 1915 and 1916, when she married Curt Alexander, an army officer, with whom she had a daughter. Four years later, Alexander's death left her a single parent with uncertain means. Moving to New York City, Bogan began her life as a writer in earnest, collaborating with such major modernist writers as William Carlos Williams, Malcolm Cowley, Lola Ridge, John Reed, Marianne Moore, and Edmund Wilson, who coached Bogan in professional reviewing that gave her an income. Her first volume of verse, *Body of This Death* (1923), mined the resources of formal lyricism in exploring the terms of her artistic survival that ranged from depression to joy. Poetry and psychoanalysis sustained Bogan during these years through her troubled marriage to writer Raymond Holden. Her turmoil is reflected in such titles as *Dark Summer* (1929) and *The Sleeping Fury* (1937). *A Poet's Alphabet: Reflections on the Literary Art and Vocation*, later published in 1970, collects the pieces Bogan wrote as a poetry reviewer for *The New Yorker* magazine. Her visibility as a reviewer and teacher of poetry is also reflected in her critical history *American Poetry, 1900–1950*. Bogan's achievement as a poet, however, did not go unrecognized, and she received a Bollingen Prize in 1955 and awards from the Academy of American Poets (1959) and the National Endowment for the Arts (1967). Following her *Collected Poems, 1923–1953*, her last volume of verse is *Estuaries: Poems 1923–1968*.

Gwendolyn Brooks (1917–2000). *See Chapter 32.*

Elizabeth Barrett Browning (1806–1861)

Born in Durham, England, Elizabeth Barrett Browning had an affluent childhood due to the wealth her father accumulated from his sugar plantations in Jamaica. In 1821, she began to suffer from a nervous disorder which was aggravated further by the death of her mother in that year. This trauma, according to her critics, left its trace in her poem "Aurora Leigh." Browning had a passion for classical learning and taught herself Hebrew in order to read the Old Testament. Hugh Stuart Boyd encouraged her in her studies of Greek authors. Her own major volume of accomplished verse appeared in 1838 under the title *The Seraphim and Other Poems*. That same year, however, the trauma of her brother Edward's drowning off the coast of Devon left her an invalid and recluse for the next five years. Nevertheless, her next volume, entitled simply *Poems*, in 1844 drew the attention of Robert Browning, and although six years younger than Elizabeth and in far better health, he courted her over the period of two years. During this time, she composed the poetry that would later make up her *Sonnets from the Portuguese*. Following the example of Percy Shelley and Mary Godwin, the couple eloped to Italy in 1846 and three years later became parents of a son, Robert, in Florence. In 1850, Elizabeth published a second edition of *Poems* including the *Sonnets from the Portuguese*. With the death of William Wordsworth that same year, she became a serious contender for the Laureateship which passed, however, to Tennyson. Her publication of the verse-novel *Aurora Leigh* in 1857 consolidated her popular readership. Toward the end of her life, her political commitment to Italian independence was reflected in *Casa Guidi Windows* (1851) and *Poems before Congress* (1860). In 1861, Robert Browning took Elizabeth to the south in an attempt to treat the disease that would nevertheless take her life that year.

Robert Browning (1812–1889)

Browning's father was a nonconformist who gave up a fortune rather than manage his family's West Indies sugar plantation. Nevertheless, as a bank clerk, Robert senior provided his son with an extensive library collection, which whetted his appetite for a life of letters. Although he attended the University of London in 1828, Browning was largely self-taught and undertook his own studies in Latin, Greek, French, and Italian authors. The eccentricity of his education, however, crept into the obscure references in his early volumes of verse such as *Pauline* (1833), *Paracelsus* (1834), and *Bells and Pomegranates* (1841–1846), which were not particularly well received by critics. It was only through the influence of the theater and such actors as William Macready that Browning turned to the dramatic monologue verse which proved to be his signature form in the *Collected Poems* (1862) and *Dramatis Persone* (1863). By then, his passionate marriage to Elizabeth Barrett Browning, begun in 1846, had been cut short by her death in 1861. Returning from Florence to London, Browning devoted the next decade to his major oeuvre *The Ring and the Book* (1869). After his death in 1889, Browning's poetic craft in such memorable dramatic monologues as "My Last Duchess" and "Soliloquy of the Spanish Cloister" had a lasting influence on the course of modern verse and particularly in the careers of its major practitioners such as T. S. Eliot and Ezra Pound.

George Gordon, Lord Byron (1788–1824)

A contemporary of English romantic poets Percy Bysshe Shelley and John Keats, Lord Byron cut an unconventional and at times heroic character. His mother's family traced its aristocratic roots back to the aristocratic Scottish Gordons. James I. Byron's father, the infamous captain "Mad Jack" Byron, abandoned the family to escape his creditors when the poet was three years old. Raised by his mother in Scotland, Byron at age ten inherited his great-uncle's title and estates. Returning to England, Byron was tutored in Nottingham and in 1801 attended Harrow and later Trinity College, where he published in 1807 two verse volumes: *Fugitive Pieces* and *Hours of Idleness*. Assuming his seat in the House of Lords in 1809, Byron responded to his harsh critics by publishing an anonymous satire, *English Bards and Scotch Reviewers*. A tour of Portugal, Spain, Malta, Albania, and Greece provided material for his autobiographical poem *Childe Harold's Pilgrimage*, which won Byron a broad readership when it was published in 1812. Of his newfound popularity, he later remarked, "I awoke one morning and found myself famous." A series of affairs culminated in Byron's troubled marriage to Anabella Milbanke in 1815. Due to mounting debt and temperamental differences, Byron left England for Europe, never to return. Touring with Percy and Mary Shelley, Byron began an affair with the stepdaughter of William Godwin, Claire

Clairmont, who would later give birth to Byron's daughter. The type of brooding romantic hero that Byron came to represent was captured in his poetic drama *Manfred* (1817), who describes mankind as "half dust, half deity, alike unfit to sink or soar." By 1818 Byron was composing his great work *Don Juan*, inspired, in part, by his affairs with Marianna Segati, a Venetian draper's wife, then Margarita Cogni, and finally Countess Teresa Guicciolo. Following the Countess to Ravenna, Byron was inducted by her father into the revolutionary secret society of the Carbonari. After Shelley's tragic drowning in 1821, Byron became a committed partisan in the Greek war of independence from Turkey. Traveling to Greece, Byron financed and participated in the planning for the assault on the Turkish fortress of Lepanto. In 1824, however, after a year spent in Greece, Byron's health steadily declined and after slipping into a coma, he died on April 19, 1824.

Lewis Carroll (1832–1898)

Charles Lutwidge Dodgson, or "Lewis Carroll," was born into a north English family in 1832. From Cheshire the family moved to Yorkshire when Charles was eleven. Home schooled early on, Charles was enrolled in Yorkshire Grammar School and the Rugby School. For his advanced study, Carroll attended his father's alma mater, Christ Chruch of Oxford. A gifted mathematician, on graduation Dodgson assumed a Christ Church mathematical lectureship and held it for the next twenty-six years. In addition to his mathematical genius, by the mid-1850s he had published several comical and satirical poems and short stories in such national journals as *The Comic Times*, and by 1856 he had also become a skilled photographer. It was also in this year that he published his first poem, "Solitude," under the pseudonym "Lewis Carroll." The genesis for his famous publication *Alice's Adventures under Ground, or Alice in Wonderland* (1865) came in 1862 in stories he invented to entertain the children of Henry Liddell, the dean of Christ Church. At the urging of Alice Liddell, Dodgson wrote out what would become *Alice in Wonderland*, which brought him his lasting reputation as an author, publishing the sequels *Through the Looking-Glass* and *What Alice Found There* (1871), as well as *The Hunting of The Snark* (1876).

Sandra Cisneros (b. 1954)

Born to a Mexican American mother and a Mexican father, Sandra Cisneros spent her early life moving between Mexico City and Chicago. When she studied creative writing as a college student in 1974, she became an active writer. After earning a degree from Chicago's Loyola University, Cisneros earned an M.A. from the creative writing program at the University of Iowa. During the late 1970s, she worked as a teacher in the Chicago barrio, where she found ample material for her writing. Cisneros's rootedness in the Chicano community is reflected in her first volume of poetry, *Bad Boys* (1980), published in a series edited by the Chicano poet Gary Soto. Her first published book of fiction, *The House on Mango Street* (1983), mixed her gift for poetic expression with fictional forms depicting, she has said, "those ghosts inside that haunt me, that will not let me sleep." Two years later, her first book won the Before Columbus American Book Award, followed in 1987 by the publication of her first volume of verse, the widely acclaimed *My Wicked Wicked Ways*. In addition, Cisneros has continued to balance her fictional and poetic forms in publishing *Woman Hollering Creek and Other Stories* (1991) and *Loose Woman: Poems* (1994).

Samuel Taylor Coleridge (1772–1834)

The youngest of fourteen children in the household of the parish vicar and master of the grammar school in Devonshire, England, Coleridge was born in 1772. Following the death of his father in 1781, Coleridge studied at Christ's Hospital School, London, and ten years later entered Jesus College, University of Cambridge. It was here that Coleridge both became an independent-minded philosopher and also where he began to accumulate the debts that would dog him throughout his life. In 1794, Coleridge met Robert Southey and for a time the two planned to emigrate to America to found a commune in Pennsylvania. This utopian scheme fell through when Southey became engaged to Edith Fricker and Coleridge met and married Sarah Fricker, Edith's younger sister. The next year Coleridge began his poetic collaboration with William Wordsworth who encouraged Coleridge to write in a more direct, natural, and colloquial form in such so-called conversation poems as "The Eolian Harp," "This Lime-Tree Bower My Prison" and other works collected in his first volume, *Poems on Various Subjects* (1796). From 1797, Coleridge lived near Wordsworth and his sister, Dorothy, in Somersetshire. Here, the two poets coauthored *Lyrical Ballads* with the famous manifesto on Romantic poetics laid out in its "Preface." Coleridge not only pioneered new colloquial forms of poetry but also worked in traditional forms such as the ode and most notably the ballad in *The Rime of the Ancient Mariner*. Subsequently, Coleridge and Wordsworth toured Europe, with Coleridge spending most of his time in Germany engaged in philosophical study of Immmanuel Kant, Jakob Boehme, A. W. Schlegel, and G. E. Lessing. After settling in Keswick in 1800, Coleridge increasingly was prone to the kind of depression recounted in his 1802 "Dejection: An Ode." Despite personal turmoil that led to his separation from his wife Sarah in 1808 and his break with Wordsworth in 1810, he turned his powers to literary criticism, philosophy, theology, and political theory until his ill health and his addiction to opium took his life in 1834. During his final decades, Coleridge published his magnum opus, *Biographica Literaria* (1817), *Sibyline Leaves* (1817), *Aids to Reflection* (1825), and *Church and State* (1830).

Countée Cullen (1903–1946)

In the 1920s, Countée Cullen became a primary figure of the Harlem Renaissance and one of its major poetic talents. Born in 1903, he was adopted by the Reverend Frederick A. and Carolyn Belle Cullen and brought up in New York

City in what the poet later described as "the conservative atmosphere of a Methodist parsonage." Such early religious influences, however ambivalently portrayed, are pronounced in Cullen's signature poem "Heritage" and in the lyrics included in *The Black Christ and Other Poems* (1929). After graduating at the top of his class at DeWitt Clinton High School in 1921, Cullen attended New York University, graduating Phi Beta Kappa in 1925. While at NYU, Cullen wrote poetry prolifically and showed an early mastery of traditional English measures in ballad stanzas, sonnets, and other fixed forms. In the mid-1920s, many of these works would appear in his early volumes of verse: *Color* (1925), *Copper Sun* (1927), and *The Ballad of the Brown Girl* (1927) which brought him the recognition of the modern literary world in such awards as the Witter Bynner Poetry Prize, *Poetry* magazine's prestigious John Reed Memorial Prize, *Crisis* magazine's Amy Spingarn Award, and a Guggenheim Fellowship. His literary fame was further capped in his highly publicized New York marriage to Yolande Du Bois, the daughter of noted black intellectual W. E. B. Du Bois. Their union proved short-lived, however, and they were divorced two years later. Cullen's productivity as a writer fell off somewhat in the 1930s owing to his teaching responsibilities as a French instructor at Frederick Douglass Junior High School, but he published a retrospective parody of the Harlem Renaissance in his novel *One Way to Heaven* (1932) and another volume of verse *The Media and Other Poems* (1935) that included a major translation of Euripides' tragedy. In 1940, Cullen married Ida Mae Roberson, and at the time of his death six years later he was collaborating with Arna Bontemps on the play *St. Louis Woman* (1946).

E. E. Cummings (1894–1962)

Poet and painter, Edward Estlin Cummings was born into the household of Unitarian minister and former Harvard professor Edward Cummings who, along with his wife, Rebecca Haswell Clarke Cummings, encouraged Cummings to pursue his creativity especially in poetry. Cummings graduated from Harvard College in 1915 and received an M.A. from Harvard the next year. His early verse was included in the collection *Eight Harvard Poets* published in 1917, the year Cummings also volunteered for the Ambulance Corps serving in France during World War I. Arrested with his friend William Slater Brown on suspicion of espionage, owing to some of Brown's pacifist letters, Cummings was held in detention at a concentration camp at La Ferté-Macé for four months, which he writes about in his autobiographical book *The Enormous Room* (1922). After serving in the 73rd Infantry until November 1918, Cummings lived in New York and exhibited his artwork modeled on cubist prinicples that also shaped the new compositional innovations to modern poetry. Making dynamic use of the page as a compositonal space, Cummings subverted the authenticity of the speaking voice in favor of visual manipulations of punctuation and typography, unusual and playful phrasings, disruption of syntax, and other unconventional formal techniques. Such early experimentation appeared in three volumes—*Tulips and Chimneys* (1923), *XLI Poems* (1925), and *&* (1925). The youthful exuberance of these first volumes was tempered by two failed marriages, the first to Elaine Orr from 1924 to 1925 and the second to Anne Barton from 1929 to 1932. A new critical temper entered his verse in the volumes *5* (1926), *ViVa* (1931), and *No Thanks* (1935). A six-week trip to the Soviet Union in 1931 provided the impetus for Cummings's parody, modeled on Dante's *Inferno*, *Purgatorio*, and *Paradiso*, of bureaucratic communism in *Eimi* (1933). In 1934, Cummings's entered into a relationship with Marion Morehouse that would last the rest of his life, much of which was spent at the poet's summer house "Joy Farm" in Madison, New Hampshire. A new optimism is evident in *50 Poems* (1940), *1 X 1* (1944), and *Xaipe* (1950) that reflects, in part, Cummings's reunion with the daughter of his first marriage, Nancy. She had lost contact with her father when Elaine Orr left Cummings, taking Nancy with her to Ireland in 1925. In his final years, Cummings received broad recognition for his poetic achievement both as a public reader of his work and in the awards of a special citation from the National Book Award Committee (1955), a Bollingen Prize (1958), and a Ford Foundation grant. Four years after his final volume of verse *95 poems* was published, Cummings died in New Hampshire after suffering a stroke at Joy Farm.

Emily Dickinson (1830–1886)

Born in 1830, Emily Dickinson grew up in a prominent nineteenth-century New England family. Her grandfather, Samuel Fowler Dickinson, founded Amherst Academy in 1814 in western Massachusetts and Amherst College seven years later. Dickinson's father was a successful Amherst lawyer who served as treasurer of the college and was elected a member of the U.S. House of Representatives. The Dickinson family home was the annual site of the Amherst College commencement receptions and a center of the community. At the heart of Amherst's social life, however, Emily Dickinson chose a life largely devoted to the solitary cultivation of her poetic imagination, becoming, in the words of her friend and editor Samuel Bowles, "the Queen Recluse." Rather than define herself through the available roles of dutiful daughter, attentive wife, devoted mother, or even devout Christian, she largely turned her back on the Amherst community in favor of an existence where, as she writes in Poem 303, the "Soul selects her own Society."

As capable as any of the great Dickinson patriarchs, Emily excelled as a student, first at Amherst Academy, where she studied under Edward Hitchcock, and later during the year she spent at Mount Holyoke Female Seminary in 1847 to 1848. It was at Holyoke that her radical independence asserted itself as she became the only student in her class not to profess a belief in Christ by the end of her year there. Similarly, by age thirty she stopped attending church services, largely cutting her ties with Amherst public life. Instead, she cultivated a rich inner spirituality and intense creative life that would produce some 1,147 poems and thousands of letters to her select circle of correspondents. Of her large corpus of poetry, however, only ten were published by the time of her death from Bright's disease in 1886. Although she courted literary editors, she was skeptical of literary fame in her own lifetime and was extremely guarded in her literary negotiations with such editors as Samuel Bowles and Thomas Wentworth Higginson. Stitched together into packets or "fascicles," Dickinson's verse in its formal innovations parts company with the conventional writing of her age and remains an important precursor for modernist poetics and also for twentieth-century feminist verse. Her use of experimental punctuation and dashes, her typographical capitalizations of key words, her unconventional phrasings and syntax, her penchant for paradox (captured in striking oxymorons such as "Heavenly Hurt" in Poem 258), the composed quality of the poem on the page, and the intertextual relations enter into the fascicle format together and broke new ground for lyric expression.

John Donne (1572–1631)

Born in London to a Roman Catholic family, John Donne lived at a time when Catholics were persecuted in England. Although Donne studied at Oxford and Cambridge, he did not receive a degree from either university because of his refusal to subscribe to Anglicanism. After his brother was convicted of Catholic loyalties and died in prison, Donne converted to avoid his brother's fate. Donne emerged as a spokesperson for a new poetic style that Samuel Johnson would later characterize, writing in the eighteenth-century, as "metaphysical poetry"—a poetics that also defines the work of George Herbert, Richard Crashaw, Andrew Marvell, and John Cleveland. Through highly ironic, extended metaphors—or metaphysical "conceits"—such verse possessed wit in the use of puns, fresh and arresting insights from sharply conceived paradoxes, subtle turns of argument, and startling insights drawn from the everyday world of things observed close at hand. Donne composed much of his metaphysical love lyrics and erotic poetry during the 1590s before becoming Sir Thomas Edgarton's private secretary in 1598. In 1601, Donne secretly married the sixteen-year-old niece of Lady Edgarton, Anne More. Disapproving of the marriage when it became public, Edgarton imprisoned Donne briefly and withheld his dowry, leaving the poet to struggle in raising what would become a large household of children. After the death of Anne during childbirth in 1617, Donne was appointed four years later by King James to the post of dean of St. Paul's Cathedral, a position he would hold until he died in 1631. In addition to breaking fresh ground in the metaphysical love lyric, Donne also explored the theological and existential implications of death and spirituality in the *Holy Sonnets* and *Devotions upon Emergent Occasions* (1624).

H. D. (Hilda Doolittle) (1886–1961)

A pioneeering figure in feminist poetics, H. D. was raised in Upper Darby, a Philadelphia suburb near the University of Pennsylvania, where her father, Charles Doolittle, an astronomer, directed the Flower Observatory. H. D. was encouraged in her creative and artistic pursuits by her mother Helen (Wolle), who was a musician. An early influence on her poetry and identity was the modernist poet Ezra Pound, to whom she was twice engaged. Her attachment to Pound was complicated by her attraction to Frances Josepha Gregg, a student enrolled at the Pennsylvania Academy of Fine Arts. Throughout her life, Doolittle would pursue a bisexual lifestyle beginning with her lifelong relationship to the shipping heiress Winifred Ellerman, who called herself Bryher. Following the failure of Doolittle's marriage to Richard Aldington and affairs with the British author D. H. Lawrence and the painter Cecil Grey (the father of Doolittle's daughter Perdita), Doolittle had a close relationship to Bryher that lasted until the poet's death in 1961. In fact, her connection to Bryher persisted through Bryher's marriages to the author Robert McAlmon and the filmmaker Kenneth Macpherson, who was also Doolittle's lover. She received her nom du plume from Ezra Pound who in 1913 sent her poems to Harriet Monroe, the editor of *Poetry Magazine*, adding the signature "H. D., Imagiste." H. D. became forever identified thereafter with the imagist movement, which stressed a concise, straightforward, and direct "treatment of the thing" at hand. Such an imagist style characterized H. D.'s first collection of verse *Sea Garden* (1916). Increasingly, however, in such mature works as *Trilogy* (1946), *Helen in Egypt* (1961), and *Hermetic Definition* (1972), H. D. devoted herself to developing a modernist "women's mythology": one that, in its epic scope, revisited and rewrote classical Greek myth. H. D.'s interest in Greek literature extended to the several translations she undertook of Sappho, Meleager, and Euripides, among others. H. D. also wrote an important and provocative memoir of her time as an analysand with Sigmund Freud, entitled *Tribute to Freud* (written in 1944 and published between 1945 and 1985). Other prose works include *End to Torment* (1979) and *The Gift* (1982), as well as *Pilate's Wife*, *Asphodel*, and *Her*, collected in *Hermione* (1981).

Rita Dove (b. 1952)

Born and raised in Akron, Ohio, Rita Dove grew up in an African American middle-class family headed by her father, who worked as a research chemist in the Akron tire industry. In 1970, Dove received a Presidential Scholar award to study at Miami University, where she later graduated Phi Beta Kappa in 1973. Following college, Dove received a Fulbright scholarship to pursue two semesters of advanced study at the Universtät Tübingen in Germany, where she met and married the German writer Fred Viebahn. Returning to the United States, Dove received an M.F.A. from the prestigious creative writing program at the University of Iowa. Her first collection of poetry was entitled *The Yellow House on the Corner* (1980), followed by *Museum* (1983). With her next volume of verse, *Thomas and Beulah* (1986), Dove became the second African American poet, after Gwendolyn Brooks, to win a Pulitzer Prize. Her subsequent volumes include *Grace Notes* (1989), *Selected Poems* (1993), *Mother Love* (1995), *On the Bus with Rosa Parks* (1999), as well as a book of short stories *Fifth Sunday* (1985) and a novel *Through the Ivory Gate* (1992), plus a book of essays entitled *The Poet's World* (1995). Her 1996 play *The Darker Face of the Earth* premiered at the Oregon Shakespeare Festival and was staged at the Kennedy Center in Washington, D.C., and the Royal National Theatre in

London. In addition to editing *Best American Poetry 2000*, she also writes a column entitled "Poet's Choice" for the *Washington Post*. In 1993, Rita Dove was the first African American to be named as Poet Laureate of the United States and consultant in poetry at the Library of Congress. Over the course of her career, Rita Dove has received numerous honorary doctorates as well as several prestigious prizes, and she is currently the Commonwealth Professor of English at the University of Virginia, Charlottesville.

T. S. Eliot (1888–1965)

Although born into a New England family, Thomas Stearns Eliot grew up in St. Louis, where his father was the president of the Hydraulic-Press Brick Company. Entering Harvard University as a freshman in 1906, Eliot studied under George Santayana and Irving Babbitt, and by 1908, he had begun studying the French symbolist verse of Jules LaForgue, who became a major modernist influence on Eliot's early poetry. Following his graduation from Harvard, Eliot lived for a year in Paris, where he met Jean Verdenal, a medical student who was later killed in the battle of the Dardenelles during World War I. Influenced by the dramatic monologue forms of Robert Browning, Eliot soon, according to the poet Ezra Pound, "trained himself and modernized himself on his own," writing his famous interior monologue "The Love Song of J. Alfred Prufrock" while in Paris in the early 1910s. By 1914, Eliot traveled to Marburg, Germany, and had intended to study at Merton College, Oxford, but soon entered into what soon would become a very difficult marriage to Vivien Haigh-Wood the following year. By 1917, Eliot had established himself in the London literary scene with the publication of *Prufrock and Other Observations* while he supported himself by working in the foreign section of Lloyds Bank. Moving in the same international literary circles as noted writers W. B. Yeats, James Joyce, Wyndham Lewis, and Filippo Tommaso Marinetti, among others, Eliot published what soon became the definitive modernist long poem, *The Waste Land* (1922). As the editor of the influential journal *The Criterion*, Eliot moved to the center of London intellectual life, becoming a literary editor at Faber and Gwyer in the mid-twenties. Not insignificantly, it was at this time that Eliot converted to the Church of England and by 1928 had famously declared himself in a book of essays called *For Lancelot Andrewes*, a "classicist in literature, royalist in politics, and anglo-catholic in religion." Eliot had already arrived as a highly influential literary critic in early 1919 with his foundational essay "Tradition and the Individual Talent." He sustained and amplified that influence in subsequent volumes of prose and authored a series of popular plays including *The Family Reunion* (1939), *The Cocktail Party* (1949), *The Confidential Clerk* (1953), and *The Elder Statesman* (1958). Among the most reputable writers of the twentieth century, Eliot was invited to deliver the Clark Lectures at Cambridge University, and the Norton Lectures at Harvard, and while a Fellow at Princeton's Institute for Advanced Study, he was awarded the Nobel Prize in literature in 1948. His late suite of poems, *Four Quartets* (1943), crowned his career as poet. In 1957,

Vasily Kandinsky, *Composition vi* (1913)

Charles Henry Demuth, *I Saw the Figure Five in Gold* (1928)

Andy Warhol, *Marilyn Monroe (Twenty Times)* (1962)

The Chicago Women's Graphics Collective, *Boycott Lettuce and Grapes* (c. 1970)

Pieter Brueghel, *Landscape with the Fall of Icarus* (1558)

Botticelli, *The Birth of Venus* (1485)

Raphael, *An Allegory: Vision of a Knight* (1504)

Michelangelo, *Leda and the Swan* (1530)

William Blake, Illuminated manuscript of "The Lamb" (1789)

Dante Gabriel Rossetti, *The Girlhood of Mary Virgin* (1848–1849)

Samuel Bak, *Thou Shalt Not Kill*, (1978)

Eliot married Valerie Fletcher and enjoyed the remainder of his life with her until his death in 1965.

Anne Finch (1661–1720)

The third child born to Sir William Kingsmill and Anne Haslewood, Anne Kingsmill Finch was five months old when her father died in 1661. Following her mother's death three years later, Anne was brought up by her grandmother, Bridget, Lady Kingsmill. After Lady Kingsmill's death in 1672, Anne was raised in the household of William Haslewood, where she studied French and Italian, Greek and Roman mythology, the Bible, and the humanities. Ten years later, Anne became a maid of honor to Mary of Modena, the wife of James, Duke of York. In 1684, Anne married Heneage Finch, who was a courtier to James. Finch retained his status at the Stuart court after the coronation of the Duke of York as King James II. After the revolution of 1688 and the coronation of William of Orange, Heneage Finch was arrested for a short period for his continuing allegiance to James II. In the 1690s, the couple lived at the estate of Charles Finch, Earl of Winchilsea. Following the succession of James II's daughter, Queen Anne, to the throne in the early 1700s, the Finches returned to London, where Anne Finch began to publish her poetry. *Miscellany Poems, on Several Occasions* appeared in 1713 and comprised eighty-six poems and Finch's play *Aristomenes: Or, The Royal Shepherd*. The previous year, her husband had become the Earl of Winchilsea. Continuing political and financial stresses, however, took their toll on Anne Finch, countess of Winchilsea, as reflected in her last poems, written during her latter years up to her death in 1720.

Robert Frost (1874–1963)

Although considered a New England poet, Robert Frost was actually born in San Francisco and lived there until the age of eleven when, after the death of his father, he moved with his mother and sister to Salem, New Hampshire. Although he graduated as a high school valedictorian, an honor he shared with future wife, Elinor White, Frost could not adjust to college life at Dartmouth and, years later, dropped out of Harvard as well. While living in Derry, New Hampshire, on the farm bequeathed to him by his grandfather, Frost split his time between farming and teaching at the Pinkerton Academy. During the decade he lived in Derry, Frost composed most of the poems that would go into his first volumes—*A Boy's Will* (1913) and *North of Boston* (1914)—which he published in England after selling the family farm and moving there in 1912. Living outside of London, Frost struck important literary friendships with the British poet Edward Thomas and the American expatriate Ezra Pound, both of whom wrote important reviews of Frost's early work and introduced him to the Irish poet W. B. Yeats. Frost returned to America in 1915 and was greeted by literary success for his next volume, *Mountain Interval* (1916), and his Pulitzer Prize–winning book *New Hampshire*

(1924). Frost would go on to win three more Pulitzers as his verse gained force and he became a leading poet of the twentieth century. Despite the steady growth of his literary reputation during the 1930s, Frost suffered domestic tragedy in the deaths of his daughter Marjorie in 1934, his wife's death in 1938, the suicide of his son Carol in 1940, and his daughter Irma's affliction with mental disorders. Several of Frost's later critics such as Randall Jarrell and Lionel Trilling would point out the tragic dimensions of his poetic vision beneath the outgoing demeanor of the good, grey New England poet. Although becoming something of an American institution culminating in his reading at President John F. Kennedy's presidential inaugural ceremony, Frost's public image further shifted after his death in 1963 owing to Lawrence Thompson's 1970 biography *Robert Frost: The Years of Triumph, 1915–1937* that depicted him as, in the critic Helen Vendler's words, a "monster of egotism." In other biographies and criticism, however, Frost received a more fairminded reception in such works as W. H. Pritchard's *A Literary Life Reconsidered* (1984) and Stanley Burnshaw's *Robert Frost Himself* (1986).

Allen Ginsberg (1926–1997)

Like Walt Whitman and William Carlos Williams, Allen Ginsberg was a New Jersey poet. Born in Newark, New Jersey, Ginsberg was introduced to literature early on by his father, Louis, himself a poet and high school English teacher. The other major influence in Ginsberg's formative years was his mother Naomi, who was a Communist Party member and also suffered from bouts of acute paranoia and mental illness, which Ginsberg records in his long poem *Kaddish*. Growing up in Paterson, New Jersey, Ginsberg took the modernist American poet William Carlos Williams as a poetic mentor, and his letters to Williams appear in the latter's long poem, *Paterson*. Ginsberg went on to study at Columbia University with such famous critics of the time as Lionel Trilling, Mark Van Doren, and Raymond Weaver. But it was also at Columbia and in New York City generally where Ginsberg met through Lucien Carr those who would become the inner core of the beat movement: William S. Burroughs, Jack Kerouac, and Neal Cassady, who all appear in Kerouac's celebrated novel *On the Road* (1957). The paradoxical connotations of the "beat" generation signified both what was down and out and spiritually beatified. That contradictory mix of urban destitution and visionary experience was memorably captured in Ginsberg's ground-breaking volume of verse, *Howl and Other Poems* (1956). Part of this book records not only Ginsberg's subterranean lifestyle but also his hospitalization in the Columbia Presbyterian Psychiactric Institute, where he met the young writer Carl Solomon. Not just a poet, Ginsberg became a cultural icon and his memorable poetry readings—including his celebrated 1955 reading at the Six Gallery in San Francisco with fellow San Francisco Renaissance poets Kenneth Rexroth, Gary Snyder, Michael McClure, Philip Whalen, and Philip LaMantia—amount to performance art. Published by Lawrence Ferlinghetti's City Lights Pocket Poets series, *Howl and Other Poems* was quickly confiscated by the San Francisco police. By the end of 1957, however, the American Civil Liberties Union successfully defended the book, convincing Judge Clayton Horn that the work had aesthetic and social value that exceeded the charges of pornography. Reviving the long line and poetic catalogue forms of Walt Whitman, whom the poet addresses in "Supermarket in California," Ginsberg went on to publish an elegy for his mother, *Kaddish and Other Poems* (1961), followed by such major volumes as *Reality Sandwiches* (1963), *Planet News, 1961–1967* (1968), *The Fall of America: Poems of These States, 1965–1971* (1973), *Plutonium Ode: Poems 1977–1980* (1982), and *Death and Fame: Last Poems 1993–1997* (1999). A winner of the National Book Award in 1974, Ginsberg combined the roles of poet and prophet in the visionary mode of William Blake, but he also was an outspoken social critic, political activist, and a distinguished professor at Brooklyn College. He died of liver cancer in New York City at the age of seventy.

Thomas Hardy (1840–1928)

Born in the rural village of Higher Bockhampton in Dorset, Thomas Hardy was the son of a stonemason. Early on, his mother encouraged his reading, and at age sixteen he apprenticed to study architecture, later traveling to London to pursue that trade at twenty-two. Although he considered taking holy orders, in London he gradually adopted a more modern skepticism toward religion owing, in part, to his reading of Charles Darwin, Herbert Spencer, and John Stuart Mill. Hardy began life as a writer by returning to Dorchester in 1867, where he worked on an unpublished novel, *The Poor Man and the Lady*. In the 1870s he emerged as a novelist with a popular following for such works of fiction as *Desperate Remedies* (1871), *Under the Greenwood Tree* (1872), *A Pair of Blue Eyes* (1873), and *Far from the Madding Crowd* (1874). Following on this successful run of fiction, he entered into a difficult marriage to Emma Gifford. His troubles with Gifford are apparent in the increasing pessimism of his themes from *The Return of the Native* (1878) followed by *The Mayor of Casterbridge* (1886), *Tess of the D'Urbervilles* (1891), and *Jude the Obscure* (1895). The latter two, in particular, were so harshly criticized by Hardy's contemporaries that he gave up fiction and turned to writing poetry, producing such notable volumes as *Wessex Poems and Other Verses* (1898), *Poems of the Past and Present* (1902), and *Satires of Circumstance, Lyrics and Reveries* (1914). Following the death of wife Emma in 1912, Hardy remarried Florence Emily Dugdale two years later. The many honors bestowed on Hardy during the final years of his life included the Order of Merit awarded by King George V, the presidency of the Society of Authors, a Nobel Prize nomination, the Gold Medal of the Royal Society of Literature, and numerous honorary degrees. Hardy died in his native Dorchester in 1928, and, after cremation, his ashes were buried in the Poet's Corner in Westminster Abbey.

Robert Hayden (1913–1980)

Robert Hayden was born in the "Paradise Valley" ghetto of Detroit to Ruth and Asa Sheffey who separated after his birth. Adopted by William and Ruth Hayden, the poet grew up in a troubled household filled with what he later described as "chronic angers." Attending Detroit City College until 1936, he then joined the Federal Writer's project, where for two years he researched African American history and folklore. Hayden married Erma Morris in 1940, which was also the year of his first publication, *Heart-Shape in the Dust*. The following year he attended the University of Michigan, where he studied with the modernist poet W. H. Auden. Graduating in 1942, Hayden remained there until 1946, when he joined the faculty of Fisk University. After he went on to enjoy a twenty-three-year career, publishing such major volumes as *The Lion and the Archer* (1948), *Figures of Time: Poems* (1955), *Night-Blooming Cereus* (1972), *Angle of Ascent* (1975), *American Journal* (1978, 1982), and his posthumous *Collected Poems* (1985). "His poetry," according to critic Mark A. Sanders, "posits race as a means through which one contemplates the expansive possibilities of language, and the transformative power of art." A master of poetic craft and modernist experimentation, Robert Hayden remains a seminal voice in American literature, and his verse spans the course of African American poetics reaching from the Harlem Renaissance through the black aesthetic movement and beyond.

Seamus Heaney (b. 1939)

Seamus Heaney has the distinction of being the only Irish poet since W. B. Yeats to have won the Nobel Prize in literature. Born and raised north of Belfast in Mossbawn, County Derry, he attended Queen's College from 1957 to 1961 and then went on to receive a teacher's certificate in English at St. Joseph's College, Belfast, where he became a lecturer while pursuing literary collaboration with such poets as Philip Hobsbaum, Derek Mahon, and Michael Longley. Four years later, he married Marie Devlin and published *Eleven Poems*, followed the next year by *Death of a Naturalist*, which brought him much recognition and such prizes as the E. C. Gregory Award, the Cholmondeley Award, Somerset Maugham Award, and Geoffrey Faber Memorial Prize. His next volume, *Door into the Dark*, became the Poetry Book Society Choice for 1969. Following a brief appointment at the University of California, Berkeley, Heaney gave up his lectureship at Queens College and took up residence in Glanmore, County Wicklow. During the 1970s, Heaney alternated giving poetry readings with a teaching position at Carysfort, publishing *North* (1975) and *Field Work* (1979), which presented the rural settings of his earlier volumes through a deeper attention to Irish history and politics. With his publication of *Station Island* in 1984, Heaney became the Boylston Professor of Rhetoric and Oratory at Harvard and in 1989 professor of poetry at Oxford University. He was awarded the Nobel Prize for literature in 1995. His recent volumes include *Seeing Things* (1991) and *The Spirit Level* (1996).

George Herbert (1593–1633)

A cousin of the Earl of Pembroke, George Herbert was born into a prominent Welsh family. His mother was a patron of the metaphysical poet John Donne, who dedicated his *Holy Sonnets* to her. Following the death of his father, Herbert attended Westminster School at age ten and then took a B.A. (1613) and an M.A. (1616) at Trinity College, Cambridge, where he later became the public orator of the University and was elected a representative to Parliament in 1624 and 1625. Herbert also received the patronage of King James I until the latter's death in 1625. After resigning his position as orator in 1627, Herbert married Jane Danvers in 1629. The following year, he took holy orders in the Church of England and assumed the duties of vicar and rector of the Bemerton parish near Salisbury. For the next three years until his death in 1633, Herbert composed the poems that would be posthumously published as *The Temple* (1633). The enormous success of this work established George Herbert's reputation among the metaphysical poets and he remains one of the major voices in seventeenth-century verse.

Robert Herrick (1591–1674)

The son of a London goldsmith, Robert Herrick apprenticed to his uncle, also in the same trade, for six years between the ages of sixteen and twenty-two before entering Saint John's College, Cambridge. After graduating in 1617, Herrick was a protégé to Ben Jonson to whom he wrote five poems. Not just a poet, Herrick took holy orders in the Church of England in 1623 and served as vicar at Dean Prior in Devonshire until 1647, when, owing to his Royalist allegiances, he was removed during the Great Rebellion. That same year, Herrick published his first volume of verse, *Noble Numbers*, which was collected in his *Herperides; or, the Works Both Human and Divine of Robert Herrick, Esq.* (1648). This major book of more than 1,200 poems includes carpe diem love lyrics, epigrams, elegies, and epistles. From his studies of Horace, Catullus, and other authors of classical antiquity, Herrick adapted the conventions of the Roman pastoral tradition to the English eclogue tradition in order to celebrate British village life and customs. With the restoration of Charles II, Herrick resumed his office of vicar at Dean Prior from 1662 until his death in 1674.

Gerard Manley Hopkins (1844–1889)

The first of nine children born to Manley and Catherine Hopkins, Gerard Manley Hopkins grew up in a household of high church Anglicans. He was not, however, the only poet in his family; the year before Gerard's birth, his father, a marine insurance adjuster, had published a volume of verse. Following in his father's footsteps, Gerard showed early promise as a poet by winning a poetry prize at Highgate, his grammar school, before going on to win a scholarship to Balliol College, Oxford, where he studied with such tutors as the famous English "Art-for-Art's-Sake" writer, Walter Pater. Another powerful mentor at Oxford was John Henry Newman, whose conversion from the Anglican church to Catholicism was an example that Hopkins followed in 1866. The following year he graduated with a "double-first" degree from Balliol and entered the Society of Jesus in 1868, eventually becoming ordained as a Jesuit priest in 1877. Although he turned away from poetry to pursue his religious vocation initally, his studies of the medieval Catholic philosopher Duns Scotus allowed him to find parallels between what the medievalist emphasized as the vivid uniqueness or haecceitas ("thisness") of experience and what Hopkins himself depicted as the perceptual intensity of poetic "inscape" in later works such as "God's Grandeur," "Pied Beauty," and "The Windhover." History, however, drew Hopkins back into poetry in the 1875 loss of the ship *Deutschland*, whose passenger list included five Franciscan nuns. Hopkins wrote his must challenging long poem, *The Wreck of the Deutschland*, in commemoration of this tragedy, although the rector who had commissioned this work actually rejected it for final publication. During the late 1870s, Hopkins served briefly in Sheffield, Oxford, as a preacher and in the early 1880s became parish priest, ministering to the working poor of Manchester, Liverpool, and Glasgow. In the late 1880s, while teaching Latin and Greek at Stonyhurst College, Hopkins wrestled with modern, religious doubt that produced the so-called terrible sonnets before his death from typhoid fever in 1889. Hopkins's major poetry did not appear in print in his lifetime, but thanks to Robert Bridges, the Poet Laureate in 1913 and Hopkins's friend from Oxford, his work was published posthumously in 1918. Subsequently, the freshness of Hopkins's experiments in language, "sprung" rhythm, as well as poetic "inscape" and "instress" became a major influence in modern verse.

Langston Hughes (1903–1967)

A Midwesterner by birth, Hughes grew up in Lawrence, Kansas, with additional time spent in Illinois, Ohio, and Mexico. Hughes received some of his impetus to write about the specific experience of African Americans, in part, from his maternal grandmother, Mary Langston, whose husband had been killed with John Brown at Harper's Ferry. Even before attending Columbia University, Hughes had published in the prestigious *Crisis* magazine what would become a signature poem, "The Negro Speaks of Rivers." After a year at Columbia, Hughes left in 1922 to work and to travel to such destinations as the West Coast of Africa and Paris. Returning to the United States in 1924, he received notoriety as the most talented and original poet of the Harlem Renaissance. His first book, *The Weary Blues* (1926), boldly celebrated the everyday lives of ordinary black folk in a vernacular poetics influenced by such American forerunners as Walt Whitman and Carl Sandburg but also based in the kind of blues lyricism, black sermon, and other expressive forms rooted in African American culture that he espoused in an important manifesto published in *The Nation* magazine: "The Negro Artist and the Racial Mountain" (1926). The following year Hughes published his second volume *Fine Clothes to the Jew* and as a student at Lincoln University received financial support from Mrs. Charlotte Mason, Hughes's patron in the arts during the next two years. Owing to irreconcilable differences in politics, taste, and personality, Hughes reached a parting of the ways with Mason when his first novel, *Not Without Laughter*, was published in 1930. Like many writers during the Depression era, Hughes became a committed political activist on the left and was involved in the worldwide struggle for social justice. During the early thirties Hughes traveled to the Soviet Union, and in addition to publishing radical left poetry, he authored a volume of short stories, *The Ways of White Folks* (1934), and the Broadway play *Mulatto* (1935), followed other dramatic productions. By 1937, Hughes had left the country again, this time to lend his support to the Internationalist cause in the Spanish Civil War, where he wrote his moving war poem "Madrid." Returning once more to America, Hughes published an original collection of radical verse entitled "A New Song" the following year. During World War II, Hughes continued to inveigh against racism, publishing the first volume of his autobiography *The Big Sea* (1940) and verse collections such as *Shakespeare in Harlem* (1942) and *Jim Crow's Last Stand* (1943). It was at this time that Hughes reached a wide popular audience in his weekly column for the *Chicago Defender* that over the next twenty years would follow the ironic insights of Hughes's comic persona, Jesse B. Semple. Following the war, Hughes continued to publish such volumes of verse as *Fields of Wonder* (1947), *One-Way Ticket* (1949), and *Montage of a Dream Deferred* (1951). By 1953, however, his earlier politics made him a target of Senator Joseph McCarthy and his House Un-American Activities Committee hearings during the Red Scare. Forced to disavow his radical stances of the 1930s, Hughes nevertheless survived McCarthy's own loss of public credibility and went on to narrate his time in the Soviet Union in the second volume of his autobiography, *I Wonder as I Wander* (1956). A series of successful musical collaborations during the 1950s brought Hughes a measure of prosperity in his late career. His reputation in the Pan-Africanist community culminated in his celebration at the 1966 First World Festival of Negro Arts in Dakar, Senegal. Hughes's final volume of verse, *The Panther and the Lash* (1967), recounted the racial struggles of the civil rights era of the 1960s and was posthumously published the year he died in 1967.

Kobayashi Issa [Yataro Nobuyuki] (1763–1827)

Born in the small town Kashiwabara in the mountainous central region of Japan, Issa lived there until the age of thirteen when he left to live in Edo (present-day Tokyo). Under the patronage of Seibi Natsume, Issa began writing Haiku poetry at the age of twenty-five after studying under his teachers Genmu and Chiku-a. Although he was elected to take the place of his teacher on the latter's death, Issa chose instead to live the life of a wanderer until 1801, when his father died. Owing to a dispute with his stepmother and half brother over his father's estate, Issa continued to travel to Kyoto, Osaka, Nagasaki, and Matsuyama until the age of fifty-one when he married a much younger woman. Tragedy marked his married life, however, with the death of each of his four children in infancy and, finally, the death of his wife from yet another childbirth. Moreover, his house burned to the ground. Nevertheless, during the last four years, Issa married again and fathered a girl who was born shortly after his death. Issa composed plainspoken haiku lyrics that reflect on the difficult circumstances of his private life, influenced as it was by Buddhist philosophy. Among Issa's most famous literary works are "The Diary at My Father's

Death" (1801) and "My Springtime" (1819). His poetry is ranked among the best haiku verse produced by such Japanese masters of the genre as Basho Matsuo, Buson Yosa, and Shiki Masaoka.

Randall Jarrell (1914–1965)

Randall Jarrell grew up in Los Angeles until his parents' divorce, when he returned to Nashville, the city of his birth. Tellingly, his Los Angeles experiences, especially his visit with his grandparents at the age of twelve, would be represented in the title piece of his last book of verse, *The Lost World*. Supported in part by a National Youth Administration scholarship, Jarrell later attended college at Vanderbilt University, where he was mentored by Robert Penn Warren, who published Jarrell's first poems, and John Crowe Ransom, who later hired Jarrell to teach freshman composition and to coach tennis at Kenyon College. At Kenyon, Jarrell befriended the emerging fiction writer Peter Taylor and, more important, the young student Robert Lowell, whose poetry Jarrell helped to encourage through his personal and professional criticism. After his time at Kenyon, Jarrell combined careers as poet, critic, and teacher. At the University of Texas, he married Mackie Langham in 1940 and then served in the U.S. Army Air Force teaching celestial navigation. Meanwhile, he published his first book of verse, *Blood for a Stranger* (1942), and had success placing poems in *The New Republic* through his connection to the critic and editor Edmund Wilson. Jarrell's air force experience would form the basis of two volumes of verse, *Little Friend, Little Friend* (1945) and *Losses* (1948). In the postwar years, Jarrell served for a year as the literary editor of *The Nation* magzine and then taught at Sarah Lawrence College. His teaching experience there would be the subject of his humorous best-selling novel lampooning the fictional Benton College in *Pictures from an Institution* (1954). Two years previously, Jarrell married his second wife, Mary von Shrader, and moved to the University of North Carolina at Greensboro. At the same time, Jarrell was making a name for himself as an incisive and influential critic of modern American poetry with his best work collected in the volume *Poetry and the Age* (1953). His reputation as a poet, however, flowered later in the sixties when he won the National Book Award for *The Woman at the Washington Zoo* (1960) and *The Lost World* (1965). Jarrell was also a translator of Goethe's *Faust, Part I*, several of Grimm's fairy tales, and Chekhov's *The Three Sisters*. In addition, he published four books of children's stories. Toward the end of his life Jarrell suffered from depression and attempted suicide by slashing his wrist. In the fall of 1965, he received treatment at a hospital in Chapel Hill, and while walking on a highway he was struck and killed by a car.

Ben Jonson (1572–1637)

The son of a minister, who died before the poet was born, Jonson was brought up by his mother and a stepfather, who was a bricklayer by trade. Raised in Westminster, Jonson attended St. Martin's parish school, where he was mentored by the classicist William Camden. After a brief stint working in his stepfather's vocation, Jonson served in the military. He returned to London in 1592 and two years later married Anne Lewis, with whom he would have two sons. In 1598, Jonson wrote his first successful play, *Every Man in His Humor,* and its 1616 production included the famous dramatist William Shakespeare in the cast. The year it opened, however, Jonson killed actor Gabriel Spencer in a duel and barely escaped the gallows for murder by pleading "benefit of clergy" owing to his ability to read and write Latin. During the first decade of the seventeenth century, Jonson enjoyed the patronage of James I and produced a number of entertaining and witty court masques such as the *Masque of Blacknesse* (1605) and the *Masque of Queens* (1608) in addition to such popular masterpieces as *Volpone* (1606) and *The Alchemist* (1610). At this time, he also presided— mainly at the Mermaid Tavern in Fleet Street and later at the Devil's Tavern— over a circle of protégés and admirers who became known as the "Tribe of Ben" and counted among its numbers such writers as Thomas Carew, Richard Lovelace, and Robert Herrick. Jonson was appointed Poet Laureate in 1616 and wrote lyric verse, odes, and epigrams in a classical mode. Among his other offices was his appointment in 1628 to City Chronologer of London. That same year, Jonson suffered a debilitating stroke; he died nine years later and was buried in Westminster Abbey under a tombstone whose epitaph "O Rare Ben Jonson!" testifies to his unique place in English letters. His final, unfinished play, *Sad Shepherd's Tale,* was published posthmously in 1641.

John Keats (1795–1821). *See Chapter 27.*

Denise Levertov (1923–1997)

Born in Ilford, Essex, England, Denise Levertov benefited from her family's rich cultural heritage. A descendant of Shneour Zalman, a Russian founder of the Habad branch of Hasidism, Levertov's father, Paul Levertoff, converted from Judaism to become an Anglican priest. The poet's mother, Beatrice Spooner-Jones Levertoff, claimed an ancestry that included the mystical teacher Angell Jones of Mold, whose son sponsored a Welch intellectual salon in the 1870s. Educated largely at home, Levertov combined a love of literature with an eclectic spirituality. Like her mother, who undertook humanitarian causes for the League of Nations Union, Denise Levertov was an activist in the cause of peace during the antiwar movements from Vietnam onwards. During World War II, Levertov served the cause of healing as a nurse in London. In 1946 she published a first volume of verse and then emigrated to America two years later. Through her husband, Mitchell Goodman, she met poets in the Black Mountain school, including Robert Creeley and Cid Corman, who published her verse in the avant-garde journal *Origin.* Her new style parted company with the formalist measures of her early poetry in favor of the free-verse forms of William Carlos Williams, Charles Olson, and Robert Duncan. In 1955 Levertov became an American citizen and during the subsequent decades in her several roles as poet, critic, and teacher, she had an important influence on a younger generation of American experimental poets. In addition to publishing fifteen volumes of verse, including her representative collection *Selected Poems* (1986), she authored two volumes of prose criticism, *The Poet in The World* (1973) and *Light Up the Cave* (1981). After teaching variously in the Boston area at Brandeis, MIT, and Tufts University, she moved to Seattle in 1989, where she combined lecturing at the University of Washington with her appointment as professor at Stanford University from 1982 to 1993. Until her death in 1997, she pursued an active schedule of public readings and carried on a dynamic correspondence with a network of other writers. A deeply sacramental author, Levertov believed, as she wrote in "Poetry, Prophecy, Survival," that her special vocation as poet was "to live with the door of one's life open to the transcendent, the numinous."

Audre Lorde (1934–1992)

The youngest of three daughters born to the West Indian immigrants Frederic Byron and Linda Belmar Lorde, Audre Lorde was raised in Manhattan during the Depression era. She attended Catholic grammar schools, St. Mark's School and St. Catherine's School, and from the eighth grade onward, she wrote poetry and identified herself as a poet. From 1954 through 1959, Audre Lorde attended Hunter College, graduating with a B.A. In 1961, she earned an M.A. in library science from Columbia University. Working as a librarian at Mount Vernon Public Library, she married lawyer Edward Ashley Rollins, and the couple had two children before divorcing in 1970. By 1966, Lorde had assumed the position of head librarian at Town School Library in New York City. Throughout the 1960s, Lorde divided her time between writing, publishing her poetry, working, raising a family, and becoming an activist in the civil rights, antiwar, and feminist movements. In 1968 she was awarded a National Endowment for the Arts grant that funded her poet-in-residence position at Tougaloo College in Mississippi. It was at Tougaloo that Lorde met her longtime companion, Frances Clayton. That year, her inaugural volume of poetry, *The First Cities*, was published by Poets Press. Two years later, she published *Cables to Rage*, depicting her lesbian identity in a poem entitled "Martha" based on her relationship with Clayton. Three years later, Broadside Press published *From a Land Where Other People Live*, which was nominated for the National Book Award for 1973. The following year, Lorde's poetry took a decidedly more political turn in *New York Head Shop and Museum*, followed in 1976 by *Coal*, which collected poetry from the first two volumes and was published by W. W. Norton. Much of Lorde's lyric poetry explores women's erotic lives. "The erotic," she has commented, "is a resource within each of us that lies in a deeply female and spiritual plane, firmly rooted in the power of our unexpressed or unrecognized feeling." *The Black Unicorn* (1978) moved beyond her earlier verse by reading Lorde's contemporary experience as a black lesbian feminist through African mythology. In addition to her poetry of the 1970s, Lorde wrote a series of essays based on her experience as an African American intellectual and as a survivor of breast cancer. "The Transformation of Silence into Language and Action," "A Black Lesbian Feminist Experience," and "Breast Cancer: Power vs. Prosthesis" were collected in her 1980 volume, *The Cancer Journals*, which won the American Library Association Gay Caucus Book of the Year Award for 1981. Lorde's cultural study of her own mastectomy was followed by what she called her "biomythography" in *Zami: A New Spelling of My Name* (1982). Six years later, in *A Burst of Light*, Lorde reflected on her diagnosis of liver cancer, the disease that would eventually take her life in 1992. In her last years, Lorde lived on St. Croix, U.S. Virgin Islands, and took the African name Gamba Adisa, which translates as "Warrior, She Who Makes Her Meaning Known." Her last publications include *Undersong: Chosen Poems Old and New* (1992) and *The Marvelous Arithmetics of Distance* (1993). In addition to receiving several awards throughout her life, Audre Lorde was Poet Laureate of New York in 1991 and a recipient of the Walt Whitman Citation of Merit.

Robert Lowell (1917–1977)

Born into an elite Boston family, Robert Lowell claimed as distant relatives both the fireside poet, James Russell Lowell, and the modern imagist poet, Amy Lowell. At St. Marks School, Lowell benefited from studying with the poet Richard Eberhart. After graduating from St. Marks, Lowell went to Harvard but stayed there for only a year before transfering to Kenyon College to study with John Crowe Ransom and Allen Tate. In 1940 Lowell graduated from Kenyon, converted to Roman Catholicism, and married the novelist Jean Stafford. Lowell would further his connections to the American New Critics by studying with Robert Penn Warren and Cleanth Brooks at Louisiana State University. Such connections helped secure a powerful critical reception for his early volumes such as the *Land of Unlikeness* (1944) and *Lord Weary's Castle* (1946), which won a Pulitzer Prize for poetry in 1947. Meanwhile, his antiwar stance as a conscientious objector to World War II had earned him in 1943 a year of jail time in New York's West Street prison, which he would later commemorate in his poem "Memories of West Street and Lepke." His stormy marriage to Stafford lasted eight years, and following his divorce, the poet met writer and editor Elizabeth (Lizzie) Hardwick at the Yaddo writer's institute. The two married the following year in 1949. Lowell went by the nickname Cal, which signified both on the cruelty of the Roman emporer Caligula and the wildness of Shakespeare's monstrous character Caliban from *The Tempest*. Lowell suffered from manic depression and was periodically institutionalized for mental illness throughout his life. Like other contemporaneous poets such as John Berryman, Theodore Roethke, and Anne Sexton, Lowell exploited his bouts of madness as material for his verse, which took on more intimate and less formal qualities in the so-called confessional poetry of *Life Studies* (1959), which received the National Book Award in 1960. Lowell's poetry during the 1960s became more politically engaged with public history as in the titlepiece of his 1964 collection *For the Union Dead*. His translations of Rilke and Rimbaud among others collected in *Imitations* (1961) won the prestigious Bollingen Prize in 1962. Later in the decade, Lowell became a vocal critic of the Vietnam War and participated in antiwar rallies, which he would record in such poems as "The March I" and "The March II" from his volume *Notebook* (1970). Lowell expanded on the work in *Notebook* in three volumes published in 1973: *History, For Lizzie and Harriet,* and *The Dolphin*. These books record his divorce from Hardwick, its effects on his daughter, Harriet, and his remarriage to Caroline Blackwood in 1972. Although critics were divided on Lowell's use of private letters in the intimate confessional verse of *The Dolphin*, this volume won the poet another Pulitzer Prize. Four years after this success, Lowell died of a heart attack in a taxi cab while enroute to Lizzie and Harriet in New York City.

Mina Loy (1882–1966)

The daughter of a second-generation Hungarian Jewish father and an English mother, Mina Gertrude Lowry was born in London and began her career as a visual artist, exhibiting her paintings in the Salon d'Automne show in Paris, 1905. A cosmopolitan modernist, she spent time in England, Paris, and Florence before moving to the United States. In 1903, at the time she married the photographer and writer Stephen Haweis, she shortened the spelling of her name to become Mina Loy. Between 1904 and 1907 she had three children and was an active friend to fellow modernists Gertrude Stein and Mabel Dodge, in whose salons she met such figures as the cubist painter Pablo Picasso, John Reed, and Carl Van Vechten. By 1913, Loy was emerging as a modern artist in her own right, in part through her connections to Italian futurists such as Filippo Tommaso Marinetti and through her published verse in Alfred Steiglitz's stylish journal *Camera Work* and in Carl Van Vechten's *Trend*. Her publication of the experimental verse collection "Love Songs" in the avant-garde magazine *Others* created a literary stir. In 1916, Loy moved to New York to take the lead role in Alfred Kreymbourg's play *Lima Beans*, and the following year met and married the surreal poet and professional boxer Alfred Cravan. Her marriage was shortlived, however, owing to Cravan's disappearance in Mexico. Returning to England, Loy gave birth to Cravan's daughter, Fabienne, in 1919 and later moved to Florence. Leaving her children there, she sailed for New York, where she became a member of the Provincetown Players. With the financial support of Peggy Guggenheim, Loy traveled to Paris three years later with Fabienne and opened a lampshade business. In that same year, Robert McAlmon's Contact Press published her book of verse *Lunar Baedecker* (1923). By 1930 Loy had given up her business in Paris and was working as the Paris agent for a New York gallery managed by Julien Levy, her son-in-law. Her last creative project of Bowery "constructions" was documented in her New York gallery exhibition and involved a series of poems and experimental artworks based on the street life of the lower Bowery, where she lived until the age of seventy-one. Loy spent the remaining decade of her life with her daughters in Colorado, where she died in Aspen at the age of eighty-four.

Andrew Marvell (1621–1678)

The son of a minister, Andrew Marvell was born in the Yorkshire town of Hull and at age twelve attended Trinity College, Cambridge. At the age of sixteen, he published poems written in Latin and Greek in an anthology of Cambridge poets. Graduating with a B.A. in 1639, Marvell began his studies toward an M.A. degree, but his advanced degree work was interrupted when his father drowned in the Hull estuary. During the 1640s, Marvell traveled on the Continent and became a tutor in the 1650s, the decade that he most likely wrote his most enduring lyrics. Owing to his friendship with the poet John Milton, Marvell was appointed his Latin secretary from 1657 to 1660, when Marvell was elected to Parliament. A consummate politician, Marvell held office under Cromwell as well as during the Restoration. His posthumously published satires present sharp and witty criticisms of loyalists of both the Royalist and Republican causes. Not just a closet satirist, however, Marvell used his political influence to free Milton from jail after the Restoration and served on diplomatic journeys to Holland, Russia, Sweden, and Denmark. Although now remembered for such masterful carpe diem lyrics as "To His Coy Mistress," pastoral lyrics such as "The Garden," and political odes such as "An Horation Ode upon Cromwell's Return from Ireland," Marvell published very little during his lifetime. It was not until 1681, three years after his death, that his nephew published Marvell's verse under the title *Miscellaneous Poems*.

Claude McKay (1889–1948)

Born into a Jamaican farm family, Festus Claudius McKay received an education at first from his oldest brother, a schoolteacher. McKay began to write poetry as early as age ten before he entered into an apprenticeship to a cabinetmaker. At eighteen, he was encouraged to write dialect poetry by an expatriate English gentleman living in Jamaica, Walter Jekyll, who later set McKay's verse to music. When he immigrated to the United States in 1912, McKay had already published two volumes of dialect verse that drew on native folkloric motifs, *Songs of Jamaica* (1912) and *Constab Ballads* (1912). On his arrival in America, McKay studied briefly at Tuskegee Institute before leaving for Kansas State College. By 1914, he had moved to New York through Jekyll's patronage, where he was briefly married to Eulalie Imelda Lewars. In 1917 he published "Invocation" and "The Harlem Dancer," which drew the attention of Max Eastman, the editor of the socialist little magazine *The Liberator*. Through his collaboration with Eastman, McKay came to edit *The Liberator* and emerged as a leading voice in the Harlem Renaissance. In 1919 he published several protest poems that showed a mastery of the sonnet form including "If We Must Die," "Baptism," "The White House," and "The Lynching." For the next three years, McKay lived in England where he worked for the *Workers' Drednought*, a British socialist magazine. The year 1922 marked the publication of two volumes of verse, *Spring in New Hampshire* and *Harlem Shadows*. For the following twelve years, Mckay traveled in Europe, the Soviet Union, and Africa, during which time he published *Home to Harlem* (1928), his first widely read novel, followed by *Banjo: A Story without a Plot* (1929), *Gingertown* (1932), and *Banana Bottom* (1933). Living in France, he became a major influence on Léopold Sédar Senghor, Aimé Cesaire, and others in the Negritude movement of French West Africa and the West Indies. Returning to the United States in 1934, McKay worked for the Federal Writers Project in 1936, finishing *A Long Way from Home*, his autobiography. Four years later, he became a citizen of the United States and later converted to Catholicism, working for the Chicago-based Catholic Youth Organization. After suffering chronic coronary disease for several years, McKay died of congestive heart failure in 1948. Remembered not just as one of the seminal voices of the Harlem Renaissance, McKay's masterful fusion of the sonnet tradition with the rhetoric of social commitment remains an important example for a subsequent generation of formalist writers including Gwendolyn Brooks and for later poets of the black aesthetic movement.

Edna St. Vincent Millay (1892–1950)

Millay was born in Rockland, Maine, to Henry Tollman Millay, a schoolteacher, and Cora Millay, who became a nurse after divorcing her husband in 1900 and moving her family to Camden, Maine. In her teen years, Millay showed early literary talent in editing her school magazine and publishing in *St. Nicholas Magazine*. Based in part on her poem "Renascence," published in *The Lyric Year*, Millay received a scholarship from the National Training School of the YWCA to attend Vassar College, where she studied literature and was active in the Vassar drama department. In 1917, the year of her graduation, she published *Renascence and Other Poems*, and became a part of the lively Bohemian community of Greenwich Village. As a member of the Provincetown Players, she befriended such notable modernist intellectuals as Edmund Wilson, Floyd Dell, and Susan Glaspell. In 1920, Millay published *A Few Figs from Thistles* followed by her Pulitzer Prize–winning volume, *The Harp Weaver* in 1923. That year Millay married Eugen Boissevain, who encouraged Millay's literary career as well as her unconventional bisexual orientation in her extramarital relations with others. Boissevain helped to promote Millay's literary career by managing her reading schedule in the mid-1920s. In 1927 Millay published a libretto for *The King's Henchman*, which had a successful premier at New York's Metropolitan Opera. That same year, Millay became committed to the leftist struggle over the murder conviction of two Italian labor agitators, Nicola Sacco and Bartolomeo Vanzetti. Millay's protest of the Sacco-Vanzetti case reflected her socialist commitments, which are evident in her 1927 poem, "Justice Denied in Massachusetts." Two years later Millay was elected to the National Institute of Arts and Letters, followed by a similar accolade in 1940 from the American Academy of Arts and Letters. Millay's antifascist stances in the Spanish Civil War and her protest of Nazism are featured in such volumes of verse as *Huntsman, What Quarry?* (1939), *Make Bright the Arrows* (1940), and *The Murder of Lidice* (1942). Owing in part to her chronic alcoholism, Millay suffered a nervous breakdown in 1944; her husband died of cancer in 1949. A year later, Millay also passed away, leaving behind a rich corpus of verse gathered in her *Collected Lyrics* (1943) and *Collected Poems* (1949, 1956).

John Milton (1609–1674)

Born in London and educated at St. Paul's School, John Milton entered Christ's College of Cambridge University in 1625. Milton received a bachelor's degree in 1629 and a master's degree three years later. Publishing his essay "On Shakespeare" in the Second Folio of Shakespeare's works, Milton went on to read widely in his family homes at Hammersmith and Horton. In 1634, his play *Comus* was performed in honor of Thomas Egerton, and it was published three years later. In 1637, Milton's mother died, and he also lost his friend and fellow student at Christ's College, Edward King, who is the subject of Milton's great elegy "Lycidas," published the following year. For 1638, Milton traveled in France and throughout Italy, returning to London the following year. During the next three years, Milton sided with Parliament against Charles I's claim to monarchical power and published such essays as "Of Reformation" and "The Reason of Church Government." In 1642, Milton married Mary Powell, who then separated from the poet during the next three years owing to her family's sympathy for the Royalist cause. By 1645, Milton had emerged as a major poet with the publication of his *Poems*. Mary returned to him that year at the time of the Battle of Naseby, which marked Charles I's decisive military defeat. In 1649, following the public execution of King Charles I, Milton was appointed to the diplomatic post of Secretary of Foreign Tongues. During the next two years, Milton wrote defenses of Charles's execution in works such as his 1651 *Defensio pro populo Anglicano* (a "defense of the English people"). The following year was marked by the death of Milton's first wife and the loss of his eyesight, most likely due to glaucoma. Curtailing his diplomatic work, Milton undertook a Latin dictionary and Greek lexicon in the mid-1650s and in 1657 married Katharine Woodcock, who died two years later. Following the death of Oliver Cromwell in 1658, Milton went into hiding from the loyalist supporters of Charles II and was arrested and imprisoned in the fall of the following year. Defended by Andrew Marvell, however, Milton was fined and released at the time of the restoration of Charles II in 1660. During the 1660s, Milton worked on the composition of *Paradise Lost*, which was published as a ten-book volume in 1667, four years after Milton had married his third wife, Elizabeth Minshully. In 1671, Milton published *Paradise Regain'd* and *Samson Agonistes*, followed by the expanded, twelve-book edition of *Paradise Lost*, published in 1674, the year Milton died.

Marianne Moore (1887–1972)

Raised by her grandfather, a Presbyterian minister, Marianne Moore moved to Carlisle, Pennsylvania in 1896 two years after his death. Moore graduated from Bryn Mawr College with a B.A. degree in 1909 and, after studying typing at the Carlisle Commercial College for a year, worked as a teacher of "commerical subjects" at the Carlisle Indian School through 1915. That year, Moore published in the little magazine *The Egoist* and moved with her mother to Chatham, New Jersey, and later to an apartment at St. Luke's Place in Greenwich Village. The 1920s marked the ascent of Moore as a poet in her collaboration with such modernists as William Carlos Williams, Wallace Stevens, and Kenneth Burke. While working as an assistant at the Hudson Park branch of the New York Public Library, she published a volume entitled *Poems* in 1920 and from 1925 through 1932 served as the editor of the influential modernist journal *The Dial.* In the 1930s, Moore won the Helen Haire Levinson Prize for Poetry (1932), published her *Selected Poems* (1935), received the Ernst Harstock Memorial Prize, and published a volume entitled *The Pangolin and Other Verse* (1936). Beginning the next decade with the Shelley Memorial Award (1940), Moore also won *Contemporary Poetry's* Patrons Prize (1944), the Harriet Monroe Poetry Prize (1944), and a Guggenheim Fellowship (1945). During this period, Moore published *What Are Years?* (1941) and *Nevertheless* (1944), followed by her *Collected Poems* (1951), which received the Pulitzer Prize, National Book Award, and the Bollingen Prize (1953). In 1955, Moore was elected to the Academy of Arts and Letters, and the National Institute of Arts and Letters observed her seventy-fifth birthday in 1962. By the end of that decade, Moore had become a popular celebrity and in addition to throwing out the first baseball of the 1968 season at Yankee Stadium at age eighty, she was named "Senior Citizen of the Year" for 1969. The following year she received an honorary degree from Harvard and published her final poems before her death in 1972 at age eighty-four.

Pat Mora (b. 1942)

A native of El Paso, Texas, Pat Mora is a Mexican American writer whose grandparents emigrated to the United States at the beginning of the twentieth century. The poet's father, an optician, was born in Chihuahua, and her mother came from El Paso. After completing her bachelor's degree in 1963 from Texas Western College—now the University of Texas, El Paso—Mora went on to receive a master's degree, also from UTEP (1967). While working as a secondary school teacher and college-level instructor, she also hosted a radio program entitled *Voices: The Mexican-American Perspective.* The mother of three children, Mora is an author of poetry and of children's literature. Mora's numerous awards include the Creative Writing Award of the National Association for Chicano Studies (1983), Women Artists and Writers of the Southwest poetry award (1984), and the Tomas Rivera Mexican American Children's Book Award (1997). In the fall of 1999, she was named Garrey Carruthers Chair in Honors, Distinguished Visiting Professor at the University of New Mexico. A self-proclaimed "daughter of the desert," Mora has explored in such works as *Chants* (1984), *Borders* (1986), *Communion* (1991), *Nepantla: Essays from the Land in the Middle* (1993), *House of Houses* (1997), and *My Own True Name: New and Selected Poems for Young Adults, 1984–1999* (2000) what Gloria Anzaldua has characterized as the "border land" of bilingual and bicultural identity as a Mexican American woman.

Sharon Olds (b. 1942)

Born and raised in San Francisco, Sharon Olds received a B.A. at Stanford and pursued graduate work in English at Columbia University. Her first volume of verse, *Satan Says* (1980), won the San Francisco Poetry Center Award for its intense and candid portrayals of desire and domestic turmoil. Influenced by the example of such precursor poets as Robert Lowell, Sylvia Plath, and Anne Sexton, Olds continued to explore the psychic terrain of family experience in her second book, *The Dead and the Living*, which received the 1983 Lamont Poetry Prize and the National Book Critics Circle Award. On the question of whether her poetry presents autobiographical or invented personae, Olds is somewhat ambiguous and compares her work with that of Emily Dickinson. "I guess," she has said, "I'm trying to lead two lives, the life of art and the life of life, and to keep them as separate as possible from each other. Emily Dickinson talks somewhere about the 'someone' in her poems. That seems to me a useful way to think about it." Olds's subsequent volumes similarly have paid unflinching attention to the sources of her desire, grief, rage, and joy in *The Gold Cell* (1987), *The Father* (1992) (a finalist for the National Book Critics' Circle Award), *The Wellspring* (1996), and *Blood, Tin, Straw* (1999). Olds's poetry is widely anthologized and translated. She is a faculty member of the graduate creative writing program at New York University. Olds was also the New York State Poet Laureate from 1998 to 2000.

Wilfred Owen (1893–1918)

The son of a railway clerk, Wilfred Owen showed early talent as a poet but, despite his mother's encouragement of his love for literature, failed in 1912 to win a scholarship to London University. Instead, he taught English the following year at a Berlitz School in Bordeaux. After the start of the Great War, Owen returned to England in 1915, where he lived for a time at the Poetry Bookshop managed by Harold Monro. Two years later, Owen joined the 2nd Manchesters Regiment, where, on the Somme, he was exposed to the trauma of trench warfare. In 1917, Owen suffered a concussion and after prolonged exposure to the violence of war on the front lines was blown into the air by a shell blast. Diagnosed with shell-shock, he recuperated near Edinburgh at Craiglockhart Hospital, where he met Siegfried Sassoon, who helped clarify Owen's poetic aims and introduced him to the author Robert Graves. By the end of 1917, Owen had received a promotion to the rank of lieutenant and published poems in *The Nation* and *The Bookman*. The next year, Owen returned to the front, where he was awarded the Military Cross a month before he was killed while leading his command across the Sambre Canal. Of his work as a poet, Owen wrote, "My subject is War, and the pity of War. The Poetry is in the pity."

Sylvia Plath (1932–1963)

Of German American descent, Sylvia Plath was born in Jamaica Plain, Massachusetts, to Otto and Aurelia Schoeber Plath. Having immigrated to America from Silesia, Otto Plath was a professor of Biology at Boston University and the author of *Bumblebees and Their Ways* published in 1934, two years after Sylvia was born. Interrupting the normal course of Sylvia's girlhood, Otto suffered a traumatic illness involving the amputation of a gangrenous leg. He died in 1940, when Sylvia was eight years old. A creative writer herself, Aurelia Plath encouraged Sylvia's interest in poetry and literature. Sylvia Plath attended Smith College on scholarship and was appointed to the College Board of *Mademoiselle* magazine in 1953. That year, Plath suffered from depression and received bipolar electroconvulsive shock treatment. In August, she attempted suicide for the first time. But after six months of therapy, she was able to return to Smith, where she graduated summa cum laude in English and won a Fulbright fellowship to Newnham College, Cambridge in 1955. There she met the British poet Ted Hughes, whom she married in June 1956. The following year, the Hugheses sailed to the United States, where Plath taught in the Smith College English Department for a year. During 1958 and 1959, Sylvia and Ted lived in Boston and, while Ted's first volume *The Hawk* received much notoriety, Sylvia attended Robert Lowell's poetry seminar at Boston University, where she met Anne Sexton and George Starbuck. After spending the fall at the writer's colony at Yaddo, New York, Plath gave birth to her daughter Frieda in April 1960. That spring the Hugheses moved from London to Devon, where Plath studied beekeeping and entered into her most creative phase as a poet. In the fall of 1960, Plath published *The Colossus and Other Poems*, and the following year, Plath authored her autobiographical novel *The Bell Jar*. Meanwhile, Ted Hughes moved to the center of England's literary world through his contacts with the BBC and T. S. Eliot. Plath's son Nicholas was born in January 1962, but Ted Hughes's infidelity led Plath to separate from her husband that fall. It was at this time that she wrote her so-called October poems, which would appear in her posthumously published volume, *Ariel* (1965). Returning to London as a single mother with two children, Plath suffered from depression and chronic flu-like symptoms in December of that year. Overwhelmed by the return of her depression, compounded by her isolation and ill health, Plath committed suicide on February 11, 1963, two weeks before the publication of *The Bell Jar*. With the publication of *Ariel*, Plath became a central poet of her generation and was awarded a Pulitzer Prize for poetry in 1982 for her posthumous volume of *Collected Poems*.

Edgar Allan Poe (1809–1847)

Poe's parents, the traveling actors David and Elizabeth Poe, died before Edgar Allan Poe reached the age of three. The poet's foster parents, John and Frances Allan, traveled with him to England, where between the age of six and eleven Poe studied in a boarding school. In 1826, Poe attended the University of Virginia, but gambling debts caused him to drop out of college. He traveled to Boston, where he published his first book of verse, *Tamerlane and Other Poems* (1827), and then had a brief appointment to West Point. Poe's second book of poems, *Al Aaraaf, Tamerlane, and Minor Poems*, appeared in 1829 before the publication of *Poems* (1831), which included such famous works as "To Helen" and "Israfel." In 1832, Poe was living in Baltimore with his aunt Maria Clemm and her daughter, Virginia. That year, he published five stories followed in 1833 by the award of a prize from the *Baltimore Satur-*

day Visitor for "Ms. Found in a Bottle." Two years later, Poe moved to Richmond, Virginia, where he assumed the position of editor of the *Southern Literary Messenger* and married Virginia Clemm in 1836. The following year, Poe moved his family to New York, where he published *The Narrative of Arthur Gordon Pym.* During the next decade—from his time in Philadelphia between 1838 and 1844 and then in New York from 1844 through 1849—Poe sought to consolidate his reputation as a journalist, poet, and fiction writer, publishing such masterpieces as "Ligeia" (1838), "The Fall of the House of Usher" (1839), "The Murders in the Rue Morgue" (1841), "The Raven" (1845), and "The Bells" (1849). Two years after the death of Virginia from tuberculosis in 1847, Poe returned to Richmond for a lecture tour, but traveling north en route to New York, Poe died in Baltimore of "acute congestion of the brain."

Alexander Pope (1688–1744)

Born to a Catholic cloth merchant in London, Pope grew up in an era of anti-Catholic prejudice and was denied a university education. Consequently, he studied under independent teachers such as the Catholic convert and former Oxford don, Thomas Deane. Pope also was a victim of tuberculosis, which left him, in the words of Sir Joshua Reynolds, "about four feet six high; very humpbacked and deformed." Nevertheless, through the encouragement he received from William Wycherley, among others, Pope grew in stature as a poet and writer with the publication of *Pastorals* in 1709, his neoclassical *Essay on Criticism* (1711), and his bawdy mock epic *The Rape of the Lock* (1712). A translator of the *Iliad* and the *Odyssey*, Pope emerged as the preeminent man of letters with his 1717 publication of his *Collected Works.* With his move to Twickenham, Pope shared an interest in horticulture with Lady Mary Wortley before entering into a lasting companionship with Martha Blount. In 1728, he published *The Dunciad*, a satiric reponse to an attack of his edition of Shakespeare, followed by his *Moral Essays* (1731) and *Essay on Man* (1733–1734). During his remaining years, Pope hosted the major literary figures of his age at his villa where he died on May 21, 1744.

Ezra Pound (1885–1972)

Born in Hailey, Idaho, Pound studied at the University of Pennsylvania for two years before graduating from Hamilton College in 1905. Following a two-year teaching stint at Wabash College, Pound traveled to Europe in 1908, where he met W. B. Yeats. By 1911, Pound had published six volumes of verse whose style reflected Pound's interests in Provençal and Italian literary models. Influenced by such modernists as Ford Madox Ford and T. E. Hulme, Pound founded the imagist movement in 1912 and later propounded the more dynamic compositional style of vorticism. Reflecting his study of Ernest Fenollosa and the Chinese written character, Pound published *Cathay* in 1915, the year after his marriage to Dorothy Shakespear. Moving to the center of London's international literary scene, Pound became the editor of the *Little Review* in 1917. Deeply troubled by the events of the First World War, Pound wrote "Homage to Sextus Propertius" (1919) and "Hugh Selwyn Mauberley" (1921), which protested what Pound criticized as the cultural decadence and wasted promise of the war generation. At this time, Pound was also editing T. S. Eliot's *The Waste Land* (1922), leading Eliot to name him as *il miglior fabbro* or "the better craftsman." By 1924, Pound had left London to settle in Rapallo, where he began to compose a long "poem including history" that would evolve into *The Cantos*. Following the publication of the first section of *The Cantos* in 1925, Pound expanded them with the release of *A Draft of XXX Cantos* (1930), followed by Cantos 31 to 70 published between 1934 and 1940. Throughout the 1930s, Pound became increasingly involved with Italian fascism, which culminated in his infamous Rome Radio addresses that promoted the dictatorship of Benito Mussolini and anti-Semitism. After Pound's six-month detention in the Disciplinary Training Centre near Pisa, he was deemed mentally unfit to stand trial for treason in 1945. Instead, Pound was diagnosed as insane and became an inmate at St. Elizabeth's Hospital in Washington, D.C. from 1946 to 1958. He continued on as poet, publishing *The Pisan Cantos* (1948), *Section: Rock-Drill* (1955), *Thrones* (1959), and *Drafts and Fragments of Cantos CX–CXVII* (1969). On his release from St. Elizabeth's, Pound lived out his remaining years in Italy, eventually settling in Venice, where he died in 1972.

Edwin Arlington Robinson (1869–1935)

Born in Head Tide, Maine, Robinson was the son of Edward Robinson, a timber merchant, and Mary Elizabeth Palmer. He grew up in the town of Gardiner, which is the setting for his poems on life in "Tilbury Town." The third of three sons, Robinson pursued poetry as early as age eleven before attending Harvard University from 1891 through 1893. During this time, Robinson's father died in 1892, and the Robinsons plummeted into backruptcy over the next seven years, forcing the poet to leave Harvard. Robinson published *The Torrent and the Night Before*, in 1896, also the year his mother died. The next year he brought out a revised version of this volume entitled *The Children of the Night*. Poems such as "Richard Cory," "Luke Havergal," and "Aaron Stark" witness to the bleak social lives and tragic circumstances of Robinson's "Tilbury Town" characters. In 1897, Robinson left Gardiner for New York City, where he lived in poverty owing to the collapse of his family finances. After publishing *Captain Craig* in 1902, Robinson made a sporatic living from temporary work, eventually receiving, through Kermit Roosevelt, a New York Customs House job in 1905 that allowed him to sustain himself while writing. In 1909, Robinson published *The Town Down the River* and quit the Customs House, spending summers at the MacDowell Colony in New Hampshire after 1911. His literary reputation grew with the publication in 1916 of *The Man Against the Sky* and with Amy Lowell's favorable chapter on his work in her book of essays entitled *Tendencies in Modern American Poetry* (1917). By 1921, he had won the first Pulitzer Prize for poetry for his *Collected Poems* followed by a second Pulitzer for *The Man Who Died Twice* (1924). Throughout the 1920s, Robinson published actively with such major volumes as *Avon's Harvest* (1921), *Roman Bartholow* (1925), *Dionysus in Doubt* (1925), *Cavender's House* (1929), *Matthias at the Door* (1931), a collection of shorter poems called *Nicodemus* (1932), *Talifer* (1933), and *Amaranth* (1934). His last volume, *King Jasper*, was published posthumously in 1935.

Theodore Roethke (1908–1963)

As a youth, Roethke literally grew up in the garden world of his parents' greenhouse business before becoming a student at Saginaw's Arthur Hill High School, where he showed early promise in a speech on the Junior Red Cross that was subsequently published in twenty-six languages. The poet's adolescent years were jarred, however, by the death of his father from cancer in 1923, a loss that would powerfully shape Roethke's psychic and creative lives. From 1925 to 1929 Roethke distinguished himself at the University of Michigan at Ann Arbor, graduating magna cum laude. Resisting family pressure to pursue a legal career, he quit law school after one semester and, from 1929 to 1931, took graduate courses at the University of Michigan and later the Harvard Graduate School, where he worked closely with the poet Robert Hillyer. The hard economic times of the Great Depression forced Roethke to leave Harvard and to take up a teaching career at Lafayette College from 1931 to 1935. Here he met Rolfe Humphries, who introduced him to Louise Bogan; during these years Roethke also found a powerful supporter, colleague, and friend in the poet Stanley Kunitz. In the fall of 1935 Roethke assumed his second teaching post, at Michigan State College at Lansing, but was soon hospitalized for what would prove to be recurring bouts of mental illness. Throughout his subsequent career Roethke used these periodic incidents of depression for creative self-exploration. During the remainder of the decade Roethke enjoyed a growing reputation as a poet. He taught at Pennsylvania State University from 1936 to 1943, publishing in such prestigious journals as *Poetry*, the *New Republic*, the *Saturday Review*, and *Sewanee Review*. He brought out his first volume of verse, *Open House*, in 1941. The year after *Open House* was published, Roethke was invited to deliver one of the prestigious Morris Gray lectures at Harvard University, and in 1943 he left Penn State to teach at Bennington College, where he joined such luminaries as Léonie Adams and Kenneth Burke. His collaboration with Burke, in particular, was crucial to the development of the second, and pivotal, volume of Roethke's career, *The Lost Son and Other Poems* (1948). The descent into the organic life of things themselves dramatized the theme of regression that is explored in psychoanalytic terms in the book's title piece. In his next volume, *Praise to the End!* (1951), Roethke's regressive aesthetic continued to explore further the prerational experience of early childhood and sexual discoveries of adolescence. The volume's title, as an allusion to Wordsworth's *The Prelude*, signaled the work's romantic celebration of the child's unity of being in the natural world. *Praise to the End!* was composed after the poet's move to the University of Washington. The early 1950s augured Roethke's growing stature with the award of a Guggenheim fellowship (1950), *Poetry* magazine's Levinson Prize

(1951), and major grants from the Ford Foundation and the National Institute of Arts and Letters in 1952. The following year Roethke married Beatrice O'Connell, whom he had met during his earlier stint at Bennington. The two spent the following spring at W. H. Auden's villa at Ischia, off the coast of Italy, where Roethke edited the galley proofs for *The Waking: Poems 1933–1953* (1953), a seminal volume that won the Pulitzer Prize the next year. Although thematically akin to Roethke's work of the late 1940s, this volume's title piece marked the poet's return to formalist verse, composed as it is in the complex villanelle pattern. Throughout 1955 and 1956 the Roethkes traveled in Italy, Europe, and England on a Fulbright grant. The following year he published a collection of works that included forty-three new poems entitled *Words for the Wind* (1957), which won the Bollingen Prize, the National Book Award, the Edna St. Vincent Millay Prize, the Longview Foundation Award, and the Pacific Northwest Writer's Award. Now at the height of his popularity and fame, Roethke balanced his teaching career with reading tours in New York and Europe, underwritten by another Ford Foundation grant. While visiting with friends at Bainbridge Island, Washington, Roethke suffered a fatal heart attack in 1963. During the last years of his life he had composed the sixty-one new poems that were published posthumously in *The Far Field* (1964)—which received the National Book Award—and in *The Collected Poems* (1966).

Christina Rossetti (1830–1894)

The daughter of Gabriele and Frances Rossetti, Christina Rossetti was also the sister of the famous Pre-Raphelite painter and sculptor Dante Gabriel Rossetti, for whom she posed as a model. At the age of eighteen, she became engaged to James Collinson, a member of Dante's Pre-Raphelite circle. After the death of her father, Christina led a reclusive life owing to her poor health that may have been a result of angina or tuberculosis. During the 1860s, Rossetti had a relationship with Charles Cayley, but she never married him due, most likely, to the fact that he was not a professed Christian. Nevertheless, Christina had a close circle of friends and admirers that included such figures as Charles Dodgson (Lewis Carroll), James Abbott McNeill Whistler, and Algernon Charles Swinburne. Moreover, she was an active member of the Society for Promoting Christian Knowedge before her death in 1894.

Carl Sandburg (1878–1967)

A native of Illinois, Carl Sandburg was born into a working-class family of Swedish immigrants. After finishing the eighth grade, Sandburg labored at a series of odd jobs before riding the rails in search of work at the age of nineteen. In 1898, he joined Company C of the Sixth Infantry Regiment of the Illinois Volunteers and was assigned to Puerto Rico during the Spanish-American War. That same year he was admitted to Lombard College on a veteran's scholarship. After leaving Lombard in 1902, Sandburg worked as a journalist in Chicago. For five years beginning in 1907, he served as a Social-Democratic Party organizer in Wisconsin, returning to journalism as a staff member for the *Chicago Evening World* in 1912. Significantly, two years later he emerged as a poet when Harriet Monroe published six of his poems in the Chicago-based journal *Poetry: A Magazine of Verse*. In 1916, Henry Holt and Company published his *Chicago Poems* followed by *Cornhuskers* two years later. The next year, he left Holt to publish later volumes such as *Smoke and Steel* (1920), *Good Morning, America* (1928), and *The People, Yes* (1936) with Harcourt, Brace & Howe. Sandburg reported on the First World War for the Newspaper Enterprise Association and became an investigative journalist for the *Chicago Daily News* thereafter until he covered World War II as a syndicated columnist. In 1950, Sandburg was awarded the Pulitzer Prize in poetry for his *Complete Poems*. He was also a collector and performer of American folk songs and published many of them in *The American Songbag* (1927). Moreover, he was a prolific author of children's books as well as a major biographer of Abraham Lincoln, publishing *Abraham Lincoln: The Prairie Years* in 1926, followed by a four-volume sequel, *Abraham Lincoln: The War Years* (1939), which was awarded the Pulitzer Prize for history. In 1952, Sandburg received the American Academy of Arts and Letters gold medal in biography and history and a year later published his own autobiography, *Always the Young Strangers*. In 1955 he collaborated with his brother-in-law, the photographer Edward Steichen, on *The Family of Man*. In 1964, Sandburg received the Presidential Medal of Freedom and his achievement as a man of American letters was celebrated by President Lyndon B. Johnson, among many others, at the Lincoln Memorial shortly after the poet's death in 1967.

Anne Sexton (1928–1974). *See Chapter 35.*

William Shakespeare (1564–1616)

The third of eight children born to the leather merchant John Shakespeare, William Shakespeare most likely was educated at Stratford Grammar School. What little is known about Shakespeare's life must be gleaned from church and legal documents as well as his writing. Shakespeare did not receive a university education, and, according to Ben Jonson, he possessed "small Latine, and less Greeke." There is almost no information on his early life until his marriage at age eighteen to Anne Hathaway, who was then twenty-six. Between 1588 and 1592, Shakespeare had left Stratford for London. The year 1593 marked his emergence as a poet with "Venus and Adonis," and "The Rape of Lucrece" was published the next year. By 1594, Shakespeare was acting as one of the Lord Chamberlain's Men (better known as the King's Men following the ascension of James I in 1603), and during the mid-1590s, Shakespeare became a proprietor of the Globe Theatre and a part owner of Blackfriar's Theatre. Shakespeare began his career as a playwright in 1595. In 1609, the Sonnets and "A Lover's Complaint" were published in *Shake-speares Sonnets*. During his lifetime eighteen of his plays were published in the quarto editions. Thirty-six of the Shakespeare canon of thirty-eight plays appeared in the 1623 *First Folio* of the collected works published by two of Shakespeare's colleagues in the King's Men, John Heminges and Henry Condell. Shakespeare retired from his writing career in 1611, returning to Stratford. Although Shakespeare's son Hamnet and his twin sister Judith both died during the bard's lifetime, his other daughter, Susanna, outlived him to marry John Hall. Shakespeare died in 1616 and was buried in the Church of the Holy Trinity, where he had been baptized fifty-two years earlier.

Percy Bysshe Shelley (1792–1822)

As the eldest son born to Elizabeth Shelley and Timothy Shelley (a member of the House of Commons), Percy Bysshe Shelley came from a venerable family whose roots reached back to the era of William of Normandy. From 1804 to 1810, Shelley was a student at Eton College and then entered Oxford University. A prolific essayist and poet, Shelley was nevertheless expelled early on from Oxford owing to an essay he coauthored with a fellow student, Thomas Jefferson Hogg, entitled "The Necessity of Atheism." At the age of nineteen, Shelley eloped to Scotland with Harriet Westbrook, three years his junior. During this time Shelley met Wordsworth, Southey, De Quincey, and Wilson, who encouraged Shelley's literary ambitions. Over the next three years, Shelley and Harriet had two children before the poet abandoned his young family. While living in the Lake District, Shelley had befriended William Godwin and Mary Wollstonecraft and eloped to Europe with their daughter, Mary Godwin, in 1814. In January 1815, Mary Godwin bore Shelley a son, and the following May, Shelley and Godwin moved to Lake Geneva, where the poet composed his allegorical poem *Alastor, or The Spirit of Solitude* while spending time with George Gordon, Lord Byron. In 1816 Harriet Shelley committed suicide by drowning herself in the Serpentine River. Although Shelley and Mary Godwin soon married thereafter, he nevertheless lost custody of his two children conceived with Harriet. Two years later, Shelley left England for good and published *The Revolt of Islam.* During the next four years, Shelley traveled in Italy and befriended Leigh Hunt and others. During this period, he produced the major works of his canon including "Prometheus Unbound," "Hellas," "The Witch of Atlas," "Adonais," and "Epipsychidion." Sailing under stormy conditions from Leghorn in 1822, Shelley drowned after his small schooner the *Don Juan* sank in the Bay of Spezia.

Gary Snyder (b. 1930)

Born in San Francisco, Gary Snyder grew up in rural Oregon and Washington. After earning a B.A. degree in anthropology from Reed College, he worked variously on logging crews and as a forest-fire lookout in Baker National Forest in the early 1950s. During this time, he pursued graduate studies in Asian languages at the University of California, Berkeley. By the decade's end, he would become a culture hero in the Beat movement, appearing as the character of Japhy Rider in Jack Kerouac's celebrated novel *The Dharma Bums.* Snyder's commitment to Asian studies extended beyond his time at Berkeley, and later in the 1960s he became a student of Buddhism in

Kyoto, Japan, under the Zen master Oda Sesso Roshi. Similar to Ezra Pound's collaborative work with Ernest Fenollosa in *The Chinese Written Character as a Medium for Poetry*, Snyder's spare imagist style in his short lyrics, such as "Mid-August at Sourdough Mountain Lookout," reflects the poet's work as a translator of classical Chinese verse and Japanese haiku poetry. Included among his numerous awards are a Guggenehim fellowship (1968) and the Pulitzer Prize for poetry (1975) for *Turtle Island* (1974). In addition to this volume, Snyder's other major books of poetry include *Riprap* (1958), *The Back Country* (1968), *Earth House Hold* (1969), *Regarding Wave* (1970), *Axe Handles* (1983), and *Mountains and Rivers without End* (1997).

Cathy Song (b. 1955)

A native of Wahiawa, Hawaii, Cathy Song was born in Honolulu to a Chinese American mother and Korean American father. At the age of seven, she moved with her family to the Waialae Kahala district of Honolulu. She began writing poetry at Kalani High School before attending the University of Hawaii at Manoa for two years, where she studied with the poet John Unterecker. In 1977, Song graduated from Wellesley College with a B.A. in English and then earned an M.A. in creative writing from Boston University in 1981. Two years later, she published her first volume of poetry, *Picture Bride*, which won the prestigious Yale Younger Poets Award. In 1987, she returned to Hawaii with her husband, Douglas Davenport, and the following year she published *Frameless Windows, Squares of Light* (1988) followed by *School Figures* (1994). She divides her time between teaching at the University of Hawaii at Manoa and working as an editor for the Bamboo Ridge Press, which is devoted to publishing the literature of Hawaii.

Gary Soto (b. 1952)

A native of Fresno, California, Gary Soto was born into a Mexican American family of farm workers. At the age of five, Soto lost his twenty-seven-year-old father in a factory accident. Soto returns to the barrio of his childhood for the setting of many of his poems. "It's important to me," he has said "to create and share new stories about my heritage. . . . That's why I write so much about growing up in the barrio. It allows me to use specific memories that are vivid for me." After graduating high school in 1970, Soto began studying geology at Fresno City College where he received an A.A. degree in 1972. Two years later, he earned a B.A. in English studying under the poet Philip Levine at California State University at Fresno. The following year, he married and received the Discovery-Nation Prize for his writing. In 1976, Soto earned an M.F.A. degree in creative writing from the University of California and won the U.S. Award of the International Poetry Forum. The following year, he published his first book of verse, *The Elements of San Joaquin.* Two years later, he published *The Tale of Sunlight* in 1978. During the 1980s and 1990s, Soto emerged as one of the most prolific poets and children's authors of his generation in such works as *Where Sparrows Work Hard* (1981), *Black Hair* (1985),

Who Will Know Us? (1990), *Home Course in Religion* (1991), *Neighborhood Odes* (1992), *Canto Familiar/Familiar Song* (1994), and *Selected Poems* (1995). He lives in Berkeley and is a Distinguished Professor at the University of California at Riverside.

Wole Soyinka (b. 1934)

Oluwole Akinwande Soyinka was born in Ijebu Isara, Western Nigeria, to a school supervisor. From 1940 through 1952, Soyinka attended primary school in Abeokuta and secondary school at the Government College, Ibadan. From 1952 through 1954, he was enrolled at University College, Ibadan, which has an affiliation with the University of London. In 1957, Soyinka received his honors degree in English literature from the University of Leeds followed by work toward an M.A. that same year; in 1973 he completed his doctorate there. The year 1958 marked the debut of Soyinka's career as a dramatist with the production of *The Swamp Dwellers* for the University of London Drama Festival followed by a run of *The Swamp Dwellers* and *The Lion and the Jewel* the next year in Ibadan. In 1959, Soyinka wrote, produced, and acted in *An Evening with Décor* at the Royal Court Theatre, London. In 1960, Soyinka was awarded a Rockefeller bursary to study African drama in Nigeria, and he also founded the theater group The 1960 Masks followed four years later by the Orisun Theatre Company. In 1965, Soyinka published the novel *The Interpreters* and recorded *The Detainee* for the BBC in London. In the mid-sixties, Soyinka became increasingly critical of dictatorships in Africa, and in 1967, he was arrested for conspiring with the Biafra rebels and detained as a political prisoner for twenty-two months. In 1971, Soyinka published a volume of poems entitled *A Shuttle in the Crypt* and gave testimony concerning the violation of student rights to the Kazeem Enquiry. The next year he published his prison memoir, *The Man Died*, followed by a second novel, *Season of Anomy* (1973). In addition to earlier volumes of verse, including *Idanre, and Other Poems* (1967) and *Poems from Prison* (1969), he edited *Poems of Black Africa* in 1975. He would go on to publish such books of poetry as *Ogun Abibiman* (1976) and *Mandela's Earth and Other Poems* (1988). Since winning the Nobel Prize for literature in 1986, Soyinka has continued to publish steadily in all genres and is the author of over forty works of literature. During this time he has also led an active, cosmopolitan life as an educator and social activitist, holding several professorships at such prestigious universities as Cambridge, Sheffield, Yale, and Emory.

William Stafford (1914–1993)

Born in Hutchinson, Kansas, to Ruby Mayher and Earl Ingersoll Stafford, William Stafford grew up in a working-class family and graduated from high school in 1933 during the middle of the Depression era. After passing through two junior colleges, Stafford earned a bachelor's degree from the University of Kansas in 1937. Over the next three years, he studied for a master's degree in English, but World War II cut short his graduate education. As a conscientious objector to the war, Stafford spent 1942 through 1946 doing community service in such areas as soil conservation, fire fighting, road maintenance, and other forms of manual labor in Arkansas, California, and Illinois. During this period, in California he married Dorothy Frantz in 1944. After the war, Stafford taught high school and worked for the Church World Service before earning his master's degree from the University of Kansas in 1947. That year, the poet's memoir of his war experiences as a conscientious objector, *Down in My Heart*, was published by Brethren Publish House. The next year Stafford moved to Portland, Oregon, to accept a teaching position at Lewis and Clark College, where he would remain for the rest of his professional career until 1980. In 1954, he earned a Ph.D. from the University of Iowa. Stafford's first volume of verse, *Traveling through the Dark*, was not published until the poet was forty-eight, but it won him the National Book Award in 1963. Other awards followed, including the Award in Literature by the American Academy and Institute of Arts and Letters, Shelley Memorial Award, a Guggenheim Fellowship, and a Western States Lifetime Achievement Award, among numerous other prizes. In 1970, he served as the consultant in poetry to the Library of Congress. Before his death at the age of seventy-nine in 1993, he had published more than sixty-five volumes of poetry, including *The Rescued Year* (1966), *Stories That Could Be True: New and Collected Poems* (1977), *Writing the Australian Crawl: Views on the Writer's Vocation* (1978), and *An Oregon Message* (1987).

Wallace Stevens (1879–1955)

Born in Reading, Pennsylvania, Wallace Stevens attended Harvard University as a special student for three years between 1897 and 1900 without graduating. Three years later, he graduated from New York law school and passed the New York bar exam the following year. During the next five years, he courted a Reading woman, Elsie Kachel, and married her in 1909. Making his way in New York as an attorney, Stevens worked as a bond lawyer, rising to the position of vice president of the New York office of the Equitable Surety Co. of St. Louis in 1914. Two years later, he joined the Hartford Accident and Indemnity Co. and moved to Hartford, Connecticut, where he lived for the rest of his life. Although Stevens began writing poetry while a student at Harvard, he did not publish his first volume, *Harmonium*, until 1923, the year before the birth of his only child, Holly Bight. It was not until 1931 that he published a second edition of *Harmonium*, which included only eight new poems. Meanwhile, Stevens advanced his professional career and assumed the position of vice president of the Hartford in 1934. Stevens's career as a poet also picked up speed in the mid-thirties with the publication of *Ideas of Order* (1935), *The Man with the Blue Guitar* (1937), and *Owl's Clover* (1937). Throughout the 1940s, Stevens would achieve a major reputation as a modern American poet based, in part, on his long, philosophical poems in such works as *Parts of a World* (1942), *Notes toward a Supreme Fiction* (1942), "Esthetique du Mal" (1945), "The Auroras of Autumn" (1947), and "An Ordinary Evening in New Haven" (1950). In 1951, Stevens published an important book of essays on

modernist aesthetics entitled *The Necessary Angel*. In it, he defined the imagination as "A violence from within that protects us from a violence without. It
is the imagination pressing back against the pressure of reality." By the time
of his death in 1955, Stevens was recognized as one of the foremost poets of
his generation.

May Swenson (1913–1989)

Born in Logan, Utah, May Swenson received a bachelor's degree from Utah
State University in 1939. It was not until 1954, however, that she published
her first volume of poetry, entitled *Another Animal*, followed by two more
books: *A Cage of Spines* (1958) and *To Mix with Time, New and Selected Poems*
(1963). During this time, from 1959 through 1966, she served as editor at New
Directions and held a number of teaching positions at Bryn Mawr, the University of North Carolina, the University of California, Riverside, Purdue University, and Utah State University. She also published a volume of translations
of contemporary Swedish poetry entitled *Iconographs* (1970). Poetry, for Swenson, allowed access to what she described as "the vastness of the unknown beyond [one's] consciousness." Until her death in 1989, she remained a prolific
writer whose books of poetry include *Poems to Solve* (1966), *Half Sun Half
Sleep* (1967), *More Poems to Solve* (1968), *New & Selected Things Taking Place*
(1978), and *In Other Words* (1987). She is a recipient of the American Introductions Prize, the Longview Foundation Award, a National Instititute of Arts
and Letters Award, Shelley Award, a Bollingen Prize for poetry, and the
MacArthur Fellowship, among other numerous awards.

Alfred, Lord Tennyson (1809–1892)

The fourth of twelve children born to George and Elizabeth Tennyson, Alfred
Tennyson was raised in Lincolnshire before he entered Trinity College, Cambridge, in 1827 to study under William Whewell. There, like his brothers, Tennyson distinguished himself as a poet and won the Chancellor's Gold Medal in
1828 for *Timbuctoo*. At Cambridge, he joined a group of student intellectuals
who called themselves "The Apostles" and included Arthur Henry Hallam, who
was Tennyson's closest friend. Hallam became engaged to Emily Tennyson, but
at the age of twenty-two he died suddenly from illness. This trauma had a formative influence on Tennyson in such major works as *In Memoriam*, "The Passing
of Arthur," "Ulysses," and "Tithonus." Although Tennyson's 1832 volume *Poems* met a mixed critical reception, he had success ten years later with his 1842
Poems. By 1850, Tennyson was named Poet Laureate and at the time of his death
in 1892 was the most popular poet of the Victorian age.

Dylan Thomas (1914–1953)

Named after the medieval Welsh word for the "sea," Dylan Thomas was born
in Swansea, Wales. At the age of twenty, he moved to London, where in 1934
he published his first book of poetry, *Eighteen Poems*. Two years later, Thomas

published *Twenty-five Poems* and met Caitlin MacNamara, whom he married the following year. In 1938, the couple moved to Laugharne, Wales, and soon had a son, Llewelyn Edouard Thomas, born in 1939, the year Thomas also published *The Map of Love* and *The World I Breathe*. In 1940, Thomas published *Portrait of the Artist as a Young Dog* and began work for Strand Films, where he would stay on throughout World War II. Thomas would have two more children during the 1940s, Aeronwyn Bryn Thomas born in 1943, followed by Colm Garan Hart Thomas in 1949. During these years, Thomas published *Deaths and Entrances* (1946), *In Country Sleep* (1951), followed by his final book *Collected Poems, 1934–1952*. A charismatic public reader of his own verse, Thomas gave a series of popular reading tours in the United States. Chronic alcoholism took its toll on the poet's health, and during his fourth tour, accompanied by a physician, Thomas collapsed in his New York hotel room and died at St. Vincent's Hospital at the age of thirty-nine. *Under Milk Wood*, a play scripted for radio broadcast and Thomas's unfinished novel, *Adventures in the Skin Trade*, were published posthumously in 1954.

Phillis Wheatley (1753–1784)

A native of West Africa, Phillis Wheatley was kidnapped at the age of seven and sold to John Wheatley, a Boston tailor, in 1761. Although Phillis Wheatley did not attend school, she received her education from Mrs. John Wheatley. According to John Wheatley, Phillis learned to read English in only sixteen months. Just four years later in 1765, Phillis also had become a proficient writer, addressing a letter to the Reverend Mr. Occom. She also learned Latin and began publishing poetry with "On Messrs. Hussey and Coffin" in 1767. Three years later, her poem "On the Death of the Rev. Mr. George Whitefield, 1770" had a broad circulation in England and in such northern cities as Boston, Newport, and Philadelphia. While traveling to England as part of her treatment for severe asthma, Phillis Wheatley identified a publisher for her first book of verse, entitled *Poems on Various Subjects, Religious and Moral* (1773). To put to rest the suspicion that Wheatly was not the sole author of her book, her publishers included a statement verifying her as the author, witnessed by a group of distinguished New England civic leaders including the governor and lieutenant-governor of Massachusettes—Thomas Hutchinson and Andrew Oliver. Wheatley's poetry reflected the major strands of her New England education in terms of its focus on religious and classical themes. On returning to Boston in 1773, John Wheatley freed Phillis although she nevertheless continued to live with Wheatley as his caretaker. During the Revolutionary period, Phillis corresponded with George Washington and wrote a poem in his honor in 1776. Two years later, John Wheatley died, and Phillis, herself now free, married John Peters, who was also a freed former slave. Living in a squalid New England bording house, the couple fell into poverty. In these adverse circumstances, Phillis gave birth to three children, all of whom died in childhood. In 1784, the year of her death at the age of thirty-one, Phillis Wheatley published a number of poems, including "To Mr. And Mrs.——, on the Death of Their Infant Son," under the name of Phillis Peters. Her poetry, however, survived her tragic end and, by the Abolitionist period of the 1830s, had achieved a recognized place in the canon of American literature.

Walt Whitman (1819–1892)

The second son in a family of nine children, Walt Whitman grew up on Long Island in a troubled household headed by the poet's alcoholic father. After failing as a carpenter and farmer, Walter Whitman Sr. moved his family to Brooklyn in 1823. After attending school in Brooklyn, Whitman worked at the age of eleven as a clerk before apprenticing as a printer at the *Patriot* and *Star* newspapers in Brooklyn. At the age of seventeen, Whitman began teaching in one-room schoolhouses on Long Island until 1841, when he turned to journalism and founded the weekly paper, *The Long Islander*. For the next seven years, he would work on a number of New York papers, including the *Aurora, Tatler*, the *Democrat*, and the *Brooklyn Daily Eagle*. In 1848, he traveled to New Orleans to become the editor of the *New Orleans Crescent*. Returning to Brooklyn that year, Whitman became the founding editor of the *Brooklyn Freeman*. By 1855, Whitman had composed and published the first edition of *Leaves of Grass*, sending a copy to Ralph Waldo Emerson, who responded with the famous reply, "I greet you at the beginning of a great career." During the American Civil War, Whitman traveled to Washington, D.C., to care for his wounded brother. Whitman's role as caregiver to the wounded and dying in the area hospitals became the basis for his "Drum Taps" section of *Leaves of Grass*. During the next eleven years, Whitman lived in Washington. For part of that time, Whitman worked as a Department of Interior clerk until he was fired by Secretary James Harlan, who was offended by the explicit sexuality of *Leaves of Grass*. At the age of forty-four in 1873, Whitman suffered a stroke from which he never fully recovered. Nevertheless, he continued to add poems to *Leaves of Grass* over the course of eight editions. In 1884, the poet bought a small house in Camden, New Jersey, and four years later another major stroke left him immobilized. By 1891, his health was failing completely, but he managed to finish *Good-Bye, My Fancy* (1891) and revise the so-called death-bed edition of *Leaves of Grass* before he died in 1892.

William Carlos Williams (1883–1963)

Born and raised in Rutherford, New Jersey, William Carlos Williams was the son of William George Williams, a New York businessman, and Raquel Hélène Hoheb, who was a native of Puerto Rico. From 1897 through 1899, Williams studied in Europe and began writing verse while attending the Horace Mann High School in New York City. Williams studied medicine and received his M.D. from the University of Pennsylvania. While there he met the painter Charles Demuth and the modernist poets Hilda Doolittle and Ezra Pound. After studying pediatrics in Leipzig, Germany, Williams returned to Rutherford in 1910 where he set up his private practice, married Flossie Herman two years later, and over time became the head pediatrician of Paterson General Hospital. At the same time, Williams also had a parallel career as poet, publishing his first volume *Poems* in 1909, followed by *The Tempers* in 1913, which he published in London largely through the efforts of Ezra Pound. Influenced by the artistic tendencies that he saw in the 1913 Armory show in New York, Williams was an active member of the New York avant-garde, publishing in such little magazines as *Others*. Williams's third volume of verse, *Al Que Quiere!* (1917), reflected his Spanish American inheritance from his mother's family. Throughout his career, Williams composed a poetry in search of an original American idiom. Influenced by the tight verbal economy of the Imagist movement, Williams's new poetic style examined the subtle life of things rooted in native place. Williams demonstrated his famous dictum "no ideas but in things" in such volumes as *Kora in Hell: Improvisations* (1920) and in his 1923 volume *Spring and All*. In addition to these significant books of poems, Williams also wrote the important essay collection *In the American Grain* (1925). Moreover, in 1926 Williams won the Dial Award for his short story "Paterson." During the Depression era, Williams would publish several short stories in such little magazines as *New Masses, Anvil, Little Review*, and other journals. These works were then collected in his 1938 book of short stories, *Life Along the Passaic*. Throughout the thirties, Williams continued to write verse, publishing in 1934 his *Complete Poems, 1921–1931* followed by *Adam & Eve & the City* in 1936, and *The Complete Collected Poems* two years later. During World War II, Williams published his collection *The Wedge* in 1944 but turned his efforts as poet to the composition of his long poem *Paterson*, whose first section *Paterson I* he published in 1946, followed by *Paterson, A Dream of Love* two years later, and *Selected Poems and Paterson III* in 1949, which won the National Book Award the next year. In 1951, Williams's career as a writer culminated in the publication of *Paterson IV*, the *Autobiography of William Carlos Williams*, and *The Collected Earlier Poems*. Despite suffering strokes in 1951 and 1952, Williams was named consultant in poetry to the Library of Congress and won the Bollingen Prize the following year. In *Desert Music* (1954), he adopted a new poetic style of composition based in what he called the "triadic line," followed the next year by his poignant love poem "Asphodel, That Greeny Flower" written for his wife Flossie. In October 1955 Williams suffered another, devastating stroke that left him partially paralyzed. Nevertheless, he published his *Selected Letters* in 1957 and *Paterson V* in 1958. A series of strokes followed during the composition of *Pictures from Brueghel and Other Poems* (1962), which was awarded a posthumous Pulitzer Prize in 1963, the year of the poet's death.

William Wordsworth (1770–1850)

The second of five children born to John and Anne Wordsworth, William Wordsworth was sent to the reputable Hawkshead Grammar School after the death of his mother in 1778. While at Hawkshead, Wordsworth became an orphan with the death of his father. After Hawkshead, Wordsworth entered St. John's College, Cambridge in 1787, the next summer he became a prodigious walker in the English countryside, and two years later he went on his famous walking tour of France, Switzerland, and Germany. After graduating from Cambridge, Wordsworth returned to France in 1791. At this time, Wordsworth entered into a relationship with Annette Vallon, with whom he fathered a daughter, Caroline, in 1792. Returning to England at the time of France's Reign of Terror, Wordsworth would not return to France for another nine years. Meanwhile, Wordsworth kept company with his sister Dorothy and met Samuel Taylor Coleridge in 1795, with whom he would collaborate on the 1798 volume *Lyrical Ballads*, whose famous "Preface" advocated a Romantic poetics based on the "common speech" of vernacular English. With the Peace of Amiens in 1802, Wordsworth returned briefly to France before marrying Mary Hutchinson. *Poems in Two Volumes* (1807) increased Wordsworth's reputation as poet, and in 1813 Wordsworth was appointed Distributor of Stamps for Westmorland, which gave him a modicum of financial security while he lived in the Lake District's Rydal Mount. With the death of Robert Southey in 1843, Wordsworth became Poet Laureate. Although completed in earlier drafts as early as 1805, Wordsworth's greatest work *The Prelude* was published posthumously the year of his death in 1850.

W. B. Yeats (1865–1939)

The son of the famous Irish painter John Butler Yeats, William Butler Yeats was born in Dublin and raised in Western Ireland. At the age of fifteen, W. B. Yeats studied in Dublin and, after following his father's painterly art, pursued the vocation of poet and man of letters. Yeats began his career as a supporter of the celtic revival that promulgated Irish art, literature, and drama against the cultural influences of England. Yeats published his first volume of verse in 1887, but he wrote drama rather than poetry in his early career. With Lady Gregory, Yeats founded the Irish Theatre in 1902 and two years later moved to the Abbey Theatre in Dublin. His early plays include *The Countess Cathleen* (1892), *The Land of Heart's Desire* (1894), *Cathleen ni Houlihan* (1902), *The King's Threshold* (1904), and *Deirdre* (1907). During these years, Yeats also met the Irish political revolutionary Maud Gonne in 1889 and was involved in a relationship with her until her marriage to another in 1903. Having met and collaborated with Ezra Pound in London, Yeats's poetry began to take on a decidedly modern style after 1910, although he still composed his verse in traditional fixed forms involving rhyme and rhythm. At the height of his powers as poet, Yeats also played a role in Irish nationalist politics through his election to the Irish Senate in 1922. Two years later, he received the Nobel Prize. In addition to Yeats's participation in the Irish literary revival, he also was a student of spiritualism and occult traditions as a member of the Theosophical Society of London and the Hermetic Order of the Golden Dawn. Reflecting these esoteric pursuits, Yeats's evolving philosophical themes and major symbols found powerful poetic expression in such volumes of verse as *The Wilde Swans at Coole* (1919), *Michael Robartes and the Dancer* (1921), *The Tower* (1928), and *The Winding Stair and Other Poems* (1933). His final volume, *Last Poems and Plays* (1940), was published posthumously a year following his death in 1939.

Ray A. Young Bear (b. 1950)

Born in Marshalltown, Iowa, Ray A. Young Bear is a member of the Mesquakie Tribal community; Mesquakie translated means "People of the Red Earth." Young Bear is the great-great-grandson of the Mesquakie Okima (or tribal chief) Maminwanike. After the tribe had been removed to Kansas, the elder Young Bear negotiated the purchase of the tribe's sacred lands, returning in 1856 to Tama, Iowa, on the Iowa River. From early on, Ray Young Bear had a close relationship to Native American culture, and he received inspiration in storytelling from his maternal grandmother Ada Kapayou Old Bear. "I'm grateful for my grandmother," he has said. "She is all of everything to me." In addition, he received an introduction to contemporary poetry writing through participating in an Upward Bound program at Luther College in Decorah in 1968. Between 1969 and 1971, Young Bear attended Pomona College and went on to study creative writing at the University of Iowa (1971), Grinnell College (1973), Northern Iowa University (1975–1976), and at Iowa State University (1980). Since completing his education, Young Bear has taught creative writing at The Institute of American Indian Art (1984), Eastern Washington University (1987), Mesquakie Indian Elementary School (1988–1989), the University of Iowa (1989), and Iowa State University (1993 and 1998). Since 1975, the year he published his first volme *Waiting to Be Fed*, Young Bear has also published *Winter of the Salamander: The Keeper of Importance* (1980), *The Invisible Musician* (1990), *Black Eagle Child* (1992), and *Remnants of the First Earth* (1996). Young Bear views his poetry as an art of connection among the various dimensions of how the Native American heritage is lived in the present. "The most interesting facet in all of this," he says, "has been the artistic interlacing of ethereality, past and present. As such there are considerations of visions, traditional healing, supernaturalism, and hallucinogen-based sacraments interposed with centuries-old philosophies and customs." In addition to his books of poetry, Young Bear is also the cofounder with his wife of the Woodland Song and Dance Troupe.

40

Critical Perspectives on Literature

Performance and Performativity

We humans love performance. From earliest times to modern times, from rituals to film, theater to spectacle, oral poetry, and even storytelling and juggling, the art of performance is something we cherish. Performance occurs whenever one person deliberately presents an act to be witnessed (visually, orally, or both) by another. The defining element of performance is a consciousness of this witnessing.

Typically, we think of performance in the context of theater, television, and film; we link it to acting. Acting is the most obvious example of one person presenting another person (or character) and at the same time enacting the techniques necessary to produce the illusion of this other person. Drama, whether on stage or screen, is performance; people present acts to be witnessed by others and in ways that situate these acts as things to be seen and heard. In film and television, extra layers of presentation are present in the camera work, editing, sound tracks, and other apparatus of the filmmaking process.

Performativity

A performative text is a text that both describes something and produces the effect it is describing at the same time. For example, in a marriage ceremony, the betrothed say, "I do." Saying "I do" accomplishes the marriage. The words of consent produce the consent and the legal tie. When stage performance also emphasizes the ways it is doing what it is saying, it becomes performance art. Performance art is a postmodern genre of theater that emphasizes improvisation and direct address to the audience. It is performative in its desire to shock, disturb, and otherwise destroy complacency.

Fiction, particularly postmodern fiction, can also be performative. In fiction, performativity refers to two slightly different, but related practices: (1) the ways stories present what they tell in the ways that they tell it, and (2) the ways stories invite the active participation of readers in the construction of the story itself. Mark Leyner's *My Cousin, My Gastroenterologist* (see

Chapter 16), an example of the first practice, performs a frenzied romp through commodity culture while it describes it. Metafictional texts, another example of the first kind of performativity, are often performative insofar as writing about writing actually produces the text we read (see, for example, Julio Cortázar's "Blow Up," in Chapter 14, and Rudolfo Anaya's "A Story," in Chapter 15). An example of the second practice where a text pushes readers to produce meaning for themselves by forcing their active intervention in putting the text or story together is Joyce Carol Oates's "How I Contemplated the World from the Detroit House of Correction and Began My Life Over Again" (see Chapter 15). Hypertexts are performative in that they require readers to engage in a constant process of selection and arrangement that actually produces narrative (see **Writing for Hypertext**).

Included in this chapter are two short pieces from contemporary performance artist Guillermo Gómez-Peña, who combines radio, television, poetry, wrestling, music, and social criticism in his work. For Gómez-Peña, the aesthetic concept of hybridity—the melding together of distinct cultural forms from various media—corresponds with his vision of a twenty-first-century America not as a "melting pot" but a "menudo chowder." The difference between the two terms in his metaphor is crucial: While the former melts away difference into a bland, colorless homogeneity, the latter maintains "stubborn chunks" of cultural and ethnic difference. The result is an exciting, multicultural America. Although we categorize literature in terms of genre—fiction, poetry, and drama—authors not only write within these generic traditions, their creative expression also can make a difference in such "wordly" multicultural contexts of social life. Literature's power to shape the imagination is not limited to the high school or college curriculum. It also plays a significant role in popular culture. Broadly defined, **popular culture** comprises the attitudes, customs, and folkways of ordinary, everyday people. In the modern period, popular culture becomes increasingly mediated by the new information technologies of phonograph, radio, television, computerization, and the Internet, representations that give shape and definition to everyday life.

Performative Poetics

More than likely, there's a coffeehouse near your school or campus where you can hear the spoken word of poetry at an open-mike night or even read your own verse in a poetry competition ("slam"). Poetry readings, jazz poetry, beat poetry, performance poetry, and shout-outs are alive and well, and they share crossover audiences with rap and popular song. What are the historical roots of these contemporary literary and performative traditions?

Key forerunners for an experimental mode of performance poetics in the twentieth century began with the language experiments of Dadaism and the sound-influenced verse of Russian *zaum* verse. Aspiring to the kind of pure sound qualities found in musical composition, *zaum* poetry relied on repeating particular syllables for onomatopoetic effects.

Marcel Duchamp, *Bicycle Wheel* (1913)

Dadaism and *zaum* verse were two modern antecedents to present-day performance poetics. But reaching back to the Homeric age and even further to prehistoric times, poetry from the beginning has been as much a performed as it is a written art. Although we now read Homer's *Iliad* and *Odyssey* between the covers of a book, the written version of Homeric epic is a latecomer. In Ancient Greece, the poet as oral reciter (*rhapsoidos*) and composer (*aoidos*) originally performed to the accompaniment of a lyre at public events. Not infrequently, the Homeric poet would compose on the spot and improvise in response to audience suggestions.

The Homeric context of poetic performance may not sound that far removed from modern-day poetry slams, spoken word fests, and jazz rap performances. But there are major differences between the two in their performative roles. In this context, giving voice to one's experience in a poetry reading involves less the "sincere" or "authentic" expression of inward and personal emotive states. Instead, stepping up to the mike at a poetry slam demands a more self-conscious and coded performance of identity including the clothing, speaking voice, props, and the like. Such performative values have always been a factor in a conventional poetry reading, but whereas the modern poet assumed cultural authority largely in resistance to popular culture, the postmodern slam rapper/urban griot blurs the boundaries between the rigor of poetic form and the mass appeal of populist representation.

Performance poetry has its grass-roots origins in the local, subcultural public sphere of bars, coffeehouses, nightclubs, and other more mundane spaces such as community libraries, bookstores, and school auditoriums. Poetry slams had their beginnings in Chicago's Green Mill bar in the 1980s, where they were first organized by Marc Smith. But the origin of slam, according to Nuyorican poet Miguel Algarín "grows out of ancient traditions of competitive and/or linked rhymes between orators—from the Greek mythological tale of Apollo and Marsyas to the African griots, from the Sanjurokunin sen, or imaginary poetry team competitions, of tenth-century Japanese court poet Fujiwara no Kinto to the African-American 'dozens.'" A major modern influence on such rap/poetry events is the Beat Movement of the 1950s in New York City and San Francisco (see Chapter 18).

Signifying

A key element of the jazz aesthetic that influenced contemporary performance poetry is the technique of **signifying,** the improvisational appropriation and reworking of mainstream melodies and popular songs. Here the jazz musician, according to Henry Louis Gates, Jr., "suggests a given structure precisely by failing to coincide with it—that is, suggests it by dissemblance." Gates cites John Coltrane's jazz version of "My Favorite Things" that signified on the song Julie Andrews popularized in *The Sound of Music.* Another influence on the "open mic" rap sessions of contemporary performance poetics is the improvisational competitions that jazz musicians called "cutting contests." These musical competitions go back to the witty games of verbal one-upmanship called the "dozens" in the African American community. The vitally inventive tradition of jazz and jazz poetics is what ties hip-hop to be-bop, according to jazz composer Quincy Jones: "I see a connection," Jones writes, "between Hip Hop and Be-Bop. They both had to invent their own language. You know: If you don't let us in your culture, then we'll start our own!" One venue that has promoted rap, hip-hop, and spoken poetry since the 1970s is the Nuyorican Poets Café founded by Miguel Algarín and Miguel Piñero. Over the past two decades, poets such as Sandra Maria Esteves, Luis Reyes Rivera, Amiri Baraka, Pedro Pietri, Tracie Morris, and Paul Beatty conceived diverse poetic voices and styles of poetic performance art. "The philosophy and purpose of the Nuyorican Poets Café," writes Miguel Algarín,

> "has always been to reveal poetry as a living art. Even as the eye scans the lines of a poem, poetry is in flux in the United States. From Baja California to Seattle to Detroit, from the dance clubs with rap lyrics booming to the schools where Gil Scott-Heron plays to the churches where poetry series thrive to community centers with poets-in-residence and coffee houses throughout the whole of the nation, the spoken word is on fire."

Much of spoken word poetry is site-specific, spontaneous, ephemeral, and performed in the moment. If Baraka's verse—as in, say, "Black Dada Nihilismus" or "Prayer for Saving"—jams popular, vernacular references to black history and black performance art, then Beatty's poetics cut and mix such signs of black expressive culture with advertising signage and consumer slogans as in "The Revolution Will Be Commercialized":

> 7 out of 10 grass root interventionists
> recommend trident missiles
> for their patients
> who eschew guns

This playful lyric signifies simultaneously on at least three disparate discursive references. Beatty jams Gil Scott-Heron's song "The Revolution Will Not Be Televised," with a pun on the U.S. Navy's Trident submarine-launched ballistic missile, spliced with the advertising slogan made famous by Trident sugarless gum: "Four out of five dentists surveyed recommend sugarless gum to their patients who chew gum." Similarly, a poem such as "Darryl Strawberry Asleep in a Field of Dreams" probes the racial politics of baseball spectatorship and Hollywood cinema. In it, Beatty places former New York Yankee left fielder and convicted cocaine offender Daryl Strawberry in the film title *Field of Dreams*, which is based on W. P. Kinsella's baseball novel *Shoeless Joe* (1982). By contrasting the film's setting in heartland Iowa with Harlem and Cabrini Green, Beatty makes the sly point that

> shoeless joe jackson was white
>   his uni was white
>   all the dead white players was white
>   takin batting practice in white home uniforms
>   under the white iowa clouds

Not only does Beatty recover the segregated contexts of baseball's pre-civil rights history, but, equally important, he shows the ways in which such racism persists in the subtle and not-so-subtle entertainment codes of Hollywood cinema.

Winner of the National Haiku Slam and the Nuyorican Grand Slam competitions, Tracie Morris's poetry, when read on the page, only begins to suggest the oral complexity and sonic richness she brings to her performance poetics. She often performs her incredible range of voiced sonic effects not just as a solo slam poet at the mike but also with her posse, the Words-N-Music band. As she suggests in her poem "Griot," the postmodern performance poet uses her voice less as the expression of personal or confessional values and more as a pure rhythmic instrument. "Work the voice," she advises, "like a drum":

> With some treble tremor
> May seem tenuous
> It's syncretic
> Mesh ascension of flesh
> Touched with a tinge of regret.
>
> What you said?

Morris's verse presents a sensuous linguistic surface that draws heavily on alliteration, assonance, and internal rhymes in playfully associative and highly "syncretic" verbal signifying. But more radically, in its hybridized patois of phonic signification, a poem like, say, "Chief Song" is meant to be heard, as well as read, on the page:

TRACIE MORRIS *(b. 1968)*

Chief Song *(1998)*

Mene
Mene lazu na guine puene

Many Bete

Mene lazu na guine puene

I am supposed to be	Noh
I am supposed to be	Noh, Noh
I am supposed to be	Noh

The lead in	Danse ce
	Danse ce paradis

Ki Yi-K
Ki Yi-K
Ki Yi-K
Ki Yi-K
Ki Yi-K

-Os?

	Noh
But. I ah	Noh, Noh

I-A-Kuko
A cool/cool/cool/kuko

The lead	Back, Bock
Cool so	Back, Bock

Teeth on edge	eje, eje

Tre chaud	sho 'nuf

show	sho' nuf
show	sho'nuf

chaud	
chaud	eau.

Hearkening back, in some ways, to the transrational, phonic experimentation of the *zaum* poets, Morris's performative verse bears a closer resemblance to the DVD or videotape media than to the inscribed text on the page. Hers is a poetry seemingly tailor-made to the digitized streaming of today's information technology.

Performance Literature

GUILLERMO GÓMEZ-PEÑA   (b. 1955)

I Could Only Fight Back in My Poetry   (1996)

Performed live as "El Quebradito," a flamboyant vaquero from northern Mexico, dressed in a fake zebra-skin tuxedo. He looks tired and crestfallen, and his voice is raspy. Soundbed: Music by guitar maestro Antonio Bribiesca plays on a ghetto blaster; the irritating voice of an evangelist preacher can be heard in the distance.

it was the spring of '87 in the city of Arlington
I tried to explain to you in my very broken English
that Texas had once been a Mexican ranch
& that truth was not a "gringo-bashing ideology"
but you had seen too many Stallone films   5
& felt obliged to let me have it, ¿que no?
so you tried to beat the Meskin out of me
of course, since you were a foot taller & 85 lbs. heavier
& not that skilled in cross-cultural diplomacy
I could only fight back in my poetry   10
in fact, I'm fighting back right now
you claimed you hated my accent & my arrogance
but the real reason you despised me
was that your wife was just about to leave you
& hit the road to sexy Mexico   15
to escape the Texan nightmare, your inflexible arms,
your smelly feet & psychotic eyes
so Mexico became the source of all your fears
the red-light district where gringos are poisoned by midget
    whores
the mountain of trash where kids with typhoid make holes to   20
    sleep in
the bus that keeps breaking down on your way to some
    generic jungle
the gentle mariachi who touched your wife like you never did
you saw all these images in my eyes before you broke my ribs
& I could only fight back in my poetry

P.S. #1   I don't harbor any resentments but I sure hope one   25
          of these days you learn to read & write

P.S. #2   See, I told you culero, I win most fights in the
          streets of my poetry

P.S. #3   I heard you joined the militia movement last
           month. . . . I must say that you are consistent in
           misplacing your anger, man

AMIRI BARAKA   *(b. 1934)*

KA 'BA   *(1969)*

A closed window looks down
on a dirty courtyard, and black people
call across or scream across or walk across
defying physics in the stream of their will

Our world is full of sound   5
Our world is more lovely than anyone's
tho we suffer, and kill each other
and sometimes fail to walk the air

We are beautiful people
with african imaginations   10
full of masks and dances and swelling chants
with african eyes, and noses, and arms,
though we sprawl in grey chains in a place
full of winters, when what we want is sun.
We have been captured,   15
brothers. And we labor
to make our getaway, into
the ancient image, into a new

correspondence with ourselves
and our black family. We need magic   20
now we need the spells, to raise up
return, destroy, and create. What will be

the sacred words?

Black Dada Nihilismus   *(1969)*

Against what light

is false what breath
sucked, for deadness.
                    Murder, the cleansed

purpose, frail, against   5
God, if they bring him
                    bleeding, I would not

forgive, or even call him
black dada nihilismus.

The protestant love, wide windows,   10
color blocked to Mondrian, and the
ugly silent deaths of jews under

the surgeon's knife. (To awake on
69th street with money and a hip
nose. Black dada nihilismus, for   15

the umbrella'd jesus. Trilby intrigue
movie house presidents sticky the floor.
B.D.N., for the secret men, Hermes, the

blacker art. Thievery (ahh, they return
those secret gold killers. Inquisitors   20
of the cocktail hour. Trismegistus,° have

them, in their transmutation, from stone
to bleeding pearl, from lead to burning
looting, dead Moctezuma, find the West

a grey hideous space.   25

2

From Sartre,° a white man, it gave
the last breath. And we beg him die,
before he is killed. Plastique, we

---

21 *Trismegistus:* Thrice-great Hermes or Thoth-Hermes, mythical inventor of language and
founder of Hermeticism.   26 *Sarte:* Jean-Paul Sartre (1905–1980), French existentialist
philosopher.

do not have, only thin heroic blades.
The razor. Our flail against them, why   30
you carry knives? Or brutaled lumps of

heart? Why you stay, where they can
reach? Why you sit, or stand, or walk
in this place, a window on a dark

warehouse. Where the minds packed in   35
straw. New homes, these towers, for those
lacking money or art. A cult of death,

need of the simple striking arm under
the streetlamp. The cutters, from under
their rented earth. Come up, black dada   40

nihilismus. Rape the white girls. Rape
their fathers. Cut the mothers' throats.
Black dada nihilismus, choke my friends

in their bedrooms with their drinks spilling
and restless for tilting hips or dark liver   45
lips sucking splinters from the master's thigh.

Black scream
and chant, scream,
and dull, un
earthly   50

hollering. Dada, bilious
what ugliness, learned
in the dome, colored holy
shit (i call them sinned

or lost   55
    burned masters
            of the lost
                nihil German killers
                    all our learned

art, 'member   60
what you said
money, God, power,
a moral code, so cruel
it destroyed Byzantium, Tenochtitlan, Commanch

                    (got it, *Baby!*   65

For tambo, willie best, dubois, patrice, mantan, the
bronze buckaroos.

For Jack Johnson, asbestos, tonto, buckwheat,
billie holiday.

For tom russ, l'overture, vesey, beau jack,   70

(may a lost god damballah, rest or save us
against the murders we intend
against his lost white children
black dada nihilismus

PAUL BEATTY   *(b. 1962)*

Darryl Strawberry Asleep in a Field of Dreams   *(1991)*

they raised the price of dreams
blue inked can of del monte creamed corn
where baseball players
are reborn

in their prime   5
to play in modern day times

and not only was the ball white

shoeless joe jackson was white
his uni was white
all the dead white players was white   10
takin batting practice in white home uniforms
under white iowa clouds

i squirmed in my seat hopin for a
warm thunder storm
that would rain down cool papa bell   15
and hell would drip off corn stalk blades

pool into a homestead grey
inna grey away uniform
flip down flip-up shades
and say   hey now lets really play   20

*got to wear your sun glasses
so you can feel cool*

but its only a movie
and in film school heaven is
where white doctors who played   25
only an inning and a half in the show
can pray for a tinker everlastin chance to groove the 0-2 sinker

      white boys steady leanin in
       truly believin this is the best movie they've ever seen
but none of em asked josh gibson to slo-dance   30

across the color line that
falls in an iowa ball field
          broken but unhealed

fathers younger than their sons play catch
onna mismatch patch   35
natural grass and james earl jonezes broad ass

      hollywoods black fat majesty
      bellows . . . *and the people will come*

    black people smiled and fell in single file
to pay to watch mel ott run through Fences   40

and put the suicide squeeze on my mothers mother
whose color
is the same
as a night game infield

        . . . *and the people will come*   45

to see that black fathers to be
   with scars on their knees
      from shinbones split in half
        and knocked off kneecaps
practice the tap dunks they will pump over their daughters n sons   50

        . . . *and the people will come*

how could daughters n fathers build
wooden bleachers
just to sit and cheer male features

if umpire pam postema dies in the minor leagues   55
ty cobb'll hook slide into heaven
and she'll call him out

and he will
get up   dust himself   call her a . . .
brush it off as a tease   60

is this heaven
    no its iowa

is this heaven
    no its harlem

is this heaven   65
    no its bedrock

is this heaven
    no its cabrini green

do they got a team
    aint sure they got dreams   70
    damn sure aint got a field
or crops that yield
        is that the sign for steal
        i approach the third base coach
        and ask is all the movies for real   75

A Three Point Shot from Andromeda   (1991)

                    rain rusted orange
                    ring of saturn
                            in urban orbit
            over an outdoor gym

        nighttime jumpers   5
        pull up to the hoop
                    dance on the rim
            bolted against a
            metal backboard sky
            riddled with   10

ninety-nine thousand
BB-sized holes
compressing fifth floor duplex
                    kitchen light
into a galaxy   15
        of 50 watt schoolyard stars

supra-flex intense constellations
                handcheck

rotate on defense
double down   20
tryin to guard

spinning playground
planetarium delirium
of black gods flyin

on neighborhood rep   25
shake n bake
pump fake
jab step
past orion

walk on air   30

and burst a reverse
on the stellar bear

MAGGIE ESTEP   *(b. 1963)*

The Stupid Jerk I'm Obsessed With   *(1994)*

THE STUPID JERK I'M OBSESSED WITH
stands so close
I can feel his breath on my neck
and smell the way he would smell
if we slept together   5
because he is THE STUPID JERK I'M OBSESSED WITH
and that is his primary function in life
to be A STUPID JERK I CAN OBSESS OVER
and to talk to that dingy bimbette blonde
as if he really wanted to hear about her   10
manicures and pedicures and New Age Ritualistic Enema Cures
and, truth be told, he probably does want to hear about it
because he is
THE STUPID JERK I'M OBSESSED WITH
and he does anything he can to lend fuel to my fire   15
he makes a point
of standing, looking over my shoulder
when I'm talking to the guy who adores me
and would **bark like a dog and wave to strangers**
if I asked him to **bark like a dog and wave to strangers**   20
but I can't ask the guy to bark like a dog or impersonate
any kind of animal at all
cause I'm too busy
looking at the way
THE STUPID JERK I'M OBSESSED WITH   25
has pants on
that perfectly define his well-shaped ass

to the point where I'm thoroughly frantic,
I'm just gonna go home
stick my head in the oven   30
overdose on nutmeg and aspirin or sit in the bathtub
reading *The Executioner's Song*
and being completely confounded by the fact that I can see
THE STUPID JERK I'M OBSESSED WITH'S face
defining itself in the peeling plaster of the wall   35
grinning
and winking
and I start yelling: "Hey, get the hell out of there, you're just a figment of
my overripe imagination, get a life and get out of my plaster and pass me
the next painful situation please."   40

But he just keeps on
grinning
and winking
he's THE STUPID JERK I'M OBSESSED WITH
and he's mine   45
in my plaster
and frankly,
I COULDN'T BE HAPPIER.

TRACIE MORRIS   *(b. 1968)*

Project Princess   *(1998)*

Teeny feet rock layered double socks
The popping side piping of
many colored loose lace-ups
Racing toe keeps up with fancy free gear,
slick slide and just pressed recently weaved hair.   5

Jeans oversized belying her hips, back, thighs that have made guys sigh
for milleni-year.

Topped by an attractive jacket
her suit's not for flacking, flunkies or punk homies on the stroll.

Her hands the mobile thrones of today's urban goddess   10
Clinking rings link dragon fingers there's no need to be modest.

One or two gap teeth coolin'
sport gold initials
Doubt you get to her name

just check from the side, 15
please chill.

Multidimensional shrimp earrings
frame her cinnamon face

Crimson with a compliment if a
comment hits the right place 20

Don't step to the place with datelines from '88
Spare your simple, fragile feelings with the same sense that you came

Color woman variation reworks the french twist
with crinkle-cut platinum frosted bangs from a spray can's mist

Never dissed, she insists: "No you can't touch this." 25
And, if pissed, bedecked fist stops boys who must persist.

She's the one. Give her some. Under fire. Smoking gun. Of which songs are
sung, raps are spun, bells are rung, rocked, pistols cocked, unwanted advances
blocked, well-stacked she's jock. It's all about you girl. You go on. Don't you
dare stop. 30

Gangsta Suite *(1998)*

I. Who Knew?

Thought I had my shit together
I was feeling fly whatever
Feather hanging with the chickies looking dope.
Hoping I was doing better snapping on them foolish fellas
looking too hard scoping this cutie, I was like, 'nope.' 5

So I hook up with some glamour picture-pretty like a camera
gangsta thought I was a hottie and he stepped to me.
He was chillin on the d.l. guess he thought I freaked.
Thinking he'd treat me like a $5 skeeza.
Please ya damn if ya don't, screwed if ya do. 10
What I know about him flippin'?
I admit kissin', tounged him down 'till he started trippin'.

But he was hard and took no shit from nobody.
Mighta been dealing. Coming to grips with the economy.
Times is tough. He was used to being Mack Daddy. 15

Groping 'till I said ease up at my throat manhandling me.
I kicked him in his dick and split.
He almost got out his jeep.

Sweetest situation suddenly got real sticky.

II. Harder

Muthafukas try and step to me to get the best of me   20
Stay one up on a C.O. Free so 5 zero come up to another with a
big gun gonna git some dread out
ballistic kicking the lead out.
Ain't a damn thing left fa me ta do.
Go to school? Got the crazy cool Urkel flava, dudes catch ya   25
later with the boom-shoot.
Get up let up make they bones off ya ass with a 12 year wanna
crack dealer trigger fast.
Mass media wanna greedy ya with the product
so black buck, buck from the project go for the gleaming objects.   30
Rocks, cars or the poom-poom honey.
Smack up with the sheep skin inner sleeve got the money.
Funny how down low folks get the set up.
Cold steel apocalyptic drug deal blows another head up.
The Feds up and give 25 if ya good.   35
Graduation from probation lock down for ya new hood.

III. Gotta Get Yours, Girl

I cried for you and I'm still crying. One finger flick spritz
downed a six packed dying.
Fine fine gonna get some gotta flex little muscle hustle for a
coup Lex front fender for the projects   40
Gotta get yours but at who's loss did you get it? warned how many
times before you died to regret it. "Don't sweat it" you said
when your mother was sweating you. First man in the fam cause
your pops was forgetting you.
There I go, there I go, there I go with the uphill stroller   45
trying to fit the token slit in the slip with the little kid in tow.
I'm brooding and breeding after your bleeding stressing on milk
and diapers I'm needing money spent on your funeral dressing.
Now you can gloat got the coat maxing got the sneaks. Flyest
corpse in the morgue eulogize shout out from ya peeps.   50
Beside me. What about our forever lasting?
Did you think about the us you threw away
when you were 9 mm. O.G. blasting?

MIGUEL PIÑERO   *(1947–1988)*

The Book of Genesis According to
St. Miguelito
                                                                            (1985)

Before the beginning
God created God
In the beginning
God created the ghettos & slums
and God saw this was good.   5
So God said,
"Let there be more ghettos & slums"
and there were more ghettos & slums.
But God saw this was plain
so   10
to decorate it
God created lead-based paint
and then
God commanded the rivers of garbage & filth
to flow gracefully through the ghettos.   15
On the third day
because on the second day God was out of town
On the third day
God's nose was running
& his jones was coming down and God   20
in his all knowing wisdom
knew he was sick
he needed a fix
so God
created the backyards of the ghettos   25
& the alleys of the slums
in heroin & cocaine
and
with his divine wisdom & grace
God created hepatitis   30
who begat lockjaw
who begat malaria
who begat degradation
who begat
    GENOCIDE   35
and God knew this was good
in fact God knew things couldn't git better
but he decided to try anyway
On the fourth day
God was riding around Harlem in a gypsy cab   40
when he created the people

and he created these beings in ethnic proportion
but he saw the people lonely & hungry
and from his eminent rectum
he created a companion for these people   45
and he called this companion
capitalism
who begat racism
who begat exploitation
who begat male chauvinism   50
who begat machismo
who begat imperialism
who begat colonialism
who begat wall street
who begat foreign wars   55
and God knew
and God saw
and God felt this was extra good
and God said
VAYAAAAAAA   60
On the fifth day
the people kneeled
the people prayed
the people begged
and this manifested itself in a petition   65
a letter to the editor
to know why? WHY? WHY? qué pasa babyyyyy?????
and God said,
"My fellow subjects
let me make one thing perfectly clear   70
by saying this about that:
No . . . . COMMENT!"
but on the sixth day God spoke to the people
he said . . . "PEOPLE!!!
the ghettos & the slums   75
& all the other great things I've created
will have dominion over thee"
and then
he commanded the ghettos & slums
and all the other great things he created   80
to multiply
and they multiplied
On the seventh day God was tired
so he called in sick
collected his overtime pay   85
a paid vacation included
But before God got on that t.w.a.
for the sunny beaches of Puerto Rico

He noticed his main man Satan
planting the learning trees of consciousness   90
around his ghetto edens
so God called a news conference
on a state of the heavens address
on a coast to coast national t.v. hookup
and God told the people   95
to be
COOL
and the people were cool
and the people kept cool
and the people are cool   100
and the people stay cool
and God said
Vaya . . .

NTOZAKE SHANGE *(b. 1948)*

Blood Rhythms–Blood Currents–Black
Blue N Stylin'   *(1994)*

(French sugar-beet farmers, overwhelmed by mulatto competitors, plastered Europe's cities with advertisements proclaiming: "Our sugar is not soiled with black blood." A popular Afro-Cuban saying is: "Sugar is made with blood," while in the South of the United States, cane growers processed natural sugar "to get the nigger out.")

Fragrant breezes in the South
melt to melodies round small fires
mount tree limbs
with bodies black
and swayin' black n croonin'   5
songs of sunsets
comin' from the fields bawdy
brazen
hard to put yr finger on
like the blues   10
like the strum of guitars on dark damp

southern nights
hard to put your finger on
like screams in the black bloody southern soil
sweet black blood echoin' thru the evenin' service   15
grindin' by the roadhouse door
sweet black blood
movin' with slow breath

outta breath
young negroes run to pick up a bale of cotton   20
run to flee southern knights
crosses *bare blazin'* signals black bloods
gone runnin'
for Chicago
for the hollow   25
for the C.C. Rider
for the new day *sweet*

blocked melodies ache in young girls' throats
rip thru their lips like the road to freedom was lit
all lit up with the grace of God and   30
Sears Tower
the Ford plane and Pontiac's vision
all lit up *sleek* fires
sheddin' the haunts of poll taxes and test questions *like*
where is America   35
cost a *finger*
a ear
a heart
a teardrop fallin' from the saggin' front porch
to the project stairway   40
from the water fountain to the chain gang

the *night train* carried *smuggled* goods *news*
of struttin' signifyin' fellas with gold teeth
neath *they feet and brawny sway* for blocks and blocks
far as the eye cd see from Biloxi to Birmingham   45
the *contraband* of freedom *seeped* thru the swamps
the air hung heavy
with the cries of "ain't gonna let nobody turn me round"
and *young* boys in nice-cut suits
who was awready standin' with they heads up   50
awready prancin' with finesse and grand stature
like men wit eyes
don't never look down
men wit eyes burstin' wit glory
from the red sedans   55
and the *seats in schools*
to the right to set wherever they want
and when the sounds of the harmonica was slowed
by snarlin' dogs and hoses
when the *washboards* and *bottleneck players*   60
was skedattlin' *out the bullets way*
up came a roarin'
force a light blue controlled fire in un-mussed lamé

pleated silk and faces
bearin' no scars   65
to say "*we ain't been touched*"
we the *sweet black fires of dreams*
& of unobfuscated beauty

like the trails of freedom
the Good Lord himself lit up   70
we gonna *take this*
new city neon light
sound
volumes for millions to hear
to love themselves   75
enough to turn back the pulse of a whippin' history
make it carry the modern black melody from L.A.
to downtown Newark City
freedom buses
freedom riders   80
freedom is the way we walk that walk
talk that talk
gotta take that *charred black body out the ground*
switch on the current to a new sound
to a new way of walkin' a new way of talkin'   85
blues

electrified
blues
boltin-the-lynchin-tree-
n-tremblin-n-chirren-   90
blues
defyin' the sound of gravity

for a people singin'
about the sashay of blood rhythms set free.

DRAMA

What Is Drama?

Part VII
Form and Content

41 What Is Drama?

What is drama? This simple question has been asked countless times over the past twenty-five hundred years. Most answers to it emphasize one of two points:

- Drama, as shaped into the form of a play, is a particular kind of *literary* text to be read.
- Drama is an essentially *performative* event, one that requires presentation before an audience.

In his *Poetics* (335 B.C.), which offers significant insight into such matters, the Greek philosopher Aristotle stresses that drama involves both action and the imitation of reality:

> [P]lays are called dramas, because the imitation is of men acting [*drôntas* from *drân*, "do, act"].

On the London stage nearly two thousand years after Aristotle considered the question, Shakespeare's character Hamlet advanced an equally well-known opinion. Here, in coaching a troupe of actors scheduled to appear at the Danish court, Hamlet discusses drama not as a work to be read, but as a text to be enacted:

> . . . Suit the action to the word,
> the word to the action, with this special observance,
> that you o'erstep not the modesty of nature:
> for any thing so o'er done is from the purpose of playing,
> whose end, both at the first and now, was and is, to
> hold as 'twere the mirror up to nature. . . . (*Hamlet* 3.2.17–22)

Considered together, these two statements identify not only several characteristics of drama, but also its challenges as a *performed* art. Both the Greek philosopher and melancholy Dane place a high value on reality and a play's reproduction of it: hold the mirror up to nature, imitate men in action. But the matter is not always so simple; first, playwrights, directors, and actors have to agree on what is "real" and how best to imitate it. And this is just the beginning of the beauty—and complexity—of drama.

Drama in production inevitably means collaboration, the interaction of artists with a variety of specific talents. To be sure, all but the most egocentric writers know that they benefit from the assistance of others—constructive criticism from editors, for example, who comment on and improve drafts of their works. Most writing also eventually finds a reader or an audience. Some kinds of writing, poetry for instance, is sometimes performed or read aloud. But no other form of fictive writing requires performance and is written with performance in mind. Drama's fictive nature is significant because although many events or moments are dramatic—a rousing political speech or the rescue of a hostage as detailed in a news report—they are not dramas. As a basic definition, then, **drama** is a fictional text composed to be presented by one or more performers to an audience.

Yet this only begins to answer the question "What is drama?" Screenplays, for example, fulfill all the criteria of this definition: They are fictional and composed to be presented to an audience. It is also true that some writers, most famously the nineteenth-century British poets Percy Shelley and Lord Byron, wrote so-called closet plays that were never intended to be performed (although in some cases they were). Such instances, however, are rare; most dramatists write for an audience, usually a very particular one. Moreover, unlike film, drama on stage takes place in—indeed, *is*—an "eternal present." Each time *Hamlet* is performed, drama critic Martin Esslin explains, "Hamlet is present and goes through the sequence of events that happened to him as if they were happening now for the first time." Drama thus enjoys a unique relationship with time that differentiates it from film; it occurs at the same moment an audience receives it. As a result, our perception of and response to drama differ considerably from our responses to film, poetry, and fiction.

This chapter outlines the formal elements of drama as a literary genre, and then moves to a brief consideration of it as a performed event. Before doing so, however, one word of caution: In separating the elements of dramatic form and considering each individually, we are in one respect distorting the experience of the *theater event*. Drama in production creates such a total experience or event that distinguishing plot from character, thought from action, is not only practically impossible, it is often unnecessary. An audience might learn as much about a character from his posture or facial expression as from what he says or does. Taken together, all of the sights and sounds of live performance, combined with the texts provided by writers (or, at times, the improvisations agreed on by a group of performers), make up the totality of the theater event.

This means that we must be attentive to the subtler elements of drama in performance. What, for example, does the concept of *theatrical production* mean? Does it mean the same thing today as it did in Shakespeare's England or Molière's seventeenth-century France? Whatever the answers, one thing is clear: What occurs in the *practice* of theatrical representation—the mounting of a play on stage before an audience—does not preclude our examination in *theory* of the parts of this totality.

This discussion begins with a consideration of dramatic **form** or the shape of the play which, like lots of complicated phenomena, might be defined as a system of relationships that make up the whole. The human body, for example, relies on numerous systems: respiratory, cardiovascular, neural, and so on; a car contains electrical, ignition, and exhaust systems; the Library of Congress has elaborated a cataloguing system that organizes library collections across the country. Similarly, drama—and for the purposes of this chapter the term is used synonymously with *play*—is a system constituted of parts or subsystems that are both enhanced and complicated by the technologies of the theater. Their functioning is precisely relational. Just as a pancreas or spark plug means very little outside the total context of the body or the automobile, the elements or sub-systems that make up dramatic form might be considered as if they were discrete and autonomous, but in production before an audience the elements that comprise dramatic form reveal their profound interdependence.

All of this leads to a kind of map this chapter attempts to traverse and illuminate: from script to actor to audience. In other words, drama progresses from the playwright's desk, to the stage or playing space, and finally to the audience's response. Our job in both this chapter and the next one on the concluding scene of Arthur Miller's play *Death of a Salesman* is to chart this progress, stopping along the way at formal conventions crucial to our understanding.

Script → Actor → Audience

> The irreducible theater event is contained in these three elements. . . . The playwright in setting down his play on paper works perforce by a code of words. The text is a coded pattern of signals to the actor, and the resulting performance is a further coded pattern of signals to the spectator. Any study of a play is impossible without an initial decoding of all signals. . . . (J. L. Styan, *Drama, Stage and Audience* [1975])

J. L. Styan's notion of the theater event provides a starting point for understanding drama in performance. Communication in the theater begins with words, with the play that becomes a script or blueprint for performance. This order would seem not only logical but inevitable. But it has not always been so. Well before the dawn of the twenty-first century, performance practices existed in which the written text enjoyed no such priority. Today, comic improvisational theater thrives on actors responding to each other and the audience, effectively eliminating the "script" from Styan's equation. Here, the emphasis shifts from the play as an aesthetic work—and the author as its god-like creator—to the ways in which meaning is produced in performance.

The simple tripartite diagram *script → actor → audience* thus actually does more than trace a network of communication in the theater. It also implies a kind of politics in which the written text occupies a privileged position as the origin of the theater event. And this politics, especially in the twentieth century, has at times proved controversial. For the Irish playwright Bernard Shaw working as a drama reviewer in London in the 1890s, a play's language formed the center of the theater event. Shaw deplored the visual excess and overly emotional acting style of late Victorian theater, even those productions that featured the leading "legitimate" actors of his day (here *legitimate* means actors who played both popular and classical roles successfully). When his friend William Archer, responding to a draft of one of Shaw's plays, complained that it was nothing but "talk," Shaw forcefully reminded him that "talk" or the skillful use of language in **dialogue**—conversation between two or more characters—or **monologue**—the spoken thoughts of a single character—*is* the business of the dramatist.

Writing some forty years later, French playwright and director Antonin Artaud advanced a totally different view. In his influential treatise *The Theater and Its Double* (1938), Artaud attacked the "exclusive dictatorship of speech" in the Western or "Occidental" theater, arguing that dialogue "does not belong specifically to the stage, it belongs to books." He asked, "How does it happen that in the theater, at least in the theater as we know it in Europe . . . everything specifically theatrical, i.e., everything that cannot be expressed in speech, in words, or, if you prefer, everything that is not contained in the dialogue . . . is left in the background?" Instead, he called for the renewed importance of **mise-en-scène:** "everything that occupies the stage" and is "addressed first of all to the senses." In this "double" of the Western theater, sight and nonverbal sound would reanimate the audience, returning the theater to a spirit of anarchy and poetic vitality.

Such debates often assume other political dimensions as well. But this is hardly surprising. Almost all drama possesses visual and verbal dimensions, the relative importance of which has often occasioned critical disagreement. All drama also advances a politics, even if at first glance it seems politically neutral. African American writer Ntozake Shange, for example, author of *for colored girls who have considered suicide/when the rainbow is enuf* (1976), insists on calling herself "a poet or writer" rather than a playwright. For Shange, the tradition of Western drama from the time of Aristotle forward contains both an aesthetic and a thematic preoccupation (a "psychology") from which she hopes to distance herself. In the interdisciplinary world in which African American artists reside, she maintains, "we must use everything we've got," the full range of sensory possibilities in the theater. Consequently, Shange refuses to call her works "plays" or "dramas," preferring instead such terms as "theater pieces" (the subtitle of her 1978 *Spell #7*) or "choreopoems." Plays belong to a different, essentially European tradition, she argues, one that leads us all the way back to Aristotle and the Greek classical theater.

What follows, then—a discussion of the **narrative structure** of drama—is again just a starting point. It marks a place to initiate our thinking about drama as a form or script. What is drama? How might we describe it as a specific kind of literary art?

Six Essential Elements of Drama

In *Poetics*, Aristotle identifies six essential elements of drama, all of which are as relevant today as they were in ancient Athens:

1. action or plot
2. character
3. thought
4. language
5. song and dance
6. spectacle or visual excess

Action or Plot

For Aristotle, a play's action is of utmost importance. By the term **unity of action,** he means that the best dramas, particularly tragedies, are imitations of an action that is unified and complete. In this instance, *unified* means that all the scenes in the play are linked together by "probability and necessity." That is to say, unlike the historian or journalist who reports events that may be the result of accident or anomaly, the skillful tragedian introduces only those incidents that follow probably or logically from those that precede them. Different plots or actions demand different kinds of characters, thought, and language, but all of these elements of drama originate in a play's action. This action is constructed in a play, which in turn provides the blueprint for performance or the **script.**

Throughout the nineteenth and twentieth centuries, writers have found much in Aristotle to admire, particularly his explanation of plot and character. In revising his 1955 play *A View from the Bridge*, Arthur Miller echoed Aristotle by observing that "nothing was permitted [in the play's action] which did not advance the progress of [the protagonist's] catastrophe in a most direct way." Aristotle's influence is equally apparent in the thought of contemporary dramatist David Mamet, arguably one of America's most significant writers. Reflecting on the relationship between action and character, Mamet asserts that *"characterization* is taken care of by the author [not the actor]," who accomplishes this by showing us *"what the character does* rather than having the character's entrance greeted with 'Well, well, if it isn't my ne'er-do-well half-brother, just returned from New Zealand.'" Here, Mamet makes a point worth our consideration: namely, the fundamental importance of dramatic action to character development.

From Aristotle to David Mamet, from ancient Greece to contemporary America, a strong consensus exists about one element of the script: Plot or action is its most significant element. To aid in this undertaking, read Terrence McNally's short play *André's Mother* reprinted here. McNally, a successful playwright since the 1960s, has contributed substantially to the American theater, winning critical praise in the 1990s for such full-length plays as *Love! Valour! Compassion!* (1995) and *Master Class* (1996). Writing *André's Mother* in 1988 as one in a series of short dramatic sketches, McNally expanded it in 1990 into an Emmy Award-winning teleplay. But even in its shorter original version, this text can teach us much about the structure or dramatic action and other components of dramatic form. We shall refer to it often in the discussion that follows.

Plot: The Case of André's Mother

TERRENCE MCNALLY

André's Mother   *(1988)*

Four people enter. They are nicely dressed and carry white helium-filled balloons on a string.

They are Cal, a young man; Arthur, his father; Penny, his sister; and André's Mother.

Cal: You know what's really terrible? I can't think of anything terrific to say. Goodbye. I love you. I'll miss you. And I'm supposed to be so great with words!

Penny: What's that over there?

Arthur: Ask your brother.

Cal: It's a theatre. An outdoor theatre. They do plays there in the summer. Shakespeare's plays. (*To André's Mother.*) God, how much he wanted to play Hamlet. It was his greatest dream. I think he would have sold his soul to play it. He would have gone to Timbuktu to have another go at that part. The summer he did it in Boston, he was so happy!

Penny: Cal, I don't think she . . . ! It's not the time. Later.

Arthur: You son was a . . . the Jews have a word for it . . .

Penny: (*Quietly appalled.*) Oh my God!

Arthur: *Mensch*, I believe it is and I think I'm using it right. It means warm, solid, the real thing. Correct me if I'm wrong.

Penny: Fine, dad, fine. Just quit while you're ahead.

Arthur: I won't say he was like a son to me. Even my son isn't always like a son to me. I mean . . . ! In my clumsy way, I'm trying to say how much I like André. And how much he helped me to know my own boy. Cal was always two hands full but André and I could talk about anything under the sun. My wife was very fond of him, too.

Penny: Cal, I don't understand about the balloons.

Cal: They represent the soul. When you let go, it means you're letting his soul ascend to heaven. That you're willing to let go. Breaking the last earthly ties.

Penny: Does the Pope know about this?

Arthur: Penny!

Penny: André loved my sense of humor. Listen, you can hear him laughing. (*She lets go of her white balloon.*) So long, you glorious, wonderful. I-know-what-Cal-means-about-words . . . *man!* God forgive me for wishing you were straight every time I laid eyes on you. But if any man was going to have you, I'm glad it was my brother! Look how fast it went up. I bet that means something. Something terrific. (*Arthur lets his balloon go.*)

Arthur: Goodbye. God speed.

Penny: Cal?

Cal: I'm not ready yet.

Penny: Okay. We'll be over there. Come on, pop, you can buy your little girl a Good Humor.

Arthur: They still make Good Humor?

Penny: Only now they're called Dove Bars and they cost 12 dollars. (*Penny takes Arthur off. Cal and André's Mother stand with their balloons.*)

Cal: I wish I knew what you were thinking. I think it would help me. You know almost nothing about me and I only know what André told me about you. I'd always had it in my mind that one day we would be friends, you and me. But if you didn't know about André and me. . . . If this hadn't happened, I wonder if he would have ever told you. When he was so sick, if I asked him once I asked him a thousand times, tell her.

She's your mother. She won't mind. But he was so afraid of hurting you and of your disapproval. I don't know which was worse. (*No response. No sighs.*) God, how many of us live in this city because we don't want to hurt our mothers and live in mortal terror of their disapproval. We loose ourselves here. Our lives aren't furtive, just our feelings towards people like you are! A city of fugitives from our parents' scorn or heart-break. Sometimes he'd seem a little down and I'd say, "What's the matter, babe!" And this funny sweet, sad smile would cross his face and he'd say, "Just a little homesick, Cal, just a little bit." I always accused him of being a country boy just playing at being a hot shot, sophisticated New Yorker. (*He sighs.*) It's bullshit. It's all bullshit. (*Still no response.*) Do you remember the comic strip *Little Lulu?* Her mother had no name, she was so remote, so formidable to all the children. She was just Lulu's mother. "Hello, Lulu's Mother," Lulu's friends would say. She was al-most anonymous in her remoteness. You remind me of her. André's mother. Let me answer the questions you can't ask and then I'll leave you alone and you won't ever have to see me again. André died of AIDS. I don't know how he got it. I tested negative. He died bravely. You would have been proud of him. The only thing that frightened him was you. I'll have everything that was his sent to you. I'll pay for it. There isn't much. You should have come up the summer he played *Hamlet.* He was magnificent. Yes, I'm bitter. I'm bitter I've lost him. I'm bitter what's happening. I'm bitter even now, after all this, I can't reach you. I'm beginning to feel your disapproval and it's making me ill. (*He looks at his balloon.*) Sorry, old friend. I blew it. (*He lets go of the balloon.*) Good night, sweet prince, and flights of angels sing thee to thy rest! (*Beat.*) Goodbye, André's mother. (*He goes. André's Mother stands alone holding her white balloon. Her lip trembles. She looks on the verge of breaking down. She is about to let go of the balloon when she pulls it down to her. She looks at it a while before she gently kisses it. She lets go of the balloon. She follows it with her eyes as it rises and rises. The lights are beginning to fade. André's Mother's eyes are still on the balloon. Blackout.*)

THE END

Let's think about plot more carefully. Most dramas, whether they present the fall of royalty (*Oedipus Rex, Hamlet*), the downfalls of less powerful char-acters (*The Emperor Jones, Trifles*), or the happier circumstance of the marriage or impending marriage of young lovers (*The Tempest, The Flying Doctor*), share a common structure of action:

Exposition → Development → Climax
Dénouement → Conclusion
(Opened/Closed)

The early scenes of most plays introduce an audience to characters and set-ting, create a tone, and transmit what some critics call "generic signals" that hint at what might occur later. To follow the play and understand the events that follow, the audience needs an exposition of basic facts: Who are the central characters? Where do they come from? What relationships exist between them? And, perhaps most important, what do they want and what, if anything, prevents them from getting what they want? Later scenes often continue this exposition as they develop the conflicts that drive the action. The consequences of these conflicts typically reach a climax in which a central conflict must be resolved, its implications unraveled in a dénouement, and the action resolved.

Consider the simple action of *André's Mother*. It seems improbable that a script of such brevity could contain all of these elements of dramatic action, but it does. Soon after the play's four characters enter, we understand that they have gathered to mourn a recent death. In the play's opening lines, Cal expresses both his love and sense of loss for someone we soon realize is André. When he explains that André wanted to play Hamlet, we realize that the deceased was an actor. We also learn that Arthur is Cal's father and Penny is his sister. Recalling Mamet's point about exposition originating from action, McNally does not have one character say, "This is my father" or "This is my sister"; rather, these points arise from the dramatic situation. McNally's revelation that the fourth character is the decedent's mother is handled even more deftly. The stage direction "(*To André's mother*)" indicates that Cal looks at her when saying, "God, how much he wanted to play Hamlet." We might infer further that Cal knew André better than his mother did: Why would he say this to her if she already knew it? What else might he know about André that his mother doesn't? What does this imply about André's relationship with his mother—and with Cal? Among other things, these opening lines establish the closeness and affection between Cal and André.

This is efficient exposition. In a minute or so, the dialogue conveys who these characters are, why they are together, and what relationships they enjoy with each other.

But one important detail remains to be discovered: We don't know what they want—or at least what one of them wants. Sadly, like McNally's characters, most of us have had to mourn the loss of loved ones and have similarly assembled to memorialize them and relate our sense of loss to each other. But, however poignant these moments might be, are they inherently dramatic? If this were all that *André's Mother* concerned—people assembled to mourn a recent death—it might prove difficult to interest an audience. For this reason, a play's action nearly always introduces a character or characters who desire something that another character or entity (law, authority, code of behavior) prevents them from obtaining, accomplishing, or achieving. Dramatic action, in other words, eventually develops conflict or, on the ancient Athenian stage, *agōn*.

Often a central character or **protagonist** is opposed by another character, an **antagonist** (both words coming from *agon*), and the dramatic action propels these opposing forces into an inevitable collision. In this respect, drama and film are remarkably similar: Hamlet fights a duel with Laertes and is opposed by Claudius in Shakespeare's *Hamlet*, Luke Skywalker battles Darth Vader (before his conversion to Jedi virtue) in the first *Star Wars* trilogy. Even

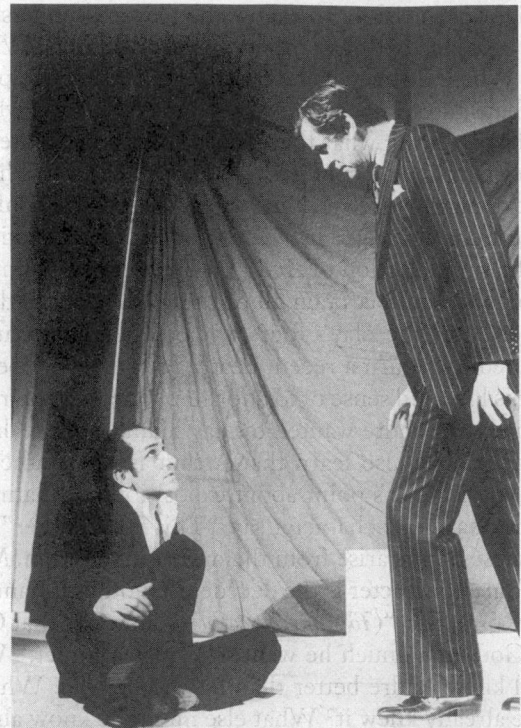

Hamlet, 1975, The Other Place. Director: Buzz
Goodbody. Ben Kingsley (*left*) as Hamlet and
George Baker (*right*) as Claudius.

comic plots that end in celebration are driven to the resolution of a conflict:
between two young lovers (Shakespeare's *The Taming of the Shrew, Much Ado
About Nothing*), between the lovers and an obstructing parent, usually a father
(*A Midsummer Night's Dream*), between a character and an unjust or repressive law. Dramatic action then typically moves to a climax, a point of "no return." Something has to happen.

André's Mother develops a conflict that is, at first, implied in several ways:
the somber tone, Cal's anxiety about initiating a conversation with André's
mother, and her silence. Then, Penny provides a crucial piece of information
when recalling André's physical attractiveness: "God forgive me for wishing
you were straight every time I laid eyes on you. But if any man was going to
have you, I'm glad it was my brother!" Cal and André, if we hadn't realized
this before, were much more than friends. They were lovers in a committed
relationship. And although Cal's father remarks about how much he enjoyed
André's company and how often they talked "about anything under the sun,"
it is equally apparent that his mother never embraced her son's relationship
with Cal. In fact, she never knew about it or her son's sexuality, as Cal's long
monologue at the end confirms.

The monologue sharpens all of these details, adding crucial exposition of the past and also refining the nature of the conflict underlying the dramatic action. Addressed to André's mother, the opening lines of Cal's monologue explain that his dead lover had hoped she would one day forge a friendship with Cal. This hope, it seems, persisted even through the days when André grew gravely ill, as did his reluctance to tell his mother about his life. Cal confronts this matter directly: "He was so afraid of hurting you and of your disapproval." Here exposition and definition of the conflict merge. He died of AIDS—something Cal later confirms—and his mother had perhaps never accepted or was never made aware of her son's sexuality. How will she respond to this news? Were André's fears justified, and will she now exhibit the disapproval he so greatly feared? Will the play end with a reconciliation between a mother and her dead son, or will it conclude in just the opposite way, with a firm denunciation of him and his sexuality?

Such questions and conflicts informed numerous plays written about the AIDS epidemic in 1980s and 1990s America, and they still do. Like his contemporaries Tony Kushner and Larry Kramer, McNally has written several plays in which AIDS in the gay community and the question of larger social or familial acceptance combine to provide dramatic conflict: *Lips Together, Teeth Apart* in 1991, for instance, and *Love! Valour! Compassion!*, later adapted for a feature film. But these are all full-length dramas in which conflicts take significant time to simmer and approach resolution. How can such a potentially deep division be reconciled in a sketch that runs for just a few minutes? How, in other words, can the play's action reach closure? In such a short play, is it possible even to locate a climax, a place in the narrative where things cannot return to the way they once were?

After Cal's remarks connect André to the role he once aspired to play by echoing Horatio's line at the end of *Hamlet*—"Good night, sweet prince, /And flights of angels sing thee to thy rest!"—Cal leaves the stage. But he doesn't do so immediately. McNally's stage directions stipulate that a *beat* occurs first, a pause to give both André's mother and the audience an opportunity to reflect on what we have just heard.

Then, she is left alone on stage with her thoughts—and her grief. What will she do? Any number of responses are possible, from outrage to acceptance. One stage direction confirms her emotion after hearing Cal's monologue: *"Her lip trembles. She looks on the verge of breaking down."* At this point, the actor's performance, the nonverbal communication so central to the theater event, grows in importance. Her body, her gestures, her lips communicate everything. Then, as she is about release the balloon she carries—earlier Cal has explained that the white balloons represent André's soul—she gently kisses it. For her, the balloon represents her son, and her kiss tells the audience all it needs to know. She loves him, and they are reconciled as the lights fade into darkness.

However moving, the resolution of McNally's play is essentially comic, reconciliation and love belonging to the comic world. The resolution of the dramatic action is one of the chief reasons some plays are called tragedies and others comedies. Both kinds suggest that the principal action of the play is closed: That is, the main conflicts are resolved conclusively, either badly or happily for the protagonist. Some plays, Anton Chekhov's *The Cherry Orchard*

(1904), for example, end on a bittersweet or tragicomic note, as the fates of the central characters are neither clearly comic nor tragic, but a subtle mixture of both. In some instances, most famously that of Samuel Beckett's *Waiting for Godot* (1953), the subtitle of which is "A Tragicomedy," the ending remains open: Nothing is resolved because the action does not conclude in a final or determinative way. In *Waiting for Godot,* two characters stand by a road waiting for a Mr. Godot to appear; both acts one and two of the play end with their remaining by the roadside waiting. Beckett's pair of characters, for all we know, are still out there waiting. As one critic quipped, *"Waiting for Godot* is a play in which nothing happens—twice!"

   Not so with *André's Mother.* Something significant occurs as the lights fade on the scene: A mother expresses her love for her son. The conflict underlying the action—whether she will still love her son after she learns about both the secrets of his life and the circumstances of his death—is resolved. The dramatic action is completed.

Character

As we have said, Aristotle believed that dramatic action was so significant that a tragedy "cannot exist without a plot, but it can without characters," citing epic poems of his age as examples. Nevertheless, the history of drama since Aristotle often appears to suggest just the opposite: that the most influential plays *are* so influential precisely because they create unique characters or "personalities." This is Harold Bloom's thesis in his widely read study of Shakespeare's works, *Shakespeare: The Invention of the Human* (1998). For Bloom, "The idea of Western character, of the self as a moral agent, has many sources: Homer and Plato, Aristotle and Sophocles, the Bible and St. Augustine, Dante and Kant . . . Personality, in our sense, is a Shakespearean invention, and is not only Shakespeare's greatest originality but also the authentic cause of his perpetual pervasiveness." The greatest of Shakespeare's plays introduce us to memorable personalities—Hamlet and Falstaff, for example— who embody "life's largeness."

   These characters have spanned the range of human possibility: from great kings or troubled emperors and generals, to clowns, drunkards, and fools. Shakespeare's uniquely tragic characters, much as McNally's Cal does, speak to us in heartfelt monologues and **soliloquies** that grant us access to their most intimate thoughts. His comic creations—characters like Falstaff or Sir Toby Belch—have entertained us with their wit, their amusing banter, and even their drunken mishaps. Some have drawn us into their confidence through **asides;** others have sung to us or spoken in blank verse. This range of characters enlivens the contemporary stage as well, although the number of kings and princes who reside there has declined considerably from Shakespeare's day. Some comic characters originate in stock or "type" figures that have proved enduringly popular for centuries: clever servants, gullible fools, lecherous old men, hypocrites, and so on, characters central to the success of Molière's *The Flying Doctor,* included later in *Understanding Literature.* Today, these types reappear on television situation comedies in the guise of the goofy next-door neighbors or the horrible in-laws.

The Flying Doctor, 1982. American Repertory
Theatre, Cambridge, MA. 1982. Director: Andrei
Serban. Thomas Derrah (*left*) as Sganarelle and
Tony Shalhoub (*right*) as Valère. (Photograph by
Richard Feldman)

As is the case in *André's Mother,* characters reveal themselves by what they
say or don't say, and by what they do or don't do. We then decide what we feel
about them. This means more than whether we like them or not, but whether
we are emotionally *engaged* in their dilemmas or *detached* from them. Most of
us sympathize with both Cal and André's mother, in large part because of their
love for André and their great sadness at his loss. At the same time, however,
we also take comfort in his mother's final gesture of affection for her dead
son, the kissing of the balloon. Insofar as it is possible in such a short play,
McNally succeeds in developing his characters sufficiently for us to respond
to their loss.

This development comes not only from what they do, but also from what
they say.

Thought and Language

Language in drama is generally communicated in one of three forms: dialogue, monologue (including asides or direct addresses to the audience), and
soliloquies. Dialogue, like that in *André's Mother,* frequently accomplishes

several things at once: It reveals something about the character speaking; it usually reveals something about his or her attitude toward the characters with whom he or she is speaking and about the topics they are discussing; it may aid in advancing the plot, either by providing necessary exposition of the past or foreshadowing of the future; it may contribute to the tone or rhythm of the play; it may help orient the audience to the fictive space in which the action occurs; it may imply a larger meaning, a topic, or issue the play will develop as the action progresses.

Recall the opening lines of *André's Mother:*

Cal: You know what's really terrible? I can't think of anything terrific to say. Goodbye. I love you. I'll miss you. And I'm supposed to be so great with words!

Penny: What's that over there?

Arthur: Ask your brother.

Cal: It's a theatre. An outdoor theatre. They do plays there in the summer. Shakespeare's plays. (*To André's Mother.*) God, how much he wanted to play Hamlet. It was his greatest dream. I think he would have sold his soul to play it. He would have gone to Timbuktu to have another go at that part. The summer he did it in Boston, he was so happy!

Cal's opening lines clearly communicate that he is mourning the loss of someone whom he loved. They also hint at other aspects of his background: that he is an articulate young man, probably well educated, who may work with words for a living as a writer or journalist.

Language and tone in McNally's play potentially reveal more than character. Aspects of the setting and time in which the action is set, for example, while not specified, might be inferred from dialogue. The opening stage directions are sparse: *"Four people enter. They are nicely dressed and carry white helium-filled balloons on a string."* "Nicely dressed" could imply various costumes; balloons are carried at zoos and amusement parks. The scene could be almost anywhere; and, in theory, the action could be set at any time. But Cal's lines add needed information about the fictional space and time in which the dramatic action unfolds. Amusement is not an issue or goal in the play, so we understand that the characters are not visiting Disney World or the National Zoo in Washington. When Penny asks Cal about a building she sees, he provides another clue both about the person he will miss and the scene: They are outside, most likely in a park or other large public space, near a theater. Such spaces exist all over the world—an outdoor theater where Shakespeare's plays are performed is located in Regents Park in London, for example—but Cal's line about André playing Shakespeare in Boston implies that the action is set in America. His closing speech specifies this even more narrowly: André played at being a "sophisticated" New Yorker. Finally, while their costumes and balloons suggest that the play takes place in the present—did characters on Shakespeare's stage or in Puritan America carry balloons?—Cal's language confirms this. "I think he would have sold his soul," among other modern idioms, has a strongly contemporary resonance.

Ensuing dialogue, not surprisingly, relates even more about these characters, about the fictive space in which the action occurs, and about the past. But the point is that, in all plays except for pantomime or mime performance, language in drama can be uttered in several distinctly different ways, some of which communicate several things at the same time. In this regard, Bernard Shaw was right to remind his friend William Archer about the value of language to drama, for "Words, words, words" (Polonius's phrase in *Hamlet*) are the business of the playwright.

Spectacle

When Aristotle denigrated "the visual adornment of the dramatic persons" as the "least artistic element" of tragic drama, he seemingly was referring to excess: to violence on stage and lavish visual displays. But, in fact, drama in performance appeals to both the eye and the ear. The next chapter takes up in greater detail the issue of sight and sound in performed drama, particularly the significance of **mise-en-scène**—set, properties, lighting, costuming, gesture, makeup, movement, and sound—to the theater event. But before there is a theater art devoted to the spectator's senses, there is a dramatic scene or

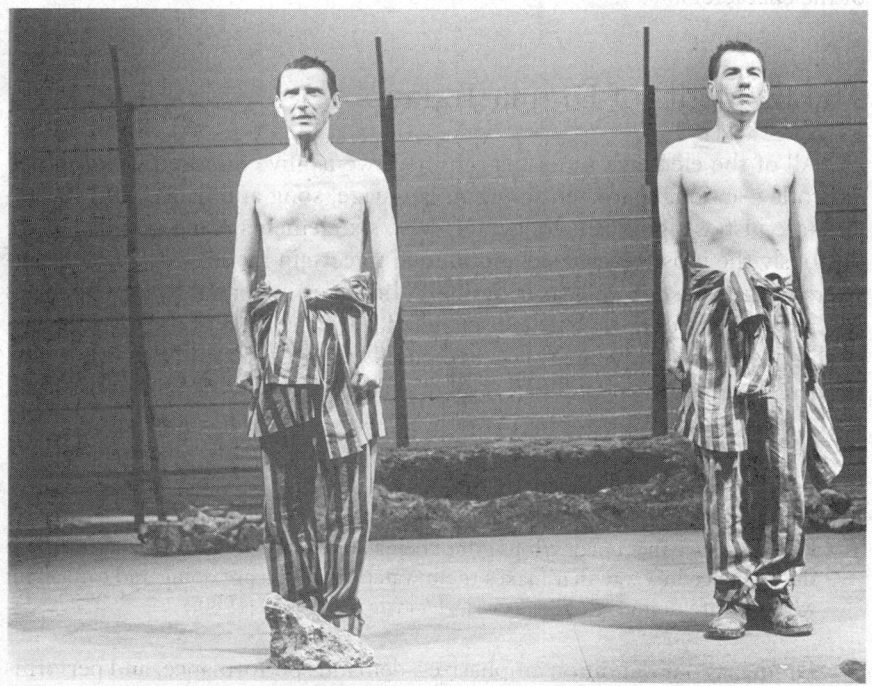

Bent, 1979. Author: Martin Sherman. Tom Bell (*left*) and Ian McKellen (*right*) in the play about homosexual love among the horrors of Hitler's concentration camps. (Photograph: John Haynes)

setting. Action, after all, has to occur somewhere; and dramatists create setting in a variety of ways, usually to relate essential pieces of information.

The description and design of the dramatic scene alone may clarify for
the audience the historical period being dramatized, the geographical location, the social class of the characters, the time of day, season of the year,
mood or atmosphere, dramatic emphasis, and so on. And it may not. The
writer or director may opt for a minimalist set that communicates very little
to the audience. The scene for Samuel Beckett's *Waiting for Godot* is a roadside
and a single tree; his play *Endgame* (1957) (see Chapter 48) takes place in a
sparsely decorated room at an unspecified time and in a nameless place. By
contrast, Cherríe Moraga's *Shadow of a Man* (1990) (see Chapter 49) is set in
a highly particularized locale: the Rodriguez family home located in Los Angeles. The time of the play is 1969, and the main sets for the play include the
family kitchen and the front porch. Although her directions mandate that
stage properties be "kept to a minimum, only what is essential to the action,"
she is in fact very specific about the garden that surrounds the porch, about
the Los Angeles sunset in the background, and about other features of the
home. Further, the exact location of such objects in the kitchen as the stove
and the all-important portable television set—the production's **proxemics**—
determines the possibilities for movement among the characters. Is the space
relatively open or tightly composed? So tightly composed as to seem claus-
trophobic? What does such a design tell us about the lives and daily routines
of the characters?

The Elements of Drama Today

All of the elements of drama outlined twenty-five hundred years ago by
Aristotle—action, character, thought, language, song and dance, and spectacle—are just as significant today. Of these six elements, song and dance are
obviously the most specialized and unique to certain kinds of drama. But answers to the question "What is drama?," however informed by new theories
and recent technologies, have not changed since the time of the Greek Classical Theater of fifth century B.C. Athens. Drama is still a fictive event performed by actors to an audience, and dramatic form still contains most or all
of the elements Aristotle recognized.

Script → **Actor** → Audience

You must have that unconscious gift of being able, while creating on stage, to grab
the audience in a way that makes them watch what you are doing and care about
what you are doing. (Robert Lewis, *Advice to the Players* [1980])

Drama, as our definition emphasizes, demands performance, and performance requires actors practicing their craft before audiences. As Robert Lewis,
innovative American director and acting teacher, envisions it, the "gift" of the
actor—a gift refined through diligent training and practice of the craft—

corresponds exactly with the primary goal of drama: to reach an audience, to delight it, and, occasionally, to teach it. On the page, drama is analogous to an architectural design for a new building: intriguing and beautiful, perhaps, but incomplete. Drama is meant to be seen and to be performed, not just to be read, and for this reason *Understanding Literature* features selections from drama reviews, photographs, and scenes from productions of the plays reprinted here.

Reading drama means visualizing the scene and actor, hearing the inflection of lines and sounds, and reaching conclusions about a host of questions. Some of these pertain directly to the narrative elements of the production already discussed: What does a character want? Why does he or she want it? What significance—psychological, social, or ideological—might be inferred from these desires? Does the character succeed or fail in this quest? How do we feel about this result and the factors that either prevented the character from reaching the goal or helped her attain it? To what extent does this fiction comment on the wider culture in which the playwright lived—and on our own?

Such questions relate to our need as readers not only to imagine the play as an event, but also to envision the actors speaking and moving. That is to say, the actor exudes meaning in every gesture, facial expression, inflection of voice, and movement; and, throughout the centuries, actors have endeavored to perfect these skills: to grab the audience, as Robert Lewis argues, to affect them emotionally. Successful performers achieve this in a myriad of ways, and audiences often carry with them to the theater vivid memories of productions they have seen. When just a child, Harold Bloom saw the great British actor Ralph Richardson play Falstaff; a half century later, the "reality" of Richardson's Falstaff was still much with him, as he recalls in his prefatory remarks to *Shakespeare: The Invention of the Human*. This is hardly surprising given the

Sarah Bernhardt in *Theodora*, 1884, Paris.

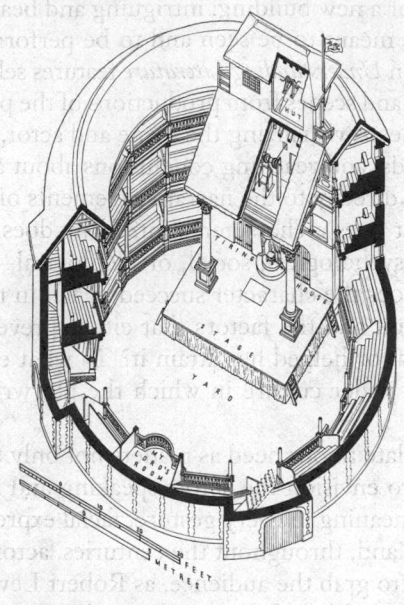

The Swan Theatre, c. 1594–1596: scale reconstruction

association of film and television actors with specific roles: Sean Connery, for many James Bond fans, *is* 007; Mike Myers *is* Austin Powers.

How an actor achieves this degree of emotional impact is another matter. Lewis ends his *Advice to the Players* with a passage from "Demands of the Actor in Ancient India" that blends physical attractiveness with more abstract virtues:

> Freshness, beauty, a pleasant broad face, red lips, beautiful teeth, a neck round as a bracelet, beautifully formed hands, graceful build, powerful hips, charm, grace, dignity, nobility, pride, not to speak of the quality of the talent.

Some theories of acting reveal more cerebral, even psychoanalytic approaches to the art of theatrical impersonation. In the first half of the twentieth century, the most influential theories were propounded by Constantin Stanislavsky in his work with the Moscow Art Theatre and in his influential book *The Actor Prepares.* When the Moscow Art Theatre made a tour of America in 1923, actors and directors stood up and took note. Stanislavsky's theory starts with the premise that plays contain a rich **sub-text,** a pattern woven from "magic ifs"—"given circumstances, all sorts of figments of the imagination, inner movements, objects of attention" and so on—to help the actor discover a character's motivation. The Stanislavsky method as refined by American prac-

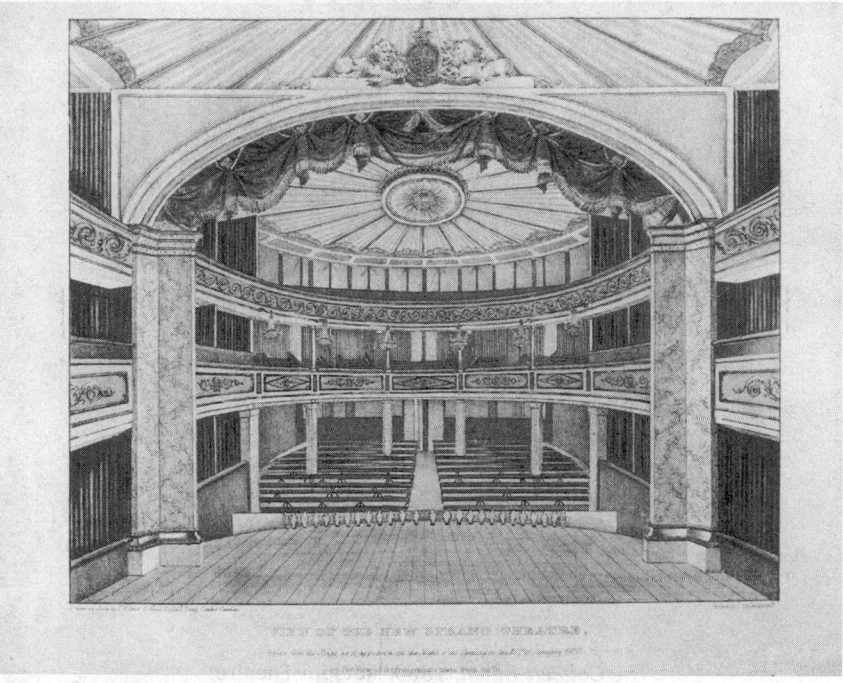

View of the new Strand Theatre taken from the stage as it appeared on the night of its opening on January 26, 1832. (Lithograph by J. W. Gear)

titioners demanded that actors' revisit their pasts, their own pain or happiness, to help "play" similar emotions in the characters they portray. Yet, like everything else in life and in the theater, actor training changes with the times. Many contemporary writers, David Mamet, for example, reject Stanislavsky's theories as "based on shame and guilt" and advocate totally different techniques in directing actors.

Other factors influence acting styles as well, the architecture of the theater, for instance. Gestures that might have proven effective at the Theatre of Dionysus in ancient Greece, an open air arena that seated up to fourteen thousand spectators, would differ from those employed in the public theaters of Shakespeare's times. Facial expression in the Theatre of Dionysus was conveyed by large masks that covered the actors' faces and communicated a sense of character to the large throng of playgoers that assembled there. The Swan Theatre, built in South London around 1596, accommodated some three thousand spectators and relied on an **open** stage with the audience sitting around it. Compare this kind of stage to that on which Henry Irving, the first British actor to be knighted in 1895, or the great American actor Edwin Booth, brother of John Wilkes Booth who assassinated President Lincoln, performed during the mid- to late 1800s. These **proscenium** stages were also known as "picture frame" stages, because the audience—separated from the stage by a heavy curtain—observed the action as if they were viewing a

I THE COLLEEN BAWN

Elly O'Connor: Save me. Don't kill me. Don't, Danny. I'll—do anything, only let
me live. *A shot rings out, and he falls from the rock* (Adelphi Theatre, 1860)

The Colleen Bawn, 1860, Adelphi Theatre.
"Elly O'Conner: Save me. Don't kill me. Don't
Danny. I'll—do anything, only let me live. *A
shot rings out, and he falls from the rock.*"

picture. To help create the effect, the border of the stage opening was often
painted in gold to resemble popular gilded frames, and audiences expected
lavish pictorial displays within them. After all, these audiences lived in a time
in which such technological advances outside the theater as photography,
plate glass windows, and illustrated newspapers were whetting the taste for
spectacle; successful theater managers catered to it.

What exactly does catering to popular taste mean? Something different in ancient Athens, Shakespeare's London, and today's Los Angeles. In
nineteenth-century New York and London, it meant staging dramas not unlike action films today that attract viewers not because of sensitive dialogue or
complex characterization, but because of visual effects and exciting action.
Victorian playwright Dion Boucicault, whose work drew large crowds in New
York, Dublin, and London throughout the latter half of the nineteenth century, was famous for plays called "melodramas" with spectacular scenes: burning steamboats, avalanches, and, a staple of many melodramas, drowning and
rescue scenes. Audiences flocked to theaters to see such effects and the plays
that featured them. Indeed, melodrama, with its stock characters of hero,
heroine, and villain, proved the perfect genre for visual sensation. Villains
could contrive horrible calamities for hapless heroines, and heroes could
overcome these obstacles to save them. In today's cinema, Bruce Willis,

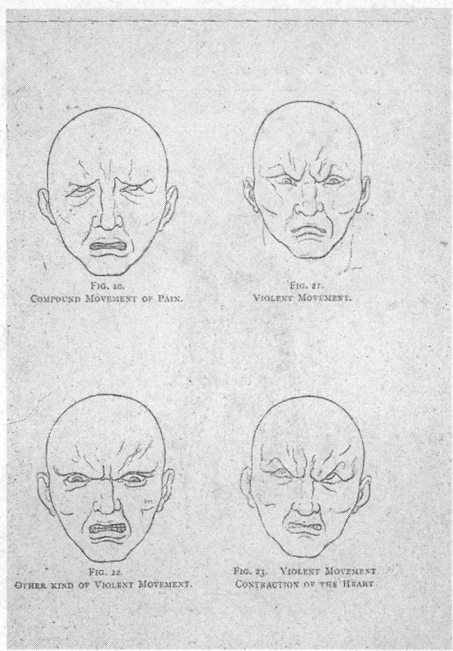

FIG. 20.
COMPOUND MOVEMENT OF PAIN.

FIG. 21.
VIOLENT MOVEMENT.

FIG. 22.
OTHER KIND OF VIOLENT MOVEMENT.

FIG. 23. VIOLENT MOVEMENT
CONTRACTION OF THE HEART.

Instructions in a nineteenth-century actors' training manual.

Sylvester Stallone, Wesley Snipes, and Arnold Schwartzenegger frequently play these kinds of heroes, battling armies of terrorists, cyborg terminators, and assorted other villains. The appeal of melodramas never seems to die, and neither does the audience's interest in having them become ever more visually spectacular and exciting.

Equally central to the success of such ventures was the acting. Given the relatively large size of the most popular theaters—Booth's held more than fifteen hundred people and Irving's about one thousand—actors throughout most of the nineteenth century were trained to make exaggerated gestures. Arms extended with heads turned away could indicate horror; an actress looking straight at the audience with her arms outstretched could convey attraction or mysterious contemplation. Acting manuals like Gustav Garcia's *The Actor's Art* (1882) provided instructions on such matters, matching poses and gestures with emotions. One illustration, for example, indicated how an actor playing Macbeth might respond to the sudden appearance of Banquo's ghost. Françoise Delsarte's *System of Expression* (1894) even provided instruction on how actors might deploy their eyebrows and hands to best effect, illustrating a range of possible emotions communicated by both.

As nineteenth-century melodrama and excess became rivaled by an emergent modern drama—plays by Henrik Ibsen, Bernard Shaw, and others—not only did the subjects and forms of plays change, but theatrical space and acting style changed with them. Ibsen's realistic plays, largely concerned with

74   THE ACTORS' ART.

FIG. 44.

" Hence, horrible shadow! unreal mockery, hence!"

From a nineteenth-century training manual
for actors: *Playing Macbeth.*

middle-class Norwegians and their familial complications, generally took place in well-appointed drawing rooms furnished to resemble their counterparts in real life. The central characters in *Hedda Gabler* (1890), for example, however much they at times resembled their predecessors in melodrama, lived in more mundane worlds absent the pyrotechnics and other excesses of popular melodrama. Acting styles became more subdued as well, with the emphasis on restraint, not wild gesticulation.

Inevitably, the restrained acting styles and meticulously decorated sets of Ibsen's realism also gave way to new ideas, some of which looked back to the Elizabethan open stage. Visionary designers like Gordon Craig who, as the son of Irving's leading actress Ellen Terry, grew up in the theater, eventually repudiated the heavy scenery of the Victorian stage in favor of an entirely different aesthetic. Craig painted with light and two or three primary colors, replacing cumbersome stage furnishings and structures with abstraction and geometric shapes. Such a radical aesthetic, labeled the **New Stagecraft** by critics, appealed not only to Stanislavsky, but also to Irish poet William Butler Yeats. In fact, Yeats carried a model Craig had built for him when lecturing about the Irish Literary Theatre, which, in 1904, became the Abbey Theatre in Dublin, where it still stands today.

The Abbey Theatre, like many theaters today, is a far more intimate space than Irving's Lyceum or Shakespeare's Globe. And, the contemporary theater, architecturally speaking, affords far more flexibility for playwrights and actors

Models for *Hamlet,* 1909. Act I, Scene 1

than Shaw or Irving enjoyed. Britain's National Theatre, opened by Queen Elizabeth II in 1976, for example, houses three theatres within it: the Olivier, named after Lord Laurence Olivier, which features an open stage and seats 1160; the Lyttleton, which has an adjustable proscenium stage, and seats 890; and the Cottesloe, an adaptable rectangular space that seats up to 400. This last space, often referred to as a **black box,** is a key part of many theater complexes and, quite obviously, exercises a major effect on acting style and scenic decoration. The Actors Theatre of Louisville's Victor Jory Theatre, for instance, seats less than half of what the Cottesloe does, fewer than 200. Imagine how different a staging of *Oedipus Rex* would look in these venues as opposed to its original production in an amphitheatre that seated thousands. How might *Hamlet* be staged differently in a black box as opposed to a proscenium or open stage? How would acting techniques be modified for these spaces?

Reading drama, therefore, means imagining performance, imagining the words and scenes from the page to a playing space, compete with sight, sounds, and actors whose voice and bodies contribute to the drama's meaning and our response. It means, finally, imagining yourself as part of an audience.

Script → Actor → **Audience**

Instead of sharing an experience the spectator must come to grips with things. (Bertolt Brecht, *The Epic Theatre and Its Difficulties* [1927])

Over the last thirty years [since the 1960s] many theatres have emerged which speak for dominated and generally marginalized peoples. . . . Many of these emergent theatres have self-consciously sought the centrality of the spectators as subject of the drama, but as a subject who can think and act. (Susan Bennett, *Theatre Audiences* [1990])

These quotations, especially the latter passage taken from Susan Bennett's study of the ways in which we "read" theatrical performance, reveal a range of understandings of the audience, the receiver and decoder, as it were, of communication in the theater. In *Poetics*, Aristotle contemplated the way an audience responds to tragedy, and many translators of Aristotle emphasize that "catharsis"—the spectator's expurgation of pity and fear—contains a significant aspect of intellectual advancement. By seeing a well-wrought tragedy, the viewer learns what is truly pitiable and fearful. But for the last century or so, students of theatrical audiences like the German playwright and theoretician Bertolt Brecht have seemed more concerned not about an audience's feeling, but about its thinking and the ways in which dramatists might heighten an audience's political responses. And Bennett is right that during the last half of the twentieth century, marginalized groups have employed drama as a call to political action and cultural transformation.

This is especially true of recent American drama. In the mid 1960s, the Black Arts movement on the East coast attempted to forge a uniquely African American aesthetic, while in northern California activist Luis Valdez founded El Teatro Campesino (The Farm Workers' Theater) in 1965. Performing short plays on flatbed trucks, Valdez took his plays right into the fields, attempting to raise the political awareness of Chicano workers, while also supporting the organizing efforts of the United Farm Workers' Union. In the 1980s and 1990s, feminist playwrights and performance artists like Karen Finley and Holly Hughes have questioned the essential voyeurism of the theater, challenging audiences to reexamine traditional notions of the feminine and the female body as the object (and captive) of a male spectator.

Unquestionably, such political projects construct an implied audience within their dramatic texts. Split Britches, a New York-based feminist-lesbian company, assumes a largely lesbian audience for its work. Chicana playwright Cherríe Moraga explains that often her work addresses a Chicano audience and the "heterosexual male" who dominates traditional Latino households; at other times, at other moments in her plays, she is explicitly addressing white feminists. Indeed, playwrights seem always to envision or imagine an audience for their plays, and this is particularly true of the kind of "emergent theaters" to which Susan Bennett alludes.

In the earlier, highly influential theory of Bertolt Brecht, written mostly in the 1920s and 1930s, these imagined audiences in turn affect the dramatic action and writing strategies political playwrights use to further their ends. Because Brecht was interested in the raising of political consciousness, of placing the audience in a more analytical position relative to the action on stage, his plays, much like Luis Valdez's earlier work and David Henry Hwang's *M. Butterfly* (1988) (see Chapter 50), endeavor to detach or **alienate** the audience emotionally from characters' predicaments. But how is this achieved? For Brecht, by "not propelling the spectator along a single track" or story; by training actors *not* to play "to the audience's heart"; by building characters whose thought is determined more by "social being" than psychology. As a consequence, the Brechtian plot is often interrupted so audiences cannot get too involved emotionally. Through his use of various devices—songs and projections, for instance—Brecht insures that the audience is aware of what actions will occur next. This way, it is less concerned with the shape of the plot and more attuned to the sociopolitical critique the action suggests.

The term *audience*, then, is not quite so simple as it seems. A great number of audiences exist: implied audiences, informed audiences, alienated audiences, marginalized audiences, and just plain fans. At times, an individual may be a part of several of these, making her responses complicated, even paradoxical or contradictory. How an audience receives stage action emotionally and intellectually is thus a matter of serious thought and, occasionally, critical disagreement. But there is no disagreement with one fact: An audience is as necessary to the theater event as plays and actors. Without audiences, there is no theater.

Coda: Reading Drama, Imagining Theater

What is drama? As this chapter attempts to demonstrate, drama is both a literary and performative text. Reading drama, therefore, is an imaginative act, one that envisions performance and, in fact, requires it. Playwrights have always known this, even if in some instances they provide little indication of how staged action is to sound or appear. For, after all, if Prospero is right in Shakespeare's *The Tempest* when he says that he and the other characters "are such stuff / As dreams are made on" (4.1.156–157), then drama is made in the imagination of the playwright, the actor, and the audience.

42   Drama on the Stage

Chapter 41 uses Terrence McNally's dramatic sketch *André's Mother* (1988) to discuss the narrative elements of drama, particularly plot or action, character, and language and thought. This chapter, by contrast, concerns itself with **mise-en-scène,** the visual and aural elements of drama as realized in theatrical production. To assist in this discussion, we examine the last scene of Arthur Miller's landmark play, *Death of a Salesman* (1949).

At the end of *Death of a Salesman,* the one thing Willy Loman's loving wife Linda and sons Biff and Happy fear the most occurs: Willy crashes his car and kills himself. And although Linda, Biff, Happy, and Willy's friend Charley have good reason to suspect the cause of the fatal wreck, we know that his death was no accident. Moments before roaring away from his house, Willy asks his brother Ben, with whom he has conducted several imaginary conversations, "Can you imagine that magnificence with twenty thousand dollars in his pocket"? That "magnificence" is Willy's shiftless son Biff, and the sum twenty thousand dollars coincides exactly with the value of Willy's life insurance policy. With this money "behind him," Willy believes, Biff will finally make a success of himself. While Linda waits fearfully for her husband and calls his name, Miller's stage directions confirm that he will not be returning: "*There is the sound of a car starting and moving away at full speed.*" Biff and Linda both shout out, but it is too late. Willy is gone. Miller's stage directions communicate the news: "*As the car speeds off, the music crashes down in a frenzy of sound, which becomes the soft pulsation of a single cello string.*" All that remains for his family and friend is to mourn his death, remember Willy Loman, and try to understand why this happened. All that remains is the Requiem, staged at the cemetery over Willy's grave. **CD-ROM**

This is the inevitable destination, it seems, for Miller's protagonist, an exhausted man in the twilight of his career no longer able, as his young employer had reminded him earlier, to do his job: "[I]t's a business, kid, and everybody's gotta pull his own weight." Willy cannot. Perhaps he never could. In this regard, as so many critics have emphasized since its New York premiere on February 10, 1949, *Death of a Salesman* concerns much more than the fate of one man. For some, it constitutes a sharp indictment of the ethos of American business, maybe even of capitalism itself. The influential Marxist scholar Raymond Williams regarded Willy as both a victim and a "conformist, the type of the society itself," who has gone from selling things to selling himself, becoming in effect "a commodity which like other commodities will at a certain point be discarded." Critic Stephen Barker regards Willy as too fervently devoted to America's false "religion of success." "I met a salesman

[Dave Singleman] in the Parker House," Willy recalls. "I realized that selling was the greatest career a man could want." And after Singleman died, wearing his green velvet slippers in the smoking car of the train businessmen used, "hundreds of salesmen and buyers" attended the funeral. There was "respect," Willy emphasizes, "and comradeship and gratitude in it." There was, in short, a professional community in which one could find not only his proper place, but also his dignity as a man.

As *Salesman* opens, however, Willy has neither been embraced by this professional community nor received its respect. Quite to the contrary. But does this fact, as those readings that underscore Miller's dismantling of the American Dream, suggest that Willy is a victim of a system in which he can neither prosper nor survive? In his own commentary on the play, Miller argues for Willy's stature as a tragic hero, not as a victim. In "The Nature of Tragedy," an essay published six weeks after *Salesman* opened in New York, Miller insisted that audiences must "discriminate between the tragic and the pathetic." And so must we, which makes the play's closing scene even more important.

The Requiem at the end of *Death of a Salesman* takes scarcely four minutes to perform. In the celebrated 1985 film adaptation starring Dustin Hoffman and John Malkovich, in which the Requiem runs about four and a half minutes, this crucial closing scene offers in concentrated form all the subtlety and paradox of the entire drama. It does so not only because of Miller's development of plot and character, but also because of his thoughtful use of the visual and aural potential of theatrical production. This skill is hardly surprising, given Miller's close collaboration with the play's first director Elia Kazan and its stage designer Jo Mielziner. As he records in his autobiography *Timebends* (1987), Miller attended rehearsals of the play in 1948, revising dialogue in reaction to actors' rendering of the lines and sharpening his vision of the material and psychological worlds Willy inhabited. So, for example, when Lee J. Cobb, who played Willy in the 1949 production, "bawled" to his wife Linda, "There's more people now. . . . There's more people!" and gestured "toward the empty upstage," a "block of apartment houses" began to "spring up in [Miller's] brain." The result was Mielziner's creation of a "romantic and dreamlike" environment that, at the same time, suggested the urban crowding of lower middle class. This environment had to convey both Willy's idealizations of a more rural past and the harsh urban realities of the present. It had to look, sound—Miller even says smell—like a modern city grown overcrowded and unlivable.

These are the contradictory and complicated realities of Willy's life, one that leads finally to the Requiem reprinted below. When reading it, pay attention not only to what is said, but how it looks.

- How do characters deliver their lines? How would you describe their tone?
- How do they appear and move? Does their appearances match the tone and subjects of their conversations?
- How is the scene described? What does it look like in terms of color, lighting, and stage image? What does it sound like?

- Which elements of the scene convey the paradoxes and complications of Willy's life? What effect does the scenic background produce?

Taken from the French, *mise-en-scène* means literally "put into the scene." Everything on stage that an audience sees and hears—set, properties, costume, makeup, lighting, music, even an actor's gestures and movements—is part of a production's mise-en-scène. And each of these elements retains significance in Miller's poignant closing scene.

The Text CD-ROM

(As the car speeds off, the music crashes down in a frenzy of sound, which becomes the soft pulsation of a single cello string. Biff slowly returns to his bedroom. He and Happy gravely don their jackets. Linda slowly walks out of her room. The music has developed into a dead march. The leaves of the day are appearing over everything. Charley and Bernard, somberly dressed, appear and knock on the kitchen door. Biff and Happy slowly descend the stairs to the kitchen as Charley and Bernard enter. All stop a moment when Linda, in clothes of mourning, bearing a little bunch of roses, comes through the draped doorway into the kitchen. She goes to Charley and takes his arm. Now all move toward the audience, through the wall-line of the kitchen. At the limit of the apron, Linda lays down the flowers, kneels, and sits back on her heels. All stare down at the grave.)

REQUIEM

Charley: It's getting dark, Linda.

> *(Linda doesn't react. She stares at the grave.)*

Biff: How about it, Mom? Better get some rest, heh? They'll be closing the gate soon.

> *(Linda makes no move. Pause.)*

Happy (*deeply angered*): He had no right to do that. There was no necessity for it. We would've helped him.

Charley (*grunting*): Hmmm.

Biff: Come along, Mom.

Linda: Why didn't anybody come?

Charley: It was a very nice funeral.

Linda: But where are all the people he knew? Maybe they blame him.

Charley: Naa. It's a rough world, Linda. They wouldn't blame him.

Linda: I can't understand it. At this time especially. First time in thirty-five years we were just about free and clear. He only needed a little salary. He was even finished with the dentist.

Charley: No man only needs a little salary.

Linda: I can't understand it.

Biff: There were a lot of nice days. When he'd come home from a trip; or on Sundays, making the stoop; finishing the cellar; putting on the new porch; when he built the extra bathroom; and put up the garage. You know something, Charley; there's more of him in that front stoop than in all the sales he ever made.

Charley: Yeah. He was a happy man with a batch of cement.

Linda: He was so wonderful with his hands.

Biff: He had the wrong dreams. All, all, wrong.

Happy (almost ready to fight Biff): Don't say that!

Biff: He never knew who he was.

Charley (stopping Happy's movement and reply. To Biff): Nobody dast blame this man. You don't understand: Willy was a salesman. And for a salesman, there is no rock bottom to the life. He don't put a bolt to a nut, he don't tell you the law or give you medicine. He's a man way out there in the blue, riding on a smile and a shoeshine. And when they start not smiling back—that's an earthquake. And then you get yourself a couple of spots on your hat, and you're finished. Nobody dast blame this man. A salesman is got to dream, boy. It comes with the territory.

Biff: Charley, the man didn't know who he was.

Happy (infuriated): Don't say that!

Biff: Why don't you come with me, Happy?

Happy: I'm not licked that easily. I'm staying right in this city, and I'm gonna beat this racket! *(He looks at Biff, his chin set.)* The Loman Brothers!

Biff: I know who I am, kid.

Happy: All right, boy. I'm gonna show you and everybody else that Willy Loman did not die in vain. He had a good dream. It's the only dream you can have—to come out number-one man. He fought it out here, and this is where I'm gonna win it for him.

Biff (with a hopeless glance at Happy, bends toward his mother): Let's go, Mom.

Linda: I'll be with you in a minute. Go on, Charley. *(He hesitates.)* I want to, just for a minute. I never had a chance to say good-by.

(Charley moves away, followed by Happy. Biff remains a slight distance up and left of Linda. She sits there, summoning herself. The flute begins, not far away, playing behind her speech.)

Linda: Forgive me, dear, I can't cry. I don't know what it is, but I can't cry. I don't understand it. Why did you ever do that? Help me, Willy, I can't cry. It seems to me that you're just on another trip. I keep expecting you. Willy, dear, I can't cry. Why did you do it? I search and search and I search, and I can't understand it, Willy. I made the last payment on the house today. Today, dear. And there'll be nobody home. *(A sob rises in her throat.)* We're free and clear. *(Sobbing more fully, released.)* We're free. *(Biff comes slowly toward her.)* We're free . . . We're free . . .

Biff lifts her to her feet and moves out up right with her in his arms. Linda sobs quietly. Bernard and Charley come together and follow them, followed by

Happy. Only the music of the flute is left on the darkening stage as over the house the hard towers of the apartment buildings rise into sharp focus, and

THE CURTAIN FALLS

As the previous chapter discusses, the central elements of dramatic form—action, characterization, and language, especially dialogue—communicate much of the complexity of this final scene. These all contribute to both the play's *story* and *plot*, terms that need to be differentiated, particularly as they pertain to the fictive time of a drama. While **story** refers to a series of events occurring in time, **plot** denotes the arrangement of these events in an order that may not necessarily follow the sequence in which they occurred. In fact, dramatists since the time of Sophocles' *Oedipus Rex* have understood that the most effective plots often begin in the middle of the story (**in medias res**); and screenwriters often employ a similar strategy. Think, for example, of the first *Star Wars* trilogy, which begins with the fourth of nine episodes, or of the innumerable detective films that begin after most of the action has occurred with the detective relating a story to the audience of what mysteries he has recently unraveled.

Time is also one of the most complicated aspects of the plot of *Death of a Salesman* because so much of the action occurs in Willy's memory. (Miller had once considered entitling the play "The Inside of his Head.") But time concerns more than plot in Miller's drama. In fact, the play's first producer warned designer Jo Mielziner beforehand that this would be a "toughie" to mount, and it was, precisely because of the element of time in the plot. "It was not only that there were so many different scenic locations," Mielziner explains, "but that the action demanded instantaneous time changes from the present to the past and back again. Actors playing a contemporaneous scene suddenly went back fifteen years in exactly the same setting—the Salesman's house." The Loman home and its surroundings thus dominated Mielziner's attention. One statement Miller made about the house struck Mielziner with particular force: "It had once been surrounded by open country, but it was now hemmed in with apartment houses. Trees that used to shade the house against the open sky and hot summer sun now were for the most part dead or dying." Not surprisingly, even though the Requiem is staged at the cemetery, Miller's description of the Lomans' changed neighborhood—and Mielziner's method of staging the urban landscape it represents—resurfaces in important ways in the play's concluding scene.

What We See and Hear in the Theater: Elements of Mise-en-Scène

Drama in theatrical production involves both visual and aural phenomena: setting, costumes, properties, lighting, sounds and the actors' movements, gestures, and intonations. Obviously of great importance when plays are staged, such elements retain their significance when a play is read, for in reading plays we actively imagine how a scene might look and sound in the theater. The word *theater*, as drama critic W. B. Worthen reminds us, comes from the Greek word *theatron*, or "seeing place"; and the play in performance becomes a theatre event, even if the performance occurs only in our imagination. This is precisely why when we are given the benefit of carefully delineated stage directions, as we are in *Death of a Salesman*, we must use them to "see" the play in our minds and hear the inflection of particularly meaningful lines, yet also be open to the possibility of their being delivered in a different way. Everything we see and hear becomes a part of this event, every color, shadow, whisper, or movement.

So, too, do acting styles and the physical presence of the actors, even their bodies. How they look, how they move, how they speak and react to other characters' lines are often crucial to our understanding of a scene. As many drama critics wondered aloud when assessing the successful revival of *Salesman* in 1999, opening fifty years to the day in New York after the play's premiere, how does our response to Willy change depending on the actor who assumes the part? Raising this question while reviewing the 1999 *Salesman*'s run in Chicago before its opening on February 10 at New York's Eugene O'Neill Theatre, *New York Times*' reviewer Ben Brantley compared this production starring Brian Dennehy to its predecessor featuring Dustin Hoffman fifteen years earlier:

> Those whose last exposure to Willy came with Dustin Hoffman's memorable scrappy bantamweight of 1984 will be shocked at first by the presence of Mr. Dennehy, a man of truly monumental proportions. . . .

In Brantley's view, Robert Falls, the play's director, productively exploits Dennehy's "imposing frame," contrasting the actor's obvious potential for physical strength with Willy's "sad, scared" gestures and pronounced inability ever to wield such power.

As Brantley's commentary suggests, understanding the final moments of *Death of a Salesman* also depends a great deal on what occurs earlier. After all, because the Requiem brings a complex view of an American family to conclusion, we might assume that it is not only crucial to our understanding of the effect of Willy's death on his family, but that visual motifs employed earlier will also reappear. And they do. To begin, Miller communicates the seriousness of the Requiem through the stage directions that form the transition between it and the play. After the frenzied music signaling Willy's crash has subsided, Biff and Happy "gravely" put on their suit jackets; Linda walks slowly away to don "clothes of mourning"; and the music develops into a somber "dead march." The Lomans are joined by Bernard and Charley, and the entire cast moves toward the audience to the stage's "apron." There, Linda places a small bouquet of roses and kneels, as if over a grave. All of them cast their eyes downward. Although the 1985 film adaptation stages this entirely differently, Charley's opening line confirms both the time of day and the lighting of the scene: "It's getting dark, Linda." Biff's suggestion that they should go indicates that we are witnessing not the beginning of Willy's funeral but the end. Further, we understand through subsequent dialogue that while the ceremony was "very nice," the funeral was sparsely attended. Linda wonders, "But where were all the people he knew?" The sad answer is clear: They were somewhere else. His passing did not merit their attention.

Linda's lines prompt yet another question, the one we want answered: Why? Why did Willy do this? Her closing speech in particular reveals not only her pain, but her sense of the irony of Willy's act. Why now? Why kill yourself when the house is finally paid off, when the major financial obligation in their lives is satisfied? Her last refrain, "We're free and clear. We're free . . . We're free . . . ," signals both this irony and one final, regrettable fact: Willy in fact *is* free at last of the burdens of paying bills and suffering the professional humiliations he has endured. Like many characters in the social dramas of one writer Miller particularly admires—those of Norwegian playwright Henrik Ibsen—Willy Loman may be viewed as achieving a paradoxical victory through death. He has finally escaped the urban landscape that entraps him and that, in Miller's final stage direction, rises to reassert its domination: "*Only the music of the flute is left on the darkening stage as over the house the hard towers of the apartment buildings rise into sharp focus.*" The play began with precisely these elements of the mise-en-scène:

> *A melody is heard, played upon a flute. It is small and fine, telling of grass and trees and the horizon. The curtain rises.*
>
> *Before us is the Salesman's house. We are aware of towering, angular shapes behind it, surrounding it on all sides.*

Taken together, these two **motifs**—one aural, one visual—represent the internal conflict Willy suffers throughout the play, the same conflict that nearly leads Biff and Happy to blows at his grave. The flute recalls Willy's father who took his family across the American prairie and onto "the open roads" of South Dakota; the towering buildings represent the urban sprawl that has stifled natural beauty and the freedom Willy once enjoyed.

This opposition is reflected here and earlier in the play by yet another visual trope in the play: the falling of leaves. Before the Requiem begins and while the Loman family dresses for the funeral, Miller's stage directions indicate that "*the leaves of day are appearing over everything.*" These same leaves appear for the first time much earlier when Willy's thoughts wander fifteen years into the past and the dramatic action shifts to the time of Biff's high school days: "*The apartment houses are fading out, and the entire house and surroundings become covered with leaves.*" Moments later, the boys appear as they did then: Happy eager to wash his father's car; Biff, the embodiment of a high school sports star with a letterman's sweater and a football.

The leaves constitute a visual cue to the audience that Willie has slipped into the past. But more than that, they also evoke a sense of sadness and of the passing of a simpler, more natural time. Mielziner was particularly emphatic about the leaves falling during the Requiem, providing a poetic replacement for the gravestone he had once contemplated using:

> The whole scene was bathed in a magic-lantern projection of autumn leaves. Here, again, leaves were symbolic. With this kind of lighting, I thought I could

completely obliterate the house in the background and evoke a sense of sadness and finality that might enable us to eliminate the gravestone itself.

The motif of colored leaves is thus the product of a kind of theatrical trick, of the combination of lighting and projectors, all of which serve to change the mood of the scene. This change becomes more evident after comparing Mielziner's drawings of the opening set and the leaf projection, for not only are the myriad lights of the surrounding apartment buildings eclipsed by the falling leaves, but the entire color scheme of the stage changes from the darker brown and black hues of the urban present to the green and golden brilliance of the past. Autumnal leaves, however close to winter and the death they symbolize, are still more beautiful than gray concrete or city asphalt.

The Requiem: Two Different Productions

Such contrasts in color—and in the tone and mood that result—distinguish the two celebrated American productions of *Death of a Salesman* discussed earlier: the Dustin Hoffman production in 1984 (adapted for film a year later) and the Brian Dennehy production of 1999 directed by Robert Falls. For the Requiem of the film version of Hoffman's *Salesman*, widely available on videotape, director Volker Schlondorff and screenwriter Michael Rudman borrow the "leaves" motif Mielziner and Miller developed to create a dramatic environment quite different from the one Miller outlines in his stage directions. Or, rather, the 1985 film emphasizes the possibility of a kind of optimism or paradoxical victory in death that Miller discusses in "Tragedy and the Common Man" when elevating Willy to the status of tragic hero.

Brightness overcomes despair, the leaves overwhelm the towering skyline in this Requiem, an emphasis that begins moments before the car crash. Instead of "uttering a gasp of fear" and rushing around crying "Shh!" at voices that seem to be "swarming" around him, as Miller's stage directions prescribe, Hoffman's Willy smiles broadly, waving the voices away and then blowing a kiss in Linda's direction. He is almost exuberant at his contrivance, running out the door, the window of which fades into a blinding white, not black, as the music cues the car crash. And it is this whiteness that fades into a late afternoon gold as the Requiem begins. Linda stands throughout, positioned squarely in front of a tree draped in orange and yellow foliage, gloriously backlit by the autumn sun. There is no animosity between Biff and Happy, no sign of anger or readiness to fight on Happy's part, only a calm confidence. Linda's closing speech is pared considerably, eliminating her repetitive—and perhaps inaccurate—claim of inability to cry and concentrating instead on Willy and their newfound freedom. Most important, no "hard towers" of apartment buildings rise "into sharp focus"; instead, the New York skyline is visible far off in the distance, but it is minuscule compared to the glorious trees and their dazzling leaves.

By stark contrast, the 1999 *Salesman* struck many reviewers as intensely dark, a darkness that not only terrifies Willy but renders the entire Loman family as more fragile and lonely. Writing in *The New York Times*, Ben Brantley praised the production's evocation of a "sense of engulfing night," as figures seemed illuminated only by "wan pools of light." For Brantley, seeing the production first in Chicago and later in New York, the darkness is "always threatening to consume, the tidal pull of depression itself." There is in this production, then, precious little relief from the "almost operatic emotional sweep" of this family tragedy, with a "desperate, mortally wounded father at its center."

Certainly, *Death of a Salesman*—and this final scene—contains these very emotional gears, these same opposing tendencies: exuberance and despair, brilliant leaves and overwhelming darkness, freedom and death. Interestingly, both the 1985 film and 1999 production began in similar ways: with the blazing headlights of a car heading straight for the audience. Yet, from this common starting point and in the face of these oppositions inherent in Miller's play, these two productions finally developed very different readings of Willy Loman, his family, and the American Dream they sought. Such readings begin with the elements of dramatic form discussed in the preceding chapter and the theatrical environment or mise-en-scène outlined here. Without considering both, without imagining the theater event as an eternal present with all its sights and sounds, rich and alive, we will miss much of the depth and emotional experience of Arthur Miller's master work, *Death of a Salesman*.

43 Kinds of Drama: Tragedy

> *[W]e must remember the enormous power of tragedy, exciting, purifying, and releasing the entire life of a people . . . ; it presents itself as the essence of all the . . . healing forces, as the mediator arbitrating between the strongest and most inherently fateful characteristics of a people.*
>
> —FRIEDRICH NIETZSCHE, THE BIRTH OF TRAGEDY *(1871)*

No commentator has ever spoken of tragedy with the passion that German philosopher Friedrich Nietzsche exhibits in his book *The Birth of Tragedy* (1871), dedicated to the great composer Richard Wagner. In his study, Nietzsche returns again and again to the grandeur of tragic drama, to its sublime combination of horror and joy, and finally to its resemblance to classical music and opera. "Tragedy," Nietzsche writes, "absorbs into itself the highest musical ecstasy so that it absolutely brings music to perfection among the Greeks, as among ourselves." In his Foreword, Nietzsche exclaims that "art is the highest task and the proper metaphysical activity of this life." It is fitting that tragedy would serve him so well as an example of this highest calling, as the zenith of the art of drama.

More recent commentators on tragedy echo Nietzsche's praise. Many also agree with Francis Fergusson, who underscores the importance of Sophocles' play *Oedipus Rex* to the evolution of tragic drama:

> There can be little doubt that *Oedipus Rex* is a crucial instance of drama, if not *the* play which best exemplifies this art in its essential nature and its completeness.

This claim, made over fifty years ago, is as accurate today as when Fergusson first made it. If anything, it may be too modest. For Sophocles' drama, based on a myth well known to his audience, has served not only to illuminate the nature of drama, especially tragedy, but also to motivate landmark intellectual work in numerous other disciplines. A roster of the thinkers influenced by *Oedipus Rex* reads like a who's who of Western thought and includes psychoanalyst Sigmund Freud, who regarded the play as depicting a universal truth about desire, the so-called Oedipus complex. Sophocles and Oedipus were so central to psychoanalytic theory that Freud and his students wore medals around their necks with likenesses of the playwright on one side, his tragic king on the other. For some anthropologists, *Oedipus Rex* reenacts the **ritual** of punishing a scapegoat; more specifically, it repeats a seasonal ritual of slaying a monarch so that a period of growth and fertility can begin. A myriad of other explanations, or readings, of Sophocles' play exist, some of which will be outlined at the end of this chapter.

The reading of *Oedipus Rex* most pertinent to students of drama, however, is that of the Greek philosopher Aristotle, who in his treatise *Poetics* (335 B.C.) formulates a definition of tragedy indebted to Sophocles' play. Before beginning with Aristotle's definition of the tragic form, we should examine the circumstances in which *Oedipus Rex* was first produced. Because plays are written to be performed, the theaters in which they are produced—and the conventions of theatrical production prevailing at the time—exert a considerable impact on how a playwright develops the play. Sophocles is no exception to this historical rule.

Athenian Drama and the Theater of Dionysus

In ancient Greece, plays like *Oedipus Rex* formed part of a religious festival held every spring in honor of Dionysus, the god of wine and, by extension, of life and revelry. By the sixth century B.C., a competition was held in which playwrights submitted a trilogy of works developing a consistent story, and a short comedy called a **satyr** typically was performed at the end of the three-day production. These facts are significant for at least two reasons. First, they suggest the longstanding relationship between drama and religion. Until the establishment of public theaters in Shakespeare's London, drama was performed almost exclusively in connection with religious observances or holy days. Shakespeare's plays, for example, were preceded in medieval England by **morality plays** and **mystery plays,** the latter of which were based on episodes of the Bible and traveled through the streets to be performed on wagons. Brief plays were also given in churches to celebrate Easter and Corpus Christi, and of course nativity pageants at Christmastime are still popular today. Second, the principal plays associated with the Dionysian festival are tragedies, with comedy—the satyr—a distant second in terms of its perceived importance.

Trilogies written for the Athenian stage concern powerful figures, familial tensions, and often violent events. Some, like Aeschylus's trilogy *The Oresteia* (458 B.C.), are based on events of the Trojan War. Other trilogies, like the one in which Euripides' play *Medea* appears, are taken from well-known mythologies, as are Sophocles' plays. Sophocles, however, is credited for breaking the tradition of submitting three plays at the same time. In fact, his "Theban Plays"—*Oedipus Rex, Oedipus at Colonus,* and *Antigone*—were not submitted as a trilogy, even though they trace Oedipus's fate through the first two plays and that of his children in the third. *Antigone* was produced first, probably in 441 B.C.; *Oedipus Rex* was staged some eleven to fifteen years later; and *Oedipus at Colonus* was produced in 404 B.C., the year after Sophocles' death. It is perhaps for this reason that *Oedipus Rex* and *Antigone* have enjoyed considerable success over the centuries as separate dramas.

Performed at the Theater of Dionysus in an amphitheatre that could accommodate fourteen thousand spectators, Greek drama was played on a stage in front of a building front or **skênê,** from which the modern word *scene* is taken. This building and its facade functioned not only as the setting, but also provided a space where actors might change costumes when necessary. The skênê also housed primitive machines, which could be used when the play demanded the sudden appearance of a god or goddess; hence, the phrase **deus ex machina** ("god from the machine") was coined to describe the last-minute appearances of a god to save a play's central characters from disaster. Unfortunately for Oedipus, no such deity intervenes to save him from his terrible fate.

All roles on the Greek stage were played by men, with the central characters wearing masks and high boots (**cothurni**) so they could be seen by the crowds that viewed them. (Today, at large concert venues, this problem is handled by Jumbotron television screens.) Equally important, the wearing of masks indicates how little facial expressions meant to play production techniques or actor training, as the size of the theater influenced costuming and acting style. Prior to Sophocles' innovation of adding a third character, Greek plays featured the dialogue of only two characters in a scene: the **protagonist,** or central character, and **antagonist,** a character who in some way blocks the desire or aim of the central character. True to the subject matter of the drama and the sociopolitical importance of the central characters of these plays, almost all the dialogue and action in Greek drama take place in public, in front of the houses of the families involved or at a specific location in the city in which the play occurs. Compare this convention to the partly public, partly private nature of Shakespearean tragedy—after all, we gain access to the most intimate of rooms in *Hamlet* and *Othello*—and the often entirely private setting of modern drama. Or, ask yourself this question: in how many films or television dramas does *all* the action take place in public?

Other factors account for some of the formal elements of Greek tragedy. The architecture of the theater, for example, often helps explain a character's actions or a writer's stage directions. Plays at the Theater of Dionysus were performed to a semicircle of spectators seated in the amphitheatre with a rounded open space called an **orchestra** separating the stage from the audience. Here, the Chorus in plays like *Oedipus Rex* chanted and performed their dance movements during the choral breaks in the play's action. A **strophe** is the first of three parts of an ode sung by the Chorus while moving in a choreographed pattern from right to left; during the **antistrophe,** the second part of a choral ode, the Chorus moves from left to right, back to its starting position. An altar located in the middle of the orchestra indicates that religious observances were central to the entire event and, in some instances, reinforces the many references to gods in plays like *Oedipus Rex*.

This is not to say that companies working today in smaller indoor venues cannot stage ancient drama. They do so all the time, often in ingenious and illuminating ways. But knowing something about the playing space, the size and configuration of the audience, and the mechanical capability of a theater can prove helpful in understanding elements of the plays produced there. Such is the case with the Theater of Dionysus. Performed in front of an audience that in number resembles that at a contemporary concert, Greek drama typically concerned larger-than-life figures such as Oedipus, the Greek general Agamemnon, and other heroes from the Trojan War in matters of social or political importance. The architecture of the theater reflects the size and philosophical scope of such plays.

Oedipus Rex: Myth and Play

When reading *Oedipus Rex*, the first task is to distinguish the **story** of the Oedipus myth from the **plot** Sophocles creates. Sophocles begins his play **in medias res** (Latin for "in the middle of things") on the last day of Oedipus's reign as king of the city of Thebes. As the plot moves forward in time, it carries us backward to the circumstances of Oedipus's assumption of the throne and marriage to Iokastê, his fatal meeting with his father Laïos, and the circumstances of Oedipus's birth. And, while the plot gradually reveals the truth about Oedipus's identity, it also prompts a number of questions, some of which are answered while others remain mysterious. Perhaps the greatest of these mysteries is how a man like Oedipus, famous for his cleverness—after all, he solved the riddle of the Sphinx that once afflicted Thebes—can be so blind to his own past and his own failings. The Sphinx's riddle and its answer—"What walks on four legs in the morning, two in the afternoon, and three in the evening?"— have often been regarded as a key to the meaning of Sophocles' play. Man, as Oedipus replied, walks these ways when proceeding from infancy to walking with the aid of a cane in old age. This is a play about being a human.

The story or myth of Oedipus, on another level, seems simple enough. Here is the version Francis Fergusson relates:

> Laïos and Iokastê, King and Queen of Thebes, want to have a child, but are told by an oracle that their son will one day kill his father and marry his mother. Ignoring the prophecy, they conceive a child anyway, a baby boy. Shortly after his birth and beginning to regard the prophecy differently, Iokastê gives the child, whose ankles have been pierced and bound, to a shepherd and instructs him to "get rid" of it. Taking pity on the helpless child, the shepherd instead takes him to Mount Kithairon. There, he gives the baby to another shepherd who cares for him before finally taking the child to Corinth, where King Polybos and Queen Merope raise him as their own.
>
> Years later, Oedipus hears about the prophecy and, to escape it, leaves Corinth. After a time, at a place where three roads intersect, he meets an old man accompanied by servants, argues with him, and eventually kills the entire party—save for one. After wandering for a time, he comes to Thebes, which is being terrorized by the Sphinx, whose riddle he solves saving the city. He is made king, marries Iokastê with whom he has four children, and rules for years. Then his city is once again threatened with disaster, which he learns is caused by the fact that Laïos's murderer remains at large. He vows to find the murderer, discovers that he himself is the criminal, blinds himself and leaves the city, only to re-appear at Colonus as a kind of seer. Subsequent to his self-imposed banishment, his two sons kill each other while battling for control of Thebes and when his daughter Antigone, in violation of the edict imposed by her uncle Kreon, decides to honor both brothers in burial—including the one who attacked the city—she is sen-

tenced to death. In the end, Antigone, her sister Ismene, and her brothers are all dead, the entire nuclear family of Oedipus destroyed.

Again, the story's closure, like that of most tragedies, lacks any ambiguity. Oedipus, unable to escape his fate, is punished for his crime and is banished from Thebes. His reversal of fortune is complete: Once the most powerful of leaders, he is sent into exile at the end of the drama, a blind man whose home and family lie in ruin.

Yet, however clear the play's resolution, important questions remain. When did the oracle prophesy that Laïos and Iokastê's son would kill his father and marry his mother? In Scene Two, Iokastê tells Oedipus that "an oracle was reported to Laïos once . . . / That his doom would be death at the hands of his own son." Why later in the story was Iokastê unable to recognize her own son? After all, Oedipus means "swollen foot," an indication that the actor playing the role would walk with a limp. Shouldn't she have known or at least suspected the truth of his birth? What makes us certain that she doesn't? And what about Oedipus? Why doesn't he consider the possibility that he might have been implicated in the death of the previous king? After all, he must have remembered killing a party of men before coming to Thebes. Perhaps the largest question originates in the nature of the prediction: Since the gods made it, should we infer, as Oedipus did when leaving Corinth, that realistically it was possible to escape it?

Sophocles' play raises these and other questions, many of which pertain not to his play but to the myth of the character on which it is based. Again, we must distinguish between the two. In some accounts, for example, Iokastê, determined to have a son and thus fulfill what was at the time the principal duty of women to bear male children, gets her husband drunk and seduces him. Some critics regard this as merely the first of a number of "sins" she has committed. In other interpretations, especially those that refute Freud's formulation of the so-called Oedipus conflict, this is not a story about the son's unconscious desire for the mother. After all, when the Thebans made Oedipus their king after he solved the riddle of the Sphinx, Iokastê was most likely a kind of bonus. He is the new ruler and as such he also acquires the previous king's wife. His desire has nothing to do with it. But what of hers? And what is her motivation in attempting to dissuade Oedipus from pursuing his investigation to its ultimate revelations?

All these questions save for the last one are not necessarily relevant to a reading of the play, precisely because many of these events occur in the *story* long before the *plot* of *Oedipus Rex* begins. We cannot know from Sophocles' play exactly how Iokastê got pregnant, why Oedipus's ankles were pierced, or why as an infant he was to have been killed in the manner the play describes. But we *can* draw conclusions from other elements of the script, for example, from Sophocles' presentation of Oedipus and from the Chorus's response to the horror of his downfall. Appropriate to the religious context of the play's production, the Chorus—which, in addition to providing dance and song often serves as a kind of model reader—sees Oedipus's fall as an object lesson in the consequences of excessive pride. In its second Ode, it observes that "haughtiness and the high hand of disdain / Tempt and outrage God's holy law." In the final moments of the play, the Choragos tells his fellow Thebans to "look upon Oedipus" and learn how even the most powerful of men should not "presume on his good fortune."

In other words, if we separate the story or myth from the play's dramatic action, if we focus on the issues presented in the play, as Aristotle attempts to do in *Poetics*, we are left with a much clearer sense of exactly what elements comprise tragedy.

Oedipus Rex: Plot and Character

> Tragedy, then, is an *imitation of an action* that is *serious, complete, and of a certain magnitude.* [Emphasis added.]

For Aristotle, tragedy is an imitation (**mimesis**) of the actions of men and women greater than ourselves. In this instance, *greater* does not mean better, nor does it suggest moral or ethical perfection. On the contrary, the central character or so-called tragic hero is a figure of political or social power who possesses both admirable and less noble characteristics, like most of us. If tragic heroes were all good, Aristotle observes, and then brought to ruin, the resulting emotion in the spectator would be merely shock, not pity and fear. If they were mostly evil, on the other hand, an audience would applaud their downfall, as movie audiences routinely do today when film villains are defeated. But **catharsis,** the expurgation of pity and fear, which Aristotle regards as the response appropriate to tragedy, requires a more complex character, an amalgam of moral strength and human weakness.

This character is involved in a dramatic action, the resolution of which signals his or her fall from power through a profound reversal of fortune. This, we might agree, is a *serious* trajectory for the action to take. But the tragic action must also be *of a certain magnitude*. A wealthy investor, for example, who loses a thousand dollars through an ill-advised stock transaction may have suffered a serious loss. But is it tragic? A Little League team losing a game in a tournament is hardly an occasion for celebration, but is it tragic? Can a dramatic action be built around a millionaire's loss of a thousand dollars or the loss of a baseball game? The "certain magnitude" phrase indicates that the dramatic action of tragedy concerns larger events and more dire conclusions.

Perhaps the most significant element of dramatic action involves the notion of completeness. A well-made tragedy must possess **unity of action,** which Aristotle describes in the *Poetics* with almost disarming simplicity: The tragic plot has a beginning, a middle, and an end, and the events it presents follow each other "according to the law of probability or necessity." In a rather strangely worded translation, Aristotle maintains that the well-constructed tragedy must not "begin or end at haphazard." An end "naturally follows" some other thing; a middle follows a beginning in a probable or necessary way—that is, in a causal way. Scenes tracing the reversal of fortune of a tragic figure are linked in cause and effect relationship. Aristotle, in fact, is so emphatic about a unified action that he compares it several times to the delicate balance of a living organism. Aesthetic beauty, he argues, depends on magnitude and order; well-written tragedies must possess both qualities, just as beauty in nature possesses both a harmony of parts and a kind of grandeur of appearance.

Aristotle's emphasis on tragedy's unity of action suggests why horrible accidents or sudden catastrophes—events that, in everyday language, we may call "tragic"—do not qualify as examples of dramatic tragedy. Tragic action, as we see in *Oedipus Rex*, may imitate the actions of paranoid or irrational people. Oedipus, given to conspiracy theory, irrationally accuses both Kreon and Teiresias of plotting against him, and is quick to anger whenever he feels information is being withheld from him. But, however outraged Oedipus becomes, the structure of the episodes in the play is highly rational. By contrast, sudden catastrophes such as explosions, hurricanes, or airline crashes strike with such an immediacy that they cannot be regarded as the culmination of a logical, cause and effect, sequence of events.

For Aristotle, character is second in importance to dramatic action, followed by language, thought, spectacle, and song. Quite obviously, popular films often invert this hierarchy, especially action films in which spectacle (explosions, gunfights, car chases) and music seem to predominate over the logic of the dramatic action and the development of the character. Indeed, some film stars seem to play the same character over and over again, muttering the same clichés and disposing of the same kinds of villains. Complexity of characterization and carefully developed plots are not requisite for a great action film; talented special effects artists and stuntmen, by comparison, are far more important.

Not so with tragedy and its protagonist, its **tragic hero**. A tragic hero is not a superstar, not a muscled Superman whose only goals are "truth, justice, and the American way," but a more complex mixture of traits. Most important, in the words of one influential critic, in the beginning scenes of a tragedy, the tragic hero occupies a position "on top of the wheel of fortune, halfway between human society on the ground and the something greater in the sky." In Sophocles' play, Oedipus's prominence is reflected in numerous ways, from the high stage boots he wears to the exposition in the play's prologue in which Theban suppliants enter pleading for his help. The Priest refers to him as "Great Oedipus" and "O mighty power," clear indications of the respect he commands. At the same time, as noted philosopher Susanne Langer describes it, although the tragic protagonist "grows mentally, emotionally, or morally by the demand of the action, which he himself initiated," the plot also leads inevitably to the "complete exhaustion of his powers, the limit of his possible development." However powerful a character like Oedipus may be, his entire being becomes focused "on one aim, one passion"—and one ultimate defeat.

Further, for Aristotle the tragic hero possesses at least four other characteristics: He or she is good (but not infallible), appropriate, true to life, and consistent. The first of these points about the moral nature of the tragic hero has led frequently to a misunderstanding of Aristotle's ideas. Later in the *Poetics* he refines the idea of the tragic hero's goodness. Tragic heroes are "not eminently good and just": their "misfortune is brought about not by vice or depravity, but by some error or frailty." "Error" and "frailty" were, at one time, translated as "tragic flaw," which is clearly not what Aristotle means. Borrowing a term from archery, Aristotle uses the word **hamartia** or "missing the mark" to describe his theory. Tragic heroes like Oedipus, Hamlet, and Othello literally miss or are unable to see the truth or to react correctly to the adversity they experience. Late-twentieth-century examples surface outside the theater in the American presidency with Richard Nixon's involvement in the Watergate cover-up and Bill Clinton's escapade with Monica Lewinsky. Like Hamlet and Othello, they were not evil men; rather, they made enormous mistakes in judgment and then based their actions on them. Nor were these powerful leaders mere victims. On occasion, tragic heroes approach the innocence of victims such as those lost to horrific events outside of their control, but not characters like Oedipus, who participate in their own downfall.

Thought and language express this culpability, and both need to be appropriate to the character. A king and responsible leader, Oedipus speaks like a politician, a rather arrogant one, in the early scenes of the play. To give him some credit, however, he is also a concerned king attempting to relieve the suffering of his people. He speaks accordingly, sometimes quite ironically. For example, he vows to "take the son's part"—"just as though I were [Laïos's] son"—in pursuing the murderer. Appropriately, and in words rich with metaphorical significance, he says in the opening scene, "Then once more I must bring what is dark to light." Such lines are rich with **dramatic irony,** the situation where the audience knows more than the character on stage. In fact, he *is* taking the son's part because he *is* Laïos's son; in fact, like the blind seer Teiresias whom he later threatens, Oedipus will produce "light" or knowledge from the darkness of ignorance.

Spectacle in *Oedipus Rex*

In *Poetics*, Aristotle ranks spectacle as the least artistic element of tragedy, a concept that might help us distinguish between early Greek tragedies and some later tragic forms. The violence in *Oedipus Rex* takes place offstage. We learn of Iokastê's suicide and see the horrific results of Oedipus's self-blinding when he is led onto the stage in the play's final scene or Exodus. But we never view the violent causes of both injuries, only their results. By contrast, Shakespeare's audience expected to see violent spectacle at the end of revenge tragedies like *Hamlet* or *Titus Andronicus*, both of which were adapted for the cinema as the twentieth century came to a close. While Shakespeare's playgoers and contemporary filmgoers, therefore, might expect to witness graphic representations of such atrocities, spectators at the Theater of Dionysus rarely did. As a result, in his theory of tragedy Aristotle regards spectacle with little enthusiasm.

Oedipus and Interpretive Theory

Because the term *tragedy* refers to a dramatic action that mirrors the inevitable decline of an individual's life, one can occur only in a society in which individual life is valued. Otherwise, the fall of an Oedipus or Hamlet would mean very little to an audience. Tragedy is thus a serious dramatic form, composed—as complex organisms are—of a highly organized system of elements. Perhaps it is for this reason that so many thinkers over the centuries—philosophers, psychoanalysts, and anthropologists, to name a few—have found in tragedy rich implications about life, religion, and the nature of both men and women. **Web**　　*www*

> Have no more fear of sleeping with your mother:
> How many men, in dreams, have lain with their mothers!
> No reasonable man is troubled by such things.

Iokastê's infamous advice to her husband-son in Scene Three of *Oedipus Rex* informs Sigmund Freud's hypotheses about desire and psychosexual development in what we now know as psychoanalysis. Freud's study *The Interpretation of Dreams* (1900) includes a sustained reading of *Oedipus Rex*. Motivated by Iokastê's lines, he proposes that Sophocles' play relates a profoundly amoral story. Why amoral and not immoral? Freud begins his explanation by noting that "the tragedy of Sophocles does not call up indignant repudiation in his audience." Why? Because *Oedipus Rex* "absolves men from moral responsibility" and "exhibits the gods as promoters of crime." Moreover, the play reveals "the impotence of the moral impulses of men which struggle against crime." Freud emphasizes that Oedipus does indeed struggle in vain to avoid the fate the gods have imposed on him and, in the end, stands guilty of the crimes he sought to avoid. He therefore is not immoral but amoral; he is not to be judged primarily on moral grounds.

But for Freud, the gods and tragic destiny are really not the crucial issues. Rather, he regards the entire myth as containing a profound psychological truth: A man may repress his evil impulses deep into the unconscious, but he is dimly aware of them nonetheless and often experiences a sense of guilt, even though he may not understand precisely why. Of what crime or desire are men and women guilty? (Recall that the Sphinx's riddle asks the large metaphysical question "What is a man?") Because the mother is the first object of the baby's affection, the first being whom a child loves and desires to possess exclusively, Sophocles' play represents universal truths of psychical life through the vehicle of Oedipus's downfall. In this way, tragic destiny replicates psychical reality. The son desires possession of the mother, and the father stands in the way of the son realizing this project. Importantly, the desire exists at the unconscious, not the conscious level; that is, it is not accessible to Oedipus or any son at the conscious level because it has been repressed. From Freud's perspective, the dramatic action of Sophocles' play follows the same trajectory as a psychoanalytic session with a patient: As the session proceeds forward, it also moves further back into the patient's past.

Such readings of Oedipus's story tend to carry us beyond the plot of Sophocles' play. Is it necessarily true that Oedipus is absolved from moral responsibility? Do the gods force him to act the way he does *in the play*? Doesn't he possess reason, the ability to choose a particular course of action? Those readers unsupportive of Freud's view tend to pose these and related questions. If Aristotle had been alive when Freud developed these theories from Sophocles' play, he doubtless would have questioned his conclusions. Because tragic heroes commit errors and possess human frailties, they are in no sense amoral puppets who are helpless to control their behavior; tragic destiny is not, finally, an excuse that absolves them of moral responsibility. No god pulls the tragic hero's strings.

For French anthropologist Claude Lévi-Strauss, an influential thinker who in the 1960s helped refine *structuralist* reading practices, the Oedipus tragedy suggests the "double-structured" nature of all myths. That is, myths have both a historical dimension—they tell a story in a linear or "diachronic" way—and an ahistorical or "synchronic" dimension revealed by repetitive structural oppositions. This latter dimension is made clear after one recognizes the "bundle of relations" between episodes in the story of Oedipus and his family. For example, each generation of Oedipus's extended family is damaged by intrafamilial violence: Oedipus kills his father, Oedipus's sons kill each other, and so on. Similarly, several generations of Oedipus's family break legal prohibitions against certain relationships between siblings or parent and child, the incestuous marriage of Oedipus and Iokastê providing the most conspicuous example. Lévi-Strauss regards these structural patterns as especially meaningful and indicative of the larger social resonance of the Oedipus myth. In the first instance, familial relationships are *under*valued (family members attack each other, ignoring or minimizing their relationship); in the second, these relationships are *over*valued, more intimate than they should be. Thus, in his reading, Oedipus's myth works in a manner typical of most myths: "Mythical thought always progresses from the awareness of oppositions toward their resolution."

Other readings of Sophocles' play take a more direct approach, linking the play not to human psychology or narrative structure but to the time and society in which it was written. For Philip Slater, *Oedipus Rex* performs significant cultural work in a society intent on preserving male dominance. As Slater explains in *The Glory of Hera*, Sophocles' play functions as a kind of parable about the danger of marrying mature women. One of the many advantages Greek men enjoyed over women was the ability to select wives—or concubines—for both personal and social gain. Fathers often gave scarcely pubescent daughters to male friends, and once these girls left their fathers' houses they were expected to raise children and manage their new homes. They had no real function outside the domestic sphere, and their most important role was to bear children, especially sons. By contrast, men ruled the social and political realms, taking multiple wives and lovers, many of them much younger than themselves.

Slater's feminist and culturally contextualized reading emphasizes that, as is the case with other artifacts of Athenian culture, in *Oedipus Rex* the older woman poses a specific danger. For this reason, the Sphinx, whose riddle

Oedipus solves to save Thebes the first time, is represented as part woman, part animal. Greek statuary and painting of the period reinforce the culture's valuation of younger women, women for whom the depilation of all bodily hair was customary. Young women like Antigone are loyal and steadfast; older women like Iokastê, Clytemnestra in Aeschylus's *Agamemnon,* and Medea are aggressive, duplicitous, even murderous. For Slater, *Oedipus Rex* confirms the culture's fear of mature women, therefore supporting the dominant ideology and the social practices stemming from it that allowed Greek men to maintain their privilege. This cultural subordination of women extended to both sides of the theater event: the vast majority of the audience attending Greek tragedies were men, as were the actors.

To return to Friedrich Nietzsche's praise, only a form as intricate and beautiful as tragedy could excite so many brilliant minds and motivate so many rich and varied readings. And these few examples barely scratch the surface. Experience *Oedipus Rex* yourself and discover in it, as so many readers from Aristotle through Lévi-Strauss have, meanings relevant to you and to the time in which you live. Some of these may resemble those discussed here; others may not. The production of new insights and fresh interpretations is part of the legacy of tragedy and of *Oedipus Rex,* which has endured for some twenty-five hundred years.

SOPHOCLES

Oedipus Rex   *(c. 430 B.C.)*

CHARACTERS

Oedipus, King of Thebes, supposed son of Polybos and Meropê, King and
     Queen of Corinth
Iokastê, wife of Oedipus and widow of the late King Laïos
Kreon, brother of Iokastê, a prince of Thebes
Teiresias, a blind seer who serves Apollo
Priest
Messenger, from Corinth
Shepherd, former servant of Laïos
Second Messenger, from the palace
Chorus of Theban Elders
Choragos, leader of the Chorus
Antigonê and Ismenê, young daughters of Oedipus and Iokastê. They appear
     in the Exodos but do not speak.
Suppliants, Guards, Servants

THE SCENE. *Before the palace of* Oedipus, *King of Thebes. A central door and two
lateral doors open onto a platform that runs the length of the facade. On the platform, right and left, are altars; and three steps lead down into the orchestra or
chorus-ground. At the beginning of the action these steps are crowded by suppliants
who have brought branches and chaplets of olive leaves and who sit in various attitudes of despair.* Oedipus *enters.*

PROLOGUE

Oedipus: My children, generations of the living
          In the line of Kadmos,° nursed at his ancient hearth:
          Why have you strewn yourselves before these <u>altars</u>
          In supplication, with your boughs and garlands?
          The breath of incense rises from the city   5
          With a sound of prayer and lamentation.
                                        Children,
          I would not have you speak through messengers,
          And therefore I have come myself to hear you—
          I, Oedipus, who bear the famous name.   10
          (*to a* Priest) You, there, since you are eldest in the company,

────

2 *Kadmos:* Founder of Thebes.

Speak for them all, tell me what preys upon you,
Whether you come in dread, or crave some blessing:
Tell me, and never doubt that I will help you
In every way I can; I should be heartless 15
Were I not moved to find you suppliant here.
Priest: Great Oedipus, O powerful king of Thebes!
You see how all the ages of our people
Cling to your altar steps: here are boys
Who can barely stand alone, and here are priests 20
By weight of age, as I am a priest of God,
And young men chosen from those yet unmarried;
As for the others, all that multitude,
They wait with olive chaplets in the squares,
At the two shrines of Pallas, and where Apollo 25
Speaks in the glowing embers.
                            Your own eyes
Must tell you: Thebes is tossed on a murdering sea
And can not lift her head from the death surge.
A rust consumes the buds and fruits of the earth; 30
The herds are sick; children die unborn,
And labor is vain. The god of plague and pyre
Raids like detestable lightning through the city,
And all the house of Kadmos is laid waste,
All emptied, and all darkened: Death alone 35
Battens upon the misery of Thebes.

You are not one of the immortal gods, we know;
Yet we have come to you to make our prayer
As to the man surest in mortal ways
And wisest in the ways of God. You saved us 40
From the Sphinx, that flinty singer, and the tribute
We paid to her so long; yet you were never
Better informed than we, nor could we teach you:
A god's touch, it seems, enabled you to help us.

Therefore, O mighty power, we turn to you: 45
Find us our safety, find us a remedy,
Whether by counsel of the gods or of men.
A king of wisdom tested in the past
Can act in a time of troubles, and act well.
Noblest of men, restore 50
Life to your city! Think how all men call you
Liberator for your boldness long ago;
Ah, when your years of kingship are remembered,
Let them not say *We rose, but later fell*—
Keep the State from going down in the storm! 55
Once, years ago, with happy augury,

You brought us fortune; be the same again!
No man questions your power to rule the land:
But rule over men, not over a dead city!
Ships are only hulls, high walls are nothing,   60
When no life moves in the empty passageways.

Oedipus: Poor children! You may be sure I know
All that you longed for in your coming here.
I know that you are deathly sick; and yet,
Sick as you are, not one is as sick as I.   65
Each of you suffers in himself alone
His anguish, not another's; but my spirit
Groans for the city, for myself, for you.

I was not sleeping, you are not waking me.
No, I have been in tears for a long while   70
And in my restless thought walked many ways.
In all my search I found one remedy,
And I have adopted it: I have sent Kreon,
Son of Menoikeus, brother of the queen,
To Delphi, Apollo's place of revelation,   75
To learn there, if he can,
What act or pledge of mine may save the city.
I have counted the days, and now, this very day,
I am troubled, for he has overstayed his time.
What is he doing? He has been gone too long.   80
Yet whenever he comes back, I should do ill
Not to take any action the god orders.

Priest: It is a timely promise. At this instant
They tell me Kreon is here.

Oedipus: O Lord Apollo!   85
May his news be fair as his face is radiant!

Priest: Good news, I gather! he is crowned with bay,
The chaplet is thick with berries.

Oedipus: We shall soon know;
He is near enough to hear us now.   90

(Enter Kreon.*)*

                                         O prince:
Brother: son of Menoikeus:
What answer do you bring us from the god?

Kreon: A strong one. I can tell you, great afflictions
Will turn out well, if they are taken well.   95

Oedipus: What was the oracle? These vague words
Leave me still hanging between hope and fear.

Kreon: Is it your pleasure to hear me with all these
Gathered around us? I am prepared to speak,
But should we not go in?   100

Oedipus: Speak to them all,
It is for them I suffer, more than for myself.

Kreon: Then I will tell you what I heard at Delphi.
In plain words
The god commands us to expel from the land of Thebes 105
An old defilement we are sheltering.
It is a deathly thing, beyond cure;
We must not let it feed upon us longer.

Oedipus: What defilement? How shall we rid ourselves of it?

Kreon: By exile or death, blood for blood. It was 110
Murder that brought the plague-wind on the city.

Oedipus: Murder of whom? Surely the god has named him?

Kreon: My lord: Laïos once ruled this land,
Before you came to govern us.

Oedipus: I know; 115
I learned of him from others; I never saw him.

Kreon: He was murdered; and Apollo commands us now
To take revenge upon whoever killed him.

Oedipus: Upon whom? Where are they? Where shall we find a clue
To solve that crime, after so many years? 120

Kreon: Here in this land, he said. Search reveals
Things that escape an inattentive man.

Oedipus: Tell me: Was Laïos murdered in his house,
Or in the fields, or in some foreign country?

Kreon: He said he planned to make a pilgrimage. 125
He did not come home again.

Oedipus: And was there no one,
No witness, no companion, to tell what happened?

Kreon: They were all killed but one, and he got away
So frightened that he could remember one thing only. 130

Oedipus: What was that one thing? One may be the key
To everything, if we resolve to use it.

Kreon: He said that a band of highwaymen attacked them,
Outnumbered them, and overwhelmed the king.

Oedipus: Strange, that a highwayman should be so daring— 135
Unless some faction here bribed him to do it.

Kreon: We thought of that. But after Laïos' death
New troubles arose and we had no avenger.

Oedipus: What troubles could prevent your hunting
down the killers? 140

Kreon: The riddling Sphinx's song
Made us deaf to all mysteries but her own.

Oedipus: Then once more I must bring what is dark to light.
It is most fitting that Apollo shows,
As you do, this compunction for the dead. 145
You shall see how I stand by you, as I should,
Avenging this country and the god as well,

And not as though it were for some distant friend,
But for my own sake, to be rid of evil.
Whoever killed King Laïos might—who knows?—   150
Lay violent hands even on me—and soon.
I act for the murdered king in my own interest.

Come, then, my children: leave the altar steps,
Lift up your olive boughs!
                              One of you go   155
And summon the people of Kadmos to gather here.
I will do all that I can; you may tell them that.

(Exit a Page.*)*

So, with the help of God,
We shall be saved—or else indeed we are lost.
Priest: Let us rise, children. It was for this we came,   160
And now the king has promised it.
Phoibos° has sent us an oracle; may he descend
Himself to save us and drive out the plague.

(Exeunt Oedipus *and* Kreon *into the palace by the central door. The* Priest *and
the* Suppliants *disperse R and L. After a short pause the* Chorus *enters the
orchestra.)*

PÁRADOS°

STROPHE 1

Chorus: What is God singing in his profound
            Delphi of gold and shadow?
            What oracle for Thebes, the Sunwhipped city?
            Fear unjoints me, the roots of my heart tremble.
            Now I remember, O Healer, your power, and wonder: 5
            Will you send doom like a sudden cloud, or weave it
            Like nightfall of the past?
            Speak to me, tell me, O
            Child of golden Hope, immortal Voice.

---

162 *Phoibos:* Apollo   *Párodos:* The song or ode chanted by the chorus on its entry. It is accompanied by dancing and music played on a flute. The chorus in this play represents elders of the
city of Thebes. Chorus members remain onstage (on a level lower than the principal actors) for
the remainder of the play. The choral odes and dances serve to separate one scene from another
(there was no curtain in Greek theater) as well as to comment on the action, reinforce the emotion, and interpret the situation. The chorus also performs dance movements during certain portions of the scenes themselves. Strophe and antistrophe are terms denoting the movement and
countermovement of the chorus from one side of its playing area to the other. When the chorus
participates in dialogue with the other characters, its lines are spoken by the Choragos, its leader.

ANTISTROPHE 1

Let me pray to Athenê, the immortal daughter of Zeus,　　　　10
And to Artemis her sister
Who keeps her famous throne in the market ring,
And to Apollo, archer from distant heaven—
O gods, descend! Like three streams leap against
The fires of our grief, the fires of darkness;　　　　15
Be swift to bring us rest!
As in the old time from the brilliant house
Of air you stepped to save us, come again!

STROPHE 2

Now our afflictions have no end,
Now all our stricken host lies down　　　　20
And no man fights off death with his mind;
The noble plowland bears no grain,
And groaning mothers can not bear—
See, how our lives like birds take wing,
Like sparks that fly when a fire soars,　　　　25
To the shore of the god of evening.

ANTISTROPHE 2

The plague burns on, it is pitiless,
Though pallid children laden with death
Lie unwept in the stony ways,
And old gray women by every path　　　　30
Flock to the strand about the altars
There to strike their breasts and cry
Worship of Phoibos in wailing prayers:
Be kind, God's golden child!

STROPHE 3

There are no swords in this attack by fire,　　　　35
No shields, but we are ringed with cries.
Send the besieger plunging from our homes
Into the vast sea-room of the Atlantic
Or into the waves that foam eastward of Thrace—
For the day ravages what the night spares—　　　　40
Destroy our enemy, lord of the thunder!
Let him be riven by lightning from heaven!

ANTISTROPHE 3

Phoibos Apollo, stretch the sun's bowstring,
That golden cord, until it sing for us,
Flashing arrows in heaven!　　　　45

                    Artemis, Huntress,
Race with flaring lights upon our mountains!
O scarlet god, O golden-banded brow,
O Theban Bacchos in a storm of Maenads,

(*Enter* Oedipus, *C.*)

Whirl upon Death, that all the Undying hate!   50
Come with blinding torches, come in joy!

SCENE I

Oedipus: Is this your prayer? It may be answered. Come,
    Listen to me, act as the crisis demands,
    And you shall have relief from all these evils.

    Until now I was a stranger to this tale,
    As I had been a stranger to the crime.   5
    Could I track down the murderer without a clue?
    But now, friends,
    As one who became a citizen after the murder,
    I make this proclamation to all Thebans:
    If any man knows by whose hand Laïos, son of Labdakos,   10
    Met his death, I direct that man to tell me everything,
    No matter what he fears for having so long withheld it.
    Let it stand as promised that no further trouble
    Will come to him, but he may leave the land in safety.

    Moreover: If anyone knows the murderer to be foreign,   15
    Let him not keep silent: he shall have his reward from me.
    However, if he does conceal it; if any man
    Fearing for his friend or for himself disobeys this edict,
    Hear what I propose to do:

    I solemnly forbid the people of this country,   20
    Where power and throne are mine, ever to receive that man
    Or speak to him, no matter who he is, or let him
    Join in sacrifice, lustration, or in prayer.
    I decree that he be driven from every house,
    Being, as he is, corruption itself to us: the Delphic   25
    Voice of Apollo has pronounced this revelation.
    Thus I associate myself with the oracle
    And take the side of the murdered king.

    As for the criminal, I pray to God—
    Whether it be a lurking thief, or one of a number—   30

I pray that that man's life be consumed in evil and wretchedness.
And as for me, this curse applies no less
If it should turn out that the culprit is my guest here,
Sharing my hearth.

           You have heard the penalty.   35
I lay it on you now to attend to this
For my sake, for Apollo's, for the sick
Sterile city that heaven has abandoned.
Suppose the oracle had given you no command:
Should this defilement go uncleansed for ever?   40
You should have found the murderer: your king,
A noble king, had been destroyed!

               Now I,
Having the power that he held before me,
Having his bed, begetting children there   45
Upon his wife, as he would have, had he lived—
Their son would have been my children's brother,
If Laïos had had luck in fatherhood!
(And now his bad fortune has struck him down)—
I say I take the son's part, just as though   50
I were his son, to press the fight for him
And see it won! I'll find the hand that brought
Death to Labdakos' and Polydoros' child,
Heir of Kadmos' and Agenor's line.°
And as for those who fail me,   55
May the gods deny them the fruit of the earth,
Fruit of the womb, and may they rot utterly!
Let them be wretched as we are wretched, and worse!

For you, for loyal Thebans, and for all
Who find my actions right, I pray the favor   60
Of justice, and of all the immortal gods.
Choragos: Since I am under oath, my lord, I swear
I did not do the murder, I can not name
The murderer. Phoibos ordained the search;
Why did he not say who the culprit was?   65
Oedipus: An honest question. But no man in the world
Can make the gods do more than the gods will.
Choragos: There is an alternative, I think—
Oedipus: Tell me.
Any or all, you must not fail to tell me.   70
Choragos: A lord clairvoyant to the lord Apollo,
As we all know, is the skilled Teiresias.
One might learn much about this from him, Oedipus.

53–54 *Labdakos'* . . . *Agenor's:* Father, grandfather, great-grandfather, and great-great-grandfather of Laïos

Oedipus: I am not wasting time:
    Kreon spoke of this, and I have sent for him—   75
    Twice, in fact; it is strange that he is not here.
Choragos: The other matter—that old report—seems useless.
Oedipus: What was that? I am interested in all reports.
Choragos: The king was said to have been killed by highwaymen.
Oedipus: I know. But we have no witnesses to that.   80
Choragos: If the killer can feel a particle of dread,
    Your curse will bring him out of hiding!
Oedipus: No.
    The man who dared that act will fear no curse.

(Enter the blind seer Teiresias, *led by a* Page.)

Choragos: But there is one man who may detect the criminal.   85
    This is Teiresias, this is the holy prophet
    In whom, alone of all men, truth was born.
Oedipus: Teiresias: seer: student of mysteries,
    Of all that's taught and all that no man tells,
    Secrets of Heaven and secrets of the earth: 90
    Blind though you are, you know the city lies
    Sick with plague; and from this plague, my lord,
    We find that you alone can guard or save us.

    Possibly you did not hear the messengers?
    Apollo, when we sent to him,   95
    Sent us back word that this great pestilence
    Would lift, but only if we established clearly
    The identity of those who murdered Laïos.
    They must be killed or exiled.
                   Can you use
    Birdflight° or any art of divination   100
    To purify yourself, and Thebes, and me
    From this contagion? We are in your hands.
    There is no fairer duty
    Than that of helping others in distress.
Teiresias: How dreadful knowledge of the truth can be   105
    When there's no help in truth! I knew this well,
    But did not act on it; else I should not have come.
Oedipus: What is troubling you? Why are your eyes so cold?
Teiresias: Let me go home. Bear your own fate, and I'll
    Bear mine. It is better so: trust what I say.   110
Oedipus: What you say is ungracious and unhelpful
    To your native country. Do not refuse to speak.

———
100 *Birdflight:* Prophets predicted the future or divined the unknown by observing the flight of birds.

Teiresias: When it comes to speech, your own is neither temperate
    Nor opportune. I wish to be more prudent.
Oedipus: In God's name, we all beg you— 115
Teiresias: You are all ignorant.
    No; I will never tell you what I know.
    Now it is my misery; then, it would be yours.
Oedipus: What! You do know something, and will not tell us?
    You would betray us all and wreck the State? 120
Teiresias: I do not intend to torture myself, or you.
    Why persist in asking? You will not persuade me.
Oedipus: What a wicked old man you are! You'd try a stone's
    Patience! Out with it! Have you no feeling at all?
Teiresias: You call me unfeeling. If you could only see 125
    The nature of your own feelings . . .
Oedipus: Why,
    Who would not feel as I do? Who could endure
    Your arrogance toward the city?
Teiresias: What does it matter? 130
    Whether I speak or not, it is bound to come.
Oedipus: Then, if "it" is bound to come, you are bound to tell me.
Teiresias: No, I will not go on. Rage as you please.
Oedipus: Rage? Why not!
                   And I'll tell you what I think: 135
    You planned it, you had it done, you all but
    Killed him with your own hands: if you had eyes,
    I'd say the crime was yours, and yours alone.
Teiresias: So? I charge you, then,
    Abide by the proclamation you have made: 140
    From this day forth
    Never speak again to these men or to me;
    You yourself are the pollution of this country.
Oedipus: You dare say that! Can you possibly think you have
    Some way of going free, after such insolence? 145
Teiresias: I have gone free. It is the truth that sustains me.
Oedipus: Who taught you shamelessness? It was not your craft.
Teiresias: You did. You made me speak. I did not want to.
Oedipus: Speak what? Let me hear it again more clearly.
Teiresias: Was it not clear before? Are you tempting me? 150
Oedipus: I did not understand it. Say it again.
Teiresias: I say that you are the murderer whom you seek.
Oedipus: Now twice you have spat out infamy. You'll pay for it!
Teiresias: Would you care for more? Do you wish to be really angry?
Oedipus: Say what you will. Whatever you say is worthless. 155
Teiresias: I say you live in hideous shame with those
    Most dear to you. You can not see the evil.
Oedipus: Can you go on babbling like this for ever?
Teiresias: I can, if there is power in truth.

Oedipus: There is: 160
  But not for you, not for you,
  You sightless, witless, senseless, mad old man!
Teiresias: You are the madman. There is no one here
  Who will not curse you soon, as you curse me.
Oedipus: You child of total night! I would not touch you;   165
  Neither would any man who sees the sun.
Teiresias: True: it is not from you my fate will come.
  That lies within Apollo's competence,
  As it is his concern.
Oedipus: Tell me, who made   170
  These fine discoveries? Kreon? or someone else?
Teiresias: Kreon is no threat. You weave your own doom.
Oedipus: Wealth, power, craft of statesmanship!
  Kingly position, everywhere admired!
  What savage envy is stored up against these,   175
  If Kreon, whom I trusted, Kreon my friend,
  For this great office which the city once
  Put in my hands unsought—if for this power
  Kreon desires in secret to destroy me!

  He has bought this decrepit fortune-teller, this   180
  Collector of dirty pennies, this prophet fraud—
  Why, he is no more clairvoyant than I am!
                              Tell us:
  Has your mystic mummery ever approached the truth?
  When that hellcat the Sphinx was performing here,   185
  What help were you to these people?
  Her magic was not for the first man who came along:
  It demanded a real exorcist. Your birds—
  What good were they? or the gods, for the matter of that?
  But I came by,   190
  Oedipus, the simple man, who knows nothing—
  I thought it out for myself, no birds helped me!
  And this is the man you think you can destroy,
  That you may be close to Kreon when he's king!
  Well, you and your friend Kreon, it seems to me,   195
  Will suffer most. If you were not an old man,
  You would have paid already for your plot.
Choragos: We can not see that his words or yours
  Have been spoken except in anger, Oedipus,
  And of anger we have no need. How to accomplish   200
  The god's will best: that is what most concerns us.
Teiresias: You are a king. But where argument's concerned
  I am your man, as much a king as you.
  I am not your servant, but Apollo's.
  I have no need of Kreon or Kreon's name.   205

Listen to me. You mock my blindness, do you?
But I say that you, with both your eyes, are blind:
You can not see the wretchedness of your life,
Nor in whose house you live, no, nor with whom.
Who are your father and mother? Can you tell me?   210
You do not even know the blind wrongs
That you have done them, on earth and in the world below.
But the double lash of your parents' curse will whip you
Out of this land some day, with only night
Upon your precious eyes.   215
Your cries then—where will they not be heard?
What fastness of Kithairon° will not echo them?
And that bridal-descant of yours—you'll know it then,
The song they sang when you came here to Thebes
And found your misguided berthing.   220
All this, and more, that you can not guess at now,
Will bring you to yourself among your children.

Be angry, then. Curse Kreon. Curse my words.
I tell you, no man that walks upon the earth
Shall be rooted out more horribly than you.   225
Oedipus: Am I to bear this from him?—Damnation
Take you! Out of this place! Out of my sight!
Teiresias: I would not have come at all if you had not asked me.
Oedipus: Could I have told that you'd talk nonsense, that
You'd come here to make a fool of yourself, and of me?   230
Teiresias: A fool? Your parents thought me sane enough.
Oedipus: My parents again!—Wait: who were my parents?
Teiresias: This day will give you a father, and break your heart.
Oedipus: Your infantile riddles! Your damned abracadabra!
Teiresias: You were a great man once at solving riddles.   235
Oedipus: Mock me with that if you like; you will find it true.
Teiresias: It was true enough. It brought about your ruin.
Oedipus: But if it saved this town?
Teiresias (to the Page):   Boy, give me your hand.
Oedipus: Yes, boy; lead him away.   240
                                —While you are here
We can do nothing. Go; leave us in peace.
Teiresias: I will go when I have said what I have to say.
How can you hurt me? And I tell you again:
The man you have been looking for all this time,   245
The damned man, the murderer of Laïos,
That man is in Thebes. To your mind he is foreign-born,
But it will soon be shown that he is a Theban,

---

217 *Kithairon:* The mountain where Oedipus was taken to be exposed as an infant.

A revelation that will fail to please.

                              A blind man,   250
Who has his eyes now; a penniless man, who is rich now;
And he will go tapping the strange earth with his staff.
To the children with whom he lives now he will be
Brother and father—the very same; to her
Who bore him, son and husband—the very same   255
Who came to his father's bed, wet with his father's blood.

Enough. Go think that over.
If later you find error in what I have said,
You may say that I have no skill in prophecy.

(*Exit* Teiresias, *led by his* Page. Oedipus *goes into the palace.*)

ODE I

STROPHE 1

Chorus: The Delphic stone of prophecies
          Remembers ancient regicide
          And a still bloody hand.
          That killer's hour of flight has come.
          He must be stronger than riderless   5
          Coursers of untiring wind,
          For the son° of Zeus armed with his father's thunder
          Leaps in lightning after him;
          And the Furies hold his track, the sad Furies.

ANTISTROPHE 1

          Holy Parnassos'° peak of snow   10
          Flashes and blinds that secret man,
          That all shall hunt him down:
          Though he may roam the forest shade
          Like a bull gone wild from pasture
          To rage through glooms of stone.   15
          Doom comes down on him; flight will not avail him;
          For the world's heart calls him desolate,
          And the immortal voices follow, for ever follow.

STROPHE 2

          But now a wilder thing is heard
          From the old man skilled at hearing Fate in the wing-beat of a bird.   20

---

7 *son:* Apollo.   10 *Parsassos':* Mountain sacred to Apollo.

Bewildered as a blown bird, my soul hovers and can not find
Foothold in this debate, or any reason or rest of mind.
But no man ever brought—none can bring
Proof of strife between Thebes' royal house,
Labdakos' line, and the son of Polybos; 25
And never until now has any man brought word
Of Laïos' dark death staining Oedipus the King.

ANTISTROPHE 2

Divine Zeus and Apollo hold
Perfect intelligence alone of all tales ever told;
And well though this diviner works, he works in his own night; 30
No man can judge that rough unknown or trust in second sight,
For wisdom changes hands among the wise.
Shall I believe my great lord criminal
At a raging word that a blind old man let fall?
I saw him, when the carrion woman° faced him of old, 35
Prove his heroic mind. These evil words are lies.

SCENE II

Kreon: Men of Thebes:
   I am told that heavy accusations
   Have been brought against me by King Oedipus.
   I am not the kind of man to bear this tamely.

   If in these present difficulties 5
   He holds me accountable for any harm to him
   Through anything I have said or done—why, then,
   I do not value life in this dishonor.
   It is not as though this rumor touched upon
   Some private indiscretion. The matter is grave. 10
   The fact is that I am being called disloyal
   To the State, to my fellow citizens, to my friends.
Choragos: He may have spoken in anger, not from his mind.
Kreon: But did you not hear him say I was the one
   Who seduced the old prophet into lying? 15
Choragos: The thing was said; I do not know how seriously.
Kreon: But you were watching him! Were his eyes steady?
   Did he look like a man in his right mind?
Choragos: I do not know.
   I can not judge the behavior of great men. 20
   But here is the king himself.

----

35 *carrion woman:* The Sphinx.

(*Enter* Oedipus.)

Oedipus: So you dared come back.
    Why? How brazen of you to come to my house,
    You murderer!
                Do you think I do not know   25
    That you plotted to kill me, plotted to steal my throne?
    Tell me, in God's name: am I coward, a fool,
    That you should dream you could accomplish this?
    A fool who could not see your slippery game?
    A coward, not to fight back when I saw it?   30
    You are the fool, Kreon, are you not? hoping
    Without support or friends to get a throne?
    Thrones may be won or bought: you could do neither.
Kreon: Now listen to me. You have talked; let me talk, too.
    You can not judge unless you know the facts.   35
Oedipus: You speak well: there is one fact; but I find it hard
    To learn from the deadliest enemy I have.
Kreon: That above all I must dispute with you.
Oedipus: That above all I will not hear you deny.
Kreon: If you think there is anything good in being stubborn   40
    Against all reason, then I say you are wrong.
Oedipus: If you think a man can sin against his own kind
    And not be punished for it, I say you are mad.
Kreon: I agree. But tell me: What have I done to you?
Oedipus: You advised me to send for that wizard, did you not?   45
Kreon: I did. I should do it again.
Oedipus: Very well. Now tell me:
    How long has it been since Laïos—
Kreon: What of Laïos?
Oedipus: Since he vanished in that onset by the road?   50
Kreon: It was long ago, a long time.
Oedipus: And this prophet,
    Was he practicing here then?
Kreon: He was; and with honor, as now.
Oedipus: Did he speak of me at that time?   55
Kreon: He never did,
    At least, not when I was present.
Oedipus: But . . . the enquiry?
    I suppose you held one?
Kreon: We did, but we learned nothing.   60
Oedipus: Why did the prophet not speak against me then?
Kreon: I do not know; and I am the kind of man
    Who holds his tongue when he has no facts to go on.
Oedipus: There's one fact that you know, and you could tell it.
Kreon: What fact is that? If I know it, you shall have it.   65
Oedipus: If he were not involved with you, he could not say
    That it was I who murdered Laïos.

Kreon: If he says that, you are the one that knows it!—
    But now it is my turn to question you.
Oedipus: Put your questions. I am no murderer.   70
Kreon: First, then: You married my sister?
Oedipus: I married your sister.
Kreon: And you rule the kingdom equally with her?
Oedipus: Everything that she wants she has from me.
Kreon: And I am the third, equal to both of you?   75
Oedipus: That is why I call you a bad friend.
Kreon: No. Reason it out, as I have done.
    Think of this first: Would any sane man prefer
    Power, with all a king's anxieties,
    To that same power and the grace of sleep?   80
    Certainly not I.
    I have never longed for the king's power—only his rights.
    Would any wise man differ from me in this?
    As matters stand, I have my way in everything
    With your consent, and no responsibilities.   85
    If I were king, I should be a slave to policy.

    How could I desire a scepter more
    Than what is now mine—untroubled influence?
    No, I have not gone mad; I need no honors,
    Except those with the perquisites I have now.   90
    I am welcome everywhere; every man salutes me,
    And those who want your favor seek my ear,
    Since I know how to manage what they ask.
    Should I exchange this ease for that anxiety?
    Besides, no sober mind is treasonable.   95
    I hate anarchy
    And never would deal with any man who likes it.
    Test what I have said. Go to the priestess
    At Delphi, ask if I quoted her correctly.
    And as for this other thing: if I am found   100
    Guilty of treason with Teiresias,
    Then sentence me to death. You have my word
    It is a sentence I should cast my vote for—
    But not without evidence!
                       You do wrong   105
    When you take good men for bad, bad men for good.
    A true friend thrown aside—why, life itself
    Is not more precious!
                 In time you will know this well:
    For time, and time alone, will show the just man,   110
    Though scoundrels are discovered in a day.
Choragos: This is well said, and a prudent man would ponder it.
    Judgments too quickly formed are dangerous.
Oedipus: But is he not quick in his duplicity?

And shall I not be quick to parry him?   115
Would you have me stand still, hold my peace, and let
This man win everything, through my inaction?
Kreon: And you want—what is it, then? To banish me?
Oedipus: No, not exile. It is your death I want,
So that all the world may see what treason means.   120
Kreon: You will persist, then? You will not believe me?
Oedipus: How can I believe you?
Kreon: Then you are a fool.
Oedipus: To save myself?
Kreon: In justice, think of me.   125
Oedipus: You are evil incarnate.
Kreon: But suppose that you are wrong?
Oedipus: Still I must rule.
Kreon: But not if you rule badly.
Oedipus: O city, city!   130
Kreon: It is my city, too!
Choragos: Now, my lords, be still. I see the queen,
Iokastê, coming from her palace chambers;
And it is time she came, for the sake of you both.
This dreadful quarrel can be resolved through her.   135

(Enter Iokastê.*)*

Iokastê: Poor foolish men, what wicked din is this?
With Thebes sick to death, is it not shameful
That you should rake some private quarrel up?
(to Oedipus*)* Come into the house.
                    —And you, Kreon, go now: 140
Let us have no more of this tumult over nothing.
Kreon: Nothing? No, sister: what your husband plans for me
Is one of two great evils: exile or death.
Oedipus: He is right.
                    Why, woman I have caught him squarely   145
Plotting against my life.
Kreon: No! Let me die
Accurst if ever I have wished you harm!
Iokastê: Ah, believe it, Oedipus!
In the name of the gods, respect this oath of his   150
For my sake, for the sake of these people here!

STROPHE I

Choragos: Open your mind to her, my lord. Be ruled by her, I beg you!
Oedipus: What would you have me do?
Choragos: Respect Kreon's word. He has never spoken like a fool,
And now he has sworn an oath.   155
Oedipus: You know what you ask?

Choragos: I do.

Oedipus: Speak on, then.

Choragos: A friend so sworn should not be baited so,
   In blind malice, and without final proof.   160

Oedipus: You are aware, I hope, that what you say
   Means death for me, or exile at the least.

STROPHE 2

Choragos: No, I swear by Helios, first in Heaven!
      May I die friendless and accurst,
      The worst of deaths, if ever I meant that!   165
         It is the withering fields
            That hurt my sick heart:
         Must we bear all these ills,
            And now your bad blood as well?

Oedipus: Then let him go. And let me die, if I must,   170
   Or be driven by him in shame from the land of Thebes.
   It is your unhappiness, and not his talk,
   That touches me.
                  As for him—
   Wherever he goes, hatred will follow him.   175

Kreon: Ugly in yielding, as you were ugly in rage!
   Natures like yours chiefly torment themselves.

Oedipus: Can you not go? Can you not leave me?

Kreon: I can.
   You do not know me; but the city knows me,   180
   And in its eyes I am just, if not in yours.

(*Exit* Kreon.)

ANTISTROPHE 1

Choragos: Lady Iokastê, did you not ask the King to go to his chambers?

Iokastê: First tell me what has happened.

Choragos: There was suspicion without evidence; yet it rankled
   As even false charges will.   185

Iokastê: On both sides?

Choragos: On both.

Iokastê: But what was said?

Choragos: Oh let it rest, let it be done with!
   Have we not suffered enough?   190

Oedipus: You see to what your decency has brought you:
   You have made difficulties where my heart saw none.

ANTISTROPHE 2

Choragos: Oedipus, it is not once only I have told you—
   You must know I should count myself unwise

To the point of madness, should I now forsake you—   195
> You, under whose hand,
>> In the storm of another time,
>> Our dear land sailed out free.
>> But now stand fast at the helm!

Iokastê: In God's name, Oedipus, inform your wife as well: 200
Why are you so set in this hard anger?

Oedipus: I will tell you, for none of these men deserves
My confidence as you do. It is Kreon's work,
His treachery, his plotting against me.

Iokastê: Go on, if you can make this clear to me.   205

Oedipus: He charges me with the murder of Laïos.

Iokastê: Has he some knowledge? Or does he speak from hearsay?

Oedipus: He would not commit himself to such a charge,
But he has brought in that damnable soothsayer
To tell his story.   210

Iokastê: Set your mind at rest.
If it is a question of soothsayers, I tell you
That you will find no man whose craft gives knowledge
Of the unknowable.

>   Here is my proof: 215

An oracle was reported to Laïos once
(I will not say from Phoibos himself, but from
His appointed ministers, at any rate)
That his doom would be death at the hands of his own son—
His son, born of his flesh and of mine!   220
Now, you remember the story: Laïos was killed
By marauding strangers where three highways meet;
But his child had not been three days in this world
Before the king had pierced the baby's ankles
And left him to die on a lonely mountainside.   225

Thus, Apollo never caused that child
To kill his father, and it was not Laïos' fate
To die at the hands of his son, as he had feared.
This is what prophets and prophecies are worth!
Have no dread of them.   230

>   It is God himself
Who can show us what he wills, in his own way.

Oedipus: How strange a shadowy memory crossed my mind,
Just now while you were speaking; it chilled my heart.

Iokastê: What do you mean? What memory do you speak of?   235

Oedipus: If I understand you, Laïos was killed
At a place where three roads meet.

Iokastê: So it was said;
We have no later story.

Oedipus: Where did it happen?   240

Iokastê: Phokis, it is called: at a place where the Theban Way
   Divides into the roads toward Delphi and Daulia.
Oedipus: When?
Iokastê: We had the news not long before you came
   And proved the right to your succession here.   245
Oedipus: Ah, what net has God been weaving for me?
Iokastê: Oedipus! Why does this trouble you?
Oedipus: Do not ask me yet.
   First, tell me how Laïos looked, and tell me
   How old he was.   250
Iokastê: He was tall, his hair just touched
   With white; his form was not unlike your own.
Oedipus: I think that I myself may be accurst
   By my own ignorant edict.
Iokastê: You speak strangely.   255
   It makes me tremble to look at you, my king.
Oedipus: I am not sure that the blind man can not see.
   But I should know better if you were to tell me—
Iokastê: Anything—though I dread to hear you ask it.
Oedipus: Was the king lightly escorted, or did he ride   260
   With a large company, as a ruler should?
Iokastê: There were five men with him in all: one was a herald.
   And a single chariot, which he was driving.
Oedipus: Alas, that makes it plain enough!
                            But who—   265
   Who told you how it happened?
Iokastê: A household servant,
   The only one to escape.
Oedipus: And is he still
   A servant of ours?   270
Iokastê: No; for when he came back at last
   And found you enthroned in the place of the dead king,
   He came to me, touched my hand with his, and begged
   That I would send him away to the frontier district
   Where only the shepherds go—   275
   As far away from the city as I could send him.
   I granted his prayer; for although the man was a slave,
   He had earned more than this favor at my hands.
Oedipus: Can he be called back quickly?
Iokastê: Easily.   280
   But why?
Oedipus: I have taken too much upon myself
   Without enquiry; therefore I wish to consult him.
Iokastê: Then he shall come.
                         But am I not one also   285
   To whom you might confide these fears of yours?
Oedipus: That is your right; it will not be denied you,

Now least of all; for I have reached a pitch
Of wild foreboding. Is there anyone
To whom I should sooner speak?   290

Polybos of Corinth is my father.
My mother is a Dorian: Meropê.
I grew up chief among the men of Corinth
Until a strange thing happened—
Not worth my passion, it may be, but strange.   295
At a feast, a drunken man maundering in his cups
Cries out that I am not my father's son!°
I contained myself that night, though I felt anger
And a sinking heart. The next day I visited
My father and mother, and questioned them. They stormed,   300
Calling it all the slanderous rant of a fool;
And this relieved me. Yet the suspicion
Remained always aching in my mind;
I knew there was talk; I could not rest;
And finally, saying nothing to my parents,   305
I went to the shrine at Delphi.

The god dismissed my question without reply;
He spoke of other things.
                        Some were clear,
Full of wretchedness, dreadful, unbearable: 310
As, that I should lie with my own mother, breed
Children from whom all men would turn their eyes;
And that I should be my father's murderer.

I heard all this, and fled. And from that day
Corinth to me was only in the stars   315
Descending in that quarter of the sky,
As I wandered farther and farther on my way
To a land where I should never see the evil
Sung by the oracle. And I came to this country
Where, so you say, King Laïos was killed.   320

I will tell you all that happened there, my lady.

There were three highways
Coming together at a place I passed;
And there a herald came towards me, and a chariot
Drawn by horses, with a man such as you describe   325
Seated in it. The groom leading the horses

---

297 *not my father's son:* Oedipus perhaps interprets this as an allegation that he is a bastard, the son
of Meropê but not of Polybos. The implication, at any rate, is that he is not of royal birth, not the
legitimate heir to the throne of Corinth.

Forced me off the road at his lord's command;
But as this charioteer lurched over towards me
I struck him in my rage. The old man saw me
And brought his double goad down upon my head   330
As I came abreast.

                He was paid back, and more!
Swinging my club in this right hand I knocked him
Out of his car, and he rolled on the ground.

                       I killed him.   335
I killed them all.
Now if that stranger and Laïos were—kin,
Where is a man more miserable than I?
More hated by the gods? Citizen and alien alike
Must never shelter me or speak to me—   340
I must be shunned by all.

                And I myself
Pronounced this malediction upon myself!

Think of it: I have touched you with these hands,
These hands that killed your husband. What defilement!   345

Am I all evil, then? It must be so,
Since I must flee from Thebes, yet never again
See my own countrymen, my own country,
For fear of joining my mother in marriage
And killing Polybos, my father.   350

                    Ah,
If I was created so, born to this fate,
Who could deny the savagery of God?
O holy majesty of heavenly powers!
May I never see that day! Never!   355
Rather let me vanish from the race of men
Than know the abomination destined me!

Choragos: We too, my lord, have felt dismay at this.
     But there is hope: you have yet to hear the shepherd.
Oedipus: Indeed, I fear no other hope is left me.   360
Iokastê: What do you hope from him when he comes?
Oedipus: This much:
     If his account of the murder tallies with yours,
     Then I am cleared.
Iokastê: What was it that I said   365
     Of such importance?
Oedipus: Why, "marauders," you said,
     Killed the king, according to this man's story.
     If he maintains that still, if there were several,
     Clearly the guilt is not mine: I was alone.   370
     But if he says one man, singlehanded, did it,
     Then the evidence all points to me.

Iokastê: You may be sure that he said there were several;
    And can he call back that story now? He can not.
    The whole city heard it as plainly as I.   375
    But suppose he alters some detail of it:
    He can not ever show that Laïos's death
    Fulfilled the oracle: for Apollo said
    My child was doomed to kill him; and my child—
    Poor baby!—it was my child that died first.   380
    No. From now on, where oracles are concerned,
    I would not waste a second thought on any.
Oedipus: You may be right.
                         But come: let someone go
    For the shepherd at once. This matter must be settled.   385
Iokastê: I will send for him.
    I would not wish to cross you in anything,
    And surely not in this.—Let us go in.

(Exeunt into the palace.)

ODE II

Chorus: Let me be reverent in the ways of right,
    Lowly the paths I journey on;
    Let all my words and actions keep
    The laws of the pure universe
    From highest Heaven handed down.   5
    For Heaven is their bright nurse,
    Those generations of the realms of light;
    Ah, never of mortal kind were they begot,
    Nor are they slaves of memory, lost in sleep:
    Their Father is greater than Time, and ages not.   10

ANTISTROPHE 1

    The tyrant is a child of Pride
    Who drinks from his great sickening cup
    Recklessness and vanity,
    Until from his high crest headlong
    He plummets to the dust of hope.   15
    That strong man is not strong.
    But let no fair ambition be denied;
    May God protect the wrestler for the State
    In government, in comely policy,
    Who will fear God, and on His ordinance wait.   20

STROPHE 2

Haughtiness and the high hand of disdain
Tempt and outrage God's holy law;
And any mortal who dares hold
No immortal Power in awe
Will be caught up in a net of pain: 25
The price for which his levity is sold.
Let each man take due earnings, then,
And keep his hands from holy things,
And from blasphemy stand apart—
Else the crackling blast of heaven   30
Blows on his head, and on his desperate heart.
Though fools will honor impious men,
In their cities no tragic poet sings.

ANTISTROPHE 2

Shall we lose faith in Delphi's obscurities,
We who have heard the world's core   35
Discredited, and the sacred wood
Of Zeus at Elis praised no more?
The deeds and the strange prophecies
Must make a pattern yet to be understood.
Zeus, if indeed you are lord of all,   40
Throned in light over night and day,
Mirror this in your endless mind:
Our masters call the oracle
Words on the wind, and the Delphic vision blind!
Their hearts no longer know Apollo,   45
And reverence for the gods has died away.

SCENE III

(*Enter* Iokastê.)

Iokastê: Princes of Thebes, it has occurred to me
To visit the altars of the gods, bearing
These branches as a suppliant, and this incense.
Our king is not himself: his noble soul
Is overwrought with fantasies of dread,   5
Else he would consider
The new prophecies in the light of the old.
He will listen to any voice that speaks disaster,
And my advice goes for nothing.

(She approaches the altar, R.)

To you, then, Apollo, 10
Lycean lord, since you are nearest, I turn in prayer.
Receive these offerings, and grant us deliverance
From defilement. Our hearts are heavy with fear
When we see our leader distracted, as helpless sailors
Are terrified by the confusion of their helmsman. 15

(Enter Messenger.*)*

Messenger: Friends, no doubt you can direct me:
    Where shall I find the house of Oedipus,
    Or, better still, where is the king himself?
Choragos: It is this very place, stranger; he is inside.
    This is his wife and mother of his children. 20
Messenger: I wish her happiness in a happy house,
    Blest in all the fulfillment of her marriage.
Iokastê: I wish as much for you: your courtesy
    Deserves a like good fortune. But now, tell me:
    Why have you come? What have you to say to us? 25
Messenger: Good news, my lady, for your house and your husband.
Iokastê: What news? Who sent you here?
Messenger: I am from Corinth.
    The news I bring ought to mean joy for you,
    Though it may be you will find some grief in it. 30
Iokastê: What is it? How can it touch us in both ways?
Messenger: The word is that the people of the Isthmus
    Intend to call Oedipus to be their king.
Iokastê: But old King Polybos—is he not reigning still?
Messenger: No. Death holds him in his sepulchre. 35
Iokastê: What are you saying? Polybos is dead?
Messenger: If I am not telling the truth, may I die myself.
Iokastê (to a Maidservant*):* Go in, go quickly; tell this to your master.

O riddlers of God's will, where are you now!
This was the man whom Oedipus, long ago, 40
Feared so, fled so, in dread of destroying him—
But it was another fate by which he died.

(Enter Oedipus, C.*)*

Oedipus: Dearest Iokastê, why have you sent for me?
Iokastê: Listen to what this man says, and then tell me
    What has become of the solemn prophecies.
Oedipus: Who is this man? What is his news for me? 45
Iokastê: He has come from Corinth to announce your father's death!

Oedipus: Is it true, stranger? Tell me in your own words.

Messenger: I can not say it more clearly: the king is dead.

Oedipus: Was it by treason? Or by an attack of illness?   50

Messenger: A little thing brings old men to their rest.

Oedipus: It was sickness, then?

Messenger: Yes, and his many years.

Oedipus: Ah!

Why should a man respect the Pythian hearth,° or   55
Give heed to the birds that jangle above his head?
They prophesied that I should kill Polybos,
Kill my own father; but he is dead and buried,
And I am here—I never touched him, never,
Unless he died of grief for my departure,   60
And thus, in a sense, through me. No. Polybos
Has packed the oracles off with him underground.
They are empty words.

Iokastê: Had I not told you so?

Oedipus: You had; it was my faint heart that betrayed me.   65

Iokastê: From now on never think of those things again.

Oedipus: And yet—must I not fear my mother's bed?

Iokastê: Why should anyone in this world be afraid,
Since Fate rules us and nothing can be foreseen?
A man should live only for the present day.   70

Have no more fear of sleeping with your mother:
How many men, in dreams, have lain with their mothers!
No reasonable man is troubled by such things.

Oedipus: That is true; only—
If only my mother were not still alive!   75
But she is alive. I can not help my dread.

Iokastê: Yet this news of your father's death is wonderful.

Oedipus: Wonderful. But I fear the living woman.

Messenger: Tell me, who is this woman that you fear?

Oedipus: It is Meropê, man; the wife of King Polybos.   80

Messenger: Meropê? Why should you be afraid of her?

Oedipus: An oracle of the gods, a dreadful saying.

Messenger: Can you tell me about it or are you sworn to silence?

Oedipus: I can tell you, and I will.
Apollo said through his prophet that I was the man   85
Who should marry his own mother, shed his father's blood
With his own hands. And so, for all these years
I have kept clear of Corinth, and no harm has come—
Though it would have been sweet to see my parents again.

Messenger: And is this the fear that drove you out of Corinth?   90

Oedipus: Would you have me kill my father?

---

55 *Pythian hearth:* Delphi.

Messenger: As for that
      You must be reassured by the news I gave you.
Oedipus: If you could reassure me, I would reward you.
Messenger: I had that in mind, I will confess: I thought   95
      I could count on you when you returned to Corinth.
Oedipus: No: I will never go near my parents again.
Messenger: Ah, son, you still do not know what you are doing—
Oedipus: What do you mean? In the name of God tell me!
Messenger: —if these are your reasons for not going home.   100
Oedipus: I tell you, I fear the oracle may come true.
Messenger: And guilt may come upon you through your parents?
Oedipus: That is the dread that is always in my heart.
Messenger: Can you not see that all your fears are groundless?
Oedipus: Groundless? Am I not my parents' son?   105
Messenger: Polybos was not your father.
Oedipus: Not my father?
Messenger: No more your father than the man speaking to you.
Oedipus: But you are nothing to me!
Messenger: Neither was he.   110
Oedipus: Then why did he call me son?
Messenger: I will tell you:
      Long ago he had you from my hands, as a gift.
Oedipus: Then how could he love me so, if I was not his?
Messenger: He had no children, and his heart turned to you.   115
Oedipus: What of you? Did you buy me? Did you find me by chance?
Messenger: I came upon you in the woody vales of Kithairon.
Oedipus: And what were you doing there?
Messenger: Tending my flocks.
Oedipus: A wandering shepherd?   120
Messenger: But your savior, son, that day.
Oedipus: From what did you save me?
Messenger: Your ankles should tell you that.
Oedipus: Ah, stranger, why do you speak of that childhood pain?
Messenger: I pulled the skewer that pinned your feet together.   125
Oedipus: I have had the mark as long as I can remember.
Messenger: That was why you were given the name you bear.
Oedipus: God! Was it my father or my mother who did it?
      Tell me!
Messenger: I do not know. The man who gave you to me   130
      Can tell you better than I.
Oedipus: It was not you that found me, but another?
Messenger: It was another shepherd gave you to me.
Oedipus: Who was he? Can you tell me who he was?
Messenger: I think he was said to be one of Laïos' people.   135
Oedipus: You mean the Laïos who was king here years ago?
Messenger: Yes; King Laïos; and the man was one of his herdsmen.
Oedipus: Is he still alive? Can I see him?

Messenger: These men here
    Know best about such things.   140
Oedipus: Does anyone here
    Know this shepherd that he is talking about?
    Have you seen him in the fields, or in the town?
    If you have, tell me. It is time things were made plain.
Choragos: I think the man he means is that same shepherd   145
    You have already asked to see. Iokastê perhaps
    Could tell you something.
Oedipus: Do you know anything
    About him, Lady? Is he the man we have summoned?
    Is that the man this shepherd means?   150
Iokastê: Why think of him?
    Forget this herdsman. Forget it all.
    This talk is a waste of time.
Oedipus: How can you say that,
    When the clues to my true birth are in my hands?   155
Iokastê: For God's love, let us have no more questioning!
    Is your life nothing to you?
    My own is pain enough for me to bear.
Oedipus: You need not worry. Suppose my mother a slave,
    And born of slaves: no baseness can touch you.   160
Iokastê: Listen to me, I beg you: do not do this thing!
Oedipus: I will not listen; the truth must be made known.
Iokastê: Everything that I say is for your own good!
Oedipus: My own good
    Snaps my patience, then! I want none of it.   165
Iokastê: You are fatally wrong! May you never learn who you are!
Oedipus: Go, one of you, and bring the shepherd here.
    Let us leave this woman to brag of her royal name.
Iokastê: Ah, miserable!
    That is the only word I have for you now.   170
    That is the only word I can ever have.

(Exit into the palace.)

Choragos: Why has she left us, Oedipus? Why has she gone
    In such a passion of sorrow? I fear this silence:
    Something dreadful may come of it.
Oedipus: Let it come!   175
    However base my birth, I must know about it.
    The Queen, like a woman, is perhaps ashamed
    To think of my low origin. But I
    Am a child of Luck; I can not be dishonored.
    Luck is my mother; the passing months, my brothers,   180
    Have seen me rich and poor.
              If this is so,

How could I wish that I were someone else?
How could I not be glad to know my birth?

ODE III

STROPHE

Chorus: If ever the coming time were known
    To my heart's pondering,
    Kithairon, now by Heaven I see the torches
    At the festival of the next full moon,
    And see the dance, and hear the choir sing   5
    A grace to your gentle shade:
    Mountain where Oedipus was found,
    O mountain guard of a noble race!
    May the god° who heals us lend his aid,
    And let that glory come to pass   10
    For our king's cradling-ground.

ANTISTROPHE

Of the nymphs that flower beyond the years,
    Who bore you,° royal child,
    To Pan of the hills or the timberline Apollo,
    Cold in delight where the upland clears,   15
    Or Hermês for whom Kyllenê's heights are piled?
    Or flushed as evening cloud,
    Great Dionysos, roamer of mountains,
    He—was it he who found you there,
    And caught you up in his own proud   20
    Arms from the sweet god-ravisher
    Who laughed by the Muses' fountains?

SCENE IV

Oedipus: Sirs: though I do not know the man,
    I think I see him coming, this shepherd we want:
    He is old, like our friend here, and the men
    Bringing him seem to be servants of my house.
    But you can tell, if you have ever seen him.   5

(Enter Shepherd *escorted by* Servants.*)*

---

9 *god:* Apollo.   13 *Who bore you:* The chorus is suggesting that perhaps Oedipus is the son of
one of the immortal nymphs and of a god—Pan, Apollo, Hermes, or Dionysos. The "sweet god-
ravisher" is the presumed mother.

Choragos: I know him, he was Laïos' man. You can trust him.

Oedipus: Tell me first, you from Corinth: is this the shepherd
    We were discussing?

Messenger: This is the very man.

Oedipus (to Shepherd*):* Come here. No, look at me. You must answer   10
    Everything I ask.—You belonged to Laïos?

Shepherd: Yes: born his slave, brought up in his house.

Oedipus: Tell me: what kind of work did you do for him?

Shepherd: I was a shepherd of his, most of my life.

Oedipus: Where mainly did you go for pasturage?   15

Shepherd: Sometimes Kithairon, sometimes the hills near-by.

Oedipus: Do you remember ever seeing this man out there?

Shepherd: What would he be doing there? This man?

Oedipus: This man standing here. Have you ever seen him before?

Shepherd: No. At least, not to my recollection.   20

Messenger: And that is not strange, my lord. But I'll refresh
    His memory: he must remember when we two
    Spent three whole seasons together, March to September,
    On Kithairon or thereabouts. He had two flocks;
    I had one. Each autumn I'd drive mine home   25
    And he would go back with his to Laïos' sheepfold.—
    Is this not true, just as I have described it?

Shepherd: True, yes; but it was all so long ago.

Messenger: Well, then: do you remember, back in those days,
    That you gave me a baby boy to bring up as my own?   30

Shepherd: What if I did? What are you trying to say?

Messenger: King Oedipus was once that little child.

Shepherd: Damn you, hold your tongue!

Oedipus: No more of that!
    It is your tongue needs watching, not this man's.   35

Shepherd: My king, my master, what is it I have done wrong?

Oedipus: You have not answered his question about the boy.

Shepherd: He does not know . . . He is only making trouble . . .

Oedipus: Come, speak plainly, or it will go hard with you.

Shepherd: In God's name, do not torture an old man!   40

Oedipus: Come here, one of you; bind his arms behind him.

Shepherd: Unhappy king! What more do you wish to learn?

Oedipus: Did you give this man the child he speaks of?

Shepherd: I did.
    And I would to God I had died that very day.   45

Oedipus: You will die now unless you speak the truth.

Shepherd: Yet if I speak the truth, I am worse than dead.

Oedipus: (to Attendant*):* He intends to draw it out, apparently—

Shepherd: No! I have told you already that I gave him the boy.

Oedipus: Where did you get him? From your house? From somewhere else?   50

Shepherd: Not from mine, no. A man gave him to me.

Oedipus: Is that man here? Whose house did he belong to?

Shepherd: For God's love, my king, do not ask me any more!
Oedipus: You are a dead man if I have to ask you again.
Shepherd: Then . . . Then the child was from the palace of Laïos.   55
Oedipus: A slave child? or a child of his own line?
Shepherd: Ah, I am on the brink of dreadful speech!
Oedipus: And I of dreadful hearing. Yet I must hear.
Shepherd: If you must be told, then . . .

                                 They said it was Laïos' child;   60
But it is your wife who can tell you about that.
Oedipus: My wife!—Did she give it to you?
Shepherd: My lord, she did.
Oedipus: Do you know why?
Shepherd: I was told to get rid of it.   65
Oedipus: Oh heartless mother!
Shepherd: But in dread of prophecies . . .
Oedipus: Tell me.
Shepherd: It was said that the boy would kill his own father.
Oedipus: Then why did you give him over to this old man?   70
Shepherd: I pitied the baby, my king,
And I thought that this man would take him far away
To his own country.

                  He saved him—but for what a fate!
For if you are what this man says you are,   75
No man living is more wretched than Oedipus.
Oedipus: Ah God!
It was true!
            All the prophecies!
                       —Now,   80
O Light, may I look on you for the last time!
I, Oedipus,
Oedipus, damned in his birth, in his marriage damned,
Damned in the blood he shed with his own hand!

(He rushes into the palace.)

ODE IV

STROPHE 1

Chorus: Alas for the seed of men.
     What measure shall I give these generations
     That breathe on the void and are void
     And exist and do not exist?
     Who bears more weight of joy   5
     Than mass of sunlight shifting in images,
     Or who shall make his thought stay on

That down time drifts away?
Your splendor is all fallen.
O naked brow of wrath and tears, 10
O change of Oedipus!
I who saw your days call no man blest—
Your great days like ghosts gone.

ANTISTROPHE 1

That mind was a strong bow.
Deep, how deep you drew it then, hard archer, 15
At a dim fearful range,
And brought dear glory down!
You overcame the stranger°—
The virgin with her hooking lion claws—
And though death sang, stood like a tower 20
To make pale Thebes take heart.
Fortress against our sorrow!
True king, giver of laws,
Majestic Oedipus!
No prince in Thebes had ever such renown, 25
No prince won such grace of power.

STROPHE 2

And now of all men ever known
Most pitiful is this man's story:
His fortunes are most changed, his state
Fallen to a low slave's 30
Ground under bitter fate.
O Oedipus, most royal one!
The great door° that expelled you to the light
Gave at night—ah, gave night to your glory:
As to the father, to the fathering son. 35
All understood too late.
How could that queen whom Laïos won,
The garden that he harrowed at his height,
Be silent when that act was done?

ANTISTROPHE 2

But all eyes fail before time's eye, 40
All actions come to justice there.
Though never willed, though far down the deep past,
Your bed, your dread sirings,
Are brought to book at last.

---

18 *the stranger:* The Sphinx. 33 *great door:* Iokastê's womb.

Child by Laïos doomed to die,   45
Then doomed to lose that fortunate little death,
Would God you never took breath in this air
That with my wailing lips I take to cry:
For I weep the world's outcast.
I was blind, and now I can tell why: 50
Asleep, for you had given ease of breath
To Thebes, while the false years went by.

EXODOS°

(Enter, from the palace, Second Messenger.)

Second Messenger: Elders of Thebes, most honored in this land,
    What horrors are yours to see and hear, what weight
    Of sorrow to be endured, if, true to your birth,
    You venerate the line of Labdakos!
    I think neither Istros nor Phasis, those great rivers,   5
    Could purify this place of all the evil
    It shelters now, or soon must bring to light—
    Evil not done unconsciously, but willed.

    The greatest griefs are those we cause ourselves.
Choragos: Surely, friend, we have grief enough already;   10
    What new sorrow do you mean?
Second Messenger: The queen is dead.
Choragos: O miserable queen! But at whose hand?
Second Messenger: Her own.
    The full horror of what happened you can not know,   15
    For you did not see it; but I, who did, will tell you
    As clearly as I can how she met her death.

    When she had left us,
    In passionate silence, passing through the court,
    She ran to her apartment in the house,   20
    Her hair clutched by the fingers of both hands.
    She closed the doors behind her; then, by that bed
    Where long ago the fatal son was conceived—
    That son who should bring about his father's death—
    We heard her call upon Laïos, dead so many years,   25
    And heard her wail for the double fruit of her marriage,
    A husband by her husband, children by her child.

Exodos: Final scene.

Exactly how she died I do not know:
For Oedipus burst in moaning and would not let us
Keep vigil to the end: it was by him   30
As he stormed about the room that our eyes were caught.
From one to another of us he went, begging a sword,
Hunting the wife who was not his wife, the mother
Whose womb had carried his own children and himself.
I do not know: it was none of us aided him,   35
But surely one of the gods was in control!
For with a dreadful cry
He hurled his weight, as though wrenched out of himself,
At the twin doors: the bolts gave, and he rushed in.
And there we saw her hanging, her body swaying   40
From the cruel cord she had noosed about her neck.
A great sob broke from him, heartbreaking to hear,
As he loosed the rope and lowered her to the ground.
I would blot out from my mind what happened next!
For the king ripped from her gown the golden brooches   45
That were her ornament, and raised them, and plunged them down
Straight into his own eyeballs, crying, "No more,
No more shall you look on the misery about me,
The horrors of my own doing! Too long you have known
The faces of those whom I should never have seen,   50
Too long been blind to those for whom I was searching!
From this hour, go in darkness!" And as he spoke,
He struck at his eyes—not once, but many times;
And the blood spattered his beard,
Bursting from his ruined sockets like red hail.   55

So from the unhappiness of two this evil has sprung,
A curse on the man and woman alike. The old
Happiness of the house of Labdakos
Was happiness enough: where is it today?
It is all wailing and ruin, disgrace, death—all   60
The misery of mankind that has a name—
And it is wholly and for ever theirs.

Choragos: Is he in agony still? Is there no rest for him?

Second Messenger: He is calling for someone to open the doors wide
So that all the children of Kadmos may look upon   65
His father's murderer, his mother's—no,
I can not say it!
                    And then he will leave Thebes,
Self-exiled, in order that the curse
Which he himself pronounced may depart from the house.   70
He is weak, and there is none to lead him,
So terrible is his suffering.
                    But you will see:

Look, the doors are opening; in a moment
You will see a thing that would crush a heart of stone.   75

(The central door is opened; Oedipus, blinded, is led in.)

Choragos: Dreadful indeed for men to see.
      Never have my own eyes
      Looked on a sight so full of fear.

      Oedipus!
      What madness came upon you, what daemon   80
      Leaped on your life with heavier
      Punishment than a mortal man can bear?
      No: I can not even
      Look at you, poor ruined one.
      And I would speak, question, ponder,   85
      If I were able. No.
      You make me shudder.
Oedipus: God. God.
      Is there a sorrow greater?
      Where shall I find harbor in this world?   90
      My voice is hurled far on a dark wind.
      What has God done to me?
Choragos: Too terrible to think of, or to see.

STROPHE I

Oedipus: O cloud of night,
      Never to be turned away: night coming on,   95
      I can not tell how: night like a shroud!
      My fair winds brought me here.
                                    O God. Again
      The pain of the spikes where I had sight,
      The flooding pain   100
      Of memory, never to be gouged out.
Choragos: This is not strange.
      You suffer it all twice over, remorse in pain,
      Pain in remorse.

ANTISTROPHE I

Oedipus: Ah dear friend   105
      Are you faithful even yet, you alone?
      Are you still standing near me, will you stay here,
      Patient, to care for the blind?
                                    The blind man!
      Yet even blind I know who it is attends me,   110

By the voice's tone—
Though my new darkness hide the comforter.
Choragos: Oh fearful act!
What god was it drove you to rake black
Night across your eyes?   115

STROPHE 2

Oedipus: Apollo. Apollo. Dear
Children, the god was Apollo.
He brought my sick, sick fate upon me.
But the blinding hand was my own!
How could I bear to see   120
When all my sight was horror everywhere?
Choragos: Everywhere; that is true.
Oedipus: And now what is left?
Images? Love? A greeting even,
Sweet to the senses? Is there anything?   125
Ah, no, friends: lead me away.
Lead me away from Thebes.
                                    Lead the great wreck
And hell of Oedipus, whom the gods hate.
Choragos: Your misery, you are not blind to that.   130
Would God you had never found it out!

ANTISTROPHE 2

Oedipus: Death take the man who unbound
My feet on that hillside
And delivered me from death to life! What life?
If only I had died,   135
This weight of monstrous doom
Could not have dragged me and my darlings down.
Choragos: I would have wished the same.
Oedipus: Oh never to have come here
With my father's blood upon me! Never   140
To have been the man they call his mother's husband!
Oh accurst! Oh child of evil,
To have entered that wretched bed—
                                    the selfsame one!
More primal than sin itself, this fell to me.   145
Choragos: I do not know what words to offer you.
You were better dead than alive and blind.
Oedipus: Do not counsel me any more. This punishment
That I have laid upon myself is just.
If I had eyes,   150
I do not know how I could bear the sight
Of my father, when I came to the house of Death,

Or my mother: for I have sinned against them both
So vilely that I could not make my peace
By strangling my own life.   155
                         Or do you think my children,
Born as they were born, would be sweet to my eyes?
Ah never, never! Nor this town with its high walls,
Nor the holy images of the gods.
                         For I,   160
Thrice miserable!—Oedipus, noblest of all the line
Of Kadmos, have condemned myself to enjoy
These things no more, by my own malediction
Expelling that man whom the gods declared
To be a defilement in the house of Laïos.   165
After exposing the rankness of my own guilt,
How could I look men frankly in the eyes?
No, I swear it,
If I could have stifled my hearing at its source,
I would have done it and made all this body   170
A tight cell of misery, blank to light and sound:
So I should have been safe in my dark mind
Beyond external evil.
                         Ah Kithairon!
Why did you shelter me? When I was cast upon you,   175
Why did I not die? Then I should never
Have shown the world my execrable birth.

Ah Polybos! Corinth, city that I believed
The ancient seat of my ancestors: how fair
I seemed, your child! And all the while this evil   180
Was cancerous within me!
                         For I am sick
In my own being, sick in my origin.
O three roads, dark ravine, woodland and way
Where three roads met: you, drinking my father's blood,   185
My own blood, spilled by my own hand: can you remember
The unspeakable things I did there, and the things
I went on from there to do?
                         O marriage, marriage!
That act that engendered me, and again the act   190
Performed by the son in the same bed—
                         Ah, the net
Of incest, mingling fathers, brothers, sons,
With brides, wives, mothers: the last evil
That can be known by men: no tongue can say   195
How evil!
            No. For the love of God, conceal me
Somewhere far from Thebes; or kill me; or hurl me
Into the sea, away from men's eyes for ever.

Come, lead me. You need not fear to touch me.   200
Of all men, I alone can bear this guilt.

(*Enter Kreon.*)

Choragos: Kreon is here now. As to what you ask,
He may decide the course to take. He only
Is left to protect the city in your place.
Oedipus: Alas, how can I speak to him? What right have I   205
To beg his courtesy whom I have deeply wronged?
Kreon: I have not come to mock you, Oedipus,
Or to reproach you, either. (*to* Attendants)
                              —You, standing there:
If you have lost all respect for man's dignity,   210
At least respect the flame of Lord Helios:
Do not allow this pollution to show itself
Openly here, an affront to the earth
And Heaven's rain and the light of day. No, take him
Into the house as quickly as you can.   215
For it is proper
That only the close kindred see his grief.
Oedipus: I pray you in God's name, since your courtesy
Ignores my dark expectation, visiting
With mercy this man of all men most execrable: 220
Give me what I ask—for your good, not for mine.
Kreon: And what is it that you turn to me begging for?
Oedipus: Drive me out of this country as quickly as may be
To a place where no human voice can ever greet me.
Kreon: I should have done that before now—only,   225
God's will had not been wholly revealed to me.
Oedipus: But his command is plain: the parricide
Must be destroyed. I am that evil man.
Kreon: That is the sense of it, yes; but as things are,
We had best discover clearly what is to be done.   230
Oedipus: You would learn more about a man like me?
Kreon: You are ready now to listen to the god.
Oedipus: I will listen. But it is to you
That I must turn for help. I beg you, hear me.

The woman in there—   235
Give her whatever funeral you think proper:
She is your sister.
                    —But let me go, Kreon!
Let me purge my father's Thebes of the pollution
Of my living here, and go out to the wild hills,   240
To Kithairon, that has won such fame with me,
The tomb my mother and father appointed for me,
And let me die there, as they willed I should.

And yet I know
Death will not ever come to me through sickness   245
Or in any natural way: I have been preserved
For some unthinkable fate. But let that be.

As for my sons, you need not care for them.
They are men, they will find some way to live.
But my poor daughters, who have shared my table,   250
Who never before have been parted from their father—
Take care of them, Kreon; do this for me.

And will you let me touch them with my hands
A last time, and let us weep together?
Be kind, my lord,   255
Great prince, be kind!
                           Could I but touch them,
They would be mine again, as when I had my eyes.

(*Enter* Antigonê *and* Ismenê, *attended.*)

          Ah, God!
Is it my dearest children I hear weeping?   260
Has Kreon pitied me and sent my daughters?
Kreon: Yes, Oedipus: I knew that they were dear to you
    In the old days, and know you must love them still.
Oedipus: My God bless you for this—and be a friendlier
    Guardian to you than he has been to me!   265

    Children, where are you?
    Come quickly to my hands: they are your brother's—
    Hands that have brought your father's once clear eyes
    To this way of seeing—
                           Ah dearest ones,   270
    I had neither sight nor knowledge then, your father
    By the woman who was the source of his own life!
    And I weep for you—having no strength to see you—,
    I weep for you when I think of the bitterness
    That men will visit upon you all your lives.   275
    What homes, what festivals can you attend
    Without being forced to depart again in tears?
    And when you come to marriageable age,
    Where is the man, my daughters, who would dare
    Risk the bane that lies on all my children?   280
    Is there any evil wanting? Your father killed
    His father; sowed the womb of her who bore him;
    Engendered you at the fount of his own existence!
    That is what they will say of you.

Then, whom   285
Can you ever marry? There are no bridegrooms for you,
And your lives must wither away in sterile dreaming.

O Kreon, son of Menoikeus!
You are the only father my daughters have,
Since we, their parents, are both of us gone for ever.   290
They are your own blood: you will not let them
Fall into beggary and loneliness;
You will keep them from the miseries that are mine!
Take pity on them; see, they are only children,
Friendless except for you. Promise me this,   295
Great prince, and give me your hand in token of it.

(Kreon *clasps his right hand.*)

Children:
I could say much, if you could understand me,
But as it is, I have only this prayer for you:
Live where you can, be as happy as you can—   300
Happier, please God, than God has made your father.
Kreon: Enough. You have wept enough. Now go within.
Oedipus: I must; but it is hard.
Kreon: Time eases all things.
Oedipus: You know my mind, then?   305
Kreon: Say what you desire.
Oedipus: Send me from Thebes!
Kreon: God grant that I may!
Oedipus: But since God hates me . . .
Kreon: No, he will grant your wish.   310
Oedipus: You promise?
Kreon: I can not speak beyond my knowledge.
Oedipus: Then lead me in.
Kreon: Come now, and leave your children.
Oedipus: No! Do not take them from me!   315
Kreon: Think no longer
That you are in command here, but rather think
How, when you were, you served your own destruction.

(Exeunt *into the house all but the* Chorus; *the* Choragos *chants directly to the*
audience.)

Choragos: Men of Thebes: look upon Oedipus.
This is the king who solved the famous riddle   320
And towered up, most powerful of men.
No mortal eyes but looked on him with envy,
Yet in the end ruin swept over him.

Let every man in mankind's frailty
Consider his last day; and let none   325
Presume on his good fortune until he find
Life, at his death, a memory without pain.

SOPHOCLES

www   *(c. 496–405 B.C.)* **Web**

One of ancient Greece's most prolific and innovative dramatists, Sophocles is
credited with expanding the number of the Greek Chorus from twelve to fifteen
and authoring some 120 plays. Only 7 of his tragedies survive, 3 comprising the
"Theban Plays" and such other works as *Ajax, Electra,* and *Philoctetes.*

TOPICS FOR CRITICAL THINKING

1. If Aristotle's definition of the tragic hero is correct, what evidence exists in the plot
   of *Oedipus Rex* to suggest Oedipus's tragic error or failing? How does he contribute
   to his own reversal of fortune?
2. Friedrich Nietzsche, among others, argues that the Chorus is far more than an
   "ideal audience," as some have claimed, and observes that the Chorus existed long
   before tragic characters did. What functions does the Chorus perform in this play?
   What would the play lack without a Chorus?
3. What part does the Choragos play? Why is he necessary?
4. Does Iokastê learn the truth before Oedipus does? What might be inferred from
   her attempts to dissuade Oedipus from learning more about his past?
5. How is the story of Oedipus appropriate to a religious festival? What moral or religious conclusions might an audience draw from the play?
6. The language of *Oedipus Rex* is often explicitly poetic, replete with metaphors and
   other figures of speech. What central metaphors does the play develop? How do
   they contribute to our understanding of the play's action?
7. How do you respond to the conclusion? Aristotle's notion of catharsis emphasizes
   pity and fear as the responses appropriate to tragedy. Do you feel either or both of
   these feelings? Why or why not?

TOPICS FOR CRITICAL WRITING

1. Read one scene of *Oedipus Rex* closely. What failings or errors does Oedipus exhibit
   in this scene? How does the scene progress? What specific aspect of the scene advances the plot in a cause and effect way? Your thesis should explain why this scene
   is significant to the play in terms resembling those developed by Aristotle.
2. Develop a thesis about the narrative function or functions of the Chorus (as opposed to its function of providing entertainment through song and movement).
   What is its principal role in the play?

Critical Perspective: On Characterization in Greek Tragedy

"Critics are always reminding us that character-drawing in Greek tragedy was a very different thing from what we meet in the modern theatre, different and (it is implied) perhaps more limited or rudimentary. But this contrast between ancient and modern is too vague to be illuminating: we need to define exactly what kind of difference it is before we can decide whether it is important. In drama meant for live performance it can hardly be a difference of *technique*, since every playwright is limited to two basic means of character-drawing, what his figures say and do and what other people say and do to them and about them. Nor can there be much significance in difference of *convention*. Of course convention counts for something: a dramatist writing for three masked male actors, who must take all the speaking roles in his play, male or female indiscriminately, using a highly formal and declamatory style of acting in a large open-air theatre, will create characters which can be rendered in these circumstances. But there is no reason why the particular conventions of his time should limit his portrayal of character in any serious way: Lady Macbeth, after all, was written to be played by a teenage boy. Surely the differences that really demand attention are those of *attitude*.

"Modern audiences . . . expect a dramatist to be primarily concerned with the unique aspect of each man's experience, with the solitary focus of consciousness which, as John Jones puts it, is 'secret, inward, interesting.' When they first read a Greek play they are naturally inclined to interpret what the characters say and do as if the ancient dramatist shared their preoccupation with idiosyncratic detail. But closer study soon makes plain that this is an anachronistic prejudice, which can all too easily lead us to irrelevant or absurd conclusions."

— P. E. Easterling, "Character in Sophocles" (1993)

Critical Perspective: On Greek Theater and Religious Ritual

"The relationship between the space of tragic performance and the space of sacrifice has great symbolic importance. Sacrifice was in a sense another dramatic mode. . . . The Greek conception of tragedy is closely linked to the idea of sacrifice, and the *Oresteia* [Aeschylus's trilogy] seems in this respect to have had a seminal influence on how this space was used. In the trilogy Agamemnon, Cassandra, and Clytaemnestra are each in turn seen as sacrificial victims, and enter the single *skênê* door to be slaughtered. The later dramatists worked many variants on the convention. In *Antigone* and *Women of Trachis*, for example, the protagonists go off to side to die, but the woman who embodies the reproductive power of the house is revealed in the end as the sacrificial victim behind the skênê door. . . . The convention of off-stage death relates to the fact that the playing area is purified, whilst the blood sacrifice takes place below and beyond the playing area."

—David Wiles, from *Tragedy in Athens* (1997)

Critical Perspective: On Greek Tragedy and Women

"Greek tragedy was written and performed by men and aimed—perhaps not exclusively if women were present in the theater—at a large, public male audience. Masculine identity and conflicts remain central to the enterprise, but the texts often explore or query these issues through female characters and the culturally more marginal positions that they occupy. Such indirection is basic to the genre as a whole. Tragic plots borrow from the whole repertoire of Greek myths, often myths about cities other than Athens, and the plays take place in the remote past. The heroic kings who dominate the cities of Greek tragedies no more directly reflect the leaders of Athenian democracy than the active and assertive women who make public choices and determine the outcome of the plot of so many Greek tragedies resemble their more restricted Athenian counterparts. At the same time, . . . the tragedies provoke an implicit dialogue between present and past, and the enduring fascination of these stories of powerful aristocratic families for a democratic *polis* (city-state) requires explanation.

"The study of tragic women is both more limited and in a sense more elusive than that of tragic men. Tragedy at least makes a pretense of knowing what women are and how they should act. . . . As a category, women are a 'tribe' apparently less differentiated as individuals than men; paradoxically, they are both more embedded in the social system and marginal to its central institutions. Ideally, their speech and action should be severely limited, since they are by nature incapable of full social maturity and independence."

—Helene P. Foley, from *Female Acts in Greek Tragedy* (2001)

44

Kinds of Drama: Comedy

Comedy. It's a word we hear all the time to describe everything from stories that make us laugh to the antics of Jim Carrey, Robin Williams, or the Wayans brothers. The term *comedy* also refers to a kind of drama that has attracted large audiences for well over two thousand years and is still going strong—in some ways, stronger than ever. Since the early years of American television in the 1940s, for example, situation comedies have enjoyed tremendous popularity: from *I Love Lucy* to *Everybody Loves Raymond*, from *Leave It to Beaver* to *Cosby*, from *My Three Sons* to *Friends*. These days, comedy on television has its own cable channel and celebrities like Jon Stewart and Ben Stein. Comedy has played an equally prominent role in the history of Hollywood and international film. Such talented clowns as Charlie Chaplin and Buster Keaton delighted audiences before movies had soundtracks, and comedians today continue to rank among Hollywood's most popular actors. In fact, many of today's film and television stars—Eddie Murphy, Ellen DeGeneres, Chris Rock, Jerry Seinfeld, and Jay Leno, to name just a few—were featured stand-up artists at comedy clubs before stepping in front of the camera.

Comedy, as these brief remarks imply, can be understood in various ways. This chapter outlines several definitions of dramatic comedy by way of *The Flying Doctor* (1658?), written by one of the European theater's most enduring talents, Jean-Baptiste Poquelin, who early in his professional career took the stage name Molière. **Web** As was the case in the previous chapter on tragedy, *www* most definitions of comedy as a distinct kind of dramatic form begin with considerations of plot and character.

The Comic Form

Comedy is as old as the Western theater itself, its laughter countering the tears of tragic drama. On the ancient Greek stage, a trilogy of tragic plays was typically accompanied by a short comic piece, a **satyr,** from which the English word *satyr* comes and which the term *satire* resembles. This etymology also suggests how closely aligned desire—a satyr in Greek mythology is a woodland deity, half goat and half man, famous for his lechery—and at least one type of comedy are. A form that Molière mastered, satire holds up social vices, repressive laws, even popular fashion to laughter or ridicule. Anyone who has ever enjoyed *Saturday Night Live*, with its irreverent portrayals of former President Bill Clinton's sexual indiscretions or George W. Bush's occasionally laughable mispronunciations, is familiar with satire.

Comedy, at its most basic level, provokes laughter and, as French critic Henri Bergson emphasizes, laughter originates in human frailty and with people to find humor in it. In other words, like all drama, comedy is an intrinsically social form that needs an audience. And it has always seemed to find one, from the works of Aristophanes in Greece and Plautus and Terence in ancient Rome, to contemporary comedies on the New York and London stages. Few comic playwrights in this history can match Molière's wit, his ability to construct and then unravel predicaments for his lead characters, and—especially— his development of clever tricksters who make such comic resolutions possible. All of these abilities are prominently on display in his early one-act farce, *The Flying Doctor*.

Plot

Like most theories of tragedy, critical thinking about comedy begins with the *Poetics* (335 B.C.), in which Aristotle compares the two forms in terms of plot and characterization. For Aristotle, dramatic action imitates real life: Tragedy concerns the actions of people better or greater than those in real life, and comedy represents the actions of characters who are worse. *Better* and *worse* are not in this instance terms of moral evaluation or assessments of ethical goodness or badness. Rather, tragic heroes are admirable figures who possess greater political and social power than the average citizen. They hail from the ranks of kings or princes (Oedipus and Hamlet), great military leaders (Macbeth and Othello), or royal families (Antigone and Electra). The central characters of comedies, by contrast, originate often in the middle or lower classes, or they are the powerless daughters of fathers who wish to control their lives in an almost tyrannical fashion. Tragic characters like Oedipus or Othello thus fall from power or greatness, while the central characters of comedy rise to fulfill their desires.

How these characters fall or rise, though, how tragic and comic plots reach their opposite conclusions, is quite different. As is the case in Molière's *The Flying Doctor*, the plots of comedies are both predictable and improbable at the same time. This is not so confused a statement as it might first appear, and Aristotle's comparison of tragedy and comedy addresses this paradox. As discussed in the preceding chapter, the best tragedies possess a **unity of action**: All the incidents in the play are linked by "probability and necessity." That is, tragedies are causally structured: Because event A occurs, consequence B follows. Once Oedipus determines to find the murderer of his father, for example, the events that ensue follow inevitably from this goal. By contrast, the typical comic plot is brought to closure almost by accident, by an unexpected "twist" that allows the conflicts driving the action to be settled happily. The conflict inherent to one perennially popular form, the **romantic comedy,** for which Shakespeare is best known, is often resolved in this surprising way: A young man or woman wants to marry, an obstacle represented by the father or a repressive law interferes with the young lover's wishes, and a twist of the plot—a coincidence or chance occurrence—allows the obstructing father or repressive law to be overcome. The result? Marriage, sometimes multiple marriages, and a celebration, dance, or family reunion to mark the joyous outcome.

The plot of *The Flying Doctor* opens in a manner typical of romantic comedy, the play's conflict originating in the desires of two young lovers to marry and the opposition of the girl's father to their union. Further, we learn in the opening dialogue that Valère's love for Lucile is imperiled by her father Gorgibus's determination to have her marry a wealthy older man. As Lucile's cousin Sabine informs us, Gorgibus had wanted to hurry this arranged marriage along and only through feigning illness has Lucile managed to delay this fate. Fortunately for the young lovers, Sabine has formulated a plan. Believing that his daughter really is ill, Gorgibus has called for a doctor and, because he will "believe almost anything," Sabine instructs Valère to have his valet Sganarelle impersonate one. While Sganarelle occupies the gullible father's attention with phony diagnoses and other foolery, Sabine arranges for the two lovers to be married. Gorgibus's intention to marry his daughter Lucile to whomever he pleases is defeated without bloodshed or other serious consequences, and the audience is entertained by the often ridiculous manner in which Sganarelle thwarts his plans.

Such an overwhelming of tragic possibility is essential to comedy's success, for the comic world, as eighteenth-century writer Oliver Goldsmith observes, will "not admit of tragic distress." Yet, for the comic outcome to be celebrated as a victory, the possibility of serious consequences must exist. Such is the case near the end of *The Flying Doctor* when Gorgibus, learning that Lucile has been married to Valère, responds angrily to the news: "I'm ruined! I'll have [Sganarelle] strung up, you dog, you knave!" His anger quickly subsides, as Sganarelle reminds Gorgibus that he has gained a wealthy son-in-law and that further opposition to his daughter's marriage will only bring him disgrace. Again, the tears of tragedy, the audience's feelings of pity for the tragic hero, are replaced by smiles and laughter. In some instances, these responses are accompanied by a keener insight into the social conditions or archaic laws that placed such an outcome in doubt in the first place. Why, for example, *should* a father be empowered to choose a husband for his daughter? What kinds of societies allow such laws to be enforced or created in the first place?

Although muted in *The Flying Doctor*, the possibility of "tragic distress" in many comedies is significant. In his later, quite controversial play *Tartuffe* (1664), for example, Molière extends such a possibility until the final scene, and it is much in evidence throughout the play's action. Distraught over the thought of marrying the imposter Tartuffe as her father Orgon commands, Mariane threatens to kill herself; later, she begs her father to send her to a convent instead of giving her in marriage to a man she despises. Her brother Damis, determined to help his sister and expose Tartuffe's villainy, is threatened with banishment and disinheritance. Orgon even calls for a stick to beat his son before disowning him and making Tartuffe his sole heir. And, although Orgon is finally made to see Tartuffe's hypocrisy, his rush to judgment has placed his family's security in jeopardy. As the legal heir to Orgon's house and wealth, Tartuffe presses his claim by forcing eviction on the very man who had befriended him. Fortunately, none of these events occur as an emissary of an anonymous Prince saves the day. All but Tartuffe live happily ever after: The lovers marry, the family is reunited, and their home is saved.

Unlike the action of tragic drama, comic plots effect such magic, overturning the ominous possibilities of dramatic conflict and allowing the more festive ones to be realized. In so doing, comedy enacts a process of wish fulfillment, much as dreams often do. In opposing the desires of the young with parental or legal obstacles to their fulfillment, the comic plot typically elevates the young over the old, the free expression of love over its restraint, and—in the best cases—effects the transformation of a repressive society into a more humane one. In such plays as *The Flying Doctor* and *Tartuffe*, the father-daughter relationship often serves to represent these oppositions. As *The Flying Doctor* further demonstrates, comic action often requires disguise, humorous pranks, and other strategies to insure the young lovers' happiness. Such a comic resolution also involves the interactions of a cast of predictable and entertaining characters.

Character

In *The Flying Doctor*, Molière combines the interests of romantic comedy with those of two other comic forms: **satire** and **commedia dell'arte**, the latter a type of comedy made popular in sixteenth-century Italy. Commedia dell'arte features predictable or **stock characters** performing customary roles that delighted audiences: young lovers, witty servants (Sganarelle), dupes or "gulls" (Gorgibus), and others. Like that of romantic comedy, the typical plot of commedia dell'arte is quite simple: A character endeavors to win a woman, a large sum of money, or both at another character's expense. A full-length play like *Tartuffe* realizes such a definition perfectly. Through his maneuvering and posturing, the hypocrite Tartuffe hopes to steal both Orgon's wife and his money. Part of the pleasure for audiences lies in their knowledge that one character is outwitting another, and, at times, such characters draw us into their confidence, making us confederates in their intrigues.

The Flying Doctor, an early play in Molière's career, exhibits many of these traits, in part by featuring such enduringly popular comic types. Initially reluctant to join Sabine and Valère in their hoodwinking of Gorgibus, Sganarelle complains that he "wouldn't know how to start" to impersonate a doctor. Loyal to Valère and eager to help him, Sganarelle finally relents, although he believes he lacks the brains for the job. He doesn't. In fact, Sganarelle manages to hoodwink his gull through his nimble wit, his physical dexterity, and a series of almost unbelievable deceptions. The result is hilarious mischief on Sganarelle's part and total confusion on Gorgibus's.

One in a long line of clever trickster-servants in Molière's drama, Sganarelle initiates his deception with a ridiculous, but nonetheless impressive sounding pronouncement: "Hippocrates has said—and Galen has confirmed it with many persuasive arguments—that when a girl is not in good health she must be sick." "Duh," we might say. Of course, if someone is not in good health, it is likely she is sick. But Gorgibus is taken in by the high-sounding rhetoric of Sganarelle's next sentence: "You are right to put your trust in me, for I am the greatest, the most brilliant, the most doctoral physician in the vegetable, mineral, and animal kingdoms." Continuing in his zany impersonation, Sganarelle, as many physicians might request, asks for a sample of his patient's urine—which he promptly drinks. Not surprisingly, Gorgibus looks on incredulously, but the audience isn't surprised as it is revealed that Lucile is filling beakers not with urine, but with white wine. Comedy then and now often deals with the body and its products, including excrement, as the installments of the popular *Austin Powers* films confirm: Dr. Evil's assistant is called Number Two, which allows Mike Myers as Austin Powers the opportunity for a long bathroom sequence in *Austin Powers: International Man of Mystery*; and in *The Spy Who Shagged Me* Austin mistakes a stool specimen for old coffee and drinks it. Such scatological or "potty humor" was as popular on the seventeenth-century stage as it is on the contemporary big screen.

Popular too was the inversion of social class. In Molière's dramatic world, class hierarchies are frequently overturned so that servants outwit masters and genuine wit exposes deceit. Like Sganarelle, the clever serving-girl Dorine in *Tartuffe* enables the comic victory as much as the Prince's officer does by his last-minute appearance. She sees through Tartuffe immediately, serves as a mediator in Mariane's Act Two lovers' quarrel with her confused boyfriend, and devises Mariane's strategy in humoring her "dunce" of a father to delay Tartuffe's plans long enough to expose him. Moreover, through several asides, Dorine relates to the audience her acute observations and strategies to outwit Tartuffe. Repulsed by Tartuffe's feigned piety, for example, she turns to the audience to exclaim, "Dear God, what affectation! What a fake!" Through such remarks, we become her allies, her confidantes, just as we are in league with Sganarelle and his co-conspirators from the beginning of *The Flying Doctor*.

By the later seventeenth century, Molière's plot and characters—foolish and domineering fathers, vulnerable daughters, and outrageous hypocrites—were familiar figures on stage. So, too, were clowns like Sganarelle and other **low comic** characters noted for their physical dexterity, linguistic ineptitude, and ability to make audiences laugh. In Shakespeare's comedies, these are most often buffoons with names that indicate their foolishness or unsophisticated background: Dogberry, Bottom, and so on. If romantic comedy satisfies the heart—all's well that end's well—low comedy and farce aim at the belly or unrestrained laughter through physical gags, mildly obscene language or jokes, and just plain nonsense. Sganarelle's portrayal of both a doctor and his twin, a ploy that tests his quickness and acting ability, constitutes a prime example of the silliness conventional to low comedy. We laugh at Gorgibus's stupidity but are also entertained by the clown's ingenuity in deceiving him.

In these and many other ways, plot or action and characterization constitute the two prime ingredients of successful comedy.

Satire: Scene, Language, Thought

Molière's plays, even short ones like *The Flying Doctor*, are not merely romantic comedies or examples of seventeenth-century commedia dell'arte. That is to say, they frequently do more than entertain an audience. Social satire was clearly Molière's aim in *Tartuffe*, for example, as several statements he made about it confirm. In three petitions to King Louis XIV urging that his controversial play be allowed to be performed, Molière reiterated that comedy's "duty" is to "to correct men by amusing them." Its "function," he argued, is "to correct men's vices." First produced in the spring of 1664, *Tartuffe* amused both the king and his wife. Its satirical representation of religious piety, however, disturbed others, including powerful Catholic clergymen and the queen mother, so much so that the play was blocked from further production for nearly five years. In early 1669, Molière wrote his third petition or "placet" to Louis XIV, calling for "la grande résurrection" of the play, which was finally granted and the interdiction on its production lifted.

Unlike so-called low comedy, employing the fake karate chops and pratfalls of Austin Powers or the elastic facial expressions of a talented comic like Jim Carrey, satire appeals to the intellect. And sometimes it does so in abrasive ways that offend some members of an audience. Perhaps the nineteenth-century British writer George Meredith puts it best: "To touch and kindle the mind through laughter demands . . . a most subtle delicacy." To "kindle the mind," to illuminate social injustices and reveal flawed value systems or repressive ideas, satirists must know the mores of a society inside out. They must also be attuned to the impostures of prominent people and the flaws of the ideologies that support their social status. Such comedy, as Meredith is quick to point out, also requires a "society of cultivated men and women": an audience, in other words, who will get the gag and understand precisely what is being ridiculed or mocked.

All of this begs the question of precisely what is being held up for comic skewering in *The Flying Doctor*. One place to start in answering these questions is the play's setting. If satire aims at exposing overly rigid societal mores and fashion—and if it requires a relatively sophisticated audience—then, not surprisingly, most satirical comedy is set in the city. Fashionable homes and neighborhoods in Paris, London, New York, and elsewhere have furnished satirists with abundant opportunities to poke fun at hypocrisy, foolish adherence to the reigning fashion, and even contemporary political debates. Most romantic comedy is set in the city as well, before it moves to a more natural setting to allow the young lovers to meet and then returns to the city later. But unlike the appeals to the heart and emotions in romantic comedy—think of plays like *A Midsummer Night's Dream* or films like *Sleepless in Seattle* and *You've Got Mail*—satire requires a more dispassionate and informed audience that recognizes the defects it attacks.

The scene of *The Flying Doctor*, for instance, is the front of Gorgibus's house in a small French town, and we quickly infer from the dialogue that the greedy father is most concerned with material wealth: in fact, he wants to force his daughter to marry a wealthy man. We also learn that Gorgibus's property includes not only a house but an appreciable garden with a pavilion where Lucile is feigning her convalescence. What sorts of families have houses complete with such large garden properties? What sorts of men have valets, as we learn a moment later about Sganarelle's relationship to Valère? Wealthy or at least upper middle class families. And many of these, as is the case here, are headed by patriarchs whose desires to accumulate wealth have overwhelmed whatever more human values they once possessed. The audience is thus compelled by this first scene to consider such questions as greed, social class, and fashion as the play progresses.

Yet another question concerns the ways in which Molière accomplishes his critique of Gorgibus's values. One answer is that, in the most cutting satire, language and the wit underlying it contribute to the satirist's objectives. So, for example, when Sganarelle asks for someone to write a prescription for Lucile, Gorgibus wonders why he can't write it himself. Sganarelle's speedy improvisation that he has too many things to think about and might forget some of them is both ridiculous and brilliant, totally disarming his adversary. Such quick-witted exchanges or **repartee** amuse and instruct throughout *The Flying Doctor*.

Satirical comedy, therefore, typically requires more than plot and character. Setting, language, and social criticism combine to amuse *and* instruct, thereby fulfilling the larger critical aims of playwrights like Molière. In so doing, in holding up social mores, class structures, and artificial values to ridicule, satire demonstrates that comedy is often a more significant, more political form than some critics have been willing to recognize.

Reading the Comic Form

Understanding comedy begins with formal analysis, with an assessment of the ways plot, characterization, setting, dialogue, and language work together to convey meaning. Comic laughter is sometimes as simple as a man slipping on a banana peel (although psychologists have often wondered why we find such accidents amusing and have devised complex theories to explain the sources of such laughter). At other times, and this is particularly true of satire, the comic form is a more intricate system, producing both pleasure and instruction in more complicated ways. Such instruction might begin with our reflection about those things we find funny and the reasons we laugh at them. Once we have puzzled over such matters, we may discover that comedy is a far more sophisticated form than it initially appears.

MOLIÈRE

The Flying Doctor   *(1658?)*

Le Médecin volant

CHARACTERS:

Gorgibus, a respectable, comfortable, credulous citizen
Lucile, his daughter
Sabine, his niece
Valère, young man in love with *Lucile*
Sganarelle, valet to *Valère*
Gros-René, valet to *Gorgibus*
A Lawyer

Scene: [*A street in a small French town.*]

[Valère, *a young man, is talking to* Sabine, *a young woman, in front of the* house of Gorgibus, *her uncle.*]

Valère: Sabine, what do you advise me to do?
Sabine: We'll have to work fast. My uncle is determined to make Lucile
   marry this rich man, Villebrequin, and he's pushed the preparations so far
   that the marriage would have taken place today if my cousin were not in
   love with you. But she is—she has told me so—and since my greedy
   uncle is forcing our hand, we've come up with a device for putting off the
   wedding. Lucile is pretending to be ill, and the old man, who'll believe
   almost anything, has sent me for a doctor. If you have a friend we can
   trust, I'll take him to my uncle and he can suggest that Lucile is not getting nearly enough fresh air. The old boy will then let her live in the
   pavilion at the end of our garden, and you can meet her secretly, marry
   her, and leave my uncle to take out his anger on Villebrequin.
Valère: But where can I find a doctor who will be sympathetic to me and risk
   his reputation? Frankly, I can't think of a single one.
Sabine: I was wondering if you could disguise your valet? It'll be easy for
   him to fool the old man.
Valère: If you knew my valet as I do— He's so dense he'll ruin everything.
   Still, I can't think of anybody else. I'll try to find him.

[Sabine *leaves.*]

Where can I start to look for the halfwit?

[Sganarelle *comes in, playing intently with a yo-yo.*]

Sganarelle, my dear boy, I'm delighted to see you. I need you for an
important assignment. But I don't know what you can do——

Sganarelle: Don't worry, Master, I can do anything. I can handle any assignment, especially important ones. Give me a difficult job. Ask me to find out what time it is. Or to check on the price of butter at the market. Or to water your horse. You'll soon see what I can do.

Valère: This is more complicated. I want you to impersonate a doctor.

Sganarelle. A doctor! You know I'll do anything you want, Master, but when it comes to impersonating a doctor, I couldn't do it if I tried—wouldn't know how to start. I think you're making fun of me.

Valère: If you care to try, I'll give you one hundred francs.

Sganarelle: One hundred whole francs, just for pretending to be a doctor? No, Master, it's impossible. You see I don't have the brains for it. I'm not subtle enough; I'm not even bright. So that's settled. I impersonate a doctor. Where?

Valère: You know Gorgibus? His daughter is lying in there ill—No, it's no use; you'll only confuse matters.

Sganarelle: I bet I can confuse matters as well as all the doctors in this town put together. Or kill patients as easily. You know the old saying, "After you're dead, the doctor comes." When I take a hand there'll be a new saying: "After the doctor comes, you're dead." Now I think it over, though, it's not that easy to play a doctor. What if something goes wrong?

Valère: What can go wrong? Gorgibus is a simple man, not to say stupid, and you can dazzle him by talking about Hippocrates and Galen. Put on a bold front.

Sganarelle: In other words, talk about philosophy and mathematics and the like. Leave it to me, Master; if he's a fool, as you say, I think I can swing it. All I need is a doctor's cloak and a few instructions. And also my license to practice, or to put it another way, those hundred francs.

[*They go out together.*]

[Gorgibus *enters with his fat valet,* Gros-René.]

Gorgibus: Hurry away and find a doctor. My daughter's sick. Hurry.

Gros-René: Hell's bells, the trouble is you're trying to marry her off to an old man when she wants a young man; that's the only thing making her sick. Don't you see any connection between the appetite and the illness?

Gorgibus: I can see that the illness will delay the wedding. Get a move on.

Gros-René: All this running about and my stomach's crying out for a new inner lining of food and now I have to wait for it. I need the doctor for myself as much as for your daughter. I'm in a desperate state.

[*He lumbers off.*]

[Sabine *comes in with* Sganarelle *behind her.*]

Sabine: Uncle, I have good news. I've brought a remarkably skilled doctor with me, a man who has traveled across the world and knows the medical secrets of Asia and Africa. He'll certainly be able to cure Lucile. As luck would have it, somebody pointed him out to me and I knew you'd

want to meet him. He's so clever that I wish I were ill myself so that he
could cure me.

Gorgibus: Where is he?

Sabine: Standing right behind me. [*She moves away.*] There he is.

Gorgibus: Thank you so much for coming, Doctor. I'll take you straight to
my daughter, who is unwell. I'm putting all my trust in you.

Sganarelle: Hippocrates has said—and Galen has confirmed it with many
persuasive arguments—that when a girl is not in good health she must
be sick. You are right to put your trust in me, for I am the greatest, the
most brilliant, the most doctoral physician in the vegetable, mineral, and
animal kingdoms.

Gorgibus: I'm overjoyed to hear it.

Sganarelle: No ordinary physician am I, no common medico. In my opinion,
all others are quacks. I have peculiar talents. I have secrets. *Salamalec*
and *shalom aleichem. Nil nisi bonum? Si, Signor. Nein, mein Herr. Para
siempre.* But let us begin.

[*He takes* Gorgibus' *pulse.*]

Sabine: He's not the patient. His daughter is.

Sganarelle: That is of no consequence. The blood of the parent and the blood
of the child are the same. *Si? Nein. Per quanto? Nada.* And by examining
the father I can reveal the daughter's malady. Monsieur Gorgibus, is there
any way in which I might scrutinize the invalid's urine?

Gorgibus: Of course. Sabine, hurry. Bring the doctor a sample of Lucile's
urine.

[Sabine *goes into the house.*]

Doctor, I'm afraid my daughter may die.

Sganarelle: Tell her to be careful. She is not supposed to amuse herself doing
things like that without a doctor's prescription.

[Sabine *comes out with a beaker full of urine and gives it to* Sganarelle, *who
drinks it.*]

It's very warm. There must be some inflammation in her intestines.
Nevertheless, she is not seriously ill.

Gorgibus: [*gaping*] You swallowed it?

Sganarelle: Not immediately. I let it wash about in my mouth first. An ordinary doctor would merely look at it, but I am extraordinary. As the liquid touches my taste buds, I can tell both the cause of the illness and its
probable development. But this was a meager specimen. I need another
bladderful.

Sabine: She had enough trouble getting that much out.

Sganarelle: I never heard of such reluctance. Tell her she must urinate freely,
copiously. As much as she can manage.

Sabine: I'll try.

[*She goes off again into the house. This time we see, through a window, how the "urine" is procured:* Sabine *is holding another beaker and* Lucile *is pouring white wine into it from a bottle.*]

Sganarelle: [*licking his beaker, aside*] If every invalid pissed like this I'd stay a doctor for the rest of my life.

[Sabine *returns with the second beaker, a tiny liqueur glass.*]

Sabine: She says this is definitely all she has available. She can't squeeze out another drop.
Sganarelle: This is scandalous. Monsieur Gorgibus, your daughter will have to learn to do better than this. She's one of the worst urinators I've encountered. I can see that I'll have to prescribe a potion that encourages her to flow more generously. Now, may I see the patient?
Sabine: She may be up by now. I'll bring her out.

[*She goes into the house and brings* Lucile *back with her.*]

Sganarelle: How do you do, Mademoiselle? So you are sick?
Lucile: Yes, Doctor.
Sganarelle: That is a striking sign that you are not well. Do you feel pains in your head, in your kidneys?
Lucile: Yes, Doctor.
Sganarelle: Very good. As one great physician has said in regard to the nature of animal life—well—he said many things. We must attribute this to the interconnections between the humors and the vapors. For example, since melancholy is the natural enemy of joy, and since the bile that spreads through the body makes us turn yellow, and since there is nothing more inimical to good health than sickness, we may conclude with that great man that your daughter is indisposed. Let me write you a prescription.
Gorgibus: Quick! A table, paper, some ink—
Sganarelle: Is there anybody here who knows how to write?
Gorgibus: Don't you?
Sganarelle: I have so many things to think of I forget half of them. Now it's obvious to me that your daughter needs fresh air and open prospects.
Gorgibus: We have a very beautiful garden and a pavilion with some rooms that look out on it. If you agree, I can have her stay there.
Sganarelle: Let us examine this dwelling.

[*They start to go out.*]

[*The* Lawyer *appears.*]

Lawyer: Monsieur Gorgibus—
Gorgibus: Your servant, Monsieur.
Lawyer: I hear that your daughter is sick. May I offer my services, as a friend of the family?
Gorgibus: I have the most scholarly doctor you ever met looking into this.

Lawyer: Really? I wonder if I might be able to meet him, however briefly?

[Gorgibus *beckons to* Sganarelle. Lucile *and* Sabine *have moved offstage.*]

Gorgibus: Doctor, I would like you to meet one of my dear friends, who is a lawyer and would like the privilege of conversing with you.

Sganarelle: I wish I could spare the time, Monsieur, but I dare not neglect my patients. Please forgive me.

[*He tries to go. The* Lawyer *holds his sleeve.*]

Lawyer: My friend Gorgibus has intimated, Monsieur, that your learning and abilities are formidable, and I am honored to make your acquaintance. I therefore take the liberty of saluting you in your noble work, and trust that it may resolve itself well. Those who excel in any branch of knowledge are worthy of all praise, but particularly those who practice medicine, not only because of its utility, but because it contains within itself other branches of knowledge, all of which render a perfect familiarity with it almost impossible to achieve. As Hippocrates so well observes in his first aphorism, "Life is short, art is long, opportunity fleeting, experiment perilous, judgment difficult: *Vita brevis, ars vero longa, occasio autem praeceps, experimentum periculosum, judicium difficile.*"

Sganarelle: [*confidentially to* Gorgibus] Ficile, bicile, uptus, downtus, inandaboutus, wrigglo, gigolo.

Lawyer: You are not one of those doctors who apply themselves to so-called rational or dogmatic medicine, and I am sure that you conduct your work with unusual success. Experience is the great teacher: *experientia magistra rerum.* The first men who practiced medicine were so esteemed that their daily cures earned them the status of gods on earth. One must not condemn a doctor who does not restore his patients to health, for healing may not be effected by his remedies and wisdom alone. Ovid remarks, "Sometimes the ill is stronger than art and learning combined." Monsieur, I will not detain you longer. I have enjoyed this dialogue and am more impressed than before with your percipience and breadth of knowledge. I take my leave, hoping that I may have the pleasure of conversing with you further at your leisure. I am sure that your time is precious, and . . .

[*He goes off, walking backwards, still talking, waving good-bye.*]

Gorgibus: How did he strike you?

Sganarelle: He's moderately well informed. If I had more time I could engage him in a spirited discussion on some sublime and elevated topic. However, I must go. What is this?

[Gorgibus *is tucking some money into his hand.*]

Gorgibus: Believe me, Doctor, I know how much I owe you.

Sganarelle: You must be joking, Monsieur Gorgibus. I am no mercenary. [*He takes the money.*] Thank you very much.

[Gorgibus *goes off, and* Sganarelle *drops his doctor's cloak and hat at the edge of the stage, just as* Valère *reappears.*]

Valère: Sganarelle, how did it go? I've been worried. I was looking for you. Did you ruin the plan?

Sganarelle: Marvel of marvels. I played the part so well that Gorgibus thought I knew what I was talking about—and paid me. I looked at his home and told him that his daughter needed air, and he's moved her into the little house at the far end of his garden. You can visit her at your pleasure.

Valère: You've made me very happy, Sganarelle. I'm going to her now.

[*He rushes away.*]

Sganarelle: That Gorgibus is a bigger dimwit than I am to let me get away with a trick like that. Save me—here he comes again. I'll have to talk fast.

[Gorgibus *returns.*]

Gorgibus: Good morning, Monsieur.

Sganarelle: Monsieur, you see before you a poor lad in despair. Have you come across a doctor who arrived in town a short while ago and cures people miraculously?

Gorgibus: Yes, I've met him. He just left my house.

Sganarelle: I am his brother. We are identical twins and people sometimes take one of us for the other.

Gorgibus: Heaven help me if I didn't nearly make the same mistake. What is your name?

Sganarelle: Narcissus, Monsieur, at your service. I should explain that once, when I was in his study, I accidentally knocked over two containers perched on the edge of his table. He flew into such a rage that he threw me out and swore he never wanted to see me again. So here I am now, a poor boy without means or connections.

Gorgibus: Don't worry; I'll put in a good word for you. I'm a friend of his; I promise to bring you together again. As soon as I see him, I'll speak to him about it.

Sganarelle: I am very much obliged to you, Monsieur.

[*He goes out and reappears in the cloak and hat, playing the doctor again and talking to himself.*]

When patients refuse to follow their doctor's advice and abandon themselves to debauchery and—

Gorgibus: Doctor, your humble servant. May I ask a favor of you?

Sganarelle: What can I do for you, Monsieur Gorgibus?

Gorgibus: I just happened to meet your brother, who is quite distressed——

Sganarelle: He's a rascal, Monsieur Gorgibus.

Gorgibus: But he truly regrets that he made you so angry, and——

Sganarelle: He's a drunkard, Monsieur Gorgibus.

Gorgibus: But surely, Doctor, you're not going to give the poor boy up?

Sganarelle: Not another word about him. The impudence of the rogue, seeking you out to intercede for him! I implore you not to mention him to me.

Gorgibus: In God's name, Doctor, and out of respect for me, too, have pity on him. I'll do anything for you in return. I promised——

Sganarelle: You plead so insistently that, even though I swore a violent oath never to forgive him—well, I'll shake your hand on it; I forgive him. You can be assured that I am doing myself a great injury and that I would not have consented to this for any other man. Good-bye, Monsieur Gorgibus.

Gorgibus: Thank you, Doctor, thank you. I'll go off and look for the boy to tell him the glad news.

[*He walks off.* Sganarelle *takes off the doctor's cloak and hat.*]

[Valère *appears.*]

Valère: I never thought Sganarelle would do his duty so magnificently. Ah, my dear boy, I don't know how to repay you. I'm so happy I——

Sganarelle: It's easy for you to talk. Gorgibus just ran into me without my doctor's outfit, and if I hadn't come up with a quick story we'd have been sunk. Here he comes again. Disappear.

[Valère *runs away.*]

[Gorgibus *returns.*]

Gorgibus: Narcissus, I've been looking everywhere for you. I spoke to your brother and he forgives you. But to be safe, I want to see the two of you patch up your quarrel in front of me. Wait here in my house, and I'll find him.

Sganarelle: I don't think you'll find him, Monsieur. Anyhow, I wouldn't dare to wait; I'm terrified of him.

Gorgibus: [*pushing* Sganarelle *inside*] Yes, you will stay. I'm locking you in. Don't be afraid of your brother. I promise you that he's not angry now.

[*He slams the door and locks it, then goes off to look for the doctor.*]

Sganarelle: [*at the upstairs window*] Serves me right; I trapped myself and there's no way out. The weather in my future looks threatening, and if there's a storm I'm afraid I'll feel a rain of blows on my back. Or else they'll brand me across the shoulders with a whip—not exactly the brand of medicine any doctor ever prescribed. Yes, I'm in trouble. But why give up when we've come this far? Let's go the limit. I can still make a bid for freedom and prove that Sganarelle is the king of swindlers.

[*He holds his nose, closes his eyes, and jumps to the ground, just as* Gros-René *comes back. Then he darts away, picking up the cloak and hat.* Gros-René *stands staring.*]

Gros-René: A flying man! What a laugh! I'll wait around and see if there's another one.

[Gorgibus *reenters with* Sganarelle *following him in the doctor's outfit.*]

Gorgibus: Can't find that doctor. Where the devil has he hidden himself?

[*He turns and* Sganarelle *walks into him.*]

There you are. Now, Doctor, I know you said you forgive your brother, but that's not enough. I won't be satisfied until I see you embrace him. He's waiting here in my house.

Sganarelle: You are joking, Monsieur Gorgibus. Have I not extended myself enough already? I wish never to see him again.

Gorgibus: Please, Doctor, for me.

Sganarelle: I cannot refuse when you ask me like that. Tell him to come down.

[*As* Gorgibus *goes into the house,* Sganarelle *drops the clothes, clambers swiftly up to the window again, and scrambles inside.*]

Gorgibus: [*at the window*] Your brother is waiting for you downstairs, Narcissus. He said he'd do what I asked.

Sganarelle: [*at the window*] Couldn't you please make him come up here? I beg of you—let me see him in private to ask his forgiveness, because if I go down there he'll show me up and say nasty things to me in front of everybody.

Gorgibus: All right. Let me tell him.

[*He leaves the window, and* Sganarelle *leaps out, swiftly puts on his outfit again, and stands waiting for* Gorgibus *outside the door.*]

Doctor, he's so ashamed of himself he wants to beg your forgiveness in private, upstairs. Here's the key. Please don't refuse me.

Sganarelle: There is nothing I would not do for you, Monsieur Gorgibus. You will hear how I deal with him.

[*He walks into the house and soon appears at the window.* Gorgibus *has his ear cocked at the door below.* Sganarelle *alternates his voice, playing the characters one at a time.*]

Sganarelle: So there you are, you scoundrel!
—Brother, listen to me, please. I'm sorry I knocked those containers over——
—You clumsy ox!
—It wasn't my fault, I swear it.
—Not your fault, you bumpkin? I'll teach you to destroy my work.
—Brother, no, please——
—I'll teach you to trade on Monsieur Gorgibus' good nature. How dare you ask him to ask me to forgive you!
—Brother, I'm sorry, but——
—Silence, you dog!

—I never wanted to hurt you or——

—Silence, I say—

Gros-René: What exactly do you think is going on up there?

Gorgibus: It's the doctor and his brother, Narcissus. They had a little disagreement, but now they're making it up.

Gros-René: Doctor and his brother? But there's only one man.

Sganarelle: [*at the window*] Yes, you drunkard, I'll thump some good behavior
into you. [*pretends to strike a blow*] Ah, he's lowering his eyes; he knows
what he's done wrong, the jailbird. And now this hypocrite wants to play
the good apostle—

Gros-René: Just for fun, tell him to let his brother appear at the window.

Gorgibus: I will. [*to* Sganarelle] Doctor, let me see your brother for a moment.

Sganarelle: He is not fit to be seen by an honest gentleman like yourself.
Besides, I cannot bear to have him next to me.

Gorgibus: Please don't say no, after all you've done for me.

Sganarelle: Monsieur Gorgibus, you have such power over me that I must
grant whatever you wish. Show yourself, beast!

[*He appears at the window as Narcissus.*]

Monsieur Gorgibus, I thank you for your kindness.

[*He reappears as the doctor.*]

Well, Monsieur, did you take a good look at that image of impurity?

Gros-René: There's only one man there, Monsieur. We can prove it. Tell
them to stand by the window together.

Gorgibus: Doctor, I want to see you at the window embracing your brother,
and then I'll be satisfied.

Sganarelle: To any other man in the world I would return a swift and negative answer, but to you, Monsieur Gorgibus, I will yield, although not
without much pain to myself. But first I want this knave to beg your
pardon for all the trouble he has caused you.

[*He comes back as* Narcissus.]

Yes, Monsieur Gorgibus, I beg your pardon for having bothered you,
and I promise you, brother, in front of Monsieur Gorgibus there, that
I'll be so good from now on that you'll never be angry with me again.
Please let bygones be bygones.

[*He embraces the cloak and hat.*]

Gorgibus: There they are, the two of them together.

Gros-René: The man's a magician.

[*He hides;* Sganarelle *comes out of the house, dressed as the doctor.*]

Sganarelle: Here is your key, Monsieur. I have left my brother inside because
I am ashamed of him. One does not wish to be seen in his company now

that one has some reputation in this town. You may release him whenever you think fit. Goodbye, Monsieur.

[*He strides off, then as* Gorgibus *goes into the house he wheels, dropping the cloak. and hat, and climbs back through the window.*]

Gorgibus: [*upstairs*] There you are, my boy, you're free. I am pleased that your brother forgave you, although I think he was rather hard on you.

Sganarelle: Monsieur, I cannot thank you enough. A brother's blessing on you. I will remember you all my life.

[*While they are upstairs,* Gros-René *has picked up the cloak. and hat, and stands waiting for them. They come out of the door.*]

Gros-René: Well, where do you think your doctor is now?

Gorgibus: Gone, of course.

Gros-René: He's right here, under my arm. And by the way, while this fellow was getting in and out of the cloak, the hat, and the window, Valère ran off with your daughter and married her.

Gorgibus: I'm ruined! I'll have you strung up, you dog, you knave! Yes, you deserve every name your brother called you—What am I saying?

Sganarelle: You don't really want to string me up, do you, Monsieur? Please listen for one second. It's true that I was having a game with you while my master was with Mademoiselle Lucile. But in serving him I haven't done you any harm. He's a most suitable partner for her, by rank and by income, by God. Believe me, if you make a row about this you'll only bring more confusion on your head. As for that porker there, let him get lost and take Villebrequin with him. Here come our loving couple.

[*Valère enters contritely with* Lucile. *They kneel to* Gorgibus.]

Valère: We apologize to you.

Gorgibus: Well, perhaps it's lucky that I was tricked by Sganarelle; he's brought me a fine son-in-law. Let's go out to celebrate the marriage and drink a toast to the health of all the company.

[*They dance off in couples:* Valère *with* Lucile, Gorgibus *with* Gros-René, *and* Sganarelle *with* Sabine.]

CURTAIN

MOLIÈRE

(1622–1673) Web   *www*

Born Jean-Baptiste Poqueline, Molière was raised in a well-connected merchant family and enjoyed what at the time was a traditional education. He joined a theater company at the age of twenty-one, starting his career as an actor. His career as a playwright of note began in the late 1650s, and his most famous comedies include *School for Husbands* (1660), *School for Wives* (1661), *The Misanthrope* (1666), *Tartuffe* (1664), *The Miser* (1668), and *The Imaginary Invalid* (1673).

Molière remained an actor throughout his life, and his company performed frequently at the court of King Louis XIV.

TOPICS FOR CRITICAL THINKING

1. If Molière's announced intention in such plays as *The Flying Doctor* includes the exposure of vice and hypocrisy, what particular vices or values seem under attack in the play? Is Gorgibus the only site of this criticism?
2. What role does social class play in *The Flying Doctor*?
3. In addition to exposing vice, plays like *The Flying Doctor* are designed to entertain. What sources of entertainment and humor exist in the play? Why are they funny?
4. Initially, Sganaralle seems doubtful that he will be able to impersonate a doctor. Is his ultimate success at doing so an indication of his modesty—he really is more skillful than he thought—or of Gorgibus's gullibility? Both?
5. Why does Gorgibus, so angry after learning that he has been deceived, quickly change his mind and embrace his daughter's marriage? Does anything prior to this moment prepare us for his change of heart?
6. Many scholars argue that romantic comedy in particular contains sympathies that we might recognize as feminist. Assuming that this view is accurate, what is feminist about *The Flying Doctor*? Another way of asking this is to acknowledge that if Sabine and Sganarelle had not contrived to help the young lovers Valère and Lucile, Gorgibus almost certainly would have successfully forced Lucile to marry a man she did not love. Why? What social conditions allow such a misalliance to occur?

TOPICS FOR CRITICAL WRITING

1. *The Flying Doctor* is set in a relatively affluent French neighborhood, but the stage directions describing it are extremely sparse. The same might be said of the characters' appearances; all we know about them is what they and other characters say. Yet, at the same time, fashion and appearance are key issues in the play. Pretend you are the director of a production of *The Flying Doctor* set in contemporary America. What do some of the central characters look like? How do you know this? Why are the issues of fashion and appearance important to a reading of the play?
2. While Gorgibus obviously provides the obstruction in *The Flying Doctor* and might thus be identified as a target of Molière's comic deflation, a number of readers suggest that French society is the real target. How so? What issues or social values are responsible for the comic predicament of the young lovers?

Critical Perspective: On the Plot of *The Flying Doctor*

"Molière has added [to the romantic comic plot] what might be called an [Alfred] Hitchcock touch to sharpen the suspense: the servant Gros-René has noticed Sganarelle's cloak and hat on the ground and will pick them up, so that the ruse of 'stealing' the personality of a doctor can go on only for so long. The question becomes not whether Sganarelle will be found out but when—and for how long he can sustain his act."

—Albert Bermel, *Molière's Theatrical Bounty: A New View of His Plays* (1990)

Critical Perspective: On Characterization: Molière and Aristotle

"It was generally agreed among theorists of drama that tragedy painted people as better than they are in real life, while comedy painted them as worse. The most important source of this view was Aristotle's remark that, as all poetry is imitation, the poet must of necessity paint men exactly as they are, better than they are, or worse than they are (*Poetics*, II, 1–7).

"There was general agreement, too, though Aristotle did not say this, that comedy should portray lower levels of society. Kings, queens and great men, it was felt, did not offer fit targets for ridicule. The natural domain of comedy . . . is 'low and trifling affairs such as take place in the private actions of people.' This view found support in the practice of Plautus and Terence, who portrayed conflicts within families, and misunderstandings and quarrels of lovers, mistresses, parents and children and, at a lower level still, of slaves, pimps and courtesans. . . .

"Molière's respectable fools, Arnolphe, Orgon, Alceste, and Philaminte . . . are in varying degrees incarnations and exaggerations of human folly and vice. The comic perspective makes them more flawed, more ludicrous than people sharing their foibles or vices might appear in real life. They fit easily into the Aristotelian definition of comic character."

—Andrew Calder, *Molière: The Theory and Practice of Comedy* (1993)

Critical Perspective: On Father and Daughters in Seventeenth-Century France

"The possibility of a recalcitrant daughter being forced into a convent [a real possibility in *Tartuffe*, for example], far from being merely a convention of comedy, was legally available as a means of parental coercion right up to the Revolution. . . . [The father in many plays] does not actually mention putting his daughter in a convent. But the extent of his legal authority is implicit. . . ."

—David Shaw, "*Tartuffe* and the Law" (1999)

45

Featured Writer

www

WILLIAM SHAKESPEARE `Web`

Seventeenth-century playwright Ben Jonson once said of him, "He was not of an age, but for all time!" Two centuries later, the romantic poet Samuel Taylor Coleridge employed more chivalric terms: "Clothed in radiant armour, and authorized by titles sure and manifold, as a poet, Shakespeare came forward to demand the throne of fame, as *the* dramatic poet of England." William Butler Yeats, winner of the Nobel Prize for Literature in 1923, claimed that "[I]f one is moved by Shakespeare . . . one is mixed with the whole spectacle of the world." And more recently, in his best-selling *Shakespeare: The Invention of the Human* (1998), Harold Bloom resorted to astronomical imagery to express his admiration:

> [Shakespeare] is a system of northern lights, an aurora borealis visible where most of us will never go. Libraries and playhouses (and cinemas) cannot contain him; he has become a spirit or "spell of light," almost too vast to apprehend.

As these accolades suggest, while selecting poets' or novelists' work for this volume was often a difficult task, choosing Shakespeare as a dramatist to study in depth was, as the saying goes, a "no-brainer." "Who else is there?" as Bloom asks in his book.

Indeed. No other dramatist's work has meant so much both to Western culture and to the history of its theater. For actors, from the time of David Garrick in the eighteenth century to that of Kenneth Branagh today, impersonating Shakespearean characters, particularly his tragic heroes, has provided a litmus test of ability and importance. In the nineteenth century, major actors like William Charles Macready, Charles Kean, Edwin Booth, and Henry Irving confirmed their significant talent playing Hamlet and Othello. In the twentieth century—on stage and in film—the list of major actors who have played in Shakespeare reads like a short list of Academy Award winners and British knights honored for their talent: Orson Welles, Laurence Olivier,

Marlon Brando, Richard Burton, Elizabeth Taylor, John Gielgud, James Earl Jones, Anthony Hopkins, Ian McKellen, Laurence Fishburne, Mel Gibson, Glenn Close, Emma Thompson, and Kenneth Branagh. Major international film directors—Welles, Olivier, Franco Zeffirelli, Roman Polanski, Peter Greenaway, Akira Kurosawa—have envisioned Shakespeare's plays as psychological thrillers, action films, tales of ancient samurai, even as Mafia yarns, as in the 1990 film *Men of Respect* starring John Turturro as a Mob-capo Macbeth, and science-fiction fables like *Forbidden Planet* (1956).

Edwin Booth as Hamlet.

Novelists, poets, composers, modern playwrights, and painters have adapted Shakespeare's plays or found in them great inspiration for their art. The Italian composer Giuseppe Verdi based several of his most enduring operas on Othello and Shakespeare's great comic creation, Sir John Falstaff; and *The Tempest* alone has received musical treatments in the later seventeenth-century by Henry Purcell, in the nineteenth century by Franz Schubert and Claude Debussy, by the French composer Hector Berlioz, and later by Jean Sibelius, Igor Stravinsky, and many more. Nineteenth-century artists Sir John Everett Millais and John Singer Sergeant, to name just two influential figures, created magnificent paintings of Ophelia, Lady Macbeth, and other Shakespearean subjects; and contemporary playwrights like Tom Stoppard—winner of an Academy Award for his coauthorship of the 1998 film *Shakespeare in Love*—Edward Bond, and Aimé Césaire have written plays inspired by Shakespeare's work. This does not even mention the number of influential novels in which Shakespearean plays are either crucial topics of discussion or inspirations, from the theories of Hamlet's father discussed in James Joyce's *Ulysses* (1922) to George Lamming's novel *Water with Berries* (1972), inspired by *The Tempest.*

Shakespeare, as his contemporary Ben Jonson so presciently described him, has been a writer "for all time" and a vital source for artists working in a myriad of cultures and artistic media. He is a playwright and a poet, a creator of intriguing characters, and a source of continuing inspiration. In the cases of the plays represented here, all of these commendations would seem especially relevant. Reading any of these three plays requires both our imagination of them in performance—this includes our study of significant productions of the plays—*and* our thoughtful engagement with their language. As is true of any well-wrought poem, the language of these plays is frequently as much figurative as it is literal. Metaphor, meter, imagery—all of these are inherent to Shakespearean language.

Orson Wells as Falstaff.

Shakespeare thus demands that we pay attention to both the visual and linguistic details of his work.

We would expect no less of a writer who has exercised such an influence on our culture and continues to do so in the twenty-first century.

Shakespeare's Stage and Career

William Shakespeare (1564–1616) moved to London from Stratford-upon-Avon in the late 1580s, a time in which the English drama had migrated as well from its former home in the church to the public stage. He married Anne Hathaway, a woman eight years his senior, in November 1582, fathering three children: Susanna, born in 1583 some six months after the marriage of her parents; and the twins Hamnet and Judith, born in February 1585. Hamnet, a variant of Hamlet, died a year later, and Shakespeare is believed to have journeyed to London at about this time (or perhaps a year earlier). A decade earlier in 1576, Shakespeare's contemporaries, the Burbages, built what many historians regard as the first public theater in London named, appropriately enough, The Theatre, and by the time Shakespeare arrived on the scene professional acting companies had been formed. Troupes of actors had existed several decades before this, but they performed mainly in inns or at the estates of wealthy noblemen. When Shakespeare arrived in London, therefore, there were both theaters and actors ready to collaborate with him.

As historians emphasize, public theaters of this time, like the Burbages' playhouse, were unroofed facilities modeled after both medieval pageant wagons, drawn by horse and then detached for performance, and bear-baiting yards. Like these popular sporting venues, most of the theaters were circular in configuration, although at least one, The Fortune, was rectangular according to theater historian Richard Leacroft. Many contained three galleries or levels for spectators to sit—cheaper standing room was allowed in a pit surrounding the stage on three sides—and the stage floor was raised off the ground a sufficient height to allow for the use of a trap door so that devils or other entities could be summoned from the depths. Several playhouses were built just south of the Thames River in London during the 1580s and 1590s—the Rose in 1587 and the Swan less than a decade later, for example. The Swan was a large structure able to seat up to three thousand spectators, and most of its competitors could accommodate between two thousand and three thousand spectators.

The most famous of these public theaters, the Globe, was built in 1599 along the south bank of the Thames, in part from used timbers from the Burbages' Theatre, which had been pulled down. Like other houses of the period, it featured a large platform stage, which historians estimate to have been twenty-seven-and-a-half feet deep and forty-three feet wide. Spectators or "groundlings" could pay a penny to stand

The Globe

on three sides of the stage, with three galleries of more expensive seating above them. Much of the dramatic action occurred downstage close to the audience, while at the back of the stage a small building or "tiring house" (short for "attiring house," where actors changed costumes) was situated. The Globe burned to the ground in 1613 during a production of *Henry VIII* and was rebuilt the following year.

Sometime around 1589, Shakespeare became associated with the Strange's and Admiral's men and turned to chronicles of English history for the sources of his first dramatic works. Between 1589 and 1593, he wrote three plays about Henry VI and one about the infamous Richard III, the first of what would become eight plays on the "Wars of the Roses" fought between two houses of nobility—the Yorks and the Lancasters—between 1400 and 1485. He wrote his first comedy, *The Comedy of Errors*, some time between 1592 and 1594, and in 1593 initiated what would eventually become a series of 154 sonnets, first published ten years later. He also produced several long narrative poems in the early 1590s, *Venus and Adonis* (1592–1593) and *The Rape of Lucrece* (1593–1594). The year 1594 marked the emergence of the Lord Chamberlain's Men, later renamed the King's Men in 1603 in honor of James the First, who assumed the throne after the death of Queen Elizabeth earlier that year. Shakespeare maintained an association with this company until his death in 1616.

Between his arrival in London in the 1580s and his death in Stratford in 1616, Shakespeare is credited with the authorship of some thirty-eight plays, two of which—*The Two Noble Kinsmen* (1613) and *Henry VIII* (1612–1613)—were most likely cowritten with his friend and fellow playwright John Fletcher. Scholars typically summarize his nondramatic achievements as including five substantial poems and 154 sonnets. His plays are usually grouped into four distinct categories or kinds: thirteen comedies, ten histories, ten tragedies, and five romances. Moreover, a group of plays of uncertain authorship, the historical drama *The Reign of King Edward the Third* (1595) for instance, are thought to be wholly or in part Shakespeare's work.

Two of Shakespeare's most enduring plays are introduced and reprinted here. As has been the case throughout *Understanding Literature*, the introductions that follow begin discussion of individual texts with the concept of *form*, in these cases particular varieties of *tragedies* and *comedies*. How do the forms of these plays compare with those of the plays that precede and follow them, with *Oedipus Rex* and *The Flying Doctor*, for example? How does a play like *The Tempest* trouble notions of a "pure" dramatic form? Later in these introductions, other relevant issues and the focuses of other interpretations—social history, ideology, gender, politics—also receive attention. The introductions to all three plays, in short, raise significantly different questions about them, questions about Shakespeare's representation of gender and race or his development of characters like Hamlet, whose motives may not necessarily be what they appear. A playwright like Shakespeare cannot be a writer "for all time," as Ben Jonson praised him, if his works do not provoke very different readings from each successive generation that discovers him. The introductions that follow are intended to move this process of discovery and rereading along into your classroom.

Hamlet

> Shakespeare is above all writers, at least above all modern writers, the poet of nature; the poet that holds up to his readers a faithful mirror of manners and life. . . . His persons act and speak by the influence of those general passions and principles by which all minds are agitated, and the whole system of life is continued in motion. In the writings of other poets a character is too often an individual; in those of Shakespeare it is commonly a species. (Samuel Johnson, *Preface to Shakespeare* [1765])

This is high praise indeed, and from a man of estimable talent himself who, in addition to writing poetry and an influential dictionary, is renowned as a preeminent thinker and critic. It is characteristic of the intellectual history of Johnson's time that he would value the universal quality of Shakespeare's characters over their individuality. For it is the representation of general passions and principles that allows audience members to learn more about themselves, even in characters quite remote from their experience. At times, Johnson's *Preface* also served as a defense of Shakespeare, as Johnson's contemporaries at times indicted Shakespeare for failing to create historically accurate characters and for mixing elements of comedy and tragedy in the same play (a topic to which we shall return in discussing *The Tempest*). In answering the latter charge, Johnson countered that when elements of tragedy and comedy coexisted in the same work, they did so to register more accurately the inevitably mixed "course of the world" and to achieve poetry's highest ambition: "to instruct by pleasing."

Hamlet (1600–1601), not surprisingly, has seldom been viewed as comic, which is not to denigrate its title character's wit and verbal dexterity. Rather, in terms of Shakespeare's career, it marks the beginning of a fertile period in which he produced a series of remarkable tragedies: *Othello* (1604), *King Lear* (1605–1606), *Macbeth* (1605–1606), and *Antony and Cleopatra* (1607). He had written *Titus Andronicus* (1593–1594), *Romeo and Juliet* (1595–1596), and *Julius Caesar* (1599) earlier, and would write *Coriolanus* (1607–1608) during this same period. But there is nothing in any playwright's work to compare with this series of plays coming near the middle of Shakespeare's career on the London stage.

In writing *Hamlet*, Shakespeare was capitalizing on the popularity of a particular genre, the **revenge tragedy,** which had drawn large audiences for over a decade (and would again later on the Jacobean stage). Thomas Kyd, whose play called *Hamlet* is regarded as the primary source or "Ur-text" of the play, had also authored the age's best-known revenge tragedy, *The Spanish Tragedy; or Hieronymo Goes Mad Again.* Kyd's play, usually dated between 1582 and 1592, with the later 1580s serving as the most likely date of composition, concerns the fate of Hieronymo, seeking justice for the murder of his son by a Spanish prince. Prompted by the Spirit of Revenge, Hieronymo is left with no recourse but to exact it himself and, like the last scene of *Hamlet*, the conclusion of *The Spanish Tragedy* is marked by the deaths of the principal characters including Hieronymo. But the Spirit of Revenge, who appears in the play's Prologue and remains on stage to oversee the bloody action, is appeased; and Hieronymo's son is able to gain admission to the Elysian Fields—in Greek mythology, a dwelling place of the virtuous after their death—because of his father's retribution.

Most scholars view such plays as evidence of the renewed popularity in Shakespeare's England of a kind of sensational tragedy made famous by the Roman playwright Seneca in the first century A.D. His bloody drama *Thyestes* served as a model for Shakespeare's earlier *Titus Andronicus*, a tragedy that includes rape, mutilation, and one of the most horrible acts of revenge played on the Elizabethan—or any other—stage. Here, the Goth Queen Tamora, Titus's bitter enemy, is served a dish made of the severed limbs of her sons, who earlier had violated Titus's daughter Lavinia. In this moment of horror, as editor G. Blakemore Evans describes it, "Certainly the famous banquet of the two sons served by Atreus to their father Thyestes in Seneca's drama of that name can scarcely have been out of Shakespeare's thoughts." Plays such as Kyd's *Spanish Tragedy* and *Titus Andronicus* paved the way for even more sophisticated and insidious revenge plays in the seventeenth century, including *Hamlet*.

Nearly all of these plays feature conflicts and characters similar to those introduced in the opening act of *Hamlet*, where much of the story's *exposition* is related. As scholar Fredson Bowers explains, blood-revenge or the system of *wergeld* was not viewed as a crime in England until the middle of the fourteenth century. Even after that, the "legal procedure of the appeal, while abolishing the system of wergeld, retained the spirit of old blood-revenge, for the nearest of kin had to take up the suit against the murderer and frequently to fight it out with him in the direct revenge of judicial combat." The action of dramatic plots based upon blood-revenge, then, has a predictable cast of characters: a victim or victims, wronged family members seeking justice, and a murderer or usurper left unpunished. All of these characters appear in *Hamlet*. On both the Elizabethan stage—and frequently on the contemporary movie screen, for that matter—avengers begin with only one task in mind: punish a murderer who, for a variety of reasons, will escape any such punishment if the revengers do not act. And act they do.

Yet, even though eventually successful, the protagonists of *Hamlet* and *The Spanish Tragedy* suffer not only enormous sorrow, but also considerable anxiety over taking up arms against what Hamlet terms a "sea of troubles." On this point, Elizabethan law followed religious teaching. "Vengeance is mine, and I will reward," says the Lord; it is not the prerogative of any person who feels him- or herself wronged. This larger religious and ethical constraint disturbs Hamlet greatly. In his soliloquy in Act Two, scene two, for instance, he wonders if the Ghost of his father "May be a [dev'l], and the [dev'l] hath power / T'assume a pleasing shape" (2.2. 535–36). Later, in his famous "To be or not to be" soliloquy, he implies that our fear of what may come after death, the "undiscover'd country," restrains our actions: "Thus conscience does make cowards [of us all]" (3.1.82). More specifically, in Act Four he invokes "godlike reason" as the internal mechanism people of conscience rely on to determine right from wrong. Some sixty-five years later in his epic poem *Paradise Lost* (1667), John Milton's God explains the fall of Adam and Eve in similar terms. Distinguishing foreknowledge from predestination,

God claims, "I made him [man] just and right, / Sufficient to have stood, though free to fall." What made Adam and Eve sufficient, able to withstand temptation? Reason, which God associates with will and "choice" in Book Three of the poem.

All of these considerations beg the larger question: How important is "godlike reason" or ethical restraint in *Hamlet*? To what extent is Hamlet's reservation about avenging his father's murder—and subsequent delay in carrying out his revenge—attributable to these moral or ethical conundrums? What other explanations of Hamlet's inaction might exist?

Not surprisingly, particularly since the rise of psychoanalysis at the beginning of the twentieth century, scholars have questioned the strength of Hamlet's ethical qualms about the morality of revenge. His madness or antic disposition, many argue, has far more to do with his own repressed desire for his mother and his ambivalent feelings toward his father than with the workings of "godlike reason." For such readers, Gertrude and, by extension, Ophelia become far more significant than Claudius in sparking Hamlet's internal conflicts. Among others, American poet and critic T. S. Eliot criticized *Hamlet* for the overreactions of its hero and for Shakespeare's attempt to combine a revenge play with a psychodrama focusing on the revenger's "guilty reaction" to his mother. For Eliot, and later for British psychoanalyst Ernest Jones, Hamlet's madness is "more than feigned." But what sort of madness is it? Jones's answer invokes a comparison between Hamlet and Oedipus, implicating both characters at the *unconscious* level in a drama of incest and forbidden desire. This reading traces Hamlet's depression back to a "tortured conscience," one that underlies his extreme reaction to Gertrude's quick marriage to Claudius:

> Within a month,
> Ere yet the salt of most unrighteous tears
> Had left the flushing in her galled eyes,
> She married—O most wicked speed: to post
> With such dexterity to incestious sheets,
> It is not, nor it cannot come to good. . . . (1.2.153–58)

And even though later in the opening act the Ghost would admonish Hamlet not to "taint" his mind with thoughts of his mother, Hamlet is unable to heed this advice. He immediately reviles her as a "pernicious woman," leading to his larger condemnation of all women, including Ophelia. More important from Jones's perspective, Hamlet reveals the deep-seated reason for his inability to exact revenge against Claudius: His father's death and mother's remarriage "represented ideas which in Hamlet's unconscious phantasy had always been closely associated." And in his fantasy, Hamlet played Claudius's role.

More recent psychoanalytic feminist critics like Linda Charnes and Jacqueline Rose urge us to stop at this point and consider two factors inherent in Hamlet's supposedly Oedipal dilemma: first, his psychical projection of not one, but two fathers or King Hamlets, one idealized and one profane; and second, Shakespeare's predictable representation of women. For Charnes, Hamlet's lofty vision of the Father as Law is tarnished when the Ghost confides that he was, in fact, an abject sinner, "confin'd to fast in fires, / Till the foul crimes done in my days of nature / Are burnt and purg'd away" (1.5.11–13). The son's idealized image of the Father, the noble Hyperion to the satyr-like Claudius, is shattered; thus, in following the Ghost's injunction to "Remember me," Hamlet is thrown into a "lassitude" or listlessness. Why act at all in such a world so far fallen from grace?

This attitude extends to Hamlet's view of Ophelia. As Jones observed in 1949, Hamlet's demand in Act Three that she get herself to a nunnery reflects his infantile tendency to view women in one of two ways: as a virginal Madonna and "inaccessible saint," or as a sensual "creature" accessible to everyone. For Rose, this Virgin–whore opposition parallels Shakespeare's failed representation of women more generally. She identifies in particular characters like Gertrude, too improperly sexualized, and the nun Isabella from *Measure for Measure* (1604), too excessively proper and sexually restrained. In both cases, according to Rose, feminine sexuality appears as something "unmanageable which cannot be held in place"; ultimately, it is a woman who is deemed the cause of "the excess and deficiency in the play" and thus bears the "chief burden of guilt."

As these readings suggest, *Hamlet* remains both an enigma to and a passion of its audiences and actors as well. The editors of this book hope it will continue to fascinate readers in the classrooms of the new millennium.

WILLIAM SHAKESPEARE

The Tragedy of Hamlet, Prince of Denmark

(1600–1601)

CHARACTERS

Claudius, King of Denmark
Hamlet, son to the late King Hamlet, and nephew to the present King
Polonius, Lord Chamberlain
Horatio, friend to Hamlet
Laertes, son to Polonius
Voltemand
Cornelius
Rosencrantz } courtiers
Guildenstern
Osric
Gentleman
Marcellus } officers
Barnardo
Francisco, a soldier
Reynaldo, servant to Polonius
Fortinbras, Prince of Norway
Norwegian Captain
Doctor of Divinity

Players
Two Clowns, grave-diggers
English Ambassadors
Gertrude, Queen of Denmark, and mother to Hamlet
Ophelia, daughter to Polonius
Ghost of Hamlet's Father
Lords, Ladies, Officers, Soldiers, Sailors, Messengers, and *Attendants*

Scene: Denmark

ACT I

SCENE I

(*Enter* Barnardo *and* Francisco, *two sentinels [meeting].*)

Barnardo: Who's there?
Francisco: Nay, answer me. Stand and unfold yourself.
Barnardo: Long live the King!
Francisco: Barnardo.
Barnardo: He.
Francisco: You come most carefully upon your hour.   5
Barnardo: 'Tis now strook twelf. Get thee to bed, Francisco.
Francisco: For this relief much thanks. 'Tis bitter cold,
     And I am sick at heart.
Barnardo: Have you had quiet guard?
Francisco: Not a mouse stirring.   10
Barnardo: Well, good night.
     If you do meet Horatio and Marcellus,
     The rivals of my watch, bid them make haste.

(*Enter* Horatio *and* Marcellus.)

Francisco: I think I hear them. Stand ho! Who is there?
Horatio: Friends to this ground.
Marcellus: And liegemen to the Dane.   15
Francisco: Give you good night.
Marcellus: O, farewell, honest [soldier].
     Who hath reliev'd you?
Francisco: Barnardo hath my place.
     Give you good night.   (*Exit* Francisco.)

———

Words and passages enclosed in square brackets in the text are either emendations of the copy-text or additions to it.
I.i. *Location:* Elsinore; a guard-platform of the castle   2 *answer me:* You answer *me*. Francisco is on watch; Barnardo has come to relieve him.   *unfold yourself:* Make known who you are.
3 *Long . . . King:* perhaps a password, perhaps simply an utterance to allow the voice to be recognized   7 *strook twelf:* struck twelve   9 *sick at heart:* in low spirits   13 *rivals:* partners
15 *liegemen . . . Dane:* loyal subjects to the king of Denmark   16 *Give:* God give

Marcellus: Holla, Barnardo!
Barnardo: Say—
    What, is Horatio there?
Horatio: A piece of him.
Barnardo: Welcome, Horatio, welcome, good Marcellus.   20
Horatio: What, has this thing appear'd again to-night?
Barnardo: I have seen nothing.
Marcellus: Horatio says 'tis but our fantasy,
    And will not let belief take hold of him
    Touching this dreaded sight twice seen of us;   25
    Therefore I have entreated him along,
    With us to watch the minutes of this night,
    That if again this apparition come,
    He may approve our eyes and speak to it.
Horatio: Tush, tush, 'twill not appear.
Barnardo: Sit down a while,   30
    And let us once again assail your ears,
    That are so fortified against our story,
    What we have two nights seen.
Horatio: Well, sit we down,
    And let us hear Barnardo speak of this.
Barnardo: Last night of all,   35
    When yond same star that's westward from the pole
    Had made his course t' illume that part of heaven
    Where now it burns, Marcellus and myself,
    The bell then beating one—

(Enter Ghost.*)*

Marcellus: Peace, break thee off! Look where it comes again!   40
Barnardo: In the same figure like the King that's dead.
Marcellus: Thou art a scholar, speak to it, Horatio.
Barnardo: Looks 'a not like the King? Mark it, Horatio.
Horatio: Most like; it [harrows] me with fear and wonder.
Barnardo: It would be spoke to.
Marcellus: Speak to it, Horatio.   45
Horatio: What art thou that usurp'st this time of night,
    Together with that fair and warlike form
    In which the majesty of buried Denmark
    Did sometimes march? By heaven I charge thee speak!
Marcellus: It is offended.

---

23 *fantasy:* imagination   29 *approve:* corroborate   36 *pole:* pole star   37 *his:* its (the commonest form of the neuter possessive singular in Shakespeare's day)   41 *like:* in the likeness of 42 *a scholar:* one who knows how best to address it   43 *'a:* he   45 *It . . . to:* A ghost had to be spoken to before it could speak.   46 *usurp'st:* The ghost, a supernatural being, has invaded the realm of nature.   48 *majesty . . . Denmark:* late king of Denmark   49 *sometimes:* formerly

Barnardo: See, it stalks away!   50
Horatio: Stay! Speak, speak, I charge thee speak!

  (*Exit* Ghost.)

Marcellus: 'Tis gone, and will not answer.
Barnardo: How now, Horatio? you tremble and look pale.
  Is not this something more than fantasy?
  What think you on't?   55
Horatio: Before my God, I might not this believe
  Without the sensible and true avouch
  Of mine own eyes.
Marcellus: Is it not like the King?
Horatio: As thou art to thyself.
  Such was the very armor he had on   60
  When he the ambitious Norway combated.
  So frown'd he once when in an angry parle
  He smote the sledded [Polacks] on the ice.
  'Tis strange.
Marcellus: Thus twice before, and jump at this dead hour,   65
  With martial stalk hath he gone by our watch.
Horatio: In what particular thought to work I know not,
  But in the gross and scope of mine opinion,
  This bodes some strange eruption to our state.
Marcellus: Good row, sit down, and tell me, he that knows,   70
  Why this same strict and most observant watch
  So nightly toils the subject of the land,
  And [why] such daily [cast] of brazen cannon,
  And foreign mart for implements of war,
  Why such impress of shipwrights, whose sore task   75
  Does not divide the Sunday from the week,
  What might be toward, that this sweaty haste
  Doth make the night joint-laborer with the day:
  Who is't that can inform me?
Horatio: That can I,
  At least the whisper goes so: our last king,   80
  Whose image even but now appear'd to us,
  Was, as you know, by Fortinbras of Norway,
  Thereto prick'd on by a most emulate pride,
  Dar'd to the combat; in which our valiant Hamlet
  (For so this side of our known world esteem'd him)   85

---

57 *sensible:* relating to the senses   *avouch:* guarantee   61 *Norway:* king of Norway   62
parle: parley   63 *sledded:* using sleds or sledges   *Polacks:* Poles   65 *jump:* precisely
67–68 *In . . . opinion:* while I have no precise theory about it, my general feeling is that; *gross* =
wholeness, totality; *scope* = range   69 *eruption:* upheaval   72 *toils:* causes to work   *subject:*
subjects   74 *foreign mart:* dealing with foreign markets   75 *impress:* forced service
77 *toward:* in preparation   83 *emulate:* emulous, proceeding from rivalry

Did slay this Fortinbras, who, by a seal'd compact
Well ratified by law and heraldy,
Did forfeit (with his life) all [those] his lands
Which he stood seiz'd of, to the conqueror;
Against the which a moi'ty competent   90
Was gaged by our king, which had [return'd]
To the inheritance of Fortinbras,
Had he been vanquisher; as by the same comart
And carriage of the article [design'd],
His fell to Hamlet. Now, sir, young Fortinbras,   95
Of unimproved mettle hot and full,
Hath in the skirts of Norway here and there
Shark'd up a list of lawless resolutes
For food and diet to some enterprise
That hath a stomach in't, which is no other,   100
As it doth well appear unto our state,
But to recover of us, by strong hand
And terms compulsatory, those foresaid lands
So by his father lost; and this, I take it,
Is the main motive of our preparations,   105
The source of this our watch, and the chief head
Of this post haste and romage in the land.
Barnardo: I think it be no other but e'en so.
Well may it sort that this portentous figure
Comes armed through our watch so like the King   110
That was and is the question of these wars.
Horatio: A mote it is to trouble the mind's eye.
In the most high and palmy state of Rome,
A little ere the mightiest Julius fell,
The graves stood [tenantless] and the sheeted dead   115
Did squeak and gibber in the Roman streets.
As stars with trains of fire, and dews of blood,
Disasters in the sun; and the moist star
Upon whose influence Neptune's empire stands
Was sick almost to doomsday with eclipse.   120

---

87 *law and heraldy:* heraldic law (governing combat)   *Heraldy* is a variant of *heraldry.*   89 *seiz'd of:* possessed of   90 *moi'ty:* portion   *competent:* adequate, equivalent   91 *gaged:* pledged   *had:* would have   92 *inheritance:* possession   93 *comart:* bargain   94 *carriage:* tenor   *design'd:* drawn up   96 *unimproved:* untried (?) or not directed to any useful end (?)   97 *skirts:* outlying territories   98 *Shark'd up:* gathered up hastily and indiscriminately   100 *stomach:* relish of danger (?) or demand for courage (?)   106 *head:* source   107 *romage:* rummage, bustling activity   109 *sort:* fit   *portentous:* ominous   114 One or more lines may have been lost between this line and the next.   118 *Disasters:* ominous signs   *moist star:* moon   119 *Neptune's empire stands:* the seas are dependent   120 *sick . . . doomsday:* almost totally darkened. When the Day of Judgment is imminent, says Matthew 24:29, "the moon shall not give her light."   *eclipse:* There were a solar and two total lunar eclipses visible in England in 1598; they caused gloomy speculation.

And even the like precurse of [fear'd] events,
As harbingers preceding still the fates
And prologue to the omen coming on,
Have heaven and earth together demonstrated
Unto our climatures and countrymen.   125

(*Enter* Ghost.)

But soft, behold! lo where it comes again!

(*It spreads his arms.*)

I'll cross it though it blast me. Stay, illusion!
If thou hast any sound or use of voice,
Speak to me.
If there be any good thing to be done   130
That may to thee do ease, and grace to me,
Speak to me.
If thou art privy to thy country's fate,
Which happily foreknowing may avoid,
O speak!   135
Or if thou hast uphoarded in thy life
Extorted treasure in the womb of earth,
For which, they say, your spirits oft walk in death,
Speak of it, stay and speak!   (*The cock crows.*)   Stop it, Marcellus.
Marcellus: Shall I strike it with my partisan?   140
Horatio: Do, if it will not stand.
Barnardo: 'Tis here!
Horatio: 'Tis here!

[*Exit* Ghost.]

Marcellus: 'Tis gone!
We do it wrong, being so majestical,
To offer it the show of violence,
For it is as the air, invulnerable,   145
And our vain blows malicious mockery.
Barnardo: It was about to speak when the cock crew.
Horatio: And then it started like a guilty thing
Upon a fearful summons. I have heard
The cock, that is the trumpet to the morn,   150
Doth with his lofty and shrill-sounding throat
Awake the god of day, and at his warning,

---

121 *precurse:* foreshadowing   122 *harbingers:* advance messengers   *still:* always   123 *omen:*
the events portended   125 *climatures:* regions   125 s.d. (stage direction) *his:* its   127
cross it: cross its path, confront it directly   *blast:* wither (by supernatural means)   134 *happily:*
haply, perhaps   138 *your:* Colloquial and impersonal; cf. I.v.186, IV.iii.23–25. Most editors
adopt *you* from F1.   140 *partisan:* long-handled spear   146 *malicious mockery:* mockery of
malice, empty pretenses of harming it.   150 *trumpet:* trumpeter

Whether in sea or fire, in earth or air,
Th' extravagant and erring spirit hies
To his confine; and of the truth herein   155
This present object made probation.

Marcellus: It faded on the crowing of the cock.
Some say that ever 'gainst that season comes
Wherein our Saviour's birth is celebrated,
This bird of dawning singeth all night long,   160
And then they say no spirit dare stir abroad,
The nights are wholesome, then no planets strike,
No fairy takes, nor witch hath power to charm,
So hallowed, and so gracious, is that time.

Horatio: So have I heard and do in part believe it.   165
But look, the morn in russet mantle clad
Walks o'er the dew of yon high eastward hill.
Break we our watch up, and by my advice
Let us impart what we have seen to-night
Unto young Hamlet, for, upon my life,   170
This spirit, dumb to us, will speak to him.
Do you consent we shall acquaint him with it,
As needful in our loves, fitting our duty?

Marcellus: Let's do't, I pray, and I this morning know
Where we shall find him most convenient.   175

(*Exeunt.*)

[SCENE II]

(*Flourish. Enter* Claudius, King of Denmark, Gertrude the Queen,
Council: *as* Polonius; *and his son* Laertes, Hamlet, *cum aliis [including* Voltemand *and* Cornelius*].*)

King: Though yet of Hamlet our dear brother's death
The memory be green, and that it us befitted
To bear our hearts in grief, and our whole kingdom
To be contracted in one brow of woe,
Yet so far hath discretion fought with nature   5
That we with wisest sorrow think on him
Together with remembrance of ourselves.
Therefore our sometime sister, now our queen,
Th' imperial jointress to this warlike state,

---

154 *extravagant:* wandering outside its proper bounds   *erring:* wandering abroad   *hies:* hastens
156 *object:* sight   *probation:* proof   158 *'gainst:* just before   162 *strike:* exert malevolent influence   163 *takes:* bewitches, charms   164 *gracious:* blessed   166 *russet:* coarse greyish-
brown cloth   I.ii. Location: the castle   o.s.d. (opening stage direction)   *Flourish:* trumpet
fanfare   *cum aliis:* with others   2 *befitted:* would befit   4 *contracted in:* (1) reduced to; (2)
knit or wrinkled in   *brow of woe:* mournful brow   9 *jointress:* joint holder

Have we, as 'twere with a defeated joy, 10
With an auspicious, and a dropping eye,
With mirth in funeral, and with dirge in marriage,
In equal scale weighing delight and dole,
Taken to wife; nor have we herein barr'd
Your better wisdoms, which have freely gone 15
With this affair along. For all, our thanks.
Now follows that you know young Fortinbras,
Holding a weak supposal of our worth,
Or thinking by our late dear brother's death
Our state to be disjoint and out of frame, 20
Co-leagued with this dream of his advantage,
He hath not fail'd to pester us with message
Importing the surrender of those lands
Lost by his father, with all bands of law,
To our most valiant brother. So much for him. 25
Now for ourself, and for this time of meeting,
Thus much the business is: we have here writ
To Norway, uncle of young Fortinbras—
Who, impotent and bedred, scarcely hears
Of this his nephew's purpose—to suppress 30
His further gait herein, in that the levies,
The lists, and full proportions are all made
Out of his subject; and we here dispatch
You, good Cornelius, and you, Voltemand,
For bearers of this greeting to old Norway, 35
Giving to you no further personal power
To business with the King, more than the scope
Of these delated articles allow.   *[Giving a paper.]*
Farewell, and let your haste commend your duty.

Cornelius, Voltemand: In that, and all things, will we show our duty. 40
King: We doubt it nothing; heartily farewell.

[Exeunt Voltemand *and* Cornelius.*]*

And now, Laertes, what's the news with you?
You told us of some suit, what is't, Laertes?
You cannot speak of reason to the Dane
And lose your voice. What wouldst thou beg, Laertes, 45
That shall not be my offer, not thy asking?
The head is not more native to the heart,

----

10 *defeated:* impaired   11 *auspicious . . . dropping:* cheerful . . . weeping   15 *freely:* fully,
without reservation   17 *know:* be informed, learn   18 *supposal:* conjecture, estimate   21
Co-leagued: joined   22 *pester . . . message:* trouble me with persistent messages (the original
sense of *pester* is "overcrowd")   23 *Importing:* having as import   24 *bands:* bonds, binding
terms   29 *impotent and bedred:* feeble and bedridden   31 *gait:* proceeding   31–33 *in . . .
subject:* since the troops are all drawn from his subjects   38 *delated:* extended, detailed (a variant of *dilated*)   41 *nothing:* not at all   45 *lose:* waste   47 *native:* closely related

The hand more instrumental to the mouth,
Than is the throne of Denmark to thy father.
What wouldst thou have, Laertes?

Laertes: My dread lord,   50
Your leave and favor to return to France,
From whence though willingly I came to Denmark
To show my duty in your coronation,
Yet now I must confess, that duty done,
My thoughts and wishes bend again toward France,   55
And bow them to your gracious leave and pardon.

King: Have you your father's leave? What says Polonius?

Polonius: H'ath, my lord, wrung from me my slow leave
By laborsome petition, and at last
Upon his will I seal'd my hard consent.   60
I do beseech you give him leave to go.

King: Take thy fair hour, Laertes, time be thine,
And thy best graces spend it at thy will!
But now, my cousin Hamlet, and my son—

Hamlet [Aside.]: A little more than kin, and less than kind.   65

King: How is it that the clouds still hang on you?

Hamlet: Not so, my lord, I am too much in the sun.

Queen: Good Hamlet, cast thy nighted color off,
And let thine eye look like a friend on Denmark.
Do not for ever with thy vailed lids   70
Seek for thy noble father in the dust.
Thou know'st 'tis common, all that lives must die,
Passing through nature to eternity.

Hamlet: Ay, madam, it is common.

Queen: If it be,
Why seems it so particular with thee?   75

Hamlet: Seems, madam? nay, it is, I know not "seems."
'Tis not alone my inky cloak, [good] mother,
Nor customary suits of solemn black,
Nor windy suspiration of forc'd breath,
No, nor the fruitful river in the eye,   80
Nor the dejected havior of the visage,
Together with all forms, moods, [shapes] of grief,
That can [denote] me truly. These indeed seem,
For they are actions that a man might play,

---

48 *instrumental:* serviceable   51 *leave and favor:* gracious permission   56 *pardon:* permission
to depart   58 *H'ath:* he hath   60 *hard:* reluctant   64 *cousin:* kinsman (used in familiar
address to any collateral relative more distant than a brother or sister; here to a nephew)   65
A little . . . kind: closer than a nephew, since you are my mother's husband; yet more distant than
a son, too (and not well disposed to you)   67 *sun:* with obvious quibble on *son*   70 *vailed:*
downcast   72 *common:* general, universal   75 *particular:* individual, personal   80 *fruitful:*
copious

But I have that within which passes show,   85
These but the trappings and the suits of woe.
King: 'Tis sweet and commendable in your nature, Hamlet,
To give these mourning duties to your father.
But you must know your father lost a father,
That father lost, lost his, and the survivor bound   90
In filial obligation for some term
To do obsequious sorrow. But to persever
In obstinate condolement is a course
Of impious stubbornness, 'tis unmanly grief,
It shows a will most incorrect to heaven,   95
A heart unfortified, or mind impatient,
An understanding simple and unschool'd:
For what we know must be, and is as common
As any the most vulgar thing to sense,
Why should we in our peevish opposition   100
Take it to heart? Fie, 'tis a fault to heaven,
A fault against the dead, a fault to nature,
To reason most absurd, whose common theme
Is death of fathers, and who still hath cried,
From the first corse till he that died to-day,   105
"This must be so." We pray you throw to earth
This unprevailing woe, and think of us
As of a father, for let the world take note
You are the most immediate to our throne,
And with no less nobility of love   110
Than that which dearest father bears his son
Do I impart toward you. For your intent
In going back to school in Wittenberg,
It is most retrograde to our desire,
And we beseech you bend you to remain   115
Here in the cheer and comfort of our eye,
Our chiefest courtier, cousin, and our son.
Queen: Let not thy mother lose her prayers, Hamlet,
I pray thee stay with us, go not to Wittenberg.
Hamlet: I shall in all my best obey you, madam.   120
King: Why, 'tis a loving and a fair reply.
Be as ourself in Denmark. Madam, come.
This gentle and unforc'd accord of Hamlet
Sits smiling to my heart, in grace whereof,
No jocund health that Denmark drinks to-day,   125
But the great cannon to the clouds shall tell,

---

92 *obsequious:* proper to obsequies   93 *condolement:* grief   95 *incorrect:* unsubmissive
99 *any . . . sense:* what is perceived to be commonest   101 *to:* against   103 *absurd:* contrary
107 *unprevailing:* unavailing   111 *dearest:* most loving   112 *impart:* impart love

And the King's rouse the heaven shall bruit again,
Respeaking earthly thunder. Come away.

(*Flourish. Exeunt all but* Hamlet.)

Hamlet: O that this too too sallied flesh would melt,
    Thaw, and resolve itself into a dew!   130
    Or that the Everlasting had not fix'd
    His canon 'gainst [self-]slaughter! O God, God,
    How [weary], stale, flat, and unprofitable
    Seem to me all the uses of this world!
    Fie on't, ah fie! 'tis an unweeded garden   135
    That grows to seed, things rank and gross in nature
    Possess it merely. That it should come [to this]!
    But two months dead, nay, not so much, not two.
    So excellent a king, that was to this
    Hyperion to a satyr, so loving to my mother   140
    That he might not beteem the winds of heaven
    Visit her face too roughly. Heaven and earth,
    Must I remember? Why, she should hang on him
    As if increase of appetite had grown
    By what it fed on, and yet, within a month—   145
    Let me not think on't! Frailty, thy name is woman!—
    A little month, or ere those shoes were old
    With which she followed my poor father's body,
    Like Niobe, all tears—why, she, [even she]—
    O God, a beast that wants discourse of reason   150
    Would have mourn'd longer—married with my uncle,
    My father's brother, but no more like my father
    Than I to Hercules. Within a month,
    Ere yet the salt of most unrighteous tears
    Had left the flushing in her galled eyes,   155
    She married—O most wicked speed: to post
    With such dexterity to incestious sheets,
    It is not, nor it cannot come to good,
    But break my heart, for I must hold my tongue.

(*Enter* Horatio, Marcellus *and* Barnardo.)

Horatio: Hail to your lordship!
Hamlet: I am glad to see you well.   160
    Horatio—or I do forget myself.

---

128 *rouse:* bumper, drink   *bruit:* loudly declare   129 *sallied:* sullied. Many editors prefer the
F1 reading, *solid.*   132 *canon:* law   134 *uses:* customs   137 *merely:* utterly   137 *to:* in
comparison with   140 *Hyperion:* the sun-god   141 *beteem:* allow   147 *or ere:* before
149 *Niobe:* She wept endlessly for her children, whom Apollo and Artemis had killed.
150 *wants . . . reason:* lacks the power of reason (which distinguishes men from beasts)   154
unrighteous: hypocritical   155 *flushing:* redness   *galled:* inflamed   157 *incestious:* incestuous.
The marriage of a man to his brother's widow was so regarded until long after Shakespeare's day.

Horatio: The same, my lord, and your poor servant ever.
Hamlet: Sir, my good friend—I'll change that name with you.
    And what make you from Wittenberg, Horatio?
    Marcellus.   165
Marcellus: My good lord.
Hamlet: I am very glad to see you.   *[to* Barnardo*]*   Good even, sir.—But
    what, in faith, make you from Wittenberg?
Horatio: A truant disposition, good my lord.
Hamlet: I would not hear your enemy say so,   170
    Nor shall you do my ear that violence
    To make it truster of your own report
    Against yourself. I know you are no truant.
    But what is your affair in Elsinore?
    We'll teach you to drink [deep] ere you depart.   175
Horatio: My lord, I came to see your father's funeral.
Hamlet: I prithee do not mock me, fellow student,
    I think it was to [see] my mother's wedding.
Horatio: Indeed, my lord, it followed hard upon.
Hamlet: Thrift, thrift, Horatio, the funeral bak'd-meats   180
    Did coldly furnish forth the marriage tables.
    Would I had met my dearest foe in heaven
    Or ever I had seen that day, Horatio!
    My father—methinks I see my father.
Horatio: Where, my lord?
Hamlet: In my mind's eye, Horatio.   185
Horatio: I saw him once, 'a was a goodly king.
Hamlet: 'A was a man, take him for all in all,
    I shall not look upon his like again.
Horatio: My lord, I think I saw him yesternight.
Hamlet: Saw, who?   190
Horatio: My lord, the King your father.
Hamlet: The King my father?
Horatio: Season your admiration for a while
    With an attent ear, till I may deliver,
    Upon the witness of these gentlemen,
    This marvel to you.
Hamlet: For God's love let me hear!   195
Horatio: Two nights together had these gentlemen,
    Marcellus and Barnardo, on their watch,
    In the dead waste and middle of the night,
    Been thus encount'red: a figure like your father,

---

163 *change:* exchange   164 *what . . . from:* what are you doing away from   169 *truant disposition:* inclination to play truant   177 *studient:* student   181 *coldly:* when cold   182 *dearest:* most intensely hated   183 *Or:* ere, before   192 *Season:* temper   *admiration:* wonder
193 *deliver:* report   198 *waste:* empty expanse

Armed at point exactly, cap-a-pe,   200
Appears before them, and with solemn march
Goes slow and stately by them; thrice he walk'd
By their oppress'd and fear-surprised eyes
Within his truncheon's length, whilst they, distill'd
Almost to jelly with the act of fear,   205
Stand dumb and speak not to him. This to me
In dreadful secrecy impart they did,
And I with them the third night kept the watch,
Where, as they had delivered, both in time,
Form of the thing, each word made true and good,   210
The apparition comes. I knew your father,
These hands are not more like.

Hamlet: But where was this?
Marcellus: My lord, upon the platform where we watch.
Hamlet: Did you not speak to it?
Horatio: My lord, I did,
But answer made it none. Yet once methought   215
It lifted up it head and did address
Itself to motion like as it would speak;
But even then the morning cock crew loud,
And at the sound it shrunk in haste away
And vanish'd from our sight.
Hamlet: 'Tis very strange.   220
Horatio: As I do live, my honor'd lord, 'tis true,
And we did think it writ down in our duty
To let you know of it.
Hamlet: Indeed, [indeed,] sirs. But this troubles me.
Hold you the watch to-night?
[Marcellus, Barnardo]:   We do, my lord.   225
Hamlet: Arm'd, say you?
[Marcellus, Barnardo]:   Arm'd, my lord.
Hamlet: From top to toe?
[Marcellus, Barnardo]:   My lord, from head to foot.
Hamlet: Then saw you not his face.
Horatio: O yes, my lord, he wore his beaver up.
Hamlet: What, look'd he frowningly?
Horatio: A countenance more   230
In sorrow than in anger.
Hamlet: Pale, or red?
Horatio: Nay, very pale.

---

200 *at point exactly:* in every particular   *cap-a-pe:* from head to foot   203 *fear-surprised:* overwhelmed by fear   204 *truncheon:* short staff carried as a symbol of military command   206
act: action, operation   207 *dreadful:* held in awe, solemnly sworn   211 *are . . . like:* do not
resemble each other more closely than the apparition resembled him   216 *it:* its   216–217
address . . . motion: begin to make a gesture   229 *beaver:* visor

Hamlet: And fix'd his eyes upon you?
Horatio: Most constantly.
Hamlet: I would I had been there.
Horatio: It would have much amaz'd you.
Hamlet: Very like, [very like]. Stay'd it long?   235
Horatio: While one with moderate haste might tell a hundredth.
Both [Marcellus, Barnardo]: Longer, longer.
Horatio: Not when I saw't.
Hamlet: His beard was grisl'd, no?
Horatio: It was, as I have seen it in his life,
    A sable silver'd.
Hamlet: I will watch to-night,   240
    Perchance 'twill walk again.
Horatio: I warr'nt it will.
Hamlet: If it assume my noble father's person,
    I'll speak to it though hell itself should gape
    And bid me hold my peace. I pray you all,
    If you have hitherto conceal'd this sight,   245
    Let it be tenable in your silence still,
    And whatsomever else shall hap to-night,
    Give it an understanding but no tongue.
    I will requite your loves. So fare you well.
    Upon the platform 'twixt aleven and twelf   250
    I'll visit you.
All: Our duty to your honor.
Hamlet: Your loves, as mine to you; farewell.

    (Exeunt [all but Hamlet*].)*

    My father's spirit—in arms! All is not well,
    I doubt some foul play. Would the night were come!
    Till then sit still, my soul. [Foul] deeds will rise,   255
    Though all the earth o'erwhelm them, to men's eyes.

    (Exit.)

[SCENE III]

    (Enter Laertes *and* Ophelia, *his sister.)*
Laertes: My necessaries are inbark'd. Farewell.
    And, sister, as the winds give benefit
    And convey [is] assistant, do not sleep,
    But let me hear from you.
Ophelia: Do you doubt that?

---

236 *tell a hundreth:* count a hundred   238 *grisl'd:* grizzled, mixed with grey   246 *tenable:*
held close   250 *aleven:* eleven   254 *doubt:* suspect   I.iii. Location: Polonius's quarters in
the castle   1 *inbark'd:* embarked, abroad   3 *convey is assistant:* means of transport is available

Laertes: For Hamlet, and the trifling of his favor, 5
    Hold it a fashion and a toy in blood,
    A violet in the youth of primy nature,
    Forward, not permanent, sweet, not lasting,
    The perfume and suppliance of a minute—
    No more. 10
Ophelia: No more but so?
Laertes: Think it no more:
    For nature crescent does not grow alone
    In thews and [bulk], but as this temple waxes,
    The inward service of the mind and soul
    Grows wide withal. Perhaps he loves you now, 15
    And now no soil nor cautel doth besmirch
    The virtue of his will, but you must fear,
    His greatness weigh'd, his will is not his own,
    [For he himself is subject to his birth:]
    He may not, as unvalued persons do, 20
    Carve for himself, for on his choice depends
    The safety and health of this whole state,
    And therefore must his choice be circumscrib'd
    Unto the voice and yielding of that body
    Whereof he is the head. Then if he says he loves you, 25
    It fits your wisdom so far to believe it
    As he in his particular act and place
    May give his saying deed, which is no further
    Than the main voice of Denmark goes withal.
    Then weigh what loss your honor may sustain 30
    If with too credent ear you list his songs,
    Or lose your heart, or your chaste treasure open
    To his unmast'red importunity.
    Fear it, Ophelia, fear it, my dear sister,
    And keep you in the rear of your affection, 35
    Out of the shot and danger of desire.
    The chariest maid is prodigal enough
    If she unmask her beauty to the moon.
    Virtue itself scapes not calumnious strokes.
    The canker galls the infants of the spring 40
    Too oft before their buttons be disclos'd,

---

6 *a fashion:* standard behavior for a young man   *toy in blood:* idle fancy of youthful passion   7 *primy:* springlike   8 *Forward:* early of growth   9 *suppliance:* pastime   12 *crescent:* growing, increasing   13 *thews:* muscles, sinews   13–15 *as . . . withal:* as the body develops, the powers of mind and spirit grow along with it   16 *soil:* stain   *cautel:* deceit   17 *will:* desire   18 *His greatness weigh'd:* considering his princely status   20 *unvalued:* of low rank   21 *Carve for himself:* indulge his own wishes   24 *voice:* vote, approval   *yielding:* consent   *that body:* the state   27 *in . . . place:* acting as he must act in the position he occupies   29 *main:* general   *goes withal:* accord with   31 *credent:* credulous   36 *shot:* range   40 *canker:* canker-worm   41 *buttons:* buds   *disclos'd:* opened

And in the morn and liquid dew of youth
Contagious blastments are most imminent.
Be wary then, best safety lies in fear:
Youth to itself rebels, though none else near.   45

Ophelia: I shall the effect of this good lesson keep
As watchman to my heart. But, good my brother,
Do not, as some ungracious pastors do,
Show me the steep and thorny way to heaven,
Whiles, [like] a puff'd and reckless libertine,   50
Himself the primrose path of dalliance treads,
And reaks not his own rede.

Laertes: O, fear me not.

(*Enter* Polonius.)

I stay too long—but here my father comes.
A double blessing is a double grace,
Occasion smiles upon a second leave.   55

Polonius: Yet here, Laertes? Aboard, aboard, for shame!
The wind sits in the shoulder of your sail,
And you are stay'd for. There—*[laying his hand on* Laertes' *head]* my
blessing with thee!
And these few precepts in thy memory   60
Look thou character. Give thy thoughts no tongue,
Nor any unproportion'd thought his act.
Be thou familiar, but by no means vulgar:
Those friends thou hast, and their adoption tried,
Grapple them unto thy soul with hoops of steel,   65
But do not dull thy palm with entertainment
Of each new-hatch'd, unfledg'd courage. Beware
Of entrance to a quarrel, but being in,
Bear't that th' opposed may beware of thee.
Give every man thy ear, but few thy voice,   70
Take each man's censure, but reserve thy judgment.
Costly thy habit as thy purse can buy,
But not express'd in fancy, rich, not gaudy,
For the apparel oft proclaims the man,
And they in France of the best rank and station   75
[Are] of a most select and generous chief in that.
Neither a borrower nor a lender [be],

---

43 *blastments:* withering blights   47 *to:* of   48 *ungracious:* graceless   50 *puff'd:* bloated
52 *reaks:* recks, heeds   *rede:* advice   *fear me not:* don't worry about me   55 *Occasion:* opportunity (here personified, as often)   *smiles upon:* graciously bestows   61 *character:* inscribe   62
unproportion'd: unfitting   63 *familiar:* affable, sociable   *vulgar:* friendly with everybody
64 *their adoption tried:* their association with you tested and proved   67 *courage:* spirited, young
blood   69 *Bear't that:* manage it in such a way that   71 *Take:* listen to   *censure:* opinion
76 *generous:* noble   *chief:* eminence (?) But the line is probably corrupt. Perhaps *of a* is intrusive,
in which case *chief* = chiefly.

For [loan] oft loses both itself and friend,
And borrowing dulleth [th'] edge of husbandry.
This above all: to thine own self be true,   80
And it must follow, as the night the day,
Thou canst not then be false to any man.
Farewell, my blessing season this in thee!

Laertes: Most humbly do I take my leave, my lord.

Polonius: The time invests you, go, your servants tend.   85

Laertes: Farewell, Ophelia, and remember well
    What I have said to you.

Ophelia: 'Tis in my memory lock'd,
    And you yourself shall keep the key of it.

Laertes: Farewell.   (*Exit* Laertes.)

Polonius: What is't, Ophelia, he hath said to you?   90

Ophelia: So please you, something touching the Lord Hamlet.

Polonius: Marry, well bethought.
    'Tis told me, he hath very oft of late
    Given private time to you, and you yourself
    Have of your audience been most free and bounteous.   95
    If it be so—as so 'tis put on me,
    And that in way of caution—I must tell you,
    You do not understand yourself so clearly
    As it behooves my daughter and your honor.
    What is between you? Give me up the truth.   100

Ophelia: He hath, my lord, of late made many tenders
    Of his affection to me.

Polonius: Affection, puh! You speak like a green girl,
    Unsifted in such perilous circumstance.
    Do you believe his tenders, as you call them?   105

Ophelia: I do not know, my lord, what I should think.

Polonius: Marry, I will teach you: think yourself a baby
    That you have ta'en these tenders for true pay,
    Which are not sterling. Tender yourself more dearly,
    Or (not to crack the wind of the poor phrase,   110
    [Wringing] it thus) you'll tender me a fool.

Ophelia: My lord, he hath importun'd me with love
    In honorable fashion.

Polonius: Ay, fashion you may call it. Go to, go to.

Ophelia: And hath given countenance to his speech, my lord,   115
    With almost all the holy vows of heaven.

---

79 *husbandry:* thrift   83 *season:* preserve (?) or ripen, make fruitful (?)   85 *invests:* besieges
tend: wait   92 *Marry:* indeed (originally the name of the Virgin Mary used as an oath)   96
put on: told to   101 *tenders:* offers   104 *Unsifted:* untried   108 *tenders:* with play on the
sense "money offered in payment" (as in *legal tender*)   109 *Tender:* hold, value   111 *Wringing:* straining, forcing to the limit   *tender . . . fool:* (1) show me that you are a fool; (2) make me
look like a fool; (3) present me with a (bastard) grandchild   113 *fashion:* See note on line 7.
115 *countenance:* authority

Polonius: Ay, springes to catch woodcocks. I do know,
When the blood burns, how prodigal the soul
Lends the tongue vows. These blazes, daughter,
Giving more light than heat, extinct in both   120
Even in their promise, as it is a-making,
You must not take for fire. From this time
Be something scanter of your maiden presence,
Set your entreatments at a higher rate
Than a command to parle. For Lord Hamlet,   125
Believe so much in him, that he is young,
And with a larger teder may he walk
Than may be given you. In few, Ophelia,
Do not believe his vows, for they are brokers,
Not of that dye which their investments show,   130
But mere [implorators] of unholy suits,
Breathing like sanctified and pious bonds,
The better to [beguile]. This is for all:
I would not, in plain terms, from this time forth
Have you so slander any moment leisure   135
As to give words or talk with the Lord Hamlet.
Look to't, I charge you. Come your ways.
Ophelia: I shall obey, my lord.

   (Exeunt.)

[Scene IV]

   (Enter Hamlet, Horatio, and Marcellus.)

Hamlet: The air bites shrowdly, it is very cold.
Horatio: It is [a] nipping and an eager air.
Hamlet: What hour now?
Horatio: I think it lacks of twelf.
Marcellus: No, it is strook.
Horatio: Indeed? I heard it not. It then draws near the season   5
Wherein the spirit held his wont to walk.

   (A flourish of trumpets, and two pieces goes off [within].)

What does this mean, my lord?

---

117 *springes:* snares *woodcocks:* proverbially gullible birds   124–25 *Set . . . parle:* Place a
higher value on your favors; do not grant interviews simply because he asks for them. Polonius
uses a military figure: *entreatments* = negotiations for surrender; *parle* = parley, discuss terms.
126 *so . . . him:* no more than this with respect to him   127 *larger teder:* longer tether   129
brokers: procurers   130 *Not . . . show:* not of the color that their garments (*investments*) exhibit;
not what they seem   131 *mere:* out-and-out   132 *bonds:* (lover's) vows or assurances. Many
editors follow Theobald in reading *bawds.*   135 *slander:* disgrace *moment:* momentary
137 *Come your ways:* come along   I.iv. Location: the guard-platform of the castle   1
shrowdly: shrewdly, wickedly   2 *eager:* sharp   6 s.d. *pieces:* cannon

Hamlet: The King doth wake to-night and takes his rouse,
 Keeps wassail, and the swagg'ring up-spring reels;
 And as he drains his draughts of Rhenish down,   10
 The kettle-drum and trumpet thus bray out
 The triumph of his pledge.
Horatio: Is it a custom?
Hamlet: Ay, marry, is't,
 But to my mind, though I am native here
 And to the manner born, it is a custom   15
 More honor'd in the breach than the observance.
 This heavy-headed revel east and west
 Makes us traduc'd and tax'd of other nations.
 They clip us drunkards, and with swinish phrase
 Soil our addition, and indeed it takes   20
 From our achievements, though perform'd at height,
 The pith and marrow of our attribute.
 So, oft it chances in particular men,
 That for some vicious mole of nature in them,
 As in their birth, wherein they are not guilty   25
 (Since nature cannot choose his origin),
 By their o'ergrowth of some complexion
 Oft breaking down the pales and forts of reason,
 Or by some habit, that too much o'er-leavens
 The form of plausive manners—that these men, 30
 Carrying, I say, the stamp of one defect,
 Being nature's livery, or fortune's star,
 His virtues else, be they as pure as grace,
 As infinite as man may undergo,
 Shall in the general censure take corruption   35
 From that particular fault: the dram of [ev'l]
 Doth all the noble substance of a doubt
 To his own scandal.

(Enter Ghost.*)*

---

8 *doth . . . rouse:* holds revels far into the night 9 *wassail:* carousal *up-spring:* wild dance
10 *Rhenish:* Rhine wine 11 *triumph . . . pledge:* accomplishment of his toast (by draining his
cup at a single draught) 15 *manner:* custom (of carousing) 16 *More . . . observance:* which
it is more honorable to break than to observe 18 *tax'd of:* censured by 19 *clip:* clepe, call
20 *addition:* titles of honor 21 *at height:* most excellently 22 *attribute:* reputation 23
particular: individual 24 *vicious . . . nature:* small natural blemish 26 *his:* its 27 *By . . .
complexion:* by the excess of some one of the humors (which were thought to govern the disposition) 28 *pales:* fences 29 *o'er-leavens:* makes itself felt throughout (as leaven works in the
whole mass of dough) 30 *plausive:* pleasing 32 *Being . . . star:* whether they were born
with it, or got it by misfortune. *Star* means "blemish." 34 *undergo:* carry the weight of, sustain 35 *general censure:* popular opinion 36 *dram:* minute amount *ev'l:* evil, with a pun
on *eale,* "yeast" (cf. *o'er-leavens* in line 31) 37 *of a doubt:* a famous crux, for which many emendations have been suggested, the most widely accepted being Steevens' *often dout* (extinguish)
37 *To . . . scandal:* so that it all shares in the disgrace

Horatio: Look, my lord, it comes!
Hamlet: Angels and ministers of grace defend us!
        Be thou a spirit of health, or goblin damn'd,   40
        Bring with thee airs from heaven, or blasts from hell,
        Be thy intents wicked, or charitable,
        Thou com'st in such a questionable shape
        That I will speak to thee. I'll call thee Hamlet,
        King, father, royal Dane. O, answer me!   45
        Let me not burst in ignorance, but tell
        Why thy canoniz'd bones, hearsed in death,
        Have burst their cerements; why the sepulchre,
        Wherein we saw thee quietly [inurn'd,]
        Hath op'd his ponderous and marble jaws   50
        To cast thee up again. What may this mean,
        That thou, dead corse, again in complete steel
        Revisits thus the glimpses of the moon,
        Making night hideous, and we fools of nature
        So horridly to shake our disposition   55
        With thoughts beyond the reaches of our souls?
        Say why is this? wherefore? what should we do?

        ([Ghost] beckons [Hamlet].)

Horatio: It beckons you to go away with it,
        As if it some impartment did desire
        To you alone.
Marcellus: Look with what courteous action   60
        It waves you to a more removed ground,
        But do not go with it.
Horatio: No, by no means.
Hamlet: It will not speak, then I will follow it.
Horatio: Do not, my lord.
Hamlet: Why, what should be the fear?
        I do not set my life at a pin's fee,   65
        And for my soul, what can it do to that,
        Being a thing immortal as itself?
        It waves me forth again, I'll follow it.
Horatio: What if it tempt you toward the flood, my lord,
        Or to the dreadful summit of the cliff   70
        That beetles o'er his base into the sea,
        And there assume some other horrible form

---

40 *of health:* wholesome, good   43 *questionable:* inviting talk   47 *canoniz'd:* buried with the prescribed rites   48 *cerements:* grave-clothes   52 *complete steel:* full armor   53 *Revisits:* The *-s* ending in the second-person singular is common.   54 *fools of nature:* the children (or the dupes) of a purely natural order, baffled by the supernatural   55 *disposition:* nature   59 *impartment:* communication   65 *fee:* worth

Which might deprive your sovereignty of reason,
And draw you into madness? Think of it.
The very place puts toys of desperation,   75
Without more motive, into every brain
That looks so many fadoms to the sea
And hears it roar beneath.
Hamlet: It waves me still.—
Go on, I'll follow thee.
Marcellus: You shall not go, my lord.
Hamlet: Hold off your hands.   80
Horatio: Be rul'd, you shall not go.
Hamlet: My fate cries out,
And makes each petty artere in this body
As hardy as the Nemean lion's nerve.
Still am I call'd. Unhand me, gentlemen.
By heaven, I'll make a ghost of him that lets me!   85
I say away!—Go on, I'll follow thee.

(*Exeunt* Ghost *and* Hamlet.)

Horatio: He waxes desperate with [imagination].
Marcellus: Let's follow. 'Tis not fit thus to obey him.
Horatio: Have after. To what issue will this come?
Marcellus: Something is rotten in the state of Denmark.   90
Horatio: Heaven will direct it.
Marcellus: Nay, let's follow him.

(*Exeunt.*)

[SCENE V]

(*Enter* Ghost *and* Hamlet.)

Hamlet: Whither wilt thou lead me? Speak, I'll go no further.
Ghost: Mark me.
Hamlet: I will.
Ghost: My hour is almost come
When I to sulph'rous and tormenting flames
Must render up myself.
Hamlet: Alas, poor ghost!
Ghost: Pity me not, but lend thy serious hearing   5
To what I shall unfold.

---

73 *deprive . . . reason:* unseat reason from the rule of your mind   75 *toys of desperation:* fancies of
desperate action, inclinations to jump off   77 *fadoms:* fathoms   82 *artere:* variant spelling of
artery; here, ligament, sinew   83 *Nemean lion:* slain by Hercules as one of his twelve labors
nerve: sinew   85 *lets:* hinders   91 *it:* the issue   I.v. Location: on the battlements of the
castle

Hamlet: Speak, I am bound to hear.
Ghost: So art thou to revenge, when thou shalt hear.
Hamlet: What?
Ghost: I am thy father's spirit,
    Doom'd for a certain term to walk the night,   10
    And for the day confin'd to fast in fires,
    Till the foul crimes done in my days of nature
    Are burnt and purg'd away. But that I am forbid
    To tell the secrets of my prison-house,
    I could a tale unfold whose lightest word   15
    Would harrow up thy soul, freeze thy young blood,
    Make thy two eyes like stars start from their spheres,
    Thy knotted and combined locks to part,
    And each particular hair to stand an end,
    Like quills upon the fearful porpentine.   20
    But this eternal blazon must not be
    To ears of flesh and blood. List, list, O, list!
    If thou didst ever thy dear father love—
Hamlet: O God!
Ghost: Revenge his foul and most unnatural murther.   25
Hamlet: Murther!
Ghost: Murther most foul, as in the best it is,
    But this most foul, strange, and unnatural.
Hamlet: Haste me to know't, that I with wings as swift
    As meditation, or the thoughts of love,   30
    May sweep to my revenge.
Ghost: I find thee apt,
    And duller shouldst thou be than the fat weed
    That roots itself in ease on Lethe wharf,
    Wouldst thou not stir in this. Now, Hamlet, hear:
    'Tis given out that, sleeping in my orchard,   35
    A serpent stung me, so the whole ear of Denmark
    Is by a forged process of my death
    Rankly abus'd; but know, thou noble youth,
    The serpent that did sting thy father's life
    Now wears his crown.
Hamlet: O my prophetic soul!   40
    My uncle?
Ghost: Ay, that incestuous, that adulterate beast,
    With witchcraft of his wits, with traitorous gifts—

---

11 *fast:* do penance   12 *crimes:* sins   17 *spheres:* eye-sockets; with allusion to the revolving spheres in which, according to the Ptolemaic astronomy, the stars were fixed   19 *an end:* on end   20 *fearful porpentine:* frightened porcupine   21 *eternal blazon:* revelation of eternal things   30 *meditation:* thought   33 *Lethe:* river of Hades, the water of which made the drinker forget the past   *wharf:* bank   35 *orchard:* garden   37 *forged process:* false account   38 *abus'd:* deceived   42 *adulterate:* adulterous

O wicked wit and gifts that have the power
So to seduce!—won to his shameful lust   45
The will of my most seeming virtuous queen.
O Hamlet, what [a] falling-off was there
From me, whose love was of that dignity
That it went hand in hand even with the vow
I made to her in marriage, and to decline   50
Upon a wretch whose natural gifts were poor
To those of mine!
But virtue, as it never will be moved,
Though lewdness court it in a shape of heaven,
So [lust], though to a radiant angel link'd,   55
Will [sate] itself in a celestial bed
And prey on garbage.
But soft, methinks I scent the morning air,
Brief let me be. Sleeping within my orchard,
My custom always of the afternoon,   60
Upon my secure hour thy uncle stole,
With juice of cursed hebona in a vial,
And in the porches of my ears did pour
The leprous distillment, whose effect
Holds such an enmity with blood of man   65
That swift as quicksilver it courses through
The natural gates and alleys of the body,
And with a sudden vigor it doth [posset]
And curd, like eager droppings into milk,
The thin and wholesome blood. So did it mine,   70
And a most instant tetter bark'd about,
Most lazar-like, with vile and loathsome crust
All my smooth body.
Thus was I, sleeping, by a brother's hand
Of life, of crown, of queen, at once dispatch'd,   75
Cut off even in the blossoms of my sin,
Unhous'led, disappointed, unanel'd,
No reck'ning made, but sent to my account
With all my imperfections on my head.
O, horrible, O, horrible, most horrible!   80
If thou hast nature in thee, bear it not,
Let not the royal bed of Denmark be
A couch for luxury and damned incest.

------

54 *shape of heaven:* angelic form   61 *secure:* carefree   62 *hebona:* ebony (which Shakespeare,
following a literary tradition, and perhaps also associating the word with *henbane*, thought the
name of a poison)   68 *posset:* curdle   69 *eager:* sour   71 *tetter:* scabby eruption   *bark'd:*
formed a hard covering, like bark on a tree   72 *lazar-like:* leperlike   75 *at once:* all at the
same time   *dispatch'd:* deprived   77 *Unhous'led:* without the Eucharist   *disappointed:* without
(spiritual) preparation   *unanel'd:* unanointed, without extreme unction   81 *nature:* natural
feeling   83 *luxury:* lust

But howsomever thou pursues this act,
Taint not thy mind, nor let thy soul contrive   85
Against thy mother aught. Leave her to heaven,
And to those thorns that in her bosom lodge
To prick and sting her. Fare thee well at once!
The glow-worm shows the matin to be near,
And gins to pale his uneffectual fire.   90
Adieu, adieu, adieu! remember me.

[Exit.]

Hamlet: O all you host of heaven! O earth! What else?
And shall I couple hell? O fie, hold, hold, my heart,
And you, my sinows, grow not instant old,
But bear me [stiffly] up. Remember thee!   95
Ay, thou poor ghost, whiles memory holds a seat
In this distracted globe. Remember thee!
Yea, from the table of my memory
I'll wipe away all trivial fond records,
All saws of books, all forms, all pressures past   100
That youth and observation copied there,
And thy commandement all alone shall live
Within the book and volume of my brain,
Unmix'd with baser matter. Yes, by heaven!
O most pernicious woman!   105
O villain, villain, smiling, damned villain!
My tables—meet it is I set it down
That one may smile, and smile, and be a villain!
At least I am sure it may be so in Denmark.   *[He writes.]*
So, uncle, there you are. Now to my word: 110
It is "Adieu, adieu! remember me."
I have sworn't.

Horatio [Within.]: My lord, my lord!
Marcellus [Within.]:   Lord Hamlet!

(*Enter* Horatio *and* Marcellus.)

Horatio: Heavens secure him!
Hamlet: So be it!
Marcellus: Illo, ho, ho, my lord!   115
Hamlet: Hillo, ho, ho, boy! Come, [bird,] come.
Marcellus: How is't, my noble lord?
Horatio: What news, my lord?

---

89 *matin:* morning   90 *gins:* begins   94 *sinows:* sinews   97 *globe:* head   98 *table:* writing tablet   99 *fond:* foolish   100 *saws:* wise sayings   *forms:* shapes, images   *pressures:* impressions   110 *word:* word of command from the Ghost   116 *Hillo . . . come:* Hamlet answers Marcellus' halloo with a falconer's cry

Hamlet: O, wonderful!

Horatio: Good my lord, tell it.

Hamlet: No, you will reveal it.

Horatio: Not I, my lord, by heaven.

Marcellus: Nor I, my lord.   120

Hamlet: How say you then, would heart of man once think it?—
    But you'll be secret?

Both [Horatio, Marcellus]: Ay, by heaven, [my lord].

Hamlet: There's never a villain dwelling in all Denmark
    But he's an arrant knave.   125

Horatio: There needs no ghost, my lord, come from the grave
    To tell us this.

Hamlet: Why, right, you are in the right,
    And so, without more circumstance at all,
    I hold it fit that we shake hands and part,
    You, as your business and desire shall point you,   130
    For every man hath business and desire,
    Such as it is, and for my own poor part,
    I will go pray.

Horatio: These are but wild and whirling words, my lord.

Hamlet: I am sorry they offend you, heartily,   135
    Yes, faith, heartily.

Horatio: There's no offense, my lord.

Hamlet: Yes, by Saint Patrick, but there is, Horatio,
    And much offense too. Touching this vision here,
    It is an honest ghost, that let me tell you.
    For your desire to know what is between us,   140
    O'ermaster't as you may. And now, good friends,
    As you are friends, scholars, and soldiers,
    Give me one poor request.

Horatio: What is't, my lord, we will.

Hamlet: Never make known what you have seen tonight.   145

Both [Horatio, Marcellus]: My lord, we will not.

Hamlet: Nay, but swear't.

Horatio: In faith,
    My lord, not I.

Marcellus: Nor I, my lord, in faith.

Hamlet: Upon my sword.

Marcellus: We have sworn, my lord, already.

Hamlet: Indeed, upon my sword, indeed.

    (Ghost *cries under the stage.*)

Ghost: Swear.   150

---

128 *circumstance:* ceremony   139 *honest:* true, genuine   144 *What is't:* whatever it is
149 *Upon my sword:* on the cross formed by the hilt

Hamlet: Ha, ha, boy, say'st thou so? Art thou there, truepenny?
    Come on, you hear this fellow in the cellarage,
    Consent to swear.
Horatio: Propose the oath, my lord.
Hamlet: Never to speak of this that you have seen,
    Swear by my sword.   155
Ghost [beneath]: Swear.
Hamlet: Hic et ubique? Then we'll shift our ground.
    Come hither, gentlemen,
    And lay your hands again upon my sword.
    Swear by my sword   160
    Never to speak of this that you have heard.
Ghost [beneath]: Swear by his sword.
Hamlet: Well said, old mole, canst work i' th' earth so fast?
    A worthy pioner! Once more remove, good friends.
Horatio: O day and night, but this is wondrous strange!   165
Hamlet: And therefore as a stranger give it welcome.
    There are more things in heaven and earth, Horatio,
    Than are dreamt of in your philosophy.
    But come—
    Here, as before, never, so help you mercy,   170
    How strange or odd some'er I bear myself—
    As I perchance hereafter shall think meet
    To put an antic disposition on—
    That you, at such times seeing me, never shall,
    With arms encumb'red thus, or this headshake,   175
    Or by pronouncing of some doubtful phrase,
    As "Well, well, we know," or "We could, and if we would,"
    Or "If we list to speak," or "There be, and if they might,"
    Or such ambiguous giving out, to note
    That you know aught of me—this do swear,   180
    So grace and mercy at your most need help you.
Ghost [beneath]: Swear.   *[They swear.]*
Hamlet: Rest, rest, perturbed spirit! So, gentlemen,
    With all my love I do commend me to you,
    And what so poor a man as Hamlet is   185
    May do t' express his love and friending to you,
    God willing, shall not lack. Let us go in together,
    And still your fingers on your lips, I pray.
    The time is out of joint—O cursed spite,

---

151 *truepenny:* trusty fellow   157 *Hic et ubique:* here and everywhere   164 *pioner:* digger,
miner (variant of *pioneer*)   166 *as . . . welcome:* give it the welcome due in courtesy to strangers
168 *your:* See note on I.i.151.   *philosophy:* natural philosophy, science   173 *put . . . on:* behave
in some fantastic manner, act like a madman   175 *encumb'red:* folded   177 *and if:* if   178
list: cared, had a mind   179 *note:* indicate   188 *still:* always

That ever I was born to set it right!   190
Nay, come, let's go together.

(Exeunt.)

ACT II

SCENE I

(Enter old Polonius *with his man* [Reynaldo].*)*

Polonius: Give him this money and these notes, Reynaldo.
Reynaldo: I will, my lord.
Polonius: You shall do marvell's wisely, good Reynaldo,
    Before you visit him, to make inquire
    Of his behavior.
Reynaldo: My lord, I did intend it.   5
Polonius: Marry, well said, very well said. Look you, sir,
    Inquire me first what Danskers are in Paris,
    And how, and who, what means, and where they keep,
    What company, at what expense; and finding
    By this encompassment and drift of question   10
    That they do know my son, come you more nearer
    Than your particular demands will touch it.
    Take you as 'twere some distant knowledge of him,
    As thus, "I know his father and his friends,
    And in part him." Do you mark this, Reynaldo?   15
Reynaldo: Ay, very well, my lord.
Polonius: "And in part him—but," you may say, "not well.
    But if't be he I mean, he's very wild,
    Addicted so and so," and there put on him
    What forgeries you please: marry, none so rank   20
    As may dishonor him, take heed of that,
    But, sir, such wanton, wild, and usual slips
    As are companions and most known
    To youth and liberty.
Reynaldo: As gaming, my lord.
Polonius: Ay, or drinking, fencing, swearing, quarreling,   25
    Drabbing—you may go so far.
Reynaldo: My lord, that would dishonor him.

---

191 *Nay . . . together:* They are holding back to let him go first. II.i. Location: Polonius's
quarters in the castle   3 *marvell's:* marvellous(ly)   7 *Danskers:* Danes   8 *keep:* lodge
10 *encompassment:* circuitousness   *drift of question:* directing of the conversation   12 *particular
demands:* direct questions   20 *forgeries:* invented charges   22 *wanton:* sportive   26 *Drab-
bing:* whoring

Polonius: Faith, as you may season it in the charge:
    You must not put another scandal on him,
    That he is open to incontinency—   30
    That's not my meaning. But breathe his faults so quaintly
    That they may seem the taints of liberty,
    The flash and outbreak of a fiery mind,
    A savageness in unreclaimed blood,
    Of general assault.
Reynaldo: But, my good lord—   35
Polonius: Wherefore should you do this?
Reynaldo: Ay, my lord,
    I would know that.
Polonius: Marry, sir, here's my drift,
    And I believe it is a fetch of wit:
    You laying these slight sallies on my son,
    As 'twere a thing a little soil'd [wi' th'] working,   40
    Mark you,
    Your party in converse, him you would sound,
    Having ever seen in the prenominate crimes
    The youth you breathe of guilty, be assur'd
    He closes with you in this consequence: 45
    "Good sir," or so, or "friend," or "gentleman,"
    According to the phrase or the addition
    Of man and country.
Reynaldo: Very good, my lord.
Polonius: And then, sir, does 'a this—'a does—what was I about to say?
    By the mass, I was about to say something.   50
    Where did I leave?
Reynaldo: At "closes in the consequence."
Polonius: At "closes in the consequence," ay, marry.
    He closes thus: "I know the gentleman.
    I saw him yesterday, or th' other day,
    Or then, or then, with such or such, and as you say,   55
    There was 'a gaming, there o'ertook in 's rouse,
    There falling out at tennis"; or, perchance,
    "I saw him enter such a house of sale,"
    Videlicet, a brothel, or so forth. See you now,
    Your bait of falsehood take this carp of truth,   60
    And thus do we of wisdom and of reach,

---

28 *Faith:* Most editors read *Faith, no,* following F1; this makes easier sense.   *season:* qualify, temper   30 *open to incontinency:* habitually profligate   31 *quaintly:* artfully   34 *unreclaimed:* untamed   34 *Of general assault:* to which young men are generally subject   38 *fetch of wit:* ingenious device   39 *sallies:* sullies, blemishes   40 *soil'd . . . working:* shopworn   43 *Having:* if he has   *prenominate crimes:* aforementioned faults   45 *closes:* falls in   *in this consequence:* as follows   47 *addition:* style of address   56 *o'ertook in 's rouse:* overcome by drink   61 *reach:* capacity, understanding

With windlasses and with assays of bias,
By indirections find directions out;
So by my former lecture and advice
Shall you my son. You have me, have you not?   65
Reynaldo: My lord, I have.
Polonius: God buy ye, fare ye well.
Reynaldo: Good my lord.
Polonius: Observe his inclination in yourself.
Reynaldo: I shall, my lord.
Polonius: And let him ply his music.   70
Reynaldo: Well, my lord.
Polonius: Farewell.

(*Exit* Reynaldo.)

(*Enter* Ophelia.)

How now, Ophelia, what's the matter?
Ophelia: O my lord, my lord, I have been so affrighted!
Polonius: With what, i' th' name of God?
Ophelia: My lord, as I was sewing in my closet,   75
Lord Hamlet, with his doublet all unbrac'd,
No hat upon his head, his stockins fouled,
Ungart'red, and down-gyved to his ankle,
Pale as his shirt, his knees knocking each other,
And with a look so piteous in purport   80
As if he had been loosed out of hell
To speak of horrors—he comes before me.
Polonius: Mad for thy love?
Ophelia: My lord, I do not know,
But truly I do fear it.
Polonius: What said he?
Ophelia: He took me by the wrist, and held me hard,   85
Then goes he to the length of all his arm,
And with his other hand thus o'er his brow,
He falls to such perusal of my face
As 'a would draw it. Long stay'd he so.
At last, a little shaking of mine arm,   90
And thrice his head thus waving up and down,
He rais'd a sigh so piteous and profound
As it did seem to shatter all his bulk

---

62 *windlasses:* roundabout methods   *assays of bias:* indirect attempts (a figure from the game of bowls, in which the player must make allowance for the curving course his bowl will take toward its mark)   63 *directions:* the way things are going   65 *have me:* understand me   66 *God buy ye:* good-bye (a contraction of *God be with you*)   68 *in:* by. Polonius asks him to observe Laertes directly, as well as making inquiries.   70 *let him ply:* see that he goes on with   75 *closet:* private room   76 *unbrac'd:* unlaced   77 *stockins fouled:* stockings dirty   78 *down-gyved:* hanging down like fetters on a prisoner's legs   93 *bulk:* body

And end his being. That done, he lets me go,
And with his head over his shoulder turn'd,   95
He seem'd to find his way without his eyes,
For out a' doors he went without their helps,
And to the last bended their light on me.

Polonius: Come, go with me. I will go seek the King.
This is the very ecstasy of love,   100
Whose violent property fordoes itself,
And leads the will to desperate undertakings
As oft as any passions under heaven
That does afflict our natures. I am sorry—
What, have you given him any hard words of late?   105

Ophelia: No, my good lord, but as you did command
I did repel his letters, and denied
His access to me.

Polonius: That hath made him mad.
I am sorry that with better heed and judgment
I had not coted him. I fear'd he did but trifle   110
And meant to wrack thee, but beshrow my jealousy!
By heaven, it is as proper to our age
To cast beyond ourselves in our opinions,
As it is common for the younger sort
To lack discretion. Come, go we to the King.   115
This must be known, which, being kept close, might move
More grief to hide, than hate to utter love.
Come.

(Exeunt.)

[Scene II]

(Flourish. Enter King *and* Queen, Rosencrantz *and* Guildenstern
[cum aliis].)

King: Welcome, dear Rosencrantz and Guildenstern!
Moreover that we much did long to see you,
The need we have to use you did provoke
Our hasty sending. Something have you heard
Of Hamlet's transformation; so call it,   5
Sith nor th' exterior nor the inward man

---

100 *ecstasy:* madness   101 *property:* quality *fordoes:* destroys   110 *coted:* observed
111 *beshrow:* beshrew, plague take   *jealousy:* suspicious mind   112 *proper . . . age:* characteristic of men of my age   113 *cast beyond ourselves:* overshoot, go too far (by way of caution)
116 *close:* secret   116–117 *move . . . love:* cause more grievous consequences by its concealment
than we shall incur displeasure by making it known   II.ii. Location: the castle   2 *Moreover . . . you:* besides the fact that we wanted to see you for your own sakes   6 *Sith:* since

Resembles that it was. What it should be,
More than his father's death, that thus hath put him
So much from th' understanding of himself,
I cannot dream of. I entreat you both   10
That, being of so young days brought up with him,
And sith so neighbored to his youth and havior,
That you voutsafe your rest here in our court
Some little time, so by your companies
To draw him on to pleasures, and to gather   15
So much as from occasion you may glean,
Whether aught to us unknown afflicts him thus,
That, open'd, lies within our remedy.

Queen: Good gentlemen, he hath much talk'd of you,
And sure I am two men there is not living   20
To whom he more adheres. If it will please you
To show us so much gentry and good will
As to expend your time with us a while
For the supply and profit of our hope,
Your visitation shall receive such thanks   25
As fits a king's remembrance.

Rosencrantz: Both your Majesties
Might, by the sovereign power you have of us,
Put your dread pleasures more into command
Than to entreaty.

Guildenstern: But we both obey,
And here give up ourselves, in the full bent,   30
To lay our service freely at your feet,
To be commanded.

King: Thanks, Rosencrantz and gentle Guildenstern.

Queen: Thanks, Guildenstern and gentle Rosencrantz.
And I beseech you instantly to visit   35
My too much changed son. Go some of you
And bring these gentlemen where Hamlet is.

Guildenstern: Heavens make our presence and our practices
Pleasant and helpful to him!

Queen: Ay, amen!

(*Exeunt* Rosencrantz *and* Guildenstern *[with some* Attendants*].*)

(*Enter* Polonius.)

Polonius: Th' embassadors from Norway, my good lord,   40
Are joyfully return'd.

---

11 *of:* from   13 *voutsafe your rest:* vouchsafe to remain   21 *more adheres:* is more attached
22 *gentry:* courtesy   24 *supply and profit:* support and advancement   30 *in . . . bent:* to our
utmost   40 *embassadors:* ambassadors

King: Thou still hast been the father of good news.
Polonius: Have I, my lord? I assure my good liege
   I hold my duty as I hold my soul,
   Both to my God and to my gracious king;   45
   And I do think, or else this brain of mine
   Hunts not the trail of policy so sure
   As it hath us'd to do, that I have found
   The very cause of Hamlet's lunacy.
King: O, speak of that, that do I long to hear.   50
Polonius: Give first admittance to th' embassadors;
   My news shall be the fruit to that great feast.
King: Thyself do grace to them, and bring them in. *[Exit Polonius.]*
   He tells me, my dear Gertrude, he hath found
   The head and source of all your son's distemper.   55
Queen: I doubt it is no other but the main,
   His father's death and our [o'erhasty] marriage.

   (*Enter [*Polonius *with* Voltemand *and* Cornelius, *the]* Embassadors.)

King: Well, we shall sift him.—Welcome, my good friends!
   Say, Voltemand, what from our brother Norway?
Voltemand: Most fair return of greetings and desires.   60
   Upon our first, he sent out to suppress
   His nephew's levies, which to him appear'd
   To be a preparation 'gainst the Polack;
   But better look'd into, he truly found
   It was against your Highness. Whereat griev'd,   65
   That so his sickness, age, and impotence
   Was falsely borne in hand, sends out arrests
   On Fortinbras, which he, in brief, obeys,
   Receives rebuke from Norway, and in fine,
   Makes vow before his uncle never more   70
   To give th' assay of arms against your Majesty.
   Whereon old Norway, overcome with joy,
   Gives him threescore thousand crowns in annual fee,
   And his commission to employ those soldiers,
   So levied, as before, against the Polack,   75
   With an entreaty, herein further shown,   *[giving a paper]*
   That it might please you to give quiet pass
   Through your dominions for this enterprise,
   On such regards of safety and allowance
   As therein are set down.

---

42 *still:* always   43 *liege:* sovereign   47 *policy:* statecraft   52 *fruit:* dessert   55 *head:* synonymous with *source distemper:* (mental) illness   56 *doubt:* suspect *main:* main cause
61 *Upon our first:* at our first representation   65 *griev'd:* aggrieved, offended   67 *borne in hand:* taken advantage of   69 *in fine:* in the end   71 *assay:* trial   79 *On . . . allowance:* with such safeguards and provisos

King: It likes us well,   80
And at our more considered time we'll read,
Answer, and think upon this business.
Mean time, we thank you for your well-took labor.
Go to your rest, at night we'll feast together.
Most welcome home!

(Exeunt Embassadors *[and* Attendants*].)*

Polonius: This business is well ended.   85
My liege, and madam, to expostulate
What majesty should be, what duty is,
Why day is day, night night, and time is time,
Were nothing but to waste night, day, and time;
Therefore, [since] brevity is the soul of wit,   90
And tediousness the limbs and outward flourishes,
I will be brief. Your noble son is mad:
Mad call I it, for to define true madness,
What is't but to be nothing else but mad?
But let that go.
Queen: More matter with less art.   95
Polonius: Madam, I swear I use no art at all.
That he's mad, 'tis true, 'tis true 'tis pity,
And pity 'tis 'tis true—a foolish figure,
But farewell it, for I will use no art.
Mad let us grant him then, and now remains   100
That we find out the cause of this effect,
Or rather say, the cause of this defect,
For this effect defective comes by cause:
Thus it remains, and the remainder thus.
Perpend.   105
I have a daughter—have while she is mine—
Who in her duty and obedience, mark,
Hath given me this. Now gather, and surmise.

[reads the salutation of the letter]

"To the celestial and my soul's idol, the most beautified Ophelia"—
That's an ill phrase, a vile phrase, "beautified" is a vile phrase. But you   110
shall hear. Thus:
"In her excellent white bosom, these, etc."
Queen: Came this from Hamlet to her?
Polonius: Good madam, stay awhile. I will be faithful.

---

80 *likes:* pleases   81 *consider'd:* suitable for consideration   86 *expostulate:* expound
90 *wit:* understanding, wisdom   95 *art:* rhetorical art   98 *figure:* figure of speech
103 *For . . . cause:* for this effect (which shows as a defect in Hamlet's reason) is not merely accidental, and has a cause we may trace   105 *Perpend:* consider   110 *beautified:* beautiful (not
an uncommon usage)

([reads the] letter)

> "Doubt thou the stars are fire,   115
>   Doubt that the sun doth move,
>   Doubt truth to be a liar,
>   But never doubt I love.

> O dear Ophelia, I am ill at these numbers. I have not art to reckon my
> groans, but that I love thee best, O most best, believe it. Adieu.   120
>   Thine evermore, most dear lady,
>   whilst this machine is to him, Hamlet."

This in obedience hath my daughter shown me,
And more [above], hath his solicitings,
As they fell out by time, by means, and place,   125
All given to mine ear.

King: But how hath she
Receiv'd his love?

Polonius: What do you think of me?

King: As of a man faithful and honorable.

Polonius: I would fain prove so. But what might you think,
When I had seen this hot love on the wing—   130
As I perceiv'd it (I must tell you that)
Before my daughter told me—what might you,
Or my dear Majesty your queen here, think,
If I had play'd the desk or table-book,
Or given my heart a [winking,] mute and dumb,   135
Or look'd upon this love with idle sight,
What might you think? No, I went round to work,
And my young mistress thus I did bespeak:
"Lord Hamlet is a prince out of thy star;
This must not be"; and then I prescripts gave her,   140
That she should lock herself from [his] resort,
Admit no messengers, receive no tokens.
Which done, she took the fruits of my advice;
And he repell'd, a short tale to make,
Fell into a sadness, then into a fast,   145
Thence to a watch, thence into a weakness,
Thence to [a] lightness, and by this declension,
Into the madness wherein now he raves,
And all we mourn for.

King: Do you think ['tis] this?

---

118 *Doubt:* suspect   119 *ill . . . numbers:* bad at versifying   *reckon:* count (with a quibble on
numbers)   122 *machine:* body   124 *more above:* furthermore   129 *fain:* willingly, gladly
134 *play'd . . . table-book:* noted the matter secretly   135 *winking:* closing of the eyes   136
idle sight: noncomprehending eyes   137 *round:* straightforwardly   138 *bespeak:* address
139 *star:* sphere, lot in life   143 *took . . . of:* profited by, carried out   144 *repell'd:* repulsed
146 *watch:* sleeplessness   147 *lightness:* lightheadedness

Queen: It may be, very like.   150

Polonius: Hath there been such a time—I would fain know that—
That I have positively said, " 'Tis so,"
When it prov'd otherwise?

King: Not that I know.

Polonius [points to his head and shoulder]: Take this from this, if this be
otherwise.   155
If circumstances lead me, I will find
Where truth is hid, though it were hid indeed
Within the centre.

King: How may we try it further?

Polonius: You know sometimes he walks four hours together
Here in the lobby.

Queen: So he does indeed.   160

Polonius: At such a time I'll loose my daughter to him.
Be you and I behind an arras then,
Mark the encounter: if he love her not,
And be not from his reason fall'n thereon,
Let me be no assistant for a state,   165
But keep a farm and carters.

King: We will try it.

(*Enter* Hamlet [*reading on a book*].)

Queen: But look where sadly the poor wretch comes reading.

Polonius: Away, I do beseech you, both away.
I'll board him presently.

(*Exeunt* King *and* Queen.)

                                        O, give me leave,
How does my good Lord Hamlet?   170

Hamlet: Well, God-a-mercy.

Polonius: Do you know me, my lord?

Hamlet: Excellent well, you are a fishmonger.

Polonius: Not I, my lord.

Hamlet: Then I would you were so honest a man.   175

Polonius: Honest, my lord?

Hamlet: Ay, sir, to be honest, as this world goes, is to be one man pick'd out
of ten thousand.

Polonius: That's very true, my lord.

Hamlet: For if the sun breed maggots in a dead dog, being a good kissing car-   180
rion—Have you a daughter?

---

157 *centre:* of the earth (which in the Ptolemaic system is also the centre of the universe)   162
arras: hanging tapestry   164 *thereon:* because of that   168 *board:* accost   *presently:* at once
171 *God-a-mercy:* thank you   173 *fishmonger:* Usually explained as slang for "bawd," but no evidence has been produced for such a usage in Shakespeare's day.   180–81 *good kissing carrion:*
flesh good enough for the sun to kiss

Polonius: I have, my lord.

Hamlet: Let her not walk i' th' sun. Conception is a blessing, but as your
daughter may conceive, friend, look to't.

Polonius [aside]: How say you by that? still harping on my daughter. Yet he   185
knew me not at first, 'a said I was a fishmonger. 'A is far gone. And truly
in my youth I suff'red much extremity for love—very near this. I'll speak
to him again.—What do you read, my lord?

Hamlet: Words, words, words.

Polonius: What is the matter, my lord?   190

Hamlet: Between who?

Polonius: I mean, the matter that you read, my lord.

Hamlet: Slanders, sir; for the satirical rogue says here that old men have grey
beards, that their faces are wrinkled, their eyes purging thick amber and
plumtree gum, and that they have a plentiful lack of wit, together with   195
most weak hams; all which, sir, though I most powerfully and potently believe, yet I hold it not honesty to have it thus set down, for yourself, sir,
shall grow old as I am, if like a crab you could go backward.

Polonius [aside]: Though this be madness, yet there is method in't.—Will you
walk out of the air, my lord?   200

Hamlet: Into my grave.

Polonius: Indeed that's out of the air. *[aside]* How pregnant sometimes his replies
are! a happiness that often madness hits on, which reason and [sanity] could
not so prosperously be deliver'd of. I will leave him, [and suddenly contrive
the means of meeting between him] and my daughter.—My lord, I will take   205
my leave of you.

Hamlet: You cannot take from me any thing that I will not more willingly part
withal—except my life, except my life, except my life.

Polonius: Fare you well, my lord.

Hamlet: These tedious old fools!   210

(*Enter* Guildenstern *and* Rosencrantz.)

Polonius: You go to seek the Lord Hamlet, there he is.

Rosencrantz [to Polonius*]:* God save you, sir!

[Exit Polonius.*]*

Guildenstern: My honor'd lord!

Rosencrantz: My most dear lord!

Hamlet: My [excellent] good friends! How dost thou, Guildenstern? Ah,   215
Rosencrantz! Good lads, how do you both?

Rosencrantz: As the indifferent children of the earth.

---

183 *Conception:* understanding (with following play on the sense "conceiving a child")
190 *matter:* subject; but Hamlet replies as if he had understood Polonius to mean "cause for a
quarrel."   197 *honesty:* a fitting thing   199 *method:* orderly arrangement, sequence of ideas
202 *out . . . air:* Outdoor air was thought to be bad for invalids.   202 *pregnant:* apt
204 *suddenly:* at once   217 *indifferent:* average

Guildenstern: Happy, in that we are not [over-]happy, on Fortune's [cap] we
   are not the very button.
Hamlet: Nor the soles of her shoe?   220
Rosencrantz: Neither, my lord.
Hamlet: Then you live about her waist, or in the middle of her favors?
Guildenstern: Faith, her privates we.
Hamlet: In the secret parts of Fortune? O, most true, she is a strumpet.
   What news?   225
Rosencrantz: None, my lord, but the world's grown honest.
Hamlet: Then is doomsday near. But your news is not true. [Let me question
   more in particular. What have you, my good friends, deserv'd at the
   hands of Fortune, that she sends you to prison hither?
Guildenstern: Prison, my lord?   230
Hamlet: Denmark's a prison.
Rosencrantz: Then is the world one.
Hamlet: A goodly one, in which there are many confines, wards, and dun-
   geons, Denmark being one o' th' worst.
Rosencrantz: We think not so, my lord.   235
Hamlet: Why then 'tis none to you; for there is nothing either good or bad,
   but thinking makes it so. To me it is a prison.
Rosencrantz: Why then your ambition makes it one. 'Tis too narrow for
   your mind.
Hamlet: O God, I could be bounded in a nutshell, and count myself a king of 240
   infinite space—were it not that I have bad dreams.
Guildenstern: Which dreams indeed are ambition, for the very substance of
   the ambitious is merely the shadow of a dream.
Hamlet: A dream itself is but a shadow.
Rosencrantz: Truly, and I hold ambition of so airy and light a quality that it is 245
   but a shadow's shadow.
Hamlet: Then are our beggars bodies, and our monarchs and outstretch'd he-
   roes the beggars' shadows. Shall we to th' court? for, by my fay, I cannot
   reason.
Both [Rosencrantz, Guildenstern]: We'll wait upon you.   250
Hamlet: No such matter. I will not sort you with the rest of my servants; for
   to speak to you like an honest man, I am most dreadfully attended.] But
   in the beaten way of friendship, what make you at Elsinore?
Rosencrantz: To visit you, my lord, no other occasion.
Hamlet: Beggar that I am, I am [even] poor in thanks—but I thank you, and 255
   sure, dear friends, my thanks are too dear a halfpenny. Were you not sent

---

223 *privates:* (1) intimate friends; (2) genitalia   224 *strumpet:* a common epithet for Fortune,
because she grants favors to all men   233 *wards:* cells   247 *bodies:* not shadows (since they
lack ambition)   *outstretch'd:* with their ambition extended to the utmost (and hence producing
stretched-out or elongated shadows)   248 *fay:* faith   250 *wait upon you:* attend you thither
251 *sort:* associate   252 *dreadfully:* execrably   256 *too . . . halfpenny:* too expensive priced at
a halfpenny; not worth much

for? is it your own inclining? is it a free visitation? Come, come, deal
justly with me. Come, come—nay, speak.

Guildenstern: What should we say, my lord?

Hamlet: Any thing but to th' purpose. You were sent for, and there is a kind   260
of confession in your looks, which your modesties have not craft enough
to color. I know the good King and Queen have sent for you.

Rosencrantz: To what end, my lord?

Hamlet: That you must teach me. But let me conjure you, by the rights of our
fellowship, by the consonancy of our youth, by the obligation of our ever-   265
preserv'd love, and by what more dear a better proposer can charge you
withal, be even and direct with me, whether you were sent for or no!

Rosencrantz [aside to Guildenstern*]:* What say you?

Hamlet [aside]: Nay then I have an eye of you!—If you love me, hold not off.

Guildenstern: My lord, we were sent for.   270

Hamlet: I will tell you why, so shall my anticipation prevent your discovery,
and your secrecy to the King and Queen moult no feather. I have of late—
but wherefore I know not—lost all my mirth, forgone all custom of exercises; and indeed it goes so heavily with my disposition, that this goodly
frame, the earth, seems to me a sterile promontory; this most excellent   275
canopy, the air, look you, this brave o'erhanging firmament, this majestical
roof fretted with golden fire, why, it appeareth nothing to me but a foul
and pestilent congregation of vapors. What [a] piece of work is a man, how
noble in reason, how infinite in faculties, in form and moving, how express
and admirable in action, how like an angel in apprehension, how like a   280
god! the beauty of the world; the paragon of animals; and yet to me what
is this quintessence of dust? Man delights not me—nor women neither,
though by your smiling you seem to say so.

Rosencrantz: My lord, there was no such stuff in my thoughts.

Hamlet: Why did ye laugh then, when I said, "Man delights not me"?   285

Rosencrantz: To think, my lord, if you delight not in man, what lenten entertainment the players shall receive from you. We coted them on the way,
and hither are they coming to offer you service.

Hamlet: He that plays the king shall be welcome—his Majesty shall have
tribute on me, the adventerous knight shall use his foil and target, the   290
lover shall not sigh gratis, the humorous man shall end his part in peace,

---

258 *justly:* honestly   260 *but:* Ordinarily punctuated with a comma preceding, to give the sense
"provided that it is"; but Q2 has no comma, and Hamlet may intend, or include, the sense "except."   261 *modesties:* sense of shame   265 *consonancy . . . youth:* similarity of our ages
266 *charge:* urge, adjure   *even:* frank, honest (cf. modern "level with me")   269 *of:* on   271
prevent your discovery: forestall your disclosure (of what the king and queen have said to you in
confidence)   272 *moult no feather:* not be impaired in the least   273–74 *custom of exercises:*
my usual athletic activities   276 *brave:* splendid   277 *fretted:* ornamented as with fretwork
278 *piece of work:* masterpiece   279–81 *how infinite . . . god:* See the Textual Notes for the different punctuation in F1.   279 *express:* exact   282 *quintessence:* finest and purest extract
287–87 *lenten entertainment:* meagre reception   287 *coted:* outstripped   290 *on:* of, from
adventerous: adventurous, wandering in search of adventure   *foil and target:* light fencing sword
and small shield   291 *gratis:* without reward   *humorous:* dominated by some eccentric trait
(like the melancholy Jaques in *As You Like It*)

[the clown shall make those laugh whose lungs are [tickle] a' th' sere,] and the lady shall say her mind freely, or the [blank] verse shall halt for't. What players are they?

Rosencrantz: Even those you were wont to take such delight in, the tragedians 295 of the city.

Hamlet: How chances it they travel? Their residence, both in reputation and profit, was better both ways.

Rosencrantz: I think their inhibition comes by the means of the late innovation.

Hamlet: Do they hold the same estimation they did when I was in the city? 300 Are they so follow'd?

Rosencrantz: No indeed are they not.

Hamlet: How comes it? do they grow rusty?

Rosencrantz: Nay, their endeavor keeps in the wonted pace; but there is, sir, an aery of children, little eyases, that cry out on the top of question, and are 305 most tyrannically clapp'd for't. These are now the fashion, and so [berattle] the common stages—so they call them—that many wearing rapiers are afraid of goose-quills and dare scarce come thither.

Hamlet: What, are they children? Who maintains 'em? How are they escoted? Will they pursue the quality no longer than they can sing? Will 310 they not say afterwards, if they should grow themselves to common players (as it is [most like], if their means are [no] better), their writers do them wrong, to make them exclaim against their own succession?

Rosencrantz: Faith, there has been much to do on both sides, and the nation holds it no sin to tarre them to controversy. There was for a while no 315 money bid for argument, unless the poet and the player went to cuffs in the question.

Hamlet: Is't possible?

---

292 *tickle . . . sere:* easily made to laugh (literally, describing a gun that goes off easily; *sere* = a catch in the gunlock; *tickle* = easily affected, highly sensitive to stimulus)   293 *halt:* limp, come off lamely (the verse will not scan if she omits indecent words)   299 *inhibition:* hindrance (to playing in the city). The word could be used of an official prohibition. See next note.   299 *innovation:* Shakespeare elsewhere uses this word of a political uprising or revolt, and lines 332–33 are often explained as meaning that the company had been forbidden to play in the city as the result of some disturbance. It is commonly conjectured that the allusion is to the Essex rebellion of 1601, but it is known that Shakespeare's company, though to some extent involved on account of the special performance of *Richard II* they were commissioned to give on the eve of the rising, were not in fact punished by inhibition. A second interpretation explains *innovation* as referring to the new theatrical vogue described in lines 320 ff., and conjectures that *inhibition* may allude to a Privy Council order of 1600 restricting the number of London playhouses to two and the number of performances to two a week.   303–321 *How . . . too:* This passage refers topically to the "War of the Theatres" between the child actors and their poet Jonson on the one side, and on the other the adults, with Dekker, Marston, and possibly Shakespeare as spokesmen, in 1600–1601. 305 *aery:* nest *eyases:* unfledged hawks *cry . . . question:* cry shrilly above others in controversy 306 *tyrannically:* outrageously *berattle:* cry down, satirize   307 *common stages:* public theatres (the children played at the Blackfriars, a private theatre)   308 *goose-quills:* pens (of satirical playwrights)   310 *escoted:* supported   310 *quality:* profession (of acting) *no . . . sing:* only until their voices change   313 *succession:* future   314 *to do:* ado   315 *tarre:* incite   316 *argument:* plot of a play   316–17 *in the question:* as part of the script

Guildenstern: O, there has been much throwing about of brains.

Hamlet: Do the boys carry it away?   320

Rosencrantz: Ay, that they do, my lord—Hercules and his load too.]

Hamlet: It is not very strange, for my uncle is King of Denmark, and those
that would make mouths at him while my father liv'd, give twenty, forty,
fifty, a hundred ducats a-piece for his picture in little. 'Sblood, there is
something in this more than natural, if philosophy could find it out.   325
(*a flourish [for the* Players*]*)

Guildenstern: There are the players.

Hamlet: Gentlemen, you are welcome to Elsinore. Your hands, come then: th'
appurtenance of welcome is fashion and ceremony. Let me comply with
you in this garb, [lest my] extent to the players, which, I tell you, must show   330
fairly outwards, should more appear like entertainment than yours. You are
welcome; but my uncle-father and aunt-mother are deceiv'd.

Guildenstern: In what, my dear lord?

Hamlet: I am but mad north-north-west. When the wind is southerly I know
a hawk from a hand-saw.   335

(*Enter* Polonius.*)

Polonius: Well be with you, gentlemen!

Hamlet [aside to them]: Hark you, Guildenstern, and you too—at each ear a
hearer—that great baby you see there is not yet out of his swaddling-clouts.

Rosencrantz: Happily he is the second time come to them, for they say an old
man is twice a child.   340

Hamlet: I will prophesy, he comes to tell me of the players, mark it. [*aloud*]
You say right, sir, a' Monday morning, 'twas then indeed.

Polonius: My lord, I have news to tell you.

Hamlet: My lord, I have news to tell you. When Roscius was an actor in
Rome—   345

Polonius: The actors are come hither, my lord.

Hamlet: Buzz, buzz!

Polonius: Upon my honor—

Hamlet: "Then came each actor on his ass"—

Polonius: The best actors in the world, either for tragedy, comedy, history,   350
pastoral,   pastoral-comical,   historical-pastoral,   [tragical-historical,

---

320 *carry it away:* win   321 *Hercules . . . too:* Hercules in the course of one of his twelve labors
supported the world for Atlas; the children do better, for they carry away the world and Hercules
as well. There is an allusion to the Globe playhouse, which reportedly had for its sign the figure
of Hercules upholding the world.   323 *mouths:* derisive faces   324 *'Sblood:* by God's
(Christ's) blood   329 *comply:* observe the formalities   330 *garb:* fashion, manner   *my extent:*
the degree of courtesy I show   331 *more . . . yours:* seem to be a warmer reception than I have
given you   335 *hawk, hand-saw:* both cutting tools; but also both birds, if *hand-saw* quibbles on
hernshaw, "heron," a bird preyed upon by the hawk   338 *swaddling-clouts:* swaddling clothes
339 *Happily:* haply, perhaps   340 *twice:* for the second time   344 *Roscius:* the most famous of
Roman actors (died 62 B.C.). News about him would be stale news indeed.   347 *Buzz:* exclamation of impatience at someone who tells news already known

tragical-comical-historical-pastoral,] scene individable, or poem unlimited; Seneca cannot be too heavy, nor Plautus too light, for the law of writ
and the liberty: these are the only men.

Hamlet: O Jephthah, judge of Israel, what a treasure hadst thou!   355

Polonius: What a treasure had he, my lord?

Hamlet: Why—

> "One fair daughter, and no more,
> The which he loved passing well."

Polonius [aside]: Still on my daughter.   360

Hamlet: Am I not i' th' right, old Jephthah?

Polonius: If you call me Jephthah, my lord, I have a daughter that I love passing well.

Hamlet: Nay, that follows not.

Polonius: What follows then, my lord?   365

Hamlet: Why—

> "As by lot, God wot,"

and then, you know,

> "It came to pass, as most like it was"—

the first row of the pious chanson will show you more, for look where   370
my abridgment comes.

(Enter the Players, *[four or five].)*
You are welcome, masters, welcome all. I am glad to see thee well. Welcome, good friends. O, old friend! why, thy face is valanc'd since I saw
thee last; com'st thou to beard me in Denmark? What, my young lady and
mistress! by' lady, your ladyship is nearer to heaven than when I saw you   375
last, by the altitude of a chopine. Pray God your voice, like a piece of uncurrent gold, be not crack'd within the ring. Masters, you are all welcome. We'll e'en to't like [French] falc'ners—fly at any thing we see; we'll
have a speech straight. Come give us a taste of your quality, come, a passionate speech.   380

[1.] Player: What speech, my good lord?

Hamlet: I heard thee speak me a speech once, but it was never acted, or if it
was, not above once; for the play, I remember, pleas'd not the million,

---

352 *scene individable:* play observing the unity of place   352–53 *poem unlimited:* play ignoring
rules such as the three unities   353 *Seneca:* Roman writer of tragedies   353 *Plautus:* Roman
writer of comedies   353–54 *for . . . liberty:* for strict observance of the rules, or for freedom
from them (with possible allusion to the location of playhouses, which were not built in properties
under city jurisdiction, but in the "liberties"—land once monastic and now outside the jurisdiction
of the city authorities)   354 *only:* very best (a frequent use)   355 *Jephthah . . . Israel:* title of a
ballad, from which Hamlet goes on to quote. For the story of Jephthah and his daughter, see
Judges 11.   370 *row:* stanza *chanson:* song, ballad   371 *abridgment:* (1) interruption; (2)
pastime   373 *valanc'd:* fringed, bearded   374 *beard:* confront boldly (with obvious pun)
375 *by' lady:* by Our Lady   376 *chopine:* thick-soled shoe   377 *crack'd . . . ring:* broken to the
point where you can no longer play female roles. A coin with a crack extending far enough in from
the edge to cross the circle surrounding the stamp of the sovereign's head was unacceptable in exchange (*uncurrent*).   379 *straight:* straightway   379 *quality:* professional skill

'twas caviary to the general, but it was—as I receiv'd it, and others, whose
judgments in such matters cried in the top of mine—an excellent play,   385
well digested in the scenes, set down with as much modesty as cunning. I
remember one said there were no sallets in the lines to make the matter
savory, nor no matter in the phrase that might indict the author of affection, but call'd it an honest method, as wholesome as sweet, and by very
much more handsome than fine. One speech in't I chiefly lov'd, 'twas Ae-   390
neas' [tale] to Dido, and thereabout of it especially when he speaks of
Priam's slaughter. If it live in your memory, begin at this line—let me see,
let me see:
"The rugged Pyrrhus, like th' Hyrcanian beast—"
'Tis not so, it begins with Pyrrhus: 395
"The rugged Pyrrhus, he whose sable arms,
Black as his purpose, did the night resemble
When he lay couched in th' ominous horse,
Hath now this dread and black complexion smear'd
With heraldy more dismal: head to foot   400
Now is he total gules, horridly trick'd
With blood of fathers, mothers, daughters, sons,
Bak'd and impasted with the parching streets,
That lend a tyrannous and a damned light
To their lord's murther. Roasted in wrath and fire,   405
And thus o'er-sized with coagulate gore,
With eyes like carbuncles, the hellish Pyrrhus
Old grandsire Priam seeks."
So proceed you.

Polonius: 'Fore God, my lord, well spoken, with good accent and good   410
discretion.

[1.] Player: "Anon he finds him
Striking too short at Greeks. His antique sword,
Rebellious to his arm, lies where it falls,
Repugnant to command. Unequal match'd,   415
Pyrrhus at Priam drives, in rage strikes wide,
But with the whiff and wind of his fell sword
Th' unnerved father falls. [Then senseless Ilium,]
Seeming to feel this blow, with flaming top

---

384 *caviary . . . general:* caviare to the common people, too choice for the multitude   385 *cried . . .
of:* were louder than, carried more authority than   387 *sallets:* salads, spicy jokes   *savory:* zesty
389–89 *affection:* affectation   390 *fine:* showily dressed (in language)   392 *Priam's slaughter:*
the slaying of Priam (at the fall of Troy)   395 *Pyrrhus:* another name for Neoptolemus,
Achilles' son   *Hyrcanian beast:* Hyrcania in the Caucasus was notorious for its tigers.   396
sable arms: The Greeks within the Trojan horse had blackened their skin so as to be inconspicu-
ous when they emerged at night.   400 *heraldy:* heraldry   *dismal:* ill-boding   401 *gules:* red
(heraldic term)   *trick'd:* adorned   403 *Bak'd:* caked   *impasted:* crusted   *with . . . streets:* by
the heat from the burning streets   406 *o'er-sized:* covered over as with a coat of sizing   407
carbuncles: jewels believed to shine in the dark   415 *Repugnant:* resistant, hostile   417 *fell:*
cruel   418 *unnerved:* drained of strength   *senseless:* insensible   *Ilium:* the citadel of Troy

Stoops to his base, and with a hideous crash   420
Takes prisoner Pyrrhus' ear; for lo his sword,
Which was declining on the milky head
Of reverent Priam, seem'd i' th' air to stick.
So as a painted tyrant Pyrrhus stood
[And,] like a neutral to his will and matter,   425
Did nothing.
But as we often see, against some storm,
A silence in the heavens, the rack stand still,
The bold winds speechless, and the orb below
As hush as death, anon the dreadful thunder   430
Doth rend the region; so after Pyrrhus' pause,
A roused vengeance sets him new a-work,
And never did the Cyclops' hammers fall
On Mars's armor forg'd for proof eterne
With less remorse than Pyrrhus' bleeding sword   435
Now falls on Priam.
Out, out, thou strumpet Fortune! All you gods,
In general synod take away her power!
Break all the spokes and [fellies] from her wheel,
And bowl the round nave down the hill of heaven   440
As low as to the fiends!"
Polonius: This is too long.
Hamlet: It shall to the barber's with your beard. Prithee say on, he's for a jig
    or a tale of bawdry, or he sleeps. Say on, come to Hecuba.
[1.] Player: "But who, ah woe, had seen the mobled queen"—   445
Hamlet: "The mobled queen"?
Polonius: That's good, ["[mobled] queen" is good].
[1.] Player: "Run barefoot up and down, threat'ning the flames
    With bisson rheum, a clout upon that head
    Where late the diadem stood, and for a robe,   450
    About her lank and all o'er-teemed loins,
    A blanket, in the alarm of fear caught up—
    Who this had seen, with tongue in venom steep'd,
    'Gainst Fortune's state would treason have pronounc'd.
    But if the gods themselves did see her then,   455
    When she saw Pyrrhus make malicious sport
    In mincing with his sword her [husband's] limbs,
    The instant burst of clamor that she made,
    Unless things mortal move them not at all,

---

423 *reverent:* reverend, aged   425 *like . . . matter:* poised midway between intention and performance   427 *against:* just before   428 *rack:* cloud-mass   431 *region:* air   433 *Cy-*
clops: giants who worked in Vulcan's smithy, where armor was made for the gods   434 *proof*
eterne: eternal endurance   435 *remorse:* pity   439 *fellies:* rims   440 *nave:* hub   443 *jig:*
song-and-dance entertainment performed after the main play   445 *mobled:* muffled   449
bisson rheum: blinding tears   *clout:* cloth   451 *o'er-teemed:* worn out by childbearing   454
state: rule, government

Would have made milch the burning eyes of heaven,   460
And passion in the gods."

Polonius: Look whe'er he has not turn'd his color and has tears in 's eyes.
Prithee no more.

Hamlet: 'Tis well, I'll have thee speak out the rest of this soon. Good my
lord, will you see the players well bestow'd? Do you hear, let them be well   465
us'd, for they are the abstract and brief chronicles of the time. After your
death you were better have a bad epitaph than their ill report while
you live.

Polonius: My lord, I will use them according to their desert.

Hamlet: God's bodkin, man, much better: use every man after his desert,   470
and who shall scape whipping? Use them after your own honor and
dignity—the less they deserve, the more merit is in your bounty. Take
them in.

Polonius: Come, sirs.

> *[Exit.]*

Hamlet: Follow him, friends, we'll hear a play tomorrow.   475

> *[Exeunt all the* Players *but the* First.*]*

Dost thou hear me, old friend? Can you play "The Murther of Gonzago"?

[1.] Player: Ay, my lord.

Hamlet: We'll ha't to-morrow night. You could for need study a speech of
some dozen lines, or sixteen lines, which I would set down and insert in't,
could you not?   480

[1.] Player: Ay, my lord.

Hamlet: Very well. Follow that lord, and look you mock him not.

> *[Exit First Player.]*

My good friends, I'll leave you [till] night. You are welcome to Elsinore.

Rosencrantz: Good my lord!

Hamlet: Ay so, God buy to you.

> *(Exeunt [*Rosencrantz *and* Guildenstern*].)*

Now I am alone.   485
O, what a rogue and peasant slave am I!
Is it not monstrous that this player here,
But in a fiction, in a dream of passion,
Could force his soul so to his own conceit
That from her working all the visage wann'd,   490
Tears in his eyes, distraction in his aspect,
A broken voice, an' his whole function suiting

---

460 *milch:* moist (literally, milky)   461 *passion:* grief   462 *Look . . . not:* note how he has
465 *bestow'd:* lodged   *us'd:* treated   470 *God's bodkin:* by God's (Christ's) little body
478 *for need:* if necessary   489 *conceit:* imaginative conception   492 *his whole function:* the
operation of his whole body

With forms to his conceit? And all for nothing,
For Hecuba!
What's Hecuba to him, or he to [Hecuba],   495
That he should weep for her? What would he do
Had he the motive and [the cue] for passion
That I have? He would drown the stage with tears,
And cleave the general ear with horrid speech,
Make mad the guilty, and appall the free,   500
Confound the ignorant, and amaze indeed
The very faculties of eyes and ears. Yet I,
A dull and muddy-mettled rascal, peak
Like John-a-dreams, unpregnant of my cause,
And can say nothing; no, not for a king,   505
Upon whose property and most dear life
A damn'd defeat was made. Am I a coward?
Who calls me villain, breaks my pate across,
Plucks off my beard and blows it in my face,
Tweaks me by the nose, gives me the lie i' th' throat   510
As deep as to the lungs? Who does me this?
Hah, 'swounds, I should take it; for it cannot be
But I am pigeon-liver'd, and lack gall
To make oppression bitter, or ere this
I should 'a' fatted all the region kites   515
With this slave's offal. Bloody, bawdy villain!
Remorseless, treacherous, lecherous, kindless villain!
Why, what an ass am I! This is most brave,
That I, the son of a dear [father] murthered,
Prompted to my revenge by heaven and hell,   520
Must like a whore unpack my heart with words,
And fall a-cursing like a very drab,
A stallion. Fie upon't, foh!
About, my brains! Hum—I have heard
That guilty creatures sitting at a play   525
Have by the very cunning of the scene
Been strook so to the soul, that presently
They have proclaim'd their malefactions:
For murther, though it have no tongue, will speak
With most miraculous organ. I'll have these players   530
Play something like the murther of my father

---

493 *forms:* actions, expressions   500 *free:* innocent   501 *amaze:* confound   503 *muddy-mettled:* dull-spirited *peak:* mope   504 *John-a-dreams:* a sleepy fellow *unpregnant of:* unquickened by   507 *defeat:* destruction   510–11 *gives . . . lungs:* calls me a liar in the extremest degree   512 *'swounds:* by God's (Christ's) wounds *should:* would certainly   513 *am . . . gall:* am constitutionally incapable of resentment. That doves were mild because they had no gall was a popular belief.   516 *offal:* entrails   517 *kindless:* unnatural   523 *stallion:* male whore. Most editors adopt the F1 reading *scullion,* "kitchen menial."   524 *About:* to work   527 *presently:* at once, then and there

Before mine uncle. I'll observe his looks,
I'll tent him to the quick. If 'a do blench,
I know my course. The spirit that I have seen
May be a [dev'l], and the [dev'l] hath power   535
T' assume a pleasing shape, yea, and perhaps,
Out of my weakness and my melancholy,
As he is very potent with such spirits,
Abuses me to damn me. I'll have grounds
More relative than this—the play's the thing   540
Wherein I'll catch the conscience of the King.

(Exit.)

ACT III

Scene I

(Enter King, Queen, Polonius, Ophelia, Rosencrantz, Guildenstern,
Lords.*)*

King: An' can you by no drift of conference
     Get from him why he puts on this confusion,
     Grating so harshly all his days of quiet
     With turbulent and dangerous lunacy?
Rosencrantz: He does confess he feels himself distracted,   5
     But from what cause 'a will by no means speak.
Guildenstern: Nor do we find him forward to be sounded,
     But with a crafty madness keeps aloof
     When we would bring him on to some confession
     Of his true state.
Queen: Did he receive you well?   10
Rosencrantz: Most like a gentleman.
Guildenstern: But with much forcing of his disposition.
Rosencrantz: Niggard of question, but of our demands
     Most free in his reply.
Queen: Did you assay him
     To any pastime?   15
Rosencrantz: Madam, it so fell out that certain players
     We o'erraught on the way; of these we told him,
     And there did seem in him a kind of joy

---

533 *tent:* probe *blench:* flinch   534 *spirits:* states of temperament   539 *Abuses:* deludes
540 *relative:* closely related (to fact), conclusive   III.i. Location: the castle   1 *An':* and
drift of conference: leading on of conversation   7 *forward:* readily willing   *sounded:* plumbed,
probed   8 *crafty madness:* mad craftiness, the shrewdness that mad people sometimes exhibit
12 *disposition:* inclination   13 *question:* conversation   *demands:* questions   14 *assay:* attempt
to win   17 *o'erraught:* passed (literally, overreached)

To hear of it. They are here about the court,
And as I think, they have already order   20
This night to play before him.
Polonius: 'Tis most true,
And he beseech'd me to entreat your Majesties
To hear and see the matter.
King: With all my heart, and it doth much content me
To hear him so inclin'd.   25
Good gentlemen, give him a further edge,
And drive his purpose into these delights.
Rosencrantz: We shall, my lord.

(*Exeunt* Rosencrantz *and* Guildenstern.)

King: Sweet Gertrude, leave us two,
For we have closely sent for Hamlet hither,
That he, as 'twere by accident, may here   30
Affront Ophelia. Her father and myself,
We'll so bestow ourselves that, seeing unseen,
We may of their encounter frankly judge,
And gather by him, as he is behav'd,
If't be th' affliction of his love or no   35
That thus he suffers for.
Queen: I shall obey you.
And for your part, Ophelia, I do wish
That your good beauties be the happy cause
Of Hamlet's wildness. So shall I hope your virtues
Will bring him to his wonted way again,   40
To both your honors.
Ophelia: Madam, I wish it may.   *[Exit* Queen.*]*
Polonius: Ophelia, walk you here.—Gracious, so please you,
We will bestow ourselves.   *[to* Ophelia*]*   Read on this book,
That show of such an exercise may color
Your [loneliness]. We are oft to blame in this—   45
'Tis too much prov'd—that with devotion's visage
And pious action we do sugar o'er
The devil himself.
King: [aside]   O, 'tis too true!
How smart a lash that speech doth give my conscience!
The harlot's cheek, beautied with plast'ring art,   50
Is not more ugly to the thing that helps it
Than is my deed to my most painted word.
O heavy burthen!

---

26 *edge:* stimulus   27 *into:* on to   29 *closely:* privately   31 *Affront:* meet   33 *frankly:*
freely   44 *exercise:* religious exercise (as the next sentence makes clear)   44–45 *color Your*
loneliness: make your solitude seem natural   46 *too much prov'd:* too often proved true
47 *action:* demeanor   51 *to . . . it:* in comparison with the paint that makes it look beautiful

Polonius: I hear him coming. Withdraw, my lord.

[*Exeunt* King *and* Polonius.]

(*Enter* Hamlet.)

Hamlet: To be, or not to be, that is the question: 55
Whether 'tis nobler in the mind to suffer
The slings and arrows of outrageous fortune,
Or to take arms against a sea of troubles,
And by opposing, end them. To die, to sleep—
No more, and by a sleep to say we end   60
The heart-ache and the thousand natural shocks
That flesh is heir to; 'tis a consummation
Devoutly to be wish'd. To die, to sleep—
To sleep, perchance to dream—ay, there's the rub,
For in that sleep of death what dreams may come,   65
When we have shuffled off this mortal coil,
Must give us pause; there's the respect
That makes calamity of so long life:
For who would bear the whips and scorns of time,
Th' oppressor's wrong, the proud man's contumely,   70
The pangs of despis'd love, the law's delay,
The insolence of office, and the spurns
That patient merit of th' unworthy takes,
When he himself might his quietus make
With a bare bodkin; who would fardels bear,   75
To grunt and sweat under a weary life,
But that the dread of something after death,
The undiscover'd country, from whose bourn
No traveller returns, puzzles the will,
And makes us rather bear those ills we have,   80
Than fly to others that we know not of?
Thus conscience does make cowards [of us all],
And thus the native hue of resolution
Is sicklied o'er with the pale cast of thought,
And enterprises of great pitch and moment   85
With this regard their currents turn awry,
And lose the name of action.—Soft you now,

---

56 *suffer:* submit to, endure patiently   62 *consummation:* completion, end   64 *rub:* obstacle
(a term from the game of bowls)   66 *shuffled off:* freed ourselves from   *this mortal coil:* the
turmoil of this mortal life   67 *respect:* consideration   68 *of . . . life:* so long-lived   69
time: the world   74 *his quietus make:* write paid to his account   75 *bare bodkin:* mere dagger
fardels: burdens   78 *undiscover'd:* not disclosed to knowledge; about which men have no information   *bourn:* boundary, region   79 *puzzles:* paralyzes   82 *conscience:* reflection (but with
some of the modern sense, too)   83 *native hue:* natural (ruddy) complexion   84 *pale cast:*
pallor   *thought:* melancholy thought, brooding   85 *pitch:* loftiness (a term from falconry, signifying the highest point of a hawk's flight)

The fair Ophelia. Nymph, in thy orisons
Be all my sins rememb'red.

Ophelia: Good my lord,
How does your honor for this many a day?   90

Hamlet: I humbly thank you, well, [well, well].

Ophelia: My lord, I have remembrances of yours
That I have longed long to redeliver.
I pray you now receive them.

Hamlet: No, not I,
I never gave you aught.   95

Ophelia: My honor'd lord, you know right well you did,
And with them words of so sweet breath compos'd
As made these things more rich. Their perfume lost,
Take these again, for to the noble mind
Rich gifts wax poor when givers prove unkind.   100
There, my lord.

Hamlet: Ha, ha! are you honest?

Ophelia: My lord?

Hamlet: Are you fair?

Ophelia: What means your lordship?   105

Hamlet: That if you be honest and fair, [your honesty] should admit no discourse to your beauty.

Ophelia: Could beauty, my lord, have better commerce than with honesty?

Hamlet: Ay, truly, for the power of beauty will sooner transform honesty from what it is to a bawd than the force of honesty can translate beauty into his   110
likeness. This was sometime a paradox, but now the time gives it proof. I
did love you once.

Ophelia: Indeed, my lord, you made me believe so.

Hamlet: You should not have believ'd me, for virtue cannot so [inoculate] our
old stock but we shall relish of it. I lov'd you not.   115

Ophelia: I was the more deceiv'd.

Hamlet: Get thee [to] a nunn'ry, why wouldst thou be a breeder of sinners? I
am myself indifferent honest, but yet I could accuse me of such things
that it were better my mother had not borne me: I am very proud, revengeful, ambitious, with more offenses at my beck than I have thoughts   120
to put them in, imagination to give them shape, or time to act them in.
What should such fellows as I do crawling between earth and heaven? We
are arrant knaves, believe none of us. Go thy ways to a nunn'ry. Where's
your father?

Ophelia: At home, my lord.   125

Hamlet: Let the doors be shut upon him, that he may play the fool no where
but in 's own house. Farewell.

---

88 *orisons:* prayers   102 *honest:* chaste   111 *sometime:* formerly   *paradox:* tenet contrary to
accepted belief   114–115 *virtue . . . it:* Virtue, engrafted on our old stock (of viciousness), cannot so change the nature of the plant that no trace of the original will remain.   118 *indifferent
honest:* tolerably virtuous

Ophelia: O, help him, you sweet heavens!

Hamlet: If thou dost marry, I'll give thee this plague for thy dowry: be thou as
chaste as ice, as pure as snow, thou shalt not escape calumny. Get thee to   130
a nunn'ry, farewell. Or if thou wilt needs marry, marry a fool, for wise
men know well enough what monsters you make of them. To a nunn'ry,
go, and quickly too. Farewell.

Ophelia: Heavenly powers, restore him!

Hamlet: I have heard of your paintings, well enough. God hath given you one   135
face, and you make yourselves another. You jig and amble, and you [lisp,]
you nickname God's creatures and make your wantonness [your] ignorance. Go to, I'll no more on't, it hath made me mad. I say we will have
no moe marriage. Those that are married already (all but one) shall live,
the rest shall keep as they are. To a nunn'ry, go.   140

(*Exit.*)

Ophelia: O, what a noble mind is here o'erthrown!
      The courtier's, soldier's, scholar's, eye, tongue, sword,
      Th' expectation and rose of the fair state,
      The glass of fashion and the mould of form,
      Th' observ'd of all observers, quite, quite down!   145
      And I, of ladies most deject and wretched,
      That suck'd the honey of his [music] vows,
      Now see [that] noble and most sovereign reason
      Like sweet bells jangled out of time, and harsh;
      That unmatch'd form and stature of blown youth   150
      Blasted with ecstasy. O, woe is me
      T' have seen what I have seen, see what I see!

[*Ophelia withdraws.*]

(*Enter* King *and* Polonius.)

King: Love? his affections do not that way tend,
      Nor what he spake, though it lack'd form a little,
      Was not like madness. There's something in his soul   155
      O'er which his melancholy sits on brood,
      And I do doubt the hatch and the disclose
      Will be some danger; which for to prevent,
      I have in quick determination
      Thus set it down: he shall with speed to England   160
      For the demand of our neglected tribute.

---

132 *monsters:* alluding to the notion that the husbands of unfaithful wives grew horns   *you:* you
women   136–37 *You . . . creatures:* you walk and talk affectedly   137–38 *make . . . ignorance:*
excuse your affectation as ignorance   139 *moe:* more   143 *expectation:* hope   *rose:* ornament   *fair:* probably proleptic: "(the kingdom) made fair by his presence"   144 *glass:* mirror
mould of form: pattern of (courtly) behavior   145 *observ'd . . . observers:* Shakespeare uses *observe*
to mean not only "behold, mark attentively" but also "pay honor to".   150 *blown:* in full bloom
151 *Blasted:* withered   *ecstasy:* madness   153 *affections:* inclinations, feelings   157 *doubt:*
fear   *disclose:* Synonymous with *hatch;* see also V.i.247.

Haply the seas, and countries different,
With variable objects, shall expel
This something-settled matter in his heart,
Whereon his brains still beating puts him thus   165
From fashion of himself. What think you on't?
Polonius: It shall do well; but yet do I believe
The origin and commencement of his grief
Sprung from neglected love.   *[Ophelia comes forward.]*
                How now, Ophelia?   170
You need not tell us what Lord Hamlet said,
We heard it all. My lord, do as you please,
But if you hold it fit, after the play
Let his queen-mother all alone entreat him
To show his grief. Let her be round with him,   175
And I'll be plac'd (so please you) in the ear
Of all their conference. If she find him not,
To England send him, or confine him where
Your wisdom best shall think.
King: It shall be so.
Madness in great ones must not [unwatch'd] go.   180

(Exeunt.)

[SCENE II]

(Enter Hamlet *and three of the* Players.*)*

Hamlet: Speak the speech, I pray you, as I pronounc'd it to you, trippingly on
the tongue, but if you mouth it, as many of our players do, I had as live
the town-crier spoke my lines. Nor do not saw the air too much with your
hand, thus, but use all gently, for in the very torrent, tempest, and, as I
may say, whirlwind of your passion, you must acquire and beget a tem-   5
perance that may give it smoothness. O, it offends me to the soul to hear
a robustious periwig-pated fellow tear a passion to totters, to very rags,
to spleet the ears of the groundlings, who for the most part are capable
of nothing but inexplicable dumb shows and noise. I would have such a
fellow whipt for o'erdoing Termagant, it out-Herods Herod, pray you   10
avoid it.
[1.] Player: I warrant your honor.
Hamlet: Be not too tame neither, but let your own discretion be your tutor.
Suit the action to the word, the word to the action, with this special observance, that you o'erstep not the modesty of nature: for any thing so   15

---

169 *neglected:* unrequited   175 *his grief:* what is troubling him   *round:* blunt, outspoken
177 *find him:* learn the truth about him.   III.ii. Location: the castle   2 *mouth:* pronounce
with exaggerated distinctness or declamatory effect   *live:* lief, willingly   7 *totters:* tatters
spleet: split   8 *groundlings:* those who paid the lowest admission price and stood on the ground
in the "yard" or pit of the theatre   *capable of:* able to take in   10 *Termagant:* a supposed god of
the Saracens, whose role in medieval drama, like that of Herod (line 10), was noisy and violent
15 *modesty:* moderation

o'erdone is from the purpose of playing, whose end, both at the first and now, was and is, to hold as 'twere the mirror up to nature: to show virtue her feature, scorn her own image, and the very age and body of the time his form and pressure. Now this overdone, or come tardy off, though it makes the unskillful laugh, cannot but make the judicious grieve; the cen- 20
sure of which one must in your allowance o'erweigh a whole theatre of others. O, there be players that I have seen play—and heard others [praise], and that highly—not to speak it profanely, that, neither having th' accent of Christians nor the gait of Christian, pagan, nor man, have so strutted and bellow'd that I have thought some of Nature's journeymen 25
had made men, and not made them well, they imitated humanity so abominably.

[1.] Player: I hope we have reform'd that indifferently with us, [sir].

Hamlet: O, reform it altogether. And let those that play your clowns speak no more than is set down for them, for there be of them that will themselves 30
laugh to set on some quantity of barren spectators to laugh too, though in the mean time some necessary question of the play be then to be consider-
er'd. That's villainous, and shows a most pitiful ambition in the fool that uses it. Go make you ready.

[Exeunt Players.*]*

(*Enter* Polonius, Guildenstern, *and* Rosencrantz.*)*

How now, my lord? Will the King hear this piece of work?   35

Polonius: And the Queen too, and that presently.

Hamlet: Bid the players make haste.   *[Exit* Polonius.*]*
Will you two help to hasten them?

Rosencrantz: Ay, my lord.   (*Exeunt they two.*)

Hamlet: What ho, Horatio!   40

(*Enter* Horatio.*)*

Horatio: Here, sweet lord, at your service.

Hamlet: Horatio, thou art e'en as just a man
As e'er my conversation cop'd withal.

Horatio: O my dear lord—

Hamlet: Nay, do not think I flatter,
For what advancement may I hope from thee   45
That no revenue hast but thy good spirits
To feed and clothe thee? Why should the poor be flatter'd?

---

16 *from:* contrary to   18 *scorn:* that which is worthy of scorn   19 *pressure:* impression (as of a seal), exact image   *tardy:* inadequately   20–21 *censure:* judgment   21 *which one:* (even) one of whom   *allowance:* estimation   23 *profanely:* irreverently   25–27 *some . . . abominably:* They were so unlike men that it seemed Nature had not made them herself, but had delegated the task to mediocre assistants.   28 *indifferently:* pretty well   30 *of them:* some of them   33 *fool:* (1) stupid person; (2) actor playing a fool's role   35 *piece of work:* masterpiece (said jocularly)   36 *presently:* at once   42 *thou . . . man:* you come as close to being what a man should be (*just* = exact, precise)   43 *my . . . withal:* my association with people has brought me into contact with

No, let the candied tongue lick absurd pomp,
And crook the pregnant hinges of the knee
Where thrift may follow fawning. Dost thou hear?   50
Since my dear soul was mistress of her choice
And could of men distinguish her election,
Sh' hath seal'd thee for herself, for thou hast been
As one in suff'ring all that suffers nothing,
A man that Fortune's buffets and rewards   55
Hast ta'en with equal thanks; and blest are those
Whose blood and judgment are so well co-meddled,
That they are not a pipe for Fortune's finger
To sound what stop she please. Give me that man
That is not passion's slave, and I will wear him   60
In my heart's core, ay, in my heart of heart,
As I do thee. Something too much of this.
There is a play to-night before the King,
One scene of it comes near the circumstance
Which I have told thee of my father's death.   65
I prithee, when thou seest that act afoot,
Even with the very comment of thy soul
Observe my uncle. If his occulted guilt
Do not itself unkennel in one speech,
It is a damned ghost that we have seen,   70
And my imaginations are as foul
As Vulcan's stithy. Give him heedful note,
For I mine eyes will rivet to his face,
And after we will both our judgments join
In censure of his seeming.
Horatio.   Well, my lord.   75
If 'a steal aught the whilst this play is playing,
And scape [detecting], I will pay the theft.

([Sound a flourish. Danish march.] Enter Trumpets and Kettle-drums, King,
Queen, Polonius, Ophelia, *[Rosencrantz, Guildenstern, and other* Lords
attendant, with his Guard *carrying torches].)*

Hamlet: They are coming to the play. I must be idle; Get you a place.
King: How fares our cousin Hamlet?
Hamlet: Excellent, i' faith, of the chameleon's dish: I eat the air, promise-   80
cramm'd—you cannot feed capons so.

---

48 *candied:* sugared, flattering   *absurd:* tasteless (Latin sense)   49 *pregnant:* moving readily
50 *thrift:* thriving, profit   57 *blood:* passions   *co-meddled:* mixed, blended   61 *my heart of
heart:* the heart of my heart   67 *very . . . soul:* your most intense critical observation   68 *occulted:* hidden   69 *unkennel:* bring into the open   70 *damned ghost:* evil spirit, devil   72
stithy: forge   75 *censure . . . seeming:* reaching a verdict on his behavior   78 *be idle:* act foolish, pretend to be crazy   79 *fares:* Hamlet takes up this word in another sense.   80
chameleon's dish: Chameleons were thought to feed on air. Hamlet says that he subsists on an
equally nourishing diet, the promise of succession. There is probably a pun on *air/heir.*

King: I have nothing with this answer, Hamlet, these words are not mine.

Hamlet: No, nor mine now. *[to* Polonius*]* My lord, you play'd once i' th' university, you say?

Polonius: That did I, my lord, and was accounted a good actor.   85

Hamlet: What did you enact?

Polonius: I did enact Julius Caesar. I was kill'd i' th' Capitol; Brutus kill'd me.

Hamlet: It was a brute part of him to kill so capital a calf there. Be the players ready?

Rosencrantz: Ay, my lord, they stay upon your patience.   90

Queen: Come hither, my dear Hamlet, sit by me.

Hamlet: No, good mother, here's metal more attractive. *[lying down at* Ophelia*'s feet]*

Polonius [to the King*]:* O ho, do you mark that?

Hamlet: Lady, shall I lie in your lap?   95

Ophelia: No, my lord.

[Hamlet: I mean, my head upon your lap?

Ophelia: Ay, my lord.]

Hamlet: Do you think I meant country matters?

Ophelia: I think nothing, my lord.   100

Hamlet: That's a fair thought to lie between maids' legs.

Ophelia: What is, my lord?

Hamlet: Nothing.

Ophelia: You are merry, my lord.

Hamlet: Who, I?   105

Ophelia: Ay, my lord.

Hamlet: O God, your only jig-maker. What should a man do but be merry, for look you how cheerfully my mother looks, and my father died within 's two hours.

Ophelia: Nay, 'tis twice two months, my lord.   110

Hamlet: So long? Nay then let the dev'l wear black, for I'll have a suit of sables. O heavens, die two months ago, and not forgotten yet? Then there's hope a great man's memory may outlive his life half a year, but, by'r lady, 'a must build churches then, or else shall 'a suffer not thinking on, with the hobby-horse, whose epitaph is, "For O, for O, the hobby-   115 horse is forgot."

(The trumpets sounds. Dumb show follows.)

(Enter a King and a Queen [very lovingly], the Queen embracing him and he her. [She kneels and makes show of protestation unto him.] He takes her up and

---

82 *have nothing with:* do not understand   *mine:* an answer to my question   88 *part:* action   99 *country matters:* indecency   107 *only:* very best   *jig-maker:* one who composed or played in the farcical song-and-dance entertainments that followed plays   109 *'s:* this   112 *let . . . sables:* To the devil with my garments; after so long a time I am ready for the old man's garb of sables (fine fur).   115 *not thinking on:* not being thought of, being forgotten   116 *For . . . forgot:* line from a popular ballad lamenting puritanical suppression of such country sports as the May-games, in which the hobby-horse, a character costumed to resemble a horse, traditionally appeared

declines his head upon her neck. He lies him down upon a bank of flowers. She, seeing him asleep, leaves him. Anon come in another man, takes off his crown, kisses it, pours poison in the sleeper's ears, and leaves him. The Queen returns, finds the King dead, makes passionate action. The pois'ner with some three or four [mutes] come in again, seem to condole with her. The dead body is carried away. The pois'ner woos the Queen with gifts; she seems harsh [and unwilling] awhile, but in the end accepts love.   [Exeunt.])

Ophelia: What means this, my lord?
Hamlet: Marry, this' [miching] mallecho, it means mischief.
Ophelia: Belike this show imports the argument of the play.

(*Enter* Prologue.)

Hamlet: We shall know by this fellow. The players cannot keep [counsel], 120
they'll tell all.
Ophelia: Will 'a tell us what this show meant?
Hamlet: Ay, or any show that you will show him. Be not you asham'd to show,
he'll not shame to tell you what it means.
Ophelia: You are naught, you are naught. I'll mark the play.   125
Prologue: For us, and for our tragedy,
        Here stooping to your clemency,
        We beg your hearing patiently.   [*Exit.*]
Hamlet: Is this a prologue, or the posy of a ring?
Ophelia: 'Tis brief, my lord.   130
Hamlet: As woman's love.

(*Enter [two* Players,*] King and* Queen.)

[P.] King: Full thirty times hath Phoebus' cart gone round
        Neptune's salt wash and Tellus' orbed ground,
        And thirty dozen moons with borrowed sheen
        About the world have times twelve thirties been,   135
        Since love our hearts and Hymen did our hands
        Unite comutual in most sacred bands.
[P.] Queen: So many journeys may the sun and moon
        Make us again count o'er ere love be done!
        But woe is me, you are so sick of late,   140
        So far from cheer and from [your] former state,
        That I distrust you. Yet though I distrust,
        Discomfort you, my lord, it nothing must,
        [For] women's fear and love hold quantity,
        In neither aught, or in extremity.   145
        Now what my [love] is, proof hath made you know,

---

118 *this' miching mallecho:* this is sneaking mischief   119 *argument:* subject, plot   120 *counsel:* secrets   123 *Be not you:* if you are not   125 *naught:* wicked   129 *posy . . . ring:* verse motto inscribed in a ring (necessarily short)   132 *Phoebus' cart:* the sun-god's chariot   133 *Tellus:* goddess of the earth   136 *Hymen:* god of marriage   137 *bands:* bonds   142 *distrust:* fear for   144 *hold quantity:* are related in direct proportion   146 *proof:* experience

And as my love is siz'd, my fear is so.
Where love is great, the littlest doubts are fear;
Where little fears grow great, great love grows there.
[P.] King: Faith, I must leave thee, love, and shortly too;   150
My operant powers their functions leave to do,
And thou shalt live in this fair world behind,
Honor'd, belov'd, and haply one as kind
For husband shalt thou—
[P.] Queen: O, confound the rest!
Such love must needs be treason in my breast.   155
In second husband let me be accurs'd!
None wed the second but who kill'd the first.
Hamlet [aside]: That's wormwood!
[P.] Queen: The instances that second marriage move
Are base respects of thrift, but none of love.   160
A second time I kill my husband dead,
When second husband kisses me in bed.
[P.] King: I do believe you think what now you speak,
But what we do determine, oft we break.
Purpose is but the slave to memory,   165
Of violent birth, but poor validity,
Which now, the fruit unripe, sticks on the tree,
But fall unshaken when they mellow be.
Most necessary 'tis that we forget
To pay ourselves what to ourselves is debt.   170
What to ourselves in passion we propose,
The passion ending, doth the purpose lose.
The violence of either grief or joy
Their own enactures with themselves destroy.
Where joy most revels, grief doth most lament;   175
Grief [joys], joy grieves, on slender accident.
This world is not for aye, nor 'tis not strange
That even our loves should with our fortunes change:
For 'tis a question left us yet to prove,
Whether love lead fortune, or else fortune love.   180
The great man down, you mark his favorite flies,
The poor advanc'd makes friends of enemies.
And hitherto doth love on fortune tend,
For who not needs shall never lack a friend,

---

151 *operant:* active, vital *leave to do:* cease to perform   154 *confound the rest:* May destruction befall what you are about to speak of—a second marriage on my part.   159 *instances:* motives *move:* give rise to   160 *respects of thrift:* considerations of advantage   166 *validity:* strength, power to last   169–70 *Most . . . debt:* Such resolutions are debts we owe to ourselves, and it would be foolish to pay such debts.   171 *passion:* violent emotion   173–74 *The violence . . . destroy:* Both violent grief and violent joy fail of their intended acts because they destroy themselves by their very violence.   176 *slender accident:* slight occasion

And who in want a hollow friend doth try,   185
Directly seasons him his enemy.
But orderly to end where I begun,
Our wills and fates do so contrary run
That our devices still are overthrown,
Our thoughts are ours, their ends none of our own: 190
So think thou wilt no second husband wed,
But die thy thoughts when thy first lord is dead.
[P.] Queen: Nor earth to me give food, nor heaven light,
  Sport and repose lock from me day and night,
  To desperation turn my trust and hope,   195
  [An] anchor's cheer in prison be my scope!
  Each opposite that blanks the face of joy
  Meet what I would have well and it destroy!
  Both here and hence pursue me lasting strife,
  If once I be a widow, ever I be a wife!   200
Hamlet: If she should break it now!
[P.] King: 'Tis deeply sworn. Sweet, leave me here a while,
  My spirits grow dull, and fain I would beguile
  The tedious day with sleep.   *[sleeps]*
[P.] Queen: Sleep rock thy brain,
  And never come mischance between us twain!   *(Exit.)*   205
Hamlet: Madam, how like you this play?
Queen: The lady doth protest too much, methinks.
Hamlet: O but she'll keep her word.
King: Have you heard the argument? is there no offense in't?
Hamlet: No, no, they do but jest, poison in jest—no offense i' th' world.   210
King: What do you call the play?
Hamlet: "The Mouse-trap." Marry, how? tropically: this play is the image of
  a murther done in Vienna; Gonzago is the duke's name, his wife, Baptista.
  You shall see anon. 'Tis a knavish piece of work, but what of that? Your
  Majesty, and we that have free souls, it touches us not. Let the gall'd jade   215
  winch, our withers are unwrung.

  (Enter Lucianus.*)*

  This is one Lucianus, nephew to the king.
Ophelia: You are as good as a chorus, my lord.

---

186 *seasons:* ripens, converts into   189 *devices:* devisings, intentions   *still:* always   196 *anchor's cheer:* hermit's fare   *my scope:* the extent of my comforts   197 *blanks:* blanches, makes pale (a symptom of grief)   209 *offense:* offensive matter (but Hamlet quibbles on the sense "crime")   210 *jest:* pretend   212 *tropically:* figuratively (with play on *trapically*—which is the reading of Q1—and probably with allusion to the children's saying *marry trap,* meaning "now you're caught")   *image:* representation   215 *free souls:* clear consciences   *gall'd jade:* chafed horse   *winch:* wince   216 *withers:* ridge between a horse's shoulders.   *unwrung:* not rubbed sore   218 *chorus:* one who explains the forthcoming action

Hamlet: I could interpret between you and your love, if I could see the pup-
pets dallying.   220
Ophelia: You are keen, my lord, you are keen.
Hamlet: It would cost you a groaning to take off mine edge.
Ophelia: Still better, and worse.
Hamlet: So you mistake your husbands. Begin, murtherer, leave thy
damnable faces and begin. Come, the croaking raven doth bellow for   225
revenge.
Lucianus: Thoughts black, hands apt, drugs fit, and time agreeing,
  [Confederate] season, else no creature seeing,
  Thou mixture rank, of midnight weeds collected,
  With Hecat's ban thrice blasted, thrice [infected],   230
  Thy natural magic and dire property
  On wholesome life usurps immediately.

[pours the poison in his ears]

Hamlet: 'A poisons him i' th' garden for his estate. His name's Gonzago, the
story is extant, and written in very choice Italian. You shall see anon how
the murtherer gets the love of Gonzago's wife.   235
Ophelia: The King rises.
[Hamlet: What, frighted with false fire?]
Queen: How fares my lord?
Polonius: Give o'er the play.
King: Give me some light. Away!   240
Polonius: Lights, lights, lights!

(Exeunt all but Hamlet *and* Horatio.*)*

Hamlet: "Why, let the strooken deer go weep,
    The hart ungalled play,
  For some must watch while some
      must sleep,   245
    Thus runs the world away."
Would not this, sir, and a forest of feathers—if the rest of my fortunes
turn Turk with me—with [two] Provincial roses on my raz'd shoes, get
me a fellowship in a cry of players?
Horatio: Half a share.   250

219–20 *I . . . dallying:* I could speak the dialogue between you and your lover like a puppet-master
(with an indecent jest).   221 *keen:* bitter, sharp   223 *better, and worse:* more pointed and less
decent   224 *So:* "for better, for worse," in the words of the marriage service   *mistake:* mistake, take wrongfully. Their vows, Hamlet suggests, prove false.   225 *faces:* facial expressions
the croaking . . . revenge: misquoted from an old play, *The True Tragedy of Richard III*
228 *Confederate season:* the time being my ally   230 *Hecat's ban:* the curse of Hecate, goddess of
witchcraft   237 *false fire:* a blank cartridge   242 *strooken:* struck, wounded   243 *ungalled:*
unwounded   244 *watch:* stay awake   247 *feathers:* the plumes worn by tragic actors   248
turn Turk: go to the bad   *Provincial roses:* rosettes designed to look like a variety of French rose
raz'd: with decorating slashing   249 *fellowship:* partnership   *cry:* company

Hamlet: A whole one, I.
    "For thou dost know, O Damon dear,
       This realm dismantled was
    Of Jove himself, and now reigns here
       A very, very"—pajock.   255

Horatio: You might have rhym'd.

Hamlet: O good Horatio, I'll take the ghost's word for a thousand pound.
    Didst perceive?

Horatio: Very well, my lord.

Hamlet: Upon the talk of the pois'ning?   260

Horatio: I did very well note him.

Hamlet: Ah, ha! Come, some music! Come, the recorders!
    For if the King like not the comedy,
    Why then belike he likes it not, perdy.
    Come, some music!   265

(Enter Rosencrantz *and* Guildenstern.*)*

Guildenstern: Good my lord, voutsafe me a word with you.

Hamlet: Sir, a whole history.

Guildenstern: The King, sir—

Hamlet: Ay, sir, what of him?

Guildenstern: Is in his retirement marvellous distemp'red.   270

Hamlet: With drink, sir?

Guildenstern: No, my lord, with choler.

Hamlet: Your wisdom should show itself more richer to signify this to the
    doctor, for for me to put him to his purgation would perhaps plunge him
    into more choler.   275

Guildenstern: Good my lord, put your discourse into some frame, and [start]
    not so wildly from my affair.

Hamlet: I am tame, sir. Pronounce.

Guildenstern: The Queen, your mother, in most great affliction of spirit, hath
    sent me to you.   280

Hamlet: You are welcome.

Guildenstern: Nay, good my lord, this courtesy is not of the right breed. If it
    shall please you to make me a wholesome answer, I will do your mother's
    commandement; if not, your pardon and my return shall be the end of
    [my] business.   285

Hamlet: Sir, I cannot.

Rosencrantz: What, my lord?

---

253 *dismantled:* divested, deprived   255 *pajock:* peacock (substituting for the rhyme-word *ass*).
The natural history of the time attributed many vicious qualities to the peacock.   264 *perdy:*
assuredly (French *pardieu,* "by God")   272 *choler:* anger (but Hamlet willfully takes up the
word in the sense "biliousness")   274 *put . . . purgation:* prescribe for what's wrong with him
276 *frame:* logical structure   283 *wholesome:* sensible, rational   284 *pardon:* permission for
departure

Hamlet: Make you a wholesome answer—my wit's diseas'd. But, sir, such answer as I can make, you shall command, or rather, as you say, my mother. Therefore no more, but to the matter: my mother, you say—   290

Rosencrantz: Then thus she says: your behavior hath strook her into amazement and admiration.

Hamlet: O wonderful son, that can so stonish a mother! But is there no sequel at the heels of this mother's admiration? Impart.

Rosencrantz: She desires to speak with you in her closet ere you go to bed.   295

Hamlet: We shall obey, were she ten times our mother. Have you any further trade with us?

Rosencrantz: My lord, you once did love me.

Hamlet: And do still, by these pickers and stealers.

Rosencrantz: Good my lord, what is your cause of distemper? You do surely   300
bar the door upon your own liberty if you deny your griefs to your friend.

Hamlet: Sir, I lack advancement.

Rosencrantz: How can that be, when you have the voice of the King himself for your succession in Denmark?

Hamlet: Ay, sir, but "While the grass grows"—the proverb is something   305
musty.

(*Enter the* Players *with recorders.*)
O, the recorders! Let me see one.—To withdraw with you—why do you go about to recover the wind of me, as if you would drive me into a toil?

Guildenstern: O my lord, if my duty be too bold, my love is too unmannerly.

Hamlet: I do not well understand that. Will you play upon this pipe?   310

Guildenstern: My lord, I cannot.

Hamlet: I pray you.

Guildenstern: Believe me, I cannot.

Hamlet: I do beseech you.

Guildenstern: I know no touch of it, my lord.   315

Hamlet: It is as easy as lying. Govern these ventages with your fingers and [thumbs], give it breath with your mouth, and it will discourse most eloquent music. Look you, these are the stops.

Guildenstern: But these cannot I command to any utt'rance of harmony. I have not the skill.   320

Hamlet: Why, look you now, how unworthy a thing you make of me! You would play upon me, you would seem to know my stops, you would pluck out the heart of my mystery, you would sound me from my lowest note to [the top of] my compass; and there is much music, excellent voice, in this little organ, yet cannot you make it speak. 'Sblood, do you think I am eas-   325
ier to be play'd on than a pipe? Call me what instrument you will, though you fret me, [yet] you cannot play upon me.

291–92 *amazement and admiration:* bewilderment and wonder   293 *stonish:* astound
295 *closet:* private room   299 *pickers and stealers:* hands, which, as the Catechism says, we must
keep "from picking and stealing"   305 *proverb:* "While the grass grows, the steed starves."
305–306 *something musty:* somewhat stale   308 *recover the wind:* get to windward   *toil:* snare
316 *ventages:* stops   325 *organ:* instrument   327 *fret:* (1) finger (an instrument); (2) vex

(*Enter* Polonius.)

God bless you, sir.

Polonius: My lord, the Queen would speak with you, and presently.

Hamlet: Do you see yonder cloud that's almost in shape of a camel?   330

Polonius: By th' mass and 'tis, like a camel indeed.

Hamlet: Methinks it is like a weasel.

Polonius: It is back'd like a weasel.

Hamlet: Or like a whale.

Polonius: Very like a whale.   335

Hamlet: Then I will come to my mother by and by. *[aside]* They fool me to the
top of my bent.—I will come by and by.

Polonius: I will say so.   *[Exit.]*

Hamlet: "By and by" is easily said. Leave me, friends.   *[Exeunt all but
Hamlet.]*   340
'Tis now the very witching time of night,
When churchyards yawn and hell itself [breathes] out
Contagion to this world. Now could I drink hot blood,
And do such [bitter business as the] day
Would quake to look on. Soft, now to my mother.   345
O heart, lose not thy nature! let not ever
The soul of Nero enter this firm bosom,
Let me be cruel, not unnatural;
I will speak [daggers] to her, but use none.
My tongue and soul in this be hypocrites—   350
How in my words somever she be shent,
To give them seals never my soul consent!

(*Exit.*)

[SCENE III]

(*Enter* King, Rosencrantz, *and* Guildenstern.)

King: I like him not, nor stands it safe with us
To let his madness range. Therefore prepare you.
I your commission will forthwith dispatch,
And he to England shall along with you.
The terms of our estate may not endure   5
Hazard so near 's as doth hourly grow
Out of his brows.

---

329 *presently:* at once   336–337 *They . . . bent:* They make me play the fool to the limit of my
ability.   337 *by and by:* at once   341 *witching:* when the powers of evil are at large   346
nature: natural affection, filial feeling   347 *Nero:* murderer of his mother   351 *shent:* rebuked   352 *give them seals:* confirm them by deeds   III.iii. Location: the castle   1 *him:*
his state of mind, his behavior   3 *dispatch:* have drawn up   5 *terms:* conditions, nature   *our
estate:* my position (as king)   7 *his brows:* the madness visible in his face (?)

Guildenstern: We will ourselves provide.
      Most holy and religious fear it is
      To keep those many many bodies safe
      That live and feed upon your Majesty.   10
Rosencrantz: The single and peculiar life is bound
      With all the strength and armor of the mind
      To keep itself from noyance, but much more
      That spirit upon whose weal depends and rests
      The lives of many. The cess of majesty   15
      Dies not alone, but like a gulf doth draw
      What's near it with it. Or it is a massy wheel
      Fix'd on the summit of the highest mount,
      To whose [huge] spokes ten thousand lesser things
      Are mortis'd and adjoin'd, which when it falls,   20
      Each small annexment, petty consequence,
      Attends the boist'rous [ruin]. Never alone
      Did the King sigh, but [with] a general groan.
King: Arm you, I pray you, to this speedy viage,
      For we will fetters put about this fear,   25
      Which now goes too free-footed.
Rosencrantz: We will haste us.

      (Exeunt Gentlemen *[Rosencrantz and* Guildenstern*].)*

      (Enter Polonius.*)*

Polonius: My lord, he's going to his mother's closet.
      Behind the arras I'll convey myself
      To hear the process. I'll warrant she'll tax him home,
      And as you said, and wisely was it said,   30
      'Tis meet that some more audience than a mother,
      Since nature makes them partial, should o'erhear
      The speech, of vantage. Fare you well, my liege,
      I'll call upon you ere you go to bed,
      And tell you what I know.
King: Thanks, dear my lord.   35

      (Exit [Polonius].*)*

      O, my offense is rank, it smells to heaven,
      It hath the primal eldest curse upon't,
      A brother's murther. Pray can I not,

---

8 *fear:* concern   11 *single and peculiar:* individual and private   13 *noyance:* injury   15 *cess:* cessation, death   16 *gulf:* whirlpool   20 *mortis'd:* fixed   22 *Attends:* accompanies   *ruin:* fall   24 *Arm:* prepare   *viage:* voyage   25 *fear:* object of fear   29 *process:* course of the talk   *tax him home:* take him severely to task   33 *of vantage:* from an advantageous position (?) or in addition (?)   37 *primal eldest curse:* God's curse on Cain, who also slew his brother

Though inclination be as sharp as will.
My stronger guilt defeats my strong intent,   40
And, like a man to double business bound,
I stand in pause where I shall first begin,
And both neglect. What if this cursed hand
Were thicker than itself with brother's blood,
Is there not rain enough in the sweet heavens   45
To wash it white as snow? Whereto serves mercy
But to confront the visage of offense?
And what's in prayer but this twofold force,
To be forestalled ere we come to fall,
Or [pardon'd] being down? then I'll look up.   50
My fault is past, but, O, what form of prayer
Can serve my turn? "Forgive me my foul murther"?
That cannot be, since I am still possess'd
Of those effects for which I did the murther:
My crown, mine own ambition, and my queen.   55
May one be pardon'd and retain th' offense?
In the corrupted currents of this world
Offense's gilded hand may [shove] by justice,
And oft 'tis seen the wicked prize itself
Buys out the law, but 'tis not so above: 60
There is no shuffling, there the action lies
In his true nature, and we ourselves compell'd,
Even to the teeth and forehead of our faults,
To give in evidence. What then? What rests?
Try what repentance can. What can it not?   65
Yet what can it, when one can not repent?
O wretched state! O bosom black as death!
O limed soul, that struggling to be free
Art more engag'd! Help, angels! Make assay,
Bow, stubborn knees, and heart, with strings of steel,   70
Be soft as sinews of the new-born babe!
All may be well.   *[He kneels.]*

(Enter Hamlet.)

Hamlet: Now might I do it [pat], now 'a is a-praying;
And now I'll do't—and so 'a goes to heaven,
And so am I [reveng'd]. That would be scann'd: 75

---

39 *Though . . . will:* though my desire is as strong as my resolve to do so   41 *bound:* committed
43 *neglect:* omit   46–47 *Whereto . . . offense:* what function has mercy except when there has
been sin   56 *th' offense:* the "effects" or fruits of the offense   57 *currents:* courses   58
gilded: bribing   59 *wicked prize:* rewards of vice   61 *shuffling:* evasion   *the action lies:* the
charge comes for legal consideration   63 *Even . . . forehead:* fully recognizing their features,
extenuating nothing   64 *rests:* remains   68 *limed:* caught (as in birdlime, a sticky substance
used for catching birds)   69 *engag'd:* entangled   75 *would be scann'd:* must be carefully considered

A villain kills my father, and for that
I, his sole son, do this same villain send
To heaven.
Why, this is [hire and salary], not revenge.
'A took my father grossly, full of bread,   80
With all his crimes broad blown, as flush as May,
And how his audit stands who knows save heaven?
But in our circumstance and course of thought
'Tis heavy with him. And am I then revenged,
To take him in the purging of his soul,   85
When he is fit and season'd for his passage?
No!
Up, sword, and know thou a more horrid hent:
When he is drunk asleep, or in his rage,
Or in th' incestious pleasure of his bed,   90
At game a-swearing, or about some act
That has no relish of salvation in't—
Then trip him, that his heels may kick at heaven,
And that his soul may be as damn'd and black
As hell, whereto it goes. My mother stays,   95
This physic but prolongs thy sickly days.   *(Exit.)*
King *[Rising]:* My words fly up, my thoughts remain below:
Words without thoughts never to heaven go.

      (Exit.)

[SCENE IV]

      (Enter [Queen] Gertrude *and* Polonius.*)*

Polonius: 'A will come straight. Look you lay home to him.
Tell him his pranks have been too broad to bear with,
And that your Grace hath screen'd and stood between
Much heat and him. I'll silence me even here;
Pray you be round [with him].   5
Queen: I'll [warr'nt] you, fear me not. Withdraw,
I hear him coming.   *[Polonius hides behind the arras.]*

      (Enter Hamlet.*)*

Hamlet: Now, mother, what's the matter?
Queen: Hamlet, thou hast thy father much offended.

---

80 *grossly:* in a gross state; not spiritually prepared   81 *crimes:* sins   *broad blown:* in full bloom
flush: lusty, vigorous   82 *audit:* account   83 *in . . . thought:* to the best of our knowledge and
belief   88 *Up:* into the sheath   *know . . . hent:* be grasped at a more dreadful time   92 *relish:* trace   96 *physic:* (attempted) remedy, prayer.   III.iv. *Location:* the queen's closet in the
castle   1 *lay . . . him:* reprove him severely   2 *broad:* unrestrained   5 *round:* plainspoken   6 *fear me not:* have no fears about my handling of the situation

Hamlet: Mother, you have my father much offended.   10
Queen: Come, come, you answer with an idle tongue.
Hamlet: Go, go, you question with a wicked tongue.
Queen: Why, how now, Hamlet?
Hamlet: What's the matter now?
Queen: Have you forgot me?
Hamlet: No, by the rood, not so:
    You are the Queen, your husband's brother's wife,   15
    And would it were not so, you are my mother.
Queen: Nay, then I'll set those to you that can speak.
Hamlet: Come, come, and sit you down, you shall not boudge;
    You go not till I set you up a glass
    Where you may see the [inmost] part of you.   20
Queen: What wilt thou do? Thou wilt not murther me?
    Help ho!
Polonius [behind]: What ho, help!
Hamlet [drawing]: How now? A rat? Dead, for a ducat, dead!   *[Kills* Polo-
    nius *through the arras.]*   25
Polonius [behind]: O, I am slain.
Queen: O me, what hast thou done?
Hamlet: Nay, I know not, is it the King?
Queen: O, what a rash and bloody deed is this!
Hamlet: A bloody deed! almost as bad, good mother,
    As kill a king, and marry with his brother.   30
Queen: As kill a king!
Hamlet: Ay, lady, it was my word.

[parts the arras and discovers Polonius*]*

    Thou wretched, rash, intruding fool, farewell!
    I took thee for thy better. Take thy fortune;
    Thou find'st to be too busy is some danger.—
    Leave wringing of your hands. Peace, sit you down,   35
    And let me wring your heart, for so I shall
    If it be made of penetrable stuff,
    If damned custom have not brass'd it so
    That it be proof and bulwark against sense.
Queen: What have I done, that thou dar'st wag thy tongue   40
    In noise so rude against me?
Hamlet: Such an act
    That blurs the grace and blush of modesty,
    Calls virtue hypocrite, takes off the rose
    From the fair forehead of an innocent love
    And sets a blister there, makes marriage vows   45

---

11 *idle:* foolish   14 *rood:* cross   18 *boudge:* budge   24 *for a ducat:* I'll wager a ducat
34 *busy:* officious, meddlesome   38 *damned custom:* the habit of ill-doing   *brass'd:* hardened,
literally, plated with brass   39 *proof:* armor   *sense:* feeling   45 *blister:* brand of shame

As false as dicers' oaths, O, such a deed
As from the body of contraction plucks
The very soul, and sweet religion makes
A rhapsody of words. Heaven's face does glow
O'er this solidity and compound mass   50
With heated visage, as against the doom;
Is thought-sick at the act.

Queen: Ay me, what act,
That roars so loud and thunders in the index?

Hamlet: Look here upon this picture, and on this,
The counterfeit presentment of two brothers.   55
See what a grace was seated on this brow:
Hyperion's curls, the front of Jove himself,
An eye like Mars, to threaten and command,
A station like the herald Mercury
New lighted on a [heaven-]kissing hill,   60
A combination and a form indeed,
Where every god did seem to set his seal
To give the world assurance of a man.
This was your husband. Look you now what follows:
Here is your husband, like a mildewed ear,   65
Blasting his wholesome brother. Have you eyes?
Could you not on this fair mountain leave to feed,
And batten on this moor? ha, have you eyes?
You cannot call it love, for at your age
The heyday in the blood is tame, it's humble,   70
And waits upon the judgment, and what judgment
Would step from this to this? Sense sure you have,
Else could you not have motion, but sure that sense
Is apoplex'd, for madness would not err,
Nor sense to ecstasy was ne'er so thrall'd   75
But it reserv'd some quantity of choice
To serve in such a difference. What devil was't
That thus hath cozen'd you at hoodman-blind?
Eyes without feeling, feeling without sight,
Ears without hands or eyes, smelling sans all,   80
Or but a sickly part of one true sense

---

47 *contraction:* the making of contracts, the assuming of solemn obligation   48 *religion:* sacred
vows   49 *rhapsody:* miscellaneous collection, jumble   *glow:* with anger   50 *this . . . mass:*
the earth; *compound* = compounded of the four elements   51 *as . . . doom:* as if for Judgment
Day   53 *index:* table of contents. The index was formerly placed at the beginning of a book.
55 *counterfeit presentment:* painted likenesses   57 *Hyperion's:* the sun-god's   *front:* forehead
59 *station:* bearing   65 *ear:* of grain   68 *batten:* gorge   70 *heyday:* excitement   72
Sense: sense perception, the five senses   74 *apoplex'd:* paralyzed   74–77 *madness . . . difference:* Madness itself could not go so far astray, nor were the senses ever so enslaved by lunacy that
they did not retain the power to make so obvious a distinction.   78 *cozen'd:* cheated   *hoodman-blind:* blindman's bluff   80 *sans:* without

Could not so mope. O shame, where is thy blush?
Rebellious hell,
If thou canst mutine in a matron's bones,
To flaming youth let virtue be as wax 85
And melt in her own fire. Proclaim no shame
When the compulsive ardure gives the charge,
Since frost itself as actively doth burn,
And reason [panders] will.

Queen: O Hamlet, speak no more!
Thou turn'st my [eyes into my very] soul, 90
And there I see such black and [grained] spots
As will [not] leave their tinct.

Hamlet: Nay, but to live
In the rank sweat of an enseamed bed,
Stew'd in corruption, honeying and making love
Over the nasty sty!

Queen: O, speak to me no more! 95
These words like daggers enter in my ears.
No more, sweet Hamlet!

Hamlet: A murtherer and a villain!
A slave that is not twentith part the [tithe]
Of your precedent lord, a Vice of kings,
A cutpurse of the empire and the rule, 100
That from a shelf the precious diadem stole,
And put it in his pocket—

Queen: No more!

(Enter Ghost *[in his night-gown].)*

Hamlet: A king of shreds and patches—
Save me, and hover o'er me with your wings,
You heavenly guards! What would your gracious figure? 105

Queen: Alas, he's mad!

Hamlet: Do you not come your tardy son to chide,
That, laps'd in time and passion, lets go by
Th' important acting of your dread command?
O, say! 110

Ghost: Do not forget! This visitation
Is but to whet thy almost blunted purpose.
But look, amazement on thy mother sits,

---

82 *mope:* be dazed   84 *mutine:* rebel   86–89 *Proclaim . . . will:* Do not call it sin when the
hot blood of youth is responsible for lechery, since here we see people of calmer age on fire for it;
and reason acts as procurer for desire, instead of restraining it. *Ardure* = ardor   91 *grained:*
fast-dyed, indelible   92 *leave their tinct:* lose their color   93 *enseamed:* greasy   98 *twentith:* twentieth   99 *precedent:* former   *Vice:* buffoon (like the Vice of the morality plays)   s.d.
night-gown: dressing gown   103 *of . . . patches:* clownish (alluding to the motley worn by
jesters) (?) or patched-up, beggarly (?)   108 *laps'd . . . passion:* "having suffered time to slip and
passion to cool" (Johnson)   109 *important:* urgent   113 *amazement:* utter bewilderment

O, step between her and her fighting soul.
Conceit in weakest bodies strongest works,   115
Speak to her, Hamlet.

Hamlet: How is it with you, lady?

Queen: Alas, how is't with you,
That you do bend your eye on vacancy,
And with th' incorporal air do hold discourse?
Forth at your eyes your spirits wildly peep,   120
And as the sleeping soldiers in th' alarm,
Your bedded hair, like life in excrements,
Start up and stand an end. O gentle son,
Upon the heat and flame of thy distemper
Sprinkle cool patience. Whereon do you look?   125

Hamlet: On him, on him! look you how pale he glares!
His form and cause conjoin'd, preaching to stones,
Would make them capable.—Do not look upon me,
Lest with this piteous action you convert
My stern effects, then what I have to do   130
Will want true color—tears perchance for blood.

Queen: To whom do you speak this?

Hamlet: Do you see nothing there?

Queen: Nothing at all, yet all that is I see.

Hamlet: Nor did you nothing hear?

Queen: No, nothing but ourselves.

Hamlet: Why, look you there, look how it steals away!   135
My father, in his habit as he lived!
Look where he goes, even now, out at the portal!

(Exit Ghost.)

Queen: This is the very coinage of your brain,
This bodiless creation ecstasy
Is very cunning in.

Hamlet: [Ecstasy?]   140
My pulse as yours doth temperately keep time,
And makes as healthful music. It is not madness
That I have utt'red. Bring me to the test,
And [I] the matter will reword, which madness
Would gambol from. Mother, for love of grace,   145
Lay not that flattering unction to your soul,
That not your trespass but my madness speaks;

---

115 *Conceit:* imagination   121 *in th' alarm:* when the call to arms is sounded   122 *excrements:* outgrowths; here, hair (also used of nails)   123 *an end:* on end   125 *patience:* self-control   127 *His . . . cause:* his appearance and what he has to say   128 *capable:* sensitive, receptive   129 *convert:* alter   130 *effects:* (purposed) actions   131 *want true color:* lack its proper appearance   136 *habit:* dress   139 *ecstasy:* madness   145 *gambol:* start, jerk away   146 *flattering unction:* soothing ointment

It will but skin and film the ulcerous place,
Whiles rank corruption, mining all within,
Infects unseen. Confess yourself to heaven,   150
Repent what's past, avoid what is to come,
And do not spread the compost on the weeds
To make them ranker. Forgive me this my virtue,
For in the fatness of these pursy times
Virtue itself of vice must pardon beg,   155
Yea, curb and woo for leave to do him good.
Queen: O Hamlet, thou hast cleft my heart in twain.
Hamlet: O, throw away the worser part of it,
And [live] the purer with the other half.
Good night, but go not to my uncle's bed—   160
Assume a virtue, if you have it not.
That monster custom, who all sense doth eat,
Of habits devil, is angel yet in this,
That to the use of actions fair and good
He likewise gives a frock or livery   165
That aptly is put on. Refrain [to-]night,
And that shall lend a kind of easiness
To the next abstinence, the next more easy;
For use almost can change the stamp of nature,
And either [. . . .] the devil or throw him out   170
With wondrous potency. Once more good night,
And when you are desirous to be blest,
I'll blessing beg of you. For this same lord,

[pointing to Polonius*]*

I do repent; but heaven hath pleas'd it so
To punish me with this, and this with me,   175
That I must be their scourge and minister.
I will bestow him, and will answer well
The death I gave him. So again good night.
I must be cruel only to be kind.
This bad begins and worse remains behind.   180
One word more, good lady.
Queen: What shall I do?

---

152 *compost:* manure   154 *pursy:* puffy, out of condition   156 *curb and woo:* bow and entreat
162 *all . . . eat:* wears away all natural feeling   163 *Of habits devil:* though it acts like a devil in
establishing bad habits. Most editors read (in lines 162–63) *eat / Of habits evil,* following
Theobald.   165–66 *frock . . . on:* a "habit" or customary garment, readily put on without need
of any decision   169 *use:* habit   170 A word seems to be wanting after *either.*   172 *desirous . . . blest:* repentant   176 *scourge and minister:* the agent of heavenly justice against human
crime. *Scourge* suggests a permissive cruelty (Tamburlaine was the "scourge of God"), but "woe to
him by whom the offense cometh"; the scourge must suffer for the evil it performs.   177 *bestow:* dispose of   *answer:* answer for   180 *behind:* to come

Hamlet: Not this, by no means, that I bid you do:
　　Let the bloat king tempt you again to bed,
　　Pinch wanton on your cheek, call you his mouse,
　　And let him, for a pair of reechy kisses,　　　　　　　　185
　　Or paddling in your neck with his damn'd fingers,
　　Make you to ravel all this matter out,
　　That I essentially am not in madness,
　　But mad in craft. 'Twere good you let him know,
　　For who that's but a queen, fair, sober, wise,　　　　　190
　　Would from a paddock, from a bat, a gib,
　　Such dear concernings hide? Who would do so?
　　No, in despite of sense and secrecy,
　　Unpeg the basket on the house's top,
　　Let the birds fly, and like the famous ape,　　　　　　195
　　To try conclusions in the basket creep,
　　And break your own neck down.
Queen: Be thou assur'd, if words be made of breath,
　　And breath of life, I have no life to breathe
　　What thou hast said to me.　　　　　　　　　　　　　200
Hamlet: I must to England, you know that?
Queen:　　　　　　　　　　　　　　　　　Alack,
　　I had forgot. 'Tis so concluded on.
Hamlet: There's letters seal'd, and my two schoolfellows,
　　Whom I will trust as I will adders fang'd,
　　They bear the mandate, they must sweep my way　　205
　　And marshal me to knavery. Let it work,
　　For 'tis the sport to have the enginer
　　Hoist with his own petar, an't shall go hard
　　But I will delve one yard below their mines,
　　And blow them at the moon. O, 'tis most sweet　　210
　　When in one line two crafts directly meet.
　　This man shall set me packing;
　　I'll lug the guts into the neighbor room.
　　Mother, good night indeed. This counsellor
　　Is now most still, most secret, and most grave,　　　215
　　Who was in life a foolish prating knave.
　　Come, sir, to draw toward an end with you.
　　Good night, mother.

(*Exeunt [severally,* Hamlet *tugging in* Polonius*].*)

---

185 *reechy:* filthy　　191 *paddock:* toad　*gib:* tom-cat　　192 *dear concernings:* matters of intense
concern　　194 *Unpeg the basket:* open the door of the cage　　195 *famous ape:* The actual story
has been lost.　　196 *conclusions:* experiments (to see whether he too can fly if he enters the cage
and then leaps out)　　197 *down:* by the fall　　206 *knavery:* some knavish scheme against me.
207 *enginer:* deviser of military "engines" or contrivances　　208 *Hoist with:* blown up by　*petar:*
petard, bomb　　211 *crafts:* plots　　212 *packing:* (1) taking on a load; (2) leaving in a hurry
217 *draw . . . end:* finish my conversation

ACT IV

SCENE I

(Enter King *and* Queen *with* Rosencrantz *and* Guildenstern.*)*

King: There's matter in these sighs, these profound heaves—
You must translate, 'tis fit we understand them.
Where is your son?
Queen: Bestow this place on us a little while.

[Exeunt Rosencrantz *and* Guildenstern.*]*

Ah, mine own lord, what have I seen to-night!   5
King: What, Gertrude? How does Hamlet?
Queen: Mad as the sea and wind when both contend
Which is the mightier. In his lawless fit,
Behind the arras hearing something stir,
Whips out his rapier, cries, "A rat, a rat!"   10
And in this brainish apprehension kills
The unseen good old man.
King: O heavy deed!
It had been so with us had we been there.
His liberty is full of threats to all,
To you yourself, to us, to every one.   15
Alas, how shall this bloody deed be answer'd?
It will be laid to us, whose providence
Should have kept short, restrain'd, and out of haunt
This mad young man; but so much was our love,
We would not understand what was most fit,   20
But like the owner of a foul disease,
To keep it from divulging, let it feed
Even on the pith of life. Where is he gone?
Queen: To draw apart the body he hath kill'd,
O'er whom his very madness, like some ore   25
Among a mineral of metals base,
Shows itself pure: 'a weeps for what is done.
King: O Gertrude, come away!
The sun no sooner shall the mountains touch,
But we will ship him hence, and this vile deed   30
We must with all our majesty and skill
Both countenance and excuse. Ho, Guildenstern!

IV.i. Location: the castle   11 *brainish apprehension:* crazy notion   16 *answer'd:* satisfactorily
accounted for to the public   17 *providence:* foresight   18 *short:* on a short leash   *out of
haunt:* away from other people   22 *divulging:* being revealed   25 *ore:* vein of gold   26
mineral: mine

(Enter Rosencrantz *and* Guildenstern.*)*

Friends both, go join you with some further aid:
Hamlet in madness hath Polonius slain,
And from his mother's closet hath he dragg'd him.   35
Go seek him out, speak fair, and bring the body
Into the chapel. I pray you haste in this.

[Exeunt Rosencrantz *and* Guildenstern.*]*

Come, Gertrude, we'll call up our wisest friends
And let them know both what we mean to do
And what's untimely done, [. . . .]   40
Whose whisper o'er the world's diameter,
As level as the cannon to his blank,
Transports his pois'ned shot, may miss our name,
And hit the woundless air. O, come away!
My soul is full of discord and dismay.   45

(Exeunt.)

[SCENE II]

(Enter Hamlet.*)*

Hamlet: Safely stow'd.
[Gentlemen. (Within.): Hamlet! Lord Hamlet!]
[Hamlet]: But soft, what noise? Who calls on Hamlet? O, here they come.

(Enter Rosencrantz *and* [Guildenstern].*)*

Rosencrantz: What have you done, my lord, with the dead body?
Hamlet: [Compounded] it with dust, whereto 'tis kin.   5
Rosencrantz: Tell us where 'tis, that we may take it thence,
    And bear it to the chapel.
Hamlet: Do not believe it.
Rosencrantz: Believe what?
Hamlet: That I can keep your counsel and not mine own. Besides, to be de-   10
    manded of a spunge, what replication should be made by the son
    of a king?
Rosencrantz: Take you me for a spunge, my lord?
Hamlet: Ay, sir, that soaks up the King's countenance, his rewards, his au-
    thorities. But such officers do the King best service in the end: he keeps   15
    them, like [an ape] an apple, in the corner of his jaw, first mouth'd, to be
    last swallow'd. When he needs what you have glean'd, it is but squeezing
    you, and, spunge, you shall be dry again.

————

40 Some words are wanting at the end of the line. Capell's conjecture, *so, haply, slander,* probably indicates the intended sense of the passage.   42 *As level:* with aim as good   *blank:* target   44 *woundless:* incapable of being hurt   IV.ii. *Location:* the castle   11–12 *demanded of:* questioned by   11 *spunge:* sponge   *replication:* reply   14 *countenance:* favor

Rosencrantz: I understand you not, my lord.

Hamlet: I am glad of it, a knavish speech sleeps in a foolish ear.   20

Rosencrantz: My lord, you must tell us where the body is, and go with us to the King.

Hamlet: The body is with the King, but the King is not with the body. The King is a thing—

Guildenstern: A thing, my lord?   25

Hamlet: Of nothing, bring me to him. [Hide fox, and all after.]

> *(Exeunt.)*

[SCENE III]

> *(Enter* King *and two or three.)*

King: I have sent to seek him, and to find the body.
How dangerous is it that this man goes loose!
Yet must not we put the strong law on him.
He's lov'd of the distracted multitude,
Who like not in their judgment, but their eyes,   5
And where 'tis so, th' offender's scourge is weigh'd,
But never the offense. To bear all smooth and even,
This sudden sending him away must seem
Deliberate pause. Diseases desperate grown
By desperate appliance are reliev'd,   10
Or not at all.

> *(Enter* Rosencrantz.*)*

How now, what hath befall'n?

Rosencrantz: Where the dead body is bestow'd, my lord,
We cannot get from him.

King: But where is he?

Rosencrantz: Without, my lord, guarded, to know your pleasure.   15

King: Bring him before us.

Rosencrantz: Ho, bring in the lord.

> *(They [*Hamlet *and* Guildenstern*] enter.)*

King: Now, Hamlet, where's Polonius?

Hamlet: At supper.

King: At supper? where?

---

20 *sleeps:* is meaningless   23 *The body . . . the body:* possibly alluding to the legal fiction that the king's dignity is separate from his mortal body   26 *Of nothing:* of no account Cf. "Man is like a thing of nought, his time passeth away like a shadow" (Psalm 144:4 in the Prayer Book version). "Hamlet at once insults the King and hints that his days are numbered" (Dover Wilson). *Hide . . . after:* probably a cry in some game resembling hide-and-seek   IV.iii. Location: the castle   4 *distracted:* unstable   6 *scourge:* punishment   7 *bear:* manage   8–9 *must . . . pause:* must be represented as a maturely considered decision

Hamlet: Not where he eats, but where 'a is eaten; a certain convocation of 20
    politic worms are e'en at him. Your worm is your only emperor for diet:
    we fat all creatures else to fat us, and we fat ourselves for maggots; your
    fat king and your lean beggar is but variable service, two dishes, but to
    one table—that's the end.

King: Alas, alas! 25

Hamlet: A man may fish with the worm that hath eat of a king, and eat of
    the fish that hath fed of that worm.

King: What dost thou mean by this?

Hamlet: Nothing but to show you how a king may go a progress through the
    guts of a beggar. 30

King: Where is Polonius?

Hamlet: In heaven, send thither to see; if your messenger find him not there,
    seek him i' th' other place yourself. But if indeed you find him not within
    this month, you shall nose him as you go up the stairs into the lobby.

King [to Attendants*]:* Go seek him there. 35

Hamlet: 'A will stay till you come.

    [Exeunt Attendants.*]*

King: Hamlet, this deed, for thine especial safety—
    Which we do tender, as we dearly grieve
    For that which thou hast done—must send thee hence
    [With fiery quickness]; therefore prepare thyself, 40
    The bark is ready, and the wind at help,
    Th' associates tend, and every thing is bent
    For England.

Hamlet: For England.

King: Ay, Hamlet.

Hamlet: Good.

King: So is it, if thou knew'st our purposes.

Hamlet: I see a cherub that sees them. But come, for England! Farewell, dear 45
    mother.

King: Thy loving father, Hamlet.

Hamlet: My mother: father and mother is man and wife, man and wife is one
    flesh—so, my mother. Come, for England!   *(Exit.)*

King: Follow him at foot, tempt him with speed aboard. 50
    Delay it not, I'll have him hence to-night.
    Away, for every thing is seal'd and done
    That else leans on th' affair. Pray you make haste.

    [Exeunt Rosencrantz *and* Guildenstern.*]*

---

21 *politic:* crafty, prying; "such worms as might breed in a politician's corpse" (Dowden)   *e'en:*
even now   *for diet:* with respect to what it eats   23 *variable service:* different courses of a meal
29 *progress:* royal journey of state   38 *tender:* regard with tenderness, hold dear   *dearly:* with
intense feeling   41 *at help:* favorable   42 *Th':* thy   *tend:* await   *bent:* made ready   45 *I . . .
them:* heaven sees them   50 *at foot:* at his heels, close behind   53 *leans on:* relates to

And, England, if my love thou hold'st at aught—
As my great power thereof may give thee sense,   55
Since yet thy cicatrice looks raw and red
After the Danish sword, and thy free awe
Pays homage to us—thou mayst not coldly set
Our sovereign process, which imports at full,
By letters congruing to that effect,   60
The present death of Hamlet. Do it, England,
For like the hectic in my blood he rages,
And thou must cure me. Till I know 'tis done,
How e'er my haps, my joys [were] ne'er [begun].

(*Exit.*)

[SCENE IV]

(*Enter* Fortinbras *with his army over the stage.*)

Fortinbras: Go, captain, from me greet the Danish king.
    Tell him that by his license Fortinbras
    Craves the conveyance of a promis'd march
    Over his kingdom. You know the rendezvous.
    If that his Majesty would aught with us,   5
    We shall express our duty in his eye,
    And let him know so.
Captain: I will do't, my lord.
Fortinbras: Go softly on.   *[Exeunt all but the* Captain.*]*

(*Enter* Hamlet, Rosencrantz, [Guildenstern,] *etc.*)

Hamlet: Good sir, whose powers are these?
Captain: They are of Norway, sir.   10
Hamlet: How purpos'd, sir, I pray you?
Captain: Against some part of Poland.
Hamlet: Who commands them, sir?
Captain: The nephew to old Norway, Fortinbras.
Hamlet: Goes it against the main of Poland, sir,   15
    Or for some frontier?
Captain: Truly to speak, and with no addition,
    We go to gain a little patch of ground
    That hath in it no profit but the name.
    To pay five ducats, five, I would not farm it;   20

---

54 *England:* king of England   56 *cicatrice:* scar   57–58 *thy . . . Pays:* your fear makes you pay voluntarily   58 *coldly set:* undervalue, disregard   59 *process:* command   60 *congruing to:* in accord with   61 *present:* immediate   62 *hectic:* continuous fever   64 *haps:* fortunes   IV.iv. Location: the Danish coast, near the castle   3 *conveyance of:* escort for   6 *eye:* presence   8 *softly:* slowly   9 *powers:* forces   15 *main:* main territory   20 *To pay:* for an annual rent of   *farm:* lease

Nor will it yield to Norway or the Pole
A ranker rate, should it be sold in fee.
Hamlet: Why then the Polack never will defend it.
Captain: Yes, it is already garrison'd.
Hamlet: Two thousand souls and twenty thousand ducats   25
Will not debate the question of this straw.
This is th' imposthume of much wealth and peace,
That inward breaks, and shows no cause without
Why the man dies. I humbly thank you, sir.
Captain: God buy you, sir.   *[Exit.]*
Rosencrantz: Will't please you go, my lord?   30
Hamlet: I'll be with you straight—go a little before.

[Exeunt all but Hamlet.*]*

How all occasions do inform against me,
And spur my dull revenge! What is a man,
If his chief good and market of his time
Be but to sleep and feed? a beast, no more.   35
Sure He that made us with such large discourse,
Looking before and after, gave us not
That capability and godlike reason
To fust in us unus'd. Now whether it be
Bestial oblivion, or some craven scruple   40
Of thinking too precisely on th' event—
A thought which quarter'd hath but one part wisdom
And ever three parts coward—I do not know
Why yet I live to say, "This thing's to do,"
Sith I have cause, and will, and strength, and means   45
To do't. Examples gross as earth exhort me:
Witness this army of such mass and charge,
Led by a delicate and tender prince,
Whose spirit with divine ambition puff'd
Makes mouths at the invisible event,   50
Exposing what is mortal and unsure
To all that fortune, death, and danger dare,
Even for an egg-shell. Rightly to be great
Is not to stir without great argument,
But greatly to find quarrel in a straw   55
When honor's at the stake. How stand I then,
That have a father kill'd, a mother stain'd,

---

22 *ranker:* higher   *in fee:* outright   26 *Will not debate:* will scarcely be enough to fight out
27 *imposthume:* abscess   32 *inform against:* denounce, accuse   34 *market:* purchase, profit
36 *discourse:* reasoning power   39 *fust:* grow mouldy   40 *oblivion:* forgetfulness   41
event: outcome   46 *gross:* large, obvious   47 *mass and charge:* size and expense   50 *Makes
mouths at:* treats scornfully   *invisible:* unforeseeable   54 *Is not to:* is *not* not to   *argument:*
cause   55 *greatly:* nobly

Excitements of my reason and my blood,
And let all sleep, while to my shame I see
The imminent death of twenty thousand men,   60
That for a fantasy and trick of fame
Go to their graves like beds, fight for a plot
Whereon the numbers cannot try the cause,
Which is not tomb enough and continent
To hide the slain? O, from this time forth,   65
My thoughts be bloody, or be nothing worth!

(Exit.)

[Scene V]

(Enter Horatio, [Queen] Gertrude, *and a* Gentleman.*)*

Queen: I will not speak with her.
Gentleman: She is importunate, indeed distract.
    Her mood will needs be pitied.
Queen: What would she have?
Gentleman: She speaks much of her father, says she hears
    There's tricks i' th' world, and hems, and beats her heart,   5
    Spurns enviously at straws, speaks things in doubt
    That carry but half sense. Her speech is nothing,
    Yet the unshaped use of it doth move
    The hearers to collection; they yawn at it,
    And botch the words up fit to their own thoughts,   10
    Which as her winks and nods and gestures yield them,
    Indeed would make one think there might be thought,
    Though nothing sure, yet much unhappily.
Horatio: 'Twere good she were spoken with, for she may strew
    Dangerous conjectures in ill-breeding minds.   15
[Queen]: Let her come in.   *[Exit* Gentleman.*]*
    [aside] To my sick soul, as sin's true nature is,
    Each toy seems prologue to some great amiss,
    So full of artless jealousy is guilt,
    It spills itself in fearing to be spilt.   20

(Enter Ophelia *[distracted, with her hair down, playing on a lute].)*

Ophelia: Where is the beauteous majesty of Denmark?

---

58 *Excitements of:* urgings by   61 *fantasy:* caprice   *trick:* trifle   63 *Whereon . . . cause:* which
isn't large enough to let the opposing armies engage upon it   64 *continent:* container   IV.v.
Location: the castle   6 *Spurns . . . straws:* spitefully takes offense at trifles   *in doubt:* obscurely
7 *Her speech:* what she says   8 *unshaped use:* distracted manner   9 *collection:* attempts to
gather the meaning   *yawn at:* gape eagerly (as if to swallow). Most editors adopt the F1 reading
aim at.   10 *botch:* patch   11 *Which:* the words   12 *thought:* inferred, conjectured   15
ill-breeding: conceiving ill thoughts, prone to think the worst   18 *toy:* trifle   *amiss:* calamity
19 *artless jealousy:* uncontrolled suspicion   20 *spills:* destroys

Queen: How now, Ophelia?

Ophelia: "How should I your true-love   (She sings.)
                know
            From another one?   25
        By his cockle hat and staff,
        And his sandal shoon."

Queen: Alas, sweet lady, what imports this song?

Ophelia: Say you? Nay, pray you mark.
            "He is dead and gone, lady,   (Song.) 30
            He is dead and gone,
        At his head a grass-green turf,
        At his heels a stone."

    O ho!

Queen: Nay, but, Ophelia—   35

Ophelia: Pray you mark.   [Sings.]
        "White his shroud as the mountain snow"—

(Enter King.)

Queen: Alas, look here, my lord.

Ophelia: "Larded all with sweet flowers,   (Song.)
            Which bewept to the ground did not go   40
            With true-love showers."

King: How do you, pretty lady?

Ophelia: Well, God dild you! They say the owl was a baker's daughter. Lord,
    we know what we are, but know not what we may be. God be at your table!

King: Conceit upon her father.   45

Ophelia: Pray let's have no words of this, but when they ask you what it
    means, say you this:
            "To-morrow is Saint Valentine's   (Song.)
                day,
            All in the morning betime,   50
            And I a maid at your window,
                To be your Valentine.
        "Then up he rose and donn'd his clo'es,
            And dupp'd the chamber-door,
        Let in the maid, that out a maid   55
                Never departed more."

23–27 These lines resemble a passage in an earlier ballad beginning "As you came from the holy
land / Of Walsingham." Probably all the song fragments sung by Ophelia were familiar to the
Globe audience, but only one other line (187) is from a ballad still extant.   26 *cockle hat:* hat
bearing a cockle shell, the badge of a pilgrim to the shrine of St. James of Compostela in Spain
staff: another mark of a pilgrim   27 *shoon:* shoes (already an archaic form in Shakespeare's day)
39 *Larded:* adorned   40 *not:* contrary to the expected sense, and unmetrical; explained as
Ophelia's alteration of the line to accord with the facts of Polonius' burial (see line 83)   43
dild: yield, reward   *owl:* alluding to the legend of a baker's daughter whom Jesus turned into an
owl because she did not respond generously to his request for bread   45 *Conceit:* fanciful
brooding   54 *dupp'd:* opened

King: Pretty Ophelia!

Ophelia: Indeed without an oath I'll make an end on't.   *[Sings.]*

   "By Gis, and by Saint Charity,
    Alack, and fie for shame!   60
   Young men will do't if they come to't,
    By Cock, they are to blame.
   "Quoth she, 'Before you tumbled me,
    You promis'd me to wed.'"

             (He answers.)

   " 'So would I 'a' done, by yonder sun,   65
    And thou hadst not come to my bed.'"

King: How long hath she been thus?

Ophelia: I hope all will be well. We must be patient, but I cannot choose but
weep to think they would lay him i' th' cold ground. My brother shall know
of it, and so I thank you for your good counsel. Come, my coach! Good   70
night, ladies, good night. Sweet ladies, good night, good night.   *[Exit.]*

King: Follow her close, give her good watch, I pray you.   *[Exit* Horatio.*]*
 O, this is the poison of deep grief, it springs
 All from her father's death—and now behold!
 O Gertrude, Gertrude,   75
 When sorrows come, they come not single spies,
 But in battalions: first, her father slain;
 Next, your son gone, and he most violent author
 Of his own just remove; the people muddied,
 Thick and unwholesome in [their] thoughts and whispers   80
 For good Polonius' death; and we have done but greenly
 In hugger-mugger to inter him; poor Ophelia
 Divided from herself and her fair judgment,
 Without the which we are pictures, or mere beasts;
 Last, and as much containing as all these,   85
 Her brother is in secret come from France,
 Feeds on this wonder, keeps himself in clouds,
 And wants not buzzers to infect his ear
 With pestilent speeches of his father's death,
 Wherein necessity, of matter beggar'd,   90
 Will nothing stick our person to arraign
 In ear and ear. O my dear Gertrude, this,
 Like to a murd'ring-piece, in many places
 Gives me superfluous death.   *(a noise within)*

[Queen: Alack, what noise is this?]*

---

59 *Gis:* contraction of *Jesus*   62 *Cock:* corruption of *God*   66 *And:* if   76 *spies:* soldiers
sent ahead of the main force to reconnoiter; scouts.   79 *muddied:* confused   81 *greenly:* un-
wisely   82 *In hugger-mugger:* secretly and hastily   87 *in clouds:* in cloudy surmise and suspicion (rather than the light of fact)   88 *wants:* lacks   *buzzers:* whispering informers   90 *of
matter beggar'd:* destitute of facts   91 *nothing . . . arraign:* scruple not at all to charge me with
the crime   93 *murd'ring-piece:* cannon firing a scattering charge

King: Attend!   95
    Where is my Swissers? Let them guard the door.

    (Enter a Messenger.*)*

    What is the matter?
Messenger: Save yourself, my lord!
    The ocean, overpeering of his list,
    Eats not the flats with more impiteous haste
    Than young Laertes, in a riotous head,   100
    O'erbears your officers. The rabble call him lord,
    And as the world were now but to begin,
    Antiquity forgot, custom not known,
    The ratifiers and props of every word,
    [They] cry, "Choose we, Laertes shall be king!"   105
    Caps, hands, and tongues applaud it to the clouds,
    "Laertes shall be king, Laertes king!" *(a noise within)*
Queen: How cheerfully on the false trail they cry!
    O, this is counter, you false Danish dogs!

    (Enter Laertes *with others.)*

King: The doors are broke.   110
Laertes: Where is this king? Sirs, stand you all without.
All: No, let's come in.
Laertes: I pray you give me leave.
All: We will, we will.
Laertes: I thank you, keep the door. *[Exeunt* Laertes' *followers.]* O thou vile
    king,   115
    Give me my father!
Queen: Calmly, good Laertes.
Laertes: That drop of blood that's calm proclaims me bastard,
    Cries cuckold to my father, brands the harlot
    Even here between the chaste unsmirched brow
    Of my true mother.
King: What is the cause, Laertes,   120
    That thy rebellion looks so giant-like?
    Let him go, Gertrude, do not fear our person:
    There's such divinity doth hedge a king
    That treason can but peep to what it would,
    Acts little of his will. Tell me, Laertes,   125
    Why thou art thus incens'd. Let him go, Gertrude.
    Speak, man.
Laertes: Where is my father?

----

96 *Swissers:* Swiss guards   98 *overpeering . . . list:* rising higher than its shores   100 *in . . .
head:* with a rebellious force   102 *as:* as if   104 *word:* pledge, promise   109 *counter:* on
the wrong scent (literally, following the scent backward)   122 *fear:* fear for   124 *would:*
would like to do

King: Dead.

Queen: But not by him.

King: Let him demand his fill.

Laertes: How came he dead? I'll not be juggled with.   130
    To hell, allegiance! vows, to the blackest devil!
    Conscience and grace, to the profoundest pit!
    I dare damnation. To this point I stand,
    That both the worlds I give to negligence,
    Let come what comes, only I'll be reveng'd   135
    Most throughly for my father.

King: Who shall stay you?

Laertes: My will, not all the world's:
    And for my means, I'll husband them so well,
    They shall go far with little.

King: Good Laertes,
    If you desire to know the certainty   140
    Of your dear father, is't writ in your revenge
    That, swoopstake, you will draw both friend and foe,
    Winner and loser?

Laertes: None but his enemies.

King: Will you know them then?

Laertes: To his good friends thus wide I'll ope my arms,   145
    And like the kind life-rend'ring pelican,
    Repast them with my blood.

King: Why, now you speak
    Like a good child and a true gentleman.
    That I am guiltless of your father's death,
    And am most sensibly in grief for it,   150
    It shall as level to your judgment 'pear
    As day does to your eye.

                (a noise within:) "Let her come in!"

Laertes: How now, what noise is that?

(Enter Ophelia.*)*

    O heat, dry up my brains! tears seven times salt
    Burn out the sense and virtue of mine eye!   155
    By heaven, thy madness shall be paid with weight
    [Till] our scale turn the beam. O rose of May!
    Dear maid, kind sister, sweet Ophelia!
    O heavens, is't possible a young maid's wits
    Should be as mortal as [an old] man's life?   160

---

134 *both . . . negligence:* I don't care what the consequences are in this world or in the next.
136 *throughly:* thoroughly   137 *world's:* world's will   142 *swoopstake:* sweeping up everything without discrimination (modern *sweepstake*)   146 *pelican:* The female pelican was believed to draw blood from her own breast to nourish her young.   148 *good child:* faithful son
150 *sensibly:* feelingly   151 *level:* plain   155 *virtue:* faculty

[Nature is fine in love, and where 'tis fine,
It sends some precious instance of itself
After the thing it loves.]

Ophelia: "They bore him barefac'd on the   (Song.)
                       bier,   165
              [Hey non nonny, nonny, hey nonny,]
              And in his grave rain'd many a tear"—
Fare you well, my dove!

Laertes: Hadst thou thy wits and didst persuade revenge,
It could not move thus.   170

Ophelia: You must sing, "A-down, a-down," and you call him a-down-a. O
how the wheel becomes it! It is the false steward, that stole his master's
daughter.

Laertes: This nothing's more than matter.

Ophelia: There's rosemary, that's for remembrance; pray you, love, remem-   175
ber. And there is pansies, that's for thoughts.

Laertes: A document in madness, thoughts and remembrance fitted.

Ophelia [to Claudius*]:* There's fennel for you, and columbines.   *[to* Gertrude*]*
There's rue for you, and here's some for me; we may call it herb of grace
a' Sundays. You may wear your rue with a difference. There's a daisy. I would   180
give you some violets, but they wither'd all when my father died. They say
'a made a good end—   *[sings]*
              "For bonny sweet Robin is all my joy."

Laertes: Thought and afflictions, passion, hell itself,
She turns to favor and to prettiness.   185

Ophelia: "And will 'a not come again?   (Song.)
              And will 'a not come again?
                   No, no, he is dead,
                   Go to thy death-bed,
              He never will come again.   190
              "His beard was as white as snow,
              [All] flaxen was his pole,
                   He is gone, he is gone,
                   And we cast away moan,
              God 'a' mercy on his soul!"   195
And of all Christians' souls, [I pray God]. God buy you.   *[Exit.]*

––––

161 *fine in:* refined or spiritualized by   162 *instance:* proof, token. So delicate is Ophelia's love
for her father that her sanity has pursued him into the grave.   169 *persuade:* argue logically for
171 *and . . . a-down-a:* "if he indeed agrees that Polonius is 'a-down,' fallen low" (Dover Wilson)
172 *wheel:* refrain (?) or spinning-wheel, at which women sang ballads (?)   174 *matter:* lucid
speech   177 *A document in madness:* a lesson contained in mad talk   178 *fennel, columbines:*
symbols respectively of flattery and ingratitude   179 *rue:* symbolic of sorrow and repentance
180 *with a difference:* to represent a different cause of sorrow. *Difference* is a term from heraldry,
meaning a variation in a coat of arms made to distinguish different members of a family.   180,
181 *daisy, violets:* symbolic respectively of dissembling and faithfulness. It is not clear who are the
recipients of these.   184 *Thought:* melancholy   185 *favor:* grace, charm   192 *flaxen:*
white   *pole:* poll, head

Laertes: Do you [see] this, O God?
King: Laertes, I must commune with your grief,
　Or you deny me right. Go but apart,
　Make choice of whom your wisest friends you will,　　　　　200
　And they shall hear and judge 'twixt you and me.
　If by direct or by collateral hand
　They find us touch'd, we will our kingdom give,
　Our crown, our life, and all that we call ours,
　To you in satisfaction; but if not,　　　　　205
　Be you content to lend your patience to us,
　And we shall jointly labor with your soul
　To give it due content.
Laertes:　　　　　　　Let this be so.
　His means of death, his obscure funeral—
　No trophy, sword, nor hatchment o'er his bones,　　　　　210
　No noble rite nor formal ostentation—
　Cry to be heard, as 'twere from heaven to earth,
　That I must call't in question.
King:　　　　　　　　So you shall,
　And where th' offense is, let the great axe fall.
　I pray you go with me.　　　　　215

　　(Exeunt.)

[Scene VI]

　　(Enter Horatio *and others.)*

Horatio: What are they that would speak with me?
Gentleman: Sea-faring men, sir. They say they have letters for you.
Horatio: Let them come in.　*[Exit* Gentleman.*]*
　I do not know from what part of the world
　I should be greeted, if not from Lord Hamlet.　　　　　5

　　(Enter Sailors.*)*

[1.] Sailor: God bless you, sir.
Horatio: Let him bless thee too.
[1.] Sailor: 'A shall, sir, and['t] please him. There's a letter for you, sir—it
　came from th' embassador that was bound for England—if your name be
　Horatio, as I am let to know it is.　　　　　10
Horatio [reads]: "Horatio, when thou shalt have overlook'd this, give these fel-
　lows some means to the King, they have letters for him. Ere we were two
　days old at sea, a pirate of very warlike appointment gave us chase. Finding
　ourselves too slow of sail, we put on a compell'd valor, and in the grapple I

---

202 *collateral:* indirect　　　203 *touch'd:* guilty　　　210 *trophy:* memorial　*hatchment:* heraldic memorial tablet　　211 *formal ostentation:* fitting and customary ceremony　　213 *That:* so that
IV.vi. Location: the castle

boarded them. On the instant they got clear of our ship, so I alone became   15
their prisoner. They have dealt with me like thieves of mercy, but they knew
what they did: I am to do a [good] turn for them. Let the King have the letters I have sent, and repair thou to me with as much speed as thou wouldest
fly death. I have words to speak in thine ear will make thee dumb, yet are
they much too light for the [bore] of the matter. These good fellows will   20
bring thee where I am. Rosencrantz and Guildenstern hold their course for
England, of them I have much to tell thee. Farewell.
                              [He] that thou knowest thine,
                                                   Hamlet."

Come, I will [give] you way for these your letters,   25
And do't the speedier that you may direct me
To him from whom you brought them.

(*Exeunt.*)

[SCENE VII]

(*Enter* King *and* Laertes.)

King: Now must your conscience my acquittance seal,
          And you must put me in your heart for friend,
          Sith you have heard, and with a knowing ear,
          That he which hath your noble father slain
          Pursued my life.
Laertes: It well appears. But tell me   5
          Why you [proceeded] not against these feats
          So criminal and so capital in nature,
          As by your safety, greatness, wisdom, all things else
          You mainly were stirr'd up.
King: O, for two special reasons,
          Which may to you perhaps seem much unsinow'd,   10
          But yet to me th' are strong. The Queen his mother
          Lives almost by his looks, and for myself—
          My virtue or my plague, be it either which—
          She is so [conjunctive] to my life and soul,
          That, as the star moves not but in his sphere,   15
          I could not but by her. The other motive,
          Why to a public count I might not go,
          Is the great love the general gender bear him,
          Who, dipping all his faults in their affection,

---

16 *thieves of mercy:* merciful thieves   20 *bore:* calibre, size (gunnery term)   IV.vii. *Location:*
the castle   1 *my acquittance seal:* ratify my acquittal; i.e., acknowledge my innocence in Polonius's death.   6 *feats:* acts   8 *safety:* regard for your own safety   9 *mainly:* powerfully
10 *unsinow'd:* unsinewed, weak   13 *either which:* one or the other   14 *conjunctive:* closely
joined   15 *in his sphere:* by the movement of the sphere in which it is fixed (as the Ptolemaic
astronomy taught)   17 *count:* reckoning   18 *the general gender:* everybody

Work like the spring that turneth wood to stone, 20
Convert his gyves to graces, so that my arrows,
Too slightly timber'd for so [loud a wind],
Would have reverted to my bow again,
But not where I have aim'd them.
Laertes: And so have I a noble father lost, 25
A sister driven into desp'rate terms,
Whose worth, if praises may go back again,
Stood challenger on mount of all the age
For her perfections—but my revenge will come.
King: Break not your sleeps for that. You must not think 30
That we are made of stuff so flat and dull
That we can let our beard be shook with danger
And think it pastime. You shortly shall hear more.
I lov'd your father, and we love ourself,
And that, I hope, will teach you to imagine— 35

(Enter a Messenger *with letters.)*

[How now? What news?
Messenger: Letters, my lord, from Hamlet:]
These to your Majesty, this to the Queen.
King: From Hamlet? Who brought them?
Messenger: Sailors, my lord, they say, I saw them not.
They were given me by Claudio. He receiv'd them 40
Of him that brought them.
King: Laertes, you shall hear them.
—Leave us.   *[Exit* Messenger.*]*
[reads] "High and mighty, You shall know I am set naked on your kingdom.
To-morrow shall I beg leave to see your kingly eyes, when I shall, first asking
you pardon thereunto, recount the occasion of my sudden [and more 45
strange] return.

                                        [Hamlet.]"

What should this mean? Are all the rest come back?
Or is it some abuse, and no such thing?
Laertes: Know you the hand?
King: 'Tis Hamlet's character. "Naked"! 50
And in a postscript here he says "alone."
Can you devise me?
Laertes: I am lost in it, my lord. But let him come,
It warms the very sickness in my heart

---

21 *gyves:* fetters   26 *terms:* condition   27 *go back again:* refer to what she was before she
went mad   28 *on mount:* preeminent   30 *for that:* for fear of losing your revenge   31 *flat:*
spiritless   32 *let . . . shook:* To ruffle or tweak a man's beard was an act of insolent defiance that
he could not disregard without loss of honor. Cf. II.ii.521.   *with:* by   43 *naked:* destitute
45 *pardon thereunto:* permission to do so   49 *abuse:* deceit   50 *character:* handwriting   52
devise me: explain it to me

That I [shall] live and tell him to his teeth,   55
"Thus didst thou."

King: If it be so, Laertes—
As how should it be so? how otherwise?—
Will you be rul'd by me?

Laertes: Ay, my lord,
So you will not o'errule me to a peace.

King: To thine own peace. If he be now returned   60
As [checking] at his voyage, and that he means
No more to undertake it, I will work him
To an exploit, now ripe in my device,
Under the which he shall not choose but fall;
And for his death no wind of blame shall breathe,   65
But even his mother shall uncharge the practice,
And call it accident.

Laertes: My lord, I will be rul'd,
The rather if you could devise it so
That I might be the organ.

King: It falls right.
You have been talk'd of since your travel much,   70
And that in Hamlet's hearing, for a quality
Wherein they say you shine. Your sum of parts
Did not together pluck such envy from him
As did that one, and that, in my regard,
Of the unworthiest siege.   75

Laertes: What part is that, my lord?

King: A very riband in the cap of youth,
Yet needful too, for youth no less becomes
The light and careless livery that it wears
Than settled age his sables and his weeds,
Importing health and graveness. Two months since   80
Here was a gentleman of Normandy:
I have seen myself, and serv'd against, the French,
And they can well on horseback, but this gallant
Had witchcraft in't, he grew unto his seat,
And to such wondrous doing brought his horse,   85
As had he been incorps'd and demi-natur'd
With the brave beast. So far he topp'd [my] thought,

---

57 *As . . . otherwise:* How can he have come back? Yet he obviously has.   59 *So:* provided that
61 *checking at:* turning from (like a falcon diverted from its quarry by other prey)   66 *uncharge the practice:* adjudge the plot no plot, fail to see the plot   69 *organ:* instrument, agent
71 *quality:* skill   72 *Your . . . parts:* all your (other) accomplishments put together   75 *unworthiest:* least important (with no implication of unsuitableness)   *siege:* status, position
79 *weeds:* (characteristic) garb   80 *Importing . . . graveness:* signifying prosperity and dignity
83 *can . . . horseback:* are excellent riders   86 *incorps'd:* made one body   *demi-natur'd:* become half of a composite animal

That I in forgery of shapes and tricks
Come short of what he did.
Laertes: A Norman was't?
King: A Norman.   90
Laertes: Upon my life, Lamord.
King: The very same.
Laertes: I know him well. He is the brooch indeed
And gem of all the nation.
King: He made confession of you,
And gave you such a masterly report   95
For art and exercise in your defense,
And for your rapier most especial,
That he cried out 'twould be a sight indeed
If one could match you. The scrimers of their nation
He swore had neither motion, guard, nor eye,   100
If you oppos'd them. Sir, this report of his
Did Hamlet so envenom with his envy
That he could nothing do but wish and beg
Your sudden coming o'er to play with you.
Now, out of this—
Laertes: What out of this, my lord?   105
King: Laertes, was your father dear to you?
Or are you like the painting of a sorrow,
A face without a heart?
Laertes: Why ask you this?
King: Not that I think you did not love your father,
But that I know love is begun by time,   110
And that I see, in passages of proof,
Time qualifies the spark and fire of it.
There lives within the very flame of love
A kind of week or snuff that will abate it,
And nothing is at a like goodness still,   115
For goodness, growing to a plurisy,
Dies in his own too much. That we would do,
We should do when we would; for this "would" changes,
And hath abatements and delays as many
As there are tongues, are hands, are accidents,   120
And then this "should" is like a spendthrift's sigh,
That hurts by easing. But to the quick of th' ulcer:

---

88 *forgery:* mere imagining   92 *brooch:* ornament (worn in the hat)   94 *made . . . you:* acknowledged your excellence   99 *scrimers:* fencers   104 *sudden:* speedy   110 *time:* a particular set of circumstances   111 *in . . . proof:* by the test of experience, by actual examples   112 *qualifies:* moderates   114 *week:* wick   115 *nothing . . . still:* nothing remains forever at the same pitch of perfection   116 *plurisy:* plethora (a variant spelling of *pleurisy,* which was erroneously related to *plus,* stem *plur,* "more, overmuch")   117 *too much:* excess   121 *spendthrift's sigh:* A sigh was supposed to draw blood from the heart.   122 *hurts by easing:* injures us at the same time that it gives us relief

Hamlet comes back. What would you undertake
To show yourself indeed your father's son
More than in words?

Laertes: To cut his throat i' th' church.   125

King: No place indeed should murther sanctuarize,
      Revenge should have no bounds. But, good Laertes,
      Will you do this, keep close within your chamber.
      Hamlet return'd shall know you are come home.
      We'll put on those shall praise your excellence,   130
      And set a double varnish on the fame
      The Frenchman gave you, bring you in fine together,
      And wager o'er your heads. He, being remiss,
      Most generous, and free from all contriving,
      Will not peruse the foils, so that with ease,   135
      Or with a little shuffling, you may choose
      A sword unbated, and in a [pass] of practice
      Requite him for your father.

Laertes: I will do't,
      And for [that] purpose I'll anoint my sword.
      I bought an unction of a mountebank,   140
      So mortal that, but dip a knife in it,
      Where it draws blood, no cataplasm so rare,
      Collected from all simples that have virtue
      Under the moon, can save the thing from death
      That is but scratch'd withal. I'll touch my point   145
      With this contagion, that if I gall him slightly,
      It may be death.

King: Let's further think of this,
      Weigh what convenience both of time and means
      May fit us to our shape. If this should fail,
      And that our drift look through our bad performance,   150
      'Twere better not assay'd; therefore this project
      Should have a back or second, that might hold
      If this did blast in proof. Soft, let me see.
      We'll make a solemn wager on your cunnings—
      I ha't!   155
      When in your motion you are hot and dry—

---

126 *sanctuarize:* offer asylum to   128 *Will . . . this:* if you want to undertake this   130 *put on those:* incite those who   131 *double varnish:* second coat of varnish   132 *in fine:* finally
133 *remiss:* careless, overtrustful   134 *generous:* noble-minded   *free . . . contriving:* innocent of sharp practices   135 *peruse:* examine   136 *shuffling:* cunning exchange   137 *unbated:* not blunted   *pass of practice:* tricky thrust   140 *unction:* ointment   *mountebank:* traveling quack-doctor   141 *mortal:* deadly   142 *cataplasm:* poultice   143 *simples:* medicinal herbs   *virtue:* curative power   146 *gall:* graze   149 *fit . . . shape:* suit our purposes best   150 *drift:* purpose   *look through:* become visible, be detected   152 *back or second:* a second plot in reserve for emergency   153 *blast in proof:* blow up while being tried (an image from gunnery)

As make your bouts more violent to that end—
And that he calls for drink, I'll have preferr'd him
A chalice for the nonce, whereon but sipping,
If he by chance escape your venom'd stuck,   160
Our purpose may hold there. But stay, what noise?

(Enter Queen.*)*

Queen: One woe doth tread upon another's heel,
    So fast they follow. Your sister's drown'd, Laertes.
Laertes: Drown'd! O, where?
Queen: There is a willow grows askaunt the brook,   165
    That shows his hoary leaves in the glassy stream,
    Therewith fantastic garlands did she make
    Of crow-flowers, nettles, daisies, and long purples
    That liberal shepherds give a grosser name,
    But our cull-cold maids do dead men's fingers call them.   170
    There on the pendant boughs her crownet weeds
    Clamb'ring to hang, an envious sliver broke,
    When down her weedy trophies and herself
    Fell in the weeping brook. Her clothes spread wide,
    And mermaid-like awhile they bore her up,   175
    Which time she chaunted snatches of old lauds,
    As one incapable of her own distress,
    Or like a creature native and indued
    Unto that element. But long it could not be
    Till that her garments, heavy with their drink,   180
    Pull'd the poor wretch from her melodious lay
    To muddy death.
Laertes: Alas, then she is drown'd?
Queen: Drown'd, drown'd.
Laertes: Too much of water hast thou, poor Ophelia,
    And therefore I forbid my tears; but yet   185
    It is our trick, Nature her custom holds,
    Let shame say what it will; when these are gone,
    The woman will be out. Adieu, my lord,
    I have a speech a' fire that fain would blaze,
    But that this folly drowns it.   *(Exit.)*
King: Let's follow, Gertrude.   190
    How much I had to do to calm his rage!

---

157 *As:* and you should   158 *preferr'd:* offered to. Most editors adopt the F1 reading *prepar'd.*
159 *nonce:* occasion   160 *stuck:* thrust (from *stoccado,* a fencing term)   165 *askaunt:* sideways
over   166 *hoary:* grey-white   167 *Therewith:* with willow branches   168 *long purples:*
wild orchids   169 *liberal:* free-spoken   170 *cull-cold:* chaste   171 *crownet:* made into
coronets   172 *envious sliver:* malicious branch   176 *lauds:* hymns   177 *incapable:* insensible   178 *indued:* habituated   186 *It:* weeping   *trick:* natural way   187 *these:* these tears
188 *The woman . . . out:* My womanish traits will be gone for good.

Now fear I this will give it start again,
Therefore let's follow.

(*Exeunt.*)

ACT V

Scene I

(*Enter two* Clowns *[with spades and mattocks].*)

1. *Clown:* Is she to be buried in Christian burial when she willfully seeks her
   own salvation?
2. *Clown:* I tell thee she is, therefore make her grave straight. The crowner
   hath sate on her, and finds it Christian burial.
1. *Clown:* How can that be, unless she drown'd herself in her own defense?   5
2. *Clown:* Why, 'tis found so.
1. *Clown:* It must be *[se offendendo]*, it cannot be else. For here lies the point: if I
   drown myself wittingly, it argues an act, and an act hath three branches—it
   is to act, to do, to perform; [argal], she drown'd herself wittingly.
2. *Clown:* Nay, but hear you, goodman delver—   10
1. *Clown:* Give me leave. Here lies the water; good. Here stands the man; good.
   If the man go to this water and drown himself, it is, will he, nill he, he goes,
   mark you that. But if the water come to him and drown him, he drowns not
   himself; argal, he that is not guilty of his own death shortens not his own
   life.   15
2. *Clown:* But is this law?
1. *Clown:* Ay, marry, is't—crowner's quest law.
2. *Clown:* Will you ha' the truth an't? If this had not been a gentlewoman, she
   should have been buried out a' Christian burial.
1. *Clown:* Why, there thou say'st, and the more pity that great folk should have   20
   count'nance in this world to drown or hang themselves, more than their
   even-Christen. Come, my spade. There is no ancient gentlemen but
   gard'ners, ditchers, and grave-makers; they hold up Adam's profession.
2. *Clown:* Was he a gentleman?
1. *Clown:* 'A was the first that ever bore arms.   25
[2. *Clown:* Why, he had none.
1. *Clown:* What, art a heathen? How dost thou understand the Scripture? The
   Scripture says Adam digg'd; could he dig without arms?] I'll put another
   question to thee. If thou answerest me not to the purpose, confess thyself—

V.i. Location: a churchyard   o.s.d. *Clowns:* rustics   3 *straight:* immediately   *crowner:* coroner
7 *se offendendo:* blunder for *se defendendo*, "in self-defense"   9 *argal:* blunder for *ergo*, "therefore"   11–15 *Here . . . life:* Alluding to a very famous suicide case, that of Sir James Hales, a
judge who drowned himself in 1554; it was long cited in the courts. The clown gives a garbled account of the defense summing-up and the verdict.   12 *nill he:* will he not   17 *quest:* inquest
22 *even-Christen:* fellow-Christians   26 *none:* no coat of arms

2. Clown: Go to. 30

1. Clown: What is he that builds stronger than either the mason, the ship-wright, or the carpenter?

2. Clown: The gallows-maker, for that outlives a thousand tenants.

1. Clown: I like thy wit well, in good faith. The gallows does well; but how does it well? It does well to those that do ill. Now thou dost ill to say the 35
gallows is built stronger than the church; argal, the gallows may do well to thee. To't again, come.

2. Clown: Who builds stronger than a mason, a shipwright, or a carpenter?

1. Clown: Ay, tell me that, and unyoke.

2. Clown: Marry, now I can tell. 40

1. Clown: To't.

2. Clown: Mass, I cannot tell.

(*Enter* Hamlet *and* Horatio *[afar off].*)

1. Clown: Cudgel thy brains no more about it, for your dull ass will not mend his pace with beating, and when you are ask'd this question next, say "a grave-maker": the houses he makes lasts till doomsday. Go get thee in, 45
and fetch me a sup of liquor.

[Exit Second Clown. First Clown digs.]

> "In youth when I did love, did love,   (*song*)
> Methought it was very sweet,
> To contract—O—the time for—a—my behove,
> O, methought there—a—was nothing—a—meet." 50

Hamlet: Has this fellow no feeling of his business? 'a sings in grave-making.

Horatio: Custom hath made it in him a property of easiness.

Hamlet: 'Tis e'en so, the hand of little employment hath the daintier sense.

1. Clown: "But age with his stealing steps   (*song*)
> Hath clawed me in his clutch, 55
> And hath shipped me into the land,
> As if I had never been such."

[throws up a shovelful of earth with a skull in it]

Hamlet: That skull had a tongue in it, and could sing once. How the knave jowls it to the ground, as if 'twere Cain's jaw-bone, that did the first mur-der! This might be the pate of a politician, which this ass now o'er- 60
reaches, one that would circumvent God, might it not?

Horatio: It might, my lord.

---

39 *unyoke:* cease to labor, call it a day   42 *Mass:* by the mass   49 *contract . . . behove:* shorten,
spend agreeably . . . advantage. The song, punctuated by the grunts of the clown as he digs, is a
garbled version of a poem by Thomas Lord Vaux, entitled "The Aged Lover Renounceth Love."
52 *Custom:* habit   *a property of easiness:* a thing he can do with complete ease of mind   53 *daintier sense:* more delicate sensitivity   59 *jowls:* dashes   60 *politician:* schemer, intriguer   *o'er-
reaches:* gets the better of (with play on the literal sense)   61 *circumvent God:* bypass God's law

Hamlet: Or of a courtier, which could say, "Good morrow, sweet lord! How
    dost thou, sweet lord?" This might be my Lord Such-a-one, that prais'd
    my Lord Such-a-one's horse when 'a [meant] to beg it, might it not?   65
Horatio: Ay, my lord.
Hamlet: Why, e'en so, and now my Lady Worm's, chopless, and knock'd about
    the [mazzard] with a sexton's spade. Here's fine revolution, and we had the
    trick to see't. Did these bones cost no more the breeding, but to play at
    loggats with them? Mine ache to think on't.   70
1. Clown: "A pickaxe and a spade, a spade,   *(song)*
                    For and a shrouding sheet:
                    O, a pit of clay for to be made
                    For such a guest is meet."

[throws up another skull]

Hamlet: There's another. Why may not that be the skull of a lawyer? Where   75
    be his quiddities now, his quillities, his cases, his tenures, and his tricks?
    Why does he suffer this mad knave now to knock him about the sconce
    with a dirty shovel, and will not tell him of his action of battery? Hum!
    This fellow might be in 's time a great buyer of land, with his statutes, his
    recognizances, his fines, his double vouchers, his recoveries. [Is this the   80
    fine of his fines, and the recovery of his recoveries,] to have his fine pate
    full of fine dirt? Will [his] 'vouchers vouch him no more of his purchases,
    and [double ones too], than the length and breadth of a pair of inden-
    tures? The very conveyances of his lands will scarcely lie in this box, and
    must th' inheritor himself have no more, ha?   85
Horatio: Not a jot more, my lord.
Hamlet: Is not parchment made of sheep-skins?
Horatio: Ay, my lord, and of calves'-skins too.
Hamlet: They are sheep and calves which seek out assurance in that. I will
    speak to this fellow. Whose grave's this, sirrah?   90
1. Clown: Mine, sir.   *[sings]*
                    "[O], a pit of clay for to be made
                    [For such a guest is meet]."
Hamlet: I think it be thine indeed, for thou liest in't.
1. Clown: You lie out on't, sir, and therefore 'tis not yours; for my part, I do   95
    not lie in't, yet it is mine.
Hamlet: Thou dost lie in't, to be in't and say it is thine. 'Tis for the dead, not
    for the quick; therefore thou liest.

---

67 *chopless:* lacking the lower jaw   68 *mazzard:* head   *revolution:* change   *and:* if   69 *trick:*
knack, ability   *Did . . . cost:* were . . . worth   70 *loggats:* a game in which blocks of wood were
thrown at a stake   76 *quiddities:* subtleties, quibbles   *quillities:* fine distinctions   *tenures:* titles
to real estate   77 *sconce:* head   80 *statutes, recognizances:* bonds securing debts by attaching
land and property   80 *fines, recoveries:* procedures for converting an entailed estate to freehold
double vouchers: documents guaranteeing title to real estate, signed by two persons   *fine:* end
84 *pair of indentures:* legal document cut into two parts which fitted together on a serrated edge.
Perhaps Hamlet thus refers to the two rows of teeth in the skull, or to the bone sutures.   *con-
veyances:* documents relating to transfer of property   84 *this box:* the skull itself   *inheritor:*
owner   90 *sirrah:* term of address to inferiors

1. Clown: 'Tis a quick lie, sir, 'twill away again from me to you.

Hamlet: What man dost thou dig it for?   100

1. Clown: For no man, sir.

Hamlet: What woman then?

1. Clown: For none neither.

Hamlet: Who is to be buried in't?

1. Clown: One that was a woman, sir, but, rest her soul, she's dead.   105

Hamlet: How absolute the knave is! we must speak by the card, or equivocation will undo us. By the Lord, Horatio, this three years I have took note of it: the age is grown so pick'd that the toe of the peasant comes so near the heel of the courtier, he galls his kibe. How long hast thou been grave-maker?

1. Clown: Of [all] the days i' th' year, I came to't that day that our last king   110
Hamlet overcame Fortinbras.

Hamlet: How long is that since?

1. Clown: Cannot you tell that? Every fool can tell that. It was that very day that young Hamlet was born—he that is mad, and sent into England.

Hamlet: Ay, marry, why was he sent into England?   115

1. Clown: Why, because 'a was mad. 'A shall recover his wits there, or if 'a do not, 'tis no great matter there.

Hamlet: Why?

1. Clown: 'Twill not be seen in him there, there the men are as mad as he.

Hamlet: How came he mad?   120

1. Clown: Very strangely, they say.

Hamlet: How strangely?

1. Clown: Faith, e'en with losing his wits.

Hamlet: Upon what ground?

1. Clown: Why, here in Denmark. I have been sexton here, man and boy, thirty   125
years.

Hamlet: How long will a man lie i' th' earth ere he rot?

1. Clown: Faith, if 'a be not rotten before 'a die—as we have many pocky corses, that will scarce hold the laying in—'a will last you some eight year or nine year. A tanner will last you nine year.   130

Hamlet: Why he more than another?

1. Clown: Why, sir, his hide is so tann'd with his trade that 'a will keep out water a great while, and your water is a sore decayer of your whoreson dead body. Here's a skull now hath lien you i' th' earth three and twenty years.

Hamlet: Whose was it?   135

1. Clown: A whoreson mad fellow's it was. Whose do you think it was?

Hamlet: Nay, I know not.

1. Clown: A pestilence on him for a mad rogue! 'a pour'd a flagon of Rhenish on my head once. This same skull, sir, was, sir, Yorick's skull, the King's jester.   140

Hamlet: This?   *[takes the skull]*

---

106 *absolute:* positive   *by the card:* by the compass, punctiliously   106–107 *equivocation:* ambiguity   108 *pick'd:* refined   109 *galls his kibe:* rubs the courtier's chilblain   128 *pocky:* rotten with venereal disease   129 *hold . . . in:* last out the burial

1. Clown: E'en that.

Hamlet: Alas, poor Yorick! I knew him, Horatio, a fellow of infinite jest, of
   most excellent fancy. He hath bore me on his back a thousand times, and
   now how abhorr'd in my imagination it is! my gorge rises at it. Here hung   145
   those lips that I have kiss'd I know not how oft. Where be your gibes now,
   your gambols, your songs, your flashes of merriment, that were wont to
   set the table on a roar? Not one now to mock your own grinning—quite
   chop-fall'n. Now get you to my lady's [chamber], and tell her, let her
   paint an inch thick, to this favor she must come; make her laugh at that.   150
   Prithee, Horatio, tell me one thing.

Horatio: What's that, my lord?

Hamlet: Dost thou think Alexander look'd a' this fashion i' th' earth?

Horatio: E'en so.

Hamlet: And smelt so? pah!   *[puts down the skull]*   155

Horatio: E'en so, my lord.

Hamlet: To what base uses we may return, Horatio! Why may not imagination trace the noble dust of Alexander, till 'a find it stopping a bunghole?

Horatio: 'Twere to consider too curiously, to consider so.

Hamlet: No, faith, not a jot, but to follow him thither with modesty enough   160
   and likelihood to lead it: Alexander died, Alexander was buried, Alexander
   returneth to dust, the dust is earth, of earth we make loam, and why of that
   loam whereto he was converted might they not stop a beer-barrel?
   Imperious Caesar, dead and turn'd to clay,
   Might stop a hole to keep the wind away.   165
   O that that earth which kept the world in awe
   Should patch a wall t' expel the [winter's] flaw!
   But soft, but soft awhile, here comes the King,

(*Enter* King, Queen, Laertes, *and [a* Doctor of Divinity, *following] the
corse, [with* Lords *attendant].*)

   The Queen, the courtiers. Who is this they follow?
   And with such maimed rites? This doth betoken   170
   The corse they follow did with desp'rate hand
   Foredo it own life. 'Twas of some estate.
   Couch we a while and mark.   *[retiring with* Horatio*]*

Laertes: What ceremony else?

Hamlet: That is Laertes, a very noble youth. Mark.   175

Laertes: What ceremony else?

Doctor: Her obsequies have been as far enlarg'd
   As we have warranty. Her death was doubtful,

---

149 *chop-fall'n:* (1) lacking the lower jaw; (2) downcast   150 *favor:* appearance   159 *curiously:* closely, minutely   160 *modesty:* moderation   162 *loam:* a mixture of moistened clay
with sand, straw, etc.   164 *Imperious:* imperial   167 *flaw:* gust   170 *maimed rites:* lack of
customary ceremony   172 *Foredo:* fordo, destroy   *it:* its   *estate:* rank   173 *Couch we:* let us
conceal ourselves   178 *doubtful:* the subject of an "open verdict"

And but that great command o'ersways the order,
She should in ground unsanctified been lodg'd   180
Till the last trumpet; for charitable prayers,
[Shards,] flints, and pebbles should be thrown on her.
Yet here she is allow'd her virgin crants,
Her maiden strewments, and the bringing home
Of bell and burial.   185

Laertes: Must there no more be done?

Doctor: No more be done:
We should profane the service of the dead
To sing a requiem and such rest to her
As to peace-parted souls.

Laertes: Lay her i' th' earth,
And from her fair and unpolluted flesh   190
May violets spring! I tell thee, churlish priest,
A minist'ring angel shall my sister be
When thou liest howling.

Hamlet: What, the fair Ophelia!

Queen [scattering flowers]: Sweets to the sweet, farewell!
I hop'd thou shouldst have been my Hamlet's wife.   195
I thought thy bride-bed to have deck'd, sweet maid,
And not have strew'd thy grave.

Laertes: O, treble woe
Fall ten times [treble] on that cursed head
Whose wicked deed thy most ingenious sense
Depriv'd thee of! Hold off the earth a while,   200
Till I have caught her once more in mine arms.

[leaps in the grave]

Now pile your dust upon the quick and dead,
Till of this flat a mountain you have made
T' o'ertop old Pelion, or the skyish head
Of blue Olympus.   205

Hamlet [coming forward]: What is he whose grief
Bears such an emphasis, whose phrase of sorrow
Conjures the wand'ring stars and makes them stand
Like wonder-wounded hearers? This is I,
Hamlet the Dane!   210

---

179 *order:* customary procedure   180 *should:* would certainly   181 *for:* instead of
183 *crants:* garland   184 *maiden strewments:* flowers scattered on the grave of an unmarried
girl   184–85 *bringing . . . burial:* burial in consecrated ground, with the bell tolling   188 *re-*
quiem: dirge   194 *Sweets:* flowers   199 *ingenious:* intelligent   204, 205 *Pelion, Olympus:*
mountains in northeastern Greece   207 *emphasis, phrase:* rhetorical terms, here used in dis-
paraging reference to Laertes' inflated language   208 *Conjures:* puts a spell upon   *wand'ring*
stars: planets   210 *the Dane:* This title normally signifies the king

[Hamlet leaps in after Laertes.]

Laertes: The devil take thy soul!   *[grappling with him]*
Hamlet: Thou pray'st not well.
     I prithee take thy fingers from my throat.
     For though I am not splenitive [and] rash,
     Yet have I in me something dangerous,
     Which let thy wisdom fear. Hold off thy hand!   215
King: Pluck them asunder.
Queen: Hamlet, Hamlet!
All: Gentlemen!
Horatio: Good my lord, be quiet.

[The Attendants part them, and they come out of the grave.]

Hamlet: Why, I will fight with him upon this theme
     Until my eyelids will no longer wag.
Queen: O my son, what theme?   220
Hamlet: I lov'd Ophelia. Forty thousand brothers
     Could not with all their quantity of love
     Make up my sum. What wilt thou do for her?
King: O, he is mad, Laertes.
Queen: For love of God, forbear him.   225
Hamlet: 'Swounds, show me what thou't do.
     Woo't weep, woo't fight, woo't fast, woo't tear thyself?
     Woo't drink up eisel, eat a crocodile?
     I'll do't. Dost [thou] come here to whine?
     To outface me with leaping in her grave?   230
     Be buried quick with her, and so will I.
     And if thou prate of mountains, let them throw
     Millions of acres on us, till our ground,
     Singeing his pate against the burning zone,
     Make Ossa like a wart! Nay, and thou'lt mouth,   235
     I'll rant as well as thou.
Queen: This is mere madness,
     And [thus] a while the fit will work on him;
     Anon, as patient as the female dove,
     When that her golden couplets are disclosed,
     His silence will sit drooping.
Hamlet: Hear you, sir,   240
     What is the reason that you use me thus?
     I lov'd you ever. But it is no matter.

---

213 *splenitive:* impetuous   226 *thou't:* thou wilt   227–28 *Woo't:* wilt thou   228 *eisel:* vinegar   *crocodile:* crocodile   232 *if . . . mountains:* referring to lines 203–205   234 *burning
zone:* sphere of the sun   235 *Ossa:* another mountain in Greece, near Pelion and Olympus
mouth: talk bombast (synonymous with *rant* in the next line)   236 *mere:* utter   238 *patient:*
calm   239 *golden couplets:* pair of baby birds, covered with yellow down   *disclosed:* hatched

Let Hercules himself do what he may,
The cat will mew, and dog will have his day.

(*Exit* Hamlet.)

King: I pray thee, good Horatio, wait upon him.   245

([*Exit*] Horatio.)

[*to* Laertes] Strengthen your patience in our last night's speech,
We'll put the matter to the present push.—
Good Gertrude, set some watch over your son.
This grave shall have a living monument.
An hour of quiet [shortly] shall we see,   250
Till then in patience our proceeding be.

(*Exeunt.*)

[SCENE II]

(*Enter* Hamlet *and* Horatio.)

Hamlet: So much for this, sir, now shall you see the other—
  You do remember all the circumstance?
Horatio: Remember it, my lord!
Hamlet: Sir, in my heart there was a kind of fighting
  That would not let me sleep. [Methought] I lay   5
  Worse than the mutines in the [bilboes]. Rashly—
  And prais'd be rashness for it—let us know
  Our indiscretion sometime serves us well
  When our deep plots do pall, and that should learn us
  There's a divinity that shapes our ends,   10
  Rough-hew them how we will—
Horatio: That is most certain.
Hamlet: Up from my cabin,
  My sea-grown scarf'd about me, in the dark
  Grop'd I to find out them, had my desire,
  Finger'd their packet, and in fine withdrew   15
  To mine own room again, making so bold,
  My fears forgetting manners, to [unseal]
  Their grand commission; where I found, Horatio—

243–44 *Let . . . day:* nobody can prevent another from making the scenes he feels he has a right to   246 *in:* by recalling   247 *present push:* immediate test   249 *living:* enduring (?) or in the form of a lifelike effigy (?)   V.ii. Location: the castle   1 *see the other:* hear the other news I have to tell you (hinted at in the letter to Horatio, IV.vi.19–20)   6 *mutines:* mutineers (but the term *mutiny* was in Shakespeare's day used of almost any act of rebellion against authority)   *bilboes:* fetters attached to a heavy iron bar   *Rashly:* on impulse   7 *know:* recognize, acknowledge   9 *pall:* lose force, come to nothing   *learn:* teach   10 *shapes our ends:* gives final shape to our designs   11 *Rough-hew them:* block them out in initial form   15 *Finger'd:* filched, "pinched"

Ah, royal knavery!—an exact command,
Larded with many several sorts of reasons,   20
Importing Denmark's health and England's too,
With, ho, such bugs and goblins in my life,
That, on the supervise, no leisure bated,
No, not to stay the grinding of the axe,
My head should be strook off.

Horatio: Is't possible?   25

Hamlet: Here's the commission, read it at more leisure.
But wilt thou hear now how I did proceed?

Horatio: I beseech you.

Hamlet: Being thus benetted round with [villainies],
Or I could make a prologue to my brains,   30
They had begun the play. I sat me down,
Devis'd a new commission, wrote it fair.
I once did hold it, as our statists do,
A baseness to write fair, and labor'd much
How to forget that learning, but, sir, now   35
I did me yeman's service. Wilt thou know
Th' effect of what I wrote?

Horatio: Ay, good my lord.

Hamlet: An earnest conjuration from the King,
As England was his faithful tributary,
As love between them like the palm might flourish,   40
As peace should still her wheaten garland wear
And stand a comma 'tween their amities,
And many such-like [as's] of great charge,
That on the view and knowing of these contents,
Without debatement further, more or less,   45
He should those bearers put to sudden death,
Not shriving time allow'd.

Horatio: How was this seal'd?

Hamlet: Why, even in that was heaven ordinant.
I had my father's signet in my purse,
Which was the model of that Danish seal;   50
Folded the writ up in the form of th' other,
[Subscrib'd] it, gave't th' impression, plac'd it safely,

---

20 *Larded:* garnished   21 *Importing:* relating to   22 *bugs . . . life:* terrifying things in
prospect if I were permitted to remain alive; *bugs* = bugaboos   23 *supervise:* perusal   *bated:* de-
ducted (from the stipulated speediness)   24 *stay:* wait for   30 *Or:* before   32 *fair:* in a
beautiful hand (such as a professional scribe would use)   33 *statists:* statesmen, public officials
34 *A baseness:* a skill befitting men of low rank   36 *yeman's:* yeoman's; solid, substantial
37 *effect:* purport, gist   42 *comma:* connective, link   43 *as's . . . charge:* (1) weighty clauses
beginning with *as;* (2) asses with heavy loads   47 *shriving time:* time for confession and absolution   48 *ordinant:* in charge, guiding   50 *model:* small copy   52 *Subscrib'd:* signed

The changeling never known. Now the next day
Was our sea-fight, and what to this was sequent
Thou knowest already.   55
Horatio: So Guildenstern and Rosencrantz go to't.
Hamlet: [Why, man, they did make love to this employment,]
They are not near my conscience. Their defeat
Does by their own insinuation grow.
'Tis dangerous when the baser nature comes   60
Between the pass and fell incensed points
Of mighty opposites.
Horatio: Why, what a king is this!
Hamlet: Does it not, think thee, stand me now upon—
He that hath kill'd my king and whor'd my mother,
Popp'd in between th' election and my hopes,   65
Thrown out his angle for my proper life,
And with such coz'nage—is't not perfect conscience
[To quit him with this arm? And is't not to be damn'd,
To let this canker of our nature come
In further evil?   70
Horatio: It must be shortly known to him from England
What is the issue of the business there.
Hamlet: It will be short; the interim's mine,
And a man's life's no more than to say "one."
But I am very sorry, good Horatio,   75
That to Laertes I forgot myself,
For by the image of my cause I see
The portraiture of his. I'll [court] his favors.
But sure the bravery of his grief did put me
Into a tow'ring passion.
Horatio: Peace, who comes here?]   80

(*Enter [young* Osric,*] a courtier.*)

Osric: Your lordship is right welcome back to Denmark.
Hamlet: I [humbly] thank you, sir.—Dost know this water-fly?
Horatio: No, my good lord.

---

53 *changeling:* Hamlet's letter, substituted secretly for the genuine letter, as fairies substituted
their children for human children   *never known:* never recognized as a substitution (unlike the
fairies' changelings)   56 *go to't:* are going to their death   58 *defeat:* ruin, overthrow
59 *insinuation:* winding their way into the affair   60 *baser:* inferior   61 *pass:* thrust   *fell:*
fierce   63 *stand . . . upon:* rest upon me as a duty   65 *election:* as king of Denmark   66 *angle:*
hook and line   *proper:* very   67 *coz'nage:* trickery   68 *quit him:* pay him back   69 *canker:*
cancerous sore   69–70 *come In:* grow into   74 *a man's . . . more:* to kill a man takes no more
time   *say "one."* Perhaps this is equivalent to "deliver one sword thrust"; see line 246 below,
where Hamlet says "One" as he makes the first hit.   77 *image:* likeness   79 *bravery:* osten-
tatious expression   82 *water-fly:* tiny, vainly agitated creature

Hamlet: Thy state is the more gracious, for 'tis a vice to know him. He hath much land, and fertile; let a beast be lord of beasts, and his crib shall stand at the King's mess. 'Tis a chough, but, as I say, spacious in the possession of dirt. 85

Osric: Sweet lord, if your lordship were at leisure, I should impart a thing to you from his Majesty.

Hamlet: I will receive it, sir, with all diligence of spirit. [Put] your bonnet to his right use, 'tis for the head. 90

Osric: I thank your lordship, it is very hot.

Hamlet: No, believe me, 'tis very cold, the wind is northerly.

Osric: It is indifferent cold, my lord, indeed.

Hamlet: But yet methinks it is very [sultry] and hot [for] my complexion. 95

Osric: Exceedingly, my lord, it is very sultry—as 'twere—I cannot tell how. My lord, his Majesty bade me signify to you that 'a has laid a great wager on your head. Sir, this is the matter—

Hamlet: I beseech you remember.

[Hamlet moves him to put on his hat.]

Osric: Nay, good my lord, for my ease, in good faith. Sir, here is newly come to court Laertes, believe me, an absolute [gentleman], full of most excellent differences, of very soft society, and great showing; indeed, to speak sellingly of him, he is the card or calendar of gentry; for you shall find in him the continent of what part a gentleman would see. 100

Hamlet: Sir, his definement suffers no perdition in you, though I know to divide him inventorially would dozy th' arithmetic of memory, and yet but yaw neither in respect of his quick sail; but in the verity of extolment, I take him to be a soul of great article, and his infusion of such dearth and rareness as, to make true diction of him, his semblable is his mirror, and who else would trace him, his umbrage, nothing more. 105 110

Osric: Your lordship speaks most infallibly of him.

Hamlet: The concernancy, sir? Why do we wrap the gentleman in our more rawer breath?

Osric: Sir?

---

84 *gracious:* virtuous   85–86 *let . . . mess:* If a beast owned as many cattle as Osric, he could feast with the King.   86 *chough:* jackdaw, a bird that could be taught to speak   90 *bonnet:* hat   94 *indifferent:* somewhat   95 *complexion:* temperament   100 *for my ease:* I am really more comfortable with my hat off (a polite insistence on maintaining ceremony).   101 *absolute:* complete, possessing every quality a gentleman should have   102 *differences:* distinguishing characteristics, personal qualities   *soft:* agreeable   *great showing:* splendid appearance   *sellingly:* like a seller to a prospective buyer; in a fashion to do full justice. Most editors follow Q3 in reading *feelingly* = with exactitude, as he deserves.   103 *card or calendar:* chart or register, compendious guide   *gentry:* gentlemanly behavior   104–110 *the continent . . . part:* one who contains every quality   105 *perdition:* loss   106 *dozy:* make dizzy   107 *yaw:* keep deviating erratically from its course (said of a ship)   *neither:* for all that   *in respect of:* compared with   *in . . . extolment:* to praise him truly   108 *article:* scope (?) or importance (?)   *infusion:* essence, quality   *dearth:* scarceness   109 *make true diction:* speak truly   *his semblable:* his only likeness or equal   110 *who . . . him:* anyone else who tries to follow him   *umbrage:* shadow   112 *concernancy:* relevance   112–13 *more rawer breath:* words too crude to describe him properly

Horatio: Is't not possible to understand in another tongue? You will to't, sir,   115
   really.

Hamlet: What imports the nomination of this gentleman?

Osric: Of Laertes?

Horatio: His purse is empty already: all 's golden words are spent.

Hamlet: Of him, sir.   120

Osric: I know you are not ignorant—

Hamlet: I would you did, sir, yet, in faith, if you did, it would not much approve me. Well, sir?

Osric: You are not ignorant of what excellence Laertes is—

Hamlet: I dare not confess that, lest I should compare with him in excellence,   125
   but to know a man well were to know himself.

Osric: I mean, sir, for [his] weapon, but in the imputation laid on him by
   them, in his meed he's unfellow'd.

Hamlet: What's his weapon?

Osric: Rapier and dagger.   130

Hamlet: That's two of his weapons—but well.

Osric: The King, sir, hath wager'd with him six Barbary horses, against the
   which he has impawn'd, as I take it, six French rapiers and poniards, with
   their assigns, as girdle, [hangers], and so. Three of the carriages, in faith,
   are very dear to fancy, very responsive to the hilts, most delicate carriages,   135
   and of very liberal conceit.

Hamlet: What call you the carriages?

Horatio: I knew you must be edified by the margent ere you had done.

Osric: The [carriages], sir, are the hangers.

Hamlet: The phrase would be more germane to the matter if we could carry   140
   a cannon by our sides; I would it [might be] hangers till then. But on: six
   Barb'ry horses against six French swords, their assigns, and three liberal-
   conceited carriages; that's the French bet against the Danish. Why is this
   all [impawn'd, as] you call it?

Osric: The King, sir, hath laid, sir, that in a dozen passes between yourself and   145
   him, he shall not exceed you three hits; he hath laid on twelve for nine;
   and it would come to immediate trial, if your lordship would vouchsafe
   the answer.

Hamlet: How if I answer no?

---

115 *in another tongue:* when someone else is the speaker   115–16 *You . . . really:* you can do it if
you try   117 *nomination:* naming, mention   122–23 *approve:* commend   125 *compare . . .
excellence:*   seem   to   claim   the   same   degree   of   excellence   for   myself
126 *but:* The sense seems to require *for:* *himself:* oneself   127–28 *in . . . them:* in popular estimation   128 *meed:* merit   133 *impawn'd:* staked   134 *assigns:* appurtenances *hangers:*
straps on which the swords hang from the girdle *carriages:* properly, gun-carriages; here used affectedly in place of *hangers*   135 *fancy:* taste *very responsive to:* matching well   136 *liberal
conceit:* elegant design   138 *must . . . margent:* would require enlightenment from a marginal
note   145 *laid:* wagered   146 *he . . . hits:* Laertes must win by at least eight to four (if none
of the "passes" or bouts are draws), since at seven to five he would be only two up. *he . . . nine:*
Not satisfactorily explained despite much discussion. One suggestion is that Laertes has raised
the odds against himself by wagering that out of twelve bouts he will win nine.   148 *answer:*
encounter (as Hamlet's following quibble forces Osric to explain in his next speech)

Osric: I mean, my lord, the opposition of your person in trial.   150

Hamlet: Sir, I will walk here in the hall. If it please his Majesty, it is the breathing time of day with me. Let the foils be brought, the gentleman willing, and the King hold his purpose, I will win for him and I can; if not, I will gain nothing but my shame and the odd hits.

Osric: Shall I deliver you so?   155

Hamlet: To this effect, sir—after what flourish your nature will.

Osric: I commend my duty to your lordship.

Hamlet: Yours.   *[Exit Osric.]*   ['A] does well to commend it himself, there are no tongues else for 's turn.

Horatio: This lapwing runs away with the shell on his head.   160

Hamlet: 'A did [comply], sir, with his dug before 'a suck'd it. Thus has he, and many more of the same breed that I know the drossy age dotes on, only got the tune of the time, and out of an habit of encounter, a kind of [yesty] collection, which carries them through and through the most [profound] and [winnow'd] opinions, and do but blow them to their trial, the bubbles   165 are out.

(Enter a Lord.*)*

Lord: My lord, his Majesty commended him to you by young Osric, who brings back to him that you attend him in the hall. He sends to know if your pleasure hold to play with Laertes, or that you will take longer time.

Hamlet: I am constant to my purposes, they follow the King's pleasure. If his   170 fitness speaks, mine is ready; now or whensoever, provided I be so able as now.

Lord: The King and Queen and all are coming down.

Hamlet: In happy time.

Lord: The Queen desires you to use some gentle entertainment to Laertes   175 before you fall to play.

Hamlet: She well instructs me.   *[Exit Lord.]*

Horatio: You will lose, my lord.

Hamlet: I do not think so; since he went into France I have been in continual practice. I shall win at the odds. Thou wouldst not think how ill all's   180 here about my heart—but it is no matter.

Horatio: Nay, good my lord—

---

152 *breathing . . . me:* my usual hour for exercise   156 *after what flourish:* with whatever embellishment of language   157 *commend my duty:* offer my dutiful respects (but Hamlet picks up the phrase in the sense "praise my manner of bowing")   160 *lapwing:* a foolish bird which upon hatching was supposed to run with part of the eggshell still over its head. (Osric has put his hat on at last.)   161 *comply . . . dug:* bow politely to his mother's nipple   162 *drossy:* worthless   163 *tune . . . time:* fashionable ways of talk   *habit of encounter:* mode of social intercourse   *yesty:* yeasty, frothy   164 *collection:* anthology of fine phrases   165 *winnow'd:* sifted, choice   *opinions:* judgments   *blow . . . trial:* test them by blowing on them; make even the least demanding trial of them   166 *out:* blown away (?) or at an end, done for (?)   170–71 *If . . . ready:* If this is a good moment for him, it is for me also.   175 *gentle entertainment:* courteous greeting

Hamlet: It is but foolery, but it is such a kind of [gain-]giving, as would perhaps trouble a woman.

Horatio: If your mind dislike any thing, obey it. I will forestall their repair   185
hither, and say you are not fit.

Hamlet: Not a whit, we defy augury. There is special providence in the fall of
a sparrow. If it be [now], 'tis not to come; if it be not to come, it will be
now; if it be not now, yet it [will] come—the readiness is all. Since no
man, of aught he leaves, knows what is't to leave betimes, let be.   190

(*A table prepar'd, [and flagons of wine on it. Enter] Trumpets, Drums, and
Officers with cushions, foils, daggers;* King, Queen, Laertes, *[Osric,] and all
the State.*)

King: Come, Hamlet, come, and take this hand from me.

[The King *puts* Laertes' *hand into* Hamlet's.*]*

Hamlet: Give me your pardon, sir. I have done you wrong,
But pardon't as you are a gentleman.
This presence knows,
And you must needs have heard, how I am punish'd   195
With a sore distraction. What I have done
That might your nature, honor, and exception
Roughly awake, I here proclaim was madness.
Was't Hamlet wrong'd Laertes? Never Hamlet!
If Hamlet from himself be ta'en away,   200
And when he's not himself does wrong Laertes,
Then Hamlet does it not, Hamlet denies it.
Who does it then? His madness. If't be so,
Hamlet is of the faction that is wronged,
His madness is poor Hamlet's enemy.   205
[Sir, in this audience,]
Let my disclaiming from a purpos'd evil
Free me so far in your most generous thoughts,
That I have shot my arrow o'er the house
And hurt my brother.

Laertes: I am satisfied in nature,   210
Whose motive in this case should stir me most
To my revenge, but in my terms of honor
I stand aloof, and will no reconcilement
Till by some elder masters of known honor

183 *gain-giving:* misgiving   188–88 *special . . . sparrow:* See Matthew 10:29.   190 *of aught:*
whatever   190 *knows . . . betimes:* knows what is the best time to leave it   s.d. *State:* nobles
194 *presence:* assembled court   195 *punish'd:* afflicted   197 *exception:* objection   207
my . . . evil: my declaration that I intended no harm   208 *Free:* absolve   210 *in nature:* so far
as my personal feelings are concerned   212 *in . . . honor:* as a man governed by an established
code of honor

I have a voice and president of peace   215
To [keep] my name ungor'd. But [till] that time
I do receive your offer'd love like love,
And will not wrong it.
Hamlet: I embrace it freely,
And will this brothers' wager frankly play.
Give us the foils. [Come on.]
Laertes: Come, one for me.   220
Hamlet: I'll be your foil, Laertes; in mine ignorance
Your skill shall like a star i' th' darkest night
Stick fiery off indeed.
Laertes: You mock me, sir.
Hamlet: No, by this hand.
King: Give them the foils, young Osric. Cousin Hamlet,   225
You know the wager?
Hamlet: Very well, my lord.
Your Grace has laid the odds a' th' weaker side.
King: I do not fear it, I have seen you both;
But since he is [better'd], we have therefore odds.
Laertes: This is too heavy; let me see another.   230
Hamlet: This likes me well. These foils have all a length?   *[Prepare to play.]*
Osric: Ay, my good lord.
King: Set me the stoups of wine upon that table.
If Hamlet give the first or second hit,
Or quit in answer of the third exchange,   235
Let all the battlements their ord'nance fire.
The King shall drink to Hamlet's better breath,
And in the cup an [union] shall he throw,
Richer than that which four successive kings
In Denmark's crown have worn. Give me the cups,   240
And let the kettle to the trumpet speak,
The trumpet to the cannoneer without,
The cannons to the heavens, the heaven to earth,
"Now the King drinks to Hamlet." Come begin;

(trumpets the while)

And you, the judges, bear a wary eye.   245
Hamlet: Come on, sir.
Laertes: Come, my lord.

215–16 *have . . . ungor'd:* can secure an opinion backed by precedent that I can make peace with
you without injury to my reputation   219 *brothers':* amicable, as if between brothers   *frankly:*
freely, without constraint   221 *foil:* thin sheet of metal placed behind a jewel to set it off
222 *Stick . . . off:* blaze out in contrast   227 *laid the odds:* wagered a higher stake (horses to
rapiers)   229 *is better'd:* has perfected his skill   *odds:* the arrangement that Laertes must take
more bouts than Hamlet to win   231 *likes:* pleases   *a length:* the same length   233 *stoups:*
tankards   235 *quit . . . exchange:* pays back wins by Laertes in the first and second bouts by taking the third   238 *union:* an especially fine pearl   241 *kettle:* kettle-drum

[They play and Hamlet *scores a hit.]*

Hamlet: One.
Laertes: No.
Hamlet: Judgment.
Osric: A hit, a very palpable hit.
Laertes: Well, again.
King: Stay, give me drink. Hamlet, this pearl is thine,
　　Here's to thy health! Give him the cup.

(Drum, trumpets [sound] flourish. A piece goes off [within].)

Hamlet: I'll play this bout first, set it by a while.　　　　　　　250
　　Come.　*[They play again.]*　　Another hit; what say you?
Laertes: [A touch, a touch,] ˙I do confess't.
King: Our son shall win.
Queen: He's fat, and scant of breath.
　　Here, Hamlet, take my napkin, rub thy brows.
　　The Queen carouses to thy fortune, Hamlet.　　　　　　　255
Hamlet: Good madam!
King: Gertrude, do not drink.
Queen: I will, my lord, I pray you pardon me.
King *[aside]*: It is the pois'ned cup, it is too late.
Hamlet: I dare not drink yet, madam; by and by.
Queen: Come, let me wipe thy face.　　　　　　　　　　　　260
Laertes: My lord, I'll hit him now.
King: I do not think't.
Laertes *[aside]*: And yet it is almost against my conscience.
Hamlet: Come, for the third, Laertes, you do but dally.
　　I pray you pass with your best violence;
　　I am sure you make a wanton of me.　　　　　　　　　　265
Laertes: Say you so? Come on.　*[They play.]*
Osric: Nothing, neither way.
Laertes: Have at you now!

[Laertes wounds Hamlet; *then, in scuffling, they change rapiers.]*

King: Part them, they are incens'd.
Hamlet: Nay, come again.

[Hamlet wounds Laertes. *The* Queen *falls.]*

Osric: Look to the Queen there ho!
Horatio: They bleed on both sides. How is it, my lord?　　　　270
Osric: How is't, Laertes?
Laertes: Why, as a woodcock to mine own springe, Osric:
　　I am justly kill'd with mine own treachery.

---

253 *fat:* sweaty　　255 *carouses:* drinks a toast　　265 *make . . . me:* are holding back in order to
let me win, as one does with a spoiled child (*wanton*)　　272 *springe:* snare

Hamlet: How does the Queen?
King: She sounds to see them bleed.
Queen: No, no, the drink, the drink—O my dear Hamlet—   275
     The drink, the drink! I am pois'ned.   *[Dies.]*
Hamlet: O villainy! Ho, let the door be lock'd!
     Treachery! Seek it out.
Laertes: It is here, Hamlet. [Hamlet,] thou art slain.
     No med'cine in the world can do thee good;   280
     In thee there is not half an hour's life.
     The treacherous instrument is in [thy] hand,
     Unbated and envenom'd. The foul practice
     Hath turn'd itself on me. Lo here I lie,
     Never to rise again. Thy mother's pois'ned.   285
     I can no more—the King, the King's to blame.
Hamlet: The point envenom'd too!
     Then, venom, to thy work.   *[hurts the King]*
All: Treason! treason!
King: O, yet defend me, friends, I am but hurt.   290
Hamlet: Here, thou incestious, [murd'rous], damned Dane,
     Drink [off] this potion! Is [thy union] here?
     Follow my mother!   *[King dies.]*
Laertes: He is justly served,
     It is a poison temper'd by himself.
     Exchange forgiveness with me, noble Hamlet.   295
     Mine and my father's death come not upon thee,
     Nor thine on me!   *[dies]*
Hamlet: Heaven make thee free of it! I follow thee.
     I am dead, Horatio. Wretched queen, adieu!
     You that look pale, and tremble at this chance,   300
     That are but mutes or audience to this act,
     Had I but time—as this fell sergeant, Death,
     Is strict in his arrest—O, I could tell you—
     But let it be. Horatio, I am dead,
     Thou livest. Report me and my cause aright   305
     To the unsatisfied.
Horatio: Never believe it;
     I am more an antique Roman than a Dane.
     Here's yet some liquor left.
Hamlet: As th' art a man,
     Give me the cup. Let go! By heaven, I'll ha't!
     O God, Horatio, what a wounded name,   310
     Things standing thus unknown, shall I leave behind me!

------

274 *sounds:* swoons   283 *Unbated:* not blunted   *foul practice:* vile plot   s.d. *hurts:* wounds
294 *temper'd:* mixed   298 *make thee free:* absolve you   301 *mutes or audience:* silent spectators   302 *fell:* cruel   *sergeant:* sheriff's officer   307 *antique Roman:* one who will commit
suicide on such an occasion

If thou didst ever hold me in thy heart,
Absent thee from felicity a while,
And in this harsh world draw thy breath in pain
To tell my story.   *(a march afar off [and a shot within])*
                              What warlike noise is this?   315

[Osric goes to the door and returns.]

Osric: Young Fortinbras, with conquest come from Poland,
    To th' embassadors of England gives
    This warlike volley.
Hamlet: O, I die, Horatio,
    The potent poison quite o'er-crows my spirit.
    I cannot live to hear the news from England,   320
    But I do prophesy th' election lights
    On Fortinbras, he has my dying voice.
    So tell him, with th' occurrents more and less
    Which have solicited—the rest is silence.   *[dies]*
Horatio: Now cracks a noble heart. Good night, sweet prince,   325
    And flights of angels sing thee to thy rest!

[march within]

Why does the drum come hither?

(Enter Fortinbras *with the* [English] *Embassadors, [with Drum, Colors,
and* Attendants*].)*

Fortinbras: Where is this sight?
Horatio: What is it you would see?
    If aught of woe or wonder, cease your search.
Fortinbras: This quarry cries on havoc. O proud death,   330
    What feast is toward in thine eternal cell,
    That thou so many princes at a shot
    So bloodily hast strook?
[1.] Embassador: The sight is dismal,
    And our affairs from England come too late.
    The ears are senseless that should give us hearing,   335
    To tell him his commandment is fulfill'd,
    That Rosencrantz and Guildenstern are dead.
    Where should we have our thanks?
Horatio: Not from his mouth,
    Had it th' ability of life to thank you.
    He never gave commandement for their death.   340
    But since so jump upon this bloody question,

---

319 *o'er-crows:* triumphs over (a term derived from cockfighting)   *spirit:* vital energy   322
voice: vote   323 *occurrents:* occurrences   324 *solicited:* instigated   330 *This . . . havoc:* this
heap of corpses proclaims a massacre   331 *toward:* in preparation   338 *his:* the king's
341 *jump:* precisely, pat   *question:* matter

You from the Polack wars, and you from England,
Are here arrived, give order that these bodies
High on a stage be placed to the view,
And let me speak to [th'] yet unknowing world   345
How these things came about. So shall you hear
Of carnal, bloody, and unnatural acts,
Of accidental judgments, casual slaughters,
Of deaths put on by cunning and [forc'd] cause,
And in this upshot, purposes mistook   350
Fall'n on th' inventors' heads: all this can I
Truly deliver.
Fortinbras: Let us haste to hear it,
And call the noblest to the audience.
For me, with sorrow I embrace my fortune.
I have some rights, of memory in this kingdom,   355
Which now to claim my vantage doth invite me.
Horatio: Of that I shall have also cause to speak,
And from his mouth whose voice will draw [on] more.
But let this same be presently perform'd
Even while men's minds are wild, lest more mischance   360
On plots and errors happen.
Fortinbras: Let four captains
Bear Hamlet like a soldier to the stage,
For he was likely, had he been put on,
To have prov'd most royal; and for his passage,
The soldiers' music and the rite of war   365
Speak loudly for him.
Take up the bodies. Such a sight as this
Becomes the field, but here shows much amiss.
Go bid the soldiers shoot.

(Exeunt [marching; after the which a peal of ordinance are shot off].)

TOPICS FOR CRITICAL THINKING

1. As the play begins, Barnardo and Francisco are on guard. Why? Why is this important to the play? Imagine the play in performance and the several ways in
which the first line—Barnardo's question "Who's there?" —might be delivered. Is
he frightened? Cold and tired? Authoritative and aggressive? What effect might
such rendering of the first scene have on the mood of the drama and our understanding of the state of Denmark?

---

344 *stage:* platform   348 *judgments:* retributions   *casual:* happening by chance   349 *put on:*
instigated   355 *of memory:* unforgotten   356 *my vantage:* my opportune presence at a moment when the throne is empty   358 *his . . . more:* the mouth of one (Hamlet) whose vote will
induce others to support your claim   359 *presently:* at once   360 *wild:* distraught
363 *put on:* put to the test (by becoming king)   364 *passage:* death   368 *Becomes . . . amiss:*
befits the battlefield, but appears very much out of place here

2. Remembering that plays like *Hamlet* are also poetic, which images developed in Act One are repeated and grow in importance throughout the action? Likely candidates might include the metaphor of Norway as an "unweeded garden," Hamlet's display of grief as "unmanly," and the dead King Hamlet as Hyperion.

3. Read Hamlet's speech in Act One in which he grapples with his mother's hasty marriage to Claudius (1.2.129–159). Exactly how long *did* Gertrude wait before marrying him? What might we infer about Hamlet's muddled exposition of this expanse of time?

4. In the same speech, Hamlet refers to his mother as a "beast" that lacks the "discourse of reason." What exactly does "reason" mean in *Hamlet*?

5. Characterize Laertes' advice to his sister Ophelia in Act One (1.3. 11–45). What does it suggest about his opinion of his sister? More broadly, *Hamlet* is a play replete with scenes of one character giving another advice. Is the advice usually worth heeding? Do women get different advice than men receive?

6. How might we account for the betrayal of Hamlet by his old friends Rosencrantz and Guildenstern? What is their motive insofar as their old friend is concerned?

7. Examine "The Mouse-trap" or play within the play in Act Three, scene two. Why does Hamlet choose a play to expose his uncle? What role does the Player Queen have in the play? How is Hamlet's commentary to Ophelia relevant to the action of "The Mouse-trap"?

8. In Act Four, scene four, Hamlet calls himself a "coward." Is this a fair indictment?

9. Review Ophelia's distracted appearance at court in Act Four, scene five. Of what significance are the lyrics she sings? How do they relate to other interchanges earlier in the play?

10. Consider the clown's appearance in Act Five. Since this scene does little to further the plot or develop main characters, why is it included? What function does it serve?

TOPICS FOR CRITICAL WRITING

1. One of the several perennial questions about *Hamlet* concerns the reasons for his inaction. Why does he delay in exacting his revenge against Claudius? How do Hamlet's soliloquies, especially those in 2.2, 3.4, and 4.4, help answer this question? What motives do they reveal? Which of these speeches seems the most revealing in explaining Hamlet's delay?

2. If early psychoanalytic critics had much to say about Hamlet's unconscious motivation, they had little to say about Gertrude's. What motive does she have for marrying Claudius? Is she, for example, as the Ghost describes her in Act One, scene five, "seeming virtuous"? Of what is she guilty, if anything?

3. Compare one specific scene from two different productions of *Hamlet*, the "To be or not to be" soliloquy, for example. What differences in staging and interpretation distinguish these two versions? How do they affect your understanding of the entire play?

Critical Perspective: On *Hamlet* as a Political Drama

"The most common interpretation of tragedy is that it is an action in which the hero is destroyed. This fact is seen as irreparable. At a simple level this is so obviously true that the formula usually gets little further examination. But it is of course still an interpretation, and a partial one. If attention is concentrated on the hero alone, such an interpretation naturally follows. We have been very aware of the kind of reading which we can describe as *Hamlet* without the Prince, but we have been almost totally unaware of the opposite and equally erroneous reading of the Prince of Denmark without the State of Denmark. It is this unity that we must now restore."

—Raymond Williams, *Modern Tragedy* (1966)

Critical Perspective: Toward a Feminist Reading of *Hamlet*

"For most critics of Shakespeare, Ophelia has been an insignificant minor character in the play, touching in her weakness and madness but chiefly interesting, of course, in what she tells us about Hamlet. And while female readers of Shakespeare have often attempted to champion Ophelia, even feminist critics have done so with a certain embarrassment. . . .

"Yet when feminist criticism allows Ophelia to upstage Hamlet, it also brings to the foreground the issues in an ongoing theoretical debate about the cultural links between femininity, female sexuality, insanity, and representation. Though she is neglected in criticism, Ophelia is probably the most frequently illustrated and cited of Shakespeare's heroines. . . . Why has she been such a potent and obsessive figure in our cultural mythology? . . . What is our responsibility towards her as character and woman?"

—Elaine Showalter, "Representing Ophelia: Women, Madness, and the Responsibilities of Feminist Criticism" (1985)

Critical Perspective: On Shakespeare's Enduring Presence in Our Culture

"William Shakespeare haunts English-speaking culture like the ghost of Hamlet's father, forever accusing us . . . of failing to rise to his own formidable standard of literary achievement. Shakespeare troubles our collective imagination in other, more complex ways as well. Our greatest writer is our greatest enigma, a historical personage about whom less is known but more has been speculated than virtually any other figure in Western literary history."

—Helen Sword, *Ghostwriting Modernism* (2002)

The Tempest

In many formal respects, *The Tempest* (1611) resembles earlier comedies like *A Midsummer Night's Dream* (1595) and, especially, *Twelfth Night* (1600), which also begins with a shipwreck and the adventures of characters newly arrived in a strange place. But it is also significantly different, so much so that influential editors of Shakespeare Alfred Harbage and G. Blakemore Evans regard *The Tempest* as a **romance,** a kind of play popular on the early seventeenth-century stage that, among other things, bordered on the seriousness of tragedy even as its central conflicts were resolved happily. Shakespeare wrote a number of these plays between 1608 and the end of his career as a working playwright. *The Tempest* has proved, by far, the most enduringly celebrated of these.

Much like Shakespeare's earlier comedies, *The Tempest* concludes with a familial reconciliation and the promised union of two attractive young lovers, Ferdinand and Miranda. The daughter of banished Milanese Duke Prospero, Miranda has spent most of her life on an enchanted island with only her father, the native Caliban, and spirits like Ariel to keep her company. Thus, in Act Three when Ferdinand flatters her as "So perfect and so peerless," Miranda is unable to comprehend the extent of his compliment. "I do not know / One of my sex," she responds, "no woman's face remember" (3.1.49–50). Yet, within moments of seeing Ferdinand for the first time, she has little difficulty appreciating *his* beauty: "I might call him / A thing divine, for nothing natural / I ever saw so noble" (1.2.418–420). Ferdinand, son of Alonso King of Naples, is a perfect match for Miranda. And, after Prospero has tested the young man's character, he announces his intention in the final scene to travel to Naples to see "the nuptial / Of these our dear-belov'd solemnized" (5.1.308–309). Like *A Midsummer Night's Dream* and such later plays as *The Winter's Tale* (1610–1611), *The Tempest* concerns the father-daughter relationship and, ultimately, the giving of the daughter in marriage. Insofar as these same conflicts and characters surface in romantic comedy—and because the play ends in a manner consistent with a world of festivity and communal celebration—*The Tempest* is a variety of romantic comedy.

But the so-called romances or "late comedies"—*Pericles, Cymbeline, The Winter's Tale, The Tempest,* and *Two Noble Kinsmen,* Shakespeare's collaboration with John Fletcher—also include severe emotional tests, trials of character, and on occasion death. By comparison to the ordeals Pericles experiences or the sixteen-year period in which Leontes in *The Winter's Tale* is both separated from his daughter and believes his wife to be dead, Ferdinand's trials seem slight: He is forced to haul wood and provoked with other "vexations" so as to prove himself worthy of Miranda's hand. More so than Ferdinand, characters in these later plays, to echo the epilogue of *Pericles* (1608), are frequently "assailed with fortune fierce and keen." This assault of fortune prominently includes Antigonus's death in *The Winter's Tale,* a turn of events that wrenches the play closer to the events of tragic drama. Emphasizing such moments, Harbage describes these later plays as comedies that, paradoxically, share "affinities" with tragedies, and alludes to Shakespeare's sometime collaborator in making the point. In describing one of his own works, John Fletcher observed that it "wants deaths, which is enough to make it no tragedy, yet brings some near it, which is enough to make it no comedy."

To many readers, especially those of our own time, *The Tempest* is "no comedy" for more political and ideological reasons. On a political level, for

example, one far removed from the infatuation of young lovers (at times referred to as "Prospero's play"), *The Tempest* concerns failed governance, conspiracy, and attempted assassination. In Act Two, Ariel disrupts Antonio's and
Sebastian's plans to murder Alonso, the King of Naples, which would allow
Sebastian, his brother, to usurp the throne (a parallel to Claudius's regicide in
Hamlet). Gonzalo, old friend of Prospero and spokesman for a reformed, idealized political state, would also have been murdered had Ariel not inter-
vened. This political, potentially tragic dimension—and, of course, the
magical dimension represented by Ariel—seems always present.

But there is more. Much recent critical attention has not so much focused
on Prospero as father or politician but as colonizer, as Caliban's "master." To
recall José David Saldívar's distinction, it is "Caliban's play" that has perhaps
most intrigued contemporary critics. For contemporary postcolonial critics
like Saldívar, Peter Brown, and Ania Loomba, *The Tempest* emerges from a
context of British colonialism and of its representations of a colonized
"Other" like Caliban. Among the sources Shakespeare used are accounts of
British conquest of the New World and what would later be termed the
"Third World": India, America, even Ireland, which in the early years of the
seventeenth century was subject to invasion and colonization by supporters of
James the First. Several pamphlets published in 1610 gave accounts of a shipwreck and sailors landing safely on Bermuda. Another published by the Virginia Company entitled *The True Declaration of the Estate of the Colony in
Virginia* detailed British colonization of America. And throughout Shakespeare's career, the relationship between England and Ireland led to strong
anti-Irish prejudice. (Indeed, as far back as The Statutes of Kilkenny in 1366,
the English view of Ireland was that, while it might be settled, the country's
pagan customs, clothing, and language should not be adopted by settlers because they would contaminate the purity of Englishness.)

This denigrative representation of the colonized subject has attracted
considerable attention. In the play's last scene, for example, one which promises a political union between Milan and Naples through marriage, the
drunken Stephano and Trinculo appear with Caliban, of whom Prospero says,
"this thing of darkness I / Acknowledge mine" (5.1.276–277). This "thing,"
this native inhabitant of the island, languishes under Prospero's rule. From
Prospero's perspective, Caliban is a "freckled whelp . . . not honor'd with / A
human shape" (1.2.283–284); he is a "poisonous" and ungrateful "slave, who
never / Yields us kind answer" (1.2.308–309); and, most important, he is the
beast who sought to "violate" Miranda's honor. Echoing her father, Miranda
reminds Caliban that she once taught him her language and pitied him; now,
she believes that "any print of goodness wilt not take" on him because he is
"capable of all ill!" (1.2.352–353). Responding to Prospero's allegation, Caliban admits that had he not been prevented from doing so, he would have
"peopled" the isle with more Calibans.

For Ania Loomba, both the accusation of rape and Caliban's admission fit
too neatly with the stereotype or myth of the black rapist who harbors within
him a "peculiar lust for white womanhood" (certainly one myth that underlies
several remarks in *Othello*). Moreover, when considering Caliban's relation-

ship to his mother, the witch Sycorax, Loomba argues that "we must read Caliban's rapacity against Sycorax's licentious black femininity and the passive purity of Miranda," whose own desire corroborates the rule of her father. For Paul Brown, Prospero's ability to govern his small colony is in part dependent on his ability to legislate and contain the desire of his subjects. This ability, as is often the case in the colonial enterprise, includes both "civilizing" instruction (in religion and language) and, when necessary, sharper repressive force (Prospero's continual physical torment of Caliban). In sum, these critics regard *The Tempest* as a historical artifact produced within a context of colonization, a political project the drama seems to legitimize. Much of the play—the depiction of Caliban as bestial and rapacious, for instance—serves finally to legitimate Prospero's rule and, in so doing, to justify European rule over "uncivilized" colonial properties.

In these ways, as Shakespeare's career as a playwright was coming to an end, plays like *The Tempest* both looked back to romantic comedy and popular romance narratives but also gazed forward to a new world and the peoples that it might include. That is, elements of the comic formula evident in *A Midsummer Night's Dream*, *As You Like It*, and even *Twelfth Night*, one of the later and in some ways more problematic of the comedies, are much in evidence in *The Tempest*. Young lovers find each other; parental or societal objections to their union are neutralized; low-comic buffoons entertain us as they find their niches in the plot. At the same time, however, the spirit of festivity with which many of the early plays concludes, if not absent, is subdued in the romances. The implications of the dramatic action seem more serious; the issues, more troublesome; and some of the consequences of an expanding world, less likely to be resolved by the application of a little magic here, a little clemency there. In these ways, Shakespeare, the man "for all ages," was also very much a man of his own age, inevitably confronting the important issues of his time. And of our own time as well.

The Tempest   *(1611)*

NAMES OF THE ACTORS

Alonso, King of Naples
Sebastian, his brother
Prospero, the right Duke of Milan
Antonio, his brother, the usurping Duke of Milan
Ferdinand, son to the King of Naples
Gonzalo, an honest old councillor
Adrian, and *Francisco*, Lords
Caliban, a salvage and deformed slave
Trinculo, a jester
Stephano, a drunken butler

Names of the Actors   *salvage:* savage

Master of a Ship
Boatswain
Mariners
Miranda, daughter to Prospero
Ariel, an airy spirit
Iris
Ceres
Juno } spirits
Nymphs
Reapers
[Other *Spirits* attending on Prospero]

The Scene: [A ship at sea;] an uninhabited island

ACT I

SCENE I

A tempestuous noise of thunder and lightning heard.

Enter a Ship-Master *and a* Boatswain.

Mast.: Boatswain!

Boats.: Here, master; what cheer?

Mast.: Good; speak to th' mariners. Fall to't, yarely, or we run ourselves aground. Bestir, bestir. *Exit.*

Enter Mariners

Boats.: Heigh, my hearts! cheerly, cheerly, my hearts! yare, yare! Take in the 5 topsail. Tend to th' master's whistle.—Blow till thou burst thy wind, if room enough!

Enter Alonso, Sebastian, Antonio, Ferdinando, Gonzalo, *and others.*

Alon.: Good boatswain, have care. Where's the master? Play the men.

Boats.: I pray now keep below.

Ant.: Where is the master, bos'n? 10

Boats.: Do you not hear him? You mar our labor. Keep your cabins; you do assist the storm.

Gon.: Nay, good, be patient.

Boats.: When the sea is. Hence! What cares these roarers for the name of king? To cabin! silence! trouble us not. 15

Gon.: Good, yet remember whom thou hast aboard.

_____

I.i. *Location:* on a ship at sea   3 *Good:* an acknowledgment of the boatswain's reply. The punctuation differentiates this from the *good* in line 13, which means "good fellow."   3 *yarely:* smartly, nimbly   6 *Tend:* attend   6–8 *Blow . . . enough:* He addresses the storm. *if room enough:* so long as we have sea-room, i.e. space in which to maneuver without going aground   8 *Play:* ply, urge on (?)   14 *roarers:* (1) turbulent waves; (2) rowdies

Boats.: None that I more love than myself. You are a councillor; if you can command these elements to silence, and work the peace of the present, we will not hand a rope more. Use your authority. If you cannot, give thanks you have liv'd so long, and make yourself ready in your cabin for 20 the mischance of the hour, if it so hap.—Cheerly, good hearts!—Out of our way, I say. *Exit.*

Gon.: I have great comfort from this fellow. Methinks he hath no drowning mark upon him, his complexion is perfect gallows. Stand fast, good Fate, to his hanging, make the rope of his destiny our cable, for our own doth little 25 advantage. If he be not born to be hang'd, our case is miserable. *Exeunt.*

Enter Boatswain.

Boats.: Down with the topmast! yare! lower, lower! bring her to try with main-course. (*A cry within.*) A plague upon this howling! they are louder than the weather, or our office.

Enter Sebastian, Antonio, *and* Gonzalo.

Yet again? What do you here? Shall we give o'er and drown? Have you a 30 mind to sink?

Seb.: A pox o' your throat, you bawling, blasphemous, incharitable dog!

Boats.: Work you, then.

Ant.: Hang, cur! hang, you whoreson, insolent noisemaker! We are less afraid to be drown'd than thou art. 35

Gon.: I'll warrant him for drowning, though the ship were no stronger than a nutshell, and as leaky as an unstanch'd wench.

Boats.: Lay her a-hold, a-hold! Set her two courses off to sea again! Lay her off.

Enter Mariners *wet.*

Mariners.: All lost! To prayers, to prayers! All lost! *[Exeunt.]* 40

Boats.: What, must our mouths be cold?

Gon.: The King and Prince at prayers, let's assist them,
For our case is as theirs.

Seb.:   I am out of patience.

Ant.: We are merely cheated of our lives by drunkards.
This wide-chopp'd rascal—would thou mightst lie drowning 45
The washing of ten tides!

Gon.:   He'll be hang'd yet,

---

17 *councillor:* member of the King's council   18 *the present:* the present occasion; but *present* may be a mistake for *presence,* i.e. the King's presence or presence chamber   23–24 *Methinks . . . gallows:* Alluding to the proverb "He that is born to be hanged need fear no drowning." 24 *complexion:* appearance (as reflecting his temperament)   25–26 *make . . . advantage:* make the rope that will hang him our anchor chain, since our actual one now does us little good 28 *bring . . . main-course:* keep her close to the wind by means of the mainsail   29 *office:* duties 30 *give o'er:* give up   36 *warrant him for:* guarantee him against   38 *a-hold:* a-hull, close to the wind   38 *Set . . . sea:* i.e. set her mainsail and foresail so as to get her out to sea   44 *merely:* utterly   45 *wide-chopp'd:* wide-jawed   45 *ten tides:* Pirates were hanged on shore and left until three tides had washed over them

Though every drop of water swear against it,
And gape at wid'st to glut him.
A confused noise within: "Mercy on us!"—
"We split, we split!"—"Farewell, my wife and children!"—   50
"Farewell, brother!"—"We split, we split, we split!"   *[Exit* Boatswain.*]*
Ant.: Let's all sink wi' th' King.
Seb.: Let's take leave of him.   *Exit [with* Antonio*].*
Gon.: Now would I give a thousand furlongs of sea for an acre of barren
   ground, long heath, brown [furze], any thing. The wills above be done! 55
   but I would fain die a dry death.   *Exit.*

Scene II

Enter Prospero *and* Miranda.

Mir.: If by your art, my dearest father, you have
   Put the wild waters in this roar, allay them.
   The sky it seems would pour down stinking pitch,
   But that the sea, mounting to th' welkin's cheek,
   Dashes the fire out. O! I have suffered   5
   With those that I saw suffer. A brave vessel
   (Who had, no doubt, some noble creature in her)
   Dash'd all to pieces! O, the cry did knock
   Against my very heart. Poor souls, they perish'd.
   Had I been any God of power, I would   10
   Have sunk the sea within the earth or ere
   It should the good ship so have swallow'd, and
   The fraughting souls within her.
Pros.:   Be collected,
   No more amazement. Tell your piteous heart
   There's no harm done.
Mir.:   O woe the day!
Pros.:   No harm: 15
   I have done nothing, but in care of thee
   (Of thee, my dear one, thee my daughter), who
   Art ignorant of what thou art, nought knowing
   Of whence I am, nor that I am more better
   Than Prospero, master of a full poor cell,   20
   And thy no greater father.
Mir.:   More to know

---

48 *gape . . . him:* open its mouth to the widest to gulp him down   55 *heath . . . furze:*
heather . . . gorse (plants that grow in poor soil)   56 *fain:* gladly   I.ii. Location: an island
before Prospero's cell   1 *art:* magic   4 *welkin's:* sky's   *cheek:* (1) face; (2) side of a grate
6 *brave:* splendid   11 *or ere:* before   13 *fraughting:* forming the cargo   *collected:* composed
14 *amazement:* terror   *piteous:* pitying   19 *more better:* of higher rank (common Elizabethan
double comparative)   20 *full:* very   21 *no greater:* i.e. of no loftier position than is implied
by his "full poor cell"

Did never meddle with my thoughts.
Pros.:   'Tis time
    I should inform thee farther. Lend thy hand,
    And pluck my magic garment from me. So,   *[Lays down his mantle.]*
    Lie there, my art. Wipe thou thine eyes, have comfort.   25
    The direful spectacle of the wrack, which touch'd
    The very virtue of compassion in thee,
    I have with such provision in mine art
    So safely ordered that there is no soul—
    No, not so much perdition as an hair   30
    Betid to any creature in the vessel
    Which thou heard'st cry, which thou saw'st sink. Sit down,
    For thou must now know farther.
Mir.:   You have often
    Begun to tell me what I am, but stopp'd
    And left me to a bootless inquisition,   35
    Concluding, "Stay: not yet."
Pros.:   The hour's now come,
    The very minute bids thee ope thine ear.
    Obey, and be attentive. Canst thou remember
    A time before we came unto this cell?
    I do not think thou canst, for then thou wast not   40
    Out three years old.
Mir.:   Certainly, sir, I can.
Pros.: By what? by any other house, or person?
    Of any thing the image, tell me, that
    Hath kept with thy remembrance.
Mir.:   'Tis far off;
    And rather like a dream than an assurance   45
    That my remembrance warrants. Had I not
    Four, or five, women once that tended me?
Pros.: Thou hadst; and more, Miranda. But how is it
    That this lives in thy mind? What seest thou else
    In the dark backward and abysm of time?   50
    If thou rememb'rest aught ere thou cam'st here,
    How thou cam'st here, thou mayst.
Mir.:   But that I do not.
Pros.: Twelve year since, Miranda, twelve year since,
    Thy father was the Duke of Milan, and
    A prince of power.
Mir.:   Sir, are not you my father?   55

---

22 *meddle with*: mingle with, enter   26 *wrack*: shipwreck   27 *virtue*: essence   28 *provision*: foresight   29 *soul—*: The sentence changes its course in what follows, but the sense is plain.   30 *perdition*: loss   31 *Betid*: happened   35 *bootless inquisition*: useless inquiry   38 *Obey*: i.e. listen   41 *Out*: fully   45 *assurance*: certainty   46 *remembrance warrants*: memory guarantees   50 *backward . . . time*: abyss of the past

Pros.: Thy mother was a piece of virtue, and
        She said thou wast my daughter; and thy father
        Was Duke of Milan, and his only heir
        And princess no worse issued.
Mir.:   O the heavens,
        What foul play had we that we came from thence?   60
        Or blessed was't we did?
Pros.:   Both, both, my girl.
        By foul play (as thou say'st) were we heav'd thence,
        But blessedly holp hither.
Mir.:   O, my heart bleeds
        To think o' th' teen that I have turn'd you to,
        Which is from my remembrance! Please you, farther.   65
Pros.: My brother and thy uncle, call'd Antonio—
        I pray thee mark me—that a brother should
        Be so perfidious!—he whom next thyself
        Of all the world I lov'd, and to him put
        The manage of my state, as at that time   70
        Through all the signories it was the first,
        And Prospero the prime duke, being so reputed
        In dignity, and for the liberal arts
        Without a parallel; those being all my study,
        The government I cast upon my brother,   75
        And to my state grew stranger, being transported
        And rapt in secret studies. Thy false uncle—
        Dost thou attend me?
Mir.:   Sir, most heedfully.
Pros.: Being once perfected how to grant suits,
        How to deny them, who t' advance, and who   80
        To trash for overtopping, new created
        The creatures that were mine, I say, or chang'd 'em,
        Or else new form'd 'em; having both the key
        Of officer and office, set all hearts i' th' state
        To what tune pleas'd his ear, that now he was   85
        The ivy which had hid my princely trunk,
        And suck'd my verdure out on't. Thou attend'st not!
Mir.: O, good sir, I do.
Pros.:   I pray thee mark me.
        I, thus neglecting worldly ends, all dedicated
        To closeness and the bettering of my mind   90

---

56 *piece:* masterpiece   *virtue:* chastity   59 *no worse issued:* no less noble in birth   63 *blessedly holp:* providentially helped   64 *teen:* sorrow, trouble   *turn'd you to:* reminded you of   65 *from:* out of   71 *signories:* city states   72 *prime:* chief, first in rank   79 *perfected:* expert in   81 *trash for overtopping:* restrain from becoming too powerful. Two images are combined here: *trash* = check a hunting dog from going too fast; *overtopping* = growing too high.   82 *or:* either   83 *key:* (1) key to office; (2) tuning key   87 *verdure:* vigor, vitality   *on't:* of it   90 *closeness:* seclusion

With that which, but by being so retir'd,
O'er-priz'd all popular rate, in my false brother
Awak'd an evil nature, and my trust,
Like a good parent, did beget of him
A falsehood in its contrary, as great   95
As my trust was, which had indeed no limit,
A confidence sans bound. He being thus lorded,
Not only with what my revenue yielded,
But what my power might else exact—like one
Who having into truth, by telling of it,   100
Made such a sinner of his memory
To credit his own lie—he did believe
He was indeed the Duke, out o' th' substitution,
And executing th' outward face of royalty
With all prerogative. Hence his ambition growing—   105
Dost thou hear?
Mir.:   Your tale, sir, would cure deafness.
Pros.: To have no screen between this part he play'd
And him he play'd it for, he needs will be
Absolute Milan—me (poor man) my library
Was dukedom large enough: of temporal royalties   110
He thinks me now incapable; confederates
(So dry he was for sway) wi' th' King of Naples
To give him annual tribute, do him homage,
Subject his coronet to his crown, and bend
The dukedom, yet unbow'd (alas, poor Milan!)   115
To most ignoble stooping.
Mir.:   O the heavens!
Pros.: Mark his condition, and th' event, then tell me
If this might be a brother.
Mir.:   I should sin
To think but nobly of my grandmother.
Good wombs have borne bad sons.
Pros.:   Now the condition.   120
This King of Naples, being an enemy
To me inveterate, hearkens my brother's suit,
Which was, that he in lieu o' th' premises,
Of homage and I know not how much tribute,
Should presently extirpate me and mine   125

---

92 *O'er-priz'd . . . rate:* had greater worth than any vulgar evaluation would place upon it   94
good parent: That a good parent often bred a bad child was proverbial.   97 *sans:* without
lorded: i.e. established in a position of power   100 *into:* unto, against (*into truth* modifies *sinner*)
102 *To:* as to   103 *out:* as a result   107–8 *no . . . for:* i.e. no separation between acting as
Duke and being Duke   109 *Absolute Milan:* actual Duke of Milan   110 *temporal royalties:*
practical administration   111 *confederates:* makes alliance   112 *dry:* thirsty   117 *condition:* compact   *event:* outcome   123 *lieu premises:* return for the pledge   125 *presently extirpate:* immediately remove

Out of the dukedom, and confer fair Milan
With all the honors on my brother; whereon,
A treacherous army levied, one midnight
Fated to th' purpose, did Antonio open
The gates of Milan, and i' th' dead of darkness   130
The ministers for th' purpose hurried thence
Me and thy crying self.

Mir.:   Alack, for pity!
I, not rememb'ring how I cried out then,
Will cry it o'er again. It is a hint
That wrings mine eyes to't.   135

Pros.:   Hear a little further,
And then I'll bring thee to the present business
Which now's upon 's; without the which this story
Were most impertinent.

Mir.:   Wherefore did they not
That hour destroy us?

Pros.:   Well demanded, wench;
My tale provokes that question. Dear, they durst not,   140
So dear the love my people bore me; nor set
A mark so bloody on the business; but
With colors fairer painted their foul ends.
In few, they hurried us aboard a bark,
Bore us some leagues to sea, where they prepared   145
A rotten carcass of a butt, not rigg'd,
Nor tackle, sail, nor mast, the very rats
Instinctively have quit it. There they hoist us,
To cry to th' sea, that roar'd to us; to sigh
To th' winds, whose pity, sighing back again,   150
Did us but loving wrong.

Mir.:   Alack, what trouble
Was I then to you!

Pros.:   O, a cherubin
Thou wast that did preserve me. Thou didst smile,
Infused with a fortitude from heaven,
When I have deck'd the sea with drops full salt,   155
Under my burden groan'd, which rais'd in me
An undergoing stomach, to bear up
Against what should ensue.

Mir.:   How came we ashore?

---

131 *ministers:* agents   134 *hint:* occasion   135 *wrings:* (1) constrains; (2) extracts moisture
from   138 *impertinent:* irrelevant   143 *With . . . ends:* i.e. undertook to accomplish the
same end by less violent means   144 *In few:* in short   146 *butt:* tub   151 *Did . . . wrong:* i.e.
only added to our discomfort   155 *deck'd:* (1) adorned; (2) covered   156 *which:* i.e. Miranda's
smile   157 *undergoing stomach:* courage to endure

Pros.:　By Providence divine.
　　Some food we had, and some fresh water, that　　　　　　160
　　A noble Neapolitan, Gonzalo,
　　Out of his charity, who being then appointed
　　Master of this design, did give us, with
　　Rich garments, linens, stuffs, and necessaries,
　　Which since have steaded much; so of his gentleness,　　　165
　　Knowing I lov'd my books, he furnish'd me
　　From mine own library with volumes that
　　I prize above my dukedom.
Mir.:　　　　　　　　　　　　　Would I might
　　But ever see that man!
Pros.:　　　　　　　　　　Now I arise. *[Puts on his robe.]*
　　Sit still, and hear the last of our sea-sorrow:　　　　　170
　　Here in this island we arriv'd, and here
　　Have I, thy schoolmaster, made thee more profit
　　Than other princess' can, that have more time
　　For vainer hours, and tutors not so careful.
Mir.:　Heavens thank you for't! And now I pray you, sir,　　175
　　For still 'tis beating in my mind, your reason
　　For raising this sea-storm?
Pros.:　　　　　　　　　　Know thus far forth:
　　By accident most strange, bountiful Fortune
　　(Now my dear lady) hath mine enemies
　　Brought to this shore; and by my prescience　　　　　180
　　I find my zenith doth depend upon
　　A most auspicious star, whose influence
　　If now I court not, but omit, my fortunes
　　Will ever after droop. Here cease more questions.
　　Thou art inclin'd to sleep; 'tis a good dullness,　　　　185
　　And give it way. I know thou canst not choose. *[Miranda sleeps.]*
　　Come away, servant, come; I am ready now.
　　Approach, my Ariel. Come.

　　Enter Ariel.

Ari.:　All hail, great master, grave sir, hail! I come
　　To answer thy best pleasure; be't to fly,　　　　　　190
　　To swim, to dive into the fire, to ride
　　On the curl'd clouds. To thy strong bidding, task
　　Ariel, and all his quality.

---

165 *steaded:* been of use　*gentleness:* character proper to one of high birth and cultivation
167 *volumes:* i.e books of magic　172 *more profit:* profit more　173 *princess':* princesses
176 *beating:* working violently　179 *my dear lady:* i.e. favorable to me　181 *zenith:* height of
fortune　182 *influence:* power (astrological term)　183 *omit:* ignore　185 *good dullness:*
timely sleepiness　187 *Come away:* come here　193 *quality:* (1) skill; (2) cohorts, minor spirits under him

Pros.:   Hast thou, spirit,
Perform'd to point the tempest that I bade thee?
Ari.: To every article.   195
I boarded the King's ship; now on the beak,
Now in the waist, the deck, in every cabin,
I flam'd amazement. Sometime I'ld divide,
And burn in many places; on the topmast,
The yards and boresprit, would I flame distinctly,   200
Then meet and join. Jove's lightning, the precursors
O' th' dreadful thunder-claps, more momentary
And sight-outrunning were not; the fire and cracks
Of sulphurous roaring the most mighty Neptune
Seem to besiege, and make his bold waves tremble,   205
Yea, his dread trident shake.
Pros.:   My brave spirit!
Who was so firm, so constant, that this coil
Would not infect his reason?
Ari.:   Not a soul
But felt a fever of the mad, and play'd
Some tricks of desperation. All but mariners   210
Plunged in the foaming brine, and quit the vessel;
Then all afire with me, the King's son, Ferdinand,
With hair up-staring (then like reeds, not hair),
Was the first man that leapt; cried, "Hell is empty,
And all the devils are here."
Pros.:   Why, that's my spirit!   215
But was not this nigh shore?
Ari.:   Close by, my master.
Pros.: But are they, Ariel, safe?
Ari.:   Not a hair perish'd;
On their sustaining garments not a blemish,
But fresher than before; and, as thou bad'st me,
In troops I have dispers'd them 'bout the isle.   220
The King's son have I landed by himself,
Whom I left cooling of the air with sighs,
In an odd angle of the isle, and sitting,
His arms in this sad knot.
Pros.:   Of the King's ship,
The mariners, say how thou hast dispos'd,   225

---

194 *to point:* in detail   196 *beak:* prow   198 *flam'd amazement:* struck terror by appearing as the flamelike phenomenon called St. Elmo's fire or the corposant   200 *boresprit:* bowsprit *distinctly:* in separate places   206 *brave:* splendid   207 *coil:* uproar   209 *of the mad:* such as madmen have   212 *Then . . . me:* Many editors repunctuate lines 211–12 so as to make this phrase modify *vessel* rather than *son.*   213 *up-staring:* standing on end   218 *sustaining garments:* garments that bore them up in the water   224 *in . . . knot:* i.e. crossed thus (Ariel illustrates with a gesture) Crossed arms indicated melancholy.

And all the rest o' th' fleet.

Ari.:   Safely in harbor
Is the King's ship, in the deep nook, where once
Thou call'dst me up at midnight to fetch dew
From the still-vex'd Bermoothes, there she's hid;
The mariners all under hatches stowed,   230
Who, with a charm join'd to their suff'red labor,
I have left asleep; and for the rest o' th' fleet
(Which I dispers'd), they all have met again,
And are upon the Mediterranean float
Bound sadly home for Naples,   235
Supposing that they saw the King's ship wrack'd,
And his great person perish.

Pros.:   Ariel, thy charge
Exactly is perform'd; but there's more work.
What is the time o' th' day?

Ari.:   Past the mid season.

Pros.: At least two glasses. The time 'twixt six and now   240
Must by us both be spent most preciously.

Ari.: Is there more toil? Since thou dost give me pains,
Let me remember thee what thou hast promis'd,
Which is not yet perform'd me.

Pros.:   How now? moody?
What is't thou canst demand?

Ari.:   My liberty.   245

Pros.: Before the time be out? No more!

Ari.:   I prithee,
Remember I have done thee worthy service,
Told thee no lies, made thee no mistakings, serv'd
Without or grudge or grumblings. Thou did promise
To bate me a full year.   250

Pros.:   Dost thou forget
From what a torment I did free thee?

Ari.:   No.

Pros.: Thou dost; and think'st it much to tread the ooze
Of the salt deep,
To run upon the sharp wind of the north,
To do me business in the veins o' th' earth   255
When it is bak'd with frost.

Ari.:   I do not, sir.

Pros.: Thou liest, malignant thing! Hast thou forgot

---

227 *nook:* inlet, small bay   229 *still-vex'd Bermoothes:* always stormy Bermuda islands   231 *with*
a charm: by means of a magic spell   *their suff'red labor:* the labor they have endured   234 *float:*
flood, sea   239 *mid season:* noon   240 *glasses:* hourglasses   242 *pains:* duties, chores
243 *remember:* remind   250 *bate:* remit   252 *ooze:* mud at sea-bottom   255 *veins:* underground streams, which were thought to correspond to veins of the body   256 *bak'd:* hardened

The foul witch Sycorax, who with age and envy
Was grown into a hoop? Hast thou forgot her?

Ari.: No, sir.

Pros.:   Thou hast. Where was she born? Speak. Tell me.   260

Ari.: Sir, in Argier.

Pros.:   O, was she so? I must
Once in a month recount what thou hast been,
Which thou forget'st. This damn'd witch Sycorax,
For mischiefs manifold, and sorceries terrible
To enter human hearing, from Argier   265
Thou know'st was banish'd; for one thing she did
They would not take her life. Is not this true?

Ari.: Ay, sir.

Pros.: This blue-ey'd hag was hither brought with child,
And here was left by th' sailors. Thou, my slave,   270
As thou report'st thyself, was then her servant,
And for thou wast a spirit too delicate
To act her earthy and abhorr'd commands,
Refusing her grand hests, she did confine thee,
By help of her more potent ministers,   275
And in her most unmitigable rage,
Into a cloven pine, within which rift
Imprison'd, thou didst painfully remain
A dozen years; within which space she died,
And left thee there, where thou didst vent thy groans   280
As fast as mill-wheels strike. Then was this island
(Save for the son that [she] did litter here,
A freckled whelp, hag-born) not honor'd with
A human shape.

Ari.:   Yes—Caliban her son.

Pros.: Dull thing, I say so; he, that Caliban   285
Whom now I keep in service. Thou best know'st
What torment I did find thee in; thy groans
Did make wolves howl, and penetrate the breasts
Of ever-angry bears. It was a torment
To lay upon the damn'd, which Sycorax   290
Could not again undo. It was mine art,
When I arriv'd and heard thee, that made gape
The pine, and let thee out.

Ari.:   I thank thee, master.

Pros.: If thou more murmur'st, I will rend an oak
And peg thee in his knotty entrails till   295

---

258 *envy:* malice   261 *Argier:* Algiers   269 *blue-ey'd:* with dark circles around the eyes
272 *for:* because   274 *hests:* commands   281 *mill-wheels:* i.e. the clappers on mill-wheels
292 *gape:* open wide   295 *his:* its

Thou hast howl'd away twelve winters.

Ari.:   Pardon, master,
   I will be correspondent to command
   And do my spriting gently.

Pros.:   Do so; and after two days
   I will discharge thee.

Ari.:   That's my noble master!
   What shall I do? say what? what shall I do?   300

Pros.:   Go make thyself like a nymph o' th' sea; be subject
   To no sight but thine and mine, invisible
   To every eyeball else. Go take this shape
   And hither come in't. Go. Hence with diligence!   *Exit* [Ariel].

   Awake, dear heart, awake! Thou hast slept well,   305
   Awake!

Mir.:   The strangeness of your story put
   Heaviness in me.

Pros.:   Shake it off. Come on,
   We'll visit Caliban my slave, who never
   Yields us kind answer.

Mir.:   'Tis a villain, sir,
   I do not love to look on.

Pros.:   But as 'tis,   310
   We cannot miss him. He does make our fire,
   Fetch in our wood, and serves in offices
   That profit us. What ho! slave! Caliban!
   Thou earth, thou! speak.

Cal. (Within):   There's wood enough within.

Pros.:   Come forth, I say, there's other business for thee.   315
   Come, thou tortoise, when?

   Enter Ariel *like a water-nymph.*

   Fine apparition! My quaint Ariel,
   Hark in thine ear.

Ari.:   My lord, it shall be done.   *Exit.*

Pros.:   Thou poisonous slave, got by the devil himself
   Upon thy wicked dam, come forth!   320

   Enter Caliban.

Cal.:   As wicked dew as e'er my mother brush'd
   With raven's feather from unwholesome fen
   Drop on you both! A south-west blow on ye,
   And blister you all o'er!

---

297 *correspondent:* obedient   298 *do . . . gently:* perform my tasks as a spirit ungrudgingly
307 *Heaviness:* drowsiness   311 *miss:* do without   316 *when:* a common expression of impatience   s.d. *like:* in the shape of   317 *quaint:* clever, ingenious   321 *wicked:* harmful
323 *south-west:* southwest wind, thought to bring pestilence

Pros.: For this, be sure, to-night thou shalt have cramps,   325
    Side-stitches, that shall pen thy breath up; urchins
    Shall, for that vast of night that they may work,
    All exercise on thee; thou shalt be pinch'd
    As thick as honeycomb, each pinch more stinging
    Than bees that made 'em.   330
Cal.:   I must eat my dinner.
    This island's mine by Sycorax my mother,
    Which thou tak'st from me. When thou cam'st first,
    Thou strok'st me and made much of me, wouldst give me
    Water with berries in't, and teach me how
    To name the bigger light, and how the less,   335
    That burn by day and night; and then I lov'd thee
    And show'd thee all the qualities o' th' isle,
    The fresh springs, brine-pits, barren place and fertile.
    Curs'd be I that did so! All the charms
    Of Sycorax, toads, beetles, bats, light on you!   340
    For I am all the subjects that you have,
    Which first was mine own king; and here you sty me
    In this hard rock, whiles you do keep from me
    The rest o' th' island.
Pros.:   Thou most lying slave,
    Whom stripes may move, not kindness! I have us'd thee   345
    (Filth as thou art) with human care, and lodg'd thee
    In mine own cell, till thou didst seek to violate
    The honor of my child.
Cal.: O ho, O ho, would't had been done!
    Thou didst prevent me; I had peopled else   350
    This isle with Calibans.
Mir.:   Abhorred slave,
    Which any print of goodness wilt not take,
    Being capable of all ill! I pitied thee,
    Took pains to make thee speak, taught thee each hour
    One thing or other. When thou didst not, savage,   355
    Know thine own meaning, but wouldst gabble like
    A thing most brutish, I endow'd thy purposes
    With words that made them known. But thy vild race
    (Though thou didst learn) had that in't which good natures
    Could not abide to be with; therefore wast thou   360
    Deservedly confin'd into this rock,
    Who hadst deserv'd more than a prison.

---

326 *urchins:* hedgehogs; here, goblins in the shape of hedgehogs   327 *for . . . work:* during that
long and desolate period of darkness during which they are permitted to perform their mischief
It was thought that malignant spirits lost their power with the coming of day.   330 *'em:* i.e.
cells of the honeycomb   345 *stripes:* lashes   346 *human:* humane   351 *s.p. Mir.:* Some
editors make Prospero the speaker.   358 *vild:* vile   *race:* nature

Cal.: You taught me language, and my profit on't
    Is, I know how to curse. The red-plague rid you
    For learning me your language! 365

Pros.:   Hag-seed, hence!
    Fetch us in fuel; and be quick, thou 'rt best,
    To answer other business. Shrug'st thou, malice?
    If thou neglect'st, or dost unwillingly
    What I command, I'll rack thee with old cramps,
    Fill all thy bones with aches, make thee roar 370
    That beasts shall tremble at thy din.

Cal.:   No, pray thee.
    [Aside.] I must obey. His art is of such pow'r,
    It would control my dam's god, Setebos,
    And make a vassal of him.

Pros.:   So, slave, hence!   *Exit* Caliban.

Enter Ferdinand; *and* Ariel, *invisible*, playing and singing.

                Ariel['s] *Song.*

Come unto these yellow sands, 375
    And then take hands:
Curtsied when you have, and kiss'd,
    The wild waves whist:
Foot it featly here and there,
And, sweet sprites, [the burthen bear]. 380
Hark, hark!
    Burthen, dispersedly, [within].   Bow-wow.
The watch dogs bark!
    [Burthen, dispersedly, within.]   Bow-wow.
Hark, hark! I hear 385
The strain of strutting chanticleer:
    Cry [within].   Cock-a-diddle-dow.

Fer.: Where should this music be? I' th' air, or th' earth?
    It sounds no more; and sure it waits upon
    Some god o' th' island. Sitting on a bank, 390
    Weeping again the King my father's wrack,
    This music crept by me upon the waters,
    Allaying both their fury and my passion
    With its sweet air; thence I have follow'd it,
    Or it hath drawn me rather. But 'tis gone. 395
    No, it begins again.

---

364 *red-plague:* plague that produces red sores   *rid:* destroy   365 *learning:* teaching   366 *thou'rt best:* you had better   369 *old:* i.e. such as old people have   370 *aches:* pronounced *aitches*   374 s.d. *invisible:* Ariel is of course visible to the audience but he wears a costume which by convention makes him invisible to other persons on the stage, except Prospero. 378 *whist:* being hushed   379 *featly:* nimbly   380 *the burthen bear:* bear the burden, i.e. the bass undersong   382 *dispersedly:* from several directions   393 *passion:* sorrow

Ariel['s] *Song.*

Full fadom five thy father lies,
   Of his bones are coral made:
Those are pearls that were his eyes:
   Nothing of him that doth fade,   400
But doth suffer a sea-change
Into something rich and strange.
Sea-nymphs hourly ring his knell:
   Burthen [within].   Ding-dong.
Hark! now I hear them—ding-dong bell.   405

Fer.: The ditty does remember my drown'd father.
This is no mortal business, nor no sound
That the earth owes. I hear it now above me.

Pros.: The fringed curtains of thine eye advance,
And say what thou seest yond.

Mir.:   What, is't a spirit?   410
Lord, how it looks about! Believe me, sir,
It carries a brave form. But 'tis a spirit.

Pros.: No, wench; it eats and sleeps, and hath such senses
As we have—such. This gallant which thou see'st
Was in the wrack; and but he's something stain'd   415
With grief (that's beauty's canker), thou mightst call him
A goodly person. He hath lost his fellows,
And strays about to find 'em.

Mir.:   I might call him
A thing divine, for nothing natural
I ever saw so noble.

Pros.:   *[Aside.]* It goes on, I see,   420
As my soul prompts it. Spirit, fine spirit, I'll free thee
Within two days for this.

Fer.:   Most sure, the goddess
On whom these airs attend! Vouchsafe, my pray'r
May know if you remain upon this island,
And that you will some good instruction give   425
How I may bear me here. My prime request,
Which I do last pronounce, is (O you wonder!)
If you be maid, or no?

Mir.:   No wonder, sir,
But certainly a maid.

Fer.:   My language heavens!
I am the best of them that speak this speech,   430

---

397 *fadom:* fathom   406 *ditty:* words of the song *remember:* commemorate   408 *owes:* owns   409 *advance:* raise   412 *brave:* excellent, splendid   415 *but:* except that *something stain'd:* somewhat disfigured   416 *canker:* worm that eats blossoms   420 *It:* i.e. the charm   423 *airs:* i.e. the music he has heard   426 *prime:* first, most important   428 *maid:* i.e. a human maiden, not a goddess   430 *best:* first in rank

Were I but where 'tis spoken.

Pros.:   How? the best?
What wert thou, if the King of Naples heard thee?

Fer.: A single thing, as I am now, that wonders
To hear thee speak of Naples. He does hear me,
And that he does I weep. Myself am Naples,   435
Who with mine eyes (never since at ebb) beheld
The King my father wrack'd.

Mir.:   Alack, for mercy!

Fer.: Yes, faith, and all his lords, the Duke of Milan
And his brave son being twain.

Pros.:   *[Aside.]* The Duke of Milan
And his more braver daughter could control thee,   440
If now 'twere fit to do't. At the first sight
They have chang'd eyes. Delicate Ariel,
I'll set thee free for this.—A word, good sir,
I fear you have done yourself some wrong; a word.

Mir.: Why speaks my father so ungently? This   445
Is the third man that e'er I saw; the first
That e'er I sigh'd for. Pity move my father
To be inclin'd my way!

Fer.:   O! if a virgin,
And your affection not gone forth, I'll make you
The Queen of Naples.

Pros.:   Soft, sir, one word more.   450
[Aside.] They are both in either's pow'rs; but this swift business
I must uneasy make, lest too light winning
Make the prize light.—One word more: I charge thee
That thou attend me. Thou dost here usurp
The name thou ow'st not, and hast put thyself   455
Upon this island as a spy, to win it
From me, the lord on't.

Fer.:   No, as I am a man.

Mir.: There's nothing ill can dwell in such a temple.
If the ill spirit have so fair a house,
Good things will strive to dwell with't.

Pros.:   Follow me.—   460
Speak not you for him; he's a traitor.—Come,
I'll manacle thy neck and feet together.
Sea-water shalt thou drink; thy food shall be

***

433 *single:* solitary (because he thinks that he and the King are one and the same), but he probably has in mind also the senses "deserted" and "helpless"   434 *Naples:* King of Naples
436 *at ebb:* dry (a part of the continued sea-imagery in the play)   439 *his brave son:* Not mentioned elsewhere in the play   440 *control:* refute   442 *chang'd eyes:* exchanged loving looks
444 *done . . . wrong:* An ironically polite way of charging him with lying   452 *uneasy:* difficult
452–53 *light . . . light:* easy . . . lightly esteemed   457 *on't:* of it

The fresh-brook mussels, wither'd roots, and husks
Wherein the acorn cradled. Follow.

Fer.:   No,   465
I will resist such entertainment till
Mine enemy has more pow'r.   *He draws, and is charmed from moving.*

Mir.:   O dear father,
Make not too rash a trial of him, for
He's gentle, and not fearful.

Pros.:   What, I say,
My foot my tutor? Put thy sword up, traitor,   470
Who mak'st a show but dar'st not strike, thy conscience
Is so possess'd with guilt. Come, from thy ward,
For I can here disarm thee with this stick,
And make thy weapon drop.

Mir.:   Beseech you, father.

Pros.: Hence! hang not on my garments.

Mir.:   Sir, have pity,   475
I'll be his surety.

Pros.:   Silence! one word more
Shall make me chide thee, if not hate thee. What,
An advocate for an impostor? Hush!
Thou think'st there is no more such shapes as he,
Having seen but him and Caliban. Foolish wench,   480
To th' most of men this is a Caliban,
And they to him are angels.

Mir.:   My affections
Are then most humble; I have no ambition
To see a goodlier man.

Pros.:   *[To* Ferdinand.*]* Come on, obey:
Thy nerves are in their infancy again   485
And have no vigor in them.

Fer.:   So they are.
My spirits, as in a dream, are all bound up.
My father's loss, the weakness which I feel,
The wrack of all my friends, nor this man's threats
To whom I am subdu'd, are but light to me,   490
Might I but through my prison once a day
Behold this maid. All corners else o' th' earth
Let liberty make use of; space enough
Have I in such a prison.

Pros.:   *[Aside.]* It works. *[To* Ferdinand.*]* Come on.— 495
Thou hast done well, fine Ariel! *[To* Ferdinand.*]* Follow me.

---

466 *entertainment:* treatment   466 s.d. *charmed:* magically prevented   468 *gentle:* of high birth *fearful:* cowardly   470 *foot:* i.e. subordinate (Miranda)   472 *ward:* position of defense   473 *stick:* staff   481 *To:* in comparison with   482 *affections:* inclinations   485 *nerves:* sinews   487 *spirits:* vital powers

[*To* Ariel.*]* Hark what thou else shalt do me.

Mir.:   Be of comfort,
My father's of a better nature, sir,
Than he appears by speech. This is unwonted
Which now came from him.

Pros.:   Thou shalt be as free   500
As mountain winds; but then exactly do
All points of my command.

Ari.:   To th' syllable.

Pros. [*To* Ferdinand.*]*: Come, follow. *[To* Miranda.*]*
Speak not for him.   *Exeunt.*

ACT II

SCENE I

    Enter Alonso, Sebastian, Antonio, Gonzalo, Adrian, Francisco, *and*
others.

Gon.: Beseech you, sir, be merry; you have cause

    (So have we all) of joy; for our escape

Is much beyond our loss. Our hint of woe
Is common: every day, some sailor's wife,
The masters of some merchant, and the merchant   5
Have just our theme of woe; but for the miracle
(I mean our preservation), few in millions
Can speak like us. Then wisely, good sir, weigh
Our sorrow with our comfort.

Alon.:   Prithee, peace.

Seb.: He receives comfort like cold porridge.   10

Ant.: The visitor will not give him o'er so.

Seb.: Look, he's winding up the watch of his wit, by and by it will strike.

Gon.: Sir—

Seb.: One. Tell.

Gon.: When every grief is entertain'd that's offer'd,   15
    Comes to th' entertainer—

Seb.: A dollar.

Gon.: Dolor comes to him indeed, you have spoken truer than you purpos'd.

Seb.: You have taken it wiselier than I meant you should.

---

497 *do me:* do for me   II.i. Location: another part of the island   3 *hint:* occasion   5 *masters . . . the merchant:* chief officers of some merchant vessel, and the owner of it   9 *with:* against   10 *porridge:* broth. There is an underlying pun on *peace* (line 9) and *pease,* i.e. peas, a common ingredient of porridge.   11 *visitor:* minister who visits the sick and bereaved, i.e. would-be comforter   14 *Tell:* count   16 *entertainer:* sufferer Sebastian puns on the sense "innkeeper"   17 *dollar:* a continental coin   18 *Dolor:* sorrow

Gon.: Therefore, my lord—   20
Ant.: Fie, what a spendthrift is he of his tongue!
Alon.: I prithee spare.
Gon.: Well, I have done. But yet—
Seb.: He will be talking.
Ant.: Which, of he or Adrian, for a good wager, first begins to crow?   25
Seb.: The old cock.
Ant.: The cock'rel.
Seb.: Done. The wager?
Ant.: A laughter.
Seb.: A match!   30
Adr.: Though this island seem to be desert—
Seb.: Ha, ha, ha!
Ant.: So: you're paid!
Adr.: Uninhabitable, and almost inaccessible—
Seb.: Yet—   35
Adr.: Yet—
Ant.: He could not miss't.
Adr.: It must needs be of subtle, tender, and delicate temperance.
Ant.: Temperance was a delicate wench.
Seb.: Ay, and a subtle, as he most learnedly deliver'd.   40
Adr.: The air breathes upon us here most sweetly.
Seb.: As if it had lungs, and rotten ones.
Ant.: Or, as 'twere perfum'd by a fen.
Gon.: Here is every thing advantageous to life.
Ant.: True, save means to live.   45
Seb.: Of that there's none, or little.
Gon.: How lush and lusty the grass looks! How green!
Ant.: The ground indeed is tawny.
Seb.: With an eye of green in't.
Ant.: He misses not much.   50
Seb.: No; he doth but mistake the truth totally.
Gon.: But the rarity of it is—which is indeed almost beyond credit—
Seb.: As many vouch'd rarieties are.
Gon.: That our garments, being (as they were) drench'd in the sea, hold
      notwithstanding their freshness and glosses, being rather new dy'd than   55
      stain'd with salt water.
Ant.: If but one of his pockets could speak, would it not say he lies?

———

26 *old cock:* i.e. Gonzalo   27 *cock'rel:* i.e. Adrian   29 *laughter:* a laugh (perhaps with pun on
the sense "a sitting of eggs," consistent with the poultry imagery)   31 *desert:* uninhabited
32 *Ha, ha, ha:* Antonio wins the bet, since Adrian spoke first. The winner was entitled to laugh.
Accordingly most editors reverse the speech prefixes for lines 32 and 33.   37 *miss't:* (1) escape
saying "yet"; (2) avoid the island   39 *temperance:* climate Antonio puns on the word as a girl's
name.   48 *tawny:* parched tan or yellow   49 *eye:* spot   52 *rarity:* Perhaps this spelling
indicates an unusual pronunciation of the word by Gonzalo, which Sebastian mimics.   53
vouch'd: guaranteed true

Seb.: Ay, or very falsely pocket up his report.

Gon.: Methinks, our garments are now as fresh as when we put them on first
   in Afric, at the marriage of the King's fair daughter Claribel to the King   60
   of Tunis.

Seb.: 'Twas a sweet marriage, and we prosper well in our return.

Adr.: Tunis was never grac'd before with such a paragon to their queen.

Gon.: Not since widow Dido's time.

Ant.: Widow? a pox o' that! How came that widow in? Widow Dido!   65

Seb.: What if he had said "widower Aeneas" too? Good Lord, how you take
   it!

Adr.: "Widow Dido," said you? You make me study of that. She was of
   Carthage, not of Tunis.

Gon.: This Tunis, sir, was Carthage.   70

Adr.: Carthage?

Gon.: I assure you, Carthage.

Ant.: His word is more than the miraculous harp.

Seb.: He hath rais'd the wall, and houses too.

Ant.: What impossible matter will he make easy next?   75

Seb.: I think he will carry this island home in his pocket, and give it his son for
   an apple.

Ant.: And, sowing the kernels of it in the sea, bring forth more islands.

Gon.: Ay.

Ant.: Why, in good time.   80

Gon.: Sir, we were talking that our garments seem now as fresh as when we
   were at Tunis at the marriage of your daughter, who is now queen.

Ant.: And the rarest that e'er came there.

Seb.: Bate, I beseech you, widow Dido.

Ant.: O, widow Dido? Ay, widow Dido.   85

Gon.: Is not, sir, my doublet as fresh as the first day I wore it? I mean, in a
   sort.

Ant.: That "sort" was well fish'd for.

Gon.: When I wore it at your daughter's marriage?

Alon.: You cram these words into mine ears against   90
   The stomach of my sense. Would I had never
   Married my daughter there! for coming thence,

---

58 *pocket up:* conceal, suppress One who failed to challenge a lie or an insult was said to "pocket up"
the injury.   63 *to:* for   64–65 *widow . . . Dido:* Antonio's vigorous reaction has been variously
explained. Dido was indeed a widow, and Aeneas a widower, when they met, and perhaps Antonio is laughing at what he considers Gonzalo's prudery in referring to her as widow rather than
as Aeneas' mistress. *Widow* could also be used of a wife separated from or deserted by her husband, and Antonio may be laughing at Gonzalo for prudish evasion of the fact that the deserted
Dido was not Aeneas' wife.   70 *This . . . Carthage:* Tunis and Carthage were separate cities,
though not far apart.   73 *miraculous harp:* the legendary harp of Amphion, which raised the
walls of Thebes. Gonzalo's error has created a whole new city.   78 *kernels:* seeds   79 *Ay:*
Probably a reassertion of the identity of the two cities. Antonio responds with a sarcastic expression of approbation.   84 *Bate:* except   87 *in a sort:* comparatively   90–91 *You . . . sense:*
The image is of someone being fed against his will; *stomach* = appetite.

My son is lost and (in my rate) she too,
Who is so far from Italy removed
I ne'er again shall see her. O thou mine heir   95
Of Naples and of Milan, what strange fish
Hath made his meal on thee?
Fran.:   Sir, he may live.
I saw him beat the surges under him,
And ride upon their backs. He trod the water,
Whose enmity he flung aside, and breasted   100
The surge most swoll'n that met him. His bold head
'Bove the contentious waves he kept, and oared
Himself with his good arms in lusty stroke
To th' shore, that o'er his wave-worn basis bowed,
As stooping to relieve him. I not doubt   105
He came alive to land.
Alon.:   No, no, he's gone.
Seb.: Sir, you may thank yourself for this great loss,
That would not bless our Europe with your daughter,
But rather loose her to an African,
Where she, at least, is banish'd from your eye,   110
Who hath cause to wet the grief on't.
Alon.:   Prithee, peace.
Seb.: You were kneel'd to, and importun'd otherwise
By all of us, and the fair soul herself
Weigh'd between loathness and obedience, at
Which end o' th' beam should bow. We have lost your son,   115
I fear for ever. Milan and Naples have
Moe widows in them of this business' making
Than we bring men to comfort them.
The fault's your own.
Alon.:   So is the dear'st of th' loss.
Gon.: My lord Sebastian,   120
The truth you speak doth lack some gentleness,
And time to speak it in. You rub the sore,
When you should bring the plaster.
Seb.:   Very well.
Ant.: And most chirurgeonly.
Gon.: It is foul weather in us all, good sir,   125
When you are cloudy.
Seb.:   Fowl weather?

---

93 *rate:* opinion   104 *his wave-worn basis:* its foundation hollowed by the action of the sea
108 *That:* you who   109 *loose:* with second (perhaps primary) sense "lose," often spelled *loose*
114–15 *Weigh'd . . . bow:* weighed in the scale her unwillingness to marry and her duty of obedience to her father, to see which would prevail   117 *Moe:* more   119 *dear'st:* most heartfelt
122 *time:* appropriate occasion   124 *chirurgeonly:* like a surgeon   126 *Fowl:* Sebastian's pun
returns to the imagery of line 25.

Ant.:　　　　　　　　　　　　Very foul.

Gon.:　Had I plantation of this isle, my lord—

Ant.:　He'd sow't with nettle-seed.

Seb.:　　　　　　　　　　　Or docks, or mallows.

Gon.:　And were the king on't, what would I do?

Seb.:　Scape being drunk, for want of wine.　　　　　　130

Gon.:　I' th' commonwealth I would, by contraries,
　　Execute all things; for no kind of traffic
　　Would I admit; no name of magistrate;
　　Letters should not be known; riches, poverty,
　　And use of service, none; contract, succession,　　　135
　　Bourn, bound of land, tilth, vineyard, none;
　　No use of metal, corn, or wine, or oil;
　　No occupation, all men idle, all;
　　And women too, but innocent and pure;
　　No sovereignty—

Seb.:　　　　　　　　　　Yet he would be king on't.　　140

Ant.:　The latter end of his commonwealth forgets the beginning.

Gon.:　All things in common nature should produce
　　Without sweat or endeavor; treason, felony,
　　Sword, pike, knife, gun, or need of any engine,
　　Would I not have; but nature should bring forth,　　145
　　Of it own kind, all foison, all abundance,
　　To feed my innocent people.

Seb.:　No marrying 'mong his subjects?

Ant.:　None, man, all idle—whores and knaves.

Gon.:　I would with such perfection govern, sir,　　　　150
　　T' excel the golden age.

Seb.:　　　　　　　'Save his Majesty!

Ant.:　Long live Gonzalo!

Gon.:　　　　　　　And—do you mark me, sir?

Alon.:　Prithee, no more; thou dost talk nothing to me.

Gon.:　I do well believe your Highness, and did it to minister occasion to these
　　gentlemen, who are of such sensible and nimble lungs that they always　155
　　use to laugh at nothing.

Ant.:　'Twas you we laugh'd at.

Gon.:　Who, in this kind of merry fooling, am nothing to you; so you may
　　continue, and laugh at nothing still.

Ant.:　What a blow was there given!　　　　　　　　　160

Seb.:　And it had not fall'n flat-long.

---

127 *plantation:* colonization, but the following speakers take up the word in the sense "planting."
131 *contraries:* the opposite of what is customary　　132 *traffic:* business, trade　　134 *Letters:*
learning, literacy　　135 *service:* servanthood, serving of some by others　*succession:* inheritance,
hereditary privilege　　136 *Bourn:* boundary, i.e. division of land among individual owners
tilth: tillage　　137 *corn:* grain　　144 *pike:* spear　*engine:* instrument of war　　146 *it:* its
foison: plenty　　151 *'Save:* God save　　154 *minister occasion:* give opportunity　　155 *sensible
and nimble:* sensitive and lively　　161 *And:* if　*flat-long:* with the sword blade flat, not on edge

Gon.:   You are gentlemen of brave mettle; you would lift the moon out of her
sphere, if she would continue in it five weeks without changing.

       Enter Ariel *[invisible], playing solemn music.*

Seb.:   We would so, and then go a-batfowling.

Ant.:   Nay, good my lord, be not angry.   165

Gon.:   No, I warrant you, I will not adventure my discretion so weakly. Will
you laugh me asleep, for I am very heavy?

Ant.:   Go sleep, and hear us.

                     [All sleep except Alonso, Sebastian, *and* Antonio.*]*

Alon.:   What, all so soon asleep! I wish mine eyes

Would, with themselves, shut up my thoughts. I find   170

They are inclin'd to do so.

Seb.:   Please you, sir,

Do not omit the heavy offer of it.

It seldom visits sorrow; when it doth,

It is a comforter.

Ant.:   We two, my lord,

Will guard your person while you take your rest,   175

And watch your safety.

Alon.:   Thank you. Wondrous heavy.

                     *[*Alonso *sleeps. Exit* Ariel.*]*

Seb.:   What a strange drowsiness possesses them!

Ant.:   It is the quality o' th' climate.

Seb.:   Why

Doth it not then our eyelids sink? I find not   180

Myself dispos'd to sleep.

Ant.:   Nor I, my spirits are nimble.

They fell together all, as by consent;

They dropp'd, as by a thunder-stroke. What might,

Worthy Sebastian, O, what might—? No more—

And yet methinks I see it in thy face,   185

What thou should'st be. The occasion speaks thee, and

My strong imagination sees a crown

Dropping upon thy head.

Seb.:   What? art thou waking?

Ant.:   Do you not hear me speak?

Seb.:   I do, and surely

It is a sleepy language, and thou speak'st   190

Out of thy sleep. What is it thou didst say?

------

164 *a-batfowling:* bird-hunting with sticks *(bats)* at night He suggests that they would use the
moon as their lantern.   166 *adventure. . . . weakly:* risk my reputation for good sense by getting
angry at such superficial fellows   167 *heavy:* drowsy   168 *hear us:* i.e. listen to our laughter
172 *omit . . . offer:* neglect the opportunity sleepiness provides   173 *visits:* See note to II.i.11.
186 *speaks thee:* calls upon you (to seize the opportunity)

This is a strange repose, to be asleep
With eyes wide open—standing, speaking, moving—
And yet so fast asleep.

Ant.:   Noble Sebastian,
Thou let'st thy fortune sleep—die, rather; wink'st   195
Whiles thou art waking.

Seb.:   Thou dost snore distinctly,
There's meaning in thy snores.

Ant.: I am more serious than my custom; you
Must be so too, if heed me; which to do
Trebles thee o'er.   200

Seb.:   Well; I am standing water.

Ant.: I'll teach you how to flow.

Seb.:   Do so. To ebb
Hereditary sloth instructs me.

Ant.:   O!
If you but knew how you the purpose cherish
Whiles thus you mock it! how, in stripping it,
You more invest it! Ebbing men, indeed,   205
Most often, do so near the bottom run
By their own fear or sloth.

Seb.:   Prithee, say on.
The setting of thine eye and cheek proclaim
A matter from thee; and a birth, indeed,
Which throes thee much to yield.   210

Ant.:   Thus, sir:
Although this lord of weak remembrance, this
Who shall be of as little memory
When he is earth'd, hath here almost persuaded
(For he's a spirit of persuasion, only
Professes to persuade) the King his son's alive,   215
'Tis as impossible that he's undrown'd,
As he that sleeps here swims.

Seb.:   I have no hope
That he's undrown'd.

Ant.:   O, out of that no hope
What great hope have you! No hope, that way, is
Another way so high a hope that even   220
Ambition cannot pierce a wink beyond,

---

195 *wink'st:* keep your eyes shut   200 *Trebles thee o'er:* triples your fortune   *standing water:* i.e indecisive, going neither forward nor back   202 *Hereditary sloth:* natural laziness   203 *cherish:* enrich   205 *invest:* dress up   208 *setting:* fixed look   210 *throes:* causes labor pains 211 *this lord:* i.e. Gonzalo   *of weak remembrance:* having a short memory (perhaps alluding to Gonzalo's lapse in identifying Tunis with Carthage); with following shift to the sense "remembered only briefly after death"   213 *earth'd:* buried   214–15 *only . . . persuade:* has no function except to persuade. Gonzalo is a privy councillor.   219 *that way:* i.e. with respect to Ferdinand's being undrowned   221 *wink:* glimpse

But doubt discovery there. Will you grant with me
That Ferdinand is drown'd?
Seb.:   He's gone.
Ant.:   Then tell me,
Who's the next heir of Naples?
Seb.:   Claribel.
Ant.: She that is Queen of Tunis; she that dwells   225
Ten leagues beyond man's life; she that from Naples
Can have no note, unless the sun were post—
The Man i' th' Moon's too slow—till new-born chins
Be rough and razorable; she that from whom
We all were sea-swallow'd, though some cast again   230
(And by that destiny) to perform an act
Whereof what's past is prologue, what to come
In yours and my discharge.
Seb.:   What stuff is this? How say you?
'Tis true, my brother's daughter 's Queen of Tunis,
So is she heir of Naples; 'twixt which regions   235
There is some space.
Ant.:   A space whose ev'ry cubit
Seems to cry out, "How shall that Claribel
Measure us back to Naples? Keep in Tunis,
And let Sebastian wake." Say this were death
That now hath seiz'd them, why, they were no worse   240
Than now they are. There be that can rule Naples
As well as he that sleeps; lords that can prate
As amply and unnecessarily
As this Gonzalo; I myself could make
A chough of as deep chat. O, that you bore   245
The mind that I do! what a sleep were this
For your advancement! Do you understand me?
Seb.: Methinks I do.
Ant.:   And how does your content
Tender your own good fortune?
Seb.:   I remember
You did supplant your brother Prospero.
Ant.:   True.   250
And look how well my garments sit upon me,
Much feater than before. My brother's servants
Were then my fellows, now they are my men.

---

222 *doubt discovery there:* is uncertain of seeing clearly even there   226 *Ten . . . life:* thirty miles
farther than a lifetime's journey   227 *note:* news *post:* messenger   229 *from:* coming from
230 *cast:* (1) cast up; (2) cast as actors   233 *discharge:* performance   236 *cubit:* measure of
about 20 inches   238 *Measure us:* i.e. travel over the cubits   239 *wake:* i.e. awake to fortune
244–45 *make . . . chat:* train a jackdaw to speak as wisely as he Jackdaws were taught to speak.
248 *content:* inclination   249 *Tender:* regard   252 *feater:* more gracefully

Seb.: But, for your conscience?

Ant.: Ay, sir; where lies that? If 'twere a kibe, 255
'Twould put me to my slipper; but I feel not
This deity in my bosom. Twenty consciences,
That stand 'twixt me and Milan, candied be they,
And melt ere they molest! Here lies your brother,
No better than the earth he lies upon, 260
If he were that which now he's like—that's dead,
Whom I with this obedient steel, three inches of it,
Can lay to bed for ever; whiles you, doing thus,
To the perpetual wink for aye might put
This ancient morsel, this Sir Prudence, who 265
Should not upbraid our course. For all the rest,
They'll take suggestion as a cat laps milk;
They'll tell the clock to any business that
We say befits the hour.

Seb.:   Thy case, dear friend,
Shall be my president: as thou got'st Milan, 270
I'll come by Naples. Draw thy sword. One stroke
Shall free thee from the tribute which thou payest,
And I the King shall love thee.

Ant.:   Draw together;
And when I rear my hand, do you the like,
To fall it on Gonzalo. 275

Seb.:   O, but one word.   *[They talk apart.]*

Enter Ariel *[invisible], with music and song.*

Ari.: My master through his art foresees the danger
That you, his friend, are in, and sends me forth
(For else his project dies) to keep them living.   *Sings in* Gonzalo's *ear.*
                              While you here do snoring lie,
                              Open-ey'd conspiracy 280
                                        His time doth take.
                              If of life you keep a care,
                              Shake off slumber, and beware.
                                        Awake! awake!

Ant.: Then let us both be sudden.

Gon. [Waking.]:   Now, good angels 285
          Preserve the King!   *[Wakes* Alonso.*]*

Alon.: Why, how now, ho! Awake? Why are you drawn?
          Wherefore this ghastly looking?

Gon.:   What's the matter?

---

255 *kibe:* chilblain   256 *put me to:* make me wear   258 *Milan:* the dukedom of Milan   *candied:* sugared   264 *wink:* sleep   267 *suggestion:* evil prompting   268 *tell . . . to:* i.e. agree that the time sorts with   270 *president:* precedent   275 *fall it:* let it fall   281 *time:* opportunity

Seb.: Whiles we stood here securing your repose,
           Even now, we heard a hollow burst of bellowing   290
           Like bulls, or rather lions. Did't not wake you?
           It strook mine ear most terribly.
Alon.:   I heard nothing.
Ant.: O, 'twas a din to fright a monster's ear,
           To make an earthquake; sure it was the roar
           Of a whole herd of lions.
Alon.:   Heard you this, Gonzalo?   295
Gon.: Upon mine honor, sir, I heard a humming
           (And that a strange one too) which did awake me.
           I shak'd you, sir, and cried. As mine eyes open'd,
           I saw their weapons drawn. There was a noise,
           That's verily. 'Tis best we stand upon our guard,   300
           Or that we quit this place. Let's draw our weapons.
Alon.: Lead off this ground, and let's make further search
           For my poor son.
Gon.:   Heavens keep him from these beasts!
           For he is sure i' th' island.
Alon.:   Lead away.
Ari.: Prospero my lord shall know what I have done.   305
           So, King, go safely on to seek thy son.   *Exeunt.*

Scene II

Enter Caliban *with a burthen of wood. A noise of thunder heard.*

Cal.: All the infections that the sun sucks up
           From bogs, fens, flats, on Prosper fall, and make him
           By inch-meal a disease! His spirits hear me,
           And yet I needs must curse. But they'll nor pinch,
           Fright me with urchin-shows, pitch me i' th' mire,   5
           Nor lead me, like a fire-brand, in the dark
           Out of my way, unless he bid 'em; but
           For every trifle are they set upon me,
           Sometime like apes that mow and chatter at me,
           And after bite me; then like hedgehogs which   10
           Lie tumbling in my barefoot way, and mount
           Their pricks at my footfall; sometime am I
           All wound with adders, who with cloven tongues
           Do hiss me into madness.—
           Enter Trinculo.

---

289 *securing:* guarding   292 *strook:* struck   298 *cried:* called out   II.ii. Location: another
part of the island   3 *By inch-meal:* inch by inch. Cf. *piecemeal*   5 *urchin-shows:* sights of goblins in the shape of hedgehogs   6 *like a fire-brand:* in the shape of a will-o'-the-wisp   9 *mow:*
make faces   13 *wound:* twined about

                              Lo, now lo,
Here comes a spirit of his, and to torment me   15
For bringing wood in slowly. I'll fall flat,
Perchance he will not mind me.

Trin.: Here's neither bush nor shrub to bear off any weather at all. And another storm brewing, I hear it sing i' th' wind. Yond same black cloud,
yond huge one, looks like a foul bumbard that would shed his liquor. If it   20
should thunder as it did before, I know not where to hide my head. Yond
same cloud cannot choose but fall by pailfuls. What have we here? a man
or a fish? dead or alive? A fish, he smells like a fish; a very ancient and fish-
like smell; a kind of, not-of-the-newest poor-John. A strange fish! Were I
in England now (as once I was) and had but this fish painted, not a holi-   25
day fool there but would give a piece of silver. There would this monster
make a man; any strange beast there makes a man. When they will not
give a doit to relieve a lame beggar, they will lay out ten to see a dead Indian. Legg'd like a man; and his fins like arms! Warm, o' my troth! I do
now let loose my opinion, hold it no longer: this is no fish, but an islander, 30
that hath lately suffer'd by thunderbolt. *[Thunder.]* Alas, the storm is
come again! My best way is to creep under his gaberdine; there is no
other shelter hereabout. Misery acquaints a man with strange bedfellows;
I will here shroud till the dregs of the storm be past.

        Enter Stephano, *singing, [a bottle in his hand].*

Ste.:   "I shall no more to sea, to sea,   35
              Here shall I die ashore—"
This is a very scurvy tune to sing at a man's funeral.
Well, here's my comfort.   *Drinks.*
(Sings.) "The master, the swabber, the boatswain, and I,
        The gunner, and his mate,   40
    Lov'd Mall, Meg, and Marian, and Margery,
        But none of us car'd for Kate;
    For she had a tongue with a tang,
        Would cry to a sailor 'Go hang!'
    She lov'd not the savour of tar nor of pitch,   45
    Yet a tailor might scratch her where'er she did itch.
        Then to sea, boys, and let her go hang!"

This is a scurvy tune too; but here's my comfort.   *Drinks.*
Cal.: Do not torment me! O!

---

17 *mind:* notice   18 *bear off:* ward off   20 *bumbard:* bombard, leather bottle   *his:* its
24 *poor-John:* cheap dried fish   25 *painted:* i.e. on a sign hung outside a booth at a fair to attract
customers, with the monster exhibited within   27 *make a man:* make a man's fortune, with obvious punning sense "be indistinguishable from an Englishman"   28 *doit:* coin of trifling value
29 *o' my troth:* by my faith   30 *hold it:* hold it back   32 *gaberdine:* cloak   34 *dregs:* lees (recurring to the image of the rain as liquor poured from a jug)   49 *Do . . . me:* Caliban takes
Stephano for a spirit sent by Prospero to plague him.

Ste.: What's the matter? Have we devils here? Do you put tricks upon 's with   50
salvages and men of Inde? Ha? I have not scap'd drowning to be afeard
now of your four legs; for it hath been said, "As proper a man as ever went
on four legs cannot make him give ground"; and it shall be said so again,
while Stephano breathes at' nostrils.

Cal.: The spirit torments me! O!   55

Ste.: This is some monster of the isle with four legs, who hath got (as I take
it) an ague. Where the devil should he learn our language? I will give him
some relief, if it be but for that. If I can recover him, and keep him tame,
and get to Naples with him, he's a present for any emperor that ever trod
on neat's-leather.   60

Cal.: Do not torment me, prithee. I'll bring my wood home faster.

Ste.: He's in his fit now, and does not talk after the wisest. He shall taste of my
bottle; if he have never drunk wine afore, it will go near to remove his fit.
If I can recover him, and keep him tame, I will not take too much for him;
he shall pay for him that hath him, and that soundly.   65

Cal.: Thou dost me yet but little hurt; thou wilt anon, I know it by thy
trembling. Now Prosper works upon thee.

Ste.: Come on your ways. Open your mouth; here is that which will give language to you, cat. Open your mouth: this will shake your shaking, I can
tell you, and that soundly. You cannot tell who's your friend. Open your   70
chaps again.   *[Caliban drinks.]*

Trin.: I should know that voice; it should be—but he is drown'd; and these are
devils. O, defend me!

Ste.: Four legs and two voices; a most delicate monster! His forward voice
now is to speak well of his friend; his backward voice is to utter foul   75
speeches and to detract. If all the wine in my bottle will recover him, I will
help his ague. Come. *[Caliban drinks again.]* Amen! I will pour some in
thy other mouth.

Trin.: Stephano!

Ste.: Doth thy other mouth call me? Mercy, mercy! This is a devil, and no   80
monster. I will leave him, I have no long spoon.

Trin.: Stephano! If thou beest Stephano, touch me, and speak to me; for I am
Trinculo—be not afeared—thy good friend Trinculo.

Ste.: If thou beest Trinculo, come forth. I'll pull thee by the lesser legs. If any
be Trinculo's legs, these are they. Thou art very Trinculo indeed! How   85
cam'st thou to be the siege of this moon-calf? Can he vent Trinculos?

---

50 *put tricks upon 's:* delude us with a conjuror's or showman's devices   *salvages:* savages   *Inde:*
India   52–53 *As . . . legs:* Stephano adapts a proverbial expression by substituting *four* for
two. Proper = handsome   54 *at':* at the   58 *for that:* i.e. because he knows our language   *re-*
cover: restore   60 *neat's-leather:* cowhide   64 *I will . . . much:* whatever I can take for him
won't be too much   65 *hath:* gets   66 *thou wilt anon:* i.e. you will hurt me more very soon
68–69 *here . . . cat:* Alluding to the proverb "Liquor will make a cat talk."   71 *chaps:* jaws
74 *delicate:* ingenious   81 *long spoon:* Alluding to the proverb "He must have a long spoon that
will eat with the devil."   86 *siege:* excrement   *moon-calf:* monstrosity, creature born misshapen
because of lunar influence   86 *vent:* emit

Trin.: I took him to be kill'd with a thunder-stroke. But art thou not drown'd, Stephano? I hope now thou art not drown'd. Is the storm overblown? I hid me under the dead moon-calf's gaberdine for fear of the storm. And art thou living, Stephano? O Stephano, two Neapolitans scap'd!　　90

Ste.: Prithee do not turn me about, my stomach is not constant.

Cal. [Aside.]: These be fine things, and if they be not sprites. That's a brave god, and bears celestial liquor. I will kneel to him.

Ste.: How didst thou scape? How cam'st thou hither? Swear by this bottle　95 how thou cam'st hither—I escap'd upon a butt of sack which the sailors heav'd o'erboard—by this bottle, which I made of the bark of a tree with mine own hands since I was cast ashore.

Cal.: I'll swear upon that bottle to be thy true subject, for the liquor is not earthly.　　100

Ste.: Here; swear then how thou escap'dst.

Trin.: Swom ashore, man, like a duck. I can swim like a duck, I'll be sworn.

Ste.: Here, kiss the book. *[Passing the bottle.]* Though thou canst swim like a duck, thou art made like a goose.

Trin.: O Stephano, hast any more of this?　　105

Ste.: The whole butt, man. My cellar is in a rock by th' sea-side, where my wine is hid. How now, moon-calf? how does thine ague?

Cal.: Hast thou not dropp'd from heaven?

Ste.: Out o' th' moon, I do assure thee. I was the Man i' th' Moon, when time was.　　110

Cal.: I have seen thee in her, and I do adore thee. My mistress show'd me thee, and thy dog, and thy bush.

Ste.: Come, swear to that; kiss the book. I will furnish it anon with new contents. Swear.　　　　　　　　　　　　*[Caliban drinks.]*

Trin.: By this good light, this is a very shallow monster! I afeard of him? A　115 very weak monster! The Man i' th' Moon? A most poor credulous monster! Well drawn, monster, in good sooth!

Cal.: I'll show thee every fertile inch o' th' island; And I will kiss thy foot. I prithee, be my god.

Trin.: By this light, a most perfidious and drunken monster! When 's god's　120 asleep, he'll rob his bottle.

Cal.: I'll kiss thy foot. I'll swear myself thy subject.

Ste.: Come on, then; down, and swear.

Trin.: I shall laugh myself to death at this puppy-headed monster. A most scurvy monster! I could find in my heart to beat him—　　125

Ste.: Come, kiss.

Trin.: But that the poor monster's in drink. An abominable monster!

---

92 *and if:* if　　96 *butt of sack:* barrel of Spanish wine　　102 *Swom:* swam　　103 *kiss the book:* Trinculo has taken his oath on the bottle, not on the customary Bible. Stephano means "Take a drink."　　109–10 *when time was:* once upon a time　　112 *dog . . . bush:* The man in the moon was placed there in punishment for gathering firewood on Sunday.　　117 *Well drawn:* that's a good long draught you've taken　*sooth:* truth

Cal.: I'll show thee the best springs; I'll pluck thee berries;
    I'll fish for thee, and get thee wood enough.
    A plague upon the tyrant that I serve!   130
    I'll bear him no more sticks, but follow thee,
    Thou wondrous man.
Trin.: A most ridiculous monster, to make a wonder of a poor drunkard!
Cal.: I prithee let me bring thee where crabs grow;
    And I with my long nails will dig thee pig-nuts;   135
    Show thee a jay's nest, and instruct thee how
    To snare the nimble marmazet. I'll bring thee
    To clust'ring filberts, and sometimes I'll get thee
    Young scamels from the rock. Wilt thou go with me?
Ste.: I prithee now lead the way without any more talking. Trinculo, the king   140
    and all our company else being drown'd, we will inherit here. Here! bear
    my bottle. Fellow Trinculo, we'll fill him by and by again.
Cal. (Sings drunkenly.): Farewell, master; farewell, farewell!
Trin.: A howling monster, a drunken monster!
Cal.: No more dams I'll make for fish,   145
        Nor fetch in firing
        At requiring,
    Nor scrape trenchering, nor wash dish.
        'Ban 'Ban, Ca-Caliban
    Has a new master, get a new man.   150
    Freedom, high-day! high-day, freedom! freedom, high-day, freedom!
Ste.: O brave monster! lead the way.   *Exeunt.*

ACT III

Scene I

Enter Ferdinand, *bearing a log.*

Fer.: There be some sports are painful, and their labor
    Delight in them [sets] off; some kinds of baseness
    Are nobly undergone; and most poor matters
    Point to rich ends. This my mean task
    Would be as heavy to me as odious, but   5
    The mistress which I serve quickens what's dead,
    And makes my labors pleasures. O, she is
    Ten times more gentle than her father's crabbed;

---

134 *crabs:* crab apples   135 *pig-nuts:* peanuts   137 *marmazet:* marmoset (a small monkey)
139 *scamels:* Meaning unknown, but apparently either shellfish or rock-inhabiting birds.
Some editors emend to *sea-mels,* i.e. sea-mews.   148 *trenchering:* trenchers, wooden plates
III.i. Location: before Prospero's cell   1 *are painful:* that are laborious   1–2 *their . . . off:*
their laboriousness increases our pleasure in them (?) or our pleasure in them offsets their laboriousness (?)   2 *baseness:* menial activity   6 *quickens:* brings to life

And he's compos'd of harshness. I must remove
Some thousands of these logs, and pile them up,   10
Upon a sore injunction. My sweet mistress
Weeps when she sees me work, and says such baseness
Had never like executor. I forget;
But these sweet thoughts do even refresh my labors,
Most [busil'est] when I do it.   15

Enter Miranda *and* Prospero *[at a distance, unseen].*

Mir.:   Alas! now pray you
Work not so hard. I would the lightning had
Burnt up those logs that you are enjoin'd to pile!
Pray set it down, and rest you. When this burns,
'Twill weep for having wearied you. My father
Is hard at study; pray now rest yourself,   20
He's safe for these three hours.
Fer.:   O most dear mistress,
The sun will set, before I shall discharge
What I must strive to do.
Mir.:   If you'll sit down,
I'll bear your logs the while. Pray give me that,
I'll carry it to the pile.
Fer.:   No, precious creature,   25
I had rather crack my sinews, break my back,
Than you should such dishonor undergo,
While I sit lazy by.
Mir.:   It would become me
As well as it does you; and I should do it
With much more ease, for my good will is to it,   30
And yours it is against.
Pros. [Aside.]:   Poor worm! thou art infected!
This visitation shows it.
Mir.:   You look wearily.
Fer.: No, noble mistress, 'tis fresh morning with me
When you are by at night. I do beseech you—   35
Chiefly that I might set it in my prayers—
What is your name?
Mir.:   Miranda.—O my father,
I have broke your hest to say so.
Fer.:   Admir'd Miranda,
Indeed the top of admiration! worth
What's dearest to the world! Full many a lady   40
I have ey'd with best regard, and many a time

---

11 *sore injunction:* harsh command   13 *like:* such, i.e. such a noble   15 *Most . . . it:* when I
am working hardest   19 *weep:* i.e. exude resin   33 *visitation:* (1) visit; (2) attack of plague
(carrying on the medical figure in *infected*)   38 *hest:* command   *Admir'd Miranda:* A pun,
since *Miranda* = admired, i.e. wondered at.   41 *best regard:* highest approval

Th' harmony of their tongues hath into bondage
Brought my too diligent ear. For several virtues
Have I lik'd several women, never any
With so full soul but some defect in her   45
Did quarrel with the noblest grace she ow'd,
And put it to the foil. But you, O you,
So perfect and so peerless, are created
Of every creature's best!

Mir.:   I do not know
One of my sex; no woman's face remember,   50
Save, from my glass, mine own; nor have I seen
More that I may call men than you, good friend,
And my dear father. How features are abroad
I am skilless of; but by my modesty
(The jewel in my dower), I would not wish   55
Any companion in the world but you;
Nor can imagination form a shape,
Besides yourself, to like of. But I prattle
Something too wildly, and my father's precepts
I therein do forget.

Fer.:   I am, in my condition,   60
A prince, Miranda; I do think, a king
(I would not so!), and would no more endure
This wooden slavery than to suffer
The flesh-fly blow my mouth. Hear my soul speak:
The very instant that I saw you, did   65
My heart fly to your service, there resides,
To make me slave to it, and for your sake
Am I this patient log-man.

Mir.:   Do you love me?

Fer.: O heaven, O earth, bear witness to this sound,
And crown what I profess with kind event   70
If I speak true! if hollowly, invert
What best is boded me to mischief! I,
Beyond all limit of what else i' th' world,
Do love, prize, honor you.

Mir.:   I am a fool
To weep at what I am glad of.

Pros.:   *[Aside.]* Fair encounter   75
Of two most rare affections! Heavens rain grace
On that which breeds between 'em!

43, 44 *several:* particular   46 *ow'd:* owned   47 *foil:* (1) contrast; (2) defeat   53 *abroad:*
elsewhere   54 *skilless:* ignorant   60 *condition:* rank   63 *wooden slavery:* being compelled
to carry wood   64 *blow:* defile   70 *kind event:* favorable outcome   71 *hollowly:* insin-
cerely   71–72 *invert . . . to mischief:* turn . . . to ill fortune   72 *boded:* destined

Fer.:   Wherefore weep you?
Mir.: At mine unworthiness, that dare not offer
    What I desire to give; and much less take
    What I shall die to want. But this is trifling,   80
    And all the more it seeks to hide itself,
    The bigger bulk it shows. Hence, bashful cunning,
    And prompt me, plain and holy innocence!
    I am your wife, if you will marry me;
    If not, I'll die your maid. To be your fellow   85
    You may deny me, but I'll be your servant,
    Whether you will or no.
Fer.:   My mistress, dearest,
    And I thus humble ever.
Mir.:   My husband then?
Fer.: Ay, with a heart as willing
    As bondage e'er of freedom. Here's my hand.   90
Mir.: And mine, with my heart in't. And now farewell
    Till half an hour hence.
Fer.:   A thousand, thousand!

                              *Exeunt [*Ferdinand *and* Miranda *severally].*

Pros.: So glad of this as they I cannot be,
    Who are surpris'd [withal]; but my rejoicing
    At nothing can be more. I'll to my book,   95
    For yet, ere supper-time must I perform
    Much business appertaining.   *Exit.*

SCENE II

    Enter Caliban, Stephano, *and* Trinculo.

Ste.: Tell not me. When the butt is out, we will drink water—not a drop be-
    fore; therefore bear up and board 'em. Servant-monster, drink to me.

Trin.: Servant-monster? the folly of this island! They say there's but five upon
    this isle: we are three of them; if th' other two be brain'd like us, the state
    totters.   5

Ste.: Drink, servant-monster, when I bid thee. Thy eyes are almost set in thy
    head.

Trin.: Where should they be set else? He were a brave monster indeed if they
    were set in his tail.

80 *want:* be without   82 *bashful cunning:* coyness   85 *maid:* handmaiden   *fellow:* mate
92 *thousand:* i.e. thousand farewells   94 *withal:* with it, i.e. by it   III.ii. Location: another
part of the island   1 *out:* empty   2 *bear . . . 'em:* stand firm and attack Stephano uses naval
jargon as an encouragement to drink.   3 *folly of:* low level of intellect on   6 *set:* sunk out of
sight. Trinculo puns on the sense "placed."

Ste.: My man-monster hath drown'd his tongue in sack. For my part, the sea 10
cannot drown me; I swam, ere I could recover the shore, five and thirty
leagues off and on. By this light, thou shalt be my lieutenant, monster, or
my standard.

Trin.: Your lieutenant if you list, he's no standard.

Ste.: We'll not run, Monsieur Monster. 15

Trin.: Nor go neither; but you'll lie like dogs, and yet say nothing neither.

Ste.: Moon-calf, speak once in thy life, if thou beest a good moon-calf.

Cal.: How does thy honor? Let me lick thy shoe. I'll not serve him, he is not
valiant.

Trin.: Thou liest, most ignorant monster, I am in case to justle a constable. 20
Why, thou debosh'd fish thou, was there ever man a coward that hath
drunk so much sack as I to-day? Wilt thou tell a monstrous lie, being but
half fish and half a monster?

Cal.: Lo, how he mocks me! Wilt thou let him, my lord?

Trin.: "Lord," quoth he? That a monster should be such a natural! 25

Cal.: Lo, lo again. Bite him to death, I prithee.

Ste.: Trinculo, keep a good tongue in your head. If you prove a mutineer—
the next tree! The poor monster's my subject, and he shall not suffer
indignity.

Cal.: I thank my noble lord. Wilt thou be pleas'd to hearken once again to the 30
suit I made to thee?

Ste.: Marry, will I; kneel, and repeat it. I will stand, and so shall Trinculo.

Enter Ariel, *invisible.*

Cal.: As I told thee before, I am subject to a tyrant,
A sorcerer, that by his cunning hath
Cheated me of the island. 35

Ari.: Thou liest.

Cal.:   Thou liest, thou jesting monkey, thou!
I would my valiant master would destroy thee.
I do not lie.

Ste.: Trinculo, if you trouble him any more in 's tale, by this hand, I will supplant some of your teeth. 40

Trin.: Why, I said nothing.

Ste.: Mum then, and no more.—Proceed.

Cal.: I say by sorcery he got this isle;
From me he got it. If thy greatness will
Revenge it on him—for I know thou dar'st, 45
But this thing dare not—

---

13 *standard:* standard-bearer   14 *no standard:* i.e. unable to stand   15 *run:* i.e. run from the
enemy   16 *go:* walk   *lie:* (1) lie down; (2) tell lies; (3) excrete (with a backward glance at *run* in
the sense "urinate" and perhaps at *standard* in the sense "conduit")   20 *case:* fit condition
21 *debosh'd:* debauched   25 *natural:* idiot. The point is that a monster is by definition "unnatural."   32 *Marry:* indeed (originally the name of the Virgin Mary used as an oath)   46 *this
thing:* i.e. Trinculo

Ste.: That's most certain.

Cal.: Thou shalt be lord of it, and I'll serve thee.

Ste.: How now shall this be compass'd? Canst thou bring me to the party?

Cal.: Yea, yea, my lord. I'll yield him thee asleep,   50
  Where thou may'st knock a nail into his head.

Ari.: Thou liest, thou canst not.

Cal.: What a pied ninny's this! Thou scurvy patch!
  I do beseech thy greatness, give him blows,
  And take his bottle from him. When that's gone,   55
  He shall drink nought but brine, for I'll not show him
  Where the quick freshes are.

Ste.: Trinculo, run into no further danger; interrupt the monster one word
  further, and by this hand, I'll turn my mercy out o' doors, and make a
  stock-fish of thee.   60

Trin.: Why, what did I? I did nothing. I'll go farther off.

Ste.: Didst thou not say he lied?

Ari.: Thou liest.

Ste.: Do I so? Take thou that.   *[Beats* Trinculo.]
  As you like this, give me the lie another time.   65

Trin.: I did not give the lie. Out o' your wits and hearing too? A pox o' your
  bottle! this can sack and drinking do. A murrain on your monster, and the
  devil take your fingers!

Cal.: Ha, ha, ha!

Ste.: Now forward with your tale.—Prithee stand further off.   70

Cal.: Beat him enough. After a little time
  I'll beat him too.

Ste.:   Stand farther.—Come, proceed.

Cal.: Why, as I told thee, 'tis a custom with him
  I' th' afternoon to sleep. There thou may'st brain him,
  Having first seiz'd his books; or with a log   75
  Batter his skull, or paunch him with a stake,
  Or cut his wezand with thy knife. Remember
  First to possess his books; for without them
  He's but a sot, as I am; nor hath not
  One spirit to command: they all do hate him   80
  As rootedly as I. Burn but his books.
  He has brave utensils (for so he calls them)
  Which when he has a house, he'll deck withal.
  And that most deeply to consider is
  The beauty of his daughter. He himself   85
  Calls her a nonpareil. I never saw a woman
  But only Sycorax my dam and she;

---

53 *pied . . . patch:* foolish . . . fool (from the multicolored garb of the professional fool)
57 *quick freshes:* fresh-water springs   60 *stock-fish:* dried cod, so stiff it had to be beaten before
cooking   67 *murrain:* a disease of cattle   76 *paunch:* stab in the belly   77 *wezand:* windpipe   79 *sot:* fool   82 *utensils:* furnishings   83 *withal:* with.

But she as far surpasseth Sycorax
As great'st does least.

Ste.:   Is it so brave a lass?

Cal.: Ay, lord, she will become thy bed, I warrant,   90
And bring thee forth brave brood.

Ste.: Monster, I will kill this man. His daughter and I will be king and queen—'save our Graces! and Trinculo and thyself shall be viceroys. Dost thou like the plot, Trinculo?

Trin.: Excellent.   95

Ste.: Give me thy hand. I am sorry I beat thee; but while thou liv'st keep a good tongue in thy head.

Cal.: Within this half hour will he be asleep.
Wilt thou destroy him then?

Ste.:   Ay, on mine honor.

Ari.: This will I tell my master.   100

Cal.: Thou mak'st me merry; I am full of pleasure,
Let us be jocund. Will you troll the catch
You taught me but while-ere?

Ste.: At thy request, monster, I will do reason, any reason. Come on, Trinculo, let us sing.   *Sings.* 105

"Flout 'em and scout 'em,
And scout 'em and flout 'em!
Thought is free."

Cal.: That's not the tune.

Ariel *plays the tune on a tabor and pipe.*

Ste.: What is this same?   110

Trin.: This is the tune of our catch, play'd by the picture of Nobody.

Ste.: If thou beest a man, show thyself in thy likeness. If thou beest a devil, take't as thou list.

Trin.: O, forgive me my sins!

Ste.: He that dies pays all debts. I defy thee. Mercy upon us!   115

Cal.: Art thou afeard?

Ste.: No, monster, not I.

Cal.: Be not afeard, the isle is full of noises,
Sounds, and sweet airs, that give delight and hurt not.
Sometimes a thousand twangling instruments   120
Will hum about mine ears; and sometime voices,
That if I then had wak'd after long sleep,
Will make me sleep again, and then in dreaming,
The clouds methought would open, and show riches
Ready to drop upon me, that when I wak'd   125
I cried to dream again.

---

102 *troll the catch:* sing the round   103 *but while-ere:* a short time ago   106 *Flout:* deride *scout:* jeer at   109 s.d. *tabor:* small drum   111 *picture of Nobody:* traditional image of a man with arms and legs but no torso; but Trinculo means an invisible agency   113 *take't . . . list:* do as you please (a challenge)   118 *noises:* musical sounds   120 *twangling:* an invented word

Ste.: This will prove a brave kingdom to me, where I shall have my music for
　　nothing.

Cal.: When Prospero is destroy'd.

Ste.: That shall be by and by. I remember the story.　　　　　　　　　130

Trin.: The sound is going away. Let's follow it, and after do our work.

Ste.: Lead, monster, we'll follow. I would I could see this taborer; he lays it on.

Trin.: Wilt come? I'll follow Stephano.　　　　　　　　　　　　*Exeunt.*

SCENE III

　　Enter Alonso, Sebastian, Antonio, Gonzalo, Adrian, Francisco, *etc.*

Gon.: By'r lakin, I can go no further, sir,
　　My old bones aches. Here's a maze trod indeed
　　Through forth-rights and meanders! By your patience,
　　I needs must rest me.

Alon.:　　　　　　　　Old lord, I cannot blame thee,
　　Who am myself attach'd with weariness　　　　　　　　　　　　5
　　To th' dulling of my spirits. Sit down, and rest.
　　Even here I will put off my hope, and keep it
　　No longer for my flatterer. He is drown'd
　　Whom thus we stray to find, and the sea mocks
　　Our frustrate search on land. Well, let him go.　　　　　　　10

Ant. [Aside to Sebastian.*]:* I am right glad that he's so out of hope.
　　Do not for one repulse forgo the purpose
　　That you resolv'd t' effect.

Seb. [Aside to Antonio.*]:* The next advantage
　　Will we take throughly.　　　　　　　　　　　　　　　　　15

Ant. [Aside to Sebastian.*]:* Let it be to-night,
　　For now they are oppress'd with travail, they
　　Will not, nor cannot, use such vigilance
　　As when they are fresh.

Seb. [Aside to Antonio.*]:* I say, to-night. No more.　　　　　　20

　　Solemn and strange music; and Prosper *on top, invisible.*

Alon.: What harmony is this? My good friends, hark!

Gon.: Marvellous sweet music!

　　Enter several strange Shapes, *bringing in a banket; and dance about it with
gentle actions of salutations; and inviting the King, etc., to eat, they depart.*

Alon.: Give us kind keepers, heavens! what were these?

Seb.: A living drollery. Now I will believe

---

130 *by and by:* immediately　　III.iii. Location: another part of the island　　1 *By'r lakin:* by our
Ladykin, i.e. the Virgin Mary　　3 *forth-rights:* straight paths　　5 *attach'd:* seized　　8 *for:* as
12 *for:* because of　　15 *throughly:* thoroughly　　20 s.d. *top:* probably the third level of the
tiring-house　　22 s.d. *banket:* banquet, i.e. light repast　　23 *kind keepers:* guardian angels
24 *living drollery:* puppet show with live actors

That there are unicorns; that in Arabia   25
There is one tree, the phoenix' throne, one phoenix
At this hour reigning there.
Ant.:   I'll believe both;
And what does else want credit, come to me,
And I'll be sworn 'tis true. Travellers ne'er did lie,
Though fools at home condemn 'em.
Gon.:   If in Naples   30
I should report this now, would they believe me?
If I should say I saw such [islanders]
(For, certes, these are people of the island),
Who though they are of monstrous shape, yet note
Their manners are more gentle, kind, than of   35
Our human generation you shall find
Many, nay, almost any.
Pros.:   *[Aside.]* Honest lord,
Thou hast said well; for some of you there present
Are worse than devils.
Alon.:   I cannot too much muse
Such shapes, such gesture, and such sound expressing   40
(Although they want the use of tongue) a kind
Of excellent dumb discourse.
Pros.:   *[Aside.]* Praise in departing.
Fran.: They vanish'd strangely.
Seb.:   No matter, since
They have left their viands behind; for we have stomachs.
Will't please you taste of what is here?
Alon.:   Not I.   45
Gon.: Faith, sir, you need not fear. When we were boys,
Who would believe that there were mountaineers,
Dew-lapp'd, like bulls, whose throats had hanging at 'em
Wallets of flesh? or that there were such men
Whose heads stood in their breasts? which now we find   50
Each putter-out of five for one will bring us
Good warrant of.
Alon.:   I will stand to, and feed,
Although my last, no matter, since I feel
The best is past. Brother, my lord the Duke,
Stand to, and do as we.   55

---

28 *want credit:* lack credence   33 *certes:* certainly   34 *monstrous:* abnormal, unnatural
39 *muse:* wonder at   42 *Praise in departing:* i.e. don't judge until you see the conclusion
(proverbial)   44 *stomachs:* appetites   48 *Dew-lapp'd:* with pouches of skin hanging from
the neck (probably alluding to travellers' tales about goiter among Swiss mountaineers)
49–50 *men . . . breasts:* A common travellers' tale.   51 *Each . . . one:* Travellers deposited a sum
of money at home to be repaid fivefold if they returned, forfeited if they did not   52 *stand to:*
take the risk.   54 *best:* i.e. best part of life

Thunder and lightning. Enter Ariel, *like a harpy, claps his wings upon the table, and with a quaint device the banquet vanishes.*

Ari.: You are three men of sin, whom Destiny,
   That hath to instrument this lower world
   And what is in't, the never-surfeited sea
   Hath caus'd to belch up you; and on this island
   Where man doth not inhabit—you 'mongst men   60
   Being most unfit to live. I have made you mad;
   And even with such-like valor men hang and drown
   Their proper selves.   *[Alonso, Sebastian, etc., draw their swords.]*
                   You fools! I and my fellows
   Are ministers of Fate. The elements,
   Of whom your swords are temper'd, may as well   65
   Wound the loud winds, or with bemock'd-at stabs
   Kill the still-closing waters, as diminish
   One dowle that's in my plume. My fellow ministers
   Are like invulnerable. If you could hurt,
   Your swords are now too massy for your strengths,   70
   And will not be uplifted. But remember
   (For that's my business to you) that you three
   From Milan did supplant good Prospero,
   Expos'd unto the sea (which hath requit it)
   Him, and his innocent child; for which foul deed   75
   The pow'rs, delaying (not forgetting), have
   Incens'd the seas and shores—yea, all the creatures,
   Against your peace. Thee of thy son, Alonso,
   They have bereft; and do pronounce by me
   Ling'ring perdition (worse than any death   80
   Can be at once) shall step by step attend
   You and your ways, whose wraths to guard you from—
   Which here, in this most desolate isle, else falls
   Upon your heads—is nothing but heart's sorrow,
   And a clear life ensuing.   85

He vanishes in thunder; then, to soft music, enter the Shapes *again, and dance, with mocks and mows, and carry out the table.*

Pros.: Bravely the figure of this harpy hast thou
   Perform'd, my Ariel; a grace it had, devouring.
   Of my instruction hast thou nothing bated

---

55 s.d. *like a harpy:* in the shape of a harpy, a rapacious monster with the face of a woman and the wings and claws of a bird of prey   *with device:* by means of an ingenious stage mechanism   57 *to:* for   62 *such-like valor:* i.e. the valor of madness, very different from true courage   63 *proper:* own   65 *whom:* which   67 *still-closing:* always closing as soon as parted   68 *dowle:* small feather   69 *like:* similarly   74 *requit it:* repaid the act (by casting you up here)   80 *perdition:* ruin   82 *whose:* i.e. those of the "pow'rs" of line 76   84 *is . . . sorrow:* there is no means except repentance   85 *clear:* sinless   s.d. *mocks and mows:* mocking gestures and grimaces   87 *devouring:* i.e. making the banquet disappear   88 *bated:* omitted

In what thou hadst to say; so with good life,
And observation strange, my meaner ministers   90
Their several kinds have done. My high charms work,
And these, mine enemies, are all knit up
In their distractions. They now are in my pow'r;
And in these fits I leave them, while I visit
Young Ferdinand, whom they suppose is drown'd,   95
And his and mine lov'd darling.   *[Exit above.]*

Gon.: I' th' name of something holy, sir, why stand you
In this strange stare?
Alon.:   O, it is monstrous! monstrous!
Methought the billows spoke, and told me of it;
The winds did sing it to me, and the thunder,   100
That deep and dreadful organ-pipe, pronounc'd
The name of Prosper; it did base my trespass.
Therefore my son i' th' ooze is bedded; and
I'll seek him deeper than e'er plummet sounded,
And with him there lie mudded.   *Exit.*
Seb.:   But one fiend at a time,   105
I'll fight their legions o'er.
Ant.:   I'll be thy second.

                    Exeunt [Sebastian and Antonio].

Gon.: All three of them are desperate: their great guilt
(Like poison given to work a great time after)
Now gins to bite the spirits. I do beseech you
(That are of suppler joints) follow them swiftly,   110
And hinder them from what this ecstasy
May now provoke them to.
Adr.:   Follow, I pray you.   *Exeunt omnes.*

ACT IV

SCENE I

Enter Prospero, Ferdinand, *and* Miranda.

Pros.: If I have too austerely punish'd you,
Your compensation makes amends, for I

---

89 *life:* realism   90 *observation strange:* exceptional care   *meaner:* i.e. inferior to Ariel
91 *several kinds:* individual parts   92–93 *knit . . . distractions:* entangled in their madness
97–98 *why . . . stare:* Gonzalo has not heard Ariel's speech   99 *it:* i.e. my sin   102 *base:* bass,
i.e. utter in a deep voice   103 *Therefore:* therefor, i.e. in consequence of his trespass
106 *o'er:* one after another   109 *gins . . . spirits:* begins to cause mental anguish   111 *ecstasy:*
fit of madness   IV.i. Location: before Prospero's cell

Have given you here a third of mine own life,
Or that for which I live; who once again
I tender to thy hand. All thy vexations   5
Were but my trials of thy love, and thou
Hast strangely stood the test. Here, afore heaven,
I ratify this my rich gift. O Ferdinand,
Do not smile at me that I boast her [off],
For thou shalt find she will outstrip all praise   10
And make it halt behind her.
Fer.:   I do believe it
Against an oracle.
Pros.: Then, as my [gift], and thine own acquisition
Worthily purchas'd, take my daughter. But
If thou dost break her virgin-knot before   15
All sanctimonious ceremonies may
With full and holy rite be minist'red,
No sweet aspersion shall the heavens let fall
To make this contract grow; but barren hate,
Sour-ey'd disdain, and discord shall bestrew   20
The union of your bed with weeds so loathly
That you shall hate it both. Therefore take heed,
As Hymen's lamps shall light you.
Fer.:   As I hope
For quiet days, fair issue, and long life,
With such love as 'tis now, the murkiest den,   25
The most opportune place, the strong'st suggestion
Our worser genius can, shall never melt
Mine honor into lust, to take away
The edge of that day's celebration,
When I shall think or Phoebus' steeds are founder'd   30
Or Night kept chain'd below.
Pros.:   Fairly spoke.
Sit then and talk with her, she is thine own.
What, Ariel! my industrious servant, Ariel!

Enter Ariel.

---

3 *a third . . . life:* Various explanations have been put forward: for example, that the other two
parts have been his dukedom and his books, or his late wife and his personal interests; or that Miranda represents his future, the other two parts being his past and his present; or that he has spent
a third of his life on Miranda's education   7 *strangely:* wonderfully well   9 *boast her off:* i.e.
praise her so highly   11 *halt:* limp   12 *Against an oracle:* even if an oracle should declare
otherwise   16 *sanctimonious:* sacred, holy   18 *aspersion:* i.e. blessing; literally, sprinkling,
as of rain that promotes fertility and growth   19 *grow:* be fruitful (as contrasted with *barren*)
21 *weeds:* Instead of the flowers with which the marriage bed was customarily strewn.
23 *As . . . you:* i.e. as you desire happiness in your marriage The symbolic torch of Hymen, god
of marriage, was supposed to promise happiness if it burned with a clear flame, the opposite
if it smoked.   26 *suggestion:* temptation   27 *Our . . . can:* our bad angel is capable of
30 *or . . . founder'd:* either the sun-god's horses have gone lame (because the day is so long)

Ari.: What would my potent master? here I am.

Pros.: Thou and thy meaner fellows your last service   35
    Did worthily perform; and I must use you
    In such another trick. Go bring the rabble
    (O'er whom I give thee pow'r) here to this place.
    Incite them to quick motion, for I must
    Bestow upon the eyes of this young couple   40
    Some vanity of mine art. It is my promise,
    And they expect it from me.

Ari.:   Presently?

Pros.: Ay, with a twink.

Ari.: Before you can say "come" and "go,"
    And breathe twice, and cry "so, so,"   45
    Each one, tripping on his toe,
    Will be here with mop and mow.
    Do you love me, master? no?

Pros.: Dearly, my delicate Ariel. Do not approach
    Till thou dost hear me call.

Ari.:   Well; I conceive.   *Exit.*   50

Pros.: Look thou be true; do not give dalliance
    Too much the rein. The strongest oaths are straw
    To th' fire i' th' blood. Be more abstenious,
    Or else good night your vow!

Fer.:   I warrant you, sir,
    The white cold virgin snow upon my heart   55
    Abates the ardor of my liver.

Pros.:   Well.
    Now come, my Ariel, bring a corollary,
    Rather than want a spirit. Appear, and pertly.
    No tongue! all eyes! Be silent.   *Soft music.*

    Enter Iris.

Iris: Ceres, most bounteous lady, thy rich leas   60
    Of wheat, rye, barley, fetches, oats, and pease;
    Thy turfy mountains, where live nibbling sheep,
    And flat meads thatch'd with stover, them to keep;
    Thy banks with pioned and twilled brims,
    Which spungy April at thy hest betrims,   65

---

37 *trick:* ingenious device (technical term in pageantry)   *rabble:* troop of inferior spirits
41 *vanity:* show, delusive appearance   42 *Presently:* immediately   43 *with a twink:* in a twinkling   47 *mop and mow:* gesture and grimace   50 *conceive:* understand   53 *abstenious:* ab-
stemious   56 *liver:* supposed seat of the passions   57 *corollary:* extra   58 *want:* lack
pertly: briskly   59 *No tongue:* Any speech from the spectators would make the spirits vanish. Cf.
lines 126–27.   s.d. *Iris:* goddess of the rainbow and Juno's messenger   60 *Ceres:* goddess of
agriculture   *leas:* meadows, cultivated land   61 *fetches:* vetch, a fodder plant   63 *stover:* hay
for winter use   64 *pioned and twilled:* undercut by the stream and retained by interwoven
branches   65 *spungy:* spongy, i.e. wet

To make cold nymphs chaste crowns; and thy broomgroves,
Whose shadow the dismissed bachelor loves,
Being lass-lorn; thy pole-clipt vineyard,
And thy sea-marge, sterile and rocky-hard,
Where thou thyself dost air—the Queen o' th' sky, 70
Whose wat'ry arch and messenger am I,
Bids thee leave these, and with her sovereign Grace,
Here on this grass-plot, in this very place,
To come and sport. [Her] peacocks fly amain.

　　　　　　　　　　　　　　Juno descends [slowly in her car].

Approach, rich Ceres, her to entertain. 75

Enter Ceres.

Cer.: Hail, many-colored messenger, that ne'er
Dost disobey the wife of Jupiter;
Who with thy saffron wings upon my flow'rs
Diffusest honey-drops, refreshing show'rs,
And with each end of thy blue bow dost crown 80
My bosky acres and my unshrubb'd down,
Rich scarf to my proud earth—why hath thy Queen
Summon'd me hither, to this short-grass'd green?
Iris: A contract of true love to celebrate,
And some donation freely to estate 85
On the bless'd lovers.
Cer.: 　　　　　　　Tell me, heavenly bow,
If Venus or her son, as thou dost know,
Do now attend the Queen? Since they did plot
The means that dusky Dis my daughter got,
Her and her blind boy's scandall'd company 90
I have forsworn.
Iris: 　　　　　　Of her society
Be not afraid. I met her Deity
Cutting the clouds towards Paphos; and her son
Dove-drawn with her. Here thought they to have done
Some wanton charm upon this man and maid, 95
Whose vows are, that no bed-right shall be paid
Till Hymen's torch be lighted; but in vain,

---

66 *cold:* chaste　*broom:* a kind of shrub bearing yellow flowers　67 *dismissed bachelor:* rejected suitor　68 *pole-clipt:* poll-clipped, i.e. with top growth pruned back (?) If *clipt* means (as often) "embraced," the sense could be "enclosed by a fence of poles" or "with poles entwined by the vines."　70 *Queen . . . sky:* Juno　74 *peacocks:* Juno's sacred birds, which drew her chariot　*amain:* swiftly　75 *entertain:* receive　81 *bosky:* wooded　*down:* upland　85 *estate:* bestow　87 *son:* Cupid, the "blind boy" of line 90　89 *Dis:* Pluto, ruler of the underworld (hence *dusky*), who carried off Ceres' daughter Proserpine to be his queen　90 *scandall'd:* scandalous　93 *Paphos:* place in Cyprus sacred to Venus　94 *Dove-drawn:* Venus' chariot was drawn by her sacred doves　94–95 *done . . . charm:* cast some unchaste spell

Mars's hot minion is return'd again;
Her waspish-headed son has broke his arrows,
Swears he will shoot no more, but play with sparrows,   100
And be a boy right out.

[*Juno alights.*]

Cer.:   Highest Queen of state,
Great Juno, comes, I know her by her gait.
Juno: How does my bounteous sister? Go with me
To bless this twain, that they may prosperous be,
And honor'd in their issue.   *They sing.* 105
Juno: Honor, riches, marriage-blessing,
Long continuance, and increasing,
Hourly joys be still upon you!
Juno sings her blessings on you.
Cer.: Earth's increase, foison plenty,   110
Barns and garners never empty;
Vines with clust'ring bunches growing,
Plants with goodly burthen bowing;
Spring come to you at the farthest
In the very end of harvest!   115
Scarcity and want shall shun you,
Ceres' blessing so is on you.
Fer.: This is a most majestic vision, and
Harmonious charmingly. May I be bold
To think these spirits?
Pros.:   Spirits, which by mine art   120
I have from their confines call'd to enact
My present fancies.
Fer.:   Let me live here ever;
So rare a wond'red father and a wise
Makes this place Paradise.

                          Juno *and* Ceres *whisper, and send* Iris *on employment.*

Pros.:   Sweet now, silence!
Juno and Ceres whisper seriously;   125
There's something else to do. Hush, and be mute,
Or else our spell is marr'd.

---

98 *hot minion:* lustful mistress Venus and Mars were lovers. *return'd:* i.e. to Paphos   99
waspish-headed: peevish   100 *sparrows:* like doves, sacred to Venus Sparrows were proverbially
lecherous.   101 *right out:* outright *Highest . . . state:* most majestic queen   102 *gait:* i.e.
regal bearing   108 *still:* always   110 *foison plenty:* plentiful abundance   115 *In . . . harvest:* i.e. without intervening winter   119 *charmingly:* enchantingly, magically
123 *wond'red:* (1) to be wondered at; (2) able to perform wonders; (3) possessed of that wonder,
Miranda (see note to III.i.37).   124 *Sweet now, silence:* Addressed to Miranda, who is about
to speak

Iris: You nymphs, call'd Naiades, of the windring brooks,
With your sedg'd crowns and ever-harmless looks,
Leave your crisp channels, and on this green land   130
Answer your summons; Juno does command.
Come, temperate nymphs, and help to celebrate
A contract of true love; be not too late.

Enter certain Nymphs.

You sunburn'd sicklemen, of August weary,
Come hither from the furrow and be merry.   135
Make holiday; your rye-straw hats put on,
And these fresh nymphs encounter every one
In country footing.

Enter certain Reapers, *properly habited: they join with the Nymphs in a
graceful dance, towards the end whereof* Prospero *starts suddenly, and speaks; after
which, to a strange, hollow, and confused noise, they heavily vanish.*

Pros. [Aside.]: I had forgot that foul conspiracy
Of the beast Caliban and his confederates   140
Against my life. The minute of their plot
Is almost come. *[To the* Spirits.*]* Well done, avoid; no more.
Fer.: This is strange. Your father's in some passion
That works him strongly.
Mir.:   Never till this day
Saw I him touch'd with anger, so distemper'd.   145
Pros.: You do look, my son, in a mov'd sort,
As if you were dismay'd; be cheerful, sir.
Our revels now are ended. These our actors
(As I foretold you) were all spirits, and
Are melted into air, into thin air,   150
And, like the baseless fabric of this vision,
The cloud-capp'd tow'rs, the gorgeous palaces,
The solemn temples, the great globe itself,
Yea, all which it inherit, shall dissolve,
And like this insubstantial pageant faded   155
Leave not a rack behind. We are such stuff
As dreams are made on; and our little life
Is rounded with a sleep. Sir, I am vex'd;
Bear with my weakness, my old brain is troubled.

---

128 *windring:* winding and wandering (apparently a coinage of Shakespeare's)   129 *ever-
harmless:* ever-innocent   130 *crisp:* rippling   132 *temperate:* chaste   137 *fresh:* young and
beautiful   *encounter:* meet   138 *footing:* dance   s.d. *heavily:* reluctantly   142 *avoid:* be
gone   144 *works:* agitates   146 *mov'd sort:* troubled state   148 *revels:* festivity, entertainment   151 *baseless fabric:* structure without physical foundation   154 *which it inherit:* who
occupy it   155 *insubstantial:* without material substance   156 *rack:* wisp of cloud   157
on: of   158 *rounded:* surrounded

Be not disturb'd with my infirmity.   160
If you be pleas'd, retire into my cell,
And there repose. A turn or two I'll walk
To still my beating mind.
Fer., Mir.:   We wish your peace.
Pros. [To Ariel.]: Come with a thought. *[To Ferdinand and* Miranda*.]* I
thank thee.   *Exeunt [Ferdinand and* Miranda*].* 165
                                                  Ariel! come!

Enter Ariel.

Ari.: Thy thoughts I cleave to. What's thy pleasure?
Pros.:   Spirit,
We must prepare to meet with Caliban.
Ari.: Ay, my commander. When I presented Ceres,
I thought to have told thee of it, but I fear'd   170
Lest I might anger thee.
Pros.: Say again, where didst thou leave these varlots?
Ari.: I told you, sir, they were red-hot with drinking,
So full of valor that they smote the air
For breathing in their faces; beat the ground   175
For kissing of their feet; yet always bending
Towards their project. Then I beat my tabor,
At which like unback'd colts they prick'd their ears,
Advanc'd their eyelids, lifted up their noses
As they smelt music. So I charm'd their ears   180
That calf-like they my lowing follow'd through
Tooth'd briers, sharp furzes, pricking goss, and thorns,
Which ent'red their frail shins. At last I left them
I' th' filthy-mantled pool beyond your cell,
There dancing up to th' chins, that the foul lake   185
O'erstunk their feet.
Pros.:   This was well done, my bird.
Thy shape invisible retain thou still.
The trumpery in my house, go bring it hither,
For stale to catch these thieves.
Ari.:   I go, I go.   *Exit.*
Pros.: A devil, a born devil, on whose nature   190
Nurture can never stick; on whom my pains,
Humanely taken, all, all lost, quite lost;
And as with age his body uglier grows,

---

164 *with:* at the summons of   169 *presented:* represented, took the part of?   172 *varlots:* var-
lets, ruffians   176–77 *bending . . . project:* pursuing their purpose—the murder of Prospero
178 *unback'd:* never ridden, unbroken   179 *Advanc'd:* raised   180 *As:* as if   182. *goss:*
gorse   184 *filthy-mantled:* covered with dirty scum   188 *trumpery:* showy finery (the "glistering apparel" of line 194 s.d.)   189 *stale:* bait

So his mind cankers. I will plague them all,
Even to roaring.

Enter Ariel, *loaden with glistering apparel, etc.*

                            Come, hang [them on] this line.   195

[Prospero and Ariel *remain, invisible.] Enter* Caliban, Stephano, *and* Trinculo, *all wet.*

Cal.: Pray you tread softly, that the blind mole may not
  Hear a foot fall; we now are near his cell.

Ste.: Monster, your fairy, which you say is a harmless fairy, has done little better than play'd the Jack with us.

Trin.: Monster, I do smell all horse-piss, at which my nose is in great in- 200
dignation.

Ste.: So is mine. Do you hear, monster? If I should take a displeasure against
you, look you—

Trin.: Thou wert but a lost monster.

Cal.: Good my lord, give me thy favor still.   205
  Be patient, for the prize I'll bring thee to
  Shall hoodwink this mischance; therefore speak softly,
  All's hush'd as midnight yet.

Trin.: Ay, but to lose our bottles in the pool—

Ste.: There is not only disgrace and dishonor in that, monster, but an infinite 210
loss.

Trin.: That's more to me than my wetting; yet this is your harmless fairy,
monster!

Ste.: I will fetch off my bottle, though I be o'er ears for my labor.

Cal.: Prithee, my king, be quiet. Seest thou here,   215
  This is the mouth o' th' cell. No noise, and enter.
  Do that good mischief which may make this island
  Thine own for ever, and I, thy Caliban,
  For aye thy foot-licker.

Ste.: Give me thy hand. I do begin to have bloody thoughts.   220

Trin.: O King Stephano! O peer! O worthy Stephano! look what a wardrobe
here is for thee!

Cal.: Let it alone, thou fool, it is but trash.

Trin.: O, ho, monster! we know what belongs to a frippery. O King Stephano!

Ste.: Put off that gown, Trinculo. By this hand, I'll have that gown.   225

Trin.: Thy Grace shall have it.

Cal.: The dropsy drown this fool! what do you mean
  To dote thus on such luggage? Let['t] alone

---

194 *cankers:* becomes malignant   195 *line:* lime tree, linden   196 *mole:* thought to have sensitive hearing   199 *Jack:* (1) knave; (2) jack-o'-lantern, i.e. will-o'-the-wisp   207 *hoodwink:* make you blind to   221 *peer:* referring to the old ballad "King Stephen was a worthy peer," quoted in *Othello*   224 *frippery:* secondhand-clothes shop   227 *drown:* suffocate   228 *luggage:* encumbering trash

And do the murther first. If he awake,
From toe to crown he'll fill our skins with pinches,   230
Make us strange stuff.

Ste.: Be you quiet, monster. Mistress line, is not this my jerkin? Now is the
jerkin under the line. Now, jerkin, you are like to lose your hair, and
prove a bald jerkin.

Trin.: Do, do; we steal by line and level, and't like your Grace.   235

Ste.: I thank thee for that jest; here's a garment for't. Wit shall not go unre-
warded while I am king of this country. "Steal by line and level" is an excellent pass of pate; there's another garment for't.

Trin.: Monster, come, put some lime upon your fingers, and away with the
rest.   240

Cal.: I will have none on't. We shall lose our time,
And all be turn'd to barnacles, or to apes
With foreheads villainous low.

Ste.: Monster, lay-to your fingers. Help to bear this away where my hogshead
of wine is, or I'll turn you out of my kingdom. Go to, carry this.   245

Trin.: And this.

Ste.: Ay, and this.

A noise of hunters heard. Enter divers Spirits *in shape of dogs and hounds,
hunting them about;* Prospero *and* Ariel *setting them on.*

Pros.: Hey, Mountain, hey!

Ari.: Silver! there it goes, Silver!

Pros.: Fury, Fury! there, Tyrant, there! hark, hark!   250
                    *[*Caliban, Stephano, *and* Trinculo *are driven out.]*
Go, charge my goblins that they grind their joints
With dry convulsions, shorten up their sinews
With aged cramps, and more pinch-spotted make them
Than pard or cat o' mountain.

Ari.:   Hark, they roar!

Pros.: Let them be hunted soundly. At this hour   255
Lies at my mercy all mine enemies.
Shortly shall all my labors end, and thou
Shalt have the air at freedom. For a little
Follow, and do me service.   *Exeunt.*

---

232 *jerkin:* a kind of jacket   *under the line:* With pun on the sense "south of the equator." The
joke involves the popular idea that travellers to tropical countries lost their hair through fevers,
or from scurvy resulting from lack of fresh food on the long voyage.   235 *Do, do:* an expression of approval, equivalent to "bravo"   *by . . . level:* with plumb-line and carpenter's level, i.e.
with professional skill (continuing the puns on *line*)   *and't like:* if it please   238 *pass:* thrust
(a fencing term)   *pate:* i.e. wit   239 *lime:* sticky substance; thieves were jokingly said to have
lime on their fingers   242 *barnacles:* a kind of geese traditionally supposed to develop from the
shellfish so named   243 *villainous:* wretchedly   245 *Go to:* expression of exhortation or reproof, equivalent to "come, come!"   250 *hark:* "sic 'em!"   252 *dry convulsions:* Precisely
what sort of painful seizure is meant here is uncertain.   253 *aged:* such as old people have
254 *pard:* leopard   *cat o' mountain:* catamount, wildcat

ACT V

SCENE I

Enter Prospero *in his magic robes, and* Ariel.

Pros.: Now does my project gather to a head:
My charms crack not; my spirits obey; and Time
Goes upright with his carriage. How's the day?
Ari.: On the sixt hour, at which time, my lord,
You said our work should cease.
Pros.:   I did say so,   5
When first I rais'd the tempest. Say, my spirit,
How fares the King and 's followers?
Ari.:   Confin'd together
In the same fashion as you gave in charge,
Just as you left them; all prisoners, sir,
In the line-grove which weather-fends your cell;   10
They cannot boudge till your release. The King,
His brother, and yours, abide all three distracted,
And the remainder mourning over them,
Brimful of sorrow and dismay; but chiefly
Him that you term'd, sir, "the good old Lord Gonzalo,"   15
His tears run down his beard like winter's drops
From eaves of reeds. Your charm so strongly works 'em
That if you now beheld them, your affections
Would become tender.
Pros.:   Dost thou think so, spirit?
Ari.: Mine would, sir, were I human.
Pros.:   And mine shall.   20
Hast thou, which art but air, a touch, a feeling
Of their afflictions, and shall not myself,
One of their kind, that relish all as sharply
Passion as they, be kindlier mov'd than thou art?
Though with their high wrongs I am strook to th' quick,   25
Yet, with my nobler reason, 'gainst my fury
Do I take part. The rarer action is
In virtue than in vengeance. They being penitent,
The sole drift of my purpose doth extend

V.i. *Location:* before Prospero's cell   3 *Goes . . . carriage:* walks upright under what he is carrying (because his burden of coming events has been greatly lightened)   4 *On:* approaching *sixt:* sixth On the time, see I.ii.240–41.   10 *weather-fends:* serves as windbreak for   11 *boudge:* budge, stir   *your release:* i.e. their release by you   12 *distracted:* out of their wits   17 *eaves of reeds:* thatched roofs   18 *affections:* inclinations, bent of mind   21 *touch:* synonymous with *feeling*   23 *relish:* experience   *all:* quite   24 *kindlier:* (1) more sympathetically; (2) more naturally (as "one of their kind")   27 *take part:* side   *rarer:* finer, nobler

Not a frown further. Go release them, Ariel.   30
My charms I'll break, their senses I'll restore,
And they shall be themselves.
Ari.:   I'll fetch them, sir.

Exit. [Prospero *traces a magic circle with his staff.*]

Pros.: Ye elves of hills, brooks, standing lakes, and groves,
And ye that on the sands with printless foot
Do chase the ebbing Neptune, and do fly him   35
When he comes back; you demi-puppets that
By moonshine do the green sour ringlets make,
Whereof the ewe not bites; and you whose pastime
Is to make midnight mushrumps, that rejoice
To hear the solemn curfew: by whose aid   40
(Weak masters though ye be) I have bedimm'd
The noontide sun, call'd forth the mutinous winds,
And 'twixt the green sea and the azur'd vault
Set roaring war; to the dread rattling thunder
Have I given fire, and rifted Jove's stout oak   45
With his own bolt; the strong-bas'd promontory
Have I made shake, and by the spurs pluck'd up
The pine and cedar. Graves at my command
Have wak'd their sleepers, op'd, and let 'em forth
By my so potent art. But this rough magic   50
I here abjure; and when I have requir'd
Some heavenly music (which even now I do)
To work mine end upon their senses that
This airy charm is for, I'll break my staff,
Bury it certain fadoms in the earth,   55
And deeper than did ever plummet sound
I'll drown my book.   *Solemn music.*

Here enters Ariel *before; then* Alonso, *with a frantic gesture, attended by*
Gonzalo; Sebastian *and* Antonio *in like manner, attended by* Adrian *and* Francisco. *They all enter the circle which* Prospero *had made, and there stand*
charm'd; which Prospero *observing, speaks.*

A solemn air, and the best comforter
To an unsettled fancy, cure thy brains,

---

36 *demi-puppets:* quasi-puppets, i.e. creatures of small size   37 *green sour ringlets:* so-called
"fairy rings" in grass, actually caused by mushrooms   39 *mushrumps:* mushrooms, supposed
because of their rapid growth to be made by elves during the night   40 *curfew:* Supposedly
spirits could be abroad only between curfew (9 p.m.) and the first cockcrow; cf. I.ii.327.
41 *Weak:* i.e. as compared with the powerful demons summoned up by black magic   45 *rifted:*
split   47 *spurs:* roots   50 *rough:* i.e. capable of producing the violent effects just described
(?)   51 *requir'd:* requested   53 *their senses that:* the senses of those whom   54 *airy charm:*
i.e. the music   57 s.d. *frantic gesture:* insane demeanor   58 *and:* i.e. which is   59 *thy*
brains: The first sentence is addressed to Alonso, the next to all six now within the circle.

Now useless, [boil'd] within thy skull! There stand,   60
For you are spell-stopp'd.
Holy Gonzalo, honorable man,
Mine eyes, ev'n sociable to the show of thine,
Fall fellowly drops. The charm dissolves apace,
And as the morning steals upon the night,   65
Melting the darkness, so their rising senses
Begin to chase the ignorant fumes that mantle
Their clearer reason. O good Gonzalo,
My true preserver, and a loyal sir
To him thou follow'st! I will pay thy graces   70
Home both in word and deed. Most cruelly
Didst thou, Alonso, use me and my daughter;
Thy brother was a furtherer in the act.
Thou art pinch'd for't now, Sebastian. Flesh and blood,
You, brother mine, that [entertain'd] ambition,   75
Expell'd remorse and nature, whom, with Sebastian
(Whose inward pinches therefore are most strong),
Would here have kill'd your king, I do forgive thee,
Unnatural though thou art.—Their understanding
Begins to swell, and the approaching tide   80
Will shortly fill the reasonable [shores]
That now lie foul and muddy. Not one of them
That yet looks on me, or would know me! Ariel,
Fetch me the hat and rapier in my cell.

>   *[Exit* Ariel, *and returns immediately.]*

I will discase me, and myself present   85
As I was sometime Milan. Quickly, spirit,
Thou shalt ere long be free.   Ariel *sings and helps to attire him.*
[Ari.:] Where the bee sucks, there suck I,
      In a cowslip's bell I lie;
         There I couch when owls do cry.   90
      On the bat's back I do fly
         After summer merrily.
Merrily, merrily shall I live now,
Under the blossom that hangs on the bough.
Pros.: Why, that's my dainty Ariel! I shall miss thee,   95
But yet thou shalt have freedom. So, so, so.
To the king's ship, invisible as thou art;
There shalt thou find the mariners asleep

---

60 *boil'd:* i.e. made useless by passion   63 *sociable:* sympathetic *show:* appearance   64 *Fall:*
let fall   67 *ignorant fumes:* fumes that make them uncomprehending   70–71 *pay . . . Home:*
reward your favors fully   76 *remorse:* pity *nature:* natural feeling   77 *therefore:* therefor, to
that end   81 *reasonable shores:* shores of reason, i.e. minds   85 *discase me:* take off my magician's robe   86 *As . . . Milan:* dressed as I formerly was as Duke of Milan   96 *So, so, so:*
Probably an expression of approval as Ariel finishes attiring him.

Under the hatches. The master and the boatswain
Being awake, enforce them to this place;   100
And presently, I prithee.
Ari.: I drink the air before me, and return
Or ere your pulse twice beat.   *Exit.*
Gon.: All torment, trouble, wonder, and amazement
Inhabits here. Some heavenly power guide us   105
Out of this fearful country!
Pros.:   Behold, sir King,
The wronged Duke of Milan, Prospero.
For more assurance that a living prince
Does now speak to thee, I embrace thy body,
And to thee and thy company I bid   110
A hearty welcome.
Alon.:   Whe'er thou beest he or no,
Or some enchanted trifle to abuse me
(As late I have been), I not know. Thy pulse
Beats as of flesh and blood; and since I saw thee,
Th' affliction of my mind amends, with which   115
I fear a madness held me. This must crave
(And if this be at all) a most strange story.
Thy dukedom I resign, and do entreat
Thou pardon me my wrongs. But how should Prospero
Be living, and be here?
Pros.:   *[To* Gonzalo.*]* First, noble friend,   120
Let me embrace thine age, whose honor cannot
Be measur'd or confin'd.
Gon.:   Whether this be,
Or be not, I'll not swear.
Pros.:   You do yet taste
Some subtleties o' th' isle, that will [not] let you
Believe things certain. Welcome, my friends all!   125
[Aside to Sebastian *and* Antonio.*]* But you, my brace of lords, were I so
          minded,
I here could pluck his Highness' frown upon you
And justify you traitors. At this time
I will tell no tales.
Seb.:   *[Aside.]* The devil speaks in him.
Pros.:   No.   130
For you, most wicked sir, whom to call brother

---

101 *presently:* at once   108 *a living prince:* i.e. not a spirit   112 *enchanted trifle:* trick of magic
abuse: deceive   116–17 *This . . . story:* this demands, if it is really taking place, an extraordinary
explanation   121 *thine age:* i.e. thy reverend self   121–22 *cannot . . . confin'd:* i.e. is immeasurable and boundless   124 *subtleties:* illusions, with play (as *taste* suggests) on the word as applied to fancy confections representing actual objects or allegorical figures   129 *justify:* prove

Would even infect my mouth, I do forgive
Thy rankest fault—all of them; and require
My dukedom of thee, which perforce, I know
Thou must restore.

Alon.:   If thou beest Prospero,   135
Give us particulars of thy preservation,
How thou hast met us here, whom three hours since
Were wrack'd upon this shore; where I have lost
(How sharp the point of this remembrance is!)
My dear son Ferdinand.

Pros.:   I am woe for't, sir.   140

Alon.: Irreparable is the loss, and patience
Says, it is past her cure.

Pros.:   I rather think
You have not sought her help, of whose soft grace
For the like loss I have her sovereign aid,
And rest myself content.

Alon.:   You the like loss?   145

Pros.: As great to me as late, and supportable
To make the dear loss, have I means much weaker
Than you may call to comfort you; for I
Have lost my daughter.

Alon.:   A daughter?   150
O heavens, that they were living both in Naples,
The King and Queen there! That they were, I wish
Myself were mudded in that oozy bed
Where my son lies. When did you lose your daughter?

Pros.: In this last tempest. I perceive these lords   155
At this encounter do so much admire
That they devour their reason, and scarce think
Their eyes do offices of truth, their words
Are natural breath; but howsoev'r you have
Been justled from your senses, know for certain   160
That I am Prospero, and that very duke
Which was thrust forth of Milan, who most strangely
Upon this shore (where you were wrack'd) was landed,
To be the lord on't. No more yet of this,
For 'tis a chronicle of day by day,   165
Not a relation for a breakfast, nor
Befitting this first meeting. Welcome, sir;
This cell's my court. Here have I few attendants,
And subjects none abroad. Pray you look in.

---

143 *of . . . grace:* by whose mercy   146 *late:* recent   147 *dear:* deeply felt   152 *That:* provided that   156 *admire:* marvel   157 *devour their reason:* Presumably referring to the open-mouthed astonishment in which their rational powers are lost.   158 *do . . . truth:* function accurately   162 *of:* from   169 *abroad:* i.e. elsewhere on the island

My dukedom since you have given me again,   170
I will requite you with as good a thing,
At least bring forth a wonder, to content ye
As much as me my dukedom.

Here Prospero *discovers* Ferdinand *and* Miranda *playing at chess.*

Mir.: Sweet lord, you play me false.
Fer.:   No, my dearest love,
    I would not for the world.   175
Mir.: Yes, for a score of kingdoms you should wrangle,
    And I would call it fair play.
Alon.:   If this prove
    A vision of the island, one dear son
    Shall I twice lose.
Seb.:   A most high miracle!
Fer.: Though the seas threaten, they are merciful;   180
    I have curs'd them without cause.   *[Kneels.]*
Alon.:   Now all the blessings
    Of a glad father compass thee about!
    Arise, and say how thou cam'st here.
Mir.:   O wonder!
    How many goodly creatures are there here!
    How beauteous mankind is! O brave new world   185
    That has such people in't!
Pros.:   'Tis new to thee.
Alon.: What is this maid with whom thou wast at play?
    Your eld'st acquaintance cannot be three hours.
    Is she the goddess that hath sever'd us,
    And brought us thus together?
Fer.:   Sir, she is mortal;   190
    But by immortal Providence she's mine.
    I chose her when I could not ask my father
    For his advice, nor thought I had one. She
    Is daughter to this famous Duke of Milan,
    Of whom so often I have heard renown,   195
    But never saw before; of whom I have
    Receiv'd a second life; and second father
    This lady makes him to me.
Alon.:   I am hers.
    But, O! how oddly will it sound that I
    Must ask my child forgiveness!
Pros.:   There, sir, stop.   200

---

173 s.d. *discovers:* discloses (by pulling aside a curtain)   176 *Yes . . . wrangle:* i.e. certainly you should do so for the world; in fact, for less than the world—for twenty kingdoms you ought to do your utmost against me   178 *vision:* i.e. illusion   188 *eld'st:* longest possible

Let us not burden our remembrances with
A heaviness that's gone.

Gon.:   I have inly wept,
Or should have spoke ere this. Look down, you gods,
And on this couple drop a blessed crown!
For it is you that have chalk'd forth the way   205
Which brought us hither.

Alon.:   I say amen, Gonzalo!

Gon.: Was Milan thrust from Milan, that his issue
Should become kings of Naples? O, rejoice
Beyond a common joy, and set it down
With gold on lasting pillars: in one voyage   210
Did Claribel her husband find at Tunis,
And Ferdinand, her brother, found a wife
Where he himself was lost; Prospero, his dukedom
In a poor isle; and all of us, ourselves,
When no man was his own.

Alon.:   *[To* Ferdinand *and* Miranda.*]* Give me your hands.   215
Let grief and sorrow still embrace his heart
That doth not wish you joy!

Gon.:   Be it so, amen!

Enter Ariel, *with the* Master *and* Boatswain *amazedly following.*

O, look, sir, look, sir, here is more of us.
I prophesied, if a gallows were on land,
This fellow could not drown. Now, blasphemy,   220
That swear'st grace o'erboard, not an oath on shore?
Hast thou no mouth by land? What is the news?

Boats.: The best news is, that we have safely found
Our king and company; the next, our ship—
Which, but three glasses since, we gave out split—   225
Is tight and yare, and bravely rigg'd as when
We first put out to sea.

Ari.:   *[Aside to* Prospero.*]* Sir, all this service
Have I done since I went.

Pros.:   *[Aside to* Ariel.*]* My tricksy spirit!

Alon.: These are not natural events, they strengthen
From strange to stranger. Say, how came you hither?   230

Boats.: If I did think, sir, I were well awake,

---

201 *heaviness:* grief   207 *Milan . . . Milan:* the Duke . . . the city   214–15 *all . . . own:* we all
found ourselves when every man was deluded   216 *still:* ever   216–17 *his heart That:* the
heart of anyone who   217 s.d. *amazedly:* as in a maze, in bewilderment   220 *blasphemy:*
blasphemous fellow Cf. *diligence* (= diligent creature) in line 243   221 *That . . . o'erboard:* who
are profane enough to make heavenly grace forsake the ship   225 *glasses:* i.e. hours   *gave out:*
reported   226 *yare:* shipshape   228 *tricksy:* ingenious, adroit   229–30 *strengthen . . .
stranger:* increase in strangeness

I'ld strive to tell you. We were dead of sleep,
And (how we know not) all clapp'd under hatches,
Where, but even now, with strange and several noises
Of roaring, shrieking, howling, jingling chains,   235
And moe diversity of sounds, all horrible,
We were awak'd; straightway, at liberty;
Where we, in all our trim, freshly beheld
Our royal, good, and gallant ship; our master
Cap'ring to eye her. On a trice, so please you,   240
Even in a dream, were we divided from them,
And were brought moping hither.

Ari.:   *[Aside to* Prospero.*]* Was't well done?

Pros. [Aside to Ariel.*]:* Bravely, my diligence. Thou shalt be free.

Alon.: This is as strange a maze as e'er men trod,
And there is in this business more than nature   245
Was ever conduct of. Some oracle
Must rectify our knowledge.

Pros.:   Sir, my liege,
Do not infest your mind with beating on
The strangeness of this business. At pick'd leisure,
Which shall be shortly, single I'll resolve you   250
(Which to you shall seem probable) of every
These happen'd accidents; till when, be cheerful
And think of each thing well. *[Aside to* Ariel.*]* Come hither, spirit.
Set Caliban and his companions free;
Untie the spell. *[Exit* Ariel.*]* How fares my gracious sir?   255
There are yet missing of your company
Some few odd lads that you remember not.

Enter Ariel, *driving in* Caliban, Stephano, *and* Trinculo *in their stol'n apparel.*

Ste.: Every man shift for all the rest, and let no man take care for himself;
for all is but fortune. *Coraggio,* bully-monster, *coraggio!*

Trin.: If these be true spies which I wear in my head, here's a goodly sight. 260

Cal.: O Setebos, these be brave spirits indeed!
How fine my master is! I am afraid
He will chastise me.

Seb.:   Ha, ha!
What things are these, my lord Antonio?
Will money buy 'em?

---

232 *of sleep:* asleep   236 *moe:* more   237 *at liberty:* i.e. no longer under hatches   240 *On:* in   242 *moping:* in a daze   246 *conduct:* conductor   247 *liege:* sovereign   248 *infest:* annoy   249 *pick'd:* i.e. convenient   250 *single:* by myself (without an oracle)   251 *probable:* satisfactory   252 *accidents:* occurrences   257 *odd:* unaccounted for   258 *Every . . . rest:* Stephano drunkenly inverts the proverbial "Every man for himself."   259 *Coraggio:* courage (Italian)   260 *true spies:* reliable observers (eyes)   262 *fine:* splendidly dressed (in his ducal robes)

Ant.: Very like; one of them   265
  Is a plain fish, and no doubt marketable.
Pros.: Mark but the badges of these men, my lords,
  Then say if they be true. This misshapen knave—
  His mother was a witch, and one so strong
  That could control the moon, make flows and ebbs,   270
  And deal in her command without her power.
  These three have robb'd me, and this demi-devil
  (For he's a bastard one) had plotted with them
  To take my life. Two of these fellows you
  Must know and own, this thing of darkness I   275
  Acknowledge mine.
Cal.: I shall be pinch'd to death.
Alon.: Is not this Stephano, my drunken butler?
Seb.: He is drunk now. Where had he wine?
Alon.: And Trinculo is reeling ripe. Where should they
  Find this grand liquor that hath gilded 'em?   280
  How cam'st thou in this pickle?
Trin.: I have been in such a pickle since I saw you last that I fear me will never
  out of my bones. I shall not fear fly-blowing.
Seb.: Why, how now, Stephano!
Ste.: O, touch me not, I am not Stephano, but a cramp.   285
Pros.: You'ld be king o' the isle, sirrah?
Ste.: I should have been a sore one then.
Alon.: This is a strange thing as e'er I look'd on.   *[Pointing to* Caliban.*]*
Pros.: He is as disproportion'd in his manners
  As in his shape. Go, sirrah, to my cell;   290
  Take with you your companions. As you look
  To have my pardon, trim it handsomely.
Cal.: Ay, that I will; and I'll be wise hereafter,
  And seek for grace. What a thrice-double ass
  Was I to take this drunkard for a god,   295
  And worship this dull fool!
Pros.: Go to, away!
Alon.: Hence, and bestow your luggage where you found it.
Seb.: Or stole it, rather.   *[Exeunt* Caliban, Stephano, *and* Trinculo.*]*
Pros.: Sir, I invite your Highness and your train
  To my poor cell, where you shall take your rest   300

---

267 *badges:* insignia for servants, indicating what master they served Stephano and Trinculo are of course dressed in stolen garments.   268 *true:* honest   271 *her command:* i.e. the moon's authority   *without her power:* beyond the moon's influence   280 *gilded 'em:* flushed their faces (a common connection between blood and gold) Possibly *grand liquor* contains an alchemical allusion to the long-sought elixir that could transform base substances to gold.   281 *pickle:* predicament   282 *pickle:* preservative (the horse urine of the pool being equivalent to vinegar) 283 *fly-blowing:* infestation by maggots (to which unpickled meat would be subject   286 *sirrah:* form of address to an inferior   287 *sore:* (1) harsh; (2) pain-wracked

For this one night; which, part of it, I'll waste
With such discourse as, I not doubt, shall make it
Go quick away—the story of my life,
And the particular accidents gone by
Since I came to this isle. And in the morn   305
I'll bring you to your ship, and so to Naples,
Where I have hope to see the nuptial
Of these our dear-belov'd solemnized,
And thence retire me to my Milan, where
Every third thought shall be my grave.

Alon.:   I long   310
To hear the story of your life, which must
Take the ear strangely.

Pros.:   I'll deliver all,
And promise you calm seas, auspicious gales,
And sail so expeditious, that shall catch
Your royal fleet far off. *[Aside to* Ariel.*]* My Ariel, chick,   315
That is thy charge. Then to the elements
Be free, and fare thou well!—Please you draw near.   *Exeunt omnes.*

EPILOGUE

Spoken by Prospero.

Now my charms are all o'erthrown,
And what strength I have's mine own,
Which is most faint. Now 'tis true,
I must be here confin'd by you,
Or sent to Naples. Let me not,   5
Since I have my dukedom got,
And pardon'd the deceiver, dwell
In this bare island by your spell,
But release me from my bands
With the help of your good hands.   10
Gentle breath of yours my sails
Must fill, or else my project fails,
Which was to please. Now I want
Spirits to enforce, art to enchant,
And my ending is despair,   15
Unless I be reliev'd by prayer,
Which pierces so, that it assaults
Mercy itself, and frees all faults.

---

301 *waste:* use up   312 *Take:* enchant   *deliver:* report   314 *sail:* voyage   317 *draw near:*
i.e. enter the cell   Epi. 9 *bands:* bonds   10 *hands:* i.e. applause The noise of clapping would
break the charm.   11 *Gentle breath:* a favorable breeze (produced by hands clapping)   13
want: lack   16 *prayer:* i.e. this petition   17 *assaults:* storms the ear of   18 *frees:* remits

As you from crimes would pardon'd be,
Let your indulgence set me free.   *Exit.*   20

TOPICS FOR CRITICAL THINKING

1. In Act One, scene two, Prospero offers a lengthy exposition of the events that precede the action of the play. How did Prospero and Miranda arrive on the island? How did he meet Ariel and Caliban? What is Prospero's relationship to them at the start of the play?

2. Caliban's mother Sycorax is described as a "hag" and "witch." What do these terms mean in the context of the play?

3. In Act Two, scene one, Gonzalo outlines his conception of an ideal commonwealth or utopia. What are its principal characteristics? What do they say about him in relation to the other Italian nobility?

4. Stephano and Trinculo are familiar comic figures on the Shakespearean stage and obvious sources of laughter. What inferences might be made from their interactions with Caliban?

5. Romances often concern the adventures of knights, the passing of tests, the swearing of oaths or vows, and the attainment of virtue. Is Ferdinand a kind of knight? Does he reveal any chivalric or knightly attributes? Is his virtue really tested?

6. Caliban is largely humiliated by the end of the play, and he seems excluded from the reconciliation that allows it to end happily. Does this ostracism seem just? Is he in any ways a sympathetic figure who deserves better?

7. A number of recent productions have "cast against type" by selecting handsome leading men to play Caliban. How does the meaning of the play change when Caliban is played not as brutish or animalistic but as exotic and attractive?

TOPICS FOR CRITICAL WRITING

1. Many contemporary critics regard *The Tempest* as reflective of European efforts to colonize America; as a result, they position Caliban as a representative of the *colonized* and Prospero as a representative of the *colonizer*. What do *colonized* and *colonizer* mean in the context of the play? Are the two terms binary opposites?

2. *The Tempest* has launched scores of paintings, novels, symphonies, and films. Choose a film based on the play—the 1956 science fiction film *Forbidden Planet*, for example, or Peter Greenaway's 1991 film *Prospero's Books*, both of which are widely available—and explain how these adaptations illuminate the play. What aspect or issue of the original is developed most clearly in this adaptation? An alternative topic would be to select a novel, painting, or play, answering the same question.

Critical Perspective: *The Tempest* and Genre

"*The Tempest* in short is a spectacular and operatic play, and when we think of other plays like it, we are more apt to think of, say, Mozart's *Magic Flute* than of ordinary stage plays."

　　　　　—Northrop Frye, *Introduction to The Tempest, Penguin Edition* (1969)

---

19 *crimes:* sins

Critical Perspective: Caliban as Colonized Subject

"Imprisoned by language and power Caliban is the paradigm of the colonial subject in colonial discourse: a 'monster' who both threatens the virginity of Miranda and, through his abortive rebellion, the life of Prospero. The conclusion to be drawn from such a presentation is the necessity of Caliban's subjection to the (self) protective power of Prospero, who must be constantly alert to the threat of treachery on the part of his slave.

"[Yet] Shakespeare's presentation of Caliban as possessing a consciousness chafing under the restraints and injustices of his position [suggests that] 'he is overpowered but not tamed, he is threatened but not convinced of his own inferiority.'"

—David Cairns and Shaun Richards,
Writing Ireland: Colonialism, Nationalism, and Culture (1988)

Critical Perspective: "The School of Caliban"

"The phrase ['The School of Caliban'] suggests a group of engaged [Latin American, Caribbean, African American, and Chicano/a] writers, scholars, and professors of literature who work under a common political influence, a group whose different (imagined) national communities and symbologies are linked by their derivation from a common and explosive reading of Shakespeare's last (pastoral and tragicomic) play, *The Tempest*."

—José David Saldívar, *The Dialectics of Our America* (1991)

46   Forms of Modern Drama

Modern, modernism, modernity—all three of these terms appear in discussions of western society and culture in the late nineteenth and first half of the twentieth centuries. Taken from a Latin word that in one form means "mode" and in another means "just now," the adjective *modern* connotes newness: a new kind of play, poem, painting, novel, or musical composition.

Historians such as German scholar Peter Szondi trace the genealogy of a "modern" drama to Shakespeare's England. Here, as a god-centered medieval world-view declined, dramatists "sought to create an artistic reality within which [a newly self-conscious being] could fix and mirror himself on the basis of interpersonal relationships alone." These interpersonal relationships get expressed in dialogue: men and women talking to, with, and about each other. In the latter half of the nineteenth century and early decades of the twentieth, dramatists experimented with innovative ways of achieving such interaction on stage, ways now recognized as part of a distinctly *modern* drama.

For the twentieth-century American poet Ezra Pound, the definition "just now" evolved into the aesthetic imperative "Make it new," which became a goal for literary modernism, implying that somehow modernist writers were revolting from older literary forms. But what counts as "old"? How is it possible for a dramatist—or any other artist, for that matter—to create something *totally* "new," especially given the public nature of theatrical performance? In their own ways, the works of each of the four playwrights in this section— Henrik Ibsen, Anton Chekhov, Susan Glaspbell, and Eugene O'Neill— address this question by inventing fresh, new elements of form while, at the same time, refining older dramatic conventions.

Their achievements originate, at least in part, in their attempts to represent the changing realities of the times and cultures in which they lived. Such realities might be attributable to "modernity," which generally does not refer to literary or dramatic form but to a kind of lived experience, as American cultural historian Marshall Berman explains:

> [Modernity] is a mode of vital experience—experience of space and time, of the self and others, of life's possibilities and perils—that is shared by men and women all over the world today . . . To be modern is to find ourselves in an environment that promises us adventure, power, joy, growth, transformation of ourselves and the world—and, at the same time, that threatens to destroy everything we have, everything we know, everything we are.

To be modern, Berman remarks, "is to be part of a universe in which, as [Karl] Marx said, 'all that is solid melts into air.'" Writing in the 1980s, Berman underscores the paradoxical quality of life from the middle of the nineteenth century through the 1970s. The period is marked, on the one hand, by the development of such technologies as the film, car, airplane, and computer, all of which have expanded the horizons of our world. Yet the same period includes the horrors of World Wars I and II, Hiroshima and Auschwitz, Korea and Vietnam. Such a metaphor of wondrous progress existing alongside seemingly inevitable catastrophe resonates even more ominously since the events of September 11 and their global repercussions.

Is it any wonder, then, that thinkers from Bernard Shaw at the end of the nineteenth century to philosopher Herbert Marcuse writing during the Cold War of the 1950s and 1960s question the notion that "modernity" is synonymous with "progress"? "Progress" and "modernity" are mottled, ambivalent concepts, with the latter possessing connotations of both real cultural advances and simultaneous limitations on human freedom. One advance occurred on stage to which the four dramatists introduced in this chapter contributed greatly.

The Rise of Modern Drama at the End of the Nineteenth Century

However accurate skepticism about modernity might be, there is little denying the progress of a distinctly modern drama as the nineteenth century came to a close. This is true throughout western Europe, Russia, Great Britain, and the United States. Moreover, as the work of the four influential playwrights represented in this chapter attests, the best drama of the period became *international*. Throughout the 1870s, 1880s and 1890s, Norwegian playwright Henrik Ibsen's works were produced in Stockholm, Copenhagen, Munich, and Berlin. By the 1880s and 1890s, Ibsen's works had become so controversial—and influential—in London, that in 1891 Bernard Shaw wrote a book about them, *The Quintessence of Ibsenism*, and in 1900 James Joyce, then a college freshman in Dublin, published his first essay, "Ibsen's New Drama." Arriving in the United States and greeted with similar objections from conservative reviewers, *A Doll House* (1879), later joined by *Hedda Gabler* (1890) and *Ghosts* (1881), were produced in New York in the 1890s. By the turn of the century, Ibsenite social realism, a topic to which we shall return, had found staunch defenders in America, and the "new drama" Joyce and Shaw so admired had firmly taken root.

Throughout Europe and America, drama and theater were on the rise. Ibsen's associate Bjørn Bjørnson became head of the Norwegian National Theatre in 1899; and William Butler Yeats, Edward Martyn, and Lady Augusta Gregory founded the Irish Literary Theatre, later the Abbey Theatre, in 1897. During the decade of the 1890s, British drama in the wake of Ibsen was being reinvigorated by Shaw's early plays and those of his countryman Oscar Wilde. In the later 1890s, the Moscow Art Theatre scored major successes with Anton Chekhov's *The Seagull* (1896) and *Uncle Vanya* (1897), paving the way for *Three Sisters* (1901) and *The Cherry Orchard* (1903; first produced in January 1904). At roughly this same time, the highly symbolic drama of Frenchman Maurice Maeterlinck began to appear throughout Europe, and Gerhart Hauptmann's social drama in Germany exercised a tremendous influence on young intellectuals like Joyce. Today, a century later, most of these writers' works are still read in college classes and produced by theater companies. This is particularly true of Shaw, Wilde, and Chekhov, whose plays are revived every year all over the world.

Such was not always the case, especially at the end of the nineteenth century. Given the public nature of the genre and the expense of theatrical production, drama requires not only playing spaces, actors, and writers, but also audiences to support them. For Londoners in the nineteenth century, this meant a theater to frequent, sufficient money to spend on entertainment, and a means of transportation to the theater and back. All of these criteria were difficult to satisfy as the nineteenth century began. London, like other major cities in Britain and America, was flooded with immigrants both from the rural countryside and other countries seeking employment in the growing industrial economy. While many attained a better standard of living than they had known previously, they did so by toiling fifteen or more hours a day in factories, which left little time or money for amusements. But for many, this was preferable to the even harsher realities of the Irish famine (1845–1851), religious intolerance in eastern Europe, or slavery in the antebellum American South. Cities like London, Manchester, Liverpool, New York, Boston, and Philadelphia became metropolises in the nineteenth century and, eventually, drama and theater grew with them.

Still, legal restrictions on theater enacted during both the Puritan restoration of the seventeenth century and the eighteenth century continued to constrain drama in early nineteenth-century England. The latter of these, the Licensing Act of 1737, required that all plays produced in England and Scotland be read by the Lord Chamberlain's Reviewer before being granted a license. Not surprisingly, Ibsen's plays and some of Shaw's were denied licenses, forcing Ibsen's works to be mounted in private club theaters. Modern drama in England, in other words, faced the considerable obstacle of censorship. Yet another legal challenge, the Patent Act of 1660, restricted the number of so-called legitimate theaters in London and was finally repealed in 1843. The result? According to historian Michael Booth, as London's population grew from 3 million in 1850 to 6.5 million in 1900, the number of playhouses increased from twenty to sixty-one. By the 1880s, Booth argues, theater became profitable as Londoners living in the suburbs could be conveyed to and from the city and the standard of living increased.

A similar pattern occurred in America, with New York ascending to the position of preeminence it enjoys today. By the middle of the nineteenth century, Boston—never before a haven for drama given its Puritan heritage—had two significant and several minor venues. St. Louis's first professional theater was founded in 1835, Chicago's in 1847. Philadelphia, the center of American drama during the late eighteenth and early nineteenth centuries, was being supplanted by New York, especially the area known as Broadway. Broadway, in fact, became so dominant and so commercial that by the early 1900s, in a trend known today as the Little Theater Movement, small companies producing experimental drama opened across the country: in Madison and Milwaukee, Wisconsin; in Detroit, Cleveland, and Fargo, North Dakota; in Dallas and Pasadena. Two of the most famous of these—Maurice Browne's Little Theatre in Chicago (founded in 1912) and especially Provincetown Massachusetts's, later New York's, Provincetown Players (1915)—helped cultivate the artistry of two figures of enduring significance to American drama: Susan Glaspell and Nobel Prize–winner Eugene O'Neill. In the twenty-first century, regional theaters in America remain as crucial to the health of contemporary drama as they were at the beginning of the last century when William Archer, British critic and translator of Ibsen, hailed them as the birthplace of a "new" American drama:

> The great hope of the future lies in the fertilization of the large by the little theater, of Broadway by Provincetown . . . In the region of Washington Square and Greenwich Village—or ultimately among the sand dunes of Cape Cod—we must look for the real birthplace of the New American drama.

This chapter sketches some of the "newness," formal and otherwise, of the plays of four highly influential modern dramatists: Henrik Ibsen, Anton Chekhov, Susan Glaspell, and Eugene O'Neill. In particular, it charts the development of realism, the emergence of modern tragicomedy, and the influence of psychoanalysis on expressionistic drama in America.

Henrik Ibsen's *Hedda Gabler*: From Melodrama to Realism

More so than the legal, demographic, and economic obstacles alluded to above, popular taste proved to be the modern drama's most formidable opponent. Throughout nineteenth-century England and America, the dominant dramatic form was *melodrama*, which, along with several varieties of comedy, musical entertainments, and revivals of earlier drama, made up the repertories at most theaters. Any fan of contemporary films—the 1999 hit *The Matrix*, for example—is familiar with the attractions of melodrama: dramatic rescues and escapes, lavishly staged battles or natural disasters, and a clear opposition between good and evil. Unlike *The Matrix*, however, where a muscular Trinity (Carrie-Ann Moss) can fend for herself, the center of dramatic action in earlier melodrama was often an innocent, even helpless, heroine who needed protection and rescuing from desperate predicaments. Fortunately, melodrama featured then—and still does—heroes like *The Matrix*'s Neo (Keanu Reeves) eager to perform these services, defeating the villains who jeopardize everything that is good in the world. Such victories and harrowing rescues, in both contemporary film and nineteenth-century melodrama, mean spectacular confrontations between the forces of good and evil, virtually guaranteeing audiences the emotional satisfactions to which such dramatic action caters.

Not surprisingly given these conditions, revivals of Shakespeare and other serious drama posed a significant financial risk for producers. Indeed, until 1870 or so, one slogan informed the thinking of most London and New York theater managers: "Shakespeare spells ruin, and Byron [the Romantic poet and playwright] bankruptcy." Now, of course, popular actors like Sean Connery are knighted quite regularly as theater and film have become legitimate and respected media, but in the later nineteenth century drama was just beginning to reemerge as a valuable cultural form. Even so, when Shakespeare was produced to popular acclaim, the original text was often severely edited both to garner more attention for the star-actors in the leading parts and to heighten the pictorial spectacle. As a result of this taste for visual extravagance, a revival of Shakespeare in the late nineteenth century could take six or more hours, as lavish sets needed to be struck and rebuilt between acts. Popular taste demanded it.

And then along came Henrik Ibsen, **Web** with such plays as *A Doll House*   *www* (1879), *Ghosts* (1881), *An Enemy of the People* (1883), *Rosmersholm* (1887), and *Hedda Gabler* (1890). *A Doll House* received its first professional production in London in 1889. Reviewing it, William Archer, translator and champion of Ibsen, reported that the "general public" has "risen heroically" to the challenge of the Norwegian dramatist and is "crying out for more." But orthodox London critics were not nearly so enthusiastic, particularly after 1891 productions of *Ghosts* and *Hedda Gabler.* One newspaper reviewer decried *A Doll House* as "morbid and unwholesome"; another condemned it as "unnatural" and "immoral." Few critics were more hostile than Clement Scott, reviewer for both *The Daily Telegraph* and, for a time, *The Illustrated London News.* Lacerating the Independent Theatre's production of *Ghosts*, he predicted that this "revolting" play could only serve the purpose of driving "decent-minded women out of the playhouse." His most indignant response was reserved for those who thought Ibsen's plays to be unconventional and "new":

> [We] are to be airily told that Ibsen and the founders of the Independent Theatre are the chosen apostles to free the neglected stage from the fetters and manacles of conventionality! A more stupendous proposition was never offered by misguided men or believed in by masculine women.

Clearly, Ibsen struck a raw nerve with the defenders of the status quo. But why? In large part, because he abandoned many of the simplifications and excesses of melodrama. Sensational plots and spectacular battles are replaced by the subtleties of middle class life in Ibsen's more realistic plays; predictable or stock characters are replaced by troubled, middle class figures whose complexity shook dominant views of gender, marriage, and the nuclear family. Scott's response was typical of those critics who were simply unprepared for the sharp interrogation of middle-class domesticity that Ibsen offered his audiences. *Hedda Gabler* is just such a play.

Realistic Form: Plot and Character in Hedda Gabler

Realistic drama begins with its plot and in its characters, in whom conflict often rages. Such is the case with Hedda Gabler, who languishes in an unhappy marriage that in no way corresponds to the grandeur of her fantasy life or the privileges of her upbringing. Such disparities are not a problem with the **flat**

characters of melodrama: The heroes are good simply because they are; the villains, greedy or lascivious because they are. Conflict in melodramatic plots is thus largely "external," developing a clear opposition between the forces of good and evil. Not so in Ibsen's plays. In fact, the psychologies of Hedda Gabler and Rebecca West in *Rosmersholm* are so complex that Sigmund Freud devoted much of an essay to them. At times, as in Oswald's case in *Ghosts*, mental disorder is associated with moral failings that were avoided on the Victorian stage—congenital syphilis, and all it suggests, for example—or self-destructive fantasies, as in Hedda's tortuous path to suicide. In this regard, Clement Scott's reference to "masculine women" is telling in that characters like Hedda transcend conventional boundaries of the womanly in Victorian culture, possessing a kind of "masculine" independence that melodramatic heroines seldom exhibited. Judge Brack's closing line in *Hedda Gabler*, here responding to Tesman's cry that she has shot herself in the head, captures this notion in dramatic fashion: "But good God! People don't *do* such things!"

They do in realistic drama. The miraculous rescues and escapes of melodrama seldom occur in the meticulously described drawing rooms in which Ibsen's realistic plays, written between 1875 and 1899, are set. There, familial and psychical conflict replaces the confrontations of heroes and villains; there, Ibsen's protagonists achieve only a "paradoxical victory" largely because, as Ibsen scholar James Hurt explains, they are unable to "preserve an identity based on will alone." In *A Doll House*, Nora can no longer play the "little skylark" to her patronizing husband, so she abandons both her marriage and her children. In *Hedda Gabler*, Hedda can no longer sustain the fantasy life she has created to escape her unexciting marriage and the dismal prospect of Thea Elvsted's visits to assist Tesman in restoring his scholarly manuscript. Her fantasies about Løvborg shattered by the threat of scandal and her freedom compromised by Judge Brack's ominous questioning about how Løvborg acquired one of her pistols, Hedda is trapped. "I'm in your power," she tells Brack moments before her suicide. "I can't bear the thought of it." She escapes this servitude by killing herself, thereby securing the paradoxical victory of gaining freedom in death.

When Ibsen's plots reached such unconventional closure on the nineteenth-century stage, orthodox views of marriage, of the relationships between men and women, and of gender were equally shaken. But again, unlike melodrama, realistic drama does not typically involve heroes or virtuous heroines, but characters more like the people one sees outside the theater. This means characters who possess both the strengths and limitations of "real" people struggling with the same issues many of us face: unhappy marriages, the suppression of one's dreams and aspirations, and stifling constructions of gender. Given that Ibsen's plays are quieter, more subtle, and less visually spectacular than melodramas, where does dramatic conflict reside? In the uneasy relationships between men and women, in the tension between orthodox morality and individual desire, and in the often sharp disparity between law and justice. Such topics do not require sensational staging and the histrionics of star-actors, but more restrained methods of acting, speaking, and stage design that were vastly different than those employed in Victorian melodrama.

Language and Mise-en-Scène

Just as crucial to realism's success as its plot and often psychologically complex protagonists are the **pictorial realism** of its **mise-en-scène**—setting, costumes, lighting, stage properties, and movement—and the more common "everyday" language contained in the dialogue. Unlike the sparsely decorated stages of Sophocles and Shakespeare, Ibsen's stage directions carefully delineate a middle class parlor or drawing room rich with implication. To signal both the social class and relative affluence of Hedda and George Tesman—to replicate the sights and sounds of contemporary life—the set of *Hedda Gabler* is an attractively furnished drawing room, complete with plush carpeting, glass doorways, étagères with ornaments, flowers, lamps, and much more. Clearly visible is a smaller room located behind the drawing room in which Hedda's piano, a portrait of General Gabler, and, as we learn, her father's dueling pistols are located. The play opens in bright morning light and grows—like the action—increasingly dark as the action progresses.

Critics have often regarded the set of realistic drama as communicating more than just the social class and financial circumstances of its protagonists. In this case, the set also serves as a metaphor of Hedda's troubled psychology: The drawing room is a social space (or prison) in which Hedda Tesman is compelled to meet visitors, even those who annoy her like George's aunt; the back room functions as a space where Hedda's memories of her father, his pistols, and her piano reside. It is the deeply private counterpoint to the more superficial social place of the drawing room. There, in this inner sanctum, she can indulge her fantasies of Eilert Løvborg or vanquish her disappointment with a bullet.

In the 2000–2001 New York production of *Hedda Gabler*, the set and the lead actress's (Kate Burton) movements helped reinforce Hedda's unhappiness and increasing desperation. One reviewer observed that Hedda "can hardly keep still, pacing in wide circles around the high-ceilinged drawing room." In the background, behind this frenetic pacing, her father's portrait looms over the stage, reminding us of his presence in her loveless marriage. Further, while the play opens in bright morning light, by the end Hedda's preference for "the gloom of pulled curtains" and closed windows conveys "the self-imposed restraints of her fear of scandal." In many productions of *Hedda Gabler*, the set seems to mimic Hedda's descent into depression. In a 1986 Los Angeles production starring Kate Mulgrew, for example, one critic observed that "as the action moved toward its inevitable conclusion, the room grew evermore suffocating, both in dimension and hue." Lighting and costuming typically follow a similar pattern when the play is revived on the contemporary stage.

The language of realism is altogether different as well. Tragedy and melodrama often represent public scenes, complete with lengthy monologues and, in the case of tragedy, soliloquies. Comedy, by contrast, or comic scenes in more serious dramas, often include asides, where characters talk to the audience. The language in realistic drama usually preserves the fiction of the action, the pretense that this event is really happening now. That is, unlike an aside that signals the theatricality of the action, language in realism replicates the vernacular of everyday middle class life. It is often entirely mundane, like that with which *Hedda Gabler* begins: the number of boxes Hedda required to hold her wardrobe, the manner in which the furniture was financed, the appearance of Tesman's embroidered bedroom slippers, and so on. To be sure, realistic drama may contain impassioned speeches of considerable length, but in general such passion will not take the form of soliloquies or poetry. Just as the set represents a kind of snapshot of a particular way of life, language in modern realism is the language of a particular culture's middle—or, at times, other—class and its everyday life.

Perhaps most important in plays like *Hedda Gabler* and *A Doll House*, Ibsen propelled a new kind of drama into motion. This drama concerns real people in real settings, not heroes in fantastical battles or predicaments; it emphasizes emotional restraint over histrionics, and language over spectacle; and, in the later nineteenth century, it dealt with subject matter that orthodox Victorians attempted to sweep under the carpet. American writers like James A. Herne and Clyde Fitch wrote realist plays in imitation of Ibsen and, by the turn of the century, realism was well established throughout Europe and America. To be sure, melodrama remained a popular theatrical form, as did comedy. But after Ibsen, most intellectuals at the time believed that a distinctly modern realistic drama had been born, one that evolved later in the twentieth century into a dominant dramatic form.

Henrik Ibsen

Translated by Rolf Fjelde

Hedda Gabler   *(1890)*

THE CHARACTERS

George Tesman, research fellow in cultural history
Hedda Tesman, his wife
Miss Juliana Tesman, his aunt
Mrs. Elvsted
Judge Brack
Eilert Løvborg
Berta, the *Tesmans'* maid

The action takes place in Tesman's *residence in the fashionable part of town.*

ACT I

A large, attractively furnished drawing room, decorated in dark colors. In the rear wall, a wide doorway with curtains drawn back. The doorway opens into a smaller room in the same style as the drawing room. In the right wall of the front room, a folding door that leads to the hall. In the left wall opposite, a glass door, with curtains similarly drawn back. Through the panes one can see part of an overhanging veranda and trees in autumn colors. In the foreground is an oval table, with tablecloth and chairs around it. By the right wall, a wide, dark porcelain stove, a high-backed armchair, a cushioned footstool, and two taborets.° In the right-hand corner, a settee with a small round table in front. Nearer, on the left and slightly out from the wall, a piano. On either side of the doorway in back, étagères° with terracotta and majolica ornaments. Against the back wall of the inner room, a sofa, a table, and a couple of chairs can be seen. Above this sofa hangs a portrait of a handsome, elderly man in a general's uniform. Over the table, a hanging lamp with an opalescent glass shade. A number of bouquets of flowers are placed about the drawing room in vases and glasses. Others lie on the tables. The floors in both rooms are covered with thick carpets. Morning light. The sun shines in through the glass door.

Miss Juliana Tesman, *wearing a hat and carrying a parasol, comes in from the hall, followed by* Berta, *who holds a bouquet wrapped in paper.* Miss Tesman *is a lady around sixty-five with a kind and good-natured look, nicely but simply dressed in a gray tailored suit.* Berta *is a maid somewhat past middle age, with a plain and rather provincial appearance.*

Miss Tesman (stops close by the door, listens, and says softly): Goodness, I don't think they're even up yet!

Berta (also softly): That's just what I said, Miss Juliana. Remember how late the steamer got in last night. Yes, and afterward! My gracious, how much the young bride had to unpack before she could get to bed.

Miss Tesman: Well, then—let them enjoy a good rest. But they must have some of this fresh morning air when they do come down. *(She goes to the glass door and opens it wide.)*

Berta (by the table, perplexed, with the bouquet in her hand): I swear there isn't a bit of space left. I think I'll have to put it here, miss. *(Places the bouquet on the piano.)*

Miss Tesman: So now you have a new mistress, Berta dear. Lord knows it was misery for me to give you up.

Berta (on the verge of tears): And for me, miss! What can I say? All those many blessed years I've been in your service, you and Miss Rina.

Miss Tesman: We must take it calmly, Berta. There's really nothing else to do. George needs you here in this house, you know that. You've looked after him since he was a little boy.

Berta: Yes, but miss, I'm all the time thinking of her lying at home. Poor thing—completely helpless. And with that new maid! She'll never take proper care of an invalid, that one.

Miss Tesman: Oh, I'll manage to teach her. And most of it, you know, I'll do myself. So you mustn't be worrying over my poor sister.

Berta: Well, but there's something else too, miss. I'm really so afraid I won't please the young mistress.

Miss Tesman: Oh, well—there might be something or other at first—

Berta: Because she's so very particular.

---

taborets: Stools without back or arms. *étagères:* Cabinets with shelves.

Miss Tesman: Well of course. General Gabler's daughter. What a life she had in the general's day! Remember seeing her out with her father—how she'd go galloping past in that long black riding outfit, with a feather in her hat?

Berta: Oh yes—I remember! But I never would have dreamed then that she and George Tesman would make a match of it.

Miss Tesman: Nor I either. But now, Berta—before I forget: from now on, you mustn't say George Tesman. You must call him Doctor Tesman.

Berta: Yes, the young mistress said the same thing—last night, right after they came in the door. Is that true, then, miss?

Miss Tesman: Yes, absolutely. Think of it, Berta—they gave him his doctor's degree. Abroad, that is—on this trip you know. I hadn't heard one word about it, till he told me down on the pier.

Berta: Well, he's clever enough to be anything. But I never thought he'd go in for curing people.

Miss Tesman: No, he wasn't made that kind of doctor. *(Nods significantly.)* But as a matter of fact, you may soon now have something still greater to call him.

Berta: Oh, really! What's that, miss?

Miss Tesman (smiling): Hm, wouldn't you like to know! *(Moved.)* Ah, dear God—if only my poor brother could look up from his grave and see what his little boy has become! *(Glancing about.)* But what's this, Berta? Why, you've taken all the slipcovers off the furniture—?

Berta: Madam told me to. She doesn't like covers on chairs, she said.

Miss Tesman: Are they going to make this their regular living room, then?

Berta: It seems so—with her. For his part—the doctor—he said nothing.

(George Tesman *enters the inner room from the right, singing to himself and carrying an empty, unstrapped suitcase. He is a youngish-looking man of thirty-three, medium sized, with an open, round, cheerful face, blond hair and beard. He is somewhat carelessly dressed in comfortable lounging clothes.*)

Miss Tesman: Good morning, good morning, George!

Tesman (in the doorway): Aunt Julie! Dear Aunt Julie! *(Goes over and warmly shakes her hand.)* Way out here—so early in the day—uh?

Miss Tesman: Yes, you know I simply had to look in on you a moment.

Tesman: And that without a decent night's sleep.

Miss Tesman: Oh, that's nothing at all to me.

Tesman: Well, then you did get home all right from the pier? Uh?

Miss Tesman: Why, of course I did—thank goodness. Judge Brack was good enough to see me right to my door.

Tesman: We were sorry we couldn't drive you up. But you saw for yourself— Hedda had all those boxes to bring along.

Miss Tesman: Yes, that was quite something, the number of boxes she had.

Berta (to Tesman*):* Should I go in and ask Mrs. Tesman if there's anything I can help her with?

Tesman: No, thanks, Berta—don't bother. She said she'd ring if she needed anything.

Berta (going off toward the right): All right.

Tesman: But wait now—you can take this suitcase with you.

Berta (taking it): I'll put it away in the attic. (*She goes out by the hall door.*)

Tesman: Just think, Aunt Julie—I had that whole suitcase stuffed full of notes. You just can't imagine all I've managed to find, rummaging through archives. Marvelous old documents that nobody knew existed—

Miss Tesman: Yes, you've really not wasted any time on your wedding trip, George.

Tesman: I certainly haven't. But do take your hat off, Auntie. Here—let me help you—uh?

Miss Tesman (as he does so): Goodness—this is exactly as if you were still back at home with us.

Tesman (turning the hat in his hand and studying it from all sides): My—what elegant hats you go in for!

Miss Tesman: I bought that for Hedda's sake.

Tesman: For Hedda's sake? Uh?

Miss Tesman: Yes, so Hedda wouldn't feel ashamed of me if we walked down the street together.

Tesman (patting her cheek): You think of everything, Aunt Julie! (*Laying the hat on a chair by the table.*) So—look, suppose we sit down on the sofa and have a little chat till Hedda comes. (*They settle themselves. She puts her parasol on the corner of the sofa.*)

Miss Tesman (takes both of his hands and gazes at him): How wonderful it is having you here, right before my eyes again, George! You—dear Jochum's own boy!

Tesman: And for me too, to see you again, Aunt Julie! You, who've been father and mother to me both.

Miss Tesman: Yes, I'm sure you'll always keep a place in your heart for your old aunts.

Tesman: But Auntie Rina—hm? Isn't she any better?

Miss Tesman: Oh no—we can hardly expect that she'll ever be better, poor thing. She lies there, just as she has all these years. May God let me keep her a little while longer! Because otherwise, George, I don't know what I'd do with my life. The more so now, when I don't have you to look after.

Tesman (patting her on the back): There, there, there—

Miss Tesman (suddenly changing her tone): No, but to think of it, that now you're a married man! And that it was *you* who carried off Hedda Gabler. The beautiful Hedda Gabler! Imagine! She, who always had so many admirers!

Tesman (hums a little and smiles complacently): Yes, I rather suspect I have several friends who'd like to trade places with me.

Miss Tesman: And then to have such a wedding trip! Five—almost six months—

Tesman: Well, remember, I used it for research, too. All those libraries I had to check—and so many books to read!

Miss Tesman: Yes, no doubt. (*More confidentially; lowering her voice.*) But now listen, George—isn't there something—something special you have to tell me?

Tesman: From the trip?

Miss Tesman: Yes.

Tesman: No, I can't think of anything beyond what I wrote in my letters. I got my doctor's degree down there—but I told you that yesterday.

Miss Tesman: Yes, of course. But I mean—whether you have any kind of—expectations—?

Tesman: Expectations?

Miss Tesman: My goodness, George—I'm your old aunt!

Tesman: Why, naturally I have expectations.

Miss Tesman: Ah!

Tesman: I have every expectation in the world of becoming a professor shortly.

Miss Tesman: Oh, a professor, yes—

Tesman: Or I might as well say, I'm sure of it. But, Aunt Julie—you know that perfectly well yourself.

Miss Tesman (with a little laugh): That's right, so I do. *(Changing the subject.)* But we were talking about your trip. It must have cost a terrible amount of money.

Tesman: Well, that big fellowship, you know—it took us a good part of the way.

Miss Tesman: But I don't see how you could stretch it enough for two.

Tesman: No, that's not so easy to see—uh?

Miss Tesman: And especially traveling with a lady. For I hear tell that's much more expensive.

Tesman: Yes, of course—it's a bit more expensive. But Hedda just had to have that trip. She *had* to. There was nothing else to be done.

Miss Tesman: No, no, I guess not. A honeymoon abroad seems to be the thing nowadays. But tell me—have you had a good look around your house?

Tesman: You can bet I have! I've been up since daybreak.

Miss Tesman: And how does it strike you, all in all?

Tesman: First-rate! Absolutely first-rate! Only I don't know what we'll do with the two empty rooms between the back parlor and Hedda's bedroom.

Miss Tesman (laughing again): Oh, my dear George, I think you can use them—as time goes on.

Tesman: Yes, you're quite right about that, Aunt Julie! In time, as I build up my library—uh?

Miss Tesman: Of course, my dear boy. It was your library I meant.

Tesman: I'm happiest now for Hedda's sake. Before we were engaged, she used to say so many times there was no place she'd rather live than here, in Secretary Falk's town house.

Miss Tesman: Yes, and then to have it come on the market just after you'd sailed.

Tesman: We really have had luck, haven't we?

Miss Tesman: But expensive, George dear! You'll find it expensive, all this here.

Tesman (looks at her, somewhat crestfallen): Yes, I suppose I will.

Miss Tesman: Oh, Lord, yes!

Tesman: How much do you think? Approximately? Hm?

Miss Tesman: It's impossible to say till the bills are all in.

Tesman: Well, fortunately Judge Brack has gotten me quite easy terms. That's what he wrote Hedda.

Miss Tesman: Don't worry yourself about that, dear. I've also put up security to cover the carpets and furniture.

Tesman: Security? Aunt Julie, dear—you? What kind of security could *you* give?

Miss Tesman: I took out a mortgage on our pension.

Tesman (jumping up): What! On your—and Auntie Rina's pension!

Miss Tesman: I saw nothing else to do.

Tesman (standing in front of her): But you're out of your mind, Aunt Julie! That pension—it's all Aunt Rina and you have to live on.

Miss Tesman: Now, now—don't make so much of it. It's only a formality; Judge Brack said so. He was good enough to arrange the whole thing for me. Just a formality, he said.

Tesman: That's all well enough. But still—

Miss Tesman: You'll be drawing your own salary now. And, good gracious, if we have to lay out a bit, just now at the start—why, it's no more than a pleasure for us.

Tesman: Oh, Aunt Julie—you never get tired of making sacrifices for me!

Miss Tesman (rises and places her hands on his shoulders): What other joy do I have in this world than smoothing the path for you, my dear boy? You, without father or mother to turn to. And now we've come to the goal, George! Things may have looked black at times; but now, thank heaven, you've made it.

Tesman: Yes, it's remarkable, really, how everything's turned out for the best.

Miss Tesman: Yes—and those who stood against you—who wanted to bar your way—they've gone down. They've fallen, George. The one most dangerous to you—he fell farthest. And he's lying there now, in the bed he made—poor, misguided creature.

Tesman: Have you heard any news of Eilert? I mean, since I went away.

Miss Tesman: Only that he's supposed to have brought out a new book.

Tesman: What's that? Eilert Løvborg? Just recently, uh?

Miss Tesman: So they say. But considering everything, it can hardly amount to much. Ah, but when *your* new book comes out—it'll be a different story, George! What will it be about?

Tesman: It's going to treat the domestic handicrafts of Brabant in the Middle Ages.

Miss Tesman: Just imagine—that you can write about things like that!

Tesman: Actually, the book may take quite a while yet. I have this tremendous collection of material to put in order, you know.

Miss Tesman: Yes, collecting and ordering—you do that so well. You're not my brother's son for nothing.

Tesman: I look forward so much to getting started. Especially now, with a comfortable home of my own to work in.

Miss Tesman: And most of all, dear, now that you've won her, the wife of your heart.

Tesman (embracing her): Yes, yes, Aunt Julie! Hedda—that's the most beautiful part of it all! *(Glancing toward the doorway.)* But I think she's coming—uh?

(Hedda *enters from the left through the inner room. She is a woman of twenty-nine. Her face and figure show breeding and distinction; her complexion is pallid and opaque. Her steel gray eyes express a cool, unruffled calm. Her hair is an attractive medium brown, but not particularly abundant. She wears a tasteful, rather loose-fitting gown.)*

Miss Tesman (going to meet Hedda*):* Good morning, Hedda dear—how good to see you!

Hedda (holding out her hand): Good morning, my dear Miss Tesman! Calling so early? This *is* kind of you.

Miss Tesman (slightly embarrassed): Well—did the bride sleep well in her new home?

Hedda: Oh yes, thanks. Quite adequately.

Tesman: Adequately! Oh, I like that, Hedda! You were sleeping like a stone when I got up.

Hedda: Fortunately. But of course one has to grow accustomed to anything new, Miss Tesman—little by little. *(Looking toward the left.)* Oh! That maid has left the door open—and the sunlight's just flooding in.

Miss Tesman (going toward the door): Well, we can close it.

Hedda: No, no—don't! *(To* Tesman.*)* There, dear, draw the curtains. It gives a softer light.

Tesman (by the glass door): All right—all right. Look, Hedda—now you have shade and fresh air both.

Hedda: Yes, we really need some fresh air here, with all these piles of flowers—But—won't you sit down, Miss Tesman?

Miss Tesman: Oh no, thank you. Now that I know that everything's fine—thank goodness—I will have to run along home. My sister's lying there waiting, poor thing.

Tesman: Give her my very, very best, won't you? And say I'll be looking in on her later today.

Miss Tesman: Oh, you can be sure I will. But what do you know, George—*(Searching in her bag.)*—I nearly forgot. I have something here for you.

Tesman: What's that, Aunt Julie? Hm?

Miss Tesman (brings out a flat package wrapped in newspaper and hands it to him*):* There, dear. Look.

Tesman (opening it): Oh, my—you kept them for me, Aunt Julie! Hedda! That's really touching! Uh!

Hedda (by the étagère on the right): Yes, dear, what is it?

Tesman: My old bedroom slippers! My slippers!

Hedda: Oh yes. I remember how often you spoke of them during the trip.

Tesman: Yes, I missed them terribly. *(Going over to her.)* Now you can see them, Hedda!

Hedda (moves toward the stove): Thanks, but I really don't care to.

Tesman (following her): Imagine—Auntie Rina lay and embroidered them, sick as she was. Oh, you couldn't believe how many memories are bound up in them.

Hedda (at the table): But not for me.

Miss Tesman: I think Hedda is right, George.

Tesman: Yes, but I only thought, now that she's part of the family—

Hedda (interrupting): We're never going to manage with this maid, Tesman.

Miss Tesman: Not manage with Berta?

Tesman: But dear—why do you say that? Uh?

Hedda (pointing): See there! She's left her old hat lying out on a chair.

Tesman (shocked; dropping the slippers): But Hedda—!

Hedda: Suppose someone came in and saw it.

Tesman: Hedda—that's Aunt Julie's hat!

Hedda: Really?

Miss Tesman (picking it up): That's right, it's mine. And what's more, it certainly is not old—Mrs. Tesman.

Hedda: I really hadn't looked closely at it, Miss Tesman.

Miss Tesman (putting on the hat): It's actually the first time I've had it on. The very first time.

Tesman: And it's lovely, too. Most attractive!

Miss Tesman: Oh, it's hardly all that, George. *(Looks about.)* My parasol—? Ah, here. *(Takes it.)* For that's mine too. *(Murmurs.)* Not Berta's.

Tesman: New hat and new parasol! Just imagine, Hedda!

Hedda: Quite charming, really.

Tesman: Yes, aren't they, huh? But Auntie, take a good look at Hedda before you leave. See how charming *she* is!

Miss Tesman: But George dear, there's nothing new in that. Hedda's been lovely all her life. *(She nods and starts out, right.)*

Tesman (following her): But have you noticed how plump and buxom she's grown? How much she's filled out on the trip?

Hedda (crossing the room): Oh, do be quiet—!

Miss Tesman (who has stopped and turned): Filled out?

Tesman: Of course, you can't see it so well when she has that dressing gown on. But I, who have the opportunity to—

Hedda (by the glass door, impatiently): Oh, you have no opportunity for anything!

Tesman: It must have been the mountain air, down in the Tyrol—

Hedda (brusquely interrupting): I'm exactly as I was when I left.

Tesman: Yes, that's your claim. But you certainly are not. Auntie, don't you agree?

Miss Tesman (gazing at her with folded hands): Hedda is lovely—lovely—lovely. *(Goes up to her, takes her head in both hands, bends it down and kisses her hair.)* God bless and keep Hedda Tesman—for George's sake.

Hedda (gently freeing herself): Oh—! Let me go.

Miss Tesman (with quiet feeling): I won't let a day go by without looking in on you two.

Tesman: Yes, please do that, Aunt Julie! Uh?

Miss Tesman: Good-bye—good-bye!

(*She goes out by the hall door.* Tesman *accompanies her, leaving the door half open. He can be heard reiterating his greetings to* Aunt Rina *and his thanks for the slippers. At the same time,* Hedda *moves about the room, raising her arms and clenching her fists as if in a frenzy. Then she flings back the curtains from the glass door and stands there, looking out. A moment later* Tesman *comes back, closing the door after him.*)

Tesman (retrieving the slippers from the floor): What are you standing and looking at, Hedda?

Hedda (again calm and controlled): I'm just looking at the leaves—they're so yellow—and so withered.

Tesman (wraps up the slippers and puts them on the table): Yes, well, we're into September now.

Hedda (once more restless): Yes, to think—that already we're in—in September.

Tesman: Didn't Aunt Julie seem a bit strange? A little—almost formal? What do you suppose was bothering her? Hm?

Hedda: I hardly know her at all. Isn't that how she usually is?

Tesman: No, not like this, today.

Hedda (leaving the glass door): Do you think this thing with the hat upset her?

Tesman: Oh, not very much. A little, just at the moment, perhaps—

Hedda: But really, what kind of manners has she—to go throwing her hat about in a drawing room! It's just not proper.

Tesman: Well, you can be sure Aunt Julie won't do it again.

Hedda: Anyhow, I'll manage to smooth it over with her.

Tesman: Yes, Hedda dear, I wish you would!

Hedda: When you go in to see them later on, you might ask her out for the evening.

Tesman: Yes, I'll do that. And there's something else you could do that would make her terribly happy.

Hedda: Oh?

Tesman: If only you could bring yourself to speak to her warmly, by her first name. For my sake, Hedda? Uh?

Hedda: No, no—don't ask me to do that. I told you this once before. I'll try to call her "Aunt." That should be enough.

Tesman: Oh, all right. I was only thinking, now that you belong to the family—

Hedda: Hm—I really don't know—(*She crosses the room to the doorway.*)

Tesman (after a pause): Is something the matter, Hedda? Uh?

Hedda: I'm just looking at my old piano. It doesn't really fit in with all these other things.

Tesman: With the first salary I draw, we can see about trading it in on a new one.

Hedda: No, not traded in. I don't want to part with it. We can put it there, in the inner room, and get another here in its place. When there's a chance, I mean.

Tesman (slightly cast down): Yes, we could do that, of course.

Hedda (picks up the bouquet from the piano): These flowers weren't here when we got in last night.

Tesman: Aunt Julie must have brought them for you.

Hedda (examining the bouquet): A visiting card. *(Takes it out and reads it.)* "Will stop back later today." Can you guess who this is from?

Tesman: No. Who? Hm?

Hedda: It says, Mrs. Elvsted.

Tesman: No, really? Sheriff Elvsted's wife. Miss Rysing, she used to be.

Hedda: Exactly. The one with the irritating hair that she was always showing off. An old flame of yours, I've heard.

Tesman (laughing): Oh, that wasn't for long. And it was before I knew you, Hedda. But imagine—that she's here in town.

Hedda: It's odd that she calls on us. I've hardly seen her since we were in school.

Tesman: Yes, I haven't seen her either—since God knows when. I wonder how she can stand living in such an out-of-the-way place. Hm?

Hedda (thinks a moment, then bursts out): But wait— isn't it somewhere up in those parts that he—that Eilert Løvborg lives?

Tesman: Yes, it's someplace right around there. *(Berta enters by the hall door.)*

Berta: She's back again, ma'am—that lady who stopped by and left the flowers an hour ago. *(Pointing.)* The ones you have in your hand, ma'am.

Hedda: Oh, is she? Good. Would you ask her to come in.

(Berta opens the door for Mrs. Elvsted and goes out. Mrs. Elvsted is a slender woman with soft, pretty features. Her eyes are light blue, large, round, and somewhat prominent, with a startled, questioning look. Her hair is remarkably light, almost a white-gold, and unusually abundant and wavy. She is a couple of years younger than Hedda. She wears a dark visiting dress, tasteful, but not quite in the latest fashion.)

Hedda (going to greet her warmly): Good morning, my dear Mrs. Elvsted. How delightful to see you again!

Mrs. Elvsted (nervously; struggling to control herself): Yes, it's a very long time since we last met.

Tesman (gives her his hand): Or since *we* met, uh?

Hedda: Thank you for your beautiful flowers—

Mrs. Elvsted: Oh, that's nothing—I would have come straight out here yesterday afternoon, but then I heard you weren't at home—

Tesman: Have you just now come to town? Uh?

Mrs. Elvsted: I got in yesterday toward noon. Oh, I was in desperation when I heard that you weren't at home.

Hedda: Desperation! Why?

Tesman: But my dear Mrs. Rysing—Mrs. Elvsted, I mean—

Hedda: You're not in some kind of trouble?

Mrs. Elvsted: Yes, I am. And I don't know another living soul down here I can turn to.

Hedda (putting the bouquet down on the table): Come, then—let's sit here on the sofa—

Mrs. Elvsted: Oh, I can't sit down. I'm really too much on edge!

Hedda: Why, of course you can. Come here.

(*She draws* Mrs. Elvsted *down on the sofa and sits beside her.*)

Tesman: Well? What is it, Mrs. Elvsted?

Hedda: Has anything particular happened at home?

Mrs. Elvsted: Yes, that's both it—and not it. Oh, I do want so much that you don't misunderstand me—

Hedda: But then the best thing, Mrs. Elvsted, is simply to speak your mind.

Tesman: Because I suppose that's why you've come. Hm?

Mrs. Elvsted: Oh yes, that's why. Well, then, I have to tell you—if you don't already know—that Eilert Løvborg's also in town.

Hedda: Løvborg—!

Tesman: What! Is Eilert Løvborg back! Just think, Hedda!

Hedda: Good Lord, I can hear.

Mrs. Elvsted: He's been back all of a week's time now. A whole week—in this dangerous town! Alone! With all the bad company that's around.

Hedda: But my dear Mrs. Elvsted, what does *he* have to do with you?

Mrs. Elvsted (*glances anxiously at her and says quickly*): He was the children's tutor.

Hedda: Your children's?

Mrs. Elvsted: My husband's. I have none.

Hedda: Your stepchildren's, then.

Mrs. Elvsted: Yes.

Tesman (*somewhat hesitantly*): But was he—I don't know quite how to put it—was he sufficiently—responsible in his habits for such a job? Uh?

Mrs. Elvsted: In these last two years, there wasn't a word to be said against him.

Tesman: Not a word? Just think of that, Hedda!

Hedda: I heard it.

Mrs. Elvsted: Not even a murmur, I can assure you! Nothing. But anyway—now that I know he's here—in this big city—and with so much money in his hands—then I'm just frightened to death for him.

Tesman: But why didn't he stay up there where he was? With you and your husband? Uh?

Mrs. Elvsted: After the book came out, he just couldn't rest content with us.

Tesman: Yes, that's right—Aunt Julie was saying he'd published a new book.

Mrs. Elvsted: Yes, a great new book, on the course of civilization—in all its stages. It's been out two weeks. And now it's been bought and read so much—and it's made a tremendous stir—

Tesman: Has it really? It must be something he's had lying around from his better days.

Mrs. Elvsted: Years back, you mean?

Tesman: I suppose.

Mrs. Elvsted: No, he's written it all up there with us. Now—in this last year.

Tesman: That's marvelous to hear. Hedda! Just imagine!

Mrs. Elvsted: Yes, if only it can go on like this!

Hedda: Have you seen him here in town?

Mrs. Elvsted: No, not yet. I had such trouble finding out his address. But this morning I got it at last.

Hedda (looks searchingly at her): I must say it seems rather odd of your husband—

Mrs. Elvsted (with a nervous start): Of my husband—! What?

Hedda: To send you to town on this sort of errand. Not to come and look after his friend himself.

Mrs. Elvsted: No, no, my husband hasn't the time for that. And then I had— some shopping to do.

Hedda (with a slight smile): Oh, that's different.

Mrs. Elvsted (getting up quickly and uneasily): I beg you, please, Mr. Tesman— be good to Eilert Løvborg if he comes to you. And he will, I'm sure. You know—you were such good friends in the old days. And you're both doing the same kind of work. The same type of research—from what I can gather.

Tesman: We were once, at any rate.

Mrs. Elvsted: Yes, and that's why I'm asking you, please—you too—to keep an eye on him. Oh, you will do that. Mr. Tesman—promise me that?

Tesman: I'll be only too glad to, Mrs. Rysing—

Hedda: Elvsted.

Tesman: I'll certainly do everything in my power for Eilert. You can depend on that.

Mrs. Elvsted: Oh, how terribly kind of you! *(Pressing his hands.)* Many, many thanks! *(Frightened.)* He means so much to my husband, you know.

Hedda (rising): You ought to write him, dear. He might not come by on his own.

Tesman: Yes, that probably would be the best, Hedda? Hm?

Hedda: And the sooner the better. Right now, I'd say.

Mrs. Elvsted (imploringly): Oh yes, if you could!

Tesman: I'll write him this very moment. Have you got his address, Mrs.— Mrs. Elvsted?

Mrs. Elvsted: Yes. *(Takes a slip of paper from her pocket and hands it to him.)* Here it is.

Tesman: Good, good. Then I'll go in—*(Looking about.)* But wait—my slippers? Ah! Here. *(Takes the package and starts to leave.)*

Hedda: Write him a really warm, friendly letter. Nice and long, too.

Tesman: Don't worry. I will.

Mrs. Elvsted: But please, not a word that I asked you to!

Tesman: No, that goes without saying. Uh? *(Leaves by the inner room, to the right.)*

Hedda (goes over to Mrs. Elvsted, *smiles, and speaks softly):* How's that! Now we've killed two birds with one stone.

Mrs. Elvsted: What do you mean?

Hedda: Didn't you see that I wanted him out of the room?

Mrs. Elvsted: Yes, to write the letter—

Hedda: But also to talk with you alone.

Mrs. Elvsted (confused): About this same thing?

Hedda: Precisely.

Mrs. Elvsted (upset): But Mrs. Tesman, there's nothing more to say! Nothing!

Hedda: Oh yes, but there is. There's a great deal more—I can see that. Come, sit here—and let's speak openly now, the two of us. *(She forces* Mrs. Elvsted *down into the armchair by the stove and sits on one of the taborets.)*

Mrs. Elvsted (anxiously glancing at her watch): But Mrs. Tesman, dear—I was just planning to leave.

Hedda: Oh, you can't be in such a rush—Now! Tell me a little about how things are going at home.

Mrs. Elvsted: Oh, that's the last thing I'd ever want to discuss.

Hedda: But with me, dear—? After all, we were in school together.

Mrs. Elvsted: Yes, but you were a class ahead of me. Oh, I was terribly afraid of you then!

Hedda: Afraid of me?

Mrs. Elvsted: Yes, terribly. Because whenever we met on the stairs, you'd always pull my hair.

Hedda: Did I really?

Mrs. Elvsted: Yes, and once you said you would burn it off.

Hedda: Oh, that was just foolish talk, you know.

Mrs. Elvsted: Yes, but I was so stupid then. And, anyway, since then—we've drifted so far—far apart from each other. We've moved in such different circles.

Hedda: Well, let's try now to come closer again. Listen, at school we were quite good friends, and we called each other by our first names—

Mrs. Elvsted: No, I'm sure you're mistaken.

Hedda: Oh, I couldn't be! I remember it clearly. And that's why we have to be perfectly open, just as we were. *(Moves the stool nearer* Mrs. Elvsted.*)* There now! *(Kissing her cheek.)* You have to call me Hedda.

Mrs. Elvsted (pressing and patting her hands): Oh, you're so good and kind—! It's not at all what I'm used to.

Hedda: There, there! And I'm going to call you my own dear Thora.

Mrs. Elvsted: My name is Thea.

Hedda: Oh yes, of course. I meant Thea. *(Looks at her compassionately.)* So you're not much used to goodness or kindness, Thea? In your own home?

Mrs. Elvsted: If only I had a home! But I don't. I never have.

Hedda (glances quickly at her): I thought it had to be something like that.

Mrs. Elvsted (gazing helplessly into space): Yes—yes—yes.

Hedda: I can't quite remember now—but wasn't it as a housekeeper that you first came up to the Elvsteds?

Mrs. Elvsted: Actually as a governess. But his wife—his first wife—she was an invalid and mostly kept to her bed. So I had to take care of the house too.

Hedda: But finally you became mistress of the house yourself.

Mrs. Elvsted (heavily): Yes, I did.

Hedda: Let me see—about how long ago was that?

Mrs. Elvsted: That I was married?

Hedda: Yes.

Mrs. Elvsted: It's five years now.

Hedda: That's right. It must be.

Mrs. Elvsted: Oh, these five years—! Or the last two or three, anyway. Oh, if you only knew, Mrs. Tesman—

Hedda (gives her hand a little slap): Mrs. Tesman! Now, Thea!

Mrs. Elvsted: I'm sorry; I'll try—Yes, if you could only understand— Hedda—

Hedda (casually): Eilert Løvborg has lived up there about three years too, hasn't he?

Mrs. Elvsted (looks at her doubtfully): Eilert Løvborg? Yes—he has.

Hedda: Had you already known him here in town?

Mrs. Elvsted: Hardly at all. Well, I mean—by name, of course.

Hedda: But up there—I suppose he'd visit you both?

Mrs. Elvsted: Yes, he came to see us every day. He was tutoring the children, you know. Because, in the long run, I couldn't do it all myself.

Hedda: No, that's obvious. And your husband—? I suppose he often has to be away?

Mrs. Elvsted: Yes, you can imagine, as sheriff, how much traveling he does around in the district.

Hedda (leaning against the chair arm): Thea—my poor, sweet Thea—now you must tell me everything—just as it is.

Mrs. Elvsted: Well, then you have to ask the questions.

Hedda: What sort of man is your husband, Thea? I mean—you know—to be with. Is he good to you?

Mrs. Elvsted (evasively): He believes he does everything for the best.

Hedda: I only think he must be much too old for you. More than twenty years older, isn't he?

Mrs. Elvsted (irritated): That's true. Along with everything else. I just can't stand him! We haven't a single thought in common. Nothing at all—he and I.

Hedda: But doesn't he care for you all the same—in his own way?

Mrs. Elvsted: Oh, I don't know what he feels. I'm no more than useful to him. And then it doesn't cost much to keep me. I'm inexpensive.

Hedda: That's stupid of you.

Mrs. Elvsted (shaking her head): It can't be otherwise. Not with him. He really doesn't care for anyone but himself—and maybe a little for the children.

Hedda: And for Eilert Løvborg, Thea.

Mrs. Elvsted (looking at her): Eilert Løvborg! Why do you think so?

Hedda: But my dear—it seems to me, when he sends you all the way into town to look after him—*(Smiles almost imperceptibly.)* Besides, it's what you told my husband.

Mrs. Elvsted (with a little nervous shudder): Really? Yes, I suppose I did. *(In a quiet outburst.)* No—I might as well tell you here and now! It's bound to come out in time.

Hedda: But my dear Thea—?

Mrs. Elvsted: All right, then! My husband never knew I was coming here.

Hedda: What! Your husband never knew—

Mrs. Elvsted: Of course not. Anyway, he wasn't at home. Off traveling some-where. Oh, I couldn't bear it any longer, Hedda. It was impossible! I would have been so alone up there now.

Hedda: Well? What then?

Mrs. Elvsted: So I packed a few of my things together—the barest necessi-ties—without saying a word. And I slipped away from the house.

Hedda: Right then and there?

Mrs. Elvsted: Yes, and took the train straight into town.

Hedda: But my dearest girl—that you could dare to do such a thing!

Mrs. Elvsted (rising and walking about the room): What else could I possibly do!

Hedda: But what do you think your husband will say when you go back home?

Mrs. Elvsted (by the table, looking at her): Back to him?

Hedda: Yes, of course.

Mrs. Elvsted: I'll never go back to him.

Hedda (rising and approaching her): You mean you've left, in dead earnest, for good?

Mrs. Elvsted: Yes. There didn't seem anything else to do.

Hedda: But—to go away so openly.

Mrs. Elvsted: Oh, you can't keep a thing like that secret.

Hedda: But what do you think people will say about you, Thea?

Mrs. Elvsted: God knows they'll say what they please. *(Sitting wearily and sadly on the sofa.)* I only did what I had to do.

Hedda (after a short silence): What do you plan on now? What kind of work?

Mrs. Elvsted: I don't know yet. I only know I have to live here, where Eilert Løvborg is—if I'm going to live at all.

Hedda (moves a chair over from the table, sits beside her, and strokes her hands): Thea dear—how did this—this friendship—between you and Eilert Løvborg come about?

Mrs. Elvsted: Oh, it happened little by little. I got some kind of power, almost, over him.

Hedda: Really?

Mrs. Elvsted: He gave up his old habits. Not because I'd asked him to. I never dared do that. But he could tell they upset me, and so he dropped them.

Hedda (hiding an involuntary, scornful smile): My dear little Thea—just as they say—you rehabilitated him.

Mrs. Elvsted: Well, he says so, at any rate. And he—on his part—he's made a real human being out of me. Taught me to think—and understand so many things.

Hedda: You mean he tutored you also?

Mrs. Elvsted: No, not exactly. But he'd talk to me—talk endlessly on about one thing after another. And then came the wonderful, happy time when I could share in his work! When I could help him!

Hedda: Could you really?

Mrs. Elvsted: Yes! Whenever he wrote anything, we'd always work on it together.

Hedda: Like two true companions.

Mrs. Elvsted (eagerly): Companions! You know, Hedda—that's what he said too! Oh, I ought to feel so happy—but I can't. I just don't know if it's going to last.

Hedda: You're no more sure of him than that?

Mrs. Elvsted (despondently): There's a woman's shadow between Eilert Løvborg and me.

Hedda (looks at her intently): Who could that be?

Mrs. Elvsted: I don't know. Someone out of his—his past. Someone he's really never forgotten.

Hedda: What has he said—about this!

Mrs. Elvsted: It's only once—and just vaguely—that he touched on it.

Hedda: Well! And what did he say!

Mrs. Elvsted: He said that when they broke off she was going to shoot him with a pistol.

Hedda (with cold constraint): That's nonsense! Nobody behaves that way around here.

Mrs. Elvsted: No. And that's why I think it must have been that redheaded singer that at one time he—

Hedda: Yes, quite likely.

Mrs. Elvsted: I remember they used to say about her that she carried loaded weapons.

Hedda: Ah—then of course it must have been her.

Mrs. Elvsted (wringing her hands): But you know what, Hedda—I've heard that this singer—that she's in town again! Oh, it has me out of my mind—

Hedda (glancing toward the inner room): Shh! Tesman's coming. (*Gets up and whispers.*) Thea—keep all this just between us.

Mrs. Elvsted (jumping up): Oh yes! In heaven's name—!

(George Tesman, *with a letter in his hand, enters from the right through the inner room.*)

Tesman: There, now—the letter's signed and sealed.

Hedda: That's fine. I think Mrs. Elvsted was just leaving. Wait a minute. I'll go with you to the garden gate.

Tesman: Hedda, dear—could Berta maybe look after this?

Hedda (taking the letter): I'll tell her to.

(Berta *enters from the hall.*)

Berta: Judge Brack is here and says he'd like to greet you and the Doctor, ma'am.

Hedda: Yes, ask Judge Brack to come in. And, here—put this letter in the mail.

Berta (takes the letter): Yes, ma'am.

(*She opens the door for* Judge Brack *and goes out.* Brack *is a man of forty-five, thickset, yet well built, with supple movements. His face is roundish, with a distinguished profile. His hair is short, still mostly black, and carefully groomed. His eyes are bright and lively. Thick eyebrows; a mustache to match, with neatly clipped ends. He wears a trimly tailored walking suit, a bit too youthful for his age. Uses a monocle, which he now and then lets fall.)*

Judge Brack (hat in hand, bowing): May one dare to call so early?

Hedda: Of course one may.

Tesman (shakes his hand): You're always welcome here. *(Introducing him.)* Judge Brack—Miss Rysing—

Hedda: Ah—!

Brack (bowing): I'm delighted.

Hedda (looks at him and laughs): It's really a treat to see you by daylight. Judge!

Brack: You find me—changed?

Hedda: Yes. A bit younger, I think.

Brack: Thank you, most kindly.

Tesman: But what do you say for Hedda, uh? Doesn't she look flourishing? She's actually—

Hedda: Oh, leave me out of it! You might thank Judge Brack for all the trouble he's gone to—

Brack: Nonsense—it was a pleasure—

Hedda: Yes, you're a true friend. But here's Thea, standing here, aching to get away. Excuse me. Judge; I'll be right back.

(Mutual good-byes. Mrs. Elvsted and Hedda go out by the hall door.)

Brack: So—is your wife fairly well satisfied, then—?

Tesman: Yes, we can't thank you enough. Of course—I gather there's some rearrangement called for here and there. And one or two things are lacking. We still have to buy a few minor items.

Brack: Really?

Tesman: But that's nothing for you to worry about. Hedda said she'd pick up those things herself. Why don't we sit down, hm?

Brack: Thanks. Just for a moment. *(Sits by the table.)* There's something I'd like to discuss with you, Tesman.

Tesman: What? Oh, I understand! *(Sitting.)* It's the serious part of the banquet we're coming to, uh?

Brack: Oh, as far as money matters go, there's no great rush—though I must say I wish we'd managed things a bit more economically.

Tesman: But that was completely impossible! Think about Hedda, Judge! You, who know her so well—I simply couldn't have her live like a grocer's wife.

Brack: No, no—that's the trouble, exactly.

Tesman: And then—fortunately—it can't be long before I get my appointment.

Brack: Well, you know—these things can often hang fire.

Tesman: Have you heard something further? Hm?

Brack: Nothing really definite—*(Changing the subject.)* But incidentally—I do have one piece of news for you.

Tesman: Well?

Brack: Your old friend Eilert Løvborg is back in town.

Tesman: I already know.

Brack: Oh? How did you hear?

Tesman: She told me. The lady that left with Hedda.

Brack: I see. What was her name again? I didn't quite catch it—

Tesman: Mrs. Elvsted.

Brack: Aha—Sheriff Elvsted's wife. Yes—it's up near them he's been staying.

Tesman: And, just think—what a pleasure to hear that he's completely stable again!

Brack: Yes, that's what they claim.

Tesman: And that he's published a new book, uh?

Brack: Oh yes!

Tesman: And it's created quite a sensation.

Brack: An extraordinary sensation.

Tesman: Just imagine—isn't that marvelous? He, with his remarkable talents—I was so very afraid that he'd really gone down for good.

Brack: That's what everyone thought.

Tesman: But I've no idea what he'll find to do now. How on earth can he ever make a living? Hm?

(During the last words, Hedda *comes in by the hall door.)*

Hedda (to Brack, *laughing, with a touch of scorn):* Tesman always goes around worrying about how people are going to make a living.

Tesman: My Lord—it's poor Eilert Løvborg we're talking of, dear.

Hedda (glancing quickly at him): Oh, really? *(Sits in the armchair by the stove and asks casually.)* What's the matter with him?

Tesman: Well—he must have run through his inheritance long ago. And he can't write a new book every year. Uh? So I was asking, really, what's going to become of him.

Brack: Perhaps I can shed some light on that.

Tesman: Oh?

Brack: You must remember that he does have relatives with a great deal of influence.

Tesman: Yes, but they've washed their hands of him altogether.

Brack: They used to call him the family's white hope.

Tesman: They used to, yes! But he spoiled all that himself.

Hedda: Who knows? *(With a slight smile.)* He's been rehabilitated up at the Elvsteds—

Brack: And then this book that he's published—

Tesman: Oh, well, let's hope they really help him some way or other. I just now wrote to him. Hedda dear, I asked him out here this evening.

Brack: But my dear fellow, you're coming to my stag party this evening. You promised down on the pier last night.

Hedda: Had you forgotten, Tesman?

Tesman: Yes, I absolutely had.

Brack: For that matter, you can rest assured that he'd never come.

Tesman: What makes you say that, hm?

Brack (hesitating, rising and leaning on the back of the chair): My dear
    Tesman—and you too, Mrs. Tesman—I can't, in all conscience, let
    you go on without knowing something that—that—
Tesman: Something involving Eilert—?
Brack: Both you and him.
Tesman: But my dear Judge, then tell us!
Brack: You must be prepared that your appointment may not come through
    as quickly as you've wished or expected.
Tesman (jumping up nervously): Has something gone wrong? Uh?
Brack: It may turn out that there'll have to be a competition for the post—
Tesman: A competition! Imagine, Hedda!
Hedda (leaning further back in the chair): Ah, there—you see!
Tesman: But with whom! You can't mean—?
Brack: Yes, exactly. With Eilert Løvborg.
Tesman (striking his hands together): No, no—that's completely unthinkable!
    It's impossible! Uh?
Brack: Hm—but it may come about, all the same.
Tesman: No, but, Judge Brack—that would just be incredibly inconsiderate,
    toward me! *(Waving his arms.)* Yes, because—you know—I'm a married
    man! We married on my prospects, Hedda and I. We went into debt.
    And even borrowed money from Aunt Julie. Because that job—my
    Lord, it was as good as promised to me, uh?
Brack: Easy now—I'm sure you'll get the appointment. But you will have to
    compete for it.
Hedda (motionless in the armchair): Just think, Tesman—it will be like a kind
    of championship match.
Tesman: But Hedda dearest, how can you take it so calmly!
Hedda (as before): I'm not the least bit calm. I can't wait to see how it turns
    out.
Brack: In any case, Mrs. Tesman, it's well that you know now how things
    stand. I mean—with respect to those little purchases I hear you've been
    threatening to make.
Hedda: This business can't change anything.
Brack: I see! Well, that's another matter. Good-bye. *(To Tesman.)* When I
    take my afternoon walk, I'll stop by and fetch you.
Tesman: Oh yes, please do—I don't know where I'm at.
Hedda (leaning back and reaching out her hand): Good-bye, Judge. And come
    again soon.
Brack: Many thanks. Good-bye now.
Tesman (accompanying him to the door): Good-bye, Judge! You really must
    excuse me—

    (Brack goes out by the hall door.)

Tesman (pacing about the room): Oh, Hedda—one should never go off and
    lose oneself in dreams, uh?
Hedda (looks at him and smiles): Do *you* do *that?*

Tesman: No use denying it. It was living in dreams to go and get married and set up house on nothing but expectations.

Hedda: Perhaps you're right about that.

Tesman: Well, at least we have our comfortable home, Hedda! The home that we always wanted. That we both fell in love with, I could almost say. Hm?

Hedda (rising slowly and wearily): It was part of our bargain that we'd live in society—that we'd keep a great house—

Tesman: Yes, of course—how I'd looked forward to that! Imagine—seeing you as a hostess—in our own select circle of friends! Yes, yes—well for a while, we two will just have to get on by ourselves, Hedda. Perhaps have Aunt Julie here now and then. Oh, you—for you I wanted to have things so—so utterly different—!

Hedda: Naturally this means I can't have a butler now.

Tesman: Oh no—I'm sorry, a butler—we can't even talk about that, you know.

Hedda: And the riding horse I was going to have—

Tesman (appalled): Riding horse!

Hedda: I suppose I can't think of that anymore.

Tesman: Good Lord, no—that's obvious!

Hedda (crossing the room): Well, at least I have one thing left to amuse myself with.

Tesman (beaming): Ah, thank heaven for that! What is it, Hedda? Uh?

Hedda (in the center doorway, looking at him with veiled scorn): My pistols, George.

Tesman (in fright): Your pistols!

Hedda (her eyes cold): General Gabler's pistols. *(She goes through the inner room and out to the left.)*

Tesman (runs to the center doorway and calls after her): No, for heaven's sake, Hedda darling—don't touch those dangerous things! For my sake, Hedda! Uh?

ACT II

The rooms at the Tesmans', *same as in the first act, except that the piano has been moved out, and an elegant little writing table with a bookcase put in its place. A smaller table stands by the sofa to the left. Most of the flowers have been removed. Mrs. Elvsted's bouquet stands on the large table in the foreground, it is afternoon.*

Hedda, *dressed to receive callers, is alone in the room. She stands by the open glass door, loading a revolver. The match to it lies in an open pistol case on the writing table.*

Hedda (looking down into the garden and calling): Good to see you again, Judge!

Brack (heard from below, at a distance): Likewise, Mrs. Tesman!

Hedda (raises the pistol and aims): And now, Judge, I'm going to shoot you!

Brack (shouting from below): No—no—no! Don't point that thing at me!

Hedda: That's what comes of sneaking in the back way. *(She fires.)*

Brack (nearer): Are you out of your mind—!

Hedda: Oh dear—I didn't hit you, did I?

Brack (still outside): Just stop this nonsense!

Hedda: All right, you can come in, Judge.

(Judge Brack, *dressed for a stag party, enters through the glass door. He carries a light overcoat on his arm.*)

Brack: Good God! Are you still playing such games? What are you shooting at?

Hedda: Oh, I was just shooting into the sky.

Brack (gently taking the pistol out of her hand): Permit me. *(Looks at it.)* Ah, this one—I know it well. *(Glancing around.)* Where's the case? Ah, here. *(Puts the pistol away and shuts the case.)* We'll have no more of that kind of fun today.

Hedda: Well, what in heaven's name do you want me to do with myself?

Brack: You haven't had any visitors?

Hedda (closing the glass door): Not a single one. All of our set are still in the country, I guess.

Brack: And Tesman isn't home either?

Hedda (at the writing table, putting the pistol case away in a drawer): No. Right after lunch he ran over to his aunts. He didn't expect you so soon.

Brack: Hm—I should have realized. That was stupid of me.

Hedda (turning her head and looking at him): Why stupid?

Brack: Because in that case I would have stopped by a little bit—earlier.

Hedda (crossing the room): Well, you'd have found no one here then at all. I've been up in my room dressing since lunch.

Brack: And there's not the least little crack in the door we could have conferred through.

Hedda: You forgot to arrange it.

Brack: Also stupid of me.

Hedda: Well, we'll just have to settle down here—and wait. Tesman won't be back for a while.

Brack: Don't worry, I can be patient.

(Hedda *sits in the corner of the sofa.* Brack *lays his coat over the back of the nearest chair and sits down, keeping his hat in his hand. A short pause. They look at each other.*)

Hedda: Well?

Brack (in the same tone): Well?

Hedda: I spoke first.

Brack (leaning slightly forward): Then let's have a nice little cozy chat, Mrs. Hedda.

Hedda (leaning further back on the sofa): Doesn't it seem like a whole eternity since the last time we talked together? Oh, a few words last night and this morning—but they don't count.

Brack: You mean, like this—between ourselves? Just the two of us?

Hedda: Well, more or less.

Brack: There wasn't a day that I didn't wish you were home again.

Hedda: And I was wishing exactly the same.

Brack: You? Really, Mrs. Hedda? And I thought you were having such a marvelous time on this trip.

Hedda: Oh, you can imagine!

Brack: But that's what Tesman always wrote.

Hedda: Oh, him! There's nothing he likes better than grubbing around in libraries and copying out old parchments, or whatever you call them.

Brack (with a touch of malice): But after all, it's his calling in life. In good part, anyway.

Hedda: Yes, that's true. So there's nothing wrong with it—But what about *me!* Oh, Judge, you don't know—I've been so dreadfully bored.

Brack (sympathetically): You really mean that? In all seriousness?

Hedda: Well, you can understand—! To go for a whole six months without meeting a soul who knew the least bit about our circle. No one that one could talk to about our kind of things.

Brack: Ah, yes—I think that would bother me too.

Hedda: But then the most unbearable thing of all—

Brack: What?

Hedda: To be everlastingly together with—with one and the same person—

Brack (nodding in agreement): Morning, noon, and night—yes. At every conceivable hour.

Hedda: I said "everlastingly."

Brack: All right. But with our good friend Tesman I really should have thought—

Hedda: My dear Judge, Tesman is—a specialist.

Brack: Undeniably.

Hedda: And specialists aren't at all amusing to travel with. Not in the long run, anyway.

Brack: Not even—the specialist that one *loves.*

Hedda: Ugh—don't use that syrupy word!

Brack (startled): What's that, Mrs. Hedda!

Hedda (half laughing, half annoyed): Well, just try it yourself! Try listening to the history of civilization morning, noon, and—

Brack: Everlastingly.

Hedda: Yes! Yes! And then all this business about domestic crafts in the Middle Ages—! That really is just too revolting!

Brack (looks searchingly at her): But tell me—I can't see how it ever came about that—? Hm—

Hedda: That George Tesman and I could make a match?

Brack: All right, let's put it that way.

Hedda: Good Lord, does it seem so remarkable?

Brack: Well, yes—and no, Mrs. Hedda.

Hedda: I really had danced myself out, Judge. My time was up. *(With a slight shudder.)* Ugh! No, I don't want to say that. Or think it, either.

Brack: You certainly have no reason to.

Hedda: Oh—reasons—*(Watching him carefully.)* And George Tesman—he is, after all, a thoroughly acceptable choice.

Brack: Acceptable and dependable, beyond a doubt.

Hedda: And I don't find anything especially ridiculous about him. Do you?

Brack: Ridiculous? No-o-o, I wouldn't say that.

Hedda: Hm. Anyway, he works incredibly hard on his research! There's every chance that, in time, he could still make a name for himself.

Brack (looking at her with some uncertainty): I thought you believed, like everyone else, that he was going to be quite famous some day.

Hedda (wearily): Yes, so I did. And then when he kept pressing and pleading to be allowed to take care of me—I didn't see why I ought to resist.

Brack: No. From that point of view, of course not—

Hedda: It was certainly more than my other admirers were willing to do for me, Judge.

Brack (laughing): Well, I can't exactly answer for all the others. But as far as I'm concerned, you know that I've always cherished a—a certain respect for the marriage bond. Generally speaking, that is.

Hedda (bantering): Oh, I never really held out any hopes for *you.*

Brack: All I want is to have a warm circle of intimate friends, where I can be of use one way or another, with the freedom to come and go as—as a trusted friend—

Hedda: Of the man of the house, you mean?

Brack (with a bow): Frankly—I prefer the lady. But the man, too, of course, in his place. That kind of—let's say, triangular arrangement—you can't imagine how satisfying it can be all around.

Hedda: Yes, I must say I longed for some third person so many times on that trip. Oh—those endless tête-à-têtes° in railway compartments—!

Brack: Fortunately the wedding trip's over now.

Hedda (shaking her head): The trip will go on—and on. I've only come to one stop on the line.

Brack: Well, then what you do is jump out—and stretch yourself a little, Mrs. Hedda.

Hedda: I'll never jump out.

Brack: Never?

Hedda: No. Because there's always someone on the platform who—

Brack (with a laugh): Who looks at your legs, is that it?

Hedda: Precisely.

Brack: Yes, but after all—

Hedda (with a disdainful gesture): I'm not interested. I'd rather keep my seat—right here, where I am. Tête-à-tête.

Brack: Well, but suppose a third person came on board and joined the couple.

Hedda: Ah! That's entirely different.

Brack: A trusted friend, who understands—

Hedda: And can talk about all kinds of lively things—

---

tête-à-tête: Face-to-face conversation.

Brack: Who's not in the least a specialist.

Hedda (with an audible sigh): Yes, that would be a relief.

Brack (hearing the front door open and glancing toward it): The triangle is complete.

Hedda (lowering her voice): And the train goes on.

(George Tesman, *in a gray walking suit and a soft felt hat, enters from the* hall. He has a good number of unbound books under his arm and in his pockets.)

Tesman (going up to the table by the corner settee): Phew! Let me tell you, that's hot work—carrying all these. *(Setting the books down.)* I'm actually sweating, Hedda. And what's this—you're already here, Judge? Hm? Berta didn't tell me.

Brack (rising): I came in through the garden.

Hedda: What are all these books you've gotten?

Tesman (stands leafing through them): They're new publications in my special field. I absolutely need them.

Hedda: Your special field?

Brack: Of course. Books in his special field, Mrs. Tesman.

(Brack *and* Hedda *exchange a knowing smile.)*

Hedda: You need still more books in your special field?

Tesman: Hedda, my dear, it's impossible ever to have too many. You have to keep up with what's written and published.

Hedda: Oh, I suppose so.

Tesman (searching among the books): And look—I picked up Eilert Løvborg's new book too. *(Offering it to her.)* Maybe you'd like to have a look at it? Uh?

Hedda: No, thank you. Or—well, perhaps later.

Tesman: I skimmed through some of it on the way home.

Hedda: Well, what do you think of it—as a specialist?

Tesman: I think it's amazing how well it holds up. He's never written like this before. *(Gathers up the books.)* But I'll take these into the study now. I can't wait to cut the pages°—! And then I better dress up a bit. *(To* Brack.) We don't have to rush right off, do we? Hm?

Brack: No, not at all. There's ample time.

Tesman: Ah, then I'll be at my leisure. *(Starts out with the books, but pauses and turns in the doorway.)* Oh, incidentally, Hedda—Aunt Julie won't be by to see you this evening.

Hedda: She won't? I suppose it's that business with the hat?

Tesman: Don't be silly. How can you think that of Aunt Julie? Imagine—! No, it's Auntie Rina—she's very ill.

Hedda: She always is.

Tesman: Yes, but today she really took a turn for the worse.

Hedda: Well, then it's only right for her sister to stay with her. I'll have to bear with it.

---

cut the pages: Book pages were printed on large sheets of paper that were folded and bound in groups of four. Readers had to trim the edges to separate the pages.

Tesman: But you can't imagine how delighted Aunt Julie was all the same— because you'd filled out so I nicely on the trip!

Hedda (under her breath; rising): Oh, these eternal aunts!

Tesman: What?

Hedda (going over to the glass door): Nothing.

Tesman: All right, then. (*He goes through the inner room and out, right.*)

Brack: What were you saying about a hat?

Hedda: Oh, it's something that happened with Miss Tesman this morning. She'd put her hat down over there on the chair. (*Looks at him and smiles.*) And I pretended I thought it was the maid's.

Brack (shaking his head): But my dear Mrs. Hedda, how could you do that! Hurt that fine old lady!

Hedda (nervously, pacing the room): Well, it's—these things come over me, just like that, suddenly. And I can't hold back. (*Throws herself down in the armchair by the stove.*) Oh, I don't know myself how to explain it.

Brack (behind the armchair): You're not really happy—that's the heart of it.

Hedda (gazing straight ahead): And I don't know why I ought to be—happy. Or maybe you can tell me why?

Brack: Yes—among other things, because you've gotten just the home you've always wanted.

Hedda (looks up at him and laughs): You believe that story too?

Brack: You mean there's nothing to it?

Hedda: Oh, yes—there's something to it.

Brack: Well?

Hedda: There's this much to it, that I used Tesman as my escort home from parties last summer—

Brack: Unfortunately—I was going in another direction then.

Hedda: How true. Yes, you had other directions to go last summer.

Brack (laughing): For shame, Mrs. Hedda! Well—so you and Tesman—?

Hedda: Yes, so one evening we walked by this place. And Tesman, poor thing, was writhing in torment, because he couldn't find anything to say. And I felt sorry for a man of such learning—

Brack (smiling skeptically): Did you? Hm—

Hedda: No, I honestly did. And so—just to help him off the hook—I came out with some rash remark about this lovely house being where I'd always wanted to live.

Brack: No more than that?

Hedda: No more that evening.

Brack: But afterward?

Hedda: Yes, my rashness had its consequences, Judge.

Brack: I'm afraid our rashness all too often does Mrs. Hedda.

Hedda: Thanks! But don't you see, it was this passion for the old Falk mansion that drew George Tesman and me together! It was nothing more than that, that brought on our engagement and the marriage and the wedding trip and everything else. Oh yes. Judge—I was going to say, you make your bed and then you lie in it.

Brack: But that's priceless! So actually you couldn't care less about all this?

Hedda: God knows, not in the least.

Brack: But even now? Now that we've made it somewhat comfortable for you here?

Hedda: Ugh—all the rooms seem to smell of lavender and dried roses. But maybe that scent was brought in by Aunt Julie.

Brack (laughing): No, I think it's a bequest from the late Mrs. Falk.

Hedda: Yes, there's something in it of the odor of death. It's like a corsage— the day after the dance. *(Folds her hands behind her neck, leans back in her chair, and looks at him.)* Oh, my dear Judge—you can't imagine how horribly I'm going to bore myself here.

Brack: But couldn't you find some goal in life to work toward? Others do, Mrs. Hedda.

Hedda: A goal—that would really absorb me?

Brack: Yes, preferably.

Hedda: God only knows what that could be. I often wonder if—*(Breaks off.)* But that's impossible too.

Brack: Who knows? Tell me.

Hedda: I was thinking—if I could get Tesman to go into politics.

Brack (laughing): Tesman! No, I can promise you—politics is absolutely out of his line.

Hedda: No, I can believe you. But even so, I wonder if I could get him into it?

Brack: Well, what satisfaction would you have in that, if he can't succeed? Why push him in that direction?

Hedda: Because, I've told you. I'm bored! *(After a pause.)* Then you think it's really out of the question that he could ever be a cabinet minister?

Brack: Hm—you see, Mrs. Hedda—to be anything like that, he'd have to be fairly wealthy to start with.

Hedda (rising impatiently): Yes, there it is! It's this tight little world I've stumbled into—*(Crossing the room.)* That's what makes life so miserable! So utterly ludicrous! Because that's what it *is.*

Brack: I'd say the fault lies elsewhere.

Hedda: Where?

Brack: You've never experienced anything that's really stirred you.

Hedda: Anything serious, you mean.

Brack: Well, you can call it that, if you like. But now perhaps it's on the way.

Hedda (tossing her head): Oh, you mean all the fuss over that wretched professorship! But that's Tesman's problem. I'm not going to give it a single thought.

Brack: No, that isn't—ah, never mind. But suppose you were to be confronted now by what—in rather elegant language—is called your most solemn responsibility. *(Smiling.)* A new responsibility, Mrs. Hedda.

Hedda (angrily): Be quiet! You'll never see me like that!

Brack (delicately): We'll discuss it again in a year's time—at the latest.

Hedda (curtly): I have no talent for such things, Judge. I won't have responsibilities!

Brack: Don't you think you've a talent for what almost every woman finds the most meaningful—

Hedda (over by the glass door): Oh, I told you, be quiet! I often think I have talent for only one thing in life.

Brack (moving closer): And what, may I ask, is that?

Hedda (stands looking out): Boring myself to death. And that's the truth. *(Turns, looks toward the inner room, and laughs.)* See what I mean! Here comes the professor.

Brack (in a low tone of warning): Ah-ah-ah, Mrs. Hedda!

(George Tesman, dressed for the party, with hat and gloves in hand, enters from the right through the inner room.)

Tesman: Hedda—there's been no word from Eilert Løvborg, has there? Hm?

Hedda: No.

Tesman: Well, he's bound to be here soon then. You'll see.

Brack: You really believe he'll come?

Tesman: Yes, I'm almost positive of it. Because I'm sure they're nothing but rumors, what you told us this morning.

Brack: Oh?

Tesman: Yes. At least Aunt Julie said she couldn't for the world believe that he'd stand in my way again. Can you imagine that!

Brack: So, then everything's well and good.

Tesman (putting his hat with the gloves inside on a chair to the right): Yes, but I really would like to wait for him as long as possible.

Brack: We have plenty of time for that. There's no one due at my place till seven or half past.

Tesman: Why, then we can keep Hedda company for a while. And see what turns up. Uh?

Hedda (taking Brack's hat and coat over to the sette): And if worst comes to worst, Mr. Løvborg can sit and talk with me.

Brack (trying to take his things himself): Ah, please, Mrs. Tesman—! What do you mean by "worst," in this case?

Hedda: If he won't go with you and Tesman.

Tesman (looks doubtfully at her): But Hedda dear—is it quite right that he stays with you here? Uh? Remember that Aunt Julie isn't coming.

Hedda: No, but Mrs. Elvsted is. The three of us can have tea together.

Tesman: Oh, well, that's all right.

Brack (smiling): And that might be the soundest plan for him too.

Hedda: Why?

Brack: Well, really, Mrs. Tesman, you've made enough pointed remarks about my little bachelor parties. You've always said they're only fit for men of the strictest principles.

Hedda: But Mr. Løvborg is surely a man of principle now. After all, a re-formed sinner—

(Berta appears at the hall door.)

Berta: Ma'am, there's a gentleman here who'd like to see you—

Hedda: Yes, show him in.

Tesman (softly): I'm sure it's him! Just think!

(Eilert Løvborg *enters from the hall. He is lean and gaunt, the same age as* Tesman, *but looks older and rather exhausted. His hair and beard are dark brown, his face long and pale, but with reddish patches over the cheekbones. He is dressed in a trim black suit, quite new, and holds dark gloves and a top hat in his hand. He hesitates by the door and bows abruptly. He seems somewhat embarrassed.*)

Tesman (crosses over and shakes his hand): Ah, my dear Eilert—so at last we meet again!

Eilert Løvborg (speaking in a hushed voice): Thanks for your letter, George! (*Approaching* Hedda.) May I shake hands with you too, Mrs. Tesman?

Hedda (taking his hand): So glad to see you, Mr. Løvborg. (*Gesturing with her hand.*) I don't know if you two gentlemen—?

Løvborg (bowing slightly): Judge Brack, I believe.

Brack (reciprocating): Of course. It's been some years—

Tesman (to Løvborg, *with his hands on his shoulders):* And now, Eilert, make yourself at home, completely! Right, Hedda? I hear you'll be settling down here in town again? Uh?

Løvborg: I plan to.

Tesman: Well, that makes sense. Listen—I just got hold of your new book. But I really haven't had time to read it yet.

Løvborg: You can save yourself the bother.

Tesman: Why? What do you mean?

Løvborg: There's very little to it.

Tesman: Imagine—you can say that!

Brack: But it's won such high praise, I hear.

Løvborg: That's exactly what I wanted. So I wrote a book that everyone could agree with.

Brack: Very sound.

Tesman: Yes, but my dear Eilert—!

Løvborg: Because now I want to build up my position again—and try to make a fresh start.

Tesman (somewhat distressed): Yes, that is what you want, I suppose. Uh?

Løvborg (smiling, puts down his hat and takes a thick manila envelope out of his pocket): But when this comes out—George Tesman—you'll have to read it. Because this is the real book—the one that speaks for my true self.

Tesman: Oh, really? What sort of book is that?

Løvborg: It's the sequel.

Tesman: Sequel? To what?

Løvborg: To the book.

Tesman: The one just out?

Løvborg: Of course.

Tesman: Yes, but my dear Eilert—that comes right down to our own time!

Løvborg: Yes, it does. And this one deals with the future.

Tesman: The future! But good Lord, there's nothing we know about that!

Løvborg: True. But there are one or two things worth saying about it all the same. (*Opens the envelope.*) Here, take a look—

Tesman: But that's not your handwriting.

Løvborg: I dictated it. *(Paging through the manuscript.)* It's divided into two sections. The first is about the forces shaping the civilization of the future. And the second part, here—*(paging further on)* suggests what lines of development it's likely to take.

Tesman: How extraordinary! It never would have occurred to me to write about anything like that.

Hedda (at the glass door, drumming on the pane): Hm—no, of course not.

Løvborg (puts the manuscript back in the envelope and lays it on the table): I brought it along because I thought I might read you a bit of it this evening.

Tesman: Ah, that's very good of you, Eilert; but this evening—*(Glancing at Brack.)* I'm really not sure that it's possible—

Løvborg: Well, some other time, then. There's no hurry.

Brack: I should explain, Mr. Løvborg—there's a little party at my place tonight. Mostly for Tesman, you understand.

Løvborg (looking for his hat): Ah—then I won't stay—

Brack: No, listen—won't you give me the pleasure of having you join us?

Løvborg (sharply and decisively): No, I can't. Thanks very much.

Brack: Oh, nonsense! Do that. We'll be a small, select group. And you can bet we'll have it "lively," as Mrs. Hed—Mrs. Tesman says.

Løvborg: I don't doubt it. But nevertheless—

Brack: You could bring your manuscript with you and read it to Tesman there, at my place. I have a spare room you could use.

Tesman: Why, of course, Eilert—you could do that, couldn't you? Uh?

Hedda (intervening): But dear, if Mr. Løvborg simply doesn't want to! I'm sure Mr. Løvborg would much prefer to settle down here and have supper with me.

Løvborg (looking at her): With you, Mrs. Tesman!

Hedda: And with Mrs. Elvsted.

Løvborg: Ah. *(Casually.)* I saw her a moment this afternoon.

Hedda: Oh, did you? Well, she'll be here soon. So it's almost essential for you to stay, Mr. Løvborg. Otherwise, she'll have no one to see her home.

Løvborg: That's true. Yes, thank you, Mrs. Tesman—I'll be staying, then.

Hedda: Then let me just tell the maid—

(She goes to the hall door and rings. Berta *enters.* Hedda *talks to her quietly and points toward the inner room.* Berta *nods and goes out again.)*

Tesman (at the same time, to Løvborg*):* Tell me, Eilert—is it this new material—about the future—that you're going to be lecturing on?

Løvborg: Yes.

Tesman: Because I heard at the bookstore that you'll be giving a lecture series here this autumn.

Løvborg: I intend to. I hope you won't be offended, Tesman.

Tesman: Why, of course not! But—?

Løvborg: I can easily understand that it makes things rather difficult for you.

Tesman (dispiritedly): Oh, I could hardly expect that for my sake you'd—

Løvborg: But I'm going to wait till you have your appointment.

Tesman: You'll wait! Yes, but—but—you're not competing for it, then? Uh?

Løvborg: No. I only want to win in the eyes of the world.

Tesman: But, my Lord—then Aunt Julie was right after all! Oh yes—I knew it all along! Hedda! Can you imagine—Eilert Løvborg won't stand in our way!

Hedda (brusquely): Our way? Leave me out of it.

(*She goes up toward the inner room where* Berta *is putting a tray with decanters and glasses on the table.* Hedda *nods her approval and comes back again.* Berta *goes out.*)

Tesman (at the same time): But you, Judge—what do you say to all this? Uh?

Brack: Well, I'd say that victory and honor—hm—after all, they're very sweet—

Tesman: Yes, of course. But still—

Hedda (regarding Tesman *with a cold smile):* You look as if you'd been struck by lightning.

Tesman: Yes—something like it—I guess—

Brack: That's because a thunderstorm just passed over us, Mrs. Tesman.

Hedda (pointing toward the inner room): Won't you gentlemen please help yourselves to a glass of cold punch?

Brack (looking at his watch): A parting cup? That's not such a bad idea.

Tesman: Marvelous, Hedda! Simply marvelous! The way I feel now, with this weight off my mind—

Hedda: Please, Mr. Løvborg, you too.

Løvborg (with a gesture of refusal): No, thank you. Not for me.

Brack: Good Lord, cold punch—it isn't poison, you know.

Løvborg: Perhaps not for everyone.

Hedda: I'll keep Mr. Løvborg company a while.

Tesman: All right, Hedda dear, you do that.

(*He and* Brack *go into the inner room, sit down, drink punch, smoke cigarettes, and talk animatedly during the following.* Løvborg *remains standing by the stove.* Hedda *goes to the writing table.*)

Hedda (slightly raising her voice): I can show you some photographs, if you like. Tesman and I traveled through the Tyrol on our way home.

(*She brings over an album and lays it on the table by the sofa, seating herself in the farthest corner.* Eilert Løvborg *comes closer, stops and looks at her. Then he takes a chair and sits down on her left, his back toward the inner room.*)

Hedda (opening the album): You see this view of the mountains, Mr. Løvborg. That's the Ortler group. Tesman's labeled them underneath. Here it is: "The Ortler group, near Meran."

Løvborg (whose eyes have never left her, speaking in a low, soft voice): Hedda— Gabler!

Hedda (with a quick glance at him): Ah! Shh!

Løvborg (repeating softly): Hedda Gabler!

Hedda (looks at the album): Yes, I used to be called that. In those days—when we two knew each other.

Løvborg: And from now on—for the rest of my life—I have to teach myself not to say Hedda Gabler.

Hedda (turning the pages): Yes, you have to. And I think you ought to start practicing it. The sooner the better, I'd say.

Løvborg (resentment in his voice): Hedda Gabler married? And to George Tesman!

Hedda: Yes—that's how it goes.

Løvborg: Oh, Hedda, Hedda—how could you throw yourself away like that!

Hedda (looks at him sharply): All right—no more of that!

Løvborg: What do you mean?

   (Tesman *comes in and over to the sofa.*)

Hedda (hears him coming and says casually): And this one, Mr. Løvborg, was taken from the Val d'Ampezzo. Just look at the peaks of those mountains. (*Looks warmly up at* Tesman.) Now what were those marvelous mountains called, dear?

Tesman: Let me see. Oh, those are the Dolomites.

Hedda: Why, of course! Those are the Dolomites, Mr. Løvborg.

Tesman: Hedda dear—I only wanted to ask if we shouldn't bring in some punch anyway. At least for you, hm?

Hedda: Yes. thank you. And a couple of *petits fours*, please.

Tesman: No cigarettes?

Hedda: No.

Tesman: Right.

   (He goes through the inner room and out to the right. Brack *remains sitting inside, keeping his eye from time to time on* Hedda *and* Løvborg.)

Løvborg (softly, as before): Answer me, Hedda—how could you go and do such a thing!

Hedda (apparently immersed in the album): If you keep on saying Hedda like that to me, I won't talk to you.

Løvborg: Can't I say Hedda even when we're alone?

Hedda: No. You can think it, but you mustn't say it like that.

Løvborg: Ah, I understand. It offends your—love for George Tesman.

Hedda (glances at him and smiles): Love? You *are* absurd!

Løvborg: Then you don't love him!

Hedda: I don't expect to be unfaithful, either. I'm not having any of that!

Løvborg: Hedda, just answer me one thing—

Hedda: Shh!

   (Tesman, *carrying a tray, enters from the inner room.*)

Tesman: Look out! Here come the goodies. (*He sets the tray on the table.*)

Hedda: Why do you do the serving?

Tesman (filling the glasses): Because I think it's such fun to wait on you, Hedda.

Hedda: But now you've poured out two glasses. And you know Mr. Løvborg doesn't want—

Tesman: Well, but Mrs. Elvsted will be along soon.

Hedda: Yes, that's right—Mrs. Elvsted—

Tesman: Had you forgotten her? Uh?

Hedda: We've been so caught up in these. *(Showing him a picture.)* Do you remember this little village?

Tesman: Oh, that's the one just below the Brenner Pass! It was there that we stayed overnight—

Hedda: And met all those lively summer people.

Tesman. Yes, that's the place. Just think—if we could have had you with us, Eilert! My! *(He goes back and sits beside* Brack.*)*

Løvborg: Answer me just one thing, Hedda—

Hedda: Yes?

Løvborg: Was there no love with respect to me, either? Not a spark—not one glimmer of love at all?

Hedda: I wonder, really, was there? To me it was as if we were two true companions—two very close friends. *(Smiling.)* You, especially, were so open with me.

Løvborg: You wanted it that way.

Hedda: When I look back on it now, there was really something beautiful and fascinating—and daring, it seems to me, about —about our secret closeness—our companionship that no one, not a soul, suspected.

Løvborg: Yes, Hedda, that's true! Wasn't there? When I'd come over to your father's in the afternoon—and the general sat by the window reading his papers—with his back to us—

Hedda: And we'd sit on the corner sofa—

Løvborg: Always with the same illustrated magazine in front of us—

Hedda: Yes, for the lack of an album.

Løvborg: Yes, Hedda—and the confessions I used to make—telling you things about myself that no one else knew of then. About the way I'd go out, the drinking, the madness that went on day and night, for days at a time. Ah, what power was it in you, Hedda, that made me tell you such things?

Hedda: You think it was some kind of power in me?

Løvborg: How else can I explain it? And all those—those devious questions you asked me—

Hedda: That you understood so remarkably well—

Løvborg: To think you could sit there and ask such questions! So boldly.

Hedda: Deviously, please.

Løvborg: Yes, but boldly, all the same. Interrogating me about—all that kind of thing!

Hedda: And to think you could answer, Mr. Løvborg.

Løvborg: Yes, that's exactly what I don't understand—now, looking back. But tell me, Hedda—the root of that bond between us, wasn't it love? Didn't you feel, on your part, as if you wanted to cleanse and absolve me— when I brought those confessions to you? Wasn't that it?

Hedda: No, not quite.

Løvborg: What was your power, then?

Hedda: Do you find it so very surprising that a young girl—if there's no chance of anyone knowing—

Løvborg: Yes?

Hedda: That she'd like some glimpse of a world that—

Løvborg: That—?

Hedda: That she's forbidden to know anything about.

Løvborg: So that was it?

Hedda: Partly. Partly that, I guess.

Løvborg: Companionship in a thirst for life. But why, then, couldn't it have
    gone on?

Hedda: But that was your fault.

Løvborg: You broke it off.

Hedda: Yes, when that closeness of ours threatened to grow more serious.
    Shame on you, Eilert Løvborg! How could you violate my trust when
    I'd been so—so bold with my friendship?

Løvborg (clenching his fists): Oh, why didn't you do what you said! Why didn't
    you shoot me down!

Hedda: I'm—much too afraid of scandal.

Løvborg: Yes, Hedda, you're a coward at heart.

Hedda: A terrible coward. *(Changing her tone.)* But that was lucky for you.
    And now you're so nicely consoled at the Elvsteds'.

Løvborg: I know what Thea's been telling you.

Hedda: And perhaps you've been telling her all about us?

Løvborg: Not a word. She's too stupid for that sort of thing.

Hedda: Stupid?

Løvborg: When it comes to those things, she's stupid.

Hedda: And I'm a coward. *(Leans closer, without looking him in the eyes, and
    speaks softly.)* But there is something now that I can tell you.

Løvborg (intently): What?

Hedda: When I didn't dare shoot you—

Løvborg: Yes?

Hedda: That wasn't my worst cowardice—that night.

Løvborg (looks at her a moment, understands, and whispers passionately): Oh,
    Hedda! Hedda Gabler! Now I begin to see it, the hidden reason why
    we've been so close! You and I—! . . . . It was the hunger for *life* in you—

Hedda (quietly, with a sharp glance): Careful! That's no way to think!

    (It has begun to grow dark. The hall door is opened from without by Berta.)

Hedda (clapping the album shut and calling out with a smile): Well, at last! Thea
    dear—please come in!

    *(Mrs. Elvsted enters from the hall. She is in evening dress. The door is closed
behind her.)*

Hedda (on the sofa, stretching her arms out toward her): Thea, my sweet—I
    thought you were never coming!

    *(In passing, Mrs. Elvsted exchanges light greetings with the gentlemen in the
inner room, then comes over to the table and extends her hand to* Hedda. Løvborg
has gotten up. He and Mrs. Elvsted *greet each other with a silent nod.)*

Mrs. Elvsted: Perhaps I ought to go in and talk a bit with your husband?

Hedda: Oh, nonsense. Let them be. They're leaving soon.

Mrs. Elvsted: They're leaving?

Hedda: Yes, for a drinking party.

Mrs. Elvsted (quickly, to Løvborg*):* But you're not?

Løvborg: No.

Hedda: Mr. Løvborg—is staying with us.

Mrs. Elvsted (taking a chair, about to sit down beside him): Oh, it's so good to be here!

Hedda: No, no, Thea dear! Not there! You have to come over here by me. I want to be in the middle.

Mrs. Elvsted: Any way you please.

(*She goes around the table and sits on the sofa to* Hedda'*s right.* Løvborg *resumes his seat.*)

Løvborg (after a brief pause, to Hedda*):* Isn't she lovely to look at?

Hedda (lightly stroking her hair): Only to look at?

Løvborg: Yes. Because we two—she and I—we really *are* true companions. We trust each other completely. We can talk things out together without any reservations—

Hedda: Never anything devious, Mr. Løvborg?

Løvborg: Well—

Mrs. Elvsted (quietly, leaning close to Hedda*):* Oh, Hedda, you don't know how happy I am! Just think—he says that I've inspired him.

Hedda (regarding her with a smile): Really, dear; did he say that?

Løvborg: And then the courage she has, Mrs. Tesman, when it's put to the test.

Mrs. Elvsted: Good heavens, me! Courage!

Løvborg: Enormous courage—where I'm concerned.

Hedda: Yes, courage—yes! If one only had that.

Løvborg: Then what?

Hedda: Then life might still be bearable. (*Suddenly changing her tone.*) But now, Thea dearest—you really must have a nice cold glass of punch.

Mrs. Elvsted: No, thank you. I never drink that sort of thing.

Hedda: Well, then you, Mr. Løvborg,

Løvborg: Thanks, not for me either.

Mrs. Elvsted: No, not for him either!

Hedda (looking intently at him): But if I insist?

Løvborg: Makes no difference.

Hedda (with a laugh): Poor me, then I have no power over you at all?

Løvborg: Not in that area.

Hedda: But seriously, I think you ought to, all the same. For your own sake.

Mrs. Elvsted: But Hedda—!

Løvborg: Why do you think so?

Hedda: Or, to be more exact, for others' sakes.

Løvborg: Oh?

Hedda: Otherwise, people might get the idea that you're not very bold at heart. That you're not really sure of yourself at all.

Mrs. Elvsted (softly): Oh, Hedda, don't—!

Løvborg: People can think whatever they like, for all I care.

Mrs. Elvsted (happily): Yes, that's right!

Hedda: I saw it so clearly in Judge Brack a moment ago.

Løvborg: What did you see?

Hedda: The contempt in his smile when you didn't dare join them for a
  drink.

Løvborg: Didn't dare! Obviously I'd rather stay here and talk with you.

Mrs. Elvsted: That's only reasonable, Hedda.

Hedda: But how could the judge know that? And besides, I noticed him
  smile and glance at Tesman when you couldn't bring yourself to go to
  their wretched little party.

Løvborg: Couldn't! Are you saying I couldn't?

Hedda: I'm not. But that's the way Judge Brack sees it.

Løvborg: All right, let him.

Hedda: Then you won't go along?

Løvborg: I'm staying here with you and Thea.

Mrs. Elvsted: Yes, Hedda—you can be sure he is!

Hedda (smiles and nods approvingly at Løvborg*):* I see. Firm as a rock. True to
  principle, to the end of time. There, that's what a man ought to be!
  (Turning to Mrs. Elvsted *and patting her.)* Well, now, didn't I tell you
  that, when you came here so distraught this morning—

Løvborg (surprised): Distraught?

Mrs. Elvsted (terrified): Hedda—! But Hedda—!

Hedda: Can't you see for yourself? There's no need at all for your going
  around so deathly afraid that—*(Changing her tone.)* There! Now we can
  all enjoy ourselves!

Løvborg (shaken): What is all this, Mrs. Tesman?

Mrs. Elvsted: Oh, God, oh, God, Hedda! What are you saying! What are
  you doing!

Hedda: Not so loud. That disgusting judge is watching you.

Løvborg: So deathly afraid? For my sake?

Mrs. Elvsted (in a low moan): Oh, Hedda, you've made me so miserable!

Løvborg (looks intently at her a moment, his face drawn): So that's how completely you trusted me.

Mrs. Elvsted (imploringly): Oh, my dearest—if you'll only listen—!

Løvborg (takes one of the glasses of punch, raises it, and says in a low, hoarse voice):
  Your health, Thea! *(He empties the glass, puts it down, and takes the other.)*

Mrs. Elvsted (softly): Oh, Hedda, Hedda—how could you want such a thing!

Hedda: Want it? I? Are you crazy?

Løvborg: And your health too, Mrs. Tesman. Thanks for the truth. Long live
  truth! *(Drains the glass and starts to refill it.)*

Hedda (laying her hand on his arm): All right—no more for now. Remember,
  you're going to a party.

Mrs. Elvsted: No, no, no!

Hedda: Shh! They're watching you.

Løvborg (putting down his glass): Now, Thea—tell me honestly—

Mrs. Elvsted: Yes!

Løvborg: Did your husband know that you followed me?

Mrs. Elvsted (wringing her hands): Oh, Hedda—listen to him!

Løvborg: Did you have it arranged, you and he, that you should come down into town and spy on me? Or maybe he got you to do it himself? Ah, yes—I'm sure he needed me back in the office! Or maybe he missed my hand at cards?

Mrs. Elvsted (softly, in anguish): Oh, Eilert, Eilert—!

Løvborg (seizing his glass to fill it): Skoal to the old sheriff, too!

Hedda (stopping him): That's enough. Don't forget, you're giving a reading for Tesman.

Løvborg (calmly, setting down his glass): That was stupid of me, Thea. I mean, taking it like this. Don't be angry at me, my dearest. You'll see—you and all the others—that if I stumbled and fell—I'm back on my feet again now! With your help, Thea.

Mrs. Elvsted (radiant with joy): Oh, thank God—!

(*Brack, in the meantime, has looked at his watch. He and* Tesman *stand up and enter the drawing room.*)

Brack (takes his hat and overcoat): Well, Mrs. Tesman, our time is up.

Hedda: I suppose it is.

Løvborg (rising): Mine too, Judge.

Mrs. Elvsted (softly pleading): Oh, Eilert—don't!

Hedda (pinching her arm): They can hear you!

Mrs. Elvsted (with a small cry): Ow!

Løvborg (to Brack*):* You were kind enough to ask me along.

Brack: Oh, then you *are* coming, after all?

Løvborg: Yes, thank you.

Brack: I'm delighted—

Løvborg (putting the manila envelope in his pocket, to Tesman*):* I'd like to show you one or two things before I turn this in.

Tesman: Just think—how exciting! But Hedda dear, how will Mrs. Elvsted get home? Uh?

Hedda: Oh, we'll hit on something.

Løvborg (glancing toward the ladies): Mrs. Elvsted? Don't worry, I'll stop back and fetch her. (*Coming nearer.*) Say about ten o'clock, Mrs. Tesman? Will that do?

Hedda: Yes. That will do very nicely.

Tesman: Well, then everything's all set. But you mustn't expect *me* that early, Hedda.

Hedda: Dear, you stay as long—just as long as you like.

Mrs. Elvsted (with suppressed anxiety): Mr. Løvborg—I'll be waiting here till you come.

Løvborg (his hat in his hand): Yes, I understand.

Brack: So, gentlemen—the excursion train is leaving! I hope it's going to be lively, as a certain fair lady puts it.

Hedda: Ah, if only that fair lady could be there, invisible—!

Brack: Why invisible?

Hedda: To hear a little of your unadulterated liveliness, Judge.

Brack (laughs): I wouldn't advise the fair lady to try.

Tesman (also laughing): Hedda, you are the limit! What an idea!

Brack: Well, good night. Good night, ladies.

Løvborg (bowing): About ten o'clock, then.

(*Brack, Løvborg, and* Tesman *go out the hall door. At the same time,* Berta *enters from the inner room with a lighted lamp, which she sets on the drawing room table, then goes out the same way.*)

Mrs. Elvsted (having risen, moving restlessly about the room): Hedda—Hedda— what's going to come of all this?

Hedda: At ten o'clock—he'll be here. I can see him now—with vine leaves in his hair—fiery and bold—

Mrs. Elvsted: Oh, how good that would be!

Hedda: And then, you'll see—he'll be back in control of himself. He'll be a free man, then, for the rest of his days.

Mrs. Elvsted: Oh, God—if only he comes as you see him now!

Hedda: He'll come back like that, and no other way! (*Gets up and goes closer.*) Go on and doubt him as much as you like. I believe in him. And now we'll find out—

Mrs. Elvsted: There's something behind what you're doing, Hedda.

Hedda: Yes, there is. For once in my life, I want to have power over a human being.

Mrs. Elvsted: But don't you have that?

Hedda: I don't have it. I've never had it.

Mrs. Elvsted: Not with your husband?

Hedda: Yes, what a bargain *that* was! Oh, if you only could understand how poor I am. And you're allowed to be so rich! (*Passionately throws her arms about her.*) I think I'll burn your hair off, after all!

Mrs. Elvsted: Let go! Let me go! I'm afraid of you, Hedda!

Berta (in the doorway to the inner room): Supper's waiting in the dining room, ma'am.

Hedda: All right, we're coming.

Mrs. Elvsted: No, no, no! I'd rather go home alone! Right away—now!

Hedda: Nonsense! First you're going to have tea, you little fool. And then— ten o'clock—Eilert Løvborg comes—with vine leaves in his hair.

(*She drags* Mrs. Elvsted, *almost by force, toward the doorway.*)

ACT III

The same rooms at the Tesmans'. *The curtains are down across the doorway to the inner room, and also across the glass door. The lamp, shaded and turned down low, is burning on the table. The door to the stove stands open; the fire has nearly gone out.*

Mrs. Elvsted, *wrapped in a large shawl, with her feet up on a footstool, lies back in the armchair close by the stove.* Hedda, *fully dressed, is asleep on the sofa, with a blanket over her. After a pause,* Mrs. Elvsted *suddenly sits straight up in the chair, listening tensely. Then she sinks wearily back again.*

Mrs. Elvsted (in a low moan): Not yet—oh, God—oh, God—not yet!

(Berta *slips in cautiously by the hall door. She holds a letter in her hand.)*

Mrs. Elvsted (turns and whispers anxiously): Yes? Has anyone come?

Berta (softly): Yes, a girl just now stopped by with this letter.

Mrs. Elvsted (quickly, reaching out her hand): A letter! Give it to me!

Berta: No, it's for the Doctor, ma'am.

Mrs. Elvsted: Oh.

Berta: It was Miss Tesman's maid that brought it. I'll leave it here on the table.

Mrs. Elvsted: Yes, do.

Berta (putting the letter down): I think I'd best put out the lamp. It's smoking.

Mrs. Elvsted: Yes, put it out. It'll be daylight soon.

Berta (does so): It's broad daylight already, ma'am.

Mrs. Elvsted: It's daylight! And still no one's come—!

Berta: Oh, mercy—I knew it would go like this.

Mrs. Elvsted: You knew?

Berta: Yes, when I saw that a certain gentleman was back here in town—and that he went off with them. We've heard plenty about that gentleman over the years.

Mrs. Elvsted: Don't talk so loud. You'll wake Mrs. Tesman.

Berta (looks toward the sofa and sighs): Goodness me—yes, let her sleep, poor thing. Should I put a bit more on the fire?

Mrs. Elvsted: Thanks, not for me.

Berta: All right. *(She goes quietly out the hall door.)*

Hedda (wakes as the door shuts and looks up): What's that?

Mrs. Elvsted: It was just the maid—

Hedda (glancing about): In here—? Oh yes, I remember now. *(Sits up on the sofa, stretches, and rubs her eyes.)* What time is it, Thea?

Mrs. Elvsted (looking at her watch): It's after seven.

Hedda: When did Tesman get in?

Mrs. Elvsted: He isn't back.

Hedda: Not back yet?

Mrs. Elvsted (getting up): No one's come in.

Hedda: And we sat here and waited up for them till four o'clock—

Mrs. Elvsted (wringing her hands): And *how* I've waited for him!

Hedda (yawns, and speaks with her hand in front of her mouth): Oh, dear—we could have saved ourselves the trouble.

Mrs. Elvsted: Did you get any sleep?

Hedda: Oh yes. I slept quite well, I think. Didn't you?

Mrs. Elvsted: No, not at all. I couldn't, Hedda! It was just impossible.

Hedda (rising and going toward her): There, there, now! There's nothing to worry about. It's not hard to guess what happened.

Mrs. Elvsted: Oh, what? Tell me!

Hedda: Well, it's clear that the party must have gone on till all hours—

Mrs. Elvsted: Oh, Lord, yes—it must have. But even so—

Hedda: And then, of course, Tesman didn't want to come home and make a commotion in the middle of the night. *(Laughs.)* Probably didn't care to show himself, either—so full of his party spirits.

Mrs. Elvsted: But where else could he have gone?

Hedda: He must have gone up to his aunts' to sleep. They keep his old room ready.

Mrs. Elvsted: No, he can't be with them. Because he just now got a letter from Miss Tesman. It's over there.

Hedda: Oh? *(Looking at the address.)* Yes, that's Aunt Julie's handwriting, all right. Well, then he must have stayed over at Judge Brack's. And Eilert Løvborg—he's sitting with vine leaves in his hair, reading away.

Mrs. Elvsted: Oh, Hedda, you say these things, and you really don't believe them at all.

Hedda: You're such a little fool, Thea.

Mrs. Elvsted: That's true; I guess I am.

Hedda: And you really look dead tired.

Mrs. Elvsted: Yes, I feel dead tired.

Hedda: Well, you just do as I say, then. Go in my room and stretch out on the bed for a while.

Mrs. Elvsted: No, no—I still wouldn't get any sleep.

Hedda: Why, of course you would.

Mrs. Elvsted: Well, but your husband's sure to be home now soon. And I've got to know right away—

Hedda: I'll call you the moment he comes.

Mrs. Elvsted: Yes? Promise me, Hedda?

Hedda: You can count on it. Just go and get some sleep.

Mrs. Elvsted: Thanks. I'll try. *(She goes out through the inner room.)*

(Hedda goes over to the glass door and draws the curtains back. Bright daylight streams into the room. She goes over to the writing table, takes out a small hand mirror, regards herself and arranges her hair. She then goes to the hall door and presses the bell. After a moment, Berta *enters.)*

Berta: Did you want something, ma'am?

Hedda: Yes, you can build up the fire. I'm freezing in here.

Berta: Why, my goodness—we'll have it warm in no time. *(She rakes the embers together and puts some wood on, then stops and listens.)* There's the front doorbell, ma'am.

Hedda: Go see who it is. I'll take care of the stove.

Berta: It'll be burning soon. *(She goes out the hall door.)*

(Hedda kneels on the footstool and lays more wood on the fire. After a moment, George Tesman *comes in from the hall. He looks tired and rather serious. He tiptoes toward the doorway to the inner room and is about to slip through the curtains.)*

Hedda (at the stove, without looking up): Good morning.

Tesman (turns): Hedda! *(Approaching her.)* But what on earth—! You're up so early? Uh?

Hedda: Yes, I'm up quite early today.

Tesman: And I was so sure you were still in bed sleeping. Isn't that something, Hedda!

Hedda: Not so loud. Mrs. Elvsted's resting in my room.

Tesman: Was Mrs. Elvsted here all night?

Hedda: Well, no one returned to take her home.

Tesman: No, I guess that's right.

Hedda (shuts the door to the stove and gets up): So did you enjoy your party?

Tesman: Were you worried about me? Hm?

Hedda: No, that never occurred to me. I just asked if you'd had a good time.

Tesman: Oh yes, I really did, for once. But more at the beginning, I'd say—
when Eilert read to me out of his book. We got there more than an
hour too soon—imagine! And Brack had so much to get ready. But then
Eilert read to me.

Hedda (sitting at the right-hand side of the table): Well? Tell me about it—

Tesman (sitting on a footstool by the stove): Really, Hedda—you can't imagine
what a book that's going to be! I do believe it's one of the most remarkable things ever written. Just think!

Hedda: Yes, I don't mean the book—

Tesman: But I have to make a confession, Hedda. When he'd finished reading—I had such a nasty feeling—

Hedda: Nasty?

Tesman: I found myself envying Eilert, that he was able to write such a book.
Can you imagine, Hedda!

Hedda: Oh yes, I can imagine!

Tesman: And then how sad to see—that with all his gifts—he's still quite
irreclaimable.

Hedda: Don't you mean that he has more courage to live than the others?

Tesman: Good Lord, no—I mean, he simply can't take his pleasures in moderation.

Hedda: Well, what happened then—at the end?

Tesman: I suppose I'd have to say it turned into an orgy, Hedda.

Hedda: Were there vine leaves in his hair?

Tesman: Vine leaves? Not that I noticed. But he gave a long, muddled
speech in honor of the woman who'd inspired his work. Yes, that was his
phrase for it.

Hedda: Did he give her name?

Tesman: No, he didn't. But it seems to me it has to be Mrs. Elvsted. Wait
and see!

Hedda: Oh? Where did you leave him?

Tesman: On the way here. We broke up—the last of us—all together. And
Brack came along with us too, to get a little fresh air. And then we did
want to make sure that Eilert got home safe. Because he really had a
load on, you know.

Hedda: He must have.

Tesman: But here's the curious part of it, Hedda. Or perhaps I should say,
the distressing part. Oh, I'm almost ashamed to speak of it—for Eilert's
sake—

Hedda: Yes, go on—

Tesman: Well, as we were walking toward town, you see, I happened to drop
    back a little behind the others. Only for a minute or two—you follow me?

Hedda: Yes, yes, so—?

Tesman: And then when I was catching up with the rest of them, what do
    you think I found on the sidewalk? Uh?

Hedda: Oh, how should I know!

Tesman: You mustn't breathe a word to anyone, Hedda—you hear me?
    Promise me that, for Eilert's sake. *(Takes a manila envelope out of his coat
    pocket.)* Just think—I found this.

Hedda: Isn't that what he had with him yesterday?

Tesman: That's right. It's the whole of his precious, irreplaceable manuscript.
    And he went and lost it—without even noticing. Can you imagine,
    Hedda! How distressing—

Hedda: But why didn't you give it right back to him?

Tesman: No, I didn't dare do that—in the state he was in—

Hedda: And you didn't tell any of the others you'd found it?

Tesman: Of course not. I'd never do that, you know—for Eilert's sake.

Hedda: Then there's no one who knows you have Eilert Løvborg's manu-
    script?

Tesman: No. And no one must ever know, either.

Hedda: What did you say to him afterwards?

Tesman: I had no chance at all to speak with him. As soon as we reached the
    edge of town, he and a couple of others got away from us and disap-
    peared. Imagine!

Hedda: Oh? I expect they saw him home.

Tesman: Yes, they probably did, I suppose. And also Brack went home.

Hedda: And where've you been carrying on since then?

Tesman: Well, I and some of the others—we were invited up by one of the
    fellows and had morning coffee at his place. Or a post-midnight snack,
    maybe—uh? But as soon as I've had a little rest—and given poor Eilert
    time to sleep it off, then I've got to take this back to him.

Hedda (reaching out for the envelope): No—don't give it back! Not yet, I
    mean. Let me read it first.

Tesman: Hedda dearest, no. My Lord, I can't do that.

Hedda: You can't?

Tesman: No. Why, you can just imagine the anguish he'll feel when he
    wakes up and misses the manuscript. He hasn't any copy of it, you know.
    He told me that himself.

Hedda (looks searchingly at him): Can't such a work be rewritten? I mean,
    over again?

Tesman: Oh, I don't see how it could. Because the inspiration, you know—

Hedda: Yes, yes—that's the thing, I suppose. *(Casually.)* Oh, by the way—
    there's a letter for you.

Tesman: No, really—?

Hedda (handing it to him): It came early this morning.

Tesman: Dear, from Aunt Julie! What could that be? *(Sets the envelope on the*

other taboret, opens the letter, skims through it, and springs to his feet.) Oh,
Hedda—she says poor Auntie Rina's dying!

Hedda: It's no more than we've been expecting.

Tesman: And if I want to see her one last time, I've got to hurry. I'll have to
hop right over.

Hedda (suppressing a smile): Hop?

Tesman: Oh, Hedda dearest, if you could only bring yourself to come with
me! Think of it!

Hedda (rises and dismisses the thought wearily): No no, don't ask me to do such
things. I don't want to look on sickness and death. I want to be free of
everything ugly.

Tesman: Yes, all right, then—*(Dashing about.)* My hat—? My overcoat—?
Oh, in the hall—I do hope I'm not there too late, Hedda! Hm?

Hedda: Oh, if you hurry—

(Berta appears at the hall door.)

Berta: Judge Brack's outside, asking if he might stop in.

Tesman: At a time like this! No, I can't possibly see him now.

Hedda: But I can. *(To* Berta.*)* Ask the judge to come in.

(Berta goes out.)

Hedda (quickly, in a whisper): Tesman, the manuscript! *(She snatches it from the
taboret.)*

Tesman: Yes, give it here!

Hedda: No, no, I'll keep it till you're back.

(She moves over to the writing table and slips it in the bookcase. Tesman *stands
flustered, unable to get his gloves on.* Brack *enters from the hall.)*

Hedda: Well, aren't you the early bird.

Brack: Yes, wouldn't you say so? *(To* Tesman.*)* Are you off and away too?

Tesman: Yes, I absolutely have to get over to my aunts'. Just think—the
invalid one, she's dying.

Brack: Good Lord, she is? But then you mustn't let me detain you. Not at a
moment like this—

Tesman: Yes, I really must run—Good-bye! Good-bye! *(He goes hurriedly out
the hall door.)*

Hedda: It would seem you had quite a time of it last night, Judge.

Brack: I've not been out of my clothes yet, Mrs. Hedda.

Hedda: Not you, either?

Brack: No, as you can see. But what's Tesman been telling you about our
night's adventures?

Hedda: Oh, some tedious tale. Something about stopping up somewhere for
coffee.

Brack: Yes, I know all about the coffee party. Eilert Løvborg wasn't with
them, I expect?

Hedda: No, they'd already taken him home.

Brack: Tesman, as well.

Hedda: No, but he said some others had.

Brack (smiles): George Tesman is really a simple soul, Mrs. Hedda.

Hedda: God knows he's that. But was there something else that went on?

Brack: Oh, you might say so.

Hedda: Well, now! Let's sit down, Judge; you'll talk more easily then.

(*She sits at the left-hand side of the table, with* Brack. *at the long side, near her.*)

Hedda: So?

Brack: I had particular reasons for keeping track of my guests—or, I should say, certain of my guests, last night.

Hedda: And among them Eilert Løvborg, perhaps?

Brack: To be frank—yes.

Hedda: Now you really have me curious—

Brack: You know where he and a couple of the others spent the rest of the night, Mrs. Hedda?

Hedda: Tell me—if it's fit to be told.

Brack: Oh, it's very much fit to be told. Well, it seems they showed up at a quite animated soiree.

Hedda: Of the lively sort.

Brack: Of the liveliest.

Hedda: Do go on, Judge—

Brack: Løvborg, and the others also, had advance invitations. I knew all about it. But Løvborg had begged off, because now, of course, he was supposed to have become a new man, as you know.

Hedda: Up at the Elvsteds', yes. But he went anyway?

Brack: Well, you see, Mrs. Hedda—unfortunately the spirit moved him up at my place last evening—

Hedda: Yes, I hear that he *was* inspired there.

Brack: To a very powerful degree, I'd say. Well, so his mind turned to other things, that's clear. We males, sad to say—we're not always so true to principle as we ought to be.

Hedda: Oh, I'm sure you're an exception, Judge. But what about Løvborg—?

Brack: Well, to cut it short—the result was that he wound up in Mademoiselle Diana's parlors.

Hedda: Mademoiselle Diana's?

Brack: It was Mademoiselle Diana who was holding the soiree. For a select circle of lady friends and admirers.

Hedda: Is she a red-haired woman?

Brack: Precisely.

Hedda: Sort of a—singer?

Brack: Oh yes—she's that too. And also a mighty huntress—of men, Mrs. Hedda. You've undoubtedly heard about her. Løvborg was one of her ruling favorites—back there in his palmy° days.

---

palmy: Prosperous.

Hedda: And how did all this end?

Brack: Less amicably, it seems. She gave him a most tender welcoming, with open arms, but before long she'd taken to fists.

Hedda: Against Løvborg?

Brack: That's right. He accused her or her friends of having robbed him. He claimed that his wallet was missing—along with some other things. In short, he must have made a frightful scene.

Hedda: And what did it come to?

Brack: It came to a regular free-for-all, the men and the women both. Luckily the police finally got there.

Hedda: The police too?

Brack: Yes. But it's likely to prove an expensive little romp for Eilert Løvborg. That crazy fool.

Hedda: So?

Brack: He apparently made violent resistance. Struck one of the officers on the side of the head and ripped his coat. So they took him along to the station house.

Hedda: Where did you hear all this?

Brack: From the police themselves.

Hedda (gazing straight ahead): So that's how it went. Then he had no vine leaves in his hair.

Brack: Vine leaves, Mrs. Hedda?

Hedda (changing her tone): But tell me, Judge—just why I do you go around like this, spying on Eilert Løvborg?

Brack: In the first place, it's hardly a matter of no concern to me, if it's brought out during the investigation that he'd come direct from my house.

Hedda: There'll be an investigation—?

Brack: Naturally. Anyway, that takes care of itself. But I felt that as a friend of the family I owed you and Tesman a full account of his nocturnal exploits.

Hedda: Why, exactly?

Brack: Well, because I have a strong suspicion that he'll try to use you as a kind of screen.

Hedda: Oh, how could you ever think such a thing!

Brack: Good Lord—we're really not blind, Mrs. Hedda. You'll see! This Mrs. Elvsted, she won't be going home now so quickly.

Hedda: Well, even supposing there were something between them, there are plenty of other places where they could meet.

Brack: Not one single home. From now on, every decent house will be closed to Eilert Løvborg.

Hedda: So mine ought to be too, is that what you mean?

Brack: Yes. I'll admit I'd find it more than annoying if that gentleman were to have free access here. If he came like an intruder, an irrelevancy, forcing his way into—

Hedda: Into the triangle?

Brack: Precisely. It would almost be like turning me out of my home.

Hedda (looks at him with a smile): I see. The one cock of the walk—that's what you want to be.

Brack (nodding slowly and lowering his voice): Yes, that's what I want to be. And that's what I'll fight for—with every means at my disposal.

Hedda (her smile vanishing): You can be a dangerous person, can't you—in a tight corner.

Brack: Do you think so?

Hedda: Yes, now I'm beginning to think so. And I'm thoroughly grateful— that you have no kind of hold over me.

Brack (with an ambiguous laugh): Ah, yes, Mrs. Hedda—perhaps you're right about that. If I had, then who knows just what I might do?

Hedda: Now you listen here. Judge! That sounds too much like a threat.

Brack (rising): Oh, nothing of the kind! A triangle, after all—is best fortified and defended by volunteers.

Hedda: There we're agreed.

Brack: Well, now that I've said all I have to say. I'd better get back to town. Good-bye, Mrs. Hedda. *(He goes toward the glass door.)*

Hedda (rising): Are you going through the garden?

Brack: Yes, I find it's shorter.

Hedda: Yes, and then it's the back way, too.

Brack: How true. I have nothing against back ways. At certain times they can be rather piquant.

Hedda: You mean, when somebody's sharpshooting?

Brack (in the doorway, laughing): Oh, people don't shoot their tame roosters!

Hedda (also laughing): I guess not. Not when there's only one—

(Still laughing, they nod good-bye to each other. He goes. She shuts the door after him, then stands for a moment, quite serious, looking out. She then goes over and glances through the curtains to the inner room. Moves to the writing table, takes Løvborg's envelope from the bookcase, and is about to page through it, when Berta's voice is heard loudly in the hall. Hedda turns and listens. She hurriedly locks the envelope in the drawer and lays the key on the inkstand. Eilert Løvborg, with his overcoat on and his hat in his hand, throws open the hall door. He looks confused and excited.)

Løvborg (turned toward the hall): And I'm telling you, I have to go in! I will, you hear me! *(He shuts the door, turns, sees Hedda, immediately gains control of himself and bows.)*

Hedda (at the writing table): Well, Mr. Løvborg, it's late to call for Thea.

Løvborg: Or rather early to call on you. You must forgive me.

Hedda: How did you know she was still with me?

Løvborg: They said at her lodgings that she'd been out all night.

Hedda (goes to the center table): Did you notice anything in their faces when they said that?

Løvborg (looking at her inquiringly): Notice anything?

Hedda: I mean, did it look like they had their own thoughts on the matter?

Løvborg (suddenly understanding): Oh yes, that's true? I'm dragging her down with me! Actually, I didn't notice anything. Tesman—I don't suppose he's up yet?

Hedda: No, I don't think so.

Løvborg: When did he get in?

Hedda: Very late.

Løvborg: Did he tell you anything?

Hedda: Well, I heard you'd had a high time of it out at Judge Brack's.

Løvborg: Anything else?

Hedda: No, I don't think so. As a matter of fact, I was terribly sleepy—

(Mrs. Elvsted *comes in through the curtains to the inner room.*)

Mrs. Elvsted (running toward him): Oh, Eilert! At last—!

Løvborg: Yes, at last. And too late.

Mrs. Elvsted (looking anxiously at him): What's too late?

Løvborg: Everything's too late now. It's over with me.

Mrs. Elvsted: Oh no, no—don't say that!

Løvborg: You'll say the same thing when you've heard—

Mrs. Elvsted: I won't hear anything!

Hedda: Maybe you'd prefer to talk with her alone. I can leave.

Løvborg: No, stay— you too. Please.

Mrs. Elvsted: But I tell you, I don't want to hear anything!

Løvborg: It's nothing about last night.

Mrs. Elvsted: What is it, then—

Løvborg: It's simply this, that from now on, we separate.

Mrs. Elvsted: Separate!

Hedda (involuntarily): I knew it!

Løvborg: Because I have no more use for you, Thea.

Mrs. Elvsted: And you can stand there and say that! No more use for me!
Then I'm not going to help you now, as I have? We're not going to go
on working together?

Løvborg: I have no plans for any more work.

Mrs. Elvsted (in desperation): Then what will I do with my life?

Løvborg: You must try to go on living as if you'd never known me.

Mrs. Elvsted: But I can't do that!

Løvborg: You must try to, Thea. You'll have to go home again—

Mrs. Elvsted (in a fury of protest): Never! No! Where you are, that's where I
want to be! I won't be driven away like this! I'm going to stay right
here—and be together with you when the book comes out.

Hedda (in a tense whisper): Ah, yes—the book!

Løvborg (looks at her): My book and Thea's—for that's what it is.

Mrs. Elvsted: Yes, that's what I feel it is. And that's why I have the right, as
well, to be with you when it comes out. I want to see you covered with
honor and respect again. And the joy—I want to share the joy of it with
you too.

Løvborg: Thea—our book's never coming out.

Hedda: Ah!

Mrs. Elvsted: Never coming out!

Løvborg: Can never come out.

Mrs. Elvsted (with anguished foreboding): Eilert— what have you done with
the manuscript?

Hedda (watching him intently): Yes, the manuscript—?

Mrs. Elvsted: Where is it!

Løvborg: Oh, Thea—don't ask me that.

Mrs. Elvsted: Yes, yes, I have to know. I've got a right to know, this minute!

Løvborg: The manuscript—well, you see—I tore the manuscript into a thousand pieces.

Mrs. Elvsted (screams): Oh no, no—!

Hedda (involuntarily): But that just isn't—!

Løvborg (looks at her): Isn't so, you think?

Hedda (composing herself): All right. Of course; if you say it yourself. But it sounds so incredible—

Løvborg: It's true, all the same.

Mrs. Elvsted (wringing her hands): Oh, God—oh, God, Hedda—to tear his own work to bits!

Løvborg: I've torn my own life to bits. So why not tear up my life's work as well—

Mrs. Elvsted: And you did this thing last night!

Løvborg: Yes, you heard me. In a thousand pieces. And scattered them into the fjord. Far out. At least there, there's clean salt water. Let them drift out to sea—drift with the tide and the wind. And after a while, they'll sink. Deeper and deeper. As I will, Thea.

Mrs. Elvsted: Do you know, Eilert, this thing you've done with the book— for the rest of my life it will seem to me as if you'd killed a little child.

Løvborg: You're right. It was like murdering a child.

Mrs. Elvsted: But how could you do it—! It was my child too.

Hedda (almost inaudible): Ah, the child—

Mrs. Elvsted (breathes heavily): Then it *is* all over. Yes, yes, I'm going now, Hedda.

Hedda: But you're not leaving town, are you?

Mrs. Elvsted: Oh, I don't know myself what I'll do. Everything's dark for me now. *(She goes out the hall door.)*

Hedda (stands waiting a moment): You're not going to take her home, then, Mr. Løvborg?

Løvborg: I? Through the streets? So people could see that she'd been with me?

Hedda: I don't know what else may have happened last night. But is it so completely irredeemable?

Løvborg: It won't just end with last night—I know that well enough. But the thing is, I've lost all desire for that kind of life. I don't want to start it again, not now. It's the courage and daring for life—that's what she's broken in me.

Hedda (staring straight ahead): To think that pretty little fool could have a man's fate in her hands. *(Looks at him.)* But still, how could you treat her so heartlessly?

Løvborg: Oh, don't say it was heartless!

Hedda: To go ahead and destroy what's filled her whole being for months and years! That's not heartless?

Løvborg: To you, Hedda—I can tell the truth.

Hedda: The truth?

Løvborg: Promise me first—give me your word that what I tell you now, you'll never let Thea know.

Hedda: You have my word.

Løvborg: Good. I can tell you, then, that what I said here just now isn't true.

Hedda: About the manuscript?

Løvborg: Yes. I didn't tear it up—or throw it in the fjord.

Hedda: No, but—where is it, then?

Løvborg: I've destroyed it all the same, Hedda. Utterly destroyed it.

Hedda: I don't understand.

Løvborg: Thea said that what I've done, for her was like killing a child.

Hedda: Yes—that's what she said.

Løvborg: But killing his child—that's not the worst thing a father can do.

Hedda: *That's* not the worst?

Løvborg: No. I wanted to spare Thea the worst.

Hedda: And what's that—the worst?

Løvborg: Suppose now, Hedda, that a man—in the early morning hours, say—after a wild, drunken night, comes home to his child's mother and says: "Listen—I've been out to this place and that—here and there. And I had our child with me. In this place and that. And I lost the child. Just lost it. God only knows what hands it's come into. Or who's got hold of it."

Hedda: Well—but when all's said and done—it was only a book—

Løvborg: Thea's pure soul was in that book.

Hedda: Yes, I understand.

Løvborg: Well, then you can understand that for her and me there's no future possible any more.

Hedda: What do you intend to do?

Løvborg: Nothing. Just put an end to it all. The sooner the better.

Hedda (coming a step closer): Eilert Løvborg—listen to me. Couldn't you arrange that—that it's done beautifully?

Løvborg: Beautifully? *(Smiles.)* With vine leaves in my hair, as you used to dream in the old days—

Hedda: No. I don't believe in vine leaves anymore. But beautifully, all the same. For this once—! Goodbye! You must go now—and never come here again.

Løvborg: Good-bye, then. And give my best to George Tesman. *(He turns to leave.)*

Hedda: No, wait. I want you to have a souvenir from me.

(She goes to the writing desk and opens the drawer and the pistol case, then comes back to Løvborg with one of the pistols.)

Løvborg (looks at her): That? Is that the souvenir?

Hedda (nods slowly): Do you recognize it? It was aimed at you once.

Løvborg: You should have used it then.

Hedda: Here! Use it now.

Løvborg (puts the pistol in his breast pocket): Thanks.

Hedda: And beautifully, Eilert Løvborg. Promise me that!

Løvborg: Good-bye, Hedda Gabler.

(*He goes out the hall door. Hedda listens a moment at the door. Then she goes over to the writing table, takes out the envelope with the manuscript, glances inside, pulls some of the sheets half out and looks at them. She then goes over to the armchair by the stove and sits, with the envelope in her lap. After a moment, she opens the stove door, then brings out the manuscript.*)

Hedda (*throwing some of the sheets into the fire and whispering to herself*): Now I'm burning your child, Thea! You, with your curly hair! (*Throwing another sheaf in the stove.*) Your child and Eilert Løvborg's. (*Throwing in the rest.*) Now I'm burning—I'm burning the child.

ACT IV

The same rooms at the Tesmans'. *It is evening. The drawing room is in darkness. The inner room is lit by the hanging lamp over the table. The curtains are drawn across the glass door.* Hedda, *dressed in black, is pacing back and forth in the dark room. She then enters the inner room, moving out of sight toward the left. Several chords are heard on the piano. She comes in view again, returning into the drawing room.* Berta *enters from the right through the inner room with a lighted lamp, which she puts on the table in front of the settee in the drawing room. Her eyes are red from crying, and she has black ribbons on her cap. She goes quietly and discreetly out to the right.* Hedda *moves to the glass door, lifts the curtains aside slightly, and gazes out into the darkness.*

Shortly after, Miss Tesman, *in mourning, with a hat and veil, comes in from the hall.* Hedda *goes toward her, extending her hand.*

Miss Tesman: Well, Hedda, here I am, all dressed in mourning. My poor sister's ordeal is finally over.

Hedda: As you see, I've already heard. Tesman sent me a note.

Miss Tesman: Yes, he promised he would. But all the same I thought that, to Hedda—here in the house of life—I ought to bear the news of death myself.

Hedda: That was very kind of you.

Miss Tesman: Ah, Rina ought not to have passed on just now. This is no time for grief in Hedda's house.

Hedda (*changing the subject*): She had a peaceful death, then, Miss Tesman?

Miss Tesman: Oh, she went so calmly, so beautifully. And so inexpressibly happy that she could see George once again. And say good-bye to him properly. Is it possible that he's still not home?

Hedda: No, he wrote that I shouldn't expect him too early. But won't you sit down?

Miss Tesman: No, thank you, my dear—blessed Hedda. I'd love to, but I have so little time. I want to see her dressed and made ready as best as I can. She should go to her grave looking her finest.

Hedda: Can't I help you with something?

Miss Tesman: Oh, you mustn't think of it. This is nothing for Hedda Tesman to put her hands to. Or let her thoughts dwell on, either. Not at a time like this, no.

Hedda: Ah, thoughts—they're not so easy to control—

Miss Tesman (continuing): Well, there's life for you. At my house now we'll be sewing a shroud for Rina. And here, too, there'll be sewing soon, I imagine. But a far different kind, praise God!

(*George Tesman enters from the hall.*)

Hedda: Well, at last! It's about time.

Tesman: Are you here, Aunt Julie? With Hedda? Think of that!

Miss Tesman: I was just this minute leaving, dear boy. Well, did you get done all you promised you would?

Tesman: No, I'm really afraid I've forgotten half. I'll have to run over and see you tomorrow. My brain's completely in a whirl today. I can't keep my thoughts together.

Miss Tesman: But George dear, you mustn't take it that way.

Tesman: Oh? Well, how should I, then?

Miss Tesman: You should rejoice in your grief. Rejoice in everything that's happened, as I do.

Tesman: Oh yes, of course. You're thinking of Auntie Rina.

Hedda: It's going to be lonely for you, Miss Tesman.

Miss Tesman: For the first few days, yes. But it won't be for long, I hope. I won't let dear Rina's little room stand empty.

Tesman: No? Who would you want to have in it? Hm?

Miss Tesman: Oh, there's always some poor invalid in need of care and attention.

Hedda: Would you really take another burden like that on yourself?

Miss Tesman: Burden! Mercy on you, child—it's been no burden for me.

Hedda: But now, with a stranger—

Miss Tesman: Oh, you soon make friends with an invalid. And I do so much need someone to live for—I, too. Well, thank God, in this house as well, there soon ought to be work that an old aunt can turn her hand to.

Hedda: Oh, forget about us—

Tesman: Yes, think how pleasant it could be for the three of us if—

Hedda: If—?

Tesman (uneasily): Oh, nothing. It'll all take care of itself. Let's hope so. Uh?

Miss Tesman: Ah, yes. Well, I expect you two have things to talk about. (*Smiles.*) And perhaps Hedda has something to tell you, George. Good-bye. I'll have to get home now to Rina. (*Turning at the door.*) Goodness me, how strange! Now Rina's both with me and with poor dear Jochum as well.

Tesman: Yes, imagine that, Aunt Julie! Hm?

(*Miss Tesman goes out the hall door.*)

Hedda (follows Tesman with a cold, probing look): I almost think you feel this death more than she.

Tesman: Oh, it's not just Auntie Rina's death. It's Eilert who has me worried.

Hedda (quickly): Any news about him?

Tesman: I stopped up at his place this afternoon, thinking to tell him that the manuscript was safe.

Hedda: Well? Didn't you see him then?

Tesman: No, he wasn't home. But afterward I met Mrs. Elvsted, and she said he'd been here early this morning.

Hedda: Yes, right after you left.

Tesman: And apparently he said he'd torn his manuscript up. Uh?

Hedda: Yes, he claimed that he had.

Tesman: But good Lord, then he must have been completely demented! Well, then I guess you didn't dare give it back to him, Hedda, did you?

Hedda: No, he didn't get it.

Tesman: But you did tell him we had it, I suppose?

Hedda: No. *(Quickly.)* Did you tell Mrs. Elvsted anything?

Tesman: No, I thought I'd better not. But you should have said something to him. Just think, if he goes off in desperation and does himself some harm! Give me the manuscript, Hedda! I'm taking it back to him right away. Where do you have it?

Hedda (cold and impassive, leaning against the armchair): I don't have it anymore.

Tesman: You don't have it! What on earth do you mean by that?

Hedda: I burned it—the whole thing.

Tesman (with a start of terror): Burned it! Burned Eilert Løvborg's manuscript!

Hedda: Stop shouting. The maid could hear you.

Tesman: Burned it! But my God in heaven—! No, no, no—that's impossible!

Hedda: Yes, but it's true, all the same.

Tesman: But do you realize what you've done, Hedda! It's illegal disposition of lost property. Just think! Yes, you can ask Judge Brack; he'll tell you.

Hedda: It would be wiser not mentioning this—either to the judge or to anyone else.

Tesman: But how could you go and do such an incredible thing! Whatever put it into your head? What got into you, anyway? Answer me! Well?

Hedda (suppressing an almost imperceptible smile): I did it for your sake, George.

Tesman: For my sake!

Hedda: When you came home this morning and told about how he'd read to you—

Tesman: Yes, yes, then what?

Hedda: Then you confessed that you envied him this book.

Tesman: Good Lord, I didn't mean it literally.

Hedda: Never mind. I still couldn't bear the thought that anyone should eclipse you.

Tesman (in an outburst of mingled doubt and joy): Hedda—is this true, what you say! Yes, but—but—I never dreamed you could show your love like this. Imagine!

Hedda: Well, then it's best you know that—that I'm going to—*(Impatiently, breaking off.)* No, no—you ask your Aunt Julie. She's the one who can tell you.

Tesman: Oh, I'm beginning to understand you, Hedda! *(Claps his hands together.)* Good heavens, no! Is it actually *that!* Can it be? Uh?

Hedda: Don't shout so. The maid can hear you.

Tesman: The maid! Oh, Hedda, you're priceless, really! The maid—but that's Berta! Why, I'll go out and tell her myself.

Hedda (clenching her fists in despair): Oh, I'll die—I'll die of all this!

Tesman: Of what, Hedda? Uh?

Hedda: Of all these—absurdities—George.

Tesman: Absurdities? What's absurd about my being so happy? Well, all right—I guess there's no point in my saying anything to Berta.

Hedda: Oh, go ahead—why not that, too?

Tesman: No, no, not yet. But Aunt Julie will have to hear. And then, that you've started to call me George, too! Imagine! Oh, Aunt Julie will be so glad—so glad!

Hedda: When she hears that I burned Eilert Løvborg's book—for your sake?

Tesman: Well, as far as that goes—this thing with the book—of course, no one's to know about that. But that you have a love that burns for me, Hedda—Aunt Julie can certainly share in that! You know, I wonder, really, if things such as this are common among young wives? Hm?

Hedda: I think you should ask Aunt Julie about that, too.

Tesman: Yes, I definitely will, when I have the chance.

(Mrs. Elvsted, *dressed as on her first visit, with hat and coat, comes in the hall door.*)

Mrs. Elvsted (greets them hurriedly and speaks in agitation): Oh, Hedda dear, don't be annoyed that I'm back again.

Hedda: Has something happened, Thea?

Tesman: Something with Eilert Løvborg? Uh?

Mrs. Elvsted: Yes, I'm so terribly afraid he's met with an accident.

Hedda (seizing her arm): Ah—you think so!

Tesman: But, Mrs. Elvsted, where did you get that idea?

Mrs. Elvsted: Well, because I heard them speaking of him at the boardinghouse, just as I came in. Oh, there are the most incredible rumors about him in town today.

Tesman: Yes, you know, I heard them too! And yet I could swear that he went right home to bed last night. Imagine!

Hedda: Well—what did they say at the boardinghouse?

Mrs. Elvsted: Oh, I couldn't get anything clearly. They either didn't know much themselves, or else—They stopped talking when they saw me. And I didn't dare to ask.

Tesman (restlessly moving about): Let's hope—let's hope you misunderstood them, Mrs. Elvsted!

Mrs. Elvsted: No, no, I'm sure they were talking of him. And then I heard them say something or other about the hospital, or—

Tesman: The hospital!

Hedda: No—but that's impossible!

Mrs. Elvsted: Oh, I'm so deathly afraid for him now. And later I went up to his lodging to ask about him.

Hedda: But was that very wise to do, Thea?

Mrs. Elvsted: What else could I do? I couldn't bear the uncertainty any longer.

Tesman: But didn't you find him there either? Hm?

Mrs. Elvsted: No. And no one had any word of him. He hadn't been in since yesterday afternoon, they said.

Tesman: Yesterday! Imagine them saying that!

Mrs. Elvsted: I think there can only be one reason—something terrible must have happened to him!

Tesman: Hedda dear—suppose I went over and made a few inquiries—?

Hedda: No, no—don't you get mixed up in this business.

(Judge Brack, *with hat in hand, enters from the hall,* Berta *letting him in and shutting the door after him. He looks grave and bows silently.*)

Tesman: Oh, is that you, Judge? Uh?

Brack: Yes, it's imperative that I see you this evening.

Tesman: I can see that you've heard the news from Aunt Julie.

Brack: Among other things, yes.

Tesman: It's sad, isn't it? Uh?

Brack: Well, my dear Tesman, that depends on how you look at it.

Tesman (eyes him doubtfully): Has anything else happened?

Brack: Yes, as a matter of fact.

Hedda (intently): Something distressing, Judge?

Brack: Again, that depends on how you look at it, Mrs. Tesman.

Mrs. Elvsted (in an uncontrollable outburst): Oh, it's something about Eilert Løvborg!

Brack (glancing at her): Now how did you hit upon that, Mrs. Elvsted? Have you, perhaps, heard something already—?

Mrs. Elvsted (in confusion): No, no, nothing like that—but—

Tesman: Oh, for heaven's sake, tell us!

Brack (with a shrug): Well—I'm sorry, but—Eilert Løvborg's been taken to the hospital. He's dying.

Mrs. Elvsted (crying out): Oh, God, oh, God—!

Tesman: To the hospital! And dying!

Hedda (involuntarily): All so soon—!

Mrs. Elvsted (wailing): And we parted in anger, Hedda!

Hedda (in a whisper): Thea—be careful, Thea!

Mrs. Elvsted (ignoring her): I have to see him! I have to see him alive!

Brack: No use, Mrs. Elvsted. No one's allowed in to see him.

Mrs. Elvsted: Oh, but tell me, at least, what happened to him! What is it?

Tesman: Don't tell me he tried to—! Uh?

Hedda: Yes, he did, I'm sure of it.

Tesman: Hedda—how can you say—!

Brack (his eyes steadily on her): Unhappily, you've guessed exactly right, Mrs.
Tesman.

Mrs. Elvsted: Oh, how horrible!

Tesman: Did it himself! Imagine!

Hedda: Shot himself!

Brack: Again, exactly right, Mrs. Tesman.

Mrs. Elvsted (trying to control herself): When did it happen, Mr. Brack?

Brack: This afternoon. Between three and four,

Tesman: But good Lord—where did he do it, then? Hm?

Brack (hesitating slightly): Where? Why—in his room, I suppose.

Mrs. Elvsted: No, that can't be right. I was there between six and seven.

Brack: Well, somewhere else, then. I don't know exactly. I only know he was
found like that. Shot—in the chest.

Mrs. Elvsted: What a horrible thought! That he should end that way!

Hedda (to Brack*):* In the chest, you say.

Brack: Yes—I told you.

Hedda: Not the temple?

Brack: In the chest, Mrs. Tesman.

Hedda: Well—well, the chest is just as good.

Brack: Why, Mrs. Tesman?

Hedda (evasively): Oh, nothing—never mind.

Tesman: And the wound is critical, you say? Uh?

Brack: The wound is absolutely fatal. Most likely, it's over already.

Mrs. Elvsted: Yes, yes, I can feel that it is! It's over! All over! Oh, Hedda—!

Tesman: But tell me now—how did you learn about this?

Brack (brusquely): One of the police. Someone I talked to.

Hedda (in a clear, bold voice): At last, something truly done!

Tesman (shocked): My God, what are you saying, Hedda?

Hedda: I'm saying there's beauty in all this.

Brack: Hm, Mrs. Tesman—

Tesman: Beauty! What an idea!

Mrs. Elvsted: Oh, Hedda, how can you talk about beauty in such a thing?

Hedda: Eilert Løvborg's settled accounts with himself. He's had the courage
to do what—what had to be done.

Mrs. Elvsted: Don't you believe it! It never happened like that. When he did
this, he was in a delirium!

Tesman: In despair, you mean.

Hedda: No, he wasn't. I'm certain of that.

Mrs. Elvsted: But he was! In delirium! The way he was when he tore up our
book.

Brack (startled): The book? His manuscript, you mean? He tore it up?

Mrs. Elvsted: Yes. Last night.

Tesman (in a low whisper): Oh, Hedda, we'll never come clear of all this.

Brack: Hm, that's very strange.

Tesman (walking about the room): To think Eilert could be gone like that! And
then not to have left behind the one thing that could have made his
name live on.

Mrs. Elvsted: Oh, if it could only be put together again!

Tesman: Yes, imagine if that were possible! I don't know what I wouldn't give—

Mrs. Elvsted: Perhaps it can, Mr. Tesman.

Tesman: What do you mean?

Mrs. Elvsted (searching in the pockets of her dress): Look here. I've kept all these notes that he used to dictate from.

Hedda (coming a step closer): Ah—!

Tesman: You've kept them, Mrs. Elvsted! Uh?

Mrs. Elvsted: Yes, here they are. I took them along when I left home. And they've stayed right here in my pocket—

Tesman: Oh, let me look!

Mrs. Elvsted (hands him a sheaf of small papers): But they're in such a mess. All mixed up.

Tesman: But just think, if we could decipher them, even so! Maybe the two of us could help each other—

Mrs. Elvsted: Oh yes! At least, we could try—

Tesman: We can do it! We *must!* I'll give my whole life to this!

Hedda: You, George. Your life?

Tesman: Yes. Or, let's say, all the time I can spare. My own research will have to wait. You can understand, Hedda. Hm! It's something I owe to Eilert's memory,

Hedda: Perhaps.

Tesman: And so, my dear Mrs. Elvsted, let's see if we can't join forces. Good Lord, there's no use brooding over what's gone by. Uh? We must try to compose our thoughts as much as we can, in order that—

Mrs. Elvsted: Yes, yes, Mr. Tesman, I'll do the best I can.

Tesman: Come on, then. Let's look over these notes right away. Where shall we sit? Here? No, in there, in the back room. Excuse us, Judge. You come with me, Mrs. Elvsted.

Mrs. Elvsted: Dear God—if only we can do this!

(*Tesman and Mrs. Elvsted go into the inner room. She takes off her hat and coat. They both sit at the table under the hanging lamp and become totally immersed in examining the papers. Hedda goes toward the stove and sits in the armchair. After a moment,* Brack *goes over by her.*)

Hedda (her voice lowered): Ah, Judge—what a liberation it is, this act of Eilert Løvborg's.

Brack: Liberation, Mrs. Hedda? Well, yes, for him; you could certainly say he's been liberated—

Hedda: I mean for me. It's liberating to know that there can still actually be a free and courageous action in this world. Something that shimmers with spontaneous beauty.

Brack (smiling): Hm—my dear Mrs. Hedda—

Hedda: Oh, I already know what you're going to say. Because you're a kind of specialist too, you know, just like—Oh, well!

Brack (looking fixedly at her): Eilert Løvborg meant more to you than you're willing to admit, perhaps even to yourself. Or am I wrong about that?

Hedda: I won't answer that sort of question. I simply know that Eilert Løvborg's had the courage to live life after his own mind. And now—this last great act, filled with beauty! That he had the strength and the will to break away from the banquet of life—so young.

Brack: It grieves me, Mrs. Hedda—but I'm afraid I have to disburden you of this beautiful illusion.

Hedda: Illusion?

Brack: One that, in any case, you'd soon be deprived of.

Hedda: And what's that?

Brack: He didn't shoot himself—of his own free will.

Hedda: He didn't—!

Brack: No. This whole affair didn't go off quite the way I described it.

Hedda (in suspense): You've hidden something? What is it?

Brack: For poor Mrs. Elvsted's sake, I did a little editing here and there.

Hedda: Where?

Brack: First, the fact that he's already dead.

Hedda: In the hospital?

Brack: Yes. Without regaining consciousness.

Hedda: What else did you hide?

Brack: That the incident didn't occur in his room.

Hedda: Well, that's rather unimportant.

Brack: Not entirely. Suppose I were to tell you that Eilert Løvborg was found shot in—in Mademoiselle Diana's boudoir.

Hedda (half rises, then sinks back again): That's impossible, Judge! He wouldn't have gone there again today!

Brack: He was there this afternoon. He went there, demanding something he said they'd stolen from him. Kept raving about a lost child—

Hedda: Ah—so that was it—

Brack: I thought perhaps that might be his manuscript. But, I hear now, he destroyed that himself. So it must have been his wallet.

Hedda: I suppose so. Then, there—that's where they found him.

Brack: Yes, there. With a discharged pistol in his breast pocket. The bullet had wounded him fatally.

Hedda: In the chest—yes.

Brack: No—in the stomach—more or less.

Hedda (stares up at him with a look of revulsion): That too! What is it, this—this curse—that everything I touch turns ridiculous and vile?

Brack: There's something else, Mrs. Hedda. Another ugly aspect to the case.

Hedda: What's that?

Brack: The pistol he was carrying—

Hedda (breathlessly): Well! What about it!

Brack: He must have stolen it.

Hedda (springs up): Stolen! That's not true! He didn't!

Brack: It seems impossible otherwise. He must have stolen it—shh!

(Tesman and Mrs. Elvsted *have gotten up from the table in the inner room and come into the drawing room.)*

Tesman (with both hands full of papers): Hedda dear—it's nearly impossible to see in there under that overhead lamp. You know?

Hedda: Yes, I know.

Tesman: Do you think it would be all right if we used your table for a while? Hm?

Hedda: Yes, I don't mind. *(Quickly.)* Wait! No, let me clear it off first.

Tesman: Oh, don't bother, Hedda. There's plenty of room.

Hedda: No, no, let me just clear it off, can't you? I'll put all this in by the piano. There!

(She has pulled out an object covered with sheet music from under the bookcase, adds more music to it, and carries the whole thing into the inner room and off left. Tesman puts the scraps of paper on the writing table and moves the lamp over from the corner table. He and Mrs. Elvsted *sit down and go on with their work.* Hedda *comes back.)*

Hedda (behind Mrs. Elvsted's *chair, gently ruffling her hair):* Well, my sweet little Thea—how is it going with Eilert Løvborg's monument?

Mrs. Elvsted (looking despondently up at her): Oh, dear—it's going to be terribly hard to set these in order.

Tesman: It's got to be done. There's just no alternative. Besides, setting other people's papers in order—it's exactly what I can do best.

(Hedda goes over by the stove and sits on one of the taborets. Brack *stands over her, leaning on the armchair.)*

Hedda (whispering): What did you say about the pistol?

Brack (softly): That he must have stolen it.

Hedda: Why, necessarily, that?

Brack: Because every other explanation would seem impossible, Mrs. Hedda.

Hedda: I see.

Brack (glancing at her): Of course, Eilert Løvborg was here this morning. Wasn't he?

Hedda: Yes.

Brack: Were you alone with him?

Hedda: Yes, briefly.

Brack: Did you leave the room while he was here?

Hedda: No.

Brack: Consider. You didn't leave, even for a moment.

Hedda: Well, yes, perhaps, just for a moment—into the hall.

Brack: And where did you have your pistol case?

Hedda: I had it put away in—

Brack: Yes, Mrs. Hedda?

Hedda: It was lying over there, on the writing table.

Brack: Have you looked since to see if both pistols are there?

Hedda: No.

Brack: No need to. I saw the pistol. Løvborg had it on him. I knew it immediately, from yesterday. And other days too.

Hedda: Do you have it, maybe?

Brack: No, the police have it.

Hedda: What will they do with it?

Brack: Try to trace it to the owner.

Hedda: Do you think they'll succeed?

Brack (bending over her and whispering): No, Hedda Gabler—as long as I
keep quiet.

Hedda (looking at him anxiously): And if you don't keep quiet—then what?

Brack (with a shrug): Counsel could always claim that the pistol was stolen.

Hedda (decisively): I'd rather die!

Brack (smiling): People *say* such things. But they don't *do* them.

Hedda (without answering): And what, then, if the pistol wasn't stolen. And
they found the owner. What would happen?

Brack: Well, Hedda—there'd be a scandal.

Hedda: A scandal!

Brack: A scandal, yes—the kind you're so deathly afraid of. Naturally, you'd
appear in court—you and Mademoiselle Diana. She'd have to explain
how the whole thing occurred. Whether it was an accident or homicide.
Was he trying to pull the pistol out of his pocket to threaten her? Is that
why it went off? Or had she torn the pistol out of his hand, shot him,
and slipped it back in his pocket again? It's rather like her to do that,
you know. She's a powerful woman, this Mademoiselle Diana.

Hedda: But all that sordid business is no concern of mine.

Brack: No. But you'll have to answer the question: Why did you give Eilert
Løvborg the pistol? And what conclusions will people draw from the
fact that you did give it to him?

Hedda (her head sinking): That's true. I hadn't thought of that.

Brack: Well, luckily there's no danger, as long as I keep quiet.

Hedda: So I'm in your power, Judge. You have your hold over me from
now on.

Brack (whispers more softly): My dearest Hedda—believe me—I won't abuse
my position.

Hedda: All the same, I'm in your power. Tied to your will and desire. Not
free. Not free, then! *(Rises impetuously.)* No—I can't bear the thought of
it. Never!

Brack (looks at her half mockingly): One usually manages to adjust to the
inevitable.

Hedda (returning his look): Yes, perhaps so. *(She goes over to the writing table.
Suppressing an involuntary smile, she imitates Tesman's intonation.)* Well?
Getting on with it, George? Uh?

Tesman: Goodness knows, dear. It's going to mean months and months of
work, in any case.

Hedda (as before): Imagine that! *(Runs her hand lightly through* Mrs. Elvsted's
hair.)* Don't you find it strange, Thea? Here you are, sitting now beside
Tesman—just as you used to sit with Eilert Løvborg.

Mrs. Elvsted: Oh, if I could only inspire your husband in the same way.

Hedda: Oh, that will surely come—in time.

Tesman: Yes, you know what, Hedda—I really think I'm beginning to feel something of the kind. But you go back and sit with Judge Brack.

Hedda: Is there nothing the two of you need from me now?

Tesman: No, nothing in the world. *(Turning his head.)* From now on, Judge, you'll have to be good enough to keep Hedda company.

Brack (with a glance at Hedda): I'll take the greatest pleasure in that.

Hedda: Thanks. But I'm tired this evening. I want to rest a while in there on the sofa.

Tesman: Yes, do that, dear. Uh?

(*Hedda goes into the inner room, pulling the curtains closed after her. Short pause. Suddenly she is heard playing a wild dance melody on the piano.*)

Mrs. Elvsted (starting up from her chair): Oh—what's that?

Tesman (running to the center doorway): But Hedda dearest—don't go playing dance music tonight! Think of Auntie Rina! And Eilert, too!

Hedda (putting her head out between the curtains): And Auntie Julie. And all the rest of them. From now on I'll be quiet. *(She closes the curtains again.)*

Tesman (at the writing table): She can't feel very happy seeing us do this melancholy work. You know what, Mrs. Elvsted—you must move in with Aunt Julie. Then I can come over evenings. And then we can sit and work *there.* Uh?

Mrs. Elvsted: Yes, perhaps that would be best—

Hedda: I can hear everything you say, Tesman. But what will I do evenings over here?

Tesman (leafing through the notes): Oh, I'm sure Judge Brack will be good enough to stop by and see you.

Brack (in the armchair, calling out gaily): I couldn't miss an evening, Mrs. Tesman! We'll have great times here together, the two of us!

Hedda (in a clear, ringing voice): Yes, you can hope so, Judge, can't you? You, the one cock of the walk—

(*A shot is heard within.* Tesman, Mrs. Elvsted, *and* Brack *start from their chairs.*)

Tesman: Oh, now she's fooling with those pistols again.

(*He throws the curtains back and runs in.* Mrs. Elvsted *follows.* Hedda *lies, lifeless, stretched out on the sofa. Confusion and cries.* Berta *comes in, bewildered, from the right.*)

Tesman (shrieking to Brack): Shot herself! Shot herself in the temple! Can you imagine!

Brack (in the armchair, prostrated): But good God! People don't *do* such things!

——— **HENRIK IBSEN** ———
(1828–1906) Web   *www*

Henrik Ibsen was born in Norway and, while in his early 20s, joined the National Theater in Christiana. At the beginning of his career, Ibsen wrote poetic plays and several dramas based on historical events and Nordic sagas. In 1877 in a kind of experiment, he wrote *The Pillars of Society* as a social critique and, in the process, gained considerable recognition for its realist style. Buoyed by this success, he turned to dramatic realism, writing such hugely influential plays as *A Doll House*, *Ghosts*, and *Hedda Gabler*. Toward the end of his career, Ibsen returned to more symbolic dramas like *When We Dead Awaken* (1899), which also found their audiences in such important modernists as the young James Joyce, whose first published work was an essay on the play.

TOPICS FOR CRITICAL THINKING

1. Given the common critical notion that no form of art is entirely new, one might expect *Hedda Gabler* to retain some elements of such prior forms as melodrama. How so? Is Eilert Løvborg, for example, a variety of melodramatic villain? Or is he more a victim himself of social forces and mores beyond his control? What about Judge Brack? In what ways does his behavior near the end of the play recall the bullying of melodramatic villains?

2. What clues about Hedda and her past given in the play's exposition are crucial to understanding her subsequent behavior? Is she simply spoiled by her father and by men taken with her beauty? What does her past tell us? Is this past in any way also related to her fear of social scandal?

3. To what extent does Ibsen's highly detailed set for *Hedda Gabler* express the play's dramatic conflict? Could the play be staged with a totally different set—or without any furnishing at all? Lighting is also very specifically prescribed by Ibsen's stage directions. Why is this important to the play's action?

4. What dramatic functions does Thea Elvsted perform? What would the play lack if such a character were removed from the text or altered extensively? What functions does her metaphorical association of Tesman's manuscript with a child serve? In what ways does she serve as a "foil" to Hedda?

5. Why is Hedda's wild piano playing near the end of the play significant? It doesn't really further the plot in a direct way, so why does Ibsen include it? Does its inclusion suggest that dramatic action in realistic drama functions differently than it does in, say, classical tragedies like *Oedipus Rex?*

TOPICS FOR CRITICAL WRITING

1. *Hedda Gabler* was revived in New York in 2000–2001 to considerable critical acclaim, but such praise does not necessarily mean that the play is still relevant to the position of women in the twenty-first century. Can it still be regarded as a feminist play, one that effectively questions gender roles, as it was when it was first produced? Explain why you think the play either does or does not speak to issues affecting women today.

2. Suppose you were asked to design this play for a contemporary production and that, to help you, the director specified that she wanted the set, costumes, sounds, light-

ing, and movement all to indicate a middle class American home in the city or town where you are attending college. What would the production look like? What furniture, for example, or costuming would you select, and why? How do these decisions relate to the action of the play transposed into twenty-first century America?

Critical Perspective: Ibsen's Nineteenth-Century Detractors

"Mr. Ibsen . . . could be borne, although, even in that aspect, he is an offence to taste and a burden to patience."

—William Winter, *Shadows of the Stage* (1892)

"The terrible ludicrousness of life—that is their [Ibsen's plays'] prevailing theme . . . If the ultimate end of art is beauty of some sort . . . he is not an artist. He shows us little but the ugliness of things."

—William Watson, *Excursions in Criticism* (1893)

Critical Perspective: On Modern Realism (Ibsen and Chekhov)

"When I say *modern realism* I am taking the term in the broad sense of the strictly photographic imitation of the human scene. In this sense modern realism is a lingua franca, a pidgin-English of the imagination which everyone can understand. The camera and the radio, continuing a process which began at least a hundred years ago, reproduce more and more accurately the surfaces, the sounds, and sights of contemporary life. . . . If we have lost our bearings . . . , we can still gossip about the neighbors and eavesdrop on other lives. It would seem that this medium, and the narrow scene of human life it implies, are too meager for drama at all. Yet Ibsen and Chekhov accepted its limitations, and made superb plays."

—Francis Fergusson, *The Idea of a Theater* (1949)

Critical Perspective: On Ibsen's Formal and Social Radicalism

"So explosive was the message of *A Doll House* [and *Hedda Gabler*]—that a marriage was not sacrosanct, that a man's authority in his home should not go unchallenged, and that the prime duty of anyone was to find out who he or she really was and to become that person—that the technical originality of the play is often forgotten. It achieved the most powerful and moving effect by the highly untraditional methods of extreme simplicity and economy of language—a kind of literary Cubism."

—Michael Meyer, *Ibsen: A Biography* (1967)

Critical Perspective: Hedda's Anxieties

"The central fact about Hedda Gabler is that she is constantly in the grip of a terrible, inescapable, paralyzing anxiety, despite her pose of easy negligence and boredom....

"What Hedda fears, above all, is the intimacy of close relationships, because she unconsciously feels that such intimacy implies being 'invaded' or 'possessed' by another person and consequently having one's ego drowned or smothered. Paradoxically, however, Hedda also seeks out close relationships of a certain kind. Complete withdrawal from others presents another ego-threat: that of complete regression into one's inner world. She therefore cultivates certain close relationships, provided they are heavily surrounded by restrictions and limitations that keep them from becoming too intimate and thus too threatening."

—James Hurt, *Catiline's Dream: An Essay on Ibsen's Plays* (1972)

Critical Perspective: On Melodrama and Realism

"Historically, melodrama and realistic dramas developed during the same period in the nineteenth and twentieth centuries. So, if we wish to define two genres, we need to recognize that right from the beginning they shared traits, forms, and practices. Like twins, they were separate yet joined identities."

—Thomas Postlewait, "From Melodrama to Realism:
The Suspect History of American Drama" (1996)

Critical Perspective: On Hedda and Gender Roles

"So much of what she is dealing with is being a woman in that society, being repressed in not having the opportunities that men had, not being able to follow a career. As the only child, both daughter and son, of the general, everything she loves—guns, horses—were virtually male."

—Kate Burton, qtd. in Iris Fanger, "Actress Likens 'Hedda'
to a Female Hamlet," *Christian Science Monitor* (2001)

Anton Chekhov: *The Cherry Orchard* and Tragicomedy

What the Moscow Art Theatre means to our stage—apart from our delight in mere proficiency—is something that is more moral and ethical than aesthetic . . . Chekhov's plays carry realism to an honest and spiritual depth and candor, and to a relentless, poignant perfection and truth.

Writing these lines in the *New Republic*, drama critic Stark Young, like much of the New York theatrical world in early 1923, was dazzled by Anton

Chekhov's plays as produced by the touring Moscow Art Theatre (MAT). This enthusiasm is even more amazing given the fact that the MAT performed Chekhov's plays in Russian. No matter. For Young, the only thing comparable to what he saw in Chekhov was Shakespeare. But while Shakespeare often employed "every freedom in the poetic method," Chekhov relied only on "words and actions that are possible in actual daily life." The emotional impact of Chekhov's writing, Young asserted, rivaled that of Shakespeare's poetry: the "tragic excitement, the vivacity and pathetic beauty. . . the thrill that comes from a sense of truth." As Ibsen's plays had done in London, Chekhov and the acting of the MAT changed the American theater, shaping acting methods in ways still seen today on stage and in film.

A prolific writer of short stories—nearly six hundred, which, as recently as 2001, scholars were still discovering—Anton Chekhov rose to prominence as a dramatist in the later 1890s with *The Seagull* (1896). Joining forces with director and theorist of acting Konstantin Stanislavsky, Chekhov completed *The Cherry Orchard* in 1903 and the Moscow Art Theatre, under Stanislavsky's direction, gave the play its premiere in January 1904. Some twenty years later, the MAT brought Chekhov's plays to New York, and the American theater would never be the same, not only because of Chekhov's artistry, but also because of Stanislavsky's theory of acting as represented in the New York productions. Both would influence the American theater, especially actor training, for decades to come.

As Stark Young makes clear, Chekhov's realism in *The Cherry Orchard* was both "spiritual" and overpowering. Like that of *Hedda Gabler*, the dramatic action of the play elevates dialogue over visual spectacle, character complexity over flat stereotype, and emotional ambiguity over simple narrative closure. Like Hedda and Eilert Løvborg, Chekhov's characters are complex and in some ways infuriating. In short, they are realistic, believable depictions of an ineffectual aristocracy on the way out and, in Lopakhin's case, an enterprising, middle class on the way up the socioeconomic ladder. Indeed, almost as if to mock melodramatic formula, the potential hero Lopakhin, a successful merchant risen from an impoverished childhood to affluence, plays the villain as well by ordering that the cherry orchard be chopped down to clear the way for new summer cottages. His is a vision of a new Russia of economic progress, development, and social change. As a result, he exclaims after announcing that he has purchased the orchard at auction, "our grandsons and great grand-sons will see a new life here."

For this new life to be born, however, an older one symbolized by the cherry orchard must be sacrificed. Returning from France after a five-year absence, Lyubov Andreyevna and her entourage have hardly lived the life of luxury to which they were accustomed. Her younger daughter Anya describes their "comfortless" place in Paris and relates to her older sister Varya, who had remained behind to manage the family estate, the spiral of poverty into which the family has sunk. In spite of this, Lyuba found it impossible to curb her spending, ordering extravagant meals and lending money to anyone who approached her with a sad story. Varya then explains to Anya that the estate and orchard must be sold to settle past mortgages. At the same time as the fate of the family home is shrouded in uncertainty, its fate creating the principal conflict that drives the plot, Chekhov provides the possibility of three romances blossoming into marriage.

But none of them does. And implicit in Lopakhin's shrewd plan, the idea of building rental cottages for the tourists who have begun to flock to the region in the summer, is the same potential for a happy ending. As he explains in Act One, the world they knew has vanished. Once, the region contained only two classes of inhabitants—"gentlefolks" and "peasants," rich and poor. Now, summer visitors come with money to spend, and he predicts that the business will continue to grow. He outlines his plan to Lyuba who, in spite of her financial dilemma, dismisses it: "Villas and summer visitors—forgive me saying so—it's so vulgar." Her feckless brother Gayev agrees. Instead, Chekhov's aristocrats continue to wallow in what British critic Raymond Williams terms "elaborate and persistent" illusion, refusing to acknowledge that the world of privilege they once enjoyed is gone forever. Reality changes and they need to change with it.

But they are unable to do so. A symbol of the past social order Lyuba embraces, the cherry orchard, which once produced fruit to be made into preserves, can no longer support the estate. As Old Firs, the ancient family valet observes, no one can even remember the recipe anymore. The orchard has outlived its time, much like the aristocracy that, since the emancipation of the peasant class, no longer can depend on an archaic social privilege. Vulgar or not, Lopakhin's plan means economic survival and a bright future, but it requires the destruction of the past.

To mark this passing, this changing of the social order, Chekhov employs an aural **motif** or significant repetition: the breaking of a harp string that, in the play's final moments, can be heard "dying away mournfully" punctuated by the sounds of the axes chopping away at the orchard. The final curtain descends on an estate now evacuated of laughter and elegance save for the lone presence of the eighty-seven-year-old Firs, forgotten and left behind. Devoid of strength, he lies in the doorway, an emblem of the old order now near death. Similarly exhausted is Lopakhin and Varya's relationship. Once headed for marriage, the pair seem as doomed to loneliness as the orchard is destined for destruction.

All of these events, the elegiac tone of the last act, and other factors led Stanislavsky to regard *The Cherry Orchard* as a tragedy, a reading with which Chekhov profoundly disagreed. He saw the play as a comedy, even a "farce" in places, one that, among other things, marked the fulfillment of Lopakhin's dream to purchase the estate on which his father and grandfather had worked as slaves. Both readings have merits. And their disagreement suggests the tragicomic form of the play and many others on the modern and contemporary stage. To be sure, tragicomedy is not a modern invention. But as drama moves into the twentieth century, the traditional categories of tragedy and comedy are made more complicated by such rare achievements as Chekhov's *The Cherry Orchard.*

Anton Chekhov

Translated from the Russian by Ann Dunnigan

The Cherry Orchard   *(1903)*

CHARACTERS

Ranevskaya, Lyubov Andreyevna, a landowner
Anya, her daughter, seventeen years old
Varya, her adopted daughter, twenty-four years old
Gayev, Leonid Andreyevich, Madame Ranevskaya's brother
Lopakhin, Yermolai Alekseyevich, a merchant
Trofimov, Pyotr Sergeyevich, a student
Semyonov-Pishchik, Boris Borisovich, a landowner
Charlotta Ivanovna, a governess
Yepikhodov, Semyon Panteleyevich, a clerk
Dunyasha, a maid
Firs, an old valet, eighty-seven years old
Yasha, a young footman
A Stranger
The Stationmaster
A Post-Office Clerk
Guests, Servants

The action takes place on Madame Ranevskaya's estate.

ACT I

(A room that is still called the nursery. One of the doors leads into Anya's room. Dawn; the sun will soon rise. It is May, the cherry trees are in bloom, but it is cold in the orchard; there is a morning frost. The windows in the room are closed. Enter Dunyasha *with a candle, and* Lopakhin *with a book in his hand.)*

Lopakhin: The train is in, thank God. What time is it?
Dunyasha: Nearly two. *(Blows out the candle.)* It's already light.
Lopakhin: How late is the train, anyway? A couple of hours at least. *(Yawns and stretches.)* I'm a fine one! What a fool I've made of myself! Came here on purpose to meet them at the station, and then overslept. . . . Fell asleep in the chair. It's annoying. . . . You might have waked me.
Dunyasha: I thought you had gone. *(Listens.)* They're coming now, I think!
Lopakhin *(listens):* No . . . they've got to get the luggage and one thing and another. *(Pause)* Lyubov Andreyevna has lived abroad for five years, I don't know what she's like now. . . . She's a fine person. Sweet-tempered, simple. I remember when I was a boy of fifteen, my late father—he had a shop in the village then—gave me a punch in the face and made my

nose bleed. . . . We had come into the yard here for some reason or other, and he'd had a drop too much. Lyubov Andreyevna—I remember it as if it were yesterday—still young, and so slender, led me to the washstand in this very room, the nursery. "Don't cry, little peasant," she said, "it will heal in time for your wedding. . . ." *(Pause)* Little peasant . . . my father was a peasant, it's true, and here I am in a white waistcoat and tan shoes. Like a pig in a pastry shop. . . . I may be rich, I've made a lot of money, but if you think about it, analyze it, I'm a peasant through and through. *(Turning pages of the book)* Here I've been reading this book, and I didn't understand a thing. Fell asleep over it. *(Pause)*

Dunyasha: The dogs didn't sleep all night: they can tell that their masters are coming.

Lopakhin: What's the matter with you, Dunyasha, you're so . . .

Dunyasha: My hands are trembling. I'm going to faint.

Lopakhin: You're much too delicate, Dunyasha. You dress like a lady, and do your hair like one, too. It's not right. You should know your place.

(Enter Yepikhodov *with a bouquet; he wears a jacket and highly polished boots that squeak loudly. He drops the flowers as he comes in.)*

Yepikhodov (picking up the flowers): Here, the gardener sent these. He says you're to put them in the dining room. *(Hands the bouquet to* Dunyasha.*)*

Lopakhin: And bring me some kvas.

Dunyasha: Yes, sir. *(Goes out.)*

Yepikhodov: There's a frost this morning—three degrees—and the cherry trees are in bloom. I cannot approve of our climate. *(Sighs.)* I cannot. Our climate is not exactly conducive. And now, Yermolai Alekseyevich, permit me to append: the day before yesterday I bought myself a pair of boots, which, I venture to assure you, squeak so that it's quite infeasible. What should I grease them with?

Lopakhin: Leave me alone. You make me tired.

Yepikhodov: Every day some misfortune happens to me. But I don't complain, I'm used to it, I even smile.

(Dunyasha enters, serves Lopakhin *the kvas.)*

Yepikhodov: I'm going. *(Stumbles over a chair and upsets it.)* There! *(As if in triumph.)* Now you see, excuse the expression . . . the sort of circumstance, incidentally. . . . It's really quite remarkable! *(Goes out.)*

Dunyasha: You know, Yermolai Alekseyich, I have to confess that Yepikhodov has proposed to me.

Lopakhin: Ah!

Dunyasha: And I simply don't know. . . . He's a quiet man, but sometimes, when he starts talking, you can't understand a thing he says. It's nice, and full of feeling, only it doesn't make sense. I sort of like him. He's madly in love with me. But he's an unlucky fellow: every day something happens to him. They tease him about it around here; they call him Two-and-twenty Troubles.

Lopakhin (listening): I think I hear them coming . . .

Dunyasha: They're coming! What's the matter with me? I'm cold all over.

Lopakhin: They're really coming. Let's go and meet them. Will she recognize me? It's five years since we've seen each other.

Dunyasha (agitated): I'll faint this very minute . . . oh, I'm going to faint!

(*Two carriages are heard driving up to the house.* Lopakhin *and* Dunyasha *go out quickly. The stage is empty. There is a hubbub in the adjoining rooms.* Firs *hurriedly crosses the stage leaning on a stick. He has been to meet* Lyubov Andreyevna *and wears old-fashioned livery and a high hat. He mutters something to himself, not a word of which can be understood. The noise offstage grows louder and louder. A voice: "Let's go through here . . ."* Enter Lyubov Andreyevna, Anya, Charlotta Ivanovna *with a little dog on a chain, all in traveling dress;* Varya *wearing a coat and kerchief;* Gayev, Semyonov-Pishchik, Lopakhin, Dunyasha *with a bundle and parasol;* Servants *with luggage—all walk through the room.*)

Anya: Let's go this way. Do you remember, Mama, what room this is?

Lyubov Andreyevna (joyfully, through tears): The nursery!

Varya: How cold it is! My hands are numb. (*To* Lyubov Andreyevna) Your rooms, both the white one and the violet one, are just as you left them, Mama.

Lyubov Andreyevna: The nursery . . . my dear, lovely nursery. . . . I used to sleep here when I was little. . . . (*Weeps.*) And now, like a child, I . . . (*Kisses her brother,* Varya, *then her brother again.*) Varya hasn't changed; she still looks like a nun. And I recognized Dunyasha. . . . (*Kisses* Dunyasha.)

Gayev: The train was two hours late. How's that? What kind of management is that?

Charlotta (to Pishchik*):* My dog even eats nuts.

Pishchik (amazed): Think of that now!

(*They all go out except* Anya *and* Dunyasha.)

Dunyasha: We've been waiting and waiting for you. . . . (*Takes off* Anya's *coat and hat.*)

Anya: I didn't sleep for four nights on the road . . . now I feel cold.

Dunyasha: It was Lent when you went away, there was snow and frost then, but now? My darling! (*Laughs and kisses her.*) I've waited so long for you, my joy, my precious . . . I must tell you at once, I can't wait another minute. . . .

Anya (listlessly): What now?

Dunyasha: The clerk, Yepikhodov, proposed to me just after Easter.

Anya: You always talk about the same thing. . . . (*Straightening her hair*) I've lost all my hairpins. . . . (*She is so exhausted she can hardly stand.*)

Dunyasha: I really don't know what to think. He loves me—he loves me so!

Anya (looking through the door into her room, tenderly): My room, my windows . . . it's just as though I'd never been away. I am home! Tomorrow morning I'll get up and run into the orchard. . . . Oh, if I could only sleep! I didn't sleep during the entire journey, I was so tormented by anxiety.

Dunyasha: Pyotr Sergeich arrived the day before yesterday.

Anya (joyfully): Petya!

Dunyasha: He's asleep in the bathhouse, he's staying there. "I'm afraid of being in the way," he said. *(Looks at her pocket watch.)* I ought to wake him up, but Varvara Mikhailovna told me not to. "Don't you wake him," she said.

(Enter Varya *with a bunch of keys at her waist.)*

Varya: Dunyasha, coffee, quickly . . . . Mama's asking for coffee.

Dunyasha: This very minute. *(Goes out.)*

Varya: Thank God, you've come! You're home again. *(Caressing her.)* My little darling has come back! My pretty one is here!

Anya: I've been through so much.

Varya: I can imagine!

Anya: I left in Holy Week, it was cold then. Charlotta never stopped talking and doing her conjuring tricks the entire journey. Why did you saddle me with Charlotta?

Varya: You couldn't have traveled alone, darling. At seventeen!

Anya: When we arrived in Paris, it was cold, snowing. My French is awful. . . . Mama was living on the fifth floor, and when I got there, she had all sorts of Frenchmen and ladies with her, and an old priest with a little book, and it was full of smoke, dismal. Suddenly, I felt sorry for Mama, so sorry. I took her head in my arms and held her close and couldn't let her go. Afterward she kept hugging me and crying. . . .

Varya (through her tears): Don't talk about it, don't talk about it. . . .

Anya: She had already sold her villa near Mentone, and she had nothing left, nothing. And I hadn't so much as a kopeck left, we barely managed to get there. But Mama doesn't understand! When we had dinner in a station restaurant, she always ordered the most expensive dishes and tipped each of the waiters a ruble. Charlotta is the same. And Yasha also ordered a dinner, it was simply awful. You know, Yasha is Mama's footman; we brought him with us.

Varya: I saw the rogue.

Anya: Well, how are things? Have you paid the interest?

Varya: How could we?

Anya: Oh, my God, my God!

Varya: In August the estate will be put up for sale.

Anya: My God!

(Lopakhin peeps in at the door and moo's like a cow.)

Lopakhin: Moo-o-o! *(Disappears.)*

Varya (through her tears): What I couldn't do to him! *(Shakes her fist.)*

Anya (embracing Varya, *softly):* Varya, has he proposed to you? *(Varya shakes her head.)* But he loves you. . . . Why don't you come to an understanding, what are you waiting for?

Varya: I don't think anything will ever come of it. He's too busy, he has no time for me . . . he doesn't even notice me. I've washed my hands of him, it makes me miserable to see him. . . . Everyone talks of our wedding, they all congratulate me, and actually there's nothing to it—it's all like a dream. . . . *(In a different tone.)* You have a brooch like a bee.

Anya (sadly): Mama bought it. *(Goes into her own room; speaks gaily, like a child.)* In Paris I went up in a balloon!

Varya: My darling is home! My pretty one has come back!

(Dunyasha has come in with the coffeepot and prepares coffee.)

Varya (stands at the door of Anya's *room):* You know, darling, all day long I'm busy looking after the house, but I keep dreaming. If we could marry you to a rich man I'd be at peace. I could go into a hermitage, then to Kiev, to Moscow, and from one holy place to another. . . . I'd go on and on. What a blessing!

Anya: The birds are singing in the orchard. What time is it?

Varya: It must be after two. Time you were asleep, darling. *(Goes into* Anya's *room.)* What a blessing!

(Yasha enters with a lap robe and a traveling bag.)

Yasha (crosses the stage mincingly): May one go through here?

Dunyasha: A person would hardly recognize you, Yasha. Your stay abroad has done wonders for you.

Yasha: Hm. . . . And who are you?

Dunyasha: When you left here I was only that high—*(indicating with her hand).* I'm Dunyasha, Fyodor Kozoyedov's daughter. You don't remember!

Yasha: Hm. . . . A little cucumber! *(Looks around, then embraces her; she cries out and drops a saucer. He quickly goes out.)*

Varya (in a tone of annoyance, from the doorway): What's going on in here?

Dunyasha (tearfully): I broke a saucer.

Varya: That's good luck.

Anya: We ought to prepare Mama: Petya is here. . . .

Varya: I gave orders not to wake him.

Anya (pensively): Six years ago Father died, and a month later brother Grisha drowned in the river . . . a pretty little seven-year-old boy. Mama couldn't bear it and went away . . . went without looking back. . . . *(Shudders.)* How I understand her, if she only knew! *(Pause)* And Petya Trofimov was Grisha's tutor, he may remind her. . . .

(Enter Firs *wearing a jacket and white waistcoat.)*

Firs (goes to the coffeepot, anxiously): The mistress will have her coffee here. *(Puts on white gloves.)* Is the coffee ready? *(To* Dunyasha, *sternly.)* You! Where's the cream?

Dunyasha: Oh, my goodness! *(Quickly goes out.)*

Firs (fussing over the coffeepot): Ah, what an addlepate! *(Mutters to himself.)* They've come back from Paris. . . . The master used to go to Paris . . . by carriage . . . *(Laughs.)*

Varya: What is it, Firs?

Firs: If you please? *(Joyfully)* My mistress has come home! At last! Now I can die. . . . *(Weeps with joy.)*

(Enter Lyubov Andreyevna, Gayev, *and* Semyonov-Pishchik, *the last wearing a sleeveless peasant coat of fine cloth and full trousers.* Gayev, *as he comes in, goes through the motions of playing billiards.)*

Lyubov Andreyevna: How does it go? Let's see if I can remember . . . cue ball into the corner! Double the rail to center table.

Gayev: Cut shot into the corner! There was a time, sister, when you and I used to sleep here in this very room, and now I'm fifty-one, strange as it may seem. . . .

Lopakhin: Yes, time passes.

Gayev: How's that?

Lopakhin: Time, I say, passes.

Gayev: It smells of patchouli here.

Anya: I'm going to bed. Good night, Mama. *(Kisses her mother.)*

Lyubov Andreyevna: My precious child. *(Kisses her hands.)* Are you glad to be home? I still feel dazed.

Anya: Good night, Uncle.

Gayev (kisses her face and hands): God bless you. How like your mother you are! *(To his sister)* At her age you were exactly like her, Lyuba.

(Anya *shakes hands with* Lopakhin *and* Pishchik *and goes out, closing the door after her.)*

Lyubov Andreyevna: She's exhausted.

Pishchik: Must have been a long journey.

Varya: Well, gentlemen? It's after two, high time you were going.

Lyubov Andreyevna (laughs): You haven't changed, Varya. *(Draws* Varya *to her and kisses her.)* I'll just drink my coffee and then we'll go. *(Firs *places a cushion under her feet.)* Thank you, my dear. I've got used to coffee. I drink it day and night. Thanks, dear old man. *(Kisses him.)*

Varya: I'd better see if all the luggage has been brought in.

Lyubov Andreyevna: Is this really me sitting here? *(Laughs.)* I feel like jumping about and waving my arms. *(Buries her face in her hands.)* What if it's only a dream! God knows I love my country, love it dearly. I couldn't look out the train window, I was crying so! *(Through tears)* But I must drink my coffee. Thank you, Firs, thank you, my dear old friend. I'm so glad you're still alive.

Firs: The day before yesterday.

Gayev: He's hard of hearing.

Lopakhin: I must go now, I'm leaving for Kharkov about five o'clock. It's so annoying! I wanted to have a good look at you, and have a talk. You're as splendid as ever.

Pishchik (breathing heavily): Even more beautiful. . . . Dressed like a Parisienne. . . . There goes my wagon, all four wheels!

Lopakhin: Your brother here, Leonid Andreich, says I'm a boor, a moneygrubber, but I don't mind. Let him talk. All I want is that you should trust me as you used to, and that your wonderful, touching eyes should look at me as they did then. Merciful God! My father was one of your father's serfs, and your grandfather's, but you yourself did so much for me once, that I've forgotten all that and love you as if you were my own kin—more than my kin.

Lyubov Andreyevna: I can't sit still, I simply cannot. (*Jumps up and walks about the room in great excitement.*) I cannot bear this joy. . . . Laugh at me, I'm silly. . . . My dear little bookcase . . . (*Kisses bookcase.*) my little table . . .

Gayev: Nurse died while you were away.

Lyubov Andreyevna (*sits down and drinks coffee*): Yes, God rest her soul. They wrote me.

Gayev: And Anastasy is dead. Petrushka Kosoi left me and is now with the police inspector in town. (*Takes a box of hard candies from his pocket and begins to suck one.*)

Pishchik: My daughter, Dashenka . . . sends her regards . . .

Lopakhin: I wish I could tell you something very pleasant and cheering. (*Glances at his watch.*) I must go directly, there's no time to talk, but . . . well, I'll say it in a couple of words. As you know, the cherry orchard is to be sold to pay your debts. The auction is set for August twenty-second, but you need not worry, my dear, you can sleep in peace, there is a way out. This is my plan. Now, please listen! Your estate is only twenty versts from town, the railway runs close by, and if the cherry orchard and the land along the river were cut up into lots and leased for summer cottages, you'd have, at the very least, an income of twenty-five thousand a year.

Gayev: Excuse me, what nonsense!

Lyubov Andreyevna: I don't quite understand you, Yermolai Alekseich.

Lopakhin: You will get, at the very least, twenty-five rubles a year for a two-and-a-half-acre lot, and if you advertise now, I guarantee you won't have a single plot of ground left by autumn, everything will be snapped up. In short, I congratulate you, you are saved. The site is splendid, the river is deep. Only, of course, the ground must be cleared . . . you must tear down all the old outbuildings, for instance, and this house, which is worthless, cut down the old cherry orchard——

Lyubov Andreyevna: Cut it down? Forgive me, my dear, but you don't know what you are talking about. If there is one thing in the whole province that is interesting, not to say remarkable, it's our cherry orchard.

Lopakhin: The only remarkable thing about this orchard is that it is very big. There's a crop of cherries every other year, and then you can't get rid of them, nobody buys them.

Gayev: This orchard is even mentioned in the *Encyclopedia*.

Lopakhin (*glancing at his watch*): If we don't think of something and come to a decision, on the twenty-second of August the cherry orchard, and the entire estate, will be sold at auction. Make up your minds! There is no other way out, I swear to you. None whatsoever.

Firs: In the old days, forty or fifty years ago, the cherries were dried, soaked, marinated, and made into jam, and they used to——

Gayev: Be quiet, Firs.

Firs: And they used to send cartloads of dried cherries to Moscow and Kharkov. And that brought in money! The dried cherries were soft and juicy in those days, sweet, fragrant. . . . They had a method then . . .

Lyubov Andreyevna: And what has become of that method now?

Firs: Forgotten. Nobody remembers. . . .

Pishchik: How was it in Paris? What's it like there? Did you eat frogs?

Lyubov Andreyevna: I ate crocodiles.

Pishchik: Think of that now!

Lopakhin: There used to be only the gentry and the peasants living in the country, but now these summer people have appeared. All the towns, even the smallest ones, are surrounded by summer cottages. And it is safe to say that in another twenty years these people will multiply enormously. Now the summer resident only drinks tea on his porch, but it may well be that he'll take to cultivating his acre, and then your cherry orchard will be a happy, rich, luxuriant——

Gayev (indignantly): What nonsense!

(*Enter* Varya *and* Yasha.)

Varya: There are two telegrams for you, Mama. (*Picks out a key and with a jingling sound opens an old-fashioned bookcase.*) Here they are.

Lyubov Andreyevna: From Paris. (*Tears up the telegrams without reading them.*) That's all over. . . .

Gayev: Do you know, Lyuba, how old this bookcase is? A week ago I pulled out the bottom drawer, and what do I see? Some figures burnt into it. The bookcase was made exactly a hundred years ago. What do you think of that? Eh? We could have celebrated its jubilee. It's an inanimate object, but nevertheless, for all that, it's a bookcase.

Pishchik: A hundred years . . . think of that now!

Gayev: Yes . . . that is something. . . . (*Feeling the bookcase*) Dear, honored bookcase, I salute thy existence, which for over one hundred years has served the glorious ideals of goodness and justice; thy silent appeal to fruitful endeavor, unflagging in the course of a hundred years, tearfully sustaining through generations of our family, courage and faith in a better future, and fostering in us ideals of goodness and social consciousness. . . .

(*A pause*)

Lopakhin: Yes . . .

Lyubov Andreyevna: You are the same as ever, Lyonya.

Gayev (somewhat embarrassed): Carom into the corner, cut shot to center table.

Lopakhin (looks at his watch): Well, time for me to go.

Yasha (hands medicine to Lyubov Andreyevna*):* Perhaps you will take your pills now.

Pishchik: Don't take medicaments, dearest lady, they do neither harm nor good. Let me have them, honored lady. (*Takes the pill box, shakes the pills into his hand, blows on them, puts them into his mouth, and washes them down with kvas.*) There!

Lyubov Andreyevna (alarmed): Why, you must be mad!
Pishchik: I've taken all the pills.
Lopakhin: What a glutton!

(Everyone laughs.)

Firs: The gentleman stayed with us during Holy Week . . . ate half a bucket
   of pickles. . . . *(Mumbles.)*
Lyubov Andreyevna: What is he saying?
Varya: He's been muttering like that for three years now. We've grown used
   to it.
Yasha: He's in his dotage.

*(Charlotta Ivanovna, very thin, tightly laced, in a white dress with a
lorgnette at her belt, crosses the stage.)*

Lopakhin: Forgive me, Charlotta Ivanovna, I haven't had a chance to say
   how do you do to you. *(Tries to kiss her hand.)*
Charlotta (pulls her hand away): If I permit you to kiss my hand you'll be
   wanting to kiss my elbow next, then my shoulder.
Lopakhin: I have no luck today. *(Everyone laughs.)* Charlotta Ivanovna, show
   us a trick!
Lyubov Andreyevna: Charlotta, show us a trick!
Charlotta: No. I want to sleep. *(Goes out.)*
Lopakhin: In three weeks we'll meet again. *(Kisses* Lyubov Andreyevna's
   hand.) Good-bye till then. Time to go. *(To* Gayev.) Good-bye. *(Kisses*
   Pishchik.) Good-bye. *(Shakes hands with* Varya, *then with* Firs *and* Yasha.)
   I don't feel like going. *(To* Lyubov Andreyevna) If you make up your
   mind about the summer cottages and come to a decision, let me know;
   I'll get you a loan of fifty thousand or so. Think it over seriously.
Varya (angrily): Oh, why don't you go!
Lopakhin: I'm going, I'm going. *(Goes out.)*
Gayev: Boor. Oh, pardon. Varya's going to marry him, he's Varya's young
   man.
Varya: Uncle dear, you talk too much.
Lyubov Andreyevna: Well, Varya, I shall be very glad. He's a good man.
Pishchik: A man, I must truly say . . . most worthy. . . . And my Dashenka . . .
   says, too, that . . . says all sorts of things. *(Snores but wakes up at once.)* In
   any case, honored lady, oblige me . . . a loan of two hundred and forty
   rubles . . . tomorrow the interest on my mortgage is due. . . .
Varya (in alarm): We have nothing, nothing at all!
Lyubov Andreyevna: I really haven't any money.
Pishchik: It'll turn up. *(Laughs.)* I never lose hope. Just when I thought
   everything was lost, that I was done for, lo and behold—the railway line
   ran through my land . . . and they paid me for it. And before you know
   it, something else will turn up, if not today—tomorrow. . . . Dashenka
   will win two hundred thousand . . . she's got a lottery ticket.
Lyubov Andreyevna: The coffee is finished, we can go to bed.
Firs (brushing Gayev's *clothes, admonishingly):* You've put on the wrong
   trousers again. What am I to do with you?

Varya (softly): Anya's asleep. *(Quietly opens the window.)* The sun has risen, it's no longer cold. Look, Mama dear, what wonderful trees! Oh, Lord, the air! The starlings are singing!

Gayev (opens another window): The orchard is all white. You haven't forgotten, Lyuba? That long avenue there that runs straight—straight as a stretched-out strap; it gleams on moonlight nights. Remember? You've not forgotten?

Lyubov Andreyevna (looking out the window at the orchard): Oh, my childhood, my innocence! I used to sleep in this nursery, I looked out from here into the orchard, happiness awoke with me each morning, it was just as it is now, nothing has changed. *(Laughing with joy)* All, all white! Oh, my orchard! After the dark, rainy autumn and the cold winter, you are young again, full of happiness, the heavenly angels have not forsaken you. . . . If I could cast off this heavy stone weighing on my breast and shoulders, if I could forget my past!

Gayev: Yes, and the orchard will be sold for our debts, strange as it may seem. . . .

Lyubov Andreyevna: Look, our dead mother walks in the orchard . . . in a white dress! *(Laughs with joy.)* It is she!

Gayev: Where?

Varya: God be with you, Mama dear.

Lyubov Andreyevna: There's no one there, I just imagined it. To the right, as you turn to the summerhouse, a slender white sapling is bent over . . . it looks like a woman.

(Enter Trofimov *wearing a shabby student's uniform and spectacles.)*

Lyubov Andreyevna: What a wonderful orchard! The white masses of blossoms, the blue sky——

Trofimov: Lyubov Andreyevna! *(She looks around at him.)* I only want to pay my respects, then I'll go at once. *(Kisses her hand ardently.)* I was told to wait until morning, but I hadn't the patience.

(Lyubov Andreyevna looks at him, puzzled.)

Varya (through tears): This is Petya Trofimov.

Trofimov: Petya Trofimov, I was Grisha's tutor. . . . Can I have changed so much?

(Lyubov Andreyevna embraces him, quietly weeping.)

Gayev (embarrassed): There, there, Lyuba.

Varya (crying): Didn't I tell you, Petya, to wait till tomorrow?

Lyubov Andreyevna: My Grisha . . . my little boy . . . Grisha . . . my son. . . .

Varya: What can we do, Mama dear? It's God's will.

Trofimov (gently, through tears): Don't, don't. . . .

Lyubov Andreyevna (quietly weeping): My little boy dead, drowned . . . Why? Why, my friend? *(In a lower voice.)* Anya is sleeping in there, and I'm talking loudly . . . making all this noise . . . But Petya, why do you look so bad? Why have you grown so old?

Trofimov: A peasant woman in the train called me a mangy gentleman.

Lyubov Andreyevna: You were just a boy then, a charming little student, and now your hair is thin—and spectacles! Is it possible you are still a student? *(Goes toward the door.)*

Trofimov: I shall probably be an eternal student.

Lyubov Andreyevna (kisses her brother, then Varya): Now, go to bed. . . . You've grown older too, Leonid.

Pishchik (follows her): Well, seems to be time to sleep. . . . Oh, my gout! I'm staying the night. Lyubov Andreyevna, my soul, tomorrow morning . . . two hundred and forty rubles. . . .

Gayev: He keeps at it.

Pishchik: Two hundred and forty rubles . . . to pay the interest on my mortgage.

Lyubov Andreyevna: I have no money, my friend.

Pishchik: My dear, I'll pay it back . . . it's a trifling sum.

Lyubov Andreyevna: Well, all right, Leonid will give it to you. . . . Give it to him, Leonid.

Gayev: Me give it to him! . . . Hold out your pocket!

Lyubov Andreyevna: It can't be helped, give it to him. . . . He needs it. . . . He'll pay it back.

(Lyubov Andreyevna, Trofimov, Pishchik, *and* Firs *go out.* Gayev, Varya, *and* Yasha *remain.)*

Gayev: My sister hasn't yet lost her habit of squandering money. *(To* Yasha.*)* Go away, my good fellow, you smell of the henhouse.

Yasha (with a smirk): And you, Leonid Andreyevich, are just the same as ever.

Gayev: How's that? *(To* Varya) What did he say?

Varya: Your mother has come from the village; she's been sitting in the servants' room since yesterday, waiting to see you. . . .

Yasha: Let her wait, for God's sakc!

Varya: Aren't you ashamed?

Yasha: A lot I need her! She could have come tomorrow. *(Goes out.)*

Varya: Mama's the same as ever, she hasn't changed a bit. She'd give away everything, if she could.

Gayev: Yes. . . . *(A pause)* If a great many remedies are suggested for a disease, it means that the disease is incurable. I keep thinking, racking my brains, I have many remedies, a great many, and that means, in effect, that I have none. It would be good to receive a legacy from someone, good to marry our Anya to a very rich man, good to go to Yaroslav and try our luck with our aunt, the Countess. She is very, very rich, you know.

Varya (crying): If only God would help us!

Gayev: Stop bawling. Auntie's very rich, but she doesn't like us. In the first place, sister married a lawyer, not a nobleman . . . *(Anya appears in the doorway.)* She married beneath her, and it cannot be said that she has conducted herself very virtuously. She is good, kind, charming, and I love her dearly, but no matter how much you allow for extenuating circumstances, you must admit she leads a sinful life. You feel it in the slightest movement.

Varya (in a whisper): Anya is standing in the doorway.

Gayev: What? *(Pause)* Funny, something got into my right eye . . . I can't see very well. And Thursday, when I was in the district court . . .

(Anya *enters.*)

Varya: Why aren't you asleep, Anya?

Anya: I can't get to sleep. I just can't.

Gayev: My little one! *(Kisses* Anya's *face and hands.)* My child. . . . *(Through tears)* You are not my niece, you are my angel, you are everything to me. Believe me, believe . . .

Anya: I believe you, Uncle. Everyone loves you and respects you, but, Uncle dear, you must keep quiet, just keep quiet. What were you saying just now about my mother, about your own sister? What made you say that?

Gayev: Yes, yes. . . . *(Covers his face with her hand.)* Really, it's awful! My God! God help me! And today I made a speech to the bookcase . . . so stupid! And it was only when I had finished that I realized it was stupid.

Varya: It's true, Uncle dear, you ought to keep quiet. Just don't talk, that's all.

Anya: If you could keep from talking, it would make things easier for you, too.

Gayev: I'll be quiet. *(Kisses* Anya's *and* Varya's *hands.)* I'll be quiet. Only this is about business. On Thursday I was in the district court, well, a group of us gathered together and began talking about one thing and another, this and that, and it seems it might be possible to arrange a loan on a promissory note to pay the interest at the bank.

Varya: If only God would help us!

Gayev: On Tuesday I'll go and talk it over again. *(To* Varya) Stop bawling. *(To* Anya) Your mama will talk to Lopakhin; he, of course, will not refuse her. . . . And as soon as you've rested, you will go to Yaroslav to the Countess, your great-aunt. In that way we shall be working from three directions—and our business is in the hat. We'll pay the interest, I'm certain of it. . . . *(Puts a candy in his mouth.)* On my honor, I'll swear by anything you like, the estate shall not be sold. *(Excitedly.)* By my happiness, I swear it! Here's my hand on it, call me a worthless, dishonorable man if I let it come to auction! I swear by my whole being!

Anya (a calm mood returns to her, she is happy): How good you are, Uncle, how clever! *(Embraces him.)* Now I am at peace! I'm at peace! I'm happy!

(Enter Firs.)

Firs (reproachfully): Leonid Andreich, have you no fear of God? When are you going to bed?

Gayev: Presently, presently. Go away, Firs. I'll . . . all right, I'll undress myself. Well, children, bye-bye. . . . Details tomorrow, and now go to sleep. *(Kisses* Anya *and* Varya.) I am a man of the eighties. . . . They don't think much of that period today, nevertheless, I can say that in the course of my life I have suffered not a little for my convictions. It is not for nothing that the peasant loves me. You have to know the peasant! You have to know from what—

Anya: There you go again, Uncle!

Varya: Uncle dear, do be quiet.

Firs (angrily): Leonid Andreich!

Gayev: I'm coming, I'm coming. . . . Go to bed. A clean double rail shot to center table. . . . *(Goes out; Firs hobbles after him.)*

Anya: I'm at peace now. I would rather not go to Yaroslav, I don't like my great-aunt, but still, I'm at peace, thanks to Uncle. *(She sits down.)*

Varya: We must get some sleep. I'm going now. Oh, something unpleasant happened while you were away. In the old servant's quarters, as you know, there are only the old people; Yefimushka, Polya, Yevstignei, and, of course, Karp. They began letting in all sorts of rogues to spend the night—I didn't say anything. But then I'd heard they'd been spreading a rumor that I'd given an order for them to be fed nothing but dried peas. Out of stinginess, you see. . . . It was all Yevstignei's doing. . . . Very well, I think, if that's how it is, you just wait. I send for Yevstignei . . . *(yawning)* he comes. . . . "How is it, Yevstignei," I say, "that you could be such a fool. . . ." *(Looks at* Anya.*)* She's fallen asleep. *(Takes her by the arm.)* Come to your little bed. . . . Come along. *(Leading her)* My little darling fell asleep. Come. . . . *(They go.)*

(In the distance, beyond the orchard, a shepherd is playing on a reed pipe. Trofimov *crosses the stage and, seeing* Varya *and* Anya, *stops.)*

Varya: Sh! She's asleep . . . asleep. . . . Come along, darling.

Anya (softly, half-asleep): I'm so tired. . . . Those bells . . . Uncle . . . dear . . . Mama and Uncle . . .

Varya: Come, darling, come along. *(They go into* Anya's *room.)*

Trofimov (deeply moved): My sunshine! My spring!

ACT II

(A meadow. An old, lopsided, long-abandoned little chapel; near it a well, large stones that apparently were once tombstones, and an old bench. A road to the Gayev *manor house can be seen. On one side, where the cherry orchard begins, tall poplars loom. In the distance a row of telegraph poles, and far, far away, on the horizon, the faint outline of a large town, which is visible only in very fine, clear weather. The sun will soon set.* Charlotta, Yasha, *and* Dunyasha *are sitting on the bench;* Yepikhodov *stands near playing something sad on the guitar. They are all lost in thought.* Charlotta *wears an old forage cap; she has taken a gun from her shoulder and is adjusting the buckle on the sling.)*

Charlotta (reflectively): I haven't got a real passport, I don't know how old I am, but it always seems to me that I'm quite young. When I was a little girl, my father and mother used to travel from one fair to another giving performances—very good ones. And I did the *salto mortale* and all sorts of tricks. Then when Papa and Mama died, a German lady took me in to live with her and began teaching me. Good. I grew up and became a governess. But where I come from and who I am—I do not know. . . . Who my parents were—perhaps they weren't even married—I don't

know. *(Takes a cucumber out of her pocket and eats it.)* I don't know anything. *(Pause)* One wants so much to talk, but there isn't anyone to talk
to . . . I have no one.

Yepikhodov (plays the guitar and sings): "What care I for the clamorous world,
what's friend or foe to me?" . . . How pleasant it is to play a mandolin!

Dunyasha: That's a guitar, not a mandolin. *(Looks at herself in a hand mirror
and powders her face.)*

Yepikhodov: To a madman, in love, it is a mandolin. . . . *(Sings.)* "Would that
the heart were warmed by the flame of requited love . . ."

(Yasha joins in.)

Charlotta: How horribly these people sing! . . . Pfui! Like jackals!

Dunyasha (to Yasha): Really, how fortunate to have been abroad!

Yasha: Yes, to be sure. I cannot but agree with you there. *(Yawns, then lights a
cigar.)*

Yepikhodov: It stands to reason. Abroad everything has long since been fully
constituted.

Yasha: Obviously.

Yepikhodov: I am a cultivated man, I read all sorts of remarkable books, but I
am in no way able to make out my own inclinations, what it is I really
want, whether, strictly speaking, to live or to shoot myself; nevertheless,
I always carry a revolver on me. Here it is. *(Shows revolver.)*

Charlotta: Finished. Now I'm going. *(Slings the gun over her shoulder.)* You're
a very clever man, Yepikhodov, and quite terrifying; women must be
mad about you. Brrr! *(Starts to go.)* These clever people are all so stupid,
there's no one for me to talk to. . . . Alone, always alone, I have no
one . . . and who I am, and why I am, nobody knows. . . . *(Goes out un-
hurriedly.)*

Yepikhodov: Strictly speaking, all else aside, I must state regarding myself,
that fate treats me unmercifully, as a storm does a small ship. If, let us
assume, I am mistaken, then why, to mention a single instance, do I
wake up this morning, and there on my chest see a spider of terrifying
magnitude? . . . Like that. *(Indicates with both hands.)* And likewise, I take
up some kvas to quench my thirst, and there see something in the highest degree unseemly, like a cockroach. *(Pause.)* Have you read Buckle?
(Pause.) If I may trouble you, Avdotya Federovna, I should like to have a
word or two with you.

Dunyasha: Go ahead.

Yepikhodov: I prefer to speak with you alone. . . . *(Sighs.)*

Dunyasha (embarrassed): Very well . . . only first bring me my little cape . . .
you'll find it by the cupboard. . . . It's rather damp here. . . .

Yepikhodov: Certainly, ma'am . . . I'll fetch it, ma'am. . . . Now I know what
to do with my revolver. . . . *(Takes the guitar and goes off playing it.)*

Yasha: Two-and-twenty Troubles! Between ourselves, a stupid fellow.
(Yawns.)

Dunyasha: God forbid that he should shoot himself. *(Pause.)* I've grown so
anxious, I'm always worried. I was only a little girl when I was taken into

the master's house, and now I'm quite unused to the simple life, and my
hands are white as can be, just like a lady's. I've become so delicate, so
tender and ladylike, I'm afraid of everything. . . . Frightfully so. And,
Yasha, if you deceive me, I just don't know what will become of my
nerves.

Yasha (kisses her): You little cucumber! Of course a girl should never forget
herself. What I dislike above everything is when a girl doesn't conduct
herself properly.

Dunyasha: I'm passionately in love with you; you're educated, you can discuss anything. *(Pause)*

Yasha [yawns]: Yes. . . . As I see it, it's like this: if a girl loves somebody, that
means she's immoral. *(Pause)* Very pleasant smoking a cigar in the open
air. . . . *(Listens.)* Someone's coming this way. . . . It's the masters. (Dunyasha *impulsively embraces him.)* You go home, as if you'd been to the
river to bathe; take that path, otherwise they'll see you and suspect me
of having a rendezvous with you. I can't endure that sort of thing.

Dunyasha (with a little cough): My head is beginning to ache from your
cigar. . . . *(Goes out.)*

(Yasha *remains, sitting near the chapel.* Lyubov Andreyevna, Gayev, *and*
Lopakhin *enter.)*

Lopakhin: You must make up your mind once and for all—time won't stand
still. The question, after all, is quite simple. Do you agree to lease the
land for summer cottages or not? Answer in one word: yes or no? Only
one word!

Lyubov Andreyevna: Who is it that smokes those disgusting cigars out here?
(Sits down.)

Gayev: Now that the railway line is so near, it's made things convenient. *(Sits
down.)* We went to town and had lunch . . . cue ball to the center! I feel
like going to the house first and playing a game.

Lyubov Andreyevna: Later.

Lopakhin: Just one word! *(Imploringly)* Do give me an answer!

Gayev (yawning): How's that?

Lyubov Andreyevna (looks into her purse): Yesterday I had a lot of money, and
today there's hardly any left. My poor Varya tries to economize by feeding everyone milk soup, and in the kitchen the old people get nothing
but dried peas, while I squander money foolishly. . . . *(Drops the purse,
scattering gold coins.)* There they go. . . . *(Vexed)*

Yasha: Allow me, I'll pick them up in an instant. *(Picks up the money.)*

Lyubov Andreyevna: Please do, Yasha. And why did I go to town for
lunch? . . . That miserable restaurant of yours with its music, and tablecloths smelling of soap. . . . Why drink so much, Lyonya? Why eat so
much? Why talk so much? Today in the restaurant again you talked too
much, and it was all so pointless. About the seventies, about the decadents. And to whom? Talking to waiters about the decadents!

Lopakhin: Yes.

Gayev (waving his hand): I'm incorrigible, that's evident. . . . *(Irritably to
Yasha.)* Why do you keep twirling about in front of me?

Yasha (laughs): I can't help laughing when I hear your voice.

Gayev (to his sister): Either he or I——

Lyubov Andreyevna: Go away, Yasha, run along.

Yasha (hands Lyubov Andreyevna *her purse):* I'm going, right away. *(Hardly able to contain his laughter.)* This very instant. . . . *(Goes out.)*

Lopakhin: That rich man, Deriganov, is prepared to buy the estate. They say he's coming to the auction himself.

Lyubov Andreyevna: Where did you hear that?

Lopakhin: That's what they're saying in town.

Lyubov Andreyevna: Our aunt in Yaroslav promised to send us something, but when and how much no one knows.

Lopakhin: How much do you think she'll send? A hundred thousand? Two hundred?

Lyubov Andreyevna: Oh . . . ten or fifteen thousand, and we'll be thankful for that.

Lopakhin: Forgive me, but I have never seen such frivolous, such queer, unbusinesslike people as you, my friends. You are told in plain language that your estate is to be sold, and it's as though you don't understand it.

Lyubov Andreyevna: But what are we to do? Tell us what to do.

Lopakhin: I tell you every day. Every day I say the same thing. Both the cherry orchard and the land must be leased for summer cottages, and it must be done now, as quickly as possible—the auction is close at hand. Try to understand! Once you definitely decide on the cottages, you can raise as much money as you like, and then you are saved.

Lyubov Andreyevna: Cottages, summer people—forgive me, but it's so vulgar.

Gayev: I agree with you, absolutely.

Lopakhin: I'll either burst into tears, start shouting, or fall into a faint! I can't stand it! You've worn me out! *(To* Gayev*)* You're an old woman!

Gayev: How's that?

Lopakhin: An old woman! *(Starts to go.)*

Lyubov Andreyevna (alarmed): No, don't go, stay, my dear. I beg you. Perhaps we'll think of something!

Lopakhin: What is there to think of?

Lyubov Andreyevna: Don't go away, please. With you here it's more cheerful somehow. . . . *(Pause.)* I keep expecting something to happen, like the house caving in on us.

Gayev (in deep thought): Double rail shot into the corner. . . . Cross table to the center. . . .

Lyubov Andreyevna: We have sinned so much. . . .

Lopakhin: What sins could you have——

Gayev (puts a candy into his mouth): They say I've eaten up my entire fortune in candies. . . . *(Laughs.)*

Lyubov Andreyevna: Oh, my sins. . . . I've always squandered money recklessly, like a madwoman, and I married a man who did nothing but amass debts. My husband died from champagne—he drank terribly— then, to my sorrow, I fell in love with another man, lived with him, and just at that time—that was my first punishment, a blow on the head—

my little boy was drowned . . . here in the river. And I went abroad, went away for good, never to return, never to see this river. . . . I closed my eyes and ran, beside myself, and *he* after me . . . callously, without pity. I bought a villa near Mentone, because he fell ill there, and for three years I had no rest, day or night. The sick man wore me out, my soul dried up. Then last year, when the villa was sold to pay my debts, I went to Paris, and there he stripped me of everything, and left me for another woman; I tried to poison myself . . . So stupid, so shameful. . . . And suddenly I felt a longing for Russia, for my own country, for my little girl. . . . *(Wipes away her tears.)* Lord, Lord, be merciful, forgive my sins! Don't punish me anymore! *(Takes a telegram out of her pocket.)* This came today from Paris. . . . He asks my forgiveness, begs me to return. . . . *(Tears up telegram.)* Do I hear music? *(Listens.)*

Gayev: That's our famous Jewish band. You remember, four violins, a flute and double bass.

Lyubov Andreyevna: It's still in existence? We ought to send for them some time and give a party.

Lopakhin *(listens):* I don't hear anything. . . . *(Sings softly.)* "The Germans, for pay, will turn Russians into Frenchmen, they say." *(Laughs.)* What a play I saw yesterday at the theater—very funny!

Lyubov Andreyevna: There was probably nothing funny about it. Instead of going to see plays you ought to look at yourselves a little more often. How drab your lives are, how full of futile talk!

Lopakhin: That's true. I must say, this life of ours is stupid. . . . *(Pause)* My father was a peasant, an idiot; he understood nothing, taught me nothing; all he did was beat me when he was drunk, and always with a stick. As a matter of fact, I'm as big a blockhead and idiot as he was. I never learned anything, my handwriting's disgusting, I write like a pig—I'm ashamed to have people see it.

Lyubov Andreyevna: You ought to get married, my friend.

Lopakhin: Yes . . . that's true.

Lyubov Andreyevna: To our Varya. She's a nice girl.

Lopakhin: Yes.

Lyubov Andreyevna: She's a girl who comes from simple people, works all day long, but the main thing is she loves you. Besides, you've liked her for a long time now.

Lopakhin: Well? I've nothing against it. . . . She's a good girl. *(Pause)*

Gayev: I've been offered a place in the bank. Six thousand a year. . . . Have you heard?

Lyubov Andreyevna: How could you! You stay where you are. . . .

(Firs enters carrying an overcoat.)

Firs *(To* Gayev): If you please, sir, put this on, it's damp.

Gayev *(puts on the overcoat):* You're a pest, old man.

Firs: Never mind. . . . You went off this morning without telling me. *(Looks him over.)*

Lyubov Andreyevna: How you have aged, Firs!

Firs: What do you wish, madam?

Lopakhin: She says you've grown very old!

Firs: I've lived a long time. They were arranging a marriage for me before your papa was born. . . . *(Laughs.)* I was already head footman when the Emancipation came. At that time I wouldn't consent to my freedom, I stayed with the masters. . . . *(Pause)* I remember, everyone was happy, but what they were happy about, they themselves didn't know.

Lopakhin: It was better in the old days. At least they flogged them.

Firs (not hearing): Of course. The peasants kept to the masters, the masters kept to the peasants; but now they have all gone their own ways, you can't tell about anything.

Gayev: Be quiet, Firs. Tomorrow I must go to town. I've been promised an introduction to a certain general who might let us have a loan.

Lopakhin: Nothing will come of it. And you can rest assured, you won't even pay the interest.

Lyubov Andreyevna: He's raving. There is no such general.

(*Enter* Trofimov, Anya, *and* Varya.)

Gayev: Here come our young people.

Anya: There's Mama.

Lyubov Andreyevna (tenderly): Come, come along, my darlings. *(Embraces* Anya *and* Varya.*)* If you only knew how I love you both! Sit beside me— there, like that.

(*They all sit down.*)

Lopakhin: Our eternal student is always with the young ladies.

Trofimov: That's none of your business.

Lopakhin: He'll soon be fifty, but he's still a student.

Trofimov: Drop your stupid jokes.

Lopakhin: What are you so angry about, you queer fellow?

Trofimov: Just leave me alone.

Lopakhin (laughs): Let me ask you something: what do you make of me?

Trofimov: My idea of you, Yermolai Alekseich, is this: you're a rich man, you will soon be a millionaire. Just as the beast of prey, which devours everything that crosses its path, is necessary in the metabolic process, so are you necessary.

(*Everyone laughs.*)

Varya: Petya, you'd better tell us something about the planets.

Lyubov Andreyevna: No, let's go on with yesterday's conversation.

Trofimov: What was it about?

Gayev: About the proud man.

Trofimov: We talked a long time yesterday, but we didn't get anywhere. In the proud man, in your sense of the word, there's something mystical. And you may be right from your point of view, but if you look at it simply, without being abstruse, why even talk about pride? Is there any sense in it if, physiologically, man is poorly constructed, if, in the vast majority of cases, he is coarse, ignorant, and profoundly unhappy? We should stop admiring ourselves. We should just work, and that's all.

Gayev: You die, anyway.

Trofimov: Who knows? And what does it mean—to die? It may mean that man has a hundred senses, and at his death only the five that are known to us perish, and the other ninety-five go on living.

Lyubov Andreyevna: How clever you are, Petya!

Lopakhin (ironically): Terribly clever!

Trofimov: Mankind goes forward, perfecting its powers. Everything that is now unattainable will some day be comprehensible and within our grasp, only we must work, and help with all our might those who are seeking the truth. So far, among us here in Russia, only a very few work. The great majority of the intelligentsia that I know seek nothing, do nothing, and as yet are incapable of work. They call themselves the intelligentsia, yet they belittle their servants, treat the peasants like animals, are wretched students, never read anything serious, and do absolutely nothing; they only talk about science and know very little about art. They all look serious, have grim expressions, speak of weighty matters, and philosophize; and meanwhile anyone can see that workers eat abominably, sleep without pillows, thirty or forty to a room, and everywhere there are bedbugs, stench, dampness, and immorality. . . . It's obvious that all our fine talk is merely to delude ourselves and others. Show me the day nurseries they are always talking about—and where are the reading rooms? They only write about them in novels, but in reality they don't exist. There is nothing but filth, vulgarity, asiaticism. . . . I'm afraid of those very serious countenances, I don't like them, I'm afraid of serious conversations. We'd do better to remain silent.

Lopakhin: You know, I get up before five in the morning, and I work from morning to night; now, I'm always handling money, my own and other people's, and I see what people around me are like. You have only to start doing something to find out how few honest, decent people there are. Sometimes, when I can't sleep, I think: "Lord, Thou gavest us vast forests, boundless fields, broad horizons, and living in their midst we ourselves ought truly to be giants. . . ."

Lyubov Andreyevna: Now you want giants! They're good only in fairy tales, otherwise they're frightening.

(Yepikhodov *crosses at the rear of the stage, playing the guitar.*)

Lyubov Andreyevna (pensively): There goes Yepikhodov . . .

Anya (pensively): There goes Yepikhodov. . .

Gayev: The sun has set, ladies and gentlemen.

Trofimov: Yes.

Gayev (in a low voice, as if reciting): Oh, Nature, wondrous Nature, you shine with eternal radiance, beautiful and indifferent; you, whom we call mother, unite within yourself both life and death, giving life and taking it away. . . .

Varya (beseechingly): Uncle dear!

Anya: Uncle, you're doing it again!

Trofimov: You'd better cue ball into the center.

Gayev: I'll be silent, silent.

(*All sit lost in thought. The silence is broken only by the subdued muttering of* Firs. *Suddenly a distant sound is heard, as if from the sky, like the sound of a snapped string mournfully dying away.*)

Lyubov Andreyevna: What was that?

Lopakhin: I don't know. Somewhere far off in a mine shaft a bucket's broken loose. But somewhere very far away.

Gayev: It might be a bird of some sort . . . like a heron.

Trofimov: Or an owl . . .

Lyubov Andreyevna (shudders): It's unpleasant somehow. . . . (*Pause*)

Firs: The same thing happened before the troubles: an owl hooted and the samovar hissed continually.

Gayev: Before what troubles?

Firs: Before the Emancipation.

Lyubov Andreyevna: Come along, my friends, let us go, evening is falling. (*To* Anya) There are tears in your eyes—what is it, my little one?

(*Embraces her.*)

Anya: It's all right, Mama. It's nothing.

Trofimov: Someone is coming.

(*A* Stranger *appears wearing a shabby white forage cap and an overcoat. He is slightly drunk.*)

Stranger: Permit me to inquire, can I go straight through here to the station?

Gayev: You can. Follow the road.

Stranger: I am deeply grateful to you. (*Coughs.*) Splendid weather. . . . (*Reciting*) "My brother, my suffering brother . . . come to the Volga, whose groans" . . . (*To* Varya) Mademoiselle, will you oblige a hungry Russian with thirty kopecks?

(*Varya, frightened, cries out.*)

Lopakhin (angrily): There's a limit to everything.

Lyubov Andreyevna (panic-stricken): Here you are—take this. . . . (*Fumbles in her purse.*) I have no silver. . . . Never mind, here's a gold piece for you. . . .

Stranger: I am deeply grateful to you. (*Goes off.*)

(*Laughter*)

Varya (frightened): I'm leaving . . . I'm leaving. . . . Oh, Mama, dear, there's nothing in the house for the servants to eat, and you give him a gold piece!

Lyubov Andreyevna: What's to be done with such a silly creature? When we get home, I'll give you all I've got. Yermolai Alekseyevich, you'll lend me some more!

Lopakhin: At your service.

Lyubov Andreyevna: Come, my friends, it's time to go. Oh, Varya, we have definitely made a match for you. Congratulations!

Varya [through tears]: Mama, that's not something to joke about.

Lopakhin: "Aurelia, get thee to a nunnery . . ."

Gayev: Look, my hands are trembling: it's a long time since I've played a game of billiards.

Lopakhin: "Aurelia, O Nymph, in thy orisons, be all my sins remember'd!"

Lyubov Andreyevna: Let us go, my friends, it will soon be suppertime.

Varya: He frightened me. My heart is simply pounding.

Lopakhin: Let me remind you, ladies and gentlemen: on the twenty-second of August the cherry orchard is to be sold. Think about that!—Think!

(*All go out except* Trofimov *and* Anya.)

Anya (laughs): My thanks to the stranger for frightening Varya, now we are alone.

Trofimov: Varya is so afraid we might suddenly fall in love with each other that she hasn't left us alone for days. With her narrow mind she can't understand that we are above love. To avoid the petty and the illusory, which prevent our being free and happy—that is the aim and meaning of life. Forward! We are moving irresistibly toward the bright star that burns in the distance! Forward! Do not fall behind, friends!

Anya (clasping her hands): How well you talk! (*Pause*) It's marvelous here today!

Trofimov: Yes, the weather is wonderful.

Anya: What have you done to me, Petya, that I no longer love the cherry orchard as I used to? I loved it so tenderly, it seemed to me there was no better place on earth than our orchard.

Trofimov: All Russia is our orchard. It is a great and beautiful land, and there are many wonderful places in it. (*Pause*) Just think, Anya: your grandfather, your great-grandfather, and all your ancestors were serf-owners, possessors of living souls. Don't you see that from every cherry tree, from every leaf and trunk, human beings are peering out at you? Don't you hear their voices? To possess living souls—that has corrupted all of you, those who lived before and you who are living now, so that your mother, you, your uncle, no longer perceive that you are living in debt, at someone else's expense, at the expense of those whom you wouldn't allow to cross your threshold. . . . We are at least two hundred years behind the times, we have as yet absolutely nothing, we have no definite attitude toward the past, we only philosophize, complain of boredom, or drink vodka. Yet it's quite clear that to begin to live we must first atone for the past, be done with it, and we can atone for it only by suffering, only by extraordinary, unceasing labor. Understand this, Anya.

Anya: The house we live in hasn't really been ours for a long time, and I shall leave it, I give you my word.

Trofimov: If you have the keys of the household, throw them into the well and go. Be as free as the wind.

Anya (in ecstasy): How well you put that!

Trofimov: Believe me, Anya, believe me! I am not yet thirty, I am young, still a student, but I have already been through so much! As soon as winter comes, I am hungry, sick, worried, poor as a beggar, and—where has not fate driven me! Where have I not been? And yet always, every minute of the day and night, my soul was filled with inexplicable premonitions. I have a premonition of happiness, Anya, I can see it . . .

Anya: The moon is rising.

(*Yepikhodov is heard playing the same melancholy song on the guitar. The moon rises. Somewhere near the poplars* Varya *is looking for* Anya *and calling:* "Anya, where are you?")

Trofimov: Yes, the moon is rising. (*Pause*) There it is—happiness . . . it's coming, nearer and nearer, I can hear its footsteps. And if we do not see it, if we do not recognize it, what does it matter? Others will see it.

Varya's voice: Anya! Where are you?

Trofimov: That Varya again! (*Angrily*) It's revolting!

Anya: Well? Let's go down to the river. It's lovely there.

Trofimov: Come on. (*They go.*)

Varya's voice: Anya! Anya!

ACT III

(*The drawing room, separated by an arch from the ballroom. The chandelier is lighted. The Jewish band that was mentioned in Act II is heard playing in the hall. It is evening. In the ballroom they are dancing a grand rond. The voice of* Semyonov-Pishchik: "Promenade à une paire!" *They all enter the drawing room:* Pishchik *and* Charlotta Ivanovna *are the first couple,* Trofimov *and* Lyubov Andreyevna *the second,* Anya *and the* Post-Office Clerk *the third,* Varya *and the* Stationmaster *the fourth, etc.* Varya, *quietly weeping, dries her tears as she dances.* Dunyasha *is in the last couple. As they cross the drawing room* Pishchik *calls:* "Grand rond, balancez!" *and* "Les cavaliers à genoux et remercier vos dames!" Firs, *wearing a dress coat, brings in a tray with seltzer water.* Pishchik *and* Trofimov *come into the drawing room.*)

Pishchik: I'm a full-blooded man, I've already had two strokes, and dancing's hard work for me, but as they say, "If you run with the pack, you can bark or not, but at least wag your tail." At that, I'm as strong as a horse. My late father—quite a joker he was, God rest his soul—used to say, talking about our origins, that the ancient line of Semyonov-Pishchik was descended from the very horse that Caligula had seated in the Senate. . . . (*Sits down.*) But the trouble is—no money! A hungry dog believes in nothing but meat. . . . (*Snores but wakes up at once.*) It's the same with me—I can think of nothing but money. . . .

Trofimov: You know, there really is something quite equine about your
    figure.
Pishchik: Well, a horse is a fine animal. . . . You can sell a horse.

(*There is the sound of a billiard game in the next room.* Varya *appears in the
archway.*)

Trofimov (teasing her): Madame Lopakhina! Madame Lopakhina!
Varya (angrily): Mangy gentleman!
Trofimov: Yes, I am a mangy gentleman, and proud of it!
Varya (reflecting bitterly): Here we've hired musicians, and what are we going
    to pay them with? (*Goes out.*)
Trofimov (To Pishchik*):* If the energy you have expended in the course of
    your life trying to find money to pay interest had gone into something
    else, ultimately, you might very well have turned the world upside down.
Pishchik: Nietzsche . . . the philosopher . . . the greatest, most renowned . . .
    a man of tremendous intellect . . . says in his works that it is possible to
    forge banknotes.
Trofimov: And have you read Nietzsche?
Pishchik: Well . . . Dashenka told me. I'm in such a state now that I'm just
    about ready for forging. . . . The day after tomorrow I have to pay three
    hundred and ten rubles . . . I've got a hundred and thirty. . . . (*Feels in his
    pocket, grows alarmed.*) The money is gone! I've lost the money! (*Tear-
    fully*) Where is my money? (*Joyfully*) Here it is, inside the lining. . . . I'm
    all in a sweat. . . .

(Lyubov Andreyevna *and* Charlotta Ivanovna *come in.*)

Lyubov Andreyevna (humming a Lezginka*):* Why does Leonid take so long?
    What is he doing in town? (*To* Dunyasha) Dunyasha, offer the musicians
    some tea.
Trofimov: In all probability, the auction didn't take place.
Lyubov Andreyevna: It was the wrong time to have the musicians, the wrong
    time to give a dance. . . . Well, never mind. . . . (*Sits down and hums
    softly.*)
Charlotta (gives Pishchik *a deck of cards):* Here's a deck of cards for you.
    Think of a card.
Pishchik: I've thought of one.
Charlotta: Now shuffle the pack. Very good. And now, my dear Mr.
    Pishchik, hand it to me. *Ein, zwei, drei!* Now look for it—it's in your side
    pocket.
Pishchik (takes the card out of his side pocket): The eight of spades—absolutely
    right! (*Amazed*) Think of that, now!
Charlotta (holding the deck of cards in the palm of her hand, to Trofimov*):*
    Quickly, tell me, which card is on top?
Trofimov: What? Well, the queen of spades.
Charlotta: Right! (*To* Pishchik) Now which card is on top?
Pishchik: The ace of hearts.
Charlotta: Right! (*Claps her hands and the deck of cards disappears.*) What lovely

weather we're having today! (*A mysterious feminine voice, which seems to come from under the floor, answers her:* "*Oh, yes, splendid weather, madam.*") You are so nice, you're my ideal. . . . (*The voice:* "*And I'm very fond of you, too, madam.*")

Stationmaster (applauding): Bravo, Madame Ventriloquist!

Pishchik (amazed): Think of that, now! Most enchanting Charlotta Ivanovna . . . I am simply in love with you. . . .

Charlotta: In love? (*Shrugs her shoulders.*) Is it possible that you can love? *Guter Mensch, aber schlechter Musikant.*

Trofimov (claps Pishchik *on the shoulder):* You old horse, you!

Charlotta: Attention, please! One more trick. (*Takes a lap robe from a chair.*) Here's a very fine lap robe; I should like to sell it. (*Shakes it out.*) Doesn't anyone want to buy it?

Pishchik (amazed): Think of that, now!

Charlotta: Ein, zwei, drei! (*Quickly raises the lap robe; behind it stands Anya, who curtseys, runs to her mother, embraces her, and runs back into the ballroom amid the general enthusiasm.*)

Lyubov Andreyevna (applauding): Bravo, bravo!

Charlotta: Once again! *Ein, zwei, drei.* (*Raises the lap robe; behind it stands* Varya, *who bows.*)

Pishchik [amazed]: Think of that, now!

Charlotta: The end! (*Throws the robe at* Pishchik, *makes a curtsey, and runs out of the room.*)

Pishchik (hurries after her): The minx! . . . What a woman! What a woman! (*Goes out.*)

Lyubov Andreyevna: And Leonid still not here. What he is doing in town so long, I do not understand! It must be all over by now. Either the estate is sold, or the auction didn't take place—but why keep us in suspense so long!

Varya (trying to comfort her): Uncle has bought it, I am certain of that.

Trofimov (mockingly): Yes.

Varya: Great-aunt sent him power of attorney to buy it in her name and transfer the debt. She's doing it for Anya's sake. And I am sure, with God's help, Uncle will buy it.

Lyubov Andreyevna: Our great-aunt in Yaroslavl sent fifteen thousand to buy the estate in her name—she doesn't trust us—but that's not even enough to pay the interest. (*Covers her face with her hands.*) Today my fate will be decided, my fate . . .

Trofimov (teasing Varya*):* Madame Lopakhina!

Varya (angrily): Eternal student! Twice already you've been expelled from the university.

Lyubov Andreyevna: Why are you so cross, Varya? If he teases you about Lopakhin, what of it? Go ahead and marry Lopakhin if you want to. He's a nice man, he's interesting. And if you don't want to, don't. Nobody's forcing you, my pet.

Varya: To be frank, Mama dear, I regard this matter seriously. He is a good man. I like him.

Lyubov Andreyevna: Then marry him. I don't know what you're waiting for!

Varya: Mama, I can't propose to him myself. For the last two years everyone has been talking to me about him; everyone talks, but he is either silent or he jokes. I understand. He's getting rich, he's absorbed in business, he has no time for me. If I had some money, no matter how little, if it were only a hundred rubles, I'd drop everything and go far away. I'd go into a nunnery.

Trofimov: A blessing!

Varya (to Trofimov*):* A student ought to be intelligent! *(In a gentle tone, tearfully)* How homely you have grown, Petya, how old! *(To* Lyubov Andreyevna, *no longer crying)* It's just that I cannot live without work, Mama. I must be doing something every minute.

(Yasha *enters.*)

Yasha (barely able to suppress his laughter): Yepikhodov has broken a billiard cue! *(Goes out.)*

Varya: But why is Yepikhodov here? Who gave him permission to play billiards? I don't understand these people. . . . *(Goes out.)*

Lyubov Andreyevna: Don't tease her, Petya. You can see she's unhappy enough without that.

Trofimov: She's much too zealous, always meddling in other people's affairs. All summer long she's given Anya and me no peace—afraid a romance might develop. What business is it of hers? Besides, I've given no occasion for it, I am far removed from such banality. We are above love!

Lyubov Andreyevna: And I suppose I am beneath love. *(In great agitation.)* Why isn't Leonid here? If only I knew whether the estate had been sold or not! The disaster seems to me so incredible that I don't even know what to think, I'm lost. . . . I could scream this very instant . . . I could do something foolish. Save me, Petya. Talk to me, say something. . . .

Trofimov: Whether or not the estate is sold today—does it really matter? That's all done with long ago; there's no turning back, the path is overgrown. Be calm, my dear. One must not deceive oneself; at least once in one's life one ought to look the truth straight in the eye.

Lyubov Andreyevna: What truth? You can see where there is truth and where there isn't, but I seem to have lost my sight, I see nothing. You boldly settle all the important problems, but tell me, my dear boy, isn't it because you are young and have not yet had to suffer for a single one of your problems? You boldly look ahead, but isn't it because you neither see nor expect anything dreadful, since life is still hidden from your young eyes? You're bolder, more honest, deeper than we are, but think about it, be just a little bit magnanimous, and spare me. You see, I was born here, my mother and father lived here, and my grandfather. I love this house, without the cherry orchard my life has no meaning for me, and if it must be sold, then sell me with the orchard. . . . *(Embraces* Trofimov *and kisses him on the forehead.)* And my son was drowned here. . . . *(Weeps.)* Have pity on me, you good, kind man.

Trofimov: You know I feel for you with all my heart.

Lyubov Andreyevna: But that should have been said differently, quite differently. . . . *(Takes out her handkerchief and a telegram falls to the floor.)* My heart is heavy today, you can't imagine. It's so noisy here, my soul quivers at every sound, I tremble all over, and yet I can't go to my room. When I am alone the silence frightens me. Don't condemn me, Petya . . . I love you as if you were my own. I would gladly let you marry Anya, I swear it, only you must study, my dear, you must get your degree. You do nothing, fate simply tosses you from place to place—it's so strange. . . . Isn't that true? Isn't it? And you must do something about your beard, to make it grow somehow. . . . *(Laughs.)* You're so funny!

Trofimov (picks up the telegram): I have no desire to be an Adonis.

Lyubov Andreyevna: That's a telegram from Paris. I get them every day. One yesterday, one today. That wild man has fallen ill again, he's in trouble again. . . . He begs my forgiveness, implores me to come, and really, I ought to go to Paris to be near him. Your face is stern, Petya, but what can one do, my dear? What am I to do? He is ill, he's alone and unhappy, and who will look after him there, who will keep him from making mistakes, who will give him his medicine on time? And why hide it or keep silent, I love him, that's clear. I love him, love him. . . . It's a millstone round my neck, I'm sinking to the bottom with it, but I love that stone, I cannot live without it. *(Presses* Trofimov's *hand.)* Don't think badly of me, Petya, and don't say anything to me, don't say anything. . . .

Trofimov (through tears): For God's sake, forgive my frankness: you know that he robbed you!

Lyubov Andreyevna: No, no, no, you mustn't say such things! *(Covers her ears.)*

Trofimov: But he's a scoundrel! You're the only one who doesn't know it! He's a petty scoundrel, a nonentity—

Lyubov Andreyevna (angry, but controlling herself): You are twenty-six or twenty-seven years old, but you're still a schoolboy!

Trofimov: That may be!

Lyubov Andreyevna: You should be a man, at your age you ought to understand those who love. And you ought to be in love yourself. *(Angrily)* Yes, yes! It's not purity with you, it's simply prudery, you're a ridiculous crank, a freak—

Trofimov (horrified): What is she saying!

Lyubov Andreyevna: "I am above love!" You're not above love, you're just an addlepate, as Firs would say. Not to have a mistress at your age!

Trofimov (in horror): This is awful! What is she saying! . . . *(Goes quickly toward the ballroom.)* This is awful . . . I can't . . . I won't stay here. . . . *(Goes out, but immediately returns.)* All is over between us! *(Goes out to the hall.)*

Lyubov Andreyevna (calls after him): Petya, wait! You absurd creature, I was joking! Petya!

(In the hall there is the sound of someone running quickly downstairs and suddenly falling with a crash. Anya *and* Varya *scream, but a moment later laughter is heard.)*

Lyubov Andreyevna: What was that?

(Anya runs in.)

Anya (laughing): Petya fell down the stairs! *(Runs out.)*
Lyubov Andreyevna: What a funny boy that Petya is!

(The Stationmaster *stands in the middle of the ballroom and recites A. Tolstoy's "The Sinner." Everyone listens to him, but he has no sooner spoken a few lines than the sound of a waltz is heard from the hall and the recitation is broken off. They all dance.* Trofimov, Anya, Varya, *and* Lyubov Andreyevna *come in from the hall.)*

Lyubov Andreyevna: Come, Petya . . . come, you pure soul . . . please, forgive me. . . . Let's dance. . . . *(They dance.)*

(Anya and Varya *dance.* Firs *comes in, puts his stick by the side door.* Yasha *also comes into the drawing room and watches the dancers.)*

Yasha: What is it, grandpa?
Firs: I don't feel well. In the old days we used to have generals, barons, admirals, dancing at our balls, but now we send for the post-office clerk and the stationmaster, and even they are none too eager to come. Somehow I've grown weak. The late master, their grandfather, dosed everyone with sealing wax, no matter what ailed them. I've been taking sealing wax every day for twenty years or more; maybe that's what's kept me alive.
Yasha: You bore me, grandpa. *(Yawns.)* High time you croaked.
Firs: Ah, you . . . addlepate! *(Mumbles.)*

(Trofimov and Lyubov Andreyevna *dance from the ballroom into the drawing room.)*

Lyubov Andreyevna: Merci. I'll sit down a while. *(Sits.)* I'm tired.

(Anya comes in.)

Anya (excitedly): There was a man in the kitchen just now saying that the cherry orchard was sold today.
Lyubov Andreyevna: Sold to whom?
Anya: He didn't say. He's gone. *(Dances with* Trofimov; *they go into the ballroom.)*
Yasha: That was just some old man babbling. A stranger.
Firs: Leonid Andreich is not back yet, still hasn't come. And he's wearing the light, between-seasons overcoat; like enough he'll catch cold. Ah, when they're young they're green.
Lyubov Andreyevna: This is killing me. Yasha, go and find out who it was sold to.

Yasha: But that old man left long ago. *(Laughs.)*

Lyubov Andreyevna (slightly annoyed): Well, what are you laughing at? What are you so happy about?

Yasha: That Yepikhodov is very funny! Hopeless! Two-and-twenty Troubles.

Lyubov Andreyevna: Firs, if the estate is sold, where will you go?

Firs: Wherever you tell me to go, I'll go.

Lyubov Andreyevna: Why do you look like that? Aren't you well? You ought to go to bed.

Firs: Yes. . . . *(With a smirk.)* Go to bed, and without me who will serve, who will see to things? I'm the only one in the whole house.

Yasha (to Lyubov Andreyevna): Lyubov Andreyevna! Permit me to make a request, be so kind! If you go back to Paris again, do me the favor of taking me with you. It is positively impossible for me to stay here. *(Looking around, then in a low voice)* There's no need to say it, you can see for yourself, it's an uncivilized country, the people have no morals, and the boredom! The food they give us in the kitchen is unmentionable, and besides, there's this Firs who keeps walking about mumbling all sorts of inappropriate things. Take me with you, be so kind!

(Enter Pishchik*).*

Pishchik: May I have the pleasure of a waltz with you, fairest lady? *(Lyubov Andreyevna goes with him.)* I really must borrow a hundred and eighty rubles from you, my charmer . . . I really must. . . . *(Dancing.)* Just a hundred and eighty rubles. . . . *(They pass into the ballroom.)*

Yasha (softly sings): "Wilt thou know my soul's unrest . . ."

(In the ballroom a figure in a gray top hat and checked trousers is jumping about, waving its arms; there are shouts of "Bravo, Charlotta Ivanovna!")

Dunyasha (stopping to powder her face): The young mistress told me to dance—there are lots of gentlemen and not enough ladies—but dancing makes me dizzy, and my heart begins to thump. Firs Nikolayevich, the post-office clerk just said something to me that took my breath away.

(The music grows more subdued.)

Firs: What did he say to you?

Dunyasha: "You," he said, "are like a flower."

Yasha (yawns): What ignorance. . . . *(Goes out.)*

Dunyasha: Like a flower. . . . I'm such a delicate girl, I just adore tender words.

Firs: You'll get your head turned.

(Enter Yepikhodov.*)*

Yepikhodov: Avdotya Fyodorovna, you are not desirous of seeing me . . . I might also be some sort of insect. *(Sighs.)* Ah, life!

Dunyasha: What is it you want?

Yepikhodov: Indubitably, you may be right. *(Sighs.)* But, of course, if one looks at it from a point of view, then, if I may so express myself, and you will forgive my frankness, you have completely reduced me to a state of mind. I know my fate, every day some misfortune befalls me, but I have long since grown accustomed to that; I look upon my fate with a smile. But you gave me your word, and although I——

Dunyasha: Please, we'll talk about it later, but leave me in peace now. Just now I'm dreaming. . . . *(Plays with her fan.)*

Yepikhodov: Every day a misfortune, and yet, if I may so express myself, I merely smile, I even laugh.

(Varya enters from the ballroom.)

Varya: Are you still here, Semyon? What a disrespectful man you are, really! *(To* Dunyasha*)* Run along, Dunyasha. *(To* Yepikhodov*)* First you play billiards and break a cue, then you wander about the drawing room as if you were a guest.

Yepikhodov: You cannot, if I may so express myself, penalize me.

Varya: I am not penalizing you, I'm telling you. You do nothing but wander from one place to another, and you don't do your work. We keep a clerk, but for what, I don't know.

Yepikhodov (offended): Whether I work, or wander about, or eat, or play billiards, these are matters to be discussd only by persons of discernment, and my elders.

Varya: You dare say that to me! *(Flaring up)* You dare? You mean to say I have no discernment? Get out of here! This instant!

Yepikhodov (intimidated): I beg you to express yourself in a more delicate manner.

Varya (beside herself): Get out, this very instant! Get out! *(He goes to the door, she follows him.)* Two-and-twenty Troubles! Don't let me set eyes on you again!

Yepikhodov (goes out, his voice is heard behind the door): I shall lodge a complaint against you!

Varya: Oh, you're coming back? *(Seizes the stick left near the door by* Firs.*)* Come, come on. . . . Come, I'll show you. . . . Ah, so you're coming, are you? Then take that— *(Swings the stick just as* Lopakhin *enters.)*

Lopakhin: Thank you kindly.

Varya (angrily and mockingly): I beg your pardon.

Lopakhin: Not at all. I humbly thank you for your charming reception.

Varya: Don't mention it. *(Walks away, then looks back and gently asks.)* I didn't hurt you, did I?

Lopakhin: No, it's nothing. A huge bump coming up, that's all.

(Voices in the ballroom: "Lopakhin has come! Yermolai Alekseich!" *Pishchik enters.)*

Pishchik: As I live and breathe! *(Kisses* Lopakhin.*)* There is a whiff of cognac about you, dear soul. And we've been making merry here, too.

(Enter Lyubov Andreyevna.*)*

Lyubov Andreyevna: Is that you, Yermolai Alekseich? What kept you so long? Where's Leonid?

Lopakhin: Leonid Andreich arrived with me, he's coming . . .

Lyubov Andreyevna (agitated): Well, what happened? Did the sale take place? Tell me!

Lopakhin (embarrassed, fearing to reveal his joy): The auction was over by four o'clock. . . . We missed the train, had to wait till half past nine. *(Sighing heavily)* Ugh! My head is swimming. . . .

(Enter Gayev; he carries his purchases in one hand and wipes away his tears with the other.)

Lyubov Andreyevna: Lyonya, what happened? Well, Lyonya? *(Impatiently, through tears.)* Be quick, for God's sake!

Gayev (not answering her; simply waves his hand. To Firs, weeping): Here, take these. . . . There's anchovies, Kerch herrings. . . . I haven't eaten anything all day. . . . What I have been through! *(The click of billiard balls is heard through the open door to the billiard room, and Yasha's voice: "Seven and eighteen!" Gayev's expression changes, he is no longer weeping.)* I'm terribly tired. Firs, help me change. *(Goes through the ballroom to his own room, followed by Firs.)*

Pishchik: What happened at the auction? Come on, tell us!

Lyubov Andreyevna: Is the cherry orchard sold?

Lopakhin: It's sold.

Lyubov Andreyevna: Who bought it?

Lopakhin: I bought it. *(Pause)*

(Lyubov Andreyevna is overcome; she would fall to the floor if it were not for the chair and table near which she stands. Varya takes the keys from her belt and throws them on the floor in the middle of the drawing room and goes out.)

Lopakhin: I bought it! Kindly wait a moment, ladies and gentlemen, my head is swimming, I can't talk. . . . *(Laughs.)* We arrived at the auction, Deriganov was already there. Leonid Andreich had only fifteen thousand, and straight off Deriganov bid thirty thousand over and above the mortgage. I saw how the land lay, so I got into the fight and bid forty. He bid forty-five. I bid fifty-five. In other words, he kept raising it by five thousand, and I by ten. Well, it finally came to an end. I bid ninety thousand above the mortgage, and it was knocked down to me. The cherry orchard is now mine! Mine! *(Laughs uproariously.)* Lord! God in heaven! The cherry orchard is mine! Tell me I'm drunk, out of my mind, that I imagine it. . . . *(Stamps his feet.)* Don't laugh at me! If my father and my grandfather could only rise from their graves and see all that has happened, how their Yermolai, their beaten, half-literate Yermolai, who used to run about barefoot in winter, how that same Yermolai has bought an estate, the most beautiful estate in the whole world! I bought the estate where my father and grandfather were slaves, where they weren't even allowed in the kitchen. I'm asleep, this is just some dream of mine, it only seems to be. . . . It's the fruit of your imagination, hidden in the darkness of uncertainty. . . . *(Picks up the keys, smiling tenderly.)* She threw down the keys, wants to show that she's not mistress here anymore. . . . *(Jingles the keys.)* Well, no matter. *(The orchestra is heard tuning up.)* Hey, musicians, play, I want to hear you! Come on, everybody, and see how Yermolai Lopakhin will lay the ax to the cherry orchard, how the trees will fall to the ground! We're going to build summer cottages, and our grandsons and great-grandsons will see a new life here. . . . Music! Strike up!

(The orchestra plays. Lyubov Andreyevna *sinks into a chair and weeps bitterly.)*

Lopakhin *(reproachfully):* Why didn't you listen to me, why? My poor friend, there's no turning back now. *(With tears.)* Oh, if only all this could be over quickly, if somehow our discordant, unhappy life could be changed!

Pishchik *(takes him by the arm; speaks in an undertone):* She's crying. Let's go into the ballroom, let her be alone. . . . Come on. . . . *(Leads him into the ballroom.)*

Lopakhin: What's happened? Musicians, play so I can hear you! Let everything be as I want it! *(Ironically)* Here comes the new master, owner of the cherry orchard! *(Accidentally bumps into a little table, almost upsetting the candelabrum.)* I can pay for everything! *(Goes out with* Pishchik.)

(There is no one left in either the drawing room or the ballroom except Lyubov Andreyevna, *who sits huddled up and weeping bitterly. The music plays softly.* Anya *and* Trofimov *enter hurriedly.* Anya *goes to her mother and kneels before her.* Trofimov *remains in the doorway of the ballroom.)*

Anya: Mama! . . . Mama, you're crying! Dear, kind, good Mama, my beautiful one, I love you . . . I bless you. The cherry orchard is sold, it's gone, that's true, true, but don't cry, Mama, life is still before you, you still have your good, pure soul. . . . Come with me, come, darling, we'll go away from here! . . . We'll plant a new orchard, more luxuriant than this one. You will see it and understand; and joy, quiet, deep joy, will sink into your soul, like the evening sun, and you will smile, Mama! Come, darling, let us go. . . .

ACT IV

(The scene is the same as Act I. There are neither curtains on the windows nor pictures on the walls, and only a little furniture piled up in one corner, as if for sale. There is a sense of emptiness. Near the outer door, at the rear of the stage, suitcases, traveling bags, etc., are piled up. Through the open door on the left the voices of Varya *and* Anya *can be heard.* Lopakhin *stands waiting.* Yasha *is holding a tray with little glasses of champagne. In the hall,* Yepikhodov *is tying up a box. Off stage, at the rear, there is a hum of voices. It is the peasants who have come to say good-bye.* Gayev's *voice: "Thanks, brothers, thank you.")*

Yasha: The peasants have come to say good-bye. In my opinion, Yermolai Alekseich, peasants are good-natured, but they don't know much.

(The hum subsides. Lyubov Andreyevna *enters from the hall with* Gayev. *She is not crying, but she is pale, her face twitches, and she cannot speak.)*

Gayev: You gave them your purse, Lyuba. That won't do! That won't do!

Lyubov Andreyevna: I couldn't help it! I couldn't help it! *(They both go out.)*

Lopakhin (in the doorway, calls after them): Please, do me the honor of having a little glass at parting. I didn't think of bringing champagne from town, and at the station I found only one bottle. Please! What's the matter, friends, don't you want any? *(Walks away from the door.)* If I'd known that, I wouldn't have bought it. Well, then I won't drink any either. (Yasha *carefully sets the tray down on a chair.)* At least you have a glass, Yasha.

Yasha: To those who are departing! Good luck! *(Drinks.)* This champagne is not the real stuff, I can assure you.

Lopakhin: Eight rubles a bottle. *(Pause)* It's devilish cold in here.

Yasha: They didn't light the stoves today; it doesn't matter, since we're leaving. *(Laughs.)*

Lopakhin: Why are you laughing?

Yasha: Because I'm pleased.

Lopakhin: It's October, yet it's sunny and still outside, like summer. Good for building. *(Looks at his watch, then calls through the door.)* Bear in mind, ladies and gentlemen, only forty-six minutes till train time! That means leaving for the station in twenty minutes. Better hurry up!

*(*Trofimov *enters from outside wearing an overcoat.)*

Trofimov: Seems to me it's time to start. The carriages are at the door. What the devil has become of my rubbers? They're lost. *(Calls through the door.)* Anya, my rubbers are not here. I can't find them.

Lopakhin: I've got to go to Kharkov. I'm taking the same train you are. I'm going to spend the winter in Kharkov. I've been hanging around here with you, and I'm sick and tired of loafing. I can't live without work, I don't know what to do with my hands; they dangle in some strange way, as if they didn't belong to me.

Trofimov: We'll soon be gone, then you can take up your useful labors again.

Lopakhin: Here, have a little drink.

Trofimov: No, I don't want any.

Lopakhin: So you're off for Moscow?

Trofimov: Yes, I'll see them in town, and tomorrow I'll go to Moscow.

Lopakhin: Yes. . . . Well, I expect the professors haven't been giving any lectures: they're waiting for you to come!

Trofimov: That's none of your business.

Lopakhin: How many years is it you've been studying at the university?

Trofimov: Can't you think of something new? That's stale and flat. *(Looks for his rubbers.)* You know, we'll probably never see each other again, so allow me to give you one piece of advice at parting: don't wave your arms about! Get out of that habit—of arm-waving. And another thing, building cottages and counting on the summer residents in time becoming independant farmers—that's just another form of arm-waving. Well, when all's said and done, I'm fond of you anyway. You have fine, delicate fingers, like an artist; you have a fine delicate soul.

Lopakhin (embraces him): Good-bye, my dear fellow. Thank you for everything. Let me give you some money for the journey, if you need it.

Trofimov: What for? I don't need it.

Lopakhin: But you haven't any!

Trofimov: I have. Thank you. I got some money for a translation. Here it is in my pocket. *(Anxiously)* But where are my rubbers?

Varya (from the next room): Here, take the nasty things! *(Flings a pair of rubbers onto the stage.)*

Trofimov: What are you so cross about, Varya? Hm. . . . But these are not my rubbers.

Lopakhin: In the spring I sowed three thousand acres of poppies, and now I've made forty thousand rubles clear. And when my poppies were in bloom, what a picture it was! So, I'm telling you, I've made forty thousand, which means I'm offering you a loan because I can afford to. Why turn up your nose? I'm a peasant—I speak bluntly.

Trofimov: Your father was a peasant, mine was a pharmacist—which proves absolutely nothing. *(Lopakhin takes out his wallet.)* No, don't—even if you gave me two hundred thousand I wouldn't take it. I'm a free man. And everything that is valued so highly and held so dear by all of you, rich and poor alike, has not the slightest power over me—it's like a feather floating in the air. I can get along without you, I can pass you by, I'm strong and proud. Mankind is advancing toward the highest truth, the highest happiness attainable on earth, and I am in the front ranks!

Lopakhin: Will you get there?

Trofimov: I'll get there. *(Pause)* I'll either get there or I'll show others the way to get there.

(The sound of axes chopping down trees is heard in the distance.)

Lopakhin: Well, good-bye my dear fellow. It's time to go. We turn up our noses at one another, but life goes on just the same. When I work for a long time without stopping, my mind is easier, and it seems to me that I, too, know why I exist. But how many there are in Russia, brother, who exist nobody knows why. Well, it doesn't matter, that's not what makes the wheels go round. They say Leonid Andreich has taken a position in the bank, six thousand a year. . . . Only, of course, he won't stick it out, he's too lazy. . . .

Anya (in the doorway): Mama asks you not to start cutting down the cherry orchard until she's gone.

Trofimov: Yes, really, not to have had the tact . . . *(Goes out through the hall.)*

Lopakhin: Right away, right away. . . . Ach, what people. . . . *(Follows* Trofimov *out.)*

Anya: Has Firs been taken to the hospital?

Yasha: I told them this morning. They must have taken him.

Anya (to Yepikhodov, *who is crossing the room):* Semyon Panteleich, please find out if Firs has been taken to the hospital.

Yasha (offended): I told Yegor this morning. Why ask a dozen times?

Yepikhodov: It is my conclusive opinion that the venerable Firs is beyond repair; it's time he was gathered to his fathers. And I can only envy him. *(Puts a suitcase down on a hatbox and crushes it.)* There you are! Of course! I knew it! *(Goes out.)*

Yasha (mockingly): Two-and-twenty Troubles!

Varya (through the door): Has Firs been taken to the hospital?

Anya: Yes, he has.

Varya: Then why didn't they take the letter to the doctor?

Anya: We must send it on after them. . . . *(Goes out.)*

Varya (from the adjoining room): Where is Yasha? Tell him his mother has come to say good-bye to him.

Yasha (waves his hand): They really try my patience.

(Dunyasha has been fussing with the luggage; now that Yasha is alone she goes up to him.)

Dunyasha: You might give me one little look, Yasha. You're going away . . . leaving me. . . . *(Cries and throws herself on his neck.)*

Yasha: What's there to cry about? *(Drinks champagne.)* In six days I'll be in Paris again. Tomorrow we'll take the express, off we go, and that's the last you'll see of us. I can hardly believe it. *Vive la France!* This place is not for me, I can't live here. . . . It can't be helped. I've had enough of this ignorance—I'm fed up with it. *(Drinks champagne.)* What are you crying for? Behave yourself properly, then you won't cry.

Dunyasha (looks into a small mirror and powders her face): Send me a letter from Paris. You know, I loved you, Yasha, how I loved you! I'm such a tender creature, Yasha!

Yasha: Here they come. *(Busies himself with the luggage, humming softly.)*

(Enter Lyubov Andreyevna, Gayev, Charlotta Ivanovna.)

Gayev: We ought to be leaving. There's not much time now. *(Looks at Yasha.)* Who smells of herring?

Lyubov Andreyevna: In about ten minutes we should be getting into the carriages. *(Glances around the room.)* Good-bye, dear house, old grandfather. Winter will pass, spring will come, and you will no longer be here, they will tear you down. How much these walls have seen! *(Kisses her daughter warmly.)* My treasure, you are radiant, your eyes are sparkling like two diamonds. Are you glad? Very?

Anya: Very! A new life is beginning, Mama!

Gayev (cheerfully): Yes, indeed, everything is all right now. Before the cherry orchard was sold we were all worried and miserable, but afterward, when the question was finally settled once and for all, everybody calmed down and felt quite cheerful. . . . I'm in a bank now, a financier . . . cue ball into the center . . . and you, Lyuba, say what you like, you look better, no doubt about it.

Lyubov Andreyevna: Yes. My nerves are better, that's true. *(Her hat and coat are handed to her.)* I sleep well. Carry out my things, Yasha, it's time. *(To*

Anya) My little girl, we shall see each other soon. . . . I shall go to Paris
and live there on the money your great-aunt sent to buy the estate—
long live Auntie!—but that money won't last long.

Anya: You'll come back soon, Mama, soon . . . won't you? I'll study hard and
pass my high-school examinations, and then I can work and help you.
We'll read all sorts of books together, Mama. . . . Won't we? *(Kisses her
mother's hand.)* We'll read in the autumn evenings, we'll read lots of
books, and a new and wonderful world will open up before us. . . .
(Dreaming) Mama, come back. . . .

Lyubov Andreyevna: I'll come, my precious. *(Embraces her.)*

(Enter Lopakhin. Charlotta Ivanovna *is softly humming a song.)*

Gayev: Happy Charlotta: she's singing!

Charlotta (picks up a bundle and holds it like a baby in swaddling clothes): Bye,
baby, bye. . . . *(A baby's crying is heard, "Wah! Wah!")* Be quiet, my darling, my dear little boy. *("Wah! Wah!")* I'm so sorry for you! *(Throws the
bundle down.)* You will find me a position, won't you? I can't go on like
this.

Lopakhin: We'll find something, Charlotta Ivanovna, don't worry.

Gayev: Everyone is leaving us, Varya's going away . . . all of a sudden nobody
needs us.

Charlotta: I have nowhere to go in town. I must go away. *(Hums.)* It doesn't
matter . . .

(Enter Pishchik.)

Lopakhin: Nature's wonder!

Pishchik (panting): Ugh! Let me catch my breath. . . . I'm exhausted. . . . My
esteemed friends. . . . Give me some water. . . .

Gayev: After money, I suppose? Excuse me, I'm fleeing from temptation. . . .
(Goes out.)

Pishchik: It's a long time since I've been to see you . . . fairest lady. . . . *(To*
Lopakhin) So you're here. . . . Glad to see you, you intellectual
giant. . . . Here . . . take it . . . four hundred rubles . . . I still owe you
eight hundred and forty . . .

Lopakhin (shrugs his shoulders in bewilderment): I must be dreaming. . . .
Where did you get it?

Pishchik: Wait . . . I'm hot. . . . A most extraordinary event. Some Englishmen came to my place and discovered some kind of white clay on my
land. *(To* Lyubov Andreyevna) And four hundred for you . . . fairest,
most wonderful lady. . . . *(Hands her the money.)* The rest later. *(Takes a
drink of water.)* Just now a young man in the train was saying that a certain . . . great philosopher recommends jumping off roofs. . . . "Jump!"
he says, and therein lies the whole problem. *(In amazement)* Think of
that, now! . . . Water!

Lopakhin: Who were those Englishmen?

Pishchik: I leased them the tract of land with the clay on it for twenty-four
years. . . . And now, excuse me, I have no time . . . I must be trotting

along . . . I'm going to Znoikov's . . . to Kardamanov's . . . I owe everybody. *(Drinks.)* Keep well . . . I'll drop in on Thursday . . .

Lyubov Andreyevna: We're just moving into town, and tomorrow I go abroad . . .

Pishchik: What? *(Alarmed)* Why into town? That's why I see the furniture . . . suitcases. . . . Well, never mind. . . . *(Through tears)* Never mind. . . . Men of the greatest intellect, those Englishmen. . . . Never mind. . . . Be happy . . . God will help you. . . . Never mind. . . . Everything in this world comes to an end. . . . *(Kisses* Lyubov Andreyevna's *hand.)* And should the news reach you that my end has come, just remember this old horse, and say: "There once lived a certain Semyonov-Pishchik, God rest his soul." . . . Splendid weather. . . . Yes. . . . *(Goes out greatly disconcerted, but immediately returns and speaks from the doorway.)* Dashenka sends her regards. *(Goes out.)*

Lyubov Andreyevna: Now we can go. I am leaving with two things on my mind. First—that Firs is sick. *(Looks at her watch.)* We still have about five minutes. . . .

Anya: Mama, Firs has already been taken to the hospital. Yasha sent him there this morning.

Lyubov Andreyevna: My second concern is Varya. She's used to getting up early and working, and now, with no work to do, she's like a fish out of water. She's grown pale and thin, and cries all the time, poor girl. . . . *(Pause)* You know very well, Yermolai Alekseich, that I dreamed of marrying her to you, and everything pointed to your getting married. *(Whispers to* Anya, *who nods to* Charlotta, *and they both go out.)* She loves you, you are fond of her, and I don't know—I don't know why it is you seem to avoid each other. I can't understand it!

Lopakhin: To tell you the truth, I don't understand it myself. The whole thing is strange, somehow. . . . If there's still time, I'm ready right now. . . . Let's finish it up—and *basta*, but without you I feel I'll never be able to propose to her.

Lyubov Andreyevna: Splendid! After all, it only takes a minute. I'll call her in at once. . . .

Lopakhin: And we even have the champagne. *(Looks at the glasses.)* Empty! Somebody's already drunk it. *(Yasha coughs.)* That's what you call lapping it up.

Lyubov Andreyevna (animatedly): Splendid! We'll leave you. . . . Yasha, *allez!* I'll call her. . . . *(At the door)* Varya, leave everything and come here. Come! *(Goes out with* Yasha.)

Lopakhin (looking at his watch): Yes. . . . *(Pause)*

(Behind the door there is smothered laughter and whispering; finally, Varya *enters.)*

Varya (looking over the luggage for a long time): Strange, I can't seem to find it . . .

Lopakhin: What are you looking for?

Varya: I packed it myself, and I can't remember . . . *(Pause)*

Lopakhin: Where are you going now, Varya Mikhailovna?

Varya: I? To the Ragulins'. . . . I've agreed to go there to look after the house . . . as a sort of housekeeper.

Lopakhin: At Yashnevo? That would be about seventy versts from here. *(Pause)* Well, life in this house has come to an end. . . .

Varya (examining the luggage): Where can it be? . . . Perhaps I put it in the trunk. . . . Yes, life in this house has come to an end . . . there'll be no more . . .

Lopakhin: And I'm off for Kharkov . . . by the next train. I have a lot to do. I'm leaving Yepikhodov here . . . I've taken him on.

Varya: Really!

Lopakhin: Last year at this time it was already snowing, if you remember, but now it's still and sunny. It's cold though. . . . About three degrees of frost.

Varya: I haven't looked. *(Pause)* And besides, our thermometer's broken. *(Pause)*

(A voice from the yard calls: "Yermolai Alekseich!")

Lopakhin (as if he had been waiting for a long time for the call): Coming! *(Goes out quickly.)*

(Varya sits on the floor, lays her head on a bundle of clothes, and quietly sobs. The door opens and Lyubov Andreyevna *enters cautiously.)*

Lyubov Andreyevna: Well? *(Pause)* We must be going.

Varya (no longer crying, dries her eyes): Yes, it's time, Mama dear. I can get to the Ragulins' today, if only we don't miss the train.

Lyubov Andreyevna (in the doorway): Anya, put your things on!

(Enter Anya, *then* Gayev *and* Charlotta Ivanovna. Gayev *wears a warm overcoat with a hood. The servants and coachmen come in.* Yepikhodov *bustles about the luggage.)*

Lyubov Andreyevna: Now we can be on our way.

Anya (joyfully): On our way!

Gayev: My friends, my dear, cherished friends! Leaving this house forever, can I pass over in silence, can I refrain from giving utterance, as we say farewell, to those feelings that now fill my whole being——

Anya (imploringly): Uncle!

Varya: Uncle dear, don't!

Gayev (forlornly): Double the rail off the white to center table . . . yellow into the side pocket. . . . I'll be quiet. . . .

(Enter Trofimov, *then* Lopakhin.)*

Trofimov: Well, ladies and gentlemen, it's time to go!

Lopakhin: Yepikhodov, my coat!

Lyubov Andreyevna: I'll sit here just one more minute. It's as though I had never before seen what the walls of this house were like, what the ceilings were like, and now I look at them hungrily, with such tender love . . .

Gayev: I remember when I was six years old, sitting on this window sill on Whitsunday, watching my father going to church . . .

Lyubov Andreyevna: Have they taken all the things?

Lopakhin: Everything, I think. *(Puts on his overcoat.)* Yepikhodov, see that everything is in order.

Yepikhodov (in a hoarse voice): Rest assured, Yermolai Alekseich!

Lopakhin: What's the matter with your voice?

Yepikhodov: Just drank some water . . . must have swallowed something.

Yasha (contemptuously): What ignorance!

Lyubov Andreyevna: When we go—there won't be a soul left here. . . .

Lopakhin: Till spring.

Varya (pulls an umbrella out of a bundle as though she were going to hit someone; Lopakhin pretends to be frightened): Why are you—I never thought of such a thing!

Trofimov: Ladies and gentlemen, let's get into the carriages—it's time now! The train will soon be in!

Varya: Petya, there they are—your rubbers, by the suitcase. *(Tearfully)* And what dirty old things they are!

Trofimov (putting on his rubbers): Let's go, ladies and gentlemen!

Gayev (extremely upset, afraid of bursting into tears): The train . . . the station . . . Cross table to the center, double the rail . . . on the white into the corner.

Lyubov Andreyevna: Let us go!

Gayev: Are we all here? No one in there? *(Locks the side door on the left.)* There are some things stored in there, we must lock up. Let's go!

Anya: Good-bye, house! Good-bye, old life!

Trofimov: Hail to the new life! *(Goes out with* Anya.*)*

(Varya *looks around the room and slowly goes out.* Yasha *and* Charlotta *with her dog go out.)*

Lopakhin: And so, till spring. Come along, my friends. . . . Till we meet! *(Goes out.)*

(Lyubov Andreyevna *and* Gayev *are left alone. As though they had been waiting for this, they fall onto each other's necks and break into quiet, restrained sobs, afraid of being heard.)*

Gayev (in despair): My sister, my sister. . . .

Lyubov Andreyevna: Oh, my dear, sweet, lovely orchard! . . . My life, my youth, my happiness, good-bye! . . . Good-bye!

Anya's voice (gaily calling): Mama!

Trofimov's voice (gay and excited): Aa-oo!

Lyubov Andreyevna: One last look at these walls, these windows. . . . Mother loved to walk about in this room. . . .

Gayev: My sister, my sister!

Anya's voice: Mama!

Trofimov's voice: Aa-oo!

Lyubov Andreyevna: We're coming! *(They go out.)*

(The stage is empty. There is the sound of doors being locked, then of the carriages driving away. It grows quiet. In the stillness, there is the dull thud of an ax on a tree, a forlorn, melancholy sound. Footsteps are heard. From the door on the right Firs *appears. He is dressed as always in a jacket and white waistcoat, and wears slippers. He is ill.)*

Firs *(goes to the door and tries the handle):* Locked. They have gone. . . . *(Sits down on the sofa.)* They've forgotten me. . . . Never mind . . . I'll sit here awhile. . . . I expect Leonid Andreich hasn't put on his fur coat and has gone off in his overcoat. *(Sighs anxiously.)* And I didn't see to it. . . . When they're young, they're green! *(Mumbles something which cannot be understood.)* I'll lie down awhile. . . . There's no strength left in you, nothing's left, nothing. . . . Ach, you . . . addlepate! *(Lies motionless.)*

(A distant sound is heard that seems to come from the sky, the sound of a snapped string mournfully dying away. A stillness falls, and nothing is heard but the thud of the ax on a tree far away in the orchard.)

——————— **ANTON CHEKHOV** ———————
www   *(1860–1904)* **Web**

Anton Chekhov grew up in poverty and eventually trained in Moscow to be a physician. Medicine, however, only provided him with a living; drama and fiction provided him a passion. He wrote some hundreds of short stories and several plays of international influence: *The Seagull* (1896), *Uncle Vanya* (1897), *Three Sisters* (1901), and *The Cherry Orchard* (1903).

TOPICS FOR CRITICAL THINKING

1. Consider the importance of the Act One set of *The Cherry Orchard* and Chekhov's description of both the climate and the orchard. Why is Chekhov so specific about these matters? How do they relate to the action of the play? Compare the opening set to the play's final stage picture, with old Firs standing alone on a bare stage.

2. The play presents the possibility that three couples might marry: Lopakhin and Varya, Anya and Trofimov, and Dunyasha—madly in love with Yasha—and Yepikhodov, who has proposed to Dunyasha before the play begins. How viable are these relationships by the end of the play? What inferences might be made about the apparent results of these relationships?

3. Among other things, Trofimov is a perpetual student given to philosophical rumblings about society, class structure, and other topics. Review his criticism of the intelligentsia and present urban conditions in Act Two. What do they say about both the character and the social climate of the play?

4. Near the end of Act Two, Trofimov maintains that "all Russia is our orchard." If this metaphor is accurate, what does it tell us about the state of Russia at the beginning of the twentieth century?

5. Compare Lopakhin's and Lyubov's reactions to the news that Lopakhin has purchased the orchard at auction. What can you infer about their differing responses?

6. What predictions might we make about the future for the play's central characters? Will Gayev make a successful banker? Will Lyubov ever find happiness? Will Trofi-

mov and Anya find happiness? What is the significance of the late announcement that "some kind of white clay" has been discovered on Piskchik's property?

7. Why is Firs left behind?

8. Review the visual and aural motifs in the play. What do they add to the play's action, characterization, or representation of dramatic conflict? How do they enhance our understanding of *The Cherry Orchard*?

TOPIC FOR CRITICAL WRITING

Take up the debate between Stanislavsky and Chekhov about the play's similarity to or difference from the more traditional genres of tragedy and comedy. Which of these two positions seems more accurate, and why? Is the play closer to tragedy or comedy?

Illustrate your answer by adducing traditional elements of these forms, then use the text of the play to support your position.

Critical Perspective: On Social Class in *The Cherry Orchard*

"I think the issue of class is fantastically important . . . that the people who owned most of the land in Chekhov's plays did not live there. Now that's an important *fact*, a material fact which leads to relationships that are on the one hand fantastically strong and passionate, because there's an 'over there' immediately, there's a Moscow . . . and on the other hand there's a fury because they're . . . exploited places."

> —Adrian Noble, director of a production of *The Cherry Orchard* by the
> Royal Shakespeare Company, Stratford-upon-Avon, England, 1995

Critical Perspective: On Repression in *The Cherry Orchard*

"I don't agree that the play is only about a lot of couples wanting to get it off with each other . . . I think it's about the repression of passion of all kinds (not only sexual) . . . Repression . . . implies a kind of passivity in the face of life . . . Love, sex, passion, freedom, change, risk."

> —Mary-Ann Gifford, director of a production of
> *The Cherry Orchard* by the New Theatre, Sydney, Australia, 1996

Critical Perspective: On Chekhov's Aesthetic Innovations

"Chekhov did not foresee, as he struggled with illness to complete the play, that *The Cherry Orchard* would be recognized as new drama. Comedy has become cruel enough to deal with tragic situations; dramatic silences (like musical rests) have acquired a parity with utterances; . . . Blurring boundaries between genres, between comedy and tragedy, between prose narrative and drama, introducing musical values—not just background music as a commentary, but also a musical structure of recurrent motifs, of an end which mirrors the beginning—Chekhov's *The Cherry Orchard* became a progenitor of radical theatre."

—Donald Rayfield, *Understanding Chekhov* (1999)

Susan Glaspell and Eugene O'Neill: Toward an American Avant-Garde

In the second decade of the twentieth century, Susan Glaspell and Eugene O'Neill were young writers honing the experimental edge of a still undistinguished American drama. While studying literature and writing mostly prose at the University of Iowa, Glaspell met her husband George Cram "Jig" Cook in 1908 and accompanied him to Chicago, where he became involved with the Little Theatre opened by Maurice Browne in 1912. Prior to this time, Glaspell had worked as both a reporter and novelist. After a brief stint in Europe, she and her husband returned to America, settling in Cape Cod, Massachusetts, and in 1915 they began staging amateur theatrical productions as the Provincetown Players.

A year later, the twenty-seven-year-old O'Neill, son of celebrated actor James O'Neill, joined the Players, who had decided to produce his one-act play *Bound East for Cardiff* (1916), written two years earlier and the first of several plays influenced by his experiences as a sailor. Up to this point in his young life, O'Neill had led a checkered past that included his expulsion from Princeton at the end of his freshman year, a premature marriage in 1909 to Kathleen Jenkins and divorce some two years later, work as a sailor in Central and South America, and—most devastating of all—prolonged periods of alcoholism. Louis Sheaffer, a distinguished biographer of O'Neill, actually poses two possible readings of O'Neill's dismissal from Princeton: failing grades in several classes that led to his being "dropped" from the school and O'Neill's own explanation that he went too far with "general hell-raising." The two were obviously connected, leading his father to exclaim in reference to O'Neill and his brother Jamie: "God deliver me from my children!"

By the time of his death in the summer of 1920, the elder O'Neill's prayer was in several respects answered. For by 1917, O'Neill and the Provincetown Players had successfully moved from Massachusetts to Greenwich Village in New York. In their first years of existence, the Players were known for their productions of new one-act plays, with Glaspell and O'Neill emerging as the company's principal writers. On February 3, 1920, the Players staged O'Neill's first full-length play *Beyond the Horizon*, a Broadway production witnessed by his parents. As Sheaffer describes it, a "show-wise audience" of critics and "theater people" assembled at the Morosco Theater for a matinee performance. Seated in a box, James O'Neill, who would suffer a stroke a week later and succumb to cancer the following August, was moved to a state of "agitated happiness" at his son's achievement. At times "tears of joy" rolled down his face, though he tried to conceal his response afterward with queries about the drama's emotional seriousness. His son was disappointed, however, by the polite applause of the audience, which seemed to suggest the production's failure.

The drama reviews the next day indicated otherwise: O'Neill and the Provincetown Players were a "triumph." The *New York Times* hailed the play as "memorable" and "significant." Writing in *The Nation* on February 21, Ludwig Lewisohn praised the play's naturalism, which "establishes America's kinship with the stage of the modern world." Theater historian Barnard Hewitt exclaimed that "with Eugene O'Neill the American drama came of age." And, quoting yet another reviewer of the play, Louis Sheaffer puts the matter of O'Neill's contributions in the 1920s perhaps most succinctly: "Before O'Neill the U.S. had theater; after O'Neill, it had drama." The Pulitzer Prize committee agreed, awarding O'Neill and *Beyond the Horizon* the prize for 1920; and in 1936 the Nobel Prize committee followed suit, making O'Neill the first American playwright to be so internationally celebrated.

Glaspell's *Trifles* (1916) and such earlier one-acts as *Suppressed Desires* (1915) established the foundation for the Players' success in New York, and she went on to write such influential full-length works as *Alison's House* (1930), which won a Pulitzer Prize. All of these plays, much like O'Neill's major works of the 1920s—*The Emperor Jones* (1920), *Desire Under the Elms* (1924), *Strange Interlude* (1927), and *Mourning Becomes Electra* (1928)—reveal the influence of one of the most widely discussed intellectual issues of the time: psychoanalysis. *Suppressed Desires*, in fact, pokes fun at the prominence of the theories of Sigmund Freud in American culture. As contemporary scholar Joel Pfister contends, psychoanalysis was a veritable "mass-culture phenomenon" in 1910s and 1920s America, discussed in scholarly tomes and popular magazines alike. It was a major topic of conversation among the artists and intellectuals that comprised the Provincetown Players; so, not surprisingly, psychoanalytic theory vitally informed the work of the company.

So did other intensely debated topics of the time, especially feminism and socialism. *Trifles* is often regarded as a prime example of the former, for at least two reasons. First, like Ibsen's *A Doll House* and Sophie Treadwell's 1928 play *Machinal*, *Trifles* scrutinizes marriage and the potential for unhappiness inherent in it; second, it illustrates the chauvinism of male investigators whose condescension toward women renders them unable to "read" a murder scene correctly. While *A Doll House* involves the dissolution of an unhappy marriage, both *Trifles* and *Machinal* are based on real cases of desperate wives murdering their husbands. Both plays employ the set in an emotionally resonant way,

Glaspell's special emphasis on the birdcage, for example. Mrs. Peters is quick to notice that one of its hinges is broken, prompting Mrs. Hale's line, "Looks as if someone must have been rough with it." Of course, they inevitably discover the former occupant of the cage, a bird with a broken neck, inside Minnie Wright's sewing box, and become immediately aware of why she might have broken her own husband's neck in revenge. In a lonely life of rough treatment and emotional starvation, a woman must seek affection and companionship where she can.

In O'Neill's *The Emperor Jones*, the emotional life of the protagonist Brutus Jones is gradually revealed as the play's action moves deeper into the tropical jungle where the action is set. To stage such emotions—indeed such deep-seated fears—O'Neill combines highly emotive character development with **expressionist** stage techniques. Driven theoretically by psychoanalytic insights, expressionism was developed by dramatists and filmmakers in Germany during the second and third decades of the twentieth century. As its name suggests, expressionism does not strive to create a photograph in the way that Ibsen's sets duplicate a middle class drawing room or parlor. In expressionist art, the mimetic or "objective" photograph is replaced by a "subjective" perspective; in other words, expressionists try to recreate reality not as it is but as the character perceives it. So, in expressionist film, if a character wakes up in the morning with a hangover, the shot capturing his condition might be overexposed or out of focus—or, in one famous shot in a silent film by the German director F. W. Murnau, a man sees multiple pictures of his wife circling before his eyes as she speaks to him. Form expresses emotional state or state of mind.

For O'Neill, this means, among other strategies, beginning the distant beat of tom-toms in Scene One "at a rate exactly corresponding to normal pulse—72 to the minute" and then accelerating the beat as Jones becomes more anxious and, finally, terrified. It also means the appearance in Scene Two of the shapeless "Little Formless Fears" as Jones flees deeper into the jungle. Even their movement or blocking is carefully detailed in O'Neill's stage directions to help represent the growing terror Jones experiences.

As the play progresses, the influence of Swiss psychoanalyst Carl Jung on O'Neill becomes apparent. Jung, who postulated the existence of a "collective," even racial unconscious, serves as the source for O'Neill's inclusion of the slave auction in Scene Five. We are to understand the auction as occurring in Jones's troubled mind, just as Jones's "fixed and stony expression" and "obsessed glare" at the beginning of Scene Seven register his mental turmoil. Both the ticket-buying public and major drama reviewers heralded the experimental form of the play a triumph. Writing for the *New York Globe*, Kenneth Macgowan praised O'Neill for transcending "the traditional forms of our drama" to create a "study of personal and racial psychology of real imaginative truth." Reviewing *The Emperor Jones* for the *Times*, Alexander Woollcott agreed, calling it "an extraordinarily striking and dramatic study of panic fear."

Expressionism, again, one of several forms associated with a modernist avant-garde in Europe, is a form within which psychical states, fears, and desires were realized on stage. *The Emperor Jones* offers one distinguished example of this form on the American stage; others include Treadwell's *Machinal* discussed above and Elmer Rice's 1923 play *The Adding Machine*. By the 1930s, other expressionist stage devices—heavy makeup, lighting effects, raked stages, and sharply angled sets—helped create similar effects in a series of popular horror films like *Frankenstein* (1931) and *Dracula* (1931). Equally important, *The Emperor Jones* propelled Eugene O'Neill into the forefront of American drama and helped establish the reputation of the Provincetown Players as one of America's most important theatrical companies.

Notes on Production

One further method of representing Brutus Jones's terror was not met with universal approval: namely, his heavy nonstandard dialect and a kind of knee-knocking trepidation that reminded Charles Gilpin, the black actor who first played Jones in New York, of the worst sort of stereotypes of African Americans. Mark Twain's Jim in *Adventures of Huckleberry Finn* (1884) was similarly superstitious and wide-eyed in terror, and Gilpin—whose performance was highly celebrated in the title role—grew to despise the potentially racist implications of such a role. He also objected to the word *nigger* in the play and began to make improvisational revisions to the script on stage, drawing O'Neill's ire and ultimately leading to his loss of the role, one that had made him both famous and financially secure.

O'Neill later called on his friend Paul Robeson, a graduate of Rutgers and a sports celebrity, to interrupt his study of the law to play Brutus Jones and star in his play *All God's Chillun Got Wings*. Robeson repeated his role in a 1933 film version of *The Emperor Jones*, which is widely available in video stores.

∽∽∽

Susan Glaspell

Trifles   (1916)

CHARACTERS

George Henderson, County Attorney
Henry Peters, Sheriff
Lewis Hale, A Neighboring Farmer
Mrs. Peters
Mrs. Hale

Scene: *The kitchen in the now abandoned farmhouse of* John Wright, *a gloomy kitchen, and left without having been put in order—unwashed pans under the sink, a loaf of bread outside the breadbox, a dish towel on the table—other signs of incompleted work. At the rear the outer door opens and the* Sheriff *comes in followed by the* County Attorney *and* Hale. *The* Sheriff *and* Hale *are men in middle life, the* County Attorney *is a young man; all are much bundled up and go at once to the stove. They are followed by two women—the* Sheriff's *wife first; she is a slight wiry woman, a thin nervous face. Mrs. Hale is larger and would ordinarily be called more comfortable looking, but she is disturbed now and looks fearfully about as she enters. The women have come in slowly, and stand close together near the door.*

County Attorney (Rubbing his hands.): This feels good. Come up to the fire, ladies.

Mrs. Peters (After taking a step forward.): I'm not—cold.

Sheriff (Unbuttoning his overcoat and stepping away from the stove as if to mark the beginning of official business.): Now, Mr. Hale, before we move things about, you explain to Mr. Henderson just what you saw when you came here yesterday morning.

County Attorney: By the way, has anything been moved? Are things just as you left them yesterday?

Sheriff (Looking about.): It's just the same. When it dropped below zero last night I thought I'd better send Frank out this morning to make a fire for us—no use getting pneumonia with a big case on, but I told him not to touch anything except the stove—and you know Frank.

County Attorney: Somebody should have been left here yesterday.

Sheriff: Oh—yesterday. When I had to send Frank to Morris Center for that man who went crazy—I want you to know I had my hands full yesterday, I knew you could get back from Omaha by today and as long as I went over everything here myself—

County Attorney: Well, Mr. Hale, tell just what happened when you came here yesterday morning.

Hale: Harry and I had started to town with a load of potatoes. We came along the road from my place and as I got here I said, "I'm going to see if I can't get John Wright to go in with me on a party telephone." I spoke to Wright about it once before and he put me off, saying folks talked too much anyway, and all he asked was peace and quiet—I guess you know about how much he talked himself; but I thought maybe if I went to the house and talked about it before his wife, though I said to Harry that I didn't know as what his wife wanted made much difference to John—

County Attorney: Let's talk about that later, Mr. Hale. I do want to talk about that, but tell now just what happened when you got to the house.

Hale: I didn't hear or see anything; I knocked at the door, and still it was all quiet inside. I knew they must be up, it was past eight o'clock. So I knocked again, and I thought I heard somebody say, "Come in." I wasn't sure, I'm not sure yet, but I opened the door—this door *(Indicating the door by which the two women are still standing)* and there in that rocker— *(Pointing to it.)* sat Mrs. Wright.

(They all look at the rocker.)

County Attorney: What—was she doing?

Hale: She was rockin' back and forth. She had her apron in her hand and was kind of—pleating it.

County Attorney: And how did she—look?

Hale: Well, she looked queer.

County Attorney: How do you mean—queer?

Hale: Well, as if she didn't know what she was going to do next. And kind of done up.

County Attorney: How did she seem to feel about your coming?

Hale: Why, I don't think she minded—one way or other. She didn't pay much attention. I said, "How do, Mrs. Wright, it's cold, ain't it?" And she said, "Is it?"—and went on kind of pleating at her apron. Well, I was surprised; she didn't ask me to come up to the stove, or to set down, but just sat there, not even looking at me, so I said, "I want to see John." And then she—laughed. I guess you would call it a laugh. I thought of Harry and the team outside, so I said a little sharp: "Can't I see John?" "No," she says, kind o' dull like. "Ain't he home?" says I. "Yes," says she, "he's home." "Then why can't I see him?" I asked her, out of patience. "Cause he's dead," says she. "*Dead?*" says I. She just nodded her head, not getting a bit excited, but rockin' back and forth. "Why—where is he?" says I, not knowing what to say. She just pointed upstairs—like that *(Himself pointing to the room above.)* I got up, with the idea of going up there. I walked from there to here—then I says, "Why, what did he die of?" "He died of a rope round his neck," says she, and just went on pleatin' at her apron. Well, I went out and called Harry. I thought I might—need help. We went up-stairs and there he was lyin'—

County Attorney: I think I'd rather have you go into that upstairs where you can point it all out. Just go on now with the rest of the story.

Hale: Well, my first thought was to get that rope off. It looked . . . *(Stops, his face twitches.)* . . . but Harry, he went up to him, and he said, "No, he's dead all right, and we'd better not touch anything." So we went back down stairs. She was still sitting that same way. "Has anybody been notified?" I asked. "No," says she, unconcerned. "Who did this, Mrs. Wright?" said Harry. He said it businesslike—and she stopped pleatin' of her apron. "I don't know," she says. "You don't *know?*" says Harry. "No," says she. "Weren't you sleepin' in the bed with him?" says Harry. "Yes," says she, "but I was on the inside." "Somebody slipped a rope round his neck and strangled him and you didn't wake up?" says Harry. "I didn't wake up," she said after him. We must 'a looked as if we didn't see how that could be, for after a minute she said, "I sleep sound." Harry was going to ask her more questions but I said maybe we ought to let her tell her story first to the coroner, or the sheriff, so Harry went fast as he could to Rivers' place, where there's a telephone.

County Attorney: And what did Mrs. Wright do when she knew that you had gone for the coroner?

Hale: She moved from that chair to this one over here *(Pointing to a small chair in the corner.)* and just sat there with her hands held together and looking down. I got a feeling that I ought to make some conversation, so I said I had come in to see if John wanted to put in a telephone, and at that she started to laugh, and then she stopped and looked at me—

scared. (*The County Attorney, who has had his notebook out, makes a note.*) I dunno, maybe it wasn't scared. I wouldn't like to say it was. Soon Harry got back, and then Dr. Lloyd came, and you, Mr. Peters, and so I guess that's all I know that you don't.

County Attorney (Looking around.): I guess we'll go upstairs first— and then out to the barn and around there. (*To the* Sheriff) You're convinced that there was nothing important here—nothing that would point to any motive.

Sheriff: Nothing here but kitchen things.

(*The* County Attorney, *after again looking around the kitchen, opens the door of a cupboard closet. He gets up on a chair and looks on a shelf. Pulls his hand away, sticky.*)

County Attorney: Here's a nice mess.

(*The women draw nearer.*)

Mrs. Peters (To the other woman.): Oh, her fruit; it did freeze. (*To the County Attorney*) She worried about that when it turned so cold. She said the fire'd go out and her jars would break.

Sheriff: Well, can you beat the women! Held for murder and worryin' about her preserves.

County Attorney: I guess before we're through she may have something more serious than preserves to worry about.

Hale: Well, women are used to worrying over trifles.

(*The two women move a little closer together.*)

County Attorney (With the gallantry of a young politician.): And yet, for all their worries, what would we do without the ladies? (*The women do not unbend. He goes to the sink, takes a dipperful of water from the pail and, pouring it into a basin, washes his hands. Starts to wipe them on the roller towel, turns it for a cleaner place.*) Dirty towels! (*Kicks his foot against the pans under the sink.*) Not much of a housekeeper, would you say, ladies?

Mrs. Hale (Stiffly.): There's a great deal of work to be done on a farm.

County Attorney: To be sure. And yet (*With a little bow to her*) I know there are some Dickson county farmhouses which do not have such roller towels.

(*He gives it a pull to expose its full length again.*)

Mrs. Hale: Those towels get dirty awful quick. Men's hands aren't always as clean as they might be.

County Attorney: Ah, loyal to your sex, I see. But you and Mrs. Wright were neighbors. I suppose you were friends, too.

Mrs. Hale (Shaking her head.): I've not seen much of her of late years. I've not been in this house—it's more than a year.

County Attorney: And why was that? You didn't like her?

Mrs. Hale: I liked her all well enough. Farmers' wives have their hands full, Mr. Henderson. And then——

County Attorney: Yes—?

Mrs. Hale (Looking about.): It never seemed a very cheerful place.

County Attorney: No—it's not cheerful. I shouldn't say she had the home-making instinct.

Mrs. Hale: Well, I don't know as Wright had, either.

County Attorney: You mean that they didn't get on very well?

Mrs. Hale: No, I don't mean anything. But I don't think a place'd be any cheerfuller for John Wright's being in it.

County Attorney: I'd like to talk more of that a little later. I want to get the lay of things upstairs now.

(He goes to the left, where three steps lead to a stair door.)

Sheriff: I suppose anything Mrs. Peters does'll be all right. She was to take in some clothes for her, you know, and a few little things. We left in such a hurry yesterday.

County Attorney: Yes, but I would like to see what you take, Mrs. Peters, and keep an eye out for anything that might be of use to us.

Mrs. Peters: Yes, Mr. Henderson.

(The women listen to the men's steps on the stairs, then look about the kitchen.)

Mrs. Hale: I'd hate to have men coming into my kitchen, snooping around and criticising.

(She arranges the pans under sink which the County Attorney *had shoved out of place.)*

Mrs. Peters: Of course it's no more than their duty.

Mrs. Hale: Duty's all right, but I guess that deputy sheriff that came out to make the fire might have got a little of this on. *(Gives the roller towel a pull.)* Wish I'd thought of that sooner. Seems mean to talk about her for not having things slicked up when she had to come away in such a hurry.

Mrs. Peters (Who has gone to a small table in the left rear corner of the room, and lifted one end of a towel that covers a pan.): She had bread set.

(Stands still.)

Mrs. Hale (Eyes fixed on a loaf of bread beside the breadbox, which is on a low shelf at the other side of the room. Moves slowly toward it.): She was going to put this in there. *(Picks up loaf, then abruptly drops it. In a manner of returning to familiar things.)* It's a shame about her fruit. I wonder if it's all gone. *(Gets up on the chair and looks.)* I think there's some here that's all right, Mrs. Peters. Yes—here; *(Holding it toward the window.)* this is cherries, too. *(Looking again.)* I declare I believe that's the only one. *(Gets down, bottle in her hand. Goes to the sink and wipes it off on the outside.)* She'll feel awful bad after all her hard work in the hot weather. I remember the afternoon I put up my cherries last summer.

(She puts the bottle on the big kitchen table, center of the room. With a sigh, is about to sit down in the rocking-chair. Before she is seated realizes what chair it is;

with a slow look at it, steps back. The chair which she has touched rocks back and forth.)

Mrs. Peters: Well, I must get those things from the front room closet. *(She goes to the door at the right, but after looking into the other room, steps back.)* You coming with me, Mrs. Hale? You could help me carry them.

(They go in the other room; reappear, Mrs. Peters carrying a dress and skirt, Mrs. Hale following with a pair of shoes.)

Mrs. Peters: My, it's cold in there.

(She puts the clothes on the big table, and hurries to the stove.)

Mrs. Hale (Examining her skirt.): Wright was close. I think maybe that's why she kept so much to herself. She didn't even belong to the Ladies Aid. I suppose she felt she couldn't do her part, and then you don't enjoy things when you feel shabby. She used to wear pretty clothes and be lively, when she was Minnie Foster, one of the town girls singing in the choir. But that—oh, that was thirty years ago. This all you was to take in?

Mrs. Peters: She said she wanted an apron. Funny thing to want, for there isn't much to get you dirty in jail, goodness knows. But I suppose just to make her feel more natural. She said they was in the top drawer in this cupboard. Yes, here. And then her little shawl that always hung behind the door. *(Opens stair door and looks.)* Yes, here it is.

(Quickly shuts door leading upstairs.)

Mrs. Hale (Abruptly moving toward her.): Mrs. Peters?
Mrs. Peters: Yes, Mrs. Hale?
Mrs. Hale: Do you think she did it?
Mrs. Peters (In a frightened voice.): Oh, I don't know.
Mrs. Hale: Well, I don't think she did. Asking for an apron and her little shawl. Worrying about her fruit.
Mrs. Peters (Starts to speak, glances up, where footsteps are heard in the room above. In a low voice.): Mr. Peters says it looks bad for her. Mr. Henderson is awful sarcastic in a speech and he'll make fun of her sayin' she didn't wake up.
Mrs. Hale: Well, I guess John Wright didn't wake when they was slipping that rope under his neck.
Mrs. Peters: No, it's strange. It must have been done awful crafty and still. They say it was such a—funny way to kill a man, rigging it all up like that.
Mrs. Hale: That's just what Mr. Hale said. There was a gun in the house. He says that's what he can't understand.
Mrs. Peters: Mr. Henderson said coming out that what was needed for the case was a motive; something to show anger, or—sudden feeling.
Mrs. Hale (Who is standing by the table.): Well, I don't see any signs of anger around here. *(She puts her hand on the dish towel which lies on the table,*

stands looking down at table, one half of which is clean, the other half messy.)
It's wiped to here. *(Makes a move as if to finish work, then turns and looks at loaf of bread outside the breadbox. Drops towel. In that voice of coming back to familiar things.)* Wonder how they are finding things upstairs. I hope she had it a little more red-up up there. You know, it seems kind of *sneaking.* Locking her up in town and then coming out here and trying to get her own house to turn against her!

Mrs. Peters: But Mrs. Hale, the law is the law.

Mrs. Hale: I s'pose 'tis. *(Unbuttoning her coat.)* Better loosen up your things, Mrs. Peters. You won't feel them when you go out.

(Mrs. Peters *takes off her fur tippet, goes to hang it on hook at back of room, stands looking at the under part of the small corner table.)*

Mrs. Peters: She was piecing a quilt.

(She brings the large sewing basket and they look at the bright pieces.)

Mrs. Hale: It's log cabin pattern. Pretty, isn't it? I wonder if she was goin' to quilt it or just knot it?

(Footsteps have been heard coming down the stairs. The Sheriff *enters followed by* Hale *and the* County Attorney.)*

Sheriff: They wonder if she was going to quilt it or just knot it!

(The men laugh; the women look abashed.)

County Attorney (Rubbing his hands over the stove.): Frank's fire didn't do much up there, did it? Well, let's go out to the barn and get that cleared up.

(The men go outside.)

Mrs. Hale (Resentfully.): I don't know as there's anything so strange, our takin' up our time with little things while we're waiting for them to get the evidence. *(She sits down at the big table smoothing out a block with decision.)* I don't see as it's anything to laugh about.

Mrs. Peters (Apologetically.): Of course they've got awful important things on their minds.

(Pulls up a chair and joins Mrs. Hale *at the table.)*

Mrs. Hale (Examining another block.): Mrs. Peters, look at this one. Here, this is the one she was working on, and look at the sewing! All the rest of it has been so nice and even. And look at this! It's all over the place! Why, it looks as if she didn't know what she was about!

(After she has said this they look at each other, then start to glance back at the door. After an instant Mrs. Hale *has pulled at a knot and ripped the sewing.)*

Mrs. Peters: Oh, what are you doing, Mrs. Hale?

Mrs. Hale: (Mildly.) Just pulling out a stitch or two that's not sewed very good. *(Threading a needle.)* Bad sewing always made me fidgety.

Mrs. Peters (Nervously.): I don't think we ought to touch things.

Mrs. Hale: I'll just finish up this end. *(Suddenly stopping and leaning forward.)* Mrs. Peters?

Mrs. Peters: Yes, Mrs. Hale?

Mrs. Hale: What do you suppose she was so nervous about?

Mrs. Peters: Oh—I don't know. I don't know as she was nervous. I sometimes sew awful queer when I'm just tired. *(Mrs. Hale starts to say something, looks at Mrs. Peters, then goes on sewing.)* Well, I must get these things wrapped up. They may be through sooner than we think. *(Putting apron and other things together.)* I wonder where I can find a piece of paper, and string.

Mrs. Hale: In that cupboard, maybe.

Mrs. Peters (Looking in cupboard.): Why, here's a birdcage. *(Holds it up.)* Did she have a bird, Mrs. Hale?

Mrs. Hale: Why, I don't know whether she did or not—I've not been here for so long. There was a man around last year selling canaries cheap, but I don't know as she took one; maybe she did. She used to sing real pretty herself.

Mrs. Peters (Glancing around.): Seems funny to think of a bird here. But she must have had one, or why would she have a cage? I wonder what happened to it.

Mrs. Hale: I s'pose maybe the cat got it.

Mrs. Peters: No, she didn't have a cat. She's got that feeling some people have about cats—being afraid of them. My cat got in her room and she was real upset and asked me to take it out.

Mrs. Hale: My sister Bessie was like that. Queer, ain't it?

Mrs. Peters (Examining the cage.): Why, look at this door. It's broke. One hinge is pulled apart.

Mrs. Hale (Looking too.): Looks as if someone must have been rough with it.

Mrs. Peters: Why, yes.

(She brings the cage forward and puts it on the table.)

Mrs. Hale: I wish if they're going to find any evidence they'd be about it. I don't like this place.

Mrs. Peters: But I'm awful glad you came with me, Mrs. Hale. It would be lonesome for me sitting here alone.

Mrs. Hale: It would, wouldn't it? *(Dropping her sewing.)* But I tell you what I do wish, Mrs. Peters. I wish I had come over sometimes when *she* was here. I—*(Looking around the room.)*—wish I had.

Mrs. Peters: But of course you were awful busy, Mrs. Hale—your house and your children.

Mrs. Hale: I could've come. I stayed away because it weren't cheerful—and that's why I ought to have come. I—I've never liked this place. Maybe because it's down in a hollow and you don't see the road. I dunno what it is but it's a lonesome place and always was. I wish I had come over to see Minnie Foster sometimes. I can see now—*(Shakes her head.)*

Mrs. Peters: Well, you mustn't reproach yourself, Mrs. Hale. Somehow we just don't see how it is with other folks until—something comes up.

Mrs. Hale: Not having children makes less work—but it makes a quiet house, and Wright out to work all day, and no company when he did come in. Did you know John Wright, Mrs. Peters?

Mrs. Peters: Not to know him; I've seen him in town. They say he was a good man.

Mrs. Hale: Yes—good; he didn't drink, and kept his word as well as most, I guess, and paid his debts. But he was a hard man, Mrs. Peters. Just to pass the time of day with him—*(Shivers.)* Like a raw wind that gets to the bone. *(Pauses, her eye falling on the cage.)* I should think she would 'a wanted a bird. But what do you suppose went with it?

Mrs. Peters: I don't know, unless it got sick and died.

(She reaches over and swings the broken door, swings it again. Both women watch it.)

Mrs. Hale: You weren't raised round here, were you? (Mrs. Peters *shakes her head.)* You didn't know—her?

Mrs. Peters: Not till they brought her yesterday.

Mrs. Hale: She—come to think of it, she was kind of like a bird herself—real sweet and pretty, but kind of timid and—fluttery. How—she—did—change. *(Silence; then as if struck by a happy thought and relieved to get back to everyday things.)* Tell you what, Mrs. Peters, why don't you take the quilt in with you? It might take up her mind.

Mrs. Peters: Why, I think that's a real nice idea, Mrs. Hale. There couldn't possibly be any objection to it, could there? Now, just what would I take? I wonder if her patches are in here—and her things.

(They look in the sewing basket.)

Mrs. Hale: Here's some red. I expect this has got sewing things in it. *(Brings out a fancy box.)* What a pretty box. Looks like something somebody would give you. Maybe her scissors are in here. *(Opens box. Suddenly puts her hand to her nose.)* Why—(Mrs. Peters *bends nearer, then turns her face away.)* There's something wrapped up in this piece of silk.

Mrs. Peters: Why, this isn't her scissors.

Mrs. Hale (Lifting the silk.): Oh, Mrs. Peters—it's—

(Mrs. Peters bends closer.)

Mrs. Peters: It's the bird.

Mrs. Hale (Jumping up.): But, Mrs. Peters—look at it! Its neck! Look at its neck! It's all—other side *to.*

Mrs. Peters: Somebody—wrung—its—neck.

(Their eyes meet. A look of growing comprehension, of horror. Steps are heard outside. Mrs. Hale *slips box under quilt pieces, and sinks into her chair. Enter* Sheriff *and* County Attorney. Mrs. Peters *rises.)*

County Attorney (As one turning from serious things to little pleasantries.): Well, ladies, have you decided whether she was going to quilt it or knot it?

Mrs. Peters: We think she was going to—knot it.

County Attorney: Well, that's interesting, I'm sure. *(Seeing the birdcage.)* Has
the bird flown?

Mrs. Hale (Putting more quilt pieces over the box.): We think the—cat got it.

County Attorney (Preoccupied.): Is there a cat?

(Mrs. Hale *glances in a quick covert way at* Mrs. Peters.)

Mrs. Peters: Well, not *now*. They're superstitious, you know. They leave.

County Attorney (To Sheriff Peters, *continuing an interrupted conversation.):*
No sign at all of anyone having come from the outside. Their own rope.
Now let's go up again and go over it piece by piece. *(They start upstairs.)*
It would have to have been someone who knew just the—

(Mrs. Peters *sits down. The two women sit there not looking at one another,
but as if peering into something and at the same time holding back. When they talk
now it is in the manner of feeling their way over strange ground, as if afraid of
what they are saying, but as if they can not help saying it.)*

Mrs. Hale: She liked the bird. She was going to bury it in that pretty box.

Mrs. Peters (In a whisper.): When I was a girl—my kitten—there was a boy
took a hatchet, and before my eyes—and before I could get there—
(Covers her face an instant.) If they hadn't held me back I would have—
(Catches herself, looks upstairs where steps are heard, falters weakly.)—hurt
him.

Mrs. Hale (With a slow look around her.): I wonder how it would seem never
to have had any children around. *(Pause.)* No, Wright wouldn't like the
bird—a thing that sang. She used to sing. He killed that, too.

Mrs. Peters (Moving uneasily.): We don't know who killed the bird.

Mrs. Hale: I knew John Wright.

Mrs. Peters: It was an awful thing was done in this house that night, Mrs.
Hale. Killing a man while he slept, slipping a rope around his neck that
choked the life out of him.

Mrs. Hale: His neck. Choked the life out of him.

(Her hand goes out and rests on the birdcage.)

Mrs. Peters (With rising voice.): We don't know who killed him. We don't
know.

Mrs. Hale (Her own feeling not interrupted.): If there'd been years and years of
nothing, then a bird to sing to you, it would be awful—still, after the
bird was still.

Mrs. Peters (Something within her speaking.): I know what stillness is. When
we homesteaded in Dakota, and my first baby died—after he was two
years old, and me with no other then—

Mrs. Hale (Moving.): How soon do you suppose they'll be through, looking
for the evidence?

Mrs. Peters: I know what stillness is. *(Pulling herself back.)* The law has got to
punish crime, Mrs. Hale.

Mrs. Hale (Not as if answering that.): I wish you'd seen Minnie Foster when
she wore a white dress with blue ribbons and stood up there in the choir

and sang. *(A look around the room.)* Oh, I *wish* I'd come over here once in a while! That was a crime! That was a crime! Who's going to punish that?

Mrs. Peters *(Looking upstairs.):* We mustn't—take on.

Mrs. Hale: I might have known she needed help! I know how things can be—for women. I tell you, it's queer, Mrs. Peters. We live close together and we live far apart. We all go through the same things—it's all just a different kind of the same thing. *(Brushes her eyes; noticing the bottle of fruit, reaches out for it.)* If I was you I wouldn't tell her her fruit was gone. Tell her it *ain't*. Tell her it's all right. Take this in to prove it to her. She—she may never know whether it was broke or not.

Mrs. Peters *(Takes the bottle, looks about for something to wrap it in; takes petticoat from the clothes brought from the other room, very nervously begins winding this around the bottle. In a false voice.):* My, it's a good thing the men couldn't hear us. Wouldn't they just laugh! Getting all stirred up over a little thing like a—dead canary. As if that could have anything to do with—with—wouldn't they *laugh!*

(The men are heard coming down stairs.)

Mrs. Hale *(Under her breath.):* Maybe they would—maybe they wouldn't.

County Attorney: No, Peters, it's all perfectly clear except a reason for doing it. But you know juries when it comes to women. If there was some definite thing. Something to show—something to make a story about— a thing that would connect up with this strange way of doing it—

(The women's eyes meet for an instant. Enter Hale *from outer door.)*

Hale: Well, I've got the team around. Pretty cold out there.

County Attorney: I'm going to stay here a while by myself. *(To the* Sheriff.*)* You can send Frank out for me, can't you? I want to go over everything. I'm not satisfied that we can't do better.

Sheriff: Do you want to see what Mrs. Peters is going to take in?

(The County Attorney *goes to the table, picks up the apron, laughs.)*

County Attorney: Oh, I guess they're not very dangerous things the ladies have picked out. *(Moves a few things about, disturbing the quilt pieces which cover the box. Steps back.)* No, Mrs. Peters doesn't need supervising. For that matter, a sheriff's wife is married to the law. Ever think of it that way, Mrs. Peters?

Mrs. Peters: Not—just that way.

Sheriff *(Chuckling.):* Married to the law. *(Moves toward the other room.)* I just want you to come in here a minute, George. We ought to take a look at these windows.

County Attorney *(Scoffingly.):* Oh, windows!

Sheriff: We'll be right out, Mr. Hale.

(Hale goes outside. The Sheriff *follows the* County Attorney *into the other room. Then Mrs. Hale rises, hands tight together, looking intensely at Mrs.*

Peters, *whose eyes make a slow turn, finally meeting* Mrs. Hale's. *A moment* Mrs. Hale *holds her, then her own eyes point the way to where the box is concealed. Suddenly* Mrs. Peters *throws back quilt pieces and tries to put the box in the bag she is wearing. It is too big. She opens box, starts to take bird out, cannot touch it, goes to pieces, stands there helpless. Sound of a knob turning in the other room.* Mrs. Hale *snatches the box and puts it in the pocket of her big coat. Enter* County Attorney *and* Sheriff.)

County Attorney *(Facetiously.):* Well, Henry, at least we found out that she was not going to quilt it. She was going to—what is it you call it, ladies?

Mrs. Hale *(Her hand against her pocket.):* We call it—knot it, Mr. Henderson.

CURTAIN

————   **SUSAN GLASPELL**   ————

www   *(1876–1948)* Web

Susan Glaspell was one of the original members of the Provincetown Players, founded in 1915 by her husband George Cram "Jig" Cook, a director and producer. Glaspell graduated from Drake University in 1899 and attended the University of Iowa's Writers' Workshop; she also worked as a journalist. Among her several plays are *Suppressed Desires* (1914), a play that satirizes the then-popular Freudian psychoanalysis; *The Verge* (1921), and *Alison's House* (1930), for which she won the Pulitzer Prize.

TOPICS FOR CRITICAL THINKING

1. In what specific ways is *Trifles* a feminist play?
2. Glaspell never allows us to meet the accused murderer, Mrs. Wright, or her dead husband. What inferences about them and their marriage can you make?
3. How do the birdcage and bird function as metaphors in the play? What other objects in the set function in such ways?
4. To what does the play's title refer? What meaning of the word *trifles* does Glaspell develop?
5. How are we to understand Mrs. Peters's and Mrs. Hale's silence at the end of the play?

Critical Perspective: On Male "Rationality" and Domination

"The idea of rationalization forms a bridge between intellectual history and the history of social and economic relationships. It describes the essence of modern social practice and thought. It is a . . . discourse. My argument is that it is a *gendered* discourse . . . This means that male domination, like class domination, is no longer a function of personal power relationships . . . but something inherent in social and cultural structures, independent of what individual men and women will.

"Thus regardless of woman's increasing participation in the public, productive sphere of society, it remains 'a man's world.' The presence of women has no effect on its rules and processes."

—Jessica Benjamin, *The Bonds of Love: Psychoanalysis, Feminism, and the Problem of Domination* (1988)

Critical Perspective: On the Maternal in *Trifles*

"The sympathy of Mrs. Hale and Mrs. Peters arises not only from sisterly solidarity but from the two women's self-identification as mothers, in contrast to the childless Minnie. Love, particularly maternal love, is associated with sound and its absence with silence. Mrs. Hale wonders 'how it would seem never to have had any children around,' and Mrs. Peters can tell her: 'I know what stillness is . . .'

"Adrienne Rich justly observes that 'powerless women have always used mothering as a channel—narrow but deep—for their own human will to power.' Similarly, Glaspell is not idealizing motherhood or maternal feelings here but demonstrating that these rural women have no outlets for expression aside from domesticity focusing on children, though Minnie Wright lacks even that . . . In a sense, as Annette Kolodny has written, Glaspell is also exploring the plight of the woman writer; her 'trifles' are as unnoticed and unappreciated by her culture as are Minnie's domestic artifacts by the investigating men."

—Veronica Makowsky, *Susan Glaspell's Century of American Women* (1993)

Critical Perspective: On the Source of *Trifles*: Glaspell as "Gonzo" Journalist

"In the process of completing research for a biography of Susan Glaspell, I discovered the historical source upon which *Trifles* and 'Jury of Her Peers' are based: the murder of a sixty-year-old farmer named John Hossack on December 2, 1900, in Indianola, Iowa. Glaspell covered the case and the subsequent trial when she was a reporter for the *Des Moines Daily News*, a position she began full-time the day after she graduated from Drake University in June, 1899, a twenty-four-year-old woman with a bachelor of philosophy (Ph.B.) degree and several years of newspaper work in Davenport and Des Moines behind her. . . .

"There was really nothing unique about such a murder in the Iowa of 1900, which, if no more violent than it is today, was certainly no less so. . . . What makes the Hossack case stand out are the extended length of the coverage and the vivid style of the reporter. Her paper seems to have charged

Glaspell with two tasks: rousing the readership and insuring that the story stay on the first page. She accomplished both.

"Employing the techniques of 'Gonzo' journalism sixty years before Hunter Thompson, Glaspell filed twenty-six stories on the Hossack case. . . ."

—Linda Ben-Zvi, *Susan Glaspell: Essays on Her Theater and Fiction* (1995)

ᕃᕑᕒ

EUGENE O'NEILL

The Emperor Jones   *(1920)*

CHARACTERS

Brutus Jones, Emperor
Henry Smithers, A Cockney Trader
An Old Native Woman
Lem, A Native Chief
Soldiers, Adherents of Lem
The Little Formless Fears; Jeff; The Negro Convicts; The Prison Guard; The
  Planters; The Auctioneer; The Slaves; The Congo Witch Doctor; The
  Crocodile God.

  The action of the play takes place on an island in the West Indies as yet not self-determined by White Marines. The form of native government is, for the time being, an Empire.

SCENES

Scene I: In the palace of the Emperor Jones. Afternoon.
Scene II: The edge of the Great Forest. Dusk.
Scene III: In the Forest. Night.
Scene IV: In the Forest. Night.
Scene V: In the Forest. Night.
Scene VI: In the Forest. Night.
Scene VII: In the Forest. Night.
Scene VIII: Same as Scene Two—the edge of the Great Forest. Dawn.

SCENE ONE

  The audience chamber in the palace of the Emperor—a spacious, high-ceilinged room with bare, whitewashed walls. The floor is of white tiles. In the rear, to the left of center, a wide archway giving out on a portico with white pillars. The palace is evidently situated on high ground for beyond the portico nothing can be seen but a vista of distant hills, their summits crowned with thick groves of palm trees. In the right wall, center, a smaller arched doorway leading to the living quarters of the palace. The room is bare of furniture with the exception of one huge chair made of uncut wood which stands at center, its back to rear. This is very apparently the Emperor's throne. It is painted a dazzling, eye-smiting scarlet. There is a brilliant orange cushion on the seat and another smaller one is placed on the floor to serve as a footstool. Strips of matting, dyed scarlet, lead from the foot of the throne to the two entrances.

It is late afternoon but the sunlight still blazes yellowly beyond the portico and there is an oppressive burden of exhausting heat in the air.

As the curtain rises, a native Negro woman sneaks in cautiously from the entrance on the right. She is very old, dressed in cheap calico, bare-footed, a red bandana handkerchief covering all but a few stray wisps of white hair. A bundle bound in colored cloth is carried over her shoulder on the end of a stick. She hesitates beside the doorway, peering back as if in extreme dread of being discovered. Then she begins to glide noiselessly, a step at a time, toward the doorway in the rear. At this moment, Smithers *appears beneath the portico.*

Smithers *is a tall, stoop-shouldered man about forty. His bald head, perched on a long neck with an enormous Adam's apple, looks like an egg. The tropics have tanned his naturally pasty face with its small, sharp features to a sickly yellow, and native rum has painted his pointed nose to a startling red. His little, washy-blue eyes are red-rimmed and dart about him like a ferret's. His expression is one of unscrupulous meanness, cowardly and dangerous. He is dressed in a worn riding suit of dirty white drill, puttees, spurs, and wears a white cork helmet. A cartridge belt with an automatic revolver is around his waist. He carries a riding whip in his hand. He sees the woman and stops to watch her suspiciously. Then, making up his mind, he steps quickly on tiptoe into the room. The woman, looking back over her shoulder continually, does not see him until it is too late. When she does* Smithers *springs forward and grabs her firmly by the shoulder. She struggles to get away, fiercely but silently.*

Smithers *(tightening his grasp—roughly):* Easy! None o' that, me birdie. You can't wiggle out, now I got me 'ooks on yer.

Woman *(seeing the uselessness of struggling, gives way to frantic terror, and sinks to the ground, embracing his knees supplicatingly):* No tell him! No tell him, Mister!

Smithers *(with great curiosity):* Tell 'im? *(Then scornfully)* Oh, you mean 'is bloomin' Majesty. What's the gaime, any'ow? What are you sneakin' away for? Been stealin' a bit, I s'pose. *(He taps her bundle with his riding whip significantly.)*

Woman *(shaking her head vehemently):* No, me no steal.

Smithers: Bloody liar! But tell me what's up. There's somethin' funny goin' on. I smelled it in the air first thing I got up this mornin'. You blacks are up to some devilment. This palace of 'is is like a bleedin' tomb. Where's all the 'ands? *(The woman keeps sullenly silent.* Smithers *raises his whip threateningly.)* Ow, yer won't, won't yer? Ill show yer what's what.

Woman *(coweringly):* I tell, Mister. You no hit. They go—all go. *(She makes a sweeping gesture toward the hills in the distance.)*

Smithers: Run away—to the 'ills?

Woman: Yes, Mister. Him Emperor—Great Father *(She touches her forehead to the floor with a quick mechanical jerk.)* Him sleep after eat. Then they go—all go. Me old woman. Me left only. Now me go too.

Smithers (his astonishment giving way to an immense, mean satisfaction): Ow! So that's the ticket! Well, I know bloody well wot's in the air—when they runs orf to the 'ills. The tom-tom'll be thumping out there bloomin' soon. *(With extreme vindictiveness)* And I'm bloody glad of it, for one! Serve 'im right! Puttin' on airs, the stinkin' nigger! 'Is Majesty! Gawd blimey! I only 'opes I'm there when they takes 'im out to shoot 'im. *(Suddenly)* 'E's still 'ere all right, ain't 'e?

Woman: Him sleep.

Smithers: 'E's bound to find out soon as 'e wakes up. 'E's cunnin' enough to know when 'is time's come. *(He goes to the doorway on right and whistles shrilly with his fingers in his mouth. The old woman springs to her feet and runs out of the doorway, rear. Smithers goes after her, reaching for his revolver.)* Stop or I'll shoot! *(Then stopping—indifferently)* Pop orf then, if yer like, yer black cow. *(He stands in the doorway, looking after her.)*

(Jones enters from the right. He is a tall, powerfully-built, full-blooded Negro of middle age. His features are typically negroid, yet there is something decidedly distinctive about his face—an underlying strength of will, a hardy, self-reliant confidence in himself that inspires respect. His eyes are alive with a keen, cunning intelligence. In manner he is shrewd, suspicious, evasive. He wears a light blue uniform coat, sprayed with brass buttons, heavy gold chevrons on his shoulders, gold braid on the collar, cuffs, etc. His pants are bright red with a light blue stripe down the side. Patent leather laced boots with brass spurs, and a belt with a long-barreled, pearl-handled revolver in a holster complete his make up. Yet there is something not altogether ridiculous about his grandeur. He has a way of carrying it off.)

Jones (not seeing anyone—greatly irritated and blinking sleepily—shouts): Who dare whistle dat way in my palace? Who dare wake up de Emperor? I'll git de hide frayled off some o' you niggers sho'!

Smithers (showing himself—in a manner half-afraid and half-defiant): It was me whistled to yer. *(As Jones frowns angrily)* I got news for yer.

Jones (putting on his suavest manner, which fails to cover up his contempt for the white man): Oh, it's you, Mister Smithers. *(He sits down on his throne with easy dignity.)* What news you got to tell me?

Smithers (coming close to enjoy his discomfiture): Don't yer notice nothin' funny today?

Jones (coldly): Funny? No. I ain't perceived nothin' of de kind!

Smithers: Then yer ain't so foxy as I thought yer was. Where's all your court? *(Sarcastically)* the Generals and the Cabinet Ministers and all?

Jones (imperturbably): Where dey mostly runs to minute I closes my eyes—drinkin' rum and talkin' big down in de town. *(Sarcastically)* How come you don't know dat? Ain't you sousin' with 'em most every day?

Smithers (stung but pretending indifference—with a wink): That's part of the day's work. I got ter—ain't I—in my business?

Jones (contemptuously): Yo' business!

Smithers (imprudently enraged): Gawd blimey, you was glad enough for me ter take yer in on it when you landed here first. You didn't 'ave no 'igh and mighty airs in them days!

Jones (his hand going to his revolver like a flash—menacingly): Talk polite, white man! Talk polite, you heah me! I'm boss heah now, is you fergettin'? (*The Cockney seems about to challenge this last statement with the facts but something in the other's eyes holds and cows him.*)

Smithers (in a cowardly whine): No 'arm meant, old top.

Jones (condescendingly): I accepts yo' apology. (*Lets his hand fall from his revolver*) No use'n you rakin' up ole times. What I was den is one thing. What I is now's another. You didn't let me in on yo' crooked work out o' no kind feelin's dat time. I done de dirty work fo' you—and most o' de brain work, too, fo' dat matter—and I was wu'th money to you, dat's de reason.

Smithers: Well, blimey, I give yer a start, didn't I?—when no one else would. I wasn't afraid to 'ire you like the rest was—'count of the story about your breakin' jail back in the States.

Jones: No, you didn't have no s'cuse to look down on me fo' dat. You been in jail you'self more'n once.

Smithers (furiously): It's a lie! (*Then trying to pass it off by an attempt at scorn*) Garn! Who told yer that fairy tale?

Jones: Dey's some tings I ain't got to be tole. I kin see 'em in folk's eyes. (*Then after a pause—meditatively*) Yes, you sho' give me a start. And it didn't take long from dat time to git dese fool, woods niggers right where I wanted dem. (*With pride*) From stowaway to Emperor in two years! Dat's goin' some!

Smithers (with curiosity): And I bet you got yer pile o' money 'id safe some place.

Jones (with satisfaction): I sho' has! And it's in a foreign bank where no pusson don't ever git it out but me no matter what come. You didn't s'pose I was holdin' down dis Emperor job for de glory in it, did you? Sho'! De fuss and glory part of it, dat's only to turn de heads o' de low-flung, bush niggers dat's here. Dey wants de big circus show for deir money. I gives it to 'em an' I gits de money. (*With a grin*) De long green, dat's me every time! (*Then rebukingly*) But you ain't got no kick agin me, Smithers. I'se paid you back all you done for me many times. Ain't I pertected you and winked at all de crooked tradin' you been doin' right out in de broad day? Sho' I has—and me makin' laws to stop it at de same time! (*He chuckles.*)

Smithers (grinning): But, meanin' no 'arm, you been grabbin' right and left yourself, ain't yer? Look at the taxes you've put on 'em! Blimey! You've squeezed 'em dry!

Jones (chuckling): No, dey ain't *all* dry yet. I'se still heah, ain't I?

Smithers (smiling at his secret thought): They're dry right now, you'll find out. (*Changing the subject abruptly*) And as for me breakin' laws, you've broke 'em all yerself just as fast as yer made 'em.

Jones: Ain't I de Emperor? De laws don't go for him. (*Judicially*) You heah
what I tells you, Smithers. Dere's little stealin' like you does, and dere's
big stealin' like I does. For de little stealin' dey gits you in jail soon or
late. For de big stealin' dey makes you Emperor and puts you in de Hall
o' Fame when you croaks. (*Reminiscently*) If dey's one thing I learns in
ten years on de Pullman ca's listenin' to de white quality talk, it's dat
same fact. And when I gits a chance to use it I winds up Emperor in two
years.

Smithers (unable to repress the genuine admiration of the small fry for the large):
Yes, yer turned the bleedin' trick, all right. Blimey, I never seen a bloke
'as 'ad the bloomin' luck you 'as.

Jones (severely): Luck? What you mean—luck?

Smithers: I suppose you'll say as that swank about the silver bullet ain't
luck—and that was what first got the fool blacks on yer side the time of
the revolution, wasn't it?

Jones (with a laugh): Oh, dat silver bullet! Sho' was luck. But I makes dat
luck, you heah? I loads de dice! Yessuh! When dat murderin' nigger ole
Lem hired to kill me takes aim ten feet away and his gun misses fire and
I shoots him dead, what you heah me say?

Smithers: You said yer'd got a charm so's no lead bullet'd kill yer. You was so
strong only a silver bullet could kill yer, you told 'em. Blimey, wasn't
that swank for yer—and plain, fat-'eaded luck?

Jones (proudly): I got brains and I uses 'em quick. Dat ain't luck.

Smithers: Yer know they wasn't 'ardly liable to get no silver bullets. And it
was luck 'e didn't 'it you that time.

Jones (laughing): And dere all dem fool bush niggers was kneelin' down and
bumpin' deir heads on de ground like I was a miracle out o' de Bible.
Oh, Lawd, from dat time on I has dem all eatin' out of my hand. I cracks
de whip and dey jumps through.

Smithers (with a sniff): Yankee bluff done it.

Jones: Ain't a man's talkin' big what makes him big—long as he makes folks
believe it? Sho', I talks large when I ain't got nothin' to back it up, but I
ain't talkin' wild just de same. I knows I kin fool 'em—I *knows* it—and
dat's backin' enough fo' my game. And ain't I got to learn deir lingo and
teach some of dem English befo' I kin talk to 'em? Ain't dat wuk? You
ain't never learned ary word er it, Smithers, in de ten years you been
heah, dough you knows it's money in yo' pocket tradin' wid 'em if you
does. But you'se too shiftless to take de trouble.

Smithers (flushing): Never mind about me. What's this I've 'eard about yer
really 'avin' a silver bullet moulded for yourself?

Jones: It's playin' out my bluff. I has de silver bullet moulded and I tells 'em
when de time comes I kills myself wid it. I tells 'em dat's 'cause I'm de
on'y man in de world big enuff to git me. No use'n deir tryin'. And dey
falls down and bumps deir heads. (*He laughs*) I does dat so's I kin take a
walk in peace widout no jealous nigger gunnin' at me from behind de
trees.

Smithers (astonished): Then you 'ad it made—'onest?

Jones: Sho' did. Heah she be. *(He takes out his revolver, breaks it, and takes the silver bullet out of one chamber.)* Five lead an' dis silver baby at de last. Don't she shine pretty? *(He holds it in his hand, looking at it admiringly, as if strangely fascinated.)*

Smithers: Let me see. *(Reaches out his hand for it)*

Jones (harshly): Keep yo' hands whar dey b'long, white man. *(He replaces it in the chamber and puts the revolver back on his hip.)*

Smithers (snarling): Gawd blimey! Think I'm a bleedin' thief, you would.

Jones: No, 'tain't dat. I knows you'se scared to steal from me. On'y I ain't 'lowin' nary body to touch dis baby. She's my rabbit's foot.

Smithers (sneering): A bloomin' charm, wot? *(Venomously)* Well, you'll need all the bloody charms you 'as before long, s' 'elp me!

Jones (judicially): Oh, I'se good for six months yit 'fore dey gits sick o' my game. Den, when I sees trouble comin', I makes my getaway.

Smithers: Ho! You got it all planned, ain't yer?

Jones: I ain't no fool. I knows dis Emperor's time is sho't. Dat why I make hay when de sun shine. Was you thinkin' I'se aimin' to hold down dis job for life? No, suh! What good is gittin' money if you stays back in dis raggedy country? I wants action when I spends. And when I sees dese niggers gittin' up deir nerve to tu'n me out, and I'se got all de money in sight, I resigns on de spot and beats it quick.

Smithers: Where to?

Jones: Nonc o' yo' business.

Smithers: Not back to the bloody States, I'll lay my oath.

Jones (suspiciously): Why don't I? *(Then with an easy laugh)* 's all talk.
of dat story 'bout me breakin' from jail back de—

Smithers (skeptically): Ho, yes!

Jones (sharply): You ain't 'sinuatin' I'se a liar. —y thinkin' o' the bloody lies

Smithers (hastily): No, Gawd strike me! I— men in the States.
you told the blacks 'ere about kill—

Jones (angered): How come dey're—d, wouldn't yer then? *(With venom)*
—althy for a black to kill a white man

Smithers: You'd 'ave been in ja' oil, don't they?
And from what I've 'eaean lynchin' 'd scare me? Well, I tells you,
in the States. They 'll one white man back dere. Maybe I does.
—er right heah 'fore long if he don't look out.

Jones (with cool deadli—augh): I was on'y spoofin' yer. Can't yer take a
Smithers, m—just sayin' you'd never been in jail.
And may—slightly boastful): Maybe I goes to jail dere for gittin'
*Smithers (it wid razors ovah a crap game. Maybe I gits twenty years
jok—lored man die. Maybe I gits in 'nother argument wid de
Jone—ard was overseer ovah us when we're wukin' de road. Maybe
—me wid a whip and I splits his head wid a shovel and runs away
files de chain off my leg and gits away safe. Maybe I does all dat an'

maybe I don't. It's a story I tells you so's you knows I'se de kind of man dat if you evah repeats one word of it, I ends yo' stealin' on dis yearth mighty damn quick!

Smithers *(terrified):* Think I'd peach on yer? Not me! Ain't I always been yer friend?

Jones *(suddenly relaxing):* Sho' you has—and you better be.

Smithers *(recovering his composure—and with it his malice):* And just to show yer I'm yer friend, I'll tell yer that bit o' news I was goin' to.

Jones: Go ahead! Shoot de piece. Must be bad news from de happy way you look.

Smithers *(warningly):* Maybe it's gettin' time for you to resign—with that bloomin' silver bullet, wot? *(He finishes with a mocking grin.)*

Jones *(puzzled):* What's dat you say? Talk plain.

Smithers: Ain't noticed any of the guards or servants about the place today, I 'aven't.

Jones *(carelessly):* Dey're all out in de garden sleepin' under de trees. When I sleeps, dey sneaks a sleep, too, and I pretends I never suspicions it. All I got to do is to ring de bell and dey come flyin', makin' a bluff dey was wukin' all de time.

Smithers *(in the same mocking tone):* Ring the bell now an' you'll bloody well see what I means.

Jones *(startled to alertness, but preserving the same careless tone):* Sho' I rings.

(He reaches below the throne and pulls out a big, common dinner bell which is painted the same vivid scarlet as the throne. He rings this vigorously—then stops to listen. Then ... goes to both doors, rings again, and looks out.)

Smithers *(watching ...*

The bloody shi... *with malicious satisfaction, after a pause—mockingly):*

Jones *(in a sudden fit of ...kin' an' the bleedin' rats 'as slung their 'ooks.* woods niggers! *(The ... rings the bell clattering into a corner):* Low-flung, suddenly bursts into a low ...g Smithers' eye on him, he controls himself and once! A man can't take de ...ng laugh.)* Reckon I overplays my hand dis sayin' I'd sit in six months ... bob-tailed flush all de time. Was I cashes in and resigns de job o... I'se changed my mind den. I

Smithers *(with real admiration):* Blime ... right dis minute.

Jones: No use'n fussin'. When I know ... a cool bird, and no mistake. out no long waits. Dey've all run off...e ... up I kisses it good-by wid-

Smithers: Yes—every bleedin' man jack of ...in't dey?

Jones: Den de revolution is at de post. And ... smokin' up de trail. *(He starts for the door in ...*

Smithers: Goin' out to look for your 'orse? Yer w...tter git his feet the 'orses first thing. Mine was gone when I we... That's wot first give me a suspicion of wot was up ...hey steals

Jones *(alarmed for a second, scratches his head, then philosoph...* mornin'. hoofs it. Feet, do yo' duty! *(He pulls out a gold watch an...* Three-thuty. Sundown's at six-thuty or dereabouts. *(Pu...* back—with cool confidence) I got plenty o' time to make it ea... I

Smithers: Don't be so bloomin' sure of it. They'll be after you 'ot and 'eavy. Ole Lem is at the bottom o' this business an' 'e 'ates you like 'ell. 'E'd rather do for you than eat 'is dinner, 'e would!

Jones (scornfully): Dat fool no-count nigger! Does you think I'se scared o' him? I stands him on his thick head more'n once befo' dis, and I does it again if he comes in my way—*(Fiercely)* And dis time I leave him a dead nigger fo' sho'!

Smithers: You'll 'ave to cut through the big forest—an' these blacks 'ere can sniff and follow a trail in the dark like 'ounds. You'd 'ave to 'ustle to get through that forest in twelve hours even if you knew all the bloomin' trails like a native.

Jones (with indignant scorn): Look-a-heah, white man! Does you think I'se a natural bo'n fool? Give me credit fo' havin' some sense, fo' Lawd's sake! Don't you s'pose I'se looked ahead and made sho' of all de chances? I'se gone out in dat big forest, pretendin' to hunt, so many times dat I knows it high an' low like a book. I could go through on dem trails wid my eyes shut. *(With great contempt)* Think dese ign'rent bush niggers dat ain't got brains enuff to know deir own names even can catch Brutus Jones? Huh, I s'pects not! Not on yo' life! Why, man, de white men went after me wid blood-hounds where I come from an' I jes' laughs at 'em. It's a shame to fool dese black trash around heah, dey're so easy. You watch me, man. I'll make dem look sick, I will. I'll be 'cross de plain to de edge of de forest by time dark comes. Once in de woods in de night, dey got a swell chance o' findin' dis baby! Dawn tomorrow I'll be out at de oder side and on de coast whar dat French gunboat is stayin'. She picks me up, takes me to Martinique when she go dar, and dere I is safe wid a mighty big bankroll in my jeans. It's easy as rollin' off a log.

Smithers (maliciously): But s'posin' somethin' 'appens wrong an' they do nab yer?

Jones (decisively): Dey don't—dat's de answer.

Smithers: But, just for argyment's sake—what'd you do?

Jones (frowning): I'se got five lead bullets in dis gun good enuff fo' common bush niggers—and after dat I got de silver bullet left to cheat 'em out o' gittin' me.

Smithers (jeeringly): Ho, I was fergettin' that silver bullet. You'll bump yourself orf in style, won't yer? Blimey!

Jones (gloomily): You kin bet yo' whole roll on one thing, white man. Dis baby plays out his string to de end and when he quits, he quits wid a bang de way he ought. Silver bullet ain't none too good for him when he go, dat's a fac'! *(Then shaking off his nervousness—with a confident laugh)* Sho'! What is I talkin' about? Ain't come to dat yit and I never will—not wid trash niggers like dese yere. *(Boastfully)* Silver bullet bring me luck anyway. I kin outguess, outrun, outfight, an' outplay de whole lot o' dem all ovah de board any time o' de day er night! You watch me! *(From the distant hills comes the faint, steady thump of a tom-tom, low and vibrating. It starts at a rate exactly corresponding to normal pulse beat—72 to the minute—*

*and continues at a gradually accelerating rate from this point uninterruptedly
to the very end of the play.)*

(Jones *starts at the sound. A strange look of apprehension creeps into his face
for a moment as he listens. Then he asks, with an attempt to regain his most casual
manner)*

What's dat drum beatin' fo'?

Smithers (with a mean grin): For you. That means the bleedin' ceremony 'as
started. I've 'eard it before and I knows.

Jones: Cer'mony? What cer'mony?

Smithers: The blacks is 'oldin' a bloody meetin', 'avin' a war dance, getting
their courage worked up b'fore they starts after you.

Jones: Let dem! Dey'll sho' need it!

Smithers: And they're there 'oldin' their 'eathen religious service—makin' no
end of devil spells and charms to 'elp 'em against your silver bullet. *(He
guffaws loudly)* Blimey, but they're balmy as 'ell!

Jones (a tiny bit awed and shaken in spite of himself): Huh! Takes more'n dat to
scare dis chicken!

Smithers (scenting the other's feeling—maliciously): Ternight when it's pitch
black in the forest, they'll 'ave their pet devils and ghosts 'oundin'
after you. You'll find yer bloody 'air'll be standin' on end before termorrow mornin'. *(Seriously)* It's a bleedin' queer place, that stinkin' forest,
even in daylight. Yer don't know what might 'appen in there, it's that
rotten still. Always sends the cold shivers down my back minute I gets
in it.

Jones (with a contemptuous sniff): I ain't no chicken-liver like you is. Trees an'
me, we'se friends, and dar's a full moon comin' bring me light. And let
dem po' niggers make all de fool spells dey'se a min' to. Does yo' s'pect
I'se silly enuff to b'lieve in ghosts an' ha'nts an' all dat ole woman's talk?
G'long, white man! You ain't talkin' to me. *(With a chuckle)* Doesn't you
know dey's got to do wid a man was member in good standin' o' de Baptist Church? Sho' I was dat when I was porter on de Pullmans, befo' I
gits into my little trouble. Let dem try deir heathen tricks. De Baptist
Church done pertect me and land dem all in hell. *(Then with more confident satisfaction)* And I'se got little silver bullet o' my own, don't forgit!

Smithers: Ho! You 'aven't give much 'eed to your Baptist Church since you
been down 'ere. I've 'eard myself you 'ad turned yer coat an' was takin'
up with their blarsted witch doctors, or whatever the 'ell yer calls the
swine.

Jones (vehemently): I pretends to! Sho' I pretends! Dat's part o' my game
from de fust. If I finds out dem niggers believes dat black is white, den I
yells it out louder 'n deir loudest. It don't git me nothin' to do missionary work for de Baptist Church. I'se after de coin, an' I lays my Jesus on
de shelf for de time bein'. *(Stops abruptly to look at his watch—alertly)* But
I ain't got de time to waste on no more fool talk wid you. I'se gwine
away from heah dis secon'. *(He reaches in under the throne and pulls out an
expensive Panama hat with a bright multi-colored band and sets it jauntily on*

his head.) So long, white man! *(With a grin)* See you in jail sometime, maybe!

Smithers: Not me, you won't. Well, I wouldn't be in yer bloody boots for no bloomin' money, but 'ere's wishin' yer luck just the same.

Jones (contemptuously): You're de frightenedest man evah I see! I tells you I'se safe's 'f I was in New York City. It takes dem niggers from now to dark to git up de nerve to start somethin'. By dat time, I'se got a head start dey never kotch up wid.

Smithers (maliciously): Give my regards to any ghosts yer meets up with.

Jones (grinning): If dat ghost got money, I'll tell him never ha'nt you less'n he wants to lose it.

Smithers (flattered): Garn! *(Then curiously)* Ain't yer takin' no luggage with yer?

Jones: I travels light when I wants to move fast. And I got tinned grub buried on de edge o' de forest. *(Boastfully)* Now say dat I don't look ahead an' use my brains! *(With a wide, liberal gesture)* I will all dat's left in de palace to you—and you better grab all you kin sneak away wid befo' dey gits here.

Smithers (gratefully): Righto—and thanks ter yer. *(As Jones walks toward the door in rear—cautioningly)* Say! Look 'ere, you ain't goin' out that way, are yer?

Jones: Does you think I'd slink out de back door like a common nigger? I'se Emperor yit, ain't I? And de Emperor Jones leaves de way he comes, and dat black trash don't dare stop him—not yit, leastways. *(He stops for a moment in the doorway, listening to the far-off but insistent beat of the tom-tom.)* Listen to dat roll-call, will you? Must be mighty big drum carry dat far. *(Then with a laugh)* Well, if dey ain't no whole brass band to see me off, I sho' got de drum part of it. So long, white man. *(He puts his hands in his pockets and with studied carelessness, whistling a tune, he saunters out of the doorway and off to the left.)*

Smithers (looks after him with a puzzled admiration): 'E's got 'is bloomin' nerve with 'im, s'elp me! *(Then angrily)* Ho—the bleedin' nigger— puttin' on 'is bloody airs! I 'opes they nabs 'im an' gives 'im what's what!

CURTAIN

SCENE TWO

The end of the plain where the Great Forest begins. The foreground is sandy, level ground dotted by a few stones and clumps of stunted bushes cowering close against the earth to escape the buffeting of the trade wind. In the rear the forest is a wall of darkness dividing the world. Only when the eye becomes accustomed to the gloom can the outlines of separate trunks of the nearest trees be made out, enormous pillars of deeper blackness. A somber monotone of wind lost in the leaves moans in the air. Yet this sound serves but to intensify the impression of the forest's relentless immobility, to form a background throwing into relief its brooding, implacable silence.

Jones *enters from the left, walking rapidly. He stops as he nears the edge of the forest, looks around him quickly, peering into the dark as if searching for some familiar landmark. Then, apparently satisfied that he is where he ought to be, he throws himself on the ground, dog-tired.*

Well, heah I is. In de nick o' time, too! Little mo' an' it'd be blacker'n de ace of spades heahabouts. *(He pulls a bandana handkerchief from his hip pocket and mops off his perspiring face.)* Sho'! Gimme air! I'se tuckered out sho' 'nuff. Dat soft Emperor job ain't no trainin' fo' a long hike ovah dat plain in de brilin' sun. *(Then with a chuckle)* Cheer up, nigger, de worst is yet to come. *(He lifts his head and stares at the forest. His chuckle peters out abruptly. In a tone of awe)* My goodness, look at dem woods, will you? Dat no-count Smithers say dey'd be black an' he sho' called de turn. *(Turning away from them quickly and looking down at his feet, he snatches at a chance to change the subject—solicitously.)* Feet, you is holdin' up yo' end fine an' I sutinly hopes you ain't blisterin' none. It's time you git a rest. *(He takes off his shoes, his eyes studiously avoiding the forest. He feels of the soles of his feet gingerly.)* You is still in de pink—on'y a little mite feverish. Cool yo'selfs. Remember you done got a long journey yit befo' you. *(He sits in a weary attitude, listening to the rhythmic beating of the tom-tom. He grumbles in a loud tone to cover up a growing uneasiness.)* Bush niggers! Wonder dey wouldn't git sick o' beatin' dat drum. Sound louder, seem like. I wonder if dey's startin' after me? *(He scrambles to his feet, looking back across the plain.)* Couldn't see dem now, nohow, if dey was hundred feet away. *(Then shaking himself like a wet dog to get rid of these depressing thoughts)* Sho', dey's miles an' miles behind. What you gittin' fidgety about? *(But he sits down and begins to lace up his shoes in great haste, all the time muttering reassuringly)* You know what? Yo' belly is empty, dat's what's de matter wid you. Come time to eat! Wid nothin' but wind on yo' stomach, o' course you feels jiggedy. Well, we eats right heah an' now soon's I gits dese pesky shoes laced up. *(He finishes lacing up his shoes.)* Dere! Now le's see! *(Gets on his hands and knees and searches the ground around him with his eyes)* White stone, white stone, where is you? *(He sees the first white stone and crawls to it with satisfaction.)* Heah you is! I knowed dis was de right place. Box of grub, come to me. *(He turns over the stone and feels in under it—in a tone of dismay.)* Ain't heah! Gorry, is I in de right place or isn't I? Dere's 'nother stone. Guess dat's it. *(He scrambles to the next stone and turns it over)* Ain't heah, neither! Grub, whar is you ? Ain't heah. Gorry, has I got to go hungry into dem woods—all de night? *(While he is talking he scrambles from one stone to another, turning them over in frantic haste. Finally, he jumps to his feet excitedly.)* Is I lost de place? Must have! But how dat happen when I was followin' de trail across de plain in broad daylight? *(Almost plaintively)* I'se hungry, I is! I gotta git my feed. Whar's my strength gonna come from if I doesn't? Gorry, I gotta find dat grub high an' low somehow! Why it come dark so quick like dat? Can't see nothin'. *(He scratches a match on his trousers and peers about him. The rate of the beat of the far-off tom-tom increases perceptibly as he does so. He mutters in a bewildered voice.)* How come all dese white stones come heah when I only remembers one? *(Suddenly, with a frightened gasp, he flings the match on the ground and stamps on it.)* Nigger, is you gone crazy mad? Is you lightin' matches to show dem whar you is? Fo' Lawd's sake, use yo' haid. Gorry, I'se got to be careful! *(He stares at the plain behind him apprehensively, his hand on his revolver.)* But how come all dese white stones? And whar's dat tin box o' grub I hid all wrapped up in oilcloth?

(While his back 'is turned, the Little Formless Fears *creep out from the deeper blackness of the forest. They are black, shapeless, only their glittering little eyes can be seen. If they have any describable form at all it is that of a grubworm about the size of a creeping child. They move noiselessly, but with deliberate, painful effort, striving to raise themselves on end, failing and sinking prone again.* Jones *turns about to face the forest. He stares up at the tops of the trees, seeking vainly to discover his whereabouts by their conformation.)*

Can't tell nothin' from dem trees! Gorry, nothin' 'round heah looks like I evah seed it befo'. I'se done lost de place sho' 'nuff! *(With mournful foreboding)* It's mighty queer! It's mighty queer! *(With sudden forced defiance—in an angry tone)* Woods, is you tryin' to put somethin' ovah on me?

(From the formless creatures on the ground in front of him comes a tiny gale of low mocking laughter like a rustling of leaves. They squirm upward toward him in twisted attitudes. Jones *looks down, leaps backward with a yell of terror, yanking out his revolver as he does so—in a quavering voice.)* What's dat? Who's dar? What is you? Git away from me befo' I shoots you up! You don't?—

(He fires. There is a flash, a loud report, then silence broken only by the far-off, quickened throb of the tom-tom. The formless creatures have scurried back into the forest. Jones *remains fixed in his position, listening intently. The sound of the shot, the reassuring feel of the revolver in his hand, have somewhat restored his shaken nerve. He addresses himself with renewed confidence.)*

Dey're gone. Dat shot fix 'em. Dey was only little animals—little wild pigs, I reckon. Dey've maybe rooted out yo' grub an' eat it. Sho', you fool nigger, what you think dey is—ha'nts? *(Excitedly)* Gorry, you give de game away when you fire dat shot. Dem niggers heah dat fo' su'tin'! Time you beat it in de woods widout no long waits. *(He starts for the forest—hesitates before the plunge—then urging himself in with manful resolution.)* Git in, nigger! What you skeered at? Ain't nothin' dere but de trees! Git in! *(He plunges boldly into the forest.)*

SCENE THREE

In the forest. The moon has just risen. Its beams, drifting through the canopy of leaves, make a barely perceptible, suffused, eerie glow. A dense low wall of underbrush and creepers is in the nearer foreground, fencing in a small triangular clearing. Beyond this is the massed blackness of the forest like an encompassing barrier. A path is dimly discerned leading down to the clearing from left, rear, and winding away from it again toward the right. As the scene opens nothing can be distinctly made out. Except for the beating of the tom-tom, which is a trifle louder and quicker than at the close of the previous scene, there is silence, broken every few seconds by a queer, clicking sound. Then gradually the figure of the Negro, Jeff, *can be discerned crouching on his haunches at the rear of the triangle. He is middle-aged, thin, brown in color, is dressed in a Pullman porter's uniform and cap. He is throwing a pair of dice on the ground before him, picking them up, shaking them, casting them out with the regular, rigid, mechanical movements of an automaton. The heavy, plodding footsteps of someone approaching along the trail from the left are heard and* Jones' *voice, pitched on a slightly higher key and strained in a cheery effort to overcome its own tremors.*

De moon's rizen. Does you heah dat, nigger? You gits more light from dis out. No mo' buttin' yo' fool head agin' de trunks an' scratchin' de hide off yo' legs in de bushes. Now you sees whar yo'se gwine. So cheer up! From now on you has a snap. *(He steps just to the rear of the triangular clearing and mops off his face on his sleeve. He has lost his Panama hat. His face is scratched, his brilliant uniform shows several large rents.)* What time's it gittin' to be, I wonder? I dassent light no match to find out. Phoo'. It's wa'm an' dat's a fac'! *(Wearily)* How long I been makin tracks in dese woods? Must be hours an' hours. Seems like fo'-evah! Yit can't be, when de moon's jes' riz. Dis am a long night fo' yo', yo' Majesty! *(With a mournful chuckle)* Majesty! Der ain't much majesty 'bout dis baby now. *(With attempted cheerfulness)* Never min'. It's all part o' de game. Dis night come to an end like everything else. And when you gits dar safe and has dat bankroll in yo' hands you laughs at all dis. *(He starts to whistle but checks himself abruptly.)* What yo' whistlin' for, you po' dope! Want all de worl' to heah you? *(He stops talking to listen.)* Heah dat ole drum! Sho' gits nearer from de sound. Dey's packin' it along wid 'em. Time fo' me to move. *(He takes a step forward, then stops—worriedly.)* What's dat odder queer clickety sound I heah? Dere it is! Sound close! Sound like—sound like—Fo' God sake, sound like some nigger was shootin' crap! *(Frightenedly)* I better beat it quick when I gits dem notions. *(He walks quickly into the clear space—then stands transfixed as he sees* Jeff—*in a terrified gasp.)* Who dar? Who dat? Is dat you, Jeff? *(Starting toward the other, forgetful for a moment of his surroundings and really believing it is a living man that he sees—in a tone of happy relief)* Jeff! I'se sho' mighty glad to see you! Dey tol' me you done died from dat razor cut I gives you. *(Stopping suddenly, bewilderedly)* But how you come to be heah, nigger? *(He stares fascinatedly at the other who continues his mechanical play with the dice.* Jones' *eyes begin to roll wildly. He stutters.)* Ain't you gwine—look up—can't you speak to me? Is you—is you—a ha'nt? *(He jerks out his revolver in a frenzy of terrified rage.)* Nigger, I kills you dead once! Has I got to kill you ag'in? You take it den. *(He fires. When the smoke clears away* Jeff *has disappeared.* Jones *stands trembling—then with a certain reassurance.)* He's gone, anyway. Ha'nt or not ha'nt, dat shot fix him. *(The beat of the far-off tom-tom is perceptibly louder and more rapid.* Jones *becomes conscious of it—with a start, looking back over his shoulder.)* Dey's gittin' near! Dey's comin' fast! And heah I is shootin' shots to let 'em know jes' whar I is! Oh, Gorry, I'se got to run. *(Forgetting the path he plunges wildly into the under-brush in the rear and disappears in the shadow.)*

SCENE FOUR

In the forest. A wide dirt road runs diagonally from right, front to left, rear. Rising sheer on both sides the forest walls it in. The moon it now up. Under its light the road glimmers ghastly and unreal. It is as if the forest had stood aside momentarily to let the road pass through and accomplish its veiled purpose. This done, the forest will fold in upon itself again and the road will be no more. Jones *stumbles in from the forest on the right. His uniform is ragged and torn. He looks about him with numbed surprise when he sees the road, his eyes blinking in the bright moonlight. He flops down exhaustedly and pants heavily for a while. Then with sudden anger.*

I'm meltin' wid heat! Runnin' an' runnin' an' runnin'! Damn dis heah coat! Like a straitjacket! (*He tears off his coat and flings it away from him, revealing himself stripped to the waist.*) Dere! Dat's better! Now I kin breathe! (*Looking down at his feet, the spurs catch his eye*) And to hell wid dese high-fangled spurs. Dey're what's been a-trippin' me up an' breakin' my neck. (*He unstraps them and flings them away disgustedly.*) Dere! I gits rid o' dem frippety Emperor trappin's an' I travels lighter. Lawd! I'se tired! (*After a pause, listening to the insistent beat of the tom-tom in the distance*) I must 'a' put some distance between myself an' dem—runnin' like dat—and yit—dat damn drum sounds jes' de same—nearer, even. Well, I guess I a'most holds my lead anyhow. Dey won't never catch up. (*With a sigh*) If on'y my fool legs stands up. Oh, I'se sorry I evah went in for dis. Dat Emperor job is sho' hard to shake. (*He looks around him suspiciously.*) How'd dis road evah git heah? Good level road, too. I never remembers seein' it befo'. (*Shaking his head apprehensively*) Dese woods is sho' full o' de queerest things at night. (*With a sudden terror*) Lawd God, don't let me see no more o' dem ha'nts! Dey gits my goat! (*Then trying to talk himself into confidence*) Ha'nts! You fool nigger, dey ain't no such things) Don't de Baptist parson tell you dat many time? Is you civilized, or is you like dese ign'rent black niggers heah? Sho'! Dat was all in yo' own head. Wasn't nothin' dere. Wasn't no Jeff! Know what? You jus' get seein' dem things 'cause yo' belly's empty and you's sick wid hunger inside. Hunger 'fects yo' head and yo' eyes. Any fool know dat. (*Then pleading fervently*) But bless God, I don't come across no more o' dem, whatever dey is! (*Then cautiously*) Rest! Don't talk! Rest! You needs it. Den you gits on yo' way again. (*Looking at the moon*) Night's half gone a'most. You hits de coast in de mawning! Den you's all safe.

(*From the right forward a small gang of Negroes enter. They are dressed in striped convict suits, their heads are shaven, one leg drags limpingly, shackled to a heavy ball and chain. Some carry picks, the others shovels. They are followed by a white man dressed in the uniform of a prison guard. A Winchester rifle is slung across his shoulders and he carries a heavy whip. At a signal from the* Guard *they stop on the road opposite where* Jones *is sitting.* Jones, *who has been staring up at the sky, unmindful of their noiseless approach, suddenly looks down and sees them. His eyes pop out, he tries to get to his feet and fly, but sinks back, too numbed by fright to move. His voice catches in a choking prayer.*)

Lawd Jesus!

(*The* Prison Guard *cracks his whip—noiselessly—and at that signal all the convicts start to work on the road. They swing their picks, they shovel, but not a sound comes from their labor. Their movements, like those of* Jeff *in the preceding scene, are those of automatons,—rigid, slow, and mechanical. The* Prison Guard *points sternly at* Jones *with his whip, motions him to take his place among the other shovelers.* Jones *gets to his feet in a hypnotized stupor. He mumbles subserviently.*)

Yes, suh! Yes, suh! I'se comin'.

(*As he shuffles, dragging one foot, over to his place, he curses under his breath with rage and hatred.*)

God damn yo' soul, I gits even wid you yit, sometime.

(*As if there were a shovel in his hands he goes through weary, mechanical gestures of digging up dirt, and throwing it to the roadside. Suddenly the* Guard *approaches him angrily, threateningly. He raises his whip and lashes* Jones *viciously across the shoulders with it.* Jones *winces with pain and cowers abjectly. The* Guard *turns his back on him and walks away contemptuously. Instantly* Jones *straightens up. With arms upraised as if his shovel were a club in his hands he springs murderously at the unsuspecting* Guard. *In the act of crashing down his shovel on the white man's skull,* Jones *suddenly becomes aware that his hands are empty. He cries despairingly.*)

Whar's my shovel? Gimme my shovel 'til I splits his damn head! (*Appealing to his fellow convicts*) Gimme a shovel, one o' you, fo' God's sake!

(*They stand fixed in motionless attitudes, their eyes on the ground. The* Guard *seems to wait expectantly, his back turned to the attacker.* Jones *bellows with baffled, terrified rage, tugging frantically at his revolver.*)

I kills you, you white debil, if it's de last thing I evah does! Ghost or debil, I kill you agin!

(*He frees the revolver and fires point blank at the* Guard's *back. Instantly the walls of the forest close in from both sides, the road and the figures of the convict gang are blotted out in an enshrouding darkness. The only sounds are a crashing in the underbrush as* Jones *leaps away in mad flight and the throbbing of the tom-tom, still far distant, but increased in volume of sound and rapidity of beat.*)

SCENE FIVE

A large circular clearing, enclosed by the serried ranks of gigantic trunks of tall trees whose tops are lost to view. In the center is a big dead stump worn by time into a curious resemblance to an auction block. The moon floods the clearing with a clear light. Jones *forces his way in through the forest on the left. He looks wildly about the clearing with hunted, fearful glances. His pants are in tatters, his shoes cut and misshapen, flapping about his feet. He slinks cautiously to the stump in the center and sits down in a tense position, ready for instant flight. Then he holds his head in his hands and rocks back and forth, moaning to himself miserably.*

Oh, Lawd, Lawd! Oh, Lawd, Lawd! (*Suddenly he throws himself on his knees and raises his clasped hands to the sky—in a voice of agonized pleading*) Lawd Jesus, heah my prayer! I'se a po' sinner, a po' sinner! I knows I done wrong, I knows it! When I cotches Jeff cheatin' wid loaded dice my anger overcomes me and I kills him dead! Lawd, I done wrong! When dat guard hits me wid de whip, my anger overcomes me, and I kills him dead. Lawd, I done wrong! And down heah whar dese fool bush niggers raises me up to the seat o' de mighty, I steals all I could grab. Lawd, I done wrong! I knows it! I'se sorry! Forgive me, Lawd! Forgive dis po' sinner! *(Then beseeching terrifiedly)* And keep dem away, Lawd! Keep dem away from me! And stop dat drum soundin' in my cars! Dat begin to sound ha'nted, too. *(He gets to his feet, evidently slightly reassured by his prayer—with attempted confidence.)* De Lawd'll preserve me from dem ha'nts after dis. *(Sits down on the stump again)* I ain't skeered o' real men. Let dem come. But dem odders—(He shudders—then looks down at his feet, working his toes inside the shoes—with a groan.)* Oh, my po' feet! Dem shoes ain't no use no more 'ceptin' to hurt. I'se better off widout dem. *(He unlaces them and pulls them off—holds the wrecks of the shoes in his hands and regards them mournfully.)* You was real, A-one patin' leather, too. Look at you now. Emperor, you'se gittin' mighty low!

(He sighs dejectedly and remains with bowed shoulders, staring down at the shoes in his hands as if reluctant to throw them away. While his attention is thus occupied, a crowd of figures silently enter the clearing from all sides. All are dressed in Southern costumes of the period of the fifties of the last century. There are middle-aged men who are evidently well-to-do planters. There is one spruce, authoritative individual—the Auctioneer. *There is a crowd of curious spectators, chiefly young belles and dandies who have come to the slave-market for diversion. All exchange courtly greetings in dumb show and chat silently together. There is something stiff, rigid, unreal, marionettish about their movements. They group themselves about the stump. Finally a batch of slaves is led in from the left by an attendant—three men of different ages, two women, one with a baby in her arms, nursing. They are placed to the left of the stump, beside* Jones.*

The white planters look them over appraisingly as if they were cattle, and exchange judgments on each. The dandies point with their fingers and make witty remarks. The belles titter bewitchingly. All this in silence save for the ominous throb of the tom-tom. The Auctioneer holds up his hand, taking his place at the stump. The groups strain forward attentively. He touches* Jones *on the shoulder peremptorily, motioning for him to stand on the stump—the auction block.*

Jones *looks up, sees the figures on all sides, looks wildly for some opening to escape, sees none, screams and leaps madly to the top of the stump to get as far away from them as possible. He stands there, cowering, paralyzed with horror. The Auctioneer begins his silent spiel. He points to* Jones, *appeals to the planters to see for themselves. Here is a good field hand, sound in wind and limb as they can see. Very strong still in spite of his being middle-aged. Look at that back. Look at those shoulders. Look at the muscles in his arms and his sturdy legs. Capable of any amount of hard labor. Moreover, of a good disposition, intelligent and tractable. Will any gentleman start the bidding? The* Planters *raise their fingers, make their bids. They are apparently all eager to possess* Jones. *The bidding is lively, the crowd interested. While this has been going on,* Jones *has been seized by the courage of desperation. He dares to look down and around him. Over his face abject terror gives way to mystification, to gradual realization—stutteringly.)*

What you all doin', white folks? What's all dis? What you all lookin' at me fo'? What you doin' wid me, anyhow? *(Suddenly convulsed with raging hatred and fear)* Is dis a auction? Is you sellin' me like dey uster befo' de war? *(Jerking out his revolver just as the* Auctioneer *knocks him down to one of the* Planters—*glaring from him to the purchaser)* And *you* sells me? And *you* buys me? I shows you I'se a free nigger, damn yo' souls! *(He fires at the* Auctioneer *and at the* Planter *with such rapidity that the two shots are almost simultaneous. As if this were a signal the walls of the forest fold in. Only blackness remains and silence broken by* Jones *as he rushes off, crying with fear—and by the quickened, ever louder beat of the tom-tom.)*

SCENE SIX

A cleared space in the forest. The limbs of the trees meet over it forming a low ceiling about five feet from the ground. The interlocked ropes of creepers reaching upward to entwine the tree trunks give an arched appearance to the sides. The space thus enclosed is like the dark noisome hold of some ancient vessel. The moonlight is almost completely shut out and only a vague wan light filters through. There is the noise of someone approaching from the left, stumbling and crawling through the undergrowth. Jones' *voice is heard between chattering moans.*

Oh, Lawd, what I gwine do now? Ain't got no bullet left on'y de silver one. If mo' o' dem ha'nts come after me, how I gwine skeer dem away? Oh, Lawd, on'y de silver one left—an' I gotta save dat fo' luck. If I shoots dat one I'm a goner sho'! Lawd, it's black heah! Whar's de moon? Oh, Lawd, don't dis night evah come to an end! *(By the sounds, he is feeling his way cautiously forward.)* Dere! Dis feels like a clear space. I gotta lie down an' rest. I don't care if dem niggers does cotch me. I gotta rest.

(He is well forward now where his figure can be dimly made out. His pants have been so torn away that what is left of them is no better than a breech cloth. He flings himself full length, face downward on the ground, panting with exhaustion. Gradually it seems to grow lighter in the enclosed space and two rows of seated figures can be seen behind Jones. *They are sitting in crumpled, despairing attitudes, hunched, facing one another with their backs touching the forest walls as if they were shackled to them. All are Negroes, naked save for loin cloths. At first they are silent and motionless. Then they begin to sway slowly forward toward each other and back again in unison, as if they were laxly letting themselves follow the long roll of a ship at sea. At the same time, a low, melancholy murmur rises among them, increasing gradually by rhythmic degrees which seem to be directed and controlled by the throb of the tom-tom in the distance, to a long, tremulous wail of despair that reaches a certain pitch, unbearably acute, then falls by slow gradations of tone into silence and is taken up again.* Jones *starts, looks up, sees the figures, and throws himself down again to shut out the sight. A shudder of terror shakes his whole body as the wail rises up about him again.*

*But the next time, his voice, as if under some uncanny compulsion, starts with the oth-
ers. As their chorus lifts he rises to a sitting posture similar to the others, swaying back
and forth. His voice reaches the highest pitch of sorrow, of desolation. The light fades
out, the other voices cease, and only darkness is left.* Jones *can be heard scrambling to
his feet and running off, his voice sinking down the scale and receding as he moves
farther and farther away in the forest. The tom-tom beats louder, quicker, with a
more insistent, triumphant pulsation.)*

SCENE SEVEN

*The foot of a gigantic tree by the edge of a great river. A rough structure of
boulders, like an altar, is by the tree. The raised river bank is in the nearer background. Beyond this the surface of the river spreads out, brilliant and unruffled in
the moonlight, blotted out and merged into a veil of bluish mist in the distance.*
Jones' *voice is heard from the left rising and falling in the long, despairing wail of
the chained slaves, to the rhythmic beat of the tom-tom. As his voice sinks into silence, he enters the open space. The expression of his face is fixed and stony, his eyes
have an obsessed glare, he moves with a strange deliberation like a sleep-walker or
one in a trance. He looks around at the tree, the rough stone altar, the moonlit surface of the river beyond, and passes his hand over his head with a vague gesture of
puzzled bewilderment. Then, as if in obedience to some obscure impulse, he sinks
into a kneeling, devotional posture before the altar. Then he seems to come to himself
partly, to have an uncertain realization of what he is doing, for he straightens up
and stares about him horrifiedly—in an incoherent mumble.*

What—what is I doin'? What is—dis place? Seems like I know dat tree—
an' dem stones—an' de river. I remember—seems like I been heah befo'.
(Tremblingly) Oh, Gorry, I'se skeered in dis place! I'se skeered. Oh, Lawd, pertect dis sinner!

*(Crawling away from the altar, he cowers close to the ground, his face hidden, his
shoulders heaving with sobs of hysterical fright. From behind the trunk of the tree, as
if he had sprung out of it, the figure of the* Congo Witch Doctor *appears. He is
wizened and old, naked except for the fur of some small animal tied about his waist,
its bushy tail hanging down in front. His body is stained all over a bright red. Antelope horns are on each side of his head, branching upward. In one hand he carries a
bone rattle, in the other a charm stick with a bunch of white cockatoo feathers tied to
the end. A great number of glass beads and bone ornaments are about his neck, ears,
wrists, and ankles. He struts noiselessly with a queer prancing step to a position in the
clear ground between* Jones *and the altar. Then with a preliminary, summoning
stamp of his foot on the earth, he begins to dance and to chant. As if in response to his
summons the beating of the tom-tom grows to a fierce, exultant boom whose throbs
seem to fill the air with vibrating rhythm.* Jones *looks up, starts to spring to his feet,
reaches a half-kneeling, half-squatting position and remains rigidly fixed there, paralyzed with awed fascination by this new apparition. The* Witch Doctor *sways,
stamping with his foot, his bone rattle clicking the time. His voice rises and falls in a
weird, monotonous croon, without articulate word divisions. Gradually his dance*

*becomes clearly one of a narrative in pantomime, his croon is an incantation, a charm
to allay the fierceness of some implacable deity demanding sacrifice. He flees, he is pursued by devils, he hides, he flees again. Ever wilder and wilder becomes his flight,
nearer and nearer draws the pursuing evil, more and more the spirit of terror gains
possession of him. His croon, rising to intensity, is punctuated by shrill cries.* Jones *has
become completely hypnotized. His voice joins in the incantation, in the cries, he beats
time with his hands and sways his body to and fro from the waist. The whole spirit
and meaning of the dance has entered into him, has become his spirit. Finally the
theme of the pantomime halts on a howl of despair, and is taken up again in a note of
savage hope. There is a salvation. The forces of evil demand sacrifice. They must be
appeased. The* Witch Doctor *points with his wand to the sacred tree, to the river beyond, to the altar, and finally to* Jones *with a ferocious command.* Jones *seems to sense
the meaning of this. It is he who must offer himself for sacrifice. He beats his forehead
abjectly to the ground, moaning hysterically.)*

Mercy, Oh, Lawd! Mercy! Mercy on dis po' sinner.

(The Witch Doctor *springs to the river bank. He stretches out his arms and
calls to some God within its depths. Then he starts backward slowly, his arms remaining out. A huge head of a crocodile appears over the bank and its eyes, glittering
greenly, fasten upon* Jones. *He stares into them fascinatedly. The* Witch Doctor
*prances up to him, touches him with his wand, motions with hideous command toward
the waiting monster.* Jones *squirms on his belly nearer and nearer, moaning continually.)*

Mercy, Lawd! Mercy!

(The crocodile heaves more of his enormous hulk onto the land. Jones *squirms
toward him. The* Witch Doctor's *voice shrills out in furious exultation, the tom-tom
beats madly.* Jones *cries out in a fierce, exhausted spasm of anguished pleading.)*

Lawd, save me! Lawd Jesus, heah my prayer!

*(Immediately, in answer to his prayer, comes the thought of the one bullet left
him. He snatches at his hip, shouting defiantly.)*

De silver bullet! You don't git me yit!

*(He fires at the green eyes in front of him. The head of the crocodile sinks back
behind the river bank, the* Witch Doctor *springs behind the sacred tree and disappears.* Jones *lies with his face to the ground, his arms outstretched, whimpering with
fear as the throb of the tom-tom fills the silence about him with a somber pulsation, a
baffled but revengeful power.)*

SCENE EIGHT

*Dawn. Same as Scene Two, the dividing line of forest and plain. The nearest
tree trunks are dimly revealed but the forest behind them is still a mass of glooming
shadow. The tom-tom seems on the very spot, so loud and continuously vibrating are
its beats.* Lem *enters from the left, followed by a small squad of his soldiers, and by
the Cockney trader,* Smithers. Lem *is a heavy-set, ape-faced old savage of the
extreme African type, dressed only in a loin cloth. A revolver and cartridge belt are
about his waist. His soldiers are in different degrees of rag-concealed nakedness. All
wear broad palm-leaf hats. Each one carries a rifle.* Smithers *is the same as in
Scene One. One of the soldiers, evidently a tracker, is peering about keenly on the*

ground. He points to the spot where Jones *entered the forest.* Lem *and* Smithers *come to look.*

Smithers *(after a glance, turns away in disgust):* That's where 'e went in right enough. Much good it'll do yer. 'E's miles orf by this an' safe to the Coast, damn 's 'ide! I tole yer yer'd lose 'im, didn't I?—wastin' the 'ole bloomin' night beatin' yer bloody drum and castin' yer silly spells! Gawd blimey, wot a pack!

Lem *(gutturally):* We cotch him. *(He makes a motion to his soldiers who squat down on their haunches in a semi-circle.)*

Smithers *(exasperatedly):* Well, ain't yer goin' in an' 'unt 'im in the woods? What the 'ell's the good of waitin'?

Lem *(imperturbably—squatting down himself):* We cotch him.

Smithers *(turning away from him contemptuously):* Aw! Garn! 'E's a better man than the lot o' you put together, I 'ates-the sight o' 'im but I'll say that for 'im. *(A sound comes from the forest. The soldiers jump to their feet, cocking their rifles alertly.* Lem *remains sitting with an imperturbable expression, but listening intently. He makes a quick signal with his hand. His followers creep quickly into the forest, scattering so that each enters at a different spot.)*

Smithers: You ain't thinkin' that would be 'im, I 'ope?

Lem *(calmly):* We cotch him.

Smithers: Blarsted fat 'eads! *(Then after a second's thought—wonderingly)* Still an' all, it might 'appen. If 'e lost 'is bloody way in these stinkin' woods 'e'd likely turn in a circle without 'is knowin' it.

Lem *(peremptorily):* Ssshh! *(The reports of several rifles sound from the forest, followed a second later by savage, exultant yells. The beating of the tom-tom abruptly ceases.* Lem *looks up at the white man with a grin of satisfaction.)* We cotch him. Him dead.

Smithers *(with a snarl):* 'Ow d'yer know it's 'im an' 'ow d'yer know 'e's dead?

Lem: My mens dey got um silver bullets. Lead bullet no kill him. He got um strong charm. I cook um money, make um silver bullet, make um strong charm, too.

Smithers *(astonished):* So that's wot you was up to all night, wot? You was scared to put after 'im till you'd moulded silver bullets, eh?

Lem *(simply stating a fact):* Yes. Him got strong charm. Lead no good.

Smithers *(slapping his thigh and guffawing):* Haw-haw! If yer don t beat all 'ell! *(Then recovering himself—scornfully)* I'll bet yer it ain't 'im they shot at all, yer bleedin' looney!

Lem *(calmly):* Dey come bring him now. *(The soldiers come out of the forest, carrying* Jones' *limp body. He is dead. They carry him to* Lem, *who examines his body with great satisfaction.* Smithers *leans over his shoulder—in a tone of frightened awe.)* Well, they did for yer right enough, Jonesey, me lad! Dead as a 'erring! *(Mockingly)* Where's yer 'igh an' mighty airs now, yer bloomin' Majesty? *(Then with a grin)* Silver bullets! Gawd blimey, but yer died in the 'eight o' style, any'ow!

CURTAIN

———— EUGENE O'NEILL ————

(1888–1953) Web

Eugene O'Neill is the only American dramatist to receive the Nobel Prize for literature, which he was awarded in 1936. Recipient of the Pulitzer Prize three times during the decade of the 1920s, O'Neill wrote plays in a number of different forms: realism, expressionism, and—in the later 1920s—modern versions of the Greek trilogy. As produced by the Provincetown Players in 1920, *The Emperor Jones* was an enormous success in New York and then went on a tour of America that lasted two years. O'Neill's later work, in particular the autobiographical plays *The Iceman Cometh* (1939), *Long Day's Journey Into Night* (1939–1941), and *A Moon for the Misbegotten* (1943), remain central to the contemporary repertoire.

TOPICS FOR CRITICAL THINKING

1. Review the expressionist elements of *The Emperor Jones*. How effective are they at revealing Brutus Jones's fears and desires?

2. Is O'Neill's representation of Jones offensive, as Charles Gilpin, the first actor to play the role, alleged in 1920? What roles do language and dialect play in this representation? Does this representation necessarily make O'Neill a racist?

3. Is Brutus Jones a tragic figure? How closely does the play follow the conventions of tragedy, particularly in terms of plot and characterization? How does a comparison of Jones with tragic protagonists affect our reading of the play?

4. What function does the Slave Auction perform in Scene Five? What would the play lack if this scene were omitted?

5. Why is Smithers important to the play? Does he possess any redeeming qualities? If so, what are they? What are we to infer from his position at the end of the play?

TOPIC FOR CRITICAL WRITING

Develop a thesis about the representation of race and ethnicity in *The Emperor Jones*. How does O'Neill represent African Americans in the play? How do his techniques of doing so compare to his methods of representing Smithers as a "Cockney," or lower class Brit?

Critical Perspective: On Modern Tragedy

"The tragedy of Man is perhaps the only significant thing about him. What I am after is to get an audience leaving the theatre with an exultant feeling from seeing somebody on the stage facing life, fighting against the eternal odds, not conquering, but perhaps inevitably being conquered. The individual life is made significant just by the struggle."

—Eugene O'Neill (1917)

Critical Perspective: On Casting Brutus Jones for the 1920 Production

"Brutus Jones was a problem [to cast], and there is some dispute as to how it was resolved. There are people who recall that [Jig] Cook was determined from the beginning to cast a Negro in the role—a decision that, as little as five years later, would probably have been an automatic one. But in 1920 no Negro had ever played a major role in an American tragedy. . . ."

—Arthur and Barbara Gelb, *O'Neill* (1960)

Critical Perspective: On the Effect of *The Emperor Jones* on O'Neill's Career

"The success [of *The Emperor Jones*] was the rock on which the Players foundered, yet their demise was inevitable from the very nature of their idealism. More important in considering the development of O'Neill's work is that *The Emperor Jones*, while it confirmed O'Neill's direction and justified his dedication, set him on a path that at its farthest end was to prove artistically perilous. For with the play, O'Neill accepted the dicta of the American Art Theatre movement and began to write plays that moved far from his realistic style. He became a writer from whom 'experiment' was expected, and one who would sometimes put the dictates of style over the development of theme and character."

—Travis Bogard, *Contour in Time* (1972)

47 Realism Revisited: Two American Writers

How many familiar sayings do you know that begin, "Old somethings never die, they just . . ."? Old generals never die, old songs never die, old dramatic forms never die—they just go somewhere else. Or, as is the case with realism in the two plays in this chapter, it becomes revitalized as gifted writers breathe new life into it.

Such an assertion should hardly seem surprising, as the best of older cultural forms never seem to die. For example, who would have thought that as the twenty-first century began two of the Top Ten albums on the *Billboard* charts would be by the Beatles? Virtually all of the songs on both albums were first performed in the 1960s, but no matter: Fans were still eager to hear them again or for the first time. Some cultural theorists, in fact, believe that at any one time three kinds of cultural formations exist: a dominant formation, a residual formation, and an emergent one. In popular music, a number of forms—hip-hop, rap, certain kinds of pop—might be considered *dominant*. Artists who successfully master these forms seem to be everywhere: on the radio, on television, in the largest concert venues. Music by the Beatles, the Kinks, Eric Clapton, Jimi Hendrix, Aretha Franklin, even Tony Bennett confirm the enduring attraction of such *residual* forms as '60s rock and roll, soul, psychedelic rock, and even World War II-era big band swing. And somewhere in America practicing right now in a garage or basement, innovative young musicians are preparing to bring a newer, *emergent* form to the public that will totally revise the music scene.

Much the same is true of dramatic form. Ibsenite realism of the later nineteenth century has never really gone away—perhaps it never will—but at times it has been transformed by later plays. Expressionist techniques employed by such writers as Eugene O'Neill in *The Emperor Jones* (1920), stylistic devices borrowed from advances in German silent film and drama, were hardly dead either by mid-century. Both of the plays in this chapter by two of the most important American dramatists of the twentieth—or any other—century demonstrate this fact. But this in no way means that either playwright simply borrowed techniques from expressionism and mixed them randomly into the aesthetic formula of realism. Tennessee Williams and Arthur Miller seized both forms and added their own innovations to create landmark plays in the history of modern drama. At the dawn of the twenty-first century, Williams and Miller remain giants of the American theater. Their plays are produced constantly and, so long as drama is seen, their works will be rediscovered by future generations of playgoers.

Tennessee Williams's "Gauzy Realism":
The Glass Menagerie

In his introductory notes to *The Glass Menagerie* (1944), Tennessee Williams discusses the evolution of dramatic form at mid-century, training his sights specifically on realism:

> The straight realistic play with its genuine frigidaire and authentic ice cubes, its characters that speak exactly as its audience speaks . . . has the same virtue of a photographic likeness. Everyone nowadays should know the unimportance of the photographic in art. . . .

Williams's remarks pertain not only to *The Glass Menagerie*, but to the modern drama more broadly. The "exhausted theatre of realistic conventions," he argues, must be replaced by a more vital "plastic theatre" able to express the "poetic imagination." To that end, in *The Glass Menagerie* Williams employs screens on which images and phrases appear, musical cues associated with individual characters, and specifically "nonrealistic" lighting effects: darkness, dim light to suggest fading memory or nostalgia, bright light on emotionally resonant objects like Laura Wingfield's glass figurines, and other devices. As Tom Wingfield, a figure for Williams himself, explains in his opening monologue, his missing father is a virtual fifth character. We never see him, so dialogue and scenic effect must convey the sense of his importance. "Nonrealistic" devices help do this.

One of these is a dropped panel made of gauze, hence the term "gauzy realism" or, equally accurate, "subjective realism." That is to say, once Tom acknowledges his intentions to pull "tricks" from his pocket and "turn back time," we understand that what follows on stage is not the *objective* or "photographic" realism of Henrik Ibsen. Instead, as he explains, what we see is a "memory play," dramatic action as mediated by his consciousness. Tom's explanation of his dual role as narrator and character *is* objectively "real": we understand it as taking place now. But what we see in the Wingfield apartment from the 1930s may or may not have happened exactly the way it transpires. Some events may be recalled as more significant than they actually were—or as less so. One way to achieve this kind of subjective or dreamy effect is through the use of a transparent scrim or gauze and lighting. A drop made of gauze representing the "portieres of the dining room arch" was lowered in the first and last scenes, and rendered transparent by strategic lighting. Even though the action is readily visible to the audience, it is not so sharply focused as it would be when the drop was raised.

In other ways, as a number of critics have observed, *The Glass Menagerie* seems almost like a film. Each scene has specific lighting and design effects like legends printed on screens; each has specific music that functions almost like the soundtrack of a film. Such devices, Williams often contended, are required if the inherent poetry of drama is to be realized on stage. And, perhaps, such devices were necessary for Williams to convey the emotion of what is, finally, a highly autobiographical play. Williams's father, like Tom's, moved his family from Mississippi to an apartment in St. Louis. Williams's mother, like Amanda

Wingfield, seemed to embody the Old South and lived in a fantastical past more refined than the vulgar present. And Rose Williams, like Laura Wingfield, was a shy, introverted young woman who eventually suffered from a variety of psychological conflicts leading to a lobotomy. Like Tom Wingfield, Thomas "Tennessee" Williams was very close to his sister. As embodied in Laura, she remains one of the American stage's most vulnerable, and fragile characters.

Williams's innovations include more than lighting effects, gauze drops, and projected legends; some concern such basic elements of dramatic form as plot, characterization, and language. Characterization in *The Glass Menagerie* and the form of the play, for example, have occupied critics for decades. Marc Robinson describes the ways in which directors' choices for staging *The Glass Menagerie* depend largely on which character they recognize as the play's "main" character. The title of the play seems to suggest that Laura is the central character. If not Laura, then Tom seems most likely because he narrates the action and serves as the character around whom the action revolves. Robinson, however, contends that Amanda actually serves this purpose; she drives the action of the play and remains a kind of enigma, a "mess of contradictions." Without her, there is little conflict or dramatic tension; without her, both the fictional present and past would be very different.

For critics and playwrights alike, Williams's language and the poetic quality of the play mark its distinctive contribution to modern drama. Irish playwright Marina Carr reserves her highest praise for Williams's ability to create poetry on stage. For her, there exists a "kind of grace and dignity" about Williams's writing that is both rare and appealing. She describes his use of metaphor on stage—the metaphor of Laura's menagerie of figurines—as merely one example of a poetic quality in his writing that she greatly admires.

The Glass Menagerie, an early play in what would become a distinguished body of dramatic work, anticipates much of what makes Williams's plays so unique in the history of the American theater. His ability to evoke the often tragic difference between a past life of leisure and a greatly diminished present so painfully evident in Tom's mother, Amanda; his depiction of working class or Depression-era families struggling to survive; his representation of the American South; his contemplation of ways to revise realism in poetic and imaginative ways—these are merely some of the things for which Thomas Lanier "Tennessee" Williams is known.

TENNESSEE WILLIAMS

The Glass Menagerie   *(1944)*

CHARACTERS

Amanda Wingfield, the mother.
> *A little woman of great but confused vitality clinging frantically to another time and place. Her characterization must be carefully created, not copied from type. She is not paranoiac, but her life is paranoia. There is much to admire in*

Amanda, *and as much to love and pity as there is to laugh at. Certainly she has endurance and a kind of heroism, and though her foolishness makes her unwittingly cruel at times, there is tenderness in her slight person.*

Laura Wingfield, her daughter.

Amanda, *having failed to establish contact with reality, continues to live vitally in her illusions, but* Laura's *situation is even graver. A childhood illness has left her crippled, one leg slightly shorter than the other, and held in a brace. This defect need not be more than suggested on the stage. Stemming from this,* Laura's *separation increases till she is like a piece of her own glass collection, too exquisitely fragile to move from the shelf.*

Tom Wingfield, her son, and the narrator of the play.

A poet with a job in a warehouse. His nature is not remorseless, but to escape from a trap he has to act without pity.

Jim O'Connor, the gentleman caller.

A nice, ordinary, young man.

Scene: An alley in St. Louis.

Part I: Preparation for a Gentleman Caller.

Part II: The Gentleman Calls.

Time: Now and the Past.

SCENE I

The Wingfield apartment is in the rear of the building, one of those vast hive-like conglomerations of cellular living-units that flower as warty growths in over-crowded urban centers of lower middle-class population and are symptomatic of the impulse of this largest and fundamentally enslaved section of American society to avoid fluidity and differentiation and to exist and function as one interfused mass of automatism.

The apartment faces an alley and is entered by a fire-escape, a structure whose name is a touch of accidental poetic truth, for all of these huge buildings are always burning with the slow and implacable fires of human desperation. The fire-escape is included in the set—that is, the landing of it and steps descending from it.

The scene is memory and is therefore nonrealistic. Memory takes a lot of poetic license. It omits some details; others are exaggerated, according to the emotional value of the articles it touches, for memory is seated predominantly in the heart. The interior is therefore rather dim and poetic.

At the rise of the curtain, the audience is faced with the dark, grim rear wall of the Wingfield tenement. This building, which runs parallel to the footlights, is flanked on both sides by dark, narrow alleys which run into murky canyons of tangled clotheslines, garbage cans and the sinister latticework of neighboring fire-escapes. It is up and down these side alleys that exterior entrances and exits are made, during the play. At the end of Tom's opening commentary, the dark tene-ment wall slowly reveals (by means of a transparency) the interior of the ground floor Wingfield apartment.

   Downstage is the living room, which also serves as a sleeping room for Laura, the sofa unfolding to make her bed. Upstage, center, and divided by a wide arch or second proscenium with transparent faded portieres (or second curtain), is the dining room. In an old-fashioned what-not in the living room are seen scores of transparent glass animals. A blown-up photograph of the father hangs on the wall of the living room, facing the audience, to the left of the archway. It is the face of a very hand-some young man in a doughboy's First World War cap. He is gallantly smiling, ineluctably smiling, as if to say, "I will be smiling forever."

   The audience hears and sees the opening scene in the dining room through both the transparent fourth wall of the building and the transparent gauze portieres of the dining-room arch. It is during this revealing scene that the fourth wall slowly ascends, out of sight. This transparent exterior wall is not brought down again until the very end of the play, during Tom's final speech.

   The narrator is an undisguised convention of the play. He takes whatever license with dramatic convention as is convenient to his purposes.

   Tom *enters dressed as a merchant sailor from alley, stage left, and strolls across the front of the stage to the fire-escape. There he stops and lights a cigarette. He addresses the audience.*

Tom: Yes, I have tricks in my pocket, I have things up my sleeve. But I am
      the opposite of a stage magician. He gives you illusion that has the ap-
      pearance of truth. I give you truth in the pleasant disguise of illusion. To
      begin with, I turn back time. I reverse it to that quaint period, the thir-
      ties, when the huge middle class of America was matriculating in a
      school for the blind. Their eyes had failed them, or they had failed their
      eyes, and so they were having their fingers pressed forcibly down by the
      fiery Braille alphabet of a dissolving economy. In Spain there was revo-
      lution. Here there was only shouting and confusion. In Spain there was
      Guernica. Here there were disturbances of labor, sometimes pretty vio-
      lent, in otherwise peaceful cities such as Chicago, Cleveland, Saint
      Louis. . . . This is the social background of the play.

(Music.)

The play is memory. Being a memory play, it is dimly lighted, it is sentimental, it is not realistic. In memory everything seems to happen to
music. That explains the fiddle in the wings. I am the narrator of the
play, and also a character in it. The other characters are my mother,
Amanda, my sister, Laura, and a gentleman caller who appears in the
final scenes. He is the most realistic character in the play, being an emissary from a world of reality that we were somehow set apart from. But
since I have a poet's weakness for symbols, I am using this character also
as a symbol; he is the long delayed but always expected something that
we live for. There is a fifth character in the play who doesn't appear
except in this larger-than-life photograph over the mantel. This is our
father who left us a long time ago. He was a telephone man who fell in

love with long distances; he gave up his job with the telephone company and skipped the light fantastic out of town . . . The last we heard of him was a picture post-card from Mazatlan, on the Pacific coast of Mexico, containing a message of two words—"Hello—Goodbye!"—and an address. I think the rest of the play will explain itself. . . .

(Amanda's voice becomes audible through the portieres.)

(Legend on screen: "Où sont les neiges.")

(He divides the portieres and enters the upstage area.
Amanda *and* Laura *are seated at a drop-leaf table. Eating is indicated by gestures without food or utensils.* Amanda *faces the audience.* Tom *and* Laura *are seated in profile.*

The interior has lit up softly and through the scrim we see Amanda *and* Laura *seated at the table in the upstage area.)*

Amanda (calling): Tom?

Tom: Yes, Mother.

Amanda: We can't say grace until you come to the table!

Tom: Coming, Mother. *(He bows slightly and withdraws, reappearing a few moments later in his place at the table.)*

Amanda (to her son): Honey, don't *push* with your *fingers*. If you have to push with something, the thing to push with is a crust of bread. And chew— chew! Animals have sections in their stomachs which enable them to digest food without mastication, but human beings are supposed to chew their food before they swallow it down. Eat food leisurely, son, and really enjoy it. A well-cooked meal has lots of delicate flavors that have to be held in the mouth for appreciation. So chew your food and give your salivary glands a chance to function!

(Tom deliberately lays his imaginary fork down and pushes his chair back from the table.)

Tom: I haven't enjoyed one bite of this dinner because of your constant directions on how to eat it. It's you that makes me rush through meals with your hawk-like attention to every bite I take. Sickening—spoils my appetite—all this discussion of animals' secretion—salivary glands— mastication!

Amanda (lightly): Temperament like a Metropolitan star! *(He rises and crosses downstage.)* You're not excused from the table.

Tom: I am getting a cigarette.

Amanda: You smoke too much.

(Laura rises.)

Laura: I'll bring in the blanc mange.

(He remains standing with his cigarette by the portieres during the following.)

Amanda (rising): No, sister, no, sister—you be the lady this time and I'll be the darky.

Laura: I'm already up.

Amanda: Resume your seat, little sister—I want you to stay fresh and
   pretty—for gentlemen callers!
Laura: I'm not expecting any gentlemen callers.
Amanda (crossing out to kitchenette; airily): Sometimes they come when they
   are least expected! Why, I remember one Sunday afternoon in Blue
   Mountain—*(enters kitchenette)*
Tom: I know what's coming!
Laura: Yes. But let her tell it.
Tom: Again?
Laura: She loves to tell it.

   (Amanda returns with bowl of dessert.)

Amanda: One Sunday afternoon in Blue Mountain—your mother
   received—*seventeen!*—gentlemen callers! Why, sometimes there weren't
   chairs enough to accommodate them all. We had to send the nigger
   over to bring in folding chairs from the parish house.
Tom (remaining at portieres): How did you entertain those gentlemen callers?
Amanda: I understood the art of conversation!
Tom: I bet you could talk.
Amanda: Girls in those days *knew* how to talk, I can tell you.
Tom: Yes?

   (Image: Amanda as a girl on a porch greeting callers.)

Amanda: They knew how to entertain their gentlemen callers. It wasn't
   enough for a girl to be possessed of a pretty face and a graceful figure—
   although I wasn't slighted in either respect. She also needed to have a
   nimble wit and a tongue to meet all occasions.
Tom: What did you talk about?
Amanda: Things of importance going on in the world! Never anything
   coarse or common or vulgar. *(She addresses Tom as though he were seated
   in the vacant chair at the table though he remains by portieres. He plays this
   scene as though he held the book.)* My callers were gentlemen—all! Among
   my callers were some of the most prominent young planters of the Mississippi Delta—planters and sons of planters!

   *(Tom motions for music and a spot of light on Amanda. Her eyes lift, her face
glows, her voice becomes rich and elegiac.)*

   (Screen legend: "Où sont les neiges.")

There was young Champ Laughlin who later became vice-president of
the Delta Planters Bank. Hadley Stevenson who was drowned in Moon
Lake and left his widow one hundred and fifty thousand in Government
bonds. There were the Cutrere brothers, Wesley and Bates. Bates was
one of my bright particular beaux! He got in a quarrel with that wild
Wainright boy. They shot it out on the floor of Moon Lake Casino.
Bates was shot through the stomach. Died in the ambulance on his way
to Memphis. His widow was also well-provided for, came into eight or
ten thousand acres, that's all. She married him on the rebound—never

loved her—carried my picture on him the night he died! And there was that boy that every girl in the Delta had set her cap for! That beautiful, brilliant young Fitzhugh boy from Green County!

Tom: What did he leave his widow?

Amanda: He never married! Gracious, you talk as though all of my old admirers had turned up their toes to the daisies!

Tom: Isn't this the first you mentioned that still survives?

Amanda: That Fitzhugh boy went North and made a fortune—came to be known as the Wolf of Wall Street! He had the Midas touch, whatever he touched turned to gold! And I could have been Mrs. Duncan J. Fitzhugh, mind you! But—I picked your *father!*

Laura (rising): Mother, let me clear the table.

Amanda: No, dear, you go in front and study your typewriter chart. Or practice your shorthand a little. Stay fresh and pretty—It's almost time for our gentlemen callers to start arriving. (*She flounces girlishly toward the kitchenette.*) How many do you suppose we're going to entertain this afternoon?

(*Tom throws down the paper and jumps up with a groan.*)

Laura (alone in the dining room): I don't believe we're going to receive any, Mother.

Amanda (reappearing, airily): What? No one—not one? You must be joking! (*Laura nervously echoes her laugh. She slips in a fugitive manner through the half-open portieres and draws them gently behind her. A shaft of very clear light is thrown on her face against the faded tapestry of the curtains. Music: "The Glass Menagerie" under faintly; lightly.*) Not one gentleman caller? It can't be true! There must be a flood, there must have been a tornado!

Laura: It isn't a flood, it's not a tornado, Mother. I'm just not popular like you were in Blue Mountain. . . . (*Tom utters another groan. Laura glances at him with a faint, apologetic smile; her voice catching a little.*) Mother's afraid I'm going to be an old maid.

(*The scene dims out with "Glass Menagerie" music.*)

SCENE II

(*"Laura, Haven't You Ever Liked Some Boy?"*)

On the dark stage the screen is lighted with the image of blue roses.
Gradually Laura's figure becomes apparent and the screen goes out.
The music subsides.
Laura *is seated in the delicate ivory chair at the small clawfoot table.*
She wears a dress of soft violet material for a kimono—her hair tied back from her forehead with a ribbon.
She is washing and polishing her collection of glass.
Amanda *appears on the fire-escape steps. At the sound of her ascent, Laura catches her breath, thrusts the bowl of ornaments away and seats herself stiffly before the diagram of the typewriter keyboard as though it held her spellbound. Something*

has happened to Amanda. *It is written in her face as she climbs to the landing: a look that is grim and hopeless and a little absurd.*

She has on one of those cheap or imitation velvety-looking cloth coats with imitation fur collar. Her hat is five or six years old, one of those dreadful cloche hats that were worn in the late twenties and she is clasping an enormous black patent-leather pocket-book with nickel clasp and initials. This is her full-dress outfit, the one she usually wears to the D.A.R.

Before entering she looks through the door.

She purses her lips, opens her eyes wide, rolls them upward, and shakes her head.

Then she slowly lets herself in the door. Seeing her mother's expression Laura *touches her lips with a nervous gesture.*

Laura: Hello, Mother, I was—*(She makes a nervous gesture toward the chart on the wall.* Amanda *leans against the shut door and stares at* Laura *with a martyred look.)*

Amanda: Deception? Deception? *(She slowly removes her hat and gloves, continuing the swift suffering stare. She lets the hat and gloves fall on the floor—a bit of acting.)*

Laura (shakily): How was the D.A.R. meeting? *(Amanda slowly opens her purse and removes a dainty white handkerchief which she shakes out delicately and delicately touches to her lips and nostrils.)* Didn't you go to the D.A.R. meeting, Mother?

Amanda (faintly, almost inaudibly): —No.—No. *(then more forcibly)* I did not have the strength—to go to the D.A.R. In fact, I did not have the courage! I wanted to find a hole in the ground and hide myself in it forever! *(She crosses slowly to the wall and removes the diagram of the typewriter keyboard. She holds it in front of her for a second, staring at it sweetly and sorrowfully—then bites her lips and tears it in two pieces.)*

Laura (faintly): Why did you do that, Mother? *(Amanda repeats the same procedure with the chart of the Gregg Alphabet.)* Why are you—

Amanda: Why? Why? How old are you, Laura?

Laura: Mother, you know my age.

Amanda: I thought that you were an adult; it seems that I was mistaken. *(She crosses slowly to the sofa and sinks down and stares at* Laura.*)*

Laura: Please don't stare at me, Mother.

(Amanda closes her eyes and lowers her head. Count ten.)

Amanda: What are we going to do, what is going to become of us, what is the future?

(Count ten.)

Laura: Has something happened, Mother? *(Amanda draws a long breath and takes out the handkerchief again; dabbing process.)* Mother, has—something happened?

Amanda: I'll be all right in a minute. I'm just bewildered—*(Count five.)*—by life. . . .

Laura: Mother, I wish that you would tell me what's happened.

Amanda: As you know, I was supposed to be inducted into my office at the D.A.R. this afternoon. (IMAGE: A SWARM OF TYPEWRITERS.) But I stopped off at Rubicam's Business College to speak to your teachers about your having a cold and ask them what progress they thought you were making down there.

Laura: Oh. . . .

Amanda: I went to the typing instructor and introduced myself as your mother. She didn't know who you were. Wingfield, she said. We don't have any such student enrolled at the school! I assured her she did, that you had been going to classes since early in January. "I wonder," she said, "if you could be talking about that terribly shy little girl who dropped out of school after only a few days' attendance?" "No," I said, "Laura, my daughter, has been going to school every day for the past six weeks!" "Excuse me," she said. She took the attendance book out and there was your name, unmistakably printed, and all the dates you were absent until they decided that you had dropped out of school. I still said, "No, there must have been some mistake! There must have been some mix-up in the records!" And she said, "No—I remember her perfectly now. Her hand shook so that she couldn't hit the right keys! The first time we gave a speed-test, she broke down completely—was sick at the stomach and almost had to be carried into the wash-room! After that morning she never showed up any more. We phoned the house but never got any answer—while I was working at Famous and Barr, I suppose, demonstrating those—Oh!" I felt so weak I could barely keep on my feet! I had to sit down while they got me a glass of water! Fifty dollars' tuition, all of our plans—my hopes and ambitions for you—just gone up the spout, just gone up the spout like that. *(Laura draws a long breath and gets awkwardly to her feet. She crosses to the victrola and winds it up.)* What are you doing?

Laura: Oh! *(She releases the handle and returns to her seat.)*

Amanda: Laura, where have you been going when you've gone out pretending that you were going to business college?

Laura: I've just been going out walking.

Amanda: That's not true.

Laura: It is. I just went walking.

Amanda: Walking? Walking? In winter? Deliberately courting pneumonia in that light coat? Where did you walk to, Laura?

Laura: All sorts of places—mostly in the park.

Amanda: Even after you'd started catching that cold?

Laura: It was the lesser of two evils, Mother. (IMAGE: WINTER SCENE IN PARK.) I couldn't go back up. I—threw up—on the floor!

Amanda: From half past seven till after five every day you mean to tell me you walked around in the park, because you wanted to make me think that you were still going to Rubicam's Business College?

Laura: It wasn't as bad as it sounds. I went inside places to get warmed up.

Amanda: Inside where?

Laura: I went in the art museum and the bird-houses at the Zoo. I visited the penguins every day! Sometimes I did without lunch and went to the movies. Lately I've been spending most of my afternoons in the Jewel-box, that big glass house where they raise the tropical flowers.

Amanda: You did all this to deceive me, just for the deception? (*Laura looks down.*) Why?

Laura: Mother, when you're disappointed, you get that awful suffering look on your face, like the picture of Jesus' mother in the museum!

Amanda: Hush!

Laura: I couldn't face it.

(*Pause. A whisper of strings.*)

(*Legend: "The crust of humility."*)

Amanda (*hopelessly fingering the huge pocketbook*): So what are we going to do the rest of our lives? Stay home and watch the parades go by? Amuse ourselves with the glass menagerie, darling? Eternally play those worn-out phonograph records your father left as a painful reminder of him? We won't have a business career—we've given that up because it gave us nervous indigestion! (*laughs wearily*) What is there left but dependency all our lives? I know so well what becomes of unmarried women who aren't prepared to occupy a position. I've seen such pitiful cases in the South—barely tolerated spinsters living upon the grudging patronage of sister's husband or brother's wife!—stuck away in some little mouse-trap of a room—encouraged by one in-law to visit another—little birdlike women without any nest—eating the crust of humility all their life! Is that the future that we've mapped out for ourselves? I swear it's the only alternative I can think of! It isn't a very pleasant alternative, is it? Of course—some girls *do marry*. (*Laura twists her hands nervously.*) Haven't you ever liked some boy?

Laura: Yes. I liked one once. (*rises*) I came across his picture a while ago.

Amanda (*with some interest*): He gave you his picture?

Laura: No, it's in the year-book.

Amanda (*disappointed*): Oh—a high-school boy.

(*Screen image: Jim as a high-school hero bearing a silver cup.*)

Laura: Yes. His name was Jim. (*Laura lifts the heavy annual from the claw-foot table.*) Here he is in *The Pirates of Penzance*.

Amanda (*absently*): The what?

Laura: The operetta the senior class put on. He had a wonderful voice and we sat across the aisle from each other Mondays, Wednesdays and Fridays in the Aud. Here he is with the silver cup for debating! See his grin?

Amanda (*absently*): He must have had a jolly disposition.

Laura: He used to call me—Blue Roses.

(*Image: Blue roses.*)

Amanda: Why did he call you such a name as that?

Laura: When I had that attack of pleurosis—he asked me what was the matter when I came back. I said pleurosis—he thought that I said Blue

Roses! So that's what he always called me after that. Whenever he saw me, he'd holler, "Hello, Blue Roses!" I didn't care for the girl that he went out with. Emily Meisenbach. Emily was the best-dressed girl at Soldan. She never struck me, though, as being sincere . . . . It says in the Personal Section—they're engaged. That's—six years ago! They must be married by now.

Amanda: Girls that aren't cut out for business careers usually wind up married to some nice man. *(gets up with a spark of revival)* Sister, that's what you'll do!

(Laura utters a startled, doubtful laugh. She reaches quickly for a piece of glass.)

Laura: But, Mother—

Amanda: Yes? *(crossing to photograph)*

Laura (in a tone of frightened apology): I'm—crippled!

(Image: Screen.)

Amanda: Nonsense! Laura, I've told you never, never to use that word. Why, you're not crippled, you just have a little defect—hardly noticeable, even! When people have some slight disadvantage like that, they cultivate other things to make up for it—develop charm—and vivacity—and—*charm!* That's all you have to do! *(She turns again to the photograph.)* One thing your father had *plenty of*—was *charm!*

(Tom motions to the fiddle in the wings.)

(The scene fades out with music.)

SCENE III

(Legend on screen: "After the fiasco—")

Tom *speaks from the fire-escape landing.*

Tom: After the fiasco at Rubicam's Business College, the idea of getting a gentleman caller for Laura began to play a more important part in Mother's calculations. It became an obsession. Like some archetype of the universal unconscious, the image of the gentleman caller haunted our small apartment. . . . (IMAGE: YOUNG MAN AT DOOR WITH FLOWERS.) An evening at home rarely passed without some allusion to this image, this spectre, this hope. . . . Even when he wasn't mentioned, his presence hung in Mother's preoccupied look and in my sister's frightened, apologetic manner—hung like a sentence passed upon the Wingfields! Mother was a woman of action as well as words. She began to take logical steps in the planned direction. Late that winter and in the early spring—realizing that extra money would be needed to properly feather the nest and plume the bird—she conducted a vigorous campaign on the telephone, roping in subscribers to one of those magazines for matrons called *The Home-maker's Companion*, the type of journal that features the serialized sublimations of ladies of letters who think in terms of delicate cup-like breasts, slim, tapering waists, rich, creamy thighs, eyes like wood-smoke in autumn, fingers that soothe and caress like strains of music, bodies as powerful as Etruscan sculpture.

(Screen image: Glamor magazine cover.)

(Amanda enters with phone on long extension cord. She is spotted in the dim stage.)

Amanda: Ida Scott? This is Amanda Wingfield! We *missed* you at the D.A.R. last Monday! I said to myself: She's probably suffering with that sinus condition! How is that sinus condition? Horrors! Heaven have mercy!— You're a Christian martyr, yes, that's what you are, a Christian martyr! Well, I just now happened to notice that your subscription to the *Companion*'s about to expire! Yes, it expires with the next issue, honey!—just when that wonderful new serial by Bessie Mae Hopper is getting off to such an exciting start. Oh, honey, it's something that you can't miss! You remember how *Gone With the Wind* took everybody by storm? You simply couldn't go out if you hadn't read it. All everybody *talked* was Scarlett O'Hara. Well, this is a book that critics already compare to *Gone With the Wind*. It's the *Gone With the Wind* of the post-World War generation!—What?—Burning?—Oh, honey, don't let them burn, go take a look in the oven and I'll hold the wire! Heavens—I think she's hung up!

(Dim out.)

(Legend on screen: "You think I'm in love with Continental Shoemakers?")

(Before the stage is lighted, the violent voices of Tom *and* Amanda *are heard. They are quarreling behind the portieres. In front of them stands* Laura *with clenched hands and panicky expression.*

A clear pool of light on her figure throughout this scene.)

Tom: What in Christ's name am I—
Amanda (shrilly): Don't you use that—
Tom: Supposed to do!
Amanda: Expression! Not in my—
Tom: Ohhh!
Amanda: Presence! Have you gone out of your senses?
Tom: I have, that's true, *driven* out!
Amanda: What is the matter with you, you—big—big—IDIOT!
Tom: Look—I've got *no thing*, no single thing—
Amanda: Lower your voice!
Tom: In my life here that I can call my OWN! Everything is—
Amanda: Stop that shouting!
Tom: Yesterday you confiscated my books! You had the nerve to—
Amanda: I took that horrible novel back to the library—yes! That hideous

book by that insane Mr. Lawrence. *(Tom laughs wildly.)* I cannot control the output of diseased minds or people who cater to them—*(Tom laughs still more wildly.)* BUT I WON'T ALLOW SUCH FILTH BROUGHT INTO MY HOUSE! No, no, no, no, no!

Tom: House, house! Who pays rent on it, who makes a slave of himself to—

Amanda (fairly screeching): Don't you DARE to—

Tom: No, no, I mustn't say things! *I've* got to just—

Amanda: Let me tell you—

Tom: I don't want to hear any more! *(He tears the portieres open. The upstage area is lit with a turgid smoky red glow.)*

(Amanda's hair is in metal curlers and she wears a very old bathrobe, much too large for her slight figure, a relic of the faithless Mr. Wingfield.

An upright typewriter and a wild disarray of manuscripts is on the dropleaf table. The quarrel was probably precipitated by Amanda's interruption of his creative labor. A chair lying overthrown on the floor.

Their gesticulating shadows are cast on the ceiling by the fiery glow.)

Amanda: You *will* hear more, you—

Tom: No, I won't hear more, I'm going out!

Amanda: You come right back in—

Tom: Out, out out! Because I'm—

Amanda: Come back here, Tom Wingfield! I'm not through talking to you!

Tom: Oh, go—

Laura (desperately): —Tom!

Amanda: You're going to listen, and no more insolence from you! I'm at the end of my patience! *(He comes back toward her.)*

Tom: What do you think I'm at? Aren't I supposed to have any patience to reach the end of, Mother? I know, I know. It seems unimportant to you, what I'm *doing*—what I *want* to do—having a little *difference* between them! You don't think that—

Amanda: I think you've been doing things that you're ashamed of. That's why you act like this. I don't believe that you go every night to the movies. Nobody goes to the movies night after night. Nobody in their right minds goes to the movies as often as you pretend to. People don't go to the movies at nearly midnight, and movies don't let out at two A.M. Come in stumbling. Muttering to yourself like a maniac! You get three hours sleep and then go to work. Oh, I can picture the way you're doing down there. Moping, doping, because you're in no condition.

Tom (wildly): No, I'm in no condition!

Amanda: What right have you got to jeopardize your job? Jeopardize the security of us all? How do you think we'd manage if you were—

Tom: Listen! You think I'm crazy *about* the *warehouse?* *(He bends fiercely toward her slight figure.)* You think I'm in love with the Continental Shoemakers? You think I want to spend fifty-five *years* down there in that—*celotex interior!* with—*fluorescent—tubes!* Look! I'd rather somebody picked up a crowbar and battered out my brains—than go back mornings! I *go!* Every time you come in yelling that God damn *"Rise and*

Shine!" "*Rise and Shine!*" I say to myself "How *lucky dead* people are!" But I get up. I *go!* For sixty-five dollars a month I give up all that I dream of doing and being *ever! And you say self—self's* all I ever think of. Why, listen, if self is what I thought of, Mother, I'd be where he is— GONE! *(pointing to father's picture)* As far as the system of transportation reaches! *(He starts past her. She grabs his arm.)* Don't grab me, Mother!

Amanda: Where are you going?

Tom: I'm going to the *movies!*

Amanda: I don't believe that lie!

Tom (crouching toward her, overtowering her tiny figure. She backs away, gasping.): I'm going to opium dens! Yes, opium dens, dens of vice and criminals' hang-outs, Mother. I've joined the Hogan gang, I'm a hired assassin, I carry a tommy-gun in a violin case! I run a string of cat-houses in the Valley! They call me Killer, Killer Wingfield, I'm leading a double-life, a simple, honest warehouse worker by day, by night, a dynamic *czar* of the *underworld, Mother.* I go to gambling casinos, I spin away fortunes on the roulette table! I wear a patch over one eye and a false mustache, sometimes I put on green whiskers. On those occasions they call me—*El Diablo!* Oh, I could tell you things to make you sleepless! My enemies plan to dynamite this place. They're going to blow us all sky-high some night! I'll be glad, very happy, and so will you! You'll go up, up on a broomstick, over Blue Mountain with seventeen gentlemen callers! You ugly— babbling old—*witch.* . . . *(He goes through a series of violent, clumsy movements, seizing his overcoat, lunging to the door, pulling it fiercely open. The women watch him, aghast. His arm catches in the sleeve of the coat as he struggles to pull it on. For a moment he is pinioned by the bulky garment. With an outraged groan he tears the coat off again, splitting the shoulders of it, and hurls it across the room. It strikes against the shelf of Laura's glass collection, there is a tinkle of shattering glass. Laura cries out as if wounded.)*

(Music legend: "The Glass Menagerie.")

Laura (shrilly): My glass!—menagerie. . . . *(She covers her face and turns away.)*

(But Amanda is still stunned and stupefied by the "ugly witch" so that she barely notices this occurrence. Now she recovers her speech.)

Amanda (in an awful voice): I won't speak to you—until you apologize! *(She crosses through portieres and draws them together behind her.* Tom *is left with* Laura. Laura *clings weakly to the mantel with her face averted.* Tom *stares at her stupidly for a moment. Then he crosses to shelf. Drops awkwardly to his knees to collect the fallen glass, glancing at* Laura *as if he would speak but couldn't.)*

"The Glass Menagerie" steals in as

(The scene dims out.)

SCENE IV

The interior is dark. Faint light in the alley.

A deep-voiced bell in a church is tolling the hour of five as the scene commences.

Tom *appears at the top of the alley. After each solemn boom of the bell in the tower, he shakes a little noise-maker or rattle as if to express the tiny spasm of man in contrast to the sustained power and dignity of the Almighty. This and the unsteadiness of his advance make it evident that he has been drinking.*

As he climbs the few steps to the fire-escape landing light steals up inside. Laura *appears in night-dress, observing* Tom's *empty bed in the front room.*

Tom *fishes in his pockets for the door-key, removing a motley assortment of articles in the search, including a perfect shower of movie-ticket stubs and an empty bottle. At last he finds the key, but just as he is about to insert it, it slips from his fingers. He strikes a match and crouches below the door.*

Tom (bitterly): One crack—and it falls through!

(Laura opens the door.)

Laura: Tom! Tom, what are you doing?

Tom: Looking for a door-key.

Laura: Where have you been all this time?

Tom: I have been to the movies.

Laura: All this time at the movies?

Tom: There was a very long program. There was a Garbo picture and a Mickey Mouse and a travelogue and a newsreel and a preview of coming attractions. And there was an organ solo and a collection for the milk-fund—simultaneously—which ended up in a terrible fight between a fat lady and an usher!

Laura (innocently): Did you have to stay through everything?

Tom: Of course! And, oh, I forgot! There was a big stage show! The headliner on this stage show was Malvolio the Magician. He performed wonderful tricks, many of them, such as pouring water back and forth between pitchers. First it turned to wine and then it turned to beer and then it turned to whiskey. I know it was whiskey it finally turned into because he needed somebody to come up out of the audience to help him, and I came up—both shows! It was Kentucky Straight Bourbon. A very generous fellow, he gave souvenirs. *(He pulls from his back pocket a shimmering rainbow-colored scarf.)* He gave me this. This is his magic scarf. You can have it, Laura. You wave it over a canary cage and you get a bowl of gold-fish. You wave it over the gold-fish bowl and they fly away canaries. . . . But the wonderfullest trick of all was the coffin trick. We nailed him into a coffin and he got out of the coffin without removing one nail. *(He has come inside.)* There is a trick that would come in handy for me—get me out of this 2 by 4 situation! *(flops onto bed and starts removing shoes)*

Laura: Tom—Shhh!

Tom: What you shushing me for?

Laura: You'll wake up Mother.

Tom: Goody, goody! Pay 'er back for all those "Rise an' Shines." *(lies down, groaning)* You know it don't take much intelligence to get yourself into a nailed-up coffin, Laura. But who in hell ever got himself out of one without removing one nail?

(As if in answer, the father's grinning photograph lights up.)

(Scene dims out.)

(Immediately following: The church bell is heard striking six. At the sixth stroke the alarm clock goes off in Amanda's *room, and after a few moments we hear her calling: "Rise and Shine! Rise and Shine! Laura, go tell your brother to rise and shine!")*

Tom (sitting up slowly): I'll rise—but I won't shine.

(The light increases.)

Amanda: Laura, tell your brother his coffee is ready.

(Laura slips into front room.)

Laura: Tom! it's nearly seven. Don't make Mother nervous. *(He stares at her stupidly, beseechingly.)* Tom, speak to Mother this morning. Make up with her, apologize, speak to her!

Tom: She won't to me. It's her that started not speaking.

Laura: If you just say you're sorry she'll start speaking.

Tom: Her not speaking—is that such a tragedy?

Laura: Please—please!

Amanda (calling from kitchenette): Laura, are you going to do what I asked you to do, or do I have to get dressed and go out myself?

Laura: Going, going—soon as I get on my coat! *(She pulls on a shapeless felt hat with nervous, jerky movement, pleadingly glancing at* Tom. *Rushes awkwardly for coat. The coat is one of* Amanda's, *inaccurately made-over, the sleeves too short for* Laura.) Butter and what else?

Amanda (entering upstage): Just butter. Tell them to charge it.

Laura: Mother, they make such faces when I do that.

Amanda: Sticks and stones may break my bones, but the expression on Mr. Garfinkel's face won't harm us! Tell your brother his coffee is getting cold.

Laura (at door): Do what I asked you, will you, will you, Tom?

(He looks sullenly away.)

Amanda: Laura, go now or just don't go at all!

Laura (rushing out): Going—going! *(A second later she cries out.* Tom *springs up and crosses to the door.* Amanda *rushes anxiously in.* Tom *opens the door.)*

Tom: Laura?

Laura: I'm all right. I slipped, but I'm all right.

Amanda (peering anxiously after her): If anyone breaks a leg on those fire-escape steps, the landlord ought to be sued for every cent he possesses! *(She shuts door, remembers she isn't speaking, and returns to other room.)*

(As Tom *enters listlessly for his coffee, she turns her back to him and stands rigidly facing the window on the gloomy gray vault of the areaway. Its light on her face with its aged but childish features is cruelly sharp, satirical as a Daumier print.)*

(Music under: "Ave Maria.")

*(*Tom *glances sheepishly but sullenly at her averted figure and slumps at the table. The coffee is scalding hot; he sips it and gasps and spits it back in the cup. At his gasp, Amanda catches her breath and half turns. Then catches herself and turns back to window.*

Tom *blows on his coffee, glancing sidewise at his mother. She clears her throat.* Tom *clears his. He starts to rise. Sinks back down again, scratches his head, clears his throat again.* Amanda *coughs.* Tom *raises his cup in both hands to blow on it, his eyes staring over the rim of it at his mother for several moments. Then he slowly sets the cup down and awkwardly and hesitantly rises from the chair.)*

Tom (hoarsely): Mother. I—I apologize. Mother. *(*Amanda *draws a quick, shuddering breath. Her face works grotesquely. She breaks into childlike tears.)* I'm sorry for what I said, for everything that I said, I didn't mean it.

Amanda (sobbingly): My devotion has made me a witch and so I make myself hateful to my children!

Tom: No, you *don't.*

Amanda: I worry so much, don't sleep, it makes me nervous!

Tom (gently): I understand that.

Amanda: I've had to put up a solitary battle all these years. But you're my right-hand bower! Don't fall down, don't fail!

Tom (gently): I try, Mother.

Amanda (with great enthusiasm): Try and you will SUCCEED! *(The notion makes her breathless.)* Why, you—you're just *full* of natural endowments! Both of my children—they're *unusual* children! Don't you think I know it? I'm so—*proud!* Happy and—feel I've—so much to be thankful for but— Promise me one thing, son!

Tom: What, Mother?

Amanda: Promise, son, you'll—never be a drunkard!

Tom (turns to her grinning): I will never be a drunkard, Mother.

Amanda: That's what frightened me so, that you'd be drinking! Eat a bowl of Purina!

Tom: Just coffee, Mother.

Amanda: Shredded wheat biscuit?

Tom: No. No, Mother, just coffee.

Amanda: You can't put in a day's work on an empty stomach. You've got ten minutes—don't gulp! Drinking too-hot liquids makes cancer of the stomach. . . . Put cream in.

Tom: No, thank you.

Amanda: To cool it.

Tom: No! No, thank you, I want it black.

Amanda: I know, but it's not good for you. We have to do all that we can to build ourselves up. In these trying times we live in, all that we have to cling to is—each other. . . . That's why it's so important to—Tom, I—I sent out your sister so I could discuss something with you. If you hadn't spoken I would have spoken to you. *(sits down)*

Tom (gently): What is it, Mother, that you want to discuss?

Amanda: Laura!

(Tom puts his cup down slowly.)

(Legend on screen: "Laura.")

(Music: "The Glass Menagerie.")

Tom: —Oh.—Laura . . .

Amanda (touching his sleeve): You know how Laura is. So quiet but—still water runs deep! She notices things and I think she—broods about them. *(Tom looks up.)* A few days ago I came in and she was crying.

Tom: What about?

Amanda: You.

Tom: Me?

Amanda: She has an idea that you're not happy here.

Tom: What gave her that idea?

Amanda: What gives her any idea? However, you do act strangely. I—I'm not criticizing, understand *that!* I know your ambitions do not lie in the warehouse, that like everybody in the whole wide world—you've had to—make sacrifices, but—Tom—Tom—life's not easy, it calls for— Spartan endurance! There's so many things in my heart that I cannot describe to you! I've never told you but I—*loved* your father. . . .

Tom (gently): I know that, Mother.

Amanda: And you—when I see you taking after his ways! Staying out late— and—well, you *had* been drinking the night you were in that—terrifying condition! Laura says that you hate the apartment and that you go out nights to get away from it! Is that true, Tom?

Tom: No. You say there's so much in your heart that you can't describe to me. That's true of me, too. There's so much in my heart that I can't describe to *you!* So let's respect each other's—

Amanda: But, why—*why,* Tom—are you always so *restless?* Where do you go to, nights?

Tom: I—go to the movies.

Amanda: Why do you go to the movies so much, Tom?

Tom: I go to the movies because—I like adventure. Adventure is something I don't have much of at work, so I go to the movies.

Amanda: But, Tom, you go to the movies *entirely* too *much!*

Tom: I like a lot of adventure.

(Amanda looks baffled, then hurt. As the familiar inquisition resumes he becomes hard and impatient again. Amanda slips back into her querulous attitude toward him.)

(Image on screen: Sailing vessel with Jolly Roger.)

Amanda: Most young men find adventure in their careers.

Tom: Then most young men are not employed in a warehouse.

Amanda: The world is full of young men employed in warehouses and offices and factories.

Tom: Do all of them find adventure in their careers?

Amanda: They do or they do without it! Not everybody has a craze for adventure.

Tom: Man is by instinct a lover, a hunter, a fighter, and none of those instincts are given much play at the warehouse!

Amanda: Man is by instinct! Don't quote instinct to me! Instinct is something that people have got away from! It belongs to animals! Christian adults don't want it!

Tom: What do Christian adults want, then, Mother?

Amanda: Superior things! Things of the mind and the spirit! Only animals have to satisfy instincts! Surely your aims are somewhat higher than theirs! Than monkeys—pigs—

Tom: I reckon they're not.

Amanda: You're joking. However, that isn't what I wanted to discuss.

Tom (rising): I haven't much time.

Amanda (pushing his shoulders): Sit down.

Tom: You want me to punch in red at the warehouse, Mother?

Amanda: You have five minutes. I want to talk about Laura.

(Legend: "Plans and provisions.")

Tom: All right! What about Laura?

Amanda: We have to be making plans and provisions for her. She's older than you, two years, and nothing has happened. She just drifts along doing nothing. It frightens me terribly how she just drifts along.

Tom: I guess she's the type that people call home girls.

Amanda: There's no such type, and if there is, it's a pity! That is unless the home is hers, with a husband!

Tom: What?

Amanda: Oh, I can see the handwriting on the wall as plain as I see the nose in front of my face! It's terrifying! More and more you remind me of your father! He was out all hours without explanation—Then *left! Goodbye!* And me with a bag to hold. I saw that letter you got from the Merchant Marine. I know what you're dreaming of. I'm not standing here blindfolded. Very well, then. Then *do* it! But not till there's somebody to take your place.

Tom: What do you mean?

Amanda: I mean that as soon as Laura has got somebody to take care of her, married, a home of her own, independent—why, then you'll be free to go wherever you please, on land, on sea, whichever way the wind blows! But until that time you've got to look out for your sister. I don't say me because I'm old and don't matter! I say for your sister because she's

young and dependent. I put her in business college—a dismal failure!
Frightened her so it made her sick to her stomach. I took her over to the
Young People's League at the church. Another fiasco. She spoke to nobody, nobody spoke to her. Now all she does is fool with those pieces of
glass and play those worn-out records. What kind of life is that for a girl
to lead?

Tom: What can I do about it?

Amanda: Overcome selfishness! Self, self, self is all that you ever think of!
(*Tom springs up and crosses to get his coat. It is ugly and bulky. He pulls on a
cap with earmuffs.*) Where is your muffler? Put your wool muffler on!
(*He snatches it angrily from the closet and tosses it around his neck and pulls
both ends tight.*) Tom! I haven't said what I had in mind to ask you.

Tom: I'm too late to—

Amanda (catching his arm—very importunately; then shyly): Down at the warehouse, aren't there some—nice young men?

Tom: No!

Amanda: There *must* be—*some* . . .

Tom: Mother—

(*Gesture.*)

Amanda: Find out one that's clean-living—doesn't drink and—ask him out
for sister!

Tom: What?

Amanda: For *sister!* To *meet!* Get *acquainted!*

Tom (stamping to door): Oh, my go-osh!

Amanda: Will you? (*He opens door; imploringly:*) Will you? (*He starts down.*)
Will you? *Will* you, dear?

Tom (calling back): Yes!

(*Amanda closes the door hesitantly and with a troubled but faintly hopeful
expression.*)

(*Screen image: Glamor magazine cover.*)

(*Spot Amanda at phone.*)

Amanda: Ella Cartwright? This is Amanda Wingfield! How are you, honey?
How is that kidney condition? (*Count five.*) Horrors! (*Count five.*) You're a
Christian martyr, yes, honey, that's what you are, a Christian martyr!
Well, I just happened to notice in my little red book that your subscrip-
tion to the *Companion* has just run out! I knew that you wouldn't want to
miss out on the wonderful serial starting in this new issue. It's by Bessie
Mae Hopper, the first thing she's written since *Honeymoon for Three.*
Wasn't that a strange and interesting story? Well, this one is even lovelier, I believe. It has a sophisticated society background. It's all about the
horsey set on Long Island!

(*Fade out.*)

SCENE V

(Legend on screen: "Annunciation.")

Fade with music.

It is early dusk of a spring evening. Supper has just been finished in the Wing-field apartment. Amanda and Laura in light colored dresses are removing dishes from the table, in the upstage area, which is shadowy, their movements formalized almost as a dance or ritual, their moving forms as pale and silent as moths.

Tom, *in white shirt and trousers, rises from the table and crosses toward the fire escape.*

Amanda *(as he passes her):* Son, will you do me a favor?

Tom: What?

Amanda: Comb your hair! You look so pretty when your hair is combed! *(Tom slouches on sofa with evening paper; enormous caption "Franco Triumphs.")* There is only one respect in which I would like you to emulate your father.

Tom: What respect is that?

Amanda: The care he always took of his appearance. He never allowed himself to look untidy. *(He throws down the paper and crosses to fire escape.)* Where are you going?

Tom: I'm going out to smoke.

Amanda: You smoke too much. A pack a day at fifteen cents a pack. How much would that amount to in a month? Thirty times fifteen is how much, Tom? Figure it out and you will be astounded at what you could save. Enough to give you a night-school course in accounting at Washington U! Just think what a wonderful thing that would be for you, son!

(Tom is unmoved by the thought.)

Tom: I'd rather smoke. *(He steps out on landing, letting the screen door slam.)*

Amanda *(sharply):* I know! That's the tragedy of it. . . . *(Alone, she turns to look at her husband's picture.)*

(Dance music: "All the world is waiting for the sunrise!")

Tom *(to the audience):* Across the alley from us was the Paradise Dance Hall. On evenings in spring the windows and doors were open and the music came outdoors. Sometimes the lights were turned out except for a large glass sphere that hung from the ceiling. It would turn slowly about and filter the dusk with delicate rainbow colors. Then the orchestra played a waltz or a tango, something that had a slow and sensuous rhythm. Couples would come outside, to the relative privacy of the alley. You could see them kissing behind ash-pits and telephone poles. This was the compensation for lives that passed like mine, without any change or adventure. Adventure and change were imminent in this year. They were waiting around the corner for all these kids. Suspended in the mist

over Berchtesgaden, caught in the folds of Chamberlain's umbrella—In
Spain there was Guernica! But here there was only hot swing music and
liquor, dance halls, bars, and movies, and sex that hung in the gloom like
a chandelier and flooded the world with brief, deceptive rainbows. . . .
All the world was waiting for bombardments!

(Amanda *turns from the picture and comes outside.*)

Amanda (*sighing*): A fire-escape landing's a poor excuse for a porch. (*She
    spreads a newspaper on a step and sits down, gracefully and demurely as if she
    were settling into a swing on a Mississippi veranda.*) What are you looking at?
Tom: The moon.
Amanda: Is there a moon this evening?
Tom: It's rising over Garfinkel's Delicatessen.
Amanda: So it is! A little silver slipper of a moon. Have you made a wish on
    it yet?
Tom: Um-hum.
Amanda: What did you wish for?
Tom: That's a secret.
Amanda: A secret, huh? Well, I won't tell mine either. I will be just as mys-
    terious as you.
Tom: I bet I can guess what yours is.
Amanda: Is my head so transparent?
Tom: You're not a sphinx.
Amanda: No, I don't have secrets. I'll tell you what I wished for on the
    moon. Success and happiness for my precious children! I wish for that
    whenever there's a moon, and when there isn't a moon, I wish for it, too.
Tom: I thought perhaps you wished for a gentleman caller.
Amanda: Why do you say that?
Tom: Don't you remember asking me to fetch one?
Amanda: I remember suggesting that it would be nice for your sister if you
    brought home some nice young man from the warehouse. I think I've
    made that suggestion more than once.
Tom: Yes, you have made it repeatedly.
Amanda: Well?
Tom: We are going to have one.
Amanda: What?
Tom: A gentleman caller!

    (*The annunciation is celebrated with music.*)

    (Amanda *rises.*)

    (*Image on screen: Caller with bouquet.*)

Amanda: You mean you have asked some nice young man to come over?
Tom: Yep. I've asked him to dinner.
Amanda: You really did?
Tom: I did!
Amanda: You did, and did he—*accept?*
Tom: He did!

Amanda: Well, well—well, well! That's—lovely!

Tom: I thought that you would be pleased.

Amanda: It's definite, then?

Tom: Very definite.

Amanda: Soon?

Tom: Very soon.

Amanda: For heaven's sake, stop putting on and tell me some things, will you?

Tom: What things do you want me to tell you?

Amanda: *Naturally* I would like to know when he's *coming!*

Tom: He's coming tomorrow.

Amanda: *Tomorrow?*

Tom: Yep. Tomorrow.

Amanda: But, Tom!

Tom: Yes, Mother?

Amanda: Tomorrow gives me no time!

Tom: Time for what?

Amanda: Preparations! Why didn't you phone me at once, as soon as you asked him, the minute that he accepted? Then, don't you see, I could have been getting ready!

Tom: You don't have to make any fuss.

Amanda: Oh, Tom, Tom, Tom, of course I have to make a fuss! I want things nice, not sloppy! Not thrown together. I'll certainly have to do some fast thinking, won't I?

Tom: I don't see why you have to think at all.

Amanda: You just don't know. We can't have a gentleman caller in a pig-sty! All my wedding silver has to be polished, the monogrammed table linen ought to be laundered! The windows have to be washed and fresh curtains put up. And how about clothes? We have to *wear* something, don't we?

Tom: Mother, this boy is no one to make a fuss over!

Amanda: Do you realize he's the first young man we've introduced to your sister? It's terrible, dreadful, disgraceful that poor little sister has never received a single gentleman caller! Tom, come inside! *(She opens the screen door.)*

Tom: What for?

Amanda: I want to ask you some things.

Tom: If you're going to make such a fuss, I'll call it off, I'll tell him not to come.

Amanda: You certainly won't do anything of the kind. Nothing offends people worse than broken engagements. It simply means I'll have to work like a Turk! We won't be brilliant, but we'll pass inspection. Come on inside. *(Tom follows, groaning.)* Sit down.

Tom: Any particular place you would like me to sit?

Amanda: Thank heavens I've got that new sofa! I'm also making payments on a floor lamp I'll have sent out! And put the chintz covers on, they'll brighten things up! Of course I'd hoped to have these walls re-papered. . . . What is the young man's name?

Tom: His name is O'Connor.

Amanda: That, of course, means fish—tomorrow is Friday! I'll have that
   salmon loaf—with Durkee's dressing! What does he do? He works at
   the warehouse?

Tom: Of course! How else would I—

Amanda: Tom, he—doesn't drink?

Tom: Why do you ask me that?

Amanda: Your father *did!*

Tom: Don't get started on that!

Amanda: He *does* drink, then?

Tom: Not that I know of!

Amanda: Make sure, be certain! The last thing I want for my daughter's a
   boy who drinks!

Tom: Aren't you being a little premature? Mr. O'Connor has not yet appeared on the scene!

Amanda: But will tomorrow. To meet your sister, and what do I know about
   this character? Nothing! Old maids are better off than wives of drunkards!

Tom: Oh, my God!

Amanda: Be still!

Tom (leaning forward to whisper): Lots of fellows meet girls whom they
   don't marry!

Amanda: Oh, talk sensibly, Tom—and don't be sarcastic! *(She has gotten
   a hairbrush.)*

Tom: What are you doing?

Amanda: I'm brushing that cow-lick down! What is this young man's position at the warehouse?

Tom (submitting grimly to the brush and the interrogation): This young man's
   position is that of a shipping clerk, Mother.

Amanda: Sounds to me like a fairly responsible job, the sort of a job *you*
   would be in if you just had more *get-up.* What is his salary? Have you
   got any idea?

Tom: I would judge it to be approximately eighty-five dollars a month.

Amanda: Well—not princely, but—

Tom: Twenty more than I make.

Amanda: Yes, how well I know! But for a family man, eighty-five dollars a
   month is not much more than you can just get by on. . . .

Tom: Yes, but Mr. O'Connor is not a family man.

Amanda: He might be, mightn't he? Some time in the future?

Tom: I see. Plans and provisions.

Amanda: You are the only young man that I know of who ignores the fact
   that the future becomes the present, the present the past, and the past
   turns into everlasting regret if you don't plan for it!

Tom: I will think that over and see what I can make of it.

Amanda: Don't be supercilious with your mother! Tell me some more about
   this—what do you call him?

Tom: James D. O'Connor. The D. is for Delaney.

Amanda: Irish on *both* sides! *Gracious!* And doesn't drink?

Tom: Shall I call him up and ask him right this minute?

Amanda: The only way to find out about those things is to make discreet inquiries at the proper moment. When I was a girl in Blue Mountain and it was suspected that a young man drank, the girl whose attentions he had been receiving, if any girl *was*, would sometimes speak to the minister of his church, or rather her father would if her father was living, and sort of feel him out on the young man's character. That is the way such things are discreetly handled to keep a young woman from making a tragic mistake!

Tom: Then how did you happen to make a tragic mistake?

Amanda: That innocent look of your father's had everyone fooled! He *smiled*—the world was *enchanted!* No girl can do worse than put herself at the mercy of a handsome appearance! I hope that Mr. O'Connor is not too good-looking.

Tom: No, he's not too good-looking. He's covered with freckles and hasn't too much of a nose.

Amanda: He's not right-down homely, though?

Tom: Not right-down homely. Just medium homely, I'd say.

Amanda: Character's what to look for in a man.

Tom: That's what I've always said, Mother.

Amanda: You've never said anything of the kind and I suspect you would never give it a thought.

Tom: Don't be suspicious of me.

Amanda: At least I hope he's the type that's up and coming.

Tom: I think he really goes in for self-improvement.

Amanda: What reason have you to think so?

Tom: He goes to night school.

Amanda (beaming): Splendid! What does he do, I mean study?

Tom: Radio engineering and public speaking!

Amanda: Then he has visions of being advanced in the world! Any young man who studies public speaking is aiming to have an executive job some day! And radio engineering? A thing for the future! Both of these facts are very illuminating. Those are the sort of things that a mother should know concerning any young man who comes to call on her daughter. Seriously or—not.

Tom: One little warning. He doesn't know about Laura. I didn't let on that we had dark ulterior motives. I just said, why don't you come have dinner with us? He said okay and that was the whole conversation.

Amanda: I bet it was! You're eloquent as an oyster. However, he'll know about Laura when he gets here. When he sees how lovely and sweet and pretty she is, he'll thank his lucky stars he was asked to dinner.

Tom: Mother, you mustn't expect too much of Laura.

Amanda: What do you mean?

Tom: Laura seems all those things to you and me because she's ours and we love her. We don't even notice she's crippled any more.

Amanda: Don't say crippled! You know that I never allow that word to be used!

Tom: But face facts, Mother. She is and—that's not all—

Amanda: What do you mean "not all"?

Tom: Laura is very different from other girls.

Amanda: I think the difference is all to her advantage.

Tom: Not quite all—in the eyes of others—strangers—she's terribly shy and lives in a world of her own and those things make her seem a little peculiar to people outside the house.

Amanda: Don't say peculiar.

Tom: Face the facts. She is.

(*The dance-hall music changes to a tango that has a minor and somewhat ominous tone.*)

Amanda: In what way is she peculiar—may I ask?

Tom (gently): She lives in a world of her own—a world of—little glass ornaments, Mother. . . . (*Gets up.* Amanda *remains holding brush, looking at him, troubled.*) She plays old phonograph records and—that's about all— (*He glances at himself in the mirror and crosses to door.*)

Amanda (sharply): Where are you going?

Tom: I'm going to the movies. (*out screen door*)

Amanda: Not to the movies, every night to the movies! (*follows quickly to screen door*) I don't believe you always go to the movies! (*He is gone.* Amanda *looks worriedly after him for a moment. Then vitality and optimism return and she turns from the door, crossing to portieres.*) Laura! Laura! (*Laura answers from kitchenette.*)

Laura: Yes, Mother.

Amanda: Let those dishes go and come in front! (*Laura appears with dish towel; gaily:*) Laura, come here and make a wish on the moon!

Laura (entering): Moon—moon?

Amanda: A little silver slipper of a moon. Look over your left shoulder, Laura, and make a wish! (*Laura looks faintly puzzled as if called out of sleep.* Amanda *seizes her shoulders and turns her at an angle by the door.*) No! Now, darling, *wish!*

Laura: What shall I wish for, Mother?

Amanda (her voice trembling and her eyes suddenly filling with tears): Happiness! Good Fortune!

(*The violin rises and the stage dims out.*)

SCENE VI

(*Image: High school hero.*)

Tom: And so the following evening I brought Jim home to dinner. I had known Jim slightly in high school. In high school Jim was a hero. He had tremendous Irish good nature and vitality with the scrubbed and polished look of white chinaware. He seemed to move in a continual spotlight. He was a star in basketball, captain of the debating club, president of the senior class and the glee club and he sang the male lead in the annual light operas. He was always running or bounding, never just walking. He seemed always at the point of defeating the law of gravity. He was shooting with such velocity through his adolescence that you would logically expect him to arrive at nothing short of the White House by the time he was thirty. But Jim apparently ran into more interference after his graduation from Soldan. His speed had definitely slowed. Six years after he left high school he was holding a job that wasn't much better than mine.

(Image: Clerk.)

He was the only one at the warehouse with whom I was on friendly terms. I was valuable to him as someone who could remember his former glory, who had seen him win basketball games and the silver cup in debating. He knew of my secret practice of retiring to a cabinet of the washroom to work on poems when business was slack in the warehouse. He called me Shakespeare. And while the other boys in the warehouse regarded me with suspicious hostility, Jim took a humorous attitude toward me. Gradually his attitude affected the others, their hostility wore off and they also began to smile at me as people smile at an oddly fashioned dog who trots across their path at some distance.

I knew that Jim and Laura had known each other at Soldan, and I had heard Laura speak admiringly of his voice. I didn't know if Jim remembered her or not. In high school Laura had been as unobtrusive as Jim had been astonishing. If he did remember Laura, it was not as my sister, for when I asked him to dinner, he grinned and said, "You know, Shakespeare, I never thought of you as having folks!"

He was about to discover that I did. . . .

(Light up stage.)

(Legend on screen: "The accent of a coming foot.")

Friday evening. It is about five o'clock of a late spring evening which comes "scattering poems in the sky."

A delicate lemony light is in the Wingfield apartment.

Amanda has worked like a Turk in preparation for the gentleman caller. The results are astonishing. The new floor lamp with its rose-silk shade is in place, a colored paper lantern conceals the broken light fixture in the ceiling, new billowing white curtains are at the windows, chintz covers are on chairs and sofa, a pair of new sofa pillows make their initial appearance.

Open boxes and tissue paper are scattered on the floor.

Laura stands in the middle with lifted arms while Amanda crouches before her, adjusting the hem of the new dress, devout and ritualistic. The dress is colored and designed by memory. The arrangement of Laura's hair is changed; it is softer and more becoming. A fragile, unearthly prettiness has come out in Laura: she is like a piece of translucent glass touched by light, given a momentary radiance, not actual, not lasting.

Amanda (impatiently): Why are you trembling?
Laura: Mother, you've made me so nervous!

Amanda: How have I made you nervous?

Laura: By all this fuss! You make it seem so important!

Amanda: I don't understand you, Laura. You couldn't be satisfied with just sitting home, and yet whenever I try to arrange something for you, you seem to resist it. *(She gets up.)* Now take a look at yourself. No, wait! Wait just a moment—I have an idea!

Laura: What is it now?

(Amanda *produces two powder puffs which she wraps in handkerchiefs and stuffs in* Laura's *bosom.)*

Laura: Mother, what are you doing?

Amanda: They call them "Gay Deceivers"!

Laura: I won't wear them!

Amanda: You will!

Laura: Why should I?

Amanda: Because, to be painfully honest, your chest is flat.

Laura: You make it seem like we were setting a trap.

Amanda: All pretty girls are a trap, a pretty trap, and men expect them to be. *(Legend: "A pretty trap.")* Now look at yourself, young lady. This is the prettiest you will ever be! I've got to fix myself now! You're going to be surprised by your mother's appearance! *(She crosses through portieres, humming gaily.)*

(Laura *moves slowly to the long mirror and stares solemnly at herself. A wind blows the white curtains inward in a slow, graceful motion and with a faint, sorrowful sighing.)*

Amanda (off stage): It isn't dark enough yet. *(She turns slowly before the mirror with a troubled look.)*

(Legend on screen: "This is my sister: celebrate her with strings!" Music.)

Amanda (laughing, off): I'm going to show you something. I'm going to make a spectacular appearance!

Laura: What is it, mother?

Amanda: Possess your soul in patience—you will see! Something I've resurrected from that old trunk! Styles haven't changed so terribly much after all. . . . *(She parts the portieres.)* Now just look at your mother! *(She wears a girlish frock of yellowed voile with a blue silk sash. She carries a bunch of jonquils—the legend of her youth is nearly revived; feverishly:)* This is the dress in which I led the cotillion. Won the cakewalk twice at Sunset Hill, wore one spring to the Governor's ball in Jackson! See how I sashayed around the ballroom, Laura? *(She raises her skirt and does a mincing step around the room.)* I wore it on Sundays for my gentlemen callers! I had it on the day I met your father—I had malaria fever all that spring. The change of climate from East Tennessee to the Delta— weakened resistance—I had a little temperature all the time—not enough to be serious—just enough to make me restless and giddy! Invitations poured in—parties all over the Delta!—"Stay in bed," said

Mother, "you have fever!"—but I just wouldn't.—I took quinine but kept on going, going!—Evenings, dances!—Afternoons, long, long, rides! Picnics—lovely!—So lovely, that country in May.—All lacy with dogwood, literally flooded with jonquils!—That was the spring I had the craze for jonquils. Jonquils became an absolute obsession. Mother said, "Honey, there's no more room for jonquils." And still I kept bringing in more jonquils. Whenever, wherever I saw them, I'd say, "Stop! Stop! I see jonquils!" I made the young men help me gather the jonquils! It was a joke, Amanda and her jonquils! Finally there were no more vases to hold them, every available space was filled with jonquils. No vases to hold them? All right, I'll hold them myself! And then I—*(She stops in front of the picture. Music.)* met your father! Malaria fever and jonquils and then—this—boy. . . . *(She switches on the rose-colored lamp.)* I hope they get here before it starts to rain. *(She crosses upstage and places the jonquils in bowl on table.)* I gave your brother a little extra change so he and Mr. O'Connor could take the service car home.

Laura (with altered look): What did you say his name was?

Amanda: O'Connor.

Laura: What is his first name?

Amanda: I don't remember. Oh, yes, I do. It was—Jim!

(Laura sways slightly and catches hold of a chair.)

(Legend on screen: "Not Jim!")

Laura (faintly): Not—Jim!

Amanda: Yes, that was it, it was Jim! I've never known a Jim that wasn't nice!

(Music: Ominous.)

Laura: Are you sure his name is Jim O'Connor?

Amanda: Yes. Why?

Laura: Is he the one that Tom used to know in high school?

Amanda: He didn't say so. I think he just got to know him at the warehouse.

Laura: There was a Jim O'Connor we both knew in high school—*(then, with effort:)* If that is the one that Tom is bringing to dinner—you'll have to excuse me, I won't come to the table.

Amanda: What sort of nonsense is this?

Laura: You asked me once if I'd ever liked a boy. Don't you remember I showed you this boy's picture?

Amanda: You mean the boy you showed me in the year book?

Laura: Yes, that boy.

Amanda: Laura, Laura, were you in love with that boy?

Laura: I don't know, Mother. All I know is I couldn't sit at the table if it was him!

Amanda: It won't be him! It isn't the least bit likely. But whether it is or not, you will come to the table. You will not be excused.

Laura: I'll have to be, Mother.

Amanda: I don't intend to humor your silliness, Laura. I've had too much

from you and your brother, both! So just sit down and compose yourself
till they come. Tom has forgotten his key so you'll have to let them in,
when they arrive.

Laura (panicky): Oh, Mother—*you* answer the door!

Amanda (lightly): I'll be in the kitchen—busy!

Laura: Oh, Mother, please answer the door, don't make me do it!

Amanda (crossing into kitchenette): I've got to fix the dressing for the salmon.
Fuss, fuss—silliness!—over a gentleman caller!

(Door swings shut. Laura is left alone.)

(Legend: "Terror!")

*(She utters a low moan and turns off the lamp—sits stiffly on the edge of the
sofa, knotting her fingers together.)*

(Legend on screen: "The opening of a door!")

*(Tom and Jim appear on the fire-escape steps and climb to landing. Hearing
their approach, Laura rises with a panicky gesture. She retreats to the portieres.
The doorbell. Laura catches her breath and touches her throat. Low drums.)*

Amanda (calling): Laura, sweetheart! The door!

(Laura stares at it without moving.)

Jim: I think we just beat the rain.

Tom: Uh-huh. *(He rings again, nervously. Jim whistles and fishes for a cigarette.)*

Amanda (very, very gaily): Laura, that is your brother and Mr. O'Connor!
Will you let them in, darling?

(Laura crosses toward kitchenette door.)

Laura (breathlessly): Mother—you go to the door!

*(Amanda steps out of kitchenette and stares furiously at Laura. She points
imperiously at the door.)*

Laura: Please, please!

Amanda (in a fierce whisper): What is the matter with you, you silly thing?

Laura (desperately): Please, you answer it, *please!*

Amanda: I told you I wasn't going to humor you, Laura. Why have you
chosen this moment to lose your mind?

Laura: Please, please, please, you go!

Amanda: You'll have to go to the door because I can't!

Laura (despairingly): I can't either!

Amanda: Why?

Laura: I'm *sick!*

Amanda: I'm sick, too—of your nonsense! Why can't you and your brother
be normal people? Fantastic whims and behavior! *(Tom gives a long
ring.)* Preposterous goings on! Can you give me one reason—*(calls out
lyrically)* COMING! JUST ONE SECOND!—why should you be afraid to open a
door? Now you answer it, Laura!

Laura: Oh, oh, oh . . . (*She returns through the portieres. Darts to the victrola and winds it frantically and turns it on.*)

Amanda: Laura Wingfield, you march right to that door!

Laura: Yes—yes, Mother!

(*A faraway, scratchy rendition of "Dardanella" softens the air and gives her strength to move through it. She slips to the door and draws it cautiously open.* Tom *enters with the caller,* Jim O'Connor.)

Tom: Laura, this is Jim. Jim, this is my sister, Laura.

Jim (stepping inside): I didn't know that Shakespeare had a sister!

Laura (retreating stiff and trembling from the door): How—how do you do?

Jim (heartily extending his hand): Okay!

(Laura *touches it hesitantly with hers.*)

Jim: Your hand's *cold*, Laura!

Laura: Yes, well—I've been playing the victrola. . . .

Jim: Must have been playing classical music on it! You ought to play a little hot swing music to warm you up!

Laura: Excuse me—I haven't finished playing the victrola. . . .

(*She turns awkwardly and hurries into the front room. She pauses a second by the victrola. Then catches her breath and darts through the portieres like a frightened deer.*)

Jim (grinning): What was the matter?

Tom: Oh—with Laura? Laura is—terribly shy.

Jim: Shy, huh? It's unusual to meet a shy girl nowadays. I don't believe you ever mentioned you had a sister.

Tom: Well, now you know. I have one. Here is the *Post Dispatch*. You want a piece of it?

Jim: Uh-huh.

Tom: What piece? The comics?

Jim: Sports! (*glances at it*) Ole Dizzy Dean is on his bad behavior.

Tom (disinterest): Yeah? (*lights cigarette and crosses back to fire-escape door*)

Jim: Where are *you* going?

Tom: I'm going out on the terrace.

Jim (goes after him): You know, Shakespeare—I'm going to sell you a bill of goods!

Tom: What goods?

Jim: A course I'm taking.

Tom: Huh?

Jim: In public speaking! You and me, we're not the warehouse type.

Tom: Thanks—that's good news. But what has public speaking got to do with it?

Jim: It fits you for—executive positions!

Tom: Awww.

Jim: I tell you it's done a helluva lot for me.

(*Image: Executive at desk.*)

Tom: In what respect?

Jim: In every! Ask yourself what is the difference between you an' me and men in the office down front? Brains?—No!—Ability?—No! Then what? Just one little thing—

Tom: What is that one little thing?

Jim: Primarily it amounts to—social poise! Being able to square up to people and hold your own on any social level!

Amanda (off stage): Tom?

Tom: Yes, Mother?

Amanda: Is that you and Mr. O'Connor?

Tom: Yes, Mother.

Amanda: Well, you just make yourselves comfortable in there.

Tom: Yes, Mother.

Amanda: Ask Mr. O'Connor if he would like to wash his hands.

Jim: Aw—no—no—thank you—I took care of that at the warehouse. Tom—

Tom: Yes?

Jim: Mr. Mendoza was speaking to me about you.

Tom: Favorably?

Jim: What do you think?

Tom: Well—

Jim: You're going to be out of a job if you don't wake up.

Tom: I am waking up—

Jim: You show no signs.

Tom: The signs are interior.

(*Image on screen: The sailing vessel with Jolly Roger again.*)

Tom: I'm planning to change. (*He leans over the rail speaking with quiet exhilaration. The incandescent marquees and signs of the first-run movie houses light his face from across the alley. He looks like a voyager.*) I'm right at the point of committing myself to a future that doesn't include the warehouse and Mr. Mendoza or even a night-school course in public speaking.

Jim: What are you gassing about?

Tom: I'm tired of the movies.

Jim: Movies!

Tom: Yes, movies! Look at them—(*a wave toward the marvels of Grand Avenue*) All of those glamorous people—having adventures—hogging it all, gobbling the whole thing up! You know what happens? People go to the *movies* instead of *moving!* Hollywood characters are supposed to have all the adventures for everybody in America, while everybody in America sits in a dark room and watches them have them! Yes, until there's a war. That's when adventure becomes available to the masses! *Everyone's* dish, not only Gable's! Then the people in the dark room come out of the dark room to have some adventures themselves—Goody, goody!—It's our turn now, to go to the South Sea Island—to make a safari—to be exotic, far-off!—But I'm not patient. I don't want to wait till then. I'm tired of the *movies* and I am *about* to *move!*

Jim (incredulously): Move?

Tom: Yes.
Jim: When?
Tom: Soon!
Jim: Where? Where?

(*Theme three music seems to answer the question, while Tom thinks it over. He searches among his pockets.*)

Tom: I'm starting to boil inside. I know I seem dreamy, but inside—well, I'm boiling! Whenever I pick up a shoe, I shudder a little thinking how short life is and what I am doing!—Whatever that means. I know it doesn't mean shoes—except as something to wear on a traveler's feet! (*finds paper*) Look—
Jim: What?
Tom: I'm a member.
Jim (reading): The Union of Merchant Seamen.
Tom: I paid my dues this month, instead of the light bill.
Jim: You will regret it when they turn the lights off.
Tom: I won't be here.
Jim: How about your mother?
Tom: I'm like my father. The bastard son of a bastard! See how he grins? And he's been absent going on sixteen years!
Jim: You're just talking, you drip. How does your mother feel about it?
Tom: Shhh!—Here comes Mother! Mother is not acquainted with my plans!
Amanda (enters portieres): Where are you all?
Tom: On the terrace, Mother.

(*They start inside. She advances to them.* Tom *is distinctly shocked at her appearance. Even* Jim *blinks a little. He is making his first contact with girlish Southern vivacity and in spite of the night-school course in public speaking is somewhat thrown off the beam by the unexpected outlay of social charm.*

Certain responses are attempted by Jim *but are swept aside by* Amanda's *gay laughter and chatter.* Tom *is embarrassed but after the first shock* Jim *reacts very warmly. Grins and chuckles, is altogether won over.*)

(*Image:* Amanda *as a girl.*)

Amanda (coyly smiling, shaking her girlish ringlets): Well, well, well, so this is Mr. O'Connor. Introductions entirely unnecessary. I've heard so much about you from my boy. I finally said to him, Tom—good gracious!— why don't you bring this paragon to supper? I'd like to meet this nice young man at the warehouse!—Instead of just hearing him sing your praises so much! I don't know why my son is so stand-offish—that's not Southern behavior! Let's sit down and—I think we could stand a little more air in here! Tom, leave the door open. I felt a nice fresh breeze a moment ago. Where has it gone? Mmm, so warm already! And not quite summer, even. We're going to burn up when summer really gets started. However, we're having—we're having a very light supper. I think light things are better fo' this time of year. The same as light clothes are. Light clothes an' light food are what warm weather calls fo'.

You know our blood gets so thick during th' winter—it takes a while fo'
us to *adjust* ou'selves!—when the season changes . . . It's come so quick
this year. I wasn't prepared. All of a sudden—heavens! Already summer!—I ran to the trunk an' pulled out this light dress—Terribly old!
Historical almost! But feels so good—so good an' co-ol, y'know. . . .

Tom: Mother—

Amanda: Yes, honey?

Tom: How about—supper?

Amanda: Honey, you go ask Sister if supper is ready! You know that Sister is
in full charge of supper! Tell her you hungry boys are waiting for it. *(to
Jim)* Have you met Laura?

Jim: She—

Amanda: Let you in? Oh, good, you've met already! It's rare for a girl as
sweet an' pretty as Laura to be domestic! But Laura is, thank heavens,
not only pretty but also very domestic. I'm not at all. I never was a bit. I
never could make a thing but angel-food cake. Well, in the South we
had so many servants. Gone, gone, gone. All vestige of gracious living!
Gone completely! I wasn't prepared for what the future brought me. All
of my gentlemen callers were sons of planters and so of course I
assumed that I would be married to one and raise my family on a large
piece of land with plenty of servants. But man proposes—and woman
accepts the proposal!—To vary that old, old saying a little bit—I married
no planter! I married a man who worked for the telephone company!—
That gallantly smiling gentleman over there! *(points to the picture)* A
telephone man who—fell in love with long-distance!—Now he travels
and I don't even know where!—But what am I going on for about my—
tribulations? Tell me yours—I hope you don't have any! Tom?

Tom (returning): Yes, Mother?

Amanda: Is supper nearly ready?

Tom: It looks to me like supper is on the table.

Amanda: Let me look—*(She rises prettily and looks through portieres.)* Oh,
lovely!—But where is Sister?

Tom: Laura is not feeling well and she says that she thinks she'd better not
come to the table.

Amanda: What?—Nonsense!—Laura? Oh, Laura!

Laura (off stage, faintly): Yes, Mother.

Amanda: You really must come to the table. We won't be seated until you
come to the table! Come in, Mr. O'Connor. You sit over there and I'll—
Laura? Laura Wingfield! You're keeping us waiting, honey! We can't say
grace until you come to the table!

(The back door is pushed weakly open and Laura *comes in. She is obviously
quite faint, her lips trembling, her eyes wide and staring. She moves unsteadily
toward the table.)*

(Legend: "Terror!")

*(Outside a summer storm is coming abruptly. The white curtains billow in-
ward at the windows and there is a sorrowful murmur and deep blue dusk.*

Laura *suddenly stumbles; she catches at a chair with a faint moan.)*

Tom: Laura!

Amanda: Laura! *(There is a clap of thunder.)* *(Legend: "Ah!")* *(despairingly:)*
Why, Laura, you *are* sick, darling! Tom, help your sister into the living
room, dear! Sit in the living room, Laura—rest on the sofa. Well! *(to the
gentleman caller:)* Standing over the hot stove made her ill!—I told her
that it was just too warm this evening, but—(Tom *comes back in.* Laura *is
on the sofa.)* Is Laura all right now?

Tom: Yes.

Amanda: What *is* that? Rain? A nice cool rain has come up! *(She gives the
gentleman caller a frightened look.)* I think we may—have grace—now . . .
(Tom looks at her stupidly.) Tom, honey—you say grace!

Tom: Oh . . . "For these and all thy mercies—" *(They bow their heads,*
Amanda *stealing a nervous glance at* Jim. *In the living room* Laura, *stretched
on the sofa, clenches her hand to her lips, to hold back a shuddering sob.)* God's
Holy Name be praised—

(The scene dims out.)

SCENE VII

(Legend: "A souvenir.")

*Half an hour later. Dinner is just being finished in the upstage area which is
concealed by the drawn portieres.*

As the curtain rises Laura *is still huddled upon the sofa, her feet drawn under
her, her head resting on a pale blue pillow, her eyes wide and mysteriously watchful.
The new floor lamp with its shade of rose-colored silk gives a soft, becoming light to
her face, bringing out the fragile, unearthly prettiness which usually escapes attention. There is a steady murmur of rain, but it is slackening and stops soon after the
scene begins; the air outside becomes pale and luminous as the moon breaks out.*

A moment after the curtain rises, the lights in both rooms flicker and go out.

Jim: Hey, there, Mr. Light Bulb!

(Amanda laughs nervously.)

(Legend: "Suspension of a public service.")

Amanda: Where was Moses when the lights went out? Ha-ha. Do you know
the answer to that one, Mr. O'Connor?

Jim: No, Ma'am, what's the answer?

Amanda: In the dark! *(Jim laughs appreciably.)* Everybody sit still. I'll light
the candles. Isn't it lucky we have them on the table? Where's a match?
Which of you gentlemen can provide a match?

Jim: Here.

Amanda: Thank you, sir.

Jim: Not at all, Ma'am!

Amanda: I guess the fuse has burnt out. Mr. O'Connor, can you tell a burnt-out fuse? I know I can't and Tom is a total loss when it comes to mechanics. *(Sound: Getting up: voices recede a little to kitchenette.)* Oh, be careful you don't bump into something. We don't want our gentleman caller to break his neck. Now wouldn't that be a fine howdy-do?

Jim: Ha-ha! Where is the fuse-box?

Amanda: Right here next to the stove. Can you see anything?

Jim: Just a minute.

Amanda: Isn't electricity a mysterious thing? Wasn't it Benjamin Franklin who tied a key to a kite? We live in such a mysterious universe, don't we? Some people say that science clears up all mysteries for us. In my opinion it only creates more! Have you found it yet?

Jim: No, Ma'am. All these fuses look okay to me.

Amanda: Tom!

Tom: Yes, Mother?

Amanda: That light bill I gave you several days ago. The one I told you we got the notices about?

Tom: Oh.—Yeah.

     (Legend: "Ha!")

Amanda: You didn't neglect to pay it by any chance?

Tom: Why, I—

Amanda: Didn't! I might have known it!

Jim: Shakespeare probably wrote a poem on that light bill, Mrs. Wingfield.

Amanda: I might have known better than to trust him with it! There's such a high price for negligence in this world!

Jim: Maybe the poem will win a ten-dollar prize.

Amanda: We'll just have to spend the remainder of the evening in the nineteenth century, before Mr. Edison made the Mazda lamp!

Jim: Candlelight is my favorite kind of light.

Amanda: That shows you're romantic! But that's no excuse for Tom. Well, we got through dinner. Very considerate of them to let us get through dinner before they plunged us into everlasting darkness, wasn't it, Mr. O'Connor?

Jim: Ha-ha!

Amanda: Tom, as a penalty for your carelessness you can help me with the dishes.

Jim: Let me give you a hand.

Amanda: Indeed you will not!

Jim: I ought to be good for something.

Amanda: Good for something? *(Her tone is rhapsodic.)* You? Why, Mr. O'Connor, nobody, *nobody's* given me this much entertainment in years—as you have!

Jim: Aw, now, Mrs. Wingfield!

Amanda: I'm not exaggerating, not one bit! But Sister is all by her lonesome. You go keep her company in the parlor! I'll give you this lovely old candelabrum that used to be on the altar at the church of the Heavenly Rest. It was melted a little out of shape when the church burnt down. Lightning struck it one spring. Gypsy Jones was holding a revival at the time and he intimated that the church was destroyed because the Episcopalians gave card parties.

Jim: Ha-ha.

Amanda: And how about coaxing Sister to drink a little wine? I think it would be good for her! Can you carry both at once?

Jim: Sure. I'm Superman!

Amanda: Now, Thomas, get into this apron!

(*The door of kitchenette swings closed on* Amanda's *gay laughter; the flickering light approaches the portieres.*

Laura *sits up nervously as he enters. Her speech at first is low and breathless from the almost intolerable strain of being alone with a stranger.*)

(*The legend: "I don't suppose you remember me at all!"*)

(*In her first speeches in his scene, before* Jim's *warmth overcomes her paralyzing shyness,* Laura's *voice is thin and breathless as though she has just run up a steep flight of stairs.*

Jim's *attitude is gently humorous. In playing this scene it should be stressed that while the incident is apparently unimportant, it is to* Laura *the climax of her secret life.*)

Jim: Hello, there, Laura.

Laura (faintly): Hello. (*She clears her throat.*)

Jim: How are you feeling now? Better?

Laura: Yes. Yes, thank you.

Jim: This is for you. A little dandelion wine. (*He extends it toward her with extravagant gallantry.*)

Laura: Thank you.

Jim: Drink it—but don't get drunk! (*He laughs heartily.* Laura *takes the glass uncertainly, laughs shyly.*) Where shall I set the candles?

Laura: Oh—oh, anywhere . . .

Jim: How about here on the floor? Any objections?

Laura: No.

Jim: I'll spread a newspaper under to catch the drippings. I like to sit on the floor. Mind if I do?

Laura: Oh, no.

Jim: Give me a pillow?

Laura: What?

Jim: A pillow!

Laura: Oh . . . (*hands him one quickly*)

Jim: How about you? Don't you like to sit on the floor?

Laura: Oh—yes.

Jim: Why don't you, then?

Laura: I—will.

Jim: Take a pillow! *(Laura does. Sits on the other side of the candelabrum.* Jim *crosses his legs and smiles engagingly at her.)* I can't hardly see you sitting way over there.

Laura: I can—see you.

Jim: I know, but that's not fair, I'm in the limelight. *(Laura moves her pillow closer.)* Good! Now I can see you! Comfortable?

Laura: Yes.

Jim: So am I. Comfortable as a cow. Will you have some gum?

Laura: No, thank you.

Jim: I think that I will indulge, with your permission. *(musingly unwraps it and holds it up)* Think of the fortune made by the guy that invented the first piece of chewing gum. Amazing, huh? The Wrigley Building is one of the sights of Chicago.—I saw it summer before last when I went up to the Century of Progress. Did you take in the Century of Progress?

Laura: No, I didn't.

Jim: Well, it was quite a wonderful exposition. What impressed me most was the Hall of Science. Gives you an idea of what the future will be in America, even more wonderful than the present time is! *(pause; smiling at her:)* Your brother tells me you're shy. Is that right, Laura?

Laura: I—don't know.

Jim: I judge you to be an old-fashioned type of girl. Well, I think that's a pretty good type to be. Hope you don't think I'm being too personal— do you?

Laura (hastily, out of embarrassment): I believe I *will* take a piece of gum, if you—don't mind. *(clearing her throat)* Mr. O'Connor, have you—kept up with your singing?

Jim: Singing? Me?

Laura: Yes, I remember what a beautiful voice you had.

Jim: When did you hear me sing?

> *(Voice off stage in the pause.)*

Voice (off stage):

> O blow, ye winds, heigh-ho,
> A-roving I will go!
> I'm off to my love
> With a boxing glove—
> Ten thousand miles away!

Jim: You say you've heard me sing?

Laura: Oh, yes! Yes, very often . . . I—don't suppose you remember me— at all?

Jim (smiling doubtfully): You know I have an idea I've seen you before. I had that idea soon as you opned the door. It seemed almost like I was about to remember your name. But the name that I started to call you—wasn't a name! And so I stopped myself before I said it.

Laura: Wasn't it—Blue Roses?

Jim (springs up, grinning): Blue Roses! My gosh, yes—Blue Roses! That's what I had on my tongue when you opened the door! Isn't it funny what tricks your memory plays? I didn't connect you with the high school somehow or other. But that's where it was; it was high school. I didn't even know you were Shakespeare's sister! Gosh, I'm sorry.

Laura: I didn't expect you to. You—barely knew me!

Jim: But we did have a speaking acquaintance, huh?

Laura: Yes, we—spoke to each other.

Jim: When did you recognize me?

Laura: Oh, right away!

Jim: Soon as I came in the door?

Laura: When I heard your name I thought it was probably you. I knew that Tom used to know you a little in high school. So when you came in the door—Well, then I was—sure.

Jim: Why didn't you *say* something, then?

Laura (breathlessly): I didn't know what to say, I was—too surprised!

Jim: For goodness' sakes! You know, this sure is funny!

Laura: Yes! Yes, isn't it, though . . .

Jim: Didn't we have a class in something together?

Laura: Yes, we did.

Jim: What class was that?

Laura: It was—singing—Chorus!

Jim: Aw!

Laura: I sat across the aisle from you in the Aud.

Jim: Aw.

Laura: Mondays, Wednesdays and Fridays.

Jim: Now I remember—you always came in late.

Laura: Yes, it was so hard for me, getting upstairs. I had that brace on my leg—it clumped so loud!

Jim: I never heard any clumping.

Laura (wincing at the recollection): To me it sounded like—thunder!

Jim: Well, well, well. I never even noticed.

Laura: And everybody was seated before I came in. I had to walk in front of all those people. My seat was in the back row. I had to go clumping all the way up the aisle with everyone watching!

Jim: You shouldn't have been self-conscious.

Laura: I know, but I was. It was always such a relief when the singing started.

Jim: Aw, yes. I've placed you now! I used to call you Blue Roses. How was it that I got started calling you that?

Laura: I was out of school a little while with pleurosis. When I came back you asked me what was the matter. I said I had pleurosis—you thought I said Blue Roses. That's what you always called me after that!

Jim: I hope you didn't mind.

Laura: Oh, no—I liked it. You see, I wasn't acquainted with many—people. . . .

Jim: As I remember you sort of stuck by yourself.

Laura: I—I—never had much luck at—making friends.

Jim: I don't see why you wouldn't.

Laura: Well, I—started out badly.

Jim: You mean being—

Laura: Yes, it sort of—stood between me—

Jim: You shouldn't have let it!

Laura: I know, but it did, and—

Jim: You were shy with people!

Laura: I tried not to be but never could—

Jim: Overcome it?

Laura: No, I—I never could!

Jim: I guess being shy is something you have to work out of kind of gradually.

Laura (sorrowfully): Yes—I guess it—

Jim: Takes time!

Laura: Yes—

Jim: People are not so dreadful when you know them. That's what you have to remember! And everybody has problems, not just you, but practically everybody has got some problems. You think of yourself as having the only problems, as being the only one who is disappointed. But just look around you and you will see lots of people as disappointed as you are. For instance, I hoped when I was going to high school that I would be further along at this time, six years later, than I am now—You remember that wonderful write-up I had in *The Torch?*

Laura: Yes! *(She rises and crosses to table.)*

Jim: It said I was bound to succeed in anything I went into! *(Laura returns with the annual.)* Holy Jeez! *The Torch!* *(He accepts it reverently. They smile across it with mutual wonder. Laura crouches beside him and they begin to turn through it. Laura's shyness is dissolving in his warmth.)*

Laura: Here you are in *Pirates of Penzance!*

Jim (wistfully): I sang the baritone lead in that operetta.

Laura (rapidly): So—*beautifully!*

Jim (protesting): Aw—

Laura: Yes, yes—beautifully—beautifully!

Jim: You heard me?

Laura: All three times!

Jim: No!

Laura: Yes!

Jim: All three performances?

Laura (looking down): Yes.

Jim: Why?

Laura: I—wanted to ask you to—autograph my program.

Jim: Why didn't you ask me to?

Laura: You were always surrounded by your own friends so much that I never had a chance to.

Jim: You should have just—

Laura: Well, I—thought you might think I was—

Jim: Thought I might think you was—what?

Laura: Oh—

Jim (with reflective relish): I was beleaguered by females in those days.

Laura: You were terribly popular!

Jim: Yeah—

Laura: You had such a—friendly way—

Jim: I was spoiled in high school.

Laura: Everybody—liked you!

Jim: Including you?

Laura: I—yes, I—I did, too—*(She gently closes the book in her lap.)*

Jim: Well, well, well!—Give me that program, Laura. *(She hands it to him. He signs it with a flourish.)* There you are—better late than never!

Laura: Oh, I—what a—surprise!

Jim: My signature isn't worth very much right now. But some day— maybe—it will increase in value! Being disappointed is one thing and being discouraged is something else. I am disappointed but I am not discouraged. I'm twenty-three years old. How old are you?

Laura: I'll be twenty-four in June.

Jim: That's not old age!

Laura: No, but—

Jim: You finished high school?

Laura (with difficulty): I didn't go back.

Jim: You mean you dropped out?

Laura: I made bad grades in my final examinations. *(She rises and replaces the book and the program; her voice strained:)* How is—Emily Meisenbach getting along?

Jim: Oh, that kraut-head!

Laura: Why do you call her that?

Jim: That's what she was.

Laura: You're not still—going with her?

Jim: I never see her.

Laura: It said in the Personal Section that you were—engaged!

Jim I know, but I wasn't impressed by that—propaganda!

Laura: It wasn't—the truth?

Jim: Only in Emily's optimistic opinion!

Laura: Oh—

(Legend: "What have you done since high school?")
(Jim lights a cigarette and leans indolently back on his elbows smiling at Laura with a warmth and charm which lights her inwardly with altar candles. She remains by the table and turns in her hands a piece of glass to cover her tumult.)

Jim (after several reflective puffs on a cigarette): What have you done since high school? *(She seems not to hear him.)* Huh? *(Laura looks up.)* I said what have you done since high school, Laura?

Laura: Nothing much.

Jim: You must have been doing something these six long years.

Laura: Yes.

Jim: Well, then, such as what?

Laura: I took a business course at business college—

Jim: How did that work out?

Laura: Well, not very—well—I had to drop out, it gave me—indigestion—

(Jim *laughs gently.*)

Jim: What are you doing now?

Laura: I don't do anything—much. Oh, please don't think I sit around doing nothing! My glass collection takes up a good deal of my time. Glass is something you have to take good care of.

Jim: What did you say—about glass?

Laura: Collection I said—I have one—*(She clears her throat and turns away again, acutely shy.)*

Jim (abruptly): You know what I judge to be the trouble with you? Inferiority complex! Know what that is? That's what they call it when someone low-rates himself! I understand it because I had it, too. Although my case was not so aggravated as yours seems to be. I had it until I took up public speaking, developed my voice, and learned that I had an aptitude for science. Before that time I never thought of myself as being outstanding in any way whatsoever! Now I've never made a regular study of it, but I have a friend who says I can analyze people better than doctors that make a profession of it. I don't claim that to be necessarily true, but I can sure guess a person's psychology, Laura! *(takes out his gum)* Excuse me, Laura. I always take it out when the flavor is gone. I'll use this scrap of paper to wrap it in. I know how it is to get it stuck on a shoe. Yep— that's what I judge to be your principal trouble. A lack of confidence in yourself as a person. You don't have the proper amount of faith in yourself. I'm basing that fact on a number of your remarks and also on certain observations I've made. For instance that clumping you thought was so awful in high school. You say that you even dreaded to walk into class. You see what you did? You dropped out of school, you gave up an education because of a clump, which as far as I know was practically non-existent! A little physical defect is what you have. Hardly noticeable even! Magnified thousands of times by imagination! You know what my strong advice to you is? Think of yourself as *superior* in some way!

Laura: In what way would I think?

Jim: Why, man alive, Laura! Just look about you a little. What do you see? A world full of common people! All of 'em born and all of 'em going to die! Which of them has one-tenth of your good points! Or mine! Or anyone else's, as far as that goes—Gosh! Everybody excels in some one thing. Some in many! *(unconsciously glances at himself in the mirror)* All you've got to do is discover in *what!* Take me, for instance. *(He adjusts his tie at the mirror.)* My interest happens to lie in electro-dynamics. I'm taking a course in radio engineering at night school, Laura, on top of a fairly responsible job at the warehouse. I'm taking that course and studying public speaking.

Laura: Ohhhh.

Jim: Because I believe in the future of television! *(turning back to her)* I wish to be ready to go up right along with it. Therefore I'm planning to get in on the ground floor. In fact, I've already made the right connections and all that remains is for the industry itself to get under way! Full steam—*(His eyes are starry.)* Knowledge—Zzzzzp! Money—Zzzzzp!—Power! That's the cycle democracy is built on! *(His attitude is convincingly dynamic. Laura stares at him, even her shyness eclipsed in her absolute wonder. He suddenly grins.)* I guess you think I think a lot of myself!

Laura: No—o-o-o, I—

Jim: Now how about you? Isn't there something you take more interest in than anything else?

Laura: Well, I do—as I said—have my—glass collection—

(A peal of girlish laughter from the kitchen.)

Jim: I'm not right sure I know what you're talking about. What kind of glass is it?

Laura: Little articles of it, they're ornaments mostly! Most of them are little animals made out of glass, the tiniest little animals in the world. Mother calls them a glass menagerie! Here's an example of one, if you'd like to see it! This one is one of the oldest. It's nearly thirteen. *(He stretches out his hand.)* *(Music: "The Glass Menagerie.")* Oh, be careful—if you breathe, it breaks!

Jim: I'd better not take it. I'm pretty clumsy with things.

Laura: Go on, I trust you with him! *(places it in his palm)* There now—you're holding him gently! Hold him over the light, he loves the light! You see how the light shines through him?

Jim: It sure does shine!

Laura: I shouldn't be partial, but he is my favorite one.

Jim: What kind of thing is this one supposed to be?

Laura: Haven't you noticed the single horn on his forehead?

Jim: A unicorn, huh?

Laura: Mmm-hmmm!

Jim: Unicorns, aren't they extinct in the modern world?

Laura: I know!

Jim: Poor little fellow, he must feel sort of lonesome.

Laura (smiling): Well, if he does he doesn't complain about it. He stays on a shelf with some horses that don't have horns and all of them seem to get along nicely together.

Jim: How do you know?

Laura (lightly): I haven't heard any arguments among them!

Jim (grinning): No arguments, huh? Well, that's a pretty good sign! Where shall I set him?

Laura: Put him on the table. They all like a change of scenery once in a while!

Jim (stretching): Well, well, well, well—Look how big my shadow is when I stretch!

Laura: Oh, oh, yes—it stretches across the ceiling!

Jim (crossing to the door): I think it's stopped raining. *(opens fire-escape door)* Where does the music come from?

Laura: From the Paradise Dance Hall across the alley.

Jim: How about cutting the rug a little, Miss Wingfield?

Amanda: Oh, I—

Jim: Or is your program filled up? Let me have a look at it. *(grasps imaginary card)* Why, every dance is taken! I'll just have to scratch some out. *(Waltz music: "La Golondrina.")* Ahhh, a waltz! *(He executes some sweeping turns by himself, then holds his arms toward* Laura.*)*

Laura (breathlessly): I—can't dance!

Jim: There you go, that inferiority stuff.

Laura: I've never danced in my life!

Jim: Come on, try!

Laura: Oh, but I'd step on you!

Jim: I'm not made out of glass.

Laura: How—how—how do we start?

Jim: Just leave it to me. You hold your arms out a little.

Laura: Like this?

Jim: A little bit higher. Right. Now don't tighten up, that's the main thing about it—relax.

Laura (laughing breathlessly): It's hard not to.

Jim: Okay.

Laura: I'm afraid you can't budge me.

Jim: What do you bet I can't? *(He swings her into motion.)*

Laura: Goodness, yes, you can!

Jim: Let yourself go, now, Laura, just let yourself go.

Laura: I'm—

Jim: Come on!

Laura: Trying!

Jim: Not so stiff—Easy does it!

Laura: I know but I'm—

Jim: Loosen th' backbone! There now, that's a lot better.

Laura: Am I?

Jim: Lots, lots better! *(He moves her about the room in a clumsy waltz.)*

Laura: Oh, my!

Jim: Ha-ha!

Laura: Goodness, yes you can!

Jim: Ha-ha-ha! *(They suddenly bump into the table.* Jim *stops.)* What did we hit on?

Laura: Table.

Jim: Did something fall off it? I think—

Laura: Yes.

Jim: I hope that it wasn't the little glass horse with the horn!

Laura: Yes.

Jim: Aw, aw, aw. Is it broken?

Laura: Now it is just like all the other horses.

Jim: It's lost its—

Laura: Horn! It doesn't matter. Maybe it's a blessing in disguise.

Jim: You'll never forgive me. I bet that that was your favorite piece of glass.

Laura: I don't have favorites much. It's no tragedy, Freckles. Glass breaks so easily. No matter how careful you are. The traffic jars the shelves and things fall off them.

Jim: Still I'm awfully sorry that I was the cause.

Laura (smiling): I'll just imagine he had an operation. The horn was removed to make him feel less—freakish! *(They both laugh.)* Now he will feel more at home with the other horses, the ones that don't have horns . . .

Jim: Ha-ha, that's very funny! *(suddenly serious:)* I'm glad to see that you have a sense of humor. You know—you're—well—very different! Surprisingly different from anyone else I know! *(His voice becomes soft and hesitant with a genuine feeling.)* Do you mind me telling you that? *(Laura is abashed beyond speech.)* You make me feel sort of—I don't know how to put it! I'm usually pretty good at expressing things, but—This is something that I don't know how to say! *(Laura touches her throat and clears it—turns the broken unicorn in her hands.) (even softer:)* Has anyone ever told you that you were pretty? *(Pause: Music)* *(Laura looks up slowly, with wonder, and shakes her head.)* Well, you are! In a very different way from anyone else. And all the nicer because of the difference, too. *(His voice becomes low and husky.* Laura *turns away, nearly faint with the novelty of her emotions.)* I wish that you were my sister. I'd teach you to have some confidence in yourself. The different people are not like other people, but being different is nothing to be ashamed of. Because other people are not such wonderful people. They're one hundred times one thousand. You're one times one! They walk all over the earth. You just stay here. They're common as—weeds, but—you—well, you're—*Blue Roses!*

(Image on screen: Blue roses.)

(Music changes.)

Laura: But blue is wrong for—roses . . .

Jim: It's right for you—You're—pretty!

Laura: In what respect am I pretty?

Jim: In all respects—believe me! Your eyes—your hair—are pretty! Your hands are pretty! *(He catches hold of her hand.)* You think I'm making this up because I'm invited to dinner and have to be nice. Oh, I could do that! I could put on an act for you, Laura, and say lots of things without being very sincere. But this time I am. I'm talking to you sincerely. I happened to notice you had this inferiority complex that keeps you from feeling comfortable with people. Somebody needs to build your confidence up and make you proud instead of shy and turning away and—blushing—Somebody ought to—Ought to—*kiss* you, Laura! *(His hand slips slowly up her arm to her shoulder.) (Music swells tumultuously.) (He suddenly turns her about and kisses her on the lips. When he releases her* Laura *sinks on the sofa with a bright, dazed look. Jim backs away and fishes in his pocket for a cigarette.) (Legend on screen: "Souvenir.")* Stumble-john! *(He lights the cigarette, avoiding her look. There is a peal of girlish laughter from* Amanda *in the kitchen.* Laura *slowly raises and opens her hand. It still contains the little broken glass animal. She looks at it with a tender, bewildered expression.)* Stumble-john! I shouldn't have done that—That was way off the beam. You don't smoke, do you? *(She looks up, smiling, not hearing the question. He sits beside her a little gingerly. She looks at him speechlessly—waiting. He coughs decorously and moves a little farther aside as he considers the situation and senses her feelings, dimly, with perturbation; gently:)* Would you—care for a—mint? *(She doesn't seem to hear him but her look grows brighter even.)* Peppermint—Life Saver? My pocket's a regular drug store—wherever I go . . . *(He pops a mint in his mouth. Then gulps and decides to make a clean breast of it. He speaks slowly and gingerly.)* Laura, you know, if I had a sister like you, I'd do the same thing as Tom. I'd bring out fellows—introduce her to them. The right type of boys of a type to—appreciate her. Only—well—he made a mistake about me. Maybe I've got no call to be saying this. That may not have been the idea in having me over. But what if it was? There's nothing wrong about that. The only trouble is that in my case—I'm not in a situation to—do the right thing. I can't take down your number and say I'll phone. I can't call up next week and—ask for a date. I thought I had better explain the situation in case you misunderstood it and—hurt your feelings. . . . *(Pause. Slowly, very slowly, Laura's look changes, her eyes returning slowly from his to the ornament in her palm.)*

(Amanda utters another gay laugh in the kitchen.)

Laura (faintly): You—won't—call again?

Jim: No, Laura, I can't. *(He rises from the sofa.)* As I was just explaining, I've—got strings on me, Laura, I've—been going steady! I go out all the time with a girl named Betty. She's a home-girl like you, and Catholic, and Irish, and in a great many ways we—get along fine. I met her last summer on a moonlight boat trip up the river to Alton, on the *Majestic.* Well—right away from the start it was—love! *(Legend: Love!)* *(Laura sways slightly forward and grips the arm of the sofa. He fails to notice, now enrapt in his own comfortable being.)* Being in love has made a new man of me! *(Leaning stiffly forward, clutching the arm of the sofa,* Laura *struggles visibly with her storm. But* Jim *is oblivious; she is a long way off.)* The power of love is really pretty tremendous! Love is something that—changes the whole world, Laura! *(The storm abates a little and* Laura *leans back. He notices her again.)* It happened that Betty's aunt took sick, she got a wire and had to go to Centralia. So Tom—when he asked me to dinner—I naturally just accepted the invitation, not knowing that you—that he—that I—(He stops awkwardly.)* Huh—I'm a stumble-john! *(He flops back on the sofa. The holy candles in the altar of* Laura's *face have been snuffed out! There is a look of almost infinite desolation.* Jim *glances at her uneasily.)* I wish that you would—say something. *(She bites her lip which was trembling and then bravely smiles. She opens her hand again on the broken glass ornament. Then she gently takes his hand and raises it level with her own. She carefully places the unicorn in the palm of his hand, then pushes his fingers closed upon it.)* What are you—doing that for? You want me to have him?—Laura? *(She nods.)* What for?

Laura: A—souvenir . . .

(She rises unsteadily and crouches beside the victrola to wind it up.)

(Legend on screen: "Things have a way of turning out so badly.")

(Or image: "Gentleman caller waving goodbye!—gaily.")

(At this moment Amanda *rushes brightly back in the front room. She bears a pitcher of fruit punch in an old-fashioned cut-glass pitcher and a plate of macaroons. The plate has a gold border and poppies painted on it.)*

Amanda: Well, well, well! Isn't the air delightful after the shower? I've made you children a little liquid refreshment. *(turns gaily to the gentleman caller)* Jim, do you know that song about lemonade?

> "Lemonade, lemonade
> Made in the shade and stirred with a spade—
> Good enough for any old maid!"

Jim (uneasily): Ha-ha! No—I never heard it.

Amanda: Why, Laura! You look so serious!

Jim: We were having a serious conversation.

Amanda: Good! Now you're better acquainted!

Jim (uncertainly): Ha-ha! Yes.

Amanda: You modern young people are much more serious-minded than my generation. I was so gay as a girl!

Jim: You haven't changed, Mrs. Wingfield.

Amanda: Tonight I'm rejuvenated! The gaiety of the occasion, Mr. O'Connor! *(She tosses her head with a peal of laughter, spills lemonade.)* Oooo! I'm baptizing myself!

Jim: Here—let me—

Amanda (setting the pitcher down): There now. I discovered we had some maraschino cherries. I dumped them in, juice and all!

Jim: You shouldn't have gone to that trouble, Mrs. Wingfield.

Amanda: Trouble, trouble? Why it was loads of fun! Didn't you hear me cutting up in the kitchen? I bet your ears were burning! I told Tom how outdone with him I was for keeping you to himself so long a time! He should have brought you over much, much sooner! Well, now that you've found your way, I want you to be a very frequent caller! Not just occasional but all the time. Oh, we're going to have a lot of gay times together! I see them coming! Mmm, just breathe that air! So fresh, and the moon's so pretty! I'll skip back out—I know where my place is when young folks are having a—serious conversation!

Jim: Oh, don't go out, Mrs. Wingfield. The fact of the matter is I've got to be going.

Amanda: Going, now? You're joking! Why, it's only the shank of the evening, Mr. O'Connor!

Jim: Well, you know how it is.

Amanda: You mean you're a young workingman and have to keep workingmen's hours. We'll let you off early tonight. But only on the condition that next time you stay later. What's the best night for you? Isn't Saturday night the best night for you workingmen?

Jim: I have a couple of time-clocks to punch, Mrs. Wingfield. One at morning, another one at night!

Amanda: My, but you *are* ambitious! You work at night, too?

Jim: No, Ma'am, not work but—Betty! *(He crosses deliberately to pick up his hat. The band at the Paradise Dance Hall goes into a tender waltz.)*

Amanda: Betty? Betty? Who's—Betty! *(There is an ominous cracking sound in the sky.)*

Jim: Oh, just a girl. The girl I go steady with! *(He smiles charmingly. The sky falls.)*

(Legend: "The sky falls.")

Amanda (a long-drawn exhalation): Ohhhh . . . Is it a serious romance, Mr. O'Connor?

Jim: We're going to be married the second Sunday in June.

Amanda: Ohhhh—how nice! Tom didn't mention that you were engaged to be married.

Jim: The cat's not out of the bag at the warehouse yet. You know how they are. They call you Romeo and stuff like that. *(He stops at the oval mirror to put on his hat. He carefully shapes the brim and the crown to give a discreetly dashing effect.)* It's been a wonderful evening, Mrs. Wingfield. I guess this is what they mean by Southern hospitality.

Amanda: It really wasn't anything at all.

Jim: I hope it don't seem like I'm rushing off. But I promised Betty I'd pick her up at the Wabash depot, an' by the time I get my jalopy down there her train'll be in. Some women are pretty upset if you keep 'em waiting.

Amanda: Yes, I know—The tyranny of women! *(extends her hand)* Goodbye, Mr. O'Connor. I wish you luck—and happiness—and success! All three of them, and so does Laura!—Don't you, Laura?

Laura: Yes!

Jim (taking her hand): Good-bye, Laura. I'm certainly going to treasure that souvenir. And don't you forget the good advice I gave you. *(raises his voice to a cheery shout)* So long, Shakespeare! Thanks again, ladies— Good night!

(He grins and ducks jauntily out.
Still bravely grimacing, Amanda *closes the door on the gentleman caller. Then she turns back to the room with a puzzled expression. She and* Laura *don't dare to face each other.* Laura *crouches beside the victrola to wind it.)*

Amanda (faintly): Things have a way of turning out so badly. I don't believe that I would play the victrola. Well, well—well—Our gentleman caller was engaged to be married! Tom!

Tom (from back): Yes, Mother?

Amanda: Come in here a minute. I want to tell you something awfully funny.

Tom (enters with a macaroon and a glass of the lemonade): Has the gentleman caller gotten away already?

Amanda: The gentleman caller has made an early departure. What a wonderful joke you played on us!

Tom: How do you mean?

Amanda: You didn't mention that he was engaged to be married.

Tom: Jim? Engaged?

Amanda: That's what he just informed us.

Tom: I'll be jiggered! I didn't know about that.

Amanda: That seems very peculiar.

Tom: What's peculiar about it?

Amanda: Didn't you call him your best friend down at the warehouse?

Tom: He is, but how did I know?

Amanda: It seems extremely peculiar that you wouldn't know your best friend was going to be married!

Tom: The warehouse is where I work, not where I know things about people!

Amanda: You don't know things anywhere! You live in a dream; you manufacture illusions! *(He crosses to door.)* Where are you going?

Tom: I'm going to the movies.

Amanda: That's right, now that you've had us make such fools of ourselves. The effort, the preparations, all the expense! The new floor lamp, the rug, the clothes for Laura! All for what? To entertain some other girl's fiancé! Go to the movies, go! Don't think about us, a mother deserted, an unmarried sister who's crippled and has no job! Don't let anything interfere with your selfish pleasure! Just go, go, go—to the movies!

Tom: All right, I will! The more you shout about my selfishness to me the quicker I'll go, and I won't go to the movies!

Amanda: Go, then! Then go to the moon—you selfish dreamer!

(Tom smashes his glass on the floor. He plunges out on the fire-escape, slamming the door; Laura screams—cut off by the door.

Dance-hall music up. Tom goes to the rail and grips it desperately, lifting his face in the chill white moonlight penetrating the narrow abyss of the alley.)

(Legend on screen: "And so good-bye . . .")

(Tom's closing speech is timed with the interior pantomime. The interior scene is played as though viewed through soundproof glass. Amanda appears to be making a comforting speech to Laura who is huddled upon the sofa. Now that we cannot hear the mother's speech, her silliness is gone and she has dignity and tragic beauty. Laura's dark hair hides her face until at the end of the speech she lifts it to smile at her mother. Amanda's gestures are slow and graceful, almost dancelike, as she comforts the daughter. At the end of her speech she glances a moment at the father's picture—then withdraws through the portieres. At close of Tom's speech, Laura blows out the candles, ending the play.)

Tom: I didn't go to the moon, I went much further—for time is the longest distance between two places—Not long after that I was fired for writing a poem on the lid of a shoe-box. I left Saint Louis. I descended the steps of this fire-escape for a last time and followed, from then on, in my father's footsteps, attempting to find in motion what was lost in space—I traveled around a great deal. The cities swept about me like dead leaves, leaves that were brightly colored but torn away from the branches. I would have stopped, but I was pursued by something. It always came upon me unawares, taking me altogether by surprise. Perhaps it was a familiar bit of music. Perhaps it was only a piece of transparent glass— Perhaps I am walking along a street at night, in some strange city, before I have found companions. I pass the lighted window of a shop where perfume is sold. The window is filled with pieces of colored glass, tiny transparent bottles in delicate colors, like bits of a shattered rainbow. Then all at once my sister touches my shoulder. I turn around and look into her eyes . . . Oh, Laura, Laura, I tried to leave you behind me, but I am more faithful than I intended to be! I reach for a cigarette, I cross the street, I run into the movies or a bar, I buy a drink, I speak to the nearest stranger—anything that can blow your candles out! (*Laura bends over the candles.*)—for nowadays the world is lit by lightning! Blow out your candles, Laura—and so good-bye. . . .

(*She blows the candles out.*)

(*The scene dissolves.*)

——— TENNESSEE WILLIAMS ———
www *(1911–1983)* Web

Tennessee Williams was born in Columbus, Mississippi, and, like Tom Wingfield, moved with his family to a tenement in St. Louis. He attended the University of Missouri for a brief period but dropped out, finally completing a degree at the State University of Iowa. He made his way on to the New York theater scene in 1940 and, after the success of *The Glass Menagerie*, wrote such influential plays as *A Streetcar Named Desire* (1947), *Summer and Smoke* (1948), and *The Rose Tattoo* (1951). At times, as in the ill-fated *Camino Real* (1953), Williams attempted an almost total departure from realism. Far more successful than *Camino Real, Cat on a Hot Tin Roof* (1955)—much like *The Glass Menagerie*—offers a more subtle blend of realism and "poetic" or imaginative effects, most of them achieved by the set. Although his career faltered at times and he suffered from a variety of personal setbacks, Williams continued to write earning a reputation as one of America's greatest playwrights.

TOPICS FOR CRITICAL THINKING

1. Much critical discussion of the play concerns Amanda, the Wingfield matriarch. To what extent is she to blame for her daughter's reticence and pathological shyness? How reliable are Amanda's reminiscences of her past in the South?

2. What effect do the screens, legends, music, and lighting create? Do they add to the emotional impact of the action or, on the contrary, do they distance the audience from it?

3. In the stage directions for Scene One, Williams refers to "poetic truth" and the "fires of human desperation." Does the play suggest repressed desire or burning passion boiling under the surface? Who possesses this desire and exactly what is the object of this longing?

4. Describe Tom and Laura's absent father. Who or what was he? How has his absence affected their lives? How has it affected Amanda's life?

5. Jim O'Connor, the "Gentleman Caller" of Scene Six, is described as a "nice, ordinary, young man" in the Cast of Characters. What exactly do these adjectives mean in the context of this play?

6. How should we respond to Tom's last speech? Does it imply that a person can never escape the past and familial experience? Is his being fired and leaving St. Louis, then, only a partial escape?

TOPIC FOR CRITICAL WRITING

Discuss the point alluded to above about characterization in *The Glass Menagerie*. Who is the protagonist or central character of the play? Make a case for either Tom, Laura, or Amanda Wingfield, explaining why the character you have selected is the most crucial to the play's dramatic action.

Critical Perspective: On Its Premiere in New York

" 'The Glass Menagerie,' written by Tennessee Williams, . . . is fragile and poignant. It is a vivid, eerie and curiously enchanting play and it is made an eventful one by the appearance of Miss [Laurette] Taylor as a faded and bedraggled Southern belle from a past long receded. 'The Glass Menagerie,' as it is acted and presented at the drama-hungry Playhouse, is something to see, to cheer about, and to see again."

—Ward Morehouse, *The New York Sun*, 2 April 1945

"The play hurts you . . . hurts you all through. It arouses in you pity and terror. That, according to Aristotle, is what tragedy is for; it is supposed to drain you of these emotions, so that you can go on living. 'The Glass Menagerie' certainly does that."

—Burton Rascoe, *The New York World-Telegram*, 2 April 1945

Critical Perspective: On Memory and Illusion

"The techniques which emphasize memory and illusion in the drama reinforce the theme of the escape from time which controls the action. The survival tactic practiced by the Wingfields is to retreat from reality into a timeless world of their own making. Amanda's reveries are so much a part of her life that she seems completely oblivious to reality when she is in the midst of one. . . . Tom, too, retreats from what is unappealing in the present. Finding his job dull and his homelife drab, he escapes into the movies. . . . Laura seeks

refuge from the painful present in her imaginative world of the glass figurines."

—Mary Ann Corrigan, "Memory, Dream, and
Myth in the Plays of Tennessee Williams" (1976)

Critical Perspective: On Williams's Expressionism

"Williams's plays insistently challenge the expressionist model . . . for the
simple reason that none of them stages the psychodynamics of a single, cen-
trifugal consciousness projecting its thoughts, emotions, and desires onto
characters, actions, and locale."
—David Savran, *Communists, Cowboys, and Queers: The Politics of Masculinity
in the Works of Arthur Miller and Tennessee Williams* (1992)

Critical Perspective: On Williams's Women

"[Women in Williams] all fear the possibility of being overwhelmed by their
unruly feelings, and the panic that escalates as each play moves on shows how
desperate are their struggles to master them. . . .

These are qualities that Williams's central characters—all women—have
in common. . . . It should go without saying that Amanda is the center of *The
Glass Menagerie. . . .*"
—Marc Robinson, *The Other American Drama* (1993)

Beyond "Straight Realism": Arthur Miller's *Death of a Salesman*

After Arthur Miller had garnered considerable acclaim for *All My Sons*
(1947)—it topped Eugene O'Neill's *The Iceman Cometh* (1946) for the New
York Drama Critics Circle Award in 1947—there would seem to have been
little reason to revise a successful formula. Yet, however considerable its triumph, *All My Sons*, as some critics have ungenerously remarked, is hardly innovative. It is a distinguished example of domestic realism much in the vein of
Henrik Ibsen, for whom Miller has often expressed his great admiration. Indeed, years after its New York premiere, scholar Robert Heilman denigrated
All My Sons as a "plotted play in the well made tradition." Its dramatic subject—the ethical dispute between a father and his son over the management of
the family business—leads to tragedy. But when the father, Joe Keller, takes
his own life before allowing his son to take him to jail, his suicide is more the
result of philosophical or social disagreement than a troubled psychology
riven by guilt and fear. *All My Sons* amounts to Miller's advocacy for social
change, a call for American business to acknowledge its larger ethical responsibilities to the world in which it exists and from which it prospers. Two years
later in *Death of a Salesman*, he returned to the issue of American business in-

tent on demonstrating both its harshness and its effects on the psyche of a man who fervently believes in its shallow promise of self-fulfillment. To do so, he needed to refine a different dramatic form.

In his essay "Tragedy and the Common Man," a critical explanation of the tragic dimensions of *Death of a Salesman*, Miller argues that tragedy springs neither from the "purely psychiatric" nor from the "purely sociologi-cal" but from a balance of the two. Nearly fifty years later in a 1999 essay that accompanied the revival of the play by director Robert Falls and starring Brian Dennehy, Miller railed against a confusion about dramatic form that is relevant not only to the representation of the sociological and the psycholog-ical, but also to our examination of the relationship between realism and other "styles" (Miller's term) of dramatic "condensation":

> "Realism" is now a put-down; "poetic" is praise. "Experimental" is attractive; "traditional" is not. . . . It is almost as if "realism" can hardly be poetic, or as if the "poetic" is not, at its best, more real than the merely "realistic."

The fact is, Miller continues, that "there is no such thing as 'reality' in any theatrical exhibition that can properly be called a play" (as opposed to, say, a piece of performance art). Often, the main reason for this is time: "street" or real time is not the same as stage time. If it were, the approximately two and one-half hours of *Death of a Salesman* would have to be expanded to sixty-two hours, the fictive time represented in the play's dramatic action. Thus, Miller concludes, the real issue ought to be not how "nonlinear," "dream-like," or "poetic" a play is, but how effective and efficient such nonrealistic devises are in communicating the writer's vision of life.

To reveal his vision of Willy Loman, Miller traveled a considerable aes-thetic distance from the form of *All My Sons*. But it was hardly a unique jour-ney. As Miller recalls, when he began writing in the 1930s, realism was the dominant form of American theater. But it quickly became evident to him, as it had for Tennessee Williams, that "straight realism" had grown "tiresome," even if audiences and critics at the time failed to recognize its staleness. As a result, *Death of a Salesman*, as the reading of the play's Requiem in Chapter 42 is intended to suggest, employs both realistic and expressionistic devices to represent the complex amalgam of Willy's rich dream life and his dispiriting failures as salesman, husband, and father.

To achieve this exposition, Miller exploits all the visual and aural capabil-ities of modern stagecraft: lighting, scenic effects, music, and so on. When, for example, a strained dinner between Willy and his sons begins to go awry in Act Two, a "single trumpet note" sounds and the "light of green leaves" stains the outlines of the house to signal a temporal shift. Immediately, the narrative shifts to the past, to a flashback that explains Biff's last line in the present before the flashback begins: "I can't talk to him!" He can't talk to his father because, as the flashback clarifies, he once caught Willy in an adulter-ous affair, thus shattering his image of his father. Similarly, when Ben appears near the end of the play, Miller's instructions call for his "idyllic music" to be played. A dream figure, a character from Willy's troubled psychology, Ben is thus associated with profound changes in the way the play looks and sounds.

In his 1999 essay in *Harper's Magazine,* Miller asserts that "theater, like politics, is always the art of the possible." And for him, dramatic form or what he calls "style" is more than a matter of taste or "novelty." Form is matched to dramatic subject; form, in the best of cases, expresses a subject in a manner that is intimately related to it. And the technological advances of the contemporary stage help make innovative forms possible. In the best plays, no other form will do, just as "straight realism" would never have matched the tragic subject of *Death of a Salesman.*

ARTHUR MILLER

Death of a Salesman   (1949)

CHARACTERS

Willy Loman
Linda
Biff
Happy
Bernard
The Woman
Charley
Uncle Ben
Howard Wagner
Jenny
Stanley
Miss Forsythe
Letta

The action takes place in Willy Loman's house and yard and in various places he visits in the New York and Boston of today.
    Throughout the play, in the stage directions, left and right mean stage left and stage right.

ACT ONE

A melody is heard, played upon a flute. It is small and fine, telling of grass and trees and the horizon. The curtain rises.
    Before us is the Salesman's house. We are aware of towering, angular shapes behind it, surrounding it on all sides. Only the blue light of the sky falls upon the house and forestage; the surrounding area shows an angry glow of orange. As more light appears, we see a solid vault of apartment houses around the small, fragile-seeming home. An air of the dream clings to the place, a dream rising out of reality. The kitchen at center seems actual enough, for there is a kitchen table with three chairs, and a refrigerator. But no other fixtures are seen. At the back of the kitchen

there is a draped entrance, which leads to the living-room. To the right of the kitchen, on a level raised two feet, is a bedroom furnished only with a brass bedstead and a straight chair. On a shelf over the bed a silver athletic trophy stands. A window opens onto the apartment house at the side.

Behind the kitchen, on a level raised six and a half feet, is the boys' bedroom, at present barely visible. Two beds are dimly seen, and at the back of the room a dormer window. (This bedroom is above the unseen living-room.) At the left a stairway curves up to it from the kitchen.

The entire setting is wholly or, in some places, partially transparent. The roof-line of the house is one-dimensional; under and over it we see the apartment buildings. Before the house lies an apron, curving beyond the forestage into the orchestra. This forward area serves as the back yard as well as the locale of all Willy's imaginings and of his city scenes. Whenever the action is in the present the actors observe the imaginary wall-lines, entering the house only through its door at the left. But in the scenes of the past these boundaries are broken, and characters enter or leave a room by stepping "through" a wall onto the forestage.

From the right, Willy Loman, *the Salesman, enters, carrying two large sample cases. The flute plays on. He hears but is not aware of it. He is past sixty years of age, dressed quietly. Even as he crosses the stage to the doorway of the house, his exhaustion is apparent. He unlocks the door, comes into the kitchen, and thankfully lets his burden down, feeling the soreness of his palms. A word-sigh escapes his lips— it might be "Oh, boy, oh, boy." He closes the door, then carries his cases out into the living-room, through the draped kitchen doorway.*

Linda, *his wife, has stirred in her bed at the right. She gets out and puts on a robe, listening. Most often jovial, she has developed an iron repression of her exceptions to Willy's behavior—she more than loves him, she admires him, as though his mercurial nature, his temper, his massive dreams and little cruelties, served her only as sharp reminders of the turbulent longings within him, longings which she shares but lacks the temperament to utter and follow to their end.*

Linda, (hearing Willy *outside the bedroom, calls with some trepidation):* Willy!
Willy: It's all right. I came back.
Linda: Why? What happened? *(Slight pause.)* Did something happen, Willy?
Willy: No, nothing happened.
Linda: You didn't smash the car, did you?
Willy, (with casual irritation): I said nothing happened. Didn't you hear me?
Linda: Don't you feel well?
Willy: I'm tired to the death. *(The flute has faded away. He sits on the bed beside her, a little numb.)* I couldn't make it. I just couldn't make it, Linda.
Linda, (very carefully, delicately): Where were you all day? You look terrible.
Willy: I got as far as a little above Yonkers. I stopped for a cup of coffee.
  Maybe it was the coffee.
Linda: What?
Willy, (after a pause): I suddenly couldn't drive any more. The car kept going off onto the shoulder, y'know?
Linda, (helpfully): Oh. Maybe it was the steering again. I don't think Angelo knows the Studebaker.

Willy: No, it's me, it's me. Suddenly I realize I'm goin' sixty miles an hour and I don't remember the last five minutes. I'm—I can't seem to—keep my mind to it.

Linda: Maybe it's your glasses. You never went for your new glasses.

Willy: No, I see everything. I came back ten miles an hour. It took me nearly four hours from Yonkers.

Linda, (resigned): Well, you'll just have to take a rest, Willy, you can't continue this way.

Willy: I just got back from Florida.

Linda: But you didn't rest your mind. Your mind is overactive, and the mind is what counts, dear.

Willy: I'll start out in the morning. Maybe I'll feel better in the morning. *(She is taking off his shoes.)* These goddam arch supports are killing me.

Linda: Take an aspirin. Should I get you an aspirin? It'll soothe you.

Willy, (with wonder): I was driving along, you understand? And I was fine. I was even observing the scenery. You can imagine, me looking at scenery, on the road every week of my life. But it's so beautiful up there, Linda, the trees are so thick, and the sun is warm. I opened the windshield and just let the warm air bathe over me. And then all of a sudden I'm goin' off the road! I'm tellin' ya, I absolutely forgot I was driving. If I'd've gone the other way over the white line I might've killed somebody. So I went on again—and five minutes later I'm dreamin' again, and I nearly— *(He presses two fingers against his eyes.)* I have such thoughts, I have such strange thoughts.

Linda: Willy, dear. Talk to them again. There's no reason why you can't work in New York.

Willy: They don't need me in New York. I'm the New England man. I'm vital in New England.

Linda: But you're sixty years old. They can't expect you to keep traveling every week.

Willy: I'll have to send a wire to Portland. I'm supposed to see Brown and Morrison tomorrow morning at ten o'clock to show the line. Goddammit, I could sell them! *(He starts putting on his jacket.)*

Linda, (taking the jacket from him): Why don't you go down to the place tomorrow and tell Howard you've simply got to work in New York? You're too accommodating, dear.

Willy: If old man Wagner was alive I'd been in charge of New York now! That man was a prince, he was a masterful man. But that boy of his, that Howard, he don't appreciate. When I went north the first time, the Wagner Company didn't know where New England was!

Linda: Why don't you tell those things to Howard, dear?

Willy, (encouraged): I will, I definitely will. Is there any cheese?

Linda: I'll make you a sandwich.

Willy No, go to sleep. I'll take some milk. I'll be up right away. The boys in?

Linda: They're sleeping. Happy took Biff on a date tonight.

Willy, (interested): That so?

Linda: It was so nice to see them shaving together, one behind the other, in the bathroom. And going out together. You notice? The whole house smells of shaving lotion.

Willy: Figure it out. Work a lifetime to pay off a house. You finally own it, and there's nobody to live in it.

Linda: Well, dear, life is a casting off. It's always that way.

Willy: No, no, some people—some people accomplish something. Did Biff say anything after I went this morning?

Linda: You shouldn't have criticized him, Willy, especially after he just got off the train. You mustn't lose your temper with him.

Willy: When the hell did I lose my temper? I simply asked him if he was making any money. Is that a criticism?

Linda: But, dear, how could he make any money?

Willy, (worried and angered): There's such an undercurrent in him. He became a moody man. Did he apologize when I left this morning?

Linda: He was crestfallen, Willy. You know how he admires you. I think if he finds himself, then you'll both be happier and not fight any more.

Willy: How can he find himself on a farm? Is that a life? A farmhand? In the beginning, when he was young, I thought, well, a young man, it's good for him to tramp around, take a lot of different jobs. But it's more than ten years now and he has yet to make thirty-five dollars a week!

Linda: He's finding himself, Willy.

Willy: Not finding yourself at the age of thirty-four is a disgrace!

Linda: Shh!

Willy: The trouble is he's lazy, goddammit!

Linda: Willy, please!

Willy: Biff is a lazy bum!

Linda: They're sleeping. Get something to eat. Go on down.

Willy: Why did he come home? I would like to know what brought him home.

Linda: I don't know. I think he's still lost, Willy. I think he's very lost.

Willy: Biff Loman is lost. In the greatest country in the world a young man with such—personal attractiveness, gets lost. And such a hard worker. There's one thing about Biff—he's not lazy.

Linda: Never.

Willy, (with pity and resolve): I'll see him in the morning; I'll have a nice talk with him. I'll get him a job selling. He could be big in no time. My God! Remember how they used to follow him around in high school? When he smiled at one of them their faces lit up. When he walked down the street . . . (*He loses himself in reminiscences.*)

Linda, (trying to bring him out of it): Willy, dear, I got a new kind of American-type cheese today. It's whipped.

Willy: Why do you get American when I like Swiss?

Linda: I just thought you'd like a change—

Willy: I don't want a change! I want Swiss cheese. Why am I always being contradicted?

Linda, (with a covering laugh): I thought it would be a surprise.

Willy: Why don't you open a window in here, for God's sake?

Linda, (with infinite patience): They're all open, dear.

Willy: The way they boxed us in here. Bricks and windows, windows and bricks.

Linda: We should've bought the land next door.

Willy: The street is lined with cars. There's not a breath of fresh air in the neighborhood. The grass don't grow any more, you can't raise a carrot in the back yard. They should've had a law against apartment houses. Remember those two beautiful elm trees out there? When I and Biff hung the swing between them?

Linda: Yeah, like being a million miles from the city.

Willy: They should've arrested the builder for cutting those down. They massacred the neighborhood. *(Lost):* More and more I think of those days, Linda. This time of year it was lilac and wisteria. And then the peonies would come out, and the daffodils. What fragrance in this room!

Linda: Well, after all, people had to move somewhere.

Willy: No, there's more people now.

Linda: I don't think there's more people. I think—

Willy: There's more people! That's what's ruining this country! Population is getting out of control. The competition is maddening! Smell the stink from that apartment house! And another one on the other side . . . How can they whip cheese?

On Willy's *last line,* Biff *and* Happy *raise themselves up in their beds, listening.*

Linda: Go down, try it. And be quiet.

Willy, (turning to Linda, *guiltily):* You're not worried about me, are you, sweetheart?

Biff: What's the matter?

Happy: Listen!

Linda: You've got too much on the ball to worry about.

Willy: You're my foundation and my support, Linda.

Linda: Just try to relax, dear. You make mountains out of molehills.

Willy: I won't fight with him any more. If he wants to go back to Texas, let him go.

Linda: He'll find his way.

Willy: Sure. Certain men just don't get started till later in life. Like Thomas Edison, I think. Or B. F. Goodrich. One of them was deaf. *(He starts for the bedroom doorway.)* I'll put my money on Biff.

Linda: And Willy—if it's warm Sunday we'll drive in the country. And we'll open the windshield, and take lunch.

Willy: No, the windshields don't open on the new cars.

Linda: But you opened it today.

Willy: Me? I didn't. *(He stops.)* Now isn't that peculiar! Isn't that a remarkable— *(He breaks off in amazement and fright as the flute is heard distantly.)*

Linda: What, darling?

Willy: That is the most remarkable thing.

Linda: What, dear?

Willy: I was thinking of the Chevvy. *(Slight pause.)* Nineteen twenty-eight . . . when I had that red Chevvy— *(Breaks off.)* That funny? I coulda sworn I was driving that Chevvy today.

Linda: Well, that's nothing. Something must've reminded you.

Willy: Remarkable. Ts. Remember those days? The way Biff used to simonize that car? The dealer refused to believe there was eighty thousand miles on it. *(He shakes his head.)* Heh! *(To* Linda*):* Close your eyes, I'll be right up. *(He walks out of the bedroom.)*

Happy, (to Biff*):* Jesus, maybe he smashed up the car again!

Linda, (calling after Willy*):* Be careful on the stairs, dear! The cheese is on the middle shelf! *(She turns, goes over to the bed, takes his jacket, and goes out of the bedroom.)*

Light has risen on the boys' room. Unseen, Willy *is heard talking to himself, "Eighty thousand miles," and a little laugh.* Biff *gets out of bed, comes downstage a bit, and stands attentively.* Biff *is two years older than his brother* Happy, *well built, but in these days bears a worn air and seems less self-assured. He has succeeded less, and his dreams are stronger and less acceptable than* Happy's. Happy *is tall, powerfully made. Sexuality is like a visible color on him, or a scent that many women have discovered. He, like his brother, is lost, but in a different way, for he has never allowed himself to turn his face toward defeat and is thus more confused and hard-skinned, although seemingly more content.*

Happy, (getting out of bed): He's going to get his license taken away if he keeps that up. I'm getting nervous about him, y'know, Biff?

Biff: His eyes are going.

Happy: No, I've driven with him. He sees all right. He just doesn't keep his mind on it. I drove into the city with him last week. He stops at a green light and then it turns red and he goes. *(He laughs.)*

Biff: Maybe he's color-blind.

Happy: Pop? Why he's got the finest eye for color in the business. You know that.

Biff, (sitting down on his bed): I'm going to sleep.

Happy: You're not still sour on Dad, are you, Biff?

Biff: He's all right, I guess.

Willy, (underneath them, in the living-room): Yes, sir, eighty thousand miles— eighty-two thousand!

Biff: You smoking?

Happy, (holding out a pack of cigarettes): Want one?

Biff, (taking a cigarette): I can never sleep when I smell it.

Willy: What a simonizing job, heh!

Happy, (with deep sentiment): Funny, Biff, y'know? Us sleeping in here again? The old beds. *(He pats his bed affectionately.)* All the talk that went across those two beds, huh? Our whole lives.

Biff: Yeah. Lotta dreams and plans.

Happy, (with a deep and masculine laugh): About five hundred women would like to know what was said in this room.

They share a soft laugh.

Biff: Remember that big Betsy something—what the hell was her name— over on Bushwick Avenue?

Happy, (combing his hair): With the collie dog!

Biff: That's the one. I got you in there, remember?

Happy: Yeah, that was my first time—I think. Boy, there was a pig! *(They laugh, almost crudely.)* You taught me everything I know about women. Don't forget that.

Biff: I bet you forgot how bashful you used to be. Especially with girls.

Happy: Oh, I still am, Biff.

Biff: Oh, go on.

Happy: I just control it, that's all. I think I got less bashful and you got more so. What happened, Biff? Where's the old humor, the old confidence? *(He shakes* Biff's *knee.* Biff *gets up and moves restlessly about the room.)* What's the matter?

Biff: Why does Dad mock me all the time?

Happy: He's not mocking you, he—

Biff: Everything I say there's a twist of mockery on his face. I can't get near him.

Happy: He just wants you to make good, that's all. I wanted to talk to you about Dad for a long time, Biff. Something's—happening to him. He— talks to himself.

Biff: I noticed that this morning. But he always mumbled.

Happy: But not so noticeable. It got so embarrassing I sent him to Florida. And you know something? Most of the time he's talking to you.

Biff: What's he say about me?

Happy: I can't make it out.

Biff: What's he say about me?

Happy: I think the fact that you're not settled, that you're still kind of up in the air . . .

Biff: There's one or two other things depressing him, Happy.

Happy: What do you mean?

Biff: Never mind. Just don't lay it all to me.

Happy: But I think if you just got started—I mean—is there any future for you out there?

Biff: I tell ya, Hap, I don't know what the future is. I don't know—what I'm supposed to want.

Happy: What do you mean?

Biff: Well, I spent six or seven years after high school trying to work myself up. Shipping clerk, salesman, business of one kind or another. And it's a measly manner of existence. To get on that subway on the hot mornings in summer. To devote your whole life to keeping stock, or making phone calls, or selling or buying. To suffer fifty weeks of the year for the sake of a two-week vacation, when all you really desire is to be outdoors, with your shirt off. And always to have to get ahead of the next fella. And still—that's how you build a future.

Happy: Well, you really enjoy it on a farm? Are you content out there?

Biff, (with rising agitation): Hap, I've had twenty or thirty different kinds of jobs since I left home before the war, and it always turns out the same. I just realized it lately. In Nebraska when I herded cattle, and the Dakotas, and Arizona, and now in Texas. It's why I came home now, I guess, because I realized it. This farm I work on, it's spring there now, see? And they've got about fifteen new colts. There's nothing more inspiring or—beautiful than the sight of a mare and a new colt. And it's cool there now, see? Texas is cool now, and it's spring. And whenever spring comes to where I am, I suddenly get the feeling, my God, I'm not gettin' anywhere! What the hell am I doing, playing around with horses, twenty-eight dollars a week! I'm thirty-four years old, I oughta be makin' my future. That's when I come running home. And now, I get here, and I don't know what to do with myself. *(After a pause):* I've always made a point of not wasting my life, and everytime I come back here I know that all I've done is to waste my life.

Happy: You're a poet, you know that, Biff? You're a—you're an idealist!

Biff: No, I'm mixed up very bad. Maybe I oughta get married. Maybe I oughta get stuck into something. Maybe that's my trouble. I'm like a boy. I'm not married, I'm not in business, I just—I'm like a boy. Are you content, Hap? You're a success, aren't you? Are you content?

Happy: Hell, no!

Biff: Why? You're making money, aren't you?

Happy, (moving about with energy, expressiveness): All I can do now is wait for the merchandise manager to die. And suppose I get to be merchandise manager? He's a good friend of mine, and he just built a terrific estate on Long Island. And he lived there about two months and sold it, and now he's building another one. He can't enjoy it once it's finished. And I know that's just what I would do. I don't know what the hell I'm workin' for. Sometimes I sit in my apartment—all alone. And I think of the rent I'm paying. And it's crazy. But then, it's what I always wanted. My own apartment, a car, and plenty of women. And still, goddammit, I'm lonely.

Biff, (with enthusiasm): Listen, why don't you come out West with me?

Happy: You and I, heh?

Biff: Sure, maybe we could buy a ranch. Raise cattle, use our muscles. Men built like we are should be working out in the open.

Happy, (avidly): The Loman Brothers, heh?

Biff, (with vast affection): Sure, we'd be known all over the counties!

Happy, (enthralled): That's what I dream about, Biff. Sometimes I want to just rip my clothes off in the middle of the store and outbox that goddam merchandise manager. I mean I can outbox, outrun, and outlift anybody in that store, and I have to take orders from those common, petty sons-of-bitches till I can't stand it any more.

Biff: I'm tellin' you, kid, if you were with me I'd be happy out there.

Happy, (enthused): See, Biff, everybody around me is so false that I'm con-
    stantly lowering my ideals . . .
Biff: Baby, together we'd stand up for one another, we'd have someone
    to trust.
Happy: If I were around you—
Biff: Hap, the trouble is we weren't brought up to grub for money. I don't
    know how to do it.
Happy: Neither can I!
Biff: Then let's go!
Happy: The only thing is—what can you make out there?
Biff: But look at your friend. Builds an estate and then hasn't the peace of
    mind to live in it.
Happy: Yeah, but when he walks into the store the waves part in front
    of him. That's fifty-two thousand dollars a year coming through the
    revolving door, and I got more in my pinky finger than he's got in
    his head.
Biff: Yeah, but you just said—
Happy: I gotta show some of those pompous, self-important executives
    over there that Hap Loman can make the grade. I want to walk into the
    store the way he walks in. Then I'll go with you, Biff. We'll be together
    yet, I swear. But take those two we had tonight. Now weren't they gor-
    geous creatures?
Biff: Yeah, yeah, most gorgeous I've had in years.
Happy: I get that any time I want, Biff. Whenever I feel disgusted. The only
    trouble is, it gets like bowling or something. I just keep knockin' them
    over and it doesn't mean anything. You still run around a lot?
Biff: Naa. I'd like to find a girl—steady, somebody with substance.
Happy: That's what I long for.
Biff: Go on! You'd never come home.
Happy: I would! Somebody with character, with resistance! Like Mom,
    y'know? You're gonna call me a bastard when I tell you this. That girl
    Charlotte I was with tonight is engaged to be married in five weeks. *(He
    tries on his new hat.)*
Biff: No kiddin'!
Happy: Sure, the guy's in line for the vice-presidency of the store. I don't
    know what gets into me, maybe I just have an overdeveloped sense of
    competition or something, but I went and ruined her, and furthermore I
    can't get rid of her. And he's the third executive I've done that to. Isn't that
    a crummy characteristic? And to top it all, I go to their weddings! *(Indig-
    nantly, but laughing):* Like I'm not supposed to take bribes. Manufacturers
    offer me a hundred-dollar bill now and then to throw an order their way.
    You know how honest I am, but it's like this girl, see. I hate myself for it.
    Because I don't want the girl, and, still I take it and—I love it!
Biff: Let's go to sleep.
Happy: I guess we didn't settle anything, heh?
Biff: I just got one idea that I think I'm going to try.
Happy: What's that?

Biff: Remember Bill Oliver?

Happy: Sure, Oliver is very big now. You want to work for him again?

Biff: No, but when I quit he said something to me. He put his arm on my shoulder, and he said, "Biff, if you ever need anything, come to me."

Happy: I remember that. That sounds good.

Biff: I think I'll go to see him. If I could get ten thousand or even seven or eight thousand dollars I could buy a beautiful ranch.

Happy: I bet he'd back you. 'Cause he thought highly of you, Biff. I mean, they all do. You're well liked, Biff. That's why I say to come back here, and we both have the apartment. And I'm tellin' you, Biff, any babe you want . . .

Biff: No, with a ranch I could do the work I like and still be something. I just wonder though. I wonder if Oliver still thinks I stole that carton of basketballs.

Happy: Oh, he probably forgot that long ago. It's almost ten years. You're too sensitive. Anyway, he didn't really fire you.

Biff: Well, I think he was going to. I think that's why I quit. I was never sure whether he knew or not. I know he thought the world of me, though. I was the only one he'd let lock up the place.

Willy, (below): You gonna wash the engine, Biff?

Happy: Shh!

Biff *looks at* Happy, *who is gazing down, listening.* Willy *is mumbling in the parlor.*

Happy: You hear that?

They listen. Willy *laughs warmly.*

Biff, (growing angry): Doesn't he know Mom can hear that?

Willy: Don't get your sweater dirty, Biff!

A look of pain crosses Biff's *face.*

Happy: Isn't that terrible? Don't leave again, will you? You'll find a job here. You gotta stick around. I don't know what to do about him, it's getting embarrassing.

Willy: What a simonizing job!

Biff: Mom's hearing that!

Willy: No kiddin', Biff, you got a date? Wonderful!

Happy: Go on to sleep. But talk to him in the morning, will you?

Biff, (reluctantly getting into bed): With her in the house. Brother!

Happy, (getting into bed): I wish you'd have a good talk with him.

The light on their room begins to fade.

Biff, (to himself in bed): That selfish, stupid . . .

Happy: Sh . . . Sleep, Biff.

Their light is out. Well before they have finished speaking, Willy's *form is dimly seen below in the darkened kitchen. He opens the refrigerator, searches in there, and takes out a bottle of milk. The apartment houses are fading out, and the entire house and surroundings become covered with leaves. Music insinuates itself as the leaves appear.*

Willy: Just wanna be careful with those girls, Biff, that's all. Don't make any promises. No promises of any kind. Because a girl, y'know, they always believe what you tell 'em, and you're very young, Biff, you're too young to be talking seriously to girls.

Light rises on the kitchen. Willy, talking, shuts the refrigerator door and comes downstage to the kitchen table. He pours milk into a glass. He is totally immersed in himself, smiling faintly.

Willy: Too young entirely, Biff. You want to watch your schooling first. Then when you're all set, there'll be plenty of girls for a boy like you. (*He smiles broadly at a kitchen chair.*) That so? The girls pay for you? (*He laughs.*) Boy, you must really be makin' a hit.

Willy is gradually addressing—physically—a point offstage, speaking through the wall of the kitchen, and his voice has been rising in volume to that of a normal conversation.

Willy: I been wondering why you polish the car so careful. Ha! Don't leave the hubcaps, boys. Get the chamois to the hubcaps. Happy, use newspaper on the windows, it's the easiest thing. Show him how to do it, Biff! You see, Happy? Pad it up, use it like a pad. That's it, that's it, good work. You're doin' all right, Hap. (*He pauses, then nods in approbation for a few seconds, then looks upward.*) Biff, first thing we gotta do when we get time is clip that big branch over the house. Afraid it's gonna fall in a storm and hit the roof. Tell you what. We get a rope and sling her around, and then we climb up there with a couple of saws and take her down. Soon as you finish the car, boys, I wanna see ya. I got a surprise for you, boys.

Biff, (offstage): Whatta ya got, Dad?

Willy: No, you finish first. Never leave a job till you're finished—remember that. (*Looking toward the "big trees"):* Biff, up in Albany I saw a beautiful hammock. I think I'll buy it next trip, and we'll hang it right between those two elms. Wouldn't that be something? Just swingin' there under those branches. Boy, that would be . . .

Young Biff and Young Happy appear from the direction Willy was addressing. Happy carries rags and a pail of water. Biff, wearing a sweater with a block "S," carries a football.

Biff, (pointing in the direction of the car offstage): How's that, Pop, professional?

Willy: Terrific. Terrific job, boys. Good work, Biff.

Happy: Where's the surprise, Pop?

Willy: In the back seat of the car.

Happy: Boy! (*He runs off.*)

Biff: What is it, Dad? Tell me, what'd you buy?

Willy, (laughing, cuffs him): Never mind, something I want you to have.

Biff, (turns and starts off): What is it, Hap?

Happy, (offstage): It's a punching bag!

Biff: Oh, Pop!

Willy: It's got Gene Tunney's signature on it!

Happy *runs onstage with a punching bag.*

Biff: Gee, how'd you know we wanted a punching bag?

Willy: Well, it's the finest thing for the timing.

Happy, (lies down on his back and pedals with his feet): I'm losing weight, you notice, Pop?

Willy, (to Happy): Jumping rope is good too.

Biff: Did you see the new football I got?

Willy, (examining the ball): Where'd you get a new ball?

Biff: The coach told me to practice my passing.

Willy: That so? And he gave you the ball, heh?

Biff: Well, I borrowed it from the locker room. *(He laughs confidentially.)*

Willy, (laughing with him at the theft): I want you to return that.

Happy: I told you he wouldn't like it!

Biff, (angrily): Well, I'm bringing it back!

Willy, (stopping the incipient argument, to Happy*):* Sure, he's gotta practice with a regulation ball, doesn't he? *(To Biff):* Coach'll probably congratulate you on your initiative!

Biff: Oh, he keeps congratulating my initiative all the time, Pop.

Willy: That's because he likes you. If somebody else took that ball there'd be an uproar. So what's the report, boys, what's the report?

Biff: Where'd you go this time, Dad? Gee, we were lonesome for you.

Willy, (pleased, puts an arm around each boy and they come down to the apron): Lonesome, heh?

Biff: Missed you every minute.

Willy: Don't say? Tell you a secret, boys. Don't breathe it to a soul. Someday I'll have my own business, and I'll never have to leave home any more.

Happy: Like Uncle Charley, heh?

Willy: Bigger than Uncle Charley! Because Charley is not—liked. He's liked, but he's not—well liked.

Biff: Where'd you go this time, Dad?

Willy: Well, I got on the road, and I went north to Providence. Met the Mayor.

Biff: The Mayor of Providence!

Willy: He was sitting in the hotel lobby.

Biff: What'd he say?

Willy: He said, "Morning!" And I said, "You got a fine city here, Mayor." And then he had coffee with me. And then I went to Waterbury. Waterbury is a fine city. Big clock city, the famous Waterbury clock. Sold a nice bill there. And then Boston—Boston is the cradle of the Revolution. A fine city. And a couple of other towns in Mass., and on to Portland and Bangor and straight home!

Biff: Gee, I'd love to go with you sometime, Dad.

Willy: Soon as summer comes.

Happy: Promise?

Willy: You and Hap and I, and I'll show you all the towns. America is full of
beautiful towns and fine, upstanding people. And they know me, boys,
they know me up and down New England. The finest people. And when
I bring you fellas up, there'll be open sesame for all of us, 'cause one
thing, boys: I have friends. I can park my car in any street in New England, and the cops protect it like their own. This summer, heh?

Biff and Happy, (together): Yeah! You bet!

Willy: We'll take our bathing suits.

Happy: We'll carry your bags, Pop!

Willy: Oh, won't that be something! Me comin' into the Boston stores with
you boys carryin' my bags. What a sensation!

Biff *is prancing around, practicing passing the ball.*

Willy: You nervous, Biff, about the game?

Biff: Not if you're gonna be there.

Willy: What do they say about you in school, now that they made you
captain?

Happy: There's a crowd of girls behind him every time the classes change.

Biff, (taking Willy's *hand):* This Saturday, Pop, this Saturday—just for you,
I'm going to break through for a touchdown.

Happy: You're supposed to pass.

Biff: I'm takin' one play for Pop. You watch me, Pop, and when I take off
my helmet, that means I'm breakin' out. Then you watch me crash
through that line!

Willy, (kisses Biff*):* Oh, wait'll I tell this in Boston!

Bernard *enters in knickers. He is younger than* Biff, *earnest and loyal, a worried boy.*

Bernard: Biff, where are you? You're supposed to study with me today.

Willy: Hey, looka Bernard. What're you lookin' so anemic about, Bernard?

Bernard: He's gotta study, Uncle Willy. He's got Regents next week.

Happy, (tauntingly, spinning Bernard *around):* Let's box, Bernard!

Bernard: Biff! *(He gets away from* Happy.*)* Listen, Biff, I heard Mr. Birnbaum
say that if you don't start studyin' math he's gonna flunk you, and you
won't graduate. I heard him!

Willy: You better study with him, Biff. Go ahead now.

Bernard: I heard him!

Biff: Oh, Pop, you didn't see my sneakers! *(He holds up a foot for* Willy *to
look at.)*

Willy: Hey, that's a beautiful job of printing!

Bernard, (wiping his glasses): Just because he printed University of Virginia
on his sneakers doesn't mean they've got to graduate him, Uncle Willy!

Willy, (angrily): What're you talking about? With scholarships to three universities they're gonna flunk him?

Bernard: But I heard Mr. Birnbaum say—

Willy: Don't be a pest, Bernard! *(To his boys):* What an anemic!

Bernard: Okay, I'm waiting for you in my house, Biff.

Bernard *goes off. The* Lomans *laugh.*

Willy: Bernard is not well liked, is he?

Biff: He's liked, but he's not well liked.

Happy: That's right, Pop.

Willy: That's just what I mean. Bernard can get the best marks in school, y'understand, but when he gets out in the business world, y'understand, you are going to be five times ahead of him. That's why I thank Almighty God you're both built like Adonises. Because the man who makes an appearance in the business world, the man who creates personal interest, is the man who gets ahead. Be liked and you will never want. You take me, for instance. I never have to wait in line to see a buyer. "Willy Loman is here!" That's all they have to know, and I go right through.

Biff: Did you knock them dead, Pop?

Willy: Knocked 'em cold in Providence, slaughtered 'em in Boston.

Happy, (on his back, pedaling again): I'm losing weight, you notice, Pop?

Linda *enters, as of old, a ribbon in her hair, carrying a basket of washing.*

Linda, (with youthful energy): Hello, dear!

Willy: Sweetheart!

Linda: How'd the Chevvy run?

Willy: Chevrolet, Linda, is the greatest car ever built. *(To the boys):* Since when do you let your mother carry wash up the stairs?

Biff: Grab hold there, boy!

Happy: Where to, Mom?

Linda: Hang them up on the line. And you better go down to your friends, Biff. The cellar is full of boys. They don't know what to do with themselves.

Biff: Ah, when Pop comes home they can wait!

Willy, (laughs appreciatively): You better go down and tell them what to do, Biff.

Biff: I think I'll have them sweep out the furnace room.

Willy: Good work, Biff.

Biff, (goes through wall-line of kitchen to doorway at back and calls down): Fellas. Everybody sweep out the furnace room! I'll be right down!

Voices: All right! Okay, Biff.

Biff: George and Sam and Frank, come out back! We're hangin' up the wash! Come on, Hap, on the double! *(He and* Happy *carry out the basket.)*

Linda: The way they obey him!

Willy: Well, that's training, the training. I'm tellin' you, I was sellin' thousands and thousands, but I had to come home.

Linda: Oh, the whole block'll be at that game. Did you sell anything?

Willy: I did five hundred gross in Providence and seven hundred gross in Boston.

Linda: No! Wait a minute, I've got a pencil. *(She pulls pencil and paper out of*

her apron pocket.) That makes your commission . . . Two hundred—my
God! Two hundred and twelve dollars!

Willy: Well, I didn't figure it yet, but . . .

Linda: How much did you do?

Willy: Well, I—I did—about a hundred and eighty gross in Providence.
Well, no—it came to—roughly two hundred gross on the whole trip.

Linda, (without hesitation): Two hundred gross. That's . . . *(She figures.)*

Willy: The trouble was that three of the stores were half closed for inventory in Boston. Otherwise I woulda broke records.

Linda: Well, it makes seventy dollars and some pennies. That's very good.

Willy: What do we owe?

Linda: Well, on the first there's sixteen dollars on the refrigerator—

Willy: Why sixteen?

Linda: Well, the fan belt broke, so it was a dollar eighty.

Willy: But it's brand new.

Linda: Well, the man said that's the way it is. Till they work themselves
in, y'know.

They move through the wall-line into the kitchen.

Willy: I hope we didn't get stuck on that machine.

Linda: They got the biggest ads of any of them!

Willy: I know, it's a fine machine. What else?

Linda: Well, there's nine-sixty for the washing machine. And for the vacuum
cleaner there's three and a half due on the fifteenth. Then the roof, you
got twenty-one dollars remaining.

Willy: It don't leak, does it?

Linda: No, they did a wonderful job. Then you owe Frank for the
carburetor.

Willy: I'm not going to pay that man! That goddam Chevrolet, they ought
to prohibit the manufacture of that car!

Linda: Well, you owe him three and a half. And odds and ends, comes to
around a hundred and twenty dollars by the fifteenth.

Willy: A hundred and twenty dollars! My God, if business don't pick up I
don't know what I'm gonna do!

Linda: Well, next week you'll do better.

Willy: Oh, I'll knock 'em dead next week. I'll go to Hartford. I'm very well
liked in Hartford. You know, the trouble is, Linda, people don't seem to
take to me.

They move onto the forestage.

Linda: Oh, don't be foolish.

Willy: I know it when I walk in. They seem to laugh at me.

Linda: Why? Why would they laugh at you? Don't talk that way, Willy.

Willy *moves to the edge of the stage.* Linda *goes into the kitchen and starts to
darn stockings.*

Willy: I don't know the reason for it, but they just pass me by. I'm not
noticed.

Linda: But you're doing wonderful, dear. You're making seventy to a hundred dollars a week.

Willy: But I gotta be at it ten, twelve hours a day. Other men—I don't know—they do it easier. I don't know why—I can't stop myself—I talk too much. A man oughta come in with a few words. One thing about Charley. He's a man of few words, and they respect him.

Linda: You don't talk too much, you're just lively.

Willy, (smiling): Well, I figure, what the hell, life is short, a couple of jokes. *(To himself):* I joke too much! *(The smile goes.)*

Linda: Why? You're—

Willy: I'm fat. I'm very—foolish to look at, Linda. I didn't tell you, but Christmas time I happened to be calling on F.H. Stewarts, and a salesman I know, as I was going in to see the buyer I heard him say something about—walrus. And I—I cracked him right across the face. I won't take that. I simply will not take that. But they do laugh at me. I know that.

Linda: Darling . . .

Willy: I gotta overcome it. I know I gotta overcome it. I'm not dressing to advantage, maybe.

Linda: Willy, darling, you're the handsomest man in the world—

Willy: Oh, no, Linda.

Linda: To me you are. *(Slight pause.)* The handsomest.

From the darkness is heard the laughter of a woman. Willy *doesn't turn to it, but it continues through* Linda's *lines.*

Linda: And the boys, Willy. Few men are idolized by their children the way you are.

Music is heard as behind a scrim, to the left of the house, The Woman, *dimly seen, is dressing.*

Willy, (with great feeling): You're the best there is, Linda, you're a pal, you know that? On the road—on the road I want to grab you sometimes and just kiss the life outa you.

The laughter is loud now, and he moves into a brightening area at the left, where The Woman *has come from behind the scrim and is standing, putting on her hat, looking into a "mirror" and laughing.*

Willy: 'Cause I get so lonely—especially when business is bad and there's nobody to talk to. I get the feeling that I'll never sell anything again, that I won't make a living for you, or a business, a business for the boys. *(He talks through* The Woman's *subsiding laughter;* The Woman *primps at the "mirror.")* There's so much I want to make for—

The Woman: Me? You didn't make me, Willy. I picked you.

Willy, (pleased): You picked me?

The Woman, (who is quite proper-looking, Willy's *age):* I did. I've been sitting at that desk watching all the salesmen go by, day in, day out. But you've got such a sense of humor, and we do have such a good time together, don't we?

Willy: Sure, sure. *(He takes her in his arms.)* Why do you have to go now?

The Woman: It's two o'clock . . .

Willy: No, come on in! *(He pulls her.)*

The Woman: . . . my sisters'll be scandalized. When'll you be back?

Willy: Oh, two weeks about. Will you come up again?

The Woman: Sure thing. You do make me laugh. It's good for me. *(She squeezes his arm, kisses him.)* And I think you're a wonderful man.

Willy: You picked me, heh?

The Woman: Sure. Because you're so sweet. And such a kidder.

Willy: Well, I'll see you next time I'm in Boston.

The Woman: I'll put you right through to the buyers.

Willy, (slapping her bottom): Right. Well, bottoms up!

The Woman, (slaps him gently and laughs): You just kill me, Willy. *(He suddenly grabs her and kisses her roughly.)* You kill me. And thanks for the stockings. I love a lot of stockings. Well, good night.

Willy: Good night. And keep your pores open!

The Woman: Oh, Willy!

The Woman *bursts out laughing, and* Linda's *laughter blends in. The* Woman *disappears into the dark. Now the area at the kitchen table brightens.* Linda *is sitting where she was at the kitchen table, but now is mending a pair of her silk stockings.*

Linda: You are, Willy. The handsomest man. You've got no reason to feel that—

Willy, (coming out of The Woman's *dimming area and going over to* Linda): I'll make it all up to you, Linda, I'll—

Linda: There's nothing to make up, dear. You're doing fine, better than—

Willy, (noticing her mending): What's that?

Linda: Just mending my stockings. They're so expensive—

Willy, (angrily, taking them from her): I won't have you mending stockings in this house! Now throw them out!

Linda *puts the stockings in her pocket.*

Bernard, (entering on the run): Where is he? If he doesn't study!

Willy, (moving to the forestage, with great agitation): You'll give him the answers!

Bernard: I do, but I can't on a Regents! That's a state exam! They're liable to arrest me!

Willy: Where is he? I'll whip him, I'll whip him!

Linda: And he'd better give back that football, Willy, it's not nice.

Willy: Biff! Where is he? Why is he taking everything?

Linda: He's too rough with the girls, Willy. All the mothers are afraid of him!

Willy: I'll whip him!

Bernard: He's driving the car without a license!

The Woman's *laugh is heard.*

Willy: Shut up!

Linda: All the mothers—

Willy: Shut up!

Bernard, (backing quietly away and out): Mr. Birnbaum says he's stuck up.

Willy: Get outa here!

Bernard: If he doesn't buckle down he'll flunk math! *(He goes off.)*

Linda: He's right, Willy, you've gotta—

Willy, (exploding at her): There's nothing the matter with him! You want him to be a worm like Bernard? He's got spirit, personality . . .

As he speaks, Linda, *almost in tears, exits into the living-room. Willy is alone in the kitchen, wilting and staring. The leaves are gone. It is night again, and the apartment houses look down from behind.*

Willy: Loaded with it. Loaded! What is he stealing? He's giving it back, isn't he? Why is he stealing? What did I tell him? I never in my life told him anything but decent things.

Happy *in pajamas has come down the stairs;* Willy *suddenly becomes aware of* Happy's *presence.*

Happy: Let's go now, come on.

Willy, (sitting down at the kitchen table): Huh! Why did she have to wax the floors herself? Everytime she waxes the floors she keels over. She knows that!

Happy: Shh! Take it easy. What brought you back tonight?

Willy: I got an awful scare. Nearly hit a kid in Yonkers. God! Why didn't I go to Alaska with my brother Ben that time! Ben! That man was a genius, that man was success incarnate! What a mistake! He begged me to go.

Happy: Well, there's no use in—

Willy: You guys! There was a man started with the clothes on his back and ended up with diamond mines!

Happy: Boy, someday I'd like to know how he did it.

Willy: What's the mystery? The man knew what he wanted and went out and got it! Walked into a jungle, and comes out, the age of twenty-one, and he's rich! The world is an oyster, but you don't crack it open on a mattress!

Happy: Pop, I told you I'm gonna retire you for life.

Willy: You'll retire me for life on seventy goddam dollars a week? And your women and your car and your apartment, and you'll retire me for life! Christ's sake, I couldn't get past Yonkers today! Where are you guys, where are you? The woods are burning! I can't drive a car!

Charley *has appeared in the doorway. He is a large man, slow of speech, laconic, immovable. In all he says, despite what he says, there is pity, and, now, trepidation. He has a robe over pajamas, slippers on his feet. He enters the kitchen.*

Charley: Everything all right?

Happy: Yeah, Charley, everything's . . .

Willy: What's the matter?

Charley: I heard some noise. I thought something happened. Can't we do something about the walls? You sneeze in here, and in my house hats blow off.

Happy: Let's go to bed, Dad. Come on.

Charley *signals to* Happy *to go.*

Willy: You go ahead, I'm not tired at the moment.
Happy, (to Willy*):* Take it easy, huh? *(He exits.)*
Willy: What're you doin' up?
Charley, (sitting down at the kitchen table opposite Willy*):* Couldn't sleep good.
   I had a heartburn.
Willy: Well, you don't know how to eat.
Charley: I eat with my mouth.
Willy: No, you're ignorant. You gotta know about vitamins and things
   like that.
Charley: Come on, let's shoot. Tire you out a little.
Willy, (hesitantly): All right. You got cards?
Charley, (taking a deck from his pocket): Yeah, I got them. Someplace. What is
   it with those vitamins?
Willy, (dealing): They build up your bones. Chemistry.
Charley: Yeah, but there's no bones in a heartburn.
Willy: What are you talkin' about? Do you know the first thing about it?
Charley: Don't get insulted.
Willy: Don't talk about something you don't know anything about.

   They are playing. Pause.

Charley: What're you doin' home?
Willy: A little trouble with the car.
Charley: Oh. *(Pause.)* I'd like to take a trip to California.
Willy: Don't say.
Charley: You want a job?
Willy: I got a job, I told you that. *(After a slight pause):* What the hell are you
   offering me a job for?
Charley: Don't get insulted.
Willy: Don't insult me.
Charley: I don't see no sense in it. You don't have to go on this way.
Willy: I got a good job. *(Slight pause.)* What do you keep comin' in here for?
Charley: You want me to go?
Willy, (after a pause, withering): I can't understand it. He's going back to
   Texas again. What the hell is that?
Charley: Let him go.
Willy: I got nothin' to give him, Charley, I'm clean, I'm clean.
Charley: He won't starve. None a them starve. Forget about him.
Willy: Then what have I got to remember?
Charley: You take it too hard. To hell with it. When a deposit bottle is bro-
   ken you don't get your nickel back.
Willy: That's easy enough for you to say.
Charley: That ain't easy for me to say.
Willy: Did you see the ceiling I put up in the living-room?
Charley: Yeah, that's a piece of work. To put up a ceiling is a mystery to me.
   How do you do it?

Willy: What's the difference?

Charley: Well, talk about it.

Willy: You gonna put up a ceiling?

Charley: How could I put up a ceiling?

Willy: Then what the hell are you bothering me for?

Charley: You're insulted again.

Willy: A man who can't handle tools is not a man. You're disgusting.

Charley: Don't call me disgusting, Willy.

Uncle Ben, *carrying a valise and an umbrella, enters the forestage from around the right corner of the house. He is a stolid man, in his sixties, with a mustache and an authoritative air. He is utterly certain of his destiny, and there is an aura of far places about him. He enters exactly as* Willy *speaks.*

Willy: I'm getting awfully tired, Ben.

Ben's *music is heard.* Ben *looks around at everything.*

Charley: Good, keep playing; you'll sleep better. Did you call me Ben?

Ben *looks at his watch.*

Willy: That's funny. For a second there you reminded me of my brother Ben.

Ben: I only have a few minutes. *(He strolls, inspecting the place.* Willy *and* Charley *continue playing.)*

Charley: You never heard from him again, heh? Since that time?

Willy: Didn't Linda tell you? Couple of weeks ago we got a letter from his wife in Africa. He died.

Charley: That so.

Ben, (chuckling): So this is Brooklyn, eh?

Charley: Maybe you're in for some of his money.

Willy: Naa, he had seven sons. There's just one opportunity I had with that man . . .

Ben: I must make a train, William. There are several properties I'm looking at in Alaska.

Willy: Sure, sure! If I'd gone with him to Alaska that time, everything would've been totally different.

Charley: Go on, you'd froze to death up there.

Willy: What're you talking about?

Ben: Opportunity is tremendous in Alaska, William. Surprised you're not up there.

Willy: Sure, tremendous.

Charley: Heh?

Willy: There was the only man I ever met who knew the answers.

Charley: Who?

Ben: How are you all?

Willy, (taking a pot, smiling): Fine, fine.

Charley: Pretty sharp tonight.

Ben: Is Mother living with you?

Willy: No, she died a long time ago.

Charley: Who?

Ben: That's too bad. Fine specimen of a lady, Mother.

Willy, (to Charley*):* Heh?

Ben: I'd hoped to see the old girl.

Charley: Who died?

Ben: Heard anything from Father, have you?

Willy, (unnerved): What do you mean, who died?

Charley, (taking a pot): What're you talkin' about?

Ben, (looking at his watch): William, it's half-past eight!

Willy, (as though to dispel his confusion he angrily stops Charley's *hand):* That's my build!

Charley: I put the ace—

Willy: If you don't know how to play the game I'm not gonna throw my money away on you!

Charley, (rising): It was my ace, for God's sake!

Willy: I'm through, I'm through!

Ben: When did Mother die?

Willy: Long ago. Since the beginning you never knew how to play cards.

Charley, (picks up the cards and goes to the door): All right! Next time I'll bring a deck with five aces.

Willy: I don't play that kind of game!

Charley, (turning to him): You ought to be ashamed of yourself!

Willy: Yeah?

Charley: Yeah! *(He goes out.)*

Willy, (slamming the door after him): Ignoramus!

Ben, (as Willy *comes toward him through the wall-line of the kitchen):* So you're William.

Willy, (shaking Ben's *hand):* Ben! I've been waiting for you so long! What's the answer? How did you do it?

Ben: Oh, there's a story in that.

Linda *enters the forestage, as of old, carrying the wash basket.*

Linda: Is this Ben?

Ben, (gallantly): How do you do, my dear.

Linda: Where've you been all these years? Willy's always wondered why you—

Willy, (pulling Ben *away from her impatiently):* Where is Dad? Didn't you follow him? How did you get started?

Ben: Well, I don't know how much you remember.

Willy: Well, I was just a baby, of course, only three or four years old—

Ben: Three years and eleven months.

Willy: What a memory, Ben!

Ben: I have many enterprises, William, and I have never kept books.

Willy: I remember I was sitting under the wagon in—was it Nebraska?

Ben: It was South Dakota, and I gave you a bunch of wild flowers.

Willy: I remember you walking away down some open road.

Ben, (laughing): I was going to find Father in Alaska.

Willy: Where is he?

Ben: At that age I had a very faulty view of geography, William. I discovered after a few days that I was heading due south, so instead of Alaska, I ended up in Africa.

Linda: Africa!

Willy: The Gold Coast!

Ben: Principally diamond mines.

Linda: Diamond mines!

Ben: Yes, my dear. But I've only a few minutes—

Willy: No! Boys! Boys! (*Young Biff and* Happy *appear.*) Listen to this. This is your Uncle Ben, a great man! Tell my boys, Ben!

Ben: Why, boys, when I was seventeen I walked into the jungle, and when I was twenty-one I walked out. (*He laughs.*) And by God I was rich.

Willy, (to the boys): You see what I been talking about? The greatest things can happen!

Ben, (glancing at his watch): I have an appointment in Ketchikan Tuesday week.

Willy: No, Ben! Please tell about Dad. I want my boys to hear. I want them to know the kind of stock they spring from. All I remember is a man with a big beard, and I was in Mamma's lap, sitting around a fire, and some kind of high music.

Ben: His flute. He played the flute.

Willy: Sure, the flute, that's right!

New music is heard, a high, rollicking tune.

Ben: Father was a very great and a very wild-hearted man. We would start in Boston, and he'd toss the whole family into the wagon, and then he'd drive the team right across the country; through Ohio, and Indiana, Michigan, Illinois, and all the Western states. And we'd stop in the towns and sell the flutes that he'd made on the way. Great inventor, Father. With one gadget he made more in a week than a man like you could make in a lifetime.

Willy: That's just the way I'm bringing them up, Ben—rugged, well liked, all-around.

Ben: Yeah? (*To* Biff): Hit that, boy—hard as you can. (*He pounds his stomach.*)

Biff: Oh, no, sir!

Ben, (taking boxing stance): Come on, get to me! (*He laughs.*)

Willy: Go to it, Biff! Go ahead, show him!

Biff: Okay! (*He cocks his fists and starts in.*)

Linda, (to Willy): Why must he fight, dear?

Ben, (sparring with Biff): Good boy! Good boy!

Willy: How's that, Ben, heh?

Happy: Give him the left, Biff!

Linda: Why are you fighting?

Ben: Good boy! (*Suddenly comes in, trips* Biff, *and stands over him, the point of his umbrella poised over* Biff's *eye.*)

Linda: Look out, Biff!

Biff: Gee!

Ben, (patting Biff's *knee):* Never fight fair with a stranger, boy. You'll never get out of the jungle that way. *(Taking* Linda's *hand and bowing):* It was an honor and a pleasure to meet you, Linda.

Linda, (withdrawing her hand coldly, frightened): Have a nice—trip.

Ben, (to Willy*):* And good luck with your—what do you do?

Willy: Selling.

Ben: Yes. Well . . . *(He raises his hand in farewell to all.)*

Willy: No, Ben, I don't want you to think . . . *(He takes* Ben's *arm to show him.)* It's Brooklyn, I know, but we hunt too.

Ben: Really, now.

Willy: Oh, sure, there's snakes and rabbits and—that's why I moved out here. Why, Biff can fell any one of these trees in no time! Boys! Go right over to where they're building the apartment house and get some sand. We're gonna rebuild the entire front stoop right now! Watch this, Ben!

Happy, (as he and Biff *run off):* I lost weight, Pop, you notice?

Charley *enters in knickers, even before the boys are gone.*

Charley: Listen, if they steal any more from that building the watchman'll put the cops on them!

Linda, (to Willy*):* Don't let Biff . . .

Ben *laughs lustily.*

Willy: You shoulda seen the lumber they brought home last week. At least a dozen six-by-tens worth all kinds a money.

Charley: Listen, if that watchman—

Willy: I gave them hell, understand. But I got a couple of fearless characters there.

Charley: Willy, the jails are full of fearless characters.

Ben, (clapping Willy *on the back, with a laugh at* Charley*):* And the stock exchange, friend!

Willy, (joining in Ben's *laughter):* Where are the rest of your pants?

Charley: My wife bought them.

Willy: Now all you need is a golf club and you can go upstairs and go to sleep. *(To* Ben*):* Great athlete! Between him and his son Bernard they can't hammer a nail!

Bernard, (rushing in): The watchman's chasing Biff!

Willy, (angrily): Shut up! He's not stealing anything!

Linda, (alarmed, hurrying off left): Where is he? Biff, dear! *(She exits.)*

Willy, (moving toward the left, away from Ben*):* There's nothing wrong. What's the matter with you?

Ben: Nervy boy. Good!

Willy, (laughing): Oh, nerves of iron, that Biff!

Charley: Don't know what it is. My New England man comes back and he's bleedin', they murdered him up there.

Willy: It's contacts, Charley, I got important contacts!

Charley, (sarcastically): Glad to hear it, Willy. Come in later, we'll shoot a little casino. I'll take some of your Portland money. *(He laughs at* Willy *and exits.)*

Willy (turning to Ben*):* Business is bad, it's murderous. But not for me, of course.

Ben: I'll stop by on my way back to Africa.

Willy, (longingly): Can't you stay a few days? You're just what I need, Ben, because I—I have a fine position here, but I—well, Dad left when I was such a baby and I never had a chance to talk to him and I still feel—kind of temporary about myself.

Ben: I'll be late for my train.

They are at opposite ends of the stage.

Willy: Ben, my boys—can't we talk? They'd go into the jaws of hell for me, see, but I—

Ben: William, you're being first-rate with your boys. Outstanding, manly chaps!

Willy, (hanging on to his words): Oh, Ben, that's good to hear! Because sometimes I'm afraid that I'm not teaching them the right kind of—Ben, how should I teach them?

Ben, (giving great weight to each word, and with a certain vicious audacity): William, when I walked into the jungle, I was seventeen. When I walked out I was twenty-one. And, by God, I was rich! *(He goes off into darkness around the right corner of the house.)*

Willy: . . . was rich! That's just the spirit I want to imbue them with! To walk into a jungle! I was right! I was right! I was right!

Ben *is gone, but* Willy *is still speaking to him as* Linda, *in nightgown and robe, enters the kitchen, glances around for* Willy, *then goes to the door of the house, looks out and sees him. Comes down to his left. He looks at her.*

Linda: Willy, dear? Willy?

Willy: I was right!

Linda: Did you have some cheese? *(He can't answer.)* It's very late, darling. Come to bed, heh?

Willy, (looking straight up): Gotta break your neck to see a star in this yard.

Linda: You coming in?

Willy: Whatever happened to that diamond watch fob? Remember? When Ben came from Africa that time? Didn't he give me a watch fob with a diamond in it?

Linda: You pawned it, dear. Twelve, thirteen years ago. For Biff's radio correspondence course.

Willy: Gee, that was a beautiful thing. I'll take a walk.

Linda: But you're in your slippers.

Willy, (starting to go around the house at the left): I was right! I was! *(Half to* Linda, *as he goes, shaking his head):* What a man! There was a man worth talking to. I was right!

Linda, (calling after Willy*):* But in your slippers, Willy!

Willy *is almost gone when* Biff, *in his pajamas, comes down the stairs and enters the kitchen.*

Biff: What is he doing out there?

Linda: Sh!

Biff: God Almighty, Mom, how long has he been doing this?

Linda: Don't, he'll hear you.

Biff: What the hell is the matter with him?

Linda: It'll pass by morning.

Biff: Shouldn't we do anything?

Linda: Oh, my dear, you should do a lot of things, but there's nothing to do, so go to sleep.

Happy *comes down the stair and sits on the steps.*

Happy: I never heard him so loud, Mom.

Linda: Well, come around more often; you'll hear him. *(She sits down at the table and mends the lining of* Willy's *jacket.)*

Biff: Why didn't you ever write me about this, Mom?

Linda: How would I write to you? For over three months you had no address.

Biff: I was on the move. But you know I thought of you all the time. You know that, don't you, pal?

Linda: I know, dear, I know. But he likes to have a letter. Just to know that there's still a possibility for better things.

Biff: He's not like this all the time, is he?

Linda: It's when you come home he's always the worst.

Biff: When I come home?

Linda: When you write you're coming, he's all smiles, and talks about the future, and—he's just wonderful. And then the closer you seem to come, the more shaky he gets, and then, by the time you get here, he's arguing, and he seems angry at you. I think it's just that maybe he can't bring himself to—to open up to you. Why are you so hateful to each other? Why is that?

Biff, (evasively): I'm not hateful, Mom.

Linda: But you no sooner come in the door than you're fighting!

Biff: I don't know why. I mean to change. I'm tryin', Mom, you understand?

Linda: Are you home to stay now?

Biff: I don't know. I want to look around, see what's doin'.

Linda: Biff, you can't look around all your life, can you?

Biff: I just can't take hold, Mom. I can't take hold of some kind of a life.

Linda: Biff, a man is not a bird, to come and go with the springtime.

Biff: Your hair . . . *(He touches her hair.)* Your hair got so gray.

Linda: Oh, it's been gray since you were in high school. I just stopped dyeing it, that's all.

Biff: Dye it again, will ya? I don't want my pal looking old. *(He smiles.)*

Linda: You're such a boy! You think you can go away for a year and . . . You've got to get it into your head now that one day you'll knock on this door and there'll be strange people here—

Biff: What are you talking about? You're not even sixty, Mom.

Linda: But what about your father?

Biff, (lamely): Well, I meant him too.

Happy: He admires Pop.

Linda: Biff, dear, if you don't have any feeling for him, then you can't have any feeling for me.

Biff: Sure I can, Mom.

Linda: No. You can't just come to see me, because I love him. *(With a threat, but only a threat, of tears):* He's the dearest man in the world to me, and I won't have anyone making him feel unwanted and low and blue. You've got to make up your mind now, darling, there's no leeway any more. Either he's your father and you pay him that respect, or else you're not to come here. I know he's not easy to get along with—nobody knows that better than me—but . . .

Willy, (from the left, with a laugh): Hey, hey, Biffo!

Biff, (starting to go out after Willy*):* What the hell is the matter with him? *(*Happy *stops him.)*

Linda: Don't—don't go near him!

Biff: Stop making excuses for him! He always, always wiped the floor with you. Never had an ounce of respect for you.

Happy: He's always had respect for—

Biff: What the hell do you know about it?

Happy, (surlily): Just don't call him crazy!

Biff: He's got no character—Charley wouldn't do this. Not in his own house—spewing out that vomit from his mind.

Happy: Charley never had to cope with what he's got to.

Biff: People are worse off than Willy Loman. Believe me, I've seen them!

Linda: Then make Charley your father, Biff. You can't do that, can you? I don't say he's a great man. Willy Loman never made a lot of money. His name was never in the paper. He's not the finest character that ever lived. But he's a human being, and a terrible thing is happening to him. So attention must be paid. He's not to be allowed to fall into his grave like an old dog. Attention, attention must be finally paid to such a person. You called him crazy—

Biff: I didn't mean—

Linda: No, a lot of people think he's lost his—balance. But you don't have to be very smart to know what his trouble is. The man is exhausted.

Happy: Sure!

Linda: A small man can be just as exhausted as a great man. He works for a company thirty-six years this March, opens up unheard-of territories to their trademark, and now in his old age they take his salary away.

Happy, (indignantly): I didn't know that, Mom.

Linda: You never asked, my dear! Now that you get your spending money someplace else you don't trouble your mind with him.

Happy: But I gave you money last—

Linda: Christmas time, fifty dollars! To fix the hot water it cost ninety-seven fifty! For five weeks he's been on straight commission, like a beginner, an unknown!

Biff: Those ungrateful bastards!

Linda: Are they any worse than his sons? When he brought them business, when he was young, they were glad to see him. But now his old friends, the old buyers that loved him so and always found some order to hand him in a pinch—they're all dead, retired. He used to be able to make six, seven calls a day in Boston. Now he takes his valises out of the car and puts them back and takes them out again and he's exhausted. Instead of walking he talks now. He drives seven hundred miles, and when he gets there no one knows him any more, no one welcomes him. And what goes through a man's mind, driving seven hundred miles home without having earned a cent? Why shouldn't he talk to himself? Why? When he has to go to Charley and borrow fifty dollars a week and pretend to me that it's his pay? How long can that go on? How long? You see what I'm sitting here and waiting for? And you tell me he has no character? The man who never worked a day but for your benefit? When does he get the medal for that? Is this his reward—to turn around at the age of sixty-three and find his sons, who he loved better than his life, one a philandering bum—

Happy: Mom!

Linda: That's all you are, my baby! *(To Biff):* And you! What happened to the love you had for him? You were such pals! How you used to talk to him on the phone every night! How lonely he was till he could come home to you!

Biff: All right, Mom. I'll live here in my room, and I'll get a job. I'll keep away from him, that's all.

Linda: No, Biff. You can't stay here and fight all the time.

Biff: He threw me out of this house, remember that.

Linda: Why did he do that? I never knew why.

Biff: Because I know he's a fake and he doesn't like anybody around who knows!

Linda: Why a fake? In what way? What do you mean?

Biff: Just don't lay it all at my feet. It's between me and him—that's all I have to say. I'll chip in from now on. He'll settle for half my pay check. He'll be all right. I'm going to bed. *(He starts for the stairs.)*

Linda: He won't be all right.

Biff, (turning on the stairs, furiously): I hate this city and I'll stay here. Now what do you want?

Linda: He's dying, Biff.

Happy *turns quickly to her, shocked.*

Biff, (after a pause): Why is he dying?

Linda: He's been trying to kill himself.

Biff, (with great horror): How?

Linda: I live from day to day.

Biff: What're you talking about?

Linda: Remember I wrote you that he smashed up the car again? In February?

Biff: Well?

Linda: The insurance inspector came. He said that they have evidence. That all these accidents in the last year—weren't—weren't—accidents.

Happy: How can they tell that? That's a lie.

Linda: It seems there's a woman . . . *(She takes a breath as)*

Biff, (sharply but contained): What woman?

Linda, (simultaneously): . . . and this woman . . .

Linda: What?

Biff: Nothing. Go ahead.

Linda: What did you say?

Biff: Nothing. I just said what woman?

Happy: What about her?

Linda: Well, it seems she was walking down the road and saw his car. She says that he wasn't driving fast at all, and that he didn't skid. She says he came to that little bridge, and then deliberately smashed into the railing, and it was only the shallowness of the water that saved him.

Biff: Oh, no, he probably just fell asleep again.

Linda: I don't think he fell asleep.

Biff: Why not?

Linda: Last month . . . *(With great difficulty):* Oh, boys, it's so hard to say a thing like this! He's just a big stupid man to you, but I tell you there's more good in him than in many other people. *(She chokes, wipes her eyes.)* I was looking for a fuse. The lights blew out, and I went down the cellar. And behind the fuse box—it happened to fall out—was a length of rubber pipe—just short.

Happy: No kidding?

Linda: There's a little attachment on the end of it. I knew right away. And sure enough, on the bottom of the water heater there's a new little nipple on the gas pipe.

Happy, (angrily): That—jerk.

Biff: Did you have it taken off?

Linda: I'm—I'm ashamed to. How can I mention it to him? Every day I go down and take away that little rubber pipe. But, when he comes home, I put it back where it was. How can I insult him that way? I don't know what to do. I live from day to day, boys. I tell you, I know every thought in his mind. It sounds so old-fashioned and silly, but I tell you he put his whole life into you and you've turned your backs on him. *(She is bent over in the chair, weeping, her face in her hands.)* Biff, I swear to God! Biff, his life is in your hands!

Happy, (to Biff): How do you like that damned fool!

Biff, (kissing her): All right, pal, all right. It's all settled now. I've been remiss. I know that, Mom. But now I'll stay, and I swear to you, I'll apply myself. *(Kneeling in front of her, in a fever of self-reproach):* It's just—you see, Mom, I don't fit in business. Not that I won't try. I'll try, and I'll make good.

Happy: Sure you will. The trouble with you in business was you never tried to please people.

Biff: I know, I—

Happy: Like when you worked for Harrison's. Bob Harrison said you were tops, and then you go and do some damn fool thing like whistling whole songs in the elevator like a comedian.

Biff, (against Happy*):* So what? I like to whistle sometimes.

Happy: You don't raise a guy to a responsible job who whistles in the elevator!

Linda: Well, don't argue about it now.

Happy: Like when you'd go off and swim in the middle of the day instead of taking the line around.

Biff, (his resentment rising): Well, don't you run off? You take off sometimes, don't you? On a nice summer day?

Happy: Yeah, but I cover myself!

Linda: Boys!

Happy: If I'm going to take a fade the boss can call any number where I'm supposed to be and they'll swear to him that I just left. I'll tell you something that I hate to say, Biff, but in the business world some of them think you're crazy.

Biff, (angered): Screw the business world!

Happy: All right, screw it! Great, but cover yourself!

Linda: Hap, Hap!

Biff: I don't care what they think! They've laughed at Dad for years, and you know why? Because we don't belong in this nuthouse of a city! We should be mixing cement on some open plain, or—or carpenters. A carpenter is allowed to whistle!

Willy *walks in from the entrance of the house, at left.*

Willy: Even your grandfather was better than a carpenter. *(Pause. They watch him.)* You never grew up. Bernard does not whistle in the elevator, I assure you.

Happy, (as though to laugh Willy *out of it):* Yeah, but you do, Pop.

Willy: I never in my life whistled in an elevator! And who in the business world thinks I'm crazy?

Biff: I didn't mean it like that, Pop. Now don't make a whole thing out of it, will ya?

Willy: Go back to the West! Be a carpenter, a cowboy, enjoy yourself!

Linda: Willy, he was just saying—

Willy: I heard what he said!

Happy, (trying to quiet Willy*):* Hey, Pop, come on now . . .

Willy, (continuing over Happy*'s line):* They laugh at me, heh? Go to Filene's, go to the Hub, go to Slattery's, Boston. Call out the name Willy Loman and see what happens! Big shot!

Biff: All right, Pop.

Willy: Big!

Biff: All right!

Willy: Why do you always insult me?

Biff: I didn't say a word. *(To* Linda*):* Did I say a word?

Linda: He didn't say anything, Willy.

Willy, (going to the doorway of the living-room): All right, good night, good night.

Linda: Willy, dear, he just decided . . .

Willy, (to Biff*):* If you get tired hanging around tomorrow, paint the ceiling I put up in the living-room.

Biff: I'm leaving early tomorrow.

Happy: He's going to see Bill Oliver, Pop.

Willy, (interestedly): Oliver? For what?

Biff, (with reserve, but trying, trying): He always said he'd stake me. I'd like to go into business, so maybe I can take him up on it.

Linda: Isn't that wonderful?

Willy: Don't interrupt. What's wonderful about it? There's fifty men in the City of New York who'd stake him. *(To* Biff*):* Sporting goods?

Biff: I guess so. I know something about it and—

Willy: He knows something about it! You know sporting goods better than Spalding, for God's sake! How much is he giving you?

Biff: I don't know, I didn't even see him yet, but—

Willy: Then what're you talkin' about?

Biff, (getting angry): Well, all I said was I'm gonna see him, that's all!

Willy, (turning away): Ah, you're counting your chickens again.

Biff, (starting left for the stairs): Oh, Jesus, I'm going to sleep!

Willy, (calling after him): Don't curse in this house!

Biff, (turning): Since when did you get so clean?

Happy, (trying to stop them): Wait a . . .

Willy: Don't use that language to me! I won't have it!

Happy, (grabbing Biff *shouts):* Wait a minute! I got an idea. I got a feasible idea. Come here, Biff, let's talk this over now, let's talk some sense here. When I was down in Florida last time, I thought of a great idea to sell sporting goods. It just came back to me. You and I, Biff—we have a line, the Loman Line. We train a couple of weeks, and put on a couple of exhibitions, see?

Willy: That's an idea!

Happy: Wait! We form two basketball teams, see? Two water-polo teams. We play each other. It's a million dollars' worth of publicity. Two brothers, see? The Loman Brothers. Displays in the Royal Palms—all the hotels. And banners over the ring and the basketball court: "Loman Brothers." Baby, we could sell sporting goods!

Willy: That is a one-million-dollar idea!

Linda: Marvelous!

Biff: I'm in great shape as far as that's concerned.

Happy: And the beauty of it is, Biff, it wouldn't be like a business. We'd be out playin' ball again . . .

Biff, (enthused): Yeah, that's . . .

Willy: Million-dollar . . .

Happy: And you wouldn't get fed up with it, Biff. It'd be the family again.
There'd be the old honor, and comradeship, and if you wanted to go off
for a swim or somethin'—well, you'd do it! Without some smart cooky
gettin' up ahead of you!

Willy: Lick the world! You guys together could absolutely lick the
civilized world.

Biff: I'll see Oliver tomorrow. Hap, if we could work that out . . .

Linda: Maybe things are beginning to—

Willy, (wildly enthused, to Linda*):* Stop interrupting! *(To* Biff*):* But don't
wear sport jacket and slacks when you see Oliver.

Biff: No, I'll—

Willy: A business suit, and talk as little as possible, and don't crack any jokes.

Biff: He did like me. Always liked me.

Linda: He loved you!

Willy, (to Linda*):* Will you stop! *(To* Biff*):* Walk in very serious. You are not
applying for a boy's job. Money is to pass. Be quiet, fine, and serious.
Everybody likes a kidder, but nobody lends him money.

Happy: I'll try to get some myself, Biff. I'm sure I can.

Willy: I see great things for you kids, I think your troubles are over. But
remember, start big and you'll end big. Ask for fifteen. How much you
gonna ask for?

Biff: Gee, I don't know—

Willy: And don't say "Gee." "Gee" is a boy's word. A man walking in for
fifteen thousand dollars does not say "Gee!"

Biff: Ten, I think, would be top though.

Willy: Don't be so modest. You always started too low. Walk in with a big
laugh. Don't look worried. Start off with a couple of your good stories
to lighten things up. It's not what you say, it's how you say it—because
personality always wins the day.

Linda: Oliver always thought the highest of him—

Willy: Will you let me talk?

Biff: Don't yell at her, Pop, will ya?

Willy, (angrily): I was talking, wasn't I?

Biff: I don't like you yelling at her all the time, and I'm tellin' you, that's all.

Willy: What're you, takin' over this house?

Linda: Willy—

Willy, (turning on her): Don't take his side all the time, goddammit!

Biff, (furiously): Stop yelling at her!

Willy, (suddenly pulling on his cheek, beaten down, guilt ridden): Give my best to
Bill Oliver—he may remember me. *(He exits through the living-room
doorway.)*

Linda, (her voice subdued): What'd you have to start that for? *(Biff turns
away.)* You see how sweet he was as soon as you talked hopefully? *(She
goes over to* Biff.*)* Come up and say good night to him. Don't let him go
to bed that way.

Happy: Come on, Biff, let's buck him up.

Linda: Please, dear. Just say good night. It takes so little to make him happy. Come. *(She goes through the living-room doorway, calling upstairs from within the living-room):* Your pajamas are hanging in the bathroom, Willy!

Happy, (looking toward where Linda *went out):* What a woman! They broke the mold when they made her. You know that, Biff?

Biff: He's off salary. My God, working on commission!

Happy: Well, let's face it: he's no hot-shot selling man. Except that sometimes, you have to admit, he's a sweet personality.

Biff, (deciding): Lend me ten bucks, will ya? I want to buy some new ties.

Happy: I'll take you to a place I know. Beautiful stuff. Wear one of my striped shirts tomorrow.

Biff: She got gray. Mom got awful old. Gee, I'm gonna go in to Oliver tomorrow and knock him for a—

Happy: Come on up. Tell that to Dad. Let's give him a whirl. Come on.

Biff, (steamed up): You know, with ten thousand bucks, boy!

Happy, (as they go into the living-room): That's the talk, Biff, that's the first time I've heard the old confidence out of you! *(From within the living-room, fading off)* You're gonna live with me, kid, and any babe you want just say the word . . . *(The last lines are hardly heard. They are mounting the stairs to their parents' bedroom.)*

Linda, (entering her bedroom and addressing Willy, *who is in the bathroom. She is straightening the bed for him):* Can you do anything about the shower? It drips.

Willy, (from the bathroom): All of a sudden everything falls to pieces! Goddam plumbing, oughta be sued, those people. I hardly finished putting it in and the thing . . . *(His words rumble off.)*

Linda: I'm just wondering if Oliver will remember him. You think he might?

Willy, (coming out of the bathroom in his pajamas): Remember him? What's the matter with you, you crazy? If he'd've stayed with Oliver he'd be on top by now! Wait'll Oliver gets a look at him. You don't know the average caliber any more. The average young man today—*(he is getting into bed)*—is got a caliber of zero. Greatest thing in the world for him was to bum around.

Biff *and* Happy *enter the bedroom. Slight pause.*

Willy, (stops short, looking at Biff*):* Glad to hear it, boy.

Happy: He wanted to say good night to you, sport.

Willy, (to Biff*):* Yeah. Knock him dead, boy. What'd you want to tell me?

Biff: Just take it easy, Pop. Good night. *(He turns to go.)*

Willy, (unable to resist): And if anything falls off the desk while you're talking to him—like a package or something—don't you pick it up. They have office boys for that.

Linda: I'll make a big breakfast—

Willy: Will you let me finish? *(To* Biff*):* Tell him you were in the business in the West. Not farm work.

Biff: All right, Dad.

Linda: I think everything—

Willy, (going right through her speech): And don't undersell yourself. No less than fifteen thousand dollars.

Biff, (unable to bear him): Okay. Good night, Mom. *(He starts moving.)*

Willy: Because you got a greatness in you, Biff, remember that. You got all kinds a greatness . . . *(He lies back, exhausted. Biff walks out.)*

Linda, (calling after Biff*):* Sleep well, darling!

Happy: I'm gonna get married, Mom. I wanted to tell you.

Linda: Go to sleep, dear.

Happy, (going): I just wanted to tell you.

Willy: Keep up the good work. *(Happy exits.)* God . . . remember that Ebbets Field game? The championship of the city?

Linda: Just rest. Should I sing to you?

Willy: Yeah. Sing to me. *(Linda hums a soft lullaby.)* When that team came out—he was the tallest, remember?

Linda: Oh, yes. And in gold.

Biff *enters the darkened kitchen, takes a cigarette, and leaves the house. He comes downstage into a golden pool of light. He smokes, staring at the night.*

Willy: Like a young god. Hercules—something like that. And the sun, the sun all around him. Remember how he waved to me? Right up from the field, with the representatives of three colleges standing by? And the buyers I brought, and the cheers when he came out—Loman, Loman, Loman! God Almighty, he'll be great yet. A star like that, magnificent, can never really fade away!

The light on Willy *is fading. The gas heater begins to glow through the kitchen wall, near the stairs, a blue flame beneath red coils.*

Linda, (timidly): Willy dear, what has he got against you?

Willy: I'm so tired. Don't talk any more.

Biff *slowly returns to the kitchen. He stops, stares toward the heater.*

Linda: Will you ask Howard to let you work in New York?

Willy: First thing in the morning. Everything'll be all right.

Biff *reaches behind the heater and draws out a length of rubber tubing. He is horrified and turns his head toward* Willy's *room, still dimly lit, from which the strains of* Linda's *desperate but monotonous humming rise.*

Willy, (staring through the window into the moonlight): Gee, look at the moon moving between the buildings!

Biff *wraps the tubing around his hand and quickly goes up the stairs.*

CURTAIN

ACT TWO

Music is heard, gay and bright. The curtain rises as the music fades away.
Willy, *in shirt sleeves, is sitting at the kitchen table, sipping coffee, his hat in his lap.* Linda *is filling his cup when she can.*

Willy: Wonderful coffee. Meal in itself.

Linda: Can I make you some eggs?

Willy: No. Take a breath.

Linda: You look so rested, dear.

Willy: I slept like a dead one. First time in months. Imagine, sleeping till ten on a Tuesday morning. Boys left nice and early, heh?

Linda: They were out of here by eight o'clock.

Willy: Good work!

Linda: It was so thrilling to see them leaving together. I can't get over the shaving lotion in this house!

Willy, (smiling): Mmm—

Linda: Biff was very changed this morning. His whole attitude seemed to be hopeful. He couldn't wait to get downtown to see Oliver.

Willy: He's heading for a change. There's no question, there simply are certain men that take longer to get—solidified. How did he dress?

Linda: His blue suit. He's so handsome in that suit. He could be a— anything in that suit!

Willy *gets up from the table.* Linda *holds his jacket for him.*

Willy: There's no question, no question at all. Gee, on the way home tonight I'd like to buy some seeds.

Linda, (laughing): That'd be wonderful. But not enough sun gets back there. Nothing'll grow any more.

Willy: You wait, kid, before it's all over we're gonna get a little place out in the country, and I'll raise some vegetables, a couple of chickens . . .

Linda: You'll do it yet, dear.

Willy *walks out of his jacket.* Linda *follows him.*

Willy: And they'll get married, and come for a weekend. I'd build a little guest house. 'Cause I got so many fine tools. All I'd need would be a little lumber and some peace of mind.

Linda, (joyfully): I sewed the lining . . .

Willy: I could build two guest houses, so they'd both come. Did he decide how much he's going to ask Oliver for?

Linda, (getting him into the jacket): He didn't mention it, but I imagine ten or fifteen thousand. You going to talk to Howard today?

Willy: Yeah. I'll put it to him straight and simple. He'll just have to take me off the road.

Linda: And Willy, don't forget to ask for a little advance, because we've got the insurance premium. It's the grace period now.

Willy: That's a hundred . . . ?

Linda: A hundred and eight, sixty-eight. Because we're a little short again.

Willy: Why are we short?

Linda: Well, you had the motor job on the car . . .

Willy: That goddam Studebaker!

Linda: And you got one more payment on the refrigerator . . .

Willy: But it just broke again!

Linda: Well, it's old, dear.

Willy: I told you we should've bought a well-advertised machine. Charley bought a General Electric and it's twenty years old and it's still good, that son-of-a-bitch.

Linda: But, Willy—

Willy: Whoever heard of a Hastings refrigerator? Once in my life I would like to own something outright before it's broken! I'm always in a race with the junkyard! I just finished paying for the car and it's on its last legs. The refrigerator consumes belts like a goddam maniac. They time those things. They time them so when you finally paid for them, they're used up.

Linda, (buttoning up his jacket as he unbuttons it): All told, about two hundred dollars would carry us, dear. But that includes the last payment on the mortgage. After this payment, Willy, the house belongs to us.

Willy: It's twenty-five years!

Linda: Biff was nine years old when we bought it.

Willy: Well, that's a great thing. To weather a twenty-five year mortgage is—

Linda: It's an accomplishment.

Willy: All the cement, the lumber, the reconstruction I put in this house! There ain't a crack to be found in it any more.

Linda: Well, it served its purpose.

Willy: What purpose? Some stranger'll come along, move in, and that's that. If only Biff would take this house, and raise a family . . . *(He starts to go.)* Good-by, I'm late.

Linda, (suddenly remembering): Oh, I forgot! You're supposed to meet them for dinner.

Willy: Me?

Linda: At Frank's Chop House on Forty-eighth near Sixth Avenue.

Willy: Is that so! How about you?

Linda: No, just the three of you. They're gonna blow you to a big meal!

Willy: Don't say! Who thought of that?

Linda: Biff came to me this morning, Willy, and he said, "Tell Dad, we want to blow him to a big meal." Be there six o'clock. You and your two boys are going to have dinner.

Willy: Gee whiz! That's really somethin'. I'm gonna knock Howard for a loop, kid. I'll get an advance, and I'll come home with a New York job. Goddammit, now I'm gonna do it!

Linda: Oh, that's the spirit, Willy!

Willy: I will never get behind a wheel the rest of my life!

Linda: It's changing, Willy, I can feel it changing!

Willy: Beyond a question. G'by, I'm late. *(He starts to go again.)*

Linda, (calling after him as she runs to the kitchen table for a handkerchief): You got your glasses?

Willy, (feels for them, then comes back in): Yeah, yeah, got my glasses.

Linda, (giving him the handkerchief): And a handkerchief.

Willy: Yeah, handkerchief.

Linda: And your saccharine?

Willy: Yeah, my saccharine.

Linda: Be careful on the subway stairs.

She kisses him, and a silk stocking is seen hanging from her hand. Willy *notices it.*

Willy: Will you stop mending stockings? At least while I'm in the house. It gets me nervous. I can't tell you. Please.

Linda *hides the stocking in her hand as she follows* Willy *across the forestage in front of the house.*

Linda: Remember, Frank's Chop House.

Willy, (passing the apron): Maybe beets would grow out there.

Linda, (laughing): But you tried so many times.

Willy: Yeah. Well, don't work hard today. *(He disappears around the right corner of the house.)*

Linda: Be careful!

As Willy *vanishes,* Linda *waves to him. Suddenly the phone rings. She runs across the stage and into the kitchen and lifts it.*

Linda: Hello? Oh, Biff! I'm so glad you called, I just . . . Yes, sure, I just told him. Yes, he'll be there for dinner at six o'clock, I didn't forget. Listen, I was just dying to tell you. You know that little rubber pipe I told you about? That he connected to the gas heater? I finally decided to go down the cellar this morning and take it away and destroy it. But it's gone! Imagine? He took it away himself, it isn't there! *(She listens.)* When? Oh, then you took it. Oh—nothing, it's just that I'd hoped he'd taken it away himself. Oh, I'm not worried, darling, because this morning he left in such high spirits, it was like the old days! I'm not afraid any more. Did Mr. Oliver see you? . . . Well, you wait there then. And make a nice impression on him, darling. Just don't perspire too much before you see him. And have a nice time with Dad. He may have big news too! . . . That's right, a New York job. And be sweet to him tonight, dear. Be loving to him. Because he's only a little boat looking for a harbor. *(She is trembling with sorrow and joy.)* Oh, that's wonderful, Biff, you'll save his life. Thanks, darling. Just put your arm around him when he comes into the restaurant. Give him a smile. That's the boy . . . Good-by, dear . . . You got your comb? . . . That's fine. Good-by, Biff dear.

In the middle of her speech, Howard Wagner, *thirty-six, wheels on a small typewriter table on which is a wire-recording machine and proceeds to plug it in.*

This is on the left forestage. Light slowly fades on Linda *as it rises on* Howard. Howard *is intent on threading the machine and only glances over his shoulder as* Willy *appears.*

Willy: Pst! Pst!

Howard: Hello, Willy, come in.

Willy: Like to have a little talk with you, Howard.

Howard: Sorry to keep you waiting. I'll be with you in a minute.

Willy: What's that, Howard?

Howard: Didn't you ever see one of these? Wire recorder.

Willy: Oh. Can we talk a minute?

Howard: Records things. Just got delivery yesterday. Been driving me crazy, the most terrific machine I ever saw in my life. I was up all night with it.

Willy: What do you do with it?

Howard: I bought it for dictation, but you can do anything with it. Listen to this. I had it home last night. Listen to what I picked up. The first one is my daughter. Get this. *(He flicks the switch and "Roll out the Barrel" is heard being whistled.)* Listen to that kid whistle.

Willy: That is lifelike, isn't it?

Howard: Seven years old. Get that tone.

Willy: Ts, ts. Like to ask a little favor if you . . .

The whistling breaks off, and the voice of Howard's *daughter is heard.*

His Daughter: "Now you, Daddy."

Howard: She's crazy for me! *(Again the same song is whistled.)* That's me! Ha! *(He winks.)*

Willy: You're very good!

The whistling breaks off again. The machine runs silent for a moment.

Howard: Sh! Get this now, this is my son.

His Son: "The capital of Alabama is Montgomery; the capital of Arizona is Phoenix; the capital of Arkansas is Little Rock; the capital of California is Sacramento . . ." *(and on, and on.)*

Howard, (holding up five fingers): Five years old, Willy!

Willy: He'll make an announcer some day!

His Son, (continuing): "The capital . . ."

Howard: Get that—alphabetical order! *(The machine breaks off suddenly.)* Wait a minute. The maid kicked the plug out.

Willy: It certainly is a—

Howard: Sh, for God's sake!

His Son: "It's nine o'clock, Bulova watch time. So I have to go to sleep."

Willy: That really is—

Howard: Wait a minute! The next is my wife.

They wait.

Howard's Voice: "Go on, say something." *(Pause.)* "Well, you gonna talk?"

His Wife: "I can't think of anything."

Howard's Voice: "Well, talk—it's turning."

His Wife, (shyly, beaten): "Hello." *(Silence.)* "Oh, Howard, I can't talk into this . . ."

Howard, (snapping the machine off): That was my wife.

Willy: That is a wonderful machine. Can we—

Howard: I tell you, Willy, I'm gonna take my camera, and my bandsaw, and all my hobbies, and out they go. This is the most fascinating relaxation I ever found.

Willy: I think I'll get one myself.

Howard: Sure, they're only a hundred and a half. You can't do without it. Supposing you wanna hear Jack Benny, see? But you can't be at home at that hour. So you tell the maid to turn the radio on when Jack Benny comes on, and this automatically goes on with the radio . . .

Willy: And when you come home you . . .

Howard: You can come home twelve o'clock, one o'clock, any time you like, and you get yourself a Coke and sit yourself down, throw the switch, and there's Jack Benny's program in the middle of the night!

Willy: I'm definitely going to get one. Because lots of times I'm on the road, and I think to myself, what I must be missing on the radio!

Howard: Don't you have a radio in the car?

Willy: Well, yeah, but who ever thinks of turning it on?

Howard: Say, aren't you supposed to be in Boston?

Willy: That's what I want to talk to you about, Howard. You got a minute? *(He draws a chair in from the wing.)*

Howard: What happened? What're you doing here?

Willy: Well . . .

Howard: You didn't crack up again, did you?

Willy: Oh, no. No . . .

Howard: Geez, you had me worried there for a minute. What's the trouble?

Willy: Well, tell you the truth, Howard. I've come to the decision that I'd rather not travel any more.

Howard: Not travel! Well, what'll you do?

Willy: Remember, Christmas time, when you had the party here? You said you'd try to think of some spot for me here in town.

Howard: With us?

Willy: Well, sure.

Howard: Oh, yeah, yeah. I remember. Well, I couldn't think of anything for you, Willy.

Willy: I tell ya, Howard. The kids are all grown up, y'know. I don't need much any more. If I could take home—well, sixty-five dollars a week, I could swing it.

Howard: Yeah, but Willy, see I—

Willy: I tell ya why, Howard. Speaking frankly and between the two of us, y'know—I'm just a little tired.

Howard: Oh, I could understand that, Willy. But you're a road man, Willy, and we do a road business. We've only got a half-dozen salesmen on the floor here.

Willy: God knows, Howard, I never asked a favor of any man. But I was
with the firm when your father used to carry you in here in his arms.

Howard: I know that, Willy, but—

Willy: Your father came to me the day you were born and asked me what I
thought of the name of Howard, may he rest in peace.

Howard: I appreciate that, Willy, but there just is no spot here for you.
If I had a spot I'd slam you right in, but I just don't have a single
solitary spot.

   He looks for his lighter. Willy *has picked it up and gives it to him. Pause.*

Willy, (with increasing anger): Howard, all I need to set my table is fifty dollars a week.

Howard: But where am I going to put you, kid?

Willy: Look, it isn't a question of whether I can sell merchandise, is it?

Howard: No, but it's a business, kid, and everybody's gotta pull his
own weight.

Willy, (desperately): Just let me tell you a story, Howard—

Howard: 'Cause you gotta admit, business is business.

Willy, (angrily): Business is definitely business, but just listen for a minute.
You don't understand this. When I was a boy—eighteen, nineteen—I
was already on the road. And there was a question in my mind as to
whether selling had a future for me. Because in those days I had a yearning to go to Alaska. See, there were three gold strikes in one month in
Alaska, and I felt like going out. Just for the ride, you might say.

Howard, (barely interested): Don't say.

Willy: Oh, yeah, my father lived many years in Alaska. He was an adventurous man. We've got quite a little streak of self-reliance in our family. I
thought I'd go out with my older brother and try to locate him, and
maybe settle in the North with the old man. And I was almost decided
to go, when I met a salesman in the Parker House. His name was Dave
Singleman. And he was eighty-four years old, and he'd drummed merchandise in thirty-one states. And old Dave, he'd go up to his room,
y'understand, put on his green velvet slippers—I'll never forget—and
pick up his phone and call the buyers, and without ever leaving his
room, at the age of eighty-four, he made his living. And when I saw that,
I realized that selling was the greatest career a man could want. 'Cause
what could be more satisfying than to be able to go, at the age of eighty-
four, into twenty or thirty different cities, and pick up a phone, and be
remembered and loved and helped by so many different people? Do you
know? when he died—and by the way he died the death of a salesman,
in his green velvet slippers in the smoker of the New York, New Haven
and Hartford, going into Boston—when he died, hundreds of salesmen
and buyers were at his funeral. Things were sad on a lotta trains for
months after that. *(He stands up.* Howard *has not looked at him.)* In those
days there was personality in it, Howard. There was respect, and comradeship, and gratitude in it. Today, it's all cut and dried, and there's no
chance for bringing friendship to bear—or personality. You see what I
mean? They don't know me any more.

Howard, (moving away, to the right): That's just the thing, Willy.

Willy: If I had forty dollars a week—that's all I'd need. Forty dollars, Howard.

Howard: Kid, I can't take blood from a stone, I—

Willy, (desperation is on him now): Howard, the year Al Smith was nominated, your father came to me and—

Howard, (starting to go off): I've got to see some people, kid.

Willy, (stopping him): I'm talking about your father! There were promises made across this desk! You mustn't tell me you've got people to see—I put thirty-four years into this firm, Howard, and now I can't pay my insurance! You can't eat the orange and throw the peel away—a man is not a piece of fruit! *(After a pause)* Now pay attention. Your father—in 1928 I had a big year. I averaged a hundred and seventy dollars a week in commissions.

Howard, (impatiently): Now, Willy, you never averaged—

Willy, (banging his hand on the desk): I averaged a hundred and seventy dollars a week in the year of 1928! And your father came to me—or rather, I was in the office here—it was right over this desk—and he put his hand on my shoulder—

Howard, (getting up): You'll have to excuse me, Willy, I gotta see some people. Pull yourself together. *(Going out)* I'll be back in a little while.

On Howard's *exit, the light on his chair grows very bright and strange.*

Willy: Pull myself together! What the hell did I say to him? My God, I was yelling at him! How could I! (Willy *breaks off, staring at the light, which occupies the chair, animating it. He approaches this chair, standing across the desk from it.)* Frank, Frank, don't you remember what you told me that time? How you put your hand on my shoulder, and Frank . . . *(He leans on the desk and as he speaks the dead man's name he accidentally switches on the recorder, and instantly)*

Howard's Son: ". . . of New York is Albany. The capital of Ohio is Cincinnati, the capital of Rhode Island is . . ." *(The recitation continues.)*

Willy, (leaping away with fright, shouting): Ha! Howard! Howard! Howard!

Howard, (rushing in): What happened?

Willy, (pointing at the machine, which continues nasally, childishly, with the capital cities): Shut it off! Shut it off!

Howard, (pulling the plug out): Look, Willy . . .

Willy, (pressing his hands to his eyes): I gotta get myself some coffee. I'll get some coffee . . .

Willy *starts to walk out.* Howard *stops him.*

Howard, (rolling up the cord): Willy, look . . .

Willy: I'll go to Boston.

Howard: Willy, you can't go to Boston for us.

Willy: Why can't I go?

Howard: I don't want you to represent us. I've been meaning to tell you for a long time now.

Willy: Howard, are you firing me?

Howard: I think you need a good long rest, Willy.

Willy: Howard—

Howard: And when you feel better, come back, and we'll see if we can work
    something out.

Willy: But I gotta earn money, Howard. I'm in no position to—

Howard: Where are your sons? Why don't your sons give you a hand?

Willy: They're working on a very big deal.

Howard: This is no time for false pride, Willy. You go to your sons and you
    tell them that you're tired. You've got two great boys, haven't you?

Willy: Oh, no question, no question, but in the meantime . . .

Howard: Then that's that, heh?

Willy: All right, I'll go to Boston tomorrow.

Howard: No, no.

Willy: I can't throw myself on my sons. I'm not a cripple!

Howard: Look, kid, I'm busy this morning.

Willy, (grasping Howard's *arm):* Howard, you've got to let me go to Boston!

Howard, (hard, keeping himself under control): I've got a line of people to see
    this morning. Sit down, take five minutes, and pull yourself together,
    and then go home, will ya? I need the office, Willy. *(He starts to go, turns,
    remembering the recorder, starts to push off the table holding the recorder.)* Oh,
    yeah. Whenever you can this week, stop by and drop off the samples.
    You'll feel better, Willy, and then come back and we'll talk. Pull yourself
    together, kid, there's people outside.

    Howard *exits, pushing the table off left.* Willy *stares into space, exhausted.*
Now the music is heard—Ben's music—first distantly, then closer, closer. As Willy
speaks, Ben *enters from the right. He carries valise and umbrella.*

Willy: Oh, Ben, how did you do it? What is the answer? Did you wind up
    the Alaska deal already?

Ben: Doesn't take much time if you know what you're doing. Just a short
    business trip. Boarding ship in an hour. Wanted to say good-by.

Willy: Ben, I've got to talk to you.

Ben, (glancing at his watch): Haven't the time, William.

Willy, (crossing the apron to Ben*):* Ben, nothing's working out. I don't know
    what to do.

Ben: Now, look here, William. I've bought timberland in Alaska and I need
    a man to look after things for me.

Willy: God, timberland! Me and my boys in those grand outdoors!

Ben: You've a new continent at your doorstep, William. Get out of these
    cities, they're full of talk and time payments and courts of law. Screw on
    your fists and you can fight for a fortune up there.

Willy: Yes, yes! Linda, Linda!

    Linda *enters as of old, with the wash.*

Linda: Oh, you're back?

Ben: I haven't much time.

Willy: No, wait! Linda, he's got a proposition for me in Alaska.

Linda: But he's got— *(To Ben)* He's got a beautiful job here.

Willy: But in Alaska, kid, I could—

Linda: You're doing well enough, Willy!

Ben, (to Linda*):* Enough for what, my dear?

Linda, (frightened of Ben and angry at him): Don't say those things to him! Enough to be happy right here, right now. *(To* Willy, *while* Ben *laughs)* Why must everybody conquer the world? You're well liked, and the boys love you, and someday,— *(to* Ben*)*—why, old man Wagner told him just the other day that if he keeps it up he'll be a member of the firm, didn't he, Willy?

Willy: Sure, sure. I am building something with this firm, Ben, and if a man is building something he must be on the right track, mustn't he?

Ben: What are you building? Lay your hand on it. Where is it?

Willy, (hesitantly): That's true, Linda, there's nothing.

Linda: Why? *(To* Ben*)* There's a man eighty-four years old—

Willy: That's right, Ben, that's right. When I look at that man I say, what is there to worry about?

Ben: Bah!

Willy: It's true, Ben. All he has to do is go into any city, pick up the phone, and he's making his living and you know why?

Ben, (picking up his valise): I've got to go.

Willy, (holding Ben *back):* Look at this boy!

Biff, *in his high school sweater, enters carrying suitcase.* Happy *carries* Biff's *shoulder guards, gold helmet, and football pants.*

Willy: Without a penny to his name, three great universities are begging for him, and from there the sky's the limit, because it's not what you do, Ben. It's who you know and the smile on your face! It's contacts, Ben, contacts! The whole wealth of Alaska passes over the lunch table at the Commodore Hotel, and that's the wonder, the wonder of this country, that a man can end with diamonds here on the basis of being liked! *(He turns to* Biff.*)* And that's why when you get out on that field today it's important. Because thousands of people will be rooting for you and loving you. *(To* Ben, *who has again begun to leave)* And Ben! when he walks into a business office his name will sound out like a bell and all the doors will open to him! I've seen it, Ben, I've seen it a thousand times! You can't feel it with your hand like timber, but it's there!

Ben: Good-by, William.

Willy: Ben, am I right? Don't you think I'm right? I value your advice.

Ben: There's a new continent at your doorstep, William. You could walk out rich. Rich! *(He is gone.)*

Willy: We'll do it here, Ben! You hear me? We're gonna do it here!

Young Bernard *rushes in. The gay music of the* Boys *is heard.*

Bernard: Oh, gee, I was afraid you left already!

Willy: Why? What time is it?

Bernard: It's half-past one!

Willy: Well, come on, everybody! Ebbets Field next stop! Where's the pennants? *(He rushes through the wall-line of the kitchen and out into the living-room.)*

Linda, (to Biff): Did you pack fresh underwear?

Happy, (who has been limbering up): I want to go!

Bernard: Biff, I'm carrying your helmet, ain't I?

Happy: No, I'm carrying the helmet.

Bernard: Oh, Biff, you promised me.

Happy: I'm carrying the helmet.

Bernard: How am I going to get in the locker room?

Linda: Let him carry the shoulder guards. *(She puts her coat and hat on in the kitchen.)*

Bernard: Can I, Biff? 'Cause I told everybody I'm going to be in the locker room.

Happy: In Ebbets Field it's the clubhouse.

Bernard: I meant the clubhouse. Biff!

Happy: Biff!

Biff, (grandly, after a slight pause): Let him carry the shoulder guards.

Happy, (as he gives Bernard *the shoulder guards):* Stay close to us now.

Willy *rushes in with the pennants.*

Willy, (handing them out): Everybody wave when *Biff* comes out on the field. (Happy *and* Bernard *run off.)* You set now, boy?

The music has died away.

Biff: Ready to go, Pop. Every muscle is ready.

Willy, (at the edge of the apron): You realize what this means?

Biff: That's right, Pop.

Willy, (feeling Biff's *muscles):* You're comin' home this afternoon captain of the All-Scholastic Championship Team of the City of New York.

Biff: I got it, Pop. And remember, pal, when I take off my helmet, that touchdown is for you.

Willy: Let's go! *(He is starting out, with his arm around* Biff, *when* Charley *enters, as of old, in knickers.)* I got no room for you, Charley.

Charley: Room? For what?

Willy: In the car.

Charley: You goin' for a ride? I wanted to shoot some casino.

Willy, (furiously): Casino? *(Incredulously)* Don't you realize what today is?

Linda: Oh, he knows, Willy. He's just kidding you.

Willy: That's nothing to kid about!

Charley: No, Linda, what's goin' on?

Linda: He's playing in Ebbets Field.

Charley: Baseball in this weather?

Willy: Don't talk to him. Come on, come on! *(He is pushing them out.)*

Charley: Wait a minute, didn't you hear the news?

Willy: What?

Charley: Don't you listen to the radio? Ebbets Field just blew up.

Willy: You go to hell! (Charley *laughs. Pushing them out*) Come on, come on! We're late.

Charley, (as they go): Knock a homer, Biff, knock a homer!

Willy, (the last to leave, turning to Charley*):* I don't think that was funny, Charley. This is the greatest day of his life.

Charley: Willy, when are you going to grow up?

Willy: Yeah, heh? When this game is over, Charley, you'll be laughing out of the other side of your face. They'll be calling him another Red Grange. Twenty-five thousand a year.

Charley, (kidding): Is that so?

Willy: Yeah, that's so.

Charley: Well, then, I'm sorry, Willy. But tell me something.

Willy: What?

Charley: Who is Red Grange?

Willy: Put up your hands. Goddam you, put up your hands!

Charley, *chuckling, shakes his head and walks away, around the left corner of the stage.* Willy *follows him. The music rises to a mocking frenzy.*

Willy: Who the hell do you think you are, better than everybody else? You don't know everything, you big, ignorant, stupid . . . Put up your hands!

Light rises, on the right side of the forestage, on a small table in the reception room of Charley's *office. Traffic sounds are heard.* Bernard, *now mature, sits whistling to himself. A pair of tennis rackets and an overnight bag are on the floor beside him.*

Willy, (offstage): What are you walking away for? Don't walk away! If you're going to say something say it to my face! I know you laugh at me behind my back. You'll laugh out of the other side of your goddam face after this game. Touchdown! Touchdown! Eighty thousand people! Touchdown! Right between the goal posts.

Bernard *is a quiet, earnest, but self-assured young man.* Willy's *voice is coming from right upstage now.* Bernard *lowers his feet off the table and listens.* Jenny, *his father's secretary, enters.*

Jenny, (distressed): Say, Bernard, will you go out in the hall?

Bernard: What is that noise? Who is it?

Jenny: Mr. Loman. He just got off the elevator.

Bernard, (getting up): Who's he arguing with?

Jenny: Nobody. There's nobody with him. I can't deal with him any more, and your father gets all upset everytime he comes. I've got a lot of typing to do, and your father's waiting to sign it. Will you see him?

Willy, (entering): Touchdown! Touch— (*He sees* Jenny.) Jenny, Jenny, good to see you. How're ya? Workin'? Or still honest?

Jenny: Fine. How've you been feeling?

Willy: Not much any more, Jenny. Ha, ha! (*He is surprised to see the rackets.*)

Bernard: Hello, Uncle Willy.

Willy, (almost shocked): Bernard! Well, look who's here! *(He comes quickly, guiltily, to* Bernard *and warmly shakes his hand.)*

Bernard: How are you? Good to see you.

Willy: What are you doing here?

Bernard: Oh, just stopped by to see Pop. Get off my feet till my train leaves. I'm going to Washington in a few minutes.

Willy: Is he in?

Bernard: Yes, he's in his office with the accountant. Sit down.

Willy, (sitting down): What're you going to do in Washington?

Bernard: Oh, just a case I've got there, Willy.

Willy: That so? *(Indicating the rackets)* You going to play tennis there?

Bernard: I'm staying with a friend who's got a court.

Willy: Don't say. His own tennis court. Must be fine people, I bet.

Bernard: They are, very nice. Dad tells me Biff's in town.

Willy, (with a big smile): Yeah, Biff's in. Working on a very big deal, Bernard.

Bernard: What's Biff doing?

Willy: Well, he's been doing very big things in the West. But he decided to establish himself here. Very big. We're having dinner. Did I hear your wife had a boy?

Bernard: That's right. Our second.

Willy: Two boys! What do you know!

Bernard: What kind of a deal has Biff got?

Willy: Well, Bill Oliver—very big sporting-goods man—he wants Biff very badly. Called him in from the West. Long distance, carte blanche, special deliveries. Your friends have their own private tennis court?

Bernard: You still with the old firm, Willy?

Willy, (after a pause): I'm—I'm overjoyed to see how you made the grade, Bernard, overjoyed. It's an encouraging thing to see a young man really—really— Looks very good for Biff—very— *(He breaks off, then):* Bernard— *(He is so full of emotion, he breaks off again.)*

Bernard: What is it, Willy?

Willy, (small and alone): What—what's the secret?

Bernard: What secret?

Willy: How—how did you? Why didn't he ever catch on?

Bernard: I wouldn't know that, Willy.

Willy, (confidentially, desperately): You were his friend, his boyhood friend. There's something I don't understand about it. His life ended after that Ebbets Field game. From the age of seventeen nothing good ever happened to him.

Bernard: He never trained himself for anything.

Willy: But he did, he did. After high school he took so many correspondence courses. Radio mechanics; television; God knows what, and never made the slightest mark.

Bernard, (taking off his glasses): Willy, do you want to talk candidly?

Willy, (rising, faces Bernard): I regard you as a very brilliant man, Bernard. I value your advice.

Bernard: Oh, the hell with the advice, Willy. I couldn't advise you. There's just one thing I've always wanted to ask you. When he was supposed to graduate, and the math teacher flunked him—

Willy: Oh, that son-of-a-bitch ruined his life.

Bernard: Yeah, but, Willy, all he had to do was go to summer school and make up that subject.

Willy: That's right, that's right.

Bernard: Did you tell him not to go to summer school?

Willy: Me? I begged him to go. I ordered him to go!

Bernard: Then why wouldn't he go?

Willy: Why? Why! Bernard, that question has been trailing me like a ghost for the last fifteen years. He flunked the subject, and laid down and died like a hammer hit him!

Bernard: Take it easy, kid.

Willy: Let me talk to you—I got nobody to talk to. Bernard, Bernard, was it my fault? Y'see? It keeps going around in my mind, maybe I did something to him. I got nothing to give him.

Bernard: Don't take it so hard.

Willy: Why did he lay down? What is the story there? You were his friend!

Bernard: Willy, I remember, it was June, and our grades came out. And he'd flunked math.

Willy: That son-of-a-bitch!

Bernard: No, it wasn't right then. Biff just got very angry, I remember, and he was ready to enroll in summer school.

Willy, (surprised): He was?

Bernard: He wasn't beaten by it at all. But then, Willy, he disappeared from the block for almost a month. And I got the idea that he'd gone up to New England to see you. Did he have a talk with you then?

Willy *stares in silence.*

Bernard: Willy?

Willy, (with a strong edge of resentment in his voice): Yeah, he came to Boston. What about it?

Bernard: Well, just that when he came back—I'll never forget this, it always mystifies me. Because I'd thought so well of Biff, even though he'd always taken advantage of me. I loved him, Willy, y'know? And he came back after that month and took his sneakers—remember those sneakers with "University of Virginia" printed on them? He was so proud of those, wore them every day. And he took them down in the cellar, and burned them up in the furnace. We had a fist fight. It lasted at least half an hour. Just the two of us, punching each other down in the cellar, and crying right through it. I've often thought of how strange it was that I knew he'd given up his life. What happened in Boston, Willy?

Willy *looks at him as at an intruder.*

Bernard: I just bring it up because you asked me.

Willy, (angrily): Nothing. What do you mean, "What happened?" What's that got to do with anything?

Bernard: Well, don't get sore.

Willy: What are you trying to do, blame it on me? If a boy lays down is that my fault?

Bernard: Now, Willy, don't get—

Willy: Well, don't—don't talk to me that way! What does that mean, "What happened?"

Charley *enters. He is in his vest, and he carries a bottle of bourbon.*

Charley: Hey, you're going to miss that train. *(He waves the bottle.)*

Bernard: Yeah, I'm going. *(He takes the bottle.)* Thanks, Pop. *(He picks up his rackets and bag.)* Good-by, Willy, and don't worry about it. You know, "If at first you don't succeed . . ."

Willy: Yes, I believe in that.

Bernard: But sometimes, Willy, it's better for a man just to walk away.

Willy: Walk away?

Bernard: That's right.

Willy: But if you can't walk away?

Bernard, (after a slight pause): I guess that's when it's tough. *(Extending his hand)* Good-by, Willy.

Willy, (shaking Bernard's *hand):* Good-by, boy.

Charley, (an arm on Bernard's *shoulder):* How do you like this kid? Gonna argue a case in front of the Supreme Court.

Bernard, (protesting): Pop!

Willy, (genuinely shocked, pained, and happy): No! The Supreme Court!

Bernard: I gotta run. 'By, Dad!

Charley: Knock 'em dead, Bernard!

Bernard *goes off.*

Willy, (as Charley *takes out his wallet):* The Supreme Court! And he didn't even mention it!

Charley, (counting out money on the desk): He don't have to—he's gonna do it.

Willy: And you never told him what to do, did you? You never took any interest in him.

Charley: My salvation is that I never took any interest in anything. There's some money—fifty dollars. I got an accountant inside.

Willy: Charley, look . . . *(With difficulty)* I got my insurance to pay. If you can manage it—I need a hundred and ten dollars.

Charley *doesn't reply for a moment; merely stops moving.*

Willy: I'd draw it from my bank but Linda would know, and I . . .

Charley: Sit down, Willy.

Willy, (moving toward the chair): I'm keeping an account of everything, remember. I'll pay every penny back. *(He sits.)*

Charley: Now listen to me, Willy.

Willy: I want you to know I appreciate . . .

Charley, (sitting down on the table): Willy, what're you doin'? What the hell is
goin' on in your head?

Willy: Why? I'm simply . . .

Charley: I offered you a job. You can make fifty dollars a week. And I won't
send you on the road.

Willy: I've got a job.

Charley: Without pay? What kind of a job is a job without pay? *(He rises.)*
Now, look, kid, enough is enough. I'm no genius but I know when I'm
being insulted.

Willy: Insulted!

Charley: Why don't you want to work for me?

Willy: What's the matter with you? I've got a job.

Charley: Then what're you walkin' in here every week for?

Willy, (getting up): Well, if you don't want me to walk in here—

Charley: I am offering you a job.

Willy: I don't want your goddam job!

Charley: When the hell are you going to grow up?

Willy, (furiously): You big ignoramus, if you say that to me again I'll rap you
one! I don't care how big you are! *(He's ready to fight.)*

Pause.

Charley, (kindly, going to him): How much do you need, Willy?

Willy: Charley, I'm strapped. I'm strapped. I don't know what to do. I was
just fired.

Charley: Howard fired you?

Willy: That snotnose. Imagine that? I named him. I named him Howard.

Charley: Willy, when're you gonna realize that them things don't mean anything? You named him Howard, but you can't sell that. The only thing
you got in this world is what you can sell. And the funny thing is that
you're a salesman, and you don't know that.

Willy: I've always tried to think otherwise, I guess. I always felt that if a man
was impressive, and well liked, that nothing—

Charley: Why must everybody like you? Who liked J. P. Morgan? Was he
impressive? In a Turkish bath he'd look like a butcher. But with his
pockets on he was very well liked. Now listen, Willy, I know you don't
like me, and nobody can say I'm in love with you, but I'll give you a job
because—just for the hell of it, put it that way. Now what do you say?

Willy: I—I just can't work for you, Charley.

Charley: What're you, jealous of me?

Willy: I can't work for you, that's all, don't ask me why.

Charley, (angered, takes out more bills): You been jealous of me all your life,
you damned fool! Here, pay your insurance. *(He puts the money in
Willy's hand.)*

Willy: I'm keeping strict accounts.

Charley: I've got some work to do. Take care of yourself. And pay your
insurance.

Willy, (moving to the right): Funny, y'know? After all the highways, and the

trains, and the appointments, and the years, you end up worth more
dead than alive.

Charley: Willy, nobody's worth nothin' dead. *(After a slight pause):* Did you
hear what I said?

Willy *stands still, dreaming.*

Charley: Willy!

Willy: Apologize to Bernard for me when you see him. I didn't mean to
argue with him. He's a fine boy. They're all fine boys, and they'll end up
big—all of them. Someday they'll all play tennis together. Wish me
luck, Charley. He saw Bill Oliver today.

Charley: Good luck.

Willy, (on the verge of tears): Charley, you're the only friend I got. Isn't that a
remarkable thing? *(He goes out.)*

Charley: Jesus!

Charley *stares after him a moment and follows. All light blacks out. Suddenly
raucous music is heard, and a red glow rises behind the screen at right.* Stanley, *a
young waiter, appears, carrying a table, followed by* Happy, *who is carrying
two chairs.*

Stanley, (putting the table down): That's all right, Mr. Loman, I can handle it
myself. *(He turns and takes the chairs from* Happy *and places them at the
table.)*

Happy, (glancing around): Oh, this is better.

Stanley: Sure, in the front there you're in the middle of all kinds a noise.
Whenever you got a party, Mr. Loman, you just tell me and I'll put you
back here. Y'know, there's a lotta people they don't like it private, because when they go out they like to see a lotta action around them because they're sick and tired to stay in the house by theirself. But I know
you, you ain't from Hackensack. You know what I mean?

Happy, (sitting down): So how's it coming, Stanley?

Stanley: Ah, it's a dog's life. I only wish during the war they'd a took me in
the Army. I coulda been dead by now.

Happy: My brother's back, Stanley.

Stanley: Oh, he come back, heh? From the Far West.

Happy: Yeah, big cattle man, my brother, so treat him right. And my father's
coming too.

Stanley: Oh, your father too!

Happy: You got a couple of nice lobsters?

Stanley: Hundred per cent, big.

Happy: I want them with the claws.

Stanley: Don't worry, I don't give you no mice. (Happy *laughs.)* How about
some wine? It'll put a head on the meal.

Happy: No. You remember, Stanley, that recipe I brought you from over-
seas? With the champagne in it?

Stanley: Oh, yeah, sure. I still got it tacked up yet in the kitchen. But that'll
have to cost a buck apiece anyways.

Happy: That's all right.

Stanley: What'd you, hit a number or somethin'?

Happy: No, it's a little celebration. My brother is—I think he pulled off a big deal today. I think we're going into business together.

Stanley: Great! That's the best for you. Because a family business, you know what I mean?—that's the best.

Happy: That's what I think.

Stanley: 'Cause what's the difference? Somebody steals? It's in the family. Know what I mean? *(Sotto voce)* Like this bartender here. The boss is goin' crazy what kinda leak he's got in the cash register. You put it in but it don't come out.

Happy, (raising his head): Sh!

Stanley: What?

Happy: You notice I wasn't lookin' right or left, was I?

Stanley: No.

Happy: And my eyes are closed.

Stanley: So what's the—?

Happy: Strudel's comin'.

Stanley, (catching on, looks around): Ah, no, there's no—

He breaks off as a furred, lavishly dressed girl enters and sits at the next table. Both follow her with their eyes.

Stanley: Geez, how'd ya know?

Happy: I got radar or something. *(Staring directly at her profile)* Ooooooooo . . . Stanley.

Stanley: I think that's for you, Mr. Loman.

Happy: Look at that mouth. Oh, God. And the binoculars.

Stanley: Geez, you got a life, Mr. Loman.

Happy: Wait on her.

Stanley, (going to the girl's table): Would you like a menu, ma'am?

Girl: I'm expecting someone, but I'd like a—

Happy: Why don't you bring her—excuse me, miss, do you mind? I sell champagne, and I'd like you to try my brand. Bring her a champagne, Stanley.

Girl: That's awfully nice of you.

Happy: Don't mention it. It's all company money. *(He laughs.)*

Girl: That's a charming product to be selling, isn't it?

Happy: Oh, gets to be like everything else. Selling is selling, y' know.

Girl: I suppose.

Happy: You don't happen to sell, do you?

Girl: No, I don't sell.

Happy: Would you object to a compliment from a stranger? You ought to be on a magazine cover.

Girl, (looking at him a little archly): I have been.

Stanley *comes in with a glass of champagne.*

Happy: What'd I say before, Stanley? You see? She's a cover girl.

Stanley: Oh, I could see, I could see.

Happy, (to the Girl*):* What magazine?

Girl: Oh, a lot of them. *(She takes the drink.)* Thank you.

Happy: You know what they say in France, don't you? "Champagne is the drink of the complexion"—Hya, Biff!

Biff *has entered and sits with* Happy.

Biff: Hello, kid. Sorry I'm late.

Happy: I just got here. Uh, Miss—?

Girl: Forsythe.

Happy: Miss Forsythe, this is my brother.

Biff: Is Dad here?

Happy: His name is Biff. You might've heard of him. Great football player.

Girl: Really? What team?

Happy: Are you familiar with football?

Girl: No, I'm afraid I'm not.

Happy: Biff is quarterback with the New York Giants.

Girl: Well, that is nice, isn't it? *(She drinks.)*

Happy: Good health.

Girl: I'm happy to meet you.

Happy: That's my name. Hap. It's really Harold, but at West Point they called me Happy.

Girl, (now really impressed): Oh, I see. How do you do? *(She turns her profile.)*

Biff: Isn't Dad coming?

Happy: You want her?

Biff: Oh, I could never make that.

Happy: I remember the time that idea would never come into your head. Where's the old confidence, Biff?

Biff: I just saw Oliver—

Happy: Wait a minute. I've got to see that old confidence again. Do you want her? She's on call.

Biff: Oh, no. *(He turns to look at the* Girl.*)*

Happy: I'm telling you. Watch this. *(Turning to the* Girl*)* Honey? *(She turns to him.)* Are you busy?

Girl: Well, I am . . . but I could make a phone call.

Happy: Do that, will you, honey? And see if you can get a friend. We'll be here for a while. Biff is one of the greatest football players in the country.

Girl, (standing up): Well, I'm certainly happy to meet you.

Happy: Come back soon.

Girl: I'll try.

Happy: Don't try, honey, try hard.

The Girl *exits.* Stanley *follows, shaking his head in bewildered admiration.*

Happy: Isn't that a shame now? A beautiful girl like that? That's why I can't get married. There's not a good woman in a thousand. New York is loaded with them, kid!

Biff: Hap, look—

Happy: I told you she was on call!

Biff, (strangely unnerved): Cut it out, will ya? I want to say something to you.

Happy: Did you see Oliver?

Biff: I saw him all right. Now look, I want to tell Dad a couple of things and I want you to help me.

Happy: What? Is he going to back you?

Biff: Are you crazy? You're out of your goddam head, you know that?

Happy: Why? What happened?

Biff, (breathlessly): I did a terrible thing today, Hap. It's been the strangest day I ever went through. I'm all numb, I swear.

Happy: You mean he wouldn't see you?

Biff: Well, I waited six hours for him, see? All day. Kept sending my name in. Even tried to date his secretary so she'd get me to him, but no soap.

Happy: Because you're not showin' the old confidence, Biff. He remembered you, didn't he?

Biff, (stopping Happy *with a gesture):* Finally, about five o'clock, he comes out. Didn't remember who I was or anything. I felt like such an idiot, Hap.

Happy: Did you tell him my Florida idea?

Biff: He walked away. I saw him for one minute. I got so mad I could've torn the walls down! How the hell did I ever get the idea I was a salesman there? I even believed myself that I'd been a salesman for him! And then he gave me one look and—I realized what a ridiculous lie my whole life has been! We've been talking in a dream for fifteen years. I was a shipping clerk.

Happy: What'd you do?

Biff, (with great tension and wonder): Well, he left, see. And the secretary went out. I was all alone in the waiting-room. I don't know what came over me, Hap. The next thing I know I'm in his office—paneled walls, everything. I can't explain it. I—Hap, I took his fountain pen.

Happy: Geez, did he catch you?

Biff: I ran out. I ran down all eleven flights. I ran and ran and ran.

Happy: That was an awful dumb—what'd you do that for?

Biff, (agonized): I don't know, I just—wanted to take something, I don't know. You gotta help me, Hap, I'm gonna tell Pop.

Happy: You crazy? What for?

Biff: Hap, he's got to understand that I'm not the man somebody lends that kind of money to. He thinks I've been spiting him all these years and it's eating him up.

Happy: That's just it. You tell him something nice.

Biff: I can't.

Happy: Say you got a lunch date with Oliver tomorrow.

Biff: So what do I do tomorrow?

Happy: You leave the house tomorrow and come back at night and say Oliver is thinking it over. And he thinks it over for a couple of weeks, and gradually it fades away and nobody's the worse.

Biff: But it'll go on forever!

Happy: Dad is never so happy as when he's looking forward to something!

Willy *enters.*

Happy: Hello, scout!

Willy: Gee, I haven't been here in years!

Stanley *has followed* Willy *in and sets a chair for him.* Stanley *starts off but* Happy *stops him.*

Happy: Stanley!

Stanley *stands by, waiting for an order.*

Happy, (going to Willy *with guilt, as to an invalid):* Sit down, Pop. You want a drink?

Willy: Sure, I don't mind.

Biff: Let's get a load on.

Willy: You look worried.

Biff: N-no. *(To* Stanley*):* Scotch all around. Make it doubles.

Stanley: Doubles, right. *(He goes.)*

Willy: You had a couple already, didn't you?

Biff: Just a couple, yeah.

Willy: Well, what happened, boy? *(Nodding affirmatively, with a smile)* Everything go all right?

Biff, (takes a breath, then reaches out and grasps Willy's *hand):* Pal . . . *(He is smiling bravely, and* Willy *is smiling too.)* I had an experience today.

Happy: Terrific, Pop.

Willy: That so? What happened?

Biff, (high, slightly alcoholic, above the earth): I'm going to tell you everything from first to last. It's been a strange day. *(Silence. He looks around, composes himself as best he can, but his breath keeps breaking the rhythm of his voice.)* I had to wait quite a while for him, and—

Willy: Oliver?

Biff: Yeah, Oliver. All day, as a matter of cold fact. And a lot of—instances— facts, Pop, facts about my life came back to me. Who was it, Pop? Who ever said I was a salesman with Oliver?

Willy: Well, you were.

Biff: No, Dad, I was a shipping clerk.

Willy: But you were practically—

Biff, (with determination): Dad, I don't know who said it first, but I was never a salesman for Bill Oliver.

Willy: What're you talking about?

Biff: Let's hold on to the facts tonight, Pop. We're not going to get any- where bullin' around. I was a shipping clerk.

Willy, (angrily): All right, now listen to me—

Biff: Why don't you let me finish?

Willy: I'm not interested in stories about the past or any crap of that kind because the woods are burning, boys, you understand? There's a big blaze going on all around. I was fired today.

Biff, (shocked): How could you be?

Willy: I was fired, and I'm looking for a little good news to tell your mother, because the woman has waited and the woman has suffered. The gist of it is that I haven't got a story left in my head, Biff. So don't give me a lecture about facts and aspects. I am not interested. Now what've you got to say to me?

Stanley *enters with three drinks. They wait until he leaves.*

Willy: Did you see Oliver?

Biff: Jesus, Dad!

Willy: You mean you didn't go up there?

Happy: Sure he went up there.

Biff: I did. I—saw him. How could they fire you?

Willy, (on the edge of his chair): What kind of a welcome did he give you?

Biff: He won't even let you work on commission?

Willy: I'm out! *(Driving):* So tell me, he gave you a warm welcome?

Happy: Sure, Pop, sure!

Biff, (driven): Well, it was kind of—

Willy: I was wondering if he'd remember you. *(To* Happy*)* Imagine, man doesn't see him for ten, twelve years and gives him that kind of a welcome!

Happy: Damn right!

Biff, (trying to return to the offensive): Pop, look—

Willy: You know why he remembered you, don't you? Because you impressed him in those days.

Biff: Let's talk quietly and get this down to the facts, huh?

Willy, (as though Biff *had been interrupting):* Well, what happened? It's great news, Biff. Did he take you into his office or'd you talk in the waiting-room?

Biff: Well, he came in, see, and—

Willy, (with a big smile): What'd he say? Betcha he threw his arm around you.

Biff: Well, he kinda—

Willy: He's a fine man. *(To* Happy*)* Very hard man to see, y'know.

Happy, (agreeing): Oh, I know.

Willy, (to Biff*):* Is that where you had the drinks?

Biff: Yeah, he gave me a couple of—no, no!

Happy, (cutting in): He told him my Florida idea.

Willy: Don't interrupt. *(To* Biff*)* How'd he react to the Florida idea?

Biff: Dad, will you give me a minute to explain?

Willy: I've been waiting for you to explain since I sat down here! What happened? He took you into his office and what?

Biff: Well—I talked. And—and he listened, see.

Willy: Famous for the way he listens, y'know. What was his answer?

Biff: His answer was— *(He breaks off, suddenly angry.)* Dad, you're not letting me tell you what I want to tell you!

Willy, (accusing, angered): You didn't see him, did you?

Biff: I did see him!

Willy: What'd you insult him or something? You insulted him, didn't you?

Biff: Listen, will you let me out of it, will you just let me out of it!
Happy: What the hell!
Willy: Tell me what happened!
Biff, (to Happy): I can't talk to him!

A single trumpet note jars the ear. The light of green leaves stains the house, which holds the air of night and a dream. Young Bernard *enters and knocks on the door of the house.*

Young Bernard, (frantically): Mrs. Loman, Mrs. Loman!
Happy: Tell him what happened!
Biff, (to Happy): Shut up and leave me alone!
Willy: No, no! You had to go and flunk math!
Biff: What math? What're you talking about?
Young Bernard: Mrs. Loman, Mrs. Loman!

Linda *appears in the house, as of old.*

Willy, (wildly): Math, math, math!
Biff: Take it easy, Pop!
Young Bernard: Mrs. Loman!
Willy, (furiously): If you hadn't flunked you'd've been set by now!
Biff: Now, look, I'm gonna tell you what happened, and you're going to listen to me.
Young Bernard: Mrs. Loman!
Biff: I waited six hours—
Happy: What the hell are you saying?
Biff: I kept sending in my name but he wouldn't see me. So finally he . . .
    (*He continues unheard as light fades low on the restaurant.*)
Young Bernard: Biff flunked math!
Linda: No!
Young Bernard: Birnbaum flunked him! They won't graduate him!
Linda: But they have to. He's gotta go to the university. Where is he? Biff! Biff!
Young Bernard: No, he left. He went to Grand Central.
Linda: Grand— You mean he went to Boston!
Young Bernard: Is Uncle Willy in Boston?
Linda: Oh, maybe Willy can talk to the teacher. Oh, the poor, poor boy!

Light on house area snaps out.

Biff, (at the table, now audible, holding up a gold fountain pen): . . . so I'm washed up with Oliver, you understand? Are you listening to me?
Willy, (at a loss): Yeah, sure. If you hadn't flunked—
Biff: Flunked what? What're you talking about?
Willy: Don't blame everything on me! I didn't flunk math—you did! What pen?
Happy: That was awful dumb, Biff, a pen like that is worth—
Willy, (seeing the pen for the first time): You took Oliver's pen?
Biff, (weakening): Dad, I just explained it to you.

Willy: You stole Bill Oliver's fountain pen!

Biff: I didn't exactly steal it! That's just what I've been explaining to you!

Happy: He had it in his hand and just then Oliver walked in, so he got nervous and stuck it in his pocket!

Willy: My God, Biff!

Biff: I never intended to do it, Dad!

Operator's Voice: Standish Arms, good evening!

Willy, (shouting): I'm not in my room!

Biff, (frightened): Dad, what's the matter? *(He and* Happy *stand up.)*

Operator: Ringing Mr. Loman for you!

Willy: I'm not there, stop it!

Biff, (horrified, gets down on one knee before Willy*):* Dad, I'll make good, I'll make good. (Willy *tries to get to his feet.* Biff *holds him down.)* Sit down now.

Willy: No, you're no good, you're no good for anything.

Biff: I am, Dad, I'll find something else, you understand? Now don't worry about anything. *(He holds up* Willy's *face)* Talk to me, dad.

Operator: Mr. Loman does not answer. Shall I page him?

Willy, (attempting to stand, as though to rush and silence the Operator*):* No, no, no!

Happy: He'll strike something, Pop.

Willy: No, no . . .

Biff, (desperately, standing over Willy*):* Pop, listen! Listen to me! I'm telling you something good. Oliver talked to his partner about the Florida idea. You listening? He—he talked to his partner, and he came to me . . . I'm going to be all right, you hear? Dad, listen to me, he said it was just a question of the amount!

Willy: Then you . . . got it?

Happy: He's gonna be terrific, Pop!

Willy, (trying to stand): Then you got it, haven't you? You got it! You got it!

Biff, (agonized, holds Willy *down):* No, no. Look, Pop. I'm supposed to have lunch with them tomorrow. I'm just telling you this so you'll know that I can still make an impression, Pop. And I'll make good somewhere, but I can't go tomorrow, see?

Willy: Why not? You simply—

Biff: But the pen, Pop!

Willy: You give it to him and tell him it was an oversight!

Happy: Sure, have lunch tomorrow!

Biff: I can't say that—

Willy: You were doing a crossword puzzle and accidentally used his pen!

Biff: Listen, kid, I took those balls years ago, now I walk in with his fountain pen? That clinches it, don't you see? I can't face him like that! I'll try elsewhere.

Page's Voice: Paging Mr. Loman!

Willy: Don't you want to be anything?

Biff: Pop, how can I go back?

Willy: You don't want to be anything, is that what's behind it?

Biff, (*now angry at* Willy *for not crediting his sympathy*): Don't take it that way! You think it was easy walking into that office after what I'd done to him? A team of horses couldn't have dragged me back to Bill Oliver!

Willy: Then why'd you go?

Biff: Why did I go? Why did I go! Look at you! Look at what's become of you!

Off left, The Woman *laughs.*

Willy: Biff, you're going to go to that lunch tomorrow, or—

Biff: I can't go. I've got no appointment!

Happy: Biff, for . . . !

Willy: Are you spiting me?

Biff: Don't take it that way! Goddammit!

Willy, (*strikes* Biff *and falters away from the table*): You rotten little louse! Are you spiting me?

The Woman: Someone's at the door, Willy!

Biff: I'm no good, can't you see what I am?

Happy, (*separating them*): Hey, you're in a restaurant! Now cut it out, both of you! (*The girls enter.*) Hello, girls, sit down.

The Woman *laughs, off left.*

Miss Forsythe: I guess we might as well. This is Letta.

The Woman: Willy, are you going to wake up?

Biff, (*ignoring* Willy): How're ya, miss, sit down. What do you drink?

Miss Forsythe: Letta might not be able to stay long.

Letta: I gotta get up very early tomorrow. I got jury duty. I'm so excited! Were you fellows ever on a jury?

Biff: No, but I been in front of them! (*The girls laugh.*) This is my father.

Letta: Isn't he cute? Sit down with us, Pop.

Happy: Sit him down, Biff!

Biff, (*going to him*): Come on, slugger, drink us under the table. To hell with it! Come on, sit down, pal.

On Biff's *last insistence,* Willy *is about to sit.*

The Woman, (*now urgently*): Willy, are you going to answer the door!

The Woman's *call pulls* Willy *back. He starts right, befuddled.*

Biff: Hey, where are you going?

Willy: Open the door.

Biff: The door?

Willy: The washroom . . . the door . . . where's the door?

Happy, (*leading* Willy *to the left*): Just go straight down.

Willy *moves left.*

The Woman: Willy, Willy, are you going to get up, get up, get up, get up?

Willy *exits left.*

Letta: I think it's sweet you bring your daddy along.

Miss Forsythe: Oh, he isn't really your father!

Biff, (at left, turning to her resentfully): Miss Forsythe, you've just seen a prince walk by. A fine, troubled prince. A hardworking, unappreciated prince. A pal, you understand? A good companion. Always for his boys.

Letta: That's so sweet.

Happy: Well, girls, what's the program? We're wasting time. Come on, Biff. Gather round. Where would you like to go?

Biff: Why don't you do something for him?

Happy: Me!

Biff: Don't you give a damn for him, Hap?

Happy: What're you talking about? I'm the one who—

Biff: I sense it, you don't give a good goddam about him. (*He takes the rolled-up hose from his pocket and puts it on the table in front of* Happy.) Look what I found in the cellar, for Christ's sake. How can you bear to let it go on?

Happy: Me? Who goes away? Who runs off and—

Biff: Yeah, but he doesn't mean anything to you. You could help him—I can't! Don't you understand what I'm talking about? He's going to kill himself, don't you know that?

Happy: Don't I know it! Me!

Biff: Hap, help him! Jesus . . . help him . . . Help me, help me, I can't bear to look at his face! (*Ready to weep, he hurries out, up right.*)

Happy, (starting after him): Where are you going?

Miss Forsythe: What's he so mad about?

Happy: Come on, girls, we'll catch up with him.

Miss Forsythe, (as Happy *pushes her out):* Say, I don't like that temper of his!

Happy: He's just a little overstrung, he'll be all right!

Willy, (off left, as The Woman *laughs):* Don't answer! Don't answer!

Letta: Don't you want to tell your father—

Happy: No, that's not my father. He's just a guy. Come on, we'll catch Biff, and, honey, we're going to paint this town! Stanley, where's the check! Hey, Stanley!

They exit. Stanley *looks toward left.*

Stanley, (calling to Happy *indignantly):* Mr. Loman! Mr. Loman!

Stanley *picks up a chair and follows them off. Knocking is heard off left.* The Woman *enters, laughing.* Willy *follows her. She is in a black slip; he is buttoning his shirt. Raw, sensuous music accompanies their speech.*

Willy: Will you stop laughing? Will you stop?

The Woman: Aren't you going to answer the door? He'll wake the whole hotel.

Willy: I'm not expecting anybody.

The Woman: Whyn't you have another drink, honey, and stop being so damn self-centered?

Willy: I'm so lonely.

The Woman: You know you ruined me, Willy? From now on, whenever you

come to the office, I'll see that you go right through to the buyers. No
waiting at my desk any more, Willy. You ruined me.

Willy: That's nice of you to say that.

The Woman: Gee, you are self-centered! Why so sad? You are the saddest,
self-centeredest soul I ever did see-saw. *(She laughs. He kisses her.)* Come
on inside, drummer boy. It's silly to be dressing in the middle of the
night. *(As knocking is heard)* Aren't you going to answer the door?

Willy: They're knocking on the wrong door.

The Woman: But I felt the knocking. And he heard us talking in here. Maybe
the hotel's on fire!

Willy, (his terror rising): It's a mistake.

The Woman: Then tell him to go away!

Willy: There's nobody there.

The Woman: It's getting on my nerves, Willy. There's somebody standing
out there and it's getting on my nerves!

Willy, (pushing her away from him): All right, stay in the bathroom here, and
don't come out. I think there's a law in Massachusetts about it, so don't
come out. It may be that new room clerk. He looked very mean. So
don't come out. It's a mistake, there's no fire.

*The knocking is heard again. He takes a few steps away from her, and she
vanishes into the wing. The light follows him, and now he is facing* Young Biff,
who carries a suitcase. Biff *steps toward him. The music is gone.*

Biff: Why didn't you answer?

Willy: Biff! What are you doing in Boston?

Biff: Why didn't you answer? I've been knocking for five minutes, I called
you on the phone—

Willy: I just heard you. I was in the bathroom and had the door shut. Did
anything happen home?

Biff: Dad—I let you down.

Willy: What do you mean?

Biff: Dad . . .

Willy: Biffo, what's this about? *(Putting his arm around* Biff*)* Come on, let's
go downstairs and get you a malted.

Biff: Dad, I flunked math.

Willy: Not for the term?

Biff: The term. I haven't got enough credits to graduate.

Willy: You mean to say Bernard wouldn't give you the answers?

Biff: He did, he tried, but I only got a sixty-one.

Willy: And they wouldn't give you four points?

Biff: Birnbaum refused absolutely. I begged him, Pop, but he won't give me
those points. You gotta talk to him before they close the school. Because
if he saw the kind of man you are, and you just talked to him in your
way, I'm sure he'd come through for me. The class came right before
practice, see, and I didn't go enough. Would you talk to him? He'd like
you, Pop. You know the way you could talk.

Willy: You're on. We'll drive right back.

Biff: Oh, Dad, good work! I'm sure he'll change it for you!

Willy: Go downstairs and tell the clerk I'm checkin' out. Go right down.

Biff: Yes, sir! See, the reason he hates me, Pop—one day he was late for class so I got up at the blackboard and imitated him. I crossed my eyes and talked with a lithp.

Willy, (laughing): You did? The kids like it?

Biff: They nearly died laughing!

Willy: Yeah? What'd you do?

Biff: The thquare root of thixthy twee is . . . (Willy *bursts out laughing; Biff joins him.*) And in the middle of it he walked in!

Willy *laughs and* The Woman *joins in offstage.*

Willy, (without hesitation): Hurry downstairs and—

Biff: Somebody in there?

Willy: No, that was next door.

The Woman *laughs offstage.*

Biff: Somebody got in your bathroom!

Willy: No, it's the next room, there's a party—

The Woman, (enters, laughing. She lisps this): Can I come in? There's something in the bathtub, Willy, and it's moving!

Willy *looks at* Biff, *who is staring open-mouthed and horrified at* The Woman.

Willy: Ah—you better go back to your room. They must be finished painting by now. They're painting her room so I let her take a shower here. Go back, go back . . . (*He pushes her.*)

The Woman, (resisting): But I've got to get dressed, Willy, I can't—

Willy: Get out of here! Go back, go back . . . (*Suddenly striving for the ordinary*) This is Miss Francis, Biff, she's a buyer. They're painting her room. Go back, Miss Francis, go back . . .

The Woman: But my clothes, I can't go out naked in the hall!

Willy, (pushing her offstage): Get outa here! Go back, go back!

Biff *slowly sits down on his suitcase as the argument continues offstage.*

The Woman: Where's my stockings? You promised me stockings, Willy!

Willy: I have no stockings here!

The Woman: You had two boxes of size nine sheers for me, and I want them!

Willy: Here, for God's sake, will you get outa here!

The Woman, (enters holding a box of stockings): I just hope there's nobody in the hall. That's all I hope. (*To Biff*) Are you football or baseball?

Biff: Football.

The Woman, (angry, humiliated): That's me too. G'night. (*She snatches her clothes from* Willy, *and walks out.*)

Willy, (after a pause): Well, better get going. I want to get to the school first thing in the morning. Get my suits out of the closet. I'll get my valise. (Biff *doesn't move.*) What's the matter? (Biff *remains motionless, tears falling.)* She's a buyer. Buys for J. H. Simmons. She lives down the hall—they're painting. You don't imagine— *(He breaks off. After a pause)* Now listen, pal, she's just a buyer. She sees merchandise in her room and they have to keep it looking just so . . . *(Pause. Assuming command)* All right, get my suits. *(Biff doesn't move.)* Now stop crying and do as I say. I gave you an order. Biff, I gave you an order! Is that what you do when I give you an order? How dare you cry! *(Putting his arm around Biff)* Now look, Biff, when you grow up you'll understand about these things. You mustn't—you mustn't overemphasize a thing like this. I'll see Birnbaum first thing in the morning.

Biff: Never mind.

Willy, (getting down beside Biff): Never mind! He's going to give you those points. I'll see to it.

Biff: He wouldn't listen to you.

Willy: He certainly will listen to me. You need those points for the U. of Virginia.

Biff: I'm not going there.

Willy: Heh? If I can't get him to change that mark you'll make it up in summer school. You've got all summer to—

Biff, (his weeping breaking from him): Dad . . .

Willy, (infected by it): Oh, my boy . . .

Biff: Dad . . .

Willy: She's nothing to me, Biff. I was lonely, I was terribly lonely.

Biff: You—you gave her Mama's stockings! *(His tears break through and he rises to go.)*

Willy, (grabbing for Biff): I gave you an order!

Biff: Don't touch me, you—liar!

Willy: Apologize for that!

Biff: You fake! You phony little fake! You fake! *(Overcome, he turns quickly and weeping fully goes out with his suitcase. Willy is left on the floor on his knees.)*

Willy: I gave you an order! Biff, come back here or I'll beat you! Come back here! I'll whip you!

Stanley *comes quickly in from the right and stands in front of* Willy.

Willy, (shouts at Stanley): I gave you an order . . .

Stanley: Hey, let's pick it up, pick it up, Mr. Loman. *(He helps Willy to his feet.)* Your boys left with the chippies. They said they'll see you home.

A second waiter watches some distance away.

Willy: But we were supposed to have dinner together.

Music is heard, Willy's theme.

Stanley: Can you make it?

Willy: I'll—sure, I can make it. *(Suddenly concerned about his clothes):* Do I—I look all right?

Stanley: Sure, you look all right. *(He flicks a speck off Willy's lapel.)*

Willy: Here—here's a dollar.

Stanley: Oh, your son paid me. It's all right.

Willy, (putting it in Stanley's *hand):* No, take it. You're a good boy.

Stanley: Oh, no, you don't have to . . . .

Willy: Here—here's some more, I don't need it any more. *(After a slight pause)* Tell me—is there a seed store in the neighborhood?

Stanley: Seeds? You mean like to plant?

As Willy *turns,* Stanley *slips the money back into his jacket pocket.*

Willy: Yes. Carrots, peas . . .

Stanley: Well, there's hardware stores on Sixth Avenue, but it may be too late now.

Willy, (anxiously): Oh, I'd better hurry. I've got to get some seeds. *(He starts off to the right.)* I've got to get some seeds, right away. Nothing's planted. I don't have a thing in the ground.

Willy *hurries out as the light goes down.* Stanley *moves over to the right after him, watches him off. The other waiter has been staring at* Willy.

Stanley, (to the waiter): Well, whatta you looking at?

The waiter picks up the chairs and moves off right. Stanley *takes the table and follows him. The light fades on this area. There is a long pause, the sound of the flute coming over. The light gradually rises on the kitchen, which is empty.* Happy *appears at the door of the house, followed by* Biff. Happy *is carrying a large bunch of long-stemmed roses. He enters the kitchen, looks around for* Linda. *Not seeing her, he turns to* Biff, *who is just outside the house door, and makes a gesture with his hands, indicating "Not here, I guess." He looks into the living-room and freezes. Inside,* Linda, *unseen, is seated,* Willy's *coat on her lap. She rises ominously and quietly and moves toward* Happy, *who backs up into the kitchen, afraid.*

Happy: Hey, what're you doing up? (Linda *says nothing but moves toward him implacably.)* Where's Pop? *(He keeps backing to the right, and now* Linda *is in full view in the doorway to the living-room.)* Is he sleeping?

Linda: Where were you?

Happy, (trying to laugh it off): We met two girls, Mom, very fine types. Here, we brought you some flowers. *(Offering them to her)* Put them in your room, Ma.

She knocks them to the floor at Biff's *feet. He has now come inside and closed the door behind him. She stares at* Biff, *silent.*

Happy: Now what'd you do that for? Mom, I want you to have some flowers—

Linda, (cutting Happy *off, violently to* Biff): Don't you care whether he lives or dies?

Happy, (going to the stairs): Come upstairs, Biff.

Biff, (with a flare of disgust, to Happy): Go away from me! *(To* Linda*)* What do you mean, lives or dies? Nobody's dying around here, pal.

Linda: Get out of my sight! Get out of here!

Biff: I wanna see the boss.

Linda: You're not going near him!

Biff: Where is he? *(He moves into the living-room and* Linda *follows.)*

Linda, (shouting after Biff*):* You invite him for dinner. He looks forward to it all day—(Biff *appears in his parents' bedroom, looks around, and exits)*—and then you desert him there. There's no stranger you'd do that to!

Happy: Why? He had a swell time with us. Listen, when I—(Linda *comes back into the kitchen)*—desert him I hope I don't outlive the day!

Linda: Get out of here!

Happy: Now look, Mom . . .

Linda: Did you have to go to women tonight? You and your lousy rotten whores!

Biff *re-enters the kitchen.*

Happy: Mom, all we did was follow Biff around trying to cheer him up! (To Biff*): Boy, what a night you gave me!*

Linda: Get out of here, both of you, and don't come back! I don't want you tormenting him any more. Go on now, get your things together! *(To* Biff*)* You can sleep in his apartment. *(She starts to pick up the flowers and stops herself.)* Pick up this stuff, I'm not your maid any more. Pick it up, you bum, you!

Happy *turns his back to her in refusal.* Biff *slowly moves over and gets down on his knees, picking up the flowers.*

Linda: You're a pair of animals! Not one, not another living soul would have had the cruelty to walk out on that man in a restaurant!

Happy, (not looking at her): Is that what he said?

Linda: He didn't have to say anything. He was so humiliated he nearly limped when he came in.

Happy: But, Mom, he had a great time with us—

Biff, (cutting him off violently): Shut up!

Without another word, Happy *goes upstairs.*

Linda: You! You didn't even go in to see if he was all right!

Biff, (still on the floor in front of Linda, *the flowers in his hand; with self-loathing)* No. Didn't. Didn't do a damned thing. How do you like that, heh? Left him babbling in a toilet.

Linda: You louse. You . . .

Biff: Now you hit it on the nose! *(He gets up, throws the flowers in the waste-basket.)* The scum of the earth, and you're looking at him!

Linda: Get out of here!

Biff: I gotta talk to the boss, Mom. Where is he?

Linda: You're not going near him. Get out of this house!

Biff, (with absolute assurance, determination): No. We're gonna have an abrupt conversation, him and me.

Linda: You're not talking to him!

Hammering is heard from outside the house, off right. Biff *turns toward the noise.*

Linda, *(suddenly pleading):* Will you please leave him alone?
Biff: What's he doing out there?
Linda: He's planting the garden!
Biff, *(quietly):* Now? Oh, my God!

Biff *moves outside,* Linda *following. The light dies down on them and comes up on the center of the apron as* Willy *walks into it. He is carrying a flashlight, a hoe, and a handful of seed packets. He raps the top of the hoe sharply to fix it firmly, and then moves to the left, measuring off the distance with his foot. He holds the flashlight to look at the seed packets, reading off the instructions. He is in the blue of night.*

Willy: Carrots . . . quarter-inch apart. Rows . . . one-foot rows. *(He measures it off.)* One foot. *(He puts down a package and measures off.)* Beets. *(He puts down another package and measures again.)* Lettuce. *(He reads the package, puts it down.)* One foot—*(He breaks off as* Ben *appears at the right and moves slowly down to him.)* What a proposition, ts, ts. Terrific, terrific. 'Cause she's suffered, Ben, the woman has suffered. You understand me? A man can't go out the way he came in, Ben, a man has to, to add up to something. You can't, you can't—*(Ben moves toward him as though to interrupt.)* You gotta consider, now. Don't answer so quick. Remember, it's a guaranteed twenty-thousand-dollar proposition. Now look, Ben, I want you to go through the ins and outs of this thing with me. I've got nobody to talk to, Ben, and the woman has suffered, you hear me?
Ben, *(standing still, considering):* What's the proposition?
Willy: It's twenty thousand dollars on the barrelhead. Guaranteed, gilt-edged, you understand?
Ben: You don't want to make a fool of yourself. They might not honor the policy.
Willy: How can they dare refuse? Didn't I work like a coolie to meet every premium on the nose? And now they don't pay off? Impossible!
Ben: It's called a cowardly thing, William.
Willy: Why? Does it take more guts to stand here the rest of my life ringing up a zero?
Ben, *(yielding):* That's a point, William. *(He moves, thinking, turns.)* And twenty thousand—that *is* something one can feel with the hand, it is there.
Willy, *(now assured, with rising power):* Oh, Ben, that's the whole beauty of it! I see it like a diamond, shining in the dark, hard and rough, that I can pick up and touch in my hand. Not like—like an appointment! This would not be another damned-fool appointment, Ben, and it changes all the aspects. Because he thinks I'm nothing, see, and so he spites me. But the funeral— *(Straightening up)* Ben, that funeral will be massive! They'll come from Maine, Massachusetts, Vermont, New Hampshire!

All the old-timers with the strange license plates—that boy will be
thunder-struck, Ben, because he never realized—I am known! Rhode
Island, New York, New Jersey—I am known, Ben, and he'll see it with
his eyes once and for all. He'll see what I am, Ben! He's in for a shock,
that boy!

Ben, (coming down to the edge of the garden): He'll call you a coward.

Willy, (suddenly fearful): No, that would be terrible.

Ben: Yes. And a damned fool.

Willy: No, no, he mustn't, I won't have that! *(He is broken and desperate.)*

Ben: He'll hate you, William.

The gay music of the Boys is heard.

Willy: Oh, Ben, how do we get back to all the great times? Used to be
so full of light, and comradeship, the sleigh-riding in winter, and
the ruddiness on his cheeks. And always some kind of good news
coming up, always something nice coming up ahead. And never even
let me carry the valises in the house, and simonizing, simonizing that
little red car! Why, why can't I give him something and not have him
hate me?

Ben: Let me think about it. *(He glances at his watch.)* I still have a little time.
Remarkable proposition, but you've got to be sure you're not making a
fool of yourself.

Ben drifts off upstage and goes out of sight. Biff comes down from the left.

*Willy, (suddenly conscious of Biff, turns and looks up at him, then begins picking up
the packages of seeds in confusion):* Where the hell is that seed? *(Indignantly)*
You can't see nothing out here! They boxed in the whole goddam neighborhood!

Biff: There are people all around here. Don't you realize that?

Willy: I'm busy. Don't bother me.

Biff, (taking the hoe from Willy): I'm saying good-by to you, Pop. *(Willy
looks at him, silent, unable to move.)* I'm not coming back any more.

Willy: You're not going to see Oliver tomorrow ?

Biff: I've got no appointment, Dad.

Willy: He put his arm around you, and you've got no appointment?

Biff: Pop, get this now, will you? Everytime I've left it's been a fight that
sent me out of here. Today I realized something about myself and I tried
to explain it to you and I—I think I'm just not smart enough to make
any sense out of it for you. To hell with whose fault it is or anything like
that. *(He takes Willy's arm.)* Let's just wrap it up, heh? Come on in, we'll
tell Mom. *(He gently tries to pull Willy to left.)*

Willy, (frozen, immobile, with guilt in his voice): No, I don't want to see her.

Biff: Come on! *(He pulls again, and Willy tries to pull away.)*

Willy, (highly nervous): No, no, I don't want to see her.

Biff, (tries to look into Willy's face, as if to find the answer there): Why don't you
want to see her?

Willy, (more harshly now): Don't bother me, will you?

Biff: What do you mean, you don't want to see her? You don't want them calling you yellow, do you? This isn't your fault; it's me, I'm a bum. Now come inside! (Willy *strains to get away.*) Did you hear what I said to you?

Willy *pulls away and quickly goes by himself into the house.* Biff *follows.*

Linda, (to Willy): Did you plant, dear?

Biff, (at the door, to Linda): All right, we had it out. I'm going and I'm not writing any more.

Linda, (going to Willy *in the kitchen):* I think that's the best way, dear. 'Cause there's no use drawing it out, you'll just never get along.

Willy *doesn't respond.*

Biff: People ask where I am and what I'm doing, you don't know, and you don't care. That way it'll be off your mind and you can start brightening up again. All right? That clears it, doesn't it? (Willy *is silent, and* Biff *goes to him.*) You gonna wish me luck, scout? (*He extends his hand.*) What do you say?

Linda: Shake his hand, Willy.

Willy, (turning to her, seething with hurt): There's no necessity to mention the pen at all, y'know.

Biff, (gently): I've got no appointment, Dad.

Willy, (erupting fiercely): He put his arm around . . . ?

Biff: Dad, you're never going to see what I am, so what's the use of arguing? If I strike oil I'll send you a check. Meantime forget I'm alive.

Willy, (to Linda): Spite, see?

Biff: Shake hands, Dad.

Willy: Not my hand.

Biff: I was hoping not to go this way.

Willy: Well, this is the way you're going. Good-by.

Biff *looks at him a moment, then turns sharply and goes to the stairs.*

Willy, (stops him with): May you rot in hell if you leave this house!

Biff, (turning): Exactly what is it that you want from me?

Willy: I want you to know, on the train, in the mountains, in the valleys, wherever you go, that you cut down your life for spite!

Biff: No, no.

Willy: Spite, spite, is the word for your undoing! And when you're down and out, remember what did it. When you're rotting somewhere beside the railroad tracks, remember, and don't you dare blame it on me!

Biff: I'm not blaming it on you!

Willy: I won't take the rap for this, you hear?

Happy *comes down the stairs and stands on the bottom step, watching.*

Biff: That's just what I'm telling you!

Willy, (sinking into a chair at the table, with full accusation): You're trying to put a knife in me—don't think I don't know what you're doing!

Biff: All right, phony! Then let's lay it on the line. *(He whips the rubber tube out of his pocket and puts it on the table.)*

Happy: You crazy—

Linda: Biff! *(She moves to grab the hose, but* Biff *holds it down with his hand.)*

Biff: Leave it there! Don't move it!

Willy, (not looking at it): What is that?

Biff: You know goddam well what that is.

Willy, (caged, wanting to escape): I never saw that.

Biff: You saw it. The mice didn't bring it into the cellar! What is this supposed to do, make a hero out of you? This supposed to make me sorry for you?

Willy: Never heard of it.

Biff: There'll be no pity for you, you hear it? No pity!

Willy, (to Linda*)*: You hear the spite!

Biff: No, you're going to hear the truth—what you are and what I am!

Linda: Stop it!

Willy: Spite!

Happy, (coming down toward Biff*)*: You cut it now!

Biff, (to Happy*)*: The man don't know who we are! The man is gonna know! *(To* Willy*)* We never told the truth for ten minutes in this house!

Happy: We always told the truth!

Biff, (turning on him): You big blow, are you the assistant buyer? You're one of the two assistants to the assistant, aren't you?

Happy: Well, I'm practically—

Biff: You're practically full of it! We all are! And I'm through with it. *(To* Willy*)*: Now hear this, Willy, this is me.

Willy: I know you!

Biff: You know why I had no address for three months? I stole a suit in Kansas City and I was in jail. *(To* Linda, *who is sobbing)* Stop crying. I'm through with it.

Linda *turns away from them, her hands covering her face.*

Willy: I suppose that's my fault!

Biff: I stole myself out of every good job since high school!

Willy: And whose fault is that?

Biff: And I never got anywhere because you blew me so full of hot air I could never stand taking orders from anybody! That's whose fault it is!

Willy: I hear that!

Linda: Don't, Biff!

Biff: It's goddam time you heard that! I had to be boss big shot in two weeks, and I'm through with it!

Willy: Then hang yourself! For spite, hang yourself!

Biff: No! Nobody's hanging himself, Willy! I ran down eleven flights with a pen in my hand today. And suddenly I stopped, you hear me? And in the middle of that office building, do you hear this? I stopped in the middle of that building and I saw—the sky. I saw the things that I love in this world. The work and the food and time to sit and smoke. And I looked at the pen and said to myself, what the hell am I grabbing this for? Why am I trying to become what I don't want to be? What am I doing in an office, making a contemptuous, begging fool of myself, when all I want is out there, waiting for me the minute I say I know who I am! Why can't I say that, Willy? *(He tries to make* Willy *face him, but* Willy *pulls away and moves to the left.)*

Willy, (with hatred, threateningly): The door of your life is wide open!

Biff: Pop! I'm a dime a dozen, and so are you!

Willy, (turning on him now in an uncontrolled outburst): I am not a dime a dozen! I am Willy Loman, and you are Biff Loman!

Biff *starts for* Willy, *but is blocked by* Happy. *In his fury,* Biff *seems on the verge of attacking his father.*

Biff: I am not a leader of men, Willy, and neither are you. You were never anything but a hard-working drummer who landed in the ash can like all the rest of them! I'm one dollar an hour, Willy! I tried seven states and couldn't raise it. A buck an hour! Do you gather my meaning? I'm not bringing home any prizes any more, and you're going to stop waiting for me to bring them home!

Willy, (directly to Biff*):* You vengeful, spiteful mut!

Biff *breaks from* Happy. Willy, *in fright, starts up the stairs.* Biff *grabs him.*

Biff, (at the peak of his fury): Pop, I'm nothing! I'm nothing, Pop. Can't you understand that? There's no spite in it any more. I'm just what I am, that's all.

Biff's *fury has spent itself, and he breaks down, sobbing, holding on to* Willy, *who dumbly fumbles for* Biff's *face.*

Willy, (astonished): What're you doing? What're you doing? *(To* Linda*):* Why is he crying?

Biff, (crying, broken): Will you let me go, for Christ's sake? Will you take that phony dream and burn it before something happens? *(Struggling to contain himself, he pulls away and moves to the stairs.)* I'll go in the morning. Put him—put him to bed. *(Exhausted,* Biff *moves up the stairs to his room.)*

Willy, (after a long pause, astonished, elevated): Isn't that—isn't that remarkable? Biff—he likes me!

Linda: He loves you, Willy!

Happy, (deeply moved): Always did, Pop.

Willy: Oh, Biff! *(Staring wildly):* He cried! Cried to me. *(He is choking with his love, and now cries out his promise)* That boy—that boy is going to be magnificent!

Ben *appears in the light just outside the kitchen.*

Ben: Yes, outstanding, with twenty thousand behind him.

Linda, (sensing the racing of his mind, fearfully, carefully): Now come to bed, Willy. It's all settled now.

Willy, (finding it difficult not to rush out of the house): Yes, we'll sleep. Come
on. Go to sleep, Hap.

Ben: And it does take a great kind of a man to crack the jungle.

In accents of dread, Ben's *idyllic music starts up.*

Happy, (his arm around Linda*):* I'm getting married, Pop, don't forget it. I'm
changing everything. I'm gonna run that department before the year is
up. You'll see, Mom. *(He kisses her.)*

Ben: The jungle is dark but full of diamonds, Willy.

Willy *turns, moves, listening to* Ben.

Linda: Be good. You're both good boys, just act that way, that's all.

Happy: 'Night, Pop. *(He goes upstairs.)*

Linda, (to Willy): Come, dear.

Ben, (with greater force): One must go in to fetch a diamond out.

Willy, (to Linda, *as he moves slowly along the edge of the kitchen, toward the
door):* I just want to get settled down, Linda. Let me sit alone for a
little.

Linda, (almost uttering her fear): I want you upstairs.

Willy, (taking her in his arms): In a few minutes, Linda. I couldn't sleep right
now. Go on, you look awful tired. *(He kisses her.)*

Ben: Not like an appointment at all. A diamond is rough and hard to
the touch.

Willy: Go on now. I'll be right up.

Linda: I think this is the only way, Willy.

Willy: Sure, it's the best thing.

Ben: Best thing!

Willy: The only way. Everything is gonna be—go on, kid, get to bed. You
look so tired.

Linda: Come right up.

Willy: Two minutes.

Linda *goes into the living-room, then reappears in her bedroom.* Willy *moves
just outside the kitchen door.*

Willy: Loves me. *(Wonderingly)* Always loved me. Isn't that a remarkable
thing? Ben, he'll worship me for it!

Ben, (with promise): It's dark there, but full of diamonds.

Willy: Can you imagine that magnificence with twenty thousand dollars in
his pocket?

Linda, (calling from her room): Willy! Come up!

Willy, (calling into the kitchen): Yes! Yes. Coming! It's very smart, you realize
that, don't you, sweetheart! Even Ben sees it. I gotta go, baby. 'By! 'By!
(Going over to Ben, *almost dancing)* Imagine? When the mail comes he'll
be ahead of Bernard again!

Ben: A perfect proposition all around.

Willy: Did you see how he cried to me? Oh, if I could kiss him, Ben!

Ben: Time, William, time!

Willy: Oh, Ben, I always knew one way or another we were gonna make it, Biff and I!

Ben, (looking at his watch): The boat. We'll be late. *(He moves slowly off into the darkness.)*

Willy, (elegiacally, turning to the house): Now when you kick off, boy, I want a seventy-yard boot, and get right down the field under the ball, and when you hit, hit low and hit hard, because it's important, boy. *(He swings around and faces the audience.)* There's all kinds of important people in the stands, and the first thing you know . . . *(Suddenly realizing he is alone)* Ben! Ben, where do I . . . ? *(He makes a sudden movement of search.)* Ben, how do I . . . ?

Linda, (calling): Willy, you coming up?

Willy, (uttering a gasp of fear, whirling about as if to quiet her): Sh! *(He turns around as if to find his way; sounds, faces, voices, seem to be swarming in upon him and he flicks at them, crying)*, Sh! Sh! *(Suddenly music, faint and high, stops him. It rises in intensity, almost to an unbearable scream. He goes up and down on his toes, and rushes off around the house.)* Shhh!

Linda: Willy?

　　There is no answer. Linda waits. Biff gets up off his bed. He is still in his clothes. Happy sits up. Biff stands listening.

Linda, (with real fear): Willy, answer me! Willy!

　　There is the sound of a car starting and moving away at full speed.

Linda: No!

Happy, (rushing down the stairs): Pop!

　　As the car speeds off, the music crashes down in a frenzy of sound, which becomes the soft pulsation of a single cello string. Biff slowly returns to his bedroom. He and Happy gravely don their jackets. Linda slowly walks out of her room. The music has developed into a dead march. The leaves of day are appearing over everything. Charley and Bernard, somberly dressed, appear and knock on the kitchen door. Biff and Happy slowly descend the stairs to the kitchen as Charley and Bernard enter. All stop a moment when Linda, in clothes of mourning, bearing a little bunch of roses, comes through the draped doorway into the kitchen. She goes to Charley and takes his arm. Now all move toward the audience, through the wall-line of the kitchen. At the limit of the apron, Linda lays down the flowers, kneels, and sits back on her heels. All stare down at the grave.

REQUIEM

Charley: It's getting dark, Linda.

　　Linda doesn't react. She stares at the grave.

Biff: How about it, Mom? Better get some rest, heh? They'll be closing the gate soon.

Linda *makes no move. Pause.*

Happy, (deeply angered): He had no right to do that. There was no necessity
for it. We would've helped him.

Charley, (grunting): Hmmm.

Biff: Come along, Mom.

Linda: Why didn't anybody come?

Charley: It was a very nice funeral.

Linda: But where are all the people he knew? Maybe they blame him.

Charley: Naa. It's a rough world, Linda. They wouldn't blame him.

Linda: I can't understand it. At this time especially. First time in thirty-five
years we were just about free and clear. He only needed a little salary.
He was even finished with the dentist.

Charley: No man only needs a little salary.

Linda: I can't understand it.

Biff: There were a lot of nice days. When he'd come home from a trip; or
on Sundays, making the stoop; finishing the cellar; putting on the new
porch; when he built the extra bathroom; and put up the garage. You
know something, Charley, there's more of him in that front stoop than
in all the sales he ever made.

Charley: Yeah. He was a happy man with a batch of cement.

Linda: He was so wonderful with his hands.

Biff: He had the wrong dreams. All, all wrong.

Happy, (almost ready to fight Biff*):* Don't say that!

Biff: He never knew who he was.

Charley, (stopping Happy's *movement and reply. To* Biff*):* Nobody dast blame
this man. You don't understand: Willy was a salesman. And for a salesman, there is no rock bottom to the life. He don't put a bolt to a nut, he
don't tell you the law or give you medicine. He's a man way out there in
the blue, riding on a smile and a shoeshine. And when they start not
smiling back—that's an earthquake. And then you get yourself a couple
of spots on your hat, and you're finished. Nobody dast blame this man.
A salesman is got to dream, boy. It comes with the territory.

Biff: Charley, the man didn't know who he was.

Happy, (infuriated): Don't say that!

Biff: Why don't you come with me, Happy?

Happy: I'm not licked that easily. I'm staying right in this city, and I'm
gonna beat this racket! *(He looks at* Biff, *his chin set.)* The Loman
Brothers!

Biff: I know who I am, kid.

Happy: All right, boy. I'm gonna show you and everybody else that Willy
Loman did not die in vain. He had a good dream. It's the only dream
you can have—to come out number-one man. He fought it out here,
and this is where I'm gonna win it for him.

Biff, (with a hopeless glance at Happy, *bends toward his mother):* Let's go, Mom.

Linda: I'll be with you in a minute. Go on, Charley. *(He hesitates.)* I want to,
just for a minute. I never had a chance to say good-by.

Charley *moves away, followed by* Happy. Biff *remains a slight distance up and left of* Linda. *She sits there, summoning herself. The flute begins, not far away, playing behind her speech.*

Linda: Forgive me, dear. I can't cry. I don't know what it is, but I can't cry. I don't understand it. Why did you ever do that? Help me, Willy, I can't cry. It seems to me that you're just on another trip. I keep expecting you. Willy, dear, I can't cry. Why did you do it? I search and search and I search, and I can't understand it, Willy. I made the last payment on the house today. Today, dear. And there'll be nobody home. (*A sob rises in her throat.*) We're free and clear. (*Sobbing more fully, released*) We're free. (Biff *comes slowly toward her.*) We're free . . . We're free . . .

Biff *lifts her to her feet and moves out up right with her in his arms.* Linda *sobs quietly.* Bernard *and* Charley *come together and follow them, followed by* Happy. *Only the music of the flute is left on the darkening stage as over the house the hard towers of the apartment buildings rise into sharp focus, and*

THE CURTAIN FALLS

——— ARTHUR MILLER ———
(b. 1915) Web   *www*

Arthur Miller was born in Manhattan to a manufacturer father and school-teacher mother. Moving to Brooklyn when he was thirteen and living there during the Great Depression, Miller and his family hovered on the brink of poverty, barely able to pay the mortgage. His older brother dropped out of college to help his father struggle in the garment business, and Miller worked for two years after graduating from high school before attending and eventually graduating from the University of Michigan. He wrote scripts for radio and then, in the early 1940s, one of his early plays received a New York production. He has gone on to win countless awards for such plays as *All My Sons, The Crucible* (1953), his parable of the Communist witch-hunts of the 1950s, *A View from the Bridge* (1955) and, more recently, *Broken Glass* (1994). His very early play *The Man Who Had All the Luck*, a failure when first produced in 1944, was revived in 2002. He has written screenplays and travel books, including an account of *Death of a Salesman* in China, and is widely considered to be one of the great dramatists in the history of the American theater.

TOPICS FOR CRITICAL THINKING

1. What specific techniques take Miller beyond "straight realism" in *Death of a Salesman*? What do these add to Miller's development of Willy?

2. Does Linda Loman in any way help perpetuate Willy's fantasies of success? Consider, for example, her lines in the play's closing scene. What do they imply about her unwillingness to face the truth of her husband's life?

3. What is the function of the scene involving Willy's adultery? Obviously, it shatters Biff's illusions about his father, but does it suggest anything else about Willy and his life?

4. Is Willy's speculation about Biff at the end of the play accurate? Could he take the life insurance money and become the kind of success Willy imagines? Could Happy?

5. Does this play constitute an indictment of capitalism or American business? Or does Willy have only himself to blame for his failures?

TOPIC FOR CRITICAL WRITING

How does *Death of a Salesman* comment on the so-called American Dream? Define this dream as presented in the play. Has it changed much since the late 1940s?

Critical Perspective: On the Appeal of *Death of a Salesman* in 1949

"Arthur Miller's play . . . appealed strongly to an undercurrent of rebellion against the Almighty Dollar. It had a special appeal to the big-city audience, for the Loman family is typical of second- and third-generation Americans of Jewish, Italian, German, Irish, or Russian origin who pursued material success with a singleness of purpose."

—Barnard Hewitt, *Theatre U.S.A.* (1959)

Critical Perspective: On Miller, Tennessee Williams, and the Great Depression

"Any account of post-war theatre in America must begin not with the war . . . , but with the Depression. It was an experience that shaped both Arthur Miller and Tennessee Williams who began to write not in the forties but the thirties, the former creating a series of protest plays, the latter working with a radical theatre company. . . . The loss of dignity and self-assurance which Miller saw as the one legacy of the [Stock Market] Crash clearly left its mark on Willy Loman as it did on Amanda Wingfield. The sense of promises turned to dust, of the individual suddenly severed from a world that had seemed secure, underlies much of their work. The shock which both writers express seems to derive from their sense of the fragility of the social world, the thinness of the membrane that separates us from chaos. That conviction was shaped by the events of a decade that began with economic débâcle and ended with war in Europe."

—C. W. E. Bigsby, *Modern American Drama, 1945–1990* (1992)

Critical Perspective: On Miller's Achievement in *Death of a Salesman*

"The balance between expressionistic and realistic moments in *Death of a Salesman* is both its essence and its highest achievement. Through this delicate balance, Miller found a form to dramatize the intermingling of individual psychology and social forces, which is one of his greatest themes. . . .

"German expressionists were involved in a political and philosophical movement as well as in an aesthetic revolution. Most were opposed to realism and naturalism because they glorified science, which the expressionists associated with industrialism and technology, tools of the materialist society they sought to change. In contrast, they criticized the neoromantics for their flight from contemporary social problems.

"*Death of a Salesman* may be seen as a summation of both the early and late stages of German expressionism."

—Barbara Lounsberry, "'The Woods Are Burning':
Expressionism in *Death of a Salesman*" (1995)

48 Absurdism

In a book on Samuel Beckett from the late 1960s, British publisher John Calder made a startling prediction: "More books have been written on Christ, Napoleon, and Wagner, in that order, than on anyone else. I predict that by A.D. 2000 Beckett may well rank fourth if the present flood of Beckett literature keeps up." Calder's prediction, of course, cannot be taken as an entirely serious one, since no statistical account has ever been constructed in support of it. If this data did exist, however, such writers as Chaucer, Shakespeare, and Proust would almost certainly be on it. Yet, if the list were limited to artists working only in the middle and last half of the twentieth century, Samuel Beckett's name would almost certainly appear right at the top.

This claim, like Calder's, may seem overstated, almost ridiculous. Yet if the field measured considered writers influenced by Beckett's career as a dramatist, the case would be compelling. It might begin with Harold Pinter, a vital force in British drama himself since the late 1950s, and Tom Stoppard; it surely would include such prolific and important American playwrights as Edward Albee, David Mamet, and Sam Shepard. Even Tennessee Williams, a celebrated dramatist by the time so-called absurdism reached America in the late 1950s and early 1960s, realized its importance and formal radicalism. And, for a time, he despaired of ever being able to compete with it. The list might also be extended to account for the famous directors, actors, and actresses associated with Beckett's plays: Billie Whitelaw, Tom Ewell, Bert Lahr, Hume Cronyn, Jessica Tandy, Alan Schneider, and Andre Gregory. Even such popular film actors as Robin Williams and Steve Martin have taken their turns on stage in Beckett's plays.

It is also true that Beckett's influential reach has much to do with his relationship to both an older *modernism* and a younger *postmodernism*, to both Anglo-Irish letters and to French literature, and to the evolution of twentieth-century fiction and drama. Educated at Dublin's Trinity College in modern languages, he traveled to Paris in the late 1920s, quickly becoming a friend of and assistant to his countryman James Joyce, who was then working on a manuscript that would eventually become *Finnegans Wake* (1939). By this time Joyce's *Ulysses* (1922) had become widely regarded as representing the cutting edge of literary modernism, and young Beckett followed his friend's lead by embarking on a career as a writer of short stories and novels. But by the time World War II began and was concluded, his career as a fiction writer had not advanced so far as he had hoped. In the early 1950s, he turned to drama with such plays as *Waiting for Godot* (1953), *Endgame* (1957), *Krapp's Last Tape* (1958), and *Happy Days* (1961), writing all of them in French first, then translating them back into English. In the process, he introduced a kind of drama the world had never seen before, one combining largely comic techniques borrowed from vaudeville with the serious philosophy of a post-war Europe reeling from a World War, the Holocaust, and the specter of nuclear annihilation.

The Philosophical Roots of Absurdism

As Martin Esslin contends in his influential book *The Theatre of the Absurd* (1961), all the substitute religions in which many mid-twentieth-century people believed—"progress, nationalism, and various totalitarian fallacies"— were "shattered" by the horrors of World War II. Building his definition from the works of writers like Albert Camus and Franz Kafka, Esslin also alludes to an insight offered by the dramatist Eugène Ionesco: "Absurd is that which is devoid of purpose. . . . Cut off from his religious, metaphysical, and transcendental roots, man is lost; his actions become senseless, absurd, useless." Religion and metaphysics, in other words, help explain what we are, offering consolations at times of disaster and death when reason proves inadequate. And one promise of both religion and metaphysics is transcendence: We will be rewarded in the next life for sacrifices we make in this one. Our existence *transcends*, extends meaningfully beyond, the here and now.

For many people, the war challenged these beliefs. For the German philosopher Theodor Adorno, Beckett's work, especially *Endgame*, reveals this sad state of affairs. "Everything," he writes, "has been destroyed. . . . Humankind continues to vegetate, creeping along after events that even the survivors cannot really survive." For Adorno, a particularly important part of plays like *Endgame* is the way it, unlike the realistic drama of Henrik Ibsen and Anton Chekhov, negates "precisely the particularity, individuation in time and space, that makes existence existence and not the mere concept of existence." That is to say, there is little question when and where *Hedda Gabler* or *The Cherry Orchard* occurs. In the former, the dramatic action takes place in the middle class home of late-nineteenth-century Norwegians; in the latter, it occurs on a family estate in turn-of-the-century Russia. By contrast, *Endgame* and most of Beckett's plays take place anywhere and everywhere: on the sides of roads, in a mound of dirt, in a room variously described as a bomb shelter or, even, the inside of a head. The life represented in Beckett's drama, then, is not British, Russian, or Norwegian; it is human existence everywhere. The essential, as Hamm gloomily remarks in the play, does not change: "there's no reason for it to change."

For Polish writer Jan Kott, *Endgame* resembles Shakespeare's *King Lear* (1605) in that neither play presents the decline of vital tragic heroes like Oedipus, Macbeth, or Othello. Instead, the tragic element of drama has been "superseded by grotesque," which is "more cruel than tragedy." In both the tragic and grotesque theaters, he argues, "situations are imposed, compulsory and inescapable." Freedom of choice or "agency" must be a part of this compulsory situation, but in the grotesque the "absolute" against which the characters struggle is "transformed into a blind mechanism." Meaningful choices do not exist—or all choices are equally bad. In this sense, following Ionesco, grotesque comedy is more hopeless than tragedy, rendering the dramatic situation absurd or futile. In such a drama, the clown takes center stage, as no room for traditional heroism exists. One sentence from *King Lear* summarizes this worldview. When Edgar encounters his blinded father Gloucester wandering on the heath, he laments: "As flies to wanton boys are we to th' gods, / They kill us for their sport" (4.1.36–37). This is the cruelty and capriciousness of a world grown absurd.

Endgame and Absurdist Form

Beckett insisted that the form and content of his drama were identical, that the form in some senses *was* its content. If so, then the form of *Endgame*— indeed, its very title alluding to the final strategies employed in a game of chess—might be construed as identical with its content. Taking place on a checkerboard floor in a shelter surrounded by death, whatever nimble pawns, rooks, and bishops that once existed are gone. All that remains are Hamm, a blind monarch who cannot stand; Clov, a servant unable to sit; and two aged parents who are completely immobile and dependent on their son Hamm's generosity. Unlike tragedy, which normally occurs at a time of personal, even national, import for its protagonists, and comedy, which usually leads to a conciliatory and happy ending—a special time like marriage—*Endgame* emphasizes the monotony of the ordinary. As Hamm observes early in the play, "It's the end of the day like any other day, isn't it, Clov?" It's another day of existence in an exhausted world running out of everything, and it's a play staged on a nearly barren stage very different from the settings of realistic and expressionistic drama.

In such a world, little things mean everything: a stuffed dog missing a leg, fresh sand at the bottom of a trash can, the possibility of a flea's existence. Perhaps the most significant of these precious commodities is language. Yet unlike language in realistic drama, dialogue in Beckett's plays does not necessarily individuate his characters or further the action. Rather, dialogue and language allow characters to indulge in whatever possibilities for humor or witticisms remain to them. Language leads to comic banter, to storytelling, and the expression of dreams or other imaginary products that sustain life in such austere circumstances. Words, which in Beckett's later works seem as sparse as material comforts are, remain to be savored and used, however imperfect they are at capturing reality.

Thus, when Nell tells Nagg in *Endgame* that "nothing is funnier than unhappiness"—that sorrow is "the most comical thing in the world" until it is experienced so often that it isn't funny anymore—she might have been describing Beckett's plays. They are often incredibly clever, loaded with physical humor and wit. They are also presentational, sparkling in performance in a way that they never do on the printed page. Indeed, some of the humor originates in the characters' obvious recognition that they are performing in a play, a recognition called **meta-theatre.** That is to say, the pretense that the action is "really" happening is occasionally broken by obvious references to the theater and stage that dispel such an illusion. Nonetheless, Beckett also emphasizes the harsh, even absurd realities of living in deteriorating bodies for a brief time before our lights, like Mother Pegg's in the play, burn out. Beckett's sense of grotesque humor—the comic elements of our failing bodies and fated lives—parallels that of the vaudeville slapstick humor he so much admired.

The action of *Endgame* nominally leads to its final tableau: Clov, who has vowed to leave Hamm, is frozen in place and "dressed for the road," while Hamm, ever the "ham actor," delivers his soliloquy. Does Clov ever leave? We don't know. And it may not really matter given the world—our world—in which this play takes place. The essential does not change. Life is lived out to its last instant. One day we are born, the next day we die. On the days in between we endure, filling in the time with whatever activities we can find to entertain us and provide us with a reason to continue. Such an existence, Beckett seems to say, is neither inherently tragic nor comic. It simply *is*—until it isn't any longer.

∞∞

SAMUEL BECKETT

Endgame (1957)
A Play in One Act

THE CHARACTERS

Nagg
Nell
Hamm
Clov

(Bare interior.)
   (Gray light.)
   (Left and right back, high up, two small windows, curtains drawn.)
   (Front right, a door. Hanging near door, its face to wall, a picture.)
   (Front left, touching each other, covered with an old sheet, two ashbins.°)
   (Center, in an armchair on casters, covered with an old sheet, Hamm.)
   (Motionless by the door, his eyes fixed on Hamm, Clov. Very red face.)
   (Brief tableau.)

   (Clov goes and stands under window left. Stiff, staggering walk. He looks up at window left. He turns and looks at window right. He goes and stands under window right. He looks up at window right. He turns and looks at window left. He goes out, comes back immediately with a small stepladder, carries it over and sets it down under window left, gets up on it, draws back curtain. He gets down, takes six

---

ashbins: trash cans

*steps (for example) towards window right, goes back for ladder, carries it over and
sets it down under window right, gets up on it, draws back curtain. He gets down,
takes three steps towards window left, goes back for ladder, carries it over and sets it
down under window left, gets up on it, looks out of window. Brief laugh. He gets
down, takes one step towards window right, goes back for ladder, carries it over and
sets it down under window right, gets up on it, looks out of window. Brief laugh. He
gets down, goes with ladder towards ashbins, halts, turns, carries back ladder and
sets it down under window right, goes to ashbins, removes sheet covering them, folds
it over his arm. He raises one lid, stoops and looks into bin. Brief laugh. He closes
lid. Same with other bin. He goes to Hamm, removes sheet covering him, folds it
over his arm. In a dressing gown, a stiff toque° on his head, a large bloodstained
handkerchief over his face, a whistle hanging from his neck, a rug over his knees,
thick socks on his feet,* Hamm *seems to be asleep.* Clov *looks over him. Brief laugh.
He goes to door, halts, turns towards auditorium.)*

Clov *(fixed gaze, tonelessly):* Finished, it's finished, nearly finished, it must be
nearly finished.

> *(Pause.)*

> Grain upon grain, one by one, and one day, suddenly, there's a heap, a
> little heap, the impossible heap.

> *(Pause.)*

> I can't be punished anymore.

> *(Pause.)*

> I'll go now to my kitchen, ten feet by ten feet by ten feet, and wait for
> him to whistle me.

> *(Pause.)*

> Nice dimensions, nice proportions, I'll lean on the table, and look at the
> wall, and wait for him to whistle me.

*(He remains a moment motionless, then goes out. He comes back immediately,
goes to window right, takes up the ladder and carries it out. Pause.* Hamm *stirs. He
yawns under the handkerchief. He removes the handkerchief from his face. Very red
face. Black glasses.)*

Hamm: Me—*(he yawns)*—to play.

(He holds the handkerchief spread out before him.)

Old stancher!°

*(He takes off his glasses, wipes his eyes, his face, the glasses, puts them on again,
folds the handkerchief and puts it back neatly in the breast pocket of his dressing
gown. He clears his throat, joins the tips of his fingers.)*

---

toque: A small, brimless, close-fitting hat.   *stancher:* Item that stops, or stanches, the flow of
blood.

Can there be misery—*(he yawns)*—loftier than mine? No doubt. Formerly. But now?

(Pause.)

My father?

(Pause.)

My mother?

(Pause.)

My . . . dog?

(Pause.)

Oh I am willing to believe they suffer as much as such creatures can suffer. But does that mean their sufferings equal mine? No doubt.

(Pause.)

No, all is a—*(he yawns)*—bsolute, *(proudly)* the bigger a man is the fuller he is.

(Pause. Gloomily.)

And the emptier.

(He sniffs.)

Clov!

(Pause.)

No, alone.

(Pause.)

What dreams! Those forests!

(Pause.)

Enough, it's time it ended, in the shelter too.

(Pause.)

And yet I hesitate, I hesitate to . . . to end. Yes there it is, it's time it ended and yet I hesitate to—*(he yawns)*—to end.

(Yawns.)

God, I'm tired, I'd be better off in bed.

(He whistles. Enter Clov *immediately. He halts beside the chair.)*

You pollute the air!

(Pause.)

Get me ready, I'm going to bed.

Clov: I've just got you up.

Hamm: And what of it?

Clov: I can't be getting you up and putting you to bed every five minutes, I have things to do.

(*Pause.*)

Hamm: Did you ever see my eyes?

Clov: No.

Hamm: Did you never have the curiosity, while I was sleeping, to take off my glasses and look at my eyes?

Clov: Pulling back the lids?

(*Pause.*)

No.

Hamm: One of these days I'll show them to you.

(*Pause.*)

It seems they've gone all white.

(*Pause.*)

What time is it?

Clov: The same as usual.

Hamm (*gesture towards window right*): Have you looked?

Clov: Yes.

Hamm: Well?

Clov: Zero.

Hamm: It'd need to rain.

Clov: It won't rain.

(*Pause.*)

Hamm: Apart from that, how do you feel?

Clov: I don't complain.

Hamm: You feel normal?

Clov (*irritably*): I tell you I don't complain.

Hamm: I feel a little queer.

(*Pause.*)

Clov!

Clov: Yes.

Hamm: Have you not had enough?

Clov: Yes!

(*Pause.*)

Of what?

Hamm: Of this . . . this . . . thing.

Clov: I always had.

(Pause.)

Not you?

Hamm (gloomily): Then there's no reason for it to change.

Clov: It may end.

(Pause.)

All life long the same questions, the same answers.

Hamm: Get me ready.

(Clov does not move.)

Go and get the sheet.

(Clov does not move.)

Clov!

Clov: Yes.

Hamm: I'll give you nothing more to eat.

Clov: Then we'll die.

Hamm: I'll give you just enough to keep you from dying. You'll be hungry all the time.

Clov: Then we won't die.

(Pause.)

I'll go and get the sheet.

(He goes towards the door.)

Hamm: No!

(Clov halts.)

I'll give you one biscuit per day.

(Pause.)

One and a half.

(Pause.)

Why do you stay with me?

Clov: Why do you keep me?

Hamm: There's no one else.

Clov: There's nowhere else.

(Pause.)

Hamm: You're leaving me all the same.

Clov: I'm trying.

Hamm: You don't love me.

Clov: No.

Hamm: You loved me once.

Clov: Once!

Hamm: I've made you suffer too much.

(*Pause.*)

Haven't I?

Clov: It's not that.

Hamm (shocked): I haven't made you suffer too much?

Clov: Yes!

Hamm (relieved): Ah you gave me a fright!

(*Pause. Coldly.*)

Forgive me.

(*Pause. Louder.*)

I said, Forgive me.

Clov: I heard you.

(*Pause.*)

Have you bled?

Hamm: Less.

(*Pause.*)

Is it not time for my painkiller?

Clov: No.

(*Pause.*)

Hamm: How are your eyes?

Clov: Bad.

Hamm: How are your legs?

Clov: Bad.

Hamm: But you can move.

Clov: Yes.

Hamm (violently): Then move!

(*Clov goes to back wall, leans against it with his forehead and hands.*)

Where are you?

Clov: Here.

Hamm: Come back!

(*Clov returns to his place beside the chair.*)

Where are you?

Clov: Here.

Hamm: Why don't you kill me?

Clov: I don't know the combination of the cupboard.

(*Pause.*)

Hamm: Go and get two bicycle wheels.

Clov: There are no more bicycle wheels.
Hamm: What have you done with your bicycle?
Clov: I never had a bicycle.
Hamm: The thing is impossible.
Clov: When there were still bicycles I wept to have one. I crawled at your feet. You told me to go to hell. Now there are none.
Hamm: And your rounds? When you inspected my paupers. Always on foot?
Clov: Sometimes on horse.

(*The lid of one of the bins lifts and the hands of* Nagg *appear, gripping the rim. Then his head emerges. Nightcap. Very white face.* Nagg *yawns, then listens.*)

I'll leave you, I have things to do.
Hamm: In your kitchen?
Clov: Yes.
Hamm: Outside of here it's death.

(*Pause.*)

All right, be off.

(*Exit* Clov. *Pause.*)

We're getting on.
Nagg: Me pap!
Hamm: Accursed progenitor!
Nagg: Me pap!
Hamm: The old folks at home! No decency left! Guzzle, guzzle, that's all they think of.

(*He whistles. Enter* Clov. *He halts beside the chair.*)

Well! I thought you were leaving me.
Clov: Oh not just yet, not just yet.
Nagg: Me pap!
Hamm: Give him his pap.
Clov: There's no more pap.
Hamm (to Nagg*):* Do you hear that? There's no more pap. You'll never get any more pap.
Nagg: I want me pap!
Hamm: Give him a biscuit.

(*Exit* Clov.)

Accursed fornicator! How are your stumps?
Nagg: Never mind me stumps.

(*Enter* Clov *with biscuit.*)

Clov: I'm back again, with the biscuit.

(*He gives biscuit to* Nagg *who fingers it, sniffs it.*)

Nagg (plaintively): What is it?
Clov: Spratt's medium.
Nagg (as before): It's hard! I can't!
Hamm: Bottle him!

(Clov *pushes Nagg* back into the bin, closes the lid.)

Clov (returning to his place beside the chair): If age but knew!
Hamm: Sit on him!
Clov: I can't sit.
Hamm: True. And I can't stand.
Clov: So it is.
Hamm: Every man his speciality.

(Pause.)

No phone calls?

(Pause.)

Don't we laugh?
Clov (after reflection): I don't feel like it.
Hamm (after reflection): Nor I.

(Pause.)

Clov!
Clov: Yes.
Hamm: Nature has forgotten us.
Clov: There's no more nature.
Hamm: No more nature! You exaggerate.
Clov: In the vicinity.
Hamm: But we breathe, we change! We lose our hair, our teeth! Our bloom!
    Our ideals!
Clov: Then she hasn't forgotten us.
Hamm: But you say there is none.
Clov (sadly): No one that ever lived ever thought so crooked as we.
Hamm: We do what we can.
Clov: We shouldn't.

(Pause.)

Hamm: You're a bit of all right, aren't you?
Clov: A smithereen.

(Pause.)

Hamm: This is slow work.

(Pause.)

Is it not time for my painkiller?
Clov: No.

(Pause.)

I'll leave you, I have things to do.

Hamm: In your kitchen?

Clov: Yes.

Hamm: What, I'd like to know.

Clov: I look at the wall.

Hamm: The wall! And what do you see on your wall? Mene, mene?° Naked bodies?

Clov: I see my light dying.

Hamm: Your light dying! Listen to that! Well, it can die just as well here, *your* light. Take a look at me and then come back and tell me what you think of *your* light.

(Pause.)

Clov: You shouldn't speak to me like that.

(Pause.)

Hamm (coldly): Forgive me.

(Pause. Louder.)

I said, Forgive me.

Clov: I heard you.

(The lid of Nagg's *bin lifts. His hands appear, gripping the rim. Then his head emerges. In his mouth the biscuit. He listens.)*

Hamm: Did your seeds come up?

Clov: No.

Hamm: Did you scratch round them to see if they had sprouted?

Clov: They haven't sprouted.

Hamm: Perhaps it's still too early.

Clov: If they were going to sprout they would have sprouted.

(Violently.)

They'll never sprout!

(Pause. Nagg takes biscuit in his hand.)*

Hamm: This is not much fun.

(Pause.)

But that's always the way at the end of the day, isn't it, Clov?

Clov: Always.

Hamm: It's the end of the day like any other day, isn't it, Clov?

———

Mene, mene: The handwriting on the wall in Daniel 5:25 indicating the end of King Belshazzar's reign: "MENE, MENE, TEKEL, and PARSIN."

Clov: Looks like it.

    (Pause.)

Hamm (anguished): What's happening, what's happening?
Clov: Something is taking its course.

    (Pause.)

Hamm: All right, be off.

    (He leans back in his chair, remains motionless. Clov does not move, heaves a great groaning sigh. Hamm sits up.)

    I thought I told you to be off.
Clov: I'm trying.

    (He goes to door, halts.)

    Ever since I was whelped.

    (Exit Clov.)

Hamm: We're getting on.

    (He leans back in his chair, remains motionless. Nagg knocks on the lid of the other bin. Pause. He knocks harder. The lid lifts and the hands of Nell appear, gripping the rim. Then her head emerges. Lace cap. Very white face.)

Nell: What is it, my pet?

    (Pause.)

    Time for love?
Nagg: Were you asleep?
Nell: Oh no!
Nagg: Kiss me.
Nell: We can't.
Nagg: Try.

    (Their heads strain towards each other, fail to meet, fall apart again.)

Nell: Why this farce, day after day?

    (Pause.)

Nagg: I've lost me tooth.
Nell: When?
Nagg: I had it yesterday.
Nell (elegiac): Ah yesterday!

    (They turn painfully towards each other.)

Nagg: Can you see me?
Nell: Hardly. And you?
Nagg: What?
Nell: Can you see me?

Nagg: Hardly.
Nell: So much the better, so much the better.
Nagg: Don't say that.

(*Pause.*)

Our sight has failed.
Nell: Yes.

(*Pause. They turn away from each other.*)

Nagg: Can you hear me?
Nell: Yes. And you?
Nagg: Yes.

(*Pause.*)

Our hearing hasn't failed.
Nell: Our what?
Nagg: Our hearing.
Nell: No.

(*Pause.*)

Have you anything else to say to me?
Nagg: Do you remember—
Nell: No.
Nagg: When we crashed on our tandem and lost our shanks.

(*They laugh heartily.*)

Nell: It was in the Ardennes.

(*They laugh less heartily.*)

Nagg: On the road to Sedan.

(*They laugh still less heartily.*)

Are you cold?
Nell: Yes, perished. And you?
Nagg:

(*Pause.*)

I'm freezing.

(*Pause.*)

Do you want to go in?
Nell: Yes.
Nagg: Then go in.

(Nell *does not move.*)

Why don't you go in?
Nell: I don't know.

(Pause.)

Nagg: Has he changed your sawdust?
Nell: It isn't sawdust.

(Pause. Wearily.)

Can you not be a little accurate, Nagg?
Nagg: Your sand then. It's not important.
Nell: It is important.

(Pause.)

Nagg: It was sawdust once.
Nell: Once!
Nagg: And now it's sand.

(Pause.)

From the shore.

(Pause. Impatiently.)

Now it's sand he fetches from the shore.
Nell: Now it's sand.
Nagg: Has he changed yours?
Nell: No.
Nagg: Nor mine.

(Pause.)

I won't have it!

(Pause. Holding up the biscuit.)

Do you want a bit?
Nell: No.

(Pause.)

Of what?
Nagg: Biscuit. I've kept you half.

(He looks at the biscuit. Proudly.)

Three quarters. For you. Here.

(He proffers the biscuit.)

No?

(Pause.)

Do you not feel well?
Hamm (wearily): Quiet, quiet, you're keeping me awake.

(Pause.)

Talk softer.

(*Pause.*)

If I could sleep I might make love. I'd go into the woods. My eyes would see . . . the sky, the earth. I'd run, run, they wouldn't catch me.

(*Pause.*)

Nature!

(*Pause.*)

There's something dripping in my head.

(*Pause.*)

A heart, a heart in my head.

(*Pause.*)

Nagg (soft): Do you hear him? A heart in his head!

(*He chuckles cautiously.*)

Nell: One mustn't laugh at those things, Nagg. Why must you always laugh at them?
Nagg: Not so loud!
Nell (without lowering her voice): Nothing is funnier than unhappiness, I grant you that. But—
Nagg (shocked): Oh!
Nell: Yes, yes, it's the most comical thing in the world. And we laugh, we laugh, with a will, in the beginning. But it's always the same thing. Yes, it's like the funny story we have heard too often, we still find it funny, but we don't laugh anymore.

(*Pause.*)

Have you anything else to say to me?
Nagg: No.
Nell: Are you quite sure?

(*Pause.*)

Then I'll leave you.
Nagg: Do you not want your biscuit?

(*Pause.*)

I'll keep it for you.

(*Pause.*)

I thought you were going to leave me.
Nell: I am going to leave you.
Nagg: Could you give me a scratch before you go?

Nell: No.

(*Pause.*)

Where?
Nagg: In the back.
Nell: No.

(*Pause.*)

Rub yourself against the rim.
Nagg: It's lower down. In the hollow.
Nell: What hollow?
Nagg: The hollow!

(*Pause.*)

Could you not?

(*Pause.*)

Yesterday you scratched me there.
Nell (elegiac): Ah yesterday!
Nagg: Could you not?

(*Pause.*)

Would you like me to scratch you?

(*Pause.*)

Are you crying again?
Nell: I was trying.

(*Pause.*)

Hamm: Perhaps it's a little vein.

(*Pause.*)

Nagg: What was that he said?
Nell: Perhaps it's a little vein.
Nagg: What does that mean?

(*Pause.*)

That means nothing.

(*Pause.*)

Will I tell you the story of the tailor?
Nell: No.

(*Pause.*)

What for?
Nagg: To cheer you up.
Nell: It's not funny.

Nagg: It always made you laugh.

(*Pause.*)

The first time I thought you'd die.
Nell: It was on Lake Como.

(*Pause.*)

One April afternoon.

(*Pause.*)

Can you believe it?
Nagg: What?
Nell: That we once went out rowing on Lake Como.

(*Pause.*)

One April afternoon.
Nagg: We had got engaged the day before.
Nell: Engaged!
Nagg: You were in such fits that we capsized. By rights we should have been drowned.
Nell: It was because I felt happy.
Nagg (indignant): It was not, it was not, it was my story and nothing else. Happy! Don't you laugh at it still? Every time I tell it. Happy!
Nell: It was deep, deep. And you could see down to the bottom. So white. So clean.
Nagg: Let me tell it again.

(*Raconteur's voice.*)

An Englishman, needing a pair of striped trousers in a hurry for the New Year festivities, goes to his tailor who takes his measurements.

(*Tailor's voice.*)

"That's the lot, come back in four days, I'll have it ready." Good. Four days later.

(*Tailor's voice.*)

"So sorry, come back in a week, I've made a mess of the seat." Good, that's all right, a neat seat can be very ticklish. A week later.

(*Tailor's voice.*)

"Frightfully sorry, come back in ten days, I've made a hash of the crotch." Good, can't be helped, a snug crotch is always a teaser. Ten days later.

(*Tailor's voice.*)

"Dreadfully sorry, come back in a fortnight, I've made a balls of the fly." Good, at a pinch, a smart fly is a stiff proposition.

(Pause. Normal voice.)

I never told it worse.

(Pause. Gloomy.)

I tell this story worse and worse.

(Pause. Raconteur's voice.)

Well, to make it short, the bluebells are blowing and he ballockses the buttonholes.

(Customer's voice.)

"God damn you to hell, Sir, no, it's indecent, there are limits! In six days, do you hear me, six days, God made the world. Yes Sir, no less Sir, the WORLD! And you are not bloody well capable of making me a pair of trousers in three months!"

(Tailor's voice, scandalized.)

"But my dear Sir, my dear Sir, look—*(disdainful gesture, disgustedly)*—at the world—*(pause)* and look—*(loving gesture, proudly)*—at my TROUSERS!"

(Pause. He looks at Nell *who has remained impassive, her eyes unseeing, breaks into a high forced laugh, cuts it short, pokes his head towards* Nell, *launches his laugh again.)*

Hamm: Silence!

(Nagg starts, cuts short his laugh.)

Nell: You could see down to the bottom.
Hamm *(exasperated)*: Have you not finished? Will you never finish?

(With sudden fury.)

Will this never finish?

(Nagg disappears into his bin, closes the lid behind him. Nell *does not move. Frenziedly.)*

My kingdom for a nightman!

(He whistles. Enter Clov.)

Clear away this muck! Chuck it in the sea!

(Clov goes to bins, halts.)

Nell: So white.
Hamm: What? What's she blathering about?

(Clov stoops, takes Nell's hand, feels her pulse.)

Nell *(to Clov)*: Desert!

(Clov lets go her hand, pushes her back in the bin, closes the lid.)

Clov (returning to his place beside the chair): She has no pulse.
Hamm: What was she driveling about?
Clov: She told me to go away, into the desert.
Hamm: Damn busybody! Is that all?
Clov: No.
Hamm: What else?
Clov: I didn't understand.
Hamm: Have you bottled her?
Clov: Yes.
Hamm: Are they both bottled?
Clov: Yes.
Hamm: Screw down the lids.

(Clov *goes towards door.*)

Time enough.

(Clov *halts.*)

My anger subsides, I'd like to pee.
Clov (with alacrity): I'll go and get the catheter.

(He *goes towards door.*)

Hamm: Time enough.

(Clov *halts.*)

Give me my painkiller.
Clov: It's too soon.

(Pause.)

It's too soon on top of your tonic, it wouldn't act.
Hamm: In the morning they brace you up and in the evening they calm you down. Unless it's the other way round.

(Pause.)

That old doctor, he's dead naturally?
Clov: He wasn't old.
Hamm: But he's dead?
Clov: Naturally.

(Pause.)

You ask *me* that?

(Pause.)

Hamm: Take me for a little turn.

(Clov *goes behind the chair and pushes it forward.*)

Not too fast!

(Clov *pushes chair.*)

Right round the world!

(Clov *pushes chair.*)

Hug the walls, then back to the center again.

(Clov *pushes chair.*)

I was right in the center, wasn't I?
Clov (*pushing*): Yes.
Hamm: We'd need a proper wheelchair. With big wheels. Bicycle wheels!

(*Pause.*)

Are you hugging?
Clov (*pushing*): Yes.
Hamm (*groping for wall*): It's a lie! Why do you lie to me?
Clov (*bearing closer to wall*): There! There!
Hamm: Stop!

(Clov *stops chair close to back wall. Hamm lays his hand against wall.*)

Old wall!

(*Pause.*)

Beyond is the . . . other hell.

(*Pause. Violently.*)

Closer! Closer! Up against!
Clov: Take away your hand.

(Hamm *withdraws his hand. Clov rams chair against wall.*)

There!

(Hamm *leans towards wall, applies his ear to it.*)

Hamm: Do you hear?

(*He strikes the wall with his knuckles.*)

Do you hear? Hollow bricks!

(*He strikes again.*)

All that's hollow!

(*Pause. He straightens up. Violently.*)

That's enough. Back!
Clov: We haven't done the round.
Hamm: Back to my place!

(Clov *pushes chair back to center.*)

Is that my place?
Clov: Yes, that's your place.

Hamm: Am I right in the center?
Clov: I'll measure it.
Hamm: More or less! More or less!
Clov (moving chair slightly): There!
Hamm: I'm more or less in the center?
Clov: I'd say so.
Hamm: You'd say so! Put me right in the center!
Clov: I'll go and get the tape.
Hamm: Roughly! Roughly!

(Clov *moves chair slightly.*)

Bang in the center!
Clov: There!

(*Pause.*)

Hamm: I feel a little too far to the left.

(Clov *moves chair slightly.*)

Now I feel a little too far to the right.

(Clov *moves chair slightly.*)

I feel a little too far forward.

(Clov *moves chair slightly.*)

Now I feel a little too far back.

(Clov *moves chair slightly.*)

Don't stay there (*i.e., behind the chair*), you give me the shivers.

(Clov *returns to his place beside the chair.*)

Clov: If I could kill him I'd die happy.

(*Pause.*)

Hamm: What's the weather like?
Clov: As usual.
Hamm: Look at the earth.
Clov: I've looked.
Hamm: With the glass?
Clov: No need of the glass.
Hamm: Look at it with the glass.
Clov: I'll go and get the glass.

(*Exit* Clov.)

Hamm: No need of the glass!

(*Enter* Clov *with telescope.*)

Clov: I'm back again, with the glass.

(He goes to window right, looks up at it.)

I need the steps.

Hamm: Why? Have you shrunk?

(Exit Clov with telescope.)

I don't like that, I don't like that.

(Enter Clov with ladder, but without telescope.)

Clov: I'm back again, with the steps.

(He sets down ladder under window right, gets up on it, realizes he has not the telescope, gets down.)

I need the glass.

(He goes towards door.)

Hamm (violently): But you have the glass!

Clov (halting, violently): No, I haven't the glass!

(Exit Clov.)

Hamm: This is deadly.

(Enter Clov with telescope. He goes towards ladder.)

Clov: Things are livening up.

(He gets up on ladder, raises the telescope, lets it fall.)

I did it on purpose.

(He gets down, picks up the telescope, turns it on auditorium.)

I see . . . a multitude . . . in transports . . . of joy.

(Pause.)

That's what I call a magnifier.

(He lowers the telescope, turns towards Hamm.)

Well? Don't we laugh?

Hamm (after reflection): I don't.

Clov (after reflection): Nor I.

(He gets up on ladder, turns the telescope on the without.)

Let's see.

(He looks, moving the telescope.)

Zero . . . *(he looks)* zero . . . *(he looks)* . . . and zero.

Hamm: Nothing stirs. All is—

Clov: Zer—

Hamm (violently): Wait till you're spoken to!

(Normal voice.)

All is . . . all is . . . all is what?

(Violently)

All is what?

Clov: What all is? In a word? Is that what you want to know? Just a moment.

(He turns the telescope on the without, looks, lowers the telescope, turns towards Hamm.*)*

Corpsed.

(Pause.)

Well? Content?

Hamm: Look at the sea.
Clov: It's the same.
Hamm: Look at the ocean!

(Clov gets down, takes a few steps towards window left, goes back for ladder, carries it over and sets it down under window left, gets up on it, turns the telescope on the without, looks at length. He starts, lowers the telescope, examines it, turns it again on the without.)

Clov: Never seen anything like that!
Hamm (anxious): What? A sail? A fin? Smoke?
Clov (looking): The light is sunk.
Hamm (relieved): Pah! We all knew that.
Clov (looking): There was a bit left.
Hamm: The base.
Clov (looking): Yes.
Hamm: And now?
Clov (looking): All gone.
Hamm: No gulls?
Clov (looking): Gulls!
Hamm: And the horizon? Nothing on the horizon?
Clov (lowering the telescope, turning towards Hamm, *exasperated):* What in
    God's name could there be on the horizon?

(Pause.)

Hamm: The waves, how are the waves?
Clov: The waves?

(He turns the telescope on the waves.)

Lead.
Hamm: And the sun?
Clov (looking): Zero.
Hamm: But it should be sinking. Look again.
Clov (looking): Damn the sun.
Hamm: Is it night already then?
Clov (looking): No.
Hamm: Then what is it?

Clov (looking): Gray.

> *(Lowering the telescope, turning towards* Hamm, *louder.)*

Gray!

> *(Pause. Still louder.)*

GRRAY!

> *(Pause. He gets down, approaches* Hamm *from behind, whispers in his ear.)*

Hamm (starting): Gray! Did I hear you say gray?
Clov: Light black. From pole to pole.
Hamm: You exaggerate.

> *(Pause.)*

Don't stay there, you give me the shivers.

> *(Clov returns to his place beside the chair.)*

Clov: Why this farce, day after day?
Hamm: Routine. One never knows.

> *(Pause.)*

Last night I saw inside my breast. There was a big sore.
Clov: Pah! You saw your heart.
Hamm: No, it was living.

> *(Pause. Anguished.)*

Clov!
Clov: Yes.
Hamm: What's happening?
Clov: Something is taking its course.

> *(Pause.)*

Hamm: Clov!
Clov (impatiently): What is it?
Hamm: We're not beginning to . . . to . . . mean something?
Clov: Mean something! You and I, mean something!

> *(Brief laugh.)*

Ah that's a good one!
Hamm: I wonder.

> *(Pause.)*

Imagine if a rational being came back to earth, wouldn't he be liable to get ideas into his head if he observed us long enough.

> *(Voice of rational being.)*

Ah, good, now I see what it is, yes, now I understand what they're at!

(Clov starts, drops the telescope and begins to scratch his belly with both hands. Normal voice.)

And without going so far as that, we ourselves . . . *(with emotion)* . . . we ourselves . . . at certain moments . . .

(Vehemently.)

To think perhaps it won't all have been for nothing!
Clov *(anguished, scratching himself):* I have a flea!
Hamm: A flea! Are there still fleas?
Clov: On me there's one.

(Scratching.)

Unless it's a crablouse.
Hamm *(very perturbed):* But humanity might start from there all over again!
Catch him, for the love of God!
Clov: I'll go and get the powder.

(Exit Clov.)

Hamm: A flea! This is awful! What a day!

(Enter Clov with a sprinkling tin.)

Clov: I'm back again, with the insecticide.
Hamm: Let him have it!

(Clov loosens the top of his trousers, pulls it forward and shakes powder into the aperture. He stoops, looks, waits, starts, frenziedly shakes more powder, stoops, looks, waits.)

Clov: The bastard!
Hamm: Did you get him?
Clov: Looks like it.

(He drops the tin and adjusts his trousers.)

Unless he's laying doggo.°
Hamm: Laying! Lying you mean. Unless he's *lying* doggo.
Clov: Ah? One says lying? One doesn't say laying?
Hamm: Use your head, can't you. If he was laying we'd be bitched.
Clov: Ah.

(Pause.)

What about that pee?
Hamm: I'm having it.
Clov: Ah that's the spirit, that's the spirit!

(Pause.)

---

doggo: In hiding.

Hamm (with ardor): Let's go from here, the two of us! South! You can
    make a raft and the currents will carry us away, far away, to other . . .
    mammals!
Clov: God forbid!
Hamm: Alone, I'll embark alone! Get working on that raft immediately.
    Tomorrow I'll be gone forever.
Clov (hastening towards door): I'll start straight away.
Hamm: Wait!

(Clov *halts.*)

Will there be sharks, do you think?
Clov: Sharks? I don't know. If there are there will be.

(He goes towards door.)

Hamm: Wait!

(Clov *halts.*)

Is it not yet time for my painkiller?
Clov (violently): No!

(He goes towards door.)

Hamm: Wait!

(Clov *halts.*)

How are your eyes?
Clov: Bad.
Hamm: But you can see.
Clov: All I want.
Hamm: How are your legs?
Clov: Bad.
Hamm: But you can walk.
Clov: I come . . . and go.
Hamm: In my house.

(Pause. With prophetic relish.)

One day you'll be blind, like me. You'll be sitting there, a speck in the
void, in the dark, forever, like me.

(Pause.)

One day you'll say to yourself, I'm tired, I'll sit down, and you'll go and
sit down. Then you'll say, I'm hungry, I'll get up and get something to
eat. But you won't get up. You'll say, I shouldn't have sat down, but since
I have I'll sit on a little longer, then I'll get up and get something to eat.
But you won't get up and you won't get anything to eat.

(Pause.)

You'll look at the wall a while, then you'll say, I'll close my eyes, perhaps
have a little sleep, after that I'll feel better, and you'll close them. And
when you open them again there'll be no wall anymore.

(Pause.)

Infinite emptiness will be all around you, all the resurrected dead of all
the ages wouldn't fill it, and there you'll be like a little bit of grit in the
middle of the steppe.

(Pause.)

Yes, one day you'll know what it is, you'll be like me, except that you
won't have anyone with you, because you won't have had pity on anyone
and because there won't be anyone left to have pity on.

(Pause.)

Clov: It's not certain.

(Pause.)

And there's one thing you forget.
Hamm: Ah?
Clov: I can't sit down.
Hamm (impatiently): Well you'll lie down then, what the hell! Or you'll
come to a standstill, simply stop and stand still, the way you are now.
One day you'll say, I'm tired, I'll stop. What does the attitude matter?

(Pause.)

Clov: So you all want me to leave you.
Hamm: Naturally.
Clov: Then I'll leave you.
Hamm: You can't leave us.
Clov: Then I won't leave you.

(Pause.)

Hamm: Why don't you finish us?

(Pause.)

I'll tell you the combination of the cupboard if you promise to finish
me.
Clov: I couldn't finish you.
Hamm: Then you won't finish me.

(Pause.)

Clov: I'll leave you, I have things to do.
Hamm: Do you remember when you came here?
Clov: No. Too small, you told me.
Hamm: Do you remember your father?

Clov (wearily): Same answer.

(Pause.)

You've asked me these questions millions of times.
Hamm: I love the old questions.

(With fervor.)

Ah the old questions, the old answers, there's nothing like them!

(Pause.)

It was I was a father to you.
Clov: Yes.

(He looks at Hamm *fixedly.)*

You were that to me.
Hamm: My house a home for you.
Clov: Yes.

(He looks about him.)

This was that for me.
Hamm (proudly): But for me *(gesture towards himself)*, no father. But for
      Hamm *(gesture towards surroundings)*, no home.

(Pause.)

Clov: I'll leave you.
Hamm: Did you ever think of one thing?
Clov: Never.
Hamm: That here we're down in a hole.

(Pause.)

But beyond the hills? Eh? Perhaps it's still green. Eh?

(Pause.)

Flora! Pomona!

(Ecstatically.)

Ceres!°

(Pause,)

Perhaps you won't need to go very far.
Clov: I can't go very far.

(Pause.)

I'll leave you.

——

Flora . . . Ceres: Three Roman goddesses—Flora, of flowers; Pomona, of fruit; Ceres, of agriculture.

Hamm: Is my dog ready?
Clov: He lacks a leg.
Hamm: Is he silky?
Clov: He's a kind of Pomeranian.
Hamm: Go and get him.
Clov: He lacks a leg.
Hamm: Go and get him!

(*Exit* Clov.)

We're getting on.

(*Enter* Clov *holding by one of its three legs a black toy dog.*)

Clov: Your dogs are here.

(*He hands the dog to* Hamm *who feels it, fondles it.*)

Hamm: He's white, isn't he?
Clov: Nearly.
Hamm: What do you mean, nearly? Is he white or isn't he?
Clov: He isn't.

(*Pause.*)

Hamm: You've forgotten the sex.
Clov (*vexed*): But he isn't finished. The sex goes on at the end.

(*Pause.*)

Hamm: You haven't put on his ribbon.
Clov (*angrily*): But he isn't finished, I tell you! First you finish your dog and
then you put on his ribbon!

(*Pause.*)

Hamm: Can he stand?
Clov: I don't know.
Hamm: Try.

(*He hands the dog to* Clov *who places it on the ground.*)

Well?
Clov: Wait!

(*He squats down and tries to get the dog to stand on its three legs, fails, lets it
go. The dog falls on its side.*)

Hamm (*impatiently*): Well?
Clov: He's standing.
Hamm (*groping for the dog*): Where? Where is he?

(*Clov holds up the dog in a standing position.*)

Clov: There.

(He takes Hamm's *hand and guides it towards the dog's head.)*

Hamm (his hand on the dog's head): Is he gazing at me?

Clov: Yes.

Hamm (proudly): As if he were asking me to take him for a walk?

Clov: If you like.

Hamm (as before): Or as if he were begging me for a bone.

(He withdraws his hand.)

Leave him like that, standing there imploring me.

(Clov straightens up. The dog falls on its side.)

Clov: I'll leave you.

Hamm: Have you had your visions?

Clov: Less.

Hamm: Is Mother Pegg's light on?

Clov: Light! How could anyone's light be on?

Hamm: Extinguished!

Clov: Naturally it's extinguished. If it's not on it's extinguished.

Hamm: No, I mean Mother Pegg.

Clov: But naturally she's extinguished!

(Pause.)

What's the matter with you today?

Hamm: I'm taking my course.

(Pause.)

Is she buried?

Clov: Buried! Who would have buried her?

Hamm: You.

Clov: Me! Haven't I enough to do without burying people?

Hamm: But you'll bury me.

Clov: No I won't bury you.

(Pause.)

Hamm: She was bonny once, like a flower of the field.

(With reminiscent leer.)

And a great one for the men!

Clov: We too were bonny—once. It's a rare thing not to have been bonny—once.

(Pause.)

Hamm: Go and get the gaff.

(Clov goes to door, halts.)

Clov: Do this, do that, and I do it. I never refuse. Why?

Hamm: You're not able to.
Clov: Soon I won't do it anymore.
Hamm: You won't be able to anymore.

(*Exit* Clov.)

Ah the creatures, the creatures, everything has to be explained to them.

(*Enter* Clov *with gaff.*)

Clov: Here's your gaff. Stick it up.

(*He gives the gaff to* Hamm *who, wielding it like a puntpole,° tries to move his chair.*)

Hamm: Did I move?
Clov: No.

(Hamm *throws down the gaff.*)

Hamm: Go and get the oilcan.
Clov: What for?
Hamm: To oil the casters.
Clov: I oiled them yesterday.
Hamm: Yesterday! What does that mean? Yesterday!
Clov (violently): That means that bloody awful day, long ago, before this
    bloody awful day. I use the words you taught me. If they don't mean
    anything anymore, teach me others. Or let me be silent.

(*Pause.*)

Hamm: I once knew a madman who thought the end of the world had
    come. He was a painter—and engraver. I had a great fondness for him. I
    used to go and see him, in the asylum. I'd take him by the hand and drag
    him to the window. Look! There! All that rising corn! And there! Look!
    The sails of the herring fleet! All that loveliness!

(*Pause.*)

He'd snatch away his hand and go back into his corner. Appalled. All he
had seen was ashes.

(*Pause.*)

He alone had been spared.

(*Pause.*)

Forgotten.

(*Pause.*)

It appears the case is . . . . was not so . . . so unusual.

————

puntpole: A pole used to propel a punt, a flat-bottomed boat, through the water.

Clov: A madman? When was that?
Hamm: Oh way back, way back, you weren't in the land of the living.
Clov: God be with the days!

(*Pause.* Hamm *raises his toque.*)

Hamm: I had a great fondness for him.

(*Pause. He puts on his toque again.*)

He was a painter—and engraver.
Clov: There are so many terrible things.
Hamm: No, no, there are not so many now.

(*Pause.*)

Clov!
Clov: Yes.
Hamm: Do you not think this has gone on long enough?
Clov: Yes!

(*Pause.*)

What?
Hamm: This . . . this . . . thing.
Clov: I've always thought so.

(*Pause.*)

You not?
Hamm (gloomily): Then it's a day like any other day.
Clov: As long as it lasts.

(*Pause.*)

All life long the same inanities.
Hamm: I can't leave you.
Clov: I know. And you can't follow me.

(*Pause.*)

Hamm: If you leave me how shall I know?
Clov (briskly): Well you simply whistle me and if I don't come running it
means I've left you.

(*Pause.*)

Hamm: You won't come and kiss me good-bye?
Clov: Oh I shouldn't think so.

(*Pause.*)

Hamm: But you might be merely dead in your kitchen.
Clov: The result would be the same.
Hamm: Yes, but how would I know, if you were merely dead in your
kitchen?

Clov: Well . . . sooner or later I'd start to stink.

Hamm: You stink already. The whole place stinks of corpses.

Clov: The whole universe.

Hamm (angrily): To hell with the universe.

　(*Pause.*)

Think of something.

Clov: What?

Hamm: An idea, have an idea.

　(*Angrily.*)

A bright idea!

Clov: Ah good.

　(*He starts pacing to and fro, his eyes fixed on the ground, his hands behind his back. He halts.*)

The pains in my legs! It's unbelievable! Soon I won't be able to think anymore.

Hamm: You won't be able to leave me.

　(*Clov resumes his pacing.*)

What are you doing?

Clov: Having an idea.

　(*He paces.*)

Ah!

　(*He halts.*)

Hamm: What a brain!

　(*Pause.*)

Well?

Clov: Wait!

　(*He meditates. Not very convinced.*)

Yes . . .

　(*Pause. More convinced.*)

Yes!

　(*He raises his head.*)

I have it! I set the alarm.

　(*Pause.*)

Hamm: This is perhaps not one of my bright days, but frankly—

Clov: You whistle me. I don't come. The alarm rings. I'm gone. It doesn't ring. I'm dead.

(Pause.)

Hamm: Is it working?

(Pause. Impatiently.)

The alarm, is it working?

Clov: Why wouldn't it be working?

Hamm: Because it's worked too much.

Clov: But it's hardly worked at all.

Hamm *(angrily):* Then because it's worked too little!

Clov: I'll go and see.

(Exit Clov. Brief ring of alarm off. Enter Clov with alarm clock. He holds it against Hamm's ear and releases alarm. They listen to it ringing to the end. Pause.)

Fit to wake the dead! Did you hear it?

Hamm: Vaguely.

Clov: The end is terrific!

Hamm: I prefer the middle.

(Pause.)

Is it not time for my painkiller?

Clov: No!

(He goes to door, turns.)

I'll leave you.

Hamm: It's time for my story. Do you want to listen to my story?

Clov: No.

Hamm: Ask my father if he wants to listen to my story.

(Clov goes to bins, raises the lid of Nagg's, stoops, looks into it. Pause. He straightens up.)

Clov: He's asleep.

Hamm: Wake him.

(Clov stoops, wakes Nagg with the alarm. Unintelligible words. Clov straightens up.)

Clov: He doesn't want to listen to your story.

Hamm: I'll give him a bonbon.

(Clov stoops. As before.)

Clov: He wants a sugarplum.

Hamm: He'll get a sugarplum.

(Clov stoops. As before.)

Clov: It's a deal.

(He goes towards door. Nagg's hands appear, gripping the rim. Then the head emerges. Clov reaches door, turns.)

Do you believe in the life to come?
Hamm: Mine was always that.

(*Exit* Clov.)

Got him that time!
Nagg: I'm listening.
Hamm: Scoundrel! Why did you engender me?
Nagg: I didn't know.
Hamm: What? What didn't you know?
Nagg: That it'd be you.

(*Pause.*)

You'll give me a sugarplum?
Hamm: After the audition.
Nagg: You swear?
Hamm: Yes.
Nagg: On what?
Hamm: My honor.

(*Pause. They laugh heartily.*)

Nagg: Two.
Hamm: One.
Nagg: One for me and one for—
Hamm: One! Silence!

(*Pause.*)

Where was I?

(*Pause. Gloomily.*)

It's finished, we're finished.

(*Pause.*)

Nearly finished.

(*Pause.*)

There'll be no more speech.

(*Pause.*)

Something dripping in my head, ever since the fontanelles.°

(*Stifled hilarity of* Nagg.)

Splash, splash, always on the same spot.

(*Pause.*)

Perhaps it's a little vein.

———
fontanelles: Soft membranes that link the incompletely developed skull bones in an infant's head.

(Pause.)

A little artery.

(Pause. More animated.)

Enough of that, it's story time, where was I?

(Pause. Narrative tone.)

The man came crawling towards me, on his belly. Pale, wonderfully pale and thin, he seemed on the point of—

(Pause. Normal tone.)

No, I've done that bit.

(Pause. Narrative tone.)

I calmly filled my pipe—the meerschaum, lit it with . . . let us say a vesta,° drew a few puffs. Aah!

(Pause.)

Well, what is it *you* want?

(Pause.)

It was an extraordinarily bitter day, I remember, zero by the thermometer. But considering it was Christmas Eve there was nothing . . . extraordinary about that. Seasonable weather, for once in a way.

(Pause.)

Well, what ill wind blows you my way? He raised his face to me, black with mingled dirt and tears.

(Pause. Normal tone.)

That should do it.

(Narrative tone.)

No no, don't look at me, don't look at me. He dropped his eyes and mumbled something, apologies I presume.

(Pause.)

I'm a busy man, you know, the final touches, before the festivities, you know what it is.

(Pause. Forcibly.)

Come on now, what is the object of this invasion?

(Pause.)

---

vesta: Wooden match.

It was a glorious bright day, I remember, fifty by the heliometer,° but already the sun was sinking down into the . . . down among the dead.

(Normal tone.)

Nicely put, that.

(Narrative tone.)

Come on now, come on, present your petition and let me resume my labors.

(Pause. Normal tone.)

There's English for you. Ah well . . .

(Narrative tone.)

It was then he took the plunge. It's my little one, he said. Tsstss, a little one, that's bad. My little boy, he said, as if the sex mattered. Where did he come from? He named the hole. A good half-day, on horse. What are you insinuating? That the place is still inhabited? No, no, not a soul, except himself and the child—assuming he existed. Good. I inquired about the situation at Kov, beyond the gulf. Not a sinner. Good. And you expect me to believe you have left your little one back there, all alone, and alive into the bargain? Come now!

(Pause.)

It was a howling wild day, I remember, a hundred by the anemometer.° The wind was tearing up the dead pines and sweeping them . . . away.

(Pause. Normal tone.)

A bit feeble, that.

(Narrative tone.)

Come on, man, speak up, what is you want from me, I have to put up my holly.

(Pause.)

Well to make it short it finally transpired that what he wanted from me was . . . bread for his brat? Bread? But I have no bread, it doesn't agree with me. Good. Then perhaps a little corn?

(Pause. Normal tone.)

That should do it.

(Narrative tone.)

---

heliometer: Ttelescope for measuring the apparent diameter of the sun.   *anemometer:* Instrument for measuring wind speed.

Corn, yes, I have corn, it's true, in my granaries. But use your head. I give you some corn, a pound, a pound and a half, you bring it back to your child and you make him—if he's still alive—a nice pot of porridge, (Nagg *reacts*) a nice pot and a half of porridge, full of nourishment. Good. The colors come back into his little cheeks—perhaps. And then?

(Pause.)

I lost patience.

(Violently.)

Use your head, can't you, use your head, you're on earth, there's no cure for that!

(Pause.)

It was an exceedingly dry day, I remember, zero by the hygrometer.° Ideal weather, for my lumbago.

(Pause. Violently.)

But what in God's name do you imagine? That the earth will awake in spring? That the rivers and seas will run with fish again? That there's manna in heaven still for imbeciles like you?

(Pause.)

Gradually I cooled down, sufficiently at least to ask him how long he had taken on the way. Three whole days. Good. In what condition he had left the child. Deep in sleep.

(Forcibly.)

But deep in what sleep, deep in what sleep already?

(Pause.)

Well to make it short I finally offered to take him into my service. He had touched a chord. And then I imagined already that I wasn't much longer for this world.

(He laughs. Pause.)

Well?

(Pause.)

Well? Here if you were careful you might die a nice natural death, in peace and comfort.

(Pause.)

---

hygrometer: Device for measuring humidity.

Well?

(Pause.)

In the end he asked me would I consent to take in the child as well—if he were still alive.

(Pause.)

It was the moment I was waiting for.

(Pause.)

Would I consent to take in the child . . .

(Pause.)

I can see him still, down on his knees, his hands flat on the ground, glaring at me with his mad eyes, in defiance of my wishes.

(Pause. Normal tone.)

I'll soon have finished with this story.

(Pause.)

Unless I bring in other characters.

(Pause.)

But where would I find them?

(Pause.)

Where would I look for them?

(Pause. He whistles. Enter Clov.*)*

Let us pray to God.
Nagg: Me sugarplum!
Clov: There's a rat in the kitchen!
Hamm: A rat! Are there still rats?
Clov: In the kitchen there's one.
Hamm: And you haven't exterminated him?
Clov: Half. You disturbed us.
Hamm: He can't get away?
Clov: No.
Hamm: You'll finish him later. Let us pray to God.
Clov: Again!
Nagg: Me sugarplum!
Hamm: God first!

(Pause.)

Are you right?
Clov (resigned): Off we go.

Hamm (to Nagg*):* And you?
Nagg (clasping his hands, closing his eyes, in a gabble): Our Father which art—
Hamm: Silence! In silence! Where are your manners?

   (Pause.)

   Off we go.

   (Attitudes of prayer. Silence. Abandoning his attitude, discouraged.)
   Well?

Clov (abandoning his attitude): What a hope! And you?
Hamm: Sweet damn all!

   (To Nagg.*)*

   And you?
Nagg: Wait!

   (Pause. Abandoning his attitude.)

   Nothing doing!
Hamm: The bastard! He doesn't exist!
Clov: Not yet.
Nagg: Me sugarplum!
Hamm: There are no more sugarplums!

   (Pause.)

Nagg: It's natural. After all I'm your father. It's true if it hadn't been me it
   would have been someone else. But that's no excuse.

   (Pause.)

   Turkish Delight,° for example, which no longer exists, we all know that,
   there is nothing in the world I love more. And one day I'll ask you for
   some, in return for a kindness, and you'll promise it to me. One must
   live with the times.

   (Pause.)

   Whom did you call when you were a tiny boy, and were frightened, in
   the dark? Your mother? No. Me. We let you cry. Then we moved you
   out of earshot, so that we might sleep in peace.

   (Pause.)

   I was asleep, as happy as a king, and you woke me up to have me listen
   to you. It wasn't indispensable, you didn't really need to have me listen
   to you.

   (Pause.)

———
Turkish Delight: Gummy candy.

I hope the day will come when you'll really need to have me listen to you, and need to hear my voice, any voice.

(Pause.)

Yes, I hope I'll live till then, to hear you calling me like when you were a tiny boy, and were frightened, in the dark, and I was your only hope.

(Pause. Nagg knocks on lid of Nell's bin. Pause.)

Nell!

(Pause. He knocks louder. Pause. Louder.)

Nell!

(Pause. Nagg sinks back into his bin, closes the lid behind him. Pause.)

Hamm: Our revels now are ended.

(He gropes for the dog.)

The dog's gone.
Clov: He's not a real dog, he can't go.
Hamm (groping): He's not there.
Clov: He's lain down.
Hamm: Give him up to me.

(Clov picks up the dog and gives it to Hamm. Hamm holds it in his arms. Pause. Hamm throws away the dog.)

Dirty brute!

(Clov begins to pick up the objects lying on the ground.)

What are you doing?
Clov: Putting things in order.

(He straightens up. Fervently.)

I'm going to clear everything away!

(He starts picking up again.)

Hamm: Order!
Clov (straightening up): I love order. It's my dream. A world where all would be silent and still and each thing in its last place, under the last dust.

(He starts picking up again.)

Hamm (exasperated): What in God's name do you think you are doing?
Clov (straightening up): I'm doing my best to create a little order.
Hamm: Drop it!

(Clov drops the objects he has picked up.)

Clov: After all, there or elsewhere.

(He goes towards door.)

Hamm (irritably): What's wrong with your feet?
Clov: My feet?
Hamm: Tramp! Tramp!
Clov: I must have put on my boots.
Hamm: Your slippers were hurting you?

(Pause.)

Clov: I'll leave you.
Hamm: No!
Clov: What is there to keep me here?
Hamm: The dialogue.

(Pause.)

I've got on with my story.

(Pause.)

I've got on with it well.

(Pause. Irritably.)

Ask me where I've got to.
Clov: Oh, by the way, your story?
Hamm (surprised): What story?
Clov: The one you've been telling yourself all your days.
Hamm: Ah you mean my chronicle?
Clov: That's the one.

(Pause.)

Hamm (angrily): Keep going, can't you, keep going!
Clov: You've got on with it, I hope.
Hamm (modestly): Oh not very far, not very far.

(He sighs.)

There are days like that, one isn't inspired.

(Pause.)

Nothing you can do about it, just wait for it to come.

(Pause.)

No forcing, no forcing, it's fatal.

(Pause.)

I've got on with it a little all the same.

(Pause.)

Technique, you know.

(Pause. Irritably.)

I say I've got on with it a little all the same.

Clov (admiringly): Well I never! In spite of everything you were able to get on with it!

Hamm (modestly): Oh not very far, you know, not very far, but nevertheless, better than nothing.

Clov: Better than nothing! Is it possible?

Hamm: I'll tell you how it goes. He comes crawling on his belly—

Clov: Who?

Hamm: What?

Clov: Who do you mean, he?

Hamm: Who do I mean! Yet another.

Clov: Ah him! I wasn't sure.

Hamm: Crawling on his belly, whining for bread for his brat. He's offered a job as gardener. Before—

(Clov bursts out laughing.)

What is there so funny about that?

Clov: A job as gardener!

Hamm: Is that what tickles you?

Clov: It must be that.

Hamm: It wouldn't be the bread?

Clov: Or the brat.

(Pause.)

Hamm: The whole thing is comical, I grant you that. What about having a good guffaw the two of us together?

Clov (after reflection): I couldn't guffaw again today.

Hamm (after reflection): Nor I.

(Pause.)

I continue then. Before accepting with gratitude he asks if he may have his little boy with him.

Clov: What age?

Hamm: Oh tiny.

Clov: He would have climbed the trees.

Hamm: All the little odd jobs.

Clov: And then he would have grown up.

Hamm: Very likely.

(Pause.)

Clov: Keep going, can't you, keep going!

Hamm: That's all. I stopped there.

(Pause.)

Clov: Do you see how it goes on?

Hamm: More or less.
Clov: Will it not soon be the end?
Hamm: I'm afraid it will.
Clov: Pah! You'll make up another.
Hamm: I don't know.

(*Pause.*)

I feel rather drained.

(*Pause.*)

The prolonged creative effort.

(*Pause.*)

If I could drag myself down to the sea! I'd make a pillow of sand for my head and the tide would come.
Clov: There's no more tide.

(*Pause.*)

Hamm: Go and see is she dead.

(Clov *goes to bins, raises the lid of* Nell's, *stoops, looks into it. Pause.*)

Clov: Looks like it.

(*He closes the lid, straightens up.* Hamm *raises his toque. Pause. He puts it on again.*)

Hamm (*with his hand to his toque*): And Nagg?

(Clov *raises lid of* Nagg's *bin, stoops, looks into it. Pause.*)

Clov: Doesn't look like it.

(*He closes the lid, straightens up.*)

Hamm (*letting go his toque*): What's he doing?

(Clov *raises lid of* Nagg's *bin, stoops, looks into it. Pause.*)

Clov: He's crying.

(*He closes lid, straightens up.*)

Hamm: Then he's living.

(*Pause.*)

Did you ever have an instant of happiness?
Clov: Not to my knowledge.

(*Pause.*)

Hamm: Bring me under the window.

(Clov *goes towards chair.*)

I want to feel the light on my face.

(Clov *pushes chair.*)

Do you remember, in the beginning, when you took me for a turn? You used to hold the chair too high. At every step you nearly tipped me out.

(*With senile quaver.*)

Ah great fun, we had, the two of us, great fun.

(*Gloomily.*)

And then we got into the way of it.

(Clov *stops the chair under window right.*)

There already?

(*Pause. He tilts back his head.*)

Is it light?
Clov: It isn't dark.
Hamm (*angrily*): I'm asking you is it light.
Clov: Yes.

(*Pause.*)

Hamm: The curtain isn't closed?
Clov: No.
Hamm: What window is it?
Clov: The earth.
Hamm: I knew it!

(*Angrily.*)

But there's no light there! The other!

(Clov *pushes chair towards window left.*)

The earth!

(Clov *stops the chair under window left.* Hamm *tilts back his head.*)

That's what I call light!

(*Pause.*)

Feels like a ray of sunshine.

(*Pause.*)

No?
Clov: No.
Hamm: It isn't a ray of sunshine I feel on my face?
Clov: No.

(*Pause.*)

Hamm: Am I very white?

(*Pause. Angrily.*)

I'm asking you am I very white!

Clov: Not more so than usual.

(*Pause.*)

Hamm: Open the window.

Clov: What for?

Hamm: I want to hear the sea.

Clov: You wouldn't hear it.

Hamm: Even if you opened the window?

Clov: No.

Hamm: Then it's not worthwhile opening it?

Clov: No.

Hamm (violently): Then open it!

(Clov *gets up on the ladder, opens the window. Pause.*)

Have you opened it?

Clov: Yes.

(*Pause.*)

Hamm: You swear you've opened it?

Clov: Yes.

(*Pause.*)

Hamm: Well . . . !

(*Pause.*)

It must be very calm.

(*Pause. Violently.*)

I'm asking you is it very calm!

Clov: Yes.

Hamm: It's because there are no more navigators.

(*Pause.*)

You haven't much conversation all of a sudden. Do you not feel well?

Clov: I'm cold.

Hamm: What month are we?

(*Pause.*)

Close the window, we're going back.

(Clov *closes the window, gets down, pushes the chair back to its place, remains standing behind it, head bowed.*)

Don't stay there, you give me the shivers!

(Clov *returns to his place beside the chair.*)

Father!

(Pause. Louder.)

Father!

(Pause.)

Go and see did he hear me.

(Clov goes to Nagg's bin, raises the lid, stoops. Unintelligible words. Clov straightens up.)

Clov: Yes.
Hamm: Both times?

(Clov stoops. As before.)

Clov: Once only.
Hamm: The first time or the second?

(Clov stoops. As before.)

Clov: He doesn't know.
Hamm: It must have been the second.
Clov: We'll never know.

(He closes lid.)

Hamm: Is he still crying?
Clov: No.
Hamm: The dead go fast.

(Pause.)

What's he doing?
Clov: Sucking his biscuit.
Hamm: Life goes on.

(Clov returns to his place beside the chair.)

Give me a rug,° I'm freezing.
Clov: There are no more rugs.

(Pause.)

Hamm: Kiss me.

(Pause.)

Will you not kiss me?
Clov: No.
Hamm: On the forehead.
Clov: I won't kiss you anywhere.

(Pause.)

---

rug: Small blanket to cover the lap, legs, and feet.

Hamm (holding out his hand): Give me your hand at least.

(*Pause.*)

Will you not give me your hand?
Clov: I won't touch you.

(*Pause.*)

Hamm: Give me the dog.

(Clov *looks round for the dog.*)
No!
Clov: Do you not want your dog?
Hamm: No.
Clov: Then I'll leave you.
Hamm (head bowed, absently): That's right.

(Clov *goes to door, turns.*)

Clov: If I don't kill that rat he'll die.
Hamm (as before): That's right.

(*Exit* Clov. *Pause.*)

Me to play.

(*He takes out his handkerchief, unfolds it, holds it spread out before him.*)

We're getting on.

(*Pause.*)

You weep, and weep, for nothing, so as not to laugh, and little by little . . . you begin to grieve.

(*He folds the handkerchief, puts it back in his pocket, raises his head.*)

All those I might have helped.

(*Pause.*)

Helped!

(*Pause.*)

Saved.

(*Pause.*)

Saved!

(*Pause.*)

The place was crawling with them!

(*Pause. Violently.*)

Use your head, can't you, use your head, you're on earth, there's no cure for that!

(Pause.)

Get out of here and love one another! Lick your neighbor as yourself!

(Pause. Calmer.)

When it wasn't bread they wanted it was crumpets.

(Pause. Violently.)

Out of my sight and back to your petting parties!

(Pause.)

All that, all that!

(Pause.)

Not even a real dog!

(Calmer.)

The end is in the beginning and yet you go on.

(Pause.)

Perhaps I could go on with my story, end it and begin another.

(Pause.)

Perhaps I could throw myself out on the floor.

(He pushes himself painfully off his seat, falls back again.)

Dig my nails into the cracks and drag myself forward with my fingers.

(Pause.)

It will be the end and there I'll be, wondering what can have brought it on and wondering what can have . . . *(he hesitates)* . . . why it was so long coming.

(Pause.)

There I'll be, in the old shelter, alone against the silence and . . . *(he hesitates)* . . . the stillness. If I can hold my peace, and sit quiet, it will be all over with sound, and motion, all over and done with.

(Pause.)

I'll have called my father and I'll have called my . . . *(he hesitates)* . . . my son. And even twice, or three times, in case they shouldn't have heard me, the first time, or the second.

(Pause.)

I'll say to myself, He'll come back.

(Pause.)

And then?

(Pause.)

And then?

(Pause.)

He couldn't, he has gone too far.

(Pause.)

And then?

(Pause. Very agitated.)

All kinds of fantasies! That I'm being watched! A rat! Steps! Breath held and then . . .

(He breathes out.)

Then babble, babble, words, like the solitary child who turns himself into children, two, three, so as to be together, and whisper together, in the dark.

(Pause.)

Moment upon moment, pattering down, like the millet grains of . . . *(he hesitates)* . . . that old Greek, and all life long you wait for that to mount up to a life.

(Pause. He opens his mouth to continue, renounces.)

Ah let's get it over!

(He whistles. Enter Clov *with alarm clock. He halts beside the chair.)*

What? Neither gone nor dead?
Clov: In spirit only.
Hamm: Which?
Clov: Both.
Hamm: Gone from me you'd be dead.
Clov: And vice versa.
Hamm: Outside of here it's death!

(Pause.)

And the rat?
Clov: He's got away.
Hamm: He can't go far.

(Pause. Anxious.)

Eh?
Clov: He doesn't need to go far.

(Pause.)

Hamm: Is it not time for my painkiller?
Clov: Yes.

Hamm: Ah! At last! Give it to me! Quick!

(Pause.)

Clov: There's no more painkiller.

(Pause.)

Hamm (appalled): Good . . . !

(Pause.)

No more painkiller!

Clov: No more painkiller. You'll never get any more painkiller.

(Pause.)

Hamm: But the little round box. It was full!

Clov: Yes. But now it's empty.

(Pause. Clov starts to move about the room. He is looking for a place to put down the alarm clock.)

Hamm (soft): What'll I do?

(Pause. In a scream.)

What'll I do?

(Clov sees the picture, takes it down, stands it on the floor with its face to the wall, hangs up the alarm clock in its place.)

What are you doing?

Clov: Winding up.

Hamm: Look at the earth.

Clov: Again!

Hamm: Since it's calling to you.

Clov: Is your throat sore?

(Pause.)

Would you like a lozenge?

(Pause.)

No.

(Pause.)

Pity.

(Clov goes, humming, towards window right, halts before it, looks up at it.)

Hamm: Don't sing.

Clov (turning towards Hamm): One hasn't the right to sing anymore?

Hamm: No.

Clov: Then how can it end?

Hamm: You want it to end?

Clov: I want to sing.

Hamm: I can't prevent you.

> (*Pause.* Clov *turns towards window right.*)

Clov: What did I do with that steps?

> (*He looks around for ladder.*)

You didn't see that steps?

> (*He sees it.*)

Ah, about time.

> (*He goes towards window left.*)

Sometimes I wonder if I'm in my right mind. Then it passes over and I'm as lucid as before.

> (*He gets up on ladder, looks out of window.*)

Christ, she's under water!

> (*He looks.*)

How can that be?

> (*He pokes forward his head, his hand above his eyes.*)

It hasn't rained.

> (*He wipes the pane, looks. Pause.*)

Ah what a fool I am! I'm on the wrong side!

> (*He gets down, takes a few steps towards window right.*)

Under water!

> (*He goes back for ladder.*)

What a fool I am!

> (*He carries ladder towards window right.*)

Sometimes I wonder if I'm in my right senses. Then it passes off and I'm as intelligent as ever.

> (*He sets down ladder under window right, gets up on it, looks out of window.*
> *He turns towards* Hamm.)

Any particular sector you fancy? Or merely the whole thing?
Hamm: Whole thing.
Clov: The general effect? Just a moment.

> (*He looks out of window. Pause.*)

Hamm: Clov.
Clov (absorbed): Mmm.
Hamm: Do you know what it is?
Clov (as before): Mmm.

Hamm: I was never there.

(*Pause.*)

Clov!

Clov (turning towards Hamm, *exasperated):* What is it?
Hamm: I was never there.
Clov: Lucky for you.

(*He looks out of window.*)

Hamm: Absent, always. It all happened without me. I don't know what's happened.

(*Pause.*)

Do you know what's happened?

(*Pause.*)

Clov!

Clov (turning towards Hamm, *exasperated):* Do you want me to look at this muckheap, yes or no?
Hamm: Answer me first.
Clov: What?
Hamm: Do you know what's happened?
Clov: When? Where?
Hamm (violently): When! What's happened? Use your head, can't you! What has happened?
Clov: What for Christ's sake does it matter?

(*He looks out of window.*)

Hamm: I don't know.

(*Pause.* Clov *turns towards* Hamm.)

Clov (harshly): When old Mother Pegg asked you for oil for her lamp and you told her to get out to hell, you knew what was happening then, no?

(*Pause.*)

You know what she died of, Mother Pegg? Of darkness.
Hamm (feebly): I hadn't any.
Clov (as before): Yes, you had.

(*Pause.*)

Hamm: Have you the glass?
Clov: No, it's clear enough as it is.
Hamm: Go and get it.

(*Pause.* Clov, *casts up his eyes, brandishes his fists. He loses balance, clutches on to the ladder. He starts to get down, halts.*)

Clov: There's one thing I'll never understand.

(He gets down.)

Why I always obey you. Can you explain that to me?

Hamm: No. . . . Perhaps it's compassion.

(Pause.)

A kind of great compassion.

(Pause.)

Oh you won't find it easy, you won't find it easy.

(Pause. Clov begins to move about the room in search of the telescope.)

Clov: I'm tired of our goings on, very tired.

(He searches.)

You're not sitting on it?

(He moves the chair, looks at the place where it stood, resumes his search.)

Hamm (anguished): Don't leave me there!

(Angrily Clov restores the chair to its place.)

Am I right in the center?

Clov: You'd need a microscope to find this—

(He sees the telescope.)

Ah, about time.

(He picks up the telescope, gets up on the ladder, turns the telescope on the without.)

Hamm: Give me the dog.

Clov (looking): Quiet!

Hamm (angrily): Give me the dog!

(Clov drops the telescope, clasps his hands to his head. Pause. He gets down precipitately, looks for the dog, sees it, picks it up, hastens towards Hamm and strikes him violently on the head with the dog.)

Clov: There's your dog for you!

(The dog falls to the ground. Pause.)

Hamm: He hit me!

Clov: You drive me mad, I'm mad!

Hamm: If you must hit me, hit me with the axe.

(Pause.)

Or with the gaff, hit me with the gaff. Not with the dog. With the gaff. Or with the axe.

(Clov picks up the dog and gives it to Hamm who takes it in his arms.)

Clov (imploringly): Let's stop playing!
Hamm: Never!

(*Pause.*)

Put me in my coffin.
Clov: There are no more coffins.
Hamm: Then let it end!

(Clov *goes towards ladder.*)

With a bang!

(Clov *gets up on ladder, gets down again, looks for telescope, sees it, picks it up, gets up ladder, raises telescope.*)

Of darkness! And me? Did anyone ever have pity on me?
Clov (lowering the telescope, turning towards Hamm*):* What?

(*Pause.*)

Is it me you're referring to?
Hamm (angrily): An aside, ape! Did you never hear an aside before?

(*Pause.*)

I'm warming up for my last soliloquy.
Clov: I warn you. I'm going to look at this filth since it's an order. But it's the last time.

(*He turns the telescope on the without.*)

Let's see.

(*He moves the telescope.*)

Nothing . . . nothing . . . good . . . . good . . . nothing goo—

(*He starts, lowers the telescope, examines it, turns it again on the without. Pause.*)

Bad luck to it!
Hamm: More complications!

(Clov *gets down.*)

Not an underplot, I trust.

(Clov *moves ladder nearer window, gets up on it, turns telescope on the without.*)

Clov (dismayed): Looks like a small boy!
Hamm (sarcastic): A small . . . boy!
Clov: I'll go and see.

(*He gets down, drops the telescope, goes towards door, turns.*)

I'll take the gaff.

(*He looks for the gaff, sees it, picks it up, hastens towards door.*)

Hamm: No!

   (Clov *halts.*)

Clov: No? A potential procreator?
Hamm: If he exists he'll die there or he'll come here. And if he doesn't . . .

   (*Pause.*)

Clov: You don't believe me? You think I'm inventing?

   (*Pause.*)

Hamm: It's the end, Clov, we've come to the end. I don't need you anymore.

   (*Pause.*)

Clov: Lucky for you.

   (*He goes towards door.*)

Hamm: Leave me the gaff.

   (Clov *gives him the gaff, goes towards door, halts, looks at alarm clock, takes it down, looks round for a better place to put it, goes to bins, puts it on lid of* Nagg's *bin. Pause.*)

Clov: I'll leave you.

   (*He goes towards door.*)

Hamm: Before you go . . .

   (Clov *halts near door.*)

   . . . say something.
Clov: There is nothing to say.
Hamm: A few words . . . to ponder . . . in my heart.
Clov: Your heart!
Hamm: Yes.

   (*Pause. Forcibly.*)

Yes!

   (*Pause.*)

With the rest, in the end, the shadows, the murmurs, all the trouble, to
end up with.

   (*Pause.*)

Clov. . . . He never spoke to me. Then, in the end, before he went, with-
out my having asked him, he spoke to me. He said . . .
Clov (*despairingly*): Ah . . . !
Hamm: Something . . . from your heart.
Clov: My heart!

Hamm: A few words . . . from your heart.

(*Pause.*)

Clov (*fixed gaze, tonelessly, towards auditorium*): They said to me, That's love, yes, yes, not a doubt, now you see how—

Hamm: Articulate!

Clov (*as before*): How easy it is. They said to me, That's friendship, yes, yes, no question, you've found it. They said to me, Here's the place, stop, raise your head and look at all that beauty. That order! They said to me, Come now, you're not a brute beast, think upon these things and you'll see how all becomes clear. And simple! They said to me, What skilled attention they get, all these dying of their wounds.

Hamm: Enough!

Clov (*as before*): I say to myself—sometimes, Clov, you must learn to suffer better than that if you want them to weary of punishing you—one day. I say to myself—sometimes, Clov, you must be there better than that if you want them to let you go—one day. But I feel too old, and too far, to form new habits. Good, it'll never end, I'll never go.

(*Pause.*)

Then one day, suddenly, it ends, it changes, I don't understand, it dies, or it's me, I don't understand, that either. I ask the words that remain—sleeping, waking, morning, evening. They have nothing to say.

(*Pause.*)

I open the door of the cell and go. I am so bowed I only see my feet, if I open my eyes, and between my legs a little trail of black dust. I say to myself that the earth is extinguished, though I never saw it lit.

(*Pause.*)

It's easy going.

(*Pause.*)

When I fall I'll weep for happiness.

(*Pause. He goes towards door.*)

Hamm: Clov!

(*Clov halts, without turning.*)

Nothing.

(*Clov moves on.*)

Clov!

(*Clov halts, without turning.*)

Clov: This is what we call making an exit.

Hamm: I'm obliged to you, Clov. For your services.
Clov (turning, sharply): Ah pardon, it's I am obliged to you.
Hamm: It's we are obliged to each other.

(*Pause. Clov goes towards door.*)

One thing more.

(*Clov halts.*)

A last favor.

(*Exit Clov.*)

Cover me with the sheet.

(*Long pause.*)

No? Good.

(*Pause.*)

Me to play.

(*Pause. Wearily.*)

Old endgame lost of old, play and lose and have done with losing.

(*Pause. More animated.*)

Let me see.

(*Pause.*)

Ah yes!

(*He tries to move the chair, using the gaff as before. Enter* Clov, *dressed for
the road. Panama hat, tweed coat, raincoat over his arm, umbrella, bag. He halts
by the door and stands there, impassive and motionless, his eyes fixed on* Hamm, *till
the end.* Hamm *gives up.*)

Good.

(*Pause.*)

Discard.

(*He throws away the gaff, makes to throw away the dog, thinks better of it.*)

Take it easy.

(*Pause.*)

And now?

(*Pause.*)

Raise hat.

(*He raises his toque.*)

Peace to our . . . arses.

(*Pause.*)

And put on again.

(*He puts on his toque.*)

Deuce.

(*Pause. He takes off his glasses.*)

Wipe.

(*He takes out his handkerchief and, without unfolding it, wipes his glasses.*)

And put on again.

(*He puts on his glasses, puts back the handkerchief in his pocket.*)

We're coming. A few more squirms like that and I'll call.

(*Pause.*)

A little poetry.

(*Pause.*)

You prayed—

(*Pause. He corrects himself.*)

You CRIED for night; it comes—

(*Pause. He corrects himself.*)

It FALLS: now cry in darkness.

(*He repeats, chanting.*)

You cried for night; it falls: now cry in darkness.

(*Pause.*)

Nicely put, that.

(*Pause.*)

And now?

(*Pause.*)

Moments for nothing, now as always, time was never and time is over, reckoning closed and story ended.

(*Pause. Narrative tone.*)

If he could have his child with him. . . .

(*Pause.*)

It was the moment I was waiting for.

(Pause.)

You don't want to abandon him? You want him to bloom while you are withering? Be there to solace your last million last moments?

(Pause.)

He doesn't realize, all he knows is hunger, and cold, and death to crown it all. But you! You ought to know what the earth is like, nowadays. Oh I put him before his responsibilities!

(Pause. Normal tone.)

Well, there we are, there I am, that's enough.

(He raises the whistle to his lips, hesitates, drops it. Pause.)

Yes, truly!

(He whistles. Pause. Louder. Pause.)

Good.

(Pause.)

Father!

(Pause. Louder.)

Father!

(Pause.)

Good.

(Pause.)

We're coming.

(Pause.)

And to end up with?

(Pause.)

Discard.

(He throws away the dog. He tears the whistle from his neck.)

With my compliments.

(He throws whistle towards auditorium. Pause. He sniffs. Soft.)

Clov!

(Long pause.)

No? Good.

(He takes out the handkerchief.)

Since that's the way we're playing it . . . *(he unfolds handkerchief)* . . . let's play it that way . . . *(he unfolds)* . . . and speak no more about it . . . *(he finishes unfolding)* . . . speak no more.

(He holds handkerchief spread out before him.)

Old stancher!

(Pause.)

You . . . remain.

(Pause. He covers his face with handkerchief, lowers his arms to armrests, remains motionless.)

(Brief tableau.)

CURTAIN

SAMUEL BECKETT
(1906–1989) Web

www

Born in Dublin, Samuel Beckett lived in Foxrock, a southern suburb of Dublin, until his graduation from Trinity College in 1928. He taught for a brief time in Dublin and Belfast before moving to Paris, where he quickly immersed himself in literary circles, particularly that led by his fellow countryman, James Joyce. Beckett wrote essays and fiction before World War II, when he fought with the French resistance. He turned to drama after the war, writing, among other works, *Waiting for Godot* (1953). He was awarded the Nobel Prize in 1969 and continued to write drama and fiction until the time of his death.

TOPICS FOR CRITICAL THINKING

1. Review names in the play, particularly Hamm and Clov. What do these names suggest about the relationships between the characters?
2. Why is Hamm angry at his parents, especially Nagg? What have they done to incur his ill will?
3. Review Nagg's long joke about the "Englishman and the trousers." What's funny about his story?
4. Why does Clov want to leave Hamm? Do you think that he eventually will one day?
5. Near the middle of the play, Clov turns his telescope to the audience and says he sees "a multitude . . . in transports . . . of joy." What irony potentially exists in this statement?
6. How are we to account for the boy Clov finally claims to see outside of Hamm's shelter? Who is this boy? Why is his appearance significant?

TOPIC FOR CRITICAL WRITING

Critics have long speculated about the set of *Endgame*. Is it, for example, a bomb shelter or even the inside of Hamm's head? Does the title of the play and the chessboard floor indicate that the play is somehow like chess? Develop an argument that describes the set and explains why it is important to the issues that Beckett develops in the play.

Critical Perspective: Beckett after Auschwitz

"After the Second World War, everything, including a resurrected culture, has been destroyed without realizing it; humankind continues to vegetate, creeping along after events that even the survivors cannot really survive, on a rubbish heap that has made even reflection on one's own damaged state useless. . . . The violence of the unspeakable is mirrored in the fear of mentioning it. Beckett keeps it nebulous.

"The catastrophes that inspire *Endgame* have shattered the individual whose substantiality and absoluteness was the common thread . . . of existentialism."

—Theodor Adorno, "Trying to Understand *Endgame*" (1961)

Critical Perspective: Beckett and Shakespeare, Tragedy and the Grotesque

"Between tragedy and grotesque there is the same conflict for or against such notions as . . . belief in the absolute, hope for the ultimate solution of the contradiction between the moral order and every-day practice. Tragedy is the theatre of priests, grotesque is the theatre of clowns.

"This conflict between two philosophies and two types of theatre becomes particularly acute in times of great upheavals. When established values have been overthrown, and there is no appeal, to God, Nature, or History, from the tortures inflicted by the cruel world, the clown becomes the central figure in the theatre. He accompanies the exiled trio—the king, the nobleman and his son—on their cruel wanderings through the cold endless night which has fallen on the world; through the 'cold night' which, as in Shakespeare's *King Lear*, 'will turn us all into fools and madmen.'"

—Jan Kott, *Shakespeare Our Contemporary* (1964)

Critical Perspective: On Beckett, Modernism, and Postmodernism

"In the context of twentieth-century theatre, his first plays mark the transition from Modernism with its preoccupation with self-reflection to Postmodernism with its insistence on pastiche, parody and fragmentation. Instead of following the tradition which demands that a play have an exposition, a climax and a dénouement, Beckett's plays have a cyclical structure which might indeed be better described as a diminishing spiral. They present images of entropy in which the world and the people in it are slowly but inexorably running down. In this spiral descending towards a final closure that can never be found in the Beckettian universe, the characters take refuge in repetition, repeating their own actions and words and often those of others—to pass the time."

—Michael Worton, "Waiting for Godot and
Endgame: Theatre as Text" (1994)

Critical Perspective: On Materiality in Beckett and Why It Matters

"Beckett's protagonists . . . are never set free from the material world—from objects and the need to take inventories—and they are always connected to the past in complicated ways. Juxtaposing these characters to the nomadic subjectivities (and memories) of postmodern and postcolonial travelers, therefore, will not simply vault them into postmodernity but will, I hope, explain their predicaments and Beckett's effacement of neat lines between modernity and postmodernity. . . ."

—Stephen Watt, *Postmodern/Drama:
Reading the Contemporary Stage* (1998)

Part VIII
Reading and Interpreting:
An Anthology of Contemporary Plays

49 Race and Gender on the American Stage

The pairing of works from the contemporary American stage in this chapter is in no way intended to suggest that the representation of race, gender, and ethnicity began in the later decades of the twentieth century. Nor is it meant to imply that only recently have dramatists of color contributed to an ongoing discourse about race in America. Far from it. Indeed, scholars Nicolás Kanellos and Jorge A. Huerta observe that Spanish American drama was most likely born sometime during the sixteenth century, when Spanish missionaries "wed their evangelical theater to the dramatic performance of the indigenous peoples of America." In his influential study *Theater U.S.A.*, historian Barnard Hewitt similarly maintains that the first plays seen in America were performed by Spanish soldiers in camps along the Rio Grande near what is now El Paso, Texas.

There is little question that plays by and about ethnic Americans have enriched the history of American drama. One of the most popular dramas of the early republic, for example, John Augustus Stone's *Metamora; or, The Last of the Wampanoags* (1829), was produced for several decades through the time of the Civil War. However barbaric or savage Metamora appeared, however much he may have been used to justify the expansion of white influence in early nineteenth-century America, he also possessed an inherent nobility that, finally, had to be recognized. In many novels of the time, James Fenimore Cooper's *The Last of the Mohicans* (1826), for example, representations of Native Americans followed a more binary logic based in part on an association of sexuality and racial identity. Such a logic dictated that, on the one hand, Cooper's Magua replicates an invidious stereotype of the racial or ethnic "Other" as barbaric and rapacious; on the other hand, Chingachgook and Uncas, the last of the Mohicans, are loyal and moral men: "noble savages." They are so, at least in part, because of their friendship with Cooper's white hero, Natty Bumppo.

In the years prior to the Civil War, not surprisingly, plays representing the lives of African American slaves enjoyed tremendous popularity in America—North and South. George L. Aiken's dramatization of Harriet Beecher Stowe's novel *Uncle Tom's Cabin* (1852) was performed over a quarter of a million times during Stowe's lifetime—and many more times on stage and in film after her death. In 1859, Irish playwright Dion Boucicault's *The Octoroon; or, Life in Louisiana* introduced the issue of miscegenation to American audiences, as a handsome white protagonist falls in love with a beautiful and tragic mulatta. Some at the time regarded the play as a kind of *Romeo and Juliet*: American star-crossed lovers doomed not by fate, but by both prejudice and an unjust law prohibiting interracial marriage. At this same time, a number of plays staged in Philadelphia, New York, and Boston concerned immigration and the immigrant's often difficult assimilation into what was becoming a multicultural America. Irish plays were especially popular, as these cities were growing at unprecedented rates because of the influx of Irish fleeing to America to escape the Great Famine (1845–1851). How would newly arrived Irish find their ways in Boston Brahmin society or in New York? Would there be room in the great melting pot of American society for the Irish, Italians, Jews, and other immigrants who poured into the country? What lives awaited African Americans who migrated from the South seeking freedom and economic opportunity in the great cities of the North?

All of these matters—race, ethnicity, interracial relationships, and a new multi-ethnic America—have received considerable attention in modern and contemporary American drama. In the 1920s, Eugene O'Neill's *The Emperor Jones* (1920) and *All God's Chillun Got Wings* (1923) featured psychologically complex African American protagonists. During the Harlem Renaissance of the same decade, novels like Nella Larsen's *Quicksand* (1928) and *Passing* (1929) revisited the issues dramatized by Boucicault of race, racism, and interracial intimacy. In 1935, Harlem Renaissance poet Langston Hughes wrote *Mulatto*, which earned the distinction of being the longest-running play ever written by an African American. But beyond writing poems and successful plays, Hughes also founded three companies to produce African American drama: the Suitcase Theatre in Harlem, the Negro Art Theatre in Los Angeles, and the Skyloft Players in Chicago. In 1955, Alice Childress's *Trouble in Mind*, a play critical of the racial stereotyping of blacks on stage, won an Obie for the best off-Broadway play; and in 1959, Lorraine Hansberry's *A Raisin in the Sun*, directed by Lloyd Richards and starring Sidney Poitier, won the New York Drama Critics Circle Award as the best play of the year.

The beginning of the twentieth century also marks the emergence of a distinctly woman's drama and feminist sensibility to the American stage. A few women, of course, wrote for the nineteenth-century theater, the most influential of whom was Anna Cora Mowatt, whose satire of wealthy New Yorkers, *Fashion* (1845), achieved considerable success. More concerned than Mowatt with such issues as women's independence and professional success, Rachel Crothers wrote *A Man's World* (1910) and *He and She* (1911), the latter of which centers around a wife's painful choice between a career and a daughter who craves—and desperately needs—her attention. Arguably the most enduring of American plays of this period, Susan Glaspell's *Trifles* (1916), appears in Chapter 46. It, like Sophie Treadwell's later *Machinal* (1928), probes the effects of loneliness on a sterile marriage, culminating in the arrest of a wife for the murder of her husband. Unlike earlier realistic drama, that of Henrik Ibsen for example, which dealt with similar social issues, both Treadwell and Glaspell experiment with nonrealistic devices to communicate more forcefully the psychological effects on women of living in a male-dominated world.

Not surprisingly, women have contributed significantly to the contemporary American stage, where issues of equal rights, male conceptions of beauty and the feminine body, racism, sexism, and—in the case of Cherríe Moraga's *Giving Up the Ghost* (1986; revised and reproduced, 1989)—lesbianism have found theatrical representation. Wendy Wasserstein, Beth Henley, and Marsha Norman, to name just three, have proved themselves playwrights of enduring quality, as have such African American dramatists as Adrienne Kennedy, Suzan-Lori Parks, Anna Deavere Smith, and Ntozake Shange. Like their predecessors earlier in the century, Kennedy and Shange in particular are responsible for tremendous formal experimentation. Shange, for example, poses the significant question of whether traditional dramatic forms, European realism for instance, is adequate to express the experience of growing up black in a predominantly white St. Louis or enduring the longstanding dilemma of racial stereotyping. Like much of Shange's work, Moraga's *Giving Up the Ghost*, a poetic drama that includes monologue, poetry, and two incarnations of the same central character—one a teenager from the past; the other, a Chicana lesbian in the present—mixes into a hybrid form a variety of narrative techniques.

Both LeRoi Jones's *Dutchman* and Cherríe Moraga's *Shadow of a Man* suggest, on the one hand, that the same questions about race and gender in America have persisted from the time the country was founded. On the other hand, both plays indicate how these social realities change with the times. As a consequence, it is hardly surprising that Jones and Moraga subject longstanding stereotypes of African Americans, Latinos, and Latinas to critical scrutiny. At the same time, these plays are rooted in the historical moments of their composition, thus revealing the supple, even fluid ways in which "Otherness" and conceptions of gender are continually being revised in America.

From LeRoi Jones to Amiri Baraka: *Dutchman* and the Black Arts Movement

Amiri Baraka was born Everett LeRoi Jones in Newark, New Jersey, and after studying at Rutgers and Howard Universities and serving in the U.S. Air Force, he became a part of the bohemian arts scene in New York in the later 1950s. In 1958, he married Jewish American Hetti Roberta Cohen and began writing and reading poetry. He was associated with both Beat and Black Mountain poets and published his first book of poetry in 1961.

After a brief trip to Cuba, Jones began to move politically and aesthetically away from the countercultural, white-dominated Beats and toward the more radically separatist **Black Arts Movement.** In the wake of Malcolm X's assassination in 1965, LeRoi Jones became Imamu Amiri Baraka and his work changed significantly. His plays *Dutchman*, *The Toilet*, and *The Slave* were all produced in 1964, the latter of which contains an autobiographical quality as a black intellectual finds himself caught between a predominantly white academic world in which his wife, children, and former colleagues live and a revolution outside of blacks seeking equal rights and social justice. The times demanded that characters like Walker Vessels and writers like Baraka make difficult choices, and both opted for allegiance to a separatist black nationalist ideology. As was the case with many such movements—in early twentieth-century Ireland, for example, or mid-century India—a militant nationalism was underwritten by a distinctly cultural nationalism. Revolution, in other words, takes place both in the streets and in the mind; its weapons include books, art, language, and thought.

Baraka's poems and plays of the mid- and later 1960s, therefore, press emphatically for both a more just society *and* a uniquely black art. And, like the streets of Detroit and Los Angeles in the later 1960s, Baraka's poems and plays are often linguistically or physically violent. Anger calcifies into resolve in his poem "Black Art," which ends with the following refrain:

> We want a black poem. And a
> Black World.
> Let the world be a Black Poem
> And let all Black People Speak This Poem
> Silently
> Or LOUD

Black art bespeaks both a cultural nationalism and an advocacy for black power, as two lines from the introductory verse to his *Four Black Revolutionary Plays* (1969) clarify:

> i am prophesying the death of white people in this land
> i am prophesying the triumph of black life in this land,
>   and over all the world

Such confrontational sentiments inform Baraka's best-known play *Dutchman*, the form of which borrows from both expressionist drama and absurdism. The opening stage directions emphasize the play's nonrealistic qualities: "*In the flying underbelly of the city. Steaming hot, and summer on top, outside. Underground. The subway heaped in modern myth.*" The myths incorporated into the play, however, are more than just "modern." The title of the play, for instance, refers to the legend of the *Flying Dutchman*, an infamous ghost ship, and, perhaps, the Dutch traders who helped bring slaves to the New World. Lula, like Eve in the Old Testament, is associated with an apple and temptation, in this case sexual temptation. She initially speaks "pure sex talk," or so her eventual victim Clay perceives it, a "come on" intended to incite his desire. And she has a bag full of apples and other inducements to overwhelm her "big-eyed prey."

At the same time, Baraka creates a substrate of references to stereotypes of black men that runs throughout the play. This includes Clay as "Black Beast," a kind of Bigger Thomas from Richard Wright's novel *Native Son* (1940), prone both to unrestrained violence and desire. Both traits are inevitably associated with manhood, which Lula in Scene Two explains has been the subject of their conversation all along: "[We've been talking] About your manhood, what do you think? What do you think we've been talking about all this time?" Her references to him later as "Uncle Tom. Thomas Woollyhead" and "Uncle Tom Big Lip" are calculated to challenge Clay's sense of manhood: "You're afraid of white people," Lula taunts. "And your father was." If anything, Clay is a young intellectual, fascinated by ideas and literature, much like Baraka himself in the 1950s. But Lula will not allow him to pursue these interests without reminding him in the most vulgar of ways about racism in America: "I bet you never once thought you were a black nigger." The play thus seems to ask: How is her racist attack on Clay related to her repeated challenges to his masculinity?

The narrative leads ultimately to Lula's ritualistic murder of Clay and the complicity of both black and white passengers—and a shuffling, deferential black conductor—in the crime. As the play ends, Lula spies another young black man to tempt, incite to anger, and then murder. The ritual continues, presumably forever.

Because such action is unrealistic, Baraka invites his audience to read the play in allegorical terms. Does Lula symbolize all white America? Is Clay representative of an optimistic and ambitious black America tempted into believing it can become intimate with white America, only to discover that the gesture of welcome is merely a cheap hustle or a death warrant? Does the art of Charlie Parker or Bessie Smith, to whom Clay alludes near the end of the play, sublimate black anger or is it an expression of it? Does the conductor at the end suggest blacks' complicity in their own destruction? How does the "mythic" express these issues? *Dutchman* remains an important play in the canon of contemporary drama in part because it prompts these—and many more—questions.

ᗰᗯᗰ

AMIRI BARAKA

Dutchman   (1964)

CHARACTERS

Clay, twenty-year-old Negro
Lula, thirty-year-old white woman
Riders of coach, white and black
Young negro
Conductor

In the flying underbelly of the city. Steaming hot, and summer on top, outside. Underground. The subway heaped in modern myth.

Opening scene is a man sitting in a subway seat, holding a magazine but looking vacantly just above its wilting pages. Occasionally he looks blankly toward the window on his right. Dim lights and darkness whistling by against the glass. (Or paste the lights, as admitted props, right on the subway windows. Have them move, even dim and flicker. But give the sense of speed. Also stations, whether the train is stopped or the glitter and activity of these stations merely flashes by the windows.)

The man is sitting alone. That is, only his seat is visible, though the rest of the car is outfitted as a complete subway car. But only his seat is shown. There might be, for a time, as the play begins, a loud scream of the actual train. And it can recur throughout the play, or continue on a lower key once the dialogue starts.

The train slows after a time, pulling to a brief stop at one of the stations. The man looks idly up, until he sees a woman's face staring at him through the window; when it realizes that the man has noticed the face, it begins very premeditatedly to smile. The man smiles too, for a moment, without a trace of self-consciousness. Almost an instinctive though undesirable response. Then a kind of awkwardness or embarrassment sets in, and the man makes to look away, is further embarrassed, so he brings back his eyes to where the face was, but by now the train is moving again, and the face would seem to be left behind by the way the man turns his head to look back through the other windows at the slowly fading platform. He smiles then; more comfortably confident, hoping perhaps that his memory of this brief encounter will be pleasant. And then he is idle again.

SCENE I

Train roars. Lights flash outside the windows.

Lula *enters from the rear of the car in bright, skimpy summer clothes and sandals. She carries a net bag full of paper books, fruit, and other anonymous articles. She is wearing sunglasses, which she pushes up on her forehead from time to time. Lula is a tall, slender, beautiful woman with long red hair hanging straight down her back, wearing only loud lipstick in somebody's good taste. She is eating an apple, very daintily. Coming down the car toward* Clay.

She stops beside Clay's *seat and hangs languidly from the strap, still managing to eat the apple. It is apparent that she is going to sit in the seat next to* Clay, *and that she is only waiting for him to notice her before she sits.*

Clay *sits as before, looking just beyond his magazine, now and again pulling the magazine slowly back and forth in front of his face in a hopeless effort to fan himself. Then he sees the woman hanging there beside him and he looks up into her face, smiling quizzically.*

Lula: Hello.
Clay: Uh, hi're you?
Lula: I'm going to sit down. . . . O.K.?
Clay: Sure.
Lula:

(Swings down onto the seat, pushing her legs straight out as if she is very weary)

Oooof! Too much weight.
Clay: Ha, doesn't look like much to me.

(Leaning back against the window, a little surprised and maybe stiff)

Lula: It's so anyway.

(And she moves her toes in the sandals, then pulls her right leg up on the left knee, better to inspect the bottoms of the sandals and the back of her heel. She appears for a second not to notice that Clay *is sitting next to her or that she has spoken to him just a second before.* Clay *looks at the magazine, then out the black window. As he does this, she turns very quickly toward him)*

Weren't you staring at me through the window?

(Wheeling around and very much stiffened)

What?

Lula: Weren't you staring at me through the window? At the last stop?

Clay: Staring at you? What do you mean?

Lula: Don't you know what staring means?

Clay: I saw you through the window. . . if that's what it means. I don't know if I was staring. Seems to me you were staring through the window at me.

Lula: I was. But only after I'd turned around and saw you staring through that window down in the vicinity of my ass and legs.

Clay: Really?

Lula: Really. I guess you were just taking those idle potshots. Nothing else to do. Run your mind over people's flesh.

Clay: Oh boy. Wow, now I admit I was looking in your direction. But the rest of that weight is yours.

Lula: I suppose.

Clay: Staring through train windows is weird business. Much weirder than staring very sedately at abstract asses.

Lula: That's why I came looking through the window . . . so you'd have more than that to go on. I even smiled at you.

Clay: That's right.

Lula: I even got into this train, going some other way than mine. Walked down the aisle . . . searching you out.

Clay: Really? That's pretty funny.

Lula: That's pretty funny. . . . God, you're dull.

Clay: Well, I'm sorry, lady, but I really wasn't prepared for party talk.

Lula: No, you're not. What are you prepared for?

(Wrapping the apple core in a Kleenex and dropping it on the floor)

Clay:

(Takes her conversation as pure sex talk. He turns to confront her squarely with this idea)

I'm prepared for anything. How about you?

Lula:

(Laughing loudly and cutting it off abruptly)

What do you think you're doing?

Clay: What?

Lula: You think I want to pick you up, get you to take me somewhere and screw me, huh?

Clay: Is that the way I look?

Lula: You look like you been trying to grow a beard. That's exactly what you look like. You look like you live in New Jersey with your parents and are trying to grow a beard. That's what. You look like you've been reading Chinese poetry and drinking lukewarm sugarless tea.

(*Laughs, uncrossing and recrossing her legs*)

You look like death eating a soda cracker.

Clay:

(*Cocking his head from one side to the other, embarrassed and trying to make some comeback, but also intrigued by what the woman is saying . . . even the sharp city coarseness of her voice, which is still a kind of gentle sidewalk throb*)

Really? I look like all that?

Lula: Not all of it.

(*She feints a seriousness to cover an actual somber tone*)

I lie a lot.

(*Smiling*)

It helps me control the world.

Clay:

(*Relieved and laughing louder than the humor*)

Yeah, I bet.

Lula: But it's true, most of it, right? Jersey? Your bumpy neck?

Clay: How'd you know all that? Huh? Really, I mean about Jersey . . . and even the beard. I met you before? You know Warren Enright?

Lula: You tried to make it with your sister when you were ten.

(Clay *leans back hard against the back of the seat, his eyes opening now, still trying to look amused*)

But I succeeded a few weeks ago.

(*She starts to laugh again*)

Clay: What're you talking about? Warren tell you that? You're a friend of Georgia's?

Lula: I told you I lie. I don't know your sister. I don't know Warren Enright.

Clay: You mean you're just picking these things out of the air?

Lula: Is Warren Enright a tall skinny black boy with a phony English accent?

Clay: I figured you knew him.

Lula: But I don't. I just figured you would know somebody like that.

(*Laughs*)

Clay: Yeah, yeah.

Lula: You're probably on your way to his house now.

Clay: That's right.

Lula:

(*Putting her hand on Clay's closest knee, drawing it from the knee up to the thigh's hinge, then removing it, watching his face very closely and continuing to laugh, perhaps more gently than before*)

Dull, dull, dull. I bet you think I'm exciting.

Clay: You're O.K.

Lula: Am I exciting you now?

Clay: Right. That's not what's supposed to happen?

Lula: How do I know?

(*She returns her hand, without moving it, then takes it away and plunges it in her bag to draw out an apple*)

You want this?

Clay: Sure.

Lula:

(*She gets one out of the bag for herself*)

Eating apples together is always the first step. Or walking up uninhabited Seventh Avenue in the twenties on weekends.

(*Bites and giggles, glancing at* Clay *and speaking in loose sing-song*)

Can get you involved . . . boy! Get us involved. Um-huh.

(*Mock seriousness*)

Would you like to get involved with me, Mister Man?

Clay:

(*Trying to be as flippant as* Lula, *whacking happily at the apple*)

Sure. Why not? A beautiful woman like you. Huh, I'd be a fool not to.

Lula: And I bet you're sure you know what you're talking about.

(*Taking him a little roughly by the wrist, so he cannot eat the apple, then shaking the wrist*)

I bet you're sure of almost everything anybody ever asked you about . . . right?

(*Shakes his wrist harder*)

Right?

Clay: Yeah, right. . . . Wow, you're pretty strong, you know? Whatta you, a lady wrestler or something?

Lula: What's wrong with lady wrestlers? And don't answer because you never knew any. Huh.

(Cynically)

That's for sure. They don't have any lady wrestlers in that part of Jersey. That's for sure.

Clay: Hey, you still haven't told me how you know so much about me.

Lula: I told you I didn't know anything about *you* . . . you're a well-known type.

Clay: Really?

Lula: Or at least I know the type very well. And your skinny English friend too.

Clay: Anonymously?

Lula:

(Settles back in seat, single-mindedly finishing her apple and humming snatches of rhythm and blues song)

What?

Clay: Without knowing us specifically?

Lula: Oh boy.

(Looking quickly at Clay*)*

What a face. You know, you could be a handsome man.

Clay: I can't argue with you.

Lula:

(Vague, off-center response)

What?

Clay:

(Raising his voice, thinking the train noise has drowned part of his sentence)

I can't argue with you.

Lula: My hair is turning gray. A gray hair for each year and type I've come through.

Clay: Why do you want to sound so old?

Lula: But it's always gentle when it starts.

(Attention drifting)

Hugged against tenements, day or night.

Clay: What?

Lula:

(Refocusing)

Hey, why don't you take me to that party you're going to?

Clay: You must be a friend of Warren's to know about the party.

Lula: Wouldn't you like to take me to the party?

(Imitates clinging vine)

Oh, come on, ask me to your party.

Clay: Of course I'll ask you to come with me to the party. And I'll bet you're a friend of Warren's.

Lula: Why not be a friend of Warren's? Why not?

(Taking his arm)

Have you asked me yet?

Clay: How can I ask you when I don't know your name?

Lula: Are you talking to my name?

Clay: What is it, a secret?

Lula: I'm Lena the Hyena.°

Clay: The famous woman poet?

Lula: Poetess! The same!

Clay: Well, you know so much about me . . . what's my name?

Lula: Morris the Hyena.

Clay: The famous woman poet?

Lula: The same.

(Laughing and going into her bag)

You want another apple?

Clay: Can't make it, lady. I only have to keep one doctor away a day.

Lula: I bet your name is . . . something like . . . uh, Gerald or Walter. Huh?

Clay: God, no.

Lula: Lloyd, Norman? One of those hopeless colored names creeping out of New Jersey. Leonard? Gag. . . .

Clay: Like Warren?

Lula: Definitely. Just exactly like Warren. Or Everett.

Clay: Gag. . . .

Lula: Well, for sure, it's not Willie.

Clay: It's Clay.

Lula: Clay? Really? Clay what?

Clay: Take your pick. Jackson, Johnson, or Williams.

Lula: Oh, really? Good for you. But it's got to be Williams. You're too pretentious to be a Jackson or Johnson.

Clay: Thass right.

Lula: But Clay's O.K.

Clay: So's Lena.

Lula: It's Lula.

Clay: Oh?

Lula: Lula the Hyena.

Clay: Very good.

Lena the Hyena: Character in Al Capp's comic strip, *L'il Abner* (1934–1977). The ugliest woman who ever lived, Lena drove anyone who looked at her instantly mad, so no sane person could reliably describe her. She was the subject of a famous national drawing contest sponsored by Capp in 1945.

Lula:

(*Starts laughing again*)

Now you say to me, "Lula, Lula, why don't you go to this party with me tonight?" It's your turn, and let those be your lines.

Clay: Lula, why don't you go to this party with me tonight, Huh?

Lula: Say my name twice before you ask, and no huh's.

Clay: Lula, Lula, why don't you go to this party with me tonight?

Lula: I'd like to go, Clay, but how can you ask me to go when you barely know me?

Clay: That is strange, isn't it?

Lula: What kind of reaction is that? You're supposed to say, "Aw, come on, we'll get to know each other better at the party."

Clay: That's pretty corny.

Lula: What are you into anyway?

(*Looking at him half sullenly but still amused*)

What thing are you playing at, Mister? Mister Clay Williams?

(*Grabs his thigh, up near the crotch*)

What are *you* thinking about?

Clay: Watch it now, you're gonna excite me for real.

Lula:

(*Taking her hand away and throwing her apple core through the window*)

I bet.

(*She slumps in the seat and is heavily silent*)

Clay: I thought you knew everything about me? What happened?

(Lula *looks at him, then looks slowly away, then over where the other aisle would be. Noise of the train. She reaches in her bag and pulls out one of the paper books. She puts it on her leg and thumbs the pages listlessly.* Clay *cocks his head to see the title of the book. Noise of the train.* Lula *flips pages and her eyes drift. Both remain silent*)

Are you going to the party with me, Lula?

Lula:

(*Bored and not even looking*)

I don't even know you.

Clay: You said you know my type.

Lula:

(*Strangely irritated*)

Don't get smart with me, Buster. I know you like the palm of my hand.

Clay: The one you eat the apples with?

Lula: Yeh. And the one I open doors late Saturday evening with. That's my
       door. Up at the top of the stairs. Five flights. Above a lot of Italians and
       lying Americans. And scrape carrots with. Also . . .

(Looks at him)

the same hand I unbutton my dress with, or let my skirt fall down. Same
hand. Lover.

Clay: Are you angry about anything? Did I say something wrong?

Lula: Everything you say is wrong.

(Mock smile)

That's what makes you so attractive. Ha. In that funnybook jacket with
all the buttons.

(More animate, taking hold of his jacket)

What've you got that jacket and tie on in all this heat for? And why're
you wearing a jacket and tie like that? Did your people ever burn witches
or start revolutions over the price of tea? Boy, those narrow-shoulder
clothes come from a tradition you ought to feel oppressed by. A three-
button suit. What right do you have to be wearing a three-button suit
and striped tie? Your grandfather was a slave, he didn't go to Harvard.

Clay: My grandfather was a night watchman.

Lula: And you went to a colored college where everybody thought they
       were Averell Harriman.°

Clay: All except me.

Lula: And who did you think you were? Who do you think you are now?

Clay:

(Laughs as if to make light of the whole trend of the conversation)

Well, in college I thought I was Baudelaire.° But I've slowed down since.

Lula: I bet you never once thought you were a black nigger.

*(Mock serious, then she howls with laughter. Clay is stunned but after initial
reaction, he quickly tries to appreciate the humor. Lula almost shrieks)*

A black Baudelaire.

Clay: That's right.

Lula: Boy, are you corny. I take back what I said before. Everything you say
       is not wrong. It's perfect. You should be on television.

Clay: You act like you're on television already.

Lula: That's because I'm an actress.

Clay: I thought so.

Averell Harriman: Wealthy U.S. businessman and public official (1891–1986). Harriman was un-
dersecretary of state in 1964, when *Dutchman* was first performed.   *Charles Baudelaire
(1821–1867):* French poet and critic unappreciated during his lifetime (he was fined for "offenses
against public morals" after the publication of one book), now considered a landmark French literary figure.

Lula: Well, you're wrong. I'm no actress. I told you I always lie. I'm nothing, honey, and don't you ever forget it.

(Lighter)

Although my mother was a Communist. The only person in my family
ever to amount to anything.

Clay: My mother was a Republican.

Lula: And your father voted for the man° rather than the party.°

Clay: Right!

Lula: Yea for him. Yea, yea for him.

Clay: Yea!

Lula: And yea for America where he is free to vote for the mediocrity of his
choice! Yea!

Clay: Yea!

Lula: And yea for both your parents who even though they differ about so
crucial a matter as the body politic still forged a union of love and sacrifice that was destined to flower at the birth of the noble Clay . . . what's
your middle name?

Clay: Clay.

Lula: A union of love and sacrifice that was destined to flower at the birth of
the noble Clay Clay Williams. Yea! And most of all yea yea for you, Clay
Clay. The Black Baudelaire! Yes!

(And with knifelike cynicism)

My Christ. My Christ.

Clay: Thank you, ma'am.

Lula: May the people accept you as a ghost of the future. And love you, that
you might not kill them when you can.

Clay: What?

Lula: You're a murderer, Clay, and you know it.

(Her voice darkening with significance)

You know goddamn well what I mean.

Clay: I do?

Lula: So we'll pretend the air is light and full of perfume.

Clay:

(Sniffing at her blouse)

It is.

Lula: And we'll pretend the people cannot see you. That is, the citizens.
And that you are free of your own history. And I am free of my history.
We'll pretend that we are both anonymous beauties smashing along
through the city's entrails.

---

the man: Slang for the "white man," or the system of institutionalized racism that oppresses black
Americans   *party:* International Communist Party, which recruited heavily among the American black population in the mid-twentieth century by promising complete racial equality.

(She yells as loud as she can)

GROOVE!

Black

SCENE II

Scene is the same as before, though now there are other seats visible in the car. And throughout the scene other people get on the subway. There are maybe one or two seated in the car as the scene opens, though neither Clay *nor* Lula *notices them.* Clay's *tie is open.* Lula *is hugging his arm.*

Clay: The party!

Lula: I know it'll be something good. You can come in with me, looking casual and significant. I'll be strange, haughty, and silent, and walk with long slow strides.

Clay: Right.

Lula: When you get drunk, pat me once, very lovingly on the flanks, and I'll look at you cryptically, licking my lips.

Clay: It sounds like something we can do.

Lula: You'll go around talking to young men about your mind, and to old men about your plans. If you meet a very close friend who is also with someone like me, we can stand together, sipping our drinks and exchanging codes of lust. The atmosphere will be slithering in love and half-love and very open moral decision.

Clay: Great. Great.

Lula: And everyone will pretend they don't know your name, and then . . .

(She pauses heavily)

later, when they have to, they'll claim a friendship that denies your sterling character.

Clay:

(Kissing her neck and fingers)

And then what?

Lula: Then? Well, then we'll go down the street, late night, eating apples and winding very deliberately toward my house.

Clay: Deliberately?

Lula: I mean, we'll look in all the shopwindows, and make fun of the queers. Maybe we'll meet a Jewish Buddhist and flatten his conceits over some very pretentious coffee.

Clay: In honor of whose God?

Lula: Mine.

Clay: Who is . . . ?

Lula: Me . . . and you?

Clay: A corporate Godhead.
Lula: Exactly. Exactly.

(*Notices one of the other people entering*)

Clay: Go on with the chronicle. Then what happens to us?
Lula:

(*A mild depression, but she still makes her description triumphant and increasingly direct*)

To my house, of course.
Clay: Of course.
Lula: And up the narrow steps of the tenement.°
Clay: You live in a tenement?
Lula: Wouldn't live anywhere else. Reminds me specifically of my novel form of insanity.
Clay: Up the tenement stairs.
Lula: And with my apple-eating hand I push open the door and lead you, my tender big-eyed prey, into my . . . God, what can I call it . . . into my hovel.
Clay: Then what happens?
Lula: After the dancing and games, after the long drinks and long walks, the real fun begins.
Clay: Ah, the real fun.

(*Embarrassed, in spite of himself*)

Which is . . . ?
Lula:

(*Laughs at him*)

Real fun in the dark house. Hah! Real fun in the dark house, high up above the street and the ignorant cowboys. I lead you in, holding your wet hand gently in my hand . . .
Clay: Which is not wet?
Lula: Which is dry as ashes.
Clay: And cold?
Lula: Don't think you'll get out of your responsibility that way. It's not cold at all. You Fascist!° Into my dark living room. Where we'll sit and talk endlessly, endlessly.
Clay: About what?
Lula: About what? About your manhood, what do you think? What do you think we've been talking about all this time?

---

tenement: Apartment house, but with connotations of overcrowding, poor sanitation, safety hazards, and discomfort. Generally used to refer to the housing of impoverished urban immigrants during the early twentieth century.   *Fascist:* Adherent of Facism, a totalitarian political system organized around fidelity to a dictatorial leader, social and economic centralization, and the violent suppression of resistance.

Clay: Well, I didn't know it was that. That's for sure. Every other thing in
    the world but that.

   *(Notices another person entering, looks quickly, almost involuntarily up and
down the car, seeing the other people in the car)*

   Hey, I didn't even notice when those people got on.
Lula: Yeah, I know.
Clay: Man, this subway is slow.
Lula: Yeah, I know.
Clay: Well, go on. We were talking about my manhood.
Lula: We still are. All the time.
Clay: We were in your living room.
Lula: My dark living room. Talking endlessly.
Clay: About my manhood.
Lula: I'll make you a map of it. Just as soon as we get to my house.
Clay: Well, that's great.
Lula: One of the things we do while we talk. And screw.
Clay:

   (Trying to make his smile broader and less shaky)

   We finally got there.
Lula: And you'll call my rooms black as a grave. You'll say, "This place is
    like Juliet's tomb."°
Clay:

   (Laughs)

   I might.
Lula: I know. You've probably said it before.
Clay: And is that all? The whole grand tour?
Lula: Not all. You'll say to me very close to my face, many, many times,
    you'll say, even whisper, that you love me.
Clay: Maybe I will.
Lula: And you'll be lying.
Clay: I wouldn't lie about something like that.
Lula: Hah. It's the only kind of thing you will lie about. Especially if you
    think it'll keep me alive.
Clay: Keep you alive? I don't understand.
Lula:

   (Bursting out laughing, but too shrilly)

   Don't understand? Well, don't look at me. It's the path I take, that's all.
   Where both feet take me when I set them down. One in front of the
   other.

Juliet's tomb: Reference to William Shakespeare's *Romeo and Juliet.* Because her parents opposed
her marriage to Romeo, Juliet feigned death with a sleeping potion in order to be reunited with
him, thus spending several days alive in her family's tomb.

Clay: Morbid. Morbid. You sure you're not an actress? All that self-aggrandizement.

Lula: Well, I told you I wasn't an actress . . . but I also told you I lie all the time. Draw your own conclusions.

Clay: Morbid. Morbid. You sure you're not an actress? All scribed? There's no more?

Lula: I've told you all I know. Or almost all.

Clay: There's no funny parts?

Lula: I thought it was all funny.

Clay: But you mean peculiar, not ha-ha.

Lula: You don't know what I mean.

Clay: Well, tell me the almost part then. You said almost all. What else? I want the whole story.

Lula:

(Searching aimlessly through her bag. She begins to talk breathlessly, with a light and silly tone)

All stories are whole stories. All of 'em. Our whole story . . . nothing but change. How could things go on like that forever? Huh?

(Slaps him on the shoulder, begins finding things in her bag, taking them out and throwing them over her shoulder into the aisle)

Except I do go on as I do. Apples and long walks with deathless intelligent lovers. But you mix it up. Look out the window, all the time. Turning pages. Change change change. Till, shit, I don't know you. Wouldn't, for that matter. You're too serious. I bet you're even too serious to be psychoanalyzed. Like all those Jewish poets from Yonkers,° who leave their mothers looking for other mothers, or others' mothers, on whose baggy tits they lay their fumbling heads. Their poems are always funny, and all about sex.

Clay: They sound great. Like movies.

Lula: But you change.

(Blankly)

And things work on you till you hate them.

(More people come into the train. They come closer to the couple, some of them not sitting, but swinging drearily on the straps, staring at the two with uncertain interest)

Clay: Wow. All these people, so suddenly. They must all come from the same place.

Lula: Right. That they do.

Clay: Oh? You know about them too?

Lula: Oh yeah. About them more than I know about you. Do they frighten you?

Yonkers: Suburb of Manhattan in southern Westchester County, New York.

Clay: Frighten me? Why should they frighten me?

Lula: 'Cause you're an escaped nigger.

Clay: Yeah?

Lula: 'Cause you crawled through the wire and made tracks to my side.

Clay: Wire?

Lula: Don't they have wire around plantations?

Clay: You must be Jewish. All you can think about is wire.° Plantations didn't have any wire. Plantations were big open whitewashed places like heaven, and everybody on 'em was grooved to be there. Just strummin' and hummin' all day.

Lula: Yes, yes.

Clay: And that's how the blues was born.

Lula: Yes, yes. And that's how the blues was born.

(Begins to make up a song that becomes quickly hysterical. As she sings she rises from her seat, still throwing things out of her bag into the aisle, beginning a rhythmical shudder and twistlike wiggle, which she continues up and down the aisle, bumping into many of the standing people and tripping over the feet of those sitting. Each time she runs into a person she lets out a very vicious piece of profanity, wiggling and stepping all the time)

And that's how the blues was born. Yes. Yes. Son of a bitch, get out of the way. Yes. Quack. Yes. Yes. And that's how the blues was born. Ten little niggers sitting on a limb, but none of them ever looked like him.°

(Points to Clay, returns toward the seat, with her hands extended for him to rise and dance with her)

And that's how blues was born. Yes. Come on, Clay. Let's do the nasty. Rub bellies. Rub bellies.

Clay:

(Waves his hands to refuse. He is embarrassed, but determined to get a kick out of the proceedings)

Hey, what was in those apples? Mirror, mirror on the wall, who's the fairest one of all? Snow White,° baby, and don't you forget it.

Lula:

(Grabbing for his hands, which he draws away)

Come on, Clay. Let's rub bellies on the train. The nasty. The nasty. Do the gritty grind, like your ol' rag-head mammy. Grind till you lose your mind. Shake it, shake it, shake it, shake it! OOOOweeee! Come on, Clay. Let's do the choo-choo train shuffle, the navel scratcher.

---

wire: Reference to the barbed wire fences surrounding Nazi concentration camps during the Holocaust.   *Ten little niggers . . . like him:* Parody of a British nursery rhyme, "Ten Little Niggers" (also known as "Ten Little Indians"), in which each of the ten is sequentially killed. For example, "Ten little niggers going out to dine/One choked his little self and then there were nine." In Lula's version, all ten are lynching victims who were hanged from a tree limb.   *Snow White:* Slang reference to cocaine.

Clay: Hey, you coming on like the lady who smoked up her grass skirt.

Lula:

(Becoming annoyed that he will not dance, and becoming more animated as if to embarrass him still further)

Come on, Clay . . . let's do the thing. Uhh! Uhh! Clay! Clay! You middle-class black bastard. Forget your social-working mother for a few seconds and let's knock stomachs. Clay, you liver-lipped white man. You would-be Christian. You ain't no nigger, you're just a dirty white man. Get up, Clay. Dance with me, Clay.

Clay: Lula! Sit down, now. Be cool.

Lula:

(Mocking him, in wild dance)

Be cool. Be cool. That's all you know . . . shaking that wildroot cream-oil on your knotty head, jackets buttoning up to your chin, so full of white man's words. Christ. God. Get up and scream at these people. Like scream meaningless shit in these hopeless faces.

(She screams at people in train, still dancing)

Red trains cough Jewish underwear for keeps! Expanding smells of silence. Gravy snot whistling like sea birds. Clay. Clay, you got to break out. Don't sit there dying the way they want you to die. Get up.

Clay: Oh, sit the fuck down.

(He moves to restrain her)

Sit down, goddamn it.

Lula:

(Twisting out of his reach)

Screw yourself, Uncle Tom.° Thomas Woolly-head.

(Begins to dance a kind of jig, mocking Clay with loud forced humor)

There is Uncle Tom . . . I mean, Uncle Thomas Woolly-Head. With old white matted mane. He hobbles on his wooden cane. Old Tom. Old Tom. Let the white man hump his ol' mama, and he jes' shuffle off in the woods and hide his gentle gray head. Ol' Thomas Woolly-Head.

(Some of the other riders are laughing now. A drunk gets up and joins Lula in her dance, singing, as best he can, her "song." Clay gets up out of his seat and visibly scans the faces of the other riders)

Clay: Lula! Lula!

(She is dancing and turning, still shouting as loud as she can. The drunk too is shouting, and waving his hands wildly)

Uncle Tom: Slang term for a servile black man, taken from the docile, pious black slave and title character of Harriet Beecher Stowe's 1852 novel *Uncle Tom's Cabin*.

Lula . . . you dumb bitch. Why don't you stop it?

(He rushes half stumbling from his seat, and grabs one of her flailing arms)

Lula: Let me go! You black son of a bitch.

(She struggles against him)

Let me go! Help!

(Clay is dragging her towards her seat, and the drunk seeks to interfere. He grabs Clay around the shoulders and begins wrestling with him. Clay clubs the drunk to the floor without releasing Lula, who is still screaming. Clay finally gets her to the seat and throws her into it)

Clay: Now you shut the hell up.

(Grabbing her shoulders)

Just shut up. You don't know what you're talking about. You don't know anything. So just keep your stupid mouth closed.

Lula: You're afraid of white people. And your father was. Uncle Tom
Big Lip!

Clay:

(Slaps her as hard as he can, across the mouth. Lula's head bangs against the back of the seat. When she raises it again, Clay slaps her again)

Now shut up and let me talk.

(He turns toward the other riders, some of whom are sitting on the edge of their seats. The drunk is on one knee, rubbing his head, and singing softly the same song. He shuts up too when he sees Clay watching him. The others go back to newspapers or stare out the windows)

Shit, you don't have any sense, Lula, nor feelings either. I could murder you now. Such a tiny ugly throat. I could squeeze it flat, and watch you turn blue, on a humble. For dull kicks. And all these weak-faced ofays° squatting around here, staring over their papers at me. Murder them too. Even if they expected it. That man there . . .

(Points to well-dressed man)

I could rip that *Times* right out of his hand, as skinny and middle-classed as I am, I could rip that paper out of his hand and just as easily rip out his throat. It takes no great effort. For what? To kill you soft idiots? You don't understand anything but luxury.

Lula: You fool!

Clay:

(Pushing her against the seat)

---

ofays: Derogatory black slang for white people.

I'm not telling you again, Tallulah Bankhead!° Luxury. In your face and your fingers. You telling me what I ought to do.

(Sudden scream frightening the whole coach)

Well, don't! Don't you tell me anything! If I'm a middle-class fake white man . . . let me be. And let me be in the way I want.

(Through his teeth)

I'll rip your lousy breasts off! Let me be who I feel like being. Uncle Tom. Thomas. Whoever. It's none of your business. You don't know anything except what's there for you to see. An act. Lies. Device. Not the pure heart, the pumping black heart. You don't ever know that. And I sit here, in this buttoned-up suit, to keep myself from cutting all your throats. I mean wantonly. You great liberated whore! You fuck some black man, and right away you're an expert on black people. What a lotta shit that is. The only thing you know is that you come if he bangs you hard enough. And that's all. The belly rub? You wanted to do the belly rub? Shit, you don't even know how. You don't know how. That ol' dipty-dip shit you do, rolling your ass like an elephant. That's not my kind of belly rub. Belly rub is not Queens. Belly rub is dark places, with big hats and overcoats held up with one arm. Belly rub hates you. Old bald-headed four-eyed ofays popping their fingers . . . and don't know yet what they're doing. They say, "I love Bessie Smith."° And don't even understand that Bessie Smith is saying, "Kiss my ass, kiss my black un- ruly ass." Before love, suffering, desire, anything you can explain, she's saying, and very plainly, "Kiss my black ass." And if you don't know that, it's you that's doing the kissing.

Charlie Parker?° Charlie Parker. All the hip white boys scream for Bird. And Bird saying, "Up your ass, feeble-minded ofay! Up your ass." And they sit there talking about the tortured genius of Charlie Parker. Bird would've played not a note of music if he just walked up to East Sixty-seventh Street and killed the first ten white people he saw. Not a note! And I'm the great would-be poet. Yes. That's right! Poet. Some kind of bastard literature . . . all it needs is a simple knife thrust. Just let me bleed you, you loud whore, and one poem vanished. A whole people of neurotics, struggling to keep from being sane. And the only thing that would cure the neurosis would be your murder. Simple as that. I mean if I murdered you, then other white people would begin to under- stand me. You understand? No. I guess not. If Bessie Smith had killed

---

Tallulah Bankhead: Flamboyant American stage and film actress (1903–1968), notorious for glam- orous parties, heavy drinking, chain smoking, and public nudity.   *Bessie Smith:* Legendary American blues singer and enormously influential musician (1895–1937) who achieved stardom in the 1920s with both black and white audiences.   *Charlie Parker:* Known as "Bird," brilliant jazz saxophonist (1920–1955) who pioneered bebop and improvisational forms, changing popu- lar music forever. Almost as well known for his lifelong drug use as for his music, Parker collab- orated with nearly every major jazz musician of the mid-twentieth century before his untimely death at 34.

some white people she wouldn't have needed that music. She could have talked very straight and plain about the world. No metaphors. No grunts. No wiggles in the dark of her soul. Just straight two and two are four. Money. Power. Luxury. Like that. All of them. Crazy niggers turning their backs on sanity. When all it needs is that simple act. Murder. Just murder! Would make us all sane.

(Suddenly weary)

Ahhh. Shit. But who needs it? I'd rather be a fool. Insane. Safe with my words, and no deaths, and clean, hard thoughts, urging me to new conquests. My people's madness. Hah! That's a laugh. My people. They don't need me to claim them. They got legs and arms of their own. Personal insanities. Mirrors. They don't need all those words. They don't need any defense. But listen, though, one more thing. And you tell this to your father, who's probably the kind of man who needs to know at once. So he can plan ahead. Tell him not to preach so much rationalism and cold logic to these niggers. Let them alone. Let them sing curses at you in code and see your filth as simple lack of style. Don't make the mistake, through some irresponsible surge of Christian charity, of talking too much about the advantages of Western rationalism, or the great intellectual legacy of the white man, or maybe they'll begin to listen. And then, maybe one day, you'll find they actually do understand exactly what you are talking about, all these fantasy people. All these blues people. And on that day, as sure as shit, when you really believe you can "accept" them into your fold, as half-white trusties late of the subject peoples. With no more blues, except the very old ones, and not a watermelon in sight, the great missionary heart will have triumphed, and all of those ex-coons will be stand-up Western men, with eyes for clean hard useful lives, sober, pious and sane, and they'll murder you. They'll murder you, and have very rational explanations. Very much like your own. They'll cut your throats, and drag you out to the edge of your cities so the flesh can fall away from your bones, in sanitary isolation.

Lula:

(Her voice takes on a different, more businesslike quality)

I've heard enough.

Clay:

(Reaching for his books)

I bet you have. I guess I better collect my stuff and get off this train. Looks like we won't be acting out that little pageant you outlined before.

Lula: No. We won't. You're right about that, at least.

(She turns to look quickly around the rest of the car)

All right!

(The others respond)

Clay:

(Bending across the girl to retrieve his belongings)

Sorry, baby, I don't think we could make it.

(As he is bending over her, the girl brings up a small knife and plunges it into Clay's chest. Twice. He slumps across her knees, his mouth working stupidly)

Lula: Sorry is right.

(Turning to the others in the car who have already gotten up from their seats)

Sorry is the rightest thing you've said. Get this man off me! Hurry, now!

(The others come and drag Clay's body down the aisle)

Open the door and throw his body out.

(They throw him off)

And all of you get off at the next stop.

(Lula busies herself straightening her things. Getting everything in order. She takes out a notebook and makes a quick scribbling note. Drops it in her bag. The train apparently stops and all the others get off, leaving her alone in the coach.

Very soon a young Negro of about twenty comes into the coach, with a couple of books under his arm. He sits a few seats in back of Lula. When he is seated she turns and gives him a long slow look. He looks up from his book and drops the book on his lap. Then an old Negro conductor comes into the car, doing a sort of restrained soft shoe, and half mumbling the words of some song. He looks at the young man, briefly, with a quick greeting)

Conductor: Hey, brother!
Young Man: Hey.

(The conductor continues down the aisle with his little dance and the mumbled song. Lula turns to stare at him and follows his movements down the aisle. The conductor tips his hat when he reaches her seat, and continues out the car)

CURTAIN

───── **AMIRI BARAKA** Web ───── *www*
(b. 1934)

Amiri Baraka was born Everett LeRoi Jones in Newark, New Jersey and, after studying at Rutgers and Howard Universities, became a well-known poet associated with the Beat movement. Publishing his first book of poetry in 1961, Baraka turned to drama in the middle and late 1960s, rising to become the best-known figure in the Black Arts Movement, in part by founding the Black Arts Repertory Theatre in Harlem and the Spirit House in Newark. The Obie

Award-winning *Dutchman* and such other plays as *The Slave* and *Slave Ship* have become part of the canon of American drama.

TOPICS FOR CRITICAL THINKING

1. What specifically does the use of the Edenic myth contribute to our understanding of *Dutchman*? What is Lula tempting Clay to do, and why must it lead to punishment?
2. The plot of *Dutchman* suggests a ritual: That is, it appears that the action we have seen will be repeated again and again. What effect does this conclusion have on our understanding of the play? How would the play be different if it ended conclusively with Clay's murder?
3. Consider Clay's long monologue near the end of the play. What is its thesis? What does it say about black art and such artists as Charlie Parker and Bessie Smith?
4. If this play is a myth, more specifically an allegory, then the characters Clay and Lula merely stand in for larger abstract principles or ideas. What are these larger notions?
5. What effect does the setting of the play exert on the action?

TOPIC FOR CRITICAL WRITING

At various moments in *Dutchman*, Clay wonders how Lula knows so much about him, how she possesses "uncanny" knowledge of his past and his desires. How does she know so much? Is this question related to the notion of stereotyping and the taunts she uses to anger him? Explain this relationship.

Critical Perspective: On Black Cultural Nationalism

"Black art, like everything else in the black community, must respond positively to the reality of revolution.

"It must become and remain a part of the revolutionary machinery that moves us to change quickly and creatively. We have always said, and continue to say, that the battle we are waging now is the battle for the minds of Black people, and that if we lose this battle, we cannot win the violent one. It becomes very important then, that art plays the role it should play in black survival and not bog itself down in the meaningless madness of the Western world wasted. In order to avoid this madness, black artists and those who wish to be artists must accept the fact that what is needed is an aesthetic, a black aesthetic. . . ."
                              —Ron Karenga, "Black Cultural Nationalism" (1968)

Critical Perspective: On Baraka, Clay, and the Need for Social Change

"Baraka's espousal of 'change' as both act and maxim has been a singular distinct constant. Both the pain felt in his early poetry and drama and the cele-

bration heard in his later works stem from the exertion of mind and body to win an expressive freedom from inherited structures, including those we have made and willed to ourselves. Clay's central speech in *Dutchman*, for example, is a major creative triumph precisely in its portrayal of the frightening yet liberating fluidity of self. His newly released imagination . . . collides catastrophically with an intractable world that will not satisfy it."
     —Kimberly W. Benston, *Imamu Amiri Baraka: A Collection of Essays* (1978)

Critical Perspective: *Dutchman* as Drama of the Self

"*Dutchman* is a drama of the self. While it is generally accepted that Clay is a Baraka-projection and -spokesman, Lula, too, expresses many of Baraka's ideas in Baraka's own language. Clay and Lula are not merely depersonalized, absurd, two-faced social symbols, but are also endowed with elements of their creator's self. Like '64' and '46,' they represent different temporal aspects of an artistic consciousness which has divided itself into opposing forces."
     —Werner Sollors, *Amiri Baraka/LeRoi Jones* (1978)

Critical Perspective: On Black Theatre and Dramatic Form

". . . i insist on calling myself a poet or writer/ rather than a playwright/ i am interested solely in the poetry of a moment/ the emotional & aesthetic impact of a character or a line. For too long now afro-americans in theater have been duped by the same artificial aesthetics that plague our white counterparts/ 'the perfect play,' as we know it to be /a truly european framework for european psychology/cannot function efficiently for those of us from this hemisphere."
     —Ntozake Shange, "Unrecovered Losses/Black Theater Traditions" (1981)

Cherríe Moraga, "Poverties," and *Shadow of a Man*

Before she was a playwright, Cherríe Moraga was both a student of and contributor to feminist thought, publishing the anthology *This Bridge Called My Back: Writings by Radical Women of Color* (1981), coedited with Gloria Anzaldúa, and *Loving in the War Years* (1983). For the former, Moraga wrote an essay, "La Güera," that identifies the factors of oppression in her life about as directly as they can be expressed: "In this country lesbianism is a poverty—as is being brown, as is being a woman, as is being just plain poor. The danger lies in ranking the oppressions." Recalling her childhood and adolescence, she emphasizes both the education she received and an upbringing that "tried to bleach" her of what "color" she possessed. As "la güerra," the fair-skinned daughter of a Mexican woman and an Anglo father, she realized how her parents' derogatory views of poorer Latino families—and their use of aspersions like "braceros" and "wetbacks"—actually served to erase her mother's own past. Her family had been poor, too, finding employment wherever they could as lowly paid farm workers.

Inspired by Ntozake Shange's work and Maxine Hong Kingston's novel *Woman Warrior* (1976), Moraga began to explore her own ethnicity, her own lesbianism, and—somewhat paradoxically—her own self-loathing and homophobia. In addition to her many poems and prose works, her three major plays—*Giving Up the Ghost* (revised production, 1989), *Shadow of a Man* (1990), and *Heroes and Saints* (1992)—tell the lives of Mexican Americans: in California's agricultural fields, in working class households, in lesbian relationships seeking both a place to survive and a newly defined sense of family.

Shadow of a Man dramatizes many of the issues that run through all three plays: the stricture of Catholicism, for example, the dominance of the father in Chicano households, and the often uneasy relationships between white and Latin societies. The most realistic of the three plays, *Shadow of a Man* is also historically specific: Los Angeles, 1969. Two young girls, a twelve-year-old enrolled in a Catholic school and her seventeen-year-old sister, watch their parents' household fall apart. Their brother is marrying a "gringa" whom their mother despises; their mother deludes herself everyday with Mexican soap operas (*telanovelas*); and their father—now virtually a shadow of his former self—is drinking himself to death. Leticia, the seventeen-year-old, announces that she has given up her virginity, in part because she could no longer bear the weight of it as prize and herself as valuable property; and Lupe, her younger sister, is struggling to understand her desire to be confirmed and renamed after one of her girlfriends.

Leticia, as Moraga describes her, is also a familiar type from the late 1960s: a Chicana activist wearing tight jeans, an army jacket, and a United Farm Workers insignia. There is something fitting about this description, as contemporary Chicano theater was galvanized by César Chavez's activism on behalf of exploited farm workers. One distinguished result of this activist politics was Luis Valdez's founding in 1965 of *El Teatro Campesino* (The Farmworkers' Theatre) in northen California. And Moraga's *Heroes and Saints*, albeit at times almost surreal in dramatic form—one character, for example, has no body and is literally a "talking head"—is based on a 1988 farm workers' boycott protesting a dangerous exposure to pesticides that had affected poor families in the San Joaquin Valley.

For Moraga, therefore, drama is both a vehicle for exposing the ideological and material forces of oppression in Chicano lives and a means of self-exploration. Her poetry, prose, and plays confront the realities or—as she terms them—the poverties she has experienced as a lesbian, as a woman of color in male-dominated Chicano culture, and as a poor woman living in a class-conscious society. Yet, as radical as they are in political trajectory, her plays also seem haunted by a sorrow as the world represented by her mother, however oppressive it may be, slowly recedes from view. This touch of the poet is evident even in a largely realist play like *Shadow of a Man*.

CHERRÍE MORAGA

Shadow of a Man　　　　　　　　　　　　　　*(1990)*

CHARACTERS

Lupe, the younger daughter, 12
Rosario, the aunt, mid-50s
Hortensia, the mother, mid-40s
Leticia, the older daughter, 17
Manuel, the father, early 50s
Conrado, the compadre, early 50s

(Compadre refers to the relationship of a godfather to the parents of his godchild. In Mexican culture, it is a very special bond, akin to that of blood ties, sometimes stronger.)

SETTING

1969. The action takes place in the home of the Rodriguez family in Los Angeles over a period of about a year.

The play opens into the interior of the house to the places chiefly inhabited by mothers and daughters. The kitchen is the central feature with the bathroom (stage right) and daughters' bedroom (stage left). Downstage is the porch, surrounded by the family garden of chiles, nopales, and roses. Props and set pieces have been kept to a minimum, only what is essential to the action. Rooms are divided by representative walls that rise about sixteen inches from the floor, yet still give the impression of providing some minimal privacy for secrets both shared and concealed. There is an exit upstage center.

The backdrop to the house is a Mexican painting of a Los Angeles sunset. As the light descends into garden, the smoggy sky takes on a faint mixture of orange and lavender, a pastel rose against the stark silhouette of cactus and palm trees; multiple plant life abounds.

ACT I

SCENE ONE

At rise, spot on Lupe, *staring with deep intensity into the bathroom mirror. She wears a Catholic school uniform. She holds a lit votive candle under her chin and a rosary with crucifix in her hand. Her face is a circle of light in the darkness. The shadow of the crucifix looms over the back wall.*

Lupe: I think there's somethin' wrong with me. I have ex-ray eyes. *(Staring.)*
I can see through Sister Genevieve's habit, through her thick black belt
with the rosary hanging from it, through her scapular and cotton slip.
She has a naked body under there. I try not to see Sister Genevieve this
way, but I can't stop. *(Pause.)* I look at other kids' faces. Their eyes are
smart like Frankie Pacheco or sleepy like Chela La Bembona, but they
seem to be seeing things purty much as they are. Not ex-ray or nuthin'.
(Pause.) Sometimes I think I should tell somebody about myself. It's a
sin to have secrets. A'least the priest is apose to find out everything that's
insida you. I try. I really do try, but no matter how many times I make
confession, no matter how many times I try to tell the priest what I hold
insida me, I know I'm still lying. Sinning. Keeping secrets. *(She pauses
before the reflection, then blows out the candle.)*

Rosario *appears in the garden. She wears a bandana around her head and an
apron around her thick middle. She picks a few chiles, tastes them. Moments later*
Lupe *enters.*

Rosario (chewing on a chile): I still say que los chiles no saben buenos aquí. I
think it's the smog. They don' taste like nut'ing. Aquí en Los Angeles
the sun has to fight its way down to the plantas . . . and to the peepo,
too. *(Takes another bite. To* Lupe:*)* No sabe a nada. Try one.

Lupe: No, these things are like fire.

Rosario: Prúebalo, gallina.

Lupe (taking the chile and very gingerly taking a bite off the top): Hmm. Not so
bad. *(Swallows.)* ¡Ay, tía! You tricked me. *(Fans her mouth.)*

Rosario: ¡Eres gringuita!

Lupe: I swear I dunno how you can eat them like they were nuthin'.

Rosario: Vas a ver when your tía is kicked the bucket and is gone, you'll
be there in your big Hollywood mansion haciendo tortillas y el
chile, nomaś to remember me. Or maybe you'll get la criada mexicana
to do it.

Lupe: I won't have a maid. I don't believe in that.

Rosario: Es trabajo like any other work. There will always be ricos, an' the
rich peepo always need someone to clean up after them. ¿Sabes qué? En
México, half the woman got criadas. Allá you don' have to be rico to
have one.

Lupe: That's why it's better here.

Rosario: ¿Por qué?

Lupe: People don't have to be maids.

Rosario: Bueno, pero la tierra no me da ni un chile verdadero. *(*Rosario
crosses to the rose bushes.) Mijita, ¿me traes el agua? Tienen tanta sed estas
rosas. I don' know why I let them go so long sin agua. *(*Lupe *brings her
the watering can.)* Gracias, mija. Make sure you cut a few of these para la
mesa. Mañana es Sábado.

Lupe: Flowers won't make this Saturday any better.

Rosario: It's your brother's wedding.

Lupe: I'm never leaving home like Rigo.

Rosario: Never say never, hija. *(She continues watering.)* Ya, ya. No 'stén enoja-
   ditas conmigo. You're thirsty ¿no, mis rositas? Tomen el agua. Ya, ya . . .

Lupe: Why do you talk to them, tía?

Rosario: To who, las plantas?

Lupe: Yeah.

Rosario: Because they got souls, the same as you and me.

Lupe: You believe that?

Rosario: It's true.

Lupe: The nuns don't say that.

Rosario: And you think the nuns are always right?

Lupe: I guess so.

Rosario: God is always right, not the Church. The Church is made by men.
   Men make mistakes, I oughta know. *(To the roses:)* ¡Ay, pobrecitas! ¡Qué
   mala madre soy, mis pobres rositas! Tomen, tomen el agua. Ya, mis hiji-
   tas . . . mis rositas.

Lupe: Tía, you know how they say that . . . that when you get that chill that
   goes through your body—

Rosario: Es el diablo que te toca.

Lupe: Yeah, the devil. He comes up and kinda brushes past you, touching
   you on the shoulder or somethin', right?

Rosario: Sí, pero es un dicho nomás.

Lupe: Pero ¿sabe qué, tía? A veces I do feel him. El diablo me entra a mí.
   He's like a shadow. I can barely tell he's there, jus' kinda get a glimpse of
   him outta the corner of my eye, like he's following me or somethin', but
   when I turn my head, he's gone. I jus' feel the brush of his tail as he goes
   by me.

Rosario: ¿Tiene cola?

Lupe: Sí.

Rosario: El diablo.

Lupe: I tole you and I get a chill all over.

Rosario: No hables así, hija. I don' know what those monjas teach you at tha'
   school sometimes.

Lupe: The nuns never tole me this.

Rosario: Well, take it out of your head. It's not good for you.

Lupe: It's not like I'm making myself think about it, it jus' keeps popping up
   in my head. It's like the more I try not to think about somethin', the
   more it stays in my head. I mean your mind jus' thinks what it wants to,
   doesn't it?

Rosario: No, you gottu train it. If you don', it could make you a very unhappy girl.

Lupe: I try, but I can't. At night, I try to stay awake cuz when I fall asleep
   that's when he sneaks inside me. I wake up con tanto miedo. It's like my
   whole body's on fire and I can hardly breathe. I try to call Lettie pero la
   voz no me sale. Nuthin' comes out of my mouth.

Rosario: You gottu stop thinking like tha'. Tu mamá y yo, we had a cousin,
   Fina, a very good-looking girl, but she thought about el diablo y la religion y todo eso so much that she went crazy. Se volvió loca, hija.

Lupe: You think I'm going to go crazy, tía?

Rosario: No, mija.

Lupe: Is it a sin to think like this?

Rosario: No sé, mija. I don' think so. Not if you can't help it.

Lupe: Sometimes I jus' feel like my eyes are too open. It's like the more you
see, the more you got to be afraid of.

Rosario: ¿Quieres saber la verdad, Lupita?

Lupe: What?

Rosario: Only los estúpidos don' know enough to be afraid. The rest of us,
we learn to live con nuestros diablitos. Tanto que if those little devils
wernt around, we woont even know who we were. *(Collecting the roses.)*
Vente. Today we think about las rosas. Sundee, cuando we go to church,
there's plenty a time to think about el diablo.

SCENE TWO

*Crossfade to the kitchen, where a "telenovela" (a Mexican soap opera) plays on
the TV.* Hortensia, *wearing a house dress and apron, is rolling out tortillas onto a
chopping block. There is a kind of grace to her movements as she alternately crosses
to the stove, where she heats the tortillas on the comal, then back to the board again.*
Lupe *and* Rosario *are seated next to each other at the kitchen table, engrossed in
the novela. For a few moments all that is heard are the muted voices coming from
the TV and the steady beat of the rolling pin.*

Hortensia: She can go to hell as far as I'm concern.

Rosario: Who, Hortensia?

Hortensia: La gringa. They didn't even get married yet, and she's already got
my son where she wants him. Ni lo conozco. He's a stranger. *(She puts
the tortilla on the comal, watches it rise.)* The other day, Rigo comes home
from the college. Manuel sees him in the door, and of course he jumps
up from the chair para darle un abrazo. And you know what Rigo does?

Rosario: What?

Hortensia: He pushes Manuel away.

Rosario: No!

Hortensia: And you know what he says?

Rosario: ¿Qué?

Hortensia: He says, "No, Dad. I'm a man now. We shake hands."

Rosario: No me digas.

Hortensia: Te digo. Does that sound like my son to you?

Rosario: No.

Hortensia: And to see the look on Manuel's face. . . . Y la girl standing there
with a smile en la cara.

Rosario: ¡Que barbaridad!

Hortensia: It's eating Manuel up. *(She gestures that* Manuel *has been drinking.)*

Rosario: Tha's not so good, Tencha.

Hortensia (intimately): Claro que no. Pero ¿qué puedo hacer yo?

Lupe: Miren. María's telling Enrique she's pregnant.

Rosario: No! ¿de veras?

> *They all stop and watch, mesmerized. Muffled voices emerge from the TV, then commercial.*

Lupe: ¡Ay, wait til he finds out quien es el padre!

Rosario: ¡Híjole!

Hortensia (resuming her work): But, I tell you one of this days I'm gointu tell esa gringuita everything I think of her. She thinks she gointu keep my son, holding him all to herself? But, they're a difernt kina peepo, los gringos, . . . gente fría. I try to tell Rigo this before they were novios que iba tener problemas con ella pero no me quiso escuchar. They might fool you with their pecas y ojos azules, but the women are cold.

Rosario: I bet her thing down there is already frozen up.

Hortensia (loving it): ¡Ay, Rosario, no digas eso!

Rosario: I may be old . . . but my thing is still good 'n' hot ¿verdad, mija? Us mexicanas keep our things muy caliente . . . as hot as tha' comal allí ¿no?

Lupe: I dunno, tía.

Rosario: ¿No sabes? ¿Tú no sabes, eh? *(Snatches playfully at* Lupe *between the legs.)* Is your fuchi fachi hot down there, too?

Lupe (jumping away): Stop, tía!

Hortensia: Chayo!

Rosario: ¡Ay, tú eres pura gallina!

Lupe *comes up behind* Hortensia *and takes a warm tortilla from the stack.* Hortensia *slaps her hand lightly.*

Hortensia: With you around, the stack never gets any bigger.

Lupe: But my panza does. *(She sticks out her stomach.)*

Rosario: Now you look like María on the novela.

> Lupe *begins to enact "la desesperada" role as* Leticia *enters. She is wearing late '60s Chicana "radical" attire: tight jeans, large looped earrings, an army jacket with a UFW (United Farm Workers) insignia on it.*

Hortensia: Allí viene la politica. *(To* Leticia:*)* I tole you I don' wan' you to wear esa chaqueta.

Rosario: Es el estilo, Tencha.

Leticia (stealing a warm tortilla from the stack): Yeah.

Hortensia: ¡Tú también!

Leticia (putting butter on the tortilla): How can you stand watching those things? Those novelas are so phony. I mean, c'mon. What do you think the percentage of blondes is in México?

Rosario: No sé.

Leticia: I mean in relation to the whole population.

Rosario: No sé.

Leticia: One percent? But no, the novelas make it look like half the population is Swedish or something. Even the maids are güeras. But, of course, the son of the patrón falls madly in love with one and they live happily ever after in luxury. Give me a break!

Hortensia: Ni modo, I enjoy them.

Rosario: Es pura fantasía. Pero mija, they got so many problemas, it gets your mind off your own.

Leticia: I guess that's the idea.

Offstage, a man's heavy, labored steps.

Manuel: Hortensia! Hortensia!

Hortensia: ¡Ay, that man's gointu make me crazy! Lupita, go see what your papi wan's.

Lupe: Sí, mami.

Hortensia: Y si te pide cigaros, don' give him none.

Lupe: Okay. *(She exits.)*

Rosario: ¿Todavía 'stá fumando?

Leticia: Like a chimney.

Hortensia: Sure! He wants to kill himself. He's not suppose to smoke. Es otro día que no trabaja. I don' know what we're gointu do if he keep missing work.

Rosario: He dint see el doctor?

Leticia: Are you kidding?

Hortensia: He's scare to death of them. He complain that he pull something in his arm on the job, que le duele mucho. But I don' believe it. I think it's his heart. The other night he woke up in the middle of the night and he could har'ly breathe. He was burning up. I had to get up to change all the sheets y sus piyamas . . . they were completely soak. Now he's gottu take the sleeping pills jus' to close his eyes for a few hours. Pero vas a ver, tonight he'll go out again.

Leticia (kissing Hortensia *on the cheek):* Pues, ay te watcho.

Hortensia: ¿A dónde vas?

Leticia: To Irma's.

Hortensia: ¿Qué vas a hacer con ésa?

Leticia: Oh, were jus' gonna hang out for a while.

Hortensia: Well, not on the street, do you hear me?

Leticia: Aw, Mom!

Hortensia: Aw, Mom!

Rosario: Déjala, Tencha.

Hortensia: Pero no la conoces, es callejera.

Leticia: Shoot, I'll be graduating in a month.

Hortensia: You think graduating makes you una mujer? Eres mujer cuando te cases. Then your husband can worry about you, not me.

Leticia: Yeah, but Rigo can come and go as he pleases whether he's married or not.

Hortensia: Claro. Es hombre.

Leticia: Es hombre. Es hombre. I'm sick of hearing that. It's not fair.

Hortensia: Well, you better get usetu things not being fair. Whoever said the world was gointu be fair?

Leticia: Well my world's going to be fair!

Leticia *exits upstage.* Rosario *and* Hortensia *stare at the air in silence.*

Hortensia: Te digo the girl scares me sometimes.
Lupe (entering): Papi wants his cigarettes.

A beat, then all three simultaneously turn their attention back to the novela. The lights fade to black while the novela continues playing in the darkness. It gradually fades out.

SCENE THREE

Late that night. Offstage, a car pulls up, then a door slams. The sound of keys being tossed and a man's heavy steps. Manuel *enters, drunk. He wears a hat and a light jacket. From the point of his entrance, the scene assumes a stylized, surreal quality. Characters' actions seem to slow down into almost ritualized movement. This scenario has replayed itself many times in the lives of the Rodríguez family.*

Manuel: Rigo, mijo. I can't touch you no more. I have to tie my hands down to keep them from reaching for you. Cuz it goes against my nature, not to touch the face of my son. *(He sits, takes off his hat.)* You usetu sit and converse with me. Your eyes were so black, I forgot myself in there sometimes. I watched the little fold of indio skin above your eyes and felt those eyes hold me to the ground. They saw. I know they saw lo que sabía mi compadre, that I am a weak man, but they did not judge me. Why do you judge me now, hijo? How does the eye turn like that so suddenly?
Hortensia (entering): ¿A quién 'stás hablando?
Manuel (as if snapping out of a trance): He doesn't got a mind no more.
Hortensia: Who?
Manuel: Who do you think? *(He looks at her.)* She's took his mind.

Hortensia *goes to* Manuel, *begins to undress him.*

Hortensia: And who's took your mind, talking to yourself como un loco?
Manuel (rising): What was my son given huevos for? Tell me. For some spoiled gabachita to come along and squeeze the blood white from them?
Hortensia: No hables cochino. Siéntate. *(*Manuel *sits, she removes his shoes.)*
Manuel: You know what they call men like that que let the women do their thinking for 'em? Pussywhipped, that's what they call 'em.
Hortensia: No seas grosero. The girls are gointu hear you.
Manuel: My son is a pussywhipped!
Hortensia: Estás borracho. I dunno how you gointu get up for the wedding tomorrow. *(She unbuttons his shirt.)*
Manuel: Ni modo. I'm not going.
Hortensia: No empieces.
Manuel: No voy.
Hortensia: Quítate la camisa.

Manuel: We're not good enough for them, that's what they think! Y tú eres igual que Rigo. You jus' want to put on the face in front a those gringos. *(Digging at her.)* They don' even let your sister come.

Hortensia: They said it's gointu be a small ceremony.

Manuel: ¡A la chingada! A small ceremony.

Hortensia (unbuckling his pants): How you think Rigo's gointu feel without his padre there?

Manuel: He's gonna feel nothing. Rigo's got no feelings no more.

Hortensia: You're not gointu do this to me ¿m'oyes?

Manuel: Where's my baby? *(He rises, hoists up his pants.)*

Hortensia: Manuel.

Manuel: Quiero verla.

Hortensia: You're not gointu leave us solitas to go into the church tomorrow.

Manuel: ¡Mija! ¡Mijiiita!

Hortensia: Leave the girls alone.

Manuel: ¡Mija! *(He tries to fasten his pants, fumbling.)*

Hortensia: Why do you think your son lef' this house?

Manuel: Because he's a gabachero!

Hortensia: Because you make him ashame, coming home smelling de los bars.

Manuel: Coming home con el cheque en la mano to feed you.

Hortensia (severely): Tiene ojos. He can see what you are.

Manuel: ¡Soy hombre! *(He takes a feeble swing at her, misses.)*

Hortensia: ¡Pégame! Es lo único que sabes.

A shot of pain rushes through Manuel's *arm. He doubles over.*

Hortensia: Your heart, te molesta.

Manuel: No.

Hortensia: Pero sigues tomando. I'm gointu get your pills. *(She starts for the bathroom.)*

Manuel: ¡No, no necesito nada!

Hortensia (with disdain): I should let you die.

Leticia *appears at the doorway.*

Manuel: Y ¿qué quieres tú?

Leticia: What did you do to her?

Manuel: I didn't touch her.

Leticia: Did he hit you?

Manuel: What I say is not good enough for you, metiche?

Hortensia: Déjala.

Manuel: You wanna defend your mother? You think cuz your brother's gone, que you're the macho around this house now?

Leticia: No.

Manuel: I'm sick of this house full of viejas.

Leticia: Why don't you leave then?

Hortensia: Leticia!

Manuel: If my compadre could see how you and Rigo turned out . . .

Hortensia: That's enough!

Manuel: Eres fría ¿sabes? You're cold as a piece of ice . . . jus' like your
mother.

Hortensia (glaring at Manuel*):* I wish I had a heart of stone.

Hortensia *goes out to the porch, takes out a cigarette and lights it.* Manuel
crosses to the girls' bedroom. Leticia *remains in the kitchen. Lights rise on* Lupe *in
bed, the covers pulled up tight around her. She clutches a rosary in one hand.*
Manuel *stands at the doorway, his shadow filling it.*

Manuel: I know la chiquita is waiting for me. She's got a soft heart, mi
niñita. She makes sure her papacito comes home safe.

Hortensia: If he doesn't give a damn about himself, why should I care?

Manuel (going to Lupe*):* Lupita! ¿'Stás durmiendo, hijita? *(He lays his huge
man's head on* Lupe*'s small shoulder.)* You'll never leave me ¿no, mijita?

Lupe: No, papi.

Manuel: Eres mi preferida ¿sabes?

Lupe: Sí, papi.

Manuel: You're different from the rest. You got a heart that was made to
love. Don't ever leave me, baby.

Lupe: No, papi. I won't.

*He begins to weep softly. Her thin arm mechanically caresses his broad back. A
muted tension falls over the scene. A few moments later* Leticia *enters the bedroom,
brings* Manuel *to his feet.*

Leticia: C'mon, Dad. Let's get you to bed now.

He gets up without resistance. Leticia *holds him up as they exit. Fade out.*

SCENE FOUR

The next morning. Leticia *is standing in front of the bathroom mirror fixing
her hair, while* Lupe *polishes a pair of white dress shoes. They are wearing
bathrobes.* Manuel *sits on the porch, drinking a beer, a six-pack next to him. It is
cloudy out. Lucha Villas "Que me lleva el tren" is playing on the radio.*

Radio:
'Estoy al punto de volver contigo.
Estoy al punto de subirme al tren . . .'

Lupe: I liked Teresa better.

Leticia: I liked Teresa, too, but Rigo thought he was too good for a Chicana,
so he's gonna marry a gringa.

Lupe: Well, he mus' love Karen.

Leticia: Right.

Lupe: Doesn't he?

Leticia (holding a bang in place): I can never get these bangs to lay right.

Lupe: Well, does he?

Leticia: Does he what?

Lupe: Love her. Does he love Karen?

Leticia: Who knows what he feels, man. Jus' forget it. Do you hear me? Don't think about him no more. He's gone. In a couple of hours he'll be married and that's it. We'll never see him again. *(Beat.)* Hand me the Dippity Do.

Lupe *gets up, gives* Leticia *the styling gel.* Leticia *begins applying it to her* bangs. Lupe *moves in front of* Leticia *into the face of the mirror. She stretches open her eyelids with her fingertips.*

Leticia: Lupe, get out the way.

Lupe: You can see yourself in there . . . in the darkest part.

Leticia: What?

Lupe: Two little faces, one in each eye. It's like you got other people living inside you. Maybe you're not really you. Maybe they're the real you and the big you is just a dream you.

Leticia: I swear you give me the creeps when you talk about this stuff. You're gonna make yourself nuts.

Lupe: But I'm not kidding. I mean how d'you know? How do you really know what's regular life and what's a sueño?

Leticia: You're talking to me, aren't you? That's no dream. *(Holds her hand up to* Lupe.) How many fingers do you see?

Lupe: Five.

Leticia: Right! *(Grabs* Lupe's *face.)* Five fingers around your fat little face. You feel this?

Lupe: Yeah. Yeah.

Leticia: That's whats real, 'manita. What you can see, taste, and touch . . . that's real.

Lupe: I still say you can't know for sure.

Leticia: Say something else. You're boring me.

Lupe (putting her shoes on): I went over to Cholo Park yesterday.

Leticia: You better not tell Mom. Some chick jus' got her lonche down there the other day. They found her naked, man, all chopped up.

Lupe: Oooh. Shaddup.

Leticia: Well, it's true. What were you doing down there?

Lupe: Nuthin'. Jus' hanging out with Frankie and her brother, Nacho.

Leticia: God, I hate that huevón. Stupid cholo. He jus' hangs out with you girls cuz nobody his own age will have anything to do with him. So, what were you guys up to?

Lupe: Nuthin'.

Leticia: C'mon. Fess up! Out with it!

Lupe: Nuthin'. The boys were jus' throwing cats.

Leticia: What?

Lupe: They was throwing cats off the hill.

Leticia: Whadda you mean?

Lupe: Well, they stand up there, grab the gatos by the colas and swing 'em above their heads and let 'em go. ¡Ay! They let out such a grito! It's horrible! It sounds like a baby being killed!

Leticia: And you watch that shit?

Lupe: They was the ones doing it! Most of the time the gatos land on their feet. But this one time this one got caught on these telephone wires. It jus' hung there in shock with its lengua así. (*She sticks out her tongue dramatically.*)

Leticia: ¡Ay! Stop it! I swear you're really sick. How can you stand to see 'em do that?

Lupe: It's hard to take your eyes off it.

Leticia: Si-ick. (*Holding her hair in place.*) Here, Lupe. Stick the bobby pin in for me.

Lupe: Where?

Leticia: Back here. C'mon, my arm's getting tired. (*Lupe does it.*) Ouch! ¡Bruta! You want to draw blood or what?

Hortensia *walks through the kitchen toward the porch. Her hair and face are done. She wears dress shoes and a house robe. She carries* Manuel's *suit.*

Hortensia: I hear too much talking in there!

Lupe: We'll be right out, mami!

Hortensia: We're gointu be late for the wedding!

Leticia (muttering): Ask me if I care.

Crossfade to Hortensia *at the screen door of the porch.*

Hortensia (to Manuel*):* I got your clothes ready.

He ignores her, turns up the volume on the radio.

Radio:
‘Voy a tratar de ser feliz como antes
y si no puedo que me lleva el tren.’

Rosario *enters from the garden.*

Rosario: If you listen too much to that music, you start to believe there's something good about suffering.

Manuel: ¿Qué dices?

Rosario: I don' believe in suffering . . . for nobody.

Manuel: Siéntate.

Rosario: You're gointu be late for la boda, Manuel.

Manuel (cracking open a beer for her): Toma.

Rosario *sits as* Hortensia *turns away. They watch her exit.*

Manuel (lowering the volume on the radio): Salud. (*They toast, clinking bottles.*) One of these days, I'm gonna get in the car, buy me a coupla six-packs and hit the road and I'm not gonna stop until I reach the desert. They got the road paved now all the way to my pueblito. I'll stop off and see my compadre in Phoenix. Conrado's got a real nice life there. He's getting rich, I bet, pouring cement holes in the ground. He's making swimming pools. Everybody's got a swimming pool out there. (*There's a slight rumbling in the sky.*)

Rosario: It's gointu rain.

Manuel (observing the sky for a moment): In Arizona, it rains when you least
   expect it. You got thunder and lightning and the whole sky lights up.
   (Thunder is heard. He takes a swig of beer.) I remember when I was a little
   esquincle, riding in the back of my tío's troque. We was coming back
   from digging ditches or something, me and a buncha primos all piled up
   in back, jus' watching the sky get darker and darker. Suddenly the lightning flashed and the whole desert lit up and you could see the mountain
   with the camel back clear as noontime. Then, crack! The thunder came
   and it started raining cats and dogs. In minutes the water soaked up all
   the dust of the road and it smelled real clean. Then right there in the
   open back of the troque, we tore off our clothes and took our showers in
   the rain. *(Another swig.)* Sometimes, you know, you want to be a boy like
   that again. The rain was better then, it cleaned something.
Lupe (standing at the screen door, dressed for the wedding): Papi?

Manuel *turns to* Lupe. *They all freeze. The lights and music fade.*

SCENE FIVE

   Days later. Afternoon. Hortensia *is sorting beans at the table while* Leticia
shows Rosario *snapshots from Rodrigo's wedding.*

Leticia: Mira, tía. Look at all the stiffs lined up in a row.
Rosario: ¡Ay, Leticia!
Leticia: You didn't miss much, tía. All they gave you was a little drop of lousy
   champagne and this white cake that stuck to the roof of your mouth.
   (Shows her a picture.) Don't we look miserable?
Rosario: I haftu admit you look like a buncha sourpusses.
Lupe (entering): What bothered me was the stupid dress I had to wear.
Hortensia: You look purty, mija.
Rosario: Wasn' tha' the dress you wore for Easter?
Lupe: Yeah.
Leticia (taking out another photo): Look. Karen's mother is spose to be
   younger than my mom and she already looks like she's ready for
   the grave!
Hortensia (to Rosario): You know how güeras' skin gets arrugas so young.
Rosario: It's true.
Leticia: Well, I feel sorry for Rigo cuz his wife is gonna be a has-been in no
   time. It runs in their genes, you can tell.
Rosario: Don' you have anyt'ing nice to say about the wedding?
Hortensia: Rigo looked real handsome. He smelled good, too. I got to say it,
   I got a good-looking boy. He had on a beautiful white . . . como lino . . .
   suit and a kina grey tie with a tiny design in it, muy fino. I think era
   de seda.
Leticia: Probably la vieja bought it for him, so he'd look classy enough for
   them.
Hortensia: Tu hermano has more class than all those peepo put together.

Leticia: You don't have to tell me that! Tell him. He's the one trying to get over.

Rosario: Déjame ver otra, Lupita.

Leticia (sarcastically): Oh, that's us standing by the "horn of plenty," the big banquet table.

Hortensia: Chayo, you could of died of starvation there. We didn't eat before cuz I thought they'd feed us at the wedding. Pero you know, the peepo that got the most are the tightest with their money.

Rosario: Tha's why they got it.

Leticia: I dunno. The cacahuates they had in the little platitos really filled me up.

Lupe (sing-songy): Ca-ca-huates. Ca-ca-huates. I like that word!

Leticia: You just like the "caca" part.

Lupe: Shad-dup.

Hortensia *shows* Rosario *another photo.* Lupe *and* Leticia *start exploring a packet of old photos.*

Hortensia: This is el marido. Not a bad-looking man, really. *(Almost proud.)* He's a doctor.

Rosario: ¿De veras?

Hortensia: I think for the babies.

Leticia: A pediatrician.

Rosario: Uh huh. Y ¿qué pasó when they saw que Manuel wasn' with you?

Hortensia: When we came in, the mother—

Leticia: She knew something was up.

Hortensia: I guess she could tell from our faces. I felt so ashame to walk in there without my husband, and I sure wasn't gointu tell her que he refuse to come. But she didn't give me a chance to say nothing. She jus' grab me by the arm and, right away like she har'ly notice, says to me, "Oh, I'm so sorry Mr. Rodriguez couldn't make it, I hope it's nothing serious." Pero muy suave.

Leticia: And then she took us into this big room, introducing us to all these stiffs, going *(very upper-class WASP),* "Isn't it a pity that Mr. Road-ree-gays had to be ill today . . . of all days!" It got me ill!

Rosario: ¿Había mucha gente?

Leticia: ¡Montones!

Hortensia: Sí. Mucha. It was a lie that there was no room for our family.

Leticia: They were afraid that if too many Mexicans got together, we'd take over the joint. Bring out the mariachi, spill guacamole over everything . . .

Hortensia: They jus' didn't want us.

Lupe: You should've been there, tía.

Rosario (a bit martyred): No importa. Y Rigo dint say nut'ing tampoco about his papá?

Hortensia: Ni una palabra.

Rosario: ¡Válgame Dios!

Hortensia: When we came into the church, me besó en la cara. "Hello, Mother," he says to me, muy formal . . . y nada más.

Rosario: ¡No me digas!

Hortensia: Te digo . . . y la girl had nothing to say to me neither. She hug me—

Leticia: Cold enough to freeze the dead.

Lupe (taking out another photo): Oooh! I like this picture of you, Lettie. What grade were you in?

Manuel *enters unnoticed, he stands behind the women.*

Leticia: What grade, mamá?

Hortensia (examining the photo): Kinnergarten.

Lupe: I like your little curly top. *(They pass it around, amused.)*

Rosario: Se parece a Chirlee Temple ¿no?

Hortensia (tossing Leticia's *hair):* Un poco.

Lupe (with another photo): Who's this, mami? *(Passes it on to* Hortensia*).*

Hortensia: Este . . . that's . . . Conrado.

Lupe: Who's that?

Rosario: A friend of your papi's, mija.

Hortensia: His compadre.

Lupe: He's really handsome. Where's he at?

Hortensia (nervously): No sé. I don' know where he is. Don' talk about him.

Lupe: Why? Is he dead or something?

Hortensia: No, he's not dead!

Lupe: God, I jus' asked.

Hortensia: Pues, no seas tan preguntona. It makes tu papi . . . *(Manuel comes up from behind and takes the photo from* Hortensia's *hand.)* . . . nervioso.

Manuel: I've been looking for this.

Hortensia (gathering up the photos, to the girls): Mira. You messed up all my pictures. Next time I wannu find something, I won' be able to. Put them away now. I can't pass the whole day here contando los chismes. Put all these fotos away now!

As the rest of the lights fade, a spot remains on Manuel *staring at the picture. A look of nostalgia passes over his face as "Sombras" by Javier Solis rises. Fade out.*

'Sombras nada más, acariciando mis manos,
sombras nada más, en el temblor de mi voz . . .'

Scene Six

Many months later. A Saturday afternoon. Hortensia *is changing Rodrigo's baby on top of the kitchen table, making the usual exclamations a grandmother does over her first grandchild.*

Hortensia: ¡Ay, mi chulito! ¡Riguito! ¡Qué precioso! . . .

Leticia (offstage): Mom, I got the car!

Hortensia: Is that you, hijas?

Lupe (entering with Leticia*):* It's so tuff, mami!

Hortensia: Miren lo que tengo aquí.

Leticia: It's jus' an old jalopy, but I can fix it up.

Lupe: Hey! When'd Sean come?

Hortensia: ¡Ay, don' call him that! It sounds like a girl's name.

Leticia: That's what they called him.

Hortensia: Well, I call him Riguito, como su papá, not . . . Shawn!

Leticia: Yeah, well jus' don't try calling him that in front of Karen. What's he doing here anyway?

Hortensia: She left me the baby to watch. Qué milagro ¿eh?

Lupe: That's for sure.

Hortensia: Una 'mergency came up. She tole me would I mind watching the baby. I said of course not. Even though they only call me when they need me.

Leticia: Where's Rigo?

Hortensia: He has the army this weekend. ¡Ay! You should of seen how handsome he look in that uniform! He remind me of your papá.

Leticia: The entire Raza's on the streets protesting the war and my brother's got to be strutting around in a uniform.

Hortensia: Es mejor que he should of gone to Vietnam?

Leticia: No, but he doesn't have to go around parading it. God, I hope nobody I know saw him.

Hortensia: No te entiendo.

Lupe: Lettie got the car, Mom.

Hortensia: I know, mija. *(To* Leticia:*)* But don' think this means you are free to go wherever you please now. Es para ir al trabajo, nomás.

Leticia: I paid for it.

Hortensia: And who's paid for you for the las' eighteen years of your life?

Leticia (doesn't respond, she dangles her car keys over the baby; then, with a thick "chola" accent): Hey, little guy. You wannu go cruising with me, ése?

Hortensia (taking out various articles from the diaper bag): She brought enough things for a week. And she gave me a long list of instructions. You think I dint already have three babies of my own. *(Changing the diaper, to the baby:)* ¡Fuchi! Apestas. *(The baby sprays her.)* ¡Ay, Dios! Miren. He soak me. *(Wiping herself.)* No mijito, you haftu learn not to shoot tu pajarito in the air. I forgot since I had you girls, Riguito usetu do the same thing. I'd get it right in the face sometimes.

Lupe: Ugh!

Hortensia: They don' know yet to control their little pipis.

Lupe: Let me have the keys, Lettie. *(*Leticia *gives them to her.)*

Leticia: He is a little cutie, but I don't know about that blond hair.

Lupe (dangling the keys over the baby): The rest of him is brown.

Hortensia: Mi güerito. He's as purty as they get to be. Miren, su pajarito es igual a de Rigo when he was a baby.

Leticia: Please, spare me.

Lupe: Really?

Hortensia: Igualito. *(To the baby:)* You got your papi's thing, mi Riguito. *(To her daughters:)* Dicen que esta parte siempre es the true color del hombre, el color de su . . . nature.

Leticia: Does that make him a real Mexican then?

Hortensia: Mira, qué lindo es . . . like a little jewel. Mi machito. That's one thing, you know, the men can never take from us. The birth of a son. Somos las creadoras. Without us women, they'd be nothing but a dream.

Leticia: Well, I don't see you getting so much credit.

Hortensia: But the woman knows. Tú no entiendes. Wait until you have your own son.

Leticia: Who knows? Maybe I won't have kids.

Hortensia: Adió. Then you should of been born a man. *(She finishes changing the baby.)*

Leticia: I'm gonna go wash the car. You want to help, Lupe?

Lupe (dangling the keys): I'll be there in a second.

Leticia: Well, give me the keys then. *(Lupe does. Leticia starts to exit.)*

Hortensia: When you're done, you can go pick up the panza from Pedro's Place. I wanna make menudo for the morning.

Leticia: All right. All right. *(She exits.)*

Hortensia: ¡Ay! They grow up so fast, Lupita. In only minutes, los muchachitos are already standing at the toilet, their legs straight like a man's. I remember sometimes being in the kitchen and hearing little Riguito, he must of been only three or so, going to the toilet by himself. The toilet seat flipped back. Bang! it would go. Then the stream from his baby's body. But the sound was like a man's, full . . . y fuerte. It gives you a kind of comfort, that sound. And I knew the time would fly so fast. In minutes, he would be a man. *(To the baby:)* You, too ¿no, mijito? You got your papi's thing. El color de la tierra. A sleeping mountain, with a little worm of life in it. Una joya. Ya ya, duérmete, mi chulito.

Lupe: Duérmete.

Fade out.

Scene Seven

Leticia *is practicing dance steps in the kitchen to the tune of "I Heard it through the Grapevine." She sings along.* Lupe *sits on the front porch, drawing.*

Leticia: 'Oh I heard it through the grapevine . . . And I'm just about to loooose my mind.'

Manuel (entering, carrying a lunch pail): Apaga la música.

Leticia (turning down the radio): You're home early.

Manuel: Apágala. *(Leticia turns it off, glaring at him.)* Don't look at me in the eyes like that. You look at your father con respeto ¿m'oyes?

Leticia: I hear you.

Manuel (muttering as he passes): If my compadre could see you now, it'd break his heart.

Leticia: I don't even remember him, Dad.

Manuel *stops, looks at her absently, then exits.*

Leticia (going out onto the porch): I bet they're gonna fire him.
Lupe: You think so, Lettie?
Leticia: Yeah.
Lupe: He's sick.
Leticia: He's not sick. He's drunk. *(She sits on the step.)*
Lupe (after a pause): I wish Rigo'd come home and take me down to the cañón like he usetu cuz everything would be better there.
Leticia: I'll take you, . . . soon as I get the car running again.
Lupe: I never told mami pero sometimes Rigo'd leave me there by myself.
Leticia: I bet when he took Carmen along.
Lupe: Yeah, *(Pause.)* but it was jus' fine with me. I'd pack a little lonche, una manzana, un taco de papas and fill a jar up with chocolate. Then I'd find my special spot by the stream and sit myself down to eat. *(Pause.)* Funny, being alone by that riyito makes everything different. It's like the cañón is a cathedral greater than any church you've ever seen. Más grande que even la misión and there you can really feel God in the incense, the viejitas kissing their rosaries . . . and just the oldness of the place. It echoes con las voces de los ancianos. But the cañón is different, even older . . . and God, a lot kinder. *(Pause.)* I can never put a face to Him out there. I just feel Him in a way that makes my whole body disappear. Not like I'm a ghost or somethin', but just that my body doesn't matter. I mean it doesn't matter any more than the little pajarito landing on the ramita or the tiny stream of water that cools my toes. And I feel so light, like an astronaut or somethin', weightless, with no worries holding me down to the ground.
Leticia: You feel free there.
Lupe: Yeah, that's how it feels, Lettie. It feels free.

The lights fade to black.

SCENE EIGHT

Hortensia *and* Rosario *are just finishing folding clothes on the kitchen table. It is a humid evening.* Hortensia *wears a light robe.*
Hortensia: For weeks now, I walk around the house and hold my breath. Conrado is the only name on Manuel's lips. He don' talk about nothing else.
Rosario: ¿Qué dice, Hortensia?
Hortensia: Estupideces. Half the time, I can't understand him. I see him sitting on the toilet, crying. I go to him, "Manuel ¿qué tienes?" Pero no responde. His heart is as closed as this. *(Makes a fist.)* I can't make him open up to me. No puedo. He miss work already two times this week. And the week before, another two days. El patrón call him this morning. He wouldn't go to the phone.
Rosario: You're going to make yourself sick, worrying so much about him.
Hortensia: How often does he have anything to do with me? Once in a blue moon. I touch his feet in bed and he freezes. No soy tan vieja. I don'

wannu give up, Chayo. If I give up, I might as well put on the black
dress and say I'm a dead man's wife.

Rosario: Then don' give up, sister. Make your husband see you. Grab his
face and make him see you. It's not that men don' love. They jus' don'
stop to see a woman. Us women do all the seeing for them. If a man
sighs for no reason, we already know the reason. We watch their faces y
sabemos cuando se vuelvan máscaras. What they hide from us, we smell
on their clothes and hear en sus sueños. We know better than them
what they feel . . . and tha's enough to make us believe it's love. Tha's
a marriage.

Hortensia: Pues para mí, ya no. It's not a marriage for me.

Rosario (after a pause): Tencha, sooner or later, we choose.

Hortensia: ¿Qué quiere decir eso?

Rosario: Bueno, I know sometimes you look at me and think there's
somet'ing wrong with me becuz I coont stay with a husband.

Hortensia: That's not true, hermana.

Rosario: But after you see the other side of a man, your heart changes. It's
harder to love. I've seen tha' side too many times, mija. *(Pause.)* Ahora,
tengo me casita, mi jardín, my kids are grown. What more do I need?

Hortensia: I need more, Chayo. *(She carries the basket of clothes upstage.)* I
think about Conrado sometimes . . . the way he walked into a room . . .
like a warrior, un gallo. His plumas bien planchadas. His shoes shined,
the crease in his pantalones sharp like swards . . . y tan perfumado, you
could smell him before you saw him. I remember how when Conrado
touch me . . . jus' to grab my hand nomás, and los vellitos on my arm
would stand straight up. *(Pause.)* I've never felt that with Manuel.

Rosario: Conrado was not the kina man you marry, hija.

Hortensia: He never ask me.

Rosario: Yo sé.

Manuel *can be seen coming up the porch steps from the garden. He carries a
caged canary.*

Rosario: Allí viene.

Manuel *sets the cage on the porch, removes his jacket. He wears a sleeveless
undershirt, sits and stares at the canary.*

Manuel: Lupita's lying to me. She knows. I know she knows. She puts her
little hand on my back and pats me real softly. "It's okay, papi," she says.
"It's okay." But I know she's just waiting for the day she can get away
from me.

Rosario: Me voy, hermana. Nos vemos mañana.

Hortensia: 'Stá bien. Buenas noches.

They embrace. Rosario *exits upstage.* Manuel *enters, still mumbling to himself. He doesn't notice* Hortensia *until she speaks.*

Hortensia: Manuel. *(He stops.)* Touch me. *(Pause.)* Yo existo. *(Pause.)* Manuel,
yo existo. Existo yo. *(He walks past her.)* Nothing's changed, has it? I look

at your back and it tells me nothing's changed. A back doesn't cry, ni tiene sonrisa, ni sabe gemir, gritar. But this is what I look at day in and day out.

He doesn't move. She approaches him.

Hortensia (tenderly): You know how good I know this back? (*Lightly touching him, he stiffens.*) I know it mejor que tú. ¿Sabes que tienes a scar right here? (*Touching it.*) ¿Y un lunar allí? (*Touching.*) ¿Y otro acá? (*Pounding his back.*) ¡Mirame, cabrón! Why don't you look at me? ¡Mirame!

Manuel (spinning around, grabbing her by the wrists): No, you take a good look at me!

Hortensia: Manuel!

Manuel: Everywhere I go, everybody's laughing at me. The girls, they're laughing at me all the time. The people I work with, the patrón . . . he's laughing, too. Nobody knows our secret, but they all know and they're all laughing at what they see inside my head.

Hortensia: ¡No es cierto!

Manuel: You don' think I hear you laughing every day at the big joke? (*Pushes her away violently.*)

Hortensia: No!

Manuel: I don' need this! I got friends. I don' need to suffer no more on account a you!

Hortensia (going to him): ¡Manuel, por favor!

He slaps her, throws her to the floor, then pulls her up by the hair.

Manuel: You make me sick ¿sabes? I can't stand for you to touch me!

He drops her to the floor, grabs his jacket and the bird and exits. Hortensia *sobs, starts crawling on the floor to the bathroom. Her face is bruised.* Lupe *enters.*

Lupe (running to her): Mami, ¿qué pasó? Did papi hurt you, mami?

Hortensia: Estoy sucia.

Lupe: No, mami.

Hortensia: Me tengo que bañar. (*Looks up at* Lupe *with glazed eyes.*) Oh, eres tú, hija. Vente, mi bebita. I haftu give you a bath.

Lupe: What, mami? I don't need a bath.

Hortensia (pulling at Lupe's *clothes):* I haftu take off your piyamita and your little diaper.

Lupe: No, mami.

Hortensia: I'll put you in the water.

Lupe: ¿Qué 'stás diciendo, mamá?

Hortensia (trying to drag Lupe *to the bathroom):* Don' worry. I'm gointu test the water first con el dedito. (*Pulls her.*)

Lupe: Stop, mami. You're hurting me.

Hortensia (catching the fear in Lupe's *eyes):* Don' look at me like that? (*Covering* Lupe's *eyes.*) ¡No puedo soportarlo! (*Lupe begins to cry.*) Conrado . . . You got his eyes. Why you gottu have his eyes?

Hortensia *buries* Lupe's *face into her lap, holds* Lupe *down, covering her face and mouth.* Lupe *struggles, cries out.*

Hortensia: I have to turn off the sound. No llores más, bebita. *(Smothering* Lupe's *cries, she pushes her head onto the floor.)* I cover your little head with my hand and push it down into the water. *(Lupe stiffens.)* Your piernitas stop kicking. Your skin turns white and your little hands float up like a toy baby. Sí. Eso. Everything is quiet.

Lupe *passes out. She lies limp on the floor. There is a pause, then* Hortensia *suddenly realizes what she has done.*

Hortensia: ¡Dios mío! ¿Qué he hecho? I killed her. ¿Para qué? For him? ¿Qué he hecho? ¿Qué he hecho?

Lupe *stirs, sits up.* Hortensia, *hysterical, rushes to the bathroom. She grabs a douche bag and a bottle of vinegar.* Leticia *enters.* Lupe *runs to her.*

Lupe: Lettie, it's mami.

Hortensia *climbs into the tub, starts to pour the vinegar into the bag, her hands shaking.* Lupe *stands back, horrified.* Leticia *goes to* Hortensia.

Leticia: Mamá, what are you doing?

Hortensia: ¡Estoy cochina! Filthy!

Leticia: Did he hit you, mamá?

Hortensia: ¡Me tengo que lavar! ¡Me voy a bañar! *(She abandons the bag, pouring vinegar directly all over herself.* Leticia *tries to get the bottle from her.)*

Leticia: No, mamá. ¡Dámela!

Hortensia: ¡Déjame sola! 'Stoy sucia! ¡Desgraciada!

Leticia: Mamá, you're gonna hurt yourself, let it go!

Hortensia: Tu padre thinks I stink, pues now I stink for sure!

Leticia: Give me it! *(She grabs the bottle.* Hortensia *slumps into the tub, holding her bruised face.)*

Hortensia: ¿Por qué no me mata tu papá? ¿Por qué no? It'd be better if he kill me!

Lupe (softly): No llores, mami.

Leticia: Let me see your eye.

Hortensia: No me toques. 'Stoy sucia.

Leticia (putting a washcloth to the bruise): C'mon, mamá. Now, hold it there. *(Removes* Hortensia's *robe.)* God, you're drenched in the stuff.

Hortensia (seeing Lupe, *to* Leticia*):* ¡Díle que se vaya! I don' want her to see me!

Leticia: Lupe, go get another bata. *(Lupe doesn't move.)*

Hortensia: ¡No quiero que me vea!

Leticia: Now! *(Lupe runs out.)*

Hortensia: I'm sorry you gottu see me así, mija.

Leticia (drying Hortensia's *shoulders):* Its okay, mamá. It's not your fault.

Hortensia: I guess all my girls are grown up now.

Leticia: Yeah.

Leticia *unties* Hortensia's *hair. Lupe enters with the robe. Leticia puts it over* Hortensia's *shoulders, dries her hair.*

Hortensia: ¿Sabes que, Leticia? Tu hermanita es una señorita now.

Lupe: ¡Ay, mami!

Leticia: I know, mamá.

Hortensia (to Lupe*):* No, ya no eres baby. You gottu behave a little difernt now, mija. Tú sabes, . . . con más vergüenza. You can't go jumping around all over the place con los chavos like before.

Lupe (soberly): Sí, mami.

Hortensia: I got no more babies. *(To* Lupe:*)* Vente.

Lupe *goes to her. They embrace.* Lupe *massages* Hortensia's *shoulders.* Leticia *sits on the edge of the tub, watching.*

Hortensia: You got good hands, hija. Now, I'm your baby ¿no, mija? Now you have to clean my nalguitas jus' like I wipe yours when you was a baby.

Lupe: ¡Ay, mami!

Hortensia: You girls are all I got in the world, you know.

Lupe: Sí, mami. Sí.

"*Sombras*" *rises as the lights gradually fade to black.*

'Sombras nada más, entre tu vida y mi vida.

Sombras nada más, entre tu amor y mi amor.'

ACT II

SCENE ONE

Sunset. A few months have passed. Rosario *sits on the porch. She fans herself.*
Lupe *sits on the step below her.* Leticia *lies on top of the bed.* "*Evil Ways*" *by Santana plays in the background.*

'Oh you got to change your evil ways, baby . . .' *(The music gradually fades.)*

Lupe: Papi keeps talking to himself all the time. Maybe he's a saint.

Rosario: Tu papá no es un santo, mija.

Lupe: He could be. He suffers inside like the saints.

Rosario: Alotta peepo, suffer. It doesn' make them saints.

Lupe: Maybe he'll die and it'll be our sin because we didn't know he was a saint.

Rosario: Don' say that. Some peepo suffer because they wannu.

Lupe: I dont wannu.

Rosario: So don'. But your papi wan's to suffer.

Lupe: He doesn't. He has something inside . . . that hurts him.

Rosario: What?

Lupe: I dunno.

Leticia (from the bedroom): Lupe!
Lupe: What?
Leticia: Are you gonna do my toenails?
Lupe: Yeah!

Manuel *enters the kitchen from upstage center, talking silently to himself. An orange color washes over the scene.* Rosario *looks to the horizon.*

Rosario: Mira. Ya se pone el sol. *(They all observe the sunset for a moment.)* This is the bes' time of the day. ¿Ves las sombras?
Lupe: They're so clear.
Rosario: En esta hora, jus' before the sun sets, you see the shadows more clear than any time of the day.

The sunset colors deepen, then fade as the sun descends into the horizon. Lupe *goes to the kitchen, pulls a chair out for her father to sit.* Rosario *exits upstage.* Lupe *sits at* Manuel's *feet, rubs some dirt off his shoe.* Manuel *takes out the photo of Conrado from the breast pocket of his shirt. He stares at it, then puts it on the table.*

Manuel: When my compadre Conrado was a little boy, he usetu shine shoes for a living. He was never ashamed of it because, like he said, it was about making a buck any way you could. He built the little shoeshine box with his own hands. I watched him do it. He sawed six perfeckly even rectangles of wood and hammered them together. He made the top piece so it could flip open and shut. Like this. *(He demonstrates.)* And then he sanded it con una piedra. He painted the box black because most of the shoes he shined were black, he said, and that way the box would never look dirty. But the Tucson streets were very dusty in those days and the polvo would seep into the cracks of the box anyway. *(Pause.)* You don't know him, Lupita. But my compadre is an American success story. He usetu live here . . . near us. But then he went back to Arizona to make it big.
Leticia: Lupe!
Lupe Yeah! . . . I'm coming! *(She starts to go.)*
Manuel: Lupita. *(Lupe stops. Manuel stares at her absently.)*
Lupe: ¿Sí, papi?

Manuel *walks out mumbling to himself. He has left the photo on the table.* Lupe *picks it up, studies it.*

Leticia: Lupe!
Lupe: Okay!

She stuffs the photo into her pocket and crosses to the bedroom. Leticia *hands her a bottle of nail polish.* Lupe *sits by the foot of the bed and starts applying polish to* Leticia's *toes.* Leticia *keeps reading.*

Lupe: What name did you choose for your confirmation, Lettie?
Leticia: Cecilia.
Lupe: Why Cecilia? Saint Cecilia was burned at the stake.
Leticia: I liked the name.

Lupe: I was thinking of Magdalena for me. . . . Naw, cuz then people call you Maggie. That's Maggie O'Connell's name. I can't stand her.

Leticia: They could call you Lena. Anyway, nobody calls anybody by their confirmation name. It's just on paper.

Lupe: Yeah, but I love the story about her.

Leticia: Who?

Lupe: Mary Magdalene. *(She rises, begins to dramatize the story.)* I love how she jus' walked right through all those phony baloney pharisees, right up to the face of Jesus. And there they were all looking down their noses at her like she was nuthin' but a . . . tú sabes, a fallen woman.

Leticia: Well, she was a prostitute.

Lupe: She doesn't look to the right or to the left, jus' keeps staring straight ahead. The pharisees try to stop her, but Jesus tells them, "Let her come forward." *(Returns to the toes.)*

Leticia: Make sure you get it all the way down to the cuticle.

Lupe: I am. *(She paints one toe, then goes back to her story.)* So the crowd opens up and makes a path for her. And then she kneels down in front of Jesus and jus' starts crying and crying for all the sins she's done. *(Sobs dramatically at the feet of "Jesus.")* And y'see his feet are dusty from all those long walks in the desert. She's crying up a storm. It's coming down in buckets all over Jesus' feet. *(Sob, sob, sob.)*

Leticia: Are you finished?

Lupe: In a minute. But suddenly the tears become like bath water, real soft and warm and soothing-like. She's got this hair, y'see, this long beautiful dark hair and it's so thick she can make a towel out of it. It's so soft, it's almost like velvet as she spreads it all over Jesus' feet. *(She pours her hair over "Jesus'" feet, then returns to* Leticia's *toes.)*

Leticia: Blow on 'em a little, will you? So they can dry faster. (Lupe *does.)*

Lupe: Can you imagine what it musta felt like to have this woman with such beautiful hair *wiping* it on you? It's jus' too much to think about. And then Jesus says . . . *(She grabs* Leticia's *hand as if* Leticia *were Mary Magdalene.)* "Rise woman and go and sin no more." Now that's what I call forgiveness. That's . . . relief.

Hortensia (offstage): Lupita! Lupe!

Rosario (offstage): Lupe! ¡Tu mamá te 'stá llamando!

Lupe: God, I'm everybody's slave around here.

Lupe *exits. "Evil Ways" rises in the background. The light and the music gradually fade out.*

SCENE TWO

Manuel *is talking to the caged canary in the garden. He drinks from a bottle of tequila. It is dusk.*

Manuel: I am a lonely man. I bring the bottle to my lips and feel the tequila pour down behind my tongue, remojando the back of my throat. Corre down la espina, until it hits my belly and burns como madre in there.

For a minute, I am filled up, contento . . . satisfecho. *(Pause.)* I look across the table and my compadre's there y me siento bien. All I gotta do is sit in my own skin in that chair. *(Pause.)* But he was leaving. I could smell it coming. I tried to make him stay. How did I let myself disappear like that? I became nothing, a ghost. I asked him, "Do you want her, compa?" And he said, "Yes." So, I told him, "What's mine is yours, compadre. Take her." *(Pause.)* I floated into the room with him. In my mind, I was him. And then, I was her too. In my mind, I imagined their pleasure, and I turned into nothing.

Black out.

Scene Three

Manuel, Leticia *and* Lupe *are seated at the kitchen table.* Lupe *wears a Catholic school uniform.* Hortensia *is making breakfast.* Lupe *and* Leticia *are eating.* Leticia *puts the food to her mouth without lifting her eyes from the college textbook she is reading.* Manuel *is writing a letter.*

Hortensia: Leticia, if you read while you eat, the food doesn't set right in your stomach.
Leticia: I'm all right.
Lupe: You got a test, Lettie?
Leticia: A mid-term.
Lupe: Is college hard?
Leticia: Uh-huh.
Hortensia: Don't bother your sister, hija. Tiene que estudiar.
Lupe: I wanna go to college, too.
Leticia: You should try to get a scholarship. Go to Harvard or something.
Lupe: Whats Harvard?
Leticia: The best.

Hortensia *puts a plate of food down for* Manuel. *He ignores it.*

Hortensia: What are you doing?
Manuel: Writing a letter.
Hortensia: You're not gointu eat?

He doesn't respond. They all took at him. After a beat, Lupe *takes a slip of paper and a pen from her book bag, goes to* Hortensia.

Lupe: Mami, I need my confirmation form signed.
Hortensia: Dásela a tu padre.
Lupe: Will you sign this for me, papi? *(*Manuel *ignores her.* Lupe *points to the signature line.)* Right here. *(He continues writing the letter.* Hortensia *signs the form.)* Thanks, mami.
Leticia: You ready, Lupe?
Lupe: Yeah.

They gather their things to leave, kiss their mother, then their father. Manuel *does not respond.*

Leticia: See ya, Dad.

Lupe: Bye, papi.

Leticia (exiting): 'Bout the time you're in college, lots of Chicanos will be going to Harvard. You'll see.

Lupe: Where's it at?

Leticia: Cambridge, Massachusetts.

Lupe: Too far.

Leticia (calling out): I'll be home late! Gotta work tonight!

Hortensia: Okay, mija!

Lupe: Bye, mami!

Hortensia: ¡Qué les vaya bien!

Hortensia *clears off the table.* Manuel *is addressing an envelope. She brings him a cup of coffee. He pushes it away very slowly the full length of his arm.*

Hortensia (after a pause): Why are you writing him?

Manuel: Because he's my compadre.

Hortensia: Y ¿quién soy yo?

Manuel: You're my wife.

Hortensia: Sí, soy tu esposa. Cuando tienes hambre, I put the food in front of you. When you're sick, I force the medicine into your mouth. I iron your pantalones and put out clean piyamas for you each night. Every time you take a bath, I wash out the ring in the tub.

Manuel *tears the page from the writing tablet.* Hortensia *takes an envelope from her apron and tosses it onto the table.*

Hortensia: You asked him to come back.

Manuel (grabbing the envelope): You read this? . . . You read my compadre's letter?

Hortensia: Sí, la leí.

Manuel: You had no right. Do you see your name on this sobre?

Hortensia: No.

Manuel: Pues, until my compadre puts your name here, you got no right to read what he writes to me.

Hortensia: Why, Manuel? Why you want that man back in our lives?

Manuel: No te importa a tí. My compadre's coming back cuz I ask him to. And when he does, we aint never even gonna talk about you. Ni una palabra. We're gonna talk about the track or the weather or my new grandson or cualquiera chingada cosa que queremos, but we aint gonna talk about you. And we aint gonna talk about my son neither. I had a compadre before you went and mess it all up. So you can forget any other ideas you got, cuz everything's gonna go back to normal. Todo está bien arreglado. Y cuando te digo que my compadre's coming for dinner, you're gonna make his favorite chile verde. I don't care what you feel ¿m'entiendes? Me vas a obedecer. And you'll put the plate of food in front of his face and you pretend that you'll feel nothing, menos que antes. Becuz if I see you give him even a little sign, like your face gets a little red o demasiada pálida or your hand shakes a little when you pour el café into la taza, recuerdas que te estoy watchando, mujer. And it's gonna be like old times and you're not going to mess it up again.

He stuffs the letter he has written into an envelope and seals it. He puts both letters into his pocket and exits. Hortensia *sits, drops her face into her hands. Fade out.*

SCENE FOUR

Lupe *is on the porch, shining* Manuel's *shoes.* Rosario *approaches, sits on the step.*

Rosario: Tu papi's getting all spruced up, eh?
Lupe: Really.
Rosario: Dáme uno. Yo te ayudo.
Lupe: Thanks, tía. (Rosario *hands* Lupe *a shoe to polish.)*
Rosario: He's going out?
Lupe: Uh-huh.
Rosario: ¿A dónde?
Lupe: To see that man.
Rosario: Who?
Lupe: Conrado.
Rosario: How do you know?
Lupe: I heard papi telling mami. She's getting his clothes ready. She's been singing all day, so she won't say nuthin' mean to him.
Rosario: She's singing?
Lupe: She's mad inside, so she sings. That way only nice things come out of her mouth.
Rosario: Tu mamá es una buena mujer.
Lupe: I know.

Hortensia *enters the kitchen singing to herself. She puts a pair of* Manuel's *dress pants and a suit coat over the back of a chair. She crosses to the ironing board, begins pressing his dress shirt.*

Manuel (offstage): Lupe! ¡Los zapatos!
Lupe: I'm coming! (Rosario *and* Lupe *rise, go into the kitchen.)*
Rosario: If they dint take the license from me we could all go out and paint the town ourselves tonight.
Lupe: In that car! Forget it, tía! It's got fins sharp enough to kill somebody.
Rosario: Pues, we got pertection then.

Lupe *exits with the shoes.* Rosario *pours herself a cup of coffee and sits at the table.*

Rosario: Conrado's back?
Hortensia: Sí. (Pause.) It's like he wants to jump right into the heart of the herida and bury himself in there. I'm his wife, but I'm not gointu jump in there with him.

Manuel *enters in boxer shorts and T-shirt, talking to himself softly. He wears a hat and holds his shoes and two ties.* Hortensia *hands him the shirt and he puts it on. The two women watch him dress in silence. He puts on the pants, examining its crease. He licks his fingers and runs them down the crease's edge. He sits down, then stands up, checking the crease again.*

Manuel: The crease doesn't stay in them. *(He looks distraught, holds up the two ties.)* La azul or the yellow one?
Hortensia: La azul.

Manuel *chooses the yellow one instead, stuffing the blue one into his pant pocket. He sits down and puts on his shoes with a shoehorn. The women continue watching him dress, their eyes never leaving him.*

Rosario: Sometimes a man thinks of another man before he thinks of nobody else. He don' think about his woman ni su madre ni los children, jus' what he gots in his head about tha' man. He closes his eyes and dreams, "If I could get inside tha' man, then I'd really be somebody!" But when he opens his eyes and sees that he's as empty as he was before, he curls his fingers into fists and knocks down whatever he thinks is standing in his way.

Manuel *stands, buttons his coat, looks at* Hortensia.

Hortensia: If you go, Manuel, you won't find me here when you get back. I don't know where you'll find me, but I won't be here.
Manuel: Fine. *(He starts for the door.)*
Hortensia: I'll take the girls, Manuel. You'll have a empty house to come home to. No 'stoy jugando. The minute you walk out that door.

Manuel *turns around, crosses to her and kisses her on the cheek. She stares back at him.*

Hortensia: No puedo aguantarlo. No puedo.
Manuel: You'll do as I say. Things will get better now. You'll see.

He goes to the door, dips his hat slightly over one eye and runs his fingers over the rim of it. He imagines himself a different man, in Conrado's image.

Manuel: Adios, mujer.

He exits. The women stare at the door in silence.

Hortensia: I don't want Lupita here when Manuel comes home tonight.
Rosario: Sí, hermana. I'll take her.
Lupe *(reentering, suddenly frightened):* Tía?
Hortensia: You're gointu go with your tía tonight, mija.
Lupe: But . . . .
Hortensia: Lettie will bring your piyamas later.

Rosario *puts her arm around* Lupe *to escort her out of the house.*

Lupe: Is it papi's friend, mami?
Hortensia: No. Everything's fine. You be a good girl now. Help your tía.

Lupe: Sí, mami.

Rosario: Good night, hermana. *(They go to the door.)*

Hortensia: Good night.

Lupe: Mami? . . .

Hortensia (goes to Lupe, *kisses her):* Nos vemos por la mañana, mija . . . muy tempranito.

Lupe *and* Rosario *exit. After a few moments,* Hortensia *goes out onto the porch, lights a cigarette, waits.*

Scene Five

It is the wee hours of the morning. Hortensia *sits out on the porch.* Leticia *enters wearing a miniskirt and boots.* Leticia *doesn't notice* Hortensia *until she speaks.*

Hortensia: It's two o'clock in the morning.

Leticia: I know. *(Leticia goes into the kitchen. Hortensia follows her.)*

Hortensia: ¿Crees que eres mujer ya?

Leticia: No.

Hortensia: Eres hombre, entonces. That's what you want, isn't it? To be free like a man.

Leticia: That wouldn't be so bad.

Hortensia: Pues, no naciste varón. If God had wanted you to be a man, he would of given you something between your legs.

Leticia: I have something between my legs.

Hortensia: Está bien. Then go wipe the streets with it if that's what you want!

Leticia: Why do you gotta talk to me like that?

Hortensia: ¡Lárgate de esta casa! ¡Si no tienes respeto a tus padres, lárgate! There's the door, señorita.

Leticia: I can see it. *(She goes to the cupboard, finds a shopping bag.)*

Hortensia: ¿A dónde vas?

Leticia: Just obeying you, mamá.

Hortensia: Go 'head. You think your pachuco boyfriend loves you so much?

Leticia: No.

Hortensia: Pues, go to him. But he'll kick you out in the street, too. He knows what you are.

Leticia: And what am I, mamá? Díme. What am I?

Hortensia: Desgraciada!

Leticia: ¿Como tú?

Hortensia (grabbing the bag from her): Maybe better I should of cut Lupita out from me! That would of made all you santos happy . . . that I would cut your sister from me and nobody had to know the difernce.

Leticia: Mamá.

Hortensia: Well, I can tell you one thing, mujer, I don' give a damn who sticks their thing inside me, that doesn't make a father. What comes out of me is my own flesh and blood! The father is the one who puts the food on the table, nomás.

Leticia (softly): I know that.

Hortensia *lights up another cigarette, sits at the table and for a few moments smokes in silence.*

Leticia: Mamá?

Hortensia: Do you think I was never young? I know what you're feeling and I can't stop you. You walk in that door and I can smell the woman coming out of you.

Leticia: What's wrong with that?

Hortensia: Maybe there's nothing wrong with that. I don' know what to tell you no more. What consejo can I give you? I marry un hombre tranquilo, a good man. And I watch his back bend, his belly blow up with beer and I see my own daughter grow to look at him con desprecio and . . . contempt.

Leticia: It's not contempt, mamá. It's pity.

Hortensia: That's worse.

There is a pause. Leticia *goes downstage, stands with her back to* Hortensia.

Leticia: I thought of you tonight. I thought of no longer being your daughter, that what I was gonna do would turn you away from me.

Hortensia: I don' wannu know.

Leticia: There they were, the Raza gods with their legs spread, popping beers, talking revolución and those things, each with its own life, its own personality and I wanted to taste them all. Each and every fruta. "Una joya," you would say. *(Pause.)* So, I opened my legs to one of them, mamá. The way a person opens her arms to take the whole world in, I opened my legs.

Hortensia: Is that what you call love?

Leticia (turning to her): It's not about love. It's power. Power we get to hold and caress and protect. Power they drop into our hands, so fragile the slightest pressure makes them weak with pain.

Hortensia: Why, mija? Why you give your virginidad away for nothing?

Leticia: I was tired of carrying it around, that weight of being a woman with a prize. Walking around with that special secret, that valuable commodity, waiting for some lucky guy to put his name on it. I wanted it to be worthless, mamá. Don't you see? Not for me to be worthless, but to know that my worth had nothing to do with it.

Hortensia (after a pause): You protect yourself, hija?

Leticia: Yeah. I'll be all right.

After a pause, Hortensia *goes to her. They embrace.* Hortensia's *anguished face can be seen over* Leticia's *shoulder.* Leticia *exits upstage.*

SCENE SIX

Crossfade to Conrado *entering the garden. The lighting assumes a dreamlike, surreal quality. Action seems to occur outside of time.* Conrado *is well dressed in a double-breasted, '40s-style suit and wears a hat dipped over one eye.* Hortensia *sits in the kitchen, still waiting for* Manuel's *return. As* Conrado *goes up the porch steps, he removes his hat, combs his hair with his fingers, replaces the hat. At the same moment,* Hortensia *takes off her bathrobe. She wears a dark evening dress. She goes to the door.*

Hortensia: ¿Dónde 'stá Manuel?

Conrado: He told me to go on ahead. He's not here yet?

Hortensia: No. *(Pause.)* Pásale. *(*Conrado *enters.)*

Conrado: Te ves igual.

Hortensia: After thirteen years?

Conrado: You look the same.

Hortensia: ¿Y tú? Are you the same?

Conrado: Pues, díme. Am I?

Hortensia: You've changed.

Conrado: I'm older. *(He laughs.)*

    They both sit.

Hortensia *(after a pause)*: Why did you come back?

Conrado: To see Manuel. *(Pause.)* He wrote me.

Hortensia: Ya lo sé.

Conrado: He told you?

Hortensia: Sí

Conrado: He said you wanted me to come back.

Hortensia: And you believe that?

Conrado: No sé. *(Pause.)* I'm broke.

Hortensia: That's why you came back?

Conrado: Pues . . .

Hortensia: So, you didn't make it so big?

Conrado: No, 'mana.

    They both smile.

Hortensia: So, here you are.

Conrado: Here I am. *(Pause.)* You remember one morning, I was standing on the corner of First and Figueroa. I was with a woman, una güera, muy alta. I was talking to her when I heard the streetcar go past behind me. I turned around and I saw you looking at me through the window. The sun was just coming up into our eyes. And I turned to la güera y la bese en la boca.

Hortensia: Yo recuerdo.

Conrado: I did that to let you go, so that you would go to him. Barely a month later and you married Manuel. *(Pause.)* He never knew what he had.

Hortensia: He's been good to me.

Conrado *(after a pause)*: In those early days I used to watch Riguito and Leticia circling around you in the kitchen. Two little satellites in your orbit. I watched the way you moved inside your apron. I wanted you, Tencha.

Hortensia: No me digas más. *(She stands. "Sunrise Serenade" by Glen Miller rises in the background.)* When we first met, you and Manuel and me . . .

we had a good time, the three of us. He was the one I was with, but I was proud of you both, tan guapos en sus uniformes. Manuel would dance a few numbers with me and then he'd say, "This one's for you, 'mano. Dance with Tencha."

Conrado *goes to* Hortensia, *takes her into his arms and they dance.* Manuel *appears upstage in shadow, watching.* Conrado *dips* Hortensia *and is about to kiss her, she turns her face away.* Conrado *spies* Manuel.

Conrado: Compadre.

Hortensia *backs away.*

Manuel (to Conrado*):* You never have enough. What I gave you was never enough.

Conrado: Nothing happened.

Manuel: ¿Ahora quieres más, compadre? It's not enough you come back to pick my pocket without a dime in your own?

Conrado: Manuel, I didn't—

Manuel: "There she is waiting for you, compadre." Isn't that what I said? "I'll give you the shirt off my back." You want my shirt? *(He starts unbuttoning his shirt.)*

Conrado: Stop it, compa.

Manuel: You want my hat? *(He shoves* Conrado *into a chair, removes* Conrado*'s hat and sticks his own hat on him.)* How about la waifa?

Manuel *grabs* Hortensia *and throws her onto* Conrado*'s lap. She crawls away.*

Manuel: After you left her como un trapo en la cama, how was I suppose to go to her? Wipe up the little that you left of her. She walked around the house like she was something special, like she *(He grabs* Conrado *by the balls.)* got a piece of you. You know what that feels like? To have your own wife hold something inside her que no es tuyo? She made me feel like I was nothing. *(Pause.)* I loved you, man. I gave you hasta mi propia mujer, but that didn't mean nothing to you. You just went and left. I gave you my fucking wife, cabrón. What does that make me? *(Pause.)* And all these years she looks at me like she knows something I don't know, like she's got something I don't got.

Hortensia: Manuel, a mí no me puedes echar la culpa. You were there that night. I heard you both coming in, laughing and crying. Conrado was leaving. And then I fell off to sleep, but when I open my eyes again, the whole house está bien bien quieto y veo esta sombra in the doorway.

Conrado *slowly moves toward* Hortensia. *He comes up behind her.*

Hortensia: You stand there in the dark sin decir nada, jus' staring at me. You come and lay down next to me. *(*Conrado *puts his arms around her.)* Pones la mano around my waist and your touch is difernt. Hablas . . .

Conrado: Hortensia.

Hortensia: And it's not your voice. I tell you que te vayas, that we can't do what you're thinking. Y me respondes . . .

Conrado: No te apures. Manuel knows. This is what he wants.

Hortensia: Y cierro los ojos, and I wrap myself around you, and nothing is the same after that. *(Pause.)* Leave us alone now, compadre.

Conrado *hesitates, looking at them each for a moment, then grabs his hat and exits. There is a pause.* Hortensia *reaches her arms out to* Manuel *in a final gesture to him. He turns his face away. She exits.*

Manuel *sits in a stupor alone in the room. He slowly rises, takes out a fresh fifth of tequila and a bottle of pills. He swallows half the pills, washing them down with the tequila.*

Manuel: Lupita! *(He goes toward the bedroom.)* She's waiting for me. *(He enters the bedroom. When he doesn't see her, he begins to panic.)* Lupe? Lupita! *(He rushes back into the kitchen.)* She's gone! ¡Miji-i-i-ta!

He slumps into the chair and begins to cry. It is a kind of labored sobbing of a man unable to reach the core of his despair.

Manuel: She took from me everything I ever loved.

Moments later, he composes himself, his face hardened, impassive. He grabs the bottle of tequila and goes out onto the porch. The sun is beginning to rise. He sits, a silhouette against the dawn's light, swallows the remainder of the pills and raises the bottle to his lips. He drinks the entire bottle down, his head thrown back. Black out. In the dark, there is the sound of his body hitting the floor.

Moments later the lights rise to reveal Manuel *in a heap an the floor.* Hortensia *enters, rushes to him, puts her ear to his heart. She looks up in horror. Black out.*

Scene Seven

Lupe *stands in her robe in front of the bathroom mirror, a rosary with crucifix in her hand. She lights a candle as at the beginning of the play, then takes out the photo of* Conrado *her father had left. She studies the image for a moment, measuring it against her own reflection in the mirror. Then she tears the small photo into pieces and drops it into the mouth of the burning candle. The shadow of the crucifix goes up in flames. Fade out.*

Scene Eight

The day of Manuel's *funeral. The women are gathered in the Rodríguez kitchen.* Hortensia *is ironing a black dress.* Rosario *mends a black rebozo.* Leticia *is painting her fingernails.* Lupe *enters, joins her sister and aunt at the table.*

Rosario: Bueno, somos puras hembras now. A house full of women nomás.

They look at one another, as if noticing for the first time.

Hortensia: I wish it were all over already. (*She hands* Leticia *the dress.*)

Leticia (blowing on her nails): Thanks, Mom.

Hortensia (with affection): And do something about your hair. I don' wan' it wild como una india.

Rosario: Ven, mija. Te hago una trenza. I got a nice cinta for it.

Leticia: All right.

Leticia *and* Rosario *exit upstage.* Hortensia *begins to iron* Lupita's *dress.*

Lupe (after a pause): Did you love papi, mami?

Hortensia (after a pause): No sé. To be with a man so long, day in and day out, it's hard to know. Your head on the pillow next to his. You feel his body, his weight, su aliento. I could know tu padre's breathing anywhere porque lo oigo hasta en mis sueños. Entra en el alma cuando uno duerme. (*Pause.*) Funny, when a man is asleep, that's when you really get to know him. You see the child's look on his face, before he wakes up and remembers he's a man again. ¿Sabes qué, mija? Tu papi siempre se despertaba con la voz de un niño.

Lupe: ¿Un niño?

Hortensia: He sound jus' like a little boy. (*Pause.*) Después de tantos años, es difícil decir, "He dug his own grave, let him lie in it." I know I could never do that with you children. No matter what you did, you would always be my children.

Lupe: Even Rigo, mami?

Hortensia: Of course, even Rigo. With a husband, it's difernt. You see, this man did not come from your body. No matter cuantas veces le das la chichi, tu marido no es tu hijo. Your blood never mixes. He stays a stranger in his own home. (*She gives* Lupe *the dress.*) Andale, mijita. You better get dressed. Rigo will be here para llevarnos purty soon.

Lupe: All right, mami.

Lupe *exits to the bathroom. She dresses.* Leticia *enters with a suitcase as* Conrado *approaches the porch. He holds a note in his hand. He removes his hat, combs his hair back with his fingers.* Leticia *gives* Hortensia *the suitcase.*

Leticia: It's Conrado.

Hortensia: Did I kill him? When you let go your child's hand and they go off to meet la Muerte in the street, es tu culpa? Or es el destino?

Leticia *exits.* Hortensia *goes to the door.*

Conrado (referring to the note): You wanted me to get his things?

Hortensia: Aquí 'stá su ropa. (*She gives him the suitcase.*)

Conrado: What should I do with them?

Hortensia: Wear them. Burn them.

Conrado *exits. Sound of car pulling up.* Rosario *enters.*

Rosario: Ya es hora. Ha llegado Rigo.

Hortensia: Lupe!

Lupe: I'm coming.

    The three women begin to file out. Rosario *stops, crosses to the table, picks up the rebozo, and goes to* Lupe.

Rosario (handing her the rebozo): Lupita, cover up ese espejo. We don' wan' your papi to come back and try and take us with him.
Lupe: Sí, señora.

    The women exit in procession. Lupe *starts to cover the mirror, then pauses for a moment before her reflection.*

Lupe: I've decided my confirmation name will be Frances cuz that's what Frankie Pacheco's name is and I wannu be in her body. When she sits, she doesn't hold her knees together like my mom and the nuns are always telling me to. She jus' lets them fly and fall wherever they want, real natural-like, like they was wings instead of knees. *(Pause.)* And she's got a laugh, a laugh that seems to come from way deep inside herself, from the bottom of her heart or something. *(Pause.)* If I could, I'd like to jus' unzip her chest and climb right inside there, next to her heart, to feel everything she's feeling and I could forget about me. *(Pause.)* It's okay if she doesn't feel the same way, . . . it's my secret.
Hortensia (offstage): Lupe!
Lupe: Ya voy.

    She covers the mirror with the rebozo. The lights fade to black.

END

www   ——— **CHERRÍE MORAGA** Web ———
(b. 1952)

Cherríe Moraga was born in Whittier, California, to a Chicana mother and Anglo father. After teaching high school in Los Angeles in the mid-1970s, she entered San Francisco State University, completing a master's degree that focused on feminist writing and submitting *This Bridge Called My Back: Writings by Radical Women of Color* (1981), coedited with Gloria Anzaldúa, as her Master's thesis. In addition to writing numerous essays and poems, including the volumes *The Sexuality of Latinas* (1993) and *The Last Generation: Prose and Poetry* (1993), Moraga has written several plays. *Shadow of a Man* was first produced in 1990 by Brava! For Women in the Arts and the Eureka Theatre Company in San Francisco.

TOPICS FOR CRITICAL THINKING

1. Moraga is very specific about the setting and time period of the play: Los Angeles in 1969. What issues in the play seem specific to the late 1960s? Are any of these still particularly relevant in the twenty-first century?
2. Does Moraga seem critical of Hortensia and Rosario, the two older women in the Rodríguez family? If so, what aspects of their characters are being criticized? If not, then what specifically distinguishes them from Leticia in particular?

3. What forces render Manuel, the patriarch of the family, a "shadow"? Or is he largely responsible for his own failures? Is there any analogy to be made between him and other failed fathers in American drama, Arthur Miller's Willy Loman, for instance?

4. What is a "compadre," and what role does he play in *Shadow of a Man*?

5. Describe the role of such institutions as Catholicism and the family in *Shadow of a Man*. What forces do they exert on Hortensia, Leticia, and—most obviously—Lupe?

6. Compare the form of *Shadow of a Man* to that of a more traditionally realistic play like Henrik Ibsen's *Hedda Gabler*. What differences, if any, exist between the two? Has realism evolved in any significant way? If so, what is the effect of this evolution?

TOPIC FOR CRITICAL WRITING

In Act One, scene two, of *Shadow of a Man*, Leticia makes fun of the *telenovela* her mother and aunt watch regularly, particularly denigrating the blond actors in the lead roles. "Whiteness," in fact, recurs in various guises throughout *Shadow of a Man*. What does whiteness or being a "gringo" or "gringuita" mean in the play? Is it necessarily a bad or oppressive thing? Does it mean the same thing to each of the characters?

Critical Perspective: On the Emergence of Chicano Theatre: A Feminist Critique

"Chicano Theatre began as a political theatre with the emergence of El Teatro Campesino (The Farmworkers' Theatre) in the grape strike of the United Farmworkers' Union at Delano, California in 1965. From 1965 to 1967 El Teatro Campesino developed short skits called actos to dramatize the issues of strike and promote support for the union. . . .

"Around 1970, El Teatro Campesino moved away from the initial goals of the Chicano theatre movement. They settled in San Juan Bautista and started working with a new form to express a religious vision of reality combining Catholicism with aspects of Aztec and Mayan philosophy. The *mitos* (myths) celebrated a mystical Indo-Hispanic identity. . . .

"[Yet] the construction of the class, 'racial' and cultural identity of the subject in the work of Valdez and El Teatro Campesino reproduced the heterosexual hierarchy reinforced by the cultural nationalism of the movement. Feminist critics have analyzed how the theatre perpetuates the power relations of sexual difference through the exclusive representation of the male subject and the relegation of women to the status of Other within the social construct of the gender 'woman.'"

—Yvonne Yarbro-Benjamin, "The Female Subject in Chicano Theatre: Sexuality, 'Race,' and Class" (1986)

Critical Perspective: On Being "La Güerra"

"I was educated, and wore it with a keen sense of pride and satisfaction, my head propped up with the knowledge, from my mother, that my life would be easier than hers. I was educated; but more than this, I was 'la güerra'—fair-skinned. Born with the features of my Chicana mother, but the skin of my Anglo father, I had it made.

    "No one ever quite told me this (that light was right), but I knew that being light was something valued in my family (who were all Chicano, with the exception of my father). In fact, everything about my upbringing (at least what occurred on a conscious level) attempted to bleach me of what color I did have. . . . For [to my mother], on a basic economic level, being Chicana meant being 'less.' It was through my mother's desire to protect her children from poverty and illiteracy that we became 'anglocized'; the more effectively we could pass in the white world, the better guaranteed our future."

—Cherríe Moraga, *This Bridge Called My Back:*
Writings by Radical Women of Color (1981)

Critical Perspective: *Shadow of a Man* in Denver, February 1995: Moraga and Arthur Miller

"Denver, capital of the only state to pass legislation forbidding the inclusion of sexual orientation in official anti-discrimination language, seems an unlikely place to stage a play by lesbian writer Cherríe Moraga, [for] theatre about AIDS, coming out stories, and plays written by openly gay authors have never been so popular here.

    "Denver's El Centro Su Teatro, one of the oldest amateur bilingual *teatro chicanos* in the United States, is Poor Theater at its best. In a partially remodeled school flanked by a Purina Dog Chow factory and Interstate 70 located in one of Denver's oldest and poorest barrios, Su Teatro has served its community for over twenty years.

    Moraga's [*Shadow of a Man*] is in many ways a radical revision of Arthur Miller's *Death of a Salesman* with the sexual tension of Miller's subtext placed in the foreground. Moraga's Willy Loman is Manuel, an alcoholic on the verge of losing his job as he watches his family authority disintegrate. The disintegration is catalyzed by the emergence into the present of sexual secrets, shadows. . . .

    Like *Salesman*, *Shadow* paints the American dream as a sexual fantasy of unrequited love and both Willy and Manuel see in their love objects . . . the embodiment of what the American male should be."

—Catherine Wiley, "Shadow of a Man" (1995)

50 Drama and (Post) Colonialism

Writing about nineteenth-century England when a vast British empire sprawled from London to Bombay, from Belfast to Hong Kong, theater historian J. L. Bratton describes how popular drama supported the politics of colonial expansion:

> Theatre contributed vividly and powerfully, but in complex and sometimes qualified ways, to the web of meaning generated and maintained by official documents, news reportage, romantic adventure stories, military and economic argument, political debate and commercial exploitation whereby the Empire was naturalized.

By "naturalized," Bratton means that a variety of cultural forms—newspaper reports, pulp fiction, popular theater—reinforced the notion that conquering other lands and subjugating their populations was good, moral, even necessary. This process, better known as *imperialism*, was also "natural," the way things ought to be. After all, Britain and other Western nations could spread democracy, Christianity, and economic progress throughout Asia and Africa. Everyone concerned, or so the logic went, particularly the indigenous people, would benefit from the Western presence. Most important, "dark" continents would become "civilized." As the nineteenth century progressed, however, many colonized nations grew weary of their status as a cultural satellite, just as America had at the end of the eighteenth century, and nationalist revolt shook Britain's hold in Ireland, India, Africa, and elsewhere. By the end of the millennium, the colonial empire would be virtually extinct, with England's tenuous rule of Northern Ireland all that remains of its former holdings.

But the process took centuries. During the mid-nineteenth century, between the American Revolution of 1776 and the Boer War in South Africa, fought between England and Dutch Boers between 1899 and 1902, an insurrection in India and the guerrilla tactics of Ireland's Fenian Brotherhood, a precursor of today's IRA, rocked the Empire. By the mid-twentieth century, India and Pakistan had achieved independence from England. Later, in the 1960s Algeria, like a number of African nations, gained its nationhood from France, and by the end of the century, Hong Kong followed suit by declaring its independence from Britain. Such colonial encounters obviously make for great drama and film, as Mel Gibson's Academy Award-winning *Braveheart* and *The Patriot* confirm. And Gibson's two films also indicate how drama representing colonial tensions can possess just the opposite political valence from the plays Bratton discusses. If popular Victorian plays justified colonial domination for their London audiences by representing the colonized country as primitive or savage and the British as altruistic, Gibson's two movies suggest just the opposite. In both films, it is the British officers who are brutal and rapacious, not the Scots clansmen of *Braveheart* or the courageous American revolutionaries in *The Patriot.*

Central to this link between drama and colonialism in both Victorian drama and recent film—and crucial to the imperialist enterprise itself—is the creation of **stereotypes.** For Homi Bhabha, an influential critic of colonialist language and culture, stereotypes perform a very specific, if at times complex, function:

> An important feature of colonial discourse is its dependence on the concept of "fixity" in the ideological construction of otherness. Fixity, as the sign of cultural/ historical/racial difference in the discourse of colonialism, is a paradoxical mode of representation: it connotes rigidity and an unchanging order as well as disorder, degeneracy. . . . Likewise the stereotype, which is its major discursive strategy, is a form of knowledge and identification that vacillates between what is always "in place," already known, and something that must be anxiously repeated . . . as if the essential duplicity of the Asiatic or the bestial sexual license of the African that needs no proof can never . . . be proved.

Stereotypes are presumed to offer a "form of knowledge" about the racial or ethnic "Other." In particular, they repeat and thereby "fix" identities for the audiences that read them. Most often, these identities are negative or derisory: that is, Africans are bestial, primitive, or sexually promiscuous; Asians are treacherous and duplicitous; Irishmen are prone to drunkenness, anger, and indolence. During the colonial regimes of the nineteenth and early twentieth centuries, occupying European powers needed to dominate native populations—sometimes by the application of physical force—while they went about the business of "civilizing" them. Negative stereotypes provided European occupiers with both a secure notion of their own superiority *and* a justification for the application of force. Because "these people" are savage and immoral, the colonialist rationalization holds, they must be suppressed, even if this means violence or imprisonment. There is no alternative.

One of the plays in this chapter, David Henry Hwang's *M. Butterfly* (1988), reminds us that stereotypes can work in the opposite direction as well. That is, if Victorian drama typically promoted negative representations of the racial or ethnic Other, some texts develop the Other as an object of fantasy and desire. During the first half of the twentieth century, for example, as burgeoning cities made life increasingly mechanical and alienating, such writers as the British novelist D. H. Lawrence and the American playwright Eugene O'Neill turned, respectively, to Africa and the South Sea Islands for images of sexual freedom, natural beauty, and a life that opposed the emotional aridity of the modern city. In such texts, the Other becomes a figure of exoticism: of enticing difference and sexual license. As these examples intimate, stereotypes of the colonized do not always function as a "phobia"—something to fear and constrain—but often serve as a "fetish" to excite desire.

Both of the plays in this chapter explore the complex relationships between the European and the Other (in Soyinka's drama, a Nigerian Other; in

Hwang's, an Asian); both explore notions of native Otherness as, alternatively, phobia and fetish; and both offer representations of an imperial governing force meeting a native culture. In addition, both dramatists employ unique and innovative dramatic forms. Soyinka's *Death and the King's Horseman* (1975), in some ways reminiscent of plays from the Greek Classical theater, includes choral songs, dance movements, even storytelling as it draws distinctions between Nigerian culture and that of the British who occupy the country. Much like Tennessee Williams's *The Glass Menagerie* (1944) (see Chapter 47), Hwang's *M. Butterfly* is a **memory play**. That is, the play begins in the present with an imprisoned narrator relating the events that led him to his downfall and imprisonment. One result of this form is Hwang's development of a split stage, where present and past coexist; as René Gallimard tells the story of his long relationship with a Chinese spy he believed to be a woman, we watch the relationship evolve on another part of the stage.

Hwang's play also moves us closer to a postcolonial world: that is, a world after colonialism or, in another definition, one in which the residents of a formerly colonized country emigrate from their ancestral homes to the metropolis that once ruled them. In *M. Butterfly*, Gallimard narrates his story in the present from the Parisian cell in which he is confined. As the play progresses, the action shifts to the past—both to Gallimard's days as a French schoolboy in the late 1940s and to his scandalous affair in China in the 1960s—and to his imagined production of the Puccini opera *Madam Butterfly*. Gallimard relives his happiness with his Chinese lover as he tells his story, bringing China and his mistress Song with him home to France.

Postcolonial literature often concerns the literal movement of colonized subjects to the Western metropolis, not merely the imaginary encounters of Gallimard and his Chinese lover. Since the 1950s, for example, and especially during the last quarter of the twentieth century, England has witnessed the influx of thousands of Indian, Pakistani, Jamaican, Irish, and other immigrants into its cities, London in particular. The postcolonial world is inevitably a multicultural one in which different peoples meet and, at times, clash. Adding to this complexity, while many immigrants strive to maintain their native culture after moving to their new homes, others disown it in an effort to assimilate into a society that is not always eager to embrace them. In the late 1970s, suggesting a kind of purity or singularity to British identity, then Prime Minister Margaret Thatcher expressed concern that England "might be rather swamped by people with a different culture." In his 1983 novel *Shame*, Salman Rushdie describes precisely the opposite situation when a Pakistani girl is murdered by her father for dating a white boy, hence being "swamped" by British ways. The girl, Anna Muhammad, wore blue jeans, not traditional dress; she understood her parents' native language, but "obstinately" refused to speak it; she regarded Mecca as a ballroom with strobe lights, not as a sacred place of religious significance.

Life after colonialism, in other words, may be preferable to colonial domination, but the negotiation of cultural difference is nevertheless difficult and at times tragic. Both Soyinka's play, set in colonial Nigeria of the 1940s, and Hwang's set in, among other places, postcolonial China, offer such tragic possibility as well. Both have much to say about colonial pasts and postcolonial presents, about cultural differences, and about stereotypes of the racial Other.

Mourning, Colonialism, and *Death and the King's Horseman*

In an authorial note to *Death and the King's Horseman*, Wole Soyinka identifies the historical incident that motivated his writing of the play and also expresses his dismay over productions that reduce it merely to a "clash of cultures." The above introduction to colonialism and drama may be accused, in fact, of succumbing to this reductionist tendency. For Soyinka's play is, as he protests, much more than a canvas on which hostile interactions between British officers and Yoruban natives are drawn. Soyinka himself calls attention to the play's "threnodic essence," by which he suggests its funereal quality. A "threnody" is a song of lamentation or mourning and, in cultivating the analogy, he recalls the connection between song and classical tragedy developed in Friedrich Nietzsche's reading of plays like *Oedipus Rex*. The action of the play follows the purposeful march to death of Elesin, chief Horseman to a recently deceased king, who in following the deceased monarch fulfills both a long-honored Yoruban ritual of sacrifice and the requirements of his sense of honor. One might argue that, by punishing himself in Sophocles' play, Oedipus fulfills a similar destiny.

Like Sophocles, Soyinka builds dramatic episodes, even explosive confrontations, around choral movements. Further, like the beginning of *Oedipus Rex*, the inaugural episode of *Death and the King's Horseman* takes place in a public setting, in this instance the market where Elesin and the Praise-Singer meet the women who will eventually form a Chorus. In the first scene, Elesin narrates the story of the "Not-I" bird who calls reluctant men and women to their deaths. One by one they do all they can to avoid him, locking their doors or their hearts to him. But not Elesin. By inviting the bird in, in other words by not cringing in fear of death, Elesin claims to be "master" of his "Fate." In accepting this fate, Elesin also displays his honor, something the women acknowledge by dressing him in rich red clothes and dancing around him.

This opening contrasts sharply with the second scene on the verandah of Simon Pilkings, the British District Officer's, home. Here, the native dance and energy of the opening scene are juxtaposed to the strained notes of music on a gramophone and the tango of Pilkings and his wife. Here, the Pilkings's colorful native attire for a social event to be held in honor of the arrival of British royalty to the colony is paralleled with the rich clothing of the horseman preparing to meet his destiny. And here, in this scene, the racism implicit in Pilkings's colonial rule becomes evident. Amusa, a native working as a police officer for the British, enters and is shocked by the Pilkings's dress or *egungun*, ancestral garb associated with death that once belonged to tribesmen Amusa has arrested. Pilkings thinks such native garb would make for an effective party costume, but his tribal policeman strenuously disagrees. The British officer attempts to "reason" with Amusa, but to no avail, prompting Pilkings' remark "It's hopeless. . . . When they get this way there is nothing you can do. It's simply hammering against a brick wall." Translation: Native beliefs are so essentially irrational that they render the believers immune to logic or reason. Even his wife's more sympathetic admonition of her husband reveals their condescension: "I think you've shocked his big pagan heart bless him."

One native Yoruban who appears to understand both British and native ways is Olunde, the Horseman's son. Against his father's objections, Olunde has traveled to England to study medicine and, realizing immediately what the recent death of the king means, returns after a four-year absence to mourn properly the impending death of his father. Olunde knows his father's death is far more than a "barbaric custom," Pilkings's characterization of the ritual. It is an act that verifies Elesin's honor and manhood. This latter assurance underlies Elesin's determination to marry before his death and is contrasted in Scene Three when the women in the market refer to Amusa as a "white man's eunuch." Native culture preserves manhood and manly honor; accession to British "civilization" destroys both. Olunde understands this as well, as he criticizes Jane Pilkings's wearing of native clothing in Scene Four. While he admires the British for their courage in fighting the Nazis, he cannot tolerate their desecration of ancestral masks to impress the visiting Prince at a party.

On the evening of the royal visit, then, "barbaric" native custom meets colonialist "decadence," as a longstanding cultural practice honoring death is juxtaposed to British denigration of death masks and the culture that produced them.

Yet there is, as Soyinka properly insists, much more to *Death and the King's Horseman* than the clash of cultures. There is sacrifice and honor, pathos and tragedy. There is formal experimentation as Soyinka weaves poetry and song, storytelling and dance, into the narrative of a fated man and his ill-fated son. All of these elements make *Death and the King's Horseman* a compelling representation of the consequences of Britain's colonial project—and much more.

WOLE SOYINKA

Death and the King's Horseman   *(1975)*

CHARACTERS

Praise-Singer
Elesin, Horseman of the King
Iyaloja, 'Mother' of the market
Simon Pilkings, District Officer
Jane Pilkings, his wife
Sergeant Amusa
Joseph, houseboy to the Pikingses

Bride
H.R.H. The Prince
The Resident
Aide-de-Camp
Olunde, eldest son of Elesin
Drummers, Women, Young Girls, Dancers at the Ball

I

A passage through a market in its closing stages. The stalls are being emptied, mats folded. A few women pass through on their way home, loaded with baskets. On a cloth-stand, bolts of cloth are taken down, display pieces folded and piled on a tray. Elesin Oba *enters along a passage before the market, pursued by his drummers and praise-singers. He is a man of enormous vitality, speaks, dances and sings with that infectious enjoyment of life which accompanies all his actions.*

Praise-Singer: Elesin o! Elesin Oba! Howu! What tryst is this the cockerel goes to keep with such haste that he must leave his tail behind?

Elesin (slows down a bit, laughing): A tryst where the cockerel needs no adornment.

Praise-Singer: O-oh, you hear that my companions? That's the way the world goes. Because the man approaches a brand new bride he forgets the long faithful mother of his children.

Elesin: When the horse sniffs the stable does he not strain at the bridle? The market is the long-suffering home of my spirit and the women are packing up to go. That Esu-harrassed day slipped into the stewpot while we feasted. We ate it up with the rest of the meat. I have neglected my women.

Praise-Singer: We know all that. Still it's no reason for shedding your tail on this day of all days. I know the women will cover you in damask and *alari*° but when the wind blows cold from behind, that's when the fowl knows his true friends.

Elesin: Olohun-iyo!

Praise-Singer: Are you sure there will be one like me on the other side?

Elesin: Olohun-iyo!

Praise-Singer: Far be it for me to belittle the dwellers of that place but, a man is either born to his art or he isn't. And I don't know for certain that you'll meet my father, so who is going to sing these deeds in accents that will pierce the deafness of the ancient ones. I have prepared my going—just tell me: Olohun-iyo, I need you on this journey and I shall be behind you.

Elesin: You're like a jealous wife. Stay close to me, but only on this side. My fame, my honour are legacies to the living; stay behind and let the world sip its honey from your lips.

---

alari: A rich, woven cloth, brightly coloured.

Praise-Singer: Your name will be like the sweet berry a child places under his tongue to sweeten the passage of food. The world will never spit it out.

Elesin: Come then. This market is my roost. When I come among the women I am a chicken with a hundred mothers. I become a monarch whose palace is built with tenderness and beauty.

Praise-Singer: They love to spoil you but beware. The hands of women also weaken the unwary.

Elesin: This night I'll lay my head upon their lap and go to sleep. This night I'll touch feet with their feet in a dance that is no longer of this earth. But the smell of their flesh, their sweat, the smell of indigo on their cloth, this is the last air I wish to breathe as I go to meet my great forebears.

Praise-Singer: In their time the world was never tilted from its groove, it shall not be in yours.

Elesin: The gods have said No.

Praise-Singer: In their time the great wars came and went, the little wars came and went; the white slavers came and went, they took away the heart of our race, they bore away the mind and muscle of our race. The city fell and was rebuilt, the city fell and our people trudged through mountain and forest to found a new home but—Elesin Oba do you hear me?

Elesin: I hear your voice Olohun-iyo.

Praise-Singer: Our world was never wrenched from its true course.

Elesin: The gods have said No.

Praise-Singer: There is only one home to the life of a river-mussel; there is only one home to the life of a tortoise; there is only one shell to the soul of man: there is only one world to the spirit of our race. If that world leaves its course and smashes on boulders of the great void, whose world will give us shelter?

Elesin: It did not in the time of my forebears, it shall not in mine.

Praise-Singer: The cockerel must not be seen without his feathers.

Elesin: Nor will the Not-I bird be much longer without his nest.

Praise-Singer (stopped in his lyric stride): The Not-I bird, Elesin?

Elesin: I said, the Not-I bird.

Praise-Singer: All respect to our elders but, is there really such a bird?

Elesin: What! Could it be that he failed to knock on your door?

Praise-Singer (smiling): Elesin's riddles are not merely the nut in the kernel that breaks human teeth; he also buries the kernel in hot embers and dares a man's fingers to draw it out.

Elesin: I am sure he called on you, Olohun-iyo. Did you hide in the loft and push out the servant to tell him you were out?

(Elesin *executes a brief, half-taunting dance. The drummer moves in and draws a rhythm out of his steps.* Elesin *dances towards the market-place as he chants the story of the Not-I bird, his voice changing dexterously to mimic his characters. He performs like a born raconteur, infecting his retinue with his humour and energy. More women arrive during his recital, including* Iyaloja.)

Death came calling.
Who does not know his rasp of reeds?
A twilight whisper in the leaves before
The great araba falls? Did you hear it?
Not I! swears the farmer. He snaps
His fingers round his head, abandons
A hard-worn harvest and begins.
A rapid dialogue with his legs.

'Not I,' shouts the fearless hunter, 'but—
It's getting dark, and this night-lamp
Has leaked out all its oil. I think
It's best to go home and resume my hunt
Another day.' But now he pauses, suddenly
Lets out a wail: 'Oh foolish mouth, calling
Down a curse on your own head! Your lamp
Has leaked out all its oil, has it?'
Forwards or backwards now he dare not move.
To search for leaves and make *etutu*°
On that spot? Or race home to the safety
Of his hearth? Ten market-days have passed
My friends, and still he's rooted there
Rigid as the plinth of Orayan.

The mouth of the courtesan barely
Opened wide enough to take a ha'penny *robo*°
When she wailed: 'Not I.' All dressed she was
To call upon my friend the Chief Tax Officer.
But now she sends her go-between instead:
'Tell him I'm ill: my period has come suddenly
But not—I hope—my time.'

Why is the pupil crying?
His hapless head was made to taste
The knuckles of my friend the Mallam:
'If you were then reciting the Koran
Would you have ears for idle noises
Darkening the trees, you child of ill omen?'
He shuts down school before its time
Runs home and rings himself with amulets.

And take my good kinsman, Ifawomi.
His hands were like a carver's, strong
And true. I saw them

---

etutu: Placatory rites or medicine.   *robo:* A delicacy made from crushed melon seeds, fried in tiny balls.

Tremble like wet wings of a fowl
One day he cast his time-smoothed *opele*°
Across the divination board. And all because
The suppliant looked him in the eye and asked,
'Did you hear that whisper in the leaves?'
'Not I,' was his reply; 'perhaps I'm growing deaf—
Good-day.' And Ifa spoke no more that day
The priest locked fast his doors,
Sealed up his leaking roof—but wait!
This sudden care was not for Fawomi
But for Osanyin, courier-bird of Ifa's
Heart of wisdom. I did not know a kite
Was hovering in the sky
And Ifa now a twittering chicken in
The brood of Fawomi the Mother Hen.

Ah, but I must not forget my evening
Courier from the abundant palm, whose groan
Became Not I, as he constipated down
A wayside bush. He wonders if Elegbara
Has tricked his buttocks to discharge
Against a sacred grove. Hear him
Mutter spells to ward off penalties
For an abomination he did not intend.
If any here
Stumbles on a gourd of wine, fermenting
Near the road, and nearby hears a stream
Of spells issuing from a crouching form,
Brother to a *sigidi*,° bring home my wine,
Tell my tapper I have ejected
Fear from home and farm. Assure him,
All is well.

Praise-Singer: In your time we do not doubt the peace of farmstead and
home, the peace of road and hearth, we do not doubt the peace of the forest.

Elesin: There was fear in the forest too.
Not-I was lately heard even in the lair
Of beasts. The hyena cackled loud Not I,
The civet twitched his fiery tail and glared:
Not I. Not-I became the answering-name
Of the restless bird, that little one
Whom Death found nesting in the leaves
When whisper of his coming ran
Before him on the wind. Not-I
Has long abandoned home. This same dawn

---

opele: String of beads used in Ifa divination.   *sigidi:* A squat, carved figure, endowed with the
powers of an incubus.

I heard him twitter in the gods' abode.
Ah, companions of his living world
What a thing this is, that even those
We call immortal
Should fear to die.

Iyaloja: But you, husband of multitudes?

Elesin: I, when that Not-I bird perched
Upon my roof, bade him seek his nest again,
Safe, without care or fear. I unrolled
My welcome mat for him to see. Not-I
Flew happily away, you'll hear his voice
No more in this lifetime—You all know
What I am.

Praise-Singer: That rock which turns its open lodes
Into the path of lighting. A gay
Thoroughbred whose stride disdains
To falter though an adder reared
Suddenly in his path.

Elesin: My rein is loosened.
I am master of my Fate. When the hour comes
Watch me dance along the narrowing path
Glazed by the soles of my great precursors.
My soul is eager. I shall not turn aside.

Women: You will not delay?

Elesin: Where the storm pleases, and when, it directs
The giants of the forest. When friendship summons
Is when the true comrade goes.

Women: Nothing will hold you back?

Elesin: Nothing. What! Has no one told you yet?
I go to keep my friend and master company.
Who says the mouth does not believe in
'No, I have chewed all that before?' I say I have.
The world is not a constant honey-pot.
Where I found little I made do with little.
Where there was plenty I gorged myself.
My master's hands and mine have always
Dipped together and, home or sacred feast,
The bowl was beaten bronze, the meats
So succulent our teeth accused us of neglect.
We shared the choicest of the season's
Harvest of yams. How my friend would read
Desire in my eyes before I knew the cause—
However rare, however precious, it was mine.

Women: The town, the very land was yours.

Elesin: The world was mine. Our joint hands
Raised houseposts of trust that withstood
The siege of envy and the termites of time.

　　　　　　　But the twilight hour brings bats and rodents—
　　　　　　　Shall I yield them cause to foul the rafters?

Praise-Singer:　Elesin Oba! Are you not that man who
　　　　　　　Looked out of doors that stormy day
　　　　　　　The god of luck limped by, drenched
　　　　　　　To the very lice that held
　　　　　　　His rags together? You took pity upon
　　　　　　　His sores and wished him fortune.
　　　　　　　Fortune was footloose this dawn, he replied,
　　　　　　　Till you trapped him in a heartfelt wish
　　　　　　　That now returns to you. Elesin Oba!
　　　　　　　I say you are that man who
　　　　　　　Chanced upon the calabash of honour
　　　　　　　You thought it was palm wine and
　　　　　　　Drained its contents to the final drop.

Elesin:　　　Life has an end. A life that will outlive
　　　　　　　Fame and friendship begs another name.
　　　　　　　What elder takes his tongue to his plate,
　　　　　　　Licks it clean of every crumb? He will encounter
　　　　　　　Silence when he calls on children to fulfill
　　　　　　　The smallest errand! Life is honour.
　　　　　　　It ends when honour ends.

Women:　　　We know you for a man of honour.

Elesin: Stop! Enough of that!

Women (puzzled, they whisper among themselves, turning mostly to Iyaloja):
　　　What is it? Did we say something to give offence? Have we slighted him
　　　in some way?

Elesin: Enough of that sound I say. Let me hear no more in that vein. I've
　　　heard enough.

Iyaloja: We must have said something wrong. (*Comes forward a little.*) Elesin
　　　Oba, we ask forgiveness before you speak.

Elesin: I am bitterly offended.

Iyaloja: Our unworthiness has betrayed us. All we can do is ask your forgive-
　　　ness. Correct us like a kind father.

Elesin: This day of all days . . .

Iyaloja: It does not bear thinking. If we offend you now we have mortified
　　　the gods. We offend heaven itself. Father of us all, tell us where we went
　　　astray. (*She kneels, the other women follow.*)

Elesin:　　　Are you not ashamed? Even a tear-veiled
　　　　　　　Eye preserves its function of sight.
　　　　　　　Because my mind was raised to horizons
　　　　　　　Even the boldest man lowers his gaze
　　　　　　　In thinking of, must my body here
　　　　　　　Be taken for a vagrant's?

Iyaloja: Horseman of the King, I am more baffled than ever.

Praise-Singer: The strictest father unbends his brow when the child is peni-
　　　tent, Elesin. When time is short, we do not spend it prolonging the

riddle. Their shoulders are bowed with the weight of fear lest they have marred your day beyond repair. Speak now in plain words and let us pursue the ailment to the home of remedies.

Elesin: Words are cheap. 'We know you for
               A man of honour.' Well tell me, is this how
               A man of honour should be seen?
               Are these not the same clothes in which
               I came among you a full half-hour ago?

(He roars with laughter and the women, relieved, rise and rush into stalls to fetch rich cloths.)

Woman: The gods are kind. A fault soon remedied is soon forgiven. Elesin Oba, even as we match our words with deed, let your heart forgive us completely.

Elesin: You who are breath and giver of my being
               How shall I dare refuse you forgiveness
               Even if the offence were real.

Iyaloja (dancing round him. Sings):
               He forgives us. He forgives us.
               What a fearful thing it is when
               The voyager sets forth
               But a curse remains behind.

Women: For a while we truly feared
               Our hands had wrenched the world adrift
               In emptiness.

Iyaloja: Richly, richly, robe him richly
               The cloth of honour is *alari*
               Sanyan° is the band of friendship
               Boa-skin makes slippers of esteem

Women: For a while we truly feared
               Our hands had wrenched the world adrift
               In emptiness.

Praise-Singer: He who must, must voyage forth
               The world will not roll backwards
               It is he who must, with one
               Great gesture overtake the world.

Women: For a while we truly feared
               Our hands had wrenched the world
               In emptiness.

Praise-Singer: The gourd you bear is not for shirking.
               The gourd is not for setting down
               At the first crossroad or wayside grove.
               Only one river may know its contents

Women: We shall all meet at the great market
               We shall all meet at the great market

———
sanyan: A richly valued woven cloth.

He who goes early takes the best bargains
But we shall meet, and resume our banter.

(Elesin *stands resplendent in rich clothes, cap, shawl, etc. His sash is of a bright red* alari *cloth. The women dance round him. Suddenly, his attention is caught by an object off-stage.*)

Elesin:	The world I know is good.
Women:	We know you'll leave it so.
Elesin:	The world I know is the bounty
	Of hives after bees have swarmed.
	No goodness teems with such open hands
	Even in the dreams of deities.
Women:	And we know you'll leave it so.
Elesin:	I was born to keep it so. A hive
	Is never known to wander. An anthill
	Does not desert its roots. We cannot see
	The still great womb of the world—
	No man beholds his mother's womb—
	Yet who denies it's there? Coiled
	To the navel of the world is that
	Endless cord that links us all
	To the great origin. If I lose my way
	The trailing cord will bring me to the roots.
Women:	The world is in your hands.

(*The earlier distraction, a beautiful young girl, comes along the passage through which* Elesin *first made his entry.*)

Elesin:	I embrace it. And let me tell you, women—
	I like this farewell that the world designed,
	Unless my eyes deceive me, unless
	We are already parted, the world and I,
	And all that breeds desire is lodged
	Among our tireless ancestors. Tell me friends,
	Am I still earthed in that beloved market
	Of my youth? Or could it be my will
	Has outleapt the conscious act and I have come
	Among the great departed?
Praise-Singer:	Elesin-Oba why do your eyes roll like a bush-rat who sees his fate like his father's spirit, mirrored in the eye of a snake? And all these questions! You're standing on the same earth you've always stood upon. This voice you hear is mine, Oluhun-iyo, not that of an acolyte in heaven.
Elesin:	How can that be? In all my life
	As Horseman of the King, the juiciest
	Fruit on every tree was mine. I saw,
	I touched, I wooed, rarely was the answer No.
	The honour of my place, the veneration I

> Received in the eye of man or woman
> Prospered my suit and
> Played havoc with my sleeping hours.
> And they tell me my eyes were a hawk
> In perpetual hunger. Split an iroko tree
> In two, hide a woman's beauty in its heartwood
> And seal it up again—Elesin, journeying by,
> Would make his camp beside that tree
> Of all the shades in the forest.

Praise-Singer: Who would deny your reputation, snake-on-the-loose in dark passages of the market! Bed-bug who wages war on the mat and receives the thanks of the vanquished! When caught with his bride's own sister he protested—but I was only prostrating myself to her as becomes a grateful in-law. Hunter who carries his powder-horn on the hips and fires crouching or standing! Warrior who never makes that excuse of the whining coward—but how can I go to battle without my trousers?—trouserless or shirtless it's all one to him. Oka-rearing-from-a-camouflage-of-leaves, before he strikes the victim is already prone! Once they told him, Howu, a stallion does not feed on the grass beneath him: he replied, true, but surely he can roll on it!

Women: Ba-a-a-ba O!

Praise-Singer: Ah, but listen yet. You know there is the leaf-knibbling grub and there is the cola-chewing beetle; the leaf-nibbling grub lives on the leaf, the cola-chewing beetle lives in the colanut. Don't we know what our man feeds on when we find him cocooned in a woman's wrapper?

Elesin: Enough, enough, you all have cause
> To know me well. But, if you say this earth
> Is still the same as gave birth to those songs,
> Tell me who was that goddess through whose lips
> I saw the ivory pebbles of Oya's river-bed.
> Iyaloja, who is she? I saw her enter
> Your stall; all your daughters I know well
> No, not even Ogun-of-the-farm toiling
> Dawn till dusk on his tuber patch
> Not even Ogun with the finest hoe he ever
> Forged at the anvil could have shaped
> That rise of buttocks, not though he had
> The richest earth between his fingers.
> Her wrapper was no disguise
> For thighs whose ripples shamed the river's
> Coils around the hills of Ilesi. Her eyes
> Were new-laid eggs glowing in the dark.
> Her skin . . .

Iyaloja: Elesin Oba . . .

Elesin: What! Where do you all say I am?

Iyaloja: Still among the living.

Elesin:	And that radiance which so suddenly
	Lit up this market I could boast
	I knew so well?
Iyaloja:	Has one step already in her husband's home. She is betrothed.
Elesin (irritated):	Why do you tell me that?

(Iyaloja *falls silent. The women shuffle uneasily.*)

Iyaloja:	Not because we dare give you offence Elesin. Today is your day and the whole world is yours. Still, even those who leave town to make a new dwelling elsewhere like to be remembered by what they leave behind.
Elesin:	Who does not seek to be remembered?
	Memory is Master of Death, the chink
	In his armour of conceit. I shall leave
	That which makes my going the sheerest
	Dream of an afternoon. Should voyagers
	Not travel light? Let the considerate traveller
	Shed, of his excessive load, all
	That may benefit the living.
Women (relieved):	Ah Elesin Oba, we knew you for a man of honour.
Elesin:	Then honour me. I deserve a bed of honour to lie upon.
Iyaloja:	The best is yours. We know you for a man of honour. You are not one who eats and leaves nothing on his plate for children. Did you not say it yourself? Not one who blights the happiness of others for a moment's pleasure.
Elesin:	Who speaks of pleasure? O women, listen!
	Pleasure palls. Our acts should have meaning.
	The sap of the plantain never dries.
	You have seen the young shoot swelling
	Even as the parent stalk begins to wither.
	Women, let my going be likened to
	The twilight hour of the plantain.
Women:	What does he mean Iyaloja? This language is the language of our elders, we do not fully grasp it.
Iyaloja:	I dare not understand you yet Elesin.
Elesin:	All you who stand before the spirit that dares
	The opening of the last door of passage,
	Dare to rid my going of regrets! My wish
	Transcends the blotting out of thought
	In one mere moment's tremor of the senses.
	Do me credit. And do me honour.
	I am girded for the route beyond
	Burdens of waste and longing.
	Then let me travel light. Let
	Seed that will not serve the stomach
	On the way remain behind. Let it take root
	In the earth of my choice, in this earth
	I leave behind.

Iyaloja (turns to women): The voice I hear is already touched by the waiting
    fingers of our departed. I dare not refuse.

Woman: But Iyaloja . . .

Iyaloja: The matter is no longer in our hands.

Woman: But she is betrothed to your own son. Tell him.

Iyaloja: My son's wish is mine. I did the asking for him, the loss can be
    remedied. But who will remedy the blight of closed hands on the day
    when all should be openness and light? Tell him, you say! You wish that
    I burden him with knowledge that will sour his wish and lay regrets on
    the last moments of his mind. You pray to him who is your intercessor
    to the other world—don't set this world adrift in your own time; would
    you rather it was my hand whose sacrilege wrenched it loose?

Woman: Not many men will brave the curse of a dispossessed husband.

Iyaloja: Only the curses of the departed are to be feared. The claims of one
    whose foot is on the threshold of their abode surpasses even the claims
    of blood. It is impiety even to place hindrances in their ways.

Elesin: What do my mothers say? Shall I step
                  Burdened into the unknown?

Iyaloja: Not we, but the very earth says No. The sap in the plantain does not
    dry. Let grain that will not feed the voyager at his passage drop here and
    take root as he steps beyond this earth and us. Oh you who fill the home
    from hearth to threshold with the voices of children, you who now be-
    stride the hidden gulf and pause to draw the right foot across and into
    the resting-home of the great forebears, it is good that your loins be
    drained into the earth we know, that your last strength be ploughed
    back into the womb that gave you being.

Praise-Singer: Iyaloja, mother of multitudes in the teeming market of the
    world, how your wisdom transfigures you!

Iyaloja (smiling broadly, completely reconciled): Elesin, even at the narrow end
    of the passage I know you will look back and sigh a last regret for the
    flesh that flashed past your spirit in flight. You always had a restless eye.
    Your choice has my blessing. *(To the women.)* Take the good news to our
    daughter and make her ready. *(Some women go off.)*

Elesin: Your eyes were clouded at first.

Iyaloja: Not for long. It is those who stand at the gateway of the great
    change to whose cry we must pay heed. And then, think of this—it
    makes the mind tremble. The fruit of such a union is rare. It will be
    neither of this world nor of the next. Nor of the one behind us. As if the
    timelessness of the ancestor world and the unborn have joined spirits to
    wring an issue of the elusive being of passage . . . . Elesin!

Elesin: I am here. What is it?

Iyaloja: Did you hear all I said just now?

Elesin: Yes.

Iyaloja: The living must eat and drink. When the moment comes, don't turn
    the food to rodents' droppings in their mouth. Don't let them taste the
    ashes of the world when they step out at dawn to breathe the morning
    dew.

Elesin: This doubt is unworthy of you Iyaloja.

Iyaloja: Eating the awusa nut is not so difficult as drinking water afterwards.

Elesin: The waters of the bitter stream are honey to a man
            Whose tongue has savoured all.

Iyaloja: No one knows when the ants desert their home; they leave the
    mound intact. The swallow is never seen to peck holes in its nest when
    it is time to move with the season. There are always throngs of human-
    ity behind the leave-taker. The rain should not come through the roof
    for them, the wind must not blow through the walls at night.

Elesin: I refuse to take offence.

Iyaloja: You wish to travel light. Well, the earth is yours. But be sure the
    seed you leave in it attracts no curse.

Elesin: You really mistake my person Iyaloja.

Iyaloja: I said nothing. Now we must go prepare your bridal chamber. Then
    these same hands will lay your shrouds.

Elesin (exasperated): Must you be so blunt? *(Recovers.)* Well, weave your
    shrouds, but let the fingers of my bride seal my eyelids with earth and
    wash my body.

Iyaloja: Prepare yourself Elesin.

(She gets up to leave. At that moment the women return, leading the Bride.
*Elesin's face glows with pleasure. He flicks the sleeves of his agbada with renewed
confidence and steps forward to meet the group. As the girl kneels before* Iyaloja,
lights fade out on the scene.)

2

*The verandah of the District Officer's bungalow. A tango is playing from an
old hand-cranked gramophone and, glimpsed through the wide windows and doors
which open onto the forestage verandah are the shapes of* Simon Pilkings *and his
wife,* Jane, *tangoing in and out of shadows in the living-room. They are wearing
what is immediately apparent as some form of fancy-dress. The dance goes on for
some moments and then the figure of a 'Native Administration' policeman emerges
and climbs up the steps onto the verandah. He peeps through and observes the dancing couple, reacting with what is obviously a long-standing bewilderment. He stiffens suddenly, his expression changes to one of disbelief and horror. In his excitement
he upsets a flowerpot and attracts the attention of the couple. They stop dancing.*

Pilkings: Is there anyone out there?

Jane: I'll turn off the gramophone.

Pilkings (approaching the verandah): I'm sure I heard something fall over.
    (The constable retreats slowly, open-mouthed as Pilkings *approaches the veran-
dah.)* Oh it's you Amusa. Why didn't you just knock instead of knocking
things over?

Amusa (stammers badly and points a shaky finger at his dress): Mista
    Pirinkin . . . Mista Pirinkin . . .

Pilkings: What is the matter with you?

Jane (emerging): Who is it dear? Oh, Amusa . . .

Pilkings: Yes it's Amusa, and acting most strangely.

Amusa (his attention now transferred to Mrs. Pilkings*):* Mammadam . . . you too!

Pilkings: What the hell is the matter with you man!

Jane: Your costume darling. Our fancy dress.

Pilkings: Oh hell, I'd forgotten all about that. *(Lifts the face mask over his head showing his face. His wife follows suit.)*

Jane: I think you've shocked his big pagan heart bless him.

Pilkings: Nonsense, he's a Moslem. Come on Amusa, you don't believe in all this nonsense do you? I thought you were a good Moslem.

Amusa: Mista Pirinkin, I beg you sir, what you think you do with that dress? It belong to dead cult, not for human being.

Pilkings: Oh Amusa, what a let down you are. I swear by you at the club you know—thank God for Amusa, he doesn't believe in any mumbo-jumbo. And now look at you!

Amusa: Mista Pirinkin, I beg you, take it off. Is not good for man like you to touch that cloth.

Pilkings: Well, I've got it on. And what's more Jane and I have bet on it we're taking first prize at the ball. Now, if you can just pull yourself together and tell me what you wanted to see me about . . .

Amusa: Sir, I cannot talk this matter to you in that dress. I no fit.

Pilkings: What's that rubbish again?

Jane: He is dead earnest too Simon. I think you'll have to handle this delicately.

Pilkings: Delicately my . . . ! Look here Amusa, I think this little joke has gone far enough hm? Let's have some sense. You seem to forget that you are a police officer in the service of His Majesty's Government. I order you to report your business at once or face disciplinary action.

Amusa: Sir, it is a matter of death. How can man talk against death to person in uniform of death? Is like talking against government to person in uniform of police. Please sir, I go and come back.

Pilkings (roars): Now! *(Amusa switches his gaze to the ceiling suddenly, remains mute.)*

Jane: Oh Amusa, what is there to be scared of in the costume? You saw it confiscated last month from those *egungun°* men who were creating trouble in town. You helped arrest the cult leaders yourself—if the juju didn't harm you at the time how could it possibly harm you now? And merely by looking at it?

Amusa (without looking down): Madam, I arrest the ring-leaders who make trouble but me I no touch *egungun*. That *egungun* itself, I no touch. And I no abuse 'am. I arrest ringleader but I treat *egungun* with respect.

Pilkings: It's hopeless. We'll merely end up missing the best part of the ball. When they get this way there is nothing you can do. It's simply hammering against a brick wall. Write your report or whatever it is on that

---

egungun: Ancestral masquerade.

pad Amusa and take yourself out of here. Come on Jane. We only upset his delicate sensibilities by remaining here.

(Amusa *waits for them to leave, then writes in the notebook, somewhat laboriously. Drumming from the direction of the town wells up. Amusa listens, makes a movement as if he wants to recall* Pilkings *but changes his mind. Completes his note and goes. A few moments later* Pilkings *emerges, picks up the pad and reads.*)

Pilkings: Jane!
Jane (from the bedroom): Coming darling. Nearly ready.
Pilkings: Never mind being ready, just listen to this.
Jane: What is it?
Pilkings: Amusa's report. Listen. 'I have to report that it come to my information that one prominent chief, namely, the Elesin Oba, is to commit death tonight as a result of native custom. Because this is criminal offence I await further instruction at charge office. Sergeant Amusa.'

(Jane *comes out onto the verandah while he is reading.*)

Jane: Did I hear you say commit death?
Pilkings: Obviously he means murder.
Jane: You mean a ritual murder?
Pilkings: Must be. You think you've stamped it all out but it's always lurking under the surface somewhere.
Jane: Oh. Does it mean we are not getting to the ball at all?
Pilkings: No-o. I'll have the man arrested. Everyone remotely involved. In any case there may be nothing to it. Just rumours.
Jane: Really? I though you found Amusa's rumours generally reliable.
Pilkings: That's true enough. But who knows what may have been giving him the scare lately. Look at his conduct tonight.
Jane (laughing): You have to admit he had his own peculiar logic. (*Deepens her voice.*) How can man talk against death to person in uniform of death? (*Laughs.*) Anyway, you can't go into the police station dressed like that.
Pilkings: I'll send Joseph with instructions. Damn it, what a confounded nuisance!
Jane: But don't you think you should talk first to the man, Simon?
Pilkings: Do you want to go to the ball or not?
Jane: Darling, why are you getting rattled? I was only trying to be intelligent. It seems hardly fair just to lock up a man—and a chief at that—simply on the er . . . what is that legal word again?—uncorroborated word of a sergeant.
Pilkings: Well, that's easily decided. Joseph!
Joseph (from within): Yes master.
Pilkings: You're quite right of course, I am getting rattled. Probably the effect of those bloody drums. Do you hear how they go on and on?
Jane: I wondered when you'd notice. Do you suppose it has something to do with this affair?

Pilkings: Who knows? They always find an excuse for making a noise . . .
(*Thoughtfully.*) Even so . . .

Jane: Yes Simon?

Pilkings: It's different Jane. I don't think I've heard this particular—sound—
before. Something unsettling about it.

Jane: I thought all bush drumming sounded the same.

Pilkings: Don't tease me now Jane. This may be serious.

Jane: I'm sorry. (*Gets up and throws her arms around his neck. Kisses him. The
houseboy enters, retreats and knocks.*)

Pilkings (wearily): Oh, come in Joseph! I don't know where you pick up all
these elephantine notions of tact. Come over here.

Joseph: Sir?

Pilkings: Joseph, are you a christian or not?

Joseph: Yessir.

Pilkings: Does seeing me in this outfit bother you?

Joseph: No sir, it has no power.

Pilkings: Thank God for some sanity at last. Now Joseph, answer me on the
honour of a christian—what is supposed to be going on in town
tonight?

Joseph: Tonight sir? You mean that chief who is going to kill himself?

Pilkings: What?

Jane: What do you mean, kill himself?

Pilkings: You do mean he is going to kill somebody don't you?

Joseph: No master. He will not kill anybody and no one will kill him. He will
simply die.

Jane: But why Joseph?

Joseph: It is native law and custom. The King die last month. Tonight is his
burial. But before they can bury him, the Elesin must die so as to accompany him to heaven.

Pilkings: I seem to be fated to clash more often with that man than with any
of the other chiefs.

Joseph: He is the King's Chief Horseman.

Pilkings (in a resigned way): I know.

Jane: Simon, what's the matter?

Pilkings: It would have to be him!

Jane: Who is he?

Pilkings: Don't you remember? He's that chief with whom I had a scrap
some three or four years ago. I helped his son get to a medical school in
England, remember? He fought tooth and nail to prevent it.

Jane: Oh now I remember. He was that very sensitive young man. What was
his name again?

Pilkings: Olunde. Haven't replied to his last letter come to think of it. The
old pagan wanted him to stay and carry on some family tradition or the
other. Honestly I couldn't understand the fuss he made. I literally had to
help the boy escape from close confinement and load him onto the next
boat. A most intelligent boy, really bright.

Jane: I rather thought he was much too sensitive you know. The kind of
person you feel should be a poet munching rose petals in Bloomsbury.

Pilkings: Well, he's going to make a first-class doctor. His mind is set on that. And as long as he wants my help he is welcome to it.

Jane (after a pause): Simon.

Pilkings: Yes?

Jane: This boy, he was his eldest son wasn't he?

Pilkings: I'm not sure. Who could tell with that old ram?

Jane: Do you know, Joseph?

Joseph: Oh yes madam. He was the eldest son. That's why Elesin cursed master good and proper. The eldest son is not supposed to travel away from the land.

Jane (giggling): Is that true Simon? Did he really curse you good and proper?

Pilkings: By all accounts I should be dead by now.

Joseph: Oh no, master is white man. And good christian. Black man juju can't touch master.

Jane: If he was his eldest, it means that he would be the Elesin to the next king. It's a family thing isn't it Joseph?

Joseph: Yes madam. And if this Elesin had died before the King, his eldest son must take his place.

Jane: That would explain why the old chief was so mad you took the boy away.

Pilkings: Well it makes me all the more happy I did.

Jane: I wonder if he knew.

Pilkings: Who? Oh, you mean Olunde?

Jane: Yes. Was that why he was so determined to get away? I wouldn't stay if I knew I was trapped in such a horrible custom.

Pilkings (thoughtfully): No, I don't think he knew. At least he gave no indication. But you couldn't really tell with him. He was rather close you know, quite unlike most of them. Didn't give much away, not even to me.

Jane: Aren't they all rather close, Simon?

Pilkings: These natives here? Good gracious. They'll open their mouths and yap with you about their family secrets before you can stop them. Only the other day . . .

Jane: But Simon, do they really give anything away? I mean, anything that really counts. This affair for instance, we didn't know they still practised that custom did we?

Pilkings: Ye-e-es, I suppose you're right there. Sly, devious bastards.

Joseph (stiffly): Can I go now master? I have to clean the kitchen.

Pilkings: What? Oh, you can go. Forgot you were still here.

(Joseph *goes.*)

Jane: Simon, you really must watch your language. Bastard isn't just a simple swear-word in these parts, you know.

Pilkings: Look, just when did you become a social anthropologist, that's what I'd like to know.

Jane: I'm not claiming to know anything. I just happen to have overheard quarrels among the servants. That's how I know they consider it a smear.

Pilkings: I thought the extended family system took care of all that. Elastic family, no bastards.

Jane (shrugs): Have it your own way.

(*Awkward silence. The drumming increases in volume.* Jane *gets up suddenly, restless.*)

That drumming Simon, do you think it might really be connected with this ritual? It's been going on all evening.

Pilkings: Let's ask our native guide. Joseph! Just a minute Joseph. (*Joseph re-enters.*) What's the drumming about?

Joseph: I don't know master.

Pilkings: What do you mean you don't know? It's only two years since your conversion. Don't tell me all that holy water nonsense also wiped out your tribal memory.

Joseph (visibly shocked): Master!

Jane: Now you've done it.

Pilkings: What have I done now?

Jane: Never mind. Listen Joseph, just tell me this. Is that drumming connected with dying or anything of that nature?

Joseph: Madam, this is what I am trying to say: I am not sure. It sounds like the death of a great chief and then, it sounds like the wedding of a great chief. It really mix me up.

Pilkings: Oh get back to the kitchen. A fat lot of help you are.

Joseph: Yes master. (*Goes.*)

Jane: Simon . . .

Pilkings: Alright, alright. I'm in no mood for preaching.

Jane: It isn't my preaching you have to worry about, it's the preaching of the missionaries who preceded you here. When they make converts they really convert them. Calling holy water nonsense to our Joseph is really like insulting the Virgin Mary before a Roman Catholic. He's going to hand in his notice tomorrow you mark my word.

Pilkings: Now you're being ridiculous.

Jane: Am I? What are you willing to bet that tomorrow we are going to be without a steward-boy? Did you see his face?

Pilkings: I am more concerned about whether or not we will be one native chief short by tomorrow. Christ! Just listen to those drums. (*He strides up and down, undecided.*)

Jane (getting up): I'll change and make up some supper.

Pilkings: What's that?

Jane: Simon, it's obvious we have to miss this ball.

Pilkings: Nonsense. It's the first bit of real fun the European club has managed to organise for over a year, I'm damned if I'm going to miss it. And it is a rather special occasion. Doesn't happen every day.

Jane: You know this business has to be stopped Simon. And you are the only man who can do it.

Pilkings: I don't have to stop anything. If they want to throw themselves off the top of a cliff or poison themselves for the sake of some barbaric custom what is that to me? If it were ritual murder or something like that I'd be duty-bound to do something. I can't keep an eye on all the potential suicides in this province. And as for that man—believe me it's good riddance.

Jane (laughs): I know you better than that Simon. You are going to have to do something to stop it—after you've finished blustering.

Pilkings (shouts after her): And suppose after all it's only a wedding. I'd look a proper fool if I interrupted a chief on his honeymoon, wouldn't I? *(Resumes his angry stride, slows down.)* Ah well, who can tell what those chiefs actually do on their honeymoon anyway? *(He takes up the pad and scribbles rapidly on it.)* Joseph! Joseph! Joseph! *(Some moments later* Joseph *puts in a sulky appearance.)* Did you hear me call you? Why the hell didn't you answer?

Joseph: I didn't hear master.

Pilkings: You didn't hear me! How come you are here then?

Joseph (stubbornly): I didn't hear master.

Pilkings (controls himself with an effort): We'll talk about it in the morning. I want you to take this note directly to Sergeant Amusa. You'll find him at the charge office. Get on your bicycle and race there with it. I expect you back in twenty minutes exactly. Twenty minutes, is that clear?

Joseph: Yes master. *(Going.)*

Pilkings: Oh er . . . Joseph.

Joseph: Yes master?

Pilkings (between gritted teeth): Er . . . forget what I said just now. The holy water is not nonsense. *I* was talking nonsense.

Joseph: Yes master. *(Goes.)*

Jane (pokes her head round the door): Have you found him?

Pilkings: Found who?

Jane: Joseph. Weren't you shouting for him?

Pilkings: Oh yes, he turned up finally.

Jane: You sounded desperate. What was it all about?

Pilkings: Oh nothing. I just wanted to apologise to him. Assure him that the holy water isn't really nonsense.

Jane: Oh? And how did he take it?

Pilkings: Who the hell gives a damn! I had a sudden vision of our Very Reverend Macfarlane drafting another letter of complaint to the Resident about my unchristian language towards his parishioners.

Jane: Oh I think he's given up on you by now.

Pilkings: Don't be too sure. And anyway, I wanted to make sure Joseph didn't 'lose' my note on the way. He looked sufficiently full of the holy crusade to do some such thing.

Jane: If you've finished exaggerating, come and have something to eat.

Pilkings: No, put it all away. We can still get to the ball.

Jane: Simon . . .

Pilkings: Get your costume back on. Nothing to worry about. I've instructed Amusa to arrest the man and lock him up.

Jane: But that station is hardly secure Simon. He'll soon get his friends to help him escape.

Pilkings: A-ah, that's where I have out-thought you. I'm not having him put

in the station cell. Amusa will bring him right here and lock him up in
my study. And he'll stay with him till we get back. No one will dare
come here to incite him to anything.

Jane: How clever of you darling. I'll get ready.

Pilkings: Hey.

Jane: Yes darling.

Pilkings: I have a surprise for you. I was going to keep it until we actually
got to the ball.

Jane: What is it?

Pilkings: You know the Prince is on a tour of the colonies don't you? Well,
he docked in the capital only this morning but he is already at the Residency. He is going to grace the ball with his presence later tonight.

Jane: Simon! Not really.

Pilkings: Yes he is. He's been invited to give away the prizes and he has
agreed. You must admit old Engleton is the best Club Secretary we ever
had. Quick off the mark that lad.

Jane: But how thrilling.

Pilkings: The other provincials are going to be damned envious.

Jane: I wonder what he'll come as.

Pilkings: Oh I don't know. As a coat-of-arms perhaps. Anyway it won't be
anything to touch this.

Jane: Well that's lucky. If we are to be presented I won't have to start looking for a pair of gloves. It's all sewn on.

Pilkings (laughing): Quite right. Trust a woman to think of that. Come on,
let's get going.

Jane (rushing off): Won't be a second. *(Stops.)* Now I see why you've been so
edgy all evening. I thought you weren't handling this affair with your
usual brilliance—to begin with that is.

Pilkings (his mood is much improved): Shut up woman and get your things on.

Jane: Alright boss, coming.

(Pilkings *suddenly begins to hum the tango to which they were dancing before.*
Starts to execute a few practice steps. Lights fade.)

3

A swelling, agitated hum of women's voices rises immediately in the
background. The lights come on and we see the frontage of a converted cloth stall in
the market. The floor leading up to the entrance is covered in rich velvets and wo-
ven cloth. The women come on stage, borne backwards by the determined progress of
Sergeant Amusa *and his two constables who already have their batons out and use*
them as a pressure against the women. At the edge of the cloth-covered floor how-
ever the women take a determined stand and block all further progress of the men.
They begin to tease them mercilessly.

Amusa: I am tell you women for last time to commot my road. I am here on
official business.

Woman: Official business you white man's eunuch? Official business is taking place where you want to go and it's a business you wouldn't understand.

Woman (makes a quick tug at the constable's baton): That doesn't fool anyone you know. It's the one you carry under your government knickers that counts. *(She bends low as if to peep under the baggy shorts. The embarrassed constable quickly puts his knees together. The women roar.)*

Woman: You mean there is nothing there at all?

Woman: Oh there was something. You know that handbell which the white-man uses to summon his servants . . . ?

Amusa (he manages to preserve some dignity throughout): I hope you women know that interfering with officer in execution of his duty is criminal offence.

Woman: Interfere? He says we're interfering with him. You foolish man we're telling you there's nothing there to interfere with.

Amusa: I am order you now to clear the road.

Woman: What road? The one your father built?

Woman: You are a Policeman not so? Then you know what they call trespassing in court. Or—*(Pointing to the cloth-lined steps)*—do you think that kind of road is built for every kind of feet.

Woman: Go back and tell the white man who sent you to come himself.

Amusa: If I go I will come back with reinforcement. And we will all return carrying weapons.

Woman: Oh, now I understand. Before they can put on those knickers the white man first cuts off their weapons.

Woman: What a cheek! You mean you come here to show power to women and you don't even have a weapon.

Amusa (shouting above the laughter): For the last time I warn you women to clear the road.

Woman: To where?

Amusa: To that hut. I know he dey dere.

Woman: Who?

Amusa: The chief who call himself Elesin Oba.

Woman: You ignorant man. It is not he who calls himself Elesin Oba, it is his blood that says it. As it called out to his father before him and will to his son after him. And that is in spite of everything your white man can do.

Woman: Is it not the same ocean that washes this land and the white man's land? Tell your white man he can hide our son away as long as he likes. When the time comes for him, the same ocean will bring him back.

Amusa: The government say dat kin' ting must stop.

Woman: Who will stop it? You? Tonight our husband and father will prove himself greater than the laws of strangers.

Amusa: I tell you nobody go prove anything tonight or anytime. Is ignorant and criminal to prove dat kin' prove.

Iyaloja (entering, from the hut. She is accompanied by a group of young girls who have been attending the Bride*):* What is it Amusa? Why do you come here to disturb the happiness of others.

Amusa: Madame Iyaloja, I glad you come. You know me. I no like trouble but duty is duty. I am here to arrest Elesin for criminal intent. Tell these women to stop obstructing me in the performance of my duty.

Iyaloja: And you? What gives you the right to obstruct our leader of men in the performance of his duty.

Amusa: What kin' duty be dat one Iyaloja.

Iyaloja: What kin' duty? What kin' duty does a man have to his new bride?

Amusa (bewildered, looks at the women and at the entrance to the hut): Iyaloja, is it wedding you call dis kin' ting?

Iyaloja: You have wives haven't you? Whatever the white man has done to you he hasn't stopped you having wives. And if he has, at least he is married. If you don't know what a marriage is, go and ask him to tell you.

Amusa: This no to wedding.

Iyaloja: And ask him at the same time what he would have done if anyone had come to disturb him on his wedding night.

Amusa: Iyaloja, I say dis no to wedding.

Iyaloja: You want to look inside the bridal chamber? You want to see for yourself how a man cuts the virgin knot?

Amusa: Madam . . .

Iyaloja: Perhaps his wives are still waiting for him to learn.

Amusa: Iyaloja, make you tell dese women make den no insult me again. If I hear dat kin' indult once more . . .

Girl (pushing her way through): You will do what?

Girl: He's out of his mind. It's our mothers you're talking to, do you know that? Not to any illiterate villager you can bully and terrorise. How dare you intrude here anyway?

Girl: What a cheek, what impertinence!

Girl: You've treated them too gently. Now let them see what it is to tamper with the mothers of this market.

Girls: Your betters dare not enter the market when the women say no!

Girl: Haven't you learnt that yet, you jester in khaki and starch?

Iyaloja: Daughters . . .

Girl: No no Iyaloja, leave us to deal with him. He no longer knows his mother, we'll teach him.

(With a sudden movement they snatch the batons of the two constables. They begin to hem them in.)

Girl: What next? We have your batons? What next? What are you going to do?

(With equally swift movements they knock off their hats.)

Girl: Move if you dare. We have your hats, what will you do about it? Didn't the white man teach you to take off your hats before women?

Iyaloja: It's a wedding night. It's a night of joy for us. Peace . . .

Girl: Not for him. Who asked him here?

Girl: Does he dare go to the Residency without an invitation?

Girl: Not even where the servants eat the left-overs.

Girls (*in turn. In an 'English' accent*): Well well it's Mister Amusa. Were you
    invited? (*Play-acting to one another. The older women encourage them with
    their titters.*)
    —Your invitation card please?
    —Who are you? Have we been introduced?
    —And who did you say you were?
    —Sorry, I didn't quite catch your name.
    —May I take your hat?
    —If you insist. May I take yours? (*Exchanging the policeman's hats.*)
    —How very kind of you.
    —Not at all. Won't you sit down?
    —After you.
    —Oh no.
    —I insist.
    —You're most gracious.
    —And how do you find the place?
    —The natives are alright.
    —Friendly?
    —Tractable.
    —Not a teeny-weeny bit restless?
    —Well, a teeny-weeny bit restless.
    —One might even say, difficult?
    —Indeed one might be tempted to say, difficult.
    —But you do manage to cope?
    —Yes indeed I do. I have a rather faithful ox called Amusa.
    —He's loyal?
    —Absolutely.
    —Lay down his life for you what?
    —Without a moment's thought.
    —Had one like that once. Trust him with my life.
    —Mostly of course they are liars.
    —Never known a native tell the truth.
    —Does it get rather close around here?
    —It's mild for this time of the year.
    —But the rains may still come.
    —They are late this year aren't they?
    —They are keeping African time.
    —Ha ha ha ha
    —Ha ha ha ha
    —The humidity is what gets me.
    —It used to be whisky.
    —Ha ha ha ha
    —Ha ha ha ha
    —What's your handicap old chap?
    —Is there racing by golly?
    —Splendid golf course, you'll like it.
    —I'm beginning to like it already.

—And a European club, exclusive.

—You've kept the flag flying.

—We do our best for the old country.

—It's a pleasure to serve.

—Another whisky old chap?

—You are indeed too too kind.

—Not at all sir. Where is that boy? *(With a sudden bellow.)* Sergeant!

Amusa (snaps to attention): Yessir!

(The women collapse with laughter.)

Girl: Take your men out of here.

Amusa (realizing the trick, he rages from loss of face): I'm give you warning . . .

Girl: Alright then. Off with his knickers! *(They surge slowly forward.)*

Iyaloja: Daughters, please.

Amusa (squaring himself for defence): The first woman wey touch me . . .

Iyaloja: My children, I beg of you . . .

Girl: Then tell him to leave this market. This is the home of our mothers. We don't want the eater of white left-overs at the feast their hands have prepared.

Iyaloja: You heard them Amusa. You had better go.

Girls: Now!

Amusa (commencing his retreat): We dey go now, but make you no say we no warn you.

Girl: Now!

Girl: Before we read the riot act—you should know all about that.

Amusa: Make we go. *(They depart, more precipitately.)*

(The women strike their palms across in the gesture of wonder.)

Women: Do they teach you all that at school?

Woman: And to think I nearly kept Apinke away from the place.

Woman: Did you hear them? Did you see how they mimicked the white man?

Woman: The voices exactly. Hey, there are wonders in this world!

Iyaloja: Well, our elders have said it: Dada may be weak, but he has a younger sibling who is truly fearless.

Woman: The next time the white man shows his face in this market I will set Wuraola on his tail.

(A woman bursts into song and dance of euphoria—'Tani l'awa o l'ogbeja? Kayi! A l'ogbeja. Omo Kekere l'ogbeja'° The rest of the women join in, some placing the girls on their back like infants, others dancing round them. The dance becomes general, mounting in excitement. Elesin appears, in wrapper only. In his hands a white velvet cloth folded loosely as if it held some delicate object. He cries out.)

'Tani . . . l'ogbeja' 'Who says we haven't a defender? Silence! We have our defenders. Little children are our champions.'

Elesin: Oh you mothers of beautiful brides! *(The dancing stops. They turn and see him, and the object in his hands.* Iyaloja *approaches and gently takes the cloth from him.)* Take it. It is no mere virgin stain, but the union of life and the seeds of passage. My vital flow, the last from this flesh is inter-mingled with the promise of future life. All is prepared. Listen! *(A steady drum-beat from the distance.)* Yes. It is nearly time. The King's dog has been killed. The King's favourite horse is about to follow his master. My brother chiefs know their task and perform it well. *(He listens again.)*

(The Bride *emerges, stands shyly by the door. He turns to her.)*

Our marriage is not yet wholly fulfilled. When earth and passage wed, the consummation is complete only when there are grains of earth on the eyelids of passage. Stay by me till then. My faithful drummers, do me your last service. This is where I have chosen to do my leave-taking, in this heart of life, this hive which contains the swarm of the world in its small compass. This is where I have known love and laughter away from the palace. Even the richest food cloys when eaten days on end; in the market, nothing ever cloys. Listen. *(They listen to the drums.)* They have begun to seek out the heart of the King's favourite horse. Soon it will ride in its bolt of raffia with the dog at its feet. Together they will ride on the shoulders of the King's grooms through the pulse centres of the town. They know it is here I shall await them. I have told them. *(His eyes appear to cloud. He passes his hand over them as if to clear his sight. He gives a faint smile.)* It promises well; just then I felt my spirit's eagerness. The kite makes for wide spaces and the wind creeps up behind its tail; can the kite say less than—thank you, the quicker the better? But wait a while my spirit. Wait. Wait for the coming of the courier of the King. Do you know friends, the horse is born to this one destiny, to bear the burden that is man upon its back. Except for this night, this night alone when the spotless stallion will ride in triumph on the back of man. In the time of my father I witnessed the strange sight. Perhaps tonight also I shall see it for the last time. If they arrive before the drums beat for me, I shall tell him to let the Alafin know I follow swiftly. If they come after the drums have sounded, why then, all is well for I have gone ahead. Our spirits shall fall in step along the great passage. *(He listens to the drums. He seems again to be falling into a state of semi-hypnosis; his eyes scan the sky but it is in a kind of daze. His voice is a little breathless.)* The moon has fed, a glow from its full stomach fills the sky and air, but I cannot tell where is that gate-way through which I must pass. My faithful friends, let our feet touch together this last time, lead me into the other market with sounds that cover my skin with down yet make my limbs strike earth like a thorough-bred. Dear mothers, let me dance into the passage even as I have lived beneath your roofs. *(He comes down progressively among them. They make a way for him, the drummers playing. His dance is one of solemn, regal motions, each gesture of the body is made with a solemn finality. The women join him, their steps a somewhat more fluid version of his. Beneath the* Praise-Singer's *exhortations the women dirge 'Alẹ lẹ lẹ, awo mi lọ'.)*

Praise-Singer:	Elesin Alafin, can you hear my voice?
Elesin:	Faintly, my friend, faintly.
Elesin:	Elesin Alafin, can you hear my call?
Elesin:	Faintly my king, faintly.
Praise-Singer:	Is your memory sound Elesin?
	Shall my voice be a blade of grass and
	Tickle the armpit of the past?
Elesin:	My memory needs no prodding but
	What do you wish to say to me?
Praise-Singer:	Only what has been spoken. Only what concerns
	The dying wish of the father of all.
Elesin:	It is buried like seed-yam in my mind
	This is the season of quick rains, the harvest
	Is this moment due for gathering.
Praise-Singer:	If you cannot come, I said, swear
	You'll tell my favourite horse. I shall
	Ride on through the gates alone.
Elesin:	Elesin's message will be read
	Only when his loyal heart no longer beats.
Praise-Singer:	If you cannot come Elesin, tell my dog.
	I cannot stay the keeper too long
	At the gate.
Elesin:	A dog does not outrun the hand
	That feeds it meat. A horse that throws its rider
	Slows down to a stop. Elesin Alafin
	Trusts no beasts with messages between
	A king and his companion.
Praise-Singer:	If you get lost my dog will track
	The hidden path to me.
Elesin:	The seven-way crossroads confuses
	Only the stranger. The Horseman of the King
	Was born in the recesses of the house.
Praise-Singer:	I know the wickedness of men. If there is
	Weight on the loose end of your sash, such weight
	As no mere man can shift; if your sash is earthed
	By evil minds who mean to part us at the last . . .
Elesin:	My sash is of the deep purple *alari*;
	It is no tethering-rope. The elephant
	Trails no tethering-rope; that king
	Is not yet crowned who will peg an elephant—
	Not even you my friend and King.
Praise-Singer:	And yet this fear will not depart from me
	The darkness of this new abode is deep—
	Will your human eyes suffice?
Elesin:	In a night which falls before our eyes
	However deep, we do not miss our way.
Praise-Singer:	Shall I now not acknowledge I have stood

> Where wonders met their end? The elephant deserves
> Better than that we say 'I have caught
> A glimpse of something'. If we see the tamer
> Of the forest let us say plainly, we have seen
> An elephant.

Elesin (his voice is drowsy):
> I have freed myself of earth and now
> It's getting dark. Strange voices guide my feet.

Praise-Singer: The river is never so high that the eyes
> Of a fish are covered. The night is not so dark
> That the albino fails to find his way. A child
> Returning homewards craves no leading by the hand.
> Gracefully does the mask regain his grove at the end
>   of day . . .
> Gracefully. Gracefully does the mask dance
> Homeward at the end of day, gracefully . . .

(Elesin's trance appears to be deepening, his steps heavier.)

Iyaloja: It is the death of war that kills the valiant,
> Death of water is how the swimmer goes
> It is the death of markets that kills the trader
> And death of indecision takes the idle away
> The trade of the cutlass blunts its edge
> And the beautiful die the death of beauty.
> It takes an Elesin to die the death of death . . .
> Only Elesin . . . dies the unknowable death of death . . .
> Gracefully, gracefully does the horseman regain
> The stables at the end of day, gracefully . . .

Praise-Singer: How shall I tell what my eyes have seen? The Horseman
gallops on before the courier, how shall I tell what my eyes have seen?
He says a dog may be confused by new scents of beings he never dreamt
of, so he must precede the dog to heaven. He says a horse may stumble
on strange boulders and be lamed, so he races on before the horse to
heaven. It is best, he says, to trust no messenger who may falter at the
outer gate; oh how shall I tell what my ears have heard? But do you hear
me still Elesin, do you hear your faithful one?

*(Elesin in his motions appears to feel for a direction of sound, subtly, but he
only sinks deeper into his trance-dance.)*

Elesin Alafin, I no longer sense your flesh. The drums are changing now
but you have gone far ahead of the world. It is not yet noon in heaven;
let those who claim it is begin their own journey home. So why must
you rush like an impatient bride: why do you race to desert your
Olohun-iyo?

*(Elesin is now sunk fully deep in his trance, there is no longer sign of any
awareness of his surroundings.)*

Does the deep voice of *gbedu*° cover you then, like the passage of royal
elephants? Those drums that brook no rivals, have they blocked the
passage to your ears that my voice passes into wind, a mere leaf floating
in the night? Is your flesh lightened Elesin, is that lump of earth I slid
between your slippers to keep you longer slowly sifting from your feet?
Are the drums on the other side now tuning skin to skin with ours in
osugbo°? Are there sounds there I cannot hear, do footsteps surround you
which pound the earth like *gbedu*, roll like thunder round the dome of
the world? Is the darkness gathering in your head Elesin? Is there now a
streak of light at the end of the passage, a light I dare not look upon?
Does it reveal whose voices we often heard, whose touches we often felt,
whose wisdoms come suddenly into the mind when the wisest have
shaken their heads and murmured; It cannot be done? Elesin Alafin,
don't think I do not know why your lips are heavy, why your limbs are
drowsy as palm oil in the cold of harmattan. I would call you back but
when the elephant heads for the jungle, the tail is too small a handhold
for the hunter that would pull him back. The sun that heads for the sea
no longer heeds the prayers of the farmer. When the river begins to
taste the salt of the ocean, we no longer know what deity to call on, the
river-god or Olokun. No arrow flies back to the string, the child does
not return through the same passage that gave it birth. Elesin Oba, can
you hear me at all? Your eyelids are glazed like a courtesan's, is it that
you see the dark groom and master of life? And will you see my father?
Will you tell him that I stayed with you to the last? Will my voice ring
in your ears awhile, will you remember Olohun-iyo even if the music on
the other side surpasses his mortal craft? But will they know you over
there? Have they eyes to gauge your worth, have they the heart to love
you, will they know what thoroughbred prances towards them in ca-
parisons of honour? If they do not Elesin, if any there cuts your yam
with a small knife, or pours you wine in a small calabash, turn back and
return to welcoming hands. If the world were not greater than the
wishes of Olohun-iyo, I would not let you go . . .

(He appears to break down. Elesin *dances on, completely in a trance. The dirge
wells up louder and stronger.* Elesin's *dance does not lose its elasticity but his gestures become, if possible, even more weighty. Lights fade slowly on the scene.)*

4

*A Masque. The front side of the stage is part of a wide corridor around the
great hall of the Residency extending beyond vision into the rear and wings. It is
redolent of the tawdry decadence of a far-flung but key imperial frontier. The couples
in a variety of fancy-dress are ranged around the walls, gazing in the same direction. The guest-of-honour is about to make an appearance. A portion of the local*

---

gbedu: A deep-timbred royal drum.   *osugbo:* Secret 'executive' cult of the Yoruba; its meeting
place.

police brass band and with its white conductor is just visible. At last, the entrance of Royalty. The band plays 'Rule Britannia', badly, beginning long before he is visible. The couples bow and curtsey as he passes by them. Both he and his companions are dressed in seventeenth century European costume. Following behind are the Resident *and his partner similarly attired. As they gain the end of the hall where the orchestra dais begins the music comes to an end. The* Prince *bows to the guests. The band strikes up a Viennese waltz and the* Prince *formally opens the floor. Several bars later the* Resident *and his companion follow suit. Others follow in appropriate pecking order. The orchestra's waltz rendition is not of the highest musical standard.*

Some time later the Prince *dances again into view and is settled into a corner by the* Resident *who then proceeds to select couples as they dance past for introduction, sometimes threading his way through the dancers to tap the lucky couple on the shoulder. Desperate efforts from many to ensure that they are recognized in spite of, perhaps, their costume. The ritual of introductions soon takes in* Pilkings *and his wife. The* Prince *is quite fascinated by their costume and they demonstrate the adaptations they have made to it, pulling down the mask to demonstrate how the* egungun *normally appears, then showing the various press-button controls they have innovated for the face flaps, the sleeves, etc. They demonstrate the dance steps and the guttural sounds made by the* egungun, *harass other dancers in the hall,* Mrs. Pilkings *playing the 'restrainer' to* Pilkings' *manic darts. Everyone is hightly entertained, the Royal Party especially who lead the applause.*

At this point a liveried footman comes in with a note on a salver and is intercepted almost absent-mindedly by the Resident *who takes the note and reads it. After polite coughs he suceeds in excusing* Pilkingses *from the* Prince *and takes them aside. The* Prince *considerately offers the* Resident's *wife his hand and dancing is resumed.*

On their way out the Resident *gives an order to his* Aide-De-Camp. *They come into the side corridor where the* Resident *hands the note to* Pilkings.

Resident: As you see it says 'emergency' on the outside. I took the liberty of opening it because His Highness was obviously enjoying the entertainment. I didn't want to interrupt unless really necessary.

Pilkings: Yes, yes of course sir.

Resident: Is it really as bad as it says? What's it all about?

Pilkings: Some strange custom they have sir. It seems because the King is dead some important chief has to commit suicide.

Resident: The King? Isn't it the same one who died nearly a month ago?

Pilkings: Yes sir.

Resident: Haven't they buried him yet?

Pilkings: They take their time about these things sir. The pre-burial ceremonies last nearly thirty days. It seems tonight is the final night.

Resident: But what has it got to do with the market women? Why are they rioting? We've waived that troublesome tax haven't we?

Pilkings: We don't quite know that they are exactly rioting yet sir. Sergeant Amusa is sometimes prone to exaggerations.

Resident: He sounds desperate enough. That comes out even in his rather quaint grammar. Where is the man anyway? I asked my aide-de-camp to bring him here.

Pilkings: They are probably looking in the wrong verandah. I'll fetch him myself.

Resident: No no you stay here. Let your wife go and look for them. Do you mind my dear . . . ?

Jane: Certainly not, your Excellency. *(Goes.)*

Resident: You should have kept me informed Pilkings. You realize how disastrous it would have been if things had erupted while His Highness was here.

Pilkings: I wasn't aware of the whole business until tonight sir.

Resident: Nose to the ground Pilkings, nose to the ground. If we all let these little things slip past us where would the empire be eh? Tell me that. Where would we all be?

Pilkings (low voice): Sleeping peacefully at home I bet.

Resident: What did you say Pilkings?

Pilkings: It won't happen again sir.

Resident: It mustn't Pilkings. It musn't. Where is that damned sergeant? I ought to get back to His Highness as quickly as possible and offer him some plausible explanation for my rather abrupt conduct. Can you think of one Pilkings?

Pilkings: You could tell him the truth sir.

Resident: I could? No no no no Pilkings, that would never do. What! Go and tell him there is a riot just two miles away from him? This is supposed to be a secure colony of His Majesty, Pilkings.

Pilkings: Yes sir.

Resident: Ah, there they are. No, these are not our native police. Are these the ring-leaders of the riot?

Pilkings: Sir, these are my police officers.

Resident: Oh, I beg your pardon officers. You do look a little . . . I say, isn't there something missing in their uniform? I think they used to have some rather colourful sashes. If I remember rightly I recommended them myself in my young days in the serice. A bit of colour always appeals to the natives, yes, I remember putting that in my report. Well well well, where are we? Make your report man.

Pilkings (moves close to Amusa, *between his teeth):* And let's have no more superstitious nonsense from you Amusa or I'll throw you in the guard-room for a month and feed you pork!

Resident: What's that? What has pork to do with it?

Pilkings: Sir, I was just warning him to be brief. I'm sure you are most anxious to hear his report.

Resident: Yes yes yes of course. Come on man, speak up. Hey, didn't we give them some colourful fez hats with all those wavy things, yes, pink tassells . . .

Pilkings: Sir, I think if he was permitted to make his report we might find that he lost his hat in the riot.

Resident: Ah yes indeed. I'd better tell His Highness that. Lost his hat in the riot, ha ha. He'll probably say well, as long as he didn't lose his head. *(Chuckles to himself.)* Don't forget to send me a report first thing in the morning young Pilkings.

Pilkings: No sir.

Resident: And whatever you do, don't let things get out of hand. Keep a cool head and—nose to the ground Pilkings. (*Wanders off in the general direction of the hall.*)

Pilkings: Yes sir.

Aide-De-Camp: Would you be needing me sir?

Pilkings: No thanks Bob. I think His Excellency's need of you is greater than ours.

Aide-De-Camp: We have a detachment of soldiers from the capital sir. They accompanied His Highness up here.

Pilkings: I doubt if it will come to that but, thanks, I'll bear it in mind. Oh, could you send an orderly with my cloak.

Aide-De-Camp: Very good sir. (*Goes.*)

Pilkings: Now Sergeant.

Amusa: Sir . . . (*Makes an effort, stops dead. Eyes to the ceiling.*)

Pilkings: Oh, not again.

Amusa: I cannot against death to dead cult. This dress get power of dead.

Pilkings: Alright, let's go. You are relieved of all further duty Amusa. Report to me first thing in the morning.

Jane: Shall I come Simon?

Pilkings: No, there's no need for that. If I can get back later I will. Otherwise get Bob to bring you home.

Jane: Be careful Simon . . . I mean, be clever.

Pilkings: Sure I will. You two, come with me. (*As he turns to go, the clock in the Residency begins to chime.* Pilkings *looks at his watch then turns, horror-stricken, to stare at his wife. The same thought clearly occurs to her. He swallows hard. An orderly brings his cloak.*) It's midnight. I had no idea it was that late.

Jane: But surely . . . they don't count the hours the way we do. The moon, or something . . .

Pilkings: I am . . . not so sure.

(*He turns and breaks into a sudden run. The two constables follow, also at a run.* Amusa, *who has kept his eyes on the ceiling throughout waits until the last of the footsteps has faded out of hearing. He salutes suddenly, but without once looking in the direction of the woman.*)

Amusa: Goodnight madam.

Jane: Oh. (*She hesitates.*) Amusa . . . (*He goes off without seeming to have heard.*) Poor Simon . . . (*A figure emerges from the shadows, a young black man dressed in a sober western suit. He peeps into the hall, trying to make out the figures of the dancers.*) Who is that?

Olunde (*emerging into the light*): I didn't mean to startle you madam. I am looking for the District Officer.

Jane: Wait a minute . . . don't I know you? Yes, you are Olunde, the young man who . . .

Olunde: Mrs Pilkings! How fortunate. I came here to look for your husband.

Jane: Olunde! Let's look at you. What a fine young man you've become. Grand but solemn. Good God, when did you return? Simon never said a word. But you do look well Olunde. Really!

Olunde: You are . . . well, you look quite well yourself Mrs. Pilkings. From what little I can see of you.

Jane: Oh, this. It's caused quite a stir I assure you, and not all of it very pleasant. You are not shocked I hope?

Olunde: Why should I be? But don't you find it rather hot in there? Your skin must find it difficult to breathe.

Jane: Well, it is a little hot I must confess, but it's all in a good cause.

Olunde: What cause Mrs Pilkings?

Jane: All this. The ball. And His Highness being here in person and all that.

Olunde (mildly): And that is the good cause for which you desecrate an ancestral mask?

Jane: Oh, so you are shocked after all. How disappointing.

Olunde: No I am not shocked Mrs Pilkings You forget that I have now spent four years among your people. I discovered that you have no respect for what you do not understand.

Jane: Oh. So you've returned with a chip on your shoulder. That's a pity Olunde. I am sorry.

(An uncomfortable silence follows.)

I take it then that you did not find your stay in England altogether edifying.

Olunde: I don't say that. I found your people quite admirable in many ways, their conduct and courage in this war for instance.

Jane: Ah yes the war. Here of course it is all rather remote. From time to time we have a black-out drill just to remind us that there is a war on. And the rare convoy passes through on its way somewhere or on manoeurvres. Mind you there is the occasional bit of excitement like that ship that was blown up in the harbour.

Olunde: Here? Do you mean through enemy action?

Jane: Oh no, the war hasn't come that close. The captain did it himself. I don't quite understand it really. Simon tried to explain. The ship had to be blown up because it had become dangerous to the other ships, even to the city itself. Hundreds of the coastal population would have died.

Olunde: Maybe it was loaded with ammunition and had caught fire. Or some of those lethal gases they've been experimenting on.

Jane: Something like that. The captain blew himself up with it. Deliberately. Simon said someone had to remain on board to light the fuse.

Olunde: It must have been a very short fuse.

Jane (shrugs): I don't know much about it. Only that there was no other way to save lives. No time to devise anything else. The captain took the decision and carried it out.

Olunde: Yes . . . I quite believe it. I met men like that in England.

Jane: Oh just look at me! Fancy welcoming you back with such morbid news. Stale too. It was at least six months ago.

Olunde: I don't find it morbid at all. I find it rather inspiring. It is an affirmative commentary on life.

Jane: What is?

Olunde: That captain's self-sacrifice.

Jane: Nonsense. Life should never be thrown deliberately away.

Olunde: And the innocent people round the harbour?

Jane: Oh, how does one know? The whole thing was probably exaggerated anyway.

Olunde: That was a risk the captain couldn't take. But please Mrs Pilkings, do you think you could find your husband for me? I have to talk to him.

Jane: Simon? Oh. *(As she recollects for the first time the full significance of Olunde's presence.)* Simon is . . . there is a little problem in town. He was sent for. But . . . when did you arrive? Does Simon know you're here?

Olunde (suddenly earnest): I need your help Mrs Pilkings. I've always found you somewhat more understanding than your husband. Please find him for me and when you do, you must help me talk to him.

Jane: I'm afraid I don't quite . . . follow you. Have you seen my husband already?

Olunde: I went to your house. Your houseboy told me you were here. *(He smiles.)* He even told me how I would recognise you and Mr Pilkings.

Jane: Then you must know what my husband is trying to do for you.

Olunde: For me?

Jane: For you. For your people. And to think he didn't even know you were coming back! But how do you happen to be here? Only this evening we were talking about you. We thought you were still four thousand miles away.

Olunde: I was sent a cable.

Jane: A cable? Who did? Simon? The business of your father didn't begin till tonight.

Olunde: A relation sent it weeks ago, and it said nothing about my father. All it said was, Our King is dead. But I knew I had to return home at once so as to bury my father. I understood that.

Jane: Well, thank God you don't have to go through that agony. Simon is going to stop it.

Olunde: That's why I want to see him. He's wasting his time. And since he has been so helpful to me I don't want him to incur the enmity of our people. Especially over nothing.

Jane (sits down open-mouthed): You . . . you Olunde!

Olunde: Mrs Pilkings, I came home to bury my father. As soon as I heard the news I booked my passage home. In fact we were fortunate. We travelled in the same convoy as your Prince, so we had excellent protection.

Jane: But you don't think your father is also entitled to whatever protection is available to him?

Olunde: How can I make you understand? He *has* protection. No one can undertake what he does tonight without the deepest protection the mind can conceive. What can you offer him in place of his peace of mind, in place of the honour and veneration of his own people? What would you think of your Prince if he had refused to accept the risk of losing his life on this voyage? This . . . showing-the-flag tour of colonial possessions.

Jane: I see. So it isn't just medicine you studied in England.

Olunde: Yet another error into which your people fall. You believe that everything which appears to make sense was learnt from you.

Jane: Not so fast Olunde. You have learnt to argue I can tell that, but I never said you made sense. However cleverly you try to put it, it is still a barbaric custom. It is even worse—it's feudal! The king dies and a chieftian must be buried with him. How feudalistic can you get!

Olunde (waves his hand towards the background. The Prince *is dancing past again—to a different step—and all the guests are bowing and curtseying as he passes):* And this? Even in the midst of a devastating war, look at that. What name would you give to that?

Jane: Therapy, British style. The preservation of sanity in the midst of chaos.

Olunde: Others would call it decadence. However, it doesn't really interest me. You white races know how to survive; I've seen proof of that. By all logical and natural laws this war should end with all the white races wiping out one another, wiping out their so-called civilisation for all time and reverting to a state of primitivism the like of which has so far only existed in your imagination when you thought of us. I thought all that at the beginning. Then I slowly realised that your greatest art is the art of survival. But at least have the humility to let others survive in their own way.

Jane: Through ritual suicide?

Olunde: Is that worse than mass suicide? Mrs Pilkings, what do you call what those young men are sent to do by their generals in this war? Of course you have also mastered the art of calling things by names which don't remotely describe them.

Jane: You talk! You people with your long-winded, roundabout way of making conversation.

Olunde: Mrs Pilkings, whatever we do, we never suggest that a thing is the opposite of what it really is. In your newsreels I heard defeats, thorough, murderous defeats described as strategic victories. No wait, it wasn't just on your newsreels. Don't forget I was attached to hospitals all the time. Hordes of your wounded passed through those wards. I spoke to them. I spent long evenings by their bedside while they spoke terrible truths of the realities of that war. I know now how history is made.

Jane: But surely, in a war of this nature, for the morale of the nation you must expect . . .

Olunde: That a disaster beyond human reckoning be spoken of as a triumph? No. I mean, is there no mourning in the home of the bereaved that such blasphemy is permitted?

Jane (after a moment's pause): Perhaps I can understand you now. The time we picked for you was not really one for seeing us at our best.

Olunde: Don't think it was just the war. Before that even started I had plenty of time to study your people. I saw nothing, finally, that gave you the right to pass judgment on other peoples and their ways. Nothing at all.

Jane (hesitantly): Was it the . . . colour thing? I know there is some discrimination.

Olunde: Don't make it so simple, Mrs Pilkings. You make it sound as if when I left, I took nothing at all with me.

Jane: Yes . . . and to tell the truth, only this evening, Simon and I agreed that we never really knew what you left with.

Olunde: Neither did I. But I found out over there. I am grateful to your country for that. And I will never give it up.

Jane: Olunde, please . . . promise me something. Whatever you do, don't throw away what you have started to do. You want to be a doctor. My husband and I believe you will make an excellent one, sympathetic and competent. Don't let anything make you throw away your training.

Olunde (genuinely surprised): Of course not. What a strange idea. I intend to return and complete my training. Once the burial of my father is over.

Jane: Oh, please . . . !

Olunde: Listen! Come outside. You can't hear anything against that music.

Jane: What is it?

Olunde: The drums. Can you hear the change? Listen.

(*The drums come over, still distant but more distinct. There is a change of rhythm, it rises to a crescendo and then, suddenly, it is cut off. After a silence, a new beat begins, slow and resonant.*)

There. It's all over.

Jane: You mean he's . . .

Olunde: Yes Mrs Pilkings, my father is dead. His will-power has always been enormous; I know he is dead.

Jane (screams): How can you be so callous! So unfeeling! You announce your father's own death like a surgeon looking down on some strange . . . stranger's body! You're just a savage like all the rest.

Aide-De-Camp (rushing out): Mrs Pilkings, Mrs Pilkings. (*She breaks down sobbing.*) Are you alright, Mrs Pilkings?

Olunde: She'll be alright. (*Turns to go.*)

Aide-De-Camp: Who are you? And who the hell asked your opinion?

Olunde: You're quite right, nobody. (*Going.*)

Aide-De-Camp: What the hell! Did you hear me ask you who you were?

Olunde: I have business to attend to.

Aide-De-Camp: I'll give you business in a moment you impudent nigger. Answer my question!

Olunde: I have a funeral to arrange. Excuse me. (*Going.*)

Aide-De-Camp: I said stop! Orderly!

Jane: No no, don't do that. I'm alright. And for heaven's sake don't act so foolishly. He's a family friend.

Aide-De-Camp: Well he'd better learn to answer civil questions when he's asked them. These natives put a suit on and they get high opinions of themselves.

Olunde: Can I go now?

Jane: No no don't go. I must talk to you. I'm sorry about what I said.

Olunde: It's nothing Mrs Pilkings. And I'm really anxious to go. I couldn't see my father before, it's forbidden for me, his heir and successor to set eyes on him from the moment of the king's death. But now . . . I would like to touch his body while it is still warm.

Jane: You will. I promise I shan't keep you long. Only, I couldn't possibly let you go like that. Bob, please excuse us.

Aide-De-Camp: If you're sure . . .

Jane: Of course I'm sure. Something happened to upset me just then, but I'm alright now. Really.

(*The* Aide-De-Camp *goes, somewhat reluctantly.*)

Olunde: I mustn't stay long.

Jane: Please, I promise not to keep you. It's just that . . . oh you saw yourself what happens to one in this place. The Resident's man thought he was being helpful, that's the way we all react. But I can't go in among that crowd just now and if I stay by myself somebody will come looking for me. Please, just say something for a few moments and then you can go. Just so I can recover myself.

Olunde: What do you want me to say?

Jane: Your calm acceptance for instance, can you explain that? It was so unnatural. I don't understand that at all. I feel a need to understand all I can.

Olunde: But you explained it yourself. My medical training perhaps. I have seen death too often. And the soldiers who returned from the front, they died on our hands all the time.

Jane: No. It has to be more than that. I feel it has to do with the many things we don't really grasp about your people. At least you can explain.

Olunde: All these things are part of it. And anyway, my father has been dead in my mind for nearly a month. Ever since I learnt of the King's death. I've lived with my bereavement so long now that I cannot think of him alive. On that journey on the boat, I kept my mind on my duties as the one who must perform the rites over his body. I went through it all again and again in my mind as he himself had taught me. I didn't want to do anything wrong, something which might jeopardise the welfare of my people.

Jane: But he had disowned you. When you left he swore publicly you were no longer his son.

Olunde: I told you, he was a man of tremendous will. Sometimes that's another way of saying stubborn. But among our people, you don't disown a child just like that. Even if I have died before him I would still be buried like his eldest son. But it's time for me to go.

Jane: Thank you. I feel calmer. Don't let me keep you from your duties.

Olunde: Goodnight Mrs Pilkings.

Jane: Welcome home. *(She holds out her hand. As he takes it footsteps are heard approaching the drive. A short while later a woman's sobbing is also heard.)*

Pilkings (off): Keep them here till I get back. *(He strides into view, reacts at the sight of* Olunde *but turns to his wife.)* Thank goodness you're still here.

Jane: Simon, what happened?

Pilkings: Later Jane, please. Is Bob still here?

Jane: Yes, I think so. I'm sure he must be.

Pilkings: Try and get him out here as quietly as you can. Tell him it's urgent.

Jane: Of course. Oh Simon, you remember . . .

Pilkings: Yes yes. I can see who it is. Get Bob out here. *(She runs off.)* At first I thought I was seeing a ghost.

Olunde: Mr Pilkings, I appreciate what you tried to do. I want you to believe that. I can only tell you it would have been a terrible calamity if you'd succeeded.

Pilkings (opens his mouth several times, shuts it): You . . . said what?

Olunde: A calamity for us, the entire people.

Pilkings (sighs): I see. Hm.

Olunde: And now I must go. I must see him before he turns cold.

Pilkings: Oh ah . . . em . . . but this is a shock to see you. I mean er thinking all this while you were in England and thanking God for that.

Olunde: I came on the mail boat. We traveled in the Prince's convoy.

Pilkings: Ah yes, a-ah, hm . . . er well . . .

Olunde: Goodnight. I can see you are shocked by the whole business. But you must know by now there are things you cannot understand—or help.

Pilkings: Yes. Just a minute. There are armed policemen that way and they have instructions to let no one pass. I suggest you wait a little. I'll er . . . yes, I'll give you an escort.

Olunde: That's very kind of you. But do you think it could be quickly arranged.

Pilkings: Of course. In fact, yes, what I'll do is send Bob over with some men to the er . . . place. You can go with them. Here he comes now. Excuse me a minute.

Aide-De-Camp: Anything wrong sir?

Pilkings (takes him to one side): Listen Bob, that cellar in the disused annexe of the Residency, you know, where the slaves were stored before being taken down to the coast . . .

Aide-De-Camp: Oh yes, we use it as a storeroom for broken furniture.

Pilkings: But it's still got the bars on it?

Aide-De-Camp: Oh yes, they are quite intact.

Pilkings: Get the keys please. I'll explain later. And I want a strong guard over the Residency tonight.

Aide-De-Camp: We have that already. The detachment from the coast . . .

Pilkings: No, I don't want them at the gates of the Residency. I want you to deploy them at the bottom of the hill, a long way from the main hall so they can deal with any situation long before the sound carries to the house.

Aide-De-Camp: Yes of course.

Pilkings: I don't want His Highness alarmed.

Aide-De-Camp: You think the riot will spread here?

Pilkings: It's unlikely but I don't want to take a chance. I made them believe I was going to lock the man up in my house, which was what I had planned to do in the first place. They are probably assailing it by now. I took a roundabout route here so I don't think there is any danger at all. At least not before dawn. Nobody is to leave the premises of course— the native employees I mean. They'll soon smell something is up and they can't keep their mouths shut.

Aide-De-Camp: I'll give instructions at once.

Pilkings: I'll take the prisoner down myself. Two policemen will stay with him throughout the night. Inside the cell.

Aide-De-Camp: Right sir. *(Salutes and goes off at the double.)*

Pilkings: Jane. Bob is coming back in a moment with a detachment. Until he gets back please stay with Olunde. *(He makes an extra warning gesture with his eyes.)*

Olunde: Please Mr Pilkings . . .

Pilkings: I hate to be stuffy old son, but we have a crisis on our hands. It has to do with your father's affair if you must know. And it happens also at a time when we have His Highness here. I am responsible for security so you'll simply have to do as I say. I hope that's understood. *(Marches off quickly, in the direction from which he made his first appearance.)*

Olunde: What's going on? All this can't be just because he failed to stop my father killing himself.

Jane: I honestly don't know. Could it have sparked off a riot?

Olunde: No. If he'd succeeded that would be more likely to start the riot. Perhaps there were other factors involved. Was there a chieftancy dispute?

Jane: None that I know of.

Elesin (an animal bellow from off): Leave me alone! Is it not enough that you have covered me in shame! White man, take your hand from my body!

(Olunde *stands frozen on the spot.* Jane *understanding at last, tries to move him.)*

Jane: Let's go in. It's getting chilly out here.

Pilkings (off): Carry him.

Elesin: Give me back the name you have taken away from me you ghost from the land of the nameless!

Pilkings: Carry him! I can't have a disturbance here. Quickly! stuff up his mouth.

Jane: Oh God! Let's go in. Please Olunde. (Olunde *does not move.)*

Elesin: Take your albino's hand from me you . . .

(Sounds of a struggle. His voice chokes as he is gagged.)

Olunde (quietly): That was my father's voice.

Jane: Oh you poor orphan, what have you come home to?

(There is a sudden explosion of rage from off-stage and powerful steps come running up the drive.)

Pilkings: You bloody fools, after him!

(Immediately Elesin, *in handcuffs, comes pounding in the direction of* Jane *and* Olunde, *followed some moments afterwards by* Pilkings *and the constables.* Elesin *confronted by the seeming statue of his son, stops dead.* Olunde *stares above his head into the distance. The constables try to grab him.* Jane *screams at them.)*

Jane: Leave him alone! Simon, tell them to leave him alone.

Pilkings: All right, stand aside you. *(Shrugs.)* Maybe just as well. It might help to calm him down.

(For several moments they hold the same position. Elesin *moves a few steps forward, almost as if he's still in doubt.)*

Elesin: Olunde? *(He moves his head, inspecting him from side to side.)* Olunde! *(He collapses slowly at* Olunde's *feet.)* Oh son, don't let the sight of your father turn you blind!

Olunde (he moves for the first time since he heard his voice, brings his head slowly down to look on him): I have no father, eater of left-overs.

(He walks slowly down the way his father had run. Light fades out on Elesin, *sobbing into the ground.)*

5

A wide iron-barred gate stretches almost the whole width of the cell in which Elesin *is imprisoned. His wrists are encased in thick iron bracelets, chained together; he stands against the bars, looking out. Seated on the ground to one side on the outside is his recent bride, her eyes bent perpetually to the ground. Figures of the two guards can be seen deeper inside the cell, alert to every movement* Elesin *makes.* Pilkings *now in a police officer's uniform enters noiselessly, observes him for a while. Then he coughs ostentatiously and approaches. Leans against the bars near a corner, his back to* Elesin. *He is obviously trying to fall in mood with him. Some moments' silence.*

Pilkings: You seem fascinated by the moon.

Elesin (after a pause): Yes, ghostly one. Your twin-brother up there engages my thoughts.

Pilkings: It is a beautiful night.

Elesin: Is that so?

Pilkings: The light on the leaves, the peace of the night . . .

Elesin: The night is not at peace, District Officer.

Pilkings: No? I would have said it was. You know, quiet . . .

Elesin: And does quiet mean peace for you?

Pilkings: Well, nearly the same thing. Naturally there is a subtle difference . . .

Elesin: The night is not at peace ghostly one. The world is not at peace. You have shattered the peace of the world for ever. There is no sleep in the world tonight.

Pilkings: It is still a good bargain if the world should lose one night's sleep as the price of saving a man's life.

Elesin: You did not save my life District Officer. You destroyed it.

Pilkings: Now come on . . .

Elesin: And not merely my life but the lives of many. The end of the night's work is not over. Neither this year nor the next will see it. If I wished you well, I would pray that you do not stay long enough on our land to see the disaster you have brought upon us.

Pilkings: Well, I did my duty as I saw it. I have no regrets.

Elesin: No. The regrets of life always come later.

(Some moments' pause.)

You are waiting for dawn white man. I hear you saying to yourself; only so many hours until dawn and then the danger is over. All I must do is keep him alive tonight. You don't quite understand it all but you know that tonight is when what ought to be must be brought about. I shall ease your mind ever more, ghostly one. It is not an entire night but a moment of the night, and that moment is past. The moon was my messenger and guide. When it reached a certain gateway in the sky, it touched that moment for which my whole life has been spent in blessings. Even I do not know the gateway. I have stood here and scanned the sky for a glimpse of that door but, I cannot see it. Human eyes are useless for a search of this nature. But in the house of *osugbo*, those who keep watch through the spirit recognised the moment, they sent word to me through the voice of our sacred drums to prepare myself. I heard them and I shed all thoughts of earth. I began to follow the moon to the abode of gods . . . servant of the white king, that was when you entered my chosen place of departure on feet of desecration.

Pilkings: I'm sorry, but we all see our duty differently.

Elesin: I no longer blame you. You stole from me my first-born, sent him to your country so you could turn him into something in your own image. Did you plan it all beforehand? There are moments when it seems part of a larger plan. He who must follow my footsteps is taken from me, sent across the ocean. Then, in my turn, I am stopped from fulfilling my destiny. Did you think it all out before, this plan to push our world from its course and sever the cord that links us to the great origin?

Pilkings: You don't really believe that. Anyway, if that was my intention with your son, I appear to have failed.

Elesin: You did not fail in the main thing ghostly one. We know the roof covers the rafters, the cloth covers blemishes; who would have known that the white skin covered our future, preventing us from seeing the death our enemies had prepared for us. The world is set adrift and its inhabitants are lost. Around them, there is nothing but emptiness.

Pilkings: Your son does not take so gloomy a view.

Elesin: Are you dreaming now white man? Were you not present at my reunion of shame? Did you not see when the world reversed itself and the father fell before his son, asking forgiveness?

Pilkings: That was in the heat of the moment. I spoke to him and . . . if you want to know, he wishes he could cut out his tongue for uttering the words he did.

Elesin: No. What he said must never be unsaid. The contempt of my own son rescued something of my shame at your hands. You may have stopped me in my duty but I know now that I did give birth to a son. Once I mistrusted him for seeking the companionship of those my spirit knew as enemies of our race. Now I understand. One should seek to obtain the secrets of his enemies. He will avenge my shame, white one. His spirit will destroy you and yours.

Pilkings: That kind of talk is hardly called for. If you don't want my consolation . . .

Elesin: No white man, I do not want your consolation.

Pilkings: As you wish. Your son anyway, sends his consolation. He asks your forgiveness. When I asked him not to despise you his reply was: I cannot judge him, and if I cannot judge him, I cannot despise him. He wants to come to you to say goodbye and to receive your blessing.

Elesin: Goodbye? Is he returning to your land?

Pilkings: Don't you think that's the most sensible thing for him to do? I advised him to leave at once, before dawn, and he agrees that is the right course of action.

Elesin: Yes, it is best. And even if I did not think so, I have lost the father's place of honour. My voice is broken.

Pilkings: Your son honours you. If he didn't he would not ask your blessing.

Elesin: No. Even a thoroughbred is not without pity for the turf he strikes with his hoof. When is he coming?

Pilkings: As soon as the town is a little quieter. I advised it.

Elesin: Yes white man, I am sure you advised it. You advise all our lives although on the authority of what gods, I do not know.

Pilkings (opens his mouth to reply, then appears to change his mind. Turns to go. Hesitates and stops again): Before I leave you, may I ask just one thing of you?

Elesin: I am listening.

Pilkings: I wish to ask you to search the quiet of your heart and tell me—do you not find great contradictions in the wisdom of your own race?

Elesin: Make yourself clear, white one.

Pilkings: I have lived among you long enough to learn a saying or two. One came to my mind tonight when I stepped into the market and saw what was going on. You were surrounded by those who egged you on with song and praises. I thought, are these not the same people who say: the elder grimly approaches heaven and you ask him to bear your greetings yonder; do you really think he makes the journey willingly? After that, I did not hesitate.

(A pause. Elesin signs. *Before he can speak a sound of running feet is heard.)*

Jane (off): Simon! Simon!
Pilkings: What on earth . . . ! *(Runs off.)*

(Elesin turns to his new wife, gazes on her for some moments.)*

Elesin: My young bride, did you hear the ghostly one? You sit and sob in
your silent heart but say nothing to all this. First I blamed the white
man, then I blamed my gods for deserting me. Now I feel I want to
blame you for the mystery of the sapping of my will. But blame is a
strange peace offering for a man to bring a world he has deeply
wronged, and to its innocent dwellers. Oh little mother, I have taken
countless women in my life but you were more than a desire of the flesh.
I needed you as the abyss across which my body must be drawn, I filled
it with earth and dropped my seed in it at the moment of preparedness
for my crossing. You were the final gift of the living to their emissary to
the land of the ancestors, and perhaps your warmth and youth brought
new insights of this world to me and turned my feet leaden on this side
of the abyss. For I confess to you, daughter, my weakness came not
merely from the abomination of the white man who came violently into
my fading presence, there was also a weight of longing on my earth-held
limbs. I would have shaken it off, already my foot had begun to lift but
then, the white ghost entered and all was defiled.

(Approaching voices of Pilkings *and his wife.)*

Jane: Oh Simon, you will let her in won't you?
Pilkings: I really wish you'd stop interfering.

(They come in view. Jane *is in a dressing-gown.* Pilkings *is holding a note to
which he refers from time to time.)*

Jane: Good gracious, I didn't initiate this. I was sleeping quietly, or trying to
anyway, when the servant brought it. It's not my fault if one can't sleep
undisturbed even in the Residency.
Pilkings: He'd have done the same if we were sleeping at home so don't
sidetrack the issue. He knows he can get round you or he wouldn't send
you the petition in the first place.
Jane: Be fair Simon. After all he has thinking of your own interests. He is
grateful you know, you seem to forget that. He feels he owes you some-
thing.
Pilkings: I just wish they'd leave this man alone tonight, that's all.
Jane: Trust him Simon. He's pledged his word it will all go peacefully.
Pilkings: Yes, and that's the other thing. I don't like being threatened.
Jane: Threatened? *(Takes the note.)* I didn't spot any threat.
Pilkings: It's there. Veiled, but it's there. The only way to prevent serious
rioting tomorrow—what a cheek!
Jane: I don't think he's threatening you Simon.

Pilkings: He's picked up the idiom alright. Wouldn't surprise me if he's been mixing with commies or anarchists over there. The phrasing sounds too good to be true. Damn! If only the Prince hadn't picked this time for his visit.

Jane: Well, even so Simon, what have you got to lose? You don't want a riot on your hands, not with the Prince here.

Pilkings (going up to Elesin*):* Let's see what he has to say. Chief Elesin, there is yet another person who wants to see you. As she is not a next-of-kin I don't really feel obliged to let her in. But your son sent a note with her, so it's up to you.

Elesin: I know who that must be. So she found out your hiding-place. Well, it was not difficult. My stench of shame is so strong, it requires no hunter's dog to follow it.

Pilkings: If you don't want to see her, just say so and I'll send her packing.

Elesin: Why should I not want to see her? Let her come. I have no more holes in my rag of shame. All is laid bare.

Pilkings: I'll bring her in. *(Goes off.)*

Jane (hesitates, then goes to Elesin*):* Please, try and understand. Everything my husband did was for the best.

Elesin (he gives her a long strange stare, as if he is trying to understand who she is): You are the wife of the District Officer?

Jane: Yes. My name, is Jane.

Elesin: That is my wife sitting down there. You notice how still and silent she sits? My business is with your husband.

(Pilkings *returns with* Iyaloja.*)*

Pilkings: Here she is. Now first I want your word of honour that you will try nothing foolish.

Elesin: Honour? White one, did you say you wanted my word of honour?

Pilkings: I know you to be an honourable man. Give me your word of honour you will receive nothing from her.

Elesin: But I am sure you have searched her clothing as you would never dare touch your own mother. And there are these two lizards of yours who roll their eyes even when I scratch.

Pilkings: And I shall be sitting on that tree trunk watching even how you blink. Just the same I want your word that you will not let her pass anything to you.

Elesin: You have my honour already. It is locked up in that desk in which you will put away your report of this night's events. Even the honour of my people you have taken already; it is tied together with those papers of treachery which make you masters in this land.

Pilkings: Alright. I am trying to make things easy but if you must bring in politics we'll have to do it the hard way. Madam, I want you to remain along this line and move no nearer to that cell door. Guards! *(They spring to attention.)* If she moves beyond this point, blow your whistle. Come on Jane. *(They go off.)*

Iyaloja: How boldly the lizard struts before the pigeon when it was the eagle itself he promised us he would confront.

Elesin: I don't ask you to take pity on me Iyaloja. You have a message for me or you would not have come. Even if it is the curses of the world, I shall listen.

Iyaloja: You made so bold with the servant of the white king who took your side against death. I must tell your brother chiefs when I return how bravely you waged war against him. Especially with words.

Elesin: I more than deserve your scorn.

Iyaloja (with sudden anger): I warned you, if you must leave a seed behind, be sure it is not tainted with the curses of the world. Who are you to open a new life when you dared not open the door to a new existence? I say who are you to make so bold? *(The* Bride *sobs and* Iyaloja *notices her. Her contempt noticeably increases as she turns back to* Elesin.*)* Oh you self-vaunted stem of the plantain, how hollow it all proves. The pith is gone in the parent stem, so how will it prove with the new shoot? How will it go with that earth that bears it? Who are you to bring this abomination on us!

Elesin: My powers deserted me. My charms, my spells, even my voice lacked strength when I made to summon the powers that would lead me over the last measure of earth into the land of the fleshless. You saw it, Iyaloja. You saw me struggle to retrieve my will from the power of the stranger whose shadow fell across the doorway and left me floundering and blundering in a maze I had never before encountered. My senses were numbed when the touch of cold iron came upon my wrists. I could do nothing to save myself.

Iyaloja: You have betrayed us. We fed you sweetmeats such as we hoped awaited you on the other side. But you said No, I must eat the world's left-overs. We said you were the hunter who brought the quarry down; to you belonged the vital portions of the game. No, you said, I am the hunter's dog and I shall eat the entrails of the game and the faeces of the hunter. We said you were the hunter returning home in triumph, a slain buffalo pressing down on his neck; you said wait, I first must turn up this cricket hole with my toes. We said yours was the doorway at which we first spy the tapper when he comes down from the tree, yours was the blessing of the twilight wine, the purl that brings night spirits out of doors to steal their portion before the light of day. We said yours was the body of wine whose burden shakes the tapper like a sudden gust on his perch. You said No, I am content to lick the dregs from each cal-abash when the drinkers are done. We said, the dew on earth's surface was for you to wash your feet along the slopes of honour. You said No, I shall step in the vomit of cats and the droppings of mice; I shall fight them for the left-overs of the world.

Elesin: Enough Iyaloja, enough.

Iyaloja: We called you leader and oh, how you led us on. What we have no intention of eating should not be held to the nose.

Elesin: Enough, enough. My shame is heavy enough.

Iyaloja: Wait. I came with a burden.

Elesin: You have more than discharged it.

Iyaloja: I wish I could pity you.

Elesin: I need neither your pity nor the pity of the world. I need understanding. Even I need to understand. You were present at my defeat. You
were part of the beginnings. You brought about the renewal of my tie to
earth, you helped in the binding of the cord.

Iyaloja: I gave you warning. The river which fills up before our eyes does
not sweep us away in its flood.

Elesin: What were warnings beside the moist contact of living earth between
my fingers? What were warnings beside the renewal of famished embers
lodged eternally in the heart of man. But even that, even if it overwhelmed one with a thousandfold temptations to linger a little while, a
man could overcome it. It is when the alien hand pollutes the source of
will, when a stranger force of violence shatters the mind's calm resolution,
this is when a man is made to commit the awful treachery of relief, commit in his thought the unspeakable blasphemy of seeing the hand of the
gods in this alien rupture of his world. I know it was this thought that
killed me, sapped my powers and turned me into an infant in the hands of
unnamable strangers. I made to utter my spells anew but my tongue
merely rattled in my mouth. I fingered hidden charms and the contact was
damp; there was no spark left to sever the life-strings that should stretch
from every finger-tip. My will was squelched in the spittle of an alien race,
and all because I had committed this blasphemy of thought—that there
might be the hand of the gods in a stranger's intervention.

Iyaloja: Explain it how you will, I hope it brings you peace of mind. The
bush-rat fled his rightful cause, reached the market and set up a lamentation. 'Please save me!'- are these fitting words to hear from an ancestral mask? 'There's a wild beast at my heels' is not becoming language
from a hunter.

Elesin: May the world forgive me.

Iyaloja: I came with a burden I said. It approaches the gates which are so
well guarded by those jackals whose spittle will from this day on be your
food and drink. But first, tell me, you who where once Elesin Oba, tell
me, you who know so well the cycles of the plantain: is it the parent
shoot which withers to give sap to the younger or, does your wisdom see
it running the other way?

Elesin: I don't see your meaning Iyaloja.

Iyaloja: Did I ask you for a meaning? I asked a question. Whose trunk withers to give sap to the other? The parent shoot or the younger?

Elesin: The parent.

Iyaloja: Ah. So you do know that. There are sights in this world which say
different Elesin. There are some who choose to reverse this cycle of our
being. Oh you emptied bark that the world once saluted for a pith-laden
being, shall I tell you what the gods have claimed of you?

(In her agitation she steps beyond the line indicated by Pilkings *and the air is rent by piercing whistles. The two* Guards *also leap forward and place safe-guarding hands on* Elesin. Iyaloja *stops, astonished.* Pilkings *comes racing in, followed by* Jane.)

Pilkings: What is it? Did they try something?

Guard: She stepped beyond the line.

Elesin (in a broken voice): Let her alone. She meant no harm.

Iyaloja: Oh Elesin, see what you've become. Once you had no need to open your mouth in explanation because evil-smelling goats, itchy of hand and foot had lost their senses. And it was a brave man indeed who dared lay hands on you because Iyaloja stepped from one side of the earth onto another. Now look at the spectacle of your life. I grieve for you.

Pilkings: I think you'd better leave. I doubt you have done him much good by coming here. I shall make sure you are not allowed to see him again. In any case we are moving him to a different place before dawn, so don't bother to come back.

Iyaloja: We foresaw that. Hence the burden I trudged here to lay beside your gates.

Pilkings: What was that you said?

Ilyaloja: Didn't our son explain? Ask that one. He knows what it is. At least we hope the man we once knew as Elesin remembers the lesser oaths he need not break.

Pilkings: Do you know what she is talking about?

Elesin: Go to the gates, ghostly one. Whatever you find there, bring it to me.

Iyaloja: Not yet. It drags behind me on the slow, weary feet of women. Slow as it is Elesin, it has long overtaken you. It rides ahead of your laggard will.

Pilkings: What is she saying now? Christ! Must your people forever speak in riddles?

Elesin: It will come white man, it will come. Tell your men at the gates to let it through.

Pilkings (dubiously): I'll have to see what it is.

Iyaloja: You will. *(Passionately.)* But this is one oath he cannot shirk. White one, you have a king here, a visitor from your land. We know of his presence here. Tell me, were he to die would you leave his spirit roaming restlessly on the surface of earth? Would you bury him here among those you consider less than human? In your land have you no ceremonies of the dead?

Pilkings: Yes. But we don't make our chiefs commit suicide to keep him company.

Iyaloja: Child, I have not come to help your understanding. *(Points to* Elesin.*)* This is the man whose weakened understanding holds us in bondage to you. But ask him if you wish. He knows the meaning of a king's passage; he was not born yesterday. He knows the peril to the race when our dead father, who goes as intermediary, waits and waits and knows he is betrayed. He knows when the narrow gate was opened and he knows it will not stay for laggards who drag their feet in dung and vomit, whose lips are reeking of the left-overs of lesser men. He knows he has condemned our king to wander in the void of evil with beings who are enemies of life.

Pilkings: Yes er . . . but look here . . .

Iyaloja: What we ask is little enough. Let him release our King so he can ride on homewards alone. The messenger is on his way on the backs of women. Let him send word through the heart that is folded up within the bolt. It is the least of all his oaths, it the easiest fulfilled.

(*The* Aide-De-Camp *runs in.*)

Pilkings: Bob?

Aide-De-Camp: Sir, there's a group of women chanting up the hill.

Pilkings (rounding on Iyaloja*):* If you people want trouble . . .

Jane: Simon, I think that's what Olunde referred to in his letter.

Pilkings: He knows damned well I can't have a crowd here! Damn it, I explained the delicacy of my position to him. I think it's about time I got him out of town. Bob, send a car and two or three soldiers to bring him in. I think the sooner he takes his leave of his father and gets out the better.

Iyaloja: Save your labour white one. If it is the father of your prisoner you want, Olunde, he who until this night we knew as Elesin's son, he comes soon himself to take his leave. He has sent the women ahead, so let them in.

(Pilkings *remains undecided.*)

Aide-De-Camp: What do we do about the invasion? We can still stop them far from here.

Pilkings: What do they look like?

Aide-De-Camp: They're not many. And they seem quite peaceful.

Pilkings: No men?

Aide-De-Camp: Mm, two or three at the most.

Jane: Honestly, Simon, I'd trust Olunde. I don't think he'll deceive you about their intentions.

Pilkings: He'd better not. Alright, let them in Bob. Warn them to control themselves. Then hurry Olunde here. Make sure he brings his baggage because I'm not returning him into town.

Aide-De-Camp: Very good sir. (*Goes.*)

Pilkings (to Iyaloja*):* I hope you understand that if anything goes wrong it will be on your head. My men have orders to shoot at the first sign of trouble.

Iyaloja: To prevent one death you will actually make other deaths? Ah, great is the wisdom of the white race. But have no fear. Your Prince will sleep peacefully. So at long last will ours. We will disturb you no further, servant of the white king. Just let Elesin fulfill his oath and we will retire home and pay homage to our King.

Jane: I believe her Simon, don't you?

Pilkings: Maybe.

Elesin: Have no fear ghostly one. I have a message to send my King and then you have nothing more to fear.

Iyaloja: Olunde would have done it. The chiefs asked him to speak the words but he said no, not while you lived.

Elesin: Even from the depths to which my spirit has sunk, I find some joy that this little has been left to me.

(*The women enter, intoning the dirge 'Alę lę lę' and swaying from side to side. On their shoulders is borne a longish object roughly like a cylindrical bolt, covered in cloth. They set it down on the spot where* Iyaloja *had stood earlier, and form a semi-circle round it. The* Praise-Singer *and* Drummer *stand on the inside of the semi-circle but the drum is not used at all. The* Drummer *intones under the* Praise-Singer's *invocations.*)

Pilkings (*as they enter*): What is *that*?

Iyaloja: The burden you have made white one, but we bring it in peace.

Pilkings: I said *what* is it?

Elesin: White man, you must let me out. I have a duty to perform.

Pilkings: I most certainly will not.

Elesin: There lies the courier of my King. Let me out so I can perform what is demanded of me.

Pilkings: You'll do what you need to do from inside there or not at all. I've gone as far as I intend to with this business.

Elesin: The worshipper who lights a candle in your church to bear a message to his god bows his head and speaks in a whisper to the flame. Have I not seen it ghostly one? His voice does not ring out to the world. Mine are no words for anyone's ears. They are not words even for the bearers of this load. They are words I must speak secretly, even as my father whispered them in my ears and I in the ears of my first-born. I cannot shout them to the wind and the open night-sky.

Jane: Simon . . .

Pilkings: Don't interfere. Please!

Iyaloja: They have slain the favourite horse of the king and slain his dog. They have borne them from pulse to pulse centre of the land receiving prayers for their king. But the rider has chosen to stay behind. Is it too much to ask that he speak his heart to heart of the waiting courier? (Pilkings *turns his back on her.*) So be it. Elesin Oba, you see how even the mere leavings are denied you. (*She gestures to the* Praise-Singer.)

Praise-Singer: Elesin Oba! I call you by that name only this last time. Remember when I said, if you cannot come, tell my horse. (*Pause.*) What? I cannot hear you? I said, if you cannot come, whisper in the ears of my horse. Is your tongue severed from the roots Elesin? I can hear no response. I said, if there are boulders you cannot climb, mount my horse's back, this spotless black stallion, he'll bring you over them. (*Pauses.*) Elesin Oba, once you had a tongue that darted like a drummer's stick. I said, if you get lost my dog will track a path to me. My memory fails me but I think you replied: My feet have found the path, Alafin.

(The dirge rises and falls.)

I said at the last, if evil hands hold you back, just tell my horse there is weight on the hem of your smock. I dare not wait too long.

(The dirge rises and falls.)

There lies on the swiftest ever messenger of a king, so set me free with the errand of your heart. There lie the head and heart of the favourite of the gods, whisper in his ears. Oh my companion, if you had followed when you should, we would not say that the horse preceded its rider. If you had followed when it was time, we would not say the dog has raced beyond and left his master behind. If you had raised your will to cut the thread of life at the summons of the drums, we would not say your mere shadow fell across the gateway and took its owner's place at the banquet. But the hunter, laden with a slain buffalo, stayed to root in the cricket's hole with his toes. What now is left? If there is a dearth of bats, the pigeon must serve us for the offering. Speak the words over your shadow which must now serve in your place.

Elesin: I cannot approach. Take off the cloth. I shall speak my message from heart to heart of silence.

Iyaloja *(moves forward and removes the covering)*: Your courier Elesin, cast your eyes on the favoured companion of the King.

(Rolled up in the mat, his head and feet showing at either end, is the body of Olunde.*)*

There lies the honour of your household and of our race. Because he could not bear to let honour fly out of doors, he stopped it with his life. The son has proved the father Elesin, and there is nothing left in your mouth to gnash but infant gums.

Praise-Singer: Elesin, we placed the reins of the world in your hands yet you watched it plunge over the edge of the bitter precipice. You sat with folded arms while evil strangers tilted the world from its course and crashed it beyond the edge of emptiness—you muttered, there is little that one man can do, you left us floundering in a blind future. Your heir has taken the burden on himself. What the end will be, we are not gods to tell. But this young shoot has poured its sap into the parent stalk, and we know this is not the way of life. Our world is tumbling in the void of strangers. Elesin.

(Elesin has stood rock-still, his knuckles taut on the bars, his eyes glued to the body of his son. The stillness seizes and paralyses everyone, including Pilkings who has turned to look. Suddenly Elesin flings one arm round his neck, once, and with the loop of the chain, strangles himself in a swift, decisive pull. The guards rush forward to stop him but they are only in time to let his body down. Pilkings has leapt to the door at the same time and struggles with the lock. He rushes within, fumbles with the handcuffs and unlocks them, raises the body to a sitting position while he tries to give resuscitation. The women continue their dirge, unmoved by the sudden event.)

Iyaloja: Why do you strain yourself? Why do you labour at tasks for which no one, not even the man lying there would give you thanks? He is gone at last into the passage but oh, how late it all is. His son will feast on the meat and throw him bones. The passage is clogged with droppings from the King's stallion; he will arrive all stained in dung.

Pilkings (in a tired voice): Was this what you wanted?

Iyaloja: No child, it is what you brought to be, you who play with strangers' lives, who even usurp the vestments of our dead, yet believe that the stain of death will not cling to you. The gods demanded only the old expired plantain but you cut down the sap-laden shoot to feed your pride. There is your board, filled to overflowing. Feast on it. *(She screams at him suddenly, seeing that* Pilkings *is about to close* Elesin's *staring eyes.)* Let him alone! However sunk he was in debt he is no pauper's carrion abandoned on the road. Since when have strangers donned clothes of indigo before the bereaved cries out his loss?

(She turns to the Bride *who has remained motionless throughout.)*

Child.

(The girl takes up a little earth, walks calmly in to the cell and closes Elesin's *eyes. She then pours some earth over each eyelid and comes out again.)*

Now forget the dead, forget even the living. Turn your mind only to the unborn.

(She goes off, accompanied by the Bride. *The dirge rises in volume and the women continue their sway. Lights fade to a black-out.)*

THE END

──────── **WOLE SOYINKA** Web ────────

(b. 1934)

Wole Soyinka was born in Nigeria and studied in England. He served as Director of the Drama School of Ibadan University until 1967, when he was arrested for political writing. He has continued to write plays and political prose, winning the Nobel Prize for Literature in 1986. He was the first African writer ever to have received this award.

TOPICS FOR CRITICAL THINKING

1. Describe the importance of honor in *Death and the King's Horseman*. How significant is it in describing Elesin's motivation? Is it also a factor in his son's actions and eventual death?

2. Is there a tragic hero in *Death and the King's Horseman*? Who is it? Why?

3. In the middle of Soyinka's play, the British disparage Elesin's suicide as a "barbaric custom" and his son Olunde calls their party a sign of "decadence." What is the difference between a "barbaric custom" and decadence?

4. Elesin tells Pilkings that British colonization has the potential to "sever the cord that links us to the great origin." How so? How does the colonial presence "shake" the Yoruban world from its "course"?

5. What functions does the Chorus of Yoruban women perform? How would the play be different without this Chorus?

6. What function does Amusa, the native Police Sergeant, perform?

7. In his note to the play, Soyinka explains that he took a 1946 incident and "set it back two or three years while the war was still on, for minor reasons." Speculate on these reasons. What does this slight shift in historical setting accomplish? Also, historical accounts of the incident do not include Elesin's desire to get married the night before his death. What does this add to the play and to our understanding of the character?

TOPICS FOR CRITICAL WRITING

1. What stereotypes does Soyinka create—or dismantle—in *Death and the King's Horseman*? What representations of Africans and the British result from this?

2. Expand question 2 above into an essay that attempts to argue the tragic qualities of the play in Aristotelian terms. Does *Death and the King's Horseman*, for example, contain a "unity of action"? Does it develop a tragic hero and, if so, what are his failings or errors in judgment?

Critical Perspective: On Colonialism and the Colonized

"The black man has two dimensions. One with his fellows, the other with the white man. . . . That this self-division is a direct result of colonial subjugation is beyond question."

—Frantz Fanon, *Black Skin, White Masks* (1967)

Critical Perspective: On the Legacy of Colonialism

"The contemporary international division of labor is a displacement of the divided field of nineteenth-century territorial imperialism. Put simply, a group of countries, generally first-world, are in the position of investing capital; another group, generally third-world, provide the field for investment. . . . In the interest of maintaining the circulation and growth of industrial capital (and of the concomitant task of administration within nineteenth-century territorial imperialism), transportation, law, and standardized education systems were developed—even as local industries were destroyed, land distribution was rearranged, and raw material was transferred to the colonized country. With so-called decolonization, the growth of multinational capital, and the relief of the administrative charge, 'development' now does not now involve wholesale legislation and establishing educational systems in a comparable way. . . . [But] maintaining the international division of labor serves to keep the supply of cheap labor in [third-world] countries."

—Gayatri Chakravorty Spivak, from "Can the Subaltern Speak?" (1988)

Critical Perspective: On Staging *Death and the King's Horseman*

"On 22 November 1990, the Royal Exchange Theatre (RET) in Manchester was the scene for the second British production of Wole Soyinka's *Death and the King's Horseman*. Although written in 1973, the play had only once before been staged in Britain, in production . . . at the University of Hull. And so far as the press were concerned, the RET production . . . was generally regarded as the British premiere.

"For Western directors the staging of the play causes problems on a formal as well as thematic level, the main obstacle being the dramaturgical importance of music and dance as the two other basic means, apart from verbal dialogue, of communication in African culture. These three elements in fact constitute the fundamental pattern of communication throughout the play, and its success or failure in production will mainly depend on how the interrelation of each of these stylistic devices to one another is established.

"The basic question is thus to what extent the unfolding of the tragic action leads to a shift within the different levels of expression—or, to put it another way, in what ways does a change within the patterns of communication reflect the development of the characters?"

—Martin Rohmer, from "Wole Soyinka's 'Death and the King's Horseman,'
Royal Exchange Theatre, Manchester" (1992)

Critical Perspective: On Political Criticism of the Play

"Criticism of *Horseman* has ranged from metaphysical interpretations . . . to dissenting 'leftocratic' political readings. The latter have construed the work as essentially historical drama in which Soyinka privileges a static, totalitarian feudal culture over more mobile and egalitarian alternatives and uses a distracting metaphysics to suppress social and ideological differences and claim a false unanimity for Oyo society. This conception is not entirely just. Unashamedly hierarchic though the play is in its interlarding of social and royal destinies, it does contain an implied critique of feudal leadership elites and ideologies, and the fact that the Western-educated Olunde, the play's agent of change, has to take charge of the ritual practice argues for the need for its modification and redefinition in a changing world. Elesin [after all] is no paragon of Oyo courage and integrity but a pretender and prevaricator who mistakes honor for cheap worldly pleasures . . . ."

—Derek Wright, from *Wole Soyinka Revisited* (1993)

D. H. Hwang's *M. Butterfly* and "The Oriental"

In a 1989 essay, David Henry Hwang considers concepts of the "Oriental" in Western culture that underlie *M. Butterfly*. By "oriental," Hwang means a derogatory stereotype of Asians as "mysterious, inscrutable, and ultimately inferior." In his play, this definition accrues even greater complexity as it is used to characterize Western fantasies about Asian women, fantasies in part connected to Cio-Cio-San, the heroine of Puccini's opera *Madam Butterfly* from which Hwang derives the play's title. While Puccini's character is beautiful and brave, she is also a commodity to be purchased, a humble woman whose very accessibility blends seamlessly with male fantasies about sexually submissive geishas who allow men to do with them "whatever they want." Sadly, this precise position induces her self-hatred and dependence on the great Western protector—her sailor-lover—who eventually abandons her.

Puccini's opera provides one context for Hwang's play about a European diplomat who conducted a lengthy affair with a Chinese agent disguised as a woman. Hwang's protagonist René Gallimard, the play's narrator, is a career French diplomat who, among other things, has suppressed his passion and checked his fantasy life so as to succeed in government service. In addition, he is trapped in a loveless marriage before being assigned to Beijing in 1960, near the beginning of what would later escalate into the Vietnam War. Here, Puccini's opera, his own fantasies, and the manipulations of a talented Chinese agent combine to ruin his career. This male agent, impersonating Song, a self-described "delicate Oriental woman," can insinuate himself easily into both the French diplomatic corps and Gallimard's affection. So, when Gallimard is assigned to revamp the intelligence division of the embassy, Song is able to exploit him to extract the information he needs. They pursue a long affair and their intimacy still preoccupies Gallimard years later, imprisoned at age sixty-five as the play opens and he begins to recount this amazing story. As is the case in most memory plays, the dramatic action occurs mostly in the past—as flashbacks or glimpses of the past—and is replayed for us on a split stage. All of the past action, however, is understood to occur in Gallimard's memory.

Based on a news story of a twenty-year relationship between a French diplomat and a Chinese transvestite convicted of espionage, *M. Butterfly* teases audiences with the logistics that baffle them most: namely, how is it possible for a man to engage in an affair for so many years without knowing the real sex of his lover? One answer, seemingly the most practical and banal one, is that Gallimard never saw him undressed. Yet this simple fact, in Hwang's exposition, connects to Western fantasies of the Oriental woman who, on the one hand, is so modest that she can only undress in darkness but, on the other, is well practiced in the multiple ways to "pleasure" her lover. Still another explanation, one advanced by Song at Gallimard's trial, is that "I am an Oriental. And being an Oriental, I could never be completely a man." Gender and ethnicity, ethnicity and gender: in imperialist ideology, the

"Other" is usually feminized, as he is in Hwang's play. In this way, we understand that *gender* is often a construction that, in extreme instances, can eclipse the reality of biological sex.

A Chinese American born in California, Hwang frequently probes issues of Asian identity, the hurdles facing immigrants assimilating into American society, and the kind of self-loathing of one's ancestry or past that informs *M. Butterfly*. In the prologue to his 1979 play *FOB*, for example, a character delivers a lecture on Chinese America and the disdain with which ABCs (American-Born Chinese) hold FOB's (Fresh-Off-the-Boat Chinese): "Before an ABC girl will be seen on Friday night with a boy FOB in Westwood, she would rather burn off her face." Like many ethnic writers, Hwang attempts to locate the place of the non-white in an America that has not always been welcoming of immigrants of color. Isolationism or separatism, one thrust of the Black Arts Movement of the 1960s, coexists in complicated ways with assimilation. Fantasies and stereotypes persist, as they do in *M. Butterfly*, and one challenge for America in the twenty-first century will be to confront these potentially divisive ideas, dismantling the most egregious aspects of the "Oriental" while retaining those life-affirming values that celebrate ethnic difference.

DAVID HENRY HWANG

M. Butterfly   (1988)

CHARACTERS

Kurogo
Rene Gallimard
Song Liling
Marc
Man 2
Consul Sharpless
Renee
Woman At Party
Pinup Girl
Comrade Chin
Suzuki
Shu-Fang
Helga
M. Toulon
Man 1
Judge

The action of the play takes place in a Paris prison in the present, and in recall, during the decade 1960 to 1970 in Beijing, and from 1966 to the present in Paris.

ACT ONE

Scene I

M. Gallimard's *prison cell. Present.*

Lights fade up to reveal Rene Gallimard, *65, in a prison cell. He wears a comfortable bathrobe, and looks old and tired. The sparsely furnished cell contains a wooden crate upon which sits a hot plate with a kettle, and a portable tape recorder. Gallimard sits on the crate staring at the recorder, a sad smile on his face.*

Upstage Song, *who appears as a beautiful woman in traditional Chinese garb, dances a traditional piece from the Peking Opera, surrounded by the percussive clatter of Chinese music.*

Then, slowly, lights and sound cross-fade; the Chinese opera music dissolves into a Western opera, the "Love Duet" from Puccini's Madame Butterfly. *Song continues dancing, now to the Western accompaniment. Though her movements are the same, the difference in music now gives them a balletic quality.*

Gallimard rises, and turns upstage towards the figure of Song, *who dances without acknowledging him.*

Gallimard: Butterfly. Butterfly . . .

(He forces himself to turn away, as the image of Song *fades out, and talks to us.)*

Gallimard: The limits of my cell are as such: four-and-a-half meters by five. There's one window against the far wall; a door, very strong, to protect me from autograph hounds. I'm responsible for the tape recorder, the hot plate, and this charming coffee table.

When I want to eat, I'm marched off to the dining room—hot, steaming slop appears on my plate. When I want to sleep, the light bulb turns itself off—the work of fairies. It's an enchanted space I occupy. The French—we know how to run a prison.

But, to be honest, I'm not treated like an ordinary prisoner. Why? Because I'm a celebrity. You see, I make people laugh.

I never dreamed this day would arrive. I've never been considered witty or clever. In fact, as a young boy, in an informal poll among my grammar school classmates, I was voted "least likely to be invited to a party." It's a title I managed to hold onto for many years. Despite some stiff competition.

But now, how the tables turn! Look at me: the life of every social function in Paris. Paris? Why be modest? My fame has spread to Amsterdam, London, New York. Listen to them! In the world's smartest parlors. I'm the one who lifts their spirits!

(With a flourish, Gallimard *directs our attention to another part of the stage.)*

SCENE II

A party. Present.

Lights go up on a chic-looking parlor, where a well-dressed trio, two men and one woman, make conversation. Gallimard *also remains lit; he observes them from his cell.*

Woman: And what of Gallimard?
Man 1: Gallimard?
Man 2: Gallimard!
Gallimard (To us.): You see? They're all determined to say my name, as if it were some new dance.
Woman: He still claims not to believe the truth.
Man 1: What? Still? Even since the trial?
Woman: Yes. Isn't it mad?
Man 2 (Laughing): He says . . . it was dark . . . and she was very modest!

(The trio break into laughter.)

Man 1: So—what? He never touched her with his hands?
Man 2: Perhaps he did, and simply misidentified the equipment. A compelling case for sex education in the schools.
Woman: To protect the National Security—the Church can't argue with that.
Man 1: That's impossible! How could he not know?
Man 2: Simple ignorance.
Man 1: For twenty years?
Man 2: Time flies when you're being stupid.
Woman: Well, I thought the French were ladies' men.
Man 2: It seems Monsieur Gallimard was overly anxious to live up to his national reputation.
Woman: Well, he's not very good-looking.
Man 1: No, he's not.
Man 2: Certainly not.
Woman: Actually, I feel sorry for him.
Man 2: A toast! To Monsieur Gallimard!
Woman: Yes! To Gallimard!
Man 1: To Gallimard!
Man 2: Vive la différence!

(They toast, laughing. Lights down on them.)

SCENE III

M. Gallimard's cell.

Gallimard (Smiling.): You see? They toast me. I've become patron saint of the socially inept. Can they really be so foolish? Men like that—they should be scratching at my door, begging to learn my secrets! For I, Rene Gallimard, you see, I have known, and been loved by . . . the Perfect Woman.

Alone in this cell, I sit night after night, watching our story play through my head, always searching for a new ending, one which redeems my honor, where she returns at last to my arms. And I imagine you—my ideal audience—who come to understand and even, perhaps just a little, to envy me.

(He turns on his tape recorder. Over the house speakers, we hear the opening phrases of Madame Butterfly.*)*

Gallimard: In order for you to understand what I did and why, I must introduce you to my favorite opera: *Madame Butterfly*. By Giacomo Puccini. First produced at La Scala, Milan, in 1904, it is now beloved throughout the Western world.

(As Gallimard *describes the opera, the tape segues in and out to sections he may be describing.)*

Gallimard: Any why not? Its heroine, Cio-Cio-San, also known as Butterfly, is a feminine ideal, beautiful and brave. And its hero, the man for whom she gives up everything, is—*(He pulls out a naval officer's cap from under his crate, pops it on his head, and struts about.)*—not very good-looking, not too bright, and pretty much a wimp: Benjamin Franklin Pinkerton of the U.S. Navy. As the curtain rises, he's just closed on two great bargains: one on a house, the other on a woman—call it a package deal.

      Pinkerton purchased the rights to Butterfly for one hundred yer— in modern currency, equivalent to about . . . sixty-six cents. So, he's feeling pretty pleased with himself as Sharpless, the American consul, arrives to witness the marriage.

(Marc, wearing an official cap to designate Sharpless, *enters and plays the character.)*

Sharpless/Marc: Pinkerton!

Pinkerton/Gallimard: Sharpless! How's it hangin'? It's a great day, just great. Between my house, my wife, and the rickshaw ride in from town, I've saved nineteen cents just this morning.

Sharpless: Wonderful. I can see the inscription on your tombstone already: "I saved a dollar, here I lie." *(He looks around.)* Nice house.

Pinkerton: It's artistic, don't you think? Like the way the shoji screens slide open to reveal the wet bar and disco mirror ball? Classy, huh? Great for impressing the chicks.

Sharpless: "Chicks"? Pinkerton, you're going to be a married man!

Pinkerton: Well, sort of.

Sharpless: What do you mean?

Pinkerton: This country—Sharpless, it is okay. You got all these geisha girls running around—

Sharpless: I know! I live here!

Pinkerton: Then, you know the marriage laws, right? I split for one month, it's annulled!

Sharpless: Leave it to you to read the fine print. Who's the lucky girl?

Pinkerton: Cio-Cio-San. Her friends call her Butterfly. Sharpless, she eats out of my hand!

Sharpless: She's probably very hungry.

Pinkerton: Not like American girls. It's true what they say about Oriental girls. They want to be treated bad!

Sharpless: Oh, please!

Pinkerton: It's true!

Sharpless: Are you serious about this girl?

Pinkerton: I'm marrying her, aren't I?

Sharpless: Yes—with generous trade-in terms.

Pinkerton: When I leave, she'll know what it's like to have loved a real man. And I'll even buy her a few nylons.

Sharpless: You aren't planning to take her with you?

Pinkerton: Huh? Where?

Sharpless: Home!

Pinkerton: You mean, America? Are you crazy? Can you see her trying to buy rice in St. Louis?

Sharpless: So, you're not serious.

(*Pause.*)

Pinkerton/Gallimard (*As* Pinkerton.): Consul, I am a sailor in port. (*As* Gallimard.) They then proceed to sing the famous duet, "The Whole World Over."

(*The duet plays on the speakers.* Gallimard, *as* Pinkerton, *lip-syncs his lines from the opera.*)

Gallimard: To give a rough translation: "The whole world over, the Yankee travels, casting his anchor wherever he wants. Life's not worth living unless he can win the hearts of the fairest maidens, then hotfoot it off the premises ASAP." (*He turns towards* Marc.) In the preceding scene, I played Pinkerton, the womanizing cad, and my friend Marc from school . . . (Marc *bows grandly for our benefit.*) played Sharpless, the sensitive soul of reason. In life, however, our positions were usually—no, always—reversed.

Scene IV

Ecole Nationale. Aix-en-Provence. 1947.

Gallimard: No, Marc, I think I'd rather stay home.

Marc: Are you crazy?! We are going to Dad's condo in Marseille! You know what happened last time?

Gallimard: Of course I do.

Marc: Of course you don't! You never know. . . . They stripped, Rene!

Gallimard: Who stripped?

Marc: The girls!

Gallimard: Girls? Who said anything about girls?

Marc: Rene, we're a buncha university guys goin' up to the woods. What are we gonna do—talk philosophy?

Gallimard: What girls? Where do you get them?

Marc: Who cares? The point is, they come. On trucks. Packed in like sardines. The back flips open, babes hop out, we're ready to roll.

Gallimard: You mean, they just—?

Marc: Before you know it, every last one of them—they're stripped and splashing around my pool. There's no moon out, they can't see what's going on, their boobs are flapping, right? You close your eyes, reach out—it's grab bag, get it? Doesn't matter whose ass is between whose legs, whose teeth are sinking into who. You're just in there, going at it, eyes closed, on and on for as long as you can stand. *(Pause.)* Some fun, huh?

Gallimard: What happens in the morning?

Marc: In the morning, you're ready to talk some philosophy. *(Beat.)* So how 'bout it?

Gallimard: Marc, I can't . . . I'm afraid they'll say no—the girls. So I never ask.

Marc: You don't have to ask! That's the beauty—don't you see? They don't have to say yes. It's perfect for a guy like you, really.

Gallimard: You go ahead . . . I may come later.

Marc: Hey, Rene—it doesn't mater that you're clumsy and got zits—they're not looking!

Gallimard: Thank you very much.

Marc: Wimp.

(Marc *walks over to the other side of the stage, and starts waving and smiling at women in the audience.*)

Gallimard (To us.): We now return to my version of *Madame Butterfly* and the events leading to my recent conviction for treason.

(Gallimard *notices* Marc *making lewd gestures.*)

Marc, what are you doing?

Marc: Huh? *(Sotto voce.)* Rene, there're a lotta great babes out there. They're probably lookin' at me and thinking, "What a dangerous guy."

Gallimard: Yes—how could they help but be impressed by your cool sophistication?

(Gallimard *pops the* Sharpless *cap on* Marc's *head, and points him offstage.* Marc *exits, leering.*)

Scene V

M. Gallimard's *cell.*

Gallimard: Next, Butterfly makes her entrance. We learn her age—fifteen . . . but very mature for her years.

(Lights come up on the area where we saw Song *dancing at the top of the play. She appears there again, now dressed as* Madame Butterfly, *moving to the "Love Duet."* Gallimard *turns upstage slightly to watch, transfixed.)*

Gallimard: But as she glides past him, beautiful, laughing softly behind her fan, don't we who are men sigh with hope? We, who are not handsome, nor brave, nor powerful, yet somehow believe, like Pinkerton, that we deserve a Butterfly. She arrives with all her possessions in the folds of her sleeves, lays them all out, for her man to do with as he pleases. Even her life itself—she bows her head as she whispers that she's not even worth the hundred yen he paid for her. He's already given too much, when we know he's really had to give nothing at all.

(Music and lights on Song *out.* Gallimard *sits at his crate.)*

Gallimard: In real life, women who put their total worth at less than sixty-six cents are quite hard to find. The closest we come is in the pages of these magazines *(He reaches into his crate, pulls out a stack of girlie magazines, and begins flipping through them.)* Quite a necessity in prison. For three or four dollars, you get seven or eight women.

   I first discovered these magazines at my uncle's house. One day, as a boy of twelve. The first time I saw them in his closest . . . all lined up— my body shook. Not with lust—no, with power. Here were women—a shelfful—who would do exactly as I wanted.

(The "Love Duet" creeps in over the speakers. Special comes up, revealing, not Song *this time, but a* Pinup Girl *in a sexy negligee, her back to us.* Gallimard *turns upstage and looks at her.)*

Girl: I know you're watching me.
Gallimard: My throat . . . it's dry.
Girl: I leave my blinds open every night before I go to bed.
Gallimard: I can't move.
Girl: I leave my blinds open and the lights on.
Gallimard: I'm shaking. My skin is hot, but my penis is soft. Why?
Girl: I stand in front of the window.
Gallimard: What is she going to do?
Girl: I toss my hair, and I let my lips part . . . barely.
Gallimard: I shouldn't be seeing this. It's so dirty. I'm so bad.
Girl: Then, slowly, I lift off my nightdress.
Gallimard: Oh, god. I can't believe it. I can't—
Girl: I toss it to the ground.
Gallimard: Now, she's going to walk away. She's going to—
Girl: I stand there, in the light, displaying myself.
Gallimard: No. She's—why is she naked?
Girl: To you.
Gallimard: In front of a window? This is wrong. No—
Girl: Without shame.
Gallimard: No, she must . . . like it.
Girl: I like it.

Gallimard: She . . . she wants me to see.

Girl: I want you to see.

Gallimard: I can't believe it! She's getting excited!

Girl: I can't see you. You can do whatever you want.

Gallimard: I can't do a thing. Why?

Girl: What would you like me to do . . . next?

(*Lights go down on her. Music off. Silence, as* Gallimard *puts away his magazines. Then he resumes talking to us.*)

Gallimard: Act Two begins with Butterfly staring at the ocean. Pinkerton's been called back to the U.S., and he's given his wife a detailed schedule of his plans. In the column marked "return date," he's written "when the robins nest." This failed to ignite her suspicions. Now, three years have passed without a peep from him. Which brings a response from her faithful servant, Suzuki.

(Comrade Chin *enters, playing* Suzuki.)

Suzuki: Girl, he's a loser. What'd he ever give you? Nineteen cents and those ugly Day-Glo stockings? Look, it's finished! Kaput! Done! And you should be glad! I mean, the guy was a woofer! He tried before, you know—before he met you, he went down to geisha central and plunked down his spare change in front of the usual candidates—everyone else gagged! These are hungry prostitutes, and they were not interested, get the picture? Now, stop slathering when an American ship sails in, and let's make some bucks—I mean, yen! We are broke!

Now, what about Yamadori? Hey, hey—don't look away—the man is a prince—figuratively, and, what's even better, literally. He's rich, he's handsome, he says he'll die if you don't marry him—and he's even willing to overlook the little fact that you've been deflowered all over the place by a foreign devil. What do you mean, "But he's Japanese?" You're Japanese! You think you've been touched by the whitey god? He was a sailor with dirty hands!

(Suzuki *stalks offstage.*)

Gallimard: She's also visited by Consul Sharpless, sent by Pinkerton on a minor errand.

(Marc *enters, as* Sharpless.)

Sharpless: I hate this job.

Gallimard: This Pinkerton—he doesn't show up personally to tell his wife he's abandoning her. No, he sends a government diplomat . . . at taxpayer's expense.

Sharpless: Butterfly? Butterfly? I have some bad—I'm going to be ill. Butterfly, I came to tell you—

Gallimard: Butterfly says she knows he'll return and if he doesn't she'll kill herself rather than go back to her own people. (*Beat.*) This causes a lull in the conversation.

Sharpless: Let's put it this way . . .

Gallimard: Butterfly runs into the next room, and returns holding—

(*Sound cue: a baby crying. Sharpless, "seeing" this, backs away.*)

Sharpless: Well, good. Happy to see things going so well. I suppose I'll be going now. Ta ta. Ciao. (*He turns away. Sound cue out.*) I hate this job. (*He exits.*)

Gallimard: At that moment, Butterfly spots in the harbor an American ship—the *Abramo Lincoln!*

(*Music cue: "The Flower Duet."* Song, *still dressed as* Butterfly, *changes into a wedding kimono, moving to the music.*)

Gallimard: This is the moment that redeems her years of waiting. With Suzuki's help, they cover the room with flowers—

(Chin, *as Suzuki, trudges onstage and drops a lone flower without much enthusiam.*)

Gallimard: —and she changes into her wedding dress to prepare for Pinkerton's arrival.

(Suzuki *helps* Butterfly *change.* Helga *enters, and helps* Gallimard *change into a tuxedo.*)

Gallimard: I married a woman older than myself—Helga.

Helga: My father was ambassador to Australia. I grew up among criminals and kangaroos.

Gallimard: Hearing that brought me to the altar—

(Helga *exits.*)

Gallimard: —where I took a vow renouncing love. No fantasy woman would ever want me, so, yes, I would settle for a quick leap up the career ladder. Passion, I banish, and in its place—practicality!

But my vows had long since lost their charm by the time we arrived in China. The sad truth is that all men want a beautiful woman, and the uglier the man, the greater the want.

(Suzuki *makes final adjustments of* Butterfly's *costume, as does* Gallimard *of his tuxedo.*)

Gallimard: I married late, at age thirty-one. I was faithful to my marriage for eight years. Until the day when, as a junior-diplomat in puritanical Peking, in a parlor at the German ambassador's house, during the "Reign of a Hundred Flowers," I first saw her . . . singing the death scene from *Madame Butterfly.*

(Suzuki *runs offstage.*)

SCENE VI

German ambassador's house. Beijing. 1960

The upstage special area now becomes a stage. Several chairs face upstage, representing seating from some twenty guests in the parlor. A few "diplomats"— Renee, Marc, Toulon—in formal dress enter and take seats.

Gallimard *also sits down, but turns towards us and continues to talk. Orchestral accompaniment on the tape is now replaced by a simple piano.* Song *picks up the death scene from the point where* Butterfly *uncovers the hara-kiri knife.*

Gallimard: The ending is pitiful. Pinkerton, in an act of great courage, stays home and sends his American wife to pick up Butterfly's child. The truth, long deferred, has come up to her door.

(Song, playing Butterfly, *sings the lines from the opera in her own voice— which, though not classical, should be decent.)*

Song: "Con onor muore/chi non puo serbar/vita con onore."
Gallimard *(Simultaneously.):* "Death with honor/Is better than life/Life with dishonor."

(The stage is illuminated; we are now completely within an elegant diplomat's residence. Song *proceeds to play out an abbreviated death scene. Everyone in the room applauds.* Song, *shyly, takes her bows. Others in the room rush to congratulate her.* Gallimard *remains with us.)*

Gallimard: They say in opera the voice is everything. That's probably why I'd never before enjoyed opera. Here . . . here was a Butterfly with little or no voice—but she had the grace, the delicacy . . . I believed this girl. I believed her suffering. I wanted to take her in my arms—so delicate, even I could protect her, take her home, pamper her until she smiled.

(Over the course of the preceding speech, Song *has broken from the upstage crowd and moved directly upstage of* Gallimard.*)*

Song: Excuse me. Monsieur . . . ?

*(*Gallimard *appears upstage, shocked.)*

Gallimard: Oh! Gallimard. Mademoiselle . . . ? A beautiful . . .
Song: Song Liling.
Gallimard: A beautiful performance.
Song: Oh, please.
Gallimard: I usually—
Song: You make me blush. I'm no opera singer at all.
Gallimard: I usually don't like *Butterfly.*
Song: I can't blame you in the least.
Gallimard: I mean, the story—
Song: Ridiculous.
Gallimard: I like the story, but . . . what?

Song: Oh, you like it?

Gallimard: I . . . what I mean is, I've always seen it played by huge women in so much bad makeup.

Song: Bad makeup is not unique to the West.

Gallimard: But, who can believe them?

Song: And you believe me?

Gallimard: Absolutely. You were utterly convincing. It's the first time—

Song: Convincing? As a Japanese woman? The Japanese used hundreds of our people for medical experiments during the war, you know. But I gather such an irony is lost on you.

Gallimard: No! I was about to say, it's the first time I've seen the beauty of the story.

Song: Really?

Gallimard: Of her death. It's a . . . a pure sacrifice. He's unworthy, but what can she do? She loves him . . . so much. It's a very beautiful story.

Song: Well, yes, to a Westerner.

Gallimard: Excuse me?

Song: It's one of your favorite fantasies, isn't it? The submissive Oriental woman and the cruel white man.

Gallimard: Well, I didn't quite mean . . .

Song: Consider it this way: what would you say if a blonde homecoming queen fell in love with a short Japanese businessman? He treats her cruelly, then goes home for three years, during which time she prays to his picture and turns down marriage from a young Kennedy. Then, when she learns he has remarried, she kills herself. Now, I believe you would consider this girl to be deranged idiot, correct? But because it's an Oriental who kills herself for a Westerner—ah!—you find it beautiful.

(Silence.)

Gallimard: Yes . . . well . . . I see your point . . .

Song: I will never do Butterfly again, Monsieur Gallimard. If you wish to see some real theatre, come to the Peking Opera sometime. Expand your mind.

(Song walks offstage.)

Gallimard (To us.): So much for protecting her in my big Western arms.

Scene VII

M. Gallimard's *apartment. Beijing. 1960.*

Gallimard *changes from his tux into a casual suit.* Helga *enters.*

Gallimard: The Chinese are an incredibly arrogant people.

Helga: They warned us about that in Paris, remember?

Gallimard: Even Parisians consider them arrogant. That's a switch.

Helga: What is it that Madame Su says? "We are a very old civilization." I never know if she's talking about her country or herself.

Gallimard: I walk around here, all I hear every day, everywhere is how *old* this culture is. The fact that "old" may be synonymous with "senile" doesn't occur to them.

Helga: You're not going to change them. "East is east, west is west, and . . ." whatever that guy said.

Gallimard: It's just that—silly. I met . . . at Ambassador Koening's tonight— you should've been there.

Helga: Koening? Oh god, no. Did he enchant you all again with the history of Bavaria?

Gallimard: No. I met, I suppose, the Chinese equivalent of a diva. She's a singer in the Chinese opera.

Helga: They have an opera, too? Do they sing in Chinese? Or maybe—in Italian?

Gallimard: Tonight, she did sing in Italian.

Helga: How'd she manage that?

Gallimard: She must've been educated in the West before the Revolution. Her French is very good also. Anyway, she sang the death scene from *Madame Butterfly.*

Helga: Madame Butterfly! Then I should have come. *(She begins humming, floating around the room as if dragging long kimono sleeves.)* Did she have a nice costume? I think it's a classic piece of music.

Gallimard: That's what *I* thought, too. Don't let her hear you say that.

Helga: What's wrong?

Gallimard: Evidently the Chinese hate it.

Helga: She hated it, but she performed it anyway? Is she perverse.

Gallimard: They hate it because the white man gets the girl. Sour grapes if you ask me.

Helga: Politics again? Why can't they just hear it as a piece of beautiful music? So, what's in their opera?

Gallimard: I don't know. But, whatever it is, I'm sure it must be *old.*

(Helga *exits.*)

SCENE VIII

Chinese opera house and the streets of Beijing. 1960.

The sound of gongs clanging fills the stage.

Gallimard: My wife's innocent question kept ringing in my ears. I asked around, but no one knew anything about the Chinese opera. It took four weeks, but my curiosity overcame my cowardice. This Chinese diva—this unwilling Butterfly—what did she do to make her so proud?

The room was hot, and full of smoke. Wrinkled faces, old women, teeth missing—a man with a growth on his neck, like a human toad. All smiling, pipes falling from their mouths, cracking nuts between their teeth, a live chicken pecking at my foot—all looking, screaming, gawking . . . at her.

(The upstage area is suddenly hit with a harsh white light. It has become the stage for the Chinese opera performance. Two dancers enter, along with Song. *Gallimard stands apart, watching.* Song *glides gracefully amidst the two dancers. Drums suddenly slam to a halt.* Song *strikes a pose, looking straight at* Gallimard. *Dancers exit. Light change. Pause, then* Song *walks right off the stage and straight up to* Gallimard.*)*

Song: Yes. You. White man. I'm looking straight at you.
Gallimard: Me?
Song: You see any other white men? It was too easy to spot you. How often does a man in my audience come in a tie?

(Song starts to remove her costume. Underneath, she wears simple baggy clothes. They are now backstage. The show is over.)

Song: So, you are an adventurous imperialist?
Gallimard: I . . . thought it would further my education.
Song: It took you four weeks. Why?
Gallimard: I've been busy.
Song: Well, education has always been undervalued in the West, hasn't it?
Gallimard *(Laughing.):* I don't think it's true.
Song: No, you wouldn't. You're a Westerner. How can you objectively judge your own values?
Gallimard: I think it's possible to achieve some distance.
Song: Do you? *(Pause.)* It stinks in here. Let's go.
Gallimard: These are the smells of your loyal fans.
Song: I love them for being my fans, I hate the smell they leave behind. I too can distance myself from my people. *(She looks around, then whispers in his ear.)* "Art for the masses" is a shitty excuse to keep artists poor. *(She pops a cigarette in her mouth.)* Be a gentleman, will you? And light my cigarette.

(Gallimard fumbles for a match.)

Gallimard: I don't . . . smoke.
Song *(Lighting her own.):* Your loss. Had you lit my cigarette, I might have blown a puff of smoke right between your eyes. Come.

(They start to walk about the stage. It is a summer night on the Beijing streets. Sounds of the city play on the house speakers.)

Song: How I wish there were even a tiny cafe to sit in. With cappuccinos, and men in tuxedos and bad expatriate jazz.
Gallimard: If my history serves me correctly, you weren't even allowed into the clubs in Shanghai before the Revolution.
Song: Your history serves you poorly, Monsieur Gallimard. True, there were signs reading "No dogs and Chinamen." But a woman, especially a delicate Oriental woman—we always go where we please. Could you imagine it otherwise? Clubs in China filled with pasty, big-thighed white women, while thousands of slender lotus blossoms wait just outside the door? Never. The clubs would be empty. *(Beat.)* We have always held a certain fascination for you Caucasian men, have we not?

Gallimard: But . . . that fascination is imperialist, or so you tell me.

Song: Do you believe everything I tell you? Yes. It is always imperialist. But sometimes . . . sometimes, it is also mutual. Oh—this is my flat.

Gallimard: I didn't even—

Song: Thank you. Come another time and we will further expand your mind.

(Song *exits.* Gallimard *continues roaming the streets as he speaks to us.*)

Gallimard: What was that? What did she mean, "Sometimes . . . it is mutual?" Women do not flirt with me. And I normally can't talk to them. But tonight, I held up my end of the conversation.

SCENE IX

Gallimard's *bedroom. Beijing. 1960.*

Helga *enters.*

Helga: You didn't tell me you'd be home late.

Gallimard: I didn't intend to. Something came up.

Helga: Oh! Like what?

Gallimard: I went to the . . . to the Dutch ambassador's home.

Helga: Again?

Gallimard: There was a reception for a visiting scholar. He's writing a six-volume treatise on the Chinese revolution. We all gathered that meant he'd have to live here long enough to actually write six volumes, and we all expressed our deepest sympathies.

Helga: Well, I had a good night too. I went with the ladies to a martial arts demonstration. Some of those men—when they break those thick boards—(*She mimes fanning herself.*) whoo-whoo!

(Helga *exits. Lights dim.*)

Gallimard: I lied to my wife. Why? I've never had any reason to lie before. But what reason did I have tonight? I didn't do anything wrong. That night, I had a dream. Other people, I've been told, have dreams where angels appear. Or dragons, or Sophia Loren in a towel. In my dream, Marc from school appeared.

(Marc *enters, in a nightshirt and cap.*)

Marc: Rene! You met a girl.

(Gallimard *and* Marc *stumble down the Beijing streets. Night sounds over the speakers.*)

Gallimard: It's not that amazing, thank you.

Marc: No! It's so monumental, I heard about it halfway around the world in my sleep!

Gallimard: I've met girls before, you know.

Marc: Name one. I've come across time and space to congratulate you. (*He hands* Gallimard *a bottle of wine.*)

Gillimard: Marc, this is expensive.

Marc: On those rare occasions when you become a formless spirit, why not steal the best?

(Marc *pops open the bottle, begins to share it with* Gallimard.)

Gallimard: You embarrass me. She . . . there's no reason to think she likes me.

Marc: "Sometimes, it is mutual?"

Gallimard: Oh.

Marc: "Mutual"? "Mutual"? What does that mean?

Gallimard: You heard!

Marc: It means the money is in the bank, you only have to write the check!

Gallimard: I am a married man!

Marc: And an excellent one too. I cheated after . . . six months. Then again and again, until now—three hundred girls in twelve years.

Gallimard: I don't think we should hold that up as a model.

Marc: Of course not! My life—it is disgusting! Phooey! Phooey! But, you— you are the model husband.

Gallimard: Anyway, it's impossible. I'm a foreigner.

Marc: Ah, yes. She cannot love you, it is taboo, but something deep inside her heart . . . she cannot help herself . . . she must surrender to you. It is her destiny.

Gallimard: How do you imagine all this?

Marc: The same way you do. It's an old story. It's in our blood. They fear us, Rene. Their women fear us. And their men—their men hate us. And, you know something? They are all correct.

(They spot a light in a window.)

Marc: There! There, Rene!

Gallimard: It's her window.

Marc: Late at night—it burns. The light—it burns for you.

Gallimard: I won't look. It's not respectful.

Marc: We don't have to be respectful. We're foreign devils.

(Enter Song, *in a sheer robe. The "One Fine Day" aria creeps in over the speakers. With her back to us,* Song *mimes attending to her toilette. Her robe comes loose, revealing her white shoulders.*)

Marc: All your life you've waited for a beautiful girl who would lay down for you. All your life you've smiled like a saint when it's happened to every other man you know. And you see them in magazines and you see them in movies. And you wonder, what's wrong with me? Will anyone beautiful ever want me? As the years pass, your hair thins and you struggle to hold onto even your hopes. Stop struggling, Rene. The wait is over. (He exits.)

Gallimard: Marc? Marc?

(At that moment, Song, *her back still towards us, drops her robe. A second of her naked back, then a sound cue: a phone ringing, very loud. Blackout, followed in the next beat by a special up on the bedroom area, where a phone now sits.* Gallimard *stumbles across the stage and picks up the phone. Sound cue out. Over the course of his conversation, area lights fill in the vicinity of his bed. It is the following morning.)*

Gallimard: Yes? Hello?
Song (Offstage.): Is it very early?
Gallimard: Why, yes.
Song (Offstage.): How early?
Gallimard: It's . . . it's 5:30. Why are you—?
Song (Offstage.): But it's light outside. Already.
Gallimard: It is. The sun must be in confusion today.

(Over the course of Song's *next speech, her upstage special comes up again. She sits in a chair, legs crossed, in a robe, telephone to her ear.)*

Song: I waited until I saw the sun. That was as much discipline as I could manage for one night. Do you forgive me?
Gallimard: Of course . . . for what?
Song: Then I'll ask you quickly. Are you really interest in the opera?
Gallimard: Why, yes. Yes I am.
Song: Then come again next Thursday. I am playing *The Drunken Beauty*. May I count on you?
Gallimard: Yes. You may
Song: Perfect. Well, I must be getting to bed. I'm exhausted. It's been a very long night for me.

(Song hangs up; special on her goes off. Gallimard *begins to dress for work.)*

SCENE X

Song Liling's *apartment. Beijing. 1960.*

Gallimard: I returned to the opera that next week, and the week after that . . . she keeps our meeting so short—perhaps fifteen, twenty minutes at most. So I am left each week with a thirst which is intensified. In this way, fifteen weeks have gone by. I am starting to doubt the words of my friend Marc. But no, not really. In my heart, I know she has . . . an interest in me. I suspect this is her way. She is outwardly bold and outspoken, yet her heart is shy and afraid. It is the Oriental in her at war with her Western education.
Song (Offstage.): I will be out in an instant. Ask the servant for anything you want.
Gallimard: Tonight, I have finally been invited to enter her apartment. Though the idea is almost beyond belief, I believe she is afraid of me.

(Gallimard looks around the room. He picks up a picture in a frame, studies it. Without his noticing, Song *enters, dressed elegantly in a black gown from the twenties. She stands in the doorway looking like Anna May Wong.)*

Song: That is my father.
Gallimard (Surprised.): Mademoiselle Song . . .

(She glides up to him, snatches away the picture.)

Song: It is very good that he did not live to see the Revolution. They would, no doubt, have made him kneel on broken glass. Not that he didn't deserve such a punishment. But he is my father. I would've hated to see it happen.

Gallimard: I'm very honored that you've allowed me to visit your home.

(Song *curtsys.*)

Song: Thank you. Oh! Haven't you been poured any tea?

Gallimard: I'm really not—

Song (To her offstage servant.): Shu-Fang! Cha! Kwai-lah! *(To* Gallimard.*)* I'm sorry. You want everything to be perfect—

Gallimard: Please.

Song: —and before the evening even begins—

Gallimard: I'm really not thirsty.

Song: —it's ruined.

Gallimard (Sharply.): Mademoiselle Song!

(Song *sits down.*)

Song: I'm sorry.

Gallimard: What are you apologizing for now?

(Pause; Song *starts to giggle.*)

Song: I don't know!

(Gallimard *laughs.*)

Gallimard: Exactly my point.

Song: Oh, I am silly. Lightheaded. I promise not to apologize for anything else tonight, do you hear me?

Gallimard: That's a good girl!

(Shu-Fang, *a servant girl, comes out with a tea tray and starts to pour.*)

Song (To Shu-Fang.*):* No! I'll pour myself for the gentleman!

(Shu-Fang, *staring at* Gallimard, *exits.*)

Song: No, I . . . I don't even know why I invited you up.

Gallimard: Well, I'm glad you did.

(Song *looks around the room.*)

Song: There is an element of danger to your presence.

Gallimard: Oh?

Song: You must know.

Gallimard: It doesn't concern me. We both know why I'm here.

Song: It doesn't concern me either. No . . . well perhaps . . .

Gallimard: What?

Song: Perhaps I am slightly afraid of scandal.

Gallimard: What are we doing?

Song: I'm entertaining you. In my parlor.

Gallimard: In France, that would hardly—

Song: France. France is a country living in the modern era. Perhaps even ahead of it. China is a nation whose soul is firmly rooted two thousand years in the past. What I do, even pouring the tea for you now . . . it has . . . implications. The walls and windows say so. Even my own heart, strapped inside this Western dress . . . even it says things—things I don't care to hear.

(Song *hands* Gallimard *a cup of tea.* Gallimard *puts his hand over both the* teacup *and* Song's *hand.*)

Gallimard: This is a beautiful dress.
Song: Don't.
Gallimard: What?
Song: I don't even know if it looks right on me.
Gallimard: Believe me—
Song: You are from France. You see so many beautiful women.
Gallimard: France? Since when are the European woman—?
Song: Oh! What am I trying to do, anyway?!

(Song *runs to the door, composes herself, then turns towards* Gallimard.)

Song: Monsieur Gallimard, perhaps you should go.
Gallimard: But . . . why?
Song: There's something wrong about this.
Gallimard: I don't see what.
Song: I feel . . . I am not myself.
Gallimard: No. You're nervous.
Song: Please. Hard as I try to be modern, to speak like a man, to hold a Western woman's strong face up to my own . . . in the end, I fail. A small, frightened heart beats too quickly and gives me away. Monsieur Gallimard, I'm a Chinese girl. I've never . . . never invited a man up to my flat before. The forwardness of my actions makes my skin burn.
Gallimard: What are you afraid of? Certainly not me, I hope.
Song: I'm a modest girl.
Gallimard: I know. And very beautiful. (He touches her hair.)
Song: Please—go now. The next time you see me, I shall again be myself.
Gallimard: I like you the way you are right now.
Song: You are a cad.
Gallimard: What do you expect? I'm a foreign devil.

(Gallimard *walks downstage.* Song *exits.*)

Gaillimard (To us.): Did you hear the way she talked about Western women? Much differently than the first night. She does—she feels inferior to them—and to me.

SCENE XI

The French embassy. Beijing. 1960.

Gallimard *moves towards a desk.*

Gallimard: I determined to try an experiment. In *Madame Butterfly*, Cio-Cio-San fears that the Western man who catches a butterfly will pierce its heart with a needle, then leave it to perish. I began to wonder: had I, too, caught a butterfly who would writhe on a needle?

(*Marc enters, dressed as a bureaucrat, holding a stack of papers. As* Gallimard *speaks,* Marc *hands papers to him. He peruses, then signs, stamps or rejects them.*)

Gallimard: Over the next five weeks, I worked like a dynamo. I stopped going to the opera, I didn't phone or write her. I knew this little flower was waiting for me to call, and, as I wickedly refused to do so, I felt for the first time that rush of power—the absolute power of a man.

(*Marc continues acting as the bureaucrat, but he now speaks as himself.*)

Marc: Rene! It's me!

Gallimard: Marc—I hear your voice everywhere now. Even in the midst of work.

Marc: That's because I'm watching you—all the time.

Gallimard: You were always the most popular guy in school.

Marc: Well, there's no guarantee of failure in life like happiness in high school. Somehow I knew I'd end up in the suburbs working for Renault and you'd be in the Orient picking exotic women off the trees. And they say there's no justice.

Gallimard: That's why you were my friend?

Marc: I gave you a little of my life, so that now you can give me some of yours. (*Pause.*) Remember Isabelle?

Gallimard: Of course I remember! She was my first experience.

Marc: We all wanted to ball her. But she only wanted me.

Gallimard: I had her.

Marc: Right. You balled her.

Gallimard: You were the only one who ever believed me.

Marc: Well, there's a good reason for that. (*Beat.*) C'mon. You must've guessed.

Gallimard: You told me to wait in the bushes by the cafeteria that night. The next thing I knew, she was on me. Dress up in the air.

Marc: She never wore underwear.

Gallimard: My arms were pinned to the dirt.

Marc: She loved the superior position. A girl ahead of her time.

Gallimard: I looked up, and there was this woman . . . bouncing up and down on my loins.

Marc: Screaming, right?

Gallimard: Screaming, and breaking off the branches all around me, and pounding my butt up and down in to the dirt.

Marc: Huffing and puffing like a locomotive.

Gallimard: And in the middle of all this, the leaves were getting into my mouth, my legs were losing circulation, I though, "God. So this is *it*?"

Marc: You thought that?

Gallimard: Well, I was worried about my legs falling off.

Marc: You didn't have a good time?

Gallimard: No, that's not what I—I had a great time!

Marc: You're sure?

Gallimard: Yeah. Really.

Marc: 'Cuz I wanted you to have a good time.

Gallimard: I did.

(*Pause.*)

Marc: Shit. (*Pause.*) When all is said and done, she was kind of a lousy lay, wasn't she? I mean, there was a lot of energy there, but you never knew what she was doing with it. Like when she yelled "I'm coming!"—hell, it was so loud, you wanted to go "Look, it's not that big a deal."

Gallimard: I got scared. I thought she meant someone was actually coming. (*Pause.*) But, Marc?

Marc: What?

Gallimard: Thanks.

Marc: Oh, don't mention it.

Gallimard: It was my first experience.

Marc: Yeah. You got her.

Gallimard: I got her.

Marc: Wait! Look at that letter again!

(Gallimard *picks up one of the papers he's been stamping, and rereads it.*)

Gallimard (To us.): After six weeks, they began to arrive. The letters.

(*Upstage special on* Song, *as* Madame Butterfly. *The scene is underscored by the "Love Duet."*)

Song: Did we fight? I do not know. Is the opera no longer of interest to you? Please come—my audiences miss the white devil in their midst.

(Gallimard *looks up from the letter, towards us.*)

Gallimard (To us.): A concession, but much too dignified. (*Beat; he discards the letter.*) I skipped the opera again that week to complete a position paper on trade.

(*The bureaucrat hands him another letter.*)

Song: Six weeks have passed since last we met. In this your practice—to leave friends in the lurch? Sometimes I hate you, sometimes I hate myself, but always I miss you.

Gallimard (To us.): Better, but I don't like the way she calls me "friend." When a woman calls a man her "friend," she's calling him a eunuch or a homosexual. (*Beat; he discards the letter.*) I was absent from the opera for the seventh week, feeling a sudden urge to clean out my files.

(*Bureaucrat hands him another letter.*)

Song: Your rudeness is beyond belief. I don't deserve this cruelty. Don't bother to call. I'll have you turned away at the door.

Gallimard (To us.): I didn't. (*He discards the letter; bureaucrat hands him an-other.*) And then finally, the letter that concluded my experiment.

Song: I am out of words. I can hide behind dignity no longer. What do you want? I have already given you my shame.

(Gallimard *gives the letter back to* Marc, *slowly. Special on* Song *fades out.*)

Gallimard (To us.): Reading it, I became suddenly ashamed. Yes, my experiment had been a success. She was turning on my needle. But the victory seemed hollow.

Marc: Hollow? Are you crazy?

Gallimard: Nothing, Marc. Please go away.

Marc (Exiting, with papers.): Haven't I taught you anything?

Gallimard: "I have already given you my shame." I had to attend a reception that evening. On the way, I felt sick. If there is a God, surely he would punish me now. I had finally gained power over a beautiful woman, only to abuse it cruelly. There must be justice in the world. I had the strange feeling that the ax would fall this very evening.

Scene XII

Ambassador Toulon's *residence. Beijing. 1960.*

Sound cue: party noises. Light change. We are now in a spacious residence.
Toulon, *the French ambassador, enters and taps* Gallimard *on the shoulder.*

Toulon: Gallimard? Can I have a word? Over here.

Gallimard (To us.): Manuel Toulon. French ambassador to China. He likes to think of us all as his children. Rather like God.

Toulon: Look, Gallimard, there's not much to say. I've liked you. From the day you walked in. You were no leader, but you were tidy and efficient.

Gallimard: Thank you, sir.

Toulon: Don't jump the gun. Okay, our needs in China are changing. It's embarrassing that we lost Indochina. Someone just wasn't on the ball there. I don't mean you personally, of course.

Gallimard: Thank you, sir.

Toulon: We're going to be doing a lot more information-gathering in the future. The nature of our work here is changing. Some people are just going to have to go. It's nothing personal.

Gallimard: Oh.

Toulon: Want to know a secret? Vice-Consul LeBon is being transferred.

Gallimard (To us.): My immediate superior!

Toulon: And most of his department.

Gallimard (To us.): Just as I feared! God has seen my evil heart—

Toulon: But not you.

Gallimard (To us.):—and he's taking her away just as . . . (*To* Toulon.) Excuse me, sir?

Toulon: Scare you? I think I did. Cheer up, Gallimard. I want you to replace LeBon as vice-consul.

Gallimard: You—? Yes, well, thank you, sir.
Toulon: Anytime.
Gallilmard: I . . . accept with great humility.
Toulon: Humility won't be part of the job. You're going to coordinate the revamped intelligence division. Want to know a secret? A year ago, you would've been out. But the past few months, I don't know how it happened, you've become this new aggressive confident . . . thing. And they also tell me you get along with the Chinese. So I think you're a lucky man, Gallimard. Congratulations.

(*They shake hands.* Toulon *exits. Party noises out.* Gallimard *stumbles across a darkened stage.*)

Gallimard: Vice-consul? Impossible! As I stumbled out of the party, I saw it written across the sky: There is no God. Or, no—say that there is a God. But that God . . . understands. Of course! God who creates Eve to serve Adam, who blesses Solomon with his harem but ties Jezebel to a burning bed—that God is a man. And he understands! At age thirty-nine, I was suddenly initiated into the way of the world.

SCENE XIII

Song Liling's *apartment. Beijing. 1960.*

Song *enters, in a sheer dressing gown.*

Song: Are you crazy?
Gallimard: Mademoiselle Song—
Song: To come here—at this hour? After . . . after eight weeks?
Gallimard: It's the most amazing—
Song: You bang on my door? Scare my servants, scandalize the neighbors?
Gallimard: I've been promoted. To vice-consul.

(*Pause.*)

Song: And what is that supposed to mean to me?
Gallimard: Are you my Butterfly?
Song: What are you saying?
Gallimard: I've come tonight for an answer: are you my Butterfly?
Song: Don't you know already?
Gallimard: I want you to say it.
Song: I don't want to say it.
Gallimard: So, that is your answer?
Song: You know how I feel about—
Gallimard: I do remember one thing.
Song: What?
Gallimard: In the letter I received today.
Song: Don't.
Gallimard: "I have already given you my shame."
Song: It's enough that I even wrote it.

Gallimard: Well, then—

Song: I shouldn't have it splashed across my face.

Gallimard: —if that's all true—

Song: Stop!

Gallimard: Then what is one more short answer?

Song: I don't want to!

Gallimard: Are you my Butterfly? *(Silence; he crosses the room and begins to touch her hair.)* I want from you honesty. There should be nothing false between us. No false pride.

> *(Pause.)*

Song: Yes, I am. I am your Butterfly.

Gallimard: Then let me be honest with you. It is because of you that I was promoted tonight. You have changed my life forever. My little Butterfly, there should be no more secrets: I love you.

> *(He starts to kiss her roughly. She resists slightly.)*

Song: No . . . no . . . gently . . . please, I've never . . .

Gallimard: No?

Song: I've tried to appear experienced, but . . . the truth is . . . no.

Gallimard: Are you cold?

Song: Yes. Cold.

Gallimard: Then we will go very, very slowly.

> *(He starts to caress her; her gown begins to open.)*

Song: No . . . let me . . . keep my clothes . . .

Gallimard: But . . .

Song: Please . . . it all frightens me. I'm a modest Chinese girl.

Gallimard: My poor little treasure.

Song: I am your treasure. Though inexperienced, I am not . . . ignorant. They teach us things, our mothers, about pleasing a man.

Gallimard: Yes?

Song: I'll do my best to make you happy. Turn off the lights.

> *(Gallimard gets up and heads for a lamp. Song, propped up on one elbow, tosses her hair back and smiles.)*

Song: Monsieur Gallimard?

Gallimard: Yes, Butterfly?

Song: "Vieni, vieni!"

Gallimard: "Come, darling."

Song: "Ah! Dolce notte!"

Gallimard: "Beautiful night."

Song: "Tutto estatico d'amor ride il ciel!"

Gallimard: "All ecstatic with love, the heavens are filled with laughter."

> *(He turns off the lamp. Blackout.)*

ACT TWO

Scene I

M. Gallimard's *cell. Paris. Present.*

Lights up on Gallimard. *He sits in his cell, reading from a leaflet.*

Gallimard: This, from a contemporary critic's commentary on *Madame But-terfly:* "Pinkerton suffers from . . . being an obnoxious bounder whom every man in the audience itches to kick." Bully for us men in the audience! Then, in the same note: "Butterfly is the most irresistibly appealing of Puccini's 'Little Women.' Watching the succession of her humiliations is like watching a child under torture." *(He tosses the pamphlet over his shoulder.)* I suggest that, while we men may all want to kick Pinkerton, very few of us would pass up the opportunity to be Pinkerton.

(Gallimard moves out of his cell.)

Scene II

Gallimard *and* Butterfly's *flat. Beijing. 1960.*

We are in a simple but well-decorated parlor. Gallimard *moves to sit on a sofa, while* Song, *dressed in a chong sam, enters and curls up at his feet.*

Gallimard (To us.): We secured a flat on the outskirts of Peking. Butterfly, as I was calling her now, decorated our "home" with Western furniture and Chinese antiques. And there, on a few stolen afternoons or evenings each week, Butterfly commenced her education.

Song: The Chinese men—they keep us down.

Gallimard: Even in the "New Society"?

Song: In the "New Society," we are all kept ignorant equally. That's one of the exciting things about loving a Western man. I know you are not threatened by a woman's education.

Gallimard: I'm no saint, Butterfly.

Song: But you come from a progressive society.

Gallimard: We're not always reminding each other how "old" we are, if that's what you mean.

Song: Exactly. We Chinese—once, I suppose, it is true, we ruled the world. But so what? How much more exciting to be part of the society ruling the world today. Tell me—what's happening in Vietnam?

Gallimard: Oh, Butterfly—you want me to bring my work home?

Song: I want to know what you know. To be impressed by my man. It's not the particulars so much as the fact that you're making decisions which change the shape of the world.

Gallimard: Not the world. At best, a small corner.

(Toulon enters, and sits at a desk upstage.)

SCENE III

French embassy. Beijing. 1961.

Gallimard *moves downstage, to* Toulon's *desk.* Song *remains upstage, watching.*

Toulon: And a more troublesome corner is hard to imagine.

Gallimard: So, the Americans plan to begin bombing.

Toulon: This is very secret, Gallimard: yes. The Americans don't have an embassy here. They're asking us to be their eyes and ears. Say Jack Kennedy signed an order to bomb North Vietnam, Laos. How would the Chinese react?

Gallimard: I think the Chinese will squawk—

Toulon: Uh-huh.

Gallimard: —but, in their hearts, they don't even like Ho Chi Minh.

(*Pause.*)

Toulon: What a bunch of jerks. Vietnam was *our* colony. Not only didn't the Americans help us fight to keep them, but now, seven years later, they've come back to grab the territory for themselves. It's very irritating.

Gallimard: With all due respect, sir, why, should the Americans have won our war for us back in '54 if we didn't have the will to win it ourselves?

Toulon: You're kidding, aren't you?

(*Pause.*)

Gallimard: The Orientals simply want to be associated with whoever shows the most strength and power. You live with the Chinese, sir. Do you think they like Communism?

Toulon: I live in China. Not with the Chinese.

Gallimard: Well, I—

Toulon: *You* live with the Chinese.

Gallimard: Excuse me?

Toulon: I can't keep a secret.

Gallimard: What are you saying?

Toulon: Only that I'm not immune to gossip. So, you're keeping a native mistress. Don't answer. It's none of my business. (*Pause.*) I'm sure she must be gorgeous.

Gallimard: Well . . .

Toulon: I'm impressed. You have the stamina to go out into the streets and hunt one down. Some of us have to be content with the wives of the expatriate community.

Gallimard: I do feel . . . fortunate.

Toulon: So, Gallimard, you've got the inside knowledge—what do the Chinese think?

Gallimard: Deep down, they miss the old days. You know, cappuccinos, men in tuxedos—

Toulon: So what do we tell the Americans about Vietnam?

Gallimard: Tell them there's a natural affinity between the West and the Orient.

Toulon: And that you speak from experience?

Gallimard: The Orientals are people too. They want the good things we can give them. If the Americans demonstrate the will to win, the Vietnamese will welcome them into a mutually beneficial union.

Toulon: I don't see how the Vietnamese can stand up to American firepower.

Gallimard: Orientals will always submit to a greater force.

Toulon: I'll note your opinions in my report. The Americans always love to hear how "welcome" they'll be. *(He starts to exit.)*

Gallimard: Sir?

Toulon: Mmmm?

Gallimard: This . . . rumor you've heard.

Toulon: Uh-huh?

Gallimard: How . . . widespread do you think it is?

Toulon: It's only widespread within this embassy. Where nobody talks because everybody is guilty. We were worried about you, Gallimard. We thought you were the only one here without a secret. Now you go and find a lotus blossom . . . and top us all. *(He exits.)*

Gallimard (To us.): Toulon knows! And he approves. I was learning the benefits of being a man. We form our own clubs, sit behind thick doors, smoke—and celebrate the fact that we're still boys. *(He starts to move downstage, towards* Song.*)* So, over the—

(Suddenly Comrade Chin *enters.* Gallimard *backs away.)*

Gallimard (To Song.*):* No! Why does she have to come in?

Song: Rene, be sensible. How can they understand the story without her? Now, don't embarrass yourself.

(Gallimard moves down center.*)*

Gallimard (To us.): Now, you will see why my story is so amusing to so many people. Why they snicker at parties in disbelief. Please—try to understand it from my point of view. We are all prisoners of our time and place. *(He exits.)*

SCENE IV

Gallimard *and* Butterfly's *flat. Beijing. 1961.*

Song (To us.): 1961. The flat Monsieur Gallimard rented for us. An evening after he has gone.

Chin: Okay, see if you find out when the Americans plan to start bombing Vietnam. If you can find out what cities, even better.

Song: I'll do my best, but I don't want to arouse his suspicions.

Chin: Yeah, sure, of course. So, what else?

Song: The Americans will increase troops in Vietnam to 170,000 soldiers with 120,000 militia and 11,000 American advisors.

Chin (Writing.): Wait, wait. 120,000 militia and—

Song: —11,000 American—

Chin: —American advisors. *(Beat.)* How do you remember so much?

Song: I'm an actor.

Chin: Yeah. *(Beat.)* Is that how come you dress like that?

Song: Like what, Miss Chin?

Chin: Like that dress! You;'re wearing a dress. And every time I come here, you're wearing a dress. Is that because you're an actor? Or what?

Song: It's a . . . disguise, Miss Chin.

Chin: Actors, I think they're all weirdos. My mother tells me actors are like gamblers or prostitutes or—

Song: It helps me in my assignment.

    (Pause.)

Chin: You're not gathering information in any way that violates Communist Party principles, are you?

Song: Why would I do that?

Chin: Just checking. Remember: when working for the Great Proletarian State, you represent our Chairman Mao in every position you take.

Song: I'll try to imagine the Chairman taking my positions.

Chin: We all think of him this way. Good-bye, comrade. *(She starts to exit.)* Comrade?

Song: Yes?

Chin: Don't forget: there is no homosexuality in China!

Song: Yes, I've heard.

Chin: Just checking. *(She exits.)*

Song (To us.): What passes for a woman in modern China.

    (Gallimard *sticks his head out from the wings.*)

Gallimard: Is she gone?

Song: Yes, Rene. Please continue in your own fashion.

Scene V

    Beijing. 1961–63.

    Gallimard *moves to the couch where* Song *still sits. He lies down in her lap, and she strokes his forehead.*

Gallimard (To us.): And so, over the years 1961, '62, '63, we settled into our routine, Butterfly and I. She would always have prepared a light snack and then, ever so delicately, and only if I agreed, she would start to pleasure me. With her hands, her mouth . . . too many ways to explain, and too sad, given my present situation. But mostly we would talk. About my life. Perhaps there is nothing more rare than to find a woman who passionately listens.

    (Song *remains upstage, listening, as* Helga *enters and plays a scene downstage with* Gallimard.)

Helga: Rene, I visited Dr. Bolleart this morning.

Gallimard: Why? Are you ill?

Helga: No, no. You see, I wanted to ask him . . . that question we've been discussing.

Gallimard: And I told you, it's only a matter of time. Why did you bring a doctor into this? We just have to keep trying—like a crapshoot, actually.

Helga: I went, I'm sorry. But listen: he says there's nothing wrong with me.

Gallimard: You see? Now, will you stop—?

Helga: Rene, he says he'd like you to go in and take some tests.

Gallimard: Why? So he can find there's nothing wrong with both of us?

Helga: Rene, I don't ask for much. One trip! One visit! And then, whatever you want to do about it—you decide.

Gallimard: You're assuming he'll find something defective!

Helga: No! Of course not! Whatever he finds—if he finds nothing, we decide what to do about nothing! But go!

Gallimard: If he finds nothing, we keep trying. Just like we do now.

Helga: But at least we'll know! *(Pause.)* I'm sorry. *(She starts to exit.)*

Gallimard: Do you really want me to see Dr. Bolleart?

Helga: Only if you want a child, Rene. We have to face the fact that time is running out. Only if you want a child. *(She exits.)*

Gallimard (To Song.*):* I'm a modern man, Butterfly. And yet, I don't want to go. It's the same old voodoo. I feel like God himself is laughing at me if I can't produce a child.

Song: You men of the West—you're obsessed by your odd desire for equality. Your wife can't give you a child, and *you're* going to the doctor?

Gallimard: Well, you see, she's already gone.

Song: And because this incompetent can't find the defect, you now have to subject yourself to him? It's unnatural.

Gallimard: Well, what is the "natural" solution?

Song: In Imperial China, when a man found that one wife was inadequate, he turned to another—to give him his son.

Gallimard: What do you—? I can't . . . marry you, yet.

Song: Please. I'm not asking you to be my husband. But I am already your wife.

Gallimard: Do you want to . . . have my child?

Song: I thought you'd never ask.

Gallimard: But, your career . . . your—

Song: Phooey on my career! That's your Western mind, twisting itself into strange shapes again. Of course I love my career. But what would I love most of all? To feel something inside me—day and night—something I know is yours. *(Pause.)* Promise me . . . you won't go to this doctor. Who is this Western quack to set himself as judge over the man I love? I know who is a man, and who is not. *(She exits.)*

Gallimard (To us.): Dr. Bolleart? Of course I didn't go. What man would?

SCENE VI

Beijing. 1963.

Party noises over the house speakers. Renee *enters, wearing a revealing gown.*

Gallimard: 1963. A party at the Austrian embassy. None of us could remember the Austrian ambassador's name, which seemed somehow appropriate. *(To Renee.)* So, I tell the Americans, Diem must go. The U.S. wants to be respected by the Vietnamese, and yet they're propping up this nobody seminarian as her president. A man whose claim to fame is his sister-in-law imposing fanatic "moral order" campaigns? Oriental women—when they're good, they're very good, but when they're bad, they're Christians.

Renee: Yeah.

Gallimard: And what do you do?

Renee: I'm a student. My father exports a lot of useless stuff to the Third World.

Gallimard: How useless?

Renee: You know. Squirt guns, confectioner's sugar, hula hoops . . .

Gallimard: I'm sure they appreciate the sugar.

Renee: I'm here for two years to study Chinese.

Gallimard: Two years?

Renee: That's what everybody says.

Gallimard: When did you arrive?

Renee: Three weeks ago.

Gallimard: And?

Renee: I like it. It's primitive, but . . . well, this is the place to learn Chinese, so here I am.

Gallimard: Why Chinese?

Renee: I think it'll be important someday.

Gallimard: You do?

Renee: Don't ask me when, but . . . that's what I think.

Gallimard: Well, I agree with you. One hundred percent. That's very far-sighted.

Renee: Yeah. Well of course, my father thinks I'm a complete weirdo.

Gallimard: He'll thank you someday.

Renee: Like when the Chinese start buying hula hoops?

Gallimard: There're a billion bellies out there.

Renee: And if they end up taking over the world—well, then I'll be lucky to know Chinese too, right?

(Pause.)

Gallimard: At this point, I don't see how the Chinese can possibly take—

Renee: You know what I *don't* like about China?

Gallimard: Excuse me? No—what?

Renee: Nothing to do at night.

Gallimard: You come to parties at embassies like everyone else.

Renee: Year, but they get out at ten. And then what?

Gallimard: I'm afraid the Chinese idea of a dance hall is a dirt floor and a man with a flute.

Renee: Are you married?

Gallimard: Yes. Why?

Renee: You wanna . . . fool around?

(Pause.)

Gallimard: Sure.

Renee: I'll wait for you outside. What's your name?

Gallimard: Gallimard. Rene.

Renee: Weird. I'm Renee too. *(She exits.)*

Gallimard (To us.): And so, I embarked on my first extra-extramarital affair. Renee was picture perfect. With a body like those girls in the magazines. If I put a tissue paper over my eyes, I wouldn't have been able to tell the difference. And it was exciting to be with someone who wasn't afraid to be seen completely naked. But is it possible for a woman to be *too* uninhibited, *too* willing, so as to seem almost too . . . masculine?

(Chuck Berry blares from the house speakers, then comes down in volume as Renee *enters, toweling her hair.)*

Renee: You have a nice weenie.

Gallimard: What?

Renee: Penis. You have a nice penis.

Gallimard: Oh. Well, thank you. That's very . . .

Renee: What—can't take a compliment?

Gallimard: No, it's very . . . reassuring.

Renee: But most girls don't come out and say it, huh?

Gallimard: And also . . . what did you call it?

Renee: Oh. Most girls don't call it a "weenie," huh?

Gallimard: It sounds very—

Renee: Small, I know.

Gallimard: I was going to say, "young."

Renee: Yeah. Young, small, same thing. Most guys are pretty, uh, sensitive about that. Like, you know, I had a boyfriend back home in Denmark. I got mad at him once and called him a little weeniehead. He got so mad! He said at least I should call him a great big weeniehead.

Gallimard: I suppose I just say "penis."

Renee: Yeah. That's pretty clinical. There's "cock," but that sounds like a chicken. And "prick" is painful, and "dick" is like you're talking about someone who's not in the room.

Gallimard: Yes. It's a . . . bigger problem than I imagined.

Renee: I—I think maybe it's because I really don't know what to do with them—that's why I call them "weenies."

Gallimard: Well, you did quite well with . . . mine.

Renee: Thanks, but I mean, really *do* with them. Like, okay, have you ever looked at one? I mean, really?

Gallimard: No, I suppose when it's part of you, you sort of take it for granted.

Renee: I guess. But, like, it just hangs there. This little . . . flap of flesh. And there's so much fuss that we make about it. Like, I think the reason we fight wars is because we wear clothes. Because no one knows—between the men, I mean—who has the bigger . . . weenie. So, if I'm a guy with a small one, I'm going to build a really big building or take over a really big piece of land or write a really long book so the other men don't know, right? But, see, it never really works, that's the problem. I mean, you conquer the country, or whatever, but you're still wearing clothes, so there's no way to prove absolutely whose is bigger or smaller. And that's what we call a civilized society. The whole world run by a bunch of men with pricks the size of pins. *(She exits.)*

Gallimard (To us.): This was simply not acceptable.

(A high-pitched chime rings through the air. Song, dressed as Butterfly, appears in the upstage special. She is obviously distressed. Her body swoons as she attempts to clip the stems of flowers she's arranging in a vase.)

Gallimard: But I kept up our affair, wildly, for several months. Why? I believe because of Butterfly. She knew the secret I was trying to hide. But, unlike a Western woman, she didn't confront me, threaten, even pout. I remembered the words of Puccini's *Butterfly:*

Song: "Noi siamo gente avvezza / alle piccole cose / umili e silenziose."

Gallimard: "I come from a people / Who are accustomed to little / Humble and silent." I saw Pinkerton and Butterfly, and what she would say if he were unfaithful . . . nothing. She would cry, alone, into those wildly soft sleeves, once full of possessions, now empty to collect her tears. It was her tears and her silence that excited me, every time I visited Renee.

Toulon (Offstage.): Gallimard!

(Toulon enters. Gallimard turns towards him. During the next section, Song, up center, begins to dance with the flowers. It is a drunken dance, where she breaks small pieces off the stems.)

Toulon: They're killing him.

Gallimard: Who? I'm sorry? What?

Toulon: Bother you to come over at this late hour?

Gallimard: No . . . of course not.

Toulon: Not after you hear my secret. Champagne?

Gallimard: Um . . . thank you.

Toulon: You're surprised. There's something that you've wanted, Gallimard. No, not a promotion. Next time. Something in the world. You're not aware of this, but there's an informal gossip circle among intelligence agents. And some of ours heard from some of the Americans—

Gallimard: Yes?

Toulon: That the U.S. will allow the Vietnamese generals to stage a coup . . . and assassinate President Diem.

(The chime rings again. Toulon *freezes.* Gallimard *turns upstage and looks at* Song, *who slowly and deliberately clips a flower off its stem.* Gallimard *turns back towards* Toulon.)

Gallimard: I think . . . that's a very wise move!

(Toulon *unfreezes.)*

Toulon: It's what you've been advocating. A toast?
Gallimard: Sure. I consider this a vindication.
Toulon: Not exactly. "To the test. Let's hope you pass."

(They drink. The chime rings again. Toulon *freezes.* Gallimard *turns upstage, and* Song *clips another flower.)*

Gallimard *(To* Toulon.): The test?
Toulon *(Unfreezing.):* It's a test of everything you've been saying. I personally think the generals probably will stop the Communists. And you'll be a hero. But if anything goes wrong, then your opinions won't be worth a pig's ear. I'm sure that won't happen. But sometimes it's easier when they don't listen to you.
Gallimard: They're your opinions too, aren't they?
Toulon: Personally, yes.
Gallimard: So we agree.
Toulon: But my opinions aren't on that report. Yours are. Cheers.

(Toulon *turns away from* Gallimard *and raises his glass. At that instant* Song *picks up the vase and hurls it to the ground. It shatters.* Song *sinks down amidst the shards of the vase, in a calm, childlike trance. She sings softly, as if reciting a child's nursery rhyme.)*

Song *(Repeat as necessary.):* "The whole world over, the white man travels, setting anchor, wherever he likes. Life's not worth living, unless he finds, the finest maidens, of every land . . ."

*(*Gallimard *turns downstage towards us.* Song *continues singing.)*

Gallimard: I shook as I left his house. That coward! That worm! To put the burden for his decisions on my shoulders!
     I started for Renee's. But no, that was all I needed. A schoolgirl who would question the role of the penis in modern society. What I wanted was revenge. A vessel to contain my humiliation. Though I hadn't seen her in several weeks, I headed for Butterfly's.

*(*Gallimard *enters* Song's *apartment.)*

Song: Oh! Rene . . . I was dreaming!
Gallimard: You've been drinking?
Song: If I can't sleep, then yes, I drink. But then, it gives me these dreams which—Rene, it's been almost three weeks since you visited me last.
Gallimard: I know. There's been a lot going on in the world.

Song: Fortunately I am drunk. So I can speak freely. It's not the world, it's you and me. And an old problem. Even the softest skin becomes like leather to a man who's touched it too often. I confess I don't know how to stop it. I don't know how to become another woman.

Gallimard: I have a request.

Song: Is this a solution? Or are you ready to give up the flat?

Gallimard: It may be a solution. But I'm sure you won't like it.

Song: Oh well, that's very important. "Like it?" Do you think I "like" lying here alone, waiting, always waiting for your return? Please—don't worry about what I may not "like."

Gallimard: I want to see you . . . naked.

(Silence)

Song: I thought you understood my modesty. So you want me to—what— strip? Like a big cowboy girl? Shiny pasties on my breasts? Shall I fling my kimono over my head and yell "ya-hoo" in the process? I thought you respected my shame!

Gallimard: I believe you gave me your shame many years ago.

Song: Yes—and it is just like a white devil to use it against me. I can't believe it. I thought myself so repulsed by the passive Oriental and the cruel white man. Now I see—we are always most revolted by the things hidden within us.

Gallimard: I just mean—

Song: Yes?

Gallimard: —that it will remove the only barrier left between us.

Song: No, Rene. Don't couch your request in sweet words. Be yourself—a cad—and know that my love is enough, that I submit—submit to the worst you can give me. *(Pause.)* Well, come. Strip me. Whatever happens, know that you have willed it. Our love, in your hands. I'm helpless before my man.

(Gallimard starts to cross the room.)

Gallimard: Did I not undress her because I knew, somewhere deep down, what I would find? Perhaps. Happiness is so rare that our mind can turn somersaults to protect it.

  At the time, I only knew that I was seeing Pinkerton stalking towards his Butterfly, ready to reward her love with his lecherous hands. The image sickened me, pulled me to my knees, so I was crawling towards her like a worm. By the time I reached her, Pinkerton . . . had vanished from my heart. To be replaced by something new, something unnatural, that flew in the face of all I'd learned in the world—something very close to love.

(He grabs her around the waist; she strokes his hair.)

Gallimard: Butterfly, forgive me.

Song: Rene . . .

Gallimard: For everything. From the start.

Song: I'm . . .

Gallimard: I want to—

Song: I'm pregnant. *(Beat.)* I'm pregnant. *(Beat.)* I'm pregnant.

(*Beat.*)

Gallimard: I want to marry you!

SCENE VII

Gallimard *and* Butterfly's *flat. Beijing. 1963.*

Downstage, Song *paces as* Comrade Chin *reads from her notepad. Upstage,* Gallimard *is still kneeling. He remains on his knees throughout the scene, watching it.*

Song: I need a baby.

Chin (From pad.): He's been spotted going to a dorm.

Song: I need a baby.

Chin: At the Foreign Language Institute.

Song: I need a baby.

Chin: The room of a Danish girl . . . What do you mean, you need a baby?!

Song: Tell Comrade Kang—last night, the entire mission, it could've ended.

Chin: What do you mean?

Song: Tell Kang—he told me to strip.

Chin: Strip?!

Song: Write!

Chin: I tell you, I don't understand nothing about this case anymore. Nothing.

Song: He told me to strip, and I took a chance. Oh, we Chinese, we know how to gamble.

Chin (Writing.): ". . . told him to strip."

Song: My palms were wet, I had to make a split-second decision.

Chin: Hey! Can you slow down?!

(*Pause.*)

Song: You write faster, I'm the artist here. Suddenly, it hit me—"All he wants is for her to submit. Once a woman submits, a man is always ready to become 'generous.'"

Chin: You're just gonna end up with rough notes.

Song: And it worked! He gave in! Now, if I can just present him with a baby. A Chinese baby with blond hair—he'll be mine for life!

Chin: Kang will never agree! The trading of babies has to be a counterrevolutionary act.

Song: Sometimes, a counterrevolutionary act is necessary to counter a counterrevolutionary act.

(*Pause.*)

Chin: Wait.

Song: I need one . . . in seven months. Make sure it's a boy.

Chin: This doesn't sound like something the Chairman would do. Maybe you'd better talk to Comrade Kang yourself.

Song: Good. I will.

(Chin *gets up to leave.*)

Song: Miss Chin? Why, in the Peking Opera, are women's roles played by men?

Chin: I don't know. Maybe, a reactionary remnant of male—

Song: No. *(Beat.)* Because only a man knows how a woman is supposed to act.

(Chin *exits.* Song *turns upstage, towards* Gallimard.)

Gallimard (Calling after Chin.*):* Good riddance! *(To* Song.*)* I could forget all that betrayal in an instant, you know. If you'd just come back and become Butterfly again.

Song: Fat chance. You're here in prison, rotting in a cell. And I'm on a plane, winging my way back to China. Your President pardoned me of our treason, you know.

Gallimard: Yes, I read about that.

Song: Must make you feel . . . lower than shit.

Gallimard: But don't you, even a little bit, wish you were here with me?

Song: I'm an artist, Rene. You were my greatest . . . acting challenge. *(She laughs.)* It doesn't matter how rotten I answer, does it? You still adore me. That's why I love you, Rene. *(She points to us.)* So—you were telling your audience about the night I announced I was pregnant.

(Gallimard *puts his arms around* Song's *waist. He and* Song *are in the positions they were in at the end of Scene 6.)*

SCENE VIII

Same.

Gallimard: I'll divorce my wife. We'll live together here, and then later in France.

Song: I feel so . . . ashamed.

Gallimard: Why?

Song: I had begun to lose faith. And now, you shame me with your generosity.

Gallimard: Generosity? No, I'm proposing for very selfish reasons.

Song: Your apologies only make me feel more ashamed. My outburst a moment ago!

Gallimard: Your outburst? What about my request?!

Song: You've been very patient dealing with my . . . eccentricities. A Western man, used to women freer with their bodies—

Gallimard: It was sick! Don't make excuses for me.

Song: I have to. You don't seem willing to make them for yourself.

(*Pause.*)

Gallimard: You're crazy.

Song: I'm happy. Which often looks like crazy.

Gallimard: Then make me crazy. Marry me.

(*Pause.*)

Song: No.

Gallimard: What?

Song: Do I sound silly, a slave, if I say I'm not worthy?

Gallimard: Yes. In fact you do. No one has loved me like you.

Song: Thank you. And no one ever will. I'll see to that.

Gallimard: So what is the problem?

Song: Rene, we Chinese are realists. We understand rice, gold, and guns. You are a diplomat. Your career is skyrocketing. Now, what would happen if you divorced your wife to marry a Communist Chinese actress?

Gallimard: That's not being realistic. That's defeating yourself before you begin.

Song: We must conserve our strength for the battles we can win.

Gallimard: That sounds like a fortune cookie!

Song: Where do you think fortune cookies come from?

Gallimard: I don't care.

Song: You do. So do I. And we should. That is why I say I'm not worthy. I'm worthy to love and even to be loved by you. But I am not worthy to end the career of one of the West's most promising diplomats.

Gallimard: It's not that great a career! I made it sound like more than it is!

Song: Modesty will get you nowhere. Flatter yourself, and you flatter me. I'm flattered to decline your offer. (*She exits.*)

Gallimard (To us.): Butterfly and I argued all night. And, in the end, I left, knowing I would never be her husband. She went away for several months—to the countryside, like a small animal. Until the night I received her call.

(*A baby's cry from offstage,* Song *enters, carrying a child.*)

He looks like you.

Gallimard: Oh! (*Beat; he approaches the baby.*) Well, babies are never very attractive at birth.

Song: Stop!

Gallimard: I'm sure he'll grow more beautiful with age. More like his mother.

Song: "Chi vide mai / a bimbo del Giappon . . ."

Gallimard: "What baby, I wonder, was ever born in Japan"— or China, for that matter—

Song: ". . . occhi azzurrini?"

Gallimard: "With azure eyes"—they're actually sort of brown, wouldn't you say?

Song: "E il labbro."

Gallimard: "And such lips!" (*He kisses* Song.) And such lips.

Song: "E i ricciolini d'oro schietto?"

Gallimard: "And such a head of golden"—if slightly patchy—"curls?"

Song: I'm going to call him "Peepee."

Gallimard: Darling, could you repeat that because I'm sure a rickshaw just flew by overhead.

Song: You heard me.

Gallimard: "Song Peepee"? May I suggest Michael, or Stephan, or Adolph?

Song: You may, but I won't listen.

Gallimard: You can't be serious. Can you imagine the time this child will have in school?

Song: In the West, yes.

Gallimard: It's worse than naming him Ping Pong or Long Dong or—

Song: But he's never going to live in the West, is he?

　　(Pause.)

Gallimard: That wasn't my choice.

Song: It is mine. And this is my promise to you: I will raise him, he will be our child, but he will never burden you outside of China.

Gallimard: Why do you make these promises? I want to be burdened! I want a scandal to cover the papers!

Song (To us.): Prophetic.

Gallimard: I'm serious.

Song: So am I. His name is as I registered it. And he will never live in the West.

　　(Song exits with the child.)

Gallimard (To us.): It is possible that her stubbornness only made me want her more. That drawing back at the moment of my capitulation was the most brilliant strategy she could have chosen. It is possible. But it is also possible that by this point she could have said, could have done . . . anything, and I would have adored her still.

Scene IX

　　Beijing. 1966.

　　A driving rhythm of Chinese percussion fills the stage.

Gallimard: And then, China began to change. Mao became very old, and his cult became very strong. And, like many old men, he entered his second childhood. So he handed over the reins of state to those with minds like his own. And children ruled the Middle Kingdom with complete caprice. The doctrine of the Cultural Revolution implied continuous anarchy. Contact between Chinese and foreigners became impossible. Our flat was confiscated. Her fame and my money now counted against us.

　　(Two dancers in Mao suits and red-starred caps enter, and begin crudely mimicking revolutionary violence, in an agitprop fashion.)

Gallimard: And somehow the American war went wrong too. Four hundred thousand dollars were being spent for every Viet Cong killed; so General Westmoreland's remark that the Oriental does not value life the way Americans do was oddly accurate. Why weren't the Vietnamese people giving in? Why were they content instead to die and die and die again?

(*Toulon enters.*)

Toulon: Congratulations, Gallimard.

Gallimard: Excuse me, sir?

Toulon: Not a promotion. That was last time. You're going home.

Gallimard: What?

Toulon: Don't say I didn't warn you.

Gallimard: I'm being transferred . . . because I was wrong about the American war?

Toulon: Of course not. We don't care about the Americans. We care about your mind. The quality of your analysis. In general, everything you've predicted here in the Orient . . . just hasn't happened.

Gallimard: I think that's premature.

Toulon: Don't force me to be blunt. Okay, you said China was ready to open to Western trade. The only thing they're trading out there are Western heads. And, yes, you said the Americans would succeed in Indochina. You were kidding, right?

Gallimard: I think the end is in sight.

Toulon: Don't be pathetic. And don't take this personally. You were wrong. It's not your fault.

Gallimard: But I'm going home.

Toulon: Right. Could I have the number of your mistress? (*Beat.*) Joke! Joke! Eat a croissant for me.

(*Toulon exits. Song, wearing a Mao suit, is dragged in from the wings as part of the upstage dance. They "beat" her, then lampoon the acrobatics of the Chinese opera, as she is made to kneel onstage.*)

Gallimard (Simultaneously.): I don't care to recall how Butterfly and I said our hurried farewell. Perhaps it was better to end our affair before it killed her.

(*Gallimard exits. Comrade Chin walks across the stage with a banner reading: "The Actor Renounces His Decadent Profession!" She reaches the kneeling* Song. *Percussion stops with a thud. Dancers strike poses.*)

Chin: Actor-oppressor, for years you have lived above the common people and looked down on their labor. While the farmer ate millet—

Song: I ate pastries from France and sweetmeats from silver trays.

Chin: And how did you come to live in such an exalted position?

Song: I was a plaything for the imperialists!

Chin: What did you do?

Song: I shamed China by allowing myself to be corrupted by a foreigner . . .

Chin: What does this mean? The People demand a full confession!

Song: I engaged in the lowest perversions with China's enemies!

Chin: What perversions? Be more clear!

Song: I let him put it up my ass!

   (Dancers look over, disgusted.)

Chin: Aaaa-ya! How can you use such sickening language?!
Song: My language . . . is only as foul as the crimes I committed . . .
Chin: Yeah. That's better. So—what do you want to do now?
Song: I want to serve the people.

   (Percussion starts up, with Chinese strings.)

Chin: What?
Song: I want to serve the people!

   (Dancers regain their revolutionary smiles, and begin a dance of victory.)

Chin: What?!
Song: I want to serve the people!

   (Dancers unveil a banner: "The Actor Is Rehabilitated!" Song remains kneeling before Chin, *as the dancers bounce around them, then exit. Music out.)*

Scene X

   A commune. Hunan Province. 1970.

Chin: How you planning to do that?
Song: I've already worked four years in the fields of Hunan, Comrade Chin.
Chin: So? Farmers work all their lives. Let me see your hands.

   (Song holds them out for her inspection.)

Chin: Goddamn! Still so smooth! How long does it take to turn you actors
      into good anythings? Hunh. You've just spent too many years in luxury
      to be any good to the Revolution.
Song: I served the Revolution.
Chin: Serve the Resolution? Bullshit! You wore dresses! Don't tell me—I
      was there. I saw you! You and your white vice-consul! Stuck up there in
      your flat, living off the People's Treasury! Yeah, I knew what was going
      on! You two . . . homos! Homos! Homos! *(Pause; she composes herself.)*
      Ah! Well . . . you will serve the people, all right. But not with the Revo-
      lution's money. This time, you use your own money.
Song: I have no money.
Chin: Shut up! And you won't stink up China anymore with your pervert
      stuff. You'll pollute the place where pollution begins—the West.
Song: What do you mean?
Chin: Shut up! You're going to France. Without a cent in your pocket. You
      find your consul's house, you make him pay your expenses—
Song: No.
Chin: And you give us weekly reports! Useful information!
Song: That's crazy. It's been four years.
Chin: Either that, or back to rehabilitation center!

Song: Comrade Chin, he's not going to support me! Not in France! He's a white man! I was just his plaything—

Chin: Oh yuck! Again with the sickening language. Where's my stick?

Song: You don't understand the mind of a man.

(Pause.)

Chin: Oh no? No I don't? Then how come I'm married, huh? How come I got a man? Five, six years ago, you always tell me those kinds of things. I felt very bad. But not now! Because what does the Chairman say? He tells us *I'm* now the smart one, you're now the nincompoop! *You're* the blackhead, the harebrain, the nitwit! You think you're so smart? You understand "The Mind of a Man"? Good! Then *you* go to France and be a pervert for Chairman Mao!

(Chin and Song *exit in opposite directions.)*

SCENE XI

Paris. 1968–70.

Gallimard *enters.*

Gallimard: And what was waiting for me back in Paris? Well, better Chinese food than I'd eaten in China. Friends and relatives. A little accounting, regular schedule, keeping track of traffic violations in the suburbs . . . And the indignity of students shouting the slogans of Chairman Mao at me—in French.

Helga: Rene? Rene? *(She enters, soaking wet.)* I've had a . . . a problem. *(She sneezes.)*

Gallimard: You're wet.

Helga: Yes, I . . . coming back from the grocer's. A group of students, waving red flags, they—

(Gallimard fetches a towel.)

Helga: —they ran by, I was caught up along with them. Before I knew what was happening—

(Gallimard gives her the towel.)

Helga: Thank you. The police started firing water cannons at us. I tried to shout, to tell them I was the wife of a diplomat, but—you know how it is . . . *(Pause.)* Needless to say, I lost the groceries. Rene, what's happening to France?

Gallimard: What's—? Well, nothing, really.

Helga: Nothing? The storefronts are in flames, there's glass in the streets, buildings are toppling—and I'm wet!

Gallimard: Nothing! . . . that I care to think about.

Helga: And is that why you stay in this room?

Gallimard: Yes, in fact.

Helga: With the incense burning? You know something? I hate incense. It
    smells so sickly sweet.
Gallimard: Well, I hate the French. Who just smell—period!
Helga: And the Chinese were better?
Gallimard: Please—don't start.
Helga: When we left, this exact same thing, the riots—
Gallimard: No, no . . .
Helga: Students screaming slogans, smashing down doors—
Gallimard: Helga—
Helga: It was all going on in China, too. Don't you remember?!
Gallimard: Helga! Please! *(Pause.)* You have never understood China, have
    you? You walk in here with these ridiculous ideas, that the West is
    falling apart, that China was spitting in our faces. You come in, dripping
    of the streets, and you leave water all over my floor. *(He grabs* Helga's
    towel, begins mopping up the floor.)
Helga: But it's the truth!
Gallimard: Helga, I want a divorce.

    (Pause; Gallimard *continues, mopping the floor.)*

Helga: I take it back. China is . . . beautiful. Incense, I like incense.
Gallimard: I had a mistress.
Helga: So?
Gallimard: For eight years.
Helga: I knew you would. I knew you would the day I married you. And now
    what? You want to marry her?
Gallimard: I can't. She's in China.
Helga: I see. You want to leave. For someone who's not here, is that right?
Gallimard: That's right.
Helga: You can't live with her, but still you don't want to live with me.
Gallimard: That's right.

    (Pause.)

Helga: Shit. How terrible that I can figure that out. *(Pause.)* I never thought
    I'd say it. But, in China, I was happy. I knew, in my own way, I knew that
    you were not everything you pretended to be. But the pretense—going
    on your arm to the embassy ball, visiting your office and the guards
    saying, "Good morning, good morning, Madame Gallimard"—the pre-
    tense . . . was very good indeed. *(Pause.)* I hope everyone is mean to you
    for the rest of your life. *(She exits.)*
Gallimard (To us.): Prophetic.

    (Marc enters with two drinks.)

Gallimard (To Marc.): In China, I was different from all other men.
Marc: Sure. You were white. Here's your drink.
Gallimard: I felt . . . touched.
Marc: In the head? Rene, I don't want to hear about the Oriental love god-
    dess. Okay? One night—can we just drink and throw up without a lot of
    conversation?

Gallimard: You still don't believe me, do you?

Marc: Sure I do. She was the most beautiful, et cetera, et cetera, blasé blasé.

(*Pause.*)

Gallimard: My life in the West has been such a disappointment.

Marc: Life in the West is like that. You'll get used to it. Look, you're driving me away. I'm leaving. Happy, now? (*He exits, then returns.*) Look, I have a date tomorrow night. You wanna come? I can fix you up with—

Gallimard: Of course. I would love to come.

(*Pause.*)

Marc: Uh—on second thought, no. You'd better get ahold of yourself first.

(*He exits;* Gallimard *nurses his drink.*)

Gallimard (To us.): This is the ultimate cruelty, isn't it? That I can talk and talk and to anyone listening, it's only air—too rich a diet to be swallowed by a mundane world. Why can't anyone understand? That in China, I once loved, and was loved by, very simply, the Perfect Woman.

(*Song enters, dressed as Butterfly in wedding dress.*)

Gallimard (To Song.): Not again. My imagination is hell. Am I asleep this time? Or did I drink too much?

Song: Rene?

Gallimard: God, it's too painful! That you speak?

Song: What are you talking about? Rene—touch me.

Gallimard: Why?

Song: I'm real. Take my hand.

Gallimard: Why? So you can disappear again and leave me clutching at the air? For the entertainment of my neighbors who—?

(*Song touches* Gallimard.)

Song: Rene?

(Gallimard *takes* Song's *hand. Silence.*)

Gallimard: Butterfly? I never doubted you'd return.

Song: You hadn't . . . forgotten—?

Gallimard: Yes, actually, I've forgotten everything. My mind, you see—there wasn't enough room in this hard head—not for the world *and* for you. No, there was only room for one. (*Beat.*) Come, look. See? Your bed has been waiting, with the Klimt poster you like, and—see? The xiang lu [incense burner] you gave me?

Song: I . . . don't know what to say.

Gallimard: There's nothing to say. Not at the end of a long trip. Can I make you some tea?

Song: But where's your wife?

Gallimard: She's by my side. She's by my side at last.

(Gallimard *reaches to embrace* Song. Song *sidesteps, dodging him.*)

Gallimard: Why?

Song (To us.): So I did return to Rene in Paris. Where I found—

Gallimard: Why do you run away? Can't we show them how we embraced that evening?

Song: Please, I'm talking.

Gallimard: You have to do what I say! I'm conjuring you up in *my* mind!

Song: Rene, I've never done what you've said. Why should it be any different in your mind? Now split—the story moves on, and I must change.

Gallimard: I welcomed you into my home! I didn't have to, you know! I could've left you penniless on the streets of Paris! But I took you in!

Song: Thank you.

Gallimard: So . . . please . . . don't change.

Song: You know I have to. You know I will. And anyway, what difference does it make? No matter what your eyes tell you, you can't ignore the truth. You already know too much.

(Gallimard *exits.* Song *turns to us.*)

Song: The change I'm going to make requires about five minutes. So I thought you might want to take this opportunity to stretch your legs, enjoy a drink, or listen to the musicians. I'll be here, when you return, right where you left me.

(Song *goes to a mirror in front of which is a wash basin of water. She starts to remove her makeup as stagelights go to half and houselights come up.*)

ACT THREE

SCENE I

A courthouse in Paris. 1986.

As he promised, Song *has completed the bulk of his transformation onstage by the time the houselights go down and the stagelights come up full. He removes his wig and kimono, leaving them on the floor. Underneath, he wears a well-cut suit.*

Song: So I'd done my job better than I had a right to expect. Well, give him some credit, too. He's right—I was in a fix when I arrived in Paris. I walked from the airport into town, then I located, by blind groping, the Chinatown district. Let me make one thing clear: whatever else may be said about the Chinese, they are stingy! I slept in doorways three days until I could find a tailor who would make me this kimono on credit. As it turns out, maybe I didn't even need it. Maybe he would've been happy to see me in a simple shift and mascara. But . . . better safe than sorry.

   That was 1970, when I arrived in Paris. For the next fifteen years, yes, I lived in a very comfy life. Some relief, believe me, after four years on the fucking commune in Nowheresville, China. Rene supported the boy and me, and I did some demonstrations around the country as part of my "cultural exchange" cover. And then there was the spying.

(Song *moves upstage, to a chair.* Toulon *enters as a* Judge, *wearing the appropriate wig and robes. He sits near* Song. *It's 1986, and* Song *is testifying in a courtroom.*)

Song: Not much at first. Rene had lost all his high-level contacts. Comrade Chin wasn't very interested in parking-ticket statistics. But finally, at my urging, Rene got a job as a courier, handling sensitive documents. He'd photograph them for me, and I'd pass them onto the Chinese embassy.

Judge: Did he understand the extent of his activity?

Song: He didn't ask. He knew that I needed those documents, and that was enough.

Judge: But he must've known he was passing classified information.

Song: I can't say.

Judge: He never asked what you were going to do with them?

Song: Nope.

(Pause.)

Judge: There is one thing that the court—indeed, that all of France—would like to know.

Song: Fire away.

Judge: Did Monsieur Gallimard know you were a man?

Song: Well, he never saw me completely naked. Ever.

Judge: But surely, he must've . . . how can I put this?

Song: Put it however you like. I'm not shy. He must've felt around?

Judge: Mmmmm.

Song: Not really. I did all the work. He just laid back. Of course we did enjoy more . . . complete union, and I suppose he *might* have wondered why I was always on my stomach, but . . . But what you're thinking is, "Of course a wrist must've brushed . . . a hand hit . . . over twenty years! Yeah. Well, Your Honor, it was my job to make him think I was a woman. And chew on this: it wasn't all that hard. See, my mother was a prostitute along the Bundt before the Revolution. And, uh, I think it's fair to say she learned a few things about Western men. So I borrowed her knowledge. In service to my country.

Judge: Would you care to enlighten the court with this secret knowledge? I'm sure we're all very curious.

Song: I'm sure you are. *(Pause.)* Okay, Rule One is: Men always believe what they want to hear. So a girl can tell the most obnoxious lies and the guys will believe them every time—"This is my first time"—"That's the biggest I've ever seen"—or *both*, which, if you really think about it, is not possible in a single lifetime. You've maybe heard those phrases a few times in your own life, yes, Your Honor?

Judge: It's not my life, Monsieur Song, which is on trial today.

Song: Okay, okay, just trying to lighten up the proceedings. Tough room.

Judge: Go on.

Song: Rule Two: As soon as a Western man comes into contact with the East—he's already confused. The West has sort of an international rape mentality towards the East. Do you know rape mentality?

Judge: Give us your definition, please.

Song: Basically, "Her mouth says no, but her eyes say yes." The West thinks of itself as masculine—big guns, big industry, big money—so the East is feminine—weak, delicate, poor . . . but good at art, and full of inscrutable wisdom—the feminine mystique.

    Her mouth says no, but her eyes say yes. The West believes the East, deep down, *wants* to be dominated—because a woman can't think for herself.

Judge: What does this have to do with my question?

Song: You expect Oriental countries to submit to your guns, and you expect Oriental women to be submissive to your men. That's why you say they make the best wives.

Judge: But why would that make it possible for you to fool Monsieur Gallimard? Please—get to the point.

Song: One, because when he finally met his fantasy woman, he wanted more than anything to believe that she was, in fact, a woman. And second, I am an Oriental. And being an Oriental, I could never be completely a man.

    (Pause.)

Judge: Your armchair political theory is tenuous, Monsieur Song.

Song: You think so? That's why you'll lose in all your dealings with the East.

Judge: Just answer my question: did he know you were a man?

    (Pause.)

Song: You know, your Honor, I never asked.

Scene II

    Same.

    Music from the "Death Scene" from Butterfly *blares over the house speakers. It is the loudest thing we've heard in this play.*

    Gallimard *enters, crawling towards* Song's *wig and kimono.*

Gallimard: Butterfly? Butterfly?

    *(*Song *remains a man, in the witness box, delivering a testimony we do not hear.)*

Gallimard (To us.): In my moment of greatest shame, here, in this courtroom—with that . . . person up there, telling the world . . . What strikes me especially is how shallow he is, how glib and obsequious . . . completely . . . without substance! The type that prowls around discos with a gold medallion stinking of garlic. So little like my Butterfly.

Yet even in this moment my mind remains agile, flip-flopping like a man on a trampoline. Even now, my picture dissolves, and I see that . . . witness . . . talking to me.

(Song *suddenly stands straight up in his witness box, and looks at* Gallimard.)

Song: Yes. You. White man.

(Song *steps out of the witness box, and moves downstage towards* Gallimard. *Light change.*)

Gallimard (To Song.*):* Who? Me?
Song: Do you see any other white men?
Gallimard: Yes. There're white men all around. This is a French courtroom.
Song: So you are an adventurous imperialist. Tell me, why did it take you so long? To come back to this place.
Gallimard: What place?
Song: This theatre in China. Where we met many years ago.
Gallimard (To us.): And once again, against my will, I am transported.

(*Chinese opera music comes up on the speakers.* Song *begins to do opera moves, as he did the night they met.*)

Song: Do you remember? The night you gave your heart?
Gallimard: It was a long time ago.
Song: Not long enough. A night that turned your world upside down.
Gallimard: Perhaps.
Song: Oh, be honest with me. What's another bit of flattery when you've already given me twenty years' worth? It's a wonder my head hasn't swollen to the size of China.
Gallimard: Who's to say it hasn't?
Song: Who's to say? And what's the shame? In pride? You think I could've pulled this off if I wasn't already full of pride when we met? No, not just pride. Arrogance. It takes arrogance, really—to believe you can will, with your eyes and your lips, the destiny of another. *(He dances.)* C'mon. Admit it. You still want me. Even in slacks and a button-down collar.
Gallimard: I don't see what the point of—
Song: You don't? Well maybe, Rene, just maybe—I want you.
Gallimard: You do?
Song: Then again, maybe I'm just playing with you. How can you tell? *(Reprising his feminine character, he sidles up to* Gallimard.*)* "How I wish there were even a small cafe to sit in. With men in tuxedos, and cappuccinos, and bad expatriate jazz." Now you want to kiss me, don't you?
Gallimard (Pulling away.): What makes you—?
Song: —so sure? See? I take the words from your mouth. Then I wait for you to come and retrieve them. *(He reclines on the floor.)*
Gallimard: Why? Why do you treat me so cruelly?
Song: Perhaps I *was* treating you cruelly. But now—I'm being nice. Come here, my little one.

Gallimard: I'm not your little one!

Song: My mistake. It's I who am *your* little one, right?

Gallimard: Yes, I—

Song: So come get your little one. If you like. I may even let you strip me.

Gallimard: I mean, you were! Before . . . but not like this!

Song: I was? Then perhaps I still am. If you look hard enough.

(*He starts to remove his clothes.*)

Gallimard: What—what are you doing?

Song: Helping you to see through my act.

Gallimard: Stop that! I don't want to! I don't—

Song: Oh, but you asked me to strip, remember?

Gallimard: What? That was years ago! And I took it back!

Song: No. You postponed it. Postponed the inevitable. Today, the inevitable has come calling.

(*From the speakers, cacophony:* Butterfly *mixed in with Chinese gongs.*)

Gallimard: No! Stop! I don't want to see!

Song: Then look away.

Gallimard: You're only in my mind! All this is in my mind! I order you! To stop!

Song: To what? To strip? That's just what I'm—

Gallimard: No! Stop! I want you—!

Song: You want me?

Gallimard: To stop!

Song: You know something, Rene? Your mouth says no, but your eyes say yes. Turn them away. I dare you.

Gallimard: I don't have to! Every night, you say you're going to strip, but then I beg you and you stop!

Song: I guess tonight is different.

Gallimard: Why? Why should that be?

Song: Maybe I've become frustrated. Maybe I'm saying "Look at me, you fool!" Or maybe I'm just feeling . . . sexy. (*He is down to his briefs.*)

Gallimard: Please. This is unnecessary. I know what you are.

Song: Do you? What am I?

Gallimard: A—a man.

Song: You don't really believe that.

Gallimard: Yes I do! I knew all the time somewhere that my happiness was temporary, my love a deception. But my mind kept the knowledge at bay. To make the wait bearable.

Song: Monsieur Gallimard—the wait is over.

(Song *drops his briefs. He is naked. Sound cue out. Slowly, we and* Song *come to the realization that what we had thought to be* Gallimard's *sobbing is actually his laughter.*)

Gallimard: Oh god! What an idiot! Of course!

Song: Rene—what?

Gallimard: Look at you! You're a man! *(He bursts into laughter again.)*

Song: I fail to see what's so funny!

Gallimard: "You fail to see—!" I mean, you never did have much of a sense of humor, did you? I just think it's ridiculously funny that I've wasted so much time on just a man!

Song: Wait. I'm not "just a man."

Gallimard: No? Isn't that what you've been trying to convince me of?

Song: Yes, but what I mean—

Gallimard: And now, I finally believe you, and you tell me it's not true? I think you must have some kind of identity problem.

Song: Will you listen to me?

Gallimard: Why?! I've been listening to you for twenty years. Don't I deserve a vacation?

Song: I'm not just any man!

Gallimard: Then, what exactly are you?

Song: Rene, how can you ask—? Okay, what about this?

(He picks up Butterfly's robes, starts to dance around. No music.)

Gallimard: Yes, that's very nice. I have to admit.

(Song holds out his arm to Gallimard.)

Song: It's the same skin you've worshiped for years. Touch it.

Gallimard: Yes, it does feel the same.

Song: Now—close your eyes.

(Song covers Gallimard's eyes with one hand. With the other, Song draws Gallimard's hand up to his face. Gallimard, like a blind man, lets his hands run over Song's face.)

Gallimard: This skin, I remember. The curve of her face, the softness of her cheek, her hair against the back of my hand . . .

Song: I'm your Butterfly. Under the robes, beneath everything, it was always me. Now, open your eyes and admit it—you adore me. *(He removes his hand from Gallimard's eyes.)*

Gallimard: You, who knew every inch of my desires—how could you, of all people, have made such a mistake?

Song: What?

Gallimard: You showed me your true self. When all I loved was the lie. A perfect lie, which you let fall to the ground—and now, it's old and soiled.

Song: So—you never really loved me? Only when I was playing a part?

Gallimard: I'm a man who loved a woman created by a man. Everything else—simply falls short.

(Pause.)

Song: What am I supposed to do now?

Gallimard: You were a fine spy, Monsieur Song, with an even finer accomplice. But now I believe you should go. Get out of my life!

Song: Go where? Rene, you can't live without me. Not after twenty years.

Gallimard: I certainly can't live with you—not after twenty years of betrayal.

Song: Don't be so stubborn! Where will you go?

Gallimard: I have a date . . . with my Butterfly.

Song: So, throw away your pride. And come . . .

Gallimard: Get away from me! Tonight, I've finally learned to tell fantasy from reality. And, knowing the difference, I choose fantasy.

Song: I'm your fantasy!

Gallimard: You? You're as real as hamburger. Now get out! I have a date with my Butterfly and I don't want your body polluting the room! *(He tosses Song's suit at him.)* Look at these—you dress like a pimp.

Song: Hey! These are Armani slacks and—! *(He puts on his briefs and slacks.)* Let's just say . . . I'm disappointed in you, Rene. In the crush of your adoration, I thought you'd become something more. More like . . . a woman.

　　　But no. Men. You're like the rest of them. It's all in the way we dress, and make up our faces, and bat our eyelashes. You really have so little imagination!

Gallimard: You, Monsieur Song? Accuse me of too little imagination? You, if anyone, should know—I am pure imagination. And in imagination I will remain. Now get out!

(Gallimard bodily removes Song from the stage, taking his kimono.)

Song: Rene! I'll never put on those robes again! You'll be sorry!

Gallimard (To Song.): I'm already sorry! *(Looking at the kimono in his hands.)* Exactly as sorry . . . as a Butterfly.

SCENE III

　　M. Gallimard's *prison cell. Paris. Present.*

Gallimard: I've played out the events of my life night after night, always searching for a new ending to my story, one where I leave this cell and return forever to my Butterfly's arms.

　　Tonight I realize my search is over. That I've looked all along in the wrong place. And now, to you, I will prove that my love was not in vain—by returning to the world of fantasy where I first met her.

(He picks up the kimono; dancers enter.)

Gallimard: There is a vision of the Orient that I have. Of slender women in chong sams and kimonos who die for the love of unworthy foreign devils. Who are born and raised to be the perfect women. Who take whatever punishment we give them, and bounce back, strengthened by love, unconditionally. It is a vision that has become my life.

(Dancers bring the wash basin to him and help him make up his face.)

Gallimard: In public, I have continued to deny that Song Liling is a man.

This brings me headlines, and is a source of great embarrassment to my French colleagues, who can now be sent into a coughing fit by the mere mention of Chinese food. But alone, in my cell, I have long since faced the truth.

And the truth demands a sacrifice. For mistakes made over the course of a lifetime. My mistakes were simple and absolute—the man I loved was a cad, a bounder. He deserved nothing but a kick in the behind, and instead I gave him . . . all my love.

Yes—love. Why not admit it all? That was my undoing, wasn't it? Love warped my judgment, blinded my eyes, rearranged the very lines on my face . . . until I could look in the mirror and see nothing but . . . a woman.

(Dancers help him put on the Butterfly wig.)

Gallimard: I have a vision. Of the Orient. That, deep within its almond eyes, there are still women. Women willing to sacrifice themselves for the love of a man. Even a man whose love is completely without worth.

(Dancers assist Gallimard *in donning the kimono. They hand him a knife.)*
Gallimard: Death with honor is better than life . . . life with dishonor. *(He sets himself center stage, in a seppuku position.)* The love of a Butterfly can withstand many things—unfaithfulness, loss, even abandonment. But how can it face the one sin that implies all others? The devastating knowledge that, underneath it all, the object of her love was nothing more, nothing less than . . . a man. *(He sets the tip of the knife against his body.)* It is 19___. And I have found her at last. In a prison on the outskirts of Paris. My name is Rene Gallimard—also known as Madame Butterfly.

(Gallimard turns upstage and plunges his knife into his body, as music from the "Love Duet" blares over the speakers. He collapses into the arms of the dancers, who lay him reverently on the floor. The image holds for several beats. Then a tight special up on Song, *who stands as a man, staring at the dead* Gallimard. *He smokes a cigarette; the smoke filters up through the lights. Two words leave his lips.)*
Song: Butterfly? Butterfly?

(Smoke rises as lights fade slowly to black.)

——— **DAVID HENRY HWANG** ———
(b. 1957) Web   *www*

Born and raised in California, David Henry Hwang graduated from Stanford University, where, by his own admission, he entered an "isolationist-nationalist" phase of writing only about Chinese America. At Stanford, he began writing a trilogy about Chinese Americans with the play *FOB* (1979), which won an Obie Award for Best Play of the Year for its New York production in 1981. He then moved on to Yale University to continue his education. After winning a Tony Award for its success on Broadway, *M. Butterfly* has proved an international success and, since its premiere in 1988, Hwang has won another Obie Award for *Golden Child* (1997).

TOPICS FOR CRITICAL THINKING

1. To what extent does Gallimard's portrayal of Pinkerton, the "womanizing cad" in Puccini's *Madame Butterfly*, help explain his fantasies about Oriental women? More generally, how does Hwang's play reflect the influence of Puccini's opera?

2. In Act Six, Song identifies "the submissive Oriental woman and the cruel white man" as one of Gallimard's "favorite fantasies." Is she right? What does "submissive" mean in this context?

3. What role does Helga play?

4. *M. Butterfly* is structured in episodes, brief scenes played largely through Gallimard's memory. What emotional effect does this structure create? What difference does the flashback structure of the play cause?

5. Does the narrative of the play prepare us adequately for its violent conclusion? What are we to make of the gender reversal in the play's final moment, that of Gallimard becoming Madame Butterfly and Song appearing as a man?

6. How would you describe Gallimard and the punishment he suffers? Is he, for example, a tragic hero? If so, does this make *M. Butterfly* a tragedy?

TOPIC FOR CRITICAL WRITING

Song's masquerade requires not only his physical dexterity, but also Gallimard's fantasies about and experiences with women. Discuss male fantasies about women and Hwang's development of women characters in the play. How are both complicitous in Song's deception? What would the play lack without them?

Critical Perspective: On D. H. Hwang's Politics in *M. Butterfly*

"[In *M. Butterfly*] Hwang teases us with our prurient curiosity: Just *how* was this man duped for decades about the gender of his partner—or did he know all along, and repress the knowledge? But these questions eventually prove less tantalizing than those Hwang emphasizes—not the "hows" of this seduction but the "whys." If we want to believe something badly enough—and if it plays directly upon our vanities and prejudices—then, the playwright suggests, nothing so prosaic as physical reality is likely to stop us."

—Scott Rosenberg, "Can We Talk?" (1994)

Critical Perspective: On Racism, Sexism, and Imperialism

"[T]hroughout the range of his plays, Hwang is trying to convey a fairly consistent view of the 'struggle that begins here now, in our hearts.' When he portrays the sadomasochistic power games people play, he would seem to be seeking to unsettle the audience, to make them reflect upon dehumanizing relationships. . . . Realizing the relationship of misogyny to racism and imperialism, Hwang says of *M. Butterfly*, 'I discovered the relationship of the "isms": racism, sexism, imperialism. These are all part of the same impulse to downgrade "the other," that person who is different from oneself.'"
—Vera Jiji, "The Plays of David Hwang: The Gaze of the Medusa" (1998)

51   The Contemporary Stage: Two Writers

This final selection of plays features the work of two shining—and very distinct—lights of the British and American stages.

www Sir Harold Pinter **Web** is, arguably, one of the most significant dramatists writing today, having contributed major works to the contemporary theater for well over forty years. He has been a director of England's National Theatre and written prolifically for film as well, inspiring a generation of drama-

www tists in the process. By contrast, Margaret Edson, **Web** a kindergarten teacher in Atlanta, spent much of the 1990s writing and refining her only complete play, *Wit*, which won the Pulitzer Prize for Drama in 1999 and was adapted in 2001 into an HBO film starring Emma Thompson (in which Pinter, returning to his theatrical roots as an actor, played a role). The enormous critical and popular success of *Wit*—it has been and continues to be performed by repertory companies across the country—is almost unprecedented in the annals of American theater.

Rather than offer sustained interpretations of the plays written by this talented pair—by this point, you are prepared to do so on your own—this introduction merely suggests a few ways in which these contemporary plays connect to texts and issues raised earlier in *Understanding Literature*. For example, both extend and revise formal innovations discussed earlier. *Wit*, for example, with its direct addresses to the audience and constant reminders of its fictiveness, recalls the **meta-theatrics** of *M. Butterfly*. *Ashes to Ashes* prompts our reconsideration of the movement in modern drama from realism to expressionism to modified or hybrid combinations of the two forms. In 1920s drama and film, in Tennessee Williams's criticism of realism in the 1940s, and more recently in dramatic theory, realism is often denigrated as an antiquated form whose time has passed. Echoing Williams, one critic of photographic realism complained that it is "stuck in a dreary dead-end . . . piled high in kitchen sinks." Perhaps it is. Yet even opponents of realism concede that many of today's most memorable plays—by David Mamet, August Wilson, Marsha Norman, to name but three—are largely realistic in terms of dramatic form. But is this realism identical with that of Henrik Ibsen or Anton Chekhov? What has happened to realism as the twentieth century evolved? Or, more to the point, how does a playwright like Pinter redefine realism at the dawn of the twenty-first century?

Such a formal question might be asked about *Ashes to Ashes*. The set of the play seems familiar enough, however vaguely it is sketched in comparison to Ibsen's meticulously detailed drawing rooms:

> A house in the country.
> Ground floor room. A large window. Garden beyond.
> Two armchairs. Two lamps.
> Early evening. Summer.

But then these descriptions follow:

> The room darkens during the course of the play.
> By the end of the play the room and the garden beyond are only dimly defined.
> The lamplight has become very bright but does not illumine the room.

To these lighting cues, Pinter adds nonrealistic aural effects to underscore the emotional trauma Rebecca has suffered. For a 1999 New York production of the play, the director began the action with a siren heard off in the distance, suggesting that the apparent serenity of the setting conceals something terrible. As Rebecca recounts the forcible separation of mothers and their children, the room literally echoes her anguish:

> Rebecca: They took us to the trains
> Echo: The trains . . .
> Rebecca: They were taking the babies away
> Echo: the babies away

The result is a painful repetition of a past that Rebecca seems scarcely to grasp but nonetheless relives, although it is never quite clear if she is recounting an event she actually experienced. Some readers discern in *Ashes to Ashes*, and in this scene in particular, an overt allusion to Nazism and the atrocities of World War II. Theatrically, this connection to a larger event or collective trauma is achieved by means developed earlier in the century as expressionist devices: by lighting, aural effects, and other aspects of the **mise-en-scène.** How different are these strategies from those Eugene O'Neill employs in *The Emperor Jones* (see Chapter 46)?

The trauma in Margaret Edson's *Wit* is equally acute and similarly painful. For her protagonist Vivian Bearing, a professor of seventeenth-century British poetry is dying of ovarian cancer. Or, rather, she is already dead and speaking to us at the beginning of the play with a clear sense of how it will conclude. Bearing, intellectually as tough as nails, relishes the linguistic challenges of one poet in particular, John Donne. She spent her scholarly life unpacking the paradoxes and intellectual puzzles—not to mention the sharp, complicated wit—of Donne's "Holy Sonnets," and teaches her classes with the same sense of lofty standards and mental toughness. By comparison to Donne, one of her doctors and a former student declares, Shakespeare "sounds like a Hallmark card." But which of these two, brilliant paradoxes or the sentiment of a Hallmark card, does one enjoy—even *need*—in the painful endgame of a terminal struggle with so implacable a foe as cancer? And how does a playwright develop an engaging play we want to watch—not to mention a conflict—out of a dramatic situation whose end is so obvious from the beginning? It requires great resourcefulness—and wit. Edson displays both virtues in abundance.

Enjoy these plays, two unique and powerful expressions of contemporary drama in the Western world, and consult the Website for biographical and critical information about these two forces in international drama in the twenty-first century.

ᗡᗡᗡ

HAROLD PINTER

Ashes to Ashes   *(1996)*

CHARACTERS

Devlin
Rebecca

Both in their forties

TIME: NOW

A house in the country.

Ground floor room. A large window.
Garden beyond.

Two armchairs. Two lamps.

Early evening. Summer.

The room darkens during the course of the play.
The lamplight intensifies.

By the end of the play the room and the garden beyond are only dimly defined.
The lamplight has become very bright but does not illumine the room.

Devlin *standing with drink.* Rebecca *sitting.*

Silence.

Rebecca: Well . . . for example . . . he would stand over me and clench his fist. And then he'd put his other hand on my neck and grip it and bring my head towards him. His fist . . . grazed my mouth. And he'd say, 'Kiss my fist.'
Devlin: And did you?
Rebecca: Oh yes. I kissed his fist. The knuckles. And then he'd open his hand and give me the palm of his hand . . . to kiss . . . which I kissed.

Pause.

And then I would speak.

Devlin: What did you say? You said what? What did you say?

Pause.

Rebecca: I said, 'Put your hand round my throat.' I murmured it through his hand, as I was kissing it, but he heard my voice, he heard it through his hand, he felt my voice in his hand, he heard it there.

Silence.

Devlin: And did he? Did he put his hand round your throat?

Rebecca: Oh yes. He did. He did. And he held it there, very gently, very gently, so gently. He adored me, you see.

Devlin: He adored you?

Pause.

What do you mean, he adored you? What do you mean?

Pause.

Are you saying he put no pressure on your throat? Is that what you're saying?

Rebecca: No.

Devlin: What then? What are you saying?

Rebecca: He put a little . . . . pressure . . . on my throat, yes. So that my head started to go back, gently but truly.

Devlin: And your body? Where did your body go?

Rebecca: My body went back, slowly but truly.

Devlin: So your legs were opening?

Rebecca: Yes.

Pause.

Devlin: Your legs were opening?

Rebecca: Yes.

Silence.

Devlin: Do you feel you're being hypnotised?

Rebecca: When?

Devlin: Now.

Rebecca: No.

Devlin: Really?

Rebecca: No.

Devlin: Why not?

Rebecca: Who by?

Devlin: By me.

Rebecca: You?

Devlin: What do you think?

Rebecca: I think you're a fuckpig.
Devlin: Me a fuckpig? Me! You must be joking.

> Rebecca *smiles.*

Rebecca: Me joking? You must be joking.

> *Pause.*

Devlin: You understand why I'm asking you these questions. Don't you? Put yourself in my place. I'm compelled to ask you questions. There are so many things I don't know. I know nothing . . . about any of this. Nothing. I'm in the dark. I need light. Or do you think my questions are illegitimate?

> *Pause.*

Rebecca: What questions?

> *Pause.*

Devlin: Look. It would mean a great deal to me if you could define him more clearly.
Rebecca: Define him? What do you mean, define him?
Devlin: Physically. I mean, what did he actually look like? If you see what I mean? Length, breadth . . . that sort of thing. Height, width. I mean, quite apart from his . . . disposition, whatever that may have been . . . or his character . . . or his spiritual . . . standing . . . I just want, well, I need . . . to have a clearer idea of him . . . well, not a clearer idea . . . just an idea, in fact . . . because I have absolutely no idea . . . as things stand . . . of what he looked like. I mean, what did he *look like?* Can't you give him a shape for me, a concrete shape? I want a concrete image of him, you see . . . an image I can carry about with me. I mean, all you can talk of are his hands, one hand over your face, the other on the back of your neck, then the first one on your throat. There must be more to him than hands. What about eyes? Did he have any eyes?
Rebecca: What colour?

> *Pause.*

Devlin: That's precisely the question I'm asking you . . . my darling.
Rebecca: How odd to be called darling. No one has ever called me darling. Apart from my lover.
Devlin: I don't believe it.
Rebecca: You don't believe what?
Devlin: I don't believe he ever called you darling.

> *Pause.*

> Do you think my use of the word is illegitimate?
Rebecca: What word?
Devlin: Darling.

Rebecca: Oh yes, you called me darling. How funny.

Devlin: Funny? Why?

Rebecca: Well, how can you possibly call me darling? I'm not your darling.

Devlin: Yes you are.

Rebecca: Well I don't want to be your darling. It's the last thing I want to be. I'm nobody's darling.

Devlin: That's a song.

Rebecca: What?

Devlin: 'I'm nobody's baby now'.

Rebecca: It's '*You're* nobody's baby now'. But anyway, I didn't use the word baby.

Pause.

I can't tell you what he looked like.

Devlin: Have you forgotten?

Rebecca: No. I haven't forgotten. But that's not the point. Anyway, he went away years ago.

Devlin: Went away? Where did he go?

Rebecca: His job took him away. He had a job.

Devlin: What was it?

Rebecca: What?

Devlin: What kind of job was it? What job?

Rebecca: I think it had something to do with a travel agency. I think he was some kind of courier. No. No, he wasn't. That was only a part-time job. I mean that was only part of the job in the agency. He was quite high up, you see. He had a lot of responsibilities.

Pause.

Devlin: What sort of agency?

Rebecca: A travel agency.

Devlin: What sort of travel agency?

Rebecca: He was a guide, you see. A guide.

Devlin: A tourist guide?

Pause.

Rebecca: Did I ever tell you about that place . . . about the time he took me to that place?

Devlin: What place?

Rebecca: I'm sure I told you.

Devlin: No. You never told me.

Rebecca: How funny. I could swear I had. Told you.

Devlin: You haven't told me anything. You've never spoken about him before. You haven't told me anything.

Pause.

What place?

Rebecca: Oh, it was a kind of factory, I suppose.

Devlin: What do you mean, a kind of factory? Was it a factory or wasn't it? And if it was a factory, what kind of factory was it?

Rebecca: Well, they were making things—just like any other factory. But it wasn't the usual kind of factory.

Devlin: Why not?

Rebecca: They were all wearing caps . . . the workpeople . . . soft caps . . . and they took them off when he came in, leading me, when he led me down the alleys between the rows of workpeople.

Devlin: They took their caps off? You mean they doffed them?

Rebecca: Yes.

Devlin: Why did they do that?

Rebecca: He told me afterwards it was because they had such great respect for him.

Devlin: Why?

Rebecca: Because he ran a really tight ship, he said. They had total faith in him. They respected his . . . purity, his . . . conviction. They would follow him over a cliff and into the sea, if he asked them, he said. And sing in a chorus, as long as he led them. They were in fact very musical, he said.

Devlin: What did they make of you?

Rebecca: Me? Oh, they were sweet. I smiled at them. And immediately every single one of them smiled back.

Pause.

The only thing was—the place was so damp. It was exceedingly damp.

Devlin: And they weren't dressed for the weather?

Rebecca: No.

Pause.

Devlin: I thought you said he worked for a travel agency?

Rebecca: And there was one other thing. I wanted to go to the bathroom. But I simply couldn't find it. I looked everywhere. I'm sure they had one. But I never found out where it was.

Pause.

He did work for a travel agency. He was a guide. He used to go to the local railway station and walk down the platform and tear all the babies from the arms of their screaming mothers.

Pause.

Devlin: Did he?

Silence.

Rebecca: By the way, I'm terribly upset.

Devlin: Are you? Why?

Rebecca: Well, it's about that police siren we heard a couple of minutes ago.

Devlin: What police siren?

Rebecca: Didn't you hear it? You must have heard it. Just a couple of minutes ago.

Devlin: What about it?

Rebecca: Well, I'm just terribly upset.

> *Pause.*

I'm just incredibly upset.

> *Pause.*

Don't you want to know why? Well, I'm going to tell you anyway. If I can't tell you who can I tell? Well, I'll tell you anyway. It just hit me so hard. You see . . . as the siren faded away in my ears I knew it was becoming louder and louder for somebody else.

Devlin: You mean that it's always being heard by somebody, somewhere? Is that what you're saying?

Rebecca: Yes. Always. Forever.

Devlin: Does that make you feel secure?

Rebecca: No! It makes me feel insecure! Terribly insecure.

Devlin: Why?

Rebecca: I hate it fading away. I hate it echoing away. I hate it leaving me. I hate losing it. I hate somebody else possessing it. I want it to be mine, all the time. It's such a beautiful sound. Don't you think?

Devlin: Don't worry, there'll always be another one. There's one on its way to you now. Believe me. You'll hear it again soon. Any minute.

Rebecca: Will I?

Devlin: Sure. They're very busy people, the police. There's so much for them to do. They've got so much to take care of, to keep their eye on. They keep getting signals, mostly in code. There isn't one minute of the day when they're not charging around one corner or another in the world, in their police cars, ringing their sirens. So you can take comfort from that, at least. Can't you? You'll never be lonely again. You'll never be without a police siren. I promise you.

> *Pause.*

Listen. This chap you were just talking about . . . I mean this chap you and I have been talking about . . . in a manner of speaking . . . when exactly did you meet him? I mean when did all this happen exactly? I haven't . . . how can I put this . . . quite got it into focus. Was it before you knew me or after you knew me? That's a question of some importance. I'm sure you'll appreciate that.

Rebecca: By the way, there's something I've been dying to tell you.

Devlin: What?

Rebecca: It was when I was writing a note, a few notes for the laundry. Well . . . to put it bluntly . . . a laundry list. Well. I put my pen on that little coffee table and it rolled off.

Devlin: No?

Rebecca: It rolled right off, onto the carpet. In front of my eyes.

Devlin: Good God.

Rebecca: This pen, this perfectly innocent pen.

Devlin: You can't know it was innocent.

Rebecca: Why not?

Devlin: Because you don't know where it had been. You don't know how many other hands have held it, how many other hands have written with it, what other people have been doing with it. You know nothing of its history. You know nothing of its parents' history.

Rebecca: A pen has no parents.

Pause.

Devlin: You can't sit there and say things like that.

Rebecca: I can sit here.

Devlin: You can't sit there and say things like that.

Rebecca: You don't believe I'm entitled to sit here? You don't think I'm entitled to sit in this chair, in the place where I live?

Devlin: I'm saying that you're not entitled to sit in that chair or in or on any other chair and say things like that and it doesn't matter whether you live here or not.

Rebecca: I'm not entitled to say things like what?

Devlin: That that pen was innocent.

Rebecca: You think it was guilty?

Silence.

Devlin: I'm letting you off the hook. Have you noticed? I'm letting you slip. Or perhaps it's me who's slipping. It's dangerous. Do you notice? I'm in a quicksand.

Rebecca: Like God.

Devlin: God? God? You think God is sinking into a quicksand? That's what I would call a truly disgusting perception. If it can be dignified by the word perception. Be careful how you talk about God. He's the only God we have. If you let him go he won't come back. He won't even look back over his shoulder. And then what will you do? You know what it'll be like, such a vacuum? It'll be like England playing Brazil at Wembley and not a sole in the stadium. Can you imagine? Playing both halves to a totally empty house. The game of the century. Absolute silence. Not a soul watching. Absolute silence. Apart from the referee's whistle and a fair bit of fucking and blinding. If you turn away from God it means that the great and noble game of soccer will fall into permanent oblivion. No score for extra time after extra time after extra time, no score for time everlasting, for time without end. Absence. Stalemate. Paralysis. A world without a winner.

Pause.

I hope you get the picture.

Pause.

Now let me say this. A little while ago you made . . . shall we say . . . you made a somewhat oblique reference to your bloke . . . your lover? . . . and babies and mothers, etc. And platforms. I inferred from this that you were talking about some kind of atrocity. Now let me ask you this. What authority do you think you yourself possess which would give you the right to discuss such an atrocity?

Rebecca: I have no such authority. Nothing has ever happened to me. Nothing has ever happened to any of my friends. I have never suffered. Nor have my friends.

Devlin: Good.

Pause.

Shall we talk more intimately? Let's talk about more intimate things, let's talk about something more personal, about something within your own immediate experience. I mean, for example, when the hairdresser takes your head in his hands and starts to wash your hair very gently and to massage your scalp, when he does that, when your eyes are closed and he does that, he has your entire trust, doesn't he? It's not just your head which is in his hands, is it, it's your life, it's your spiritual . . . welfare.

Pause.

So you see what I wanted to know was this . . . when your lover had his hand on your throat, did he remind you of your hairdresser?

Pause.

I'm talking about your lover. The man who tried to murder you.

Rebecca: Murder me?

Devlin: Do you to death.

Rebecca: No, no. He didn't try to murder me. He didn't want to murder me.

Devlin: He suffocated you and strangled you. As near as makes no difference. According to your account. Didn't he?

Rebecca: No, no. He felt compassion for me. He adored me.

Pause.

Devlin: Did he have a name, this chap? Was he a foreigner? And where was I at the time? What do you want me to understand? Were you unfaithful to me? Why didn't you confide in me? Why didn't you confess? You would have felt so much better. Honestly. You could have treated me like a priest. You could have put me on my mettle. I've always wanted to be put on my mettle. It used to be one of my lifetime ambitions. Now I've missed my big chance. Unless all this happened before I met you. In which case you have no obligation to tell me anything. Your past is not my business. I wouldn't dream of telling you about my past. Not that I had one. When you lead a life of scholarship you can't be bothered with the humorous realities, you know, tits, that kind of thing. Your mind is on other things, have you got an attentive landlady, can she come up with bacon and eggs after eleven o'clock at night, is the bed warm, does the sun rise in the right direction, is the soup cold? Only once in a blue moon do you wobble the chambermaid's bottom, on the assumption there is one—chambermaid not bottom—but of course none of this applies when you have a wife. When you have a wife you let thought, ideas and reflection take their course. Which means you never let the best man win. Fuck the best man, that's always been my motto. It's the man who ducks his head and moves on through no matter what wind or weather who gets there in the end. A man with guts and application.

Pause.

A man who doesn't give a shit.
A man with a rigid sense of duty.

Pause.

There's no contradiction between those last two statements. Believe me.

Pause.

Do you follow the drift of my argument?

Rebecca: Oh yes, there's something I've forgotten to tell you. It was funny. I looked out of the garden window, out of the window into the garden, in the middle of summer, in that house in Dorset, do you remember? Oh no, you weren't there. I don't think anyone else was there. No. I was all by myself. I was alone. I was looking out of the window and I saw a whole crowd of people walking through the woods, on their way to the sea, in the direction of the sea. They seemed to be very cold, they were wearing coats, although it was such a beautiful day. A beautiful, warm, Dorset day. They were carrying bags. There were . . . guides . . . ushering them, guiding them along. They walked through the woods and I could see them in the distance walking across the cliff and down to the sea. Then I lost sight of them. I was really quite curious so I went upstairs to the highest window in the house and I looked way over the top of the treetops and I could see down to the beach. The guides . . . were ushering all these people across the beach. It was such a lovely day. It was so still and the sun was shining. And I saw all these people walk into the sea. The tide covered them slowly. Their bags bobbed about in the waves.

Devlin: When was that? When did you live in Dorset? I've never lived in Dorset.

Pause.

Rebecca: Oh by the way somebody told me the other day that there's a condition known as mental elephantiasis.

Devlin: What do you mean, 'somebody told you'? What do you mean, 'the other day'? What are you talking about?

Rebecca: This mental elephantiasis means that when you spill an ounce of gravy, for example, it immediately expands and becomes a vast sea of gravy. It becomes a sea of gravy which surrounds you on all sides and you suffocate in a voluminous sea of gravy. It's terrible. But it's all your own fault. You brought it upon yourself. You are not the *victim* of it, you

are the *cause* of it. Because it was you who spilt the gravy in the first
place, it was you who handed over the bundle.

Pause.

Devlin: The what?
Rebecca: The bundle.

Pause.

Devlin: So what's the question? Are you prepared to drown in your own
gravy? Or are you prepared to die for your country? Look. What do
you say, sweetheart? Why don't we go out and drive into town and take
in a movie?
Rebecca: That's funny, somewhere in a dream . . . a long time ago . . . I heard
someone calling me sweetheart.

Pause.

I looked up. I'd been dreaming. I don't know whether I looked up in
the dream or as I opened my eyes. But in this dream a voice was calling.
That I'm certain of. This voice was calling me. It was calling me
sweetheart.

Pause.

Yes.

Pause.

I walked out into the frozen city. Even the mud was frozen. And the snow
was a funny colour. It wasn't white. Well, it was white but there were
other colours in it. It was as if there were veins running through it. And it
wasn't smooth, as snow is, as snow should be. It was bumpy. And when I
got to the railway station I saw the train. Other people were there.

Pause.

And my best friend, the man I had given my heart to, the man I knew
was the man for me the moment we met, my dear, my most precious
companion, I watched him walk down the platform and tear all the babies from the arms of their screaming mothers.

Silence.

Devlin: Did you see Kim and the kids?

She looks at him.

You were going to see Kim and the kids today.

She stares at him.

Your sister Kim and the kids.
Rebecca: Oh, Kim! And the kids, yes. Yes. Yes, of course I saw them. I had tea
with them. Didn't I tell you?

Devlin: No.
Rebecca: Of course I saw them.

Pause.

Devlin: How were they?
Rebecca: Ben's talking.
Devlin: Really? What's he saying?
Rebecca: Oh, things like 'My name is Ben'. Things like that. And 'Mummy's name is Mummy'. Things like that.
Devlin: What about Betsy?
Rebecca: She's crawling.
Devlin: No, really?
Rebecca: I think she'll be walking before we know where we are. Honestly.
Devlin: Probably talking too. Saying things like 'My name is Betsy'.
Rebecca: Yes, of course I saw them. I had tea with them. But oh . . . my poor sister . . . she doesn't know what to do.
Devlin: What do you mean?
Rebecca: Well, he wants to come back . . . you know . . . he keeps phoning and asking her to take him back. He says he can't bear it, he says he's given the other one up, he says he's living quite alone, he's given the other one up.
Devlin: Has he?
Rebecca: He says he has. He says he misses the kids.

Pause.

Devlin: Does he miss his wife?
Rebecca: He says he's given the other one up. He says it was never serious, you know, it was only sex.
Devlin: Ah.

Pause.

And Kim?

Pause.

And Kim?
Rebecca: She'll never have him back. Never. She says she'll never share a bed with him again. Never. Ever.
Devlin: Why not?
Rebecca: Never ever.
Devlin: But why not?
Rebecca: Of course I saw Kim and the kids. I had tea with them. Why did you ask? Did you think I didn't see them?
Devlin: No. I didn't know. It's just that you said you were going to have tea with them.
Rebecca: Well, I did have tea with them! Why shouldn't I? She's my sister.

Pause.

Guess where I went after tea? To the cinema. I saw a film.

Devlin: Oh? What?

Rebecca: A comedy.

Devlin: Uh-huh? Was it funny? Did you laugh?

Rebecca: Other people laughed. Other members of the audience. It was funny.

Devlin: But you didn't laugh?

Rebecca: Other people did. It was a comedy. There was a girl . . . you know . . . and a man. They were having lunch in a smart New York restaurant. He made her smile.

Devlin: How?

Rebecca: Well . . . he told her jokes.

Devlin: Oh, I see.

Rebecca: And then in the next scene he took her on an expedition to the desert, in a caravan. She'd never lived in a desert before, you see. She had to learn how to do it.

Pause.

Devlin: Sounds very funny.

Rebecca: But there was a man sitting in front of me, to my right. He was absolutely still throughout the whole film. He never moved, he was rigid, like a body with rigor mortis, he never laughed once, he just sat like a corpse. I moved far away from him, I moved as far away from him as I possibly could.

Silence.

Devlin: Now look, let's start again. We live here. You don't live . . . in Dorset . . . or *anywhere else*. You live here with me. This is our house. You have a very nice sister. She lives close to you. She has two lovely kids. You're their aunt. You like that.

Pause.

You have a wonderful garden. You love your garden. You created it all by yourself. You have truly green fingers. You also have beautiful fingers.

Pause.

Did you hear what I said? I've just paid you a compliment. In fact I've just paid you a number of compliments. Let's start again.

Rebecca: I don't think we can start again. We started . . . a long time ago. We started. We can't start *again*. We can end again.

Devlin: But we've never ended.

Rebecca: Oh, we have. Again and again and again. And we can end again. And again and again. And again.

Devlin: Aren't you misusing the word 'end'? End means end. You can't end 'again'. You can only end once.

Rebecca: No. You can end once and then you can end again.

Silence.

(singing softly) 'Ashes to ashes'—
Devlin: 'And dust to dust'—
Rebecca: 'If the women don't get you'—
Devlin: 'The liquor must.'

Pause.

I always knew you loved me.
Rebecca: Why?
Devlin: Because we like the same tunes.

Silence.

Listen.

Pause.

Why have you never told me about this lover of yours before this? I have the right to be very angry indeed. Do you realise that? I have the right to be very angry indeed. Do you understand that?

Silence.

Rebecca: Oh by the way there's something I meant to tell you. I was standing in a room at the top of a very tall building in the middle of town. The sky was full of stars. I was about to close the curtains but I stayed at the window for a time looking up at the stars. Then I looked down. I saw an old man and a little boy walking down the street. They were both dragging suitcases. The little boy's suitcase was bigger than he was. It was a very bright night. Because of the stars. The old man and the little boy were walking down the street. They were holding each other's free hand. I wondered where they were going. Anyway, I was about to close the curtains but then I suddenly saw a woman following them, carrying a baby in her arms.

Pause.

Did I tell you the street was icy? It was icy. So she had to tread very carefully. Over the bumps. The stars were out. She followed the man and the boy until they turned the corner and were gone.

Pause.

She stood still. She kissed her baby. The baby was a girl.

Pause.

She kissed her.

Pause.

She listened to the baby's heartbeat. The baby's heart was beating.

The light in the room has darkened. The lamps are very bright.

Rebecca *sits very still.*

The baby was breathing.

Pause.

I held her to me. She was breathing. Her heart was beating.

Devlin goes to her. He stands over her and looks down at her.

He clenches his fist and holds it in front of her face.

He puts his left hand behind her neck and grips it. He brings her head towards his fist. His fist touches her mouth.

Devlin: Kiss my fist.

She does not move.

He opens his hand and places the palm of his hand on her mouth.

She does not move.

Devlin: Speak. Say it. Say 'Put your hand round my throat.'

She does not speak.

Ask me to put my hand round your throat.

She does not speak or move.

He puts his hand on her throat. He presses gently. Her head goes back.

They are still.

She speaks. There is an echo. His grip loosens.

Rebecca: They took us to the trains
Echo: the trains

He takes his hand from her throat.

Rebecca: They were taking the babies away
Echo: the babies away

Pause.

Rebecca: I took my baby and wrapped it in my shawl
Echo: my shawl
Rebecca: And I made it into a bundle
Echo: a bundle
Rebecca: And I held it under my left arm
Echo: my left arm

Pause.

Rebecca: And I went through with my baby
Echo: my baby

Pause.

Rebecca: But the baby cried out

Echo: cried out
Rebecca: And the man called me back
Echo: called me back
Rebecca: And he said what do you have there
Echo: have there
Rebecca: He stretched out his hand for the bundle
Echo: for the bundle
Rebecca: And I gave him the bundle
Echo: the bundle
Rebecca: And that's the last time I held the bundle
Echo: the bundle

Silence.

Rebecca: And we got on the train
Echo: the train
Rebecca: And we arrived at this place
Echo: this place
Rebecca: And I met a woman I knew
Echo: I knew
Rebecca: And she said what happened to your baby
Echo: your baby
Rebecca: Where is your baby
Echo: your baby
Rebecca: And I said what baby
Echo: what baby
Rebecca: I don't have a baby
Echo: a baby
Rebecca: I don't know of any baby
Echo: of any baby

Pause.

Rebecca: I don't know of any baby

Long silence.

BLACKOUT

⤜⤛

MARGARET EDSON

Wit　　*(1999)*

CHARACTERS

Vivian Bearing, Ph.D.
50; professor of seventeenth-century poetry at the university

Harvey Kelekian, M.D.
50; chief of medical oncology, University Hospital

Jason Posner, M.D.
28; clinical fellow, Medical Oncology Branch

Susie Monahan, R.N., B.S.N.
28; primary nurse, Cancer Inpatient Unit

E.M. Ashford, D.Phil.
80; professor emerita of English literature

Mr. Bearing
Vivian's father

Lab Technicians
Clinical Fellows
Students
Code Team

The play may be performed with a cast of nine: the four Technicians, Fellows,
Students, *and* Code Team Members *should double;* Dr. Kelekian *and* Mr.
Bearing *should double.*

NOTES

*Most of the action, but not all, takes place in a room of the University Hospital
Comprehensive Cancer Center. The stage is empty, and furniture is rolled on and
off by the technicians.*

*Jason and Kelekian wear lab coats, but each has a different shirt and tie every
time he enters. Susie wears white jeans, white sneakers, and a different blouse
each entrance.*

*Scenes are indicated by a line rule in the script; there is no break in the action
between scenes, but there might be a change in lighting. There is no intermission.*

*Vivian has a central-venous-access catheter over her left breast, so the IV tub-
ing goes there, not into her arm. The IV pole, with a Port-a-Pump attached, rolls
easily on wheels. Every time the IV pole reappears, it has a different configuration
of bottles.*

(Vivian Bearing *walks on the empty stage pushing her IV pole. She is fifty, tall
and very thin, barefoot, and completely bald. She wears two hospital gowns—one*

*tied in the front and one tied in the back—a baseball cap, and a hospital ID bracelet.
The house lights are at half strength.* Vivian *looks out at the audience, sizing
them up.)*

Vivian *(In false familiarity, waiving and nodding to the audience):* Hi. How are
you feeling today? Great. That's just great. *(In her own professorial tone)*
This is not my standard greeting, I assure you.

I tend toward something a little more formal, a little less inquisitive,
such as, say, "Hello."

But it is the standard greeting here.

There is some debate as to the correct response to this salutation.
Should one reply "I feel good," using "feel" as a copulative to link the
subject, "I," to its subjective complement, "good"; or "I feel well," modifying with an adverb the subject's state of being?

I don't know. I am a professor of seventeenth-century poetry, spe-
cializing in the Holy Sonnets of John Donne.

So I just say, "Fine."

Of course it is not very often that I do feel fine.

I have been asked "How are you feeling today?" while I was throwing up into a plastic washbasin. I have been asked as I was emerging
from a four-hour operation with a tube in every orifice, "How are you
feeling today?"

I am waiting for the moment when someone asks me this question
and I am dead.

I'm a little sorry I'll miss that.

It is unfortunate that this remarkable line of inquiry has come to me
so late in my career. I could have exploited its feigned solicitude to great
advantage: as I was distributing the final examination to the graduate
course in seventeenth-century textual criticism—"Hi. How are you
feeling today?"

Of course I would not be wearing this costume at the time, so the
question's *ironic significance* would not be fully apparent.

As I trust it is now.

Irony is a literary device that will necessarily be deployed to great
effect.

I ardently wish this were not so. I would prefer that a play about me
be cast in the mythic-heroic-pastoral mode; but the facts, most notably
stage-four metastatic ovarian cancer, conspire against that. *The Faerie
Queene* this is not.

And I was dismayed to discover that the play would contain elements of . . . *humor.*

I have been, at best, an *unwitting* accomplice. *(She pauses.)* It is not
my intention to give away the plot; but I think I die at the end.

They've given me less than two hours.

If I were poetically inclined, I might employ a threadbare
metaphor—the sands of time slipping through the hourglass, the two-
hour glass.

Now our sands are almost run;
More a little, and then dumb.

Shakespeare. I trust the name is familiar.
At the moment, however, I am disinclined to poetry.
I've got less than two hours. Then: curtain.

(She disconnects herself from the IV pole and shoves it to a crossing
Technician. *The house lights go out.)*

Vivian: I'll never forget the time I found out I had cancer.

(Dr. Harvey Kelekian enters at a big desk piled high with papers.)

Kelekian: You have cancer.

Vivian (To audience): See? Unforgettable. It was something of a shock. I had
to sit down. *(She plops down.)*

Kelekian: Please sit down. Miss Bearing, you have advanced metastatic ovarian cancer.

Vivian: Go on.

Kelekian: You are a professor, Miss Bearing.

Vivian: Like yourself, Dr. Kelekian.

Kelekian: Well, yes. Now then. You present with a growth that, unfortunately,
went undetected in stages one, two, and three. Now it is an insidious
adenocarcinoma, which has spread from the primary adnexal mass—

Vivian: "Insidious"?

Kelekian: "Insidious" means undetectable at an—

Vivian: "Insidious" *means* treacherous.

Kelekian: Shall I continue?

Vivian: By all means.

Kelekian: Good. In invasive epithelial carcinoma, the most effective treatment modality is a chemotherapeutic agent. We are developing an experimental combination of drugs designed for primary-site ovarian, with a target specificity of stage three-and-beyond administration. Am I going too fast? Good. You will be hospitalized as an in-patient for treatment each cycle. You will be on complete	*Vivian:* Insidious. Hmm. Curious word choice. Cancer. Cancel. "By cancer nature's changing course untrimmed." No—that's not it. *(To Kelekian)* No. Must read something about cancer. Must get some books,

intake-and-output measurement for three days after each treatment to monitor kidney function. After the initial eight cycles, you will have another battery of tests.	articles. Assemble a bibliography.
	Is anyone doing research on cancer?
The antineoplastic will inevitably affect some healthy cells, including those lining the gastrointestinal tract from the lips to the anus, and the hair follicles. We will of course be relying on your resolve to withstand some of the more pernicious side effects.	Concentrate. Antineoplastic. Anti: against. Neo: new. Plastic. To mold. Shaping. Antineoplastic. Against new shaping.
	Hair follicles. My resolve.
	"Pernicious" That doesn't seem—

Kelekian: Miss Bearing?

Vivian: I beg your pardon?

Kelekian: Do you have any questions so far?

Vivian: Please, go on.

Kelekian: Perhaps some of these terms are new. I realize—

Vivian: No, no. Ah. You're being very thorough.

Kelekian: I make a point of it. And I always emphasize it with my students—

Vivian: So do I. "Thoroughness"—I always tell my students, but they are constitutionally averse to painstaking work.

Kelekian: Yours, too.

Vivian: Oh, it's worse every year.

Kelekian: And this is not dermatology, it's medical oncology, for Chrissake.

Vivian: My students read through a text once—*once!*—and think it's time for a break.

Kelekian: Mine are blind.

Vivian: Well, mine are deaf.

Kelekian (Resigned, but warmly): You just have to hope . . .

Vivian (Not so sure): I suppose.

(Pause)

Kelekian: Where were we, Dr. Bearing?

Vivian: I believe I was being thoroughly diagnosed.

Kelekian: Right. Now. The tumor is spreading very quickly, and this treatment is very aggressive. So far, so good?

Vivian: Yes.

Kelekian: Better not teach next semester.

Vivian (Indignant): Out of the question.

Kelekian: The first week of each cycle you'll be hospitalized for chemotherapy; the next week you may feel a little tired; the next two weeks'll be fine, relatively. This cycle will repeat eight times, as I said before.

Vivian: Eight months like that?

Kelekian: This treatment is the strongest thing we have to offer you. And, as research, it will make a significant contribution to our knowledge.

Vivian: Knowledge, yes.

Kelekian (Giving her a piece of paper): Here is the informed-consent form. Should you agree, you sign there, at the bottom. Is there a family member you want me to explain this to?

Vivian (Signing): That won't be necessary.

Kelekian (Taking back the paper): Good. The important thing is for you to take the full dose of chemotherapy. There may be times when you'll wish for a lesser dose, due to the side effects. But we've got to go full-force. The experimental phase has got to have the maximum dose to be of any use. Dr. Bearing—

Vivian: Yes?

Kelekian: You must be very tough. Do you think you can be very tough?

Vivian: You needn't worry.

Kelekian: Good. Excellent.

(Kelekian *and the desk exit as* Vivian *stands and walks forward.*)

Vivian (Hesitantly): I should have asked more questions, because I know there's going to be a test.

I have cancer, insidious cancer, with pernicious side effects—no, the *treatment* has pernicious side effects.

I have stage-four metastatic ovarian cancer. There is no stage five. Oh, and I have to be very tough. It appears to be a matter, as the saying goes, of life and death.

I know all about life and death. I am, after all, a scholar of Donne's Holy Sonnets, which explore mortality in greater depth than any other body of work in the English language.

And I know for a fact that I am tough. A demanding professor. Uncompromising. Never one to turn from a challenge. That is why I chose, while a student of the great E. M. Ashford, to study Donne.

(Professor E. M. Ashford, *fifty-two, enters, seated at the same desk as* Kelekian *was. The scene is twenty-eight years ago.* Vivian *suddenly turns twenty-two, eager and intimidated.*)

Vivian: Professor Ashford?

E.M.: Do it again.

Vivian (To audience): It was something of a shock. I had to sit down. (*She plops down.*)

E.M.: Please sit down. Your essay on Holy Sonnet Six, Miss Bearing, is a melodrama, with a veneer of scholarship unworthy of you—to say nothing of Donne. Do it again.

Vivian: I, ah . . .

E.M.: You must begin with a text, Miss Bearing, not with a feeling.

Death be not proud, though some have called thee
Mighty and dreadfull, for, thou art not soe.

You have entirely missed the point of the poem, because, I must tell you, you have used an edition of the text that is inauthentically punctuated. In the Gardner edition—

Vivian: That edition was checked out of the library—

E.M.: Miss Bearing!

Vivian: Sorry.

E.M.: You take this too lightly, Miss Bearing. This is Metaphysical Poetry, not The Modern Novel. The standards of scholarship and critical reading which one would apply to any other text are simply insufficient. The effort must be total for the results to be meaningful. Do you think the punctuation of the last line of this sonnet is merely an insignificant detail?

The sonnet begins with a valiant struggle with death, calling on all the forces of intellect and drama to vanquish the enemy. But it is ultimately about overcoming the seemingly insuperable barriers separating life, death, and eternal life.

In the edition you chose, this profoundly simple meaning is sacrificed to hysterical punctuation:

And Death—*capital D*—shall be no more—*semicolon!*
Death—*capital D*—comma—thou shalt die—*exclamation point!*

If you go in for this sort of thing, I suggest you take up Shakespeare. Gardner's edition of the Holy Sonnets returns to the Westmoreland manuscript source of 1610—not for sentimental reasons, I assure you, but because Helen Gardner is a *scholar.* It reads:

And death shall be no more, *comma*, Death thou shalt die.

(As she recites this line, she makes a little gesture at the comma.)

Nothing but a breath—a comma—separates life from life everlasting. It is very simple really. With the original punctuation restored, death is no longer something to act out on a stage, with exclamation points. It's a comma, a pause.

This way, the *uncompromising* way, one learns something from this poem, wouldn't you say? Life, death. Soul, God. Past, present. Not insuperable barriers, not semicolons, just a comma.

Vivian: Life, death . . . I see. *(Standing)* It's a metaphysical conceit. It's wit! I'll go back to the library and rewrite the paper—

E.M. (Standing, emphatically): It is *not wit*, Miss Bearing. It is truth. *(Walking around the desk to her)* The paper's not the point.

Vivian: It isn't?

E.M. (Tenderly): Vivian. You're a bright young woman. Use your intelligence. Don't go back to the library. Go out. Enjoy yourself with your friends. Hmm?

(Vivian walks away. E.M. slides off.)

Vivian (As she gradually returns to the hospital): I, ah, went outside. The sun was very bright. I, ah, walked around, past the . . . There were students on the lawn, talking about nothing, laughing. The insuperable barrier between one thing and another is . . . just a comma? Simple human truth, uncompromising scholarly standards? They're *connected?* I just couldn't . . .

    I went back to the library.

    Anyway.

    All right. Significant contribution to knowledge.

    Eight cycles of chemotherapy. Give me the full dose, the full dose every time.

(In a burst of activity, the hospital scene is created.)

Vivian: The attention was flattering. For the first five minutes. Now I know how poems feel.

(Susie Monahan, Vivian's primary nurse, gives Vivian her chart, then puts her in a wheelchair and takes her to her first appointment: chest x-ray. This and all other diagnostic tests are suggested by light and sound.)

Technician 1: Name.

Vivian: My name? Vivian Bearing.

Technician 1: Huh?

Vivian: Bearing. B-E-A-R-I-N-G. Vivian. V-I-V-I-A-N.

Technician 1: Doctor.

Vivian: Yes, I have a Ph.D.

Technician 1: Your doctor.

Vivian: Oh. Dr. Harvey Kelekian.

(Technician 1 positions her so that she is leaning forward and embracing the metal plate, then steps offstage.)

Vivian: I am a doctor of philosophy—

Technician 1 (From offstage): Take a deep breath, and hold it. *(Pause, with light and sound)* Okay.

Vivian: —a scholar of seventeenth-century poetry.

Technician 1 (From offstage): Turn sideways, arms behind your head, and hold it. *(Pause)* Okay.

Vivian: I have made an immeasurable contribution to the discipline of English literature. *(Technician 1 returns and puts her in the wheelchair.)* I am, in short, a force.

(Technician 1 rolls her to upper GI series, where Technician 2 picks up.)

Technician 2: Name.

Vivian: Lucy, Countess of Bedford.

Technician 2 (Checking a printout): I don't see it here.

Vivian: My name is Vivian Bearing. B-E-A-R-I-N-G. Dr. Kelekian is my doctor.

Technician 2: Okay. Lie down. *(Technician 2 positions her on a stretcher and leaves. Light and sound suggest the filming.)*

Vivian: After an outstanding undergraduate career, I studied with Professor E. M. Ashford for three years, during which time I learned by instruction and example what it means to be a scholar of distinction.

As her research fellow, my principal task was the alphabetizing of index cards for Ashford's monumental critical edition of Donne's *Devotions upon Emergent Occasions*.

(During the procedure, another Technician *takes the wheelchair away.)*

I am thanked in the preface: "Miss Vivian Bearing for her able assistance."

My dissertation, "Ejaculations in Seventeenth-Century Manuscript and Printed Editions of the Holy Sonnets: A Comparison," was revised for publication in the *Journal of English Texts*, a very prestigious venue for a first appearance.

Technician 2: Where's your wheelchair?

Vivian: I do not know. I was busy just now.

Technician 2: Well, how are you going to get out of here?

Vivian: Well, I do not know. Perhaps you would like me to stay.

Technician 2: I guess I got to go find you a chair.

Vivian (Sarcastically): Don't inconvenience yourself on my behalf. *(Technician 2 leaves to get a wheelchair.)*

My second article, a classic explication of Donne's sonnet "Death be not proud," was published in *Critical Discourse*.

The success of the essay prompted the University Press to solicit a volume on the twelve Holy Sonnets in the 1633 edition, which I produced in the remarkably short span of three years. My book, entitled *Made Cunningly*, remains an immense success, in paper as well as cloth.

In it, I devote one chapter to a thorough examination of each sonnet, discussing every word in extensive detail.

(Technician 2 returns with a wheelchair.)

Technician 2: Here.

Vivian: I summarize previous critical interpretations of the text and offer my own analysis. It is exhaustive.

(Technician 2 deposits her at CT scan.)

Bearing. B-E-A-R-I-N-G. Kelekian.

(Technician 3 has Vivian lie down on a metal stretcher. Light and sound suggest the procedure.)

Technician 3: Here. Hold still.

Vivian: For how long?

Technician 3: Just a little while. *(Technician 3 leaves. Silence)*

Vivian: The scholarly study of poetic texts requires a capacity for scrupulously detailed examination, particularly the poetry of John Donne.

The salient characteristic of the poems is wit: "Itchy outbreaks of far-fetched wit," as Donne himself said.

To the common reader—that is to say, the undergraduate with a B-plus or better average—wit provides an invaluable exercise for sharpening the mental faculties, for stimulating the flash of comprehension that can only follow hours of exacting and seemingly pointless scrutiny.

(*Technician 3 puts* Vivian *back in the wheelchair and wheels her toward the unit. Partway,* Technician 3 *gives the chair a shove and* Susie Monahan, Vivian's *primary nurse, takes over.* Susie *rolls* Vivian *to the exam room.*)

To the scholar, to the mind comprehensively trained in the subtleties of seventeenth-century vocabulary, versification, and theological, historical, geographical, political, and mythological allusions, Donne's wit is . . . a way to see how good you really are.

After twenty years, I can say with confidence, no one is quite as good as I.

(*By now,* Susie *has helped* Vivian *sit on the exam table.* Dr. Jason Posner, *clinical fellow, stands in the doorway.*)

Jason: Ah, Susie?

Susie: Oh, hi.

Jason: Ready when you are.

Susie: Okay. Go ahead. Ms. Bearing, this is Jason Posner. He's going to do your history, ask you a bunch of questions. He's Dr. Kelekian's fellow.

(Susie *is busy in the room, setting up for the exam.*)

Jason: Hi, Professor Bearing. I'm Dr. Posner, clinical fellow in the medical oncology branch, working with Dr. Kelekian.

    Professor Bearing, I, ah, I was an undergraduate at the U. I took your course in seventeenth-century poetry.

Vivian: You did?

Jason: Yes. I thought it was excellent.

Vivian: Thank you. Were you an English major?

Jason: No. Biochemistry. But you can't get into medical school unless you're well-rounded. And I made a bet with myself that I could get an A in the three hardest courses on campus.

Susie: Howdja do, Jace?

Jason: Success.

Vivian (Doubtful): Really?

Jason: A minus. It was a very tough course. (*To* Susie) I'll call you.

Susie: Okay. (*She leaves.*)

Jason: I'll just pull this over. (*He gets a little stool on wheels.*) Get the proxemics right here. There. (*Nervously*) Good. Now. I'm going to be taking your history. It's a medical interview, and then I give you an exam.

Vivian: I believe Dr. Kelekian has already done that.

Jason: Well, I know, but Dr. Kelekian wants *me* to do it, too. Now. I'll be taking a few notes as we go along.

Vivian: Very well.

Jason: Okay. Let's get started. How are you feeling today?

Vivian: Fine, thank you.

Jason: Good. How is your general health?

Vivian: Fine.

Jason: Excellent. Okay. We know you are an academic.

Vivian: Yes, we've established that.

Jason: So we don't need to talk about your interesting work.

Vivian: No.

(The following questions and answers go extremely quickly.)

Jason: How old are you?

Vivian: Fifty.

Jason: Are you married?

Vivian: No.

Jason: Are your parents living?

Vivian: No.

Jason: How and when did they die?

Vivian: My father, suddenly, when I was twenty, of a heart attack. My mother, slowly, when I was forty-one and forty-two, of cancer. Breast cancer.

Jason: Cancer?

Vivian: Breast cancer.

Jason: I see. Any siblings?

Vivian: No.

Jason: Do you have any questions so far?

Vivian: Not so far.

Jason: Well, that about does it for your life history.

Vivian: Yes, that's all there is to my life history.

Jason: Now I'm going to ask you about your past medical history. Have you ever been hospitalized?

Vivian: I had my tonsils out when I was eight.

Jason: Have you ever been pregnant?

Vivian: No.

Jason: Ever had heart murmurs? High blood pressure?

Vivian: No.

Jason: Stomach, liver, kidney problems?

Vivian: No.

Jason: Venereal diseases? Uterine infections?

Vivian: No.

Jason: Thyroid, diabetes, cancer?

Vivian: No—cancer, yes.

Jason: When?

Vivian: Now.

Jason: Well, not including now.

Vivian: In that case, no.

Jason: Okay. Clinical depression? Nervous breakdowns? Suicide attempts?

Vivian: No.

Jason: Do you smoke?

Vivian: No.

Jason: Ethanol?

Vivian: I'm sorry?

Jason: Alcohol.

Vivian: Oh. Ethanol. Yes, I drink wine.

Jason: How much? How often?

Vivian: A glass with dinner occasionally. And perhaps a Scotch every now and then.

Jason: Do you use substances?

Vivian: Such as.

Jason: Marijuana, cocaine, crack cocaine, PCP, ecstasy, poppers—

Vivian: No.

Jason: Do you drink caffeinated beverages?

Vivian: Oh, yes!

Jason: Which ones?

Vivian: Coffee. A few cups a day.

Jason: How many?

Vivian: Two . . . to six. But I really don't think that's immoderate—

Jason: How often do you undergo routine medical checkups?

Vivian: Well, not as often as I should, probably, but I've felt fine, I really have.

Jason: So the answer is?

Vivian: Every three to . . . five years.

Jason: What do you do for exercise?

Vivian: Pace.

Jason: Are you having sexual relations?

Vivian: Not at the moment.

Jason: Are you pre- or post-menopausal?

Vivian: Pre.

Jason: When was the first day of your last period?

Vivian: Ah, ten days—two weeks ago.

Jason: Okay. When did you first notice your present complaint?

Vivian: This time, now?

Jason: Yes.

Vivian: Oh, about four months ago. I felt a pain in my stomach, in my abdomen, like a cramp, but not the same.

Jason: How did it feel?

Vivian: Like a cramp.

Jason: But not the same?

Vivian: No, duller, and stronger. I can't describe it.

Jason: What came next?

Vivian: Well, I just, I don't know, I started noticing my body, little things. I would be teaching, and feel a sharp pain.

Jason: What kind of pain?

Vivian: Sharp, and sudden. Then it would go away. Or I would be tired.

Exhausted. I was working on a major project, the article on John Donne for *The Oxford Encyclopedia of English Literature*. It was a great honor. But I had a very strict deadline.

Jason: So you would say you were under stress?

Vivian: It wasn't so much more stress than usual, I just couldn't withstand it this time. I don't know.

Jason: So?

Vivian: So I went to Dr. Chin, my gynecologist, after I had turned in the article, and explained all this. She examined me, and sent me to Jefferson the internist, and he sent me to Kelekian because he thought I might have a tumor.

Jason: And that's it?

Vivian: Till now.

Jason: Hmmm. Well, that's very interesting.

(Nervous pause)

Well, I guess I'll start the examination. It'll only take a few minutes. Why don't you, um, sort of lie back, and—oh—relax.

(He helps her lie back on the table, raises the stirrups out of the table, raises her legs and puts them in the stirrups, and puts a paper sheet over her.)

Be very relaxed. This won't hurt. Let me get this sheet. Okay. Just stay calm. Okay. Put your feet in these stirrups. Okay. Just. There. Okay? Now. Oh, I have to go get Susie. Got to have a girl here. Some crazy clinical rule. Um. I'll be right back. Don't move.

(Jason leaves. Long pause. He is seen walking quickly back and forth in the hall, and calling Susie's name as he goes by.)

Vivian (To herself): I wish I had given him an A. *(Silence)*
Two times one is two.
Two times two is four.
Two times three is six.
Um.
Oh.

Death be not proud, though some have called thee
Mighty and dreadfull, for, thou art not soe,
For, those, whom thou think'st, thou dost overthrow,
Die not, poore death, nor yet canst thou kill mee . . .

Jason (In the hallway): Has anybody seen Susie?

Vivian (Losing her place for a second): Ah.

Thou'art slave to Fate, chance, kings, and desperate men,
And dost with poyson, warre, and sicknesse dwell,
And poppie,' or charmes can make us sleepe as well,
And better than thy stroake; why swell'st thou then?

Jason (In the hallway): She was here just a minute ago.

Vivian:

> One short sleepe past, wee wake eternally,
> And death shall be no more—*comma*—Death thou shalt die.

(Jason *and* Susie *return.*)

Jason: Okay. Here's everything. Okay.

Susie: What is this? Why did you leave her—

Jason (To Susie): I had to find you. Now, come on. (*To* Vivian*)* We're ready, Professor Bearing. (*To himself, as he puts on exam gloves*) Get these on. Okay. Just lift this up. Ooh. Okay. (*As much to himself as to her*) Just relax. (*He begins the pelvic exam, with one hand on her abdomen and the other inside her, looking blankly at the ceiling as he feels around.*) Okay. (*Silence*) Susie, isn't that interesting, that I had Professor Bearing.

Susie: Yeah. I wish I had taken some literature. I don't know anything about poetry.

Jason (Trying to be casual): Professor Bearing was very highly regarded on campus. It looked very good on my transcript that I had taken her course. (*Silence*) They even asked me about it in my interview for med school—(*He feels the mass and does a double take.*) Jesus! (*Tense silence. He is amazed and fascinated.*)

Susie: What?

Vivian: What?

Jason: Um. (*He tries for composure.*) Yeah. I survived Bearing's course. No problem. Heh. (*Silence*) Yeah, John Donne, those metaphysical poets, that metaphysical wit. Hardest poetry in the English department. Like to see *them* try biochemistry. (*Silence*) Okay. We're about done. Okay. That's it. Okay, Professor Bearing. Let's take your feet out, there. (*He takes off his gloves and throws them away.*) Okay. I gotta go. I gotta go.

(Jason *quickly leaves.* Vivian *slowly gets up from this scene and walks stiffly away.* Susie *cleans up the exam room and exits.*)

––––––––––

Vivian (Walking downstage to audience): That . . . was . . . hard. That . . . was . . .

> One thing can be said for an eight-month course of cancer treatment: it is highly educational. I'm learning to suffer.
>
> Yes, it is mildly uncomfortable to have an electrocardiogram, but the . . . agony . . . of a proctosigmoidoscopy sweeps it from memory. Yes, it was embarrassing to have to wear a nightgown all day long—two nightgowns!—but that seemed like a positive privilege compared to watching myself go bald. Yes, having a former student give me a pelvic exam was thoroughly *degrading*—and I use the term deliberately—but I could not have imagined the depths of humiliation that—
>
> Oh, God— (Vivian *runs across the stage to her hospital room, dives onto the bed, and throws up into a large plastic washbasin.*) Oh, God. Oh. Oh.

(She lies slumped on the bed, fastened to the IV, which now includes a small bottle with a bright orange label.) Oh, God. It can't be. *(Silence)* Oh, God. Please. Steady. Steady. *(Silence)* Oh—Oh, no! *(She throws up again, moans, and retches in agony.)* Oh, God. What's left? I haven't eaten in two days. What's left to puke?

You may remark that my vocabulary has taken a turn for the Anglo-Saxon.

God, I'm going to barf my brains out.

(She begins to relax.) If I actually did barf my brains out, it would be a great loss to my discipline. Of course, not a few of my colleagues would be relieved. To say nothing of my students.

It's not that I'm controversial. Just uncompromising. Ooh— *(She lunges for the basin. Nothing)* Oh. *(Silence)* False alarm. If the word went round that Vivian Bearing had barfed her brains out . . .

Well, first my colleagues, most of whom are my former students, would scramble madly for my position. Then their consciences would flare up, so to honor *my* memory they would put together a collection of their essays about John Donne. The volume would begin with a warm introduction, capturing my most endearing qualities. It would be short. But sweet.

Published *and* perished.

Now, watch this. I have to ring the bell *(She presses the button on the bed)* to get someone to come and measure this emesis, and record the amount on a chart of my intake and output. This counts as output.

(Susie enters.)

Susie *(Brightly):* How you doing, Ms. Bearing? You having some nausea?
Vivian *(Weakly):* Uhh, yes.
Susie: Why don't I take that? Here.
Vivian: It's about 300 cc's.
Susie: That all?
Vivian: It was very hard work.

(Susie takes the basin to the bathroom and rinses it.)

Susie: Yup. Three hundred. Good guess. *(She marks the graph.)* Okay. Anything else I can get for you? Some Jell-O or anything?
Vivian: Thank you, no.
Susie: You okay all by yourself here?
Vivian: Yes.
Susie: You're not having a lot of visitors, are you?
Vivian *(Correcting):* None, to be precise.
Susie: Yeah, I didn't think so. Is there somebody you want me to call for you?
Vivian: That won't be necessary.
Susie: Well, I'll just pop my head in every once in a while to see how you're coming along. Kelekian and the fellows should be in soon. *(She touches Vivian's arm.)* If there's anything you need, you just ring.

Vivian (Uncomfortable with kindness): Thank you.
Susie: Okay. Just call. (Susie *disconnects the IV bottle with the orange label and takes it with her as she leaves.* Vivian *lies still. Silence.*)

Vivian: In this dramatic structure you will see the most interesting aspects of my tenure as an in-patient receiving experimental chemotherapy for advanced metastatic ovarian cancer.

But as I am a *scholar* before . . . an impresario, I feel obliged to document what it is like here most of the time, between the dramatic climaxes. Between the spectacles.

In truth, it is like this:

(She ceremoniously lies back and stares at the ceiling.)

You cannot imagine how time . . . can be . . . so still.
It hangs. It weighs. And yet there is so little of it.
It goes so slowly, and yet it is so scarce.
If I were writing this scene, it would last a full fifteen minutes. I would lie here, and you would sit there.

(She looks at the audience, daring them.)

Not to worry. Brevity is the soul of wit.
But if you think eight months of cancer treatment is tedious for the *audience,* consider how it feels to play my part.
All right. All right. It is Friday morning: Grand Rounds. *(Loudly, giving a cue)* Action.

(Kelekian enters, followed by Jason *and four other* Fellows.*)*

Kelekian: Dr. Bearing.
Vivian: Dr. Kelekian.
Kelekian: Jason.

*(*Jason *moves to the front of the group.)*

Jason: Professor Bearing. How are you feeling today?
Vivian: Fine.
Jason: That's great. That's just great. *(He takes a sheet and carefully covers her legs and groin, then pulls up her gown to reveal her entire abdomen. He is barely audible, but his gestures are clear.)*
Vivian: "Grand Rounds."

The term is theirs. Not "Grand" in the traditional sense of sweeping or magnificent. Not "Rounds" as in a musical canon, or a *round* of applause (though either would be refresh-	*Jason:* Very late detection. Staged as a four upon admission. Hexamethophosphacil with Vinplatin to potentiate. Hex at 300 mg. per meter squared, Vin at 100. Today is cycle two, day

ing at this point). Here, "Rounds" seems to signify darting *around* the main issue . . . which I suppose would be the struggle for life . . . *my* life . . . with heated discussions of side effects, other complaints, additional treatments.

Grand Rounds is not Grand Opera. But compared to lying here, it is positively *dramatic*.

Full of subservience, hierarchy, gratuitous displays, sublimated rivalries—I feel right at home. It is just like a graduate seminar.

With one important difference: in Grand Rounds, *they* read *me* like a book. Once I did the teaching, now I am taught.

This is much easier. I just hold still and look cancerous. It requires less acting every time.

Excellent command of details.

three. Both cycles at the *full dose. (The* Fellows *are impressed.)*

The primary site is—*here (He puts his finger on the spot on her abdomen)*, behind the left ovary. Metastases are suspected in the peritoneal cavity— here. And—here. *(He touches those spots.)*

Full lymphatic involvement. *(He moves his hands over her entire body.)*

At the time of first-look surgery, a significant part of the Tumor was de-bulked, mostly in this area— here. *(He points to each organ, poking her abdomen.)* Left, right ovaries. Fallopian Tubes. Uterus. All out.

Evidence of primary-site shrinkage. Shrinking in metastatic tumors has not been documented. Primary mass frankly palpable in pelvic exam, frankly, all through here—*here*. *(Some* Fellows *reach and press where he is pointing.)*

Kelekian: Excellent command of details.
Vivian *(To herself)*: I taught him, you know—
Kelekian: Okay. Problem areas with Hex and Vin. *(He addresses all the* Fellows, *but* Jason *answers first and they resent him.)*
Fellow 1: Myselosu—
Jason *(Interrupting)*: Well, first of course is myelosuppression, a lowering of

blood-cell counts. It goes without saying. With this combination of agents, nephrotoxicity will be next.

Kelekian: Go on.

Jason: The kidneys are designed to filter out impurities in the bloodstream. In trying to filter the chemotherapeutic agent out of the bloodstream, the kidneys shut down.

Kelekian: Intervention.

Jason: Hydration.

Kelekian: Monitoring.

Jason: Full recording of fluid intake and output, as you see here on these graphs, to monitor hydration and kidney function. Totals monitored daily by the clinical fellow, as per the protocol.

Kelekian: Anybody else. Side effects.

Fellow 1: Nausea and vomiting.

Kelekian: Jason.

Jason: Routine.

Fellow 2: Pain while urinating.

Jason: Routine. *(The* Fellows *are trying to catch* Jason.*)*

Fellow 3: Psychological depression.

Jason: No way.

(The Fellows *are silent.)*

Kelekian (Standing by Vivian *at the head of the bed):* Anything else. Other complaints with Hexamethophosphacil and Vinplatin. Come on. *(Silence.* Kelekian *and* Vivian *wait together for the correct answer.)*

Fellow 4: Mouth sores.

Jason: Not yet.

Fellow 2 (Timidly): Skin rash?

Jason: Nope.

Kelekian (Sharing this with Vivian*):* Why do we waste our time, Dr. Bearing?

Vivian (Delighted): I do not know, Dr. Kelekian.

Kelekian (To the Fellows*):* Use your eyes. *(All* Fellows *look closely at* Vivian.*)* Jesus God. Hair loss.

Fellows: *(All protesting.* Vivian *and* Kelekian *are amused.)*

    —Come on.

    —You can see it.

    —It doesn't count.

    —No fair.

Kelekian: Jason.

Jason (Begrudgingly): Hair loss after first cycle of treatment.

Kelekian: That's better. *(To* Vivian*)* Dr. Bearing. Full dose. Excellent. Keep pushing the fluids.

(The Fellows *leave.* Kelekian *stops* Jason.*)*

Kelekian: Jason.

Jason: Huh?

Kelekian: Clinical.

Jason: Oh, right. *(To* Vivian) Thank you, Professor Bearing. You've been
 very cooperative. *(They leave with her stomach uncovered.)*

Vivian: Wasn't that . . . Grand? *(She gets up without the IV pole.)* At times, this
 obsessively detailed examination, this *scrutiny* seems to me to be a nefar-
 ious business. On the other hand, what is the alternative? Ignorance?
 Ignorance may be . . . bliss; but it is not a very noble goal.

   So I play my part.

(Pause)

   I receive chemotherapy, throw up, am subjected to countless indig-
nities, feel better, go home. Eight cycles. Eight neat little strophes. Oh,
there have been the usual variations, subplots, red herrings: hepatotoxic-
ity (liver poison), neuropathy (nerve death).

   (Righteously) They are medical terms. I look them up.

   It has always been my custom to treat words with respect.

   I can recall the time—the very hour of the very day—when I knew
words would be my life's work.

––––––––––––––––

(A pile of six little white books appears, with Mr. Bearing, *Vivian's father,
seated behind an open newspaper.)*

   It was my fifth birthday.

(Vivian, now a child, flops down to the books.)

   I liked that one best.

Mr. Bearing (Disinterested but tolerant, never distracted from his newspaper):
 Read another.

Vivian: I think I'll read . . . *(She takes a book from the stack and reads its spine
 intently) The Tale of the Flopsy Bunnies. (Reading the front cover) The Tale of
 the Flopsy Bunnies.)* It has little bunnies on the front.

(Opening to the title page) The Tale of the Flopsy Bunnies by Beatrix Potter.
(She turns the page and begins to read.)

   It is said that the effect of eating too much lettuce is sopor—sop—or—
what is that word?

Mr. Bearing: Sound it out.

Vivian: Sop—or—fic. Sop—or—i—fic. Soporific. What does that mean?

Mr. Bearing: Soporific. Causing sleep.

Vivian: Causing sleep.

Mr. Bearing: Makes you sleepy.

Vivian: "Soporific" means "makes you sleepy"?

Mr. Bearing: Correct.

Vivian: "Soporific" means "makes you sleepy." Soporific.

Mr. Bearing: Now use it in a sentence. What has a soporific effect on *you?*

Vivian: A soporific effect on me.

Mr. Bearing: What makes you sleepy?

Vivian: Aahh—nothing.

Mr. Bearing: Correct.

Vivian: What about you?

Mr. Bearing: What has a soporific effect on me? Let me think: boring conversation, I suppose, after dinner.

Vivian: Me too, boring conversation.

Mr. Bearing: Carry on.

Vivian: It is said that the effect of eating too much lettuce is soporific.

The little bunnies in the picture are asleep! They're sleeping! Like you said, because of *soporific!*

(She stands up, and Mr. Bearing *exits.)*

The illustration bore out the meaning of the word, just as he had explained it. At the time, it seemed like magic.

So imagine the effect that the words of John Donne first had on me: ratiocination, concatenation, coruscation, tergiversation.

Medical terms are less evocative. Still, I want to know what the doctors mean when they . . . anatomize me. And I will grant that in this particular field of endeavor they possess a more potent arsenal of terminology than I. My only defense is the acquisition of vocabulary.

(Susie enters and puts her arm around Vivian's *shoulders to hold her up.* Vivian *is shaking, feverish, and weak.)*

Vivian (All at once): Fever and neutropenia.

Susie: When did it start?

Vivian (Having difficulty speaking): I—I was at home—reading—and I—felt so bad. I called. Fever and neutropenia. They said to come in.

Susie: You did the right thing to come. Did somebody drive you?

Vivian: Cab. I took a taxi.

Susie (She grabs a wheelchair and helps Vivian *sit. As Susie speaks, she takes* Vivian's *temperature, pulse, and respiration rate.):* Here, why don't you sit? Just sit there a minute. I'll get Jason. He's on call tonight. We'll get him to give you some meds. I'm glad I was here on nights. I'll make sure you get to bed soon, okay? It'll just be a minute. I'll get you some juice, some nice juice with lots of ice.

(Susie leaves quickly. Vivian *sits there, agitated, confused, and very sick.* Susie *returns with the juice.)*

Vivian: Lights. I left all the lights on at my house.

Susie: Don't you worry. It'll be all right.

(Jason enters, roused from his sleep and not fully awake. He wears surgical scrubs and puts on a lab coat as he enters.)

Jason (Without looking at Vivian*):* How are you feeling, Professor Bearing?

Vivian: My teeth—are chattering.

Jason: Vitals.

Susie (Giving Vivian *juice and a straw, without looking at Jason):* Temp 39.4. Pulse 120. Respiration 36. Chills and sweating.

Jason: Fever and neutropenia. It's a "shake and bake." Blood cultures and urine, stat. Admit her. Prepare for reverse isolation. Start with acetaminophen. Vitals every four hours. *(He starts to leave.)*

Susie (Following him): Jason—I think you need to talk to Kelekian about lowering the dose for the next cycle. It's too much for her like this.

Jason: Lower the dose? No way. Full dose. She's tough. She can take it. Wake me up when the counts come from the lab.

(He pads off. Susie *wheels* Vivian *to her room, and* Vivian *collapses on the bed.* Susie *connects* Vivian's *IV, then wets a washcloth and rubs her face and neck.* Vivian *remains delirious.* Susie *checks the IV and leaves with the wheelchair.*

After a while, Kelekian *appears in the doorway holding a surgical mask near his face.* Jason *is with him, now dressed and clean-shaven.)*

Kelekian: Good morning, Dr. Bearing. Fifth cycle. Full dose. Definite progress. Everything okay.

Vivian (Weakly): Yes.

Kelekian: You're doing swell. Isolation is no problem. Couple of days. Think of it as a vacation.

Vivian: Oh.

*(Jason *starts to enter, holding a mask near his face, just like* Kelekian.)*

Kelekian: Jason.

Jason: Oh, Jesus. Okay, okay.

(He returns to the doorway, where he puts on a paper gown, mask, and gloves. Kelekian *leaves.)*

Vivian (To audience): In isolation, I am isolated. For once I can use a term literally. The chemotherapeutic agents eradicating my cancer have also eradicated my immune system. In my present condition, every living thing is a health hazard to me . . .

*(Jason *comes in to check the intake-and-output.)*

Jason (Complaining to himself): I really have not got time for this . . .

Vivian: . . . particularly health-care professionals.

Jason (Going right to the graph on the wall): Just to look at the I&O sheets for one minute, and it takes me half an hour to do precautions. Four, seven, eleven. Two-fifty twice. Okay. *(Remembering)* Oh, Jeez. Clinical. Professor Bearing. How are you feeling today?

Vivian (Very sick): Fine. Just shaking sometimes from the chills.

Jason: IV will kick in anytime now. No problem. Listen, gotta go. Keep pushing the fluids.

(As he exits, he takes off the gown, mask, and gloves.)

Vivian (Getting up from bed with her IV pole and resuming her explanation): I am not in isolation because I have cancer, because I have a tumor the size of a grapefruit. No. I am in isolation because I am being treated for cancer. My treatment imperils my health.

Herein lies the paradox. John Donne would revel in it. I would revel in it, if he wrote a poem about it. My students would flounder in it, because paradox is too difficult to understand. Think of it as a puzzle, I would tell them, an intellectual game.

(She is trapped.) Or, I *would have* told them. Were it a game. Which it is not.

(Escaping) If they were here, if I were lecturing: How I would *perplex* them! I could work my students into a frenzy. Every ambiguity, every shifting awareness. I could draw so much from the poems.

I could be so powerful.

———————

(Vivian stands still, as if conjuring a scene. Now at the height of her powers, she grandly disconnects herself from the IV. Technicians remove the bed and hand her a pointer.

Vivian: The poetry of the early seventeenth century, what has been called the metaphysical school, considers an intractable mental puzzle by exercising the outstanding human faculty of the era, namely *wit*.

The greatest wit—the greatest English poet, some would say— was John Donne. In the Holy Sonnets, Donne applied his capacious, agile wit to the larger aspects of the human experience: life, death, and God.

In his poems, metaphysical quandaries are addressed, but never resolved. Ingenuity, virtuosity, and a vigorous intellect that jousts with the most exalted concepts: these are the tools of wit.

(The lights dim. A screen lowers, and the sonnet "If poysonous mineralis," from the Gardner edition, appears on it. Vivian recites.)

> If poysonous mineralis, and if that tree.
> Whose fruit threw death on else immortall us,
> If lecherous goats, if serpents envious
> Cannot be damn'd; Alas; why should I bee?
> Why should intent or reason, borne in mee,
> Make sinnes, else equall, in mee, more heinous?
> And mercy being easie, 'and glorious
> To God, in his sterne wrath, why threatens hee?
> But who am I, that dare dispute with thee?
> O God, Oh! of thine onely worthy blood,
> And my teares, make a heavenly Lethean flood,
> And drowne in it my sinnes blacke memorie.
> That thou remember them, some claime as debt,
> I thinke it mercy, if thou wilt forget.

(Vivian occasionally whacks the screen with a pointer for emphasis. She moves around as she lectures.)

Aggressive intellect. Pious melodrama. And a final, fearful point. Donne's Holy Sonnet Five, 1609. From the Ashford edition, based on Gardner.

The speaker of the sonnet has a brilliant mind, and he plays the part convincingly; but in the end he finds God's *forgiveness* hard to believe, so he crawls under a rock to *hide.*

If arsenic and serpents are not damned, then why is he? In asking the question, the speaker turns eternal damnation into an intellectual game. Why would God choose to do what is *hard*, to condemn, rather than what is *easy*, and also *glorious*—to show mercy?

(Several scholars have disputed Ashford's third comma in line six, but none convincingly.)

But. Exception. Limitation. Contrast. The argument shifts from cleverness to melodrama, an unconvincing eruption of piety: "O" "God" "Oh!"

A typical prayer would plead "Remember me, O Lord." (This point is nicely explicated in an article by Richard Strier—a former student of mine who once sat where you do now, although I dare say he was *awake*—in the May 1989 issue of *Modern Philology*.) True believers ask to be *remembered* by God. The speaker of this sonnet asks God to forget. *(Vivian moves in front of the screen, and the projection of the poem is cast directly upon her.)* Where is the hyperactive intellect of the first section? Where is the histrionic outpouring of the second? When the speaker considers his own *sins*, and the inevitability of God's *judgment*, he can conceive of but one resolution: to *disappear. (Vivian moves away from the screen.)* Doctrine assures us that no sinner is denied *forgiveness*, not even one whose sins are overweening *intellect* or overwrought *dramatics*. The speaker does not need to *hide* from God's *judgment*, only to accept God's *forgiveness*. It is very simple. Suspiciously simple.

We want to correct the speaker, to remind him of the assurance of salvation. But it is too late. The poetic encounter is over. We are left to our own consciences. Have we outwitted Donne? Or have we been outwitted?

(Susie comes on.)

Susie: Ms. Bearing?
Vivian (Continuing): Will the po—
Susie: Ms. Bearing?
Vivian (Crossly): What is it?
Susie: You have to go down for a test. Jason just called. They want another ultrasound. They're concerned about a bowel obstruction— Is it okay if I come in?
Vivian: No. Not now.
Susie: I'm sorry, but they want it now.
Vivian: Not right now. It's not *supposed* to be now.

Susie: Yes, they want to do it now. I've got the chair.

Vivian: It should not be now. I am in the middle of—this. I have *this* planned for now, not ultrasound. No more tests. We've covered that.

Susie: I know, I know, but they need for it to be now. It won't take long, and it isn't a bad procedure. Why don't you just come along.

Vivian: I do not want to go now!

Susie: Ms. Bearing.

(*Silence.* Vivian *raises the screen, walks away from the scene, hooks herself to the IV, and gets in the wheelchair.* Susie *wheels* Vivian, *and a* Technician *takes her.*)

Technician: Name.

Vivian: B-E-A-R-I-N-G. Kelekian.

Technician: It'll just be a minute.

Vivian: Time for your break.

Technician: Yup.

(*The* Technician *leaves.*)

Vivian (Mordantly): Take a break!

――――――――――

(Vivian *sits weakly in the wheelchair.*)

Vivian:

> This is my playes last scene, here heavens appoint
> My pilgrimages last mile; and my race
> Idly, yet quickly runne, hath this last pace,
> My spans last inch, my minutes last point,
> And gluttonous death will instantly unjoynt
> My body, 'and soule
> John Donne. 1609.

I have always particularly liked that poem. In the abstract. Now I find the image of "my minute's last point" a little too, shall we say, *pointed.*

I don't mean to complain, but I am becoming very sick. Very, very sick. Ultimately sick, as it were.

In everything I have done, I have been steadfast, resolute—some would say in the extreme. Now, as you can see, I am distinguishing myself in illness.

I have survived eight treatments of Hexamethophosphacil and Vinplatin at the *full* dose, ladies and gentlemen. I have broken the record. I have become something of a celebrity. Kelekian and Jason are simply delighted. I think they foresee celebrity status for themselves upon the appearance of the journal article they will no doubt write about me.

But I flatter myself. The article will not be about *me,* it will be about my ovaries. It will be about my peritoneal cavity, which, despite their best intentions, is now crawling with cancer.

What we have come to think of as *me* is, in fact, just the specimen jar, just the dust jacket, just the white piece of paper that bears the little black marks.

My next line is supposed to be something like this:

"It is such a *relief* to get back to my room after those infernal tests."

This is hardly true.

It would be *a relief* to be a cheerleader on her way to Daytona Beach for Spring Break.

To get back to my room after those infernal tests is just the next thing that happens.

(She returns to her bed, which now has a commode next to it. She is very sick.)

Oh, God. It is such a relief to get back to my goddamn room after those goddamn tests.

(Jason enters.)

Jason: Professor Bearing. Just want to check the I&O. Four-fifty, six, five. Okay. How are you feeling today? *(He makes notations on his clipboard throughout the scene.)*

Vivian: Fine.

Jason: That's great. Just great.

Vivian: How are my fluids?

Jason: Pretty good. No kidney involvement yet. That's pretty amazing, with Hex and Vin.

Vivian: How will you know when the kidneys are involved?

Jason: Lots of in, not much out.

Vivian: That simple.

Jason: Oh, no way. Compromised kidney function is a highly complex reaction. I'm simplifying for you.

Vivian: Thank you.

Jason: We're supposed to.

Vivian: Bedside manner.

Jason: Yeah, there's a whole course on it in med school. It's required. Colossal waste of time for researchers. *(He turns to go.)*

Vivian: I can imagine. *(Trying to ask something important)* Jason?

Jason: Huh?

Vivian (Not sure of herself): Ah, what . . . *(Quickly)* What were you just saying?

Jason: When?

Vivian: Never mind.

Jason: Professor Bearing?

Vivian: Yes.

Jason: Are you experiencing confusion? Short-term memory loss?

Vivian: No.

Jason: Sure?

Vivian: Yes. *(Pause)* I was just wondering: why cancer?

Jason: Why cancer?

Vivian: Why not open-heart surgery?

Jason: Oh yeah, why not *plumbing*. Why not run a *lube rack*, for all the surgeons know about *Homo sapiens sapiens*. No way. Cancer's the only thing I ever wanted.

Vivian (Intrigued): Huh.

Jason: No, really. Cancer is . . . *(Searching)*

Vivian (Helping): Awesome.

Jason (Pause): Yeah. Yeah, that's right. It is. It is awesome. How does it do it? The intercellular regulatory mechanisms—especially for proliferation and differentiation—the malignant neoplasia just don't get it. You grow normal cells in tissue culture in the lab, and they replicate just enough to make a nice, confluent monolayer. They divide twenty times, or fifty times, but eventually they conk out. You grow cancer cells, and they never stop. No contact inhibition whatsoever. They just pile up, just keep replicating forever. *(Pause)* That's got a funny name. Know what it is?

Vivian: No. What?

Jason: Immortality in culture.

Vivian: Sounds like a symposium.

Jason: It's an error in judgment, in a molecular way. But *why?* Even on the protistic level the normal cell–cell interactions are so subtle they'll take your breath away. Golden-brown algae, for instance, the lowest multicellular life form on earth—they're *idiots*—and it's incredible. It's perfect. So what's up with the cancer cells? Smartest guys in the world, with the best labs, funding—they don't know what to make of it.

Vivian: What about you?

Jason: Me? Oh, I've got a couple of ideas, things I'm kicking around. Wait till I get a lab of my own. If I can survive this . . . *fellowship*.

Vivian: The part with the human beings.

Jason: Everybody's got to go through it. All the great researchers. They want us to be able to converse intelligently with the clinicians. As though *researchers* were the impediments. The clinicians are such troglodytes. So smarmy. Like we have to hold hands to discuss creatinine clearance. Just cut the crap, I say.

Vivian: Are you going to be sorry when I— Do you ever miss people?

Jason: Everybody asks that. Especially girls.

Vivian: What do you tell them?

Jason: I tell them yes.

Vivian: Are they persuaded?

Jason: Some.

Vivian: Some. I see. *(With great difficulty)* And what do you say when a patient is . . . apprehensive . . . frightened.

Jason: Of who?

Vivian: I just . . . Never mind.

Jason: Professor Bearing, who is the President of the United States?

Vivian: I'm fine, really. It's all right.

Jason: You sure? I could order a test—

Vivian: No! No, I'm fine. Just a little tired.

Jason: Okay. Look. Gotta go. Keep pushing the fluids. Try for 2,000 a
day, okay?

Vivian: Okay. To use your word. Okay.

> (Jason *leaves.*)

Vivian (Getting out of bed, without her IV): So. The young doctor like the
senior scholar, prefers research to humanity. At the same time the senior
scholar, in her pathetic state as a simpering victim, wishes the young
doctor would take more interest in personal contact.

> Now I suppose we shall see, through a series of flashbacks, how the
senior scholar ruthlessly denied her simpering students the touch of
human kindness she now seeks.

> (Students *appear, sitting at chairs with writing desks attached to the*
right arm.)

Vivian (Commanding attention): How then would you characterize (*pointing
to a student*)—you.

Student 1: Huh?

Vivian: How would you characterize the animating force of this sonnet?

Student 1: Huh?

Vivian: In this sonnet, what is the principal poetic device? I'll give you a
hint. It has nothing to do with football. What propels this sonnet?

Student 1: Um.

Vivian (Speaking to the audience): Did I say (*tenderly*) "You are nineteen years
old. You are so young. You don't know a sonnet from a steak sandwich."
(*Pause*) By no means.

> (*Sharply, to* Student 1) You can come to this class prepared, or you
can excuse yourself from this class, this department, and this university.
Do not think for a moment that I will tolerate anything in between.

> (*To the audience, defensively*) I was teaching him a lesson. (*She walks*
away from Student 1, *then turns and addresses the class.*)

> So we have another instance of John Donne's agile wit at work:
not so much *resolving* the issues of life and God as *reveling* in their
complexity.

Student 1: But why?

Vivian: Why what?

Student 2: Why does Donne make everything so *complicated*? (*The other*
Students *laugh in agreement.*) No, really, *why*?

Vivian (To the audience): You know, someone asked me that every year. And
it was always one of the smart ones. What could I say? (*To* Student 2)
What do you think?

Student 2: I think it's like he's hiding. I think he's really confused, I don't
know, maybe he's scared, so he hides behind all this complicated stuff,
hides behind this *wit*.

Vivian: *Hides* behind *wit?*

Student 2: I mean, if it's really something he's sure of, he can say it more simple—simply. He doesn't have to be such a brain, or such a performer. It doesn't have to be such a big deal.

(*The other* Students *encourage him.*)

Vivian: Perhaps he is suspicious of simplicity.

Student 2: Perhaps, but that's pretty stupid.

Vivian (To the audience): That observation, despite its infelicitous phrasing, contained the seed of a perspicacious remark. Such an unlikely occurrence left me with two choices. I could draw it out, or I could allow the brain to rest after that heroic effort. If I pursued, there was the chance of great insight, or the risk of undergraduate banality. I could never predict. (*To* Student 2) Go on.

Student 2: Well, if he's trying to figure out God, and the meaning of life, and big stuff like that, why does he keep running away, you know?

Vivian (To the audience, moving closer to Student 2): So far so good, but they can think for themselves only so long before they begin to self-destruct.

Student 2: Um, it's like, the more you hide, the less—no, wait—the more you are getting closer—although you don't know it—and the simple thing is there—you see what I mean?

Vivian (To the audience, looking at Student 2, *as suspense collapses):* Lost it.

(*She walks away and speaks to the audience.*) I distinctly remember an exchange between two students after my lecture on pronunciation and scansion. I overheard them talking on their way out of class. They were young and bright, gathering their books and laughing at the expense of seventeenth-century poetry, at *my* expense.

(*To the class*) To scan the line properly, we must take advantage of the contemporary flexibility in "i-o-n" endings, as in "expansion." The quatrain stands:

> Our two souls therefore, which are one,
> > Though I must go, endure not yet
> A breach, but an ex-*pan*-see-on,
> > Like gold to airy thinness beat.

Bear this in mind in your reading. That's all for today.

(*The* Students *get up in a chaotic burst.* Student 3 *and* Student 4 *pass by* Vivian *on their way out.*)

Student 3: I hope I can get used to this pronuncia-see-on.

Student 4: I know. I hope I can survive this course and make it to gradua-see-on.

(*They laugh.* Vivian *glowers at them. They fall silent, embarrassed.*)

Vivian (To the audience): That was a witty little exchange, I must admit. It showed the mental acuity I would praise in a poetic text. But I admired only the studied application of wit, not its spontaneous eruption.

(Student 1 *interrupts.*)

Student 1: Professor Bearing? Can I talk to you for a minute?
Vivian: You may.
Student 1: I need to ask for an extension on my paper. I'm really sorry, and I
    know your policy, but see—
Vivian: Don't tell me. Your grandmother died.
Student 1: You knew.
Vivian: It was a guess.
Student 1: I have to go home.
Vivian: Do what you will, but the paper is due when it is due.

(*As* Student 1 *leaves and the classroom disappears,* Vivian *watches. Pause*)

Vivian: I don't know. I feel so much—what is the word? I look back, I see
    these scenes, and I . . .

(*Long silence.* Vivian *walks absently around the stage, trying to think of something. Finally, giving up, she trudges back to bed.*)

———————————

Vivian: It was late at night, the graveyard shift. Susie was on. I could hear
    her in the hall.
        I wanted her to come and see me. So I had to create a little emer-
    gency. Nothing dramatic.

(Vivian *pinches the IV tubing. The pump alarm beeps.*)

It worked.

(Susie *enters, concerned.*)

Susie: Ms. Bearing? Is that you beeping at four in the morning? (*She checks
    the tubing and presses buttons on the pump. The alarm stops.*) Did that wake
    you up? I'm sorry. It just gets occluded sometimes.
Vivian: I was awake.
Susie: You were? What's the trouble, sweetheart?
Vivian (*To the audience, roused*): Do not think for a minute that anyone calls
    me "Sweetheart." But then . . . I allowed it. (*To* Susie) Oh, I don't know.
Susie: You can't sleep?
Vivian: No. I just keep thinking.
Susie: If you do that too much, you can get kind of confused.
Vivian: I know. I can't figure things out. I'm in a . . . *quandary*, having
    these . . . *doubts.*
Susie: What you're doing is very hard.
Vivian: Hard things are what I like best.
Susie: It's not the same. It's like it's out of control, isn't it?
Vivian (*Crying, in spite of herself*): I'm scared.
Susie (*Stroking her*): Oh, honey, of course you are.
Vivian: I want . . .
Susie: I know. It's hard.

Vivian: I don't feel sure of myself anymore.

Susie: And you used to feel sure.

Vivian (Crying): Oh, yes, I used to feel sure.

Susie: Vivian. It's all right. I know. It hurts. I know. It's all right. Do you want a tissue? It's all right. *(Silence)* Vivian, would you like a Popsicle?

Vivian (Like a child): Yes, please.

Susie: I'll get it for you. I'll be right back.

Vivian: Thank you.

(Susie *leaves.*)

Vivian (Pulling herself together): The epithelial cells in my GI tract have been killed by the chemo. The cold Popsicle feels good, it's something I can digest, and it helps keep me hydrated. For your information.

(Susie *returns with an orange two-stick Popsicle. Vivian unwraps it and breaks it in half.*)

Vivian: Here.

Susie: Sure?

Vivian: Yes.

Susie: Thanks. (Susie *sits down on the commode by the bed. Silence)* When I was a kid, we used to get these from a truck. The man would come around and ring his bell and we'd all run over. Then we'd sit on the curb and eat our Popsicles.

   Pretty profound, huh?

Vivian: It sounds nice.

(Silence)

Susie: Vivian, there's something we need to talk about, you need to think about.

(Silence)

Vivian: My cancer is not being cured, is it.

Susie: Huh-uh.

Vivian: They never expected it to be, did they.

Susie: Well, they thought the drugs would make the tumor get smaller, and it has gotten a lot smaller. But the problem is that it started in new places too. They've learned a lot for their research. It was the best thing they had to give you, the strongest drugs. There just isn't a good treatment for what you have yet, for advanced ovarian. I'm sorry. They should have explained this—

Vivian: I knew.

Susie: You did.

Vivian: I read between the lines.

Susie: What you have to think about is your "code status." What you want them to do if your heart stops.

Vivian: Well.

Susie: You can be "full code," which means that if your heart stops, they'll call a Code Blue and the code team will come and resuscitate you and take you to Intensive Care until you stabilize again. Or you can be "Do Not Resuscitate," so if your heart stops we'll . . . well, we'll just let it. You'll be "DNR." You can think about it, but I wanted to present both choices before Kelekian and Jason talk to you.

Vivian: You don't agree about this?

Susie: Well, they like to save lives. So anything's okay, as long as life continues. It doesn't matter if you're hooked up to a million machines. Kelekian is a great researcher and everything. And the fellows, like Jason, they're really smart. It's really an honor for them to work with him. But they always . . . want to know more things.

Vivian: I always want to know more things. I'm a scholar. Or I was when I had shoes, when I had eyebrows.

Susie: Well, okay then. You'll be full code. That's fine.

(Silence)

Vivian: No, don't complicate the matter.

Susie: It's okay. It's up to you—

Vivian: Let it stop.

Susie: Really?

Vivian: Yes.

Susie: So if your heart stops beating—

Vivian: Just let it stop.

Susie: Sure?

Vivian: Yes.

Susie: Okay. I'll get Kelekian to give the order, and then—

Vivian: Susie?

Susie: Uh-huh?

Vivian: You're still going to take care of me, aren't you?

Susie: 'Course, sweetheart. Don't you worry.

(As Susie *leaves,* Vivian *sits upright, full of energy and rage.)*

Vivian: That certainly was a *maudlin* display. Popsicles? "Sweetheart"? I can't believe my life has become so . . . *corny.*

But it can't be helped. I don't see any other way. We are discussing life and death, and not in the abstract, either; we are discussing *my* life and *my* death, and my brain is dulling, and poor Susie's was never very sharp to begin with, and I can't conceive of any other . . . *tone.*

(Quickly) Now is not the time for verbal swordplay, for unlikely flights of imagination and wildly shifting perspectives, for metaphysical conceit, for wit.

And nothing would be worse than a detailed scholarly analysis. Erudition. Interpretation. Complication.

(Slowly) Now is a time for simplicity. Now is a time for, dare I say it, kindness.

(Searchingly) I thought being extremely smart would take care of it. But I see that I have been found out. Ooohhh.

I'm scared. Oh, God. I want . . . I want . . . No. I want to hide. I just want to curl up in a little ball. (*She dives under the covers.*)

(*Vivian wakes in horrible pain. She is tense, agitated, fearful. Slowly she calms down and addresses the audience.*)

Vivian (*Trying extremely hard*): I want to tell you how it feels. I want to explain it, to use *my* words. It's as if . . . I can't . . . There aren't . . . I'm like a student and this is the final exam and I don't know what to put down because I don't understand the question and I'm *running out of time.*

The time for extreme measures has come. I am in terrible pain. Susie says that I need to begin aggressive pain management if I am going to stand it.

"It": such a little word. In this case, I think "it" signifies "being alive."

I apologize in advance for what this palliative treatment modality does to the dramatic coherence of my play's last scene. It can't be helped. They have to do something. I'm in terrible pain.

Say it, Vivian. *It hurts like hell. It really does.*

(*Susie enters. Vivian is writhing in pain.*)

Oh, God. Oh, God.

Susie: Sshh. It's okay. Sshh. I paged Kelekian up here, and we'll get you some meds.

Vivian: Oh, God, it is so painful. So painful. So much pain. So much pain.

Susie: I know, I know, it's okay. Sshh. Just try and clear your mind. It's all right. We'll get you a Patient-Controlled Analgesic. It's a little pump, and you push a little button, and you decide how much medication you want. (*Importantly*) It's very simple, and it's up to you.

(*Kelekian storms in; Jason follows with chart.*)

Kelekian: Dr. Bearing. Susie.

Susie: Time for Patient-Controlled Analgesic. The pain is killing her.

Kelekian: Dr. Bearing, are you in pain? (*Kelekian holds out his hand for chart; Jason hands it to him. They read.*)

Vivian (*Sitting up, unnoticed by the staff*): Am I in pain? I don't believe this. Yes, I'm in goddamn pain. (*Furious*) I have a fever of 101 spiking to 104. And I have bone metastases in my pelvis and both femurs. (*Screaming*) There is cancer eating away at my goddamn bones, and I did not know there could be such pain on this earth.

(*She flops back on the bed and cries audibly to them.*) Oh, God.

Kelekian (*Looking at* Vivian *intently*): I want a morphine drip.

Susie: What about Patient-Controlled? She could be more alert—

Kelekian (*Teaching*): Ordinarily, yes. But in her case, no.

Susie: But—

Kelekian (*To* Susie): She's earned a rest. (*To* Jason) Morphine, ten push now, then start at ten an hour. (*To* Vivian) Dr. Bearing, try to relax. We're going to help you through this, don't worry. Dr. Bearing? Excellent. *(He squeezes* Vivian's *shoulder. They all leave.)*

Vivian (Weakly, painfully, leaning on her IV pole, she moves to address the audience.): Hi. How are you feeling today?

(Silence)

> These are my last coherent lines. I'll have to leave the action to the professionals.
>
> It came so quickly, after taking so long. Not even time for a proper conclusion.

(Vivian concentrates with all her might, and she attempts a grand summation, as if trying to conjure her own ending.)

> And Death—*capital D*—shall be no more—semi-colon.
> Death—*capital D*—thou shalt die—*ex-cla-mation point!*

(She looks down at herself, looks out at the audience, and sees that the line doesn't work. She shakes her head and exhales with resignation.)

> I'm sorry.

(She gets back into bed as Susie *injects morphine into the IV tubing.* Vivian *lies down and, in a final melodramatic gesture, shuts the lids of her own eyes and folds her arms over her chest.)*

Vivian: I trust this will have a soporific effect.
Susie: Well, I don't know about that, but it sure makes you sleepy.

(This strikes Vivian *as delightfully funny. She starts to giggle, then laughs out loud.* Susie *doesn't get it.)*

Susie: What's so funny? *(Vivian keeps laughing).* What?
Vivian: Oh! It's that—"Soporific" *means* "makes you sleepy."
Susie: It does?
Vivian: Yes. *(Another fit of laughter)*
Susie (Giggling): Well, that was pretty dumb—
Vivian: No! No, no! It was *funny!*
Susie (Starting to catch on): Yeah, I guess so. *(Laughing)* In a dumb sort of way. *(This sets them both off laughing again)* I never would have gotten it. I'm glad you explained it.
Vivian (Simply): I'm a teacher.

(They laugh a little together. Slowly the morphine kicks in, and Vivian's *laughs become long sighs. Finally she falls asleep.* Susie *checks everything out, then leaves. Long silence)*

(Jason and Susie *chat as they enter to insert a catheter.)*

Jason: Oh, yeah. She was a great scholar. Wrote tons of books, articles,

was the head of everything. *(He checks the I&O sheet.)* Two hundred.
Seventy-five. Five-twenty. Let's up the hydration. She won't be drinking
anymore. See if we can keep her kidneys from fading. Yeah, I had a lot
of respect for her, which is more than I can say for the *entire* biochemistry department.

Susie: What do you want? Dextrose?

Jason: Give her saline.

Susie: Okay.

Jason: She gave a hell of a lecture. No notes, not a word out of place. It was
pretty impressive. A lot of students hated her, though.

Susie: Why?

Jason: Well, she wasn't exactly a cupcake.

Susie (Laughing, fondly): Well, she hasn't exactly been a cupcake here, either.
(Leaning over Vivian *and talking loudly and slowly in her ear)* Now, Ms.
Bearing, Jason and I are here, and we're going to insert a catheter to
collect your urine. It's not going to hurt, don't you worry. *(During the
conversation she inserts the catheter.)*

Jason: Like she can hear you.

Susie: It's just nice to do.

Jason: Eight cycles of Hex and Vin at the full dose. Kelekian didn't think it
was possible. I wish they could all get through it at full throttle. Then
we could really have some data.

Susie: She's not what I imagined. I thought somebody who studied poetry
would be sort of dreamy, you know?

Jason: Oh, not the way she did it. It felt more like boot camp than English
class. This guy John Donne was incredibly intense. Like your whole
brain had to be in knots before you could get it.

Susie: He made it hard on purpose?

Jason: Well, it has to do with the subject. The Holy Sonnets we worked on
most, they were mostly about Salvation Anxiety. That's a term I made
up in one of my papers, but I think it fits pretty well. Salvation Anxiety.
You're this brilliant guy, I mean, brilliant—this guy makes Shakespeare
sound like a Hallmark card. And you know you're a sinner. And there's
this promise of salvation, the whole religious thing. But you just can't
deal with it.

Susie: How come?

Jason: It just doesn't stand up to scrutiny. But you can't face life without it
either. So you write these screwed-up sonnets. Everything is brilliantly
convoluted. Really tricky stuff. Bouncing off the walls. Like a game, to
make the puzzle so complicated.

(The catheter is inserted. Susie *puts things away.)*

Susie: But what happens in the end?

Jason: End of what?

Susie: To John Donne. Does he ever get it?

Jason: Get what?

Susie: His Salvation Anxiety. Does he ever understand?

Jason: Oh, no way. The puzzle takes over. You're not even trying to solve it anymore. Fascinating, really. Great training for lab research. Looking at things in increasing levels of complexity.

Susie: Until what?

Jason: What do you mean?

Susie: Where does it end? Don't you get to solve the puzzle?

Jason: Nah. When it comes right down to it, research is just trying to quantify the complications of the puzzle.

Susie: But you *help* people! You save lives and stuff.

Jason: Oh, yeah, I save some guy's life, and then the poor slob gets hit by a bus!

Susie (Confused): Yeah, I guess so. I just don't think of it that way. Guess you can tell I never took a class in poetry.

Jason: Listen, if there's one thing we learned in Seventeenth-Century Poetry, it's that you can forget about that sentimental stuff. *Enzyme Kinetics* was more poetic than Bearing's class. Besides, you can't think about that *meaning-of-life* garbage all the time or you'd go nuts.

Susie: Do you believe in it?

Jason: In what?

Susie: Umm. I don't know, the meaning-of-life garbage. *(She laughs a little.)*

Jason: What do they *teach* you in nursing school? *(Checking* Vivian's *pulse)* She's out of it. Shouldn't be too long. You done here?

Susie: Yeah, I'll just . . . tidy up.

Jason: See ya. *(He leaves.)*

Susie: Bye, Jace. *(She thinks for a minute, then carefully rubs baby oil on* Vivian's *hands. She checks the catheter, then leaves.)*

———————————

(Professor E. M. Ashford, *now eighty, enters.)*

E.M.: Vivian? Vivian? It's Evelyn. Vivian?

Vivian (Waking, slurred): Oh, God. *(Surprised)* Professor Ashford. Oh, God.

E.M: I'm in town visiting my great-grandson, who is celebrating his fifth birthday. I went to see you at your office, and they directed me here. *(She lays her jacket, scarf, and parcel on the bed.)* I have been walking all over town. I had forgotten how early it gets chilly here.

Vivian (Weakly): I feel so bad.

E.M.: I know you do. I can see. (Vivian *cries.)* Oh, dear, there, there. There, there. *(Vivian cries more, letting the tears flow.)* Vivian, Vivian. *(E.M. looks toward the hall, then furtively slips off her shoes and swings up on the bed. She puts her arm around Vivian.)* There, there. There, there, Vivian. *(Silence)*

It's a windy day. *(Silence)*

Don't worry, dear. *(Silence)*

Let's see. Shall I recite to you? Would you like that? I'll recite something by Donne.

Vivian (Moaning): Nooooooo.

Set design for *Death of a Salesman* by Jo Mielziner

Sir John Everett Millais, *Ferdinand Lured by Ariel* (1849)

E.M.: Very well. *(Silence)* Hmmm. *(Silence)* Little Jeffrey is very sweet. Gets into everything.

(Silence. E.M. takes a children's book out of the paper bag and begins reading. Vivian nestles in, drifting in and out of sleep.)

Let's see. *The Runaway Bunny.* By Margaret Wise Brown. Pictures by Clement Hurd. Copyright 1942. First Harper Trophy Edition, 1972. Now then.
Once there was a little bunny who wanted to run away.
So he said to his mother, "I am running away."
"If you run away," said his mother, "I will run after you. For you are my little bunny."
"If you run after me," said the little bunny, "I will become a fish in a trout stream and I will swim away from you."
"If you become a fish in a trout stream," said his mother, "I will become a fisherman and I will fish for you."
(Thinking out loud) Look at that. A little allegory of the soul. No matter where it hides, God will find it. See, Vivian?
Vivian (Moaning): Uhhhhhh.
E.M.: "If you become a fisherman," said the little bunny, "I will be a bird and fly away from you."
"If you become a bird and fly away from me," said his mother, " I will be a tree that you come home to."
(To herself) Very clever.
"Shucks," said the little bunny, "I might just as well stay where I am and be your little bunny."
And so he did.
"Have a carrot," said the mother bunny.
(To herself) Wonderful.

(Vivian is now fast asleep. E.M. slowly gets down and gathers her things. She leans over and kisses her.)

It's time to go. And flights of angels sing thee to thy rest. *(She leaves.)*

(Jason strides in and goes directly to the I&O sheet without looking at Vivian.)

Jason: Professor Bearing. How are you feeling today? Three p.m. IV hydration totals. Two thousand in. Thirty out. Uh-oh. That's it. Kidneys gone.
(He looks at Vivian.) Professor Bearing? Highly unresponsive. Wait a second—*(Puts his head down to her mouth and chest to listen for heartbeat and breathing)* Wait a sec—Jesus Christ! *(Yelling)* CALL A CODE!

(Jason throws down the chart, dives over the bed, and lies on top of her body as he reaches for the phone and punches in the numbers.)

(To himself) Code: 4-5-7-5. *(To operator)* Code Blue, room 707. Code Blue, room 707. Dr. Posner—P-O-S-N-E-R. Hurry up!

(*He throws down the phone and lowers the head of the bed.*)

      Come on, come on, COME ON.

(*He begins CPR, kneeling over* Vivian, *alternately pounding frantically and giving mouth-to-mouth resuscitation. Over the loudspeaker in the hall, a droning voice repeats "Code Blue, room 707. Code Blue, room 707."*)

      One! Two! Three! Four! Five! (*He breathes in her mouth.*)

(Susie, *hearing the announcement, runs into the room.*)

Susie: WHAT ARE YOU DOING?
Jason: A GODDAMN CODE. GET OVER HERE!
Susie: She's DNR! (*She grabs him.*)
Jason (*He pushes her away.*): She's Research!
Susie: She's NO CODE!

(Susie *grabs* Jason *and hurls him off the bed.*)

Jason: Ooowww! Goddamnit, Susie!
Susie: She's no code!
Jason: Aaargh!
Susie: Kelekian put the order in—you saw it! You were right there, Jason!
      Oh, God, the code! (*She runs to the phone. He struggles to stand.*) 4-5-7-5.

(*The* Code Team *swoops in. Everything changes. Frenzy takes over. They knock* Susie *out of the way with their equipment.*)

Susie (*At the phone*): Cancel code, room 707. Sue Monahan, primary nurse.
      Cancel code. Dr. Posner is here.
Jason (*In agony*): Oh, God.
Code Team: —Get out of the way!
              —Unit staff out!
              —Get the board!
              —Over here!

(*They throw* Vivian's *body up at the waist and stick a board underneath for CPR. In a whirlwind of sterile packaging and barked commands, one team member attaches a respirator, one begins CPR, and one prepares the defibrillator.* Susie *and* Jason *try to stop them but are pushed away. The loudspeaker in the hall announces "Cancel code, room 707. Cancel code, room 707."*)

Code Team: —Bicarb amp!
              —I got it! (*To* Susie) Get out!
              —One, two, three, four, five!
              —Get ready to shock! (*To* Jason) Move it!
Susie (*Running to each person, yelling*): STOP! Patient is DNR!
Jason (*At the same time, to the* Code Team): No, no! Stop doing this. STOP!
Code Team: —Keep it going!
              —What do you get?
              —Bicarb amp!
              —No pulse!

Susie: She's NO CODE! Order was given— *(She dives for the chart and holds it up as she cries out)* Look! Look at this! DO NOT RESUSCITATE. KELEKIAN.
Code Team: (As they administer electric shock, Vivian's body arches and bounces back down.)
　　　　—Almost ready!
　　　　—Hit her!
　　　　—CLEAR!
　　　　—Pulse? Pulse?
Jason (Howling): I MADE A MISTAKE!

(Pause. The Code Team *looks at him. He collapses on the floor.)*

Susie: No code! Patient is no code.
Code Team Head: Who the hell are you?
Susie: Sue Monahan, primary nurse.
Code Team Head: Let me see the goddamn chart. CHART!
Code Team: (Slowing down)
　　　　—What's going on?
　　　　—Should we stop?
　　　　—What's it say?
Susie (Pushing them away from the bed): Patient is no code. Get away from her!

(Susie lifts the blanket.) Vivian *steps out of the bed.*	*Code Team Head: (Reading)* Do Not Resuscitate. Kelekian. Shit.
She walks away from the scene, toward a little light.	*(The* Code Team *stops working.)*
She is now attentive and eager, moving slowly toward the light.	*Jason: (Whispering)* Oh, God.
She takes off her cap and lets it drop.	*Code Team Head:* Order was put in yesterday.
She slips off her bracelet.	*Code Team:*
She loosens the ties and the top gown slides to the floor. She lets the second gown fall.	—It's a doctor fuck-up. —What is he, a resident? —Got us up here on a DNR.
The instant she is naked, and beautiful, reaching for the light—	—Called a code on a no-code. *Jason:* Oh, God.
Lights out.)	*(The bedside scene fades.)*

SUSIE: She's NO CODE! Order was given — (She dives for the chart and both it up and reads it over.) Look! Look at this! DO NOT RESUSCITATE.

KELEKIAN

CODE TEAM: (As they administer electric shock, Vivian's body arches and bounces from the table.)

—Almost ready—

—Hit her!

—CLEAR—

—Pulse? Pulse?

JASON: (Horrified) I MADE A MISTAKE!

(Pause. The Code Team looks at him. He collapses on the floor.)

SUSIE: No code! Patient is no code.

CODE TEAM HEAD: Who the hell are you?

SUSIE: Susie Monahan, primary nurse.

CODE TEAM HEAD: Let me see the goddamn chart. CHART!

CODE TEAM: (Slowing down)

—What's going on?

—Should we stop?

—What's it say?

SUSIE: (Pushing them away from the bed) Patient is no code. Get away from her!

(Susie lifts the blanket.)
Vivian steps out of the bed.

She walks away from the scene, toward a small light.

She is now attentive and eager, moving slowly toward the light.

She takes off her cap and lets it drop.

She slips off her bracelet.

She loosens the ties of her top gown and lets it go to the floor. She lets the second gown fall.

The instrument is naked and beautiful, reaching for the light—

Lights out.

CODE TEAM HEAD: (Reading) Do Not Resuscitate. Kelekian. Shit.

(The Code Team stops working.)

JASON: (Despairing) Oh, God.

CODE TEAM HEAD: Order was put in yesterday.

CODE TEAM:

—It's a doctor fuck-up.

—What is it, a resident?

—Got us up here on a DNR.

—Called a code on a no-code.

JASON: Oh, God.

(The bedside scene fades.)

WRITING

Part IX
Writing about Literature

52   Writing about Literature

A well-known writer was once asked his opinion about a topic. He responded by saying that he could not possibly answer the question until he saw what he had written about it. The point is a particularly cogent one and very relevant to the composition of papers on literary topics: Essay-writing affords a reader the opportunity to organize ideas or responses, and to meditate deeply on the text or texts under consideration. Writing clarifies not only what is important about a text, illuminating what really matters to its construction, language, or meaning, but also what is important to the reader herself.

An essay, true to its origin in the French verb *essayer*, meaning "to try or attempt," communicates its author's efforts to convey his or her reflections about a text or group of texts. At the same time, these reflections constitute an attempt to persuade an audience of their interpretive validity and explanatory power. Writing about literature, therefore, is also writing about reading. But how to begin? What plan of attack will be most effective in conveying your ideas?

Getting Ready, Making Decisions

As your instructor will explain and as we outline in greater detail in Chapter 56, "Writing a Research Paper," a writer needs to consider a number of questions before typing the first word: What audience am I addressing? What do they know about the text I want to discuss? What language will be most effective or appropriate in communicating to this audience? In other words, what assumptions should I make about the *rhetorical situation?* A writer always weighs these and other questions carefully before beginning, considering each point of the triangle below.

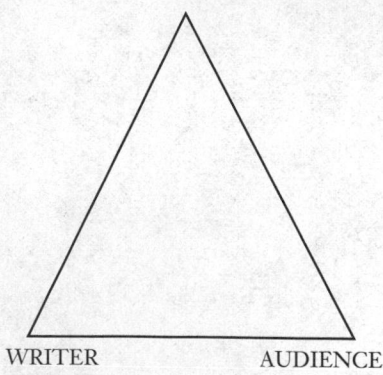

WRITER   AUDIENCE

In preparing to write essays on literary topics, you should consider, among other things, who will read the paper and why. Assume that your audience is already familiar with the work you intend to discuss; thus, there is little reason to summarize the plot or rehearse the attractions or shortcomings of central characters if you are writing about a play or short story. Your audience knows, for example, that Hamlet meets a tragic fate and that Oedipus' last day as king of Thebes is not a happy one. What kind of language and evidence will be most effective in addressing this audience? What role do you as writer play? Generally, the answer is none at all. You are not a professor or academician, nor are you talking to a personal friend. You aren't in a locker room either, so select terms appropriate both to the occasion of the composition and the audience. This is especially true when crafting your thesis, the most significant aspect of your essay that your audience does *not* know.

The thesis embodies your purpose in writing the paper in the first place. Unlike, say, the occupation of a drama or film reviewer in a newspaper, your job in writing about literature is to persuade your audience of the significance of your topic to an understanding of the text you are discussing. The single statement most crucial to this enterprise is your *thesis statement*.

Thesis Statements

The thesis statement provides focus and purpose for the entire essay. Because it represents the most direct expression of your "big idea" about the literature you have read, the thesis statement may take longer to formulate than any other sentence you prepare. And it may take some time, some experimentation, and some trial-and-error before you arrive at the precise point you want to make. As we discuss in detail in Chapter 54, "Writing about Poetry," you may want to try such techniques as *freewriting* or *brainstorming*, where you put down on paper as quickly as you can whatever thoughts enter your mind about a topic. Don't stop to worry about punctuation or spelling—these can be corrected later. In a freewriting exercise, sometimes called "automatic writing," simply transcribe your thoughts into words on a page or screen, revising them later into more precise and compelling statements. The purpose of this exercise is invention: You are trying to purge your mind of thoughts on a topic, one of which may be refined later into a thesis statement.

You might also consider the thesis statement as the culmination of a process that narrows the topic: from a text to discuss, to a topic in or about the text, to a specific issue or reading. So, for example, if the text is William Blake's poem "London," the subject or topic might be the poem's imagery and image patterns; the thesis might argue for the importance of images of confinement, regulation, or imprisonment. Or, suppose you are afforded an opportunity to write about any aspect of Arthur Miller's drama *Death of a Salesman*. The subject might be characterization and the thesis might focus on questions about Linda, Willy Loman's wife. Does she aid Willy in his delusion, making his fantasies more extreme than they might otherwise be? Or, given what happens to Willy, another kind of thesis might argue that he stands as symptomatic of a capitalism run amok, one in which the "little guy" or "low man" has little chance of success. Same play, different subject and thesis, and the same process of narrowing the scope of what will become your *argument*.

Argument in this context *is* the correct term. You should select a topic that you can develop into a persuasive argument, which begins with articulating a coherent, concise, and arguable thesis statement. Thesis statements have several distinctive features or criteria, as the following six points summarize. Test the thesis statement for your paper against these characteristics: Does your thesis meet all of the following? If not, what adjustments will make the statement more specific, more forceful, or more significant?

1. Thesis statements are statements of opinion, not statements of fact or intention.

Statement of Fact

> In William Shakespeare's tragedy *Othello*, Iago does a number of evil, reprehensible things.

As any reader of *Othello* will readily concede, Iago *does* act maliciously and destructively. Consequently, a research paper cannot be organized around a statement of this fact. Iago is an evil man, Boston is located in Massachusetts, the Beatles are still popular—these facts do not require discussion or the presentation of evidence. They are self-evident.

Statement of Intention

> In my essay, I want to show you that Iago commits evil deeds.

This sentence is no better than the first one. It not only fails to advance an opinion, but also is wordier than the statement of fact: "In my essay, I want to show you that" is particularly ineffective and verbose.

Statement of Opinion

> Since the plot of *Othello* is Iago's plot, improvisation by Iago constitutes the tragedy's heart and center.

This sentence, taken from Harold Bloom's popular and controversial book *Shakespeare: The Invention of the Human* (1998), actually contains two opinions: that Iago drives the plot of *Othello* and that the play's structure results largely from his improvised manipulations. The latter assertion in particular is one with which a number of readers of the play might disagree, locating the "heart" of the tragedy in jealousy, racism, cultural sexism, and so on. Often, abstract terms like *heart* and *center* in thesis statements spark disagreement or simple confusion, so be careful when inserting abstractions into theses. Nonetheless, Bloom's assertion fits the first criterion of an effective thesis statement by stating an opinion, not a fact or intention.

2. A thesis statement advances an opinion about which informed and reasonable people might disagree.   As is the case with Bloom's reading of

Iago as a figure of universal evil, a thesis furthers an understanding about which informed readers might disagree. What would be the point of re-searching a topic about which everyone already possesses the same opinion? What would a reader of the paper learn that he or she does not know already? Thus, one way of testing a thesis is to present it to your classmates and deter-mine if they all share your view. If they do, you need to keep working.

3. A thesis statement often contains an underlying rhetorical premise. By *rhetorical premise* we mean a concept or mode of understanding that im-plicitly structures or organizes the rest of the paper. In the 1960s, the rhetori-cian Randall Decker published a widely used textbook called *Patterns of Exposition*, which included chapters on comparison, process analysis, causality, definition, classification, and other rhetorical modes or premises. Such prem-ises are frequently imbedded in the articulation of theses: "Willy Loman's col-lapse in Arthur Miller's *Death of a Salesman* progresses through three distinct stages" (this essay will follow the organizational strategy of process analysis); "The young boy's sudden insight at the end of James Joyce's 'Araby' is caused by the deflation of his fantasy" (this essay uses the organizational strategy of causality), and so on.

4. A thesis statement predicts, obligates, and controls what follows it. Rhetorician William Irmscher once made this point in a composition text-book, and its implications are still relevant today. Much like the title, a thesis suggests to a reader what course a research paper—or any essay, for that matter—will take. It *predicts*. It also *obligates* the writer to present evidence and discussion of the evidence consistent with the assertion; a writer cannot begin by claiming that Willy Loman experiences three distinct stages of psycholog-ical collapse and then later argue that there are, in fact, five stages to his downfall. Finally, a thesis *controls* the kinds of evidence relevant to the essay's purpose. If the thesis addresses Willy's troubled psychology, then long diag-noses of his wife's or sons' emotional problems would seem digressive unless they can be shown to affect his emotional state and decline.

5. A thesis statement takes on a topic of significance, often the answer to an implicit question. Many graduate students we know, parodying a well-known Victorian writer's phrases the "Everlasting Yea" and the "Ever-lasting Nay," talk about the "The Everlasting So What?" This means, simply, that a thesis should argue a point of importance. "Willy's decline progresses through three distinct stages"—so what? Why is this important? Notice, too, that all the examples we have used answer an unasked or implicit question, a "how" or "why" question: Why is the young boy in "Araby" so self-critical at the story's conclusion?

6. A thesis statement reflects theoretical or other assumptions that un-derlie your reading and, finally, the argument of the essay. All of the sample theses so far are based more or less on *formalist* premises: How is the plot constructed? How might a character's actions be explained? Why or how is an image, scene, or even a single word important to our understanding? Such questions quite properly involve close reading of the literary text, as they address one or more aspects of literary form. But, of course, as many of the chapters of *Understanding Literature* outline, other kinds of readings—and other premises for thesis statements—exist. They arise, in part, by asking different questions of the text: How is race or sexuality represented? How is social class or capitalism depicted? How does psychoanalytic theory, Marx's social theory, or feminist thought help explain a character's action or predicament? In other words, literature is more than a self-contained aesthetic object—or, to borrow a metaphor—it is more than an exceptionally "well-wrought urn." A literary text is also a social text, a historical artifact, a product made in a specific place, time, and culture. It can tell us much about these cultures and times as well.

These are, admittedly, difficult concepts that often lead to difficult questions and challenging thesis statements. But they must be asked and answered, because no writer—or reader—wants to waste his or her time on a topic of little consequence. If your paper addresses the actions of an important character, the implications of a major event or a significant *motif* (repetition in a poem, play, or story), then this close reading is likely to be important enough to make. If your essay concerns a matter of representation—how Africans are portrayed in Joseph Conrad's *Heart of Darkness*, how the city is represented in modernist fiction, how women are portrayed in Shakespeare's plays—the chances are you can focus this interest into a significant thesis statement and thus respond effectively to the "Everlasting So What?"

And there's one other bit of good news, too—you're probably ready to write.

Writing

But how do you begin? If you're at all like the authors of this textbook, then you've probably asked yourself this very question scores of times. A thesis statement might be introduced in any number of ways, but it is actually easier to identify ways *not* to begin. The advice of rhetorician William Irmscher is again helpful in explaining three opening strategies to avoid at all costs.

1. The "Panoramic" Historical Gesture. We've all read sentences like this one and tried to suppress our groans: "Since the dawn of time, man has pondered the nature of _____." This sentence is so trite and predictable that you can fill in the blank with any number of terms: *love*, *men*, *women*, *life*, and so on. But if it really is true that humans have puzzled over such weighty and complex matters for millennia, what chance do you have of resolving the matter in three to five pages? Obviously, this opening strategy—and that's what we are discussing, a strategy or tactic to present the thesis—has now lapsed into a parody of a profound utterance more likely to elicit laughter than respect.

The problem is, when you've stared into a blank computer screen for an hour, a sentence like this one starts to sound better and better—better than nothing. It isn't.

2. The Appeal to Mr. Webster. Whenever a writer is really strapped for an opening gambit, this sentence starts to sound better as well: "According to *Webster's Dictionary*, tragedy is defined as . . ." Like the "panoramic" opener—and the "fact" that grandparents tend to die on the very day papers are due in a class like this one—this strategy has been overused. More important, the dictionary provides only a basic understanding of a term, its common meanings or denotations. Literary perceptions of a term like *tragedy* are far more complex and historically contingent than the definitions in most dictionaries.

3. Irrelevant Biographical Detail. Young writers sometimes feel that literary understanding always begins with the biography of the author; consequently, they begin essays with hackneyed sentences: "Langston Hughes was born in Joplin, Missouri, in 1902." Fine. But save in the specific instance in which biography impinges directly upon reading, such a fact is not only superfluous, but irrelevant.

This was not always the case, which perhaps explains why the appeal to biography remains an attractive option for some students. In early twentieth-century British and American literary criticism, for example, biography often comprised the center around which interpretation revolved. In *The Human Approach to Literature* (1933), for example, William Freeman began a discussion of Chaucer's *Canterbury Tales* this way: "Geoffrey Chaucer, the sturdily-built man with the friendly brown eyes, was not merely a widely traveled Englishman who had passionately preserved his nationality, but a Londoner by birth and breeding."

Today, such opening strategies fail to introduce the real purpose of the essay and seem, well, almost silly. Chaucer's buff physique might be interesting, but surely it is not pertinent to a reading of his work. So why go there?

Fortunately, some devices *are* effective in introducing a thesis. You might begin with an epigraph, a brief quotation that encapsulates issues you feel are important to the text, and return to it in your opening paragraph (and later). You might start with a sensational detail, an anecdote, or a brief exchange of dialogue when discussing a play. Or, you might follow the instructions of countless composition texts by replicating the narrowing process discussed earlier, moving from a general subject, to a topic, to a specific statement.

The point is this: Thesis statements require introductions. The background of your "big idea" needs to be elaborated early in the essay and then, after your thesis is stated, you are ready to build a support structure for it. This is the body or argument of the essay.

Arguments and Admissible Evidence: Paraphrase and Quotation

Much like a lawyer in a criminal case who introduces materials into evidence and then "reads" the evidence in an attempt to persuade a judge or jury, writers of literary criticism marshal evidence carefully and discuss its implications. Persuasive arguments rely on well-chosen pieces of evidence and incisive analysis. The best kind of evidence is located in the literary text itself, parts of which will need to be summarized and paraphrased in the argument. For further discussion of paraphrase, see Chapter 56, "Writing a Research Paper."

But perhaps the most difficult task facing writers of all ages and experience is quoting from the text; that is, there will be occasions when a paraphrase or summary will not serve your needs. You will need to quote the original. But when? How much should you quote? What are the most graceful methods of integrating quoted excerpts into your own prose?

Let's take up this last question. In general, the same formula that makes for a good legal argument—evidence + analysis = guilt or innocence—applies in writing essays about literature. A prosecutor, for example, doesn't throw a weapon on a table and claim, "You see—that proves the defendant is guilty." Rather, a prosecutor examines the evidence, then builds an argument about it: Forensic analysis proves this is the murder weapon; the gun is registered to the defendant, who had a motive to kill the victim; the defendant was witnessed at the scene of the murder minutes before, and so on. If the lawyer is lucky, she might have eyewitnesses to depose, hair fibers or DNA evidence to present and discuss, and more: evidence + analysis = case. The same is true of building literary arguments: textual evidence (quotations or paraphrases) + your analysis = an argument.

To bring this to an even smaller, more precise case, consider the following:

your writing + quoted excerpts = complete sentence.

In other words, when quoting from a literary text don't simply drop a quotation between sentences; work to incorporate it into your sentence just as you attempt to integrate the piece of evidence into a larger argument. A citation should appear at the end of a quoted passage of any length (over a phrase or two), and usually this means that the citation appears at the end of a sentence. That is, try not to interrupt the sense of the sentence by placing page citations in the middle of clauses.

There are at least three proven ways of quoting effectively from a literary text.

1. Identification of the speaker + quotation. This method is employed in both popular and academic writing, usually for passages of four lines or less. Example: In Margaret Edson's *Wit*, Vivian Bearing explains, "I have cancer, insidious cancer, with pernicious side effects—no the *treatment* has pernicious side effects" (12). The positioning of the identification may be manipulated in any way that reads smoothly, for example: "I have cancer," Vivian Bearing explains in *Wit*, "insidious cancer, with pernicious side effects—no the *treatment* has pernicious side effects" (12). Again, variety of structure will enhance the readability of your essay. Don't begin every quotation with "Vivian says" or "Iago says."

Because the introduction of the quotation specifies the origin of the passage, there is no need to identify it a second time by citing the author's name or the work's title in parenthesis. If, however, the identification fails to make this clear, then the author's name should appear in the citation. A full bibliographic entry should appear at the end of your paper in a section entitled "Works Cited."

2. The "block quotation" for longer excerpts. Any passage greater than four lines should be set off from the paragraph by indenting on the left side, a method that renders quotation marks themselves superfluous. Lines taken from poems should be quoted exactly as they appear in the original—line by line—as should dialogue in blank verse from plays like Shakespeare's. Line numbers, not page numbers, should be cited for poems; and it is conventional to cite act, scene, and line numbers from plays edited with line numbers. For example:

> Toward the end of *The Tempest*, Prospero reveals to his visitors both the magical qualities of his island and his penchant for philosophy:
>
> Our revels now are ended. These our actors
> (As I foretold you) were all spirits, and
> Are melted into air, into thin air,
> And like the baseless fabric of this vision,
> The cloud-capp'd towers, the gorgeous palaces,
> The solemn temples, the great globe itself,
> Yea, all which it inherit, shall dissolve,
> And like this insubstantial pageant faded
> Leave not a rack behind. (4.1.148–56)

Or, to take another example, here is a passage from John Milton's elegy "Lycidas," written in memory of a friend who had drowned. Note that, as in the above cases, you must introduce the quotation, not simply "drop" it in the sentence.

> In "Lycidas," Milton's speaker searches for consolation in the sudden death of his friend and finds it, in part, in his faith:
>
> So Lycidas sunk low, but mounted high,
> Through the dear might of Him that walked the waves;
> Where other groves, and other streams along,
> With nectar pure his oozy locks he laves,
> And hears the unexpressive nuptial song,
> In the blest kingdoms meek of joy and love. (172–77)

In all of these examples, longer quotations are introduced by a complete sentence. But your responsibilities do not end here, because the quotation needs to be considered or "unpacked" thoroughly. After all, if the passage did not contain specific language that supports your argument, you would not have introduced it into evidence in the first place. Here, again, a balance between admissible evidence and your analysis is important. Remember: Quoting at length generally means discussing at length. This is entirely consistent with the logic that should inform your selection of the passage to quote: The very issues that led you to select the passage need to be conveyed to your reader.

3. Quoted phrases or "sound bites." Often you may want to quote only a word or phrase from the original. No problem. In these instances, take bits or "bites" of texts and work them smoothly into the syntax of your sentence. One suggestion might help: After quoting the bites, pretend that the quotation marks aren't there—that the bits are merely words in your sentence. Does it read smoothly and clearly as a sentence? If so, you have probably integrated the quoted excerpts well into your prose.

Examples

> Since the late 1950s, Bruce Conner has been an "important but shadowy" figure in the world of American art and film, a kind of "home-grown" artist with strong connections to California (Boswell 26).

> Recalling the orthodox mores that Beat culture attempted to overthrow, Joyce Johnson describes sex in the 1950s as a "serious and anxious act" (89).

> In *M. Butterfly*, Gallimard describes Butterfly in Puccini's opera as a "feminine ideal," and later he expresses his dismay that such an ideal could be debased by a "womanizing cad" (7, 9).

Note here that all three examples, in addition to crafting sentences that accommodate the quotations, employ different strategies of citation. The first example includes both a name and page number because the context does not identify the author of the quotation. The second example includes only a page number because the author's name—Joyce Johnson—is specified. The citation for the third example explains that the two phrases appear on different pages in the original.

In conclusion, select evidence carefully and present it in a meaningful pattern or logical order: Have you arranged it chronologically, in the order events occur in the literature you are discussing? Or have you elected to present the evidence in another way: from the least compelling example to the most compelling? From the easiest point to prove to the most difficult? In some other way? Paraphrase or summarize events as part of your argument— relevant events that provide a background or context for the specific argument you hope to build. When the language of the original is striking or so perfectly stated for your argument that you want to introduce it into evidence, follow the instructions we have just outlined. Last but not least, make certain that you have quoted *accurately:* word for word, punctuation mark for punctuation mark. Also, use the quotation fairly; in other words, make sure that it represents what you take to be the intent of the original.

If you do all of these things, there is an excellent chance the argument of your essay—your attempt at persuading your reader of the validity and importance of your thesis—will be successful.

Concluding

Like the creation of an effective introduction, the drafting of effective conclusions often poses a challenge. And, like trite introductions, ineffective conclusions are fairly easy to describe. Here's the worst:

> And, in conclusion, I have just shown you that John Milton's speaker in "Lycidas" derives consolation from his religious beliefs.

Why is this such a weak statement? For several reasons. First, in a brief paper of three to five pages, it's fairly easy to determine that you are heading for a conclusion; you don't need to announce this. Second, the reader will decide whether you've made the case or not; the statement "I have just shown you" may in fact be inaccurate, because you might *not* have succeeded in making the case persuasively. Last, other than bringing the argument to a close, what is gained by this kind of sentence?

Fortunately, better concluding strategies exist. You might restate the thesis and offer a brief suggestion of its implications—or of matters related to the thesis that could not be admitted into your argument. Why is the thesis significant? What intellectual purchase or insight does it allow your reader? Such a tactic should not lead to a lengthy digression; rather, a strong thesis possesses a quality of interpretive richness that often exceeds the limits of the essay. Thus, in your conclusion you might outline briefly what other kinds of issues will be better understood because of your thesis statement. You might return to the epigraph or startling fact with which your essay began (assuming you employed one of these strategies). Or you might speculate briefly on how the field of evidence might have been expanded had you been afforded the opportunity of doing so.

Whatever strategy you use, remember that, like introductions, your conclusion for a short essay need not be overly elaborate. But you *do* need to bring the argument to closure.

Revision and Final Thoughts

Be sure to leave ample time to proofread your essay, which—we know—is advice easier to give than follow. Procrastination is the great enemy of revision. If you wait to begin your paper the night before it is due, the revision process will inevitably be compromised—or just totally nuked! So, get started early.

Then, after you have produced a rough draft, begin your revision process strategically. Does your essay satisfy the requirement of the assignment your instructor gave you? Is the title effective? Next, proceed to the largest elements of composition: arguments and paragraphs. Is the argument delineated in a logical and persuasive order? Are the paragraphs coherent, with immediately relevant topic sentences, evidence, and analysis? Is there an effective balance between evidence and discussion? Have you varied the lengths of quotations and your methods of introducing them? Have you created effective transitions between paragraphs and points of the argument?

Then, move to smaller matters, beginning with the problems your instructor has identified in previous essays. These differ from one writer to the next. Some have difficulty with sentence construction, others with phrasing and word choice, still others with spelling and punctuation. Recognize those areas of composition that have caused you difficulty in the past and revise them carefully. When writing on literary topics, again, accuracy is a crucial matter: Check every quotation against the original and make certain the citations are accurate. Also, be sure that you have followed your instructor's requirements in terms of pagination, presentation, and so on.

With any luck, this essay will prove a learning experience for you. How will you know what you think until you've seen what you have written?

53 Writing about Fiction

Just as any kind of writing helps writers clarify what they might think about a question, anyone who writes about fiction writes to explain, illuminate, enrich, deepen, connect, or even admire stories and novels. When scholars and literary critics write about fiction, they pose questions: What does this mean? How does this work? How is this fiction related to other works? How is this story related to its social and historical contexts? How does a work employ or describe sexual, gender, class, or racial relations? What does this fiction tell us about fiction in general or the act of reading or writing?

Experienced writers tend to answer such questions by providing a conclusion about how specific elements of a story or novel might express or convey an idea or produce an aesthetic effect. Like all good writers, they base their view on evidence from the specific fictional works under discussion, and perhaps from its historical context.

Another way writers offer ideas about understanding a story comes from using a particular set of assumptions that belong to one or another of the critical theories about literature. In this book, you have seen presented many different approaches (or theories) about literature including formalism, close reading, psychoanalytic criticism, feminist criticism, Marxist criticism, deconstruction, and reader response criticism. These critical approaches depend on slightly different sets of assumptions about how literary texts do what they do or arise partly from asking different questions about texts. For example, writers who want to study how a story's various parts—character, narrator, imagery, and style—work together to produce certain effects engage in analyses based on close reading. Writers exploring a psychoanalytic view ask how a story might reflect various tenets of psychoanalysis or illustrate or enact certain relationships in terms best understood through psychoanalytic categories.

Thoughtful writing about fiction enriches our understanding of how a story works. Such a thesis is seldom the only "truth" to be discovered about a story, since fiction is rich, embodies a broad range of values, and is open to multiple and even contradictory interpretations. Those who write about fiction, including students, join in an ongoing conversation about a text or the work of a writer.

An Ongoing Conversation

Criticism of fiction occurs in classrooms, among friends, and as part of a written exchange that takes place in newspapers, magazines, scholarly journals, and books. While some of this criticism takes the form of reviews in which a critic evaluates the quality of a story or novel, other criticism is more concerned with the questions listed above—with how stories work as stories. (See "Writing a Research Paper".) As more and more critics write about a particular text, other critics and students of literature read what they have written. Sometimes critics agree with one another; in that case, critics who have read and agree with what a previous critic has said will often cite the work of that critic as a part of their own arguments. Incorporating points another critic has already made enables scholars to build on what they have said to make other observations. Sometimes, however, critics will not agree with what another critic has said. In that case, scholars might merge a disagreement with another critic into the presentation of their own points.

Not all writing about fiction must become a part of this conversation. Essays for class sometimes ask you to engage with a literary work in various ways; the purpose of such assignments is to enable you to improve your reading, writing, and analytical skills. In this kind of writing, what is important is evidence that comes from the text as it is presented in a cogent argument with a clear, limited, specific thesis.

Drafting Your Essay

The conventional form for a discussion of a fictional text is an essay in which the writer presents a thesis and maps supporting arguments in the introductory paragraph or paragraphs, provides textual evidence throughout the essay's body, and concludes at the end. The introductory paragraphs are important because they indicate to readers what they can expect. If your thesis is clear and specific and if you map your supporting arguments, readers will know where you are going and will be gratified when you actually fulfill your promise. Introductory material is like a contract writers make with readers; it primes readers' expectations, makes them happy when the promises are fulfilled, and makes them angry or frustrated when the essay deviates from what it has promised.

The essay's body paragraphs present textual evidence incorporated into logical forms called arguments. These arguments may take several forms. They may be inductive (reasoning from a specific case to a more general conclusion) or deductive (reasoning from the general to the specific). In other words, writers may begin with a specific example—a character, an event in a story, an image—and in analyzing it, draw more general conclusions about the story. Or they may begin with a general principle or observation about a text and "prove" it by providing several more specific examples. Whether writers organize their arguments inductively or deductively, they always make certain assumptions about the nature of fiction and the ways stories work that affect not only the thesis they formulate, but the kinds of examples they use.

Essays on fiction end with a conclusion. In short essays, this conclusion should not simply reiterate what the writer has said, but also address the question "so what?" A conclusion might also help incorporate more specific material into a more general thesis (in an inductively organized essay) or might return to a restatement and clarification of a general principle (in a deductive essay).

Admissible Evidence

There are many kinds of evidence that writers can produce to support a thesis. Good evidence, however, is material that supports the thesis and provides some insight about the text under scrutiny. Good evidence is relevant to the thesis, is clear, or can be made clear through analysis. Kinds of evidence might include portions of the text itself, historical or biographical evidence, and conclusions of other critics. Evidence from primary texts (the story you are writing about) must often be analyzed to provide evidence. For example, if a particular image is the subject of the essay, then the writer must locate and sometimes analyze the appearances and uses of the image in the text. If the thesis involves a reading of gender or race or uses psychoanalytic principles, you may want to summarize examples taken from the story from the perspective of such a focus.

The presentation of evidence is crucial. Not only should its connection to the thesis be made absolutely clear in a topic sentence (which indicates the purpose and argument of a paragraph), its presentation must also be accurate. The passage should be exact and material that is elided or cut out should not be material that changes the meaning of a sentence or eliminates contrary evidence. Evidence should also be inserted at points where it best illustrates the point being made about it.

Textual evidence should be presented economically; that is, enough evidence should be there to make the point, but whole chunks of text inserted without commentary force readers to do the writer's work by making them locate what might be important in a quoted passage. Writers should always make the argument as easily accessible as possible. Don't make the reader do the work.

Summaries of narrative or character can be valuable rhetorical tools. Summaries are ways writers can organize aspects of a text that help make their argument. To be convincing, however, summaries should not distort the text too much; they should instead be a ground for agreement between the writer and the reader that at the same time provide a pretext for discussion and the development of further argument.

Outside sources may also provide evidence, as can historical context, biographical information, examples from other texts, or statements of authorial intent. In the case of any kind of evidence, the critic should ask the following questions:

1. What am I trying to show?
2. What does this evidence show?
3. Is this evidence relevant?
4. Does this evidence add something new to my argument?
5. Is this evidence consistent with the assumptions of my argument?

Though it may seem obvious that questions 1 and 2 should match, not asking these questions sometimes results in the presentation of evidence that does not relate to a thesis. Asking if evidence is relevant and if it adds something new are not only ways of double-checking 1 and 2, but also addresses the problem of too much evidence that provides too little support. Question 5 asks the writer to consider the kind of evidence being offered and prevents such problems as biographical evidence being used as support for an argument about textual language, for example, or material from another author being adduced as evidence of a text's use of a particular image. If a writer assumes, for example, that a text forms a consistent world in and of itself, how is evidence of historical context consistent with that kind of close reading? If a writer assumes that all of the relations within a story can be explained through the use of a class and economic analysis, how would the addition of an argument about psychoanalysis be consistent?

Final Thoughts

The purposes of writing about fiction, of course, are ultimately to learn something about how a particular story works as a story: how it makes its various meanings, how it composes its style, how its various formal parts (plot, character, narrator, point of view, imagery, structure) work together, how it reflects on its own sociohistorical context, how it might present views that either challenge or underwrite the status quo (or both).

Sample Student Essay

The sample essay below is an excellent example of a close reading of Colette's story, "The Hidden Woman," which appears in Chapter 13.

Ann Telford

English 50

Prof. Roof

May 12, 2002

When Reading Is about Writing:

Desire and Perception in Colette's

"The Hidden Woman"

He thinks the eel-like Pierrot is his wife. He

follows her through the party, watching her dance with

one, kiss another, drink champagne, put her hands on

the neck of a woman. At the end he comforts himself

with the idea that none of the Pierrot's gestures mean

anything. Instead, she is merely being alone, "unknown,

Telford 2

forever solitary and without shame, whom a little mask
and a hermetic costume had restored to her irremediable
solitude and her immodest innocence" (153). This husband, from whose point of view "The Hidden Woman" is
narrated, is caught in his lie. Not only has he lied to
his wife about attending the masked ball, he lies to
himself about his wife's nature—and perhaps even about
whether the Pierrot he follows is really his wife at
all. For the husband, believing is seeing; what he sees
is a reflection of his own guilt and desires. As he interprets the Pierrot as his wife and reads her actions
as ultimately harmless (ultimately unthreatening to
him), he shows the degree to which interpretation is
more about the desires of the interpreter.

Why does the husband think he has the truth when
the whole affair began with lies? After situating the
husband at the masked ball, the story relates a flashback where the husband told his wife he would be out
of town for the ball. The wife, with "shivers of disgust which made her hair, her delicate hands, and her
chest in her white dress shudder at the sight of a
slug or some filthy passer-by" performed her revulsion
at the idea of attending (151). Since the story begins
with the husband at the ball, we can only assume that
he lied in order to be free to attend by himself. Like
the husband, the story's readers must guess at why the
wife lied, if the Pierrot is indeed the wife. But why
would the husband suspect that she is his wife? What
function does the Pierrot serve for him?

The husband thinks the Pierrot is his wife because he is guilty about his lie. In making his wife
present as well, he makes her a partner in his own deceit. The evidence that the Pierrot is his wife is
that she utters a little "ahem" "typical of his wife,"

Telford 3

and she pulls out a gold box like one he had given his
wife, and she addresses him in a voice that sounds
like hers "thinly disguised" (151-52). There is also,
however, evidence to the contrary; the Pierrot is
unidentifiable and it scratches "its thigh, with a free
and uninhibited gesture" so unlike the wife that the
husband is momentarily relieved. He encounters the
Pierrot after he has been gazing at a scene of domination, a woman grasped by "the enormous square hands"
of a Venetian lord (151). The husband's ability to
penetrate the Pierrot's disguise is like the Lord
grasping the woman with his hands. The husband is indeed the "Domino," the lord, the name used by the
Pierrot to address him. But it is also possible—a possibility the husband ignores—that if the Pierrot is
indeed his wife, she recognizes him.

　　The husband's interpretation of his wife's
actions is one that initially worries him. He thinks
"she's here for someone, with someone" (152). He follows her through the party, interpreting every meeting
as a romantic tryst—her dance with the warrior, the
Byzantine she kisses, the tussle with the wrestler, the
dalliance with the Dutch girl. At the end of the story
the husband comforts himself by interpreting all of
these actions as meaningless. He has seen his wife as
she would be if she thinks she's alone and she isn't
unfaithful, but free and unfettered and perhaps more
sensual than he thought (and certainly more than her
first squeamish presentation). Finding a text in the
suggestive Pierrot, the husband "reads" her actions and
concludes that she is as he would want her. He also
concludes that she is doing exactly what he is. If his
initial identification of the Pierrot comes through
guilt, his final analysis forgives them both.

Telford 4

   As readers of this story, we are also asked to
interpret the Pierrot's actions; through point of view
we are aligned with the husband's perspective. We see
his desire, but do we see our own? If we are
sympathetic to the husband, we might not see the
story's edge of irony that brings the astuteness of
the husband's ideas into doubt. It is entirely possible, for example, that if the Pierrot/wife recognizes
the husband, her actions are deliberate attempts to
mislead and enrage him. She would also see him as a
liar and might pay him back for his mendacity. After
all, the Pierrot approaches the husband, not he her.
If the Pierrot's actions are all accomplished with the
idea that she has an audience, they gain an entirely
different meaning, one the guilty hopeful husband cannot see. If we read from the side of the woman and if
we assume she has knowledge, then her actions may mean
nothing in themselves, but are deliberate attempts to
show the husband what he deserves to see: her freedom,
perversity, lack of discrimination, and unladylike
character. He cannot fault her later without admitting
he lied, but she will have taught him a lesson.

   What lesson do the readers of the story learn?
Do we know the ways we, too, are implicated in desire?
If we see from the husband's perspective, we see that
the Pierrot is as he thinks. If we stand apart from
him, we might see that he is fooling himself. If we
imagine events from the perspective of the Pierrot/
wife, we play a little trick on him that will catch
him with his own guilt. Perhaps readings of this story
depend on the critics' desire to see the husband or
wife vindicated, or perhaps, like the husband, our desire is for the text to be simple and fall into place.

Thomas Edison—the modern inventor of the wireless telegraph, phonograph, and the light bulb (with Joseph Swan)—once remarked that "thinking is hard work." "Genius," he famously quipped, "is one percent inspiration and ninety-nine percent perspiration." We might want to modify this truism for the composition process to say that good writing is 40 percent invention and 60 percent presentation—give or take a few percentage points.

From the very beginning of your writing process, invention is your first step toward finished modes of rhetorical presentation. There is no presentation without invention because the stuff of writing—language—is not just a static vehicle or tool for thought. Instead, the very act of working with language, as a discursive practice, is a way of thinking. The British empiricist philosopher John Locke asserted as much in his *Essay Concerning Human Understanding* (1690) when he said, "there is so close a connection between ideas and WORDS . . . that it is impossible to speak clearly and distinctly of our knowledge, which all consists of propositions, without considering, first, the nature, use, and signification of Language."

If thinking always already takes place in language, then you can use that linguistic process to help you arrive at your "idea" or thesis and its proper presentational format for the essay assignment. Your completed essay might purposefully present a comparison/contrast pattern of development; it might define and classify a poem's key tropes and how they function together. You might even explain how particular combinations of alliteration and assonance cause certain sound effects based on, say, **onomatopoeia.** But in each case—whether you use the rhetorical modes of comparison/contrast, or classification, or cause/effect—your essay's presentation, ideally, will emerge from your engagement with the poem at hand in a prior process of invention.

Invention is, arguably, even more crucial to writing successfully about poetry than other literary genres. For one thing, there is less information on the page when we are reading a poem than, say, a Charles Dickens novel or Shakespearean romance. Moreover, what information is there often denies its status as information. "A poem," as Archibald MacLeish has it, "should not mean / But be." A poem's mode of being is defined, in part, not through its communication of meaning but, rather, through its artful resistance to paraphrased meaning.

The poet will almost never lay out a poem's message in the straightforward mode of the journalist's questions: who? what? when? where? how? and why? The poet's job, in fact, contradicts that of the newspaper reporter. "Do not forget," the philosopher Ludwig Wittgenstein once said, "that a poem, even though it is composed in the language of information, is not used in the language-game of giving information." Poetry, W. H. Auden wrote in his famous elegy "In Memory Of W. B. Yeats," "survives / In the valley of its making where executives / Would never want to tamper." So, if we are to analyze a poem—to tamper with its form, meaning, techniques, mode of address, and so on—we must first arrive "in the valley of its making": We must make an imaginative effort to understand the poem in its unique mode of utterance.

Two things that distinguish writing about poetry from writing about short stories or plays are length and arrangement. Take, for example, a fourteen-line sonnet like, say, Shakespeare's Sonnet 73: "That time of year thou mayst in me behold." It comprises 121 words. By contrast, Nathaniel Hawthorne's "Young Goodman Brown," a relatively brief short story, has over 5,000 words. Nevertheless, your instructor may ask you to write the same amount of material—say, anywhere from 750 to 1000 words of your own—regardless of whether it's on a 100-word poem or a 100,000-word novel. The artful presentation of language is important in both of these genres. Obviously, however, the individual words and their particular arrangement will matter in your analysis of the sonnet in ways that are far more crucial than in your reading of the novel. Poetry entails an incredibly compressed use of language when compared to a story, play, or novel. In poetry, then, less is more.

Second, whether composed in a fixed form like a sonnet, villanelle, sestina, ballad stanza, or even in free verse, a poem involves a highly stylized arrangement of language on the page. William Carlos Williams defined a poem as a "machine made out of words." The mechanics of a poem's visual presentation—its spacings, its line lengths, its pattern of enjambment, its typography, and so on—all go into the makeup of the kind of verbal mechanisms that Williams had in mind. Moreover, the ways in which the grammatical syntax and punctuation play against and across the line length in patterns of end-stopped utterances or in the artful use of enjambment further complicate a poem's presentation. Add to this the sonic dimension of poetry's rhyme scheme, alliteration, assonance, and onomatopoeia—not to mention the musical qualities of its meter and rhythm—and you confront a very different reading experience and interpretive situation when approaching a poem rather than, say, a newspaper article.

One way of understanding a poem—of entering into "the valley of its making"—is to read it aloud. Some practicing poets will tell you that they often compose poems out loud first by intoning certain unconscious rhythms and sounds orally even before the conscious sense of a particular line or composed stanza takes shape later on the page. Moreover, most poets will test their poems "on the air" by performing them at poetry readings before they are actually published in a magazine, anthology, or book. Reading the poem out loud several times will help you appreciate the cadences, sounds, and music of the work. Memorizing a short lyric will also give you a special sense of ownership of a poem that may help you later in interpreting it with confidence and care.

An analogous technique to reading verse aloud is to copy your poem out on the page or computer screen. In closely comparing your copy to the original, you may find discrepancies where you "got it wrong" or assumed a particular phrasing that wasn't exactly how the poet had it. This process, again, will attune you to a poem's particular verbal character and its formal arrangement as such. Copying the poem out may help you assume a greater sense of mastery over the material. That is, such close attention to the poem's crafted details may help you in the writing situation of dealing with the poem's language, imagery, form, and themes in the more advanced stages of your composing process later on.

If you are a writer who can effortlessly compose complete and polished sentences, consider yourself very unique. Most of us aren't this lucky; we typically don't write this way or at least for very long. Composition theorists agree that for the vast majority of authors, writing is a repetitive and recursive process full of fits and starts, blockages and flows, blindnesses and insights. Trying to "get it right" in composing phrases, sentences, paragraphs, or entire essay formats is seldom easy. Moreover, there is no final arbiter of successful writing. W. S. Merwin, in a poem about his former mentor John Berryman, recalls asking him how you could tell if a poem you wrote was actually "any good at all":

> . . . and he said you can't
> you can't you can never be sure
> you die without knowing
> whether anything you wrote was any good
> if you have to be sure don't write

The point here is not to agonize over the quality of your prose up front but to prime the compositional process by simply beginning to write, even if it's not your best writing. As it happens, there are several generative methods that can help you get material out on the page for later revision, arrangement, and polishing.

To begin with, you might photocopy the poem and annotate it. That is, circle key words and jot down in the margins any thoughts you have on their significance or on their relationships to other significant details and phrasings. In poetry especially, the compression and brevity of the poem's utterance, its gaps, line lengths, and sound patterning together suggest rather than insist on particular meanings. The reader has a greater collaborative role to play in the act of interpreting a poem. This is not to say that "anything goes" in responding to a poem. To be plausible, our interpretations must be rhetorically coherent, well argued, and pragmatically convincing for other readers. But before your reading of a poem arrives at that level of interpretive competence, you should give yourself time to experience the poem psychically. In this regard, you may want to take into account any of the following in generating your theme and organizational plan.

- Pay attention, perhaps in a journal, to your personal encounter with the particulars of the poem and to how your interpretative reading changes over time.
- Explore the differences between your historical moment and that of the poem. Are you coming from a very different historical moment than the time period in which the poem is written? Would it be helpful for your understanding to research that period difference?

- Does the poem address a particular gender or a particular race or class position and, if so, to what extent can you relate or empathize with the poem's take on these markers of identity? To what extent are you alienated by the work's assumption about audience?
- Are there significant language barriers—say, Old English, Middle English, or Shakespearean dialogue, modern experimental uses of syntax, or contemporary performative slang terms—that get in the way of your reading experience? Allow yourself extra time to look up difficult terms in a reference resource such as the *Oxford English Dictionary*. What role does etymology play in enriching your reading experience of a poem's particular diction choices and its unique idiom?
- How might you rewrite the poem and to what effect?
- What questions would you put to the poem?

Once you have generated your freewriting and brainstormed the relations that you see among key phrasings, you are ready to begin shaping your essay's thematic focus.

One way to start is to take some of the questions that you generated about the work and begin to answer them in sentence units. Here you can also build into your sentences some of the phrasings that you generated from your freewriting. Using these sentence openers, expand them into larger units, gradually assuming paragraph length based perhaps on the major ideas that you generated through your cluster map. Go on to develop your paragraph units with supporting illustration and evidence drawn from the text of the poem. In addition, you may find that quoted material from the author, historical and/or biographical contexts, secondary criticism, and so on may also lend themselves to the developing plan of your essay. Consult with your instructor on how much material beyond the text of the poem would be appropriate for your topic. Remember to document any primary or secondary summaries, paraphrases, or direct quotes that helped you develop your essay (see documentation under "Writing a Research Paper").

Handling Quotations

Handling quotes in writing about poetry entails special considerations that are unique to this genre. When quoting fewer than four lines of verse, format the quote in the body of your essay, indicating the line breaks with space followed by forward slash (/) and another space moving into the next line. In the student essay below, Jamie uses this technique:

> Man is constantly thrown into unpleasant situations. By climbing ". . . up a snow-white trunk / *Toward* heaven, till the tree could bear no more, / But dipped me [Frost] down again" (55–57), he would be able to escape briefly from life's difficulties and return unharmed. The tree represents an elevation away from complications, bringing the ascender closer to divinity for a moment yet without him having to die.

Always provide line numbers for your quoted excerpts of poetry. Notice that Jane gives the line numbers for her quote in her lead into the excerpt.

> In line 13, Dickinson combines onomatopoeia and synaesthesia to portray the fly "With Blue—uncertain stumbling Buzz—."

An alternative format for providing the line numbers is to present them in parentheses at the end of the quote. To indicate a stanza break while quoting in the body of your text, use two forward slashes (//) as in this example:

> In describing the ecstasy of horseback riding in her poem "Ariel," Plath depicts how "The furrow, // Splits and passes, sister to / The brown arc" (6–8).

For quotes of four or more lines, set the quote up in block format by indenting it ten spaces from the left-hand margin. Format the lines exactly as they appear in the original and double-space them. Cite the line numbers, again, in parentheses at the end of the quote. If you decide to leave certain lines out, indicate these omissions with a running line of spaced periods approximating the length of the lines you are quoting as follows:

> In the first and fourth stanzas of Theodore Roethke's poem "My Papa's Waltz," the poet employs an extra syllable to the iambic trimeter meter in the second and fourth lines of each stanza:

> The whiskey on your breath
> Could make a small boy dizzy;
> But I hung on like death:
> Such waltzing was not easy.
> . . . .
> The hand that held my wrist
> Was battered on one knuckle;
> At every step you missed
> My right ear scraped a buckle. (1–4, 9–12)

As you revise subsequent drafts of your essay, continue to go over the recursive stages of revision to refine your essay's

- Overall arrangement
- Paragraph order and modes of paragraph development
- Thesis statement and conclusion strategy
- Integration of quoted material
- Exactness of quoted material
- Diction choices and phrasing
- Syntax and grammar
- Punctuation
- Spelling
- Formatting mechanics (margins, line spacings, title, name, course, date, and so on)

Naturally, to carry out all—or even some—of the steps outlined above will demand your most precious resource: time. Writing, as we have seen, is hard work that like, say, power-lifting cannot be attained overnight. Any weight trainer will tell you that you need to wait at least twenty-four hours between lifting sessions to give your muscles enough time to grow and strengthen. No one starts out by bench pressing his or her body weight, but over time, you can get there. Similarly, in writing, give yourself the time to make discoveries, to formulate your thesis, to draft successive revisions, to get to the next level. Successful writing takes practice.

Best Advice: Don't try to write your paper the night before it's due.

Sample Student Essay

To assist you further in drafting your essay, the following section provides a student essay with commentary from the instructor. The student chose to interpret Robert Frost's "Birches" through an **explication** of the poem's developing drama and argument. Literally meaning an "unfolding," an explication accounts for the significant features of a poem allowing the poet's narrative presentation of the work from beginning to middle to end to dictate the paper's order of arrangement. But an explication will not just restate the poem's meaning and themes in the manner of a paraphrase. More importantly, it will consider how significant formal features of the work perform that meaning in original ways at the level of poetic technique. Depending on the work at hand, explication could take into account such elements as a poem's rhyme scheme, its meter and rhythm, its figurative language (metaphor, simile, personification, metonymy, and synecdoche), its symbolism, alliteration, assonance, internal rhyme, onomatopoeia, and so on.

ROBERT FROST   *(1874–1963)*

Birches   *(1916)*

When I see birches bend to left and right   .
Across the lines of straighter darker trees,
I like to think some boy's been swinging them.
But swinging doesn't bend them down to stay
As ice-storms do. Often you must have seen them   5
Loaded with ice a sunny winter morning
After a rain. They click upon themselves
As the breeze rises, and turn many-colored
As the stir cracks and crazes their enamel.
Soon the sun's warmth makes them shed crystal shells   10
Shattering and avalanching on the snowcrust—
Such heaps of broken glass to sweep away
You'd think the inner dome of heaven had fallen.
They are dragged to the withered bracken by the load,
And they seem not to break; though once they are bowed   15

So low for long, they never right themselves:
You may see their trunks arching in the woods
Years afterwards, trailing their leaves on the ground
Like girls on hands and knees that throw their hair
Before them over their heads to dry in the sun.   20
But I was going to say when Truth broke in
With all her matter-of-fact about the ice-storm,
I should prefer to have some boy bend them
As he went out and in to fetch the cows—
Some boy too far from town to learn baseball,   25
Whose only play was what he found himself,
Summer or winter, and could play alone.
One by one he subdued his father's trees
By riding them down over and over again
Until he took the stiffness out of them,   30
And not one but hung limp, not one was left
For him to conquer. He learned all there was
To learn about not launching out too soon
And so not carrying the tree away
Clear to the ground. He always kept his poise   35
To the top branches, climbing carefully
With the same pains you use to fill a cup
Up to the brim, and even above the brim.
Then he flung outward, feet first, with a swish,
Kicking his way down through the air to the ground.   40
So was I once myself a swinger of birches.
And so I dream of going back to be.
It's when I'm weary of considerations,
And life is too much like a pathless wood
Where your face burns and tickles with the cobwebs   45
Broken across it, and one eye is weeping
From a twig's having lashed across it open.
I'd like to get away from earth awhile
And then come back to it and begin over.
May no fate willfully misunderstand me   50
And half grant what I wish and snatch me away
Not to return. Earth's the right place for love:
I don't know where it's likely to go better.
I'd like to go by climbing a birch tree,
And climb black branches up a snow-white trunk,   55
Toward heaven, till the tree could bear no more,
But dipped its top and set me down again.
That would be good both going and coming back.
One could do worse than be a swinger of birches.

Jamie Stein
English 101
Prof. Kalaidjian
April 10, 2002

Frost's "Birches"

   Robert Frost opens his poem "Birches" by
describing crippled birch trees bent against a set of
straighter neighbors. He then thinks of a hypothetical
boy swinging down from birch trees as he used to in
his earlier days. For a moment, in fact, he allows
himself to believe the child's vitality has been the
cause of the misshapen trees, but he remembers that
children do not have so much force. Time and winter
ice are the ultimate causes of the warped birches,
and Frost finds this tragic. Through the violent and
dissonant descriptions of the harmful ice, Frost
demonstrates his wish that the trees be altered in
some other method. The poem quickly shifts, however,
away from the ice and back again to the image of
swinging boys. Frost informs the reader of his former
childhood occupation as a birch swinger, and how he
wishes he could still perform such an act of youth.
Frost's masterful use of figurative language and setting transforms the tree from an amusement to a means
of rebirth. If he could, he would climb the tree to
escape from life when reality becomes too harsh. The
tree carries one towards heaven, yet transports one
back to the ground when the height becomes too great.
The climb provides a brief apotheosis, yet most important, one that is free of death.

   Frost organizes his poem in an interesting manner. Speaking entirely in the first person, he decides
not to break the poem in stanzas. Thus, the poem reads
like a monologue. It has a "spoken" quality to it,
giving Frost much versatility in the various

Stein 2

directions he takes. Within the first twenty lines, it
seems as if Frost's main theme will be the destructive
force of winter and life's ultimate deference to the
coldness. Frost masterfully employs cacophonous language to describe the destructive ice that eternally
handicaps the tree. Listening to the birches, Frost
notices how:

> . . . They click upon themselves
>   As the breeze rises, and turn many-colored
>   As the stir cracks and crazes their enamel.
>   Soon the sun's warmth makes them shed crystal
>   shells
>   Shattering and avalanching on the snow crust—
>   (7-11)

Fricatives and plosives in this quote give the reader
a strong sense of sound. The hard consonants of the
words "cracks," "crazes," and "click," along with the
words "shattering" and "avalanching," fill the reader's
ears with the onomatopoeia of fracturing ice. These
words are loud and violent, perfectly imitating ice's
crashing sound; Frost's diction is masterful. He goes
on to describe that the "glass," figurative for ice,
upon the ground is so plentiful that one would "think
the inner dome of heaven had fallen." It is appropriate that he likens the ice from the trees to glass
from heaven, for later in the poem the tree acts as a
means for becoming closer to heaven. These slightly
divine trees have "fallen" from their heights (like
the "heavenly dome") and are now forever bowed to the
ground along with the "glass."

Frost, however, unexpectedly breaks his discus-

sion of the ice storm and recedes back to his original
thought of boys swinging from birches:

> But I was going to say when Truth broke in
> With all her matter-of-fact about the ice-storm
> I should prefer to have some boy bend them (21-23)

It is strange that Frost wonderfully describes the
deadly ice only to return to the image of a swinging
boy. His poem goes in a circle. Frost personifies
"Truth" and blames her for the break in discussion.
Ironically, *he* is the one to blame. The "Truth" is an
abstraction that Frost chooses to address; no one
forces him to discuss life's tendency to grow frail
during the winter. Thus, there must be a purpose in
including the "ice" section—for if it is only a side
track, as implied from the previous passage, why discuss it in such detail?

Frost is a master of his craft, and the
relevance of the ice is revealed later in the poem,
but first he must revisit the theme of boyhood vitality
within a natural setting:

> I should prefer to have some boy bend them
> . . . .
> By riding them down over and over again
> Until he took the stiffness out of them,
> And not one but hung limp, not one was left
> For him to conquer. . . . (23, 29-31)

Frost would rather a boy bend the trees than the ice.
In his mind, an energetic boy with the ambition and
persistence to humble a birch tree is more pleasing

Stein 4

than winter's harsh "Truth" causing the deformity. Instead of the tree being a symbol of life's frailty,
the bent birch would be a testament to the human
spirit.

Frost, after giving an account on the skills of
birch swinging, recalls his former adventures with
such trees:

> So I was once myself a swinger of birches.
> And so I dream of going back to be.
> It's when I'm weary of considerations,
> And life's too much like a pathless wood
> Where your face burns and tickles with cobwebs
> . . . .
> I'd like to get away from earth awhile
> And then come back to it and begin over. (41–45,
>   48–49)

It is finally within this passage where the reader begins to understand Frost's purpose in describing the
ice storm. Frost explains that from time to time, he
would like to go back to his youth when he could climb
trees and swoop down from them. This desire only occurs, however, when he is "weary of life's considerations." Observing crippled and bent birch trees and
realizing that an icy and deadly storm has stripped
the tree of its magnificence is exactly one of those
"considerations" that lead to weariness. By
understanding the depressing "Truth," Frost does not
allow himself to believe that an innocent and
energetic boy caused the trees' deformities. Death and
coldness are instead the explanations.

Life's sad realities, as documented by bent

birches, inevitably lead to times of frustration, which Frost periodically wishes to escape. Earth can be seen as difficult and agonizing. Frost analogizes the more painful aspects of life to a directionless wood filled with "pain" and "confusion." The pathless wood, which symbolizes existence in a most disturbing and chaotic setting, gives the reader insight as to why Frost wishes to return to his youthful birch swinging days. Humanity is constantly thrown into unpleasant situations. By climbing ". . . up a snow-white trunk / *Toward* heaven, till the tree could bear no more, / But dipped me [Frost] down again" (55–57), he would be able to escape briefly from life's difficulties and re-turn unharmed. The tree represents an elevation away from complications, bringing the ascender closer to divinity for a moment yet without him having to die. In fact, the key to this poem is that, despite the hardships, Frost in no way wants to escape the world:

> May no fate willfully misunderstand me
> And half grant what I wish and snatch me away
> Not to return. Earth's the right place for love:
> I don't know where it's likely to go better
> (50–53)

Even with the imperfections, life is good to him, and he does not wish to leave but instead to transcend earth from time to time. "Fate" is of course figurative for death, and death is not appealing. Love invokes a desire to stay, and there is no telling if love exists past the grave. These few lines shift the poem from one that critiques life to one that celebrates it. The pains of earth are by no means cause enough to forfeit

Stein 6

existence. The reader finally realizes from these few
lines that Frost does not wish to return to childhood
merely to bask in endless innocence; nor does he wish
to stop time altogether. He just wants to escape sometimes by getting close to the uncomplicated heavens,
like he could do as a boy by climbing a birch and then
swinging down. Atop the tree, one achieves godlike
status, observing the world from up high, detached and
safe from dangers. Upon return, life's gifts are much
easier to appreciate; one feels renewed. Unfortunately,
Frost is now too old to perform the rebirth that birch
swinging could provide.

Frost fully understands the paradox of life. The
earth is saturated with pain and hardship, yet it is
also "the right place for love." He knows that the
earth is a beautiful place to live; the only problem
is that sometimes hardships seem to outweigh the joy.
These are the times when Frost wishes he could return
to his state of youthful vitality, but there is no way
to reverse time. Frost accepts this as a fact of life,
and he is willing to follow the rules. Ice may cause
some birches to hunch forever, but there will always
be some trees somewhere that a boy will find climbable,
and he will swing from these branches as Frost once
did. Thus, the world trudges forward. Life is
ultimately a sweet and enjoyable journey if approached
correctly. As stated at the end of the poem, "One
could do worse than be a swinger of birches" (59).

Commentary

In "Frost's Birches," Jamie Stein begins with a general explication of the poem's setting and situation in paragraph one. In it, he captures the thematic oscillation the poem stages between signs of life's tragedy and nature's violence versus moments and memories of ascent and escape from reality. In getting to the point of the essay's thesis, however, Jamie could compress this paragraph somewhat by editing down the opening paraphrase of the poem's plot narrative. Jamie should assume that his reader already knows the general story line of the poem. The second paragraph notes the poem's first-person, dramatic monologue format and makes a transition to Frost's onomatopoeia in capturing the cacophonous sound of breaking ice. Notice that Jamie does not just use the block quote for illustration but also explicates the sound elements he quotes at some length. The fourth paragraph focuses on the poem's personification of Truth that voices the reality of nature's violence that has broken the tree. The fifth paragraph makes a transition from the personified figure of Truth to the tree itself as a symbol both of "life's frailty" and the resistant "human spirit" depending on the poet's point of view. The sixth paragraph further probes the tension between truth and fiction in Frost's digression to childhood memory.

Notice in the next two paragraphs how Jamie mixes his presentational format both to incorporate quotes into the syntax of his own sentences and to set off key passages in block quote formats. The conclusion paragraph returns to the level of thematic generality that begins the essay but also frames the poem's central paradox through a new insistence that, however hard, earth is nevertheless "the right place for love." In this manner, then, the essay's overall rhetorical strategy follows the poem's unfolding narrative. Along the way, Jamie signals the key techniques of alliteration and assonance, personification, symbolism, and paradox as they shape and perform Frost's musings in "Birches."

55 Writing about Drama

In many respects, writing about drama differs very little from composing a critical essay on poetry or fiction. For a "critical essay" discussing any genre—or one on nonliterary topics, for that matter—contains many of the same elements: a *thesis statement* that is effectively introduced, an *argument* developed in support of the thesis that presents evidence in a persuasive fashion, and a *conclusion* that not only brings the analysis to completion but also suggests its larger significance. Like essays on other kinds of literature, one on drama conveys a reading, and this volume outlines various interpretive alternatives or *kinds* of reading. Other chapters in this book continue this discussion with advice on "Writing about Literature" (Chapter 52) and "Writing a Research Paper" (Chapter 56) in which thesis statements, methods of quoting and paraphrasing, and accurate citation forms are considered at length.

While these and other similarities exist between writing assignments, it is also true that writing about drama and theater presents unique challenges as well. This is true because many papers on drama also try to account for the theatrical event, the play as performed text. Although Chapter 41, "What Is Drama?," explains some of the reasons for drama's uniqueness, it might prove helpful to review this issue, because the dramatic text marks the beginning of theatrical presentation, not the end. For this reason, when writing about drama, an author has to imagine the play as performed, as completed by live actors appearing before an audience. This imaginative effort makes writing about drama a kind of report on a play production that occurs inside the essay writer's head—and often leads to comparisons between this kind of idealized reconstruction of the text and one or more actual productions from the archive of theater (or film) history.

It is, in short, the genesis and evolution of the performance event that make writing about drama and theater so challenging—and so rewarding as well.

Drama → Script → Theater → Performance

The drama is the domain of the author, the composer . . . ; the script is the domain of the teacher, guru, master; the theater is the domain of the performers; the performance is the domain of the audience.

What Richard Schechner, who teaches at the Tisch School of the Arts at New York University, means by these distinctions is that most books on literature, this one included, consider drama in a privileged position relative to performance. A drama is a very particular kind of script that, in Europe and

America, occupies a special status in the theater. This is not the case, as Schechner emphasizes, in many non-Western cultures, where performance begins with an "active sense of script"—the director's reimagining of a dramatic work or, more radically, something nonwritten that "pre-exists any given enactment, which persists from enactment to enactment." This ensemble of nonwritten elements includes movement, dance, gesture, bodily position, social expression, and so on that mean something to actors and an audience but is not written down. It is simply known or understood. Consider, for example, how in everyday life we read a person's body language, gestures, even clothing. All of these can communicate meaning without the person saying a word, and theatrical performance is no exception.

"Performance," if viewed as a site on a continuum, resides at a pole opposite of drama: If a drama is a written blueprint that guides theatrical production, performance's "only life is in the present." "Drama" and "performance" mark the range of topics you might select to write about. That is to say, you could write an essay about a play's narrative progress, how and why something happens, or why the dramatic action concludes the way it does; about a character's motives, relationships, or psychology; or about the effect of the set on the tone or mood of the drama. Comparative analysis of dramatic texts can also yield significant insights: How does Cherríe Moraga's *Shadow of a Man* revise Arthur Miller's depiction of the American family? How do the presentational or "meta-theatric" styles of *M. Butterfly* and *Wit* affect our reading of the central characters' dilemmas? Considering the other pole, a more performative one, intriguing papers are written all the time about how a production—or a single performance—presents Willy Loman's psychology, Hamlet's "antic disposition," or Hedda Gabler's profound unhappiness. How does Mel Gibson's Hamlet differ from Laurence Olivier's some forty years earlier? How would *Dutchman* be played to a contemporary audience in the twenty-first century? How did a specific production of the play in 2002 differ from one in the 1960s?

On the continuum between these poles resides the script, the "domain" of the "guru" in some societies and the director in today's theater (and certainly analogies might be made between powerful directors and wise gurus). How does a director shape a play into a script? Why, for example, did the influential director Elia Kazan want Tennessee Williams to write a new ending for *Cat on a Hot Tin Roof*? Why in his version of *Death of a Salesman* did Dustin Hoffman elect, in several key respects, to play Willy in a manner *not* indicated by Arthur Miller's very specific stage directions? What interpretations or readings of the drama are thus made possible by such scripts? What readings are minimized or rendered less important?

Any one of these questions about drama, script, and performance—and many more—might serve as the springboard for a successful essay on drama. And, at times, these categories are not easily separated, as Charlene Owens's sample essay on Harold Pinter's play *Ashes to Ashes* demonstrates at the end of this chapter. Clearly, her main interest is in the play—specifically, Rebecca's troubled psychology and the traumas she has endured; nonetheless, reviews of specific productions contribute to her understanding of Pinter's character.

Quoting Dialogue

One other significant difference when writing papers about drama and performance is the necessity from time to time to quote dialogue as part of the evidentiary structure of the argument. For excerpts over four lines, these should be indented on the left margin and, when necessary, the identity of the speakers should be identified, as in the following example from the opening lines of *Ashes to Ashes:*

> *Devlin standing with a drink. Rebecca sitting.*
>
> *Silence.*
>
> *Rebecca:* Well . . . for example . . . he would stand over me and clench his fist. And then he'd put his other hand on my neck and grip it and bring my head towards him. His fist . . . grazed my mouth. And he'd say, 'Kiss my fist.'
>
> *Devlin:* And did you?
>
> *Rebecca:* Oh, yes. [. . .] (3)

Stage directions are rendered here to allow the reader of the essay to envision the scene as it is written, and the identity of the speakers allows for the same kind of clarity. The use of bracketed ellipsis points indicates that they have been added by the writer; the unbracketed ellipsis points in Rebecca's lines indicate that they appear in Pinter's original.

It is crucial that lines from texts be quoted *exactly* as they are rendered in the original, a matter that on the surface seems an easy task. But often it isn't. The phone rings, you get in a hurry, you're beginning to feel tired—any number of things can distract you from the task at hand and inaccuracy often results. Here's a tip: At the proofreading stage, compare every quoted excerpt to its textual original—word for word, punctuation mark for punctuation mark. This procedure will help keep mistakes to a minimum.

Final Thoughts

Other than these particular considerations, writing an essay on drama and performance requires much the same care and construction, the same careful prewriting and revision, as any other essay. At the same time, because of drama's unique relationship to performance, writing about drama may take you to the exciting and often provocative worlds of film and theater. In consultation with your instructor, you decide just how far you want to travel from the page to the stage, from drama to performance.

Sample Student Essay

To help you with your own writing assignment, the following section provides a student essay about drama. This particular essay is also an example of a research paper.

Charlene Owens

English L365

Professor Watt

April 17, 2002

Historical Hysteria

Harold Pinter's 1995 play *Ashes to Ashes* appears to investigate the domestic relationship of Rebecca and Devlin, who share an English country house, and are romantically involved, if not married. The play chronicles Devlin's frustrated attempts to get Rebecca to explain what her past experiences have been. However, the dramatic tension only appears to emerge from Devlin's investigations. As the play progresses, its momentum depends more and more on the impossibility of knowing what has come before. Furthermore, when we find out the details of Rebecca's past—or, at least, what she remembers as her past—we realize, ironically, that we are *already familiar with the relevant past*. For, in "remembering" the Holocaust in the final moments of *Ashes to Ashes*, Rebecca claims as her own a collective, cultural past. As the realization that Nazi brutality dominates her memory dawns on us, we find ourselves in the same position as the two characters, simultaneously struggling to bring the past to light yet also guilty of keeping it hidden. The result is that, in framing his narrative, Pinter presents his audience not with an Aristotelian drama of clear events in cause-effect relationships; rather, he offers us a "traumatic" narrative that imitates Sigmund Freud's methods for revealing and treating hysteria and its attendant neurosis and implicates the audience partly as analysts, partly as hysterics.

This "bait-and-switch" technique, setting up the audience with false expectations and then dashing them against a sudden and shocking revelation, is

Owens 2

characteristic of Pinter's earlier drama in that it
offers nothing in the way of concrete exposition, but,
like *The Room, The Caretaker,* or, more recently, *Mountain Language* and *One for the Road,* begins *in medias
res.* Beginning "in the middle of things," these plays
present special challenges to readers and audiences
alike, since Pinter gives them no reliable character
history or plot background and demands that we orient
ourselves to the action, dialogue, and themes immediately and without warning. Specifically, *Ashes to Ashes*
proceeds without establishing the past events relevant
to the present action; in fact, it is this lack of exposition that provides the bulk of *Ashes to Ashes'*
dramatic tension.

Freud's published papers on his own clinical
psychoanalytical undertakings provide the critical
foundation for this analysis. In taking the role of
analyst, observing patients who manifest psychic symptoms, and in piecing together a coherent case history
that would explain the origins of his patients' illnesses, Freud cast himself as a critical spectator.
Pinter asks his audience to take the same critical
stance toward his work: for, like Freud confronted
with bizarre and apparently inexplicable symptoms, we
watch the action of *Ashes to Ashes* unfold without any
prior explanation of why it occurs. We as readers and
spectators must judge the validity of what we see and
hear on stage, take into account details as they
emerge during the performance or reading, and finally
piece them together into a narrative we are capable of
understanding.

Ashes to Ashes lends itself readily to a spectatorship analogous to clinical psychoanalysis. It's

opening moments seem to replicate a session of
psychotherapy, with Devlin asking questions in order
to elicit details and reminiscences from Rebecca, and
Rebecca struggling to recount her own past as if, like
a neurotic, she had repressed some fundamental event
that she is psychologically incapable of facing fully.
But in this critical analogy, equating the audience
with the analyst, the patient is not Rebecca. That is,
the audience must not be duped into focusing all its
energies into diagnosing Rebecca. Rather, the patient
is *Western cultural history*. We are asked to make
sense not of Rebecca alone—for she is a fictional construction with no real "past"—but instead of the wider
culture that she represents and that the text implies;
for, though the story is fiction, the cultural context
in which the text was written and in which the
performance is put on is quite real: It confronts us
head on and demands interpretation. Along with making
demands, the play as a narrative about our present
historical moment may, like the faulty memory of
Freud's patients, deceive us at first, and may even lay
"traps" for us, red herrings that could lead us off
course.

    Pinter's work has traditionally confounded audi-
ences, critics, and scholars alike. In the first decade
and a half of Pinter's career, scholars expended a
great deal of energy simply trying to figure out *how* to
make sense of Pinter without fully interpreting his
plays. Often, critics who tried to fit Pinter into
recognizable "categories"—realist, surrealist, or
absurdist—found that such categorization did little to
help understand his texts. Austin E. Quigley's seminal
book *The Pinter Problem,* published in 1975, marked the

Owens 4

beginning of a new understanding of Pinter. Quigley
argued that critics who attempted to categorize Pinter
with an easy-to-understand "label" failed to ask the
most fundamental question about his work: How do Pinter's characters make meaning out of language? Critics
before Quigley certainly recognized that Pinter's
characters do not use language in conventional ways,
that meaning is often confused or occluded by the word
choice, syntax, or passive-aggressive manipulations of
language. Quigley, however, suggested that understanding Pinter required understanding *how meaning emerges
from dramatic language.* To do so, he focused on dis-
continuities, apparently irrelevant statements, and
half-finished or confusingly phrased statements and
questions, arguing that these moments in the text help
reveal the fundamental meaning of Pinter's dialogue.

This essay follows Quigley's lead, adopting a
Freudian critical framework precisely because it uses
methods of analysis similar to those Quigley
recommended. More precisely, it attempts to rescue meaning by focusing on details of an account or narrative
that do not seem to fit or seem to keep something hidden
and basing an interpretation on those Freudian slips.
For, in *Ashes to Ashes,* such moments predominate. To try
to make conventional "sense" of them, taking words and
statements at face value, would only lead to the interpretive difficulties scholars and critics prior to
Quigley's intervention experienced. For, on the surface,
Devlin's questions and Rebecca's replies seem almost
nonsensical. Only in considering what this apparent nonsense reveals about their relation to each other and to
Western cultural history can we begin to understand what
is at stake fundamentally in the play.

Owens 5

Despite its abrupt beginning, *Ashes to Ashes* presents a deceptively straightforward situation. The stage directions suggest a familiar domestic atmosphere: "*A house in the country. Ground floor room. A large window. Garden beyond. Two armchairs. Two lamps. Early evening. Summer*" (1). So far, we might as well be faced with a "well-made piece" in the tradition of Henrik Ibsen, George Bernard Shaw, or Oscar Wilde. Indeed, according to Katherine Burkman, who reviewed The Roundabout Theatre Company's March 30, 1999, performance of *Ashes to Ashes* at New York's Gramercy Theater, director Karel Reisz explicitly put the play in that tradition. Instead of simply "*A house in the country,*" The Roundabout's program "suggests that [the play] takes place in '*A university town outside of London*'" (Burkman 154). Burkman describes the set as "elaborate, giving full detail to the room with twin chairs, twin lamps, window seat, tables, bar, and large window looking out on a garden," critiquing the director and set designer's failure to adhere to the sparseness the text stipulates (154). Burkman's critique seems to highlight a fundamental flaw in any reading of *Ashes to Ashes* that posits conformity to the traditions of the "well-made play": namely, that *Ashes to Ashes* finally subverts those traditional expectations and gains much of its dramatic force from that subversion. For a director and set designer to buy into the realist "setup," without seeing the play's attempt to frustrate that setup, is to encourage the audience to view the play with expectations of character, plot, and structural unity.

Further, unlike a reader or a performer, the theater audience would not even have the benefit of the

complete stage directions and therefore would not be
alerted in advance of the action of the disorienting
symbolism of the lighting effects:

> *The room darkens during the course of the play.
> The lamplight intensifies.*
>
> *By the end of the play the room and the garden
> beyond are only dimly defined.*
>
> *The lamplight has become very bright but does
> not illumine the room.* (1)

Though as readers we become aware of the importance of
lighting because the stage directions appear before
the dialogue, the theater audience would experience
the intensification of the lamplight and concurrent
dimming of the twilight while the trauma of Rebecca's
memories unfold, not beforehand.

So, for The Roundabout Theatre Company audience,
the well-made appearance of the play does not waver
even when Rebecca utters her first line: "Well . . . for
example . . . he would stand over me and clench his fist.
And then he'd put his other hand on my neck and grip
it and bring my head towards him. His fist . . . grazed
my mouth. And he'd say, 'Kiss my fist'" (3). At this
point, whether readers or viewers, though we wonder
what this scene of domination could mean, how it informs the action ahead of us, we do not despair of a
clear resolution to the many questions surrounding Rebecca's strange, disorienting narrative. As Devlin
questions Rebecca further about the unnamed man and
the actions to which she alludes, and as Rebecca accordingly responds to Devlin's questions, it appears
certain, in fact, that soon enough we will have the
entire exposition and the plot will begin in earnest.

Our certainties are dashed, however, when

Devlin, only a few minutes into the dialogue, abruptly
asks "Do you feel you're being hypnotised?" (7). His
non sequitur question derails the line of inquiry already established and suggests that deeper psychological issues are at stake; and the promise of
psychological depth is fulfilled soon into the play.
For it becomes clear that Rebecca is either unwilling
or, more likely, unable to recount more than mere
half-remembered fragments of her past. Further, the
play is marked by Freudian slips-of-the-tongue that
reveal an underlying anxiety about motherhood. For instance, she refuses to be called "darling" by Devlin,
and claims "I'm nobody's darling." "That's a song,"
Devlin replies: "'I'm nobody's baby now'" (17). But
Rebecca does not immediately notice that he has substituted the word "baby" for "darling." Instead, she
corrects his use of the pronoun "I": "It's 'You're nobody's baby now.'" Then, almost as an afterthought,
she adds dismissively, "But anyway, I didn't use the
word baby" (17). This important denial characterizes
the more general repression Rebecca seems to suffer
throughout the play.

 Later, Rebecca makes a similar slip-of-the-
tongue, this time referring to the "bundle," which, we
later learn, she believes she has used to protect her
infant child from abduction. Tellingly, her mention of
the bundle comes as if out of nowhere during her explanation of a mental condition she calls "mental
elephantiasis":

 This mental elephantiasis means that when you
   spill an ounce of gravy, for example, it immediately expands and becomes a vast sea of gravy.

Owens 8

> It becomes a sea of gravy which surrounds you on
> all sides and you suffocate in a voluminous sea
> of gravy. It's terrible. But it's all your own
> fault. You brought it upon yourself. You are not
> the *victim* of it, you are the *cause* of it. Be-
> cause it was you who spilt the gravy in the first
> place, it was you who handed over the bundle.
>
> (51; Pinter's emphasis)

Though her explanation constructs an allegory for the
same kind of hysterical fear Rebecca herself suffers—
namely, the exaggeration of a trifling mistake that,
caught in the subconscious network as a repressed
trauma, emerges as a dominating, irrational fear or
fantasy threatening to engulf the neurotic's sense of
identity—she herself seems not to recognize the therapeutic potential of "mental elephantiasis" as a diagnosis of her own condition. Nevertheless, we glimpse
the real workings of her psyche when, without explanation, she makes the leap from "gravy" to "bundle." It
seems likely that Rebecca's explanation has hit close
enough to home to elicit a Freudian slip, if not to
alert her to the true nature of her neurosis.

Sigmund Freud's early work on psychoanalysis,
along with his essay "The Uncanny," helps to explain
the eerie, sinister nature of Rebecca's slips-of-the-
tongue. In his analysis of "Dora," an early case history of psychoanalysis, Freud lays out some of his
foundational ideas about repression, neurosis, and
hysteria. Unable to come to terms with either her own
sexual orientation or with the aggressive sexual over-
tures foisted on her by one of her father's friends,
Dora represses her memories associated with sexuality

and denies knowledge even of the precise nature of the
sex act. However, Freud deduces that the physical and
mental symptoms she exhibits—loss of voice, loss of
memory, and localized acute pain—are, in fact, symptoms that Dora subconsciously associates with her sexual trauma and that her subconscious uses as
expressions of her repressed homosexual desires and
her fear of those desires (Freud *Dora* 55).

Citing Dora's case here is not meant to suggest
that Rebecca's repressions are the same as Dora's.
Rather, it is to point out a general mechanism of repression and expression, which Freud outlines in his
"Postscript" to *Dora,* a mechanism that helps to
explain the often confusing, disorienting, and even
alienating progress of *Ashes to Ashes.* For Freud, the
neurotic is plagued by repressions, memories or
desires that are so discomforting that the mind never
allows them to emerge consciously. Nevertheless, the
subconscious craves to express those repressions, and
it does so by disguising them in forms, images, ideas,
and sensations only distantly associated with them. It
is by tracing these symptoms back to their source and
forcing the patient to come to terms with what she has
repressed that the analyst is able to bring his
patient to terms with her own desires and her own past
(Freud *Dora* 103–112 *passim*). We can understand
Rebecca's plight and the general trajectory of *Ashes
to Ashes* by reading it as part of the same structure
of repression and symptom formation.

Already I have pointed out two moments in *Ashes
to Ashes* seemingly symptomatic of Rebecca's condition:
her denial of having used the word "baby" and her sudden reference to "the bundle." However, for the reader

Owens 10

or audience approaching the work for the first time,
the significance of these symptoms does not become
clear until the end of the play, just as for the psychoanalyst, the meaning of a patient's symptoms cannot
be understood until the analysis has pieced together
the clues they offer. Hence, when, at the end of the
play, Rebecca begins narrating her traumatic past,
prompted by a disembodied "Echo," the story she tells
helps to explain retroactively the significance of her
earlier symptoms. Rebecca recites her memory of waiting, with her infant, for a train to take them away.
She is careful to conceal the infant in a bundle, but
she explains that "the baby cried out [. . .] And the
man called me back [. . .] He stretched out his hand
for the bundle [. . .] And I gave him the bundle" (79,
81). However, as if this abduction of her child by
"the man," who resembles the Nazi guards responsible
for deporting Jews to concentration camps, were not
eerie enough, Rebecca goes on to tell of a haunting
denial: "And I met a woman I knew [. . .] And she said
what happened to your baby [. . .] Where is your baby
[. . .] And I said what baby [. . .] I don't have a
baby [. . .] I don't know of any baby" (81, 83). This
denial, this repression of her maternal grief, has instigated the symptoms earlier in the play, the uncanny
way Rebecca's statements keep coming around to the
topic of the "baby" or "the bundle."

Freud discusses at some length the way repression returns to conscious thought in his essay "The
Uncanny." An uncanny event or sight is one that is simultaneously familiar and unfamiliar. On the one hand,
we seem to recognize an uncanny experience because it
reminds us, either by similarity or by association, of

something our minds have repressed. On the other hand, the uncanny seems strange and unfamiliar because our minds' repression is so effective that we cannot fully recognize the event's familiarity or psychical signifi- cance. The uncanny, then, haunts us with our own past; it does not bring the past to light, but nevertheless reminds us indirectly of its lurking, potentially threatening existence in the subconscious.

The final narration of abduction and denial that occurs at the end of *Ashes to Ashes* precisely exempli- fies the uncanny. The memory of genocidal atrocity re- turns abruptly and hauntingly in the voice of the echo and the vague but recognizable events Rebecca recounts. However, this instance of the uncanny dif- fers from Freud's notion in one important respect. For Freud, the uncanny, like other psychical phenomena, is confined to the mind and perception of a single indi- vidual: One man's uncanny is another man's commonplace. Rebecca's recitation, though, invokes not her own experience (she is too young to have experi- enced the Holocaust first-hand), but a cultural experi- ence. Somehow, the repressed, forgotten, or overlooked *first-hand* horror of genocide speaks, returns uncannily, through a single, isolated, and historically uninvolved individual.

This emphasis on the return of a collective and inaccessible past differentiates *Ashes to Ashes* from Arthur Miller's *Broken Glass,* written precisely con- temporaneously with it. Miller treats similar themes and structures in *Broken Glass,* focusing on an Ameri- can woman who suffers hysterical paralysis as a result of the almost brutal domination her husband foists on her, combined with reports of atrocities committed

Owens 12

against Jews in Fascist Germany. However, Miller's
play ends with the dominating husband's death and the
woman's resulting recovery. That turn of events, the
happy ending, reduces the global and historical import
of atrocity to a merely domestic tension resolved in a
coincidental death. Further, because the play is set
during the rise of Nazism in Germany, it limits the
influence of historical atrocity to its own time. Pinter's play, however, succeeds in indicting contemporary readers because it allows the cultural
significance of Rebecca's trauma to prevail over its
private, domestic significance, and because the Holocaust's significance reaches beyond the limits of its
own time to affect those of later generations.

The force of this haunting juxtaposition of a
cultural memory with individual recollection is that it
makes an important claim about the status of history in
general and the status of atrocity more specifically. For
the play seems to argue that a late-twentieth-century
culture that looks to the power and responsibility of
the autonomous individual is at heart a hysterical,
neurotic culture: It overlooks the general human cost
of, and complicity in, the horrors of the past. *Ashes
to Ashes,* then, uses Freudian psychoanalytic structures
to suggest that the past cannot remain locked safely
away in history books, documentary film, or on the West
End stage; rather, the past breaks the rules of time
because it remains present, inherent in the state of
the world today. Hence, the play suggests, as humans
alive in that world, we must take responsibility for
our collective past or face the consequences of living
dishonestly, dysfunctionally, and neurotically in the
false isolation of the present.

Works Cited

Burkman, Katherine H. "*Ashes to Ashes* in New York."

   The Pinter Review: Collected Essays 1997 and

   1998. Ed. Francis Gillen and Stephen Gale.

   Tampa: U of Tampa P, 1999.

Freud, Sigmund. *Dora: An Analysis of a Case of Hysteria.*

———. "The Uncanny." [1919] *The Complete Psychological*

   Works of Sigmund Freud. Trans. James Strachey et

   al. Vol. XVII. London: Hogarth, 1955.

Pinter, Harold. *Ashes to Ashes.* New York: Grove P, 1996.

Quigley, Austin E. *The Pinter Problem.* Princeton:

   Princeton UP, 1975.

Commentary

Charlene Owens's essay is an ambitious one, the product of a mature writer with an uncommonly strong background in drama and theater (indeed, she has significant acting experience for an undergraduate). This paper was written near the end of an academic term in which the entire class had read a variety of plays. The assignment required students to discuss a play read during the term in part by using at least three sources found at the library to construct the argument. In other words, again, this is a research paper.

Charlene starts by identifying a feature common to many of Harold Pinter's plays: the impossibility of knowing exactly what has occurred before the dramatic action begins. This insight leads to a forceful restatement of the problem at the end of paragraph two: "Specifically, *Ashes to Ashes* proceeds without establishing the past events relevant to the present action; in fact, it is this lack of exposition that provides the bulk of *Ashes to Ashes'* dramatic tension." This is a cogent point: exposition is generally used to reveal facts that an audience needs to know. In *Hamlet,* for example, we understand fairly quickly why guards have been posted: Old King Hamlet is dead and Denmark is especially susceptible to invasion. We learn from the opening of *The Tempest* how and why Prospero arrived on the island in which the play is set. Not so with *Ashes to Ashes.*

As a result, Charlene argues that the position of the spectator is thus altered by Pinter's method of exposition; to be precise, at the end of her opening paragraph, she asserts that the audience's position resembles that of the psychoanalyst listening to a "hysterical" narrative from a patient. What does this entail? She explains in paragraphs three and four that, like the analyst, we need to "piece" together bits of information from the dialogue into a coherent narrative; more specifically, as she explains in paragraphs five and six, we might follow the critical lead of a well-known scholar by "focusing on details of an account . . . that do not seem to fit or seem to keep something hidden." This is excellent advice, and by following it we are likely to arrive at insights into the aptness of the parallel between spectatorship and psychoanalysis that Owens announces in her opening paragraph.

At this point, however, we might ask two questions: Is this essay strengthened by what is essentially a six-paragraph introduction? Couldn't these points have been made more concisely? And, second, if attention needs to be paid to the characters' language, why does she move immediately to aspects of *mise-en-scène* and a specific production of the play? Paragraphs seven and eight do not engage the play's language, and only in paragraphs nine to eleven does she return to the investigative strategy recommended in paragraphs five and six. Then, in the paragraphs that follow, Charlene develops a more direct comparison between Freud's hysterics and Pinter's characters, especially Rebecca (note that this approach has very little to say about the play's other character, Devlin).

In sum, this is a fine effort by a strong student-writer. The writing is generally quite lucid and only a few minor errors surface ("It's" instead of "Its" in paragraph four, for instance). A few phrases might have been redrafted ("As the realization that Nazi brutality dominates her memory dawns on us" in paragraph one seems awkward because of the positioning of "dawns on us"; "As we begin to realize that Nazi brutality dominates her memory" might have been better). More significant areas for revision would include the protracted introduction, the structure of the argument and shift to aspects of *mise-en-scène* at paragraph seven, and the need for a more careful attention to the very linguistic issues raised in paragraphs five and six. Still, this is an impressive essay.

56 Writing a Research Paper

> *Not to interpret is impossible, as refraining from thinking is impossible.*
>
> —ITALO CALVINO, *MR. PALOMAR* (1983)

This epigraph from Italo Calvino's novel, one chapter of which appears earlier in this book, seems uncannily accurate. For many of the phenomena we encounter in everyday life, however subtly, demand interpretation: menus, clothing styles, even the facial expressions of people we meet, to name just three. The interpretive process begins with reading, then moves to larger speculations, and, in the best of cases, leads to the formulation of answers to specific questions. What salad would go well with this entree? Why is this person frowning at me? What image does this suit or jacket and slacks ensemble project? In fact, many popular styles or recent "subcultures"—the Beat Movement, "Goth" culture, or the so-called punk rock movement of the 1970s—comprise a larger text to be read and interpreted. How is this music connected to that fashion, hairstyle, or lifestyle? What larger social or political statement is this subculture making, or not making? Consider, for example, all the things a term like *hip-hop* or *heavy metal* means. The list of things that might be interpreted is potentially endless.

Calvino's character Mr. Palomar, a compulsive reader and interpreter, knows this all too well. He contemplates waves, bodies on beaches, stellar constellations, the flight patterns of migrating birds—just about everything. Therein resides his problem: He has no rules to limit his interpretive activities; as a consequence, he drives himself to distraction by "reading" everything from the blades of grass and sea of weeds in his lawn to the kind of cheese he buys at a store. He is, in other words, both obsessed and adrift, a player immersed in a readerly game devoid of any organizing rules. And a game without rules quickly leads to chaos, which is one of the inferences *Mr. Palomar* seems to promote.

Fortunately, writing research papers on literature is a highly "ruleful" enterprise. Unlike Mr. Palomar's chaotic lawn, topics selected for research papers need to have clearly marked limits. Setting these boundaries, however, often poses one of the most difficult problems a writer faces, and this is merely one of the many decisions a research project demands. Some of these are relatively large, potentially complicated matters like "what is my topic?" and, even more central to most kinds of research papers, "what is my thesis statement?" Other decisions, like the one we just made about whether to quote directly or paraphrase a line from Calvino's novel, concern the smaller issues of a single sentence or paragraph. What would a paraphrase of this sentence sound like, and how should it be cited? Would it be more effective to render the passage as it appeared in the original?

This essay considers all of these questions and more. Throughout, however, as is the case in writing about literature without the benefit of research, we want to emphasize that at each step of the process—during the prewriting, writing, and revision stages—the composition of successful research papers depends on the writer's thoughtful decision making, the careful organization of reference materials, and a sincere effort to use these materials accurately. The best research writing is driven by the writer's intellectual curiosity about a subject, for writing based on research should result in increased knowledge for both the writer and reader of the paper.

As we described in Chapter 52, "Writing about Literature," the decisions that most influence the purpose and ultimate structure of a research paper are made during prewriting, before the first sentence is even drafted.

Prewriting

After being informed about the length of the assignment and its due date, the first question to be answered about a research project is this: What kind of essay am I being asked to write, a *review* or an interpretive *argument*? Most instructors will assign the latter, and the distinction between the two is crucial because it helps define your purpose in researching and writing about a topic, it determines who you are as a writer, and it suggests the kind of audience your paper is addressing. As in virtually every writing situation, from letters home to papers written for courses to portions of typical job applications, a writer at the prewriting stage needs to define as specifically as possible the purpose of the writing and the audience to whom it is directed.

The author of a *review*, a film review for example, regards his or her audience as *uninformed*. Because the audience has not seen the movie, the reviewer's job is largely descriptive and, finally, evaluative. For this reason, a reviewer of a feature film will almost always summarize the central plot or action, mention such features as the central characters, the actors' performances, and maybe even the film's musical score before rendering an opinion. And this opinion almost always pertains to the film's quality, its goodness or badness. That's the purpose of a review. The most influential reviewers, like Roger Ebert and the late Gene Siskel, can either breathe life into a movie's financial future or sound its death knell by giving it a "thumb's up" or a "thumb's down" verdict.

Reviewers, like all writers, make other decisions as well. What is the reading level of my audience? What language will most effectively communicate ideas to such readers? What other elements of my essay, such as the length and complexity of sentences or paragraphs, ought to be shaped for this particular group of readers? What kinds of evidence will be most persuasive in this particular rhetorical situation, and how should this evidence be presented?

By contrast, writers of critical essays define their audiences and purpose for writing quite differently. Such essays are addressed to *informed* readers, and the writer's task does not generally include commentary on a text's goodness or badness—indications of whether the writer liked it or not—but rather develops an idea, an opinion, about the text or texts under discussion. Because the reader of the essay, by definition, is familiar with the text, knows who the characters are and so on, the writers of research papers—and, indeed, most papers on literary topics—are not required to provide long summaries of the plot or action, descriptions of the central characters, and other features of the text. Instead, the paper attempts to advance a *reading*, an interpretation, of some aspect or aspects of the play, story, or poem by making a case for the validity of a particular understanding or intellectual "purchase" of the topic. This means that a research paper has to have a thesis statement.

Thesis Statements

The sentence that conveys the thrust of the writer's purpose—and, in fact, organizes the entire essay—is called the *thesis statement*. And while it is often the case that a precise thesis statement is formulated after a rough draft is produced, all research writing begins with at least some ideas about the topic to be undertaken and the direction the paper will take. But, as every writer also knows, finding that topic and refining the thesis are among the most difficult jobs a writer undertakes during prewriting.

By way of a brief review, here are the characteristics of a good thesis statement.

- A thesis statement is a statement of opinion, not a fact or statement of intention.
- A thesis statement offers an opinion about which reasonable people might disagree.
- A thesis statement usually possesses a rhetorical premise (comparison, process, classification, definition, and so on).
- A thesis statement predicts the progress of the paper and controls the evidence to be admitted.
- A thesis statement addresses a topic of interpretive significance, not a minor point.
- A thesis statement relies on theoretical or aesthetic assumptions.

All of these issues are described in greater detail in Chapter 52, "Writing about Literature." But when writing an essay based on research, one other component of thesis statements becomes relevant.

- A thesis statement enters its author into a critical conversation with other readers.

Unlike papers written solely from your own experience of a poem, short story, film, or play, a research paper inevitably leads to your consultation of other opinions. How have other readers before you understood Shakespeare's Hamlet, Joseph Conrad's Marlow and Kurtz, or Susan Glaspell's Iowa farmers? In some ways, this quality of a thesis statement becomes the most intimidating because, after all, if something is published in a book or academic journal, it must be correct. Right?

Wrong. A published essay or chapter of a book that analyzes the topic you want to explore need not be regarded as unimpeachable or exhaustive. In the case of materials printed on non-refereed Web sites, it may not even be any good. But such readings *do* exist and, as we will see, if you borrow anything from them—in any form—your indebtedness must be cited appropriately. The thesis of a research paper, in fact, responds in part to what "outside" sources you have found. But the best papers achieve more than a reiteration of source materials. They add to them, modify them, refocus them, even refute them. The sources you uncover during your research are much like the voices in a conversation into which your voice—your thesis statement—enters.

But how do you find this conversation in the first place? You start the research process by heading for the library.

Finding and Evaluating Sources

Your instructor will most likely stipulate the number of sources you need to consult for this assignment and may also restrict the kinds of materials you may use. One of the most controversial sources of information, whatever might be said of its convenience, is the World Wide Web, which can be "surfed" on topics ranging from Sophocles to Emily Dickinson, Edgar Allan Poe to performance artist Karen Finley. Several realities make information taken from the Web potentially problematic: the possibility that it has not been "refereed," for instance, and the fact that information on Web sites may exist in cyberspace today and be gone tomorrow. By "refereed," we mean that an essay appearing in most academic books and journals has undergone "peer review": It has been evaluated and approved by experts in the field before being published. In the case of most academic presses, a book has not only been recommended for publication by experts, but also endorsed by a review board at the press. Unfortunately, most Web sites cannot guarantee such quality in the materials they post, with the exception of such refereed online publications as *Postmodern Culture* and *Workplace: The Journal of Academic Labor.*

In general, at least two factors can help you decide the quality of the material you have found: its date of publication and the reputation of the publisher. Journals and books published at reputable institutions (that is, colleges and universities you have heard of) have undergone peer review, as have books accepted by such major publishers as Houghton Mifflin, Norton, Macmillan, John Wiley, Harcourt Brace, and others. When in doubt about a potential source, ask your instructor.

Also, it is generally advisable—not to mention, efficient—to begin your search with recently published books and journal articles. Not because the last thing written is necessarily the best thing written, but because the bibliographies in these publications will lead you to potential sources published earlier. Obviously, starting your research with earlier materials will not be similarly enhancing of your bibliography. Here, again, exceptions exist. If, for example, you are interested in how New York audiences responded to the first production of Eugene O'Neill's *The Emperor Jones* in 1920 or how reviewers in the 1890s responded to several of Thomas Hardy's novels, then your investigation would most likely begin with the review of materials published then.

Finally, a number of indexes and bibliographies are helpful both in leading you to sources and in evaluating the sources you find. For example, the Modern Language Association (MLA) publishes the annual *MLA International Bibliography*, which lists works published about most American, British, and Western European authors during a given year. The *Reader's Guide to Periodical Literature* is similarly useful, because it indexes the contents of popular magazines, and the gateway site *Voice of the Shuttle: Web Page for Humanities Research* (if Internet sources are permissible for your assignment) can assist you in locating relevant materials on the Web. Most major city newspapers like the *New York Times* and the *Washington Post* are indexed and can prove indispensable sources for such materials as theater and film reviews. The *MLA Handbook for Writers of Research Papers*, 5th ed. (1999), whose documentation system we will summarize below, also recommends the *Book Review Index* and *Book Review Digest* as places you can go to find reviews of books you might want to consult. If you are preparing a research paper on a topic in American literature or culture, the annual volume *American Literary Scholarship* (*ALS*) could also prove valuable to you.

All of these reference books and much, much more are available in college and university libraries. And reference librarians are there to make your search for materials as painless and productive as possible; if you need assistance, don't hesitate to ask one for help.

Taking Notes from Sources

Remember that whatever sources you decide to use, it is your responsibility to paraphrase or quote from them accurately. Accuracy down to the last word or punctuation mark sounds like an easy enough goal to achieve, but it isn't. Imagine taking notes from a source when the phone rings, or when your roommate comes in and invites you to a party, or when someone next door puts on Eminem or Jimi Hendrix at high volume—any of these distractions could compromise your ability to record information accurately from a source. Further, after a week, a month, or more of reviewing and evaluating sources, it's easy to get confused about where certain material originated. If essential information from and about a source is not written down—and checked carefully—the possibilities of making mistakes increase dramatically. Of course, factors beyond your control may complicate your research: a book you are relying on may be called back to the library; a journal issue you found easily today may be missing tomorrow; and, as we have already mentioned, the Web site you discovered today may be quite different tomorrow.

For all of these reasons, it is essential that your note-taking system include at least the following information.

1. A *full* citation for every source. This means the author's complete name, title, publication information and, for articles or chapters of collected books, the full page run of the essay you intend to cite.
2. An indication for each entry that reminds you whether the information is a brief summary, an extended paraphrase of the original, or a direct quotation. The distinction between a paraphrase and a direct quotation is a crucial one and is discussed in the next section below.
3. A page number—or paragraph number for some Internet sites—for each note you take.
4. A note to yourself of exactly where you found the source, just in case you need to consult it later.

Quoting, Paraphrasing, and Avoiding Plagiarism

Once you have found sources relevant to your project and begin note-taking, you will need to decide whether to make a brief summary of the material, write a more extended paraphrase, or quote directly. Of course, you will probably do a combination of all three for many of the sources you find. The decision to quote or paraphrase involves several factors. Is the language of the original so striking that its precise phrasing is nearly as striking as its content? A sentence commonly found in histories of British drama like "The public theatre in England began in the later 1570s" might convey significant information, but its wording is hardly exceptional and need not be quoted. Whereas, Hamlet's famous soliloquy that begins "To be, or not to be, that is the question" (3.1.57) might prove awkward to restate and ineffective as well. "Should I, like, kill myself or maybe I shouldn't is what I'm trying to figure out" fails to capture the elegance of Shakespeare's line. Some passages, like the opening sentence of Samuel Beckett's novel *Murphy* (1957), are too cleverly phrased to be reduced to paraphrase: "The sun shone, having no alternative, on the nothing new." Others, like Salman Rushdie's description of the shame of colonized peoples from his novel *Shame* (1983), contain such vivid metaphors that you will probably want to quote it directly:

> Imagine shame as a liquid, let's say a sweet fizzy tooth-rotting drink stored in a vending machine. Push the right button and a cup plops down under a pissing stream of the liquid. How to push the button? Nothing to it. Tell a lie, sleep with a white boy, get born the wrong sex. (125)

You decide how best to use the material you find. Whether you quote or paraphrase, remember that you are obliged to explain the implications of this material when you write your paper.

When paraphrasing a passage, make certain that you not only convey its meaning accurately, but that you also restate it in your own words. This means, at the very least, revising the descriptive language of the original into your own prose. If you consciously recall taking a paraphrase from a source and using it in your essay, it must be cited, just as you would cite a direct quotation. Consider the following example, taken from Terry Eagleton's book *Crazy John and the Bishop and Other Essays on Irish Culture* (1998), which discusses the changing forms of modern art after World War II. Pay particular attention to the language Eagleton employs at the end of the excerpt to define aesthetic innovations and their origins.

Original Passage

It is as though we can now recognize that, for example, simply because of the sharpening contradictions of naturalistic drama, there would have been a thrust beyond such theatrical realism, even if its names had not turned out to be Beckett or Pirandello or Ionesco. Someone, we feel, would have had to come up with free verse or musical dissonance or showing a face from five different angles simultaneously, just as once you have a variety of liquors it is hard not to think that cocktails were somehow preordained. Every cultural period provides us with a [host] of possibilities. . . . In post-war Europe, there were those authors gripped by a sense of spiritual exhaustion, writers who carved out a niche of anti-heroic debunkery, artistic exiles adrift between languages, and avant-garde experimenters in theatrical form. (Eagleton 297)

Paraphrase

Naturalistic or realistic drama at the beginning of the twentieth century contained a number of ever-sharpening contradictions, so some innovative playwright inevitably would have gone beyond theatrical realism in terms of dramatic form. The same is true of all art in the period; someone would have had to come up with free verse in poetry, musical dissonance in composition, or showing a face from five different angles in filmmaking. Lots of aesthetic possibilities exist in every period. This is particularly true of Europe after World War II, where many authors, gripped by a sense of spiritual exhaustion, felt adrift between languages and led avant-garde experimentation, especially in a new theatre of anti-heroic debunkery.

Although this paraphrase accurately summarizes the original, it verges on *plagiarism* for at least two reasons: Highly descriptive phrases from the original appear without quotations marks, and no citation at the end identifies the source of these ideas. Notice that the quotation is followed by "(Eagleton 297)," signaling the origin of this material. If previous sentences clarified that Eagleton's book was the source, then only "(297)" would be necessary. But, again, *any material that you consciously recall taking from a source must be accompanied by a citation*. And, of course, fuller information about the source should appear in the "Works Cited" section at the end of the paper.

But this is only half of the problem with the above paraphrase. An equally significant failing is the writer's inability to rephrase important descriptions in Eagleton's paragraph: "sharpening contradictions," "gripped by a sense of spiritual exhaustion," "anti-heroic debunkery" and so on. Again, some language is, by its very nature, so basic and colorless that it really cannot be paraphrased. For example, "Abraham Lincoln was born in Kentucky and moved to Illinois when he was a small child" contains little descriptive language to rephrase. You cannot replace "born" with "came into this world" without risking verbosity; "moved" need not be changed to "migrated" or "transported." But phrases like "gripped by a sense of spiritual exhaustion" or "anti-heroic debunkery" in the original must be restated in your own words. The following paraphrase suggests one way to do this.

Paraphrase

> Contemporary scholars like Terry Eagleton emphasize the decline of dramatic realism in the early decades of the twentieth century, and the aesthetic experimentation that eventually took place not only in play writing, but in such other areas as poetry, musical composition, and filmmaking as well. So-called "free verse" in poetry and "musical dissonance" in musical composition were followed, in the years of soul-searching in Europe after World War II, by a variety of formal experiments in drama such as the writing of plays around anti-heroes and the creation of a dramatic mood on stage that matched the pessimism of the times. (297)

You may elect, as we have in the above paraphrase, to quote and paraphrase in the same paragraph. No problem—so long as the quoted portions are identified and are integrated smoothly into the syntax of your sentence. If you are at all confused about methods of quoting from the original, please review "Arguments and Admissible Evidence: Paraphrase and Quotation" in Chapter 52, "Writing about Literature."

Once you have formulated a thesis, however tentative and subject to refinement or tweaking; have found, evaluated, and taken notes from sources; and have made preliminary decisions about paraphrasing and quoting, you are probably ready to begin a rough draft. Of course, this stage of the research writing process means making more decisions, some of which are outlined in the following section.

Writing

Your trips to the library have helped you refine a thesis in which you feel confident; you have tested it against the criteria listed above and have asked informed readers (your classmates or instructor) to comment on its potential. After consulting the card catalogue at the library, indexes and bibliographies, and—perhaps—online sources, you have assembled a set of high-quality sources and taken accurate notes from them. You have read carefully the literary text or texts you intend to discuss, deciding what passages to incorporate into your argument; you have even made some preliminary decisions about which excerpts might be paraphrased and which should be quoted. Most important, you have allowed yourself sufficient time to write, rewrite, and revise some more. You are aware of the citation system you are supposed to follow and any other formal requirements outlined by your instructor: the recommended length of the essay, the placement of page numbers, and so on. You are well rested and comfortable.

You're ready to go! Well, almost.

Before you begin, reconsider the basic equation formulated in Chapter 52 and the ways in which your research will modify it. Here's the previous equation:

Your "reading" + textual evidence (paraphrase + quotation) = argument.

Writing that includes research material extends this equation as follows:

Your "reading" + textual evidence (paraphrase + quotation) + research (paraphrase + quotation) = argument.

Note that in both cases *your* analysis comes first, supported by concrete textual evidence. As we remarked earlier, a *balance* between your analysis and the evidence is crucial to the success of your paper. An argument with no evidence is no argument; an argument with only pieces of evidence left unexplained amounts to a mere patchwork of quotations and paraphrases. Effective arguments require both your organization and explanation of evidence—and, of course, the evidence itself must be presented clearly and concisely.

Most important, remember that the research you conduct only *supplements* your argument. That is to say, as is the case in writing any essay on a literary topic, your argument rests on your abilities to articulate a thesis statement and mount a convincing evidentiary case for it. Part of this evidence originates in the references you have consulted, but only a part and not necessarily the major part. And this prompts one more question:

What is your attitude toward this research and how does this affect your presentation of it in your argument?

As we mentioned earlier, not everything you read will be of equal quality, and you may not agree with everything you read. Fine. The question is, how do you present this information in your paper? The first answer is "with respect" and verbal grace.

After that, a number of possibilities exist. One common rhetorical tactic, for example, is called the "straw man" or "straw critic" approach in which a writer repeats a critical assertion only to modify or refute it. The purpose of the strategy is to create a "space" for the thesis or point of the argument by way of negation. Professional literary critics employ this strategy all the time, as the following passage from Richard H. Rodino's essay ("Authors, Characters, and Readers in *Gulliver's Travels*," *PMLA* 106 [October 1991]: 1054–70) on conflicting interpretations of Jonathan Swift's *Gulliver's Travels* suggests. Here, Rodino cites another scholar whose reading of the book, while incisive and useful, needs to be extended:

> Even a preliminary exploration of [conflicting views of *Gulliver's Travels*] requires an unusually complex understanding of the rhetorical relations involved. We must, for instance, go beyond Everett Zimmerman's pioneering description of the *Travels* as "a book not about a man who undergoes certain experiences but about a man who writes a book about experiences he has undergone"—a view that regards the reader simply as a receiver of meaning. . . . (1057)

In this passage Rodino expresses his admiration of Zimmerman's work ("pioneering description"), while at the same time insisting that his conception of the reader ought to be revised ("go beyond," "reader simply as a receiver"). The result is a respectful, yet strong statement of interpretive difference, which Rodino elaborates in his close reading of Swift's text.

On other occasions, broad critical agreement might exist, yet this consensus does not consider a text in which you are interested. Or, if it has been considered in such conversations, its significance hasn't been properly assessed. In such instances, you might indicate the principal parties in the conversation and then "clear a space" for your participation in the dialogue. This is the strategy Megan Sullivan uses to introduce her essay on recent women's films in Northern Ireland ("Orla Walsh's *The Visit* (1992): Incarceration and Feminist Cinema in Northern Ireland," *New Hibernia Review* 2 [Summer 1998]: 85–99):

> Following Pat Murphy, Anne Crilly, Margo Harkin, and Orla Walsh each have used film to critique nationalism and women's place in it. They also have taken great pains to suggest that nationalism itself is no longer women's primary concern; rather, they are concerned with day-to-day or material problems: censorship, the women's movement, class structure, and reproductive choice. Importantly, Crilly, Harkin, and Walsh invoke the site of the prison to suggest these concerns, and Murphy herself relies on the trope of incarceration to signal a young woman's emerging feminist consciousness. . . . Because her twenty-two minute film *The Visit* centers on the protagonist's physical and mental journey to visit her husband in prison, Walsh's film progresses furthest to argue for the significance of incarceration for nationalist women in Northern Ireland. (85)

This excerpt accomplishes several things at once. By alluding to several examples, it lends a sense of authority to the argument, suggesting that the writer really knows her subject. Like the "straw critic" approach, this more positive tactic also clears a discursive space for the writer's thesis. And, by returning to key terms in the essay's title, this passage reiterates elements crucial to the progress of the argument: "feminist cinema," Northern Ireland, and the importance of images of incarceration in these films.

However you choose to weave critical opinions into the fabric of your argument, do not let them overwhelm your presentation and analysis of textual detail. Introduce and enunciate the thesis statement, develop the evidence, and conclude—much as you would any other essay.

Revision

One unfortunate reality of research assignments is that while writers may spend weeks researching a topic and writing, many devote too little time to revising the argument, polishing the prose, and proofreading for mistakes. The revision stage, in fact, seems almost doomed to be given short shrift in most varieties of writing, yet its importance to the quality of the final product is indisputable. This is especially true of research papers.

Why? Because, as we have implied above, the process of conducting and writing a research paper is particularly vulnerable to human error. It isn't hard to understand why. Research writing includes more documents to read than most other kinds of writing, more material to process and organize, more quotations and decisions, more citations to foul up.

Our advice, consistent with that we have given earlier, is to read your draft carefully, checking in particular for some of the writing problems that have surfaced in earlier essays. This could mean checking all the transitions or topic sentences of paragraphs, sharpening the precision of your word selection, looking for spelling errors, and so on. By the time you write your research paper, you should have a fairly clear idea of the things you do well and those elements of your writing that need improvement. Remember that the root of word *revise* comes from the Latin meaning "look again," not "glance again" or "hurry through again." The very word, therefore, denotes a careful review of the entire project.

Research papers also add two significant elements to your list of "things to do" at the revision stage: Check the accuracy of every quotation in the essay—word by word, punctuation mark by punctuation mark—and verify that each entry in your "Notes" and "Works Cited" sections follow the *exact* format specified by your instructor. We are following the documentation system outlined in the *MLA Handbook for Writers of Research Papers*, 5th edition. If questions arise at any time in the process of researching or writing your paper, the *MLA Handbook* probably contains an answer. It is generally available in the reference section of college libraries or may be purchased from the Modern Language Association of America.

Because "Notes" and Works Cited" generally appear at the end of research papers, we will conclude with a brief discussion of their function and a listing of citation formats for the most common kinds of sources. The sample research paper at the end of Chapter 55, "Writing about Drama, provides an example of the kind of essay we have been outlining here.

Notes and Works Cited

In the MLA citation system, "footnotes" and "endnotes" are greatly simplified. Why? Because instead of supplying a superscripted number for each citation and then listing each of these at the foot of the page or at the end of the essay, in the MLA system each reference in the text is followed by a parenthesis identifying the source and page number. So, to take the paraphrase from Terry Eagleton's book mentioned earlier, if the author of the excerpt is clear from the context—or if his name is specifically mentioned—you need only supply the page number at the end of the excerpt: thus, "(297)." If the source is *not* made clear by the context, then you must cite the author's last name and the page number: thus, "(Eagleton 297)." And, in cases in which you refer to two or more works by the same author, and the context does not specify the source of the excerpt, you must include the author's last name, an abbreviated title, and a page number: thus, "(Eagleton, *Crazy John* 297)."

That's about it. In this system of parenthetical or "internal" citation, the

"Notes" section includes only extra information or brief asides—comments you might wish to make about a point raised in the essay that, in your judgment, is not important enough to include in the body of the argument. So, for example, suppose you had consulted several sources on literary experimentation after World War II, good sources but ones not so effective as Eagleton in explaining the topic. You might place a superscript after the passage from Eagleton and in your "Notes" section at the end of the paper direct your reader to these sources: thus,

Notes

[1]For further discussion of the origins of late modernist aesthetics and mid-twentieth-century "exhaustion," see Esslin and Miller.

You might even want to add a sentence or two to this entry distinguishing one source from another. Whatever the case, even if you only mention their names in one note, full information on Esslin and Miller must appear in the "Works Cited."

In the MLA documentation system of parenthetical citations, therefore, it is entirely possible to write a fine research paper without any notes at all. Not so with "Works Cited." Every work mentioned in notes, paraphrased or quoted in the body of the essay—and, of course, this includes the literary texts that form the nexus of your argument—must appear in the "Works Cited" at the end of the paper. Entries should be organized in alphabetical order by the author's last name (for a book written or edited by more than one person, you should use the last name of the first person listed on the title page). If an author is not listed for an article or essay, the first letter of the first major word in the title dictates its position in your "Works Cited."

Citation forms for the most commonly used kinds of sources follows.

A SINGLE-AUTHORED BOOK

Chávez, John R. *The Lost Land: The Chicano Image of the Southwest.* Albuquerque: U of New Mexico P, 1984.

TWO OR MORE BOOKS BY THE SAME AUTHOR

Jameson, Fredric. *The Political Unconscious: Narrative as a Socially Symbolic Act.* Ithaca: Cornell UP, 1981.

———. *Postmodernism, or, The Cultural Logic of Late Capitalism.* Durham, NC: Duke UP, 1991.

AN EDITED BOOK BY TWO OR MORE AUTHORS

Bérubé, Michael, and Cary Nelson, eds. *Higher Education Under Fire: Politics, Economics, and the Crisis of the Humanities.* New York: Routledge, 1995.

A TRANSLATED BOOK

Baudrillard, Jean. *Fatal Strategies*. Trans. Philip
    Beitchman and W. G. J. Niesluchowski. Ed. Jim Flem-
    ing. New York/London: Semiotext(e)/Pluto, 1990.

AN ARTICLE IN A SCHOLARLY JOURNAL

Newman, Karen. "Portia's Ring: Unruly Women and Struc-
    tures of Exchange in *The Merchant of Venice*."
    Shakespeare Quarterly 38 (1987): 19-33.

AN ARTICLE IN A MAGAZINE

Schlosser, Eric. "The Taking of the Presidency 2000."
    Rolling Stone 1 Feb. 2001: 36-38, 64.

AN ESSAY IN AN ANTHOLOGY

Onkey, Lauren. "The Passion Machine Theatre Company's
    Everyday Life." *A Century of Irish Drama: Widening
    the Stage*. Ed. Stephen Watt, Eileen Morgan, and
    Shakir Mustafa. Bloomington: Indiana UP, 2000.
    223-35.

A MULTIVOLUME WORK

Lauter, Paul, et al., eds. *The Heath Anthology of Ameri-
    can Literature*. 4th ed. 2 vols. Boston: Houghton
    Mifflin, 2002.

A FILM

North by Northwest. Dir. Alfred Hitchcock. Perf. Cary
    Grant, Eva Marie Saint, James Mason, Martin Landau,
    and Leo G. Carroll. MGM, 1959.

A LECTURE

Burke, Cynthia. "Tomorrow's English Majors." MLA Conven-
    tion. Hynes Auditorium, Boston. 25 Apr. 2002.

AN INTERVIEW

Harold Bloom. Interview with Anthony Perro. *Weekend
    Edition*. Natl. Public Radio. WBUR, Boston. 10
    June 1995.

AN E-MAIL

Tuttle, Robert. E-mail to the author. 2 May 2002.

CD-ROM

"Dickinson, Emily." *Discovering Authors*. Vers. 2.0. CD-
    ROM. Detroit: Gale, 1999.

A DOCUMENT WITHIN A DATABASE

"City Profile: San Francisco." *CNN Interactive*. 19 June
    1998. Cable News Network. 19 June 1998.<http://
    www.cnn.com/TRAVEL/CITY.GUIDES/WTR/
    north.america.profiles/nap.san francisco.html>

WEB SITE

Internet Public Library. 1 May 2002. 6 July 2002.
    <http://www.ipl.org/>.

Sample Student Essay

See the sample student essay at the end of Chapter 55, "Writing about
Drama," for an example of a thoughtful research paper.

Glossary

absurdism   See *theater of the absurd*.

accentual meter   The strong stress meter characteristic of Old English poetry.

accentual syllabic meter   Reaching back to the fourteenth century, this tradition of versification is based on the number of accents and syllables per line.

alienate   To detach. German dramatist Bertolt Brecht (1898–1956) coined the term *theater of alienation* to describe plays and acting styles that detach the audience emotionally. This process is also described as *detachment*.

allegory   A symbolic representation of a character for a concept, position, or one aspect of personality. The term comes from the Greek words meaning "other" (*allos*) and "to speak" (*agoreuein*)—to speak in terms of something other.

allegorical   Pertaining to an allegory.

allusion   A reference in a text to a passage or figure from literary, popular, or religious traditions.

analepsis   A literary term for shifts in chronology from the present to the past. In film, this practice is called a *flashback*.

anapest   A poetic foot comprising two unaccented syllables followed by an accented syllable.

antagonist   A character who opposes the protagonist or whose actions conflict with the protagonist's aims or desires.

antistrophe   The second part of a choral ode.

apostrophe   A special performative instance of *prosopopoeia* (addressing an inanimate thing or a person who is absent or deceased).

archetype   The basic model for a particular character in a myth. Stemming from the Greek word *archetypos*, meaning "original pattern," an archetype in literature describes a symbolic image that is basic to the human experience of birth, death, fertility, disease, war, quest, and so on.

aside   A moment in a play during which a character talks directly to the audience, bringing them into a pact or confidence. Unlike a soliloquy, in which the actor is alone on stage, an aside can be delivered to the audience in the midst of dialogue.

Black Arts Movement   A radically separatist cultural movement in the 1960s, led by such figures as Amiri Baraka, that advocated a negation of white aesthetics and the embrace of more authentic African and African American forms. Baraka founded the Black Arts Repertory Theatre School in Harlem in 1965.

black box   An adaptable rectangular theatrical space that typically accommodates a small audience of less than 200.

blank verse   Unrhymed iambic pentameter.

blazon A traditional poetic form where a male poet pays tribute to a woman by complimenting the details of her face or body.

blocking The movement of actors on stage. Effective blocking is purposeful, calculated by the director to accompany dialogue, monologue, or other stage activity in a meaningful way.

cacophony A sound that is unpleasant and grating.

caesura A pause. From the Latin *caedere*, meaning "to cut."

catharsis The expurgation of pity and fear. Taken from Aristotle's *Poetics*, this term describes the audience response that is appropriate to tragedy.

climax The moment of greatest emotional tension in a narrative. Usually, after events lead up to this point, they are resolved in the *denouement*.

close reading An engaged analysis and interpretation of a literary text that moves beyond a simple summary of the ideas or actions expressed in the work. A close reading often focuses on the specific words or figurative language used in a passage.

cognate A word that has the same root as a word from a different language.

commedia dell'arte A type of comedy in which stock characters perform customary roles that delight audiences, made popular in sixteenth-century Italy.

concrete poetry Poetry that explores the visual possibilities of pattern in calligraphy, typewriter art, stamp art, and typographical design. The concrete poetry movement began in the 1950s.

connotation The values, qualities, associations, and shades of meaning that a word acquires in contextual usage over time.

consonance A similarity in beginning or ending consonant sounds but different vowel sounds.

cothurni High boots worn by actors on the ancient Greek and Roman stages.

couplet A pair of rhyming lines.

dactyl A poetic foot comprising one accented syllable followed by two unaccented syllables.

deconstruction The examination of how structures, language, and imagery work against or contradict themselves or other aspects of a story's expression.

denotation The literal meaning of a word or group of words rather than additional meanings those words might suggest (see *connotation*).

denouement The final resolution of a plot's conflict, generally occurring after the *climax* of the narrative.

deus ex machina God from the machine (Latin). An artificial device or character introduced to resolve a plot issue. It refers to the machinery that carried a Roman or Greek god to the stage to "save the day" at the last moment.

dialogism A method of interpreting culture as responsive, as individuals act in a particular time and space and react to the past and to the expected future. Key words can be examined for their open-ended rather than closed nature. It is a key concept that New Historicism takes from the Russian thinker Mikhail Bakhtin (1895–1975).

dialogue The conversation between two or more characters.

diction The choice of words in prose, fiction, poetry, and drama.

diegesis The world of the story.

dimeter A line of verse consisting of two metrical feet.

drama A composition that is intended for representation by one or more performers to an audience.

dramatic irony The disparity created when readers (or viewers) know more than the characters.

El Teatro Campesino (Farmworkers' Theater) A theater founded in California by playwright and political activist, Luis Valdéz, in 1965 to produce works by Chicano and Chicana writers; some feminist critics regard the company as not providing an adequate forum for women writers.

end rhyme A rhyme that comes at the end of a line of verse.

enjambment The movement of syntactic phrasing from the end of one line to the beginning of the next.

epiphany A sudden and overwhelming insight or recognition of a truth.

euphony The impression of sounds that are pleasing to the ear.

explication A critical interpretation of a text.

exposition The beginning of a story or drama in which the characters and circumstances of the narrative are introduced.

expressionism An early twentieth-century movement in the arts that attempted to express subjective or psychological realities. In German drama and silent film of the 1910s and 1920s, for example, expressionist techniques included distorted make-up or camera angles, slanted stages and settings, and other means to represent an interior or psychological reality.

feminine rhyme A rhyming of words of two or more syllables where the final syllable is unstressed.

feminist criticism The criticism that focuses on the politics and aesthetics of female experience and representation, as well as of gender generally.

figurative language Words and descriptions, including metaphor, simile, and personification, that differ from purely denotative, or literal, meanings to suggest comparisons between two or more terms or things.

first-person narrator See *narrator.*

flat characters Characters that behave in predictable and uncomplicated ways, in part because they are thinly developed emotionally. Frequently found in melodrama, flat characters are often stereotypes. Their opposites, so-called rounded characters, possess the complications and contradictions of real people.

foot A unit of poetic meter consisting of stressed and unstressed syllables.

formalism A kind of literary analysis that emphasizes using elements of form to interpret meaning.

frame narrator See *narrator.*

free verse A kind of poetry that varies in length, typography, rhythms, and stanza patterns to fit the particular style and content of the work at hand.

gay and lesbian criticism   Analysis that focuses on issues of sexuality or the politics and aesthetics of gay experience and representation. It is part of a larger investigation of sexuality and gender called *queer theory*.

half rhyme   Rhymes that have minor or dissonant tonalities.

hamartia   Tragic flaw or error (Greek). The tragic error leads to the protagonist's downfall. In his *Poetics*, Aristotle describes the downfall of a character brought about not by the character's vice or depravity but by some error or frailty.

hemistich   A half line of poetry.

heptameter   A metrical unit consisting of seven feet.

heroic couplet   In poetry, rhyming couplets composed in iambic pentameter. These couplets were a popular form in the eighteenth century.

hexameter   A metrical unit consisting of six feet.

high comedy   In drama, the kind of humor created through clever verbal means, wit, and intellectual sophistication; see also *low comedy*.

hybridity   The multicultural reality of contemporary America. As discussed by Guillermo Goméz-Peña and other commentators on contemporary culture, identity and culture are now composed of different national and ethnic phenomena, as once firm cultural borders topple or disappear.

hyperbole   A figure of speech using exaggeration for emphasis or effect. An example is Andrew Marvell's pledge to his lover that "An hundred years should go to praise / Thine eyes, and on thy forehead gaze; / Two hundred to adore each breast."

hypertext   Internet-based writing that contains links to other resources. Hypertext is performative because it requires readers to engage in a constant process of selection and arrangement that produces narrative.

iambic foot   A metrical unit of verse based on the iamb, which comprises an unaccented syllable followed by an accented one.

iambic pentameter   The most typical metrical line in English constructed of five iambic feet per line.

image   A suggestion of sensory phenomena.

imagery   The use of language to evoke sensory experience.

in medias res   In the middle of the thing (Latin). This term refers to starting a narrative in the middle of events rather than at the beginning.

internal rhyme   A pair of words that rhyme within and across adjacent lines.

intertextuality   The various ways that texts refer to other texts.

irony   A situation (dramatic irony) or phrasing (verbal irony) that performs something contrary to expectation. Dramatic irony occurs when the audience knows more about an incident than a character in a play does.

literary movement   A set of ideas formulated by authors and critics about what literature should do and how it should be done.

low comedy   In drama, the kind of humor generated by characters noted for their physical dexterity, linguistic ineptitude, and ability to make an audience laugh; for example, the antics of a clown or jester. Some critics call this physical comedy.

Marxist criticism   A form of analysis that studies representations of class, the ways literature enacts the effects of economic disparity, and the material conditions and contexts in which literature is produced. It is based on a labor theory of value advanced by the nineteenth-century German philosopher, historian, social scientist, and revolutionary Karl Marx.

masculine rhyme   A rhyme made on a masculine ending. Masculine rhyme describes rhyming words of more than one syllable when the rhyming sound falls on the final, unstressed syllable.

memory play   A play in the present with a narrator relating events that occurred in the past. Examples in this book include *The Glass Menagerie* and *M. Butterfly*.

metafiction   A story about a story.

metanarrative   A story that draws attention to the mechanisms of telling stories.

metaphor   Figurative language that compares one word or thing in terms of another word or thing by way of direct transference.

metatheatrics   The elements of a play that recognize the play's own fictiveness, including characters' direct addresses to the audience or references to the "staged" nature of the play.

metonymy   Figurative language that describes a word substituted for another word associated with it. For instance, the metonymy of "the crown" is often used to refer to the regal authority of the king or queen who wears it. See also *synecdoche*.

mimesis   An imitation.

mise-en-scène   Put in the scene (French). Everything that a drama audience sees and hears, including set, costume, lighting, movement, and sound effects.

modernism   A term used to describe various aesthetic movements in the late nineteenth and twentieth centuries, especially those prior to World War II. Modernism reacted against realistic representations of nineteenth-century literature as well as the conformity of commercial culture, in part by emphasizing stylistic experimentation.

monologue   The spoken thoughts of a single character.

monometer   A verse consisting of a single metrical foot.

mood   The atmosphere or feeling produced in a text, usually through descriptive language of places, people, and events.

morality plays   In medieval England, the plays that taught audiences clear moral lessons.

motif   Any significant repetition of images, symbols, language, actions, or other elements of a literary work.

myth criticism   An approach to literary studies that analyzes characters and events as representative parts of archetypal, mythical patterns.

narrative   A structure by which we make sense out of events by ordering them in a chain of cause-and-effect relations that play out in space and time.

narrator   The voice of the person telling the story. Typically, the author selects a dominant narrative mode for each literary work, though some works may include multiple narrators and multiple narrative modes. A *first-person narrator* is a participating character in the story identified through the narrator's use of *I* or occasionally *we*. A *third-person narrator* is not explicitly present in the story but appears to re-count events from a position outside the story, which is not explained or accounted for by the story. A *third-person omniscient narrator* is a narrator who has a complete, nearly godlike range of knowledge, including the thoughts and emotions of all char-acters. A *third-person limited narrator* is a narrator whose implied knowledge is lim-ited to his or her subjective experiences. If a story involves more than one narrator, the first narrator is called the *frame narrator* (see Conrad's *Heart of Darkness* as an ex-ample).

naturalism   A literary movement in which writers sought to render a realistic or sci-entific view of the human species.

near rhyme   Rhymes with minor or dissonant tonalities.

New Criticism   An approach to literary criticism that was followed by a group of American critics of the early and middle twentieth century who believed that ana-lyzing the elements of a work was all that was necessary to understand it.

New Historicism   An approach to literary analysis that focuses on the historical and cultural aspects of a text, asserting the importance of context and treating the text as a cultural document, not a literary icon.

octameter   A unit of verse having eight feet per poetic line.

octave   The first eight lines of a sonnet.

onomatopoeia   The verbal sounds or words that are meant to mimic things imagi-natively heard in the world, such as *buzz* and *plop*.

open form verse   Poetry that varies in length, typography, rhythms, and stanza pat-terns to fit the particular style and content of the work at hand.

open stage   A stage that an audience can sit around in a circle.

orchestra   A rounded open space separating the stage from the audience.

Orientalism   An approach to cultural analysis that stereotypes Eastern or Asian peoples and rationalizes Western values as superior. Based on Edward Said's *Orien-talism*. See D. H. Hwang's play *M. Butterfly*.

Other   The different. In both race and postcolonial criticism, the other is often con-structed as a negation of white, European values. At times, the other is also made into an exotic or alluring figure of desire.

ottava rima   The eight-line stanza pattern rhyming *abababcc* (Italian).

oxymoron   A rhetorical figure that combines contradictory terms—a blending of op-posites. It is derived from the Greek roots meaning sharp (*oxus*) and foolish (*moros*).

paradigms   The models or patterns that make up the events in a story.

paradox   A contradictory experience, insight, or truth that cuts across the grain of our conventional expectations. It is derived from the Greek root words meaning be-yond (*para*) and opinion (*doxos*).

paraphrase   A restatement in your own words of the main ideas, arguments, and thematic elements of a poem.

parataxis   A technique in which images are set directly side by side. In experimental film, this might be a quick cut from one scene or image to another; in poetry, setting phrases side by side without an obvious or logical connection.

pastoral   Relating to the natural landscapes of Greece and Rome, found in much of traditional English love poetry representing desire.

patriarchy   The social and cultural relations that have historically empowered men at the expense of women. It is drawn from the Greek root *patriarkhes* and the Latin word *pater* or father.

pattern poetry   A version of fixed form verse that presents the typography and arrangement of lines on the page as a visual icon for its subject matter.

pentameter   A metrical measure of verse made up of five feet per line, as in the iambic pentameter measure of Shakespeare's sonnets.

personification   A figure of speech in which nonhuman objects or creatures are endowed with human characteristics.

plot   The purposeful arrangement of events in a story or play and the order in which they are presented. This arrangement of events may not necessarily follow the sequence in which they occurred but are usually presented for affective or causal reasons.

poetic foot   A unit of verse measurement based on a metrical pattern of accented and unaccented syllables.

point of view   The perspective from which people, events, and other details of a literary work are described.

popular culture   The attitudes, customs, and folkways of ordinary, everyday people.

postcolonial criticism   A set of theoretical issues emerging from the literature and culture of Europe's former colonies as they rebelled against colonial rule and asserted their own cultural and political independence, often by appropriating and recoding colonial discourse, national symbols, and other linguistic conventions of social distinction (see *hybridity*).

postmodernism   A term used variously to characterize sets of aesthetic practices that break up any idea of unity, consistency, or singularity or that employs pastiche or other modes of borrowing. This term may also refer to postmodernist aesthetic practices or textual features.

prolepsis   A flashforward.

proscenium stage   A stage that is separated from the audience by a heavy curtain and that presents the stage action as if it were a framed picture.

prosopopoeia   The figurative rhetoric that attributes human aspects to what are otherwise inanimate objects, abstractions, or nonhuman animals.

protagonist   A character that serves as the primary actor in a literary work and with whom readers are often invited to sympathize.

psychoanalytic criticism   A critical approach that investigates the ways literary texts embody, enact, or illustrate dynamic relations within or among characters using concepts taken from psychoanalysis, particularly the work of Sigmund Freud and Jacques Lacan.

psychological criticism   A critical approach that focuses on interpreting the psychological motivations of characters. Such an approach may adopt vocabularies from any of several psychological "schools" of thought such as the work of Sigmund Freud, Carl Jung, or D. W. Winnicott.

pure rhyme   The heard likeness and differences linking two or more words.

pyrrhic   A metrical foot comprising two unaccented syllables.

quatrain   A four-line stanza unit.

queer theory   See *gay and lesbian theory*.

race criticism   An approach to literary analysis that focuses on how racial difference is represented in the themes, characterizations, symbolism, settings, diction, and formal properties of literary texts.

reader response criticism   An approach to literary analysis that focuses on the individual's response to literary texts and investigates the social conventions of reading that make up broader interpretive communities.

realism   A literary movement and style that focuses on reproducing objective portraits of normal life through the use of a rigorous observation of human behavior in its social and material contexts.

reliability   The degree to which readers can trust representations made by a narrator.

representation   The act of using a word, image or pictorial sign to stand for something else. Representations have a shaping role in society insofar as they communicate perceptions, influence opinions, and build consensus, as well as determine attitudes and beliefs.

revenge tragedy   A popular drama on the Elizabethan and Jacobean stages. In revenge tragedies like Shakespeare's *Hamlet*, a wronged party attempts to avenge harm done to him or his family.

rhyme royal   A seven-stanza rhyming unit patterned *ababbcc*.

romance   A kind of play known for bordering on the seriousness of tragedy even as its central conflicts are resolved happily. Shakespeare's later plays are often referred to as romances. The term is also used to describe medieval narratives in prose or verse—and written in Middle English or a Romance language such as French—that feature the adventures of knights or other heroes (*Sir Gawain and the Green Knight*, for example).

romantic comedy   A comic plot in which young lovers wish to be married and are prevented from doing so, usually by an intervening father or a harsh law. The conflict is brought to closure almost by accident, often by an unexpected twist that allows the conflicts driving the action to be settled happily.

satire   A literary work in which a person or group's vices, hypocrisies, or vanities are held up for ridicule or other comic criticism.

scansion   The process of noting the metrics of a line by counting the number of feet it contains and by charting both accents and syllables.

Scottish stanza   A six-line rhyming unit patterned *aaabab* that was popularized by Robert Burns.

script   The written text of a play, including the dialogue, stage directions, notes from the director, and so on.

semiotics   The study of how various signs (or signifiers) relate to one another in complex webs of meaning.

sestet   The last six lines of a sonnet.

setting The physical, environmental, social, historical, and cultural contexts described in a story as the scene of its action.

simile A figure of speech that makes an explicit comparison between two things by using words such as *like* or *as*. For instance, "She sings like a bird" is a simile.

slant rhyme A rhyme with minor or dissonant tonalities.

soliloquy A speech or lines in a drama in which an actor is alone, revealing his innermost thoughts to the audience.

sonnet The most widely written and read fixed form of poetry, which came into English from the Italian influence of Petrarch.

Spenserian stanza A distinctive nine-line stanza of poetry named after Spenser's "The Faerie Queen."

spondee A metrical foot of poetry consisting of two long or stressed syllables.

stanza A unit or grouping of poetry lines that have the same or similar patterns of meter, rhythm, and end rhyme.

stereotypes A character who represents a familiar type.

stock character A character that fills a predictable role that is conventional to certain kinds of drama. Westerns, for example, predictably offer readers and viewers a hero, a bad guy, a kind-hearted woman who either gambles or works in a saloon, and stereotypes of Native Americans.

story The collection of events that belong to the space and time of the world created by the text as well as events that are only suggested or implied in the text.

strophe A choral song in classical Greek drama accompanied by a movement from the right to the left of the stage.

structuralist criticism Criticism that focuses on a story's structure as a way to understand how the story works.

style The distinctive manner of expression an author uses in a literary text.

subsystem A coherent group within a story.

symbol A concrete image, word, or thing, that refers to an abstract idea or condition. For instance, a wedding ring is a symbol of marriage.

synaesthesia A literary device that uses one of the perceptual senses (sight, hearing, smell, taste, and touch) to portray figuratively another perceptual sense. For example, Dylan Thomas describes smoke as "tunes from the chimneys."

synecdoche A type of metonymy that substitutes a part of something for the whole designated. "Counting heads" is a synecdoche for taking attendance in a classroom.

tercet A group of three lines of verse, often rhyming together or with another triplet.

terza rima A well-known tercet pattern that takes the middle rhyme of each stanza and uses it as the envelope frame for the next stanza unit to rhyme (Italian).

tetrameter A line of verse consisting of four metrical feet.

theater of the absurd A term developed by drama critic Martin Esslin in a 1961 book of the same title. It refers to post-World War II drama like Samuel Beckett's *Waiting for Godot* that emphasizes life's meaninglessness, the decline of religious faith, and other aspects of man's existence.

theme   The central idea or ideas suggested by a literary work.

third-person limited narrator   See *narrator*.

third-person narrator   See *narrator*.

third-person omniscient narrator   See *narrator*.

tone   A literary concept analogous to the tone of voice in spoken language.

tragedy   A narrative in which the central character or protagonist suffers a fall, often death.

tragic hero   The protagonist of a tragedy.

trimeter   A line of poetry made up of three feet.

trochee   A metrical foot of poetry having two syllables where the accent falls on the first syllable rather than on the second, as it does in the iamb.

unity of action   An element of a tragedy privileged by Aristotle in *Poetics*. A unified plot has a beginning, middle, and end, the events of which are linked together by probability and necessity.

unreliability   The adjective applies to narrators whom readers may not trust to deliver unbiased information.

vers libre   Free verse (French). Verse that varies in length, typography, rhythms and stanza patterns to fit the particular style and content of the work at hand.

Credits

TEXT CREDITS

FICTION

Achebe, Chinua, "The Sacrificial Egg": From *Girls at War and Other Stories* by Chinua Achebe, copyright © 1972, 1973 by Chinua Achebe. Used by permission of Doubleday, a division of Random House, Inc.

Anaya, Rudolfo, "A Story": From *The Silence of the Llano*. Copyright © 1982 by Rudolfo Anaya. Originally published by TQS Publications. Reprinted by permission of Susan Bergholz Literary Services, New York. All rights reserved.

Auster, Paul, *Ghosts*: Paul Auster, *Ghosts* (Los Angeles: Sun & Moon Press, 1986). Copyright © 1986 by Paul Auster. Reprinted with the permission of the publisher.

Baldwin, James, "Previous Condition": Originally published in *Commentary*. Collected in *Going to Meet the Man* © 1965 by James Baldwin. Copyright renewed. Published by Vintage Books. Reprinted by arrangement with the James Baldwin estate; "Sonny's Blues": Originally published in *Partisan Review*. Collected in *Going to Meet the Man* © 1965 by James Baldwin. Copyright renewed. Published by Vintage Books. Reprinted by arrangement with the James Baldwin estate.

Balzac, Honoré de, "Sarrasine": From *S/Z* by Roland Barthes, translated by Richard Miller. Translation copyright © 1986 by Farrar, Straus & Giroux, Inc. Reprinted by permission of Hill and Wang, a division of Farrar, Straus & Giroux, LLC.

Beckett, Samuel, "The Calmative": From *Complete Short Prose: 1929–1989* by Samuel Beckett. Copyright © 1946 by Samuel Beckett. Used by permission of Grove/Atlantic, Inc.

Borges, Jorge Luis, "The Shape of the Sword": Translated by Donald A. Yates, from *Labyrinths*, copyright © 1962, 1964 by New Directions Publishing Corporation. Reprinted by permission of New Directions Publishing Corporation.

Calvino, Italo, "Mr. Palomar on the Beach: Reading a Wave": From *Mr. Palomar* by Italo Calvino, copyright © 1983 by Giulio Einaudi editore, s.p.a., Torino, English translation by William Weaver copyright © 1985 by Harcourt, Inc. reprinted by permission of Harcourt, Inc.

Cather, Willa, "Paul's Case": Reprinted from *Willa Cather's Collected Short Fiction, 1892–1912* edited by Virginia Faulkner by permission of the University of Nebraska Press. Copyright © renewed 1992, 1998 by the University of Nebraska Press.

Chekhov, Anton, "The Lady with the Dog": From *My Life and Other Stories*, translated by Constance Garnett. Copyright © 1992. Reprinted by permission of Everyman's Library.

Cliff, Michelle, "The Store of a Million Items": From *The Store of a Million Items*. Copyright © 1998 by Michelle Cliff. Reprinted by permission of Hougton Mifflin Company. All rights reserved.

Colette, Sidonie-Gabrielle, "The Hidden Woman": Reprinted with the permission of Simon & Schuster, Inc. from *The Other Woman* by Colette, translated by Margaret Crosland. Copyright © 1972 by The Bobbs-Merrill Company, Inc.

Cortázar, Julio, "Blow-Up": From *End of the Game and Other Stories* by Julio Cortázar, translated by Paul Blackburn, copyright © 1967 by Random House, Inc. Used by permission of Pantheon Books, a division of Random House, Inc.

Desai, Anita, "Studies in the Park": Copyright © Anita Desai 1978. Reproduced by permission of the author c/o Rogers, Coleridge & White Ltd., 20 Powis Mews, London W11 1JN.

Faulkner, William, "A Rose for Emily": Copyright 1930 and renewed 1958 by William Faulkner, from *Collected Stories of William Faulkner* by William Faulkner. Used by permission of Random House, Inc.; "Barn Burning": Copyright 1950 by Random House, Inc. Copyright renewed 1977 by Jill Faulkner Summers, from *Collected Stories of William Faulkner* by William Faulkner. Used by permission of

Random House, Inc.; "Golden Land": Copyright 1935 by Random House, Inc., from *Collected Stories of William Faulkner* by William Faulkner. Used by permission of Random House, Inc.

Fitzgerald, F. Scott, "Babylon Revisited": Reprinted with permission of Scribner, a Division of Simon & Schuster, Inc., from *The Short Stories of F. Scott Fitzgerald*, edited by Mattew J. Bruccoli. Copyright 1931 by The Curtis Publishing Company. Copyright renewed © 1959 by Frances Scott Fitzgerald Lanahan.

Forster, E. M., "The Road from Colonus": From *Collected Tales of E. M. Forster* by E. M. Forster, copyright 1974 by Alfred A. Knopf, a division of Random House, Inc. Used by permission of Alfred A. Knopf, a division of Random House, Inc.

Gilman, Charlotte Perkins, "The Yellow Wall-Paper": Reprinted by The Feminist Press in 1973.

Hemingway, Ernest: "Hills Like White Elephants": Reprinted with permission of Scribner, a Division of Simon & Schuster, Inc., from *The Short Stories of Ernest Hemingway*. Copyright 1927 by Charles Scribner's Sons. Copyright renewed 1955 by Ernest Hemingway.

Himes, Chester, "Lunching at the Ritzmore": From the book *The Collected Stories of Chester Himes* by Chester Himes. Copyright © 1990 by Thunder's Mouth Press. Appears by permission of the publisher, Thunder's Mouth Press.

Hurston, Zora Neale, "Sweat": As taken from *The Complete Short Stories* by Zora Neale Hurston. Introduction copyright © 1995 by Henry Louis Gates, Jr. and Sieglinde Lemke. Compilation copyright © 1995 by Vivian Bowden, Lois J. Hurston Gaston, Clifford Hurston, Lucy Ann Hurston, Winifred Hurston Clark, Zora Mack Goins, Edgar Hurston, Sr., and Barbara Hurston Lewis. Afterword and Bibliography copyright © 1995 by Henry Louis Gates. Reprinted by permission of HarperCollins Publishers, Inc. "Sweat" was originally published in Fire, November 1926.

Joyce, James, "Araby": From *Dubliners* by James Joyce, copyright 1916 by B. W. Heubsch. Definitive text copyright © 1967 by the Estate of James Joyce. Used by permission of Viking Penguin, a division of Penguin Putnam, Inc.

Kafka, Franz, "A Hunger Artist": From *Franz Kafka: The Complete Stories* by Franz Kafka, edited by Nahum N. Glatzer, copyright 1946, 1947, 1948, 1949, 1954, 1958, 1971 by Schocken Books. Used by permission of Schocken Books, a division of Random House, Inc.

Kureishi, Hanif, "Blue, Blue Pictures of You": Copyright © Hanif Kureishi, 1997. Reproduced by permission of the author c/o Rogers, Coleridge & White, Ltd., 20 Powis Mews, London W11 1JN.

Lawrence, D. H., "The Horse-Dealer's Daughter": From D. H. Lawrence, *The Collected Short Stories*. Copyright © 1974. Reprinted by permission of Laurence Pollinger Limited and the Estate of Frieda Lawrence Ravagli.

Lessing, Doris, "A Woman on the Roof": Copyright © 1963 Doris Lessing. Reprinted by kind permission of Jonathan Clowes Ltd., London, on behalf of Doris Lessing.

Leyner, Mark, Selections from *My Cousin, My Gastroenterologist* by Mark Leyner, copyright © 1990 by Mark Leyner. Used by permission of Harmony Books, a division of Random House, Inc.

London, Jack, "The Law of Life"and "To Build a Fire": Reprinted with the permission of Scribner, a Division of Simon & Schuster, Inc., from *Jack London Short Stories, Authorized Edition with Definitive Texts*, edited by Earle Labor, Robert C. Leitz III, I. Milo Shepard. Copyright © 1991 by Macmillan Publishing Company.

Mansfield, Katherine, "The Garden-Party" and "This Flower": From *The Short Stories of Katherine Mansfield* by Katherine Mansfield, copyright 1923 by Alfred A. Knopf, a division of Random House, Inc. and renewed 1951 by John Middleton Murray. Used by permission of Alfred A. Knopf, a division of Random House, Inc.

Márquez, Gabriel García, "The Handsomest Drowned Man in the World": Entire text from "The Handsomest Drowned Man in the World" from *Leaf Storm and Other Stories* by Gabriel García Márquez. Copyright © 1971 by Gabriel García Márquez. Reprinted by permission of HarperCollins Publishers Inc.

Melville, Herman, "Bartleby the Scrivener": From *Complete Stories*, ed. Jay Leyda, 1949, pp. 3–47, published by Random House, Inc.

Mena, María Cristina, "The Vine-Leaf": Reprinted with permission from the publisher of *The Collected Stories of María Cristina Mena* (Houston: Arte Publico Press—University of Houston, 1997).

Oates, Joyce Carol, "How I Contemplated the World from the Detroit House of Correction and Began My Life Over Again": Copyright by the Ontario Review, Inc., 1993. Reprinted by permission of the author.

O'Connor, Flannery, "A Good Man Is Hard to Find": From *A Good Man Is Hard to Find and Other Stories*, copyright 1953 by Flannery O'Connor and renewed 1981 by Regina O'Connor, reprinted by permission of Harcourt, Inc.

POETRY

DRAMA

PHOTO CREDITS

FICTION

POETRY

DRAMA

WRITING

Index of Literary Terms

Index of First Lines

Index of Authors and Titles

Index of Terms

Page numbers indicate discussion of term in anthology. A page number in bold indicates entry in the **Glossary of Literary Terms**. For a complete list of terms, please refer to the **Index of Literary Terms**.